Tugce Tasdemir

PASSWORD ®

2nd EDITION

listen

MODULO

K DICTIONARIES

We acknowledge the financial support of the government of Canada through the Book Publishing Development Program for our publishing activity.

Password®, 2nd edition—English Dictionary for Speakers of French
This dictionary is based on the semi-bilingual approach to lexicography for foreign language learners developed by Lionel Kernerman, and is part of the K Dictionaries series.

© 2000, K Dictionaries Ltd
www.kdictionaries.com

Translation: Guy Jean Forgue

French Canadian Editing Team
Chief Editor: Michèle Morin
Editors: André Payette, Pierrette Mayer, Marie-Claude Désorcy, Renée Théorêt, Stéphane Lépine, François Morin, Dolène Schmidt
Proofreading: Kathleen Beaumont, Renée Léo Guimont, Nicole Labrecque, Kristina Turner, Judy Yelon
Illustrations: Diane Blais, Monique Chaussé, Marc Delafontaine, Sylvie Gautron
Cover Design: Marguerite Gouin

PASSWORD®, 2nd edition
This semi-bilingual edition
published by arrangment with W & R Chambers
and based upon *Chambers Concise Usage Dictionary*
© 1985 and 1986 by W & R Chambers Ltd

© Modulo Éditeur, 1989 and 2000

MODULO

5800, rue Saint-Denis, bureau 900
Montréal (Québec) H2S 3L5 Canada
Téléphone : 514 273-1066
Télécopieur : 514 276-0324 ou 1 800 814-0324
info.modulo@tc.tc   www.groupemodulo.com

Dépôt légal — Bibliothèque nationale du Québec, 2000
Bibliothèque nationale du Canada, 2000
ISBN 978-2-89113-733-1 (format poche)

Printed in Canada
12 13 14 15 16   M   18 17 16 15 14

PREFACE

We are proud to present to the French Canadian community the very first English learner's dictionary designed explicitly for users whose native language is French. The number of English-French and French-English dictionaries runs into the hundreds, but none of them is quite like this one. **Password** has an English-English core, which means that the entry word, part of speech, definition, examples of usage and points of grammar are all in English. A French equivalent for each usage of each entry follows the English.

Upon first encounter, this change may appear small. However, it is really very significant, and is likely to influence profoundly the concept of dictionaries for students of foreign languages. In order to understand fully the significance of this innovation, it is necessary to review some aspects of the development of foreign language learning.

Before the 1950s the language of instruction for teaching foreign languages was the students' native tongue. Thus, English was taught, or rather explained, to French speakers in French. Consequently, little English was actually taught; quite a bit was taught, however, **about** English. This was called the translation or indirect method of teaching a foreign language.

The dictionaries used by these learners of foreign languages were bilingual dictionaries. These dictionaries presented — and still present — lists (sometimes very long lists) of possible translations of each entry word — in the learner's native tongue. The user then has no choice but to judge or guess which of the words provided is the most appropriate translation. One might guess wrong with resulting embarrassment. In fact, teachers of English as a second language frequently recount humourous sentences written by pupils who have used misguided translations which they so conscientiously sought in their bilingual dictionaries.

After the Second World War the trend in the West moved toward the direct method of foreign language teaching: total immersion in the target language. Translation was avoided as much as possible, creating a situation in which the learner was forced **to think in the new language.**

The use of bilingual dictionaries was frowned upon, and, in fact, proved counterproductive in such an approach. What was needed was a monolingual dictionary — in this case, English-English — in which everything is explained in the target language. But existing monolingual dictionaries, intended only for native language speakers, were too difficult to be used by learners. This problem gave rise to the monolingual learner's dictionary.

A monolingual learner's dictionary takes into account the fact that the language of the dictionary is not the native language of the person who is using it. Therefore, even though the dictionary might contain over 50,000 headwords, it uses a limited vocabulary (usually 2,000-2,500 words) to explain the meanings of all the words. Secondly, it offers exemplary phrases and sentences which serve to illustrate the most typical use of the entry words. Thirdly, it usually points out common grammatical and spelling errors, and gives information about grammar and usage not ordinarily found in a monolingual dictionary.

But the monolingual learner's dictionary, while avoiding much of the ambiguity of the bilingual dictionary, is still only a monolingual dictionary. In spite of the definition being in easy English, the user might not be able to understand the meaning. Furthermore, he or she might misunderstand the meaning. What worse situation for the authors of a dictionary !

By providing a brief equivalent in the user's native language, **Password** incorporates the advantages of both monolingual and bilingual dictionaries. A kind of hybrid, this dictionary simultaneously promotes the strengths of its predecessors and avoids their weaknesses. Gone are the possibilities of not understanding or misunderstanding and the resulting uncertainty from guessing at words and their definitions.

In developing the semi-bilingual learner's dictionary, we have come to recognize the importance of visual presentation. In this regard, we have designed the text to be easily readable (not crowded and claustrophobic like many dictionaries), with the typography slightly larger than usual and crystal clear. Each usage of every entry, sub-entry, derivative, idiom and expression begins on a new line. Signs, symbols and abbreviations have been eliminated (except i.e., e.g., etc., which are all accepted parts of formal writing). Even the name of the parts of speech are written out in full. We have not spared clarity for space.

The user is relieved of the burden of reading a lengthy introduction on how to use this dictionary. **Password** is truly a user-friendly dictionary, and no preparation for its use is required.

The Editor

Table of Illustrations

Human Body	54
Clothing	93
My Family Tree	197
Foods	216
Fruits	226
Kinds of Home	273
Outside the House	279
Inside the House	280-281
Household Objects	282
Mammals	353
Musical Instruments	382
Common Objects	398
Occupations	400
Transportation	641
Vegetables	666

Pronunciation Guide

symbol	example		symbol	example	
a	[bag]	**bag**	t	['teibl]	**table**
aː	[baːθ]	**bath**	d	[dog]	**dog**
e	[hed]	**head**	k	[kik]	**kick**
i	[milk]	**milk**	g	[get]	**get**
iː	[fiːl]	**feel**	m	[mad]	**mad**
o	[boks]	**box**	n	[neim]	**name**
oː	[hoːl]	**hall**	ŋ	[baŋ]	**bang**
u	[fut]	**foot**	l	[leik]	**lake**
uː	[bluː]	**blue**	r	[reis]	**race**
ʌ	[lʌv]	**love**	f	[fiːt]	**feet**
ə	['ribən]	**ribbon**	v	[vois]	**voice**
əː	[fəːst]	**first**	θ	[θiŋ]	**thing**
ai	[fain]	**fine**	ð	[ðou]	**though**
au	[laud]	**loud**	s	[seif]	**safe**
ei	[pein]	**pain**	z	[zuː]	**zoo**
eə	[heə]	**hair**	ʃ	[ʃip]	**ship**
iə	[hiə]	**here**	ʒ	['meʒə]	**measure**
oi	[dʒoin]	**join**	h	[haːf]	**half**
ou	[gou]	**go**	w	[weit]	**wait**
uə	[puə]	**poor**	j	[jʌŋ]	**young**
p	[peidʒ]	**page**	tʃ	[tʃiːz]	**cheese**
b	[boːl]	**ball**	dʒ	['dʒakit]	**jacket**

Aa

a, an [ə(n)] *indef. article* (**a** is used before words beginning with a consonant *eg a boy*, or consonant sound *eg a union*; **an** is used before words beginning with a vowel *eg an owl*, or vowel sound *eg an honour*.) **1** one: *There is a boy in the garden.* □ **un, une**
2 any; every: *An owl can see in the dark.* □ **un, une**
3 for each; per: *We earn $6 an hour.* □ **par; de**

> **a** before **hotel, historian.**
> **an** before **heir, honest, honour, hour.**

A-Z/A to Z [eitəˈzed] *noun* a small book of information in alphabetical order, *especially* a guide to the streets of a town or city. □ **répertoire alphabétique**
aback [əˈbak]: **taken aback** surprised and *usually* rather upset: *She was taken aback by his rudeness.* □ **déconcerté**
abandon [əˈbandən] *verb* **1** to leave, not intending to return to: *They abandoned the stolen car.* □ **abandonner**
2 to give (oneself) completely to: *He abandoned himself to despair.* □ **s'abandonner (à)**
a'bandoned *adjective* **1** shameless: *an abandoned young man.* □ **dévergondé**
2 having been left without any intention of returning to or reclaiming: *The police found the abandoned car.* □ **abandonné**
a'bandonment *noun: Lack of money led to the abandonment of this plan.* □ **abandon**
abashed [əˈbaʃt] *adjective* (*negative* **unabashed**) embarrassed: *She was abashed at the compliments she received.* □ **confus**
abate [əˈbeit] *verb* to become less: *The storm abated.* □ **diminuer**
a'batement *noun.* □ **diminution**
abattoir [ˈabətwar] *noun* a place where animals are killed for food; a slaughterhouse. □ **abattoir**
abbess *see* **abbot.**
abbey [ˈabi] *noun* **1** the building(s) in which a Christian (*usually* Roman Catholic) group of monks or nuns lives. □ **abbaye**
2 the church now or formerly belonging to it: *Westminster Abbey.* □ **abbaye**
abbot [ˈabət] – *feminine* **abbess** [ˈabes] – *noun* the head of an abbey. □ **abbé, abbesse**
abbreviate [əˈbriːvieit] *verb* to shorten (a word, phrase *etc*): *Frederick is often abbreviated to Fred.* □ **abréger**
ab,brevi'ation *noun* a shortened form of a word *etc*: *Math is an abbreviation of mathematics.* □ **abréviation**
ABC [eibiːˈsiː] *noun* **1** the alphabet: *The child has not learnt his ABC.* □ **alphabet**
2 the simplest and most basic knowledge: *the ABC of engineering.* □ **rudiments, b. a.-ba**
abdicate [ˈabdikeit] *verb* **1** to give up or give up the position and authority of a king or queen: *The king abdicated (the throne) in favour of his son.* □ **abdiquer**
2 to leave or give up (responsibility, power *etc*): *She abdicated all responsibility for the work to her elder son.* □ **abdiquer**

,abdi'cation *noun.* □ **abdication**
abdomen [ˈabdəmən] *noun* the part of the body between the hips and the lower ribs. □ **abdomen**
ab'dominal [-ˈdo-] *adjective.* □ **abdominal**
abduct [əbˈdʌkt] *verb* to take (someone) away against his will *usually* by trickery or violence; to kidnap: *The president has been abducted.* □ **enlever**
ab'duction [-ʃən] *noun.* □ **enlèvement**
abet [əˈbet] – *past tense, past participle* **a'betted** – *verb* to help or encourage to do something wrong: *He abetted his cousin in robbing the bank.* □ **inciter (à)**
abeyance [əˈbeiəns]: **in abeyance** left undecided *usually* for a short time: *The matter was left in abeyance.* □ **en suspens**
abhor [əbˈhoɪ] – *past tense, past participle* **ab'horred** – *verb* to hate very much: *The headmaster abhors violence.* □ **abhorrer**
ab'horrence [-ˈho-] *noun.* □ **horreur**
ab'horrent [-ˈho-] *adjective* (*with* **to**) hateful: *Fighting was abhorrent to her.* □ **odieux (à)**
abide [əˈbaid] *verb* to put up with; to tolerate: *I can't abide noisy people.* □ **supporter**
a'bide by – *past tense, past participle* **a'bided** – to act according to; to be faithful to: *They must abide by the rules of the game.* □ **se conformer (à)**
ability [əˈbiləti] – *plural* **a'bilities** – *noun* **1** the power, knowledge *etc* to do something: *I shall do the job to the best of my ability.* □ **capacité**
2 a skill: *a man of many abilities.* □ **habileté**
abject [ˈabdʒekt] *adjective* miserable; wretched: *abject poverty.* □ **misérable**
'abjectly *adverb.* □ **misérablement**
ablaze [əˈbleiz] *adjective* **1** burning strongly: *The building was ablaze when the fire brigade arrived.* □ **en flammes**
2 very bright: *The street was ablaze with lights.* □ **resplendissant**
able [ˈeibl] *adjective* **1** having enough strength, knowledge *etc* to do something: *She was able to open the door; He will come if he is able.* □ **capable**
2 clever and skilful; capable: *a very able nurse.* □ **compétent**
'ably *adverb.* □ **habilement**
abnormal [abˈnoɪ zməl] *adjective* not normal: *Her behaviour is abnormal for a child of her age.* □ **anormal**
abnor'mality [-ˈma-] *noun.* □ **caractère anormal**
ab'normally *adverb.* □ **anormalement**
aboard [əˈboɪd] *adverb, preposition* on(to) or in(to) (a means of transport): *We were aboard for several hours; He went aboard the ship/train/aircraft.* □ **à bord (de)**
abolish [əˈboliʃ] *verb* to put an end to (a custom, law *etc*): *We must abolish the death penalty.* □ **abolir**
,abo'lition [a-] *noun.* □ **abolition**
A-bomb [ˈeibom] *noun* an atomic bomb. □ **bombe atomique**
abominable [əˈbominəbl] *adjective* very bad; terrible: *What abominable weather!* □ **abominable**
a'bominably *adverb.* □ **abominablement**
abominate [əˈbomineit] *verb* to detest: *She abominates cruelty.* □ **abominer**

a,bomi'nation *noun.* □ **abomination**

aborigine [abə'ridʒini] *noun* an original inhabitant of a country, *especially* of Australia. □ **aborigène**
,abo'riginal *adjective.* □ **autochtone**

abort [ə'bɔːt] *verb* 1 to lose or bring about the loss of (an unborn child) from the womb. □ **avorter**
2 (of a plan *etc*) to (cause to) come to nothing. □ **faire avorter**
3 to stop or abandon (a space mission, *eg* the firing of a rocket) before it is completed. □ **interrompre**
a'bortion [-ʃən] *noun.* □ **avortement**
a'bortive [-tiv] *adjective* unsuccessful: *an abortive attempt to climb the mountain.* □ **raté**

abound [ə'baund] *verb* 1 (*with* in or with) to have plenty of: *The east coast abounds in good farming land.* □ **abonder en**
2 to be very plentiful: *Fish abound in these waters.* □ **regorger (de)**

about [ə'baut] *preposition* on the subject of: *We talked about our plans; What's the book about?* □ **sur; de**
■ *preposition, adverb* 1 (*sometimes* **round about**) near (in place, time, size *etc*): *about five kilometres away; (around) about six o'clock; just about big enough.* □ **environ**
2 in different directions; here and there: *The children ran about (the garden).* □ **ici et là**
3 in or on some part (of a place *etc*): *You'll find her somewhere about (the office).* □ **quelque part**
4 around or surrounding: *She wore a coat about her shoulders; He lay with his clothes scattered about.* □ **autour**
■ *adverb* (in military commands *etc*) in the opposite direction: *About turn!* □ **demi-tour**
be about to to be going to (perform an action): *I am about to leave the office.* □ **être sur le point de**

above [ə'bʌv] *preposition* 1 in a higher position than: *a picture above the fireplace.* □ **au-dessus de**
2 greater than: *The child's intelligence is above average.* □ **au-dessus de**
3 too good for: *The police must be above suspicion.* □ **au-dessus de**
■ *adverb* 1 higher up: *seen from above.* □ **en haut**
2 (in a book *etc*) earlier or higher up on the page: *See above.* □ **plus haut**
a,bove-'board *adjective and adverb* open and honourable; not secret: *Her dealings are all above-board.* □ **franc**
above all most importantly: *He is strong, brave and, above all, honest.* □ **par-dessus tout**

abrasion [ə'breiʒən] *noun* an injury caused by scraping or grazing the skin: *minor abrasions.* □ **écorchure**
a'brasive [-siv] *adjective and adverb* tending to make surfaces rough when rubbed on to them: *An abrasiv material is unsuitable for cleaning baths.* □ **abrasif**
■ *noun* something used for scraping or rubbing a surface: *Sandpaper is an abrasive.* □ **abrasif**

abreast [ə'brest] *adverb* side by side: *They walked along the road three abreast.* □ **côte à côte**
keep abreast of to remain up to date with: *keeping abreast of recent scientific developments.* □ **se tenir au**

courant de

abridge [ə'bridʒ] *verb* to make (*especially* a book) shorter. □ **abréger**
a'bridged *adjective.* □ **abrégé**
a'bridg(e)ment *noun.* □ **résumé**

abroad [ə'brɔːd] *adverb* 1 in or to another country: *She lived abroad for many years.* □ **à l'étranger**
2 current; going around: *There's a rumour abroad that she is leaving.* □ **qui court**

abrupt [ə'brʌpt] *adjective* 1 sudden; unexpected: *The car came to an abrupt halt.* □ **soudain**
2 (of a person's manner of speaking *etc*) rude or sharp. □ **brusque**
a'bruptly *adverb.* □ **brusquement**
a'bruptness *noun.* □ **brusquerie**

abscess ['abses] *noun* a painful swelling, containing pus: *He has a bad abscess under that tooth.* □ **abcès**

absent ['absənt] *adjective* not present: *Johnny was absent from school with a cold.* □ **absent**
■ [ab'sent] *verb* to keep (oneself) away: *She absented herself from the meeting.* □ **s'absenter**
'absence *noun* 1 the condition of not being present: *His absence was noticed.* □ **absence**
2 a time during which a person *etc* is not present: *After an absence of five years he returned home.* □ **absence**
,absen'tee *noun* a person who is not present, *especially* frequently (*eg* at work, school *etc*). □ **absentéiste**
,absen'teeism *noun* being often absent from work *etc* without good reason: *Absenteeism is a problem in some industries.* □ **absentéisme**
,absent-'minded *adjective* not noticing what is going on around one because one is thinking deeply: *an absent-minded professor.* □ **distrait**
,absent'mindedly *adverb.* □ **distraitement**
,absent-'mindedness *noun.* □ **distraction**

absolute ['absəluːt] *adjective* complete: *absolute honesty.* □ **absolu**
,abso'lutely *adverb* completely: *It is absolutely impossible for me to go.* □ **absolument**

absolution *see* **absolve.**

absolve [əb'zolv] *verb* to make free or release (from a promise, duty or blame): *She was absolved of all blame.* □ **absoudre**
absolution [absə'luːʃən] *noun* forgiveness, *especially* of sins: *The priest granted the man absolution.* □ **absolution**

absorb [əb'zɔːb] *verb* 1 to soak up: *The cloth absorbed the ink I had spilled.* □ **absorber**
2 to take up the whole attention of (a person): *She was completely absorbed in her book.* □ **absorber**
ab'sorbent *adjective* able to soak up: *absorbent paper.* □ **absorbant**
ab'sorption [-'zɔːp-] *noun.* □ **absorption**

abstain [əb'stein] *verb* (*often with* from) not to do, take *etc*: *He abstained (from voting in the election); He abstained from alcohol.* □ **s'abstenir (de)**
ab'stention [-'sten-] *noun* the act of abstaining: *At the election of the new chairman the voting was six for, three against, and two abstentions.* □ **abstention**

abstemious [əb'stiːmiəs] *adjective* taking little food,

drink *etc*: *She was being very abstemious as she was trying to lose weight; an abstemious young man.* □ **sobre**
ab'stemiously *adverb.* □ **sobrement**
ab'stemiousness *noun.* □ **sobriété**
abstention *see* **abstain.**
abstinence ['abstinəns] *noun* the act or habit of abstaining, *especially* from alcohol. □ **abstinence**
abstract ['abstrakt] *adjective* **1** (of a noun) referring to something which exists as an idea and which is not physically real: *Truth, poverty and bravery are abstract nouns.* □ **abstrait**
2 (of painting, sculpture *etc*) concerned with colour, shape, texture *etc* rather than showing things as they really appear: *an abstract sketch of a vase of flowers.* □ **abstrait**
■ *noun* a summary (of a book, article *etc*). □ **résumé**
abstruse [əb'struːs] *adjective* difficult to understand: *abstruse reasoning.* □ **abstrus**
ab'struseness *noun.* □ **complexité**
absurd [əb'səːd] *adjective* unreasonable or ridiculous: *These demands are absolutely absurd.* □ **absurde**
ab'surdly *adverb.* □ **absurdement**
ab'surdity (*plural* **ab'surdities**) *noun.* □ **absurdité**
ab'surdness *noun.* □ **absurdité**
abundance [ə'bʌndəns] *noun* a large amount: *an abundance of food*; *There was food in abundance.* □ **abondance**
a'bundant *adjective* plentiful: *abundant proof.* □ **abondant**
a'bundantly *adverb.* □ **abondamment**
abuse [ə'bjuːz] *verb* **1** to use wrongly, *usually* with harmful results: *She abused her privileges by taking too long a holiday.* □ **abuser de**
2 to insult or speak roughly to: *He abused the servants.* □ **injurier**
■ [ə'bjuːs] *noun* **1** insulting language: *He shouted abuse at her.* □ **injure**
2 the wrong use of something: *This toy has been subjected to a lot of abuse.* □ **usage abusif**
a'busive [-siv] *adjective* using insulting language: *He wrote an abusive letter to the manager.* □ **injurieux**
a'busively *adverb.* □ **injurieusement**
a'busiveness *noun.* □ **grossièreté verbale**
abysmal [ə'bizməl] *adjective* very great (in a bad sense); very bad: *abysmal ignorance*; *The weather is abysmal.* □ **insondable**
a'bysmally *adverb.* □ **abominablement**
abyss [ə'bis] *noun* a very deep or bottomless hole or chasm. □ **abîme**
academy [ə'kadəmi] – *plural* **a'cademies** – *noun* **1** a higher school for special study: *Academy of Music.* □ **académie**
2 a society to encourage science, art *etc*: *The Royal Academy.* □ **académie**
3 a type of senior school. □ **collège**
academic [akə'demik] *adjective* of or concerning study *especially* in schools, colleges *etc*: *an academic career.* □ **universitaire**
■ *noun* a university or college teacher. □ **universitaire**
aca'demically [akə'de-] *adverb.* □ **académiquement**

accede [ək'siːd]: **accede to** to agree to: *She acceded to my request.* □ **accéder (à)**
accelerate [ək'seləreit] *verb* **1** to increase speed: *The driver accelerated to pass the other car.* □ **accélérer**
2 to make (something) happen sooner: *Worry accelerated his death.* □ **hâter**
ac,cele'ration *noun.* □ **accélération**
ac'celerator *noun* a pedal, lever *etc* that controls the speed or acceleration of a machine. □ **accélérateur**
accent ['aksənt] *noun* **1** (a mark used to show) the stress on a syllable: *The accent is on the second syllable.* □ **accent (tonique)**
2 a mark used to show the pronunciation of a letter in certain languages: *Put an accent on the e in début.* □ **accent**
3 emphasis: *The accent must be on hard work.* □ **accent**
4 a special way of pronouncing words in a particular area *etc*: *an American accent.* □ **accent**
■ [ak'sent] *verb* to pronounce with stress or emphasis: *The second syllable is accented.* □ **accentuer**
accept [ək'sept] *verb* **1** to take (something offered): *He accepted the gift.* □ **accepter**
2 to believe in, agree to or acknowledge: *We accept your account of what happened*; *Their proposal was accepted*; *He accepted responsibility for the accident.* □ **accepter**
ac'ceptable *adjective* **1** satisfactory: *The decision should be acceptable to most people.* □ **acceptable**
2 pleasing: *a very acceptable gift.* □ **bienvenu**
ac'ceptably *adverb.* □ **acceptablement**
ac'ceptance *noun*: *We have had few acceptances to our invitation.* □ **acceptation**
ac'cepted *adjective* generally recognized: *It is an accepted fact that the world is round.* □ **reconnu**
access ['akses] *noun* **1** way or right of approach or entry: *We gained access to the house through a window.* □ **accès**
2 way or right to meet (someone) or use (something): *Senior students have access to the library at weekends.* □ **accès**
ac'cessible *adjective* (of a person or place) able to be reached or approached easily: *Her house is not accessible by car.* □ **accessible**
ac,cessi'bility *noun.* □ **accessibilité**
accession [ək'seʃən] *noun* **1** a coming to the position of king or queen: *in the year of the Queen's accession (to the throne).* □ **avènement**
2 an addition: *There are several new accessions to the library.* □ **acquisition**
accessory [ək'sesəri] – *plural* **ac'cessories** – *noun* **1** something additional (*eg* a handbag, scarf, shoes *etc* to the main part of a woman's clothing, or a radio, seat-covers *etc* to a car): *She wore matching accessories.* □ **accessoire**
2 (*legal*) a person who helps somebody, *especially* a criminal. □ **complice**
accident ['aksidənt] *noun* **1** an unexpected happening, often harmful, causing injury *etc*: *There has been a road accident.* □ **accident**

2 chance: *I met her by accident.* □ **(par) hasard**

,acci'dental [-'den-] *adjective* happening by chance or accident: *an accidental discovery.* □ **accidentel**

,acci'dentally [-'den-] *adverb.* □ **par hasard**

acclaim [ə'kleim] *verb* 1 to applaud or welcome enthusiastically: *The footballer was acclaimed by the fans.* □ **acclamer**

2 to declare (someone) ruler, winner *etc* by enthusiastic approval: *They acclaimed him king.* □ **acclamer**

■ *noun* enthusiastic approval. □ **acclamation**

acclamation [aklə'meiʃən] *noun* a noisy demonstration of applause, agreement, approval *etc*. □ **acclamation**

acclimatize, acclimatise [ə'klaimətaiz] *verb* to make or become accustomed to a new climate, new surroundings *etc*: *It took her several months to become acclimatized to the heat.* □ **(s')acclimater (à)**

ac,climati'zation, ac,climati'sation *noun.* □ **acclimatation**

accommodate [ə'komədeit] *verb* 1 to find or be a place for: *The house could accommodate two families.* □ **loger**

2 to oblige: *They did their best to accommodate him by carrying out his wishes.* □ **obliger**

ac'commodating *adjective* obliging; helpful. □ **accommodant**

ac,commo'dation *noun* 1 room(s) in a house or hotel in which to live, *especially* for a short time: *It is difficult to find accommodation in London in August.* □ **logement**

2 space for something: *There is accommodation for your car behind the hotel.* □ **place**

---

accommodate has two cs and two ms.

---

accompany [ə'kʌmpəni] *verb* 1 to go with (someone or something): *He accompanied her to the door.* □ **accompagner**

2 to play a musical instrument to go along with (a singer *etc*): *He accompanied her on the piano.* □ **accompagner**

ac'companiment *noun* something that accompanies: *I'll play the piano accompaniment while you sing.* □ **accompagnement**

ac'companist *noun* a person who plays a musical accompaniment. □ **accompagnateur, trice**

accomplice [ə'komplis] *noun* a person who helps another, *especially* in crime: *The thief's accomplice warned him that the police were coming.* □ **complice**

accomplish [ə'kompliʃ] *verb* 1 (*with* **with**) to complete (something) successfully: *Have you accomplished your task?* □ **accomplir**

ac'complished *adjective* skilled: *an accomplished singer.* □ **accompli**

ac'complishment *noun* 1 completion. □ **accomplissement**

2 a special skill: *She has many different accomplishments.* □ **talent**

accord [ə'koːd] *verb* 1 (*with* **with**) to agree with: *Her story accords with what I saw happen.* □ **concorder (avec)**

2 to grant or give to (a person): *They accorded the president great respect.* □ **accorder**

■ *noun* agreement: *That is not in accord with your origi-*nal statement.* □ **accord**

ac'cordance: in accordance with in agreement with: *The money will be given out in accordance with his instructions.* □ **conformément (à)**

ac'cordingly *adverb* 1 in agreement (with the circumstances *etc*): *Find out what has happened and act accordingly.* □ **en conséquence**

2 therefore: *She was very worried about the future of the firm and accordingly she did what she could to help.* □ **en conséquence**

according to 1 as said or told by: *According to John, the bank closes at 3:00 p.m.* □ **d'après**

2 in agreement with: *She acted according to her promise.* □ **selon**

3 in the order of: *books arranged according to their subjects.* □ **selon; par**

4 in proportion to: *You will be paid according to the amount of work you have done.* □ **selon**

of one's own accord of one's own free will: *He did it of his own accord, without being forced to.* □ **de plein gré**

with one accord (everybody) in agreement: *With one accord they stood up to cheer him.* □ **d'un commun accord**

accordion [ə'koːdiən] *noun* a musical instrument with bellows and a keyboard. □ **accordéon**

accost [ə'kost] *verb* to approach and speak to, *especially* in an unfriendly way: *I was accosted in the street by four men with guns.* □ **accoster**

account [ə'kaunt] *noun* 1 a statement of money owing: *Send me an account.* □ **compte**

2 (*usually in plural*) a record of money received and spent: *You must keep your accounts in order;* (*also adjective*) *an account book.* □ **comptes**

3 an arrangement by which a person keeps his money in a bank: *I have (opened) an account with the local bank.* □ **compte**

4 an arrangement by which a person makes a regular (*eg* monthly) payment instead of paying at the time of buying: *I have an account at Smith's.* □ **compte**

5 a description or explanation (of something that has happened): *a full account of his holiday.* □ **compte rendu**

ac'countancy *noun* the work of an accountant: *She is studying accountancy.* □ **comptabilité**

ac'countant *noun* a keeper or inspector of (money) accounts: *She employs an accountant to deal with her income tax.* □ **comptable**

account for to give a reason for; to explain: *I can account for the mistake.* □ **rendre compte de**

on account of because of: *She stayed indoors on account of the bad weather.* □ **à cause de**

on my, his *etc* **account** because of me, him *etc* or for my, his *etc* sake: *You don't have to leave early on my account.* □ **à cause de**

on no account not for any reason: *On no account must you open that door.* □ **en aucun cas**

take (something) into account, take account of (something) to consider (something which is part of the problem *etc*): *We must take his illness into account when*

accredited / across

assessing his work. □ **tenir compte de**

accredited [ə'kreditid] *adjective* officially recognized: *He is an accredited accountant.* □ **accrédité**

accumulate [ə'kjuːmjuleit] *verb* (*usually* of things) to gather or be gathered together in a large quantity: *Rubbish accumulates very quickly in our house.* □ **(s')accumuler**

ac'cumulation *noun.* □ **accumulation**

ac'cumulator *noun* a type of electric battery. □ **accumulateur**

accurate [a'kjurət] *adjective* 1 exactly right: *an accurate drawing.* □ **exact**

2 making no mistakes: *an accurate memory.* □ **fidèle**

'**accurately** *adverb.* □ **exactement**

accuracy *noun.* □ **exactitude**

accursed [ə'kɔːsid] *adjective* 1 under a curse. □ **maudit** 2 hateful. □ **exécrable**

accuse [ə'kjuːz] *verb* (*with* of) to charge (someone) with having done something wrong: *They accused him of stealing the car.* □ **accuser (de)**

,**accu'sation** [a-] *noun.* □ **accusation**

the accused the person(s) accused in a court of law: *The accused was found not guilty.* □ **accusé, ée**

accustom [ə'kʌstəm] *verb* to make (*especially* oneself) familiar with or used to: *He soon accustomed himself to the idea.* □ **(s')habituer (à)**

ac'customed *adjective* usual: *his accustomed seat.* □ **habituel**

accustomed to familiar with or used to: *I am not accustomed to being treated like this.* □ **habitué à**

ace [eis] *noun* 1 the one in playing cards: *the ace of spades.* □ **as**

2 a person who is expert at anything: *She's an ace with a rifle.* □ **as**

3 a serve in tennis in which the ball is not touched by the opposing player. □ **as**

ache [eik] *noun* a continuous pain: *I have a stomach ache.* □ **douleur**

■ *verb* 1 to be in continuous pain: *My tooth aches.* □ **faire mal**

2 to have a great desire: *I was aching to tell him the news.* □ **brûler de**

achieve [ə'tʃiːv] *verb* to gain or reach successfully: *She has achieved her ambition.* □ **réaliser**

a'chievement *noun: his academic achievements; the achievement of her ambition.* □ **réussite**

acid ['asid] *adjective* 1 (of taste) sharp or sour: *Lemons and limes are acid fruits.* □ **acide**

2 sarcastic: *acid humour.* □ **mordant**

■ *noun* a substance, containing hydrogen, which will dissolve metals *etc: She spilled some acid which burned a hole in her dress.* □ **acide**

a'cidity *noun* the quality of containing acid or too much acid. □ **acidité**

acknowledge [ək'nolidʒ] *verb* 1 to admit as being fact: *He acknowledged defeat; He acknowledged that I was right.* □ **reconnaître**

2 to say (*usually* in writing) that one has received (something): *She acknowledged the letter.* □ **accuser réception (de)**

3 to give thanks for: *He acknowledged their help.* □ **se montrer reconnaissant de**

4 to greet someone: *He acknowledged her by waving.* □ **saluer**

acknowledg(e)ment *noun.* □ **reconnaissance**

acme ['akmi] *noun* the highest point: *the acme of perfection.* □ **comble**

acne ['akni] *noun* a common skin disease with pimples: *Acne is common among young people.* □ **acné**

acoustic [ə'kuːstik] *adjective* having to do with hearing or with sound: *This hall has acoustic problems.* □ **acoustique**

a'coustics 1 *noun plural* the characteristics of a room or hall that affect the quality of sound. □ **acoustique** 2 *noun singular* the science of sound. □ **acoustique**

acquaint [ə'kweint] *verb* 1 to make (*usually* oneself) familiar (with): *You must acquaint yourself with the routine of the office.* □ **se mettre au courant de**

2 to inform (a person) of: *Have you acquainted her with your plans?* □ **aviser**

acquaintance *noun* 1 a person whom one knows slightly. □ **connaissance**

2 (with **with**) knowledge: *My acquaintance with the works of Shakespeare is slight.* □ **connaissance (de)**

be acquainted with to know or be familiar with: *I'm not acquainted with her father.* □ **connaître**

make someone's acquaintance to get to know someone: *I made her acquaintance when on holiday in France.* □ **faire la connaissance de qqn**

acquiesce [akwi'es] *verb* to agree: *After a lot of persuasion, he finally acquiesced.* □ **acquiescer**

acqui'escence *noun.* □ **consentement**

acqui'escent *adjective.* □ **consentant**

acquire [ə'kwaiə] *verb* to get: *She acquired a knowledge of English.* □ **acquérir**

acquisition [akwi'ziʃən] *noun* 1 the act of acquiring: *the acquisition of more land.* □ **acquisition**

2 something acquired: *Her recent acquisitions included a piano.* □ **acquisition**

acquisitive [ə'kwizətiv] *adjective* eager to get possessions: *an acquisitive child.* □ **avide**

ac'quisitiveness *noun.* □ **instinct de possession**

acquit [ə'kwit] – *past tense, past participle* **ac'quitted** – *verb* to declare (an accused person) to be innocent: *The judge acquitted her of murder.* □ **acquitter**

ac'quittal *noun: She was released from prison following her acquittal.* □ **acquittement**

acrid ['akrid] *adjective* harsh in smell or taste: *The acrid smell of smoke filled the room.* □ **âcre**

acrobat ['akrəbat] *noun* a person in a circus *etc* who performs gymnastics. □ **acrobate**

,**acro'batic** *adjective.* □ **acrobatique**

,**acro'batics** *noun plural* acrobatic performances. □ **acrobatie(s)**

across [ə'kros] *preposition* 1 to the other side (of); from one side to the other side of: *He took her across the road.* □ **de l'autre côté de**

2 at the other side (of): *The butcher's shop is across the street.* □ **de l'autre côté de**

■ *adverb* to the other side or to the speaker's side: *She dived in off the river-bank and swam across.* □ **de l'autre côté**

act [akt] *verb* **1** to do something: *It's time the government acted to lower taxes.* □ **agir**

2 to behave: *He acted foolishly at the meeting.* □ **se comporter**

3 to perform (a part) in a play: *He has acted (the part of Romeo) in many theatres; I thought he was dying, but he was only acting* (= pretending). □ **jouer**

■ *noun* **1** something done: *Running away is an act of cowardice; He committed many cruel acts.* □ **acte**

2 (*often with capital*) a law: *Acts of Parliament.* □ **loi**

3 a section of a play: *'Hamlet' has five acts.* □ **acte**

4 an entertainment: *an act called 'The Smith Family'.* □ **divertissement**

acting *adjective* temporarily carrying out the duties of: *She is acting president of the society.* □ **suppléant**

'actor – *feminine also* **'actress** – *noun* a performer in a play. □ **acteur, trice**

act as to do the work or duties of: *He acts as head of department when his boss is away.* □ **faire fonction de**

act on **1** to do something following the advice *etc* of someone: *I am acting on the advice of my lawyer.* □ **suivre**

2 to have an effect on: *Certain acids act on metal.* □ **agir (sur)**

act on behalf of/act for to do something for (someone else); to act as the representative of (someone): *My lawyer is acting on my behalf; He is also acting on behalf of my mother; She is acting for the headmaster in his absence.* □ **représenter**

in the act (of) at the exact moment (of doing something): *He was caught in the act (of stealing my car).* □ **sur le fait**

put on an act to pretend: *I thought she had hurt herself but she was only putting on an act.* □ **jouer la comédie**

action ['akʃən] *noun* **1** something done: *Action, not talking, is necessary if we are to defeat the enemy; Take action immediately; The firemen are ready to go into action.* □ **action**

2 movement: *Tennis needs a good wrist action.* □ **jeu**

3 a legal case: *She brought an action for divorce against her husband.* □ **action (en justice)**

4 the events (of a play, film *etc*): *The action of the play takes place on an island.* □ **intrigue**

5 a battle; fighting: *He was killed in action; Our troops fought an action against the enemy.* □ **combat**

in action working: *Is your machine still in action?* □ **en état de marche**

out of action not working: *My car's out of action this week.* □ **hors d'usage**

activate ['aktiveit] *verb* to put into force or operation: *The smoke activated the fire alarms.* □ **déclencher**

active ['aktiv] *adjective* **1** energetic or lively; able to work *etc*: *At seventy, he's no longer very active.* □ **actif**

2 (busily) involved: *She is an active supporter of women's rights.* □ **actif**

3 causing an effect or effects: *Yeast is an active ingredient in bread-making.* □ **actif**

4 in force: *The rule is still active.* □ **en vigueur**

5 (of volcanoes) still likely to erupt. □ **en activité**

6 of the form of a verb in which the subject performs the action of the verb: *The dog bit the man.* □ **actif**

'activeness *noun.* □ **activité**

'actively *adverb*: *actively engaged in politics.* □ **activement**

ac'tivity – *plural* **ac'tivities** – *noun* **1** the state of being active or lively: *The streets are full of activity this morning.* □ **activité**

2 something which one does as a pastime, as part of one's job *etc*: *Her activities include fishing and golf.* □ **activité(s)**

actor, actress *see* **act**.

actual ['aktʃuəl] *adjective* real; existing; not imaginary: *In actual fact he is not as stupid as you think he is.* □ **réel**

,actu'ality [-'a-] *noun* (a) reality: *the actuality of the situation.* □ **réalité**

'actually *adverb* **1** really: *She actually saw the accident happen.* □ **réellement**

2 in fact: *Actually, I'm doing something else this evening.* □ **en fait**

acupuncture ['akjupʌŋktʃə] *noun* a method of treating illness *etc* by sticking needles into the patient's skin at certain points. □ **acupuncture**

acute [ə'kjuːt] *adjective* **1** (of a disease *etc*) severe but not lasting very long: *They think his illness is acute rather than chronic.* □ **aigu**

2 very great: *There is an acute shortage of teachers.* □ **critique**

3 quick-witted: *As a businessman, he's very acute.* □ **avisé**

4 (of the senses) keen: *acute hearing.* □ **fin**

a'cutely *adverb.* □ **vivement**

a'cuteness *noun.* □ **acuité**

acute angle an angle of less than ninety degrees. □ **angle aigu**

ad [ad] short for **advertisement**: *I'll put an ad in the newspaper.* □ **annonce**

adamant ['adəmənt] *adjective* determined or insistent: *an adamant refusal.* □ **inflexible**

adapt [ə'dapt] *verb* to change or alter (so as to fit a different situation *etc*): *She always adapted easily to new circumstances; She has adapted the play for television.* □ **(s')adapter (à)**

,adap'tation [a-] *noun.* □ **adaptation**

a'daptable *adjective* willing or able to change to fit in with different circumstances: *Children are usually very adaptable.* □ **adaptable**

a,dapta'bility *noun.* □ **adaptabilité**

a'daptor *noun* a device which enables an electrical plug of one type to be used in a socket of another type, or several plugs to be used in the same socket at the same time. □ **adaptateur**

add [ad] *verb* **1** (*often with* **to**) to put (one thing) to or with (another): *She added water to her whisky.* □ **ajouter**

2 (*often with* **to, together, up**) to find the total of (various numbers): *Add these figures together; Add 124 to 356; He added up the figures.* □ **additionner**

3 to say something extra: *He explained, and added that*

he was sorry. □ **ajouter (à)**
4 (*with* **to**) to increase: *His illness had added to their difficulties.* □ **ajouter (à)**
ad'dition *noun* **1** the act of adding: *The child is not good at addition.* □ **addition**
2 something added: *They've had an addition to the family; They've put an addition on the house.* □ **nouveau venu; nouvelle partie**
ad'ditional *adjective*: *This has meant additional work for me.* □ **supplémentaire**
addict ['adikt] *noun* a person who has become dependent on something, *especially* drugs: *a drug addict; a television addict.* □ **intoxiqué, ée, toxicomane**
ad'dicted *adjective* (*often with* **to**) dependent on (*especially* a drug): *He is addicted to alcohol.* □ **adonné (à)**
ad'diction [-ʃən] *noun*. □ **dépendance**
addition *see* **add.**
address [ə'dres] *verb* **1** to put a name and address on (an envelope *etc*): *Address the parcel clearly.* □ **mettre l'adresse sur**
2 to speak or write to: *I shall address my remarks to you only.* □ **adresser à**
■ [ə'dres] *noun* **1** the name of the house, street, town *etc* where a person lives: *Her address is 30 Main St., Edinburgh.* □ **adresse**
2 a speech: *He made a long and boring address.* □ **discours**
,addres'see [ad-] *noun* the person to whom a letter *etc* is addressed. □ **destinataire**
adept [ə'dept] *adjective* highly skilled: *She's very adept at keeping her balance.* □ **expert (à/en)**
■ ['adept] *noun* an expert. □ **expert, erte**
adequate ['adikwət] *adjective* sufficient; enough: *He does not earn a large salary but it is adequate for his needs.* □ **suffisant**
'**adequately** *adverb*. □ **suffisamment**
'**adequacy** *noun*. □ **justesse**
adhere [əd'hiə] *verb* **1** (*often with* **to**) to stick (to): *This tape doesn't adhere (to the floor) very well.* □ **coller à**
2 (*with* **to**) to remain loyal (to): *I'm adhering to my principles.* □ **adhérer à**
ad'herence *noun*. □ **adhésion**
ad'herent *noun* a follower; supporter: *an adherent of Marx.* □ **partisan, ane**
adhesion [əd'hiːʒən] *noun* the act or quality of adhering (to). □ **adhérence, adhésion**
ad'hesive [-siv] *adjective* able to adhere; sticky: *adhesive tape.* □ **adhésif**
■ *noun* a substance which makes things stick: *The tiles would not stick as he was using the wrong adhesive.* □ **adhésif**
adjacent [ə'dʒeisənt] *adjective* (*often with* **to**) lying next (to): *We had adjacent rooms in the hotel; They have bought the house adjacent to mine.* □ **adjacent**
adjective ['adʒiktiv] *noun* a word which describes a noun: *a red flower; air which is cool.* □ **adjectif**
,**adjec'tival** [-'tai-] *adjective*. □ **adjectival**
adjoin [ə'dʒoin] *verb* to be next to or joined to: *Her house adjoins the hotel.* □ **toucher (à)**
adjourn [ə'dʒəːn] *verb* to stop (a meeting *etc*), intend-

ing to continue it at another time or place: *We shall adjourn (the meeting) until Wednesday.* □ **ajourner (à)**
a'djournment *noun*. □ **ajournement**
adjudicate [ə'dʒuːdikeit] *verb* to act as a judge (in an artistic competition *etc*). □ **juger**
a,djudi'cation *noun*. □ **décision**
a'djudicator *noun*. □ **juge**
adjust [ə'dʒʌst] *verb* **1** (*often with* **to**) to change so as to make or be better suited: *He soon adjusted to his new way of life.* □ **ajuster (à)**
2 to change (the position of, setting of): *Adjust the setting of the alarm clock.* □ **régler**
a'djustable *adjective* able to be adjusted: *This car has adjustable seats.* □ **réglable**
a'djustment *noun*. □ **réglage**
administer [əd'ministə] *verb* **1** to govern or manage: *She administers the finances of the company.* □ **gérer**
2 to carry out (the law *etc*). □ **appliquer**
3 to give (medicine, help *etc*): *The doctor administered drugs to the patient.* □ **administrer**
ad'ministrate [-streit] *verb* to govern or manage. □ **administrer**
ad,mini'stration *noun* **1** management: *She's in charge of administration at the hospital.* □ **administration**
2 (the people who carry on) the government of a country *etc*. □ **gouvernement**
administrative [-streitiv] *adjective*: *an administrative post; administrative ability.* □ **administratif**
ad'ministrator [-strei-] *noun*. □ **administrateur, trice**
admirable *see* **admire.**
admiral ['admərəl] *noun* (*with capital in titles*) the commander of a navy. □ **amiral, ale**
admire [əd'maiə] *verb* **1** to look at with great pleasure and often to express this pleasure: *I've just been admiring your new car.* □ **admirer**
2 to have a very high opinion of (something or someone): *I admire John's courage.* □ **admirer**
'**admirable** ['admə-] *adjective* extremely good: *His behaviour during the riot was admirable.* □ **admirable**
'**admirably** ['admə-] *adverb* extremely well: *She's admirably suited to the job.* □ **admirablement**
admiration [admi'reiʃən] *noun*: *They were filled with admiration at the team's performance.* □ **admiration**
ad'mirer *noun* **1** one who admires (someone or something): *He is an admirer of Mozart.* □ **admirateur, trice**
2 a man who is attracted by a particular woman: *She has many admirers.* □ **admirateur**
ad'miring *adjective*: *an admiring glance.* □ **admirateur**
ad'miringly *adverb*. □ **admirativement**
admission *see* **admit.**
admit [əd'mit] – *past tense, past participle* **ad'mitted** – *verb* **1** to allow to enter: *This ticket admits one person.* □ **laisser entrer**
2 to say that one accepts as true: *He admitted (that) he was wrong.* □ **admettre**
ad'missible [-səbl] *adjective* allowable: *admissible evidence.* □ **acceptable**
ad'mission [-ʃən] *noun* **1** being allowed to enter; entry: *They charge a high price for admission.* □ **entrée**
2 (an) act of accepting the truth of (something): *an ad-*

mission of guilt. □ **aveu**

ad'mittance *noun* the right or permission to enter: *The notice said 'No admittance'.* □ **entrée**

ad'mittedly *adverb* as is generally accepted: *Admittedly, she is not well.* □ **de l'aveu général**

admonish [əd'mɔniʃ] *verb* to scold or rebuke: *The judge admonished the young man for fighting in the street.* □ **réprimander**

,**admo'nition** [ad-] *noun.* □ **réprimande**

adolescent [adə'lesnt] *adjective* in the stage between childhood and adulthood. □ **adolescent**

■ *noun* a person at this stage of life: *Adolescents often quarrel with their parents.* □ **adolescent, ente**

,**ado'lescence** *noun.* □ **adolescence**

adopt [ə'dɔpt] *verb* 1 to take (a child of other parents) as one's own: *Since they had no children of their own they decided to adopt a little girl.* □ **adopter**

2 to take (something) as one's own: *After going to France she adopted the French way of life.* □ **adopter**

a'**doption** [-ʃən] *noun.* □ **adoption**

a'**doptive** [-tiv] *adjective: her adoptive father.* □ **adoptif**

adore [ə'dɔː] *verb* 1 to love or like very much: *He adores his children.* □ **adorer**

2 to worship. □ **adorer**

a'**dorable** *adjective: an adorable little baby.* □ **adorable**

a'**dorably** *adverb.* □ **adorablement**

,**ado'ration** [adə-] *noun* worship or great love. □ **adoration**

a'**doring** *adjective: adoring parents.* □ **rempli d'adoration**

a'**doringly** *adverb.* □ **avec adoration**

adorn [ə'dɔːn] *verb* to make beautiful, with decorations *etc: Their house is adorned with beautiful antique ornaments.* □ **orner**

a'**dornment** *noun.* □ **ornement**

adrift [ə'drift] *adjective, adverb* drifting: *adrift on the open sea.* □ **à la dérive**

adroit [ə'droit] *adjective* skilful: *her adroit handling of the boat.* □ **adroit**

a'**droitly** *adverb.* □ **adroitement**

a'**droitness** *noun.* □ **adresse**

adulation [adju'leiʃən] *noun* foolishly excessive praise: *The teenager's adulation of the pop-group worried her parents.* □ **adulation**

'**adulatory** *adjective.* □ **louangeur**

adult [ə'dʌlt, 'adʌlt] *adjective* 1 fully grown: *an adult gorilla.* □ **adulte**

2 mature: *adult behaviour.* □ **adulte**

■ *noun* a fully grown human being: *That film is suitable only for adults.* □ **adulte**

adultery [ə'dʌltəri] *noun* sexual intercourse between a husband and a woman who is not his wife or between a wife and a man who is not her husband. □ **adultère**

advance [əd'vɑːns] *verb* 1 to move forward: *The army advanced towards the town; Our plans are advancing well; He married the boss's daughter to advance* (= improve) *his chances of promotion.* □ **(faire) avancer**

2 to supply (someone) with (money) on credit: *The bank will advance you $500.* □ **avancer**

■ *noun* 1 moving forward or progressing: *We've halted*

the enemy's advance; *Great advances in medicine have been made in this century.* □ **progrès**

2 a payment made before the normal time: *Can I have an advance on my salary?* □ **avance**

3 (*usually in plural*) an attempt at (*especially* sexual) seduction. □ **avance(s)**

■ *adjective* 1 made *etc* before the necessary or agreed time: *an advance payment.* □ **anticipé**

2 made beforehand: *an advance booking.* □ **à l'avance**

3 sent ahead of the main group or force: *the advance guard.* □ **avant-garde**

advanced *adjective* having made a lot of progress; at a high level: *an advanced computer course; in the advanced stages of the illness.* □ **avancé**

in advance 1 before(hand): *Can you pay me in advance?* □ **d'avance**

2 in front: *I've been sent on in advance (of the main force).* □ **en éclaireur**

advantage [əd'vɑːntidʒ] *noun* 1 (a) gain or benefit: *There are several advantages in being self-employed.* □ **avantage**

2 in tennis, the first point gained after deuce. □ **avantage**

advantageous [advən'teidʒəs] *adjective* having or giving an advantage: *Because of her experience she was in an advantageous position for promotion.* □ **avantageux**

,**advan'tageously** *adverb.* □ **avantageusement**

have an/the advantage (over) to be in a better or more advantageous position (than): *As she already knew French, she had an advantage over the rest of the class.* □ **avoir l'avantage (sur)**

take advantage of to make use of (a situation, person *etc*) in such a way as to benefit oneself: *She took full advantage of all her business opportunities.* □ **profiter de**

advent ['advent] *noun* coming or arrival: *the advent of space travel.* □ **avènement**

adventure [əd'ventʃə] *noun* a bold or exciting undertaking or experience: *He wrote a book about his adventures in the Antarctic.* □ **aventure**

ad'**venturer** *noun* a person who seeks adventure or fortune. □ **aventurier, ière**

ad'**venturous** *adjective* liking or eager for adventure(s). □ **aventureux**

ad'**venturously** *adverb.* □ **aventureusement**

adverb ['advəːb] *noun* a word used before or after a verb, before an adjective or preposition, or with another adverb to show time, manner, place, degree *etc: Yesterday he looked more carefully in the box, and there he found a very small key with a hole right through it.* □ **adverbe**

ad'**verbial** *adjective.* □ **adverbial**

ad'**verbially** *adverb.* □ **adverbialement**

adversary ['advəsəri] – *plural* '**adversaries** – *noun* an opponent; an enemy: *his adversary in the chess match.* □ **adversaire**

adverse ['advəːs] *adjective* unfavourable: *adverse criticism.* □ **défavorable**

'**adversely** *adverb.* □ **défavorablement**

ad'**versity** *noun* misfortune or hardship. □ **adversité**

advert ['advə:t] short for **advertisement**: *I saw your advert in yesterday's newspaper.* □ **annonce**

advertise ['advətaiz] *verb* to make (something) known to the public by any of various methods: *I've advertised (my house) in the newspaper; They advertised on TV for volunteers.* □ **annoncer**
advertisement [əd'və:tismənt, advər'taizmənt] *noun (also* **ad** [ad], **advert** ['advə:t]) a film, newspaper announcement, poster *etc* making something known, *especially* in order to persuade people to buy it: *an advertisement for toothpaste on television; He replied to my advertisement for a private tutor.* □ **réclame**
'**advertiser** *noun* a person who advertises. □ **annonceur, euse**

advice [əd'vais] *noun* suggestions to a person about what he should do: *You must seek legal advice if you want a divorce; Let me give you a piece of advice.* □ **conseil(s)**
advise [əd'vaiz] *verb* **1** to give advice to; to recommend: *My lawyer advises me to buy the house.* □ **conseiller (de)**
2 (*with of*) to inform: *This letter is to advise you of our interest in your proposal.* □ **informer (de)**
ad'visable *adjective* (of actions) wise: *The doctor does not think it advisable for you to drink alcohol.* □ **conseillé**
ad,visa'bility *noun.* □ **opportunité**
ad'viser, ad'visor *noun* a person who advises. □ **conseiller, ère**
ad'visory *adjective* giving advice: *an advisory leaflet; He acted in an advisory capacity.* □ **consultatif**

---

advice is a noun and never used in the plural: *to give advice/a piece of advice/some advice.*
advise is a verb: *She advises us not to go.*

---

advocate ['advəkət] *noun* a supporter, a person who is in favour (of): *an advocate of reform.* □ **défenseur**
■ [-keit] *verb* to recommend: *She advocated increasing the charges.* □ **recommander (de)**
aerial ['eəriəl] *adjective* in or from the air: *aerial photography.* □ **aérien**
aerobatics [eərə'batiks] *noun plural* acrobatics performed by an aircraft or high in the air. □ **acrobatie(s) aérienne(s)**
aerodrome ['eərədroum] *noun* a place (*usually* private or military) where aircraft are kept and from which they fly. □ **aérodrome**
aeronautics [eərə'nɔːtiks] *noun singular* the science or practice of flying: *Aeronautics is a popular science.* □ **aéronautique**
,**aero'nautical** *adjective.* □ **aéronautique**
aerosol ['eərəsol] *noun* a mixture of liquid or solid particles and gas under pressure which is released from a container in the form of a mist: *Many deodorants come in the form of aerosols;* (*also adjective*) *an aerosol spray.* □ **aérosol**
afar [ə'faː] *adverb* from, at or to a distance: *The three wise men came from afar.* □ **loin**
affable ['afəbl] *adjective* pleasant and easy to talk to: *an affable young man.* □ **affable**
'**affably** *adverb.* □ **aimablement**

,**affa'bility** *noun.* □ **affabilité**
affair [ə'feə] *noun* **1** happenings *etc* which are connected with a particular person or thing: *the Suez affair.* □ **affaire**
2 a thing: *The new machine is a weird-looking affair.* □ **chose**
3 (*often in plural*) business; concern(s): *financial affairs; Where I go is entirely my own affair.* □ **affaire(s)**
4 a love relationship: *His wife found out about his affair with another woman.* □ **liaison**
affect [ə'fekt] *verb* **1** to act or have an effect on: *Rain affects the grass; His kidneys have been affected by the disease.* □ **affecter, influer sur**
2 to move the feelings of: *She was deeply affected by the news of his death.* □ **affecter**
affection [ə'fekʃən] *noun* liking or fondness: *I have great affection for her, but she never shows any affection towards me.* □ **affection**
af'fectionate [-nət] *adjective* having or showing affection: *an affectionate child; She is very affectionate towards her mother.* □ **affectueux**
af'fectionately *adverb.* □ **affectueusement**
affiliated [ə'filieitid] *adjective* connected with or joined to (a larger group *etc*) as a member: *an affiliated branch of the union.* □ **affilié**
af,fili'ation *noun* a connection with (an organization *etc*): *What are his political affiliations?* □ **affiliation**
affirm [ə'fə:m] *verb* to state something positively and firmly: *Despite all the policeman's questions the lady continued to affirm that she was innocent.* □ **affirmer**
,**affir'mation** [a-] *noun.* □ **affirmation**
af'firmative [-tiv] *adjective, noun* saying or indicating yes to a question, suggestion *etc*: *He gave an affirmative nod; a reply in the affirmative.* □ **affirmatif**
affix [ə'fiks] *verb* to attach (something) to an object *etc*: *Affix the stamp to the envelope.* □ **apposer**
afflict [ə'flikt] *verb* to give pain or distress to (a person *etc*): *He is continually afflicted by/with headaches.* □ **affliger**
af'fliction [-ʃən] *noun*: *Her deafness is a great affliction to her.* □ **affliction**
affluent ['afluənt] *adjective* wealthy: *She is becoming more and more affluent.* □ **riche**
'**affluence** *noun* wealth. □ **richesse**
afford [ə'fɔːd] *verb* **1** (*usually with* **can, could**) to be able to spend money, time *etc* on or for something: *I can't afford (to buy) a new car.* □ **avoir les moyens (de)**
2 (*usually with* **can, could**) to be able to do (something) without causing oneself trouble, difficulty *etc*: *She can't afford to be rude to her employer no matter how rude she is to her.* □ **pouvoir se permettre (de)**
affront [ə'frʌnt] *noun* an insult, *usually* one made in public: *His remarks were obviously intended as an affront to her.* □ **affront**
■ *verb* to insult or offend: *We were affronted by the offhand way in which they treated us.* □ **offenser**
afloat [ə'flout] *adjective* floating: *We've got the boat afloat at last.* □ **à flot**

afoot [ə'fut] *adjective* in progress or happening: *There is* *a scheme afoot to improve recreational facilities in the area*. □ **en préparation**

aforesaid [ə'fɔːsed] *adjective* said, named *etc* before (*usually* in an earlier part of a document). □ **susdit**

afraid [ə'freid] *adjective* 1 feeling fear or being frightened (of a person, doing *etc*): *The child is not afraid of the dark; She was afraid to go*. □ **effrayé**
2 sorry (to have to say that): *I'm afraid I don't agree with you*. □ **désolé**

Afro- [afrou] (*as part of a word*) African: ,*Afro-A'merican*. □ **Afro-, afro**

after ['ɑːftə] *preposition* 1 later in time or place than: *After the car came a bus*. □ **après**
2 following (*often indicating repetition*): *one thing after another; night after night*. □ **après**
3 behind: *Shut the door after you!* □ **derrière**
4 in search or pursuit of: *She ran after the bus*. □ **après**
5 considering: *After all I've done you'd think he'd thank me; It's sad to fail after all that work*. □ **après**
6 (*in telling the time*) past: *It's a quarter after ten*. □ **(dix heures quinze)**
■ *adverb* later in time or place: *They arrived soon after*. □ **après**
■ *conjunction* later than the time when: *After she died we moved house twice*. □ **après (que)**

'**aftermath** [-mɑθ] *noun* the situation *etc* resulting from an important, *especially* unpleasant, event: *The country is still suffering from the aftermath of the war*. □ **suites**

'**afterthought** *noun* a later thought. □ **pensée après coup**

'**afterwards** *adverb* later or after something else has happened or happens: *He told me afterwards that he had not enjoyed the film*. □ **par la suite**

after all 1 (used when giving a reason for doing something *etc*) taking everything into consideration: *I won't invite him. After all, I don't really know him*. □ **après tout**
2 in spite of everything that has/had happened, been said *etc*: *It turns out he went by plane after all*. □ **en fin de compte**

be after to be looking for something: *What are you after?; The police are after him*. □ **être à la recherche de**

afternoon [ɑːftə'nuːn] *noun* the time between morning and evening: *tomorrow afternoon; She works for us three afternoons a week; Tuesday afternoon*; (*also adjective*) *afternoon tea*. □ **après-midi**

again [ə'gen] *adverb* once more or another time: *He never saw her again; He hit the child again and again; Don't do that again!; He has been abroad but he is home again now*. □ **encore; de nouveau**

against [ə'genst] *preposition* 1 in opposition to: *They fought against the enemy; Dropping litter is against the law* (= illegal). □ **contre**
2 in contrast to: *The trees were black against the evening sky*. □ **sur**
3 touching or in contact with: *She stood with her back against the wall; The rain beat against the window*. □ **contre**
4 in order to protect against: *vaccination against tuber-*

culosis. □ **contre**

age [eidʒ] *noun* 1 the amount of time during which a person or thing has existed: *She went to school at the age of six (years); What age is she?* □ **âge**
2 (*often with capital*) a particular period of time: *This machine was the wonder of the age; the Middle Ages*. □ **époque, âge**
3 the quality of being old: *This wine will improve with age; With the wisdom of age he regretted the mistakes he had made in his youth*. □ **âge**
4 (*usually in plural*) a very long time: *We've been waiting (for) ages for a bus*. □ **éternité**
■ *verb – present participle* '**ag(e)ing** – to (cause to) grow old or look old: *He has aged a lot since I last saw him; His troubles have aged him*. □ **vieillir**

aged *adjective* 1 ['eidʒid] old: *an aged man*. □ **vieux**
2 [eidʒd] of the age of: *a child aged five*. □ **âgé de**

'**ageless** *adjective* never growing old or never looking older: *ageless beauty*. □ **sans âge**

'**age-old** *adjective* done, known *etc* for a very long time: *an age-old custom*. □ **séculaire**

the aged ['eidʒid] old people: *care for the aged*. □ **gens âgés**

(come) of age (to become) old enough to be considered legally an adult. □ **atteindre sa majorité**

agency *see* agent.

agenda [ə'dʒendə] *noun* a list of things to be done, *especially* at a meeting: *What's on the agenda this morning?* □ **ordre du jour**

agent ['eidʒənt] *noun* 1 a person or thing that acts: *detergents and other cleaning agents*. □ **agent, ente**
2 a person who acts for someone in business *etc*: *our agent in London; a theatrical agent*. □ **représentant, ante**
3 (*especially* **secret agent**) a spy: *an agent for the Russians*. □ **agent, ente**

'**agency** – *plural* '**agencies** – *noun* the office or business of an agent: *an advertising agency*. □ **bureau**

by/through the agency of by the action of: *The meeting was arranged through the agency of a friend*. □ **par l'entremise de**

aggravate ['agrəveit] *verb* 1 to make worse: *His bad temper aggravated the situation*. □ **aggraver**
2 to make (someone) angry or impatient: *She was aggravated by the constant questions*. □ **exaspérer**
,**aggra'vation** *noun*. □ **exaspération**

aggregate ['agrigət] *noun* a total: *What is the aggregate of goals from the two football matches?* □ **total**

aggressive [ə'gresiv] *adjective* ready to attack or oppose; quarrelsome: *He's a most aggressive boy – he is always fighting at school*. □ **agressif**
ag'gressively *adverb*. □ **agressivement**
ag'gressiveness *noun*. □ **agressivité**
ag'gression [-ʃən] *noun* (a feeling of) hostility. □ **agression**
ag'gressor *noun* (in a war *etc*) the party which attacks first. □ **agresseur**

aggrieved [ə'griːvd] *adjective* unhappy or hurt because of unjust treatment: *He felt aggrieved at his friend's distrust*. □ **chagriné**

aghast [ə'gɑːst] *adjective* struck with horror: *She was aghast at the mess.* □ **atterré**

agile ['adʒail] *adjective* able to move quickly and easily: *The antelope is very agile.* □ **agile**

a'gility [-'dʒi-] *noun.* □ **agilité**

agitate ['adʒiteit] *verb* **1** to make (someone) excited and anxious: *The news agitated her.* □ **agiter**

2 to try to arouse public feeling and action: *That group is agitating for prison reform.* □ **mener campagne**

3 to shake: *The tree was agitated by the wind.* □ **secouer**

'**agitated** *adjective.* □ **agité**

,**agi'tation** *noun.* □ **agitation**

'**agitator** *noun* a person who tries constantly to stir up public feeling: *a political agitator.* □ **agitateur, trice**

ago [ə'gou] *adverb* at a certain time in the past: *two years ago; Long ago, men lived in caves; How long ago did she leave?* □ **il y a**

agog [ə'gog] *adjective* eager and excited: *We were all agog at the news.* □ **en émoi**

agony ['agəni] – *plural* '**agonies** – *noun* great pain or suffering: *The dying man was in agony; agonies of regret.* □ **agonie; douleur intense**

'**agonized,** '**agonised** *adjective* showing agony: *She had an agonized expression on her face as she lost the match.* □ **d'angoisse**

'**agonizing,** '**agonising** *adjective* causing agony: *an agonizing pain.* □ **atroce**

agonizingly, agonisingly *adverb.* □ **atrocement**

agree [ə'griː] – *past tense, past participle* a'**greed** – *verb* **1** (*often with* **with**) to think or say the same (as): *I agreed with them that we should try again; The newspaper report does not agree with what she told us.* □ **être d'accord avec**

2 to say that one will do or allow something: *He agreed to go; She agreed to our request.* □ **consentir (à)**

3 (*with* **with**) to be good for (*usually* one's health): *Cheese does not agree with me.* □ **réussir à qqn**

4 to be happy and friendly together: *John and his wife don't agree.* □ **bien s'entendre**

a'**greeable** *adjective* pleasant: *She is a most agreeable person.* □ **agréable**

a'**greeably** *adverb.* □ **agréablement**

a'**greement** *noun* **1** the state of agreeing: *We are all in agreement.* □ **accord**

2 a business, political *etc* arrangement, spoken or written: *You have broken our agreement; We have signed an agreement.* □ **accord**

agriculture ['agrikʌltʃə] *noun* (the science of) the cultivation of land: *She is studying agriculture.* □ **agriculture**

,**agri'cultural** *adjective.* □ **agricole**

aground [ə'graund] *adjective, adverb* (of ships) (stuck) on the bed of the sea *etc* in shallow water: *Our boat ran aground.* □ **échoué**

ahead [ə'hed] *adverb* (*often with* **of**) in front; in advance: *He went on ahead of me; We are well ahead (of our rivals).* □ **en avant (de)**

aid [eid] *noun* help: *Rich countries give aid to developing countries; The teacher uses visual aids; He came to my aid when my car broke down.* □ **aide**

■ *verb* to help: *I was aided in my search by the library staff.* □ **aider**

in aid of as a financial help to (a charity *etc*): *The collection is in aid of the blind.* □ **au profit de**

AIDS [eidz] (Acquired Immune Deficiency Syndrome) a life-threatening disease that destroys the ability to fight off infection or disease and is spread through contaminated blood or body fluids: *If you do not practice safe sex you are at risk of getting AIDS.* □ **sida**

ail [eil] *verb* **1** to be ill: *The old lady has been ailing for some time.* □ **souffrir**

2 to trouble: *What ails you?* □ **tracasser**

'**ailment** *noun* an illness, *usually* not serious or dangerous: *Children often have minor ailments.* □ **petits maux**

aim [eim] *verb* **1** (*usually with* **at, for**) to point or direct something at; to try to hit or reach *etc*: *She picked up the rifle and aimed it at the target.* □ **viser**

2 (*with* **to, at**) to plan, intend or to have as one's purpose: *He aims at finishing tomorrow; We aim to please our customers.* □ **viser à**

■ *noun* **1** the act of or skill at aiming: *His aim is excellent.* □ **habileté à viser**

2 what a person intends to do: *My aim is to become prime minister.* □ **ambition**

'**aimless** *adjective* without purpose: *an aimless life.* □ **sans ambition**

'**aimlessly** *adverb.* □ **sans but**

'**aimlessness** *noun.* □ **manque d'ambition**

take aim to aim: *She took aim at the target.* □ **viser**

air [eə] *noun* **1** the mixture of gases we breathe; the atmosphere: *Mountain air is pure.* □ **air**

2 the space above the ground; the sky: *Birds fly through the air.* □ **air(s)**

3 appearance: *The house had an air of neglect.* □ **air**

4 a tune: *She played a simple air on the piano.* □ **air**

■ *verb* **1** to expose to the air in order to dry or make more fresh *etc*: *to air linen.* □ **aérer**

2 to make known: *He loved to air his opinions.* □ **exprimer**

'**airily** *adverb* in a light-hearted manner: *She airily dismissed all objections.* □ **avec désinvolture**

'**airiness** *noun.* □ **désinvolture**

'**airing** *noun* a short walk *etc* in the open air: *He took the baby for an airing.* □ **promenade au grand air**

'**airless** *adjective* **1** (of weather) still and windless: *It was a hot, airless night.* □ **sans air**

2 (of a room *etc*) stuffy and without fresh air. □ **renfermé**

'**airy** *adjective* **1** with plenty of (fresh) air: *an airy room.* □ **bien aéré**

2 light-hearted and not serious: *an airy disregard for authority.* □ **désinvolte**

'**airborne** *adjective* in the air or flying: *We were airborne five minutes after boarding the plane; airborne germs.* □ **en vol, en suspension (dans l'air)**

,**air-con'ditioned** *adjective* having air conditioning: *an air-conditioned building.* □ **climatisé**

,**air con'ditioner** *noun* an apparatus providing air conditioning. □ **climatiseur**

,**air con'ditioning** *noun* a method of providing a room, building *etc* with air of a controlled temperature and humidity. □ **climatisation**

'aircraft – *plural* **'aircraft** – *noun* any of several types of machine for flying in the air: *Enemy aircraft have been sighted.* □ **appareil; avion**

aircraft carrier a ship which carries aircraft and which aircraft can use for landing and taking off. □ **porte-avions**

'airfield *noun* an area of ground (with buildings *etc*) where (*usually* military) aircraft are kept and from which they fly. □ **terrain d'aviation**

air force the part of the armed services which uses aircraft: *the army, navy and air force.* □ **armée de l'air**

'air gun *noun* a gun that is worked by air under pressure. □ **carabine/pistolet à air comprimé**

air hostess a woman who looks after passengers in an aircraft. □ **hôtesse de l'air**

air letter a sheet of light paper that forms its own envelope for sending by airmail. □ **aérogramme**

'airlift *noun* an operation to move cargo or people, carried out by air. □ **pont aérien**

'airline *noun* (a company that owns) a regular air transport service: *Which airline are you travelling by?* □ **compagnie aérienne**

'airliner *noun* a (*usually* large) aircraft for carrying passengers. □ **avion de ligne**

'airlock *noun* a bubble in a pipe which prevents liquid from flowing along it. □ **bouchon d'air**

'airmail *noun* a system of carrying mail by air: *Send this parcel by airmail*; (*also adjective*) *an airmail letter.* □ **poste aérienne**

'airman *noun* a member of an air force. □ **aviateur militaire**

'airport *noun* a place where passenger aircraft arrive and depart, with buildings for customs, waiting-rooms *etc*. □ **aéroport**

'air pump *noun* a pump for forcing air in or out of something. □ **compresseur**

'air raid *noun* an attack by aircraft. □ **raid aérien**

'airship *noun* an aircraft that is lighter than air and can be steered *etc*. □ **dirigeable; aéronef**

'airtight *adjective* (of a container *etc*) into or through which air cannot pass: *an airtight seal on a bottle.* □ **hermétique**

'airway *noun* a regular course followed by aircraft. □ **voie aérienne**

on the air broadcasting (regularly) on radio or television. □ **à l'antenne**

put on airs/give oneself airs to behave as if one is better or more important than others: *She gives herself such airs that everyone dislikes her.* □ **se donner des airs**

airplane ['eərplein] *noun* (*often abbreviated to* **plane**) a machine for flying which is heavier than air and has wings. □ **avion**

aisle [ail] *noun* a passage between rows of seats *etc* in a church, cinema *etc*. □ **allée**

ajar [ə'dʒaː] *adjective* partly open: *The door was ajar when I returned.* □ **entrouvert**

akin [ə'kin] *adjective* (*often with* **to**) similar in nature: *This problem is akin to the one we had last year.* □ **apparenté (à)**

alacrity [ə'lakrəti] *noun* quick and cheerful willingness: *He obeyed with alacrity.* □ **empressement**

alarm [ə'laːm] *noun* **1** sudden fear: *We did not share her alarm at the suggestion.* □ **inquiétude(s)**

2 something that gives warning of danger, attracts attention *etc*: *Sound the alarm!*; *a fire-alarm*; (*also adjective*) *an alarm clock.* □ **alerte, signal d'alarme; réveil (-matin)**

■ *verb* to make (someone) afraid: *The least sound alarms the old lady.* □ **alarmer**

a'larming *adjective* disturbing or causing fear: *alarming news.* □ **alarmant**

a'larmingly *adverb.* □ **de façon alarmante**

alarm clock *noun* a clock set to ring or buzz at a specific time: *Susan's alarm clock woke her at 6:00 a.m.* □ **réveille-matin**

alas! [ə'las] *interjection* used to express grief: *Alas, he died young!* □ **hélas!**

album ['albəm] *noun* **1** a book with blank pages for holding photographs, stamps *etc*. □ **album**

2 a long-playing gramophone record: *I haven't got the group's latest album.* □ **disque, album**

alcohol ['alkəhol] *noun* liquid made by the fermentation or distillation of sugar, present in intoxicating drinks, used also as a fuel, and in thermometers: *I never drink alcohol – I drink orange juice.* □ **alcool**

,alco'holic *adjective* **1** of or containing alcohol: *Is cider alcoholic?* □ **alcoolisé, alcoolique**

2 caused by alcohol: *an alcoholic stupor.* □ **alcoolique, éthylique**

■ *noun* a person who suffers from a dependence on alcohol. □ **alcoolique**

'alcoholism *noun* the condition suffered by an alcoholic. □ **alcoolisme**

alcove ['alkouv] *noun* a small section of a room *etc* formed by part of the wall being set back. □ **alcôve**

ale [eil] *noun* the name given to certain kinds of beer: *one litre of ale.* □ **ale**

alert [ə'ləːt] *adjective* **1** quick-thinking: *She's very old but still very alert.* □ **alerte**

2 (*with* **to**) watchful and aware: *You must be alert to danger.* □ **vigilant, attentif (à)**

■ *noun* a signal to be ready for action. □ **alerte**

■ *verb* to make (someone) alert; to warn: *The sound of gunfire alerted us to our danger.* □ **alerter**

a'lertly *adverb.* □ **prestement**

a'lertness *noun.* □ **promptitude; vigilance**

on the alert on the watch (for): *We were on the alert for any sound that might tell us where he was.* □ **sur le qui-vive**

algae ['aldʒiː] *noun plural* a group of simple plants which includes seaweed. □ **algues**

algebra ['aldʒibrə] *noun* a method of calculating using letters and signs to represent numbers. □ **algèbre**

,alge'braic [-breiik] *adjective.* □ **algébrique**

alias ['eiliəs] *noun* a false name: *What alias did the crook use this time?* □ **faux nom**

■ *adverb* otherwise known as: *John Smith, alias Peter Jones.* □ **alias**

alibi ['alibai] *noun* the fact or a statement that a person accused of a crime was somewhere else when it was committed: *Has she an alibi for the night of the murder?* □ **alibi**

alien ['eiliən] *adjective* foreign: *alien customs.* □ **étranger**
■ *noun* a foreigner: *Aliens are not welcome there.* □ **étranger, ère**

'**alienate** [-neit] *verb* to make someone feel unfriendly to one: *He alienated his wife by his cruelty to her.* □ **s'aliéner**
,alie'**nation** *noun.* □ **aliénation, désaffection**

alight[1] [ə'lait] – *past tense, past participle* a'**lighted** – *verb* 1 to get down from or out of: *to alight from a bus.* □ **descendre (de)**
2 (*with* on) to settle or land on: *The bird alighted on the fence.* □ **se poser sur**

alight[2] [ə'lait] *adjective* burning; very bright: *The bonfire was still alight*; *His eyes were alight with joy.* □ **embrasé, allumé**

align [ə'lain] *verb* 1 to put in a straight line or in parallel lines. □ **aligner**
2 to attach (oneself) to one side in an argument, politics *etc*: *She aligned herself with the rebels.* □ **s'aligner (sur)**

alike [ə'laik] *adjective* like one another; similar: *Twins are often very alike.* □ **semblable**
■ *adverb* in the same way: *He treated all his children alike.* □ **pareillement**

alimentary [ali'mentəri]: **alimentary canal** the passage for the digestion of food in animals, including the gullet, stomach and intestines. □ **alimentaire, tube digestif**

alive [ə'laiv] *adjective* 1 living and not dead: *My grandmother was still alive in 1900.* □ **vivant**
2 full of activity: *The town was alive with policemen on the day of the march.* □ **grouillant de**
alive to aware of: *She was alive to the dangers of the situation.* □ **conscient de**

alkali ['alkəlai] *noun* a substance, the opposite of acid, such as soda. □ **alcali**
'**alkaline** [-lain] *adjective.* □ **alcalin**

all [ɔːl] *adjective, pronoun* 1 the whole (of): *He ate all the cake*; *She has spent all of her money.* □ **tout**
2 every one (of a group) when taken together: *They were all present*; *All men are equal.* □ **tous**
■ *adverb* 1 entirely: *all alone*; *dressed all in white.* □ **tout**
2 (*with* the) much; even: *Your low pay is all the more reason to find a new job*; *I feel all the better for a shower.* □ **d'autant plus/mieux**

'**all around** *adjective* 1 including or applying to every part, person, thing *etc*: *an all around pay rise.* □ **général**
2 good at all parts of a subject *etc*: *an all around sportsman.* □ **complet**

,**all-'clear** *noun* (*usually with* the) a signal or formal statement that a time of danger *etc* is over: *They sounded the all-clear after the air raid.* □ **fin d'alerte**

'**all-out** *adjective* using the greatest effort possible: *an all-out attempt.* □ **maximum, suprême**

,**all-'rounder** *noun* a person who is good at many kinds of work, sport *etc*. □ **bonne en tout**

all along the whole time (that something was happening): *I knew the answer all along.* □ **depuis le début**

all at once 1 all at the same time: *Don't eat those cakes all at once!* □ **d'un seul coup**
2 suddenly: *All at once the light went out.* □ **tout à coup**
all in with everything included: *Is that the price all in?* □ **tout compris**
all in all considering everything: *We haven't done badly, all in all.* □ **à tout prendre**
all over 1 over the whole of (a person, thing *etc*): *My car is dirty all over.* □ **d'un bout à l'autre**
2 finished: *The excitement's all over now.* □ **terminé**
3 everywhere: *We've been looking all over for you!* □ **partout**
all right 1 unhurt; not ill or in difficulties *etc*: *You look ill. Are you all right?* □ **très bien**
2 an expression of agreement to do something: *'Will you come?' 'Oh, all right.'* □ **d'accord!**
in all in total, when everything is added up: *I spent three hours in all waiting for buses last week.* □ **en tout**

Write **all right** (not **alright**).

all the more so especially since; to a greater degree: *The movie was sad and all the more so because it was a true story.* □ **d'autant plus que**

allay [ə'lei] *verb* to make less: *She allayed his fears.* □ **modérer**

allege [ə'ledʒ] *verb* to say, *especially* in making a legal statement, without giving proof: *He alleged that I had been with the accused on the night of the murder.* □ **alléguer, prétendre**
allegation [ali'geiʃən] *noun.* □ **allégation**

allegiance [ə'liːdʒəns] *noun* loyalty to a person, group, idea *etc*: *I have no allegiance to any political party.* □ **fidélité**

allergy ['alədʒi] – *plural* '**allergies** – *noun* an unusual sensitiveness of the body which causes certain people to be affected in a bad way by something *usually* harmless: *The rash on her face is caused by an allergy to grass.* □ **allergie**
allergic [-'ləː-] *adjective* (*with* to) affected in a bad way by (certain) things: *She is allergic to certain flowers.* □ **allergique**

alleviate [ə'liːvieit] *verb* to make an improvement by lessening (pain *etc*): *The drugs will alleviate the pain.* □ **soulager**
al,levi'ation *noun.* □ **soulagement**

alley ['ali] *noun* 1 (*often* '**alleyway**) a narrow street in a city *etc* (*usually* not wide enough for vehicles). □ **ruelle**
2 a long narrow area used for the games of bowling or skittles: *a bowling alley.* □ **allée**

alliance, allied *see* **ally.**

alligator ['aligeitə] *noun* a kind of large reptile closely related to the crocodile, found mainly in the rivers of the warmer parts of America. □ **alligator**

allocate ['aləkeit] *verb* 1 to give (to someone) for his own use: *She allocated a room to each student.* □ **allouer (à)**
2 to set apart (for a particular purpose): *They allocated $500 to the project.* □ **affecter (à)**
,**allo'cation** *noun.* □ **allocation**

allot [ə'lot] – *past tense, past participle* al'**lotted** – *verb* to give (each person) a fixed share of or place in (something): *They have allotted all the money to the various people who applied.* □ **attribuer**

al'lotment *noun* a small part of a larger piece of public ground rented to a person to grow vegetables *etc.* □ **parcelle**

allow [ə'lau] *verb* 1 not to forbid or prevent: *She allowed me to enter; Playing football in the street is not allowed.* □ **permettre**

2 (*with* **for**) to take into consideration when judging or deciding: *These figures allow for price rises.* □ **tenir compte de**

3 to give, *especially* for a particular purpose or regularly: *His mother allows him too much money.* □ **donner, allouer**

al'lowance *noun* 1 a fixed sum or quantity given regularly: *His mother made him an allowance of $20 a month.* □ **allocation**

2 something (*usually* a quantity) allowed: *This dress pattern has a seam allowance of 1 cm.* □ **marge**

make allowance for to take into consideration when deciding *etc*: *We've made allowance for the fact that everyone has different tastes.* □ **tenir compte de**

alloy ['aloi] *noun* a mixture of two or more metals. □ **alliage**

allude [ə'luːd] *verb* (*with* **to**) to mention: *He did not allude to the remarks made by the previous speaker.* □ **faire allusion (à)**

al'lusion [-ʒən] *noun* (the act of making) a mention or reference: *The prime minister made no allusion to the war in his speech.* □ **allusion**

alluring [ə'ljuəriŋ] *adjective* attractive, tempting. □ **séduisant**

allusion *see* **allude.**

ally [ə'lai] *verb* to join by political agreement, marriage, friendship *etc*: *Small countries must ally themselves with larger countries in order to survive.* □ **s'allier (à, avec)**

■ ['alai] *noun* a state, person *etc* allied with another: *The two countries were allies at that time.* □ **allié(e)**

al'liance *noun*: *the alliance between Britain and France; The three countries entered into an alliance.* □ **alliance**

'allied ['a-] *adjective* 1 joined by political agreement or treaty: *The allied forces entered the country.* □ **allié**

2 (*with* **with**) joined together with; joined to: *Her beauty allied with her intelligence made her a successful model.* □ **joint à**

3 (*with* **to**) related to; resembling: *The ape is closely allied to man.* □ **proche parent de**

almanac ['ɔːlmənak] *noun* a calendar *usually* with information about the phases of the moon *etc*. □ **almanach**

almighty [ɔːl'maiti] *adjective* having complete power; very great: *almighty God.* □ **tout-puissant**

almond ['aːmənd] *noun* 1 (*also* **almond tree**) a kind of tree related to the peach. □ **amandier**

2 the kernel of its fruit: *The cake had raisins and almonds in it.* □ **amande**

almost ['ɔːlmoust] *adverb* nearly but not quite: *She is almost five years old; She almost fell under a moving car.* □ **presque, quasiment**

alms [aːmz] *noun plural* money *etc* given to the poor. □

aumône

aloft [ə'loft] *adverb* high up; overhead: *He held the banner aloft.* □ **en l'air**

alone [ə'loun] *adverb* 1 with no one else; by oneself: *She lived alone; She is alone in believing that he is innocent.* □ **seul**

2 only: *He alone can remember.* □ **seul**

all alone completely by oneself: *He has been all alone since the death of his wife.* □ **tout seul**

along [ə'loŋ] *preposition* 1 from one end to the other: *He walked along several streets; The wall runs along the river.* □ **le long de**

2 at a point at the end or on the length of: *There's a post-box somewhere along this street.* □ **quelque part**

■ *adverb* 1 onwards or forward: *She ran along beside me; Come along, please!* □ **en avant (avec)**

2 to the place mentioned: *I'll come along in five minutes.* □ **ici, là**

3 in company, together: *I took a friend along with me.* □ **avec**

a,long'side *preposition, adverb* beside or close to (the side of a ship, a pier *etc*): *She berthed alongside her friend's boat.* □ **le long de**

aloof [ə'luːf] *adverb* apart or at a distance from other people: *I kept aloof from the whole business.* □ **à l'écart (de)**

■ *adjective* not sociable and friendly: *People find the new teacher rather aloof.* □ **distant**

a'loofness *noun*. □ **réserve**

aloud [ə'laud] *adverb* so as can be heard: *She read the letter aloud.* □ **à haute voix**

alphabet ['alfəbit] *noun* the letters of a written language arranged in order: *I have learned all the letters of the Greek alphabet.* □ **alphabet**

,alpha'betical [-'be-] *adjective: in alphabetical order.* □ **alphabétique**

,alpha'betically *adverb*. □ **alphabétiquement**

alpine ['alpain] *adjective* of the Alps or other high mountains: *alpine flowers.* □ **alpin; alpestre**

already [ɔːl'redi] *adverb* 1 before a particular time; previously: *I had already gone when Mary arrived; I don't want that book – I've read it already.* □ **déjà**

2 before the expected time: *Are you leaving already?; He hasn't gone already, has he?* □ **déjà**

also ['ɔːlsou] *adverb* in addition or besides; too: *He is studying German but he is also studying French; They know him and I know him also.* □ **aussi**

altar ['ɔːltə] *noun* 1 in some Christian churches the table on which the bread and wine are consecrated during the celebration of communion: *The bride and groom stood before the priest at the altar.* □ **autel**

2 a table *etc* on which offerings are made to a god. □ **autel**

alter ['ɔːltə] *verb* to make or become different; to change: *Will you alter this dress (to fit me)?; The town has altered a lot in the last two years.* □ **modifier, changer**

,alte'ration *noun: The alterations he has made to the play have not improved it.* □ **modification**

alternate ['ɔːltəneit] *verb* to use, do *etc* by turns, repeatedly, one after the other: *Lucy alternates between* *teaching and studying; He tried to alternate red and yellow tulips along the path as he planted them.* □ **(faire) alterner**

■ [ˈɔːltəːnət] *adjective* 1 coming, happening *etc* in turns, one after the other: *The water came in alternate bursts of hot and cold.* □ **alterné**

2 every second (day, week *etc*): *My friend and I take the children to school on alternate days.* □ **tous les deux**

al'ternately [-ˈtəːnət-] *adverb*: *She felt alternately hot and cold.* □ **tour à tour**

alter'nation *noun*. □ **alternance**

alternative [ɔːlˈtəːnətiv] *adjective* offering a choice of a second possibility: *An alternative arrangement can be made if my plans don't suit you.* □ **autre**

■ *noun* a choice between two (or sometimes more) things or possibilities: *You leave me no alternative but to dismiss you; I don't like fish. Is there an alternative on the menu?* □ **alternative**

al'ternatively *adverb*. □ **sinon, ou bien**

although [ɔːlˈðou] *conjunction* in spite of the fact that: *Although he hurried, the shop was closed when he got there.* □ **bien que; quoique, toutefois**

---

although should not be followed by but: *Although she is poor, she is honest* (not *Although she is poor but she is honest*).

---

altitude [ˈaltitjuːd] *noun* height above sea-level: *What is the altitude of the town?* □ **altitude**

alto [ˈaltou] – *plural* 'altos – *noun* (a singer having) the highest male singing voice, above tenor. □ **alto**

altogether [ɔːltəˈgeðə] *adverb* 1 completely: *I'm not altogether satisfied.* □ **entièrement**

2 on the whole and considering everything: *I'm wet, I'm tired and I'm cold. Altogether I'm not feeling very cheerful.* □ **dans l'ensemble**

aluminum [əˈluːminəm] *noun, adjective* (of) an element, a light, silver-coloured metal used in making saucepans *etc: pans made of aluminum; aluminum foil, rivet, tray.* □ **aluminium**

always [ˈɔːlweiz] *adverb* 1 at all times: *I always work hard; I'll always remember her.* □ **toujours**

2 continually or repeatedly: *He is always making mistakes.* □ **constamment, sans arrêt**

am *see* **be**.

amass [əˈmas] *verb* to gather or collect in a large quantity: *She amassed an enormous quantity of information.* □ **accumuler**

amateur [ˈamətə, -tʃər] *noun* 1 a person who takes part in a sport *etc* without being paid for it: *The tennis tournament was open only to amateurs.* □ **amateur, trice**

2 someone who does something for the love of it and not for money: *For an amateur, she was quite a good photographer.* □ **amateur**

■ *adjective: an amateur golfer; amateur photography.* □ **amateur**

,ama'teurish [-ˈtəː-] *adjective* not very skilful: *an amateurish drawing.* □ **d'amateur**

amaze [əˈmeiz] *verb* to surprise greatly: *I was amazed at his stupidity.* □ **stupéfier**

a'mazement *noun* great surprise: *To my amazement, he had never heard of her.* □ **stupéfaction**

a'mazing *adjective: an amazing sight.* □ **stupéfiant, renversant**

a'mazingly *adverb*. □ **étonnamment**

ambassador [amˈbasədə] – *feminine* am'bassadress – *noun* the government minister appointed to act for his government in another country: *the Canadian Ambassador to Italy.* □ **ambassadeur, drice**

am,bassa'dorial [-ˈdoː-] *adjective*. □ **d'ambassadeur**

amber [ˈambə] *noun, adjective* (of) a hard yellow or brownish substance, formed from resin, used in making jewellery *etc: made of amber; an amber brooch.* □ **(d')ambre**

ambiguous [amˈbigjuəs] *adjective* having more than one possible meaning: *After the cat caught the mouse, it died is an ambiguous statement* (ie it is not clear whether *it* = the cat or = the mouse). □ **ambigu**

am'biguously *adverb*. □ **de façon ambiguë**

,ambi'guity [-ˈgjuː-] *noun*. □ **ambiguïté**

ambition [amˈbiʃən] *noun* 1 the desire for success, fame, power *etc: He is full of ambition and energy.* □ **ambition**

2 the desire eventually to become or do something special: *Her ambition is to be Prime Minister.* □ **ambition**

am'bitious *adjective: She is very ambitious; That plan is too ambitious.* □ **ambitieux**

am'bitiously *adverb*. □ **ambitieusement**

am'bitiousness *noun*. □ **ambition**

amble [ˈambl] *verb* to walk without hurrying: *We were ambling along enjoying the scenery.* □ **marcher tranquillement**

ambulance [ˈambjuləns] *noun* a vehicle for carrying the sick and injured to hospital *etc: Call an ambulance – this man is very ill!* □ **ambulance**

---

ambulance ends in -ance (not -ence).

---

ambush [ˈambuʃ] *verb* to wait in hiding for and make a surprise attack on: *They planned to ambush the enemy as they marched towards the capital.* □ **tendre une embuscade à**

■ *noun* 1 an attack made in this way. □ **embuscade**

2 the group of people making the attack. □ **(troupes) embusquées**

amend [əˈmend] *verb* to correct or improve: *We shall amend the error as soon as possible.* □ **corriger**

make amends to do something to improve the situation after doing something wrong, stupid *etc: He gave her a present to make amends for his rudeness.* □ **réparer, racheter**

amenity [əˈmiːnəti] – *plural* a'menities – *noun* something that makes life more pleasant or convenient: *This part of town has a lot of amenities – good shops, parks etc.* □ **commodités**

American [əˈmeəikan] *adjective* of the United States of America or its inhabitants: *American dollars are all green in colour.* □ **américain, aine**

■ *noun* someone who is a citizen of the United States of America: *Pete is an American, born in Boston.* □ **Américain, aine**

amiable [ˈeimiəbl] *adjective* likeable; pleasant and good-

tempered. □ **aimable**
,amia'bility *noun*. □ **gentillesse**
'amiably *adverb*. □ **aimablement**
amicable ['amikǝbl] *adjective* friendly: *The dispute was finally settled in a very amicable manner*. □ **amical**
'amicably *adverb*. □ **à l'amiable**
amid, amidst [ǝ'mid(st)] *preposition* in the middle of; among: *Amid all the confusion, the real point of the meeting was lost*; *amidst the shadows*. □ **dans; parmi**
amiss [ǝ'mis] *adjective* wrong: *Their plans went amiss*. □ **de travers**
ammo ['amou] *short for* **ammunition**.
ammonia [ǝ'mouniǝ] *noun* 1 a strong-smelling gas made of hydrogen and nitrogen. □ **ammoniac**
2 a solution of this gas in water, used for cleaning *etc*. □ **ammoniaque**
ammunition [amju'niʃǝn] *noun* things used in the firing of a gun *etc* (*eg* bullets, gunpowder, shells): *How long will the soldiers' ammunition last?* □ **munitions**
amnesia [am'niːziǝ] *noun* loss of memory: *After falling on his head he suffered from amnesia*. □ **amnésie**
amnesty ['amnǝsti] – *plural* **'amnesties** – *noun* a general pardon given to people who have done wrong *especially* against the government: *The murderer was released under the amnesty declared by the new president*. □ **amnistie**
amok [ǝ'mok], **amuck** [ǝ'mʌk]: **run amok/amuck** to rush about madly, attacking everybody and everything: *The prisoner ran amok and killed two prison officers*. □ **devenir fou furieux**
among, amongst [ǝ'mʌŋ(st)] *preposition* 1 in the middle of: *a house among the trees*. □ **parmi**
2 in shares or parts to each person (in a group *etc*): *Divide the chocolate amongst you*. □ **entre**

see also **between**.

amount [ǝ'maunt] *verb* (*with* to) 1 to add up to: *The bill amounted to $15*. □ **se monter à**
2 to be equal to: *Borrowing money and not returning it amounts to stealing*. □ **revenir à, équivaloir**
■ *noun* a quantity, *especially* of money: *a large amount of money in the bank*. □ **somme**
ampere ['ampeǝ] *noun* (*also* **amp** [amp]) (*often abbreviated to* **A** *when written*) the unit by which an electric current is measured. □ **ampère**
amphibian [am'fibiǝn] *noun* 1 a creature that spends part of its life on land and part in water: *Frogs are amphibians*. □ **amphibie**
2 a vehicle designed to move on land or in the water. □ **véhicule amphibie**
3 an aircraft designed to fly from land or water. □ **avion amphibie**
am'phibious *adjective*. □ **amphibie**
amphitheatre, amphitheater ['amfiθiǝtǝ] *noun* an oval or circular building with rows of seats surrounding a central space, used as a theatre or arena. □ **amphithéâtre**
ample ['ampl] *adjective* (more than) enough: *There is ample space for four people*. □ **largement assez (de)**
'amply *adverb*. □ **amplement**
amplify ['amplifai] *verb* 1 to make larger, *especially* by

adding details to. □ **développer**
2 to make (the sound from a radio, record player *etc*) louder by using an amplifier. □ **amplifier**
,amplifi'cation [-fi-] *noun*. □ **amplification**
'amplifier *noun* a piece of equipment for increasing the strength or power-level of electric currents *especially* so as to increase loudness: *You need a new amplifier for your stereo equipment*. □ **amplificateur**
amputate ['ampjuteit] *verb* (of a surgeon *etc*) to cut off (an arm or leg *etc*): *They are going to have to amputate (her left leg)*. □ **amputer**
,ampu'tation *noun*. □ **amputation**
amuse [ǝ'mjuːz] *verb* 1 to make (someone) laugh: *I was amused at the monkey's antics*. □ **amuser**
2 to interest or give pleasure to (for a time): *They amused themselves playing cards*. □ **(s')amuser**
a'musement *noun* 1 the state of being amused or of finding something funny: *a smile of amusement*. □ **amusement**
2 an entertainment or interest: *surfing and other holiday amusements*. □ **distraction**
a'musing *adjective* rather funny or humorous: *an amusing story*. □ **amusant**
a'musingly *adverb*. □ **d'une manière amusante**
an *see* **a**.
anaesthetic, anesthetic [anǝs'θetik] *noun* a substance, used in surgery *etc*, that causes lack of feeling in a part of the body or unconsciousness. □ **anesthésique**
,anaes'thesia [-'θiːziǝ, -ʒǝ] *noun* loss of consciousness or of feeling caused by an anaesthetic. □ **anesthésie**
anaesthetist [ǝ'niːsθǝtist, ǝ'nes-] *noun* the doctor responsible for giving an anaesthetic to the patient during a surgical operation. □ **anesthésiste**
anaesthetize, anaesthetise [ǝ'niːsθǝtaiz, ǝ'nes-] *verb* to make (someone) unable to feel pain *etc* (by giving an anaesthetic to). □ **anesthésier**
analysis [ǝ'nalǝsis] – *plural* **a'nalyses** [-siːz] – *noun* 1 (a) detailed examination of something (a sentence, a chemical compound *etc*) *especially* by breaking it up into the parts of which it is made up: *The chemist is making an analysis of the poison*; *close analysis of the situation*. □ **analyse**
2 psychoanalysis: *He is undergoing analysis for his emotional problems*. □ **psychanalyse**
analyze, analyse ['analaiz] *verb* to examine the nature of (something) *especially* by breaking up (a whole) into parts: *The doctor analyzed the blood sample*. □ **analyser**
analyst ['analist] *noun* 1 a person who analyzes: *a chemical analyst*. □ **analyste**
2 a psychiatrist. □ **(psych)analyste**
analytical [anǝ'litikl] *adjective*. □ **analytique**
anarchy ['anǝki] *noun* 1 the absence or failure of government: *Total anarchy followed the defeat of the government*. □ **anarchie**
2 disorder and confusion. □ **anarchie**
'anarchist *noun* 1 a person who believes that governments are unnecessary or undesirable. □ **anarchiste**
2 a person who tries to overturn the government by vio-

lence. □ **anarchiste**
'**anarchism** *noun*. □ **anarchisme**
anatomy [ə'natəmi] *noun* the science of the structure of the (*usually* human) body, *especially* the study of the body by cutting up dead animal and human bodies. □ **anatomie**
anatomical [anə'tomikl] *adjective*. □ **anatomique**
,**ana'tomically** *adverb*. □ **anatomiquement**
a'**natomist** *noun* a person who specializes in anatomy. □ **anatomiste**
ancestor ['ansestə] – *feminine* '**ancestress** – *noun* a person who was a member of one's family a long time ago and from whom one is descended. □ **ancêtre**
an'**cestral** [-'ses-] *adjective*. □ **ancestral**
'**ancestry** – *plural* '**ancestries** – *noun* a line of ancestors coming down to one's parents: *She is of noble ancestry*. □ **ascendance**
anchor ['aŋkə] *noun* 1 something, *usually* a heavy piece of metal with points which dig into the sea-bed, used to hold a boat in one position. □ **ancre**
2 something that holds someone or something steady. □ **attache**
■ *verb* to hold (a boat *etc*) steady (with an anchor): *They have anchored (the boat) near the shore*; *He used a stone to anchor his papers*. □ **ancrer**
'**anchorage** [-ridʒ] *noun* a place which is safe, or used, for anchoring boats: *a sheltered anchorage*. □ **mouillage**
at anchor (of a ship) anchored: *The ship lay at anchor in the bay*. □ **à l'ancre**
ancient ['einʃənt] *adjective* 1 relating to times long ago, *especially* before the collapse of Rome: *ancient history*. □ **ancien**
2 very old: *an ancient sweater*. □ **très vieux**
and [and, ənd] *conjunction* 1 joining two statements, pieces of information *etc*: *I opened the door and went inside*; *The hat was blue and red*; *a mother and child*. □ **et**
2 in addition to: *2 and 2 makes 4*. □ **et; plus**
3 as a result of which: *Try harder and you will succeed*. □ **et**
4 used instead of 'to' with a verb: *Do try and come!* □ **de**
anecdote ['anikdout] *noun* a short amusing story, *especially* a true one: *She told us anecdotes about politicians that she knew*. □ **anecdote**
anemia [ə'niːmiə] *noun* a medical condition caused by not having enough red cells in the blood. □ **anémie**
a'**nemic** *adjective* suffering from anemia. □ **anémique**
anesthetic *see* **anaesthetic**.
angel ['eindʒəl] *noun* 1 a messenger or attendant of God: *The angels announced the birth of Christ to the shepherds*. □ **ange**
2 a very good or beautiful person: *She's an absolute angel about helping us*. □ **ange**
angelic [an'dʒelik] *adjective* like an angel. □ **angélique**
an'**gelically** *adverb*. □ **angéliquement**
'**angel-fish** *noun* a brightly-coloured tropical fish with spiny fin. □ **chétodon**
anger ['aŋgə] *noun* a violent, bitter feeling (against some-

one or something): *She was filled with anger about the way she had been treated*. □ **colère**
■ *verb* to make someone angry: *His words angered her very much*. □ **mettre en colère**
'**angry** *adjective* 1 feeling or showing anger: *He was so angry that he was unable to speak*; *angry words*; *She is angry with him*; *The sky looks angry – it is going to rain*. □ **en colère**
2 red and sore-looking: *He has an angry cut over his left eye*. □ **irrité**
'**angrily** *adverb*. □ **avec colère**

---

angry at something: *We were angry at the delay.*
angry with someone: *He is angry with his sister.*

---

angle[1] ['aŋgl] *noun* 1 the (amount of) space between two straight lines or surfaces that meet: *an angle of 90°*. □ **angle**
2 a point of view: *from a journalist's angle*. □ **point de vue**
3 a corner. □ **coin**
angular ['aŋgjulə] *adjective* 1 having (sharp) angles: *an angular building*. □ **anguleux**
2 (of a person) thin and bony: *She is tall and angular*. □ **osseux**
angularity [-'la-] *noun*. □ **angularité**
angle[2] ['aŋgl] *verb* to use a rod and line to try to catch fish: *angling for trout*. □ **pêcher (à la ligne)**
'**angler** *noun* a person who fishes with a rod and line. □ **pêcheur, euse (à la ligne)**
'**angling** *noun*. □ **pêche à la ligne**
Anglican ['aŋglikən] *noun, adjective* (a member) of the Church of England. □ **anglican, ane**
anglicize, anglicise ['aŋglisaiz] *verb* to make English or more like English: *After living in England for ten years, he had become very anglicized*. □ **angliciser**
Anglo- [aŋglou] (*as part of a word*) English: *Anglo-American*. □ **anglo-**
angry *see* **anger**.
angsana [aŋ'saːnə] *noun* a large tropical tree with sweet-smelling yellow flowers. □ **angsana**
anguish ['aŋgwiʃ] *noun* very great pain of body or mind; agony: *The woman suffered terrible anguish when her child died*. □ **angoisse**
angular, angularity *see* **angle**[1].
animal ['animəl] *noun* 1 a living being which can feel things and move freely: *man and other animals*. □ **animal**
2 an animal other than man: *a book on man's attitude to animals*; (*also adjective*) *animal behaviour*. □ **animal**
animal eater an animal that eats only other animals: *Tigers and lions are animal eaters*. □ **carnivore**
animate ['animeit] *verb* to make lively: *Joy animated his face*. □ **animer**
■ [-mət] *adjective* living. □ **vivant**
'**animated** [-mei-] *adjective* 1 lively: *An animated discussion*. □ **animé**
2 made to move as if alive: *animated dolls/cartoons*. □ **animé**
,**ani'mation** *noun*. □ **animation**

animator [animeitə] *noun* **1** an artist who draws cartoons or characters that appear to be moving: *A good animator can make any object in a movie appear to be alive.* □ **animateur, trice**
2 someone who helps generate group participation in various activities. □ **animateur, trice**
animosity [ani'mosəti] *noun* (a) strong dislike or hatred: *The rivals regarded one another with animosity.* □ **animosité**
ankle ['aŋkl] *noun* the (area around the) joint connecting the foot and leg: *She has broken her ankle.* □ **cheville**
annals ['anlz] *noun plural* yearly historical accounts of events: *This king is mentioned several times in annals of the period.* □ **annales**
annex [ə'neks] *verb* to take possession of (*eg* a country). □ **annexer**
■ ['aneks] (*also* 'annexe) *noun* a building added to, or used as an addition to, another building: *a hotel annexe.* □ **annexe**
,annex'ation [a-] *noun.* □ **annexion**
annihilate [ə'naiəleit] *verb* to destroy completely: *The epidemic annihilated the population of the town.* □ **anéantir**
an,nihi'lation *noun.* □ **anéantissement**
anniversary [anə'vəːsəri] – *plural* anni'versaries – *noun* the day of the year on which something once happened and is remembered: *We celebrated our fifth wedding anniversary.* □ **anniversaire**
announce [ə'nauns] *verb* **1** to make known publicly: *Mary and John have announced their engagement.* □ **annoncer**
2 to make known the arrival or entrance of: *She announced the next singer.* □ **annoncer**
an'nouncement *noun*: *an important announcement.* □ **annonce**
an'nouncer *noun* a person who introduces programs or reads the news on radio or television. □ **présentateur, trice**
annoy [ə'noi] *verb* to make (someone) rather angry or impatient: *Please go away and stop annoying me!* □ **importuner**
an'noyance *noun* **1** something which annoys: *That noise has been an annoyance to me for weeks!* □ **désagrément**
2 the state of being annoyed: *She was red in the face with annoyance.* □ **mécontentement**
an'noyed *adjective* made angry: *My mother is annoyed with me; He was annoyed at her remarks.* □ **agacé**
an'noying *adjective*: annoying habits. □ **agaçant**
an'noyingly *adverb.* □ **de manière agaçante**
annual ['anjuəl] *adjective* **1** happening every year: *an annual event.* □ **annuel**
2 of one year: *What is his annual salary?* □ **annuel**
■ *noun* **1** a book of which a new edition is published every year: *children's annuals.* □ **publication annuelle**
2 a plant that lives for only one year. □ **plante annuelle**
'annually *adverb*: *Her salary is increased annually.* □ **annuellement**
annul [ə'nʌl] – *past tense, past participle* an'nulled – *verb* to declare (that something is) not valid and cancel (*especially* a marriage or legal contract). □ **annuler**

an'nulment *noun.* □ **annulation**
anoint [ə'noint] *verb* to smear or cover with ointment or oil *especially* in a religious ceremony: *anointed by a priest.* □ **oindre**
anon [ə'non] short for **anonymous**, when used instead of the name of the author of a poem *etc.* □ **anon.**
anonymous [ə'nonəməs] *adjective* without the name of the author, giver *etc* being known or given: *The donor wished to remain anonymous; an anonymous poem.* □ **anonyme**
a'nonymously *adverb.* □ **anonymement**
anonymity [anə'niməti] *noun.* □ **anonymat**
another [ə'nʌðə] *adjective, pronoun* **1** a different (thing or person): *This letter isn't from Tom – it's from another friend of mine; The coat I bought was dirty, so the shop gave me another.* □ **un, une autre**
2 (one) more of the same kind: *Have another biscuit!; You didn't tell me you wanted another of those!* □ **un(e) autre**
answer ['aːnsə] *noun* **1** something said, written or done that is caused by a question *etc* from another person: *She refused to give an answer to his questions.* □ **réponse**
2 the solution to a problem: *The answer to your transport difficulties is to buy a car.* □ **solution**
■ *verb* **1** to make an answer to a question, problem, action *etc*: *Answer my questions, please; Why don't you answer the letter?* □ **répondre (à)**
2 to open (the door), pick up (the telephone) *etc* in response to a knock, ring *etc*: *He answered the telephone as soon as it rang; Could you answer the door, please?* □ **ouvrir; répondre**
3 to be suitable or all that is necessary (for): *This will answer my requirements.* □ **satisfaire**
4 (*often with* to) to be the same as or correspond to (a description *etc*): *The police have found a man answering (to) that description.* □ **correspondre à**
'answerable *adjective* (*usually with* to, for) to have the responsibility: *I will be answerable to you for his good behaviour; She is answerable for the whole project.* □ **responsable (de)**
answer for 1 (*often with* to) to bear the responsibility or be responsible for (something): *I'll answer to your mother for your safety.* □ **répondre de**
2 to suffer or be punished (for something): *You'll answer for your rudeness one day!* □ **payer pour**
answering machine [aːnsəːrŋ mə'ʃiːn] *noun* a special tape recorder that answers the telephone and takes messages: *Marcie was out when I called so I left a message on her answering machine.* □ **répondeur**
ant [ant] *noun* a type of small insect, related to bees, wasps *etc*, thought of as hard-working. □ **fourmi**
'anteater *noun* any of several toothless animals with long snouts, that feed on ants. □ **fourmilier**
'anthill *noun* a mound of earth built as a nest by ants. □ **fourmilière**
antagonist [an'tagonist] *noun* an opponent or enemy. □ **antagoniste**
an'tagonism *noun* unfriendliness, hostility. □ **antagonisme**

an,tago'nistic *adjective.* □ **antagoniste**
an,tago'nistically *adverb.* □ **de manière antagoniste**
an'tagonize, an'tagonise *verb* to make an enemy of (someone): *You are antagonizing her by your rudeness.* □ **contrarier**

Antarctic [ant'aːktik] *adjective, noun* (with **the**) (of) the area round the South Pole. □ **antarctique**

antelope ['antəloup] – *plurals* 'antelopes, 'antelope – *noun* any of several types of quick-moving, graceful, horned animal related to the goat and cow: *a herd of antelope.* □ **antilope**

antenna [an'tenə] *noun* 1 (*plural* an'tennae [-niː]) a feeler of an insect. □ **antenne**
2 (*plural* an'tennas) a wire or rod (or a set of these) able to send or receive radio waves *etc*: *a television antenna.* □ **antenne**

anthem ['anθəm] *noun* 1 a piece of music for a church choir *usually* with words from the Bible. □ **motet**
2 a song of praise: *a national anthem.* □ **hymne**

anthology [an'θolədʒi] – *plural* an'thologies – *noun* a collection of pieces of poetry or prose: *an anthology of love poems.* □ **anthologie**

anthracite ['anθrəsait] *noun* a kind of very hard coal that burns almost without any smoke or flames. □ **anthracite**

anthropology [anθrə'polədʒi] *noun* the study of human society, customs, beliefs *etc*. □ **anthropologie**
anthropo'logical [-'lo-] *adjective.* □ **anthropologique**
,anthro'pologist *noun.* □ **anthropologue**

anti- [anti] (*as part of a word*) 1 against, as in **anti-aircraft.** □ **anti-**
2 the opposite of, as in **anticlockwise.** □ **inverse**

anti-aircraft [anti'eəkraːft] *adjective* used against enemy aircraft: *anti-aircraft defences.* □ **antiaérien**

antibiotic ['antibai'otik] *noun* a medicine which is used to kill the bacteria that cause disease. □ **antibiotique**

anticipate [an'tisəpeit] *verb* 1 to expect (something): *I'm not anticipating any trouble.* □ **s'attendre à**
2 to see what is going to be wanted, required *etc* in the future and do what is necessary: *A businesswoman must try to anticipate what her customers will want.* □ **prévoir**
an,tici'pation *noun*: *I'm looking forward to the concert with anticipation* (= expectancy, excitement). □ **plaisir anticipé**

anticlimax [anti'klaimaks] *noun* a dull or disappointing ending to a play, activity *etc* after increasing excitement: *After the weeks of preparation, the concert itself was a bit of an anticlimax.* □ **déception**

anti clockwise *see* **counter-clockwise.**

antics ['antiks] *noun plural* odd or amusing behaviour: *The children laughed at the monkey's antics.* □ **bouffonneries**

antidote ['antidout] *noun* a medicine *etc* which is given to a poison acting on a person *etc*: *If you are bitten by a poisonous snake, you have to be given an antidote.* □ **antidote**

antifreeze ['antifriːz] *noun* a substance which is added to a liquid, *usually* water (*eg* in the radiator of a car engine), to prevent it from freezing. □ **antigel**

antique [an'tiːk] *adjective* 1 old and *usually* valuable: *an antique chair.* □ **ancien**
2 old or old-fashioned: *That car is positively antique.* □ **antique**
3 (of a shop *etc*) dealing in antiques: *an antique business.* □ **d'antiquités**
■ *noun* something made long ago (*usually* more than a hundred years ago) which is valuable or interesting: *He collects antiques.* □ **antiquités**

antiquated ['antikweitid] *adjective* old or out of fashion: *an antiquated car.* □ **vieillot**

antiquity [an'tikwəti] *noun* 1 ancient times, *especially* those of the ancient Greeks and Romans: *the gods and heroes of antiquity.* □ **antiquité**
2 great age: *a statue of great antiquity.* □ **très ancien**
3 (*plural* an'tiquities) something remaining from ancient times (*eg* a statue, a vase): *Roman antiquities.* □ **antiquité**

antiseptic [anti'septik] *noun, adjective* (of) a substance that destroys bacteria (*eg* in a wound): *You ought to put some antiseptic on that cut; an antiseptic cream.* □ **antiseptique**

antisocial [anti'souʃəl] *adjective* 1 against the welfare of the community *etc*: *It is antisocial to drop rubbish in the street.* □ **antisocial**
2 not wanting the company of others: *Since his wife died, he has become more and more antisocial.* □ **sauvage**

antler ['antlə] *noun* a deer's horn. □ **bois**

antonym ['antənim] *noun* a word opposite in meaning to another word: *Big and small are antonyms.* □ **antonyme**

anvil ['anvil] *noun* a block, *usually* of iron, on which metal objects (*eg* horse-shoes) are hammered into shape: *the blacksmith's anvil.* □ **enclume**

anxiety *see* **anxious.**

anxious ['aŋkʃəs] *adjective* 1 worried about what may happen or have happened: *She is anxious about her father's health.* □ **anxieux**
2 causing worry, fear or uncertainty: *an anxious moment.* □ **angoissant**
3 wanting very much (to do *etc* something): *He's very anxious to please.* □ **(très) désireux de**
'anxiously *adverb.* □ **avec inquiétude**
anxiety [aŋ'zaiəti] *noun*: *His health is a great anxiety to me; filled with anxiety about her child's health.* □ **anxiété**

any ['eni] *pronoun, adjective* 1 one, some, no matter which: *'Which dress shall I wear?' 'Wear any (dress)'; 'Which dresses shall I pack?' 'Pack any (dresses)'.* □ **n'importe quel**
2 (in questions and negative sentences *etc*) one, some: *John has been to some interesting places but I've never been to any; Have you been to any interesting places?; We have hardly any coffee left.* □ **aucun, une; quelque...**
■ *adjective* every: *Any schoolboy could tell you the answer.* □ **n'importe quel**
■ *adverb* at all; (even) by a small amount: *Is this book any better than the last one?; His writing hasn't improved any.* □ **du tout**

'anybody, 'anyone *pronoun* 1 (in questions, and negative sentences *etc*) some person: *Is anybody there?* □ quelqu'un

2 any person, no matter which: *Get someone to help - anyone will do.* □ **n'importe qui**

3 everyone: *Anyone could tell you the answer to that.* □ **n'importe qui**

'anyhow *adverb* 1 anyway: *Anyhow, even if the problem does arise, it won't affect us.* □ **de toute façon**

2 in a careless, untidy way: *Books piled anyhow on shelves.* □ **n'importe comment**

'anything *pronoun* 1 (in questions, and negative sentences *etc*) some thing: *Can you see anything?; I can't see anything.* □ **quelque chose; rien**

2 a thing of any kind: *You can buy anything you like; 'What would you like for your birthday?' 'Anything will do.'* □ **tout ce que, n'importe quoi**

'anyway *adverb* nevertheless; in spite of what has been or might be said, done *etc*: *My mother says I mustn't go but I'm going anyway; Anyway, she can't stop you.* □ **quand même, de toute façon**

'anywhere *adverb* in any place at all: *Have you seen my gloves anywhere?; I can't find them anywhere; 'Where will I put these?' 'Anywhere will do.'* □ **quelque part; nulle part; n'importe où**

at any rate at least: *It's a pity it has started to rain, but at any rate we can still enjoy ourselves at the cinema; The Premier is coming to see us – at any rate, that's what John says.* □ **au/du moins**

in any case nevertheless: *I don't believe the story but I'll check it in any case.* □ **en tout cas, quand même**

apart [ə'paːt] *adverb* separated by a certain distance: *The trees were planted three metres apart; with his feet apart; Their policies are far apart; She sat apart from the other people.* □ **à/de distance, écarté, éloigné de**

apart from except for: *I can't think of anything I need, apart from a car.* □ **sauf, à part**

come apart to break into pieces: *The book came apart in my hands.* □ **se défaire**

take apart to separate (something) into the pieces from which it is made: *She took the engine apart.* □ **démonter**

tell apart (*usually with* can, cannot *etc*) to recognize the difference between; to distinguish: *I cannot tell the twins apart.* □ **distinguer (l'un de l'autre)**

apartment [ə'paːtmənt] *noun* 1 a room or rooms, *usually* rented as a residence, in a building. □ **appartement**

2 a set of rooms on one floor, with kitchen and bathroom, in a larger building or block: *Does he live in a house or in an apartment?* □ **appartement**

3 a single room in a house: *a five-apartment house.* □ **pièce**

apathy ['apəθi] *noun* a lack of interest or enthusiasm: *his apathy towards his work.* □ **apathie**

,apa'thetic [-'θe-] *adjective*. □ **apathique**

,apa'thetically *adverb*. □ **avec indifférence**

ape [eip] *noun* a large monkey with little or no tail. □ **(grand) singe (sans queue)**

aperture ['apətjuə] *noun* 1 an opening or hole. □ **ouverture**

2 (the size of) the opening (*eg* in a camera) through

which light passes. □ **ouverture**

apex ['eipeks] *noun* the highest point or tip (of something): *the apex of a triangle; the apex of a person's career.* □ **sommet**

aphid ['eifid] *noun* a very small insect that lives on plants, *especially* a greenfly. □ **puceron**

apiary ['eipiəri] – *plural* 'apiaries – *noun* a place (containing several hives) where bees are kept. □ **rucher**

apiece [ə'piːs] *adverb* to, for, by *etc* each one of a group: *They got two chocolates apiece.* □ **chacun, une**

apologetic *see* apologize.

apologize, apologise [ə'polədʒaiz] *verb* to say that one is sorry, for having done something wrong, for a fault *etc*: *I must apologize to her for my rudeness.* □ **s'excuser (de/pour)**

a,polo'getic [-'dʒetik] *adjective* showing regret or saying one is sorry for having done something wrong *etc*: *an apologetic letter.* □ **d'excuse**

a,polo'getically *adverb*. □ **en s'excusant**

a'pology – *plural* a'pologies – *noun: Please accept my apology for not arriving on time; She made her apologies for not attending the meeting.* □ **excuse(s)**

apostle [ə'posl] *noun* (*often with capital*) a man sent out to preach the gospel in the early Christian church, *especially* one of the twelve disciples of Christ: *Matthew and Mark were apostles.* □ **apôtre**

apostolic [apə'stolik] *adjective*. □ **apostolique**

apostrophe [ə'postrəfi] *noun* a mark (') which is used to show that a letter or letters has/have been omitted from a word, and which is also used in possessive phrases and in the plurals of letters: *the boy's coat; the boys' coats; There are two n's in 'cannot' but only one in 'can't'.* □ **apostrophe**

appall, appal [ə'poːl] – *past tense, past participle* ap'palled – *verb* to horrify or shock: *We were appalled by the bomb damage.* □ **épouvanter**

ap'palling *adjective*. □ **épouvantable, révoltant**

ap'pallingly *adverb*. □ **épouvantablement**

apparatus [apə'reitəs] – *plurals* ,appa'ratus, ,appa'ratuses – *noun* machinery, tools or equipment: *chemical apparatus; gymnastic apparatus.* □ **appareil; équipement**

apparent [ə'parənt] *adjective* 1 easy to see; evident: *It is quite apparent to all of us that you haven't done your work properly.* □ **évident**

2 seeming but perhaps not real: *her apparent unwillingness.* □ **apparent**

ap'parently *adverb* it seems that; I hear that: *Apparently he is not feeling well.* □ **apparemment**

appeal [əːpiːl] *verb* 1 (*often with* to) to ask earnestly for something: *He appealed (to her) for help.* □ **en appeler à; supplier**

2 to take a case one has lost to a higher court *etc*; to ask (a referee, judge *etc*) for a new decision: *She appealed against a three-year sentence.* □ **faire appel (de)**

3 (*with* to) to be pleasing: *This place appeals to me.* □ **plaire à**

■ *noun* 1 (the act of making) a request (for help, a decision *etc*): *The appeal raised $500 for charity; a last appeal for help; The judge rejected his appeal.* □ **appel**

2 attraction: *Music holds little appeal for me.* □ **attrait**

ap'pealing *adjective* **1** pleasing: *an appealing little girl.* □ **attachant**

2 showing that a person wishes help *etc*: *an appealing glance.* □ **suppliant**

appear [ə'piə] *verb* **1** to come into view: *A man suddenly appeared around the corner.* □ **apparaître**

2 to arrive (at a place *etc*): *He appeared in time for dinner.* □ **arriver**

3 to come before or present oneself/itself before the public or a judge *etc*: *She is appearing on television today*; *He appeared before Judge Scott.* □ **paraître, comparaître**

4 to look or seem as if (something is the case): *It appears that he is wrong*; *He appears to be wrong.* □ **sembler**

ap'pearance *noun* **1** what can be seen (of a person, thing *etc*): *From his appearance he seemed very wealthy.* □ **apparence**

2 the act of coming into view or coming into a place: *The thieves ran off at the sudden appearance of two policemen.* □ **apparition**

3 the act of coming before or presenting oneself/itself before the public or a judge *etc*: *her first appearance on the stage.* □ **apparition; comparution**

appease [ə'piːz] *verb* to calm or satisfy (a person, desire *etc*) usually by giving what was asked for or is needed: *She appeased his curiosity by explaining the situation to him.* □ **apaiser**

ap'peasement *noun.* □ **apaisement**

appendicitis [əpendi'saitis] *noun* the inflammation of the appendix in the body which *usually* causes pain and often requires the removal of the appendix by surgery. □ **appendicite**

appendix [ə'pendiks] *noun* **1** (*plural* sometimes **ap'pendices** [-siːz]) a section, *usually* containing extra information, added at the end of a book, document *etc*. □ **appendice**

2 a narrow tube leading from the large intestine: *She's had her appendix removed.* □ **appendice**

appetite ['apitait] *noun* a desire for food: *Exercise gives you a good appetite.* □ **appétit**

'appetizer, 'appetiser *noun* (*especially American*) something eaten or drunk before or at the beginning of a meal in order to increase the appetite: *They ate smoked salmon as an appetizer.* □ **amuse-gueule, apéritif**

'appetizing, 'appetising *adjective* which increases the appetite: *an appetizing smell.* □ **appétissant**

applaud [ə'plɔːd] *verb* to praise or show approval, by clapping the hands: *to applaud a speech/a singer.* □ **applaudir**

ap'plause [-z] *noun* praise or approval, expressed by clapping: *The President received great applause at the end of his speech.* □ **applaudissements**

apple ['apl] *noun* a round fruit (*usually* with a green or red skin) which can be eaten: *an apple tree*; *a slice of apple.* □ **pomme**

the apple of someone's eye a person or thing which is greatly loved: *She is the apple of her father's eye.* □ **la prunelle des yeux (de qqn)**

upset the apple cart to bring into disorder: *The football team were doing very well when their best player upset the apple cart by breaking his leg.* □ **tout chambouler**

apply [ə'plai] *verb* **1** (*with* **to**) to put (something) on or against something else: *to apply ointment to a cut.* □ **appliquer (sur)**

2 (*with* **to**) to use (something) for some purpose: *He applied his wits to planning their escape.* □ **se servir de**

3 (*with* **for**) to ask for (something) formally: *You could apply (to the manager) for a job.* □ **s'adresser à (pour obtenir), postuler**

4 (*with* **to**) to concern: *This rule does not apply to her.* □ **s'appliquer à**

5 to be in force: *The rule doesn't apply at weekends.* □ **être valable**

ap'pliance [ə'plai-] *noun* an instrument or tool used for a particular job: *washing-machines and other electrical appliances.* □ **appareil, électroménager**

'applicable ['apli-] *adjective*: *This rule is not applicable (to me) any longer.* □ **applicable (à)**

,applica'bility *noun.* □ **applicabilité**

'applicant ['apli-] *noun* a person who applies (for a job *etc*): *There were two hundred applicants for the job.* □ **candidat, ate**

,appli'cation [apli-] *noun* **1** a formal request; an act of applying: *several applications for the new job*; *The syllabus can be obtained on application to the headmaster.* □ **candidature; demande**

2 hard work: *She has got a good job through sheer application.* □ **application**

3 an ointment *etc* applied to a cut, wound *etc*. □ **application**

apply oneself, one's mind (*with* **to**) to give one's full attention or energy (to a task *etc*): *If he would apply himself he could pass his exams.* □ **s'appliquer (à)**

appoint [ə'point] *verb* **1** to give (a person) a job or position: *They appointed him manager*; *They have appointed a new manager.* □ **nommer**

2 to fix or agree on (a time for something): *to appoint a time for a meeting.* □ **fixer**

ap'pointed *adjective*: *She arrived before the appointed time.* □ **convenu**

ap'pointment *noun* **1** (an) arrangement to meet someone; *I made an appointment to see him.* □ **rendez-vous**

2 the job or position to which a person is appointed: *Her appointment was for one year only.* □ **nomination**

appreciate [ə'priːʃieit] *verb* **1** to be grateful for (something): *I appreciate all your hard work.* □ **être reconnaissant (de)**

2 to value (someone or something) highly: *Mothers are very often not appreciated.* □ **apprécier (à sa juste valeur)**

3 understand; to be aware of: *I appreciate your difficulties but I cannot help.* □ **se rendre (bien) compte de**

4 to increase in value: *My house has appreciated (in value) considerably over the last ten years.* □ **prendre de la valeur**

ap'preciable [-ʃəbl] *adjective* noticeable; considerable:

an appreciable increase. □ **appréciable**

ap'preciably [-ʃəbli] *adverb.* □ **sensiblement**

ap,preci'ation *noun* 1 gratefulness: *I wish to show my appreciation for what you have done.* □ **reconnaissance**
2 the state of valuing or understanding something: *a deep appreciation of poetry.* □ **sensibilité (à)**
3 the state of being aware of something: *He has no appreciation of our difficulties.* □ **idée (de)**
4 an increase in value. □ **augmentation**
5 a written article *etc* which describes the qualities of something: *an appreciation of the new book.* □ **critique**

ap'preciative [-ʃətiv] *adjective* giving due thanks or praise; grateful: *an appreciative audience.* □ **appréciateur**

ap'preciatively *adverb.* □ **avec appréciation**

apprehend [apri'hend] *verb* 1 to arrest: *The police apprehended the thief.* □ **appréhender**
2 to understand. □ **comprendre**

,appre'hension [-ʃən] *noun* 1 fear. □ **appréhension**
2 understanding. □ **compréhension**

,appre'hensive [-siv] *adjective* anxious; worried: *an apprehensive expression.* □ **appréhensif**

,appre'hensively *adverb.* □ **avec appréhension**

,appre'hensiveness *noun.* □ **appréhension**

apprentice [ə'prentis] *noun* a (*usually* young) person who is learning a trade. □ **apprenti, ie**

■ *verb* to make (someone) an apprentice: *Her father apprenticed her to an engineer.* □ **mettre en apprentissage (chez)**

ap'prenticeship *noun* the state of being, or the time during which a person is, an apprentice: *He is serving his apprenticeship as a mechanic.* □ **apprentissage**

approach [ə'prəutʃ] *verb* to come near (to): *The car approached (the traffic lights) at top speed; Christmas is approaching.* □ **(s')approcher (de)**

■ *noun* 1 the act of coming near: *The boys ran off at the approach of a policeman.* □ **approche**
2 a road, path *etc* leading to a place: *All the approaches to the village were blocked by fallen rock.* □ **voies d'accès**
3 an attempt to obtain or attract a person's help, interest *etc*: *They have made an approach to the government for help; That fellow makes approaches to (= he tries to become friendly with) every woman he meets.* □ **démarche(s), avances**

ap'proachable *adjective* 1 friendly. □ **accessible**
2 that can be reached: *The village is not approachable by road.* □ **accessible**

ap'proaching *adjective: the approaching dawn.* □ **qui (s')approche**

approbation [aprə'beiʃən] *noun* approval: *Her bravery received the approbation of the whole town.* □ **approbation**

appropriate [ə'prəupriət] *adjective* suitable; proper: *Her clothes were appropriate to the occasion; Complain to the appropriate authority.* □ **approprié (à)**

ap'propriateness *noun.* □ **opportunité**

ap'propriately *adverb* suitably: *appropriately dressed for the occasion.* □ **convenablement**

approve [ə'pruːv] *verb* 1 (often with of) to be pleased with or think well of (a person, thing *etc*): *I approve of your decision.* □ **approuver**
2 to agree to (something): *The committee approved the plan.* □ **approuver**

ap'proval *noun* the act or state of agreeing to or being pleased with (a person, thing *etc*): *This proposal meets with my approval.* □ **approbation**

on approval to be sent or given back to a shop *etc* if not satisfactory: *She bought two dresses on approval.* □ **sous condition**

approximate [ə'proksimət] *adjective* very nearly correct or accurate; not intended to be absolutely correct: *Give me an approximate answer!; Can you give me an approximate price for the job?* □ **approximatif**

ap'proximately *adverb* nearly; more or less: *There will be approximately five hundred people present.* □ **approximativement**

ap,proxim'ation *noun* 1 a figure, answer *etc* which is not (intended to be) exact: *This figure is just an approximation.* □ **approximation**
2 the process of estimating a figure *etc*: *We decided on a price by a process of approximation.* □ **approximation**

apricot ['eiprikot] *noun* an orange-coloured fruit like a small peach. □ **abricot**

April ['eiprəl] *noun* the fourth month of the year, the month following March. □ **avril**

apron ['eiprən] *noun* 1 a piece of cloth, plastic *etc* worn over the front of the clothes for protection against dirt *etc*: *He tied on his apron before preparing the dinner.* □ **tablier**
2 something like an apron in shape, *eg* a hard surface for aircraft on an airfield. □ **aire de manœuvre**
3 (also 'apron-stage) the part of the stage in a theatre which is in front of the curtain. □ **avant-scène**

apt [apt] *adjective* 1 (with to) likely: *He is apt to get angry if you ask a lot of questions.* □ **susceptible de**
2 suitable: *an apt remark.* □ **pertinent**
3 clever; quick to learn: *an apt student.* □ **doué**

'aptly *adverb.* □ **pertinemment**

'aptness *noun.* □ **à-propos, justesse**

aptitude ['aptitjuːd] *noun* (*sometimes* with for) (a) talent or ability: *an aptitude for mathematics.* □ **aptitude (à), disposition(s) (pour)**

aqualung ['akwəlʌŋ] *noun* an apparatus worn by divers on their backs which supplies them with oxygen to breathe. □ **scaphandre autonome**

aquarium [ə'kweəriəm] – *plurals* a'quariums, a'quaria – *noun* a glass tank, or a building containing tanks, for keeping fish and other water animals. □ **aquarium**

aquatic [ə'kwatik] *adjective* living, growing, or taking place in water: *aquatic plants/sports.* □ **aquatique**

Arabic ['arəbik]: Arabic numerals 1, 2 *etc*, as opposed to Roman numerals, I, II *etc.* □ **arabe**

arable ['arəbl] *adjective* on which crops are grown: *arable land.* □ **arable**

arbitrary ['aːbitrəri] *adjective* not decided by rules or laws but by a person's own opinion: *She made a rather arbitrary decision to close the local cinema without consulting other people.* □ **arbitraire** 'arbitrarily *adverb*. □ **arbitrairement**

arbitrate ['aːbitreit] *verb* to act as an arbitrator in a dispute *etc*: *She has been asked to arbitrate in the dispute between the workers and management*. □ **arbitrer**

,arbi'tration *noun* the making of a decision by an arbitrator: *The dispute has gone/was taken to arbitration*. □ **arbitrage**

'arbitrator *noun* a person who makes a judgment in a dispute *etc*. □ **arbitre**

arc [aːk] *noun* a part of the line which forms a circle or other curve. □ **arc**

arcade [aː'keid] *noun* a covered passage or area *usually* with shops, stalls *etc*: *a shopping arcade*; *an amusement arcade*. □ **galerie (marchande)**

arch [aːtʃ] *noun* 1 the top part of a door *etc* or a support for a roof *etc* which is built in the shape of a curve. □ **voûte**

2 a monument which is shaped like an arch: *the Arc de Triomphe is an example of a triumphal arch*. □ **arc**

3 anything that is like an arch in shape: *The rainbow formed an arch in the sky*. □ **arc**

4 the raised part of the sole of the foot. □ **cambrure**

■ *verb* to (cause to) be in the shape of an arch: *The cat arched its back*. □ **arquer**

arched *adjective*: *an arched doorway*. □ **cintré**

'archway *noun* an arched passage, door or entrance. □ **porche**

archaeology [aːki'olədʒi] *noun* the study of objects belonging to ancient times (*eg* buildings, tools *etc* found in the earth). □ **archéologie**

archae'ologist *noun*. □ **archéologue**

,archaeo'logical [-'lo-] *adjective*: *archaeological research/remains*. □ **archéologique**

archangel [aːkeindʒel] *noun* a chief angel. □ **archange**

archbishop [aːtʃ'biʃəp] *noun* a chief bishop. □ **archevêque**

archer ['aːtʃə] *noun* a person who shoots with a bow and arrows. □ **archer, ère**

'archery *noun* the art or sport of shooting with a bow. □ **tir à l'arc**

archipelago [aːki'peləgou] – *plural* ,archi'pelago(e)s – *noun* a group of islands. □ **archipel**

architect ['aːkitekt] *noun* a person who designs buildings *etc*. □ **architecte**

'architecture [-tʃə] *noun* the art of designing buildings: *She's studying architecture*; *modern architecture*. □ **architecture**

,archi'tectural *adjective*. □ **architectural**

archives ['aːkaivz] *noun plural* (a place for keeping) old documents, historical records *etc*. □ **archives**

'archivist [-ki-] *noun* a person who looks after archives. □ **archiviste**

archway *see* **arch**.

Arctic ['aːktik] *adjective* 1 of the area around the North Pole: *the Arctic wilderness*. □ **arctique**

2 (*no capital*) very cold: *arctic conditions*. □ **glacial**

the Arctic the area around the North Pole. □ **l'Arctique**

ardent ['aːdənt] *adjective* enthusiastic; passionate: *an ardent supporter of a political party*. □ **ardent**

'ardently *adverb*. □ **ardemment**

ardour, ardor ['aːdə] *noun* enthusiasm; passion. □ **ardeur**

arduous ['aːdʒuəs,-dju-] *adjective* difficult; needing hard work: *an arduous task*. □ **ardu**

'arduously *adverb*. □ **laborieusement**

'arduousness *noun*. □ **difficulté**

are *see* **be**.

area ['eəriə] *noun* 1 the extent or size of a flat surface: *This garden is twelve square metres in area*. □ **aire, superficie**

2 a place; part (of a town *etc*): *Do you live in this area?* □ **secteur, quartier, zone**

arena [ə'riːnə] *noun* any place for a public show contest *etc*: *a sports arena*. □ **arène**

aren't *see* **be**.

argue ['aːgjuː] *verb* 1 (*with* with someone, about something) to quarrel with (a person) or discuss (something) with a person in a not very friendly way: *I'm not going to argue*; *Will you children stop arguing with each other about whose toy that is!* □ **se disputer (sur/à propos de)**

2 (*with* for, against) to suggest reasons for or for not doing something: *I argued for/against accepting the plan*. □ **plaider (pour, contre)**

3 (*with* into, out of) to persuade (a person) (not) to do something: *I'll try to argue him into going*; *He argued her out of buying the house*. □ **persuader (de, de ne pas)**

4 to discuss, giving one's reasoning: *She argued the point very cleverly*. □ **soutenir**

'arguable *adjective* able to be put forward in argument: *It is arguable that he would have been better to go*. □ **défendable**

'argument *noun* 1 a quarrel or unfriendly discussion: *They are having an argument about/over whose turn it is*. □ **querelle**

2 a set of reasons; a piece of reasoning: *The argument for/against going*; *a philosophical argument*. □ **argument**

,argu'mentative [-'mentətiv] *adjective* fond of arguing. □ **raisonneur**

arid ['arid] *adjective* dry: *The soil is rather arid*. □ **aride**

a'ridity *noun*. □ **aridité**

'aridness *noun*. □ **aridité**

arise [ə'raiz] – *past tense* arose [ə'rouz]: *past participle* arisen [ə'rizn] – *verb* 1 to come into being: *These problems have arisen as a result of your carelessness*; *Are there any matters arising from our earlier discussion?* □ **survenir**

2 to get up or stand up. □ **se lever**

aristocracy [arə'stokrəsi] *noun* in some countries, the nobility and others of the highest social class, who *usually* own land. □ **aristocratie**

'aristocrat [-krat, (*American*) ə'ristəkrat] *noun* a member of the aristocracy. □ **aristocrate**

,aristo'cratic [-'kra-, (*American*) ə,ristə'kratik] *adjective* (of people, behaviour *etc*) proud and noble-looking: *an aristocratic manner*. □ **aristocratique**

,aristo'cratically *adverb*. □ **aristocratiquement**

arithmetic [ə'riθmətik] *noun* the art of counting by numbers. □ **arithmétique**

arithmetical [ariθ'metikl] *adjective*. □ **arithmétique**

arm¹ [aːm] *noun* **1** the part of the body between the shoulder and the hand: *She has broken both her arms.* □ **bras** **2** anything shaped like or similar to this: *She sat on the arm of the chair.* □ **bras, accoudoir**

'**armful** *noun* as much as a person can hold in one arm or in both arms: *an armful of flowers/clothes.* □ **brassée**

'**armband** *noun* a strip of cloth *etc* worn around the arm: *The people all wore black armbands as a sign of mourning.* □ **brassard**

'**armchair** *noun* a chair with arms at each side. □ **fauteuil**

'**armpit** *noun* the hollow under the arm at the shoulder. □ **aisselle**

,**arm-in-'arm** *adverb* (of two or more people) with arms linked together: *They walked along arm-in-arm.* □ **bras dessus, bras dessous**

keep at arm's length to avoid becoming too friendly with someone: *She keeps her new neighbours at arm's length.* □ **tenir (qqn) à distance**

with open arms with a very friendly welcome: *He greeted them with open arms.* □ **à bras ouverts**

arm² [aːm] *verb* **1** to give weapons to (a person *etc*): *to arm the police.* □ **armer** **2** to prepare for battle, war *etc*: *They armed for battle.* □ **s'armer**

armed *adjective* having a weapon or weapons: *An armed man robbed the bank; Armed forces entered the country.* □ **armé**

arms *noun plural* **1** weapons: *Does the police force carry arms?* □ **armes** **2** a design *etc* which is used as the symbol of the town, family *etc* (*see also* **coat of arms**). □ **armoiries**

be up in arms to be very angry and make a great protest (about something): *She is up in arms about the decision to close the road.* □ **s'élever (contre)**

take up arms (*often with* **against**) to begin fighting: *The peasants took up arms against the dictator.* □ **s'insurger (contre)**

armament ['aːməmənt] *noun* (*usually in plural*) equipment for war, *eg* the guns *etc* of a ship, tank *etc*. □ **armement**

armistice ['aːmistis] *noun* (an agreement) stopping fighting (in a war, battle *etc*): *An armistice was declared.* □ **armistice**

armour, armor ['aːmə] *noun* **1** formerly, a metal suit worn by knights *etc* as a protection while fighting: *a suit of armour.* □ **armure** **2** a metal covering to protect ships, tanks *etc* against damage from weapons. □ **blindage**

'**armoured** *adjective* **1** (of vehicles *etc*) protected by armour: *an armoured car.* □ **blindé** **2** made up of armoured vehicles: *an armoured division of an army.* □ **blindé**

'**armoury** – *plural* '**armouries** – *noun* the place where weapons are made or kept. □ **arsenal**

army ['aːmi] – *plural* '**armies** – *noun* **1** a large number of men armed and organized for war: *The two armies met at dawn.* □ **armée**

2 a large number (of people *etc*): *an army of tourists.* □ **foule**

aroma [ə'roumə] *noun* the (*usually* pleasant) smell that a substance has or gives off: *the aroma of coffee.* □ **arôme**

aromatic [arə'matik] *adjective*: *aromatic herbs.* □ **aromatique**

arose *see* **arise.**

around [ə'raund] *preposition, adverb* **1** on all sides of or in a circle about (a person, thing *etc*): *Flowers grew around the tree; They danced around the fire; There were flowers all around.* □ **autour, alentour** **2** here and there (in a house, room *etc*): *Clothes had been left lying around (the house); I wandered around.* □ **ici et là**

■ *preposition* near to (a time, place *etc*): *around three o'clock.* □ **vers, aux alentours de**

■ *adverb* **1** in the opposite direction: *Turn around!* □ **demi-tour** **2** near-by: *If you need me, I'll be somewhere around.* □ **dans les parages**

arouse [ə'rauz] *verb* to cause or give rise to (something): *His actions aroused my suspicions.* □ **éveiller**

arrange [ə'reindʒ] *verb* **1** to put in some sort of order: *Arrange these books in alphabetical order; He arranged the flowers in a vase.* □ **ranger; arranger** **2** to plan or make decisions (about future events): *We have arranged a meeting for next week; I have arranged to meet him tomorrow.* □ **prévoir (de)** **3** to make (a piece of music) suitable for particular voices or instruments: *music arranged for choir and orchestra.* □ **adapter**

ar'rangement *noun*: *I like the arrangement of the furniture; flower-arrangements; They've finally come to some sort of arrangement about sharing expenses; a new arrangement for guitar and orchestra.* □ **arrangement**

ar'rangements *noun plural* plans; preparations: *Have you made any arrangments for a meeting with her?; funeral arrangements.* □ **préparatifs**

array [ə'rei] **1** things, people *etc* arranged in some order: *an impressive array of fabrics.* □ **collection** **2** clothes: *in fine array.* □ **atours**

■ *verb* **1** to put (things, people *etc*) in some order for show *etc*: *goods arrayed on the counter.* □ **disposer, étaler** **2** to dress (oneself) *eg* in fine clothes. □ **se parer**

arrears [ə'riəz] *noun plural* money which should have been paid because it is owed but which has not been paid: *rent arrears.* □ **arriéré**

in arrears not up to date (*eg* in payments): *He is in arrears with his rent.* □ **en retard**

arrest [ə'rest] *verb* **1** to capture or take hold of (a person) because he or she has broken the law: *The police arrested the thief.* □ **arrêter** **2** to stop: *Economic difficulties arrested the growth of industry.* □ **arrêter**

■ *noun* **1** the act of arresting; being arrested: *The police made several arrests; She was questioned after her arrest.* □ **arrestation**

2 a stopping of action: *Cardiac arrest is another term for heart failure.* □ **arrêt**

under arrest in the position of having been arrested: *The thief was placed under arrest.* □ **en état d'arrestation**

arrive [ə'raiv] *verb* to reach (a place, the end of a journey *etc*): *They arrived home last night; The parcel arrived yesterday.* □ **arriver**

ar'rival *noun* **1** the act of arriving: *I was greeted by my sister on my arrival.* □ **arrivée**

2 a person, thing *etc* that has arrived: *I wish he would stop calling our baby the new arrival.* □ **nouveau venu, nouvelle venue**

arrive at to reach: *The committee failed to arrive at a decision.* □ **parvenir à**

arrogant ['arəgənt] *adjective* extremely proud; thinking that one is much more important than other people. □ **arrogant**

'**arrogantly** *adverb.* □ **avec arrogance**
'**arrogance** *noun.* □ **arrogance**

arrow ['arou] *noun* **1** a thin, straight stick with a point, which is fired from a bow. □ **flèche**

2 a sign shaped like an arrow *eg* to show which way to go: *You can't get lost – just follow the arrows.* □ **flèche**
arrowhead *noun* **1** a water plant with leaves shaped like an arrowhead. □ **marante**

2 the tip of an arrow, shaped to a point. □ **pointe de flèche**

arsenal ['a:sənl] *noun* a factory or store for weapons, ammunition *etc*. □ **arsenal**

arsenic [a:snik] *noun* **1** an element used to make certain poisons. □ **arsenic**

2 a poison made with arsenic. □ **arsenic**

arson ['a:sn] *noun* the crime of setting fire to (a building *etc*) on purpose. □ **incendie criminel**

art [a:t] *noun* **1** painting and sculpture: *I'm studying art at school; Do you like modern art?*; (*also adjective*) *an art gallery, an art college.* □ **art(s), beaux-arts**

2 any of various creative forms of expression: *painting, music, dancing, writing and the other arts.* □ **art**

3 an ability or skill; the (best) way of doing something: *the art of conversation/war.* □ **art**

'**artful** *adjective* clever; having a lot of skill (*usually* in a bad sense): *an artful thief.* □ **rusé**

'**artfully** *adverb.* □ **astucieusement**
'**artfulness** *noun.* □ **astuce**

arts *noun plural* (*often with capital*) languages, literature, history, as opposed to scientific subjects. □ **lettres**

artery ['a:təri] – *plural* '**arteries** – *noun* **1** a blood-vessel that carries the blood from the heart through the body. □ **artère**

2 a main route of travel and transport. □ **artère**

arterial [a:'tiəriəl] *adjective*: *arterial disease; arterial roads.* □ **artériel**

artful *see* art.

arthritis [a:'θraitis] *noun* pain and swelling in the joints of the body. □ **arthrite**

ar'thritic [-'θri-] *adjective*. □ **arthritique**

artichoke ['a:ti:tʃouk] *noun* a thistle-like plant or its flower that is used as a green vegetable: *There is a good*

recipe for artichoke dip. □ **artichaut**

article ['a:tikl] *noun* **1** a thing or an object: *This shop sells articles of all kinds; articles of clothing.* □ **article**

2 a piece of writing in a newspaper or magazine: *She has written an article on the new sports centre for a local magazine.* □ **article, reportage**

3 the (the definite article) or a/an (the indefinite article). □ **article**

articulate [a:'tikjuleit] *verb* to speak or pronounce: *The teacher articulated (his words) very carefully.* □ **articuler**

■ [-lət] *adjective* able to express one's thoughts clearly: *He's unusually articulate for a three-year-old child.* □ **qui s'exprime bien**

ar'ticulately [-lət-] *adverb.* □ **avec aisance**
ar'ticulateness [-lət-] *noun.* □ **facilité d'élocution**
ar,ticu'lation *noun.* □ **articulation**

artificial [a:ti'fiʃəl] *adjective* made by man; not natural; not real: *artificial flowers; Did you look at the colour in artificial light or in daylight?* □ **artificiel**

art'ficially *adverb.* □ **artificiellement**
,**artifici'ality** [-ʃi'a-] *noun.* □ **manque de naturel**

artificial respiration the process of forcing air into and out of the lungs *eg* of a person who has almost drowned. □ **respiration artificielle**

artillery [a:'tiləri] *noun* **1** large guns. □ **artillerie**

2 (*often with capital*) the part of an army which looks after and fires such guns. □ **artillerie**

artisan ['a:ti,zan] *noun* a skilled workman. □ **artisan, ane**

artist ['a:tist] *noun* **1** a person who paints pictures or is a sculptor or is skilled at one of the other arts. □ **artiste**

2 a singer, dancer, actor *etc*; an artiste: *She announced the names of the artists who were taking part in the show.* □ **artiste**

ar'tistic *adjective* **1** liking or skilled in painting, music *etc*: *She draws and paints – she's very artistic.* □ **artiste**

2 created or done with skill and good taste: *That flower-arrangement looks very artistic.* □ **artistique**

ar'tistically *adverb.* □ **artistiquement**
'**artistry** *noun* artistic skill: *the musician's artistry.* □ **art**

artiste [a:'ti:st] *noun* a person who performs in a theatre, circus *etc*: *a troupe of circus artistes.* □ **artiste**

as [az] *conjunction* **1** when; while: *I met Mary as I was coming home; We'll be able to talk as we go.* □ **tandis que; comme; en**

2 because: *As I am leaving tomorrow, I've bought you a present.* □ **comme**

3 in the same way that: *If you are not sure how to behave, do as I do.* □ **comme**

4 used to introduce a statement of what the speaker knows or believes to be the case: *As you know, I'll be leaving tomorrow.* □ **comme**

5 though: *Old as I am, I can still fight; Much as I want to, I cannot go.* □ **malgré (que)**

6 used to refer to something which has already been stated and apply it to another person: *Tom is English, as are Dick and Harry.* □ **ainsi que**

■ *adverb* used in comparisons, *eg* the first *as* in the following example: *The bread was as hard as a brick.* □ **aussi (que)**

■ *preposition* 1 used in comparisons, *eg* the second *as* in the following example: *The bread was as hard as a brick.* □ **que**

2 like: *He was dressed as a woman.* □ **en**

3 with certain verbs *eg* **regard, treat, describe, accept**: *I am regarded by some people as a bit of a fool; He treats the children as adults.* □ **comme**

4 in the position of: *She is greatly respected both as a person and as a politician.* □ **en tant que**

as for with regard to; concerning: *The thief was caught by the police almost immediately: As for the stolen jewels, they were found in a dustbin.* □ **quant à**

as if/as though in the way one would expect if: *He acted as if he were mad; She spoke as though she knew all about our plans; He opened his mouth as if to speak; You look as if you are going to faint.* □ **comme (si, pour)**

as to as far as (something) is concerned; with regard to: *I'm willing to read his book, but as to publishing it, that's a different matter.* □ **quant à; pour ce qui est de**

asbestos [az'bestos] *noun, adjective* (of) a mineral that will not burn which can protect against fire: *an asbestos suit.* □ **amiante**

ascend [ə'send] *verb* to climb, go, or rise up: *The smoke ascended into the air.* □ **s'élever**

a'scendancy/a'scendency *noun* control or power (over): *They have the ascendancy over the other political groups.* □ **ascendant**

a'scent [-t] *noun* 1 the act of climbing or going up: *The ascent of Mount Everest.* □ **ascension**

2 a slope upwards: *a steep ascent.* □ **montée**

ascend the throne to be crowned king or queen. □ **monter sur le trône**

ascertain [asə'tein] *verb* to find out: *We shall never ascertain the truth.* □ **établir**

,**ascer'tainable** *adjective*. □ **vérifiable**

ascetic [ə'setik] *adjective* avoiding pleasure and comfort, *especially* for religious reasons: *Monks lead ascetic lives.* □ **ascétique**

■ *noun* an ascetic person. □ **ascète**

a'scetically *adverb*. □ **ascétiquement**

a'sceticism [-sizəm] *noun*. □ **ascétisme**

ascribe [ə'skraib] *verb* to think of as done or caused by someone or something: *He ascribed his success to the help of his friends.* □ **attribuer (à)**

ash [aʃ] *noun* the dust *etc* that remains after anything is burnt: *cigarette ash; the ashes of the bonfire.* □ **cendre**

'**ashen** *adjective* (of someone's face *etc*) very pale with shock *etc*. □ **terreux**

'**ashes** *noun plural* the remains of a human body after cremation: *Her ashes were scattered at sea.* □ **cendres**

'**ashtray** *noun* a dish or other container for cigarette ash. □ **cendrier**

ashamed [ə'ʃeimd] *adjective* feeling shame: *He was ashamed of his bad work, ashamed to admit his mistake, ashamed of himself.* □ **honteux**

ashore [ə'ʃoː] *adverb* on or on to the shore: *The sailor went ashore.* □ **à terre**

Asian ['eiʒən] *adjective* of Asia or its inhabitants: *Asian pottery has beautiful designs on it.* □ **asiatique**

■ *noun* someone who is a native of Asia: *Asians often travel to France for a holiday.* □ **Asiatique**

aside [ə'said] *adverb* on or to one side: *They stood aside to let her pass; I've put aside two tickets for you to collect.* □ **de côté**

■ *noun* words spoken (*especially* by an actor) which other people (on the stage) are not supposed to hear: *She whispered an aside to him.* □ **aparté**

put aside (*often with* **for**) to keep (something) for a particular person or occasion: *Would you put this book aside for me and I'll collect it later; We have put aside the dress you ordered.* □ **mettre de côté**

ask [aːsk] *verb* 1 to put a question: *She asked me what the time was; Ask the price of that scarf; Ask her where to go; Ask him about it; If you don't know, ask.* □ **demander**

2 to express a wish to someone for something: *I asked her to help me; I asked (him) for a day off; He rang and asked for you; Can I ask a favour of you?* □ **demander**

3 to invite: *She asked him to her house for lunch.* □ **inviter**

ask after to make inquiries about the health *etc* of: *She asked after his father.* □ **demander des nouvelles de**

ask for 1 to express a wish to see or speak to (someone): *When he telephoned her you; She is very ill and keeps asking for his daughter.* □ **demander, réclamer**

2 to behave as if inviting (something unpleasant): *Going for a swim when you have a cold is just as asking for trouble.* □ **chercher**

for the asking you may have (something) simply by asking for it; *This table is yours for the asking.* □ **il n'y a qu'à le demander**

asleep [ə'sliːp] *adjective* 1 sleeping: *The baby is asleep.* □ **endormi**

2 of arms and legs *etc*, numb: *My foot's asleep.* □ **engourdi**

fall asleep: *She fell asleep eventually.* □ **s'endormir**

asparagus [əzpaːɾəgəz] *noun* a green plant with long-stemmed and bushy-tipped shoots that are used as a vegetable: *Mom made roast beef with asparagus and potatoes for dinner.* □ **asperge**

aspect ['aspekt] *noun* 1 a part of something to be thought about: *We must consider every aspect of the problem.* □ **aspect**

2 a side of a building *etc* or the direction it faces in. □ **exposition**

3 look or appearance: *His face had a frightening aspect.* □ **mine, air**

asphalt ['asfalt] *noun, adjective* (of) a mixture containing tar, used to make roads, pavements *etc*: *The workmen are laying asphalt; an asphalt playground.* □ **asphalte**

aspire [ə'spaiə] *verb* (*usually with* **to**) to try very hard to reach (something difficult, ambitious *etc*): *She aspired to the position of president.* □ **aspirer à**

,**aspi'ration** [aspi-] *noun* (*often in plural*) an ambition: *aspirations to become a writer.* □ **aspiration**

aspirin ['aspərin] *noun* a (tablet of a) kind of pain-killing drug: *The child has a fever – give her some/an aspirin.* □ **(comprimé d')aspirine**

ass [as] *noun* 1 a donkey. □ **âne**
2 a stupid person. □ **idiot, idiote**

assail [ə'seil] *verb* to attack, torment: *She was assailed with questions; assailed by doubts.* □ **accabler (de)**
as'sailant *noun* a person who attacks: *His assailant came up behind him in the dark.* □ **agresseur, euse**

assassinate [ə'sasineit] *verb* to murder, *especially* for political reasons: *The president was assassinated by terrorists.* □ **assassiner**
as,sassi'nation *noun.* □ **assassinat**
as'sassin *noun* a person who assassinates. □ **assassin**

assault [ə'soːlt] *verb* 1 to attack, *especially* suddenly: *The youths assaulted the night watchman.* □ **agresser**
2 to attack sexually; to rape. □ **violenter**
■ *noun* 1 a (sudden) attack: *a night assault on the fortress; His speech was a vicious assault on his opponent.* □ **assaut, attaque**
2 a sexual attack; a rape. □ **(tentative de) viol**

assemble [ə'sembl] *verb* 1 (of people) to come together: *The crowd assembled in the hall.* □ **s'assembler**
2 to call or bring together: *He assembled his family and told them of his plan.* □ **rassembler**
3 to put together (a machine *etc*): *She assembled the model airplane.* □ **monter, assembler**
as'sembly *noun* 1 a collection of people (*usually* for a particular purpose): *a legislative assembly; The school meets for morning assembly at 8.30.* □ **assemblée, rassemblement**
2 the act of assembling or putting together. □ **rassemblement**

assent [ə'sent] *noun* agreement: *The House of Commons gave assent to the bill.* □ **assentiment**
■ *verb* (*with* **to**) to agree: *They assented to the proposal.* □ **donner son accord (à)**

assert [ə'səːt] *verb* 1 to say definitely: *She asserted that she had not borrowed his book.* □ **affirmer**
2 to insist on: *She should assert her independence.* □ **revendiquer**
as'sertion [-ʃən] *noun.* □ **assertion**
as'sertive [-tiv] *adjective* (too) inclined to assert oneself. □ **assuré**
assert oneself to state one's opinions confidently and act in a way that will make people take notice of one: *You must assert yourself more if you want promotion.* □ **s'affirmer**

assess [ə'ses] *verb* 1 to estimate or judge the quality or quantity of: *Can you assess my chances of winning?* □ **évaluer**
2 to estimate in order to calculate tax due on: *My income has been assessed wrongly.* □ **évaluer**
as'sessment *noun.* □ **évaluation**
as'sessor *noun.* □ **expert, erte, contrôleur, euse**

asset ['aset] *noun* anything useful or valuable; an advantage: *She is a great asset to the school.* □ **atout**
'assets *noun plural* the total property, money *etc* of a person, company *etc*. □ **actif**

assign [ə'sain] *verb* 1 to give to someone as his share or duty: *They assigned the task to us.* □ **assigner (à)**
2 to order or appoint: *She assigned three men to the job.* □ **affecter (à)**
as'signment *noun* a duty assigned to someone: *You must complete this assignment by tomorrow.* □ **tâche**

assimilate [ə'simǝleit] *verb* to take in and digest: *Plants assimilate food from the earth; I can't assimilate all these facts at once.* □ **assimiler**
as,simi'lation *noun.* □ **assimilation**

assist [ə'sist] *verb* to help: *The junior doctor assisted the surgeon at the operation.* □ **aider, assister**
as'sistance *noun* help: *Do you need assistance?* □ **aide**
as'sistant *noun* 1 a person who assists; a helper: *a laboratory assistant*; (*also adjective*) *an assistant headmaster.* □ **assistant, ante**
2 a person who serves in a shop. □ **vendeur, euse**

associate [ə'sousieit] *verb* 1 to connect in the mind: *He always associated the smell of tobacco with his father.* □ **associer**
2 (*usually with* **with**) to join (with someone) in friendship or work: *They don't usually associate (with each other) after office hours.* □ **(se) fréquenter**
■ [-et] *adjective* 1 having a lower position or rank: *an associate professor.* □ **associé**
2 joined or connected: *associate organizations.* □ **affilié**
■ *noun* a colleague or partner; a companion. □ **associé, ée**
association *noun* 1 a club, society *etc*. □ **société**
2 a friendship or partnership. □ **amicale, association**
3 a connection in the mind: *The house had associations with her dead husband.* □ **association d'idées**
in association with together with: *We are acting in association with the London branch of our firm.* □ **de concert avec**

assorted [ə'soːtid] *adjective* mixed; of or containing various different kinds: *assorted colours; assorted sweets.* □ **assorti; au choix**
as'sortment *noun* a mixture or variety: *an assortment of garments.* □ **assortiment**

assume [ə'sjuːm] *verb* 1 to take or accept as true: *I assume (that) you'd like time to decide.* □ **supposer**
2 to take upon oneself or accept (authority, responsibility *etc*): *She assumed the rôle of leader in the emergency.* □ **assumer**
3 to put on (a particular appearance *etc*): *He assumed a look of horror.* □ **prendre, affecter**
as'sumed *adjective* pretended; not genuine: *assumed astonishment; She wrote under an assumed name* (= not using her real name). □ **feint, d'emprunt**
as'sumption [-'sʌmp-] *noun* something assumed: *On the assumption that we can produce four pages an hour, the work will be finished tomorrow.* □ **hypothèse**

assure [ə'ʃuə] *verb* 1 to tell positively: *I assured her (that) the house was empty.* □ **assurer**
2 to make (someone) sure: *You may be assured that we shall do all we can to help.* □ **assurer**
as'surance *noun* 1 confidence: *an air of assurance.* □ **assurance**
2 a promise: *He gave me his assurance that he would help.* □ **assurance**

3 insurance: *life assurance.* □ **assurance(s)**

as'sured *adjective* certain and confident: *an assured young woman.* □ **plein d'assurance**

asterisk ['astərisk] *noun* a star-shaped mark (*) used in printing to draw attention to a note *etc.* □ **astérisque**

asthma ['azmə] *noun* an illness which causes difficulty in breathing out, resulting from an allergy *etc.* □ **asthme**

asthmatic [az'matik] *adjective.* □ **asthmatique**

astonish [ə'stoniʃ] *verb* to surprise greatly: *I was astonished by his ignorance.* □ **étonner**

a'stonishing *adjective: an astonishing sight.* □ **étonnant**

a'stonishment *noun: To my astonishment he burst into tears.* □ **étonnement**

astound [ə'staund] *verb* to make (someone) very surprised: *I was astounded to hear of her imprisonment.* □ **stupéfier**

a'stounding *adjective: an astounding piece of news.* □ **stupéfiant**

astray [ə'strei] *adjective, adverb* away from the right direction; missing, lost: *The letter has gone astray; We were led astray by the inaccurate map.* □ **égaré, perdu**

astride [ə'straid] *preposition* with legs on each side of: *She sat astride the horse.* □ **à califourchon**

■ *adverb* (with legs) apart: *He stood with legs astride.* □ **les jambes écartées (debout)**

astrology [ə'strolədʒi] *noun* the study of the stars and their influence on people's lives: *I don't have faith in astrology.* □ **astrologie**

a'strologer *noun.* □ **astrologue**

astrological [astrə'lodʒikl] *adjective.* □ **astrologique**

astronaut ['astrənɔːt] *noun* a person who travels in space: *Who was the first astronaut to land on the moon?* □ **astronaute**

astronomy [ə'stronəmi] *noun* the study of the stars and their movements: *She is studying astronomy.* □ **astronomie**

a'stronomer *noun.* □ **astronome**

astronomic(al) [astrə'nomik(l)] *adjective* **1** (of numbers or amounts very large): *The cost of the new building was astronomical.* □ **astronomique**

2 of astronomy: *astronomical observations.* □ **astronomique**

astute [ə'stjuːt] *adjective* clever: *an astute businessman.* □ **avisé, astucieux**

a'stuteness *noun.* □ **astuce**

asylum [ə'sailəm] *noun* **1** safety; protection: *He was granted political asylum.* □ **asile**

2 an old name for a home for people who are mentally ill. □ **asile (d'aliénés)**

at [at] *preposition* showing **1** position: *They are not at home; She lives at 33 Forest Road.* □ **à**

2 direction: *He looked at her; She shouted at the boys.* □ **à; vers; contre**

3 time: *He arrived at ten o'clock; The children came at the sound of the bell.* □ **à**

4 state or occupation: *The countries are at war; She is at work.* □ **en; à**

5 pace or speed: *He drove at 120 kilometres per hour.* □ **à**

6 cost: *bread at $1.20 a loaf.* □ **à**

at all in any way: *I don't like it at all.* □ **du tout**

atap *see* **attap.**

ate *see* **eat.**

atheism ['eiθiizəm] *noun* the belief that there is no God. □ **athéisme**

'atheist *noun* a person who does not believe in God. □ **athée**

,athe'istic *adjective.* □ **athée**

athlete ['aθliːt] *noun* a person who is good at sport, especially running, jumping *etc*: *Hundreds of athletes took part in the games.* □ **athlète**

ath'letic [-'le-] *adjective* **1** of athletics: *She is taking part in the athletic events.* □ **d'athlétisme**

2 good at athletics; strong and able to move easily and quickly: *She looks very athletic.* □ **athlétique; sportif**

ath'letics [-'le-] *noun singular* the sports of running, jumping *etc* or competitions in these: *Athletics was my favourite activity at school.* □ **athlétisme**

atlas ['atləs] *noun* a book of maps: *My atlas is out of date.* □ **atlas**

atmosphere ['atməsfiə] *noun* **1** the air surrounding the earth: *The atmosphere is polluted.* □ **atmosphère**

2 any surrounding feeling: *There was a friendly atmosphere in the village.* □ **atmosphère**

,atmos'pheric [-'fe-] *adjective: atmospheric disturbances.* □ **atmosphérique**

atom ['atəm] *noun* **1** the smallest part of an element. □ **atome**

2 anything very small: *There's not an atom of truth in what she says.* □ **parcelle**

a'tomic [-'to-] *adjective.* □ **atomique**

atom(ic) bomb a bomb using atomic energy. □ **bombe atomique**

atomic energy very great energy obtained by breaking up the atoms of some substances. □ **énergie atomique**

atomic power power (for making electricity *etc*) obtained from atomic energy. □ **énergie nucléaire**

atrocious [ə'trouʃəs] *adjective* **1** very bad: *Your handwriting is atrocious.* □ **affreux**

2 extremely cruel: *an atrocious crime.* □ **atroce**

a'trociousness *noun.* □ **atrocité**

atrocity [ə'trosəti] *noun* an extremely cruel and wicked act: *The invading army committed many atrocities.* □ **atrocité**

attach [ə'tatʃ] *verb* to fasten or join: *I attached a label to my bag.* □ **attacher**

at'tached *adjective* (with **to**) fond of: *I'm very attached to my sister.* □ **attaché (à)**

at'tachment *noun* **1** something extra attached: *There are several attachments for this food-mixer.* □ **accessoire**

2 (*with* **for/to**) liking or affection: *I feel attachment for this town.* □ **attachement (à)**

attack [ə'tak] *verb* **1** to make a sudden, violent attempt to hurt or damage: *He attacked me with a knife; The village was attacked from the air.* □ **attaquer**

2 to speak or write against: *The Prime Minister's policy was attacked in the newspapers.* □ **attaquer**

3 (in games) to attempt to score a goal. □ **attaquer**

4 to make a vigorous start on: *It's time we attacked that* *pile of work.* □ **s'attaquer à**

■ *noun* **1** an act or the action of attacking: *The brutal attack killed the old man; They made an air attack on the town.* □ **attaque**

2 a sudden bout of illness: *heart attack; an attack of 'flu.* □ **crise, attaque**

attain [ə'tein] *verb* to gain; to achieve: *She attained all her ambitions.* □ **atteindre, réaliser**

attap, atap ['atap] *noun* the nipah palm, whose leaves are used for thatching. □ **palme**

attempt [ə'tempt] *verb* to try: *He attempted to reach the dying man, but did not succeed; He did not attempt the last question in the exam.* □ **tenter, s'attaquer à**

■ *noun* **1** a try: *They failed in their attempt to climb Everest; She made no attempt to run away.* □ **tentative**

2 an attack: *They made an attempt on his life but he survived.* □ **attentat**

attend [ə'tend] *verb* **1** to go to or be present at: *She attended the meeting; He will attend school till he is sixteen.* □ **assister à, suivre**

2 (*with* **to**) to listen or give attention to: *Attend carefully to what the teacher is saying!* □ **prêter attention à**

3 to deal with: *I'll attend to that problem tomorrow.* □ **s'occuper de**

4 to look after; to help or serve: *Two doctors attended her all through her illness; The queen was attended by four ladies.* □ **soigner, s'occuper de**

at'tendance *noun: His attendance* (= the number of times he attends) *at school is poor; Attendance* (= the number of people attending) *at the concerts went down after the price of tickets increased.* □ **assiduité; assistance**

at'tendant *noun* a person employed to look after someone or something: *a parking lot attendant.* □ **gardien, ienne; préposé, ée**

in attendance in the position of helping or serving: *There was no doctor in attendance at the road accident.* □ **présent, là, de service**

---
attendance ends in -ance (not -ence).
---

attention [ə'tenʃən] *noun* **1** notice: *She tried to attract my attention; Pay attention to your teacher!* □ **attention**

2 care: *That broken leg needs urgent attention.* □ **soins**

3 concentration of the mind: *His attention wanders.* □ **attention**

4 (in the army *etc*) a position in which one stands very straight with hands by the sides and feet together: *She stood to attention.* □ **(au) garde-à-vous**

at'tentive [-tiv] *adjective* giving attention: *The children were very attentive when the teacher was speaking; attentive to her needs.* □ **attentif (à)**

at'tentively [-tiv-] *adverb*: *They listened attentively.* □ **attentivement**

at'tentiveness *noun*. □ **prévenance(s)**

attic ['atik] *noun* a room at the top of a house under the roof: *They store old furniture in the attic.* □ **grenier**

attire [ə'taiə] *noun* clothing: *in formal attire.* □ **habillement**

■ *verb* to dress: *attired in silk.* □ **vêtir, parer (de)**

attitude ['atitjuːd] *noun* **1** a way of thinking or acting *etc: What is your attitude to politics?* □ **attitude (envers)**

2 a position of the body: *The artist painted the model in various attitudes.* □ **attitude**

attorney [ə'təːni] *noun* **1** a person who has the legal power to act for another person. □ **mandataire**

2 a lawyer. □ **avoué, ée**

attract [ə'trakt] *verb* **1** to cause (someone or something) to come towards: *A magnet attracts iron; I tried to attract her attention.* □ **attirer**

2 to arouse (someone's) liking or interest: *She attracted all the young men in the neighbourhood.* □ **attirer**

at'traction [-ʃən] *noun* **1** the act or power of attracting: *magnetic attraction.* □ **attraction; attirance**

2 something that attracts: *The attractions of the hotel include a golf-course.* □ **attraction**

at'tractive [-tiv] *adjective* **1** pleasant and good-looking: *an attractive man; young and attractive.* □ **séduisant**

2 likeable; tempting: *an attractive personality; He found the proposition attractive.* □ **attrayant**

at'tractively *adverb*. □ **d'une manière séduisante**

at'tractiveness *noun*. □ **attrait, charme**

be attracted to to be physically, sexually or emotionally drawn to someone or something: *Mark liked Rosemary, but she was attracted to Steven.* □ **se sentir attiré**

attribute [ə'tribjut] *verb* **1** to think of as being written, made *etc* by: *The play is attributed to Shakespeare.* □ **attribuer (à)**

2 to think of as being caused by: *He attributed his illness to the cold weather.* □ **attribuer (à)**

■ ['atribjuːt] *noun* a quality that is a particular part of a person or thing: *Intelligence is not one of his attributes.* □ **attribut**

ATV (all-terrain vehicle) [eitiːviː] *noun* a motor vehicle having three or more wheels fitted with large tires, designed chiefly for recreational use over rugged terrain: *ATV's were first used by the military in order to cross rugged territory.* □ **VTT**

auction ['oːkʃən] *noun* a public sale in which each thing is sold to the person who offers the highest price: *They held an auction; She sold the house by auction.* □ **(vente aux) enchères; encan**

■ *verb* to sell something in this way: *He auctioned all his furniture before emigrating.* □ **vendre aux enchères**

,auctio'neer *noun* a person who is in charge of selling things at an auction. □ **commissaire-priseur, euse**

audacious [oː'deiʃəs] *adjective* bold and daring: *an audacious plan.* □ **audacieux**

au'dacity [-'dasə-] *noun*. □ **audace**

audible ['oːdebl] *adjective* able to be heard: *When the microphone broke her voice was barely audible.* □ **audible**

,audi'bility *noun*. □ **audibilité**

audience ['oːdiəns] *noun* **1** a group of people watching or listening to a performance *etc: The audience at the concert; a television audience.* □ **auditoire; public**

2 a formal interview with someone important *eg* a king:

an audience with the Pope. □ **audience**

---
audience ends in **-ence** (not **-ance**).
---

audio- [ɔːdiou] (*as part of a word*) of sound or hearing. □ **audio-**

audiotypist [ˈɔːdioutaipist] *noun* a typist who types from a recording on a tape-recorder *etc*. □ **audiotypiste**

audiovisual [ɔːdiouˈviʒuəl]: **audiovisual aids** *noun plural* films, recordings *etc* used in teaching. □ **(support) audio-visuel**

audit [ˈɔːdit] *noun* an official examination of financial accounts. □ **vérification des comptes**
■ *verb* to examine financial accounts officially. □ **vérifier les comptes**
'auditor *noun* a person who audits accounts. □ **vérificateur, trice**

audition [ɔːˈdiʃən] *noun* a trial performance for an actor, singer, musician *etc*: *She had an audition for a part in the television play.* □ **audition**

auditorium [ɔːdiˈtɔːriəm] *noun* the part of a theatre *etc* where the audience sits. □ **salle**

augment [ɔːgˈment] *verb* to increase in amount or make bigger in size or number. □ **augmenter**
,augmen'tation *noun*. □ **augmentation**

August [ˈɔːgəst] *noun* the eighth month of the year. □ **août**

august [ɔːˈgʌst] *adjective* full of nobility and dignity. □ **majestueux**

aunt [aːnt] *noun* the sister of one's father or mother, or the wife of one's uncle: *My Aunt Anne died last week; The child went to the circus with her favourite aunt.* □ **tante**
'auntie, 'aunty [ˈaːnti] *noun* an aunt: *Auntie Jean; Where's your auntie?* □ **tata**

aura [ˈɔːrə] *noun* a particular feeling or atmosphere: *An aura of mystery surrounded her.* □ **aura**

aural [ˈɔːrəl] *adjective* of the ear or hearing: *an aural test.* □ **auditif; auriculaire**

auspices [ˈɔːspisiz]: **under the auspices of** arranged or encouraged by (a society *etc*): *This exhibition is being held under the auspices of the Montreal Museum of Fine Arts.* □ **(sous les) auspices (de)**
au'spicious [-ʃəs] *adjective* giving hope of success: *You haven't made a very auspicious start to your new job.* □ **de bon augure**

austere [ɔːˈstiə] *adjective* severely simple and plain; without luxuries or unnecessary expenditure: *an austere way of life.* □ **austère**
au'sterity [-ˈste-] *noun*. □ **austérité**

authentic [ɔːˈθentik] *adjective* true, real or genuine: *an authentic signature.* □ **authentique**
,authen'ticity [-sə-] *noun*. □ **authenticité**

author [ˈɔːθə] – *feminine sometimes* **'authoress** – *noun* the writer of a book, article, play *etc*: *He used to be a well-known author but his books are out of print now.* □ **auteur, eure**
'authorship *noun* the state or fact of being an author. □ **profession d'écrivain**

authority [ɔːˈθorəti] – *plural* **au'thorities** – *noun* **1** the power or right to do something: *She gave me authority*

to act on her behalf. □ **autorité**
2 a person who is an expert, or a book that can be referred to, on a particular subject: *She is an authority on Roman history.* □ **autorité**
3 (*usually in plural*) the person or people who have power in an administration *etc*: *The authorities would not allow public meetings.* □ **(les) autorités**
4 a natural quality in a person which makes him able to control and influence people: *a man of authority.* □ **autorité**
au,thori'tarian *adjective* considering obedience to authority more important than personal freedom: *an authoritarian government.* □ **autoritaire**
au'thoritative [-tətiv, (*American*) -teitiv] *adjective* said or written by an expert or a person in authority: *an authoritative opinion.* □ **autorisé**

authorize, authorise [ˈɔːθəraiz] *verb* to give the power or right to do something: *She authorized him to sign the documents; I authorized the payment of $100 to John Smith.* □ **autoriser**
,authori'zation, ,authori'sation *noun*. □ **autorisation**

auto- [ɔːtou] (*as part of a word*) **1** for or by oneself or itself. □ **auto(-)**
2 Same as **auto**.

auto [ˈɔːtou] short for **automobile** or **automatic**.

autobiography [ɔːtəbaiˈogrəfi] *noun* the story of a person's life written by himself. □ **autobiographie**
,autobio'graphic(al) [-ˈgra-] *adjective*. □ **autobio-graphique**

autocrat [ˈɔːtəkrat] *noun* a ruler who has total control: *The Tsars of Russia were autocrats.* □ **autocrate**
autocracy [ɔːˈtokrəsi] *noun* government by an autocrat. □ **autocratie**
,auto'cratic *adjective* **1** having absolute power: *an autocratic government.* □ **autocratique**
2 expecting complete obedience: *a very autocratic father.* □ **autocratique**

autograph [ˈɔːtəgraːf] *noun* a person's signature, especially as a souvenir: *She collected autographs of film stars.* □ **autographe**
■ *verb* to write one's name on (*especially* for a souvenir): *The actor autographed her program.* □ **dédicacer**

automatic [ɔːtəˈmatik] *adjective* **1** (of a machine *etc*) working by itself: *an automatic washing-machine.* □ **automatique**
2 (of an action) without thinking: *an automatic response.* □ **machinal**
■ *noun* a self-loading gun: *She has two automatics and a rifle.* □ **automatique**
'automated [-mei-] *adjective* working by automation. □ **automatisé**
,auto'matically *adverb*: *This machine works automatically; He answered automatically.* □ **automatiquement, machinalement**
,auto'mation *noun* (in factories *etc*) the use of machines, especially to work other machines: *Automation has resulted in people losing their jobs.* □ **automatisation; automation**
automaton [ɔːˈtomətən] – *plurals* **au'tomata** [-tə], **au'tomatons** – *noun* a human-shaped machine that can

be operated to move by itself. □ **automate**

automobile ['oːtəməbiːl] *noun* (*abbreviation* 'auto ['oːtou] – *plural* 'autos) a car. □ **automobile**

autonomy [oːˈtonəmi] *noun* the power or right of a country *etc* to govern itself. □ **autonomie**
au'**tonomous** *adjective* self-governing. □ **autonome**

autopsy ['oːtopsi] – *plural* 'autopsies – *noun* a medical examination of a body after death. □ **autopsie**

autumn ['oːtəm] *noun* the season of the year when leaves change colour and fall and fruits ripen, September to October or November in cooler northern regions; fall. □ **automne**
au'**tumnal** [oːˈtʌmnəl] *adjective*. □ **d'automne**

auxiliary [oːgˈziljəri] *adjective* helping; additional: *auxiliary forces*; *an auxiliary nurse*. □ **auxiliaire**
■ *noun* – *plural* au'**xiliaries** – 1 an additional helper. □ **auxiliaire**
2 a soldier serving with another nation. □ **auxiliaire**

avail [əˈveil]: **of no avail, to no avail** of no use or effect: *He tried to revive her but to no avail*; *His efforts were of no avail*. □ **sans effet**

available [əˈveiləbl] *adjective* able or ready to be used: *The ball is available on Saturday night*; *All the available money has been used*. □ **disponible**
a,vaila'**bility** *noun*. □ **disponibilité**

avalanche ['avəlaːnʃ] *noun* a fall of snow and ice down a mountain: *Two skiers were buried by the avalanche*. □ **avalanche**

avarice ['avəris] *noun* strong desire for money *etc*; greed. □ **avarice**
,ava'**ricious** [-ʃəs] *adjective*. □ **avare**

avenge [əˈvendʒ] *verb* to take revenge for a wrong on behalf of someone else: *She avenged her brother/her brother's death*. □ **venger**
a'**venger** *noun*. □ **vengeur, geresse**

avenue ['avinjuː] *noun* 1 a road, often with trees along either side. □ **avenue**
2 (*often abbreviated to Ave. when written*) a word used in the names of certain roads or streets: *Her address is 14 Swan Avenue*. □ **av.**

average ['avəridʒ] *noun* the result of adding several amounts together and dividing the total by the number of amounts: *The average of 3, 7, 9 and 13 is 8* (= 32÷4). □ **moyenne**
■ *adjective* 1 obtained by finding the average of amounts *etc*: *average price*; *the average temperature for the week*. □ **moyen**
2 ordinary; not exceptional: *The average person is not wealthy*; *His work is average*. □ **moyen**
■ *verb* to form an average: *Her expenses averaged (out at) 15 dollars a day*. □ **atteindre en moyenne**

averse [əˈvoːs] *adjective* (with **to**) having a dislike for: *averse to hard work*. □ **opposé à**
a'**version** [-ʒən] *noun* a feeling of dislike. □ **aversion**

avert [əˈvoːt] *verb* 1 to turn away, *especially* one's eyes: *She averted her eyes from the dead animal*. □ **détourner**
2 to prevent: *to avert disaster*. □ **prévenir**

aviary ['eiviəri] – *plural* 'aviaries – *noun* a place in which birds are kept. □ **volière**

aviation [eiviˈeiʃən] *noun* 1 (the science or practice of) flying in aircraft. □ **aviation**
2 the industry concerned with aircraft manufacture, design *etc*. □ **aéronautique**

avid ['avid] *adjective* eager: *avid for information*; *an avid reader*. □ **avide (de)**
'**avidly** *adverb*. □ **avidement**
a'**vidity** *noun*. □ **avidité**

avocado [avəˈkaːdou] – *plural* ,avo'**cados** – *noun* (*also* **avocado pear**) a kind of pear-shaped tropical fruit. □ **avocat**

avoid [əˈvoid] *verb* to keep away from (a place, person or thing): *He drove carefully to avoid the holes in the road*; *Avoid the subject of money*. □ **éviter**
a'**voidance** *noun*. □ **action d'éviter**

await [əˈweit] *verb* to wait for: *We await your arrival with expectation*. □ **attendre**

awake [əˈweik] – *past tense* **awoke** [əˈwouk]: *past participles* a'**waked**, a'**woken** – *verb* to wake from sleep: *She was awoken by a noise*; *He awoke suddenly*. □ **(se) réveiller; (s')éveiller**
■ *adjective* not asleep: *Is he awake?* □ **(r)éveillé**
a'**waken** *verb* 1 to awake: *I was awakened by the song of the birds*. □ **(r)éveiller**
2 to start (a feeling of interest, guilt *etc*): *Her interest was awakened by the lecture*. □ **éveillé**
a'**wakening** *noun* the arousal from sleep: *The awakening of a sound sleeper takes a long time every morning*. □ **réveil**
■ *adjective* an increased awareness or revival of interest: *I am experiencing an awakening interest in music and have bought a violin*. □ **réveil**

award [əˈwoːd] *verb* 1 to give (someone something that he has won or deserved): *They awarded her first prize*. □ **décerner**
2 to give: *He was awarded damages of $5,000*. □ **accorder**
■ *noun* a prize *etc* awarded: *The film awards were presented annually*. □ **récompense**

aware [əˈweə] *adjective* knowing; informed; conscious (of): *Is he aware of the problem?*; *Are they aware that I'm coming?* □ **conscient (de)**
a'**wareness** *noun*. □ **conscience (de qqch.)**

away [əˈwei] *adverb* 1 to or at a distance from the person speaking or the person or thing spoken about: *He lives three kilometres away (from the town)*; *Go away!*; *Take it away!* □ **(au) loin**
2 in the opposite direction: *She turned away so that he would not see her tears*. □ **de l'autre côté**
3 (gradually) into nothing: *The noise died away*. □ **complètement**
4 continuously: *They worked away until dark*. □ **sans arrêt**
5 (of a football match *etc*) not on the home ground: *The team is playing away this weekend*; (*also adjective*) *an away match*. □ **à l'extérieur**

awe [oː] *noun* wonder and fear: *The child looked in awe at the movie star*. □ **crainte révérentielle**
■ *verb* to fill with awe: *He was awed by his new school*. □ **inspirer une crainte respectueuse (à)**
'**awe-inspiring**, '**awesome** *adjective* causing awe: *The*

waterfall was awe-inspiring; *an awesome sight*. □ **d'une majesté grandiose**

'**awestruck** *adjective* filled with awe: *awestruck by the mountains*. □ **frappé d'une crainte révérentielle**

awful ['ɔːful] *adjective* **1** very great: *an awful rush*. □ **terrible**

2 very bad: *This book is awful*; *an awful experience*. □ **épouvantable**

3 severe: *an awful headache*. □ **terrible**

'**awfully** *adverb* very: *awfully silly*. □ **terriblement**

'**awfulness** *noun*. □ **caractère terrible**

awhile [ə'wail] *adverb* for a short time: *Wait awhile*. □ **un moment**

awkward ['ɔːkwəd] *adjective* **1** not graceful or elegant: *an awkward movement*. □ **maladroit; malhabile**

2 difficult or causing difficulty, embarrassment *etc*: *an awkward question*; *an awkward silence*; *Her cut is in an awkward place*. □ **gênant**

'**awkwardly** *adverb*. □ **maladroitement**

'**awkwardness** *noun*. □ **maladresse**

awoke(n) *see* **awake**.

axe [aks] *noun* a tool with a (long) handle and a metal blade for cutting down trees and cutting wood *etc* into pieces. □ **hache**

■ *verb* **1** to get rid of; to dismiss: *They've axed 50% of their staff*. □ **mettre à pied**

2 to reduce (costs, services *etc*): *Government spending in education has been axed*. □ **sabrer (dans)**

axiom ['aksiəm] *noun* a fact or statement which is definitely true and accepted as a principle or rule. □ **axiome**

axis ['aksis] – *plural* **axes** ['aksiːz] – *noun* **1** the real or imaginary line on which a thing turns (as the axis of the earth, from North Pole to South Pole, around which the earth turns). □ **axe**

2 a fixed line used as a reference, as in a graph: *She plotted the temperatures on the horizontal axis*. □ **axe**

axle ['aksl] *noun* the rod on which a wheel turns: *the back axle of the car*. □ **essieu**

Bb

babble ['babl] *verb* 1 to talk indistinctly or foolishly: *What are you babbling about now?* □ **bafouiller, bavarder**
2 to make a continuous and indistinct noise: *The stream babbled over the pebbles.* □ **gazouiller**
■ *noun* such talk or noises. □ **babil(lage)**

babe [beib] *noun* 1 a baby: *a babe in arms* (= a small baby not yet able to walk). □ **petit enfant**
2 *see* **baby**.

baboon [bə'buːn, bə-] *noun* a kind of large monkey with a dog-like face. □ **babouin**

baby ['beibi] – *plural* '**babies** – *noun* 1 a very young child: *Some babies cry during the night*; (*also adjective*) *a baby boy.* □ **bébé**
2 (*slang babe*) a girl or young woman. □ **mignonne, jolie fille**
'**babyish** *adjective* like a baby; not mature: *a babyish child that cries every day at school.* □ **enfantin**
baby buggy/carriage a pram. □ **landau**
baby grand a small grand piano. □ **(piano) demi-queue**
'**babysit** *verb* to remain in a house to look after a child while its parents are out: *He babysits for his friends every Saturday.* □ **faire de la garde d'enfants**
'**babysitter** *noun.* □ **garde d'enfants**
'**babysitting** *noun.* □ **garde d'enfants**

bachelor ['batʃələ] *noun* an unmarried man: *He's a confirmed bachelor* (= he has no intention of ever marrying); (*also adjective*) *a bachelor flat* (= a flat suitable for one person). □ **célibataire; garçonnière**

back [bak] *noun* 1 in man, the part of the body from the neck to the bottom of the spine: *She lay on her back.* □ **dos**
2 in animals, the upper part of the body: *She put the saddle on the horse's back.* □ **dos**
3 that part of anything opposite to or furthest from the front: *the back of the house*; *She sat at the back of the hall.* □ **arrière**
■ *adjective* of or at the back: *the back door.* □ **de derrière**
■ *adverb* 1 to, or at, the place or person from which a person or thing came: *I went back to the shop*; *She gave the car back to its owner.* □ **de retour**
2 away (from something); not near (something): *Move back! Let the ambulance get to the injured man*; *Keep back from me or I'll hit you!* □ **en arrière**
3 towards the back (of something): *Sit back in your chair.* □ **en arrière**
4 in return; in response to: *When the teacher is scolding you, don't answer back.* □ **en retour**
5 to, or in, the past: *Think back to your childhood.* □ **en arrière**
■ *verb* 1 to (cause to) move backwards: *He backed (his car) out of the garage.* □ **faire marche arrière**
2 to help or support: *Will you back me against the others?* □ **soutenir**
3 to bet or gamble on: *I backed your horse to win.* □ **miser sur**
'**backer** *noun* a person who supports someone or something, *especially* with money: *the backer of the new theatre.* □ **commanditaire**
'**backbite** *verb* to criticize a person when he is not present. □ **médire de**
'**backbiting** *noun*: *Constant backbiting by her colleagues led to her resignation.* □ **médisance**
'**backbone** *noun* 1 the spine: *the backbone of a fish.* □ **colonne vertébrale, épine dorsale**
2 the chief support: *The older employees are the backbone of the industry.* □ **pivot**
'**backbreaking** *adjective* (of a task *etc*) very difficult or requiring very hard work: *Digging the garden is a backbreaking job.* □ **éreintant**
,**back'date** *verb* 1 to put an earlier date on (a cheque *etc*): *She should have paid her bill last month and so she has backdated the cheque.* □ **antidater**
2 to make payable from a date in the past: *Our rise in pay was backdated to April.* □ **payer rétroactivement**
,**back'fire** *verb* 1 (of a car *etc*) to make a loud bang because of unburnt gases in the exhaust system: *The car backfired.* □ **avoir un retour de flamme**
2 (of a plan *etc*) to have unexpected results, often opposite to the intended results: *His scheme backfired (on him), and he lost money.* □ **échouer**
'**background** *noun* 1 the space behind the principal or most important figures or objects of a picture *etc*: *She always paints ships against a background of stormy skies*; *trees in the background of the picture.* □ **fond**
2 happenings that go before, and help to explain, an event *etc*: *the background to a situation.* □ **arrière-plan**
3 a person's origins, education *etc*: *He was ashamed of his humble background.* □ **origines**
'**backhand** *noun* 1 in tennis *etc*, a stroke or shot with the back of one's hand turned towards the ball: *a clever backhand*; *His backhand is very strong.* □ **revers**
2 writing with the letters sloping backwards: *I can always recognize her backhand.* □ **écriture penchée à gauche**
■ *adverb* using backhand: *She played the stroke backhand*; *She writes backhand.* □ **en revers, penché à gauche**
'**backlog** *noun* a pile of uncompleted work *etc* which has collected: *a backlog of orders because of the strike.* □ **accumulation**
,**back-'number** *noun* an out-of-date copy or issue of a magazine *etc*: *She collects back-numbers of comic magazines.* □ **vieux numéro**
'**backside** *noun* the bottom or buttocks: *He sits on his backside all day long and does no work.* □ **derrière**
'**backstroke** *noun* in swimming, a stroke made when lying on one's back in the water: *The child is good at backstroke.* □ **nage sur le dos**
'**backwash** *noun* 1 a backward current *eg* that following a ship's passage through the water: *the backwash of the steamer.* □ **remous; ressac**
2 the unintentional results of an action, situation *etc*: *The backwash of that firm's financial troubles affected several other firms.* □ **remous**
'**backwater** *noun* 1 a stretch of river not in the main stream. □ **bras de décharge, bras mort**

2 a place not affected by what is happening in the world outside. *That village is rather a backwater.* □ **coin tranquille**

,back'yard *noun* a garden at the back of a house *etc*: *He grows vegetables in his backyard.* □ **arrière-cour**

back down to give up one's opinion, claim *etc*: *She backed down in the face of strong opposition.* □ **reculer (devant)**

back of behind: *He parked in back of the store.* □ **derrière**

back on to (of a building *etc*) to have its back next to (something): *My house backs on to the racecourse.* □ **donner (par derrière) sur**

back out 1 to move out backwards: *She opened the garage door and backed (her car) out.* □ **sortir en marche arrière, à reculons**

2 to withdraw from a promise *etc*: *You promised to help – you mustn't back out now!* □ **(se) dérober**

back up to support or encourage: *The new evidence backed up my arguments.* □ **soutenir**

have one's back to the wall to be in a very difficult or desperate situation: *He certainly has his back to the wall as he has lost his job and cannot find another one.* □ **être au pied du mur**

put someone's back up to anger someone: *He put my back up with his boasting.* □ **irriter qqn**

take a back seat to take an unimportant position: *At these discussions he always takes a back seat and listens to others talking.* □ **s'effacer**

backpack ['bakpak] *noun* bag carried by straps on the back, a knapsack: *The strap of my packpack broke, so I had to carry it over one shoulder; Paul's backpack holds all of his school books.* □ **sac à dos**

backward ['bakwəd] *adjective* **1** aimed or directed backwards: *She left with a backward glance.* □ **en arrière, vers l'arrière**

2 less advanced in mind or body than is normal for one's age: *a backward child.* □ **arriéré**

3 late in developing a modern culture, mechanization *etc*: *That part of Canada is still very backward; the backward peoples of the world.* □ **arriéré**

'backwardness *noun*. □ **arriération**

'backwards *adverb* **1** towards the back: *He glanced backwards.* □ **vers l'arrière**

2 with one's back facing the direction one is going in: *The child walked backwards into a lamp-post.* □ **à reculons**

3 in the opposite way to that which is usual: *Can you count from 1 to 10 backwards?* (= starting at 10 and counting to 1). □ **à l'envers**

backwards and forwards in one direction and then in the opposite direction: *The dog ran backwards and forwards across the grass.* □ **de long en large**

bend/fall over backwards to try very hard: *She bent over backwards to get us tickets for the concert.* □ **se mettre en quatre (pour)**

bacon ['beikən] *noun* the flesh of the back and sides of a pig, salted and dried, used as food. □ **bacon**

bacteria [bak'tiəriə] – *singular* **bac'terium** [-əm] – *noun plural* organisms not able to be seen except under a

microscope, found in rotting matter, in air, in soil and in living bodies, some being the germs of disease: *a throat infection caused by bacteria.* □ **bactérie(s)**

bac,teri'ology [-'olədʒi] *noun* the study of bacteria. □ **bactériologie**

bac,terio'logical ['lo-] *adjective*. □ **bactériologiste**

bac,teri'ologist *noun*. □ **bactériologue**

bactrian *see* **camel**.

bad [bad] – *comparative* **worse** [wəːs]: *superlative* **worst** [wəːst] – *adjective* **1** not good; not efficient: *He is a bad driver; His eyesight is bad; They are bad at tennis* (= they play tennis badly). □ **mauvais**

2 wicked; immoral: *a bad man; He has done some bad things.* □ **méchant**

3 unpleasant: *bad news.* □ **mauvais**

4 rotten: *This meat is bad.* □ **pourri**

5 causing harm or injury: *Smoking is bad for your health.* □ **mauvais**

6 (of a part of the body) painful, or in a weak state: *She has a bad heart; I have a bad head* (= headache) *today.* □ **malade, sale**

7 unwell: *I am feeling quite bad today.* □ **mal**

8 serious or severe: *a bad accident; a bad mistake.* □ **grave**

9 (of a debt) not likely to be paid: *The firm loses money every year from bad debts.* □ **douteux**

bad luck *noun* misfortune; when everything seems to go wrong: *Carol had bad luck all day; she broke her leg, failed a test and lost her cat.* □ **malchance**

'badly – *comparative* **worse**: *superlative* **worst** – *adverb* **1** not well, efficiently or satisfactorily: *He plays tennis very badly.* □ **mal**

2 to a serious or severe extent: *He badly needs a haircut; The dress is badly stained.* □ **sérieusement**

'badness *noun*. □ **méchanceté**

badly off not having much *especially* money: *We can't go on holiday – we are too badly off.* □ **être dans la gêne**

feel bad (about something) to feel upset or ashamed about something: *I feel bad about forgetting to telephone you.* □ **être embêté (à propos de)**

go from bad to worse to get into an even worse condition *etc* than before: *Things are going from bad to worse for the firm – not only are we losing money but there's going to be a strike as well.* □ **empirer**

not bad quite good: *'Is she a good swimmer?' 'She's not bad.'* □ **pas mauvais**

too bad unfortunate: *It's too bad that she has left.* □ **dommage (que)**

bade *see* **bid**.

badge [badʒ] *noun* a mark, emblem or ornament showing rank, occupation, or membership of a society, team *etc*: *a school badge on a blazer.* □ **insigne**

badger ['badʒə] *noun* a burrowing animal of the weasel family. □ **blaireau**

■ *verb* to annoy or worry: *She badgered the authorities until they gave her a new passport.* □ **harceler**

badminton ['badmintən] *noun* a game played on a court with a shuttlecock and rackets. □ **badminton**

■ *adjective*: *a badminton match.* □ **de badminton**

baffle ['bafl] *verb* to puzzle (a person): *I was baffled by her attitude towards her husband.* □ **déconcerter**

baffling *adjective*: *a baffling crime.* □ **déroutant**

bag [bag] *noun* 1 a container made of soft material (*eg* cloth, animal skin, plastic *etc*): *She carried a small bag.* □ **sac**

2 a quantity of fish or game caught: *Did you get a good bag today?* □ **(bonne) pêche, (bonne) chasse**

■ *verb* – *past tense, past participle* **bagged** – 1 to put into a bag. □ **mettre en sac**

2 to kill (game). □ **tuer**

'**baggy** *adjective* loose, like an empty bag: *He wears baggy trousers.* □ **bouffant**

bags of a large amount of: *She's got bags of money.* □ **des tas de**

in the bag as good as done or complete (in the desired way): *Your appointment is in the bag.* □ **dans la poche**

baggage ['bagidʒ] *noun* luggage: *She sent her baggage on in advance.* □ **bagages**

bagpipes ['bagpaips] *noun plural* a wind instrument consisting of a bag fitted with pipes, played in Scotland *etc*: *She wants to learn to play the bagpipes.* □ **cornemuse**

bail¹ [beil] *noun* a sum of money which is given to a court of law to get an untried prisoner out of prison until the time of his trial, and which acts as security for his return: *bail of $500.* □ **caution**

bail out to set (a person) free by giving such money to a court of law: *He was bailed out by his father.* □ **fournir une caution pour qqn**

■ *See also* **bale out** *under* **bale².**

bail² [beil] *noun* one of the cross-pieces laid on the top of the wicket in cricket. □ **bâtonnet**

bail³ *see* **bale².**

bait [beit] *noun* food used to attract fish, animals *etc* which one wishes to catch, kill *etc*: *Before he went fishing he dug up some worms for bait.* □ **appât**

■ *verb* to put bait on or in (a hook, trap *etc*): *She baited the mousetrap with cheese.* □ **appâter**

baize [beiz] *noun* a type of coarse woollen cloth, often green, *usually* used for covering card-tables *etc*. □ **tapis vert**

bake [beik] *verb* 1 to cook in an oven: *I'm going to bake (bread) today; He baked the ham.* □ **(faire) cuire au four**

2 to dry or harden by heat: *The sun is baking the ground dry.* □ **dessécher**

baked *adjective*: *baked ham; freshly baked bread.* □ **cuit au four**

'**baker** *noun* 1 a person who bakes: *He is a qualified baker; She is a good baker.* □ **boulanger, ère**

2 a baker's shop. □ **boulangerie**

'**bakery** – *plural* '**bakeries** – *noun* a place where baking is done and/or where bread, cakes *etc* are sold: *I bought some cakes at the bakery.* □ **boulangerie**

'**baking** *noun* the act or art of cooking bread, cakes *etc*. □ **cuisson**

baking powder a powder used to make cakes *etc* rise: *This sponge cake is very flat – you can't have used*

enough baking powder. □ **levure**

a baker's dozen thirteen. □ **treize à la douzaine**

balance ['baləns] *noun* 1 a weighing instrument. □ **balance**

2 a state of physical steadiness: *The child was walking along the wall when he lost his balance and fell.* □ **équilibre**

3 state of mental or emotional steadiness: *The balance of her mind was disturbed.* □ **équilibre**

4 the amount by which the two sides of a financial account (money spent and money received) differ: *I have a balance* (= amount remaining) *of $100 in my bank account; a large bank balance.* □ **solde**

■ *verb* 1 (of two sides of a financial account) to make or be equal: *I can't get these accounts to balance.* □ **(s')équilibrer**

2 to make or keep steady: *She balanced the jug of water on her head; The girl balanced on her toes.* □ **maintenir en équilibre**

balance sheet a paper showing a summary and balance of financial accounts. □ **bilan**

in the balance in an undecided or uncertain state: *Her fate is (hanging) in the balance.* □ **en balance**

off balance not steady: *She hit me while I was off balance.* □ **en déséquilibre**

on balance having taken everything into consideration: *On balance I think Miss Smith is a better tennis player than my sister.* □ **à tout prendre**

balcony ['balkəni] – *plural* '**balconies** – *noun* 1 a platform built out from the wall of a building: *Many hotel rooms have balconies.* □ **balcon**

2 in theatres *etc*, an upper floor: *We sat in the balcony of the movie theatre;* (*also adjective*) *balcony seats.* □ **(de) balcon**

bald [bo:ld] *adjective* 1 (of people) with little or no hair on the head: *a bald head; He is going bald* (= becoming bald). □ **chauve**

2 (of birds, animals) without feathers, fur *etc*: *a bald patch on the dog's back.* □ **dépourvu de plumes, de poils**

3 bare or plain: *a bald statement of the facts.* □ **sans ornements**

'**baldness** *noun*. □ **calvitie**

'**balding** *adjective* becoming bald. □ **devenant chauve**

'**baldly** *adverb* in a plain or bare way: *He answered her questions baldly.* □ **sèchement**

bale¹ [beil] *noun* a large bundle of goods or material (cloth, hay *etc*) tied together: *a bale of cotton.* □ **balle**

bale² [beil] *verb* (*also* **bail**) to clear (water out of a boat with buckets *etc*): *Several litres of water were baled out of the boat.* □ **écoper**

bale out to parachute from a plane in an emergency. □ **sauter en parachute**

■ *See also* **bail out** *under* **bail¹.**

baleful ['beilful] *adjective* evil or harmful: *a baleful influence.* □ **sinistre**

'**balefully** *adverb*. □ **sinistrement**

ball¹ [bo:l] *noun* 1 anything roughly round in shape: *a ball of wool.* □ **boule, pelote**

2 a round object used in games: *a tennis ball.* □ **balle,**

ballon
,**ball 'bearings** *noun plural* in machinery *etc*, small steel balls that help the revolving of one part over another. □ **roulement à billes**
'**ballcock** *noun* a valve in a cistern. □ **robinet à flotteur**
'**ballpoint** *noun* a pen having a tiny ball as the writing point. □ **stylo bille**
■ *adjective*: *a ballpoint pen*. □ **à bille**
on the ball quick, alert and up-to-date: *The new manager is really on the ball*. □ **à la hauteur**
start/set, keep the ball rolling to start or keep something going, *especially* a conversation: *He can be relied on to start the ball rolling at parties*. □ **lancer, soutenir la conversation**

ball² [bɔːl] *noun* a formal dance: *a ball at the palace*. □ **bal**
'**ballroom** *noun* a large room for a formal dance. □ **salle de bal**
■ *adjective*: *ballroom dancing*. □ **de bal**

ballad ['baləd] *noun* a simple, often sentimental, song: *Older people prefer ballads to pop music*. □ **romance**

ballerina [balə'riːnə] *noun* a female (often principal) ballet-dancer: *Pavlova was a famous ballerina*. □ **ballerine**

ballet ['balei, ba'lei] *noun* 1 a theatrical performance of dancing with set steps and mime, often telling a story: *Swan Lake is my favourite ballet*. □ **ballet**
2 the art of dancing in this way: *She is taking lessons in ballet*; (*also adjective*) *a ballet class*. □ **(de) ballet**
'**ballet-dancer** *noun*. □ **danseur, euse de ballet**

ballistic missile [ba'listik 'misail] *a missile guided for part of its course but falling like an ordinary bomb*. □ **engin balistique**

balloon [bə'luːn] *noun* a large bag, made of light material and filled with a gas lighter than air: *They decorated the dance-hall with balloons*. □ **ballon**

ballot ['balət] *noun* a method of voting in secret by marking a paper and putting it into a box: *They held a ballot to choose a new chairman*; *The question was decided by ballot*. □ **vote, scrutin**

ballyhoo ['bali,huː, ,bali'huː] *noun* noisy or sensational advertising or publicity: *a lot of ballyhoo about the filmstar's visit*. □ **battage**

balm [baːm] *noun* something that soothes: *The music was balm to my ears*. □ **baume**
'**balmy** *adjective*. □ **adoucissant**
'**balminess** *noun*. □ **adoucissement**

balsa ['bɔːlsə] *noun* 1 (*also* **balsa tree**) a tropical American tree. □ **balsa**
2 (*often* '**balsa-wood**) its very lightweight wood: *Her model airplane is made of balsa*. □ **balsa**

balsam ['bɔːlsəm] *noun* a pleasant-smelling substance obtained from certain trees: *He inhaled balsam when he had a bad cold*. □ **baume**

bamboo [bam'buː] *noun, adjective* (of) a type of gigantic grass with hollow, jointed, woody stems: *furniture made of bamboo*; *bamboo furniture*. □ **bambou**

bamboozle [bam'buːzl] *verb* to confuse completely: *The motorist was completely bamboozled by the road-signs*. □ **mystifier**

ban [ban] *noun* an order that a certain thing may not be done: *a ban on smoking*. □ **interdiction**
■ *verb* – past tense, past participle **banned** – to forbid: *The government banned publication of his book*. □ **interdire**

banana [bə'naːnə] *noun* the long curved fruit, yellow-skinned when ripe, of a type of very large tropical tree. □ **banane**
banana tree *noun* large tropical plant that bears clusters of long yellow fruit called bananas: *Ripe bananas were picked off the banana tree, peeled and eaten*. □ **bananier**

band¹ [band] *noun* 1 a strip of material to put around something: *a rubber band*. □ **bande**
2 a stripe of a colour *etc*: *a skirt with a band of red in it*. □ **bande**
3 in radio *etc*, a group of frequencies or wavelengths: *the medium waveband*. □ **bande**

band² [band] *noun* 1 a number of persons forming a group: *a band of robbers*. □ **bande**
2 a body of musicians: *a brass band*; *a dance band*. □ **orchestre**
■ *verb* to unite or gather together for a purpose: *They banded together to oppose the building of the garage*. □ **se liguer**

bandage ['bandidʒ] *noun* (a piece of) cloth for binding up a wound, or a broken bone: *She had a bandage on her injured finger*. □ **pansement**
■ *verb* to cover with a bandage: *The doctor bandaged the boy's foot*. □ **mettre un pansement à**

bandit ['bandit] *noun* an outlaw or robber, *especially* as a member of a gang: *They were attacked by bandits in the mountains*. □ **bandit**

bandy ['bandi] *adjective* (of legs) bent outwards at the knee: *She wears long skirts to hide her bandy legs*. □ **arqué**
bandy-'legged [-legid] *adjective*. □ **arqué**

bang [baŋ] *noun* 1 a sudden loud noise: *The door shut with a bang*. □ **claquement**
2 a blow or knock: *a bang on the head from a falling branch*. □ **coup (violent)**
■ *verb* 1 to close with a sudden loud noise: *He banged the door*. □ **claquer**
2 to hit or strike violently, often making a loud noise: *The child banged his drum*; *She banged the book down angrily on the table*. □ **frapper violemment**
3 to make a sudden loud noise: *We could hear the fireworks banging in the distance*. □ **éclater, péter**
'**banger** *noun* an explosive firework: *The child was frightened by the bangers at the firework display*. □ **pétard**

bangle ['baŋgl] *noun* a bracelet worn on the arm or leg: *gold bangles*. □ **bracelet**

bangs [baŋz] *noun* hair cut to hang over the forehead: *You should have your bangs cut before it covers your eyes*. □ **frange**

banish ['baniʃ] *verb* to send away (*usually* from a country), *especially* as a punishment: *He was banished (from the country) for treason*. □ **bannir**
'**banishment** *noun*. □ **bannissement**

banister ['banistə] *noun* **1** (*often plural*) the handrail of a staircase and the posts supporting it. □ **rampe**
2 one of the posts supporting the handrail. □ **barreau**

banjo ['bandʒou] – *plural* **'banjo(e)s** – *noun* a stringed musical instrument similar to the guitar: *She plays the banjo*; *Play me a tune on the banjo.* □ **banjo**

bank¹ [baŋk] *noun* **1** a mound or ridge (of earth *etc*): *The child climbed the bank to pick flowers.* □ **talus**
2 the ground at the edge of a river, lake *etc*: *The river overflowed its banks.* □ **rive**
3 a raised area of sand under the sea: *a sand-bank.* □ **banc**
■ *verb* **1** (*often with* **up**) to form into a bank or banks: *The earth was banked up against the wall of the house.* □ **remblayer**
2 to tilt (an aircraft *etc*) while turning: *The plane banked steeply.* □ **virer (sur l'aile)**

bank² [baŋk] *noun* **1** a place where money is lent or exchanged, or put for safety and/or to acquire interest: *She has plenty of money in the bank*; *I must go to the bank today.* □ **banque**
2 a place for storing other valuable material: *A blood bank.* □ **banque**
■ *verb* to put into a bank: *She banks her wages every week.* □ **déposer à la banque**
'banker *noun* a person who owns or manages a bank. □ **banquier, ière**
bank book a book recording money deposited in, or withdrawn from, a bank. □ **livret de banque**
bank card a plastic card used to access an account at automated teller machines. □ **carte bancaire**
bank holiday a day on which banks are closed (and which is often also a public holiday). □ **jour férié**
'banknote *noun* a piece of paper issued by a bank, used as money. □ **billet de banque**
bank on to rely on: *Don't bank on me – I'll probably be late.* □ **compter sur**

bank³ [baŋk] *noun* a collection of rows (of instruments *etc*): *The modern pilot has banks of instruments.* □ **rangée**

bankrupt ['baŋkrʌpt] *adjective* unable to pay one's debts: *She has been declared bankrupt.* □ **en faillite**
■ *noun* a person who is unable to pay his debts. □ **failli, ie**
■ *verb* to make bankrupt: *His extravagance soon bankrupted him.* □ **ruiner**
'bankruptcy *noun*. □ **faillite**

banner ['banə] *noun* **1** a military flag. □ **bannière**
2 a large strip of cloth bearing a slogan *etc*: *Many of the demonstrators were carrying banners.* □ **banderole**

banquet ['baŋkwit] *noun* a feast or ceremonial dinner at which speeches are often made. □ **banquet**

bantam ['bantəm] *noun* a small variety of domestic fowl: *She keeps bantams*; (*also adjective*) *a bantam cock.* □ **coq nain, poule naine**

banter ['bantə] *noun* friendly teasing: *The sick boy was cheered up by the noisy banter of his friends.* □ **taquinerie(s)**

banyan ['banjən] *noun* a tree that grows on wet land. Its branches have hanging roots that grow down and start new trunks. □ **banian**

baptize, baptise [bap'taiz] *verb* to dip (a person) in water, or sprinkle (someone) with water, as a symbol of acceptance into the Christian church, *usually* also giving him a name: *She was baptized Mary but calls herself Jane.* □ **baptiser**
'baptism [-tizəm] *noun* (an act of) baptizing: *the baptism of the baby.* □ **baptême**
bap'tismal *adjective*. □ **baptismal, de baptême**

bar [baː] *noun* **1** a rod or oblong piece (*especially* of a solid substance): *a gold bar*; *a bar of chocolate*; *iron bars on the windows.* □ **barre; tablette; barreau**
2 a broad line or band: *The blue material had bars of red running through it.* □ **rayure**
3 a bolt: *a bar on the door.* □ **bâcle**
4 a counter at which or across which articles of a particular kind are sold: *a snack bar*; *Your whisky is on the bar.* □ **bar, comptoir**
5 a pub, public house. □ **bar**
6 a measured division in music: *Sing the first ten bars.* □ **mesure**
7 something which prevents (something): *His carelessness is a bar to his promotion.* □ **obstacle**
8 the rail at which the prisoner stands in court: *The prisoner at the bar collapsed when he was sentenced to ten years' imprisonment.* □ **barre**
■ *verb* – *past tense, past participle* **barred** – **1** to fasten with a bar: *Bar the door.* □ **bâcler une porte**
2 to prevent from entering: *He's been barred from the club.* □ **exclure (de)**
3 to prevent (from doing something): *My lack of money bars me from going on holiday.* □ **empêcher (de faire qqch.)**
■ *preposition* except: *All bar one of the family had measles.* □ **sauf**
'barmaid, 'barman, 'bartender [-tendə] *noun* a person who serves drinks at a bar. □ **barmaid, barman**

barb [baːb] *noun* **1** a backward-facing point on an arrowhead, fishing-hook *etc*. □ **barbillon, barbelure**
2 a hurtful remark. □ **parole acerbe**
barbed *adjective*: *a barbed arrow/remark.* □ **acéré**
barbed wire wire with sharp points at intervals: *I tore my skirt on that barbed wire*; (*also adjective with hyphen*) *a barbed-wire fence.* □ **(fil de fer) barbelé**

barbarous ['baːbərəs] *adjective* **1** uncultured and uncivilized: *barbarous habits.* □ **barbare**
2 brutal: *a barbarous assault.* □ **barbare**
'barbarousness *noun*. □ **barbarie**
bar'barian [-'beəriən] *noun* an uncultured and uncivilized person. □ **barbare**
■ *adjective*: *barbarian customs.* □ **barbare**

barbecue ['baːbikjuː] *noun* **1** a framework for grilling meat *etc* over a charcoal fire: *We cooked the steak on a barbecue.* □ **barbecue**
2 a party in the open air, at which food is barbecued. □ **barbecue**
■ *verb* to cook on a barbecue: *She barbecued a chicken.* □ **griller au feu de bois**

barber ['baːbə] *noun* a person who cuts men's hair, shaves their beards *etc*. □ **coiffeur**

bare [beə] *adjective* **1** uncovered or naked: *bare skin*; *bare floors.* □ **nu**

2 empty: *bare shelves.* □ **vide**

3 of trees *etc*, without leaves. □ **dénudé**

4 worn thin: *The carpet is a bit bare.* □ **usé**

5 basic; essential: *the bare necessities of life.* □ **essentiel**

■ *verb* to uncover: *The dog bared its teeth in anger.* □ **montrer**

'**barely** *adverb* scarcely or only just: *We have barely enough food.* □ **tout juste**

'**bareness** *noun.* □ **nudité**

'**bareback** *adverb, adjective* without a saddle: *I enjoy riding bareback.* □ **à nu**

'**barefaced** *adjective* openly impudent: *a barefaced lie.* □ **impudent**

'**barefoot(ed)** *adjective, adverb* not wearing shoes or socks *etc*: *The children go barefoot on the beach.* □ **nu-pieds**

,**bare'headed** *adjective, adverb* not wearing a hat *etc*. □ **nu-tête**

bargain ['baːgin] *noun* **1** something bought cheaply and giving good value for money: *This carpet was a real bargain.* □ **(bonne) affaire**

2 an agreement made between people: *I'll make a bargain with you.* □ **marché**

■ *verb* to argue about or discuss a price *etc*: *I bargained with her and finally got the price down.* □ **marchander**

bargain for to expect or take into consideration: *I didn't bargain for everyone arriving at once.* □ **s'attendre à**

barge [baːdʒ] *noun* **1** a flat-bottomed boat for carrying goods *etc*. □ **chaland**

2 a large power-driven boat. □ **péniche**

■ *verb* **1** to move (about) clumsily: *He barged about the room.* □ **se déplacer avec maladresse**

2 to bump (into): *He barged into me.* □ **rentrer dans**

3 (*with* **in(to)**) to push one's way (into) rudely: *She barged in without knocking.* □ **faire brutalement irruption (dans)**

baritone ['baritoun] *noun* (a singer with) a deep male voice between bass and tenor. □ **bariton**

bark[1] [baːk] *noun* the short, sharp cry of a dog, fox *etc*. □ **aboiement**

■ *verb* **1** to make this sound: *The dog barked at the stranger.* □ **aboyer**

2 to utter abruptly: *She barked a reply.* □ **dire d'un ton brutal**

bark[2] [baːk] *noun* the covering of the trunk and branches of a tree: *He stripped the bark off the branch.* □ **écorce**

■ *verb* to take the skin off (part of the body) by accident: *I barked my skin on the table.* □ **écorcher**

barley ['baːli] *noun* a type of grain used for food and for making beer and whisky: *The farmer has harvested the barley.* □ **orge**

barley sugar a kind of hard sweet made by melting and cooling sugar. □ **sucre d'orge**

barmaid, barman *see* **bar.**

barn [baːn] *noun* a building in which grain, hay *etc* are stored: *The farmer keeps his tractor in the barn.* □ **grange**

barnacle ['baːnəkl] *noun* a kind of small shellfish that

sticks to rocks and the bottoms of ships. □ **bernacle**

barometer [bə'romitə] *noun* an instrument which indicates changes of weather: *The barometer is falling – it is going to rain.* □ **baromètre**

barometric [barə'metrik] *adjective*: *barometric pressure.* □ **barométrique**

baron ['barən] – *feminine* '**baroness** – *noun* **1** a nobleman: *He was made a baron*; *Baron Rothschild.* □ **baron, onne**

2 an important, powerful person: *a newspaper baron.* □ **magnat**

barracks ['baraks] *noun singular or plural* a building or buildings for housing soldiers: *confined to barracks* (= not allowed to leave the barracks). □ **caserne**

barrage [bə'raːʒ] *noun* **1** something that keeps back an enemy: *a barrage of gunfire.* □ **tir de barrage**

2 an overwhelming number: *a barrage of questions.* □ **déluge**

3 a man-made barrier across a river. □ **barrage**

barrel ['barəl] *noun* **1** a container of curved pieces of wood or of metal: *The barrels contain beer.* □ **tonneau; baril**

2 a long, hollow, cylindrical shape, *especially* the tube-shaped part of a gun: *The bullet jammed in the barrel of the gun.* □ **canon**

barren ['barən] *adjective* not able to produce crops, fruit, young *etc*: *barren soil*; *a barren fruit-tree*; *a barren woman.* □ **stérile; infécond**

'**barrenness** *noun.* □ **stérilité**

barricade [bari'keid] *noun* a barrier put up to block a street *etc*: *There were barricades keeping back the crowds.* □ **barricade**

■ *verb* to block something (*eg* a street) with a barricade. □ **barricader**

barrier ['bariə] *noun* **1** something put up as a defence or protection: *a barrier between the playground and the busy road.* □ **barrière**

2 something that causes difficulty: *His deafness was a barrier to promotion.* □ **obstacle**

barrister ['baristə] *noun* a lawyer qualified to present cases in court. □ **avocat**

barrow ['barou] *noun* **1** a wheelbarrow. □ **brouette**

2 a small (*usually* two-wheeled) cart. □ **diable**

bartender *see* **bar.**

barter ['baːtə] *verb* to trade by giving (one thing) in exchange (for another): *The bandits bartered gold for guns.* □ **troquer (contre)**

■ *noun* goods used in bartering: *Some tribes use sea-shells as barter.* □ **troc**

basalt ['basoːlt] *noun* any of certain types of dark-coloured rock. □ **basalte**

base[1] [beis] *noun* **1** the foundation, support, or lowest part (of something), or the surface on which something is standing: *the base of the statue*; *the base of the triangle*; *the base of the tree.* □ **base**

2 the main ingredient of a mixture: *This paint has oil as a base.* □ **base**

3 a headquarters, starting-point *etc*: *an army base.* □ **base**

■ *verb* (*often with* **on**) to use as a foundation, starting-

point *etc*: *I base my opinion on evidence*; *Our group was based in Paris.* □ **baser (sur/à)**
'**baseless** *adjective* without foundation or reason: *a baseless claim.* □ **sans fondement**
base² [beis] *adjective* wicked or worthless: *base desires.* □ **bas, abject**
'**basely** *adverb.* □ **bassement**
'**baseness** *noun.* □ **bassesse**
baseball ['beisbɔːl] *noun* an American game played with bat and ball. □ **baseball**
basement ['beismənt] *noun* the lowest floor of a building, *usually* below ground level: *She lives in a basement*; (*also adjective*) *a basement flat.* □ **sous-sol**
bash [baʃ] *verb* (*sometimes with* **in**) to beat or smash (in): *The soldiers bashed in the door.* □ **défoncer, enfoncer**
■ *noun* 1 a heavy blow: *a bash with his foot.* □ **coup**
2 a dent: *a bash on the car's nearside door.* □ **bosse**
bash on/ahead (**with**) to go on doing something *especially* in a careless or inattentive way: *In spite of his father's advice he bashed on with the painting.* □ **continuer à faire qqch. de façon négligente**
have a bash at to make an attempt at: *Although he was not a handyman, he had a bash at mending the lock.* □ **s'essayer à**
bashful ['baʃful] *adjective* shy: *a bashful boy*; *a bashful smile.* □ **timide**
bashfully *adverb.* □ **timidement**
'**bashfulness** *noun.* □ **timidité**
basic ['beisik] *adjective* 1 of, or forming, the main part or foundation of something: *Your basic theory is wrong.* □ **de base**
2 restricted to a fundamental level, elementary: *a basic knowledge of French.* □ **élémentaire**
'**basically** *adverb* fundamentally: *She seems strict, but basically* (= in reality) *she's very nice*; *Her job, basically, is to deal with foreign customers.* □ **au fond**
basil ['beizl] *noun* a fragrant herb used in cooking: *The chef sprinkled basil leaves into the soup to give it flavour.* □ **basilic**
basin ['beisn] *noun* 1 a bowl for washing oneself in: *a wash basin.* □ **cuvette**
2 a bathroom sink. □ **lavabo**
3 the area drained by a river: *the basin of the Nile.* □ **bassin**
4 the deep part of a harbour: *There were four yachts anchored in the harbour basin.* □ **bassin**
basis ['beisis] *plural* '**bases** [-siːz] – *noun* that on which a thing rests or is founded: *This idea is the basis of my argument.* □ **base**
bask [baːsk] *verb* to lie (*especially* in warmth or sunshine): *The seals basked in the warm sun.* □ **(se) dorer**
basket ['baːskit] *noun* a container made of strips of wood, rushes *etc* woven together: *She carried a large basket.* □ **panier**
'**basketball** *noun* a game in which goals are scored by throwing a ball into a net on a high post. □ **basket(-ball)**
■ *adjective*: *a basketball court.* □ **de basket(-ball)**
'**basketry** *noun* basketwork. □ **vannerie**

'**basketwork** *noun* articles made of plaited rushes *etc*. □ **(articles de) vannerie**
■ *adjective*: *a basketwork chair.* □ **de vannerie**
bass¹ [beis] – *plural* '**basses** – *noun* (a singer having) a male voice of the lowest pitch. □ **basse**
bass² [bas] – *plural* **bass**, (*rare*) '**basses** – *noun* a type of fish of the perch family. □ **perche**
bassoon [bə'suːn] *noun* a woodwind musical instrument which gives a very low sound. □ **basson**
bastard ['baːstəd] *noun* a child born of parents not married to each other. □ **bâtard**
■ *adjective*: *a bastard son.* □ **bâtard**
bastion ['bastjən] *noun* a person, place or thing which acts as a defence: *He's one of the last bastions of the old leisurely way of life.* □ **bastion**
bat¹ [bat] *noun* a shaped piece of wood *etc* for striking the ball in cricket, baseball, table-tennis *etc*. □ **bâton, raquette**
■ *verb* – *past tense, past participle* **batted** – 1 to use a bat: *He bats with his left hand.* □ **manier le bâton, la raquette**
2 to strike (the ball) with a bat: *She batted the ball.* □ **frapper avec une batte**
bat² [bat] *noun* a mouse-like animal which flies, *usually* at night. □ **chauve-souris**
'**batty** *adjective* crazy: *a batty old man.* □ **cinglé**
batch [batʃ] *noun* a number of things made, delivered *etc*, all at one time: *a batch of bread*; *The letters were sent out in batches.* □ **tas, paquet**
bated ['beitid]: **with bated breath** breathing only slightly, due to anxiety, excitement *etc*: *The crowd watched the rescue of the child with bated breath.* □ **en retenant son souffle**
bath [baːθ] – *plural* **baths** [baːðz] – *noun* 1 a large container for holding water in which to wash the whole body: *I'll fill the bath with water for you.* □ **baignoire**
2 an act of washing in a bath: *I had a bath last night.* □ **bain**
3 a container of liquid *etc* in which something is immersed: *a bird bath.* □ **vasque**
■ *verb* to wash in a bath: *I'll bath the baby.* □ **donner un bain à**
,**bath'chair** *noun* a kind of wheeled chair for an invalid. □ **fauteuil roulant**
'**bathroom** *noun* 1 a room in a house *etc* which contains a bath. □ **salle de bains**
2 (*especially North American*) a lavatory. □ **toilettes**
'**bathtub** *noun* a bath (for washing in). □ **baignoire**
bathe [beið] *verb* 1 to put into water: *He bathed his feet*; *I'll bathe your wounds.* □ **baigner**
2 to go swimming: *She bathes in the sea every day.* □ **se baigner**
■ *noun* an act of swimming: *a midnight bathe.* □ **bain**
'**bather** *noun.* □ **baigneur, euse**
'**bathing** *noun.* □ **baignade**
batik ['batik] *noun* a method of dyeing patterns on cloth by waxing certain areas so that they remain uncoloured. □ **batik**
baton [ba'ton] *noun* 1 a short, heavy stick, carried by a policeman as a weapon. □ **bâton, matraque**

2 a light, slender stick used when conducting an orchestra or choir: *The conductor raised his baton.* □ **baguette**

battalion [bə'taljən] *noun* a large body of foot soldiers forming part of a brigade. □ **bataillon**

batten ['batn] *noun* a piece of wood used for keeping other pieces in place: *These strips are all fastened together with a batten.* □ **latte, planche**

batter ['batə] *verb* to beat with blow after blow: *He was battered to death with a large stick.* □ **rouer de coups**

battery ['batəri] – *plural* **'batteries** – *noun* 1 a series of two or more electric cells arranged to produce, or store, a current: *a flashlight battery.* □ **pile(s)**
2 an arrangement of cages in which laying hens *etc* are kept. □ **batterie**
3 a group of large guns (and the people manning them). □ **batterie**
4 a long series: *a battery of questions.* □ **pluie**

battle ['batl] *noun* a fight between opposing armies or individuals: *the last battle of the war.* □ **bataille**
■ *verb* to fight. □ **(se) battre**

'battlefield *noun* the place where a battle is, or was, fought: *dead bodies covered the battlefield.* □ **champ de bataille**

'battleship *noun* a heavily armed and armoured warship. □ **cuirassé**

batty *see* bat[2].

bawdy ['bɔːdi] *adjective* vulgar and coarse: *bawdy jokes.* □ **obscène**

bawl [bɔːl] *verb* to shout or cry loudly: *He bawled something rude*; *The baby has bawled all night.* □ **brailler**
bawl out *verb* to tell off, yell at or scold somebody: *The teacher bawled Karen out for being late.* □ **gueuler**

bay[1] [bei] *noun* a wide inward bend of a coastline: *anchored in the bay*; *Botany Bay.* □ **baie**

bay[2] [bei] *noun* a separate compartment, area or room *etc* (*usually* one of several) set aside for a special purpose: *a bay in a library.* □ **travée**
bay window a window jutting out from a room. □ **fenêtre en saillie**

bay[3] [bei] *adjective* (of horses) reddish-brown in colour. □ **bai**
■ [bei] *noun* (*also* **bay tree**) the laurel tree, the leaves of which are used for seasoning and in victory wreaths. □ **laurier**
■ [bei] *verb* (*especially* of large dogs) to bark: *The hounds bayed at the fox.* □ **aboyer**

bayonet ['beiənit] *noun* a knife-like instrument of steel fixed to the end of a rifle barrel. □ **baïonnette**

bazaar [bə'zaː] *noun* 1 an Eastern market place. □ **bazar**
2 a sale of goods of various kinds, *especially* home-made or second-hand. □ **vente de charité**

be [biː] – *present tense* **am** [am], **are** [aː], **is** [iz]: *past tense* **was** [woz], **were** [wəː]: *present participle* **'being**: *past participle* **been** [biːn, bin]: *subjunctive* **were** [wəː]: *short forms* **I'm** [aim] (**I am**), **you're** [juə] (**you are**), **he's** [hiːz] (**he is**), **she's** [ʃiːz] (**she is**), **it's** [its] (**it is**), **we're** [wiə] (**we are**), **they're** [ðeə] (**they are**): *negative short forms* **isn't** ['iznt] (**is not**), **aren't** [aːnt] (**are not**), **wasn't** ['woznt] (**was not**), **weren't** [wəːnt] (**were not**) – *verb* 1 used with a present participle to form the progressive or continuous tenses: *I'm reading*; *I am being followed*; *What were you saying?* □ **être**
2 used with a present participle to form a type of future tense: *I'm going to Quebec City.*
3 used with a past participle to form the passive voice: *He was shot.* □ **être**
4 used with an infinitive to express several ideas, *eg* necessity (*When am I to leave?*), purpose (*The letter is to tell us he's coming*), a possible future happening (*If she were to lose, I'd win*) *etc.* □ **devoir; aller**
5 used in giving or asking for information about something or someone: *I am Mr. Smith*; *Is he alive?*; *She wants to be an actress*; *The money will be ours*; *They are being silly.* □ **être**

'being *noun* 1 existence: *When did the Roman Empire come into being?* □ **existence**
2 any living person or thing: *beings from outer space.* □ **créature**

the be-all and end-all the final aim apart from which nothing is of any real importance: *This job isn't the be-all and end-all of existence.* □ **le but suprême de**

beach [biːtʃ] *noun* the sandy or stony shore of a sea or lake: *Children love playing on the beach.* □ **plage**
■ *verb* to drive or pull (a boat *etc*) on to a beach: *We'll beach the boat here and continue on foot.* □ **tirer à sec, échouer**

beacon ['biːkən] *noun* 1 a type of light, fire *etc* that warns of danger, *eg* the light in a lighthouse. □ **signal lumineux**
2 a radio station or transmitter that sends out signals to guide shipping or aircraft. □ **balise**

bead [biːd] *noun* a little ball of glass *etc* strung with others in a necklace *etc*: *She's wearing two strings of wooden beads.* □ **perle**
'beady *adjective* (of eyes) small and bright: *the beady eyes of the bird.* □ **vrille**

beak [biːk] *noun* the hard, horny (*usually* pointed) part of a bird's mouth: *The bird had a worm in its beak.* □ **bec**

beaker ['biːkə] *noun* 1 a large drinking-glass or mug: *a beaker of hot milk.* □ **gobelet**
2 a deep glass container used in chemistry. □ **vase à bec**

beam [biːm] *noun* 1 a long straight piece of wood, often used in ceilings. □ **poutre**
2 a ray of light *etc*: *a beam of sunlight.* □ **rayon**
3 the greatest width of a ship or boat. □ **largeur**
■ *verb* 1 to smile broadly: *She beamed with delight.* □ **rayonner**
2 to send out (rays of light, radio waves *etc*): *This transmitter beams radio waves all over the country.* □ **diffuser**

bean [biːn] *noun* 1 any one of several kinds of pod-bearing plant or its seed: *black beans*; *green beans*; *red beans.* □ **haricot; fève**
2 the bean-like seed of other plants: *coffee beans.* □ **grain**

bear[1] [beə] – *past tense* **bore** [bɔː]: *past participle* **borne** [bɔːn] – *verb* 1 (*usually with* **cannot, could not** *etc*) to put up with or endure: *I couldn't bear it if she left.* □ **supporter**
2 to be able to support: *Will this old table bear my*

weight? □ **supporter**

3 (*past participle in passive* **born** [bɔːn]) to produce (children): *She has borne* (*him*) *several children; She was born on July 7.* □ **donner naissance à; naître**

4 to carry: *He was borne shoulder-high after his victory.* □ **porter**

5 to have: *The cheque bore her signature.* □ **porter**

6 to turn or fork: *The road bears left here.* □ **tourner, aller vers**

'bearable *adjective* able to be endured. □ **supportable**

'bearer *noun* a person or thing that bears: *the bearer of bad news.* □ **porteur, euse**

'bearing *noun* **1** manner, way of standing *etc*: *a military bearing.* □ **allure**

2 (*usually in plural*: sometimes short for **,ball-'bearings**) a part of a machine that has another part moving in or on it. □ **palier**

'bearings *noun plural* location, place on a map *etc*; *The island's bearings are 10° North, 24° West.* □ **position**

bear down on 1 to approach quickly and often threateningly: *The angry teacher bore down on the child.* □ **fondre sur**

2 to exert pressure on: *The weight is bearing down on my chest.* □ **accabler**

bear fruit to produce fruit. □ **porter des fruits**

bear out to support or confirm: *This bears out what you said.* □ **confirmer**

bear up to keep up courage, strength *etc* (under strain): *She's bearing up well after her shock.* □ **tenir le coup**

bear with to be patient with (someone): *Bear with me for a minute, and you'll see what I mean.* □ **supporter patiemment**

find/get one's bearings to find one's position with reference to *eg* a known landmark: *If we can find this hill, I'll be able to get my bearings.* □ **(se) repérer**

lose one's bearings to become uncertain of one's position: *She's confused me so much that I've lost my bearings completely.* □ **être désorienté**

bear[2] [beə] *noun* a large heavy animal with thick fur and hooked claws. □ **ours**

'bearskin *noun, adjective* (of) the skin of a bear. □ **(en) peau d'ours**

beard [biəd] *noun* **1** the hair that grows on the chin: *a man's beard; a goat's beard.* □ **barbe**

2 a group of hair-like tufts on an ear of corn: *the beard on barley.* □ **barbe, arête**

'bearded *adjective*: *bearded men.* □ **barbu**

beast [biːst] **1** a four-footed (*especially* large) animal: *beasts of the jungle.* □ **bête (à quatre pattes)**

2 a cruel, brutal person. □ **brute**

3 an unpleasant person: *Arthur is a beast for refusing to come!* □ **brute**

'beastly *adjective* **1** like a beast. □ **bestial**

2 disagreeable: *What a beastly thing to do!* □ **dégoûtant**

'beastliness *noun*. □ **bestialité**

beat [biːt] – *past tense* **beat**: *past participle* **'beaten** – *verb* **1** to strike or hit repeatedly: *Beat the drum.* □ **battre**

2 to win against: *She beat me in a contest.* □ **battre**

3 to mix thoroughly: *to beat an egg.* □ **battre**

4 to move in a regular rhythm: *My heart is beating faster*

than usual. □ **battre**

5 to mark or indicate (musical time) with a baton *etc*: *A conductor beats time for an orchestra.* □ **battre (la mesure)**

■ *noun* **1** a regular stroke or its sound: *I like the beat of that song.* □ **rythme**

2 a regular or usual course: *a policewoman's beat.* □ **ronde**

'beater *noun*. □ **batteur**

'beating *noun*. □ **raclée**

'beaten *adjective* **1** overcome; defeated: *the beaten team*; *He looked tired and beaten.* □ **battu**

2 mixed thoroughly: *beaten egg.* □ **battu**

beat about the bush to approach a subject in an indirect way, without coming to the point or making any decision. □ **tourner autour du pot**

beat down 1 (of the sun) to give out great heat: *The sun's rays beat down on us.* □ **taper (dur) sur**

2 to (force to) lower a price by bargaining: *We beat the price down; We beat him down to a good price.* □ **faire baisser**

beat it to go away: *Beat it, or I'll hit you!; She told her little brother to beat it.* □ **filer**

beat off to succeed in overcoming or preventing: *The old man beat off the youths who attacked him; She beat the attack off easily.* □ **repousser**

beat a (hasty) retreat to go away in a hurry: *The children beat a hasty retreat when he appeared.* □ **battre en retraite**

beat up to punch, kick or hit (a person) severely and repeatedly: *He beat up an old lady.* □ **rouer de coups**

off the beaten track away from main roads, centres of population *etc*. □ **hors des sentiers battus**

beautician ['buːtəʃən] *noun* someone who owns or works in a beauty salon: *After Sue had a haircut, the beautician showed her how to apply makeup.* □ **esthéticien, ienne**

beauty ['bjuːti] – *plural* **'beauties** – *noun* **1** a quality very pleasing to the eye, ear *etc*: *His beauty is undeniable.* □ **beauté**

2 a woman or girl having such a quality: *She was a great beauty in her youth.* □ **beauté**

3 something or someone remarkable: *Her new car is a beauty!* □ **merveille**

'beautiful *adjective*: *a beautiful picture; Those roses are beautiful.* □ **beau**

'beautifully *adverb*. □ **admirablement**

'beautify [-fai] *verb* to make beautiful: *He beautified the room with flowers.* □ **embellir**

beauty queen a girl or woman who is voted the most beautiful in a contest. □ **reine de beauté**

beauty spot 1 a place of great natural beauty: *a famous beauty spot.* □ **site touristique**

2 a mark (often artificial) on the face, intended to emphasize beauty. □ **grain de beauté**

beaver ['biːvə] *noun* **1** an animal with strong front teeth, noted for its skill in damming streams. □ **castor**

2 its fur. □ **castor**

became *see* **become**.

because [bi'koz] *conjunction* for the reason that: *I can't*

go because I am ill. □ **parce que**
because of on account of: *I can't walk because of my broken leg.* □ **à cause de**
beck [bek]: **at someone's beck and call** always ready to carry out someone's wishes: *He has servants at his beck and call.* □ **au doigt et à l'œil**
beckon ['bekən] *verb* to summon (someone) by making a sign with the fingers. □ **faire signe (à)**
become [bi'kʌm] – *past tense* **became** [bi'keim]: *past participle* **be'come** – *verb* **1** to come or grow to be: *Her coat has become badly torn; She has become even more beautiful.* □ **devenir**
2 to qualify or take a job as: *She became a doctor.* □ **devenir**
3 (*with of*) to happen to: *What became of his son?* □ **advenir de**
4 to suit: *That dress really becomes her.* □ **bien aller à**
be'coming *adjective* attractive: *a very becoming dress.* □ **seyant**
be'comingly *adverb.* □ **admirablement**
bed [bed] *noun* **1** a piece of furniture, or a place, to sleep on: *The child sleeps in a small bed; a bed of straw.* □ **lit**
2 the channel (of a river) or floor (of a sea) *etc.* □ **lit**
3 a plot in a garden: *a bed of flowers.* □ **parterre**
4 layer: *a bed of chalk below the surface.* □ **couche**
-bedded (*as part of a word*) having (a certain number or type of) bed(s): *a double-bedded room.* □ **à (...) lits**
'bedding *noun* mattress, bedclothes *etc.* □ **literie**
'bedbug *noun* a small blood-sucking insect that lives in houses, especially beds. □ **punaise**
'bedclothes [-klouz, -klouðz] *noun plural* sheets, blankets *etc.* □ **literie (de dessus)**
'bedcover *noun* a top cover for a bed. □ **couvre-lit**
'bedridden *adjective* in bed for a long period because of age or sickness: *He has been bedridden since the car accident.* □ **cloué au lit**
'bedroom *noun* a room for sleeping in. □ **chambre (à coucher)**
'bedside *noun* the place or position next to a person's bed: *He was at her bedside when she died;* (*also adjective*) *a bedside table.* □ **(de) chevet**
'bedspread *noun* a top cover for a bed: *Please remove the bedspread before you get into bed.* □ **couvre-lit**
'bedtime *noun* the time at which one normally goes to bed: *Seven o'clock is the children's bedtime;* (*also adjective*) *a bedtime story.* □ **heure du coucher**
bed and breakfast lodging for the night, and breakfast only (not lunch or dinner). □ **chambre avec petit déjeuner**
bed of roses an easy or comfortable place, job *etc: Life is not a bed of roses.* □ **partie de plaisir**
go to bed 1 to get into bed: *I'm sleepy – I think I'll go to bed now; What time do you usually go to bed?* □ **(aller) se coucher**
2 (*often with* **with**) to have sexual intercourse with; to have a love affair with. □ **coucher avec**
bedlam ['bedləm] *noun* (a place of) noise, confusion or uproar: *Their house is bedlam.* □ **chahut**
bee [biː] *noun* **1** a four-winged insect that makes honey. □ **abeille**

2 (*especially North American*) a meeting for combined work and enjoyment: *a knitting bee.* □ **corvée**
'beehive *noun* a box in which bees are kept, and where they store their honey. □ **ruche**
'beeswax ['biːzwaks] *noun* the yellowish solid substance produced by bees for making their cells, and used in polishing wood. □ **cire d'abeille**
a bee in one's bonnet an idea which has become fixed in one's mind: *She has a bee in her bonnet about going to America.* □ **marotte**
make a beeline for to take the most direct way to; to go immediately to: *Fred always makes a beeline for the prettiest girl at a party.* □ **se diriger droit sur**
beech [biːtʃ] *noun* **1** (*also* **beech tree**) a kind of forest tree with smooth silvery bark and small nuts: *That tree is a beech;* (*also adjective*) *a beech forest.* □ **hêtre**
2 its wood. □ **hêtre**
beef [biːf] *noun* the flesh of a bull, cow or ox, used as food. □ **bœuf**
beefy *adjective* **1** of or like beef: *a beefy taste.* □ **de bœuf**
2 having a lot of fat or muscle: *a beefy man.* □ **costaud**
beehive *see* bee.
been *see* be.
beep [biːp] *noun* a short, high-pitched burst of sound which serves as a warning. □ **bip**
■ *verb* to make a short, high-pitched sound, *usually* by electronic means: *The robot beeped as it circled the room.* □ **biper**
'beeper *noun* a small instrument for making this sound: *The sound of the beeper alerted him to call his office.* □ **bip**
beer [biə] *noun* a type of alcoholic drink made from malted barley flavoured with hops. □ **bière**
beeswax *see* bee.
beet [biːt] *noun* a hard red vegetable that grows in the ground: *Harry cut up and boiled the freshly picked beets for his meal.* □ **betterave**
beetle ['biːtl] *noun* an insect with four wings. □ **coléoptère; scarabée**
befall [bi'fɔːl] – *past tense* **befell** [bi'fel]: *past participle* **be'fallen** – *verb* to happen to (a person or thing): *A disaster has befallen her.* □ **arriver (à)**
before [bi'fɔː] *preposition* **1** earlier than: *before the war; She'll come before very long.* □ **avant**
2 in front of: *She was before me in the queue.* □ **avant, devant**
3 rather than: *Honour before wealth.* □ **avant**
■ *adverb* earlier: *I've seen you before.* □ **déjà, auparavant**
■ *conjunction* earlier than the time when: *Before I go, I must phone my parents.* □ **avant (de/que)**
be'forehand [-hand] *adverb* before the time when something else is done: *If you're coming, let me know beforehand.* □ **d'avance**
befriend [bi'frend] *verb* to take as a friend: *The old woman befriended her when she was lonely.* □ **traiter en ami(e)**
beg [beg] – *past tense, past participle* **begged** – *verb* **1** to ask (someone) for (money, food *etc*): *The old man was*

so poor that he had to beg in the street; *He begged (me) for money*. □ **mendier**

2 to ask (someone) desperately or earnestly: *I beg you not to do it*. □ **supplier (de)**

'**beggar** *noun* a person who lives by begging: *The beggar asked for money for food*. □ **mendiant, ante**

■ *verb* to make very poor: *She was beggared by the collapse of her firm*. □ **ruiner**

beggar description to be so great in some way that it cannot be described: *Her intelligence beggars description*. □ **défier**

beg to differ to disagree: *You may think that he should get the job but I beg to differ*. □ **être d'un autre avis**

began *see* **begin**.

beggar *see* **beg**.

begin [bi'gin] – *present participle* be'**ginning**: *past tense* **began** [bi'gan]: *past participle* **begun** [bi'gʌn] – *verb* to come or bring, into being, to start: *He began to talk*; *The meeting began early*. □ **commencer (à)**

be'**ginning** *noun*. □ **commencement**

be'**ginner** *noun* someone who is just learning how to do something: *'Does he paint well?' 'He's not bad for a beginner'*. □ **débutant, ante**

to begin with 1 at first: *I didn't like her to begin with, but now she's one of my best friends*. □ **au début**

2 firstly: *There are many reasons why I don't like him – to begin with, he doesn't tell the truth*. □ **d'abord**

begonia [bi'gouniə] *noun* a tropical plant with pink flowers and often coloured leaves. □ **bégonia**

begrudge [bi'grʌdʒ] *verb* to envy (someone something): *I begrudge her her success*. □ **envier (qqch. à qqn)**

beguile [bi'gail] *verb* **1** to occupy (time) pleasantly: *He beguiled the time with gardening*. □ **tromper**

2 to charm or amuse (a person): *She beguiled the children with stories*. □ **amuser**

be'**guiling** *adjective* charming: *a beguiling smile*. □ **enjôleur**

be'**guilingly** *adverb*. □ **d'une manière séduisante**

begun *see* **begin**.

behalf [bi'haːf]: **on behalf of (someone)** for, or in the interests of: *on behalf of all our members*; *I'm collecting on behalf of the blind*. □ **au nom de, pour**

behave [bi'heiv] *verb* **1** to act in a suitable way, to conduct oneself (well): *If you come, you must behave (yourself)*; *The child always behaves (himself) at his grandmother's*. □ **(se) conduire bien**

2 to act or react: *He always behaves like a gentleman*; *Metals behave in different ways when heated*. □ **(se) comporter**

be'**haviour**, be'**havior** [-jə] *noun* **1** way of behaving: *the behaviour of the pupils*. □ **conduite**

2 actions or reactions: *the behaviour of rats*; *the behaviour of metals in acids*. □ **comportement**

,**well**-, ,**badly**- *etc* be'**haved** *adjective* good (bad *etc*) in manners or conduct: *badly-behaved children*. □ **(bien/mal) élevé**

beheld *see* **behold**.

behind [bi'haind] *preposition* **1** at or towards the back of: *behind the door*. □ **derrière**

2 remaining after: *The tourists left their litter behind*

them. □ **derrière**

3 in support: *We're right behind her on this point*. □ **avec**

■ *adverb* **1** at the back: *following behind*. □ **derrière**

2 (*also* be'**hindhand** [-hand]) not up to date: *behind with her work*. □ **en retard**

3 remaining: *She left her book behind*; *We stayed behind after the party*. □ **laisser; rester**

■ *noun* the buttocks: *a smack on the behind*. □ **derrière**

behind someone's back without someone's knowledge or permission: *He sometimes bullies his sister behind his mother's back*. □ **derrière le dos (de qqn)**

behold [bi'hould] – *past tense, past participle* **beheld** [bi'held] – *verb* to see: *What a sight to behold!* □ **voir**

beige [beiʒ] *noun* a pale pinkish-yellow colour. □ **beige**

■ *adjective*: *a beige hat*. □ **beige**

being *see* **be**.

belated [bi'leitid] *adjective* happening *etc*, late or too late: *a belated birthday card*; *belated thanks*. □ **en retard**

be'**latedly** *adverb*. □ **un peu tard**

belch [beltʃ] *verb* **1** to give out air noisily from the stomach through the mouth: *He belched after eating too much*. □ **roter**

2 (*often with out*) (of a chimney *etc*) to throw (out) violently: *factory chimneys belching (out) smoke*. □ **cracher**

■ *noun* an act of belching. □ **rot**

beleaguered [bi'liːgəd] *adjective* under attack: *a beleaguered castle*; *The city was beleaguered*. □ **assiégé**

belfry ['belfri] – *plural* '**belfries** – *noun* the part of a (church) tower in which bells are hung. □ **clocher**

belie [bi'lai] – *present participle* be'**lying**: *past participle* be'**lied** – *verb* to give a false idea or impression of (something): *His innocent face belies his cunning*. □ **démentir**

belief *see* **believe**.

believe [bi'liːv] *verb* **1** to regard (something) as true: *I believe her story*. □ **croire**

2 to trust (a person), accepting what he says as true: *I believe you*. □ **croire**

3 to think (that): *I believe he's ill*. □ **croire (que)**

be'**lievable** *adjective*. □ **croyable**

be'**lief** [-f] *noun* **1** faith or trust: *I have no belief in his ability*. □ **foi, confiance**

2 (*often in plural*) something believed: *Christian beliefs*. □ **croyance(s)**

be'**liever** *noun* a person who has (*especially* religious) beliefs: *a true believer*. □ **croyant, ante**

believe in to accept the existence or recognize the value of (something): *Do you believe in ghosts?*; *He believes in capital punishment*. □ **croire (à/en)**

belittle [bi'litl] *verb* to make to seem unimportant (*usually* by harsh criticism): *He belittled her achievements*. □ **déprécier**

bell [bel] *noun* **1** a hollow object, *usually* of metal, which gives a ringing sound when struck by the clapper inside: *church bells*. □ **cloche**

2 any other mechanism for giving a ringing sound: *Our doorbell is broken*. □ **sonnette, timbre**

bellicose ['belikous] *adjective* warlike or quarrelsome:

a bellicose nation. □ **belliqueux**

belligerent [bɪˈlɪdʒərənt] *adjective* **1** unfriendly; hostile: *a belligerent stare; She is very belligerent and quarrelsome.* □ **agressif**

2 waging war: *belligerent nations.* □ **belligérant**
bel'ligerence *noun.* □ **belligérance**
bel'ligerently *adverb.* □ **de manière agressive**

bellow [ˈbelou] *verb* to roar like a bull: *The headmaster bellowed at the children.* □ **hurler**

■ *noun* an act of roaring. □ **hurlement**

bellows [ˈbelouz] *noun plural* an instrument for making a current of air. □ **soufflet**

belly [ˈbeli] – *plural* ˈ**bellies** – *noun* the part of the body between the breast and the thighs, containing the bowels: *the horse's belly; I've a pain in my belly.* □ **ventre**
belly button *noun* the mark or indentation in the middle of the abdomen where the umbilical cord was attached to the mother; the navel: *The baby's belly button has to be kept dry for a few days after birth.* □ **nombril**
ˈ**belly laugh** *noun* a loud, deep laugh: *the belly laughs of the hockey players in the bar.* □ **gros rire**

belong [bɪˈlɔŋ] *verb* **1** (*with* **to**) to be the property of: *This book belongs to me.* □ **appartenir à**

2 (*with* **to**) to be a native, member *etc* of: *I belong to the sailing club.* □ **faire partie de**

3 (*with* **with**) to go together with: *This shoe belongs with that shoe.* □ **aller avec**
be'longings *noun plural* personal possessions: *She can't have gone away – all her belongings are still here.* □ **affaires**

beloved [bɪˈlʌvɪd] *adjective* much loved: *my beloved country.* □ **(bien)-aimé**

■ *noun* a person very dear to one: *My beloved left me for another.* □ **(bien)-aimé, ée**

below [bəˈlou] *preposition* lower in position, rank, standard *etc* than: *She hurt her leg below the knee; His work is below standard.* □ **au-dessous de**

■ *adverb* in a lower place: *We looked at the houses (down) below.* □ **plus bas**

belt [belt] *noun* **1** a long (narrow) piece of leather, cloth *etc* worn around the waist: *a trouser-belt; He tightened his belt.* □ **ceinture**

2 a similar object used to set wheels in motion: *the belt of a vacuum-cleaner.* □ **courroie**

3 a zone of country *etc*: *a belt of trees; an industrial belt.* □ **zone**

■ *verb* **1** to fasten with a belt: *He belted his trousers on.* □ **ceinturer**

2 to strike (with or without a belt): *She belted the disobedient dog.* □ **donner une râclée**
ˈ**belted** *adjective.* □ **ceinturé**

bemused [bɪˈmjuːzd] *adjective* bewildered or greatly puzzled: *a bemused look.* □ **stupéfait**

bench [bentʃ] *noun* **1** a long (*usually* wooden) seat: *a park bench.* □ **banc**

2 a work-table for a carpenter *etc*: *tools on the workbench.* □ **établi**

bend [bend] – *past tense, past participle* **bent** [bent] – *verb* **1** to make, become, or be, angled or curved: *Bend*

your arm; She bent down to pick up the coin; The road bends to the right; He could bend an iron bar. □ **plier, (se) courber, tourner, tordre**

2 to force (someone) to do what one wants: *She bent me to her will.* □ **plier**

■ *noun* a curve or angle: *a bend in the road.* □ **courbe; virage**

the bends agonizing pains, *especially* in the joints, affecting divers when they surface too quickly. □ **mal des caissons**

bent on determined on: *bent on winning.* □ **déterminé à**

beneath [bɪˈniːθ] *preposition* **1** in a lower position than; under; below: *beneath the floorboards; beneath her coat.* □ **sous, au-dessous de**

2 not worthy of: *It is beneath my dignity to do that.* □ **au-dessous de**

■ *adverb* below or underneath: *They watched the boat breaking up on the rocks beneath.* □ **au-dessous**

benediction [benəˈdikʃən] *noun* a prayer giving blessing. □ **bénédiction**

benefactor [ˈbenəfaktə] *noun* a person who gives friendly help, often in the form of money: *the benefactor of the school.* □ **bienfaiteur, trice**

beneficial [benəˈfiʃəl] *adjective* having good effects: *Fresh air is beneficial to your health.* □ **bon (pour)**
ˌbeneˈficiary [-ʃieri, -ʃəri] – *plural* ˌbeneˈficiaries – *noun* a person who receives a gift *etc* (*usually* in a will). □ **bénéficiaire**

benefit [ˈbenəfit] *noun* something good to receive, an advantage: *the benefit of experience; the benefits of fresh air and exercise.* □ **bienfaits**

■ *verb* – *past tense, past participle* ˈ**benefited** – **1** (*usually with* **from** *or* **by**) to gain advantage: *She benefited from the advice.* □ **tirer profit de**

2 to do good to: *The long rest benefited her.* □ **faire du bien à**

give (someone) the benefit of the doubt to assume that someone is telling the truth because one cannot be sure that he is not doing so. □ **laisser le bénéfice du doute (à qqn)**

| **benefited** and **benefiting** have one **t**. |
---

benevolence [bɪˈnevələns] *noun* generosity and desire to do good. □ **bienveillance**
be'nevolent *adjective*: *a benevolent father.* □ **bienveillant**
be'nevolently *adverb.* □ **avec bienveillance**

benign [bɪˈnain] *adjective* **1** kind, well-wishing: *a benign smile.* □ **bienveillant**

2 not fatal: *a benign tumour.* □ **bénin**
be'nignly *adverb*: *smiling benignly.* □ **avec bienveillance**

bent[1] *see* **bend**.

bent[2] [bent] *noun* a natural inclination: *a bent for mathematics.* □ **aptitude**

bequeath [bɪˈkwiːð] *verb* to leave (personal belongings) by will: *She bequeathed her art collection to the town.* □ **léguer**

bequest [bɪˈkwest] *noun* something bequeathed in a will:

I received a bequest in my uncle's will. □ **legs**

bereaved [bi'ri:vd] *adjective* having lost, through death, someone dear: *a bereaved mother.* □ **en deuil**

be'reavement *noun: The family has suffered two bereavements recently.* □ **deuil**

bereft [bi'reft] *adjective (with of)* having had something taken away: *bereft of speech.* □ **privé de**

berry ['beri] – *plural* **'berries** – *noun* a kind of small (often juicy) fruit: *holly berry; ripe strawberries; Those berries are poisonous.* □ **baie**

berth [bɔːθ] *noun* 1 a sleeping-place in a ship *etc.* □ **couchette**

2 a place in a port *etc* where a ship can be moored. □ **poste d'amarrage**

■ *verb* to moor (a ship): *The ship berthed last night.* □ **amarrer**

beseech [bi'si:tʃ] – *past tense, past participles* **besought** [bi'sɔːt], **be'seeched** – *verb* to beg: *Don't kill him – I beseech you!* □ **supplier**

beset [bi'set] – *past tense, past participle* **be'set** – *verb* to attack on all sides: *beset by thieves.* □ **assaillir**

beside [bi'said] *preposition* 1 by the side of or near: *beside the window; She sat beside her sister.* □ **auprès de, à côté de**

2 compared with: *She looks ugly beside her sister.* □ **à côté de**

be'sides *preposition* in addition to: *Is anyone coming besides John?* □ **à part**

■ *adverb* also: *These shoes are expensive – besides, they're too small; He has three sons and an adopted one besides.* □ **de plus**

be beside oneself (with) to be in a state of very great, uncontrolled emotion: *She was beside herself with excitement as her holiday approached.* □ **ne plus se tenir (de)**

be beside the point to be irrelevant: *You will have to go. Whether you want to go is beside the point.* □ **être hors de propos**

besiege [bi'si:dʒ] *verb* 1 to surround (*eg* a town) with an army. □ **assiéger**

2 (*with* **with**) to overwhelm with: *The reporters besieged me with questions about the plane crash.* □ **assaillir**

---
besiege is spelt with **-ie-**.
---

besought *see* **beseech**.

best [best] *adjective, pronoun* (something which is) good to the greatest extent: *the best book on the subject; the best (that) I can do; She is my best friend; Which method is (the) best?; The flowers are at their best just now.* □ **le/la meilleur, eure**

■ *adverb* in the best manner: *She sings best (of all).* □ **le mieux**

■ *verb* to defeat: *She was bested in the argument.* □ **avoir le dessous**

best man the bridegroom's attendant at a wedding. □ **garçon d'honneur**

,best'seller *noun* something (*usually* a book) which sells very many copies: *Ernest Hemingway wrote several bestsellers.* □ **best-seller**

the best part of most of; nearly (all of): *I've read the best part of two hundred books on the subject.* □ **la plupart de**

do one's best to try as hard as possible: *He'll do his best to be here on time.* □ **faire de son mieux**

for the best intended to have the best results possible: *We don't want to send the child away to school but we're doing it for the best.* □ **pour le mieux**

get the best of to win, or get some advantage from, (a fight, argument *etc*): *He was shouting a lot, but I think I got the best of the argument.* □ **avoir le dessus**

make the best of it to do all one can to turn a failure *etc* into something successful: *He is disappointed at not getting into university but he'll just have to make the best of it and find a job.* □ **(s')accommoder de**

bestow [bi'stou] *verb (with on)* to give (*especially* a title, award *etc*) to someone: *The Queen bestowed a knighthood on him.* □ **conférer à**

be'stowal *noun.* □ **octroi**

bet [bet] – *past tense, past participles* **bet, 'betted** – *verb* (*often with* **on**) to gamble (*usually* with money) *eg* on a racehorse: *I'm betting on that horse.* □ **parier (sur); gager**

■ *noun* 1 an act of betting: *I won my bet.* □ **pari; gageure**

2 a sum of money betted: *Place your bets.* □ **pari**

an even bet an equal chance. □ **pari à une chance sur deux**

take a bet (*often with* **on**) to bet: *Are you willing to take a bet on whether he'll come or not?* □ **accepter un pari**

you bet certainly; of course. □ **et comment!**

betray [bi'trei] *verb* 1 to act disloyally or treacherously towards (*especially* a person who trusts one): *He betrayed his own brother (to the enemy).* □ **trahir**

2 to give away (a secret *etc*): *Never betray a confidence!.* □ **trahir**

3 to show (signs of): *His pale face betrayed his fear.* □ **trahir**

be'trayal *noun.* □ **trahison**

be'trayer *noun.* □ **traître, traîtresse**

betroth [bi'trouð] *verb* to promise in marriage: *She was betrothed to her husband at the age of twenty.* □ **fiancer (à, avec)**

be'trothal *noun.* □ **fiançailles**

be'trothed *noun* the person to whom one is betrothed: *May I introduce you to my betrothed?* □ **fiancé, ée**

better ['betə] *adjective* 1 good to a greater extent: *Her new car is better than her old one.* □ **mieux; meilleur**

2 stronger in health; recovered (from an illness): *I feel better today; She's better now.* □ **mieux**

3 preferable: *Better to do it now than later.* □ **préférable**

■ *adverb* well to a greater extent: *She sings better now than she did before.* □ **mieux**

■ *pronoun* someone or something which is good to a greater extent than the other (of two people or things): *He's the better of the two.* □ **le/la meilleur, eure (de)**

■ *verb* to improve (on): *She's bettered all previous records; The situation has bettered a little.* □ **(s')améliorer**

better off richer; happier in some way: *He'd be better off working as a miner; You'd be better off without him.* □ **plus riche, mieux**

the better part of most of: *He talked for the better part of an hour.* □ **près de**
get the better of to overcome; to win (against): *She got the better of her opponent/the argument.* □ **l'emporter sur**

> *He is better today* (not *He is more better*). *He is much better* is correct.
> *You had better come/You'd better come* (not *You better come*).

between [bi'twiːn] *preposition* 1 in, to, through or across the space dividing two people, places, times *etc*: *between the car and the pavement; between 2 o'clock and 2:30; between meals.* □ **entre**
2 concerning the relationship of two things or people: *the difference between right and wrong.* □ **entre**
3 by the combined action of; working together: *They managed it between them.* □ **à (eux, elles) deux**
4 part to one (person or thing), part to (the other): *Divide the chocolate between you.* □ **entre (vous)**
between you and me/between ourselves in confidence: *Between you and me, I think he's rather nice.* □ **entre nous, de vous à moi**

> **between** is usually used for two.
> **among** is usually used for more than two.

bevel ['bevəl] *noun* a slanting edge (rather than a sharp corner): *A chisel has a bevel on its cutting edge.* □ **biseau**
'bevelled *adjective*: *bevelled glass.* □ **biseauté**
beverage ['bevəridʒ] *noun* a drink, *especially* tea, coffee, or other non-alcoholic drink. □ **boisson (non alcoolisée)**
beware [bi'weə] – used mostly in the imperative and the infinitive – *verb* 1 (*usually with* **of**) to be careful (of): *Beware of the dog.* □ **attention (à)**
2 to be careful: *She told them to beware.* □ **prendre garde**
bewilder [bi'wildə] *verb* to amaze or puzzle: *She was bewildered when her husband suddenly left her; bewildered by the instructions.* □ **déconcerter**
be'wilderment *noun.* □ **confusion**
bewitch [bi'witʃ] *verb* to cast a spell on, to charm: *He bewitched us with his smile.* □ **ensorceler**
be'witching *adjective.* □ **enchanteur**
beyond [bi'jond] *preposition* 1 on the farther side of: *My house is just beyond those trees.* □ **de l'autre côté de**
2 farther on than (something) in time or place: *I cannot plan beyond tomorrow.* □ **au-delà de**
3 out of the range, power *etc* of: *beyond help.* □ **au-delà de, hors de**
4 other than: *What is there to say beyond what's already been said?* □ **d'autre que**
beyond compare having no equal: *Her achievements are beyond compare.* □ **sans pareil**
beyond one's means too expensive(ly): *A painting by Picasso is beyond my means; He lives well beyond his means* (= he spends more money than he earns). □ **au-dessus de ses moyens**
bi-annual [bai'anjuəl] *adjective* happening twice a year: *a bi-annual event; The dinner is bi-annual, not annual.* □

□ **semestriel**
bi-'annually *adverb.* □ **semestriellement**
bias ['baiəs] *noun* 1 favouring of one or other (side in an argument *etc*) rather than remaining neutral: *a bias against people of other religions.* □ **parti pris**
2 a weight on or in an object (*eg* a ball for lawn bowling) making it move in a particular direction. □ **déviation**
■ *verb* – *past tense, past participle* 'bias(s)ed – to influence (*usually* unfairly): *He was biased by the report in the newspapers.* □ **influencer**
'bias(s)ed *adjective* (*negative* unbias(s)ed) favouring one side rather than another: *a biased judgment.* □ **partial**
bib [bib] *noun* 1 a cloth *etc* tied under a child's chin to catch spilt food *etc*. □ **bavette**
2 the top part of an apron or overalls, covering the chest. □ **bavette**
Bible ['baibl] *noun* (*with* **the**) the sacred writings of the Christian Church, consisting of the Old and New Testaments. □ **Bible**
biblical ['biblikəl] *adjective* (*often with capital*) of or like the Bible: *biblical references.* □ **biblique**
bibliography [bibli'ogrəfi] – *plural* bibli'ographies – *noun* a list of books. □ **bibliographie**
bicentenary [bai'sentəneri, baisen'tiːnəri] (*plural* bicen'tenaries), **bicentennial** [baisen'teniəl] *noun* a two-hundredth anniversary: *the bicentenary of American independence.* □ **bicentenaire**
biceps ['baiseps] *noun plural* the large muscles in the front of the upper arm: *The boxer has enormous biceps.* □ **biceps**
bicycle ['baisikl] *noun* (*often abbreviated to* **bike** [baik], **cycle** ['saikl]) a pedal-driven vehicle with two wheels and a seat. □ **bicyclette**
■ *verb* (*usually abbreviated to* 'cycle) to ride a bicycle: *She bicycled slowly up the hill.* □ **aller à bicyclette**
bicycle path (*also called* bike path) a specific lane or trail for bicycles that automobiles can not use: *Ottawa has many bicycle paths where bikers can ride without being in traffic.* □ **piste cyclable**
bid [bid] *verb* 1 – *past tense, past participle* bid – to offer (an amount of money) at an auction: *John bid ($1,000) for the painting.* □ **faire une enchère (de)**
2 (*with* **for**) – *past tense, past participle* bid – to state a price (for a contract): *My firm is bidding for the contract for the new road.* □ **faire une offre (pour)**
3 – *past tense* bade [bad], *past participle* 'bidden – to tell (someone) to (do something): *She bade me enter.* □ **enjoindre (de)**
4 – *past tense* bade [bad], *past participle* 'bidden – to express a greeting *etc* (to someone): *He bade me farewell.* □ **dire**
■ *noun* 1 an offer of a price: *a bid of $20.* □ **offre**
2 an attempt (to obtain): *a bid for freedom.* □ **tentative (pour obtenir)**
'bidder *noun.* □ **offrant**
'bidding *noun.* □ **enchère**
'biddable *adjective* obedient: *a biddable child.* □ **obéissant**

bide [baid]: **bide one's time** to wait for a good opportunity: *I'm just biding my time until he makes a mistake.* □ **attendre (le bon moment)**

biennial [bai'eniəl] *adjective* (of plants *etc*) lasting for two years: *Foxglove is biennial; a biennial plant.* □ **bisannuel**

bifocal [bai'foukəl] *adjective* (of lenses) having two points of focus, which help people to see things close at hand and things far away. □ **à double foyer**

big [big] *adjective* 1 large in size: *a big car.* □ **gros; grand** 2 important: *a big event.* □ **grand**
big game large animals (*usually* lions, tigers *etc*) that are hunted: *She hunts big game in Africa; a big game hunter.* □ **gros gibier**

bigamy ['bigəmi] *noun* marriage to two wives or two husbands at once (a crime in some countries): *He's been charged with committing bigamy.* □ **bigamie**
'**bigamist** *noun.* □ **bigame**
'**bigamous** *adjective.* □ **bigame**

bigot ['bigət] *noun* a person who constantly and stubbornly holds a particular point of view *etc*: *a religious bigot.* □ **bigot**
'**bigoted** *adjective.* □ **bigot**
'**bigotry** *noun* bigoted attitude or behaviour. □ **bigoterie**

bike *see* **bicycle.**

bikini [bi'ki:ni] *noun* a brief two-piece swimming costume for women. □ **bikini**

bilateral [bai'latərəl] *adjective* affecting, signed, or agreed, by two sides, countries *etc*: *a bilateral agreement.* □ **bilatéral**

bile [bail] *noun* 1 a yellowish thick bitter fluid in the liver. □ **bile**
2 anger or irritability. □ **mauvaise humeur**
bilious ['biljəs] *adjective* of, or affected by, too much bile: *a bilious attack.* □ **bilieux**
'**biliousness** *noun.* □ **état/tempérament bilieux**

bilingual [bai'liŋgwəl] *adjective* 1 written or spoken in two languages: *a bilingual dictionary.* □ **bilingue**
2 speaking two languages equally well: *a bilingual waiter.* □ **bilingue**

bill[1] [bil] *noun* a bird's beak: *a bird with a yellow bill.* □ **bec**

bill[2] [bil] *noun* 1 an account of money owed for goods *etc*: *an electricity bill.* □ **facture**
2 (*North American*) a banknote: *a five-dollar bill.* □ **billet**
3 a poster used for advertising. □ **affiche**
■ *verb* to send an account (to someone): *We'll bill you next month for your purchases.* □ **facturer (à)**
'**billboard** *noun* a large board on which advertising posters are displayed: *She stuck posters on the billboard.* □ **panneau d'affichage**
'**billfold** *noun* (*North American*) a wallet: *a billfold full of dollars.* □ **portefeuille**
fill the bill to be suitable; to be exactly what is required: *We are looking for a new car and this will fill the bill.* □ **faire l'affaire**

billet ['bilit] *noun* a private house *etc* where soldiers are given food and lodging. □ **logement (chez l'habitant)**
■ *verb* – *past tense, past participle* '**billeted** – to give

lodging to (*eg* soldiers): *The men are billeted in the church hall.* □ **cantonner**

billiards ['biljədz] *noun singular* a game played with long thin sticks (**cues**) and balls, on a table. □ **billard**

billion ['biljən] – *plurals* '**billion (1, 3)**, '**billions (2, 3)** – *noun* 1 in the Canada, and often in the United Kingdom, the number 1 000 000 000: *a billion; several billion.* □ **milliard**
2 in the Canada and often in the United Kingdom, the figure 1 000 000 000. □ **milliard**
3 a billion dollars: *The sum involved amounts to several billion(s).* □ **milliard**
■ *adjective* in the Canada and often in the United Kingdom, 1 000 000 000 in number: *a few billion stars.* □ **milliard**
'**billionth** *noun* one of a billion equal parts. □ **milliardième**

billow ['bilou] *noun* a large wave. □ **lame**
'**billowy** *adjective.* □ **houleux**
billow out to move in a way similar to large waves: *The sails billowed out in the strong wind; Her skirt billowed out in the breeze.* □ **(se) gonfler**

billy-goat ['biligout] *noun* a male (*usually* adult) goat. □ **bouc**

bi-monthly [bai'mʌnθli] *adjective, adverb* 1 (happening) once in every two months. □ **bimestriel**
2 (happening) twice a month. □ **bimensuel**

bin [bin] *noun* a container (*usually* metal or plastic, often large) in which corn *etc* is stored or rubbish is collected: *a waste-paper bin.* □ **coffre, boîte, corbeille, poubelle**

binary ['bainəri]: **the binary system** the system of writing and calculating with numbers which uses only two digits (0 and 1) and has 2 as a base (101 = 1 four, 0 twos, 1 unit = 5). □ **binaire**

bind [baind] – *past tense, past participle* **bound** [baund] – *verb* 1 to tie up: *The doctor bound up the patient's leg with a bandage; The robbers bound up the bank manager with rope.* □ **lier**
2 to fasten together and put a cover on the pages of (a book): *Bind this book in leather.* □ **relier**
'**binding** *noun* the covering in which the leaves of a book are fixed: *leather binding.* □ **reliure**
-bound (as part of a word) prevented from making progress by a particular thing: *The ship was fogbound.* □ **retenu (par)**

bingo ['biŋgou] *noun* a gambling game using cards with numbered squares. □ **bingo**

binoculars [bi'nokjuləz] *noun plural* an instrument for making distant objects look nearer, with separate eye-pieces for each eye: *He looked at the ship on the horizon through his binoculars.* □ **jumelles**

biochemistry [baiə'kemistri] *noun* the chemistry of living things: *She is studying the biochemistry of the blood;* (*also adjective*) *a biochemistry lecture.* □ **biochimie**
,**bio'chemical** [-mikəl] *adjective.* □ **biochimique**
,**bio'chemist** *noun.* □ **biochimiste**

biodegradable [baiaudəgreidəbl] *adjective* made up of materials that decay or break down in the environment: *The lunch was packed in a biodegradable container so* *there would be less garbage over time.* □ **biodégradable**

biography [bai'ɔgrəfi] – *plural* **bi'ographies** – *noun* a written account by someone of another person's life: *a biography of René Lévesque.* □ **biographie**
bi'ographer *noun.* □ **biographe**
,bio'graphic(al) [-'gra-] *adjective.* □ **biographique**

biology [bai'ɔlədʒi] *noun* the science of living things: *human biology*; *(also adjective) a biology lesson.* □ **(de) biologie**
bio'logical [-'lo-] *adjective.* □ **biologique**
bio'logically [-'lo-] *adverb.* □ **biologiquement**
bi'ologist *noun.* □ **biologiste**
biological warfare the use of germs as a weapon. □ **guerre bactériologique**

bionics [bai'oniks] *noun singular* the use of biological principles in the design of computers *etc.* □ **bionique**
bi'onic *adjective* of or using bionics. □ **bionique**

biped ['baiped] *noun* an animal with two feet (*eg* man). □ **bipède**

birch [bəːtʃ] *noun* 1 (*also* **birch tree**) a kind of small tree with pointed leaves valued for its wood: *That tree is a birch*; *(also adjective) birch leaves.* □ **bouleau**
2 its wood: *a desk made of birch*; *(also adjective) a birch desk.* □ **bouleau**

bird [bəːd] *noun* a two-legged feathered creature, with a beak and two wings, with which most can fly: *Kiwis and ostriches are birds which cannot fly.* □ **oiseau**
bird's-eye view a general view from above: *a bird's-eye view of the town from an airplane.* □ **vue d'ensemble**

birth [bəːθ] *noun* 1 (an) act of coming into the world, being born: *the birth of his son*; *deaf since birth.* □ **naissance**
2 the beginning: *the birth of civilization.* □ **naissance**
birth control prevention of the conception of children. □ **limitation/contrôle des naissances**
'birthday *noun* the anniversary of the day on which a person was born: *Today is his birthday*; *(also adjective) a birthday party.* □ **anniversaire**
'birthmark *noun* a permanent mark on the skin at or from birth: *She has a red birthmark on her face.* □ **tache de vin**
'birthplace *noun* the place where a person *etc* was born: *Shakespeare's birthplace.* □ **lieu de naissance**
'birthrate *noun* the number of births per head of population over a given period. □ **(taux de) natalité**
give birth (to) (of a mother) to produce (a baby) from the womb: *She has given birth to two sets of twins.* □ **donner naissance (à)**

biscuit ['biskit] *noun* a piece of dough baked in small hard or crisp flat cakes: *dog biscuit*; *ship's biscuit* (hardtack). □ **biscuit**

bisect [bai'sekt] *verb* to cut into two equal parts: *A diagonal line across a square bisects it.* □ **couper en deux**

bishop ['biʃəp] *noun* 1 a Christian clergyman in charge of a group of churches, *usually* in a large city or area: *the Bishop of Montreal*; *He was made a bishop two years ago.* □ **évêque**
2 one of the pieces in chess. □ **fou**

bison ['baisn] – *plurals* **'bison**, (*rare*) **'bisons** – *noun* 1 the American buffalo: *a herd of bison.* □ **bison**

2 the large European wild ox. □ **bison**

bit¹ [bit] *noun* 1 a small piece: *a bit of bread.* □ **(petit) morceau**
2 a piece of any size: *a bit of advice.* □ **petit**
3 a short time: *Wait a bit longer.* □ **un peu**
bit by bit gradually: *Move the pile of rocks bit by bit.* □ **peu à peu**
do one's bit to take one's share in a task: *Each of us will have to do his bit if we are to finish the job soon.* □ **faire sa part**
in, to bits in(to) *usually* small pieces: *The broken mirror lay in bits on the floor*; *She loves taking her car to bits.* □ **en morceaux/pièces (détachées)**

bit² *see* **bite.**

bit³ [bit] *noun* the part of a bridle which a horse holds in its mouth. □ **mors**

bitch [bitʃ] *noun* 1 the female of the dog, wolf or fox. □ **chienne, louve, renarde**
2 a (bad-tempered or unpleasant) woman. □ **garce**
'bitchy *adjective* (*usually* of women) fond of making unpleasant comments about people: *He is sometimes very bitchy about his colleagues.* □ **vache**

bite [bait] – *past tense* **bit** [bit]: *past participle* **bitten** ['bitn] – *verb* to seize, grasp or tear (something) with the teeth or jaws: *The dog bit his leg*; *He was bitten by a mosquito.* □ **mordre, piquer**
■ *noun* 1 an act of biting or the piece or place bitten: *a bite from the apple*; *a mosquito bite.* □ **morsure, bouchée, piqûre**
2 the nibble of a fish on the end of one's line: *I've been fishing for hours without a bite.* □ **prise**
'biting *adjective* 1 very cold and causing discomfort: *a biting wind.* □ **mordant**
2 wounding or hurtful: *a biting remark.* □ **cinglant**
bite the dust to fail; to be unsuccessful: *That's another scheme that's bitten the dust.* □ **mordre la poussière**

bitter ['bitə] *adjective* 1 having a sharp, acid taste like lemons *etc*, and sometimes unpleasant: *a bitter orange.* □ **amer; acide**
2 full of pain or sorrow: *She learned from bitter experience*; *bitter disappointment.* □ **amer**
3 hostile: full of hatred or opposition: *bitter enemies.* □ **acharné**
4 very cold: *a bitter wind.* □ **glacial**
'bitterness *noun.* □ **amertume**
'bitterly *adverb*: *bitterly disappointed*; *bitterly cold.* □ **amèrement**
'bittergourd *noun* a long, fleshy, bitter-tasting fruit usually used as a vegetable. □ **coloquinte**

bitumen ['bitjumin] *noun* a black, sticky substance obtained from petroleum. □ **bitume**
bi'tuminous [-'tjuːmi-] *adjective.* □ **bitumineux**

bi-weekly [bai'wiːkli] *adjective, adverb* 1 (happening *etc*) once every two weeks. □ **bimensuel**
2 (happening *etc*) twice each week. □ **bihebdomadaire**

bizarre [bi'zaː] *adjective* odd or very strange: *a bizarre turn of events.* □ **bizarre**

black [blak] *adjective* 1 of the colour in which these words are printed: *black paint.* □ **noir**
2 without light: *a black night*; *The night was black and*

starless. □ **noir**

3 dirty: *Your hands are black!*; *black hands from lifting coal.* □ **noir**

4 without milk: *black coffee.* □ **noir**

5 evil: *black magic.* □ **noir**

6 coloured; also relating to culture of the African people (used by people of African descent to refer to themselves). □ **noir**

■ *noun* **1** the colour in which these words are printed: *Black and white are opposites.* □ **noir**

2 something (*eg* paint) black in colour: *I've used up all the black.* □ **noir**

■ *verb* to make black. □ **noircir**

'blackness *noun.* □ **noirceur**

'blacken *verb* **1** to make or become black: *The sky blackened before the storm.* □ **noircir, (s')assombrir**

2 to make to seem bad: *She blackened his character.* □ **noircir**

3 to clean with black polish: *He blackened his boots.* □ **passer au cirage noir**

black art/magic magic performed for evil reasons: *He tries to practise black magic.* □ **magie noire**

'blackbird *noun* a dark-coloured bird of the thrush family. □ **merle**

'blackboard *noun* a dark-coloured board for writing on in chalk (used *especially* in schools). □ **tableau (noir)**

black box a built-in machine for automatic recording of the details of a plane's flight: *They found the black box two kilometres away from the wreckage of the crashed plane.* □ **boîte noire**

black eye an eye with bad bruising around it (*eg* from a punch): *George gave me a black eye.* □ **œil au beurre noir**

'blackhead *noun* a small black-topped lump in a pore of the skin, *especially* of the face. □ **point noir**

'blacklist *noun* a list of people who are out of favour *etc.* □ **liste noire**

■ *verb* to put (a person *etc*) on such a list. □ **mettre sur une/la liste noire**

'blackmail *verb* to obtain money illegally from (a person), *usually* by threatening to make known something which the victim wants to keep secret. □ **faire chanter**

■ *noun* the act of blackmailing: *money got by blackmail.* □ **chantage**

'blackmailer *noun.* □ **maître-chanteur**

Black Maria [mə'raiə] a prison van: *The policewoman took the three suspects to the police station in a Black Maria.* □ **panier à salade**

black market (a place for) the illegal buying and selling, at high prices, of goods that are scarce, rationed *etc: coffee on the black market.* □ **marché noir**

black marketeer a person who sells goods on the black market. □ **trafiquant du marché noir**

'blackout *noun* **1** a period of darkness produced by putting out all lights: *Accidents increase during a blackout.* □ **panne de courant**

2 a ban (on news *etc*): *a blackout of news about the coup.* □ **black-out**

3 a period of unconsciousness: *He has had several blackouts during his illness.* □ **syncope**

black sheep a member of a family or group who is unsatisfactory in some way: *My sister is the black sheep of the family.* □ **brebis galeuse**

'blacksmith *noun* a person who makes and repairs by hand things made of iron: *The blacksmith made a new shoe for the horse.* □ **forgeron**

black and blue badly bruised: *After the fight the boy was all black and blue.* □ **couvert de bleus**

black out to lose consciousness: *He blacked out for almost a minute.* □ **tomber sans connaissance**

in black and white in writing or print: *Would you put that down in black and white?* □ **noir sur blanc**

bladder ['bladə] *noun* the bag-like part of the body in which the urine collects. □ **vessie**

blade [bleid] *noun* **1** the cutting part of a knife *etc: Her penknife has several different blades.* □ **lame**

2 the flat part of a leaf *etc: a blade of grass.* □ **limbe, brin (d'herbe)**

3 the flat part of an oar. □ **pale**

blame [bleim] *verb* **1** to consider someone or something responsible for something bad: *I blame the wet road for the accident.* □ **blâmer**

2 to find fault with (a person): *I don't blame you for wanting to leave.* □ **reprocher (qqch. à qqn)**

■ *noun* the responsibility (for something bad): *He takes the blame for everything that goes wrong.* □ **responsabilité**

'blameless *adjective* innocent: *a blameless life.* □ **irréprochable**

bland [bland] *adjective* **1** (of food *etc*) mild, tasteless: *That soup is very bland.* □ **(doux et) insipide**

2 (of people, their actions *etc*) showing no emotion: *a bland smile.* □ **affable**

'blandly *adverb.* □ **avec affabilité**

'blandness *noun.* □ **douceur**

blank [blaŋk] *adjective* **1** (of paper) without writing or marks: *a blank sheet of paper.* □ **blanc, vierge**

2 expressionless: *a blank look.* □ **vide; inexpressif**

3 (of a wall) having no door, window *etc.* □ **aveugle**

■ *noun* **1** (in forms *etc*) a space left to be filled (with a signature *etc*): *Fill in all the blanks!* □ **espace (à remplir)**

2 a blank cartridge: *The soldier fired a blank.* □ **cartouche à blanc**

'blankly *adverb* with a blank expression: *He looked at me blankly.* □ **sans expression**

'blankness *noun.* □ **vide (du regard)**

blank cartridge a cartridge without a bullet. □ **cartouche à blanc**

blank cheque a signed cheque on which the sum to be paid has not been entered. □ **chèque en blanc**

go blank to become empty: *My mind went blank when the police questioned me.* □ **avoir un trou**

blanket ['blaŋkit] *noun* **1** a warm covering made of wool *etc: a blanket on the bed.* □ **couverture**

2 something which covers like a blanket: *a blanket of mist.* □ **manteau**

■ *adjective* covering all of a group of things: *a blanket instruction.* □ **général**

■ *verb* – *past tense, past participle* **'blanketed** – to cover, as if with a blanket: *The hills were blanketed in mist.* □ **recouvrir**

blare [bleə] *verb* (*often with* **out**) to make a loud, harsh sound: *The radio blared* (*out music*). □ **retentir**

■ *noun: the blare of trumpets.* □ **bruit éclatant**

blasphemous ['blasfəməs] *adjective* (of speech or writing about God, religion *etc*) irreverent and without respect. □ **blasphématoire**

blast [blaːst] *noun* **1** a strong, sudden stream (of air): *a blast of cold air.* □ **souffle**

2 a loud sound: *a blast on the horn.* □ **coup**

3 an explosion: *the blast from a bomb.* □ **explosion**

■ *verb* **1** to tear (apart *etc*) by an explosion: *The door was blasted off its hinges.* □ **faire sauter**

2 (*often with* **out**) to come or be sent out, very loudly: *Music* (*was being*) *blasted out from the radio.* □ **hurler**

'**blasting** *noun* in mining *etc*, the breaking up of rock *etc* by explosives. □ **tir de mines**

blast furnace *noun* a furnace for melting iron ore using blasts of hot air. □ **haut fourneau**

at full blast at full power, speed *etc*: *She had the radio going at full blast* (= as loud as possible). □ **à plein volume**

blast off (of rockets, spacecraft *etc*) to take off and start to rise (*noun* '**blast-off**). □ **décoller; décollage**

blatant ['bleitənt] *adjective* very obvious; shameless: *a blatant lie; blatant disrespect.* □ **flagrant**

'**blatantly** *adverb.* □ **d'une manière flagrante**

blaze[1] [bleiz] *noun* **1** a bright light or fire: *A neighbour rescued her from the blaze.* □ **brasier**

2 an outburst (of anger, emotion *etc*): *a blaze of fury.* □ **explosion**

3 a bright display: *a blaze of colour.* □ **flamboiement**

■ *verb* (of a fire, the sun) to burn, shine brightly. □ **resplendir**

'**blazing** *adjective* **1** burning brightly: *a blazing fire.* □ **ardent**

2 extremely angry: *a blazing row.* □ **furieux**

blaze[2] [bleiz]: **blaze a trail** to lead or show the way towards something new: *She blazed a trail in the field of nuclear power.* □ **frayer le chemin**

blazer ['bleizə] *noun* a type of jacket, often part of a school uniform. □ **blazer**

bleach [bliːtʃ] *noun* liquid *etc* used for whitening clothes *etc*. □ **eau de javel**

■ *verb* to lose colour; to whiten: *The sun has bleached her red shirt; Her hair bleached in the sun.* □ **(se) décolorer**

bleak [bliːk] *adjective* **1** cold and unsheltered: *a bleak landscape.* □ **désolé**

2 not hopeful: *a bleak outlook for the future.* □ **triste**

bleat [bliːt] *verb* to make the noise of a sheep, lamb or goat: *The lamb bleated for its mother.* □ **bêler**

bleed [bliːd] – *past tense, past participle* **bled** [bled] – *verb* to lose blood: *Her nose was bleeding badly.* □ **saigner**

'**bleeding** *adjective* losing blood: *a bleeding wound.* □ **saignant**

bleep [bliːp] *noun* **1** a short, high-pitched burst of sound. □ **bip**

2 (*also* '**bleeper**) a small instrument for making this sound: *Call Dr. Smith on his bleep!* □ **bip**

■ *verb* to make a short, high-pitched sound, *usually* by electronic means: *Satellites bleep as they circle the earth.* □ **biper**

blemish ['blemiʃ] *noun* a stain, mark or fault: *a blemish on an apple.* □ **défaut, tache**

■ *verb* to spoil. □ **gâter**

blend [blend] *verb* to mix together: *Blend the eggs and milk together; These two colours blend well.* □ **(se) mélanger**

■ *noun* a mixture. □ **mélange**

'**blender** *noun* a machine for mixing things together, *especially* in cooking. □ **mélangeur**

bless [bles] – *past tense* **blessed**: *past participles* **blessed, blest** – to ask God to show favour to: *Bless this ship.* □ **bénir**

blessed ['blesid] *adjective* holy: *the Blessed Virgin.* □ **saint**

'**blessedly** [-sid-] *adverb.* □ **d'une manière bénie**

'**blessedness** [-sid-] *noun.* □ **félicité**

'**blessing** *noun* **1** a wish or prayer for happiness or success: *The priest gave them his blessing.* □ **bénédiction**

2 any cause of happiness: *His son was a great blessing to him.* □ **(grand) bonheur**

a blessing in disguise something that has proved to be fortunate after seeming unfortunate. □ **bienfait insoupçonné**

blew *see* **blow**[2].

blight [blait] *noun* a disease in plants that withers them: *potato blight.* □ **rouille**

blind [blaind] *adjective* **1** not able to see: *a blind woman.* □ **aveugle**

2 (*with* **to**) unable to notice: *She is blind to his faults.* □ **aveugle (à)**

3 hiding what is beyond: *a blind corner.* □ **sans visibilité**

4 of or for blind people: *a blind school.* □ **pour les aveugles**

■ *noun* **1** (*often in plural*) a screen to prevent light coming through a window *etc*: *The sunlight is too bright – pull down the blinds!* □ **store**

2 something intended to mislead or deceive: *She did that as a blind.* □ **feinte**

■ *verb* to make blind: *He was blinded in the war.* □ **rendre aveugle**

'**blinding** *adjective* **1** tending to make blind: *a blinding light.* □ **aveuglant**

2 sudden: *He realized, in a blinding flash, that she was the murderer.* □ **aveuglant**

'**blindly** *adverb.* □ **aveuglément**

'**blindness** *noun.* □ **cécité**

blind alley a situation without any way out: *This is a blind alley of a job.* □ **impasse**

'**blindfold** *noun* a piece of cloth *etc* put over the eyes to prevent someone from seeing: *The kidnappers put a blindfold over the child's eyes.* □ **bandeau**

■ *verb* to put a blindfold on (some person or animal). □ **bander les yeux (à/de)**

■ *adjective, adverb* with the eyes covered by a cloth *etc*: *She came blindfold into the room.* □ **les yeux bandés**

blind spot 1 any matter about which one always shows lack of understanding: *He seems to have a blind spot about physics.* □ **refuser de comprendre/voir clair**
2 an area which is impossible or difficult to see due to an obstruction. □ **endroit sans visibilité**
the blind leading the blind one inexperienced or incompetent person telling another about something: *My teaching you about politics will be a case of the blind leading the blind.* □ **l'aveugle conduisant l'aveugle**

blink [bliŋk] *verb* to move (the eyelids) rapidly up and down: *It is impossible to stare for a long time without blinking.* □ **cligner des yeux**
■ *noun* a rapid movement of the eyelids. □ **clignotement (des yeux)**

bliss [blis] *noun* very great happiness: *the bliss of a young married couple.* □ **félicité**
'**blissful** *adjective*. □ **bienheureux**
'**blissfully** *adverb*. □ **merveilleusement heureux**

blister ['blistə] *noun* **1** a thin bubble on the skin, containing liquid: *My feet have blisters after walking so far.* □ **ampoule**
2 a similar spot on any surface: *blisters on paintwork.* □ **cloque**
■ *verb* to (cause to) rise in a blister or blisters. □ **former des ampoules/cloques**

blithe [blaið] *adjective* happy and light-hearted: *She is merry and blithe.* □ **allègre**
'**blithely** *adverb*. □ **allègrement**

blitz [blits] *noun* a sudden, vigorous attack, *originally* in war. □ **attaque éclair**
■ *verb* to make an attack on (*usually* in war): *They blitzed London during the war.* □ **bombarder**

blizzard ['blizəd] *noun* a blinding storm of wind and snow: *Two climbers are missing after yesterday's blizzard.* □ **blizzard; poudrerie**

blob [blob] *noun* a (*usually* small) shapeless mass of liquid *etc*: *a blob of paint*; *a blob of wax.* □ **grosse goutte**

bloc [blok] *noun* a group of nations *etc* who have an interest or purpose in common: *the European trade bloc.* □ **bloc**

block [blok] *noun* **1** a flat-sided mass of wood or stone *etc*: *blocks of stone.* □ **bloc**
2 a piece of wood used for certain purposes: *a chopping-block.* □ **billot**
3 a connected group of houses, offices *etc*: *a block of flats*; *an office block.* □ **immeuble**
4 a barrier: *a road block.* □ **barrage routier**
5 (*especially North American*) a group of buildings bounded by four streets: *a walk around the block.* □ **îlot**
■ *verb* to make (progress) difficult or impossible: *The crashed cars blocked the road.* □ **bloquer**
bloc'kade [-'keid] *noun* something which blocks every approach to a place by land or sea. □ **blocus**
■ *verb*: *The ships blockaded the town.* □ **bloquer**
'**blockage** [-kidʒ] *noun* something causing a pipe *etc* to be blocked: *a blockage in the pipe.* □ **obstruction**
blocked *adjective* obstructed: *I have a bad cold – my nose is blocked.* □ **bouché**
block capital/letter a capital letter written in imitation of printed type, *eg* the letters in NAME. □ **majuscule d'imprimerie**

'**blockhead** *noun* a stupid person. □ **crétin, ine**

blond [blond] – *feminine* **blonde** – *adjective* having light-coloured hair: *a blond child.* □ **blond**
blonde *noun* a woman with light-coloured hair. □ **blonde**

blood [blʌd] *noun* **1** the red fluid pumped through the body by the heart: *Blood poured from the wound in his side.* □ **sang**
2 descent or ancestors: *She is of royal blood.* □ **sang**
'**bloodless** *adjective* **1** without the shedding of blood: *a bloodless victory.* □ **sans effusion de sang**
2 anemic: *She is definitely bloodless.* □ **anémié**
'**bloody** *adjective* **1** stained with blood: *a bloody shirt*; *His clothes were torn and bloody.* □ **ensanglanté**
2 bleeding: *a bloody nose.* □ **en sang**
3 murderous and cruel: *a bloody battle.* □ **sanglant**
4 used vulgarly for emphasis: *That bloody car ran over my foot!* □ **damné, ée**
'**bloodcurdling** *adjective* terrifying and horrible: *a blood-curdling scream.* □ **à (vous) figer le sang**
blood donor a person who gives blood for use by another person in transfusion *etc*. □ **donneur, euse de sang**
blood group/type any one of the types into which human blood is classified: *Her blood group is O.* □ **groupe sanguin**
'**blood poisoning** *noun* an infection of the blood: *He is suffering from blood poisoning.* □ **empoisonnement du sang**
blood pressure the (amount of) pressure of the blood on the walls of the blood vessels: *The excitement will raise his blood pressure.* □ **tension artérielle**
'**bloodshed** *noun* deaths or shedding of blood: *There was much bloodshed in the battle.* □ **effusion de sang**
'**bloodshot** *adjective* (of eyes) full of red lines and inflamed with blood. □ **injecté de sang**
'**bloodstained** *adjective* stained with blood: *a blood-stained bandage.* □ **taché de sang**
'**bloodstream** *noun* the blood flowing through the body: *The poison entered her bloodstream.* □ **système sanguin**
'**bloodthirsty** *adjective* **1** eager to kill people: *a blood-thirsty warrior.* □ **assoiffé de sang**
2 (of a film *etc*) full of scenes in which there is much killing. □ **sanguinaire**
'**bloodthirstiness** *noun*. □ **cruauté sanguinaire**
'**blood vessel** *noun* any of the tubes in the body through which the blood flows: *She has burst a blood vessel.* □ **vaisseau sanguin**
in cold blood while free from excitement or passion: *He killed his son in cold blood.* □ **de sang-froid**

bloom [bluːm] *noun* **1** a flower: *These blooms are withering now.* □ **fleur**
2 the state of flowering: *The flowers are in bloom.* □ **floraison**
3 freshness: *in the bloom of youth.* □ **fleur**
■ *verb* to flower or flourish: *Daffodils bloom in the spring.* □ **fleurir**

blossom ['blosəm] *noun* flowers, *especially* of a fruit tree: *beautiful blossom*; *apple blossom.* □ **fleur**
■ *verb* **1** to develop flowers: *My plant has blossomed.* □

fleurir
2 to flourish: *She blossomed into a beautiful woman.* □ **(s')épanouir**
'**blossoming** *adjective.* □ **épanouissement**

blot [blot] *noun* 1 a spot or stain (often of ink): *an exercise book full of blots.* □ **pâté, tache**
2 something ugly: *a blot on the landscape.* □ **tache**
■ *verb – past tense, past participle* '**blotted** – 1 to spot or stain, *especially* with ink: *I blotted this sheet of paper in three places when my nib broke.* □ **tacher**
2 to dry with blotting paper: *Blot your signature before you fold the paper.* □ **sécher**
'**blotter** *noun* a pad or sheet of blotting paper. □ **buvard**
'**blotting paper** *noun* soft paper used for drying up ink. □ **(papier-)buvard**
blot one's copybook to make a bad mistake: *He has really blotted his copybook by being late for the interview.* □ **faire un accroc à sa réputation**
blot out to hide from sight: *The rain blotted out the view.* □ **masquer**

blotch [blotʃ] *noun* a discoloured mark: *Those red blotches on her face are very ugly.* □ **tache**

blouse [blauz] *noun* a woman's (often loose) garment for the upper half of the body: *a skirt and blouse.* □ **chemisier**

blow¹ [bləu] *noun* 1 a stroke or knock: *a blow on the head.* □ **coup**
2 a sudden misfortune: *Her husband's death was a real blow.* □ **coup (dur)**

blow² [bləu] – *past tense* **blew** [blu]: *past participle* **blown** – *verb* 1 (of a current of air) to be moving: *The wind blew more strongly.* □ **souffler**
2 (of *eg* wind) to cause (something) to move in a given way: *The explosion blew off the lid.* □ **faire (s'en)voler**
3 to be moved by the wind *etc*: *The door must have blown shut.* □ **être poussé par le vent**
4 to drive air (upon or into): *Please blow into this tube!* □ **souffler**
5 to make a sound by means of (a musical instrument *etc*): *She blew the horn loudly.* □ **souffler dans**
'**blowhole** *noun* a breathing-hole (through the ice for seals *etc*) or a nostril (*especially* on the head of a whale *etc*). □ **évent**
'**blowout** *noun* 1 the bursting of a car tire: *That's the second blowout I've had with this car.* □ **éclatement**
2 (on *eg* an oil rig) a violent escape of gas *etc*. □ **éruption**
'**blowpipe** *noun* a tube from which a dart (often poisonous) is blown. □ **sarbacane**
'**blowtorch** *noun* a lamp for aiming a very hot flame at a particular spot: *The painter burned off the old paint with a blowtorch.* □ **chalumeau**
blow one's nose *verb* to dislodge fluid from the nose into a handkerchief or facial tissue: *Nooria was sick with a cold and had to blow her nose to breathe.* □ **se moucher**
blow one's top to become very angry: *She blew her top when he arrived home late.* □ **éclater**
blow out to extinguish or put out (a flame *etc*) by blowing: *The wind blew out the candle; The child blew out the match.* □ **éteindre (en soufflant)**

blow over to pass and become forgotten: *The trouble will soon blow over.* □ **passer**
blow up 1 to break into pieces, or be broken into pieces, by an explosion: *The bridge blew up/was blown up.* □ **sauter**
2 to fill with air or a gas: *He blew up the balloon.* □ **gonfler**
3 to lose one's temper: *If he says that again I'll blow up.* □ **exploser**

blubber ['blʌbə] *noun* the fat of whales and other sea animals. □ **blanc de baleine**

blue [bluː] *adjective* 1 of the colour of a cloudless sky: *blue paint; Her eyes are blue.* □ **bleu**
2 sad or depressed: *I'm feeling blue today.* □ **déprimé**
■ *noun* 1 the colour of a cloudless sky: *That is a beautiful blue.* □ **bleu**
2 a blue paint, material *etc*: *We'll have to get some more blue.* □ **bleu**
3 the sky or the sea: *The balloon floated off into the blue.* □ **ciel**
'**blueness** *noun*. □ **bleu**
'**bluish** *adjective* quite blue; close to blue: *a bluish green.* □ **bleuâtre**
blueberry *noun* a small, round dark blue fruit that grows on a bush: *Michel picked a litre of blueberries to make blueberry pie for dessert.* □ **bleuet**
'**bluebottle** *noun* a kind of large house-fly with a blue abdomen. □ **mouche bleue**
'**bluecollar** *adjective* (of workers) wearing overalls and working in factories *etc*: *Blue collar workers are demanding the same pay as office staff.* □ **col bleu**
'**blueprint** *noun* a detailed photographic plan of work to be carried out: *the blueprints for a new aircraft.* □ **bleu**
once in a blue moon very seldom: *He visits his mother once in a blue moon.* □ **tous les trente-six du mois**
out of the blue without warning: *She arrived out of the blue, without phoning first.* □ **à l'improviste**
the blues low spirits; depression: *He's got the blues today but he's usually cheerful.* □ **cafard**

bluff¹ [blʌf] *adjective* rough, hearty and frank: *a bluff and friendly manner.* □ **direct**

bluff² [blʌf] *verb* to try to deceive by pretending to have something that one does not have: *He bluffed his way through the exam without actually knowing anything.* □ **bluffer**
■ *noun* an act of bluffing. □ **bluff**

blunder ['blʌndə] *verb* 1 to stumble (about or into something): *She blundered into the door.* □ **(se) cogner dans**
2 to make a (bad) mistake: *He really blundered when he insulted the boss's wife.* □ **gaffer**
■ *noun* a (bad) mistake. □ **gaffe**

blunt [blʌnt] *adjective* 1 (of objects) having no point or sharp edge: *a blunt knife.* □ **émoussé**
2 (of people) (sometimes unpleasantly) straightforward or frank in speech: *She was very blunt, and said that she did not like him.* □ **brutal**
■ *verb* to make less sharp: *This knife has been blunted by years of use.* □ **émousser**
'**bluntly** *adverb*. □ **sans ménagements**

'**bluntness** *noun*. □ **brusquerie**

blur [blə:] *noun* something not clearly seen: *Everything is just a blur when I take my spectacles off.* □ **image floue**

■ *verb – past tense, past participle* **blurred** – to make or become unclear: *The rain blurred my vision.* □ **brouiller**

blurt [blə:t]: **blurt out** to say (something) suddenly: *She blurted out the whole story.* □ **lâcher**

blush [blʌʃ] *noun* **1** a red glow on the skin caused by shame, embarrassment *etc.* □ **rougeur**
2 a cosmetic which gives a pink glow to the skin. □ **fard**

■ *verb* to show shame, embarrassment *etc* by growing red in the face: *That boy blushes easily.* □ **rougir**

'**blustery** ['blʌstəri] *adjective* (of the wind) blowing in irregular, strong gusts: *a blustery day.* □ **en bourrasques**

boa ['bouə] *noun* (*usually* **boa constrictor**) **1** a large snake that kills by winding itself around its prey. □ **boa**
2 a long scarf made of feathers or fur: *A boa around her neck completed her costume.* □ **boa**

boar [bo:] *noun* a male pig (*especially* the wild variety). □ **sanglier**

board [bo:d] *noun* **1** a strip of timber: *The floorboards of the old house were rotten.* □ **planche**
2 a flat piece of wood *etc* for a special purpose: *notice-board; chessboard.* □ **panneau**
3 meals: *board and lodging.* □ **pension (complète)**
4 an official group of persons administering an organization *etc: the board of directors.* □ **conseil**

■ *verb* **1** to enter, or get on to (a vehicle, ship, plane *etc*): *This is where we board the bus.* □ **monter dans**
2 to live temporarily and take meals (in someone else's house): *He boards at Mrs. Smith's during the week.* □ **être en pension chez**

'**boarder** *noun* a person who temporarily lives, and takes his meals, in someone else's house. □ **pensionnaire**

'**boarding-house** *noun* a house where people live and take meals as paying guests. □ **pension**

'**boarding-school** *noun* a school which provides accommodation and food as well as instruction. □ **pensionnat**

across the board applying in all cases: *They were awarded wage increases across the board; (also adjective) an across-the-board increase.* □ **général**

go by the board to be abandoned: *All my plans went by the board when I lost my job.* □ **tomber à l'eau**

boast [boust] *verb* to talk with too much pride: *He was always boasting about how clever his son was.* □ **se vanter (de)**

■ *noun* the words used in talking proudly about something: *Her boast is that she has never yet lost a match.* □ **objet d'orgueil**

'**boastful** *adjective*. □ **vantard**

'**boastfully** *adverb*. □ **avec vantardise**

'**boastfulness** *noun*. □ **vantardise**

'**boasting** *noun*. □ **vantardise**

boat [bout] *noun* **1** a small vessel for travelling over water: *We'll cross the stream by boat.* □ **bateau**
2 a larger vessel for the same purpose; a ship: *to cross the Atlantic in a passenger boat.* □ **navire**

3 a serving-dish shaped like a boat: *a gravy-boat.* □ **saucière**

■ *verb* to sail about in a small boat for pleasure: *They are boating on the river.* □ **faire du bateau**

'**boatman** *noun* a man in charge of a small boat in which fare-paying passengers are carried. □ **loueur de canots**

in the same boat in the same, *usually* difficult, position or circumstances: *We're all in the same boat as far as low wages are concerned.* □ **dans la même galère**

boatswain, bosun ['bousn] *noun* an officer who looks after a ship's boats, ropes, sails *etc.* □ **maître d'équipage**

bob [bob] – *past tense, past participle* **bobbed** – *verb* to move (up and down): *The cork was bobbing about in the water.* □ **monter et descendre (sur place)**

bobbin ['bobin] *noun* a (*usually* wooden) reel or spool for winding thread *etc: There's no thread left on the bobbin.* □ **bobine**

bobsleigh ['bobslei], **bobsled** ['bobsled] *nouns* a vehicle on metal runners used in crossing (and sometimes racing on) snow and ice. □ **bobsleigh**

bode [boud]: **bode ill/well** to be an omen of or to foretell bad or good fortune: *This bodes well for the future.* □ **présager**

bodice ['bodis] *noun* the upper part of a woman's or child's dress: *The dress had an embroidered bodice.* □ **corsage**

bodily *see* body.

body ['bodi] – *plural* '**bodies** – *noun* **1** the whole frame of a man or animal including the bones and flesh: *Athletes have to look after their bodies.* □ **corps**
2 a dead person: *The battlefield was covered with bodies.* □ **cadavre**
3 the main part of anything: *the body of the hall.* □ **corps, partie principale**
4 a mass: *a huge body of evidence.* □ **masse**
5 a group of persons acting as one: *professional bodies.* □ **corps**

'**bodily** *adjective* of the body: *bodily needs.* □ **du corps, physique**

■ *adverb* by the entire (physical) body: *They lifted him bodily and carried him off.* □ **à bras-le-corps**

'**bodyguard** *noun* a guard or guards to protect (*especially* an important person): *the president's bodyguard.* □ **garde du corps**

'**bodywork** *noun* the outer casing of a car *etc: The bodywork of her new car has rusted already.* □ **carrosserie**

bog [bog] *noun* very wet ground; marsh. □ **marécage**

'**boggy** *adjective: boggy ground.* □ **marécageux**

be bogged down to be hindered in movement; to be prevented from making progress: *The tractor is bogged down in the mud.* □ **être embourbé**

bogeyman ['bo:gi,man] *noun* an imaginary evil spirit, especially invoked to frighten children. □ **croque-mitaine**

bogus ['bougəs] *adjective* false; not genuine: *She was fooled by his bogus identity card.* □ **faux**

boil[1] [boil] *verb* **1** to turn rapidly from liquid to vapour when heated: *I'm boiling the water; The water's boiling.* □ **bouillir**
2 to cook by boiling in water *etc: I've boiled the pota-*

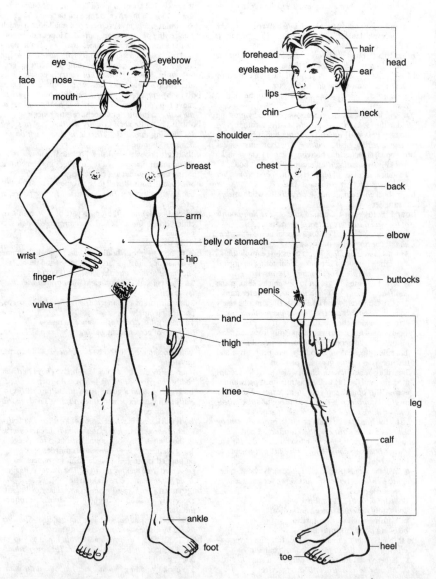

face
eye
nose
mouth
eyebrow
cheek

forehead
eyelashes
lips
chin
hair
ear
head
neck

shoulder

breast

chest
back

arm

belly or stomach

wrist
finger

hip

elbow

buttocks

vulva

penis

hand

thigh

knee

leg

calf

ankle

foot

heel

toe

toes. □ **faire bouillir**

'**boiler** *noun* a vessel in which water is heated or steam is produced. □ **chaudière**

'**boiling point** *noun* the temperature at which something boils. □ **point d'ébullition**

boil over to boil and overflow: *The pan of water boiled over and spilt on the floor.* □ **déborder**

boil[2] [boil] *noun* an inflamed swelling on the skin: *His neck is covered with boils.* □ **furoncle**

boisterous ['boistərəs] *adjective* wild and noisy: *a boisterous child.* □ **turbulent**

bold [bould] *adjective* **1** daring or fearless: *a bold plan of attack.* □ **hardi**

2 striking and well-marked: *a dress with bold stripes.* □ **frappant**

3 (of type) thick and clear, like this. □ **gras**

'**boldly** *adverb.* □ **hardiment**

'**boldness** *noun.* □ **audace**

bold as brass very cheeky: *She walked in late as bold as brass.* □ **avec impudence**

bolero ['bolərou] – *plural* '**boleros** – *noun* a short jacket with no fastening. □ **boléro**

bollard ['bolɑːd] *noun* a short post on a wharf or ship around which ropes are fastened. □ **borne d'amarrage**

bolster ['boulstə] *noun* a long, often round pillow. □ **traversin**

■ *verb* – *past tense, past participle* '**bolstered** – (*often with* up) to prop up: *We're getting a loan to bolster (up) the economy.* □ **soutenir**

bolt [boult] *noun* **1** a bar to fasten a door *etc*: *We have a bolt as well as a lock on the door.* □ **verrou**

2 a round bar of metal, often with a screw thread for a nut: *nuts and bolts.* □ **boulon**

3 a flash of lightning. □ **éclair**

4 a roll (of cloth): *a bolt of silk.* □ **rouleau**

■ *verb* **1** to fasten with a bolt: *She bolted the door.* □ **verrouiller**

2 to swallow hastily: *The child bolted her food.* □ **engloutir (sans mâcher)**

3 to go away very fast: *The horse bolted in terror.* □ **(s')emballer**

,**bolt(-)**'**upright** *adverb* absolutely upright: *She sat bolt upright in the chair with her back very straight.* □ **droit comme un piquet**

a bolt from the blue a sudden, unexpected happening: *His resignation was a bolt from the blue.* □ **un coup de tonnerre dans un ciel bleu**

bomb [bom] *noun* a hollow case containing explosives *etc*: *The enemy dropped a bomb on the factory and blew it up.* □ **bombe**

■ *verb* **1** to drop bombs on: *London was bombed several times.* □ **bombarder**

2 to fail miserably: *The play bombed on the first night.* □ **foirer**

'**bomber** *noun* **1** an airplane built for bombing. □ **bombardier**

2 a person who bombs: *Bombers have caused many deaths in Northern Ireland.* □ **poseur, euse de bombes**

'**bombshell** *noun* a piece of startling news: *Her resignation was a real bombshell.* □ **(véritable) bombe**

bombard [bom'bɑːd] *verb* **1** to attack with artillery: *They bombarded the town.* □ **bombarder**

2 to direct questions *etc* at: *The reporters bombarded the film star with questions.* □ **assaillir (de)**

bom'bardment *noun.* □ **bombardement**

bonanza [bə'nanzə] *noun* a sudden increase (in profits *etc*): *Shopkeepers in seaside towns enjoy a bonanza in hot summers.* □ **mine d'or**

bond [bond] *noun* **1** something used for tying (*especially* a person): *They released the prisoner from his bonds.* □ **chaînes**

2 something that unites or joins people together: *a bond of friendship.* □ **lien**

bonded store/warehouse a warehouse where goods are kept until customs or other duty on them is paid. □ **entrepôt des douanes**

bondage ['bondidʒ] *noun* slavery. □ **esclavage**

bone [boun] *noun* **1** the hard substance forming the skeleton of man, animals *etc*: *Bone decays far more slowly than flesh.* □ **os**

2 a piece of this substance: *She broke two of the bones in her foot.* □ **os**

■ *verb* to take the bones out of (fish *etc*). □ **désosser**

'**bony** *adjective* **1** like bone: *a bony substance.* □ **osseux**

2 full of bones: *This fish is very bony.* □ **plein d'arêtes/d'os**

3 thin: *bony fingers.* □ **décharné**

bone china china in whose manufacture the ashes of burnt bones are used. □ **porcelaine**

bone idle very lazy: *He could find a job but he's bone idle.* □ **fainéant**

a bone of contention a cause of argument or quarrelling: *Ownership of the boat was a bone of contention between the two women for many years.* □ **pomme de discorde**

have a bone to pick with (someone) to have something to argue about with (a person). □ **avoir un compte à régler avec qqn**

to the bone 1 thoroughly and completely: *I was chilled to the bone.* □ **jusqu'aux os**

2 to the minimum: *I've cut my expenses to the bone.* □ **au (strict) minimum**

bonfire ['bonfaiə] *noun* a large fire in the open air, often built to celebrate something. □ **feu (de joie)**

bonnet ['bonit] *noun* (*usually* baby's or (old) woman's) head-dress fastened under the chin *eg* by strings. □ **bonnet**

bonsai ['bonsai] *noun* a small decorative evergreen shrub or tree grown in a pot, which has been prevented from growing to its usual size by various methods. □ **bonsaï**

bonus ['bounəs] *noun* **1** an addition to the sum due as interest, dividend, or wages. □ **prime**

2 something unexpected or extra: *The extra two days holiday was a real bonus.* □ **aubaine**

bony *see* bone.

boo [buː] – *plural* **boos** – *noun* a derisive shout, made *eg* by a disapproving crowd: *the boos of the disappointed football supporters.* □ **huées**

■ *verb* – *past tense, past participle* **booed** – to make such a sound at a person *etc*: *The crowd booed (him).* □

huer

boob [buːb] *noun* a mistake: *Forgetting to invite her to the party was a real boob.* □ **gaffe**
■ *verb* to make a mistake. □ **faire une gaffe**

booby ['buːbi] – *plural* 'boobies – *noun* a stupid person. □ **nigaud**

booby prize a prize for the lowest score *etc*: *John came last and got the booby prize.* □ **prix de consolation**

book [buk] *noun* 1 a number of sheets of paper (*especially* printed) bound together: *an exercise book.* □ **cahier**

2 a piece of writing, bound and covered: *I've written a book on Charlotte Brontë.* □ **livre**

3 a record of bets. □ **livre de paris**
■ *verb* 1 to buy or reserve (a ticket, seat *etc*) for a play *etc*: *I've booked four seats for Friday's concert.* □ **réserver**

2 to hire in advance: *We've booked the hall for Saturday.* □ **retenir**

'**bookable** *adjective* able to be reserved in advance: *Are these seats bookable?* □ **qu'on peut réserver**

'**booking** *noun* a reservation. □ **réservation**

'**booklet** [-lit] *noun* a small, thin book: *a booklet about the history of the town.* □ **petit livre**

'**bookbinding** *noun* putting the covers on books. □ **reliure**

'**bookbinder** *noun*. □ **relieur, euse**

'**bookcase** *noun* a set of shelves for books. □ **bibliothèque**

'**bookmaker** *noun* a professional betting man who takes bets and pays winnings. □ **bookmaker**

'**bookmark** *noun* something put in a book to mark a particular page. □ **signet**

'**bookseller** *noun* a person who sells books. □ **libraire**

'**bookshelf** *noun* a shelf on which books are kept. □ **rayon**

'**bookshop**, '**bookstore** *noun* a shop which sells books. □ **librairie**

'**bookworm** *noun* a person who reads a lot. □ **rat de bibliothèque**

booked up having every ticket sold: *The theatre is booked up for the season.* □ **à guichets fermés**

by the book strictly according to the rules: *She always does things by the book.* □ **selon les règles**

boom¹ [buːm] *noun* a sudden increase in a business *etc*: *a boom in the sales of TV sets.* □ **forte hausse**
■ *verb* to increase suddenly (and profitably): *Business is booming this week.* □ **grimper en flèche**

boom² [buːm] *verb* (*often with* out) to make a hollow sound, like a large drum or gun: *Her voice boomed out over the loudspeaker.* □ **tonner**
■ *noun* such a sound. □ **grondement**

boomerang ['buːməraŋ] *noun* a curved piece of wood used by Australian aborigines which, when thrown, returns to the thrower. □ **boomerang**

boon [buːn] *noun* a blessing: *It's been a real boon to have a car this week.* □ **aubaine**

boor [buə] *noun* a coarse, ill-mannered person. □ **butor**

'**boorish** *adjective*. □ **grossier**

boost [buːst] *verb* to expand; to make greater; to improve: *We've boosted the sales figures; It's boosted her reputation.* □ **gonfler, renforcer**
■ *noun* a piece of help, encouragement *etc*: *This publicity will give our sales a real boost.* □ **regain de vigueur**

'**booster** *noun* 1 a person or thing that boosts: *That was a real morale booster for me* (= That made me feel more cheerful and optimistic). □ **congédier**

2 a device for increasing power, force *etc*: *I've fixed a booster on the TV antenna to improve the signal.* □ **amplificateur**

3 the first stage of a rocket that works by several stages. □ **fusée de lancement**

boot [buːt] *noun* a covering for the foot and lower part of the leg, *usually* made of leather *etc*: *a pair of suede boots.* □ **botte, bottine**
■ *verb* to kick: *She booted the ball out of the goal.* □ **lancer du pied**

give, get the boot to dismiss (someone) or to be dismissed (*usually* from a job): *He got the boot for always being late.* □ **congédier**

bootee [buː'tiː] *noun* a (*usually* knitted) woollen boot for a baby. □ **petit chausson**

booth [buːθ] *noun* 1 a tent or stall, *especially* at a fair: *the fortune teller's booth.* □ **baraque**

2 a small compartment for a given purpose: *a phone booth; a polling-booth.* □ **cabine, isoloir**

booty ['buːti] *noun* goods taken from *eg* an enemy by force (*especially* in wartime): *The soldiers shared the booty among themselves; the burglars' booty.* □ **butin**

booze [buːz] *noun* alcoholic drink: *Have you got enough booze for the party?* □ **boisson alcoolisée**
■ *verb* to drink alcoholic drinks. □ **boire (comme un trou)**

border ['boːdə] *noun* 1 the edge of a particular thing: *the border of a picture/handkerchief.* □ **bord(ure)**

2 the boundary of a country: *They'll ask for your passport at the border.* □ **frontière**

3 a flower bed around the edge of a lawn *etc*: *a flower border.* □ **plate-bande**
■ *verb* (*with* on) to come near to or lie on the border of: *Germany borders on France.* □ **toucher à, être limitrophe de**

'**borderline** *adjective* doubtful; on the border between one thing and another: *He was a borderline case, so we gave him an additional exam to see if he would pass it.* □ **cas limite**
■ *noun* the border between one thing and another: *She was on the borderline between passing and failing.* □ **limite**

bore¹ [boː] *verb* to make (a hole *etc* in something): *They bored a tunnel under the sea.* □ **faire un trou dans, forer**
■ *noun* the size of the hollow barrel of a gun. □ **calibre**

'**borehole** *noun* a hole made by boring, *especially* to find oil *etc*. □ **trou de sonde**

bore² [boː] *verb* to make (someone) feel tired and uninterested, by being dull *etc*: *He bores everyone with stories about his travels.* □ **ennuyer**
■ *noun* a dull, boring person or thing. □ **raseur, euse**

'boredom *noun* the state of being bored. □ **ennui**

'boring *adjective*: *a boring job*; *This book is boring*. □ **ennuyeux**

bore³ *born, borne see* bear¹.

borrow ['borou] *verb* to take (something, often money) temporarily with the intention of returning it: *She borrowed a book from the library*. □ **emprunter**

'borrower *noun*. □ **emprunteur, euse**

'borrowing *noun*. □ **emprunt**

---

borrow from: *I borrow money from a friend.*
lend to: *My friend lends money to me/My friend lends me money.*

---

bosom ['buzəm] *noun* 1 a woman's breasts: *She has a large bosom*. □ **poitrine**

2 the chest: *She held him tenderly to her bosom.* □ **poitrine, sein**

3 the innermost part: *in the bosom of his family.* □ **sein**

■ *adjective* intimate; close: *a bosom friend*. □ **intime**

boss [bos] *noun* the master or manager: *the boss of the factory.* □ **patron, onne**

■ *verb* (*usually with* **about/around**) to order: *Stop bossing everyone about!* □ **mener à la baguette**

'bossy *adjective* liking to order others about. □ **autoritaire**

'bossily *adverb*. □ **de manière autoritaire**

'bossiness *noun*. □ **autoritarisme**

bosun *see* boatswain.

botany ['botəni] *noun* the scientific study of plants. □ **botanique**

bo'tanic(al) [-'ta-] *adjective*. □ **botanique**

'botanist *noun* a person who studies botany. □ **botaniste**

botanic(al) garden(s) *noun singular or plural* a public park for the growing of native and foreign plants. □ **jardin botanique**

both [bouθ] *adjective, pronoun* the two; the one and the other: *We both went*; *Both* (the) *men are dead*; *The men are both dead*; *Both are dead*. □ **tous (les) deux**

bother ['boðə] *verb* 1 to annoy or worry: *The noise bothered the old woman*. □ **ennuyer, déranger**

2 to take the trouble: *Don't bother to write – it isn't necessary*. □ **se donner la peine (de)**

■ *noun* 1 trouble, nuisance or worry. □ **ennui**

2 something or someone that causes bother: *What a bother all this is!* □ **ennui**

'bothersome *adjective* causing bother or annoyance: *a bothersome cough*. □ **gênant**

bottle ['botl] *noun* a hollow narrow-necked container for holding liquids *etc*: *a lemonade bottle*. □ **bouteille**

■ *verb* to put into bottles. □ **mettre en bouteille(s)**

'bottleneck *noun* a place where slowing down or stopping of traffic, progress *etc* occurs: *a bottleneck caused by roadworks*. □ **bouchon**

bottle up to prevent (*eg* one's feelings) from becoming obvious: *Don't bottle up your anger*. □ **refouler**

bottom ['botəm] *noun* 1 the lowest part of anything: *the bottom of the sea*. □ **fond**

2 the part of the body on which a person sits. □ **derrière**

'bottomless *adjective* very deep: *a bottomless pit*. □ **sans fond**

be at the bottom of to be the cause of (*usually* something bad): *Who's at the bottom of these rumours?* □ **être à l'origine de**

get to the bottom of to discover the explanation or the real facts of (a mystery *etc*). □ **aller jusqu'au fond de**

bougainvillea [buːgən'viliə] *noun* a vine with small flowers and purple or red leaves. □ **bougainvillée**

bough [bau] *noun* a branch of a tree: *the bough of an apple tree*. □ **branche**

bought *see* buy.

boulder ['bouldə] *noun* a large rock or stone: *a boulder on the hillside*. □ **(gros) rocher (arrondi)**

bounce [bauns] *verb* 1 to (cause to) spring or jump back from a solid surface. □ **(faire) rebondir**

2 (of a cheque) to be sent back unpaid, because of lack of money in a bank account. □ **être refusé pour provisions insuffisantes**

■ *noun* 1 (of a ball *etc*) an act of springing back: *With one bounce the ball went over the net*. □ **(re)bond**

2 energy: *She has a lot of bounce*. □ **allant**

'bouncing *adjective* strong and lively: *a bouncing baby*. □ **beau**

bound¹ *see* bind.

bound² [baund]: **-bound** (*as part of a word*) going in a particular direction: *westbound traffic*. □ **vers, à destination de**

bound for on the way to: *bound for Africa*. □ **en route pour**

bound to 1 certain to: *She's bound to notice your mistake*. □ **forcé de**

2 obliged to: *I felt bound to mention it*. □ **obligé de/à**

See also -bound *under* bind.

bound³ [baund] *noun* (*usually in plural*) limits of some kind: *beyond the bounds of coincidence*. □ **limite**

'boundless *adjective* having no limit: *boundless energy*. □ **illimité**

out of bounds outside the permitted area or limits: *The movie theatre was out of bounds for the boys from the local boarding-school*. □ **interdit (à)**

bound⁴ [baund] *noun* a spring; a leap: *She reached me in one bound*. □ **bond**

■ *verb* to move in this way: *The dog bounded over eagerly to where I was sitting*. □ **bondir**

boundary ['baundəri] – *plural* 'boundaries – *noun* an often imaginary line separating one thing from another: *the boundary between two towns*. □ **frontière**

boundless *see* bound³.

bounty ['baunti] *noun* 1 generosity in giving. □ **générosité**

2 (*plural* 'bounties) something given out of generosity. □ **don**

bouquet [bu'kei] *noun* 1 a bunch of flowers: *The bride carried a bouquet of roses*. □ **bouquet**

2 the perfume of wine. □ **bouquet**

bout [baut] *noun* 1 a period (of): *a bout of coughing*. □ **accès**

2 a (*usually* boxing) contest: *a bout of fifteen five-minute rounds*. □ **combat**

boutique [buːˈtiːk] *noun* a fashionable, *usually* small shop, *especially* one selling clothes: *She prefers small* *boutiques to large stores.* □ **boutique (de luxe)**

bow¹ [bau] *verb* **1** to bend (the head and often also the upper part of the body) forwards in greeting a person *etc*: *He bowed to the ladies*; *They bowed their heads in prayer.* □ **(s')incliner devant**

2 (*with* **to**) to accept: *I bow to your superior knowledge.* □ **s'incliner devant**

■ *noun* a bowing movement: *He made a bow to the ladies.* □ **salut**

bowed *adjective* (often with **down**) bent downwards, *eg* by the weight of something: *The trees were bowed down with fruit.* □ **ployé (sous)**

bow² [bou] *noun* **1** a springy curved rod bent by a string, by which arrows are shot. □ **arc**

2 a rod with horsehair stretched along it, by which the strings of a violin *etc* are sounded. □ **archet**

3 a looped knot of material: *Her dress is decorated with bows.* □ **nœud**

■ [bau] *noun* (*often in plural*) the front of a ship or boat: *The waves broke over the bows.* □ **proue**

bowel ['bauəl] *noun* **1** (*usually in plural*) the part of the digestive system below the stomach; the intestines: *The surgeon removed part of her bowel.* □ **intestin(s)**

2 (*in plural*) the inside of something, *especially* when deep: *the bowels of the earth.* □ **entrailles**

bowl¹ [boul] *noun* a wooden ball rolled along the ground in playing bowls. *See also* **bowls** *below.* □ **boule**

■ *verb* **1** to play bowls. □ **jouer aux boules**

2 to deliver or send (a ball) towards the batsman in cricket. □ **lancer la balle à**

3 to put (a batsman) out by hitting the wicket with the ball: *Smith was bowled for eighty-five* (= Smith was put out after making eighty-five runs). □ **mettre hors jeu**

'bowler *noun.* □ **joueur, euse de boules**

'bowling *noun* the game of skittles, bowls or something similar. □ **jeu de boules, de quilles**

bowls *noun singular* a game played on a smooth green with bowls having a bias: *a game of bowls.* □ **boules**

'bowling-alley *noun* **1** a long narrow set of wooden boards along which one bowls at skittles. □ **salle de quilles**

2 a building which contains several of these. □ **salle de quilles**

bowl over to knock down: *I was bowled over in the rush for the door*; *His generosity bowled me over.* □ **renverser, stupéfier**

bowl² [boul] *noun* **1** a round, deep dish *eg* for mixing or serving food *etc*: *a mixing bowl*; *a soup bowl.* □ **bol**

2 a round hollow part, *especially* of a tobacco pipe, a spoon *etc*: *The bowl of this spoon is dirty.* □ **fourneau, creux**

bowler¹ *see* **bowl¹.**

bowler² ['boulə] *noun* (*also* **bowler hat**) a type of hard, round felt hat. □ **(chapeau) melon**

box¹ [boks] *noun* **1** a case for holding something: *a wooden box*; *a matchbox.* □ **boîte**

2 in a theatre *etc*, a group of seats separated from the rest of the audience. □ **loge**

■ *verb* to put (something) into boxes: *Will you box these apples?* □ **mettre en boîte, emballer**

Boxing day December 26, the day after Christmas Day. □ **le lendemain de Noël**

box number a number used *eg* in a newspaper advertisement instead of a full address. □ **boîte postale**

box office a ticket office in a theatre, concert hall *etc*: *There's a queue at the box office for tonight's show.* □ **guichet (de location)**

box² [boks] *verb* to fight (someone) with the fists: *Years ago, fighters used to box without wearing padded gloves.* □ **boxer**

■ *noun* a blow on the ear with the hand. □ **claque**

'boxer *noun: He's a champion boxer.* □ **boxeur**

'boxing *noun* the sport of fighting with the fists. □ **boxe**

'boxing glove *noun* a boxer's padded glove. □ **gant de boxe**

'boxing match *noun.* □ **match de boxe**

boy [boi] *noun* **1** a male child: *She has three girls and one boy.* □ **(petit) garçon**

2 (*as part of another word*) a male (often adult) who does a certain job: *a cowboy*; *a paper-boy.* □ **cow-boy, livreur de journaux**

'boyhood *noun* the time of being a boy: *a happy boyhood*; (*also adjective*) *boyhood memories.* □ **enfance (d'un garçon)**

'boyfriend *noun* a girl's favourite male friend. □ **(petit) ami**

boycott ['boikot] *verb* to refuse to have any dealings with (a firm, country *etc*). □ **boycotter**

■ *noun* a refusal to deal with a firm *etc*. □ **boycottage**

bra [braː] short for **brassière.**

brace [breis] *noun* **1** something that draws together and holds tightly: *a brace to straighten teeth.* □ **attache**

2 a pair *usually* of game-birds: *a brace of pheasants.* □ **paire**

■ *verb* to make (often oneself) firm or steady: *She braced herself for the struggle.* □ **se préparer (mentalement) pour**

'braces *noun plural* (su'spenders) straps over the shoulders for holding up the trousers. □ **bretelles**

'bracing *adjective* healthy: *bracing sea air.* □ **vivifiant**

bracelet ['breislit] *noun* an ornament worn around the wrist or arm: *a gold bracelet.* □ **bracelet**

bracket ['brakit] *noun* **1** (*usually in plural*) marks (such as ( ), [ ], { } *etc*) used to group together one or more words *etc*. □ **accolade(s)**

2 a support for a shelf *etc*: *The shelf fell down because the brackets were not strong enough.* □ **support**

■ *verb* – *past tense, past participle* '**bracketed** – **1** to enclose (words *etc*) by brackets. □ **mettre entre crochets/parenthèses**

2 (*sometimes with* **together**) to group together (similar or equal people or things). □ **mettre dans la même catégorie**

bracket fungus a round, flat fungus that grows out horizontally on the trunks of trees. □ **polypore**

brackish ['brakiʃ] *adjective* (of water) tasting slightly of salt, often unpleasantly. □ **saumâtre**

brag [brag] – *past tense, past participle* **bragged** – *verb* to boast. □ **(se) vanter**

braid [breid] *verb* to wind together (*especially* strands

of hair). □ **tresser**
■ *noun* threads twisted together and used as decoration on uniforms *etc*: *gold braid on the admiral's uniform.* □ **tresse**

braille [breil] *noun* a system of printing for the blind, using raised dots. □ **braille**

brain [brein] *noun* **1** the centre of the nervous system: *an injury to the brain*; (*also adjective*) *brain surgery*; *brain damage.* □ **(au/du) cerveau**
2 (*often in plural*) cleverness: *a good brain*; *You've plenty of brains.* □ **intelligence**
3 a clever person: *She's one of the best brains in the country.* □ **cerveau**
'**brainless** *adjective* stupid: *a brainless idiot.* □ **stupide**
'**brainy** *adjective* clever: *She's a brainy child.* □ **doué**
'**brainchild** *noun* a favourite theory, invention *etc* thought up by a particular person: *This entire process is Dr. Smith's brainchild.* □ **idée personnelle**
brain drain the loss of experts to another country (*usually* in search of better salaries *etc*): *As a result of the brain drain Britain does not have enough doctors.* □ **exode des cerveaux**
'**brainwash** *verb* to force (a person) to confess *etc* by putting great (psychological) pressure on him: *The terrorists brainwashed him into believing in their ideals.* □ **faire un lavage de cerveau à**
'**brainwave** *noun* a sudden bright idea. □ **idée géniale**

braise [breiz] *verb* to stew (meat *etc*) slowly in a closed dish. □ **braiser**

brake [breik] *verb* to slow down or stop: *She braked (the car) suddenly.* □ **freiner**
■ *noun* (*often in plural*) a device for doing this: *She put on the brake(s).* □ **frein**

branch [braːntʃ] *noun* **1** an arm-like part of a tree: *He cut some branches off the oak tree.* □ **branche**
2 an offshoot from the main part (of a business, railway *etc*): *There isn't a branch of that store in this town*; (*also adjective*) *That train runs on the branch line.* □ **succursale, ligne secondaire**
■ *verb* (*usually with* **out/off**) to spread out like, or into, a branch or branches: *The road to the coast branches off here.* □ **bifurquer**

brand [brand] *noun* **1** a maker's name or trademark: *a new brand*; (*also adjective*) *a brand name.* □ **marque (de fabrique)**
2 a variety: *He has his own brand of humour.* □ **(bien) personnel**
3 a mark on cattle *etc* to show who owns them, made with a hot iron. □ **marque**
■ *verb* **1** to mark cattle *etc* with a hot iron. □ **marquer (au fer rouge)**
2 to make a permanent impression on: *Her name is branded on my memory.* □ **graver**
3 to attach (permanent) disgrace to: *branded for life as a thief.* □ **étiqueter, stigmatiser**
,**brand** '**new** *adjective* completely new: *a brand new dress.* □ **flambant neuf**

brandish ['brandiʃ] *verb* to wave (*especially* a weapon) about: *He brandished the stick above his head.* □ **brandir**

brandy ['brandi] – *plural* '**brandies** – *noun* a type of strong alcoholic spirit made from wine: *Brandy is usually drunk after dinner.* □ **brandy**

brash [braʃ] *adjective* cheekily self-confident and impolite: *a brash young man.* □ **effronté**

brass [braːs] *noun* **1** an alloy of copper and zinc: *This plate is made of brass*; (*also adjective*) *a brass doorknocker.* □ **(de) laiton**
2 wind musical instruments which are made of brass or other metal. □ **cuivres**
'**brassy** *adjective.* □ **cuivré**
brass band a band of players of (mainly) brass wind instruments. □ **fanfare**
brass neck shameless cheeck or impudence: *After breaking off the engagement she had the brass neck to keep the ring.* □ **culot**
get down to brass tacks to deal with basic principles or matters: *Let's stop arguing about nothing and get down to brass tacks.* □ **en venir au fait**

brassière [brəˈziːr] (*usually abbreviated to* **bra** [braː]) *noun* a woman's undergarment supporting the breasts. □ **soutien-gorge**

bravado [brəˈvaːdou] *noun* (a show of) daring: *He's full of bravado, but really he's a coward.* □ **bravade**

brave [breiv] *adjective* without fear of danger, pain *etc*: *a brave soldier*; *a brave deed*; *You're very brave*; *It was brave of him to fight such an enemy.* □ **brave**
■ *verb* to meet or face boldly: *They braved the cold weather.* □ **braver**
■ *noun* a North American Indian warrior. □ **guerrier amérindien**
'**bravely** *adverb*: *He met his death bravely.* □ **bravement**
'**bravery** *noun.* □ **bravoure**

bravo ['braːˈvou, braːˈvou] *interjection* (when applauding a performer *etc*) well done! □ **bravo**

brawl [broːl] *noun* a noisy quarrel or physical fight: *The police were called out to a brawl in the street.* □ **bagarre**
■ *verb* to fight noisily. □ **(se) bagarrer**

brawn [broːn] *noun* muscle or physical strength. □ **muscle(s)**
'**brawny** *adjective.* □ **musclé**

bray [brei] *noun* the cry of an ass. □ **braiement**
■ *verb* to make such a cry. □ **braire**

brazen ['breizn] *adjective* impudent or shameless: *a brazen young woman.* □ **effronté**
brazen it out to face a situation with impudent boldness: *She knew her deception had been discovered but decided to brazen it out.* □ **crâner**

breach [briːtʃ] *noun* **1** a breaking (of a promise *etc*). □ **manquement à**
2 a gap, break or hole: *a breach in the castle wall*; *a breach in security.* □ **brèche, infraction**
■ *verb* to make an opening in or break (someone's defence). □ **ouvrir une brèche dans**
breach of the peace a riot, disturbance or public fight: *guilty of breach of the peace.* □ **attentat à l'ordre public**

bread [bred] *noun* **1** a type of food made of flour or meal baked: *bread and butter.* □ **pain**
2 one's living: *This is how I earn my daily bread.* □

pain
'breadcrumbs *noun plural* very tiny pieces of bread: *Dip the fish in egg and breadcrumbs.* □ **miette(s) de pain, chapelure; panure**
'breadwinner *noun* a person who earns money to keep a family: *When her father died she had to become the breadwinner.* □ **soutien (de famille)**
bread and butter (a way of earning) one's living: *Writing novels is my bread and butter.* □ **gagne-pain**
on the breadline with barely enough to live on: *The widow and her children are on the breadline.* □ **être sans le sou**

---
bread and butter takes a singular verb.
---

breadth [bredθ] *noun* 1 width; size from side to side: *the breadth of a table.* □ **largeur**
2 scope or extent: *breadth of outlook.* □ **largeur, ampleur**
3 a distance equal to the width (of a swimming pool *etc*). □ **largeur**
break [breik] – *past tense* **broke** [brouk]: *past participle* **broken** ['broukən] – *verb* 1 to divide into two or more parts (by force). □ **briser, casser**
2 (*usually with* **off/away**) to separate (a part) from the whole (by force). □ **casser**
3 to make or become unusable. □ **casser**
4 to go against, or not act according to (the law *etc*): *He broke his appointment at the last minute.* □ **désobéir à, manquer à**
5 to do better than (a sporting *etc* record). □ **battre**
6 to interrupt: *She broke her journey in Saskatoon.* □ **interrompre**
7 to put an end to: *She broke the silence.* □ **rompre**
8 to make or become known: *They gently broke the news of his death to his wife.* □ **annoncer**
9 (of a boy's voice) to fall in pitch. □ **muer**
10 to soften the effect of (a fall, the force of the wind *etc*). □ **amortir**
11 to begin: *The storm broke before they reached shelter.* □ **éclater**
■ *noun* 1 a pause: *a break in the conversation.* □ **pause**
2 a change: *a break in the weather.* □ **changement**
3 an opening. □ **brèche, ouverture**
4 a chance or piece of (good or bad) luck: *This is your big break.* □ **chance**
'breakable *adjective* (*negative* **unbreakable**) likely to break: *breakable toys.* □ **fragile**
■ *noun* (*usually in plural*) something likely to break. □ **objet fragile**
'breakage [-kidʒ] *noun* the act of breaking, or its result(s). □ **cassure**
'breaker *noun* a (large) wave which breaks on rocks or the beach. □ **brisant**
'breakdown *noun* 1 (*often* **nervous breakdown**) a mental collapse. □ **dépression (nerveuse)**
2 a mechanical failure causing a stop: *The car has had another breakdown. See also* **break down.** □ **panne**
break in *see* **break in(to).**
'breakneck *adjective* (*usually* of speed) dangerous: *She drove at breakneck speed.* □ **de casse-cou**

breakout *see* **break out.**
'breakthrough *noun* a sudden solution of a problem leading to further advances, *especially* in science. □ **percée**
'breakwater *noun* a barrier to break the force of the waves. □ **brise-lames**
break away to escape from control: *The dog broke away from its owner.* □ **échapper (à)**
break down 1 to use force on (a door *etc*) to cause it to open. □ **enfoncer**
2 to stop working properly: *My car has broken down.* □ **tomber en panne**
3 to fail: *The talks have broken down.* □ **échouer**
4 to be overcome with emotion: *He broke down and wept.* □ **craquer**
break in(to) 1 to enter (a house *etc*) by force or unexpectedly (*noun* **'break in**: *The Smiths have had two break ins recently*). □ **entrer par effraction (dans)**
2 to interrupt (someone's conversation *etc*). □ **interrompre**
break loose to escape from control: *The dog has broken loose.* □ **(s')échapper**
break off to stop: *She broke off in the middle of a sentence.* □ **(s')arrêter (net)**
break out 1 to appear or happen suddenly: *War has broken out.* □ **éclater**
2 to escape (from prison, restrictions *etc*): *A prisoner has broken out* (*noun* **'breakout**). □ **(s')évader; évasion**
break the ice to overcome the first shyness *etc*: *Let's break the ice by inviting our new neighbours for a meal.* □ **briser la glace**
break up 1 to divide, separate or break into pieces: *He broke up the old furniture and burnt it; John and Mary broke up* (= separated from each other) *last week.* □ **casser, se séparer, rompre**
2 to finish or end: *The meeting broke up at 4:40.* □ **(se) terminer**
make a break for it to make an (attempt to) escape: *When the guard is not looking, make a break for it.* □ **prendre la fuite**
breakfast ['brekfəst] *noun* the first meal of the day: *What time do you serve breakfast?; I have coffee and toast at breakfast; I never eat breakfast.* □ **petit déjeuner**
■ *verb* to have breakfast: *They breakfasted on the train.* □ **prendre le petit déjeuner**
'breakfast time *noun*: *I'll deal with that at breakfast time.* □ **petit déjeuner**
breast [brest] *noun* 1 either of a woman's two milk-producing glands on the front of the upper body. □ **sein**
2 the front of a body between the neck and belly: *He clutched the child to his breast; This recipe needs three chicken breasts.* □ **poitrine**
■ *verb* 1 to face or oppose: *breast the waves.* □ **affronter**
2 to come to the top of: *As we breasted the hill we saw the enemy in the distance.* □ **atteindre le sommet de**
'breastfeed *verb* to feed (a baby) with milk from the breast. □ **allaiter**
'breastfed *adjective.* □ **nourri au sein**
'breaststroke *noun* a style of swimming in which the arms are pushed out in front and then sweep backwards.

□ **brasse**

breath [breθ] *noun* **1** the air drawn into, and then sent out from, the lungs: *My dog's breath smells terrible.* □ **haleine**

2 an act of breathing: *Take a deep breath.* □ **respiration, inspiration**

'**breathless** *adjective* having difficulty in breathing normally: *His asthma makes him breathless*; *He was breathless after climbing the hill.* □ **essoufflé**

'**breathlessly** *adverb*. □ **en haletant**

'**breathlessness** *noun*. □ **essoufflement**

hold one's breath to stop breathing (often because of anxiety or to avoid being heard): *She held her breath as she watched the daring acrobat.* □ **retenir son souffle**

out of breath breathless (through running *etc*): *I'm out of breath after climbing all these stairs.* □ **essoufflé**

under one's breath in a whisper: *She swore under her breath.* □ **à voix basse**

> **breath** is a noun: *She held her breath.*
> **breathe** is a verb: *She found it difficult to breathe.*

breathe [briːð] *verb* **1** to draw in and let out (air *etc*) from the lungs: *He was unable to breathe because of the smoke*; *She breathed a sigh of relief.* □ **respirer**

2 to tell (a secret): *Don't breathe a word of this to anyone.* □ **souffler**

'**breather** *noun* a short rest or break from work *etc*: *I must have a breather before I do any more.* □ **(moment de) répit**

bred *see* **breed**.

breech [briːtʃ] *noun* the back part of a gun, where it is loaded. □ **culasse**

breeches ['briːtʃiz] *noun plural* trousers, *especially* ones coming just below the knee: *riding breeches.* □ **culotte**

breed [briːd] – *past tense, past participle* **bred** [bred] – *verb* **1** to produce young: *Rabbits breed often.* □ **se reproduire**

2 to keep animals for the purpose of breeding young: *I breed dogs and sell them as pets.* □ **élever**

■ *noun* a type, variety or species (of animal): *a breed of dog.* □ **race**

bred [bred] *adjective* (*often as part of a word*) **1** (of people) brought up in a certain way or place: *a well-bred young lady*; *American born and bred.* □ **élevé**

2 (of animals) brought up or reared in a certain way: *a pure-bred dog.* □ **de race**

'**breeding** *noun* education and training; good manners: *a man of good breeding.* □ **éducation**

breeze [briːz] *noun* a gentle wind: *There's a lovely cool breeze today.* □ **brise**

'**breezy** *adjective* **1** windy: *a breezy day.* □ **frais, venteux**

2 (of people *etc*) bright, lively: *She's always so bright and breezy; a breezy young man.* □ **jovial**

brethren *see* **brother**.

brevity *see* **brief**.

brew [bruː] *verb* **1** to make (beer, ale *etc*): *She brews beer at home.* □ **brasser**

2 to make (tea *etc*): *He brewed another pot of tea.* □ **faire (infuser)**

3 to prepare: *There's a storm brewing.* □ **(être) dans**

l'air

'**brewer** *noun*. □ **brasseur, euse**

'**brewery** – *plural* '**breweries** – *noun* a place for brewing beer *etc*. □ **brasserie**

bribe [braib] *noun* a gift offered to persuade a person to do something, *usually* dishonest: *Policemen are not allowed to accept bribes.* □ **pot-de-vin**

■ *verb* to give (someone) a bribe: *He bribed the guards to let him out of prison.* □ **soudoyer**

'**bribery** *noun*. □ **corruption**

brick [brik] *noun* (a block of) baked clay used for building: *a pile of bricks*; (*also adjective*) *a brick wall.* □ **(de/en) brique**

'**brickbat** *noun* an insult: *They hurled brickbats at the politician throughout his speech.* □ **insultes**

'**bricklayer** *noun* a person who builds (houses *etc*) with bricks. □ **maçon, maçonne**

bride [braid] *noun* a woman about to be married, or newly married: *The bride wore a white dress.* □ **(jeune/future) mariée**

'**bridal** *adjective* **1** of a wedding: *the bridal feast.* □ **de noce**

2 of a bride: *bridal finery.* □ **de mariée**

'**bridegroom** *noun* a man about to be married, or newly married. □ **(jeune/futur) marié**

bridesmaid ['braidzmeid] *noun* an unmarried woman attending the bride at a wedding. □ **demoiselle d'honneur**

bridge [bridʒ] *noun* **1** a structure carrying a road or railway over a river *etc*. □ **pont**

2 the narrow raised platform for the captain of a ship. □ **passerelle**

3 the bony part (of the nose). □ **arête**

4 the support of the strings of a violin *etc*. □ **chevalet**

5 a card game for four players derived from whist. □ **bridge**

■ *verb* **1** to build a bridge over: *They bridged the stream.* □ **construire un pont sur**

2 to close a gap, pause *etc*: *She bridged the awkward silence with a funny remark.* □ **remplir, meubler**

bridle ['braidl] *noun* the harness on a horse's head to which the reins are attached. □ **bride**

brief [briːf] *adjective* not long; short: *a brief visit; a brief account.* □ **bref**

■ *noun* a short statement of facts (*especially* in a lawsuit, of a client's case): *a lawyer's brief.* □ **dossier**

■ *verb* to give detailed instructions to (*especially* a barrister, group of soldiers *etc*): *The astronauts were briefed before the space mission.* □ **donner des instructions à**

'**briefing** *noun* instructions and information: *The pilots were given a briefing before they left.* □ **instructions**

'**briefly** *adverb*: *She told me briefly what she knew.* □ **brièvement**

briefs *noun plural* (used *especially* in shops) women's pants or men's underpants: *a pair of briefs.* □ **slip**

brevity ['brevəti] *noun* shortness (of speech, writing, time *etc*): *She is well known for the brevity of her speeches.* □ **concision**

'**briefcase** *noun* a light case for papers, made of leather *etc.*: *businesswoman's briefcase* □ **porte-documents**

in brief in a few words: *In brief, we have been successful.* □ **en résumé**

brigade [bri'geid] *noun* **1** a body of troops. □ **brigade**
2 a uniformed group of people organized for a particular purpose: *Call the fire brigade!* □ **brigade**
brigadier [brigə'diə] *noun* in the army, the commander of a brigade. □ **général de brigade**

bright [brait] *adjective* **1** shining with much light: *bright sunshine.* □ **brillant, éclatant**
2 (of a colour) strong and bold: *a bright red car.* □ **vif**
3 cheerful: *a bright smile.* □ **radieux**
4 clever: *bright children.* □ **intelligent**
'brightly *adverb.* □ **avec éclat**
'brightness *noun.* □ **éclat**
'brighten *verb (often with* up*)* to make or become bright or brighter: *The new wallpaper brightens up the room.* □ **(s')aviver, (s')éclairer**

brilliant ['briljənt] *adjective* **1** very bright: *the bird's brilliant feathers.* □ **éclatant**
2 very clever: *a brilliant scholar.* □ **brillant**
'brilliantly *adverb.* □ **brillamment**
'brilliance *noun* **1** brightness: *the brilliance of the moon.* □ **éclat**
2 cleverness: *her brilliance as a surgeon.* □ **brillant**

brim [brim] *noun* **1** the top edge of a cup, glass *etc*: *The jug was filled to the brim.* □ **bord**
2 the edge of a hat: *She pulled the brim of her hat down over her eyes.* □ **bord**
■ *verb* – *past tense, past participle* **brimmed** – to be, or become, full to the brim: *His eyes were brimming with tears.* □ **se remplir de**

brine [brain] *noun* very salty water: *a jar of olives in brine.* □ **saumure**
'briny *adjective* (of water) very salty. □ **salé, saumâtre**

bring [briŋ] – *past tense, past participle* **brought** [broːt] – *verb* **1** to make (something or someone) come (to or towards a place): *I'll bring plenty of food with me; Bring him to me!* □ **apporter (qqch.); amener (qqn)**
2 to result in: *This medicine will bring you relief.* □ **apporter**
bring about to cause: *His disregard for danger brought about his death.* □ **entraîner**
bring around to bring back from unconsciousness: *Fresh air brought him around.* □ **ranimer**
bring back to (cause to) return: *She brought back the umbrella she borrowed; Her singing brings back memories of my mother.* □ **rapporter, rappeler, ramener**
bring down to cause to fall: *The storm brought all the trees down.* □ **abattre**
bring home to to prove or show (something) clearly to (someone): *His illness brought home to her how much she depended on him.* □ **(bien) faire comprendre (à)**
bring off to achieve (something attempted): *They brought off an unexpected victory.* □ **réussir, remporter**
bring up 1 to rear or educate: *Her parents brought her up to be polite.* □ **élever**
2 to introduce (a matter) for discussion: *Bring the matter up at the next meeting.* □ **soulever**

bring towards the speaker: *Mary, bring me some coffee.*
take away from the speaker: *Take these cups away.*
fetch from somewhere else and bring to speaker: *Fetch me my book from the bedroom.*

brink [briŋk] *noun* the edge or border of a steep, dangerous place or of a river. □ **bord (d'un à-pic)**

brisk [brisk] *adjective* active or fast moving: *a brisk walk; Business was brisk today.* □ **vif**
'briskly *adverb.* □ **vivement**

bristle ['brisl] *noun* a short, stiff hair on an animal or brush: *The dog's bristles rose when it was angry.* □ **poil**
'bristly *adjective* having bristles; rough: *a bristly moustache.* □ **hérissé**

brittle ['britl] *adjective* hard but easily broken: *brittle materials.* □ **cassant**
'brittleness *noun.* □ **fragilité**

broad [broːd] *adjective* **1** wide; great in size from side to side: *a broad street.* □ **large**
2 from side to side: *two metres broad.* □ **de large**
3 general; not detailed: *We discussed the plans in broad outline.* □ **général**
'broaden *verb* to make or become broad or broader. □ **(s')élargir**
'broadly *adverb* generally: *Broadly speaking, I'd say your chances are poor.* □ **en gros**
broad daylight full daylight: *The child was attacked in broad daylight.* □ **plein jour**
,broad-'minded *adjective* ready to allow others to think or act as they choose without criticizing them: *a broad-minded headmaster.* □ **large d'esprit**
broadside on sideways: *The ships collided broadside on.* □ **par le travers**

broadcast ['broːdkɑːst] – *past tense, past participle* **'broadcast** – *verb* **1** to send out (radio and TV programs *etc*): *He broadcasts regularly.* □ **diffuser**
2 to make (something) widely known. □ **diffuser**
■ *noun* a television or radio program: *I heard her broadcast last night.* □ **émission**
'broadcaster *noun.* □ **(radio/télé) reporter**
'broadcasting *noun.* □ **radiodiffusion**

brocade [brou'keid] *noun, adjective* (of) a (*usually* silk) material having a raised design on it: *curtains made of blue brocade; brocade curtains.* □ **brocart**

broccoli [bro'kəliz] *noun* a green vegetable that resembles cauliflower with edible stems and flower-like tops: *Many restaurants serve steamed broccoli with beef and rice.* □ **brocoli**

brochure ['brouʃuə] *noun* a short booklet giving information about holidays, products *etc*: *Get some brochures from the travel agent.* □ **brochure**

broil [broil] *verb* (*North American*) to grill (food): *She broiled the chicken.* □ **(faire) griller**

broke [brouk] *verb see* **break.**
■ *adjective* completely without money: *I'm broke till pay day.* □ **fauché**

broken ['broukən] *adjective* **1** *see* **break:** *a broken window; My watch is broken.* □ **cassé**
2 interrupted: *broken sleep.* □ **interrompu**

3 uneven: *broken ground.* □ **accidenté**

4 (of language) not fluent: *He speaks broken English.* □ **mauvais**

5 ruined: *The children come from a broken home* (= their parents are no longer living together). □ **désuni**

,broken-'hearted *adjective* overcome by grief. □ **au cœur brisé**

broker ['brəukə] *noun* a person employed to buy and sell (*especially* shares *etc*) for others: *an insurance broker; a stockbroker.* □ **courtier**

bronchitis [broŋ'kaitis] *noun* inflammation of the air passages in the lungs, causing difficulty in breathing: *Wet weather makes his bronchitis worse.* □ **bronchite**

bron'chitic *adjective.* □ **bronchitique**

bronze [bronz] *noun, adjective* 1 (of) an alloy of copper and tin: *The medal is (made of) bronze.* □ **bronze**

2 (of) its reddish brown colour. □ **(couleur) bronze**

3 (a work of art) made of bronze: *an exhibition of bronzes.* □ **bronze**

bronzed *adjective* suntanned: *a bronzed face.* □ **bronzé**

bronze medal in athletics competitions, the medal awarded as third prize. □ **médaille de bronze**

brooch [brəutʃ] *noun* a decoration, *especially* for a woman's dress, fastened by a pin: *She wore a brooch on the collar of her dress.* □ **broche**

brood [bruːd] *verb* 1 (of birds) to sit on eggs. □ **couver**

2 to think (about something) anxiously for some time: *There's no point in brooding about what happened.* □ **ruminer (sur)**

■ *noun* the number of young hatched at one time. □ **nichée**

brook¹ [bruk] *noun* a small stream. □ **ruisseau**

brook² [bruk] *verb* to put up with: *She will not brook any interference.* □ **tolérer**

broom [bruːm] *noun* 1 a wild shrub of the pea family with (*usually* yellow) flowers: *The hillside was covered in broom.* □ **genêt**

2 a type of brush with a long handle that is used for sweeping floors *etc*. □ **balai-brosse**

broth [broːə] *noun* a liquid made by boiling meat in water, then used as the base for soup: *A nutritious soup can be made by adding vegetables to chicken broth.* □ **bouillon**

brother ['brʌðə] *noun* 1 the title given to a male child to describe his relationship to the other children of his parents: *I have two brothers.* □ **frère**

2 a fellow member of any group (*also adjective*): *brother officers.* □ **compagnon**

3 (*plural also* **brethren** ['breðrən]) a member of a religious group: *The brothers of the order prayed together; The brethren met daily.* □ **frère**

'brotherhood *noun* 1 the state of being a brother: *the ties of brotherhood.* □ **fraternité**

2 an association of men for a certain purpose. □ **confrérie, société**

'brother-in-law – *plural* **'brothers-in-law** – *noun* 1 the brother of one's husband or wife. □ **beau-frère**

2 the husband of one's sister. □ **beau-frère**

brought *see* bring.

brow [brau] *noun* 1 the eyebrow: *huge, bushy brows.* □

sourcil

2 the forehead. □ **front**

3 the top (of a hill): *over the brow of the hill.* □ **sommet**

brown [braun] *adjective* 1 of a dark colour between red and yellow: *brown paint; Her eyes are brown.* □ **marron; brun**

2 suntanned: *He was very brown after his holiday in Greece.* □ **bronzé**

■ *noun* 1 (any shade of) a colour similar to toasted bread, tanned skin, coffee *etc*. □ **brun**

2 something (*eg* paint, polish *etc*) brown in colour: *I prefer the brown to the green.* □ **brun**

■ *verb* to make or become brown. □ **brunir**

browned off 1 bored: *I feel really browned off in this wet weather.* □ **tanné de**

2 annoyed: *I'm browned off with his behaviour.* □ **ennuyé de**

brownie ['brauni] *noun* 1 (*with capital: short for* **Brownie Guide**) a junior Girl Guide. □ **jeannette**

2 a sweet chocolate and nut cake. □ **carré au chocolat**

browse [brauz] *verb* 1 (of people) to glance through a book *etc* casually: *I don't want to buy a book – I'm just browsing.* □ **feuilleter**

2 (of animals) to feed (on shoots or leaves of plants). □ **brouter**

■ *noun* an act of browsing. □ **broutement; flânerie**

bruise [bruːz] *noun* an injury caused by a blow to a person or a fruit, turning the skin a dark colour: *bruises all over his legs; apples covered in bruises.* □ **bleu, ecchymose, meurtrissure**

■ *verb* to cause or develop such a mark on the skin: *She bruised her forehead; She bruises easily.* □ **(se) couvrir d'ecchymoses**

brunette [bruː'net] *noun* a woman with brown or dark hair: *He prefers blondes to brunettes.* □ **brune**

brunt [brʌnt]: **bear the brunt of** to bear the worst of the effect of (a blow, attack *etc*): *I bore the brunt of his abuse/the storm.* □ **le (plus) gros de**

brush [brʌʃ] *noun* 1 an instrument with bristles, wire, hair *etc* for cleaning, scrubbing *etc*: *a toothbrush; She sells brushes.* □ **brosse**

2 an act of brushing. □ **brossage**

3 a bushy tail of a fox. □ **queue**

4 a disagreement: *a slight brush with the law.* □ **ennuis (avec)**

■ *verb* 1 to rub with a brush: *He brushed his jacket.* □ **brosser**

2 to remove (dust *etc*) by sweeping with a brush: *brush the floor.* □ **balayer**

3 to make tidy by using a brush: *Brush your hair!* □ **brosser**

4 to touch lightly in passing: *The leaves brushed her face.* □ **frôler**

brush aside to pay no attention to: *She brushed aside my objections.* □ **balayer**

brush away to wipe off: *She brushed away a tear; She brushed it away.* □ **essuyer**

brush up (*with* **on**) to refresh one's knowledge of (*eg* a language): *He brushed up his Spanish before he went on holiday.* □ **réviser**

give, get the brush-off to reject or be rejected abruptly. □ **(se faire) envoyer promener**

brusque [brʌsk, brusk] *adjective* blunt and abrupt in manner: *a brusque reply*. □ **brusque**
'brusquely *adverb*. □ **brusquement**
'brusqueness *noun*. □ **brusquerie**

brute [bruːt] *noun* 1 an animal other than man: *My dog died yesterday, the poor brute*; (*also adjective*) *brute force*. □ **bête, brutal**
2 a cruel person. □ **brute**
'brutal *adjective* very cruel or severe: *a brutal beating*. □ **brutal**
bru'tality [-'ta-] *noun*. □ **brutalité**
'brutish *adjective* of, or like, a brute: *brutish manners*. □ **de brute**

bubble ['bʌbl] *noun* a floating ball of air or gas: *bubbles in lemonade*. □ **bulle**
■ *verb* to form or rise in bubbles: *The champagne bubbled in the glass*. □ **pétiller**
'bubbly *adjective* having bubbles. □ **pétillant**
bubble over to be full (with happiness *etc*): *bubbling over with excitement*. □ **déborder de**

buccaneer [bʌkə'niə] *noun* a type of pirate. □ **boucanier**

buck [bʌk] *noun* the male of the deer, hare, rabbit *etc*: *a buck and a doe*. □ **mâle**
■ *verb* (of a horse or mule) to make a series of rapid jumps into the air. □ **lancer une/des ruade(s)**
'buckskin *noun, adjective* (of) a soft leather made of deerskin or sheepskin. □ **peau de daim**
buck up to cheer up: *She bucked up when she heard the news*. □ **être ragaillardi**
pass the buck to pass on responsibility (to someone else): *Whenever he is blamed for anything, he tries to pass the buck*. □ **refiler une responsabilité à qqn**

bucket ['bʌkit] *noun* a container for holding water, milk *etc*: *We carried water in buckets to the burning house*. □ **seau**

buckle ['bʌkl] *noun* a fastening for a strap or band: *a belt with a silver buckle*. □ **boucle**
■ *verb* 1 to fasten with a buckle: *He buckled on his sword*. □ **attacher**
2 (*usually* of something metal) to make or become bent or crushed: *The metal buckled in the great heat*. □ **se déformer**

bud [bʌd] *noun* a shoot of a tree or plant, containing undeveloped leaves or flower(s) or both: *Are there buds on the trees yet?*; *a rosebud*. □ **bourgeon**
■ *verb – past tense, past participle* **'budded** – to begin to grow: *The trees are budding*. □ **bourgeonner**
'budding *adjective* just beginning to develop: *a budding poet*. □ **en herbe**
in bud producing buds: *The flowers are in bud*. □ **en bouton**

Buddhism ['budizəm, 'budizəm] *noun* the religion founded by Gautama or Buddha. □ **Bouddhisme**
'Buddhist *noun* a believer in Buddhism. □ **Bouddhiste**
■ *adjective*: *a Buddhist monk*. □ **bouddhiste**

buddy ['bʌdi] – *plural* **'buddies** – *noun* (*especially North American*) a friend. □ **copain, copine**

budge [bʌdʒ] *verb* to (cause to) move, even slightly: *I can't budge it*; *It won't budge!* □ **(faire) bouger**

budgerigar ['bʌdʒərigaː] (*abbreviation* '**budgie** ['bʌdʒi]) *noun* a type of small (*originally* Australian) brightly-coloured bird, often kept as a pet. □ **perruche**

budget ['bʌdʒit] *noun* any plan showing how money is to be spent: *my budget for the month*. □ **budget**
■ *verb – past tense, past participle* '**budgeted** – 1 to make a plan showing this: *We must try to budget or we shall be in debt*. □ **faire un budget**
2 (*with* **for**) to allow for (something) in a budget: *I hadn't budgeted for a new car*. □ **prévoir qqch. dans son budget**

budgie *see* **budgerigar**.

buff [bʌf] *noun* a dull yellow colour. □ **chamois**
■ *adjective*: *a buff envelope*. □ **chamois**

buffalo ['bʌfəlou] – *plurals* **'buffalo, 'buffalo(e)s** – *noun* 1 a large kind of ox, *especially* the Asian and African varieties. □ **buffle**
2 the American variety of ox; the bison. □ **bison**

buffer ['bʌfə] *noun* an apparatus for lessening the force with which a moving object strikes something. □ **tampon**

buffet¹ ['bʌfit] *noun* a blow with the hand or fist: *a buffet on the side of the head*. □ **claque**
■ *verb – past tense, past participle* '**buffeted** – 1 to strike with the fist. □ **frapper (de la main/du poing)**
2 to knock about: *The boat was buffeted by the waves*. □ **ballotter**

buffet² [bə'fei, 'bufei] *noun* 1 a refreshment bar, *especially* in a railway station or on a train *etc*: *We'll get some coffee at the buffet*. □ **buffet**
2 a (*usually* cold) meal set out on tables from which people help themselves. □ **buffet**
■ *adjective*: *a buffet supper*. □ **buffet**

bug [bʌg] *noun* 1 an insect that lives in dirty houses and beds: *a bedbug*. □ **punaise**
2 an insect: *There's a bug crawling up your arm*. □ **insecte**
3 a germ or infection: *a stomach bug*. □ **microbe**
4 a small hidden microphone. □ **micro caché**
■ *verb – past tense, past participle* **bugged** –1 to place small hidden microphones in (a room *etc*): *The spy's bedroom was bugged*. □ **cacher des micros (dans)**
2 to annoy: *What's bugging him?* □ **tracasser**

buggy ['bʌgi] – *plural* '**buggies** – *noun* a light, open, one-horse vehicle. □ **boghei**

bugle ['bjuːgl] *noun* a musical wind instrument *usually* made of brass, used chiefly for military signals: *She plays the bugle*. □ **clairon**
'bugler *noun*. □ **(joueur, euse de) clairon**

build [bild] – *past tense, past participle* built [-t] – *verb* to form or construct from parts: *build a house/railway/bookcase*. □ **bâtir, construire**
■ *noun* physical form: *a man of heavy build*. □ **carrure**
'builder *noun* a person who builds houses *etc*: *The builder who built our house has gone bankrupt*. □ **constructeur, trice**
'building *noun* 1 the art or business of putting up (houses *etc*) (*also adjective*): *a building contractor*. □ **(de) construction**

2 anything built: *The new supermarket is a very ugly building.* □ **bâtiment, bâtisse, immeuble**
,built-'in *adjective* forming a permanent part of the building *etc*: *Built-in cupboards save space.* □ **encastré**
,built-'up *adjective* covered with houses *etc*: *a built-up area.* □ **urbanisé**
build up 1 to increase (the size or extent of): *The traffic begins to build up around five o'clock.* □ **(s')accroître**
2 to strengthen gradually (a business, one's health, reputation *etc*): *Her father built up that grocery business from nothing.* □ **créer, monter**
bulb [bʌlb] *noun* **1** the ball-shaped part of the stem of certain plants, *eg* onions, tulips *etc*, from which their roots grow. □ **bulbe**
2 (*also* **'light bulb**) a pear-shaped glass globe surrounding the element of an electric light. □ **ampoule**
3 the pear-shaped end of a thermometer. □ **cuvette**
'bulbous *adjective* like a bulb, *especially* in shape: *a bulbous nose.* □ **bulbeux, gros**
bulbul ['bulbul] *noun* a songbird of Asia or Africa. □ **bulbul**
bulge [bʌldʒ] *noun* a swelling: *the bulge of her hips.* □ **renflement**
■ *verb* to swell out: *His muscles bulged.* □ **gonfler**
bulk [bʌlk] *noun* **1** the greater part: *The bulk of his money was spent on food.* □ **la majeure partie de**
2 (great) size or mass: *the bulk of a parcel*; *His huge bulk appeared around the corner.* □ **masse, volume**
■ *adjective* in bulk: *bulk buying.* □ **en gros**
'bulky *adjective* large in size, awkward to carry *etc*: *a bulky parcel*; *This is too bulky to send by post.* □ **volumineux**
in bulk in large quantities: *Huge tankers now carry oil in bulk*; *They like to buy goods in bulk.* □ **en gros**
bulkhead ['bʌlkhed] *noun* a division between one part of a ship's interior and another. □ **cloison**
bull [bul] *noun* **1** the male of the ox family and of the whale, walrus, elephant *etc*. □ **mâle**
2 a bull's eye. □ **centre d'une cible**
'bullock [-lək] *noun* **1** a young bull. □ **bouvillon**
2 a castrated bull, an ox, often used to pull **bullock carts**. □ **bœuf**
'bullfight *noun* in Spain *etc* a fight between a bull and men on horseback and on foot. □ **corrida**
'bullfighter *noun*. □ **torero**
'bullring *noun* the enclosed area where a bullfight takes place. □ **arène**
'bull's eye *noun* the centre of a target, *especially* in archery, darts *etc*. □ **mille**
bulldozer ['buldouzə] *noun* a (*usually* large) tractor for clearing obstacles and levelling ground. □ **bouteur**
'bulldoze *verb* to use a bulldozer on: *They bulldozed the building site.* □ **passer au bouteur**
bullet ['bulit] *noun* a piece of metal *etc* fired from certain hand guns: *He was killed by machine-gun bullets.* □ **balle**
bulletin ['bulətin] *noun* **1** an official (verbal) report of news: *a bulletin about the teachers' strike.* □ **communiqué**
2 a printed information-sheet: *a monthly bulletin of lo-*

cal news. □ **bulletin**
bullfight *see* **bull**.
bullion ['buliən] *noun* gold or silver in bulk, not made into coins. □ **lingot**
bullock *see* **bull**.
bully ['buli] – *plural* **'bullies** – *noun* a person who hurts or frightens other, weaker people: *The fat boy was a bully at school.* □ **brute (tyrannique)**
■ *verb* to act like a bully towards. □ **brutaliser**
bulrush ['bulrʌʃ] *noun* a tall strong water plant. □ **jonc**
bulwark ['bulwək] *noun* a wall built as a defence, often made of earth. □ **rempart**
bum¹ [bʌm] *noun* the buttocks. □ **cul**
bum² [bʌm] *noun* a tramp or worthless person: *He doesn't work – he's just a bum.* □ **vaurien**
■ *adjective* worthless: *a bum job.* □ **minable**
bumblebee ['bʌmblbiː] *noun* a kind of large bee with a hairy body. □ **bourdon**
bump [bʌmp] *verb* to knock or strike (something): *She bumped into me*; *I bumped my head against the ceiling.* □ **(se) cogner (contre/dans)**
■ *noun* **1** (the sound of) a blow or knock: *We heard a loud bump.* □ **coup (sourd)**
2 a swelling or raised part: *a bump on the head*; *This road is full of bumps.* □ **bosse**
'bumper *noun* a bar on a motor vehicle to lessen damage when it collides with anything. □ **pare-chocs**
■ *adjective* excellent in some way, *especially* by being large: *a bumper crop.* □ **exceptionnel**
'bumpy *adjective* uneven: *a bumpy road.* □ **accidenté, raboteux**
bump into to meet (someone) by accident: *I bumped into her in the street.* □ **tomber sur**
bumpkin ['bʌmpkin] *noun* a clumsy or stupid country person: *a country bumpkin.* □ **rustre**
bumptious ['bʌmpʃəs] *adjective* full of one's own importance: *a very bumptious young man.* □ **suffisant**
bun [bʌn] *noun* a kind of sweet cake: *a currant bun.* □ **brioche**
bunch [bʌntʃ] *noun* a number of things fastened or growing together: *a bunch of bananas.* □ **paquet, botte, grappe, régime**
■ *verb* (*often with* **up** *or* **together**) to come or put together in bunches, groups *etc*: *Traffic often bunches on an expressway.* □ **(s')entasser**
bundle ['bʌndl] *noun* a number of things bound together: *a bundle of rags.* □ **ballot**
■ *verb* **1** (*often with* **up** *or* **together**) to make into bundles: *Bundle up all your things and bring them with you.* □ **empaqueter**
2 to go, put or send (away) in a hurried or disorderly way: *They bundled him out of the room.* □ **pousser dehors**
bung [bʌŋ] *noun* the stopper of the hole in a barrel, a small boat *etc*. □ **bonde**
■ *verb* to block with such a stopper. □ **boucher**
bungalow ['bʌŋgəlou] *noun* a (*usually* small) house of one storey: *They live in a small bungalow.* □ **bungalow**
bungle ['bʌŋgl] *verb* to do (something) clumsily or badly: *Someone has bungled.* □ **gâcher (le travail)**

bunk [bʌŋk] *noun* a sleeping-berth in a ship's cabin. □ **couchette**

bunker ['bʌŋkə] *noun* **1** a hollow containing sand on a golf course. □ **fosse de sable**
2 an underground shelter against bombs *etc*. □ **abri (anti-nucléaire)**

bunsen ['bʌnsn]: **bunsen (burner)** *noun* a gas burner which produces a smokeless flame of great heating power: *Several of the bunsens in the chemistry laboratory are out of order.* □ **bec Bunsen**

bunting ['bʌntiŋ] *noun* flags for use in celebrations. □ **drapeaux**

buoy [boi, 'buːi] *noun* a floating anchored mark, acting as a guide, warning or mooring point for boats. □ **bouée** *See also* **lifebuoy.**
'**buoyancy** *noun* the ability to float on water or in the air: *the buoyancy of a balloon.* □ **flottabilité**
'**buoyant** *adjective*. □ **qui peut flotter**

burden ['bəːdn] *noun* **1** something to be carried: *She carried a heavy burden up the hill; The ox is sometimes a beast of burden* (= an animal that carries things). □ **fardeau**
2 something difficult to carry or withstand: *the burden of taxation.* □ **poids écrasant**
■ *verb* to put a responsibility *etc* on (someone): *burdened with cares.* □ **charger de**

bureau ['bjuərou] – *plurals* '**bureaux** [-z], '**bureaus** – *noun* **1** a writing-desk with drawers. □ **bureau**
2 (*North American*) a chest of drawers. □ **commode**
3 an office for collecting and supplying information *etc*: *a travel bureau.* □ **bureau**

bureaucracy [bju'rokrəsi] *noun* **1** a system of government by officials working for a government. □ **bureaucratie**
2 a country having such a government which uses such officials. □ **État bureaucratique**
,**bureau'cratic** *adjective*. □ **bureaucratique**

burglar ['bəːglə] *noun* a person who enters a house *etc* illegally to steal: *The burglar stole her jewellery.* □ **cambrioleur, euse**
'**burglary** – *plural* '**burglaries** – *noun* (an act of) illegally entering a house *etc* to steal: *He has been charged with burglary.* □ **cambriolage**
'**burgle** *verb*: *Our house has been burgled.* □ **cambrioler**
burial *see* **bury.**

burly ['bəːli] *adjective* (of a person) big, strong and heavy: *a big burly farmer.* □ **robuste**

burn [bəːn] – *past tense, past participles* **burned, burnt** [-t] – *verb* **1** to destroy, damage or injure by fire, heat, acid *etc*: *The fire burned all my papers; I've burnt the meat.* □ **brûler**
2 to use as fuel. □ **brûler**
3 to make (a hole *etc*) by fire, heat, acid *etc*: *The acid burned a hole in my dress.* □ **faire un trou (dans)**
4 to catch fire: *Paper burns easily.* □ **brûlé**
■ *noun* an injury or mark caused by fire *etc*: *His burns will take a long time to heal; a burn in the carpet.* □ **brûlure**
'**burner** *noun* any device producing a flame: *I'll have to use a burner to get this paint off.* □ **bec (de gaz),** chalumeau

burnish ['bəːniʃ] *verb* to make (metal) bright by polishing: *They burnished the silver.* □ **polir**

burnt *see* **burn.**

burp [bəːp] – *verb* to give out air noisily from the stomach through the mouth: *He burped after eating too much.* □ **roter**
■ *noun* an act of burping. □ **rot**

burrow ['bʌrou] *noun* a hole dug for shelter: *a rabbit burrow.* □ **terrier**
■ *verb* to make holes underground or in a similar place for shelter *etc*; *The mole burrows underground; She burrowed under the bedclothes.* □ **creuser**

burst [bəːst] – *past tense, past participle* **burst** – *verb* **1** to break open or in pieces suddenly: *The bag/balloon burst.* □ **éclater**
2 (*with* **in, into, through** *etc*) to come or go suddenly or violently: *He burst in without knocking; He burst into the room; He burst into tears.* □ **faire irruption**
3 (of rivers) to overflow or flood (the banks): *The river has burst its banks.* □ **rompre**
■ *noun* **1** a break or explosion: *a burst in the pipes.* □ **éclatement**
2 an (often sudden and short) outbreak: *a burst of applause.* □ **salve**
burst open to open suddenly or violently: *The door burst open and she rushed in.* □ **(s')ouvrir violemment**

bury ['beri] *verb* **1** to place (a dead body) in a grave, the sea *etc*. □ **enterrer**
2 to hide (under the ground *etc*): *My socks are buried somewhere in this drawer.* □ **enfouir**
'**burial** *noun* (an instance of) burying (a dead body) in a grave *etc*: *my grandfather's burial:* (*also adjective*) *a burial service.* □ **(d')enterrement**
bury the hatchet to stop quarrelling: *Let's bury the hatchet and be friends.* □ **enterrer la hache de guerre**

bus [bʌs] *noun* a large road vehicle for carrying passengers: *He came by bus.* □ **autobus**
■ *verb* – *present participle* '**bus(s)ing**: *past tense, past participle* **bus(s)ed** – to carry by bus. □ **transport en autobus**
bus stop a place where buses stop to let passengers on or off. □ **arrêt d'autobus**

bush [buʃ] *noun* **1** a growing thing between a tree and a plant in size: *a rose bush.* □ **buisson**
2 (in Australia, Africa *etc*) wild uncultivated country. □ **brousse**
'**bushy** *adjective* thick and spreading: *bushy eyebrows; a bushy tail.* □ **touffu**

business ['biznis] *noun* **1** occupation; buying and selling: *Selling china is my business; The shop does more business at Christmas than at any other time.* □ **métier; affaire(s)**
2 a shop, a firm: *She owns her own business.* □ **commerce**
3 concern: *Make it your business to help him; Let's get down to business* (= Let's start the work *etc* that must be done). □ **affaire**
'**businesslike** *adjective* practical; alert and prompt: *a businesslike approach to the problem; She is very busi-*

nesslike. □ **sérieux, professionnel**
'**businessman** – *feminine* '**businesswoman** – *noun* a person who makes a living from some form of trade or commerce, not from one of the professions. □ **homme/femme d'affaires**
on business in the process of doing business or something official. □ **pour affaires**
bust [bʌst] *noun* **1** a woman's chest: *She has a very small bust*. □ **poitrine**
2 a sculpture of a person's head and shoulders: *a bust of Julius Caesar*. □ **buste**
bustle ['bʌsl] *verb* (*often with* **about**) to busy oneself (often noisily or fussily): *She bustled about doing things all day*. □ **(se) démener**
■ *noun* hurry, fuss or activity. □ **remue-ménage**
busy ['bizi] *adjective* **1** having a lot (of work *etc*) to do: *I am very busy*. □ **occupé**
2 full of traffic, people, activity *etc*: *The roads are busy*; *a busy time of year*. □ **animé**
3 (of a telephone line) engaged: *All the lines to New York are busy*. □ **occupé**
■ *verb* (*sometimes with* **with**) to occupy (oneself) with: *He busied himself preparing the meal*. □ **s'occuper (à)**
'**busily** *adverb*. □ **activement**
but [bʌt] *conjunction* used to show a contrast between two or more things: *John was there but Peter was not*. □ **mais**
■ *preposition* except (for): *no one but me*; *the next road but one*. □ **sauf**
butcher ['butʃə] *noun* a person whose business is to kill cattle *etc* for food and/or sell their flesh. □ **boucher, ère**
■ *verb* **1** to kill for food. □ **abattre**
2 to kill cruelly: *All the prisoners were butchered by the dictator*. □ **massacrer**
butcher shop *noun* a small store where fresh meat and poultry are sold: *Ms. Mitchell bought lamb chops, steak and chicken breast at the butcher shop*. □ **boucherie**
butt¹ [bʌt] *verb* to strike (someone or something) with the head: *He fell over when the goat butted him*. □ **donner un coup de tête à/dans**
butt in to interrupt or interfere: *Don't butt in while I'm speaking!* □ **interrompre**
butt² [bʌt] *noun* someone whom others criticize or tell jokes about: *He's the butt of all his jokes*. □ **cible**
■ [bʌt] *noun* **1** the thick and heavy end (*especially* of a rifle). □ **crosse**
2 the end of a finished cigar, cigarette *etc*: *His cigarette butt was the cause of the fire*. □ **mégot**
butter ['bʌtə] *noun* a fatty substance made from cream by churning. □ **beurre**
■ *verb* to spread with butter: *She buttered the bread*. □ **beurrer**
'**buttery** *adjective*: *a buttery knife*. □ **beurré, couvert de beurre**
'**butterfingers** *noun* a person who is likely to drop things which he or she is carrying. □ **empoté, ée**
'**butterscotch** [-skotʃ] *noun* a kind of hard toffee made with butter. □ **caramel écossais**
butter up to flatter (someone) *usually* because one

wants him to do something for one. □ **passer de la pommade à**
butterfly ['bʌtəflai] – *plural* '**butterflies** – *noun* a type of insect with large (often coloured) wings. □ **papillon**
buttock ['bʌtək] *noun* (*usually in plural*) either half of the part of the body on which one sits: *He smacked the child on the buttocks*. □ **fesse**
button ['bʌtn] *noun* **1** a knob or disc used as a fastening: *I lost a button off my coat*. □ **bouton**
2 a small knob pressed to operate something: *This button turns the radio on*. □ **bouton**
■ *verb* (often with **up**) to fasten by means of buttons. □ **boutonner**
'**buttonhole** *noun* the hole or slit into which a button is put. □ **boutonnière**
■ *verb* to catch someone's attention and hold him in conversation: *He buttonholed me and began telling me the story of his life*. □ **accrocher**
buttress ['bʌtris] *noun* a support built on to the outside of a wall. □ **contrefort**
buxom ['bʌksəm] *adjective* (of a woman) plump and usually attractive: *a buxom blonde*. □ **plantureux**
buy [bai] – *present participle* '**buying**: *past tense, past participle* **bought** [boːt] – *verb* to get (something) by exchanging it for money: *He has bought a car*. □ **acheter**
buzz [bʌz] *verb* **1** (of an insect) to make a noise by beating its wings *eg* when flying: *The bees buzzed angrily*. □ **bourdonner**
2 to be filled with or make a similar noise: *My ears are buzzing*; *The crowd was buzzing with excitement*. □ **bourdonner**
■ *noun* (*sometimes with* **a**) a buzzing sound: *a buzz of conversation*. □ **bourdonnement**
'**buzzer** *noun* an electrical or other apparatus producing a buzzing sound. □ **timbre, sonnerie**
by [bai] *preposition* **1** next to; near; at the side of: *by the door*; *He sat by his sister*. □ **(au)près de**
2 past: *going by the house*. □ **(en passant) devant**
3 through; along; across: *We came by the main road*. □ **par**
4 used (in the passive voice) to show the person or thing which performs an action: *struck by a stone*. □ **par**
5 using: *She's going to contact us by letter*; *We travelled by train*. □ **par, en**
6 from; through the means of: *I met her by chance*; *by post*. □ **par**
7 (of time) not later than: *by 6 o'clock*. □ **(...) au plus tard**
8 during the time of. □ **de**
9 to the extent of: *taller by ten centimetres*. □ **de**
10 used to give measurements *etc*: *4 metres by 2 metres*. □ **sur**
11 in quantities of: *fruit sold by the kilogram*. □ **au/à la/aux**
12 in respect of: *a teacher by profession*. □ **de**
■ *adverb* **1** near: *They stood by and watched*. □ **près, à proximité**
2 past: *A dog ran by*. □ **par là**
3 aside; away: *money put by for an emergency*. □ **de côté**

'**bygones: let bygones be bygones** to forgive and forget past causes of ill-feeling. □ **il faut oublier le passé**
'**bypass** *noun* a road which avoids an obstruction or a busy area: *Take the bypass around the city.* □ **dérivation**
■ *verb* to avoid (a place) by taking such a road. □ **contourner**
'**by-product** *noun* something obtained or formed during the making of something else: *Coal tar is a by-product of the process of obtaining gas from coal.* □ **sous-produit**
'**bystander** *noun* a person who watches but does not take part. □ **spectateur, trice**

by and by after a short time: *By and by, everyone went home.* □ **(un peu) plus tard**
by and large mostly; all things considered: *Things are going quite well, by and large.* □ **à tout prendre**
by oneself 1 alone: *He was standing by himself at the bus-stop.* □ **tout(e) seul(e)**
2 without anyone else's help: *She did the job (all) by herself.* □ **tout(e) seul(e)**
by the way incidentally: *By the way, have you a moment to spare?* □ **à propos**

---

by is used for forms of transport: *by train*; *by airplane*; *by land*; *by sea*.

Cc

cab [kab] *noun* **1** a taxi: *Could you call a cab for me?* □ **taxi**

2 the driver's compartment of a railway engine, truck *etc.* □ **cabine**

cabaret ['kabərei] *noun* an entertainment given in a restaurant *etc*: *a singer in a cabaret.* □ **spectacle de cabaret**

cabbage ['kabidʒ] *noun* a type of vegetable with edible (*usually* green) leaves: *She bought a cabbage.* □ **chou**

cabin ['kabin] *noun* **1** a small house or hut (made *eg* of logs): *a log cabin.* □ **cabane**

2 a (small) room in a ship for sleeping in: *We've a four-berth cabin.* □ **cabine**

3 the part of an aircraft containing seating for passengers. □ **cabine**

cabinet ['kabinit] *noun* **1** a piece of furniture with shelves and doors or drawers: *a filing cabinet.* □ **meuble de rangement**

2 in Canada and some other countries the group of chief ministers who govern a country: *The Prime Minister has chosen a new Cabinet.* □ **cabinet (ministériel)**

cabinet maker *noun* someone who is skilled at making fine woodwork, especially furniture with drawers or intricate designs: *A cabinet maker was hired to build kitchen cupboards.* □ **ébéniste**

cable ['keibl] *noun* **1** (a) strong rope or chain for hauling or tying anything, *especially* a ship. □ **câble**

2 (a set of) wires for carrying electric current or signals: *They are laying (a) new cable.* □ **câble**

3 (a rope made of) strands of metal wound together for supporting a bridge *etc.* □ **câble**

4 (*also* '**cablegram**) a telegram sent by cable. □ **câblogramme**

■ *verb* to telegraph by cable: *I cabled news of my mother's death to our relations in Vancouver.* □ **câbler**

cabomba [kə'bombə] *noun* an aquatic plant with feathery leaves. □ **cabomba**

cacao [kə'kaːou, kə'keiou] *noun* the tropical tree from whose seeds cocoa and chocolate are made. □ **cacaotier**

cackle ['kakl] *noun* **1** the sound made by a hen or goose. □ **caquet**

2 a laugh which sounds like this: *an evil cackle.* □ **gloussement**

■ *verb* to make such a sound. □ **glousser**

cactus ['kaktəs] – *plurals* '**cacti** [-tai], '**cactuses** – *noun* a prickly plant whose stem stores water. □ **cactus**

caddie, caddy[1] ['kadi] *noun* a person who carries clubs for a golfer. □ **caddie**

caddy[2] ['kadi] – *plural* '**caddies** – *noun* a small box for keeping tea-leaves in. □ **boîte à thé**

cadet [kə'det] *noun* **1** a student in a military, naval or police school: *an army cadet; a police cadet.* □ **élève officier**

2 a schoolboy taking military training. □ **élève suivant la préparation militaire**

■ *adjective*: *a school cadet force.* □ **d'élève officier**

café [ka'fei] *noun* a (*usually* small) shop where meals

and (non-alcoholic) drinks are served. □ **café-restaurant**

cafeteria [kafə'tiəriə] *noun* a self-service restaurant: *This department store has a cafeteria.* □ **cafétéria**

caffeine [ka'fiːn] *noun* a drug found in coffee and tea. □ **caféine**

caftan, kaftan ['kaftan] *noun* a type of long flowing dress or robe sometimes brightly-coloured. □ **caftan**

cage [keidʒ] *noun* **1** a box of wood, wire *etc* for holding birds or animals: *The lion has escaped from its cage; a bird-cage.* □ **cage**

2 a lift in a mine. □ **cage**

■ *verb* to put in a cage: *Some people think that it is cruel to cage wild animals.* □ **mettre en cage**

'**cagebird** *noun* a bird, *eg* a canary, suitable for keeping in a cage. □ **oiseau de volière**

cagey ['keidʒi] *adjective* secretive: *She's very cagey about her plans.* □ **cachottier**

'**caginess** *noun.* □ **circonspection**

cajole [kə'dʒoul] *verb* to coax (someone into doing something), often by flattery: *The little boy cajoled his father into buying him a new toy.* □ **cajoler**

cake [keik] *noun* **1** a food made by baking a mixture of flour, fat, eggs, sugar *etc*: *a piece of cake; a plate of cream cakes; a Christmas cake.* □ **gâteau**

2 a piece of other food pressed into shape: *fishcakes; oatcakes.* □ **croquette, galette d'avoine**

3 a flattened hard mass: *a cake of soap.* □ **pain**

■ *verb* to cover in the form of a dried mass: *Her shoes were caked with mud.* □ **former une croûte**

calamity [kə'laməti] – *plural* **ca'lamities** – *noun* a great misfortune: *It will be a calamity if he fails his exam.* □ **calamiteux**

ca'lamitous *adjective.* □ **désastreux**

calcium ['kalsiəm] *noun* an element of which one compound (**calcium carbonate**) forms limestone, chalk *etc.* □ **calcium**

calculate ['kalkjuleit] *verb* to count or estimate, using numbers: *Calculate the number of days in a century.* □ **calculer**

'**calculable** *adjective.* □ **calculable**

,**calcu'lation** *noun.* □ **calcul**

'**calculator** *noun* a machine for calculating: *Use a calculator for adding all those numbers.* □ **calculatrice**

calendar ['kaləndə] *noun* **1** a table showing the months and days of the year: *Look at the calendar and tell me which day of the week November 22nd is.* □ **calendrier**

2 a list of important dates or events: *The football team's calendar is complete now.* □ **calendrier**

---

calendar ends in **-ar** (not **-er**).

---

calf[1] [kaːf] – *plural* **calves** [kaːvz] – *noun* **1** the young of a cow, elephant, whale *etc.* □ **veau, éléphanteau, baleineau**

2 (*also* '**calfskin**) leather made from the skin of the young of a cow. □ **(cuir de) veau**

calve [kaːv] *verb* to give birth to a calf: *The cow calved last night.* □ **vêler**

calf[2] [kaːf] – *plural* **calves** [kaːvz] – *noun* the thick fleshy back part of the leg below the knee: *She has slim ankles* *but fat calves.* □ **mollet**

caliber *see* **calibre.**

calibrate ['kalibreit] *verb* **1** to mark out the scale on (a measuring instrument). □ **graduer**

2 to correct or adjust (the scale or instrument): *He calibrated the weighing machine.* □ **rectifier**

calibre, caliber ['kaliba] *noun* **1** the inner diameter of a gun barrel *etc.* □ **calibre**

2 (of a person) quality of character; ability: *a salesman of extremely high calibre.* □ **calibre**

call [koːl] *verb* **1** to give a name to: *My name is Alexander but I'm called Sandy by my friends.* □ **appeler**

2 to regard (something) as: *I saw you turn that card over – I call that cheating.* □ **appeler**

3 to speak loudly (to someone) to attract attention *etc*: *Call everyone over here*; *She called louder so as to get his attention.* □ **appeler**

4 to summon; to ask (someone) to come (by letter, telephone *etc*): *They called her for an interview for the job*; *He called a doctor.* □ **convoquer**

5 to make a visit: *I shall call at your house this evening*; *You were out when I called.* □ **passer**

6 to telephone: *I'll call you at 6:00.* □ **téléphoner à**

7 (in card games) to bid. □ **annoncer, demander**

■ *noun* **1** an exclamation or shout: *a call for help.* □ **appel**

2 the song of a bird: *the call of a blackbird.* □ **cri**

3 a (*usually* short) visit: *The teacher made a call on the boy's parents.* □ **visite**

4 the act of calling on the telephone: *I've just had a call from the police.* □ **coup de fil**

5 (*usually with* **the**) attraction: *the call of the sea.* □ **appel**

6 a demand: *There's less call for coachmen nowadays.* □ **demande**

7 a need or reason: *You've no call to say such things!* □ **besoin, raison**

'**caller** *noun.* □ **visiteur, euse**

'**calling** *noun* a trade or profession: *Teaching is a worthwhile calling.* □ **métier**

'**call box** *noun* a direct telephone line for reporting emergencies. □ **cabine téléphonique**

call for 1 to demand or require: *This calls for quick action.* □ **exiger**

2 to collect: *I'll call for you at eight o'clock.* □ **passer prendre**

call off to cancel: *The party's been called off.* □ **annuler**

call on to visit: *I'll call on him tomorrow.* □ **aller voir**

call up to telephone (someone): *He called me up from the airport.* □ **téléphoner à**

give (someone) a call to telephone (someone): *I'll give you a call tomorrow.* □ **téléphoner à**

on call keeping (oneself) ready to come out to an emergency: *Which of the doctors is on call tonight?* □ **de garde**

calligraphy [kə'ligrəfi] *noun* (the art of) beautiful, decorative handwriting. □ **calligraphie**

callous ['kaləs] *adjective* unfeeling; cruel: *a callous person/attack.* □ **dur**

'**callously** *adverb.* □ **durement**

'**callousness** *noun.* □ **dureté**

calm [kaːm] *adjective* **1** still or quiet: *a calm sea*; *The weather was calm.* □ **calme**

2 not anxious or excited: *a calm person/expression*; *Please keep calm!* □ **calme**

■ *noun* **1** (a period of) absence of wind and large waves. □ **calme**

2 peace and quiet: *She enjoyed the calm of the library.* □ **calme**

■ *verb* to make calm: *Calm yourself!* □ **(se) calmer**

'**calmly** *adverb.* □ **calmement**

'**calmness** *noun.* □ **calme**

calm down to make or become calm: *She tried to calm him down by giving him some brandy*; *Calm down!* □ **(se) calmer**

calorie ['kalori] *noun* (*abbreviated to* **cal** *when written*) **1** a unit of heat. □ **calorie**

2 a unit of energy given by food: *My diet allows me 1200 calories per day.* □ **calorie**

,**calo'rific** *adjective.* □ **calorifique**

calve, calves *see* **calf¹, calf²·**

calypso [kə'lipsou] – *plural* **ca'lypsos** – *noun* a West Indian folk-song, telling of a current event and sometimes made up as the singer goes along. □ **calypso**

came *see* **come.**

camel ['kaməl] *noun* a desert animal with one (**dromedary** ['dromədəri]) or two (**bactrian (camel)** ['baktriən]) humps on its back, used for carrying goods and/or people. □ **chameau**

camellia [kə'miːliə] *noun* (the red or white flower of) an evergreen shrub from eastern Asia. □ **camélia**

cameo ['kamiou] – *plural* '**cameos** – *noun* an engraved stone with a raised design, used as jewellery. □ **camée**

camera ['kamərə] *noun* **1** an apparatus for taking still or ('**movie-camera**) moving photographs. □ **appareil-photo; caméra**

2 in television, an apparatus which receives a picture and turns it into electrical impulses for transmitting. □ **caméra (de télévision)**

camouflage ['kaməflaːʒ] *noun* something, *eg* protective colouring, that makes an animal, person, building *etc* difficult for enemies to see against the background: *The tiger's stripes are an effective camouflage in the jungle*; *The soldiers wound leaves and twigs round their helmets as camouflage.* □ **camouflage**

■ *verb* to conceal with camouflage. □ **camoufler**

camp [kamp] *noun* **1** a piece of ground with tents pitched on it. □ **camp(ement)**

2 a collection of buildings, huts or tents in which people stay temporarily for a certain purpose: *a holiday camp.* □ **camp**

3 a military station, barracks *etc.* □ **camp**

4 a party or side: *They belong to different political camps.* □ **camp**

■ *verb* (*also* **go camping**) to set up, and live in, a tent/tents: *We camped on the beach*; *We go camping every year.* □ **camper**

'**camper** *noun* **1** a person who goes camping. □ **campeur, euse**

2 a van or trailer equipped for camping. □ **caravane**

'**camping** *noun.* □ **camping**

camp bed (cot) a light folding bed (not only for camping): *The visitor will have to sleep on a camp bed.* □ **lit de camp**

camp-fire *noun* the fire on which campers cook, and round which they sit in the evening *etc.* □ **feu de camp**

'campsite *noun* a piece of land on which tents may be pitched. □ **terrain de camping**

campaign [kam'pein] *noun* **1** the operations of an army while fighting in one area or for one purpose: *the Burma campaign in the Second World War.* □ **campagne**

2 a series of organized actions in support of a cause: *a campaign against smoking.* □ **campagne**

■ *verb* to take part in a campaign: *He has campaigned against smoking for years.* □ **faire campagne**

cam'paigner *noun.* □ **militant, ante**

camphor ['kamfə] *noun* a strongly scented whitish substance, used for various medical and industrial purposes: *Mothballs contain camphor.* □ **camphre**

campus ['kampəs] *noun* college or university grounds: *The new library was built in the centre of the campus.* □ **campus**

can[1] [kan] – *negative* **can't** [kaɪnt], **cannot** ['kanɔt] – *verb*

1 to be able to: *You can do it if you try hard.* □ **pouvoir**

2 to know how to: *Can you drive a car?* □ **savoir**

3 (*usually* **may**) to have permission to: *You can go if you behave yourself.* □ **pouvoir**

4 used in questions to indicate surprise, disbelief *etc*: *What can he be doing all this time?* □ **pouvoir**

can[2] [kan] *noun* a metal container for liquids and many types of food: *oil-can*; *beer-can*; *six cans of beer.* □ **bidon, boîte de conserve**

■ *verb* – *past tense, past participle* **canned** – to put (*especially* food) into cans, *usually* to preserve it: *a factory for canning raspberries.* □ **mettre en conserve**

canned *adjective* put in cans: *canned peas.* □ **en conserve**

'cannery – *plural* **'canneries** – *noun* a factory where goods are canned. □ **conserverie**

can opener *noun* any of several types of tool or device for opening tins of food. □ **ouvre-boîte(s)**

Canadian [kəneidiːən] *adjective* of Canada or its inhabitants: *The beaver is a Canadian emblem; A Canadian citizen won the award.* □ **canadien, ienne**

■ *noun* a native or citizen from Canada: *Many Canadians love hockey.* □ **Canadien, ienne**

canal [kə'nal] *noun* **1** a (*usually* narrow) man-made waterway: *barges on the canal; the Panama Canal.* □ **canal**

2 a passage in the body carrying fluids, food *etc.* □ **canal**

canary [kə'neəri] – *plural* **ca'naries** – *noun* a type of small, yellow, singing bird, kept as a pet. □ **canari**

cancan ['kankan]: **the cancan** a type of high-kicking dance. □ **cancan**

cancel ['kansəl] – *past tense, past participle* 'cancelled, 'canceled – *verb* **1** to decide or announce that (something already arranged *etc*) will not be done *etc*: *He cancelled his appointment.* □ **annuler**

2 to mark (stamps) with a postmark. □ **oblitérer**

3 to stop payment of (a cheque, subscription *etc*). □

annuler

,cancel'lation *noun.* □ **annulation**

cancel out to undo the effect of: *We don't want our profits to be cancelled out by extra expenses.* □ **annuler**

cancer ['kansə] *noun* **1** a diseased growth in the body, often fatal: *The cancer has spread to her stomach.* □ **cancer**

2 the (often fatal) condition caused by such diseased growth(s): *He is dying of cancer.* □ **cancer**

'cancerous *adjective.* □ **cancéreux**

candid ['kandid] *adjective* saying just what one thinks, without hiding anything: *Do you like my hairstyle? Be candid.* □ **sincère**

'candidly *adverb.* □ **sincèrement**

'candour [-də] *noun.* □ **franchise**

'candidness *noun.* □ **sincérité**

candidate ['kandideit, -dət] *noun* a person who enters for a competition or examination (for a job, prize *etc*): *a candidate for the job of manager; a parliamentary candidate.* □ **candidat, ate**

'candidacy [-dəsi], **'candidature** [-dətʃə] *noun* being a candidate. □ **candidature**

candied *see* **candy.**

candle ['kandl] *noun* a moulded piece of wax with a wick in the centre, for giving light: *We had to use candles when the electric lights went out.* □ **bougie, chandelle**

'candle-light *noun* the light from a candle: *We had dinner by candle-light.* □ **lumière de chandelle**

'candlestick *noun* a holder for a candle. □ **chandelier**

candour *see* **candid.**

candy ['kandi] – *plural* 'candies – *noun* **1** sugar formed into a solid mass by boiling. □ **sucre candi**

2 a sweet or sweets; (a piece of) confectionery: *That child eats too much candy; Have a candy!* □ **bonbon(s)**

'candied *adjective* covered with sugar: *candied fruits.* □ **confit**

candy floss (cotton candy) flavoured sugar spun into a fluffy ball on the end of a stick. □ **barbe à papa**

cane [kein] *noun* **1** the stem of certain types of plant (*eg* sugar plant, bamboo *etc*). □ **canne**

2 a stick used as an aid to walking or as an instrument of punishment: *He beat the child with a cane.* □ **canne**

■ *verb* to beat with a cane: *The schoolmaster caned the boy.* □ **corriger (avec une canne)**

cane sugar sugar obtained from the sugar cane. □ **sucre de canne**

canine ['keinain] *adjective* like, or of, a dog or dogs: *canine characteristics.* □ **canin**

canine teeth in man, the four sharp-pointed teeth. □ **canine**

canister ['kanistə] *noun* a box or case *usually* of metal. □ **boîte (en métal)**

cannabis ['kanəbis] *noun* a drug made from Indian hemp, whose use is illegal in many countries: *He is hooked on* (= addicted to) *cannabis.* □ **cannabis**

cannibal ['kanibəl] *noun* **1** a person who eats human flesh. □ **cannibale**

2 an animal *etc* which eats others of its own species. □ **cannibale**

'cannibalism *noun.* □ **cannibalisme**

,canniba'listic *adjective*. □ **cannibale**

cannon ['kanən] – *plurals* '**cannons**, '**cannon** – *noun* a type of large gun used formerly, mounted on a carriage. □ **canon**

■ *verb* (*with* **into**) to hit or collide with: *She came rushing round the corner and cannoned into me.* □ **rentrer (de)dans**

'**cannonball** *noun* a ball of iron, shot from a cannon. □ **boulet de canon**

cannot *see* can¹.

canoe [kə'nuː] *noun* a light narrow boat driven by a paddle or paddles. □ **canoé**

■ *verb* to travel by canoe: *She canoed over the rapids.* □ **faire du canoé**

ca'noeist *noun*. □ **canoéiste**

canon ['kanən] *noun* **1** a rule (*especially* of the church). □ **canon**

2 a clergyman belonging to a cathedral. □ **chanoine**

3 a list of saints. □ **canon**

4 a musical composition in which one part enters after another in imitation. □ **canon**

ca'nonical [-'no-] *adjective*. □ **canonique**

'**canonize**, '**canonise** *verb* to place in the list of saints: *Joan of Arc was canonized in 1920.* □ **canoniser**

,**canoni'zation**, ,**canoni'sation** *noun*. □ **canonisation**

canopy ['kanəpi] – *plural* '**canopies** – *noun* a covering hung over a throne, bed *etc* or (on poles) as a shelter. □ **dais, baldaquin**

cant [kant] *noun* **1** insincere talk: *politicians' cant.* □ **langage hypocrite**

2 the special slang of a particular group of people: *thieves' cant.* □ **jargon**

can't *see* can¹.

cantankerous [kan'taŋkərəs] *adjective* quarrelsome: *a cantankerous old man.* □ **revêche**

canteen [kan'tiːn] *noun* **1** a place where meals are sold in a factory, barracks *etc*. □ **cantine**

2 a case for, or of, cutlery. □ **ménagère**

3 a small container used by soldiers for holding water *etc*. □ **bidon**

canter ['kantə] *noun* (of a horse) an easy gallop: *He went off at a canter.* □ **petit galop**

■ *verb* to gallop easily: *The horse cantered over the meadow.* □ **aller au petit galop**

canvas ['kanvəs] – *plural* '**canvases** – *noun* **1** (*also adjective*) (of) a coarse cloth made of hemp or flax *etc*, used for sails, tents *etc*, and for painting on: *canvas sails.* □ **toile**

2 (a piece of canvas for) a painting: *She painted twenty canvases.* □ **toile**

under canvas in tents: *living under canvas.* □ **sous la tente**

canvass ['kanvəs] *verb* to go round (an area) asking (people) for (support, votes, custom *etc*): *We're canvassing for the Conservative Party candidate.* □ **faire campagne pour**

'**canvasser** *noun*. □ **agent électoral**

canyon ['kanjən] *noun* a deep valley between high steep banks, *usually* containing a river: *the Grand Canyon.* □ **canyon**

cap [kap] *noun* **1** a hat with a peak: *a chauffeur's cap.* □ **casquette**

2 a covering for the head, not with a peak: *a swimming cap*; *a nurse's cap.* □ **bonnet; coiffe**

3 a cover or top (of a bottle, pen *etc*): *Replace the cap after you've finished with the pen.* □ **capsule; capuchon**

capped *adjective* having a cap or covering: *snow-capped mountains.* □ **couronné**

capable ['keipəbl] *adjective* **1** clever *especially* in practical ways: *She'll manage somehow – she's so capable!* □ **capable**

2 (*with* **of**) clever enough to; likely to; able to: *She is capable of doing better; He is quite capable of cheating us.* □ **capable (de)**

'**capably** *adverb*. □ **avec compétence**

,**capa'bility** *noun*. □ **capacité**

capacious [kə'peiʃəs] *adjective* roomy, holding a lot: *a capacious handbag.* □ **vaste**

capacity [kə'pasəti] – *plural* **ca'pacities** – *noun* **1** ability to hold, contain *etc*: *This tank has a capacity of 300 litres.* □ **capacité (de)**

2 ability: *his capacity for remembering facts.* □ **capacité (de)**

3 position: *in his capacity as a leader.* □ **qualité de**

cape¹ [keip] *noun* a long, loose, sleeveless outer garment hanging from the shoulders and fastening at the neck: *a waterproof cycling cape.* □ **cape**

cape² [keip] *noun* a headland sticking out into the sea: *The fishing-boat rounded the cape; Cape Breton.* □ **cap**

caper ['keipə] *verb* to leap or jump about: *The child was capering about.* □ **gambader**

■ *noun* **1** a frisky jump. □ **gambade**

2 a piece of playful behaviour. □ **farce(s)**

capillary [kə'piləri] – *plural* **capillaries** – *noun* a tube with a very small diameter, *especially* (in *plural*) the tiny vessels that join veins to arteries. □ **capillaire**

capital¹ ['kapitl] *noun* **1** the chief town or seat of government: *Paris is the capital of France.* □ **capitale**

2 (*also* **capital letter**) any letter of the type found at the beginning of sentences, proper names *etc*: *THESE ARE CAPITAL LETTERS/CAPITALS.* □ **majuscule**

3 money (for investment *etc*): *You need capital to start a new business.* □ **capital**

■ *adjective* **1** involving punishment by death: *a capital offence.* □ **capital**

2 excellent: *a capital idea.* □ **excellent**

3 (of a city) being a capital: *Paris and other capital cities.* □ **capitale**

'**capitalism** *noun* a system of economics in which money and business are controlled by capitalists. □ **capitalisme**

'**capitalist** *noun* a person who has much money in business concerns. □ **capitaliste**

'**capitalist**, ,**capita'listic** *adjective*. □ **capitaliste**

capital² ['kapitl] *noun* in architecture, the top part of a column of a building *etc*. □ **chapiteau**

capitulate [kə'pitjuleit] *verb* to surrender *usually* on agreed conditions: *We capitulated to the enemy.* □ **capituler**

ca,pitu'lation *noun*. □ **capitulation**

caprice [kə'priːs] *noun* **1** an *especially* unreasonable sudden change of mind *etc*; a whim: *I'm tired of the old man and his caprices.* □ **caprice**

2 a fanciful and lively piece of music *etc*. □ **capriccio**

capricious [kə'priʃəs] *adjective* changeable: *She may change her mind – she's very capricious.* □ **capricieux ca'priciously** *adverb.* □ **capricieusement ca'priciousness** *noun.* □ **humeur capricieuse**

capsize [kap'saiz] *verb* (of a boat) to overturn, often sinking afterwards. □ **chavirer**

capstan ['kapstən] *noun* a drum-shaped machine, used for winding *eg* a ship's anchor-cable. □ **cabestan**

capsule ['kapsl, -sjuːl] *noun* **1** a small gelatin case containing a dose of medicine *etc*. □ **capsule**

2 a closed metal container: *a space capsule.* □ **capsule**

captain ['kaptən] *noun* **1** the commander of a ship, an aircraft, or a group of soldiers. □ **capitaine**

2 (*abbreviated to* **Capt.**, *when written in titles*) the leader of a team or club. □ **capitaine**

■ *verb* to be captain of (something non-military): *John captained the football team last year.* □ **être le capitaine de**

'captaincy *noun* the job of captain: *the captaincy of the team.* □ **commandement d'une équipe**

caption ['kapʃən] *noun* a title or short note written on or beneath an illustration, cartoon, cinema or TV film *etc*: *a witty caption.* □ **légende**

captivate ['kaptiveit] *verb* to charm, fascinate, or hold the attention of: *He was captivated by her beauty.* □ **captiver**

captive ['kaptiv] *noun* a prisoner: *Two of the captives escaped.* □ **captif, ive**

■ *adjective* kept prisoner: *captive soldiers*; *The children were taken/held captive.* □ **prisonnier**

cap'tivity *noun* a state of being a prisoner, caged *etc*: *animals in captivity in a zoo.* □ **captivité**

'captor *noun* a person who captures someone: *He managed to escape from his captors.* □ **ravisseur, euse**

'capture [-tʃə] *verb* **1** to take by force, skill *etc*: *The soldiers captured the castle*; *Several animals were captured.* □ **capturer**

2 to take possession of (a person's attention *etc*): *The story captured his imagination.* □ **captiver**

■ *noun* **1** the act of capturing. □ **capture**

2 something caught: *A kangaroo was his most recent capture.* □ **capture**

car [kaː] *noun* **1** (**,automo'bile**) a (*usually* privately-owned) motor vehicle on wheels for carrying people: *What kind of car do you have?*; *'Did you go by car?'* □ **auto**

2 a section for passengers in a train *etc*: *a dining-car.* □ **voiture**

3 a railway carriage for goods or people: *a freight car.* □ **wagon**

car park (**parking lot**) a piece of land or a building where cars may be parked. □ **parc de stationnement**

car wash *noun* a place where cars are washed and waxed using automated and specialized equipment: *Samuel's car was sparkling clean when he drove away from the car wash.* □ **lave-auto**

carafe [kə'raf] *noun* a glass bottle for serving water, wine

etc. □ **carafe**

caramel ['karəmel] *noun* **1** sugar melted and browned, used for flavouring: *This sauce is flavoured with caramel.* □ **caramel**

2 a sweet made with sugar, butter *etc*, a toffee. □ **caramel**

carat ['karət] *noun* **1** a measure of weight for precious stones. □ **carat**

2 a unit for stating the purity of gold: *an eighteen-carat gold ring.* □ **carat**

caravan ['karəvan] *noun* **1** a vehicle on wheels for living in, now pulled by car *etc*, formerly by horse: *a holiday caravan*; *a gypsy caravan.* □ **caravane**

2 a group of people travelling together for safety *especially* across a desert on camels: *a caravan of merchants.* □ **caravane**

carbohydrate [kaːbə'haidreit] *noun* (any of a group of) substances containing carbon, hydrogen and oxygen, *especially* the sugars and starches found in food: *Potatoes are full of carbohydrate.* □ **hydrate de carbone**

carbon ['kaːbən] an element occurring as diamond and graphite and also in coal *etc*. □ **carbone**

carbon copy a copy of writing or typing made by means of carbon paper. □ **carbone**

carbon dioxide [dai'oksaid] a gas present in the air, breathed out by man and other animals. □ **gaz carbonique**

carbon monoxide [mə'noksaid] a colourless, very poisonous gas which has no smell: *Carbon monoxide is given off by car engines.* □ **oxyde de carbone**

carbon paper a type of paper coated with carbon *etc* which makes a copy when placed between the sheets being written or typed. □ **papier carbone**

carburetor, carburettor ['kaːbəreitə] *noun* a part of an internal-combustion engine in which air is mixed with fuel. □ **carburateur**

carcass ['kaːkəs] *noun* a dead body, *usually* animal, not human: *The carcasses of various animals hung in the butcher's shop.* □ **carcasse**

card [kaːd] *noun* **1** thick paper or thin board: *shapes cut out from card.* □ **carton**

2 (*also* **'playing card**) a small piece of such paper *etc* with designs, used in playing certain games: *a pack of cards.* □ **carte**

3 a similar object used for *eg* sending greetings, showing membership of an organization, storing information *etc*: *a birthday card*; *a membership card*; *a business card.* □ **carte (de)**

cards *noun singular* the game(s) played with playing cards: *He cheats at cards.* □ **cartes**

'cardboard *noun, adjective* (of) a stiff kind of paper often made up of several layers: *a cardboard box.* □ **carton**

cardiac ['kaːdiak] *adjective* of the heart: *This patient has a cardiac complaint*; *cardiac failure.* □ **cardiaque**

cardigan ['kaːdigən] *noun* a knitted jacket which buttons up the front. □ **gilet (de laine)**

cardinal ['kaːdənl] *adjective* chief; principal: *cardinal sins.* □ **cardinal**

■ *noun* (the status of) one of the men next in rank to the

Pope in the Roman Catholic Church. □ **cardinal**
cardinal numbers numbers expressing quantity (1, 2,
3 *etc*). *See also* **ordinal numbers.** □ **nombres**
cardinaux

care [keə] *noun* **1** close attention: *Do it with care.* □ **soin**
2 keeping; protection: *Your belongings will be safe in*
my care. □ **sous la garde de**
3 (a cause for) worry: *free from care*; *all the cares of the*
world. □ **souci**
■ *verb* **1** to be anxious or concerned: *Don't you care if*
you fail?; *I couldn't care less* (= It's of no importance to
me); *She really cares about her career.* □ **se soucier**
(de)
2 to be willing (to): *Would you care to have dinner with*
me? □ **vouloir (bien)**
'**careful** *adjective* **1** taking care; being cautious: *Be care-*
ful when you cross the street; *a careful driver.* □ **pru-**
dent
2 thorough: *a careful search.* □ **complet**
'**carefully** *adverb.* □ **soigneusement**
'**carefulness** *noun.* □ **attention**
'**careless** *adjective* not careful (enough): *This work is*
careless; *a careless worker.* □ **négligé, négligent**
'**carelessly** *adverb.* □ **négligemment**
'**carelessness** *noun.* □ **négligence**
'**carefree** *adjective* light-hearted: *a carefree attitude.* □
insouciant
'**caretaker** *noun* a person who looks after a building
etc. □ **concierge**
'**careworn** *adjective* worn out by worry: *a careworn*
face. □ **rongé par les soucis**
'**care for 1** to look after (someone): *The nurse will care*
for you. □ **s'occuper de**
2 to be fond of: *I don't care for him enough to marry*
him. □ **aimer**
care of (*usually written* **c/o**) at the house or address of.
□ **aux soins de**
take care to be cautious, watchful, thorough *etc*: *Take*
care or you will fall! □ **faire attention**
take care of to look after: *Their uncle took care of them*
when their parents died. □ **prendre soin de, soigner**

career [kə'riə] *noun* **1** a way of making a living (*usually*
professional): *a career in publishing.* □ **carrière**
2 course; progress (through life): *The present govern-*
ment is nearly at the end of its career. □ **carrière**
■ *verb* to move rapidly and dangerously: *The brakes*
failed and the car careered down the hill. □ **aller à toute**
vitesse

caress [kə'res] *verb* to touch gently and lovingly: *He*
caressed the horse's neck. □ **caresser**
■ *noun* an act of touching in this way: *a loving caress.*
□ **caresse**

cargo ['ka:gou] – *plural* '**cargoes** – *noun* a load of goods
carried by a ship *etc*: *a cargo of cotton.* □ **cargaison**

caricature ['karikətjuə] *noun* a drawing or imitation (of
someone or something) which is so exaggerated as to
appear ridiculous: *Caricatures of politicians appear in*
the newspapers every day. □ **caricature**
'**caricaturist** *noun* a person who makes caricatures. □
caricaturiste

caries ['keərii:z] *noun* decay or rottenness of the teeth. □
carie

carnage ['ka:nidʒ] *noun* the slaughter of great numbers
of people: *the carnage of war.* □ **carnage**

carnival ['ka:nivəl] *noun* a public entertainment, often
involving processions of people in fancy dress *etc*: *a*
winter carnival. □ **carnaval**

carnivore ['ka:nivo:] *noun* a flesh-eating animal: *The*
lion is a carnivore. □ **carnassier**
car'nivorous *adjective.* □ **carnivore**

carol ['karəl] *noun* a song of joy or praise, *especially* for
Christmas. □ **chant de Noël**

carouse [kə'rauz] *verb* to take part in a noisy drinking
session. □ **faire la bombe**
ca'rousal *noun.* □ **beuverie**

carousel [karə'sel] *noun* **1** a merry-go-round. □ **manège**
2 conveyor belt for luggage, especially at an airport. □
carrousel

carp [ka:p] – *plural* **carp** – *noun* a freshwater fish found
in ponds and rivers. □ **carpe**

carpenter ['ka:pəntə] *noun* a craftsman in wood. □
charpentier, ière, menuisier, ière
'**carpentry** *noun* the work of a carpenter. □ **charpenterie**

carpet ['ka:pit] *noun* a woven covering for floors *etc*. □
tapis
■ *verb* to cover with a carpet: *They haven't carpeted*
the floor yet. □ **recouvrir d'un tapis**

carriage ['karidʒ] *noun* **1** the act or cost of conveying
and delivering goods: *Does that price include carriage?*
□ **transport**
2 a vehicle for carrying (*especially* in Britain, railway
passengers): *the carriage nearest the engine*; *a railway*
carriage. □ **wagon**
3 *especially* formerly, a horse-drawn passenger vehicle. □ **voiture**
4 the part of a typewriter which moves back and forwards, carrying the paper. □ **chariot**
5 posture; way of walking. □ **maintien**

carrion ['kariən] *noun* dead animal flesh, eaten by other
animals: *Vultures feed on carrion.* □ **charogne**

carrot ['karət] *noun* (a vegetable with) an edible, orange,
pointed root. □ **carotte**

carry ['kari] *verb* **1** to take from one place *etc* to another:
He carried the child over the river; *Flies carry disease.*
□ **(trans)porter**
2 to go from one place to another: *Sound carries better*
over water. □ **porter**
3 to support: *These stone columns carry the weight of*
the whole building. □ **supporter**
4 to have or hold: *This job carries great responsibility.*
□ **comporter**
5 to approve (a bill *etc*) by a majority of votes: *The par-*
liamentary bill was carried by forty-two votes. □ **voter,**
faire passer
6 to hold (oneself) in a certain way: *He carries himself*
like a soldier. □ **avoir le port/maintien de**
7 to add (a number from one column of figures to
the next): *I forgot to carry the 2.* □ **retenir**
be/get carried away to be overcome by one's feelings:
I was/got carried away by the excitement. □ **être**

emporté
carry off to take away by carrying: *She carried off the screaming child.* □ **emporter**
carry on 1 to continue: *You must carry on working*; *Carry on with your work.* □ **continuer**
2 to manage (a business *etc*): *She carries on a business as a grocer.* □ **diriger**
carry out to accomplish: *He carried out the plan.* □ **mener à bien**
carry weight to have influence: *Her opinion carries a lot of weight around here.* □ **compter**

cart [kaːt] *noun* **1** a two-wheeled (*usually* horse-drawn) vehicle for carrying loads: *a farm cart.* □ **charrette**
2 a small wheeled vehicle pushed by hand, for carrying groceries (shopping cart), golf clubs (golf cart) *etc*. □ **chariot**
■ *verb* **1** to carry (in a cart): *He carted the manure into the field.* □ **charrier**
2 to carry: *I don't want to cart this luggage around all day.* □ **trimballer**
'cartwheel *noun* **1** a wheel of a cart. □ **roue de charrette**
2 a sideways somersault. □ **(la) roue**

cartilage ['kaːtəlidʒ] *noun* a firm elastic substance found in the bodies of men and animals. □ **cartilage**

cartography [kaːˈtogrəfi] *noun* map-making. □ **cartographie**
car'tographer *noun*. □ **cartographe**
,carto'graphic [-'gra-] *adjective*. □ **cartographique**

carton ['kaːtən] *noun* a cardboard or plastic container: *orange juice sold in cartons.* □ **(boîte en) carton**

cartoon [kaːˈtuːn] *noun* **1** a drawing making fun of someone or something: *a cartoon of the Prime Minister in the newspaper.* □ **dessin humoristique**
2 a film consisting of a series of drawings in which the people and animals give the impression of movement: *a Walt Disney cartoon.* □ **dessin animé**
car'toonist *noun* a person who draws cartoons. □ **caricaturiste**

cartridge ['kaːtridʒ] *noun* **1** a case containing the explosive charge (and *usually* a bullet) for a gun. □ **cartouche**
2 a stylus of a record player and its holder. □ **cellule**
3 a plastic container of photographic film or recording tape. □ **chargeur**
4 a tube containing ink for loading a fountain pen. □ **cartouche**

carve [kaːv] *verb* **1** to make designs, shapes *etc* by cutting a piece of wood *etc*: *A figure carved out of wood.* □ **sculpter (dans)**
2 to cut up (meat) into slices: *I carved the joint.* □ **découper**
'carving *noun* a design, ornament *etc* carved from wood, stone *etc*. □ **sculpture**
carve out to achieve or gain (something): *She carved out a career for herself.* □ **se tailler**

cascade [kas'keid] *noun* a waterfall: *a magnificent cascade.* □ **cascade**
■ *verb* to fall in or like a waterfall: *Water cascaded over the rock*; *Dishes cascaded off the table.* □ **tomber en cascade**

case¹ [keis] *noun* **1** an instance or example: *another case of child-beating*; *a bad case of measles.* □ **cas**
2 a particular situation: *It's different in my case.* □ **cas**
3 a legal trial: *The judge in this case is very fair.* □ **affaire**
4 an argument or reason: *There's a good case for thinking he's wrong.* □ **raison(s)**
5 (*usually with* **the**) a fact: *I don't think that's really the case.* □ **cas**
6 a form of a pronoun (*eg* **he** or **him**), noun or adjective showing its relation to other words in the sentence. □ **cas**
in case in order to guard against a possibility: *I'll take an umbrella in case (it rains).* □ **au cas où**
in case of if (a particular thing) happens: *In case of fire, telephone the fire brigade.* □ **en cas de**
in that case if that should happen or should have happened: *You're leaving? In that case, I'm leaving too.* □ **dans ce cas**

case² [keis] *noun* **1** a container or outer covering: *a case of medical instruments*; *a suitcase.* □ **boîte, étui, trousse, valise**
2 a crate or box: *six cases of whisky.* □ **caisse**
3 a piece of furniture for displaying or containing things: *a glass case full of china*; *a bookcase.* □ **vitrine, bibliothèque**

cash [kaʃ] *noun* **1** coins or paper money, not cheques, credit cards *etc*: *Do you wish to pay cash?* □ **(en) espèces**
2 payment by money or cheque as opposed to payment by account: *Cash or charge, madam?* □ **comptant**
3 money in any form: *She has plenty of cash.* □ **argent (liquide)**
■ *verb* to turn into, or exchange for, money: *You may cash a traveller's cheque here*; *Can you cash a cheque for me?* □ **encaisser**
cashier [ka'ʃiə] *noun* a person who receives and pays out money (*eg* in a bank), works at a cash register *etc*: *a bank cashier*; *a cashier in a supermarket.* □ **caissier, ière**
,cash and 'carry *noun* a store where goods are sold more cheaply for cash and taken away by the buyer. □ **libre service, solderie**
cash (register) a machine for holding money, which records the amount put in. □ **caisse (enregistreuse)**
cash in to exchange for money: *I've cashed in all my shares.* □ **réaliser, vendre**
cash in on to take financial or other advantage of (a situation *etc*): *He is the sort of person who cashes in on other people's misfortunes.* □ **tirer profit de**

cashew ['kaʃuː] *noun* a type of small nut: *Is that a cashew?* □ **noix de cajou**
■ *adjective*: *a cashew nut.* □ **de cajou**

cashier¹ *see* **cash**.

cashier² [ka'ʃiə] *verb* to dismiss (a military officer) from a post in disgrace. □ **casser**

cashmere ['kaʒmiər, kaʃ'miə] *noun, adjective* (of) a type of material made from fine goats' hair: *a cashmere sweater.* □ **cachemire**

casino [kə'siːnou] – *plural* **ca'sinos** – *noun* a building with gambling tables *etc*. □ **casino**

cask [kaːsk] *noun* a barrel for holding liquids, *usually* wine: *three casks of sherry*. □ **tonneau**

casket ['kɑːskit] *noun* **1** a small case for holding jewels *etc*. □ **coffret**

2 a coffin. □ **cercueil**

cassava [kə'sɑːvə] *noun* (*also* **tapioca plant**) a tropical plant, whose roots yield tapioca. □ **manioc**

casserole ['kasəroul] *noun* **1** a covered dish in which food is both cooked and served: *an earthenware casserole*. □ **cocotte**

2 the food cooked in a casserole: *I've made a casserole for dinner*. □ **plat en cocotte**

cassette [kə'set] *noun* a plastic container holding photographic film or magnetic tape: *I've put a new cassette in my camera*; *I bought a cassette of Scottish music*; (*also adjective*) *a cassette recorder*. □ **cassette**

cassia ['kasiə, 'kaʃə] *noun* any of several types of tropical tree or shrub of the pea family with small yellow or pink flowers. □ **casse**

cassock ['kasək] *noun* a long robe worn by clergymen and church choir-singers. □ **soutane**

cast [kɑːst] – *past tense, past participle* **cast** – *verb* **1** to throw: *The angler cast his line into the river*; *These facts cast new light on the matter*; *She cast him a look of hatred*. □ **jeter**

2 to get rid of; to take off: *Some snakes cast their skins*. □ **se dépouiller de**

3 to shape (metal *etc*) by pouring into a mould: *Metal is melted before it is cast*. □ **couler**

4 to give a part in a play *etc* to: *She was cast as Lady Macbeth*. □ **donner le rôle de**

5 to select the actors for (a film *etc*): *The director is casting (the film) tomorrow*. □ **faire la distribution**

6 to give (a vote): *I cast my vote for the younger candidate*. □ **voter**

■ *noun* **1** a throw: *At his third cast he caught a fish*. □ **lancer**

2 something made by moulding: *The doctor put a plaster cast on his broken leg*. □ **plâtre**

3 a mould: *The hot metal is poured into a cast*. □ **moule**

4 the complete set of actors in a play, opera *etc*: *the whole cast of the play*. □ **distribution**

5 something that is ejected by certain animals, *eg* the earthworm: *worm casts all over the grass*. □ **déjections**

'castaway *noun* a shipwrecked person. □ **naufragé, ée**

casting vote the deciding vote of the chairman of a meeting when the other votes are equally divided. □ **voix prépondérante**

cast iron unpurified iron melted and shaped in a mould. □ **fonte**

'cast-iron *adjective* **1** made of cast iron: *a cast-iron frying-pan*. □ **en fonte**

2 very strong: *cast-iron muscles*. □ **d'acier**

'cast-off *noun, adjective* (a piece of clothing *etc*) no longer needed: *cast-off clothes*; *I don't want my sister's cast-offs*. □ **vieilles fringues**

cast off 1 to untie (the mooring lines of a boat). □ **larguer (les amarres)**

2 (*also* **cast aside**) to reject as unwanted. □ **(re)jeter**

3 in knitting, to finish (the final row of stitches). □ **arrêter**

cast on in knitting, to make the first row of stitches. □ **monter les mailles**

castanets [kastə'nets] *noun plural* two hollow pieces of ivory or hard wood struck together as a rhythm for (*especially* Spanish) dances. □ **castagnettes**

caste [kɑːst] *noun* a social class *especially* in India: *the lowest caste*; (*also adjective*) *the caste system*. □ **caste**

caster¹ ['kɑːstə]: **caster sugar** fine sugar used in baking *etc*. □ **sucre en poudre**

caster² *see* **castor**.

castle ['kɑːsl] *noun* **1** a large building strengthened against attack: *the Norman castles of England and Wales*; *Windsor Castle*. □ **château**

2 (*also* **rook**) a piece in chess. □ **tour**

castor, caster ['kɑːstə] *noun* a small wheel on the legs of furniture to make it easier to move. □ **roulette**

castor oil ['kɑːstərɔil] an oil from a tropical plant, used in medicine *etc*. □ **huile de ricin**

castrate ['kastreit] *verb* to remove the sexual organs of (a male animal): *The bull has been castrated*. □ **castrer**

ca'stration *noun*. □ **castration**

casual ['kaʒuəl] *adjective* **1** not careful: *I took a casual glance at the book*. □ **rapide, en passant**

2 informal: *casual clothes*. □ **sport**

3 happening by chance: *a casual remark*. □ **fortuit**

4 not regular or permanent: *casual labour*. □ **temporaire**

'casually *adverb*. □ **par hasard**

'casualness *noun*. □ **désinvolture**

casualty ['kaʒuəlti] – *plural* **'casualties** – *noun* a person who is wounded or killed in a battle, accident *etc*: *There were hundreds of casualties when the factory went on fire*. □ **victime**

casuarina [kaʒuə'riːnə] *noun* a tall, feathery tree with drooping, jointed, green branches and scale-like leaves. □ **casuarina**

cat [kat] *noun* **1** a small, four-legged, fur-covered animal often kept as a pet: *a Siamese cat*. □ **chat, chatte**

2 a large wild animal of the same family (*eg* tiger, lion *etc*): *the big cats*. □ **félin**

'catty *adjective* spiteful, malicious: *He's catty even about his best friend*; *catty remarks*. □ **méchant**

'catcall *noun* a shrill whistle showing disagreement or disapproval: *the catcalls of the audience*. □ **sifflet**

'catfish *noun* any of a family of scaleless fish with long feelers round the mouth. □ **poisson-chat**

'catgut *noun* a kind of cord made from the intestines of sheep *etc*, used for violin strings *etc*. □ **catgut**

,Cat's 'Eye® *noun* a small, thick piece of glass fixed in the surface of a road to reflect light and guide drivers at night. □ **catadioptre**

'catsuit *noun* a woman's close-fitting one-piece trouser suit. □ **combinaison-pantalon**

'cattail *noun* a tall plant that grows in wet places, with flowers shaped like a cat's tail. □ **massette**

let the cat out of the bag to let a secret become known unintentionally. □ **vendre la mèche**

cataclysm ['katəklizəm] *noun* a violent disaster or upheaval: disaster. □ **cataclysme**

,cata'clysmic *adjective*. □ **cataclysmique**

catalogue ['katəlog] *noun* (a book containing) an ordered list of names, goods, books *etc*: *a library catalogue.* □ **catalogue**

■ *verb* to put in an ordered list: *She catalogued the books in alphabetical order of author's name.* □ **cataloguer**

catalyst [ˈkatəlist] *noun* **1** a substance which causes or assists a chemical change in another substance without itself undergoing any permanent chemical change. □ **catalyseur**

2 someone or something that helps bring about a change. □ **catalyseur**

,cata'lytic *adjective.* □ **catalytique**

catamaran [katəməˈran] *noun* a sailing-boat with two parallel hulls. □ **catamaran**

catapult [ˈkatəpʌlt] *verb* to throw violently: *The driver was catapulted through the windshield when his car hit the wall.* □ **catapulter**

cataract [ˈkatərakt] *noun* a clouding of the lens of the eye causing difficulty in seeing. □ **cataracte**

catarrh [kəˈtɑː] *noun* inflammation of the lining of the nose and throat causing a discharge of thick fluid. □ **rhume chronique**

catastrophe [kəˈtastrəfi] *noun* a sudden great disaster: *earthquakes and other natural catastrophes; Her brother's death was a catastrophe for the family.* □ **catastrophe**

catastrophic [katəˈstrofik] *adjective.* □ **catastrophique** ,cata'strophically *adverb.* □ **de façon catastrophique**

catcall *see* **cat.**

catch [katʃ] – *past tense, past participle* **caught** [kɔːt] – *verb* **1** to stop and hold (something which is moving); to capture: *She caught the cricket ball; The cat caught a mouse; Did you catch any fish?; I tried to catch his attention.* □ **attraper**

2 to be in time for, or get on (a train, bus *etc*): *I'll have to catch the 9:45 (train) to Ottawa.* □ **arriver à temps pour (prendre)**

3 to surprise (someone) in the act of: *I caught them stealing (my vegetables).* □ **surprendre**

4 to become infected with (a disease or illness): *I caught flu.* □ **attraper**

5 to (cause to) become accidentally attached or held: *The child caught her fingers in the car door.* □ **(se) prendre**

6 to hit: *The punch caught me on the chin.* □ **flanquer un coup**

7 to manage to hear: *Did you catch what she said?* □ **comprendre**

8 to start burning: *I dropped a match on the pile of wood and it caught (fire) immediately.* □ **prendre (feu)**

■ *noun* **1** an act of catching: *I took a fine catch behind the wicket.* □ **arrêt (au vol)**

2 a small device for holding (a door *etc*) in place: *The catch on my suitcase is broken.* □ **loquet, serrure, fermoir**

3 the total amount (of *eg* fish) caught: *the largest catch of mackerel this year.* □ **prise**

4 a trick or problem: *There's a catch in this question.* □ **attrape**

'catching *adjective* infectious: *Is chicken-pox catching?* □ **contagieux**

'catchy *adjective* (of a tune) attractive and easily remembered. □ **facile à retenir**

'catchphrase, 'catchword *nouns* a phrase or word in popular use for a time. □ **rengaine, slogan accrocheur**

catch a cold to become ill with a virus that causes coughing, sneezing, stuffy nose and sore throat: *Namisha caught a cold and was up all night coughing and blowing her nose.* □ **s'enrhumer**

catch someone's eye to attract someone's attention: *The advertisement caught my eye; I couldn't catch the waiter's eye and so we were last to be served.* □ **attirer l'attention de**

catch on 1 to become popular: *The fashion caught on.* □ **prendre**

2 to understand: *He's a bit slow to catch on.* □ **piger**

catch out 1 to put out (a batsman) at cricket by catching the ball after it has been hit and before it touches the ground. □ **mettre hors jeu à balle attrapée**

2 to cause (someone) to fail by means of a trick, a difficult question *etc*: *The last question in the exam caught them all out.* □ **prendre au dépourvu**

catch up to come level (with): *We caught up with him at the corner; Ask the taxi-driver if he can catch up with that truck; We waited for him to catch up; She had a lot of schoolwork to catch up on after her illness.* □ **rattraper**

catechism [ˈkatikizəm] *noun* **1** a book (*especially* religious) of instructions by means of question and answer. □ **catéchisme**

2 a series of searching questions on any subject. □ **catéchisme**

category [ˈkatəgəri] – *plural* 'categories – *noun* a class or division of things (or people): *various categories of goods on sale.* □ **catégorie**

'categorize, 'categorise *verb* to put (things or people) into a category. □ **classer par catégories**

cater [ˈkeitə] *verb* **1** to provide food *etc*: *We cater for all types of functions.* □ **fournir des repas**

2 to supply what is needed: *We cater for all educational needs.* □ **pourvoir à**

'caterer *noun.* □ **traiteur, euse**

'catering *noun.* □ **approvisionnement**

caterpillar [ˈkatəpilə] *noun* the larva of a butterfly or moth that feeds upon the leaves of plants: *There's a caterpillar on this lettuce.* □ **chenille**

■ *adjective* moving on endless belts: *a caterpillar tractor.* □ **à chenilles**

catfish, catgut *see* **cat.**

cathedral [kəˈθiːdrəl] *noun* the principal church of a district under a bishop. □ **cathédrale**

catholic [ˈkaθəlik] *adjective* **1** wide-ranging in one's taste *etc*: *a catholic taste in books.* □ **éclectique**

2 (*with capital*) Roman Catholic. □ **catholique**

■ *noun* (*with capital*) a Roman Catholic. □ **catholique**

Catholicism [kəˈθolisizəm] *noun* Roman Catholicism. □ **catholicisme**

catsuit, cattail *see* **cat.**

cattle [ˈkatl] *noun plural* grass-eating animals, *especially* cows, bulls and oxen: *That farmer does not keep sheep but he keeps several breeds of cattle.* □ **bovins**

caught *see* **catch**.

cauldron ['kɔːldrən] *noun* a large deep pot (used *especially* by witches) for boiling things in. □ **chaudron**

cauliflower ['kɒliflauə] a vegetable of the cabbage family whose white flower-head is used as food. □ **chou-fleur**

cause [kɔːz] *noun* 1 something or someone that produces an effect or result: *Having no money is the cause of all my misery.* □ **cause**

2 a reason for an action; a motive: *You had no cause to treat your son so badly.* □ **raison**

3 an aim or concern for which an individual or group works: *cancer research and other deserving causes; in the cause of peace.* □ **cause**

■ *verb* to make (something) happen; to bring about; to be the means of: *What caused the accident?; He caused me to drop my suitcase.* □ **causer, occasionner**

causeway ['kɔːzwei] *noun* a raised pathway, road *etc* over wet ground or shallow water. □ **chaussée**

caustic ['kɔːstik] *adjective* 1 burning by chemical action: *caustic soda.* □ **caustique**

2 (of remarks) bitter or sarcastic: *caustic comments.* □ **mordant**

'**caustically** *adverb.* □ **d'un ton mordant**

cauterize, cauterise ['kɔːtəraiz] *verb* to burn (a wound) with a caustic substance or a hot iron (to destroy infection). □ **cautériser**

caution ['kɔːʃən] *noun* 1 carefulness (because of possible danger *etc*): *Exercise caution when crossing this road.* □ **prudence**

2 in law, a warning: *The policewoman gave her a caution for speeding.* □ **avertissement**

■ *verb* to give a warning to: *He was cautioned for drunken driving.* □ **avertir**

'**cautionary** *adjective.* □ **d'avertissement**

'**cautious** *adjective* having or showing caution; careful: *She used to trust everyone but she's more cautious now; a cautious driver.* □ **prudent, avisé**

'**cautiously** *adverb.* □ **prudemment**

cavalcade [kavəl'keid] *noun* a ceremonial procession. □ **cortège**

cavalier [kavə'liə] *noun* in former times, a horseman or knight. □ **cavalier**

cavalry ['kavəlri] *noun or noun plural* (the part of an army consisting of) horse-soldiers: *The cavalry were/was ordered to advance.* □ **cavalerie**

cave [keiv] *noun* a large natural hollow in rock or in the earth: *The children explored the caves.* □ **grotte**

'**caveman** [-man] *noun* in prehistoric times, a person who lived in a cave: *Cavemen dressed in the skins of animals.* □ **homme des cavernes**

cave in (of walls *etc*) to collapse. □ **s'effondrer**

cavern ['kavən] *noun* a large cave. □ **caverne**

'**cavernous** *adjective* huge and hollow: *a cavernous hole.* □ **caverneux**

caviar ['kavi,aː] *noun* the pickled eggs (roe) of a certain large fish, used as food. □ **caviar**

cavity ['kavəti] – *plural* '**cavities** – *noun* a hollow place; a hole: *The dentist said she had three cavities in her teeth; The thief hid the necklace in a cavity in the wall.* □ **cavité**

cease [siːs] *verb* to stop or (bring to an) end: *They were ordered to cease firing; That department has ceased to exist; This foolishness must cease!; Cease this noise!* □ **cesser**

'**ceaseless** *adjective* continuous; never ceasing: *ceaseless noise.* □ **continuel**

'**ceaselessly** *adverb.* □ **sans arrêt**

ceasefire [siːsfaiə] *noun* a truce; an agreement to stop fighting for a while, made by both sides in a conflict: *The guns stopped at the exact hour of the ceasefire* □ **cessez-le-feu**

cedar ['siːdə] *noun* 1 a cone-bearing evergreen tree. □ **cèdre**

2 (*also* '**cedarwood**) its hard, sweet-smelling wood. □ **cèdre**

ceiling ['siːliŋ] *noun* the inner roof (of a room *etc*): *Paint the ceiling before you paint the walls.* □ **plafond**

celebrate ['seləbreit] *verb* to mark by giving a party *etc* in honour of (a happy or important event): *I'm celebrating (my birthday) today.* □ **fêter**

'**celebrated** *adjective* famous: *a celebrated actress.* □ **célèbre**

,**cele'bration** *noun: birthday celebrations.* □ **fêtes**

ce'lebrity [-'le-] – *plural* **ce'lebrities** – *noun* a well-known person: *celebrities from the world of entertainment.* □ **célébrité**

celery ['seləri] *noun* the long juicy edible stalks of a type of vegetable, used in salads *etc.* □ **céleri**

celestial [sə'lestiəl] *adjective* of heaven or the skies: *Stars are celestial bodies.* □ **céleste**

celibacy ['selibəsi] *noun* the state of being unmarried or of refraining from sexual intercourse, *especially* in obedience to religious vows. □ **célibat**

'**celibate** [-bət] *adjective.* □ **célibataire**

cell [sel] *noun* 1 a small room (*especially* in a prison or monastery). □ **cellule**

2 a very small piece of the substance of which all living things are made; the smallest unit of living matter: *The human body is made up of cells.* □ **cellule**

3 (the part containing the electrodes in) an electrical battery. □ **élément (de pile)**

4 one of many small compartments making up a structure: *the cells of a honeycomb.* □ **cellule**

cellular ['seljulə] *adjective* 1 consisting of cells: *cellular tissue.* □ **cellulaire**

2 containing tiny hollow spaces: *Foam rubber is a cellular substance.* □ **alvéolé**

cellar ['selə] *noun* a room, *especially* underground, *especially* for stores of coal or wine. □ **cave**

cello, 'cello ['tʃelou] *noun* (short for '**violoncello**) a stringed musical instrument similar to, but much larger than, a violin. □ **violoncelle**

'**cellist, 'cellist** *noun* a person who plays the cello. □ **violoncelliste**

Cellophane® ['seləfein] *noun* a type of clear wrapping material: *flowers wrapped in Cellophane*; (*also adjective*) *Cellophane wrapping.* □ **cellophane**

cellular *see* **cell**.

cellulose ['seljulous] *noun* the chief substance in the cell walls of plants, also found in woods, used in the making of plastic, paper *etc*. □ **cellulose**

Celsius ['selsiəs] *adjective* (*often abbreviated to* **C** *when written*) centigrade: *twenty degrees Celsius*; *20°C*. □ **Celsius**

Celsius ends in -sius (not -cius)
---

cement [sə'ment] *noun* **1** a mixture of clay and lime (*usually* with sand and water added) used for sticking things (*eg* bricks) together in building and to make concrete for making very hard surfaces. □ **ciment**
2 any of several types of glue. □ **ciment**
3 a substance used to fill cavities in teeth. □ **amalgame**
■ *verb* to join firmly with cement. □ **cimenter**
cement mixer a machine with a revolving drum in which water and cement are mixed together. □ **bétonnière**

cemetery ['seməteri] – *plural* **'cemeteries** – *noun* a piece of ground, *usually* not round a church, where people are buried. □ **cimetière**

cenotaph ['senətɑːf] *noun* a monument to a person or people buried elsewhere, *especially* a monument built in memory of soldiers *etc* killed in war. □ **cénotaphe**

censor ['sensə] *noun* **1** an official who examines films *etc* and has the power to remove any of the contents which might offend people: *Part of his film has been banned by the censor.* □ **censeur, eure**
2 an official (*eg* in the army) who examines letters *etc* and removes information which the authorities do not wish to be made public for political reasons *etc*. □ **censeur**
■ *verb*: *This film has been censored*; *The soldiers' letters are censored.* □ **censurer**
cen'sorious [-'sɔː-] *adjective* very critical: *She is censorious about the behaviour of young people.* □ **hypercritique**
'censorship *noun* the policy of censoring: *Some people disapprove of censorship.* □ **censure**

censure ['senʃə] *verb* to criticize or blame: *He was censured for staying away from work.* □ **blâmer**
■ *noun* criticism or blame. □ **blâme**

census ['sensəs] – *plural* **'censuses** – *noun* an official counting *especially* of a country's inhabitants: *When was the last census in Canada?* □ **recensement**

cent [sent] *noun* a coin equal to the hundredth part of a dollar, rupee, rand *etc*. □ **cent**

centenary [sen'tɑneri] (*plural* **cen'tenaries**), **centennial** [sen'teniəl] *noun* a hundredth anniversary: *The firm is celebrating its centenary this year.* □ **centenaire**
centenarian [sentə'neriən] *noun* a person who is a hundred or more years old. □ **centenaire**

centigrade ['sentigreid] *adjective* (*often abbreviated to* **C** *when written*) as measured on a centigrade thermometer: *twenty degrees centigrade*; *20°C*. □ **centigrade**
centigrade thermometer a thermometer which shows the temperature at which water freezes as 0°, and that at which it boils as 100°. □ **thermomètre centigrade**

centimetre ['sentimiːtə] *noun* a unit of length equal to one-hundredth of a metre. □ **centimètre**

centipede ['sentipiːd] *noun* a type of very small worm-like animal with many legs. □ **mille-pattes**

central ['sentrəl] *adjective* **1** belonging to or near the centre (*eg* of a town): *My flat is very central.* □ **central**
2 principal or most important: *the central point of his argument.* □ **central**
'centralize, 'centralise *verb* to bring under one control. □ **centraliser**
,centrali'zation, ,centrali'sation *noun*. □ **centralisation**
'centrally *adverb*: *centrally situated.* □ **centralement**
central heating heating of a building by water, steam or air through pipes from one central boiler *etc*. □ **chauffage central**

centre, center ['sentə] *noun* **1** the middle point, or middle of anything; the point or area farthest from the edge: *the centre of a circle*; *the city centre.* □ **centre**
2 a place having, or designed for, a particular activity, interest *etc*: *a centre of industry*; *a shopping-centre*; *a sports-centre.* □ **centre**
3 the main point (of interest *etc*): *the centre of attention.* □ **centre**
■ *verb* **1** to place, or to be, at the centre. □ **centrer**
2 (*with* **on**) to concentrate round: *His plans always centre on his child.* □ **se concentrer (sur)**

centrifugal [sen'trifjugəl] *adjective* tending to move away from a centre: *centrifugal force.* □ **centrifuge**

century ['sentʃuri] *noun* – *plural* **'centuries** – **1** a (period of a) hundred years: *the 19th century*; *for more than a century.* □ **siècle**
2 in cricket, a hundred runs: *He has just made his second century this year.* □ **centaine (de points)**

ceramic [sə'ramik] *adjective* (of the art) of pottery. □ **en céramique**
■ *noun* something made of pottery: *She sells ceramics, but they are very expensive.* □ **objet en céramique**
ce'ramics *noun singular* the art of pottery. □ **céramique**

cereal ['siəriəl] *noun* **1** a kind of grain used as food: *Wheat and barley are cereals*; (*also adjective*) *cereal crops.* □ **céréale; céréalier**
2 a type of breakfast food prepared from such grain. □ **céréales**

cerebral [sə'riːbrəl, 'serəbrəl] *adjective* of the brain. □ **cérébral**

ceremony ['serəmouni] – *plural* **'ceremonies** – *noun* **1** a sacred or formal act, *eg* a wedding, funeral *etc*: *a marriage ceremony.* □ **cérémonie**
2 solemn display and formality: *pomp and ceremony.* □ **cérémonie**
,cere'monial [-'mou-] *adjective* formal or official: *a ceremonial occasion such as the opening of parliament.* □ **cérémonial**
,cere'monially *adverb*. □ **avec cérémonie**
,cere'monious [-'mou-] *adjective* (*negative* **unceremonious**) carefully formal or polite. □ **cérémonieux**
,cere'moniously *adverb*. □ **solennellement**

certain ['səːtn] *adjective* **1** true or without doubt: *It's certain that the world is round.* □ **certain**
2 sure: *I'm certain she'll come*; *He is certain to forget*; *Being late is a certain way of losing one's job.* □ **certain**
3 one or some, not definitely named: *certain doctors*; *a certain Mrs. Smith*; (*also pronoun*) *certain of his friends.*

□ **certain**
4 slight; some: *a certain hostility in his manner*; *a certain amount*. □ **certain**

'**certainly** *adverb* 1 definitely: *I can't come today, but I'll certainly come tomorrow*. □ **certainement**
2 of course: *You may certainly have a chocolate*. □ **certainement**
■ *interjection* of course: *'May I borrow your typewriter?' 'Certainly!'*; *'Certainly not!'* □ **certainement**

'**certainty** – *plural* '**certainties** – *noun* 1 something which cannot be doubted: *It's a certainty that she will win*. □ **certitude**
2 freedom from doubt: *Is there any certainty of success?* □ **certitude**
for certain definitely: *She may come but she can't say for certain*. □ **avec certitude**
make certain to act so that, or check that, something is sure: *Make certain you arrive early*; *I think he's dead but you'd better make certain*. □ **s'assurer que**

certificate [sə'tifikət] *noun* a written official declaration of some fact: *a marriage certificate*. □ **certificat**

certify ['sɔːtifai] *verb* 1 to declare formally (*eg* that something is true): *I certify that I witnessed the signing of his will*. □ **certifier**
2 to declare officially that (someone) is insane. □ **déclarer qqn atteint d'aliénation mentale**

cer,tifi'cation *noun*. □ **certification, homologation**

cessation [se'seiʃən] *noun* stopping or ceasing: *the cessation of activities*. □ **cessation**

chafe [tʃeif] *verb* 1 to make warm by rubbing with the hands. □ **frictionner**
2 to make or become sore by rubbing: *These tight shoes chafe my feet*. □ **irriter**
3 to become impatient: *Everyone's chafing at the delay*. □ **s'impatienter**

chagrin [ʃə'grin] *noun* disappointment and annoyance. □ **contrariété, déception**

chain [tʃein] *noun* 1 a series of (*especially* metal) links or rings passing through one another: *The dog was fastened by a chain*; *She wore a silver chain round her neck*. □ **chaîne**
2 a series: *a chain of events*. □ **série**
■ *verb* to fasten or bind with chains: *The prisoner was chained to the wall*. □ **enchaîner**
chain mail armour made of iron links. □ **cotte de mailles**
chain store one of a series of shops (often department stores) under the same ownership. □ **magasin (à succursales multiples)**

chair [tʃeə] *noun* 1 a movable seat for one, with a back to it: *a table and four chairs*. □ **chaise**
2 the position of a person who is chairman at a meeting *etc*: *Who is in the chair?* □ **présidence**
3 the office of a university professor: *She holds the chair of History at this university*. □ **chaire**
■ *verb* to be chairman at (a meeting *etc*): *I chaired the meeting last night*. □ **présider**

'**chairlift** *noun* a set of seats hanging from a cable, used to take skiers *etc* up a mountain. □ **télésiège**

'**chairman, chairperson, chairwoman** *nouns* a person who takes charge of or directs a meeting. □ **président, ente**

'**chairmanship** *noun*. □ **présidence**

Address a male chairman as **Mr. Chairman**, and a female chairman as **Madam Chairman**.

chalet [ʃa'lei] *noun* 1 in Switzerland, a summer hut in the mountains for shepherds *etc*. □ **chalet**
2 a small (wooden) house used by travellers *etc*. □ **chalet**

chalice ['tʃalis] *noun* a wine-cup, *especially* one used in religious services. □ **calice**

chalk [tʃɔːk] *noun* 1 a white rock; a type of limestone. □ **craie**
2 (a piece of) a chalk-like substance used for writing (*especially* on blackboards): *a box of chalk*. □ **craie**

'**chalky** *adjective* 1 of or like chalk: *a chalky substance*. □ **crayeux**
2 white or pale: *Her face looked chalky*. □ **pâle**

'**chalkboard** *noun* a smooth board, *usually* green, for writing or drawing on with crayon or chalk. □ **tableau**

challenge ['tʃalindʒ] *verb* 1 to ask (someone) to take part in a contest: *He challenged his brother to a round of golf*. □ **défier**
2 to question (someone's authority or right, the truth of a statement *etc*). □ **mettre en doute**
■ *noun* 1 an invitation to a contest: *He accepted his brother's challenge to a fight*. □ **défi**
2 the act of questioning someone's right, a statement *etc*. □ **mise en question**

'**challenger** *noun*. □ **provocateur, trice**

'**challenging** *adjective* demanding effort; difficult: *a challenging job/idea*. □ **qui met au défi**

chamber ['tʃeimbə] *noun* 1 a room. □ **pièce**
2 the place where an assembly (*eg* Parliament) meets: *There were few members left in the chamber*. □ **chambre**
3 such an assembly: *the Upper and Lower Chambers*. □ **chambre**
4 an enclosed space or cavity *eg* the part of a gun which holds the bullets: *Many pistols have chambers for six bullets*. □ **chambre**

'**chambermaid** *noun* a female servant or hotel worker in charge of bedrooms. □ **femme de chambre**

chamber music music for a small group of players, suitable for a room rather than a large hall. □ **musique de chambre**

chameleon [kə'miːliən] *noun* a small lizard which is able to change colour. □ **caméléon**

chamois ['ʃamwaː, ʃami] – *plural* '**chamois** – *noun* 1 a small antelope living in mountainous country. □ **chamois**
2 (*also* **shammy** ['ʃami] – *plural* '**shammies**) (a piece of) soft washing leather *originally* made from its skin. □ **peau de chamois**

champ [tʃamp] *verb* (*especially* of horses) to chew noisily. □ **mâchonner**
champ at the bit impatient. □ **ronger son frein**

champagne [ʃam'pein] *noun* a type of white sparkling wine, *especially* from Champagne in France, often drunk at celebrations *etc*. □ **champagne**

81

champion ['tʃæmpiən] *noun* **1** in games, competitions *etc*, a competitor who has defeated all others: *this year's golf champion*; (*also adjective*) *a champion boxer*. □ **champion, onne**

2 a person who defends a cause: *a champion of human rights*. □ **champion, onne**

■ *verb* to defend or support: *She championed the cause of human rights for many years.* □ **se faire le champion de**

'**championship 1** a contest held to decide who is the champion: *The tennis championship will be decided this afternoon.* □ **championnat**

2 the act of defending or supporting: *her championship of civil rights.* □ **défense**

chance [tʃɑːns] *noun* **1** luck or fortune: *It was by chance that I found out the truth.* □ **hasard**

2 an opportunity: *Now you have a chance to do well.* □ **occasion**

3 a possibility: *He has no chance of winning.* □ **chance**

4 (a) risk: *There's an element of chance in this business deal.* □ **risque**

■ *verb* **1** to risk: *I may be too late but I'll just have to chance it.* □ **risquer le coup**

2 to happen accidentally or unexpectedly: *I chanced to see her last week.* □ **se produire par hasard**

■ *adjective* happening unexpectedly: *a chance meeting.* □ **inattendu**

'**chancy** *adjective* risky or uncertain: *a chancy arrangement.* □ **risqué**

chance on, upon 1 to meet by accident: *I chanced on a friend of yours.* □ **rencontrer par hasard**

2 to discover by accident: *I chanced upon some information.* □ **tomber sur**

by any chance used in enquiring about the possibility of something: *Are you by any chance free tonight?* □ **par hasard**

by chance by luck; without planning: *They met by chance.* □ **par (un heureux) hasard**

an even chance equal probability for and against: *We have an even chance of success.* □ **une chance sur deux**

the chances are it is likely (that): *The chances are I can't come tomorrow.* □ **il est (très) probable que**

chancellor ['tʃɑːnsələ] *noun* **1** a state or legal official of various kinds: *The Lord Chancellor is the head of the English legal system.* □ **chancelier, ière**

2 the head of a university. □ **recteur, rectrice**

chandelier [ʃandə'liə] *noun* a frame with many holders for lights, which hangs from the ceiling. □ **lustre**

change [tʃeindʒ] *verb* **1** to make or become different: *They have changed the time of the train; He has changed since I saw him last.* □ **changer**

2 to give or leave (one thing *etc* for another): *She changed my library books for me.* □ **échanger**

3 (*sometimes with* **into**) to remove (clothes *etc*) and replace them by clean or different ones: *I'm just going to change* (*my shirt*); *I'll change into an old pair of trousers.* □ **(se) changer, mettre**

4 (*with* **into**) to make into or become (something different): *The prince was changed into a frog.* □ **(se) changer (en)**

5 to give or receive (one kind of money for another): *Could you change this banknote for cash?* □ **changer**

■ *noun* **1** the process of becoming or making different: *The town is undergoing change.* □ **changement**

2 an instance of this: *a change in the program.* □ **changement**

3 a substitution of one thing for another: *a change of clothes.* □ **changement**

4 coins rather than paper money: *I'll have to give you a note – I have no change.* □ **monnaie**

5 money left over or given back from the amount given in payment: *She paid with a dollar and got 20 cents change.* □ **monnaie**

6 a holiday, rest *etc*: *He has been ill – the change will do him good.* □ **changement**

'**changeable** *adjective* changing often; liable to change often: *changeable moods.* □ **changeant**

change hands to pass into different ownership: *This car has changed hands three times.* □ **changer de main**

a change of heart a change in attitude. □ **changement d'avis**

change one's mind to alter one's intention or opinion (about something): *He was going to go to France but he changed his mind.* □ **changer d'avis**

for a change to be different; for variety: *We're tired of the car, so we'll walk for a change.* □ **pour changer**

changeling ['tʃeindʒliŋ] *noun* a child secretly left in place of another by the fairies *etc*. □ **enfant substitué, ée (par les fées)**

channel ['tʃanl] *noun* **1** the bed of a stream or other way through which liquid can flow: *a sewage channel.* □ **chenal**

2 a passage of deeper water in a river, through which ships can sail. □ **canal**

3 a narrow stretch of water joining two seas: *the English Channel.* □ **détroit**

4 a means of sending or receiving information *etc*: *We got the information through the usual channels.* □ **filière**

5 (in television, radio *etc*) a band of frequencies for sending or receiving signals: *My favourite show is broadcast on channel 3.* □ **chaîne**

■ *verb* – *past tense, past participle* '**channelled**, (*American*) '**channeled** – **1** to make a channel in. □ **creuser un canal dans**

2 to direct into a particular course: *He channelled all his energies into the project.* □ **canaliser**

chant [tʃɑːnt] *verb* **1** to recite in a singing manner: *The monks were chanting their prayers.* □ **psalmodier**

2 to repeat (a phrase, slogan *etc*) over and over out loud: *The crowd was chanting 'We want more!'* □ **scander**

■ *noun* **1** a kind of sacred song. □ **psalmodie**

2 a phrase or slogan constantly repeated: *'Stop the cuts!' was the chant.* □ **slogan (scandé)**

chaos ['keios] *noun* complete disorder or confusion: *The place was in utter chaos after the burglary.* □ **chaos**

cha'otic [-tik] *adjective.* □ **chaotique**

cha'otically *adverb.* □ **chaotiquement**

chap [tʃap] *noun* a man: *He's a nice chap.* □ **type**

chapel ['tʃapəl] *noun* **1** a place of Christian worship *eg* attached to an institution: *a college chapel.* □ **chapelle**

2 a part of a larger church, with its own altar. □ **chapelle**

chaperone ['ʃapəroun] *noun* someone, *especially* an older lady, who accompanies a girl in public. □ **chaperon**

■ *verb*: *Their aunt chaperoned the two girls at the ball.* □ **chaperonner**

chaplain ['tʃaplin] *noun* a clergyman attached to a ship, regiment *etc.* □ **aumônier**

chapped [tʃapt] *adjective* (of skin) cracked and rough: *chapped lips.* □ **gercé**

chapter ['tʃaptə] *noun* a main division of a book: *There are fifteen chapters in his new book.* □ **chapitre**
a chapter of accidents a whole series of disasters. □ **kyrielle de malheurs**

char [tʃaː] – *past tense, past participle* **charred** – *verb* to burn or turn black by fire or heat: *The wood was charred by the intense heat.* □ **carboniser**

character ['karəktə] *noun* **1** the set of qualities that make someone or something different from others; type: *You can tell a man's character from his handwriting; Publicity of this character is not good for the firm.* □ **caractère; genre**
2 a set of qualities that are considered admirable in some way: *She showed great character in dealing with the danger.* □ **caractère**
3 reputation: *They tried to damage her character.* □ **réputation**
4 a person in a play, novel *etc*: *Rosencrantz is a minor character in Shakespeare's 'Hamlet'.* □ **personnage**
5 an odd or amusing person: *This fellow's quite a character!* □ **numéro**
6 a letter used in typing *etc*: *Some characters on this typewriter are broken.* □ **caractère**
,character'istic *adjective* (*negative* **uncharacteristic**) typical (of a person *etc*): *He spoke with characteristic shyness; That kind of behaviour is characteristic of him.* □ **typique**
■ *noun* a typical quality: *It is one of his characteristics to be obstinate.* □ **caractéristique**
,characte'ristically *adverb.* □ **typiquement**
'characterize, 'characterise *verb* **1** to be the obvious feature of: *The giraffe is characterized by its long neck.* □ **caractériser**
2 to describe (as): *She characterized him as weak and indecisive.* □ **décrire**
,characteri'zation, ,characteri'sation *noun.* □ **caractérisation**

charade [ʃə'reid] *noun* a piece of ridiculous pretence which is so obvious that it does not deceive anyone. □ **parodie**
cha'rades *noun singular* a game in which each syllable of a word, and then the whole word, is acted and the audience has to guess the word. □ **charade**

charcoal ['tʃaːkoul] *noun* the black part of partly burned wood *etc*, used as fuel and for drawing. □ **charbon de bois, fusain**

charge [tʃaːdʒ] *verb* **1** to ask as the price (for something): *They charge 50 cents for a litre of milk, but they don't charge for delivery.* □ **faire payer**
2 to make a note of (a sum of money) as being owed:

Charge the bill to my account. □ **mettre sur le compte de qqn**
3 (*with* **with**) to accuse (of something illegal): *I was charged with theft.* □ **accuser**
4 to attack by moving quickly (towards): *We charged (towards) the enemy on horseback.* □ **charger**
5 to rush: *The children charged down the hill.* □ **foncer**
6 to make or become filled with electricity: *Please charge my car battery.* □ **charger**
7 to load (a gun *etc*). □ **charger**
8 to make (a person) responsible for (a task *etc*): *She was charged with seeing that everything went well.* □ **charger (qqn) de**
■ *noun* **1** a price or fee: *What is the charge for a telephone call?* □ **prix, coût**
2 something with which a person is accused: *He faces three charges of murder.* □ **accusation**
3 an attack made by moving quickly: *the charge of the Light Brigade.* □ **charge**
4 the electricity in something: *a positive or negative charge.* □ **charge**
5 someone one takes care of: *These children are my charges.* □ **personne à charge**
6 a quantity of gunpowder: *Put the charge in place and light the fuse.* □ **charge**
'charger *noun* formerly, a horse used in battle. □ **cheval de bataille**
in charge of responsible for: *I'm in charge of thirty men.* □ **responsable de**
in someone's charge in the care of someone: *You can leave the children in my charge.* □ **à la garde de**
take charge 1 (*with* **of**) to begin to control, organize *etc*: *The department was in chaos until he took charge (of it).* □ **prendre la direction**
2 (*with* **of**) to take into one's care: *The policeman took charge of the gun.* □ **se charger de**

chariot ['tʃariət] *noun* a two-wheeled vehicle used in ancient warfare or racing. □ **char**
chario'teer *noun* a chariot driver. □ **conducteur, trice de char**

charity ['tʃarəti] – *plural* **'charities** – *noun* **1** kindness (*especially* in giving money to poor people): *She gave clothes to the gypsies out of charity.* □ **charité**
2 an organization set up to collect money for the needy, for medical research *etc*: *Many charities sent money to help the victims of the disaster.* □ **œuvre de bienfaisance**
'charitable *adjective* **1** (*negative* **uncharitable**) kind. □ **charitable**
2 of a charity: *a charitable organization.* □ **de bienfaisance**
'charitably *adverb.* □ **charitablement**

charm [tʃaːm] *noun* **1** (a) pleasant quality or attraction: *Her charm made up for her lack of beauty.* □ **charme**
2 a magical spell: *The witch recited a charm.* □ **sortilège**
3 something believed to have the power of magic or good luck: *You wore a lucky charm.* □ **fétiche**
■ *verb* **1** to attract and delight: *He can charm anyone.* □ **charmer**
2 to influence by magic: *I charmed the snake from its basket.* □ **charmer**

'**charming** *adjective* very attractive: *a charming smile.* □ **charmant**

'**charmingly** *adverb.* □ **de façon charmante**

chart [tʃɑːt] *noun* **1** a map of part of the sea. □ **carte (marine)**
2 a table or diagram giving information: *a weather chart.* □ **carte, graphique**
■ *verb* **1** to make a chart of: *She charted the Black Sea.* □ **dresser la carte de**
2 to make a table of information about: *I'm charting our progress.* □ **faire le graphique de**

charter ['tʃɑːtə] *noun* a formal document giving rights or privileges. □ **charte**
■ *verb* to let or hire (a ship, aircraft *etc*) on contract: *The travel company had chartered three aircraft for their holiday flights.* □ **affréter**
■ *adjective: a charter plane; a charter flight.* □ **vol nolisé**

chary ['tʃeəri] *adjective* (with **of**) cautious: *Be chary of lending money to someone you don't know very well.* □ **prudent**

chase [tʃeis] *verb* **1** to run after; to pursue: *He chased after them but did not catch them; We chased them by car.* □ **poursuivre**
2 (*with* **away, off** *etc*) to cause to run away: *I often have to chase the boys away from my fruit trees.* □ **chasser**
■ *noun* **1** an act of chasing: *We caught her after a 120 km/h chase.* □ **poursuite**
2 hunting (of animals): *the pleasures of the chase.* □ **chasse**
give chase to chase: *The thieves ran off and the policeman gave chase.* □ **poursuivre**

chasm ['kazəm] *noun* a deep opening between high rocks *etc*: *The climber could not cross the chasm.* □ **abîme**

chassis ['ʃasi] – *plural* '**chassis** [-z] – *noun* the frame of a car *etc*. □ **châssis**

chaste [tʃeist] *adjective* pure and virtuous. □ **chaste**
chastity ['tʃastəti] *noun.* □ **chasteté; pudeur**
'**chasteness** *noun.* □ **chasteté**

chasten ['tʃeisn] *verb* to humble by punishment, suffering *etc.* □ **châtier**

chastise [tʃas'taiz] *verb* to punish by beating *etc.* □ **châtier**
chastisement ['tʃastizmənt] *noun.* □ **châtiment**

chastity *see* **chaste.**

chat [tʃat] – *past tense, past participle* '**chatted** – *verb* to talk in a friendly and informal way: *They chatted about the weather.* □ **bavarder**
■ *noun* (a) friendly and informal talk: *a chat over coffee; friend's chat.* □ **brin de causette**
'**chatty** *adjective* **1** fond of chatting: *a chatty old friend.* □ **bavard**
2 having a friendly style: *a chatty letter.* □ **familier**

chatter ['tʃatə] *verb* **1** to talk quickly and noisily about unimportant things: *The children chattered among themselves.* □ **jacasser**
2 (of teeth) to knock together with the cold *etc*: *teeth chattering with terror.* □ **claquer**
■ *noun* rapid, noisy talk: *childish chatter.* □ **jacassement**
'**chatterbox** *noun* a talkative person. □ **moulin à paroles**

chauffeur ['ʃoufər, ʃou'fəːr] *noun* a person employed as a car-driver for a rich or important person. □ **chauffeur**

chauvinism ['ʃouvinizəm] *noun* unthinking enthusiasm for a particular country, cause *etc.* □ **chauvinisme**
'**chauvinist** *noun.* □ **chauvin, ine**
,**chauvi'nistic** *adjective.* □ **chauvin**
male chauvinist a man who believes that women are inferior to men. □ **phallocrate**

cheap [tʃiːp] *adjective* **1** low in price: *Eggs are cheap just now.* □ **bon marché**
2 of poor quality; vulgar; contemptible: *cheap jewellery; a cheap trick.* □ **de mauvaise qualité, minable**
'**cheaply** *adverb.* □ **à bon marché**
'**cheapness** *noun.* □ **bas prix**

cheat [tʃiːt] *verb* to act dishonestly to gain an advantage: *They cheat at cards; He was cheated (out of ten dollars).* □ **tricher**
■ *noun* **1** a person who cheats: *He only wins because he is a cheat.* □ **tricheur, euse**
2 a dishonest trick. □ **tricherie**

check [tʃek] *verb* **1** to see if something (*eg* a sum) is correct or accurate: *Will you check my addition?* □ **vérifier**
2 to see if something (*eg* a machine) is in good condition or working properly: *Have you checked the engine (over)?* □ **vérifier**
3 to hold back; to stop: *We've checked the flow of water from the burst pipe.* □ **arrêter**
■ *noun* **1** an act of testing or checking. □ **vérification**
2 something which prevents or holds back: *a check on imports.* □ **frein**
3 in chess, a position in which the king is attacked: *She put her opponent's king in check.* □ **échec**
4 a pattern of squares: *I like the red check on that material.* □ **carreaux**
5 a ticket received in return for handing in baggage *etc.* □ **bulletin de consigne**
6 a bill: *The check please, waiter!* □ **addition**
7 (*American*) a cheque. □ **chèque**
checked *adjective* having a pattern of check: *She wore a checked skirt; Is the material checked or striped?* □ **à carreaux**
'**checkbook** *noun* (*American*) a chequebook. □ **carnet de chèques**
'**checkmate** *noun* in chess, a position from which the king cannot escape. □ **échec et mat**
■ *verb* to put (an opponent's king) in this position. □ **faire échec et mat**
'**checkout** *noun* a place where payment is made for goods bought in a supermarket. □ **caisse (de sortie)**
'**checkpoint** *noun* a barrier where cars, passports *etc* are inspected, or a point that contestants in a race must pass. □ **contrôle**
'**checkup** *noun* a medical examination to discover the state of a person's health: *my annual checkup.* □ **bilan de santé**
check in to arrive (at a hotel) and sign the register: *We checked in last night.* □ **s'inscrire (à un hôtel)**
check out 1 to leave (a hotel), paying one's bill *etc*: *You must check out before 12 o'clock.* □ **régler la note**

2 to test: *I'll check out your story.* □ **vérifier**

check up (on) to investigate to see if (someone or something) is reliable, honest, true *etc*: *Have you been checking up on me?* □ **se renseigner sur**

checkers *noun* 1 *singular* a game for two people, played on a board (a '**checkerboard**') exactly like a chessboard, with twenty-four disks. □ **(jeu de) dames**
2 *plural* the discs. □ **dames, pions**

cheek [tʃiːk] *noun* 1 the side of the face below the eye: *pink cheeks.* □ **joue**
2 impudence or disrespectful behaviour: *He had the cheek to refuse me entrance.* □ **culot**
'**cheeky** *adjective* impudent: *a cheeky remark.* □ **effronté**
'**cheekiness** *noun.* □ **effronterie**
cheekbone *noun* the prominent bone of the face directly below the eye: *Some girls wear blush to make their cheekbones stand out.* □ **pommette**

cheep [tʃiːp] *verb* to make the shrill sound of a young bird. □ **piauler**
■ *noun* 1 such a sound. □ **piaulement**
2 a single sound or word: *I have not heard a cheep from the baby since he went to bed.* □ **bruit**

cheer [tʃiə] *noun* 1 a shout of approval, encouragement or welcome: *Three cheers for the newlyweds!* □ **acclamation(s)**
2 mood: *Be of good cheer.* □ **courage**
■ *verb* to give a shout of approval *etc* (to): *The crowd cheered the new champion.* □ **encourager**
'**cheerful** *adjective* full of, or causing, happiness: *a cheerful smile; cheerful news.* □ **joyeux**
'**cheerfully** *adverb.* □ **joyeusement**
'**cheerfulness** *noun.* □ **gaieté**
'**cheerless** *adjective* gloomy: *a cheerless room.* □ **triste**
cheers! *interjection* 1 used as a toast when drinking. □ **à la votre**
2 cheerio! □ **salut!**
3 thanks! □ **merci!**
'**cheery** *adjective* lively and happy. □ **joyeux**
'**cheerily** *adverb.* □ **gaiement**
'**cheeriness** *noun.* □ **gaieté**
cheer up to make or become (more cheerful): *He cheered up when he saw her; The flowers will cheer you up.* □ **s'égayer**

cheerio! [tʃəri'ou] *interjection* used when leaving someone. □ **au revoir!**

cheese [tʃiːz] *noun* (any type of) a food prepared from the curd of milk and *usually* pressed into a mass or shape: *Cheese is full of protein.* □ **fromage**
'**cheesecake** *noun* a type of sweet food made with cheese *etc*. □ **gâteau au fromage**
cheesed off bored. □ **découragé**

cheetah ['tʃiːtə] *noun* a very swift-running animal of the cat family. □ **guépard**

chef [ʃef] *noun* a head cook, in a hotel *etc*. □ **chef**

chemical, chemist *see* **chemistry.**

chemistry ['kemistri] *noun* (the science that deals with) the nature of substances and the ways in which they act on, or combine with, each other: *Chemistry was his favourite subject; the chemistry of the blood.* □ **chimie**
'**chemical** *adjective* of chemistry: *a chemical reaction.*
□ **chimique**
■ *noun* a substance used in or obtained by a chemical process: *Some chemicals give off harmful fumes.* □ **produit chimique**
'**chemist** *noun* a scientist who studies or works in chemistry: *an industrial chemist.* □ **chimiste**

cheongsam [tʃi'oŋ'sam] *noun* a close-fitting garment with a high, round collar and slits on the skirt, worn by women in China. □ **robe-fourreau chinoise**

cheque, (*American*) **check** [tʃek] *noun* a written order on a printed form telling a bank to pay money to the person named: *to pay by cheque.* □ **chèque**
'**chequebook** *noun* a book of cheque forms. □ **chéquier**

cherish ['tʃeriʃ] *verb* 1 to protect and love (a person): *She cherishes that child.* □ **chérir**
2 to keep (a hope, idea *etc*) in the mind: *She cherishes the hope that they will return.* □ **nourrir**

cherry ['tʃeri] – *plural* '**cherries** – *noun* a type of small *usually* red fruit with a stone. □ **cerise**
cherry tree *noun* a woody plant with a trunk and branches that bear leaves, cherry blossoms and small single-stoned fruit called cherries: *Kyle climbed the cherry tree to pick cherries for a pie.* □ **cerisier**

cherub ['tʃerəb] *noun* an angel with wings and the plump face and body of a child. □ **chérubin**
che'rubic [-'ruː-] *adjective.* □ **angélique**

chess [tʃes] *noun* a game for two played with thirty-two (*usually* black and white) pieces ('**chessmen**') on a board ('**chessboard**') with sixty-four (*usually* black and white) squares. □ **échecs**
chessboard *noun* the flat surface resembling a checkerboard where the game of chess is played: *Andrea's king was the last chess piece on the chessboard, so she won the game.* □ **échiquier**

chest[1] [tʃest] *noun* the part of the body between the neck and waist, containing the heart and the lungs: *a severe pain in his chest.* □ **poitrine**
get something off one's chest to tell the truth about something that is worrying one. □ **dire ce qu'on a sur le cœur**

chest[2] [tʃest] *noun* a large, strong wooden or metal box: *The sheets were kept in a wooden chest.* □ **coffre**
chest of drawers a piece of furniture fitted with several drawers. □ **commode**

chestnut ['tʃesnʌt] 1 a reddish-brown nut (one type being edible). □ **châtaigne**
2 a reddish-brown horse. □ **alezan**
3 a boring old joke or story. □ **blague éculée**
■ *adjective* of the colour of ripe chestnuts: *chestnut hair.* □ **châtain**

chew [tʃuː] *verb* to break (food *etc*) with the teeth before swallowing: *If you chew your food properly it is easier to digest.* □ **mâcher**
'**chewing-gum** *noun* a type of sweet made from sweetened and flavoured gum. □ **gomme à mâcher**

chic [ʃiːk] *adjective* stylish: *They look very chic.* □ **chic**

chick [tʃik] *noun* a baby bird: *One of the chicks fell out of the blackbird's nest.* □ **oisillon, poussin**

chicken ['tʃikin] *noun* 1 a young bird, *especially* a young hen: *She keeps chickens.* □ **poulet(te)**

2 its flesh used as food: *a plate of fried chicken.* □ **poulet**

,**chicken-'hearted** *adjective* cowardly. □ **peureux**

'**chicken-pox** *noun* an infectious disease with fever and red itchy spots. □ **varicelle**

chicken out to avoid doing something because of cowardice: *He chickened out at the last minute.* □ **se dégonfler**

chicory ['tʃikəri] *noun* a plant whose leaves are used in salads and whose root is ground and mixed with coffee. □ **chicorée**

chide [tʃaid] *verb* to scold. □ **gronder**

chief [tʃiːf] *adjective* greatest in importance *etc*: *the chief cause of disease.* □ **principal**

■ *noun* the head of a clan or tribe, or a department, business *etc.* □ **chef**

'**chiefly** *adverb* mainly: *She became ill chiefly because she did not eat enough.* □ **surtout**

'**chieftain** [-tən] *noun* the head of a clan, tribe *etc.* □ **chef**

chiffon [ʃi'fon] *noun, adjective* (of) a thin, light material made from silk *etc*: *a chiffon dress.* □ **mousseline (de soie)**

chiku, ciku ['tʃiːkuː] *noun* a sweet tropical fruit with a thin brown skin. □ **sorte de fruit tropical**

child [tʃaild] – *plural* **children** ['tʃildrən] – *noun* 1 a young human being of either sex. □ **enfant**

2 a son or daughter: *His youngest child is five years old.* □ **enfant**

'**childhood** *noun* the state or time of being a child: *Her childhood was a time of happiness.* □ **enfance**

'**childish** *adjective* like a child; silly: *a childish remark.* □ **enfantin, puéril**

'**childishly** *adverb.* □ **puérilement**

'**childishness** *noun.* □ **enfantillage, puérilité**

'**childless** *adjective* having no children: *the childless couple.* □ **sans enfants**

'**childlike** *adjective* innocent; like a child: *childlike faith; trustful and childlike.* □ **pur, innocent**

'**childbirth** *noun* the act of giving birth to a child: *She died in childbirth.* □ **accouchement**

child's play something very easy: *Climbing that hill will be child's play.* □ **jeu d'enfant**

chili, chilli ['tʃili] – *plurals* '**chili(e)s, 'chilli(e)s** – *noun* the hot-tasting pod of a type of pepper, often dried, powdered and used in sauces *etc.* □ **piment fort**

chill [tʃil] *noun* 1 coldness: *There's a chill in the air.* □ **froid**

2 an illness which causes shivering: *I think I've caught a chill.* □ **refroidissement**

■ *adjective* cold: *a chillwind.* □ **froid**

■ *verb* to make cold (without freezing): *Have you chilled the wine?* □ **(mettre à) rafraichir**

'**chilly** *adjective* cold: *a chilly day.* □ **froid**

'**chilliness** *noun.* □ **froid**

chime [tʃaim] *noun* (the ringing of) a set of tuned bells: *the chime of the clock.* □ **carillon**

■ *verb* 1 to (cause to) ring: *The church bells chimed.* □ **carillonner**

2 (of a clock) to indicate the time by chiming: *The clock chimed 9 o'clock.* □ **sonner**

chimney ['tʃimni] *noun* a passage for the escape of smoke *etc* from a fireplace or furnace: *a factory chimney.* □ **cheminée**

chimpanzee [tʃimpən'ziː] *noun* a type of small African ape. □ **chimpanzé**

chin [tʃin] *noun* the part of the face below the mouth: *His beard completely covers his chin.* □ **menton**

china ['tʃainə] *noun* a fine kind of baked and glazed clay; porcelain: *a plate made of china*; (*also adjective*) *a china vase.* □ **(de) porcelaine**

Chinese [tʃainiːz] *adjective* of China or its inhabitants: *Chinese celebrations often include fireworks.* □ **chinois, oise**

■ *noun* the people or standard language of China: *The Chinese believe that the dragon is a symbol of strength; It is difficult for foreigners to learn how to speak Chinese.* □ **Chinois, oise**

chink [tʃiŋk] *noun* a narrow opening: *a chink in the curtains; There was no chink of light in the room.* □ **fente**

chip [tʃip] – *past tense, past participle* **chipped** – *verb* to knock or strike small pieces off: *This glass (was) chipped when I knocked it over.* □ **ébrécher**

■ *noun* 1 a place from which a small piece is broken: *There's a chip in the edge of this saucer.* □ **ébréchure**

2 a counter representing a certain value, used in gambling. □ **jeton**

chip in 1 to interrupt: *She chipped in with a remark.* □ **intervenir**

2 to give (money): *He'll chip in with a dollar.* □ **contribuer**

chipmunk [tʃipmʌŋk] *noun* a type of North American squirrel with a bushy tail and black and white-striped back. □ **tamia**

chiropodist [ki'ropədist] *noun* a person who treats minor disorders of the feet. □ **pédicure**

chi'ropody *noun* the work of a chiropodist. □ **podologie, soins du pied**

chirp [tʃəːp], **chirrup** ['tʃirəp] *nouns* the sharp, shrill sound of certain birds and insects. □ **gazouillis**

■ *verb* to make such a sound. □ **gazouiller**

chirpy ['tʃəːpi] *adjective* lively and happy: *a chirpy tune; I'm feeling chirpy today.* □ **de bonne humeur**

chisel ['tʃizl] *noun* a tool with a cutting edge at the end. □ **ciseau**

■ *verb* – *past tense, past participle* '**chiselled, (American)** '**chiseled** – to cut or carve (wood *etc*) with a chisel. □ **ciseler**

chit [tʃit] *noun* a brief note: *You must hand in a chit stating your expenses before you receive any money.* □ **note**

chivalry ['ʃivəlri] *noun* 1 kindness and courteousness *especially* towards women or the weak. □ **courtoisie**

2 the principles of behaviour of medieval knights. □ **les règles de la chevalerie**

'**chivalrous** *adjective* (*negative* **unchivalrous**). □ **chevaleresque**

chlorine ['kloːriːn] *noun* an element, a yellowish-green gas with a suffocating smell, used as a disinfectant *etc*: *They put too much chlorine in the swimming pool.* □ **chlore**

chloroform ['klorəfoːm] *noun* a liquid, the vapour of

which, when breathed in, causes unconsciousness. □ chloroforme

chlorophyll ['klɔrəfil] *noun* the colouring matter of the green parts of plants. □ **chlorophylle**

chocolate ['tʃɒkələt] *noun* **1** a paste made from the seeds of the cacao tree. □ **chocolat**
2 a sweet or drink made from it: *Have a chocolate*; *a cup of chocolate*. □ **chocolat**
■ *adjective* of, made from, covered with, chocolate: *chocolate ice cream*; *chocolate biscuits*. □ **au/en/de chocolat**

choice [tʃɔis] *noun* **1** an act or the power of choosing: *You have no choice – you must do it*. □ **choix**
2 a thing chosen: *Which car was your original choice?* □ **choix**

choir ['kwaiə] *noun* a group of singers: *I used to sing in the church choir*. □ **chœur**

choke [tʃouk] *verb* **1** to (cause to) stop, or partly stop, breathing: *The gas choked him*; *She choked to death*. □ **suffoquer, étouffer**
2 to block: *This pipe was choked with dirt*. □ **boucher**
■ *noun* an apparatus in a car engine *etc* to prevent the passage of too much air when starting the engine. □ **étrangleur**

cholera ['kɒlərə] *noun* a highly infectious, often fatal disease occurring in hot countries. □ **choléra**

choose [tʃuːz] – *past tense* **chose** [tʃouz]: *past participle* **chosen** ['tʃouzn] – *verb* **1** to take (one thing rather than another from a number of things) according to what one wants: *Always choose (a book) carefully*. □ **choisir**
2 to decide (on one course of action rather than another): *If he chooses to resign, let him do so*. □ **décider (de)**
nothing/not much to choose between hardly any difference between: *There's not much to choose between the two methods*. □ **se valoir**

chop[1] [tʃɒp] – *past tense, past participle* **chopped** – *verb* (*sometimes with* **up**) to cut (into small pieces): *He chopped up the vegetables*. □ **hacher**
■ *noun* a slice of mutton, pork *etc* containing a rib. □ **côtelette**
'chopper *noun* **1** an instrument for chopping. □ **hachoir 2** a helicopter. □ **hélicoptère**
'choppy *adjective* (of the sea) rough. □ **agité**
'choppiness *noun*. □ **agitation (de la mer)**
chop and change to keep changing (*especially* one's mind). □ **être une vraie girouette**
chop down to cause (*especially* a tree) to fall by cutting it with an axe: *She chopped down the fir tree*. □ **abattre**

chop[2] [tʃɒp] *noun* (*in plural*) the jaws or mouth, *especially* of an animal: *the wolf's chops*. □ **mâchoire(s)**

chopper, choppy *see* chop[1].

chopsticks ['tʃɒpstiks] *noun plural* two small sticks of wood, ivory *etc* used by the Chinese *etc* to eat with. □ **baguettes**

choral ['kɔːrəl] *adjective* of, for, or to be sung by, a choir: *choral music*. □ **choral**

chord [kɔːd] *noun* in music, a number of notes played together. □ **accord**

chore [tʃɔː] *noun* a piece of housework or other hard or

dull job. □ **corvée**

chorister ['kɒristə] *noun* a member of a (church) choir, *especially* a boy. □ **choriste**

chorus ['kɔːrəs] – *plural* **'choruses** – *noun* **1** a group of singers: *the festival chorus*. □ **chœur**
2 a group of singers and dancers in a musical show. □ **troupe**
3 part of a song repeated after each verse: *The audience joined in the chorus*. □ **refrain**
4 something said or shouted by a number of people together: *He was greeted by a chorus of cheers*. □ **concert**
■ *verb* to sing or say together: *The children chorused 'Goodbye, Miss Smith'*. □ **chanter/dire en chœur**

chose, chosen *see* choose.

Christ [kraist] *noun* Jesus. □ **le Christ**

christen ['krisn] *verb* **1** to baptize into the Christian church: *The priest christened three babies today*. □ **baptiser**
2 to give (a name) to: *She was christened Joanna*. □ **nommer**

Christian ['kristʃən] *noun* a follower of or a believer in Christ. □ **chrétien, ienne**
■ *adjective*: *She had a Christian upbringing*. □ **chrétien**
,Christi'anity [-'anəti] *noun* the religion of Christ. □ **christianisme**
Christian name (**given name**) the personal name given in addition to the surname: *Peter is his Christian name*. □ **nom de baptême**

Christmas ['krisməs] *noun* an annual festival in memory of the birth of Christ, held on December 25, Christmas Day. □ **Noël**
Christmas Eve December 24. □ **veille de Noël**
'Christmas tree *noun* a (*usually* fir) tree on which decorations and Christmas gifts are hung. □ **arbre de Noël**

chromatic [krou'matik]: **chromatic scale** a series of musical notes, each separated from the next by a semitone. □ **chromatique**

chrome [kroum] *noun* an alloy of chromium and steel used for car-fittings *etc*. □ **chrome**

chromium ['kroumiəm] *noun* a metallic element used in various metal alloys. □ **chrome**

chronic ['krɒnik] *adjective* (*especially* of a disease) lasting a long time: *a chronic illness*. □ **chronique**
'chronically *adverb*. □ **chroniquement**

chronicle ['krɒnikl] *noun* a record of (*especially* historical) events in order of time. □ **chronique**
■ *verb* to make such a record. □ **faire la chronique de**
'chronicler *noun*. □ **chroniqueur, euse**

chronology [krə'nɒlədʒi] *noun* (a list illustrating) the order of events in time. □ **chronologie**
chronological [krɒnə'lɒdʒikəl] *adjective*. □ **chronologique**
,chrono'logically *adverb*. □ **chronologiquement**

chrysalis ['krisəlis] *noun* the form taken by some insects (*eg* butterflies) at an early stage in their development. □ **chrysalide**

chrysanthemum [kri'sanθəməm] *noun* a type of garden flower with a large, bushy head. □ **chrysanthème**

chubby ['tʃʌbi] *adjective* plump: *a baby's chubby face*.

87

□ potelé

chuck [tʃʌk] *verb* to throw: *Chuck this rubbish in the garbage-can.* □ **jeter**

chuckle ['tʃʌkl] *verb* to laugh quietly: *She sat chuckling over a funny book.* □ **glousser**

■ *noun* such a laugh. □ **petit rire (étouffé)**

chum [tʃʌm] *noun* a close friend: *a school chum.* □ **copain**

chunk [tʃʌŋk] *noun* a thick piece of anything, as wood, bread *etc*: *chunks of meat.* □ **gros morceau**

'**chunky** *adjective* **1** solid and strong: *a chunky body.* □ **trapu**

2 containing chunks. □ **qui contient de gros morceaux**

church [tʃəːtʃ] *noun* **1** a building for public Christian worship. □ **église**

2 a group of Christians considered as a whole: *the Catholic Church.* □ **Eglise**

'**churchyard** *noun* the burial ground around a church. □ **cimetière**

churn [tʃəːn] *noun* a machine for making butter. □ **baratte**

chute [ʃuːt] *noun* **1** a sloping channel for sending down water, rubbish *etc*. □ **descente**

2 a similar structure in a playground, for children to slide down. □ **glissoire**

3 a parachute. □ **parachute**

chutney ['tʃʌtni] *noun* a sauce made from fruit, vegetables and spices: *tomato chutney.* □ **chutney**

cicada [si'kɑːdə] *noun* an insect that makes a loud chirping noise. □ **cigale**

cider ['saidə] *noun* an alcoholic drink made from apples. □ **cidre**

cigar [si'gɑː] *noun* a roll of tobacco leaves for smoking. □ **cigare**

cigarette [sigə'ret, 'sigəret] *noun* a tube of finely cut tobacco rolled in thin paper. □ **cigarette**

cigarette butt *noun* the small, useless piece of a cigarette that remains after it has been smoked: *The ashtray was full of cigarette butts.* □ **mégot**

ciku *see* **chiku.**

cinch [sintʃ] *noun* **1** a certainty: *It's a cinch!* □ **certitude**

2 something easy. □ **jeu d'enfant**

cinder ['sində] *noun* a piece of burnt coal, wood *etc*: *the cinders in the fireplace.* □ **cendre**

cine-camera ['sinikamərə] *noun* a camera for taking moving pictures. □ **caméra**

cinema ['sinəmə] *noun* a building in which films are shown: *She enjoys going to the cinema but she prefers the theatre.* □ **cinéma**

cinnamon ['sinəmən] *noun* the bark of a tree of the laurel family, used as a spice. □ **cannelle**

cipher ['saifə] *noun* secret writing; a code: *The message was written in cipher.* □ **code**

circle ['səːkl] *noun* **1** a figure (O) bounded by one line, every point on which is equally distant from the centre. □ **cercle**

2 something in the form of a circle: *He was surrounded by a circle of admirers.* □ **cercle**

3 a group of people: *a circle of close friends*; *wealthy circles.* □ **cercle, milieu**

4 a balcony in a theatre *etc*: *We sat in the circle at the opera.* □ **balcon**

■ *verb* **1** to move in a circle around something: *The cows circled around the farmer who was bringing their food.* □ **tourner autour de**

2 to draw a circle around: *Please circle the word you think is wrong.* □ **encercler**

circuit ['səːkit] *noun* **1** a journey or course around something: *the earth's circuit around the sun*; *three circuits of the race-track.* □ **tour**

2 a race-track, running-track *etc*. □ **circuit**

3 the path of an electric current and the parts through which it passes. □ **circuit**

4 a journey or tour made regularly and repeatedly *eg* by salesmen, sportsmen *etc*. □ **tournée**

circuitous [səː'kjuitəs] *adjective* round-about; not direct: *a circuitous route.* □ **détourné**

circular ['səːkjulə] *adjective* **1** having the form of a circle: *a circular piece of paper.* □ **circulaire**

2 leading back to the point from which it started: *a circular road.* □ **circulaire**

■ *noun* a notice *etc*, especially advertising something, sent to a number of persons: *We often get circulars advertising holidays.* □ **circulaire**

circu'larity [-'la-] *noun.* □ **circularité**

circulate ['səːkjuleit] *verb* **1** to (cause to) go around in a fixed path coming back to a starting-point: *Blood circulates through the body.* □ **circuler**

2 to (cause to) spread or pass around (news *etc*): *There's a rumour circulating that she is getting married.* □ **(faire) circuler**

,**circu'lation** *noun.* □ **circulation**

'**circulatory** [-lə-] *adjective.* □ **circulatoire**

circumcise ['səːkəmsaiz] *verb* to remove the foreskin of (a man). □ **circoncire**

,**circum'cision** [-'siʒən] *noun.* □ **circoncision**

circumference [sə'kʌmfərəns] *noun* (the length of) the boundary line of a circle or anything circular in shape: *the circumference of a circle/wheel.* □ **circonférence**

circumnavigate [səːkəm'navigeit] *verb* to sail around (especially the world). □ **naviguer autour de**

,**circum,navi'gation** *noun.* □ **circumnavigation**

circumstance ['səːkəmstəns] *noun* a condition (time, place *etc*) connected with an event: *In the circumstances, I don't see what else I could have done.* □ **circonstance**

circus ['səːkəs] – *plural* '**circuses** – *noun* a travelling show with performances by horsemen, acrobats, animals *etc*: *The children went to the circus.* □ **cirque**

cistern ['sistən] *noun* a tank *etc* for storing water (especially for a lavatory). □ **citerne**

citadel ['sitədl] *noun* a fortress, especially in or near a city. □ **citadelle**

citizen ['sitizn] *noun* **1** an inhabitant of a city or town: *a citizen of London.* □ **habitant, ante**

2 a member of a state or country: *a Canadian citizen*; *a citizen of the USA.* □ **citoyen, enne**

'**citizenship** *noun* the status, rights and duties of a citizen, especially of a particular country *etc*: *He has applied for Canadian citizenship.* □ **citoyenneté**

citric ['sitrik]: **citric acid** the acid which gives lemons and certain other fruits their sourness. □ **citrique**

citrus fruit ['sitrəs] a type of fruit including the lemon, orange, lime *etc.* □ **agrumes**

city ['siti] – *plural* 'cities – *noun* **1** a very large town. □ **grande ville, cité**

2 a town, *usually* with a cathedral, granted special rights. □ **ville épiscopale**

civic ['sivik] *adjective* of or belonging to a city or citizen: *Our offices are in the new civic centre*; *civic duties*. □ **civique**

civil ['sivl] *adjective* **1** polite, courteous. □ **poli**

2 of the state or community: *civil rights*. □ **civique**

3 ordinary; not military or religious: *civil life*. □ **civil**

4 concerned with law cases which are not criminal. □ **civil**

civilian [si'viljən] *noun* a person who has a civil job, not in the armed forces. □ **civil, ile**

civility [si'viləti] *noun* politeness: *Treat strangers with civility*. □ **courtoisie**

'**civilly** *adverb* politely. □ **courtoisement**

civil engineer *see* **engineer**.

civil liberties/rights the rights of a citizen according to the law of the country. □ **libertés civiques**

civil servant a member of the civil service. □ **fonctionnaire**

civil service the organization which runs the administration of a state. □ **fonction publique**

civil war (a) war between citizens of the same state: *the American Civil War*. □ **guerre civile**

civilize, civilise ['sivilaiz] *verb* to change the ways of (a primitive people) to those found in a more advanced type of society: *The Romans tried to civilize the ancient Britons*. □ **civiliser**

,**civili'zation,** ,**civili'sation** *noun* **1** the act of civilizing, or process or state of being civilized. □ **civilisation**

2 a civilized people and their way of life: *the ancient civilizations of Egypt and Greece*. □ **civilisation**

clad [klad] *adjective* **1** clothed: *clad in silk*; *leather-clad motorcyclists*. □ **vêtu (de)**

2 covered: *iron-clad warships*. □ **revêtu**

claim [kleim] *verb* **1** to say that something is a fact: *He claims to be the best runner in the class*. □ **prétendre**

2 to demand as a right: *You must claim your money back if the goods are damaged*. □ **réclamer**

3 to state that one is the owner of: *Does anyone claim this book?* □ **revendiquer**

■ *noun* **1** a statement (that something is a fact): *Her claim that she was the millionaire's daughter was disproved*. □ **affirmation**

2 (a demand for) a payment of compensation *etc*: *a claim for damages against her employer*. □ **réclamation**

3 a demand for something which (one says) one owns or has a right to: *a rightful claim to the money*. □ **revendication**

'**claimant** *noun* a person who makes a claim: *a claimant to the throne*. □ **prétendant, ante**

clair'voyance [kleə'vviəns] *noun* the power of seeing things not able to be perceived by the normal senses (*eg* details about life after death). □ **voyance**

clair'voyant *noun, adjective*. □ **voyant, ante**

clam [klam] *noun* a shellfish with two shells joined together, used as food. □ **palourde**

clamber ['klambə] *verb* to climb by holding on with hands and feet: *clambering over the rocks*. □ **grimper**

clammy ['klami] *adjective* damp and sticky: *clammy hands*. □ **moite**

clamour, clamor ['klamə] *noun* (a) loud uproar. □ **clameur**

■ *verb* (*especially* of a crowd demanding something) to make such an uproar *etc*: *They're all clamouring to get their money back*. □ **demander à cor et à cri**

'**clamorous** *adjective*. □ **vociférant**

clamp [klamp] *noun* a piece of wood, iron *etc* used to fasten things together or to strengthen them. □ **attache**

■ *verb* to bind together with a clamp: *They clamped the iron rods together*. □ **cramponner**

clamp down (*with* **on**) to check or control strictly. □ **serrer la vis (à)**

clan [klan] *noun* a tribe or group of families (*especially* Scottish) under a single chief, *usually* all having one surname. □ **clan**

clandestine [klan'destin] *adjective* secret or hidden. □ **clandestin**

clang [klaŋ] *verb* to produce a loud ringing sound: *The heavy gate clanged shut*. □ **faire un bruit métallique**

■ *noun* such a sound: *a loud clang*. □ **son métallique**

clank [klaŋk] *verb* to produce a sound like that made by heavy pieces of metal striking each other: *The chains clanked*. □ **cliqueter**

■ *noun* such a noise: *the clank of pans in the kitchen*. □ **cliquetis**

clap [klap] – *past tense, past participle* **clapped** – *verb* **1** to strike the palms of the hands together *eg* to show approval, to mark a rhythm, or to gain attention *etc*: *When the singer appeared, the audience started to clap loudly*; *Clap your hands in time to the music*. □ **applaudir; battre des mains**

2 to strike (someone) with the palm of the hand, often in a friendly way: *I clapped him on the back and congratulated him*. □ **donner une tape**

3 to put suddenly (into prison, chains *etc*): *They clapped him in jail*. □ **flanquer**

■ *noun* **1** a sudden noise (of thunder). □ **claquement**

2 an act of clapping: *She gave me a clap on the back*. □ **tape**

clarify ['klarəfai] *verb* to make or become clear (in meaning *etc*): *Would you please clarify your last statement?* □ **clarifier**

,**clarifi'cation** [-fi] *noun*. □ **clarification**

clarinet [klarə'net] *noun* a type of musical wind instrument, *usually* made of wood, and played by means of keys and fingers covering combinations of holes. □ **clarinette**

,**clari'netist** (*British* ,**clari'nettist**) *noun*. □ **clarinettiste**

clarity ['klarəti] *noun* **1** the state of being clear or easy to see through: *water remarkable for its clarity*. □ **limpidité**

2 the state of being easy to see, hear or understand: *She spoke with great clarity*. □ **clarté**

clash [klaʃ] *noun* **1** a loud noise, like *eg* swords striking together: *the clash of metal on metal*. □ **choc métallique**

2 a serious disagreement or difference: *a clash of personalities.* □ **conflit**

3 a battle: *a clash between opposing armies.* □ **affrontement**

4 (of two or more things) an act of interfering with each other because of happening at the same time: *a clash between classes.* □ **coïncidence fâcheuse**

■ *verb* to strike together noisily: *The cymbals clashed.* □ **s'entrechoquer**

2 to fight (in battle): *The two armies clashed at the mouth of the valley.* □ **s'affronter**

3 to disagree violently: *They clashed over wages.* □ **être en désaccord (sur)**

4 to interfere (with something or each other) because of happening at the same time: *The two lectures clash.* □ **tomber en même temps**

5 (of colours) to appear unpleasant when placed together: *The (colour of the) jacket clashes with the (colour of the) skirt.* □ **jurer (avec)**

clasp [klaːsp] *noun* a fastening made of two parts which link together (*eg* on a necklace). □ **fermoir**

■ *verb* to grasp, hold tightly: *She clasped the money in her hand.* □ **serrer**

class [klaːs] – *plural* 'classes – *noun* **1** a group of people or things that are alike in some way: *The dog won first prize in its class in the dog show.* □ **classe**

2 (the system according to which people belong to) one of a number of social groups: *the upper class*; *the middle class*; *the working class*; (*also adjective*) *the class system.* □ **classe**

3 a grade or rank (of merit): *musicians of a high class.* □ **classe**

4 a number of students or scholars taught together: *John and I are in the same class.* □ **classe**

5 a school lesson or college lecture *etc*: *a French class.* □ **cours**

■ *verb* to regard as being of a certain type: *He classes everybody as stupid.* □ **classer**

'**classmate** *noun* a pupil in the same school class. □ **camarade de classe**

'**classroom** *noun* a room in a school where a class is taught. □ **classe**

classical ['klasikəl] *adjective* **1** (*especially* of literature, art *etc*) of ancient Greece and Rome: *classical studies.* □ **classique**

2 (of music) having the traditional, established harmony and/or form: *She prefers classical music to popular music.* □ **classique**

3 (of literature) considered to be of the highest class. □ **classique**

'**classic** *adjective* **1** standard or best: *the classic example.* □ **classique**

2 (of literature, art *etc*) of the highest quality. □ **classique**

3 (of dress *etc*) simple, elegant and traditional. □ **classique**

■ *noun* **1** an established work of literature of high quality: *I have read all the classics.* □ **classique**

2 (*in plural*) the language and literature of Greece and Rome: *He is studying classics.* □ **humanités**

classify ['klasifai] *verb* to put into, or be in, a particular class or group: *How are the books in the library classified?* □ **classer**

,**classifi'cation** [-fi-] *noun.* □ **classification**

clatter ['klatə] *noun* a loud noise like hard objects falling, striking against each other *etc*: *the clatter of children climbing the stairs.* □ **fracas**

■ *verb* to (cause to) make such a noise: *I clattered the dishes in the sink.* □ **entrechoquer bruyamment**

clause [kloːz] *noun* **1** a part of a sentence having its own subject and predicate, *eg* either of the two parts of this sentence: *Mary has a friend/who is rich.* □ **proposition**

2 a paragraph in a contract, will, or act of parliament. □ **clause**

claustrophobia [kloːstrə'foubiə] *noun* fear of narrow, small or enclosed places. □ **claustrophobie**

,**claustro'phobic** *adjective.* □ **claustrophobe**

claw [kloː] *noun* **1** one of the hooked nails of an animal or bird: *The cat sharpened its claws on the tree-trunk.* □ **griffe**

2 the foot of an animal or bird with hooked nails: *The owl held the mouse in its claw.* □ **griffe**

3 (the pointed end of) the leg of a crab *etc*. □ **pince**

■ *verb* to scratch or tear (at something) with claws or nails: *The two cats clawed at each other.* □ **griffer**

clay [klei] *noun* a soft, sticky type of earth which is often baked into pottery, china, bricks *etc*. □ **argile**

clean [kliːn] *adjective* **1** free from dirt, smoke *etc*: *a clean window*; *a clean dress.* □ **propre**

2 neat and tidy in one's habits: *Cats are very clean animals.* □ **propre**

3 unused: *a clean sheet of paper.* □ **vierge**

4 free from evil or indecency: *a clean life*; *keep your language clean!* □ **pur**

5 neat and even: *a clean cut.* □ **net**

■ *adverb* completely: *I got clean away.* □ **complètement**

■ *verb* to (cause to) become free from dirt *etc*: *Will you clean the windows?* □ **nettoyer**

'**cleaner** *noun.* □ **nettoyeur, euse**

'**cleanly**[1] *adverb*: *The knife cut cleanly through the cheese.* □ **nettement**

cleanly[2] ['klenli] *adjective* clean in personal habits. □ **propre**

'**cleanliness** ['klen-] *noun.* □ **propreté**

clean up to clean (a place) thoroughly: *He cleaned (the room) up after they went home.* □ **nettoyer (à fond)**

a clean bill of health a certificate saying that a person, the crew of a ship *etc* is entirely healthy (*especially* after being ill): *I've been off work but I've got a clean bill of health now.* □ **en parfait état de santé**

a clean slate a fresh start: *After being in prison he started his new job with a clean slate.* □ **nouveau départ**

come clean to tell the truth about something, often about something about which one has previously lied. □ **révéler qqch.**

make a clean sweep to get rid of everything unnecessary or unwanted: *The new manager made a clean sweep of all the lazy people in the department.* □ **faire table rase de**

cleanse [klenz] *verb* to make clean: *This cream will cleanse your skin*; *cleansed of guilt.* □ **nettoyer; purifier**

'cleanser *noun* something which cleans, *especially* a cosmetic used to clean the face. □ **démaquillant**

clear [kliə] *adjective* 1 easy to see through; transparent: *clear glass*. □ **transparent**
2 free from mist or cloud: *Isn't the sky clear!* □ **dégagé**
3 easy to see, hear or understand: *a clear explanation*; *The details on that photograph are very clear*. □ **clair**
4 free from difficulty or obstacles: *a clear road ahead*. □ **libre**
5 free from guilt *etc*: *a clear conscience*. □ **tranquille**
6 free from doubt *etc*: *Are you quite clear about what I mean?* □ **bien comprendre**
7 (*often with* of) without (risk of) being touched, caught *etc*: *Is the ship clear of the rocks? clear of danger*. □ **à l'écart de**
8 (*often with* of) free: *clear of debt*; *clear of all infection*. □ **libre de**
■ *verb* 1 to make or become free from obstacles *etc*: *I cleared the table*; *I cleared my throat*; *She cleared the path of debris*. □ **débarrasser**
2 (*often with* of) to prove the innocence of; to declare to be innocent: *She was cleared of all charges*. □ **innocenter**
3 (of the sky *etc*) to become bright, free from cloud *etc*. □ **se dégager**
4 to get over or past something without touching it: *I cleared the jump easily*. □ **franchir**

'clearance *noun* 1 the act of clearing or removing: *The clearance of these trees from the front of the window will give you more light*. □ **enlèvement**
2 the clear area between two objects: *You can drive the truck under the bridge – there's a clearance of half a metre*. □ **dégagement**
3 (a certificate) giving permission for something to be done. □ **autorisation**

'clearing *noun* a piece of land cleared of wood *etc* for cultivation: *a clearing in the forest*. □ **clairière**

'clearly *adverb*. □ **clairement**

'clearness *noun*. □ **transparence**

,clear-'cut *adjective* having a clear outline; plain and definite: *clear-cut features*. □ **net**

clear off to go away: *She cleared off without saying a word*. □ **décamper**

clear out 1 to get rid of: *I cleared the rubbish out of the attic*. □ **enlever**
2 to make tidy by emptying *etc*: *He has cleared out the attic*. □ **débarrasser**

clear up 1 to make clear, tidy *etc*: *Clear up this mess!* □ **ranger**
2 to become better *etc*: *If the weather clears up, we'll go for a picnic*. □ **s'éclaircir**

in the clear no longer under suspicion, in danger *etc*. □ **au-dessus de tout soupçon; hors de danger**

cleave¹ [kliːv] – *past tense* cleft [kleft], cleaved, clove [klouv]: *past participles* cleft, cloven ['klouvn] – *verb* to split or divide. □ **fendre**

'cleavage [-vidʒ] *noun* the act of splitting; a split. □ **clivage**

'cleaver *noun* a butcher's knife. □ **couperet**

cloven hoof a hoof, like those of cows, sheep *etc*, which has a split up the centre. □ **sabot fendu**

cleave² [kliːv] – *past tense, past participle* cleaved: **cleave to** to stick to. □ **coller à**

clef [klef] *noun* in music, a sign (*eg* 𝄞 *or* 𝄢) on the stave fixing the pitch of the notes. □ **clef**

cleft [kleft] *noun* an opening made by splitting: *a cleft in the rocks*. □ **fissure**

clement ['klemənt] *adjective* 1 (of weather *etc*) mild. □ **clément**
2 merciful. □ **clément**

'clemency *noun*. □ **clémence**

clench [klentʃ] *verb* to close tightly together: *He clenched his teeth/fist*. □ **serrer**

clergy ['kləːdʒi] *noun* the ministers, priests *etc* of the Christian religion: *the clergy of the Church of England*. □ **clergé**

'clergyman *noun* one of the clergy; a priest, minister *etc*. □ **ecclésiastique**

clerical¹ ['klerikəl] *adjective* of the clergy: *He is wearing a clerical collar*. □ **clérical**

clerical² ['klerikəl] *adjective* of a clerk or of his work: *a clerical error*. □ **de bureau**

clerk [klɔːk] *noun* 1 a person who deals with letters, accounts *etc* in an office. □ **employé, ée (de bureau)**
2 a public official in charge of the business affairs of the town council *etc*: *the town clerk*. □ **secrétaire de municipalité**
3 a shop-assistant. □ **vendeur, euse**

clever ['klevə] *adjective* 1 quick to learn and understand: *a clever child*. □ **intelligent, malin**
2 skilful: *a clever carpenter*. □ **habile**
3 (of things) showing cleverness: *a clever idea*. □ **ingénieux**

'cleverly *adverb*. □ **ingénieusement**

'cleverness *noun*. □ **ingéniosité**

cliché [kliːˈʃei, ˈkliːʃei] *noun* a phrase which has been used too often, and has become meaningless. □ **cliché**

click [klik] *noun* a short, sharp sound, like that of a light-switch being turned on: *the click of the camera*. □ **déclic**
■ *verb* to (cause to) make such a sound: *The soldier clicked his heels together*; *The gate clicked*. □ **cliqueter**

client ['klaiənt] *noun* 1 a person who receives professional advice from a lawyer, accountant *etc*. □ **client, ente**
2 a customer: *That hairdresser is very popular with his clients*. □ **client, ente**

clientèle [kliːɔnˈtel] *noun* a group or type of clients: *a bank's clientèle*. □ **clientèle**

cliff [klif] *noun* a high steep rock, *especially* one facing the sea. □ **falaise**

climate ['klaimət] *noun* 1 the weather conditions of a region (temperature, moisture *etc*): *Coastal British Columbia has a temperate climate*. □ **climat**
2 the conditions in a country *etc*: *the economic/moral climate*. □ **climat**

cli'matic [-'ma-] *adjective*. □ **climatique**

climax ['klaimaks] – *plural* 'climaxes – *noun* the highest point; the most dramatic moment: *the climax of the novel*. □ **point culminant**

climb [klaim] *verb* 1 (of a person *etc*) to go up or to-

wards the top of (a mountain, wall, ladder *etc*): *We climbed to the top of the hill; She climbed up the ladder; The child climbed the tree.* □ **grimper, escalader**
2 to rise or ascend. □ **monter**
■ *noun* **1** an act of going up: *a rapid climb to the top of his profession.* □ **montée**
2 a route or place to be climbed: *The guide showed us the best climb.* □ **montée**
'**climber** *noun.* □ **grimpeur, euse**
climbing *noun* a sport or pastime using both hands and feet to scale rocks or the side of mountains: *Francis took up climbing and went to British Columbia to climb the Rocky Mountains.* □ **escalade**
clinch [klintʃ] *verb* to settle or come to an agreement about (an argument or a bargain): *The businessmen clinched the deal.* □ **conclure**
cling [kliŋ] – *past tense, past participle* **clung** [klʌŋ] – *verb* (*usually with* **to**) to stick (to); to grip tightly: *The mud clung to her shoes; She clung to her husband as he said goodbye; He clings to an impossible hope; The boat clung to* (= stayed close to) *the coastline.* □ **s'accrocher (à)**
clinic ['klinik] *noun* a place or part of a hospital where a particular kind of medical treatment or advice is given: *He is attending the skin clinic.* □ **clinique**
'**clinical** *adjective* **1** of a clinic. □ **clinique**
2 based on observation of the patient. □ **clinique**
clink [kliŋk] *noun* a ringing sound: *the clink of coins.* □ **tintement**
■ *verb* to (cause to) make such a sound: *They clinked their glasses together.* □ **faire tinter**
clip[1] [klip] – *past tense, past participle* **clipped** – *verb* **1** to cut (foliage, an animal's hair *etc*) with scissors or shears: *The shepherd clipped the sheep; The hedge was clipped.* □ **couper; tondre**
2 to strike sharply: *She clipped him over the ear.* □ **frapper**
■ *noun* **1** an act of clipping. □ **taille, tonte**
2 a sharp blow: *a clip on the ear.* □ **taloche**
'**clipper** *noun* **1** (*in plural*) a tool for clipping: *hedge-clippers; nail-clippers.* □ **tondeuse**
2 a type of fast sailing-ship. □ **clipper**
'**clipping** *noun* a thing clipped off or out of something, *especially* a newspaper: *She collects clippings about Céline Dion.* □ **coupure (de presse)**
clip[2] [klip] – *past tense, past participle* **clipped** – *verb* to fasten with a clip: *Clip these papers together.* □ **attacher**
■ *noun* something for holding things together or in position: *a paper-clip; a hair-clip; bicycle-clips* (= round pieces of metal *etc* for holding the bottom of trouser legs close to the leg). □ **attache, pince**
clique [kliːk] *noun* a group of people who are friendly with each other but exclude others: *the golf-club clique.* □ **clique**
'**cliqu(e)y, 'cliquish** *adjective.* □ **exclusif**
cloak [klouk] *noun* a loose outer garment without sleeves, covering most of the body; something that conceals: *a woollen cloak; They arrived under cloak of darkness.* □ **grande cape**
■ *verb* to cover or hide: *He used a false name to cloak*

his activities. □ **masquer**
'**cloakroom** *noun* **1** a room for coats, hats *etc*. □ **vestiaire**
2 a lavatory: *the ladies' cloakroom.* □ **toilettes**
clock [klok] *noun* **1** an instrument for measuring time, but not worn on the wrist like a watch: *We have five clocks in our house; an alarm clock* (= a clock with a ringing device for waking one up in the morning). □ **horloge**
2 an instrument for measuring speed of a vehicle or distance travelled by a vehicle: *My car has 120 000 kilometres on the clock.* □ **compteur**
■ *verb* to register (a time) on a stopwatch *etc*. □ **chronométrer**
around the clock the whole day and the whole night: *to work round the clock.* □ **ving-quatre heures d'affilée**
'**clockwise** *adverb* in the direction of the movement of the hands of a clock: *The children moved clockwise around the room, then counter-clockwise.* □ **dans le sens des aiguilles d'une montre**
'**clockwork** *noun* machinery similar to that of a clock: *a toy which works by clockwork.* □ **mécanisme**
clock in, out/on, off to register or record time of arriving at or leaving work. □ **pointer**
clock up to register on an odometer *etc*: *I've clocked up eight thousand kilometres this year in my car.* □ **faire (au compteur)**
like clockwork very smoothly and without faults: *Everything went like clockwork.* □ **comme sur des roulettes**
clod [klod] *noun* a thick lump, *especially* of earth. □ **motte**
clog[1] [klog] *noun* **1** a shoe made entirely of wood: *Dutch clogs.* □ **sabot**
2 a shoe with a wooden sole. □ **socque**
clog[2] [klog] – *past tense, past participle* **clogged** – (*often with* **up**) to make or become blocked: *The drain is clogged* (up) *with hair.* □ **boucher, bloquer**
cloister ['kloistə] *noun* a covered walk forming part of a monastery, church or college. □ **cloître**
close[1] [klous] *adverb* **1** near in time, place *etc*: *He stood close to his mother; Follow close behind.* □ **près (de)**
2 tightly; neatly: *a close-fitting dress.* □ **étroitement**
■ *adjective* **1** near in relationship: *a close friend.* □ **intime**
2 having a narrow difference between winner and loser: *a close contest; The result was close.* □ **serré**
3 thorough: *a close examination of the facts; Keep a close watch on them.* □ **rigoureux**
4 tight: *a close fit.* □ **ajusté**
5 without fresh air: *a close atmosphere; The weather was close and thundery.* □ **étouffant**
6 mean: *He's very close (with his money).* □ **regardant**
7 secretive: *They're keeping very close about the business.* □ **renfermé**
'**closely** *adverb*: *Look closely at him; She resembles her father closely.* □ **de près, étroitement**
'**closeness** *noun.* □ **proximité**
close call/shave a narrow (often lucky) escape: *That was a close shave – that car nearly ran you over.* □ **l'échapper belle**
,**close-'set** *adjective* (of eyes *etc*) positioned very near each other. □ **rapproché**

'close-up *noun* a photograph or film taken near the subject and thus big in scale: *The close-up of the model showed her beautiful skin.* □ **gros plan**

close at hand nearby; not far off: *My mother lives close at hand.* □ **à proximité**

close on almost; nearly: *She's close on sixty.* □ **pas loin de**

close to 1 near in time, place, relationship *etc*: *close to 3 o'clock*; *close to the hospital*; *close to his mother.* □ **près de**

2 almost; nearly: *close to fifty years of age.* □ **près de**

close² [klouz] *verb* **1** to make or become shut, often by bringing together two parts so as to cover an opening: *The baby closed her eyes*; *Close the door*; *The shops close on Sundays.* □ **fermer**

2 to finish; to come or bring to an end: *The meeting closed with everyone in agreement.* □ **finir**

3 to complete or settle (a business deal). □ **conclure**

■ *noun* a stop, end or finish: *the close of day*; *towards the close of the nineteenth century.* □ **fin**

close down 1 (of a business) to close permanently: *High levels of taxation have caused many firms to close down.* □ **fermer (définitivement)**

2 (of a TV or radio station *etc*) to stop broadcasting for the day (*noun* **'closedown**). □ **terminer les émissions**

close up 1 to come or bring closer together: *I closed up the space between the lines of print.* □ **rapprocher**

2 to shut completely: *He closed up the house when he went on holiday.* □ **fermer (complètement)**

closet ['klozit] *noun* a cupboard: *a clothes closet.* □ **placard**

'closeted *adjective* engaged in a private conversation in a separate room from other people: *They're closeted in his office.* □ **enfermé**

closure ['klouʒə] *noun* an act of closing: *the closure of a factory.* □ **fermeture**

clot [klot] *noun* **1** soft or fluid matter (*especially* blood) formed into a solid mass: *a clot of blood.* □ **caillot**

2 a fool or an idiot. □ **imbécile**

■ *verb* – *past tense, past participle* **'clotted** – to form into clots: *Most people's blood clots easily.* □ **coaguler**

cloth [kloθ] – *plural* **cloths** [kloθs, kloːðz] – *noun* (a piece of) woven material from which clothes and many other items are made: *a tablecloth*; *a face-cloth*; *a floor-cloth*; *Woollen cloth is often more expensive than other cloths.* □ **tissu**

clothe [klouð] – *past tense, past participle* **clothed** – *verb* **1** to provide with clothes: *The widow did not have enough money to clothe her children.* □ **habiller**

2 to put clothes on: *She was clothed in silk*; *He clothed himself in the most expensive materials.* □ **s'habiller**

clothes [klouz, klouðz] *noun plural* **1** things worn as coverings for various parts of the body: *He wears beautiful clothes.* □ **vêtements**

2 bedclothes: *The child pulled the clothes up tightly.* □ **draps (et couvertures)**

'clothing *noun* clothes: *warm clothing.* □ **vêtements**

there is no singular form for **clothes**.

cloud [klaud] **1** a mass of tiny drops of water floating in the sky: *white clouds in a blue sky*; *The hills were hidden in cloud.* □ **nuage**

2 a great number or quantity of anything small moving together: *a cloud of flies.* □ **nuée**

3 something causing fear, depression *etc*: *a cloud of sadness.* □ **nuage**

■ *verb* **1** (*often with* **over**) to become cloudy: *The sky clouded over and it began to rain.* □ **s'ennuager**

2 to (cause to) become blurred or not clear: *Her eyes were clouded with tears.* □ **(s')embuer**

3 to (cause to) become gloomy or troubled: *Her face clouded at the unhappy news.* □ **(s')assombrir**

'cloudless *adjective* free from clouds: *a cloudless sky.* □ **sans nuages**

'cloudy *adjective* **1** full of, having, or covered with clouds: *It is a bit cloudy today.* □ **nuageux**

2 not clear: *a cloudy photograph/memory.* □ **flou**

'cloudburst *noun* a sudden heavy shower of rain. □ **trombe d'eau**

under a cloud in trouble or disgrace. □ **en butte aux soupçons**

clove¹ [klouv] *noun* the flower bud of a tropical tree dried for use as a spice. □ **clou de girofle**

clove² [klouv] *noun* a section of a bulb: *a clove of garlic.* □ **gousse**

clove³, cloven *see* **cleave¹.**

clover ['klouvə] *noun* a plant with leaves in three parts, used as food for cattle *etc*. □ **trèfle**

clown [klaun] *noun* **1** a person who works in a circus, performing funny acts (*usually* ridiculously dressed). □ **clown**

2 any person who behaves ridiculously. □ **clown**

■ *verb* to behave ridiculously: *Stop clowning.* □ **faire le clown**

'clownish *adjective*. □ **bouffon**

club [klʌb] *noun* **1** a heavy stick *etc* used as a weapon. □ **gourdin**

2 a bat or stick used in certain games (*especially* golf): *Which club will you use?* □ **club**

3 a number of people meeting for study, pleasure, games *etc*: *the local tennis club.* □ **club**

4 the place where these people meet: *She goes to the club every Friday.* □ **cercle**

5 one of the playing cards of the suit clubs. □ **trèfle**

■ *verb* – *past tense, past participle* **clubbed** – to beat or strike with a club: *They clubbed him to death.* □ **matraquer**

clubs *noun plural* (sometimes treated as *noun singular*) one of the four card suits: *the six of clubs.* □ **trèfle**

cluck [klʌk] *noun* (a sound like) the call of a hen. □ **gloussement**

■ *verb* to make such a sound. □ **glousser**

clue [kluː] *noun* anything that helps to solve a mystery, puzzle *etc*: *The car number was a clue to the identity of the murderer*; *I can't answer the second clue in this crossword.* □ **indice**

'clueless *adjective* (of a person) stupid: *They're quite clueless about art.* □ **ignare**

blazer

jacket

shirt

underwear

skirt

dress

pullover

shorts

blouse

tie

jeans

dressing gown

sweater

socks

suit

overalls

t-shirt

coat

cap

pyjama

nightgown

swimsuit

shoes

hat

gloves

tights

sandals

boots

scarf

not to have a clue to be ignorant: *'How does that work?'* *'I haven't a clue.'* □ **n'avoir pas la moindre idée (de)**

clump[1] [klʌmp] *noun* a group (*eg* of trees or bushes). □ **bouquet, massif**

clump[2] [klʌmp] *verb* to walk heavily and noisily. □ **marcher à pas lourds**

clumsy ['klʌmzi] *adjective* awkward in movement *etc*: *He's very clumsy – he's always dropping things.* □ **maladroit**

'**clumsily** *adverb*. □ **maladroitement**

'**clumsiness** *noun*. □ **maladresse**

clung *see* **cling**.

cluster ['klʌstə] *noun* a closely-packed group (of people or things): *a cluster of berries*; *They stood in a cluster.* □ **groupe**

■ *verb* (*often with* **around**) to group together in clusters: *They clustered around the door.* □ **se grouper (autour de)**

clutch [klʌtʃ] *verb* 1 (*with* **at**) to try to take hold of: *I clutched at a floating piece of wood to save myself from drowning.* □ **se raccrocher (à)**

2 to hold tightly (in the hands): *She was clutching a 50-cent piece.* □ **tenir bien serré**

■ *noun* 1 control or power: *He fell into the clutches of the enemy.* □ **(sous les) griffes**

2 (the pedal operating) a device by means of which two moving parts of an engine may be connected or disconnected: *She released the clutch and the car started to move.* □ **(pédale d')embrayage**

clutch at straws to hope that something may help one in a hopeless situation. □ **se raccrocher à n'importe quoi**

clutter ['klʌtə] *noun* state of untidiness: *The house is in a clutter.* □ **désordre**

'**cluttered** *adjective* untidy; too full of furniture *etc*: *Some people think it's a beautiful room but it's too cluttered for my taste.* □ **encombré**

co- [kou] (*as part of a word*) 1 joint or working *etc* together, as in **co-author**. □ **co(-)**

2 with or together, as in **co-exist**. □ **co(-)**

coach [koutʃ] *noun* 1 a railway car: *The last two coaches of the train were derailed.* □ **wagon**

2 a bus for tourists *etc*. □ **(auto)car**

3 a trainer in athletics, sport *etc*: *the tennis coach.* □ **entraîneur, euse**

4 a four-wheeled horsedrawn vehicle. □ **carrosse**

■ *verb* to prepare (a person) for an examination, contest *etc*: *He coached his friend for the Latin exam.* □ **préparer qqn à**

'**coachbuilder** *noun* a person or business concerned with building the bodies for modern vehicles. □ **carrossier, ière**

'**coachman** *noun* the driver of a horsedrawn carriage. □ **cocher, ère**

coal [koul] *noun* a black mineral burned for fuel, heat *etc*. □ **charbon**

'**coalfield** *noun* an area where there is coal to be mined. □ **bassin houiller**

'**coalmine** *noun* a mine from which coal is dug. □ **mine de charbon**

haul (someone) over the coals to scold. □ **passer un savon à**

coalition [kouə'liʃən] *noun* a *usually* temporary union or alliance, *especially* of states or political parties. □ **coalition**

coarse [koːs] *adjective* 1 rough in texture or to touch; not fine: *This coat is made of coarse material.* □ **grossier**

2 rude, vulgar or unrefined: *coarse jokes.* □ **grossier**

'**coarsely** *adverb*. □ **grossièrement**

'**coarseness** *noun*. □ **grossièreté**

'**coarsen** *verb* to (cause to) become coarse: *The laundry-work coarsened her hands.* □ **rendre rude**

coast [koust] *noun* the side or border of land next to the sea: *The coast was very rocky.* □ **côte, littoral**

■ *verb* to travel downhill (in a vehicle, on a bicycle *etc*) without the use of any power such as the engine or pedalling: *I coasted for two miles after the car ran out of gas.* □ **aller en roue libre**

'**coastal** *adjective* of or near the coast: *a coastal town.* □ **côtier, littoral**

'**coaster** *noun* 1 a vessel that sails along near the coast. □ **caboteur**

2 a small mat for putting under a drinking-glass *etc*. □ **dessous (de verre)**

'**coastguard** *noun* a person or group of people, employed to watch the coast for smugglers, ships in distress *etc*. □ **garde-côte**

coat [kout] *noun* 1 an item of outdoor clothing, with sleeves, that covers from the shoulders *usually* to the knees: *a coat and hat.* □ **manteau**

2 a jacket: *a man's coat and trousers.* □ **veste**

3 the hair or wool of an animal: *Some dogs have smooth coats.* □ **pelage**

4 a covering (*eg* of paint): *This wall will need two coats of paint.* □ **couche**

■ *verb* to cover: *I coated the biscuits with chocolate.* □ **couvrir**

'**coating** *noun* (a) covering: *chocolate coating.* □ **couche**

coat of arms a family badge or crest. □ **armoiries**

coax [kouks] *verb* to persuade by flattery, by patient and gentle treatment *etc*: *He coaxed her into going to the dance by saying she was the best dancer he knew*; *He coaxed some money out of his mother.* □ **cajoler**

cobalt ['koubɔːlt] *noun* a silver-white metal element with compounds that give a blue colouring. □ **cobalt**

cobble[1] ['kobl] *noun* a rounded stone formerly used in paving streets. □ **pavé rond**

cobble[2] ['kobl] *verb* 1 to mend (shoes). □ **réparer**

2 to make or repair badly or roughly. □ **rafistoler**

'**cobbler** *noun* a person who mends shoes. □ **cordonnier, ière**

cobra ['koubrə] *noun* a poisonous snake found in India and Africa. □ **cobra**

cobweb ['kobweb] *noun* a spider's web: *You can't have cleaned this room – there are cobwebs in the corner.* □ **toile d'araignée**

cocaine [kə'kein] *noun* an addictive drug formerly used to deaden pain. □ **cocaïne**

cock [kok] *noun* 1 the male of birds, *especially* of the domestic fowl: *a cock and three hens*; (*also adjective*)

a cock sparrow. □ **coq**
2 a kind of tap for controlling the flow of liquid, gas *etc.* □ **robinet**
3 a slang word for the penis. □ **queue**
■ *verb* 1 to cause to stand upright or to lift: *The dog cocked its ears.* □ **dresser**
2 to draw back the hammer of (a gun). □ **armer**
3 to tilt up or sideways (*especially* a hat). □ **incliner**
cockerel ['kokərəl] *noun* a young farmyard cock. □ **jeune coq**
'**cocky** *adjective* conceited; over-confident: *a cocky attitude.* □ **suffisant**
cock-and-bull story an absurd, unbelievable story. □ **histoire à dormir debout**
'**cock crow** *noun* early morning: *She gets up at cock crow.* □ **(à)l'aube**
'**cockeyed** *adjective* ridiculous: *a cockeyed idea.* □ **absurde**
,**cock'sure** *adjective* very or too confident: *He was cocksure about passing the exam.* □ **outrecuidant**
cockade [kə'keid] *noun* formerly, a knot of ribbon worn as a hat-badge. □ **cocarde**
cockatoo [kokə'tuː] – *plural* **cocka'toos** – *noun* a parrot with a large crest. □ **cacatoès**
cockerel *see* **cock.**
cockney ['kokni] *noun* 1 a native of the City of London. □ **Cockney**
2 his speech: *I spoke cockney;* (*also adjective*) *a cockney accent.* □ **cockney**
cockpit ['kokpit] *noun* a compartment in which the pilot of an airplane, driver of a racing-car *etc* sits: *She climbed into the cockpit and drove off.* □ **cockpit**
cockroach ['kokroutʃ] – *plural* **cockroaches** – *noun* a beetle-like insect which is a household pest. □ **blatte**
cocksure *see* **cock.**
cocktail ['kokteil] 1 an alcoholic drink mixed from various spirits *etc.* □ **coquetel**
2 a mixed dish of a number of things: *a fruit cocktail.* □ **salade**
cocky *see* **cock.**
cocoa ['koukou] *noun* 1 (a powder made from) the crushed seeds of the cacao tree, used in making chocolate. □ **cacao**
2 a drink made from the powder: *a cup of cocoa.* □ **cacao**
coconut ['koukənʌt] *noun* 1 a large nut containing a white solid lining and a clear liquid. □ **noix de coco**
2 its lining, used as food. □ **noix de coco**
cocoon [kə'kuːn] *noun* a silk covering spun by many insect larvae, and in which they live while turning into butterflies. □ **cocon**
cod [kod] – *plural* **cod** – a type of edible fish found in northern seas. □ **morue**
cod-liver oil an oil obtained from cod's liver, rich in vitamins A and D. □ **huile de foie de morue**
coddle ['kodl] *verb* to treat with great care like an invalid; to pamper: *He tended to coddle his youngest child.* □ **dorloter**
code [koud] *noun* 1 a collection of laws or rules: *a code of behaviour.* □ **code**

2 a (secret) system of words, letters, or symbols: *the Morse Code; The message was in code; We have deciphered the enemy's code.* □ **code**
3 a system of symbols *etc* for translating one type of language into another: *There are a number of codes for putting English into a form usable by a computer.* □ **code**
■ *verb* to put into (secret, computer *etc*) code: *Have you coded the material for the computer?* □ **coder**
coeducational [kouedjuˈkeiʃənl] (*abbreviation* **co-ed** ['koued]) *adjective* of the education of pupils or students of both sexes in the same school or college: *a coeducational school.* □ **mixte**
coerce [kou'əːs] *verb* to force (a person into doing something). □ **contraindre**
co'ercion [-ʃən] *noun.* □ **cercition**
coexist [kouig'zist] *verb* (*especially* of nations, races *etc*) to exist side by side (*especially* peacefully). □ **coexister**
coex'istence *noun.* □ **coexistence**
coffee ['kofi] *noun* (a drink made from) the ground beans of a shrub grown in *eg* Brazil. □ **café**
■ *adjective* the colour of the drink when mixed with milk. □ **café au lait**
'**coffee pot** *noun* a container from which to serve coffee. □ **cafetière**
'**coffee shop** *noun* a café serving coffee *etc.* □ **café**
coffee table *noun* a low table usually standing in front of a sofa: *Help yourself to the snacks on the coffee table; Take your feet off the coffee table.* □ **table basse**
coffin ['kofin] *noun* ('**casket**) a box for a dead body to be buried or cremated in: *The coffin was placed in the grave.* □ **cercueil**
cog [kog] *noun* one of a series of teeth around the edge of a wheel which fits into one of a similar series in a similar wheel (or into a chain as in a bicycle) causing motion: *The cogs in the gear-wheels of a car get worn down.* □ **dent**
cogitate ['kodʒiteit] *verb* to think carefully. □ **réfléchir**
,**cogi'tation** *noun.* □ **réflexion**
cognac ['konjak] a kind of high-quality French brandy. □ **cognac**
coherent [kə'hiərənt] *adjective* clear and logical: *He was able to give a coherent account of what had happened.* □ **cohérent**
co'herently *adverb.* □ **avec cohérence**
co'herence *noun.* □ **cohérence**
cohort ['kouhoːt] *noun* 1 companion, colleague: *One of his cohorts was fired at the age of 50.* □ **acolyte**
2 a group of people: *His supporters followed him in cohorts.* □ **cohorte**
coiffure [kwa'fjuə] *noun* a hairstyle: *an elaborate coiffure.* □ **coiffure**
coil [koil] *verb* to wind into loops: *The snake coiled (itself) around the tree.* □ **enrouler**
■ *noun* 1 a length of something wound into a loop or loops: *a coil of rope; a coil of hair.* □ **rouleau**
2 a wound length of wire for conducting electricity: *the coil in an electric fire.* □ **bobine**
coin [koin] *noun* a piece of metal used as money: *a handful of coins.* □ **pièce**

■ *verb* 1 to make metal into (money): *When was that dollar coined?* □ **frapper**

2 to invent (a word, phrase *etc*): *The scientist coined a word for the new process.* □ **inventer**

'**coinage** [-nidʒ] *noun* 1 the process of coining. □ **frappe**

2 the money (system) used in a country: *Britain now uses decimal coinage.* □ **système monétaire**

coincide [kouin'said] *verb* 1 to occupy (often by accident) the same space or time: *Her arrival coincided with his departure.* □ **coïncider (avec)**

2 to agree: *This coincides with what he told us; Their tastes in music coincide.* □ **coïncider (avec)**

coincidence [kou'insidəns] *noun* (an) accidental happening of one event at the same time as another: *By a strange coincidence we were both on the same train.* □ **coïncidence**

co,inci'dental [-'den-] *adjective.* □ **de coïncidence**

coke [kouk] *noun* a type of fuel obtained from coal. □ **coke**

colander ['kʌləndə] *noun* a bowl with small holes in it for draining water off vegetables. □ **passoire**

cold [kould] *adjective* 1 low in temperature: *cold water; cold meat and salad.* □ **froid**

2 lower in temperature than is comfortable: *I feel cold.* □ **froid**

3 unfriendly: *His manner was cold.* □ **froid**

■ *noun* 1 the state of being cold or of feeling the coldness of one's surroundings: *She has gone to live in the South of France because she cannot bear the cold in Canada; She was blue with cold.* □ **froid**

2 an illness with running nose, coughing *etc*: *He has a bad cold; She has caught a cold; You might catch cold.* □ **rhume**

'**coldly** *adverb* in an unfriendly way: *She looked at me coldly.* □ **froidement**

'**coldness** *noun.* □ **froideur**

,**cold-'blooded** *adjective* 1 having blood (like that of a fish) which takes the same temperature as the surroundings of the body: *cold-blooded creatures.* □ **à sang froid**

2 cruel and unfeeling: *cold-blooded murder.* □ **sans pitié**

cold cuts *noun* sliced assorted meats used as filling for sandwiches: *One of my favourite cold cuts is smoked ham.* □ **viandes froides**

cold war a major, *especially* political, struggle between nations which involves military threats but not fighting. □ **guerre froide**

get cold feet to lose courage: *I was going to apply for the job but I got cold feet.* □ **se dégonfler**

give (someone) the cold shoulder (*also* ,**cold-'shoulder** *verb*) to show that one is unwilling to be friendly with (a person): *All the neighbours gave her the cold shoulder; He cold-shouldered all his sister's friends.* □ **se montrer froid envers qqn**

in cold blood deliberately and unemotionally: *He killed them in cold blood.* □ **de sang-froid**

coleslaw ['koulslɔ:] a salad made with finely-cut raw cabbage. □ **salade de chou**

coleus ['kouliəs] *noun* a type of plant with variegated leaves. □ **coleus**

colic ['kolik] *noun* severe pain in the abdomen. □

colique(s)

collaborate [kə'labəreit] *verb* 1 to work together (with someone) on a piece of work: *She and her brother collaborated on a book about airplanes.* □ **collaborer**

2 to work along (with someone) to betray secrets *etc*: *He was known to have collaborated with the enemy.* □ **collaborer**

col,labo'ration *noun.* □ **collaboration**

col'laborator *noun.* □ **collaborateur, trice**

collage [ko'la:ʒ] *noun* a design made by pasting pieces of paper, cloth, photographs *etc* on to a surface. □ **collage**

collapse [kə'laps] *verb* 1 to fall down and break into pieces: *The bridge collapsed under the weight of the traffic.* □ **s'écrouler**

2 (of a person) to fall down *especially* unconscious, because of illness, shock *etc*: *She collapsed with a heart attack.* □ **s'effondrer**

3 to break down, fail: *The talks between the two countries have collapsed.* □ **s'écrouler**

4 to fold up or to (cause to) come to pieces (intentionally): *Do these chairs collapse?* □ **se plier**

col'lapsible *adjective* able to be folded up *etc*: *These chairs are collapsible.* □ **pliant**

collar ['kolə] *noun* 1 the part of a garment at the neck *especially* of a shirt, jacket *etc*: *This collar is too tight.* □ **col**

2 something worn around the neck: *The dog's name was on its collar.* □ **collier**

■ *verb* to seize, get hold of: *I collared the speaker as he left the room.* □ **intercepter**

'**collar-bone** *noun* either of two bones joining breastbone and shoulder-blade. □ **clavicule**

colleague ['koli:g] *noun* a person with whom one is associated in a profession or occupation: *She gets on well with her colleagues.* □ **collègue**

collect [kə'lekt] *verb* 1 to bring or come together; to gather: *People are collecting in front of the house; I collect stamps; I'm collecting (money) for cancer research; He's trying to collect his thoughts.* □ **(se) rassembler; recueillir**

2 to call for and take away: *She collects the children from school each day.* □ **aller chercher**

col'lected *adjective* 1 gathered together in one book *etc*: *the collected poems of Robert Burns.* □ **recueil (de)**

2 composed; cool: *She appeared quite calm and collected.* □ **maître de soi**

col'lection [-ʃən] *noun* 1 (an) act of collecting: *Your letter won't get to Halifax tomorrow – you've missed the last collection (= of mail from a mailbox) for today.* □ **ramassage**

2 a set of objects *etc* collected: *a stamp collection.* □ **collection**

col'lective [-tiv] *adjective* 1 of a number of people *etc* combined into one group: *This success was the result of a collective effort.* □ **collectif**

2 of a noun, taking a singular verb but standing for many things taken as a whole: *'Cattle' is a collective noun.* □ **collectif**

■ *noun* a farm or organization run by a group of workers for the good of all of them. □ **collectif**

col'lectively adverb: They were collectively responsible for the man's death. □ **collectivement**

col'lector noun a person who collects, as a job or as a hobby: a ticket-collector/stamp-collector. □ **collectionneur, euse**

college ['kɒlidʒ] noun (any or all of the buildings housing) a higher-education institution: He is at agricultural college. □ **établissement d'enseignement supérieur**

collide [kə'laid] verb to strike together (usually accidentally) with great force: The cars collided in the fog; The van collided with a truck. □ **entrer en collision**

collision [kə'liʒən] noun a crash; a violent striking together (of eg two vehicles): Ten people were injured in the collision between the bus and the car. □ **collision**

collier ['kɒliə] noun a person who works in a coalmine: Collier is another word for a coalminer. □ **mineur (de charbon)**

'colliery – plural **'collieries** – noun a coalmine. □ **mine (de charbon)**

collision see collide.

colloquial [kə'loukwiəl] adjective of or used in everyday informal, especially spoken, language: a colloquial expression. □ **familier**

col'loquially adverb. □ **familièrement**

col'loquialism noun an expression used in colloquial language. □ **expression familière**

cologne see eau-de-cologne.

colon[1] ['koulən] noun the punctuation mark (:), used eg to separate sentence-like units within a sentence, or to introduce a list etc. □ **deux-points**

colon[2] ['koulən] noun a part of the large intestine. □ **colon**

colonel ['kəːnl] noun (often abbreviated to **Col.** when written) an army officer ranking below a brigadier general and above a lieutenant colonel. □ **colonel, elle**

colonial etc see colony.

colonnade [kɒlə'neid] noun a row of pillars. □ **colonnade**

colony ['kɒləni] – plural **'colonies** – noun 1 (a group of people who form) a settlement in one country etc which is under the rule of another country: France used to have many colonies in Africa. □ **colonie**

2 a group of people having the same interests, living close together: a colony of artists. □ **colonie**

3 a collection of animals, birds etc, of one type, living together: a colony of gulls. □ **colonie**

co'lonial [-'lou-] adjective: Britain was formerly a colonial power. □ **colonial**

co'lonialism noun. □ **colonialisme**

co'lonialist noun and adjective. □ **colonialiste**

'colonize, 'colonise verb to establish a colony in (a place): The English colonized New England in 1620. □ **coloniser**

'colonist noun. □ **colon**

,coloni'zation, ,coloni'sation noun. □ **colonisation**

colossal [kə'losəl] adjective very big; enormous: a colossal increase in the price of books. □ **colossal**

colour, color ['kʌlə] noun 1 a quality which objects have, and which can be seen, only when light falls on them:

What colour is her dress?; Red, blue and yellow are colours. □ **couleur**

2 paint(s): That artist uses water-colours. □ **peinture**

3 (a) skin-colour varying with race: people of all colours. □ **couleur**

4 vividness; interest: There's plenty of colour in his stories. □ **couleur**

■ adjective (of photographs etc) in colour, not black and white: colour film; colour television. □ **en couleur**

■ verb to put colour on; to paint: They coloured the walls yellow. □ **peindre**

'coloured adjective 1 having colour: She prefers white baths to coloured baths. □ **coloré**

2 belonging to a dark-skinned race: There are only two white families living in this street – the rest are coloured. □ **de couleur**

■ noun a dark-skinned person especially of Negro origin. □ **personne de couleur**

'colourful adjective 1 full of colour: a colourful pattern. □ **vif**

2 vivid and interesting: a colourful account of his experiences. □ **coloré**

'colouring noun 1 something used to give colour: She put pink colouring in the icing. □ **colorant**

2 complexion: She had very high colouring (= a very pink complexion). □ **teint**

'colourless adjective 1 without colour: Water is colourless. □ **incolore**

2 not lively or interesting: a colourless young woman. □ **terne**

'colours noun plural 1 a flag: Army regiments salute the colours when on parade. □ **drapeau**

2 a tunic of certain colours worn by a jockey to show that his race-horse belongs to a certain person. □ **couleurs**

'colour-blind adjective unable to tell the difference between certain colours: As he was colour-blind he could not distinguish between red and green. □ **daltonien**

'colour scheme noun an arrangement or choice of colours in decorating a house etc. □ **combinaison de couleurs**

,off-'colour adjective slightly indecent or obscene: She made an off-colour joke. □ **osé, ée**

colour in to put colour into (drawings etc): I coloured in all the oblong shapes on the page. □ **colorier**

show oneself in one's true colours to show or express one's real character, opinion etc: He pretends to be very generous but he showed his true colours when he refused to give money to charity. □ **se révéler tel que l'on est vraiment**

with flying colours with great success: He passed his exam with flying colours. □ **haut la main**

colt [koult] noun a young horse. □ **poulain**

column ['kɒləm] noun 1 a stone or wooden pillar used to support or adorn a building: the carved columns in the temple. □ **colonne**

2 something similar in shape: a column of smoke. □ **colonne**

3 a vertical row (of numbers): He added up the column (of figures) to find the answer. □ **colonne**

4 a vertical section of a page of print: *a newspaper column*. □ **colonne**

5 a section in a newspaper, often written regularly by a particular person: *She writes a daily column about sport*. □ **chronique**

6 a long file of soldiers marching in short rows: *a column of infantry*. □ **colonne**

7 a long line of vehicles *etc*, one behind the other. □ **colonne**

columnist ['koləmnist] *noun* a person who writes regular articles for a newspaper. □ **chroniqueur, euse**

coma ['koumə] *noun* a long-continuing unconscious state: *She was in a coma for several days after the accident*. □ **coma**

comb [koum] *noun* 1 a toothed instrument for separating or smoothing hair *etc*. □ **peigne**

2 an object (often decorative) of similar appearance worn by some women to keep a hair-style in place. □ **peigne**

3 the honey cells made by bees: *a honeycomb*. □ **rayon (de miel)**

4 the crest of some birds. □ **crête**

■ *verb* 1 to arrange and smooth with a comb: *Comb your hair!* □ **peigner**

2 to search (a place) thoroughly (for something): *They combed the hills for the missing climber*. □ **passer au peigne fin**

combat ['kombat,] *noun* (an act of) fighting: *The two knights met each other in single combat*. □ **combat**

■ *verb* to fight against; to oppose: *The residents of the town tried to combat the government's plans to build an expressway*. □ **combattre**

combatant [kəm'batənt, 'kombətənt] *noun* a person who is fighting: *They eventually separated the combatants*. □ **combattant, ante**

combine [kəm'bain] *verb* to join together in one whole; to unite: *They combined (forces) to fight the enemy; The chemist combined calcium and carbon*. □ **combiner**

■ ['kombain] *noun* an association of trading companies: *a large manufacturing combine*. □ **cartel**

,combi'nation [-bi-] *noun* 1 (the result of) combining or being combined: *The town was a combination of old and new architecture*. □ **combinaison**

2 a set of numbers used to open certain types of lock: *She couldn't open the safe as she had forgotten the combination*; (*also adjective*) *a combination lock*. □ **combinaison**

combine harvester a machine that both harvests and threshes crops. □ **moissonneuse-batteuse**

combustible [kəm'bʌstəbl] *adjective* liable to catch fire and burn: *combustible materials*. □ **combustible**

combustion [kəm'bʌstʃən] *noun* burning: *the combustion of gases*. □ **combustion**

come [kʌm] – *past tense* **came** [keim], *past participle* **come** – *verb* 1 to move *etc* towards the person speaking or writing, or towards the place being referred to by him: *Come here!; Are you coming to the dance?; John has come to see me; Have any letters come for me?* □ **venir, arriver**

2 to become near or close to something in time or space: *Christmas is coming soon*. □ **approcher**

3 to happen or be situated: *The letter 'd' comes between 'c' and 'e' in the alphabet*. □ **venir**

4 (*often with* **to**) to happen (by accident): *How did you come to break your leg?* □ **se faire que**

5 to arrive at (a certain state *etc*): *What are things coming to? We have come to an agreement*. □ **aboutir**

6 (*with* **to**) (of numbers, prices *etc*) to amount (to): *The total comes to 51*. □ **se monter à**

■ *interjection* expressing disapproval, drawing attention *etc*: *Come, come! That was very rude of you!* □ **allons!**

'**comer** *noun*: *late-comers will not be admitted; We welcome all comers*. □ **arrivant, ante**

'**coming** *noun*: *the comings and goings of the people in the street*. □ **venue**

'**comeback** *noun* a return (*especially* to show business): *The actress made a comeback years after retiring*. □ **rentrée**

'**comedown** *noun* a fall in dignity *etc*: *The smaller car was a bit of a comedown after the Rolls-Royce*. □ **déchéance**

come about to happen: *How did that come about?* □ **arriver**

come across to meet or find by chance: *He came across some old friends*. □ **tomber sur**

come along 1 to come with or accompany the person speaking *etc*: *Come along with me!* □ **accompagner**

2 to progress: *How are things coming along?* □ **avancer**

come around 1 to visit: *Come around and see us soon*. □ **passer**

2 to regain consciousness: *He won't come around for twenty minutes at least*. □ **reprendre connaissance**

come by to get: *How did you come by that black eye?* □ **attraper**

come down to decrease; to become less: *Tea has come down in price*. □ **baisser**

come from to originate from; to be a part of the whole of something: *The Picasso painting on display at the university comes from the museum's collection*. □ **provenir**

come into one's own to have the opportunity of showing what one can do *etc*: *He has at last come into his own as a pop-singer*. □ **se réaliser**

come off 1 to fall off: *Her shoe came off*. □ **tomber**

2 to turn out (well); to succeed: *The gamble didn't come off*. □ **réussir**

come on 1 to appear on stage or on the screen: *They waited for the comedian to come on*. □ **entrer en scène**

2 hurry up!: *Come on – we'll be late for the party!* □ **allons!**

3 don't be ridiculous!: *Come on, you don't really expect me to believe that!* □ **allons!**

come out 1 to become known: *The truth finally came out*. □ **être révélé**

2 to be published: *This newspaper comes out once a week*. □ **paraître**

3 to strike: *The men have come out (on strike)*. □ **débrayer**

4 (of a photograph) to be developed: *This photograph has come out very well*. □ **venir (bien ou mal)**

5 to be removed: *This dirty mark won't come out.* □ **partir**

come round 1 (*also* **come around**) to visit: *Come round and see us soon.* □ **passer**

2 to regain consciousness: *I won't come round for twenty minutes at least.* □ **reprendre connaissance**

come to to regain consciousness: *When will he come to after the operation?* □ **reprendre connaissance**

come to light to be discovered: *The theft only came to light when the owners returned from holiday.* □ **être découvert**

come upon to meet, find or discover by chance: *She came upon a solution to the problem.* □ **tomber sur**

come up with to think of; to produce: *She's come up with a great idea.* □ **sortir**

come what may whatever happens: *I'll give you my support, come what may!* □ **quoi qu'il arrive**

to come (in the) future: *in the days to come.* □ **à venir**

comedy ['kɔmədi] – *plural* '**comedies** – *noun* **1** a play of a pleasant or amusing kind: *We went to see a comedy last night.* □ **comédie**

2 humour: *They all saw the comedy of the situation.* □ **comique**

comedian [kə'miːdiən] – *feminine* **comedienne** [kə,miːdi'ən] – *noun* a performer who tells jokes or acts in comedies. □ **comique**

comely ['kʌmli] *adjective* pleasant to look at. □ **gracieux** '**comeliness** *noun*. □ **charme**

comet ['kɔmit] *noun* a type of heavenly body which leaves a trail of light behind it as it moves. □ **comète**

comfort ['kʌmfət] *noun* **1** a pleasant condition of being physically or mentally relaxed, happy, warm *etc*: *They now live in comfort.* □ **confort**

2 anything that provides a little luxury, or makes one feel happier, or better able to bear misfortune: *I enjoyed the comforts of the hotel; Her presence was a comfort to him in his grief; words of comfort.* □ **(ré)confort**

comfort *verb* to console; to try and make someone who is sad feel better: *We tried to comfort Yvonne when her father died.* □ **réconforter**

'**comfortable** *adjective* **1** in comfort; pleasantly relaxed: *He looked very comfortable in his chair.* □ **à l'aise**

2 producing a good physical feeling: *a comfortable chair.* □ **confortable**

3 financially secure without being rich: *a comfortable standard of living.* □ **aisé**

'**comfortably** *adverb*. □ **confortablement**

'**comforting** *adjective* producing a pleasant or relaxed feeling: *a comforting thought.* □ **réconfortant**

be comfortably off to have enough money to live in comfort. □ **être à l'aise**

comic ['kɔmik] *adjective* **1** of comedy: *a comic actor; comic opera.* □ **comique**

2 causing amusement: *comic remarks.* □ **drôle**

■ *noun* **1** an amusing person, *especially* a professional comedian. □ **comique**

2 a children's periodical containing funny stories, adventures *etc* in the form of comic strips. □ **journal de bandes dessinées**

'**comical** *adjective* funny: *It was comical to see the chim-*

panzee pouring out a cup of tea. □ **comique**

comic strip a series of small pictures showing stages in an adventure. □ **bande dessinée**

comma ['kɔmə] *noun* the punctuation mark (,) used to show a slight pause *etc*. □ **virgule**

command [kə'maːnd] *verb* **1** to order: *I command you to leave the room immediately!* □ **ordonner**

2 to have authority over: *He commanded a regiment of soldiers.* □ **commander**

3 to have by right: *She commands great respect.* □ **imposer**

■ *noun* **1** an order: *They obeyed his commands.* □ **ordre**

2 control: *She was in command of the operation.* □ **à la tête de**

commandant [,kɔmən'dant, 'kɔməndant] *noun* an officer who has the command of a place or of a body of troops. □ **commandant, ante**

com'mander *noun* **1** a person who commands: *He was the commander of the expedition.* □ **chef**

2 in the navy, an officer of the rank next below the captain. □ **capitaine de frégate**

com'manding *adjective* **1** impressive: *He has a commanding appearance.* □ **imposant**

2 with a wide view: *The house had a commanding position on the hill.* □ **dominant**

com'mandment *noun* a command given by God, *especially* one of the ten given to Moses. □ **commandement**

com,mander-in-'chief *noun* the officer in supreme command of an army, or of the entire forces of the state. □ **commandant en chef**

commandeer [kɔmən'diə] *verb* to seize (private property) for use by the army *etc* during wartime: *They commandeered the castle.* □ **réquisitionner**

commando [kə'maːndou] – *plural* **com'mandos** – *noun* (a member of) a unit of troops specially trained for tasks requiring special courage and skill. □ **commando**

commemorate [kə'meməreit] *verb* **1** (of people) to honour the memory of (someone) by a solemn celebration: *We always commemorate his birthday.* □ **célébrer**

2 (of things) to serve as a memorial to (someone or something): *This inscription commemorates those who died.* □ **commémorer**

com'memorative [-tiv] *adjective*. □ **commémoratif** **com,memor'ation** *noun*. □ **commémoration**

commence [kə'mens] *verb* to begin: *the church service commenced with a hymn.* □ **commencer**

com'mencement *noun*. □ **commencement**

commend [kə'mend] *verb* **1** to praise: *Her ability was commended.* □ **louer**

2 to give (someone or something) to be looked after: *I commend him to your care.* □ **recommander**

com'mendable *adjective* praiseworthy: *Her courage during the storm was commendable.* □ **louable** ,**commen'dation** [ko-] *noun* praise. □ **louange**

comment ['kɔment] *noun* (a) spoken or written remark: *He made several comments about your untidy appearance.* □ **commentaire**

■ *verb* (*with* on) to make such a remark: *He commented on my appearance.* □ **commenter qqch.**

'**commentary** – *plural* '**commentaries** – *noun* (*also*

running commentary) a series of broadcast comments by a reporter at a ceremony, sports event *etc*. □ **commentaire**

'**commentate** [-teit] *verb* to give a commentary: *Who is commentating on the football match?* □ **commenter** '**commentator** *noun*. □ **commentateur, trice**

commerce ['kɔmə:s] *noun* the exchange of goods between nations or people; trade on a large scale: *She is engaged in commerce.* □ **commerce**

commercial [kə'mə:ʃəl] *adjective* **1** connected with commerce: *Private cars are allowed to use this road but not commercial vehicles.* □ **commercial**

2 (likely to be) profitable: *a commercial proposition.* □ **d'affaires**

3 paid for by advertisements: *commercial television.* □ **commercial**

■ *noun* a TV or radio advertisement: *I enjoyed the play but the commercials irritated me.* □ **publicité**

commercialize, commercialise [kə'mə:ʃəlaiz] *verb* to try to make (something) a source of profit: *Christmas has become commercialized.* □ **commercialiser**

commercialism [kə'mə:ʃəlizəm] *noun.* □ **mercantilisme**

commercial traveller a travelling representative of a business firm. □ **voyageur, euse de commerce**

commiserate [kə'mizəreit] *verb* to express sympathy (with). □ **témoigner de la sympathie à** **com,mise'ration** *noun.* □ **commisération**

commission [kə'miʃən] **1** money earned by a person who sells things for someone else. □ **commission**

2 an order for a work of art: *a commission to paint the president's portrait.* □ **commande**

3 an official paper giving authority, *especially* to an army officer *etc*: *My son got his commission last year.* □ **brevet**

4 an official group appointed to report on a specific matter: *the Royal Commission on Education.* □ **commission**

■ *verb* **1** to give an order (*especially* for a work of art) to: *She was commissioned to paint the mayor's portrait.* □ **passer une commande à**

2 to give a military commission to. □ **nommer à un commandement**

com'missioner *noun* a representative of the government in a district or department. □ **commissaire**

in/out of commission in, or not in, a usable, working condition. □ **en/hors de service**

commit [kə'mit] – *past tense, past participle* **com'mitted** – *verb* **1** to perform; to do (*especially* something illegal): *He committed the murder when he was drunk.* □ **commettre**

2 to hand over (a person) to an institution *etc* for treatment, safekeeping *etc*: *committed to prison.* □ **faire interner**

3 to put (oneself) under a particular obligation: *She has committed herself to finishing the book this year.* □ **s'engager (à)**

com'mitment *noun* obligation: *She could not take the job because of family commitments.* □ **obligation**

com'mittal *noun* the act of committing (to an institu-

tion). □ **internement**

com'mitted *adjective* pledged to do, or to support, something: *He was committed to looking after his uncle; She is a committed socialist.* □ **engagé (à)**

commit suicide to kill oneself; to take one's own life: *Martha became more and more depressed until she no longer wanted to live and tried to commit suicide.* □ **se suicider**

committee [kə'miti] *noun or noun plural* a number of persons, selected from a larger body, to deal with some special business, *eg* the running of the larger body's affairs: *The committee meet(s) today; (also adjective) a committee meeting.* □ **comité**

---

committee is spelt with **-mm-, -tt-, -ee-**.

---

commodious [kə'moudiəs] *adjective* spacious. □ **spacieux**

commodity [kə'modəti] – *plural* **com'modities** – *noun* an article which is bought or sold: *soap, toothpaste and other household commodities.* □ **marchandise**

commodore ['kɔmədo:] *noun* in the Canadian and British navies, (of) the rank next above captain. □ **commodore**

common ['kɔmən] *adjective* **1** seen or happening often; quite normal or usual: *a common occurrence; These birds are not so common nowadays.* □ **courant, banal**

2 belonging equally to, or shared by, more than one: *This knowledge is common to all of us; We share a common language.* □ **commun**

3 publicly owned: *common property.* □ **public**

4 coarse or impolite: *She uses some very common expressions.* □ **vulgaire**

5 of ordinary, not high, social rank: *the common people.* □ **du commun**

6 of a noun, not beginning with a capital letter (except at the beginning of a sentence): *The house is empty.* □ **commun**

■ *noun* (a piece of) public land for everyone to use, with few or no buildings: *the village common.* □ **terrain communal**

'**commoner** *noun* a person who is not of high rank: *The royal princess married a commoner.* □ **roturier, ière**

common knowledge something known to everyone or to most people: *Surely you know that already – it's common knowledge.* □ **de notoriété publique**

'**commonplace** *adjective* very ordinary and uninteresting: *commonplace remarks.* □ **banal**

'**common room** *noun* in a college, school *etc* a sitting-room for the use of a group. □ **salle commune**

common sense practical good sense: *If he has any common sense he'll change jobs.* □ **sens commun, bon sens**

common market an association of countries to establish free trade (without duty, tariffs *etc*) among them. □ **marché commun**

the (House of) Commons the lower house of the Canadian parliament. □ **les communes**

in common (of interests, attitudes, characteristics *etc*) shared or alike: *They have nothing in common – I don't know why they're getting married.* □ **en commun**

commonwealth ['kɔmənwelθ] *noun* an association of

states who have joined together for their common good: *the Commonwealth of Australia*. □ **confédération, commonwealth**

commotion [kə'mouʃən] *noun* (a) confused, noisy uproar: *He was woken by a commotion in the street*. □ **tumulte**

communal *see* commune.

commune ['komjuːn] *noun* a group of people living together and sharing everything they own. □ **commune** 'communal *adjective* **1** of a community: *The communal life suited them*. □ **communautaire**
2 shared: *a communal television antenna*. □ **communautaire**

communicate [kə'mjuːnikeit] *verb* **1** to tell (information *etc*): *She communicated the facts to him*. □ **communiquer**
2 to get in touch (with): *It's difficult to communicate with her now that she has left the country*. □ **communiquer (avec)**
com,muni'cation *noun* **1** (an act, or means, of) conveying information: *Communication is difficult in some remote parts of the country*. □ **communication**
2 a piece of information given, a letter *etc*: *I received your communication in this morning's post*. □ **message**
com,muni'cations *noun plural* means of sending messages or of transporting (*eg* troops and supplies). □ **liaison**
com'municative [-tiv] *adjective* (*negative* **uncommunicative**) talkative; sociable: *She's not very communicative this morning*. □ **communicatif**

communion [kə'mjuːnjən] *noun* the sharing of thoughts and feelings; fellowship. □ **communion**
(Holy) Communion in the Christian Church, the service which commemorates the meal taken by Christ with His disciples before His crucifixion. □ **communion**

communiqué [kə'mjuːnikei] *noun* an official announcement. □ **communiqué**

communism ['komjunizəm] *noun* (*often with capital*) a system of government under which there is no private industry and (in some forms) no private property, most things being state-owned. □ **communisme**
'communist *noun* (*often with capital*) a person who believes in communism: *He is a Communist*; (*also adjective*) *a Communist leader*. □ **communiste**

community [kə'mjuːnəti] – *plural* com'munities – *noun*
1 a group of people *especially* having the same religion or nationality and living in the same general area: *the Chinese community in Toronto*. □ **communauté**
2 the public in general: *You did it for the good of the community*; (*also adjective*) *a community worker, a community centre*. □ **communauté; collectivité**

commute [kə'mjuːt] *verb* **1** to travel regularly between two places, *especially* between home in the suburbs and work in the city. □ **faire la navette (entre)**
2 to change (a criminal sentence) for one less severe: *His death sentence was commuted to life imprisonment*. □ **commuer**
com'muter *noun* a person who travels to work daily. □ **banlieusard, arde**

compact¹ [kəm'pakt] *adjective* fitted neatly together in a small space: *Our new house is very compact*. □ **compact**
■ ['kompakt] *noun* a small container for women's face-powder: *a powder-compact with a mirror*. □ **poudrier**

compact² ['kompakt] *noun* an agreement: *The management and trade union leaders finally signed a compact*. □ **convention**

companion [kəm'panjən] *noun* **1** a person *etc* who accompanies another person as a friend *etc*: *She was his constant companion in his childhood*. □ **compagnon, compagne**
2 a helpful handbook on a particular subject: *The Gardening Companion*. □ **manuel**
com'panionable *adjective* pleasantly friendly. □ **sociable**
com'panionship *noun* state of being or of having companion(s): *She enjoys the companionship of young people*. □ **compagnie**

company ['kʌmpəni] – *plural* 'companies – *noun* **1** a number of people joined together for a (commercial) purpose: *a glass-manufacturing company*. □ **société**
2 guests: *I'm expecting company tonight*. □ **de la visite**
3 companionship: *I was grateful for her company*; *She's always good company*. □ **compagnie**
4 a group of companions: *He got into bad company*. □ **fréquentation**
5 a large group of soldiers, *especially* part of an infantry battalion. □ **compagnie**
keep (someone) company to go, stay *etc* with (someone): *I'll come too, and keep you company*. □ **tenir compagnie à qqn**
part company (with) to leave or separate: *They parted company (with each other) at the bus stop*. □ **(se) quitter**

comparable, comparative *see* compare.

compare [kəm'peə] *verb* **1** to put (things *etc*) side by side in order to see to what extent they are the same or different: *If you compare his work with hers you will find hers more accurate*; *This is a good essay compared with your last one*. □ **comparer**
2 to describe as being similar to: *She compared him to a monkey*. □ **comparer (à)**
3 to be near in standard or quality: *He just can't compare with Mozart*. □ **se comparer**
comparable ['kompərəbl] *adjective* of the same kind, on the same scale *etc*: *The houses were not at all comparable in size*. □ **comparable**
comparative [kəm'parətiv] *adjective* **1** judged by comparing with something else: *the comparative quiet of the suburbs*. □ **relatif**
2 (of an adjective or adverb used in comparisons) between positive and superlative, as the following underlined words: *a bigger book*; *a better man*; *Blacker is a comparative adjective*; (*also noun*) *What is the comparative of 'bad'?* □ **comparatif**
com'paratively *adverb*: *This house was comparatively cheap*. □ **relativement**
comparison [kəm'parisn] *noun* (an act of) comparing: *There's no comparison between Beethoven and pop music*; *Living here is cheap in comparison with Lon-*

don. □ **comparaison**

> **compare with** is used to bring out similarities and differences between two things of the same type: *He compared his pen with mine and decided mine was better.*
> **compare to** is used when pointing out a similarity between two different things: *Stars are often compared to diamonds.*

compartment [kəm'paːtmənt] *noun* a separate part or division *eg* of a railway carriage: *We couldn't find an empty compartment in the train; The drawer was divided into compartments.* □ **compartiment**

compass ['kʌmpəs] *noun* **1** an instrument with a magnetized needle, used to find directions: *If he had carried a compass he would not have lost his way in the hills.* □ **boussole**
2 (*in plural*) an instrument with two movable legs, for drawing circles *etc.* □ **compas**
3 scope or range. □ **portée, étendue**
compass rose the circular drawing showing directions on a plan or map. □ **rose des vents**

compassion [kəm'paʃən] *noun* sorrow or pity for the sufferings of another person. □ **compassion**
com'passionate [-nət] *adjective.* □ **compatissant**

compatible [kəm'patəbl] *adjective* able to agree or exist successfully side by side. □ **compatible (avec)**
com,pati'bility *noun.* □ **compatibilité**
com'patibly *adverb.* □ **d'une manière compatible**

compatriot [kəm'peitriət] *noun* a fellow-countryman: *Many of his compatriots were killed in the war.* □ **compatriote**

compel [kəm'pel] – *past tense, past participle* **com'pelled** – *verb* to force: *They compelled me to betray my country.* □ **contraindre**

compensate ['kompənseit] *verb* **1** to give money to (someone) or to do something else to make up for loss or wrong they have experienced: *This payment will compensate (her) for the loss of her job.* □ **dédommager**
2 to undo the effect of a disadvantage *etc*: *The love the child received from his grandmother compensated for the cruelty of his parents.* □ **compenser**
compensatory [kəm'pensətəri] *adjective.* □ **compensateur**
,compen'sation *noun* payment *etc* given for loss or injury: *He received a large sum of money as compensation when he was injured at work.* □ **indemnité**

compete [kəm'piːt] *verb* to try to beat others in a contest, fight *etc*: *We are competing against them in the next round; Are you competing with her for the job?* □ **rivaliser (avec)**
competition [kompə'tiʃən] *noun* **1** the act of competing; rivalry: *Competition makes children try harder.* □ **rivalité**
2 people competing for a prize *etc*: *There's a lot of competition for this job.* □ **concurrence**
3 a contest for a prize: *Have you entered the tennis competition?* □ **concours, compétition**
competitive [kəm'petətiv] *adjective* **1** (of a person) enjoying competition: *a competitive child.* □ **qui a l'esprit de compétition**

2 (of a price *etc*) not expensive, therefore able to compete successfully with the prices *etc* of rivals. □ **concurrentiel**
3 (of sport *etc*) organized in such a way as to produce a winner: *I prefer hill-climbing to competitive sports.* □ **de compétition**
competitor [kəm'petitə] *noun* a person *etc* who takes part in a competition; a rival: *All the competitors finished the race.* □ **concurrent, ente**

competent ['kompətənt] *adjective* capable; skilled: *a competent pianist; competent to drive a car.* □ **compétent**
'**competence** *noun.* □ **compétence**
'**competently** *adverb.* □ **avec compétence**

competition, competitive, competitor *see* **compete.**

compile [kəm'pail] *verb* to make (a book, table *etc*) from information collected from other books *etc*: *She compiled a French dictionary.* □ **composer (par compilation)**
compilation [kompi'leiʃən] *noun.* □ **compilation**
com'piler *noun.* □ **compilateur, trice**

complacent [kəm'pleisnt] *adjective* showing satisfaction with one's own situation: *a complacent attitude.* □ **suffisant**
com'placence, com'placency *noun.* □ **contentement de soi, suffisance**
com'placently *adverb.* □ **avec suffisance**

complain [kəm'plein] *verb* **1** to state one's displeasure, dissatisfaction *etc*: *I'm going to complain to the police about the noise.* □ **se plaindre**
2 (*with of*) to state that one has (pain, discomfort *etc*): *She's complaining of difficulty in breathing.* □ **se plaindre (de)**
com'plaint *noun* **1** (a statement of one's) dissatisfaction: *The customer made a complaint about the lack of hygiene in the food shop.* □ **plainte**
2 a sickness, disease, disorder *etc*: *He's always suffering from some complaint or other.* □ **maladie**

complement ['kompləmənt] *noun* **1** in a sentence, the words of the predicate, not including the verb. □ **complément**
2 (something added to make) a complete number or amount. □ **complément**
■ *verb* to complete, fill up. □ **compléter**
comple'mentary *adjective.* □ **complémentaire**

> the **complement** (not **compliment**) of a verb.

complete [kəm'pliːt] *adjective* **1** whole; with nothing missing: *a complete set of Shakespeare's plays.* □ **complet**
2 thorough: *My car needs a complete overhaul; a complete surprise.* □ **complet**
3 finished: *My picture will soon be complete.* □ **achevé**
■ *verb* to finish; to make complete: *When will he complete the job?; This stamp completes my collection.* □ **terminer; compléter**
com'pletely *adverb*: *I am not completely satisfied.* □ **complètement**
com'pleteness *noun.* □ **plénitude**

com'pletion [-ʃən] *noun* finishing or state of being finished: *You will be paid on completion of the work.* □ **achèvement**

complex ['kompleks] *adjective* 1 composed of many parts: *a complex piece of machinery.* □ **complexe** 2 complicated or difficult: *a complex problem.* □ **complexe**

■ ['kompleks] *noun* 1 something made up of many different pieces: *The leisure complex will include a swimming pool, tennis courts, a library etc.* □ **ensemble** 2 (*often used loosely*) an abnormal mental state caused by experiences in one's past which affect one's behaviour: *He has a complex about his weight; inferiority complex.* □ **complexe**

complexity [kəm'pleksəti] – *plural* com'plexities – *noun* 1 the quality of being complex. □ **complexité** 2 something complex. □ **complexité**

complexion [kəm'plekʃən] *noun* the colour or appearance of the skin *especially* of the face: *a beautiful complexion.* □ **teint**

complexity *see* complex.

compliance, compliant *see* comply.

complicate ['komplikeit] *verb* to make difficult: *His illness will complicate matters.* □ **compliquer** 'complicated *adjective* (*negative* uncomplicated) difficult to understand: *complicated instructions.* □ **compliqué** ,compli'cation *noun* 1 something making a situation *etc* more difficult: *Taking the dog with us on holiday will be an added complication.* □ **complication** 2 a development (in an illness *etc*) which makes things worse. □ **complication**

compliment ['kompləmənt] *noun* an expression of praise or flattery: *He's always paying her compliments.* □ **compliment** ■ [kompli'ment] *verb* to praise or flatter: *She complimented him on his cooking.* □ **complimenter** ,compli'mentary [-'men-] *adjective* (*negative* uncomplimentary) 1 flattering or praising: *complimentary remarks.* □ **flatteur** 2 given free: *a complimentary ticket.* □ **à titre gracieux** with compliments used when sending a gift *etc*: *'With compliments from a secret admirer'.* □ **avec les hommages de**

to pay a **compliment** (not **complement**).

comply [kəm'plai] *verb* to act in the way that someone else has commanded or wished: *You must comply (with her wishes).* □ **se soumettre (à)** com'pliance *noun*. □ **conformité** com'pliant *adjective* willing to comply. □ **accommodant**

component [kəm'pounənt] *noun* a part of a machine (*eg* a car), instrument (*eg* a radio) *etc*: *He bought components for the television set he was repairing.* □ **pièce**

compose [kəm'pouz] *verb* 1 to form by putting parts together: *A word is composed of several letters.* □ **composer** 2 to write (*eg* music, poetry *etc*): *Mozart began to compose when he was six years old.* □ **composer**

3 to control (oneself) after being upset. □ **se calmer** com'posed *adjective* (of people) quiet and calm: *She looked quite composed.* □ **calme** com'poser *noun* a writer, *especially* of a piece of music. □ **compositeur, trice**

composition [kompə'ziʃən] *noun* 1 something composed, *eg* music: *his latest composition.* □ **composition** 2 the act of composing: *the difficulties of composition.* □ **composition** 3 an essay written as a school exercise: *The children had to write a composition about their holiday.* □ **rédaction** 4 the parts of which a thing is made: *Have you studied the composition of the chemical?* □ **composition** com'posure [-ʒə] *noun* calmness: *I admired her composure.* □ **calme**

composition *see* compose.

compost ['kompoust] *noun* rotting vegetable matter *etc* used as fertilizer. □ **compost**

composure *see* compose.

compound[1] ['kompaund] *adjective* composed of a number of parts: *a compound substance.* □ **composé** ■ *noun* a substance, word *etc* formed from two or more elements: *The word racetrack is a compound; chemical compounds.* □ **composé**

compound[2] ['kompaund] *noun* a fenced or walled-in area, *eg* around a factory, school *etc.* □ **enceinte**

comprehend [kompri'hend] *verb* 1 to understand. □ **comprendre** 2 to include. □ **comprendre** ,compre'hensible *adjective* capable of being understood. □ **compréhensible** ,compre'hension [-ʃən] *noun* the act or power of understanding: *After reading the passage the teacher asked questions to test the children's comprehension.* □ **compréhension** 'compre'hensive [-siv] *adjective* including many things: *The school curriculum is very comprehensive.* □ **vaste; complet** ,compre'hensively *adverb*. □ **très largement** ,compre'hensiveness *noun*. □ **étendue** comprehensive school one that provides education for children of all abilities. □ **collège d'enseignement général**

compress [kəm'pres] *verb* to press together; to force into a narrower space: *All her belongings were compressed into a very small suitcase.* □ **comprimer** com'pressible *adjective*. □ **compressible** com'pression [-ʃən] *noun*. □ **compression** compressed air air which is at a pressure higher than atmospheric pressure: *Deep sea divers breathe compressed air.* □ **air comprimé**

comprise [kəm'praiz] *verb* to contain or consist of: *Her family comprises two sons and a daughter.* □ **comprendre**

The team **comprises** (not **comprises of**) five members.

compromise ['komprəmaiz] *noun* (a) settlement of differences in which each side gives up something it has previously demanded: *We argued for a long time but finally arrived at a compromise.* □ **compromis**

compulsion [kəm'pʌlʃən] *noun* compelling or being compelled: *You are under no compulsion to go.* □ **contrainte**

com'pulsory *adjective* which must be done or carried out: *Is it compulsory for me to attend the class?*; *a compulsory examination.* □ **obligatoire**

com'pulsorily *adverb.* □ **obligatoirement**

compute [kəm'pjuːt] *verb* to calculate or estimate. □ **calculer**

,compu'tation [kom-] *noun.* □ **calcul**

computer [kəm'pjuːtə] *noun* an electronic machine that performs high-speed mathematical operations or that processes information: *The computer crashed at work today so all the employees had to take down information by hand.* □ **ordinateur**

com'puterize, com'puterise *verb* to put (information *etc*) into a form suitable for use by a computer: *Are you intending to computerize your book-ordering system?* □ **informatiser**

computer science [kəmpjuːtə saiəns] *noun* a course of study involving all aspects of computers: *Otto took a computer science course at university to learn how computers are made and how computer hardware and software works.* □ **informatique**

comrade ['komrad] *noun* a close companion: *his comrades in battle.* □ **camarade**

'comradeship *noun*: *the comradeship of the office.* □ **camaraderie**

con [kon] – *past tense, past participle* **conned** – *verb* to trick or persuade dishonestly: *He conned her into giving him money.* □ **escroquer**

■ *noun* a dishonest trick. □ **escroquerie, attrape-nigaud**

'con man *noun* someone who cons people. □ **escroc**

concave [kon'keiv] *adjective* (of an object or surface) curved inwards: *Spoons are concave.* □ **concave**

con'cavity [-'ka-] *noun.* □ **concavité**

conceal [kən'siːl] *verb* to hide or keep secret: *He concealed his disappointment from his friends.* □ **dissimuler**

con'cealment *noun.* □ **dissimulation**

concede [kən'siːd] *verb* **1** to admit: *He conceded that he had been wrong.* □ **reconnaître que**

2 to grant (*eg* a right). □ **accorder**

conceit [kən'siːt] *noun* too much pride in oneself: *He's full of conceit about his good looks.* □ **vanité**

con'ceited *adjective* having too much pride in oneself: *She's conceited about her artistic ability.* □ **vaniteux, orgueilleux**

> **conceit** is spelt with **- ei-**.

conceive [kən'siːv] *verb* **1** to form (an idea *etc*) in the mind. □ **concevoir**

2 to imagine: *I can't conceive why you did that.* □ **comprendre**

3 (of a woman) to become pregnant. □ **concevoir**

con'ceivable *adjective* able to be imagined or thought of. □ **concevable**

con'ceivably *adverb.* □ **de façon concevable**

> **conceive** is spelt with **-ei-**.

concentrate ['konsəntreit] *verb* **1** to give all one's energies, attention *etc* to one thing: *I wish you'd concentrate (on what I'm saying).* □ **se concentrer**

2 to bring together in one place: *He concentrated his soldiers at the gateway.* □ **concentrer**

3 to make (a liquid) stronger by boiling to reduce its volume. □ **concentrer**

'concentrated *adjective* (of a liquid *etc*) made stronger; not diluted: *concentrated orange juice.* □ **concentré**

,concen'tration *noun*: *She lacks concentration – she will never pass the exam.* □ **concentration**

concentric [kən'sentrik] *adjective* (of circles) having a common centre. □ **concentrique**

concept ['konsept] *noun* an idea or theory: *Her design was a new concept in town-planning.* □ **concept**

conception [kən'sepʃən] *noun* **1** the act of conceiving. □ **conception**

2 an idea grasped or understood: *We can have no conception of the size of the universe.* □ **conception**

concern [kən'səːn] *verb* **1** to have to do with: *This order doesn't concern us; So far as I'm concerned, you can do what you like.* □ **concerner**

2 (*with* **for** *or* **about**) to make (*usually* oneself) uneasy: *Don't concern yourself about her.* □ **s'inquiéter de**

3 (*with* **with** *or* **in**) to interest (oneself) in: *He doesn't concern himself with unimportant details.* □ **s'intéresser à**

■ *noun* **1** something that concerns or belongs to one: *Your problems are not my concern.* □ **responsabilité**

2 anxiety: *The condition of the patient is giving rise to concern.* □ **inquiétude**

3 a business: *a shoe-manufacturing concern.* □ **entreprise**

con'cerning *preposition* about: *He wrote to me concerning a business arrangement.* □ **à propos de**

concert ['konsət] *noun* a musical entertainment: *an orchestral concert.* □ **concert**

in concert together: *to act in concert.* □ **de concert avec**

concerted [kən'səːtid] *adjective* carried out by people acting together: *a concerted effort.* □ **concerté**

concertina [konsə'tiːnə] *noun* a portable musical wind instrument with bellows and a keyboard. □ **concertina**

concerto [kən'tʃəːtou] – *plural* **con'certos** – *noun* a piece of music written for one or more solo instruments and orchestra: *a piano concerto.* □ **concerto**

concession [kən'seʃən] *noun* something granted: *As a concession we were given a day off work to go to the wedding.* □ **concession**

conciliate [kən'silieit] *verb* to win over or regain the support, friendship *etc* of. □ **se concilier**

con,cili'ation *noun.* □ **conciliation**

con'ciliatory *adjective.* □ **conciliant**

concise [kən'sais] *adjective* brief but comprehensive: *a clear concise statement.* □ **concis**

con'cisely *adverb.* □ **avec concision**

con'ciseness *noun.* □ **concision**

conclave ['konkleiv] *noun* a private, secret meeting; the place where such a meeting is held. □ **conclave**

conclude [kən'kluːd] *verb* **1** to come or bring to an end: *to conclude a meeting*; *She concluded by thanking everyone.* □ **conclure**

2 to come to believe: *We concluded that you weren't coming.* □ **conclure (que)**

con'clusion [-ʒən] *noun* **1** an end: *the conclusion of his speech.* □ **conclusion**

2 a judgment: *I came to the conclusion that the house was empty.* □ **conclusion**

con'clusive [-siv] *adjective* convincing: *conclusive proof.* □ **concluant**

con'clusively *adverb.* □ **de façon concluante**

con'clusiveness *noun.* □ **caractère probant**

concoct [kən'kokt] *verb* to put together, make up or invent: *I've concocted a new drink for you to try*; *The child concocted a story about having been attacked.* □ **inventer**

con'coction [-ʃən] *noun.* □ **préparation**

concord ['koŋkoːd] *noun* agreement; state of peace. □ **entente**

concrete ['koŋkriːt] *adjective* **1** made of concrete: *concrete slabs.* □ **en béton**

2 able to be seen and felt; real or definite: *A wooden table is a concrete object.* □ **concret**

■ *noun* a mixture of cement with sand *etc* used in building. □ **béton**

■ *verb* to spread with concrete: *We'll have to concrete the garden path.* □ **bétonner**

'concreteness *noun.* □ **caractère concret**

concur [kən'kəːr] – *past tense, past participle* **con'curred** – *verb* to agree; to come together, or coincide. □ **être d'accord (avec)**

con'currence [-'kəːr-] *noun.* □ **simultanéité**

concurrent [kən'kəːrənt] *adjective.* □ **simultané**

con'currently *adverb.* □ **simultanément**

concussed [kən'kʌst] *adjective* suffering from concussion: *He was concussed for several hours.* □ **commotionné**

con'cussion [-ʃən] *noun* temporary harm to the brain caused by a heavy blow on the head: *suffering from concussion.* □ **commotion (cérébrale)**

condemn [kən'dem] *verb* **1** to criticize as morally wrong or evil: *Everyone condemned her for being cruel to her child.* □ **condamner**

2 to sentence to (a punishment): *She was condemned to death.* □ **condamner (à)**

3 to declare (a building) to be unfit to use: *These houses have been condemned.* □ **condamner**

condemnation [kondem'neiʃən] *noun.* □ **condamnation**

condemned cell a cell for a prisoner under sentence of death. □ **cellule des condamnés**

condense [kən'dens] *verb* **1** to make smaller: *They have produced a condensed version of the book for children.* □ **condenser**

2 to make (a liquid) thicker, stronger or more concentrated: *condensed milk.* □ **concentrer**

3 (of vapour) to turn to liquid: *Steam condensed on the kitchen windows.* □ **se condenser**

,conden'sation [konden-] *noun* **1** the act of condensing. □ **condensation**

2 liquid formed from vapour: *I can't see out because of the condensation on the window.* □ **condensation**

condescend [kondi'send] *verb* to agree graciously (to do something). □ **condescendre (à)**

,conde'scending *adjective* giving the impression that one is superior: *a condescending manner.* □ **condescendant**

,conde'scendingly *adverb.* □ **avec condescendance**

,conde'scension [-ʃən] *noun.* □ **condescendance**

condiment ['kondimənt] *noun* a seasoning (*especially* salt or pepper). □ **condiment**

condition [kən'diʃən] **1** state or circumstances in which a person or thing is: *The house is not in good condition*; *She is in no condition to leave hospital*; *under ideal conditions*; *living conditions*; *variable conditions.* □ **condition**

2 something that must happen or be done before some other thing happens or is done; a term or requirement in an agreement: *It was a condition of his going that he should pay his own expenses*; *That is one of the conditions in the agreement.* □ **condition**

■ *verb* **1** to affect or control: *behaviour conditioned by circumstances.* □ **conditionner**

2 to put into the required state: *air-conditioned buildings*; *Well-conditioned hair.* □ **mis en état**

con'ditional *adjective* depending on certain conditions: *This offer of a university place is conditional on your being able to pass your final school exams*; *a conditional offer.* □ **conditionnel**

con'ditionally *adverb.* □ **conditionnellement**

con'ditioner *noun* something which helps in conditioning: *hair conditioner.* □ **lotion capillaire**

on condition that if, and only if (something is done): *You will be paid tomorrow on condition that the work is finished.* □ **à condition que**

condolence [kən'douləns] *noun* sympathy: *a letter of condolence.* □ **condoléances**

condom [kondəm] *noun* a thin protective covering worn on the penis during sexual intercourse and used as birth control and to prevent the spread of infection and disease: *Doctors are recommending that men wear condoms to prevent pregnancy and reduce the risk of AIDS.* □ **condom**

condone [kən'doun] *verb* to excuse or forgive: *She could not condone lying.* □ **pardonner**

conduct [kən'dʌkt] *verb* **1** to lead or guide: *We were conducted down a narrow path by the guide*; *a conducted tour.* □ **conduire**

2 to carry or allow to flow: *Most metals conduct electricity.* □ **être conducteur de**

3 to direct (an orchestra, choir *etc*). □ **diriger**

4 to behave (oneself): *He conducted himself well at the reception.* □ **se conduire**

5 to manage or carry on (a business). □ **diriger**

■ ['kondʌkt] *noun* **1** behaviour: *Her conduct at school was disgraceful.* □ **conduite**

2 the way in which something is managed, done *etc*: *the conduct of the affair.* □ **conduite**

con'duction [-ʃən] *noun* transmission of heat *etc* by a conductor. □ **conduction**

con'ductor *noun* **1** a thing that conducts heat or electricity: *Copper is a good conductor of heat.* □ **conducteur**

2 a director of an orchestra, choir *etc*. □ **chef d'orchestre**

3 a person in charge of a train. □ **chef de train**

cone [koun] *noun* **1** a solid figure with a point and a base in the shape of a circle or oval. □ **cône**

2 the fruit of the pine, fir *etc: fir-cones.* □ **cocotte**

3 a pointed holder for ice cream; *an ice cream cone.* □ **cornet**

4 a warning sign placed next to roadworks *etc* or where parking is not allowed. □ **cône de signalisation**

conical ['konikəl] *adjective* cone-shaped. □ **conique**

confectioner [kən'fekʃənə] *noun* a person who makes or sells sweets or cakes. □ **pâtissier, ière; confiseur, euse**

con'fectionery *noun* **1** sweets, chocolates *etc*. □ **confiseries; pâtisseries**

2 the shop or business of a confectioner. □ **pâtisserie-confiserie**

confederate [kən'fedərət] *noun* a person who has agreed to work with others (*eg* on something dishonest): *He and his confederates were found with stolen money in their possession.* □ **complice**

con'federacy [-rəsi] – *plural* con'federacies – *noun* a league or alliance (of states *etc*). □ **confédération**

con,fede'ration *noun* (the forming of) a league or alliance, *especially* of states *etc*. □ **confédération**

confer [kən'fəː] – *past tense, past participle* con'ferred – *verb* **1** (*often with* **with**) to consult each other: *The staff conferred (with the headmaster) about the new timetable.* □ **s'entretenir (avec)**

2 (*with* **on**) to give (an honour) to someone: *The university conferred degrees on two famous scientists.* □ **conférer (un titre à qqn)**

conference ['konfərəns] *noun* a meeting for discussion: *The conference of heart specialists was held in New York.* □ **congrès**

confess [kən'fes] *verb* to make known that one is guilty, wrong *etc*; to admit: *He confessed (to the crime); He confessed that he had broken the vase; It was stupid of me, I confess.* □ **avouer**

con'fession [-ʃən] *noun* **1** acknowledgment of a crime or fault: *The youth made a confession to the police officer.* □ **aveu**

2 (an) act of confessing one's sins to a priest: *She went to confession every Friday.* □ **confession**

con'fessional [-ʃə-] *noun* the seat *etc* where a priest sits when hearing confessions. □ **confessionnal**

con'fessor *noun* a priest who hears confessions. □ **confesseur**

confetti [kən'feti] *noun* small pieces of coloured paper thrown in celebration at weddings. □ **confettis**

confide [kən'faid] *verb* to tell one's private thoughts to someone: *He confided in his brother; He confided his fears to his brother.* □ **confier (à)**

confidence ['konfidəns] *noun* **1** trust or belief in someone's ability: *I have great confidence in you.* □ **confiance**

2 belief and faith in one's own ability: *She shows a great deal of confidence for her age.* □ **confiance en soi**

confident ['konfidənt] *adjective* having a great deal of trust (*especially* in oneself): *She is confident that she will win; a confident girl.* □ **assuré**

confidential [konfi'denʃəl] *adjective* **1** secret; not to be told to others: *confidential information.* □ **confidentiel**

2 trusted to keep secrets: *a confidential secretary.* □ **de confiance**

confidentiality ['konfidenʃi'aləti] *noun*. □ **caractère confidentiel**

,confi'dentially *adverb* secretly; not wishing to have the information passed on to anyone else: *She could not tell me what he said – he was speaking confidentially.* □ **confidentiellement**

con'fiding *adjective* trustful. □ **confiant**

con'fidingly *adverb*. □ **avec confiance**

in confidence as a secret; confidentially: *He told me the story in (strictest) confidence.* □ **confidentiellement**

confine [kən'fain] *verb* **1** to keep within limits; to stop from spreading: *They succeeded in confining the fire to a small area.* □ **contenir**

2 to shut up or imprison: *The prince was confined in the castle for three years.* □ **enfermer**

con'fined *adjective* **1** (*with* **to**) kept in or shut up in: *confined to bed with a cold.* □ **confiné**

2 narrow, small: *a confined space.* □ **restreint**

con'finement *noun* **1** state of being shut up or imprisoned: *solitary confinement.* □ **emprisonnement**

2 (the time of) the birth of a child: *her third confinement.* □ **accouchement**

'confines ['kon-] *noun plural* limits or boundaries: *within the confines of the city.* □ **limites**

confirm [kən'fəːm] *verb* **1** to establish or make quite certain: *They confirmed their hotel booking by letter.* □ **confirmer**

2 to admit to full membership of certain Christian churches. □ **confirmer**

,confir'mation [kon-] *noun*. □ **confirmation**

con'firmed *adjective* settled in a habit or way of life: *a confirmed bachelor/drunkard.* □ **invétéré**

confiscate ['konfiskeit] *verb* to seize or take (something) away, *usually* as a penalty: *The teacher confiscated the boy's comic which he was reading in class.* □ **confisquer**

,confi'scation *noun*. □ **confiscation**

conflagration [konflə'greiʃən] *noun* a great fire: *Ten people perished in the conflagration.* □ **incendie**

conflict ['konflikt] *noun* **1** (a) disagreement: *There was considerable conflict about which plan should be accepted.* □ **conflit (d'opinions)**

2 a fight or battle. □ **combat**

■ [kən'flikt] *verb* to contradict each other; to disagree: *The two accounts of what had happened conflicted (with each other).* □ **être en conflit**

confluence ['konfluəns] *noun* a flowing together of two rivers. □ **confluence**

conform [kən'fɔːm] *verb* **1** to behave, dress *etc* in the way that most other people do. □ **se conformer**

2 (*with* **to**) to act according to; to be in agreement with: *Your clothes must conform to the regulation school pat-*

tern. □ **se conformer (à)**

con'formity *noun.* □ **conformité**

confound [kən'faund] *verb* to puzzle and surprise greatly.
□ confondre

confront [kən'frʌnt] *verb* 1 to bring face to face with:
He was confronted with the evidence of his crime. □
confronter (avec)
2 to face in a hostile manner; to oppose: *They confronted
the enemy at dawn.* □ **affronter**
,confron'tation [kon-] *noun.* □ **confrontation**

confuse [kən'fjuːz] *verb* 1 to put in disorder: *I confused
the arrangements by arriving late.* □ **bouleverser**
2 to mix up in one's mind: *I always confuse John and
his twin brother.* □ **confondre**
3 to make puzzled: *He completely confused me by his
questions.* □ **embrouiller**
con'fused *adjective* 1 mixed up: *The message I received
was rather confused.* □ **confus**
2 mixed up in the mind: *in a confused state of mind.* □
troublé
con'fusedly [-zidli] *adverb.* □ **confusément**
con'fusion [-ʒən] *noun.* □ **confusion**

congeal [kən'dʒiːl] *verb* (*especially* of blood, grease *etc*)
to solidify when cooled. □ **(se) figer**

congenial [kən'dʒiːniəl] *adjective* agreeable; pleasant.
□ sympathique

congenital [kən'dʒenitl] *adjective* (of diseases or de-
formities) existing at or before birth. □ **congénital**
con'genitally *adverb.* □ **congénitalement**

congested [kən'dʒestid] *adjective* over-crowded; over-
full. □ **encombré**
con'gestion [-tʃən] *noun.* □ **encombrement**

con,glome'ration [kəngloməˈreiʃən] *noun* a mixed heap
or collection: *a conglomeration of old clothes.* □
groupement

congratulate [kən'gratjuleit] *verb* (*often with* on) to
express pleasure and joy to (a person) at a happy event,
a success *etc*: *They congratulated her on passing her
driving test.* □ **féliciter (qqn de qqch.)**
con'gratulatory [-lə-] *adjective.* □ **de félicitations**
con,gratu'lation *noun* (*usually in plural*): *Warmest congratulations on the birth of your baby; a message of
congratulation.* □ **félicitations**

congregate ['kɔŋgrigeit] *verb* to come or bring together:
A large crowd congregated in the street. □ **se rassembler**
,congre'gation *noun* a group gathered together, *especially* people in a church for a service, or belonging to a
church: *The minister visited all the members of his congregation.* □ **assemblée (des fidèles)**

congress ['kɔŋgres] *noun* 1 a formal meeting, *especially*
an assembly of delegates *etc*. □ **congrès**
2 a law-making body or parliament, *especially* that of
the United States: *She has been elected to Congress.* □
Congrès
con'gressional [-ʃənl] *adjective.* □ **du Congrès**
'congressman *noun.* □ **membre du Congrès, député**
'congresswoman *noun.* □ **membre du Congrès,
députée**

congruent ['kɔŋgruənt] *adjective* of two or more geometrical figures, touching at all points when one is fit-

ted on top of the other: *congruent triangles.* □ **congruent**
con'gruity [-'gruː-] *noun.* □ **congruité**

conical *see* cone.

conifer ['kɔnifə,'kou-] *noun* a cone-bearing tree, *eg* the
fir: *The larch tree is a conifer.* □ **conifère**
co'niferous *adjective* cone-bearing. □ **conifère**

conjecture [kən'dʒektʃə] *noun* (an) opinion formed on
slight evidence; a guess: *He made several conjectures
about where his son might be.* □ **conjecture**
■ *verb* to guess. □ **conjecturer**
con'jectural *adjective.* □ **conjectural**

conjugal ['kɔndʒugəl] *adjective* of marriage. □ **conjugal**

conjugate ['kɔndʒugeit] *verb* to give the different parts
of (a verb). □ **conjuguer**
,conju'gation *noun.* □ **conjugaison**

conjunction [kən'dʒʌŋkʃən] *noun* a word that connects
sentences, clauses or words: *John sang and Mary
danced; I'll do it if you want.* □ **conjonction**
in conjunction (with) (acting) together (with). □
conjointement avec

conjure ['kɔndʒə, 'kʌn-] *verb* to perform tricks (con-
juring tricks) that seem magical, as an entertainment.
□ faire de la prestidigitation
'conjuror, 'conjurer *noun.* □ **prestidigitateur, trice**

connect [kə'nekt] *verb* 1 to join or be joined in some
way; to tie or fasten or link together: *She connected the
radio to the mains; This road connects the two farms; a
connecting link; This telephone line connects with the
President.* □ **relier**
2 to associate in the mind: *People tend to connect money
with happiness.* □ **associer (à)**
con'nection [-ʃən] *noun* 1 something that connects or
is connected: *a faulty electrical connection.* □ **connexion**
2 (a) state of being connected or related: *My connection
with their family is very slight; I wish to talk to you in
connection with my daughter's career.* □ **rapports**
3 a useful person whom one can contact, *especially* in
business: *her connections in the clothing trade.* □ **relation**
4 a train, bus *etc* to which one changes from another in
the course of a journey: *As the local train was late, I
missed the connection to Toronto.* □ **correspondance**

connive [kə'naiv] *verb* (*with* at) to make no attempt to
hinder (something wrong or illegal): *Her mother con-
nived at the child's truancy.* □ **fermer les yeux sur**
con'nivance *noun.* □ **connivence**

connoisseur [kɔnə'səː] *noun* an expert judge of *eg* art,
music, wine *etc*: *Let her choose the wine – she's the
connoisseur.* □ **connaisseur, euse**

conquer ['kɔŋkə] *verb* to overcome or defeat: *The
Normans conquered England in the eleventh century;
You must conquer your fear of the dark.* □ **conquérir,
vaincre**
'conqueror *noun.* □ **conquérant, ante**

conquest ['kɔŋkwest] *noun* (an) act of conquering: *The
Norman Conquest; He's impressed with you – you've
made a conquest.* □ **conquête**

conscience ['kɔnʃəns] *noun* (that part of one's mind
which holds one's) knowledge or sense of right and

wrong: *The injured man was on her conscience because she was responsible for the accident; She had a bad conscience about the injured man; He had no conscience about dismissing the men.* □ **conscience**

conscientious [konʃi'enʃəs] *adjective* careful and hard-working: *a conscientious pupil.* □ **consciencieux** ,**consci'entiously** *adverb.* □ **consciencieusement** ,**consci'entiousness** *noun.* □ **conscience**

conscious ['konʃəs] *adjective* **1** aware of oneself and one's surroundings; not asleep or in a coma or anaesthetized *etc*: *The patient was conscious.* □ **conscient** **2** (*sometimes with* **of**) aware or having knowledge (of): *They were conscious of his disapproval.* □ **conscient (de)** '**consciously** *adverb.* □ **consciemment** '**consciousness** *noun: The patient soon regained consciousness.* □ **connaissance**

conscript ['konskript] *noun* a person legally ordered by the state to serve in the armed forces *etc*. □ **conscrit, ite** ■ [kən'skript] *verb* legally to order (someone) to serve in the armed forces *etc*: *He was conscripted into the army.* □ **enrôler** **con'scription** [-ʃən] *noun.* □ **conscription**

consecrate ['konsikreit] *verb* to set apart for a holy use; to dedicate to God: *The bishop consecrated the new church.* □ **consacrer** ,**conse'cration** *noun.* □ **consécration**

consecutive [kən'sekjutiv] *adjective* following one after the other in regular order: *She visited us on two consecutive days, Thursday and Friday.* □ **consécutif** **con'secutively** *adverb.* □ **consécutivement**

consensus [kən'sensəs] *noun* the feeling of most people: *The consensus of opinion is that we should do this.* □ **consensus**

consent [kən'sent] *verb* to give permission or agree (to): *I consent to that plan.* □ **consentir (à)** ■ *noun* agreement; permission: *You have my consent to leave.* □ **consentement**

consequence ['konsikwəns] *noun* **1** a result: *This decision will have important consequences.* □ **conséquence** **2** importance: *A small error is of no consequence.* □ **conséquence** '**consequently** *adverb* therefore: *She didn't explain it clearly – consequently, I didn't understand.* □ **par conséquent**

conservation, conservatism *etc see* **conserve.**

conservatory [kən'sɜːvətɔːri, -tri] – *plural* **con'servatories** – *noun* **1** a kind of greenhouse, or a glass-walled part of a building, in which plants are grown. □ **serre** **2** a school of music, art *etc*. □ **conservatoire**

conserve [kən'sɜːv] *verb* to keep from changing, being damaged or lost: *We must conserve the country's natural resources; This old building should be conserved.* □ **préserver** ■ *noun* something preserved, *eg* fruits in sugar, jam *etc*. □ **conserve** ,**conser'vation** [kon-] *noun* the act of conserving *especially* wildlife, the countryside, old buildings *etc*. □ **défense de l'environnement**

,**conser'vationist** [kon-] *noun* a person who is interested in conservation. □ **partisan, ane de la défense de l'environnement**

con'servatism [-vətizəm] *noun* dislike of change. □ **conservatisme**

con'servative [-tiv] *adjective* **1** disliking change: *Older people tend to be conservative in their attitudes; conservative opinions.* □ **conservateur, trice** **2** in politics, wanting to avoid major changes and to keep business and industry in private hands. □ **conservateur**

consider [kən'sidə] *verb* **1** to think about (carefully): *He considered their comments.* □ **réfléchir à** **2** to feel inclined towards: *I'm considering leaving this job.* □ **penser à** **3** to take into account: *You must consider other people's feelings.* □ **tenir compte de** **4** to regard as being: *They consider him unfit for that job.* □ **considérer** **con'siderable** *adjective* great: *considerable wealth; a considerable number of people.* □ **considérable** **con'siderably** *adverb: Considerably fewer people came than I expected.* □ **considérablement**

considerate [kən'sidərət] *adjective* thoughtful about others: *She is always considerate to elderly people.* □ **prévenant (envers)** **con,side'ration** *noun* **1** (the act of) thinking about something, *especially* the needs or feelings of other people: *He stayed at home out of consideration for his mother.* □ **considération** **2** a fact to be taken into account in making a decision *etc*: *The cost of the journey is our main consideration.* □ **préoccupation** **con'sidering** *preposition* taking into account; despite: *Considering her deafness she manages to understand very well.* □ **étant donné** **take into consideration** to allow for (in considering a situation or problem): *You must take his illness into consideration before dismissing him.* □ **prendre en considération**

consign [kən'sain] *verb* to put into or deliver to: *The body was consigned with reverence to the grave.* □ **confier** **con'signment** *noun* a load (of goods): *the latest consignment of books.* □ **envoi**

consist [kən'sist] *verb* (*with* **of**) to be composed or made up: *The house consists of six rooms.* □ **consister (en)** **con'sistency**[1] *noun* the degree of thickness or firmness: *of the consistency of dough.* □ **consistance**

consistent [kən'sistənt] *adjective* **1** (*often with* **with**) in agreement (with): *The two statements are not consistent; The second statement is not consistent with the first.* □ **compatible** **2** always (acting, thinking or happening) according to the same rules or principles; the same or regular: *He was consistent in his attitude; a consistent style of writing.* □ **cohérent** **con'sistency**[2] *noun: the consistency of her work.* □ **cohérence** **con'sistently** *adverb: Her work is consistently good.* □ **régulièrement**

console [kən'soul] *verb* to comfort: *She could not console the weeping child.* □ **consoler**
,conso'lation [kon-] *noun* **1** the act of consoling. □ **consolation**
2 something that consoles: *His great wealth was no consolation for the loss of his reputation;* (*also adjective*) *a consolation prize* (for someone who just failed to win). □ **(de) consolation**
consolidate [kən'solideit] *verb* to make or become solid; to strengthen. □ **consolider**
con,soli'dation *noun.* □ **consolidation**
consonant ['konsənənt] *noun* any letter of the alphabet except *a,e,i,o,u.* □ **consonne**
consort ['konsoːt] *noun* a (*especially* royal) wife or husband: *prince consort* (= the husband of a reigning queen). □ **époux, ouse, (prince) consort**
■ ['konsoːt] *verb* (*with* **with**) to have dealings or associations (*with, usually* in a bad sense): *You've been consorting with drug-addicts.* □ **frayer avec qqn**
consortium [kən'soːtiəm, -ʃiəm] *noun* an association, union, *especially* of bankers or businessmen. □ **consortium**
conspicuous [kən'spikjuəs] *adjective* very noticeable: *His blond hair made him conspicuous in the crowd.* □ **voyant**
con'spicuously *adverb.* □ **remarquablement**
con'spicuousness *noun.* □ **visibilité**
conspire [kən'spaiə] *verb* to plot or secretly make plans together: *They conspired with the terrorists to overthrow the government.* □ **conspirer**
con'spiracy [-'spi-] – *plural* **con'spiracies** – *noun* (a plan made by) conspiring: *The government discovered the conspiracy in time.* □ **conspiration**
con'spirator [-'spi-] *noun* a person who conspires. □ **conspirateur, trice**
constable ['konstəbl] *noun* a policeman, *especially* one not of high rank. □ **agent, e de police**
constant ['konstənt] *adjective* **1** never stopping: *a constant noise.* □ **incessant**
2 unchanging: *It must be kept at a constant temperature.* □ **constant**
3 faithful: *I remained constant.* □ **fidèle**
'constantly *adverb.* □ **sans cesse**
'constancy *noun.* □ **constance**
constellation [konstə'leiʃən] *noun* a named group of stars: *The Plough and Orion are constellations.* □ **constellation**
consternation [konstə'neiʃən] *noun* astonishment or dismay: *To my consternation, when I reached home I found I had lost the key of the house.* □ **consternation**
constipated ['konstipeitid] *adjective* having difficulty in passing waste matter (as regularly as normal) from the bowels. □ **constipé**
,consti'pation *noun.* □ **constipation**
constituent [kən'stitjuənt] *noun* **1** a necessary part: *Hydrogen is a constituent of water.* □ **élément constitutif**
2 a voter from a particular member of parliament's constituency: *He deals with all his constituents' problems.* □ **électeur, trice**
■ *adjective:* *He broke it down into its constituent parts.*

□ **constitutif; constituant**
con'stituency – *plural* **con'stituencies** – *noun* the group of voters, or the area in which they live, represented by a member of parliament. □ **circonscription**
constitute ['konstitjuːt] *verb* to form; to make up; to be: *Nuclear waste constitutes a serious danger.* □ **constituer**
,consti'tution *noun* **1** a set of rules governing an organization; the supreme laws and rights of a country's people *etc: the constitution of the country.* □ **constitution**
2 physical characteristics, health *etc: He has a strong constitution.* □ **constitution**
,consti'tutional *adjective* legal according to a given constitution: *The proposed change would not be constitutional.* □ **constitutionnel**
,consti'tutionally *adverb.* □ **constitutionnellement**
constrict [kən'strikt] *verb* to press tightly; to cramp: *The tight collar was constricting his neck.* □ **(re)serrer**
construct [kən'strʌkt] *verb* to build; to put together: *They are planning to construct a new supermarket near our house; Construct a sentence containing 'although'.* □ **construire**
con'struction [-ʃən] *noun* **1** (a way of) constructing or putting together: *The bridge is still under construction.* □ **construction**
2 something built: *That construction won't last long.* □ **construction**
con'structive [-tiv] *adjective* helpful; having to do with making, not with destroying: *Constructive criticism tells you both what is wrong and also what to do about it.* □ **constructif**
con'structively *adverb.* □ **de manière constructive**
con'structor *noun* a person who constructs: *a constructor of bridges.* □ **constructeur, trice**
construction site a building site. □ **chantier**
construction worker a builder. □ **ouvrier, ière du bâtiment**
consul ['konsəl] *noun* **1** an agent who looks after his country's residents in (part of) a foreign country: *the Canadian Consul in Berlin.* □ **consul, ule**
2 either of the two chief magistrates in ancient Rome. □ **consul**
'consular [-sju-] *adjective.* □ **consulaire**
consulate ['konsələt, -sjulət] *noun* the office or residence of a consul. □ **consulat**
consult [kən'sʌlt] *verb* **1** to seek advice or information from: *Consult your doctor; He consulted his watch; He consulted with me about what we should do next.* □ **consulter**
2 (of a doctor *etc*) to give professional advice: *She consults on Mondays and Fridays.* □ **donner des consultations**
con'sultant *noun* **1** a person who gives professional advice: *She is consultant to a firm of engineers;* (*also adjective*) *a consultant engineer.* □ **expert-conseil, experte-conseil**
2 a senior hospital doctor specializing in a particular branch of medicine: *His condition is so serious that they have sent for the consultant;* (*also adjective*) *a consultant physician.* □ **spécialiste**
,consul'tation [kon-] *noun: How much does she charge*

for a consultation? □ **consultation**

consume [kən'sjuːm] *verb* 1 to eat or drink: *He consumes a huge amount of food.* □ **consommer**

2 to use: *How much electricity do you consume per month?* □ **consommer**

3 to destroy, *eg* by fire: *The entire building was consumed by fire.* □ **consumer**

con'sumer *noun* a person who eats, uses, buys things *etc*: *The average consumer spends 12 dollars per year on toothpaste.* □ **consommateur, trice**

consumption [kən'sʌmpʃən] *noun* the act of consuming: *The consumption of coffee has increased.* □ **consommation**

consumer goods goods which can be used immediately to satisfy human needs, *eg* clothing, food, TV sets *etc*. □ **biens de consommation**

consummate ['kɔnsəmeit] *verb* to complete or fulfil. □ **consommer**

■ [-mət] *adjective* complete; perfect. □ **accompli**

,consum'mation *noun*. □ **consommation**

consumption *see* **consume.**

contact ['kɔntakt] *noun* 1 physical touch or nearness: *Her hands came into contact with acid; Has she been in contact with measles?* □ **contact**

2 communication: *I've lost contact with all my old friends; We have succeeded in making (radio) contact with the ship; How can I get in contact with him?* □ **contact**

3 a person with influence, knowledge *etc* which might be useful: *I made several good contacts in Toronto.* □ **relation(s)**

4 (a place where) a wire *etc* carrying electric current (may be attached): *the contacts on the battery.* □ **contact**

5 a person who has been near someone with an infectious disease: *We must trace all known contacts of the cholera victim.* □ **contaminateur, trice possible**

6 a person or thing that provides a means of communicating with someone: *His radio is his only contact with the outside world.* □ **lien**

■ *verb* to get in touch with in order to give or share information *etc*: *I'll contact you by telephone.* □ **contacter**

contact lens a small plastic lens on the eyeball worn, instead of spectacles, to improve sight. □ **verre de contact**

contagious [kən'teidʒəs] *adjective* spreading from one person to another by physical contact: *Is that skin disease contagious?* □ **contagieux**

con'tagion *noun* an infection. □ **contagion**

contain [kən'tein] *verb* 1 to keep or have inside: *This box contains a pair of shoes; How much milk does this jug contain?* □ **contenir**

2 to control: *He could hardly contain his excitement.* □ **maîtriser**

con'tainer *noun* 1 something made to contain things: *He brought his lunch in a plastic container.* □ **récipient**

2 a very large sealed metal box for carrying goods on a truck, ship *etc*: *The ship carried twenty containers; (also*

adjective) a container ship. □ **conteneur**

contaminate [kən'tamineit] *verb* to make impure: *The town's water-supply has been contaminated by chemicals from the factory.* □ **contaminer**

con,tami'nation *noun*. □ **contamination**

contemplate ['kɔntəmpleit] *verb* 1 to think seriously (about): *I was contemplating* (= feeling inclined towards) *having a holiday; She contemplated her future gloomily.* □ **envisager**

2 to look thoughtfully at: *He was contemplating the ceiling.* □ **contempler**

,contem'plation *noun*. □ **contemplation**

contemplative [kən'templətiv] *adjective*. □ **contemplatif**

con'templatively *adverb*. □ **contemplativement**

contemporary [kən'tempərəri] *adjective* 1 living at, happening at or belonging to the same period: *That chair and the painting are contemporary – they both date from the seventeenth century.* □ **contemporain**

2 of the present time; modern: *contemporary art.* □ **contemporain**

■ *noun – plural* **con'temporaries** – a person living at the same time: *She was one of my contemporaries at university.* □ **contemporain, aine**

contempt [kən'tempt] *noun* 1 very low opinion; scorn: *She spoke with utter contempt of her husband's behaviour.* □ **mépris**

2 disregard for the law. □ **outrage**

con'temptible *adjective* deserving contempt: *His behaviour was contemptible.* □ **méprisable**

con'temptibly *adverb*. □ **de façon méprisable**

con'temptuous [-tʃuəs] *adjective* showing contempt: *a contemptuous sneer.* □ **dédaigneux**

con'temptuously *adverb*. □ **avec dédain**

contend [kən'tend] *verb* 1 (*usually with* **with**) to struggle against. □ **lutter (contre)**

2 (*with* **that**) to say or maintain (that). □ **soutenir (que)**

con'tender *noun* a person who has entered a competition (for a title *etc*). □ **prétendant, ante**

con'tention *noun* 1 an opinion put forward. □ **assertion**

2 argument; disagreement. □ **contestation**

con'tentious [-ʃəs] *adjective* quarrelsome. □ **querelleur**

content[1] [kən'tent] *adjective* satisfied; quietly happy: *He doesn't want more money – he's content with what he has.* □ **satisfait**

■ *noun* the state of being satisfied or quietly happy: *You're on holiday – you can lie in the sun to your heart's content.* □ **contentement**

■ *verb* to satisfy: *As the TV's broken, you'll have to content yourself with listening to the radio.* □ **se contenter (de)**

con'tented *adjective* satisfied; quietly happy: *a contented sigh.* □ **satisfait**

con'tentedly *adverb*. □ **avec contentement**

con'tentment *noun*. □ **contentement**

content[2] ['kɔntent] *noun* 1 the subject matter (of a book, speech etc): *the content of his speech.* □ **contenu**

2 the amount of something contained: *Oranges have a*

high vitamin C content. □ **teneur**

'**contents** *noun plural* **1** the things contained in something: *He drank the contents of the bottle.* □ **contenu**
2 a list of the things contained *especially* in a book: *Look up the contents at the beginning of the book.* □ **table des matières**

contention, contentious *see* **contend**.

contest ['kontest] *noun* a struggle, competition *etc* to gain an advantage or victory: *a sporting contest.* □ **compétition**
con'testant *noun* a person who takes part in a contest: *She is the youngest contestant in the swimming competition.* □ **concurrent, ente**

context ['kontekst] *noun* the parts directly before or after a word or phrase (written or spoken) which affect its meaning: *This statement, taken out of its context, gives a wrong impression of the speaker's opinions.* □ **contexte**

continence *see* **continent²**.

continent¹ ['kontinənt] *noun* **1** one of the great divisions of the land surface of the world – Europe, America, Australia, Asia or Africa. □ **continent**
2 Europe excluding Britain: *We are going to the continent for our holidays.* □ **Europe (continentale)**
,**conti'nental** [-'nen-] *adjective.* □ **continental**
continental breakfast a light breakfast of rolls and coffee. □ **petit déjeuner**

continent² ['kontinənt] *adjective* able to control especially the bladder and/or bowel. □ **continent**
'**continence** *noun.* □ **continence**

contingent [kən'tindʒənt] *noun* a number or group, especially of soldiers. □ **contingent**
con'tingency – *plural* **con'tingencies** – *noun* a chance happening: *We're prepared for all contingencies.* □ **éventualité**

continue [kən'tinjuː] *verb* **1** to go on being, doing *etc*; to last or keep on: *She continued to run; They continued running; He will continue in his present job; The noise continued for several hours; The road continues for 150 kilometres.* □ **continuer**
2 to go on (with) often after a break or pause: *He continued his talk after the interval; This story is continued on p. 53.* □ **reprendre**
con'tinual *adjective* very frequent; repeated many times: *continual interruptions.* □ **continuel**
con'tinually *adverb.* □ **sans cesse**
con,tinu'ation *noun* the act of continuing, often after a break or pause: *the continuation of his studies.* □ **reprise**
2 something which carries on, *especially* a further part of a story *etc*: *This is a continuation of what he said last week.* □ **suite**
,**conti'nuity** [kon-] *noun* **1** the state of being continuous or logically related: *It is important to children to have some continuity in their education.* □ **continuité**
2 the detailed arrangement of the parts of a story *etc* for a film script *etc.* □ **continuité**
con'tinuous *adjective* joined together, or going on, without interruption: *a continuous series; continuous rain; continuous movement.* □ **continu**

con'tinuously *adverb*: *It rained continuously all day.* □ **continuellement**

---
continual means frequent, again and again.
continuous means non-stop, without interruption.
---

contort [kən'toːt] *verb* to twist or turn violently: *Her face was contorted with pain.* □ **crisper**
con'tortion [-ʃən] *noun.* □ **contorsion**
con'tortionist *noun* an entertainer who contorts his body. □ **contorsionniste**

contour ['kontuə] *noun* **1** an outline: *the contours of the coastline.* □ **contour**
2 (*also* **contour line**) on a map, a line joining points at the same height or depth. □ **courbe de niveau**

contraband ['kontrəband] *noun* goods which are legally forbidden to be brought into a country. □ **contrebande**
■ *adjective: contraband cigarettes.* □ **de contrebande**

contraception [kontrə'sepʃən] *noun* the prevention of conceiving children; birth-control. □ **contraception**
,**contra'ceptive** [-tiv] *noun* (a pill *etc*) preventing pregnancy. □ **contraceptif**

contract [kən'trakt] *verb* **1** to make or become smaller, less, shorter, tighter *etc*: *Metals expand when heated and contract when cooled; 'I am' is often contracted to 'I'm'; Muscles contract.* □ **contracter**
2 ['kontrakt] to promise legally in writing: *They contracted to supply us with cable.* □ **s'engager (par contrat) (à)**
3 to become infected with (a disease): *He contracted malaria.* □ **contracter**
4 to promise (in marriage). □ **s'engager**
■ ['kontrakt] *noun* a legal written agreement: *She has a four-year contract (of employment) with us; The firm won a contract for three new aircraft.* □ **contrat**
con'traction [-ʃən] *noun* **1** an act of contracting: *contraction of metals; contraction of muscles.* □ **contraction**
2 a word shortened in speech or spelling: *'I'm' is a contraction of 'I am'.* □ **contraction**
con'tractor *noun* a person or firm that promises to do work or supply goods at a fixed rate: *a building contractor.* □ **entrepreneur, eure**

contradict [kontrə'dikt] *verb* to say the opposite of; to argue or disagree with: *It's unwise to contradict your boss.* □ **contredire**
,**contra'diction** [-ʃən] *noun.* □ **contradiction**
,**contra'dictory** *adjective.* □ **contradictoire**

contraption [kən'trapʃən] *noun* a strange machine or apparatus: *He tried to fly over the Atlantic in a home-made contraption.* □ **machin, bidule**

contrary¹ ['kontrəri] *adjective* (*often with* **to**) opposite (to) or in disagreement (with): *That decision was contrary to my wishes; Contrary to popular belief he is an able politician.* □ **contraire (à); contrairement (à)**
■ *noun* (*with* **the**) the opposite. □ **contraire**
on the contrary the very opposite (is true): *'Are you busy?' 'No, on the contrary, I'm out of work.'* □ **au contraire**

contrary² [kən'treəri] *adjective* obstinate; unreasonable. □ **contrariant**

con'trariness *noun*. □ **esprit de contradiction**
contrast [kən'traːst] *verb* 1 to show marked difference from: *His words contrast with his actions.* □ **contraster (avec)**
2 to compare so as to show differences: *Contrast fresh and frozen vegetables and you'll find the fresh ones taste better.* □ **mettre en contraste**
■ ['kontraːst] *noun* 1 difference(s) in things or people that are compared: *The contrast between their attitudes is very marked.* □ **contraste**
2 a thing or person that shows a marked difference (to another): *She's a complete contrast to her sister.* □ **contraste**
contravene [kontrə'viːn] *verb* to go against or break (a law, principle *etc*). □ **contrevenir (à)**
,contra'vention [-'venʃən] *noun*. □ **infraction**
contribute [kən'tribjut] *verb* 1 to give (money, help *etc*) along with others: *Have you contributed (any money) to this charity?*; *I've been contributing (articles) to this paper for many years.* □ **contribuer**
2 (*with* to) to help to cause to happen: *His gambling contributed to his downfall.* □ **contribuer à**
,contri'bution [kon-] *noun* 1 the act of contributing. □ **contribution**
2 something contributed, *especially* money: *Would you like to make a contribution to this charity?* □ **don**
con'tributor *noun*. □ **donateur; trice; collaborateur, trice**
contrite ['kontrait] *adjective* deeply sorry for something one has done. □ **contrit**
'contriteness, contrition [kən'triʃən] *noun*. □ **contrition**
contrive [kən'traiv] *verb* 1 to manage (to do something): *He contrived to remove the money from her bag.* □ **trouver moyen de**
2 to make in a clever way: *He contrived a tent from an old sack.* □ **trouver moyen de faire**
con'trivance *noun* 1 the act of contriving. □ **invention**
2 something contrived (*especially* something mechanical): *a contrivance for making the door open automatically.* □ **dispositif**
control [kən'troul] *noun* 1 the right of directing or of giving orders; power or authority: *She has control over all the decisions in that department; She has no control over that dog.* □ **pouvoir; autorité**
2 the act of holding back or restraining: *control of prices; I know you're angry but you must not lose control (of yourself).* □ **contrôle, maîtrise de soi**
3 (*often in plural*) a lever, button *etc* which operates (a machine *etc*): *The clutch and accelerator are foot controls.* □ **commande(s)**
4 a point or place at which an inspection takes place: *passport control.* □ **contrôle**
■ *verb – past tense, past participle* con'trolled – 1 to direct or guide; to have power or authority over: *The captain controls the whole ship; Control your dog!* □ **être maître de**
2 to hold back; to restrain (oneself or one's emotions *etc*): *Control yourself!* □ **(se) maîtriser**
3 to keep to a fixed standard: *The government is con-*

trolling prices. □ **contrôler**
con'troller *noun* a person or thing that controls: *an air-traffic controller.* □ **contrôleur, euse**
con'trol tower *noun* a building at an airport from which take-off and landing instructions are given. □ **tour de contrôle**
in control (of) in charge (of): *She is very much in control (of the situation).* □ **maître de**
out of control not under the authority or power of someone: *The brakes failed and the car went out of control; Those children are completely out of control (= wild and disobedient).* □ **fou, déchaîné**
under control: *Keep your dog under control!; Everything's under control now.* □ **bien en main**
controversy ['kontrəvəːsi, kən'trovəsi] – *plural* controversies – *noun* (an) argument between opposing points of view: *the controversy over the appointment of the new chairman.* □ **controverse**
controversial [kontrə'vəːʃəl] *adjective* causing controversy: *His new book is very controversial.* □ **sujet à controverse**
,contro'versially *adverb*. □ **de manière prêtant à controverse**
convalesce [konvə'les] *verb* to recover health and strength after an illness: *He is convalescing in the country.* □ **être en convalescence**
,conva'lescent *noun* a person who is recovering from an illness: *Convalescents often need a special diet.* □ **convalescent, ente**
■ *adjective* 1 recovering health and strength after illness. □ **convalescent**
2 for convalescents: *a convalescent home.* □ **de convalescence**
,conva'lescence *noun*. □ **convalescence**
convection [kən'vekʃən] *noun* the passing of heat through liquids or gases by means of currents. □ **convection**
convene [kən'viːn] *verb* to (cause to) assemble or come together: *to convene a meeting.* □ **convoquer**
con'vener *noun*. □ **président, ente (de commission)**
convenient [kən'viːnjənt] *adjective* 1 suitable; not causing trouble or difficulty: *When would it be convenient for me to come?* □ **commode**
2 easy to use, run *etc*: *a convenient size of house.* □ **commode**
3 easy to reach *etc*; accessible: *Keep this in a convenient place.* □ **pratique**
con'veniently *adverb*. □ **commodément**
con'venience *noun* 1 the state or quality of being convenient; freedom from trouble or difficulty: *the convenience of living near the office.* □ **commodité**
2 any means of giving ease or comfort: *the conveniences of modern life.* □ **commodité(s)**
3 (*also* **public convenience**) a public lavatory. □ **toilettes**
convent ['konvənt, -vent] *noun* a building in which nuns live. □ **couvent**
convent school one run by nuns. □ **couvent**
convention [kən'venʃən] *noun* 1 a way of behaving that has become usual; (an) established custom: *Shaking hands when meeting people is a normal convention in*

many countries; *She does not care about convention.* □
usage
2 in the United States a meeting of delegates from a
political party for nominating a presidential candidate.
□ **convention**
3 an assembly of people of a particular profession *etc*.
□ **congrès**
con'ventional *adjective* (*negative* **unconventional**)
according to the accepted standards *etc*; not outrageous
or eccentric: *conventional dress*; *the more conventional
forms of art.* □ **conventionnel**
con,ventio'nality [-'na-] *noun.* □ **usage(s) admis**
converge [kən'vɔːdʒ] *verb* to (cause to) move towards
or meet at one point: *The roads converge in the centre
of town.* □ **converger**
con'vergence *noun.* □ **convergence**
con'vergent *adjective.* □ **convergent**
conversation [konvə'seiʃən] *noun* talk between people:
to carry on a conversation. □ **conversation**
,conver'sational *adjective* 1 informal or colloquial: *conversational English.* □ **de la conversation**
2 fond of talking: *He's in a conversational mood.* □ **en
veine de conversation**
converse[1] [kən'vɔːs] *verb* to talk: *It is difficult to converse with people who do not speak your language.* □
converser
converse[2] ['konvɔːs] *noun* the opposite; the contrary. □
contraire
conversely [kon'vɔːsli] *adverb.* □ **à l'inverse**
conversion [kən'vɔːʒən] *noun* the act of converting: *his
conversion to Christianity*; *the conversion of the house
into a hotel.* □ **conversion, transformation**
convert [kən'vɔːt] *verb* 1 to change from one thing into
another: *He has converted his house into four separate
flats*; *This sofa converts into a bed.* □ **transformer**
2 to change from one religion *etc* to another: *She was
converted to Christianity.* □ **(se) convertir (à)**
■ ['konvɔːt] *noun* a person who has been converted to a
particular religion *etc*: *a convert to Buddhism.* □
converti, ie
con'vertible *adjective* that may or can be converted: *a
convertible sofa.* □ **transformable**
■ *noun* a car with a folding or detachable top. □
décapotable
con,verti'bility *noun.* □ **convertibilité**
convex ['konveks] *adjective* (of an object or surface)
curved outwards, like the surface of the eye: *a convex
lens.* □ **convexe**
con'vexity *noun.* □ **convexité**
convey [kən'vei] *verb* 1 to carry: *Huge ships convey oil
from the Middle East.* □ **transporter**
2 to transfer the ownership of (property by legal means).
□ **transférer**
con'veyance *noun* 1 the act of conveying: *the conveyance of goods.* □ **transport**
2 a vehicle of any kind: *A bus is a public conveyance.* □
moyen de transport
con'veyancing *noun* the branch of the law dealing with
transfer of property. □ **procédure translative (de
propriété)**

con'veyor *noun* a person or thing that conveys. □
transporteur, euse
conveyor belt an endless, moving belt carrying articles
from one place to another in a factory *etc*: *She put nuts
on the chocolates as they went down the conveyor belt.*
□ **convoyeur**
convict [kən'vikt] *verb* to prove or declare (someone)
guilty: *She was convicted of theft.* □ **déclarer coupable**
■ ['konvikt] *noun* a person serving a sentence for a
crime: *Two of the convicts have escaped from prison.* □
détenu, ue
con'viction [-ʃən] *noun* 1 the passing of a sentence on a
guilty person: *She has had two convictions for drunken
driving.* □ **condamnation**
2 (a) strong belief: *It's my conviction that he's right.* □
conviction
convince [kən'vins] *verb* to persuade (a person) that
something is true: *Her smile convinced me that she was
happy*; *She is convinced of his innocence.* □ **convaincre**
con'vincing *adjective* (*negative* **unconvincing**) having
the power to convince: *a convincing argument.* □
convaincant
convivial [kən'viviəl] *adjective* pleasantly sociable and
friendly. □ **jovial**
con'vivially *adverb.* □ **jovialement**
con,vivi'ality [-'a-] *noun.* □ **jovialité**
convoy ['konvoi] *noun* 1 a group of ships, trucks, cars
etc travelling together: *an army convoy.* □ **convoi**
2 a fleet of merchant ships escorted for safety by warships. □ **convoi**
convulse [kən'vʌls] *verb* to shake violently: *convulsed
with laughter.* □ **(se) convulser**
con'vulsive [-siv] *adjective.* □ **convulsif**
con'vulsively *adverb.* □ **convulsivement**
con'vulsion [-ʃən] *noun* (*often in plural*) a sudden stiffening or jerking of the muscles of the body. □ **convulsion**
cook [kuk] *verb* to prepare (food) or become ready by
heating: *He cooked the chicken*; *The chicken is cooking
in the oven.* □ **(faire) cuire**
■ *noun* a person who cooks, *especially* for a living: *She
was employed as a cook at the embassy.* □ **cuisinier,
ière**
'cook-book a book of instructions on how to prepare
and cook various dishes. □ **livre de cuisine**
'cooker *noun* 1 an apparatus on which food is cooked:
He has an electric cooker. □ **cuisinière**
2 an apple *etc* used in cooking, not for eating raw. □
(pomme) à cuire
'cookery *noun* the art or practice of cooking food: *He
was taught cookery at school*; (*also adjective*) *cookery
classes.* □ **(art de la) cuisine; de cuisine**
cook up to invent or make up a false story *etc*: *He cooked
up a story about his car having broken down.* □ **inventer**
cookie ['kuki] *noun* a sweet biscuit. □ **gâteau sec**
cool [kuːl] *adjective* 1 slightly cold: *cool weather.* □ **frais**
2 calm or not excitable: *She's very cool in a crisis.* □
calme
3 not very friendly: *He was very cool towards me.* □
froid

■ *verb* 1 to make or become less warm: *The jelly will cool better in the refrigerator*; *She cooled her hands in the stream.* □ **refroidir**
2 to become less strong: *His affection for her has cooled*; *Her anger cooled.* □ **(se) refroidir**
■ *noun* cool air or atmosphere: *the cool of the evening.* □ **fraîcheur**
'**coolly** *adverb.* □ **calmement**
'**coolness** *noun.* □ **fraîcheur; froideur; sang-froid**
cool-'**headed** *adjective* able to act calmly. □ **calme**
cool down 1 to make or become less warm: *Let your food cool down a bit!* □ **refroidir**
2 to make or become less excited or less emotional: *He was very angry but he's cooled down now.* □ **se calmer**
keep one's cool not to become over-excited or confused: *If you keep your cool you won't fail.* □ **garder son sang-froid**
lose one's cool not to keep one's cool. □ **perdre son sang-froid**
coop [kuːp] *noun* a box or cage for keeping fowls or small animals in: *a chicken-coop.* □ **cage, poulailler**
coop up to shut into a small place: *We've been cooped up in this tiny room for hours.* □ **claquemurer**
co-operate [kou'opəreit] *verb* to work together: *They have promised to co-operate (with us) in the planning of the exhibition.* □ **coopérer**
co-ope'ration *noun* 1 the act of working together. □ **coopération**
2 willingness to act or work together: *I would be grateful for your co-operation.* □ **concours**
co-'operative [-tiv] *adjective*: *a helpful and co-operative pupil.* □ **coopératif**
co-ordinate [kou'oːdineit] *verb* to adjust (a movement or action) so that it fits in or works smoothly (with other movements or actions): *In swimming the movement of one's arms and legs must be co-ordinated.* □ **coordonner**
co-ordi'nation *noun.* □ **coordination**
cop [kop] *noun* a slang abbreviation of **copper²**. □ **flic**
cope [koup] *verb* to manage; to deal with successfully: *I can't cope with all this work.* □ **faire face (à)**
copious ['koupiəs] *adjective* plentiful: *a copious supply.* □ **copieux**
'**copiously** *adverb.* □ **copieusement**
'**copiousness** *noun.* □ **abondance**
copper¹ ['kopə] *noun* 1 an element, a metal of a brownish-red colour: *This pipe is made of copper.* □ **cuivre**
2 (a piece of) money made of copper or a substitute: *Have you any coppers in your change?* □ **petite pièce**
■ *adjective* 1 made of copper: *a copper pipe.* □ **de cuivre**
2 (*also* '**copper-coloured**) of the colour of copper. □ **cuivre**
copper² ['kopə] *noun* a nickname for a policeman: *Run – there's a copper after you!* □ **flic**
copra ['koprə] *noun* the dried kernel of the coconut which gives coconut oil. □ **copra**
copy ['kopi] – *plural* '**copies** – *noun* 1 an imitation or reproduction: *That dress is a copy of one I saw at a Paris fashion show*; *He made eight copies of the pamphlet on the photocopier.* □ **copie**
2 a single book, newspaper *etc*: *Can I have six copies of*

this dictionary, please? □ **exemplaire**
3 written or typed material for publishing: *She writes copy for advertisements.* □ **manuscrit**
■ *verb* to make an imitation or reproduction of (something): *Copy the way I speak*; *Copy this passage into your notebook.* □ **copier**
'**copier** *noun* a photocopier. □ **photocopieur, euse**
'**copyright** *noun* (*usually abbreviated to* ©) the sole right to reproduce a literary, dramatic, musical or artistic work, and also to perform, translate, film, or record such a work. □ **droit d'auteur**
coral ['korəl] *noun, adjective* 1 (of) a hard substance of various colours, made up of skeletons of a kind of tiny animal: *a necklace made of coral*; *a coral reef.* □ **(de) corail**
2 (of) an orange-pink colour. □ **corail**
cord [koːd] *noun* 1 (a piece of) thin rope or thick string: *The burglars tied up the nightwatchman with thick cord.* □ **corde**
2 a string-like part of the body: *the spinal cord*; *the vocal cords.* □ **moëlle épinière; corde (vocale)**
3 a length of electric cable or flex attached to an electrical appliance: *the cord of his electric razor.* □ **fil**
4 a kind of velvet fabric with a ribbed appearance; (*in plural*) trousers made of this: *a pair of cords.* □ **(pantalons en) velours côtelé**
cordial ['koːrdʒl, 'koːrdiəl] *adjective* (of greetings *etc*) warm and affectionate: *a cordial welcome.* □ **cordial**
■ *noun* a refreshing drink: *lime juice cordial.* □ **cordial**
,**cordi'ality** [-'a-] *noun.* □ **cordialité**
'**cordially** *adverb.* □ **cordialement**
cordon ['koːdn] *noun* a line of sentries or policemen to prevent people from entering an area: *They've put a cordon around the house where the bomb is planted.* □ **cordon (de police)**
cordon off to enclose with a cordon: *The police cordoned off the area where the gunman was.* □ **interdire l'accès à**
core [koː] *noun* the innermost part of something, *especially* fruit: *an apple-core*; *the core of the earth.* □ **cœur**
■ *verb* to take out the core of (fruit): *Core the apples.* □ **enlever le cœur de**
cork [koːk] *noun* 1 the outer bark of the cork tree (an oak of South Europe, North Africa *etc*): *Cork floats well*; (*also adjective*) *cork floor-tiles.* □ **liège; (en) liège**
2 a stopper for a bottle *etc* made of cork: *Put the cork back in the wine-bottle.* □ **bouchon (en liège)**
■ *verb* to put a cork or stopper in: *He corked the bottle.* □ **boucher**
'**corkscrew** *noun* a tool with a screw-like spike, used for drawing corks from bottles. □ **tire-bouchon**
corn¹ [koːn] *noun* a cereal plant with usually yellow seeds which are arranged in rows on a cob. □ **blé d'inde, maïs**
corned beef salted beef (*usually* cooked and canned). □ **corned-beef**
'**cornflower** *noun* a blue-flowered plant. □ **bleuet**
'**cornstarch** *noun* finely ground cornflour. □ **farine de maïs**
corn on the cob *noun* the center part of the corn plant with the seeds: *Krista says canned and frozen corn are*

not as good as corn on the cob. □ **épi de maïs**
corn² [kɔːn] *noun* a little bump of hard skin found on the foot: *I have a corn on my little toe.* □ **cor**
cornea ['kɔːnɪə] *noun* the transparent covering of the eyeball. □ **cornée**
corner ['kɔːnə] *noun* **1** a point where two lines, walls, roads *etc* meet: *the corners of a cube; the corner of the street.* □ **coin**
2 a place, *usually* a small quiet place: *a secluded corner.* □ **coin**
3 in football, a free kick from the corner of the field: *We've been awarded a corner.* □ **corner**
■ *verb* **1** to force (a person or animal) into a place from which it is difficult to escape: *The thief was cornered in an alley.* □ **acculer**
2 to turn a corner: *He cornered on only three wheels; This car corners very well.* □ **prendre un virage**
'cornered *adjective* **1** having (a given number of) corners: *a three-cornered hat.* □ **à (...) coins**
2 forced into a position from which it is difficult to escape: *A cornered animal can be very dangerous.* □ **acculé**
cut corners to use less money, effort, time *etc* when doing something than was thought necessary, often giving a poorer result. □ **travailler à l'économie**
turn the corner 1 to go around a corner. □ **tourner le/ au coin (d'une rue)**
2 to get past a difficulty or danger: *He was very ill but he's turned the corner now.* □ **passer le moment critique**
cornet [kɔː'net] *noun* a brass musical instrument similar to the trumpet. □ **cornet (à pistons)**
cornflower, cornstarch *see* **corn¹.**
corny ['kɔːnɪ] *adjective* not original or interesting: *a corny joke.* □ **banal**
coronary ['kɔrənərɪ] *adjective* (of arteries) supplying blood to the heart. □ **coronaire**
■ *noun – plural* **'coronaries –** an attack of coronary thrombosis. □ **infarctus (du myocarde)**
coronary thrombosis a heart disease caused by blockage of one of the coronary arteries. □ **infarctus (du myocarde)**
coronation [kɔrə'neiʃən] *noun* the act or ceremony of crowning a king or queen. □ **couronnement**
coroner ['kɔrənə] *noun* an official who inquires into the causes of accidental or sudden, unexpected deaths. □ **coroner**
coronet ['kɔrənit] *noun* **1** a small crown. □ **couronne; diadème**
2 an ornamental headdress: *a coronet of flowers.* □ **couronne**
corporal¹ ['kɔːpərəl] *noun* (*often abbreviated to* **Corp.** *when written*) (a person of) the rank above private and below master corporal. □ **caporal, ale**
corporal² ['kɔːpərəl] *adjective* of the body: *The headmaster disapproves of caning and all other forms of corporal punishment.* □ **corporel**
corporate ['kɔːpərət] *adjective* united: *corporate effort.* □ **unifié**
,corpo'ration *noun* a body of people acting as one indi-

vidual *eg* for administration or business purposes: *the Canadian Broadcasting Corporation.* □ **société (commerciale)**
corps [kɔː] – *plural* **corps** [kɔːz] – *noun* **1** a division of an army: *The Royal Armoured Corps.* □ **corps**
2 a group or company: *the diplomatic corps.* □ **corps**
corpse [kɔːps] *noun* a dead body, *especially* of a human being: *Don't move the corpse before you send for the police.* □ **cadavre**
corpulent ['kɔːpjulənt] *adjective* fat: *a corpulent old lady.* □ **corpulent**
'corpulence *noun.* □ **corpulence**
corpuscle ['kɔːpʌsl] *noun* one of the red or white cells in the blood. □ **globule sanguin**
correct [kə'rekt] *verb* **1** to remove faults and errors from: *These spectacles will correct his eye defect.* □ **corriger**
2 (of a teacher *etc*) to mark errors in: *I have fourteen exercise books to correct.* □ **corriger**
■ *adjective* **1** free from faults or errors: *This sum is correct.* □ **exact**
2 right; not wrong: *Did I get the correct idea from what you said?; You are quite correct.* □ **juste; avoir raison**
cor'rection [-ʃən] *noun.* □ **correction**
cor'rective [-tiv] *adjective* setting right: *corrective treatment.* □ **correctif**
cor'rectly *adverb.* □ **correctement**
cor'rectness *noun.* □ **correction**
correspond [kɔrə'spond] *verb* **1** (*with* **to**) to be similar; to match: *A bird's wing corresponds to the arm and hand in humans.* □ **correspondre (à)**
2 (*with* **with**) to be in agreement with; to match. □ **s'accorder (avec)**
3 to communicate by letter (with): *Do they often correspond (with each other)?* □ **correspondre (avec)**
,corre'spondence *noun* **1** agreement; similarity or likeness. □ **correspondance**
2 (communication by) letters: *I must deal with that (big pile of) correspondence.* □ **courrier**
,corre'spondent *noun* **1** a person with whom one exchanges letters: *He has correspondents all over the world.* □ **correspondant(e)**
2 a person who contributes news to a newspaper *etc*: *She's foreign correspondent for 'The National Post'.* □ **correspondant, ante**
,corre'sponding *adjective* similar, matching: *The rainfall this month is not as high as for the corresponding month last year.* □ **correspondant**
correspondence course a course of lessons by post: *a correspondence course in accountancy.* □ **cours par correspondance**
corridor ['kɔridɔː] *noun* a passageway, *especially* one off which rooms open: *Go along the corridor and up the stairs.* □ **corridor**
corroborate [kə'robəreit] *verb* to support or confirm (evidence *etc* already given): *She corroborated her sister's story.* □ **confirmer**
cor,robo'ration *noun.* □ **confirmation**
cor'roborative [-rətiv] *adjective.* □ **qui confirme**
corrode [kə'roud] *verb* to destroy or eat away (as rust, chemicals *etc* do). □ **corroder**

cor'rosion [-ʒən] *noun*. □ **corrosion**
cor'rosive [-siv] *adjective* tending to corrode. □ **corrosif**
corrugated ['korəgeitid] *adjective* shaped into ridges: *corrugated iron.* □ **ondulé**
corrupt [kə'rʌpt] *verb* to make or become evil or bad: *He was corrupted by the bad influence of two friends.* □ **corrompre**
■ *adjective* 1 bad or evil: *The government is corrupt.* □ **corrompu**
2 impure: *a corrupt form of English.* □ **altéré**
cor'ruptible *adjective*. □ **corruptible**
cor,rupti'bility *noun*. □ **corruptibilité**
cor'ruption [-ʃən] *noun* 1 the act of corrupting. □ **corruption**
2 a word that has changed considerably from its original form: *Caterpillar is probably a corruption of the Old French word 'chatepelose' meaning 'hairy cat'.* □ **forme corrompue**
corset ['kɔːsit] *noun* a close-fitting stiff undergarment to support the body. □ **corset**
cortège [kɔː'teʒ] *noun* a procession, *especially* at a funeral. □ **cortège**
cosily, cosiness *see* **cozy**.
cosmetic [koz'metik] *adjective* designed to increase the beauty and hide the defects of something, *especially* the face: *He had cosmetic surgery to improve the shape of his nose.* □ **esthétique**
■ *noun* a preparation for this purpose: *She's quite pretty – she does not need to wear so many cosmetics* (= lipstick, eye-shadow *etc*). □ **produit(s) de beauté**
cosmic ['kozmik] *adjective* having to do with the universe or outer space: *cosmic rays.* □ **cosmique**
'**cosmonaut** [-nɔːt] *noun* a person who travels in space; an astronaut. □ **cosmonaute**
the cosmos ['kozmos, -məs] the universe. □ **cosmos**
cosmopolitan [kozmə'politən] *adjective* belonging to all parts of the world: *The population of Montreal is very cosmopolitan.* □ **cosmopolite**
cosmos *see* **cosmic**.
cosset ['kosit] – *past tense, past participle* '**cosseted** – *verb* to treat with too much kindness; to pamper. □ **dorloter**
cost [kost] – *past tense, past participle* **cost** – *verb* 1 to be obtainable at a certain price: *This jacket costs 75 dollars; The victory cost two thousand lives.* □ **coûter**
2 (*past tense, past participle* '**costed**) to estimate the cost of (a future project). □ **évaluer le coût de**
■ *noun* the price to be paid (for something): *What is the cost of this coat?* □ **prix**
'**costly** *adjective* costing much: *a costly wedding-dress.* □ **coûteux**
'**costliness** *noun*. □ **cherté**
costs *noun plural* the expenses of a legal case: *He won his case and was awarded costs of $500.* □ **dépens**
at all costs no matter what the cost or outcome may be: *We must prevent disaster at all costs.* □ **à tout prix**
costume ['kostjuːm] *noun* 1 an outfit, *especially* for a particular purpose: *swimming-costume.* □ **costume**
2 dress, clothes: *eighteenth-century costume.* □ **costume**
cot [kot] *noun* a folding bed: *One of the wooden legs of*

the cot is broken. □ **lit de camp**
cottage ['kotidʒ] *noun* a small house, *especially* in the country or in a village: *a cottage in the Laurentians.* □ **cottage, chalet**
cotton[1] ['kotn] *noun* 1 a soft substance got from the seeds of the cotton plant, used in making thread or cloth. □ **(de/en) coton**
2 the yarn or cloth made from this: *a reel of cotton; This shirt is made of cotton;* (*also adjective*) *a cotton shirt.* □ **coton**
absorbent cotton loose cotton pressed into a mass, for absorbing liquids, wiping or protecting an injury *etc*: *She bathed the wound with absorbent cotton.* □ **ouate**
cotton candy candy floss. □ **barbe à papa**
cotton[2]['kotn]: **cotton on** *verb* to understand: *He'll soon cotton on (to what you mean).* □ **piger**
couch[1] [kautʃ] *noun* a type of sofa for sitting or lying on: *The doctor asked him to lie on the couch.* □ **canapé**
couch[2] [kautʃ] *verb* to express (in words): *She couched her reply in vague terms.* □ **formuler**
cougar ['kuːgə] *noun* a puma. □ **puma**
cough [kof] *verb* to make a harsh sound when bringing air or harmful matter from the lungs or throat: *He's coughing badly because he has a cold.* □ **tousser**
■ *noun* 1 an act of coughing: *She gave a cough.* □ **toux**
2 an illness causing coughing: *a smoker's cough.* □ **toux**
'**cough syrup** *noun* a medicine used for relieving coughing. □ **sirop pour la toux**
cough up a slang expression for to pay: *It's time you coughed up (the money I lent you).* □ **cracher**
could [kud] – *negative short form* **couldn't** ['kudnt] – *verb* 1 *past tense of* **can**: *They asked if I could drive a car; I said I couldn't; She asked if she could go.*
2 used to express a possibility: *I could go but I'm not going to; I could do it next week if you helped me.*
could have used to express a possibility in the past: *We could have gone, but we didn't.*
council ['kaunsəl] *noun* 1 a group of people formed in order to advise *etc*: *The mayor formed a council of advisors; the Council for Recreation.* □ **conseil**
2 a body of people elected to control the workings of local government in a county, region, district *etc*. □ **assemblée**
'**councillor** *noun* a person who is elected to serve on a council. □ **conseiller, ère**
counsel ['kaunsəl] *noun* 1 advice: *He'll give you good counsel on your problems.* □ **conseil**
2 a lawyer or lawyers: *counsel for the defence.* □ **avocat, ate**
■ *verb* – *past tense, past participle* – '**counselled,** '**counseled** – to advise; to recommend. □ **conseiller**
'**counsellor, counselor** *noun* 1 a person who gives advice. □ **conseiller, ère**
2 a person who supervises children in a summer camp. □ **moniteur**
count[1] [kaunt] *noun* nobleman in certain countries, equal in rank to a British earl. □ **comte**
'**countess** *noun* 1 the wife or widow of an earl or count. □ **comtesse**
2 a woman of the same rank as an earl or count in her

own right. □ **comtesse**

count² [kaunt] *verb* **1** to name the numbers up to: *Count (up to) ten.* □ **compter**

2 to calculate using numbers: *Count (up) the number of pages; Count how many people there are; There were six people present, not counting the chairwoman.* □ **compter**

3 to be important or have an effect or value: *What he says doesn't count; All these essays count towards my final mark.* □ **compter**

4 to consider: *Count yourself lucky to be here.* □ **estimer**

■ *noun* **1** an act of numbering: *They took a count of how many people attended.* □ **compte**

2 a charge brought against a prisoner *etc*: *She faces three counts of theft.* □ **chef d'accusation**

■ *adjective see* **countable**.

'**countable** *adjective* **1** capable of being numbered: *Millionths of a second are countable only on very complicated instruments.* □ **qui peut être compté**

2 (*negative* **uncountable**: *also* **count**) (of a noun) capable of forming a plural and using the definite or indefinite article: *Table is a count(able) noun, but milk is an uncountable noun.* □ **distributif**

'**counter¹** *noun* a token used in numbering or playing certain games; *counters for playing ludo etc*. □ **jeton**

'**countless** *adjective* very many: *Countless pebbles.* □ **innombrable**

'**countdown** *noun* (used *originally* of a rocket) a counting backwards to check the time remaining until the beginning of an event, regarded as zero: *It's five minutes to countdown.* □ **compte à rebours**

count on to rely on (a person or happening): *I'm counting on you to persuade her.* □ **compter sur**

out for the count 1 (of a boxer) still not standing after the count of ten. □ **être K.O.**

2 exhausted; asleep: *He was out for the count for several hours after his long walk.* □ **avoir son compte**

countenance ['kauntinəns] *noun* the face. □ **mine**

■ *verb* to encourage or accept: *We can't possibly countenance the spending of so much money.* □ **approuver**

counter¹ *see* **count²**.

counter² ['kauntə] *adverb* (with **to**) in the opposite direction or manner to: *The election is running counter to the forecasts.* □ **à l'encontre de**

■ *verb* to meet or answer (a stroke or move *etc* by another): *He successfully countered all criticisms.* □ **contrer**

counter- against or opposite: *counter-clockwise.* □ **contre-**

counter³ ['kauntə] *noun* a kind of table or surface on which goods are laid: *Can you get me some sweets from the confectionery counter?* □ **comptoir**

counteract [kauntər'akt] *verb* to undo or prevent the effect of: *the government's efforts to counteract inflation.* □ **contrebalancer**

,**counter'action** *noun*. □ **action contraire**

counterattack ['kauntərətak] *noun* an attack in reply to an attack: *The enemy made a counterattack.* □ **contre-attaque**

■ *verb* to make such an attack (on): *Our troops counterattacked.* □ **contre-attaquer**

counter-clockwise ['kauntəklokwaiz] *adverb, adjective* moving in the opposite direction to that in which the hands of a clock move: *The wheels turn counter-clockwise; in a counter-clockwise direction.* □ **dans le sens inverse des aiguilles d'une montre**

counterfeit ['kauntəfit] *adjective* **1** copied or made in imitation *especially* with a dishonest purpose: *counterfeit money.* □ **faux**

2 not genuine or not real. □ **faux**

■ *verb* **1** to make a copy of for dishonest purposes: *to counterfeit banknotes.* □ **contrefaire**

2 to pretend: *She counterfeited friendship.* □ **feindre**

counterfoil ['kauntəfoil] *noun* a section able to be detached or removed from a cheque *etc* and kept by the giver as a receipt. □ **talon**

counterpane ['kauntəpein] *noun* a top cover for a bed. □ **courtepointe**

counterpart ['kauntəpaːt] *noun* a person or thing equivalent to another in position *etc*: *Canadian teenagers and their American counterparts.* □ **homologue**

countess *see* **count¹**.

country ['kʌntri] – *plural* '**countries** – *noun* **1** any of the nations of the world; the land occupied by a nation: *Canada is a larger country than Spain.* □ **pays**

2 the people of a country: *The whole country is in agreement with your views.* □ **pays**

3 (*usually with* **the**) districts where there are fields *etc* as opposed to towns and areas with many buildings: *a quiet holiday in the country; (also adjective) country districts.* □ **(de) campagne**

4 an area or stretch of land: *hilly country.* □ **région**

country dance a (style of) dance in which partners are arranged in parallel lines. □ **danse folklorique**

'**countryman** – *feminine* '**countrywoman** – *noun* a person born in the same country as another: *Churchill and Chamberlain were fellow countrymen.* □ **compatriote**

'**countryside** *noun* country areas: *the English countryside.* □ **campagne**

county ['kaunti] – *plural* '**counties** – *noun* a large administrative unit of local government in England and Wales and in the United States. □ **comté**

coup [kuː] *noun* **1** a sudden successful action: *She achieved a real coup by completing this deal.* □ **(beau) coup**

2 a coup d'état: *There's been a coup in one of the African republics.* □ **coup d'État**

coup d'état [kuːdei'taː] – *plural* **coups d'état** [kuːdei] – a sudden and violent change in government: *The president was killed during the coup d'état.* □ **coup d'État**

coupe ['kuːp] *noun* a two-door car with a fixed roof. □ **coupé**

couple ['kʌpl] *noun* **1** two; a few: *Can I borrow a couple of chairs?; I knew a couple of people at the party, but not many.* □ **(environ) deux**

2 a man and wife, or a boyfriend and girlfriend: *a married couple; The young couple have a child.* □ **couple**

■ *verb* to join together: *The coaches were coupled (together), and the train set off.* □ **atteler**

'**couplet** [-lit] *noun* two lines of verse, one following the other, which rhyme with each other. □ **distique**

'**coupling** *noun* a link for joining things together: *The railway car was damaged when the coupling broke.* □ **attelage**

coupon ['ku:pon] *noun* a piece of paper *etc* giving one the right to something, *eg* a gift or discount price: *This coupon gives 50 cents off your next purchase.* □ **coupon**

courage ['kʌridʒ] *noun* the quality that makes a person able to meet dangers without fear; bravery: *It took courage to sail the Atlantic singlehanded.* □ **courage**
 courageous [kə'reidʒəs] *adjective* having courage: *a courageous soldier.* □ **courageux**
 cou'rageously *adverb.* □ **courageusement**

courier ['kuriə] *noun* **1** a guide who travels with, and looks after, parties of tourists: *a courier on a bus trip.* □ **accompagnateur, trice**
 2 a messenger. □ **messager, ère**

course [ko:s] *noun* **1** a series (of lectures, medicines *etc*): *I'm taking a course (of lectures) in sociology*; *She's having a course of treatment for her leg.* □ **cours, série de**
 2 a division or part of a meal: *Now we've had the soup, what's (for) the next course?* □ **plat**
 3 the ground over which a race is run or a game (*especially* golf) is played: *a racecourse; a golf-course.* □ **terrain**
 4 the path or direction in which something moves: *the course of the Nile.* □ **cours**
 5 the progress or development of events: *Things will run their normal course despite the strike.* □ **cours**
 6 a way (of action): *What's the best course of action in the circumstances?* □ **ligne de conduite**
 in the course of during: *In the course of our talk, she told me about the accident.* □ **au cours de**
 in due course at the appropriate or normal time: *In due course, this seed will grow into a tree.* □ **à la longue; en temps voulu**
 of course naturally or obviously: *Of course, she didn't tell me any secrets*; *Of course I can swim.* □ **bien sûr**
 off, on course (not) heading in the right direction: *to drift off course*; *We're back on course.* □ **hors du cap fixé; sur le bon cap**

court [ko:t] *noun* **1** a place where legal cases are heard: *a provincial court; the Supreme Court.* □ **tribunal**
 2 the judges and officials of a legal court: *The accused is to appear before the court on Friday.* □ **cour**
 3 a marked-out space for certain games: *a tennis-court; a squash court.* □ **court**
 4 the officials, councillors *etc* of a king or queen: *the court of King James.* □ **cour**
 5 the palace of a king or queen: *Hampton Court.* □ **cour**
 6 an open space surrounded by houses or by the parts of one house.* □ **cour**
 ■ *verb* **1** to try to win the love of; to woo. □ **courtiser**
 2 to try to gain (admiration *etc*). □ **solliciter**
 3 to seem to be deliberately risking (disaster *etc*). □ **aller au-devant de**

'**courtier** [-tiə] *noun* a member of the court of a king or

queen: *He was one of King James' courtiers.* □ **courtisan, dame de la cour**

'**courtly** *adjective* having fine manners. □ **raffiné**
'**courtliness** *noun.* □ **courtoisie**

'**courtship** *noun* courting or wooing. □ **cour**

'**courthouse** *noun* a building where legal cases are held. □ **palais de justice**

,**court** '**martial** – *plural* ,**courts** '**martial** – *noun* a court held by officers of the armed forces to try offences against discipline. □ **conseil de guerre**

'**courtyard** *noun* a court or enclosed ground beside, or surrounded by, a building: *the courtyard of the castle.* □ **cour**

courteous ['kə:tiəs] *adjective* polite; considerate and respectful: *It was courteous of him to write a letter of thanks.* □ **poli**
 '**courteously** *adverb.* □ **poliment**
 '**courteousness** *noun.* □ **politesse**

courtesy ['kə:təsi] *noun* politeness; considerate and respectful behaviour: *Everyone appreciates courtesy.* □ **courtoisie**

courtier *see* **court.**

cousin ['kʌzn] *noun* a son or daughter of one's uncle or aunt. □ **cousin, ine**
 first/full cousin a son or daughter of one's uncle or aunt. □ **cousin, cousine, germain, germaine**

cove [kouv] *noun* a small bay or inlet of the sea: *They bathed in a quiet cove.* □ **anse**

covenant ['kʌvənənt] *noun* an agreement between two people or two parties to do, or not to do, something: *She signed a covenant to give money to the school fund.* □ **engagement solennel**

cover ['kʌvə] *verb* **1** to put or spread something on, over or in front of: *They covered (up) the body with a sheet*; *My shoes are covered in paint.* □ **(re)couvrir**
 2 to be enough to pay for: *Will 10 dollars cover your expenses?* □ **couvrir**
 3 to travel: *We covered forty kilometres in one day.* □ **parcourir**
 4 to stretch over a length of time *etc*: *Her diary covered three years.* □ **couvrir**
 5 to protect: *Are we covered by your car insurance?* □ **couvrir**
 6 to report on: *I'm covering the race for the local newspaper.* □ **assurer le reportage de**
 7 to point a gun at: *I had him covered.* □ **tenir sous la menace (d'une arme à feu)**
 ■ *noun* **1** something which covers, *especially* a cloth over a table, bed *etc*: *a table-cover; a bed-cover; They replaced the cover on the manhole.* □ **couverture, nappe, couvercle**
 2 something that gives protection or shelter: *The soldiers took cover from the enemy gunfire; insurance cover.* □ **abri, couverture**
 3 something that hides: *He escaped under cover of darkness.* □ **à la faveur de**

'**coverage** [-ridʒ] *noun* **1** the amount of protection given by insurance: *insurance coverage.* □ **couverture**
 2 the extent of the inclusion of items in a news report *etc*: *The TV coverage of the Olympic Games was exten-*

sive. □ **couverture**

'**covering** *noun*: *My car has a covering of dirt.* □ **couche**

'**cover girl** *noun* a girl pictured on a magazine cover. □ **cover-girl**

'**cover-up** *noun* an attempt to hide or conceal (something illegal or dishonest). □ **dissimulation**

coverlet ['kʌvəlit] *noun* a top cover for a bed. □ **couvre-lit**

covet ['kʌvit] – *past tense, past participle* '**coveted** – *verb* to desire or wish for eagerly (*especially* something belonging to someone else): *I coveted her fur coat.* □ **convoiter**

'**covetous** *adjective.* □ **avide**

'**covetously** *adverb.* □ **avidement**

'**covetousness** *noun.* □ **convoitise**

cow[1] [kau] *noun* 1 the female of cattle used for giving milk: *She has ten cows and a bull.* □ **vache**

2 the female of certain other animals *eg* the elephant, whale. □ **femelle**

'**cowboy** *noun* in the United States, a man who looks after cattle on a ranch. □ **cow-boy**

'**cowherd** *noun* a person who looks after cows. □ **vacher, ère**

'**cowhide** *noun, adjective* (of) the skin of a cow made into leather: *a bag made of cowhide; a cowhide bag.* □ **peau de vache**

cow[2] [kau] *verb* to subdue or frighten: *She looked slightly cowed after her interview with the headmaster.* □ **intimider**

coward ['kauəd] *noun* a person who shows fear easily or is easily frightened: *I am such a coward – I hate going to the dentist.* □ **poltron, onne; peureux, euse**

'**cowardly** *adjective.* □ **poltron**

'**cowardice** [-dis] *noun.* □ **lâcheté**

'**cowardliness** *noun.* □ **lâcheté**

cower ['kauə] *verb* to draw back and crouch in fear: *He was cowering away from the fierce dog.* □ **se tapir**

cowl [kaul] *noun* (a cap or hood like) a monk's hood. □ **capuchon**

coxswain ['koksn] *noun* 1 (*often abbreviated to* **cox** [koks]) a person who steers a (small, *usually* racing) boat. □ **barreur, euse**

2 a petty officer in charge of a boat and crew. □ **patron, ne**

coy [koi] *adjective* (pretending to be) shy: *She gave her brother's friend a coy smile.* □ **qui fait l'effarouché, ée**

'**coyly** *adverb.* □ **timidement**

'**coyness** *noun.* □ **timidité**

cozy, cosy ['kouzi] *adjective* warm and comfortable: *a cozy chat; a cozy armchair.* □ **douillet**

■ *noun* a covering for a teapot ('**tea-cozy**), to keep it warm. □ **couvre-théière**

'**cozily** *adverb.* □ **douillettement**

'**coziness** *noun.* □ **confort**

crab [krab] *noun* an edible sea animal with a shell and five pairs of legs, the first pair having claws. □ **crabe**

crack [krak] *verb* 1 (cause to) break partly without falling to pieces: *The window cracked down the middle.* □ **(se) fêler**

2 to break (open): *He cracked the peanuts between his*

finger and thumb. □ **casser**

3 to make a sudden sharp sound of breaking: *The twig cracked as I stood on it.* □ **craquer**

4 to make (a joke): *She's always cracking jokes.* □ **sortir**

5 to open (a safe) by illegal means. □ **percer**

6 to solve (a code). □ **déchiffrer**

7 to give in to torture or similar pressures: *The spy finally cracked under their questioning and told them everything she knew.* □ **craquer**

■ *noun* 1 a split or break: *There's a crack in this cup.* □ **fêlure**

2 a narrow opening: *The door opened a crack.* □ **entrebâillement**

3 a sudden sharp sound: *the crack of whip.* □ **claquement**

4 a blow: *a crack on the jaw.* □ **coup (sec)**

5 a joke: *He made a crack about my big feet.* □ **plaisanterie**

■ *adjective* expert: *a crack racing-driver.* □ **d'élite**

cracked *adjective* 1 damaged by cracks: *a cracked cup.* □ **fêlé**

2 crazy: *She must be cracked!* □ **cinglé**

'**cracker** *noun* 1 a thin crisp biscuit. □ **craquelin**

2 a small exploding firework: *fire cracker.* □ **pétard**

3 a decorated paper tube, containing paper hats *etc,* which gives a loud crack when pulled apart. □ **diablotin**

'**crackers** *adjective* crazy: *You must be crackers to believe that!* □ **maboule**

get cracking to get moving quickly. □ **s'y mettre**

have a crack (at) to have a try at. □ **tenter de**

crackle ['krakl] *verb* to make a continuous cracking noise: *The dry branches crackled under my feet.* □ **crépiter**

■ *noun: the crackle of burning wood.* □ **crépitement**

'**crackling** *noun* the crisp rind of roast pork. □ **couenne rissolée**

'**crackly** *adjective: The radio reception is very crackly here.* □ **grésillant**

cradle ['kreidl] *noun* 1 a child's bed *especially* one in which it can be rocked. □ **berceau**

2 a frame of similar shape, *eg* one under a ship that is being built or repaired. □ **ber**

■ *verb* to hold or rock as if in a cradle: *She cradled the child in her arms.* □ **bercer dans ses bras**

craft [krɑːft] *noun* 1 an art or skill: *the craft of woodcarving.* □ **métier**

2 (*plural* **craft**) a boat or ship: *sailing craft.* □ **embarcation**

3 cunning or trickery: *craft and deceit.* □ **ruse**

'**crafty** *adjective* cunning and sly. □ **rusé**

'**craftily** *adverb.* □ **avec ruse**

'**craftiness** *noun.* □ **ruse**

'**craftsman** ['krɑːftsmən] *noun* a person who is skilled at making things (*especially* by hand). □ **artisan, ane**

'**craftsmanship** ['krɑːfts-] *noun.* □ **(connaissance d'un) métier**

crag [krag] *noun* a rough, steep mountain or rock. □ **rocher escarpé**

'**craggy** *adjective* rocky; rugged, irregular. □ **escarpé**

cram [kram] – *past tense, past participle* **crammed** – *verb* 1 to fill very full: *The drawer was crammed with*

papers. □ **bourrer**
2 to push or force: *He crammed food into his mouth.* □ **fourrer**
3 to prepare (someone) in a short time for an examination: *She is being crammed for her university entrance exam.* □ **potasser**
cramp [kramp] *noun* (a) painful stiffening of the muscles: *The swimmer got a cramp and drowned.* □ **crampe**
■ *verb* 1 to put into too small a space: *We were all cramped together in a tiny room.* □ **entasser**
2 to restrict; *Lack of money cramped our efforts.* □ **gêner**
crane [krein] *noun* a machine with a long arm and a chain, for raising heavy weights. □ **grue**
■ *verb* to stretch out (the neck, to see around or over something): *He craned his neck in order to see around the corner.* □ **tendre (le cou)**
'**crane driver** *noun* a person operating a crane. □ **grutier, ière**
crank [kraŋk] *noun* a person with strange or odd ideas. □ **excentrique**
'**cranky** *adjective*. □ **excentrique; grincheux**
'**crankiness** *noun*. □ **excentricité; humeur difficile**
cranny *see* **nook**.
crash [kraʃ] *noun* 1 a noise as of heavy things breaking or falling on something hard: *I heard a crash, and looked around to see that he'd dropped all the plates.* □ **fracas**
2 a collision: *There was a crash involving three cars.* □ **accident**
3 a failure of a business *etc*: *the Wall Street crash.* □ **faillite**
■ *verb* 1 to (cause to) fall with a loud noise: *The glass crashed to the floor.* □ **(se) fracasser**
2 to drive or be driven violently (against, into): *He crashed (his car); Her car crashed into a wall.* □ **(faire) percuter**
3 (of aircraft) to land or be landed in such a way as to be damaged or destroyed: *His plane crashed in the mountains.* □ **s'écraser**
4 (of a business) to fail. □ **faire faillite**
5 to force one's way noisily (through, into): *He crashed through the undergrowth.* □ **passer à travers qqch. avec fracas**
■ *adjective* rapid and concentrated: *a crash course in computer technology.* □ **intensif**
'**crash-helmet** *noun* a covering for the head, worn for protection by racing-motorists, motorcyclists *etc*. □ **casque**
,**crash-'land** *verb* to land (an aircraft), *usually* in an emergency, with the undercarriage up. □ **se poser en catastrophe**
crass [kras] *adjective* 1 very obvious or very great: *a crass mistake.* □ **grossier**
2 stupid. □ **épais**
3 insensitive. □ **épais**
crate [kreit] *noun* a container *usually* made of wooden slats, for carrying goods, fruit *etc*: *three crates of bananas.* □ **caisse**
crater ['kreitə] *noun* 1 the bowl-shaped mouth of a volcano. □ **cratère**
2 a hollow made in the ground by a bomb *etc*. □ **cratère**

cravat [krə'vat] *noun* a kind of scarf worn instead of a tie around the neck. □ **foulard**
crave [kreiv] *verb* 1 to beg for. □ **implorer**
2 to long for, desire extremely. □ **désirer ardemment**
'**craving** *noun* a desire or longing: *a craving for adventure.* □ **désir ardent**
craven ['kreivən] *adjective* cowardly. □ **lâche**
crawfish *see* **crayfish**.
crawl [krɔːl] *verb* 1 to move slowly along the ground: *The injured dog crawled away.* □ **ramper**
2 (of people) to move on hands and knees or with the front of the body on the ground: *The baby can't walk yet, but she crawls everywhere.* □ **marcher à quatre pattes**
3 to move slowly: *The traffic was crawling along at ten kilometres per hour.* □ **se traîner**
4 to be covered with crawling things: *His hair was crawling with lice.* □ **grouiller (de)**
■ *noun* 1 a very slow movement or speed: *We drove along at a crawl.* □ **(au) pas**
2 a style of swimming in which the arms make alternate overarm movements: *She's better at the crawl than she is at the breaststroke.* □ **crawl**
crayfish ['kreifiʃ] – *plural* '**crayfish** – (*also* **crawfish** ['krɔːfiʃ] – *plural* '**crawfish**) a type of edible shellfish. □ **écrevisse**
crayon ['kreiən] *noun* a coloured pencil or stick of chalk *etc* for drawing with. □ **crayon de couleur**
■ *verb* to use crayons to draw a picture *etc*. □ **colorier (au crayon)**
craze [kreiz] *noun* a (*usually* temporary) fashion; great (but temporary) enthusiasm: *the current craze for cutting one's hair extremely short.* □ **engouement**
'**crazy** *adjective* 1 insane: *He must be going crazy; a crazy idea.* □ **fou**
2 very enthusiastic: *She's crazy about her new job.* □ **fou (de)**
'**crazily** *adverb*. □ **follement**
'**craziness** *noun*. □ **folie**
creak [kriːk] *verb* to make a sharp grating sound: *That chair is creaking beneath your weight.* □ **grincer**
■ *noun* such a sound: *The strange creaks in the old house kept the girl awake.* □ **grincement**
'**creaky** *adjective*. □ **grinçant; qui grince**
'**creakiness** *noun*. □ **état de ce qui grince**
cream [kriːm] *noun* 1 the yellowish-white oily substance that forms on the top of milk, and from which butter and cheese are made. □ **crème**
2 any of many substances made of, or similar to, cream: *ice cream; face-cream.* □ **crème**
3 the best part; the top people: *the cream of the medical profession.* □ **crème**
4 (*also adjective*) (of) a yellowish-white colour: *cream paint.* □ **crème**
■ *verb* 1 to make into a cream-like mixture: *Cream the eggs, butter and sugar together.* □ **battre**
2 to take the cream off: *She creamed the milk.* □ **écrémer**
3 (with **off**) to select (the best): *The best pupils will be creamed off for special training.* □ **écrémer**
'**creamy** *adjective* 1 full of, or like, cream: *creamy milk.*

□ **crémeux**
2 smooth and white: *a creamy complexion.* □ **velouté**
'**creaminess** *noun.* □ **velouté**
cream of tartar an ingredient in baking powder. □
crème de tartre
crease [kriːs] *noun* a mark made by folding or doubling
something: *a smart crease in his trousers; My dress was
full of creases after being in my suitcase.* □ **pli**
■ *verb* to make or become creased: *You've creased my
newspaper; This fabric creases easily.* □ (se) **froisser**
create [kriˈeit] *verb* 1 to cause to exist; to make: *How
was the earth created?; The circus created great excitement.* □ **créer**
2 to give (a rank *etc* to): *Sir John was created a knight
in 1958.* □ **créer**
cre'ation *noun* 1 the act of creating: *the creation of the
world.* □ **création**
2 something created: *The dress designer is showing her
latest creations.* □ **création**
cre'ative [-tiv] *adjective* having or showing the power
and imagination to create: *a creative dress-designer.* □
créateur
cre'atively *adverb.* □ **d'une façon créatrice**
cre'ativeness *noun.* □ **esprit de création**
,crea'tivity [kriːə-] *noun.* □ **créativité**
cre'ator *noun* a person who creates. □ **créateur, trice**
the Creator God. □ **le Créateur**
creature ['kriːtʃə] *noun* 1 an animal or human being: *all
God's creatures.* □ **créature**
2 a term of contempt or pity: *The poor creature could
hardly stand.* □ **créature**
crèche [kreʃ] *noun* a nursery for babies whose mothers
are at work *etc*: *Some factories have crèches for the
children of their workers.* □ **garderie**
credible ['kredəbl] *adjective* that may be believed: *The
story she told was barely credible.* □ **croyable**
'**credibly** *adverb.* □ **de manière crédible**
,credi'bility *noun.* □ **crédibilité**
credit ['kredit] *noun* 1 time allowed for payment of goods
etc after they have been received: *We don't give credit
at this shop.* □ **crédit**
2 money loaned (by a bank). □ **crédit**
3 trustworthiness regarding ability to pay for goods *etc*:
Your credit is good. □ **solvabilité**
4 (an entry on) the side of an account on which payments received are entered: *Our credits are greater than
our debits.* □ **crédit**
5 the sum of money which someone has in an account
at a bank: *Your credit amounts to 2,014 dollars.* □
compte créditeur
6 belief or trust: *This theory is gaining credit.* □
crédibilité
7 a certificate to show that a student has completed a
course which counts towards his degree. □ **unité**
■ *verb* 1 to enter (a sum of money) on the credit side (of
an account): *This cheque was credited to your account
last month.* □ **créditer**
2 (*with* **with**) to think of (a person or thing) as having: *I
was credited with magical powers.* □ **attribuer à**
3 to believe (something) to be possible: *Well, would you

credit that!* □ **croire**
'**creditable** *adjective* bringing honour or respect: *creditable effort.* □ **honorable**
'**creditably** *adverb.* □ **honorablement**
'**creditor** *noun* a person to whom a debt is owed. □
créancier, ière
'**credits** *noun plural* the list of names of the actors, producer, director *etc* given at the beginning or end of a
film. □ **générique**
credit card a card which allows the holder to buy goods
etc on credit: *to pay by credit card.* □ **carte de crédit**
be a credit to (someone), do (someone) credit to bring
honour or respect to (someone or something): *Your son
is a credit to his school; Your honesty does you credit.* □
faire honneur à
give (someone) credit (for something) to acknowledge
and praise (someone for a good piece of work *etc*): *She
was given credit for completing the work so quickly.* □
rendre hommage (à qqn pour qqch.)
on credit payment being made after the date of sale:
Do you sell goods on credit? □ **à crédit**
take (the) credit (for something) to accept the praise
given (for something): *I did all the work, and he took
all the credit.* □ **s'attribuer le mérite de**
credulous [' kredjuləs] *adjective* believing too easily. □
crédule
'**credulousness, cre'dulity** [-'djuː-] *noun.* □ **crédulité**
creed [kriːd] *noun* (a short statement of) one's (*especially* religious) beliefs. □ **credo**
creek [kriːk] *noun* 1 a small inlet, especially off a river.
□ **anse**
2 a small river. □ **ruisseau**
creep [kriːp] – *past tense, past participle* **crept** [krept] –
verb 1 to move slowly, quietly or secretly: *She crept
into the bedroom.* □ **se glisser (sans bruit)**
2 to move on hands or knees or with the body close to
the ground: *The cat crept towards the bird.* □ **ramper**
3 (of plants) to grow along the ground, up a wall *etc*. □
grimper
'**creeper** *noun* a creeping plant. □ **plante grimpante**
'**creepy** *adjective* causing feelings of fear *etc*: *The house
is rather creepy at night.* □ **qui donne la chair de poule**
'**creepily** *adverb.* □ **à donner la chair de poule**
'**creepiness** *noun.* □ **caractère effrayant**
,creepy-'crawly – *plural* **,creepy-'crawlies** – *noun* a
small creeping insect. □ **bestiole (qui rampe)**
creep up on to approach slowly and stealthily: *Old age
creeps up on us all.* □ **surprendre**
make someone's flesh creep to scare or horrify someone. □ **donner la chair de poule**
cremate ['kriːmeit, kriˈmeit] *verb* to burn dead (human)
bodies: *She asked to be cremated, not buried.* □
incinérer
cre'mation *noun.* □ **incinération**
crematorium [kriːmə'toːriəm] *noun* a place where cremation is carried out. □ **crématorium**
creosote ['kriəsout] *noun* an oily liquid obtained from
coal tar, used in preserving wood. □ **créosote**
crêpe [kreip] *noun, adjective* (of) a thin silk-like fabric
with a wrinkled surface. □ **crêpe**

crêpe paper paper with a similar surface. □ **(papier) crépon**

crept *see* **creep.**

crescendo [kri'ʃendou] – *plural* **cres'cendos** – *noun* (*especially* in music) a gradual and continuous increase in loudness. □ **crescendo**

crescent ['kresnt] *noun* **1** (*also adjective*) (having) the curved shape of the growing moon: *the crescent moon; crescent-shaped earrings.* □ **croissant**
2 (*abbreviated to* **Cres.** when written in street-names) a curved street. □ **rue (en arc de cercle)**

cress [kres] *noun* any of several edible plants with sharptasting leaves used in salads. □ **cresson**

crest [krest] *noun* **1** the comb or tuft on the head of a cock or other bird. □ **crête**
2 the summit or highest part: *the crest of a wave.* □ **crête**
3 feathers on the top of a helmet. □ **cimier**
4 a badge or emblem: *the family crest.* □ **armoiries**
'**crested** *adjective* having a tuft on the head. □ **huppé**

crestfallen ['krestfɔːlən] *adjective* very disappointed: *He was crestfallen at his failure.* □ **déconfit**

cretin ['kretin] *noun* **1** a person who is mentally subnormal and physically deformed. □ **crétin, ine**
2 an idiot, used as a term of contempt and abuse. □ **idiot, ote**

crevasse [kri'vas] *noun* a very deep crack or split in a glacier. □ **crevasse**

crevice ['krevis] *noun* a crack or narrow opening (in a wall, rock *etc*): *Plants grew in the crevices.* □ **lézarde**

crew[1] [kruː] *noun* **1** the group of people who work or operate a ship, airplane, bus *etc*. □ **équipage**
2 used jokingly, a group of people: *What an odd crew!* □ **équipe**
■ *verb* (*usually with* **for**) to act as a crew member (for someone). □ **faire partie de l'équipe (de)**
'**crewcut** *noun* a very short hairstyle. □ **cheveux en brosse**

crew[2] *see* **crow.**

crib [krib] *noun* **1** a cradle. □ **berceau**
2 a child's bed. □ **petit lit (d'enfant)**
3 a translation used when studying a text in a foreign language. □ **traduction (non autorisée)**
4 a manger. □ **crèche**
■ *verb* – *past tense, past participle* **cribbed** – to copy: *She cribbed the answer from her friend's work.* □ **copier**

cricket[1] ['krikit] *noun* an outdoor game played with bats, a ball and wickets, between two sides of eleven each. □ **cricket**
'**cricketer** *noun*. □ **joueur, euse de cricket**
not cricket unfair; not sportsmanlike. □ **qui n'est pas loyal**

cricket[2] ['krikit] *noun* an insect related to the grasshopper, the male of which makes a chirping noise. □ **grillon**

crime [kraim] *noun* **1** act(s) punishable by law: *Murder is a crime; Crime is on the increase.* □ **crime, criminalité**
2 something wrong though not illegal: *What a crime to cut down those trees!* □ **crime**

criminal ['kriminl] *adjective* **1** concerned with crime: *criminal law.* □ **criminel**
2 against the law: *Theft is a criminal offence.* □ **criminel**
3 very wrong; wicked: *a criminal waste of food.* □ **c'est un crime de**
■ *noun* a person who has been found guilty of a crime. □ **criminel(le)**
'**criminally** *adverb*. □ **criminellement**

crimson ['krimzn] *noun, adjective* (of) a deep red colour: *He went crimson with embarrassment.* □ **cramoisi**

cringe [krindʒ] *verb* to shrink back in fear, terror *etc*: *The dog cringed when his cruel master raised his hand to strike him.* □ **reculer (devant)**

crinkle ['krinkl] *verb* to (cause to) wrinkle or curl: *The paper crinkled in the heat of the sun.* □ **se froisser**
'**crinkly** *adjective*: *grey crinkly hair.* □ **crépu**

cripple ['kripl] *verb* **1** to make lame or disabled: *She was crippled by a fall from a horse.* □ **estropier**
2 to make less strong, less efficient *etc*: *The war has crippled the country's economy.* □ **paralyser**
■ *noun* a lame or disabled person: *He's been a cripple since the car accident.* □ **invalide**

crisis ['kraisis] – *plural* '**crises** [-siːz] – *noun* **1** a deciding moment or turning-point (*especially* of an illness): *Although she is still very ill, she has passed the crisis.* □ **crise**
2 a time of great danger or difficulty: *a crisis such as the recent flooding; You can rely on her in a crisis.* □ **situation critique**

crisp [krisp] *adjective* **1** stiff and dry enough to break easily: *crisp biscuits.* □ **croustillant**
2 (of vegetables *etc*) firm and fresh: *a crisp lettuce.* □ **croquant**
3 (of manner, speech *etc*) firm and clear. □ **précis; cassant**
'**crisply** *adverb*. □ **d'un ton cassant**
'**crispness** *noun*. □ **netteté**
'**crispy** *adjective*. □ **crépu**

criss-cross ['kriskros] *adjective* made of lines which cross each other repeatedly: *a criss-cross pattern.* □ **entrecroisé**

criterion [krai'tiəriən] – *plural* **cri'teria** [-ə] – *noun* a standard used or referred to in judging something: *What are your criteria for deciding which words to include in this dictionary?* □ **critère**

critic ['kritik] *noun* **1** a person who judges or comments on books, art *etc*: *She is the book critic for the local newspaper.* □ **critique**
2 a person who finds fault: *His critics would say that he is unsuitable for the job.* □ **détracteur, trice**
'**critical** *adjective* **1** judging and analyzing: *She has written several critical works on Robertson Davies.* □ **critique**
2 fault-finding: *She tends to be critical of her children.* □ **critique (envers)**
3 of, at or having the nature of, a crisis; very serious: *a critical shortage of food; After the accident, his condition was critical.* □ **critique**
'**critically** *adverb*. □ **de façon critique**
'**criticize**, '**criticise** [-saiz] *verb* **1** to find fault (with): *He's always criticizing her.* □ **critiquer**
2 to give an opinion of or judgment on a book *etc*. □

faire la critique de
'criticism *noun*. □ critique
croak [krouk] *verb* to utter a low hoarse sound like that of a frog: *I could hear the frogs croaking.* □ coasser
■ *noun* such a sound. □ coassement
crochet [krou'∫ei, 'krou∫ei] – *present participle* 'crocheting: *past tense, past participle* 'crocheted – *verb* to knit using a single small needle with a hooked end (a **crochet hook**). □ faire au crochet
■ *noun* work done in this way: *We enjoy doing crochet.*
□ travail au crochet
crock [krok] *noun* 1 an earthenware pot or jar. □ cruche
2 an old and decrepit person or thing: *That car's an old crock.* □ guimbarde
crocodile ['krokədail] *noun* a large reptile found in the rivers of Asia, Africa, South America and northern Australia. □ crocodile
crocodile tears pretended tears of grief. □ larmes de crocodile
crocus ['kroukəs] *noun* a plant growing from a bulb and having brilliant yellow, purple or white flowers. □ crocus
croissant ['krwa:sâ] *noun* a crescent-shaped bread roll. □ croissant
crony ['krouni] – *plural* 'cronies – *noun* a close companion: *He spent the evening drinking with his cronies.* □ copain, copine
crook [kruk] *noun* 1 a (shepherd's or bishop's) stick, bent at the end. □ houlette
2 a criminal: *The two crooks stole the old woman's jewels.* □ escroc, voleuse, malfaiteur, trice
3 the inside of the bend (of one's arm at the elbow): *She held the puppy in the crook of her arm.* □ creux
■ *verb* to bend (*especially* one's finger) into the shape of a hook: *She crooked her finger to beckon him.* □ (re)courber
'crooked [-kid] *adjective* 1 badly shaped: *a crooked little man.* □ courbé
2 not straight: *That picture is crooked* (= not horizontal). □ de travers
3 dishonest: *a crooked dealer.* □ malhonnête
'crookedly [-kid-] *adverb*. □ tortueusement
'crookedness [-kid-] *noun*. □ difformité; malhonnêteté
croon [kru:n] *verb* 1 to sing or hum in a low voice: *She crooned a lullaby.* □ fredonner
2 to sing in a quiet, sentimental style. □ fredonner
'crooner *noun*. □ chanteur, euse de charme
crop [krop] *noun* 1 a plant which is farmed and harvested: *a fine crop of rice; We grow a variety of crops, including cabbages, wheat and barley.* □ récolte; produits agricoles
2 a short whip used when horse-riding. □ cravache
3 a (short) haircut: *a crop of red hair.* □ courte chevelure
4 (of certain birds) the first stomach, which hangs like a bag from the neck. □ jabot
■ *verb* – *past tense, past participle* **cropped** – to cut or nibble short: *The sheep crop the grass.* □ brouter
crop up to happen unexpectedly: *I'm sorry I'm late, but something important cropped up.* □ survenir
croquet ['kroukei, krou'kei] *noun* a game in which

wooden balls are driven by mallets through a series of hoops stuck in the ground. □ croquet
cross[1] [kros] *adjective* angry: *I get very cross when I lose something.* □ fâché
'crossly *adverb*. □ avec (mauvaise) humeur
cross[2] [kros] – *plural* 'crosses – *noun* 1 a symbol formed by two lines placed across each other, *eg* + or ×. □ croix
2 two wooden beams placed thus (+), on which Christ was nailed. □ croix
3 the symbol of the Christian religion. □ croix
4 a lasting cause of suffering *etc*: *Your rheumatism is a cross you will have to bear.* □ croix
5 the result of breeding two varieties of animal or plant: *This dog is a cross between an alsatian and a labrador.* □ hybride
6 a monument in the shape of a cross. □ croix
7 any of several types of medal given for bravery *etc*: *the Victoria Cross.* □ croix
■ *verb* 1 to go from one side to the other: *Let's cross (the street); This road crosses the swamp.* □ traverser
2 (*negative* **uncross**) to place (two things) across each other: *He sat down and crossed his legs.* □ croiser
3 to go or be placed across (each other): *The roads cross in the centre of town.* □ se croiser
4 to meet and pass: *Our letters must have crossed in the post.* □ se croiser
5 to put a line across: *Cross your 't's'.* □ barrer
6 to breed (something) from two different varieties: *I've crossed two varieties of rose.* □ croiser
7 to go against the wishes of: *If you cross me, you'll regret it!* □ contrarier
cross- 1 going or placed across: *cross-winds; cross-pieces.* □ de travers, traverse
2 of mixed variety: *a crossbreed.* □ hybride
'crossing *noun* 1 a place where a road *etc* may be crossed: *a pedestrian-crossing; a level-crossing.* □ intersection
2 a journey over the sea: *I was seasick as it was a very rough crossing.* □ traversée
'crossbow *noun* a medieval type of bow fixed to a shaft with a mechanism for pulling back and releasing the string. □ arbalète
'crossbreed *noun* an animal bred from two different breeds. □ hybride
'crossbred *adjective*. □ métissé, ée
cross-'country *adjective* across fields *etc*, not on roads: *a cross-country run.* □ à travers champs
,cross-ex'amine *verb* in a court of law, to test or check the previous evidence of (a witness) by questioning him. □ faire subir un contre-interrogatoire (à)
'cross-ex,ami'nation *noun*. □ contre-interrogatoire
,cross-'eyed *adjective* having a squint. □ qui louche
'crossfire *noun* the crossing of lines of gunfire from two or more points. □ feux croisés
at cross-purposes of two or more people, confused about what they are saying or doing because of misunderstanding one another: *I think we're talking at cross-purposes.* □ (il y a) malentendu
,cross-re'fer *verb* to give a cross-reference (to): *In this dictionary went is cross-referred to go.* □ renvoyer à

,cross-'reference *noun* a reference from one part of a book, list *etc* to another, *eg* **crept** *see* **creep**. □ **renvoi**

'crossroads *noun singular* a place where two or more roads cross or meet: *At the crossroads we'll have to decide which road to take*. □ **carrefour**

,cross-'section *noun* **1** (a drawing *etc* of) the area or surface made visible by cutting through something, *eg* an apple. □ **coupe transversale**

2 a sample as representative of the whole: *He interviewed a cross-section of the audience to get their opinion of the play*. □ **échantillon**

crossword (puzzle) a square word-puzzle in which the blanks in a pattern of blank and solid checks are to be filled with words reading across and down, the words being found from clues. □ **mots croisés**

cross one's fingers to place a finger across the one next to it, for good luck. □ **faire une petite prière**

cross out to draw a line through: *She crossed out all her mistakes*. □ **biffer**

crotch [krotʃ] *noun* in humans, the place where the legs meet together and join the body. □ **entre-jambes**

crotchety ['krotʃəti] *adjective* bad-tempered. □ **grincheux**

crouch [krautʃ] *verb* **1** to stand with the knees well bent; to squat: *She crouched behind the bush*. □ **s'accroupir**

2 (of animals) to lie close to the ground, in fear, readiness for action *etc*: *The tiger was crouching ready to spring on its prey*. □ **se tapir**

croupier ['kruːpiei] *noun* a person who takes and pays bets at a gambling table in a casino *etc*. □ **croupier, ière**

croûton ['kruːton] *noun* a small piece of fried or toasted bread, served in soup *etc*. □ **croûton**

crow [krou] *noun* **1** the name given to a number of large birds, generally black. □ **corneille**

2 the cry of a cock. □ **chant du coq**

■ *verb* **1** (*past tense* **crew**) to utter the cry of a cock. □ **chanter**

2 to utter a cry of delight *etc*: *The baby crowed with happiness*. □ **gazouiller**

,crow's 'nest *noun* a shelter at the masthead of a ship, used as a lookout post. □ **nid de pie**

crowbar ['kroubaː] *noun* a large iron stake with a bend at the end, used to lift heavy stones *etc*. □ **levier**

crowd [kraud] *noun* **1** a number of persons or things gathered together: *A crowd of people gathered in the street*. □ **foule**

2 a group of friends, *usually* known to one another: *John's friends are a nice crowd*. □ **(petite) bande**

■ *verb* **1** to gather in a large group: *They crowded around the injured motorcyclist*. □ **s'attrouper**

2 to fill too full by coming together in: *Sightseers crowded the building*. □ **s'entasser (dans)**

'crowded *adjective* having or containing a lot of people or things: *crowded buses*. □ **bondé**

crown [kraun] *noun* **1** a circular, often jewelled, headdress, *especially* one worn as a mark of royalty or honour: *the queen's crown*. □ **couronne**

2 (*with capital*) the king or queen or governing power in a monarchy: *revenue belonging to the Crown*. □ **Couronne**

3 the top *eg* of a head, hat, hill *etc*: *We reached the crown of the hill*. □ **faîte**

4 (an artificial replacement for) the part of a tooth which can be seen. □ **couronne**

■ *verb* **1** to make (someone) king or queen by placing a crown on his or her head: *The archbishop crowned the queen*. □ **couronner**

2 to form the top part of (something): *an iced cake crowned with a cherry*. □ **couronner**

3 to put an artificial crown on (a tooth). □ **couronner**

4 to hit (someone) on the head: *If you do that again, I'll crown you!* □ **flanquer un coup sur la tête**

crown prince the heir to the throne. □ **prince héritier**

crown princess 1 the wife of a crown prince. □ **princesse royale/impériale**

2 the female heir to the throne. □ **princesse héritière**

crucial ['kruːʃəl] *adjective* involving a big decision; of the greatest importance: *He took the crucial step of asking her to marry him*; *The next game is crucial – if we lose it we lose the match*. □ **crucial**

crucible ['kruːsibl] *noun* a pot in which metals *etc* may be melted: *She heated the chemicals in a crucible in the laboratory*. □ **creuset**

crucify ['kruːsifai] *verb* to put to death by fixing the hands and feet to a cross: *Christ was crucified*. □ **crucifier**

'crucifix [-fiks] *noun* a figure of Christ on the cross. □ **crucifix**

,cruci'fixion [-'fikʃən] *noun* (a) death on the cross, especially that of Christ. □ **crucifixion**

crude [kruːd] *adjective* **1** unrefined: *crude oil*. □ **brut**

2 rough or primitive: *a crude shelter*. □ **rudimentaire, rude**

'crudeness *noun*. □ **grossièreté**

'crudity *noun*. □ **crudité**

cruel ['kruːəl] *adjective* **1** pleased at causing pain; merciless: *She was cruel to her dog*. □ **cruel (envers)**

2 causing distress: *a cruel disappointment*. □ **cruel**

'cruelly *adverb*. □ **cruellement**

'cruelty *noun*. □ **cruauté**

cruet ['kruːit] *noun* **1** a small jar or bottle for salt, pepper, vinegar *etc*. □ **salière, poivrière, vinaigrier**

2 (*also* 'cruet-stand) a holder for such jars *etc*, often with them on it. □ **huilier**

cruise [kruːz] *verb* **1** to sail for pleasure: *We're going cruising in the Mediterranean*. □ **être en croisière**

2 to go at a steady, comfortable speed: *The plane is cruising at an altitude of 10 000 metres*. □ **aller à sa vitesse de croisière**

■ *noun* a voyage from place to place made for pleasure and relaxation: *They went on a cruise*. □ **croisière**

'cruiser *noun* **1** a high-speed battleship. □ **croiseur**

2 (*also* 'cabin cruiser) a motor yacht with living quarters. □ **yacht de plaisance**

crumb [krʌm] *noun* a tiny piece, *especially* of bread: *She puts crumbs for the birds on her window-sill*. □ **miette**

crumble ['krʌmbl] *verb* to break into crumbs or small pieces: *She crumbled the bread*; *The building had crumbled into ruins*; *Her hopes of success finally crumbled*.

□ (s')émietter, s'effondrer
'crumbly adjective. □ friable

crumple ['krʌmpl] verb to make or become wrinkled or creased: This material crumples easily; She crumpled up the piece of paper. □ (se) froisser, (se) friper

crunch [krʌntʃ] verb to crush noisily (something hard), with the teeth, feet etc: She crunched sweets all through the film. □ croquer (avec bruit)
■ noun: the crunch of gravel under the car wheels. □ crissement
'crunchy adjective: thick crunchy biscuits. □ croquant

crusade [kruːˈseid] noun 1 in medieval times, a military expedition of Christians to win back the Holy Land from the Turks. □ croisade
2 a campaign in support of a good cause: the crusade against cigarette advertising. □ campagne
■ verb to take part in a crusade. □ faire une croisade (pour, contre)
cru'sader noun. □ croisé, ée

crush [krʌʃ] verb 1 to squash by squeezing together etc: The car was crushed between the two trucks. □ écraser
2 to crease: That material crushes easily. □ se froisser
3 to defeat: He crushed the rebellion. □ écraser
4 to push, press etc together: We (were) all crushed into the tiny room. □ entasser
■ noun squeezing or crowding together: There's always a crush in the supermarket on Saturdays. □ cohue
'crushing adjective overwhelming: a crushing defeat. □ écrasant

crust [krʌst] noun 1 (a piece of) the hard outside coating of bread: The child would not eat the crusts. □ croûte
2 pastry: He makes excellent crust. □ pâte à tarte
3 a hard surface especially the outer layer of the earth. □ écorce
'crusty adjective 1 having a crust: crusty bread. □ qui a une forte croûte
2 surly or irritable. □ bourru; hargneux
'crustily adverb. □ d'un ton hargneux/bourru
'crustiness noun. □ texture croustillante; humeur bourrue

crustacean [krʌˈsteiʃən] noun, adjective (of) any of a group of animals, including crabs, lobsters, shrimps etc, whose bodies are covered with a hard shell. □ crustacé
crusty see crust.

crutch [krʌtʃ] noun a stick with a bar at the top to support a lame person: He can walk only by using crutches. □ béquille

crux [krʌks] – plural 'cruxes – noun a difficult or essential point: That is the crux of the matter. □ nœud, point crucial

cry [krai] verb 1 to let tears come from the eyes; to weep: She cried when she heard of the old man's death. □ pleurer
2 (often with out) to shout out (a loud sound): She cried out for help. □ crier
■ noun – plural cries – 1 a shout: a cry of triumph. □ cri
2 a time of weeping: The baby had a little cry before he went to sleep. □ pleurs
3 the sound made by some animals: the cry of a wolf. □

cri
a far cry a long way (from): Our modern clothes are a far cry from the animal skins worn by our ancestors. □ (bien) loin de
cry off to cancel (an engagement or agreement). □ annuler

crypt [kript] noun an underground chapel beneath a church. □ crypte

cryptic ['kriptik] adjective intentionally very difficult to understand or make sense of: a cryptic message. □ énigmatique

crystal ['kristl] noun 1 a small part of a solid substance (eg salt or ice) which has a regular shape. □ cristal
2 a special kind of very clear glass: This bowl is made of crystal. □ cristal
'crystalline [-lain] adjective (of minerals etc) formed into crystals: Salt is a crystalline substance. □ cristallin
'crystallize, 'crystallise verb 1 to form (into) crystals: He crystallized the salt from the sea water. □ (se) cristalliser
2 to cover with a coating of sugar crystals: crystallized fruits. □ confire
3 to make or become definite or clear: He tried to crystallize his ideas. □ fixer
,crystalli'zation, ,crystalli'sation noun. □ cristallisation
crystal ball a glass ball used in fortune-telling. □ boule de cristal
crystal clear absolutely clear: My instructions were crystal clear. □ limpide

cub [kʌb] noun 1 the young of certain animals such as foxes, lions etc: a bear cub. □ petit (d'un animal)
2 (with capital: short for Cub Scout) a member of the junior branch of the Scouts. □ louveteau

cubbyhole ['kʌbihoul] noun a very small room, cupboard etc. □ cagibi

cube [kjuːb] noun 1 a solid body having six equal square faces. □ cube
2 the result of multiplying a number by itself twice: The cube of 4 = 4 × 4 × 4 = 4³ = 64. □ cube
■ verb 1 to calculate the cube of (a number): If you cube 2, you will get the answer 8. □ élever au cube
2 to make into a cube or cubes: She cubed the beef. □ découper en cubes
'cubic adjective shaped like a cube. □ cubique
cube root the number of which a given number is the cube: The cube root of 64 is 4. □ racine cubique
cubic centimetre (abbreviation cc), metre etc the volume of, or the volume equivalent to, a cube whose sides measure one centimetre, metre etc: This jug holds 500 cubic centimetres. □ (centimètre, etc.) cube

cubicle ['kjuːbikl] noun a small room etc closed off in some way from a larger one: Please use the (changing-) cubicle to change into your swimming trunks. □ cabine

cuckoo ['kukuː] – plural 'cuckoos – noun a bird, named after its call, which lays eggs in the nests of other birds. □ coucou

cucumber ['kjuːkʌmbə] noun a type of creeping plant with long green edible fruit, often used in salads etc. □ concombre

cud [kʌd]: chew the cud (of cows etc) to bring food

from the stomach back into the mouth and chew it again. □ **ruminer**

cuddle ['kʌdl] *verb* to hug affectionately: *The father cuddled the child until she fell asleep.* □ **câliner**
■ *noun* an affectionate hug. □ **câlin**
'**cuddly** *adjective*: *a cuddly teddy bear.* □ **doux**

cudgel ['kʌdʒəl] *noun* a heavy stick or club. □ **gourdin**
■ *verb – past tense, past participle* '**cudgelled**, *(American)* '**cudgeled** – to beat with a cudgel. □ **donner des coups de bâton à**

cue¹ [kjuː] *noun* the last words of another actor's speech *etc*, serving as a sign to an actor to speak *etc*: *Your cue is '– whatever the vicar says!'* □ **réplique**

cue² [kjuː] *noun* a stick which gets thinner towards one end and the point of which is used to strike the ball in playing billiards. □ **queue**

cuff¹ [kʌf] *noun* **1** the end of the sleeve (of a shirt, coat *etc*) near the wrist: *Does your shirt have buttons on the cuffs?* □ **manchette**
2 the turned-up part of a trouser leg. □ **revers**
'**cufflinks** *noun plural* two ornamental buttons *etc* joined by a small bar, chain *etc* used to fasten a shirt cuff. □ **bouton(s) de manchette**

cuff² [kʌf] *noun* a blow with the open hand: *a cuff on the ear.* □ **gifle**
■ *verb* to give such a blow: *He cuffed him on the head.* □ **gifler**

cuisine [kwiˈziːn] *noun* style of cooking: *French cuisine.* □ **cuisine**

cul-de-sac ['kʌldəsak] *noun* a street closed at one end. □ **cul-de-sac**

culinary ['kʌlinəri] *adjective* of or used in the kitchen or in cookery: *culinary herbs.* □ **de cuisine**

cull [kʌl] *verb* **1** to gather or collect. □ **cueillir**
2 to select and kill (surplus animals): *They are culling the seals.* □ **éliminer**
■ *noun* an act of killing surplus animals. □ **élimination**

culminate ['kʌlmineit] *verb* (*with* **in**) to reach the highest or most important point: *The celebrations culminated in a fireworks display in the local park.* □ **culminer**
,**culmi'nation** *noun*. □ **point culminant**

culotte [kjuˈʒlot] *noun* (*usually in plural*) women's knee-length trousers cut so as to look like a skirt. □ **jupe-culotte**

culpable ['kʌlpəbl] *adjective* deserving blame; guilty: *She was the one who committed the crime but he was culpable also.* □ **coupable**
,**culpa'bility** *noun*. □ **culpabilité**

culprit ['kʌlprit] *noun* a person responsible for something wrong, unpleasant *etc*: *As soon as she saw the broken window she began to look for the culprit.* □ **coupable**

cult [kʌlt] *noun* a particular system of (religious) belief or worship: *a strange new religious cult; Physical fitness has become a cult with you.* □ **culte**

cultivate ['kʌltiveit] *verb* **1** to prepare (land) for crops. □ **cultiver**
2 to grow (a crop in a garden, field *etc*): *She cultivates mushrooms in the cellar.* □ **cultiver**

'**cultivated** *adjective* **1** (of fields *etc*) prepared for crops; used for growing crops: *cultivated land.* □ **cultivé**
2 grown in a garden *etc*; not wild: *a cultivated variety of raspberries.* □ **de culture**
3 having good manners; educated: *a cultivated young lady; She has cultivated tastes in music.* □ **distingué**
,**culti'vation** *noun*. □ **culture**

'**cultivator** *noun* a tool or machine for breaking up ground and removing weeds. □ **motoculteur**

culture ['kʌltʃə] *noun* **1** a form or type of civilization of a certain race or nation: *the Jewish culture.* □ **culture**
2 improvement of the mind *etc* by education *etc*: *I am an enthusiastic seeker of culture.* □ **culture**
3 educated taste in art, literature, music *etc*: *He thinks that anyone who dislikes Bach is lacking in culture.* □ **culture**
4 (a) cultivated growth of bacteria *etc*. □ **culture**
5 the commercial rearing of fish, certain plants *etc*. □ **élevage**
'**cultural** *adjective*. □ **culturel**
'**cultured** *adjective* (*negative* **uncultured**) well-educated. □ **cultivé**

cumbersome ['kʌmbəsəm] *adjective* (of things) heavy and clumsy: *a cumbersome piece of furniture.* □ **encombrant**

cumulative ['kjuːmjulətiv] *adjective* becoming greater by stages or additions: *This drug has a cumulative effect.* □ **cumulatif**

cunning ['kʌniŋ] *adjective* **1** sly; clever in a deceitful way: *cunning tricks.* □ **rusé**
2 clever: *a cunning device.* □ **astucieux**
■ *noun* slyness or deceitful cleverness: *full of cunning.* □ **ruse**
'**cunningly** *adverb*: *cunningly disguised.* □ **astucieusement**

cup [kʌp] *noun* **1** a *usually* round hollow container to hold liquid for drinking, often with a handle: *a teacup; a cup of tea.* □ **tasse**
2 an ornamental vessel, *usually* of silver or other metal, given as a prize in sports events *etc*: *They won the Stanley Cup.* □ **coupe**
■ *verb – past tense, past participle* **cupped** – **1** to form (one's hands) into the shape of a cup: *He cupped his hands around his mouth and called.* □ **mettre ses mains autour (de)**
2 to hold (something) in one's cupped hands: *He cupped the egg in his hands.* □ **entourer de ses mains**
'**cupful** *noun*: *three cupfuls of water.* □ **tasse**

cupboard ['kʌbəd] *noun* ('closet) a cabinet of any size up to that of a small room for storing anything: *Put the food in the cupboard; a broom cupboard.* □ **placard**

cup final the final match in a soccer competition in which the prize is a cup. □ **finale de la coupe**

'**cup-tie** *noun* one of a series of games in a soccer competition in which the prize is a cup. □ **match de coupe**

one's cup of tea the sort of thing one likes or prefers: *Classical music is not my cup of tea.* □ **au goût de qqn**

cur [kəː] *noun* a dog of mixed breed. □ **bâtard**

curable *see* **cure**.

curate ['kjuərət] *noun* a clergyman in the Church of England assisting a rector or vicar. □ **vicaire**

curative *see* **cure.**

curator [kjuəˈreitə] *noun* a person in charge of a museum *etc.* □ **conservateur, trice**

curb [kəːb] *noun* **1** something which restrains or controls: *We'll have to put a curb on her enthusiasm.* □ **frein**
2 the edge of a sidewalk nearest the gutter. □ **bord du trottoir**
■ *verb* to hold back, restrain or control: *You must curb your spending.* □ **restreindre, modérer**
'**curbstone** *noun* the stone or concrete edge of a sidewalk. □ **bord (du trottoir)**

curd [kəːd] *noun* (*also* **curds** *noun plural*) the solid substance formed when milk turns sour, used in making cheese. □ **lait caillé**

curdle [ˈkəːdl] *verb* to turn into curd: *The heat has curdled the milk; This milk has curdled.* □ **cailler**

cure [kjuə] *verb* **1** to make better: *That medicine cured me; That will cure him of his bad habits.* □ **guérir**
2 to get rid of (an illness *etc*): *That pill cured my headache.* □ **guérir**
3 to preserve (bacon *etc*) by drying, salting *etc.* □ **sécher; saler; fumer**
■ *noun* something which cures: *They're trying to find a cure for cancer.* □ **remède**
'**curable** *adjective* able to be cured: *a curable form of cancer.* □ **guérissable**
curative [ˈkjuərətiv] *adjective* intended to, or likely to, cure: *curative treatment.* □ **curatif**

curfew [ˈkəːfjuː] *noun* an order forbidding people to be in the streets after a certain hour: *There's a curfew in force from ten o'clock tonight.* □ **couvre-feu**

curio [ˈkjuəriou] – *plural* '**curios** – *noun* an article valued for its oddness or its rareness. □ **curiosité**

curious [ˈkjuəriəs] *adjective* **1** strange; odd: *a curious habit.* □ **curieux**
2 anxious or interested (to learn): *I'm curious (to find out) whether he passed his exams.* □ **curieux (de)**
'**curiously** *adverb.* □ **curieusement**
,**curi'osity** [-ˈo-] – *plural* ,**curi'osities** – *noun* **1** eagerness to learn: *I was very unpopular because of my curiosity about other people's affairs.* □ **curiosité**
2 something strange and rare: *That old chair is quite a curiosity.* □ **curiosité**

curl [kəːl] *verb* **1** to twist or turn (*especially* hair) into small coils or rolls: *My hair curls easily.* □ **friser**
2 (*sometimes with* **up**) to move in curves; to bend or roll: *The paper curled (up) at the edges.* □ **s'enrouler**
■ *noun* **1** a coil of hair *etc.* □ **boucle**
2 the quality of being curled: *My hair has very little curl in it.* □ **ondulation**
'**curler** *noun* an object around which hair is rolled to make it curl, fastened in the hair. □ **rouleau**
'**curly** *adjective: curly hair.* □ **bouclé**
'**curliness** *noun.* □ **ondulation**
curl up to move or roll into a position or shape: *The hedgehog curled (itself) up into a ball.* □ **se mettre en boule**

currant [ˈkʌrənt] *noun* **1** a small black raisin or dried

seedless grape: *This cake has currants in it.* □ **raisin sec**
2 any of several types of small berry: *a redcurrant/blackcurrant.* □ **groseille; cassis**

a packet of **currants** (not **currents**).

currency [ˈkʌrənsi,] – *plural* '**currencies** – *noun* the money (notes and coins) of a country: *the currencies of the world; foreign currency.* □ **monnaie**

current [ˈkʌrənt] *adjective* of or belonging to the present: *current affairs; the current month; the current temperature.* □ **courant; actuel**
■ *noun* **1** (the direction of) a stream of water or air: *the current of a river.* □ **courant**
2 (a) flow of electricity: *an electrical current.* □ **courant**
'**currently** *adverb* at the present time: *Mary is currently working as a bus-driver.* □ **actuellement**
current account an account with a bank from which money may be withdrawn by cheque. □ **compte courant**

electric **current** (not **currant**); **current** (not **currant**) affairs.

curriculum [kəˈrikjuləm] – *plural* **cur'ricula** [-lə] – *noun* a course, *especially* of study at school or university: *They are changing the curriculum.* □ **programme (des études)**

curry[1] [ˈkʌri] – *plural* '**curries** – *noun* (an *originally* Indian dish of) meat, vegetables *etc* cooked with spices: *chicken curry.* □ **curry**
■ *verb* to cook in this way: *Are you going to curry this meat?* □ **accommoder au curry**
'**curried** *adjective: curried chicken.* □ **au curry**
curry powder a selection of spices ground together and used in making a curry. □ **curry**

curry[2] [ˈkʌri] *verb* to rub down or comb and clean (a horse). □ **étriller**
curry favour (*with* **with**) to seek (a) favour by flattery: *She's currying favour with the boss.* □ **chercher à gagner la faveur de**

curse [kəːs] *verb* **1** to wish that evil may fall upon: *I curse the day that I was born!; The witch cursed him.* □ **maudire**
2 to use violent language; to swear: *He cursed (at his own stupidity) when he dropped the hammer on his toe.* □ **sacrer**
■ *noun* **1** an act of cursing, or the words used: *the witch's curse.* □ **malédiction**
2 a thing or person which is cursed: *Having to work is the curse of my life.* □ **malheur**
cursed with having the misfortune to have: *He's cursed with a troublesome brother-in-law.* □ **affligé**

cursive [ˈkəːsiv] *adjective* (of handwriting) with letters joined. □ **cursif**

cursory [ˈkəːsəri] *adjective* hurried: *a cursory glance.* □ **hâtif**
'**cursorily** *adverb.* □ **hâtivement**

curt [kəːt] *adjective* rudely brief: *a curt reply.* □ **brusque**
'**curtly** *adverb.* □ **avec brusquerie**
'**curtness** *noun.* □ **brusquerie**

curtail [kəːˈteil] *verb* make less, shorter *etc* (than was originally intended): *I've had to curtail my visit.* □ **écourter**

cur'tailment *noun.* □ **raccourcissement**

curtain ['kɔːtn] *noun* a piece of material hung up to act as a screen at a window, on a theatre stage *etc*: *The maid drew the curtains*; *The curtain came down at the end of the play.* □ **rideau**

curtain call an appearance by actors, singers *etc* after a performance for the purpose of receiving applause: *After the play the actors took ten curtain calls.* □ **rappel**

curtain off to separate or enclose with a curtain: *I curtained off the alcove.* □ **diviser par un rideau**

curtsy, curtsey ['kɔːtsi] – *plural* 'curtsies – *noun* a bow made by women by bending the knees. □ **révérence**

■ *verb* to make a curtsy: *She curtsied to the queen.* □ **faire une révérence (à)**

curvature ['kɔːvətʃuər] *noun* the condition or extent of being curved: *the curvature of the earth.* □ **courbure**

curve [kɔːv] *noun* **1** a line which is not straight at any point, like part of the edge of a circle. □ **courbe**
2 anything shaped like this: *a curve in the road.* □ **tournant**

■ *verb* to bend in a curve: *The road curves east.* □ **tourner**

curved *adjective*: *a curved blade.* □ **courbé**

'curvy *adjective*. □ **courbe, sinueux**

cushion ['kuʃən] *noun* **1** a bag of cloth *etc* filled with soft material, *eg* feathers *etc*, used for support or to make a seat more comfortable: *I'll sit on a cushion on the floor.* □ **coussin**
2 any similar support: *A hovercraft travels on a cushion of air.* □ **coussin**

■ *verb* to lessen the force of a blow *etc*: *The soft sand cushioned my fall.* □ **amortir**

cushy ['kuʃi] *adjective* easy and comfortable: *a cushy job.* □ **tranquille**

custard ['kʌstəd] *noun* **1** milk, eggs *etc* cooked together and flavoured. □ **crème renversée**
2 a sauce made of milk, sugar and cornflour for sweet dishes. □ **crème anglaise**

custody ['kʌstədi] *noun* **1** care or keeping: *The mother was awarded custody of the children by the court.* □ **garde**
2 the care of police or prison authorities: *The accused man is in custody.* □ **détention**

cu'stodian [-'stou-] *noun* a person who guards or takes care of something: *the custodian of an art collection.* □ **conservateur, trice**

custom ['kʌstəm] *noun* **1** what a person *etc* is in the habit of doing or does regularly: *It's my custom to go for a walk on Saturday mornings*; *religious customs.* □ **habitude**
2 the regular buying of goods at the same shop *etc*; trade or business: *The new supermarkets take away custom from the small shops.* □ **clientèle**

'customary *adjective* habitual; usually done *etc*: *It is customary to eat turkey for Christmas dinner.* □ **habituel, traditionnel**

'customarily *adverb.* □ **habituellement**

'customer *noun* **1** a person who buys from a shop *etc*:

our regular customers. □ **client, ente**
2 used jokingly for a person: *a strange customer.* □ **individu**

'customs *noun plural* **1** (the government department that collects) taxes paid on goods coming into a country: *Did you have to pay customs on those watches?*; *He works for the customs*; (*also adjective*) *customs duty.* □ **(droits de) douane**
2 the place at a port *etc* where these taxes are collected: *I was searched when I came through customs at the airport.* □ **douane**

customs officer a government official who works at a border crossing and verifies that people are entering the country and bringing in merchandise legally: *The customs officer examines passports and searches suitcases for illegal drugs.* □ **douanier, ière**

cut [kʌt] – *present participle* 'cutting: *past tense, past participle* cut – *verb* **1** to make an opening in, *usually* with something with a sharp edge: *He cut the paper with a pair of scissors.* □ **couper**
2 to separate or divide by cutting: *She cut a slice of bread*; *The child cut out the pictures*; *She cut up the meat into small pieces.* □ **(dé)couper**
3 to make by cutting: *She cut a hole in the cloth.* □ **faire**
4 to shorten by cutting; to trim: *to cut hair*; *I'll cut the grass.* □ **couper, tondre**
5 to reduce: *They cut my wages by ten per cent.* □ **réduire**
6 to remove: *They cut several passages from the film.* □ **supprimer**
7 to wound or hurt by breaking the skin (of): *I cut my hand on a piece of glass.* □ **couper**
8 to divide (a pack of cards). □ **couper**
9 to stop: *When the actress said the wrong words, the director ordered 'Cut!'* □ **couper**
10 to take a short route or way: *He cut through/across the park on his way to the office*; *A van cut in in front of me on the highway.* □ **couper par**
11 to meet and cross (a line or geometrical figure): *An axis cuts a circle in two places.* □ **couper**
12 to stay away from (a class, lecture *etc*): *He cut school and went to the cinema.* □ **sécher**
13 (*also* cut dead) to ignore completely: *She cut me dead on Sherbrooke Street.* □ **faire semblant de ne pas voir**

■ *noun* **1** the result of an act of cutting: *a cut on the head*; *a power-cut* (= stoppage of electrical power); *a haircut*; *a cut in prices.* □ **coupure, coupe, réduction**
2 the way in which something is tailored, fashioned *etc*: *the cut of the jacket.* □ **coupe**
3 a piece of meat cut from an animal: *a cut of beef.* □ **morceau**

'cutter *noun* **1** a person or thing that cuts: *a wood-cutter*; *a glass-cutter.* □ **tailleur, euse; sécateur**
2 a type of small sailing ship. □ **cotre**

'cutting *noun* **1** a piece of plant cut off and replanted to form another plant. □ **bouture**
2 an article cut out from a newspaper *etc*: *She collects cuttings about filmstars.* □ **coupure**
3 a trench dug through a hillside *etc*, in which a railway, road *etc* is built. □ **tranchée**

■ *adjective* insulting or offending: *a cutting remark.* □ **blessant**

cut glass glass with ornamental patterns cut on the surface, used for drinking glasses *etc*. □ **cristal taillé**

'**cut-price** cheaper than normal: *cut-price goods*; *a cut-price store.* □ **au rabais**

'**cutthroat** *noun* a murderer. □ **assassin**
■ *adjective* fierce; ruthless: *cutthroat business competition.* □ **sans merci**

a cut above (obviously) better than: *She's a cut above the average engineer.* □ **supérieur à**

cut and dried fixed and definite: *cut-and-dried opinions.* □ **tout fait**

cut back to reduce considerably: *The government cut back (on) public spending* (*noun* '**cutback**). □ **réduire**

cut both ways to affect both parts of a question, both people involved, good and bad points *etc*: *That argument cuts both ways!* □ **(être) à double tranchant**

cut a dash to have a smart or striking appearance: *He cuts a dash in his purple suit.* □ **faire de l'effet**

cut down 1 to cause to fall by cutting: *He has cut down the apple tree.* □ **abattre**
2 to reduce (an amount taken *etc*): *I haven't given up smoking but I'm cutting down.* □ **réduire**

cut in to interrupt: *She cut in with a remark.* □ **intervenir**

cut it fine to allow barely enough time, money *etc* for something that must be done. □ **ne pas laisser de marge**

cut no ice to have no effect: *This sort of flattery cuts no ice with me.* □ **ne faire aucun effet (sur)**

cut off 1 to interrupt or break a telephone connection: *I was cut off in the middle of the telephone call.* □ **couper**
2 to separate: *They were cut off from the rest of the army.* □ **séparer**
3 to stop or prevent delivery of: *They've cut off our supplies of coal.* □ **couper**

cut one's losses to decide to spend no more money, effort *etc* on something which is proving unprofitable. □ **faire la part du feu**

cut one's teeth to grow one's first teeth: *The baby's cutting his first tooth.* □ **faire ses dents**

cut out 1 to stop working, sometimes because of a safety device: *The engines cut out* (*noun* '**cut-out**). □ **caler**
2 to stop: *I've cut out smoking.* □ **arrêter de**

cut short 1 to make shorter than intended: *He cut short his holiday to deal with the crisis.* □ **interrompre**
2 to cause (someone) to stop talking by interrupting them: *I tried to apologize but he cut me short.* □ **couper la parole à**

cute [kjuːt] *adjective* **1** (*especially North American*) attractive or pleasing in any way: *a cute baby.* □ **mignon**
2 cunningly clever: *You think you're pretty cute, don't you!* □ **malin**

cuticle ['kjuːtikl] *noun* the dead skin at the inner edge of a fingernail or toenail. □ **petites peaux, cuticules**

cutlass ['kʌtləs] *noun* a short, broad, slightly curved sword with one cutting edge. □ **coutelas**

cutlery ['kʌtləri] *noun* knives, forks and spoons. □ **service de couverts**

cutlet ['kʌtlit] *noun* a small slice of meat (mutton, veal, pork) on a rib or other bone: *lamb cutlets.* □ **côtelette**

cutter, cutting *see* **cut.**

cuttlefish ['kʌtlifiʃ] – *plural* '**cuttlefish** – *noun* a sea-creature like the squid, able to squirt an inky liquid. □ **seiche**

cyanide ['saiənaid] *noun* a deadly type of poison. □ **cyanure**

cycle[1] ['saikl] *verb* to go by bicycle: *She cycles to work every day.* □ **aller à/en bicyclette**
■ *noun* shortened form of **bicycle**: *They bought the child a cycle for his birthday.* □ **vélo**

'**cyclist** *noun* a person who rides a bicycle. □ **cycliste**

cycle[2] ['saikl] *noun* **1** a number of events happening one after the other in a certain order: *the life-cycle of the butterfly.* □ **cycle**
2 a series of poems, songs *etc* written about one main event *etc*: *a song cycle.* □ **cycle**
3 (of alternating current, radio waves *etc*) one complete series of changes in a regularly varying supply, signal *etc*. □ **cycle**

'**cyclic** *adjective*. □ **cyclique**

'**cyclically** *adverb*. □ **d'une manière cyclique**

cyclist *see* **cycle**[1].

cyclone ['saikloun] *noun* a violent wind-storm: *The cyclone ripped the roofs off houses and tore up trees.* □ **cyclone**

cygnet ['signit] *noun* a young swan: *a swan with three cygnets.* □ **jeune cygne**

cylinder ['silində] *noun* **1** a solid shape or object with a circular base and top and straight sides. □ **cylindre**
2 any of several pieces of machinery of this shape, solid or hollow: *The brake cylinder of her car is leaking.* □ **cylindre**
3 a container in the shape of a cylinder: *two cylinders of oxygen.* □ **bouteille**

cy'lindrical *adjective* shaped like a cylinder: *A beer-can is cylindrical.* □ **cylindrique**

cymbal ['simbəl] *noun* a brass musical instrument like a plate with a hollow in the centre, two of which are struck together to produce a noise: *The cymbals clashed.* □ **cymbale**

cynical ['sinikəl] *adjective* inclined to believe the worst, *especially about people*: *a cynical attitude.* □ **cynique**

'**cynically** *adverb*. □ **cyniquement**

'**cynic** *noun* a person who believes the worst about everyone: *He is a cynic – he thinks no one is really unselfish.* □ **cynique**

'**cynicism** [-sizəm] *noun*. □ **cynisme**

cypress ['saipris] *noun* a type of evergreen tree. □ **cyprès**

cyst [sist] *noun* a kind of liquid-filled blister on an internal part of the body or just under the skin. □ **kyste**

czar *see* **tsar.**

Dd

dab [dab] – *past tense, past participle* **dabbed** – *verb* to touch gently with something soft or moist: *He dabbed the wound gently with absorbent cotton.* □ **tamponner**
■ *noun* 1 a small lump of anything soft or moist: *a dab of butter.* □ **un petit peu (de)**
2 a gentle touch: *a dab with a wet cloth.* □ **coup léger**

dabble ['dabl] *verb* 1 to play, or trail, in water: *He dabbled his feet in the river.* □ **barboter**
2 to do anything in a half-serious way or as a hobby: *He dabbles in chemistry.* □ **faire un peu de (en amateur)**

dachshund ['daːkshund] *noun* a type of small dog with a long body and very short legs. □ **basset allemand**

dad [dad], **daddy** ['dadi] (*plural* **'daddies**) *noun* children's words for father: *Where is your daddy?*; *What are you doing, Daddy?* □ **papa**

daffodil ['dafədil] *noun* a kind of yellow spring flower which grows from a bulb. □ **jonquille**

dagger ['dagə] *noun* a knife or short sword for stabbing. □ **poignard**

daily ['deili] *adjective* happening *etc* every day: *a daily walk*; *This is part of our daily lives.* □ **quotidien**
■ *adverb* every day: *Our cream is fresh daily.* □ **quotidiennement**
■ *noun – plural* **'dailies** – 1 a newspaper published every day: *We take three dailies.* □ **quotidien**
2 (*also* **daily help**) a person who is paid to come regularly and help with housework: *Our daily (help) comes on Mondays.* □ **femme, homme de ménage**

dainty ['deinti] *adjective* small or fragile and attractive: *a dainty little girl.* □ **mignon**
'daintily *adverb.* □ **délicatement**
'daintiness *noun.* □ **délicatesse**

dairy ['deəri] – *plural* **'dairies** – *noun* 1 a shop supplying milk, butter, cheese *etc*: *We bought milk at the dairy.* □ **crémerie**
2 the place on a farm *etc* where milk is kept and butter and cheese are made. □ **laiterie**
dairy cow – *plural* **dairy cows/cattle** – a cow kept for its milk. □ **vache laitière**
dairy farm a farm specializing in producing dairy and milk products. □ **ferme laitière**

daisy ['deizi] – *plural* **'daisies** – *noun* a type of small common flower with a yellow centre and *usually* white petals: *The field was full of daisies.* □ **marguerite**

dally ['dali] *verb* to go *etc* slowly: *Don't dally – do hurry up!* □ **lambiner**

dam [dam] *noun* 1 a bank or wall of earth, concrete *etc* to keep back water: *A new dam was being built at the mouth of the valley.* □ **barrage**
2 the water kept back. □ **réservoir**
■ *verb – past tense, past participle* **dammed** – (*sometimes with* **up**) – to hold back by means of a dam: *The river has been dammed up.* □ **endiguer**

damage ['damidʒ] *noun* 1 injury or hurt, *especially* to a thing: *The storm did/caused a lot of damage*; *She suffered brain damage as a result of the accident.* □ **dommage, dégât**
2 (*in plural*) payment for loss or injury suffered: *The court awarded her $5,000 damages.* □ **dommages et intérêts**
■ *verb* to make less effective or less usable *etc*; to spoil: *The bomb damaged several buildings*; *The book was damaged in the post.* □ **endommager, abîmer**
'damaged *adjective* (*negative* **undamaged**): *a damaged table.* □ **endommagé**

dame [deim] *noun* 1 (the status of) a lady of the same rank as a knight: *There were several dames at the royal wedding.* □ **dame**
2 (*slang*) a woman. □ **nana**

dammed *see* **dam.**

damn [dam] *verb* 1 to sentence to unending punishment in hell: *His soul is damned.* □ **damner**
2 to cause to be condemned as bad, unacceptable *etc*: *That film was damned by the critics.* □ **condamner**
■ *interjection* expressing anger, irritation *etc*: *Damn! I've forgotten my purse.* □ **zut!**
■ *noun* something unimportant or of no value: *It's not worth a damn*; *I don't give a damn!* (= I don't care in the least). □ **deux fois rien**
damned *adjective* 1 sentenced to unending punishment in hell. □ **damné**
2 annoying, greatly disliked *etc*: *Get that damned dog out of here!* □ **sacré**
'damning *adjective* showing faults, sins *etc*: *The evidence was damning.* □ **accablant**

damp [damp] *adjective* slightly wet: *This towel is still damp.* □ **humide**
■ *noun* slight wetness, *especially* in the air: *The walls were brown with (the) damp.* □ **humidité**
'dampen *verb* 1 to make damp. □ **humecter**
2 to make or become less fierce or strong (interest *etc*): *The rain dampened everyone's enthusiasm considerably.* □ **(se) refroidir**
'damper *noun* 1 something which lessens the strength of enthusiasm, interest *etc*: *Her presence cast a damper on the proceedings.* □ **douche (froide)**
2 a movable plate for controlling the draught *eg* in a stove. □ **registre**
'dampness *noun* slight wetness. □ **humidité**
damp down 1 to make (a fire) burn more slowly. □ **réduire**
2 to reduce, make less strong: *I was trying to damp down their enthusiasm.* □ **modérer**

damsel ['damzəl] *noun* a young girl: *a damsel in distress.* □ **damoiselle**
'damselfly *noun* an insect with a long thin body found near water. □ **libellule**

dance [daːns] *verb* 1 to move in time to music by making a series of rhythmic steps: *She began to dance*; *Can you dance the waltz?* □ **danser**
2 to move quickly up and down: *The father was dancing the baby on his knee.* □ **(faire) sauter**
■ *noun* 1 a series of fixed steps made in time to music: *Have you done this dance before?*; (*also adjective*) *dance music.* □ **danse; de danse**
2 a social gathering at which people dance: *We're going to a dance next Saturday.* □ **bal**

'dancer *noun*: *a ballet dancer.* □ **danseur, euse**

'dancing *noun*: *She likes dancing*; (*also adjective*) *dancing shoes.* □ **la danse, de danse**

dandelion ['dandilaiən] *noun* a kind of common wild plant with jagged leaves and a yellow flower. □ **pissenlit**

dandruff ['dandrʌf] *noun* dead skin under the hair which falls off in small pieces. □ **pellicule**

danger ['deindʒə] *noun* 1 something that may cause harm or injury: *The canal is a danger to children.* □ **danger** 2 a state or situation in which harm may come to a person or thing: *He is in danger*; *The bridge is in danger of collapse.* □ **(en) danger**

'dangerous *adjective* very unsafe and likely to be the cause of danger: *a dangerous road*; *a dangerous enemy.* □ **dangereux**

dangle ['dangl] *verb* to (cause to) hang loosely: *She dangled her scarf out of the car window.* □ **(laisser) pendre**

Danish [deiniʃ] *adjective* someone or something from Denmark: *Can a Danish citizen travel to Sweden without a passport?*; *There is nothing George enjoys more than Danish pastry.* □ **danois**

■ *noun* the language of Denmark: *When we went to Denmark, we learned a few words in Danish.* □ **danois**

Dane *noun* a native of Denmark: *A Canadian switched jobs with a Dane so both could visit a foreign country.* □ **Danois, -oise**

dare [deə] – *negative short form* daren't – *verb* 1 to be brave enough (to do something): *I daren't go*; *I don't dare (to) go*; *He wouldn't dare do a thing like that*; *Don't you dare say such a thing again!* □ **oser** 2 to challenge: *I dare you to do it.* □ **défier**

■ *noun* a challenge: *She went into the lion's cage for a dare.* □ **défi**

'daring *adjective* bold; courageous: *She was a daring pilot*; *a daring attempt to rescue the climber.* □ **audacieux**

■ *noun* boldness: *We admired his daring.* □ **audace**

'daredevil *noun* a bold or reckless person. □ **casse-cou**

■ *adjective*: *a daredevil motorcyclist.* □ **téméraire**

I dare say (*also* I ,dare'say) I suppose (so): *I dare say you're right*; *'Will you be there?' 'Oh, I daresay.'* □ **sans doute**

dark [daːk] *adjective* 1 without light: *a dark room*; *It's getting dark*; *the dark* (= not cheerful) *side.* □ **noir** 2 blackish or closer to black than white: *a dark red colour*; *a dark* (= not very white or fair) *complexion*; *Her hair is dark.* □ **foncé** 3 evil and *usually* secret: *dark deeds*; *a dark secret.* □ **noir**

■ *noun* absence of light: *in the dark*; *afraid of the dark*; *He never goes out after dark*; *We are in the dark* (= we have no knowledge) *about what is happening.* □ **noir**

'darken *verb* to make or become dark or darker. □ **s'assombrir**

'darkness *noun* the state of being dark. □ **obscurité, ténèbres**

keep it dark to keep something a secret: *They're engaged to be married but they want to keep it dark.* □ **garder secret**

darling ['daːliŋ] *noun* 1 a dearly loved person (often used as a term of endearment): *Is that you, darling?* □ **chéri, ie** 2 a lovable person: *Mary really is a darling!* □ **amour**

■ *adjective* 1 much loved: *My darling child!* □ **chéri** 2 lovable; pretty and appealing: *What a darling little girl!* □ **adorable**

dart [daːt] *noun* 1 a pointed arrow-like weapon for throwing or shooting: *a poisoned dart.* □ **dard** 2 a sudden and quick movement. □ **élan**

■ *verb* to move suddenly and quickly: *The mouse darted into a hole.* □ **foncer**

darts *noun singular* a game in which darts are thrown at a board ('**dart-board**') which has a series of numbers on it by which one scores: *a game of darts*; (*also adjective*) *a darts match.* □ **jeu de fléchettes; de jeu de fléchettes**

dash [daʃ] *verb* 1 to move with speed and violence: *A man dashed into a shop.* □ **se précipiter** 2 to knock, throw *etc* violently, *especially* so as to break: *He dashed the bottle to pieces against the wall.* □ **heurter/lancer violemment** 3 to bring down suddenly and violently or to make very depressed: *Our hopes were dashed.* □ **anéantir**

■ *noun* 1 a sudden rush or movement: *The child made a dash for the door.* □ **mouvement brusque en avant** 2 a small amount of something, *especially* liquid: *whisky with a dash of soda.* □ **soupçon** 3 (in writing) a short line (–) to show a break in a sentence *etc.* □ **tiret** 4 energy and enthusiasm: *All his activities showed the same dash and spirit.* □ **entrain**

'dashing *adjective* smart and lively: *a dashing young man*; *She looks very dashing in her new clothes.* □ **fringant**

dash off 1 to write quickly: *to dash off a letter.* □ **écrire en vitesse** 2 to leave hastily: *to dash off to the shops.* □ **partir en coup de vent**

dashboard ['daʃbɔːd] *noun* a board *etc* with dials, switches *etc* in front of the driver's seat in a car. □ **tableau de bord**

data ['deitə] *noun plural* or *noun singular* facts or information (*especially* the information given to a computer): *All the data has/have been fed into the computer.* □ **données**

'data-bank *noun* a large amount of information which is stored in a computer. □ **banque de données**

,data-'processing *noun* the handling and processing of information by computer. □ **informatique**

date[1] [deit] *noun* 1 (a statement on a letter *etc* giving) the day of the month, the month and year: *I can't read the date on this letter.* □ **date** 2 the day and month and/or the year in which something happened or is going to happen: *What is your date of birth?* □ **date** 3 an appointment or engagement, *especially* a social one with a member of the opposite sex: *He asked her for a date.* □ **rendez-vous**

■ *verb* 1 to have or put a date on: *This letter isn't dated.* □ **dater**

2 (*with* from *or* back) to belong to; to have been made, written *etc* at (a certain time): *Their quarrel dates back to last year.* □ **dater de**

3 to become obviously old-fashioned: *His books haven't dated much.* □ **dater**

'**dated** *adjective* old-fashioned: *Her clothes looked very dated.* □ **démodé**

'**dateline** *noun* a north-south line drawn on maps through the Pacific Ocean, east and west of which the date is different. □ **ligne de changement de date**

out of date 1 old-fashioned: *This coat is out of date.* □ **démodé**

2 no longer able to be (legally) used; no longer valid: *Your ticket is out of date/very out-of-date; an out-of-date directory.* □ **périmé**

to date up to the present time: *This is the best entry we've received to date.* □ **à ce jour**

up to date 1 completed *etc* up to the present time: *Is the catalogue up to date?; an up-to-date catalogue.* □ **à jour**

2 modern and in touch with the latest ideas: *This method is up to date/very up-to-date; an up-to-date method.* □ **moderne**

date² [deit] *noun* the brown, sticky fruit of the **date palm**, a kind of tree growing in the tropics. □ **datte**

daughter ['dɔːtə] *noun* a female child (when spoken of in relation to her parents): *That is Mary's daughter; He has two daughters.* □ **fille**

'**daughter-in-law** – *plural* '**daughters-in-law** – *noun* a son's wife. □ **belle-fille**

dawdle ['dɔːdl] *verb* to waste time *especially* by moving slowly: *Hurry up, and don't dawdle!* □ **flâner**

'**dawdler** *noun.* □ **flâneur, euse**

'**dawdling** *noun.* □ **flânerie**

dawn [dɔːn] *verb* (*especially* of daylight) to begin to appear: *A new day has dawned. See also* **dawn on** *below.* □ **poindre**

■ *noun* **1** the very beginning of a day; very early morning: *We must get up at dawn.* □ **aube, aurore**

2 the very beginning of something: *the dawn of civilization.* □ **naissance**

'**dawning** *noun* the act of beginning: *the dawning of a new day/a new age.* □ **naissance**

dawn on to become suddenly clear to (a person): *It suddenly dawned on me what he had meant.* □ **venir subitement à l'esprit**

day [dei] *noun* **1** the period from sunrise to sunset: *She worked all day; The days are warm but the nights are cold.* □ **jour**

2 a part of this period *eg* that part spent at work: *How long is your working day?; The school day ends at 3 o'clock; I see him every day.* □ **journée**

3 the period of twenty-four hours from one midnight to the next: *How many days are in the month of September?* □ **jour**

4 (*often in plural*) the period of, or of the greatest activity, influence, strength *etc* of (something or someone): *in my grandfather's day; in the days of steam-power.* □ **(du) temps (de)**

'**daybreak** *noun* dawn; the first appearance of light: *We left at daybreak.* □ **lever du jour**

'**daydream** *noun* a dreaming or imagining of pleasant events; the making of unreal plans *etc* while awake. □ **rêverie**

■ *verb: She often daydreams.* □ **rêvasser, songer**

'**daylight** *noun* **1** (*also adjective*) (of) the light given by the sun: *daylight hours.* □ **(lumière du) jour; de jour**

2 dawn: *To get there on time we must leave before daylight.* □ **lever du jour**

day school a school whose pupils attend only during the day and live at home. □ **externat**

'**daytime** *noun* the time when it is day. □ **le jour**

call it a day to bring (something) to an end; to stop (*eg* working): *I'm so tired that I'll have to call it a day.* □ **s'en tenir là**

day by day every day: *He's getting better day by day.* □ **jour après jour**

day in, day out *see* **in**.

make someone's day to make someone very happy: *That baby's smile made my day.* □ **réjouir**

one day 1 at some time in the future: *She hopes to go to America one day.* □ **un jour (ou l'autre)**

2 on a day in the past: *I saw her one day last week.* □ **un jour**

some day at some time in the future: *He hopes to get married some day.* □ **un jour (ou l'autre)**

the day after tomorrow 48 hours from this point in time; two days from now: *Ross leaves the day after tomorrow so that gives him 2 days to pack.* □ **après-demain**

the day before yesterday 48 hours before this point in time; two days earlier: *If today is Friday then the day before yesterday was Wednesday.* □ **avant-hier**

the other day not long ago: *I saw Mr. Smith the other day.* □ **l'autre jour**

daycare [deikeə] *adjective* a type of care that is provided to babies and young children outside their home: *A daycare centre was opened for children at the university so students with children could attend courses.* □ **garderie**

■ *noun* the practice of providing care outside the home for babies and young children: *If women are to advance in the workforce, adequate daycare is needed for their children.* □ **garderie**

daze [deiz] *verb* to make confused (*eg* by a blow or a shock): *She was dazed by the news.* □ **étourdir**

■ *noun* a bewildered or absent-minded state: *She's been going around in a daze all day.* □ **stupéfaction**

dazed *adjective* confused (by a blow *etc*): *She came in looking dazed with shock.* □ **hébété**

dazzle ['dazl] *verb* **1** (of a strong light) to prevent from seeing properly: *I was dazzled by the car's headlights.* □ **aveugler**

2 to affect the ability of making correct judgments: *I was dazzled by your charm.* □ **éblouir**

'**dazzling** *adjective* **1** extremely bright: *a dazzling light.* □ **aveuglant**

2 colourful; impressive: *a dazzling display of wit.* □ **éblouissant**

dead [ded] *adjective* **1** without life; not living: *a dead body; Throw out those dead flowers.* □ **mort**

2 not working and not giving any sign of being about to work: *The phone/engine is dead.* □ **en panne**

3 absolute or complete: *There was dead silence at his words; He came to a dead stop.* □ **total**

■ *adverb* completely: *dead drunk.* □ **complètement**

'**deaden** *verb* to lessen, weaken or make less sharp, strong *etc*: *That will deaden the pain.* □ **amortir**

'**deadly** *adjective* 1 causing death: *a deadly poison.* □ **mortel**

2 very great: *He is in deadly earnest* (= He is completely serious). □ **le plus grand**

3 very dull or uninteresting: *What a deadly job this is.* □ **assommant**

■ *adverb* extremely: *deadly dull; deadly serious.* □ **mortellement**

dead end a road closed off at one end. □ **cul-de-sac**

'**dead-end** *adjective* leading nowhere: *a dead-end job.* □ **sans avenir**

dead heat a race, or a situation happening in a race, in which two or more competitors cross the finish line together. □ **(arrivée) ex æquo**

dead language a language no longer spoken, *eg* Latin. □ **langue morte**

'**deadline** *noun* a time by which something must be done or finished: *Monday is the deadline for handing in this essay.* □ **date limite**

'**deadlock** *noun* a situation in which no further progress towards an agreement is possible: *Talks between the two sides ended in deadlock.* □ **impasse**

to set a **deadline** (not **dateline**) for finishing a job.

deaf [def] *adjective* 1 unable to hear: *She has been deaf since birth.* □ **sourd**

2 (*with* to) refusing to understand or to listen: *He was deaf to all arguments.* □ **sourd**

'**deafness** *noun.* □ **surdité**

'**deafen** *verb* to make hearing difficult; to have an unpleasant effect on the hearing: *I was deafened by the noise in there!* □ **assourdir**

'**deafening** *adjective* very loud: *the deafening roar of the engine.* □ **assourdissant**

,**deaf-'mute** *noun* a person who is deaf and dumb. □ **sourd-muet, sourde-muette**

fall on deaf ears (of a warning *etc*) to be ignored. □ **tomber dans l'oreille d'un sourd**

turn a deaf ear to deliberately to ignore: *They turned a deaf ear to my advice.* □ **faire la sourde oreille à**

deal [di:l] *noun* 1 a bargain or arrangement: *a business deal.* □ **marché, affaire**

2 the act of dividing cards among players in a card game. □ **donne**

■ *verb – past tense, past participle* **dealt** [delt] – 1 to do business, *especially* to buy and sell: *I think she deals in stocks and shares.* □ **faire le commerce de**

2 to distribute (cards). □ **donner**

'**dealer** *noun* 1 a person who buys and sells: *a dealer in antiques.* □ **marchand, ande**

2 the person who distributes the cards in a card game. □ **donneur, euse**

'**dealing** *noun* (*usually in plural*) contact (often in busi-

ness), bargaining, agreement *etc* made (between two or more people or groups): *fair/honest dealing; dealing on the stock market; I have no dealings with her.* □ **relations, transactions**

deal with 1 to be concerned with: *This book deals with methods of teaching English.* □ **traiter de**

2 to take action about, *especially* in order to solve a problem, get rid of a person, complete a piece of business *etc*: *She deals with all the inquiries.* □ **s'occuper de**

a good deal/a great deal much or a lot: *They made a good deal of noise; She spent a great deal of money on it.* □ **beaucoup (de)**

dean [di:n] *noun* 1 the chief clergyman in a cathedral church. □ **doyen**

2 an important official in a university. □ **doyen, enne**

dear [diə] *adjective* 1 high in price: *Cabbages are very dear this week.* □ **cher**

2 very lovable: *He is such a dear little boy.* □ **adorable**

3 (*with* to) much loved: *She is very dear to me.* □ **cher**

4 used as a polite way of addressing someone, *especially* in a letter: *Dear Sir.* □ **cher**

■ *noun* 1 a person who is lovable or charming: *He is such a dear!* □ **amour**

2 a person who is loved or liked (*especially* used to address someone): *Come in, dear.* □ **cher, ère**

'**dearly** *adverb* very much or very strongly: *I would dearly like to see you; She loved you dearly.* □ **infiniment, tendrement**

dear, dear!/oh dear! mild expressions of regret, sorrow, pity *etc*: *Oh dear! I've forgotten my key.* □ **oh là là!**

death [deθ] *noun* 1 the act of dying: *There have been several deaths in the town recently; Most people fear death.* □ **mort, décès**

2 something which causes one to die: *Smoking too much was the death of her.* □ **mort**

3 the state of being dead: *eyes closed in death.* □ **mort**

'**deathly** *adjective, adverb* as if caused by death: *a deathly silence; It was deathly quiet.* □ **de mort**

'**deathbed** *noun* the bed in which a person dies. □ **lit de mort**

'**death certificate** an official piece of paper signed by a doctor stating the cause of someone's death. □ **acte de décès**

at death's door on the point of dying. □ **à l'agonie**

catch one's death (of cold) to get a very bad cold: *If you go out in that rain without a coat you'll catch your death (of cold).* □ **attraper son coup de mort**

put to death to cause to be killed: *The criminal was put to death by hanging.* □ **exécuter**

to death very greatly: *I'm sick to death of you.* □ **à mourir**

debate [di'beit] *noun* a discussion or argument, *especially* a formal one in front of an audience: *a Parliamentary debate.* □ **débat**

■ *verb* 1 to hold a formal discussion (about): *Parliament will debate the question tomorrow.* □ **débattre**

2 to think about or talk about something before coming to a decision: *We debated whether to go by bus or train.*

□ **se demander, discuter**

de'batable *adjective* doubtful; able to be argued about: *a debatable point.* □ **discutable**

debauched [di'bɔːtʃt] *adjective* inclined to debauchery. □ **débauché**

de'bauchery *noun* too much indulgence in pleasures *usually* considered immoral, *especially* sexual activity and excessive drinking: *a life of debauchery.* □ **débauche**

debilitate [di'biliteit] *verb* to make weak. □ **débiliter**

de'bility *noun* bodily weakness: *Despite his debility, he leads a normal life.* □ **faiblesse**

debit ['debit] *noun* an entry on the side of an account which records what is owed: *His debits outnumbered his credits.* □ **débit**

■ *verb – past tense, past participle* **'debited** – to enter or record on this side of an account. □ **débiter**

debris [də'briː] *noun* 1 the remains of something broken, destroyed *etc*: *The fireman found a corpse among the debris.* □ **décombres**

2 rubbish: *There was a lot of debris in the house after the builder had left.* □ **débris**

debt [det] *noun* what one person owes to another: *Her debts amount to over $3,000; a debt of gratitude.* □ **dette**

'debtor *noun* a person who owes a debt. □ **débiteur, trice**

in debt owing money. □ **endetté**

debut, début [dei'bjuː, 'deibjuː] *noun* a first public appearance on the stage *etc*: *She made her stage debut at the age of eight.* □ **début(s)**

decade ['dekeid, de'keid] *noun* a period of ten years: *the first decade of this century* (= 1900–09.) □ **décennie**

decadence ['dekədəns] *noun* 1 a falling from high to low standards in morals or the arts: *the decadence of the late Roman empire.* □ **décadence**

2 the state of having low or incorrect standards of behaviour; immorality: *He lived a life of decadence.* □ **décadence**

'decadent *adjective*: *a decadent young man.* □ **décadent**

decadence ends in -ence (not –ance).

decaffeinated [diː'kafəneitid] *adjective* a drink such as coffee, tea or cola which does not contain caffeine; having the caffeine removed: *Mr. Franks drank decaffeinated coffee because regular coffee kept him awake at night.* □ **décaféiné**

decapitate [di'kapiteit] *verb* to cut the head from (*especially* a person): *He was decapitated in the accident.* □ **décapiter**

de,capi'tation *noun*. □ **décapitation**

decay [di'kei] *verb* to (cause to) become rotten or ruined: *Sugar makes your teeth decay.* □ **(faire) pourrir**

■ *noun* the act or process of decaying: *tooth decay; in a state of decay.* □ **pourrissement, carie**

deceased [di'siːst] *adjective* dead: *Her parents, now deceased, were very wealthy.* □ **décédé**

the deceased in law, the dead person already mentioned, *especially* one who has recently died: *Were you a friend of the deceased?* □ **le défunt, la défunte**

deceit [di'siːt] *noun* (an act of) deceiving: *She was too honest to be capable of deceit.* □ **tromperie**

de'ceitful *adjective* deceiving or insincere: *He's such a deceitful child!* □ **trompeur**

de'ceitfully *adverb*. □ **faussement**

de'ceitfulness *noun*. □ **fausseté**

deceit is spelt with -ei-.

deceive [di'siːv] *verb* to mislead or cause to make mistakes, *usually* by giving or suggesting false information: *She was deceived by his innocent appearance.* □ **tromper**

deceive is spelt with -ei-.

decelerate [diː'seləreit] *verb* to slow down, *especially* in a car *etc*: *You must decelerate before a crossroads.* □ **ralentir**

de,cele'ration *noun*. □ **ralentissement**

December [di'sembə] *noun* the twelfth month of the year, the month following November. □ **décembre**

decent ['diːsnt] *adjective* 1 fairly good; of fairly good quality: *a decent standard of living.* □ **convenable**

2 kindly, tolerant or likeable: *He's a decent enough fellow.* □ **bien**

3 not vulgar or immoral; modest: *Keep your language decent!* □ **décent**

'decency *noun* (the general idea of) what is proper, fitting, moral *etc*; the quality or act of being decent: *In the interests of decency, we have banned nude bathing; He had the decency to admit that it was his fault.* □ **décence, bienséance**

'decently *adverb* in a manner acceptable to the general idea of what is proper or suitable: *You're not going out unless you're decently dressed.* □ **convenablement**

deception [di'sepʃən] *noun* (an act of) deceiving: *Deception is difficult in these circumstances.* □ **tromperie**

de'ceptive [-tiv] *adjective* deceiving; misleading: *Appearances may be deceptive.* □ **trompeur**

de'ceptively *adjective*: *He is deceptively shy.* □ **trompeusement**

decibel ['desibel] *noun* (abbreviation **db**) the main unit of measurement of the loudness of a sound: *Traffic noise is measured in decibels.* □ **décibel**

decide [di'said] *verb* 1 to (cause to) make up one's mind: *I have decided to retire; What decided you against going?* □ **(se) décider (de)**

2 to settle or make the result (of something) *etc* certain: *The last goal decided the match.* □ **décider (de)**

deciduous [di'sidjuəs, -djuəs] *adjective* (of trees) having leaves that fall in autumn: *Oaks are deciduous trees.* □ **décidu**

decilitre [desi'liːtə] *noun* a measure of (liquid) capacity equal to one-tenth of a litre. □ **décilitre**

decimal ['desiməl] *adjective* numbered by tens: *the decimal system.* □ **décimal**

■ *noun* a decimal fraction: *Convert these fractions to decimals.* □ **décimale**

'decimalize, 'decimalise *verb* to convert from a non-decimal to a decimal form. □ **décimaliser**

,decimali'zation, ,decimali'sation *noun*. □ **décimalisation**

decimal currency a system of money in which each coin or note is either a tenth of or ten times another in value. □ **monnaie décimale**

decimal fraction a fraction expressed as so many tenths, hundredths, thousandths *etc* and written with a decimal point, like this: 0.1 (= 1/10), 2.33 (= 233/100). □ **fraction décimale**

decimate ['desimeit] *verb* (of disease, battle *etc*) to reduce greatly in number: *The population was decimated by the plague.* □ **décimer**

,**deci'mation** *noun.* □ **décimation**

decipher [di'saifə] *verb* 1 to translate (writing in code) into ordinary, understandable language: *They deciphered the spy's letter.* □ **décoder**

2 to make out the meaning of (something which is difficult to read): *I can't decipher her handwriting.* □ **déchiffrer**

decision [di'siʒən] *noun* the act of deciding; a judgment: *a time/moment of decision*; *I think you made the wrong decision.* □ **décision**

decisive [di'saisiv] *adjective* 1 final; putting an end to a contest, dispute *etc*: *The battle was decisive.* □ **décisif**

2 showing decision and firmness: *She's very decisive.* □ **décidé**

de'cisiveness *noun.* □ **fermeté**

de'cisively *adverb*: *She acted very decisively.* □ **sans hésiter**

deck [dek] *noun* 1 a platform extending from one side of a ship *etc* to the other and forming the floor: *The cars are on the lower deck.* □ **pont**

2 a floor in a bus: *Let's go on the top deck.* □ **impériale**

3 a pack of playing cards: *The gambler used her own deck of cards.* □ **jeu (de cartes)**

'**deck chair** *noun* a light collapsible chair: *They were sitting in deck chairs on the beach.* □ **chaise-longue**

declaim [di'kleim] *verb* to make (a speech) in an impressive and dramatic manner: *She declaimed against immorality.* □ **déclamer**

declare [di'kleə] *verb* 1 to announce publicly or formally: *War was declared this morning.* □ **déclarer**

2 to say firmly: *'I don't like him at all,' she declared.* □ **déclarer**

3 to make known (goods on which duty must be paid, income on which tax should be paid *etc*): *He decided to declare his untaxed earnings to the tax office.* □ **déclarer**

declaration [deklə'reiʃən] *noun* a formal announcement: *a declaration of marriage/war.* □ **déclaration**

decline [di'klain] *verb* 1 to say no to (an invitation *etc*); to refuse: *We declined his offer of a lift.* □ **refuser**

2 to become less strong or less good *etc*: *His health has declined recently*; *Our profits have temporarily declined.* □ **baisser**

■ *noun* a gradual lessening or worsening (of health, standards, quantity *etc*): *There has been a gradual decline in the birthrate.* □ **déclin**

decode [diː'koud] *verb* to translate (a coded message) into ordinary understandable language. □ **décoder**

decompose [diːkəm'pouz] *verb* (of vegetable or animal matter) to (cause to) decay or rot: *Corpses decompose quickly in heat.* □ **(se) décomposer**

decomposition [diːkompə'ziʃən] *noun.* □ **décomposition**

,**decom'poser** *noun* something that causes a substance to rot or break up into simpler parts. □ **agent de décomposition**

décor ['deikɔː, dəi'kɔːr] *noun* the decoration of a room *etc* and the arrangement of the objects in it: *It was a comfortable room but I didn't like the décor.* □ **décoration (intérieure)**

decorate ['dekəreit] *verb* 1 to add some kind of ornament *etc* to (something) to make more beautiful, striking *etc*: *We decorated the Christmas tree with glass balls.* □ **décorer**

2 to put paint, paper *etc* on the walls, ceiling and woodwork of (a room): *He spent a week decorating the living room.* □ **peindre (et tapisser)**

3 to give a medal or badge to (someone) as a mark of honour: *She was decorated for her bravery.* □ **décorer**

,**deco'ration** *noun* 1 something used to decorate: *Christmas decorations.* □ **décoration**

2 the act of decorating: *The decoration of the house will be a long job.* □ **décoration**

'**decorative** [-rətiv] *adjective* ornamental or beautiful (*especially* if not useful): *a decorative arrangement of flowers.* □ **décoratif**

'**decorator** *noun* a person who decorates rooms, houses *etc*: *She was a painter and decorator.* □ **décorateur, trice**

decorous ['dekərəs] *adjective* (behaving in a manner which is) acceptable, *especially* quiet and dignified: *behaving in a decorous manner.* □ **digne**

'**decorously** *adverb.* □ **convenablement**

decorum [di'kɔːrəm] *noun* quiet, dignified and proper behaviour: *The man behaved with decorum in the old lady's presence.* □ **décorum**

decoy ['diːkoi] *noun* anything intended to lead someone or something into a trap: *The policewoman acted as a decoy when the police were trying to catch the murderer.* □ **piège**

decrease [di'kriːs] *verb* to make or become less: *Their numbers had decreased over the previous year.* □ **diminuer**

■ ['diːkriːs] *noun* a growing less: *a decrease of fifty per cent*; *a gradual decrease in unemployment.* □ **diminution**

decree [di'kriː] *noun* 1 an order or law: *a decree forbidding hunting.* □ **décret, arrêté**

2 a ruling of a court of civil law. □ **arrêt**

■ *verb* – *past tense, past participle* **de'creed** – to order, command or decide (something): *The court decreed that he should pay the fine in full.* □ **décréter, ordonner**

dedicate ['dedikeit] *verb* 1 to give up wholly to; to devote to: *He dedicated his life to good works.* □ **(se) consacrer**

2 to set apart, *especially* for a holy or sacred purpose: *He decided to dedicate a chapel to his wife's memory.* □ **dédier**

3 (of an author *etc*) to state that (a book *etc*) is in honour of someone: *She dedicated the book to her father*; *She dedicated that song to her.* □ **dédier**

'dedicated *adjective* spending a great deal of one's time and energy on a subject, one's job *etc*: *She's a dedicated teacher; She is dedicated to music.* □ **dévoué**

,dedi'cation *noun* 1 the quality of being dedicated; the act of dedicating: *dedication to duty; the dedication of the church.* □ **attachement, consécration**

2 the words dedicating a book to someone: *We can put the dedication at the top of the page.* □ **dédicace**

deduce [di'djuːs] *verb* to work out from facts one knows or guesses: *From the height of the sun I deduced that it was about ten o'clock.* □ **déduire**

deduction¹ [di'dʌkʃən] *noun* 1 the act of deducing. □ **déduction**

2 something that has been deduced: *Is this deduction accurate?* □ **déduction**

deduct [di'dʌkt] *verb* to subtract; to take away: *They deducted the expenses from her salary.* □ **déduire**

de'duction² [-ʃən] *noun* something that has been deducted: *There were a lot of deductions from my salary this month.* □ **déduction**

deed [diːd] *noun* something done; an act: *a good deed.* □ **action**

deem [diːm] *verb* to judge or think: *He deemed it unwise to tell her the truth.* □ **juger**

deep [diːp] *adjective* 1 going or being far down or far into: *a deep lake; a deep wound.* □ **profond**

2 going or being far down by a named amount: *a hole six feet deep.* □ **profond de**

3 occupied or involved to a great extent: *He is deep in debt.* □ **absorbé**

4 intense; strong: *The sea is a deep blue colour; They are in a deep sleep.* □ **intense**

5 low. in pitch: *His voice is very deep.* □ **grave**

■ *adverb* far down or into: *deep into the wood.* □ **profondément**

'deepen *verb* 1 to make or become deeper: *She deepened the hole.* □ **(s')approfondir**

2 to increase: *His troubles were deepening.* □ **augmenter**

'deeply *adverb* very greatly: *We are deeply grateful to you.* □ **profondément**

'deepness *noun* the quality of being deep. □ **profondeur**

,deep-'freeze *noun* a type of refrigerator which freezes food quickly and can keep it for a long time. □ **congélateur**

■ *verb* to freeze and keep (food) in this. □ **congeler**

'deep-sea *adjective* of, for, or in the deeper parts of the sea: *deep-sea diving; deep-sea fishing.* □ **sous-marin**

in deep water in difficulties or trouble: *She found herself in deep water when she took over the management of the firm.* □ **dans de beaux draps**

deer [diə] – *plural* **deer** – *noun* a kind of large, grass-eating animal, the male of which sometimes has antlers: *a herd of deer.* □ **cervidé**

deface [di'feis] *verb* to spoil the appearance of: *The statue had been defaced with red paint.* □ **défigurer, dégrader**

defeat [di'fiːt] *verb* to win a victory over: *They defeated our team by three goals; We will defeat the enemy eventually.* □ **battre**

■ *noun* the loss of a game, battle, race *etc*: *His defeat in the last race depressed him; We suffered yet another*

defeat. □ **défaite**

de'feated *adjective* (*negative* **undefeated**): *a defeated enemy.* □ **battu**

de'featism *noun* a state of mind in which one expects and accepts defeat too easily: *The defeatism of the captain affects the rest of the players.* □ **défaitisme**

de'featist *noun, adjective* (of) a person who gives up too easily and is too easily discouraged: *She is such a defeatist; She has a defeatist attitude to life.* □ **défaitiste**

defect [di'fekt] *noun* a fault or flaw: *It was a basic defect in her character; a defect in the china.* □ **défaut**

■ [di'fekt] *verb* to leave a country, political party *etc* to go and join another; to desert: *She defected to the West.* □ **passer à, déserter**

de'fection [-ʃən] *noun* (an act of) desertion. □ **défection**

de'fective [-tiv] *adjective* having a fault or flaw: *a defective machine; He is mentally defective.* □ **défectueux, déficient**

defence, defense [di'fens] *noun* 1 the act or action of defending against attack: *the defence of Rome; He spoke in defence of the plans.* □ **défense**

2 the method or equipment used to guard or protect: *The walls will act as a defence against flooding.* □ **défense**

3 a person's answer to an accusation *especially* in a lawcourt: *What is your defence?* □ **défense**

de'fenceless *adjective* helpless or without protection. □ **sans défense**

the defence the case on behalf of a person who is accused in a law court: *the counsel for the defence.* □ **la défense**

defend [di'fend] *verb* 1 to guard or protect against attack: *The soldiers defended the castle; I am prepared to defend my opinions.* □ **défendre**

2 to conduct the defence of (a person) in a law-court. □ **défendre**

de'fendant *noun* a person accused or sued in a lawcourt. □ **accusé, ée, défendeur, deresse**

de'fender *noun* a person who defends (someone or something): *the defenders of the castle.* □ **défenseur**

de'fensive [-siv] *adjective* protective or resisting attack: *a defensive attitude; defensive action.* □ **défensif**

defer¹ [di'fəː] – *past tense, past participle* **de'ferred** – *verb* to put off to another time: *They can defer their departure.* □ **différer**

defer² [di'fə] – *past tense, past participle* **de'ferred** – *verb* (*with* **to**) to act according to the wishes or opinions of another or the orders of authority: *I defer to your greater knowledge of the matter.* □ **déférer à**

deference ['defərəns] *noun* 1 willingness to consider the wishes *etc* of others: *He always treats his mother with deference.* □ **déférence**

2 the act of deferring. □ **déférence**

in deference to showing respect for: *I let him speak first, in deference to his authority.* □ **par égard pour**

defiance [di'faiəns] *noun* open disobedience; challenging or opposition: *He went in defiance of my orders.* □ **défi**

de'fiant *adjective* hostile; showing or feeling defiance: *a defiant attitude.* □ **de défi**

de'fiantly *adverb*. □ **d'un air de défi**

deficient [di'fiʃənt] *adjective* lacking in what is needed: *Their food is deficient in vitamins*. □ **défectueux**
de'ficiency – *plural* de'ficiencies – *noun* (a) shortage or absence of what is needed. □ **manque**

deficit ['defisit] *noun* the amount by which an amount (of money *etc*) is less than the amount required: *a deficit of several hundred dollars*. □ **déficit**

define [di'fain] *verb* to fix or state the exact meaning of: *Words are defined in a dictionary*. □ **définir**
de'finable *adjective*. □ **définissable**
definition [defi'niʃən] *noun* an explanation of the exact meaning of a word or phrase: *Is that definition accurate?* □ **définition**

definite ['definit] *adjective* clear; fixed or certain: *I'll give you a definite answer later*. □ **déterminé**
'definitely *adverb* clearly or certainly: *She definitely said I wasn't to wait*; *Her dress is definitely not red*. □ **nettement**
definite article the name given to the word **the**. □ **article défini**
definition *see* **define**.

deflate [di'fleit] *verb* **1** to let gas out of (a tire *etc*). □ **dégonfler**
2 to reduce (a person's) importance, self-confidence *etc*: *He was completely deflated by his failure*. □ **démonter**
de'flation *noun*. □ **déflation, dégonflement**

deflect [di'flekt] *verb* to turn aside (from a fixed course or direction): *He deflected the blow with his arm*. □ **(faire) dévier**
de'flection [-ʃən] *noun*. □ **déviation**

deforestation [diːfouristeəʃən] *noun* the practice of clearing or cutting down forests or trees: *Environmentalists are concerned that deforestation will affect the earth's supply of oxygen*. □ **déboisement**

deform [di'foːm] *verb* to spoil the shape of: *Heat deforms plastic*. □ **déformer**
de'formed *adjective* twisted out of the correct shape: *His foot was deformed*. □ **déformé**
de'formity – *plural* de'formities – *noun* **1** the state of being badly shaped or formed: *Drugs can cause deformity*. □ **difformité**
2 a part which is not the correct shape: *A twisted foot is a deformity*. □ **difformité**

defrost [diː'frost] *verb* **1** to remove frost or ice from (*eg* a refrigerator): *I keep forgetting to defrost the freezer*. □ **dégivrer**
2 (of frozen food *etc*) to thaw (out): *Make sure you defrost the chicken thoroughly*. □ **décongeler**

deft [deft] *adjective* skilful, quick and neat: *her deft handling of the situation*. □ **adroit**
'deftly *adverb*. □ **adroitement**
'deftness *noun*. □ **adresse**

defuse [diː'fjuːz] *verb* **1** to remove the fuse from (a bomb *etc*). □ **désamorcer**
2 to make harmless or less dangerous: *She succeeded in defusing the situation*. □ **désamorcer**

defy [di'fai] *verb* **1** to dare (someone to act); to challenge: *I defy you to try and stop me!* □ **défier**
2 to resist boldly or openly: *Are you defying my authority?* □ **défier**

degenerate [di'dʒenərət] *adjective* having become immoral or inferior: *the degenerate son of well-respected parents*. □ **dégénéré**
■ *noun* a person, plant *etc* that is degenerate. □ **dégénéré, ée**
■ [-reit] *verb* to become much less good or admirable: *The discussion degenerated into insults*. □ **dégénérer**

degrade [di'greid] *verb* to disgrace or make contemptible: *She felt degraded by having to ask for money*. □ **dégrader**
de'grading *adjective* tending to make lower in rank *etc* or to disgrace: *a degrading occupation*. □ **dégradant**

degree [di'griː] *noun* **1** (an) amount or extent: *There is still a degree of uncertainty*; *The degree of skill varies considerably from person to person*. □ **degré**
2 a unit of temperature: *20°* (= 20 degrees) *Celsius*. □ **degré**
3 a unit by which angles are measured: *at an angle of 90°* (= 90 degrees). □ **degré**
4 a title or certificate given by a university *etc*: *He took a degree in chemistry*. □ **diplôme**
by degrees gradually: *We reached the desired standard of efficiency by degrees*. □ **petit à petit**
to some degree to a small extent: *I agree with you to some degree, but I have doubts about your conclusions*. □ **jusqu'à un certain point**

dehydrate [diːhai'dreit] *verb* to remove water from or dry out (*especially* foodstuffs): *Vegetables take up less space if they have been dehydrated*. □ **déshydrater**
,dehy'dration *noun*. □ **déshydratation**

deity ['diːəti, 'deiəti] – *plural* 'deities – *noun* a god or goddess: *Bacchus was one of the Roman deities*. □ **dieu, déesse**

> **deity** is spelt with **-ei-**.

dejected [di'dʒektid] *adjective* gloomy or miserable: *He looked rather dejected*. □ **abattu**
de'jectedly *adverb*. □ **d'un air abattu**
de'jection [-ʃən] *noun*. □ **abattement**

delay [di'lei] *verb* **1** to put off to another time: *We have delayed publication of the book till the spring*. □ **retarder**
2 to keep or stay back or slow down: *I was delayed by the traffic*. □ **retarder**
■ *noun* (something which causes) keeping back or slowing down: *She came without delay*; *My work is subject to delays*. □ **retardement**

delegate ['deləgeit] *verb* to give (a piece of work, power *etc*) to someone else: *She delegates a great deal of work to her assistant*. □ **déléguer**
■ [-gət] *noun* an elected representative (to a conference, Parliament, committee *etc*): *The delegates met in the conference room*. □ **délégué, ée**
,dele'gation *noun* a body of delegates. □ **délégation**

delete [di'liːt] *verb* to rub or strike out (*eg* a piece of writing): *Delete his name from the list*. □ **rayer**
de'letion *noun*. □ **suppression, rature**

deliberate [di'libərət] *adjective* **1** intentional and not by accident: *That was a deliberate insult*. □ **voulu**

2 cautious and not hurried: *She had a very deliberate way of walking.* □ **mesuré**

de'liberately [-rət-] *adverb* **1** on purpose: *You did that deliberately!* □ **exprès**

2 carefully and without hurrying: *She spoke quietly and deliberately.* □ **posément**

delicate ['delikət] *adjective* **1** requiring special treatment or careful handling: *delicate china; a delicate situation/problem.* □ **délicat**

2 of fine texture *etc*; dainty: *a delicate pattern ; the delicate skin of a child.* □ **fin**

3 able to do fine, accurate work: *a delicate instrument.* □ **délicat**

4 subtle: *a delicate wine; a delicate shade of blue.* □ **délicat**

'**delicately** *adverb*. □ **délicatement**

'**delicacy** – *plural* '**delicacies** – *noun* **1** the state or quality of being delicate. □ **délicatesse**

2 something delicious and special to eat: *Caviare is a delicacy.* □ **mets délicat**

delicatessen [delikə'tesn] *noun* (a shop selling) foods prepared ready for the table, *especially* cooked meats and *usually* unusual and foreign foods: *I bought some smoked sausage at the delicatessen.* □ **charcuterie**

delicious [di'liʃəs] *adjective* highly pleasing to the taste: *a delicious meal.* □ **délicieux**

de'liciously *adverb*. □ **délicieusement**

de'liciousness *noun*. □ **goût délicieux**

delight [di'lait] *verb* **1** to please greatly: *I was delighted by/at the news*; *They were delighted to accept the invitation.* □ **enchanter**

2 to have or take great pleasure (from): *She delights in teasing me.* □ **prendre plaisir à**

■ *noun* (something which causes) great pleasure: *Peacefulness is one of the delights of country life.* □ **délice**

de'lightful *adjective* causing delight: *a delightful person/party.* □ **charmant**

de'lightfully *adverb*. □ **délicieusement**

delinquent [diliŋkwənt] *noun* someone, usually a young person, who is guilty of an offence: *Matt was a juvenile delinquent who joined a rough crowd at school and started to steal.* □ **délinquant**

delirious [di'liriəs] *adjective* **1** wandering in the mind and talking complete nonsense (*usually* as a result of fever): *The sick man was delirious and nothing he said made sense.* □ **délirant**

2 wild with excitement: *She was delirious with happiness at the news.* □ **fou de joie**

de'liriously *adverb*: *deliriously happy.* □ **frénétiquement**

deliver [di'livə] *verb* **1** to give or hand over (something) to the person for whom it is intended: *The postman delivers letters.* □ **livrer**

2 to give: *She delivered a long speech.* □ **prononcer**

3 to assist (a woman) at the birth of (a child): *The doctor delivered the twins safely.* □ **accoucher**

de'livery – *plural* **de'liveries** – *noun* **1** (an act of) handing over (letters, parcels *etc*): *There are two parcel deliveries a week.* □ **livraison**

2 the process of the birth of a child: *the delivery of the twins.* □ **accouchement**

delta ['deltə] *noun* a roughly triangular area of land formed at the mouth of a river which reaches the sea in two or more branches: *the delta of the Nile.* □ **delta**

delude [di'luːd] *verb* to deceive or mislead (*usually* without actually telling lies): *She deluded herself into thinking he cared for her.* □ **(se) tromper**

de'lusion [-ʒən] *noun* a false belief, *especially* as a symptom of mental illness: *The young man was suffering from delusions.* □ **hallucination**

deluge ['deljuːdʒ] *noun* a great quantity of water: *Few people survived the deluge.* □ **déluge**

■ *verb* to fill or overwhelm with a great quantity: *We've been deluged with orders for our new book.* □ **inonder**

delusion *see* **delude**.

deluxe [də'luks] *adjective* very luxurious or elegant; special (*especially* with extra qualities not found in an ordinary version of something): *a deluxe model of a car.* □ **de luxe**

demand [di'maːnd] *verb* **1** to ask or ask for firmly and sharply: *I demanded an explanation.* □ **exiger**

2 to require or need: *This demands careful thought.* □ **réclamer**

■ *noun* **1** a request made so that it sounds like a command: *They refused to meet the workers' demands for more money.* □ **revendication**

2 an urgent claim: *The children make demands on my time.* □ **exigence**

3 willingness or desire to buy or obtain (certain goods *etc*); a need for (certain goods *etc*): *There's no demand for books of this kind.* □ **demande**

de'manding *adjective* requiring a lot of effort, ability *etc*: *a demanding job.* □ **exigeant**

on demand when asked for: *I'm expected to supply meals on demand.* □ **sur demande**

demeanour, demeanor [dimiːnə] *noun* manner; bearing; the way one behaves. □ **comportement**

demo *see* **demonstration**.

democracy [di'mokrəsi] – *plural* **de'mocracies** – *noun* (a country having) a form of government in which the people freely elect representatives to govern them: *Which is the world's largest democracy?*; *She believes in democracy.* □ **démocratie**

democrat ['deməkrat] *noun* one who believes in democracy as a principle: *She likes to pretend she's a democrat.* □ **démocrate**

democratic [demə'kratik] *adjective* (*negative* **undemocratic**) **1** belonging to, governed by or typical of democracy: *a democratic country.* □ **démocratique**

2 believing in equal rights and privileges for all: *The boss is very democratic.* □ **démocrate**

democratically [demə'kratikəli] *adverb* (*negative* **undemocratically**) following democratic principles: *The issue was decided democratically by taking a general vote.* □ **démocratiquement**

demolish [di'moliʃ] *verb* to pull or tear down: *They're demolishing the old buildings in the centre of town.* □ **démolir**

,**demo'lition** [demə-] *noun*. □ **démolition**

demon ['diːmən] *noun* an evil spirit; a devil: *demons* *from Hell.* □ **démon**

demonstrate ['demənstreit] *verb* **1** to show clearly: *This demonstrates his ignorance of the situation.* □ **démontrer**

2 to show how (something) works: *He demonstrated the new vacuum cleaner.* □ **faire une démonstration de**

3 to express an opinion (*usually* political) by marching, showing banners *etc* in public: *A crowd collected to demonstrate against the new taxes.* □ **manifester**

,demon'stration *noun* **1** a display or exhibition (of how something works *etc*): *I'd like a demonstration of this dishwasher.* □ **démonstration**

2 (*also* 'demo ['demou] – *plural* 'demos) a public expression of opinion by holding meetings and processions, showing placards *etc*. □ **manif(estation)**

'demonstrator *noun* **1** a person who takes part in a public demonstration. □ **manifestant, ante**

2 a teacher or assistant who helps students with practical work. □ **préparateur, trice**

demonstrative *adjective/pronoun* any one of the words **this, that, these** or **those**. □ **adjectif/pronom démonstratif**

demoralize, demoralise [di'morəlaiz] *verb* to take away the confidence and courage of: *The army was demoralized by its defeat.* □ **démoraliser**

demote [di'mout] *verb* to reduce to a lower rank: *He was demoted for misconduct.* □ **rétrograder**

de'motion *noun*. □ **rétrogradation**

demure [di'mjuə] *adjective* quiet, shy, modest and well behaved (sometimes deceptively): *She looked too demure ever to do such a bold thing.* □ **réservé**

de'murely *adverb*. □ **avec réserve**

de'mureness *noun*. □ **modestie (affectée)**

den [den] *noun* **1** the home of a wild beast: *a lion's den.* □ **tanière, repaire**

2 a private room for working in *etc*. □ **bureau**

denial *see* deny.

denigrate ['denigreit] *verb* to attack the reputation *etc* of: *I'm not trying to denigrate her achievement.* □ **dénigrer**

,deni'gration *noun*. □ **dénigrement**

denim ['denim] *noun, adjective* (of) a kind of cotton cloth, often blue, used for making jeans, overalls *etc*. □ **jean**

'denims *noun plural* clothes, *especially* jeans, made of denim: *She wore blue denims; a pair of denims.* □ **jeans**

denomination [dinomi'neiʃən] *noun* **1** a value (of a stamp, coin *etc*): *banknotes of all denominations.* □ **valeur**

2 a group of people with the same religious beliefs: *This service is open to people of all denominations.* □ **secte**

denote [di'nout] *verb* to be the sign of or to mean: *Do you think his silence denotes guilt?* □ **dénoter**

denounce [di'nauns] *verb* to accuse publicly (of a crime *etc*): *He was denounced as a murderer.* □ **dénoncer**

denunciation [dinʌnsi'eiʃən] *noun*. □ **dénonciation**

dense [dens] *adjective* **1** thick and close: *We made our way through dense forest; The fog was so dense that we could not see anything.* □ **dense**

2 very stupid: *He's so dense I have to tell him every-*

thing twice. □ **bête**

'densely *adverb* very closely together: *The crowd was densely packed.* □ **à forte densité**

'density *noun* **1** the number of items, people *etc* found in a given area compared with other areas *especially* if large: *the density of the population.* □ **densité**

2 the quantity of matter in each unit of volume: *the density of a gas.* □ **densité**

dent [dent] *noun* a small hollow made by pressure or a blow: *My car has a dent where it hit a tree.* □ **bosse**

■ *verb* to make such a hollow in: *The car was dented when it hit a wall.* □ **bosseler**

dental ['dentl] *adjective* of or for the teeth: *Regular dental care is essential for healthy teeth.* □ **dentaire**

dentist ['dentist] *noun* a person who cares for diseases *etc* of the teeth, by filling or removing them *etc*: *Our dentist is very careful; I hate going to the dentist.* □ **dentiste**

'dentistry *noun* a dentist's work. □ **dentisterie**

dentures ['dentʃəz] *noun plural* a set of artificial teeth: *Do you wear dentures?* □ **dentier**

denunciation *see* denounce.

deny [di'nai] *verb* **1** to declare not to be true: *He denied the charge of theft.* □ **nier**

2 to refuse (to give or grant someone something); to say no to: *He was denied admission to the house.* □ **refuser**

de'nial *noun* **1** (an act of) declaring that something is not true: *Do you accept her denial?* □ **dénégation**

2 (an act of) refusing someone something: *a denial of his request.* □ **refus**

deodorant [diː'oudərənt] *noun* a substance that destroys or conceals unpleasant (body) smells: *She perspires a lot – she should use (a) deodorant.* □ **désodorisant**

depanneur (*also* **convenience store**) [depanə] *noun* a shop that sells everyday items such as bread and milk: *Nicolas stopped the car and ran into the depanneur for a cola, a loaf of bread and a lottery ticket* □ **dépanneur**

depart [di'paːt] *verb* **1** to go away: *The tour departed from the station at 9:00.* □ **partir**

2 (*with* **from**) to cease to follow (a course of action): *We departed from our original plan.* □ **s'écarter de**

de'parture [-tʃə] *noun* an act of departing: *The departure of the train was delayed.* □ **départ**

department [di'paːtmənt] *noun* a part or section of a government, university, office or shop: *The Department of Justice; the sales department.* □ **département, service, rayon**

,depart'mental *adjective: a departmental manager.* □ **de département, de service, de rayon**

department store a large shop with many different departments selling a wide variety of goods. □ **grand magasin**

---

department (not **departmental**) store.

---

departure *see* depart.

depend [di'pend] *verb* (*with* **on**) **1** to rely on: *You can't depend on his arriving on time.* □ **se fier à**

2 to rely on receiving necessary (financial) support from: *The school depends for its survival on money from the Church.* □ **dépendre de**

3 (of a future happening *etc*) to be decided by: *Our success depends on everyone working hard.* □ **dépendre de**

de'pendable *adjective* (*negative* **undependable**) trustworthy or reliable: *I know he'll remember to get the wine – he's very dependable.* □ **digne de confiance**

de'pendant *noun* a person who is kept or supported by another: *She has five dependants to support.* □ **personne à charge**

de'pendent *adjective* **1** relying on (someone *etc*) for (financial) support: *He is totally dependent on his parents.* □ **à charge**

2 (of a future happening *etc*) to be decided by: *Whether we go or not is dependent on whether we have enough money.* □ **dépendant (de)**

it/that depends, it all depends what happens, is decided *etc*, will be affected by something else: *I don't know if I'll go to the party – it all depends.* □ **cela dépend**

to look after one's **dependants** (not **dependents**).
to be **dependent** (not **dependant**) on one's parents.

depict [di'pikt] *verb* **1** to paint, draw *etc*. □ **représenter**
2 to describe: *Her novel depicts the life of country people.* □ **décrire**

deplete [di'pliːt] *verb* to make smaller in amount, number *etc*: *Our supplies of food are rather depleted.* □ **réduire**
de'pletion *noun*. □ **réduction**

deplore [di'ploː] *verb* to express disapproval and regret about (something): *We all deplore the actions of murderers.* □ **déplorer**
de'plorable *adjective* very bad: *deplorable behaviour.* □ **déplorable**

deport [di'poːt] *verb* (of a government *etc*) to send (a person) out of the country *eg* because he has committed a crime or because he is not officially supposed to be there: *He is being deported on a charge of murder.* □ **expulser**
,depor'tation [diːpoː-] *noun*. □ **expulsion**

depose [di'pouz] *verb* to remove from a high position (*eg* from that of a king): *They have deposed the emperor.* □ **destituer**

deposit [di'pozit] *verb* **1** to put or set down: *She deposited her shopping bags in the kitchen.* □ **(dé)poser**
2 to put in for safe keeping: *She deposited the money in the bank.* □ **déposer**
■ *noun* **1** an act of putting money in a bank *etc*: *She made several large deposits at the bank during that month.* □ **dépôt**
2 an act of paying money as a guarantee that money which is or will be owed will be paid: *We have put down a deposit on a house in the country.* □ **versement d'un acompte**
3 the money put into a bank or paid as a guarantee in this way: *We decided we could not afford to go on holiday and managed to get back the deposit which we had paid.* □ **acompte**
4 a quantity of solid matter that has settled at the bottom of a liquid, or is left behind by a liquid: *The floodwater left a yellow deposit over everything.* □ **dépôt(s)**
5 a layer (of coal, iron *etc*) occurring naturally in rock:

rich deposits of iron ore. □ **gisement**

depot ['diːpou, 'de-] *noun* **1** the place where railway engines, buses *etc* are kept and repaired: *a bus depot.* □ **dépôt**
2 a storehouse or warehouse. □ **dépôt**
3 a military station or headquarters. □ **dépôt**

depress [di'pres] *verb* **1** to make sad or gloomy: *I am always depressed by wet weather.* □ **déprimer**
2 to make less active: *This drug depresses the action of the heart.* □ **déprimer**
de'pressed *adjective* **1** sad or unhappy: *The news made me very depressed.* □ **déprimé**
2 made less active: *the depressed state of the stock market.* □ **languissant**
de'pressing *adjective* tending to make one sad or gloomy: *What a depressing piece of news!* □ **déprimant**
de'pression [-ʃən] *noun* **1** a state of sadness and low spirits: *She was treated by the doctor for depression.* □ **dépression**
2 lack of activity in trade: *the depression of the 1930s.* □ **crise**
3 an area of low pressure in the atmosphere: *The bad weather is caused by a depression.* □ **dépression (atmosphérique)**
4 a hollow. □ **creux**

deprive [di'praiv] *verb* (*with* **of**) to take something away from: *They deprived her of food and drink.* □ **priver (de)**
deprivation [depri'veiʃən] *noun* **1** (a condition of) loss, hardship *etc*. □ **privation**
2 (an) act of depriving. □ **privation**
de'prived *adjective* suffering from hardship *etc*, underprivileged: *deprived areas of the city.* □ **défavorisé**

depth [depθ] *noun* **1** the distance from the top downwards or from the surface inwards *especially* if great: *Coal is mined at a depth of 1000 m.* □ **profondeur**
2 intensity or strength *especially* if great: *The depth of colour was astonishing*; *The depth of his feeling prevented him from speaking.* □ **intensité**
depths *noun plural* a part far under the surface or in the middle of something: *the depths of the sea*; *the depths of winter.* □ **profondeurs**
'in-depth *adjective* (of a survey *etc*) deep and thorough: *an in-depth report on alcoholism.* □ **en profondeur**
in depth deeply and thoroughly: *I have studied the subject in depth.* □ **à fond**

depute [di'pjuːt] *verb* **1** to appoint a person to take over a task *etc*. □ **déléguer**
2 to hand over (a task *etc*) to someone else to do for one. □ **déléguer**
,depu'tation [depju-] *noun* a group of people appointed to represent others: *The miners sent a deputation to the Prime Minister.* □ **délégation**
deputize, deputise ['depju-] *verb* to act as a deputy: *She deputized for her mother at the meeting.* □ **représenter**
deputy ['depjuti] *noun* someone appointed to help a person and take over some of his jobs if necessary: *While the boss was ill, her deputy ran the office.* □ **adjoint, ointe**

deranged [di'reindʒd] *adjective* insane: *His mind had become deranged as a result of his ordeal*; *mentally deranged.* □ **aliéné**
de'rangement *noun.* □ **aliénation mentale**
derelict [derilikt] *adjective* abandoned and left to fall to pieces: *a derelict airfield.* □ **abandonné**
deride [di'raid] *verb* to laugh at; to mock. □ **rire de**
derision [di'riʒən] *noun* mockery or laughter which shows scorn and contempt: *His remarks were greeted with shouts of derision.* □ **dérision**
de'risive [-siv] *adjective* 1 mocking; showing scorn: *derisive laughter.* □ **moqueur**
2 causing or deserving scorn: *The salary they offered me was derisive.* □ **dérisoire**
de'risory [-səri] *adjective* ridiculous: *His attempts were derisory.* □ **dérisoire**
derive [di'raiv] *verb* (with **from**) 1 to come or develop from: *The word 'derives' is derived from an old French word.* □ **dériver (de)**
2 to draw or take from (a source or origin): *We derive comfort from his presence.* □ **tirer (de)**
‚deri'vation [deri-] *noun* 1 the source or origin (of a word *etc*). □ **dérivation**
2 the process of deriving. □ **dérivation**
derivative [di'rivətiv] *adjective* derived from something else and not original. □ **sans originalité**
■ *noun* a word, substance *etc* formed from another word, substance *etc*: *'Reader' is a derivative of 'read'.* □ **dérivé**
derrick ['derik] *noun* an apparatus like a mechanical crane for lifting weights: *The ship was unloaded, using the large derricks on the quay.* □ **mât de charge**
descend [di'send] *verb* 1 to go or climb down from a higher place or position: *He descended the staircase.* □ **descendre**
2 to slope downwards: *The hills descend to the sea.* □ **descendre**
3 (with **on**) to make a sudden attack on: *The soldiers descended on the helpless villagers.* □ **se jeter (sur)**
de'scendant *noun* the child, grandchild, great-grand-child *etc* of a person: *This is a photograph of my grand-mother with all her descendants.* □ **descendant, ante**
de'scent [-t] *noun* 1 the act of descending: *The descent of the hill was quickly completed.* □ **descente**
2 a slope: *That is a steep descent.* □ **pente**
3 family; ancestry: *She is of royal descent.* □ **origine**
be descended from to be a descendant of. □ **descendre de**

the noun **descendant** ends in **-ant** (not **-ent**).

describe [di'skraib] *verb* 1 to give an account of in words; to tell in words what something or someone is like: *He described what had happened*; *Would you describe her as beautiful?* □ **décrire**
2 to say that one is something: *He describes himself as a salesman.* □ **se dire**
de'scription [-'skrip-] *noun* 1 (an) act of describing: *I recognized her from your description.* □ **description**
2 an account of anything in words: *He gave a descrip-tion of his holiday.* □ **description**
3 a sort or kind: *She carried a gun of some description.*

□ **sorte**

to **describe** (not **describe about**) a scene.

desert[1] [di'zə:t] *verb* 1 to go away from and leave with-out help *etc*; to leave or abandon: *Why did you desert us?* □ **abandonner**
2 to run away, *usually* from the army: *She was shot for trying to desert.* □ **déserter**
de'serted *adjective* 1 with no people *etc*: *The streets are completely deserted.* □ **désert**
2 abandoned: *his deserted wife and children.* □ **abandonné**
de'serter *noun* a man who deserts from the army *etc*. □ **déserteur**
de'sertion [-ʃən] *noun* (an) act of deserting. □ **désertion**
desert[2] ['dezət] *noun* an area of barren country, *usually* hot, dry and sandy, where there is very little rain: *Parts of the country are almost desert*; (*also adjective*) *desert plants.* □ **désert; désertique**

the Sahara **desert** (not **dessert**).

deserve [di'zə:v] *verb* to have earned as a right by one's actions; to be worthy of: *He deserves recognition of his achievements.* □ **mériter**
de'serving *adjective* (*negative* **undeserving**) 1 worthy or suitable (to be given charity *etc*): *I only give money to deserving causes.* □ **méritoire**
2 (with **of**) worthy of: *She is deserving of better treat-ment than this.* □ **digne de**
desiccated ['desikeitid] *adjective* completely dried out: *desiccated coconut.* □ **(des)séché**
design [di'zain] *verb* to invent and prepare a plan of (something) before it is built or made: *A famous archi-tect designed this building.* □ **concevoir**
■ *noun* 1 a sketch or plan produced before something is made: *a design for a dress.* □ **dessin**
2 style; the way in which something has been made or put together: *It is very modern in design; I don't like the design of that building.* □ **conception**
3 a pattern *etc*: *The curtains have a flower design on them.* □ **motif**
4 a plan formed in the mind; (an) intention: *Our holi-days coincided by design and not by accident.* □ **dessein**
de'signer *noun* a person who makes designs or patterns: *She is the designer of the yacht.* □ **créateur, trice**
de'signing *noun* the art of making designs or patterns: *dress-designing.* □ **stylisme**
designate ['dezigneit] *verb* 1 to call or name: *It was des-ignated a conservation area.* □ **nommer**
2 to point out or identify: *She has been designated our next Prime Minister.* □ **désigner (comme/pour)**
■ *adjective* (*placed immediately after noun*) appointed to an office *etc* but not yet having begun it: *the ambas-sador designate.* □ **désigné**
‚desig'nation *noun* a name or title. □ **désignation**
designer *etc see* **design.**
desire [di'zaiə] *noun* a wish or longing: *I have a sudden desire for a bar of chocolate*; *I have no desire ever to see him again.* □ **désir**
■ *verb* to long for or feel desire for: *After a day's work,*

all I desire is a hot bath. □ **désirer**

de'sirable *adjective* pleasing or worth having: *a desirable residence.* □ **désirable**

de,sira'bility *noun* the extent to which something is desirable. □ **attrait**

desk [desk] *noun* a piece of furniture, often like a table, for sitting at while writing, reading *etc*: *She kept the pile of letters in a drawer in her desk.* □ **bureau, pupitre**

desolate ['desələt] *adjective* **1** (of landscapes, areas *etc*) very lonely or barren: *desolate moorland.* □ **désolé**
2 (of people) very sad, lonely and unhappy. □ **délaissé**
deso'lation *noun.* □ **désolation**

despair [di'speə] *verb* to lose hope (of): *I despair of ever teaching my son anything.* □ **(se) désespérer (de)**
■ *noun* **1** the state of having given up hope: *He was filled with despair at the news.* □ **désespoir**
2 (*with* **the**) something which causes someone to despair: *He is the despair of his mother.* □ **désespoir**

desperate ['despərət] *adjective* **1** (*sometimes used loosely*) despairingly reckless or violent: *She was desperate to get into university; a desperate criminal.* □ **prêt à tout**
2 very bad or almost hopeless: *We are in a desperate situation.* □ **désespéré**
3 urgent and despairing: *He made a desperate appeal for help.* □ **désespéré**
'desperately *adverb.* □ **désespérément**
,despe'ration *noun*: *In desperation we asked the police for help.* □ **désespoir**

despise [di'spaiz] *verb* **1** to look upon with scorn and contempt: *I know he despises me for being stupid.* □ **mépriser**
2 to refuse to have, use *etc*; to scorn: *She despises such luxuries as fur boots.* □ **dédaigner**
despicable [di'spikəbl] *adjective* contemptible, worthless and deserving to be despised: *His behaviour was despicable.* □ **méprisable**
de'spicably *adverb.* □ **bassement**

despite [di'spait] *preposition* in spite of: *He didn't get the job despite all his qualifications.* □ **malgré**

despondent [di'spondənt] *adjective* feeling miserable, unhappy, gloomy *etc*: *She was utterly despondent at her failure.* □ **découragé**
de'spondently *adverb.* □ **avec découragement**
de'spondency *noun.* □ **découragement**

despot ['despot] *noun* a person (*usually* the king or ruler of a country) with absolute power, often a tyrant. □ **despote**
de'spotic *adjective.* □ **despotique**
de'spotically *adverb.* □ **despotiquement**
'despotism [-pə-] *noun* absolute power or tyranny. □ **despotisme**

dessert [di'zəːt] *noun* **1** the sweet course in a meal; pudding: *We had ice cream for dessert.* □ **entremets**
2 fruits, sweets *etc* served at the end of dinner. □ **dessert**

to eat a **dessert** (not **desert**).

destination [desti'neiʃən] *noun* the place to which someone or something is going: *I think we've arrived at our*

destination at last. □ **destination**

destined ['destind] *adjective* **1** (having a future) organized or arranged beforehand (by a person or by fate): *She was destined for success.* □ **destiné à**
2 bound or heading (for a place): *destined for Singapore.* □ **à destination de**

destiny ['destəni] – *plural* '**destinies** – *noun* the power which appears or is thought to control events; fate: *We are all subject to the tricks played by destiny.* □ **destin**

destitute ['destitjuːt] *adjective* in great need of food, shelter *etc*: *They were left destitute when she died.* □ **sans ressources**

destroy [di'stroi] *verb* **1** to put an end to or make useless; to ruin: *Vandals destroyed the painting.* □ **détruire**
2 to kill (animals): *This poison destroys rats.* □ **tuer**
de'stroyer *noun* a type of small fast warship: *naval destroyers.* □ **contre-torpilleur**

destruction [di'strʌkʃən] *noun* **1** the act or process of destroying or being destroyed: *the destruction of the city.* □ **destruction**
2 the state of being destroyed; ruin: *a scene of destruction.* □ **destruction**
des'tructive [-tiv-] *adjective* **1** causing or able to cause destruction: *Small children can be very destructive.* □ **destructeur**
2 (of criticism *etc*) pointing out faults *etc* without suggesting improvements. □ **destructif**
de'structively *adverb.* □ **de façon destructrice**
de'structiveness *noun.* □ **effet/penchant destructeur**

detach [di'tatʃ] *verb* to unfasten or remove (from): *I detached the bottom part of the form and sent it back.* □ **détacher**
de'tachable *adjective* able to be detached. □ **détachable**
de'tached *adjective* **1** standing *etc* apart or by itself: *a detached house.* □ **détaché**
2 not personally involved or showing no emotion or prejudice: *a detached attitude to the problem.* □ **détaché**
de'tachment *noun* **1** the state of not being influenced by emotion or prejudice. □ **détachement**
2 the act of detaching. □ **séparation**
3 a group (*especially* of soldiers): *A detachment was sent to guard the supplies.* □ **détachement**

detail ['diːteil, di'teil] *noun* **1** a small part or an item: *She paid close attention to the small details.* □ **détail**
2 all the small features and parts considered as a whole: *Look at the amazing detail in this drawing!* □ **détails**
'detailed *adjective* giving many details with nothing left out: *His instructions were very detailed.* □ **détaillé**
in detail item by item, giving attention to the details: *I'll tell you the story in detail.* □ **en détail**

detain [di'tein] *verb* **1** to hold back and delay: *I won't detain you – I can see you're in a hurry.* □ **retenir**
2 (of the police *etc*) to keep under guard: *Three suspects were detained at the police station.* □ **détenir**
,detai'nee *noun* a person who is detained (by the police *etc*). □ **détenu, ue**
de'tention [-'ten-] *noun* the state of being imprisoned: *The criminals are in detention.* □ **détention**

detect [di'tekt] *verb* to notice or discover: *She thought she could detect a smell of gas.* □ **détecter**

de'tective [-tiv] *noun* a person who tries to find criminals or watches suspected persons: *She was questioned by detectives.* □ **policier, ière; détective**

detention *see* **detain**.

deter [di'tə:] – *past tense, past participle* **de'terred** – *verb* to make less willing or prevent by frightening: *She was not deterred by his threats.* □ **décourager**
de'terrent [-'tə:-] *noun, adjective* (something) that deters: *The possession of nuclear weapons by nations is thought to be a deterrent against nuclear war itself; a deterrent effect.* □ **moyen de dissuasion; préventif**
detergent [di'tə:dʒənt] *noun* a (soapless) substance used for cleaning: *She poured detergent into the washing-machine.* □ **détergent**
deteriorate [di'tiəriəreit] *verb* to grow worse: *His work has deteriorated recently.* □ **(se) détériorer**
de,terio'ration *noun.* □ **détérioration**
determine [di'tə:min] *verb* **1** to fix or settle; to decide: *He determined his course of action.* □ **déterminer**
2 to find out exactly: *He tried to determine what had gone wrong.* □ **établir**
de,termi'nation *noun* **1** firmness of character or stubbornness: *She showed her determination by refusing to give way.* □ **détermination**
2 the act of determining. □ **détermination**
de'termined *adjective* **1** having one's mind made up: *She is determined to succeed.* □ **décidé (à)**
2 stubborn: *She's very determined.* □ **résolu**
3 fixed or settled: *Our route has already been determined.* □ **déterminé**
deterrent *see* **deter**.
detest [di'test] *verb* to hate intensely: *I detest cruelty.* □ **détester**
de'testable *adjective* extremely hateful. □ **détestable**
detonate ['detəneit] *verb* to (cause to) explode violently: *This device detonates the bomb.* □ **(faire) détoner**
,deto'nation *noun* an explosion. □ **détonation**
'detonator *noun* something (*especially* a piece of equipment) that sets off an explosion. □ **détonateur**
detour ['di:tuə] *noun* a wandering from the direct way: *We made a detour through the mountains.* □ **détour**
detriment ['detrimənt] *noun* harm, damage or disadvantage: *to the detriment of his health.* □ **détriment**
,detri'mental [-'men-] *adjective* causing harm or damage. □ **nuisible**
devalue [di:'valju:] *verb* to reduce the value of (*especially* a currency): *The government devalued the dollar.* □ **dévaluer**
,devalu'ation [di:val-] *noun* the act of devaluing. □ **dévaluation**
devastate ['devəsteit] *verb* **1** to leave in ruins: *The fire devastated the countryside.* □ **dévaster**
2 to overwhelm (a person) with grief: *She was devastated by the terrible news.* □ **terrasser**
'devastating *adjective* overwhelming: *a devastating flood; The news was devastating.* □ **dévastateur, accablant**
develop [di'veləp] – *past tense, past participle* **de'veloped** – *verb* **1** to (cause to) grow bigger or to a more advanced state: *The plan developed slowly in his mind; It has de-*

veloped into a very large city. □ **(se) développer**
2 to acquire gradually: *He developed the habit of getting up early.* □ **acquérir**
3 to become active, visible *etc*: *Spots developed on her face.* □ **(se) manifester**
4 to use chemicals to make (a photograph) visible: *My brother develops all his own films.* □ **développer**
de'velopment *noun* **1** the process or act of developing: *a crucial stage in the development of a child.* □ **développement**
2 something new which is the result of developing: *important new developments in science.* □ **progrès**
deviate ['di:vieit] *verb* to turn aside, *especially* from a right, normal or standard course: *She will not deviate from her routine.* □ **s'écarter**
,devi'ation *noun.* □ **écart, déviation**
device [di'vais] *noun* **1** something made for a purpose, *eg* a tool or instrument: *a device for opening cans.* □ **appareil**
2 a plan or system of doing something, sometimes involving trickery: *This is a device for avoiding income tax.* □ **truc**

> **device**, unlike **advice**, can be used in the plural: *ingenious devices.*
> **devise** is a verb: *to devise a scheme.*

devil ['devl] *noun* **1** the spirit of evil; Satan: *He does not worship God – he worships the Devil.* □ **diable**
2 any evil or wicked spirit or person: *That man is a devil!* □ **démon**
3 a person who is bad or disapproved of: *She's a lazy devil.* □ **diable, diablesse**
4 an unfortunate person for whom one feels pity: *Poor devils! I feel really sorry for them.* □ **pauvre diable**
devious ['di:viəs] *adjective* not direct; not straightforward: *We climbed the hill by a devious route; He used devious methods to get what he wanted.* □ **détourné**
'deviously *adverb.* □ **d'une façon détournée**
'deviousness *noun.* □ **détours, sournoiserie**
devise [di'vaiz] *verb* to invent; to put together: *A shelter/new scheme was hurriedly devised.* □ **inventer, combiner**
devoid [di'void] *adjective* (*with* **of**) free from or lacking: *That is devoid of any meaning.* □ **dépourvu (de)**
devote [di'vout] *verb* (*with* **to**) to give up wholly to or use entirely for: *She devotes her life to music.* □ **consacrer (à)**
de'voted *adjective* **1** (*sometimes with* **to**) loving and loyal: *a devoted friend; I am devoted to him.* □ **attaché (à)**
2 (*with* **to**) given up (to): *He is devoted to his work.* □ **dévoué (à)**
devotee [devə'ti:] *noun* a keen follower; an enthusiast: *a devotee of football.* □ **partisan, ane**
de'votion *noun* **1** great love: *her undying devotion for her children.* □ **dévouement**
2 the act of devoting or of being devoted: *devotion to duty.* □ **dévouement**
devour [di'vauə] *verb* to eat up greedily: *He was devoured by a lion; She devoured the chocolates.* □

dévorer

devout [di'vaut] *adjective* **1** earnest or sincere: *Please accept my devout thanks.* □ **fervent**
2 religious: *a devout Christian.* □ **dévot**

dew [djuː] *noun* tiny drops of moisture coming from the air as it cools, *especially* at night: *The grass is wet with early-morning dew.* □ **rosée**

dexterity [dek'sterəti] *noun* skill and/or quickness, *especially* with the hands: *I showed my dexterity with a needle and thread.* □ **dextérité**
'**dext(e)rous** *adjective* skilful, *especially* with the hands: *She is a very dexterous surgeon.* □ **habile**

diabetes [daiə'biːtiːz] *noun* a disease in which there is usually too much sugar in the blood. □ **diabète**
,**dia'betic** [-'be-] *noun* a person who suffers from diabetes: *He is a diabetic.* □ **diabétique**
■ *adjective* relating to or suffering from diabetes: *a diabetic patient.* □ **diabétique**

diagnose [daiəg'nous, -'nouz] *verb* to say what is wrong (with a sick person *etc*) after making an examination; to identify (an illness *etc*): *The doctor diagnosed her illness as flu.* □ **diagnostiquer**
,**diag'nosis** [-sis] – *plural* **diag'noses** [-siːz] – *noun* a conclusion reached by diagnosing: *What diagnosis did the doctor make?* □ **diagnostic**

diagonal [dai'agənl] *noun* a line going from one corner to the opposite corner: *The two diagonals of a rectangle cross at the centre.* □ **diagonale**
di'agonally *adverb* in a diagonal line: *He walked diagonally across the field.* □ **en diagonale**

diagram ['daiəgram] *noun* a drawing used to explain something that is difficult to understand: *This book has diagrams showing the parts of a car engine.* □ **diagramme**

dial ['daiəl] *noun* **1** the face of a watch or clock: *My watch has a dial you can see in the dark.* □ **cadran**
2 the turning disc over the numbers on a telephone. □ **cadran**
3 any disc *etc* bearing numbers *etc* used to give information: *the dial on a radio.* □ **cadran**
■ *verb* – *past tense, past participle* '**dialled** – to turn a telephone dial to get a number: *She dialled the wrong number.* □ **composer**

dialect ['daiəlekt] *noun* a way of speaking found only in a certain area or among a certain group or class of people: *They were speaking in dialect.* □ **dialecte**

dialogue, (*American*) **dialog(ue)** ['daiəlog] *noun* (a) talk between two or more people, *especially* in a play or novel. □ **dialogue**

diameter [dai'amitə] *noun* (the length of) a straight line drawn from side to side of a circle, passing through its centre: *Could you measure the diameter of that circle?* □ **diamètre**

diamond ['daiəmənd] *noun* **1** a very hard, colourless precious stone: *Her brooch had three diamonds in it; (also adjective) a diamond ring.* □ **diamant; de diamant**
2 a piece of diamond (often artificial) used as a tip on *eg* a record player stylus. □ **diamant**
3 a kind of four-sided figure or shape; ◊: *There was a pattern of red and yellow diamonds on the floor.* □

losange
4 one of the playing cards of the suit diamonds, which have red symbols of this shape on them. □ **carreau**
'**diamonds** *noun plural* (sometimes treated as *noun singular*) one of the four card suits: *the five of diamonds.* □ **carreau**

diaper ['daiəpə] *noun* a piece of cloth or paper put between a baby's legs to soak up urine *etc*. □ **couche**

diarrhea, diarrhoea [daiə'riə] *noun* too much liquid in and too frequent emptying of the bowels: *He has diarrhoea.* □ **diarrhée**

diary ['daiəri] – *plural* '**diaries** – *noun* a (small book containing a) record of daily happenings: *The explorer kept a diary of her adventures.* □ **journal**

dice [dais] – *plural* **dice** – *noun* (*American* **die** [dai]) a small cube, *usually* with numbered sides or faces, used in certain games: *It is your turn to throw the dice.* □ **dé**
■ *verb* **1** to cut (vegetables *etc*) into small cubes: *I diced the carrots for the soup.* □ **couper en cubes**
2 to compete (with someone) at throwing dice; to gamble. □ **jouer aux dés**
'**dicey** *adjective* uncertain; risky: *a dicey situation.* □ **risqué**
dice with death to do something very risky (and dangerous): *He diced with death every time he took a short cut across the main railway line.* □ **risquer sa vie**
the die is cast the decisive step has been taken – there is no going back. □ **le sort en est jeté**

dictate ['dikteit, dik'teit] *verb* **1** to say or read out (something) for someone else to write down: *He always dictates his letters (to his secretary).* □ **dicter**
2 to state officially or with authority: *He dictated the terms of our offer.* □ **dicter**
3 to give orders to; to command: *I certainly won't be dictated to by you* (= I won't do as you say). □ **faire la loi**
dic'tation *noun* something read for another to write down: *The secretary is taking dictation.* □ **dictée**
dic'tator *noun* an all-powerful ruler: *As soon as he became dictator, he made all political parties illegal and governed the country as he liked.* □ **dictateur, trice**
dic'tatorship *noun* **1** the authority of a dictator: *His dictatorship is threatened by the terrorists.* □ **dictature**
2 a state ruled by a dictator: *That country is a dictatorship now.* □ **dictature**

diction ['dikʃən] *noun* the manner of speaking: *Her diction is always very clear.* □ **diction**

dictionary ['dikʃənəri] – *plural* '**dictionaries** – *noun* a book containing the words of a language alphabetically arranged, with their meanings *etc*: *This is an English dictionary.* □ **dictionnaire**
2 a book containing other information alphabetically arranged: *a dictionary of place names.* □ **dictionnaire**

did *see* do.

didn't *see* do.

die[1] [dai] – *present participle* **dying** ['daiiŋ]: *past tense, past participle* **died** – *verb* **1** to lose life; to stop living and become dead: *Those flowers are dying; She died of old age.* □ **mourir**
2 to fade; to disappear: *The daylight was dying fast.* □ **disparaître**

3 to have a strong desire (for something or to do something): *I'm dying for a drink*; *I'm dying to see her.* □ **avoir une envie folle de**

diehard *noun* a person who resists new ideas. □ **conservateur, trice (à tout crin)**

die away to fade from sight or hearing: *The sound died away into the distance.* □ **s'éteindre**

die down to lose strength or power: *I think the wind has died down a bit.* □ **tomber**

die hard to take a long time to disappear: *Old habits die hard.* □ **avoir la vie dure**

die off to die quickly or in large numbers: *Herds of cattle were dying off because of the drought.* □ **mourir les uns après les autres**

die out to cease to exist anywhere: *The custom died out during the last century.* □ **disparaître**

die[2] [dai] *noun* a stamp or punch for making raised designs on money, paper *etc*. □ **matrice**

die[3] *see* **dice.**

diesel engine ['di:zəl] an internal-combustion engine in trucks *etc*, in which a heavy form of oil is used. □ **moteur diesel**

diesel fuel/oil heavy oil used as fuel for a diesel engine. □ **gas-oil**

diet ['daiət] *noun* food, *especially* a course of recommended foods, for losing weight or as treatment for an illness *etc*: *a diet of fish and vegetables*; *a salt-free diet*; *He went on a diet to lose weight.* □ **régime**

■ *verb* to eat certain kinds of food to lose weight: *She has to diet to stay slim.* □ **suivre un régime**

differ ['difə] – *past tense, past participle* **'differed** – *verb* **1** (*often with* **from**) to be not like or alike: *Our views differ*; *Her house differs from mine.* □ **différer (de)**

2 to disagree (with): *I think we will have to agree to differ.* □ **ne pas être d'accord**

---

differed and **differing** have one **r**.

---

difference ['difrəns] *noun* **1** what makes one thing unlike another: *I can't see any difference between these two pictures*; *It doesn't make any difference to me whether you go or stay*; *There's not much difference between them.* □ **différence**

2 an act of differing, *especially* a disagreement: *We had a difference of opinion*; *Have they settled their differences?* (= Have they stopped arguing?). □ **désaccord**

3 the amount by which one quantity or number is greater than another: *If you buy it for me I'll give you $6 now and make up the difference later.* □ **différence**

'different *adjective* (*often with* **from**) not the same: *These gloves are not a pair – they're different*; *My ideas are different from his.* □ **différent (de)**

,diffe'rentiate [-'renʃieit] *verb* **1** to see or be able to tell a difference (between): *I cannot even differentiate a blackbird and a starling.* □ **distinguer**

2 (*with* **between**) to treat differently: *She does not differentiate between her two children although one is adopted.* □ **faire la différence (entre)**

'diffe,renti'ation *noun*. □ **différenciation**

---

different is followed by **from** (not **than**).

---

difficult ['difikəlt] *adjective* **1** hard to do or understand; not easy: *difficult sums*; *a difficult task*; *It is difficult to know what to do for the best.* □ **laborieux; difficile, pénible**

2 hard to deal with or needing to be treated *etc* in a special way: *a difficult child.* □ **difficile**

'difficulty – *plural* **'difficulties** – *noun* **1** the state or quality of being hard (to do) or not easy: *I have difficulty in understanding him.* □ **difficulté**

2 an obstacle or objection: *He has a habit of foreseeing difficulties.* □ **difficulté**

3 (*especially in plural*) trouble, *especially* money trouble: *The firm was in difficulties.* □ **embarras**

diffident ['difidənt] *adjective* not confident. □ **qui manque d'assurance**

'diffidently *adverb*. □ **timidement**

'diffidence *noun*. □ **manque d'assurance**

diffuse [di'fju:z] *verb* to (cause to) spread in all directions. □ **(se) diffuser, (se) répandre**

dig [dig] – *present participle* **'digging**: *past tense, past participle* **dug** [dʌg] – *verb* **1** to turn up (earth) with a spade *etc*: *to dig the garden.* □ **bêcher**

2 to make (a hole) in this way: *The child dug a tunnel in the sand.* □ **creuser**

3 to poke: *He dug his brother in the ribs with his elbow.* □ **enfoncer**

■ *noun* a poke: *a dig in the ribs*; *I knew that his remarks were a dig at me* (= a joke directed at me). □ **coup de poing/coude, allusion**

'digger *noun* a machine for digging. □ **excavatrice**

dig out **1** to get out by digging: *We had to dig the car out of the mud.* □ **déterrer, sortir de**

2 to find by searching: *I'll see if I can dig out that photo.* □ **dénicher**

dig up: *We dug up that old tree*; *They dug up a skeleton*; *They're digging up the road yet again.* □ **arracher, déterrer**

digest [dai'dʒest] *verb* **1** to break up (food) in the stomach *etc* and turn it into a form which the body can use: *The invalid had to have food that was easy to digest.* □ **digérer**

2 to take in and think over (information *etc*): *It took me some minutes to digest what he had said.* □ **digérer, assimiler**

di'gestible *adjective* able to be digested: *This food is scarcely digestible.* □ **digestible**

di'gestion [-tʃən] *noun* **1** the act of digesting food. □ **digestion**

2 the ability of one's body to digest food: *poor digestion.* □ **digestion**

di'gestive [-tiv] *adjective* of digestion: *the human digestive system.* □ **digestif**

digit ['didʒit] *noun* **1** any of the figures 0 to 9: *105 is a number with three digits.* □ **chiffre**

2 a finger or toe. □ **doigt; orteil**

'digital *adjective* (of a computer *etc*) using the numbers 0–9. □ **numérique**

digital clock/watch a clock or watch which shows the time in numbers instead of on a dial. □ **horloge/montre à affichage numérique**

dignified ['dignifaid] *adjective (negative* **undignified)** stately, serious or showing dignity: *She decided that it would not be dignified to run for the bus.* □ **digne**

dignitary ['dignitəri] – *plural* **'dignitaries** – *noun* a person who has a high rank or office. □ **dignitaire**

dignity ['dignəti] *noun* **1** stateliness or seriousness of manner: *Holding her head high, she retreated with dignity.* □ **dignité**

2 importance or seriousness: *the dignity of the occasion.* □ **dignité**

3 a privilege *etc* indicating rank: *He had risen to the dignity of an office of his own.* □ **dignité**

4 one's personal pride: *He had wounded her dignity.* □ **dignité**

digress [dai'gres] *verb* to wander from the point, or from the main subject in speaking or writing. □ **faire une digression**

di'gression [-ʃən] *noun.* □ **digression**

dike, dyke [daik] *noun* an embankment built as a barrier against the sea *etc.* □ **digue**

dilate [dai'leit] *verb* to make or become larger: *The sudden darkness made the pupils of his eyes dilate.* □ **(se) dilater**

dilemma [di'lemə] *noun* a position or situation giving two choices, neither pleasant: *His dilemma was whether to leave the party early so as to get a lift in his friend's car, or to stay and walk eight kilometres home.* □ **dilemme**

diligent ['dilidʒənt] *adjective* conscientious; hardworking: *a diligent student.* □ **appliqué**

'diligently *adverb.* □ **avec soin**

'diligence *noun.* □ **application**

dilly-dally [dili'dali] *verb* to waste time *especially* by stopping often: *She's always dilly-dallying on the way to school.* □ **traîner**

dilute [dai'ljuːt] *verb* to lessen the strength *etc* of by mixing *especially* with water: *You are supposed to dilute that lime juice with water.* □ **diluer**

■ *adjective* reduced in strength; weak: *dilute acid.* □ **dilué**

di'lution *noun.* □ **dilution**

dim [dim] *adjective* **1** not bright or distinct: *a dim light in the distance; a dim memory.* □ **faible, vague**

2 (of a person) not intelligent: *She's a bit dim!* □ **borné**

■ *verb* – *past tense, past participle* **dimmed** – to make or become dim: *Tears dimmed her eyes; She dimmed the lights in the theatre.* □ **réduire, brouiller**

'dimly *adverb.* □ **faiblement**

'dimness *noun.* □ **faiblesse, vague**

dime [daim] *noun* the tenth part of a dollar; 10 cents. □ **(pièce de) dix cents**

dimension [di'menʃən] *noun* a measurement in length, breadth, or thickness: *The dimensions of the box are 20 cm by 10 cm by 4 cm.* □ **dimension**

-dimensional of (a certain number of) dimensions: *a three-dimensional figure.* □ **à (...) dimension(s)**

diminish [di'miniʃ] *verb* to make or become less: *Our supplies are diminishing rapidly.* □ **diminuer**

di'minished *adjective (negative* **undiminished).** □ **diminué**

diminution [dimi'njuːʃən] *noun* lessening: *a diminution in the birth rate.* □ **diminution**

diminutive [di'minjutiv] *adjective* very small: *a diminutive child.* □ **minuscule**

dimple ['dimpl] *noun* a small hollow *especially* on the surface of the skin: *She has a dimple in her cheek when she smiles.* □ **fossette**

din [din] *noun* a loud continuous noise: *What a terrible din that machine makes!* □ **vacarme**

dine [dain] *verb* to have dinner: *We shall dine at half-past eight.* □ **dîner**

'diner *noun* a person who dines: *The diners ran from the restaurant when the fire started.* □ **dîneur, euse**

dining car *noun* a restaurant car on a train. □ **wagon-restaurant**

'dining-room *noun* a room used mainly for eating in. □ **salle à manger**

'dining-table *noun* a table around which people sit to eat. □ **table de salle à manger**

dine on to have for one's dinner: *They dined on lobster and champagne.* □ **dîner de**

dine out to have dinner somewhere other than one's own house *eg* in a restaurant or at the house of friends *etc.* □ **dîner en ville/dehors**

ding-dong ['diŋdoŋ] *adjective* crazy or foolish. □ **acharné**

■ *noun* the sound of a bell or bells. □ **engueulade**

dinghy ['diŋgi] – *plural* **'dinghies** – *noun* **1** a small boat carried on a larger boat to take passengers ashore. □ **canot, youyou**

2 a small sailing or rowing boat. □ **dériveur, canot**

dingo ['diŋgou] – *plural* **'dingoes** – *noun* a type of wild dog found in Australia. □ **dingo**

dingy ['dindʒi] *adjective* dull; faded and dirty-looking: *This room is so dingy.* □ **minable**

'dinginess *noun.* □ **aspect minable**

dinner ['dinə] *noun* **1** the main meal of the day eaten *usually* in the evening: *Is it time for dinner yet?* □ **dîner**

2 a formal party in the evening, when such a meal is eaten: *They asked me to dinner; She was the guest of honour at the dinner; (also adjective) a dinner party.* □ **banquet; de soirée**

'dinnerjacket *noun* a man's formal jacket for wear in the evening. □ **smoking**

dinosaur ['dainəsoːr] *noun* any of several types of extinct giant reptile. □ **dinosaure**

dint [dint] *noun* a hollow made by a blow; a dent. □ **bosse**

by dint of by means of: *He succeeded by dint of sheer hard work.* □ **à force de**

diocese ['daiəsis] *noun* the district over which a bishop has authority. □ **diocèse**

dip [dip] – *past tense, past participle* **dipped** – *verb* **1** to lower into any liquid for a moment: *He dipped his bread in the soup.* □ **tremper**

2 to slope downwards: *The road dipped just beyond the crossroads.* □ **descendre**

3 to lower the beam of (car headlights): *He dipped his lights as the other car approached.* □ **(se) mettre en code**

4 (of a ship) to lower (a flag) briefly in salute. □ **saluer**

(avec le pavillon)

■ *noun* **1** a hollow (in a road *etc*): *The car was hidden by a dip in the road.* □ **creux**

2 a soft, savoury mixture in which raw vegetables *etc* can be dipped: *a cheese dip.* □ **trempette**

3 a short swim: *a dip in the sea.* □ **baignade**

dip into 1 to withdraw amounts from (a supply, *eg* of money): *I've been dipping into my savings recently.* □ **puiser (dans)**

2 to look briefly at (a book) or to study (a subject) in a casual manner: *I've dipped into his book on Trudeau, but I haven't read it thoroughly.* □ **feuilleter**

diphtheria [dif'θiəriə] *noun* an infectious disease of the throat. □ **diphtérie**

diphthong ['difθoŋ] *noun* two vowel sounds pronounced as one syllable: *The vowel sound in 'out' is a diphthong.* □ **diphtongue**

diploma [di'ploumə] *noun* a written statement saying that one has passed a certain examination *etc*: *She has a diploma in teaching.* □ **diplôme**

diplomacy [di'ploumɔsi] *noun* **1** the business of making agreements, treaties *etc* between countries; the business of looking after the affairs of one's country *etc* in a foreign country. □ **diplomatie**

2 skill and tact in dealing with people, persuading them *etc*: *Use a little diplomacy and she'll soon agree to help.* □ **diplomatie**

diplomat ['diplomat] *noun* a person engaged in diplomacy: *She is a diplomat at the American embassy.* □ **diplomate**

diplomatic [diplə'matik] *adjective* **1** concerning diplomacy: *a diplomatic mission.* □ **diplomatique**

2 tactful: *a diplomatic remark.* □ **diplomate, diplomatique**

,diplo'matically *adverb.* □ **avec tact, diplomatiquement**

dire ['daiə] *adjective* dreadful; perilous. □ **terrible**

direct [di'rekt] *adjective* **1** straight; following the quickest and shortest way: *Is this the most direct route?* □ **direct**

2 (of manner *etc*) straightforward and honest: *a direct answer.* □ **franc**

3 occurring as an immediate result: *His dismissal was a direct result of his rudeness to the manager.* □ **direct**

4 exact; complete: *Her opinions are the direct opposite of his.* □ **absolu**

5 in an unbroken line of descent from father to son *etc*: *She is a direct descendant of Napoleon.* □ **en ligne directe**

■ *verb* **1** to point, aim or turn in a particular direction: *He directed my attention towards the notice.* □ **diriger**

2 to show the way to: *She directed her to the station.* □ **indiquer le chemin de**

3 to order or instruct: *We will do as you direct.* □ **ordonner**

4 to control or organize: *A policeman was directing the traffic*; *to direct a film.* □ **diriger**

di'rection [-ʃən] *noun* **1** (the) place or point to which one moves, looks *etc*: *What direction did she go in?*; *They were heading in my direction* (= towards me); *I'll find my way all right – I've a good sense of direction.* □ **direction**

2 guidance: *They are under your direction.* □ **direction**

3 (*in plural*) instructions (*eg* on how to get somewhere, use something *etc*): *We asked the policeman for directions*; *I have lost the directions for this washing-machine.* □ **instructions**

4 the act of aiming or turning (something or someone) towards a certain point. □ **orientation**

di'rectional *adjective.* □ **directionnel**

di'rective [-tiv] *noun* a general instruction from a higher authority about what is to be done *etc*. □ **directive**

di'rectly *adverb* **1** in a direct manner: *I went directly to the office.* □ **directement**

2 almost at once: *She will be here directly.* □ **immédiatement**

di'rectness *noun.* □ **franchise**

di'rector *noun* a person or thing that directs, *eg* one of a group of persons who manage the affairs of a business or a person who is in charge of the making of a film, play *etc*: *She is on the board of directors of our firm*; *The producer and the director quarrelled about the film.* □ **directeur, trice, réalisateur, trice, guide**

di'rectory – *plural* **di'rectories** – *noun* a type of book giving names and addresses *etc*: *a telephone directory.* □ **annuaire**

dirt [dəːt] *noun* any unclean substance, such as mud, dust, dung *etc*: *Her shoes are covered in dirt.* □ **saleté**

'dirty *adjective* **1** not clean: *dirty clothes.* □ **sale, malpropre**

2 mean or unfair: *a dirty trick.* □ **sale**

3 offensive; obscene: *dirty books.* □ **pornographique**

4 (of weather) stormy: *dirty books.* □ **mauvais**

■ *verb* to make or become dirty: *He dirtied his hands/shoes.* □ **(se) salir**

'dirtiness *noun.* □ **saleté**

,dirt-'cheap *adjective, adverb* very cheap. □ **très bon marché, pour rien**

dirt track an earth track for motor-racing. □ **(piste en) cendrée**

disable [dis'eibl] *verb* to reduce the ability or strength of; to cripple: *She was disabled during the war.* □ **estropier**

disability [disə'biləti] – *plural* **disa'bilities** – *noun* something which disables: *He has a disability which prevents him from walking very far.* □ **infirmité**

dis'abled *adjective* lacking ability or strength; crippled: *a disabled soldier.* □ **handicapé**

dis'ablement *noun.* □ **invalidité**

disadvantage [disəd'vaːntidʒ] *noun* something which makes a difficulty or which is an unfavourable circumstance: *There are several disadvantages to this plan.* □ **désavantage**

disadvantageous [disadvən'teidʒəs] *adjective.* □ **désavantageux**

at a disadvantage in an unfavourable position: *His power was strengthened by the fact that he had us all at a disadvantage.* □ **en position désavantageuse**

disagree [disə'griː] *verb* **1** (*sometimes with* **with**) to hold different opinions *etc* (from someone else): *We disa-*

gree about everything; I disagree with you on that point. □ **être en désaccord (avec)**

2 to quarrel: We never meet without disagreeing. □ **se brouiller**

3 (with **with**) (of food) to be unsuitable (to someone) and cause pain: Onions disagree with me. □ **ne pas convenir (à)**

,disa'greeable adjective unpleasant: a disagreeable task; a most disagreeable person. □ **désagréable**

,disa'greeably adverb. □ **désagréablement**

,disa'greement noun **1** disagreeing: disagreement between the two witnesses to the accident. □ **désaccord**

2 a quarrel: a violent disagreement. □ **brouille**

disallow [disə'lau] verb to refuse to allow (a claim etc). □ **rejeter**

disappear [disə'piə] verb **1** to vanish from sight: The sun disappeared slowly below the horizon. □ **disparaître**

2 to fade out of existence: This custom had disappeared by the end of the century. □ **disparaître**

3 to go away so that other people do not know where one is: A search is being carried out for the boy who disappeared from his home on Monday. □ **disparaître**

,disap'pearance noun. □ **disparition**

disappoint [disə'point] verb to fail to fulfil the hopes or expectations of: The Far North disappointed her after all she had heard about it. □ **décevoir**

,disap'pointed adjective: I was disappointed to hear that the party had been cancelled; a group of disappointed children. □ **déçu**

disap'pointing adjective: disappointing results. □ **décevant**

,disap'pointment noun: Her disappointment was obvious from her face; His failure was a great disappointment to his wife. □ **déception**

disapprove [disə'pruːv] verb to have an unfavourable opinion (of): Her mother disapproved of her behaviour. □ **désapprouver**

,disap'proval noun: She frowned to show her disapproval. □ **désapprobation**

,disap'proving adjective: a disapproving look. □ **désapprobateur**

,disap'provingly adverb. □ **d'un air désapprobateur**

disarm [dis'aːm] verb **1** to take away weapons from: She crept up from behind and managed to disarm the gunman. □ **désarmer**

2 to get rid of weapons of war: Not until peace was made did the victors consider it safe to disarm. □ **désarmer**

3 to make less hostile; to charm. □ **désarmer**

dis'armament noun the act of doing away with war-weapons. □ **désarmement**

dis'arming adjective charming: a disarming smile. □ **désarmant**

dis'armingly adverb. □ **de façon désarmante**

disarrange [disə'reindʒ] verb to throw out of order; to make untidy: The strong wind had disarranged her hair. □ **mettre en désordre**

,disar'rangement noun. □ **désordre**

disarray [disə'rei] noun disorder: The army was in complete disarray after the battle. □ **désarroi**

disaster [di'zaːstə] noun a terrible event, especially one that causes great damage, loss etc: The earthquake was the greatest disaster the country had ever experienced. □ **désastre**

di'sastrous adjective. □ **désastreux**

di'sastrously adverb. □ **désastreusement**

disband [dis'band] verb to (cause a group, eg a military force to) break up: The regiment disbanded at the end of the war. □ **(se) disperser**

disbelieve [disbi'liːv] verb not to believe: He was inclined to disbelieve her story. □ **ne pas croire**

,disbe'lief [-f] noun the state of not believing: She stared at him in disbelief. □ **incrédulité**

disc see **disk**

discard [di'skaːd] verb to throw away as useless: They discarded the empty bottles. □ **jeter**

discern [di'səːn] verb to see or realize; to notice: We could discern from his appearance that he was upset. □ **discerner**

discharge [dis'tʃaːdʒ] verb **1** to allow to leave; to dismiss: The prisoner was at last discharged; She was discharged from hospital. □ **libérer, renvoyer**

2 to fire (a gun): He discharged his gun at the policeman. □ **tirer**

3 to perform (a task etc): He discharges his duties well. □ **s'acquitter de**

4 to pay (a debt). □ **payer**

5 to (cause to) let or send out: The chimney was discharging clouds of smoke; The drain discharged into the street. □ **(se) déverser, émettre**

■ ['distʃaːdʒ] noun **1** (an) act of discharging: He was given his discharge from the army; the discharge of one's duties. □ **libération, accomplissement**

2 pus etc coming from eg a wound. □ **suppuration**

disciple [di'saipl] noun a person who believes in the teaching of another, especially one of the original followers of Christ: Jesus and his twelve disciples. □ **disciple**

discipline ['disiplin] noun **1** training in an orderly way of life: All children need discipline. □ **discipline**

2 strict self-control (amongst soldiers etc). □ **discipline**

■ verb **1** to bring under control: You must discipline yourself so that you do not waste time. □ **(se) discipliner**

2 to punish: The students who caused the disturbance have been disciplined. □ **punir**

'disciplinary adjective **1** of discipline. □ **disciplinaire**

2 intended as punishment: disciplinary action. □ **disciplinaire**

disclaim [dis'kleim] verb to refuse to have anything to do with; to deny: I disclaimed all responsibility. □ **(re)nier**

disclose [dis'klouz] verb to uncover, reveal or make known: She refused to disclose his identity. □ **révéler**

dis'closure [-ʒə] noun. □ **révélation**

disco ['diskou] short for **discotheque**.

discolour, discolor [dis'kʌlə] verb to (cause to) change colour or become stained: The paintwork had discoloured with the damp. □ **(se) décolorer**

dis,colou'ration noun. □ **décoloration**

discomfit [dis'kʌmfit] verb to embarrass: He realized

that his remarks had succeeded in discomfiting her. □
déconcerter
dis'comfiture [-tʃə] *noun.* □ **embarras**
discomfort [dis'kʌmfət] *noun* **1** the state of being uncomfortable; pain: *Her broken leg caused her great discomfort.* □ **inconfort, chagrin**
2 something that causes lack of comfort: *the discom-
forts of living in a tent.* □ **incommodité**
disconcert [diskən'sə:t] *verb* to embarrass or take aback:
He was disconcerted by the amount he had to pay. □
déconcerter
disconnect [diskə'nekt] *verb* to separate; to break the
connection (*especially electrical*) with: *Our phone has
been disconnected.* □ **débrancher**
,discon'nection [-ʃən] *noun.* □ **désassemblage**
discontent [diskən'tent] *noun* the state of not being contented; dissatisfaction: *There is a lot of discontent among
young people.* □ **mécontentement**
,discon'tented *adjective* dissatisfied or not happy: *She's
discontented with her life*; *a discontented expression.* □
mécontent
,discon'tentedly *adverb.* □ **sans joie**
,discon'tentment *noun.* □ **mécontentement**
discontinue [diskən'tinju] *verb* to stop or put an end to:
I have discontinued my visits there. □ **interrompre**
'discon,tinu'ation *noun.* □ **interruption**
discord ['disko:d] *noun* **1** disagreement or quarrelling.
□ **discorde**
2 in music, a group of notes played together which give
a jarring sound. □ **dissonance**
dis'cordant *adjective.* □ **discordant**
discotheque ['diskətek] *noun* (*usually abbreviated to
disco* ['diskou]) a place, or a type of entertainment, at
which recorded music is played for dancing. □
discothèque
discount ['diskaunt] *noun* a (small) sum taken off the
price of something: *She gave me a discount of 20%.* □
rabais
■ [dis'kaunt] *verb* to leave aside as something not to be
considered: *You can discount most of what he says – it's
nearly all lies!* □ **ne pas tenir compte de**
discourage [dis'kʌridʒ] *verb* **1** to take away the confidence, hope etc of: *His lack of success discouraged him.*
□ **décourager**
2 to try to prevent (by showing disapproval etc): *She
discouraged all his attempts to get to know her.* □
décourager
3 (*with* **from**) to persuade against: *The rain discouraged him from going camping.* □ **décourager (de)**
dis'couragement *noun.* □ **découragement**
discourteous [dis'kə:tiəs] *adjective* not polite; rude: *a
discourteous remark.* □ **impoli**
dis'courtesy [-təsi] *noun.* □ **impolitesse**
discover [dis'kʌvə] *verb* **1** to find by chance, *especially*
for the first time: *Columbus discovered America; Marie
Curie discovered radium.* □ **découvrir**
2 to find out: *Try to discover what's going on!* □
découvrir
discoverer *noun* someone who finds or learns something that was previously unknown: *The early discov-*

*erers sailed across the ocean in search of a new land;
Madame Curie was one of the discoverers of radium.* □
découvreur
dis'covery – *plural* **dis'coveries** – *noun: a voyage of
discovery*; *She made several startling discoveries.* □
découverte

We **discover** something that existed but was not yet known: *She discovered a cave.*   We **invent** something that was not in existence: *They invented a new machine.*

discredit [dis'kredit] *noun* (something that causes) loss
of good reputation. □ **discrédit**
■ *verb* **1** to show (a story etc) to be false. □ **discréditer**
2 to disgrace. □ **déconsidérer**
dis'creditable *adjective* bringing discredit or disgrace.
□ **déshonorant**
dis'creditably *adverb.* □ **de façon indigne**
discreet [di'skri:t] *adjective* wise, cautious and not saying anything which might cause trouble: *My secretary
won't let the secret out – he's very discreet.* □ **sage**
di'screetness *noun.* □ **discrétion**
di'scretion [-'skre-] *noun* **1** discreetness: *A secretary
needs discretion and tact.* □ **discrétion**
2 personal judgment: *I leave the arrangements entirely
to your discretion*; *The money will be distributed at the
discretion of the management.* □ **sagesse, discrétion**
discrepancy [di'skrepənsi] – *plural* **di'screpancies** –
noun disagreement or difference. □ **désaccord**
discretion *see* **discreet.**
discriminate [di'skrimineit] *verb* **1** (*with* **between**) to
make or see a difference between: *It is difficult to discriminate between real and pretended cases of poverty.*
□ **distinguer (entre)**
2 (often with **against**) to treat a certain kind of people
differently: *He was accused of discriminating against
some employees.* □ **établir une discrimination (contre)**
dis,crimi'nation *noun.* □ **discrimination**
discus ['diskəs] *noun* a heavy disc of metal etc thrown in
a type of athletic competition. □ **disque**
discuss [di'skʌs] *verb* to talk about: *We had a meeting to
discuss our plans for the future.* □ **discuter**
di'scussion [-ʃən] *noun* (an act of) talking about something: *I think there has been too much discussion of this
subject*; *Discussions between the heads of state took
place in strict security.* □ **discussion**

to **discuss** (not **discuss about**) a problem.

disdain [dis'dein] *noun* scorn or pride: *a look of disdain.*
□ **dédain**
■ *verb* **1** to be too proud (to do something). □ **dédaigner**
2 to look down on (something): *She disdains our company.* □ **dédaigner**
dis'dainful *adjective.* □ **dédaigneux**
dis'dainfully *adverb.* □ **dédaigneusement**
disease [di'zi:z] *noun* (an) illness: *She's suffering from a
disease of the kidneys*; *poverty and disease.* □ **maladie**
disembark [disim'ba:k] *verb* to (cause to) go from a
ship on to land: *We disembarked soon after breakfast.* □
débarquer

,disembar'kation *noun*. □ **débarquement**

disembodied [disim'bodid] *adjective* (of *eg* a spirit, soul *etc*) separated from the body: *A disembodied voice*. □ **désincarné**

disengage [disin'geidʒ] *verb* to separate or free (one thing from another): *to disengage the gears; He disengaged himself from her embrace*. □ **(se) dégager**

disentangle [disin'tangl] *verb* to free from being tangled; to unravel: *The bird could not disentangle itself from the net*. □ **(se) démêler**
,disen'tanglement *noun*. □ **démêlage**

disfavour, disfavor [dis'feivə] *noun* 1 the state of being out of favour: *He was in disfavour because he had stayed out late*. □ **défaveur**
2 displeasure or disapproval. □ **défaveur, désapprobation**

disfigure [dis'figə, -'figjər] *verb* to spoil the beauty of: *That scar will disfigure her for life*. □ **défigurer**
dis'figurement *noun*. □ **défiguration**

disgorge [dis'goːdʒ] *verb* to bring up from the stomach; to throw out or up: *The chimney was disgorging clouds of black smoke*. □ **vomir**

disgrace [dis'greis] *noun* 1 the state of being out of favour: *He is in disgrace because of his behaviour*. □ **disgrâce**
2 a state of being without honour and regarded without respect: *There seemed to be nothing ahead of you but disgrace and shame*. □ **déshonneur**
3 something which causes or ought to cause shame: *Your clothes are a disgrace!* □ **honte**
■ *verb* 1 to bring shame upon: *Did you have to disgrace me by appearing in those clothes?* □ **faire honte (à)**
2 to dismiss from a position of importance: *He was publicly disgraced*. □ **disgracier**
dis'graceful *adjective* very bad or shameful: *disgraceful behaviour; The service in that hotel was disgraceful*. □ **honteux**
dis'gracefully *adverb*. □ **honteusement**

disgruntled [dis'grʌntld] *adjective* sulky and dissatisfied. □ **mécontent**

disguise [dis'gaiz] *verb* 1 to hide the identity of by altering the appearance *etc*: *He disguised himself as a policeman; She disguised her voice with a foreign accent*. □ **(se) déguiser**
2 to hide (*eg* one's intentions *etc*): *He tried hard to disguise his feelings*. □ **dissimuler**
■ *noun* 1 a disguised state: *He was in disguise*. □ **déguisement**
2 a set of clothes, make-up *etc* which disguises: *He was wearing a false beard as a disguise*. □ **déguisement**

disgust [dis'gʌst] *verb* to cause feelings of dislike or sickness in: *The smell of that soup disgusts me; She was disgusted by your behaviour*. □ **écœurer, dégoûter**
■ *noun* the state or feeling of being disgusted: *She left the room in disgust*. □ **écœurement**
dis'gusting *adjective*: *What a disgusting smell!'; Her house is in a disgusting mess*. □ **écœurant**
dis'gustingly *adverb*. □ **d'une manière dégoûtante**

dish [diʃ] *noun* 1 a plate, bowl *etc* in which food is brought to the table: *a large shallow dish*. □ **plat**

2 food mixed and prepared for the table: *She served us an interesting dish containing chicken and almonds*. □ **plat, mets**
dishes *noun (plural)* plates, cutlery, containers and platters used to prepare, cook, serve and eat food or drink beverages: *Jack filled the sink with soap and water then washed all the dishes from supper*. □ **vaisselle**
'dish-washing *noun* the job of washing used dishes. □ **plonge**
'dishwater *noun* water that has been used for this job. □ **eau de vaisselle**
dish out to distribute or give to people: *He dished out the potatoes*. □ **distribuer**

dishearten [dis'haːtn] *verb* to take courage or hope away from: *The failure of her first attempt disheartened her*. □ **décourager**

dishevelled, disheveled [di'ʃevəld] *adjective* untidy: *She had been gardening and looked rather dishevelled*. □ **débraillé**

dishonest [dis'onist] *adjective* not honest; deceitful: *She was dishonest about her qualifications when she applied for the job*. □ **malhonnête**
dis'honestly *adverb*. □ **malhonnêtement**
dis'honesty *noun* the state or quality of being dishonest: *I would not have expected such dishonesty from him*. □ **malhonnêteté**

dishonour [dis'onə] *noun* disgrace; shame. □ **déshonneur**
■ *verb* to cause shame to: *You have dishonoured your family by your actions!* □ **déshonorer**
dis'honourable *adjective*: *a dishonourable action*. □ **déshonorant**
dis'honourably *adverb*. □ **de façon déshonorante**

disillusion [disi'luːʒən] *verb* to destroy the false but pleasant beliefs held by (a person): *I thought his job sounded interesting, but he soon disillusioned me*. □ **désabuser**
disil'lusionment *noun*. □ **désabusement**

disinclination [disinkli'neiʃən] *noun* unwillingness: *a disinclination to work*. □ **répugnance**
,disin'clined [-'klaind] *adjective* unwilling (to do something): *I am disinclined to help*. □ **peu disposé**

disinfect [disin'fekt] *verb* to destroy disease-causing germs in: *This sink should be disinfected regularly*. □ **désinfecter**
,disin'fectant *noun* a substance that destroys germs. □ **désinfectant**

disintegrate [dis'intigreit] *verb* to (cause to) fall to pieces: *The paper bag was so wet that the bottom disintegrated and all the groceries fell out*. □ **(se) désintégrer/désagréger**
dis,inte'gration *noun*. □ **désintégration**

disinterested [dis'intristid] *adjective* not influenced by private feelings or selfish motives: *a disinterested judgment*. □ **désintéressé**

disk, disc [disk] *noun* 1 a flat, thin, circular object: *From the earth, the full moon looks like a silver disk*. □ **disque**
2 a gramophone record. □ **disque**
3 in computing, a disk-shaped file. □ **disque**
disk jockey a person employed to present a program of

music (*usually* pop music) on the radio *etc*, from gramophone records. □ **animateur, trice**

dislike [dis'laik] *verb* not to like; to have strong feelings against: *I know she dislikes me.* □ **détester**
■ *noun* strong feeling directed against a thing, person or idea: *He doesn't go to football matches because of his dislike of crowds*; *She has few dislikes.* □ **aversion**
take a dislike to to begin to dislike: *The boss has taken a dislike to me.* □ **prendre en grippe**

dislocate ['dislɔukeit] *verb* to put (a bone) out of joint; to displace: *She dislocated her hip when she fell.* □ **disloquer**
,dislo'cation *noun.* □ **dislocation**

dislodge [dis'lɔdʒ] *verb* to knock out of place: *She accidentally dislodged a stone from the wall.* □ **faire tomber**

disloyal [dis'lɔiəl] *adjective* unfaithful or not loyal: *He has been very disloyal to his friends.* □ **déloyal**
dis'loyally *adverb.* □ **déloyalement**
dis'loyalty *noun.* □ **déloyauté**

dismal ['dizməl] *adjective* gloomy: *dismal news*; *Don't look so dismal!* □ **lugubre**
'dismally *adverb.* □ **lugubrement**

dismantle [dis'mantl] *verb* to pull down or take to pieces: *The wardrobe was so large we had to dismantle it to get it down the stairs.* □ **démonter**

dismay [dis'mei] *verb* to shock or upset: *We were dismayed by the bad news.* □ **consterner**
■ *noun* the state of being shocked or upset: *a shout of dismay.* □ **consternation**

dismiss [dis'mis] *verb* 1 to send or put away: *She dismissed him with a wave of the hand*; *Dismiss the idea from your mind!* □ **congédier, écarter, licencier**
2 to remove from office or employment: *He was dismissed from his post for being lazy.* □ **renvoyer**
3 to stop or close (a law-suit *etc*): *Case dismissed!* □ **rendre une fin de non-recevoir**
dis'missal *noun.* □ **renvoi**

dismount [dis'maunt] *verb* to get off a horse, bicycle *etc*: *I dismounted and pushed my bicycle up the hill.* □ **descendre**

disobey [disə'bei] *verb* to fail or refuse to do what is commanded: *He disobeyed my orders not to go into the road*; *He disobeyed his mother.* □ **désobéir**
,diso'bedience [-'biːdjəns] *noun* failing or refusing to obey: *You must be punished for your disobedience!* □ **désobéissance**
,diso'bedient [-'biːdjənt] *adjective* failing or refusing to obey: *a disobedient child.* □ **désobéissant**
,diso'bediently *adverb.* □ **en désobéissant**

disorder [dis'ɔːdə] *noun* 1 lack of order; confusion or disturbance: *The strike threw the whole country into disorder*; *scenes of disorder and rioting.* □ **désordre**
2 a disease: *a disorder of the lungs.* □ **trouble(s)**
dis'orderly *adjective* 1 not neatly arranged; in confusion: *His clothes lay in a disorderly heap.* □ **désordonné**
2 lawless; causing trouble: *a disorderly group of people.* □ **tumultueux**

disorganized, disorganised [dis'ɔːgənaizd] *adjective* in confusion or not organized: *a disorganized person*; *The meeting was very disorganized.* □ **désorganisé**

dis,organi'zation, dis,organi'sation *noun.* □ **désorganisation**

disown [dis'oun] *verb* to refuse to acknowledge as belonging to oneself: *to disown one's son.* □ **désavouer, renier**

dispatch [di'spatʃ] *verb* 1 to send off: *He dispatched several letters asking for financial help.* □ **expédier**
2 to finish off or deal with quickly: *She dispatched several pieces of business within the hour.* □ **expédier**
■ *noun* 1 a written official report: *a dispatch from the commanding officer.* □ **dépêche**
2 an act of sending away. □ **expédition**
3 haste. □ **rapidité**
dispatch rider a carrier of military dispatches by motorcycle. □ **estafette**

dispel [di'spel] – *past tense, past participle* **di'spelled** – *verb* to drive away: *Her words dispelled her fears.* □ **dissiper**

dispense [di'spens] *verb* 1 to give or deal out. □ **dispenser**
2 to prepare (medicines, *especially* prescriptions) for giving out. □ **préparer**
di'spensary – *plural* **di'spensaries** – *noun* a place especially in a hospital where medicines are given out. □ **pharmacie**
di'spenser *noun.* □ **dispensateur, trice, pharmacien, enne**
dispense with to get rid of or do without: *We could economize by dispensing with two assistants.* □ **se passer de**

disperse [di'spɔːs] *verb* 1 to (cause to) scatter in all directions: *Some seeds are dispersed by the wind.* □ **(se) disperser**
2 to (cause to) spread (news *etc*): *Information is dispersed by volunteers who distribute leaflets.* □ **(se) répandre**
3 to (cause to) vanish: *By this time the crowd had dispersed.* □ **(se) disperser**
di'spersal *noun.* □ **dispersion**

dispirited [di'spiritid] *adjective* sad and discouraged. □ **découragé**

displace [dis'pleis] *verb* 1 to disarrange or put out of place. □ **déplacer**
2 to take the place of: *The dog had displaced her doll in the little girl's affections.* □ **remplacer**
dis'placement *noun.* □ **déplacement, remplacement**
displaced person a person forced to leave his own country as a result of war *etc*. □ **personne déplacée**

display [di'splei] *verb* 1 to set out for show: *The china was displayed in a special cabinet.* □ **exposer**
2 to show: *She displayed a talent for mimicry.* □ **montrer**
■ *noun* 1 (an) act of showing or making clear: *a display of military strength.* □ **démonstration**
2 an entertainment *etc* intended to show the ability *etc* of those taking part: *a dancing display.* □ **manifestation**
3 something which shows or sets out something else: *an advertising display.* □ **exposition, étalage**

displease [dis'pliːz] *verb* to offend or annoy: *The children's behaviour displeased their father.* □ **déplaire**

dis'pleased *adjective*: *She was displeased with him for being late.* □ **fâché**

displeasure [dis'pleʒə] *noun* disapproval: *She showed her displeasure by leaving at once.* □ **déplaisir**

dispose [di'spouz] *verb* 1 to make inclined: *I am not disposed to help her.* □ **disposer**

2 to arrange or settle. □ **disposer**

di'sposable *adjective* intended to be thrown away or destroyed after use: *disposable cups/plates.* □ **jetable**

di'sposal *noun* the act of getting rid of something: *the disposal of waste paper.* □ **enlèvement, destruction**

at one's disposal available for one's use: *They put a car at his disposal during his stay.* □ **à la disposition de**

dispose of to get rid of: *I've disposed of your old coat.* □ **se débarrasser de**

disposition [dispə'ziʃən] *noun* personality: *She has a naturally calm disposition.* □ **caractère**

dispossess [dispə'zes] *verb* to take (property) away from: *He was dispossessed of all his lands.* □ **déposséder**

disproportionate [disprə'poːʃənət] *adjective* (*often with* **to**) too large or too small in relation to something else: *His head looks disproportionate (to his body).* □ **disproportionné (à/avec)**

,dispro'portionately *adverb*. □ **de façon disproportionnée**

disprove [dis'pruːv] *verb* to prove to be false or wrong: *Her theories have been disproved by modern scientific research.* □ **réfuter**

dispute [di'spjuːt] *verb* 1 to argue against or deny: *I'm not disputing what you say.* □ **contester**

2 to argue (about): *They disputed the ownership of the land for years.* □ **se disputer**

■ *noun* (an) argument or quarrel: *a dispute over wages.* □ **dispute**

di'sputable *adjective* able to be argued about: *Whether this change was an improvement is disputable.* □ **discutable**

,dispu'tation *noun* a formal argument. □ **débat**

disqualify [dis'kwolifai] *verb* 1 to put out of a competition *etc* for breaking rules: *She was disqualified for being too young.* □ **disqualifier**

2 to make unfit for some purpose: *His colour-blindness disqualified him for the air force.* □ **rendre inapte**

dis,qualifi'cation [-fi-] *noun*. □ **disqualification**

disquiet [dis'kwaiət] *noun* uneasiness: *a feeling of disquiet.* □ **inquiétude**

■ *verb* to make uneasy. □ **inquiéter**

disregard [disrə'gaːd] *verb* to ignore: *She disregarded my warnings.* □ **ne tenir aucun compte de**

■ *noun* lack of concern: *He has a complete disregard for his own safety.* □ **indifférence; mépris**

disrepair [disrə'peə] *noun* the state of needing repair: *The old house has fallen into disrepair.* □ **délabrement**

disrepute [disrə'pjuːt] *noun* bad reputation: *He has brought the family into disrepute.* □ **discrédit**

dis'reputable [-'repju-] *adjective* 1 not respectable, *especially* in appearance: *a disreputable old coat.* □ **miteux**

2 of bad reputation: *He's rather a disreputable charac-*ter. □ **peu recommandable**

disrespect [disrə'spekt] *noun* rudeness or lack of respect: *He spoke of his parents with disrespect.* □ **irrespect**

,disre'spectful *adjective* showing disrespect: *Never be disrespectful to older people.* □ **irrespectueux**

,disre'spectfully *adverb*. □ **irrespectueusement**

disrupt [dis'rʌpt] *verb* to break up or put into a state of disorder: *Rioters disrupted the meeting*; *Traffic was disrupted by floods.* □ **perturber**

dis'ruption [-ʃən] *noun*. □ **perturbation**

dis'ruptive [-tiv] *adjective* causing disorder: *a disruptive child.* □ **perturbateur**

dissatisfy [di'satisfai] *verb* to fail to satisfy or to displease: *The teacher was dissatisfied with the pupil's work.* □ **mécontenter**

dis,satis'faction [-'fakʃən] *noun*. □ **mécontentement**

dissect [di'sekt] *verb* to cut (*eg* an animal's body) into parts for (scientific) examination. □ **disséquer**

dis'section [-ʃən] *noun*. □ **dissection**

dissent [di'sent] *noun* disagreement: *There was a murmur of dissent.* □ **dissentiment**

■ *verb* (with **from**) to disagree: *I dissent from the general opinion.* □ **différer d'opinion (avec)**

dis'sension [-ʃən] *noun* disagreement: *The proposal caused a great deal of dissension.* □ **dissension**

dissertation [disə'teiʃən] *noun* a long formal talk or piece of writing (for a university degree *etc*). □ **exposé, mémoire**

disservice [dis'səːvis] *noun* an action which is not helpful. □ **mauvais service**

dissident ['disidənt] *noun, adjective* (a person) disagreeing, *especially* with a ruling group or form of government: *a demonstration by a large number of dissidents.* □ **dissident, ente; dissident**

'dissidence *noun*. □ **dissidence**

dissimilar [di'similə] *adjective* unlike or unalike: *The two cases are not dissimilar*; *The sisters have very dissimilar characters.* □ **dissemblable**

dis,simi'larity [-'la-] *noun*. □ **dissemblance**

dissociate [di'sousieit] *verb* 1 to separate, *especially* in thought. □ **dissocier**

2 to refuse to connect (oneself) (any longer) with: *I'm dissociating myself completely from their actions.* □ **se dissocier**

dissolute ['disəluːt] *adjective* bad or immoral: *dissolute behaviour.* □ **débauché**

'dissoluteness *noun*. □ **débauche**

dissolution *see* **dissolve**.

dissolve [di'zolv] *verb* 1 to (cause to) melt or break up, *especially* by putting in a liquid: *He dissolved the pills in water*; *The pills dissolved easily in water.* □ **(se) dissoudre**

2 to put an end to (a parliament, a marriage *etc*). □ **dissoudre**

dissolution [disə'luːʃən] *noun*: *the dissolution of Parliament.* □ **dissolution**

dissuade [di'sweid] *verb* to stop (from doing something) by advice or persuasion: *I tried to dissuade him from his foolish intention.* □ **dissuader**

dis'suasion [-ʒən] *noun*. □ **dissuasion**

distance ['distəns] *noun* **1** the space between things, places *etc*: *Some of the children have to walk long distances to school; It's quite a distance to the bus stop; It is difficult to judge distance when driving at night; What's the distance from here to Winnipeg?* □ **distance**
2 a far-off place or point: *We could see the town in the distance; He disappeared into the distance; The picture looks better at a distance.* □ **lointain**
'**distant** *adjective* **1** far away or far apart, in place or time: *the distant past; a distant country; Our house is two kilometres distant from the school.* □ **éloigné**
2 not close: *a distant relation.* □ **éloigné**
3 not friendly: *Her manner was rather distant.* □ **distant**
distaste [dis'teist] *noun* dislike (of something unpleasant): *She looked at the untidy room with distaste.* □ **dégoût**
dis'tasteful *adjective* disagreeable: *a distasteful job.* □ **désagréable**
dis'tastefully *adverb.* □ **avec dégoût**
dis'tastefulness *noun.* □ **caractère désagréable**
distemper [di'stempə] *noun* a kind of paint used on walls. □ **détrempe**
distended [di'stendəd] *adjective* stretched; swollen. □ **dilaté**
distill, distil [di'stil] – *past tense, past participle* **di'stilled** – *verb* **1** to get (a liquid) in a pure state by heating to steam or a vapour and cooling again. □ **distiller**
2 to obtain alcoholic spirit from anything by this method: *Whisky is distilled from barley.* □ **distiller**
,**distil'lation** *noun.* □ **distillation**
di'stiller *noun* a person or firm that distils and makes spirits: *a firm of whisky-distillers.* □ **distillateur**
di'stillery – *plural* **di'stilleries** – *noun* a place where distilling (of whisky, brandy *etc*) is carried on. □ **distillerie**
distinct [di'stiŋkt] *adjective* **1** easily seen, heard or noticed: *There are distinct differences between the two; Her voice is very distinct.* □ **clair**
2 separate or different: *Those two birds are quite distinct – you couldn't confuse them.* □ **distinct**
di'stinctly *adverb*: *He pronounces his words very distinctly; I distinctly heard him tell you to wait!* □ **distinctement**
di'stinctness *noun.* □ **clarté**
di'stinction [-ʃən] *noun* **1** (the making of) a difference: *He makes no distinction between male and female employees.* □ **distinction**
2 a grade awarded that indicates outstanding ability or achievement: *She passed her exams with distinction.* □ **mention**
di'stinctive [-tiv] *adjective* different and easily identified: *I recognized her from a long way off – she has a very distinctive walk!* □ **distinctif**
di'stinctively *adverb.* □ **distinctivement**
distinguish [di'stiŋgwiʃ] *verb* **1** (*often with* **from**) to mark as different: *What distinguishes this café from all the others?* □ **distinguer (de)**
2 to identify or make out: *He could just distinguish the figure of a man running away.* □ **distinguer**

3 (*sometimes with* **between**) to recognize a difference: *I can't distinguish (between) the two types – they both look the same to me.* □ **distinguer (entre)**
4 to make (oneself) noticed through one's achievements: *She distinguished herself at school by winning a prize in every subject.* □ **se distinguer**
di'stinguishable *adjective.* □ **distinguable**
di'stinguished *adjective* famous or outstanding: *a distinguished scientist.* □ **distingué**
distort [di'stoːt] *verb* **1** to make or become twisted out of shape: *Her face was distorted with pain; Metal distorts under stress.* □ **(se) déformer**
2 to make (sound) indistinct and unnatural: *Her voice sounded distorted on the telephone.* □ **déformer**
di'stortion [-ʃən] *noun.* □ **déformation**
distract [di'strakt] *verb* **1** to draw aside (the mind or attention of): *He was constantly being distracted from his work by the noisy conversation of his colleagues.* □ **distraire**
di'stracted *adjective* **1** turned aside (from what one is doing or thinking): *He had slipped out while her attention was distracted.* □ **distrait**
2 out of one's mind; mad: *a distracted old woman.* □ **égaré, fou**
3 distressed: *The distracted mother couldn't reach her child in the burning house.* □ **affolé**
di'straction [-ʃən] *noun* **1** something that takes the mind off other *especially* more serious affairs: *There are too many distractions here to allow one to work properly.* □ **distraction**
2 anxiety and confusion: *in a state of complete distraction.* □ **confusion, affolement**
distraught [di'stroːt] *adjective* very worried and upset. □ **angoissé**
distress [di'stres] *noun* **1** great sorrow, trouble or pain: *She was in great distress over his disappearance; Is your leg causing you any distress?; The loss of all their money left the family in acute distress.* □ **détresse**
2 a cause of sorrow: *My inability to draw has always been a distress to me.* □ **affliction**
■ *verb* to cause pain or sorrow to: *I'm distressed by your lack of interest.* □ **affliger**
di'stressing *adjective.* □ **affligeant**
di'stressingly *adverb.* □ **douloureusement**
distribute [di'stribjut] *verb* **1** to divide (something) among several (people); to deal out: *He distributed sweets to all the children in the class.* □ **partager, vendre**
2 to spread out widely: *Our shops are distributed all over the city.* □ **répandre, répartir**
,**distri'bution** [-'bjuː-] *noun.* □ **distribution**
district ['distrikt] *noun* an area of a country, town *etc*: *He lives in a poor district of Halifax; Public transport is often infrequent in country districts.* □ **région, quartier**
distrust [dis'trʌst] *noun* suspicion; lack of trust or faith: *He has always had a distrust of electrical gadgets.* □ **méfiance**
■ *verb* to have no trust in: *He distrusts his own judgment.* □ **se méfier**

dis'trustful *adjective.* □ **méfiant**
dis'trustfully *adverb.* □ **avec méfiance**
dis'trustfulness *noun.* □ **défiance**
disturb [di'stəːb] *verb* **1** to interrupt or take attention away from: *I'm sorry, am I disturbing you?* □ **déranger**
2 to worry or make anxious: *This news has disturbed me very much.* □ **troubler**
3 to stir up or throw into confusion: *A violent storm disturbed the surface of the lake.* □ **troubler, remuer**
di'sturbance *noun* **1** a noisy or disorderly happening: *She was thrown out of the meeting for causing a disturbance.* □ **tapage**
2 an interruption: *I've done quite a lot of work, despite several disturbances.* □ **dérangement**
3 an act of disturbing: *He was arrested for disturbance of the peace.* □ **trouble**
disturbing *adjective* upsetting, troubling or unsettling: *Joe's mother was unable to sleep after the disturbing news that Joe had been in an accident.* □ **inquiétant**
disuse [dis'juːs] *noun* the state of not being used: *The canal fell into disuse.* □ **abandon, désuétude**
dis'used [-'juːzd] *adjective: a disused warehouse.* □ **abandonné**
ditch [ditʃ] *noun* a long narrow hollow dug in the ground *especially* one to drain water from a field, road *etc*: *He climbed over the fence and fell into a ditch.* □ **fossé**
■ *verb* to get rid of: *The stolen car had been ditched by the thieves several kilometres away.* □ **abandonner**
ditty ['diti] – *plural* 'ditties – *noun* a simple little song. □ **chansonnette**
divan [di'van] *noun* a long, low couch without back or arms, *usually* able to be used as a bed. □ **divan**
dive [daiv] *verb* **1** to plunge headfirst into water or down through the air: *She dived off a rock into the sea.* □ **plonger**
2 to go quickly and suddenly out of sight: *She dived down a back street and into a shop.* □ **plonger, s'engouffrer**
■ *noun* an act of diving: *She did a beautiful dive into the deep end of the pool.* □ **plongeon**
'diver *noun* a person who dives, *especially* one who works under water using special breathing equipment. □ **plongeur, euse**
'diving board *noun* a platform from which to dive, erected beside a swimming pool. □ **plongeoir**
great diving beetle a water insect that carries a bubble of air under its wing cover for breathing when it is under water. □ **dytique**
diverge [dai'vəːdʒ] *verb* **1** to separate and go in different directions: *The roads diverge three kilometres further on.* □ **diverger**
2 to differ (from someone or something else); to go away (from a standard): *This is where our opinions diverge.* □ **diverger**
di'vergence *noun.* □ **divergence**
di'vergent *adjective.* □ **divergent**
diverse [dai'vəːs] *adjective* different; of various kinds. □ **divers**
di'versely *adverb.* □ **diversement**
di'verseness *noun.* □ **diversité**

di'versify [-fai] *verb* to make or become varied or different. □ **(se) diversifier**
di'versity *noun* variety. □ **diversité**
diversion [dai'vəːʃən] *noun* **1** an alteration to a traffic route: *There's a diversion at the end of the road.* □ **déviation**
2 (an act of) diverting attention. □ **diversion**
3 (an) amusement. □ **distraction**
diversity *see* **diverse**.
divert [dai'vəːt] *verb* **1** to cause to turn aside or change direction: *Traffic had to be diverted because of the accident.* □ **détourner**
2 to amuse or entertain. □ **diverter**
divide [di'vaid] *verb* **1** to separate into parts or groups: *The wall divided the garden in two; The group divided into three when we got off the bus; We are divided (= We do not agree) as to where to spend our holidays.* □ **(se) diviser**
2 (*with* **between** *or* **among**) to share: *We divided the sweets between us.* □ **diviser (entre)**
3 to find out how many times one number contains another: *6 divided by 2 equals 3.* □ **diviser**
di'viders *noun plural* a measuring instrument used in geometry. □ **compas**
divisible [di'vizəbl] *adjective* able to be divided: *100 is divisible by 4.* □ **divisible**
division [di'viʒən] *noun* **1** (an) act of dividing. □ **division**
2 something that separates; a dividing line: *a ditch marks the division between their two fields.* □ **séparation**
3 a part or section (of an army *etc*): *She belongs to B division of the local police force.* □ **division**
4 (a) separation of thought; disagreement. □ **désaccord**
5 the finding of how many times one number is contained in another. □ **division**
divisional [di'viʒənl] *adjective* of a division: *The soldier contacted divisional headquarters.* □ **divisionnaire**
dividend ['dividend] *noun* the interest paid on shares *etc*: *a dividend of 2%.* □ **dividende**
divine [di'vain] *adjective* **1** of or belonging to God or a god: *divine wisdom.* □ **divin**
2 very good or excellent: *What divine weather!* □ **divin, admirable**
■ *verb* to find out by keen understanding: *I managed to divine the truth.* □ **deviner**
,divi'nation [divi-] *noun.* □ **divination**
di'viner *noun* a person who has or claims a special ability to find hidden water or metals. □ **devin, devineresse, sourcier, ière**
di'vining *noun* discovering the presence of underground water, metal *etc* by holding a **di'vining rod** which moves when held directly above the water *etc*: *water-divining.* □ **radiesthésie**
di'vinity [-'vi-] – *plural* **di'vinities** – *noun* **1** religious studies. □ **théologie**
2 a god or goddess: *The ancient Greeks worshipped many divinities.* □ **divinité**
3 the state of being divine: *the divinity of God.* □ **divinité**
divisible, division *etc see* **divide**.
divorce [di'vɔːs] *noun* the legal ending of a marriage:

Divorce is becoming more common nowadays. □ **divorce**

■ *verb* **1** to end one's marriage (with): *He's divorcing her for desertion; They were divorced two years ago.* □ **divorcer (d'avec)**

2 to separate: *You can't divorce these two concepts.* □ **séparer**

dizzy ['dizi] *adjective* **1** giddy or confused: *If you spin around and around like that, you'll make yourself dizzy.* □ **pris de vertige**

2 causing dizziness: *dizzy heights.* □ **vertigineux**

'**dizzily** *adverb.* □ **vertigineusement**

'**dizziness** *noun.* □ **vertige(s)**

do [duː] – *3rd person singular present tense* **does** [dʌz]: *past tense* **did** [did]: *past participle* **done** [dʌn]: *negative short forms* **don't** [dount], **doesn't** ['dʌznt], **didn't** ['didnt] – *verb* **1** used with a more important verb in questions and negative statements: *Do you smoke?*

2 used with a more important verb for emphasis: *I do think you should apologize; I did see him after all.*

3 used to avoid repeating a verb which comes immediately before: *I thought she wouldn't come, but she did.*

4 used with a more important verb after **seldom**, **rarely** and **little**: *Little did he know what was in store for him.*

5 to carry out or perform: *What shall I do?; That was a terrible thing to do.* □ **faire**

6 to manage to finish or complete: *When you've done that, you can start on this; We did a hundred kilometres in an hour.* □ **faire, finir**

7 to perform some obvious action concerning: *to do the washing; to do the garden/the windows.* □ **faire**

8 to be enough or suitable for a purpose: *Will this piece of fish do two of us?; That'll do nicely; Do you want me to look for a blue one or will a pink one do?; Will next Saturday do for our next meeting?* □ **aller**

9 to work at or study: *She's doing sums; He's at university doing science.* □ **faire, étudier**

10 to manage or prosper: *How's your wife doing?; My son is doing well at school.* □ **aller**

11 to put in order or arrange: *She's doing her hair.* □ **arranger**

12 to act or behave: *Why don't you do as we do?* □ **faire, agir**

13 to give or show: *The whole family gathered to do her honour.* □ **faire**

14 to cause: *What damage did the storm do?; It won't do him any harm.* □ **faire**

15 to see everything and visit everything in: *They tried to do New York in four days.* □ **visiter, faire**

■ *noun* – *plural* **do's** – an affair or a festivity, especially a party: *The school is having a do for Christmas.* □ **réception, fête**

'**doer** *noun* a person who does something: *an evildoer; a doer of good deeds.* □ **auteur, eure d'une action**

'**doings** *noun plural* the things which a person does: *He tells me about all your doings.* □ **faits et gestes**

done [dʌn] *adjective* **1** finished or complete: *That's that job done at last.* □ **fini, accompli**

2 (of food) completely cooked and ready to eat: *I don't think the meat is quite done yet.* □ **cuit**

3 socially accepted: *the done thing.* □ **qui se fait**

,**do-it-your'self** *noun, adjective* (of) the art or practice of doing one's own decorating, repairs *etc*: *I've just bought a book on do-it-yourself so I can try to tile the bathroom; a do-it-yourself job.* □ **bricolage, de bricolage**

to-'do a fuss: *a tremendous to-do about the missing papers.* □ **histoire, affaire**

I, he *etc* **could be doing with/could do with** it would be better if I, he *etc* had or did (something): *I could do with a cup of coffee.* □ **avoir envie/besoin de**

do away with to get rid of: *They did away with uniforms at that school years ago.* □ **supprimer**

do for to kill or cause the end of: *That attack of flu almost did for him.* □ **démolir, tuer**

done for ruined, defeated or about to be killed *etc*: *The police are coming – run for it or we're done for!* □ **fichu**

done in exhausted. □ **claqué**

do out to clean thoroughly: *The room's tidy – I did it out yesterday.* □ **nettoyer (à fond)**

do out of to prevent from getting, *especially* by using dishonest methods: *My boss tried to do me out of a day's holiday.* □ **frustrer (de)**

do's and don'ts [dounts] rules or advice for action: *If you want to lose weight, I can give you a list of do's and don'ts.* □ **ce qu'il faut faire et ne pas faire**

do someone a favour *verb* to do a kindness for someone without expecting anything in return: *Do me a favour and buy a coffee when you're out.* □ **rendre service**

do without to manage without and accept the lack of: *We'll just have to do without a phone; If you're too lazy to fetch the ice cream you can just do without; I can do without your opinion, if you don't mind.* □ **se passer de**

to do with 1 (*with* have) to have dealings with: *I never had anything to do with the neighbours.* □ **avoir affaire à**

2 (*with* have) to be involved in, *especially* to be (partly) responsible for: *Did you have anything to do with her death?* □ **être mêlé à**

3 (*with* have) to be connected with: *Has this decision anything to do with what I said yesterday?* □ **avoir un rapport avec**

4 (*with* be *or* have) to be about or concerned with: *This letter is/has to do with Bill's plans for the summer.* □ **concerner, avoir rapport à**

5 (*with* have) to be the concern of: *I'm sorry, but that question has nothing to do with me; What has that (got) to do with him?* □ **avoir (qqch.) à voire (avec)**

what are you *etc* **doing with 1** why or how have you *etc* got: *What are you doing with my umbrella?* □ **Que faites-vous avec**

2 what action are you *etc* taking about: *What are they doing with the children during the day if they're both working?* □ **Que faites-vous de**

docile ['dousail, 'dosl] *adjective* (of a person or animal) quiet and easy to manage: *a docile child/pony.* □ **docile**

'**docilely** *adverb.* □ **docilement**

do'cility [də'si-] *noun.* □ **docilité**

dock¹ [dok] *noun* **1** a deepened part of a harbour *etc* where ships go for loading, unloading, repair *etc*: *The ship was in dock for three weeks.* □ **bassin**

2 the area surrounding this: *He works down at the docks.* □ **quais**

3 the box in a law court where the accused person sits or stands. □ **banc des accusés**

■ *verb* to (cause to) enter a dock and tie up alongside a quay: *The liner docked in Southampton this morning.* □ **(se) mettre à quai**

'**docker** *noun* a person who works in the docks. □ **débardeur, euse**

'**dockyard** *noun* a naval harbour with docks, stores *etc*. □ **chantier naval**

dock² [dok] *verb* to cut short or remove part from: *The dog's tail had been docked*; *Her wages were docked to pay for the broken window.* □ **couper, retenir**

dockyard *see* **dock¹**.

doctor ['dokta] *noun* **1** (*often abbreviated to* **Dr.** *when written in titles*) a person who is trained to treat ill people: *Doctor Davidson*; *You should call the doctor if you are ill*; *I'll have to go to the doctor.* □ **docteur, eure, médecin**

2 (*often abbreviated to* **Dr.** *when written in titles*) a person who has gained the higest university degree in any subject. □ **docteur, eure**

■ *verb* **1** to interfere with; to add something to: *Someone had doctored her drink.* □ **trafiquer**

2 to treat with medicine *etc*: *I'm doctoring my cold with aspirin.* □ **soigner**

'**doctorate** [-rət] *noun* the degree of Doctor. □ **doctorat**

doctrine ['doktrin] *noun* a belief or set of beliefs which is taught: *religious doctrines.* □ **doctrine**

document ['dokjumənt] *noun* a written statement giving information, proof, evidence *etc*: *She signed several legal documents relating to the sale of her house.* □ **document**

,**docu'mentary** [-'men-] *adjective* of or found in documents: *documentary evidence.* □ **documentaire**

■ *noun – plural* **docu'mentaries** – a film, program *etc* giving information on a certain subject: *a documentary on the political situation in Argentina.* □ **documentaire**

dodge [dodʒ] *verb* to avoid (something) by a sudden and/or clever movement: *She dodged the blow*; *He dodged around the corner out of sight*; *Politicians are very good at dodging difficult questions.* □ **esquiver**

■ *noun* **1** an act of dodging. □ **mouvement de côté**

2 a trick: *You'll never catch him – he knows every dodge there is.* □ **truc, combine**

doe [dou] *noun* the female of certain deer, and of the rabbit, hare *etc*. □ **biche, lapine, hase**

doer, does, doesn't *see* **do**.

dog [dog] *noun* a domestic, meat-eating animal related to the wolf and fox. □ **chien**

■ *adjective* (*usually* of members of the dog family) male: *a dog-fox.* □ **mâle**

■ *verb – past tense, past participle* **dogged** – to follow closely as a dog does: *She dogged his footsteps.* □ **talonner**

dogged ['dogid] *adjective* keeping on at what one is doing in a determined and persistent manner: *his dogged perseverance.* □ **tenace**

'**doggedly** [-gid-] *adverb*: *He went doggedly on with his work despite the interruptions.* □ **avec ténacité**

'**doggedness** [-gid-] *noun*. □ **ténacité**

'**dog biscuit** *noun* a small hard biscuit fed to dogs. □ **biscuit pour chien**

'**dog collar** a stiff round collar worn by a clergyman. □ **col de pasteur**

'**dog-eared** *adjective* (of a book) having the pages turned down at the corner: *dog-eared volumes*; *Several pages were dog-eared.* □ **écorné**

,**dog-'tired** *adjective* very tired: *I'm dog-tired this morning after sitting up all night in the train.* □ **crevé**

a dog's life a wretched existence: *He leads a dog's life.* □ **vie de chien**

go to the dogs to be ruined, *especially* to ruin oneself. □ **péricliter**

in the doghouse in disgrace: *I forgot my friend's birthday, so I'm in the doghouse.* □ **en disgrâce**

not a dog's chance no chance at all: *He hasn't a dog's chance of getting a ticket.* □ **pas la moindre chance**

dogged *see* **dog**.

doggerel ['dogərəl] *noun* bad poetry. □ **vers de mirliton**

doggo ['dogou]: **to lie doggo** to remain in hiding without giving any sign of one's presence. □ **faire le mort**

dogma ['dogmə] *noun* opinions settled or fixed by an authority, *eg* the Church. □ **dogme**

dogmatic [dog'matik] *adjective* tending to force one's own opinions on other people: *She's very dogmatic on this subject.* □ **autoritaire**

dog'matically *adverb*. □ **dogmatiquement**

doings *see* **do**.

dole [doul] *verb* (*usually with* **out**) to hand or give out shares of: *She doled out the food.* □ **distribuer parcimonieusement**

■ *noun* (*with* **the**) a slang word for the payment made by the state to an unemployed person: *She's on the dole.* □ **(au) chômage**

doleful ['doulful] *adjective* sorrowful: *a doleful expression.* □ **triste**

'**dolefully** *adverb*. □ **tristement**

'**dolefulness** *noun*. □ **tristesse**

doll [dol] *noun* a toy in the shape of a small human being: *a china doll.* □ **poupée**

dollar ['dolə] *noun* (*usually abbreviated to* **$** *when written*) the standard unit of currency in several countries, *eg* Canada, the United States, Australia, Singapore: *It costs ten dollars/$10.* □ **dollar**

dolly ['doli] – *plural* '**dollies** – *noun* a child's word for a doll. □ **poupée**

dolphin ['dolfin] *noun* a type of sea-animal about two and a half to three metres long, closely related to the porpoise. □ **dauphin**

domain [də'mein] *noun* **1** an old word for the lands which belong to a person: *the king's domains.* □ **domaine**

2 one's area of interest or of knowledge: *That question is outside my domain.* □ **domaine**

dome [doum] *noun* a roof shaped like half a ball: *the dome of the cathedral.* □ **dôme**

domed *adjective* having or resembling a dome: *a domed forehead.* □ **bombé**

domestic [də'mestik] *adjective* **1** of or in the house or home: *a domestic servant*; *domestic utensils.* □ **de maison**

2 concerning one's private life or family: *domestic problems.* □ **familial**

3 (of animals) tame and living with or used by people. □ **domestique**

4 not foreign: *a government's domestic policy.* □ **intérieur**

do'mesticated [-keitid] *adjective* **1** (of animals) accustomed to living near and being used by people: *Cows and sheep have been domesticated for many thousands of years.* □ **domestiqué**

2 good at doing jobs associated with running a house: *My husband has become very domesticated since I've been ill.* □ **d'intérieur**

do,mesti'cation *noun.* □ **domestication**

domesticity [doume'stisəti] *noun* (fondness for) home life. □ **vie de famille**

domestic help (a person paid to give) assistance with housework *etc.* □ **employé, ée de maison**

dominant ['dominənt] *adjective* ruling; most important; strongest: *the dominant group in society*; *Green was the dominant colour in the room.* □ **dominant**

'dominance *noun.* □ **(pré)dominance**

'dominate [-neit] *verb* **1** to have command or influence (over): *The stronger man dominates the weaker.* □ **dominer**

2 to be most strong or most noticeable *etc* (in): *The skyline is dominated by the castle.* □ **dominer**

,domi'nation *noun.* □ **domination**

domineering [domi'niəriŋ] *adjective* tending to order people about: *a domineering older brother.* □ **dominateur**

dominion [də'minjən] *noun* **1** rule or power: *There was no one left to challenge his dominion.* □ **domination**

2 a self-governing country of the British Commonwealth: *the Dominion of Canada.* □ **dominion**

domino ['dominou] – *plural* **'dominoes** – *noun* an oblong piece of wood *etc* marked with spots with which the game of **'dominoes** is played. □ **domino**

donate ['douneit, -'neit] *verb* to give to a fund *etc*: *She donated $100 to the fund.* □ **faire don de**

do'nation *noun* a gift of money or goods to a fund or collection: *All donations are welcome.* □ **don**

donor ['dounə] *noun* a giver of a gift or of a part of the body used to replace a diseased part of someone else's body: *The new piano in the hall is the gift of an anonymous donor*; *a kidney donor*; *a blood donor.* □ **donateur, trice; donneur, euse**

done *see* **do.**

donkey ['doŋki] *noun* **1** a domesticated animal with long ears related to the horse but smaller. □ **âne, ânesse**

2 a stupid person: *Don't be such a donkey!* □ **âne, imbécile**

'donkey work *noun* hard, uninteresting work: *We have a computer now, which saves us a lot of donkey work.* □ **le gros travail**

donkey's years/ages a very long time: *It's donkey's years since I was last there.* □ **une éternité**

donor *see* **donate.**

don't *see* **do.**

doodle ['duːdl] *verb* to make meaningless drawings and scribbles, *usually* while thinking, talking on the telephone *etc.* □ **griffonner (distraitement)**

■ *noun* a drawing of this sort. □ **griffonnage (distrait)**

doom [duːm] *noun* fate, *especially* something terrible and final which is about to happen (to one): *The whole place had an atmosphere of doom*; *Her doom was inevitable.* □ **ruine, perte**

■ *verb* to condemn; to make certain to come to harm, fail *etc*: *His crippled leg doomed him to long periods of unemployment*; *The project was doomed to failure*; *He was doomed from the moment he first took drugs.* □ **condamner**

door [doːz] *noun* **1** the *usually* hinged barrier, *usually* of wood, which closes the entrance of a room, house *etc*: *She knocked loudly on the door.* □ **porte**

2 a means of achieving something: *the door to success.* □ **porte, voie**

'doorknob *noun* a knob-shaped handle for opening and closing a door. □ **poignée de porte**

'doorman *noun* a man on duty at the door of a hotel, store *etc.* □ **portier**

'doormat *noun* a mat kept in front of the door for people to wipe their feet on. □ **paillasson**

'doorstep *noun* a raised step just outside the door of a house. □ **pas de porte**

'doorway *noun* the space usually filled by a door: *She was standing in the doorway.* □ **(embrasure de) porte**

on one's doorstep very close to where one lives: *The Laurentians are on our doorstep.* □ **à la porte de (qqn)**

dope [doup] *noun* any drug or drugs: *He was accused of stealing dope from the chemist.* □ **drogue**

■ *verb* to drug: *They discovered that the racehorse had been doped.* □ **doper**

'dopey *adjective* made stupid (as if) by drugs: *I was dopey from lack of sleep.* □ **abruti**

dormant ['doːmənt] *adjective* not dead but not active: *a dormant volcano.* □ **en veilleuse**

dormitory ['doːmitori] – *plural* **'dormitories** – *noun* a room used for sleeping in, with many beds. □ **dortoir**

dorsal ['doːsəl] *adjective* of the back: *a shark's dorsal fin.* □ **dorsal**

dose [dous] *noun* **1** the quantity of medicine *etc* to be taken at one time: *It's time you had a dose of your medicine.* □ **dose**

2 an unpleasant thing (*especially* an illness) which one is forced to suffer: *a nasty dose of flu.* □ **attaque**

■ *verb* to give medicine to: *She dosed him with aspirin.* □ **administrer (un médicament)**

'dosage [-sidʒ] *noun* the size of, or method of giving, a dose of medicine *etc*: *What is the dosage for a child of five?* □ **posologie**

dossier ['dosiei] *noun* a set of papers containing information *etc* about a person or a particular matter. □ **dossier**

dot [dot] *noun* a small, round mark: *She marked the pa-*

per with a dot. □ **point**

'dotted *adjective* **1** consisting of dots: *a dotted line.* □ **pointillé**

2 having dots: *dotted material.* □ **à pois**

dote [dout]: **dote on** to be fond of to an extent which is foolish: *He just dotes on that child!* □ **raffoler de**

dotted *see* **dot.**

double ['dʌbl] *adjective* **1** of twice the (usual) weight, size *etc*: *A double whisky, please.* □ **double**

2 two of a sort together or occurring in pairs: *double doors.* □ **double**

3 consisting of two parts or layers: *a double thickness of paper*; *a double meaning.* □ **double**

4 for two people: *a double bed.* □ **pour deux personnes**

■ *adverb* **1** twice: *I gave her double the usual quantity.* □ **deux fois**

2 in two: *The coat had been folded double.* □ **en deux**

■ *noun* **1** a double quantity: *Whatever you earn, I earn double.* □ **le double**

2 someone who is exactly like another: *He is my father's double.* □ **sosie**

■ *verb* **1** to (cause to) become twice as large or numerous: *He doubled his income in three years*; *Road accidents have doubled since 1960.* □ **doubler**

2 to have two jobs or uses: *This sofa doubles as a bed.* □ **servir aussi de**

'doubles *noun singular* or *noun plural* in tennis *etc*, a kind of match with two players on each side: *I enjoy playing doubles*; *(also adjective) a doubles match.* □ **double; de double**

double agent a spy paid by each of two countries hostile to each other. □ **agent, ente double**

double bass [beis] a type of large stringed instrument, the largest and deepest in sound of the violin family. □ **contrebasse**

,double-'bedded *adjective* containing a double bed: *a double-bedded room.* □ **à grand lit**

,double-'cross *verb* to betray (someone for whom one has already arranged to do something deceitful). □ **trahir, doubler**

,double-'dealing *noun* cheating and deceitfulness. □ **double jeu**

■ *adjective* cheating: *You double-dealing liar!* □ **hypocrite, faux**

,double-'decker *noun* a bus *etc* having two decks or levels. □ **autobus à impériale**

■ *adjective: a double-decker bus.* □ **à impériale**

double figures the numbers between 10 and 99: *The number of times you have been late is well into double figures.* □ **nombre à deux chiffres**

,double-'quick *adjective, adverb* very quick(ly): *Get here double-quick/in double-quick time!* □ **(en un temps) record**

at (or on) the double very quickly: *She came up the road at the double and rushed into the house.* □ **au pas de course**

double back to turn and go back the way one came: *The fox doubled back and went down a hole.* □ **revenir sur ses pas**

double up 1 to (cause to) bend or collapse suddenly at

the waist: *We (were) doubled up with laughter*; *He received a blow in the stomach which doubled him up.* □ **(se) plier (en deux)**

2 to join up in pairs: *There weren't enough desks, so some pupils had to double up.* □ **partager**

see double to see two images of everything instead of only one: *When I first met the twins, I thought I was seeing double, they were so alike.* □ **voir double**

doubt [daut] *verb* **1** to feel uncertain about, but inclined not to believe: *I doubt if he'll come now*; *She might have a screwdriver, but I doubt it.* □ **douter (que/de)**

2 not to be sure of the reliability of: *Sometimes I doubt your intelligence!* □ **avoir des doutes sur**

■ *noun* a feeling of not being sure and sometimes of being suspicious: *There is some doubt as to what happened*; *I have doubts about that place.* □ **doute**

'doubtful *adjective* **1** feeling doubt; uncertain what to think, expect *etc*: *She is doubtful about the future of the school.* □ **incertain**

2 able to be doubted; not clear: *The meaning is doubtful*; *a doubtful result.* □ **incertain, indécis**

3 uncertain but rather unlikely, unhopeful *etc*: *It is doubtful whether this will work*; *a doubtful improvement.* □ **douteux**

4 suspicious: *He's rather a doubtful character.* □ **louche**

'doubtfully *adverb.* □ **d'une manière douteuse**

'doubtfulness *noun.* □ **incertitude**

'doubtless *adverb* probably: *John has doubtless told you about me.* □ **sans aucun doute**

beyond (a) doubt certain(ly): *Beyond doubt, they will arrive tomorrow*; *Her honesty is beyond doubt.* □ **indubitable; indubitablement**

in doubt uncertain: *The result of the dispute is still in doubt.* □ **indécis**

no doubt surely; probably: *No doubt you would like to see your bedroom*; *He will come back again tomorrow, no doubt.* □ **sans doute**

dough [dou] *noun* a mass of flour moistened and kneaded but not baked. □ **pâte**

'doughnut, donut [-nʌt] *noun* a small ring-shaped cake, with a hole in the middle, fried in fat. □ **beigne**

dove [dʌv] *noun* a kind of pigeon. □ **colombe**

dowdy ['daudi] *adjective* (of dress *etc*) not smart; unfashionable. □ **démodé**

down[1] [daun] *adverb* **1** towards or in a low or lower position, level or state: *She climbed down to the bottom of the ladder.* □ **vers le bas, en bas**

2 on or to the ground: *The little boy fell down and cut his knee.* □ **par terre**

3 from earlier to later times: *The recipe has been handed down in our family for years.* □ **jusqu'à**

4 from a greater to a smaller size, amount *etc*: *Prices have been going down steadily.* □ **en/de moins**

5 towards or in a place thought of as being lower, especially southward or away from a centre: *We drove down from Montreal to Burlington.*

■ *preposition* **1** in a lower position on: *Their house is halfway down the hill.* □ **plus bas**

2 to a lower position on, by, through or along: *Water poured down the drain.* □ **vers le/en bas**

3 along: *The teacher's gaze travelled slowly down the line of children.* □ **le long de**

■ *verb* to finish (a drink) very quickly, *especially* in one gulp: *She downed a large glass of beer.* □ **s'envoyer**

'downward *adjective* leading, moving *etc* down: *a downward curve.* □ **descendant**

'downward(s) *adverb* towards a lower position or state: *The path led downward(s) towards the sea.* □ **vers le bas**

down-and-'out *noun, adjective* (a person) having no money and no means of earning a living: *a hostel for down-and-outs.* □ **clochard, arde; sans le sou**

,down-at-'heel *adjective* shabby, untidy and not well looked after or well-dressed. □ **miteux**

'downcast *adjective* (of a person) depressed; in low spirits: *a downcast expression.* □ **abattu**

'downfall *noun* a disastrous fall, *especially* a final failure or ruin: *the downfall of our hopes.* □ **chute, ruine**

,down'grade *verb* to reduce to a lower level, *especially* of importance: *His job was downgraded.* □ **déclasser**

,down'hearted *adjective* depressed and in low spirits, *especially* lacking the inclination to carry on with something: *Don't be downhearted! – we may yet win.* □ **découragé**

,down'hill *adverb* **1** down a slope: *The road goes downhill all the way from our house to yours.* □ **en descendant**

2 towards a worse and worse state: *We expected him to die, I suppose, because he's been going steadily downhill for months.* □ **sur le déclin**

,down-in-the-'mouth *adjective* miserable; in low spirits. □ **abattu**

down payment a payment in cash, *especially* to begin the purchase of something for which further payments will be made over a period of time. □ **acompte**

'downpour *noun* a very heavy fall of rain. □ **averse**

'downright *adverb* plainly; there's no other word for it: *I think she was downright rude!* □ **franchement**

■ *adjective*: *He is a downright nuisance!* □ **direct, absolu**

'downstairs *adjective*, **,down'stairs** *adverb* on or towards a lower floor: *She walked downstairs; I left my book downstairs; a downstairs flat.* □ **du bas; en bas**

,down'stream *adverb* further along a river towards the sea: *We found/rowed the boat downstream.* □ **en aval**

,down-to-'earth *adjective* practical and not concerned with theories, ideals *etc*: *She is a sensible, down-to-earth person.* □ **terre-à-terre**

'downtown *adjective* the part (of a city) containing the main centres for business and shopping: *downtown Manhattan.* □ **du centre (ville)**

,down'town *adverb* in or towards this area: *to go downtown; I was downtown yesterday.* □ **en ville**

'downtrodden *adjective* badly treated; treated without respect: *a downtrodden wife.* □ **opprimé**

be/come down with to be or become ill with: *The children all came down with measles.* □ **tomber malade de**

down on one's luck having bad luck. □ **malchanceux**

down tools to stop working: *When she was sacked her*

fellow workers downed tools and walked out. □ **débrayer**

down with get rid of: *Down with the dictator!* □ **à bas**

get down to to begin working seriously at or on: *I must get down to some letters!* □ **se mettre à**

suit (someone) down to the ground to suit perfectly: *That arrangement will suit me down to the ground.* □ **aller comme un gant**

down² [daun] *noun* small, soft feathers: *a quilt filled with down.* □ **duvet**

'downy *adjective* soft, like feathers: *the baby's downy hair.* □ **duveteux**

dowry ['dauəri] – *plural* **'dowries** – *noun* money and property brought by a woman to her husband when they marry. □ **dot**

doze [douz] *verb* to sleep lightly for short periods: *The old lady dozed in her chair.* □ **sommeiller**

■ *noun* a short sleep. □ **petit somme**

doze off to go into a light sleep. □ **s'assoupir**

dozen ['dʌzn] – *plurals* **'dozens**, (after a number or a word signifying a quantity) **'dozen** – *noun* a group of twelve: *two dozen handkerchiefs; These eggs are 50 cents a dozen; Half-a-dozen eggs, please.* □ **douzaine**

dozens (of) very many: *I've been there dozens of times.* □ **des douzaines (de)**

drab [drab] *adjective* dull and uninteresting, *especially* in colour: *drab clothes.* □ **terne**

'drably *adverb.* □ **de façon terne**

'drabness *noun.* □ **aspect/caractère terne**

drachma ['drakmə] *noun* the standard unit of Greek currency. □ **drachme**

draft [draːft] *noun* **1** a rough sketch or outline of something, *especially* written: *a rough draft of my speech.* □ **brouillon**

2 a group (of soldiers *etc*) taken from a larger group. □ **détachement**

3 a movement of air, *especially* one which causes discomfort in a room or which helps a fire to burn: *We increase the heat in the furnace by increasing the draft; There's a dreadful draft in this room!* □ **tirage, courant d'air**

4 an order (to a bank *etc*) for the payment of money: *a draft for $80.* □ **mandat**

5 a quantity of liquid drunk at once without stopping: *He took a long draft of beer.* □ **trait, gorgée**

6 the amount of water a ship requires to float it: *a draft of half a metre.* □ **tirant d'eau**

7 conscription: *He emigrated to avoid the draft.* □ **conscription**

■ *verb* **1** to make in the form of a rough plan: *Could you draft a report on this?* □ **esquisser**

2 In the US, to conscript into the army *etc*: *He was drafted into the navy.* □ **incorporer**

'drafty *adjective* full of draughts of air: *a drafty room.* □ **plein de courants d'air**

draftsman, draftswoman ['draːftsmən, 'draːftswumən] – *plural* **'draftsmen**, **'draftswomen** – *noun* a person who is good at or employed in making drawings: *My friend is a draftswoman in a firm of engineers.* □ **dessinateur, trice**

drag [drag] – *past tense, past participle* **dragged** – *verb* 1 to pull, *especially* by force or roughly: *She was dragged screaming from her car.* □ tirer, entraîner
2 to pull (something) slowly (*usually* because heavy): *She dragged the heavy table across the floor.* □ traîner
3 to (cause to) move along the ground: *His coat was so long it dragged on the ground at the back.* □ traîner
4 to search (the bed of a lake *etc*) by using a net or hook: *Police are dragging the canal to try to find the body.* □ draguer
5 to be slow-moving and boring: *The evening dragged a bit.* □ traîner en longueur
■ *noun* 1 something which slows something down: *He felt that his lack of education was a drag on his progress.* □ entrave
2 an act of drawing in smoke from a cigarette *etc*: *He took a long drag at his cigarette.* □ bouffée
3 something or someone that is dull and boring: *Washing up is a drag.* □ corvée, casse-pieds
4 a slang word for women's clothes when worn by men. □ vêtements de travesti

dragon ['dragən] *noun* a mythical beast, a *usually* large, winged, fire-breathing reptile: *St. George and the dragon.* □ dragon

dragonfly ['dragənflai] *noun* a kind of insect with a long body and double wings. □ libellule

drain [drein] *verb* 1 to clear (land) of water by the use of ditches and pipes: *There are plans to drain the marsh.* □ drainer
2 (of water) to run away: *The water drained away/off into the ditch.* □ s'écouler
3 to pour off the water *etc* from or allow the water *etc* to run off from: *Would you drain the vegetables?*; *He drained the fuel tank; The blood drained from her face.* □ égoutter
4 to drink everything contained in: *He drained his glass.* □ vider
5 to use up completely (the money, strength *etc* of): *The effort drained all her energy.* □ épuiser
■ *noun* 1 something (a ditch, trench, waterpipe *etc*) designed to carry away water: *The heavy rain has caused several drains to overflow.* □ canal/tuyau d'écoulement
2 something which slowly exhausts a supply, *especially* of one's money or strength: *His car is a constant drain on his money.* □ saignée, hémorragie
'**drainage** [-nidʒ] *noun* the process, method or system of carrying away extra water: *The town's drainage is very efficient.* □ drainage, système d'égouts
'**draining-board** *noun* the area at the side of a sink grooved and sloping to allow water from dishes to drain away. □ égouttoir
'**drainpipe** *noun* a pipe which carries water from the roof of a building to the ground. □ gouttière
down the drain wasted: *We had to scrap everything and start again – six months' work down the drain!* □ fichu

drake [dreik] *noun* a male duck. □ canard mâle

drama ['dra:mə] *noun* 1 a play for acting on the stage: *She has just produced a new drama.* □ pièce de théâtre
2 plays for the stage in general: *modern drama.* □ théâtre

3 the art of acting in plays: *He studied drama at college.* □ art dramatique
4 exciting events: *Life here is full of drama.* □ drame
dramatic [drə'matik] *adjective* 1 of or in the form of a drama: *a dramatic entertainment.* □ dramatique
2 vivid or striking: *a dramatic improvement; She made a dramatic entrance.* □ spectaculaire
3 (of a person) showing (too) much feeling or emotion: *She's very dramatic about everything.* □ théâtral
dra'**matically** *adverb.* □ de manière théâtrale
'**dramatist** ['dra-] *noun* a writer of plays. □ dramaturge
'**dramatize**, '**dramatise** ['dra-] *verb* 1 to turn into the form of a play: *She dramatized the novel for television.* □ adapter pour la scène
2 to make real events seem like things that happen in a play: *He dramatizes everything so!* □ dramatiser
drama ti'**zation** *noun.* □ dramatisation

drank *see* **drink**.

drape [dreip] *verb* 1 to hang cloth in folds (about): *We draped the sofa in red velvet.* □ draper
2 to hang in folds: *We draped sheets over the boxes to hide them.* □ draper
'**drapery** – *plural* '**draperies** – *noun* cloth used for draping: *walls hung with blue drapery.* □ tenture
drapes *noun plural* curtains. □ rideaux

drastic ['drastik] *adjective* violent, severe and having a wide effect: *At this point they decided to take drastic action.* □ énergique, radical
'**drastically** *adverb.* □ radicalement

draw [dro:] – *past tense* **drew** [dru:]: *past participle* **drawn** – *verb* 1 to make a picture or pictures (of), *usually* with a pencil, crayons *etc*: *During her stay in hospital she drew a great deal; Shall I draw a cow?* □ dessiner
2 to pull along, out or towards oneself: *She drew the child towards her; He drew a gun suddenly and fired; All water had to be drawn from a well; The cart was drawn by a pony.* □ tirer
3 to move (towards or away from someone or something): *The car drew away from the curb; Christmas is drawing closer.* □ s'éloigner; s'approcher
4 to play (a game) in which neither side wins: *The match was drawn/We drew at 1–1.* □ faire match nul
5 to obtain (money) from a fund, bank *etc*: *to draw a pension/an allowance.* □ retirer
6 to open or close (curtains). □ tirer
7 to attract: *She was trying to draw my attention to something.* □ attirer
■ *noun* 1 a drawn game: *The match ended in a draw.* □ match nul
2 an attraction: *The acrobats' act should be a real draw.* □ attraction
3 the selecting of winning tickets in a raffle, lottery *etc*: *a prize draw.* □ tirage
4 an act of drawing, *especially* a gun: *He's quick on the draw.*
'**drawing** *noun* (the art of making) a picture made with a pencil, crayon *etc*: *the drawings of Leonardo da Vinci; I am no good at drawing.* □ dessin
drawn *adjective* 1 (of curtains) pulled together or closed:

The curtains were drawn, although it was still daylight. □ **fermé**

2 (of a game *etc*) neither won nor lost: *a drawn match.* □ **nul**

3 (of a blade *etc*) pulled out of its sheath: *a drawn sword.* □ **à nu, au clair**

4 (of a person) strained and tired: *Her face was pale and drawn.* □ **hagard**

'**drawback** *noun* a disadvantage: *There are several drawbacks to his plan.* □ **inconvénient**

'**drawbridge** *noun* a bridge (at the entrance to a castle) which can be pulled up or let down. □ **pont-levis**

'**drawstring** *noun* a cord threaded through the top of a bag *etc* for closing it. □ **cordon**

draw a blank to be unsuccessful in a search, inquiry *etc.* □ **échouer**

draw a conclusion from to come to a conclusion after thinking about (what one has learned): *Don't draw any hasty conclusions from what I've said!* □ **tirer une conclusion de**

draw in (of a car *etc*) to come to a halt at the side of the road. □ **s'arrêter le long du trottoir**

draw the line to fix a limit *especially* for what one is prepared to do. □ **(se) fixer une limite**

draw/cast lots to decide who is to do *etc* something by drawing names out of a box *etc*: *Five of us drew lots for the two pop-concert tickets.* □ **tirer au sort**

draw off to pour out (liquid) from a large container: *The bartender drew off a litre of beer.* □ **(sou)tirer**

draw on[1] to use (money, strength, memory *etc*) as a source: *I'll have to draw on my savings.* □ **faire appel à**

draw on[2] **1** to pull on: *She drew on her gloves.* □ **enfiler**

2 to come nearer: *Night drew on.* □ **approcher**

draw out 1 to take (money) from a bank: *I drew out $40 yesterday.* □ **retirer**

2 to make longer: *We drew out the journey as much as we could but we still arrived early.* □ **faire durer**

3 (of a car *etc*) to move into the middle of the road from the side. □ **démarrer**

draw up 1 (of a car *etc*) to stop: *We drew up outside their house.* □ **(s')arrêter**

2 to arrange in an acceptable form or order: *They drew up the soldiers in line*; *The lawyer drew up a contract for them to sign.* □ **aligner, dresser**

3 to move closer: *Draw up a chair!* □ **approcher**

4 to extend (oneself) into an upright position: *He drew himself up to his full height.* □ **(se) redresser**

long drawn out going on for a long time: *The meeting was long drawn out*; *a long-drawn-out meeting/scream.* □ **interminable**

drawer [drɔː] *noun* a sliding box without a lid which fits into a chest, table *etc*: *the bottom drawer of my desk.* □ **tiroir**

drawing *see* **draw.**

drawing room ['drɔːɪŋrum] *noun* a sitting-room. □ **salon**

drawl [drɔːl] *verb* to speak or say in a slow, lazy manner: *He drawled his words in an irritating manner.* □ **parler d'une voix traînante**

■ *noun* a slow, lazy manner of speaking: *She spoke in a*

drawl. □ **voix traînante**

drawn, drawstring *see* **draw.**

dread [dred] *noun* great fear: *She lives in dread of her child being drowned in the canal*; *Her voice was husky with dread.* □ **terreur**

■ *verb* to fear greatly: *We were dreading his arrival.* □ **redouter**

'**dreadful** *adjective* **1** terrible: *a dreadful accident.* □ **épouvantable**

2 very bad or annoying: *What dreadful children!* □ **insupportable**

'**dreadfulness** *noun.* □ **caractère redoutable**

'**dreadfully** *adverb* extremely: *dreadfully ill*; *dreadfully clever.* □ **terriblement**

dream [driːm] *noun* **1** thoughts and pictures in the mind that come mostly during sleep: *I had a terrible dream last night.* □ **rêve, songe**

2 a state of being completely occupied by one's own thoughts: *Don't sit there in a dream!* □ **rêverie**

3 something perfect or very beautiful: *Your house is a dream!* □ **merveille**

4 an ambition or hope: *It's my dream to win a Nobel Prize.* □ **rêve**

■ *verb – past tense, past participles* **dreamed, dreamt** [dremt] *– (sometimes with* of*)* to see visions and pictures in the mind, *especially* when asleep: *For years I dreamed of being a great artist*; *I dreamt last night that the house had burnt down.* □ **rêver (de/que)**

'**dreamer** *noun* a person who is often occupied with his thoughts: *I'm afraid my son is a bit of a dreamer and not very practical.* □ **rêveur, euse**

'**dreamless** *adjective* (of sleep) sound; not disturbed by dreams. □ **sans rêves**

'**dreamy** *adjective* as if of a person who is not quite awake: *a dreamy smile*; *She is too dreamy.* □ **rêveur**

'**dreamily** *adverb.* □ **rêveusement**

'**dreaminess** *noun.* □ **(état de) rêverie**

dream up to invent: *I'm sure he'll dream up some silly plan.* □ **imaginer**

dreary ['driəri] *adjective* **1** gloomy: *What dreary weather!* □ **triste**

2 very dull: *I've got to go to another dreary meeting tomorrow.* □ **ennuyeux**

'**drearily** *adverb.* □ **tristement**

'**dreariness** *noun.* □ **tristesse**

dredge[1] [dredʒ] *verb* to deepen or clear the bed of a (a river *etc*) by bringing up mud. □ **draguer**

'**dredger** *noun* a boat with apparatus for dredging. □ **dragueur**

dredge[2] [dredʒ] *verb* to sprinkle (food with sugar *etc*): *pancakes dredged with sugar.* □ **saupoudrer**

dregs [dregz] *noun plural* **1** the solid matter which is left at the bottom of a container when the liquid is all used up: *the dregs of the wine.* □ **lie**

2 anything worthless: *the dregs of society.* □ **rebut**

drench [drentʃ] *verb* to soak completely: *They went out in the rain and were drenched to the skin.* □ **tremper**

dress [dres] *verb* **1** to put clothes or a covering on: *We dressed in a hurry and I dressed the children.* □ **(s')habiller, (se) vêtir**

2 to prepare (food *etc*) to be eaten: *He dressed a salad.* □ **apprêter**

3 to treat and bandage (wounds): *He was sent home from hospital after his burns had been dressed.* □ **panser**

■ *noun* 1 what one is wearing or dressed in: *She has strange tastes in dress.* □ **vêtements**

2 a piece of women's clothing with a top and skirt in one piece: *Shall I wear a dress or a blouse and skirt?* □ **robe**

dressed *adjective* wearing (clothes): *Don't come in – I'm not dressed!*; *She was dressed in black*; *Get dressed immediately*; *a well-dressed man.* □ **habillé**

'**dresser** *noun* a kitchen sideboard for holding dishes. □ **vaisselier**

'**dressing** *noun* 1 something put on as a covering: *We gave the rose-bed a dressing of manure.* □ **apprêt**

2 a sauce added *especially* to salads: *oil and vinegar dressing.* □ **sauce, assaisonnement**

3 a bandage *etc* used to dress a wound: *He changed the patient's dressing.* □ **pansement**

'**dressing gown** *noun* a loose garment worn over pyjamas *etc*. □ **robe de chambre**

'**dressing room** *noun* a room (in a theatre *etc*) for actors *etc* to change in. □ **loge, vestiaire**

'**dressing table** *noun* a table in a bedroom with a mirror and drawers. □ **coiffeuse**

'**dressmaker** *noun* a person who makes clothes for women. □ **couturier, ière**

dress rehearsal a full rehearsal of a play *etc* with costumes *etc*. □ **(répétition) générale**

dress up to put on special clothes, *eg* fancy dress: *She dressed up as a clown for the party.* □ **s'endimancher**

drew *see* **draw**.

dribble ['dribl] *verb* 1 to fall in small drops: *Water dribbled out of the tap.* □ **tomber goutte à goutte**

2 (of a baby *etc*) to allow saliva to run from the mouth. □ **baver**

3 in football, hockey *etc* to kick or hit (the ball) along little by little: *He dribbled up the field.* □ **dribbler**

■ *noun* a small quantity of liquid: *A dribble ran down her chin.* □ **goutte**

dried, drier *see* **dry**.

drift [drift] *noun* 1 a heap of something driven together, *especially* snow: *His car stuck in a snowdrift.* □ **amoncellement, congère**

2 the direction in which something is going; the general meaning: *I couldn't hear you clearly, but I did catch the drift of what you said.* □ **sens (général)**

■ *verb* 1 to (cause to) float or be blown along: *Sand drifted across the road*; *The boat drifted down the river.* □ **dériver, être emporté**

2 (of people) to wander or live aimlessly: *She drifted from job to job.* □ **flâner, aller à la dérive**

'**drifter** *noun* 1 a fishing-boat that uses a net which floats near the surface of the water. □ **drifter**

2 a person who drifts. □ **personne qui se laisse aller**

'**driftwood** *noun* wood floating on or cast up on the shore by the sea: *We made a fire with driftwood.* □ **bois flotté**

drill [dril] *verb* 1 to make (a hole) with a drill: *She drilled*

holes in the wood; *to drill for oil.* □ **percer**

2 (of soldiers *etc*) to exercise or be exercised: *The soldiers drilled every morning.* □ **faire l'exercice**

■ *noun* 1 a tool for making holes: *a hand-drill*; *an electric drill.* □ **perceuse**

2 exercise or practice, *especially* of soldiers: *We do half-an-hour of drill after tea.* □ **exercice**

drily *see* **dry**.

drink [driŋk] – *past tense* **drank** [draŋk]: *past participle* **drunk** [drʌŋk] – *verb* 1 to swallow (a liquid): *She drank a litre of water*; *He drank from a bottle.* □ **boire**

2 to take alcoholic liquids, *especially* in too great a quantity. □ **boire**

■ *noun* 1 (an act of drinking) a liquid suitable for swallowing: *She had/took a drink of water*; *Lemonade is a refreshing drink.* □ **boisson**

2 (a glassful *etc* of) alcoholic liquor: *He likes a drink when he returns home from work*; *Have we any drink in the house?* □ **verre, alcool**

drinkable *adjective* suitable or all right to drink: *Is the water from the well drinkable or should we boil it first?* □ **potable**

drink in to take in eagerly: *They listened eagerly, drinking in every detail.* □ **avaler**

drink to/drink (to) the health of to offer good wishes to; or wish well, while drinking: *to drink someone's health*; *Raise your glasses and drink to the bride and groom.* □ **boire à (la santé de)**

drink up to finish by drinking: *Drink up your milk!* □ **vider son verre**

drip [drip] – *past tense, past participle* **dripped** – *verb* to (cause to) fall in single drops: *Rain dripped off the roof*; *His hand was dripping blood.* □ **dégoutter, dégouliner**

■ *noun* 1 a small quantity (of liquid) falling in drops: *A drip of water ran down her arm.* □ **goutte**

2 the noise made by dripping: *I can hear a drip somewhere.* □ **bruit de l'eau qui tombe goutte à goutte**

3 an apparatus for passing a liquid slowly and continuously into a vein of the body. □ **goutte-à goutte**

'**dripping** *noun* fat obtained from meat while it is roasting *etc*. □ **graisse (de rôti)**

,**drip-'dry** *adjective* (of a garment *etc*) requiring no ironing if allowed to dry by hanging up. □ **nécessitant aucun repassage**

■ *verb* to dry in this manner.

drive [draiv] – *past tense* **drove** [drouv]: *past participle* **driven** ['drivn] – *verb* 1 to control or guide (a car *etc*): *Do you want to drive (the car), or shall I?* □ **conduire**

2 to take, bring *etc* in a car: *My mother is driving me to the airport.* □ **conduire (en voiture)**

3 to force or urge along: *Two men and a dog were driving a herd of cattle across the road.* □ **chasser (devant soi)**

4 to hit hard: *He drove a nail into the door*; *She drove a golf-ball from the tee.* □ **enfoncer**

5 to cause to work by providing the necessary power: *This mill is driven by water.* □ **actionner**

■ *noun* 1 a journey in a car, *especially* for pleasure: *We decided to go for a drive.* □ **promenade en voiture**

2 a private road leading from a gate to a house *etc*: *The drive is lined with trees.* □ **allée**

3 energy and enthusiasm: *I think he has the drive needed for this job.* □ **dynamisme**

4 a special effort: *We're having a drive to save electricity.* □ **drive**

5 in sport, a hard stroke (with a golf club, a cricket bat *etc*). □ **drive**

'**driver** *noun* a person who drives a car *etc*: *a bus driver.* □ **conducteur, trice**

'**drive-in** *adjective* (of a movie theatre, café etc, *especially* in North America) catering for people who remain in their cars while watching a film, eating *etc*: *a drive-in movie.* □ **restauvolant**

■ *noun* an outdoor theatre where a movie is shown on a large screen and moviegoers watch from their automobiles: *It was difficult to see the movie at the drive-in because our car was parked behind a large van.* □ **ciné-parc**

be driving at to be trying to say or suggest: *I don't know what you're driving at.* □ **vouloir en venir (à)**

drive off 1 to leave or go away in a car *etc*: *He got into a van and drove off.* □ **partir (en voiture)**

2 to keep away: *to drive off flies.* □ **chasser**

3 in golf, to make the first stroke from the tee. □ **driver**

drive on 1 to carry on driving a car *etc*: *Drive on – we haven't time to stop!* □ **continuer sa route**

2 to urge strongly forward: *It was ambition that drove him on.* □ **pousser**

drizzle ['drizl] *verb* (*only with* **it** *as subject*) to rain in small drops. □ **bruiner**

■ *noun* fine, light rain. □ **bruine**

dromedary *see* **camel**.

drone [droun] *noun* 1 the male of the bee. □ **faux-bourdon**

2 a person who is lazy and idle. □ **fainéant, ante**

3 a deep, humming sound: *the distant drone of traffic.* □ **bourdonnement**

■ *verb* 1 to make a low, humming sound: *An airplane droned overhead.* □ **bourdonner**

2 to speak in a dull, boring voice: *The lecturer droned on and on.* □ **parler d'une voix endormante**

droop [druːp] *verb* 1 to (cause to) hang down: *The willows drooped over the pond.* □ **(se) pencher**

2 (of a plant) to flop from lack of water: *a vase of drooping flowers.* □ **commencer à se faner**

drop [drop] *noun* 1 a small round or pear-shaped blob of liquid, *usually* falling: *a drop of rain.* □ **goutte**

2 a small quantity (of liquid): *If you want more wine, there's a drop left.* □ **goutte**

3 an act of falling: *a drop in temperature.* □ **baisse, chute**

4 a vertical descent: *From the top of the mountain there was a sheer drop of a five hundred metres.* □ **descente**

■ *verb – past tense, past participle* **dropped** – 1 to let fall, *usually* accidentally: *She dropped a box of pins all over the floor.* □ **laisser tomber**

2 to fall: *The coin dropped through the grating; The cat dropped* (=jumped down) *on to its paws.* □ **(re)tomber**

3 to give up (a friend, a habit *etc*): *I think she's dropped the idea of going abroad.* □ **abandonner**

4 to set down from a car *etc*: *The bus dropped me at the end of the road.* □ **déposer, débarquer**

5 to say or write in an informal and casual manner: *I'll drop her a note.* □ **écrire/envoyer (un petit mot)**

'**droplet** [-lit] *noun* a tiny drop: *droplets of rain.* □ **gouttelette**

'**droppings** *noun plural* excrement (of animals or birds). □ **crottes, chiures**

'**dropout** 1 *noun* someone who quits high school before graduating: *Paul left school after grade nine and became a dropout.* □ **décrocheur, euse**

2 *noun* a person who withdraws, *especially* from a course at a university *etc* or the normal life of society. □ **marginal, ale**

drop a brick/drop a clanger unknowingly to say or do something extremely tactless. □ **faire une gaffe**

drop back to slow down; to fall behind: *I was at the front of the crowd but I dropped back to speak to Bill.* □ **se laisser distancer**

drop by to visit someone casually and without being invited: *I'll drop by at his house on my way home.* □ **passer voir**

drop in to arrive informally to visit someone: *Do you drop in (on me) if you happen to be passing!* □ **passer voir**

drop off 1 to become separated or fall off: *The door-handle dropped off; This button dropped off your coat.* □ **se détacher**

2 to fall asleep: *I was so tired I dropped off in front of the television.* □ **s'endormir**

3 to allow to get off a vehicle: *Drop me off at the corner.* □ **déposer**

drop out (*often with* **of**) to withdraw from a group, from a high school *etc.*, or from the normal life of society: *There are only two of us going to the theatre now Mary has dropped out; She's dropped out of Westmount High School.* □ **vivre en marge de la société**

drought [draut] *noun* (a period of) lack of rain: *The reservoir dried up completely during the drought.* □ **sécheresse**

drown [draun] *verb* 1 to (cause to) sink in water and so suffocate and die: *She drowned in the river; He tried to drown the cat.* □ **(se) noyer**

2 to cause (a sound) not to be heard by making a louder sound: *His voice was drowned by the roar of the traffic.* □ **couvrir**

drowning *noun* a death caused by suffocating or having the lungs filled with water: *The newspaper reported that a drowning had occurred at the lake.* □ **noyade**

drowsy ['drauzi] *adjective* sleepy: *drowsy children.* □ **somnolent**

'**drowsily** *adverb.* □ **à demi endormi**

'**drowsiness** *noun.* □ **somnolence**

drudge [drʌdʒ] *verb* to do dull, very hard or humble work. □ **trimer**

■ *noun* a person who does such work. □ **homme, femme de peine**

'**drudgery** *noun* hard or humble work. □ **corvée**

drug [drʌg] *noun* 1 any substance used in medicine: *She has been prescribed a new drug for her stomach-pains.* □ **médicament**

2 a substance, sometimes one used in medicine, taken by some people to achieve a certain effect, *eg* great happiness or excitement: *I think she takes drugs*; *He behaves as though he is on drugs.* □ **drogue, stupéfiant**

■ *verb* – *past tense, past participle* **drugged** – to make to lose consciousness by giving a drug: *She drugged him and tied him up.* □ **droguer**

'**druggist** *noun* a person who sells medicines *etc*; a pharmacist. □ **pharmacien, enne**

'**drug-,addict** *noun* a person who has formed the habit of taking drugs. □ **toxicomane**

'**drugstore** *noun* (*American*) a shop which sells various articles (*eg* cosmetics, newpapers and soft drinks) as well as medicines. □ **pharmacie**

drum [drʌm] *noun* 1 a musical instrument constructed of skin *etc* stretched on a round frame and beaten with a stick: *She plays the drums.* □ **tambour**

2 something shaped like a drum, *especially* a container: *an oil-drum.* □ **tonneau**

3 an eardrum. □ **tympan**

■ *verb* – *past tense, past participle* **drummed** – 1 to beat a drum. □ **battre du tambour**

2 to tap continuously *especially* with the fingers: *Stop drumming (your fingers) on the table!* □ **tambouriner**

3 to make a sound like someone beating a drum: *The rain drummed on the metal roof.* □ **tambouriner**

'**drummer** *noun* a person who plays the drums. □ **batteur, eure**

'**drumstick** *noun* 1 a stick used for beating a drum. □ **baguette de tambour**

2 the lower part of the leg of a cooked chicken *etc*. □ **pilon**

drum in/into to force someone to remember (something) by repeating it constantly: *You never remember anything unless I drum it in/into you.* □ **seriner, rebattre les oreilles de qqn**

drunk [drʌŋk] *verb see* **drink.**

■ *adjective* overcome by having too much alcohol: *A drunk man fell off the bus*; *drunk with success.* □ **soûl, ivre**

■ *noun* a drunk person, *especially* one who is often drunk. □ **ivrogne, ivrognesse**

'**drunkard** [-kəd] *noun* a person who is often drunk: *I'm afraid he's turning into a drunkard.* □ **alcoolique**

'**drunken** *adjective* 1 drunk: *drunken soldiers.* □ **soûl, ivre**

2 caused by being drunk: *a drunken sleep.* □ **d'ivrogne**

'**drunkenness** *noun.* □ **ivresse**

dry [drai] *adjective* 1 having little, or no, moisture, sap, rain *etc*: *The ground is very dry*; *The leaves are dry and withered*; *I need to find dry socks for the children.* □ **sec**

2 uninteresting and not lively: *a very dry book.* □ **aride**

3 (of humour or manner) quiet, restrained: *a dry wit.* □ **pince-sans-rire**

4 (of wine) not sweet. □ **sec**

■ *verb* – *past tense, past participle* **dried** – to (cause to) become dry: *I prefer drying dishes to washing them*; *The clothes dried quickly in the sun.* □ **essuyer, sécher**

'**dried** *adjective* (of food) having had moisture removed for the purpose of preservation. □ **séché**

'**dryer**, '**drier** *noun* 1 a machine *etc* that dries: *a spin-dryer*; *a hair-drier.* □ **séchoir**

2 *noun* a machine which dries clothes by spinning them around and around and forcing the water out of them. □ **séchoir à linge**

'**dryly**, '**drily** *adverb* in a quiet, restrained (and humorous) manner: *He commented dryly on the untidiness of the room.* □ **d'un air pince-sans-rire**

'**dryness** *noun.* □ **sécheresse**

,**dry** '**clean** *verb* to clean (clothes *etc*) with chemicals, not with water. □ **nettoyer à sec**

dry land the land as opposed to the sea *etc*. □ **terre ferme**

dry off to make or become completely dry: *She climbed out of the swimming pool and dried off in the sun.* □ **(se) sécher**

dry out to have the water or dampness removed, usually by wind or sun: *There has been no rain and the sun has dried out the soil.* □ **assécher**

dry up 1 to lose water; to cease running *etc* completely: *All the rivers dried up in the heat.* □ **se dessécher, se tarir**

2 to become used up: *Supplies of bandages have dried up.* □ **se tarir**

3 to make dry: *The sun dried up the puddles in the road.* □ **sécher**

4 (of a speaker) to forget what he is going to say: *He dried up in the middle of his speech.* □ **rester sec**

dual ['djuəl] *adjective* double; twofold; made up of two: *a gadget with a dual purpose*; *The driving instructor's car has dual controls.* □ **double**

dub[1] [dʌb] – *past tense, past participle* **dubbed** – *verb* 1 to give (a film) a new soundtrack (*eg* in a different language). □ **doubler**

2 to add sound effects or music to (a film *etc*). □ **postsynchroniser**

'**dubbing** *noun.* □ **doublage, postsynchronisation**

dub[2] [dʌb] – *past tense, past participle* **dubbed** – *verb* to nickname: *He was dubbed Shorty because of his size.* □ **surnommer**

dubious ['djuːbiəs] *adjective* 1 doubtful: *I am dubious about the wisdom of this action.* □ **hésitant, incertain**

2 probably not honest: *dubious behaviour.* □ **douteux, suspect**

dubiety [dju'baiəti] *noun.* □ **doute**

'**dubiousness** *noun.* □ **incertitude**

ducal *see* **duke.**

duchess ['dʌtʃis] *noun* 1 the wife of a duke. □ **duchesse**

2 a woman of the same rank as a duke. □ **duchesse**

duck[1] [dʌk] *verb* 1 to push briefly under water: *They splashed about, ducking each other.* □ **plonger dans l'eau, faire boire la tasse**

2 to lower the head suddenly as if to avoid a blow: *He ducked as the ball came at him.* □ **esquiver**

duck[2] [dʌk] – *plurals* **ducks, duck** – *noun* 1 a kind of wild or domesticated water bird with short legs and a broad flat beak. □ **canard**

2 a female duck. *See also* **drake.** □ **cane**

3 in cricket, a score of nil by a batsman: *She was out for a duck.* □ **zéro**

'**duckling** [-liŋ] *noun* a baby duck. □ **caneton, canette**

duct [dʌkt] *noun* a tube or pipe for fluids *etc*: *a ventilation duct.* □ **conduit(e)**

ductile ['dʌktail] *adjective* (of metals) able to be drawn out into wire *etc*. □ **ductile**

dud [dʌd] *noun* something which is useless, does not work *etc*: *This light bulb is a dud.* □ **rebut**
■ *adjective* useless or not working: *a dud battery.* □ **de rebut**

due [djuː] *adjective* 1 owed: *I think I'm still due some pay*; *Our thanks are due to the doctor.* □ **dû**
2 expected according to timetable, promise *etc*: *The bus is due in three minutes.* □ **attendu**
3 proper: *Take due care.* □ **bon, qui convient**
■ *adverb* directly: *sailing due east.* □ **plein**
■ *noun* 1 what is owed, *especially* what one has a right to: *I'm only taking what is my due.* □ **dû**
2 (*in plural*) charge, fee or toll: *She paid the dues on the cargo.* □ **droits**
'**duly** *adverb* properly; as expected: *The bus duly arrived.* □ **en temps voulu**
'**due to** brought about by: *Her success was due to hard work.* □ **dû à, attribuable à**
give (someone) his due to be fair to someone. □ **rendre justice à qqn**

see also **owe**.

duel ['djuəl] *noun* 1 a fight (with swords or pistols) between two people over a matter of honour *etc*. □ **duel**
2 any contest between two people or two sides: *a duel for first place.* □ **duel**
■ *verb* – *past tense, past participle* '**duelled** – to fight a duel. □ **se battre en duel**

duet [dju'et] *noun* a musical piece for two singers or players: *a piano duet.* □ **duo**

duffle coat, duffel coat ['dʌfəlkout] *noun* a coat of coarse woollen cloth *usually* with a hood. □ **duffel-coat**
duffle bag a large bag with a round bottom, straight sides and drawstring. □ **sac de marin**

dug *see* **dig**.

duke [djuːk] *noun* a nobleman of the highest rank. □ **duc**
ducal ['djuːkəl] *adjective*. □ **ducal**
'**dukedom** *noun* the rank or territories of a duke. □ **titre de duc; duché**

dull [dʌl] *adjective* 1 slow to learn or to understand: *The clever children help the dull ones.* □ **borné**
2 not bright or clear: *a dull day.* □ **maussade**
3 not exciting or interesting: *a very dull book.* □ **ennuyeux**
'**dully** *adverb*. □ **d'une manière ennuyeuse**
'**dullness** *noun*. □ **caractère ennuyeux**

duly *see* **due**.

dumb [dʌm] *adjective* 1 without the power of speech: *She was born deaf and dumb*; *We were struck dumb with astonishment.* □ **muet**
2 silent: *On this point he was dumb.* □ **muet**
3 very stupid: *What a dumb thing to do!* □ **bête**
'**dumbness** *noun*. □ **mutisme**
'**dumbly** *adverb*. □ **en silence**

dum(b)found [dʌm'faund] *verb* to make speechless with amazement: *I'm completely dumbfounded!* □ **abasourdir**

dummy ['dʌmi] – *plural* '**dummies** – *noun* 1 an artificial substitute looking like the real thing: *The packets of cigarettes on display were dummies.* □ **chose fausse, factice**
2 a model of a human used for displaying clothes *etc*: *a dressmaker's dummy.* □ **mannequin**
3 an artificial teat put in a baby's mouth to comfort it. □ **tétine**

dump [dʌmp] *verb* 1 to set (down) heavily: *She dumped the heavy shopping bag on the table.* □ **déposer (sans précautions)**
2 to unload and leave (*eg* rubbish): *People dump things over our wall.* □ **jeter, décharger**
■ *noun* a place for leaving or storing unwanted things: *a rubbish dump.* □ **dépotoir**

dumpiness *see* **dumpy**.

dumpling ['dʌmpliŋ] *noun* (a) thick pudding or ball of cooked dough: *stewed beef and dumplings.* □ **boulette (de pâte)**

dumpy ['dʌmpi] *adjective* short and thick or fat: *a dumpy little man.* □ **boulot**
'**dumpiness** *noun*. □ **apparence boulotte**

dunce [dʌns] *noun* a person who is slow at learning or stupid: *I was an absolute dunce at school.* □ **cancre**

dune [djuːn] *noun* (*also* '**sand-dune**) a low hill of sand. □ **dune**

dung [dʌŋ] *noun* the waste matter passed out of an animal's body, *especially* when used as manure. □ **fumier**

dungarees [dʌŋgə'riːz] *noun plural* trousers with a bib: *a pair of dungarees.* □ **salopette**

dungeon ['dʌndʒən] *noun* a dark underground prison. □ **cachot (souterrain)**

dupe [djuːp] *noun* a person who is cheated or deceived: *She had been the dupe of a dishonest rogue.* □ **dupe**

duplex ['duːpleks, 'djuːpleks] *noun* a house divided horizontally or vertically, containing separate apartments for two families: *My neighbours live on the second floor of our duplex while I live on the main floor.* □ **duplex**
■ *verb* to deceive or trick: *He duped me into thinking he had gone home.* □ **duper**

duplicate ['djuːplikət] *adjective* exactly the same as something else: *a duplicate key.* □ **(en) double**
■ *noun* 1 another thing of exactly the same kind: *He managed to find a perfect duplicate of the ring she had lost.* □ **double**
2 an exact copy of something written: *She gave everyone a duplicate of her report.* □ **copie exacte**
■ *verb* to make an exact copy or copies of: *He duplicated the letter.* □ **faire un double de**
,**dupli'cation** *noun*. □ **reproduction**
'**duplicator** [-kei-] *noun* a machine for making copies. □ **duplicateur**

durable ['djuərəbl] *adjective* 1 lasting or able to last: *a durable peace.* □ **durable**
2 wearing well: *durable material.* □ **résistant**
,**dura'bility** *noun*. □ **durabilité**

duration [dju'reiʃən] *noun* the length of time anything continues: *We all had to stay indoors for the duration of the storm.* □ **durée**

durian ['duːriən] *noun* a large green fruit with a hard, prickly rind and seeds covered with cream-coloured pulp. □ **durione**

during ['djuəriŋ] *preposition* **1** throughout the time of: *We couldn't get cigarettes during the war.* □ **durant**
2 at a particular time within: *He died during the war.* □ **pendant**

dusk [dʌsk] *noun* (the time of) partial darkness after the sun sets; twilight. □ **crépuscule**
'**dusky** *adjective* dark-coloured. □ **sombre**
'**duskiness** *noun*. □ **obscurité**

dust [dʌst] *noun* **1** fine grains of earth, sand *etc*: *The furniture was covered in dust.* □ **poussière**
2 anything in the form of fine powder: *gold-dust*; *sawdust.* □ **poussière**
■ *verb* to free (furniture *etc*) from dust: *He dusts (the house) once a week.* □ **épousseter**
'**duster** *noun* a cloth for removing dust. □ **chiffon**
'**dusty** *adjective*: *a dusty floor.* □ **poussiéreux**
'**dustiness** *noun*. □ **état poussiéreux**
dust jacket ['dʌsdʒakit] *noun* the loose paper cover of a book. □ **jaquette**
dustpan ['dʌspan] *noun* a type of flat container with a handle, used for holding dust swept from the floor. □ **pelle à poussière**
'**dust-up** *noun* a quarrel: *There was a bit of a dust-up between the two men.* □ **bagarre**
dust down to remove the dust from with a brushing action: *She picked herself up and dusted herself down.* □ **épousseter**
throw dust in someone's eyes to try to deceive someone. □ **jeter de la poudre aux yeux de qqn**

Dutch [dʌtʃ] *adjective* of the Netherlands or its inhabitants: *Emery bought Dutch chocolate in Holland.* □ **hollandais**
■ *noun* the people or language of the Netherlands: *The Dutch are very proud of their war efforts; Although Joanne's ancestors were from Holland, she didn't speak Dutch.* □ **Hollandais, hollandais**

duty ['djuːti] – *plural* '**duties** – *noun* **1** what one ought morally or legally to do: *He acted out of duty*; *I do my duty as a responsible citizen.* □ **devoir**
2 an action or task requiring to be done, *especially* one attached to a job: *I had a few duties to perform in connection with my job.* □ **obligation**
3 (a) tax on goods: *You must pay duty when you bring wine into the country.* □ **taxe**
'**dutiable** *adjective* (of goods) on which tax is to be paid. □ **taxable**
'**dutiful** *adjective* (*negative* **undutiful**) careful to do what one should: *a dutiful daughter.* □ **respectueux**
,**duty-'free** *adjective* free from tax: *duty-free wines.* □ **hors-taxe**
off duty not actually working and not liable to be asked to do so: *The doctor's off duty this weekend*; (*also adjective*) *He spends her off-duty hours at home.* □ **qui n'est pas de garde, libre**
on duty carrying out one's duties or liable to be asked to do so during a certain period: *I'm on duty again this evening.* □ **de garde, de service**

duvet ['duːvei] *noun* a type of quilt stuffed with feathers, down *etc*, used on a bed instead of blankets. □ **couette**

dwarf [dwoːf] – *plurals* **dwarfs**, (*rare*) **dwarves** [dwoːvz] – *noun* **1** an animal, plant or person much smaller than normal. □ **nain, naine**
2 in fairy tales *etc*, a creature like a tiny man, with magic powers: *Snow White and the seven dwarfs.* □ **nain, naine**
■ *verb* to make to appear small: *The cathedral was dwarfed by the surrounding skyscrapers.* □ **écraser**

dwell [dwel] – *past tense, past participles* **dwelt** [-t], **dwelled** – *verb* to live (in a place): *She dwelt in the middle of a dark forest.* □ **habiter**
'**dwelling** *noun* a house, flat *etc*. □ **habitation**
dwell on to think or speak about something for a long time: *It isn't a good thing to dwell on your problems.* □ **revenir (sans cesse) sur**

dwindle ['dwindl] *verb* to grow less: *His money dwindled away.* □ **diminuer**

dye [dai] – *past tense, past participle* **dyed**: *present participle* '**dyeing** – *verb* to give a permanent colour to (clothes, cloth *etc*): *I've just dyed my coat green*; *I'm sure he dyes his hair.* □ **teindre**
■ *noun* a powder or liquid for colouring: *a bottle of green dye.* □ **teinture**

dying see **die**[1].

dynamic [dai'namik] *adjective* **1** concerned with force. □ **dynamique**
2 (of a person) forceful and very energetic. □ **dynamique**
dy'namically *adverb*. □ **dynamiquement**
dy'namics *noun singular* the science that deals with movement and force. □ **dynamique**

dynamite ['dainəmait] *noun* a type of powerful explosive. □ **dynamite**

dynamo ['dainəmou] – *plural* '**dynamos** – *noun* a machine that produces electric currents. □ **dynamo**

dynasty ['dinəsti] – *plural* '**dynasties** – *noun* a succession or series of rulers of the same family: *the Ming dynasty.* □ **dynastie**
dy'nastic [-'nas-] *adjective*. □ **dynastique**

dysentery ['disəntri] *noun* an infectious disease with severe diarrhea. □ **dysenterie**

Ee

each [iːtʃ] *adjective* every (thing, person *etc*) of two or more, considered separately: *each house in this street.* □ **chaque**

■ *pronoun* every single one, of two or more: *They each have 50 cents.* □ **chacun, une**

■ *adverb* to or for each one; apiece: *I gave them an apple each.* □ **(à) chacun, une**

each other used as the object when an action takes place between two (loosely, more than two) people *etc*: *They wounded each other.* □ **l'un l'autre, l'une l'autre, les uns les autres, les unes les autres**

> **each** is singular: *Each of them has (not have) a bag in his hand.*

eager ['iːgə] *adjective* full of desire, interest *etc*; keen; enthusiastic: *She is always eager to win.* □ **désireux de**
'**eagerness** *noun.* □ **désir ardent (de)**
'**eagerly** *adverb.* □ **ardemment**

eagle ['iːgl] *noun* a kind of large bird of prey noted for its good eyesight. □ **aigle**

ear¹ [iə] *noun* 1 the part of the head by means of which we hear, or its external part only: *Her new hairstyle covers her ears.* □ **oreille**
2 the sense or power of hearing *especially* the ability to hear the difference between sounds: *sharp ears*; *She has a good ear for music.* □ **oreille**
'**earache** *noun* pain in the inner part of the ear. □ **mal d'oreille(s)**
'**eardrum** *noun* the layer of tissue separating the inner from the outer ear. □ **tympan**
'**earmark** *verb* to set aside (for a particular purpose): *This money is earmarked for our holiday.* □ **réserver (pour)**
'**earring** *noun* an ornament worn attached to the ear: *silver earrings.* □ **boucle d'oreille**
'**earshot** *noun* the distance at which sound can be heard: *He did not hear her last remark as he was out of earshot.* □ **portée de voix**
be all ears to listen with keen attention: *The children were all ears when their father was describing the car crash.* □ **être tout oreilles**
go in one ear and out the other not to make any lasting impression: *I keep telling that child to work harder but my words go in one ear and out the other.* □ **entrer par une oreille et sortir par l'autre**
play by ear to play (music) without looking at and without having memorized printed music. □ **jouer d'oreille**
up to one's ears (in) deeply involved (in): *I'm up to my ears in work.* □ **par-dessus la tête**

ear² [iə] *noun* the part of a cereal plant which contains the seed: *ears of corn.* □ **épi**

earl [əːl] *noun* a British nobleman between a marquis and a viscount in rank. □ **comte**

early ['əːli] *adverb* 1 near the beginning (of a period of time *etc*): *early in my life*; *early in the afternoon.* □ **tôt**
2 sooner than others; sooner than usual; sooner than expected or than the appointed time: *He arrived early*;

She came an hour early. □ **de bonne heure, en avance**
■ *adjective* 1 belonging to, or happening, near the beginning of a period of time *etc*: *early morning*; *in the early part of the century.* □ **tôt, au début de**
2 belonging to the first stages of development: *early musical instruments.* □ **ancien**
3 happening *etc* sooner than usual or than expected: *the baby's early arrival*; *It's too early to get up yet.* □ **prématuré, tôt**
4 prompt: *I hope for an early reply to my letter.* □ **prompt**
'**earliness** *noun.* □ **heure peu avancée; précocité**
early bird someone who gets up early or who acts before others do. □ **personne matinale**

earmark *see* ear¹.

earn [əːn] *verb* 1 to gain (money, wages, one's living) by working: *He earns $200 a week*; *He earns his living by cleaning shoes*; *You can afford a car now that you're earning.* □ **gagner (sa vie)**
2 to deserve: *I've earned a rest.* □ **mériter**
'**earnings** *noun plural* money *etc* earned: *Her earnings are not sufficient to support her family.* □ **salaire**

earnest ['əːnist] *adjective* 1 serious or over-serious: *an earnest student*; *She wore an earnest expression.* □ **sérieux**
2 showing determination, sincerity or strong feeling: *He made an earnest attempt to improve his work.* □ **sérieux**
'**earnestness** *noun.* □ **sérieux**
'**earnestly** *adverb.* □ **sérieusement**
in earnest 1 serious; not joking: *I am in earnest when I say this.* □ **sérieux, sans rire**
2 seriously; with energy and determination: *He set to work in earnest.* □ **sérieusement**

earring, earshot *see* ear¹.

earth [əːθ] *noun* 1 the third planet in order of distance from the Sun; the planet on which we live: *Is Earth nearer the Sun than Mars is?*; *the geography of the earth.* □ **terre**
2 the world as opposed to heaven: *heaven and earth.* □ **terre**
3 soil: *Fill the plant-pot with earth.* □ **terre**
4 dry land; the ground: *the earth, sea and sky.* □ **terre**
5 a burrow or hole of an animal, *especially* of a fox. □ **tanière**
'**earthen** *adjective* (of a floor *etc*) made of earth. □ **en/de terre**
'**earthly** *adjective* 1 of or belonging to this world; not heavenly or spiritual: *this earthly life.* □ **terrestre**
2 possible: *This car is no earthly use.* □ **aucun**
'**earthenware** *noun, adjective* (of) a kind of pottery coarser than china: *an earthenware dish.* □ **faïence, en faïence**
'**earthquake** *noun* a shaking of the earth's surface: *The village was destroyed by an earthquake.* □ **tremblement de terre**
'**earthworm** *noun* (*usually* **worm**) a kind of small animal with a ringed body and no backbone, living in damp earth. □ **ver de terre**
on earth used for emphasis: *What on earth are you doing?*; *the stupidest man on earth.* □ **diable, du/au monde**

run to earth to find (something or someone) after a long search: *He ran his friend to earth in the pub.* □ **dénicher**

earwig ['iəwig] *noun* a kind of insect with pincers at the end of its body. □ **perce-oreille**

ease [izz] *noun* 1 freedom from pain or from worry or hard work: *a lifetime of ease.* □ **bien-être**

2 freedom from difficulty: *She passed her exam with ease.* □ **facilité**

3 naturalness: *ease of manner.* □ **naturel**

■ *verb* 1 to free from pain, trouble or anxiety: *A hot bath eased his tired limbs.* □ **soulager**

2 (*often with* **off**) to make or become less strong, less severe, less fast *etc*: *The pain has eased (off); The driver eased off as he approached the town.* □ **(se) calmer, ralentir**

3 to move (something heavy or awkward) gently or gradually in or out of position: *They eased the wardrobe carefully up the narrow staircase.* □ **(mouvoir) doucement**

'easily *adverb* 1 without difficulty: *She won the race easily.* □ **facilement**

2 by far: *This is easily the best book I've read this year.* □ **de loin**

3 very probably: *It may easily rain tomorrow.* □ **bien**

'easiness *noun.* □ **facilité**

'easy *adjective* 1 not difficult: *This is an easy job (to do).* □ **facile**

2 free from pain, trouble, anxiety *etc*: *She had an easy day at the office.* □ **tranquille**

3 friendly: *an easy manner/smile.* □ **naturel**

4 relaxed; leisurely: *The farmer walked with an easy stride.* □ **modéré**

■ *interjection* a command to go or act gently: *Easy! You'll fall if you run too fast.* □ **doucement**

easy chair a chair that is soft and comfortable, *eg* an armchair. □ **fauteuil**

,easy-'going *adjective* not inclined to worry. □ **qui ne s'en fait pas**

at ease free from anxiety or embarrassment: *She is completely at ease among strangers.* □ **à l'aise**

easier said than done more difficult than it at first seems: *Getting seats for the theatre is easier said than done.* □ **c'est vite dit!**

go easy on to be careful with: *Go easy on the wine – there won't be enough for the rest of the guests.* □ **ne pas trop en mettre**

stand at ease (*eg* soldiers) to stand with legs apart and hands clasped behind the back. □ **se tenir au repos**

take it easy not to work *etc* hard or energetically; to avoid using much effort: *The doctor told her to take it easy.* □ **ne pas se fatiguer**

take one's ease to make oneself comfortable; to relax: *There he was – taking his ease in his father's chair!* □ **prendre ses aises**

easel ['izl] *noun* a (hinged) stand for supporting a blackboard, an artist's picture *etc*. □ **chevalet**

east [izst] *noun* 1 the direction from which the sun rises, or any part of the earth lying in that direction: *The wind is blowing from the east; The village is to the east of*

Canton; in the east of England. □ **est**

2 (*also* **E**) one of the four main points of the compass: *He took a direction 10° E of N/east of north.* □ **est**

■ *adjective* 1 in the east: *the east coast.* □ **est, oriental**

2 from the direction of the east: *an east wind.* □ **d'est**

■ *adverb* towards the east: *The house faces east.* □ **à/ vers l'est**

'easterly *adjective* 1 (of a wind, breeze *etc*) coming from the east: *an easterly wind.* □ **d'est**

2 looking, lying *etc* towards the east: *We are travelling in an easterly direction.* □ **vers l'est**

'eastern *adjective* of the east or the East: *an eastern custom.* □ **oriental**

'easternmost *adjective* being furthest east: *the easternmost city in America.* □ **le plus à l'est**

'eastward *adjective* towards the east: *in an eastward direction.* □ **à l'est**

'eastward(s) *adverb* towards the east: *They are travelling eastwards.* □ **vers l'est**

the East 1 the countries east of Europe: *the Middle/Far East.* □ **l'Orient; le Moyen-Orient, l'Extrême-Orient**

2 (*sometimes without* **the**) the former USSR, the countries of Eastern Europe, the People's Republic of China: *the different political systems of (the) East and (the) West.* □ **les pays de l'Est**

Easter ['izstə] *noun* a Christian festival held in the spring, to celebrate Christ's coming back to life after the Crucifixion. □ **Pâques**

Easter egg a decorated egg, *especially* one made of chocolate, eaten at Easter. □ **œuf de Pâques**

easy *see* **ease.**

eat [izt] – *past tense* **ate** [eit, et]: *past participle* **'eaten** – *verb* to (chew and) swallow; to take food: *They are forbidden to eat meat; They ate up all the cakes; We must eat to live.* □ **manger**

'eatable (*negative* **uneatable**) *adjective* fit to be eaten: *The meal was scarcely eatable.* □ **mangeable**

■ *noun* (*in plural*) food: *Cover all eatables to keep mice away.* □ **victuailles**

eat into to destroy or waste gradually: *Acid eats into metal; The school fees have eaten into our savings.* □ **attaquer, ronger**

eat one's words to admit humbly that one was mistaken in saying something: *I'll make him eat his words!* □ **(se) rétracter**

eau de cologne [oudəkə'loun] (*also* **co'logne**) *noun* a type of perfume first made at Cologne. □ **eau de Cologne**

eaves [izvz] *noun plural* the edge of the roof sticking out beyond the wall: *There are birds nesting under the eaves.* □ **avant-toit**

eavesdrop ['izvzdrop] – *past tense, past participle* **'eavesdropped** – *verb* (*with* **on**) to listen in order to overhear a private conversation: *The child eavesdropped on her parents' discussion.* □ **écouter (indiscrètement)**

'eavesdropper *noun.* □ **oreille indiscrète**

ebb [eb] 1 (of the tide) to go out from the land: *The tide began to ebb.* □ **descendre**

2 to become less: *His strength was ebbing fast.* □

décliner

ebb tide the ebbing tide: *They sailed on the ebb tide.* □ **marée descendante**

at a low ebb in a poor or depressed state: *She was at a low ebb after the operation.* □ **bien bas**

on the ebb ebbing or getting less: *His power is on the ebb.* □ **en déclin**

ebony ['ebəni] **1** *noun, adjective* (of) a type of wood, *usually* black and almost as heavy and hard as stone. □ **ébène**

2 *adjective* black as ebony. □ **noir d'ébène**

eccentric [ik'sentrik] *adjective* (of a person, his behaviour *etc*) odd; unusual: *He is growing more eccentric every day; She had an eccentric habit of collecting stray cats.* □ **excentrique**

■ *noun* an eccentric person. □ **excentrique, hurluberlu**

ec'centrically *adverb.* □ **de manière excentrique**

eccentricity [eksen'trisəti] *noun* oddness of behaviour or an example of this. □ **excentricité**

ec,clesi'astic(al) [ikliːzi'astik(l)] *adjective* of the church or clergy. □ **ecclésiastique**

echo ['ekou] – *plural* '**echoes** – *noun* the repeating of a sound caused by its striking a surface and coming back: *The children shouted loudly in the cave so that they could hear the echoes.* □ **écho**

■ *verb – past tense* '**echoed** – **1** to send back an echo or echoes: *The cave was echoing with shouts; The hills echoed his shout.* □ **renvoyer**

2 to repeat (a sound or a statement): *She always echoes her husband's opinion.* □ **faire écho à**

eclair [i'klea] *noun* a long iced cake *usually* with cream filling and chocolate icing. □ **éclair**

eclipse [i'klips] *noun* the disappearance of the whole or part of the sun when the moon comes between it and the earth, or of the moon when the earth's shadow falls across it: *When was the last total eclipse of the sun?* □ **éclipse**

■ *verb* **1** to obscure or cut off the light or sight of (the sun or moon): *The sun was partially eclipsed at 9:00.* □ **éclipser**

2 to be much better than: *Her great success eclipsed her brother's achievements.* □ **éclipser**

eco- [iːkou] (*as part of a word*) concerned with living things in relation to their environment: *the eco-system.* □ **éco-**

ecology [i'kolədʒi] *noun* (the study of) living things considered in relation to their environment: *Pollution has a disastrous effect on the ecology of a region.* □ **écologie**

e'cologist *noun.* □ **écologiste**

,**eco'logical** [iː-] *adjective.* □ **écologique**

,**eco'logically** *adverb.* □ **écologiquement**

economy [i'konəmi] *noun* **1** the thrifty, careful management of money *etc* to avoid waste: *Please use the water with economy; We must make economies in household spending.* □ **économie**

2 organization of money and resources: *the country's economy; household economy.* □ **économie**

economic [iːkə'nomik] *adjective* **1** of or concerned with (an) economy: *the country's economic future.* □ **économique**

2 likely to bring a profit: *an economic rent.* □ **rentable**

economical [iːkə'nomikəl] *adjective* thrifty; not extravagant: *This car is very economical on gas.* □ **économe; économique**

,**eco'nomically** *adverb.* □ **économiquement**

economics [iːkə'nomiks] *noun singular* the study of production and distribution of money and goods: *She is studying economics.* □ **économie politique**

e'conomist *noun* a person who is an expert in economics. □ **économiste**

e'conomize, e'conomise *verb* to spend money or goods carefully: *We must economize on fuel.* □ **économiser**

ecstasy ['ekstəsi] – *plural* '**ecstasies** – *noun* (a feeling of) very great joy or other overwhelming emotion. □ **extase**

ec'static [-'sta-] *adjective: an ecstatic mood.* □ **extasié**

ec'statically *adverb.* □ **avec extase**

ecumenical [ekju'menikəl, iːk-] *adjective* bringing together branches of the whole Christian church. □ **œcuménique**

eczema ['eksimə] *noun* a type of skin disease in which there is an itchy rash. □ **eczéma**

eddy ['edi] – *plural* '**eddies** – *noun* a current of water or air running back against the main stream or current. □ **tourbillon**

■ *verb* to move around and around: *The water eddied around the pier; The crowds eddied to and fro in the square.* □ **tourbillonner**

edge [edʒ] *noun* **1** the part farthest from the middle of something; a border: *Don't put that cup so near the edge of the table – it will fall off; the edge of the lake; the water's edge.* □ **bord**

2 the cutting side of something sharp, *eg* a knife or weapon: *the edge of the sword.* □ **tranchant**

3 keenness; sharpness: *The chocolate took the edge off his hunger.* □ **calmer**

■ *verb* **1** to form a border to: *a handkerchief edged with lace.* □ **border**

2 to move or push little by little: *He edged his chair nearer to her; She edged her way through the crowd.* □ **(faire) avancer petit à petit**

'**edging** *noun* a border or fringe around a garment: *gold edging.* □ **bordure**

'**edgy** *adjective* irritable: *That actress is always edgy before a performance.* □ **énervé**

'**edgily** *adverb.* □ **d'un air agacé**

'**edginess** *noun.* □ **énervement**

have the edge on/over to have an advantage over: *he had the edge over his opponent.* □ **l'emporter (de justesse) sur**

on edge uneasy; nervous: *She was on edge when waiting for her exam results.* □ **énervé**

on the edge of positioned at the very limit; on the border: *The dog was on the edge of the cliff and nearly fell off.* □ **au bord de**

edible ['edəbl] *adjective* fit to be eaten: *Are these berries edible?* □ **comestible**

,**edi'bility** *noun.* □ **comestibilité**

edict ['iːdikt] *noun* an order or command from someone in authority; a decree. □ **décret**

edification *see* edify.

edifice ['edifis] *noun* a building: *The new cathedral is a magnificent edifice.* □ **édifice**

edit ['edit] *verb* to prepare (a book, manuscript, newspaper, program, film etc) for publication, or for broadcasting etc, *especially* by correcting, altering, shortening etc. □ **préparer, mettre au point (pour la publication)**

edition [i'diʃn] *noun* a number of copies of a book etc printed at a time, or the form in which they are produced: *the third edition of the book*; *a paperback edition*; *the evening edition of the newspaper.* □ **édition**

'editor *noun* 1 a person who edits books etc: *a dictionary editor.* □ **rédacteur, trice**

2 a person who is in charge of (part of) a newspaper, journal etc: *The editor of The Gazette*; *She has been appointed fashion editor.* □ **rédacteur, trice en chef**

,edi'torial [-'tɔː-] *adjective* of or belonging to editors: *editorial work/staff.* □ **de (la) rédaction**

■ *noun* an article in a newspaper which gives the opinion of the editor. □ **éditorial**

educate ['edjukeit] *verb* to train and teach: *She was educated at a private school.* □ **instruire, éduquer**

,edu'cation *noun* instruction and teaching, *especially* of children and young people in schools, universities etc: *His lack of education prevented him from getting a good job.* □ **études**

,edu'cational *adjective* 1 of education: *educational methods.* □ **pédagogique**

2 providing information: *Our visit to the zoo was educational as well as enjoyable.* □ **éducatif**

,edu'cation(al)ist *noun* an expert in methods of educating. □ **pédagogue**

eel [iːl] *noun* a kind of fish with a long smooth cylindrical or ribbon-shaped body. □ **anguille**

eerie ['iəri] *adjective* causing fear; weird: *an eerie silence.* □ **inquiétant**

'eerily *adverb.* □ **étrangement**

'eeriness *noun.* □ **étrangeté**

efface [i'feis] *verb* 1 to rub out; to remove: *You must try to efface the event from your memory.* □ **effacer**

2 to avoid drawing attention to (oneself): *She did her best to efface herself at parties.* □ **(s')effacer**

effect [i'fekt] *noun* 1 a result or consequence: *He is suffering from the effects of over-eating*; *Her discovery had little effect at first.* □ **effet**

2 an impression given or produced: *The speech did not have much effect (on them)*; *a pleasing effect.* □ **effet**

■ *verb* to make happen; to bring about: *He tried to effect a reconciliation between his parents.* □ **effectuer**

ef'fective [-tiv] *adjective* 1 having power to produce, or producing, a desired result: *These new teaching methods have proved very effective.* □ **efficace**

2 striking or pleasing: *an effective display of flowers.* □ **qui fait de l'effet**

3 in operation; working; active: *The new law becomes effective next week.* □ **en vigueur**

ef'fectively [-tivli] *adverb.* □ **efficacement**

ef'fects *noun plural* 1 property; goods: *She left few personal effects when she died.* □ **biens**

2 in drama etc, devices for producing suitable sounds, lighting etc to accompany a play etc: *sound effects.* □ **effets (de), bruitage**

ef'fectual [-tʃuəl] *adjective* successful in producing the desired results: *He was not very effectual as an organizer.* □ **efficace**

come into effect (of a law etc) to begin to operate: *The law came into effect last month.* □ **entrer en vigueur**

for effect for the sake of making an impression: *You don't mean that – you only said it for effect.* □ **pour impressionner**

in effect 1 (of a rule etc) in operation: *That law is no longer in effect.* □ **en vigueur**

2 in truth or in practical terms: *In effect our opinions differed very little.* □ **en réalité**

put into effect to put (a law etc) into operation: *She has begun to put her theories into effect.* □ **mettre en application**

take effect to begin to work; to come into force: *When will the drug take effect?* □ **faire son effet; entrer en vigueur**

effeminate [i'feminət] *adjective* (of a man) unmanly or womanish. □ **efféminé**

effervesce [efə'ves] *verb* to give off bubbles of gas; to fizz: *The champagne effervesced in the glasses.* □ **pétiller**

,effer'vescence *noun.* □ **effervescence**

,effer'vescent *adjective.* □ **effervescent**

efficacious [efi'keiʃəs] *adjective* producing the result intended: *The medicine was most efficacious.* □ **efficace**

efficacy ['efikəsi] *noun.* □ **efficacité**

efficient [i'fiʃənt] *adjective* 1 (of a person) capable; skilful: *a very efficient secretary.* □ **efficace**

2 (of an action, tool etc) producing (quick and) satisfactory results: *The new bread knife is much more efficient than the old one.* □ **efficace**

ef'ficiently *adverb.* □ **efficacement**

ef'ficiency *noun.* □ **efficacité**

effigy ['efidʒi] *noun* a likeness of a person, animal etc (in wood, stone etc): *effigies of Buddha.* □ **effigie**

effluent ['efluənt] *noun* (a flowing out of) waste matter from a factory etc. □ **effluent**

effort ['efət] *noun* 1 hard work; energy: *Learning a foreign language requires effort*; *The effort of climbing the hill made the old man very tired.* □ **effort**

2 a trying hard; a struggle: *The government's efforts to improve the economy were unsuccessful*; *Please make every effort to be punctual.* □ **effort**

3 the result of an attempt: *Your drawing was a good effort.* □ **essai**

'effortless *adjective* done without (apparent) effort: *The dancer's movements looked effortless.* □ **aisé**

'effortlessly *adverb.* □ **sans effort**

effrontery [i'frʌntəri] *noun* impudence: *He had the effrontery to call me a liar.* □ **effronterie**

effusive [i'fjuːsiv] *adjective* showing too much feeling; emotional: *an effusive letter.* □ **expansif**

ef'fusively *adverb.* □ **avec effusion**

egg[1] [eg] *noun* 1 an oval object *usually* covered with shell, laid by a bird, reptile etc, from which a young one is

hatched: *The female bird is sitting on the eggs in the nest.* □ **œuf**
2 such an object laid by a hen, used as food: *Would you rather have boiled, fried or scrambled eggs?* □ **œuf**
3 in the female mammal, the cell from which the young one is formed; the ovum: *The egg is fertilized by the male sperm.* □ **ovule**
'**egg cup** *noun* a small cup-shaped container for holding a boiled egg while it is being eaten. □ **coquetier**
'**eggplant** *noun* a dark purple fruit used as a vegetable. □ **aubergine**
'**eggshell** *noun* the fragile covering of an egg. □ **coquille d'œuf**
eggs over easy fried eggs that have been turned over in the pan to form a thin covering over a soft, runny yolk: *Khaled ordered eggs over easy, but the yolk was too solid.* □ **œufs tournés**
eggs sunny side up fried eggs that have not been turned over so the yolk remains visible and soft: *The cook said my eggs were sunny side up but the yellow yolks were not showing.* □ **œufs au miroir**
put all one's eggs in one basket to depend entirely on the success of one scheme, plan *etc*: *You should apply for more than one job – don't put all your eggs in one basket.* □ **mettre tous ses œufs dans le même panier**
teach one's grandmother to suck eggs to try to show someone more experienced than oneself how to do something. □ **ce n'est pas aux vieux singes qu'on apprend à faire des grimaces**
egg² [eg] *(urb)*: **egg on** to urge (somebody) on (to do something): *He egged his friend on to steal the radio.* □ **pousser à**
ego ['iːgou] *noun* **1** personal pride: *Her criticism wounded my ego.* □ **égo**
2 the part of a person that is conscious and thinks; the self. □ **le moi**
egocentric [iːgou'sentrik] *adjective* interested in oneself only. □ **égocentrique**
egoism [iː-] *noun* selfishness. □ **égoïsme**
egoist ['iː-] *noun*. □ **égoïste**
,**ego'istic, ego'istical** *adjective*. □ **égoïste**
Egyptian [idʒpʃən] *adjective* of Egypt or its inhabitants: *The pyramids were filled with ancient Egyptian treasures.* □ **égyptien, ienne**
■ *noun* a native or citizen of Egypt: *Cleopatra was an Egyptian.* □ **Égyptien, ienne**
eiderdown ['aidədaun] *noun* a bedcover made of the down or soft feathers of the **eider duck** (a northern sea duck). □ **édredon**
eight [eit] *noun* **1** the number or figure 8: *Four and four are/is/make eight.* □ **huit**
2 the age of 8: *children of eight and over.* □ **huit ans**
3 the crew of an eight-oared racing boat: *Did the Cambridge eight win?* □ **équipe de huit**
■ *adjective* **1** 8 in number: *eight people; She is eight years old.* □ **huit**
2 aged 8: *He is eight today.* □ **(âgé de) huit ans**
eight- having eight (of something): *an eight-sided figure.* □ **à huit (...), octo-**
eighth [eitθ] *noun* **1** one of eight equal parts: *They each*

received an eighth of the money. □ **huitième**
2 (*also adjective*) (the) last of eight (people, things *etc*); (the) next after the seventh: *His horse was eighth in the race; Are you having another cup of coffee? That's your eighth (cup) this morning; Henry VIII* (said as 'Henry the Eighth'). □ **huitième, huit**
'**eight-year-old** a person or animal that is eight years old: *Is this game suitable for an eight-year-old?* □ **enfant de huit ans**
■ *adjective: an eight-year-old child.* □ **de huit ans**
figure eight a pattern *etc* in the shape of the figure 8: *The skater did a figure eight.* □ **huit**
eighteen [ei'tiːn] *noun* **1** the number or figure 18. □ **dix-huit**
2 the age of 18: *a girl of eighteen.* □ **dix-huit ans**
■ *adjective* **1** 18 in number: *eighteen horses.* □ **dix-huit**
2 aged 18: *He is eighteen now.* □ **dix-huit ans**
eighteen- having eighteen: *an eighteen-page booklet.* □ **de dix-huit (...)**
,**eigh'teenth** *noun* **1** one of eighteen equal parts: *seventeen eighteenths.* □ **dix-huitième**
2 (*also adjective*) (the) last of eighteen (people, things *etc*); (the) next after the seventeenth: *She was eighteenth in the competition; the eighteenth storey.* □ **dix-huitième**
,**eigh'teen-year-old** *noun: He is married to an eighteen-year-old.* □ **individu, etc. âgé de dix-huit ans**
■ *adjective: an eighteen-year-old girl.* □ **de dix-huit ans**
eighty ['eiti] *noun* **1** the number or figure 80. □ **quatre-vingts**
2 the age of 80. □ **quatre-vingts ans**
■ *adjective* **1** 80 in number. □ **quatre-vingts**
2 aged 80. □ **de quatre-vingts ans**
'**eighties** *noun plural* **1** the period of time between one's eightieth and ninetieth birthdays: *He is in his eighties.* □ **entre quatre-vingts et quatre-vingt-dix ans**
2 the period of time between the eightieth and ninetieth years of a century: *life in the 'eighties/'80s.* □ **les années quatre-vingt**
'**eightieth** *noun* **1** one of eighty equal parts: *eleven eightieths.* □ **quatre-vingtième**
2 (*also adjective*) (the) last of eighty (people, things *etc*); (the) next after the seventy-ninth. □ **quatre-vingtième**
eighty- having eighty: *an eighty-page book.* □ **de quatre-vingts (...)**
'**eighty-year-old** *noun: a lively eighty-year-old.* □ **octogénaire**
■ *adjective: an eighty-year-old widow.* □ **octogénaire**
either ['aiðə, 'iːðə(r)] *pronoun* the one or the other of two: *You may borrow either of these books; I offered her coffee or tea, but she didn't want either.* □ **l'un(e) ou l'autre; l'un(e) et l'autre; ni l'un(e) ni l'autre**
■ *adjective* **1** the one or the other (of two things, people *etc*): *She can write with either hand.* □ **l'un ou l'autre, l'une ou l'autre; n'importe lequel, laquelle des deux**
2 the one and the other (of two things, people *etc*); both: *at either side of the garden.* □ **chaque**
■ *adverb* **1** used for emphasis: *If you don't go, I won't either.* □ **non plus**

2 moreover; besides: *I used to sing, and I hadn't a bad voice, either.* □ **d'ailleurs**

either ... or introducing alternatives: *Either you must go to see him or send an apology.* □ **ou (bien)... ou (bien)...**

either way in the one case or the other: *Either way he wins.* □ **de toute façon**

---

either ... or the verb usually matches the noun or pronoun that comes closest to it: *Either John or Mary is to blame/Either John or his brothers are going to the show.*

---

ejaculate [i'dʒakjuleit] *verb* 1 to utter or exclaim suddenly. □ **s'exclamer**

2 to release or expel semen through the head of the penis during an erection: *During sexual intercourse, the male ejaculates into the vagina of the female.* □ **éjaculer**

e,jacu'lation *noun.* □ **exclamation**

eject [i'dʒekt] *verb* 1 to throw out with force; to force to leave: *They were ejected from their house for not paying the rent.* □ **expulser**

2 to leave an aircraft in an emergency by causing one's seat to be ejected: *The pilot had to eject when his plane caught fire.* □ **(s')éjecter**

e'jection [-ʃən] *noun.* □ **expulsion**

eke [iːk]: **eke out** 1 to make (a supply of something) last longer *eg* by adding something else to it: *You could eke out the meat with potatoes.* □ **faire durer**

2 to manage with difficulty to make (a living, livelihood *etc*): *The artist could scarcely eke out a living from his painting.* □ **subsister avec peine**

elaborate [i'labəreit] *verb* 1 to work out or describe (a plan *etc*) in detail: *She elaborated her theory.* □ **entrer dans les détails de**

2 (*especially with* on) to discuss details: *She elaborated on the next day's menu.* □ **donner des détails sur**

■ [-rət] *adjective* 1 very detailed or complicated: *an elaborate design.* □ **compliqué**

2 carefully planned: *elaborate plans for escape.* □ **minutieux**

e'laborately *adverb.* □ **minutieusement**

e,labo'ration *noun.* □ **élaboration**

elapse [i'laps] *verb* (of time) to pass: *A month had elapsed since our last meeting.* □ **(s')écouler**

elastic [i'lastik] *adjective* 1 (of a material or substance) able to return to its original shape or size after being pulled or pressed out of shape: *an elastic bandage*; *Rubber is an elastic substance.* □ **élastique**

2 able to be changed or adapted: *This is a fairly elastic arrangement.* □ **élastique**

■ *noun* a type of cord containing strands of rubber: *Her hat was held on with a piece of elastic.* □ **élastique**

elasticity [ilastisəti, ,iː-] *noun.* □ **élasticité**

elastic band (*also* **rubber band**) a small thin piece of rubber for holding things together or in place: *She put an elastic band around the papers.* □ **élastique**

elated [i'leitid] *adjective* very cheerful: *She felt elated after winning.* □ **transporté de joie**

e'lation *noun.* □ **allégresse**

elbow ['elbou] *noun* the joint where the arm bends: *He*

leant forward on his elbows.* □ **coude**

■ *verb* to push with the elbow: *He elbowed his way through the crowd.* □ **jouer des coudes**

'elbow room *noun* space enough for doing something: *Get out of my way and give me some elbow room!* □ **de la place**

at one's elbow close to one: *The journalist always works with a dictionary at his elbow.* □ **à portée de la main**

elder[1] ['eldə] *adjective* 1 (often of members of a family) older; senior: *He has three elder sisters*; *He is the elder of the two.* □ **aîné**

■ *noun* 1 a person who is older: *Take the advice of your elders.* □ **aîné, ée**

2 an office-bearer in Presbyterian churches. □ **membre du conseil (d'une église presbytérienne)**

'elderly *adjective* (rather) old: *an elderly lady.* □ **assez âgé**

'eldest *adjective* oldest: *She is the eldest of the three children.* □ **aîné**

the elderly people who are (rather) old: *It is important for the elderly to take some exercise.* □ **les gens d'un certain âge**

elder[2] ['eldə] *noun* a kind of shrub or tree with purple-black fruit (**'elderberries**). □ **sureau**

elect [i'lekt] *verb* 1 to choose by vote: *He was elected chairman*; *elected to the committee.* □ **élire**

2 to choose (to do something): *They elected to go by taxi.* □ **choisir de faire qqch.**

■ *adjective* (*placed immediately after noun*) chosen for office but not yet in it: *the president elect.* □ **futur**

e'lection [-ʃən] *noun* the choosing, or choice, (*usually* by vote) of person(s) for office: *When do the elections take place?*; *She is standing for election again.* □ **élection(s)**

e,lectio'neer [-ʃə-] *verb* to work to bring about the election of a candidate. □ **mener une campagne électorale**

e'lector *noun* a person who has the right to vote at an election: *Not all the electors bothered to vote.* □ **électeur, trice**

e'lectoral *adjective* of elections or electors: *The names of all electors are listed in the electoral roll.* □ **électoral**

e'lectorate [-rət] *noun* all electors taken together: *Half of the electorate did not vote.* □ **électorat**

electricity [elek'trisəti] *noun* a form of energy used to give heat, light, power *etc*: *worked by electricity*; *Don't waste electricity.* □ **électricité**

electric [ə'lektrik] *adjective* 1 of, produced by, or worked by electricity: *electric light.* □ **électrique**

2 full of excitement: *The atmosphere in the theatre was electric.* □ **y avoir de l'électricité dans l'air**

e'lectrical *adjective* related to electricity: *electrical engineering*; *electrical goods*; *an electrical fault.* □ **électrique, d'électricité**

e'lectrically *adverb*: *Is this machine electrically operated?* □ **électriquement**

,elec'trician [-ʃən] *noun* a person whose job is to make, install, repair *etc* electrical equipment: *The electrician mended the electric fan.* □ **électricien, ienne**

e'lectrified [-faid] *adjective* supplied or charged with electricity: *an electrified fence.* □ **électrifié, électrisé**

e'lectrify [-fai] *verb* 1 to convert (a railway *etc*) to the use of electricity as the moving power. □ **électrifier**
2 to excite or astonish: *The news electrified us.* □ **électriser**
e,lectrifi'cation [-fi] *noun*. □ **électrification**
e'lectrifying *adjective: an electrifying speech.* □ **électrisant**
electric chair a chair used to execute criminals by sending a powerful electric current through them. □ **chaise électrique**
electrocute [i'lektrəkjuːt] *verb* 1 to kill (a person *etc*) accidentally by electricity: *The child was electrocuted when she touched an uncovered electric wire.* □ **électrocuter**
2 to put (a person) to death by means of electricity. □ **électrocuter**
electrode [i'lektroud] *noun* a conductor through which a current of electricity enters or leaves a battery *etc*. □ **électrode**
electromagnetic waves [ilektroumag'netik] *noun plural* waves of energy travelling through space *etc*, *eg* light waves, X-rays, radio waves. □ **onde électromagnétique**
electron [i'lektron] *noun* a very small particle within the atom. □ **électron**
electronic [elək'tronik] *adjective* 1 worked or produced by devices built or made according to the principles of electronics: *an electronic calculator.* □ **électronique**
2 concerned or working with such machines: *an electronic engineer.* □ **électronicien**
electronics [elək'troniks] *noun singular* the branch of science that deals with the study of the movement and effects of electrons and with their application to machines *etc*. □ **électronique**
elegant ['eligənt] *adjective* having or showing stylishness: *elegant clothes; You look elegant today.* □ **élégant**
'**elegance** *noun*. □ **élégance**
elegy ['elidʒi] *noun* a song or poem of mourning. □ **élégie**
element ['eləmənt] *noun* 1 an essential part of anything: *Sound teaching of grammar is one of the elements of a good education.* □ **élément**
2 a substance that cannot be split by chemical means into simpler substances: *Hydrogen, chlorine, iron and uranium are elements.* □ **corps simple**
3 surroundings necessary for life: *Water is a fish's natural element.* □ **milieu**
4 a slight amount: *an element of doubt.* □ **élément**
5 the heating part in an electric kettle *etc*. □ **résistance**
,ele'mentary [-'men-] *adjective* very simple; not advanced: *elementary mathematics.* □ **élémentaire**
elementary school *noun* a primary school. □ **école primaire**
'**elements** *noun plural* 1 the first things to be learned in any subject: *the elements of musical theory.* □ **rudiments**
2 the forces of nature, as wind and rain. □ **éléments**
in one's element in the surroundings that are most natural or pleasing to one. □ **dans son élément**
elephant ['elifənt] *noun* a very large type of animal with very thick skin, a trunk and two tusks. □ **éléphant**
elevate ['eliveit] *verb* 1 to raise to a higher position or to

a higher rank *etc*: *elevated to the post of manager.* □ **promouvoir**
2 to improve (a person's mind *etc*): *an elevating book.* □ **exalter**
,ele'vation *noun* 1 the act of elevating, or state of being elevated. □ **élévation**
2 height above sea-level: *at an elevation of 1500 metres.* □ **altitude**
3 an architect's drawing of one side of a building. □ **vue en élévation**
'**elevator** *noun* 1 a machine for raising persons, goods *etc* to a higher floor: *There is no elevator in this shop – you will have to climb the stairs.* □ **ascenseur**
2 a tall storehouse for grain. □ **silo**
eleven [i'levn] *noun* 1 the number or figure 11. □ **onze**
2 the age of 11. □ **onze ans**
3 in football *etc*, a team of eleven players: *He plays for the school's first eleven.* □ **onze**
■ *adjective* 1 11 in number. □ **onze**
2 aged 11. □ **(âgé de) onze ans**
eleven- having eleven (of something): *an eleven-page booklet.* □ **de onze (...)**
e'**leventh** *noun* 1 one of eleven equal parts. □ **onzième**
2 (*also adjective*) (the) last of eleven (people, things *etc*); (the) next after the tenth. □ **onzième**
e'**leven-year-old** *noun* a person or animal that is eleven years old. □ **individu, etc. âgé de onze ans**
■ *adjective* (of a person, animal or thing) that is eleven years old. □ **de onze ans**
at the eleventh hour at the last possible moment; only just in time: *The child was saved from the kidnappers at the eleventh hour.* □ **à la dernière minute**
elf [elf] – *plural* **elves** [elvz] – *noun* a tiny and mischievous fairy. □ **lutin**
'**elfin** *adjective* of or like an elf. □ **de lutin**
elicit [i'lisit] *verb* to succeed in getting (information *etc*) from a person, usually with difficulty. □ **tirer de**
eligible ['elidʒəbl] *adjective* 1 suitable or worthy to be chosen: *the most eligible candidate.* □ **qualifié, acceptable**
2 qualified or entitled: *Is he eligible to join the Scouts?* □ **admissible**
,eligi'bility *noun*. □ **admissibilité**
eliminate [i'limineit] *verb* to get rid of; to omit or exclude: *She was eliminated from the tennis match in the first round.* □ **éliminer**
e,limi'nation *noun*. □ **élimination**
élite [i'liːt, ei-] *noun* (with **the**) the best or most important people *especially* within society. □ **élite**
elixir [i'liksə] *noun* a liquid that would supposedly make people able to go on living for ever, or a substance that would turn the cheaper metals into gold: *the elixir of life.* □ **élixir**
elk [elk] – *plurals* **elks, elk** – *noun* the largest of all deer, found in the north of Europe and Asia. □ **élan**
ellipse [i'lips] *noun* a geometrical figure that is a regular oval. □ **ellipse**
el'**liptical** *adjective*. □ **elliptique**
elm [elm] *noun* a kind of tall tree with tough wood and corrugated bark. □ **orme**

elocution [eləˈkjuːʃən] *noun* the art of speaking clearly and effectively. □ **élocution**

elongated [iːˈlɔŋeitid] *adjective* (made) long and narrow; stretched out: *An oval looks like an elongated circle.* □ **allongé**
,**elon'gation** *noun.* □ **allongement**

elope [iˈloup] *verb* to run away secretly, *especially* with a lover. □ **s'enfuir (ensemble)**
e'lopement *noun.* □ **fugue (amoureuse)**

eloquence [ˈeləkwəns] *noun* the power of expressing feelings or thoughts in words that impress or move other people: *a speaker of great eloquence.* □ **éloquence**
'**eloquent** *adjective*: *an eloquent speaker/speech.* □ **éloquent**
'**eloquently** *adverb.* □ **éloquemment**

else [els] *adjective, adverb* besides; other than that already mentioned: *What else can I do? Can we go anywhere else?; He took someone else's pencil.* □ **(d')autre, de plus**
,**else'where** *adverb* in, or to, another place; somewhere or anywhere else: *You must look elsewhere if you want a less tiring job.* □ **ailleurs**
or else otherwise: *He must have missed the train – or else he's ill.* □ **sinon**

elucidate [iˈluːsideit] *verb* to explain. □ **expliquer**
e,luci'dation *noun.* □ **explication**

elude [iˈluːd] *verb* 1 to escape or avoid by quickness or cleverness: *He eluded his pursuers.* □ **échapper à**
2 to be too difficult *etc* for (a person) to understand or remember: *The meaning of this poem eludes me.* □ **échapper à**
e'lusive [-siv] *adjective* escaping or vanishing, often or cleverly: *an elusive criminal.* □ **insaisissable**

elves *see* **elf**.

emaciated [iˈmeisieitid] *adjective* having become very thin (through illness, starvation *etc*). □ **amaigri**
e,maci'ation *noun.* □ **amaigrissement**

emanate [ˈeməneit] *verb* to flow out; to come out (from some source). □ **provenir (de)**
,**ema'nation** *noun.* □ **émanation**

emancipate [iˈmansipeit] *verb* to set free from slavery or other strict or unfair control. □ **émanciper**
e,manci'pation *noun.* □ **émancipation**

embalm [imˈbaːm] *verb* to preserve (a dead body) from decay by treatment with spices or drugs: *The Egyptians embalmed the corpses of their kings.* □ **embaumer**

embankment [imˈbaŋkmənt] *noun* a bank or ridge made *eg* to keep back water or to carry a railway over low-lying places *etc*. □ **digue, talus**

embargo [imˈbaːgou] – *plural* **em'bargoes** – *noun* an official order forbidding something, *especially* trade with another country. □ **embargo**

embark [imˈbaːk] *verb* to go, or put, on board ship: *Passengers should embark early.* □ **(s')embarquer**
,**embar'kation** [em-] *noun.* □ **embarquement**
embark on to start or engage in: *She embarked on a new career.* □ **se lancer dans**

embarrass [imˈbarəs] *verb* 1 to cause to feel uneasy or self-conscious: *She was embarrassed by his praise.* □ **embarrasser**
2 to involve in (*especially* financial) difficulties: *embarrassed by debts.* □ **gêner**
em'barrassment *noun.* □ **embarras**
em'barrassed *adjective*: *He was embarrassed when the teacher asked him to read his essay to the class.* □ **gêné**
em'barrassing *adjective*: *an embarrassing question.* □ **embarrassant**

embassy [ˈembəsi] – *plural* '**embassies** – *noun* (the official residence of) an ambassador and his staff: *the American embassy in Ottawa.* □ **ambassade**

embed [imˈbed] – *past tense, past participle* **em'bedded** – *verb* to fix deeply (in something): *The bullet was embedded in the wall.* □ **enfoncer**

embellish [imˈbeliʃ] *verb* 1 to increase the interest of (a story *etc*) by adding (untrue) details: *The soldier embellished the story of his escape.* □ **enjoliver**
2 to make beautiful with ornaments *etc*: *uniform embellished with gold braid.* □ **orner (de)**
em'bellishment *noun.* □ **ornement**

embers [ˈembəz] *noun plural* the sparking or glowing remains of a fire. □ **braise**

embezzle [imˈbezl] *verb* to take dishonestly (money that has been entrusted to oneself): *As the firm's accountant, he embezzled $20,000 in two years.* □ **détourner**
em'bezzlement *noun.* □ **détournement de fonds**
em'bezzler *noun.* □ **fraudeur, euse**

embitter [imˈbitə] *verb* to make bitter and resentful: *embittered by poverty and failure.* □ **aigrir**

emblem [ˈembləm] *noun* an object chosen to represent an idea, a quality, a country *etc*: *The dove is the emblem of peace.* □ **emblème**
,**emble'matic** [-ˈmatik] *adjective.* □ **emblématique**

embody [imˈbodi] *verb* to represent. □ **exprimer**
em'bodiment *noun.* □ **personnification**

embossed [imˈbost] *adjective* (of metal, leather *etc*) ornamented with a raised design: *an embossed silver spoon.* □ **travaillé en relief**

embrace [imˈbreis] *verb* to take (a person *etc*) in the arms; to hug: *She embraced her brother warmly.* □ **étreindre**
■ *noun* a clasping in the arms; a hug: *a loving embrace.* □ **étreinte**

embroider [imˈbroidə] *verb* to decorate with designs in needlework: *The child embroidered her name on her handkerchief; an embroidered tablecloth.* □ **broder**
em'broidery *noun*: *Embroidery is one of her hobbies; What a beautiful piece of embroidery!* □ **broderie**

embroil [imˈbroil] *verb* to involve (a person) in a quarrel or in a difficult situation: *I do not wish to become embroiled in their family quarrels.* □ **mêler à**

embryo [ˈembriou] – *plural* '**embryos** – *noun* 1 a young animal or plant in its earliest stages in seed, egg or womb: *An egg contains the embryo of a chicken; (also adjective) the embryo child.* □ **embryon; embryonnaire**
2 (*also adjective*) (of) the beginning stage of anything: *The project is still at the embryo stage.* □ **embryonnaire**
,**embry'ology** [-ˈolədʒi] *noun* the science of the formation and development of the embryo. □ **embryologie**
,**embryo'logical** [-ˈlo-] *adjective.* □ **embryologique**
,**embry'ologist** *noun.* □ **embryologiste**
,**embry'onic** [-ˈonik] *adjective* in an early stage of de-

velopment. □ **embryonnaire**

emend [i:'mend] *verb* to correct errors in (a book *etc*): *The editor emended the manuscript.* □ **corriger**

,emen'dation *noun.* □ **correction**

emerald ['emərəld] *noun* 1 a type of precious stone, green in colour. □ **émeraude**

2 (*also* emerald green) its colour (*also adjective*): *She has an emerald (green) coat.* □ **(vert) émeraude**

emerge [i'mə:dʒ] *verb* 1 to come out; to come into view: *The swimmer emerged from the water*; *He was already thirty before his artistic talent emerged.* □ **émerger, apparaître**

2 to become known: *It emerged that they had had a disagreement.* □ **apparaître (que)**

e'mergence *noun.* □ **apparition**

e'mergent *adjective* being in the process of emerging or developing: *the emergent nations.* □ **en voie de développement**

emergency [i'mə:dʒənsi] – *plural* e'mergencies – *noun* an unexpected, *especially* dangerous happening or situation: *Call the doctor – it's an emergency*; *You must save some money for emergencies*; (*also adjective*) *an emergency exit.* □ **cas urgent/imprévu; de secours**

emergent *see* emerge.

emery ['eməri] *noun* a very hard kind of mineral, used as a powder *etc* for polishing. □ **émeri**

emery board a small flat strip of wood or card coated with emery powder and used for filing the fingernails. □ **lime à ongles**

emigrate ['emigreit] *verb* to leave one's country and settle in another: *Many doctors have emigrated from Canada to the United States.* □ **émigrer**

'emigrant *noun, adjective* (a person) emigrating or having emigrated: *The numbers of emigrants are increasing*; *emigrant doctors.* □ **émigrant, ante**

,emi'gration *noun.* □ **émigration**

eminent ['eminənt] *adjective* outstanding; distinguished; famous: *an eminent lawyer.* □ **éminent**

'eminence 1 distinction; fame. □ **distinction, éminence**

2 a title of honour used to or of a cardinal: *His Eminence Cardinal Kelly.* □ **Eminence**

'eminently *adverb* very: *eminently suitable.* □ **parfaitement**

emission *see* emit.

emit [i'mit] – *past tense, past participle* e'mitted – *verb* to give out (light, heat, a sound, a smell *etc*). □ **émettre, dégager**

e'mission [-ʃən] *noun.* □ **émission**

emolument [i'moljumənt] *noun* profit made from employment, salary, fees *etc.* □ **rémunération**

emotion [i'mouʃən] *noun* 1 a (strong) feeling of any kind: *Fear, joy, anger, love, jealousy are all emotions.* □ **émotion**

2 the moving or upsetting of the mind or feelings: *He was overcome by/with emotion.* □ **émotion**

e'motional *adjective* 1 of the emotions: *Emotional problems are affecting his work.* □ **souligner**

2 (*negative* unemotional) causing or showing emotion: *an emotional farewell.* □ **chargé d'émotion**

3 (*negative* unemotional) (of a person) easily affected

by joy, anger, grief *etc*: *He is a very emotional person*; *She is very emotional.* □ **émotif**

e'motionally *adverb.* □ **avec émotion**

emperor ['empərə] – *feminine* 'empress – *noun* the head of an empire: *Charlemagne was emperor of a large part of the world*; *the Emperor Napoleon.* □ **empereur, impératrice**

emphasis ['emfəsis] – *plural* 'emphases [-si:z] – *noun* 1 stress put on certain words in speaking *etc*; greater force of voice used in words or parts of words to make them more noticeable: *In writing we sometimes underline words to show emphasis.* □ **accent, accentuation**

2 force; firmness: *'I do not intend to go,' she said with emphasis.* □ **force**

3 importance given to something: *He placed great emphasis on this point.* □ **insistance, importance**

'emphasize, 'emphasise *verb* to lay or put emphasis on: *You emphasize the word 'too' in the sentence 'Are you going too?'*; *She emphasized the importance of working hard.* □ **souligner**

em'phatic [-'fa-] *adjective* (*negative* unemphatic) expressed with emphasis; firm and definite: *an emphatic denial*; *He was most emphatic about the importance of arriving on time.* □ **catégorique**

em'phatically *adverb.* □ **catégoriquement**

---

to **emphasize** (not **emphasize on**) a point.

---

empire ['empaiə] *noun* 1 a group of states *etc* under a single ruler or ruling power: *the Roman empire.* □ **empire**

2 a large industrial organization controlling many firms: *She owns a washing-machine empire.* □ **empire**

employ [im'ploi] *verb* 1 to give (*especially* paid) work to: *He employs three typists*; *She is employed as a teacher.* □ **employer**

2 to occupy the time or attention of: *She was busily employed (in) writing letters.* □ **occuper**

3 to make use of: *You should employ your time better.* □ **employer**

em'ployed *adjective* having a job; working. □ **employé**

em'ployee, ,employ'ee [em-] *noun* a person employed for wages, a salary *etc*: *That firm has fifty employees.* □ **employé, ée**

em'ployer *noun* a person who employs others: *His employer dismissed him.* □ **employeur, euse**

em'ployment *noun* the act of employing or state of being employed: *She was in my employment*; *This will give employment to more men and women.* □ **emploi**

emporium [em'po:riəm] *noun* 1 a trading centre. □ **centre commercial**

2 a large shop. □ **grand magasin**

empty ['empti] *adjective* 1 having nothing inside: *an empty box*; *an empty cup.* □ **vide**

2 unoccupied: *an empty house.* □ **vide**

3 (*with* of) completely without: *a street quite empty of people.* □ **vide (de)**

4 having no practical result; (likely to be) unfulfilled: *empty threats.* □ **vain**

■ *verb* 1 to make or become empty: *He emptied the jug*; *The movie theatre emptied quickly at 10:30*; *He emp-*

tied out his pockets. □ (se) vider

2 to tip, pour, or fall out of a container: *She emptied the milk into a pan*; *The rubbish emptied on to the ground.* □ verser, (se) répandre

■ *noun* an empty bottle *etc*: *Take the empties back to the shop.* □ bouteille consignée

'emptiness *noun.* □ vide

,empty-'handed *adjective* carrying nothing: *I went to collect my wages but returned empty-handed.* □ les mains vides

,empty-'headed *adjective* brainless: *an empty-headed young man.* □ sans cervelle

emu ['iːmjuː] *noun* a type of Australian bird which cannot fly. □ émeu

emulate ['emjuleit] *verb* to try hard to equal or be better than. □ essayer d'égaler

,emu'lation *noun.* □ émulation

emulsion [i'mʌlʃən] *noun* a milky liquid prepared by mixing *eg* oil and water. □ émulsion

emulsion paint a paint mixed with water rather than oil. □ peinture à l'eau

enable [i'neibl] *verb* to make able by giving means, power or authority (to do something): *The money I inherited enabled me to go on a world cruise.* □ rendre qqn capable de

enact [i'nakt] *verb* to act (a rôle, scene *etc*) not necessarily on stage. □ jouer

e'nactment *noun.* □ promulgation

enamel [i'naməl] *noun* 1 a variety of glass applied as coating to a metal or other surface and made hard by heating: *This pan is covered with enamel*; (*also adjective*) *an enamel plate.* □ (d'/en) émail

2 the coating of the teeth. □ émail

3 a glossy paint. □ peinture laquée

■ *verb – past tense, past participle* e'namelled, e'nameled – to cover or decorate with enamel. □ émailler

enamoured [i'naməd]: enamoured of/with delighted with: *I am not enamoured of the idea of going abroad.* □ enchanté de

encampment [in'kampmənt] *noun* a place where troops *etc* are settled in or camp. □ campement

encase [in'keis] *verb* to enclose (as if) in a case: *The nuts were encased in hard outer coverings.* □ enfermer dans

enchant [in'tʃaːnt] *verb* 1 to delight: *I was enchanted by the children's concert.* □ charmer

2 to put a magic spell on: *A wizard had enchanted her.* □ ensorceler

en'chanted *adjective*: *an enchanted castle.* □ enchanté

en'chanter – *feminine* en'chantress – *noun* a person who enchants. □ enchanteur, teresse

en'chantment *noun* 1 the act of enchanting or state of being enchanted: *a look of enchantment on the children's faces.* □ ravissement

2 a magic spell. □ ensorcèlement

3 charm; attraction: *the enchantment(s) of a big city.* □ charme ensorceleur

encircle [in'səːkl] *verb* to surround: *Enemies encircled him.* □ encercler

enclose [in'klouz] *verb* 1 to put inside a letter or its enve-

lope: *I enclose a cheque for $4.00.* □ joindre (à)

2 to shut in: *The garden was enclosed by a high wall.* □ entourer

en'closure [-ʒə] *noun* 1 the act of enclosing. □ clôture

2 land surrounded by a fence or wall: *She keeps a donkey in that enclosure.* □ enclos

3 something put in along with a letter: *I received your enclosure with gratitude.* □ pièce jointe

encore ['ɒŋkoː] *noun, interjection* (a call from an audience for) a repetition of a performance, or (for) a further performance: *The audience cried 'Encore!'*; *The singer gave two encores.* □ bis

encounter [in'kauntə] *verb* 1 to meet *especially* unexpectedly: *She encountered the manager in the hall.* □ rencontrer

2 to meet with (difficulties *etc*): *I expect to encounter many difficulties in the course of this job.* □ éprouver

■ *noun* 1 a meeting: *I feel that I know him quite well, even after a brief encounter.* □ rencontre

2 a fight: *The encounter between the armies was fierce.* □ affrontement

encourage [in'kʌridʒ] *verb* 1 to give support, confidence or hope to: *The general tried to encourage the troops*: *You should not encourage him in his extravagance*; *I felt encouraged by his praise.* □ encourager

2 to urge (a person) to do something: *You must encourage him to try again.* □ encourager (à)

en'couraging *adjective.* □ encourageant

en'couragingly *adverb.* □ d'une manière encourageante

en'couragement *noun*: *words of encouragement*; *He must be given every encouragement.* □ encouragement

---

the opposite of encourage is discourage.

---

encroach [in'kroutʃ]: en'croach on to advance into; invade: *to encroach on someone's land/rights.* □ empiéter sur

en'croachment *noun.* □ empiètement (sur)

encyclop(a)edia [insaiklə'piːdiə] *noun* a reference work containing information on every branch of knowledge, or on one particular branch: *an encyclopaedia of jazz*; *If you do not know the capital city of Hungary, look it up in an encyclopaedia.* □ encyclopédie

en,cyclo'p(a)edic *adjective.* □ encyclopédique

end [end] *noun* 1 the last or farthest part of the length of something: *the house at the end of the road*; *both ends of the room*; *Put the tables end to end* (= with the end of one touching the end of another); (*also adjective*) *We live in the end house.* □ bout, extrémité; dernier

2 the finish or conclusion: *the end of the week*; *The talks have come to an end*; *The affair is at an end*; *She is at the end of her strength*; *They fought bravely to the end*; *If she wins the prize we'll never hear the end of it* (= she will often talk about it). □ fin, conclusion, end

3 death: *The soldiers met their end bravely.* □ mort

4 an aim: *What end have you in view?* □ but

5 a small piece left over: *cigarette ends.* □ bout

■ *verb* to bring or come to an end: *The scheme ended in disaster*; *How does the play end?*; *How should I end (off) this letter?* □ finir '**ending** *noun* the end, *especially* of a story, poem *etc*: *Fairy stories have happy endings.* □ **fin**

'**endless** *adjective* 1 going on for ever or for a very long time: *endless arguments.* □ **interminable**

2 continuous, because of having the two ends joined: *an endless chain.* □ **sans fin**

at a loose end with nothing to do: *He went to the movies because he was at a loose end.* □ **ne pas trop savoir quoi faire**

end up 1 to reach or come to an end, *usually* unpleasant: *I knew that he would end up in prison.* □ **(se) retrouver**

2 to do something in the end: *He refused to believe her but he ended up apologizing.* □ **finir par**

in the end finally: *He had to work very hard but he passed his exam in the end.* □ **en fin de compte**

make (both) ends meet not to get into debt: *The widow and her four children found it difficult to make ends meet.* □ **joindre les deux bouts**

no end (of) very much: *I feel no end of a fool.* □ **énormément**

on end 1 upright; erect: *Stand the table on end; The cat's fur stood on end.* □ **debout, hérissé**

2 continuously; without a pause: *For days on end we had hardly anything to eat.* □ **d'affilée**

put an end to to cause to finish; to stop: *The government put an end to public execution.* □ **mettre fin à**

the end the limit (of what can be borne or tolerated): *His behaviour is the end!* □ **le comble**

endanger [in'deindʒə] *verb* to put in danger: *Drunk drivers endanger the lives of others.* □ **mettre en danger**

endear [in'diə] *verb* to make dear or more dear (to): *His loyalty endeared him to me.* □ **rendre cher (à)**

en'**dearing** *adjective* arousing feelings of affection: *his endearing innocence.* □ **attachant**

en'**dearment** *noun* a word of love. □ **parole affectueuse**

endeavour [in'devə] *verb* to attempt; to try (to do something): *She endeavoured to attract the waiter's attention.* □ **s'efforcer (de)**

■ *noun* an attempt: *She succeeded in her endeavour to climb Everest.* □ **tentative (pour)**

endemic [en'demik] *adjective* (of a disease *etc*) regularly found in people or a district owing to local conditions: *Malaria is endemic in/to certain tropical countries.* □ **endémique**

endorse [in'dɔːs] *verb* 1 to write one's signature on the back of (a cheque). □ **endosser**

2 to make a note of an offence on (a driving licence). □ **porter une contravention à**

3 to give one's approval to (a decision, statement *etc*): *The court endorsed the judge's decision.* □ **approuver**

en'**dorsement** *noun*. □ **approbation**

endow [in'dau] *verb* to provide: *She was endowed with great beauty.* □ **doter (de)**

en'**dowment** *noun*. □ **dotation**

endure [in'djuə] *verb* 1 to bear patiently; to tolerate: *She endures her troubles bravely; I can endure her rudeness no longer.* □ **supporter**

2 to remain firm; to last: *You must endure to the end; The memory of her great acting has endured.* □ **tenir, durer**

en'**durable** *adjective* (*negative* **unendurable**) able to be borne or tolerated: *This pain is scarcely endurable.* □ **supportable**

en'**durance** *noun* the power or ability to bear or to last: *He has amazing (power of) endurance; Her rudeness is beyond endurance; (also adjective) endurance tests.* □ **endurance; de résistance**

enema ['enəmə] *noun* the injection of a liquid into the rectum: *He was given an enema to clean out the bowels before his operation.* □ **lavement**

enemy ['enəmi] – *plural* '**enemies** – *noun* 1 a person who hates or wishes to harm one: *She is so good and kind that she has no enemies.* □ **ennemi, ie**

2 (*also noun plural*) troops, forces, a nation *etc* opposed to oneself in war *etc*: *He's one of the enemy; The enemy was/were encamped on the hillside; (also adjective) enemy forces.* □ **ennemi**

energy ['enədʒi] – *plural* '**energies** – *noun* 1 the ability to act, or the habit of acting, strongly and vigorously: *She has amazing energy for her age; That child has too much energy; I must devote my energies to gardening today.* □ **énergie**

2 the power, *eg* of electricity, of doing work: *electrical energy; nuclear energy.* □ **énergie**

,**ener'getic** [-'dʒetik] *adjective* 1 vigorous; very active: *an energetic child.* □ **actif**

2 requiring energy: *an energetic walk.* □ **énergique**

,**ener'getically** *adverb*. □ **énergiquement**

enforce [in'fɔːs] *verb* to cause (a law, a command, one's own will *etc*) to be carried out: *There is a law against dropping litter but it is rarely enforced.* □ **appliquer**

en'**forcement** *noun*. □ **mise en application**

engage [in'geidʒ] *verb* 1 to begin to employ (a workman *etc*): *He engaged him as his assistant.* □ **embaucher**

2 to book; to reserve: *He has engaged an entertainer for the children's party.* □ **engager**

3 to take hold of or hold fast; to occupy: *to engage someone's attention.* □ **éveiller**

4 to join battle with: *The two armies were fiercely engaged.* □ **être aux prises**

5 to (cause part of a machine *etc* to) fit into and lock with another part: *The driver engaged second gear.* □ **s'engrenner**

en'**gaged** *adjective* 1 bound by promise (*especially* to marry): *She became engaged to John.* □ **fiancé**

2 (*with* **in**) employed or occupied: *She is engaged in social work.* □ **occupé (à)**

3 busy; not free; occupied: *Please come if you are not already engaged for that evening; The room/telephone line is engaged.* □ **occupé**

en'**gagement** *noun*: *the engagement of three new assistants; When shall we announce our engagement?; Have you any engagements tomorrow?; a naval engagement (= battle); (also adjective) an engagement ring.* □ **recrutement, fiançailles, rendez-vous, combat; de fiançailles**

en'**gaging** *adjective* attractive: *an engaging smile.* □ **engageant**

engine ['endʒin] *noun* 1 a machine in which heat or other energy is used to produce motion: *The car has a new engine.* □ **moteur**

2 a railway engine: *She likes to sit in a seat facing the engine.* □ **locomotive**

,**engi'neer** *noun* **1** a person who designs, makes, or works with, machinery: *an electrical engineer.* □ **ingénieur, eure; technicien, ienne**

2 (*usually* **civil engineer**) a person who designs, constructs, or maintains roads, railways, bridges, sewers *etc.* □ **ingénieur civil, ingénieure civile**

3 an officer who manages a ship's engines. □ **mécanicien, ienne (de la marine)**

4 a person who drives a railway engine. □ **mécanicien, ienne**

■ *verb* to arrange by skill or by cunning means: *He engineered my promotion.* □ **être l'artisan de**

,**engi'neering** *noun* the art or profession of an engineer: *She is studying engineering at university.* □ **ingénierie**

English ['iŋgliʃ] *adjective* of England or its inhabitants: *three English people*; *the English language.* □ **anglais**

■ *noun* the main language of England and the rest of Britain, North America, a great part of the British Commonwealth and some other countries: *She speaks English.* □ **anglais**

Englishman – *feminine* '**Englishwoman** – *noun* a person born in England. □ **Anglais, aise**

engrave [in'greiv] *verb* **1** to cut (letters or designs) on stone, wood, metal *etc*: *They engraved his initials on the silver cup.* □ **graver**

2 to decorate (metal *etc*) in this way: *He engraved the silver cup.* □ **graver**

en'graver *noun.* □ **graveur, euse**

engrossed [in'groust] *adjective* (*often with* **in**) having one's attention and interest completely taken up: *She is completely engrossed in her work.* □ **absorbé**

engulf [in'gʌlf] *verb* (of waves, flames *etc*) to swallow up completely: *Flames engulfed him.* □ **engloutir**

enhance [in'haːns] *verb* to make to appear greater or better. □ **mettre en valeur**

enigma [i'nigmə] *noun* anything difficult to understand; a mystery. □ **énigme**

enigmatic [enig'matik] *adjective* puzzling; mysterious: *an enigmatic smile.* □ **énigmatique**

,**enig'matically** *adverb.* □ **mystérieusement**

enjoy [in'dʒoi] *verb* **1** to find pleasure in: *He enjoyed the meal.* □ **aimer**

2 to experience; to be in the habit of having (*especially* a benefit): *he enjoyed good health all his life.* □ **jouir (de)**

en'joyable *adjective*: *an enjoyable book*; *That was most enjoyable.* □ **agréable**

en'joyment *noun*: *the enjoyment of life.* □ **plaisir**

enjoy oneself to experience pleasure or happiness: *She enjoyed herself at the party.* □ **(s')amuser**

> **enjoy** must be followed by an object: *He enjoys reading/We enjoyed ourselves.*

enlarge [in'laːdʒ] *verb* **1** to make larger: *He enlarged the garden.* □ **agrandir**

2 to reproduce on a larger scale (a photograph *etc*): *We had the photograph enlarged.* □ **agrandir**

en'largement *noun* **1** something enlarged, *especially* a photograph. □ **agrandissement**

2 the act of enlarging or state of being enlarged: *Enlargement of the glands in the neck is usually a sign of illness.* □ **dilatation**

enlarge on to speak, write *etc* in more detail: *Would you like to enlarge on your original statement?* □ **développer**

enlighten [in'laitn] *verb* to give more information to (a person): *Will someone please enlighten me as to what is happening?* □ **éclairer (qqn sur qqch.)**

en'lightened *adjective* wise through knowledge; free from prejudice: *an enlightened headmaster*; *an enlightened decision.* □ **éclairé**

en'lightenment *noun.* □ **éclaircissement(s)**

enlist [in'list] *verb* **1** to join an army *etc*: *My father enlisted on the day after war was declared.* □ **(s')engager**

2 to obtain the support and help of: *He has enlisted George to help him organize the party.* □ **recruter**

3 to obtain (support and help) from someone: *They enlisted the support of five hundred people for their campaign.* □ **(s')assurer le concours de**

enliven [in'laivn] *verb* to make (more) lively: *I tried to think of something that might enliven the class.* □ **animer**

enmity ['enməti] *noun* unfriendliness; hatred. □ **hostilité**

enormous [i'noːməs] *adjective* very large: *The new building is enormous*; *We had an enormous lunch.* □ **énorme**

e'normousness *noun.* □ **grandeur démesurée**

e'normity *noun* **1** great wickedness. □ **crime très grave**

2 hugeness. □ **énormité**

enough [i'nʌf] *adjective* in the number or quantity *etc* needed: *Have you enough money to pay for the books?*; *food enough for everyone.* □ **assez**

■ *pronoun* the amount needed: *He has had enough to eat*; *I've had enough of her rudeness.* □ **assez**

■ *adverb* **1** to the degree needed: *Is it hot enough?*; *She swam well enough to pass the test.* □ **assez**

2 one must admit; you must agree: *She's pretty enough, but not beautiful*; *Oddly enough, it isn't raining.* □ **assez**

enquire, enquiry *see* **inquire.**

enrage [in'reidʒ] *verb* to make very angry: *His son's rudeness enraged him.* □ **faire enrager**

enrapture [in'raptʃə] *verb* to give delight to. □ **enchanter**

enrich [in'ritʃ] *verb* to improve the quality of: *Fertilizers enrich the soil*; *Reading enriches the mind*; *an enriching* (= useful and enjoyable) *experience.* □ **enrichir**

enrol, enroll [in'roul] – *past tense, past participle* **en'rolled** – *verb* to add (someone), or have oneself added, to a list (as a pupil at a school, a member of a club *etc*): *Can we enrol for this class?*; *You must enrol your child before the start of the school term.* □ **(s')inscrire, (s')enrôler**

en'rolment *noun.* □ **inscription**

> **enrolment** is spelt with one **-l-**.

en route [onruːt] *adverb* on the way: *I'm en route for my office*; *en route from Quebec City to Montreal.* □ **en**

route (pour)

ensemble [on'sobl, on'sombl] *noun* **1** a woman's complete outfit of clothes. □ **ensemble**
2 in opera *etc*, a passage performed by all the singers, musicians *etc* together. □ **ensemble**
3 a group of musicians performing regularly together. □ ensemble
4 all the parts of a thing taken as a whole. □ **ensemble**

ensnare [in'sneə] *verb* to trap: *He was ensnared by her beauty.* □ **séduire**

ensue [in'sjuː] *verb* to come after; to result (from): *the panic that ensued from the false news report.* □ **résulter (de)**
en'**suing** *adjective* coming after; happening as a result: *She was killed in the ensuing riots.* □ **qui s'ensuit**

ensure [in'ʃuə] *verb* to make sure: *Ensure that your television set is switched off at night.* □ **(s')assurer (que)**

entail [in'teil] *verb* to bring as a result; to require: *These alterations will entail great expense.* □ **occasionner**

entangle [in'taŋgl] *verb* to cause (something) to become twisted or tangled with something else: *Her long scarf entangled itself in the bicycle wheel*; *entangled in an unhappy love affair.* □ **emmêler**
en'**tanglement** *noun.* □ **enchevêtrement, complications**

enter ['entə] *verb* **1** to go or come in: *Enter by this door.* □ **entrer**
2 to come or go into (a place): *She entered the room.* □ **entrer (dans)**
3 to give the name of (another person or oneself) for a competition *etc*: *She entered for the race; I entered my pupils for the examination.* □ **(s')inscrire (à)**
4 to write (one's name *etc*) in a book *etc*: *Did you enter your name in the visitors' book?* □ **inscrire**
5 to start in: *She entered his employment last week.* □ **entrer en service**
enter into 1 to take part in: *She entered into an agreement with the film director.* □ **participer (à)**
2 to take part enthusiastically in: *They entered into the Christmas spirit.* □ **entrer dans le jeu**
3 to begin to discuss: *We cannot enter into the question of salaries yet.* □ **entrer dans**
4 to be a part of: *The price did not enter into the discussion.* □ **entrer (en ligne de compte) dans**
enter on/upon to begin: *We have entered upon the new term.* □ **commencer**

| to enter (not enter into) a room. |

enterprise ['entəpraiz] *noun* **1** something that is attempted or undertaken (*especially* if it requires boldness or courage): *business enterprises; a completely new enterprise.* □ **entreprise**
2 willingness to try new lines of action: *We need someone with enterprise and enthusiasm.* □ **esprit d'initiative**
'**enterprising** *adjective* (*negative* **unenterprising**) full of enterprise; adventurous. □ **plein d'initiative**

entertain [entə'tein] *verb* **1** to receive, and give food *etc* to (guests): *They entertained us to dinner.* □ **recevoir**
2 to amuse: *Her stories entertained us for hours.* □

amuser
3 to hold in the mind: *She entertained the hope that she would one day be Prime Minister.* □ **nourrir**
enter'**tainer** *noun* one who gives amusing performances professionally. □ **artiste**
,enter'**taining** *adjective* amusing: *entertaining stories.* □ **divertissant, distrayant**
,enter'**tainment** *noun* **1** something that entertains, *eg* a theatrical show *etc*. □ **spectacle**
2 the act of entertaining. □ **distraction**
3 amusement; interest: *There is no lack of entertainment in the city at night.* □ **divertissement**

enthrall, enthral [in'θroːl] – *past tense, past participle* en'**thralled** – *verb* to delight greatly: *His stories enthralled the children.* □ **captiver**
en'**thralling** *adjective.* □ **passionnant**
en'**thrallment** *noun.* □ **charme**

enthrone [in'θroun] *verb* to place on a throne; to crown (as a king, queen, bishop *etc*): *The queen was enthroned with great ceremony.* □ **introniser**
en'**thronement** *noun.* □ **intronisation**

enthuse [in'θjuːz] *verb* **1** to be enthusiastic. □ **être emballé (par)**
2 to fill with enthusiasm. □ **enthousiasmer**

enthusiasm [in'θjuːziazəm] *noun* strong or passionate interest: *She has a great enthusiasm for travelling; He did not show any enthusiasm for our new plans.* □ **enthousiasme**
en'**thusiast** *noun* a person filled with enthusiasm: *a computer enthusiast.* □ **enthousiaste**
en,thusi'**astic** *adjective* (*negative* **unenthusiastic**) full of enthusiasm or approval: *an enthusiastic mountaineer.* □ **enthousiaste**
en,thusi'**astically** *adverb.* □ **avec enthousiasme**

entice [in'tais] *verb* to attract or tempt: *Goods are displayed in shop windows to entice people into the shop.* □ **attirer**
en'**ticement** *noun.* □ **attrait**
en'**ticing** *adjective* attractive: *an enticing smell.* □ **attrayant**

entire [in'taiə] *adjective* whole: *I spent the entire day on the beach.* □ **entier**
en'**tirely** *adverb* completely: *a house entirely hidden by trees; not entirely satisfactory; entirely different.* □ **entièrement**
en'**tirety** [-rəti] *noun* completeness. □ **totalité**

entitle [in'taitl] *verb* **1** to give (a person) a right (to, or to do, something): *You are not entitled to free school lunches; He was not entitled to borrow money from the cash box.* □ **autoriser (à)**
2 to give to (a book *etc*) as a title or name: *a story entitled 'The White Horse'.* □ **intituler**
en'**titlement** *noun.* □ **droit(s)**

entourage [ontu'raːʒ] *noun* a group of followers, *especially* of a person of high rank. □ **entourage**

entrails ['entreilz] *noun plural* the internal parts of the body, *especially* the intestines: *a chicken's entrails.* □ **entrailles**

entrance¹ ['entrəns] *noun* **1** a place of entering, *eg* an opening, a door *etc*: *the entrance to the tunnel; The*

church has an impressive entrance. □ **entrée**
2 (an) act of entering: *Hamlet now makes his second entrance.* □ **entrée**
3 the right to enter: *She has applied for entrance to university*; (*also adjective*) *an entrance exam.* □ **(d')admission**
'**entrant** *noun* one who enters (*eg* a competition): *There were sixty entrants for the musical competition.* □ **candidat, ate**
entrance² [in'traːns] *verb* to fill with great delight: *The audience were entranced by her singing.* □ **transporter**
entrant *see* **entrance¹**.
entreat [in'triːt] *verb* to ask (a person) earnestly and seriously (to do something). □ **supplier**
en'treaty – *plural* **en'treaties** – *noun* (an) earnest request or plea. □ **supplication**
entrée ['ontrei] *noun* a dish served at dinner as, or before, the main course. □ **entrée**
entrepot ['ontrəpou] *noun* a seaport through which exports and imports pass without incurring duty: *Singapore is an entrepot.* □ **port franc**
entrepreneur [ontrəprə'nəː] *noun* a person who starts or organizes a business company, *especially* one involving risk: *What this company needs is a real entrepreneur.* □ **entrepreneur, eure**
entrust [in'trʌst] *verb* to give into the care of another; to trust (somebody with something): *I entrusted this secret to her*; *I entrusted him with the duty of locking up.* □ **confier à qqn**
entry ['entri] – *plural* '**entries** – *noun* **1** (an) act of coming in or going in: *They were silenced by the entry of the teacher; Britain's entry into the European Common Market.* □ **entrée**
2 the right to enter: *We can't go in – the sign says 'No Entry'.* □ **entrée**
3 place of entrance, *especially* a passage or small entrance hall: *Don't bring your bike in here – leave it in the entry.* □ **entrée**
4 a person or thing entered for a competition *etc*: *There are forty-five entries for the painting competition.* □ **candidat, ate; inscription**
5 something written in a list in a book *etc*: *Some of the entries in the cash-book are inaccurate.* □ **écriture**
entwine [in'twain] *verb* to wind around. □ **(s')entrelacer**
enumerate [i'njuːməreit] *verb* to give a list of: *She enumerated my faults – laziness, vanity etc.* □ **énumérer**
e,nume'ration *noun.* □ **énumération**
enunciate [i'nʌnsieit] *verb* to pronounce clearly and distinctly: *He carefully enunciated each syllable of the word.* □ **articuler**
e,nunci'ation *noun.* □ **articulation**
envelop [in'veləp] – *past tense, past participle* **en'veloped** – *verb* to cover by wrapping; to surround completely: *He enveloped himself in a long cloak.* □ **envelopper**

---

envelop, without an -e, is a verb.
envelope, with an -e, is a noun.

---

envelope ['envəloup] *noun* a thin, flat wrapper or cover, *especially* for a letter: *The letter arrived in a long envelope.* □ **enveloppe**

enviable, envious *see* **envy**.
environment [in'vaiərənmənt] *noun* (a set of) surrounding conditions, *especially* those influencing development or growth: *An unhappy home environment may drive a teenager to crime; We should protect the environment from destruction by modern chemicals etc.* □ **milieu, environnement**
en,viron'mental [-'men-] *adjective.* □ **du milieu**
envisage [in'vizidʒ] *verb* to picture in one's mind and consider: *This was the plan that we envisaged for the future.* □ **envisager**
envoy ['envoi] *noun* a messenger, *especially* one sent to deal with a foreign government: *He was sent to France as the king's envoy.* □ **envoyé, ée**
envy ['envi] *noun* a feeling of discontent at another's good fortune or success: *She could not conceal her envy of me/at my success.* □ **jalousie**
■ *verb* **1** to feel envy towards (someone): *He envied me; She envied him his money.* □ **envier**
2 to feel envy because of: *I've always envied that dress of yours.* □ **envier**
'**enviable** *adjective* (*negative* **unenviable**) that is to be envied: *She spoke in public with enviable ease.* □ **enviable**
'**envious** *adjective* feeling or showing envy: *I'm envious of her talents.* □ **jaloux (de)**
the envy of something envied by: *His piano-playing was the envy of his sisters.* □ **envie (de)**
epic ['epik] *noun* **1** a long poem telling a story of great deeds. □ **épopée**
2 a long story, film *etc* telling of great deeds *especially* historic. □ **épopée**
epidemic [epi'demik] *noun* an outbreak of a disease that spreads rapidly and attacks very many people: *an epidemic of measles/influenza.* □ **épidémie**
epilepsy ['epilepsi] *noun* a disease of the nervous system causing attacks of unconsciousness, *usually* with violent movements of the body. □ **épilepsie**
,**epi'leptic** [-tik] *noun, adjective* (a person who is) suffering from epilepsy. □ **épileptique**
■ *adjective* of, or caused by, epilepsy: *He has epileptic fits.* □ **d'épilepsie**
epilogue, epilog ['epilog] *noun* the closing section of a book, program *etc*. □ **épilogue**
episode ['episoud] *noun* **1** an incident, or series of events, occurring in a longer story *etc*: *The episode of/about the donkeys is in Chapter 3; That is an episode in her life that she wishes to forget.* □ **épisode, péripétie**
2 a part of a radio or television serial that is broadcast at one time: *This is the last episode of the serial.* □ **épisode**
epistle [i'pisl] *noun* a letter, *especially* in the Bible from an apostle: *The epistles of St. Paul.* □ **épître**
epitaph ['epitaːf] *noun* something written or said about a dead person, *especially* something written on a tombstone. □ **épitaphe**
epoch ['iːpok, 'epək] *noun* (the start of) a particular period of history, development *etc*: *The invention of printing marked an epoch in the history of education.* □ **époque**
equal ['iːkwəl] *adjective* the same in size, amount, value

etc: *four equal slices; coins of equal value; Are these pieces equal in size? Women want equal wages with men.* □ **égal**

■ *noun* one of the same age, rank, ability *etc*: *I am not his equal at running.* □ **égal, ale**

■ *verb – past tense, past participle* '**equalled**, '**equaled** – to be the same in amount, value, size *etc*: *I cannot hope to equal him; She equalled his score of twenty points; Five and five equals ten.* □ **égaler**

equality [i'kwolǝti] *noun* the state of being equal: *Women want equality of opportunity with men.* □ **égalité**

'**equalize,** '**equalise** *verb* to make or become equal: *Our team were winning by one goal – but the other side soon equalized.* □ **égaliser**

'**equally** *adverb*: *All are equally good; She divided her chocolate equally between us.* □ **également**

equal to fit or able for: *I didn't feel equal to telling him the truth.* □ **capable de**

equate [i'kweit] *verb* to regard as the same in some way: *She equates money with happiness.* □ **mettre sur le même pied**

e'**quation** [-ʒǝn] *noun* **1** a statement that two things are equal or the same: $xy + xy = 2xy$ *is an equation.* □ **équation**

2 a formula expressing the action of certain substances on others: $2H_2 + O_2 = 2H_2O$ *is an equation.* □ **équation**

equator [i'kweitǝ] *noun* (*with* **the**) an imaginary line (or one drawn on a map *etc*) passing around the globe, at an equal distance from the North and South poles: *Singapore is almost on the equator.* □ **équateur**

equatorial [ekwǝ'toːriǝl] *adjective* of or near the equator: *an equatorial climate.* □ **équatorial**

equestrian [i'kwestriǝn] *adjective* of the art of horse-riding. □ **équestre**

equilateral [iːkwi'latǝrǝl] *adjective* having all sides equal: *an equilateral triangle.* □ **équilatéral**

equilibrium [iːkwi'libriǝm] *noun* a state of equal balance between weights, forces *etc*. □ **équilibre**

equinox ['ekwinoks] *noun* the time when the sun crosses the equator, about March 21 and September 23. □ **équinoxe**

equip [i'kwip] – *past tense, past participle* e'**quipped** – *verb* to fit out or provide with everything needed: *She was fully equipped for the journey; The school is equipped with four computers.* □ **équiper (de)**

e'**quipment** *noun* **1** the clothes, machines, tools *etc* necessary for a particular kind of work, activity *etc*: *The mechanic could not repair the car because she did not have the right equipment; The boy could not afford the equipment necessary for mountaineering.* □ **équipement, matériel**

2 the act of equipping. □ **équipement**

equitable ['ekwitǝbl] *adjective* fair and just. □ **équitable**

'**equitably** *adverb*. □ **équitablement**

equity ['ekwǝti] *noun* fairness; justice. □ **équité**

equivalent [i'kwivǝlǝnt] *adjective* equal in value, power, meaning *etc*: *A metre is not quite equivalent to a yard; Would you say that 'bravery' and 'courage' are exactly equivalent?* □ **équivalent**

■ *noun* something or someone that is equivalent to

something or someone else: *This word has no equivalent in French.* □ **équivalent**

era ['iǝrǝ] *noun* **1** a number of years counting from an important point in history: *the Victorian era.* □ **époque**

2 a period of time marked by an important event or events: *an era of social reform.* □ **ère**

eradicate [i'radikeit] *verb* to get rid of completely: *Smallpox has almost been eradicated.* □ **supprimer**

e,**radi'cation** *noun*. □ **suppression**

erase [i'reis] *verb* to rub out (pencil marks *etc*): *The typist tried to erase the error.* □ **effacer**

e'**raser** *noun* something that erases, *especially* a piece of rubber *etc* for erasing pencil *etc*. □ **gomme**

erect [i'rekt] *adjective* upright: *He held his head erect.* □ **droit**

■ *verb* **1** to set up; to put up or to build: *They erected a statue in her memory; They plan to erect an office block there.* □ **dresser, ériger**

2 to set upright (a mast *etc*). □ **dresser**

e'**rection** [-ʃǝn] *noun*. □ **construction**

e'**rectly** *adverb*. □ **(tout) droit**

e'**rectness** *noun*. □ **attitude droite**

ermine [ǝrmin] *noun* a type of animal similar to a weasel. □ **hermine**

erode [i'roud] *verb* to eat or wear away (metals *etc*); to destroy gradually: *Acids erode certain metals; Water has eroded the rock; The individual's right to privacy is being eroded.* □ **ronger, éroder**

e'**rosion** [-ʒǝn] *noun*. □ **érosion**

erotic [i'rotik] *adjective* of, or arousing, sexual love or desire. □ **érotique**

err [ǝː] *verb* to make a mistake; to be wrong; to do wrong. □ **(se) tromper**

err on the side of to be guilty of what might be seen as a fault in order to avoid an opposite and greater fault: *It is better to err on the side of leniency when punishing a child.* □ **pécher par excès de**

errand ['erǝnd] *noun* **1** a short journey made in order to get something or do something *especially* for someone else: *He has sent the child on an errand; The child will run errands for you.* □ **commission**

2 the purpose of such a journey: *She accomplished her errand.* □ **commission**

erratic [i'ratik] *adjective* inclined to be irregular; not dependable: *Her behaviour/work is erratic.* □ **irrégulier**

er'**ratically** *adverb*. □ **irrégulièrement**

erratum [i'raːtǝm] – *plural* er'**rata** [-tǝ] – *noun* an error in writing or printing: *The errata are listed at the beginning of the book.* □ **erratum**

erroneous [i'rouniǝs] *adjective* (not used of a person) wrong; incorrect: *an erroneous statement.* □ **faux**

er'**roneously** *adverb*. □ **faussement**

er'**roneousness** *noun*. □ **fausseté**

error ['erǝ] **1** *noun* a mistake: *Her written work is full of errors.* □ **erreur**

2 the state of being mistaken: *I did it in error.* □ **erreur**

erupt [i'rʌpt] *verb* (of a volcano) to throw out lava *etc*: *When did Mount Etna last erupt?; The demonstration started quietly but suddenly violence erupted.* □ **faire éruption, exploser**

e'ruption [-ʃən] *noun*. □ éruption

escalate ['eskəleit] *verb* to increase or enlarge rapidly: *Prices are escalating.* □ grimper

,esca'lation *noun*. □ escalade

escalator ['eskəleitə] *noun* a moving staircase in a shop, metro *etc*. □ escalier roulant

escapade [eskə'peid] *noun* a daring or adventurous act, often one that is disapproved of by others: *Have you heard about his latest escapade?* □ fredaine

escape [i'skeip] *verb* 1 to gain freedom: *He escaped from prison.* □ s'évader (de)

2 to manage to avoid (punishment, disease *etc*): *She escaped the infection.* □ échapper (à)

3 to avoid being noticed or remembered by; to avoid (the observation of): *The fact escaped me/my notice*; *His name escapes me/my memory.* □ échapper (à)

4 (of a gas, liquid *etc*) to leak; to find a way out: *Gas was escaping from a hole in the pipe.* □ (s')échapper

■ *noun* (act of) escaping; state of having escaped: *Make your escape while the guard is away*; *There have been several escapes from that prison*; *Escape was impossible*; *The explosion was caused by an escape of gas.* □ évasion; fuite

e'scapism *noun* the tendency to escape from unpleasant reality into daydreams *etc*. □ évasion (du réel)

e'scapist *noun*, adjective. □ d'évasion

escort ['eskɔːt] *noun* person(s), ship(s) *etc* accompanying for protection, guidance, courtesy *etc*: *She offered to be my escort around the city*; *The transport supplies were under military/police escort.* □ cavalier; hôtesse; escorte

■ [i'skɔːt] – *verb* to accompany or attend as escort: *He offered to escort her to the dance*; *Four police motorcyclists escorted the president's car along the route.* □ escorter

especial [i'speʃəl] *adjective* more than the ordinary; particular: *You must treat this with especial care.* □ spécial

e'specially *adverb* particularly: *These insects are quite common, especially in hot countries.* □ particulièrement, spécialement

espionage ['espiənaːʒ] *noun* the activity of spying: *She has never been involved in espionage.* □ espionnage

esplanade [esplə'neid] *noun* a level space for walking or driving *especially* at the seaside: *Our hotel is on the esplanade and overlooks the sea.* □ esplanade

essay ['esei] *noun* a written composition; a piece of written prose: *The examination consists of four essays*; *Write an essay on/about your holiday.* □ rédaction, essai

essence ['esns] 1 the most important part or quality: *Tolerance is the essence of friendship.* □ essence (meme)

2 a substance obtained from a plant, drug *etc*: *vanilla essence.* □ essence

essential [i'senʃəl] *adjective* absolutely necessary: *Strong boots are essential for mountaineering*; *It is essential that you arrive punctually.* □ essentiel

■ *noun* a thing that is fundamental or necessary: *Everyone should learn the essentials of first aid*; *Is a television set an essential?* □ rudiments

es'sentially *adverb* basically: *She is an essentially selfish person.* □ essentiellement

establish [i'stabliʃ] *verb* 1 to settle firmly in a position (*eg* a job, business *etc*): *She established herself (in business) as a jeweller.* □ (s')établir

2 to found; to set up (*eg* a university, a business): *How long has the firm been established?* □ fonder

3 to show to be true; to prove: *The police established that he was guilty.* □ établir

e'stablished *adjective* settled or accepted: *established customs.* □ établi

e'stablishment *noun* 1 the act of establishing. □ constitution

2 an institution or organization: *All employees of this establishment get a bonus at New Year.* □ établissement

3 a person's residence or household: *a bachelor's establishment.* □ ménage

estate [i'steit] *noun* 1 a large piece of land owned by one person or a group of people *etc*: *They have an estate in Ireland.* □ propriété

2 a piece of land developed for building *etc*: *a housing/industrial estate.* □ lotissement

3 a person's total possessions (property, money *etc*): *Her estate was divided among her sons.* □ biens

real estate agent a person whose job is to sell houses and land. □ agent, ente, immobilier, ière

esteem [i'stiːm] *verb* to value or respect. □ estimer

■ *noun* favourable opinion; respect: *His foolish behaviour lowered him in my esteem*; *He was held in great esteem by his colleagues.* □ estime

esthetic *see* aesthetic.

estimate ['estimeit] *verb* 1 to judge size, amount, value *etc*, especially roughly or without measuring: *He estimated that the journey would take two hours.* □ estimer

2 to form an idea or judgment of how good *etc* something is: *I did not estimate my chances of escape very highly.* □ évaluer

■ [-mət] *noun* a calculation (*eg* of the probable cost *etc* of something): *She gave us an estimate of the cost of repairing the stonework*; *a rough estimate.* □ estimation

,esti'mation *noun* judgment; opinion: *In my estimation, he is the more gifted artist of the two.* □ avis

estuary ['estjuəri] – *plural* 'estuaries – *noun* the wide lower part of a river up which the tide flows: *the Thames estuary.* □ estuaire

et cetera [et'setrə] (*usually abbreviated to* etc *or* &c *when written*) a Latin phrase meaning 'and the rest', 'and so on': *The refugees need food, clothes, blankets etc.* □ et caetera

etch [etʃ] *verb* to make (designs) on metal, glass *etc* using an acid to eat out the lines. □ graver à l'eau forte

eternal [i'təːnl] *adjective* 1 without end; lasting for ever; unchanging: *God is eternal*; *eternal life.* □ éternel

2 never ceasing: *I am tired of your eternal complaints.* □ continuel

e'ternally *adverb*. □ éternellement

e'ternity *noun* 1 time without end. □ éternité

2 a seemingly endless time: *She waited for an eternity.* □ éternité

3 the state or time after death. □ éternité

ether ['iːθə] *noun* a colourless liquid used to dissolve fats *etc*, and, medically, as an anaesthetic. □ **éther**

ethics ['eθiks] *noun singular* the study or the science of morals. □ **morale**

■ *noun plural* rules or principles of behaviour. □ **morale**

'**ethical** *adjective* **1** of or concerning morals, justice or duty. □ **moral**

2 (*negative* **unethical**) morally right. □ **moral**

'**ethically** *adverb*. □ **selon l'éthique**

ethnic ['eθnik] *adjective* of nations or races of mankind or their customs, dress, food *etc*: *ethnic groups/dances*. □ **ethnique**

ethnology [eθ'nolədʒi] *noun* the study of the different races of mankind. □ **ethnologie**

,**ethno'logical** [-'lo-] *adjective*. □ **ethnologique**

eth'nologist *noun*. □ **ethnologue**

etiquette ['etiket] *noun* rules for correct or polite behaviour between people, or within certain professions: *medical/legal etiquette*. □ **convenances**

eucalyptus [juːkə'liptəs] – *plurals* ,**euca'lyptuses**, ,**euca'lypti** [-tai] – a type of large Australian evergreen tree, giving timber, gum and an oil that is used in the treatment of colds. □ **eucalyptus**

eulogy ['juːlədʒi] – *plural* **'eulogies** – *noun* (a speech or piece of writing containing) high praise. □ **panégyrique**

euphemism ['juːfəmizəm] *noun* a pleasant name for something that is unpleasant: *'Pass on' is a euphemism for 'die'*. □ **euphémisme**

,**euphe'mistic** *adjective*. □ **euphémique**

euphoria [juːfouriːə] *noun* an extreme feeling of wellbeing: *The euphoria Helga experienced when she first took the drug did not last*. □ **euphorie**

European [juːrəpiːən] *adjective* of Europe or its inhabitants: *The European countries won medals for skating*. □ **européen, enne**

■ *noun* a person from Europe: *The Europeans were great explorers*. □ **Européen, enne**

euthanasia [juːθə'neiziə] *noun* the painless killing of someone who is suffering from a painful and incurable illness: *Many old people would prefer euthanasia to the suffering they have to endure*. □ **euthanasie**

evacuate [i'vakjueit] *verb* **1** to leave or withdraw from (a place), *especially* because of danger: *The troops evacuated their position because of the enemy's advance*. □ **évacuer**

2 to cause (inhabitants *etc*) to leave a place, *especially* because of danger: *Children were evacuated from the city to the country during the war*. □ **évacuer**

e,vacu'ation *noun*. □ **évacuation**

evade [i'veid] *verb* to escape or avoid by *eg* trickery or skill. □ **éviter**

e'vasion [-ʒən] *noun*. □ **fuite**

e'vasive [-siv] *adjective* **1** having the purpose of evading. □ **évasif**

2 not frank and direct: *He gave evasive answers*. □ **évasif**

e'vasively *adverb*. □ **évasivement**

e'vasiveness *noun*. □ **caractère évasif**

evaluate [i'valjueit] *verb* **1** to form an idea of the worth of: *It is difficult to evaluate her as a writer*. □ **évaluer**

2 to work out the numerical value of: *If x = 1 and y = 2*

we can evaluate $x^2 + y^2$. □ **évaluer**

e,valu'ation *noun*. □ **évaluation**

evangelical [iːvan'dʒelikəl] *adjective* seeking to convert people, *especially* to Christianity. □ **évangélique**

e'vangelist [-i-] *noun* a person who preaches Christianity *especially* at large public meetings. □ **évangéliste**

evaporate [i'vapəreit] *verb* to (cause to) change into vapour and disappear: *The small pool of water evaporated in the sunshine*; *His enthusiasm soon evaporated*. □ **(s')évaporer**

e'vaporated *adjective* having had some moisture removed by evaporation: *evaporated milk*. □ **concentré**

e,vapo'ration *noun*. □ **évaporation**

evasion, evasive *see* **evade**.

eve [iːv] *noun* **1** the day or evening before a festival: *Christmas Eve*; *New Year's Eve*. □ **veille**

2 the time just before an event: *on the eve of (the) battle*. □ **veille**

3 evening. □ **soir**

even[1] [iːvən] *adjective* **1** level; the same in height, amount *etc*: *Are the table legs even?*; *an even temperature*. □ **égal**

2 smooth: *Make the path more even*. □ **plat**

3 regular: *She has a strong, even pulse*. □ **régulier**

4 divisible by 2 with no remainder: *2, 4, 6, 8, 10 etc are even numbers*. □ **pair**

5 equal (in number, amount *etc*): *The teams have scored one goal each and so they are even now*. □ **à égalité**

6 (of temperament *etc*) calm: *She has a very even temper*. □ **égal**

■ *verb* – *past tense, past participle* '**evened** – **1** to make equal: *Smith's goal evened the score*. □ **égaliser**

2 to make smooth or level. □ **niveler**

'**evenly** *adverb*. □ **également**

'**evenness** *noun*. □ **égalité**

be/get even with to be revenged on: *He tricked me, but I'll get even with him*. □ **(se) venger de**

an even chance *see* **chance**.

even out 1 to become level or regular: *The road rose steeply and then evened out*; *His pulse began to even out*. □ **(s')égaliser**

2 to make smooth: *He raked the soil to even it out*. □ **égaliser**

3 to make equal: *If Jane would do some of Mary's typing, that would even the work out*. □ **égaliser**

even up to make equal: *Mary did better in the math exam than Jim and that evened up their marks*. □ **égaliser**

even[2] [iːvən] *adverb* **1** used to point out something unexpected in what one is saying: *'Have you finished yet?' 'No, I haven't even started.'*; *Even the winner got no prize*. □ **même**

2 yet; still: *My boots were dirty, but his were even dirtier*. □ **encore (plus)**

even if no matter whether: *Even if I leave now, I'll be too late*. □ **même si**

even so in spite of that: *It rained, but even so we enjoyed the day*. □ **malgré tout**

even though in spite of the fact that: *I like the job even though it's badly paid*. □ **quand bien même**

evening [iːvniŋ] *noun* **1** the part of the day between the afternoon and the night: *She leaves the house in the morning and returns in the evening; summer evenings; tomorrow evening; on Tuesday evening; early evening;* (*also adjective*) *the evening performance.* □ **soir(ée)**
2 the last part (of one's life *etc*): *in the evening of her life.* □ **soir**

evening dress 1 clothes worn for formal occasions in the evening. □ **tenue de soirée**
2 a formal dress worn by a woman in the evening. □ **robe du soir**

event [i'vent] *noun* **1** something that happens; an incident or occurrence: *That night a terrible event occurred.* □ **événement**
2 an item in a program of sports *etc*: *The long jump was to be the third event.* □ **épreuve**

e'ventful *adjective* (*negative* **uneventful**) full of events; exciting: *We had an eventful day.* □ **mouvementé**

at all events/at any event in any case: *At all events, we can't make things worse than they already are.* □ **en tout cas**

in that event if that happens: *In that event you must do as she says.* □ **dans ce cas**

in the event in the end, as it happened/happens/may happen: *In the event, I did not need to go to hospital.* □ **en fin de compte**

in the event of if (something) occurs: *In the event of his death, you will inherit his money.* □ **au cas où**

eventual [i'ventʃuəl] *adjective* happening in the end: *their quarrel and eventual reconciliation.* □ **qui s'ensuit**

e,ventu'ality [-'a-] – *plural* **eventu'alities** – *noun* a possible happening: *We are ready for all eventualities.* □ **éventualité**

e'ventually *adverb* finally; at length: *I thought he would never ask her to marry him, but he did eventually.* □ **finalement**

ever ['evə] *adverb* **1** at any time: *Nobody ever visits us; She hardly ever writes; Have you ever ridden on an elephant?; If I ever/If ever I see him again I shall get my revenge; better than ever; the brightest star they had ever seen.* □ **jamais**
2 always; continually: *They lived happily ever after; I've known her ever since she was a baby.* □ **toujours; depuis**
3 used for emphasis: *The new doctor is ever so gentle; Whatever shall I do?* □ **comme tout; bien**

ever- always; continually: *the ever-increasing traffic.* □ **toujours**

'evergreen *adjective* (of trees *etc*) having green leaves all the year round: *Holly is evergreen.* □ **à feuilles persistantes**
■ *noun* an evergreen tree: *Firs and pines are evergreens.* □ **arbre à feuilles persistantes**

ever'lasting *adjective* endless; continual; unchanging: *I'm tired of your everlasting grumbles; everlasting life/flowers.* □ **continuel; immortel**

,ever'lastingly *adverb.* □ **éternellement**

,ever'more *adverb* for all time: *He said that he would love her (for) evermore.* □ **à tout jamais**

for ever/for'ever *adverb* **1** continually: *She was forever looking at this watch.* □ **continuellement**
2 for all time: *I'll love you for ever (and ever).* □ **pour toujours**

every ['evri] *adjective* **1** each one of or all (of a certain number): *Every room is painted white; Not every family has a car.* □ **tout; chaque**
2 each (of an indefinite number or series): *Every hour brought the two countries nearer war; He attends to her every need.* □ **chaque; chacun de**
3 the most absolute or complete possible: *We have every reason to believe that she will get better.* □ **tout**
4 used to show repetition after certain intervals of time or space: *I go to the supermarket every four or five days; Every second house in the row was bright pink; 'Every other day' means 'every two days' or 'on alternate days'.* □ **tous les**

'everybody, 'everyone *pronoun* every person: *Everyone thinks I'm mad.* □ **tout le monde**

'everyday *adjective* **1** happening, done used *etc* daily: *her everyday duties.* □ **quotidien**
2 common or usual: *an everyday event.* □ **de tous les jours**

'everything *pronoun* all things: *Have you everything you want?* □ **tout**

'everywhere *adverb* (in or to) every place: *The flies are everywhere; Everywhere I go, he follows me.* □ **partout (où)**

every bit as just as: *You're every bit as clever as he is.* □ **tout aussi**

every now and then/every now and again/every so often occasionally: *We get a letter from her every now and then.* □ **de temps à autre**

every time 1 always; invariably: *We use this method every time.* □ **chaque fois**
2 whenever: *Every time he comes, we quarrel.* □ **chaque fois que**

---

everybody, everyone are singular: *Everybody is* (not *are*) *tired/Everyone should buy his own ticket.*

---

evict [i'vikt] *verb* to put out from house or land *especially* by force of law. □ **expulser (de)**

e'viction [-ʃən] *noun.* □ **expulsion**

evidence ['evidəns] *noun* **1** information *etc* that gives reason for believing something; proof (*eg* in a law case): *Have you enough evidence (of her guilt) to arrest her?* □ **preuve(s)**
2 (an) indication; a sign: *Her bag on the table was the only evidence of her presence.* □ **signe**

evident ['evidənt] *adjective* clearly to be seen or understood: *his evident satisfaction; It is evident that you have misunderstood me.* □ **évident**

'evidently *adverb* **1** as far as can be seen: *Evidently he disagrees.* □ **manifestement**
2 clearly or obviously: *She was quite evidently furious.* □ **de toute évidence**

evil ['iːvl] *adjective* very bad; wicked; sinful: *evil intentions; an evil man; He looks evil; evil deeds; an evil tongue.* □ **mauvais**
■ *noun* **1** wrong-doing, harm or wickedness: *He tries to ignore all the evil in the world; Do not speak of*

anyone. □ **mal**
2 anything evil, *eg* crime, misfortune *etc*: *London in the eighteenth century was a place of crime, filth, poverty and other evils.* □ **fléau**
evil-: *evil-minded*; *evil-smelling.* □ **mal-**
'**evilly** *adverb.* □ **avec malveillance**
'**evilness** *noun.* □ **méchanceté**
,**evil-'doer** *noun* a wicked or sinful person. □ **méchant, ante**
evocation, evocative *see* **evoke.**
evoke [i'vouk] *verb* 1 to cause or produce (*especially* a response, reaction *etc*): *Her letter in the newspaper evoked a storm of protest.* □ **susciter**
2 to bring into the mind: *A piece of music can sometimes evoke (memories of) the past.* □ **évoquer**
,**evo'cation** [evə-] *noun.* □ **évocation**
evocative [i'vokətiv] *adjective* tending to evoke memories *etc.* □ **évocateur**
evolution, evolutionary *see* **evolve.**
evolve [i'volv] *verb* to (cause to) develop gradually: *Man evolved from the apes.* □ **évoluer**
evolution [evə'luːʃən, iː-] *noun* 1 gradual working out or development: *the evolution of our form of government.* □ **évolution**
2 the development of the higher kinds of animals (*eg* man), plants *etc*, from the lower kinds: *Darwin's theory of evolution.* □ **évolution**
evolutionary [evə'luːʃənəri, iː-] *adjective.* □ **évolutionniste**
ewe [juː] *noun* a female sheep: *The ewe had two lambs.* □ **brebis**
exact [ig'zakt] *adjective* 1 absolutely accurate or correct in every detail; the same in every detail; precise: *What are the exact measurements of the room?*; *For this recipe the quantities must be absolutely exact*; *an exact copy*; *What is the exact time?*; *She walked in at that exact moment.* □ **exact**
2 (of a person, his mind *etc*) capable of being accurate over small details: *Accountants have to be very exact.* □ **rigoureux**
■ *verb* to force the payment of or giving of: *We should exact fines from everyone who drops litter on the streets.* □ **imposer**
ex'acting *adjective* requiring much effort or work from a person: *a very exacting job.* □ **astreignant**
ex'actly *adverb* 1 just; quite; absolutely: *He's exactly the right man for the job.* □ **exactement**
2 in accurate detail; precisely: *Work out the prices exactly*; *What exactly did you say?* □ **avec précision, précisément**
3 used as a reply meaning 'I quite agree'. □ **tout juste**
ex'actness *noun.* □ **exactitude**
exaggerate [ig'zadʒəreit] *verb* 1 to make (something) appear to be, or describe it as, greater *etc* than it really is: *You seem to be exaggerating his faults*; *That dress exaggerates her thinness.* □ **exagérer**
2 to go beyond the truth in describing something *etc*: *You can't trust him. He always exaggerates.* □ **exagérer**
ex,agge'ration *noun* 1 the act of exaggerating. □ **exagération**

2 an exaggerated description, term *etc*: *To say she is beautiful is an exaggeration, but she does have nice eyes.* □ **exagération**
exalted [ig'zoːltid] *adjective* high in rank, position *etc*; noble; important. □ **haut placé**
exam *see* **examine.**
examine [ig'zamin] *verb* 1 to look at closely; to inspect closely: *They examined the animal tracks and decided that they were those of a fox.* □ **examiner**
2 (of a doctor) to inspect the body of thoroughly to check for disease *etc*: *The doctor examined the child and said she was healthy.* □ **examiner**
3 to consider carefully: *The police must examine the facts.* □ **examiner**
4 to test the knowledge or ability of (students *etc*): *She examines pupils in mathematics.* □ **interroger**
5 to question: *The lawyer examined the witness in the court case.* □ **interroger**
ex,ami'nation *noun* 1 (a) close inspection: *Make a thorough examination of the area where the crime took place*; *On examination the patient was discovered to have appendicitis.* □ **examen**
2 (*also* **ex'am**) a test of knowledge or ability: *school examinations*; *She is to take a French/dancing exam*; (*also adjective*) *examination/exam papers*; *He failed/passed the English exam.* □ **examen**
3 (a) formal questioning (*eg* of a witness). □ **interrogatoire**
ex'aminer *noun* a person who examines. □ **examinateur, trice**
example [ig'zaːmpl] *noun* 1 something that represents other things of the same kind; a specimen: *an example of his handwriting.* □ **spécimen**
2 something that shows clearly or illustrates a fact *etc*: *Can you give me an example of how this word is used?* □ **exemple (de)**
3 a person or thing that is a pattern to be copied: *She was an example to the rest of the class.* □ **exemple (pour)**
4 a warning to be heeded: *Let this be an example to you, and never do it again!* □ **exemple**
for example (*often abbreviated to* **eg** [iː'dʒiː]) for instance; as an example: *Several European countries have no sea-coast – for example, Switzerland and Austria.* □ **par exemple**
make an example of to punish as a warning to others: *The judge decided to make an example of the young thief and sent him to prison for five years.* □ **faire un exemple de**
set (someone) an example to act in such a way that other people will copy one's behaviour: *Teachers must set a good example to their pupils.* □ **donner l'exemple**
exasperate [ig'zaːspəreit] *verb* to irritate (someone) very much indeed: *She was exasperated by the continual interruptions.* □ **exaspérer**
ex,aspe'ration *noun*: *She hit the child in exasperation.* □ **exaspération**
excavate ['ekskəveit] *verb* 1 to dig up (a piece of ground *etc*) or to dig out (a hole) by doing this. □ **creuser**
2 in archaeology, to uncover or open up (a structure *etc*

remaining from earlier times) by digging: *The archaeologist excavated an ancient fortress.* □ **faire des fouilles (dans)**

,exca'vation *noun.* □ **fouille(s); excavation**

'excavator *noun* a machine or person that excavates. □ **excavatrice; fouilleur, euse**

exceed [ik'siːd] *verb* to go beyond; to be greater than: *His expenditure exceeds his income; He exceeded the speed limit on the highway.* □ **dépasser**

ex'ceedingly *adverb* very: *exceedingly nervous.* □ **extrêmement**

excel [ik'sel] – *past tense, past participle* **ex'celled** – *verb* **1** to stand out beyond others (in some quality *etc*); to do very well (in or at some activity): *He excelled in mathematics/at football.* □ **exceller (en)**

2 to be better than: *She excels them all at swimming.* □ **surpasser**

'excellence ['ek-] *noun* unusual goodness or worth: *this man's excellence as a teacher.* □ **excellence**

'Excellency ['ek-] – *plural* **'Excellencies** – *noun* (with **His, Your** *etc*) a title of honour, used *eg* for ambassadors: *His/Your Excellency; Their Excellencies.* □ **Excellence**

'excellent ['ek-] *adjective* unusually good: *an excellent plan.* □ **excellent**

'excellently *adverb.* □ **parfaitement**

except [ik'sept] *preposition* leaving out; not including: *They're all here except him; Your essay was good except that it was too long.* □ **sauf (que)**

■ *verb* to leave out or exclude. □ **exclure (de)**

ex'cepted *adjective: all European countries, Denmark excepted* (= except Denmark). □ **sauf**

ex'cepting *preposition* leaving out or excluding: *Those cars are all reliable, excepting the old red one.* □ **sauf**

ex'ception [-ʃən] *noun* **1** something or someone not included: *They all work hard, without exception; With the exception of Jim we all went home early.* □ **exception**

2 something not according to the rule: *We normally eat nothing at lunchtime, but Sunday is an exception.* □ **exception**

ex'ceptional *adjective* (*negative* **unexceptional**) unusual; remarkable: *exceptional loyalty; Her ability is exceptional.* □ **exceptionnel**

ex'ceptionally *adverb* unusually: *exceptionally stupid.* □ **exceptionnellement**

except for 1 apart from: *We enjoyed the holiday except for the expense.* □ **à part**

2 except: *Except for John, they all arrived punctually.* □ **à l'exception de**

take exception to/at to object to: *The old lady took exception to the rudeness of the children.* □ **(s')offusquer de**

excerpt ['eksɔːpt] *noun* a part taken from a book *etc*: *I heard an excerpt from his latest novel on the radio.* □ **extrait**

excess [ik'ses] *noun* **1** the (act of) going beyond normal or suitable limits: *She ate well, but not to excess.* □ **excès**

2 an abnormally large amount: *He had consumed an excess of alcohol.* □ **trop (de)**

3 an amount by which something is greater than something else: *He found he had paid an excess of $5.00 over what was actually on the bill.* □ **excédent**

■ *adjective* extra; additional (to the amount needed, allowed or usual): *She had to pay extra for her excess baggage on the aircraft.* □ **excédent (de)**

ex'cessive [-siv] *adjective* beyond what is right and proper: *The manager expects them to do an excessive amount of work.* □ **excessif**

ex'cessively *adverb.* □ **excessivement**

ex'cessiveness *noun.* □ **manque de mesure**

in excess of more than: *Her salary is in excess of $45,000 a year.* □ **qui dépasse**

exchange [iks'tʃeindʒ] *verb* **1** to give, or give up, in return for something else: *Can you exchange a dollar note for two 50-cent pieces?* □ **changer**

2 to give and receive in return: *They exchanged amused glances.* □ **échanger**

■ *noun* **1** the giving and taking of one thing for another: *He gave me a pencil in exchange for the marble; An exchange of opinions is helpful.* □ **échange**

2 a conversation or dispute: *An angry exchange took place between the two brothers when their father's will was read.* □ **échange de mots**

3 the act of exchanging the money of one country for that of another. □ **change**

4 the difference between the value of money in different countries: *What is the rate of exchange between the U.S. dollar and the mark?* □ **change**

5 a place where business shares are bought and sold or international financial dealings carried on. □ **bourse**

6 (*also* **telephone exchange**) a central telephone system where lines are connected. □ **central**

ex'changeable *adjective.* □ **échangeable (contre)**

exchequer [iks'tʃekə] *noun* **1** the government department in charge of the nation's finances. □ **ministère des Finances**

2 the national or public money supply. □ **Trésor public**

excise[1] ['eksaiz] *noun* the tax on goods *etc* made and sold within a country. □ **taxe**

excise[2] [ik'saiz] *verb* to cut out or off. □ **retrancher**

excision [ik'siʒən] *noun.* □ **suppression**

excite [ik'sait] *verb* **1** to cause or rouse strong feelings of expectation, happiness *etc* in: *The children were excited at the thought of the party.* □ **exciter**

2 to cause or rouse (feelings, emotions *etc*): *The book did not excite my interest.* □ **susciter**

ex'citable *adjective* easily becoming excited or upset. □ **nerveux**

ex,cita'bility *noun.* □ **excitabilité**

ex'cited *adjective.* □ **excité**

ex'citedly *adverb.* □ **d'une manière agitée**

ex'citement *noun: Her arrival caused great excitement; the excitement of travel.* □ **excitation**

ex'citing *adjective: an exciting adventure.* □ **excitant, palpitant**

exclaim [ik'skleim] *verb* to call out, or say, suddenly and loudly: *'Good!' he exclaimed; She exclaimed in astonishment.* □ **s'exclamer, s'écrier**

exclamation [eksklə'meiʃən] *noun* an expression of surprise or other sudden feeling: *He gave an exclama-*

tion of anger. □ **exclamation**

exclamation mark the mark (!) following and showing an exclamation. □ **point d'exclamation**

exclude [ik'sklu:d] *verb* **1** to prevent (someone) from sharing or taking part in something: *They excluded her from the meeting.* □ **exclure (de)**

2 to shut out; to keep out: *Fill the bottle to the top so as to exclude all air.* □ **chasser, exclure**

3 to leave out of consideration: *We cannot exclude the possibility that he was lying.* □ **exclure**

ex'clusion [-ʒən] *noun.* □ **exclusion**

ex'cluding *preposition* not counting; without including: *The club's expenses, excluding the cost of stationery, amounted to $251.* □ **à l'exclusion de**

exclusive [ik'sklu:siv] *adjective* **1** tending to exclude. □ **exclusif**

2 (of a group *etc*) not easily or readily mixing with others or allowing others in: *a very exclusive club.* □ **fermé**

3 given to only one individual or group *etc*: *The story is exclusive to this newspaper.* □ **publié en exclusivité (dans)**

4 fashionable and expensive: *exclusive shops/restaurants.* □ **sélect**

ex'clusively *adverb.* □ **exclusivement, uniquement**

ex'clusiveness *noun.* □ **caractère exclusif (de)**

exclusive of excluding: *That is the price of the meal exclusive of service charge.* □ **non compris**

excrement ['ekskrəmənt] *noun* matter, *especially* solid, discharged from the body; feces; dung: *The streets are filthy with dogs' excrement.* □ **excrément**

excrete [ik'skri:t] *verb* to discharge (waste matter) from the body. □ **excréter**

ex'cretion [-ʃən] *noun.* □ **excrétion**

excruciating [ik'skru:ʃieitiŋ] *adjective* causing extreme bodily or mental pain: *an excruciating headache.* □ **atroce**

excursion [ik'skəːʃən] *noun* a trip; an outing: *an excursion to the seaside.* □ **excursion**

excuse [ik'skju:z] *verb* **1** to forgive or pardon: *Excuse me – can you tell me the time?*; *I'll excuse your carelessness this time.* □ **excuser**

2 to free (someone) from a task, duty *etc*: *May I be excused from writing this essay?* □ **dispenser (de)**

■ [ik'skju:s] *noun* a reason (given by oneself) for being excused, or a reason for excusing: *He has no excuse for being so late.* □ **excuse**

excusable [ik'skju:zəbl] *adjective* pardonable. □ **excusable**

execute ['eksikju:t] *verb* **1** to put to death by order of the law: *After the war many traitors were executed.* □ **exécuter**

2 to carry out (instructions etc). □ **exécuter**

3 to perform (a movement *etc usually* requiring skill). □ **exécuter**

,**exe'cution** [-ʃən] *noun* **1** (an act of) killing by law: *The judge ordered the execution of the murderer.* □ **exécution**

2 the act of executing (orders or skilled movements *etc*). □ **exécution**

,**exe'cutioner** *noun* a person whose duty is to put to death condemned persons. □ **bourreau**

executive [ig'zekjutiv] *adverb* **1** (in a business organization *etc*) concerned with management: *executive skills.* □ **de direction**

2 concerned with the carrying out of laws *etc*: *executive powers.* □ **exécutif**

■ *noun* **1** the branch of the government that puts the laws into effect. □ **(pouvoir) exécutif**

2 a person or body of people in an organization *etc* that has power to direct or manage: *She is an executive in an insurance company.* □ **administrateur, trice**

executor [ig'zekjutə] *noun* a person appointed to see to the carrying out of what is stated in a will: *His two brothers are his executors.* □ **exécuteur, trice testamentaire**

exemplary [ig'zempləri] *adjective* worth following as an example: *Her behaviour is always exemplary.* □ **exemplaire**

> **exemplary** is spelt with **-em-** (not **-am-**).

exemplify [ig'zemplifai] *verb* to be an example of; to show by means of an example: *Her originality as a composer is exemplified by the following group of songs.* □ **illustrer**

exempt [ig'zempt] *verb* to free (a person) from a duty that other people have to carry out: *He was exempted from military service.* □ **exempter (de)**

■ *adjective* free (from a duty *etc*): *Children under 16 are exempt from the usual charges for dental treatment.* □ **exempté (de)**

ex'emption [-ʃən] *noun.* □ **exemption**

exercise ['eksəsaiz] *noun* **1** training or use (*especially* of the body) through action or effort: *Swimming is one of the healthiest forms of exercise*; *Take more exercise.* □ **exercice**

2 an activity intended as training: *ballet exercises*; *spelling exercises.* □ **exercice**

3 a series of tasks, movements *etc* for training troops *etc*: *His battalion is on an exercise in the mountains.* □ **manœuvre**

■ *verb* **1** to train or give exercise to: *Dogs should be exercised frequently*; *I exercise every morning.* □ **(faire) faire de l'exercice**

2 to use; to make use of: *She was given the opportunity to exercise her skill as a pianist.* □ **exercer**

exert [ig'zəːt] *verb* **1** to bring forcefully into use or action: *He likes to exert his authority.* □ **exercer**

2 to force (oneself) to make an effort: *Please exert yourselves.* □ **(s')efforcer**

ex'ertion [-ʃən] *noun* **1** the act of bringing forcefully into use: *the exertion of one's influence.* □ **exercice**

2 (an) effort: *They failed in spite of their exertions.* □ **effort**

exhale [eks'heil] *verb* to breathe out. □ **expirer**

exhalation [eksə'leiʃən] *noun.* □ **exhalation**

exhaust [ig'zɔːst] *verb* **1** to make very tired: *She was exhausted by her long walk.* □ **épuiser**

2 to use all of; to use completely: *We have exhausted our supplies*; *You're exhausting my patience.* □ **épuiser**

3 to say all that can be said about (a subject *etc*): *We've exhausted that topic.* □ **épuiser**

■ *noun* (an outlet from the engine of a car, motorcycle

etc for) fumes and other waste. □ **échappement**

ex'hausted *adjective* extremely tired. □ **épuisé**

ex'haustion *noun*: *He collapsed from exhaustion.* □ **épuisement**

ex'haustive [-tiv] *adjective* complete; very thorough: *an exhaustive search.* □ **complet**

exhibit [ig'zibit] *verb* 1 to show; to display to the public: *My picture is to be exhibited in the art gallery.* □ **exposer**

2 to show (a quality *etc*): *He exhibited a complete lack of concern for others.* □ **montrer**

■ *noun* 1 an object displayed publicly (*eg* in a museum): *One of the exhibits is missing.* □ **objet exposé**

2 an object or document produced in court as part of the evidence: *The blood-stained scarf was exhibit number one in the murder trial.* □ **pièce à conviction**

exhibition [eksi'biʃən] *noun* 1 a public display (*eg* of works of art, industrial goods *etc*): *an exhibition of children's books.* □ **exposition**

2 an act of showing or revealing: *What an exhibition of bad temper!* □ **démonstration**

ex'hibitor *noun* a person who provides an exhibit for a display *etc*: *She is one of the exhibitors at the flower show.* □ **exposant, ante**

exhilarate [ig'ziləreit] *verb* to make (a person) feel happy and lively: *He was exhilarated by the walk.* □ **ragaillardir**

ex,hila'ration *noun*. □ **allégresse**

ex'hilarating *adjective*: *an exhilarating walk.* □ **vivifiant**

exhort [ig'zoːt] *verb* to urge strongly and earnestly. □ **exhorter**

,exhor'tation [egzoː-] *noun*. □ **exhortation**

exhume [ig'zjuːm] *verb* to dig out (*especially* a body from a grave). □ **exhumer**

exhumation [eksju'meiʃən] *noun*. □ **exhumation**

exile ['eksail] *noun* 1 a person who lives outside his or her own country either from choice or because he or she is forced to do so: *an exile from his native land.* □ **exilé, ée**

2 a (*usually* long) stay in a foreign land (*eg* as a punishment): *She was sent into exile.* □ **exil**

■ *verb* to send away or banish (a person) from his own country. □ **exiler**

exist [ig'zist] *verb* 1 to be something real or actual: *Do ghosts really exist?* □ **exister**

2 to stay alive; to continue to live: *It is possible to exist on bread and water.* □ **subsister**

ex'istence *noun* 1 the state of existing: *She does not believe in the existence of God; How long has this rule been in existence?* □ **existence**

2 (a way of) life: *an uneventful existence.* □ **existence**

exit ['egzit] *noun* 1 a way out of a building *etc*: *the emergency exit.* □ **sortie, issue**

2 an actor's departure from the stage: *Macbeth's exit.* □ **sortie**

3 an act of going out or departing: *She made a noisy exit.* □ **sortie**

■ *verb* (used as a stage direction to one person) (he/ she) goes off the stage: *Exit Hamlet.* □ **sortir**

exodus ['eksədəs] *noun* a going away of many people: *There was a general exodus from the room.* □ **exode**

exorbitant [ig'zoːbitənt] *adjective* (of prices or demands) very high or unreasonable. □ **exorbitant**

ex'orbitantly *adverb*. □ **démesurément**

ex'orbitance *noun*. □ **énormité**

exorcize, exorcise ['eksoːsaiz] *verb* to drive away (an evil spirit); to rid (a house *etc*) of an evil spirit. □ **exorciser**

'exorcism *noun* (an) act of exorcizing. □ **exorcisme**

'exorcist *noun* a person who exorcizes. □ **exorciste**

exotic [ig'zotik] *adjective* 1 unusual or colourful: *exotic clothes.* □ **exotique**

2 brought or introduced from a foreign country: *exotic plants.* □ **exotique**

expand [ik'spand] *verb* to make or grow larger; to spread out wider: *Metals expand when heated; He does exercises to expand his chest; The school's activities have expanded to include climbing and mountaineering.* □ **(se) dilater; (se) développer**

ex'panse [-s] *noun* a wide area or extent: *an expanse of water.* □ **étendue**

ex'pansion [-ʃən] *noun* the act or state of expanding: *the expansion of metals.* □ **dilatation**

expansive *adjective* wide-ranging or extensive: *There was an expansive view of the ocean from the window of the beach house.* □ **expansif**

expatriate [eks'peitriət] *noun, adjective* (a person) living outside his own country. □ **expatrié, ée**

expect [ik'spekt] *verb* 1 to think of as likely to happen or come: *I'm expecting a letter today; We expect her on tomorrow's train.* □ **attendre**

2 to think or believe (that something will happen): *She expects to be home tomorrow; I expect that he will go; 'Will she go too?' 'I expect so'/'I don't expect so'/'I expect not.'* □ **croire**

3 to require: *They expect high wages for skilled work; You are expected to tidy your own room.* □ **exiger/ attendre (qqch. de qqn)**

4 to suppose or assume: *I expect (that) you're tired.* □ **supposer (que)**

ex'pectancy *noun* the state of expecting or hoping: *a feeling/look/air of expectancy.* □ **attente**

ex'pectant *adjective* full of hope or expectation: *the expectant faces of the audience.* □ **qui attend**

2 expecting (a baby): *an expectant mother.* □ **enceinte**

ex'pectantly *adverb*. □ **dans l'attente**

,expec'tation [ekspek-] *noun* 1 the state of expecting: *In expectation of a wage increase, he bought a washing-machine.* □ **attente**

2 what is expected: *He failed his exam, contrary to expectation(s); Did the concert come up to your expectations?* □ **espérance(s)**

expedient [ik'spiːdiənt] *adjective* convenient or advisable: *It would not be expedient to pay him what he asks.* □ **opportun**

ex'pedience *noun*. □ **opportunité**

ex'pediency *noun*. □ **convenance**

expedite ['ekspidait] *verb* to hasten or speed up (a work process *etc*). □ **accélérer**

,expe'ditious [-'di∫əs] *adjective* quick (and efficient). □ **expéditif**

expe'ditiously *adverb*. □ **expéditivement**

expedition [ekspi'di∫ən] *noun* **1** an organized journey with a purpose: *an expedition to the South Pole*. □ **expédition**

2 a group making such a journey: *He was a member of the expedition which climbed Mount Everest*. □ **expédition**

expe'ditionary *adjective* (*especially* of troops) forming, or sent on, an expedition *eg* to fight abroad. □ **expéditionnaire**

expel [ik'spel] – *past tense, past participle* ex'pelled – *verb* **1** to send away in disgrace (a person from a school *etc*): *The child was expelled for stealing.* □ **renvoyer (de), expulser (de)**

2 to get rid of: *an electric fan for expelling kitchen smells.* □ **évacuer**

expulsion [ik'spʌl∫ən] *noun*: *Any child found disobeying this rule will face expulsion from the school*. □ **renvoi, expulsion**

expend [ik'spend] *verb* to use or spend (supplies *etc*). □ **dépenser**

ex'penditure [-t∫ə] *noun* the act of spending: *the expenditure of money and resources*; *Her expenditure(s) amounted to $500*. □ **dépenses**

ex'pense [-s] *noun* **1** the spending of money *etc*; cost: *I've gone to a lot of expense to educate you well.* □ **frais**

2 a cause of spending: *What an expense clothes are!* □ **cause de dépense**

ex'penses [-siz] *noun plural* money spent in carrying out a job *etc*: *Her firm paid her travelling expenses.* □ **frais**

ex'pensive [-siv] *adjective* costing a great deal: *expensive clothes*. □ **cher**

at the expense of 1 being paid for by; at the cost of: *He equipped the expedition at his own expense*; *At the expense of her health she finally completed the work.* □ **aux frais de; aux dépens de**

2 making (a person) appear ridiculous: *She told a joke at her husband's expense.* ■ **aux dépens de**

experience [ik'spiəriəns] *noun* **1** (knowledge, skill or wisdom gained through) practice in some activity, or the doing of something: *Learn by experience – don't make the same mistake again*; *Has she had experience in teaching?* □ **expérience**

2 an event that affects or involves a person *etc*: *The earthquake was a terrible experience.* □ **épreuve**

■ *verb* to have experience of; to feel: *I have never before experienced such rudeness!* □ **éprouver**

ex'perienced *adjective* having gained knowledge from experience; skilled: *an experienced mountaineer*. □ **expérimenté**

experiment [ik'sperimənt] *noun* a test done in order to find out something, *eg* if an idea is correct: *She performs chemical experiments*; *experiments in traffic control*; *We shall find out by experiment.* □ **expérience**

■ *verb* (*with* **on** *or* **with**) to try to find out something by making tests: *He experimented with various medicines*

to find the safest cure; *The doctor experiments on animals.* □ **expérimenter**

ex,peri'mental [-'mentl] *adjective* of, or used for an experiment: *experimental teaching methods.* □ **expérimental**

ex,peri'mentally *adverb*. □ **expérimentalement**

ex,perimen'tation *noun* the practice of making experiments. □ **expérimentation**

expert ['ekspɔːt] *adjective* (*with* **at** *or* **on**) skilled through training or practice: *an expert car designer*; *I'm expert at map-reading*; *Get expert advice on plumbing.* □ **expert**

■ *noun* a person who is an expert: *an expert in political history/on ancient pottery.* □ **expert, erte**

'expertly *adverb*. □ **de façon experte**

'expertness *noun*. □ **compétence (en)**

expire [ik'spaiə] *verb* **1** (of a limited period of time) to come to an end: *Her three weeks' leave expires tomorrow.* □ **expirer**

2 (of a ticket, licence *etc*) to go out of date: *My driving licence expired last month.* □ **expirer**

3 to die. □ **expirer**

expiration [ekspi'rei∫ən] *noun*. □ **expiration**

ex'piry *noun* the end of a period of time or of an agreement *etc* with a time limit: *The date of expiry is shown on your driving licence.* □ **expiration**

explain [ik'splein] *verb* **1** to make (something) clear or easy to understand: *Can you explain the railway timetable to me?*; *Did she explain why she was late?* □ **expliquer**

2 to give, or be, a reason for: *I cannot explain his failure*; *That explains his silence.* □ **expliquer**

explanation [eksplə'nei∫ən] *noun* **1** the act or process of explaining: *Let me give a few words of explanation.* □ **explication**

2 a statement or fact that explains: *There are several possible explanations for the explosion.* □ **explication**

ex'planatory [-'splanə-] *adjective* giving an explanation: *There are explanatory notes in this book.* □ **explicatif**

explain away to get rid of (difficulties *etc*) by clever explaining: *She could not explain away the missing money.* □ **justifier**

explicable [ek'splikəbl] *adjective* capable of being explained. □ **explicable**

explicit [ik'splisit] *adjective* stated, or stating, fully and clearly: *explicit instructions*; *Can you be more explicit?* □ **clair**

ex'plicitly *adverb*. □ **explicitement**

ex'plicitness *noun*. □ **clarté**

explode [ik'sploud] *verb* **1** to (cause to) blow up with a loud noise: *The bomb exploded*; *The police exploded the bomb where it could cause no damage.* □ **(faire) exploser**

2 suddenly to show strong feeling: *The teacher exploded with anger*; *The children exploded into laughter.* □ **éclater**

3 to prove (a theory *etc*) wrong. □ **démontrer la fausseté (de)**

ex'plosion [-ʒən] *noun* **1** a blowing up, or the noise

caused by this: *a gas explosion*; *The explosion could be heard a long way off.* □ **explosion**

2 the action of exploding: *the explosion of the atom bomb.* □ **explosion**

3 a sudden showing of strong feelings *etc*: *an explosion of laughter.* □ **explosion**

4 a sudden great increase: *an explosion in food prices.* □ **explosion**

ex'plosive [-siv] *adjective* likely to explode: *Hydrogen is a dangerously explosive gas.* □ **explosif**

■ *noun* (a) material that is likely to explode: *gelignite and other explosives.* □ **explosif**

exploit ['eksploit] *noun* a (daring) deed or action: *stories of his military exploits.* □ **exploit**

■ [ik'sploit] *verb* **1** to make good or advantageous use of: *to exploit the country's natural resources.* □ **exploiter**

2 to use (*eg* a person) unfairly for one's own advantage. □ **exploiter**

,exploi'tation *noun*. □ **exploitation**

explore [ik'splo:] *verb* **1** to search or travel through (a place) for the purpose of discovery: *The oceans have not yet been fully explored*; *Let's go exploring in the caves.* □ **explorer**

2 to examine carefully: *I'll explore the possibilities of getting a job here.* □ **étudier**

exploration [eksplə'reiʃən] *noun*: *a journey of exploration.* □ **exploration**

ex'ploratory [-'splorə-] *adjective* for the purpose of exploration or investigation: *an exploratory expedition.* □ **d'exploration**

ex'plorer *noun* a person who explores unknown regions: *explorers in space.* □ **explorateur, trice**

explosion, explosive *see* explode.

expo *see* exposition.

exponent [ik'spounənt] *noun* **1** a person able to demonstrate skilfully a particular art or activity: *She was an accomplished exponent of Bach's flute sonatas.* □ **interprète**

2 a person who explains and supports (a theory or belief *etc*): *He was one of the early exponents of Marxism.* □ **chef de file**

export [ek'spo:t] *verb* to send (goods) to another country for sale: *Costa Rica exports bananas to Canada.* □ **exporter**

■ ['ekspo:t] *noun* **1** the act or business of exporting: *the export of rubber.* □ **exportation**

2 something which is exported: *Paper is an important Swedish export.* □ **(produit d')exportation**

,expor'tation [ek-] *noun*. □ **exportation**

ex'porter *noun* a person who exports goods: *Her father was a tobacco exporter.* □ **exportateur, trice**

expose [ik'spouz] *verb* **1** to uncover; to leave unprotected from (*eg* weather, danger, observation *etc*): *Paintings should not be exposed to direct sunlight*; *Don't expose children to danger.* □ **exposer**

2 to discover and make known (*eg* criminals or their activities): *It was a newspaper that exposed his spying activities.* □ **dévoiler, démasquer**

3 by releasing the camera shutter, to allow light to fall on (a photographic film). □ **exposer**

ex'posure [-ʒə] *noun* **1** (an) act of exposing or state of being exposed: *Prolonged exposure of the skin to hot sun can be harmful.* □ **exposition**

2 one frame of a photographic film *etc*: *I have two exposures left.* □ **pose**

exposition [ekspə'ziʃən] *noun* **1** a detailed explanation (of a subject). □ **exposé**

2 (*abbreviation* 'expo) an exhibition: *a trade exposition.* □ **exposition**

exposure *see* expose.

expound [ik'spaund] *verb* to explain in detail. □ **expliquer**

express [ik'spres] *verb* **1** to put into words: *She expressed her ideas very clearly.* □ **exprimer**

2 (with **oneself** *etc*) to put one's own thoughts into words: *You haven't expressed yourself clearly.* □ **(s')exprimer**

3 to show (thoughts, feelings *etc*) by looks, actions *etc*: *She nodded to express her agreement.* □ **exprimer**

4 to send by fast (postal) delivery: *Will you express this letter, please?* □ **expédier par exprès**

■ *adjective* **1** travelling, carrying goods *etc*, especially fast: *an express train*; *express delivery.* □ **express; exprès**

2 clearly stated: *You have disobeyed my express wishes.* □ **explicite**

■ *adverb* by express train or fast delivery service: *Send your letter express.* □ **exprès**

■ *noun* **1** an express train: *the Montreal to Toronto express.* □ **express**

2 the service provided *eg* by the post office for carrying goods *etc* quickly: *The parcel was sent by express.* □ **(par) exprès**

ex'pressly *adverb* in clear, definite words: *I expressly forbade you to do that.* □ **expressément**

ex'pression [-ʃən] *noun* **1** a look on one's face that shows one's feelings: *He always has a bored expression.* □ **expression**

2 a word or phrase: *'Dough' is a slang expression for 'money'.* □ **expression**

3 (a) showing of thoughts or feelings by words, actions *etc*: *This poem is an expression of his grief.* □ **expression**

4 the showing of feeling when *eg* reciting, reading aloud or playing a musical instrument: *Put more expression into your playing!* □ **expression**

ex'pressionless *adjective* (of a face or voice) showing no feeling: *a cold, expressionless tone.* □ **sans expression**

ex'pressive [-siv] *adjective* showing meaning or feeling clearly: *She has an expressive face.* □ **expressif**

ex'pressiveness *noun*. □ **expressivité**

ex'pressively *adverb*. □ **avec expression**

ex'pressway *noun* a divided highway. □ **voie express**

expulsion *see* expel.

exquisite ['ekskwizit] *adjective* very beautiful or skilful: *exquisite embroidery.* □ **exquis**

'exquisitely *adverb*. □ **d'une façon exquise**

extant ['ekstənt, ek'stant] *adjective* still existing. □ **qui existe encore**

extempore [ik'stempəri] *adverb* without previous thought or preparation: *to speak extempore.* □ **sans préparation**

extend [ik'stend] *verb* 1 to make longer or larger: *He extended his vegetable garden.* □ **agrandir**
2 to reach or stretch: *The school grounds extend as far as this fence.* □ **(s')étendre**
3 to hold out or stretch out (a limb *etc*): *He extended his hand to her.* □ **tendre**
4 to offer: *May I extend a welcome to you all?* □ **offrir à**

ex'tension [-ʃən] *noun* 1 an added part: *She built an extension to her house*; *a two-day extension to the holiday.* □ **extension**
2 the process of extending. □ **extension**

ex'tensive [-siv] *adjective* large in area or amount: *extensive plantations*; *She suffered extensive injuries in the accident.* □ **vaste, étendu**

ex'tent [-t] *noun* 1 the area or length to which something extends: *The bird's wings measured 20 centimetres at their fullest extent*; *The garden is nearly a kilometre in extent*; *A vast extent of grassland.* □ **étendue**
2 amount; degree: *What is the extent of the damage?*; *To what extent can we trust him?* □ **ampleur, degré**
to a certain extent/to some extent partly but not completely. □ **jusqu'à un certain point**

exterior [ik'stiəriə] *adjective* on or from the outside; outer: *an exterior wall of a house.* □ **extérieur**
■ *noun* the outside (of something or someone): *On the exterior she was charming, but she was known to have a violent temper.* □ **extérieur**

exterminate [ik'stə:mineit] *verb* to get rid of or destroy completely: *Rats must be exterminated from a building or they will cause disease.* □ **exterminer**
ex,termi'nation *noun.* □ **extermination**

external [ik'stə:nl] *adjective* of, for, from, or on, the outside: *Manufacturers often label skin creams 'For external use only'.* □ **externe**
ex'ternally *adverb.* □ **extérieurement**

extinct [ik'stiŋkt] *adjective* 1 (of a type of animal *etc*) no longer in existence: *Mammoths became extinct in prehistoric times.* □ **disparu**
2 (of a volcano) no longer active: *That volcano was thought to be extinct until it suddenly erupted ten years ago.* □ **éteint**

extinction [ik'stiŋkʃən] *noun* 1 making or becoming extinct: *the extinction of the species.* □ **disparition**
2 the act of putting out or extinguishing (fire, hope *etc*). □ **extinction**

extinguish [ik'stiŋgwiʃ] *verb* to put out (a fire *etc*): *Please extinguish your cigarettes.* □ **éteindre**
ex'tinguisher *noun* a spraying apparatus containing chemicals for putting out fire. □ **extincteur**

extol [ik'stoul] – *past tense, past participle* **ex'tolled** – *verb* to praise highly. □ **exalter**

extort [ik'sto:t] *verb* to obtain (from a person) by threats or violence: *They extorted a confession from him by torture.* □ **extorquer**
ex'tortion [-ʃən] *noun.* □ **extorsion**
ex'tortionate [-nət] *adjective* (of a price) much too high:

That restaurant's prices are extortionate! □ **exorbitant**

extra ['ekstrə] *adjective* additional; more than usual or necessary: *They demand an extra $10 a week*; *We need extra men for this job.* □ **supplémentaire**
■ *adverb* unusually: *an extra-large box of chocolates.* □ **très grand**
■ *pronoun* an additional amount: *The book costs $6.90 but we charge extra for postage.* □ **supplément**
■ *noun* 1 something extra, or something for which an extra price is charged: *The college fees cover teaching only – stationery and other equipment are extras.* □ **en plus**
2 in movies or television, an actor employed in a small part, *eg* as a person in a crowd. □ **figurant, ante**
3 a special edition of a newspaper containing later or special news. □ **édition spéciale**

extract [ik'strakt] *verb* 1 to pull out, or draw out, especially by force or with effort: *I have to have a tooth extracted*; *Did you manage to extract the information from her?* □ **arracher, tirer (de)**
2 to select (passages from a book *etc*). □ **extraire**
3 to take out (a substance forming part of something else) by crushing or by chemical means: *Vanilla essence is extracted from vanilla beans.* □ **extraire**
■ ['ekstrakt] *noun* 1 a passage selected from a book *etc*: *a short extract from his novel.* □ **extrait**
2 a substance obtained by an extracting process: *beef/yeast extract*; *extract of malt.* □ **extrait**
ex'traction [-ʃən] *noun* 1 race or parentage: *She is of Greek extraction.* □ **origine**
2 (an) act of extracting *eg* a tooth. □ **extraction**

extradite ['ekstrədait] *verb* to give (someone) up to the police of another country (for a crime committed there). □ **extrader**
,extra'dition [-'di-] *noun.* □ **extradition**

extramural [ekstrə'mjuərəl] *adjective* 1 (of teaching, lectures *etc*) for people who are not full-time students at a college *etc*: *extramural lectures.* □ **public**
2 separate from or outside the area of one's studies (in a university *etc*): *extramural activities.* □ **hors faculté**

extraordinary [ik'stro:dənəri] *adjective* surprising; unusual: *What an extraordinary thing to say!*; *He wears the most extraordinary clothes.* □ **extraordinaire**
extraordinarily [ik'stro:dənərəli] *adverb.* □ **extraordinairement**

extraterrestrial [ekstrətə'restriəl] *noun, adjective* (a person *etc*) not living on or coming from the planet Earth. □ **extraterrestre**

extravagant [ik'stravəgənt] *adjective* 1 using or spending too much; wasteful: *He's extravagant with money*; *an extravagant use of materials/energy.* □ **dépensier; gaspilleur**
2 (of ideas, emotions *etc*) exaggerated or too great: *extravagant praise.* □ **excessif**
ex'travagantly *adverb.* □ **d'une manière extravagante**
ex'travagance *noun*: *Her husband's extravagance reduced them to poverty*; *Food is a necessity, but wine is an extravagance.* □ **dépense excessive**

extreme [ik'stri:m] *adjective* 1 very great, *especially* much more than usual: *extreme pleasure*; *She is in ex-*

treme pain. □ **extrême**

2 very far or furthest in any direction, *especially* out from the centre: *the extreme southwestern tip of the peninsula; Politically, he belongs to the extreme left.* □ **extrême**

3 very violent or strong; not ordinary or usual: *She holds extreme views on education.* □ **extrémiste**

■ *noun* **1** something as far, or as different, as possible from something else: *the extremes of sadness and joy.* □ **extrême**

2 the greatest degree of any state, *especially* if unpleasant: *The extremes of heat in the desert make life uncomfortable.* □ **extrême**

ex'tremely *adverb* very: *extremely kind.* □ **extrêmement**

ex'tremism *noun* the holding of views which are as far from being moderate as possible. □ **extrémisme**

ex'tremist *noun, adjective.* □ **extrémiste**

ex'tremity [-'stre-] – *plural* **ex'tremities** – *noun* **1** the farthest point: *The two poles represent the extremities of the earth's axis.* □ **extrémité**

2 an extreme degree; the quality of being extreme: *Their suffering reached such extremities that many died.* □ **extrémité**

3 a situation of great danger or distress: *They need help in this extremity.* □ **extrémité**

4 the parts of the body furthest from the middle *eg* the hands and feet. □ **extrémités**

in the extreme very: *dangerous in the extreme.* □ **à l'extrême**

to extremes very far, *especially* further than is thought to be reasonable: *She can never express an opinion without going to extremes.* □ **aux extrêmes**

extricate ['ekstrikeit] *verb* to set free: *He extricated her from her difficulties.* □ **tirer (de)**

,**extri'cation** *noun.* □ **dégagement**

extrovert ['ekstrəvɔːt] *noun, adjective* (a person) more interested in what happens around him than his own ideas and feelings: *An extrovert (person) is usually good company.* □ **extroverti, ie**

exuberant [ig'zjuːbərənt] *adjective* happy and excited or in high spirits: *an exuberant mood.* □ **exubérant, e**

ex'uberance *noun.* □ **exubérance**

exude [ig'zjuːd] *verb* to give off (eg sweat) or show (a quality *etc*) strongly. □ **suinter, exsuder**

exult [ig'zʌlt] *verb* (*with* **in** *or* **at**) to be very happy; to rejoice: *They exulted in their victory/at the news of their victory.* □ **(se) réjouir (de)**

ex'ultant *adjective* very happy (at a victory or success *etc*): *exultant football fans.* □ **triomphant**

,**exul'tation** [eg-] *noun.* □ **exultation**

eye [ai] *noun* **1** the part of the body with which one sees: *Open your eyes; She has blue eyes.* □ **œil**

2 anything like or suggesting an eye, *eg* the hole in a needle, the loop or ring into which a hook connects *etc.* □ **trou**

3 a talent for noticing and judging a particular type of thing: *He has an eye for detail/colour/beauty.* □ **(avoir l')œil (pour)**

■ *verb* to look at, observe: *The boys were eyeing the*

girls at the dance; The thief eyed the policeman warily. □ **observer**

'**eyeball** *noun* **1** the whole rounded structure of the eye. □ **globe oculaire**

2 the part of the eye between the eyelids. □ **pupille (de l'œil)**

'**eyebrow** *noun* the curved line of hair above each eye. □ **sourcil**

'**eye-catching** *adjective* striking or noticeable, *especially* if attractive: *an eye-catching advertisement.* □ **tape-à-l'œil; attrayant**

'**eyelash** *noun* one of the (rows of) hairs that grow on the edge of the eyelids: *She looked at him through her eyelashes.* □ **cil**

'**eyelet** [-lit] *noun* a small hole in fabric *etc* for a cord *etc.* □ **œillet**

'**eyelid** *noun* the movable piece of skin that covers or uncovers the eye. □ **paupière**

'**eye-opener** *noun* something that reveals an unexpected fact *etc*: *Our visit to their office was a real eye-opener – they were so inefficient!* □ **révélation**

'**eye-piece** *noun* the part of a telescope *etc* to which one puts one's eye. □ **oculaire**

'**eyeshadow** *noun* a kind of coloured make-up worn around the eyes. □ **fard à paupières**

'**eyesight** *noun* the ability to see: *I have good eyesight.* □ **vue**

'**eyesore** *noun* something (*eg* a building) that is ugly to look at. □ **horreur**

'**eyewitness** *noun* a person who sees something (*eg* a crime) happen: *Eyewitnesses were questioned by the police.* □ **témoin oculaire**

before/under one's very eyes in front of one, *usually* with no attempt at concealment: *It happened before my very eyes.* □ **sous les yeux (de)**

be up to the eyes in to be very busy or deeply involved in or with: *She's up to the eyes in work.* □ **être dans...jusqu'au cou**

close one's eyes to to ignore (*especially* something wrong): *He closed his eyes to the children's misbehaviour.* □ **fermer les yeux sur**

in the eyes of in the opinion of: *You've done no wrong in my eyes.* □ **aux yeux de**

keep an eye on **1** to watch closely: *Keep an eye on the patient's temperature.* □ **suivre de près**

2 to look after: *Keep an eye on the baby while I am out!* □ **surveiller**

lay/set eyes on to see, *especially* for the first time: *I wish I'd never set eyes on her!* □ **poser son regard sur**

raise one's eyebrows to (lift one's eyebrows in order to) show surprise. □ **hausser les sourcils**

see eye to eye to be in agreement: *We've never seen eye to eye about this matter.* □ **voir les choses du même œil**

with an eye to something with something as an aim: *He's doing this with an eye to promotion.* □ **en vue de**

with one's eyes open with full awareness of what one is doing: *I knew what the job would involve – I went into it with my eyes open.* □ **en connaissance de cause**

Ff

fable ['feibl] *noun* **1** a story (*usually* about animals) that teaches a lesson about human behaviour: *Aesop's fables.* □ **fable**
2 a legend or untrue story: *fact or fable?* □ **légende**
fabulous ['fabjuləs] *adjective* **1** wonderful: *a fabulous idea.* □ **formidable**
2 existing (only) in a fable: *The phoenix is a fabulous bird.* □ **fabuleux**
'**fabulously** *adverb.* □ **fabuleusement**
fabric ['fabrik] *noun* **1** (a type of) cloth or material: *Nylon is a man-made fabric.* □ **tissu**
fabricate ['fabrikeit] *verb* to make up something that is not true (a story, accusation *etc*): *to fabricate an excuse.* □ **inventer**
,**fabri'cation** *noun* **1** a lie: *Your account of the accident was a complete fabrication.* □ **invention**
2 the act of fabricating. □ **fabrication**
fabulous *see* fable.
façade [fə'saːd] *noun* **1** the front of a building: *the façade of the temple.* □ **façade**
2 a pretended show: *In spite of his bold façade, he was very frightened.* □ **façade**
face [feis] *noun* **1** the front part of the head, from forehead to chin: *a beautiful face.* □ **visage**
2 a surface *especially* the front surface: *a rock face.* □ **face**
3 in mining, the end of a tunnel *etc* where work is being done: *a coal face.* □ **front d'attaque**
■ *verb* **1** to be opposite to: *My house faces the park.* □ **donner sur**
2 to turn, stand *etc* in the direction of: *She faced him across the desk.* □ **être en face de**
3 to meet or accept boldly: *to face one's fate.* □ **affronter**
-**faced** *adjective* having a face of a certain kind: *a baby-faced man.* □ **à visage de**
facial ['feiʃəl] *adjective* of the face: *facial expressions.* □ **facial**
facing *preposition* opposite: *The hotel is facing the church.* □ **en face de**
'**facelift** *noun* **1** an operation to smooth and firm the face: *You have had a facelift.* □ **déridage**
2 a process intended to make a building *etc* look better: *This village will be given a facelift.* □ **rénovation**
'**face powder** *noun* a type of makeup in the form of a fine powder: *She put on face powder to stop her nose shining.* □ **poudre de riz**
'**face-saving** *adjective* of something which helps a person not to look stupid or not to appear to be giving in: *He agreed to everything we asked and as a face-saving exercise we offered to consult him occasionally.* □ **qui sauve la face**
'**face value** the value stated on the face of a coin *etc*: *Some old coins are now worth a great deal more than their face value.* □ **valeur nominale**
at face value being as valuable *etc* as it appears: *You must take this offer at face value.* □ **au pied de la lettre**
face the music to accept punishment or responsibility

for something one has done: *The child had to face the music after being rude to the teacher.* □ **faire face (à)**
face to face in person; in the actual presence of one another: *I'd like to meet him face to face some day – I've heard so much about him.* □ **face à face**
face up to to meet or accept boldly: *She faced up to her difficult situation.* □ **faire face à**
in the face of having to deal with and in spite of: *She succeeded in the face of great difficulties.* □ **en dépit de**
lose face to suffer a loss of respect or reputation: *You will really lose face if you are defeated.* □ **perdre la face**
make/pull a face to twist one's face into a strange expression: *She pulled faces at the baby to make it laugh.* □ **grimacer**
on the face of it as it appears at first glance, *usually* deceptively: *On the face of it, the problem was easy.* □ **à première vue**
put a good face on it to give the appearance of being satisfied *etc* with something when one is not: *Now it's done we'll have to put a good face on it.* □ **faire contre mauvaise fortune bon cœur**
save one's face to avoid appearing stupid or wrong: *I refuse to accept the reponsibility for that error just to save your face – it's your fault.* □ **sauver la face**
facet ['fasit] *noun* **1** a side of a many-sided object, *especially* a cut jewel: *the facets of a diamond.* □ **facette**
2 an aspect or view of a subject: *There are several facets to this question.* □ **facette**
facetious [fə'siːʃəs] *adjective* not serious; intended to be funny or humorous: *a facetious remark.* □ **facétieux**
fa'cetiously *adverb.* □ **facétieusement**
fa'cetiousness *noun.* □ **caractère facétieux**
facial *see* face.
facility [fə'siləti] *noun* **1** ease or quickness: *She showed great facility in learning languages.* □ **facilité**
2 a skill: *He has a great facility for always being right.* □ **aisance**
■ *noun plural* **fa'cilities** the means to do something: *There are facilities for cooking.* □ **installations**
facing *see* face.
facsimile [fak'siməli] *noun* an exact copy. □ **fac-similé**
■ *adjective*: *a facsimile edition of an eighteenth-century book.* □ **en fac-similé**
fact [fakt] *noun* **1** something known or believed to be true: *It is a fact that smoking is a danger to health.* □ **fait**
2 reality: *fact or fiction.* □ **réel**
factual ['faktʃuəl] *adjective* of or containing facts: *a factual account.* □ **basé sur des/les faits**
'**factually** *adverb.* □ **en s'en tenant aux faits**
as a matter of fact, in fact, in point of fact actually or really: *She doesn't like him much – in fact I think she hates him!* □ **en fait**
faction ['fakʃən] *noun* a group or party that belongs to, and *usually* dissents from, a larger group. □ **faction**
factor ['faktə] *noun* **1** something, *eg* a fact, which has to be taken into account or which affects the course of events: *There are various factors to be considered.* ◻

facteur
2 a number which exactly divides into another: *3 is a factor of 6.* □ **diviseur**
factory ['faktəri] – *plural* **'factories** – *noun* a workshop where manufactured articles are made in large numbers: *a car factory*; *(also adjective) a factory worker.* □ **usine, manufacture**
factual *see* **fact.**
faculty ['fakəlti] – *plural* **'faculties** – *noun* 1 a power of the mind: *the faculty of reason.* □ **faculté**
2 a natural power of the body: *the faculty of hearing.* □ **faculté**
3 ability or skill: *She has a faculty for saying the right thing.* □ **talent**
4 *(often with capital)* a section of a university: *the Faculty of Arts/Science.* □ **faculté**
fad [fad] *noun* a trend or popular and short-lived style or activity: *The latest fad in sports equipment often comes from the United States.* □ **lubie**
fade [feid] *verb* to (make something) lose strength, colour, loudness *etc*: *The noise gradually faded (away).* □ **(s')affaiblir**
faeces *see* **feces.**
fag [fag] *noun* a slang word for a cigarette: *I'm dying for a fag.* □ **cigarette**
fagged out very tired: *I'm completely fagged out after that long walk.* □ **crevé**
Fahrenheit ['farənhait] *adjective* *(often abbreviated to* **F** *when written)* as measured on a Fahrenheit thermometer: *fifty degrees Fahrenheit (50°F).* □ **Fahrenheit**
fail [feil] *verb* 1 to be unsuccessful (in); not to manage (to do something): *They failed in their attempt; I failed my exam; I failed to post the letter.* □ **échouer (à)**
2 to break down or cease to work: *The brakes failed.* □ **tomber en panne**
3 to be insufficient or not enough: *His courage failed (him).* □ **manquer (à)**
4 (in a test, examination *etc*) to reject (a candidate): *The examiner failed half the class.* □ **recaler**
5 to disappoint: *They did not fail him in their support.* □ **manquer (à)**
'failing *noun* a fault or weakness: *He may have his failings, but he has always treated his children well.* □ **défaut**
■ *preposition* if (something) fails or is lacking: *Failing his help, we shall have to try something else.* □ **à défaut de**
'failure [-jə] *noun* 1 the state or act of failing: *She was upset by her failure in the exam; failure of the electricity supply.* □ **échec; panne**
2 an unsuccessful person or thing: *He felt he was a failure.* □ **raté, ée**
3 inability, refusal *etc* to do something: *his failure to reply.* □ **incapacité**
without fail definitely or certainly: *I shall do it tomorrow without fail.* □ **sans faute**
faint [feint] *adjective* 1 lacking in strength, brightness, courage *etc*: *The sound grew faint; a faint light.* □ **faible**
2 physically weak and about to lose consciousness: *Suddenly he felt faint.* □ **faible**

■ *verb* to lose consciousness: *She fainted on hearing the news.* □ **s'évanouir**
■ *noun* loss of consciousness: *His faint gave everybody a fright.* □ **évanouissement**
'faintly *adverb* 1 in a faint manner: *A light shone faintly.* □ **faiblement**
2 slightly; rather: *She looked faintly surprised.* □ **légèrement**
'faintness *noun.* □ **faiblesse**
fair¹ [feə] *adjective* 1 light-coloured; with light-coloured hair and skin: *fair hair; Scandinavian people are often fair.* □ **blond**
2 just; not favouring one side: *a fair test.* □ **juste**
3 (of weather) fine; without rain: *a fair afternoon.* □ **beau**
4 quite good; neither bad nor good: *Her work is only fair.* □ **passable**
5 quite big, long *etc*: *a fair size.* □ **beau**
6 beautiful: *a fair maiden.* □ **beau**
'fairness *noun.* □ **blondeur; justice**
'fairly *adverb* 1 justly; honestly: *fairly judged.* □ **impartialement**
2 quite or rather: *The work was fairly hard.* □ **assez**
fair play honest treatment; an absence of cheating, biased actions *etc*: *He's not involved in the contest – he's only here to see fair play.* □ **franc jeu**
fair² [feə] *noun* 1 a collection of entertainments that travels from town to town: *She won a large doll at the fair.* □ **foire**
2 a large market held at fixed times: *A fair is held here every spring.* □ **foire**
3 an exhibition of goods from different countries, firms *etc*: *a trade fair.* □ **foire**
fairy ['feəri] – *plural* **'fairies** – *noun* an imaginary creature in the form of a very small (often winged) human, with magical powers: *Children often believe in fairies*; *(also adjective) fairy-land.* □ **fée; (de) fée**
'fairy story *noun* 1 an old, or children's, story of fairies, magic *etc*: *a book of fairy stories.* □ **conte de fées**
2 an untrue statement; a lie: *I don't want to hear any fairy stories!* □ **histoire invraisemblable; mensonge**
'fairy tale *noun* a fairy story: *to tell fairy tales*; *(also adjective) the fairy-tale appearance of the countryside.* □ **conte de fées**
faith [feiθ] *noun* 1 trust or belief: *She had faith in her ability.* □ **confiance**
2 religious belief: *Years of hardship had not caused him to lose his faith.* □ **foi**
3 loyalty to one's promise: *to keep/break faith with someone.* □ **parole**
'faithful *adjective* 1 loyal and true; not changing: *a faithful friend; faithful to his promise.* □ **fidèle**
2 true or exact: *a faithful account of what had happened.* □ **fidèle**
'faithfully *adverb.* □ **fidèlement**
'faithfulness *noun.* □ **fidélité**
'faithless *adjective.* □ **déloyal**
'faithlessness *noun.* □ **déloyauté**
in (all) good faith sincerely: *She made the offer in good faith.* □ **en toute bonne foi**

fake [feik] *noun* **1** a worthless imitation (*especially* intended to deceive); a forgery: *That picture is a fake.* □ **faux**

2 a person who pretends to be something he is not: *He pretended to be a doctor, but he was a fake.* □ **imposteur**

■ *adjective* **1** made in imitation of something more valuable, *especially* with the intention of deceiving: *fake diamonds.* □ **faux**

2 pretending to be something one is not: *a fake clergyman.* □ **faux**

■ *verb* to pretend or imitate in order to deceive: *to fake a signature.* □ **contrefaire**

falcon ['foːlkən, 'fal-] *noun* a kind of bird of prey sometimes used for hunting. □ **faucon**

fall [foːl] – *past tense* **fell** [fel]: *past participle* 'fallen' – *verb* **1** to go down from a higher level *usually* unintentionally: *The apple fell from the tree; Her eye fell on an old book.* □ **tomber**

2 (*often with* **over**) to go down to the ground *etc* from an upright position, *usually* by accident: *She fell (over).* □ **tomber**

3 to become lower or less: *The temperature is falling.* □ **baisser**

4 to happen or occur: *Easter falls early this year.* □ **tomber**

5 to enter a certain state or condition: *She fell asleep; They fell in love.* □ **tomber**

6 (*formal: only with* **it** *as subject*) to come as one's duty *etc*: *It falls to me to take care of the children.* □ **incomber à**

■ *noun* **1** the act of falling: *He had a fall.* □ **chute**

2 (a quantity of) something that has fallen: *a fall of snow.* □ **chute**

3 capture or (political) defeat: *the fall of Rome.* □ **chute**

4 the autumn: *Leaves change colour in the fall.* □ **automne**

falls *noun plural* a waterfall: *the Niagara Falls.* □ **chutes**

'fallout *noun* radioactive dust from a nuclear explosion *etc*. □ **retombées radioactives**

his, her *etc* **face fell** he, she *etc* looked suddenly disappointed. □ **(s')allonger**

fall away 1 to become less in number: *The crowd began to fall away.* □ **diminuer**

2 to slope downwards: *The ground fell away steeply.* □ **(s')affaisser**

fall back to move back or stop moving forward. □ **reculer**

fall back on to use, or to go to for help, finally when everything else has been tried: *Whatever happens you have your father's money to fall back on.* □ **avoir recours à**

fall behind 1 to be slower than (someone else): *Hurry up! You're falling behind (the others); He is falling behind in his schoolwork.* □ **prendre du retard**

2 (*with* **with**) to become late in regular payment, letter-writing *etc*: *Don't fall behind with the rent!* □ **être en retard**

fall down (*sometimes with* **on**) to fail (in): *He's falling down on his job.* □ **ne pas être à la hauteur**

fall flat (*especially* of jokes *etc*) to fail completely or to

have no effect: *Her joke fell flat.* □ **tomber à plat**

fall for 1 to be deceived by (something): *I made up a story to explain why I had not been at work and he fell for it.* □ **tomber dans le panneau**

2 to fall in love with (someone): *He has fallen for your sister.* □ **tomber amoureux (de)**

fall in with 1 to join with (someone) for company: *On the way home we fell in with some friends.* □ **rencontrer**

2 to agree with (a plan, idea *etc*): *They fell in with our suggestion.* □ **accepter**

fall off to become smaller in number or amount: *Audiences often fall off during the summer.* □ **décroître**

fall on/upon to attack: *He fell on the old man and beat him; They fell hungrily upon the food.* □ **(se) jeter sur**

fall out (*sometimes with* **with**) to quarrel: *I have fallen out with my sister.* □ **se fâcher (avec)**

fall short (*often with* **of**) to be not enough or not good enough *etc*): *The money we have falls short of what we need.* □ **manquer (de)**

fall through (of plans *etc*) to fail or come to nothing: *Our plans fell through.* □ **échouer**

fallacy ['faləsi] – *plural* 'fallacies – *noun* a wrong idea or belief, *usually* one that is generally believed to be true; false reasoning: *That belief is just a fallacy.* □ **sophisme**

fallacious [fə'leiʃəs] *adjective* wrong, mistaken or showing false reasoning: *a fallacious argument.* □ **fallacieux**

fallible ['faləbl] *adjective* able or likely to make mistakes: *Human beings are fallible.* □ **faillible**

fallow ['falou] *adjective* (of land) left to its own natural growth and not planted with seeds: *We will let this field lie fallow for a year; fallow fields.* □ **en friche**

false [foːls] *adjective* **1** not true; not correct: *He made a false statement to the police.* □ **faux**

2 not genuine; intended to deceive: *She has a false passport.* □ **faux**

3 artificial: *false teeth.* □ **faux**

4 not loyal: *false friends.* □ **faux**

'falsehood *noun* (the telling of) a lie: *She is incapable of (uttering a) falsehood.* □ **mensonge**

'falsify [-fai] *verb* to make false: *He falsified the accounts.* □ **falsifier**

,falsifi'cation [-fi-] *noun.* □ **falsification**

'falsity *noun.* □ **fausseté**

false alarm a warning of something which in fact does not happen. □ **fausse alerte**

false start in a race, a start which is declared not valid and therefore has to be repeated. □ **faux départ**

falsetto [foːl'setou] – *plural* **fal'settos** – *noun* an unnaturally high (singing) voice in men, or a man with such a voice: *He was singing in falsetto; He is a falsetto.* □ **fausset**

■ *adverb*: *He sings falsetto.* □ **(en) fausset**

falter ['foːltə] *verb* **1** to stumble or hesitate: *She walked without faltering.* □ **hésiter**

2 to speak with hesitation: *Her voice faltered.* □ **hésiter**

'faltering *adjective.* □ **hésitant**

'falteringly *adverb.* □ **d'un pas mal assuré; d'une voix tremblante**

fame [feim] *noun* the quality of being well-known: *Her* *novels brought her fame.* □ **renom(mée)**

'famous *adjective* well-known (for good or worthy reasons): *She is famous for her strength.* □ **célèbre**

'famously *adverb* very well. □ **à merveille**

familiar [fə'miljə] *adjective* **1** well-known: *The house was familiar to him; She looks very familiar (to me).* □ **familier**

2 (*with* **with**) knowing about: *Are you familiar with the plays of Shakespeare?* □ **familier (avec)**

3 too friendly: *You are much too familiar with my wife!* □ **familier**

fa'miliarly *adverb.* □ **familièrement**

fa,mili'arity [-li'a-] – *plural* **fa,mili'arities** – *noun* **1** the state of being familiar: *I was surprised by her familiarity with our way of life.* □ **familiarité**

2 an act of (too) friendly behaviour: *You must not allow such familiarities.* □ **familiarité**

fa'miliarize, fa'miliarise *verb* (*with* **with**) to make something well known to (someone): *You must familiarize yourself with the rules.* □ **familiariser (avec)**

fa,miliari'zation, fa,miliari'sation *noun.* □ **accoutumance (à)**

family ['faməli] – *plural* **'families** – *noun* **1** (*singular* or *plural*) a man, his wife and their children: *These houses were built for families; The (members of the) Smith family are all very athletic;* (*also adjective*) *a family holiday.* □ **famille**

2 a group of people related to each other, including cousins, grandchildren *etc: He comes from a wealthy family;* (*also adjective*) *the family home.* □ **famille**

3 the children of a man and his wife: *When I get married I should like a large family.* □ **famille**

4 a group of plants, animals, languages *etc* that are connected in some way: *In spite of its name, a koala bear is not a member of the bear family.* □ **famille**

family planning controlling or limiting the number of children that people have *especially* by using a means of contraception: *a family planning clinic.* □ **limitation des naissances**

family tree (a plan showing) a person's ancestors and relations. □ **arbre généalogique**

famine ['famin] *noun* (a) great lack or shortage *especially* of food: *Some parts of the world suffer regularly from famine.* □ **famine**

famished ['famiʃt] *adjective* very hungry: *I was famished after my long walk.* □ **affamé**

famous, famously *see* fame.

fan[1] [fan] *noun* **1** a flat instrument held in the hand and waved to direct a current of air across the face in hot weather: *Ladies used to carry fans to keep themselves cool.* □ **éventail**

2 a mechanical instrument causing a current of air: *He has had a fan fitted in the kitchen for extracting smells.* □ **ventilateur**

■ *verb* – *past tense, past participle* **fanned** – **1** to cool (as if) with a fan: *She sat in the corner, fanning herself.* □ **(s')éventer**

2 to increase or strengthen (a fire) by directing air towards it with a fan *etc: They fanned the fire until it burst into flames.* □ **attiser**

fan[2] [fan] *noun* an enthusiastic admirer of a sport, hobby or well-known person: *I'm a great fan of his; football fans;* (*also adjective*) *fan mail/letters* (= letters *etc* sent by admirers). □ **admirateur**

fanatic [fə'natik] *noun* a person who is (too) enthusiastic about something: *a religious fanatic.* □ **fanatique**

fa'natic(al) *adjective* (too) enthusiastic: *He is fanatical about physical exercise.* □ **fanatique**

fa'natically *adverb.* □ **fanatiquement**

fa'naticism [-sizəm] *noun* (too) great enthusiasm, *especially* about religion: *Fanaticism is the cause of most religious hatred.* □ **fanatisme**

fancy ['fansi] – *plural* **'fancies** – *noun* **1** a sudden (often unexpected) liking or desire: *The child had many peculiar fancies.* □ **envie**

2 the power of the mind to imagine things: *She had a tendency to indulge in flights of fancy.* □ **imagination**

3 something imagined: *He had a sudden fancy that he could see spring approaching.* □ **impression**

■ *adjective* decorated; not plain: *fancy cakes.* □ **de fantaisie**

■ *verb* **1** to like the idea of having or doing something: *I fancy a cup of tea.* □ **avoir envie (de)**

2 to think or have a certain feeling or impression (that): *I fancied (that) you were angry.* □ **croire (que)**

3 to have strong sexual interest in (a person): *He fancies her a lot.* □ **se sentir attiré (par/vers)**

'fanciful *adjective* **1** inclined to have fancies, *especially* strange, unreal ideas: *She's a very fanciful girl.* □ **fantasque**

2 imaginary or unreal: *That idea is rather fanciful.* □ **extravagant**

'fancifully *adverb.* □ **d'une manière extravagante/fantasque**

fancy dress clothes representing a particular character, nationality, historical period *etc: He went to the party in fancy dress;* (*also adjective*) *a fancy-dress party.* □ **déguisement**

take a fancy to to become fond of, often suddenly or unexpectedly: *They bought that house because they took a fancy to it.* □ **prendre goût à**

take one's fancy to be liked or wanted by (someone): *When I go shopping I just buy anything that takes my fancy.* □ **avoir envie (de)**

fanfare ['fanfeə] *noun* a short piece of music played by trumpets *etc* at the entry of a king or queen during a ceremony *etc.* □ **fanfare**

fang [fan] *noun* **1** a long pointed tooth *especially* of a fierce animal: *The wolf bared its fangs.* □ **croc**

2 the poison-tooth of a snake. □ **crochet**

fantasy ['fantəsi] – *plural* **'fantasies** – *noun* an imaginary (*especially* not realistic) scene, story *etc: He was always having fantasies about becoming rich and famous;* (*also adjective*) *He lived in a fantasy world.* □ **(de) fantaisie**

fantastic [fan'tastik] *adjective* **1** unbelievable and like a fantasy: *She told me some fantastic story about her father being a Grand Duke!* □ **extraordinaire, prodigieux**

2 wonderful; very good: *You look fantastic!* □

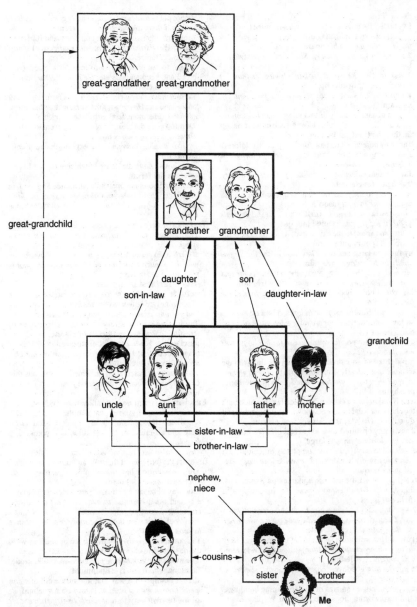

fantastique
fan'tastically *adverb*. □ **extraordinairement**
far [faː] *adverb* **1** indicating distance, progress *etc*: *How far is it from here to his house?* □ **loin**
2 at or to a long way away: *She went far away/off.* □ **loin**
3 very much: *She was a far better swimmer than her friend (was).* □ **beaucoup**
■ *adjective* **1** distant; a long way away: *a far country.* □ **lointain**
2 more distant (*usually* of two things): *He lives on the far side of the lake.* □ **plus loin; à l'autre bout de**
farther, farthest *see* **further.**
'faraway *adjective* **1** distant: *faraway places.* □ **lointain**
2 not paying attention; dreamy: *She had a faraway look in her eyes.* □ **absent**
,far-'fetched *adjective* very unlikely: *a far-fetched story.* □ **tiré par les cheveux**
as far as 1 to the place or point mentioned: *We walked as far as the lake.* □ **jusqu'à**
2 (*also* **so far as**) as great a distance as: *He did not walk as far as his friends.* □ **aussi loin que**
3 (*also* **so far as**) to the extent that: *As far as I know she is well.* □ **(pour) autant que**
by far by a large amount: *They have by far the largest family in the village.* □ **de loin**
far and away by a very great amount: *She is far and away the cleverest girl in the class!* □ **de très loin**
far from 1 not only not, but: *Far from liking him, I hate him.* □ **loin de**
2 not at all: *He was far from helpful.* □ **loin de**
so far 1 until now: *So far we have been quite successful.* □ **jusqu'ici**
2 up to a certain point: *We can get so far but no further without more help.* □ **jusqu'ici**
far-sighted of an individual who can see things in the distance more clearly than those close by: *I need glasses to read because I am far-sighted* □ **hypermétrope; presbyte**
farce [faːs] *noun* **1** a (kind of) comic play in which both the characters and the events shown are improbable and ridiculous: *The play is a classic farce.* □ **farce**
2 any funny or stupid situation in real life: *The meeting was an absolute farce.* □ **farce**
farcical ['faːsikəl] *adjective* completely ridiculous, and therefore *usually* humorous: *The whole idea was farcical.* □ **grotesque**
fare [feə] *noun* **1** the price of a journey on a train, bus, ship *etc*: *He hadn't enough money for his bus fare.* □ **(prix du) billet**
2 a paying passenger in a hired vehicle, *especially* in a taxi: *The taxi driver was asked by the police where her last fare got out.* □ **client, ente**
farewell [feə'wel] *noun* an act of saying goodbye: *They said their farewells at the station; (also adjective) a farewell dinner.* □ **(d')adieu**
■ *interjection* goodbye: *'Farewell for ever!' she cried.* □ **adieu!**
farm [faːm] *noun* **1** an area of land, including buildings, used for growing crops, breeding and keeping cows,

sheep, pigs *etc*: *Much of England is good agricultural land and there are many farms.* □ **ferme**
2 the farmer's house and the buildings near it in such a place: *We visited the farm; (also adjective) a farm kitchen.* □ **ferme**
■ *verb* to cultivate (the land) in order to grow crops, breed and keep animals *etc*: *He farms (5000 acres) in the south.* □ **cultiver**
'farmer *noun* the owner or tenant of a farm who works on the land *etc*: *How many farmworkers does that farmer employ?* □ **fermier, ière, cultivateur, trice**
'farming *noun* the business of owning or running a farm: *There is a lot of money involved in farming; (also adjective) farming communities.* □ **exploitation (agricole); rural**
'farmhouse *noun* the house in which a farmer lives. □ **(maison de) ferme**
'farmyard *noun* the open area surrounded by the farm buildings: *There were several hens loose in the farmyard; (also adjective) farmyard animals.* □ **(de) basse-cour**
fart [faːt] *noun* gas that has been expelled from the body: *The old man's fart left an unpleasant odour in the room.* □ **pet**
■ *verb* to expel or force gas out of the body: *Raman was in so much pain from gas in his stomach that he tried to fart.* □ **péter**
farther, farthest *see* **further.**
fascinate ['fasineit] *verb* to charm; to attract or interest very strongly: *She was fascinated by the strange clothes and customs of the country people.* □ **fasciner**
'fascinating *adjective* very charming, attractive or interesting: *a fascinating story.* □ **fascinant**
,fasci'nation *noun* **1** the act of fascinating or state of being fascinated: *the look of fascination on the children's faces.* □ **fascination**
2 the power of fascinating or something that has this: *Old books have/hold a fascination for him.* □ **fascination**
Fascism ['faʃizəm] *noun* a nationalistic and anti-Communist system of government like that of Italy 1922-43, where all aspects of society are controlled by the state and all criticism or opposition is suppressed. □ **fascisme**
'fascist (*also with capital*) *adjective*. □ **fasciste**
fashion ['faʃən] *noun* **1** the style and design of clothes: *Are you interested in fashion?; (also adjective) a fashion magazine.* □ **(de) mode**
2 the way of behaving, dressing *etc* which is popular at a certain time: *Fashions in music and art are always changing.* □ **mode**
3 a way of doing something: *She spoke in a very strange fashion.* □ **façon**
'fashionable *adjective* following, or in keeping with, the newest style of dress, way of living *etc*: *a fashionable woman; a fashionable part of town.* □ **à la mode**
'fashionably *adverb*. □ **élégamment**
after a fashion in a way, but not very well: *She can speak French after a fashion.* □ **tant bien que mal**
all the fashion very fashionable: *Long skirts were all*

the fashion last year. □ **la grande mode**

in fashion fashionable: *Tweed jackets are in fashion.* □ **à la mode**

out of fashion not fashionable: *Long skirts are out of fashion at present.* □ **démodé**

fast¹ [faːst] *adjective* **1** quick-moving: *a fast car.* □ **rapide 2** quick: *a fast worker.* □ **rapide 3** (of a clock, watch *etc*) showing a time in advance of the correct time: *My watch is five minutes fast.* □ **en avance**

■ *adverb* quickly: *She speaks so fast I can't understand her.* □ **vite**

'fastness *noun.* □ **rapidité**

fast food(s) food that can be quickly prepared, *eg* hamburgers *etc*. □ **prêt-à-manger, aliments prêts à manger**

fast² [faːst] *verb* to go without food, *especially* for religious or medical reasons: *Muslims fast during the festival of Ramadan.* □ **jeûner**

■ *noun* a time or act of fasting: *She has just finished two days' fast.* □ **jeûne**

'fasting *noun.* □ **jeûne**

fast³ [faːst] *adjective* **1** (of a dye) fixed; that will not come out of a fabric when it is washed. □ **bon teint résistant 2** firm; fixed: *She made her end of the rope fast to a tree.* □ **attaché**

fast asleep completely asleep: *The baby fell fast asleep in my arms.* □ **profondément endormi**

fasten ['faːsn] *verb* to fix or join (together): *Fasten the gate!; She fastened a flower to the front of her dress; He fastened his eyes upon her face.* □ **attacher**

'fastener *noun* something that fastens things (together): *A zipper is a kind of fastener.* □ **attach**

fastidious [fəˈstidiəs] *adjective* very critical and difficult to please: *She is so fastidious about her food that she will not eat in a restaurant.* □ **difficile**

faˈstidiously *adverb.* □ **dédaigneusement**

faˈstidiousness *noun.* □ **goût difficile**

fat [fat] *noun* **1** an oily substance made by the bodies of animals and by some plants: *This meat has got a lot of fat on it.* □ **gras 2** a kind of such substance, used *especially* for cooking: *There are several good cooking fats on the market.* □ **matière grasse**

■ *adjective* **1** having a lot of fat on one's body; large, heavy and round in shape: *He was a very fat child.* □ **gros 2** large or abundant: *Her business made a fat profit; A fat lot of good that is!* (= That is no good at all). □ **gros**

'fatness *noun.* □ **embonpoint**

'fatten *verb* (*often with* **up**) to make or become fat: *They are fattening up a chicken to eat at Christmas.* □ **engraisser**

'fatty *adjective* containing, or like, fat: *This meat is very fatty.* □ **gras**

'fattiness *noun.* □ **graisse**

'fat-head *noun* a stupid person. □ **imbécile**

fatal ['feitl] *adjective* **1** causing death: *a fatal accident.* □ **fatal 2** disastrous: *She made the fatal mistake of not inviting him to the party.* □ **fatal**

'fatally *adverb.* □ **fatalement**

fatality [fəˈtaləti] – *plural* **faˈtalities** – *noun* (an accident causing) death: *fatalities on the roads.* □ **accident mortel**

fate [feit] *noun* **1** (*sometimes with capital*) the supposed power that controls events: *Who knows what fate has in store* (= waiting for us in the future)? □ **destin 2** a destiny or doom, *eg* death: *A terrible fate awaited her.* □ **sort**

'fatalism *noun* the belief that fate controls everything, and man cannot change it. □ **fatalisme**

'fatalist *noun* a person who believes in fatalism: *He is a complete fatalist – he just accepts everything that happens to him.* □ **fataliste**

ˌfataˈlistic *adjective.* □ **fataliste**

'fated *adjective* controlled or intended by fate: *He seemed fated to arrive late wherever he went.* □ **destiné (à)**

'fateful *adjective* involving important decisions, results *etc*: *At last the fateful day arrived.* □ **fatidique**

father ['faːðə] *noun* **1** a male parent, *especially* human: *Mr. Smith is her father.* □ **père 2** (*with capital*) the title of a (*usually* Roman Catholic) priest: *I met Father Sullivan this morning.* □ **(révérend) Père 3** a person who begins, invents or first makes something: *King Alfred was the father of the English navy.* □ **père**

■ *verb* to be the father of: *King Charles II fathered a number of children.* □ **engendrer**

'fatherhood *noun* the state or condition of being a father: *Now that the children are older I am enjoying fatherhood.* □ **paternité**

'fatherly *adjective* like a father: *He showed a fatherly interest in his friend's child.* □ **paternel**

'father-in-law *noun* the father of one's wife or husband. □ **beau-père**

fathom ['faðəm] *noun* a measure of depth of water (6 feet or 1.8 metres): *The water is 8 fathoms deep.* □ **brasse**

■ *verb* to understand (a mystery *etc*): *I cannot fathom why she should have left home.* □ **comprendre**

fatigue [fəˈtiːɡ] *noun* **1** great tiredness (caused *especially* by hard work or effort): *He was suffering from fatigue.* □ **fatigue 2** (*especially* in metals) weakness caused by continual use: *metal fatigue.* □ **usure**

faˈtigued *adjective* made very tired: *She was fatigued by the constant questioning.* □ **épuisé**

fatten, fatty *see* **fat.**

fault [fɔːlt] *noun* **1** a mistake; something for which one is to blame: *The accident was your fault.* □ **faute 2** an imperfection; something wrong: *There is a fault in this machine; a fault in his character.* □ **défaut 3** a crack in the rock surface of the earth: *faults in the earth's crust.* □ **faille**

■ *verb* to find fault with: *I couldn't fault him/his piano-playing.* □ **reprocher**

'faultless *adjective* without fault; perfect: *a faultless*

performance. □ **irréprochable**
'**faultlessly** *adverb.* □ **irréprochablement**
'**faulty** *adjective* (*usually* of something mechanical) not made or working correctly. □ **défectueux**
at fault wrong or to blame: *She was at fault.* □ **fautif**
find fault with to criticize or complain of: *She is always finding fault with the way he eats.* □ **reprocher**
to a fault to too great an extent: *She was generous to a fault.* □ **à l'excès**
faun [fɔːn] *noun* an imaginary creature, half man and half goat. □ **faune**
fauna ['fɔːnə] *noun* the animals of a district or country as a whole: *She is interested in South American fauna.* □ **faune**
favour, favor ['feivə] *noun* **1** a kind action: *Will you do me a favour and lend me your car?* □ **service**
2 kindness or approval: *She looked on him with great favour.* □ **approbation**
3 preference or too much kindness: *By doing that he showed favour to the other side.* □ **préférence**
4 a state of being approved of: *He was very much in favour with the Prime Minister.* □ **(en) faveur**
■ *verb* to support or show preference for: *Which side do you favour?* □ **appuyer**
'**favourable** *adjective* **1** showing approval: *Was her reaction favourable or unfavourable?* □ **favorable**
2 helpful or advantageous: *a favourable wind.* □ **favorable**
'**favourably** *adverb.* □ **favorablement**
'**favourite** [-rit] *adjective* best-liked; preferred: *his favourite city.* □ **favori**
■ *noun* a person or thing that one likes best: *Of all her paintings that is my favourite.* □ **préféré, ée**
'**favouritism** [-ri-] *noun* preferring or supporting one person *etc* more than another: *I can't be accused of favouritism – I voted for everyone!* □ **favoritisme**
in favour of in support of: *I am in favour of higher pay.* □ **en faveur de**
in one's favour to one's benefit or advantage: *The wind was in our favour.* □ **pour**

> **favour,** noun, ends in **-our.**
> The adjective **favourable** is also spelt with **-our-.**

fawn[1] [fɔːn] *noun* **1** a young deer. □ **faon**
2 (*also adjective*) (of) its colour, a light yellowish brown: *a fawn sweater.* □ **fauve**
fawn[2] [fɔːn] *verb* **1** (of dogs) to show affection (by wagging the tail, rolling over *etc*). □ **faire fête à**
2 (*with* upon) to be too humble or to flatter (someone) in a servile way: *The new employee fawned over the boss.* □ **lécher les bottes de**
fear [fiə] *noun* (a) feeling of great worry or anxiety caused by the knowledge of danger: *The soldier tried not to show his fear; fear of water.* □ **peur, crainte**
■ *verb* **1** to feel fear because of (something): *She feared her father when he was angry; I fear for my father's safety* (= I am worried because I think he is in danger). □ **avoir peur (de)**
2 to regret: *I fear you will not be able to see him today.* □ **craindre (que)**

'**fearful** *adjective* **1** afraid: *a fearful look.* □ **craintif**
2 terrible: *The lion gave a fearful roar.* □ **effrayant**
3 very bad: *a fearful mistake!* □ **épouvantable**
'**fearfully** *adverb.* □ **terriblement; craintivement**
'**fearless** *adjective* without fear; brave: *a fearless soldier.* □ **intrépide**
'**fearlessly** *adverb.* □ **intrépidement**
for fear of so as not to: *She would not go swimming for fear of catching a cold.* □ **de peur de**
in fear of in a state of being afraid of: *He lived in fear of his mother.* □ **dans la crainte de**
feasible ['fiːzəbl] *adjective* able to be done: *a feasible solution to the problem.* □ **faisable, réalisable**
feasi'bility *noun.* □ **faisabilité**
feast [fiːst] *noun* **1** a large and rich meal, *usually* eaten to celebrate some occasion: *The king invited them to a feast in the palace.* □ **festin**
2 (*sometimes with capital*) a particular day on which some (*especially* religious) person or event is remembered and celebrated: *Today is the feast of St. Stephen.* □ **fête**
■ *verb* to eat (as if) at a feast: *We feasted all day.* □ **festoyer**
feather ['feðə] *noun* one of the things that grow from a bird's skin that form the covering of its body: *They cleaned the oil off the seagull's feathers.* □ **plume**
■ *verb* to line, cover or decorate with feathers: *The eagle feathers its nest with down from its own breast.* □ **emplumer**
'**feathered** *adjective.* □ **emplumé**
'**feathery** *adjective* **1** of, like, or covered in, a feather or feathers: *a feathery hat.* □ **doux comme la plume; en plumes**
2 soft and light: *a feathery touch.* □ **plumeux**
a feather in one's cap something one can be proud of: *Winning the race was quite a feather in his cap.* □ **un fleuron à sa couronne**
feature ['fiːtʃə] *noun* **1** a mark by which anything is known; a quality: *The use of bright colours is one of the features of her painting.* □ **caractéristique**
2 one of the parts of one's face (eyes, nose *etc*): *She has very regular features.* □ **trait**
3 a special article in a newspaper: *'The Gazette' is doing a feature on holidays.* □ **manchette**
4 the main film in a cinema program *etc*: *The feature begins at 7:30*; (*also adjective*) *a feature film.* □ **grand film; long métrage**
■ *verb* to give or have a part (*especially* an important one): *That film features the best of the Canadian actresses.* □ **mettre en vedette(s)**
February ['februəri] *noun* the second month of the year, the month following January. □ **février**
feces, faeces ['fiːsiːz] *noun plural* solid waste matter passed out from the body. □ **fèces**
fed *see* **feed.**
federal ['fedərəl] *adjective* (of a government or group of states) joined together, *usually* for national and external affairs only: *the federal government of the United States of America.* □ **fédéral**
'**federated** [-rei-] *adjective* joined by a treaty, agree-

ment *etc*. □ **fédéré**

,fede'ration *noun* people, societies, unions, states *etc* joined together for a common purpose: *the International Federation of Actors*. □ **fédération**

fee [fiː] *noun* the price paid for work done by a doctor, lawyer *etc* or for some special service or right: *the lawyer's fee; an entrance fee; university fees*. □ **honoraires, droit, frais (de scolarité)**

feeble ['fiːbl] *adjective* weak: *The old lady has been rather feeble since her illness; a feeble excuse*. □ **faible**
'**feebly** *adverb*. □ **faiblement**

feed [fiːd] – *past tense, past participle* **fed** [fed] – *verb* 1 to give food to: *He fed the child with a spoon*. □ **nourrir**
2 (*with* **on**) to eat: *Cows feed on grass*. □ **se nourrir (de)**

■ *noun* food *especially* for a baby or animals: *Have you given the baby his feed?*; *cattle feed*. □ **biberon, fourrage**

fed up tired; bored and annoyed: *I'm fed up with all this work!* □ **en avoir assez**

feel [fiːl] – *past tense, past participle* **felt** [felt] – *verb* 1 to become aware of (something) by the sense of touch: *She felt his hand on her shoulder*. □ **sentir**
2 to find out the shape, size, texture *etc* of something by touching, *usually* with the hands: *She felt the parcel carefully*. □ **palper, tâter**
3 to experience or be aware of (an emotion, sensation *etc*): *He felt a sudden anger*. □ **ressentir**
4 to think (oneself) to be: *She feels sick*; *How does she feel about her work?* □ (**se**) **sentir, penser de**
5 to believe or consider: *She feels that the firm treated her badly*. □ **avoir l'impression (que)**
'**feeler** *noun* (in certain animals, insects *etc*) an organ for touching, *especially* one of the two thread-like parts on an insect's head. □ **antenne**
'**feeling** *noun* 1 power and ability to feel: *I have no feeling in my little finger*. □ **sensation**
2 something that one feels physically: *a feeling of great pain*. □ **sensation**
3 (*usually in plural*) something that one feels in one's mind: *His angry words hurt my feelings*; *a feeling of happiness*. □ **sentiment**
4 an impression or belief: *I have a feeling that the work is too hard*. □ **impression**
5 affection: *He has no feeling for her now*. □ **sentiment**
6 emotion: *He spoke with great feeling*. □ **émotion**

feel as if/as though to have the sensation (physical or mental) or feeling that: *I feel as if I am going to be sick*; *She feels as though she has known him for years*. □ **avoir l'impression de**

feel like 1 to have the feelings that one would have if one were: *I feel like a princess in this beautiful dress*; *He felt like an idiot* (= He felt very foolish). □ (**se**) **sentir**
2 to feel that one would like to have (to have, do *etc*): *I feel like a drink*; *Do you feel like going to the movies?* □ **avoir envie (de)**

feel one's way to find one's way by feeling: *I had to feel my way to the door in the dark*. □ **avancer à tâtons**

feel sorry for to pity or have compassion for a person or animal: *Ryan feels sorry for Mandy's dog because*

no one ever takes it out for a walk. □ **apitoyer**

feel sorry for oneself to feel extreme pity for oneself: *No one hurt your feelings on purpose so stop sulking and feeling sorry for yourself*. □ **s'apitoyer**

get the feel of to become accustomed to: *to get the feel of a new job*. □ **se faire à**

feet *see* **foot**.

feign [fein] *verb* to pretend to feel: *He feigned illness*. □ **faire semblant (de)**
feigned *adjective* pretended: *feigned happiness*. □ **simulé**

felicity [fə'lisəti] *noun* happiness. □ **félicité**
fe,lici'tations *noun plural* congratulations. □ **félicitations**

feline ['fiːlain] *adjective* of or like a cat: *a feline appearance*. □ **félin**

fell[1] *see* **fall**.

fell[2] [fel] *verb* to cut or knock down to the ground: *They are felling all the trees in this area*. □ **abattre**

fellow ['felou] *noun* 1 a man: *He's quite a nice fellow but I don't like him*. □ **homme**
2 (*often as part of a word*) a companion and equal: *She is playing with her schoolfellows*. □ **camarade**

■ *adjective* belonging to the same group, country *etc*: *a fellow student*; *a fellow music-lover*. □ **camarade (de)**
'**fellowship** *noun* 1 an association (of people with common interests): *a youth fellowship* (= a club for young people). □ **association**
2 friendliness. □ **camaraderie**
,**fellow 'feeling** *noun* sympathy (*especially* for someone in a similar situation, of similar tastes *etc*): *I had a fellow feeling for the other patient with the broken leg*. □ **sympathie**

felon ['felən] *noun* a person who is guilty of a serious crime. □ **criminel, elle**
'**felony** – *plural* '**felonies** – *noun* a serious crime: *He committed a felony*. □ **crime**

felt[1] *see* **feel**.

felt[2] [felt] *noun, adjective* (of) a type of cloth made of wool that has been pressed together not woven: *She bought a metre of felt to re-cover the card table* (= table for playing cards on); *a felt hat*. □ **feutre**

female ['fiːmeil] *noun, adjective* 1 (a person, animal *etc*) of the sex that gives birth to children, produces eggs *etc*: *a female blackbird*; *the female of the species*. □ **femelle**
2 (a plant) that produces seeds. □ **femelle**

feminine ['feminin] *adjective* 1 of a woman: *a feminine voice*. □ **féminin**
2 with all the essential qualities of a woman: *She was a very feminine person*. □ **féminin**
3 in certain languages, of one of *usually* two or three genders of nouns *etc*. □ **féminin**
,**femi'ninity** *noun* the quality of being feminine: *She never used her femininity to win the argument*. □ **féminité**
'**feminism** *noun* the thought and actions of people who want to make women's (legal, political, social *etc*) rights equal to those of men. □ **féminisme**
'**feminist** *noun* a supporter of feminism. □ **féministe**

femur ['fiːmə] *noun* the thigh bone. □ **fémur**

fen [fen] *noun* an area of low marshy land often covered with water. □ **marécage**

fence[1] [fens] *noun* a line of wooden or metal posts joined by wood, wire *etc* to stop people, animals *etc* moving on to or off a piece of land: *The garden was surrounded by a wooden fence.* □ **clôture**

■ *verb* to enclose (an area of land) with a fence *eg* to prevent people, animals *etc* from getting in: *We fenced off the lake.* □ **clôturer**

'**fencing**[1] *noun* (the material used for) a fence: *a hundred metres of fencing.* □ **matériaux pour clôture**

fence[2] [fens] *verb* **1** to fight with (blunted) swords as a sport. □ **faire de l'escrime**

2 to avoid answering questions: *He fenced with me for half an hour before I got the truth.* □ **se dérober**

'**fencing**[2] *noun* the sport of fighting with (blunted) swords: *I used to be very good at fencing.* □ **escrime**

fend [fend]: **fend for oneself** to look after oneself: *He is old enough to fend for himself.* □ **se débrouiller**

fender ['fendə] *noun* **1** anything used to protect a boat from touching another, a pier *etc*: *She hung old car tires over the side of the boat to act as fenders.* □ **bourrelet de défense**

2 a low guard around a fireplace to prevent coal *etc* from falling out. □ **garde-feu**

3 the part of a motor vehicle which is around the wheel. □ **aile**

ferment [fə'ment] *verb* **1** to (make something) go through a particular chemical change (as when yeast is added to dough in the making of bread): *Grape juice must be fermented before it becomes wine.* □ **(faire) fermenter**

2 to excite or be excited: *He is the kind of person to ferment trouble.* □ **fomenter**

■ ['fɜːment] *noun* a state of excitement: *The whole city was in a ferment.* □ **effervescence**

,**fermen'tation** [fɜːmen-] *noun* the chemical change occurring when something ferments or is fermented. □ **fermentation**

fern [fɜːn] *noun* a kind of plant with no flowers and delicate feather-like leaves. □ **fougère**

ferocious [fə'rouʃəs] *adjective* fierce or savage: *a ferocious animal.* □ **féroce**

fe'rociously *adverb.* □ **férocement**

ferocity [fə'rosəti] *noun.* □ **férocité**

ferret ['ferit] *noun* a type of small, weasel-like animal used to chase rabbits out of their holes. □ **furet**

ferret (about) *verb* to search busily and persistently: *He ferreted about in the cupboard.* □ **fureter**

ferro- [ferou] of or containing iron: *ferro-concrete.* □ **ferro-**

ferry ['feri] *verb* to carry (people, cars *etc*) from one place to another by boat (or plane): *She ferried us across the river in a small boat.* □ **(faire) traverser**

■ *noun – plural* '**ferries** – a boat which ferries people, cars *etc* from one place to another: *We took the cross-channel ferry.* □ **bac, traversier**

fertile ['fɜːtail] *adjective* **1** producing a lot: *fertile fields; a fertile mind/imagination.* □ **fertile**

2 able to produce fruit, children, young animals *etc*: *fer-tile seed.* □ **fécond**

fer'tility [-'ti-] *noun* the state or condition of being fertile. □ **fertilité**

fertilize, fertilise [-ti-] *verb* to make fertile: *He fertilized his fields with manure; An egg must be fertilized before it can develop.* □ **fertiliser**

,**fertili'zation,** ,**fertili'sation** *noun.* □ **fertilisation**

'**fertilizer,** '**fertiliser** [-ti-] *noun* a substance (manure, chemicals *etc*) used to make land (more) fertile. □ **engrais**

fervent ['fɜːvənt] *adjective* enthusiastic and very sincere: *fervent hope.* □ **fervent**

'**fervently** *adverb.* □ **avec ferveur**

fervour, fervor ['fɜːvə] *noun* enthusiasm and strength of emotion: *He spoke with fervour.* □ **ferveur**

fester ['festə] *verb* (of an open injury *eg* a cut or sore) to become infected: *The wound began to fester.* □ **(s')envenimer**

festival ['festəvəl] *noun* **1** an occasion of public celebration: *In Italy, each village holds a festival once a year.* □ **fête**

2 a season of musical, theatrical *etc* performances: *Every three years the city holds a drama festival; (also adjective) a festival program.* □ **(de) festival**

festive ['festiv] *adjective* happy and (as if) celebrating: *a festive atmosphere.* □ **de fête**

fe'stivity [-'sti-] – *plural* **fe'stivities** – *noun* a celebration: *Come and join in the festivities.* □ **festivité**

fetch [fetʃ] *verb* **1** to go and get (something or someone) and bring it: *Fetch me some bread.* □ **aller chercher**

2 to be sold for (a certain price): *The picture fetched $100.* □ **rapporter**

---

see also **bring.**

---

fête [feit] *noun* an entertainment, *especially* in the open air, with competitions, displays, the selling of goods *etc* usually to raise money, *especially* for charity: *We are holding a summer fête in aid of charity.* □ **kermesse**

fetid ['fiːtid] *adjective* having a bad smell; stinking: *a fetid pool of water.* □ **fétide**

fetish ['fetiʃ] *noun* **1** an object worshipped, *especially* because a spirit is supposed to lodge in it. □ **fétiche**

2 something which is regarded with too much reverence or given too much attention: *It is good to dress well, but there is no need to make a fetish of it.* □ **obsession**

fetter ['fetə] *noun* a chain that holds the foot or feet of a prisoner, animal *etc* to prevent running away: *The prisoner was in fetters.* □ **chaînes, fers**

■ *verb* to fasten with a fetter: *She fettered the horse.* □ **entraver**

fetus ['fiːtəs] *noun* a young human being, animal, bird *etc* in the early stages of development before it is born or hatched. □ **fœtus**

'**fetal,** '**foetal** *adjective* of a fetus: *in a fetal position.* □ **fœtal**

feud [fjuːd] *noun* a long-lasting quarrel or war between families, tribes *etc*: *There has been a feud between our two families for two hundred years.* □ **querelle**

feudal ['fjuːdl] *adjective* of the system by which people

gave certain services *eg* military support to a more powerful man in return for lands, protection *etc*. □ **féodal**
'**feudalism** *noun*. □ **féodalité; féodalisme**

fever ['fiːvə] *noun* (an illness causing) high body temperature and quick heartbeat: *She is in bed with a fever; a fever of excitement*. □ **fièvre**
'**feverish** *adjective* **1** having a slight fever: *She seems a bit feverish tonight*. □ **fiévreux**
2 restlessly excited: *a feverish air*. □ **fébrile**
'**feverishly** *adverb* quickly and excitedly: *He wrote feverishly*. □ **fiévreusement**
at fever pitch at a level of great excitement: *The crowd's excitement was at fever pitch as they waited for the filmstar to appear*. □ **paroxysme**

few [fjuː] *adjective, pronoun* not many (emphasizing the smallness of the number): *Few people visit me nowadays; every few minutes* (= very frequently); *Such opportunities are few*. □ **peu (nombreux)**
a few a small number (emphasizing that there are indeed some): *There are a few books in this library about geology; We have only a few left*. □ **quelques (-un(e)s)**
few and far between very few: *Interesting jobs are few and far between*. □ **rare**

---

few means 'not many'.
a few means 'some'.
see also **less**.

---

fez [fez] *noun* a type of brimless hat with a tassel, *usually* red and worn by some Muslims. □ **fez**

fiancé [fiɒnsei,fiːɒn'sei] – *feminine* **fi'ancée** – *noun* a person to whom one is engaged to be married. □ **fiancé, ée**

fiasco [fi'askou] – *plural* **fi'ascos** – *noun* a complete failure: *The party was a fiasco*. □ **fiasco**

fib [fib] *noun* an unimportant lie: *to tell fibs*. □ **mensonge**
■ *verb – past tense, past participle* **fibbed** – to tell a fib: *He fibbed about his age*. □ **raconter des blagues**

fibre, fiber ['faibə] *noun* **1** a fine thread or something like a thread: *a nerve fibre*. □ **fibre**
2 a material made up of fibres: *coconut fibre*. □ **fibre**
3 character: *A girl of strong moral fibre*. □ **nature**
'**fibrous** *adjective*. □ **fibreux**
'**fibreglass** *noun, adjective* **1** (of) very fine threadlike pieces of glass, used for insulation, in materials *etc*: *fibreglass curtains*. □ **fibre de verre**
2 (of) a plastic material reinforced with such glass, used for many purposes *eg* building boats. □ **en fibre de verre**

fickle ['fikl] *adjective* always changing (one's mind, likes and dislikes *etc*): *I think that they are fickle*. □ **inconstant**
'**fickleness** *noun*. □ **inconstance**

fiction ['fikʃən] *noun* stories *etc* which tell of imagined, not real, characters and events: *I prefer reading fiction to hearing about real events*. □ **roman(s)**
'**fictional** *adjective*. □ **imaginaire**
fictitious [fik'tiʃəs] *adjective* **1** not true: *a fictitious account*. □ **fictif**
2 not real or based on fact: *All the characters in the book are fictitious*. □ **imaginaire**

fiddle ['fidl] *noun* **1** a violin: *She played the fiddle*. □ **violon**

2 a dishonest business arrangement: *He's working a fiddle over his taxes*. □ **combine**
■ *verb* **1** to play a violin: *He fiddled while they danced*. □ **jouer du violon**
2 (with **with**) to make restless, aimless movements: *Stop fiddling with your pencil!* □ **tripoter**
3 to manage (money, accounts *etc*) dishonestly: *She has been fiddling the accounts for years*. □ **traficoter**
'**fiddler** *noun*. □ **violoneux, euse**
fiddler crab a small crab, the male of which has an enlarged claw. □ **crabe appelant**
on the fiddle dishonest: *He's always on the fiddle*. □ **malhonnête**

fidelity [fi'deləti] *noun* faithfulness or loyalty: *his fidelity to his wife; fidelity to a promise*. □ **fidélité**

fidget ['fidʒit] – *past tense, past participle* '**fidgeted** – *verb* to move (the hands, feet *etc*) restlessly: *Stop fidgeting while I'm talking to you!* □ **bouger (sans cesse)**
■ *noun* a person who fidgets: *She's a terrible fidget!* □ **énervé, ée**
the fidgets nervous restlessness. □ **bougeotte**

field [fiːld] *noun* **1** a piece of land enclosed for growing crops, keeping animals *etc*: *Our house is surrounded by fields*. □ **champ**
2 a wide area: *playing fields* (= an area for games, sports *etc*). □ **terrain**
3 a piece of land *etc* where minerals or other natural resources are found: *an oil field; a coalfield*. □ **gisement**
4 an area of knowledge, interest, study *etc*: *in the fields of literature/economic development; her main fields of interest*. □ **domaine**
5 an area affected, covered or included by something: *a magnetic field; in his field of vision*. □ **champ**
6 an area of battle: *the field of Waterloo*; (*also adjective*) *a field-gun*. □ **champ**
■ *verb* (in cricket, basketball *etc*) to catch (the ball) and return it. □ **attraper et relancer**
'**field glasses** *noun plural* binoculars. □ **jumelles**
'**fieldwork** *noun* work done outside the laboratory, office *etc* (*eg* collecting information). □ **enquête sur le terrain**

fiend [fiːnd] *noun* **1** a devil: *the fiends of hell*. □ **démon**
2 a wicked or cruel person: *She's an absolute fiend when she's angry*. □ **monstre**
3 a person who is very enthusiastic about something: *a fresh air fiend; a fiend for work*. □ **mordu, maniaque (de)**
'**fiendish** *adjective* **1** wicked or devilish: *a fiendish temper*. □ **diabolique**
2 very difficult, clever *etc*: *a fiendish plan*. □ **démoniaque**
'**fiendishly** *adverb* **1** wickedly. □ **diaboliquement**
2 very: *fiendishly difficult*. □ **abominablement**

fierce [fiəs] *adjective* **1** very angry and likely to attack: *a fierce dog; a fierce expression*. □ **féroce**
2 intense or strong: *fierce rivals*. □ **implacable**
'**fiercely** *adverb*. □ **férocement**

fiery ['faiəri] *adjective* **1** like fire: *a fiery light*. □ **rougeoyant**
2 angry: *a fiery temper*. □ **violent**

fiesta [fi'estə] *noun* 1 a (religious) holiday, *especially* in Roman Catholic countries. □ **fiesta**
2 a festival or celebration. □ **fiesta**

fife [faif] *noun* a type of small flute. □ **fifre**

fifteen [fif'ti:n] *noun* 1 the number or figure 15. □ **quinze**
2 the age of 15. □ **quinze ans**
3 a team containing fifteen members: *a rugby fifteen.* □ **quinze**
■ *adjective* 1 15 in number. □ **quinze**
2 aged 15. □ **de quinze ans**
fifteen- having fifteen (of something): *a fifteen-page report.* □ **de/à quinze (...)**
,**fif'teenth** *noun* 1 one of fifteen equal parts. □ **quinzième**
2 (*also adjective*) (the) last of fifteen (people, things etc); (the) next after the fourteenth. □ **quinzième**
,**fif'teen-year-old** *noun* a person or animal that is fifteen years old. □ **(individu, etc.) âgé de quinze ans**
■ *adjective* (of a person, animal or thing) that is fifteen years old. □ **de quinze ans**

fifth [fifθ] *noun* 1 one of five equal parts. □ **cinquième**
2 (*also adjective*) the last of five (people *etc*); the next after the fourth. □ **cinquième**

fifty ['fifti] *noun* 1 the number or figure 50. □ **cinquante**
2 the age of 50. □ **cinquante ans**
■ *adjective* 1 50 in number. □ **cinquante**
2 aged 50. □ **de cinquante ans**
'**fifties** *noun plural* 1 the period of time between one's fiftieth and sixtieth birthdays. □ **cinquantaine**
2 the range of temperatures between fifty and sixty degrees. □ **températures entre cinquante et soixante degrés (Fahrenheit)**
3 the period of time between the fiftieth and sixtieth years of a century. □ **les années cinquante**
'**fiftieth** *noun* 1 one of fifty equal parts. □ **cinquantième**
2 (*also adjective*) (the) last of fifty (people, things *etc*); (the) next after the forty-ninth. □ **cinquantième**
fifty- having fifty (of something): *a fifty-page book.* □ **de cinquante (...)**
'**fifty-year-old** *noun* a person or animal that is fifty years old. □ **(individu, etc.) âgé de cinquante ans**
■ *adjective* (of a person, animal or thing) that is fifty years old. □ **de cinquante ans**
,**fifty-'fifty** *adverb* half and half: *We'll divide the money fifty-fifty.* □ **moitié-moitié**
■ *adjective* equal: *a fifty-fifty chance.* □ **égal**

fig [fig] *noun* a type of soft pear-shaped fruit, often eaten dried. □ **figue**

fight [fait] – *past tense, past participle* **fought** [fɔːt] – *verb* 1 to act against (someone or something) with physical violence: *The two boys are fighting over* (= because of) *some money they found.* □ **(se) battre**
2 to resist strongly; to take strong action to prevent: *to fight a fire; We must fight against any attempt to deprive us of our freedom.* □ **combattre**
3 to quarrel: *His parents were always fighting.* □ **(se) disputer, (se) quereller**
■ *noun* 1 an act of physical violence between people, countries *etc*: *There was a fight going on in the street.* □ **bataille**
2 a struggle; action involving effort: *the fight for free-*

dom of speech; *the fight against disease.* □ **lutte**
3 the will or strength to resist: *There was no fight left in him.* □ **résistance**
4 a boxing match. □ **combat**
'**fighter** *noun* 1 a person who fights. □ **combattant, ante**
2 a small fast aircraft designed to shoot down other aircraft. □ **chasseur**
fight back to defend oneself against an attack, or attack in return. □ **riposter, se défendre**
fight it out to fight on to a decisive end: *Although they were both exhausted the armies fought it out until the attackers were victorious at dawn; Fight it out among yourselves which of you is to go.* □ **lutter jusqu'au bout**
fight off to drive away by fighting: *She managed to fight off her attacker; I'll fight this cold off by going to bed early.* □ **repousser**
fight one's way to make one's way with difficulty: *She fought her way through the crowd.* □ **(se) frayer un passage**
fight shy of to avoid: *He fought shy of introducing her to his wife.* □ **éviter à tout prix**
put up a good fight to fight well and bravely. □ **bien se défendre**

figment ['figmənt]: **a figment of the/one's imagination** something one has imagined and which has no reality. □ **invention**

figure ['figjər, 'figə] *noun* 1 the form or shape of a person: *A mysterious figure came towards me; That girl has got a good figure.* □ **silhouette**
2 a (geometrical) shape: *The page was covered with a series of triangles, squares and other geometrical figures.* □ **figure**
3 a symbol representing a number: *a six-figure telephone number.* □ **chiffre**
4 a diagram or drawing to explain something: *The parts of a flower are shown in figure 3.* □ **figure**
■ *verb* 1 to appear (in a story *etc*): *She figures largely in the story.* □ **figurer**
2 to think, estimate or consider: *I figured that you would arrive before half past eight.* □ **penser**
'**figurative** [-rətiv] *adjective* of or using figures of speech: *figurative language.* □ **figuré**
'**figuratively** *adverb.* □ **métaphoriquement**
'**figurehead** *noun* 1 a person who is officially a leader but who does little or has little power: *She is the real leader of the party – he is only a figurehead.* □ **prête-nom**
2 an ornamental figure (*usually* of carved wood) attached to the front of a ship. □ **figure de proue**
figure of speech one of several devices (*eg* metaphor, simile) for using words not with their ordinary meanings but to make a striking effect. □ **façon de parler**
figure out to understand: *I can't figure out why he said that.* □ **arriver à comprendre**

figurine ['figjəri:n] *noun* a small statue of a person: *china figurines of Spanish ladies.* □ **figurine**

filament ['filəmənt] *noun* something very thin shaped like a thread, *especially* the thin wire in an electric light bulb. □ **filament**

file[1] [fail] *noun* a line of soldiers *etc* walking one behind the other. □ **file**

■ *verb* to walk in a file: *They filed across the road.* □ **marcher en file indienne**

in single file (moving along) singly, one behind the other: *They went downstairs in single file.* □ **à la file**

file² [fail] *noun* **1** a folder, loose-leaf book *etc* to hold papers. □ **dossier**

2 a collection of papers on a particular subject (kept in such a folder). □ **dossier**

3 in computing, a collection of data stored *eg* on a disc. □ **fichier**

■ *verb* **1** to put (papers *etc*) in a file: *He filed the letter under P.* □ **classer**

2 to bring (a suit) before a law court: *to file (a suit) for divorce.* □ **intenter (une action)**

'filing cabinet *noun* a piece of furniture with drawers *etc* for holding papers. □ **classeur**

file³ [fail] *noun* a steel tool with a rough surface for smoothing or rubbing away wood, metal *etc*. □ **lime**

■ *verb* to cut or smooth with a file: *She filed her nails.* □ **(se) limer**

'filings *noun plural* pieces of wood, metal *etc* rubbed off with a file: *iron filings.* □ **sciure, limaille**

filial ['filiəl] *adjective* of or suitable to a son or daughter: *filial piety.* □ **filial**

fill [fil] *verb* **1** to put (something) into (until there is no room for more); to make full: *to fill a cupboard with books; The news filled him with joy.* □ **remplir**

2 to become full: *His eyes filled with tears.* □ **(se) remplir**

3 to satisfy (a condition, requirement *etc*): *Does he fill all our requirements?* □ **répondre à**

4 to put something in a hole (in a tooth *etc*) to stop it up: *The dentist filled two of my teeth yesterday.* □ **plomber**

■ *noun* as much as fills or satisfies someone: *She ate her fill.* □ **à sa faim**

filled *adjective* having been filled. □ **rempli**

'filler *noun* **1** a tool or instrument used for filling something, *especially* for conveying liquid into a bottle. □ **entonnoir**

2 material used to fill cracks in a wall *etc*. □ **bouche-pores**

'filling *noun* anything used to fill: *The filling has come out of my tooth; He put an orange filling in the cake.* □ **plombage, garniture**

fill in 1 to add or put in (whatever is needed to make something complete): *to fill in the details.* □ **remplir, compléter**

2 to complete (forms, application *etc*) by putting in the information required: *Have you filled in your tax form yet?* □ **remplir**

3 to give (someone) all the necessary information: *I've been away – can you fill me in on what has happened?* □ **mettre au courant**

4 to occupy (time): *She had several drinks in the bar to fill in time until the train left.* □ **passer**

5 to do another person's job temporarily: *I'm filling in for her secretary.* □ **remplacer**

fill up to make or become completely full: *Fill up the gas tank, please.* □ **faire le plein**

fillet ['filit] *noun* a piece of meat or fish without bones: *fillet of veal; cod fillet; (also adjective) fillet steak.* □ **filet**

■ *verb* – *past tense, past participle* **'filleted** – to remove the bones from (meat or fish). □ **désosser, découper en filets**

filly ['fili] – *plural* **'fillies** – *noun* a young female horse. □ **pouliche**

film [film] *noun* **1** (a thin strip of) celluloid made sensitive to light on which photographs are taken: *photographic film.* □ **pellicule**

2 a story, play *etc* shown as a motion picture in a movie theatre, on television *etc*: *to make a film; (also adjective) a film version of the novel.* □ **film**

3 a thin skin or covering: *a film of dust.* □ **pellicule**

■ *verb* **1** to make a motion picture (of): *They are going to film the race.* □ **filmer**

2 (*usually with* **over**) to cover with a film: *Her eyes gradually filmed (over) with tears.* □ **se couvrir**

'filmy *adjective* very light and thin: *a dress of filmy material.* □ **vaporeux**

'filmstar *noun* a famous actor or actress in films. □ **étoile de cinéma**

filter ['filtə] *noun* **1** a strainer or other device through which liquid, gas, smoke *etc* can pass, but not solid material: *A filter is used to make sure that the oil is clean and does not contain any dirt; (also adjective) filter paper.* □ **filtre**

2 a kind of screening plate used to change or correct certain colours: *If you are taking photographs in sun and snow, you should use a blue filter.* □ **filtre**

■ *verb* **1** (of liquids) to (become) clean by passing through a filter: *The rainwater filtered into a tank.* □ **filtrer**

2 to come bit by bit or gradually: *The news filtered out.* □ **(s')infiltrer**

,filter 'tip *noun* (a cigarette with) a filter. □ **(à bout) filtre**

filth [filθ] *noun* anything very dirty or foul: *Look at that filth on your boots!* □ **saleté**

'filthy *adjective* **1** very dirty: *The whole house is absolutely filthy.* □ **crasseux**

2 obscene: *a filthy story.* □ **obscène**

fin [fin] *noun* **1** a thin movable part on a fish's body by which it balances, moves, changes direction *etc*. □ **nageoire**

2 anything that looks or is used like a fin: *the tail-fin of an airplane.* □ **dérive, empennage**

final ['fainl] *adjective* **1** the very last: *the final chapter of the book.* □ **dernier**

2 (of a decision *etc*) definite; decided and not to be changed: *The judge's decision is final.* □ **sans appel, définitif**

■ *noun* the last part of a competition: *The first parts of the competition will take place throughout the country, but the final will be in Halifax.* □ **finale**

'finally *adverb* **1** as the last (of many): *The lion tamer marched past, then came the acrobats, and finally the clowns.* □ **enfin**

2 at last, after a long time: *The train finally arrived.* □

finalement

'**finalist** *noun* a person who reaches the final stage in a competition: *It was difficult to decide which of the two finalists was the better tennis player.* □ **finaliste**

fi'**nality** [-'na-] *noun*. □ **finalité**

'**finalize, 'finalise** *verb* to make a final decision about plans, arrangements *etc*: *We must finalize the arrangements by Friday.* □ **finaliser**

,**finali'zation, ,finali'sation** *noun*. □ **dernière mise au point**

'**finals** *noun plural* the last examinations for a university degree *etc*: *I am sitting/taking my finals in June.* □ **examen(s) (de fins d'études)**

finale [fi'naːli] *noun* the last part of anything, *especially* a concert, opera, musical show *etc*: *The whole cast of the concert appeared in the finale.* □ **finale**

finance [fai'nans] *noun* 1 (the study or management of) money affairs: *He is an expert in finance.* □ **finance**
2 (*often in plural*) the money one has to spend: *The government is worried about the state of the country's finances.* □ **finances**
■ *verb* to give money for (a plan, business *etc*): *Will the company finance your trip abroad?* □ **financer**

fi'**nancial** [-ʃəl] *adjective* concerning money: *financial affairs.* □ **financier**

fi'**nancially** *adverb*. □ **financièrement**

fi'**nancier** [fainan'siər] *noun* a person who manages large sums of money. □ **financier, ière**

finch [fintʃ] *noun* one of several kinds of small bird: *a greenfinch.* □ **pinson**

find [faind] – *past tense, past participle* **found** [faund] – *verb* 1 to come upon or meet with accidentally or after searching: *Look what I've found!* □ **trouver**
2 to discover: *I found that I couldn't do the work.* □ **découvrir**
3 to consider; to think (something) to be: *I found the Canadian weather very cold.* □ **trouver**
■ *noun* something found, *especially* something of value or interest: *That old book is quite a find!* □ **trouvaille**

find one's feet to become able to cope with a new situation: *She found the new job difficult at first but she soon found her feet.* □ **(s')adapter**

find out 1 to discover: *I found out what was troubling her.* □ **découvrir**
2 to discover the truth (about someone), *usually* that he has done wrong: *He had been stealing for years, but eventually they found him out.* □ **démasquer**

fine¹ [fain] *adjective* 1 (*usually* of art *etc*) very good; of excellent quality: *fine paintings; a fine performance.* □ **beau**
2 (of weather) bright; not raining: *a fine day.* □ **beau**
3 well; healthy: *I was ill yesterday but I am feeling fine today!* □ **bien**
4 thin or delicate: *a fine material.* □ **fin**
5 careful; detailed: *Fine workmanship is required for such delicate embroidery.* □ **délicat**
6 made of small pieces, grains *etc*: *fine sand; fine rain.* □ **fin**
7 slight; delicate: *a fine balance; a fine distinction.* □ **subtil**

8 perfectly satisfactory: *There's nothing wrong with your work – it's fine.* □ **très bien**
■ *adverb* satisfactorily: *This arrangement suits me fine.* □ **très bien**
■ *interjection* good; well done *etc*: *You've finished already – fine!* □ **très bien**

'**finely** *adverb*. □ **magnifiquement**

'**finery** *noun* beautiful clothes, jewellery *etc*: *I arrived in all my finery.* □ **atours**

fine art that appeals immediately to the senses, *eg* painting, sculpture, music *etc*: *Painting is one of the fine arts.* □ **beaux-arts**

fine² [fain] *noun* money which must be paid as a punishment: *I had to pay a fine.* □ **amende**
■ *verb* to make (someone) pay a fine: *She was fined $10.* □ **donner/infliger une contravention/amende à**

finesse [fines] *noun* cleverness and skill in dealing with a situation *etc*: *She managed that situation with great finesse.* □ **finesse**

finger ['fiŋgə] *noun* 1 one of the five end parts of the hand, sometimes excluding the thumb: *She pointed a finger at the thief.* □ **doigt**
2 the part of a glove into which a finger is put. □ **doigt**
3 anything made, shaped, cut *etc* like a finger: *a finger of toast.* □ **doigt**
■ *verb* to touch or feel with the fingers: *She fingered the material.* □ **toucher**

'**fingernail** *noun* the nail at the tip of the finger. □ **ongle**

'**fingerprint** *noun* the mark made by the tip of the finger, often used by the police *etc* as a means of identification: *The thief wiped his fingerprints off the safe.* □ **empreinte digitale**

'**fingertip** *noun* the very end of a finger: *He burnt his fingertips on the stove.* □ **bout des doigts**

be all fingers and thumbs/my *etc* **fingers are all thumbs** to be very awkward or clumsy in handling or holding things: *He was so excited that his fingers were all thumbs and he dropped the cup.* □ **être empoté**

have (something) at one's fingertips to know all the details of (a subject) thoroughly: *He has the history of the firm at his fingertips.* □ **savoir (qqch.) sur le bout des doigts**

have a finger in the pie/in every pie to be involved in everything that happens: *She likes to have a finger in every pie in the village.* □ **être mêlé à tout**

put one's finger on to point out or describe exactly; to identify: *She put her finger on the cause of our financial trouble.* □ **mettre le doigt sur**

finicky ['finiki] *adjective* too much concerned with detail: *She is a very finicky person.* □ **tatillon, méticuleux**

finish ['finiʃ] *verb* 1 to bring or come to an end: *She's finished her work; The music finished.* □ **finir**
2 to use, eat, drink *etc* the last of: *Have you finished your tea?* □ **finir**
■ *noun* 1 the last touch (of paint, polish *etc*) that makes the work perfect: *The wood has a beautiful finish.* □ **fini**
2 the last part (of a race *etc*): *It was a close finish.* □ **arrivée**

'**finished** *adjective* 1 ended: *Her chances of success are* *finished.* □ **fini, fichu**

2 (*negative* **unfinished**) done; completed: *a finished product.* □ **fini**

3 having been completely used, eaten *etc*: *The food is finished – there's none left.* □ **fini**

finish off 1 to complete: *She finished off the job yesterday.* □ **compléter**

2 to use, eat *etc* the last of: *We've finished off the cake.* □ **terminer**

3 to kill (a person): *His last illness nearly finished him off.* □ **achever**

finish up 1 to use, eat *etc* the last of; to finish: *Finish up your meal as quickly as possible.* □ **finir (de manger)**

2 to end: *It was no surprise to me when he finished up in jail; The car finished up in the dump.* □ **se retrouver**

finite ['fainait] *adjective* **1** having an end or limit: *Human knowledge is finite, divine knowledge infinite.* □ **fini**

2 (of a verb) having a subject: *He speaks; I ran; She fell.* □ **personnel**

fir [fəː] *noun* a kind of evergreen tree that bears cones ('**fir-cones**) and is often grown for its wood. □ **sapin**

fire ['faiə] *noun* **1** anything that is burning, whether accidentally or not: *a warm fire in the kitchen; Several houses were destroyed in a fire.* □ **feu**

2 an apparatus for heating: *a gas fire; an electric fire.* □ **radiateur**

3 the heat and light produced by burning: *Fire is one of man's greatest benefits.* □ **feu**

4 enthusiasm: *with fire in his heart.* □ **ardeur**

5 attack by gunfire: *The soldiers were under fire.* □ **(essuyer le) feu**

■ *verb* **1** (of china, pottery *etc*) to heat in an oven, or kiln, in order to harden and strengthen: *The pots must be fired.* □ **cuire**

2 to make (someone) enthusiastic; to inspire: *The story fired his imagination.* □ **enflammer**

3 to operate (a gun *etc*) by discharging a bullet *etc* from it: *He fired his revolver three times.* □ **faire feu**

4 to send out or discharge (a bullet *etc*) from a gun *etc*: *He fired three bullets at the target.* □ **tirer**

5 (*often with* **at** *or* **on**) to aim and operate a gun at; to shoot at: *They suddenly fired on us; She fired at the target.* □ **tirer (sur)**

6 to send away someone from his/her job; to dismiss: *He was fired from his last job for being late.* □ **renvoyer**

fire alarm an apparatus (*eg* a bell) to give warning of a fire: *Everyone had to leave the building when the fire alarm rang.* □ **avertisseur d'incendie**

'**firearm** *noun* any type of gun: *In certain countries you need a licence to keep firearms.* □ **arme à feu**

'**fire cracker** *noun* a kind of firework which makes a loud noise. □ **pétard**

'**fire department** *noun* a company of firemen: *Call the fire department!* □ **(sapeurs-)pompiers**

'**fire engine** (*also* **fire truck**) *noun* a vehicle carrying firemen and their equipment. □ **pompe à incendie**

'**fire escape** *noun* a means of escape from a building in case of fire, *usually* in the form of a metal staircase on the outside of the building: *Hotels should have fire es-*

capes. □ **escalier de secours**

'**fire extinguisher** *noun* an apparatus (*usually* containing chemicals) for putting out fires: *There must be fire extinguishers in every room.* □ **extincteur**

'**firefighter** *noun* a person whose job is to put out accidental fires or those caused deliberately as a criminal act. □ **pompier, ière**

'**fireguard** *noun* a metal framework placed in front of a fireplace for safety. □ **pare-étincelles**

fire hydrant *noun* an upright water pipe with a spout used by firemen to fight fires: *In case of city fires, there should be a fire hydrant on every block.* □ **borne-fontaine**

'**fireplace** *noun* a space in a room (*usually* in a wall) with a chimney above, for a fire: *a wide stone fireplace.* □ **foyer**

fireproof *adjective* nearly unburnable; made of material that resists fire: *Hank wore a fireproof vest and gloves when he volunteered to fight the forest fire.* □ **ignifuge**

'**fireside** *noun* a place beside a fireplace: *The old man slept by the fireside; (also adjective) a fireside chair.* □ **au coin du feu, chauffeuse**

'**fire station** *noun* the building or buildings where fire-engines and other pieces of equipment used by firemen are kept. □ **caserne de pompiers**

'**firewood** *noun* wood that is suitable for burning as fuel: *I went into the garden to cut firewood.* □ **bois de chauffage**

'**firework** *noun* a small exploding device giving off a colourful display of lights: *Rockets are my favourite fireworks; (also adjective) a firework display; If your sister finds out, there'll be fireworks* (= a display of anger)! □ **feu d'artifice; grabuge**

'**firing squad** *noun* a group of soldiers with guns, to execute a prisoner: *He must face the firing squad.* □ **peloton d'exécution**

catch fire to begin to burn: *Dry wood catches fire easily.* □ **(s')enflammer**

on fire burning: *The building is on fire!* □ **en feu/ flammes**

open fire (*usually with* **on**) to begin shooting at: *The enemy opened fire (on us).* □ **ouvrir le feu (sur)**

play with fire to do something dangerous or risky: *Putting all your money into that business is playing with fire!* □ **jouer avec le feu**

set fire to (something)/set (something) on fire to cause (something) to begin burning *usually* accidentally or deliberately as a criminal act: *They set fire to the ambassador's house; She has set the house on fire.* □ **mettre le feu à**

under fire 1 being shot at: *We have been under fire from the enemy all day.* □ **sous le feu de**

2 being criticized or blamed: *The government is under fire.* □ **(vivement) critiqué**

firm[1] [fəːm] *adjective* **1** (fixed) strong and steady: *a firm handshake.* □ **solide**

2 decided; not changing one's mind: *a firm refusal.* □ **résolu**

'**firmly** *adverb*. □ **fermement**

firm² [fə:m] *noun* a business company: *an engineering firm.* □ **firme**

firmament ['fə:məmənt] *noun* the sky; the heavens: *The stars shine in the endless firmament.* □ **firmament**

first [fə:st] *adjective, adverb* before all others in place, time or rank: *the first person to arrive; The boy spoke first.* □ **premier, première**

■ *adverb* before doing anything else: *'Shall we eat now?' 'Wash your hands first!* □ **d'abord**

■ *noun* the person, animal *etc* that does something before any other person, animal *etc: the first to arrive.* □ **premier, ière**

'**firstly** *adverb* in the first place: *I have three reasons for not going – firstly, it's cold, secondly, I'm tired, and thirdly, I don't want to!* □ **en premier lieu**

first aid treatment of a wounded or sick person before the doctor's arrival: *We should all learn first aid; (also adjective) first-aid treatment.* □ **premiers soins**

'**first-born** *adjective, noun* (one's) oldest (child). □ **premier-né**

,**first-'class** *adjective* **1** of the best quality: *a first-class hotel.* □ **de première classe**

2 very good: *This food is first-class!* □ **de première qualité**

3 (for) travelling in the best and most expensive part of the train, plane, ship *etc: a first-class passenger ticket; (also adverb) She always travels first-class.* □ **en première classe**

,**first-'hand** *adjective, adverb* (of a story, description *etc*) obtained directly, not through various other people: *a first-hand account; I heard the story first-hand.* □ **de première main**

first name *noun* the informal name given to every person at birth, the name used directly before the family name: *Ms. Smith's first name is Susan, so her full name is Susan Smith.* □ **prénom**

,**first-'rate** *adjective* of the best quality: *She is a first-rate architect.* □ **de premier ordre**

at first at the beginning: *At first I didn't like him.* □ **au début**

at first glance 1 initially; in the beginning; without too much consideration: *At first glance the test looked easy, but Maxine soon found it very difficult.* □ **de prime abord**

2 the instant something or someone is seen: *I recognized Carl's suitcase at first glance.* □ **à première vue**

at first hand obtained *etc* directly: *I was able to acquire information at first hand.* □ **de première main**

first and foremost first of all. □ **en tout premier lieu**

first of all to begin with; the most important thing is: *First of all, let's clear up the mess; First of all, the scheme is impossible – secondly, we can't afford it.* □ **tout d'abord**

fish [fiʃ] – *plurals* **fish**, (*rare*) '**fishes** – *noun* **1** a kind of creature that lives in water and breathes through gills: *There are plenty of fish around the coast.* □ **poisson**

2 its flesh eaten as food: *Do you prefer meat or fish?* □ **poisson**

■ *verb* **1** to (try to) catch fish (in): *She likes fishing; He fished the river all day.* □ **pêcher**

2 (*usually with* **for**) to search for: *She fished around in her handbag for a handkerchief.* □ **fouiller**

3 (*usually with* **for**) to try to get by indirect means: *He is always fishing for compliments.* □ **chercher**

'**fishy** *adjective* **1** of or like a fish: *a fishy smell.* □ **de poisson**

2 odd or suspicious: *There's something fishy about that man.* □ **louche**

'**fishball** *noun* mashed fish shaped into a ball and cooked. □ **boulette de poisson**

'**fisherman** *noun* a person who fishes either as a job or as a hobby. □ **pêcheur**

fish farmer a person who breeds fish. □ **pisciculteur, trice**

'**fishing line** *noun* a fine strong thread, now *usually* made of nylon, used with a rod, hooks *etc* for catching fish. □ **ligne**

'**fishing rod** *noun* a long thin flexible rod used with a fishing-line and hooks *etc* for catching fish. □ **canne à pêche**

fish market a shop that sells mainly fish: *I must go down to the fish market.* □ **poissonnerie**

fish merchant a fishmonger. □ **poissonnier, ière**

'**fishmonger** *noun* a person who sells fish. □ **poissonnier, ière**

feel like a fish out of water to feel uncomfortable or out of place in a situation. □ **se sentir complètement dépaysé**

fish out to pull something out with some difficulty: *At last he fished out the letter he was looking for.* □ **extirper**

The plural **fish** is never wrong, but sometimes **fishes** is used in talking about different individuals or species: *How many fish did you catch?; the fishes of the Indian Ocean; the story of two little fishes.*

---

fission ['fiʃən]: **nuclear fission** *noun* the splitting of the nuclei of atoms. □ **fission**

fissure [fiʃə] *noun* a split between two parts; a narrow gap: *The earthquake caused a fissure in the ground.* □ **fissure**

fist [fist] *noun* a tightly closed hand: *He shook his fist at me in anger.* □ **poing**

fit¹ [fit] *adjective* **1** in good health: *I am feeling very fit.* □ **en forme**

2 suitable; correct for a particular purpose or person: *a dinner fit for a king.* □ **convenable**

■ *noun* the right size or shape for a particular person, purpose *etc: Your dress is a very good fit.* □ **(bon) ajustement**

■ *verb* – *past tense, past participle* '**fitted** – **1** to be the right size or shape (for someone or something): *The coat fits (you) very well.* □ **bien aller à**

2 to be suitable for: *Her speech fitted the occasion.* □ **convenir à**

3 to put (something) in position: *You must fit a new lock on the door.* □ **installer**

4 to supply with; to equip with: *She fitted the cupboard with shelves.* □ **équiper**

'**fitter** *noun* a person who puts the parts of a machine together. □ **monteur, euse**

'**fitting** *adjective* suitable: *a fitting occasion.* □ **approprié**

■ *noun* **1** something, *eg* a piece of furniture, which is fixed, *especially* in a house *etc*: *kitchen fittings.* □ **installations**

2 the trying-on of a dress *etc* and altering to make it fit: *I am having a fitting for my wedding dress tomorrow.* □ **essayage**

fit in (*often with* **with**) to be able to live, exist *etc* in agreement or harmony: *She doesn't fit in with the other children.* □ **s'entendre avec**

fit out to provide with everything necessary (clothes, equipment *etc*): *The shop fitted them out with everything they needed for their journey.* □ **équiper**

see/think fit to consider that some action is right, suitable *etc*: *You must do as you see fit (to do).* □ **trouver bon (de)**

fit^2 [fit] *noun* **1** a sudden attack of illness, *especially* epilepsy: *She suffers from fits.* □ **attaque**

2 something which happens as suddenly as this: *a fit of laughter/coughing.* □ **accès**

by fits and starts irregularly; often stopping and starting again: *He did his work by fits and starts.* □ **par à-coups**

five [faiv] *noun* **1** the number or figure 5. □ **cinq**

2 the age of 5. □ **cinq ans**

■ *adjective* **1** 5 in number. □ **cinq**

2 aged 5. □ **de cinq ans**

five- having five (of something): *a five-apartment house.* □ **à cinq (...)**

'**fiver** *noun* (a banknote worth) $5: *It cost me a fiver.* □ **billet de cinq dollars**

'**five-year-old** *noun* a person or animal that is five years old. □ **(individu, etc.) âgé de cinq ans**

■ *adjective* (of a person, animal or thing) that is five years old. □ **de cinq ans**

fix [fiks] *verb* **1** to make firm or steady: *She fixed the post firmly in the ground; He fixed his eyes on the door.* □ **enfoncer, fixer du regard**

2 to attach; to join: *He fixed the shelf to the wall.* □ **fixer**

3 to mend or repair: *She has succeeded in fixing my watch.* □ **réparer**

4 to direct (attention, a look *etc*) at: *She fixed all her attention on me.* □ **fixer**

5 (*often with* **up**) to arrange; to settle: *to fix a price; We fixed (up) a meeting.* □ **fixer, décider**

6 to make (something) permanent by the use of certain chemicals: *to fix a photographic print.* □ **fixer**

7 to prepare; to get ready: *I'll fix dinner tonight.* □ **préparer**

■ *noun* trouble; a difficulty: *I'm in a terrible fix!* □ **embarras**

fix'ation *noun* a strong idea or opinion for or against something that one does not or cannot change: *She has a fixation about travelling alone.* □ **fixation**

fixed *adjective* **1** arranged in advance; settled: *a fixed price.* □ **fixe**

2 steady; not moving: *a fixed gaze/stare.* □ **fixe**

3 arranged illegally or dishonestly: *The result was fixed.* □ **truqué**

fixedly ['fiksidli] *adverb* steadily: *He stared fixedly.* □ **fixement**

fixture ['fikstʃə] *noun* a fixed piece of furniture or a light *etc*: *We can't move the cupboard – it's a fixture; The light fixtures went with the house.* □ **installation à demeure**

fix on to decide on, choose: *Have you fixed on a date for the wedding?* □ **décider**

fix (someone) up with (something) to provide (someone) with (something): *Can you fix me up with a car for tomorrow?* □ **procurer**

fizz [fiz] *verb* (of a liquid) to release or give off many small bubbles: *I like the way champagne fizzes.* □ **pétiller**

■ *noun* the sound made or the feeling in the mouth produced by this: *This lemonade has lost its fizz.* □ **pétillement**

'**fizzy** *adjective.* □ **pétillant**

fizzle ['fizl] **fizzle out** to fail, to come to nothing: *The fire fizzled out.* □ **ne pas aboutir, avorter**

flabbergasted ['flabəgaːstid] *adjective* very surprised: *She was quite flabbergasted when we told her.* □ **éberlué**

flabby ['flabi] *adjective* loose and fat; not firm: *flabby cheeks.* □ **flasque**

flag^1 [flag] *noun* a piece of cloth with a particular design representing a country, party, association *etc*: *the French flag.* □ **drapeau**

'**flag-pole/'flagstaff** *nouns* the pole on which a flag is hung. □ **mât**

flag down – *past tense, past participle* **flagged** – *verb* to wave at (a car *etc*) in order to make it stop: *We flagged down a taxi.* □ **faire signe (à)**

flag^2 [flag] – *past tense, past participle* **flagged** – *verb* to become tired or weak: *Halfway through the race he began to flag.* □ **faiblir**

flagrant ['fleigrənt] *adjective* (*usually* of something bad) very obvious; easily seen: *flagrant injustice.* □ **flagrant**

'**flagrantly** *adverb.* □ **d'une manière flagrante**

'**flagrancy** *noun.* □ **énormité**

---

flagrant (not fragrant) disobedience.

---

flair [fleə] *noun* a natural ability or cleverness for (doing) something: *She has a flair for (learning) languages.* □ **flair, don**

flake [fleik] *noun* a very small piece: *a snowflake.* □ **flocon**

■ *verb* (*usually with* **off**) to come off in flakes: *The paint is flaking.* □ **(s')écailler**

'**flaky** *adjective.* □ **floconneux**

flamboyant [flam'boiənt] *adjective* intended to attract notice: *flamboyant clothes.* □ **flamboyant**

flam'boyance *noun.* □ **caractère flamboyant**

flame [fleim] *noun* the bright light of something burning: *A small flame burned in the lamp.* □ **flamme**

■ *verb* **1** to burn with flames: *His eyes flamed with anger.* □ **jeter des flammes, flamber**

2 to become very hot, red *etc*: *His cheeks flamed with embarrassment.* □ **s'empourprer**

'**flaming** *adjective.* □ **flamboyant**

flammable ['flaməbl] *adjective* able or likely to burn:

flammable material. □ **inflammable**

see also **inflammable.**

flamingo [flə'miŋgou] – *plural* **fla'mingo(e)s** – *noun* a type of long-legged wading bird, pink or bright red in colour. □ **flamant**

flange [flandʒ] *noun* a raised edge on the rim of a wheel *etc*. □ **rebord**

flank [flaŋk] *noun* the side of anything *especially* an animal's body or an army: *the horse's flank*; *They marched around the enemy's flank.* □ **flanc**

■ *verb* 1 to be at the side of: *The prisoner appeared, flanked by two policemen.* □ **flanquer**

2 to come around the side of: *The troops flanked the enemy forces.* □ **prendre (l'ennemi) de flanc**

flannel ['flanl] *noun* loosely woven woollen cloth: *blankets made of flannel*; *(also adjective) a flannel petticoat.* □ **(de) flannelle**

flap [flap] *noun* 1 anything broad or wide that hangs loosely: *a flap of canvas*. □ **pan**

2 the sound made when such a thing moves: *We could hear the flap of the flag blowing in the wind.* □ **battement**

3 great confusion or panic: *They are all in a terrible flap.* □ **panique**

■ *verb* – *past tense, past participle* **flapped** – 1 to (make something) move with the sound of a flap: *the leaves were flapping in the breeze*; *The bird flapped its wings.* □ **battre (des ailes)**

2 to become confused; to get into a panic: *There is no need to flap.* □ **paniquer**

flare [fleə] *verb* 1 to burn with a bright unsteady light: *The firelight flared.* □ **flamboyer**

2 (of a skirt, trousers *etc*) to become wider at the bottom edge: *a flared skirt.* □ **(s')évaser**

flare up suddenly to burn strongly: *A quarrel flared up between them (noun* **'flare-up***).* □ **(s')enflammer**

flash [flaʃ] *noun* 1 a quick showing of a bright light: *a flash of lightning.* □ **éclair**

2 a moment; a very short time: *He was with her in a flash.* □ **en un clin d'œil**

3 a flashlight. □ **flash**

4 *(often* **'news flash***)* a brief news report sent by radio, television *etc*: *Did you hear the flash about the plane crash?* □ **nouvelle-éclair**

■ *verb* 1 (of a light) to (cause to) shine quickly: *He flashed a torch.* □ **projeter (un rayon de lumière)**

2 *(usually with* **by** *or* **past**) to pass quickly: *The days flashed by*; *The cars flashed past.* □ **passer comme un éclair**

3 to show; to display: *She flashed a card and was allowed to pass.* □ **exhiber rapidement**

'flashing *adjective*: *flashing lights.* □ **clignotant**

'flashy *adjective* big, bright *etc* but cheap and of poor quality: *flashy clothes.* □ **tapageur**

'flashily *adverb*. □ **d'une manière tapageuse**

'flashlight *noun* 1 a portable, battery-powered light. □ **lampe de poche**

2 *(often abbreviated to* **flash***)* an instrument which produces a sudden bright light for taking photographs. □

flash

flask [flɑːsk] *noun* 1 a container in which drinks can be carried: *a flask of whisky.* □ **flacon**

2 a vacuum flask: *The workmen carried flasks of tea.* □ **thermos**

3 a bottle, *usually* with a narrow neck. □ **fiole**

flat [flat] *adjective* 1 level; without rise or fall: *a flat surface.* □ **plat**

2 dull; without interest: *She spent a very flat weekend.* □ **ennuyeux**

3 (of something said, decided *etc*) definite; emphatic: *a flat denial.* □ **net**

4 (of a tire) not inflated, having lost most of its air: *His car had a flat tire.* □ **à plat**

5 (of drinks) no longer fizzy: *flat lemonade*; *(also adverb) My beer has gone flat.* □ **éventé**

6 slightly lower than a musical note should be: *That last note was flat*; *(also adverb) The choir went very flat.* □ **en dessous du ton**

■ *adverb* stretched out: *She was lying flat on her back.* □ **à plat**

■ *noun* 1 (**a'partment**) a set of rooms on one floor, with kitchen and bathroom, in a larger building or block: *Do you live in a house or a flat?* □ **appartement**

2 (in musical notation) a sign (♭) which makes a note a semitone lower. □ **bémol**

3 a level, even part: *the flat of her hand.* □ **plat**

4 *(usually in plural)* an area of flat land, *especially* beside the sea, a river *etc*: *mud flats.* □ **marécages, basfonds**

'flatly *adverb* definitely; emphatically: *She flatly denied it.* □ **catégoriquement**

'flatten *verb* (*often with* **out**) to make or become flat: *The countryside flattened out as they came near the sea.* □ **(s')aplanir**

flat rate a fixed amount, *especially* one that is the same in all cases: *He charged a flat rate for the work.* □ **prix/taux fixe**

flat out as fast, energetically *etc* as possible: *She worked flat out.* □ **à toute allure**

flatter ['flatə] *verb* 1 to praise too much or insincerely: *Flatter him by complimenting him on his singing.* □ **flatter**

2 to show, describe *etc* someone or something as being better than someone *etc* really is: *The photograph flatters her.* □ **flatter**

3 to be pleased to say about (oneself) (that one can do something): *I flatter myself that I can speak French perfectly.* □ **se flatter (de)**

'flatterer *noun*. □ **flatteur, euse**

'flattery *noun* insincere praise. □ **flatterie**

flaunt [flɔːnt] *verb* to show off in order to attract attention to oneself: *He flaunted his expensive clothes.* □ **faire étalage de**

flautist ['flɔːtist] *noun* a flute player. □ **flûtiste**

flavour, flavor ['fleivə] *noun* 1 taste: *The tea has a wonderful flavour.* □ **saveur**

2 atmosphere; quality: *an Eastern flavour.* □ **atmosphère**

■ *verb* to give flavour to: *He flavoured the cake with*

lemon. □ **parfumer**

'flavouring *noun* anything used to give a particular taste: *lemon flavouring.* □ **parfum**

flaw [flɔː] *noun* a fault; something which makes something not perfect: *a flaw in the material.* □ **défaut, défectuosité**

flawed *adjective* having a flaw: *This china is flawed.* □ **défectueux**

'flawless *adjective* perfect: *her flawless beauty.* □ **impeccable**

flea [fliː] *noun* a type of small blood-sucking insect that jumps instead of flying and lives on the bodies of animals or people. □ **puce**

fleck [flek] *noun* a spot: *a fleck of dust.* □ **particule**

flecked *adjective* marked with spots: *a flecked pattern.* □ **moucheté**

fled *see* **flee.**

fledg(e)ling ['fledʒliŋ] *noun* a young bird ready to fly. □ **oisillon**

flee [fliː] – *past tense, past participle* **fled** [fled] – *verb* to run away (from danger): *She fled the danger.* □ **fuir**

fleece [fliːs] *noun* a sheep's coat of wool. □ **toison**

■ *verb* to cut wool from (sheep). □ **tondre**

'fleecy *adjective* soft and woolly: *a fleecy blanket.* □ **laineux**

fleet [fliːt] *noun* **1** a number of ships or boats under one command or sailing together: *a fleet of fishing boats.* □ **flotte**

2 the entire navy of a country: *the Canadian fleet.* □ **marine**

flesh [fleʃ] *noun* **1** the soft substance (muscles *etc*) that covers the bones of animals. □ **chair**

2 the soft part of fruit: *the golden flesh of a peach.* □ **pulpe**

'fleshy *adjective* fat: *a fleshy face.* □ **charnu**

flesh and blood 1 relations; family: *She is my own flesh and blood.* □ **la chair de sa chair**

2 human nature: *It is more than flesh and blood can tolerate.* □ **nature humaine**

in the flesh actually present: *I have seen him on television, but never in the flesh.* □ **en chair et en os**

flew *see* **fly**[2].

flex [fleks] *verb* to bend, *especially* in order to test: *to flex one's joints.* □ **fléchir**

■ *noun* (a piece of) thin insulated wire for carrying electricity: *That lamp has a long flex.* □ **fil**

'flexible *adjective* **1** that can be bent easily: *flexible metal.* □ **flexible**

2 able or willing to change according to circumstances *etc*: *My holiday plans are very flexible.* □ **souple**

,flexi'bility *noun.* □ **souplesse**

flick [flik] *noun* a quick, sharp movement: *a flick of the wrist.* □ **petit mouvement rapide**

■ *verb* to make this kind of movement (to or with something): *He flicked open a packet of cigarettes.* □ **ouvrir (en un tournemain)**

flicker ['flikə] *verb* **1** to burn unsteadily: *the candle flickered.* □ **vaciller**

2 to move quickly and unsteadily: *A smile flickered across her face.* □ **voltiger**

■ *noun* an unsteady light or flame: *the flicker of an oil lamp.* □ **lumière tremblotante**

flier *see* **fly**[2].

flight[1] [flait] *noun* **1** act of flying: *the flight of a bird.* □ **vol**

2 a journey in a plane: *How long is the flight to New York?* □ **vol**

3 a number of steps or stairs: *A flight of steps.* □ **escalier**

4 a number of birds *etc* flying or moving through the air: *a flight of geese; a flight of arrows.* □ **volée**

'flighty *adjective* (*usually* of girls and women) with easily changed ideas; not thinking deeply; always looking for amusement. □ **écervelé**

flight attendant the person that looks after passengers in an aircraft. □ **agent, ente de bord**

flight deck 1 the upper deck of an aircraft carrier where planes take off or land. □ **pont d'envol**

2 the forward part of an airplane where the pilot and crew sit. □ **cabine de pilotage**

in flight flying: *Have you seen the geese in flight?* □ **en vol**

See also **fly**[2].

flight[2] [flait] *noun* the act of fleeing or running away from an enemy, danger *etc*: *The general regarded the flight of his army as a disgrace.* □ **fuite**

put to flight to cause (someone) to flee or run away: *the army put the rebels to flight.* □ **mettre en fuite**

flimsy ['flimzi] *adjective* **1** thin and light: *You'll be cold in those flimsy clothes.* □ **léger**

2 not very well made; likely to break: *a flimsy boat.* □ **fragile**

flinch [flintʃ] *verb* to make a sudden movement back or away in fear, pain *etc*: *He flinched away from the sudden heat.* □ **tressaillir**

fling [fliŋ] – *past tense, past participle* **flung** [flʌŋ] – *verb* **1** to throw with great force: *She flung a brick through the window.* □ **lancer**

2 to rush: *He flung out of the house.* □ **se précipiter**

■ *noun* a lively Scottish dance: *They danced a Highland fling.* □ **danse écossaise**

flint [flint] *noun* **1** (*also adjective*) (of) a kind of very hard stone: *Prehistoric man used flint knives.* □ **silex**

2 a piece of hard mineral from which sparks can be struck: *I must buy a new flint for my cigarette-lighter.* □ **pierre**

flip [flip] – *past tense, past participle* **flipped** – *verb* **1** to throw (something) in the air (so that it turns): *They flipped a coin to see which side it landed on.* □ **lancer (en l'air)**

2 (*sometimes with* **over**) to turn over quickly: *She flipped over the pages of the book.* □ **feuilleter**

■ *noun* an act of flipping. □ **chiquenaude**

flippant ['flipənt] *adjective* not serious enough about important matters: *a flippant reply.* □ **désinvolte**

flip'pantly *adverb.* □ **avec désinvolture**

'flippancy *noun.* □ **désinvolture**

flipper ['flipə] *noun* **1** a limb for swimming, *especially* of a seal, walrus *etc.* □ **nageoire**

2 a kind of rubber or plastic shoe, worn when swimming, which is shaped like the flipper of a seal *etc.* □

palme(s)

flirt [fləːt] *verb* (*often with* **with**) to behave (towards someone) as though one were in love but without serious intentions: *She flirts with every man she meets.* □ **flirter**

■ *noun* a person who behaves in this way. □ **flirteur, coquette**

flir'tation *noun* act of flirting. □ **flirt**

flir'tatious [-ʃəs] *adjective.* □ **flirteur**

flir'tatiously *adverb.* □ **en manière de flirt**

flit [flit] – *past tense, past participle* **'flitted** – *verb* to move quickly and lightly from place to place: *Butterflies flitted around in the garden.* □ **voltiger**

'flitting *noun.* □ **voltigement**

float [fləut] *verb* to (make something) stay on the surface of a liquid: *A piece of wood was floating in the stream.* □ **flotter**

■ *noun* something that floats on a fishing line: *If the float moves, there is probably a fish on the hook.* □ **flotteur**

floating population a section of the population not permanently resident in a place. □ **population instable**

floating restaurant a restaurant on a boat or other floating structure. □ **restaurant flottant**

flock [flok] *noun* a number of certain animals or birds together: *a flock of sheep.* □ **troupeau**

■ *verb* (*with* **to, into** *etc*) to gather or go somewhere together in a group or crowd: *People flocked to the movies.* □ **affluer**

flog [flog] – *past tense, past participle* **flogged** – *verb* to beat; to whip: *You will be flogged for stealing the money.* □ **fouetter**

'flogging *noun.* □ **flagellation**

flog a dead horse to try to create interest in something after all interest in it has been lost. □ **s'acharner inutilement**

flood [flʌd] *noun* 1 a great overflow of water: *If it continues to rain like this, we shall have floods.* □ **inondation**

2 any great quantity: *a flood of letters.* □ **déluge**

■ *verb* to (cause something to) overflow with water: *He left the water running and flooded the kitchen.* □ **inonder**

'floodlight *noun* a kind of very strong light often used to light up the outside of buildings *etc*: *There were floodlights in the sports stadium.* □ **projecteur**

■ *verb* – *past tense, past participle* **'floodlit** [-lit] – to light with floodlights. □ **éclairer (aux projecteurs)**

'floodlighting *noun.* □ **illumination (par projecteurs)**

'floodlit *adjective.* □ **illuminé (par des projecteurs)**

,flood-'tide *noun* the rising tide. □ **marée montante**

floor [floː] *noun* 1 the surface in a room *etc* on which one stands or walks. □ **plancher**

2 all the rooms on the same level in a building: *My office is on the third floor.* □ **étage**

■ *verb* 1 to make or cover a floor: *We've floored the kitchen with plastic tiles.* □ **recouvrir**

2 to knock down: *He floored him with a powerful blow.* □ **terrasser**

-floored having a floor or floors (of a particular kind):

a stone-floored kitchen. □ **à sol de/en**

'floorboard *noun* one of the narrow boards used to make a floor. □ **latte (de plancher)**

'flooring *noun* material for making or covering floors. □ **recouvrement de sol**

flop [flop] – *past tense, past participle* **flopped** – *verb* 1 to fall or sit down suddenly and heavily: *She flopped into an armchair.* □ **(s')affaler**

2 to hang or swing about loosely: *Her hair flopped over her face.* □ **flotter**

3 (of a theatrical production) to fail; to be unsuccessful: *the play flopped.* □ **faire un flop**

■ *noun* 1 (a) flopping movement. □ **chute**

2 a failure: *The show was a complete flop.* □ **flop**

'floppy *adjective* tending to flop; flopping: *a floppy hat.* □ **flasque**

floppy disk [flopiː disk] *noun* a thin, flat magnetic disk that is inserted into a computer drive and used to back up, store or transport data from the hard drive: *Copy your work onto a floppy disk and bring it to the computer at school.* □ **disquette**

flora ['floːrə] *noun* the plants of a district or country as a whole: *the flora and fauna of Borneo.* □ **flore**

floral ['floːrəl] *adjective* made of, or having a pattern of, flowers: *floral decorations; a floral dress.* □ **floral**

florist ['florist] *noun* a person who (grows and) sells flowers. □ **fleuriste**

flotilla [flə'tilə] *noun* a fleet of small ships: *A flotilla of yachts.* □ **flotille**

flounce[1] [flauns] *verb* (*usually with* **out, away** *etc*) to move (away) in anger, impatience *etc*: *She flounced out of the room.* □ **sortir/entrer (dans un mouvement d'indignation)**

flounce[2] [flauns] *noun* a decorative strip of material *usually* frilled: *There are flounces at the bottom of her evening skirt.* □ **volant**

flounced *adjective* decorated with a flounce. □ **à volants**

flounder ['flaundə] *verb* to move one's legs and arms violently and with difficulty (in water, mud *etc*): *She floundered helplessly in the mud.* □ **patauger**

flour ['flauə] *noun* wheat, or other cereal, ground into a powder and used for cooking, baking *etc*. □ **farine**

flourish ['flʌriʃ, 'floː-] *verb* 1 to be healthy; to grow well; to thrive: *My plants are flourishing.* □ **être florissant**

2 to be successful or active: *Her business is flourishing.* □ **prospérer**

3 to hold or wave something as a show, threat *etc*: *He flourished his sword.* □ **brandir**

■ *noun* 1 an ornamental stroke of the pen in writing: *His writing was full of flourishes.* □ **fioriture**

2 an impressive, sweeping movement (with the hand or something held in it): *He bowed and made a flourish with his hat.* □ **grand geste**

3 an ornamental passage of music: *There was a flourish on the trumpets.* □ **fanfare**

'flourishing *adjective* 1 successful: *a flourishing business.* □ **prospère**

2 growing well: *flourishing crops.* □ **florissant**

flout [flaut] *verb* to refuse to respect or obey: *He flouted the headmaster's authority.* □ **se moquer de**

flow [flou] *verb* 1 to move along in the way that water does: *The river flowed into the sea.* □ **couler**

2 (of the tide) to rise: *The boat left the harbour when the tide began to flow.* □ **monter**

■ *noun* the act of flowing: *a flow of blood; the flow of traffic.* □ **circulation**

flower ['flauə] *noun* the part of a plant or tree from which fruit or seed grows, often brightly coloured and sometimes including the stem on which it grows: *a bunch of flowers.* □ **fleur**

■ *verb* (of plants *etc*) to produce flowers: *This plant flowers in early May.* □ **fleurir**

'**flowered** *adjective* having a pattern of flowers: *flowered material.* □ **fleuri**

'**flowery** *adjective* 1 having, or decorated with, flowers: *a flowery hat.* □ **fleuri, orné de fleurs**

2 (of language) using ornamental words and phrases; poetic: *a flowery speech.* □ **fleuri**

'**flower bed** *noun* a piece of earth prepared and used for the growing of plants. □ **plate-bande, parterre**

'**flowerpot** *noun* a container made of earthenware, plastic *etc* in which a plant is grown. □ **pot (à fleurs)**

in flower (of a plant) having flowers in bloom: *These trees are in flower in May.* □ **en fleur**

flown *see* **fly**².

flu [flu:] short for **influenza**.

fluent ['fluənt] *adjective* 1 (of a language *etc*) smoothly and skilfully spoken: *He spoke fluent French.* □ **facile, fluide**

2 (of a person) able to express oneself easily: *She is fluent in English.* □ **qui s'exprime couramment**

'**fluency** *noun* ease in speaking or expressing: *Her fluency surprised her colleagues.* □ **aisance (à s'exprimer)**

'**fluently** *adverb*: *He speaks Spanish fluently.* □ **couramment**

fluff [flʌf] *noun* small pieces of soft, wool-like material from blankets *etc*: *My coat is covered with fluff.* □ **peluche**

■ *verb* 1 (*often with* **out** *or* **up**) to make full and soft like fluff: *The bird fluffed out its feathers; Fluff up the pillows and make the invalid more comfortable.* □ **hérisser, faire bouffer**

2 to make a mistake in doing (something): *The actress fluffed her lines; The golfer fluffed his stroke.* □ **rater**

'**fluffy** *adjective* 1 soft and woolly: *a fluffy kitten.* □ **duveteux**

2 soft, light and full of air: *She cooked a fluffy omelette.* □ **léger**

fluid ['fluid] *noun* 1 a substance (liquid or gas) whose particles can move about freely. □ **fluide**

2 any liquid substance: *cleaning fluid.* □ **liquide**

■ *adjective* 1 able to flow like a liquid: *a fluid substance.* □ **liquide**

2 smooth and graceful: *fluid movements.* □ **fluide**

3 (of arrangements, plans *etc*) able to be changed easily: *My holiday plans are fluid.* □ **indécis**

flu'idity *noun*. □ **fluidité**

fluke [flu:k] *noun* a chance success: *Passing the exam was a fluke – I had done no work.* □ **coup de chance**

flung *see* **fling**.

flunk [flʌŋk] *verb* a slang word for to fail in an examination: *I flunked (math).* □ **rater**

fluorescent [fluə'resnt] *adjective* giving off a certain kind of light: *fluorescent light; fluorescent paint.* □ **fluorescent**

fluo'rescence *noun*. □ **fluorescence**

fluoride ['fluəraid] *noun* any of several substances containing fluorine, *especially* one which helps to prevent tooth decay. □ **fluor**

fluorine ['fluəri:n] *noun* an element, a pale greenish-yellow gas. □ **fluor**

flurry ['flʌri] – *plural* '**flurries** – *noun* 1 a sudden rush (of wind *etc*): *A flurry of wind made the door bang.* □ **rafale**

2 a confusion: *He was in a flurry.* □ **émoi**

flush [flʌʃ] *noun* 1 a flow of blood to the face, making it red: *A slow flush covered her face.* □ **rougeur**

2 (the device that works) a rush of water which cleans a toilet: *a flush toilet.* □ **chasse (d'eau)**

■ *verb* 1 to become red in the face: *He flushed with embarrassment.* □ **rougir**

2 to clean by a rush of water: *to flush a toilet.* □ **tirer la chasse (d'eau)**

3 (*usually with* **out**) to cause (an animal *etc*) to leave a hiding place: *The police flushed out the criminal.* □ **débusquer**

flushed *adjective* red in the face: *You look very flushed.* □ **rouge**

(**in**) **the first flush of** (in) the early stages of (something) when a person is feeling fresh, strong, enthusiastic *etc*: *in the first flush of youth.* □ **dans l'euphorie de**

fluster ['flʌstə] *noun* excitement and confusion caused by hurry: *She was in a terrible fluster when unexpected guests arrived.* □ **émoi**

■ *verb* to cause to be worried or nervous; to agitate: *Don't fluster me!* □ **troubler**

flute [flu:t] *noun* a type of high-pitched woodwind musical instrument. □ **flûte**

flutter ['flʌtə] *verb* 1 to (cause to) move quickly: *A leaf fluttered to the ground.* □ **(faire) voltiger**

2 (of a bird, insect *etc*) to move the wings rapidly and lightly: *The moth fluttered around the light.* □ **battre des ailes**

■ *noun* 1 a quick irregular movement (of a pulse *etc*): *She felt a flutter in her chest.* □ **palpitation**

2 nervous excitement: *He was in a great flutter.* □ **émoi**

flux [flʌks] *noun* continual change: *Events are in a state of flux.* □ **flux, changement continuel**

fly¹ [flai] – *plural* **flies** – *noun* 1 a type of small winged insect. □ **mouche**

2 a fish hook made to look like a fly so that a fish will take it in its mouth: *Which fly should I use to catch a trout?* □ **mouche (artificielle)**

3 (*often in plural*) a piece of material with buttons or a zipper, *especially* at the front of trousers. □ **braguette**

a fly in the ointment something that spoils one's enjoyment. □ **ombre au tableau**

fly² [flai] – *past tense* **flew** [flu:]: *past participle* **flown** [floun] – *verb* 1 to (make something) go through the air on wings *etc* or in an airplane: *The pilot flew (the plane)* *across the sea.* □ **voler, piloter (un avion)**

2 to run away (from): *He flew (the country).* □ **s'enfuir (de)**

3 (of time) to pass quickly: *The days flew past.* □ **filer, passer vite**

fly away *verb* to leave by travelling through the air; to go to another place propelled by the flapping of wings: *The bird landed on a tree branch for a minute then quickly flew away.* □ **s'envoler**

'**flyer**, '**flier** *noun* a person who flies an airplane *etc*. □ **aviateur, trice**

flying saucer a strange flying object thought possibly to come from another planet. □ **soucoupe volante**

flying visit a very short, often unexpected, visit: *She paid her mother a flying visit.* □ **(faire un) saut (chez)**

'**flyleaf** *noun* a blank page at the beginning or end of a book. □ **page de garde**

fly in the face of to oppose or defy; to treat with contempt: *He flew in the face of danger.* □ **lancer un défi à**

fly into suddenly to get into (a rage, a temper *etc*). □ **se mettre en**

fly off the handle to lose one's temper. □ **sortir de ses gonds**

get off to a flying start to have a very successful beginning: *Our new shop has got off to a flying start.* □ **prendre un départ en flèche**

let fly (*often with* **at**) to throw, shoot or send out violently: *He let fly (an arrow) at the target.* □ **décocher**

send (someone/something) flying to hit or knock someone or something so that he or it falls down or falls backwards: *She hit him and sent him flying.* □ **envoyer rouler (qqn)**

foal [foul] *noun* a young horse. □ **poulain**
■ *verb* to give birth to a foal: *The mare should foal this week.* □ **mettre bas**

foam [foum] *noun* a mass of small bubbles on the surface of liquids *etc*. □ **mousse, écume**
■ *verb* to produce foam: *the beer foamed in the glass.* □ **mousser, écumer**

foam rubber a form of rubber with a sponge-like appearance, used for stuffing chairs *etc*. □ **caoutchouc mousse**

fob [fob]: **fob (someone) off with (something)** to get (someone) to accept (something worthless): *He fobbed me off with promises.* □ **refiler (qqch. à qqn)**

focus ['foukəs] – *plurals* '**focuses, foci** ['fousai] – *noun* **1** the point at which rays of light meet after passing through a lens. □ **foyer**

2 a point to which light, a look, attention *etc* is directed: *She was the focus of everyone's attention.* □ **point de mire**
■ *verb* – *past tense, past participle* '**focus(s)ed** – **1** to adjust (a camera, binoculars *etc*) in order to get a clear picture: *Remember to focus the camera/the picture before taking the photograph.* □ **mettre au point**

2 to direct (attention *etc*) to one point: *The accident focussed public attention on the danger.* □ **concentrer**

'**focal** *adjective*. □ **focal**

in, out of focus giving or not giving a clear picture: *These photographs are out of focus.* □ **net; flou**

fodder ['fodə] *noun* food for farm animals. □ **fourrage**

foe [fou] *noun* an enemy: *He fought against the foe.* □ **ennemi, ie**

fog [fog] *noun* a thick cloud of moisture or water vapour in the air which makes it difficult to see: *I had to drive very slowly because of the fog.* □ **brouillard**
■ *verb* – *past tense, past participle* **fogged** – (*usually with* **up**) to cover with fog: *His glasses were fogged up with steam.* □ **embuer**

'**foggy** *adjective* full of, or covered with, fog: *It is very foggy tonight.* □ **brumeux**

'**fog-bound** *adjective* unable to move or function because of fog: *The plane is fog-bound.* □ **pris dans la brume**

'**foghorn** *noun* a horn used as a warning to or by ships in fog. □ **corne de brume**

foil[1] [foil] *verb* to defeat; to disappoint: *She was foiled in her attempt to become president.* □ **faire échouer**

foil[2] [foil] *noun* **1** extremely thin sheets of metal that resemble paper: *silver foil.* □ **feuille/papier d'aluminium**

2 a dull person or thing against which someone or something else seems brighter: *She acted as a foil to her beautiful sister.* □ **repoussoir**

foil[3] [foil] *noun* a blunt sword with a button at the end, used in the sport of fencing. □ **fleuret**

fold[1] [fould] *verb* **1** to double over (material, paper *etc*): *She folded the paper in half.* □ **plier**

2 to lay one on top of another: *She folded her hands in her lap.* □ **joindre**

3 to bring in (wings) close to the body: *The bird folded its wings.* □ **replier**
■ *noun* **1** a doubling of one layer of material, paper *etc* over another: *Her dress hung in folds.* □ **pli**

2 a mark made *especially* on paper *etc* by doing this; a crease: *There was a fold in the page.* □ **pli**

'**folded** *adjective*. □ **(re)plié**

'**folder** *noun* a cover for keeping loose papers together: *He kept the notes for his speech in a folder.* □ **chemise**

'**folding** *adjective* that can be folded: *a folding chair.* □ **pliant**

fold[2] [fould] *noun* a place surrounded by a fence or wall, in which sheep are kept: *a sheep fold.* □ **parc à moutons**

foliage ['fouliidʒ] *noun* leaves: *This plant has dark foliage.* □ **feuillage**

folio ['fouliou] – *plural* '**folios** – *noun* **1** a sheet of paper folded once. □ **folio**

2 a book in which the pages are made of sheets of paper folded once: *Shakespeare's plays were first printed in folio.* □ **in-folio**

folk [fouk] *noun plural* (*especially American* **folks**) people: *The folk in this town are very friendly.* □ **gens**
■ *adjective* (of the traditions) of the common people of a country: *folk customs; folk dance; folk music.* □ **populaire, folklorique**

folks *noun plural* one's family: *My folks all live nearby.* □ **famille**

'**folklore** *noun* the study of the customs, beliefs, stories, traditions *etc* of a particular people: *the folklore of the American Indians.* □ **folklore**

follow ['folou] *verb* **1** to go or come after: *I will follow* *(you)*. □ **suivre**

2 to go along (a road, river *etc*): *Follow this road.* □ **suivre**

3 to understand: *Do you follow (my argument)?* □ **suivre**

4 to act according to: *I followed his advice.* □ **suivre**

'**follower** *noun* a person who follows, *especially* the philosophy, ideas *etc* of another person: *She is a follower of Plato* (= Plato's theories). □ **disciple**

'**following** *noun* supporters: *He has a great following among the poorer people.* □ **partisan(s)**

■ *adjective* **1** coming after: *the following day.* □ **suivant**

2 about to be mentioned: *You will need the following things.* □ **suivant**

■ *preposition* after; as a result of: *Following his illness, his hair turned white.* □ **à la suite de**

■ *pronoun* things about to be mentioned: *You must bring the following – pen, pencil, paper and rubber.* □ **les choses suivantes**

'**follow-up** *noun* further reaction or response: *Was there any follow-up to the letter you wrote to the newspaper?* □ **suite**

follow up 1 to go further in doing something: *The police are following up a clue.* □ **poursuivre**

2 to find out more about (something): *I followed up the news.* □ **suivre (de près)**

folly ['foli] – *plural* '**follies** – *noun* foolishness: *the follies of youth.* □ **folie**

fond [fond] *adjective* **1** loving: *fond looks; a fond husband.* □ **tendre**

2 (of wishes, hopes *etc*) unlikely to be fulfilled: *His fond ambition was to be a film star.* □ **le plus cher, naïf**

'**fondly** *adverb.* □ **affectueusement, naïvement**

'**fondness** *noun* (*especially with* **for**) affection; liking: *her fondness for children.* □ **affection (pour)**

fond of having a liking for: *She is very fond of dogs.* □ **friand de**

fondle ['fondl] *verb* to touch, stroke *etc* affectionately: *He fondled the dog's ears.* □ **caresser**

food [fuːd] *noun* what living things eat: *Horses and cows eat different food from dogs.* □ **nourriture**

'**foodstuff** *noun* a material used for food: *frozen foodstuffs.* □ **aliment(s)**

fool [fuːl] *noun* a person without sense or intelligence: *He is such a fool he never knows what to do.* □ **fou, folle**

■ *verb* **1** to deceive: *She completely fooled me with her story.* □ **berner**

2 (*often with* **about** *or* **around**) to act like a fool or playfully: *Stop fooling about!* □ **faire l'imbécile**

'**foolish** *adjective* **1** having no sense: *He is a foolish young man.* □ **étourdi, stupide**

2 ridiculous: *He looked very foolish.* □ **ridicule**

'**foolishly** *adverb.* □ **stupidement**

'**foolishness** *noun.* □ **stupidité**

'**foolhardy** *adjective* taking foolish risks; rash: *She made a foolhardy attempt to climb the mountain in winter.* □ **téméraire**

'**foolhardiness** *noun.* □ **témérité**

'**foolproof** *adjective* unable to go wrong: *His new plan seems completely foolproof.* □ **à toute épreuve**

make a fool of to make (someone) appear ridiculous or stupid: *They made a real fool of you while spending all your money.* □ **ridiculiser**

make a fool of oneself to act in such a way that people consider one ridiculous or stupid: *She made a fool of herself at the party.* □ **se rendre ridicule**

play the fool to act in a foolish manner, *especially* with the intention of amusing other people: *She always played the fool when the teacher left the classroom.* □ **faire le pitre**

foot [fut] – *plural* **feet** [fiːt] – *noun* **1** the part of the leg on which a person or animal stands or walks: *My feet are very sore from walking so far.* □ **pied**

2 the lower part of anything: *at the foot of the hill.* □ **pied**

3 (*plural* often **foot**; *often abbreviated to* **ft** *when written*) a measure of length equal to twelve inches (30.48 cm): *She is five feet/foot six inches tall; a four-foot wall.* □ **pied**

'**footing** *noun* **1** balance: *It was difficult to keep his footing on the narrow path.* □ **équilibre**

2 foundation: *The business is now on a firm footing.* □ **base**

'**football** *noun* **1** a game played by kicking a large ball: *The children played football*; (*also adjective*) *a football fan.* □ **football**

2 the ball used in this game. □ **ballon (de football)**

'**foothill** *noun* a small hill at the foot of a mountain: *the foothills of the Alps.* □ **contrefort**

'**foothold** *noun* a place to put one's feet when climbing: *to find footholds on the slippery rock.* □ **prise pour le pied**

'**footlight** *noun* (in a theatre) a light which shines on the actors *etc* from the front of the stage. □ **rampe**

'**footman** – *plural* '**footmen** – *noun* a male servant wearing a uniform: *The footman opened the door.* □ **valet de pied**

'**footmark** *noun* a footprint: *She left dirty footmarks.* □ **empreinte (de pied)**

'**footnote** *noun* a note at the bottom of a page: *The footnotes referred to other chapters of the book.* □ **note en bas de page**

'**footpath** *noun* a path or way for walking, not for cars, bicycles *etc*: *You can go by the footpath.* □ **sentier (pédestre)**

'**footprint** *noun* the mark or impression of a foot: *She followed his footprints through the snow.* □ **empreinte (de pied)**

'**footsore** *adjective* with painful feet from too much walking: *He arrived, tired and footsore.* □ **qui a mal aux pieds**

'**footstep** *noun* the sound of a foot: *She heard his footsteps on the stairs.* □ **(bruit de) pas**

'**footwear** *noun* boots, shoes, slippers *etc*: *He always buys expensive footwear.* □ **chaussures**

follow in someone's footsteps to do the same as someone has done before one: *When she joined the police force she was following in her father's footsteps.* □ **marcher sur les traces de**

foot the bill to be the person who pays the bill. □ **payer**

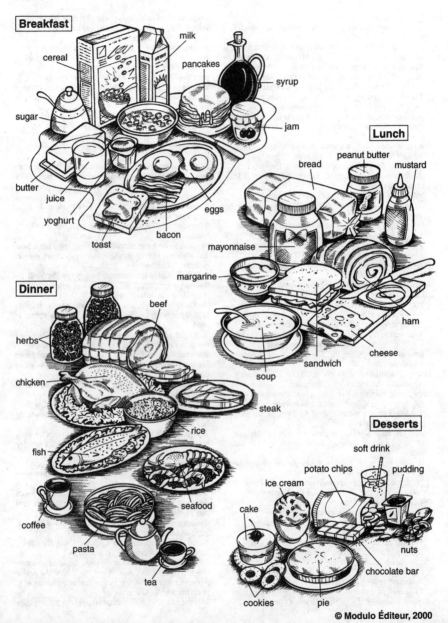

Breakfast

cereal
milk
pancakes
syrup
sugar
jam
butter
juice
yoghurt
eggs
toast
bacon

Lunch

bread
peanut butter
mustard
mayonnaise
margarine
ham
cheese
sandwich
soup

Dinner

beef
herbs
chicken
steak
rice
fish
seafood
coffee
pasta
tea

Desserts

soft drink
potato chips
pudding
ice cream
cake
nuts
cookies
chocolate bar
pie

© Modulo Éditeur, 2000

la note
on foot walking: *She arrived at the house on foot.* □ **à pied**
put one's foot down to be firm about something: *I put my foot down and refused.* □ **faire acte d'autorité**
put one's foot in it to say or do something stupid: *I really put my foot in it when I asked about his wife – she has just run away with his friend!* □ **(se) mettre les pieds dans les plats**

for [foː] *preposition* **1** to be given or sent to: *This letter is for you.* □ **pour**
2 towards; in the direction of: *We set off for Lac St. Jean.* □ **pour**
3 through a certain time or distance: *for three hours; for three kilometres.* □ **pendant; sur**
4 in order to have, get, be *etc*: *He asked me for some money; Go for a walk.* □ **pour**
5 in return; as payment: *She paid $2 for her ticket.* □ **pour**
6 in order to be prepared: *He's getting ready for the journey.* □ **pour**
7 representing: *He is the member of parliament for Hull.* □ **pour**
8 on behalf of: *Will you do it for me?* □ **pour**
9 in favour of: *Are you for or against the plan?* □ **pour**
10 because of: *for this reason.* □ **pour**
11 having a particular purpose: *She gave her money for her bus fare.* □ **pour**
12 indicating an ability or an attitude to: *a liking for peace; an ear for music.* □ **pour**
13 as being: *They mistook him for someone else.* □ **pour**
14 considering what is used in the case of: *It is quite warm for January* (= considering that it is January when it is *usually* cold). □ **pour**
15 in spite of: *For all his money, he didn't seem happy.* □ **malgré**
■ *conjunction* because: *It must be late, for I have been here a long time.* □ **car**

forage ['foridʒ] *verb* (*often with* **about**) to search thoroughly: *He foraged about in the cupboard; She foraged for food in the cupboard.* □ **fouiller (pour trouver)**
■ *noun* food for horses and cattle. □ **fourrage**

forbade *see* **forbid**.

for'bearance [fə'beərəns] *noun* patience; control of temper: *She showed great forbearance.* □ **patience**
for'bearing *adjective* patient: *a patient and forbearing friend.* □ **patient**

forbears *see* **forebears**.

forbid [fə'bid] – *past tense* **forbade** [fə'bad]: *past participle* **for'bidden** – *verb* to tell (someone) not to do something: *She forbade him to go.* □ **défendre (de)**
for'bidden *adjective* not allowed: *Smoking is forbidden.* □ **interdit**
for'bidding *adjective* rather frightening: *a forbidding appearance.* □ **rébarbatif**

force [foːs] *noun* **1** strength or power that can be felt: *the force of the wind.* □ **force**
2 a person or thing that has great power: *the forces of Nature.* □ **force**
3 (*sometimes with capital*) a group of men prepared for

action: *the police force; the air force.* □ **force**
■ *verb* **1** to make (someone or something) do something, go somewhere *etc*, often against his *etc* will: *He forced me to give him money.* □ **forcer (à)**
2 to achieve by strength or effort: *He forced a smile despite his grief.* □ **contraindre**
forced *adjective* done with great effort: *a forced march.* □ **forcé**
'forceful *adjective* powerful: *a forceful argument.* □ **vigoureux**
'forcefully *adverb.* □ **vigoureusement**
'forces *noun plural* the army, navy and air force considered together: *The Forces played a large part in the parade.* □ **forces (armées)**
in, into force in or into operation; working or effective: *The new law is now in force.* □ **en vigueur**

forceps ['foːseps] *noun plural* a medical instrument used for holding things firmly: *a pair of forceps.* □ **forceps**

ford [foːd] *noun* a shallow crossing place in a river. □ **gué**
■ *verb* to cross (water) on foot *etc*: *They forded the river.* □ **passer à gué**

forearm ['foːraːm] *noun* the lower part of the arm (between wrist and elbow). □ **avant-bras**

forebears, forbears ['foːbeəz] *noun plural* ancestors: *My forebears lived in that castle.* □ **ancêtres**

foreboding [foː'boudiŋ] *noun* a feeling that something bad is going to happen: *He has a strange foreboding that he will die young.* □ **pressentiment**

forecast ['foːkaːst] – *past tense, past participle* **'forecast** *or* **'forecasted** – *verb* to tell about (something) before it happens: *She forecast good weather for the next three days.* □ **prévoir**
■ *noun* a statement about what is going to happen; a prediction: *forecasts about the economy.* □ **prévision**

forefathers ['foːfaːðəz] *noun plural* ancestors: *His forefathers emigrated to America.* □ **ancêtres**

forefinger ['foːfiŋgə] *noun* the finger next to the thumb. □ **index**

forefront ['foːfrʌnt]: **in the 'forefront** at or in the very front: *in the forefront of the battle.* □ **au premier rang de**

foregone ['foːgon]: **a foregone conclusion** a result that is so obvious that it can be seen before it happens: *It is a foregone conclusion who will win.* □ **prévu d'avance**

foreground ['foːgraund] *noun* the part of a view or picture nearest to the person looking at it: *a landscape, with two horses in the foreground.* □ **premier plan**

forehand ['foːhand] *noun* in tennis *etc*, (the ability to make) a stroke or shot with the palm of one's hand turned towards the ball: *a strong forehand;* (*also adjective*) *a forehand stroke.* □ **coup droit**

forehead ['forid] *noun* the part of the face above the eyebrows and below the hairline; the brow: *Her hair covers her forehead.* □ **front**

foreign ['forən] *adjective* **1** belonging to a country other than one's own: *a foreign passport.* □ **étranger**
2 (*with* **to**) not naturally part of: *Anger was foreign to her nature.* □ **étranger (à)**
'foreigner *noun* **1** a person from another country. □

étranger, ère
2 an unfamiliar person. □ **étranger, ère**

foreleg ['fɔːleg] *noun* an animal's front leg. □ **jambe/ patte de devant**

foreman, forewoman ['fɔːmən, -wumən] – *plural* '**foremen, forewomen** – *noun* the supervisor or leader of a group, *especially* of workmen or a jury: *The foreman here is in charge of twenty workmen.* □ **contremaître, contremaîtresse; président, ente (du jury)**

foremost ['fɔːmoust] *adjective* most famous or important: *the foremost modern artist.* □ **le plus en vue**

forensic [fə'rensik] *adjective* of or concerning courts of law: *forensic medicine.* □ **légal, judiciaire**

forerunner ['fɔːrʌnə] *noun* a person or thing which is a sign of what is to follow: *Penicillin was the forerunner of modern antibiotics.* □ **précurseur**

foresee [fɔː'siː] – *past tense* fore'saw [-'sɔː]: *past participle* fore'seen – *verb* to see or know about before or in advance: *He could foresee the difficulties.* □ **prévoir**
fore'seeable *adjective* able to be foreseen: *in the foreseeable future* (= soon; within a short space of time). □ **prévisible**
'foresight [-sait] *noun* the ability to see in advance what may happen and to plan for it: *She had the foresight to drive carefully in case the roads were icy.* □ **prévoyance**

foreskin ['fɔːskin] *noun* the skin that covers the end of the penis. □ **prépuce**

forest ['forist] *noun* 1 (a large piece of) land covered with trees. □ **forêt**
2 an area of land in which animals, *especially* deer, are kept: *a deer forest.* □ **réserve**
'forested *adjective* covered with forest. □ **couvert de forêts**
'forester *noun* a person who works in a forest or is involved in forestry. □ **garde forestier, ière**
'forestry *noun* (the science of) growing and looking after forests. □ **sylviculture**
■ *adjective: a forestry worker.* □ **forestier**

foretaste ['fɔːteist] *noun* a small sample or experience of something before it happens: *This cold weather is just a foretaste of winter.* □ **avant-goût**

foretell [fɔː'tel] – *past tense, past participle* fore'told [-'tould] – *verb* to tell (about something) before it has happened: *to foretell the future from the stars.* □ **prédire**

forethought ['fɔːθɔːt] *noun* thought about, or concern for, the future: *They acted without sufficient forethought.* □ **prévoyance**

forever *see* **ever**.

foreword ['fɔːwəːd] *noun* a piece of writing as an introduction at the beginning of a book; a preface: *The foreword was written by a famous scholar.* □ **avant-propos**

to write a **foreword** (not **forward**) to a book.

forfeit ['fɔːfit] *noun* something that must be given up because one has done something wrong, *especially* in games: *If you lose the game you will have to pay a forfeit.* □ **gage**
■ *verb* to lose (something) because one has done something wrong: *He forfeited our respect by telling lies.* □ **perdre**

■ *adjective* forfeited: *Her former rights are forfeit now.* □ **confisqué, perdu**

forgave *see* **forgive**.

forge[1] [fɔːdʒ] *noun* a very hot oven in which metals are melted *etc*; a furnace: *Steel is manufactured in a forge.* □ **forge**
■ *verb* to shape metal by heating and hammering: *He forged a horse-shoe out of an iron bar.* □ **forger**

forge[2] [fɔːdʒ] *verb* to copy (*eg* a letter or a signature) and pretend that it is genuine, usually for illegal purposes: *He forged my signature.* □ **contrefaire**
'forgery – *plural* 'forgeries – *noun* 1 (the crime of) copying pictures, documents, signatures *etc* and pretending they are genuine: *He was sent to prison for forgery.* □ **faux, contrefaçon**
2 a picture, document *etc* copied for this reason: *The painting was a forgery.* □ **faux**

forge[3] [fɔːdʒ] *verb* to move steadily: *they forged ahead with their plans.* □ **pousser de l'avant**

forget [fə'get] – *past tense* forgot [fə'got]: *past participle* forgotten [fə'gotn] – *verb* 1 to fail to remember: *She has forgotten my name.* □ **oublier**
2 to leave behind accidentally: *She has forgotten her handbag.* □ **oublier**
3 to lose control of (oneself), act in an undignified manner: *She forgot herself so far as to criticize her boss.* □ **(s')oublier**
for'getful *adjective* often forgetting: *He is a very forgetful person.* □ **étourdi, négligent**
for'getfully *adverb.* □ **dans un moment d'étourderie**

forgive [fə'giv] – *past tense* forgave [fə'geiv]: *past participle* for'given – *verb* 1 to stop being angry with (someone who has done something wrong): *He forgave her for stealing his watch.* □ **pardonner**
2 to stop being angry about (something that someone has done): *He forgave her angry words.* □ **pardonner**
forgiveness [fə'givnis] *noun* the act of forgiving: *He asked for forgiveness.* □ **pardon**
2 readiness to forgive: *She showed great forgiveness towards them.* □ **clémence**
for'giving *adjective* ready to forgive (often): *a forgiving person.* □ **indulgent**

forgot, forgotten *see* **forget**.

fork [fɔːk] *noun* 1 an instrument with two or more pointed pieces for piercing and lifting things: *We usually eat with a knife, fork and spoon.* □ **fourchette**
2 the point at which a road, river *etc* divides into two or more branches or divisions: *a fork in the river.* □ **embranchement**
3 one of the branches or divisions of a road, river *etc* into which the road, river *etc* divides: *Take the left fork (of the road).* □ **embranchement**
■ *verb* 1 (of a road, river *etc*) to divide into (usually two) branches or divisions: *The main road forks here.* □ **bifurquer**
2 (of a person or vehicle) to follow one of the branches or divisions into which a road has divided: *The car forked left.* □ **prendre**
3 to lift or move with a fork: *The farmer forked the hay.* □ **soulever/remuer à la fourche**

forked *adjective* divided into two branches or divisions: *A snake has a forked tongue.* □ **fourchu**

fork-lift truck a small power-driven machine with an arrangement of steel prongs which can lift, raise up high and carry heavy packages and stack them where required. □ **chariot élévateur**

fork out to pay or give *especially* unwillingly: *You have to fork out (money) for so many charities these days.* □ **allonger ((de l'argent)**

forlorn [fə'lɔːn] *adjective* pitiful; unhappy because left alone: *She seems rather forlorn since he left.* □ **triste, délaissé**

for'lornly *adverb.* □ **tristement**

form [fɔːm] *noun* **1** (a) shape; outward appearance: *He saw a strange form in the darkness.* □ **forme, silhouette** **2** a kind, type or variety: *What form of ceremony usually takes place?* □ **genre** **3** a document containing certain questions, the answers to which must be written on it: *an application form.* □ **formulaire** **4** a fixed way of doing things: *forms and ceremonies.* □ **convenances**

■ *verb* **1** to make; to cause to take shape: *They decided to form a drama group.* □ **former** **2** to come into existence; to take shape: *An idea slowly formed in his mind.* □ **prendre forme** **3** to organize or arrange (oneself or other people) into a particular order: *The women formed (themselves) into three groups.* □ **(s')organiser** **4** to be; to make up: *These lectures form part of the medical course.* □ **faire partie (de)**

for'mation *noun* **1** the act of forming or making: *He agreed to the formation of a music society.* □ **formation, création** **2** (a) particular arrangement or order: *The planes flew in formation.* □ **formation**

be in good form to be in good spirits or health: *She's in good form after her holiday.* □ **être en forme**

in the form of having the shape, character, style *etc* of: *She wrote a novel in the form of a diary.* □ **sous forme de**

formal ['fɔːməl] *adjective* **1** done *etc* according to a fixed and accepted way: *a formal letter.* □ **officiel** **2** suitable or correct for occasions when things are done according to a fixed and accepted way: *You must wear formal dress.* □ **de cérémonie/soirée** **3** (of behaviour, attitude *etc*) not relaxed and friendly: *formal behaviour.* □ **compassé** **4** (of language) exactly correct by grammatical *etc* rules but not conversational: *Her English was very formal.* □ **soigné** **5** (of designs *etc*) precise and following a fixed pattern rather than occurring naturally: *formal gardens.* □ **classique**

'formally *adverb.* □ **cérémonieusement**

for'mality [-'ma-] *noun* **1** something which is done for appearance but has little meaning: *The chairwoman's speech was only a formality.* □ **formalité** **2** unrelaxed correctness of behaviour: *His formality made him appear unfriendly.* □ **raideur**

format ['fɔːmat] *noun* shape and size, *eg* that of a book, magazine *etc.* □ **format**

■ *verb* to prepare or make ready either by hand or electronically: *Brandon formatted a plan to return home; Jessica had to format the disk before adding computer data.* □ **form**

former ['fɔːmə] *adjective* of an earlier time: *In former times people did not travel so much.* □ **ancien**

'formerly *adverb* in earlier times: *Formerly this large town was a small village.* □ **autrefois**

the former the first of two things mentioned: *We visited America and Australia, staying longer in the former than in the latter.* □ **le premier**

formidable ['fɔːmidəbl] *adjective* **1** rather frightening: *a formidable appearance.* □ **terrible** **2** very difficult to overcome: *formidable difficulties.* □ **redoutable**

'formidably *adverb.* □ **formidablement**

formula ['fɔːmjulə] – *plurals* **'formulae** [-liː], **'formulas** – *noun* **1** an arrangement of signs or letters used in chemistry, arithmetic *etc* to express an idea briefly: *The formula for water is H_2O.* □ **formule** **2** a recipe or set of instructions for making something: *The shampoo was made to a new formula.* □ **formule**

forsake [fə'seik] – *past tense* **forsook** [fə'suk]: *past participle* **for'saken** – *verb* to leave alone; to abandon: *He was forsaken by his friends.* □ **abandonner**

forswear [fɔː'sweə] – *past tense* **forswore** [fɔː'swɔː]: *past participle* **forsworn** [fɔː'swɔːn] – *verb* to give up; to stop: *He has forsworn all his bad habits.* □ **renoncer à**

fort [fɔːt] *noun* a building which is built so that it can be defended against an enemy. □ **fort**

forth [fɔːθ] *adverb* forward; onward: *They went forth into the desert.* □ **en avant**

back and forth first in one direction and then in the other; backwards and forwards: *We had to go back and forth many times before we moved all our furniture to the new house.* □ **de va-et-vient, de long en large**

forthcoming [fɔːθ'kʌmiŋ] *adjective* **1** happening or appearing soon: *forthcoming events.* □ **prochain** **2** (of a person) open and willing to talk: *She wasn't very forthcoming about her work; not a very forthcoming personality.* □ **communicatif**

forthright ['fɔːθrait] *adjective* honest and straightforward: *He is a very forthright young man.* □ **direct**

fortify ['fɔːtifai] *verb* **1** to prepare (a building, city *etc*) for an attack by strengthening and arming it: *The soldiers fortified the castle against the attacking armies.* □ **fortifier** **2** to strengthen or enrich (*eg* food, drink): *Sherry is a fortified wine.* □ **augmenter la teneur en alcool (de)**

,fortifi'cation [-fi-] *noun* **1** walls *etc* built to strengthen an army, city, nation *etc* against attack: *Fortifications surrounded the city.* □ **fortification(s)** **2** the act of fortifying. □ **fortification**

fortitude ['fɔːtitjuːd] *noun* courage and endurance: *He showed great fortitude during his long illness.* □ **courage**

fortnight ['fɔːtnait] *noun* two weeks: *It's a fortnight since*

I last saw her. □ **quinzaine**

'fortnightly *adjective, adverb* every fortnight: *a fortnightly visit; He is paid fortnightly.* □ **bimensuel; bimensuellement**

fortress ['fo:tris] *noun a (usually* large) fort or fortified building. □ **forteresse**

fortune ['fo:tʃən] *noun* 1 whatever happens by chance or (good or bad) luck: *whatever fortune may bring.* □ **hasard**

2 a large amount of money: *That ring must be worth a fortune!* □ **fortune**

'fortunate [-nət] *adjective* having good fortune; lucky: *It was fortunate that no one was killed in the accident.* □ **heureux**

'fortunately *adverb.* □ **heureusement**

'fortune-teller *noun* someone who tells fortunes. □ **diseur, eure de bonne aventure**

tell (someone's) fortune to foretell what will happen to someone in the future: *He told my fortune.* □ **dire la bonne aventure**

forty ['fo:ti] *noun* 1 the number or figure 40. □ **quarante**

2 the age of 40. □ **quarante ans**

■ *adjective* 1 40 in number. □ **quarante**

2 aged 40. □ **de quarante ans**

'forties *noun plural* 1 the period of time between one's fortieth and fiftieth birthdays. □ **quarantaine**

2 the period of time between the fortieth and fiftieth years of a century. □ **les années quarante**

'fortieth *noun* 1 one of forty equal parts. □ **quarantième**

2 (*also adjective*) the last of forty (people, things *etc*); the next after the thirty-ninth. □ **quarantième**

forty- having forty (of something): *a forty-page index.* □ **de quarante (...)**

'forty-year-old *noun, adjective* (a person or animal) that is forty years old. □ **(individu, etc.) âgé de quarante ans**

forty winks a short sleep: *She always has forty winks after dinner.* □ **roupillon**

forty (not **fourty**).

forum ['fo:rəm] *noun* 1 any public place in which discussions take place, speeches are made *etc*: *In modern times the television studio is as much a forum for public opinion as the marketplaces of ancient Rome used to be.* □ **forum**

2 a marketplace in ancient Roman cities and towns. □ **forum**

forward ['fo:wəd] *adjective* 1 moving on; advancing: *a forward movement.* □ **en avant**

2 at or near the front: *The forward part of a ship is called the 'bows'.* □ **avant**

■ *adverb* 1 (*also* **'forwards**) moving towards the front: *A pendulum swings backward(s) and forward(s).* □ **en avant**

2 to a later time: *from this time forward.* □ **à partir de**

■ *noun* (in certain team games, *eg* football, hockey) a player in a forward position. □ **avant**

■ *verb* to send (letters *etc*) on to another address: *I have asked the post office to forward my mail.* □ **faire suivre**

bring forward 1 (*also* **put forward**) to bring to people's attention; to cause to be discussed *etc*: *They will consider the suggestions which you have brought/put forward.* □ **avancer**

2 to make to happen at an earlier date; to advance in time: *They have brought forward the date of their wedding by one week.* □ **avancer**

to move **forward** (not **foreword**).

fossil ['fosl] *noun* the hardened remains of an animal or vegetable found in rock: *Fossils have been found here which may be a million years old.* □ **fossile**

'fossilize, 'fossilise *verb* to change into a fossil: *Time had fossilized the animal remains in the river-bed.* □ **fossiliser**

foster ['fostə] *verb* 1 to look after for a period of time; to bring up a child that is not one's own: *She fostered the children for several months.* □ **élever**

2 to encourage or give help to (ideas *etc*): *She fostered the child's talents.* □ **favoriser**

'foster brother, 'foster sister *nouns* a child that has been fostered in another child's family. □ **frère adoptif, sœur adoptive**

'foster child *noun* a child fostered by a family. □ **enfant adoptif, ive**

'foster parent (**'foster father, 'foster mother**) *noun* a person who looks after a child not his or her own. □ **parent adoptif/nourricier**

fought *see* **fight.**

foul [faul] *adjective* 1 (*especially* of smell or taste) causing disgust: *a foul smell.* □ **infect**

2 very unpleasant; nasty: *a foul mess.* □ **dégoûtant**

■ *noun* an action *etc* which breaks the rules of a game: *The other team committed a foul.* □ **coup interdit**

■ *verb* 1 to break the rules of a game (against): *He fouled his opponent.* □ **commettre une faute contre**

2 to make dirty, *especially* with faeces: *Dogs often foul the pavement.* □ **souiller**

foul play a criminal act, *especially* involving murder: *A man has been found dead and the police suspect foul play.* □ **crime**

found¹ *see* **find.**

found² [faund] *verb* 1 to start or establish: *The school was founded by the Minister of Education.* □ **fonder**

2 (*with* **on/upon**) to base on: *The story was founded upon fact.* □ **baser**

'founding *noun.* □ **fondation**

foun'dation *noun* 1 the act of founding: *the foundation of a new university.* □ **fondation**

2 the base on which something is built: *First they laid the foundations, then they built the walls.* □ **fondation(s)**

3 an amount of money to be used for a special purpose or the organization that manages it: *The Canadian Cancer Foundation* □ **fondation**

'founder *noun* a person who founds a school, college, organization *etc*: *We commemorate the founder of the school.* □ **fondateur, trice**

foundry ['faundri] – *plural* **'foundries** – *noun* a place where metal or glass is formed by melting and pouring into moulds. □ **fonderie**

fountain ['fauntin] *noun* 1 an often ornamental structure which produces a spring of water that rises into the air: *Rome is famous for its beautifully carved stone fountains.* □ **fontaine**

2 the water coming from such a structure: *It was so hot that I stood under the fountain to get cool.* □ **fontaine**

3 a source: *God is the fountain of all goodness.* □ **source**

fountain pen a kind of pen with a nib and containing a supply of ink which is released as one writes. □ **stylo**

four [foː] *noun* **1** the number or figure 4. □ **quatre**

2 the age of 4. □ **quatre ans**

■ *adjective* **1** 4 in number. □ **quatre**

2 aged 4. □ **de quatre ans**

four- having four (of something): *a four-man team.* □ **de quatre (...)**

fourth *noun* **1** one of four equal parts. □ **quatrième**

2 (*also adjective*) the last of four (people, things *etc*); the next after the third. □ **quatrième**

'foursome *noun* a group of four people, *especially* for playing games, *eg* golf: *We'll play in a foursome.* □ **à quatre**

'four-year-old *noun* a person or animal that is four years old. □ **(individu, etc.) âgé de quatre ans**

■ *adjective* (of a person, animal or thing) that is four years old. □ **de quatre ans**

on all fours on hands and knees: *He went up the steep path on all fours.* □ **à quatre pattes**

fourteen [foːˈtiːn] *noun* **1** the number or figure 14. □ **quatorze**

2 the age of 14. □ **quatorze ans**

■ *adjective* **1** 14 in number. □ **quatorze**

2 aged 14. □ **de quatorze ans**

fourteen- having fourteen (of something): *a fourteen-volume encyclopaedia.* □ **de quatorze (...)**

four'teenth *noun* **1** one of fourteen equal parts. □ **quatorzième**

2 (*also adjective*) the last of fourteen (people things *etc*); the next after the thirteenth. □ **quatorzième**

,four'teen-year-old *noun* a person or animal that is fourteen years old. □ **(individu, etc.) âgé de quatorze ans**

■ *adjective* (of a person, animal or thing) that is fourteen years old. □ **de quatorze ans**

fowl [faul] – *plurals* **fowl, fowls** – *noun* a bird, *especially* domestic, *eg* hens, ducks, geese *etc*: *She keeps fowls and a few pigs.* □ **oiseau de basse-cour**

fox [foks] – *plural* **'foxes** – *noun* a type of reddish-brown wild animal which looks like a dog. □ **renard**

■ *adjective: fox-fur.* □ **de renard**

■ *verb* to puzzle or confuse: *She was completely foxed.* □ **mystifier, tromper**

'foxy *adjective* **1** clever in a deceitful way: *He's a foxy fellow.* □ **malin**

2 like a fox: *She had rather foxy features.* □ **roux**

'foxhound *noun* a kind of dog trained to chase foxes. □ **chien courant**

fox terrier a kind of dog formerly trained to drive foxes out of their holes in the ground. □ **fox-terrier**

foyer [ˈfoiei] *noun* an entrance hall to a theatre, hotel *etc*: *I'll meet you in the foyer.* □ **hall**

fraction [ˈfrakʃən] *noun* **1** a part; not a whole number *eg* *1/4, 5/8, 7/8 etc.* □ **fraction**

2 a small part: *He has only a fraction of his brother's intelligence.* □ **petite portion**

'fractional *adjective* very small: *a fractional amount.* □ **infime**

fracture [ˈfraktʃə] *noun* a break of anything hard, *especially* a bone: *a fracture of the left thigh bone.* □ **fracture**

■ *verb* to break: *The metal pipes (were) fractured.* □ **briser, fracturer**

fragile [ˈfradʒail] *adjective* easily broken: *a fragile glass vase.* □ **fragile**

fra'gility [-ˈdʒi-] *noun.* □ **fragilité**

fragment [ˈfragmənt] *noun* **1** a piece broken off: *The floor was covered with fragments of glass.* □ **morceau, fragment**

2 something which is not complete: *a fragment of poetry.* □ **fragment**

■ [fragˈment] *verb* to break into pieces: *The glass is very strong but will fragment if hit by something sharp.* □ **(se) fragmenter**

'fragmentary *adjective* made of pieces; incomplete: *a fragmentary account of what happened.* □ **fragmentaire**

fragrant [ˈfreigrənt] *adjective* having a sweet smell: *fragrant flowers.* □ **odorant**

'fragrance *noun* (a) sweet smell: *all the fragrance(s) of the East.* □ **parfum**

> a **fragrant** (not **flagrant**) plant.

frail [freil] *adjective* weak, *especially* in health: *a frail old lady.* □ **frêle**

'frailty – *plural* **'frailties** – *noun* physical weakness or (a) moral failing: *She loved him in spite of his frailties.* □ **fragilité, faiblesse**

frame [freim] *noun* **1** a hard main structure around which something is built or made: *the steel frame of the aircraft.* □ **structure**

2 something to enclose something: *a picture frame; a window frame.* □ **cadre**

3 the human body: *He has a slight frame.* □ **ossature**

■ *verb* **1** to put a frame around: *to frame a picture.* □ **encadrer**

2 to act as a frame for: *Her hair framed her face.* □ **encadrer**

3 to arrange false evidence so as to make (someone) seem guilty of a crime *etc* (*noun* **'frame-up**). □ **monter un coup (contre); coup monté**

'framework *noun* the basic supporting structure of anything: *The building will be made of concrete on a steel framework.* □ **charpente**

frame of mind mental state: *He is in a strange frame of mind.* □ **disposition d'esprit**

franc [fraŋk] *noun* the standard unit of currency in France, Belgium, Switzerland and several other countries, *eg* in some parts of Africa where French is spoken. □ **franc**

franchise [ˈfrantʃaiz] *noun* the right to vote: *Women did not get the franchise until the twentieth century.* □ **droit de vote**

franchise holder [ˈfrantʃaiz houldə] *noun* someone who has been given the legal right to distribute a product or operate a business such as a chain restaurant: *As a fran-*

chise holder, Roy had permission to open the fast-food restaurant at the mall. □ **concessionnaire**

Franco- ['fraŋkou] (*as part of a word*) French: ,*Franco-* '*Scottish*. □ **franco-**

frank [fraŋk] *adjective* saying or showing openly what is in one's mind; honest: *a frank person; a frank reply.* □ **franc**

■ *verb* to mark a letter by machine to show that postage has been paid. □ **affranchir**

'**frankly** *adverb.* □ **sincèrement**

frankness *noun* plain, clear or open speech: *Frankness is the best way to handle a problem, so just state your concern honestly.* □ **franchise**

frankfurter ['fraŋkfɜːtə] *noun* a kind of smoked sausage. □ **saucisse de Francfort**

frantic ['frantik] *adjective* **1** anxious or very worried: *The frantic father searched for his child.* □ **fou d'inquiétude**

2 wildly excited: *the frantic pace of modern life.* □ **trépidant**

'**frantically** *adverb.* □ **frénétiquement**

fraternal [frə'tɜːnl] *adjective* of or like a brother: *a fraternal greeting.* □ **fraternel**

fra'ternally *adverb.* □ **fraternellement**

fra'ternity – *plural* **fra'ternities** – *noun* **1** a company of people who regard each other as equals, *eg* monks. □ **confrérie**

2 a company of people with the same interest, job *etc*: *the banking fraternity.* □ **confrérie**

fraud [frɔːd] *noun* **1** (an act of) dishonesty: *He was sent to prison for fraud.* □ **fraude**

2 a person who pretends to be something that he isn't: *That man is not a famous writer, he's a fraud.* □ **imposteur**

'**fraudulent** [-djulənt] *adjective* dishonest or intending to deceive: *fraudulent behaviour.* □ **frauduleux**

'**fraudulently** *adverb.* □ **frauduleusement**

'**fraudulence** *noun.* □ **caractère frauduleux**

fray [frei] *verb* (of cloth, rope *etc*) to make or become worn at the ends or edges, so that the threads or fibres come loose: *This material frays easily.* □ **(s')effilocher**

freak [friːk] *noun* **1** an unusual or abnormal event, person or thing: *A storm as bad as that one is a freak of nature;* (*also adjective*) *a freak result.* □ **phénomène; extraordinaire**

2 a person who is wildly enthusiastic about something: *a film-freak.* □ **mordu (de)**

freak out to become very excited, *especially* because of having taken drugs (*noun* '**freak-out**). □ **se défoncer**

freckle ['frekl] *noun* a small brown spot on the skin: *In summer her face was always covered with freckles.* □ **tache de rousseur**

■ *verb* to cover with small brown spots. □ **marquer de taches de rousseur**

'**freckled,** '**freckly** *adjective.* □ **taché de rousseur**

free [friː] *adjective* **1** allowed to move where one wants; not shut in, tied, fastened *etc*: *The prison door opened, and he was a free man.* □ **libre**

2 not forced or persuaded to act, think, speak *etc* in a particular way: *free speech; You are free to think what*

you like. □ **libre**

3 (*with* **with**) generous: *He is always free with his money/ advice.* □ **généreux**

4 frank, open and ready to speak: *a free manner.* □ **ouvert**

5 costing nothing: *a free gift.* □ **gratuit**

6 not working or having another appointment; not busy: *I shall be free at five o'clock.* □ **libre**

7 not occupied, not in use: *Is this table free?* □ **libre**

8 (*with* **of** *or* **from**) without or no longer having (*especially* something or someone unpleasant *etc*): *She is free from pain now; free of charge.* □ **débarrassé de, gratuit**

■ *verb* – *past tense, past participle* **freed** – **1** to make or set (someone) free: *He freed all the prisoners.* □ **libérer**

2 (*with* **from** *or* **of**) to rid or relieve (someone) of something: *She was able to free herself of her debts by working very hard.* □ **(se) libérer/débarrasser de**

'**freedom** *noun* the state of not being under control and being able to do whatever one wishes: *The prisoner was given his freedom.* □ **liberté**

'**freely** *adverb* **1** in a free manner: *to give freely to charity; to speak freely.* □ **librement**

2 willingly; readily: *I freely admit it was my fault.* □ **volontiers**

,**free-for-'all** *noun* a contest, debate *etc* in which anyone can take part. □ **ouvert à tous**

'**freehand** *adjective, adverb* (of a drawing *etc*) (done) without any instruments (*eg* a ruler) to guide the hand. □ **à main levée**

'**freehold** *adjective* (of land, property *etc*) belonging completely to the owner, not just for a certain time. □ **en toute propriété**

'**freelance** *noun, adjective* (of or done by) a person who is working on his own, not for any one employer: *a freelance journalist; freelance work.* □ **à la pige, de pigiste**

■ *verb* to work in this way: *She is freelancing now.* □ **travailler à la pige**

free speech the right to express an opinion freely: *I believe in free speech.* □ **liberté de parole**

free trade trade with foreign countries without customs duties, taxes *etc.* □ **libre-échange**

'**freeway** *noun* an expressway. □ **autoroute (sans péage)**

,**free'wheel** *verb* to travel (downhill) on a bicycle, in a car *etc* without using mechanical power. □ **être/aller en roue libre**

free will the ability to choose and act freely: *He did it of his own free will.* □ **libre arbitre**

a free hand freedom to do whatever one likes: *He gave her a free hand with the servants.* □ **carte blanche**

set free to make (someone) free: *The soldiers set the terrorists' prisoners free.* □ **relâcher**

freeze [friːz] – *past tense* **froze** [frouz]; *past participle* **frozen** ['frouzn] – *verb* **1** to make into or become ice: *It's so cold that the river has frozen over.* □ **geler**

2 (of weather) to be at or below freezing point: *If it freezes again tonight all my plants will die.* □ **geler** •

3 to make or be very cold: *If you had stayed out all night in the snow you might have frozen to death* (= died of exposure to cold). □ **geler, (mourir de froid)**

4 to make (food) very cold in order to preserve it: *You*

can freeze the rest of that food and eat it later. □ **congeler**
5 to make or become stiff, still or unable to move (with fear *etc*): *She froze when she heard the strange noise.* □ **figer sur place, rester figé**
6 to fix prices, wages *etc* at a certain level: *If the situation does not improve, wages will be frozen again.* □ **geler (des crédits, des devises)**
■ *noun* a period of very cold weather when temperatures are below freezing point: *How long do you think the freeze will last?* □ **gel**
'**freezer** *noun* a cabinet for keeping food at, or bringing it down to, a temperature below freezing point. □ **congélateur**
'**freezing** *adjective* very cold: *This room's freezing.* □ **glacial**
'**frozen** *adjective*. □ **(con)gelé**
'**freezing point** *noun* the temperature at which a liquid becomes solid: *The freezing point of water is 0° centigrade.* □ **point de congélation**
freezing rain *noun* rain that has ice in it: *Lesley took her car out in the freezing rain but the wet ice hitting her windshield made it hard to see.* □ **grésil**
freeze up to stop moving or functioning because of extreme cold: *The car engine froze up.* □ **geler**
freight [freit] *noun* 1 goods being carried from place to place: *air-freight*; *(also adjective) a freight train.* □ **fret**
2 the money charged for carrying such goods: *He charged me $100 freight.* □ **transport**
'**freighter** *noun* a ship (or aircraft) that carries freight rather than passengers. □ **cargo**
French [frentʃ] *adjective* of France or its inhabitants: *The French flag is red, white and blue; A French waiter suggested we try this wine.* □ **français, aise**
■ *noun* 1 the people of France or their descendants; the main language of France and Québec: *The French are famous for their cooking; Most people from Québec speak French.* □ **Français, français**
2 **French fries** [fraiz] strips of deep-fried potatoes. □ **frites**
French beans the long green edible pods of a type of bean. □ **haricot(s) vert(s)**
frenzy ['frenzi] – *plural* '**frenzies** – *noun* a state of great excitement, fear *etc*: *She waited in a frenzy of anxiety.* □ **frénésie**
'**frenzied** *adjective*. □ **fou, frénétique**
'**frenziedly** *adverb*. □ **frénétiquement**
frequent ['friːkwənt] *adjective* happening often: *She made frequent journeys.* □ **fréquent**
■ [fri'kwent] *verb* to visit often: *He used to frequent the George Hotel.* □ **fréquenter**
'**frequency** – *plural* '**frequencies** – *noun* 1 the state of happening often: *The frequency of her visits surprised him.* □ **fréquence**
2 (in electricity, radio *etc*) the number of waves, vibrations *etc* per second: *At what frequency does the sound occur?* □ **fréquence**
3 a set wavelength on which radio stations regularly broadcast: *All the radio stations changed their frequencies.* □ **fréquence**
'**frequently** *adverb* often: *He frequently arrived late.* □

fréquemment
fresco ['freskou] – *plural* '**fresco(e)s** – *noun* a picture painted on a wall while the plaster is still wet. □ **fresque**
fresh [freʃ] *adjective* 1 newly made, gathered, arrived *etc*: *fresh fruit* (= fruit that is not tinned, frozen *etc*); *fresh flowers.* □ **frais**
2 (of people *etc*) healthy; not tired: *You are looking very fresh this morning.* □ **frais (comme une rose)**
3 another; different; not already used, begun, worn, heard *etc*: *a fresh piece of paper; fresh news.* □ **nouveau**
4 (of weather *etc*) cool; refreshing: *a fresh breeze; fresh air.* □ **frais**
5 (of water) without salt: *The swimming pool has fresh water in it, not sea water.* □ **doux**
'**freshen** *verb* 1 to become fresh or cool: *The wind began to freshen.* □ **fraîchir**
2 (*often with* up) to (cause to) become less tired or untidy looking: *I must freshen up before dinner.* □ **faire un brin de toilette**
'**freshly** *adverb* newly; recently: *freshly gathered plums; freshly arrived.* □ **nouvellement**
freshness *noun* that which is soft, recent or newly made: *If bread is left out on the counter it loses its freshness and becomes dried out and stale.* □ **fraîcheur**
'**fresh-water** *adjective* of inland rivers or lakes; not of the sea: *fresh-water fish.* □ **d'eau douce**
fret [fret] – *past tense, past participle* '**fretted** – *verb* to worry or show anxiety or discontentment: *She was always fretting about something or other.* □ **(se) tracasser (pour)**
'**fretful** *adjective* cross; discontented: *fretful children.* □ **grognon**
friction ['frikʃən] *noun* 1 the rubbing together of two things: *The friction between the head of the match and the matchbox causes a spark.* □ **frottement**
2 the resistance felt when one object is moved against another (or through liquid or gas): *There is friction between the wheels of a car and the road surface.* □ **friction**
3 quarrelling; disagreement: *There seems to be some friction between the workmen and the manager.* □ **désaccord**
Friday ['fraidei] *noun* the sixth day of the week, the day following Thursday: *She arrived on Friday; (also adjective) Friday evening.* □ **vendredi**
fridge [fridʒ] short for **refrigerator**.
friend [frend] *noun* 1 someone who knows and likes another person very well: *He is my best friend.* □ **ami, ie**
2 a person who acts in a friendly and generous way to people *etc* he or she does not know: *a friend to animals.* □ **ami, ie**
'**friendless** *adjective* without friends: *alone and friendless.* □ **délaissé**
'**friendly** *adjective* kind and willing to make friends: *She is very friendly to everybody.* □ **amical**
'**friendship** *noun* 1 the state of being friends: *Friendship is a wonderful thing.* □ **amitié**
2 a particular relationship between two friends: *Our friendship grew through the years.* □ **amitié**

make friends (with) to start a friendly relationship; to become friends with someone: *The child tried to make friends with the dog.* □ **devenir ami, ie avec**

frieze [friːz] *noun* a narrow strip around the walls of a room, building *etc* near the top, *usually* decorated with pictures, carving *etc*: *The walls were decorated with a frieze of horses.* □ **frise**

fright [frait] *noun* 1 a sudden fear: *the noise gave me a terrible fright.* □ **peur**

2 a person who looks ridiculous: *She looks a fright in those clothes.* □ **épouvantail**

'**frighten** *verb* to make (someone) afraid: *He was frightened by a large dog.* □ **effrayer**

'**frightened** *adjective*. □ **effrayé**

'**frightful** *adjective* 1 terrible or frightening: *I had a frightful experience.* □ **effroyable**

2 very bad: *He is a frightful liar.* □ **épouvantable**

'**frightening** *adjective*. □ **effrayant**

'**frightfully** *adverb* very: *She's frightfully clever.* □ **terriblement**

take fright to become frightened *usually* suddenly and quickly: *She took fright and ran away.* □ **prendre peur**

frigid ['fridʒid] *adjective* 1 cold and unemotional: *He behaves in a frigid manner.* □ **froid**

2 frozen: *the frigid zones of the world* (= the Arctic and Antarctic). □ **glacial**

'**frigidly** *adverb*. □ **glacialement**

fri'gidity *noun*. □ **grande froideur**

frill [fril] *noun* 1 a decorative edging to a piece of cloth, made of a strip of cloth gathered along one side and sewn on: *I sewed a frill along the bottom of the skirt.* □ **volant**

2 (*often in plural*) something unnecessary added as decoration: *the frills of business* (= having expensive dinners *etc*). □ **accessoires, à-côtés**

frilled, 'frilly *adjective* decorated with frills: *a frilled curtain; a frilly dress.* □ **à volants**

fringe [frindʒ] *noun* 1 a border of loose threads on a carpet, shawl *etc*: *Her red shawl has a black fringe.* □ **frange**

2 the outer area; the edge; the part farthest from the main part or centre of something: *on the fringe of the city.* □ **bordure**

■ *verb* to make or be a border around: *Trees fringed the pond.* □ **border**

frisk [frisk] *verb* to jump about playfully: *The lambs are frisking in the fields.* □ **folâtrer**

'**frisky** *adjective*. □ **fringant**

'**friskily** *adverb*. □ **folâtrement**

fritter ['fritə] *verb* (*often with* **away**) to throw away or waste gradually: *He frittered (away) all his money on gambling.* □ **gaspiller**

frivolous ['frivələs] *adjective* not serious; playful: *He wasted his time on frivolous pleasures.* □ **frivole**

'**frivolously** *adverb*. □ **frivolement**

'**frivolousness** *noun*. □ **frivolité**

fri'volity [-'vo-] – *plural* **fri'volities** – *noun* 1 frivolousness: *The frivolity of his behaviour.* □ **frivolité**

2 a frivolous action or thought: *I have no time for frivolities.* □ **frivolité**

frizz [friz] *verb* to (cause hair to) form a mass of tight curls: *The hairdresser frizzed her hair.* □ **friser**

'**frizzy** *adjective* (of hair) in very small curls: *He had frizzy red hair.* □ **crépu**

frock [frok] *noun* a woman's or girl's dress: *She wore a summer frock.* □ **robe**

frog [frog] *noun* a small jumping animal, without a tail, that lives on land and in water. □ **grenouille**

'**frogman** *noun* an underwater swimmer who uses breathing apparatus and flippers. □ **homme-grenouille**

frolic ['frolik] – *past tense, past participle* '**frolicked** – *verb* (of children, young animals *etc*) to play happily: *The puppies frolicked in the garden.* □ **folâtrer**

from [from] *preposition* 1 used before the place, thing, person, time *etc* that is the point at which an action, journey, period of time *etc* begins: *from Europe to Asia; from Monday to Friday; a letter from her father.* □ **de**

2 used to indicate that from which something or someone comes: *a quotation from Jane Austen.* □ **de**

3 used to indicate separation: *Take it from him.* □ **de**

4 used to indicate a cause or reason: *He is suffering from a cold.* □ **de**

from beginning to end completely, thoroughly: *We worked very hard on the project from beginning to end.* □ **du début à la fin**

from now on starting from this point in time and continuing forever: *You have bought the groceries so far, but from now on I'll go for them;* (often refers to an abrupt change in behaviour or opinion) *From now on I won't believe what you say because you have lied to me.* □ **dorénavant**

front [frʌnt] *noun* 1 the part of anything (intended to be) nearest the person who sees it; *usually* the most important part of anything: *the front of the house; the front of the picture;* (*also adjective*) *the front page.* □ **devant, première (page)**

2 the foremost part of anything in the direction in which it moves: *the front of the ship;* (*also adjective*) *the front seat of the bus.* □ **avant, de devant**

3 the part of a city or town that faces the sea: *We walked along the (sea) front.* □ **bord de mer**

4 (in war) the line of soliers nearest the enemy: *They are sending more soldiers to the front.* □ **front**

5 a boundary separating two masses of air of different temperatures: *A cold front is approaching from the Atlantic.* □ **front**

6 an outward appearance: *He put on a brave front.* □ **contenance**

7 a name sometimes given to a political movement: *the Popular Front for Liberation.* □ **front**

'**frontage** [-tidʒ] *noun* the front part of a building *etc*. □ **façade**

'**frontal** *adjective* from the front: *a frontal attack.* □ **frontal**

at the front of (standing *etc*) in the front part of something: *at the front of the house; They stood at the front of the crowd.* □ **devant**

in front (of) (placed, standing, moving *etc*) outside something on its front or forward-facing side: *There is a garden in front (of the house).* □ **devant**

frontier [frʌn'tiər] *noun* 1 a boundary between countries: *We crossed the frontier*; (*also adjective*) *a frontier town.* □ **frontière**

2 the farthest area of land on which people live and work, before the country becomes wild and deserted: *Many families went to make a new life on the frontier.* □ **frontière**

3 the limits or boundaries (of knowledge *etc*): *the frontiers of scientific knowledge.* □ **frontière**

frontispiece ['frʌntispiːs] *noun* a picture at the very beginning of a book. □ **frontispice**

frost [frost] *noun* 1 frozen dew, vapour *etc*: *The ground was covered with frost this morning.* □ **givre**

2 the coldness of weather needed to form ice: *There'll be (a) frost tomorrow.* □ **gel(ée)**

■ *verb* (*often with* **over** *or* **up**) to become covered with frost: *The windscreen of my car frosted up last night.* □ **(se) givrer**

'**frosty** *adjective* 1 covered with frost: *the frosty countryside.* □ **couvert de givre**

2 of behaviour, very unfriendly: *a frosty manner.* □ **glacial**

'**frostily** *adverb*. □ **glacialement**

frostbite *noun* injury caused to the body by very great cold: *He was suffering from frostbite in his feet.* □ **gelure**

'**frostbitten** *adjective*. □ **gelé**

froth [froθ] *noun* a mass of small bubbles on the top of a liquid *etc*: *Some types of beer have more froth than others.* □ **mousse**

■ *verb* to have or produce froth: *Mad dogs froth at the mouth.* □ **écumer**

'**frothy** *adjective* 1 containing froth: *frothy beer.* □ **mousseux**

2 light, like froth: *frothy silk dresses.* □ **vaporeux**

frown [fraun] *verb* to make the forehead wrinkle and the eyebrows move down (as a sign of worry, disapproval, deep thought *etc*): *He frowned at your bad behaviour.* □ **froncer les sourcils**

■ *noun* such a movement of the forehead and eyebrows: *a frown of disapproval.* □ **froncement de sourcils**

frown on/upon to disapprove of (something): *My family frowns (up)on smoking and drinking.* □ **désapprouver**

froze, frozen *see* **freeze.**

fruit [fruːt] *noun* 1 the part of a plant that produces the seed, *especially* when eaten as food: *The fruit of the vine is the grape.* □ **fruit**

2 a result; something gained as a result of hard work *etc*: *the fruit of his hard work.* □ **fruit**

■ *verb* to produce fruit: *This tree fruits early.* □ **donner (des fruits)**

'**fruitful** *adjective* producing (good) results: *a fruitful meeting.* □ **fructueux**

fruition [fru'iʃən] *noun* an actual result; the happening of something that was thought of, hoped for *etc*: *Her dreams came to fruition.* □ **réalisation**

'**fruitless** *adjective* useless; with no results: *a fruitless attempt.* □ **vain**

'**fruitlessly** *adverb*. □ **vainement**

'**fruity** *adjective* of or like fruit: *a fruity taste; a fruity drink.* □ **fruité**

fruit is a collective noun taking a singular verb: *Fruit is good for you*; *The tree bears fruit* (not *fruits*). The plural **fruits** is used in talking about different types of fruit: *oranges, mangoes and other fruits.*

frustrate ['frʌstreit] *verb* 1 to make (someone) feel disappointed, useless *etc*: *Staying at home all day frustrated her.* □ **frustrer**

2 to make useless: *His efforts were frustrated.* □ **faire échouer**

fru'stration *noun*. □ **frustration**

frus'trated *adjective* 1 disappointed; unhappy; not satisfied: *She is very unhappy and frustrated as a teacher.* □ **insatisfait**

2 unable to have the kind of job, career *etc* that one would like: *Literary critics are often frustrated writers.* □ **frustré**

fry[1] [frai] *verb* to cook in hot oil or fat: *Shall I fry the eggs or boil them?* □ **faire frire**

'**frying pan**, '**fry pan** *noun* a shallow pan, *usually* with a long handle, for frying food in. □ **poêle à frire**

out of the frying pan into the fire from a difficult or dangerous situation into a worse one: *His first marriage was unhappy but his second was even more unhappy – it was a real case of out of the frying pan into the fire.* □ **de Charybde en Scylla**

fry[2] [frai] *noun* a swarm of young, *especially* of fish. □ **fretin**

small fry unimportant people or things: *The local politicians are just small fry.* □ **menu fretin**

fudge [fʌdʒ] *noun* a type of soft, sugary sweet: *chocolate fudge*; *Would you like a piece of fudge?* □ **fondant**

fuel ['fjuəl] *noun* any substance by which a fire, engine *etc* is made to work (*eg* coal, oil, gasoline): *The machine ran out of fuel.* □ **combustible, carburant**

■ *verb* – *past tense, past participle* **'fuelled, fueled** – to give or take fuel: *The tanker will leave when it has finished fuelling/being fuelled.* □ **(se) ravitailler en combustible**

fugitive ['fjuːdʒətiv] *noun* a person who is running away (from the police *etc*): *a fugitive from justice.* □ **fugitif, ive**

fulfill, fulfil [ful'fil] – *past tense, past participle* **ful'filled** – *verb* 1 to carry out or perform (a task, promise *etc*): *He always fulfills his promises.* □ **accomplir**

2 to satisfy (requirements): *He fulfilled all the requirements for the job.* □ **satisfaire à**

ful'filled *adjective* (of a person) satisfied, having achieved everything he or she needs to have and to do: *With her family and her career, she is a very fulfilled person.* □ **comblé**

ful'fillment, ful'filment *noun*. □ **accomplissement**

---

fulfill, fulfil begins with **ful-** (not **full-**) and ends with **-fill** or **-fil**; the past tense is **fulfilled** and present participle **fulfilling.**

---

full [ful] *adjective* 1 holding or containing as much as possible: *My basket is full.* □ **plein**

2 complete: *a full year; a full account of what happened.*

grapefruit

blueberry

avocado

grapes

kiwi

orange

raspberry

pumpkin

pineapple

strawberry

cherry

raisin

lemon

plum

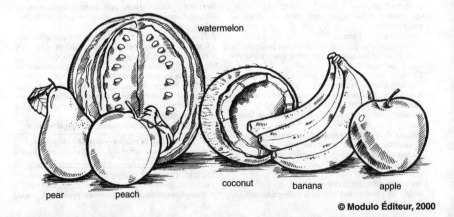

watermelon

pear

peach

coconut

banana

apple

□ **entier**
3 (of clothes) containing a large amount of material: *a full skirt*. □ **ample**
■ *adverb* 1 completely: *Fill the gas tank full*; *a full-length novel*. □ **complètement**
2 exactly; directly: *She hit him full in the face*. □ **en plein**
'**fully** *adverb* 1 completely: *He was fully aware of what was happening*; *fully-grown dogs*. □ **pleinement**
2 quite; at least: *It will take fully three days*. □ **au moins**
,full-'length *adjective* 1 complete; of the usual or standard length: *a full-length novel*. □ **pleine longueur**
2 down to the feet: *a full-length portrait*. □ **en pied**
full moon (the time of) the moon when it appears at its most complete: *There is a full moon tonight*. □ **pleine lune**
,full-'scale *adjective* of the same size as the subject: *a full-scale drawing of a flower*. □ **grandeur nature**
full stop a written or printed point (.) marking the end of a sentence; a period. □ **point**
,full-'time *adjective, adverb* occupying one's working time completely: *a full-time job*; *She works full-time now*. □ **à plein temps**
fully-fledged *adjective* 1 (as in bird) having grown its feathers and ready to fly. □ **qui a toutes ses plumes**
2 fully trained, qualified *etc*: *He's now a fully-fledged teacher*. □ **à part entière**
full of 1 filled with; containing or holding very much or very many: *The bus was full of people*. □ **plein de**
2 completely concerned with: *She rushed into the room full of the news*. □ **plein de**
in full completely: *Write your name in full*; *He paid his bill in full*. □ **en entier**
to the full to the greatest possible extent: *to enjoy life to the full*. □ **à fond**
fumble ['fʌmbl] *verb* to use one's hands awkwardly and with difficulty: *He fumbled with the key*; *She fumbled about in her bag for her key*. □ **tâtonner**
fume [fjuːm] *noun* smoke or vapour which can be seen or smelled: *He smelled the gas fumes*. □ **fumée, vapeur (de)**
■ *verb* to be very angry whilst trying not to show it: *He was fuming (with rage)*. □ **fulminer**
fun [fʌn] *noun* enjoyment; a good time: *They had a lot of fun at the party*; *Isn't this fun!* □ **plaisir**
'**funny** *adjective* 1 amusing; making one laugh: *a funny story*. □ **amusant**
2 strange; peculiar: *I heard a funny noise*. □ **drôle (de)**
'**funnily** *adverb*. □ **bizarrement**
for fun as a joke; for amusement: *The children threw stones for fun*. □ **pour s'amuser**
in fun as a joke; not seriously: *I said it in fun*. □ **pour rire**
make fun of to laugh at (someone, *usually* unkindly): *They made fun of her*. □ **se moquer de**
function ['fʌŋkʃən] *noun* a special job, use or duty (of a machine, part of the body, person *etc*): *The function of the brake is to stop the car*. □ **fonction**
■ *verb* (of a machine *etc*) to work; to operate: *This typewriter isn't functioning very well*. □ **fonctionner**

'**functional** *adjective* 1 designed to be useful rather than to look beautiful: *functional clothes*; *a functional building*. □ **fonctionnel**
2 able to operate: *It's an old car, but it's still functional*. □ **en état de marche**
fund [fʌnd] *noun* 1 a sum of money for a special purpose: *Have you given money to the repair fund?* □ **fonds**
2 a store or supply: *She has a fund of funny stories*. □ **répertoire**
funds *noun plural* money ready to spend: *Have you enough funds for your journey?* □ **argent**
fundamental [fʌndə'mentl] *adjective* of great importance; essential; basic: *Respect for law and order is fundamental to a peaceful society*. □ **fondamental**
■ *noun* a basic or essential part of any thing: *Learning to read is one of the fundamentals of education*. □ **fondement(s)**
,funda'mentally *adverb*: *He was fundamentally honest*. □ **foncièrement**
funeral ['fjuːnərəl] *noun* the ceremony before the burying or cremation of a dead body: *A large number of people attended the president's funeral*; (*also adjective*) *a funeral procession*. □ **funérailles**
funereal [fju'niəriəl] *adjective* mournful; suitable for a funeral: *to speak in funereal tones*. □ **funèbre**
fungus ['fʌŋgəs] – *plurals* '**fungi** [-gai], '**funguses** – *noun* any of several kinds of soft spongy plants without any leaves or green part: *edible fungi*; *That tree has a fungus growing on it*. □ **champignon**
'**fungicide** [-dʒisaid] *noun* a substance used to kill fungus. □ **fongicide**
funicular [fju'nikjulə]: **funicular** (**railway**) *noun* a kind of railway in which carriages are pulled uphill by cable *etc*. □ **funiculaire**
funk [fʌŋk] *noun* (a state of) fear: *He was in a funk over his exam*. □ **trouille**
■ *verb* not to do (something) because one is afraid: *She funked the appointment*. □ **se dégonfler**
funnel ['fʌnl] *noun* 1 a wide-mouthed tube through which liquid can be poured into a narrow bottle *etc*: *You will need a funnel if you are going to pour gasoline into that can*. □ **entonnoir**
2 a chimney on a ship *etc* through which smoke escapes. □ **cheminée**
funnily, funny *etc see* **fun**.
fur [fəː] *noun* 1 the thick, short, fine hair of certain animals. □ **poil, pelage**
2 the skin(s) of these animals, often used to make or decorate clothes *etc* for people: *a hat made of fur*; (*also adjective*) *a fur coat*. □ **fourrure**
3 a coat, cape *etc* made of fur: *She was wearing her fur*. □ **fourrure(s)**
furrier ['fʌriə] *noun* a person who (makes and) sells furs. □ **fourreur, euse**
'**furry** *adjective* 1 covered with fur: *a furry animal*. □ **à poil**
2 like fur: *furry material*. □ **doux comme de la fourrure**
furious, furiously *see* **fury**.
furl [fəːl] *verb* to roll up (a flag, sail or umbrella). □ **ferler (une voile), rouler (un parapluie)**

furnace ['fəːnis] *noun* a very hot oven or closed-in fireplace for melting iron ore, making steam for heating *etc*. □ **chaudière**

furnish ['fəːniʃ] *verb* 1 to provide (a house *etc*) with furniture: *We spent a lot of money on furnishing our house.* □ **meubler**

2 to give (what is necessary); to supply: *They furnished the library with new books.* □ **pourvoir (de)**

'**furnished** *adjective: a furnished flat.* □ **meublé**

'**furnishings** *noun plural* furniture, equipment *etc*: *The office had very expensive furnishings.* □ **ameublement**

'**furniture** [-tʃə] *noun* things in a house *etc* such as tables, chairs, beds *etc*: *Susan has to buy furniture for her new apartment.* □ **mobilier**

> **furniture** is a collective noun taking a singular verb: *His furniture is rather old.*

furrier *see* **fur**.

furrow ['fʌrou, 'fəː-] *noun* 1 a line cut into the earth by a plough: *The farmer planted potatoes in the furrows.* □ **sillon**

2 a line in the skin of the face; a wrinkle: *The furrows in his forehead made him look older.* □ **ride**

■ *verb* to make furrows in: *Her face was furrowed with worry.* □ **rider**

'**furrowed** *adjective.* □ **creusé de rides**

furry *see* **fur**.

further ['fəːðə] *adverb (sometimes* '**farther** ['faː-]) at or to a great distance or degree: *I cannot go any further.* □ **plus loin**

■ *adverb, adjective* more; in addition: *I cannot explain further; There is no further news.* □ **davantage**

■ *verb* to help (something) to proceed or go forward quickly: *He furthered our plans.* □ **favoriser**

,**further'more** [-'moː] *adverb* in addition (to what has been said): *Furthermore, I should like to point out.* □ **de plus**

'**furthest** *adverb (also* '**farthest** ['faː-]) at or to the greatest distance or degree: *Who lives furthest away?* □ **le plus loin**

furtive ['fəːtiv] *adjective* secretive; avoiding attention: *a furtive action/look.* □ **furtif**

fury ['fjuəri] – *plural* '**furies** – *noun* very great anger; rage: *She was in a terrible fury.* □ **fureur**

'**furious** *adjective* 1 very angry: *She was furious with him about it.* □ **furieux**

2 violent: *a furious argument.* □ **acharné**

like fury with great effort, enthusiasm *etc*: *He drove like fury.* □ **furieusement, avec acharnement**

fuse[1] [fjuːz] *verb* 1 to melt (together) as a result of great heat: *Copper and tin fuse together to make bronze.* □ **fusionner**

2 (of an electric circuit or appliance) to (cause to) stop working because of the melting of a fuse: *Suddenly all the lights fused; He fused all the lights.* □ **(faire) sauter**

■ *noun* a piece of easily-melted wire included in an electric circuit so that a dangerously high electric current will break the circuit and switch itself off: *She mended the fuse.* □ **fusible**

fusion ['fjuːʒən] *noun* 1 the act of melting together: *fusion of the metal pieces.* □ **fusion**

2 a very close joining of things: *the fusion of her ideas.* □ **fusion**

fuse[2] [fjuːz] *noun* a piece of material, a mechanical device *etc* which makes a bomb *etc* explode at a particular time: *He lit the fuse and waited for the explosion.* □ **détonateur**

fuselage ['fjuːzəlaːʒ] *noun* the body of an airplane: *Repairs were needed to the fuselage.* □ **fuselage**

fusion *see* **fuse**[1].

fuss [fʌs] *noun* unnecessary excitement, worry or activity, often about something unimportant: *Don't make such a fuss.* □ **histoires**

■ *verb* to be too concerned with or pay too much attention to (unimportant) details: *She fusses over children.* □ **faire des histoires**

'**fussy** *adjective* 1 too concerned with details; too particular; difficult to satisfy: *She is very fussy about her food.* □ **tatillon**

2 (of clothes *etc*) with too much decoration: *a very fussy hat.* □ **tarabiscoté**

'**fussily** *adverb.* □ **de façon tatillonne**

make a fuss of to pay a lot of attention to: *He always makes a fuss of his grandchildren.* □ **faire des tas d'histoires au sujet de**

futile ['fjuːtail] *adjective* useless; having no effect: *a futile attempt.* □ **futile**

fu'tility [-'ti-] *noun* uselessness: *He realized the futility of trying to continue his journey.* □ **futilité**

future ['fjuːtʃə] *noun* 1 (what is going to happen in) the time to come: *She was afraid of what the future might bring; (also adjective) his future wife.* □ **avenir; futur**

2 (a verb in) the future tense. □ **futur**

■ *adjective* (of a tense of a verb) indicating an action which will take place at a later time. □ **futur**

in future *adverb* after this; from now on: *Don't do that in future.* □ **à l'avenir**

fuzz [fʌz] *noun* a mass of soft, light material such as fine light hair *etc*: *The peaches were covered with fuzz.* □ **duvet**

'**fuzzy** *adjective* 1 covered with fuzz: *fuzzy material.* □ **floconneux**

2 indistinct; blurred; not clear: *The television picture was fuzzy.* □ **flou**

'**fuzzily** *adverb.* □ **flou**

'**fuzziness** *noun.* □ **flou**

Gg

gabble ['gabl] *verb* to talk very quickly and not very clearly. □ **bredouiller**

■ *noun* fast, incoherent talk. □ **bredouillement**

gable ['geibl] *noun* the triangular part of a wall of a building between the sloping parts of the roof. □ **pignon**

'**gabled** *adjective*: *a gabled roof*. □ **à pignon(s)**

gad [gad] – *past tense, past participle* '**gadded**: **gad about/around** *verb* to go around to one place after another (*usually* in order to amuse oneself): *They're forever gadding about now that the children are at school*. □ **vadrouiller**

gadget ['gadʒit] *noun* a *usually* small tool, machine *etc*: *a useful gadget for loosening bottle lids*. □ **gadget**

gaffe [gaf] *noun* something which ought not to have been said, done *etc*, a blunder. □ **gaffe**

gag [gag] – *past tense, past participle* **gagged** – *verb* 1 to prevent (a person) talking or making a noise, by putting something in or over his mouth: *The guards tied up and gagged the prisoners*. □ **bâillonner**

2 to choke and almost be sick. □ **avoir des haut-le-cœur**

■ *noun* something which is put in or over a person's mouth to prevent him talking or making a noise. □ **bâillon**

gage *see* **gauge.**

gaiety, gaily *see* **gay.**

gain [gein] *verb* 1 to obtain: *She quickly gained experience*. □ **gagner**

2 (*often with* **by** *or* **from**) to get (something good) by doing something: *What have I to gain by staying here?* □ **gagner (à)**

3 to have an increase in (something): *He gained strength after his illness*. □ **prendre**

4 (of a clock or watch) to go too fast: *This clock gains (four minutes a day)*. □ **avancer (de)**

■ *noun* 1 an increase (in weight *etc*): *a gain of one kilogram*. □ **gain, augmentation**

2 profits, advantage, wealth *etc*: *Her loss was my gain*; *He'd do anything for gain*. □ **profit, gain**

gain ground 1 to make progress. □ **gagner du terrain**

2 to become more influential: *Her views were once unacceptable but are now gaining ground rapidly*. □ **s'imposer**

gain on to get or come closer to (a person, thing *etc* that one is chasing): *Drive faster – the police car is gaining on us*. □ **rattraper**

gait [geit] *noun* (*plural rare*) the way in which a person or animal walks: *the old woman's shuffling gait*. □ **démarche**

gala ['gɑːlə, 'geilə] *noun* an occasion of entertainment and enjoyment out of doors: *a children's gala*. □ **gala, fête**

galaxy ['galəksi] – *plural* '**galaxies** – *noun* 1 a very large group of stars. □ **galaxie**

2 a large group of famous, impressive *etc* people, things *etc*: *a galaxy of entertainers*; *a galaxy of new cars*. □ **constellation**

the **Galaxy** *see* the **Milky Way** *under* **milk.**

gale [geil] *noun* a strong wind: *Many trees were blown down in the gale*. □ **grand vent**

gale force the speed or strength of a gale: *The winds reached gale force*; (*also adjective*) *gale force winds*. □ **force d'un vent; en tempête**

gall [gɔːl] *noun* 1 a bitter liquid which is stored in the gall bladder. □ **bile**

2 impudence: *He had the gall to say he was my friend after being so rude to me*. □ **effronterie**

■ *verb* to annoy (a person) very much: *It galls me to think that they are earning so much money*. □ **exaspérer**

gall bladder an organ of the body attached to the liver, in which gall is stored. □ **vésicule biliaire**

'**gallstone** *noun* a small hard object that is sometimes formed in the gall bladder. □ **calcul biliaire**

gallant ['galənt] *adjective* 1 brave: *a gallant soldier*. □ **brave**

2 which looks splendid or fine: *a gallant ship*. □ **superbe**

'**gallantly** *adverb*. □ **bravement**

'**gallantry** *noun* 1 bravery: *He won a medal for gallantry*. □ **bravoure**

2 politeness and attention to ladies: *The young man was noted for gallantry*. □ **galanterie**

galleon ['galiən] *noun* in former times, a large, *usually* Spanish, sailing-ship. □ **galion**

gallery ['galəri] – *plural* '**galleries** – *noun* 1 a large room or building in which paintings, statues *etc* are on show: *an art gallery*. □ **galerie**

2 an upper floor of seats in a church, theatre *etc*, especially (in a theatre) the top floor. □ **tribune, dernier balcon**

■ *adjective*: *gallery seats*. □ **de/du dernier balcon**

galley ['gali] *noun* 1 in former times, a long low ship with one deck, moved by oars (and often sails). □ **galère**

2 a ship's kitchen. □ **cuisine**

gallon ['galən] *noun* a measure for liquids equal to 4.55 litres. □ **gallon**

gallons (of) (*loosely*) a large amount (of something liquid): *The children drank gallons of orange juice*. □ **des litres et des litres de**

gallop ['galəp] *noun* (a period of riding at) the fastest pace of a horse: *She took the horse out for a gallop*; *The horse went off at a gallop*. □ **galop**

■ *verb* 1 (of a horse) to move at a gallop: *The horse galloped around the field*. □ **galoper**

2 (*with* **through**) to do, say *etc* (something) very quickly: *She galloped through the work*. □ **faire (qqch.) au galop**

'**galloping** *adjective* increasing very quickly: *galloping inflation*. □ **galopant**

gallows ['galouz] *noun singular* a wooden frame on which criminals were hanged. □ **gibet**

galore [gə'lɔː] *adjective* (*placed immediately after noun*) in large amounts, numbers: *There are bookshops galore in this town*. □ **en abondance**

galvanize, galvanise ['galvənaiz] *verb* 1 to cover (iron or steel) with a thin layer of zinc to prevent it rusting. □ **galvaniser**

2 (*with* **into**) to cause or move (a person) to do something: *The threat of losing their jobs galvanized the men*

into action. □ **galvaniser**

gambit ['gambit] *noun* **1** a first move in a game, *especially* chess. □ **gambit**

2 (*usually* **opening gambit**) a starting remark in a conversation. □ **manœuvre d'approche**

gamble ['gambl] *verb* to risk losing money on the result of a horse-race *etc.* □ **jouer**

■ *noun* (something which involves) a risk: *The whole business was a bit of a gamble.* □ **entreprise risquée**

'**gambler** *noun.* □ **joueur, euse**

'**gambling** *noun.* □ **jeu (d'argent)**

take a gamble to do something risky in the hope that it will succeed. □ **prendre un risque**

gambol ['gambl] – *past tense, past participle* '**gambolled**, '**gamboled** – *verb* (*usually* only of lambs) to jump around playfully. □ **gambader**

game [geim] *noun* **1** an enjoyable activity, which *eg* children play: *a game of pretending.* □ **jeu**

2 a competitive form of activity, with rules: *Football, tennis and chess are games.* □ **jeu**

3 a match or part of a match: *a game of tennis; winning (by) three games to one.* □ **partie**

4 (the flesh of) certain birds and animals which are killed for sport: *She's very fond of game;* (*also adjective*) *a game bird.* □ **(à/de) gibier**

■ *adjective* brave; willing; ready: *a game old guy; game for anything.* □ **prêt à**

'**gamely** *adverb* courageously. □ **courageusement**

games *noun plural* an athletic competition, sometimes with other sports: *the Olympic Games.* □ **jeux**

'**gamekeeper** *noun* a person who looks after game. □ **garde-chasse**

game point a winning point. □ **balle de match**

game reserve an area of land set aside for the protection of animals. □ **parc à gibier**

game warden a person who looks after a game reserve or, in the United States, game. □ **garde-chasse**

the game is up the plan or trick has failed or has been found out. □ **tout est fichu**

gamma ['gamə]: **gamma rays** a powerful form of radiation. □ **rayons gamma**

gander ['gandə] *noun* a male goose. □ **jars**

gang [gaŋ] *noun* **1** a number (of workmen *etc*) working together: *a gang of men working on the railway.* □ **équipe**

2 a group (of people), *usually* formed for a bad purpose: *a gang of jewel thieves.* □ **bande, gang**

'**gangster** *noun* a member of a gang of criminals. □ **gangster**

gang up on to join or act with a person *etc* against (some other person *etc*). □ **se liguer (avec... contre...)**

gang up with to join or act with. □ **s'allier avec**

gangling ['gaŋgliŋ] *adjective* tall, very thin and *usually* awkward. □ **dégingandé**

gangplank ['gaŋplaŋk] *noun* (*also* '**gangway**) a movable bridge by which to get on or off a boat. □ **passerelle**

gangrene ['gaŋgriːn] *noun* the decay of a part of the body of a living person, animal *etc*, because the blood supply to that part of the body has stopped. □ **gangrène**

'**gangrenous** [-grə-] *adjective.* □ **gangreneux**

gangster *see* **gang**.

gantry ['gantri] – *plural* '**gantries** – *noun* a bridge like structure which supports a crane, railway signals *etc*. □ **portique**

gap [gap] *noun* a break or open space: *a gap between his teeth.* □ **espace, vide**

gape [geip] *verb* to stare with open mouth, *eg* in surprise: *The children gaped at the monkeys.* □ **rester bouche bée**

'**gaping** *adjective* wide open: *a gaping hole.* □ **béant**

garage [gəˈraːʒ] *noun* **1** a building in which a car *etc* is kept: *a house with a garage; Please park the car in the garage when you come home.* □ **garage**

2 a building where cars are repaired and *usually* gasoline, oil *etc* is sold: *She has taken her car to the garage to be repaired.* □ **garage**

garbage ['gaːbidʒ] *noun* waste material, refuse, rubbish. □ **ordures**

■ *adjective*: *There is a garbage chute at the end of the corridor.* □ **à ordures**

garbage-can trash can; a container for waste material. □ **poubelle**

garbled ['gaːbld] *adjective* (of a story *etc*) mixed up: *The child gave a garbled account of the accident.* □ **embrouillé, confus**

garden ['gaːdn] *noun* a piece of ground on which flowers, vegetables *etc* are grown: *a small garden at the front of the house;* (*also adjective*) *a garden slug.* □ **(de) jardin**

■ *verb* to work in a garden, *usually* as a hobby: *The old lady does not garden much.* □ **jardiner**

'**gardener** *noun* a person who works in, and looks after, a garden. □ **jardinier, ière**

'**gardening** *noun* the work of looking after a garden: *Gardening is his favourite hobby;* (*also adjective*) *gardening clothes/tools.* □ **(de) jardinage**

'**gardens** *noun singular or plural* a park, *especially* one where animals are kept or special trees or flowers are grown: *zoological/botanical gardens.* □ **jardin, parc**

garden party a large (*usually* formal) party, held in the garden of a house *etc*: *They planned a garden party in order to raise money for sick children.* □ **garden party**

gargle ['gaːgl] *verb* to wash the throat *eg* with a soothing liquid, by letting the liquid lie in the throat and breathing out against it. □ **se gargariser**

garish ['geəriʃ] *adjective* unpleasantly bright or showy: *His shirts are very garish.* □ **criard**

'**garishly** *adverb.* □ **avec un luxe criard**

'**garishness** *noun.* □ **aspect tapageur**

garland ['gaːlənd] *noun* flowers or leaves tied or woven into a circle: *The islanders wore garlands of flowers around their heads.* □ **guirlande**

garlic ['gaːlik] *noun* a plant with a bulb shaped like an onion, which has a strong taste and smell and is used in cooking: *The sauce is flavoured with garlic.* □ **ail**

garment ['gaːmənt] *noun* an article of clothing: *This shop sells ladies' garments.* □ **vêtement**

garnish ['gaːniʃ] *verb* to decorate (a dish of food): *Parsley is often used to garnish salads.* □ **garnir**

■ *noun* (an) edible decoration added to food. □

garniture

garret ['garət] *noun* a *usually* small and sometimes dark room just under the roof of a house: *She was poor and lived in a garret.* □ **grenier**

garrison ['garisn] *noun* a number of soldiers, for guarding a fortress, town *etc*. □ **garnison**
■ *adjective: a garrison town.* □ **de garnison**
■ *verb* to supply (a town *etc*) with troops to guard it. □ **placer une garnison dans**

garrulous ['garələs] *adjective* fond of talking: *a garrulous old man.* □ **bavard**
'garrulously *adverb*. □ **avec volubilité**
gar'rulity [-'ruː-] *noun*. □ **loquacité**
'garrulousness *noun*. □ **loquacité**

gas [gas] *noun* **1** a substance like air: *Oxygen is a gas.* □ **gaz**
2 any gas which is used for heating, cooking *etc*. □ **gaz**
3 a gas which is used by dentists as an anaesthetic. □ **gaz**
4 a poisonous or irritating gas used in war *etc*: *The police used tear gas to control the riot.* □ **gaz de combat**
5 gasoline □ **essence**
■ *verb – past tense, past participle* **gassed** – to poison or kill (a person or animal) with gas: *He was gassed during World War I.* □ **asphyxier, gazer**

gaseous ['gasiəs] *adjective* of or like (a) gas: *a gaseous substance.* □ **gazeux**
'gassy *adjective* full of gas: *gassy lemonade.* □ **gazeux**
'gassiness *noun*. □ **nature/aspect gazeux**

gas chamber a room in which people are killed by means of gas: *Many people were sent to the gas chamber in World War II.* □ **chambre à gaz**

gas mask something which is used to cover the face to prevent a person breathing poisonous gas. □ **masque à gaz**

gas meter an instrument which measures the amount of gas which is used. □ **compteur à gaz**

gasoline ['gasəliːn] *noun* (*also* **gas**) a petroleum product used as a fuel for motor vehicles. □ **essence**

gas station a place where gasoline is sold. □ **poste d'essence, station service**

'gasworks *noun singular* a place where gas is made: *The gasworks is rather an ugly building.* □ **usine à gaz**

gash [gaʃ] *noun* a deep, open cut or wound: *a gash on her cheek.* □ **balafre**

gasp [gaːsp] *noun* the sound made by suddenly breathing in, *eg* because of surprise or sudden pain: *a gasp of fear.* □ **hoquet**
■ *verb: He gasped with pain.* □ **haleter**
be gasping for to want (something) very much: *I'm gasping for a cigarette.* □ **mourir d'envie de**

gastric ['gastrik] *adjective* of the stomach: *a gastric ulcer.* □ **gastrique**

gastronomic [gastrə'nomik] *adjective* of good food: *the gastronomic delights of France.* □ **gastronomique**

gate [geit] *noun* (a metal, wooden *etc* doorlike object which closes) the opening in a wall, fence *etc* through which people *etc* pass: *I'll meet you at the park gate(s).* □ **porte, barrière**

'gate crash *verb* to enter or go to (a party, meeting *etc*) without being invited or without paying. □ **faire l'intrus**

'gate crasher *noun*. □ **intrus, use**

'gate post *noun* a post to which a gate is fixed. □ **montant de porte**

'gateway *noun* an opening or entrance into a city *etc*, which contains a gate. □ **porte, portail**

gather ['gaðə] *verb* **1** to (cause to) come together in one place: *A crowd of people gathered near the accident.* □ **(s')assembler, (se) rassembler**
2 to learn (from what has been seen, heard *etc*): *I gather you are leaving tomorrow.* □ **conclure**
3 to collect or get: *He gathered flowers; She gathered her things and went off.* □ **cueillir, amasser**
4 to pull (material) into small folds and stitch together: *She gathered the skirt at the waist.* □ **froncer**
■ *noun* a fold in material, a piece of clothing *etc*. □ **fronce**

'gathering *noun* a meeting of people: *a family gathering.* □ **réunion**

gather around to come together around a person, thing *etc*: *Will everyone please gather around?* □ **se rassembler autour (de)**

gather together to come or bring together, in a group: *She gathered her books and papers together.* □ **(se) rassembler**

gauche [gouʃ] *adjective* awkward and clumsy: *a gauche young man.* □ **gauche**

gaudy ['goːdi] *adjective* very bright in colour: *a bird's gaudy plumage; gaudy clothes.* □ **criard**

gauge, (*also, especially American*) **gage** [geidʒ] *verb* **1** to measure (something) very accurately: *They gauged the hours of sunshine.* □ **mesurer**
2 to estimate, judge: *Can you gauge his willingness to help?* □ **évaluer**
■ *noun* **1** an instrument for measuring amount, size, speed *etc*: *a gas gauge.* □ **jauge**
2 a standard size (of wire, bullets *etc*): *gauge wire.* □ **calibre**
3 the distance between the rails of a railway line. □ **écartement**

gaunt [goːnt] *adjective* (of a person) thin or thin-faced: *a gaunt old woman.* □ **émacié**
'gauntness *noun*. □ **émaciation**

gauze [goːz] *noun* thin cloth used *eg* to cover wounds: *a length of gauze*; (*also adjective*) *a gauze bandage.* □ **(de) gaze**

gave *see* **give**.

gawky ['goːki] *adjective* (of a person) looking clumsy or awkward: *She is tall and gawky.* □ **gauche**

gay [gei] *adjective* **1** happy or making people happy: *The children were gay and cheerful; gay music.* □ **gai**
2 bright: *gay colours.* □ **gai**
'gaily *adverb*. □ **gaiement**

gaiety ['geiəti] *noun* **1** (an occasion of) fun or happiness: *They joined in the gaiety.* □ **amusement**
2 the state of being gay: *the gaiety of the music.* □ **gaieté**

gaze [geiz] *verb* to look steadily (at) for some time, *usually* in surprise, out of interest *etc*. □ **fixer**
■ *noun* a long steady look. □ **regard fixe**

gazelle [gə'zel] – *plurals* **ga'zelles, ga'zelle** – *noun* a type of small antelope. □ **gazelle**

gazette [gə'zet] *noun* a type of newspaper that has lists of government notices. □ **journal officiel**

gazetteer [gazə'tiə] *noun* a dictionary of geographical names. □ **répertoire géographique**

gear [giə] *noun* **1** (*usually in plural*) a set of toothed wheels which act together to carry motion: *a car with automatic gears.* □ **engrenage**
2 a combination of these wheels, *eg* in a car: *The car is in first gear.* □ **changement de vitesse**
3 a mechanism used for a particular purpose: *an airplane's landing gear.* □ **mécanisme**
4 the things needed for a particular job, sport *etc*: *sports gear.* □ **équipement**
'**gearbox** *noun* the part of a car *etc* which has the gears in it. □ **boîte de vitesses**
gear shift (*North American*), **gear lever/change/stick** (*British*) the apparatus in a car *etc* which is used to change gear. □ **levier de vitesse**

geese *see* **goose**.

geisha ['geiʃə] *noun* (*often* **geisha girl**) a Japanese girl trained to entertain (men) by her conversation, dancing *etc*. □ **geisha**

gelatin(e) ['dʒelətin] *noun* a jelly like substance made from hooves, animal bones *etc* and used in food. □ **gélatine**

gelignite ['dʒelignait] *noun* an explosive: *The bandits blew up the bridge with gelignite.* □ **plastic**

gem [dʒem] *noun* **1** a precious stone *especially* when cut into a particular shape, *eg* for a ring or necklace. □ **pierre précieuse**
2 anything or anyone thought to be especially good: *This picture is the gem of my collection.* □ **joyau**
'**gemstone** *noun* a precious or semi-precious stone *especially* before it is cut into shape. □ **pierre gemme**

gender ['dʒendə] *noun* any of a number of classes into which nouns and pronouns can be divided (*eg* masculine, feminine, neuter). □ **genre**

gene [dʒiːn] *noun* any of the basic elements of heredity, passed from parents to their offspring: *If the children are red-haired, one of their parents must have a gene for red hair.* □ **gène**

genetic [dʒə'netik] *adjective* of genes or genetics: *a genetic abnormality.* □ **génétique**
genetics [dʒə'netiks] *noun singular* the science of heredity. □ **génétique**

genealogy [dʒiːni'alədʒi] – *plural* **gene'alogies** – **1** *noun* the history of families from generation to generation: *the genealogy of the Tremblay family.* □ **généalogie**
2 a plan, list *etc* of the ancestors of a person or family. □ **généalogie**
,**genea'logical** [-'lo-] *adjective*. □ **généalogique**
,**gene'alogist** *noun* a person who studies or makes genealogies. □ **généalogiste**

general ['dʒenərəl] *adjective* **1** of, involving *etc* all, most or very many people, things *etc*: *The general feeling is that he is stupid; His general knowledge is good although he is not good at mathematics.* □ **général**
2 covering a large number of cases: *a general rule.* □ **général**

3 without details: *I'll just give you a general idea of the plan.* □ **général**
4 (as part of an official title) chief: *the Postmaster General.* □ **général**
■ *noun* in the Canadian army, (a person of) the highest rank: *General Smith.* □ **général, ale**
'**generalize**, '**generalise** *verb* **1** to make a general rule *etc* that can be applied to many cases, based on a number of cases: *She's trying to generalize from only two examples.* □ **généraliser**
2 to talk (about something) in general terms: *We should stop generalizing and discuss each problem separately.* □ **dire des généralités**
,**generali'zation**, ,**generali'sation** *noun*. □ **généralisation**
'**generally** *adverb* usually; by most people; on the whole: *She is generally disliked; She generally wins.* □ **généralement**
general election an election in which the voters in every constituency are involved. □ **élections générales**
general store a shop that sells a wide range of goods. □ **grand magasin**
as a general rule usually; in most cases: *As a general rule, we don't employ unskilled workers.* □ **en règle générale**
in general usually; in most cases; most of (a group of people *etc*): *People in general were not very sympathetic; People were in general not very sympathetic.* □ **en général**
the general public the people of a town, country *etc*, considered as a group. □ **le grand public**

generate ['dʒenəreit] *verb* to cause or produce: *This machine generates electricity; His suggestions generated a lot of ill-feeling.* □ **produire, susciter**
,**gene'ration** *noun* **1** one stage in the descent of a family: *All three generations – children, parents and grandparents – lived together quite happily.* □ **génération**
2 people born at about the same time: *People of my generation all think the same way about this.* □ **génération**
'**generator** *noun* a machine which produces electricity, gas *etc*: *The hospital has an emergency generator.* □ **génératrice**

generic [dʒə'nerik] *adjective* (of a name, term *etc*) referring to several similar objects *etc*: *'Furniture' is a generic term for chairs, tables etc.* □ **générique**

generous ['dʒenərəs] *adjective* (*negative* **ungenerous**)
1 willing to give a lot of money, time *etc* for some purpose: *a generous giver; It is very generous of you to pay for our holiday.* □ **généreux**
2 large; larger than necessary: *a generous sum of money; a generous piece of cake.* □ **généreux**
3 kind, willing to forgive: *Try to be generous and forgive; a person's generous nature/remarks.* □ **généreux**
'**generously** *adverb*. □ **généreusement**
,**gene'rosity** [-'rosəti] *noun*. □ **générosité**

genetic, genetics *see* **gene**.

genial ['dʒiːniəl] *adjective* kindly; friendly; good-natured: *a genial person.* □ **aimable**
'**genially** *adverb*. □ **aimablement**
,**geni'ality** [-'a-] *noun*. □ **amabilité**

genitive ['dʒenitiv] *noun* (the case or form of) a noun, pronoun *etc* which shows possession: *In John's hat, 'John's' is in the genitive/is a genitive*; (*also adjective*) *the genitive case.* □ **génitif**

genius ['dʒiːnjəs] – *plural* '**geniuses** – *noun* a person who is very clever: *The new professor of mathematics has been described as a genius.* □ **génie**

genocide ['dʒenəsaid] *noun* the deliberate killing of a race of people. □ **génocide**

gent, gents *see* **gentleman.**

genteel [dʒən'tiːl] *adjective* acting, talking *etc* with a very great (often too great) attention to the rules of polite behaviour: *He was laughed at for being too genteel.* □ **maniéré**
gen'teelly *adverb.* □ **de façon maniérée**
gen'teelness *noun.* □ **manières affectées**

gentile ['dʒentail] *noun, adjective* (*also with capital: especially* in the Bible) (of) anyone who is not a Jew. □ **Gentil, ile; des Gentils**

gentility [dʒən'tiləti] *noun* good manners, often to too great an extent: *She was laughed at for her gentility.* □ **manières affectées**

gentle ['dʒentl] *adjective* **1** (of people) behaving, talking *etc* in a mild, kindly, pleasant way: *a gentle old lady*; *The doctor was very gentle.* □ **doux**
2 not strong or rough: *a gentle breeze.* □ **doux**
3 (of hills) rising gradually: *a gentle slope.* □ **doux**
'**gently** *adverb.* □ **doucement**
'**gentleness** *noun.* □ **douceur**

gentleman ['dʒentlmən] – *plural* '**gentlemen** – *noun* (*abbreviation* **gent**) **1** a polite word for a man: *Two gentlemen arrived this morning.* □ **monsieur**
2 a polite, well-mannered man: *He's a real gentleman.* □ **gentleman**
'**gentlemanly** *adjective* (of men) polite; well-mannered: *gentlemanly behaviour.* □ **distingué**
gents *noun* (usually with **the**) a public toilet for men: *Where's the nearest gents?* □ **toilettes (pour hommes)**

gently *see* **gentle.**

genuine ['dʒenjuin] *adjective* **1** real; not fake or artificial: *a genuine pearl; a genuine antique.* □ **authentique**
2 honest; sincere: *She shows a genuine desire to improve.* □ **sincère**
'**genuinely** *adverb*: *He was genuinely pleased to see her.* □ **sincèrement**

geography [dʒi'ogrəfi] *noun* the science that describes the surface of the earth and its inhabitants: *She is studying geography.* □ **géographie**
ge'ographer *noun* a person who studies geography. □ **géographe**
geographic(al) [dʒiə'grafik(əl)] *adjective*: *a geographical study of the area.* □ **géographique**
,geo'graphically *adverb.* □ **géographiquement**

geology [dʒi'olədʒi] *noun* the science of the history and development of the earth as shown by rocks *etc*: *He is studying geology.* □ **géologie**
geological [dʒiə'lodʒikəl] *adjective*: *a geological survey.* □ **géologique**
,geo'logically *adverb.* □ **géologiquement**
ge'ologist *noun.* □ **géologue**

geometry [dʒi'omətri] *noun* a branch of mathematics dealing with the study of lines, angles *etc*: *She is studying geometry.* □ **géométrie**
geometric(al) [dʒiə'metrik(əl)] *adjective* made up of lines, circles *etc* and with a regular shape: *a geometrical design on wallpaper.* □ **géométrique**
,geo'metrically *adverb.* □ **géométriquement**

geriatrics [dʒeri'atriks] *noun singular* the branch of medicine concerned with the diseases of old age. □ **gériatrie**
,geri'atric *adjective* for the very old (and ill): *a geriatric hospital.* □ **gériatrique**

germ [dʒəːm] *noun* **1** a very tiny animal or plant that causes disease: *Disinfectant kills germs.* □ **microbe**
2 the small beginning (of anything): *the germ of an idea.* □ **germe**

German ['dʒəːmən] *adjective* of Germany or its inhabitants: *German beer was served during the harvest celebrations.* □ **allemand, ande**
■ *noun* someone who is a native of Germany; the language of Germany: *A German wearing a dark coat and hat was given the part in the play; Greta is the friend who taught me how to speak German.* □ **Allemand, allemand**

germinate ['dʒəːmineit] *verb* to (cause *eg* a seed to) begin to grow. □ **(faire) germer**
,germi'nation *noun.* □ **germination**

gesticulate [dʒe'stikjuleit] *verb* to wave one's hands and arms about when speaking: *He gesticulates wildly when he is angry.* □ **gesticuler**

gesture ['dʒestʃə] *noun* a movement of the head, hand *etc* to express an idea *etc*: *The speaker emphasized her words with violent gestures.* □ **geste**
■ *verb* to make a gesture or gestures: *I gestured to them to keep quiet.* □ **faire signe à**

get [get] – *past tense* **got** [got]: *past participle* **got** or **gotten** ['gotn] – *verb* **1** to receive or obtain: *I got a letter this morning.* □ **recevoir**
2 to bring or buy: *Please get me some food.* □ **procurer, aller chercher**
3 to (manage to) move, go, take, put *etc*: *He couldn't get across the river; I got the book down from the shelf.* □ **(faire) parvenir**
4 to cause to be in a certain condition *etc*: *You'll get me into trouble.* □ **(se) placer**
5 to become: *You're getting old.* □ **devenir**
6 to persuade: *I'll try to get him to go.* □ **persuader**
7 to arrive: *When did they get home?* □ **arriver**
8 to succeed (in doing) or to happen (to do) something: *I'll soon get to know the neighbours; I got the book read last night.* □ **arriver à**
9 to catch (a disease *etc*): *She got measles last week.* □ **attraper**
10 to catch (someone): *The police will soon get the thief.* □ **attraper**
11 to understand: *I didn't get the point of their story.* □ **comprendre**

'**getaway** *noun* an escape: *The thieves made their getaway in a stolen car*; (*also adjective*) *a getaway car.* □ **(de) fuite**

'get-together *noun* an informal meeting. □ **réunion**

'get-up *noun* clothes, *usually* odd or unattractive: *She wore a very strange get-up at the party.* □ **accoutrement**

be getting on for to be close to (a particular age, time *etc*): *He must be getting on for sixty at least.* □ **avoir/être près de**

get about 1 (of stories, rumours *etc*) to become well known: *I don't know how the story got about that she was leaving.* □ **se répandre**

2 to be able to move or travel about, often of people who have been ill: *She didn't get about much after her operation.* □ **se déplacer**

get across to be or make (something) understood: *This is something which rarely gets across to the general public.* □ **(se) faire comprendre**

get ahead to make progress; to be successful: *If you want to get ahead, you must work hard.* □ **avancer, faire des progrès**

get along (*often with* **with**) to be friendly or on good terms (with someone): *I get along very well with her*; *The children just cannot get along together.* □ **s'entendre (avec)**

get around 1 (of stories, rumours *etc*) to become well known: *I don't know how the story got around that she was getting married.* □ **circuler**

2 (of people) to be active or involved in many activities: *She really gets around, doesn't she!* □ **être actif**

3 to persuade (a person *etc*) to do something to one's own advantage: *We can always get around our grandfather by giving him a big smile.* □ **embobiner**

4 to solve (a problem *etc*): *We can easily get around these few difficulties.* □ **(con)tourner**

get around to to manage to (do something): *I don't know when I'll get around to (painting) the door.* □ **arriver à**

get at 1 to reach (a place, thing *etc*): *The farm is very difficult to get at.* □ **atteindre**

2 to suggest or imply (something): *What are you getting at?* □ **sous-entendre**

3 to point out (a person's faults) or make fun of (a person): *He's always getting at me.* □ **s'en prendre à**

get away 1 to (be able to) leave: *I usually get away (from the office) at four-thirty.* □ **(être libre de) partir**

2 to escape: *The thieves got away in a stolen car.* □ **s'échapper**

get away with to do (something bad) without being punished for it: *Murder is a serious crime and one rarely gets away with it.* □ **s'en tirer (sans ennuis)**

get back 1 to move away: *The policeman told the crowd to get back.* □ **reculer**

2 to retrieve: *She eventually got back the book she had lent him.* □ **récupérer**

get by to manage: *I can't get by on such a small salary.* □ **se débrouiller**

get down to make (a person) sad: *Working in this place really gets me down.* □ **déprimer**

get down to to begin to work (hard) at: *I must get down to work tonight, as the exams start next week.* □ **se mettre à**

get in to send for (a person): *The television is broken –*

we'll need to get somebody in to repair it. □ **faire venir**

get into 1 to put on (clothes *etc*): *Get into your pyjamas.* □ **mettre**

2 to begin to be in a particular state or behave in a particular way: *He got into a temper.* □ **se mettre (en colère)**

3 to affect strangely: *I don't know what has got into him* (= I don't know why he is behaving the way he is). □ **obséder**

get nowhere to make no progress: *You'll get nowhere if you follow his instructions.* □ **n'arriver à rien**

get off 1 to take off or remove (clothes, marks *etc*): *I can't get my boots off; I'll never get these stains off (my dress).* □ **enlever**

2 to change (the subject which one is talking, writing *etc* about): *We've rather got off the subject.* □ **s'éloigner (de)**

get on 1 to make progress or be successful: *How are you getting on in your new job?* □ **progresser**

2 to work, live *etc* in a friendly way: *We get on very well together; I get on well with her.* □ **(bien) s'entendre (avec)**

3 to grow old: *Our doctor is getting on a bit now.* □ **se faire vieux**

4 to put (clothes *etc*) on: *Go and get your coat on.* □ **mettre**

5 to continue doing something: *I must get on, so please don't interrupt me; I must get on with my work.* □ **continuer**

get out 1 to leave or escape: *No one knows how the lion got out.* □ **sortir, s'échapper**

2 (of information) to become known: *I've no idea how word got out that you were leaving.* □ **se répandre**

get out of to (help a person *etc* to) avoid doing something: *I wonder how I can get out of washing the dishes; How can I get him out of going to the party?* □ **(se) soustraire à**

get over 1 to recover from (an illness, surprise, disappointment *etc*): *I've got over my cold now; I can't get over her leaving so suddenly.* □ **se remettre**

2 to manage to make (oneself or something) understood: *We must get our message over to the general public.* □ **(se) faire comprendre**

3 (*with* **with**) to do (something one does not want to do): *I'm not looking forward to this meeting, but let's get it over (with).* □ **en finir avec**

get there to succeed or make progress: *There have been a lot of problems but we're getting there.* □ **réussir**

get through 1 to finish (work *etc*): *We got through a lot of work today.* □ **terminer**

2 to pass (an examination). □ **réussir**

3 to arrive, *usually* with some difficulty: *The food got through to the fort despite the enemy's attempts to stop it.* □ **parvenir**

4 to make oneself understood: *I just can't get through to her any more.* □ **se faire comprendre**

get together to meet: *We usually get together once a week.* □ **se réunir**

get up 1 to (cause to) get out of bed: *I got up at seven o'clock; Get John up at seven o'clock.* □ **se/faire lever**

2 to stand up. □ **(se) lever**

3 to increase (*usually* speed). □ **prendre (de la vitesse)**
4 to arrange, organize or prepare (something): *We must get up some sort of celebration for her when she leaves.* □ **organiser**

get worse and worse *verb* to deteriorate gradually; to have more and more adverse effects: *Ralph's behaviour got worse and worse until he was expelled from school; Alzheimer patients lose their memory completely as their disease gets worse and worse.* □ **aller de mal en pis**

geyser ['gaizə] *noun* an underground spring that produces and sends out hot water and steam: *There are geysers in Iceland and New Zealand.* □ **geyser**

ghastly ['gɑːstli] *adjective* **1** very bad, ugly *etc*: *a ghastly mistake.* □ **affreux**
2 horrible; terrible: *a ghastly murder; a ghastly experience.* □ **horrible**
3 ill; upset: *I felt ghastly when I had flu.* □ **horriblement mal**
'**ghastliness** *noun.* □ **horreur**

ghetto ['getou] – *plural* '**ghetto(e)s** – *noun* a (poor) part of a city *etc* in which a certain group of people (*especially* immigrants) lives: *Large cities like New York have many ghettoes.* □ **ghetto**

ghost [goust] *noun* a spirit, *usually* of a dead person: *Do you believe in ghosts?; Hamlet thought he saw his father's ghost.* □ **fantôme**
'**ghostly** *adjective* of or like a ghost or ghosts: *a ghostly figure.* □ **fantomatique**
give up the ghost to die. □ **rendre l'âme**

giant ['dʒaiənt] – *feminine* '**giantess** – *noun* **1** (in fairy stories *etc*) a huge person: *Jack met a giant when he climbed the beanstalk.* □ **géant, ante**
2 a person of unusually great height and size. □ **géant, ante**
3 a person of very great ability or importance: *Einstein is one of the giants of twentieth century science.* □ **géant, ante**
■ *adjective* of unusually great height or size: *a giant cod; a giant fern.* □ **géant**

gibber ['dʒibə] *verb* to make meaningless noises: *He was gibbering with fear.* □ **bégayer**
'**gibberish** [-riʃ] *noun* nonsense: *His explanations are just gibberish to me.* □ **charabia**

gibbet ['dʒibit] *noun* a gallows in the shape C on which criminals used to be executed or hung up after execution. □ **gibet**

gibbon ['gibən] *noun* a type of ape with long arms. □ **gibbon**

gibe *see* **jibe.**

giblets ['dʒiblits] *noun plural* the eatable parts from inside a chicken *etc*, *eg* heart and liver. □ **abats**

giddy ['gidi] *adjective* feeling that one is going to fall over, or that everything is spinning around: *I was dancing around so fast that I felt quite giddy; a giddy feeling.* □ **pris de vertige**
'**giddily** *adverb.* □ **vertigineusement**
'**giddiness** *noun.* □ **vertige**

gift [gift] *noun* **1** something given willingly, *eg* as a present: *a birthday gift.* □ **cadeau**
2 a natural ability: *She has a gift for music.* □ **don**
■ *verb* to give or present as a gift: *This painting was gifted by our former chairwoman.* □ **offrir**
'**gifted** *adjective* having very great natural ability: *a gifted musician/child.* □ **doué**
gift of the gab the ability to talk fluently and persuasively. □ **faconde**

gigantic [dʒai'gantik] *adjective* very large: *a gigantic wave.* □ **gigantesque**

giggle ['gigl] *verb* to laugh in a nervous or silly way. □ **rire nerveusement**
■ *noun* a laugh of this kind. □ **petit rire nerveux**
'**giggler** *noun.* □ **personne qui rit nerveusement**
'**giggly** *adjective* giggling often: *a giggly young child.* □ **qui rit nerveusement**

gild [gild] *verb* to cover with gilt: *We could gild the frame of that picture.* □ **dorer**

gill [gil] *noun* **1** one of the openings on the side of a fish's head through which it breathes. □ **ouïes (pl.)**
2 a leaf-like structure on the lower side of the top of a mushroom. □ **lamelle**
gill cover a fold of skin protecting the gills. □ **opercule**

gilt [gilt] *noun* a gold or gold-like substance: *a tiny vase covered with gilt*; (*also adjective*) *a gilt brooch.* □ **dorure; doré**
,**gilt-'edged** *adjective* safe to invest in and certain to produce interest: *gilt-edged stocks.* □ **de tout repos**

gimmick ['gimik] *noun* something used to attract attention to something or someone: *an advertising gimmick.* □ **astuce**
'**gimmicky** *adjective.* □ **plein d'astuces**

gin [dʒin] *noun* a type of alcoholic drink made from grain and flavoured with juniper berries. □ **gin**

ginger ['dʒindʒə] *noun* a hot-tasting root which is used as a spice. □ **gingembre**
■ *adjective* **1** flavoured with ginger. □ **au gingembre**
2 reddish-brown in colour: *a ginger cat.* □ **roux**
ginger ale, ginger beer a type of non-alcoholic drink flavoured with ginger. □ **soda au gingembre**
'**gingerbread** *noun* a cake flavoured with treacle and ginger. □ **pain d'épice**

gingerly ['dʒindʒəli] *adverb* very gently and carefully: *He gingerly moved his injured foot.* □ **délicatement**

gipsy *see* **gypsy.**

giraffe [dʒi'rɑːf] – *plurals* **gi'raffes, gi'raffe** – *noun* an African animal with a very long neck, long legs and spots. □ **girafe**

---
giraffe is spelt with one **r** and two **fs**.
---

girder ['gəːdə] *noun* a large beam of steel *etc*, *eg* to support a road or bridge: *The girders of the bridge have collapsed.* □ **poutre(lle)**

girdle ['gəːdl] *noun* a belt or cord worn around the waist: *She wore a girdle around her tunic.* □ **ceinture**

girl [gəːl] *noun* **1** a female child: *Her new baby is a girl.* □ **fille**
2 a young *usually* unmarried woman. □ **jeune fille**
'**girlish** *adjective* of or like a girl: *girlish look.* □ **de jeune fille/de fillette**
'**girl friend** *noun* a girl or woman who is often in the

company of a particular man or boy: *He is taking his girl friend to the movies tonight.* □ **petite amie**

Girl Guide (*also* **Guide**), (*American*) **Girl Scout** (*also no capitals*) a member of an organization for girls which is aimed at developing character *etc.* □ **guide**

girth [gə:θ] *noun* **1** the measurement around a tree, a person's waist *etc.* □ **ciconférence, tour**

2 the strap that holds a saddle on a horse. □ **sangle**

gist [dʒist]: **the gist** the main points (of an argument *etc*): *Just give me the gist of what she said.* □ **essentiel**

give [giv] – *past tense* **gave** [geiv]: *past participle* '**given** – *verb* **1** to cause to have: *My aunt gave me a book for Christmas*; *Can you give me an opinion on this?* □ **donner**

2 to produce (something): *Cows give milk but horses do not*; *He gave a talk on his travels.* □ **donner**

3 to yield, bend, break *etc*: *This lock looks solid, but it will give under pressure.* □ **céder**

4 to organize (some event *etc*): *We're giving a party next week.* □ **donner**

■ *noun* the ability to yield or bend under pressure: *This chair has a lot of give in it.* □ **élasticité**

'**given** *adjective* **1** stated: *to do a job at a given time.* □ **donné**

2 (*with* **to**) in the habit of (doing) something: *He's given to making stupid remarks.* □ **enclin à**

3 taking (something) as a fact: *Given that x equals three, x plus two equals five.* □ **étant donné**

given name a personal or Christian name. □ **prénom**

give and take willingness to allow someone something in return for being allowed something oneself. □ **donnant donnant**

give away 1 to give *etc* (something) to someone (*eg* because one no longer wants it): *I'm going to give all my money away.* □ **donner**

2 to cause or allow (information *etc*) to become known *usually accidentally*: *He gave away our hiding-place.* □ **révéler**

■ *noun* '**giveaway**: *the lingering smell was a giveaway.* □ **révélation involontaire**

give back to return something: *She gave me back the book that she borrowed last week.* □ **rendre**

give in 1 to stop fighting and admit defeat; to yield: *The soldiers were outnumbered and gave in to the enemy.* □ **se rendre**

2 to hand or bring (something) to someone (often a person in authority): *Do we have to give in our books at the end of the lesson?* □ **remettre**

give off to produce: *That fire is giving off a lot of smoke.* □ **émettre**

give or take allowing for the addition or subtraction of: *I weigh sixty-five kilograms, give or take a little* (= approximately sixty-five kilograms). □ **plus ou moins**

give out 1 to give, *usually* to several people: *The headmistress gave out the school prizes.* □ **distribuer**

2 to come to an end: *My patience gave out.* □ **manquer**

3 to produce: *The fire gave out a lot of heat.* □ **dégager**

give rise to to cause: *This gives rise to a large number of problems.* □ **donner lieu (à)**

give up 1 to stop, abandon: *I must give up smoking*;

They gave up the search. □ **cesser (de)**

2 to stop using *etc*: *You'll have to give up cigarettes*; *I won't give up all my hobbies for you.* □ **renoncer à**

3 to hand over (*eg* oneself or something that one has) to someone else. □ **(se (rendre), (se) livrer**

4 to devote (time *etc*) to doing something: *He gave up all his time to gardening.* □ **consacrer**

5 (*often with* **as** *or* **for**) to consider (a person, thing *etc*) to be: *You took so long to arrive that we had almost given you up (for lost).* □ **considérer comme**

give way 1 to stop in order to allow *eg* traffic to pass: *Give way to traffic coming from the right.* □ **céder**

2 to break, collapse *etc* under pressure: *The bridge will give way any day now.* □ **s'effondrer**

3 to agree against one's will: *I have no intention of giving way to demands like that.* □ **céder (à)**

glacé ['glasei,gla'sei] *adjective* iced or sugared: *glacé cherries.* □ **glacé, confit**

glacier ['gleiʃər] *noun* a mass of ice, formed from the snow on mountains. □ **glacier**

glad [glad] *adjective* pleased or happy: *I'm very glad that you are here*; *the glad smiles of the children.* □ **joyeux, heureux**

'**gladden** *verb* to make glad: *The news gladdened her.* □ **réjouir**

'**gladly** *adverb*: *I'd gladly help but I have too many other things to do.* □ **avec plaisir**

'**gladness** *noun.* □ **joie**

glad rags a person's best clothes, worn for special occasions: *I'll get my glad rags on for the party.* □ **beaux atours**

gladiator ['gladieitə] *noun* in ancient Rome, a man trained to fight with other men or with animals for the amusement of spectators. □ **gladiateur**

glamour, glamor ['glamə] *noun* **1** the often false or superficial beauty or charm which attracts: *the glamour of a career in films.* □ **charme**

2 great beauty or charm, achieved with the aid of make-up, beautiful clothes *etc*: *the glamour of film stars.* □ **séduction**

'**glamorize, 'glamorise** *verb* to make glamorous: *This film attempts to glamorize war.* □ **peindre sous de belles couleurs**

'**glamorous** *adjective* having glamour. □ **séduisant**

'**glamorously** *adverb.* □ **séduisante**

---

glamour, noun, ends in **-our**.
glamorous, adjective is spelt with **-or-**.

---

glance [gla:ns] *verb* to look very quickly: *He glanced at the book*; *She glanced over the accounts.* □ **jeter un coup d'œil (à/sur)**

■ *noun* a brief or quick look: *I had a glance at the books last night.* □ **coup d'œil**

'**glancing** *adjective* which hits and glances off: *a glancing blow.* □ **(en) oblique**

at a glance at once: *I could tell at a glance that something was wrong.* □ **d'un coup d'œil**

glance off to hit and bounce off to one side: *The ball glanced off the edge of her bat.* □ **ricocher**

gland [gland] *noun* a part of the body that takes substances from the blood and stores them for use or in order that the body may get rid of them: *a sweat gland*; *He has swollen glands in his neck.* □ **glande**

'**glandular** [-dʒulər] *adjective* of the glands: *glandular fever.* □ **glandulaire**

glare [gleə] *verb* 1 to stare fiercely and angrily: *She glared at the little boy.* □ **foudroyer du regard**
2 to shine very brightly, *usually* to an unpleasant extent: *The sun glared down on us as we crossed the desert.* □ **aveugler**
■ *noun* 1 a fierce or angry look: *a glare of displeasure.* □ **regard furieux**
2 unpleasantly bright light: *the glare of the sun.* □ **éclat aveuglant**

'**glaring** *adjective* 1 unpleasantly bright; too bright: *the glaring sun*; *glaring colours.* □ **aveuglant**
2 obvious: *a glaring error.* □ **flagrant**

'**glaringly** *adverb.* □ **avec trop d'éclat**

glass [glɑːs] *noun* 1 a hard *usually* breakable transparent substance: *The bottle is made of glass*; (*also adjective*) *a glass bottle.* □ **(en/de) verre**
2 a *usually* tall hollow object made of glass, used for drinking: *There are six glasses on the tray*; *sherry-glasses.* □ **verre**
3 (also '**looking-glass**) a mirror. □ **glace, miroir**
4 a barometer, or the atmospheric pressure shown by one: *The glass is falling.* □ **baromètre**

'**glasses** *noun plural* spectacles. □ **lunettes**

'**glassful** *noun* the amount that a drinking-glass will hold: *Pour in two glassfuls of water.* □ **(plein) verre**

'**glassy** *adjective* 1 not showing any expression: *a glassy stare.* □ **vitreux**
2 like glass: *a glassy sea.* □ **uni comme un miroir**

'**glassiness** *noun.* □ **aspect vitreux**

> **glasses**, meaning spectacles, is plural: *His reading glasses are broken.*
> but **a pair of glasses** takes a singular verb: *A pair of glasses has been found.*

glaze [gleiz] *verb* 1 to fit glass into: *to glaze a window.* □ **vitrer**
2 to cover with glass or a glaze: *The potter glazed the vase.* □ **vernisser**
3 (of eyes) to become blank or dull. □ **devenir vitreux**
■ *noun* 1 a glassy coating put on pottery *etc*: *a pink glaze on the grey vase.* □ **vernis**
2 a shiny coating *eg* of sugar on fruit *etc*. □ **glaçage**

'**glazier** [-ziə, -ʒər] *noun* a person who puts glass in window frames *etc*. □ **vitrier, ière**

gleam [gliːm] *verb* to shine faintly: *a light gleaming in the distance.* □ **luire**
■ *noun* 1 a faint glow: *the gleam of her eyes.* □ **lueur**
2 a slight sign or amount: *a gleam of hope.* □ **lueur**

glean [gliːn] *verb* to collect or pick up (news, facts *etc*). □ **glaner**

glee [gliː] *noun* great delight: *The children shouted with glee when they saw their presents.* □ **joie**

'**gleeful** *adjective.* □ **joyeux**

'**gleefully** *adverb.* □ **joyeusement**

glib [glib] *adjective* 1 speaking persuasively but *usually*

without sincerity: *The salesman was a very glib talker.* □ **qui a du bagou**
2 (of a reply *etc*) quick and ready, but showing little thought: *glib excuses.* □ **désinvolte**

'**glibly** *adverb.* □ **avec désinvolture**

glide [glaid] *verb* 1 to move smoothly and easily: *The dancers glided across the floor.* □ **(faire) glisser**
2 to travel by or fly a glider. □ **faire du vol à voile**
■ *noun* a gliding movement. □ **glissement**

'**glider** *noun* a small, light airplane which has no engine. □ **planeur**

'**gliding** *noun* the flying of gliders: *I enjoy gliding.* □ **vol à voile**

glimmer ['glimər] *verb* to shine faintly: *A single candle glimmered in the darkness.* □ **luire faiblement**
■ *noun* 1 a faint light. □ **faible lueur**
2 a slight sign or amount: *a glimmer of hope.* □ **(faible) lueur**

glimpse [glimps] *noun* a very brief look: *He caught a glimpse of the burglar.* □ **coup d'œil**
■ *verb* to get a brief look at. □ **jeter un coup d'œil**

glint [glint] *verb* to gleam or sparkle: *The windows glinted in the sunlight.* □ **luire**
■ *noun* a gleam or sparkle: *the glint of steel*; *a glint of anger in her eyes.* □ **éclat**

glisten ['glisn] *verb* to shine faintly or sparkle: *His skin glistened with sweat.* □ **reluire**

glitter ['glitə] *verb* to sparkle: *Her diamonds glittered in the light.* □ **scintiller**
■ *noun* the quality of glittering: *the glitter of her diamonds.* □ **scintillement**

'**glittering** *adjective*: *glittering jewels.* □ **scintillant**

gloat [glout] *verb* to look at or think about with wicked pleasure: *He gloated over his rival's failure.* □ **contempler avec un plaisir mauvais**

globe [gloub] *noun* 1 (*usually with* **the**) the earth: *I've travelled to all parts of the globe.* □ **globe, terre**
2 a ball with a map of the earth on it. □ **globe (terrestre)**
3 an object shaped like a globe: *The chemicals were crushed in a large metal globe.* □ **sphère**

'**global** *adjective* affecting the whole world: *War is now a global problem.* □ **universal**

'**globally** *adverb.* □ **globalement**

globular ['globjulə] *adjective* shaped like a globe. □ **globulaire**

'**globetrotter** *noun* a person who goes sightseeing all over the world. □ **globe-trotter**

'**globe-trotting** *noun.* □ **voyages à travers le monde**

gloom [gluːm] *noun* 1 a state of not quite complete darkness: *I could not tell the colour of the car in the gloom.* □ **demi-jour**
2 sadness: *The Prime Minister's death cast a gloom over the whole country.* □ **tristesse**

'**gloomy** *adjective* 1 sad or depressed: *Don't look so gloomy.* □ **triste**
2 depressing: *gloomy news.* □ **sombre**
3 dim; dark: *gloomy rooms.* □ **sombre**

'**gloominess** *noun.* □ **assombrissement**

glory ['gloːri] – *plural* '**glories** – *noun* 1 fame or honour: *glory on the field of battle*; *She took part in the compe-*

tition for the glory of the school. □ **honneur**
2 a source of pride, fame *etc*: *This building is one of the many glories of Venice.* □ **gloire**
3 the quality of being magnificent: *The sun rose in all its glory.* □ **splendeur**
■ *verb* to take great pleasure in: *She glories in her work as an architect.* □ **savourer**
'**glorify** [-fai] *verb* **1** to make (something) seem better than it is: *That book glorified war.* □ **exalter**
2 to praise. □ **glorifier**
,**glorifi'cation** [-fi-] *noun.* □ **glorification**
'**glorious** *adjective* **1** splendid; deserving great praise: *a glorious career/victory.* □ **glorieux**
2 very pleasant; delightful: *glorious weather; Isn't the sunshine glorious?* □ **superbe**
'**gloriously** *adverb.* □ **glorieusement**
gloss [glos] *noun* brightness or shininess on the surface: *Her hair has a lovely gloss; (also adjective) gloss paint.* □ **brillant**
'**glossary** [-səri] – *plural* '**glossaries** – *noun* a list of words *etc* with their meanings: *a glossary of technical terms; a Shakespeare glossary.* □ **glossaire**
'**glossy** *adjective* smooth and shining: *The dog has a glossy coat.* □ **lustré**
'**glossiness** *noun.* □ **lustre**
gloss over to try to hide (a mistake *etc*): *He glossed over the fact that he had forgotten the previous appointment by talking about his accident.* □ **dissimuler**
glove [glʌv] *noun* a covering for the hand: *a pair of gloves.* □ **gant**
fit like a glove to fit perfectly: *This suit fits like a glove.* □ **aller comme un gant (à)**
glow [glou] *verb* **1** to give out heat or light without any flame: *The coal was glowing in the fire.* □ **rougeoyer**
2 to have red cheeks because of heat, cold, emotion *etc*: *The little girl glowed with pride.* □ **rayonner**
■ *noun* the state of glowing: *the glow of the coal in the fire.* □ **rougeoiement**
'**glowing** *adjective*: *glowing colours.* □ **rutilant**
'**glow-worm** *noun* a kind of beetle whose tail glows in the dark. □ **ver luisant**
glower ['glauər] *verb* to stare angrily: *He glowered at me.* □ **lancer des regards noirs à**
'**glowering** *adjective* angry; threatening: *a glowering look.* □ **noir, menaçant**
'**gloweringly** *adverb.* □ **d'un air menaçant**
glucose ['gluːkous] *noun* a kind of sugar found in the juice of fruit. □ **glucose**
glue [gluː] *noun* a substance used for sticking things together: *That glue will not stick plastic to wood.* □ **colle**
■ *verb* to join (things) with glue. □ **coller**
glum [glʌm] *adjective* gloomy and sad: *a glum expression.* □ **maussade**
'**glumly** *adverb.* □ **d'un air maussade**
'**glumness** *noun.* □ **air maussade**
glut [glʌt] *noun* too great a supply: *There has been a glut of apples this year.* □ **surabondance**
glutinous ['gluːtinəs] *adjective* sticky, like glue: *glutinous rice.* □ **gluant**
glutton ['glʌtən] *noun* **1** a person who eats too much:

That child is fat because he is such a glutton. □ **glouton, onne**
2 a person who is always eager for more of something *usually* unpleasant: *He's a glutton for work.* □ **bourreau (de travail)**
'**gluttony** *noun* greediness in eating. □ **gloutonnerie, gourmandise**
glycerin(e) ['glisə,rin] *noun* a sweet, sticky, colourless liquid. □ **glycérine**
gnarled [naːrld] *adjective* (of trees, branches *etc*) twisted. □ **noueux**
gnash [naʃ] *verb* to rub (the teeth) together in anger *etc*. □ **grincer (des dents)**
gnat [nat] *noun* a very small, *usually* blood-sucking, fly. □ **moucheron**
gnaw [noː] *verb* to bite or chew with a scraping movement: *The dog was gnawing a large bone; The mice have gnawed holes in the walls of this room.* □ **ronger**
gnu [nuː] – *plurals* **gnus, gnu** – *noun* a type of large African antelope. □ **gnou**
go [gou] – *3rd person singular present tense* **goes**: *past tense* **went** [went]: *past participle* **gone** [gon] – *verb* **1** to walk, travel, move *etc*: *She is going across the field; Go straight ahead; When did he go out?* □ **aller**
·**2** to be sent, passed on *etc*: *Complaints have to go through the proper channels.* □ **être transmis**
3 to be given, sold *etc*: *The prize goes to Joan Smith; The table went for $100.* □ **être donné, se vendre**
4 to lead to: *Where does this road go?* □ **mener**
5 to visit, to attend: *He goes to school every day; I decided not to go to the movie.* □ **aller**
6 to be destroyed *etc*: *This wall will have to go.* □ **disparaître**
7 to proceed, be done: *The meeting went very well.* □ **se passer**
8 to move away: *I think it is time you were going.* □ **partir**
9 to disappear: *My purse has gone!* □ **disparaître**
10 to do (some action or activity): *I'm going for a walk; I'm going hiking next week-end.* □ **aller**
11 to fail *etc*: *I think the clutch on this car has gone.* □ **lâcher**
12 to be working *etc*: *I don't think that clock is going.* □ **marcher**
13 to become: *These apples have gone bad.* □ **devenir**
14 to be: *Many people in the world regularly go hungry.* □ **être/avoir**
15 to be put: *Spoons go in that drawer.* □ **se mettre**
16 to pass: *Time goes quickly when you are enjoying yourself.* □ **passer**
17 to be used: *All their pocket money goes on sweets.* □ **passer (à)**
18 to be acceptable *etc*: *Anything goes in this office.* □ **être permis**
19 to make a particular noise: *Dogs go woof, not miaow.* □ **faire**
20 to have a particular tune *etc*: *How does that song go?* □ **sonner**
21 to become successful *etc*: *She always makes a party go.* □ **réussir**

■ *noun – plural* **goes** – **1** an attempt: *I'm not sure how to do it, but I'll have a go.* □ **essai**
2 energy: *She's full of go.* □ **allant**
'going *noun* **1** an act of leaving, moving away *etc*: *the comings and goings of the people in the street.* □ **départ**
2 the conditions under which something is done: *Walking was heavy going because of all the mud.* □ **état du terrain**
■ *adjective* in existence at present: *the going rate for typing manuscripts.* □ **courant**
'go-ahead *noun* permission: *We'll start as soon as we get the go-ahead.* □ **feu vert**
,go-'getter *noun* a person with a great deal of energy, ability *etc* who gets what he wants. □ **fonceur, euse**
,going-'over *noun* a study or examination: *He gave the accounts a thorough going-over.* □ **révision**
,goings-'on *noun plural* (*usually* strange) happenings or behaviour. □ **manigances**
,no-'go *adjective* (of a district *etc*) which a person *etc* is not allowed to enter: *a no-go area.* □ **interdit**
be going on (for) to be near or close to (a time, age *etc*): *He must be going on (for) eighty.* □ **aller sur**
be going strong to be successful, healthy *etc*: *Our business/grandmother is still going strong.* □ **être solide**
from the word go from the very beginning. □ **depuis le tout début**
get going to get started: *If you want to finish that job you'd better get going.* □ **s'y mettre**
give the go-by to ignore in an unfriendly way: *I think we'll give all his stupid suggestions the go-by.* □ **ignorer**
go about 1 to (begin to) work at: *I don't know the best way to go about the job!* □ **se mettre à**
2 (of a ship) to change direction or turn around. □ **virer de bord**
go after 1 to try to win: *She's going after that prize.* □ **essayer d'avoir**
2 to follow or chase: *Go after him and apologize.* □ **courir après**
go against 1 to oppose or refuse to act on: *A child should never go against his parents' wishes.* □ **aller à l'encontre de**
2 to be unacceptable to: *This goes against my conscience.* □ **heurter**
go along 1 to go: *I think I'll go along to that meeting.* □ **aller**
2 to proceed or progress: *Check your work as you go along.* □ **avancer**
go along with to agree with: *I'm afraid I can't go along with you on that.* □ **être d'accord avec**
go around 1 (of stories, rumours *etc*) to be passed from one person to another: *There's a rumour going around that you are leaving.* □ **courir**
2 to be enough for everyone: *Is there enough food to go around?* □ **suffir pour tout le monde**
go around with to be friendly with: *I don't like the group of friends you're going around with.* □ **fréquenter**
go at 1 to attack: *The little boys went at each other with their fists.* □ **se jeter sur**
2 to do with enthusiasm: *She really went at the job of*

painting the wall. □ **s'attaquer à**
go back to return to an earlier time, topic of conversation *etc*: *Let's go back for a minute to what we were talking about earlier.* □ **revenir à**
go back on to fail to do (something one has promised to do): *I never go back on my promises.* □ **revenir sur**
go by 1 to base an opinion on: *We can't go by what he says.* □ **(se) fonder sur**
2 to be guided by: *I always go by the instructions.* □ **suivre**
go down 1 (*with* well/badly) to be approved or disapproved of: *The story went down well (with them).* □ **être bien/mal reçu**
2 (of a ship) to sink: *They were lost at sea when the ship went down.* □ **sombrer**
3 (of the sun or moon) to go below the horizon. □ **se coucher**
4 to be remembered: *Your bravery will go down in history.* □ **entrer dans l'histoire**
5 (of places) to become less desirable: *This part of town has gone down in the last twenty years.* □ **se dégrader**
go far to be successful: *If you keep on working as hard as this, I'm sure you'll go far.* □ **aller loin**
go for to attack physically or in words: *The two dogs went for each other as soon as they met.* □ **se jeter sur**
go in (of the sun or moon) to become covered by cloud. □ **se cacher**
go in for 1 to take part in: *I'm not going in for the 1,000 metres race.* □ **prendre part à**
2 to do (something) as a hobby, career *etc*: *My daughter is going in for medicine; She goes in for collecting postcards.* □ **se consacrer à, s'intéresser à**
go into 1 to make a careful study of (something): *We'll need to go into this plan in detail.* □ **examiner**
2 to discuss in detail: *I don't want to go into the problems at the moment.* □ **étudier en détail**
go off 1 (of a bomb *etc*) to explode: *The little boy was injured when the firework went off in his hand.* □ **exploser**
2 (of an alarm) to ring: *When the alarm went off the thieves ran away.* □ **sonner**
3 to leave: *He went off yesterday.* □ **(re)partir**
4 to cease a habit: *I've gone off cigarettes.* □ **cesser**
5 to become rotten: *That meat has gone off.* □ **s'avarier**
go on 1 to continue: *Go on reading – I won't disturb you.* □ **continuer (de)**
2 to talk a great deal, *usually* too much: *She goes on and on about her health.* □ **être intarissable**
3 to happen: *What is going on here?* □ **se passer**
4 to base one's investigations *etc* on: *The police had very few clues to go on in their search for the murderer.* □ **s'appuyer sur**
go on about to repeat over and over or give too many details about something until it becomes boring: *Don't go on about the money you lent me anymore since I already said I would pay you back tomorrow.* □ **aller de mal en**
go on at to nag at: *Her mother went on at her for coming home late after the dance.* □ **s'en prendre à**
go out 1 to become extinguished: *The light has gone*

out. □ **s'éteindre**

2 to go to parties, concerts, meetings *etc*: *We don't go out as much as we did when we were younger.* □ **sortir**

3 to be frequently in the company of (a person, *usually* of the opposite sex): *I've been going out with her for months.* □ **sortir avec**

go over 1 to study or examine carefully: *I want to go over the work you have done before you do any more.* □ **revoir**

2 to repeat (a story *etc*): *I'll go over the whole lesson again.* □ **répéter**

3 to list: *We went over all their faults.* □ **récapituler**

4 (of plays, behaviour *etc*) to be received (well or badly): *The play didn't go over at all well the first night.* □ **être bien/mal reçu**

go slow (of workers in a factory *etc*) to work less quickly than usual, *eg* as a form of protest. □ **faire la grève perlée**

go steady to have a close friendly relationship with someone of the opposite sex: *My girlfriend and I have been going steady for a year.* □ **(se) fréquenter**

go through 1 to search in: *I've gone through all my pockets but I still can't find my key.* □ **fouiller (dans)**

2 to suffer: *You have no idea what I went through to get this finished in time.* □ **subir**

3 to use up: *We went through a lot of money on holiday.* □ **dépenser**

4 to complete: *to go through certain formalities.* □ **remplir**

5 to be completed: *After long hours of negotiations, the deal went through.* □ **être conclu**

go through with to finish doing: *I'm going to go through with this in spite of what you say.* □ **aller jusqu'au bout (de)**

go too far to do something which is so bad as to be unacceptable. □ **aller trop loin**

go towards to help to buy *etc*: *The money we collect will go towards a new roof.* □ **servir à**

go up 1 to increase in size, value *etc*: *The temperature/ price has gone up.* □ **monter**

2 to be built: *There are office blocks going up all over town.* □ **se construire**

go up in smoke/flames to catch fire; to be destroyed or damaged by fire *etc*: *The building across the street went up in flames.* □ **prendre feu**

go with 1 to be sold with, be part of *etc*: *The carpets will go with the house.* □ **aller avec**

2 to look *etc* well with: *The carpet goes with the wall-paper.* □ **aller avec**

go without to manage without: *If you can't afford a new dress, you'll have to go without (one).* □ **se passer de**

keep going to continue doing what one is doing; to survive: *The snow was falling heavily, but we had to keep going; Business is bad at the moment, but we'll manage to keep going.* □ **continuer (à/de)**

make a go (of something) to make a success (of something): *She has never owned a shop before, but I think she'll make a go of it.* □ **réussir (qqch.)**

on the go very busy or active: *He's always on the go,*

from morning to night. □ **sur la brèche**

goad [goud] *verb* to urge or force (a person *etc*) to do something by annoying (him *etc*): *I was goaded into being rude to him.* □ **harceler**

■ *noun* a sharp-pointed stick used for driving cattle *etc*. □ **aiguillon**

goal [goul] *noun* **1** in football, rugby, soccer *etc* the act of kicking, hitting *etc* a ball between the goalposts; the point gained by doing this: *He scored six goals.* □ **but**

2 an aim or purpose: *My goal in life is to write a book.* □ **but**

'**goalkeeper** *noun* a player, *eg* in hockey or soccer, whose job is to prevent members of the other team from scoring goals. □ **gardien, ienne de but**

'**goalpost** *noun* one of the two upright posts which form the goal in football, rugby, hockey *etc*. □ **poteau (de but)**

goat [gout] *noun* an animal of the sheep family, with horns and a long-haired coat. □ **chèvre, bouc**

gobble ['gobl] *verb* **1** to swallow food *etc* quickly: *You'll be sick if you keep gobbling your meals like that.* □ **engloutir**

2 (of turkeys) to make a noise in the throat: *We could hear the turkeys gobbling in the farmyard.* □ **glouglouter**

goblet ['goblit] *noun* a drinking-cup with a thin stem: *He served the wine in goblets.* □ **verre à pied**

goblin ['goblin] *noun* a mischievous, ugly spirit: *a frightening fairy story about goblins.* □ **lutin**

goby ['goubi] – *plurals* '**gobies**, '**goby** – *noun* a bony coastal fish with fins that form a sucker by which it clings to rocks. □ **gobie**

god [god] *noun* **1** (*with capital*) the creator and ruler of the world (in the Christian, Jewish *etc* religions). □ **Dieu**

2 (*feminine* '**goddess**) a supernatural being who is worshipped: *the gods of Greece and Rome.* □ **dieu, déesse**

'**godly** *adjective* religious: *a godly man/life.* □ **pieux**

'**godliness** *noun.* □ **piété**

'**godchild**, '**goddaughter**, '**godson** *nouns* a child who has a godparent or godparents. □ **filleul, eule**

'**godfather**, '**godmother**, '**godparent** *nouns* a person who, at a child's baptism, promises to take an active interest in its welfare. □ **parrain, marraine**

'**godsend** *noun* a very welcome piece of unexpected good luck: *Your cheque was an absolute godsend.* □ **bénédiction**

godown [gou'daun] *noun* in India and East Asia, a warehouse, or a storehouse for goods at a port. □ **comptoir**

goggle ['gogl] *verb* to have wide, staring eyes (*eg* because of surprise): *He goggled at the amount of money he received.* □ **rouler de gros yeux**

goggles ['goglz] *noun plural* a type of spectacles used to protect the eyes from dust, water *etc*: *Many swimmers wear goggles in the water.* □ **lunettes de protection**

gold [gould] *noun* **1** an element, a precious yellow metal used for making jewellery *etc*: *This watch is made of gold*; (*also adjective*) *a gold watch.* □ **or; en or, d'or**

2 coins, jewellery *etc* made of gold. □ **or**

3 the colour of the metal: *the browns and golds of autumn leaves*; (*also adjective*) *a gold carpet.* □ **or; doré**

'**golden** *adjective* **1** of gold or the colour of gold: *golden* *hair.* □ **d'or, doré**

2 (of a wedding anniversary, jubilee *etc*) fiftieth: *They will celebrate their golden wedding (anniversary) next month.* □ **d'or**

'**goldfish** – *plural* '**goldfish** – *noun* a small golden yellow fish often kept as a pet: *The child kept a goldfish in a bowl.* □ **poisson rouge**

,**gold-'leaf** *noun* gold beaten into a very thin sheet: *a brooch made of gold-leaf.* □ **feuille d'or**

gold medal in competitions, the medal awarded as first prize. □ **médaille d'or**

'**gold mine** *noun* **1** a place where gold is mined. □ **mine d'or**

2 a source of wealth or profit: *That clothes shop is an absolute gold mine.* □ **mine d'or**

'**gold rush** *noun* a rush of people to a part of a country where gold has been discovered. □ **ruée vers l'or**

'**goldsmith** *noun* a person who makes jewellery, ornaments *etc* of gold. □ **orfèvre**

as good as gold very well-behaved. □ **sage comme une image**

golden opportunity a very good opportunity. □ **occasion unique**

golf [golf] *noun* a game in which a small white ball is hit across open ground and into small holes by means of golf-clubs: *He plays golf every Sunday.* □ **golf**

■ *verb* to play golf. □ **jouer au golf**

'**golfing** noun. □ **le golf**

'**golfer** *noun* a person who plays golf: *a keen golfer.* □ **golfeur, euse**

'**golf club** *noun* **1** the long thin stick used to hit the ball in golf: *She bought a new set of golf clubs.* □ **bâton (de golf)**

2 a society of people who play golf, or the place where they meet: *the local golf club.* □ **club de golf**

golf course the place where golf is played. □ **(terrain de) golf**

gondola ['gondələ] *noun* **1** a long narrow boat used on the canals of Venice. □ **gondole**

2 a kind of safety cage for people who are working on the outside of a tall building to stand in. □ **nacelle**

gondo'lier [-'liə] *noun* a person who rows a gondola. □ **gondolier, ière**

gone *see* go.

gong [gɒŋ] *noun* a metal plate which, when struck, gives a ringing sound: *a dinner gong.* □ **gong**

good [gud] – *comparative* **better** ['betə]: *superlative* **best** [best] – *adjective* **1** well-behaved; not causing trouble *etc*: *Be good!; He's a good baby.* □ **sage**

2 correct, desirable *etc*: *She was a good wife; good manners; good English.* □ **bon, dévoué**

3 of high quality: *good food/literature; Her singing is very good.* □ **bon**

4 skilful; able to do something well: *a good doctor; good at tennis; good with children.* □ **compétent**

5 kind: *You've been very good to him; a good father.* □ **bon**

6 helpful; beneficial: *What a good night's sleep!; Cheese is good for you.* □ **bon**

7 pleased, happy *etc*: *in a good mood today.* □ **bien**

8 pleasant; enjoyable: *to read a good book; Ice cream is good to eat.* □ **bon**

9 considerable; enough: *a good salary; She talked a good deal of nonsense.* □ **bon, grand**

10 suitable: *a good woman for the job.* □ **qualifié**

11 sound, fit: *good health; good eyesight; a car with good brakes.* □ **bon**

12 sensible: *Can you think of one good reason for doing that?* □ **bon**

13 showing approval: *We've had very good reports about you.* □ **bon**

14 thorough: *a good clean.* □ **bon**

15 well: *I don't feel very good this morning.* □ **bien**

■ *noun* **1** advantage or benefit: *He worked for the good of the poor; for your own good; What's the good of a broken-down car?* □ **bien, avantage**

2 goodness: *I always try to see the good in people.* □ **bien**

■ *interjection* an expression of approval, gladness *etc*. □ **bien! bon!**

'**goodness** *noun* the state of being good. □ **bonté**

■ *interjection* (*also* **my goodness**) an expression of surprise *etc*. □ **mon Dieu!**

goods *noun plural* **1** objects *etc* for sale, products: *leather goods.* □ **articles**

2 articles sent by rail, not road, sea or air: *This station is for passengers and goods;* (*also adjective*) *a goods train/station.* □ **(de) marchandises**

'**goody** – *plural* '**goodies** – *noun* (*usually in plural*) any food (*eg* cake, ice cream) which is particularly enjoyable to eat: *the goodies at a children's party.* □ **gâteries**

good'bye [-'bai] *interjection, noun* an expression used when leaving someone: *Goodbye – it was good of you to visit us; sad goodbyes.* □ **au revoir, adieu**

good-day, good evening *see* **good morning**.

good-for-'nothing *adjective, noun* (a person who is) useless or lazy: *That boy's a lazy good-for-nothing (rascal).* □ **bon à rien, bonne à rien**

good humour kindliness and cheerfulness. □ **bonne humeur**

good-'humoured *adjective*: *a good-humoured smile.* □ **de bonne humeur**

good-'humouredly *adverb*. □ **avec bonne humeur**

good-'looking *adjective* handsome; attractive: *a good-looking girl; He is very good-looking.* □ **beau**

good morning, good afternoon, good-'day, good evening, good night *interjections, nouns* words used (depending on the time of day) when meeting or leaving someone: *Good morning, Mrs. Brown; Good night, everyone – I'm going to bed.* □ **bonjour, bonsoir, bonne nuit**

good-'natured *adjective* pleasant; not easily made angry: *a good-natured fellow.* □ **facile à vivre**

,**good'will, good will** *noun* **1** the good reputation and trade with customers that a business firm has: *We are selling the goodwill along with the shop.* □ **clientèle**

2 friendliness: *She has always shown a good deal of goodwill towards us.* □ **bienveillance**

good works *noun plural* acts of charity: *He is known throughout the city for his good works.* □ **bonnes œuvres**

as good as almost: *The job's as good as done.* □ **pratiquement**

be as good as one's word to keep one's promises. □ **n'avoir qu'une parole**

be up to no good to be doing something wrong: *I'm sure he's up to no good.* □ **mijoter un mauvais coup**

deliver the goods to do what one has promised to do. □ **tenir parole**

for good (*sometimes* **for good and all**) permanently: *She's not going to France for a holiday – she's going for good.* □ **pour de bon**

for goodness' sake an expression of annoyance: *For goodness' sake, will you stop that noise!* □ **par pitié**

good for 1 certain to last: *These houses are good for another hundred years at least.* □ **capable de tenir**

2 certain to pay (a sum of money): *He's good for $50.* □ **bon pour**

3 certain to cause: *That story is always good for a laugh.* □ **qui provoque**

good for you, him *etc* an expression of approval: *You've passed your exam – good for you!* □ **bravo!**

Good Friday the Friday before Easter Sunday: *Christ was crucified on Good Friday.* □ **Vendredi saint**

good gracious, good heavens expressions of surprise. □ **bonté divine!**

goodness gracious, goodness me expressions of surprise. □ **juste ciel!**

good old an expression used to show approval *etc*: *Good old Fred! I knew he would help us out.* □ **bravo!**

make good 1 to be successful: *Through hard work and ability, she soon made good.* □ **prospérer, réussir**

2 to repair or compensate for (loss, damages *etc*): *The damage you caused to my car must be made good.* □ **compenser**

no good useless; pointless: *It's no good crying for help – no one will hear you*; *This penknife is no good – the blades are blunt.* □ **bon à rien, fichu**

put in a good word for to praise or recommend: *Put in a good word for me when you see the boss.* □ **glisser un mot en faveur de**

take (something) in good part not to be upset, offended or annoyed (*eg* by a joke, remark *etc*): *John took the jokes about his accident with the pot of paint all in good part.* □ **prendre en bonne part**

thank goodness an expression used to show that a person is glad that something is all right: *Thank goodness it isn't raining.* □ **Dieu merci!**

to the good richer: *After buying and selling some of these paintings, we finished up $500 to the good.* □ **de bénéfice**

goose [guːs] – *plural* **geese** [giːs] – *noun* a web-footed animal like a duck, but larger: *The farmer keeps geese.* □ **oie**

'**goosebumps** *noun plural* small bumps on the skin caused by cold or fear: *He was so afraid he broke out in goosebumps.* □ **chair de poule**

he *etc* **wouldn't say boo to a goose** he *etc* is very timid. □ **c'est une poule mouillée**

gooseberry ['guːsbəri, 'guz-] – *plural* '**gooseberries** – *noun* a round, whiskery, edible green berry. □ **groseille verte**

gore [goː] *noun* blood (*especially* when it is thick and solid): *After the battle, the knight was covered in gore.* □ **sang (coagulé)**

■ *verb* (of an animal) to pierce with its horns, tusks *etc*: *The bull gored the farmer to death.* □ **encorner**

'**gory** *adjective* with a lot of blood or bloodshed: *a gory battle*; *a gory tale.* □ **sanglant**

gorge [goːdʒ] *noun* a deep narrow valley: *A river ran along the bottom of the gorge.* □ **gorge**

■ *verb* to eat greedily until one is full: *I gorged myself on fruit at the party.* □ **se gorger de**

gorgeous ['goːdʒəs] *adjective* **1** beautiful; splendid: *a gorgeous dress*; *gorgeous plumage*; *These colours are gorgeous.* □ **splendide**

2 very pleasant: *a gorgeous meal.* □ **sensationnel**

gorilla [gə'rilə] *noun* the largest type of ape: *Two gorillas have escaped from the zoo.* □ **gorille**

gory *see* gore.

gosh [goʃ] *interjection* an expression of surprise. □ **mince alors!**

gosling ['gozliŋ] *noun* a young goose. □ **oison**

gospel ['gospəl] *noun* (one of the four descriptions in the Bible of) the life and teaching of Christ: *the Gospel according to St. Luke*; *The parable of the sower is in one of the gospels.* □ **évangile**

gossamer ['gosəmə] *noun* the fine threads made by a spider which float in the air or lie on bushes. □ **fils de la Vierge**

■ *adjective* like gossamer: *a blouse of a gossamer material.* □ **arachnéen**

gossip ['gosip] *noun* **1** talk about other people's affairs, not always truthful: *I never pay any attention to gossip.* □ **commérages**

2 a chat: *She dropped in for a cup of coffee and a gossip.* □ **brin de causette**

3 a person who listens to and passes on gossip: *He's a dreadful gossip.* □ **commère**

■ *verb* **1** to pass on gossip. □ **commérer**

2 to chat. □ **bavarder**

'**gossipy** *adjective* fond of gossiping: *gossipy neighbours.* □ **cancanier**

gossip column an article in a newspaper *etc* containing gossip about famous people. □ **échos**

got, gotten *see* get.

gouge [gaudʒ] *verb* **1** to make (a groove or hole) with a tool: *She gouged (out) a hole in the wood.* □ **gouger, creuser**

2 to take or force out: *The tyrant gouged out the prisoner's eyes.* □ **arracher**

■ *noun* a type of chisel for making grooves *etc*. □ **gouge**

gourd [gurd] *noun* a type of large fruit, or the plant on which it grows. □ **gourde**

gourmet ['guəmei] *noun* a person who enjoys and knows a lot about good food and wines. □ **gourmet**

govern ['gʌvən] *verb* **1** to rule: *The empress governed (the country) wisely and well.* □ **gouverner**

2 to influence: *Our policy is governed by three factors.* □ **régir**

government ['gʌvəmənt] *noun* **1** the people who rule a country or state: *the Canadian Government.* □ **gouvernement**

2 the way in which a country or state is ruled: *Democracy is one form of government.* □ **gouvernement**

3 the act or process of governing. □ **administration**

governmental [gʌvn'mentl] *adjective.* □ **gouvernemental**

'**governor** *noun* **1** in the United States, the head of a state: *the Governor of Ohio.* □ **gouverneur, eure**

2 a member of the committee of people who govern a school, hospital *etc*: *She is on the board of governors.* □ **administrateur, trice**

3 a person who governs a province or colony. □ **gouverneur, eure**

'**governorship** *noun.* □ **fonctions de gouverneur**

gown [gaun] *noun* **1** a woman's dress, especially one of high quality for dances, parties *etc.* □ **robe (de soirée)**

2 a loose robe worn by clergymen, lawyers, teachers *etc.* □ **toge**

grab [grab] – *past tense, past participle* **grabbed** – *verb*
1 to seize, grasp or take suddenly: *He grabbed a biscuit.* □ **saisir**

2 to get by rough or illegal means: *Many people tried to grab land when oil was discovered in the district.* □ **se saisir de**

■ *noun* a sudden attempt to grasp or seize: *I made a grab at the child.* □ **mouvement vif (pour attraper)**

grab at to try to grasp, seize or take, not necessarily successfully: *I grabbed at the child; She grabbed at the chance to leave.* □ **essayer de saisir**

grace [greis] *noun* **1** beauty of form or movement: *The dancer's movements had very little grace.* □ **grâce**

2 a sense of what is right: *At least he had the grace to leave after his dreadful behaviour.* □ **politesse**

3 a short prayer of thanks for a meal. □ **bénédicité**

4 a delay allowed as a favour: *You should have paid me today but I'll give you a week's grace.* □ **répit**

5 the title of a duke, duchess or archbishop: *Your/His/Her Grace.* □ **Monsieur le duc, Madame la duchesse, Monseigneur l'Archevêque**

6 mercy: *by the grace of God.* □ **grâce**

'**graceful** *adjective* having or showing beauty of form or movement: *a graceful dancer.* □ **gracieux**

'**gracefully** *adverb.* □ **gracieusement**

'**gracefulness** *noun.* □ **grâce**

'**gracious** [-ʃəs] *adjective* **1** kind or polite: *a gracious smile.* □ **courtois**

2 (of God) merciful. □ **miséricordieux**

■ *interjection* an exclamation of surprise. □ **juste ciel!**

'**graciously** *adverb: She smiled graciously.* □ **avec grâce**

'**graciousness** *noun.* □ **bienveillance**

with (a) good/bad grace (un)willingly: *She accepted his apology with good grace.* □ **de bonne/mauvaise grâce**

grade [greid] *noun* **1** one level in a scale of qualities, sizes *etc*: *several grades of sandpaper; a high-grade ore.* □ **qualité**

2 (the pupils in) a class or year at school: *We're in the fifth grade now.* □ **classe**

3 a mark for an examination, term paper *etc*: *She al-*

ways got good grades at school. □ **note**

4 the slope of a railway *etc*; gradient. □ **pente**

■ *verb* **1** to sort into grades: *to grade eggs.* □ **classer**

2 to move through different stages: *Red grades into purple as blue is added.* □ **passer graduellement à**

gradation [grə'deiʃən] *noun* **1** (one stage or degree in) a series of gradual and successive stages: *There are various gradations of colour between red and purple.* □ **gradation**

2 the act or process of grading. □ **classification**

'**grade school** *noun* a primary school. □ **école primaire**

make the grade to do as well as necessary: *That new apprentice will never make the grade as a trained mechanic.* □ **être à la hauteur**

gradient ['greidiənt] *noun* **1** the amount of slope (*eg* of a road, a railway): *a gradient of 1 in 4.* □ **inclinaison**

2 a slope. □ **pente**

gradual ['gradjuəl] *adjective* happening gently and slowly: *a gradual rise in temperature.* □ **graduel**

'**gradually** *adverb: Her health is gradually improving.* □ **graduellement**

graduate ['gradjueit] *verb* **1** to receive a degree, diploma *etc*: *She graduated in German and French.* □ **obtenir son diplôme**

2 to mark out with regular divisions: *A thermometer is graduated in degrees.* □ **graduer**

■ [-ət] *noun* a person who has been awarded a degree or diploma: *a graduate in French.* □ **diplômé, ée**

,**gradu'ation** *noun* **1** the act or ceremony of graduating from a college, university *etc: The graduation will be held in the large hall; (also adjective) a graduation ceremony.* □ **remise des diplômes**

2 a marked division: *the graduations on a thermometer.* □ **graduation**

graffiti [grə'fiːti] *noun plural or noun singular* words or drawings scratched or painted on a wall *etc.* □ **graffiti**

graft[1] [graːft] *verb* to fix (skin, bone *etc*) from one part of the body on to or into another part of the body: *The doctor treated her burns by grafting skin from her leg on to her back.* □ **greffer**

■ *noun* a piece of skin, bone *etc* which is grafted: *a skin graft.* □ **greffe**

graft[2] [graːft] *noun* **1** dishonesty in obtaining profit or good position. □ **corruption**

2 hard work. □ **dure besogne**

grain [grein] *noun* **1** a seed of wheat, oats *etc.* □ **grain**

2 corn in general: *Grain is ground into flour.* □ **blé**

3 a very small, hard particle: *a grain of sand.* □ **grain**

4 the way in which the lines of fibre run in wood, leather *etc.* □ **fil**

5 a very small amount: *There isn't a grain of truth in that story.* □ **grain**

go against the grain to be against a person's wishes, feelings *etc: It goes against the grain for me to tell lies.* □ **à l'encontre de**

gram [gram] *noun* the basic unit of mass in the metric system. □ **gramme**

grammar ['gramə] *noun* **1** the rules for forming words and for combining words to form sentences: *She's an expert on French grammar.* □ **grammaire**

2 a description or collection of the rules of grammar: *Could you lend me your Latin grammar?*; (*also adjective*) *a grammar book.* □ **(de) grammaire**

3 a person's use of grammatical rules: *This essay is full of bad grammar.* □ **(faute de) grammaire**

gram'matical [-'ma-] *adjective* **1** (*negative* **ungrammatical**) correct according to the rules of grammar: *a grammatical sentence.* □ **grammatical**

2 of (a) grammar: *a grammatical rule.* □ **grammatical**

gram'matically *adverb.* □ **grammaticalement**

---
grammar ends in **-ar** (not **-er**).
---

gramophone ['gramɔfoun] *noun* the old name for a record player. □ **phonographe**

granary ['granɔri] – *plural* 'granaries – *noun* a store-house for grain. □ **grenier (à blé)**

grand [grand] *adjective* **1** splendid; magnificent: *a grand procession.* □ **magnifique**

2 proud: *She gives herself grand airs.* □ **de grandeur**

3 very pleasant: *a grand day at the seaside.* □ **formidable**

4 highly respected: *a grand old woman.* □ **grand**

■ *noun* – *plural* **grand** – a slang term for $1,000: *I paid five grand for that car.* □ **mille dollars**

grand finale the final act or scene in a show *etc*, usually with all the actors, singers *etc* on the stage. □ **apothéose**

grand jury in the United States, a jury which decides whether there is enough evidence for a person to be brought to trial. □ **jury d'accusation**

grand piano a type of piano with a large flat top shaped like a harp. □ **piano à queue**

'grandstand *noun* rows of raised seats at a sports ground *etc*: *We watched the sports meeting from the grandstand*; (*also adjective*) *grandstand seats*; *We had a grandstand* (= a very good) *view of the parade.* □ **tribunes**

grand total the final total; the total of several smaller totals. □ **somme globale**

grandchild ['grantʃaild], **grand-daughter** ['grandɔːtə], **grandson** ['gransʌn] *nouns* the child, daughter or son, of one's son or daughter. □ **petits-enfants, petite-fille, petit-fils**

grandad ['grandad] *noun* a grandfather. □ **grand-papa**

grand-daughter *see* **grandchild**.

grandeur ['grandʒə] *noun* great and impressive beauty: *the grandeur of the Alps.* □ **splendeur**

grandfather ['granfaːðə], **grandmother** ['granmʌðə], **grandparent** ['granpeərənt] *noun* the father or mother of one's father or mother. □ **grand-père, grand-mère, grands-parents (pl.)**

grandfather clock a clock with a tall *usually* wooden case which stands on the floor. □ **horloge de parquet**

grandiose ['grandious] *adjective* impressive to an excessive or foolish degree: *He produced several grandiose schemes for a holiday resort but no resort was ever built.* □ **grandiose**

grandmother *see* **grandfather**.

grandparent *see* **grandfather**.

grandson *see* **grandchild**.

granite ['granit] *noun, adjective* (of) a type of hard usu-

ally grey or red rock used for building: *buildings of granite*: *granite hills.* □ **(de) granit**

granny (*plural* 'grannies), **grannie** ['grani] *noun* a grand-mother: *I have two grannies*; *Hello, Granny!* □ **grand-maman, mamie**

grant [graːnt] *verb* **1** to agree to, to give: *Would you grant me one favour*; *He granted the man permission to leave.* □ **accorder**

2 to agree or admit: *I grant (you) that it was a stupid thing to do.* □ **reconnaître**

■ *noun* money given for a particular purpose: *She was awarded a grant for studying abroad.* □ **subvention, bourse**

'granted, 'granting (even) if; assuming: *Granted that you are right, we will have to move fast.* □ **en admettant que**

take for granted 1 to assume without checking: *I took it for granted that you had heard the story.* □ **considérer comme admis**

2 to treat casually: *People take electricity for granted until their supply is cut off.* □ **tenir pour acquis**

granule ['granjuːl] *noun* a very small particle: *a granule of sugar.* □ **granule**

'granular *adjective.* □ **granuleux**

'granulated [-lei-] *adjective* broken into tiny particles: *granulated sugar.* □ **granulé**

grape [greip] *noun* a green or black smooth-skinned eatable berry from which wine is made. □ **raisin**

'grapevine *noun* **1** an informal means of passing news from person to person: *I hear through the grapevine that he is leaving.* □ **rumeur publique**

2 a vine. □ **vigne**

sour grapes saying or pretending that something is not worth having because one cannot obtain it. □ **ils sont trop verts!**

grapefruit ['greipfruːt] – *plurals* 'grapefruit, 'grape-fruits – *noun* (the flesh of) a large yellow-skinned fruit similar to an orange. □ **pamplemousse**

graph [graf] *noun* a diagram consisting of a line or lines drawn to show changes in some quantity: *a graph of temperature changes.* □ **graphique**

'graphic *adjective* **1** vivid: *a graphic description of an accident.* □ **pittoresque**

2 of painting, drawing *etc*: *the graphic arts.* □ **graphique**

'graphically *adverb.* □ **graphiquement**

graph paper paper covered in small squares used for drawing graphs on. □ **papier quadrillé/millimétré**

graphite ['grafait] *noun* a form of carbon used in the leads of pencils. □ **graphite**

grapple ['grapl] *verb* (with **with**) **1** to grasp and fight with: *He grappled with the thief.* □ **en venir aux mains/ prises avec**

2 to (try to) deal with (a problem *etc*): *She enjoys grappling with riddles.* □ **s'attaquer à**

grasp [graːsp] *verb* **1** to take hold of *especially* by putting one's fingers or arm(s) around: *He grasped the rope*; *She grasped the opportunity to ask for a higher salary.* □ **empoigner, saisir**

2 to understand: *I can't grasp what he's getting at.* □ **saisir**

■ *noun* **1** a grip with one's hand *etc*: *Have you got a good grasp on that rope?* □ **prise**

2 the ability to understand: *Her ideas are quite beyond my grasp.* □ **compréhension**

'**grasping** *adjective* greedy (*especially* for money): *a grasping old man.* □ **avare**

grass [grɑːs] *noun* **1** the green plant which covers fields, garden lawns *etc*. □ **herbe**

2 any species of grass, including also corn and bamboo: *She studies grasses.* □ **graminée**

'**grassy** *adjective*: *a grassy bank/slope.* □ **herbeux**

'**grasshopper** *noun* a type of insect which jumps and which makes a noise by rubbing its wings. □ **sauterelle**

'**grassland** *noun* land covered with grass, used as pasture for animals. □ **prairie**

grass snake *noun* a small, slender, non-poisonous snake: *Although harmless, some people dislike grass snakes as much as rattlesnakes.* □ **couleuvre**

grate[1] [greit] *noun* a framework of iron bars for holding a fire in a fireplace. □ **grille (de foyer)**

grate[2] [greit] *verb* **1** to rub (cheese, vegetables *etc*) into small pieces by means of a grater. □ **râper**

2 to irritate: *His voice grates on me.* □ **taper sur les nerfs**

'**grater** *noun* an instrument with a rough surface on which cheese, vegetables *etc* can be grated. □ **râpe**

'**grating** *adjective* (of sounds) unpleasant. □ **grinçant**

grateful ['greitful] *adjective* feeling thankful: *I am grateful to you for your help.* □ **reconnaissant**

'**gratefully** *adverb*: *She accepted her offer gratefully.* □ **avec reconnaissance**

gratified ['gratifaid] *adjective* pleased: *I was gratified at the response to my letter.* □ **content**

'**gratifying** *adjective* causing pleasure or satisfaction: *a gratifying result.* □ **(très) agréable**

grating[1] *see* **grate**[2].

grating[2] ['greitiŋ] *noun* a framework of iron *etc* bars: *a grating in the road.* □ **grillage,**

gratitude ['gratitjuːd] *noun* the state of feeling grateful: *I wish there was some way of showing my gratitude for all you have done for me.* □ **gratitude**

gratuity [grə'tjuəti] – *plural* **gra'tuities** – *noun* a small sum of money given as a reward for good service; a tip. □ **pourboire**

gra'tuitous *adjective* **1** (*derogatory*) done, said *etc* without good reason or excuse or when not wanted: *gratuitous insults.* □ **gratuit**

2 done, given *etc* without payment: *gratuitous advice.* □ **gratuit**

gra'tuitously *adverb*. □ **gratuitement**

gra'tuitousness *noun*. □ **gratuité**

grave[1] [greiv] *noun* a plot of ground, or the hole dug in it, in which a dead person is buried: *He laid flowers on the grave.* □ **tombe**

'**gravedigger** *noun* a person whose job is digging graves. □ **fossoyeur**

'**gravestone** *noun* a stone placed at a grave on which the dead person's name *etc* is written. □ **pierre tombale**

'**graveyard** *noun* a place where the dead are buried. □ **cimetière**

grave[2] [greiv] *adjective* **1** important: *a grave responsibility; grave decisions.* □ **grave**

2 serious, dangerous: *grave news.* □ **grave**

3 serious, sad: *a grave expression.* □ **sérieux**

'**gravely** *adverb*. □ **gravement**

'**gravity** ['gra-] *noun*: *The gravity of the situation was clear to us all.* □ **gravité**

gravel ['gravəl] *noun* very small stones: *gravel for the garden path.* □ **gravier**

gravity[1] *see* **grave**[2].

gravity[2] ['gravəti] *noun* the force which attracts things towards the earth and causes them to fall to the ground. □ **pesanteur**

gravy ['greivi] – *plural* '**gravies** – *noun* (a sauce made from) the juices from meat that is cooking. □ **(sauce au) jus**

gray *see* **grey**.

graze[1] [greiz] *verb* (of animals) to eat grass *etc* which is growing. □ **brouter**

graze[2] [greiz] *verb* **1** to scrape the skin from (a part of the body): *I've grazed my hand on that stone wall.* □ **écorcher**

2 to touch lightly in passing: *The bullet grazed the car.* □ **frôler**

■ *noun* the slight wound caused by grazing a part of the body: *a graze on one's hand.* □ **écorchure**

grease [griːs] *noun* **1** soft, thick, animal fat. □ **graisse**

2 any thick, oily substance: *She put grease on the squeaking hinge.* □ **graisse**

■ *verb* to put grease on, over or in: *The mechanic greased the car's axle.* □ **graisser**

'**greasy** *adjective* **1** of or like grease: *greasy food.* □ **graisseux**

2 covered in grease: *greasy hands.* □ **graisseux**

3 slippery, as if covered in grease: *greasy roads.* □ **glissant**

'**greasiness** *noun*. □ **état graisseux**

great [greit] *adjective* **1** of a better quality than average; important: *a great writer; Golda Meir was a great woman.* □ **grand**

2 very large, larger *etc* than average: *a great crowd of people at the football match.* □ **grand**

3 of a high degree: *Take great care of that book.* □ **grand**

4 very pleasant: *We had a great time at the party.* □ **merveilleux**

5 clever and expert: *John's great at football.* □ **doué pour**

'**greatly** *adverb*: *I was greatly impressed by her singing.* □ **grandement**

'**greatness** *noun*: *her greatness as an athlete.* □ **importance, grandeur**

great- [greit] separated by one generation more than (an uncle, grandfather *etc*): *A great-uncle is one's father's or mother's uncle; a great-grandchild.* □ **grand-, arrière-**

greed [griːd] *noun* a (too) great desire for food, money *etc*: *Eating five cakes is just sheer greed.* □ **avidité, gloutonnerie**

'**greedy** *adjective*. □ **avide; gourmand**

'**greedily** *adverb*. □ **avidement**

'**greediness** *noun*. □ **avidité**

Greek [griːk] *adjective* of Greece or its inhabitants: *Souvlaki is a Greek dish made with lamb.* □ **grec, grecque**

■ *noun* a person from Greece or the standard language of Greece: *Aristotle was a Greek philosopher; The best way to learn to speak Greek is to take a class.* □ **Grec**

green [griːn] *adjective* **1** of the colour of growing grass or the leaves of most plants: *a green hat.* □ **vert**

2 not ripe: *green bananas.* □ **vert**

3 without experience: *Only someone as green as you would believe a story like that.* □ **inexpérimenté**

4 looking as if one is about to be sick; very pale: *He was green with envy* (= very jealous). □ **vert**

■ *noun* **1** the colour of grass or the leaves of plants: *the green of the trees in summer.* □ **vert**

2 something (*eg* paint) green in colour: *I've used up all my green.* □ **vert**

3 an area of grass: *a village green.* □ **pelouse**

4 an area of grass on a golf course with a small hole in the centre. □ **vert**

'**greenish** *adjective* close to green: *a greenish dress.* □ **verdâtre**

greens *noun plural* green vegetables: *Children are often told that they must eat their greens.* □ **légumes verts**

'**greenfly** – *plural* '**greenfly** – *noun* a type of small, green insect: *The leaves of this rose tree have been eaten by greenfly.* □ **puceron**

'**greengage** [-geidʒ] *noun* a greenish-yellow type of plum. □ **reine-claude**

'**greengrocer** *noun* a person who sells fruit and vegetables. □ **marchand, ande de légumes**

'**greenhouse** *noun* a building *usually* of glass, in which plants are grown. □ **serre**

the green light permission to begin: *We can't start until they give us the green light.* □ **feu vert**

greet [griːt] *verb* to welcome: *She greeted me when I arrived.* □ **saluer; accueillir**

'**greeting** *noun* friendly words or actions used in welcome. □ **salutation**

'**greetings** *noun plural* a friendly message: *Christmas greetings.* □ **vœux**

gregarious [griˈgeəriəs] *adjective* **1** liking the company of other people: *a gregarious person.* □ **sociable**

2 (of animals, birds *etc*) living in groups: *Geese are gregarious.* □ **grégaire**

grenade [grəˈneid] *noun* a small bomb, *especially* one thrown by hand. □ **grenade**

grew *see* **grow**.

grey, (*especially American*) **gray** [grei] *adjective* **1** of a mixture of colour between black and white: *a grey dress.* □ **gris**

2 grey-haired: *He's turning/going grey.* □ **grisonnant**

■ *noun* **1** (any shade of) a colour between black and white: *Grey is rather a dull colour.* □ **gris**

2 something grey in colour: *I never wear grey.* □ **gris**

■ *verb* to become grey or grey-haired. □ **grisonner**

'**greyish** *adjective* close to grey: *a greyish dress.* □ **grisâtre**

greyhound [ˈgreihaund] *noun* a breed of dog which can

run very fast: *She breeds greyhounds for racing;* (*also adjective*) *greyhound racing.* □ **lévrier, levrette; de lévrier**

grid [grid] *noun* **1** a set of vertical and horizontal lines drawn on a map. □ **grille**

2 a framework of iron bars. □ **grille**

grief [griːf] *noun* great sorrow or unhappiness: *She was filled with grief at the news of her sister's death.* □ **chagrin**

'**grief-stricken** *adjective* overcome by very great grief: *the grief-stricken widow.* □ **affligé**

come to grief to meet disaster; to fail: *The project came to grief.* □ **tourner mal**

grievance [ˈgriːvəns] *noun* a cause or reason for complaint: *a list of grievances.* □ **grief**

grieve [griːv] *verb* **1** to cause to feel great sorrow: *Your wickedness grieves me deeply.* □ **affliger**

2 to feel sorrow. □ **avoir du chagrin**

'**grievous** *adjective* severe or very bad: *He was found guilty of inflicting grievous bodily harm* (= very serious injuries) *on the old man.* □ **grave**

grill [gril] *verb* **1** to cook directly under heat: *to grill chops.* □ **(faire) griller**

2 to question (a person) closely: *The police grilled the man they thought was the murderer.* □ **cuisiner**

■ *noun* **1** the part of a cooker used for grilling. □ **gril**

2 a frame of metal bars for grilling food on. □ **gril**

3 a dish of grilled food: *a mixed grill.* □ **grillade**

grim [grim] *adjective* **1** horrible; very unpleasant: *The soldiers had a grim task looking for bodies in the wrecked houses.* □ **sinistre**

2 angry; fierce-looking: *The boss looks a bit grim this morning.* □ **menaçant**

3 stubborn, unyielding: *grim determination.* □ **inflexible**

'**grimness** *noun*. □ **aspect sinistre**

'**grimly** *adverb*: *She held on grimly to the rope.* □ **sinistrement**

like grim death with great determination. □ **de toutes ses forces**

grime [graim] *noun* dirt which is difficult to remove. □ **crasse**

'**grimy** *adjective*: *grimy buildings.* □ **encrassé**

grin [grin] – *past tense, past participle* **grinned** – *verb* to smile broadly: *The children grinned happily for the photographer.* □ **sourire d'une oreille à l'autre**

■ *noun* a broad smile. □ **sourire épanoui**

grin and bear it to put up with something unpleasant without complaining: *He doesn't like his present job but he'll just have to grin and bear it till he finds another.* □ **faire contre mauvaise fortune bon cœur**

grind [graind] – *past tense, past participle* **ground** [graund] – *verb* **1** to crush into powder or small pieces: *This machine grinds coffee.* □ **moudre, broyer**

2 to rub together, *usually* producing an unpleasant noise: *He grinds his teeth.* □ **grincer**

3 to rub into or against something else: *He ground his heel into the earth.* □ **enfoncer**

■ *noun* boring hard work: *Learning vocabulary is a bit of a grind.* □ **corvée** 'grinder *noun* a person or machine that grinds: *a cof-fee-grinder.* □ **broyeur, euse**

'grinding *adjective* 1 with a sound of grinding: *The train came to a grinding stop.* □ **grinçant**
2 severe: *grinding poverty.* □ **écrasant**

'grindstone *noun* a wheel-shaped stone against which knives are sharpened as it turns. □ **meule (à aiguiser)**

grind down to crush: *She was ground down by poverty.* □ **écraser**

grind up to grind into powder or small pieces: *This machine grinds up rocks.* □ **pulvériser**

keep (some)one's nose to the grindstone to (force someone to) work hard, without stopping. □ **(faire) travailler sans relâche**

grip [grip] – *past tense, past participle* gripped – *verb* to take a firm hold of: *I gripped the stick; The speaker gripped (the attention of) her audience.* □ **empoigner**
■ *noun* 1 a firm hold: *I had a firm grip on the stick; He has a very strong grip; in the grip of the storm.* □ **prise**
2 a bag used by travellers: *I carried my sports equipment in a large grip.* □ **valise**
3 understanding: *She has a good grip of the subject.* □ **connaissance**

'gripping *adjective* which holds the attention: *a gripping story.* □ **passionnant**

come to grips with to deal with (a problem, difficulty *etc*). □ **s'attaquer à**

lose one's grip to lose understanding or control. □ **perdre la maîtrise de**

grisly ['grizli] *adjective* horrible: *a grisly sight.* □ **maca-bre**

gristle ['grisl] *noun* a tough, rubbery substance found in meat: *There's too much gristle in this steak.* □ **cartilage**
'gristly *adjective*. □ **croquant**

grit [grit] *noun* 1 very small pieces of stone: *She's got a piece of grit in her eye.* □ **poussière**
2 courage: *She's got a lot of grit.* □ **cran**
■ *verb* – *past tense, past participle* 'gritted – to keep (the teeth) tightly closed together: *He gritted his teeth to stop himself crying out in pain.* □ **serrer les dents**
'gritty *adjective*: *a gritty substance.* □ **graveleux**

grizzly ['grizli] – *plural* 'grizzlies – *noun* (*usually* griz-zly bear) a large fierce North American bear. □ **ours gris (d'Amérique), grizzly**

groan [groun] *verb* to produce a deep sound (because of pain, unhappiness *etc*): *He groaned when he heard that he had failed his exam; The table was groaning with food* (= there was a great deal of food on it). □ **gémir**
■ *noun* a deep sound: *a groan of despair.* □ **gémissement**

grocer ['grousə] *noun* a person who sells certain kinds of food and household supplies. □ **épicier, ière**
'groceries *noun plural* food *etc* sold in a grocer's shop. □ **provisions**

grocery store *noun* a place where food and other household products are sold: *Wendy's refrigerator was empty so she went to the grocery store for food.* □ **épicerie**

groggy ['grogi] *adjective* weak and walking unsteadily: *I'm not seriously hurt – I just feel a bit groggy.* □ **chancelant**
'grogginess *noun*. □ **titubation**

groin [groin] *noun* the part of the front of the body where the inner part of the thigh joins the rest of the body. □ **aine**

groom [gruːm] *noun* 1 a person who looks after horses: *a groom at the stables.* □ **garçon d'écurie**
2 a bridegroom. □ **jeune/futur marié**
■ *verb* 1 to clean, brush *etc* a horse's coat: *The horses were groomed for the horse show.* □ **panser**
2 to prepare for some task, purpose *etc*: *She's being groomed as a possible successor to our head of department.* □ **préparer**

groove [gruːv] *noun* a long, narrow cut made in a surface: *the groove in a record.* □ **rainure, sillon**
grooved *adjective*: *grooved edges.* □ **cannelé**

grope [group] *verb* to search for something by feeling with one's hands: *She groped her way through the smoke; He groped for the door.* □ **tâtonner**

gross [grous] *adjective* 1 very bad: *gross errors/indecency.* □ **grossier**
2 vulgar: *gross behaviour/language.* □ **grossier**
3 too fat: *a large, gross person.* □ **obèse**
4 total: *The gross weight of a parcel is the total weight of the contents, the box, the wrapping etc.* □ **brut**
■ *noun* the total amount (of several things added together). □ **total**
'grossly *adverb*: *grossly underpaid; He behaved grossly.* □ **grossièrement**

grotesque [grou'tesk] *adjective* very strange-looking: *a grotesque figure.* □ **grotesque**
gro'tesquely *adverb*. □ **grotesquement**

grouch [grautʃ] *verb* to complain: *She's quite happy in her job although she's always grouching (about it).* □ **rouspéter**
■ *noun* 1 a person who complains. □ **rouspéteur, euse**
2 a complaint. □ **rouspétance**
'grouchy *adjective*. □ **grognon**

ground[1] *see* grind.

ground[2] [graund] *noun* 1 the solid surface of the earth: *lying on the ground; high ground.* □ **sol**
2 a piece of land used for some purpose: *a football ground.* □ **terrain**
3 (a wire that provides) an electrical connection with the earth. □ **terre**
■ *verb* 1 to base: *His argument is grounded on a series of wrong assumptions.* □ **fonder**
2 to connect to earth elecrically: *Is your washing machine properly grounded?* □ **mettre à la terre**
3 to (cause a ship to) hit the seabed or shore and remain stuck. □ **(faire) s'échouer**
4 to prevent (an airplane, pilot) from flying: *All planes have been grounded because of the fog.* □ **interdire de vol**

'grounding *noun* the teaching of the basic facts of a subject: *a good grounding in mathematics.* □ **enseigne-ment des bases d'un sujet**

'groundless *adjective* without reason: *Your fears are groundless.* □ **sans fondement**

grounds *noun plural* 1 the garden or land around a large house *etc*: *the castle grounds.* □ **parc**
2 good reasons: *Have you any grounds for calling her a*

liar? □ **motif**

3 the powder which remains in a cup (*eg* of coffee) which one has drunk: *coffee grounds.* □ **marc (de café)**

ground floor *the rooms of a building which are at street level: My office is on the ground floor; (also adjective) a ground-floor flat.* □ **rez-de-chaussée**

groundnut *see* peanut.

'groundwork *noun* work done in preparation for beginning a project *etc.* □ **travail préparatoire**

break new ground to deal with a subject for the first time. □ **innover**

cover ground to deal with a certain amount of work *etc*: *We've covered a lot of ground at this morning's meeting.* □ **faire du bon travail**

get (something) off the ground to get (a project *etc*) started. □ **faire démarrer (qqch.)**

hold one's ground to refuse to move back or retreat when attacked: *Although many were killed, the soldiers held their ground.* □ **tenir bon**

lose ground to (be forced to) move back or retreat: *The general sent in reinforcements when he saw that his troops were losing ground.* □ **perdre du terrain**

group [gruːp] *noun* **1** a number of persons or things together: *a group of boys.* □ **groupe**

2 a group of people who play or sing together: *a pop group*; *a folk group.* □ **groupe, ensemble**

■ *verb* to form into a group or groups: *The children grouped around the teacher.* □ **(se) grouper**

grouse[1] [graus] – *plural* **grouse** – *noun* a kind of game bird. □ **grouse**

grouse[2] [graus] *verb* to complain: *He's grousing about his job again.* □ **rouspéter**

■ *noun* a complaint. □ **grief**

grovel ['grovl] – *past tense, past participle* **'grovelled**, **'groveled** – *verb* to make oneself (too) humble: *He grovelled before his leader.* □ **s'aplatir**

grow [grou] – *past tense* **grew** [gruː]: *past participle* **grown** – *verb* **1** (of plants) to develop: *Carrots grow well in this soil.* □ **pousser, croître**

2 to become bigger, longer *etc*: *My hair has grown too long; Our friendship grew as time went on.* □ **grandir**

3 to cause or allow to grow: *He has grown a beard.* □ **laisser pousser**

4 (with **into**) to change into, in becoming mature: *Your daughter has grown into a beautiful woman.* □ **devenir**

5 to become: *It's growing dark.* □ **devenir**

'grower *noun* a person who grows (plants *etc*): *a tomato-grower.* □ **producteur, trice**

grown *adjective* adult: *a grown woman; fully grown.* □ **adulte**

growth [-θ] *noun* **1** the act or process of growing, increasing, developing *etc*: *the growth of trade unionism.* □ **croissance**

2 something that has grown: *a week's growth of beard.* □ **pousse**

3 the amount by which something grows: *to measure the growth of a plant.* □ **croissance**

4 something unwanted which grows: *a cancerous growth.* □ **excroissance**

'grown-'up *noun* an adult. □ **adulte**

grown-up mature; adult; fully grown: *Her children are grown up now; a grown-up daughter.* □ **grand, adulte**

grow on to gradually become liked: *I didn't like the painting at first, but it has grown on me.* □ **finir par plaire**

grow up to become an adult: *I'm going to be an engine-driver when I grow up.* □ **devenir adulte**

growl [graul] *verb* to make a deep, rough sound: *The dog growled angrily (at the postwoman); He growled out a command.* □ **grogner**

■ *noun* a deep, rough sound. □ **grognement**

grown, growth *see* grow.

grub [grʌb] *noun* **1** the form of an insect after it hatches from its egg: *A caterpillar is a grub.* □ **larve**

2 a slang term for food: *Have we enough grub to eat?* □ **bouffe**

■ *verb* – *past tense, past participle* **grubbed** – to search by digging: *The pigs were grubbing around for roots.* □ **fouiller**

grubby ['grʌbi] *adjective* dirty: *a grubby little child.* □ **crasseux, malpropre**

'grubbiness *noun.* □ **saleté**

grudge [grʌdʒ] *verb* **1** to be unwilling to do, give *etc*; to do, give *etc* unwillingly: *I grudge wasting time on this, but I suppose I'll have to do it; She grudges the dog even the little food she gives it.* □ **rechigner à, accorder à contrecœur**

2 to feel resentment against (someone) for: *I grudge her her success.* □ **en vouloir (à qqn)**

■ *noun* a feeling of anger *etc*: *He has a grudge against me.* □ **rancune**

'grudging *adjective* said, done *etc* unwillingly: *grudging admiration.* □ **à contrecœur**

'grudgingly *adverb.* □ **de mauvaise grâce**

gruelling, grueling ['gruelin] *adjective* exhausting: *a gruelling race.* □ **épuisant**

gruesome ['gruːsəm] *adjective* horrible: *a gruesome sight.* □ **horrible**

gruff [grʌf] *adjective* **1** deep and rough: *a gruff voice.* □ **bourru**

2 (seeming to be) unfriendly: *a gruff old woman.* □ **brusque**

'gruffly *adverb.* □ **d'un ton bourru**

'gruffness *noun.* □ **ton bourru**

grumble ['grʌmbl] *verb* **1** to complain in a bad-tempered way: *She grumbled at the way she had been treated.* □ **bougonner (contre)**

2 to make a low and deep sound: *Thunder grumbled in the distance.* □ **gronder**

■ *noun* **1** a complaint made in a bad-tempered way. □ **ronchonnement**

2 a low, deep sound: *the grumble of thunder.* □ **grondement**

grumpy ['grʌmpi] *adjective* bad-tempered: *a grumpy old man.* □ **bougon**

'grumpily *adverb.* □ **bougonnant**

'grumpiness *noun.* □ **mauvaise humeur**

grunt [grʌnt] *verb* **1** to make a low, rough sound: *The pigs grunted when I brought their food.* □ **grogner**

2 (of people) to say in a way that sounds like grunting:

He grunted that he was too busy to talk to me. □
grommeler
■ *noun* a low, rough sound: *a grunt of disapproval.* □
grognement
guarantee [garən'tiː] *noun* **1** a statement by the maker
that something will work for a certain period of time:
This guarantee is valid for one year. □ **garantie**
2 a thing that makes something likely or certain: *It is no
guarantee against failure.* □ **garantie**
■ *verb* **1** to act as, or give, a guarantee: *This watch is
guaranteed for six months.* □ **garantir**
2 to state that something is true, definite *etc*: *I can't guarantee that what he told me is correct.* □ **garantir**
guard [gaːd] *verb* **1** to protect from danger or attack:
*The soldiers were guarding the Prime Minister's resi-
dence.* □ **garder**
2 to prevent (a person) escaping, (something) happening: *The soldiers guarded their prisoners*; *to guard
against mistakes.* □ **surveiller**
■ *noun* **1** someone who or something which protects: *a
guard around the Prime Minister; a guard in front of
the fire.* □ **garde**
2 someone whose job is to prevent (a person) escaping:
*There was a guard with the prisoner every hour of the
day.* □ **garde**
3 the act or duty of guarding. □ **surveillance**
'**guarded** *adjective* cautious: *She gave guarded replies.*
□ **prudent**
'**guardedly** *adverb.* □ **prudemment**
guard of honour soldiers or other people who are lined
up as an honour to someone important: *A guard of honour greeted the new President at the airport.* □ **garde
d'honneur**
keep guard (on): *The soldiers kept guard (on the prisoner).* □ **surveiller**
off guard unprepared: *He hit me while I was off guard*;
to catch someone off guard. □ **au dépourvu**
on guard prepared: *Be on your guard against his tricks.*
□ **sur ses gardes**
stand guard to be on duty as a guard: *He stood guard
at the gates.* □ **monter la garde**
guardian ['gaːdiən] *noun* **1** a person who has the legal
right to take care of a child (*usually* an orphan): *I became the child's guardian when her parents died.* □
tuteur, trice
2 a person who looks after something: *the guardian of
the castle.* □ **gardien, ienne**
'**guardianship** *noun* the state or duty of being a guardian. □ **tutelle**
guava ['gwaːvə] *noun* the yellow pear-shaped fruit of a
type of tropical tree. □ **goyave**
guer(r)illa [gə'rilə] *noun* a member of a small group of
fighters who make sudden attacks on an enemy. □
guérillero
■ *adjective*: *guerrilla warfare.* □ **de guérilla**
guess [ges] *verb* **1** to say what is likely to be the case:
*I'm trying to guess the height of this building; If you
don't know the answer, just guess.* □ **deviner**
2 to suppose: *I guess I'll have to leave now.* □ **supposer**
■ *noun* an opinion, answer *etc* got by guessing: *My guess

is that she's not coming.* □ **supposition**
'**guesswork** *noun* the process or result of guessing: *I
got the answer by guesswork.* □ **conjecture**
anybody's guess a matter of complete uncertainty: *Who
will win is anybody's guess.* □ **pure conjecture**
guest [gest] *noun* a visitor received in a house, in a hotel
etc: *We are having guests for dinner,* (*also adjective*) *a
guest bedroom.* □ **invité, ée, client, ente**
'**guesthouse** *noun* a small hotel. □ **pension de famille**
guffaw [gə'fɔː] *verb* to laugh loudly. □ **rire bruyamment**
■ *noun* a loud laugh. □ **éclat de rire**
guide [gaid] *verb* **1** to lead, direct or show the way: *I
don't know how to get to your house – I'll need someone to guide me; Your comments guided me in my final
choice.* □ **guider**
2 to control the movement of: *The teacher guided the
child's hand as she wrote.* □ **guider**
■ *noun* **1** a person who shows the way to go, points out
interesting things *etc*: *A guide will show you around the
castle.* □ **guide**
2 (*also* '**guidebook**) a book which contains information
for tourists: *a guide to Rome.* □ **guide**
3 (*usually with capital*) a Girl Guide. □ **guide**
4 something which informs, directs or influences. □
guide
'**guidance** *noun* advice towards doing something: *a
project prepared under the guidance of the professor.* □
conseils
'**guideline** *noun* (*usually in plural*) an indication as to
how something should be done. □ **directive(s)**
guided missile an explosive rocket which can be guided
to its target by radio waves. □ **missile téléguidé**
guilder ['gildə] *noun* the standard unit of Dutch currency.
□ **florin**
guile [gail] *noun* the ability to deceive or trick people: *I
used guile to get what I wanted.* □ **ruse**
'**guileless** *adjective* honest; sincere: *a guileless person/
smile.* □ **sincère**
'**guilelessly** *adverb.* □ **sincèrement**
'**guilelessness** *noun.* □ **sincérité**
guillotine ['gilətiːn] *noun* **1** in France, an instrument for
cutting criminals' heads off. □ **guillotine**
2 a machine for cutting paper. □ **massicot**
■ *verb* to cut the head off (a person) or to cut (paper)
with a guillotine. □ **guillotiner; massicoter**
guilt [gilt] *noun* **1** a sense of shame: *a feeling of guilt.* □
culpabilité
2 the state of having done wrong: *Fingerprints proved
the murderer's guilt.* □ **culpabilité**
'**guilty** *adjective* having, feeling, or causing guilt: *The
jury found the prisoner guilty; a guilty conscience.* □
coupable, chargé
'**guiltiness** *noun.* □ **culpabilité**
'**guiltily** *adverb*: *He looked at his mother guiltily.* □ **d'un
air coupable**
guinea pig ['ginipig] *noun* **1** a small animal, like a rabbit, with short ears and often kept as a pet. □ **cochon
d'Inde**
2 a person used as the subject of an experiment: *He was
used as a guinea pig for the new drug.* □ **cobaye**

guise [gaiz] *noun* a disguised or false appearance: *The thieves entered the house in the guise of workmen.* □ **apparence, déguisement**

guitar [gi'taː] *noun* a type of musical instrument with *usually* six strings. □ **guitare**
gui'tarist *noun*. □ **guitariste**

gulf [gʌlf] *noun* a part of the sea with land around a large part of it: *the Gulf of Mexico.* □ **golfe**

gull [gʌl] *noun* (*often* '**seagull**) a type of web-footed sea bird, *usually* black and white or grey and white. □ **mouette**

gullet ['gʌlit] *noun* the tube by which food passes from the mouth to the stomach. □ **œsophage**

gullible ['gʌləbl] *adjective* easily tricked or fooled: *He is so gullible that he believes everything you tell him.* □ **crédule**
,**gulli'bility** *noun*. □ **crédulité**

gully ['gʌli] – *plural* '**gullies** – *noun* a channel worn by running water *eg* on a mountain side. □ **ravine**

gulp [gʌlp] *verb* to swallow eagerly or in large mouthfuls: *She gulped down a sandwich.* □ **engloutir**
■ *noun* 1 a swallowing movement: *"There's a ghost out there," he said with a gulp.* □ **serrement de gorge**
2 the amount of food swallowed: *a gulp of coffee.* □ **bouchée**

gum[1] [gʌm] *noun* (*usually in plural*) the firm flesh in which the teeth grow. □ **gencive(s)**
'**gumboil** *noun* a painful swelling in the gum. □ **abcès à la gencive**

gum[2] [gʌm] *noun* 1 a sticky juice got from some trees and plants. □ **gomme**
2 a glue: *We can stick these pictures into the book with gum.* □ **colle**
3 a type of sweet: *a fruit gum.* □ **boule de gomme**
4 chewing-gum: *She chews gum when she is working.* □ **gomme (à mâcher)**
■ *verb* – *past tense, past participle* **gummed** – to glue with gum: *I'll gum this bit on to the other one.* □ **coller**
'**gummy** *adjective*. □ **gommeux**
'**gumminess** *noun*. □ **viscosité**

gun [gʌn] *noun* any weapon which fires bullets or shells: *I fired a gun at the burglar.* □ **arme à feu**
'**gunboat** *noun* a small warship with large guns. □ **canonnière**
'**gunfire** *noun* the firing of guns: *I could hear the sound of gunfire in the distance.* □ **coups de feu, fusillade**
'**gunman** *noun* a criminal who uses a gun to kill or rob people: *Three gunmen robbed the bank.* □ **bandit armé**
'**gunpowder** *noun* an explosive in the form of a powder. □ **poudre (à canon)**
'**gunshot** *noun* the sound of a gun firing: *I heard a gunshot and a woman dropped dead.* □ **coup de feu**
■ *adjective* caused by the bullet from a gun: *a gunshot wound.* □ **par balle**
stick to one's guns to hold to one's position in an argument *etc*: *No one believed her story but she stuck to her guns.* □ **ne pas démordre (de)**

guppy ['gʌpi] – *plural* '**guppies** – *noun* a small brightly-coloured fresh-water fish, often kept in aquariums. □ **guppy**

gush [gʌʃ] *verb* 1 (of liquids) to flow out suddenly and in large amounts: *Blood gushed from its wound.* □ **jaillir**
2 to exaggerate one's enthusiasm *etc* while talking: *They kept gushing about their success.* □ **en remettre**
■ *noun* a sudden flowing (of a liquid): *a gush of water.* □ **jaillissement**
'**gushing** *adjective* speaking or spoken in an exaggerated manner: *gushing remarks; She's a bit too gushing for me.* □ **exubérant**
'**gushingly** *adverb*. □ **avec exubérance**

gust [gʌst] *noun* a sudden blast (of wind): *gusts of wind of up to eighty kilometres an hour.* □ **rafale**
'**gusty** *adjective*: *a gusty day.* □ **venteux**
'**gustily** *adverb*. □ **par rafales**
'**gustiness** *noun*. □ **intensité des rafales**

gusto ['gʌstou] *noun* enthusiasm or enjoyment: *The girl was blowing her trumpet with great gusto.* □ **entrain**

gut [gʌt] *noun* 1 the tube in the lower part of the body through which food passes. □ **intestin**
2 a strong thread made from the gut of an animal, used for violin strings *etc*. □ **(corde de) boyau**
■ *verb* – *past tense, past participle* '**gutted** – 1 to take the guts out of: *Her job was to gut fish.* □ **vider**
2 to destroy completely, except for the outer frame: *The fire gutted the house.* □ **ne laisser que la carcasse (de)**
guts *noun plural* 1 the gut, liver, kidneys *etc*. □ **entrailles**
2 courage: *He's got a lot of guts.* □ **cran**

gutter ['gʌtə] *noun* a channel for carrying away water, *especially* at the edge of a road or roof: *The gutters are flooded with water.* □ **gouttière; caniveau**

guy [gai] *noun* 1 a man: *I don't know the guy you're talking about.* □ **type, gars**
2 (*also* '**guy-rope**) a rope which keeps a tent *etc* steady. □ **corde de tente**

gym [dʒim] short for **gymnasium** and **gymnastics**: *The children have gym on Thursdays; (also adjective) a gym teacher.* □ **gymnase, gym; de gym**
gym shoe a light, canvas *usually* rubber-soled shoe worn for gymnastics. □ **chaussure de gymnastique**

gymkhana [dʒim'kɑːnə] *noun* a meeting for sports competitions *usually* for horse-riders. □ **gymkhana**

gymnasium [dʒim'neiziəm] – *plurals* **gym'nasiums, gym'nasia** [-ə] – *noun* a building or room with equipment for physical exercise. □ **gymnase**

gymnast ['dʒimnast] *noun* a person who does gymnastics. □ **gymnaste**
gym'nastic [-'nas-] *adjective* of gymnastics. □ **gymnastique**
gym'nastics [-'nas-] *noun singular* physical exercises *usually* done in a gymnasium with certain types of equipment. □ **gymnastique**

gynecology, gynaecology [gainə'kolədʒi] *noun* the branch of medicine which deals with the diseases of women. □ **gynécologie**
gynecologist, ,gynae'cologist *noun*. □ **gynécologue**

gypsy, gipsy ['dʒipsi] – *plurals* '**gypsies**, '**gipsies** – *noun* a member of a race of wandering people. □ **bohémien, ienne, gitan, ane**
■ *adjective*: *a gypsy caravan.* □ **de bohémien/gitan**

Hh

ha! [ha, haː] *interjection* an expression of surprise, triumph *etc*: *Ha! I've found it!* □ **ah!; ha!**
See also **ha! ha!**

habit ['habit] *noun* **1** something which a person does usually or regularly: *the habit of going for a walk before bed; an irritating habit of interrupting.* □ **(par) habitude**
2 a tendency to do the same things that one has always done: *I did it out of habit.* □ **(par) habitude**
3 clothes: *a monk's habit.* □ **habit(s)**
habitual [həˈbitjuəl] *adjective* **1** having a habit of doing, being *etc* (something): *He's a habitual drunkard.* □ **habituel**
2 done *etc* regularly: *He took his habitual walk before bed.* □ **habituel**
habitually [həˈbitjuəli] *adverb*. □ **habituellement**
from force of habit because one is used to doing (something): *I took the cigarette from force of habit.* □ **par habitude**
get (someone) into, out of the habit of to make (a person) start or stop doing (something) as a habit: *I wish I could get out of the habit of biting my nails; You must get your children into the habit of cleaning their teeth.* □ **habituer à, (faire) perdre l'habitude de**
habitable ['habitəbl] *adjective* (*negative* **unhabitable**) (*usually* of buildings) fit to be lived in: *The house is no longer habitable – the roof is collapsing.* □ **habitable**
'habitat [-tat] *noun* the natural home of an animal or plant: *The Antarctic is the penguin's natural habitat.* □ **habitat**
,habi'tation *noun* the act of living in (a building *etc*): *These houses are not fit for human habitation.* □ **habitation**

habitual *see* **habit.**

hack [hak] *verb* **1** to cut or chop up roughly: *The butcher hacked the beef into large pieces.* □ **hacher**
2 to cut (a path *etc*) roughly: *She hacked her way through the jungle; She hacked (out) a path through the jungle.* □ **se tailler... à coups de**
■ *noun* **1** a rough cut made in something: *He marked the tree by making a few hacks on the trunk.* □ **entaille**
2 a horse, or in the United States, a car, for hire. □ **cheval de selle; taxi**
'hacking *adjective* (of a cough) rough and dry: *He has had a hacking cough for weeks.* □ **(toux) sèche**
'hacksaw *noun* a saw for cutting metals. □ **scie à métaux**
hackles ['haklz] *noun plural* the hair on a dog's neck or the feathers on the neck of a farmyard cock. □ **poils/plumes du cou**
hackney ['hakni]: **hackney carriage/cab** *noun* a taxi. □ **voiture de louage, taxi**
hacksaw *see* **hack.**
had *see* **have.**
haddock ['hadək] – *plurals* **'haddock, 'haddocks** – *noun* a kind of small sea fish. □ **églefin**
hadn't *see* **have.**
haemoglobin *see* **hemoglobin.**
haemorrhage *see* **hemorrhage.**

hag [hag] *noun* an ugly old woman. □ **(vieille) sorcière**
haggard ['hagəd] *adjective* (of a person) looking very tired and thin-faced, because of pain, worry *etc*: *She looked haggard after a sleepless night.* □ **hagard, défait**
haggle ['hagl] *verb* to argue about the price of something, or about the terms of an agreement. □ **marchander**
ha! ha! [haːˈhaː] *interjection* an expression of laughter, sometimes used as a sneer: *Ha! ha! That's a good joke!* □ **ah! ah!; ha! ha!**
hail[1] [heil] *noun* **1** small balls of ice falling from the clouds: *There was some hail during the rainstorm last night.* □ **grêle**
2 a shower (of things): *a hail of arrows.* □ **pluie**
■ *verb* to shower hail: *It was hailing as I drove home.* □ **grêler**
'hailstone *noun* a ball of hail: *Hailstones battered against the window.* □ **grêlon**
hail[2] [heil] *verb* **1** to shout to in order to attract attention: *We hailed a taxi; The captain hailed the passing ship.* □ **héler**
2 to greet or welcome (a person, thing *etc*) as something: *Her discoveries were hailed as a great step forward in medicine.* □ **saluer**
■ *noun* a shout (to attract attention): *Give that ship a hail.* □ **appel**
■ *interjection* an old word of greeting: *Hail, O King!* □ **salut**
hail from to come from or belong to (a place): *She hails from Texas.* □ **être originaire de**
hair [heə] *noun* **1** one of the mass of thread-like objects that grow from the skin: *She brushed the dog's hairs off her jacket.* □ **poil**
2 the mass of these, *especially* on a person's head: *He's got brown hair.* □ **cheveux**
-haired having (a certain kind of) hair: *a fair-haired girl.* □ **aux cheveux (...)**
'hairy *adjective* covered in hair or having a lot of hair: *a hairy chest.* □ **velu, poilu**
'hairiness *noun*. □ **aspect hirsute**
'hair('s) breadth *noun* a very small distance: *That knife missed me by a hair's-breadth.* □ **(d')un cheveu**
'hairbrush *noun* a brush for arranging and smoothing the hair. □ **brosse à cheveux**
'haircut *noun* the act or style of cutting a person's hair: *Go and get a haircut.* □ **coupe de cheveux**
'hair do – *plurals* **'hair-dos, 'hair-do's** – *noun* a hairstyle: *I like her new hair-do.* □ **coiffure**
'hairdresser *noun* a person who cuts, washes, styles *etc* a person's hair. □ **coiffeur, euse**
'hairdressing *noun*. □ **coiffure**
'hair dryer *noun* an electrical apparatus which dries a person's hair by blowing hot air over it. □ **sèche-cheveux**
'hairline *noun* the line along the forehead where the hair begins to grow. □ **naissance des cheveux**
'hair oil *noun* a scented, oily lotion for smoothing down the hair. □ **huile capillaire**
'hairpin *noun* a bent wire for keeping a woman's hair in place. □ **épingle à cheveux**
■ *adjective* (of a bend in a road) sharp and U-shaped,

especially on a mountain or a hill. □ **en épingle à cheveux**

'**hair-raising** *adjective* terrifying: *hair-raising stories.* □ **à faire se dresser les cheveux sur la tête**

'**hairstyle** *noun* the result of cutting, styling *etc* a person's hair: *a simple hairstyle.* □ **coiffure**

let one's hair down to behave in a free and relaxed manner. □ **se laisser aller**

make (someone's) hair stand on end to terrify (a person). □ **faire dresser les cheveux sur la tête**

split hairs to worry about unimportant details. □ **couper les cheveux en quatre**

tear one's hair to show great irritation or despair. □ **s'arracher les cheveux**

half [hɑːf] – *plural* **halves** [hɑːvz] – *noun* **1** one of two equal parts of anything: *She tried to stick the two halves together again; half a kilogram of sugar; a kilogram and a half of sugar.* □ **moitié, demi**

2 one of two equal parts of a game (*eg* in football, hockey) *usually* with a break between them: *Rangers scored three goals in the first half.* □ **demie**

■ *adjective* **1** being (equal to) one of two equal parts (of something): *a half bottle of wine.* □ **demi**

2 being made up of two things in equal parts: *A centaur is a mythical creature, half man and half horse.* □ **mi (mi-)**

3 not full or complete: *a half smile.* □ **demi-**

■ *adverb* **1** to the extent of one half: *This cup is only half full; It's half empty.* □ **à demi**

2 almost; partly: *I'm half hoping she won't come; half dead from hunger.* □ **à moitié**

half-: *a half-dozen; a half-kilogram of tea.* □ **demi**

halve [hɑːv] *verb* **1** to divide (something) into two equal parts: *He halved the apple.* □ **couper en deux**

2 to make half as great as before; to reduce by half: *By going away early in the year, we nearly halved the cost of our holiday.* □ **diminuer de moitié**

,**half-and-'half** *adverb, adjective* in equal parts: *We can split the costs between us half-and-half.* □ **moitié-moitié**

'**half-back** *noun* in football, hockey *etc*, (a player in) a position directly behind the forwards. □ **demi**

'**half-brother,** '**half-sister** *nouns* a brother or sister by one parent only: *My father has been married twice, and I have two half-brothers.* □ **demi-frère, demi-sœur**

,**half-'hearted** *adjective* not eager; done without enthusiasm: *a half-hearted cheer/attempt.* □ **sans enthousiasme**

,**half-'heartedly** *adverb.* □ **sans conviction**

,**half-'heartedness** *noun.* □ **tiédeur**

,**half-'hourly** *adjective, adverb* done *etc* every half-hour: *at half-hourly intervals; The buses to town run half-hourly.* □ **toutes les demi-heures**

,**half-'term** *noun* (the period when students are given)a holiday about the middle of a term: *We get a week's holiday at half-term;* (*also adjective*) *a half-term holiday.* □ **congé de mi-trimestre**

,**half-'time** *noun* a short rest between two halves of a game (of football *etc*): *the players ate oranges at half-time.* □ **mi-temps**

,**half-'way** *adjective, adverb* of or at a point equally far

from the beginning and the end: *We have reached the half-way point; We are half-way through the work now.* □ **à mi-chemin**

'**half-wit** *noun* a fool or idiot. □ **idiot, idiote**

,**half-'witted** *adjective* foolish or idiotic. □ **simple d'esprit**

,**half-'yearly** *adjective, adverb* done *etc* every six months: *a half-yearly report; We balance our accounts half-yearly.* □ **semestriel; semestriellement**

at half mast (of flags) flying at a position half-way up a mast *etc* to show that someone of importance has died: *The flags are (flying) at half mast.* □ **en berne**

by half by a long way: *He's too clever by half.* □ **beaucoup trop**

do things by halves to do things in an incomplete way: *She never does things by halves.* □ **faire les choses à moitié**

go halves with to share the cost with. □ **partager également**

half past three, four, seven *etc* at thirty minutes past the hour stated: *I'm leaving at half past six.* □ **et demie**

in half in(to) two equal parts: *He cut the cake in half; The pencil broke in half.* □ **en deux**

not half a slang expression for very much: *'Are you enjoying yourself?' 'Not half!'* □ **tu parles!**

hall [hɔːl] *noun* **1** a room or passage at the entrance to a house: *We left our coats in the hall.* □ **entrée, hall**

2 (a building with) a large public room, used for concerts, meetings *etc*: *a community hall.* □ **salle**

3 a building with offices where the administration of a town *etc* is carried out: *the city hall.* □ **hôtel de ville**

4 a passageway through a building; a corridor. □ **corridor**

5 a building of a university, college *etc*, especially one in which students *etc* live. □ **pavillon**

'**hallmark** *noun* a mark put on gold and silver articles to show the quality of the gold or silver. □ **cachet de contrôle**

'**hallway** *noun* a hall or passage. □ **vestibule, couloir**

hallowed ['hæloud] *adjective* holy: *hallowed ground.* □ **saint**

hallucination [həluːsi'neiʃən] *noun* the seeing of something that is not really there: *I had hallucinations after I took drugs.* □ **hallucination**

hallway *see* **hall.**

halo ['heilou] – *plural* '**halo(e)s** – *noun* **1** a ring of light around the sun or moon. □ **halo**

2 a similar ring of light around the head of a holy person in a picture *etc*. □ **auréole**

halt [hɔːlt] *verb* to (cause to) stop walking, marching, running *etc*: *The driver halted the train; The train halted at the signals.* □ **(s')arrêter**

■ *noun* **1** a complete stop: *The train came to a halt.* □ **arrêt**

2 a short stop (on a march *etc*). □ **halte**

3 a small railway station. □ **halte**

call a halt (to) to stop; to put an end (to): *It's time to call a halt to these stupid arguments.* □ **mettre un terme à**

halter ['hɔːltə] *noun* a rope for holding and leading a horse by its head. □ **licou**

halve, halves *see* **half.**

ham [ham] *noun* the top of the back leg of a pig, salted and dried. □ **jambon**

hamburger ['hambɔːgə] *noun* 1 a round cake of minced beef, *usually* fried. □ **bifteck haché**

2 a bread roll containing one of these. □ **hambourgeois**

hammer ['hamə] *noun* 1 a tool with a heavy *usually* metal head, used for driving nails into wood, breaking hard substances *etc*: *a joiner's hammer.* □ **marteau**

2 the part of a bell, piano, clock *etc* that hits against some other part, so making a noise. □ **marteau**

3 in sport, a metal ball on a long steel handle for throwing. □ **marteau**

■ *verb* 1 to hit, beat, break *etc* (something) with a hammer: *She hammered the nail into the wood.* □ **marteler/enfoncer à coups de marteau**

2 to teach a person (something) with difficulty, by repetition: *Grammar was hammered into us at school.* □ **faire entrer qqch. dans la tête de qqn**

give (someone) a hammering to hammer (= beat) (a person): *His mother gave him a hammering for stealing.* □ **rosser**

hammer home to make great efforts to make a person realize: *We'll have to hammer home to them the importance of secrecy.* □ **faire bien comprendre (à force d'insistance)**

hammer out to produce (an agreement *etc*) with a great deal of effort and discussion: *to hammer out a solution.* □ **élaborer**

hammock ['hamək] *noun* a long piece of netting, canvas *etc* hung up by the corners and used as a bed, *eg* in a ship. □ **hamac**

hamper ['hampə] *verb* to make it difficult for (someone) to do something: *I tried to run away but I was hampered by my long dress.* □ **entraver**

■ *noun* a large basket with a lid: *a picnic hamper.* □ **panier**

hamster ['hamstə] *noun* a small animal, rather like a fat rat without a tail, often kept as a pet. □ **hamster**

hand [hand] *noun* 1 the part of the body at the end of the arm. □ **main**

2 a pointer on a clock, watch *etc*: *Clocks usually have an hour hand and a minute hand.* □ **aiguille**

3 a person employed as a helper, crew member *etc*: *a farm hand; All hands on deck!* □ **ouvrier, ière, membre de l'équipage**

4 help; assistance: *Can I lend a hand?; Give me a hand with this box, please.* □ **coup de main**

5 a set of playing cards dealt to a person: *I had a very good hand so I thought I had a chance of winning.* □ **main, jeu**

6 a measure (*approximately*) 10 centimetres) used for measuring the height of horses: *a horse of 14 hands.* □ **paume**

7 handwriting: *written in a neat hand.* □ **écriture**

■ *verb* (*often with* **back, down, up** *etc*) 1 to give (something) to someone by hand: *I handed him the book; He handed it back to me; I'll go up the ladder, and you can hand the tools up to me.* □ **donner, rendre, transmettre**

2 to pass, transfer *etc* into another's care *etc*: *That is the end of my report from Paris. I'll now hand you back to Fred Smith in the television studio in London.* □ **remettre, retourner**

'**handful** *noun* 1 as much as can be held in one hand: *a handful of sweets.* □ **poignée**

2 a small number: *Only a handful of people came to the meeting.* □ **poignée**

3 a person *etc* difficult to control: *Her three children are a (bit of a) handful.* □ **(personne) qui donne du fil à retordre**

'**handbag** *noun* a small bag carried by women, for personal belongings. □ **sac à main**

'**handbill** *noun* a small printed notice. □ **prospectus**

'**handbook** *noun* a small book giving information about (how to do) something: *a handbook of European birds; a bicycle-repair handbook.* □ **manuel**

'**handbrake** *noun* (in a car, bus *etc*) a brake operated by the driver's hand. □ **frein à main**

'**handcuff** *verb* to put handcuffs on (a person): *The police handcuffed the criminal.* □ **passer les menottes à**

'**handcuffs** *noun plural* steel rings, joined by a short chain, put around the wrists of prisoners: *a pair of handcuffs.* □ **menottes**

,**hand'made** *adjective* made with a person's hands or with tools held in the hands, rather than by machines: *hand-made furniture.* □ **fait à la main**

hand-'operated *adjective: hand-operated switches.* □ **actionné à la main**

'**hand-out** *see* **hand out** *below.*

,**hand'picked** *adjective* chosen very carefully: *a hand-picked team of workers.* □ **trié sur le volet**

'**handshake** *noun* the act of grasping (a person's) hand *eg* as a greeting. □ **poignée de main**

'**handstand** *noun* the gymnastic act of balancing one's body upright in the air with one's hands on the ground. □ **arbre droit**

'**handwriting** *noun* 1 writing with a pen or pencil: *Today we will practise handwriting.* □ **écriture**

2 the way in which a person writes: *Your handwriting is terrible!* □ **écriture**

'**handwritten** *adjective: The letter was handwritten, not typed.* □ **manuscrit**

at hand 1 (*with* **close** *or* **near**) near: *The bus station is close at hand.* □ **tout près**

2 available: *Help is at hand.* □ **disponible**

at the hands of from, or by the action of: *He received very rough treatment at the hands of the terrorists.* □ **entre les mains de**

be hand in glove (with someone) to be very closely associated with someone, *especially* for a bad purpose. □ **être de mèche avec**

by hand 1 with a person's hand or tools held in the hands, rather than with machinery: *furniture made by hand.* □ **à la main**

2 not by post but by a messenger *etc*: *This parcel was delivered by hand.* □ **par porteur**

fall into the hands (of someone) to be caught, found, captured *etc* by someone: *He fell into the hands of bandits; The documents fell into the wrong hands (= were* found, captured *etc* by someone who was not supposed to see them). □ **tomber entre les mains de**

force someone's hand to force someone to do something either which he does not want to do or sooner than he wants to do it. □ **forcer la main (à)**

get one's hands on 1 to catch: *If I ever get my hands on him, I'll make him sorry for what he did!* □ **mettre la main sur**

2 to get or obtain: *I'd love to get my hands on a car like that.* □ **trouver, dénicher**

give/lend a helping hand to help or assist: *I'm always ready to give/lend a helping hand.* □ **donner un coup de main**

hand down to pass on from one generation to the next: *These customs have been handed down from father to son since the Middle Ages.* □ **transmettre**

hand in to give or bring to a person, place *etc*: *The teacher told the children to hand in their exercise-books.* □ **remettre**

hand in hand with one person holding the hand of another: *The boy and girl were walking along hand in hand; Poverty and crime go hand in hand.* □ **la main dans la main**

hand on to give to someone: *When you have finished reading these notes, hand them on to me.* □ **passer à**

hand out to give to several people; to distribute: *The teacher handed out books to all the pupils; They were handing out leaflets in the street.* □ **distribuer**

hand-out *noun* a leaflet. □ **prospectus**

hand over to give or pass; to surrender: *We know you have the jewels, so hand them over; They handed the thief over to the police.* □ **remettre, livrer**

hand over fist in large amounts, *usually* quickly: *He's making money hand over fist.* □ **comme de l'eau**

hands down very easily: *You'll win hands down.* □ **haut la main**

hands off! do not touch! □ **bas les pattes!**

hands up! raise your hands above your head: *'Hands up!' shouted the gunman.* □ **haut les mains!**

hand to hand with one individual fighting another at close quarters: *The soldiers fought the enemy hand to hand; (also adjective) hand-to-hand fighting.* □ **(au) corps-à-corps**

have a hand in (something) to be one of the people who have caused, done *etc* (something): *Did you have a hand in the building of this boat/in the success of the project?* □ **être pour qqch. dans**

have/get/gain the upper hand to (begin to) win, beat the enemy *etc*: *The enemy made a fierce attack but failed to get the upper hand.* □ **prendre l'avantage/le dessus (sur)**

hold hands (with someone) to be hand in hand with someone: *The boy and girl walked along holding hands (with each other).* □ **se tenir par la main**

in good hands receiving care and attention: *The patient is in good hands.* □ **en bonnes mains**

in hand 1 not used *etc*; remaining: *We still have $10 in hand.* □ **disponible**

2 being dealt with: *We have received your complaint and the matter is now in hand.* □ **bien en main**

in the hands of being dealt with by: *This matter is now in the hands of my solicitor.* □ **entre les mains de**

keep one's hand in to remain good or skilful at doing something by doing it occasionally: *I still sometimes play a game of billiards, just to keep my hand in.* □ **garder la main**

off one's hands no longer needing to be looked after *etc*: *You'll be glad to get the children off your hands for a couple of weeks.* □ **qui n'est plus à la charge de**

on hand near; present; ready for use *etc*: *We always keep some candles on hand in case there's a power failure.* □ **sous la main, à la portée de la main**

(on the one hand) ... on the other hand an expression used to introduce two opposing parts of an argument *etc*: *(On the one hand) we could stay and help you, but on the other hand, it might be better if we went to help her instead.* □ **d'une part... d'autre part...**

out of hand unable to be controlled: *The angry crowd was getting out of hand.* □ **incontrôlable**

shake hands with (someone)/ shake someone's hand to grasp a person's (*usually* right) hand, in one's own (*usually* right) hand, as a form of greeting, as a sign of agreement *etc*. □ **(se) serrer la main**

a show of hands at a meeting, debate *etc*, a vote expressed by people raising their hands. □ **à main levée**

take in hand to look after, discipline or train. □ **prendre en main**

handicap ['handikap] *noun* 1 something that makes doing something more difficult: *The loss of a finger would be a handicap for a pianist.* □ **handicap**

2 (in a race, competition *etc*) a disadvantage of some sort (*eg* having to run a greater distance in a race) given to the best competitors so that others have a better chance of winning. □ **désavantage**

3 a race, competition *etc* in which this happens. □ **handicap**

4 (a form of) physical or mental disability: *children with physical handicaps.* □ **anomalie**

■ *verb* – *past tense, past participle* **'handicapped** – to make something (more) difficult for: *He wanted to be a pianist, but was handicapped by his deafness.* □ **handicaper**

'handicapped *adjective*: *She is physically handicapped and cannot walk; a handicapped child.* □ **handicapé**

handicraft ['handikraːft] *noun* skilled work done by hand, *eg* knitting, pottery, model-making *etc*. □ **travail manuel**

handiwork ['handiwəːk] *noun* 1 thing(s) made by hand: *Examples of the pupils' handiwork were on show.* □ **travail, ouvrage**

2 something bad caused by a particular person: *The broken window was Sarah's handiwork.* □ **œuvre**

handkerchief ['haŋkətʃif] – *plurals* **'handkerchiefs, 'handkerchieves** [-tʃiːvz] – *noun* (*abbreviation* **hanky** (*plural* **'hankies**), **hankie** ['haŋki]) a small *usually* square piece of cloth or paper tissue used for wiping or blowing one's nose into. □ **mouchoir**

handle ['handl] *noun* the part of an object by which it may be held or grasped: *I've broken the handle off this cup; You've got to turn the handle in order to open the* *door.* □ **anse, poignée**

■ *verb* **1** to touch or hold with the hand: *Please wash your hands before handling food.* □ **manipuler, manier**
2 to control, manage or deal with: *He'll never make a good teacher – he doesn't know how to handle children.* □ **s'y prendre avec**
3 to buy or sell; to deal in: *I'm afraid we do not handle such goods in this shop.* □ **tenir, vendre**
4 to treat in a particular way: *Never handle animals roughly.* □ **traiter**
-handled: *a long-handled knife.* □ **à manche (...)**
'handler *noun* a person who trains and controls an animal (*especially* a dog): *a police dog and its handler.* □ **dresseur, euse (de chiens)**
'handlebars *noun plural* the bar at the front of a bicycle *etc* which is held by the rider and by which the bicycle *etc* is steered: *The cyclist was thrown over the handlebars when the bike crashed.* □ **guidon**
handsome ['hansəm] *adjective* **1** (*usually* of men) good-looking: *a handsome prince.* □ **beau**
2 very large; generous: *She gave a handsome sum of money to charity.* □ **joli, généreux**
'handsomely *adverb*. □ **généreusement, élégamment**
'handsomeness *noun*. □ **beauté, libéralité**
handstand, handwriting *see* **hand**.
handy ['handi] *adjective* **1** ready (to use); in a convenient place: *I like to keep my tools handy; This house is handy for the shops.* □ **à portée (de la main)**
2 easy to use; useful: *a handy tool.* □ **pratique**
'handiness *noun*. □ **habileté, commodité**
'handyman ['man] *noun* a man who does jobs, for himself or other people, *especially* around the house. □ **homme à tout faire**
come in handy to be useful: *I'll keep these bottles – they might come in handy.* □ **servir**
hang [haŋ] – *past tense, past participle* **hung** [hʌŋ] – *verb* **1** to put or fix, or to be put or fixed, above the ground *eg* by a hook: *We'll hang the picture on that wall; The picture is hanging on the wall.* □ **suspendre, être accroché**
2 to fasten (something), or to be fastened, at the top or side so that it can move freely but cannot fall: *A door hangs by its hinges.* □ **accrocher, être accroché**
3 (*past tense, past participle* **hanged**) to kill, or to be killed, by having a rope put around the neck and being allowed to drop: *Murderers used to be hanged in the United Kingdom, but hangs for murder now.* □ **pendre, être pendu**
4 (*often with* **down** *or* **out**) to be bending, drooping or falling downwards: *The dog's tongue was hanging out; Her hair was hanging down.* □ **pendre**
5 to bow (one's head): *He hung his head in shame.* □ **baisser**
'hanger *noun* (*usually* '**coat-hanger**) a shaped metal, wooden or plastic frame with a hook on which jackets, dresses *etc* are hung up. □ **cintre**
'hanging *noun* the (act of) killing a criminal by hanging. □ **pendaison**
'hangings *noun plural* curtains or material hung on walls for decoration. □ **tentures, draperies**

'hangman *noun* a man whose job it is to hang criminals. □ **bourreau**
'hangover *noun* the unpleasant effects of having had too much alcohol: *He woke up with a hangover.* □ **gueule de bois**
get the hang of to learn or begin to understand how to do (something): *It may seem difficult at first, but you'll get the hang of it after a few weeks.* □ **saisir le truc (pour faire qqch.)**
hang about/around 1 to stand around, doing nothing: *I don't like to see all these youths hanging about (street-corners).* □ **traîner**
2 to be close to (a person) frequently: *I don't want you hanging around my daughter.* □ **tourner autour (de)**
hang back to hesitate or be unwilling: *The soldiers all hung back when the sergeant asked for volunteers.* □ **hésiter**
hang in the balance to be in doubt: *The success of this project is hanging in the balance.* □ **rester en suspens**
hang on 1 to wait: *Will you hang on a minute – I'm not quite ready.* □ **attendre**
2 (*often with* **to**) to hold: *Hang on to that rope.* □ **s'accrocher à**
3 to keep; to retain: *She likes to hang on to her money.* □ **s'accrocher à**
hang together to agree or be consistent: *His statements just do not hang together.* □ **(s')accorder**
hang up 1 to hang (something) on something: *Hang up your coat in the cupboard.* □ **suspendre**
2 (*often with* **on**) to put the receiver back after a telephone conversation: *I tried to talk to her, but she hung up (on me).* □ **raccrocher (au nez de)**

> She **hung** the picture up.
> The murderer was **hanged**.

hangar ['haŋə] *noun* a shed for airplanes. □ **hangar**
hank [haŋk] *noun* a coil or loop of rope, wool, string *etc*: *hanks of knitting-wool.* □ **écheveau**
hanker ['haŋkə] *verb* (*with* **after** *or* **for**) to want (something): *He was hankering after the bright lights of the city.* □ **désirer ardemment (qqch.)**
have a hankering for: *I have a hankering for a strawberry ice cream.* □ **avoir envie de**
hankie, hanky ['haŋki] short for **handkerchief**.
haphazard [hap'hazəd] *adjective* depending on chance; without planning or system: *a haphazard arrangement.* □ **au petit bonheur**
hap'hazardly *adverb*. □ **au hasard**
happen ['hapən] *verb* **1** to take place or occur; to occur by chance: *What happened next?; It just so happens/As it happens, I have the key in my pocket.* □ **arriver, se passer**
2 (*usually with* **to**) to be done to (a person, thing *etc*): *She's late – something must have happened to her.* □ **arriver à**
3 to do or be by chance: *I happened to find him; She happens to be my friend.* □ **le hasard a voulu que, il se trouve que**
'happening *noun* an occurrence: *strange happenings.* □ **événement**

happen (up)on to find by chance: *She happened upon the perfect solution to the problem just as she was about to give up her research.* □ **tomber sur**

happy ['hapi] *adjective* 1 having or showing a feeling of pleasure or contentment: *a happy smile; I feel happy today.* □ **heureux**

2 willing: *I'd be happy to help you.* □ **heureux**

3 lucky: *By a happy chance I have the key with me.* □ **heureux**

'**happiness** *noun.* □ **bonheur**

'**happily** *adverb*: *The child smiled happily; Happily,* (= *Fortunately,*) *she arrived home safely.* □ **joyeusement; par bonheur**

,**happy-go-'lucky** *adjective* not worrying about what might happen: *cheerful and happy-go-lucky.* □ **insouciant**

happy medium a sensible middle course between two extreme positions: *I need to find the happy medium between starving and over-eating.* □ **moyen terme**

harangue [hə'raŋ] *noun* a long loud speech: *a harangue from the headmaster on good behaviour.* □ **harangue**

■ *verb* to give a harangue to. □ **haranguer**

harass ['harəs] *verb* 1 to annoy or trouble (a person) constantly or frequently: *The children have been harassing me all morning.* □ **harceler**

2 to make frequent sudden attacks on (an enemy): *The army was constantly harassed by groups of terrorists.* □ **harceler**

'**harassed** *adjective*: *a harassed mother.* □ **tracassé**

'**harassment** *noun*: *He complained of harassment by the police.* □ **harcèlement**

harbour, ['haːbə] *noun* a place of shelter for ships: *All the ships stayed in* (the) *harbour during the storm.* □ **port**

■ *verb* 1 to give shelter or refuge to (a person): *It is against the law to harbour criminals.* □ **donner asile (à)**

2 to have (*usually* bad) thoughts in one's head: *He harbours a grudge against me.* □ **nourrir**

'**harbour-master** *noun* the official in charge of a harbour. □ **capitaine de port**

hard [haːd] *adjective* 1 firm; solid; not easy to break, scratch *etc*: *The ground is too hard to dig.* □ **dur**

2 not easy to do, learn, solve *etc*: *Is English a hard language to learn?; He is a hard man to please.* □ **difficile**

3 not feeling or showing kindness: *a hard master.* □ **dur**

4 (of weather) severe: *a hard winter.* □ **rigoureux**

5 having or causing suffering: *a hard life; hard times.* □ **difficile**

6 (of water) containing many chemical salts and so not easily forming bubbles when soap is added: *The water is hard in this part of the country.* □ **dur**

■ *adverb* 1 with great effort: *She works very hard; Think hard.* □ **dur, sérieusement**

2 with great force; heavily: *Don't hit him too hard; It was raining hard.* □ **fort, à verse**

3 with great attention: *He stared hard at the man.* □ **fixement**

4 to the full extent; completely: *The car turned hard right.* □ **à droite toute**

'**harden** *verb* to make or become hard: *Don't touch the toffee till it hardens; Try to harden your heart against her.* □ **(en)durcir**

'**hardness** *noun.* □ **dureté**

'**hardship** *noun* (something which causes) pain, suffering *etc*: *a life full of hardship.* □ **épreuve(s)**

'**hard-and-fast** *adjective* (of rules) that can never be changed or ignored. □ **strict**

'**hard-back** *noun* a book with a hard cover: *Hard-backs are more expensive than paperbacks.* □ **livre relié**

,**hard-'boiled** *adjective* (of eggs) boiled until the white and the yolk are solid. □ **(œuf) dur**

'**hard-earned** *adjective* earned by hard work or with difficulty: *I deserve every penny of my hard-earned wages.* □ **bien mérité**

,**hard-'headed** *adjective* practical; shrewd; not influenced by emotion: *a hard-headed businessman.* □ **pratique**

,**hard-'hearted** *adjective* not feeling or showing pity or kindness: *a hard-hearted employer.* □ **impitoyable**

'**hardware** *noun* metal goods such as pots, tools *etc*: *This shop sells hardware.* □ **quincaillerie**

hardware dealer *noun* a person whose business is selling metal or hardware items such as tools, nails, and locks: *The hardware dealer told us what equipment we would need to install a lock.* □ **quincaillier**

,**hard-'wearing** *adjective* that will not wear out easily: *a hard-wearing fabric.* □ **solide**

be hard on 1 to punish or criticize severely: *Don't be too hard on the boy – he's too young to know that he was doing wrong.* □ **être dur avec**

2 to be unfair to: *If you punish all the children for the broken window it's a bit hard on those who had nothing to do with it.* □ **être injuste envers**

hard at it busy doing (something): *I've been hard at it all day, trying to get this report finished.* □ **attelé à (qqch.)**

hard done by unfairly treated: *You should complain to the headmaster if you feel hard done by.* □ **injustement traité**

hard luck bad luck: *Hard luck! I'm afraid you haven't won this time; It's hard luck that she broke her leg.* □ **pas de chance**

hard of hearing rather deaf: *She is a bit hard of hearing now.* □ **dur d'oreille**

a hard time (of it) trouble, difficulty, worry *etc*: *The audience gave the speaker a hard time of it at the meeting; The speaker had a hard time (of it) trying to make himself heard.* □ **du fil à retordre**

hard up not having much *especially* money: *I'm a bit hard up at the moment; I'm hard up for envelopes.* □ **avoir grand besoin (de qqch.)**

hardly ['haːdli] *adverb* 1 almost no, none, never *etc*: *Hardly any small businesses are successful nowadays; I hardly ever go out.* □ **presque**

2 only just; almost not: *My feet are so sore, I can hardly walk; I had hardly got on my bicycle when I got a puncture.* □ **à peine**

3 probably not: *He's hardly likely to forgive you after what you said about him.* □ **pas précisément**

hardship, hardware *see* **hard**.

hardy ['haːdi] *adjective* tough; strong; able to bear cold, tiredness *etc*: *She's very hardy – she takes a cold shower every morning.* □ **robuste**
'**hardiness** *noun.* □ **robustesse**

hare [heə] *noun* an animal with long ears, like a rabbit but slightly larger. □ **lièvre**

harem ['heərəm] *noun* **1** the part of a Muslim house occupied by the women. □ **harem**
2 the women themselves. □ **harem**

hark! [haːk] *interjection* listen! □ **écoute(z)!**

harm [haːm] *noun* damage; injury; distress: *I'll make sure you come to no harm; She meant no harm; It'll do you no harm to go.* □ **mal, tort**
■ *verb* to cause (a person) harm: *There's no need to be frightened – she won't harm you.* □ **faire du mal à**
'**harmful** *adjective* doing harm: *Medicines can be harmful if you take too much of them.* □ **nuisible**
'**harmless** *adjective* not dangerous or liable to cause harm: *Don't be frightened of that snake – it's harmless.* □ **inoffensif**
'**harmlessly** *adverb.* □ **innocemment**
'**harmlessness** *noun.* □ **innocuité**
out of harm's way in a safe place: *I'll put this glass vase out of harm's way, in case it gets broken.* □ **en lieu sûr**

harmonic *see* **harmony**.

harmonica [haːˈmonikə] *noun* a kind of small musical instrument played with the mouth. □ **harmonica**

harmony ['haːməni] – *plural* '**harmonies** – *noun* **1** (of musical sounds, colours *etc*) (the state of forming) a pleasing combination: *The singers sang in harmony.* □ **harmonie**
2 the agreement of people's feelings, opinions *etc*: *Few married couples live in perfect harmony.* □ **harmonie**
har'**monic** [-ˈmo-] *adjective* of, or concerned with, *especially* musical harmony. □ **harmonique**
har'**monious** [-ˈmou-] *adjective* **1** pleasant-sounding: *a harmonious melody.* □ **harmonieux**
2 pleasant to the eye: *a harmonious colour scheme.* □ **harmonieux**
3 without disagreement or bad feeling: *a harmonious relationship.* □ **harmonieux**
har'**moniously** *adverb.* □ **harmonieusement**
har'**moniousness** *noun.* □ **harmonie**
'**harmonize**, '**harmonise** *verb* **1** to sing or play musical instruments in harmony. □ **chanter/jouer en harmonie**
2 to add different parts to (a melody) to form harmonies. □ **harmoniser**
3 to (cause to) be in harmony or agreement: *The colours in this room harmonize nicely.* □ **(s')harmoniser**
harmoni'**zation**, harmoni'**sation** *noun.* □ **harmonisation**

harness ['haːnis] *noun* the leather straps *etc* by which a horse is attached to a cart *etc* which it is pulling and by means of which it is controlled. □ **harnais**
■ *verb* **1** to put the harness on (a horse). □ **harnacher**
2 to make use of (a source of power, *eg* a river) for some purpose, *eg* to produce electricity or to drive machinery: *Attempts are now being made to harness the sun as a source of heat and power.* □ **exploiter**

harp [haːp] *noun* a *usually* large musical instrument which is held upright, and which has many strings which are plucked with the fingers. □ **harpe**
'**harpist** *noun.* □ **harpiste**

harp on (about) to keep on talking about: *He's forever harping on (about his low wages); She keeps harping on his faults.* □ **revenir sur**

harpoon [haːˈpuːn] *noun* a spear fastened to a rope, used *especially* for killing whales. □ **harpon**
■ *verb* to strike with a harpoon: *He has harpooned the whale.* □ **harponner**

harpsichord ['haːpsikoːd] *noun* a type of early keyboard musical instrument. □ **clavecin**

harrowing ['harouiŋ] *adjective* extremely distressing: *a harrowing experience.* □ **déchirant**

harry ['hari] *verb* to torment or worry frequently. □ **harceler**

harsh [haːʃ] *adjective* **1** (of people, discipline *etc*) very strict; cruel: *That is a very harsh punishment to give a young child.* □ **sévère**
2 rough and unpleasant to hear, see, taste *etc*: *a harsh voice; harsh colours.* □ **dur (au toucher), âpre (au goût), strident (à l'oreille)**
'**harshly** *adverb.* □ **durement**
'**harshness** *noun.* □ **dureté**

harvest ['haːvist] *noun* the gathering in of ripened crops: *the rice harvest.* □ **récolte**
■ *verb* to gather in (crops *etc*): *We harvested the apples yesterday.* □ **récolter**
'**harvester** *noun* a person or machine that harvests corn. □ **moissonneur, euse**

has, has-been *see* **have**.

hashish ['haʃiːʃ] *noun* (a drug made from) the dried leaves, flowers *etc* of the hemp plant, *usually* smoked or chewed; cannabis. □ **haschisch**

hasn't *see* **have**.

hassle ['hasl] *noun* **1** trouble or fuss: *It's such a hassle to get to work on time; Travelling with children is such a hassle.* □ **histoire**
2 a fight or argument: *I got into a bit of a hassle with a couple of thugs.* □ **bagarre**
■ *verb* **1** to argue or fight: *It seemed pointless to hassle over such a small matter.* □ **(se) chamailler**
2 to annoy (a person): *I don't like people hassling me.* □ **embêter**

haste [heist] *noun* (too much) speed: *Your work shows signs of haste – there are too many mistakes in it.* □ **hâte**

hasten ['heisn] *verb* **1** to (cause to) move with speed: *She hastened towards me; We must hasten the preparations.* □ **(se) hâter**
2 to do at once: *She hastened to add an explanation.* □ **s'empresser (de)**
'**hasty** *adjective* **1** done *etc* in a hurry: *a hasty snack.* □ **fait à la hâte**
2 acting or done with too much speed and without thought: *She is too hasty – she should think carefully before making such an important decision; a hasty decision.* □ **irréfléchi**

3 easily made angry: *a hasty temper*. □ **emporté**
'**hastily** *adverb*. □ **à la hâte**
'**hastiness** *noun*. □ **précipitation**
in haste in a hurry; quickly: *I am writing in haste before leaving for the airport*. □ **à la hâte**
make haste to hurry. □ **faire vite**

hat [hat] *noun* a covering for the head, *usually* worn out of doors: *He raised his hat as the lady approached*. □ **chapeau**
'**hatter** *noun* a person who makes or sells hats. □ **chapelier, ière**
hat trick (in football) three goals scored by one player in a match. □ **tour du chapeau**
keep (something) under one's hat to keep (something) secret: *Keep it under your hat but I'm getting married next week*. □ **garder pour soi**
pass/send around the hat to ask for or collect money on someone's behalf. □ **faire la quête**
take one's hat off to to admire (someone) for doing something. □ **tirer son chapeau à**
talk through one's hat to talk nonsense. ■ **parler à tort et à travers**

hatch[1] [hatʃ] *noun* (the door or cover of) an opening in a wall, floor, ship's deck *etc*: *There are two hatches between the kitchen and dining room for serving food*. □ **passe-plats**
'**hatchway** *noun* an opening, *especially* in a ship's deck. □ **écoutille**

hatch[2] [hatʃ] *verb* 1 to produce (young birds *etc*) from eggs: *My hens have hatched ten chicks*. □ **faire éclore**
2 to break out of the egg: *These chicks hatched this morning*. □ **éclore**
3 to become young birds: *Four of the eggs have hatched*. □ **éclore**
4 to plan (something, *usually* bad) in secret: *to hatch a plot*. □ (**se**) **tramer**

hatchet ['hatʃit] *noun* a small axe held in one hand. □ **hachette**

hatchway *see* **hatch**[1].

hate [heit] *verb* to dislike very much: *I hate them for their cruelty to my father*; *I hate getting up in the morning*. □ **détester, haïr**
■ *noun* great dislike: *a look of hate*. □ **haine**
'**hateful** *adjective* very bad; very unpleasant: *That was a hateful thing to do to her*; *What a hateful person!* □ **odieux**
'**hatefully** *adverb*. □ **odieusement**
'**hatefulness** *noun*. □ **caractère odieux (de qqch.)**
hatred ['heitrid] *noun* great dislike: *There was a look of hatred in his eyes*; *I have a deep-seated hatred of liars*. □ **haine**

hatter *see* **hat**.

haughty ['hɔːti] *adjective* very proud: *a haughty look*; *a haughty young woman*. □ **hautain**
'**haughtily** *adverb*. □ **avec hauteur**
'**haughtiness** *noun*. □ **hauteur, morgue**

haul [hɔːl] *verb* 1 to pull with great effort or difficulty: *Horses are used to haul barges along canals*. □ **tirer**
2 to carry by some form of transport: *Coal is hauled by road and rail*. □ **transporter**

■ *noun* 1 a strong pull: *She gave the rope a haul*. □ **effort**
2 the amount of anything, *especially* fish, that is got at one time: *The fishermen had a good haul*; *The thieves got away from the jeweller's with a good haul*. □ **prise, butin**
'**haulage** [-lidʒ] *noun* (money charged for) the carrying of goods by road, rail *etc*. □ **frais de transport**
'**hauler** [-liə] *noun* a person who owns trucks which carry goods for other people. □ **transporteur, euse, routier, ière**
a long haul a long or tiring job, journey *etc*. □ **longue étape**

haunch [hɔːntʃ] *noun* 1 (*usually in plural*) the fleshy part of the hip: *The children were squatting on their haunches*. □ **hanche, derrière**
2 the leg and lower part of the body of a deer *etc*, as meat: *a haunch of venison*. □ **cuissot**

haunt [hɔːnt] *verb* 1 (of a ghost) to inhabit: *A ghost is said to haunt this house*. □ **hanter**
2 (of an unpleasant memory) to keep coming back into the mind of: *Her look of misery haunts me*. □ **hanter, obséder**
3 to visit very often: *He haunts that café*. □ **fréquenter**
■ *noun* a place one often visits: *This is one of my favourite haunts*. □ **lieu fréquenté**
'**haunted** *adjective* inhabited by ghosts: *a haunted castle*; *The old house is said to be haunted*. □ **hanté**

have [hav] – *3rd person singular present tense* **has** [haz]: *past tense, past participle* **had** [had]: *short forms* **I've** [aiv] (**I have**), **you've** [juːv] (**you have**), **he's** [hizz] (**he has**), **she's** [ʃizz] (**she has**), **it's** [its] (**it has**), **we've** [wiːv] (**we have**), **they've** [ðeiv] (**they have**), **I'd** [aid] (**I had**), **you'd** [juːd] (**you had**), **he'd** [hiːd] (**he had**), **she'd** [ʃiːd] (**she had**), **it'd** ['itəd] (**it had**), **we'd** [wiːd] (**we had**), **they'd** [ðeid] (**they had**): *negative short forms* **hadn't** ['hadnt] (**had not**), **hasn't** ['haznt] (**has not**), **haven't** ['havnt] (**have not**) – *verb* 1 used with *past participle* of other verbs to show that an action is in the past and has been completed: *I've bought a new dictionary*; *Has he gone yet?* □ **avoir**
2 (*also* **have got**) to hold or possess (something which belongs to oneself or to someone else): *I have a book of yours at home*; *He's got your book*; *I don't have any books by Sir Walter Scott*. □ **avoir**
3 (*also* **have got**) to possess something as part of oneself or in some way connected with oneself: *She has blue eyes*; *Our house has six rooms*; *I've got a pain in my stomach*. □ **avoir**
4 (*sometimes with* **back**) to receive or get: *Have you had any news of your brother?*; *Thank you for lending me the book – you can have it back next week*. □ **avoir**
5 to produce: *He does have some good ideas*; *She has had a baby*. □ **avoir**
6 to cause to be done: *I'm having a tooth (taken) out*; *Have Smith come and see me*.
7 to enjoy or suffer: *We had a lovely holiday*. □ **avoir**
8 to do or take: *I'll have a drink*; *Let me have a try*.
9 to allow: *I will not have you wearing clothes like that!* □ **permettre**

10 (*with* **back, in, over** *etc*) to ask to one's house as a guest or to do a job: *We're having friends over for dinner*; *We're having someone in to paint this room*. □ **recevoir, faire venir**

11 to think or feel: *I have some doubts about this project*. □ **avoir**

12 to trick: *You've been had!* □ **avoir**

'**has-been** *noun* a person who is no longer famous and important. □ **vieux**

have done with to stop or put an end to: *Let's have done with all this quarrelling*. □ **en finir avec**

have had it to be dead, ruined *etc*: *The bullet went into his brain – he's had it, I'm afraid*. □ **être fichu**

have it in oneself *etc* to have the courage or ability to do something: *I hear she told her boss to stop shouting at her – I didn't think she had it in her*. □ **être capable de**

have it out (*often with* **with**) to argue with (a person) in order to put an end to some disagreement: *I'm going to have it out with her once and for all*. □ **s'expliquer (avec)**

have on 1 (*also* **have got on**) to wear: *That's a nice suit you have on*. □ **porter**

2 to fool (someone): *You're having me on – that's not really true, is it?* □ **faire marcher quelqu'un**

3 (*also* **have got on**) to be busy with: *Have you* (*got*) *anything on this afternoon?* □ **être pris**

have to (*also* **have got to**) to be obliged to (do something): *I don't want to do this, but I have to*; *Do you have to go so soon?*; *I've got to leave soon*; *You didn't have to do that, did you?* □ **être obligé (de)**

have to do with (a person or thing), (*also* **have got to do with**) to be of importance or concern to (a person or thing): *What have these letters to do with you?*; *Your remarks have* (*got*) *nothing to do with the subject we are discussing*. □ **avoir un rapport avec**

have up (*usually with* **for**) to make (a person) appear in court to answer some charge: *He was had up for drunken driving*. □ **convoquer**

have what it takes, (*also* **have got what it takes**) to have the qualities or ability that one needs to do something: *He has* (*got*) *what it takes to make a good officer*. □ **avoir ce qu'il faut/les compétences pour**

I have it!, (*also* **I've got it!**) I have found the answer (to a problem *etc*). □ **j'ai trouvé!**

haven ['heivn] *noun* a harbour; a place of safety or rest. □ **havre**

haven't *see* **have**.

haversack ['havəsak] *noun* a bag worn over one shoulder by a walker *etc* for carrying food *etc*. □ **sac à dos**

havoc ['havək] *noun* great destruction or damage: *The hurricane created havoc over a wide area*. □ **ravage**

hawk[1] [hoːk] *noun* a type of bird of prey. □ **faucon**

'**hawk-'eyed** *adjective* having very good eye-sight. □ **au regard perçant**

hawk[2] [hoːk] *verb* to carry goods around for sale. □ **colporter**

'**hawker** *noun*. □ **colporteur, euse**

hawser ['hoːzə] *noun* a thick rope or a steel cable for towing ships or tying them to a dock *etc*. □ **câble de**

remorque

hawthorn ['hoːθoːn] *noun* a small tree with thorns and white or pink blossoms. □ **aubépine**

hay [hei] *noun* grass, cut and dried, used as food for cattle *etc*. □ **foin**

,**hay-'fever** *noun* an illness like a bad cold, caused by the pollen of flowers *etc*. □ **rhume des foins**

'**hayrick** [-rik], '**hay-stack** *nouns* hay built up into a large pile. □ **meule de foin**

'**haywire** *adjective* in a state of disorder; crazy: *Our computer has gone haywire*. □ **détraqué**

hazard ['hazəd] *noun* (something which causes) a risk of harm or danger: *the hazards of mountain-climbing*. □ **danger**

■ *verb* **1** to risk; to be prepared to do (something, the result of which is uncertain): *Are you prepared to hazard your life for the success of this mission?* □ **risquer**

2 to put forward (a guess *etc*). □ **risquer, hasarder (une opinion)**

'**hazardous** *adjective* dangerous: *a hazardous journey*. □ **périlleux**

'**hazardousness** *noun*. □ **péril**

haze [heiz] *noun* a thin mist: *The mountains were dim through the haze*. □ **brume (légère)**

'**hazy** *adjective* **1** misty: *a hazy view of the mountains*. □ **brumeux**

2 not clear or certain: *a hazy idea*; *I'm a bit hazy about what happened*. □ **vague**

'**haziness** *noun*. □ **flou, état brumeux**

hazel ['heizl] *noun* a kind of small tree on which nuts grow. □ **noisetier**

■ *adjective* of a light-brown colour: *hazel eyes*. □ **noisette**

'**hazel-nut** *noun* the edible nut of the hazel. □ **noisette**

H-bomb ['eitʃbom] short for **hydrogen bomb**. □ **bombe H**

he [hiː] *pronoun* (used as the subject of a verb) **1** a male person or animal already spoken about: *When I spoke to John, he told me he had seen you*. □ **il**

2 any (male) person: *He who hesitates is lost*. □ **celui (qui)**

■ *noun* a male person or animal: *Is a cow a he or a she?* □ **mâle**

'**he-man** [-man] – *plural* '**he-men** – *noun* a very strong, powerful man. □ **homme dominateur**

head [hed] *noun* **1** the top part of the human body, containing the eyes, mouth, brain *etc*; the same part of an animal's body: *The stone hit him on the head*; *She scratched her head in amazement*. □ **tête**

2 a person's mind: *An idea came into my head last night*. □ **esprit**

3 the height or length of a head: *The horse won by a head*. □ **tête**

4 the chief or most important person (of an organization, country *etc*): *Kings and presidents are heads of state*; (*also adjective*) *a head waiter*; *the head office*. □ **chef; principal**

5 anything that is like a head in shape or position: *the head of a pin*; *The boy knocked the heads off the flowers*. □ **tête**

6 the place where a river, lake *etc* begins: *the head of the Nile.* □ **source**
7 the top, or the top part, of anything: *Write your address at the head of the paper; the head of the table.* □ **tête, haut, bout**
8 the front part: *She walked at the head of the procession.* □ **(en) tête (de)**
9 a particular ability or tolerance: *He has no head for heights; She has a good head for figures.* □ **bosse**
10 a headmaster or headmistress: *You'd better ask the Head.* □ **directeur, trice**
11 (for) one person: *This dinner costs $10 a head.* □ **par personne**
12 a headland: *Beachy Head.* □ **cap**
13 the foam on the top of a glass of beer *etc.* □ **faux col**
■ *verb* 1 to go at the front of or at the top of (something): *The procession was headed by the band; Whose name headed the list?* □ **venir en tête (de)**
2 to be in charge of; to be the leader of: *She heads a team of scientists investigating cancer.* □ **être à la tête (de)**
3 (*often with* for) to (cause to) move in a certain direction: *The explorers headed south; The girls headed for home; You're heading for disaster!* □ **se diriger (vers)**
4 to put or write something at the begining of: *His report was headed 'Ways of Preventing Industrial Accidents'.* □ **intituler**
5 (in football) to hit the ball with the head: *She headed the ball into the goal.* □ **renvoyer d'un coup de tête**
-headed having (a certain number or type of) head(s): *a two-headed monster; a bald-headed man.* □ **à tête (...)**
'**header** *noun* 1 a fall or dive forwards: *He slipped and took a header into the mud.* □ **plongeon**
2 (in football) the act of hitting the ball with the head: *He scored with a great header.* □ **coup de tête**
'**heading** *noun* what is written at the top of a page *etc*: *The teacher said that essays must have a proper heading.* □ **en-tête**
heads *noun, adverb* (on) the side of a coin with the head of a king, president *etc* on it: *She tossed the penny and it came down heads.* □ **face**
'**headache** *noun* 1 a pain in the head: *Bright lights give me a headache.* □ **mal de tête**
2 something worrying: *Lack of money is a real headache.* □ **problème**
'**headband** *noun* a strip of material worn around the head to keep one's hair off one's face. □ **bandeau**
'**head-dress** *noun* something, *usually* ornamental, which is worn on, and covers, the head: *The tribesmen were wearing head-dresses of fur and feathers.* □ **coiffure**
,**head'first** *adverb* with one's head in front or bent forward: *He fell headfirst into a pool of water.* □ **la tête la première**
'**headgear** *noun* anything that is worn on the head: *Hats, caps and helmets are headgear.* □ **couvre-chef**
'**headlamp** *noun* a headlight. □ **phare**
'**headland** *noun* a point of land which sticks out into the sea. □ **promontoire**
'**headlight** *noun* a powerful light at or on the front of a

car, truck, train, ship, airplane *etc*: *As it was getting dark, the driver switched on her headlights.* □ **feu avant, phare**
'**headline** *noun* the words written in large letters at the top of newspaper articles: *I never read a paper in detail – I just glance at the headlines.* □ **(gros) titre, manchette**
'**headlines** *noun plural* a brief statement of the most important items of news, on television or radio: *the news headlines.* □ **principaux titres**
'**headlong** *adjective, adverb* 1 moving forwards or downwards, with one's head in front: *a headlong dive into the pool of water; She fell headlong into a pool of water.* □ **tête baissée, la tête la première**
2 (done) without thought or delay, often foolishly: *a headlong rush; She rushes headlong into disaster.* □ **à toute allure**
head louse a type of louse that infests the human head. □ **pou**
head'master – *feminine* **head'mistress** – *noun* the person in charge of a school; the principal. □ **directeur**
,**head-'on** *adverb, adjective* (*usually* of cars *etc*) with the front of one car *etc* hitting the front of another car *etc*: *a head-on collision; The two cars crashed head-on.* □ **de plein fouet; frontal**
'**headphones** *noun plural* (*also* '**earphones**) a pair of electronic instruments held over a person's ears, by a metal band over the head, which are connected to a radio: *a set of headphones.* □ **écouteurs**
,**head'quarters** *noun singular or plural* (*often abbreviated to* **HQ** [eitʃ'kjuːz] *noun*) the place from which the chief officers or leaders of an organization (*especially* an army) direct and control the activities of that organization: *During the election, his house was used as the campaign headquarters.* □ **quartier général, état-major**
'**headrest** *noun* a sort of small cushion which supports a person's head, *eg* as fitted to a dentist's chair, a car seat. □ **appui-tête**
'**head scarf**, *noun* a *usually* square scarf worn by women over or around the head. □ **foulard**
'**headstone** *noun* a stone put at a grave, *usually* with the name of the dead person on it, the date of his birth and death *etc.* □ **pierre tombale**
'**headstrong** *adjective* (of people) difficult to persuade or control; always doing or wanting to do what they themselves want: *a headstrong, obstinate child.* □ **volontaire**
'**headwind** *noun* a wind which is blowing towards one. □ **vent contraire**
above someone's head too difficult (for someone) to understand: *Her lecture was well above their heads.* □ **qui dépasse (qqn)**
go to someone's head 1 (of alcohol) to make someone slightly drunk: *Champagne always goes to my head.* □ **monter à la tête**
2 (of praise, success *etc*) to make someone arrogant, foolish *etc*: *Don't let success go to your head.* □ **monter à la tête**
head off 1 to make (a person, animal *etc*) change direc-

tion: *One group of the soldiers rode across the valley to head the bandits off.* □ **détourner**

2 to go in some direction: *He headed off towards the river.* □ **partir vers**

head over heels 1 completely: *He fell head over heels in love.* □ **éperdument**

2 turning over completely; headfirst: *She fell head over heels into a pond.* □ **cul par-dessus tête**

heads or tails? used when tossing a coin, *eg* to decide which of two people does, gets *etc* something: *Heads or tails? Heads you do the dishes, tails I do them.* □ **pile ou face?**

keep one's head to remain calm and sensible in a crisis *etc*. □ **garder la tête froide**

lose one's head to become angry or excited, or to act foolishly in a crisis. □ **perdre la tête**

make head or tail of to understand: *I can't make head or tail of these instructions.* □ **s'y retrouver**

make headway to make progress: *We're not making much headway with this new scheme.* □ **progresser**

heal [hiːl] *verb* (*often with* **up**) (*especially* of cuts, wounds *etc*) to make or become healthy; to (cause to) return to a normal state or condition: *That scratch will heal (up) in a couple of days; this ointment will soon heal your cuts.* □ **guérir**

'**healer** *noun* a person or thing that heals: *Time is the great healer.* □ **guérisseur, euse**

health [helθ] *noun* **1** the state of being well or ill: *She is in good/poor health.* □ **santé**

2 the state of being well: *I may be getting old, but so long as I keep my health, I'll be happy.* □ **(bonne) santé**

'**healthy** *adjective* **1** (generally) having good health: *I'm rarely ill – I'm really a very healthy person; My bank balance is healthier than it was.* □ **en bonne santé**

2 causing or helping to produce good health: *a healthy climate.* □ **salubre**

3 resulting from good health: *a healthy appetite.* □ **robuste**

4 showing a sensible concern for one's own well-being *etc*: *She shows a healthy respect for the law.* □ **salutaire**

'**healthiness** *noun.* □ **salubrité**

health service (the organization which runs) all the medical services of a country which are available to the public. □ **service de santé**

drink (to) someone's health to drink a toast to someone, wishing him good health. □ **boire à la santé de**

heap [hiːp] *noun* **1** a large amount or a large number, in a pile: *a heap of sand/apples.* □ **tas**

2 (*usually in plural with* **of**) many, much or plenty: *We've got heaps of time; I've done that heaps of times.* □ **des tas de**

■ *verb* **1** to put, throw *etc* in a heap: *I'll heap these stones (up) in a corner of the garden.* □ **entasser**

2 to fill or cover with a heap: *He heaped his plate with vegetables; He heaped insults on his opponent.* □ **empiler (de), accabler (de)**

heaped *adjective* having enough (of something) on it to form a heap: *A heaped spoonful of sugar.* □ **comble**

hear [hiə] – *past tense, past participle* **heard** [həːd] – *verb* **1** to (be able to) receive (sounds) by ear: *I don't*

hear very well; Speak louder – I can't hear you; I didn't hear you come in. □ **entendre**

2 to listen to for some purpose: *A judge hears court cases; Part of a manager's job is to hear workers' complaints.* □ **écouter**

3 to receive information, news *etc*, not only by ear: *I've heard that story before; I hear that you're leaving; 'Have you heard from your sister?' 'Yes, I got a letter from her today'; I've never heard of him – who is he? This is the first I've heard of the plan.* □ **entendre (dire), avoir des nouvelles (de), entendre (parler de)**

'**hearing** *noun* **1** the ability to hear: *My hearing is not very good.* □ **ouïe**

2 the distance within which something can be heard: *I don't want to tell you when so many people are within hearing; I think we're out of hearing now.* □ **à portée de voix**

3 an act of listening: *We ought to give his views a fair hearing.* □ **audition**

4 a court case: *The hearing is tomorrow.* □ **audition, audience**

'**hearing aid** *noun* a small electronic instrument which helps deaf people to hear better by making sounds louder by means of an amplifier. □ **appareil acoustique**

'**hearsay** [-sei] *noun* that which one has been told about by others but for which one has otherwise no evidence: *I never trust anything that I learn by hearsay.* □ **ouï-dire**

hear! hear! a shout to show that one agrees with what a speaker has said (*eg* in Parliament or at a meeting). □ **bravo!**

I, he *etc* **will, would not hear of** I, he *etc* will or would not allow: *She would not hear of her going home alone, and insisted on going with her.* □ **ne pas vouloir entendre parler de**

hearsay *see* **hear**.

hearse [həːs] *noun* a car used for carrying a dead body in a coffin to a cemetery *etc*. □ **corbillard**

heart [haːt] *noun* **1** the organ which pumps blood through the body: *How fast does a person's heart beat?*; (*also adjective*) *heart disease*; *a heart specialist.* □ **cœur**

2 the central part: *I live in the heart of the city*; *in the heart of the forest*; *the heart of a lettuce*; *Let's get straight to the heart of the matter/problem.* □ **cœur**

3 the part of the body where one's feelings, *especially* of love, conscience *etc* are imagined to arise: *She has a kind heart*; *You know in your heart that you ought to go*; *He has no heart* (= He is not kind). □ **cœur**

4 courage and enthusiasm: *The soldiers were beginning to lose heart.* □ **courage**

5 a symbol supposed to represent the shape of the heart;: *a white dress with little pink hearts on it*; *heart-shaped.* □ **(de) cœur**

6 one of the playing cards of the suit hearts, which have red symbols of this shape on them. □ **cœur**

-hearted: *kind-hearted*; *hard-hearted*; *broken-hearted.* □ **au cœur (...)**

'**hearten** *verb* to encourage or cheer up: *We were greatly heartened by the good news.* □ **encourager**

'**heartless** *adjective* cruel; very unkind: *a heartless re-*

mark. □ **cruel**

'**heartlessly** *adverb*. □ **sans pitié**

'**heartlessness** *noun*. □ **insensibilité**

hearts *noun plural* (sometimes treated as *noun singular*) one of the four card suits: *the two of hearts*. □ **cœur**

'**hearty** *adjective* 1 very friendly: *a hearty welcome*. □ **cordial**

2 enthusiastic: *a hearty cheer*. □ **chaleureux**

3 very cheerful; too cheerful: *a hearty person/laugh*. □ **gros, franc**

4 (of meals) large: *She ate a hearty breakfast*. □ **copieux**

5 (of a person's appetite) large. □ **solide**

'**heartily** *adverb*. □ **de tout cœur**

'**heartiness** *noun*. □ **cordialité**

'**heartache** *noun* (a feeling of) great sadness. □ **chagrin**

heart attack a sudden failure of the heart to function correctly, sometimes causing death: *My sister has had a slight heart attack*. □ **crise cardiaque**

'**heartbeat** *noun* (the sound of) the regular movement of the heart. □ **battement de cœur**

'**heartbreak** *noun* (something which causes) great sorrow: *I have suffered many heartbreaks in my life*. □ **(immense) chagrin**

'**heartbroken** *adjective* feeling very great sorrow: *a heartbroken widow*. □ **qui a le cœur brisé**

'**heartburn** *noun* a burning feeling in the chest caused by indigestion: *She suffers from heartburn after meals*. □ **brûlures d'estomac**

heart failure the sudden stopping of the heart's beating: *the old man died of heart failure*. □ **arrêt du cœur**

'**heartfelt** *adjective* sincere: *heartfelt thanks*. □ **sincère**

,**heart-to-'heart** *adjective* open and sincere, *usually* in private: *I'm going to have a heart-to-heart talk with her*. □ **à cœur ouvert**

■ *noun* an open and sincere talk, *usually* in private: *After our heart-to-heart I felt more cheerful*. □ **entretien à cœur ouvert**

'**heart-warming** *adjective* causing a person to feel pleasure: *It was heart-warming to see the happiness of the children*. □ **réconfortant**

at heart really; basically: *He seems rather stern but he is at heart a very kind man*. □ **au fond**

break someone's heart to cause someone great sorrow: *If you leave her, it'll break her heart*. □ **briser le cœur de**

by heart from memory; by memorizing: *The children know their multiplication tables by heart*; *Actors must learn their speeches (off) by heart*. □ **par cœur**

from the bottom of one's heart very sincerely: *She thanked him from the bottom of her heart*. □ **du fond du cœur**

have a change of heart to change a decision *etc*, *usually* to a better, kinder one: *He's had a change of heart – he's going to help us after all*. □ **se raviser**

have a heart! show some pity! □ **avez pitié!**

have at heart to have a concern for or interest in: *She has the interest of her workers at heart*. □ **avoir (qqch.) à cœur**

heart and soul with all one's attention and energy: *She*

devoted herself heart and soul to caring for her husband. □ **corps et âme**

lose heart to become discouraged. □ **perdre courage**

not have the heart to not to want or be unkind enough to (do something unpleasant): *I don't have the heart to tell him that everyone laughed at his suggestions*. □ **ne pas avoir le cœur de**

set one's heart on/have one's heart set on to want very much: *He had set his heart on winning the prize*; *She had her heart set on winning*. □ **vouloir à tout prix**

take heart to become encouraged or more confident. □ **(re)prendre courage**

take to heart 1 to be made very sad or upset by: *You mustn't take her unkind remarks to heart*. □ **prendre (trop) à cœur**

2 to pay attention to: *He's taken my criticism to heart – his work has improved*. □ **prendre au sérieux/à cœur**

to one's heart's content as much as one wants: *She could play in the big garden to her heart's content*. □ **tout son soûl**

with all one's heart very willingly or sincerely: *I hope with all my heart that you will be happy*. □ **de tout cœur**

hearth [haːθ] *noun* (the part of a room beside) the fireplace: *He was cleaning the hearth*. □ **foyer, âtre**

heartily *etc see* **heart**.

heat [hiːt] *noun* 1 the degree of hotness (of something), *especially* of things which are very hot: *Test the heat of the water before you bath the baby*. □ **température**

2 the warmth from something which is hot: *The heat from the fire will dry your coat*; *the effect of heat on metal*; *the heat of the sun*. □ **chaleur**

3 the hottest time: *the heat of the day*. □ **au plus chaud de**

4 anger or excitement: *He didn't mean to be rude – he just said that in the heat of the moment*. □ **dans le feu (de l'action)**

5 in a sports competition *etc*, one of two or more contests from which the winners go on to take part in later stages of the competition: *Having won his heat he is going through to the final*. □ **épreuve éliminatoire**

■ *verb* (sometimes with **up**) to make or become hot or warm: *We'll heat (up) the soup*; *The day heats up quickly once the sun has risen*. □ **(faire) chauffer**

'**heated** *adjective* 1 having been made hot: *a heated swimming pool*. □ **chauffé**

2 showing anger, excitement *etc*: *a heated argument*. □ **passionné**

'**heatedly** *adverb*. □ **avec chaleur**

'**heatedness** *noun*. □ **chaleur**

'**heater** *noun* an apparatus which gives out heat in order to warm a room *etc*, or which heats water *etc eg* in a water-tank. □ **chauffe-eau, radiateur**

'**heating** *noun* the system of heaters *etc* which heat a room, building *etc*: *We turn the heating off in the summer*. □ **chauffage**

heat wave a period of very hot weather. □ **vague de chaleur**

in/on heat (of female animals) in a condition for mating. □ **en chaleur**

See also **hot**.

heathen ['hi:ðən] *noun, adjective* (of) a person who believes in a less advanced form of religion, *especially* one with many gods: *Missionaries tried to convert the heathens to Christianity.* □ **païen, ïenne**

heather ['heðə] *noun* a plant with small purple or white flowers growing in hilly parts of Britain. □ **bruyère**

heave [hi:v] *verb* 1 to (try to) lift or to pull, with great effort: *They heaved with all their strength, but could not move the rock; They heaved the wardrobe up into the truck.* □ **(sou)lever, tirer (avec effort)**

2 to throw (something heavy): *Someone heaved a stone through my window.* □ **lancer**

3 to rise, or rise and fall again several times: *The earthquake made the ground heave.* □ **(se) soulever**

■ *noun* the act of heaving: *She gave one heave and the rock moved; the heave of the waves.* □ **poussée, houle**

heave a sigh to sigh: *She heaved a sigh of relief when she reached safety.* □ **pousser un soupir**

heaven ['hevn] *noun* 1 in some religions, the place where God or the gods live, and where good people go when they die. □ **paradis**

2 the sky: *He raised his eyes to heaven/the heavens.* □ **ciel**

3 (something which brings) great happiness: *'This is heaven', she said, lying on the beach in the sun.* □ **paradis**

'heavenly *adverb* 1 very pleasant; beautiful: *What a heavenly colour!* □ **divin**

2 of or from heaven. □ **céleste**

'heavenliness *noun.* □ **caractère céleste**

'heavens (*also* **good heavens**) (*interjection*) an expression of surprise, dismay *etc*: *Heavens! I forgot to buy your birthday present.* □ **mon Dieu!**

heavenly bodies the sun, moon, planets, stars. □ **corps célestes**

,heaven-'sent *adjective* very lucky or convenient: *a heaven-sent opportunity.* □ **providentiel**

for heaven's sake an expression used to show anger, surprise *etc*: *For heaven's sake, stop making that noise!* □ **pour l'amour du ciel/de Dieu!**

heaven knows 1 I don't know: *Heaven knows what she's trying to do.* □ **Dieu (seul) sait**

2 certainly: *Heaven knows I've tried to help.* □ **Dieu sait (que)**

thank heavens an expression used to show that a person is glad something has (not) happened: *Thank heavens he isn't coming!; Thank heavens for that!* □ **Dieu merci!**

heavy ['hevi] *adjective* 1 having great weight; difficult to lift or carry: *a heavy parcel.* □ **lourd**

2 having a particular weight: *I wonder how heavy our little baby is.* □ **lourd**

3 of very great amount, force *etc*: *heavy rain; a heavy blow; The ship capsized in the heavy seas; heavy taxes.* □ **gros, lourd**

4 doing something to a great extent: *He's a heavy smoker/drinker.* □ **gros**

5 dark and dull; looking or feeling stormy: *a heavy sky/atmosphere.* □ **lourd**

6 difficult to read, do, understand *etc*: *Books on phi-losophy are too heavy for me.* □ **difficile**

7 (of food) hard to digest: *rather heavy pastry.* □ **lourd**

8 noisy and clumsy: *heavy footsteps.* □ **lourd, pesant**

'heavily *adverb.* □ **lourdement**

'heaviness *noun.* □ **lourdeur**

,heavy-'duty *adjective* made to stand up to very hard wear or use: *heavy-duty tires.* □ **à grand rendement**

heavy industry industries such as coal mining, shipbuilding *etc* which involve the use of large or heavy machines or which produce large or heavy products. □ **industrie lourde**

'heavyweight *adjective, noun* (a person) in the heaviest of the various classes into which competitors in certain sports (*eg* boxing, wrestling) are divided according to their weight: *a heavyweight boxer.* □ **poids lourd**

heavy going difficult to make any progress with: *I found this book very heavy going.* □ **difficile à (…)**

a heavy heart a feeling of sadness: *She obeyed with a heavy heart.* □ **cœur gros**

make heavy weather of to find surprising difficulty in doing: *He said he'd finish the job in half an hour, but he's making rather heavy weather of it.* □ **s'en tirer avec peine**

hectare ['hekta:] *noun* a metric unit of area, 10 000 square metres. □ **hectare**

hectic ['hektik] *adjective* very busy; rushed: *Life is hectic these days.* □ **trépidant**

he'd *see* **have, would.**

hedge [hedʒ] *noun* a line of bushes *etc* planted so closely together that their branches form a solid mass, grown around the edges of gardens, fields *etc*. □ **haie**

■ *verb* 1 to avoid giving a clear answer to a question. □ **chercher des faux-fuyants**

2 (with **in** or **off**) to enclose (an area of land) with a hedge. □ **enclore**

'hedgehog *noun* a small brown prickly-backed animal. □ **hérisson**

'hedgerow [-rou] *noun* a row of bushes forming a hedge, *especially* in the country. □ **haie**

heed [hi:d] *verb* to pay attention to: *She refused to heed my warning; Heed what I say!* □ **faire attention à**

'heedful *adjective* (with **of**) paying attention to; responding to: *heedful of danger.* □ **vigilant**

'heedless *adjective* (*especially* with **of**) careless; paying no attention: *Heedless of the danger, she ran into the burning building to rescue the girl.* □ **insouciant (de)**

'heedlessly *adverb.* □ **à la légère**

pay heed to, take heed of: *Take heed of my warning; She paid no heed to me.* □ **faire attention à**

heel [hi:l] *noun* 1 the back part of the foot: *I have a blister on my heel.* □ **talon**

2 the part of a sock *etc* that covers this part of the foot: *I have a hole in the heel of my sock.* □ **talon**

3 the part of a shoe, boot *etc* under or around the heel of the foot: *The heel has come off this shoe.* □ **talon**

■ *verb* 1 to put a heel on (a shoe *etc*). □ **remettre un talon (à)**

2 (*usually* with **over**) (of ships) to lean to one side: *The boat heeled over in the strong wind.* □ **gîter**

-heeled: *high-heeled shoes.* □ **à talons (...)**

at/on one's heels close behind one: *The thief ran off with the policeman close on his heels.* □ **sur les talons**

kick one's heels to be kept waiting: *I was left kicking my heels for half an hour.* □ **poireauter**

take to one's heels to run away: *The thief took to his heels.* □ **prendre ses jambes à son cou**

to heel (of dogs *etc*) at a person's heel: *You must teach your dog to heel in a busy street.* □ **rester au pied**

turn on one's heel to turn one's back (and walk off). □ **tourner les talons**

hefty ['hefti] *adjective* 1 (of people) big and strong: *Her husband is pretty hefty.* □ **costaud**

2 (of punches *etc*) powerful: *a hefty kick.* □ **solide**

heifer ['hefə] *noun* a young cow. □ **génisse**

height [hait] *noun* 1 the distance from the bottom to the top of something: *What is the height of this building?*; *She is 1.75 metres in height.* □ **hauteur**

2 the highest, greatest, strongest *etc* point: *She is at the height of her career*; *The storm was at its height.* □ **sommet, apogée**

3 the peak or extreme: *dressed in the height of fashion*; *His actions were the height of folly.* □ **comble**

4 a high place: *We looked down from the heights at the valley beneath us.* □ **hauteur, sommet**

'**heighten** *verb* 1 to make or become higher: *to heighten the garden wall.* □ **(sur)élever**

2 to increase (an effect *etc*). □ **intensifier**

heir [eə] – *feminine* '**heiress** – *noun* a person who by law receives wealth, property *etc* when the owner dies: *A person's eldest son is usually his heir*; *A king's eldest son is the heir to the throne.* □ **héritier, ière**

'**heirloom** [-luːm] *noun* something valuable that has been handed down in a family from generation to generation: *This brooch is a family heirloom.* □ **héritage**

held *see* **hold.**

helicopter ['helikɒptə] *noun* a flying-machine kept in the air by large propellors fixed on top of it which go around very fast. □ **hélicoptère**

helium ['hiːliəm] *noun* an element, a very light gas which does not burn and which is used *eg* in balloons. □ **hélium**

hell [hel] *noun* (according to some religions) the place or state of punishment of the wicked after death with much pain, misery *etc*. □ **enfer**

for the hell of it for no particular reason; just for fun: *The boys said they had set fire to the house just for the hell of it.* □ **pour le plaisir**

,**hell'-bent on** determined on: *I've told him it will be dangerous, but he's hellbent on going.* □ **acharné (à)**

he'll *see* **will.**

hello [hə'lou] *interjections, nouns* a word used as a greeting, to attract attention, or to express surprise: *Say hello to your aunt*; *'Hello,' I said to myself, 'What's going on here?'* □ **salut!, hello**

helm [helm] *noun* the wheel or handle by which a ship is steered: *She asked me to take the helm* (= steer the ship). □ **barre**

'**helmsman** ['helmz-] *noun* a person who steers a ship. □ **homme de barre**

helmet ['helmit] *noun* a metal, leather *etc* covering to protect the head: *Soldiers wear helmets when fighting.* □ **casque**

help [help] *verb* 1 to do something with or for someone that he cannot do alone, or that he will find useful: *Will you help me with this translation?*; *Will you please help me (to) translate this poem?*; *Can I help?*; *He fell down and I helped him up.* □ **aider**

2 to play a part in something; to improve or advance: *Bright posters will help to attract the public to the exhibition*; *Good exam results will help his chances of a job.* □ **aider**

3 to make less bad: *An aspirin will help your headache.* □ **soulager**

4 to serve (a person) in a shop: *Can I help you, sir?* □ **aider**

5 (*with* can(not), could (not)) to be able not to do something or to prevent something: *He looked so funny that I couldn't help laughing*; *Can I help it if it rains?* □ **pouvoir, ne pas pouvoir s'empêcher de**

■ *noun* 1 the act of helping, or the result of this: *Can you give me some help?*; *Your digging the garden was a big help*; *Can I be of help to you?* □ **aide**

2 someone or something that is useful: *You're a great help to me.* □ **secours**

3 a servant, farmworker *etc*: *She has hired a new help.* □ **domestique, employé, ée**

4 (*usually with* no) a way of preventing something: *Even if you don't want to do it, the decision has been made – there's no help for it now.* □ **on n'y peut rien**

Help! an urgent cry for assistance: *"Help! Help!" Ursula yelled from the roof of the burning building.* □ **au secours !**

'**helper** *noun*: *We need several helpers for this job.* □ **assistant, ante**

'**helpful** *adjective*: *a very helpful boy*; *You may find this book helpful.* □ **utile**

'**helpfully** *adverb*. □ **utilement**

'**helpfulness** *noun*. □ **utilité**

'**helping** *noun* the amount of food one has on one's plate: *a large helping of pudding.* □ **portion**

'**helpless** *adjective* needing the help of other people; unable to do anything for oneself: *A baby is almost completely helpless.* □ **faible, impuissant**

'**helplessly** *adverb*. □ **faiblement, sans ressource**

'**helplessness** *noun*. □ **faiblesse, abandon**

help oneself 1 (*with* to) to give oneself or take (food *etc*): *Help yourself to another cake*; *'Can I have a pencil?' 'Certainly – help yourself*; *He helped himself to* (= stole) *my jewellery.* □ **(se) servir (de)**

2 (*with* cannot, could not) to be able to stop (oneself): *I burst out laughing when he told me – I just couldn't help myself.* □ **ne pouvoir s'empêcher de**

help out to help (a person), *usually* for a short time because the person is in some difficulty: *I help out in the shop from time to time*; *Could you help me out by looking after the baby?* □ **dépanner**

helter-skelter ['heltə'skeltə] *adverb* in great hurry and confusion. □ **en désordre**

hem [hem] *noun* the border of a piece of clothing, folded over and sewn. □ **ourlet**

■ *verb – past tense, past participle* **hemmed** – to make a hem on (a piece of clothing): *I've hemmed the skirt.* □ **ourler**

hem in to surround (someone): *The soldiers were hemmed in on all sides by the enemy.* □ **encercler**

hemisphere ['hemisfiə] *noun* one half of the Earth: *Singapore and the British Isles are in the northern hemisphere.* □ **hémisphère**

,hemi'spherical [-'sfe-] *adjective* like half a ball in shape. □ **hémisphérique**

hemoglobin [hi:mə'gloubin] *noun* the oxygen-carrying substance in red blood cells. □ **hémoglobine**

hemorrhage ['hemoridʒ] *noun* bleeding in large amounts, from damaged blood vessels. □ **hémorragie**

hemp [hemp] *noun* (a plant from which is obtained) a coarse fibre used to make rope, bags, sails *etc* and the drug cannabis (hashish or marijuana). □ **chanvre**

hen [hen] *noun* 1 the female farmyard fowl: *Hens lay eggs.* □ **poule**
2 the female of any bird: *The hen is sitting on the nest;* (*also adjective*) *a hen blackbird.* □ **femelle**

'henpecked [-pekt] *adjective* (of a man) ruled by his wife: *a henpecked husband.* □ **mené par le bout du nez**

hence [hens] *adverb* 1 for this reason: *Hence, I shall have to stay.* □ **donc, par conséquent**
2 from this time: *a year hence.* □ **dans**
3 away from this place. □ **d'ici**

hence'forth *adverb* from now on: *Henceforth I shall refuse to work with him.* □ **désormais**

henchman ['hentʃmən] – *plural* **'henchmen** – *noun* a loyal supporter: *a politician/gangster and his henchmen.* □ **acolyte**

henpecked *see* **hen**.

her [həz] *pronoun* (used as the object of a verb or preposition) a female person or animal already spoken about: *I'll ask my mother when I see her; He came with her.* □ **elle, la**
■ *adjective* belonging to such a person or animal: *My mother bought her car, so it's her car; a cat and her kittens.* □ **son, sa, ses**

hers [həzz] *pronoun* something which belongs to a female person or animal already spoken about: *It's not your book – it's hers; Hers is on that shelf.* □ **le sien, la sienne, les siens, les siennes**

her'self *pronoun* 1 used as the object of a verb or preposition when a female person or animal is the object of an action she performs: *The cat licked herself; She bought herself a car.* □ **elle-même, se**
2 used to emphasize **she, her,** or the name of a female person or animal: *She herself played no part in this; Mary answered the letter herself.* □ **elle-même**
3 without help *etc*: *She did it all herself.* □ **elle-même**

herald ['herəld] *noun* formerly, a person who carries and reads important messages and notices (*eg* from a king): *The king sent out heralds to announce the new law.* □ **héraut, messager, ère**
■ *verb* to announce or be a sign of: *A sharp wind often heralds a storm.* □ **annoncer**

he'raldic [-'ral-] *adjective* of heraldry. □ **héraldique**

'heraldry *noun* the study of coats of arms, crests *etc* and of the history of the families who have the right to use them. □ **art héraldique**

herb [həzb] *noun* a *usually* small plant used to flavour food or to make medicines: *herbs and spices.* □ **herbe (aromatique, médicinale)**

'herbal *adjective* of herbs, *especially* herbs used to make medicines: *a herbal remedy.* □ **d'herbes**

'herbalist *noun* a person who deals in herbs, *especially* those used to make medicines. □ **herboriste**

herd [həzd] *noun* a group of animals of one kind that stay, or are kept, together: *a herd of cattle; a herd of elephant(s).* □ **troupeau**
■ *verb* to gather together, or be brought together, in a group: *The dogs herded the sheep together; The tourists were herded into a tiny room.* □ **(se) rassembler (en troupeau)**

-herd a person who looks after a herd of certain kinds of animals: *a goat-herd.* □ **gardien, ienne (de troupeau)**

'herdsman ['həzdz-] *noun* a person who looks after a herd of animals. □ **pâtre**

the herd instinct the tendency to behave, think *etc* like everyone else. □ **instinct grégaire**

here [hiə] *adverb* 1 (at, in or to) this place: *She's here; Come here; He lives not far from here; Here they come; Here is/Here's your lost book.* □ **ici; voici**
2 at this time; at this point in an argument: *Here she stopped speaking to wipe her eyes; Here is where I disagree with you.* □ **là**
3 beside one: *My colleague here will deal with the matter.* □ **que voici**
■ *interjection* 1 a shout of surprise, disapproval *etc*: *Here! what do you think you're doing?* □ **hé là!**
2 a shout used to show that one is present: *Shout 'Here!' when I call your name.* □ **présent**

,herea'bout(s) *adverb* near this place: *She lives somewhere hereabouts.* □ **par ici**

here'after *adverb* especially in legal language, after this; from now on: *This concerns the will of John Smith, hereafter referred to as 'the deceased'.* □ **ci-après**

,here'by *adverb* especially in legal language, now, by means of (*eg* this statement): *I hereby declare that I will not be responsible for any of her debts.* □ **par la présente**

,here'in *adverb* especially in legal language, in this (letter *etc*): *Please complete the form enclosed herein.* □ **ci-inclus**

here'with *adverb* with this (letter *etc*): *I am returning your passport herewith.* □ **ci-joint**

here and there in, or to, various places: *Books were scattered here and there.* □ **çà et là, par-ci par-là**

here goes I'm going to do something now: *I've never tried diving before, but here goes!* □ **allons-y!**

here's to *interjection* used as a toast to the health, success *etc* of someone or something: *Here's to the success of the new company.* □ **à la santé de**

here, there and everywhere in, or to, a larger number of places; in all directions: *People were running around here, there and everywhere.* □ **un peu partout**

here you are here is what you want *etc*: *Here you are.*

This is the book you were looking for. □ **vous voici! tenez!**

neither here nor there not important: *His opinion is neither here nor there.* □ **sans importance**

heredity [hi'redəti] *noun* the passing on of qualities (*eg* appearance, intelligence) from parents to children. □ **hérédité**

he'reditary *adjective* (able to be) passed on in this way: *Is musical ability hereditary?* □ **héréditaire**

herein *see* **here.**

heresy ['herəsi] *noun* (the holding or teaching of) an (*especially* religious) opinion which differs from the official opinion. □ **hérésie**

'**heretic** [-tik] *noun* a person who holds or teaches such an opinion. □ **hérétique**

heretical [hə'retikl] *adjective.* □ **hérétique**

heritage ['heritidʒ] *noun* things (*especially* valuable things such as buildings, literature *etc*) which are passed on from one generation to another: *We must all take care to preserve our national heritage.* □ **patrimoine**

hermit ['hɜːmit] *noun* a person who lives alone, *especially* to devote himself to religion. □ **ermite**

'**hermitage** [-tidʒ] *noun* the place where a hermit lives. □ **ermitage**

hermit crab a soft-bodied crab that inhabits the empty shells of other creatures. □ **bernard-l'ermite**

hero ['hiərou] – *plural* '**heroes**: *feminine* **heroine** ['herouin] – *noun* **1** a person admired (by many people) for his or her brave deeds: *The boy was regarded as a hero for saving his friend's life.* □ **héros, héroïne**

2 the chief person in a story, play *etc*: *The hero of this book is a young American boy called Tom Sawyer.* □ **héros, héroïne**

heroic [hi'rouik] *adjective* **1** very brave: *heroic deeds.* □ **héroïque**

2 of heroes: *heroic tales.* □ **héroïque**

he'roically *adverb.* □ **héroïquement**

heroism ['herouizm] *noun* great bravery: *The policeman was given a medal in recognition of his heroism.* □ **héroïsme**

'**hero-worship** *noun* very great, sometimes too great, admiration for a person. □ **culte des héros**

■ *verb* to show such admiration for (someone): *The girl hero-worshipped the woman astronaut.* □ **idolâtrer**

> the **heroine** (not **heroin**) of the story.

heroin ['herouin] *noun* a drug obtained from opium. □ **héroïne**

> to take **heroin** (not **heroine**).

heroine, heroism *see* **hero.**

heron ['herən] *noun* a type of large water-bird, with long legs and a long neck. □ **héron**

herring ['heriŋ] – *plurals* '**herring**, '**herrings** – *noun* a small, edible kind of sea fish. □ **hareng**

hers, herself *see* **her.**

hertz [hɜːts] – *plural* **hertz** – *noun* (*often abbreviated to* **Hz** *when written*) a unit of frequency used of radio waves *etc.* □ **hertz**

he's *see* **be, have.**

hesitate ['heziteit] *verb* **1** to pause briefly *eg* because of uncertainty: *She hesitated before answering; The diver hesitated for a minute on the diving-board.* □ **hésiter**

2 to be unwilling (to do something) *eg* because one is not sure it is right: *I hesitate to say he lied but he certainly misled me; Don't hesitate to tell me if you have any complaints.* □ **hésiter (à)**

'**hesitancy** *noun* the tendency to hesitate. □ **hésitation**

'**hesitant** *adjective* making or having frequent hesitations: *a hesitant speaker; I'm hesitant to tell her she's wrong.* □ **hésitant, irrésolu**

'**hesitantly** *adverb.* □ **avec hésitation**

,**hesi'tation** *noun* **1** an act of hesitating. □ **hésitation**

2 unwillingness or uncertainty. □ **hésitation**

hew [hjuː] – *past tense* **hewed**; *past participle* **hewed, hewn** [hjuːn] – *verb* **1** to cut with an axe, sword *etc*: *He hewed down the tree.* □ **abattre**

2 to cut out or shape with an axe, sword *etc*: *She hewed a path through the forest.* □ **(se) tailler (à coups de...)**

hexagon ['heksəgən] *noun* a six-sided figure. □ **hexagone**

hey [hei] *interjection* a shout expressing joy, or a question, or used to attract attention: *Hey! What are you doing there?* □ **hé!**

heyday ['heidei] *noun* the time when a particular person or thing had great importance and popularity: *The 1950's were the heyday of rock and roll.* □ **beaux jours**

hi [hai] *interjection* a word of greeting: *Hi! How are you?* □ **salut!**

hibernate ['haibəneit] *verb* (of certain animals, *eg* hedgehogs) to pass the winter in a condition like sleep. □ **hiberner**

,**hiber'nation** *noun.* □ **hibernation**

hibiscus [hi'biskəs] *noun* a tropical plant with brightly-coloured flowers. □ **hibiscus**

hiccup ['hikʌp] *noun* **1** (the sound caused by) a sudden brief stopping of the breath caused by *eg* eating or drinking too much, too quickly. □ **hoquet**

2 (*in plural*) the frequent repetition of this, at intervals of a few seconds: *an attack of hiccups; I've got the hiccups.* □ **hoquet**

■ *verb* – *past tense, past participle* '**hiccuped** – to make a hiccup or hiccups. □ **avoir le hoquet**

hide[1] [haid] – *past tense* **hid** [hid]: *past participle* **hidden** ['hidn] – *verb* to put (a person, thing *etc*) in a place where it cannot be seen or easily found: *I'll hide the children's presents; You hide, and I'll come and look for you; She hid from her father; He tries to hide his feelings.* □ **(se) cacher**

'**hidden** *adjective* (made in such a way as to be) difficult to see or find: *a hidden door; a hidden meaning.* □ **caché**

hide-and-seek *noun* a children's game in which one person searches for other people who have hidden themselves. □ **cache-cache**

'**hide out** *noun* a place where one can hide or is hiding: *The police searched for the bandits' hide-out.* □ **repaire**

'**hiding**[1] *noun*: *He has gone into hiding because he knows the police are looking for him; Is she still in hiding?; The burglar came out of hiding when the police car drove off.* □ **cachette** '**hiding place** *noun* a place where a person or thing can be or is hidden: *We'll have to find a safe hiding-place for our jewels.* □ **cachette**

hide² [haid] *noun* the skin of an animal: *She makes coats out of animal hides*; *cow-hide.* □ **peau**

'**hiding²** *noun* a beating on the buttocks (*usually* of a child as punishment): *He got a good hiding.* □ **fessée**

hideous ['hidiəs] *adjective* extremely ugly: *a hideous vase.* □ **hideux**

'**hideously** *adverb.* □ **hideusement**

'**hideousness** *noun.* □ **hideur**

hierarchy ['haiəraːki] *noun* (an) arrangement (of *usually* people in a group, also things *etc*) in order of rank, importance *etc.* □ **hiérarchie**

hie'rarchical [-'raː-] *adjective.* □ **hiérarchique**

Notice the second **r** in **hierarchy**.

hieroglyphics [haiərə'glifiks] *noun plural* a form of writing used *eg* in ancient Egypt, in which pictures represent words and sounds. □ **hiéroglyphe(s)**

hi-fi ['haifai] (short for **high fidelity**) *noun* (a record player *etc* producing) high quality and great accuracy in the reproduction of sound. □ **haute-fidélité**

■ *adjective*: *hi-fi equipment.* □ **haute-fidélité**

high [hai] *adjective* **1** at, from, or reaching up to, a great distance from ground-level, sea-level *etc*: *a high mountain*; *a high dive*; *a dive from the high diving-board.* □ **haut**

2 having a particular height: *This building is about 20 metres high*; *a little man only one metre high*; *My horse is fifteen hands high.* □ **de haut**

3 great; large; considerable: *The car was travelling at high speed*; *He has a high opinion of her work*; *They charge high prices*; *high hopes*; *The child has a high fever/temperature.* □ **grand**

4 most important; very important: *the high altar in a church*; *Important criminal trials are held at the High Court*; *a high official.* □ **haut**

5 noble; good: *high ideals.* □ **noble**

6 (of a wind) strong: *The wind is high tonight.* □ **violent**

7 (of sounds) at or towards the top of a (musical) range: *a high note.* □ **aigu**

8 (of voices) like a child's voice (rather than like a man's): *He still speaks in a high voice.* □ **haut**

9 (of food, *especially* meat) beginning to go bad. □ **gâté**

10 having great value: *Aces and kings are high cards.* □ **fort**

■ *adverb* at, or to, a great distance from ground-level, sea-level *etc*: *The plane was flying high in the sky*; *She'll rise high in her profession.* □ **haut**

'**highly** *adverb* **1** very; very much: *highly delighted*; *highly paid*; *I value the book highly.* □ **extrêmement**

2 with approval: *She thinks/speaks very highly of you.* □ **en bien (de)**

'**highness** *noun* **1** the state or quality of being high. □ **hauteur**

2 a title of a prince, princess *etc*: *Your Highness*; *Her Highness.* □ **Altesse**

'**high chair** *noun* a chair with long legs, used by a baby or young child at mealtimes. □ **chaise haute**

,**high-'class** *adjective* of high quality: *This is a high-class hotel.* □ **de grande classe**

higher education education beyond the level of secondary school education, *eg* at a university. □ **enseignement supérieur**

high fidelity high quality and great accuracy (in the reproduction of sound). *See also* **hi-fi.** □ **haute-fidélité**

,**high-'handed** *adjective* done, acting, without consultation of, or consideration for, other people: *a high-handed decision*; *A new headmaster should try not to be too high-handed.* □ **tyrannique**

,**high-'handedly** *adverb.* □ **tyranniquement**

,**high-'handedness** *noun.* □ **tyrannie**

high jump a sports contest in which people jump over a bar which is raised until no one can jump over it. □ **saut en hauteur**

'**highlands** *noun plural* a mountainous part of certain countries, *especially* (*with capital*) of Scotland. □ **région montagneuse**

'**high-level** *adjective* involving important people: *high-level talks.* □ **de haut niveau**

'**highlight** *noun* the best or most memorable event, experience, part of something *etc*: *The highlight of our holiday was a trip to a brewery.* □ **clou**

■ *verb* to draw particular attention to (a person, thing *etc*). □ **mettre en vedette**

,**highly-'strung** *adjective* very nervous; very easily upset or excited. □ **nerveux**

,**high-'minded** *adjective* having or showing good or noble ideals, principles *etc*. □ **à l'âme noble**

,**high-'mindedness** *noun.* □ **noblesse de sentiments**

,**high-'pitched** *adjective* (of sounds, voices *etc*) high, sharp: *a high-pitched, childish voice.* □ **aigu**

,**high-'powered** *adjective* (with an engine which is) very powerful: *a high-powered motorboat/engine.* □ **de haute puissance**

'**high-rise** *adjective* with many storeys: *She does not like living in a high-rise flat as the children cannot get out to play easily.* □ **tour (d'habitation)**

high school a secondary school: *She goes to high school next year.* □ **école secondaire**

,**high-'spirited** *adjective* showing high spirits: *a high-spirited horse.* □ **fougueux**

high spirits enthusiasm, cheerfulness and energy: *He's in high spirits today.* □ **vivacité**

high tide the time when the tide is farthest up the shore: *High tide today is at 15:46*; *They set sail at high tide.* □ **marée haute**

high treason *see* **treason.**

high water the time at which the tide or other water (*eg* a river) is at its highest point. □ **marée haute; haute mer**

'**highway** *noun* a road specially made for fast traffic: *They are building a new motorway to link the two cities.* □ **autoroute**

Highway Code in Britain, (a booklet containing) a set of official rules for road users. □ **code de la route**

'**highwayman** – *plural* '**highwaymen** – *noun* in earlier times, a man *usually* on horseback, who attacked and robbed people travelling in coaches *etc* on public roads.

□ **bandit de grand chemin**
high wire *see* **wire**.
high and dry 1 (of boats) on the shore; out of the water: *The boat was left high and dry of the beach.* □ **échoué**
2 in difficulties: *I was left high and dry without any money.* □ **en plan**
high and low everywhere: *I've searched high and low for that book.* □ **partout**
high and mighty behaving as if one thinks one is very important: *Don't be so high and mighty – you're no one special.* □ **qui se donne de grands airs**
the high seas the open seas; far from land. □ **haute mer**
it is *etc* **high time** something ought to be done or have been done *etc* by now: *It is high time that this job was finished*; *It's high time someone spanked that child.* □ **il est grand temps (que)**

see also **tall**.

hijack ['haidʒak] *verb* **1** to take control of (an airplane) while it is moving and force the pilot to fly to a particular place. □ **détourner**
2 to stop and rob (a vehicle): *Thieves hijacked a truck carrying $20,000 worth of whisky.* □ **arrêter et piller**
3 to steal (something) from a vehicle: *Thieves hijacked $20,000 worth of whisky from a truck.* □ **s'emparer de**
■ *noun* the act of hijacking. □ **détournement**
'**hijacker** *noun*. □ **pirate (de la route, de l'air)**
hike [haik] *noun* a long walk, *usually* in the country: *twenty kilometre hike.* □ **randonnée**
■ *verb* to go on a hike or hikes: *She has hiked all over Nepal.* □ **excursionner (à pied)**
'**hiker** *noun*. □ **excursionniste**
hilarious [hi'leəriəs] *adjective* very funny: *a hilarious comedy.* □ **hilare**
hi'lariously *adverb*. □ **avec hilarité**
hi'larity [-'la-] *noun* amusement; laughter. □ **hilarité**
hill [hil] **1** *noun* a piece of high land, smaller than a mountain: *We went for a walk in the hills yesterday.* □ **colline**
2 a slope on a road: *This car has difficulty going up steep hills.* □ **pente**
'**hillock** [-lək] *noun* a small hill. □ **butte**
'**hilly** *adjective* having many hills: *hilly country.* □ **montagneux**
'**hillside** *noun* the side or slope of a hill: *The hillside was covered with new housing.* □ **(flanc de) coteau**
hilt [hilt] *noun* the handle, *especially* of a sword. □ **poignée (d'épée)**
him [him] *pronoun* (used as the object of a verb or preposition) a male person or animal already spoken about: *I saw him yesterday; I gave him a book; I came with him.* □ **lui, le**
him'self *pronoun* **1** used as the object of a verb or preposition when a male person or animal is the object of an action he performs: *He kicked himself; He looked at himself in the mirror.* □ **lui-même, se**
2 used to emphasize **he, him** or the name of a male person or animal: *John himself played no part in this.* □ **lui-même**

3 without help *etc*: *He did it himself.* □ **lui-même**
See also **he, his**.
hind[1] [haind] *noun* a female deer, *especially* of the red deer. □ **biche**
hind[2] [haind] *adjective* at the back (*usually* of an animal): *a hind leg.* □ **de derrière, postérieur**
hinder ['hində] *verb* to delay or prevent; to make difficult: *All these interruptions hinder my work; All the interruptions hinder me from working.* □ **gêner**
'**hindrance** [-drəns] *noun* a person, thing *etc* that hinders: *I know you are trying to help but you're just being a hindrance.* □ **obstacle**
hindquarters ['haindkwoːtəz] *noun plural* (of an animal) the back legs and the part of the body above them: *I think our dog has injured its hindquarters – it is limping.* □ **arrière-train**
hindrance *see* **hinder**.
hindsight ['haindsait] *noun* wisdom or knowledge got only after something (*usually* bad) has happened. □ **sagesse (rétrospective)**
Hindu [hin'duː] *noun, adjective* (of) a person who believes in, and lives according to the rules of, the religion of 'Hinduism. □ **hindou, oue**
hinge [hindʒ] *noun* the joint by means of which a door is fastened to a door-frame, a lid is fastened to a box *etc* and on which the door, lid *etc* turns when it opens or closes: *I must oil the hinges.* □ **gond**
hinge on to depend on: *The result of the whole competition hinges on the last match.* □ **dépendre de**
hint [hint] *noun* **1** a statement that passes on information without giving it openly or directly: *He didn't actually say he wanted more money, but he dropped a hint.* □ **allusion**
2 a helpful suggestion: *I can give you some useful gardening hints.* □ **conseil**
3 a very small amount; a slight impression: *There was a hint of fear in his voice.* □ **soupçon**
■ *verb* to (try to) pass on information without stating it openly or directly: *He hinted that he would like more money; She hinted at possible changes.* □ **laisser entendre (que)**
take a/the hint to understand a hint and act on it: *I keep making jokes to my secretary about her coming to work late every day, but she never takes the hint.* □ **saisir l'allusion**
hinterland ['hintəland] *noun* the district lying inland from the coast. □ **arrière-pays**
hip [hip] *noun* **1** (the bones in) either of the two sides of the body just below the waist: *She fell and broke her left hip.* □ **hanche**
2 (the measurement around) the body at the level of the hips and buttocks: *This exercise is good for the hips; What (size of) hip are you?* □ **hanches**
hippie, hippy ['hipi] – *plural* '**hippies** – *noun, adjective* (of) a *usually* young person who does not wish to live by the normal rules of society and who shows his rejection of these rules by his unusual clothes, habits *etc*: *The farm cottage was bought by a group of young hippies*; (*also adjective*) *hippy clothes.* □ **hippie**
hippopotamus [hipə'potəməs] *noun* a large African

animal with very thick skin living in or near rivers. □
hippopotame

hire ['haiə] *verb* 1 to employ (a workman *etc*): *They have
hired a team of labourers to dig the road.* □ **embaucher**
2 (*often with* **from**) to get the use of by paying money:
He's hiring a car (from us) for the week. □ **louer**
■ *noun* (money paid for) hiring: *Is this hall for hire?*;
How much is the hire of the hall?; *We don't own this
crane – it's on hire.* □ **location**
'**hirer** *noun.* □ **personne qui loue**

his [hiz] *adjective, pronoun* belonging to a male person
already spoken about: *John says it's his book*; *He says
the book is his*; *No, his is on the table.* □ **son, sa, ses**

hiss [his] *verb* (of snakes, geese, people *etc*) to make a
sound like that of the letter *s* [s], *eg* to show anger or
displeasure: *The children hissed (at) the witch when she
came on stage*; *The geese hissed at the dog.* □ **siffler**
■ *noun* such a sound: *The speaker ignored the hisses of
the angry crowd.* □ **siffle(men)t**

history ['histəri] – *plural* '**histories** – *noun* 1 the study of
events *etc* that happened in the past: *She is studying
Canadian history*; *(also adjective) a history lesson/book.*
□ **(d')histoire**
2 a description *usually* in writing of past events, ways
of life *etc*: *I'm writing a history of Scotland.* □ **histoire**
3 (the description of) the *usually* interesting events *etc*
associated with (something): *This desk/word has a very
interesting history.* □ **histoire**
hi'**storian** [-'stoː-] *noun* a person who studies (and writes
about) history. □ **historien, ienne**
hi'**storic** [-'sto-] *adjective* famous or important in history: *a historic battle.* □ **historique**
hi'**storical** [-'sto-] *adjective* 1 of or about history; of or
about people or events from history: *historical research*;
historical novels. □ **historique**
2 that actually happened or existed, not legendary or
mythical: *Was Shakespeare's character Macbeth a historical person?* □ **historique**
hi'**storically** [-'sto-] *adverb.* □ **historiquement**
make history to do something very important, *especially* to be the first to do something: *The Wright brothers made history when they were the first to fly an
airplane.* □ **entrer dans l'histoire**

hit [hit] – *present participle* '**hitting**: *past tense, past
participle* **hit** – *verb* 1 to (cause or allow to) come into
hard contact with: *The ball hit him on the head*; *He hit
his head on/against a low branch*; *The car hit a lamppost*; *She hit me on the head with a bottle*; *He was hit by
a bullet*; *That boxer can certainly hit hard!* □ **frapper,
heurter**
2 to make hard contact with (something), and force or
cause it to move in some direction: *The batsman hit the
ball (over the wall).* □ **envoyer**
3 to cause to suffer: *The farmers were badly hit by the
lack of rain*; *Her husband's death hit her hard.* □ **toucher**
4 to find; to succeed in reaching: *Her second arrow hit
the bull's-eye*; *Take the path across the fields and you'll
hit the road*; *She used to be a famous soprano but she
cannot hit the high notes now.* □ **atteindre**
■ *noun* 1 the act of hitting: *That was a good hit.* □ **coup**

2 a point scored by hitting a target *etc*: *She scored five
hits.* □ **coup réussi**
3 something which is popular or successful: *The play/
record is a hit*; *(also adjective) a hit song.* □ **(à) succès**
,**hit-and-'run** *adjective* (of a driver) causing injury to a
person and driving away without stopping or reporting
the accident. □ **coupable du délit de fuite**
hit and run *noun* (of an accident) caused by such a
driver. □ **délit de fuite**
,**hit-or-'miss** *adjective* without any system or planning;
careless: *hit-or-miss methods.* □ **n'importe comment**
hit back to hit (someone by whom one has been hit):
He hit me, so I hit him back. □ **rendre son coup (à)**
hit below the belt to hit in an unfair way. □ **frapper
au-dessous de la ceinture**
hit it off to become friendly: *We hit it off as soon as we
met*; *I hit it off with her.* □ **s'entendre bien avec**
hit on to find (an answer *etc*): *We've hit on the solution
at last.* □ **trouver**
hit out (*often with* **against** *or* **at**) to attempt to hit: *The
injured man hit out blindly at his attackers.* □ **se débattre**
make a hit with to make oneself liked or approved of
by: *That young man has made a hit with your daughter.*
□ **faire sensation**

hitch [hitʃ] *verb* 1 to fasten to something: *She hitched
her horse to the fence-post*; *He hitched his car to his
caravan.* □ **attacher**
2 to hitch-hike: *I can't afford the train fare – I'll have to
hitch.* □ **faire du stop**
■ *noun* 1 an unexpected problem or delay: *The job was
completed without a hitch.* □ **anicroche**
2 a kind of knot. □ **nœud**
3 a sudden, short pull upwards: *She gave her skirt a
hitch.* □ **secousse**
'**hitch hike** *verb* to travel by means of free rides in other
people's cars: *She has hitch-hiked all over Britain.* □
faire du stop
'**hitch hiker** *noun.* □ **auto-stoppeur, euse**
hitch a lift/ride to get a free ride in someone else's car.
□ **profiter d'une occasion**
hitch up to pull up or raise with a sudden short pull: *He
hitched up his trousers.* □ **remonter (d'une saccade)**

hither ['hiðə] *adverb* to this place. □ **ici**
,**hither'to** *adverb* up to this time: *Hitherto, this information has been kept secret.* □ **jusqu'ici**
hither and thither in various directions: *People were
running hither and thither.* □ **çà et là**

hive [haiv] *noun* 1 a box *etc* where bees live and store up
honey: *She's building a hive so that she can keep bees.*
□ **ruche**
2 the bees that live in such a place: *The whole hive flew
after the queen bee.* □ **essaim**

hoard [hoːd] *noun* a (sometimes hidden) store (of treasure, food *etc*): *When I was supposed to be on a diet I
secretly kept a hoard of potato crisps in a cupboard.* □
réserve
■ *verb* to store up or keep large quantities of (something), often in secret: *His mother told him to stop hoarding old newspapers.* □ **stocker**
'**hoarder** *noun.* □ **personne qui accumule**

hoarding ['hɔːdiŋ] *noun* a temporary fence of boards, *eg* around a place where a building is being knocked down or built. □ **palissade**

hoarse [hɔːs] *adjective* **1** (of voices, shouts *etc*) rough; harsh: *a hoarse cry*; *His voice sounds hoarse.* □ **enroué** **2** having a hoarse voice, *usually* because one has a cold or cough, or because one has been shouting: *You sound hoarse – have you a cold?*; *The spectators shouted themselves hoarse.* □ **enroué**

'hoarseness *noun.* □ **enrouement**

hoax [houks] *noun* a trick played to deceive people: *There was not a bomb in the school at all – it was just a hoax.* □ **tour**

■ *verb* to trick: *They found that they had been hoaxed.* □ **monter un bateau**

play a hoax on to carry out a trick on. □ **jouer un tour**

hobble ['hobl] *verb* to walk with difficulty, *usually* taking short steps (*eg* because one is lame or because one's feet are sore): *The old lady hobbled along with a stick.* □ **traîner la jambe**

hobby ['hobi] – *plural* **'hobbies** – *noun* something a person enjoys doing (*usually* frequently) in his spare time: *Stamp-collecting is a popular hobby.* □ **passe-temps**

hobo ['houbou] – *plural* **'hobo(e)s** – *noun* a tramp. □ **vagabond**

hock [hok] *noun* a joint on the hind leg of an animal, below the knee: *The horse has an injured hock.* □ **jarret**

hockey ['hoki] *noun* a game for two teams of eleven players, played with clubs which are bent at one end ('**hockey-sticks**) and a ball, or in **ice hockey**, a round flat disk called a puck. □ **hockey; bâton (de hockey)**

hocus-pocus [houkəs'poukəs] *noun* trickery; words, actions *etc* which are intended to deceive or mislead (someone): *The people were not deceived by the political hocus-pocus of the prospective candidate.* □ **tour de passe-passe, baratin**

hoe [hou] *noun* a long-handled tool with a metal blade used for removing or destroying weeds *etc*. □ **binette**

■ *verb* – *present participle* **'hoeing** – to use a hoe *eg* to remove or destroy weeds: *This morning I hoed the garden/weeds.* □ **sarcler**

hog [hog] *noun* a pig. □ **porc**

■ *verb* – *past tense, past participle* **hogged** – **1** to gobble up greedily. □ **se goinfrer** **2** to take or use more of than one ought to; to keep or use longer than one ought to: *She's hogging the spade and no one else can use it.* □ **accaparer**

'hogwash *noun* nonsense. □ **foutaise**

go the whole hog to do something completely: *I've bought a new dress – I think I'll go the whole hog and buy a complete outfit.* □ **aller jusqu'au bout**

hoist [hoist] *verb* **1** to lift (something heavy): *She hoisted the sack on to her back*; *He hoisted the child up on to his shoulders.* □ **hisser** **2** to raise or lift by means of some apparatus, a rope *etc*: *The cargo was hoisted on to the ship*; *They hoisted the flag.* □ **hisser**

■ *noun* **1** an apparatus for lifting *usually* heavy objects: *a luggage hoist.* □ **treuil** **2** a lift or push up: *Give me a hoist over this wall, will*

you! □ **poussée**

hold¹ [hould] – *past tense, past participle* **held** [held] – *verb* **1** to have in one's hand(s) or between one's hands: *She was holding a knife*; *Hold that dish with both hands*; *He held the little boy's hand*; *She held the mouse by its tail.* □ **tenir**

2 to have in a part, or between parts, of the body, or between parts of a tool *etc*: *He held the pencil in his teeth*; *She was holding a pile of books in her arms*; *Hold the stamp with tweezers.* □ **tenir**

3 to support or keep from moving, running away, falling *etc*: *What holds that shelf up?*; *She held the door closed by leaning against it*; *Hold your hands above your head*; *Hold his arms so that he can't struggle.* □ **retenir**

4 to remain in position, fixed *etc* when under strain: *I've tied the two pieces of string together, but I'm not sure the knot will hold*; *Will the anchor hold in a storm?* □ **tenir**

5 to keep (a person) in some place or in one's power: *The police are holding a man for questioning in connection with the murder*; *She was held captive.* □ **détenir**

6 to (be able to) contain: *This jug holds two litres*; *You can't hold water in a handkerchief*; *This drawer holds all my shirts.* □ **contenir**

7 to cause to take place: *The meeting will be held next week*; *We'll hold the meeting in the hall.* □ **tenir, avoir lieu**

8 to keep (oneself), or to be, in a particular state or condition: *We'll hold ourselves in readiness in case you send for us*; *She holds herself very erect.* □ **(se) tenir**

9 to have or be in (a job *etc*): *He held the position of company secretary for five years.* □ **occuper**

10 to think strongly; to believe; to consider or regard: *I hold that this was the right decision*; *He holds me (to be) responsible for everyone's mistakes*; *She is held in great respect*; *He holds certain very odd beliefs.* □ **tenir, croire**

11 to continue to be valid or apply: *Our offer will hold until next week*; *These rules hold under all circumstances.* □ **être valable**

12 (*with* **to**) to force (a person) to do something he has promised to do: *I intend to hold him to his promises.* □ **obliger (qqn) à tenir ses engagements**

13 to defend: *They held the castle against the enemy.* □ **défendre**

14 not to be beaten by: *The general realized that the soldiers could not hold the enemy for long.* □ **résister**

15 to keep (a person's attention). □ **retenir**

16 to celebrate: *The festival is held on 24 June.* □ **avoir lieu**

17 to be the owner of: *She holds shares in this company.* □ **posséder**

18 (of good weather) to continue: *I hope the weather holds until after the school sports.* □ **(se) maintenir**

19 (*also* **hold the line**) (of a person who is making a telephone call) to wait: *Mrs. Brown is busy at the moment – will you hold or would you like her to call you back?* □ **patienter**

20 to continue to sing: *Please hold that note for four* *whole beats.* □ **tenir**

21 to keep (something): *They'll hold your luggage at the station until you collect it.* □ **garder**

22 (of the future) to be going to produce: *I wonder what the future holds for me?* □ **réserver à**

■ *noun* **1** the act of holding: *She caught/got/laid/took hold of the rope and pulled; Keep hold of that rope.* □ **prise**

2 power; influence: *He has a strange hold over that man.* □ **emprise**

3 (in wrestling *etc*) a manner of holding one's opponent: *The wrestler invented a new hold.* □ **prise**

-holder a person or thing that holds something: *a penholder; a ticket-holder* (= a person who has a ticket for something). □ **porte-(...); détenteur, trice**

get hold of 1 to manage to speak to: *I've been trying to get hold of you by phone all morning.* □ **joindre**

2 to get, buy or obtain: *I've been trying to get hold of a copy of that book for years.* □ **dénicher**

hold back 1 to refuse to tell someone (something): *The police were convinced I was holding something back.* □ **cacher (qqch. à qqn)**

2 to prevent from happening, being seen *etc*, with an effort: *The little boy succeeded in holding back his tears.* □ **retenir**

3 to prevent from making progress: *I meant to finish cleaning the house but the children have held me back all morning.* □ **retarder**

hold down to keep or be allowed to stay in (a job): *He is incapable of holding down a job.* □ **garder**

hold forth to talk or give one's opinions, often loudly, at great length: *The prime minister held forth for hours on the success of her government.* □ **pérorer**

hold it! to stop or wait: *Hold it! Don't start till I tell you to.* □ **ne bougez plus !**

hold off 1 (of weather) to stay away: *I hope the rain holds off.* □ **(se) maintenir**

2 to keep off; to fight successfully against: *The soldiers managed to hold off the enemy.* □ **contenir**

hold on 1 (*often with* **to**) to keep (a grip on) (something): *She held on to me to stop herself slipping; I couldn't hold on any longer, so I let go of the rope.* □ **(se) tenir (à)**

2 to stop or wait: *Hold on – I'm not quite ready yet; The receptionist asked the caller to hold on while she connected him.* □ **patienter**

hold out 1 to continue to survive *etc* until help arrives: *The rescue team hoped the men in the boat could hold out till they arrived.* □ **(sou)tenir**

2 to continue to fight against an enemy attack: *The soldiers held out for eight days.* □ **tenir**

3 to be enough to last: *Will our supplies hold out till the end of the month?* □ **suffire**

hold one's own to be as successful in a fight, argument *etc* as one's opponent: *His opponents tried to prove his arguments wrong but he managed to hold his own.* □ **tenir bon**

hold one's tongue to remain silent or stop talking: *There were a lot of things I wanted to say, but I thought I'd better just hold my tongue.* □ **tenir sa langue**

hold true to be true or valid; to apply: *Does that rule hold good in every case?* □ **rester valable**

hold up 1 to stop or slow the progress of: *I'm sorry I'm late – I got held up at the office.* □ **retenir**

2 to stop and rob: *The bandits held up the stagecoach.* □ **attaquer (à main armée)**

'hold-up *noun.* □ **vol à main armée**

hold with to approve of: *She doesn't hold with smoking.* □ **approuver**

hold² [hould] *noun* (in ships) the place, below the deck, where cargo is stored. □ **cale**

hole [houl] *noun* **1** an opening or gap in or through something: *a hole in the fence; holes in my socks.* □ **trou**

2 a hollow in something solid: *a hole in my tooth; Many animals live in holes in the ground.* □ **brèche; trou**

3 (in golf) (the point scored by the player who takes the fewest strokes to hit his ball over) any one of the *usually* eighteen sections of the golf course between the tees and the holes in the middle of the greens: *She won by two holes; We played nine holes.* □ **trou**

■ *verb* **1** to make a hole in: *The ship was badly holed when it hit the rock.* □ **trouer**

2 to hit (a ball *etc*) into a hole: *The golfer holed his ball from twelve metres away.* □ **envoyer la balle dans le trou**

hole out *verb* to hit a golfball into a hole. □ **envoyer la balle dans le trou**

holiday ['holədi] *noun* **1** a day when one does not have to work: *Next Monday is a holiday.* □ **(jour de) congé; jour férié**

2 (*often in plural*) a period of time when one does not have to work: *The summer holidays will soon be here; We're going to Sweden for our holiday(s); I'm taking two weeks' holiday in June;* (*also adjective*) *holiday clothes.* □ **(de) vacances**

on holiday not working; having a holiday: *.Mr. Smith has gone on holiday; She is on holiday in France.* □ **en vacances**

holler ['holə] *verb* to shout: *He hollered at the boy to go away; She's hollering about the cost of gasoline again.* □ **crier**

holiness *see* **holy.**

hollow ['holou] *adjective* **1** having an empty space in it: *a hollow tree; Bottles, pipes and tubes are hollow.* □ **creux**

2 (of a sound) strangely deep, as if made in something hollow: *a hollow voice.* □ **caverneux**

■ *noun* **1** something hollow: *hollows in her cheeks.* □ **creux**

2 a small valley; a dip in the ground: *You can't see the farm from here because it's in a hollow.* □ **creux**

'hollowness *noun.* □ **creux**

beat hollow to beat thoroughly at a game *etc*: *The local team were beaten hollow by eight goals to one on Saturday.* □ **battre à plate couture**

hollow out to make hollow: *They hollowed out a treetrunk to make a boat.* □ **creuser, évider**

holly ['holi] *noun* a type of evergreen tree or bush with prickly leaves and red berries. □ **houx**

holocaust ['holəkoːst] *noun* great destruction, *usually* by fire, *especially* of people's lives. □ **holocauste**

holster ['houlstə] *noun* the *usually* leather case for a pistol, *usually* worn on a person's hips. □ **étui de revolver**

holy ['houli] *adjective* **1** (worthy of worship or respect because) associated with God, Jesus, a saint *etc*; sacred: *the Holy Bible*; *holy ground*. □ **saint**

2 good; pure; following the rules of religion: *a holy life*. □ **saint**

'**holiness** *noun* **1** the state of being holy. □ **sainteté**

2 (*with capital*: *with* **His, Your** *etc*) a title of the Pope. □ **Sa/Votre Sainteté**

the Holy Father the Pope. □ **le Saint-Père**

homage ['homidʒ] *noun* (a sign of) great respect shown to a person: *We pay homage to this great man by laying a wreath yearly on his grave*. □ **hommage**

home [houm] *noun* **1** the house, town, country *etc* where a person *etc* usually lives: *I work in London but my home is in Bournemouth*; *When I retire, I'll make my home in Bournemouth*; *Africa is the home of the lion*; *We'll have to find a home for the kitten*. □ **maison; habitat**

2 the place from which a person, thing *etc* comes originally: *America is the home of jazz*. □ **patrie**

3 a place where children without parents, old people, people who are ill *etc* live and are looked after: *an old folk's home*; *a nursing home*. □ **foyer**

4 a place where people stay while they are working: *a nurses' home*. □ **foyer**

5 a house: *Crumpy Construction build fine homes for fine people*; *He invited me over to his home*. □ **maison**

■ *adjective* **1** of a person's home or family: *home comforts*. □ **du foyer**

2 of the country *etc* where a person lives: *home produce*. □ **du pays**

3 (in football) playing or played on a team's own ground: *the home team*; *a home game*. □ **qui reçoit, à domicile**

■ *adverb* **1** to a person's home: *I'm going home now*; *Hello – I'm home!* □ **chez (soi)**

2 completely; to the place, position *etc* a thing is intended to be: *She drove the nail home*; *Few of his punches went home*; *These photographs of the war brought home to me the suffering of the soldiers*. □ **à fond; au but**

'**homeless** *noun plural, adjective* (people) without a place to live in: *This charity was set up to help the homeless*; *homeless people*. □ **sans-abri**

'**homely** *adjective* **1** simple but pleasant: *homely food*. □ **sans prétentions/façons**

2 making a person feel he is at home: *a homely atmosphere*. □ **accueillant**

3 (of a person) not attractive; ugly. □ **laid**

'**homeliness** *noun*. □ **simplicité; (E.-U) laideur**

'**homing** *adjective* **1** (of pigeons *etc*) which (can) fly home when set free a long way from home. □ **(pigeon) voyageur**

2 able to take a missile *etc* to its target: *These torpedoes have homing devices in their noses*. □ **à tête chercheuse**

'**homecoming** *noun* the return home of a person (who has been away for some time): *We had a party to celebrate her homecoming*. □ **retour**

,**home'grown** *adjective* grown in one's own garden or

in one's own country: *These tomatoes are homegrown*. □ **du jardin/pays**

'**homeland** *noun* a person's native land: *Immigrants often weep for their homeland*. □ **patrie**

,**home'made** *adjective* made by a person at home; not professionally made: *homemade jam*; *homemade furniture*. □ **fait à la maison**

home rule the government of a country or part of a country by its own citizens. □ **autonomie**

'**homesick** *adjective* missing one's home: *When the boy first went to boarding-school he was very homesick*. □ **qui a le mal du pays**

'**homesickness** *noun*. □ **mal du pays**

'**homestead** [-sted] *noun* a house, *especially* a farm, with the land and other buildings (*eg* barns) which belong to it, *especially* in the United States, Australia *etc*. □ **ferme (avec dépendances)**

home truth a plain statement of something which is unpleasant but true (about a person, his behaviour *etc*) said directly to the person: *It's time someone told him a few home truths*. □ **ses quatre vérités (à qqn)**

'**homeward** *adjective* going home: *her homeward journey*. □ **de/du retour**

'**homeward(s)** *adverb* towards home: *his journey homeward*; *She journeyed homewards*. □ **vers la maison/patrie**

'**homework** *noun* work or study done at home, *especially* by a school pupil: *Finish your homework!* □ **devoirs (à la maison)**

at home 1 in one's home: *I'm afraid he's not at home*. □ **chez (soi)**

2 (in football *etc*) in one's own ground: *The team is playing at home today*. □ **à domicile**

be/feel at home to feel as relaxed as one does in one's own home or in a place or situation one knows well: *I always feel at home in France*; *He's quite at home with cows – he used to live on a farm*. □ **se sentir à l'aise**

home in on to move towards (a target *etc*): *The missile is designed to home in on aircraft*. □ **(se) diriger (automatiquement) sur/vers**

leave home 1 to leave one's house: *I usually leave home at 7:30*. □ **sortir (de chez soi)**

2 to leave one's home to go and live somewhere else: *She left home at the age of fifteen to get a job in Australia*. □ **quitter la maison**

make oneself at home to make oneself as comfortable and relaxed as one would at home: *Make yourself at home!* □ **se mettre à l'aise**

nothing to write home about not very good: *The concert was nothing to write home about*. □ **pas de quoi faire un plat**

homicide ['homisaid] *noun* the killing of one person by another: *He has been found guilty of homicide*. □ **homicide**

,**homi'cidal** *adjective*. □ **homicide**

homonym ['homənim] *noun* a word having the same sound as another word, but a different meaning: *The words 'there' and 'their' are homonyms*. □ **homonyme**

homosexual [homə'sekʃuəl] *adjective, noun* **1** a person who is sexually attracted to people of the same sex. □

skyscraper

hotel

apartment building

bungalow

motel

mobile home

cottage

castle

semi-detached

tent

hut

igloo

homosexuel, elle

2 *adjective* of or concerning a homosexual or homosexuals: *a homosexual relationship.* □ **homosexuel**
'homo,sexu'ality [-'a-] *noun.* □ **homosexualité**

honest ['onist] *adjective* 1 (of people or their behaviour, statements *etc*) truthful; not cheating, stealing *etc*: *My secretary is absolutely honest; Give me an honest opinion.* □ **honnête**
2 (of a person's appearance) suggesting that he is honest: *an honest face.* □ **honnête**
3 (of wealth *etc*) not gained by cheating, stealing *etc*: *to earn an honest living.* □ **honnête**
'honestly *adverb* 1 in an honest way: *She gained her wealth honestly.* □ **honnêtement**
2 used to stress the truth of what a person is saying: *Honestly, that's exactly what she said; I honestly don't think it's possible.* □ **franchement**
■ *interjection* used to express mild anger *etc*: *Honestly! That was a stupid thing to do!* □ **tout de même!**
'honesty *noun*: *Surely, if you own up to something, you should be praised for your honesty, not punished.* □ **honnêteté**

honey ['hʌni] *noun* 1 a sweet, thick fluid made by bees from the nectar of flowers: *bread and honey.* □ **miel**
2 darling (used when speaking to someone one loves). □ **chéri, ie**
'honeybee *noun* a bee in a hive, bred for producing honey. □ **abeille**
'honeycomb *noun* the mass formed by rows of wax cells in which bees store their honey. □ **rayon de miel**
'honeymoon *noun* a holiday spent immediately after one's marriage: *We went to London for our honeymoon;* (*also adjective*) *a honeymoon couple.* □ **lune de miel; de jeunes mariés**

honk [hoŋk] *noun* (a sound like) the cry of a goose or the sound of a car horn. □ **cri (de l'oie); coup de klaxon**
■ *verb* 1 to make such a noise: *Don't honk that horn any more – you'll disturb the neighbours.* □ **klaxonner**
2 to sound the horn of a car *etc*: *The driver honked the horn at the cyclist in her way.* □ **klaxonner**

honorary *see* **honour.**

honour, ['onə] *noun* 1 respect for truth, honesty *etc*: *a man of honour.* □ **honneur**
2 (the keeping or increasing of) a person's, country's *etc* good reputation: *We must fight for the honour of our country.* □ **honneur**
3 fame; glory: *He won honour on the field of battle.* □ **gloire**
4 respect: *This ceremony is being held in honour of those who died in the war.* □ **en l'honneur de**
5 something which a person feels to be a reason for pride *etc*: *It is a great honour to be asked to address this meeting.* □ **honneur**
6 a title, degree *etc* given to a person as a mark of respect for his services, work, ability *etc*: *She has received many honours for her research into cancer.* □ **distinction**
7 (*with capital*: *with* **His, Your** *etc*) a title of respect used when talking to or about judges, mayors *etc*: *My client wishes to plead guilty, Your Honour.* □ **Son/Votre**

Honneur
■ *verb* 1 to show great respect to (a person, thing *etc*): *We should honour the Queen.* □ **honorer**
2 to do, say *etc* something which is a reason for pride, satisfaction *etc* to: *Will you honour us with your presence at the meeting?* □ **faire l'honneur de**
3 to give (someone) a title, degree *etc* as a mark of respect for his ability *etc*: *He was honoured for his work with the mentally handicapped.* □ **décerner une distinction**
4 to fulfil (a promise *etc*): *We'll honour our agreement.* □ **honorer**
'honorary *adjective* 1 (*often abbreviated to* **Hon.** *in writing*) (of an official position) not having any payment: *the Honorary Secretary of the Darts Association.* □ **honoraire**
2 given to a person as a mark of respect for his ability *etc*: *an honorary degree.* □ **honoris causa, honorifique**
'honourable *adjective* having, showing, bringing or deserving honour: *an honourable person.* □ **honorable**
'honours *noun plural* 1 (*sometimes with capital: sometimes abbreviated to* **Hons** *when written*) a degree awarded by universities, colleges *etc* to students who achieve good results in their final degree examinations, or who carry out specialized study or research; the course of study leading to the awarding of such a degree: *She got First Class Honours in French*; (*also adjective*) *an honours degree, an honors course.* □ **(avec) mention**
2 ceremony, when given as a mark of respect: *The dead soldiers were buried with full military honours.* □ **honneurs**
(in) honour bound forced (to do something) not by law, but because one knows it is right: *I said I would go if she sent for me, and I feel honour bound to do as I promised.* □ **tenu par l'honneur à**
on one's honour an expression used to emphasize the truth and solemnity of something which is said: *Do you swear, on your honour, never to reveal what you see here?* □ **sur l'honneur**
word of honour a promise which cannot be broken without loss of honour: *I give you my word of honour that I'll do it.* □ **parole d'honneur**

> **honour,** noun, ends in **-our.**
> **honorary,** adjective, drops the **u.**
> **honourable,** adjective, keeps the **u.**

hood [hud] *noun* 1 a *usually* loose covering for the whole head, often attached to a coat, cloak *etc*: *The monk pulled his hood over his head.* □ **capuchon**
2 a folding cover on a car, pram *etc*: *Put the hood of the pram up – the baby is getting wet.* □ **capot(e)**
3 the bonnet of a car: *She raised the hood to look at the engine.* □ **capot**
4 a fold of cloth representing a hood, worn by university graduates over their gowns on ceremonial occasions: *The professors and lecturers all wore their gowns and hoods for the graduation ceremony.* □ **épitoge**
'hooded *adjective* fitted with, or wearing, a hood. □ **encapuchonné**

hoodlum ['huːdləm] *noun* **1** a destructive person. □ **voyou**

2 (*especially American*) a criminal. □ **gangster**

hoodwink ['hudwiŋk] *verb* to trick or deceive. □ **tromper qqn**

hoof [huːf] – *plurals* **hooves** [huːvz], **hoofs** – *noun* the horny part of the feet of horses, cows *etc*: *That horse has an injured hoof.* □ **sabot**

hook [huk] *noun* **1** a small piece of metal shaped like a J fixed at the end of a fishing-line used for catching fish *etc*: *a fish-hook.* □ **hameçon**

2 a bent piece of metal used for hanging coats, cups *etc* on, or a smaller one sewn on to a garment, for fastening it: *Hang your jacket on that hook behind the door*; *hooks and eyes.* □ **crochet, agrafe**

3 in boxing, a kind of punch with the elbow bent: *a left hook.* □ **crochet**

■ *verb* **1** to catch (a fish *etc*) with a hook: *She hooked a large salmon.* □ **prendre**

2 to fasten or to be fastened by a hook or hooks: *He hooked the ladder on* (*to the branch*); *This bit hooks on to that bit*; *Could you hook my dress up down the back?* □ **accrocher**

3 in golf, to hit (the ball) far to the left of where it should be (or to the right if one is left-handed). □ **coup tiré**

hooked *adjective* **1** curved like a hook: *a hooked nose.* □ **crochu**

2 (*with* **on**) slang for very interested in, or showing a great liking for; addicted to: *She's hooked on modern art*; *He's hooked on marijuana.* □ **accroché**

by hook or by crook by some means or another; in any way possible: *I'll get her to sell that dog, by hook or by crook.* □ **coûte que coûte**

off the hook free from some difficulty or problem: *If he couldn't keep the terms of the contract, he shouldn't have signed it – I don't see how we can get him off the hook now.* □ **tiré d'affaire**

hooligan ['huːligən] *noun* a young violent, destructive or badly-behaved person. □ **voyou**

'hooliganism *noun* violent or destructive behaviour *especially* by young people. □ **délinquance**

hoop [huːp] *noun* a thin ring of metal, wood *etc*: *At the circus we saw a dog jumping through a hoop.* □ **cerceau**

hooping-cough *see* **whooping-cough.**

hoorah, hooray *see* **hurrah.**

hoot [huːt] *verb* **1** to sound the horn of a car *etc*: *The driver hooted* (*her horn*) *at the old lady.* □ **klaxonner**

2 (of car *etc* horns, sirens *etc*) to make a loud noise, as a warning, signal *etc*: *You can't leave the factory till the siren hoots.* □ **mugir**

3 (of owls) to call out: *An owl hooted in the wood.* □ **hululer**

4 (of people) to make a loud noise of laughter or disapproval: *They hooted with laughter.* □ **huer; s'esclaffer**

■ *noun* **1** the sound of a car *etc* horn, a siren *etc*. □ **coup de klaxon, de sirène**

2 the call of an owl. □ **hululement**

3 a loud shout of laughter or disapproval. □ **huée; éclat de rire**

not care a hoot/two hoots not to care in the least: *She*

doesn't care two hoots what anyone thinks of her. □ **se ficher de**

hooves *see* **hoof.**

hop¹ [hop] – *past tense, past participle* **hopped** – *verb* **1** (of people) to jump on one leg: *The children had a competition to see who could hop the farthest*; *He hopped about in pain when the hammer fell on his foot.* □ **sauter à cloche-pied**

2 (of certain small birds, animals and insects) to jump on both or all legs: *The sparrow/frog hopped across the lawn.* □ **sautiller**

3 to jump: *She hopped* (*over*) *the fence and ran away*; *He hopped out of bed.* □ **sauter**

4 (*with* **in(to), out (of)**) to get into or out of a car *etc*: *The car stopped and the driver told the hikers to hop in*; *I'll hop out of the car at the next intersection.* □ **monter/descendre**

■ *noun* **1** a short jump on one leg. □ **saut (à cloche-pied)**

2 (of certain small birds, animals and insects) a short jump on both or all legs: *The sparrow crossed the lawn in a series of hops.* □ **sautillement**

'hopscotch [-skotʃ] *noun* a game played *usually* by children in which they hop into a series of squares drawn on the ground: *The children are playing hopscotch on the pavement.* □ **marelle**

catch (someone) on the hop to do something to (someone) when he is not prepared. □ **prendre au dépourvu**

keep (someone) hopping to keep (someone) busy, active *etc*. □ **ne pas laisser chômer**

hop² [hop] *noun* a climbing plant, the bitter fruits of which (**hops**) are used in brewing beer. □ **houblon**

hope [houp] *verb* to want something to happen and have some reason to believe that it will or might happen: *He's very late, but we are still hoping he will come*; *I hope to be in London next month*; *We're hoping for some help from other people*; *It's unlikely that she'll come now, but we keep on hoping*; *'Do you think it will rain?' 'I hope so/not'.* □ **espérer**

■ *noun* **1** (any reason or encouragement for) the state of feeling that what one wants will or might happen: *She has lost all hope of becoming the president*; *He came to see me in the hope that I would help him*; *She has hopes of winning a scholarship*; *The rescuers said there was no hope of finding anyone alive in the mine.* □ **espoir, espérance**

2 a person, thing *etc* that one is relying on for help *etc*: *He's my last hope – there is no one else I can ask.* □ **espoir**

3 something hoped for: *My hope is that he will get married and settle down soon.* □ **espoir**

'hopeful *adjective* **1** (*negative* **unhopeful**) full of hope: *The police are hopeful that they will soon find the killer*; *hopeful faces*; *She is hopeful of success.* □ **plein d'espoir**

2 giving a reason or encouragement for hope: *That's a hopeful sign – perhaps she is going to change her mind after all.* □ **encourageant**

3 likely to be pleasant, successful *etc*: *The future looks quite hopeful.* □ **prometteur**

'hopefulness *noun*. □ **confiance**

'hopefully *adverb* 1 in a hopeful way: *The dog looked hopefully at the joint of meat.* □ **avec espoir**
2 it is to be hoped that: *Hopefully, that will never happen.* □ **espérons-le**
'hopeless *adjective* 1 not likely to be successful: *It's hopeless to try to persuade her; a hopeless attempt; The future looks hopeless.* □ **sans espoir**
2 (*with* at) not good: *I'm a hopeless pianist; He's hopeless at French.* □ **nul**
3 unable to be stopped, cured *etc*: *The doctors considered the patient's case hopeless; He's a hopeless liar/idiot.* □ **désespéré**
'hopelessly *adverb*. □ **sans espoir**
'hopelessness *noun*. □ **désespoir**
hope against hope to continue hoping when there is no (longer any) reason for hope. □ **espérer en dépit de tout**
hope for the best to hope that something will succeed, that nothing bad will happen *etc*. □ **avoir bon espoir**
not (have) a hope (to be) completely unlikely (to succeed in something): *He hasn't a hope of getting the job*; *'Will she get the job?' 'Not a hope!'* □ **aucune chance**
raise someone's hopes to cause someone to hope, *usually* when there is no good reason to. □ **susciter l'espoir chez**
horde [hoːd] *noun* a crowd or large number (of people *etc*): *Hordes of tourists thronged the temple.* □ **horde**
horizon [hə'raizn] *noun* the line at which the earth and the sky seem to meet: *The sun went down below the horizon; A ship could be seen on the horizon.* □ **horizon**
horizontal [hori'zontl] *adjective* at right angles to vertical; parallel to the horizon; lying level or flat: *a horizontal line; a horizontal surface.* □ **horizontal**
,hori'zontally *adverb*. □ **horizontalement**
hormone ['hoːmoun] *noun* a substance produced by certain glands of the body, which makes some organ of the body active: *Adrenalin is a hormone.* □ **hormone**
horn [hoːn] *noun* 1 a hard object which grows (*usually* in pairs) on the head of a cow, sheep *etc*: *A ram has horns.* □ **corne**
2 the material of which this is made: *spoons made of horn*; (*also adjective*) *horn spoons.* □ **(de/en) corne**
3 something which is made of horn: *a shoehorn.* □ **corne**
4 something which looks like a horn in shape: *a snail's horns.* □ **corne**
5 the apparatus in a car *etc* which gives a warning sound: *The driver blew his horn.* □ **klaxon**
6 an instrument, formerly an animal's horn but now made of brass, that is blown to produce a musical sound: *a hunting-horn.* □ **cor**
7 (*also* **French horn**) the type of coiled brass horn that is played in orchestras *etc*. □ **cor d'harmonie**
horned *adjective* having a horn or horns: *a horned animal.* □ **cornu**
-horned: *a long-horned antelope.* □ **à cornes (...)**
'horny *adjective* 1 like horn: *a horny substance.* □ **corné**
2 as hard as horn: *horny hands.* □ **calleux**
hornet ['hoːnit] *noun* a kind of large wasp. □ **frelon**
horoscope ['horəskoup] *noun* the prediction of a person's future based on the position of the stars and planets at the time of his birth. □ **horoscope**

horrible, horrid *etc see* **horror**.
horror ['horə] *noun* 1 great fear or dislike: *He has a horror of spiders; She looked at me in horror.* □ **horreur**
2 a disagreeable person or thing: *Her little boy is an absolute horror.* □ **monstre**
'horrible *adjective* 1 causing horror; dreadful: *a horrible sight.* □ **horrible**
2 unpleasant: *What a horrible day!* □ **affreux**
'horribleness *noun*. □ **caractère horrible**
'horribly *adverb*. □ **horriblement**
'horrid [-rid] *adjective* 1 unpleasant: *That was a horrid thing to say.* □ **affreux**
2 dreadful: *a horrid shriek.* □ **horrible**
horrific [hə'rifik] *adjective* terrible; terrifying: *a horrific accident; a horrific journey.* □ **terrifiant**
'horrify [-fai] *verb* to shock greatly: *Mrs. Smith was horrified to find that her son had grown a beard.* □ **horrifier**
'horrifying *adjective*. □ **horrifiant**
hors d'oeuvre [oː'dɔːvr] – *plural* **hors d'oeuvre(s)** [oː'dɔːvr] – *noun* food *eg* olives, sardines *etc* served before or at the beginning of a meal in order to increase the appetite. □ **hors-d'œuvre**
horse [hoːs] *noun* 1 a large four-footed animal which is used to pull carts *etc* or to carry people *etc*. □ **cheval**
2 a piece of apparatus used for jumping, vaulting *etc* in a gymnasium. □ **cheval d'arçons**
'horse-box *noun* an enclosed vehicle *etc* used for carrying horses. □ **fourgon à chevaux**
'horsefly *noun* a large fly that bites horses *etc*. □ **taon**
'horsehair *noun, adjective* (of) the hair from a horse's mane or tail: *The mattress is stuffed with horsehair; a horsehair mattress.* □ **(de/en) crin**
'horseman – *feminine* 'horsewoman – *noun* a rider, *especially* a skilled one: *She is a very competent horsewoman.* □ **cavalier, ière**
'horseplay *noun* rough and noisy behaviour or play. □ **jeu brutal**
'horsepower (*usually* abbreviated to **h.p.** *when written*) *noun* a standard unit used to measure the power of engines, cars *etc*. □ **cheval-vapeur**
'horseriding *noun*. □ **équitation**
horseshoe ['hoːʃʃuː] *noun* 1 a curved iron shoe for a horse. □ **fer à cheval**
2 something in the shape of a horseshoe: *The bride was presented with a lucky silver horseshoe.* □ **fer à cheval**
on horseback riding on a horse: *The soldiers rode through the town on horseback.* □ **à cheval**
(straight) from the horse's mouth from a well-informed and reliable source: *I got that story straight from the horse's mouth.* □ **de source sûre**
horticulture ['hoːtikʌltʃə] *noun* the science and art of gardening. □ **horticulture**
,horti'cultural *adjective*. □ **horticole**
hose [houz] 1 a rubber, plastic *etc* tube which bends and which is used to carry water *etc*: *a garden hose; a fireman's hose.* □ **tuyau (d'arrosage); lance (d'incendie)**
2 an older word for stockings or socks: *woollen hose.*

bas

■ *verb* to apply water to by means of a hose: *I'll go and hose the garden/car.* □ **arroser au jet**

hosiery ['houziəri] *noun* knitted goods, *especially* stockings, socks and tights. □ **bonneterie**

hose reel a revolving drum for carrying hoses. □ **dévidoir**

hose down to clean (*eg* a car) by means of water brought by a hose. □ **passer au jet**

hospitable [hə'spitəbl] *adjective* showing kindness to guests: *She is one of the most hospitable people I know.* □ **hospitalier**

ho'spitably *adverb.* □ **avec hospitalité**

ho'spitableness *noun.* □ **hospitalité**

hospitality [hospi'taləti] *noun* a friendly welcome for guests or strangers, which often includes offering them food, drink *etc.* □ **hospitalité**

hospital ['hospitl] *noun* a building or group of buildings where people who are ill or injured are given treatment: *After the train crash, the injured people were taken to hospital.* □ **hôpital**

'**hospitalize**, '**hospitalise** *verb* to keep (a person) in hospital for treatment. □ **hospitaliser**

,**hospitali'zation**, ,**hospitali'sation** *noun.* □ **hospitalisation**

host[1] [houst] *noun* 1 (*feminine* '**hostess**) a person who entertains someone else as his guest, *usually* in his own house: *Our host/hostess introduced us at the party.* □ **hôte, hôtesse**

2 an animal or plant on which another lives as a parasite. □ **hôte**

host[2] [houst] *noun* a very large number of people or things. □ **foule**

hostage ['hostidʒ] *noun* a person who is held prisoner in order to ensure that the captor's demands *etc* will be carried out: *The terrorists took three people with them as hostages; They took/were holding three people hostage.* □ **otage**

take, hold (someone) hostage to take or keep (someone) as a hostage: *The police were unable to attack the terrorists because they were holding three people hostage.* □ **prendre/garder en otage**

hostel ['hostəl] *noun* 1 a building with simple accommodation, *especially* for young people, hikers *etc*: *a youth hostel.* □ **auberge de jeunesse**

2 a building where students *etc* may live: *a nurses' hostel.* □ **foyer**

hostess *see* host.

hostile ['hostail] *adjective* 1 unfriendly; warlike: *hostile tribesmen.* □ **hostile**

2 belonging to an enemy: *a hostile army.* □ **ennemi**

3 showing dislike or opposition to something: *a hostile attitude.* □ **hostile**

ho'stilities [-'sti-] *noun plural* acts of war; battles: *The two countries were engaged in hostilities.* □ **hostilités**

ho'stility [-'sti-] *noun* unfriendliness; opposition. □ **hostilité**

hot [hot] *adjective* 1 having or causing a great deal of heat: *a hot oven; That water is hot.* □ **chaud**

2 very warm: *a hot day; Running makes me feel hot.* □

chaud

3 (of food) having a sharp, burning taste: *a hot curry.* □ **épicé**

4 easily made angry: *a hot temper.* □ **emporté**

5 recent; fresh: *hot news.* □ **frais**

'**hotly** *adverb* 1 eagerly; quickly: *The thieves were hotly pursued by the police.* □ **activement**

2 angrily; passionately: *The accusations were hotly denied.* □ **vivement**

hot air boastful words, promises that will not be kept *etc*: *Most of what he said was just hot air.* □ **du vent**

,**hot-'blooded** *adjective* passionate; having strong feelings: *hot-blooded young men.* □ **passionné**

hot dog a hot sausage sandwich. □ **chien-chaud**

'**hotfoot** *adverb* in a great hurry: *She arrived hotfoot from the meeting.* □ **à toute allure**

'**hothead** *noun* a hotheaded person. □ **exalté, ée**

,**hot'headed** *adjective* easily made angry; inclined to act suddenly and without sufficient thought. □ **impétueux**

'**hothouse** *noun* a glass-house kept warm for growing plants in: *He grows orchids in his hothouse.* □ **serre (chaude)**

'**hot-plate** *noun* a portable heated plate of metal *etc* for keeping plates of food *etc* hot. □ **chauffe-plats**

be in, get into hot water to be in or get into trouble. □ **être/se mettre dans le pétrin**

in hot pursuit chasing as fast as one can: *The thief ran off, with the shopkeeper in hot pursuit.* □ **aux trousses (de)**

like hot cakes very quickly: *These books are selling like hot cakes.* □ **comme des pains chauds**

hotel [hə'tel] *noun* a *usually* large house or building where travellers *etc* may receive food, lodging *etc* in return for payment: *The new hotel has over five hundred bedrooms.* □ **hôtel**

ho'telier [-liə] *noun* a person who owns, and sometimes manages, a hotel. □ **hôtelier, ière**

hound [haund] *noun* a hunting-dog: *The fox threw the hounds off the scent and escaped.* □ **chien (de mente)**

■ *verb* to pursue or hunt (someone): *The film star was constantly hounded by newspaper reporters.* □ **pourchasser**

hour ['auə] *noun* (*sometimes abbreviated to* **hr** *when written*) 1 sixty minutes, the twenty-fourth part of a day: *She spent an hour trying to start the car this morning; She'll be home in half an hour; a five hour delay.* □ **heure**

2 the time at which a particular thing happens: *when the hour for action arrives; He helped me in my hour of need; You can consult her during business hours.* □ **heure**

'**hourly** *adjective, adverb* (happening or done) every hour: *Take his temperature hourly; hourly reports.* □ **horaire; toutes les heures**

'**hourglass** *noun* a device that measures time in hours by passing sand from one glass container through a narrow tube into a lower container. □ **sablier**

hour hand the smaller of the two hands of a watch or clock, which shows the time in hours. □ **petite aiguille**

at all hours at irregular times, *especially* late at night: *He comes home at all hours.* □ **à toute/n'importe quelle heure**

for hours for a very long time: *We waited for hours for the train.* □ **des heures**

on the hour at exactly one, two, three *etc* o'clock: *Buses leave here for London on the hour until 10 o'clock in the evening.* □ **à l'heure juste**

house [haus] – *plural* **houses** ['hauziz] – *noun* **1** a building in which people, *especially* a single family, live: *Andrew's family is building a new house out in the country; The family is moving from an apartment to a house.* □ **maison**

2 a place or building used for a particular purpose: *a hen-house; a public house.* □ **maison**

3 a theatre, or the audience in a theatre: *There was a full house for the first night of the play.* □ **salle**

4 a family, *usually* important or noble, including its ancestors and descendants: *the house of David.* □ **maison**

■ [hauz] *verb* **1** to provide with a house, accommodation or shelter: *All these people will have to be housed; The animals are housed in the barn.* □ **loger**

2 to store or keep somewhere: *The generator for the electricity is housed in the garage.* □ **placer**

'housing [-ziŋ] *noun* **1** houses: *These flats will provide housing for the immigrants.* □ **logement**

2 the hard cover around a machine *etc.* □ **boîtier**

house arrest a type of arrest in which a person is not allowed to leave his own house: *He was kept under house arrest.* □ **assignation à résidence**

'houseboat *noun* a type of boat, *usually* with a flat bottom, which is built to be lived in. □ **bateau-maison**

'housebreaker *noun* a person who breaks into a house in order to steal. □ **cambrioleur, euse**

'housebreaking *noun.* □ **cambriolage**

'house-fly *noun* the common fly, found throughout the world. □ **mouche (commune)**

'household *noun* the people who live together in a house, including their servants: *How many people are there in this household?* □ **maison(née)**

'householder *noun* the person who owns a house or pays the rent for it. □ **propriétaire; locataire**

household word something which is well-known to everyone: *Her name is a household word throughout the country.* □ **connu de tous**

'housekeeper *noun* a person who is paid to look after the management of a house. □ **gouvernante**

'housekeeping *noun* the management of a house. □ **tenu de maison**

'housetrain *verb* to train (a dog, cat *etc*) to be clean inside the house. □ **dresser à la propreté**

'housewarming *noun* a party given after moving into a new house. □ **pendaison de crémaillère**

■ *adjective*: *a housewarming party.* □ **pendaison de crémaillère**

'housewife – *plural* **'housewives** – *noun* a woman who looks after her house, her husband and her family, and who *usually* does not have a job outside the home. □ **ménagère**

'housework *noun* the work of keeping a house clean

and tidy: *I have someone to help me with the housework.* □ **ménage**

like a house on fire 1 very well: *The two children got on with each other like a house on fire.* □ **comme larrons en foire**

2 very quickly: *I'm getting through this job like a house on fire.* □ **à toute allure**

hovel ['hovəl] *noun* a small, dirty house. □ **taudis**

hover ['hovə] *verb* **1** (of a bird, insect *etc*) to remain in the air without moving in any direction. □ **voltiger, planer**

2 to move around while still remaining near a person *etc*: *I wish she'd stop hovering around me and go away.* □ **rôder autour de**

3 (*with* **between**) to be undecided: *She hovered between leaving and staying.* □ **hésiter**

'hovercraft *noun* a vehicle which is able to move over land or water, supported by a cushion of air. □ **aéroglisseur**

how [hau] *adverb, conjunction* **1** in what way: *How do you make bread?* □ **comment**

2 to what extent: *How do you like my new hat?*; *How far is Paris from London?* □ **comment; à quelle distance**

3 by what means: *I've no idea how he came here.* □ **comment**

4 in what condition: *How are you today?*; *How do I look?* □ **comment**

5 for what reason: *How is it that I am the last to know about this?* □ **comment**

how'ever *adverb* **1** in spite of that: *It would be nice if we had more money; However, I suppose we'll manage with what we have.* □ **cependant**

2 (*also* **how'ever**) in what way; by what means: *However did you get here?*; *However did you do that?* □ **comment, de quelle manière**

3 to no matter what extent: *However hard I try, I still can't do it.* □ **de quelque manière que; avoir beau**

■ *conjunction* in no matter what way: *This painting still looks wrong however you look at it.* □ **de quelque façon que**

how about 1 I would like to suggest: *'Where shall we go tonight?' 'How about the cinema?'* □ **et si, que diriez-vous de**

2 what is he, are you *etc* going to do?; what does he, do you *etc* think?: *We're going to the cinema tonight; How about you?*; *I rather like that picture; How about you?* □ **et vous**

how come for what reason: *How come I didn't get any cake?* □ **comment se fait-il que**

how do you do? words that are said by a person to someone he is being introduced to: *'How do you do? My name is Smith,' he said, shaking her hand.* □ **enchanté**

how much an expression to ask the cost of something: *How much is a hamburger and an order of fries?* □ **combien**

however *see* **how.**

howl [haul] *verb* **1** to make a long, loud cry: *The wolves howled; She howled with pain; We howled with laugh-*

attic window
chimney
roof
window
balcony
garage
fence
hedge
flower box
backyard
garbage can
driveway
patio
garden hose
front door
front steps
porch
lawn chair
garden
lawn
mailbox
sidewalk

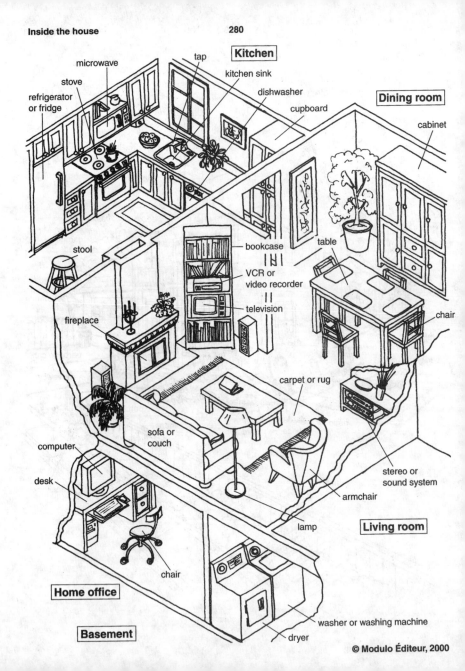

Kitchen

microwave

tap

kitchen sink

stove

dishwasher

refrigerator or fridge

cupboard

Dining room

cabinet

stool

bookcase

table

VCR or video recorder

television

fireplace

chair

carpet or rug

computer

sofa or couch

stereo or sound system

desk

armchair

lamp

Living room

Home office

chair

Basement

washer or washing machine

dryer

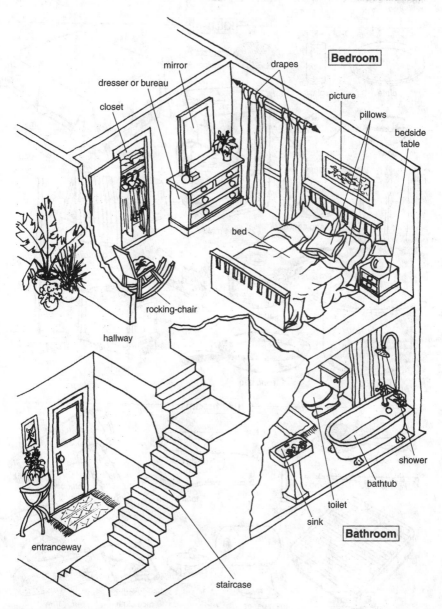

Bedroom

mirror
dresser or bureau
closet
drapes
picture
pillows
bedside table
bed
rocking-chair
hallway

entranceway
staircase

toilet
sink
shower
bathtub
Bathroom

Kitchen

plate

glass

strainer

bowl

teapot

knife fork spoon

cup and saucer

coffee maker

mug

tablecloth

napkin

dishtowel

pot

saucepan

can opener

toaster

broom

frying pan

Bathroom

hairbrush or brush

comb

razor

toothpaste

toothbrush

hair dryer

scale

toilet paper

soap

washcloth or face cloth

towel

2 (of wind) to make a similar sound: *The wind howled through the trees.* □ **mugir**

■ *noun* such a cry: *a howl of pain; howls of laughter.* □ **hurlement**

'**howler** *noun* a mistake so bad as to be funny: *an exam paper full of howlers.* □ **bourde**

hub [hʌb] *noun* 1 the centre of a wheel. □ **moyeu**

2 a centre of activity or business. □ **centre (d'activité)**

hubcap a metal, disk-shaped cover that attaches to the hub or centre of a tire: *Andy bought four new tires with shiny hubcaps for his car.* □ **enjoliveur**

hubbub ['hʌbʌb] *noun* 1 a confused noise of many sounds *especially* voices. □ **brouhaha**

2 uproar; protest. □ **tohu-bohu**

huddle ['hʌdl] *verb* 1 (*often with* **together**) to crowd closely together: *The cows (were) huddled together in the corner of the field.* □ **se serrer (les uns contre les autres)**

2 to curl up in a sitting position: *The old man (was) huddled near the fire to keep warm.* □ **se blottir**

■ *noun* a number of people, things *etc* crowded together: *a huddle of people around the injured man.* □ **ramassis**

hue [hjuː] *noun* colour: *flowers of many hues.* □ **teinte**

huff [hʌf]: **in(to) a huff** being or becoming silent because one is angry, displeased *etc*: *She is in a huff; She went into a huff.* □ **froissé**

'**huffy** *adjective* 1 in a huff. □ **froissé**

2 easily offended, and likely to go into a huff. □ **susceptible**

'**huffily** *adverb.* □ **avec mauvaise humeur**

'**huffiness** *noun.* □ **mauvaise humeur, susceptibilité**

hug [hʌg] – *past tense, past participle* **hugged** – *verb* 1 to hold close to oneself with the arms, *especially* to show love: *She hugged her son when he returned from the war.* □ **étreindre**

2 to keep close to: *During the storm, the ships all hugged the shore.* □ **longer**

■ *noun* a tight grasp with the arms, *especially* to show love: *As they said good bye she gave him a hug.* □ **étreinte**

huge [hjuːdʒ] *adjective* very large: *a huge dog; a huge sum of money; Their new house is huge.* □ **énorme**

'**hugeness** *noun.* □ **énormité**

'**hugely** *adverb* very much; greatly. □ **énormément**

hulk [hʌlk] *noun* 1 the body of an old ship from which everything has been taken away. □ **carcasse**

2 something or someone enormous and clumsy. □ **mastodonte**

hull [hʌl] *noun* the frame or body of a ship: *The hull of the ship was painted black.* □ **coque**

hullabaloo [hʌləbə'luː] *noun* 1 an uproar: *The teacher told the pupils to stop making such a hullabaloo.* □ **vacarme**

2 a loud public protest. □ **protestations**

hum [hʌm] – *past tense, past participle* **hummed** – *verb* 1 to make a musical sound with closed lips: *He was humming a tune to himself.* □ **fredonner**

2 to make a similar sound: *The bees were humming around the hive.* □ **bourdonner**

3 to be active: *Things are really humming around here.* □ **marcher rondement**

■ *noun* such a sound: *I could hear the hum of the machines; a hum of conversation.* □ **bourdonnement**

'**hummingbird** *noun* a small brightly-coloured American bird which makes a humming sound with its wings. □ **oiseau-mouche**

human ['hjuːmən] *adjective* of, natural to, concerning, or belonging to, mankind: *human nature; The dog was so clever that he seemed almost human.* □ **humain**

■ *noun* a person: *Humans are not as different from animals as we might think.* □ **(être) humain**

'**humanly** *adverb* within human power: *If it is humanly possible, she will do it.* □ **humainement**

human being a person: *Animals may behave like that, but human beings shouldn't.* □ **être humain**

humane [hju'mein] *adjective* kind; not cruel: *a humane man; a humane way to kill rats and mice.* □ **humain**

hu'manely *adverb.* □ **avec humanité**

hu'maneness *noun.* □ **humanité**

humanity [hju'manəti] *noun* 1 kindness: *a person of great humanity.* □ **humanité**

2 people in general: *all humanity.* □ **humanité**

See also **humane.**

humble ['hʌmbl] *adjective* 1 not having a high opinion of oneself *etc*: *You have plenty of ability but you're too humble.* □ **humble**

2 unimportant; having a low position in society *etc*: *a man of humble origins.* □ **modeste**

■ *verb* to make (someone) humble: *He was humbled by his failure.* □ **humilier**

'**humbly** *adverb.* □ **humblement**

'**humbleness** *noun.* □ **humilité**

See also **humility.**

humdrum ['hʌmdrʌm] *adjective* dull: *a humdrum life.* □ **monotone**

humid ['hjuːmid] *adjective* damp: *a humid climate.* □ **humide**

hu'midity *noun.* □ **humidité**

humiliate [hju'milieit] *verb* to make (someone) feel ashamed: *I was humiliated to find that you could run faster than I could.* □ **humilier**

hu'miliating *adjective.* □ **humiliant**

hu,mili'ation *noun.* □ **humiliation**

humility [hju'miləti] *noun* modesty; humbleness: *Despite her powerful position in the government, she was still a woman of great humility.* □ **humilité**

See also **humble.**

humour ['hjuːmə] *noun* 1 the ability to amuse people; quickness to spot a joke: *He has a great sense of humour.* □ **humour**

2 the quality of being amusing: *the humour of the situation.* □ **humour**

■ *verb* to please (someone) by agreeing with him or doing as he wishes: *There is no point in telling him he is wrong – just humour him instead.* □ **ne pas contrarier**

'**humorist** *noun* a person who writes or tells amusing stories, jokes *etc*. □ **humoriste**

'**humorous** *adjective* funny; amusing: *a humorous situation/remark.* □ **humoristique**

'humorously *adverb*. □ **avec humour**
'humorousness *noun*. □ **humour**
-humoured having, or showing, feelings or a personality of a particular sort: *a good-humoured person*; *an ill-
humoured remark*. □ **de (...) humeur**

> humour, noun, ends in **-our**.
> humorous, adjective, drops the **u**.

hump [hʌmp] *noun* 1 a large lump on the back of an
animal, person *etc*: *a camel's hump*. □ **bosse**
2 part of a road *etc* which rises and falls in the shape of
a hump. □ **bosse**
'humpback *noun* a back with a hump. □ **bossu, ue**
■ *adjective* rising and falling in the shape of a hump: *a
humpback bridge*. □ **en dos d'âne**
'humpbacked *adjective* having a hump on the back. □
bossu

humus ['hjuːməs] *noun* a substance like earth, made of
decayed plants, leaves *etc*. □ **humus**

hunch [hʌntʃ] *noun* an idea or belief based on one's
feelings or suspicions rather than on clear evidence: *I
have a hunch he'll be late*. □ **intuition**
'hunchback *noun* a person with a hump on his back. □
bossu, ue
'hunchbacked *adjective* having a hump on one's back.
□ **bossu**
hunched up with one's back and shoulders bent forward: *She sat hunched up near the fire*. □ **voûté**

hundred ['hʌndrəd] *noun* 1 (*plural* 'hundred) the
number 100: *Ten times ten is a hundred*; *more than one/
a hundred*; *There must be at least six hundred of them
here*. □ **cent(aine)**
2 the figure 100. □ **cent**
3 the age of 100: *She's over a hundred*; *a man of a hundred*. □ **cent ans**
4 (*plural* 'hundred) a hundred dollars: *I lost several
hundred at the casino last night*. □ **cent(aine) (de...)**
■ *adjective* 1 100 in number: *six hundred people*; *a few
hundred dollars*. □ **cent(aine)**
2 aged 100: *He is a hundred today*. □ **cent ans**
'hundred-: *a hundred-dollar bill*. □ **de cent (...)**
'hundredfold *adjective, adverb* one hundred times as
much or as great: *Production has increased a hundredfold*. □ **(au) centuple**
'hundredth *noun* 1 one of a hundred equal parts. □
centième
2 (*also adjective*) (the) last of a hundred (people, things
etc) or (the person, thing *etc*) in an equivalent position.
□ **centième**
'hundreds of 1 several hundred: *She has hundreds of
dollars in the bank*. □ **des centaines de**
2 very many: *I've got hundreds of things to do*. □ **des
tas de**

hung *see* hang.

hunger ['hʌŋgə] *noun* 1 the desire for food: *A cheese
roll won't satisfy my hunger*. □ **faim**
2 the state of not having enough food: *Poor people in
many parts of the world are dying of hunger*. □ **faim**
3 any strong desire: *a hunger for love*. □ **faim**
■ *verb* (*usually with* **for**) to long for (*eg* affection, love).

□ **avoir faim de**
'hungry *adjective* wanting or needing food *etc*: *a hungry baby*; *I'm hungry – I haven't eaten all day*; *She's
hungry for adventure*. □ **affamé**
'hungrily *adverb*. □ **voracement**
'hungriness *noun*. □ **faim**
hunger strike a refusal to eat, as a form of protest or to
force (someone) to agree to certain demands *etc*: *The
prisoners went on hunger strike as a protest against
prison discipline*. □ **grève de la faim**

hunk [hʌŋk] *noun* a lump of something broken or cut
off from a larger piece: *a hunk of cheese/bread*. □ **bout,
morceau**

hunt [hʌnt] *verb* 1 to chase (animals *etc*) for food or for
sport: *He spent the whole day hunting (deer)*. □ **chasser**
2 to pursue or drive out: *The murderer was hunted from
town to town*. □ **pourchasser**
■ *noun* 1 the act of hunting animals *etc*: *a tiger hunt*. □
chasse
2 a search: *I'll have a hunt for that lost necklace*. □ **recherche**
'hunter – *feminine* 'huntress – *noun* a person who hunts.
□ **chasseur, euse/chasseresse**
'hunting *noun* the activity of chasing animals *etc* for
food or for sport. □ **chasse**
'huntsman ['hʌnts-] *noun* a hunter. □ **chasseur**
hunt down to search for (someone or something) until
found: *The police hunted down the escaped prisoner*. □
traquer
hunt for to search for: *I've been hunting for that shoe
all morning*. □ **chercher**
hunt high and low to search everywhere. □ **chercher
dans tous les coins**
hunt out to search for (something that has been put
away) until it is found: *I'll hunt out that old photograph
for you*. □ **dénicher**

hurdle ['həːdl] *noun* 1 a frame to be jumped in a race. □
haie
2 a problem or difficulty: *There are several hurdles to
be overcome in this project*. □ **obstacle**
■ *verb* to run in a race in which hurdles are used: *She
has hurdled since she was twelve*. □ **faire de la course
de haies**
'hurdler *noun*. □ **coureur, euse (de courses de haies)**
'hurdling *noun*. □ **courses de haies**

hurl [həːl] *verb* to throw violently: *He hurled himself to
the ground*; *They hurled rocks/insults at their attackers*. □ **lancer (violemment)**

hurrah, hurray, hoorah, hooray [hu'rei] *noun, interjection* a shout of joy, enthusiasm *etc*: *Hurrah! We're
getting an extra day's holiday!* □ **hourra**

hurricane ['hʌrikən] *noun* a violent storm with winds
blowing at over 120 kilometres per hour. □ **ouragan**

hurry ['hʌri] *verb* 1 to (cause to) move or act quickly,
often too quickly: *You'd better hurry if you want to catch
that bus*. □ **se dépêcher, se hâter**
2 to convey quickly: *After the accident, the injured man
was hurried to the hospital*. □ **transporter d'urgence**
■ *noun* 1 the act of doing something quickly, often too
quickly: *In her hurry to leave, she fell and broke her*

arm. □ **hâte**

2 the need to do something quickly: *Is there any hurry for this job?* □ **nécessité de se presser**

'hurried *adjective* **1** done quickly, often too quickly: *This was a very hurried piece of work.* □ **fait à la hâte**

2 (*negative* **unhurried**) forced to do something quickly, often too quickly: *I hate feeling hurried.* □ **bousculé**

'hurriedly *adverb.* □ **à la hâte**

in a hurry 1 acting quickly: *I did this in a hurry.* □ **à la hâte**

2 wishing or needing to act quickly: *I'm in a hurry.* □ **pressé**

3 soon; easily: *You won't untie this knot in a hurry.* □ **rapidement**

4 eager: *I'm in a hurry to see my new house.* □ **impatient (de)**

hurry up to (cause to) move quickly: *Hurry her up, will you; Do hurry up!* □ **se dépêcher**

hurt [hɔːt] – *past tense, past participle* **hurt** – *verb* **1** to injure or cause pain to: *I hurt my hand on that broken glass.* □ **blesser**

2 to upset (a person or his feelings): *You hurt me/my feelings by ignoring me.* □ **blesser**

3 to be painful: *My tooth hurts.* □ **faire souffrir**

4 to do harm (to) or have a bad effect (on): *It wouldn't hurt you to work late just once.* □ **faire du mal (à)**

■ *adjective* **1** upset; distressed: *She felt very hurt at/by his behaviour; her hurt feelings.* □ **blessé**

2 injured: *Are you badly hurt?* □ **blessé**

'hurtful *adjective* causing distress: *a hurtful remark.* □ **blessant**

'hurtfully *adverb.* □ **d'une manière blessante**

'hurtfulness *noun.* □ **nocivité**

hurtle ['hɔːtl] *verb* to move very quickly and violently: *The car hurtled down the hill at top speed.* □ **aller à toute allure**

husband ['hʌzbənd] *noun* a man to whom a woman is married. □ **mari**

■ *verb* to spend or use carefully, a little at a time: *He needs to husband his strength.* □ **ménager**

'husbandry *noun* management, *especially* of a farm or animals. □ **agriculture; gestion**

hush [hʌʃ] *interjection* be quiet; silence: *Hush! Don't wake the baby.* □ **chut!**

■ *noun* silence: *A hush came over the room.* □ **silence**

hushed *adjective* silent, still: *a hushed room/crowd.* □ **silencieux**

hush up to prevent from becoming known to the general public: *The affair was hushed up.* □ **étouffer**

husk [hʌsk] *noun* the dry thin covering of certain fruits and seeds: *coconut husk.* □ **enveloppe**

■ *verb* to remove the husk from (a fruit or seed). □ **décortiquer**

husky[1] ['hʌski] *adjective* (of a voice) rough in sound: *You sound husky – have you a cold?* □ **enroué**

'huskiness *noun.* □ **enrouement**

'huskily *adverb.* □ **d'une voix enrouée**

husky[2] ['hʌski] – *plural* **'huskies** – *noun* a North American dog used for pulling sleds. □ **chien de traîneau**

hustle ['hʌsl] *verb* **1** to push quickly and roughly: *The man was hustled out of the office.* □ **bousculer**

2 to make (someone) act quickly: *Hustle the students off the property.* □ **presser**

■ *noun* quick and busy activity. □ **grande activité**

hut [hʌt] *noun* a small house or shelter, *usually* made of wood. □ **hutte**

hutch [hʌtʃ] *noun* a box with a wire front in which rabbits are kept. □ **clapier**

hyacinth ['haiəsinθ] *noun* a plant, a member of the lily family, growing from a bulb and having a sweet-smelling flower. □ **jacinthe**

hyaena *see* hyena.

hydrant ['haidrənt] *noun* a pipe connected to the main water supply *especially* in a street, to which a hose can be attached in order to draw water off *eg* to put out a fire. □ **bouche d'incendie**

hydraulic [hai'drɔːlik] *adjective* **1** worked by the pressure of water or some other liquid: *hydraulic brakes.* □ **hydraulique**

2 relating to hydraulics: *a hydraulic engineer.* □ **hydraulique**

hy'draulically *adverb.* □ **hydrauliquement**

hy'draulics *noun singular* the study of the behaviour of moving liquids (*eg* of water in pipes). □ **hydraulique**

hydroelectricity ['haidrouelek'trisəti] *noun* electricity produced by means of water-power. □ **hydro-électricité**

,hydro'lectric [-'lek-] *adjective*: *hydroelectric power stations.* □ **hydro-électrique**

hydrogen ['haidrədʒən] *noun* an element, the lightest gas, which burns and which, when combined with oxygen, produces water. □ **hydrogène**

hydrogen bomb (*also* **H-bomb** ['eitʃbom]) a very powerful bomb in which the explosion is caused by turning hydrogen into helium at a very high temperature. □ **bombe à hydrogène**

hyena, hyaena [hai'iːnə] *noun* a dog-like animal with a howl which sounds like human laughter. □ **hyène**

hygiene ['haidʒiːn] *noun* (the rules or science of) cleanliness whose aim is to preserve health and prevent the spread of disease. □ **hygiène**

hy'gienic [-'dʒiː-] *adjective* (*negative* **unhygienic**) free from germs or dirt: *Hygienic conditions are essential in a hospital.* □ **hygiénique**

hy'gienically [-'dʒiː-] *adverb.* □ **hygiéniquement**

hymn [him] *noun* a (*usually* religious) song of praise. □ **cantique**

hyphen ['haifən] *noun* a short stroke (-) which is used to join two parts of a word or phrase, as in *co-exist; a sleeping-bag; a well-thought-out plan.* □ **trait d'union**

hypnosis [hip'nousis] *noun* a sleep-like state caused by the action of another person who can then make the sleeper obey his commands. □ **hypnose**

hyp'notic [-'no-] *adjective.* □ **hypnotique**

'hypnotize, 'hypnotise *verb* **1** to put in a state of hypnosis: *The hypnotist hypnotized three people from the audience.* □ **hypnotiser**

2 to fascinate completely: *Her intelligence hypnotized him.* □ **hypnotiser**

'hypnotism *noun* the art of producing hypnosis. □ **hypnotisme**

'**hypnotist** *noun*. □ **hypnotiseur**

hypocrisy [hi'pokrəsi] *noun* the act or state of pretending to be better than one is or to have feelings or beliefs which one does not actually have. □ **hypocrisie**
hypocrite ['hipəkrit] *noun* a person who is guilty of hypocrisy. □ **hypocrite**
,**hypo'critical** [hipə'kri-] *adjective*. □ **hypocrite**
,**hypo'critically** *adverb*. □ **hypocritiquement**
hypodermic [haipə'dɔːmik] *noun, adjective* (an instrument) used for injecting a drug under the skin. □ **hypodermique**
hypothesis [hai'poθəsis] – *plural* **hy'potheses** [-siːz] – *noun* an unproved theory or point of view put forward, *eg* for the sake of argument. □ **hypothèse**

hypothetical [haipə'θetikəl] *adjective* imaginary; supposed. □ **hypothétique**
hypothetically [haipə'θetikəli] *adverb*. □ **hypothétiquement**
hysteria [hi'stiəriə] *noun* **1** a severe nervous upset which causes *eg* uncontrolled laughing or crying, imaginary illnesses *etc*. □ **hystérie**
2 uncontrolled excitement, *eg* of a crowd of people: *mass hysteria*. □ **hystérie (collective)**
hy'sterical [-'ste-] *adjective* of or suffering from hysteria. □ **hystérique**
hy'sterically [-'ste-] *adverb*. □ **hystériquement**
hy'sterics [-'ste-] *noun plural* a fit of hysteria. □ **crise de nerfs**

Ii

I [ai] *pronoun* (only as the subject of a verb) the word used by a speaker or writer in talking about himself or herself: *I can't find my book*; *John and I have always been friends.* □ **je, moi**

ice [ais] *noun* **1** frozen water: *The pond is covered with ice.* □ **glace**
2 an ice cream: *What flavour of ice cream do you prefer?* □ **crème glacée**
■ *verb* to cover with icing: *She iced the cake.* □ **glacer**
'**icing** *noun* a mixture of sugar, white of egg, water *etc* used to cover or decorate cakes. □ **glaçage**
'**icy** *adjective* **1** very cold: *icy winds.* □ **glacé**
2 covered with ice: *icy roads.* □ **verglacé**
3 unfriendly: *an icy tone of voice.* □ **glacial**
'**icily** *adverb.* □ **d'un air/ton glacial**
'**iciness** *noun.* □ **froideur glaciale**
ice age a time when a great part of the earth's surface was covered with ice. □ **période glaciaire**
ice axe a type of axe used by mountain climbers to cut holds in ice for their hands and feet. □ **piolet**
'**iceberg** *noun* a huge mass of ice floating in the sea. □ **iceberg**
,**ice 'cream** *noun* cream or a mixture of creamy substances, flavoured and frozen. □ **crème glacée**
'**ice cube** *noun* a small cube of ice used for cooling drinks *etc.* □ **glaçon**
ice rink a large room or building with a floor of ice for skating. □ **patinoire**
ice tray a metal or plastic tray for making ice cubes in a refrigerator. □ **bac à glaçons**
ice over/up to become covered with ice: *The pond iced over during the night*; *The windows have iced up.* □ **geler; givrer**
ice storm [ais stourm] *noun* ice that is created when rain freezes as soon as it falls: *The ice storm completely coated the tree branches and telephone wires with a layer of ice.* □ **verglas**
icicle ['aisikl] *noun* a long hanging piece of ice formed by the freezing of dripping water: *icicles hanging from the roof.* □ **glaçon**
icing *see* **ice.**
icon ['aikon] *noun especially* in the Orthodox Churches, a painting *etc* of Christ or a saint. □ **icône**
icy *see* **ice.**
I'd *see* **have, would.**
idea [ai'diə] *noun* **1** opinion; belief: *I have an idea that it won't work.* □ **idée**
2 a plan: *I've an idea for solving this problem.* □ **idée**
3 mental picture: *This will give you an idea of what I mean.* □ **idée**
ideal [ai'diəl] *adjective* perfect: *This tool is ideal for the job I have in mind.* □ **idéal**
■ *noun* **1** a person, thing *etc* that is looked on as being perfect: *She was clever and beautiful – in fact she was his ideal of what a woman should be.* □ **idéal**
2 a person's standard of behaviour *etc*: *a man of high ideals.* □ **idéal**

i'**dealist** *noun* a person having (too) high ideals of behaviour *etc.* □ **idéaliste**
i'**dealism** *noun.* □ **idéalisme**
,**idea'listic** [aidiə-] *adjective.* □ **idéaliste**
i'**dealize, i'dealise** *verb* to regard as perfect: *Children tend to idealize their parents.* □ **idéaliser**
i,**deali'zation, i,deali'sation** *noun.* □ **idéalisation**
i'**deally** *adverb* **1** perfectly: *He is ideally suited to this job.* □ **parfaitement**
2 under perfect conditions: *Ideally, we should check this again, but we haven't enough time.* □ **idéalement**
identical [ai'dentikəl] *adjective* **1** the same in every detail: *They wore identical dresses.* □ **identique**
2 the very same: *That is the identical car that I saw outside the bank just before the robbery.* □ **exactement le/la même**
i'**dentically** *adverb.* □ **identiquement**
i'**denticalness** *noun.* □ **caractère identique**
identify [ai'dentifai] *verb* **1** to recognize as being a certain person *etc*: *Would you be able to identify the man who robbed you?*; *She identified the coat as her brother's.* □ **identifier**
2 to think of as being the same: *He identifies beauty with goodness.* □ **assimiler (à)**
i,**dentifi'cation** [-fi] *noun.* □ **identification**
i'**dentify with** to feel in sympathy with (*eg* a character in a story). □ **(s')identifier avec**
i'**dentify oneself with/be i'dentified with** to be associated with or give one's full support or interest to (a political party *etc*). □ **s'identifier à**
identity [ai'dentəti] *noun* who or what a person is: *The police are still uncertain of the murderer's identity.* □ **identité**
i'**dentity card** a named card (often with a photograph) which is carried by a person to show or prove who he or she is. □ **carte d'identité**
idiocy *see* **idiot.**
idiom ['idiəm] *noun* **1** an expression with a meaning that cannot be guessed from the meanings of the individual words: *His mother passed away* (= died) *this morning.* □ **locution idiomatique**
2 the expressions of a language in general: *English idiom.* □ **idiome**
,**idio'matic** [-'matik] *adjective* (*negative* **unidiomatic**)
1 using an idiom: *an idiomatic use of this word.* □ **idiomatique**
2 using appropriate idioms: *We try to teach idiomatic English.* □ **idiomatique**
,**idio'matically** *adverb.* □ **de façon idiomatique**
idiot ['idiət] *noun* **1** a foolish person: *He was an idiot to give up such a good job.* □ **idiot, idiote**
2 a person with very low intelligence. □ **idiot, idiote**
'**idiocy** *noun.* □ **imbécillité**
,**idi'otic** [-'otik] *adjective.* □ **idiot**
,**idi'otically** *adverb.* □ **idiotement**
idle ['aidl] *adjective* **1** not working; not in use: *ships lying idle in the harbour.* □ **au repos**
2 lazy: *He has work to do, but he's idle and just sits around.* □ **fainéant**
3 having no effect or result: *idle threats.* □ **vain**

4 unnecessary; without good reason or foundation: *idle fears*; *idle gossip*. □ **sans fondement, futile**

■ *verb* 1 to be idle or do nothing: *On holiday they just idled from morning till night.* □ **paresser**

2 of an engine *etc*, to run gently without doing any work: *They kept the car engine idling while they checked their position with the map.* □ **(faire) tourner au ralenti**

'idler *noun* a lazy person. □ **paresseux, euse**

'idleness *noun*. □ **paresse**

'idly *adverb*. □ **paresseusement**

idle away to spend (time) doing nothing: *idling the hours away.* □ **perdre son temps**

idol ['aidl] *noun* 1 an image of a god, which is worshipped: *The tribesmen bowed down before their idol.* □ **idole**

2 a greatly loved person, thing *etc*: *The singer was the idol of thousands of teenagers.* □ **idole**

idolatry [ai'dolatri] *noun* 1 the worship of idols. □ **idolâtrie**

2 too great admiration, *especially* of a person. □ **idolâtrie**

i'dolatrous *adjective*. □ **idolâtre**

i'dolatrously *adverb*. □ **d'une manière idolâtre**

'idolize, 'idolise *verb* to love or admire a person *etc* greatly or too much: *She idolized her older brother.* □ **adorer**

if [if] *conjunction* 1 in the event that; on condition that: *She will have to go into hospital if her illness gets any worse*; *I'll only stay if you can stay too.* □ **si**

2 supposing that: *If he were to come along now, we would be in trouble.* □ **si**

3 whenever: *If I sneeze, my nose bleeds.* □ **si, chaque fois que**

4 although: *They are happy, if poor.* □ **bien que**

5 whether: *I don't know if I can come or not.* □ **si**

if 'only I wish that: *If only I were rich!* □ **si seulement**

igloo ['igluː] – *plural* 'igloos – *noun* an Inuit hut, *usually* built of blocks of snow. □ **igloo**

ignite [ig'nait] *verb* to (cause to) catch fire: *Gasoline is easily ignited.* □ **(s')enflammer**

ignition [ig'niʃən] *noun* 1 the instrument in a car *etc* which ignites the gasoline in the engine: *She switched on the car's ignition.* □ **allumage**

2 the act of igniting. □ **allumage**

ignoble [ig'noubl] *adjective* shameful: *an ignoble action.* □ **ignoble**

ig'nobleness *noun*. □ **caractère ignoble**

ig'nobly *adverb*. □ **ignoblement**

ignorant ['ignərənt] *adjective* 1 knowing very little: *He's really very ignorant – he ought to read more*; *I'm ignorant about money matters.* □ **ignorant**

2 (*with of*) unaware: *She continued on her way, ignorant of the dangers which lay ahead.* □ **ignorant (de)**

'ignorantly *adverb*. □ **par ignorance**

'ignorance *noun*. □ **ignorance**

ignore [ig'noː] *verb* to take no notice of: *He ignored all my warnings.* □ **ne tenir aucun compte de, ignorer**

iguana [i'gwaːnə] *noun* a tropical American lizard that lives in trees. □ **iguane**

ill [il] – *comparative* worse [wəːs]: *superlative* worst [wəːst] – *adjective* 1 not in good health; not well: *She was ill for a long time.* □ **malade**

2 bad: *ill health*; *These pills have no ill effects.* □ **mauvais**

3 evil or unlucky: *ill luck.* □ **mauvais**

■ *adverb* not easily: *We could ill afford to lose that money.* □ **difficilement**

■ *noun* 1 evil: *I would never wish anyone ill.* □ **mal**

2 trouble: *all the ills of this world.* □ **mal**

ill- badly: *ill-equipped*; *ill-used*. □ **mal (...)**

'illness *noun* a state or occasion of being unwell: *There is a lot of illness in the village just now*; *childhood illnesses.* □ **maladie**

,ill at 'ease *adjective* uncomfortable; embarrassed: *She feels ill at ease at parties.* □ **mal à l'aise**

,ill-'fated *adjective* ending in, or bringing, disaster: *an ill-fated expedition.* □ **malheureux**

,ill 'feeling *noun* (an) unkind feeling (towards another person): *The two men parted without any ill feeling(s).* □ **rancune**

,ill-'mannered/,ill-'bred *adjectives* having bad manners: *He's an ill-mannered young man.* □ **mal élevé**

,ill-'tempered/,ill-'natured *adjectives* having or showing bad temper: *Don't be so ill-natured just because you're tired.* □ **désagréable**

,ill-'treat *verb* to treat badly or cruelly: *She often ill-treated her children.* □ **maltraiter**

,ill-'treatment *noun*. □ **mauvais traitement**

,ill-'use [-'juːz] *verb* to ill-treat. □ **maltraiter**

,ill 'will *noun* unkind feeling: *I bear you no ill will.* □ **malveillance**

be taken ill to become ill: *He was taken ill at the party and was rushed to hospital.* □ **tomber malade**

---

ill means unwell: *She was very ill when she had pneumonia.*

sick means vomiting or inclined to vomit: *He was sick twice in the car*; *I feel sick.*

I'll *see* will, shall.

illegal [i'liːgəl] *adjective* not allowed by the law; not legal: *It is illegal to park a car here.* □ **illégal**

il'legally *adverb*. □ **illégalement**

illegality [ili'galəti] *noun*. □ **illégalité**

illegible [i'ledʒəbl] *adjective* (almost) impossible to read; not legible: *Her writing is illegible.* □ **illisible**

il'legibly *adverb*. □ **illisiblement**

il,legi'bility *noun*. □ **illisibilité**

illegitimate [ili'dʒitəmət] *adjective* 1 born of parents not married to each other. □ **illégitime**

2 unacceptable or not allowed (*especially* by law). □ **illégitime**

,ille'gitimately *adverb*. □ **illégitimement**

,ille'gitimacy *noun*. □ **illégitimité**

illicit [i'lisit] *adjective* unlawful or not permitted. □ **illicite**

il'licitly *adverb*. □ **illicitement**

il'licitness *noun*. □ **caractère illicite**

illiterate [i'litərət] *adjective* 1 unable to read and write. □ **illettré**

2 having little or no education. □ **ignorant**

il'literacy *noun*. □ **analphabétisme**

illness *see* ill.

illogical [i'lodʒikəl] *adjective* not logical; not based on, or showing, sound reasoning. □ **illogique**
il'logically *adverb.* □ **illogiquement**
il,logi'cality [-'ka-] *noun.* □ **illogisme**
illuminate [i'luːmineit] *verb* to light up: *The gardens were illuminated by rows of lamps.* □ **illuminer**
il'luminated *adjective* (of a manuscript) decorated with ornamental lettering or illustrations. □ **enluminé**
il'luminating *adjective* helping to make something clear: *an illuminating discussion.* □ **éclairant**
il,lumi'nation *noun* **1** the act of illuminating. □ **illumination; enluminure**
2 (*in plural*) the decorative lights in a town *etc*: *Go to Blackpool and see the illuminations.* □ **illumination(s)**
illusion [i'luːʒən] *noun* (something that produces) a false impression, idea or belief: *an optical illusion.* □ **illusion**
il'lusionist *noun* a conjuror. □ **illusionniste**
illustrate ['iləstreit] *verb* **1** to provide (a book, lecture *etc*) with pictures, diagrams *etc*. □ **illustrer**
2 to make (a statement *etc*) clearer by providing examples *etc*: *Let me illustrate my point; This diagram will illustrate what I mean.* □ **illustrer**
'illustrated *adjective* having pictures *etc*: *an illustrated catalogue.* □ **illustré**
,illu'stration *noun* **1** a picture: *coloured illustrations.* □ **illustration**
2 an example. □ **exemple**
3 the act of illustrating. □ **illustration**
'illustrative [-strətiv] *adjective.* □ **explicatif**
'illustrator *noun* a person who draws pictures *etc* for books *etc*. □ **illustrateur, trice**
illustrious [i'lʌstriəs] *adjective* of a very high quality, ability *etc*; famous: *an illustrious career; He is the most illustrious of a famous family.* □ **illustre**
il'lustriousness *noun.* □ **gloire**
I'm *see* **be**.
image ['imidʒ] *noun* **1** a likeness or copy of a person *etc* made of wood, stone *etc*: *images of the saints.* □ **statue**
2 a close likeness: *She's the very image of her sister.* □ **portrait**
3 reflection: *She looked at her image in the mirror.* □ **image, reflet**
4 mental picture: *I have an image of the place in my mind.* □ **image**
5 the general opinion that people have about a person, company *etc*: *our public image.* □ **image**
imagine [i'madʒin] *verb* **1** to form a mental picture of (something): *I can imagine how you felt.* □ **imaginer**
2 to see or hear *etc* (something which is not true or does not exist): *Children often imagine that there are frightening animals under their beds; You're just imagining things!* □ **(s')imaginer**
3 to think; to suppose: *I imagine (that) he will be late.* □ **supposer**
i'maginary *adjective* existing only in the mind or imagination; not real: *Her illnesses are usually imaginary.* □ **imaginaire**
i,magi'nation *noun* **1** (the part of the mind which has) the ability to form mental pictures: *I can see it all in my imagination.* □ **imagination**
2 the creative ability of a writer *etc*: *This book shows a lot of imagination.* □ **imagination**
3 the seeing *etc* of things which do not exist: *There was no one there – it was just your imagination.* □ **imagination**
i'maginative [-nətiv] *adjective* (*negative* **unimaginative**) having, or created with, imagination: *an imaginative writer; This essay is interesting and imaginative.* □ **imaginatif**
imbecile ['imbəsiːl] *noun* **1** a stupid person; a fool. □ **imbécile**
2 a person of very low intelligence who cannot look after himself. □ **imbécile**
,imbe'cility [-'si-] *noun.* □ **imbécillité**
imitate ['imiteit] *verb* to (try to) be, behave or look the same as (a person *etc*): *Children imitate their friends rather than their parents; He could imitate the song of many different birds.* □ **imiter**
,imi'tation *noun* **1** the act of imitating: *Children learn how to speak by imitation.* □ **imitation**
2 a copy: *an imitation of an ancient statue.* □ **imitation, copie**
■ *adjective* made to look like something else: *imitation wood.* □ **d'imitation**
'imitative [-tətiv] *adjective.* □ **imitatif**
'imitativeness *noun.* □ **esprit d'imitation**
'imitator *noun* a person who imitates. □ **imitateur, trice**
immaculate [i'makjulət] *adjective* **1** perfectly clean; spotless. □ **immaculé**
2 perfectly correct; faultless. □ **impeccable**
immature [imə'tjuə] *adjective* **1** childish and behaving like someone much younger. □ **qui manque de maturité**
2 not fully grown or fully developed; not ripe. □ **vert, jeune**
,imma'turity *noun.* □ **immaturité**
immeasurable [i'meʒərəbl] *adjective* **1** very great. □ **incommensurable**
2 too great *etc* to be measured. □ **infini**
im'measurably *adverb.* □ **infiniment**
immediate [i'miːdiət] *adjective* **1** happening at once and without delay: *an immediate response.* □ **immédiat**
2 without anyone *etc* coming between: *Her immediate successor was Bill Jones.* □ **immédiat**
3 close: *our immediate surroundings.* □ **immédiat**
im'mediately *adverb* at once: *He answered immediately.* □ **immédiatement**
■ *conjunction* as soon as: *You may leave immediately you finish your work.* □ **dès que, aussitôt que**
immense [i'mens] *adjective* very large or very great: *an immense forest; immense amounts of money.* □ **immense**
im'mensely *adverb.* □ **immensément**
im'mensity *noun.* □ **immensité**
immerse [i'məːs] *verb* to put completely under the surface of a liquid: *She immersed the vegetables in boiling water.* □ **immerger**
im'mersion [-ʃən] *noun.* □ **immersion**
immigrant ['imigrənt] *noun, adjective* (a person) who has come into a foreign country to live there perma-

nently, not as a tourist or visitor: *The eastern part of the city is inhabited by immigrants*; *the immigrant population.* □ **immigrant, ante**

immigrate [iməgreit] *verb* to come into and set up residence in a new country: *Nick immigrated to Canada last year and has lived here ever since.* □ **immigrer**
,**immi'gration** *noun* the act of entering a country in order to settle there. □ **immigration**

imminent ['iminənt] *adjective* (*especially* of something unpleasant) likely to happen *etc* very soon: *A storm is imminent.* □ **imminent**
'**imminence** *noun.* □ **imminence**

immobile [i'moubail] *adjective* **1** not able to move or be moved: *His leg was put in plaster and he was immobile for several weeks.* □ **immobile, immobilisé**
2 not moving; motionless: *She crouched there immobile until they had gone.* □ **immobile**
,**immo'bility** [-'bi-] *noun.* □ **immobilité**
im'mobilize, im'mobilise [-bi-] *verb* to make immobile: *He immobilized the car by removing part of the engine.* □ **immobiliser**

immodest [i'modist] *adjective* shameless or indecent; not modest. □ **impudique**
im'modestly *adverb.* □ **impudiquement**
im'modesty *noun.* □ **impudeur**

immoral [i'morəl] *adjective* wrong or wicked: *immoral conduct.* □ **immoral**
im'morally *adverb.* □ **immoralement**
,**immo'rality** [-'ra-] *noun.* □ **immoralité**

immortal [i'mo:tl] *adjective* living forever and never dying: *A person's soul is said to be immortal*; *the immortal works of Shakespeare.* □ **immortel**
,**immor'tality** [-'ta-] *noun.* □ **immortalité**
im'mortalize, im'mortalise *verb* to make (a person *etc*) famous forever: *She wrote a song immortalizing the battle.* □ **immortaliser**

immovable [i'mu:vəbl] *adjective* **1** impossible to move: *an immovable object.* □ **fixe**
2 not allowing one's feelings or attitude to be changed. □ **inébranlable**

immune [i'mju:n] *adjective* (*with* **to** *or* **from**) protected against, or naturally resistant to, *eg* a disease: *immune to measles*; *immune from danger.* □ **immunisé (contre)**
im'munity *noun.* □ **immunité**
'**immunize, 'immunise** ['imju-] *verb* to make immune to a disease, *especially* by an injection of a weak form of the disease. □ **immuniser (contre)**
,**immuni'zation, immuni'sation** *noun.* □ **immunisation**

imp [imp] *noun* **1** a small devil or wicked spirit. □ **diablotin**
2 a mischievous child: *Her son is a little imp.* □ **petit diable**
'**impish** *adjective.* □ **espiègle**

impact ['impakt] *noun* **1** (the force of) one object *etc* hitting against another: *The bomb exploded on impact.* □ **impact**
2 a strong effect or impression: *The film had quite an impact on television viewers.* □ **impact**

impair [im'peə] *verb* to damage, weaken or make less

good: *He was told that smoking would impair his health.* □ **détériorer**
im'pairment *noun.* □ **détérioration**

impale [im'peil] *verb* to fix on, or pierce with, a long pointed object such as a spear *etc.* □ **empaler (sur)**

impart [im'pa:t] *verb* to give (*eg* information): *She said she had vital information to impart.* □ **communiquer**

impartial [im'pa:ʃəl] *adjective* not favouring one person *etc* more than another: *an impartial judge.* □ **impartial**
im'partially *adverb.* □ **impartialement**
im,parti'ality [-ʃi'a-] *noun.* □ **impartialité**

impassable [im'pa:səbl] *adjective* not able to be passed through or travelled along: *The road is impassable because of flooding.* □ **impraticable**

impassive [im'pasiv] *adjective* not feeling or showing emotion: *an impassive face.* □ **impassible**
im'passively *adverb.* □ **impassiblement**

impatient [im'peiʃənt] *adjective* not willing to wait or delay; not patient: *Don't be so impatient – it will soon be your turn.* □ **impatient**
im'patience *noun.* □ **impatience**
im'patiently *adverb.* □ **impatiemment**

impeach [im'pi:tʃ] *verb* to accuse of a crime, *especially* to accuse a person who works for the government of a crime against the State. □ **mettre en accusation (en vue de destituer)**
im'peachment *noun.* □ **mise en accusation (en vue d'une destitution)**

impede [im'pi:d] *verb* to prevent or delay the start or progress of: *Progress on the building of the road was impeded by a fall of rock.* □ **entraver**
impediment [im'pedimənt] *noun* **1** something that delays or prevents. □ **obstacle**
2 a small fault in a person's speech: *A stammer is a speech impediment.* □ **défaut (d'élocution)**

impel [im'pel] – *past tense, past participle* **im'pelled** – *verb* to urge or force: *Hunger impelled the boy to steal.* □ **pousser (à)**

impenetrable [im'penitrəbl] *adjective* **1** that cannot be penetrated, entered or passed through: *impenetrable jungle.* □ **impénétrable**
2 impossible to understand: *an impenetrable mystery.* □ **insondable**

imperative [im'perətiv] *noun, adjective* used of verbs that are expressing a command: *In the sentence 'Come here!', 'come' is an imperative (verb).* □ **impératif**

imperfect [im'pə:fikt] *adjective* **1** having a fault: *This coat is being sold at half-price because it is imperfect.* □ **imparfait**
2 (*also noun*) (a verb) of the tense expressing an action or state in the past which is not completed: *The verb 'go' in 'I was going' is in the imperfect tense.* □ **imparfait**
im'perfectly *adverb.* □ **imparfaitement**
,**imper'fection** [-'fekʃən] *noun* (the state of having) a fault or defect. □ **imperfection**

imperial [im'piəriəl] *adjective* of an empire or an emperor: *the imperial crown.* □ **impérial**
im'perialism *noun* (belief in) the policy of having or

extending control over the territory of other nations. □ **impérialisme**

im'perialist *noun, adjective.* □ **impérialiste**

imperious [im'piəriəs] *adjective* proud, behaving as if expecting to be obeyed: *an imperious manner.* □ **impérieux**

im'periousness *noun.* □ **ton impératif**

impersonal [im'pəːsənl] *adjective* **1** not showing, or being affected by, personal feelings: *His manner was formal and impersonal.* □ **impersonnel**

2 (of a verb) having a subject which does not refer to a person, thing *etc*: *'It is raining' is an example of an impersonal verb.* □ **impersonnel**

im'personally *adverb.* □ **impersonnellement**

im,perso'nality [-'na-] *noun.* □ **impersonnalité**

impersonate [im'pəːsəneit] *verb* to copy the behaviour *etc* of or pretend to be (another person), sometimes in order to deceive: *The comedian impersonated the prime minister.* □ **personnifier; se faire passer pour (qqn)**

im,perso'nation *noun.* □ **personnification**

impertinent [im'pəːtinənt] *adjective* impudent or rude: *She was impertinent to her teacher.* □ **impertinent (envers)**

im'pertinently *adverb.* □ **avec impertinence**

im'pertinence *noun.* □ **impertinence**

impetuous [im'petjuəs] *adjective* acting in a hasty manner and without thinking. □ **impétueux**

im'petuously *adverb.* □ **impétueusement**

im,petu'osity [-'o-] *noun.* □ **impétuosité**

impetus ['impətəs] *noun* the force or energy with which something moves. □ **force d'impulsion**

implacable [im'plakəbl] *adjective* not able to be satisfied or won over: *an implacable enemy.* □ **implacable**

im'placably *adverb.* □ **implacablement**

implant [im'plaːnt] *verb* **1** to put (ideas *etc*) into a person's mind. □ **inculquer**

2 to put (*eg* human tissue, a device *etc*) permanently into a part of the body. □ **implanter**

implan'tation *noun.* □ **implantation**

implement ['implimənt] *noun* a tool or instrument: *kitchen/garden implements.* □ **outil, ustensile**

implicit [im'plisit] *adjective* unquestioning; complete: *implicit obedience.* □ **aveugle**

im'plicitly *adverb.* □ **aveuglément**

implore [im'ploː] *verb* to ask earnestly: *She implored her husband to give up his life of crime*; *He implored her forgiveness.* □ **implorer**

im'ploringly *adverb.* □ **d'un air/ton suppliant**

imply [im'plai] *verb* to suggest or hint without actually stating: *Are you implying that I am a liar?* □ **insinuer**

impli'cation *noun.* □ **insinuation**

impolite [impə'lait] *adjective* not polite; rude: *You must not be impolite to the teacher.* □ **impoli**

,impo'litely *adverb.* □ **impoliment**

,impo'liteness *noun.* □ **impolitesse**

import [im'poːt] *verb* to bring in (goods *etc*) from abroad usually for sale: *We import wine from France.* □ **importer**

■ ['impoːt] *noun* **1** something which is imported from abroad: *Our imports are greater than our exports.* □

importation(s)

2 the act of bringing in goods from abroad: *the import of wine.* □ **importation**

,impor'tation *noun.* □ **importation**

im'porter *noun.* □ **importateur, trice**

important [im'poːtənt] *adjective* (*negative* **unimportant**) having great value, influence or effect: *an important book/person/occasion*; *It is important that you arrive here on time.* □ **important**

im'portantly *adverb.* □ **d'une manière importante**

im'portance *noun*: *matters of great importance.* □ **importance**

impose [im'pouz] *verb* **1** to place (a tax, fine, task *etc*) on someone or something: *The government have imposed a new tax on cigarettes.* □ **taxer**

2 to force (oneself, one's opinions *etc*) on a person: *The headmaster liked to impose his authority on the teachers.* □ **imposer**

3 (*often with* **on**) to ask someone to do something which he should not be asked to do or which he will find difficult to do: *I hope I'm not imposing (on you) by asking you to help.* □ **abuser de la bonté de**

imposition [impə'ziʃən] *noun.* □ **imposition**

imposing [im'pouziŋ] *adjective* making a great impression; large and handsome: *an imposing building.* □ **imposant**

impossible [im'posəbl] *adjective* **1** that cannot be or be done: *It is impossible to sing and drink at the same time*; *an impossible task.* □ **impossible**

2 hopelessly bad or wrong: *That child's behaviour is quite impossible.* □ **insupportable**

im'possibly *adverb.* □ **de façon impossible**

im,possi'bility *noun.* □ **impossibilité**

impostor [im'postə] *noun* a person who pretends to be someone else, or to be something he or she is not, in order to deceive another person. □ **imposteur**

impoverish [im'povəriʃ] *verb* to make poor. □ **appauvrir**

im'poverishment *noun.* □ **appauvrissement**

impracticable [im'praktikəbl] *adjective* not able to be put into practice, used, done *etc*: *a completely impracticable idea.* □ **irréalisable, impraticable**

im,practica'bility *noun.* □ **impraticabilité**

impractical [im'praktikəl] *adjective* lacking common sense: *an impractical person/suggestion.* □ **peu pratique**

imprecise [impri'sais] *adjective* not clear; vague: *Her directions were so imprecise that we lost our way.* □ **imprécis**

,impre'cision *noun.* □ **imprécision**

impress [im'pres] *verb* **1** to cause feelings of admiration *etc* in (a person): *I was impressed by his good behaviour.* □ **impressionner**

2 (*with* **on** *or* **upon**) to stress (something to someone): *I must impress upon you the need for silence.* □ **faire bien comprendre (qqch. à qqn)**

3 to fix (a fact *etc* in the mind): *She re-read the plans in order to impress the details on her memory.* □ **graver (dans)**

4 make (a mark) on something by pressing: *a footprint*

impressed in the sand. □ **imprimer**

im'pression [-ʃən] *noun* **1** the idea or effect produced in someone's mind by a person, experience *etc*: *The film made a great impression on me.* □ **impression**
2 a vague idea: *I have the impression that he's not pleased.* □ **impression**
3 the mark left by an object on another object: *The dog left an impression of its paws in the wet cement.* □ **empreinte**
4 a single printing of a book *etc.* □ **tirage**

im'pressive [-siv] *adjective* (*negative* **unimpressive**) making a great impression on a person's mind, feelings *etc*: *an impressive ceremony.* □ **impressionnant**
im'pressively *adverb.* □ **de façon impressionnante**
im'pressiveness *noun.* □ **caractère impressionnant**
be under the impression (that) to have the (often wrong) feeling or idea that: *I was under the impression that you were paying for this meal.* □ **avoir l'impression que**

imprint ['imprint] *noun* a mark made by pressure: *She saw the imprint of a foot in the sand.* □ **empreinte**
■ [im'print] *verb* to make (a mark) on something by pressure; to fix permanently (in the mind or memory). □ **imprimer, graver**

imprison [im'prizn] *verb* to put in prison; to take or keep prisoner: *He was imprisoned for twenty years for his crimes.* □ **emprisonner**
im'prisonment *noun.* □ **emprisonnement**

improbable [im'probəbl] *adjective* **1** not likely to happen or exist; not probable: *Although death at her age was improbable, she had already made her will.* □ **improbable**
2 hard to believe: *an improbable explanation.* □ **invraisemblable**
im'probably *adverb.* □ **invraisemblablement**
im,proba'bility *noun.* □ **invraisemblance**

impromptu [im'promptjuː] *adjective, adverb* (made or done) without preparation beforehand: *an impromptu speech; He spoke impromptu for ten minutes.* □ **impromptu**

improper [im'propə] *adjective* (of behaviour *etc*) not acceptable; indecent; wrong: *improper suggestions.* □ **déplacé, indécent**
impropriety [imprə'praiəti] *noun.* □ **inconvenance**
improper fraction a fraction which is larger than 1: *7/5 is an improper fraction.* □ **expression fractionnaire**

improve [im'pruːv] *verb* to (cause to) become better, of higher quality *etc*: *His work has greatly improved; They recently improved the design of that car.* □ (**s')améliorer**
im'provement *noun* **1** the state or act of improving or being improved: *There has been a great improvement in her work; The patient's condition shows some improvement.* □ **amélioration**
2 something which improves, or adds beauty, value *etc*: *I've made several improvements to the house.* □ **amélioration**
improve on to produce something which is better, more useful *etc* than: *I think I can improve on that suggestion.* □ **améliorer**

improvise ['imprəvaiz] *verb* **1** to compose and perform

(a poem, tune *etc*) without preparation: *The pianist forgot her music and had to improvise.* □ **improviser**
2 to make (something) from materials that happen to be available, often materials that are not normally used for that purpose: *They improvised a shelter from branches and blankets.* □ **improviser**
,improvi'sation *noun.* □ **improvisation**

imprudent [im'pruːdənt] *adjective* not having or showing good sense; unwise. □ **imprudent**
im'prudently *adverb.* □ **imprudemment**
im'prudence *noun.* □ **imprudence**

impudent ['impjudənt] *adjective* rude; disrespectful: *an impudent child/suggestion.* □ **effronté**
'impudently *adverb.* □ **effrontément**
'impudence *noun.* □ **effronterie**

impulse ['impʌls] *noun* **1** a sudden desire to do something, without thinking about the consequences: *I bought the dress on impulse – I didn't really need it.* □ **impulsion**
2 a sudden force or stimulation: *an electrical impulse.* □ **impulsion**
im'pulsive [-siv] *adjective* done, or likely to act, suddenly, without careful thought: *an impulsive action; You're far too impulsive!* □ **impulsif**
im'pulsively *adverb.* □ **impulsivement**
im'pulsiveness *noun.* □ **impulsivité**

impure [im'pjue] *adjective* dirty, with other substances mixed in; not pure: *impure air; The water is impure.* □ **impur**
im'purity *noun* **1** something which is mixed into another substance, but which should not be: *There are too many impurities in this steel.* □ **impureté**
2 the state of being impure: *Complaints were made about the impurity of the milk.* □ **impureté**

in [in] *preposition* **1** describing the position of a thing *etc* which is surrounded by something else: *My mother is in the house; in London; in bed.* □ **en, à, dans**
2 showing the direction of movement: *He put his hand in his pocket.* □ **dans**
3 describing the time at, after or within which something happens: *in the morning; I'll be back in a week.* □ **dans**
4 indicating amount or relative number: *They arrived in large numbers.* □ **en**
5 expressing circumstances, state, manner *etc* of an event, person *etc*: *dressed in a brown coat; walking in the rain; in a hurry; written in English; He is in the army; books tied up in bundles; She is in her sixties.* □ **de, sous, en, dans**
■ *adverb, adjective* **1** expressing the position of a person *etc, usually* at or to a place where the person *etc* is expected to be, *eg* home, office, station: *Is Mr. Smith in?; Is the train in yet?; Is she coming in today?* □ **là, à l'intérieur**
2 describing something which is fashionable or popular: *Short skirts are in at the moment.* □ **à la mode**
3 (of the tide) with the water at, or moving to, its highest level: *The tide is (coming) in.* □ (**à marée**) **haute**
-in describing an activity *usually* carried out by groups of people as a form of protest *etc*: *a sit-in; a work-in.* □

manifestation

inmost *see* **innermost** *under* **inner**.

day *etc* **in, day** *etc* **out** day *etc* after day *etc* without a break: *I do the same boring job day in, day out; Last summer it rained week in, week out.* □ **jour après jour**

inasmuch as because; in consideration of the fact that: *It would not be true to say he had retired from this firm, inasmuch as he still does a certain amount of work for us.* □ **vu que**

in for likely to experience (*especially* something bad): *We're in for some bad weather; You're in for it if you broke that window!* □ **pouvoir s'attendre à**

ins and outs the complex details of a plan *etc*: *She knows all the ins and outs of this scheme.* □ **les moindres détails**

insofar as to the degree or extent that: *I gave him the details insofar as I knew them.* □ **dans la mesure où**

in that because; from the fact that: *This is not a good plant for your garden in that its seeds are poisonous.* □ **vu que**

inability [inə'biləti] *noun* the lack of power, means, ability *etc* (to do something): *I was surprised at his inability to read.* □ **incapacité**

inaccessible [inək'sesəbl] *adjective* not able to be (easily) approached, reached or obtained: *The village is inaccessible by car because of flooding.* □ **inaccessible**
'inac,cessi'bility [-sesə] *noun.* □ **inaccessibilité**

inaccurate [in'akjurət] *adjective* containing errors; not correct or accurate: *inaccurate translation/addition.* □ **inexact**
in'accuracy *noun* (*plural* **in'accuracies**). □ **inexactitude**

inactive [in'aktiv] *adjective* (*formal*) 1 not taking much exercise: *You're fat because you're so inactive.* □ **inactif** 2 no longer working, functioning *etc*; not active: *an inactive volcano.* □ **inactif, éteint**
in'action *noun.* □ **inaction**
inac'tivity *noun.* □ **inactivité**

inadequate [in'adikwət] *adjective* not sufficient; not adequate: *inadequate supplies; Our equipment is inadequate for this job.* □ **insuffisant**
in'adequacy *noun.* □ **insuffisance**

inadmissible [inəd'misəbl] *adjective* not allowable. □ **inadmissible**
'inad,missi'bility *noun.* □ **inadmissibilité**

inadvertent [inəd'vəːtənt] *adjective* not done on purpose: *an inadvertent insult.* □ **(fait) par inadvertance**
,inad'vertently *adverb.* □ **par inadvertance, par mégarde**

inadvisable [inəd'vaizəbl] *adjective* unwise; not advisable: *It would be inadvisable for you to go alone.* □ **déconseillé (de)**
'inad,visa'bility [-vai-] *noun.* □ **inopportunité**

inanimate [in'animət] *adjective* not living: *A rock is an inanimate object.* □ **inanimé**

inappropriate [inə'proupriət] *adjective* (*sometimes with* **to** *or* **for**) not appropriate or suitable: *inappropriate clothes (for a wedding); His speech was inappropriate to the occasion.* □ **peu approprié, déplacé**
,inap'propriateness *noun.* □ **caractère peu approprié**

inasmuch as *see* **in**.

inattentive [inə'tentiv] *adjective* not paying attention; not attentive: *This pupil is very inattentive in class; an inattentive audience.* □ **inattentif**
,inat'tention *noun.* □ **inattention**
,inat'tentiveness *noun.* □ **inattention**

inaudible [in'ɔːdəbl] *adjective* not loud or clear enough to be heard: *Her voice was inaudible because of the noise.* □ **inaudible**
in'audibly *adverb.* □ **de manière inaudible**
in,audi'bility *noun.* □ **imperceptibilité**

inaugurate [i'nɔːgjureit] *verb* 1 to place (a person) in an official position with great ceremony: *to inaugurate a president.* □ **investir de ses fonctions** 2 to make a ceremonial start to: *This meeting is to inaugurate our new Social Work scheme.* □ **inaugurer** 3 to open (a building, exhibition *etc*) formally to the public: *The Queen inaugurated the new university buildings.* □ **inaugurer**
i,naugu'ration *noun.* □ **inauguration**
i'naugural *adjective.* □ **inaugural**

inborn ['in'bɔːn] *adjective* natural; possessed by a person from birth: *an inborn ability to paint.* □ **inné**

incalculable [in'kalkjuləbl] *adjective* not able to be calculated; very great. □ **incalculable**

incandescent [inkan'desnt] *adjective* glowing white with heat. □ **incandescent**

incantation [inkan'teiʃən] *noun* words said or sung as a spell. □ **incantation**

incapable [in'keipəbl] *adjective* (*with* **of**) not able (to do something): *incapable of learning anything.* □ **incapable (de)**
in,capa'bility *noun.* □ **incapacité (de)**

incarnate [in'kaːnət] *adjective* (of God, the devil *etc*) having taken human form: *a devil incarnate.* □ **incarné**
incarnation [inkaːˈneiʃən] *noun* (the) human form taken by a divine being *etc*: *Most Christians believe that Christ was the incarnation of God.* □ **incarnation**

incautious [in'kɔːʃəs] *adjective* acting or done without thinking; not cautious: *an incautious action/remark/ person.* □ **imprudent**
in'cautiousness *noun.* □ **imprudence**

incendiary [in'sendiəri] *adjective* used for setting (a building *etc*) on fire: *an incendiary bomb.* □ **incendiaire**
■ *noun* – *plural* **in'cendiaries** – 1 a person who sets fire to buildings *etc* unlawfully. □ **incendiaire** 2 an incendiary bomb. □ **bombe/engin incendiaire**

incense ['insens] *noun* a substance which is burned *especially* in religious services, and which gives off a pleasant smell: *We bought a stick of incense to give a sweet smell to the room.* □ **encens**

incentive [in'sentiv] *noun* something that encourages *etc*: *Hope of promotion was an incentive to hard work.* □ **encouragement**

incessant [in'sesnt] *adjective* going on without stopping: *incessant noise.* □ **incessant**
in'cessantly *adverb.* □ **sans cesse**

inch [intʃ] *noun* 1 (*often abbreviated to* **in** *when written*) a measure of length, the twelfth part of a foot (2.54 centimetres). □ **pouce**

2 a small amount: *There is not an inch of room to spare.* □ **pouce, centimètre**

■ *verb* to move slowly and carefully: *She inched (her way) along the narrow ledge.* □ **avancer petit à petit**

within an inch of almost; very near(ly): *He came within an inch of failing the exam.* □ **à deux doigts de**

incident ['insidənt] *noun* an event or happening: *There was a strange incident in the supermarket today.* □ **incident**

,inci'dental [-'den-] *adjective* 1 occurring *etc* by chance in connection with something else: *an incidental remark.* □ **fortuit**

2 accompanying (something) but not forming part of it: *She wrote the incidental music for the play.* □ **d'accompagnement**

,inci'dentally [-'den-] *adverb* by the way: *Incidentally, where were you last night?* □ **à propos**

incinerate [in'sinəreit] *verb* to burn to ashes. □ **incinérer**

in,cine'ration *noun.* □ **incinération**

in'cinerator *noun* a furnace or other container for burning rubbish *etc*. □ **incinérateur**

incision [in'siʒən] *noun* 1 a cut, *especially* one made in a person's body by a surgeon. □ **incision**

2 the act of cutting *especially* by a surgeon. □ **incision**

incisor [in'saizə] *noun* one of the four front cutting teeth in the upper or lower jaw. □ **incisive**

incite [in'sait] *verb* 1 to urge (someone) to do something: *He incited the people to rebel against the king.* □ **inciter (à)**

2 to stir up or cause: *They incited violence in the crowd.* □ **provoquer**

in'citement *noun.* □ **incitation (à)**

incivility [insi'viləti] *noun* impoliteness. □ **impolitesse**

incline [in'klain] *verb* to bow (one's head *etc*). □ **baisser**

■ ['inklain] *noun* a slope. □ **pente**

inclination [inklə'neiʃən] *noun* 1 a tendency or slight desire to do something: *Has she any inclinations towards engineering?; I felt an inclination to thank him.* □ **penchant, envie (de)**

2 (an act of) bowing (the head *etc*). □ **inclination**

be inclined to 1 to have a tendency to (do something): *She is inclined to be a bit lazy.* □ **avoir tendance à**

2 to have a slight desire to (do something): *I am inclined to accept their invitation.* □ **être disposé à**

include [iŋ'kluːd] *verb* to take in or consider along with (other people, things *etc*) as part of a group, set *etc*: *Am I included in the team?; Your duties include making the tea.* □ **inclure, comprendre**

in'clusion [-ʒən] *noun.* □ **inclusion**

including *preposition: The whole family has been ill, including the baby.* □ **(y) compris**

in'clusive [-siv] *adjective* counting both the first and last in a series: *May 7 to May 9 inclusive is three days.* □ **inclus**

■ **not included** □ **non compris**

incognito [iŋkog'niːtou] *adverb, adjective* without letting people know who one is, *eg* by using a false name: *He travelled incognito to Paris.* □ **incognito**

incoherent [inkə'hiərənt] *adjective* talking, writing *etc* in a way which is not easy to follow: *He was quite in-coherent with rage.* □ **incohérent**

,inco'herently *adverb.* □ **sans cohérence**

,inco'herence *noun.* □ **incohérence**

incombustible [inkəm'ʌstəbl] *adjective* not able to be burned: *That new building material is quite incombustible.* □ **incombustible**

income ['iŋkəm] *noun* money received by a person as wages *etc*: *She can support her family on her income.* □ **revenu**

income tax a tax paid on income over a certain amount. □ **impôt sur le revenu**

incoming ['inkʌmiŋ] *adjective* which is coming in; approaching: *the incoming tide; incoming telephone calls.* □ **qui arrive**

incomparable [in'kompərəbl] *adjective* without equal; not comparable: *incomparable skill.* □ **incomparable**

in'comparably *adverb.* □ **incomparablement**

incompatible [inkəm'patəbl] *adjective* 1 (of people) certain to disagree, fight *etc*. □ **irréconciliable**

2 (of statements *etc*) not in agreement with one another. □ **incompatible**

'incom,pati'bility *noun.* □ **incompatibilité**

incompetent [in'kompitənt] *adjective* not good enough at doing a job *etc*: *a very incompetent mechanic.* □ **incompétent**

in'competence *noun.* □ **incompétence**

incomplete [inkəm'pliːt] *adjective* not complete or finished; with some part missing: *Her novel was incomplete when she died; an incomplete pack of cards.* □ **incomplet**

incomprehensible [inkompri'hensəbl] *adjective* impossible to understand: *an incomprehensible statement.* □ **incompréhensible**

inconceivable [inkən'siːvəbl] *adjective* not able to be imagined or believed: *inconceivable wickedness.* □ **inconcevable**

inconclusive [inkən'kluːsiv] *adjective* not leading to a definite decision, result *etc*: *inconclusive evidence.* □ **peu concluant**

incongruous [in'koŋgruəs] *adjective* unsuitable or out of place; odd: *Boots would look incongruous with an evening dress.* □ **incongru**

incon'gruity, in'congruousness *noun.* □ **incongruité**

inconsiderate [inkən'sidərət] *adjective* not showing thought for the feelings, rights *etc* of other people; thoughtless: *It was inconsiderate of you to arrive without telephoning first.* □ **sans égards, sans gêne**

,incon'siderateness *noun.* □ **manque d'égards**

inconsistent [inkən'sistənt] *adjective* 1 (*often with* **with**) contradictory in some way; not in agreement: *What you're saying today is quite inconsistent with the statement you made yesterday.* □ **en contradiction (avec)**

2 changeable, *eg* in standard: *His work is inconsistent.* □ **inégal**

,incon'sistency *noun* (*plural* **incon'sistencies**). □ **inconsistance**

inconsolable [inkən'souləbl] *adjective* not able to be comforted: *the inconsolable widow.* □ **inconsolable**

inconspicuous [inkən'spikjuəs] *adjective* not noticeable or conspicuous: *The detective tried to be as inconspicu-*

ous as possible. □ **inapparent**

,**incon'spicuousness** *noun.* □ **caractère effacé**

inconstant [in'konstənt] *adjective* (of people) having feelings, intentions *etc* which change frequently. □ **inconstant**

inconvenient [inkən'viːnjənt] *adjective* causing trouble or difficulty; awkward: *He has come at a very inconvenient time.* □ **mal choisi**

,**incon'venience** *noun* (something which causes) trouble or difficulty: *He apologized for the inconvenience caused by his late arrival.* □ **dérangement, inconvénient**

■ *verb* to cause trouble or difficulty to: *I hope I haven't inconvenienced you.* □ **déranger**

incorporate [in'koːpəreit] *verb* to contain or include as part of the whole: *The shopping centre incorporates a library and a bank.* □ **incorporer**

in'corporated *adjective* (*often abbreviated to* **Inc., inc.**) formed into a company, corporation *etc*: *The name of our company is 'Field Services, Incorporated'.* □ **constitué en société (par actions), inc.**

incorrect [inkə'rekt] *adjective* **1** not accurate or correct; wrong: *incorrect translation of a word.* □ **incorrect**

2 (of behaviour *etc*) not acceptable; wrong. □ **incorrect**

,**incor'rectness** *noun.* □ **incorrection**

incorrigible [in'koridʒəbl] *adjective* too bad to be corrected or improved. □ **incorrigible**

incorruptible [inkə'rʌptəbl] *adjective* not able to be bribed; honest: *The police should be incorruptible.* □ **incorruptible**

'**incor,rupti'bility** *noun.* □ **incorruptibilité**

increase [in'kriːs] *verb* to (cause to) grow in size, number *etc*: *The number of children in this school has increased greatly in recent years.* □ **(s')accroître, grandir**

■ ['inkriːs] *noun* (the amount, number *etc* added by) growth: *There has been some increase in business; The increase in the population over the last ten years was 40 000.* □ **accroissement**

in'creasingly *adverb* more and more: *It became increasingly difficult to find helpers.* □ **de plus en plus**

on the increase becoming more frequent or becoming greater: *Acts of violence are on the increase.* □ **aller croissant**

incredible [in'kredəbl] *adjective* **1** hard to believe: *She does an incredible amount of work.* □ **incroyable**

2 impossible to believe; not credible: *I found his story incredible.* □ **incroyable, inouï**

in'credibly *adverb.* □ **incroyablement**

in,credi'bility *noun.* □ **incrédibilité**

incredulous [in'kredjuləs] *adjective* unwilling to believe: *She listened to him with an incredulous expression.* □ **incrédule**

,**incre'dulity** [-'djuː-] *noun.* □ **incrédulité**

increment ['inkrəmənt] *noun* an increase *especially* in salary. □ **augmentation**

incriminate [in'krimineit] *verb* (of evidence) to show the involvement of (someone) in a crime *etc.* □ **incriminer**

in'criminating *adjective.* □ **compromettant**

in,crimi'nation *noun.* □ **accusation**

incubate ['inkjubeit] *verb* **1** to produce (young birds) from eggs by sitting on them or by keeping them warm by some other means. □ **couver**

2 (of germs or disease) to develop until signs of the disease appear: *How long does chickenpox take to incubate?* □ **incuber**

,**incu'bation** *noun.* □ **incubation**

'**incubator** *noun* a heated box-like apparatus for hatching eggs or a similar one for rearing premature babies *etc.* □ **couveuse**

incur [in'kəː] – *past tense, past participle* **in'curred** – *verb* **1** to bring (something unpleasant) on oneself: *to incur someone's displeasure.* □ **(s')attirer**

2 to become liable to pay (a debt): *to incur enormous debts.* □ **contracter**

incurable [in'kjuərəbl] *adjective* not able to be cured or corrected; not curable: *an incurable disease/habit.* □ **incurable**

indebted [in'detid] *adjective* (*with* **to**) having reason to be grateful to: *I am indebted to you for your help.* □ **redevable (à qqn de qqch.)**

in'debtedness *noun.* □ **dette(s)**

indecent [in'diːsnt] *adjective* offending against accepted standards of sexual or moral behaviour; not modest: *indecent clothing.* □ **indécent**

in'decency *noun.* □ **indécence**

indecipherable [indi'saifərəbl] *adjective* impossible to read or understand; not decipherable: *indecipherable handwriting*; *This code is indecipherable.* □ **indéchiffrable**

indecision [indi'siʒən] *noun* the state of not being able to decide; hesitation. □ **indécision, incertitude**

,**inde'cisive** [-'saisiv] *adverb* **1** not producing a clear decision or a definite result: *an indecisive battle.* □ **indécis**

2 unable to make firm decisions: *indecisive person.* □ **irrésolu**

indeed [in'diːd] *adverb* **1** really; in fact; as you say; of course *etc*: *'He's very talented, isn't he?' He is indeed*; *'Do you remember your grandmother?' 'Indeed I do!'* □ **en effet**

2 used for emphasis: *Thank you very much indeed*; *He is very clever indeed.* □ **vraiment**

■ *interjection* used to show surprise, interest *etc*: *'John said your idea was stupid.' 'Indeed!'* □ **vraiment?**

indefinite [in'definit] *adjective* **1** not fixed or exact; without clearly marked outlines or limits: *She invited her mother to stay for an indefinite length of time.* □ **indéterminé**

2 vague; uncertain: *His plans are indefinite at the moment.* □ **indéfini**

in'definiteness *noun.* □ **caractère vague**

in'definitely *adverb* for an indefinite period of time: *The match was postponed indefinitely.* □ **à une date indéterminée**

indefinite article the name given to the words **a** and **an**. □ **article indéfini**

indelible [in'deləbl] *adjective* (making a mark) that cannot be removed: *indelible ink*; *The events of that day have left an indelible impression on my mind.* □

indélébile

indent [in'dent] *verb* to begin (a line of writing) farther in from the margin than the other lines. □ **renforcer**

■ ['indent] *noun* (*also* ,**inden'tation**) the space left at the beginning of a line, *eg* the first line of a paragraph. □ **renfoncement**

,**inden'tation** [inden-] *noun* **1** a V-shaped cut (in the edge or outline of an object). □ **dentelure**

2 an indent. □ **alinéa**

3 a deep inward curve in a coastline. □ **échancrure(s)**

in'dented *adjective* having an edge, outline *etc* with V-shaped cuts or inward curves. □ **dentelé**

independent [indi'pendənt] *adjective* **1** not controlled by other people, countries *etc*: *an independent country*; *That country is now independent of Britain.* □ **indépendant (de)**

2 not willing to accept help: *an independent old lady.* □ **indépendant**

3 having enough money to support oneself: *She is completely independent and receives no money from her family; She is now independent of her parents.* □ **indépendant (de)**

4 not relying on, or affected by, something or someone else: *an independent observer; to arrive at an independent conclusion.* □ **indépendant**

inde'pendence *noun.* □ **indépendance**

inde'pendently *adverb.* □ **indépendamment (de)**

indestructible [indi'strʌktəbl] *adjective* not able to be destroyed: *an indestructible toy.* □ **indestructible**

index ['indeks] *noun* **1** an alphabetical list of names, subjects *etc eg* at the end of a book. □ **index**

2 (*plural* **indices** ['indisiːz]) in mathematics the figure which indicates the number of times a figure *etc* must be multiplied by itself *etc*: *In 6^3 and 7^5, the figures 3 and 5 are the indices.* □ **exposant**

index finger the finger next to the thumb: *She pointed at the map with her index finger.* □ **index**

Indian ['indiən] *noun* **1** a native inhabitant of North America, Central or South America. □ **Amérindien, ienne**

2 a person born in India or having Indian citizenship. □ **Indien, ienne**

■ *adjective* of India or of Indians. □ **indien**

indicate ['indikeit] *verb* to point out or show: *We can paint an arrow here to indicate the right path.* □ **indiquer**

,**indi'cation** *noun*: *There are clear indications that the war will soon be over; He had given no indication that he was intending to resign.* □ **indication**

indicative [in'dikətiv] *adjective, noun* describing verbs which occur as parts of statements and questions: *In 'I ran home' and 'Are you going?' 'ran' and 'are going' are indicative (verbs).* □ **indicatif**

'**indicator** *noun* a pointer, sign, instrument *etc* which indicates something or gives information about something: *the indicator on the gas gauge of a car.* □ **aiguille**

indices *see* **index**.

indifferent [in'difrənt] *adjective* **1** (*often with* **to**) showing no interest in or not caring about (opinions, events *etc*): *She is quite indifferent to other people's suffering.*

□ **indifférent (à)**

2 not very good: *He is a rather indifferent card-player.* □ **médiocre**

in'differently *adverb.* □ **indifféremment**

in'difference *noun* the state of showing no interest in, or concern about, something: *She showed complete indifference to the cries of the baby.* □ **indifférence**

indigestion [indi'dʒestʃən] *noun* (discomfort or pain which is caused by) difficulty in digesting food: *She suffers from indigestion after eating fatty food.* □ **indigestion**

,**indi'gestible** *adjective* not easily digested: *This food is quite indigestible.* □ **indigeste**

'**indi,gesti'bility** *noun.* □ **caractère indigeste**

indignant [in'dignənt] *adjective* angry, *usually* because of some wrong that has been done to oneself or others: *I feel most indignant at the rude way I've been treated; The indignant customer complained to the manager.* □ **indigné**

in'dignantly *adverb*: *'Take your foot off my toe!' she said indignantly.* □ **avec indignation**

,**indig'nation** *noun.* □ **indignation**

indirect [indi'rekt] *adjective* **1** not leading straight to the destination; not direct: *We arrived late because we took rather an indirect route.* □ **indirect**

2 not straightforward: *I asked her several questions but she kept giving me indirect answers.* □ **détourné**

3 not intended; not directly aimed at: *an indirect result.* □ **indirect**

,**indi'rectness** *noun.* □ **caractère indirect**

indirect object the word in a sentence which stands for the person or thing to or for whom something is given, done *etc*: *In 'Give me the book', 'Tell the children a story', 'Boil John an egg', me, the children and John are indirect objects.* □ **complément indirect**

indirect speech a person's words as they are reported rather than in the form in which they were said: *He said that he would come is the form in indirect speech of He said 'I will come'.* □ **discours indirect**

indiscipline [in'disəplin] *noun* bad behaviour; unwillingness to obey orders. □ **indiscipline**

indiscreet [indi'skriːt] *adjective* **1** giving too much information away: *an indiscreet remark.* □ **indiscret**

2 not wise or cautious: *indiscreet behaviour.* □ **imprudent**

,**indi'scretion** [-'skreʃən] *noun.* □ **indiscrétion**

indispensable [indi'spensəbl] *adjective* necessary; that cannot be done without: *A dictionary should be considered an indispensable possession.* □ **indispensable**

indisposed [indi'spouzd] *adjective* (slightly) ill: *The princess is indisposed and has cancelled her engagements.* □ **souffrant**

'**in,dispo'sition** *noun.* □ **malaise**

indisputable [indi'spjuːtəbl] *adjective* not able to be denied. □ **incontestable**

indistinct [indi'stiŋkt] *adjective* not clear to the eye, ear or mind; not distinct: *an indistinct outline of a ship; His speech is rather indistinct.* □ **indistinct**

,**indi'stinctly** *adverb.* □ **indistinctement**

,**indi'stinctness** *noun.* □ **manque de netteté**

indistinguishable [indi'stiŋgwiʃəbl] *adjective* not able to be seen as different or separate: *This copy is indistinguishable from the original; The twins are almost indistinguishable.* □ **indifférenciable (de)**

individual [indi'vidjuəl] *adjective* **1** single; separate: *Put price labels on each individual item.* □ **individuel; séparé**
2 intended for, used by *etc* one person *etc*: *Customers in shops should be given individual attention.* □ **particulier**
3 special to one person *etc*, showing or having special qualities: *Her style of dress is very individual.* □ **personnel**
■ *noun* **1** a single person in contrast to the group to which he belongs: *the rights of the individual in society.* □ **individu**
2 a person: *He's an untidy individual.* □ **personne**
'indi,vidu'ality [-'a-] *noun* the qualities that distinguish one person *etc* from others. □ **individualité**
,indi'vidually *adverb* each separately: *I'll deal with each question individually.* □ **séparément**

indivisible [indi'vizəbl] *adjective* not able to be divided or separated. □ **indivisible**
'indi,visi'bility *noun.* □ **indivisibilité**

indoctrinate [in'doktrineit] *verb* to fill with a certain teaching or set of opinions, beliefs *etc*: *The dictator tried to indoctrinate schoolchildren with the ideals of his party.* □ **endoctriner; inculquer (qqch. à qqn)**
in,doctri'nation *noun.* □ **endoctrinement**

indoor ['indoː] *adjective* used, done *etc* inside a building: *indoor games; an indoor swimming pool.* □ **(d')intérieur**
,in'doors *adverb* in or into a building: *Stay indoors till you've finished your homework; She went indoors when the rain started.* □ **à l'intérieur**

indulge [in'dʌldʒ] *verb* **1** to allow (a person) to do or have what he wishes: *You shouldn't indulge that child.* □ **gâter**
2 to follow (a wish, interest *etc*): *He indulges his love of food by dining at expensive restaurants.* □ **donner libre cours à**
3 to allow (oneself) a luxury *etc*: *Life would be very dull if we never indulged (ourselves).* □ **se faire plaisir**
in'dulgence *noun.* □ **indulgence; satisfaction**
in'dulgent *adjective* willing to allow people to do or have what they wish (often to too great an extent): *an indulgent parent.* □ **indulgent**
indulge in to give way to (an inclination, emotion *etc*): *She indulged in tears/in a fit of temper.* □ **se laisser aller à**

industry ['indəstri] – *plural* **'industries** – *noun* **1** (any part of) the business of producing or making goods: *the ship-building industry; The government should invest more money in industry.* □ **industrie**
2 hard work or effort: *She owed her success to both ability and industry.* □ **travail**
in'dustrial [-'dʌs-] *adjective* having, concerning *etc* industries or the making of goods: *That area of the country is industrial rather than agricultural.* □ **industriel**
in'dustrialist [-'dʌs-] *noun* a person who takes part in

the running of a large industrial organization: *a wealthy industrialist.* □ **industriel, elle**
in'dustrialized, in'dustrialised [-'dʌs] *adjective* (of a country) having a large number of industries. □ **industrialisé**
in,dustriali'zation, in,dustriali'sation *noun.* □ **industrialisation**
in'dustrious [-'dʌs-] *adjective* busy and hard-working: *industrious pupils.* □ **travailleur**
industrial estate an area of a town *etc* set aside for (the building of) factories. □ **zone industrielle**
industrial relations the relationship between the management and the workers in a factory *etc.* □ **relations industrielles**

inedible [in'edibl] *adjective* not fit or suitable to be eaten: *The meal was inedible.* □ **immangeable**

ineffective [ini'fektiv] *adjective* useless; not producing any result or the result desired: *ineffective methods.* □ **inefficace**
,inef'fectiveness *noun.* □ **inefficacité**

ineffectual [ini'fektʃuəl] *adjective* **1** not producing any result or the desired result: *His attempts to keep order in the classroom were quite ineffectual.* □ **inefficace**
2 (of a person) not confident or able to lead people; not able to get things done: *an ineffectual teacher.* □ **incompétent**
,inef'fectualness *noun.* □ **inefficacité**

inefficient [ini'fiʃənt] *adjective* not working or producing results *etc* in the best way and so wasting time, energy *etc*: *an inefficient workman; old-fashioned, inefficient machinery.* □ **inefficace**
,inef'ficiently *adverb.* □ **inefficacement**
,inef'ficiency *noun.* □ **inefficacité**

inelegant [in'eligənt] *adjective* not graceful; not elegant: *She was sprawled in a chair in a most inelegant fashion.* □ **inélégant**
in'elegantly *adverb.* □ **sans élégance**
in'elegance *noun.* □ **manque d'élégance**

ineligible [in'elidʒəbl] *adjective* not eligible: *Children under eighteen years of age are ineligible to vote in elections.* □ **qui n'a pas le droit (de)**
in,eligi'bility *noun.* □ **inéligibilité**

inequality [ini'kwoləti] *noun* (a case of) the existence of differences in size, value *etc* between two or more objects *etc*: *There is bound to be inequality between a manager's salary and a workman's wages.* □ **inégalité**

inert [i'noːt] *adjective* **1** without the power to move: *A stone is an inert object.* □ **inerte**
2 (of people) not wanting to move, act or think: *lazy, inert people.* □ **apathique**
i'nertness *noun.* □ **inactivité**
i'nertia [-ʃiə] *noun* the state of being inert: *It was difficult to overcome the feeling of inertia that the wine and heat had brought on.* □ **inertie**

inescapable [ini'skeipəbl] *adjective* (*formal*) that cannot be avoided: *an inescapable conclusion.* □ **inévitable**

inessential [inə'senʃəl] *noun, adjective* (something) which is not essential: *We have no money for inessentials; inessential luxuries.* □ **superflu**

inevitable [in'evitəbl] *adjective* that cannot be avoided;

certain to happen, be done, said, used *etc*: *The Prime Minister said that war was inevitable*. □ **inévitable**
in,evita'bility *noun*. □ **inévitabilité**
in'evitably *adverb* as you might expect: *Inevitably the train was late*. □ **inévitablement**
inexact [inig'zakt] *adjective* not quite correct, exact or true: *an inexact description*. □ **inexact**
,inex'actness *noun*. □ **inexactitude**
inexcusable [inik'skju:zəbl] *adjective* too bad *etc* to be excused or justified; not excusable: *inexcusable rudeness*. □ **inexcusable**
,inex'cusably *adverb*. □ **inexcusablement**
inexhaustible [inig'zɔːstəbl] *adjective* very large; not likely to be used up: *an inexhaustible supply*; *Her energy seems inexhaustible*. □ **inépuisable, intarissable**
,inex'haustibly *adverb*. □ **d'une manière inépuisable**
'inex,hausti'bility *noun*. □ **nature inépuisable**
inexpensive [inik'spensiv] *adjective* not costly; not expensive: *inexpensive clothes*. □ **bon marché**
,inex'pensively *adverb*. □ **à bon marché**
inexperience [inik'spiəriəns] *noun* lack of experience or skilled knowledge: *He seems good at the job in spite of his youth and inexperience*. □ **inexpérience**
,inex'perienced *adjective* lacking knowledge, skill and experience: *Inexperienced climbers should not attempt this route*. □ **inexpérimenté**
inexpert [in'ekspəːt] *adjective* unskilled or clumsy: *inexpert attempts at dressmaking*. □ **maladroit**
in'expertly *adverb*. □ **maladroitement**
inexplicable [inik'splikəbl] *adjective* impossible to explain or understand: *His inexplicable absence worried all of us*. □ **inexplicable**
,inex'plicably *adverb*. □ **inexplicablement**
inexpressible [inik'spresəbl] *adjective* that cannot be expressed or described: *inexpressible delight*. □ **inexprimable**
,inex'pressibly *adverb*. □ **indiciblement**
inextricable [inekstrəkəbl] *adjective* perplexing or extremely involved, unable to be untangled: *How to bring about peace without using force is an inextricable problem*. □ **inextricable**
infallible [in'faləbl] *adjective* **1** (of a person or his judgment *etc*) never making a mistake. □ **infaillible**
2 (of a remedy *etc*) always successful: *infallible cures*. □ **infaillible**
in,falli'bility *noun*. □ **infaillibilité**
in'fallibly *adverb*. □ **infailliblement**
infamous ['infəməs] *adjective* **1** (of something bad) well-known; notorious. □ **infâme**
2 disgraceful. □ **abominable**
'infamy *noun*. □ **infamie**
infant ['infənt] *noun* a baby or very young child: *the baptism of infants*; (*also adjective*) *an infant school*. □ **nourrisson; de maternelle**
'infancy *noun* the state or time of being a baby: *They had two children who died in infancy*. □ **petite enfance**
infantry ['infəntri] *noun or noun plural* (the part of an army consisting of) foot-soldiers: *The infantry was/were sent on ahead, with the artillery following in the rear*. □ **infanterie**

infect [in'fekt] *verb* to fill with germs that cause disease; to give a disease to: *You must wash that cut on your knee in case it becomes infected*; *She had a bad cold last week and has infected the rest of the class*. □ **infecter**
in'fection [-ʃən] *noun* **1** the process of infecting or state of being infected: *You should wash your hands after handling raw meat to avoid infection*. □ **infection**
2 a disease: *a throat infection*. □ **infection**
in'fectious [-ʃəs] *adjective* likely to spread to others: *Measles is an infectious disease*. □ **contagieux**
in'fectiously *adverb*. □ **de manière contagieuse**
infer [in'fəː] – *past tense, past participle* **in'ferred** – *verb* to judge (from facts or evidence): *I inferred from your silence that you were angry*. □ **déduire**
'inference *noun*. □ **déduction**
inferior [in'fiəriə] *adjective* (*sometimes with* to) **1** of poor, or poorer, quality *etc*: *This carpet is inferior to that*. □ **inférieur à**
2 lower in rank: *Is a colonel inferior to a brigadier?* □ **subalterne**
in,feri'ority [-'o-] *noun*. □ **infériorité**
infertile [in'fəːtail] *adjective* **1** (of soil *etc*) not fertile or producing good crops: *The land was stony and infertile*. □ **infertile**
2 (of persons or animals) unable to have young. □ **stérile**
,infer'tility [-'ti-] *noun*. □ **infertilité**
infest [in'fest] *verb* (of something bad) to swarm over and cover or fill: *The dog was infested with fleas*. □ **infester (de)**
,infe'station [infe-] *noun*. □ **infestation**
infidelity [infi'deləti] *noun* disloyalty or unfaithfulness (*eg* to one's husband or wife). □ **infidélité**
infiltrate ['infiltreit] *verb* **1** (of soldiers) to get through enemy lines a few at a time: *to infiltrate (into) enemy territory*. □ **(s')infiltrer (dans)**
2 (of a group of persons) to enter (an organization) gradually so as to be able to influence decisions *etc*. □ **(s')infiltrer (dans)**
infinite ['infinit] *adjective* **1** without end or limits: *We believe that space is infinite*. □ **infini**
2 very great: *Infinite damage could be caused by such a mistake*. □ **infini**
'infinitely *adverb* extremely; to a very great degree: *The time at which our sun will finally cease to burn is infinitely far away*. □ **infiniment**
'infiniteness *noun*. □ **infinitude**
in'finity [-'fi-] *noun* **1** space, time or quantity that is without limit, or is immeasurably great or small. □ **infini(té)**
2 in mathematics, an indefinitely large number, quantity or distance: *Parallel lines meet at infinity*. □ **infini**
infinitive [in'finətiv] *noun* the part of the verb used in English with or without *to*, that expresses an action but has no subject: *The sentence 'You need not stay if you want to go' contains two infinitives,' stay and go*. □ **infinitif**
infinity *see* **infinite**.
infirm [in'fəːm] *adjective* (of a person) weak or ill: *elderly and infirm people*. □ **infirme**
in'firmary – *plural* **in'firmaries** – *noun* a name given

to some hospitals. □ **hôpital, infirmerie**

in'firmity – *plural* in'firmities – *noun* weakness or illness. □ **infirmité**

inflame [in'fleim] *verb* to cause (feelings *etc*) to become violent. □ **enflammer**

in'flamed *adjective* hot and red *especially* because of infection: *Her throat was very inflamed.* □ **enflammé**

inflammable [in'flaməbl] *adjective* easily set on fire: *Paper is highly inflammable.* □ **inflammable**

in,flamma'bility *noun.* □ **inflammabilité**

inflammation [inflə'meiʃən] *noun* (a place in the body where there is) development of heat with pain, redness and swelling: *Tonsillitis is inflammation of the tonsils.* □ **inflammation**

---

inflammable means the same as **flammable**: *a highly inflammable gas.*

---

inflate [in'fleit] *verb* to blow up or expand (*especially* a balloon, tire or lungs with air): *He used a bicycle pump to inflate the ball.* □ **gonfler**

in'flatable *adjective* (of *eg* a cushion, ball *etc*) that can be filled with air for use: *an inflatable beach ball.* □ **gonflable**

in'flation *noun* 1 the process of inflating or being inflated. □ **gonflement**

2 a situation in country's economy where prices and wages keep forcing each other to increase. □ **inflation**

in'flationary *adjective* relating to economic inflation. □ **inflationniste**

inflexible [in'fleksəbl] *adjective* 1 (of a person) never yielding or giving way. □ **inflexible**

2 not able to bend. □ **rigide**

in'flexibly *adverb.* □ **inflexiblement**

in,flexi'bility *noun.* □ **inflexibilité**

inflict [in'flikt] *verb* (*with* on) to give or impose (something unpleasant and unwanted): *Was it necessary to inflict such a punishment on him?*; *She is always inflicting her company on me.* □ **infliger (qqch. à qqn)**

in'fliction [-ʃən] *noun.* □ **infliction**

influence ['influəns] *noun* 1 the power to affect people, actions or events: *He used his influence to get her the job*; *He should not have driven the car while under the influence of alcohol.* □ **influence**

2 a person or thing that has this power: *She is a bad influence on him.* □ **influence**

■ *verb* to have an effect on: *The weather seems to influence her moods.* □ **influer sur**

,influ'ential [-'enʃəl] *adjective* having much influence: *He is in quite an influential job*; *She was influential in getting the plan accepted.* □ **influent**

,influ'entially *adverb.* □ **avec une grande influence**

influenza [influ'enzə] (*usually abbreviated to* flu *or* 'flu [fluː]) *noun* a type of infectious illness *usually* causing headache, fever, a cold *etc.* □ **grippe**

influx ['inflʌks] *noun* an arrival of something in great quantities or numbers: *an influx of tourists.* □ **afflux**

inform [in'foːm] *verb* 1 to tell; to give knowledge to: *Please inform me of your intentions in this matter*; *I was informed that you were absent from the office.* □ **informer, avertir (de)**

2 (*with* against *or* on) to tell facts to *eg* the police about (a criminal *etc*): *He informed against his fellow thieves.* □ **dénoncer**

in'formant *noun* someone who tells or informs: *She passed on the news to us, but would not say who her informant had been.* □ **informateur, trice**

,infor'mation *noun* facts told or knowledge gained or given: *Can you give me any information about this writer?*; *the latest information on the progress of the war*; *He is full of interesting bits of information.* □ **renseignement, information**

in'formative [-mətiv] *adjective* giving useful information: *an informative book.* □ **instructif**

in'former *noun* a person who informs against a criminal *etc.* □ **indicateur, trice**

---

information does not have a plural: *some information*; *any information.*

---

informal [in'foːml] *adjective* 1 not formal or official; friendly and relaxed: *The two prime ministers will meet for informal discussions today*; *Will the party be formal or informal?*; *friendly, informal manners.* □ **informel**

2 (of speech or vocabulary) used in conversation but not *usually* when writing formally, speaking in public *etc*: *'Won't' and 'can't' are informal forms of 'will not' and 'cannot'.* □ **familier**

,infor'mality [-'ma-] *noun.* □ **simplicité**

in'formally *adverb.* □ **sans cérémonie**

infrared [infrə'red] *adjective* (of rays) below the red end of the spectrum. □ **infrarouge**

infrequent [in'friːkwənt] *adjective* not frequent: *His visits grew infrequent.* □ **rare**

in'frequency *noun.* □ **rareté**

infringe [in'frindʒ] *verb* to break (a law *etc*) or interfere with (a person's freedom or rights). □ **enfreindre, empiéter (sur), transgresser**

in'fringement *noun.* □ **transgression**

infuriate [in'fjuərieit] *verb* to make very angry: *I was infuriated by her words.* □ **rendre furieux**

in'furiating *adjective*: *I find his silly jokes infuriating.* □ **exaspérant**

in'furiatingly *adverb.* □ **de façon exaspérante**

ingenious [in'dʒiːnjəs] *adjective* 1 (of a person or his personality *etc*) clever at inventing: *He was ingenious at making up new games for the children.* □ **ingénieux**

2 (of an object or idea) cleverly made or thought out: *an ingenious plan/machine.* □ **ingénieux**

in'geniously *adverb.* □ **ingénieusement**

in'geniousness *noun.* □ **ingéniosité**

ingenuity [indʒə'njuːti] *noun.* □ **ingéniosité**

ingot ['ingət] *noun* a mass of metal (*eg* gold or silver) cast in a mould: *The gold was transported as ingots.* □ **lingot**

ingratitude [in'gratitjuːd] *noun* lack of gratitude: *I felt hurt by his ingratitude.* □ **ingratitude**

ingredient [in'griːdiənt] *noun* one of the things that go into a mixture: *Could you give me a list of the ingredients of the cake?* □ **ingrédient**

inhabit [in'habit] *verb* (of people, animals *etc*) to live in (a region *etc*): *Polar bears inhabit the Arctic region; That house is now inhabited by a Polish family.* □ **habiter**

in'**habitable** *adjective* (negative **uninhabitable**) fit to be lived in: *The building was no longer inhabitable.* □ **habitable**

in'**habitant** *noun* a person or animal that lives permanently in a place: *the inhabitants of the village; tigers, leopards and other inhabitants of the jungle.* □ **habitant, ante**

inhale [in'heil] *verb* to breathe in: *She inhaled deeply; It is very unpleasant to have to inhale the smoke from other people's cigarettes.* □ **respirer**

inhalation [in(h)ə'leiʃən] *noun.* □ **inhalation**

in'**haler** *noun* a *usually* small apparatus by means of which people inhale certain medicines. □ **inhalateur**

inherit [in'herit] *verb* 1 to receive (property *etc* belonging to someone who has died): *He inherited the house from his mother; She inherited four thousand dollars from her father.* □ **hériter (de)**

2 to have (qualities) the same as one's parents *etc*: *She inherits her quick temper from her father.* □ **tenir (qqch. de qqn)**

in'**heritance** *noun* 1 money *etc* inherited: *He spent most of his inheritance on drink.* □ **héritage**

2 the act of inheriting: *The property came to her by inheritance.* □ **héritage**

inhibit [in'hibit] *verb* to stop or hinder (*eg* someone from doing something). □ **empêcher (qqn de)**

in'**hibited** *adjective* unable to relax and express one's feelings in an open and natural way. □ **inhibé**

inhibition [ini'biʃən] *noun.* □ **inhibition**

inhospitable [inhə'spitəbl] *adjective* not welcoming guests; not friendly towards strangers: *She could not refuse to invite them in without seeming inhospitable.* □ **inhospitalier**

inhuman [in'hjuːmən] *adjective* extremely cruel or brutal; not seeming to be human: *His treatment of his children was quite inhuman.* □ **inhumain**

,inhu'**manity** [-'ma-] *noun* cruelty or lack of pity. □ **inhumanité**

inhumane [inhju'mein] *adjective* unkind or cruel: *inhumane treatment of prisoners-of-war.* □ **cruel**

,inhu'**manely** *adverb.* □ **inhumainement**

iniquity [i'nikwiti] – *plural* i'**niquities** – *noun* (an act of) wickedness. □ **iniquité**

initial [i'niʃəl] *adjective* of, or at, the beginning: *There were difficulties during the initial stages of building the house.* □ **initial**

■ *noun* the letter that begins a word, *especially* a name: *The picture was signed with the initials JJB, standing for John James Brown.* □ **initiale(s)**

■ *verb* – *past tense, past participle* i'**nitialled** – to mark or sign with initials of one's name: *Any alteration on a cheque should be initialled.* □ **parapher**

i'**nitially** *adverb* at the beginning; at first: *This project will cost a lot of money initially but will eventually make a profit.* □ **au début**

i'**nitiate**[1] [-ʃieit] *verb* 1 to start (*eg* a plan, scheme, changes, reforms *etc*): *She initiated a scheme for help-*

ing old people with their shopping. □ **instaurer**

2 to take (a person) into a society *etc, especially* with secret ceremonies: *No one who had been initiated into the society ever revealed the details of the ceremony.* □ **initier**

i'**nitiate**[2] [-ʃiət] *noun* a person who has been initiated (into a society *etc*). □ **initié, ée**

i,niti'**ation** [-ʃi'ei-] *noun* the act of initiating or process of being initiated. □ **initiation**

i'**nitiative** [-ʃətiv] *noun* 1 a first step or move that leads the way: *He took the initiative in organizing a search party to look for the girl; A move to start peace talks is sometimes called a peace initiative.* □ **initiative**

2 the ability to lead or make decisions for oneself: *He is quite good at his job, but lacks initiative; My son actually went to the hairdresser's on his own initiative!* □ **initiative**

inject [in'dʒekt] *verb* to force (a liquid *etc*) into the body of (a person) by means of a needle and syringe: *The doctor injected the antibiotic into her arm; He has to be injected twice daily with an antibiotic.* □ **faire une injection**

in'**jection** [-ʃən] *noun*: *The medicine was given by injection; She has regular injections of insulin.* □ **piqûre, injection**

injure ['indʒə] *verb* to harm or damage: *He injured his arm when he fell; They were badly injured when the car crashed; A story like that could injure her reputation; His pride has been injured.* □ **blesser, nuire (à)**

'**injured** *adjective* 1 (also *noun*) (people who have been) wounded or harmed: *The injured (people) were all taken to hospital after the accident.* □ **blessé**

2 (of feelings, pride *etc*) hurt: *'Why didn't you tell me before?' she said in an injured voice.* □ **offensé**

injurious [in'dʒuəriəs] *adjective* (with **to**) harmful: *Smoking is injurious to one's health.* □ **nuisible (à)**

'**injury** – *plural* '**injuries** – *noun* (an instance of) harm or damage: *Badly designed chairs can cause injury to the spine; The motorcyclist received severe injuries in the crash.* □ **lésion, blessure**

injustice [in'dʒʌstis] *noun* (an instance of) unfairness or the lack of justice: *He complained of injustice in the way he had been treated; They agreed that an injustice had been committed.* □ **injustice**

do (someone) an injustice to treat or regard (someone) unfairly: *You do me an injustice if you think I could tell such a lie.* □ **être injuste envers**

ink [iŋk] *noun* a black or coloured liquid used in writing, printing *etc*: *Please sign your name in ink rather than pencil; I spilt red ink all over my dress.* □ **encre**

'**inky** *adjective* 1 covered with ink: *inky fingers; Don't touch that wall – your hands are inky.* □ **taché d'encre**

2 like ink; black or very dark: *inky blackness.* □ **noir d'encre**

'**inkpot, 'inkwell** *nouns* a small pot for ink. □ **encrier**

inkling ['iŋkliŋ] *noun* a slight idea or suspicion (about something that is happening): *I had no inkling of what was going on until she told me all about it.* □ **idée, soupçon**

inky *see* **ink**.

inlaid *see* **inlay.**

inland ['inlənd] *adjective* **1** not beside the sea: *inland areas*. □ **intérieur**

2 done *etc* inside a country: *inland trade*. □ **intérieur**

■ [in'land] *adverb* in, or towards, the parts of the land away from the sea: *These flowers grow better inland*. □ **à l'intérieur (des terres)**

in-law ['inlɔː] – *plural* '**in-laws** – *noun* a person related to one by marriage *eg* one's brother-in-law, mother-in-law *etc*. □ **belle-famille; beau-frère, belle-mère**

inlay ['inlei] *noun* material set into the surface of *eg* a table to form a design: *The top of the table had an inlay of ivory*. □ **incrustation**

,**in'laid** *adjective* decorated in this way: *an inlaid table*. □ **incrusté**

inlet ['inlit] *noun* a small bay in the coastline of a sea, lake *etc*: *There are several pretty inlets suitable for bathing*. □ **anse**

inmate ['inmeit] *noun* one of the people living in an institution, *especially* a prison or mental hospital. □ **détenu, ue, interné, ée**

inmost *see* **innermost** *under* **inner.**

inn [in] *noun* **1** a name given to some small hotels or public houses *especially* in villages or the countryside. □ **auberge**

2 in former times, a house providing food and lodging for travellers. □ **auberge**

'**innkeeper** *noun* a person who owned or ran such a house. □ **aubergiste**

inner ['inə] *adjective* **1** placed *etc* on the inside or further in: *The inner tube of her tire was punctured*. □ **intérieur; chambre à air**

2 (of feelings *etc*) secret or hidden: *I could not guess what his inner thoughts might be*. □ **profond**

'**innermost** *adjective* **1** placed *etc* furthest from the edge or outside: *the innermost parts of the castle*. □ **le plus profond**

2 (*also* **inmost**) most secret or hidden: *his innermost feelings*; *in the inmost corners of his heart*. □ **le plus secret**

innocent ['inəsnt] *adjective* **1** not guilty (of a crime, misdeed *etc*): *A man should be presumed innocent of a crime until he is proved guilty*; *They hanged an innocent woman*. □ **innocent**

2 (of an action *etc*) harmless or without harmful or hidden intentions: *innocent games and amusements*; *an innocent remark*. □ **innocent**

3 free from, or knowing nothing about, evil *etc*: *an innocent child*; *You can't be so innocent as to believe what advertisements say!* □ **innocent**

'**innocently** *adverb*. □ **innocemment**

'**innocence** *noun*: *He at last managed to prove his innocence*; *the innocence of a child*. □ **innocence**

innocuous [i'nokjuəs] *adjective* harmless: *This drug was at first mistakenly thought to be innocuous*. □ **inoffensif**

innovation [inə'vei∫ən] *noun* (the act of making) a change or a new arrangement *etc*: *The new system in the school cafeteria was a welcome innovation*. □ **innovation**

'**innovator** *noun*. □ **innovateur, trice**

innumerable [i'njuːmərəbl] *adjective* too many to be counted; a great many: *innumerable difficulties*. □ **innombrable**

inoculate [i'nokjuleit] *verb* to give (a person *etc*) a mild form of a disease, *usually* by injecting germs into his body, so as to prevent him from catching a more serious form: *Has she been inoculated against diphtheria?* □ **vacciner (contre)**

i,nocu'lation *noun*. □ **vaccination, inoculation**

inoffensive [inə'fensiv] *adjective* harmless; not likely to offend: *an inoffensive remark*. □ **inoffensif**

inoperable [in'opərəbl] *adjective* not suitable for a surgical operation: *inoperable cancer*. □ **inopérable**

inorganic [inɔː'ganik] *adjective* not having the special characteristics of living bodies; not organic: *Stone, metal and other minerals are inorganic*. □ **inorganique**

in-patient ['inpei∫ənt] *noun* a patient living in, as well as receiving treatment in, a hospital. □ **malade hospitalisé, ée**

input ['input] *noun* **1** something, *eg* an amount of electrical energy, that is supplied to a machine *etc*. □ **puissance, consommation**

2 information put into a computer for processing. □ **données d'entrée**

inquest ['inkwest] *noun* a legal inquiry into a case of sudden and unexpected death. □ **enquête (criminelle)**

inquire, enquire [in'kwaiə] *verb* **1** to ask: *He inquired the way to the art gallery*; *She inquired what time the bus left*. □ **demander**

2 (*with* **about**) to ask for information about: *They inquired about trains to London*. □ **(s')informer (sur)**

3 (*with* **after**) to ask for information about the state of (*eg* a person's health): *He enquired after her mother*. □ **demander des nouvelles (de)**

4 (*with* **for**) to ask to see or talk to (a person): *Someone called inquiring for you, but you were out*. □ **demander**

5 (*with* **for**) to ask for (goods in a shop *etc*): *Several people have been inquiring for the new catalogue*. □ **demander**

6 (*with* **into**) to try to discover the facts of: *The police are inquiring into the matter*. □ **enquêter (sur)**

in'quiry ['inkwəri], **en'quiry** ['enkwəri] – *plural* **inquiries, enquiries** – *noun* **1** (an act of) asking or investigating: *His inquiries led him to her hotel*; (*also adjective*) *All questions will be dealt with at the inquiry desk*. □ **(demande de) renseignement(s)**

2 an investigation: *An inquiry is being held into her disappearance*. □ **enquête**

make inquiries to ask for information. □ **se renseigner**

inquisitive [in'kwizətiv] *adjective* eager to find out about other people's affairs: *He was rather inquisitive about the cost of our house*; *inquisitive neighbours*. □ **(trop) curieux**

in'quisitively *adverb*. □ **avec curiosité**

in'quisitiveness *noun*. □ **curiosité (indiscrète)**

insane [in'sein] *adjective* **1** mad; mentally ill. □ **dément**

2 extremely foolish: *It was insane to think she would give you the money*. □ **insensé**

in'sanity [-'sa-] *noun*. □ **folie, insanité**

insanitary [in'sanətəri] *adjective* so dirty as to be a dan-

ger to health: *living in crowded, insanitary conditions.*
□ **insalubre**
in'sanitariness *noun.* □ **insalubrité**
insatiable [in'seiʃəbl] *adjective* not able to be satisfied:
an insatiable desire for adventure. □ **insatiable**
in'satiably *adverb.* □ **insatiablement**
in'satiableness *noun.* □ **insatiabilité**
inscribe [in'skraib] *verb* to carve or write: *The monument was inscribed with the names of the men who died
in the war; She carefully inscribed her name in her new
book.* □ **inscrire**
inscription [in'skripʃən] *noun* something written, *eg*
on a gravestone or on a coin: *The coin was so worn that
the inscription could scarcely be read.* □ **inscription**
insect ['insekt] *noun* any of many kinds of small six-
legged creatures with wings and a body divided into
sections: *We were bothered by flies, wasps and other
insects.* □ **insecte**
insecticide [in'sektisaid] *noun* a substance (*usually* in
powder or liquid form) for killing insects. □ **insecticide**
,insec'tivorous [-'tivərəs] *adjective* (of plants or animals)
feeding (mainly) on insects. □ **insectivore**
insecure [insi'kjuə] *adjective* **1** unsure of oneself or lacking confidence: *Whenever he was in a crowd of people
he felt anxious and insecure.* □ **inquiet**
2 not safe or firmly fixed: *This chair's leg is insecure;
an insecure lock.* □ **peu sûr**
,inse'curely *adverb.* □ **sans sécurité**
,inse'curity *noun.* □ **insécurité**
insensible [in'sensəbl] *adjective* unconscious: *She lay
on the floor insensible.* □ **inconscient**
insensitive [in'sensətiv] *adjective* (*with* **to**) **1** not noticing or not sympathetic towards (*eg* others' feelings):
He was insensitive to her grief. □ **insensible (à)**
2 (*with* **to**) not feeling or not reacting to (touch, light
etc): *The dentist's injection numbed the nerves and made
the tooth insensitive to the drill.* □ **insensible (à)**
in,sensi'tivity *noun.* □ **insensibilité**
inseparable [in'sepərəbl] *adjective* not to be separated
or parted: *inseparable companions.* □ **inséparable**
insert [in'sɔːt] *verb* to put or place (something) in: *She
inserted the money in the parking meter; An extra chapter has been inserted into the book; They inserted the
announcement in the newpaper.* □ **insérer**
in'sertion [-ʃən] *noun.* □ **insertion**
inset ['inset] *noun* a small map, picture *etc* that has been
put in the corner of a larger one: *In a map of a coastline, there may be an inset to show offshore islands.* □
médaillon
inshore [in'ʃɔː] *adverb* near or towards the shore. □ **près
de la côte; vers la côte**
■ ['inʃɔː] *adjective* near the shore: *inshore fishing.* □ **côtier**
inside [in'said] *noun* **1** the inner side, or the part or space
within: *The inside of this apple is quite rotten.* □ **intérieur**
2 the stomach and bowels: *He ate too much and got a
pain in his inside(s).* □ **ventre**
■ ['insaid] *adjective* being on or in the inside: *the inside*

*pages of the newspaper; The inside traffic lane is the
one nearest to the curb.* □ **intérieur**
■ [in'said] *adverb* **1** to, in, or on, the inside: *The door
was open and he went inside; She shut the door but left
her key inside by mistake.* □ **à l'intérieur**
2 in a house or building: *You should stay inside in such
bad weather.* □ **dans, à l'intérieur**
■ ['in'said] *preposition* **1** (*sometimes with* **of**) within; to
or on the inside of: *She is inside the house; He went
inside the shop.* □ **à l'intérieur (de), dedans**
2 (*sometimes with* **of**) in less than, or within, a certain
time: *She finished the work inside (of) two days.* □ **en
moins de**
inside out 1 with the inner side out: *Haven't you got
your shirt on inside out?* □ **à l'envers**
2 very thoroughly: *She knows the plays of Shakespeare
inside out.* □ **à fond**
insight ['insait] *noun* (the quality of having) an understanding of something: *He shows remarkable insight
(into children's problems).* □ **perspicacité**
insignia [in'signiə] *noun plural* symbols worn or carried
as a mark of high office: *The crown and sceptre are the
insignia of a king.* □ **insignes**
insignificant [insig'nifikənt] *adjective* of little value or
importance; not significant: *They paid me an insignificant sum of money; an insignificant person.* □
insignifiant
,insig'nificance *noun.* □ **insignifiance**
insincere [insin'siə] *adjective* not sincere; not genuine:
His praise was insincere; insincere promises. □ **de
mauvaise foi**
,insin'cerely *adverb.* □ **sans sincérité**
,insin'cerity [-'se-] *noun.* □ **manque de sincérité**
insist [in'sist] *verb* **1** (*with* **that** *or* **on**) to state, emphasize, or hold firmly to (an opinion, plan *etc*): *She insists
that I was to blame for the accident; I insisted on driving him home.* □ **soutenir (que), insister (pour)**
2 (*often with* **on** *or* **that**) to demand or urge: *He insists
on punctuality/obedience; She insisted on coming with
me; He insisted that I should go.* □ **vouloir absolument
(que)**
in'sistence *noun* (the act of) insisting: *She went to see
the doctor at her husband's insistence.* □ **demande
pressante**
in'sistent *adjective.* □ **pressant**
insofar as *see* **in.**
insolent ['insələnt] *adjective* (of a person or his/her behaviour) insulting or offensive: *an insolent stare/remark.*
□ **insolent**
'insolently *adverb.* □ **insolemment**
'insolence *noun.* □ **insolence**
insoluble [in'soljubl] *adjective* **1** (of a substance) impossible to dissolve: *This chemical is insoluble (in water).* □ **insoluble**
2 (of a problem or difficulty) impossible to solve. □ **insoluble**
insolu'bility *noun.* □ **insolubilité**
insomnia [in'somniə] *noun* inability to sleep: *He takes
sleeping-pills as he suffers from insomnia.* □ **insomnie**
in'somniac [-ak] *noun, adjective* (of) a person who suf-

fers from insomnia. □ **insomniaque**

inspect [in'spekt] *verb* **1** to look at, or examine, carefully or formally: *She inspected the bloodstains.* □ **examiner (de près)**

2 to visit (*eg* a restaurant or school) officially, to make sure that it is properly run: *Cafés must be regularly inspected to find out if they are kept clean.* □ **inspecter**

3 to look at (troops *etc*) ceremonially: *The Queen will inspect the regiment.* □ **passer en revue**

in'spection [-ʃən] *noun.* □ **inspection, revue**

in'spector *noun* **1** a person appointed to inspect: *a school inspector.* □ **inspecteur, trice**

2 a police officer below a superintendent and above a sergeant in rank. □ **inspecteur, trice**

inspire [in'spaiə] *verb* **1** to encourage by filling with *eg* confidence, enthusiasm *etc*: *The players were inspired by the loyalty of their supporters and played better football than ever before.* □ **stimuler**

2 to be the origin or source of a poetic or artistic idea: *An incident in his childhood inspired the poem.* □ **inspirer**

inspiration [inspə'reiʃən] *noun.* □ **inspiration**

instability [instə'biləti] *noun* lack of stability or steadiness *eg* of personality. □ **instabilité**

install [in'stɔːl] *verb* **1** to put in place ready for use: *When was the telephone/electricity installed (in this house)?* □ **installer**

2 to put (a thing, oneself or another person) in a place or position: *She was installed as president yesterday; They soon installed themselves in the new house.* □ **(s')installer (dans)**

installation [instə'leiʃən] *noun* **1** the act of installing. □ **installation**

2 a piece of equipment that has been installed: *The cooker, fridge and other electrical installations are all in working order.* □ **installation**

in'stalment *noun* **1** one payment out of a number of payments into which an amount of money, *especially* a debt, is divided: *The new carpet is being paid for by monthly instalments.* □ **versement**

2 a part of a story that is printed one part at a time *eg* in a weekly magazine, or read in parts on the radio: *Did you hear the final instalment last week?* □ **épisode**

instance ['instəns] *noun* an example, *especially* of a condition or circumstance: *As a social worker, he saw many instances of extreme poverty.* □ **exemple**

for instance for example: *Some birds, penguins for instance, cannot fly at all.* □ **par exemple**

instant ['instənt] *adjective* **1** immediate: *Anyone disobeying these rules will face instant dismissal; Her latest play was an instant success.* □ **immédiat**

2 (of food *etc*) able to be prepared *etc* almost immediately: *instant coffee/potato.* □ **instantané**

■ *noun* **1** a point in time: *He climbed into bed and at that instant the telephone rang; She came the instant (that) she heard the news.* □ **instant**

2 a moment or very short time: *It all happened in an instant; I'll be there in an instant.* □ **instant**

'instantly *adverb* immediately: *She went to bed and instantly fell asleep.* □ **immédiatement**

this instant straight away; at this very moment: *Give it back this instant!* □ **immédiatement**

instantaneous [instən'teiniəs] *adjective* done, happening or acting in an instant or very quickly: *The effect of this poison is instantaneous.* □ **instantané**

,instan'taneously *adverb.* □ **instantanément**

instead [in'sted] *adverb* as a substitute; in place of something or someone: *I don't like coffee. Could I please have tea instead?* □ **à la place**

instead of in place of: *Please take me instead of him; You should have been working instead of watching television.* □ **à la place, au lieu de**

instep ['instep] *noun* the arched upper part of the foot: *The strap of that shoe is too tight across the instep.* □ **cou-de-pied**

instigate ['instigeit] *verb* to suggest and encourage (a wrong action, a rebellion *etc*). □ **être l'instigateur, trice de**

insti'gation *noun.* □ **instigation**

instil [in'stil] *– past tense, past participle* **in'stilled** *– verb* to put (ideas *etc*) into the mind of a person: *The habit of punctuality was instilled into me early in life.* □ **inculquer (à qqn)**

instinct ['instiŋkt] *noun* a natural tendency to behave or react in a particular way, without thinking and without having been taught: *As winter approaches, swallows fly south from Britain by instinct; He has an instinct for saying the right thing.* □ **instinct**

in'stinctive [-tiv] *adjective* arising from instinct or from a natural ability: *Blinking our eyes is an instinctive reaction when something suddenly comes close to them; I couldn't help putting my foot on the brake when I saw the other car coming towards me – it was instinctive.* □ **instinctif**

in'stinctively *adverb.* □ **instinctivement**

institute ['institjuːt] *noun* a society or organization, or the building it uses: *There is a lecture at the Philosophical Institute tonight.* □ **institut**

■ *verb* to start or establish: *When was the Red Cross instituted?* □ **fonder**

,insti'tution *noun* **1** the act of instituting or process of being instituted. □ **fondation**

2 (the building used by) an organization *etc* founded for a particular purpose, *especially* care of people, or education: *schools, hospitals, prisons and other institutions.* □ **établissement**

,insti'tutional *adjective.* □ **institutionnel**

instruct [in'strakt] *verb* **1** to teach or train (a person in a subject or skill): *Girls as well as boys should be instructed in woodwork.* □ **apprendre (qqch. à qqn)**

2 to order or direct (a person *especially* to do something): *He was instructed to come here at nine o'clock; I have already instructed you how to cook the meat.* □ **donner des instructions à**

in'struction [-ʃən] *noun* **1** the act of instructing (*especially* in a school subject or a skill) or the process of being instructed: *She sometimes gives instruction in gymnastics.* □ **enseignement, instruction**

2 an order or direction: *You must learn to obey instructions.* □ **instruction(s)**

3 (*in plural*) (a book *etc* giving) directions, *eg* about the use of a machine *etc*: *Could I look at the instructions, please?* □ **instructions**

in'structive [-tiv] *adjective* giving knowledge or information: *She gave an instructive talk about electrical repair work.* □ **instructif**

in'structively *adverb*. □ **d'une manière instructive**

in'structiveness *noun*. □ **caractère instructif**

in'structor – *feminine* **in'structress** – *noun* a person who gives instruction (in a skill *etc*): *a ski-instructor.* □ **entraîneur, euse, moniteur, trice**

instrument ['instrəmənt] *noun* **1** a tool, *especially* if used for delicate scientific or medical work: *medical/surgical/mathematical instruments.* □ **instrument**

2 (*also* **musical instrument**) an apparatus for producing musical sounds: *He can play the piano, violin and several other instruments.* □ **instrument (de musique)**

,instru'mental [-'men-] *adjective* performed on, or written for, musical instrument(s) rather than voices: *She likes instrumental music.* □ **instrumental**

,instru'mentalist [-'men-] *noun* a person who plays a musical instrument: *There are three instrumentalists and one singer in the group.* □ **instrumentiste**

insubordinate [insə'bɔːdənət] *adjective* (of a person or his behaviour) disobedient or rebellious: *an insubordinate employee.* □ **indiscipliné**

'insu,bordi'nation [-bɔː-] *noun*. □ **insubordination**

insufficient [insə'fiʃənt] *adjective* not enough: *The prisoner was released because the police had insufficient proof of his guilt.* □ **insuffisant**

,insuf'ficiently *adverb*. □ **insuffisamment**

,insuf'ficiency *noun*. □ **insuffisance**

insular ['insjulə] *adjective* of, or belonging to, an island or islands: *There are some plants that grow only in an insular climate.* □ **insulaire**

insulate ['insjuleit] *verb* to cover, protect or separate (something) with a material that does not let *especially* electrical currents or heat *etc* pass through it: *Rubber and plastic are used for insulating electric wires and cables.* □ **isoler**

,insu'lation *noun*. □ **isolation**

insulin ['insjulin] *noun* a substance used in the treatment of the disease diabetes. □ **insuline**

insult [in'sʌlt] *verb* to treat (a person) rudely or contemptuously: *He insulted her by telling her she was not only ugly but stupid too.* □ **insulter, injurier**

■ ['insʌlt] *noun* (a) comment or action that insults: *He took it as an insult that she did not shake hands with him.* □ **insulte, injure**

in'sulting *adjective* contemptuous or offensive: *insulting words.* □ **insultant, injurieux**

insuperable [in'sjuːpərəbl] *adjective* (of a problem *etc*) that cannot be overcome: *insuperable difficulties.* □ **insurmontable**

insure [in'ʃuə] *verb* to arrange for the payment of a sum of money in the event of the loss of (something) or accident or injury to (someone): *Is your car insured?*; *Employers have to insure employees against accident.* □ **assurer**

in'surance *noun* the promise of a sum of money in event of loss *eg* by fire or other disaster, given in compensation by a company *etc* in return for regular payments: *Have you paid the insurance on your jewellery?*; (*also adjective*) *insurance companies.* □ **(d')assurance(s)**

insurance policy (a document setting out) an agreement with an insurance company. □ **police d'assurance**

insurgent [in'sɜːdʒənt] *adjective* rising up in rebellion: *an insurgent population.* □ **insurgé**

■ *noun* a rebel: *the leading insurgents.* □ **insurgé, ée**

intact [in'takt] *adjective* undamaged or whole: *The box was washed up on the beach with its contents still intact.* □ **intact**

intake ['inteik] *noun* **1** the thing or quantity taken in: *This year's intake of students is smaller than last year's.* □ **admission(s)**

2 a place at which *eg* water is taken into a channel *etc*: *The ventilation system broke down when something blocked the main air intake.* □ **prise**

3 the act of taking in: *an intake of breath.* □ **prise**

integrate ['intigreit] *verb* to (cause to) mix freely with other groups in society *etc*: *The immigrants are not finding it easy to integrate into the life of our cities.* □ **(s')intégrer**

,inte'gration *noun*. □ **intégration**

integrity [in'tegrəti] *noun* honesty: *He is a man of absolute integrity.* □ **intégrité**

intellect ['intilekt] *noun* the thinking power of the mind: *She was a person of great intellect.* □ **intelligence**

,intel'lectual [-'lektʃuəl] *adjective* of, or appealing to, the intellect: *He does not play football – his interests are mainly intellectual.* □ **intellectuel**

intelligent [in'telidʒənt] *adjective* (*negative* **unintelligent**) **1** clever and quick at understanding: *an intelligent child*; *That dog is so intelligent.* □ **intelligent**

2 showing these qualities: *an intelligent question.* □ **intelligent**

in'telligently *adverb*. □ **intelligemment**

in'telligence *noun* **1** the quality of being intelligent: *It requires a high degree of intelligence to do this job well.* □ **intelligence**

2 news or information given. □ **renseignement(s)**

3 a department of state or of the army *etc* which deals with secret information: *She works in Intelligence.* □ **service de renseignements**

intelligible [in'telidʒəbl] *adjective* (*negative* **unintelligible**) able to be understood: *His answer was barely intelligible because he was speaking through a mouthful of food.* □ **intelligible**

in,telligi'bility *noun*. □ **intelligiblement**

in'telligibly *adverb*. □ **intelligibilité**

intend [in'tend] *verb* **1** to mean or plan (to do something or that someone else should do something): *Do you still intend to go?*; *Do you intend them to go?*; *Do you intend that they should go too?* □ **avoir l'intention de**

2 to mean (something) to be understood in a particular way: *Her remarks were intended to be a compliment.* □ **vouloir dire**

3 (with **for**) to direct at: *That letter/bullet was intended for me.* □ **être destiné à**

in'tent [-t] *adjective* **1** (with **on**) meaning, planning or wanting to do (something): *She's intent on going; He's intent on marrying the girl.* □ **décidé (à)**
2 (*with* **on**) concentrating hard on: *She was intent on the job she was doing.* □ **absorbé (par)**
■ *noun* purpose; what a person means to do: *He broke into the house with intent to steal.* □ **intention**

in'tention [-ʃən] *noun* what a person plans or intends to do: *He has no intention of leaving; She went to see the boss with the intention of asking for a raise; If I have offended you, it was quite without intention; good intentions.* □ **intention**

in'tentional [-ʃənl] *adjective* (*negative* **unintentional**) done, said *etc* deliberately and not by accident: *I'm sorry I offended you – it wasn't intentional; intentional cruelty.* □ **intentionnel**

in'tentionally *adverb.* □ **intentionnellement**

in'tently *adverb* with great concentration: *He was watching her intently.* □ **attentivement**

intense [in'tens] *adjective* very great: *intense heat; intense hatred.* □ **intense**

in'tensely *adverb* very much: *I dislike that sort of behaviour intensely.* □ **intensément**

in'tenseness *noun.* □ **intensité**

in'tensity *noun* the quality of being intense: *the intensity of the heat.* □ **intensité**

in'tensive [-siv] *adjective* very great; showing or having great care *etc*: *The police began an intensive search for the murderer; The hospital has just opened a new intensive care unit.* □ **intensif**

in'tensively *adverb.* □ **intensivement**

in'tensiveness *noun.* □ **intensité**

intent, intention *etc see* **intend.**

inter [in'təː] – *past tense, past participle* **in'terred** – *verb* to bury (a person *etc*). □ **enterrer**

in'terment *noun.* □ **enterrement**

interact [intər'akt] *verb* (of two or more people, things *etc*) to act, or have some effect, on each other. □ **(ré)agir réciproquement**

,inter'action [-ʃən] *noun.* □ **interaction**

intercede [intə'siːd] *verb* **1** to try to put an end to a fight, argument *etc* between two people, countries *etc*: *All attempts to intercede between the two nations failed.* □ **intercéder**
2 to try to persuade someone not to do something to someone else: *The condemned murderer's family interceded (with the President) on his behalf.* □ **intervenir (auprès de)**

,inter'cession [-'seʃən] *noun.* □ **intercession**

intercept [intə'sept] *verb* to stop or catch (a person, thing *etc*) before he, she, it *etc* arrives at the place to which he, she, it *etc* is going, being sent *etc*: *The messenger was intercepted on his way to the king.* □ **intercepter**

,inter'ception *noun.* □ **interception**

intercession *see* **intercede.**

interchange ['intətʃeindʒ] *noun* **1** a place where two or more main roads or highways at different levels are joined by means of several small roads, so allowing cars *etc* to move from one road to another. □ **échangeur**
2 (an) exchange: *an interchange of ideas.* □ **échange**

,inter'changeable *adjective* able to be used, put *etc* in the place of each other without a difference in effect, meaning *etc*: *'Great' and 'big' are not completely interchangeable.* □ **interchangeable**

intercom ['intəkom] *noun* a system of communication within an airplane, factory *etc usually* by means of microphones and loudspeakers: *The pilot spoke to the passengers over the intercom.* □ **interphone**

intercourse ['intəkoːs] *noun* **1** sexual intercourse. □ **rapports (sexuels)**
2 conversation, business dealings, trade *etc* between two or more people, countries *etc*. □ **relations**

interest ['intrəst] *noun* **1** curiosity; attention; *That newspaper story is bound to arouse interest.* □ **intérêt**
2 a matter, activity *etc* that is of special concern to one: *Gardening is one of my main interests.* □ **chose qui intéresse (qqn)**
3 money paid in return for borrowing a *usually* large sum of money: *The (rate of) interest on this loan is eight per cent; (also adjective) the interest rate.* □ **intérêt**
4 (a share in the ownership of) a business firm *etc*: *She bought an interest in the nightclub.* □ **participation**
5 a group of connected businesses which act together to their own advantage: *I suspect that the scheme will be opposed by the banking interest* (= all the banks acting together). □ **intérêts**
■ *verb* **1** to arouse the curiosity and attention of; to be of importance or concern to: *Political arguments don't interest me at all.* □ **intéresser**
2 (*with* **in**) to persuade to do, buy *etc*: *Can I interest you in (buying) this dictionary?* □ **intéresser (à)**

'interested *adjective* **1** (*often with* **in**) showing attention or having curiosity: *He's not interested in anything; Don't tell me any more – I'm not interested; I'll be interested to see what happens next week.* □ **intéressé (par)**
2 (*often with* **in**) willing, or wanting, to do, buy *etc*: *Are you interested in (buying) a used car?* □ **intéressé (par)**
3 personally involved in a particular business, project *etc* and therefore likely to be anxious about decisions made regarding it: *You must consult the other interested parties* (= the other people involved). □ **intéressé**

'interesting (*negative* **uninteresting**) *adjective*: *an interesting book.* □ **intéressant**

'interestingly *adverb.* □ **de façon intéressante**

in one's (own) interest bringing, or in order to bring, advantage, benefit, help *etc* to oneself *etc*: *It would be in our own interest to help him, as he may be able to help us later.* □ **dans son (propre) intérêt**

in the interest(s) of in order to get, achieve, increase *etc*: *The political march was banned in the interests of public safety.* □ **dans l'intérêt de**

lose interest to stop being interested: *She used to be very active in politics, but she's lost interest now.* □ **se désintéresser de**

take an interest to be interested: *I take a great interest in everything they do.* □ **s'intéresser (à)**

interfere [intə'fiə] *verb* **1** (*often with* **in, with**) to (try to) become involved in *etc*, when one's help *etc* is not wanted: *I wish you would stop interfering (with my* *plans*); *Don't interfere in other people's business!* □ **(se) mêler (de)**

2 (*with* **with**) to prevent, stop or slow down the progress of: *He doesn't let anything interfere with his game of golf on Saturday mornings.* □ **empêcher**

,**inter'ference** *noun* **1** the act of interfering: *She was infuriated by my interference in her holiday arrangements.* □ **ingérence**

2 (the spoiling of radio or television reception by) the noise caused by programs from another station, bad weather *etc*: *This television picks up a lot of interference.* □ **parasites**

,**inter'fering** *adjective*: *an interfering person.* □ **qui se mêle de tout**

interior [in'tiəriə] *adjective* on, of *etc*, the inside of (something): *the interior walls of a building.* □ **intérieur**

■ *noun* **1** the inside of a building *etc*: *The interior of the house was very attractive.* □ **intérieur**

2 the part of a country away from the coast, borders *etc*: *The explorers landed on the coast, and then travelled into the interior.* □ **intérieur**

interior decoration the art and process of designing, decorating, furnishing *etc* the insides of houses, offices *etc*. □ **décoration intérieure**

interior decorator a person who does interior decoration. □ **décorateur, trice**

interjection [intə'dʒekʃən] *noun* **1** a word or words, or some noise, used to express surprise, dismay, pain or other feelings and emotions: *Oh dear! I think I've lost my key; Ouch! That hurts!* □ **interjection**

2 the act of interjecting something. □ **exclamation**

,**inter'ject** *verb* to say (something) which interrupts what one, or someone else, is saying. □ **interrompre**

interlock [intə'lok] *verb* (of two or more pieces or parts) to fit or fasten together: *The pieces of a jigsaw puzzle interlock; interlocking pieces.* □ **(s')enclencher, (s')emboîter**

interlude ['intəluːd] *noun* a *usually* short period or gap, *eg* between the acts of a play: *We bought an ice cream during the interlude; an interlude of calm during the violence.* □ **intermède**

intermarry [intə'mari] *verb* (of tribes, families *etc*) to marry one another: *The invaders intermarried with the local population; The two families intermarried.* □ **(se) marier (entre soi)**

,**inter'marriage** [-ridʒ] *noun.* □ **intermariage**

intermediary [intə'miːdiəri] – *plural* **inter'mediaries** – *noun* a person who takes messages from one person to another in a dispute *etc*, *especially* in order to settle the dispute. □ **intermédiaire**

intermediate [intə'miːdiət] *adjective* in the middle; placed between two things, stages *etc*: *An intermediate English course is more advanced than a beginners' course, but not as difficult as an advanced course.* □ **intermédiaire**

interment *see* **inter**.

intermission [intə'miʃən] *noun* a *usually* short pause or gap between two (television or radio) programs, parts of a program, play *etc*. □ **pause, entracte**

intermittent [intə'mitənt] *adjective* happening occasion-

ally; stopping for a while and then starting again: *an intermittent pain.* □ **intermittent**

,**inter'mittently** *adverb*. □ **par intervalles**

intern¹ [in'təːn] *verb* during a war, to keep (someone who belongs to an enemy nation but who is living in one's own country) a prisoner. □ **interner**

in'ternment *noun*. □ **internement**

intern², interne ['intəːn] *noun* a junior doctor resident in a hospital. □ **interne**

internal [in'təːnl] *adjective* **1** of, on or in the inside of something (*eg* a person's body): *The man suffered internal injuries in the accident.* □ **interne**

2 concerning what happens within a country *etc*, rather than its relationship with other countries *etc*: *The prime ministers agreed that no country should interfere in another country's internal affairs.* □ **intérieur**

in'ternally *adverb*. □ **intérieurement**

internal combustion a means of producing power *eg* in the engine of a car by the burning of a fuel gas (*eg* gasoline vapour) inside the cylinder(s) of the engine. □ **combustion interne**

international [intə'naʃənl] *adjective* involving, or done by, two or more nations: *international trade; an international football match.* □ **international**

■ *noun* **1** a football *etc* match played between teams from two countries. □ **international**

2 (*also* ,**inter'nationalist**) a player in such a match. □ **international**

,**inter'nationally** *adverb*. □ **internationalement**

interne *see* **intern²**.

internment *see* **intern¹**.

interpret [in'təːprit] *verb* **1** to translate a speaker's words, while he or she is speaking, into the language of his or her hearers: *He spoke to the audience in French and she interpreted.* □ **faire l'interprète**

2 to explain the meaning of: *How do you interpret these lines of the poem?* □ **interpréter**

3 to show or bring out the meaning of (*eg* a piece of music) in one's performance of it: *The sonata was skilfully interpreted by the pianist.* □ **interpréter**

in,terpre'tation *noun*. □ **interprétation**

in'terpreter *noun* a person who translates the words of a speaker into the language of his hearers. □ **interprète**

interrogate [in'terəgeit] *verb* to question (a person) thoroughly: *The police spent five hours interrogating the prisoner.* □ **interroger**

in,terro'gation *noun*. □ **interrogation, interrogatoire**

in'terrogator *noun*. □ **interrogateur, trice**

interrogative [intə'rogətiv] *adjective, noun* (a word) that asks a question: *'Who ?' is an interrogative (pronoun).* □ **interrogatif**

interrupt [intə'rʌpt] *verb* **1** to stop a person while he is saying or doing something, *especially* by saying *etc* something oneself: *He interrupted her while she was speaking; He interrupted her speech; Listen to me and don't interrupt!* □ **interrompre**

2 to stop or make a break in (an activity *etc*): *She interrupted her work to eat her lunch; You interrupted my thoughts.* □ **interrompre**

3 to cut off (a view *etc*): *A block of flats interrupted* *their view of the sea.* □ **cacher**

‚inter'ruption [-ʃən] *noun* **1** the act of interrupting or state of being interrupted: *His failure to complete the job was due to constant interruption.* □ **interruption**
2 something that interrupts: *I get too many interruptions in my work.* □ **interruption**

intersect [intə'sekt] *verb* to divide (*eg* lines or roads) by cutting or crossing: *The line AB intersects the line CD at X; Where do the two roads intersect?* □ **(s')intersecter, (se) croiser**
‚inter'section [-ʃən] *noun* **1** the act of intersecting. □ **intersection**
2 a place where lines, roads *etc* intersect: *The crash occurred at the intersection (between the two roads).* □ **carrefour**

interval ['intəvəl] *noun* **1** a time or space between: *She returned home after an interval of two hours.* □ **intervalle**
2 a short break in a play, concert *etc*: *We had ice cream in the interval.* □ **entracte**
at intervals here and there; now and then: *Trees grew at intervals along the road.* □ **par intervalles**

intervene [intə'viːn] *verb* **1** to interfere in a quarrel: *He intervened in the dispute.* □ **intervenir (dans)**
2 to be or come between, in place or time: *A week intervened before our next meeting.* □ **s'écouler**
‚inter'vention [-'venʃən] *noun* (an) act of intervening (in a quarrel *etc*). □ **intervention**

interview ['intəvjuː] *noun* a formal meeting and discussion with someone, *eg* a person applying for a job, or a person with information to broadcast on radio or television. □ **entrevue, interview**
■ *verb* to question (a person) in an interview: *They interviewed seven people for the job; She was interviewed by reporters about her policies.* □ **interviewer**
'interviewer *noun.* □ **interviewer, euse**

intestine [in'testin] *noun* (*often in plural*) the lower part of the food passage in man and animals. □ **intestin**
intestinal [intes'tainl, in'testinl] *adjective.* □ **intestinal**

intimate ['intimət] *adjective* **1** close and affectionate: *intimate friends.* □ **intime**
2 private or personal: *the intimate details of his correspondence.* □ **intime**
3 (of knowledge of a subject) deep and thorough. □ **approfondi**
■ *noun* a close friend. □ **intime**
■ [-meit] *verb* to give information or announce. □ **annoncer**
‚inti'mation [-'mei-] *noun.* □ **annonce**
'intimacy [-məsi] *noun* **1** the quality of being intimate. □ **intimité**
2 close friendship. □ **amitié intime**
'intimately [-mət-] *adverb.* □ **intimement**

intimidate [in'timideit] *verb* to frighten *eg* by threatening violence. □ **intimider**
in‚timi'dation *noun.* □ **intimidation**

into ['intu] *preposition* **1** to or towards the inside of; to within: *The eggs were put into the box; They disappeared into the mist.* □ **dans**
2 against: *The car ran into the wall.* □ **dans**

3 to the state or condition of: *A tadpole turns into a frog; I've sorted the books into piles.* □ **en**
4 expressing the idea of division: *Two into four goes twice.* □ **divisé (par, en)**

intolerable [in'tolərəbl] *adjective* that cannot be endured or borne: *intolerable pain; This delay is intolerable.* □ **intolérable**
in'tolerably *adverb.* □ **intolérablement**

in'tolerant *adjective* (*often with* **of**) unwilling to endure or accept *eg* people whose ideas *etc* are different from one's own, members of a different race or religion *etc*: *an intolerant attitude; He is intolerant of others' faults.* □ **intolérant (de)**
in'tolerance *noun.* □ **intolérance**

intonation [intə'neiʃən] *noun* the rise and fall of the voice in speech. □ **intonation**

intoxicate [in'toksikeit] *verb* to make drunk. □ **(s')enivrer**
in‚toxi'cation *noun* drunkeness; a state of having consumed too much alcohol: *Karen drank too much at the party and was arrested for intoxication as she drove home.* □ **ébriété, ivresse**
in'toxicating *adjective.* □ **enivrant, alcoolique**

intransitive [in'transitiv] *adjective* (of a verb) that does not have an object: *The baby lay on the floor and kicked; Go and fetch the book!* □ **intransitif**
in'transitively *adverb.* □ **intransitivement**

intrepid [in'trepid] *adjective* bold and fearless: *an intrepid explorer.* □ **intrépide**
in'trepidly *adverb.* □ **intrépidement**
‚intre'pidity [-'pi-] *noun.* □ **intrépidité**

intricate ['intrikət] *adjective* complicated: *an intricate knitting pattern; intricate details.* □ **compliqué**
'intricately *adverb.* □ **de façon compliquée**
'intricacy – *plural* **'intricacies** – *noun.* □ **complexité**

intrigue [in'triːg, 'intriːg] *noun* the activity of plotting or scheming; a plot or scheme: *He became president as a result of (a) political intrigue.* □ **intrigue**
■ [in'triːg] *verb* **1** to fascinate, arouse the curiosity of or amuse: *The book intrigued me.* □ **intriguer**
2 to plot or scheme. □ **intriguer**
in'triguing *adjective* curious or amusing: *an intriguing idea.* □ **intrigant**

introduce [intrə'djuːs] *verb* **1** (*often with* **to**) to make (people) known by name to each other: *He introduced the guests (to each other); Let me introduce you to my mother; May I introduce myself? I'm John Brown.* □ **présenter**
2 (*often with* **into**) to bring in (something new): *Grey squirrels were introduced into Britain from Canada; Why did you introduce such a boring subject (into the conversation)?* □ **introduire**
3 to propose or put forward: *She introduced a bill in Parliament for the abolition of income tax.* □ **présenter**
4 (*with* **to**) to cause (a person) to get to know (a subject *etc*): *Children are introduced to algebra at about the age of eleven.* □ **initier (à)**
‚intro'duction [-'dʌkʃən] *noun* **1** the act of introducing, or the process of being introduced: *the introduction of new methods.* □ **introduction**

2 an act of introducing one person to another: *The hostess made the introductions and everyone shook hands.* □ **présentation**

3 something written at the beginning of a book explaining the contents, or said at the beginning of a speech *etc*. □ **introduction**

,intro'ductory [-'dʌktəri] *adjective* giving an introduction: *He made a few introductory remarks about the film before showing it.* □ **d'introduction**

introvert ['intrəvəːt] *noun* a person who is more concerned with his own thoughts and feelings than with other people or happenings outside him. □ **introverti, ie**

intrude [in'truːd] *verb* (*sometimes with* on) to enter, or cause (something) to enter, when unwelcome or unwanted: *He opened her door and said 'I'm sorry to intrude'; I'm sorry to intrude on your time.* □ **déranger, empiéter (sur)**

in'truder *noun* a person who intrudes, *eg* a burglar: *Place a good lock on your door to keep out intruders.* □ **intrus, use**

in'trusion [-ʒən] *noun* (an) act of intruding: *Please forgive this intrusion.* □ **intrusion**

intuition [intju'iʃən] *noun* **1** the power of understanding or realizing something without thinking it out: *He knew by intuition that she was telling him the truth.* □ **intuition**

2 something understood or realized by this power: *Her intuitions are always right.* □ **intuition**

intuitive [in'tjuːətiv] *adjective*. □ **intuitif**

inundate ['inʌndeit] *verb* to flood (a place, building *etc*). □ **inonder**

,inun'dation *noun*. □ **inondation**

invade [in'veid] *verb* (of an enemy) to enter (a country *etc*) with an army: *Britain was twice invaded by the Romans.* □ **envahir**

in'vader *noun* a person, or (*sometimes in singular with* the) an armed force *etc*, that invades: *Our armies fought bravely against the invader(s).* □ **envahisseur, euse**

in'vasion [-ʒən] *noun*. □ **invasion**

invalid[1] [in'valid] *adjective* (of a document or agreement *etc*) having no legal force; not valid: *Your passport is out of date and therefore invalid.* □ **non valable**

in'validate [-deit] *verb* to make invalid. □ **annuler**

invalidity [invə'lidəti] *noun*. □ **invalidité**

invalid[2] ['invəlid] *noun* a person who is ill or disabled: *During her last few years, she was a permanent invalid.* □ **malade, invalide**

invaluable [in'valjuəbl] *adjective* of value too great to be estimated: *Thank you for your invaluable help.* □ **inestimable**

invariable [in'veəriəbl] *adjective* unchanging; not variable. □ **invariable**

in'variably *adverb* always: *They invariably quarrel when he comes home.* □ **invariablement**

invasion *see* invade.

invent [in'vent] *verb* **1** to be the first person to make or use (*eg* a machine, method *etc*): *Who invented the microscope?; When was printing invented?* □ **inventer**

2 to make up or think of (*eg* an excuse or story): *I'll*

have to invent some excuse for not going with him. □ **inventer**

in'vention [-ʃən] *noun* **1** the act of inventing or the ability to invent: *She had great powers of invention.* □ **invention**

2 something invented: *What a marvellous invention the sewing machine was!* □ **invention**

in'ventive [-tiv] *adjective* good at inventing: *an inventive mind.* □ **inventif**

in'ventiveness *noun*. □ **esprit d'invention**

in'ventor *noun* a person who invents: *Alexander Graham Bell was the inventor of the telephone.* □ **inventeur, trice**

see also **discover**.

inventory ['invəntri] – *plural* 'inventories – *noun* a formal and detailed list of goods *eg* house furniture. □ **inventaire**

invert [in'vəːt] *verb* to turn upside down or reverse the order of. □ **inverser**

in'version [-ʃən] *noun*. □ **inversion, renversement**

inverted commas single or double commas, the first (set) of which is turned upside down (" ", ' '), used in writing to show where direct speech begins and ends: *"It is a lovely day," she said.* □ **guillemets**

invertebrate [in'vəːtibrət] *adjective, noun* (an animal *eg* a worm or insect) not having a backbone. □ **invertébré**

invest[1] [in'vest] *verb* (*with* in) to put (money) into (a firm or business) *usually* by buying shares in it, in order to make a profit: *He invested (two hundred dollars) in a building firm.* □ **investir, placer**

in'vestment *noun* **1** the act of investing. □ **investissement, placement**

2 a sum of money invested. □ **investissement, placement**

in'vestor *noun* a person who invests money. □ **investisseur, euse**

invest[2] [in'vest] *verb* to establish (a person) officially in a position of authority *etc*: *The governor will be invested next week.* □ **investir**

in'vestiture [-titʃə] *noun* (a ceremony of) giving (the robes *etc* of) high rank or office to someone. □ **investiture**

investigate [in'vestigeit] *verb* to examine or inquire into carefully: *The police are investigating the mystery.* □ **enquêter (sur)**

in,vesti'gation *noun*. □ **enquête**

in'vestigator *noun* a person, *eg* a detective, who investigates. □ **enquêteur, euse**

investment *see* invest[1].

invigilate [in'vidʒileit] *verb* to supervise students while they are doing an examination: *I am going to invigilate (the candidates) (at) the English exam.* □ **surveiller**

in,vigi'lation *noun*. □ **surveillance**

in'vigilator *noun*. □ **surveillant, ante**

invigorate [in'vigəreit] *verb* to strengthen or refresh: *The shower invigorated her.* □ **vivifier**

in'vigorating *adjective*. □ **vivifiant**

invincible [in'vinsəbl] *adjective* that cannot be overcome

or defeated: *That general thinks that his army is invincible.* □ **invincible**
in'vincibly *adverb.* □ **invinciblement**
in,vinci'bility *noun.* □ **invincibilité**
invisible [in'vizəbl] *adjective* not able to be seen: *Only in stories can people make themselves invisible.* □ **invisible**
in'visibly *adverb.* □ **invisiblement**
in,visi'bility *noun.* □ **invisibilité**
invite [in'vait] *verb* 1 to ask (a person) politely to come (*eg* to one's house, to a party *etc*): *They have invited us to dinner tomorrow.* □ **inviter (à)**
2 to ask (a person) politely to do something: *She was invited to speak at the meeting.* □ **inviter**
3 to ask for (another person's suggestions *etc*): *He invited proposals from members of the society.* □ **solliciter**
invitation [invi'teiʃən] *noun* 1 a (written) request to come or go somewhere: *Have you received an invitation to their party?*; *We had to refuse the invitation to the wedding.* □ **invitation**
2 the act of inviting: *She attended the committee meeting on the invitation of the chairman.* □ **invitation**
in'viting *adjective* (*negative* **uninviting**) attractive or tempting: *There was an inviting smell coming from the kitchen.* □ **invitant**
invocation *see* **invoke.**
invoice ['invois] *noun* a list sent with goods giving details of price and quantity. □ **facture**
invoke [in'vouk] *verb* to appeal to (some power, *eg* God, the law *etc*) for help *etc.* □ **invoquer**
invocation [invə'keiʃən] *noun.* □ **invocation**
involuntary [in'voləntəri] *adjective* (of an action *etc*) not intentional: *He gave an involuntary cry.* □ **involontaire**
in'voluntarily *adverb.* □ **involontairement**
involve [in'volv] *verb* 1 to require; to bring as a result: *Her job involves a lot of travelling.* □ **nécessiter**
2 (*often with* **in** or **with**) to cause to take part in or to be mixed up in: *She has always been involved in/with the theatre*; *Don't ask my advice – I don't want to be/get involved.* □ **mêler (à)**
in'volved *adjective* complicated: *My schedule for Friday is becoming very involved.* □ **compliqué**
in'volvement *noun.* □ **engagement**
invulnerable [in'vʌlnərəbl] *adjective* that cannot be wounded, damaged or successfully attacked: *As a friend of the manager, he is in an invulnerable position.* □ **invulnérable**
inward ['inwəd] *adjective* 1 being within, *especially* in the mind: *his inward thoughts.* □ **intime**
2 moving towards the inside: *an inward curve in the coastline.* □ **vers l'intérieur**
'inward, 'inwards *adverb* towards the inside or the centre: *When one of the eyes turns inwards, we call the effect a squint.* □ **vers l'intérieur**
'inwardly *adverb* in one's thoughts; secretly: *He was inwardly pleased when she failed*; *She was laughing/groaning inwardly.* □ **en son for intérieur**
iodine ['aiədi:n] *noun* 1 an element used in medicine and photography, forming black crystals. □ **iode**

2 a liquid form of the element used as an antiseptic. □ **(teinture d')iode**
irascible [i'rasibl] *adjective* irritable; easily made angry. □ **irascible**
i'rascibly *adverb.* □ **avec colère**
i,rasci'bility *noun.* □ **irascibilité**
irate [ai'reit] *adjective* angry. □ **furieux**
iridescent [iri'desnt] *adjective* shining or glittering with the colours of the rainbow: *Soap bubbles are iridescent.* □ **irisé**
,iri'descence *noun.* □ **irisation**
iris ['aiəris] *noun* 1 the coloured part of the eye. □ **iris**
2 a kind of brightly coloured flower with sword shaped leaves. □ **iris**
Irish [aiərəʃ] *adjective* of Ireland or its inhabitants: *Margaret has a dishtowel made of Irish linen*; *My Irish grandmother visited Montreal for the first time last year.* □ **irlandais, irlandaise**
■ *noun* the people of Ireland: *The Irish have a reputation for being superstitious.* □ **Irlandais**
iron ['aiən] *noun* 1 (*also adjective*) (of) an element that is the most common metal, is very hard, and is widely used for making tools *etc*: *Steel is made from iron*; *The ground is as hard as iron*; *iron railings*; *iron determination* (= very strong determination). □ **fer**
2 a flat-bottomed instrument that is heated up and used for smoothing clothes *etc*: *I've burnt a hole in my dress with the iron.* □ **fer (à repasser)**
3 a type of golf-club. □ **fer**
■ *verb* to smooth (clothes *etc*) with an iron: *This dress needs to be ironed*; *I've been ironing all afternoon.* □ **repasser**
'ironing *noun* clothes *etc* waiting to be ironed, or just ironed: *What a huge pile of ironing!* □ **repassage**
'irons *noun plural* formerly, a prisoner's chains: *They put him in irons.* □ **fers**
'ironing board *noun* a padded board on which to iron clothes. □ **planche à repasser**
have several, too many *etc* **irons in the fire** to be involved in, or doing, several *etc* things at the same time. □ **mener trop d'affaires de front, courir deux lièvres à la fois**
iron out 1 to get rid of (creases *etc*) by ironing. □ **faire disparaître au fer**
2 to get rid of (difficulties *etc*) so that progress becomes easier. □ **aplanir**
strike while the iron is hot to act *etc* while the situation is favourable. □ **battre le fer pendant qu'il est chaud**
irony ['aiərəni] – *plural* 'ironies – *noun* 1 a form of deliberate mockery in which one says the opposite of what is obviously true. □ **ironie**
2 seeming mockery in a situation, words *etc*: *The irony of the situation was that he stole the money which she had already planned to give him.* □ **ironie**
ironic(al) [ai'ronik(l)] *adjective.* □ **ironique**
i'ronically *adverb.* □ **ironiquement**
irregular [i'regjulə] *adjective* 1 not happening *etc* regularly: *His attendance at classes was irregular.* □ **irrégulier**

2 not formed smoothly or evenly: *irregular handwriting*. □ **irrégulier**
3 contrary to rules. □ **irrégulier**
4 (in grammar) not formed *etc* in the normal way: *irregular verbs*. □ **irrégulier**
ir'**regularly** *adverb*. □ **irrégulièrement**
ir'**regu'larity** [-'la-] *noun* (*plural* irregu'larities). □ **irrégularité**
irrelevant [i'relivənt] *adjective* not connected with the subject that is being discussed *etc*: *irrelevant comments*. □ **sans rapport avec la question**
ir'**relevantly** *adverb*. □ **hors de propos**
ir'**relevance** *noun*. □ **manque d'à-propos**
ir'**relevancy** *noun*. □ **manque d'à-propos**
irreparable [i'repərəbl] *adjective* (of damage *etc*) that cannot be put right. □ **irréparable**
ir'**reparably** *adverb*. □ **irrémédiablement**
irreplaceable [iri'pleisəbl] *adjective* too good, rare *etc* to be able to be replaced if lost or damaged. □ **irremplaçable**
irrepressible [iri'presəbl] *adjective* not able to be subdued; very cheerful. □ **irrésistible**
irresistible [iri'zistəbl] *adjective* too strong, delightful, tempting *etc* to be resisted: *He had an irresistible desire to call her.* □ **irrésistible**
,irre'**sistibly** *adverb*. □ **irrésistiblement**
'irre,sisti'**bility** *noun*. □ **caractère irrésistible**
irrespective [iri'spektiv]: **irrespective of** without consideration of: *The pupils are all taught together, irrespective of age or ability.* □ **sans tenir compte de**
irresponsible [iri'sponsəbl] *adjective* (of a person or his behaviour) not reliable, trustworthy or sensible; not responsible: *irresponsible parents/conduct.* □ **irresponsable**
'irre,sponsi'**bility** *noun*. □ **irresponsabilité**
,irre'**sponsibly** *adverb*. □ **irresponsablement**
irretrievable [iri'triːvəbl] *adjective* (of *eg* a loss or mistake) that cannot be recovered or put right. □ **irréparable**
,irre'**trievably** *adverb*. □ **irréparablement**
irreverent [i'revərənt] *adjective* showing no respect or reverence (*eg* for holy things, or people and things generally considered important). □ **irrévérencieux**
ir'**reverently** *adverb*. □ **irrévérencieusement**
ir'**reverence** *noun*. □ **irrévérence**
irreversible [iri'vəːsəbl] *adjective* that cannot be reversed or changed back; (of damage) permanent. □ **irréversible**
irrigate ['irigeit] *verb* to supply water to (land), *especially* by canals or other artificial means. □ **irriguer**
,irri'**gation** *noun*. □ **irrigation**
irritate ['iriteit] *verb* 1 to annoy or make angry: *The children's chatter irritated him.* □ **agacer**
2 to make (a part of the body) sore, red, itchy *etc*: *Soap can irritate a baby's skin.* □ **irriter**
'irritable *adjective* easily annoyed: *She was in an irritable mood.* □ **irritable**
'irritably *adverb*. □ **avec irritation**
,irrita'**bility** *noun*. □ **mauvais caractère**
'irritableness *noun*. □ **irritabilité**

'irritating *adjective*: *She has an irritating voice.* □ **agaçant**
,irri'tation *noun*. □ **irritation**
is *see* **be**.
Islam ['izlaːm] *noun* the Muslim religion. □ **Islam**
Is'lamic [-'la-] *adjective* of Islam: *Islamic festivals.* □ **islamique**
island ['ailənd] *noun* 1 a piece of land surrounded by water: *The island lay a kilometre off the coast.* □ **île**
2 (*also* **traffic island**) a traffic-free area, built in the middle of a street, for pedestrians to stand on. □ **refuge**
'islander *noun*. □ **insulaire**
isle [ail] *noun* (used mostly in place-names) an island: *the Isle of Wight.* □ **île**
isn't *see* **be**.
isolate ['aisəleit] *verb* to separate, cut off or keep apart from others: *Several houses have been isolated by the flood water; A child with an infectious disease should be isolated.* □ **isoler**
'isolated *adjective* lonely; standing alone. □ **isolé**
,iso'lation *noun*. □ **isolement**
issue ['iʃuː] *verb* 1 to give or send out, or to distribute, *especially* officially: *The police issued a description of the criminal; Rifles were issued to the troops.* □ **distribuer**
2 to flow or come out (from something): *A strange noise issued from the room.* □ **sortir (de)**
■ *noun* 1 the act of issuing or process of being issued: *Stamp collectors like to buy new stamps on the day of issue.* □ **émission**
2 one number in the series of a newspaper, magazine *etc*: *Have you seen the latest issue of that magazine?* □ **numéro**
3 a subject for discussion and argument: *The question of pay is not an important issue at the moment.* □ **question**
isthmus ['isməs] *noun* a narrow strip of land joining two larger pieces: *the Isthmus of Panama.* □ **isthme**
it [it] *pronoun* 1 (used as the subject of a verb or object of a verb or preposition) the thing spoken of, used *especially* of lifeless things and of situations, but also of animals and babies: *If you find my pencil, please give it to me; The dog is in the garden, isn't it?; I picked up the baby because it was crying; He decided to run a kilometre every morning but he couldn't keep it up.* □ **il, elle, le, la, lui**
2 used as a subject in certain kinds of sentences *eg* in talking about the weather, distance or time: *Is it raining very hard?; It's cold; It is five o'clock; Is it the fifth of March?; It's two kilometres to the village; Is it your turn to make the tea?; It is impossible for her to finish the work; It was nice of you to come; Is it likely that he would go without us?* □ **il, ce**
3 (*usually* as the subject of the verb **be**) used to give emphasis to a certain word or phrase: *It was you (that) I wanted to see, not Mary.* □ **ce**
4 used with some verbs as a direct object with little meaning: *The car broke down and we had to walk it.* □ **ça**
its *adjective* belonging to it: *The bird has hurt its wing.*

□ **son, sa, ses**

itself *pronoun* **1** used as the object of a verb or preposition when an object, animal *etc* is the object of an action it performs: *The cat looked at itself in the mirror; The cat stretched itself by the fire.* □ **lui-même, elle-même**

2 used to emphasize **it** or the name of an object, animal *etc*: *The house itself is quite small, but the garden is big.* □ **lui-même, elle-même**

3 without help *etc*: *'How did the dog get in?' 'Oh, it can open the gate itself.'* □ **tout seul**

---

its is an adjective or pronoun expressing possession: *a cat and its kittens.*

it's is short for **it is** or **it has**: *It's raining heavily.*

Italian [əta:ljən] *adjective* of Italy or its inhabitants: *When you are in Italy be sure to go to an Italian opera; My sister married an Italian artist who was painting in Canada.* □ **italien, italienne**

■ *noun* a native of Italy or the language of Italy: *Two Italians rented the house on the beach; Shaun's wife speaks English, French and Italian.* □ **Italien**

italic [i'talik] *adjective* (of print) of the sloping kind used *eg* to show emphasis and for the examples in this dictionary: *This example is printed in italic type.* □ **italique**

i'talicize, i'talicise [-saiz] *verb* to put (words) in italics. □ **mettre en italique**

i'talics *noun plural* italic print: *This example is printed in italics.* □ **italique**

itch [itʃ] *noun* an irritating feeling in the skin that makes one want to scratch: *She had an itch in the middle of her back and could not scratch it easily.* □ **démangeaison**

■ *verb* **1** to have an itch: *Some plants can cause the skin to itch.* □ **démanger**

2 to have a strong desire (for something, or to be something): *I was itching to go.* □ **mourir d'envie de**

'itchy *adjective* itching: *an itchy rash; I feel itchy all over.* □ **qui démange**

'itchiness *noun.* □ **démangeaison**

it'd *see* **have, would**.

item ['aitəm] *noun* **1** a separate object, article *etc*, especially one of a number named in a list: *He ticked the items as he read through the list.* □ **article**

2 a separate piece of information or news: *Did you see the item about dogs in the newspaper?* □ **article**

itinerant [i'tinərənt] *adjective* travelling from place to place, *eg* on business: *an itinerant preacher.* □ **itinérant**

itinerary [ai'tinərəri] *noun* a route for a journey. □ **itinéraire**

it'll *see* **will**.

its, itself *see* **it**.

it's *see* **be, have**.

I've *see* **have**.

ivory ['aivəri] *noun, adjective* (of) the hard white substance forming the tusks of an elephant, walrus *etc*: *Ivory was formerly used to make piano keys; ivory chessmen.* □ **(en/d')ivoire**

ivy ['aivi] *noun* a type of climbing evergreen plant with small shiny leaves that grows up trees and walls. □ **lierre**

Jj

jab [dʒab] – *past tense, past participle* **jabbed** – *verb* to poke or prod: *He jabbed me in the ribs with his elbow*; *She jabbed the needle into her finger.* □ **enfoncer, planter**
■ *noun* a sudden hard poke or prod: *He gave me a jab with his finger*; *a jab of pain.* □ **coup**

jabber [dʒabə] *verb* to talk idly, rapidly and indistinctly: *These persons are always jabbering with one another.* □ **bredouiller**

jack [dʒak] *noun* 1 an instrument for lifting up a car or other heavy weight: *You should always keep a jack in the car in case you need to change a wheel.* □ **cric**
2 the playing-card between the ten and queen, sometimes called the **knave**: *The jack, queen and king are the three face cards.* □ **valet**
jack up to raise (a car *etc*) and keep it supported, with a jack: *You need to jack up the car before you try to remove the wheel.* □ **soulever avec un cric**

jackal [dʒakɔːl] *noun* a type of wild animal similar to a dog or wolf. □ **chacal**

jackass [dʒakas] *noun* 1 a male ass. □ **âne**
2 a stupid person: *the silly jackass!* □ **idiot, idiote**
laughing jackass a type of Australian bird that sounds as if it is laughing. □ **dacélo**

jackboot [dʒakbuːt] *noun* a type of tall *especially* military boot that reaches above the knee. □ **bottes à l'écuyère**

jackdaw [dʒakdɔː] *noun* a type of bird of the crow family that sometimes steals bright objects. □ **choucas**

jacket [dʒakit] *noun* 1 a short coat: *He wore brown trousers and a blue jacket.* □ **veston**
2 a covering, *especially* a loose paper cover for a book: *I like the design on this (book-)jacket.* □ **jaquette**

jack-in-the-box [dʒakinðəboks] *noun* a toy consisting of a figure, fixed to a spring inside a box, which comes out suddenly when the lid is opened. □ **boîte à surprise**

jack-knife [dʒaknaif] *noun* a large folding knife. □ **couteau de poche**
■ *verb* (of *eg* a truck and its trailer) to swing together so that the trailer is at a sharp angle to the cab: *The truck skidded and jack-knifed, blocking the road.* □ **se mettre en travers**

jackpot [dʒakpot] *noun* in playing cards, some competitions *etc*, a fund of prize-money that goes on increasing until it is won. □ **gros lot**
hit the jackpot to win or obtain a lot of money or success: *She must have hit the jackpot with the sales of her last gramophone record.* □ **gagner le gros lot**

jade [dʒeid] *noun, adjective* (of) a type of hard stone, *usually* green in colour: *a piece of jade; jade ornaments.* □ **(de) jade**

jaded [dʒeidid] *adjective* (of *eg* a person or his interest, appetite *etc*) worn out and made tired and dull. □ **épuisé**

jagged [dʒagid] *adjective* having rough or sharp and uneven edges: *jagged rocks.* □ **déchiqueté**
jaggedly *adverb.* □ **en dents de scie**
jaggedness *noun.* □ **aspect déchiqueté**

jaguar [dʒagjuə] *noun* a South American beast of prey of the cat family, resembling the leopard. □ **jaguar**

jail [dʒeil] *noun* (a) prison: *You ought to be sent to jail for doing that.* □ **prison**
■ *verb* to put in prison: *He was jailed for two years.* □ **emprisonner**
jailer, jailor *noun* a person who has charge of a jail or of prisoners: *The jailer was knocked unconscious in the riot.* □ **gardien, ienne de prison**
jailbird *noun* a person who is or has often been in jail. □ **récidiviste**

to put a criminal in **jail**.

jam¹ [dʒam] *noun* a thick sticky substance made of fruit *etc* preserved by being boiled with sugar: *raspberry jam*; *(also adjective) a jam sandwich.* □ **confiture**
jammy *adjective* covered with jam: *jammy fingers.* □ **collant**

jam² [dʒam] – *past tense, past participle* **jammed** – *verb* 1 to crowd full: *The gateway was jammed with angry people.* □ **bloquer**
2 to squeeze, press or wedge tightly or firmly: *She jammed her foot in the doorway.* □ **coincer**
3 to stick and (cause to) be unable to move: *The door/steering wheel has jammed.* □ **(se) bloquer**
4 (of a radio station) to cause interference with (another radio station's broadcast) by sending out signals on a similar wavelength. □ **brouiller**
■ *noun* 1 a crowding together of vehicles, people *etc* so that movement is difficult or impossible: *traffic jams.* □ **embouteillage**
2 a difficult situation: *I'm in a bit of a jam – I haven't got enough money to pay for this meal.* □ **pétrin**
jam on to put (brakes *etc*) on with force and haste: *When the dog ran in front of his car he jammed on his brakes and skidded.* □ **bloquer**

jamboree [dʒambəriː] *noun* 1 a large and lively gathering. □ **réjouissances**
2 a rally of Boy Scouts, Girl Guides *etc*. □ **jamboree**
jammed *see* **jam²**.
jammy *see* **jam¹**.

jangle [dʒaŋgl] *verb* to (cause to) give a harsh (ringing) sound: *The bell jangled noisily.* □ **retentir (avec un bruit de ferraille)**

janitor [dʒanitə] *noun* a caretaker or a doorkeeper. □ **concierge**

January [dʒanjuəri] *noun* the first month of the year, the month following December. □ **janvier**

Japanese [dʒapəniːz] *adjective* of Japan or its inhabitants: *A Japanese skier placed first in the downhill race; The traditional Japanese kimono is a robe with wide loose sleeves.* □ **Japonais**
■ *noun* the people or language of Japan: *The Japanese eat a diet that is low in fat; Although Kim worked in Tokyo, she never learned how to speak Japanese.* □ **Japonais**

jar¹ [dʒaː] *noun* 1 a kind of bottle made of glass or pottery, with a wide mouth: *He poured the jam into large jars; jam jars.* □ **pot, bocal**
2 a container that has a wide opening and is usually

made of glass: *When Mom makes pickles, she stores them in sterilized mason jars.* □ **bocal**

jar² [dʒɑːr] – *past tense, past participle* **jarred** – *verb* 1 (*with* on) to have a harsh and startling effect (on): *Her sharp voice jarred on my ears.* □ **écorcher**

2 to give a shock to: *The car accident had jarred her nerves.* □ **ébranler**

'jarring *adjective* startling or harsh: *The orange curtains with the purple carpet had a jarring effect.* □ **discordant**

jargon ['dʒɑːrgən] *noun* special words or phrases used within a group, trade or profession *etc*: *legal jargon*; *medical jargon*; *Thieves use a special jargon in order to confuse passing hearers.* □ **jargon**

jarred, jarring *see* **jar²**.

jaundice ['dʒɔːndis] *noun* a diseased state of the body in which the skin and whites of the eyes become yellow. □ **jaunisse**

jaunt [dʒɔːnt] *noun* a brief trip or journey made for pleasure: *Did you enjoy your jaunt to Paris?* □ **balade**

jaunty ['dʒɔːnti] *adjective* cheerful, bright, lively: *a jaunty mood/hat.* □ **désinvolte**

'jauntily *adverb.* □ **avec désinvolture**

'jauntiness *noun.* □ **désinvolture**

javelin ['dʒavəlin] *noun* a light spear for throwing *eg* as an event in an athletic competition. □ **javelot**

jaw [dʒɔː] *noun* 1 either of the two bones of the mouth in which the teeth are set: *the upper/lower jaw*; *His jaw was broken in the fight.* □ **mâchoire**

2 (*in plural*) the mouth (*especially* of an animal): *The crocodile's jaws opened wide.* □ **mâchoires, gueule**

jaywalker ['dʒeiwɔːkə] *noun* a person who walks carelessly among traffic: *She never looks to see if there's a car coming before she crosses the road – she's a jaywalker.* □ **piéton indiscipliné**

'jaywalking *noun*: *The police were concerned about the number of accidents involving jaywalking.* □ **indiscipline des piétons**

jazz [dʒaz] *noun* popular music of American Negro origin: *She prefers jazz to classical music*; (*also adjective*) *a jazz musician.* □ **(de) jazz**

'jazzy *adjective* 1 bright or bold in colour or design: *a jazzy shirt.* □ **voyant**

2 of or like jazz: *jazzy music.* □ **(de) jazz**

jealous ['dʒeləs] *adjective* 1 (*with* of) feeling or showing envy: *She is jealous of her sister.* □ **jaloux (de)**

2 having feelings of dislike for any possible rivals (*especially* in love): *a jealous husband.* □ **jaloux**

'jealously *adverb.* □ **jalousement**

'jealousy *noun.* □ **jalousie**

jeans [dʒiːnz] *noun plural* trousers, *usually* tight-fitting, made of denim. □ **jean**

jeep [dʒiːp] *noun* a kind of small motor vehicle used *especially* by the armed forces. □ **jeep**

jeer [dʒiə] *verb* 1 to shout at or laugh at rudely or mockingly: *He was jeered as he tried to speak to the crowds.* □ **huer**

2 (*with* at) to make fun of (someone) rudely: *He's always jeering at you.* □ **(se) moquer (de)**

■ *noun* a rude or mocking shout: *the jeers and boos of*

the audience. □ **huée**

'jeering *adjective* mocking or scornful. □ **railleur**

'jeeringly *adverb.* □ **d'un ton railleur**

jelly ['dʒeli] – *plural* **'jellies** – *noun* 1 the juice of fruit boiled with sugar until it is firm, used like jam, or served with meat. □ **gelée**

2 a transparent, smooth food, *usually* fruit-flavoured: *I've made raspberry jelly for the party.* □ **gelée**

3 any jellylike substance: *Frogs' eggs are enclosed in a kind of jelly.* □ **gelée**

4 same as **jam¹**.

'jellyfish – *plurals* **'jellyfish, 'jellyfishes** – *noun* a kind of sea animal with a jellylike body: *The child was stung by a jellyfish.* □ **méduse**

jeopardy ['dʒepədi] *noun* danger. □ **danger**

'jeopardize, 'jeopardise *verb* to put in danger: *Bad spelling could jeopardize your chances of passing the exam.* □ **compromettre**

jerk [dʒəːk] *noun* a short, sudden movement: *We felt a jerk as the train started.* □ **secousse**

■ *verb* to move with a jerk or jerks: *He grasped my arm and jerked me around*; *The car jerked to a halt.* □ **mouvoir par saccades**

'jerky *adjective* jerking; full of jerks: *a jerky movement*; *a jerky way of speaking.* □ **saccadé**

'jerkily *adverb.* □ **par saccades**

'jerkiness *noun.* □ **allure saccadée**

jersey ['dʒəːzi] *noun* a sweater or pullover. □ **jersey**

jest [dʒest] *noun* a joke; something done or said to cause amusement. □ **plaisanterie**

■ *verb* to joke. □ **plaisanter**

'jester *noun* in former times, a man employed in the courts of kings, nobles *etc* to amuse them with jokes *etc.* □ **bouffon**

in jest as a joke; not seriously: *speaking in jest.* □ **pour rire**

jet¹ [dʒet] *noun, adjective* (of) a hard black mineral substance, used for ornaments *etc*: *The beads are made of jet*; *a jet brooch.* □ **(de) jais**

jet-'black *adjective* very black: *jet-black hair.* □ **noir de jais**

jet² [dʒet] *noun* 1 a sudden, strong stream or flow (of liquid, gas, flame or steam), forced through a narrow opening: *Firemen have to be trained to direct the jets from their hoses accurately.* □ **jet**

2 a narrow opening in an apparatus through which a jet comes: *This gas jet is blocked.* □ **gicleur**

3 an airplane driven by jet propulsion: *We flew by jet to America.* □ **avion à réaction**

'jet lag *noun* symptoms such as tiredness and lack of concentration caused by flying a long distance in a short period of time. □ **fatigue due au décalage horaire**

jet-pro'pelled *adjective* driven by jet propulsion: *jet-propelled racing-cars.* □ **à réaction**

jet propulsion a method of producing very fast forward motion (for aircraft, missiles *etc*) by sucking air or liquid *etc* into a **jet engine** and forcing it out from behind. □ **propulsion par réaction**

jettison ['dʒetisn] *verb* to throw (cargo *etc*) overboard to lighten a ship, aircraft *etc* in times of danger: *When one* *of the engines failed, the airplane crew jettisoned the luggage.* □ **larguer**

jetty ['dʒeti] – *plural* '**jetties** – *noun* a small pier for use as a landing-place. □ **embarcadère, débarcadère**

jewel ['dʒuːəl] *noun* a precious stone: *rubies, emeralds and other jewels.* □ **pierre précieuse**

'**jewelled** *adjective* ornamented with jewels: *a jewelled crown.* □ **orné de pierreries**

'**jeweller** *noun* a person who makes, or deals in, ornaments and other articles made of precious stones and metals. □ **bijoutier, ière**

'**jewellery** *noun* articles made or sold by a jeweller, and worn for personal adornment, *eg* bracelets, necklaces, brooches, rings *etc.* □ **bijoux**

jib [dʒib] *noun* 1 a three-cornered sail on the front mast of a ship. □ **foc**

2 the jutting-out arm of a crane. □ **flèche**

jibe, gibe [dʒaib] *noun* a cruel or unkind remark or taunt: *cruel jibes.* □ **moquerie**

■ *verb* (*with* **at**) to make fun (of) unkindly. □ **se moquer de**

jiffy ['dʒifi] *noun* a moment: *I'll be back in a jiffy.* □ **en moins de deux**

jig [dʒig] *noun* (a piece of music for) a type of lively dance. □ **gigue**

■ *verb* – *past tense, past participle* **jigged** – to jump (about): *Stop jigging about and stand still!* □ **sautiller**

jiggle ['dʒigl] *verb* to (cause to) jump (about) or move jerkily: *The television picture kept jiggling up and down.* □ **sautiller**

jigsaw (puzzle) ['dʒigsɔː] *noun* a puzzle made up of many differently-shaped pieces that fit together to form a picture. □ **casse-tête**

jilt [dʒilt] *verb* to reject or send away (someone with whom one has been in love): *After being her boyfriend for two years, he suddenly jilted her.* □ **laisser tomber**

jingle ['dʒingl] *noun* 1 a slight metallic ringing sound (made *eg* by coins or by small bells): *The dog pricked up its ears at the jingle of its master's keys.* □ **cliquetis**

2 a simple rhyming verse or tune: *nursery rhymes and other little jingles; advertising jingles.* □ **refrain (publicitaire)**

■ *verb* to (cause to) make a clinking or ringing sound; *He jingled the coins in his pocket.* □ **faire tinter**

jittery ['dʒitəri] *adjective* very nervous and easily upset: *She has become very jittery since her accident.* □ **froussard**

job [dʒob] *noun* 1 a person's daily work or employment: *She has a job as a bank-clerk; Some of the unemployed men have been out of a job for four years.* □ **travail, emploi**

2 a piece of work or a task: *I have several jobs to do before going to bed.* □ **tâche**

give up as a bad job to decide that (something) is not worth doing, or impossible to do, and so stop doing it. □ **renoncer**

a good job a lucky or satisfactory state of affairs: *It's a good job that she can't hear what you're saying; He has lost his trumpet, and a good job too!* □ **c'est une chance (que)**

have a job to have difficulty: *You'll have a job finishing all this work tonight.* □ **avoir du mal (à)**

just the job entirely suitable: *These gloves are just the job for gardening.* □ **justement ce qu'il faut**

make the best of a bad job to do one's best in difficult circumstances. □ **faire contre mauvaise fortune bon cœur**

jockey ['dʒoki] *noun* a person employed to ride horses in races. □ **jockey**

jodhpurs ['dʒodpəz] *noun plural* riding breeches that fit tightly from the knee to the ankle. □ **culotte de cheval**

jog [dʒog] – *past tense, past participle* **jogged** – *verb* 1 to push, shake or knock gently: *He jogged my arm and I spilt my coffee; I have forgotten, but something may jog my memory later on.* □ **secouer**

2 to travel slowly: *The cart jogged along the rough track.* □ **aller cahin-caha**

3 to run at a gentle pace, *especially* for the sake of exercise: *She jogs/goes jogging around the park for half an hour every morning.* □ **faire du jogging**

at a jog-trot at a gentle running pace: *Every morning he goes down the road at a jog-trot.* □ **au petit trot**

joggle ['dʒogl] *verb* to (cause to) shake or move slightly from side to side: *Don't joggle the table!* □ **secouer**

join [dʒoin] *verb* 1 (*often with* **up, on** *etc*) to put together or connect: *The electrician joined the wires (up) incorrectly; You must join this piece (on) to that piece; She joined the two stories together to make a play; The island is joined to the mainland by a sandbank at low tide.* □ **joindre, raccorder**

2 to connect (two points) *eg* by a line, as in geometry: *Join point A to point B.* □ **relier**

3 to become a member of (a group): *Join our club!* □ **devenir membre de**

4 (*sometimes with* **up**) to meet and come together (with): *This lane joins the main road; Do you know where the two rivers join?; They joined up with us for the remainder of the holiday.* □ **(se) rejoindre, (se) joindre (à)**

5 to come into the company of: *I'll join you later in the restaurant.* □ **rejoindre**

■ *noun* a place where two things are joined: *You can hardly see the joins in the material.* □ **joint**

join forces to come together for united work or action: *We would do better if we joined forces (with each other).* □ **s'unir (pour)**

join hands to clasp one another's hands (*eg* for dancing): *Join hands with your partner; They joined hands in a ring.* □ **se donner la main**

join in to take part (in): *We're playing a game – do join in!; He would not join in the game.* □ **prendre part à**

join up to become a member of an armed force: *He joined up in 1940.* □ **s'engager**

joint [dʒoint] *noun* 1 the place where two or more things join: *The plumber tightened up all the joints in the pipes.* □ **raccord**

2 a part of the body where two bones meet but are able to move in the manner of *eg* a hinge: *The shoulders, elbows, wrists, hips, knees and ankles are joints.* □ **articulation**

3 a piece of meat for cooking containing a bone: *A leg*

of mutton is a fairly large joint. □ **rôti**

■ *adjective* **1** united; done together: *the joint efforts of the whole team.* □ **conjugué**

2 shared by, or belonging to, two or more: *She and her husband have a joint bank account.* □ **commun**

■ *verb* to divide (an animal *etc* for cooking) at the, or into, joints: *Joint the chicken before cooking it.* □ **dépecer**

'**jointed** *adjective* **1** having (*especially* movable) joints: *a jointed doll.* □ **articulé**

2 (of an animal *etc* for cooking) divided into joints or pieces: *a jointed chicken.* □ **dépecé**

'**jointly** *adverb* together: *They worked jointly on this book.* □ **ensemble**

out of joint (of a limb *etc*) not in the correct place; dislocated: *She put her shoulder out of joint when she moved the wardrobe.* □ **démis**

See also **join.**

joke [dʒouk] *noun* **1** anything said or done to cause laughter: *He told/made the old joke about the elephant in the refrigerator*; *She dressed up as a ghost for a joke*; *He played a joke on us and dressed up as a ghost.* □ **blague**

2 something that causes laughter or amusement: *The children thought it a huge joke when the cat stole the fish.* □ **tour**

■ *verb* **1** to make a joke or jokes: *They joked about my mistake for a long time afterwards.* □ **plaisanter, (se) moquer (de)**

2 to talk playfully and not seriously: *Don't be upset by what she said – she was only joking.* □ **plaisanter**

'**joker** *noun* **1** in a pack of playing cards, an extra card (*usually* having a picture of a jester) used in some games. □ **joker**

2 a person who enjoys telling jokes, playing tricks *etc*. □ **blagueur, euse; farceur, ceuse**

'**jokingly** *adverb*: *She looked out at the rain and jokingly suggested a walk.* □ **en plaisantant**

it's no joke it is a serious or worrying matter: *It's no joke when water gets into the gas tank.* □ **ce n'est pas drôle**

joking aside let us stop joking and talk seriously: *I feel like going to Timbuctoo for the weekend – but, joking aside, I do need a rest!* □ **blague à part**

take a joke to be able to accept or laugh at a joke played on oneself: *The trouble with him is that he can't take a joke.* □ **entendre à rire**

jolly ['dʒoli] *adjective* merry and cheerful: *She's in quite a jolly mood today.* □ **jovial**

■ *adverb* very: *Taste this – it's jolly good!* □ **très**

'**jolliness, 'jollity** *noun.* □ **gaieté**

jolt [dʒoult] *verb* **1** to move jerkily: *The bus jolted along the road.* □ **avancer en cahotant**

2 to shake or move suddenly: *I was violently jolted as the train stopped.* □ **secouer**

■ *noun* **1** a sudden movement or shake: *The car gave a jolt and started.* □ **à-coup**

2 a shock: *He got a jolt when he heard the bad news.* □ **choc**

joss stick ['dʒosstik] a stick of incense used *eg* to give a sweet smell to a room. □ **bâton d'encens**

jostle ['dʒosl] *verb* to push roughly: *We were jostled by the crowd; I felt people jostling against me in the dark.* □ **bousculer, (se) cogner (à)**

jot [dʒot] *noun* a small amount: *I haven't a jot of sympathy for him.* □ **brin**

■ *verb – past tense, past participle* '**jotted** – (*usually* with **down**) to write briefly or quickly: *She jotted (down) the telephone number in her notebook.* □ **noter**

journal ['dʒəːnl] *noun* **1** a magazine or other regularly published paper (*eg* of a society): *the Canadian Medical Journal.* □ **revue**

2 a diary giving an account of each day's activities. □ **journal**

'**journalism** *noun* the business of running, or writing for, newspapers or magazines. □ **journalisme**

'**journalist** *noun* a writer for a newspaper, magazine *etc*. □ **journaliste**

journa'listic *adjective* (of style of writing) like that of a journalist, colourful and racy. □ **journalistique**

journey ['dʒəːni] *noun* a distance travelled, *especially* over land; an act of travelling: *By train, it is a two hour journey from here to the coast*; *I'm going on a long journey.* □ **voyage, trajet**

■ *verb* to travel. □ **voyager**

jovial ['dʒouviəl] *adjective* full of good humour: *She seems to be in a very jovial mood this morning.* □ **jovial**

jovi'ality [-'a-] *noun.* □ **jovialité**

'**jovially** *adverb.* □ **jovialement**

joy [dʒoi] *noun* **1** great happiness: *The children jumped for joy when they saw the new toys.* □ **joie**

2 a cause of great happiness: *Our son is a great joy to us.* □ **joie**

'**joyful** *adjective* filled with, showing or causing joy: *a joyful mood*; *joyful faces/news.* □ **joyeux**

'**joyfully** *adverb.* □ **joyeusement**

'**joyfulness** *noun.* □ **humeur joyeuse**

'**joyous** *adjective* joyful. □ **joyeux**

'**joyously** *adverb.* □ **joyeusement**

jubilant ['dʒuːbilənt] *adjective* showing and expressing triumphant joy: *Jubilant crowds welcomed the victorious team home.* □ **jubilant**

'**jubilantly** *adverb.* □ **avec joie**

jubi'lation [-'lei-] *noun* (*sometimes in plural*) (triumphant) rejoicing: *There was great jubilation over the victory*; *The jubilations went on till midnight.* □ **réjouissances**

jubilee ['dʒuːbiliː] *noun* a celebration of a special anniversary (*especially* the 25th, 50th or 60th) of some event, *eg* the succession of a king or queen: *The king celebrated his golden jubilee* (= fiftieth anniversary of his succession) *last year.* □ **jubilé**

judge [dʒʌdʒ] *verb* **1** to hear and try (cases) in a court of law: *Who will be judging this murder case?* □ **juger**

2 to decide which is the best in a competition *etc*: *Is she going to judge the singing competition again?*; *Who will be judging the vegetables at the flower show?*; *Who is judging at the horse show?* □ **être juge (à)**

3 to consider and form an idea of; to estimate: *You can't judge a man by his appearance*; *Watch how a cat judges*

the distance before it jumps; She couldn't judge whether he was telling the truth. □ **juger, apprécier**
4 to criticize for doing wrong: We have no right to judge her – we might have done the same thing ourselves. □ **juger**

■ noun 1 a public officer who hears and decides cases in a law court: The judge asked if the jury had reached a verdict. □ **juge**
2 a person who decides which is the best in a competition etc: The judge's decision is final (= you cannot argue with the judge's decision); He was asked to be on the panel of judges at the beauty contest. □ **juge**
3 a person who is skilled at deciding how good etc something is: He says she's honest, and he's a good judge of character; She seems a very fine pianist to me, but I'm no judge. □ **connaisseur, euse**

'**judgment, judgement** noun 1 the decision of a judge in a court of law: It looked as if he might be acquitted but the judgment went against him. □ **jugement**
2 the act of judging or estimating: Faulty judgment when passing is a common cause of traffic accidents. □ **jugement**
3 the ability to make right or sensible decisions: You showed good judgment in choosing this method. □ **jugement**
4 (an) opinion: In my judgment, he is a very good actor. □ **(à mon) avis**

'**judging from/to judge from** if one can use (something) as an indication: Judging from the sky, there'll be a storm soon. □ **à en juger par**

'**pass judgment (on)** to criticize or condemn: Do not pass judgment (on others) unless you are perfect yourself. □ **porter un jugement (sur)**

judicial [dʒuː'diʃəl] adjective of a judge or court of law: judicial powers; She might bring judicial proceedings against you. □ **judiciaire**
ju'**dicially** adverb. □ **juridiquement**

judicious [dʒuː'diʃəs] adjective showing wisdom and good sense: a judicious choice of words. □ **judicieux**
ju'**diciously** adverb. □ **judicieusement**
ju'**diciousness** noun. □ **discernement**

judo ['dʒuːdou] noun a Japanese form of wrestling: She learns judo at the sports centre. □ **judo**

jug [dʒʌg] noun a deep container for liquids, usually with a handle and a shaped lip for pouring: a milk jug. □ **cruche**

juggle ['dʒʌgl] verb to keep throwing in the air and catching a number of objects (eg balls or clubs): He entertained the audience by juggling with four balls and four plates at once. □ **jongler (avec)**
'**juggler** noun. □ **jongleur, euse**

juice [dʒuːs] noun 1 the liquid part of fruits or vegetables: She squeezed the juice out of the orange; tomato juice. □ **jus**
2 (often in plural) the fluid contained in meat: Roasting meat in tin foil helps to preserve the juices. □ **jus**
3 (in plural) fluid contained in the organs of the body, eg to help digestion: digestive/gastric juices. □ **suc**
'**juicy** adjective. □ **juteux**
'**juiciness** noun. □ **caractère juteux**

jukebox ['dʒuːkbɒks] noun a machine that plays selected records automatically when coins are put into it. □ **jukebox**

July [dʒu'lai] noun the seventh month of the year, the month following June. □ **juillet**

jumble ['dʒʌmbl] verb (often with up or together) to mix or throw together without order: In this puzzle, the letters of all the words have been jumbled (up); His shoes and clothes were all jumbled (together) in the cupboard. □ **mélanger, emmêler**
■ noun a confused mixture: He found an untidy jumble of things in the drawer. □ **fouillis, magma**

jump [dʒʌmp] verb 1 to (cause to) go quickly off the ground with a springing movement: He jumped off the wall/across the puddle/over the fallen tree/into the swimming pool; Don't jump the horse over that fence! □ **(faire) sauter**
2 to rise; to move quickly (upwards): She jumped to her feet; He jumped into the car. □ **sauter**
3 to make a startled movement: The noise made me jump. □ **sursauter**
4 to pass over (a gap etc) by bounding: He jumped the stream easily. □ **franchir (d'un bond)**
■ noun 1 an act of jumping: She crossed the stream in one jump. □ **bond**
2 an obstacle to be jumped over: Her horse fell at the third jump. □ **saut**
3 a jumping competition: the high jump. □ **saut**
4 a startled movement: She gave a jump when the door suddenly banged shut. □ **sursaut**
5 a sudden rise, eg in prices: There has been a jump in the price of potatoes. □ **montée en flèche**

'**jumpy** adjective nervous; easily upset: He has been very jumpy and irritable lately. □ **nerveux**

jump at to take or accept eagerly: She jumped at the chance to go to Germany for a fortnight. □ **sauter (sur)**

jump for joy to show great pleasure. □ **sauter de joie**

jump on to make a sudden attack on: He was waiting around the corner and jumped on me in the dark. □ **sauter (sur)**

jump the gun to start before the proper time: We shouldn't be going on holiday till tomorrow, but we jumped the gun and caught today's last flight. □ **prendre les devants**

jump the line to move ahead of others in a queue without waiting for one's proper turn: Many wealthy or important people try to jump the line for hospital beds. □ **resquiller**

jump to conclusions/jump to the conclusion that to form an idea without making sure of the facts: She saw my case in the hall and jumped to the conclusion that I was leaving. □ **conclure tout de suite que**

jump to it to hurry up: If you don't jump to it you'll miss the train. □ **se grouiller**

jumper ['dʒʌmpə] noun a kind of dress without sleeves, to be worn over a blouse or sweater. □ **chasuble**

junction ['dʒʌŋkʃən] noun a place at which things (eg railway lines) join: a railway junction; There was an accident at the junction of Park Road and School Lane. □ **jonction**

juncture ['dʒʌŋktʃə]: **at this/that juncture** at this or that moment or point: *At this juncture the chairman declared the meeting closed.* □ **à ce moment-là**

June [dʒuːn] *noun* the sixth month of the year, the month following May. □ **juin**

jungle ['dʒʌŋgl] *noun* a thick growth of trees and plants in tropical areas: *the Amazon jungle; Tigers are found in the jungles of Asia;* (*also adjective*) *soldiers trained in jungle warfare.* □ **jungle**

junior ['dʒuːnjə] *noun, adjective* (a person who is) younger in years or lower in rank or authority: *She is two years my junior; The school sent two juniors and one senior to take part; junior pupils; She is junior to me in the firm; the junior school.* □ **cadet, ette, subalterne, junior**
■ *adjective* (*often abbreviated to* **Jr.** *when written*) used to indicate the son of a person who is still alive and who has the same name: *John Jones Junior.* □ **fils**
■ *noun* a name for the child (*usually* a son) of a family: *Do bring Junior!* □ **le petit**

> younger than but junior to.

juniper ['dʒuːnipə] *noun* a type of evergreen shrub with berries and prickly leaves. □ **genévrier**

junk¹ [dʒʌŋk] *noun* unwanted or worthless articles; rubbish: *That cupboard is full of junk;* (*also adjective*) *This vase was bought in a junk shop* (= a shop that sells junk). □ **bric-à-brac**

junk² [dʒʌŋk] *noun* a Chinese flat-bottomed sailing ship, high in the bow and stern. □ **jonque**

junket ['dʒʌŋkit] *noun* a dish made of curdled and sweetened milk. □ **(lait) caillé**

junkie ['dʒʌŋki] *noun* a slang word for a person who is addicted to drugs, *especially* heroin. □ **drogué, ée**

junta ['dʒʌntə] *noun* a group of army officers that has taken over the administration of a country by force. □ **junte**

jurisdiction [dʒuəris'dikʃən] *noun* legal power; authority. □ **juridiction**

jurisprudence [dʒuəris'pruːdəns] *noun* the science of law. □ **jurisprudence**

jury ['dʒuəri] – *plural* 'juries – *noun* **1** a group of people legally selected to hear a case and to decide what are the facts, *eg* whether or not a prisoner accused of a crime is guilty: *The verdict of the jury was that the prisoner was guilty of the crime.* □ **jury**
2 a group of judges for a competition, contest *etc*: *The jury recorded their votes for the song contest.* □ **jury**
'**juror,** '**juryman** *nouns* a member of a jury in a law court. □ **juré, ée**

just¹ [dʒʌst] *adjective* **1** right and fair: not favouring one more than another: *a fair and just decision.* □ **juste**
2 reasonable; based on one's rights: *She certainly has a just claim to the money.* □ **juste**
3 deserved: *He got his just reward when he crashed the stolen car and broke his leg.* □ **juste**
'**justly** *adverb*: *He was justly blamed for the accident.* □ **à juste titre**
'**justness** *noun*. □ **justice; justesse**

just² [dʒʌst] *adverb* **1** (*often with* **as**) exactly or precisely:

This penknife is just what I needed; He was behaving just as if nothing had happened; The house was just as I'd remembered it. □ **exactement**
2 (*with* **as**) quite: *This dress is just as nice as that one.* □ **tout aussi**
3 very lately or recently: *He has just gone out of the house.* □ **venir de**
4 on the point of; in the process of: *She is just coming through the door.* □ **sur le point de, en train de**
5 at the particular moment: *The telephone rang just as I was leaving.* □ **à l'instant (où)**
6 (*often with* **only**) barely: *We have only just enough milk to last till Friday; I just managed to escape; You came just in time.* □ **(tout) juste**
7 only; merely: *They waited for six hours just to get a glimpse of the Queen; 'Where are you going?' 'Just to the post office'; Could you wait just a minute?* □ **juste, rien que**
8 used for emphasis, *eg* with commands: *Just look at that mess!; That just isn't true!; I just don't know what to do.* □ **donc, (tout) simplement**
9 absolutely: *The weather is just marvellous.* □ **absolument**
just about more or less: *Is your watch just about right?* □ **à peu près**
just now 1 at this particular moment: *I can't do it just now.* □ **pour l'instant**
2 a short while ago: *She fell and banged her head just now, but she feels better again.* □ **tout à l'heure**
just then 1 at that particular moment: *He was feeling rather hungry just then.* □ **à ce moment-là**
2 in the next minute: *She opened the letter and read it. Just then the door bell rang.* □ **à ce moment-là**

justice ['dʒʌstis] *noun* **1** fairness or rightness in the treatment of other people: *Everyone has a right to justice; I don't deserve to be punished – where's your sense of justice?* □ **justice**
2 the law or the administration of it: *Their dispute had to be settled in a court of justice.* □ **justice**
3 a judge. □ **juge**
bring to justice to arrest, try and sentence (a criminal): *The murderer escaped but was finally brought to justice.* □ **traduire en justice**
do (someone/something) justice/do justice to (someone/something) 1 to treat fairly or properly: *It would not be doing him justice to call him lazy when he's so ill.* □ **être juste envers**
2 to fulfil the highest possibilities of; to get the best results from; to show fully or fairly: *I was so tired that I didn't do myself justice in the exam.* □ **se montrer à sa juste valeur**
in justice to (him, her *etc***)/to do (him, her** *etc***) justice** if one must be fair (to him, her *etc*): *To do her justice, I must admit that she was only trying to help when she broke the cup.* □ **pour être juste envers**

justify ['dʒʌstifai] *verb* **1** to prove or show (a person, action, opinion *etc*) to be just, right, desirable or reasonable: *How can the government justify the spending of millions of dollars on weapons when there is so much poverty in the country?* □ **justifier**

2 to be a good excuse for: *Your state of anxiety does not justify your being so rude to me.* □ **justifier**

justi'fiable *adjective* (*negative* **unjustifiable**) able to be justified: *Is dishonesty ever justifiable?* □ **justifiable**

justifi'cation [-fi-] *noun* 1 (the act of) justifying or excusing. □ **justification**

2 something that justifies: *You have no justification for criticizing him in that way.* □ **raison valable**

jut [dʒʌt] – *past tense, past participle* '**jutted** – *verb* (*usually with* **out**) to stick out or project: *His top teeth jut out.* □ **faire saillie**

jute [dʒuːt] *noun, adjective* (of) the fibre of certain plants found in Pakistan and India, used for making sacks *etc.* □ **(de, en) jute**

jutted *see* jut.

juvenile ['dʒuːvənail] *adjective* 1 (*also noun*) (a person who is) young or youthful: *She will not be sent to prison – she is still a juvenile; juvenile offenders.* □ **jeune, mineur**

2 childish: *juvenile behaviour.* □ **puéril**

Kk

kaftan *see* caftan.

kaleidoscope [kə'laidəskoup] *noun* a tube shaped toy in which loose coloured pieces of glass *etc* reflected in two mirrors form changing patterns. □ **kaléidoscope** **ka,leido'scopic** [-'sko-] *adjective* with many changing colours, sights, impressions *etc*. □ **kaléidoscopique**

kangaroo [kaŋgə'ruː] – *plural* **kanga'roos** – *noun* a type of large Australian animal with very long hind legs and great power of leaping, the female of which carries her young in a pouch on the front of her body. □ **kangourou**

kapok ['keipok] *noun* a very light waterproof fibre fluff obtained from a type of tropical tree and used to stuff toys *etc*. □ **kapok**

karate [kə'raːti] *noun* a Japanese form of unarmed fighting, using blows and kicks. □ **karaté**

kayak ['kaiak] *noun* an open canoe, *especially* an Inuit canoe made of sealskins stretched over a frame. □ **kayak**

kebab [ki'bab] *noun* small pieces of meat *etc*, *usually* cooked on a skewer: *They ate kebabs and rice in the Indian restaurant*. □ **brochette**

kedgeree [kedʒə'riː] *noun* a dish made with rice, fish and other ingredients. □ **pilaf de poisson**

keel [kiːl] *noun* the long supporting piece of a ship's frame that lies lengthways along the bottom: *The boat's keel stuck in the mud near the shore*. □ **quille**

keel over to fall over *usually* suddenly or unexpectedly *eg* in a faint. □ **tomber dans les pommes**

be/keep on an even keel to be, keep or remain in a calm and untroubled state. □ **être/rester calme**

keen [kiːn] *adjective* 1 eager or enthusiastic: *He is a keen golfer; I'm keen to succeed*. □ **fervent**

2 sharp: *Her eyesight is as keen as ever*. □ **perçant**

3 (of wind *etc*) very cold and biting. □ **piquant**

'**keenly** *adverb*. □ **ardemment**

'**keenness** *noun*. □ **finesse**

keen on very enthusiastic about, interested in or fond of: *She's been keen on sailing; She's been keen on that boy for years*. □ **passionné de**

keep [kiːp] – *past tense, past participle* **kept** [kept] – *verb* 1 to have for a very long or indefinite period of time: *He gave me the picture to keep*. □ **garder**

2 not to give or throw away; to preserve: *I kept the most interesting books; Can you keep a secret?* □ **conserver, garder**

3 to (cause to) remain in a certain state or position: *I keep this gun loaded; How do you keep cool in this heat?; Will you keep me informed of what happens?* □ **garder, tenir**

4 to go on (performing or repeating a certain action): *He kept walking*. □ **continuer à**

5 to have in store: *I always keep a tin of baked beans for emergencies*. □ **garder**

6 to look after or care for: *She keeps the garden beautifully; I think they keep hens*. □ **entretenir**

7 to remain in good condition: *That meat won't keep in this heat unless you put it in the fridge*. □ **se conserver, (se) garder**

8 to make entries in (a diary, accounts *etc*): *She keeps a diary to remind her of her appointments; He kept the accounts for the club*. □ **tenir**

9 to hold back or delay: *Sorry to keep you*. □ **retenir**

10 to provide food, clothes, housing for (someone): *He has three children to keep*. □ **entretenir**

11 to act in the way demanded by: *She kept her promise*. □ **tenir**

■ *noun* food and lodging: *She gives her mother money every week for her keep; Our cat really earns her keep – she kills all the mice in the house*. □ **entretien, nourriture**

'**keeper** *noun* a person who looks after something, *eg* animals in a zoo: *The lion has killed its keeper*. □ **gardien, ienne**

'**keeping** *noun* care or charge: *The money had been given into his keeping*. □ **garde**

,**keep 'fit** *noun* a series or system of exercises, *usually* simple, intended to improve the physical condition of ordinary people, *especially* women: *She's very keen on keeping fit but it doesn't do her much good*. □ **(de) gymnastique**

'**keepsake** [-seik] *noun* something given or taken to be kept in memory of the giver: *She gave him a piece of her hair as a keepsake*. □ **souvenir**

for keeps permanently: *You can have this necklace for keeps*. □ **pour de bon**

in keeping with suited to: *He has moved to a house more in keeping with his position as a headmaster*. □ **en rapport avec**

keep away to (cause to) remain at a distance: *Keep away – it's dangerous!* □ **ne pas s'approcher (de)**

keep back 1 not to (allow to) move forward: *She kept the child back on the edge of the crowd; Every body keep back from the door!* □ **ne pas s'approcher (de)**

2 not to tell or make known: *I feel he's keeping the real story back for some reason*. □ **cacher**

3 not to give or pay out: *Part of my allowance is kept back to pay for my meals; Will they keep it back every week?* □ **retenir**

keep one's distance to stay quite far away: *The deer did not trust us and kept their distance*. □ **se tenir à distance**

keep down 1 not to (allow to) rise up: *Keep down – they're shooting at us!* □ **ne pas bouger**

2 to control or put a limit on: *They are taking steps to keep down the rabbit population*. □ **limiter**

3 to digest without vomiting: *He has eaten some food but he won't be able to keep it down*. □ **garder, digérer**

keep one's end up to perform one's part in something just as well as all the others who are involved. □ **faire sa part (d'une tâche)**

keep from to stop oneself from (doing something): *I could hardly keep from hitting him*. □ **se retenir de**

keep going to go on doing something despite difficulties. □ **continuer**

keep hold of not to let go of: *Keep hold of those tickets!* □ **ne pas lâcher/perdre**

keep house (for) to do the cooking, housework *etc* (for): *She keeps house for her sister*. □ **tenir la maison (de)**

keep in 1 not to allow to go or come out or outside: *The teacher kept him in till he had finished the work.* □ **empêcher qqn de sortir**
2 to stay close to the side of a road *etc.* □ **rester bien au bord (à droite)**
keep in mind to remember and take into consideration later. □ **se souvenir que**
keep it up to carry on doing something at the same speed or as well as one is doing it at present: *Your work is good – keep it up!* □ **continuer**
keep off 1 to stay away: *There are notices around the bomb warning people to keep off; The rain kept off and we had sunshine for the wedding.* □ **ne pas s'approcher**
2 to prevent from getting to or on to (something): *This umbrella isn't pretty, but it keeps off the rain.* □ **protéger (de)**
keep on to continue (doing something or moving): *He just kept on writing; They kept on until they came to a gas station.* □ **continuer (à, de)**
keep oneself to oneself to tell others very little about oneself, and not to be very friendly or sociable. □ **se tenir à l'écart**
keep out not to (allow to) enter: *The notice at the building site said 'Keep out!'; This coat keeps out the wind.* □ **empêcher qqn d'entrer**
keep out of not to become involved in: *Do try to keep out of trouble!* □ **rester à l'écart de**
keep time (of a clock *etc.*) to show the time accurately: *Does this watch keep (good) time?* □ **donner l'heure exacte**
keep to not to leave or go away from: *Keep to this side of the park!; We kept to the roads we knew.* □ **ne pas s'écarter de**
keep (something) to oneself not to tell anyone (something): *He kept his conclusions to himself.* □ **garder pour soi**
keep up 1 to continue, or cause to remain, in operation: *I enjoy our friendship and try to keep it up.* □ **entretenir**
2 (*often with* **with**) to move fast enough not to be left behind (by): *Even the children managed to keep up; Don't run – I can't keep up with you.* □ **ne pas se laisser distancer**
keep up with the Joneses ['dʒəunziz] to have everything one's neighbours have: *She didn't need a new cooker – she just bought one to keep up with the Joneses.* □ **faire concurrence aux voisins**
keep watch to have the task of staying alert and watching for danger. □ **monter la garde**
kennel ['kenl] *noun* **1** a type of small hut for a dog. □ **niche**
2 (*usually in plural*) a place where dogs can be looked after. □ **chenil**
kept *see* keep.
kernel ['kə:nl] *noun* **1** the softer substance inside the shell of a nut, or the stone of a fruit such as a plum, peach *etc.* □ **amande**
2 the central, most important part of a matter. □ **fond (du problème)**
kerosene ['kerəsi:n] *noun* paraffin oil, obtained from petroleum or from coal: *The jet plane refuelled with*

kerosene; (*also adjective*) *a kerosene lamp/stove.* □ **kérosène**
ketchup ['ketʃəp] *noun* a flavouring sauce made from tomatoes or mushrooms *etc.* □ **ketchup**
kettle ['ketl] *noun* a metal pot, *usually* with a special part for pouring and a lid, for heating liquids: *a kettle full of boiling water.* □ **bouilloire**
'kettledrum *noun* a type of drum made of a brass or copper bowl covered with a stretched skin *etc.* □ **timbale**
key [ki:] *noun* **1** an instrument or tool by which something (*eg* a lock or a nut) is turned: *Have you the key for this door?* □ **clef**
2 in musical instruments, one of the small parts pressed to sound the notes: *piano keys.* □ **touche**
3 in a typewriter, calculator *etc*, one of the parts which one presses to cause a letter *etc* to be printed, displayed *etc.* □ **touche**
4 the scale in which a piece of music is set: *What key are you singing in?; the key of F.* □ **ton**
5 something that explains a mystery or gives an answer to a mystery, a code *etc*: *the key to the whole problem.* □ **clef**
6 in a map *etc*, a table explaining the symbols *etc* used in it. □ **légende**
■ *adjective* most important: *key industries; He is a key man in the firm.* □ **-clef**
key ring *noun* a band, usually made of metal, that holds keys: *Lucy put my keys on her key ring so she wouldn't lose them.* □ **porte-clé**
'keyboard *noun* the keys in a piano, typewriter *etc* arranged along or on a flat board: *The pianist sat down at the keyboard and began to play; A computer keyboard looks like that of a typewriter; (also adjective) harpsichords and other early keyboard instruments.* □ **(à) clavier**
'keyhole *noun* the hole in which a key of a door *etc* is placed: *The child looked through the keyhole to see if his teacher was still with his parents.* □ **trou de serrure**
'keynote *noun* **1** the chief note in a musical key. □ **tonique**
2 the chief point or theme (of a lecture *etc*). □ **idée dominante**
keyed up excited; tense. □ **tendu**
khaki ['ka:ki] *noun, adjective* (of) a dull brownish or greenish yellow: *a khaki uniform; The café was full of men in khaki.* □ **kaki**
kick [kik] *verb* **1** to hit or strike out with the foot: *The child kicked his brother; She kicked the ball into the next garden; She kicked at the locked door; He kicked open the gate.* □ **donner un coup de pied (à, dans)**
2 (of a gun) to jerk or spring back violently when fired. □ **reculer**
■ *noun* **1** a blow with the foot: *The boy gave him a kick on the ankle; She was injured by a kick from a horse.* □ **coup de pied**
2 the springing back of a gun after it has been fired. □ **recul**
3 a pleasant thrill: *She gets a kick out of making people happy.* □ **plaisir**
kick about/around to treat badly or bully: *The bigger*

boys are always kicking him around. □ **brutaliser**
kick off to start a football game by kicking the ball: *We kick off at 2:30.* (*noun* '**kick-off**: *The kick-off is at 2:30*). □ **(donner le) coup d'envoi**
kick up to cause or start off (a fuss *etc*). □ **faire**
kid[1] [kid] *noun* **1** a popular word for a child or teenager: *They've got three kids now, two boys and a girl; More than a hundred kids went to the disco last night;* (*also adjective*) *his kid brother* (= younger brother). □ **enfant**
2 a young goat. □ **chevreau, chevrette**
3 (*also adjective*) (of) the leather made from its skin: *slippers made of kid; kid gloves.* □ **de chevreau**
kid[2] [kid] – *past tense, past participle* '**kidded** – *verb* to deceive or tease, *especially* harmlessly: *We were kidding him about the girl who keeps calling him; He kidded his wife into thinking he'd forgotten her birthday; She didn't mean that – she was only kidding!* □ **plaisanter, faire marcher**
kidnap ['kidnap] – *past tense, past participle* '**kidnapped** – *verb* to carry off (a person) by force, often demanding money in exchange for his safe return: *He is very wealthy and lives in fear of his children being kidnapped.* □ **kidnapper**
'**kidnapper** *noun.* □ **ravisseur, euse**
kidney ['kidni] *noun* one of a pair of organs in the body which remove waste matter from the blood and produce urine: *The kidneys of some animals are used as food.* □ **rein**
kill [kil] *verb* to cause the death of: *She killed the rats with poison; The outbreak of typhoid killed many people; The flat tire killed our hopes of getting home before midnight.* □ **tuer**
■ *noun* an act of killing: *The hunter was determined to make a kill before returning to the camp.* □ **mise à mort**
'**killer** *noun* a person, animal *etc* that kills: *There is a killer somewhere in the village;* (*also adjective*) *a killer disease.* □ **tueur, euse**
kill off to destroy completely: *So many deer have been shot that the species has almost been killed off.* □ **exterminer**
kill oneself *verb* to commit suicide; to take your own life: *A man tried to kill himself by jumping in front of the train.* □ **se suicider**
kill time to find something to do to use up spare time: *I'm just killing time until I hear whether I've got a job or not.* □ **tuer le temps**
kiln [kiln] *noun* a type of large oven for baking pottery or bricks, drying grain *etc*. □ **four**
kilogram ['kiləgram] (*often abbreviated to* **kilo** ['kiːlou] – *plural* '**kilos**) *noun* a unit of weight equal to 1000 grams. □ **kilo(gramme)**
kilometre ['kiləmiːtə, ki'lomitə] *noun* a unit of length, equal to 1000 metres. □ **kilomètre**
kilowatt ['kiləwot] *noun* (*often abbreviated to* **kW** *when written*) a measure of power, 1000 watts. □ **kilowatt**
kilt [kilt] *noun* an item of Scottish national dress, a pleated tartan skirt reaching to the knees and traditionally worn by men. □ **kilt**
kimono [ki'mounou] – *plural* **ki'monos** – *noun* a loose

Japanese robe, fastened with a sash. □ **kimono**
kin [kin] *noun plural* persons of the same family; one's relations. □ **famille**
■ *adjective* related. □ **parent**
'**kinsfolk** ['inz-] *noun plural* one's relations. □ **parents, famille**
'**kinsman** ['kinz-], '**kinswoman** ['kinz-] – *plurals* '**kinsmen**, '**kinswomen** – *nouns* a man or a woman of the same family as oneself. □ **parent(e)**
next of kin one's nearest relative(s). □ **le plus proche parent**
kind[1] [kaind] *noun* a sort or type: *What kind of car is it?; He is not the kind of man who would be cruel to children.* □ **sorte, espèce, genre**
kind[2] [kaind] *adjective* ready or anxious to do good to others; friendly: *He's such a kind man; It was very kind of you to look after the children yesterday.* □ **gentil**
'**kindly** *adverb* **1** in a kind manner: *She kindly lent me a handkerchief.* □ **gentiment, aimablement**
2 please: *Would you kindly stop talking!* □ **avoir l'obligeance de**
■ *adjective* having or showing a gentle and friendly nature: *a kindly smile; a kindly old lady.* □ **bienveillant**
'**kindliness** *noun.* □ **bienveillance**
'**kindness** *noun* the quality of being kind: *I'll never forget her kindness; Thank you for all your kindness.* □ **gentillesse**
,**kind-'hearted** *adjective* having or showing kindness: *She is too kind-hearted to hurt an animal.* □ **qui a bon cœur**
kindergarten ['kindəgaːtn] *noun* a school for very young children. □ **école maternelle**
kindle ['kindl] *verb* to (cause to) catch fire: *I kindled a fire using twigs and grass; The fire kindled easily; His speech kindled the anger of the crowd.* □ **allumer, enflammer**
'**kindling** *noun* dry wood *etc* for starting a fire. □ **petit bois**
kindliness, kindly, kindness *see* **kind.**
kindred ['kindrid] *noun plural* one's relatives. □ **parents**
■ *adjective* of the same sort: *climbing and kindred sports.* □ **du même genre**
kinetic [ki'netik] *adjective* of motion. □ **cinétique**
king [kiŋ] *noun* **1** a male ruler of a nation, who inherits his position by right of birth: *He became king when his father died; King Charles III.* □ **roi**
2 the playing card with the picture of a king: *I have two cards – the ten of spades and the king of diamonds.* □ **roi**
3 the most important piece in chess. □ **roi**
'**kingdom** *noun* **1** a state having a king (or queen) as its head: *The United Kingdom of Great Britain and Northern Ireland; She rules over a large kingdom.* □ **royaume**
2 any of the three great divisions of natural objects: *the animal, vegetable and mineral kingdoms.* □ **règne**
'**kingly** *adjective* of, relating to, or suitable for a king: *kingly robes; a kingly feast.* □ **royal**
'**kingliness** *noun.* □ **noblesse (digne d'un roi)**
'**kingfisher** *noun* a type of bird with brilliant blue feathers which feeds on fish. □ **martin-pêcheur**

'king-size(d) *adjective* of a large size; larger than normal: *a king-size(d) bed* ; *king-size cigarettes*. □ **de grand format, extra-long**

kink [kiŋk] *noun* a twist or bend, *eg* in a string, rope *etc*. □ **entortillement**

kinsman, kinswoman *etc see* **kin**.

kiosk ['kiːɔsk] *noun* a small roofed stall, either out of doors or in a public building *etc*, for the sale of newspapers, confectionery *etc*: *I bought a magazine at the kiosk at the station*. □ **kiosque**

kipper ['kipə] *noun* a herring split down the back and smoked, used as food. □ **hareng fumé et salé**

kiss [kis] *verb* to touch with the lips as a sign of affection: *She kissed him when he arrived home*; *The child kissed her parents goodnight*; *The film ended with a shot of the lovers kissing*. □ **(s')embrasser**

■ *noun* an act of kissing: *He gave her a kiss*. □ **baiser**

kiss of life a mouth-to-mouth method of restoring breathing. □ **bouche-à-bouche**

kit [kit] **1** (an outfit of) tools, clothes *etc* for a particular purpose: *He carried his tennis kit in a bag*; *a repair kit for mending punctures in bicycle tires*. □ **équipement, trousse**

2 a collection of the materials *etc* required to make something: *She bought a model airplane kit*. □ **kit**

'kitbag *noun* a strong bag for holding (*usually* a soldier's) kit. □ **sac (de voyage)**

kitchen ['kitʃin] *noun* a room where food is cooked: *A smell of burning was coming from the kitchen*; (*also adjective*) *a kitchen table*. □ **(de) cuisine**

,kitche'nette [-'net] *noun* a small kitchen. □ **petite cuisine**

kite [kait] *noun* a light frame covered with paper or other material, and with string attached, for flying in the air: *The children were flying their kites in the park*. □ **cerf-volant**

kitted *see* **kit**.

kitten ['kitn] *noun* a young cat: *The cat had five kittens last week*. □ **chaton**

'kittenish *adjective* playful. □ **enjoué**

kitty ['kiti] – *plural* **'kitties** – *noun* (a container holding) a sum of money kept for a particular purpose, to which members of a group jointly contribute: *The three friends shared a flat and kept a kitty for buying food*. □ **cagnotte**

kiwi ['kiːwiː] *noun* **1** a type of bird which is unable to fly, found in New Zealand. □ **kiwi**

2 fruit with a thin brown, hairy skin and an inner green flesh with small black seeds: *Kiwis are wonderful added to fruit salad*. □ **kiwi**

knack [nak] *noun* the ability to do something skilfully and easily: *It took me some time to get the knack of making pancakes*. □ **truc**

knapsack ['napsak] *noun* a small bag for food, clothes *etc* slung on the back. □ **sac à dos, havresac**

knave [neiv] *noun* a jack in a pack of playing cards: *the knave of diamonds*. □ **valet**

knead [niːd] *verb* to press together and work (dough *etc*) with the fingers: *His mother was kneading (dough) in the kitchen*. □ **pétrir**

knee [niː] *noun* **1** the joint at the bend of the leg: *He fell and cut his knee*; *The child sat on her father's knee*; *She was on her knees weeding the garden*; *He fell on his knees and begged for mercy*. □ **genou**

2 the part of an article of clothing covering this joint: *He has a hole in the knee of his trousers*. □ **genou**

'kneecap *noun* the flat, round bone on the front of the knee joint. □ **rotule**

,knee-'deep *adjective* reaching up to, or covered up to, one's knees: *knee-deep water*; *He is knee-deep in water*. □ **(jusqu') aux genoux**

kneel [niːl] – *past tense, past participle* **knelt** [nelt] – *verb* (often with **down**) to be in, or move into, a position in which both the foot and the knee of one or both legs are on the ground: *She knelt (down) to fasten the child's shoes*; *She was kneeling on the floor cutting out a dress pattern*. □ **s'agenouiller**

knell [nel] *noun* the sound of a bell giving warning of a death or funeral. □ **glas**

knelt *see* **kneel**.

knew *see* **know**.

knickers ['nikəz] *noun plural* women's and girls' pants, *especially* if loose-fitting and gathered in at the thigh. □ **culotte, knickers**

knife [naif] – *plural* **knives** [naivz] – *noun* **1** an instrument for cutting: *He carved the meat with a large knife*. □ **couteau**

2 such an instrument used as a weapon: *She stabbed him with a knife*. □ **couteau**

■ *verb* to stab with a knife: *He knifed her in the back*. □ **donner un coup de couteau**

knight [nait] *noun* **1** in earlier times, a man of noble birth who is trained to fight, *especially* on horseback: *King Arthur and his knights*. □ **chevalier**

2 a man of rank, having the title 'Sir': *Sir John Brown was made a knight in 1969*. □ **chevalier**

3 a piece used in chess, *usually* shaped like a horse's head. □ **cavalier**

■ *verb* to make (a person) a knight: *He was knighted for his services to industry*. □ **faire chevalier**

'knighthood *noun* the rank or title of a knight: *He received a knighthood from the Queen*. □ **titre de chevalier**

knit [nit] – *past tense, past participle* **'knitted** – *verb* **1** to form (a garment) from yarn (of wool *etc*) by making and connecting loops, using knitting needles: *She is teaching children to knit and sew*; *She knitted him a sweater for Christmas*. □ **tricoter**

2 (of broken bones) to grow together: *The bone in his arm took a long time to knit*. □ **se souder**

'knitter *noun*: *She's a very good knitter*. □ **tricoteur, euse**

'knitting *noun* **1** the work of a knitter: *She was occupied with her knitting*. □ **tricot**

2 the material made by knitting: *a piece of knitting*. □ **tricot**

'knitting needle *noun* a thin rod of steel or plastic *etc*, used in knitting. □ **aiguille à tricoter**

knit one's brows to frown. □ **froncer les sourcils**

knives *see* **knife**.

knob [nob] *noun* **1** a hard rounded part standing out from the main part: *a bedstead with brass knobs on*. □ **pomme, bouton**

2 a rounded handle on or for a door or drawer: *wooden doorknobs*. □ **poignée, bouton**

'**knobbly** *adjective* having knobs or lumps: *a knobbly walking stick*. □ **noueux**

knock [nok] *verb* 1 to make a sharp noise by hitting or tapping, *especially* on a door *etc* to attract attention: *Just then, someone knocked at the door*. □ **frapper, cogner**

2 to cause to move, *especially* to fall, by hitting (often accidentally): *She knocked a vase on to the floor while she was dusting*. □ **renverser**

3 to put into a certain state or position by hitting: *He knocked the other man senseless*. □ **assommer**

4 (*often with* **against, on**) to strike against or bump into: *She knocked against the table and spilt his cup of coffee*; *I knocked my head on the car door*. □ **se cogner, heurter**

■ *noun* 1 an act of knocking or striking: *She gave two knocks on the door*; *He had a nasty bruise from a knock he had received playing football*. □ **coup**

2 the sound made by a knock, *especially* on a door *etc*: *Suddenly they heard a loud knock*. □ **coup**

'**knocker** *noun* a piece of metal *etc* fixed to a door and used for knocking. □ **heurtoir**

,**knock-'kneed** *adjective* having legs that curve inwards abnormally at the knee. □ **cagneux**

knock about/around 1 to treat in a rough and unkind manner, *especially* to hit repeatedly: *I've heard that her husband knocks her about*. □ **maltraiter**

2 to move about (in) in a casual manner without a definite destination or purpose: *He spent six months knocking around before getting a job*. □ **vagabonder**

3 (*with* **with**) to be friendly with: *I don't like the boys he knocks about with*. □ **(se) tenir avec**

knock back to drink, *especially* quickly and in large quantities: *He knocked back three pints of beer in ten minutes*. □ **s'envoyer (un verre)**

knock down 1 to cause to fall by striking: *He was so angry with the man that he knocked him down*; *The old lady was knocked down by a van as she crossed the street*. □ **étendre, renverser**

2 to reduce the price of (goods): *She bought a coat that had been knocked down to half price*. □ **abaisser**

knock off to stop working: *I knocked off at six o'clock after studying for four hours*; *What time do you knock off in this factory?* □ **cesser le travail**

knock out 1 to make unconscious by a blow, or (in boxing) unable to recover within the required time: *The boxer knocked his opponent out in the third round*. □ **assommer**

2 to defeat and cause to retire from a competition: *That team knocked us out in the semifinals* (*noun* '**knock-out**). □ **éliminer**

knock over to cause to fall from an upright position: *The dog knocked over a chair as it rushed past*. □ **renverser**

knot [not] *noun* 1 a lump or join made in string, rope *etc* by twisting the ends together and drawing tight the loops

formed: *She fastened the string around the parcel, tying it with a knot*. □ **nœud**

2 a lump in wood at the join between a branch and the trunk: *This wood is full of knots*. □ **nœud**

3 a group or gathering: *a small knot of people*. □ **groupe**

4 a measure of speed for ships (about 1.85 km per hour). □ **nœud**

■ *verb – past tense, past particple* '**knotted** – to tie in a knot: *She knotted the rope around the post*. □ **nouer**

'**knotty** *adjective* 1 containing knots. □ **noueux**

2 (of a problem *etc*) difficult: *a knotty problem*. □ **épineux**

know [nou] – *past tense* **knew** [njuː]: *past participle* **known** – *verb* 1 to be aware of or to have been informed about: *He knows everything*; *I know he is at home because his car is in the driveway*; *He knows all about it*; *I know of no reason why you cannot go*. □ **savoir, connaître**

2 to have learned and to remember: *He knows a lot of poetry*. □ **savoir, connaître**

3 to be aware of the identity of; to be friendly with: *I know Mrs Smith – she lives near me*. □ **connaître**

4 to (be able to) recognize or identify: *You would hardly know her now – she has become very thin*; *He knows a good car when he sees one*. □ **reconnaître**

'**knowing** *adjective* showing secret understanding: *She gave him a knowing look*. □ **entendu**

'**knowingly** *adverb* 1 in a knowing manner: *She smiled knowingly*. □ **d'un air entendu**

2 deliberately or on purpose: *He would not knowingly insult her*. □ **sciemment**

'**know-it-all** *noun* an unkind name for a person who thinks he knows everything. □ **un(e) je-sais-tout**

'**know-how** *noun* the practical knowledge and skill to deal with something: *She has acquired a lot of know-how about cars*. □ **connaissances techniques**

in the know having information possessed only by a small group of people: *People in the know tell me that she is the most likely person to get the job*. □ **au courant**

know backwards to know extremely well or perfectly: *He knows his history backwards*. □ **savoir sur le bout des doigts**

know better to be too wise or well-taught (to do something): *She should know better at her age!*; *He should have known better than to trust them*. □ **bien se garder de**

know how to to have learned the way to: *She already knew how to read when she went to school*. □ **savoir**

know nothing about to have no knowledge of; to be unaware of or ignorant of: *The burglar claimed he had broken into a few houses but knew nothing about the bank robbery*. □ **ignorer**

know the ropes to understand the detail and procedure of a job *etc*. □ **connaître les ficelles**

knowledge ['nolidʒ] *noun* 1 the fact of knowing: *She was greatly encouraged by the knowledge that she had won first prize in the competition*. □ **connaissance**

2 information or what is known: *He had a vast amount of knowledge about boats*. □ **connaissances**

3 the whole of what can be learned or found out: *Sci-*

ence is a branch of knowledge about which I am rather *ignorant*. □ **savoir**

'knowledgeable *adjective* having a great deal of information: *He is very knowledgeable about the history of the city*. □ **bien informé**

general knowledge knowledge about a wide range of subjects: *The teacher sometimes tests our general knowledge*. □ **culture générale**

known *see* **know**.

knuckle ['nʌkl] *noun* a joint of a finger: *She hit her hand against the wall and grazed her knuckles*. □ **jointure**

koala (bear) [kou'aːlə] *noun* a type of Australian tree-climbing animal like a small bear, the female of which carries her baby in a pouch. □ **koala**

Koran [ko'raːn] *noun* the holy book of the Muslims. □ **Coran**

Ll

lab *see* **laboratory**.

label ['leibl] *noun* a small written note fixed on or near anything to tell its contents, owner *etc*: *luggage labels*; *The label on the blouse said 'Do not iron'*. □ **étiqueter**
■ *verb – past tense, past participle* **'labelled** – *verb* to attach a label to: *She labelled all the boxes of books carefully.* □ **étiqueter**

laboratory [lə'borətəri] – *plural* **la'boratories** – *noun* (*abbreviated to* **lab** [lab]) a place where scientific experiments are carried on or where drugs *etc* are prepared: *Samples of her blood were sent to the hospital lab(oratory) for testing.* □ **laboratoire**

labour ['leibə] *noun* **1** hard work: *The building of the cathedral involved considerable labour over two centuries; People engaged in manual labour are often badly paid.* □ **travail**
2 workmen on a job: *The firm is having difficulty hiring labour.* □ **main-d'œuvre**
3 (in a pregnant woman *etc*) the process of childbirth: *She was in labour for several hours before the baby was born.* □ **(en) travail**
4 used (*with capital*) as a name for the Socialist party in the United Kingdom. □ **travailliste**
■ *verb* **1** to be employed to do hard and unskilled work: *He spends the summer labouring on a building site.* □ **travailler**
2 to move or work *etc* slowly or with difficulty: *They laboured through the deep undergrowth in the jungle; the car engine labours a bit on steep hills.* □ **peiner**
laborious [lə'bɔːriəs] *adjective* difficult; requiring hard work: *Moving house is always a laborious process.* □ **laborieux**
la'boriously *adverb*. □ **laborieusement**
la'boriousness *noun*. □ **caractère laborieux**
'labourer *noun* a workman who is employed to do heavy work requiring little skill: *the labourers on a building site.* □ **ouvrier**
'labour-saving *adjective* intended to lessen work: *washing machines and other labour-saving devices.* □ **électro-ménager**

labyrinth ['labərinθ] *noun* a place full of long, winding passages; a maze. □ **labyrinthe**

lace [leis] *noun* **1** a string or cord for fastening shoes *etc*: *I need a new pair of laces for my tennis shoes.* □ **lacet**
2 delicate net-like decorative fabric made with fine thread: *Her dress was trimmed with lace*; (*also adjective*) *a lace shawl.* □ **(de) dentelle**
■ *verb* to fasten or be fastened with a lace which is threaded through holes: *Lace (up) your boots firmly.* □ **lacer**

lack [lak] *verb* to have too little or none of: *He lacked the courage to join the army.* □ **manquer de qqch.**
■ *noun* the state of not having any or enough: *our lack of money.* □ **manque**
be lacking (*with in*) **1** to be without or not to have enough: *He is lacking in intelligence.* □ **être dépourvu de**
2 to be absent; to be present in too little an amount:

Money for the project is not lacking but enthusiasm is. □ **qui manque, qui fait défaut**

lacquer ['lakə] *noun* a type of varnish: *He painted the iron table with black lacquer.* □ **laque**
■ *verb* to cover with lacquer. □ **laquer**

lad [lad] *noun* a boy or a youth: *I knew him when he was a lad.* □ **garçon, jeune homme**

ladder ['ladə] *noun* a set of rungs or steps between two long supports, for climbing up or down: *She was standing on a ladder painting the ceiling; the ladder of success.* □ **échelle**

laden ['leidn] *adjective* carrying a lot; heavily loaded (with): *People left the shops laden with purchases; Several laden trucks turned out of the yard.* □ **chargé**

ladle ['leidl] *noun* a bowl-like spoon with a long handle fixed to it at right angles, for lifting out liquid from a container: *a soup ladle.* □ **louche**
■ *verb* to lift and deal out with a ladle: *He ladled soup into the plates.* □ **servir (à la louche)**
'ladleful *noun*: *two ladlefuls of soup.* □ **pleine louche (de)**

lady ['leidi] *noun* **1** a more polite form of **woman**: *Tell that child to stand up and let that lady sit down; The lady in the flower shop said that roses are expensive just now; Ladies' shoes are upstairs in this shop*; (*also adjective*) *a lady doctor.* □ **dame; femme**
2 a woman of good manners and refined behaviour: *Be quiet! Ladies do not shout in public.* □ **dame**
3 in the United Kingdom, used as the title of, or a name for, a woman of noble rank: *Sir James and Lady Brown*; *lords and ladies.* □ **lady**
'ladylike *adjective* like a lady in manners: *She is too ladylike to swear.* □ **bien élevée**
'Ladyship *noun* (*with* **Her, Your** *etc*) a word used in speaking to, or about, a woman with the title 'Lady': *Thank you, Your Ladyship; Ask Her Ladyship for permission.* □ **Madame**
'ladybug *noun* a type of little round beetle, usually red with black spots. □ **coccinelle**
lady's fingers *noun plural* the long sticky green pods of a tropical plant, used as a vegetable. □ **gombo**

lag [lag] – *past tense, past participle* **lagged** – *verb* (often with **behind**) to move too slowly and become left behind: *We waited for the smaller children, who were lagging behind the rest.* □ **traîner derrière**
■ *noun* an act of lagging or the amount by which one thing is later than another: *There is sometimes a time-lag of several seconds between our seeing the lightning and our hearing the thunder.* □ **décalage**

lager ['laːgə] *noun* a light-coloured beer. □ **bière blonde (de type allemand)**

lagoon [lə'guːn] *noun* a shallow stretch of water separated from the sea by sandbanks, coral reefs *etc*. □ **lagune**

laid *see* **lay¹**.

lain *see* **lie²**.

lair [leə] *noun* the den of a wild beast: *The bear had its lair among the rocks at the top of the valley.* □ **tanière**

lake [leik] *noun* a large area of water surrounded by land: *They go swimming in/sailing on the lake; Lake Michi-*

gan. □ **lac**

lamb [lam] *noun* **1** a young sheep: *The ewe has had three lambs.* □ **agneau**

2 its flesh eaten as food: *a roast leg of lamb.* □ **agneau**

3 a lovable or gentle person, *usually* a child. □ **ange**

'**lambskin** *noun, adjective* (of) the skin of a lamb with the wool left on it: *a lambskin coat.* □ **(peau d')agneau**

'**lambswool** ['lamz-] *noun, adjective* (of) a fine type of wool obtained from a lamb: *a lambswool sweater.* □ **(en) laine d'agneau**

lame [leim] *adjective* **1** unable to walk properly: *He was lame for weeks after his fall.* □ **boiteux**

2 not satisfactory; unacceptable: *a lame excuse.* □ **piètre**

■ *verb* to make unable to walk properly: *He was lamed by a bullet in the ankle.* □ **estropier**

'**lamely** *adverb.* □ **maladroitement**

'**lameness** *noun.* □ **boiterie**

lament [lə'ment] *verb* to feel or express regret for: *We all lament his death*; *He sat lamenting over his past failures.* □ **(se) lamenter sur**

■ *noun* **1** a poem or piece of music which laments something: *This song is a lament for those killed in battle.* □ **lamentation**

2 a show of grief, regret *etc*: *I'm not going to sit listening to her laments all day.* □ **lamentation**

,**lamen'tation** [lamən-] *noun* (an) act of lamenting: *the lamentations of the widow.* □ **lamentation**

lamp [lamp] *noun* a (glass-covered) light: *an oil lamp*; *a table lamp*; *a street lamp.* □ **lampe**

'**lamppost** *noun* the pillar supporting a street lamp. □ **réverbère**

'**lampshade** *noun* a cover for a light bulb, made of *eg* cloth, paper or metal, which lessens, softens or directs the light coming from it. □ **abat-jour**

lance [laːns] *noun* a weapon of former times with a long shaft or handle of wood, a spearhead and often a small flag. □ **lance**

■ *verb* to cut open (a boil *etc*) with a knife: *The doctor lanced the boil on my neck.* □ **percer**

land [land] *noun* **1** the solid part of the surface of the Earth which is covered by the sea: *We had been at sea a week before we saw land.* □ **terre**

2 a country: *foreign lands.* □ **pays**

3 the ground or soil: *He never made any money at farming as his land was poor and stony.* □ **terre**

4 an estate: *He owns land/lands in Scotland.* □ **terrain, terre(s)**

■ *verb* **1** to come or bring down from the air upon the land: *The plane landed in a field*; *They managed to land the helicopter safely*; *She fell six metres, but landed without injury.* □ **(faire) atterrir**

2 to come or bring from the sea on to the land: *After being at sea for three months, they landed at Plymouth*; *He landed the big fish with some help.* □ **débarquer; amener à terre**

3 to (cause to) get into a particular (*usually* unfortunate) situation: *Don't drive so fast – you'll land (yourself) in hospital/trouble!* □ **se retrouver**

'**landing** *noun* **1** (an act of) coming or bringing to shore or to ground: *an emergency landing*; (*also adjective*) a

landing place. □ **débarquement; atterrissage**

2 a place for coming ashore. □ **débarcadère**

3 the level part of a staircase between flights of steps: *Her room was on the first floor, across the landing from mine.* □ **palier**

'**landing gear** *noun* the parts of an aircraft that carry the load when it lands: *The accident was caused by the failure of the plane's landing gear.* □ **train d'atterrissage**

'**landing-stage** *noun* a platform, fixed or floating, on which to land passengers or goods from a boat. □ **débarcadère**

'**landlocked** *adjective* enclosed by land: *a landlocked bay*; *That area is completely landlocked.* □ **entouré de terre**

'**landlord** – *feminine* '**landlady** (*plural* '**landladies**) – *noun* **1** a person who has tenants or lodgers: *My landlady has just put up my rent.* □ **propriétaire**

2 a person who keeps a public house: *The landlord of the 'Swan' is Mr. Smith.* □ **patron, onne**

'**landmark** *noun* **1** an object on land that serves as a guide to seamen or others: *The church tower is a landmark for sailors because it stands on the top of a cliff.* □ **(point de) repère**

2 an event of great importance. □ **date mémorable**

land mine a mine laid on or near the surface of the ground, which is set off by something passing over it. □ **mine (terrestre)**

'**landowner** *noun* a person who owns land, *especially* a lot of land. □ **propriétaire terrien/foncier**

'**landslide** *noun* a piece of land that falls down from the side of a hill: *His car was buried in the landslide.* □ **glissement de terrain**

land up to get into a particular, *usually* unfortunate, situation, *especially* through one's own fault: *If you go on like that, you'll land up in jail.* □ **finir par se retrouver à/en**

land with to burden (someone) with (an unpleasant task): *She was landed with the job of telling him the bad news.* □ **charger qqn d'une tâche désagréable**

see how the land lies to take a good look at the circumstances before making a decision. □ **tâter le terrain**

landscape ['landskeip] *noun* **1** the area of land that a person can look at all at the same time: *He stood on the hill surveying the landscape.* □ **paysage**

2 a picture showing a view of the countryside: *She paints landscapes.* □ **paysage**

■ *verb* to do landscape gardening on: *We are having our back garden landscaped.* □ **dessiner**

landscape gardening the art of planning and laying out gardens, parks *etc*. □ **paysagisme**

landscape gardener *noun.* □ **jardinier, ière paysagiste**

landslide [landslaid] *noun* the downward movement or slipping of large amounts of earth or rocks usually caused by severe storms: *The house at the foot of the hill was completely buried by a landslide.* □ **glissement**

lane [lein] **1** a narrow road or street: *a winding lane.* □ **chemin, ruelle**

2 used in the names of certain roads or streets: *His address is 12 Penny Lane.* □ **rue**

3 a division of a road for one line of traffic: *The new highway has three lanes in each direction.* □ **voie**
4 a regular course across the sea taken by ships: *a regular shipping lane.* □ **route, couloir (aérien)**

language ['læŋgwiʤ] *noun* 1 human speech: *the development of language in children.* □ **langage, langue**
2 the speech of a particular nation: *She is very good at (learning) languages; Russian is a difficult language.* □ **langue**
3 the words and way of speaking, writing *etc* usually connected with a particular group of people *etc*: *the language of journalists; medical language.* □ **langue, langage**
bad language *noun* swearing. □ **grossièreté**

languid ['læŋgwid] *adjective* without liveliness or energy. □ **languissant**
'**languidly** *adverb.* □ **languissamment**

languish ['læŋgwiʃ] *verb* to grow weak; to waste away. □ **(se)languir**

lank [læŋk] *adjective* (of hair) straight, thin, and *usually* greasy. □ **plat**
'**lanky** *adjective* thin, tall and not elegant: *He is tall and lanky.* □ **efflanqué**
'**lankiness** *noun.* □ **aspect efflanqué**

lantern ['læntən] *noun* a case for holding or carrying a light. □ **lanterne**

lap[1] [læp] – *past tense, past participle* **lapped** – *verb* 1 to drink by licking with the tongue: *The cat lapped milk from a saucer.* □ **laper**
2 (of a liquid) to wash or flow (against): *Water lapped the side of the boat.* □ **clapoter (contre)**
lap up to drink eagerly by lapping: *The dog lapped up the water.* □ **laper**

lap[2] [læp] *noun* 1 the part from waist to knees of a person who is sitting: *The baby was lying in its mother's lap.* □ **genoux**
2 one round of a racecourse or other competition track: *The runners have completed five laps, with three still to run.* □ **tour de piste**
lap dog a small pet dog. □ **petit chien (de salon)**
the lap of luxury very luxurious conditions: *living in the lap of luxury.* □ **luxe inouï**

lapel [lə'pel] *noun* the part of a coat joined to the collar and folded back against the chest: *Narrow lapels are in fashion.* □ **revers**

lapse [læps] *verb* 1 to cease to exist, often because of lack of effort: *Her insurance policy had lapsed and was not renewed.* □ **expirer**
2 to slip, fall, be reduced: *As he could think of nothing more to say, he lapsed into silence; I'm afraid our standards of tidiness have lapsed.* □ **(re)tomber dans**
■ *noun* 1 a mistake or failure (in behaviour, memory *etc*): *a lapse of memory.* □ **faute, défaillance**
2 a passing away (of time): *I saw him again after a lapse of five years.* □ **intervalle**

larch [lɑːtʃ] *noun* a type of cone-bearing, deciduous tree related to pines and firs. □ **mélèze**

lard [lɑːd] *noun* the melted fat of the pig, used in cooking. □ **saindoux**
■ *verb* to put lard on; to cover with lard. □ **larder (de), barder**

larder ['lɑːdə] *noun* a room or cupboard where food is stored in a house. □ **garde-manger**

large ['lɑːʤ] *adjective* great in size, amount *etc*; not small: *a large number of people; a large house; a large family; This house is too large for two people.* □ **grand, gros**
'**largely** *adverb* mainly; to a great extent: *This success was largely due to her efforts; Our methods have been largely successful.* □ **dans une large mesure**
'**largeness** *noun.* □ **grandeur, grosseur**
at large 1 (of prisoners *etc*) free: *Despite the efforts of the police, the escaped prisoner is still at large.* □ **en liberté**
2 in general: *the country/the public at large.* □ **en général**

lark[1] [lɑːk] *noun* a general name for several types of singing bird, *especially* the skylark, which flies high into the air as it sings. □ **alouette**

lark[2] [lɑːk] *noun* a piece of fun or mischief. □ **blague**

larva ['lɑːvə] – *plural* '**larvae** [-viː] – *noun* a developing insect in its first stage after coming out of the egg; a grub or caterpillar. □ **larve**
'**larval** *adjective.* □ **larvaire**

laser ['leizə] *noun* (an instrument that produces) a narrow and very intense beam of light: *The men were cutting the sheets of metal with a laser;* (*also adjective*) *a laser beam.* □ **laser**

lash [læʃ] *noun* 1 an eyelash: *She looked at him through her thick lashes.* □ **cil**
2 a stroke with a whip *etc*: *The sailor was given twenty lashes as a punishment.* □ **coup de fouet**
3 a thin piece of rope or cord, *especially* of a whip: *a whip with a long, thin lash.* □ **lanière**
■ *verb* 1 to strike with a lash: *She lashed the horse with her whip.* □ **fouetter**
2 to fasten with a rope or cord: *All the equipment had to be lashed to the deck of the ship.* □ **attacher**
3 to make a sudden or restless movement (with) (a tail): *The tiger crouched in the tall grass, its tail lashing from side to side.* □ **fouetter**
4 (of rain) to come down very heavily. □ **tomber à verse**
lash out (*often with* at) to hit out violently: *He lashed out with his fists.* □ **donner de violents coups à**

lass [læs] *noun* a girl. □ **jeune fille**

lasso [la'suː] – *plural* **las'so(e)s** – *noun* a long rope with a loop which tightens when the rope is pulled, used for catching wild horses *etc*. □ **lasso**
■ *verb* – *present tense* **las'soes**: *past tense, past participle* **las'soed** – to catch with a lasso: *The cowboy lassoed the horse.* □ **prendre au lasso**

last[1] [lɑːst] *adjective* 1 coming at the end: *We set out on the last day of November; He was last in the race; He caught the last bus home.* □ **dernier**
2 most recent; next before the present: *Our last house was much smaller than this; last year/month/week.* □ **dernier**
3 coming or remaining after all the others: *She was the last guest to leave.* □ **dernier**
■ *adverb* at the end of or after all the others: *He took his turn last.* □ **en dernier**

'lastly adverb finally: *Lastly, I would like to thank you all for listening so patiently to what I have been saying.* □ **enfin**

at (long) last in the end, *especially* after a long delay: *Oh, there he is at (long) last!* □ **enfin**

hear, see etc **the last of** to be finished with, be able to forget: *You haven't heard the last of this!* □ **en finir avec**

the last person a person who is very unlikely or unwilling to do a particular thing, or to whom it would be unwise or dangerous to do a particular thing: *I'm the last person to make a fuss, but you should have told me all the same; She's the last person you should offend.* □ **le/la dernier, ière, les derniers, ières**

the last straw a fact, happening etc which, when added to all other facts or happenings, makes a situation finally impossible to bear. □ **la goutte qui fait déborder le vase**

the last thing something very unlikely, unwanted, not intended etc: *It's the last thing you would think of looking for; The last thing I want is to hurt anyone.* □ **la dernière chose que...**

the last word 1 the final remark in an argument etc: *She always must have the last word!* □ **le dernier mot** 2 the final decision: *The last word rests with the chairman.* □ **le dernier mot** 3 something very fashionable or up to date: *Her hat was the last word in elegance.* □ **le dernier cri**

on one's last legs very near to falling down or collapsing with exhaustion, old age etc. □ **au bout du rouleau**

to the last until the very end: *She kept her courage to the last.* □ **jusqu'au bout**

last² [laːst] verb 1 to continue to exist: *This situation lasted until she got married; I hope this fine weather lasts.* □ **durer**

2 to remain in good condition or supply: *This carpet has lasted well; The bread won't last another two days – we'll need more; This coat will last me until I die.* □ **durer**

'lasting adjective: *A good education is a lasting benefit.* □ **durable**

last out to be or have enough to survive or continue to exist (until the end of): *I hope the gas lasts out until we reach a garage; They could only last out another week on the little food they had; The sick man was not expected to last out the night.* □ **tenir, suffire**

latch [latʃ] noun a catch of wood or metal used to fasten a door etc: *She lifted the latch and walked in.* □ **loquet**

'latchkey noun a small front door key: *She put her latchkey in the lock.* □ **clef (de la porte d'entrée)**

late [leit] adjective 1 coming etc after the expected or usual time: *The train is late tonight; I try to be punctual but I am always late.* □ **en retard** 2 far on in the day or night: *late in the day; late at night; It was very late when I got to bed.* □ **tard** 3 dead, *especially* recently: *the late king.* □ **le/la regretté(e)** 4 recently, but no longer, holding an office or position: *Mr. Allan, the late chairman, made a speech.* □ **ancien**
■ adverb 1 after the expected or usual time: *She ar-*

rived late for her interview. □ **en retard** 2 far on in the day or night: *They always go to bed late.* □ **tard**

'lateness noun. □ **retard**

'lately adverb in the recent past or not long ago: *Have you seen her lately?* □ **récemment**

later on at a later time: *He hasn't arrived yet but no doubt he'll be here later on.* □ **plus tard**

of late lately: *He thought she had been less friendly of late.* □ **ces temps-ci**

later see **latter**.

latent ['leitənt] adjective hidden or undeveloped, but capable of being developed: *a latent talent for music.* □ **latent**

lateral ['latərəl] adjective of, at, to or from the side: *lateral movement.* □ **latéral**

'laterally adverb. □ **latéralement**

latex ['leiteks] noun the milky juice of some plants *especially* rubber trees. □ **latex**

lath [laiθ] noun a thin strip of wood: *The laths were placed crosswise and made into latticework for the top of the fence.* □ **latte**

lathe [leið] noun a machine for shaping wood, metal etc, which turns the piece of wood etc which is to be shaped around and around against a tool held steady by the operator. □ **tour**

lather ['laːðə] noun 1 foam made up of soap bubbles: *Add the detergent to the water and work up a good lather.* □ **mousse** 2 a foam of sweat appearing eg on a horse's neck. □ **écume**

Latin ['latin] noun, adjective 1 (of) the language spoken in ancient Rome: *We studied Latin at school; a Latin lesson.* □ **latin** 2 (a person) who speaks a language derived from Latin. □ **Latin, ine**

Latin America the countries of Central and South America, where the official language is usually a form of either Spanish or Portuguese. □ **Amérique latine**

Latin American noun, adjective. □ **latino-américain**

latitude ['latitjuːd] noun 1 the distance, measured in degrees on the map, that a place is north or south of the Equator: *What is the latitude of London?* □ **latitude** 2 freedom of choice or action. □ **latitude**

latrine [lə'triːn] noun a lavatory, *especially* one used by soldiers etc. □ **latrines**

latter ['latə] adjective towards the end: *the latter part of our holiday.* □ **deuxième, dernier**

'latterly adverb 1 recently; lately. □ **récemment** 2 towards the end. □ **sur le tard**

the latter the second of two things etc mentioned: *John and Mary arrived, the latter wearing a green wool dress.* □ **celui/celle/ceux/celles-ci**

to choose the second or **latter** (not **later**) of two alternatives.

laudable ['loːdəbl] adjective worthy of being praised: *a laudable effort.* □ **louable**

'laudably adverb. □ **louablement**

laugh [lɑːf] *verb* to make sounds with the voice in showing happiness, amusement, scorn *etc*: *We laughed at the funny photographs*; *Children were laughing in the garden as they played.* □ **rire**

■ *noun* an act or sound of laughing: *She gave a laugh*; *a loud laugh.* □ **rire**

'**laughable** *adjective* **1** ridiculous or deserving scorn: *Her attempts at drawing were laughable.* □ **risible**

2 amusing; comical. □ **comique**

'**laughably** *adverb.* □ **ridiculement**

'**laughingly** *adverb* as a joke: *She suggested laughingly that he should try it himself.* □ **par plaisanterie**

'**laughter** *noun* the act or sound of laughing: *We could hear laughter/the sound of laughter from the next room.* □ **rire**

'**laughing-stock** *noun* someone who is laughed at: *If I wear that hat, I'll be a laughing-stock.* □ **risée**

laugh at to make it obvious that one regards something or someone as humorous, ridiculous or deserving scorn: *Everyone will laugh at me if I wear that dress!*; *The others laughed at his fears.* □ **se moquer de**

launch[1] [lɔːntʃ] *verb* **1** to make (a boat or ship) slide into the water or (a rocket) leave the ground: *As soon as the alarm was given, the lifeboat was launched*; *The Russians have launched a rocket.* □ **lancer**

2 to start (a person, project *etc*) off on a course: *His success launched him on a brilliant career.* □ **lancer**

3 to throw. □ **lancer**

■ *noun* (an) act of launching. □ **lancement**

'**launching-pad** *noun* a platform from which a rocket can be launched. □ **rampe de lancement**

launch into to begin eagerly: *He launched into an enthusiastic description of the play.* □ **se lancer dans**

launch out to throw oneself freely into some new activity (often involving spending money). □ **se lancer dans**

launch[2] [lɔːntʃ] *noun* a large, power-driven boat, *usually* used for short trips or for pleasure: *We cruised around the bay in a motorboat.* □ **bateau de plaisance**

launder ['lɔːndə] *verb* to wash and iron: *to launder clothes.* □ **blanchir**

laund(e)rette [lɔːn'dret] *noun* a shop where customers may wash clothes in washing machines. □ **laverie automatique**

'**laundress** *noun* a woman employed to launder. □ **blanchisseur, euse**

'**laundry** – *plural* **laundries** – *noun* **1** a place where clothes *etc* are washed, *especially* in return for payment: *She took the sheets to the laundry; a hospital laundry.* □ **blanchisserie**

2 clothes *etc* which have been, or are to be, washed: *a bundle of laundry.* □ **lessive**

laurel ['lɔrəl] *noun* a type of tree, once used for making wreaths to crown winners of races or competitions *etc*. □ **laurier**

rest on one's laurels to depend too much on one's past successes and therefore make no further effort. □ **(se) reposer sur ses lauriers**

lava ['lɑːvə] *noun* liquid, melted rock *etc* thrown out from a volcano and becoming solid as it cools. □ **lave**

lavatory ['lavətəri] – *plural* '**lavatories** – *noun* (a room containing) a receptacle for waste matter from the body. □ **toilettes**

lavender ['lavində] *noun* **1** a type of plant with sweet smelling pale bluish-purple flowers. □ **lavande**

2 (*also adjective*) (of) the colour of the flowers: *a lavender dress.* □ **lavande**

lavish ['laviʃ] *verb* to spend or give very freely: *She lavishes too much money on that child.* □ **dépenser/donner sans compter**

■ *adjective* **1** (of a person) spending or giving generously and sometimes too freely: *a lavish host*; *You have certainly been lavish with the brandy in this cake.* □ **prodigue**

2 given generously or too freely: *lavish gifts.* □ **copieux, somptueux**

'**lavishly** *adverb.* □ **sans compter**

'**lavishness** *noun.* □ **prodigalité**

law [lɔː] *noun* **1** the collection of rules according to which people live or a country *etc* is governed: *Such an action is against the law; law and order.* □ **loi(s), législation**

2 any one of such rules: *A new law has been passed by Parliament.* □ **loi**

3 (in science) a rule that says that under certain conditions certain things always happen: *the law of gravity.* □ **loi**

'**lawful** *adjective* **1** (*negative* **unlawful**) allowed by law: *He was attacked while going about his lawful business.* □ **légitime**

2 just or rightful: *She is the lawful owner of the property.* □ **légitime**

'**lawfully** *adverb.* □ **légalement**

'**lawless** *adjective* paying no attention to, and not keeping, the law: *In its early days, the American West was full of lawless men.* □ **sans loi**

'**lawlessly** *adverb.* □ **d'une manière illégale**

'**lawlessness** *noun.* □ **illégalité**

lawyer ['lɔːjə] *noun* a person whose work it is to know about and give advice and help to others concerning the law: *If you want to make your will, consult a lawyer.* □ **avocat, ate**

'**law-abiding** *adjective* obeying the law: *a law-abiding citizen.* □ **respectueux des lois**

law court (*also* **court of law**) a place where people accused of crimes are tried and legal disagreements between people are judged. □ **cour de justice**

'**lawsuit** *noun* a quarrel or disagreement taken to a court of law to be settled. □ **procès**

be a law unto oneself to be inclined not to obey rules or follow the usual customs and conventions. □ **ne connaître d'autre loi que la sienne**

the law the police: *The thief was still in the building when the law arrived.* □ **la police**

the law of the land the established law of a country. □ **les lois du pays**

lay down the law to state something in a way that indicates that one expects one's opinion and orders to be accepted without argument. □ **(essayer de) faire la loi**

lawn [lɔːn] *noun* an area of smooth, short grass, *especially* as part of a garden: *He is mowing the lawn.* □

pelouse

lax [laks] *adjective* careless or not strict in discipline or morals: *Pupils have been rather lax about some of the school rules recently.* □ **relâché**
'**laxity** *noun.* □ **relâchement**
'**laxness** *noun.* □ **relâchement**

laxative ['laksǝtiv] *noun, adjective* (a medicine) which makes it easier to pass waste matter from the bowels. □ **laxatif**

lay¹ [lei] – *past tense, past participle* **laid** [leid] – *verb* **1** to place, set or put (down), often carefully: *She laid the clothes in a drawer/on a chair; He laid down his pencil; She laid her report before the committee.* □ **poser**
2 to place in a lying position: *She laid the baby on his back.* □ **coucher**
3 to put in order or arrange: *He went to lay the table for dinner; to lay one's plans/a trap.* □ **mettre, préparer**
4 to flatten: *The animal laid back its ears; The wind laid the corn flat.* □ **coucher**
5 to cause to disappear or become quiet: *to lay a ghost/doubts.* □ **dissiper**
6 (of a bird) to produce (eggs): *The hen laid four eggs; My hens are laying well.* □ **pondre**
'**layer** *noun* **1** a thickness or covering: *The ground was covered with a layer of snow; There was a layer of clay a few metres under the ground.* □ **couche**
2 something which lays, *especially* a hen: *a good layer.* □ **pondeuse**
■ *verb* to put, cut or arrange in layers: *She had her hair layered by the hairdresser.* □ **couper en dégradé**
'**layabout** *noun* a lazy, idle person. □ **fainéant, ante**
'**layout** *noun* the manner in which something is displayed or laid out: *the layout of the building.* □ **plan, disposition**
laid up ill in bed: *When I caught flu, I was laid up for a fortnight.* □ **alité**
lay aside to put away or to one side, *especially* to be used or dealt with at a later time: *She laid the books aside for later use.* □ **mettre de côté**
lay bare to show clearly; to expose to view: *They dug up the road and laid bare the water pipe; Shy people don't like to lay bare their feelings.* □ **mettre à nu**
lay down 1 to give up: *They laid down their arms; The soldiers laid down their lives in the cause of peace.* □ **déposer; sacrifier**
2 to order or instruct: *The rule book lays down what should be done in such a case.* □ **établir**
lay (one's) hands on 1 to find or be able to obtain: *I wish I could lay (my) hands on that book!* □ **mettre la main sur**
2 to catch: *The police had been trying to lay hands on the criminal for months.* □ **mettre la main sur**
lay off to dismiss (employees) temporarily: *Because of a shortage of orders, the firm has laid off a quarter of its workforce.* □ **licencier**
lay out 1 to arrange over a wide area (*especially* according to a plan): *He was the architect who laid out the public gardens.* □ **dessiner**
2 to spread so as to be easily seen: *He laid out the contents of the box on the table.* □ **étaler**

3 to knock unconscious. □ **assommer**
4 to spend (money). □ **dépenser**
5 to prepare (a dead body) to be buried. □ **faire la toilette d'un mort**
lay up to put (a ship) out of use in a dock. □ **mettre en rade**
lay waste to make (a piece of land) into barren country by burning and plundering. □ **dévaster**

> **lay** needs an object and has **laid** as its past tense and past participle: *He (had) laid his book down; He will be laying his proposals before the committee tomorrow.*
> **lie** takes no object and has **lying** as its present participle, **lay** as its past tense and **lain** as its past participle: *Please lie down; He lay down; He had lain there for hours.*
> **lie**, to be untruthful, has **lying** as its present participle, and **lied** as its past tense and past participle: *He (has always) lied about his age.*

lay² *see* **lie².**

lay³ [lei] *adjective* **1** not a member of the clergy: *lay preachers.* □ **laïque**
2 not an expert or a professional (in a particular subject): *Doctors tend to use words that lay people don't understand.* □ **profane**
'**layman** *noun* a lay person. □ **laïc, profane**

layer *see* **lay¹.**

layman *see* **lay³.**

layout *see* **lay¹.**

lazy ['leizi] *adjective* too inclined to avoid hard work, exercise *etc*: *I take the bus to work as I'm too lazy to walk; Lazy people tend to become fat.* □ **paresseux**
'**lazily** *adverb.* □ **paresseusement**
'**laziness** *noun.* □ **paresse**
'**lazy-bones** *noun* a name for a lazy person. □ **fainéant, ante**

lead¹ [liːd] – *past tense, past participle* **led** [led] – *verb* **1** to guide or direct or cause to go in a certain direction: *Follow my car and I'll lead you to the highway; She took the child by the hand and led him across the road; He was leading the horse into the stable; The sound of hammering led us to the garage; You led us to believe that we would be paid!* □ **conduire, mener**
2 to go or carry to a particular place or along a particular course: *A small path leads through the woods.* □ **mener**
3 (*with* **to**) to cause or bring about a certain situation or state of affairs: *The heavy rain led to serious floods.* □ **entraîner**
4 to be first (in): *An official car led the procession; She is still leading in the competition.* □ **mener**
5 to live (a certain kind of life): *She leads a pleasant existence on a Greek island.* □ **mener**
■ *noun* **1** the front place or position: *He has taken over the lead in the race.* □ **tête**
2 the state of being first: *We have a lead over the rest of the world in this kind of research.* □ **avance**
3 the act of leading: *We all followed his lead.* □ **exemple**
4 the amount by which one is ahead of others: *He has a*

lead of twenty metres (over the man in second place). □ **avance**

5 a leather strap or chain for leading a dog *etc*: *All dogs must be kept on a lead.* □ **laisse**

6 a piece of information which will help to solve a mystery *etc*: *The police have several leads concerning the identity of the thief.* □ **piste**

7 a leading part in a play *etc*: *Who plays the lead in that film?* □ **rôle principal**

'leader *noun* **1** a person who is in front or goes first: *The fourth runner is several kilometres behind the leaders.* □ **meneur, euse**

2 a person who is the head of, organizes or is in charge (of something): *The leader of the expedition is a scientist.* □ **chef**

3 an article in a newspaper *etc* written to express the opinions of the editor. □ **éditorial**

'leadership *noun* **1** the state of being a leader: *He took over the leadership of the Labour party two years later.* □ **direction**

2 the quality of being able to be a leader: *The post requires a person who combines leadership and energy.* □ **qualités de chef**

lead on **1** to deceive with false expectations. □ **faire marcher qqn**

2 to go first; to show the way: *Lead on!* □ **ouvrir la marche**

lead up the garden path to deceive. □ **mener en bateau**

lead up to to progress towards; to contribute to: *to lead up to a climax; the events leading up to the First World War.* □ **conduire à**

lead the way to go first (*especially* to show the way): *She led the way upstairs.* □ **passer devant**

lead² [led] *noun* **1** (*also adjective*) (of) an element, a soft, heavy, bluish grey metal: *lead pipes; Are these pipes made of lead or copper?* □ **plomb**

2 the part of a pencil that leaves a mark: *The lead of my pencil has broken.* □ **mine**

'leaden *adjective* **1** lead-coloured: *leaden skies.* □ **de plomb**

2 made of lead. □ **de/en plomb**

leaf [li:f] – *plural* **leaves** [li:vz] – *noun* **1** a part of a plant growing from the side of a stem, *usually* green, flat and thin, but of various shapes depending on the plant: *Many trees lose their leaves in autumn.* □ **feuille**

2 something thin like a leaf, *especially* the page of a book: *Several leaves had been torn out of the book.* □ **page**

3 an extra part of a table, either attached to one side with a hinge or added to the centre when the two ends are apart. □ **rallonge**

'leaflet [-lit] *noun* a small, printed sheet containing information *etc*. □ **prospectus, dépliant**

'leafy *adjective* having many leaves: *a leafy plant.* □ **feuillu**

turn over a new leaf to begin a new and better way of behaving, working *etc*. □ **changer de conduite**

league¹ [li:g] *noun* **1** a union of persons, nations *etc* for the benefit of each other: *the League for the Protection of Shopkeepers.* □ **ligue**

2 a grouping of sports clubs for games. □ **division**

be in league with to be allied to. □ **être ligué avec qqn**

league² [li:g] *noun* an old measure of distance (about 4.8 km). □ **lieue**

leak [li:k] *noun* **1** a crack or hole through which liquid or gas escapes: *Water was escaping through a leak in the pipe.* □ **fuite**

2 the passing of gas, water *etc* through a crack or hole: *a gas leak.* □ **fuite**

3 a giving away of secret information: *a leak of Government plans.* □ **fuite**

■ *verb* **1** to have a leak: *This bucket leaks; The boiler leaked hot water all over the floor.* □ **fuir**

2 to (cause something) to pass through a leak: *Gas was leaking from the cracked pipe; He was accused of leaking secrets to the enemy.* □ **fuir, divulguer**

'leakage [-kidʒ] *noun* (an act of) leaking: *Leakages in several water mains had been reported; a leakage of information.* □ **fuite**

'leaky *adjective*: *a leaky boat.* □ **qui fuit, percé**

lean¹ [li:n] – *past tense, past participles* **leant** [lent], **leaned** – *verb* **1** to slope over to one side; not to be upright: *The lamppost had slipped and was leaning across the road.* □ **pencher**

2 to rest (against, on): *She leaned the ladder against the wall; Don't lean your elbows on the table; He leant on the gate.* □ **(s')appuyer (à/contre/sur)**

'leaning *noun* a liking or preference: *She has a leaning towards the arts.* □ **penchant (pour)**

lean² [li:n] *adjective* **1** thin; not fat: *a tall, lean man.* □ **maigre**

2 not containing much fat: *lean meat.* □ **maigre**

3 poor; not producing much: *a lean harvest.* □ **maigre**

'leanness *noun*. □ **maigreur**

leant *see* **lean¹**.

leap [li:p] – *past tense, past participles* **leapt** [lept], **leaped** – *verb* **1** to jump: *He leapt into the boat.* □ **sauter**

2 to jump over: *The dog leapt the wall.* □ **sauter par-dessus**

3 to rush eagerly: *She leaped into his arms.* □ **sauter**

■ *noun* an act of leaping: *The cat jumped from the roof and reached the ground in two leaps.* □ **bond**

'leapfrog *noun* a game in which one person vaults over another's bent back, pushing off from his hands. □ **saute-mouton**

leap year every fourth year, which consists of 366 days, February having 29, *ie* 1976, 1980, 1984 *etc*. □ **année bissextile**

by leaps and bounds extremely rapidly and successfully: *improving by leaps and bounds.* □ **à pas de géant**

learn [lə:n] – *past tense, past participles* **learned, learnt** – *verb* **1** to get to know: *It was then that I learned that she was dead.* □ **apprendre**

2 to gain knowledge or skill (in): *A child is always learning; to learn French; She is learning (how) to swim.* □ **apprendre**

'learned [-nid] *adjective* having or showing great learning: *a learned professor.* □ **savant**

'learner *noun* a person who is in process of learning: *Be patient – I'm only a learner; (also adjective) a learner* *driver.* □ **débutant, ante**

'learning *noun* knowledge which has been gained by learning: *The professor was a man of great learning.* □ **savoir**

lease [liːs] *noun* (the period of) an agreement giving the use of a house *etc* on payment of rent: *We signed the lease yesterday; a twenty year lease.* □ **bail**

■ *verb* to give or acquire a house *etc* in this way: *He leases the land from the local council.* □ **louer**

leash [liːʃ] *noun* a strip of leather or piece of chain attached to a collar around its neck by which a dog *etc* is held. □ **laisse**

least [liːst] *adjective, pronoun* (something) which is the smallest or the smallest amount that exists, is possible *etc: I think the least you can do is apologize!; She wanted to know how to do it with the least amount of bother.* □ **le moins (de/que)**

■ *adverb* (*sometimes with* **the**) to the smallest or lowest degree: *I like her (the) least of all the girls; That is the least important of our problems.* □ **le moins**

at least at any rate; anyway: *I think she's well – at least she was when I saw her last.* □ **du moins**

not in the least not at all: *You're not disturbing me in the least!* □ **pas le moins du monde**

leather ['leðə] *noun, adjective* (of) the skin of an animal prepared for making clothes, luggage *etc: shoes made of leather; a leather jacket/case.* □ **(de) cuir**

'leathery *adjective* like leather, *especially* tough: *The plant had broad, leathery leaves.* □ **tanné**

leave[1] [liːv] – *past tense, past participle* **left** [left] – *verb* 1 to go away or depart from, often without meaning to return: *She left the room for a moment; They left at about six o'clock; I have left that job.* □ **quitter, partir**

2 to go without taking: *She left her gloves in the car; He left his children behind when he went to France.* □ **laisser**

3 to allow to remain in a particular state or condition: *She left the job half-finished.* □ **laisser**

4 to let (a person or a thing) do something without being helped or attended to: *I'll leave the meat to cook for a while.* □ **laisser**

5 to allow to remain for someone to do, make *etc: Leave that job to the experts!* □ **laisser**

6 to make a gift of in one's will: *She left all her property to her son.* □ **léguer**

leave alone not to disturb, upset or tease: *Why can't you leave your little brother alone?* □ **laisser tranquille**

leave out not to include or put in: *You've left out a word in that sentence.* □ **oublier**

leftover not used; extra: *When everyone took a partner there was one person leftover; We divided out the leftover food.* □ **de trop, de reste**

leave[2] [liːv] *noun* 1 permission to do something, *eg* to be absent: *Have I your leave to go?* □ **permission**

2 (*especially* of soldiers, sailors *etc*) a holiday: *He is home on leave at the moment.* □ **permission**

take one's leave (of) to say goodbye (to): *I took my leave (of the others) and went out.* □ **prendre congé (de)**

leavened ['levnd] *adjective* (*negative* **unleavened**) containing yeast to make it rise: *leavened bread.* □ **levé**

leaves *see* **leaf**.

lectern ['lektən] *noun* a stand for holding a book *etc* to be read from, *especially* for a lecture or in a church. □ **lutrin**

lecture ['lektʃə] *noun* 1 a formal talk given to students or other audiences: *a history lecture.* □ **conférence, cours**

2 a long and boring or irritating speech, warning or scolding: *The teacher gave the children a lecture for running in the corridor.* □ **réprimande**

■ *verb* to give a lecture: *He lectures on Roman Art; She lectured him on good behaviour.* □ **donner un cours/ une leçon**

'lecturer *noun* a person who lectures, *especially* to students: *She is a lecturer in the English department.* □ **conférencier, ière, professeur, eure**

led *see* **lead**[1].

ledge [ledʒ] *noun* a shelf or an object that sticks out like a shelf: *He keeps plant pots on the window ledge; They stopped on a ledge halfway up the cliff.* □ **rebord, corniche**

ledger ['ledʒə] *noun* the book of accounts of an office or shop. □ **grand livre**

lee [liː] *noun* the sheltered side, away from the wind: *We sat in the lee of the rock.* □ **côté sous le vent**

'leeway *noun* 1 the drifting of a ship *etc* away from its true course, or the amount of this. □ **dérive**

2 lost time: *He has a lot of leeway to make up at school after being away ill.* □ **retard (à rattraper)**

3 extra space, time *etc* allowed: *Book the later flight so as to allow yourself some leeway in case you're delayed.* □ **marge (de sécurité)**

leech [liːtʃ] *noun* a kind of bloodsucking worm. □ **sangsue**

leek [liːk] *noun* a type of vegetable related to the onion with green leaves and a white base. □ **poireau**

leer [liə] *noun* an unpleasant kind of smile. □ **regard mauvais**

■ *verb* to give this kind of smile. □ **lorgner**

left[1] *see* **leave**[1].

left[2] [left] *adjective* on, for, or belonging to, the side of the body that in most people has the less skilful hand (the side of a person or thing which is toward the west when that person or thing is facing north–opposite to **right**): *She wore an engagement ring on her left hand; They drive on the left side of the road in Britain.* □ **gauche**

■ *adverb* to or towards this side: *He turned left at the end of the road.* □ **à gauche**

■ *noun* 1 the left side, part *etc: He sat on her left; She turned to her left; Take the first road on the left; Keep to the left!* □ **gauche**

2 within a political party, Parliament *etc*, the most radical or socialist group. □ **gauche**

'left-hand *adjective* 1 at the left; to the left of something else: *the bottom left-hand drawer of the desk.* □ **à/ de gauche**

2 towards the left: *a left-hand bend in the road.* □ **à gauche**

left-'handed *adjective* having the left hand more skilful than the right. □ **gaucher**

left-'handedness *noun*. □ **fait d'être gaucher**
left-'wing *adjective* (having opinions which are) radical, socialist or communist. □ **de gauche**
left wing the left of a political party. □ **gauche**
leg [leg] *noun* **1** one of the limbs by which animals and man walk: *The horse injured a front leg; She stood on one leg.* □ **patte, jambe**
2 the part of an article of clothing that covers one of these limbs closely: *He has torn the leg of his trousers.* □ **jambe**
3 a long, narrow support of a table *etc*: *One of the legs of the chair was broken.* □ **pied**
4 one stage in a journey, competition *etc*: *the last leg of the trip; the second leg of the contest.* □ **étape**
-legged [legid] *adjective*: *a long-legged girl; a four-legged animal.* □ **à/aux... jambes (...)**
pull someone's leg to try as a joke to make someone believe something which is not true: *You haven't really got a black mark on your face – he's only pulling your leg.* □ **faire marcher qqn**
legacy ['legəsi] – *plural* '**legacies** – *noun* something left in a will by someone who has died: *He was left a legacy by his great-aunt.* □ **héritage**
legal ['liːgəl] *adjective* **1** lawful; allowed by the law: *Is it legal to bring gold watches into the country?*; *a legal contract.* □ **légal**
2 concerned with or used in the law: *the legal profession.* □ **légal, juridique**
'**legally** *adverb*. □ **légalement**
le'gality [-'ga-] *noun*. □ **légalité**
'**legalize**, '**legalise** *verb* to make legal or lawful. □ **légaliser**
legation [li'geiʃən] *noun* (the headquarters of) an official group of people acting on behalf of the government of their own country *etc* in another country. □ **légation**
legend ['ledʒənd] *noun* a myth or traditional story, handed down from one generation to another: *the legend of St George.* □ **légende**
'**legendary** *adjective* **1** mentioned *etc* in legend: *legendary heroes.* □ **légendaire**
2 very famous because very great, good *etc*: *His generosity is legendary.* □ **légendaire**
legible ['ledʒəbl] *adjective* clear enough to be read: *The writing was faded but still legible.* □ **lisible**
'**legibly** *adverb*. □ **lisiblement**
,**legi'bility** *noun*. □ **lisibilité**
legion ['liːdʒən] *noun* **1** in ancient Rome, a body of from three to six thousand soldiers. □ **légion**
2 a great many or a very large number. □ **légion**
'**legislate** ['ledʒisleit] *verb* to make laws: *The government plan to legislate against the import of foreign cars.* □ **légiférer**
,**legi'slation** *noun* **1** the act of legislating. □ **élaboration des lois**
2 a law or group of laws. □ **loi, législation**
'**legislative** [-lətiv] *adjective* law-making: *a legislative assembly; legislative powers.* □ **législatif**
'**legislator** a person who makes laws. □ **législateur, trice**

'**legislature** [-lətʃə] *noun* the part of the government which has the power of making laws. □ **corps législatif**
legitimate [li'dʒitimət] *adjective* **1** lawful: *Is this procedure perfectly legitimate?* □ **légitime**
2 (of a child) born to parents who are married to each other. □ **légitime**
le'gitimately *adverb*. □ **légitimement**
le'gitimacy *noun*. □ **légitimité**
leisure ['leʒə] *noun* time which one can spend as one likes, *especially* when one does not have to work: *I seldom have leisure to watch television.* □ **loisir**
'**leisurely** *adjective, adverb* not hurrying; taking plenty of time: *She had a leisurely bath.* □ **sans se presser**
lemon ['lemən] *noun, adjective* **1** (of) a type of oval, juicy, citrus fruit with pale yellow skin and very sour juice: *She added the juice of a lemon to the pudding; a lemon drink.* □ **citron**
2 (of) the colour of this fruit: *a pale lemon dress.* □ **citron**
lemo'nade [-'neid] *noun* a (fizzy) drink flavoured with lemons. □ **citronnade, limonade**
lemon grass a tough grass with a strong scent, used to flavour food. □ **citronnelle**
lend [lend] – *past tense, past participle* **lent** [lent] – *verb* **1** to give (someone) the use of for a time: *She had forgotten her umbrella so I lent her mine to go home with.* □ **prêter**
2 to give or add (a quality) to: *Desperation lent him strength.* □ **donner**
lend itself to to be suitable for or adapt easily to: *The play lends itself to performance by children.* □ **(se) prêter à**

see also **borrow.**

length [leŋθ] *noun* **1** the distance from one end to the other of an object, period of time *etc*: *What is the length of your car?*; *Please note down the length of time it takes you to do this.* □ **longueur; durée**
2 a piece of something, *especially* cloth: *I bought a (3-metre) length of silk.* □ **coupon**
3 in racing, the measurement from end to end of a horse, boat *etc*: *He won by a length; The other boat is several lengths in front.* □ **longueur**
'**lengthen** *verb* to make or become longer: *I'll have to lengthen this skirt; The days are lengthening now that the spring has come.* □ **(r)allonger**
'**lengthways**/'**lengthwise** *adverb* in the direction of the length: *She folded the towels lengthways.* □ **dans le sens de la longueur**
'**lengthy** *adjective* of great, often too great, length: *This essay is interesting but lengthy.* □ **(trop) long**
at length 1 in detail; taking a long time: *She told us at length about her accident.* □ **en long et en large**
2 at last: *At length the walkers arrived home.* □ **enfin**
go to any lengths to do anything, no matter how extreme, dishonest, wicked *etc*, to achieve a particular aim: *She'd go to any lengths to get herself promoted.* □ **ne reculer devant rien pour**
lenient ['liːniənt] *adjective* merciful or punishing only lightly: *You are much too lenient with wrongdoers.* □ **indulgent**

'leniently adverb. □ avec indulgence
'lenience, 'leniency noun. □ indulgence

lens [lenz] noun 1 a piece of glass etc curved on one or both sides and used in spectacles, microscopes, cameras etc: I need new lenses in my spectacles; The camera lens is dirty. □ verre, lentille
2 a similar part of the eye: The disease has affected the lens of his left eye. □ cristallin

> lens is singular; the plural is lenses.

lent see lend.

lentil ['lentil] noun the small orange seed of a pod-bearing plant, used in soups etc. □ lentille

leopard ['lepəd] noun a type of large spotted member of the cat family. □ léopard

leotard ['liətɑːd] noun a kind of tight-fitting garment worn for dancing, gymnastics etc. □ maillot (de danse)

leper ['lepə] noun a person who has leprosy. □ lépreux, euse
'leprosy [-rəsi] noun a contagious skin disease, causing serious and permanent damage to the body, including loss of fingers, nose etc. □ lèpre

lesbian [ləzbiən] noun a woman whose sexual preference is women: Mary is a lesbian and not attracted to men. □ lesbienne

less [les] adjective (often with than) not as much (as): Think of a number less than forty; He drank his tea and wished he had put less sugar in it; The salary for that job will be not less than $40,000. □ plus petit que, moins (de)
■ adverb not as much or to a smaller extent: I like her less every time I see her; You should smoke less if you want to remain healthy. □ moins
■ pronoun a smaller part or amount: He has less than I have. □ moins (que)
■ preposition minus: He earns $280 a week less $90 income tax. □ moins
'lessen verb to make or become less: The fan lessened the heat a little; When the children left, the noise lessened considerably. □ diminuer
'lesser adjective smaller or not as important: the lesser of the two towns. □ le/la moindre
■ adverb less: the lesser-known streets of London. □ moins
the less ... the less/more etc: The less I see of him, the better (pleased I'll be)!; The less I practise, the less confident I become; The less I try, the more I succeed. □ moins...moins/plus
no less a person etc than: as great a person etc as: I had tea with no less a person than the Prime Minister (= with the Prime Minister himself). □ rien (de) moins que

> less is used in speaking about quantity or amount: People should eat less fat; I've less than $100 in the bank.
> fewer sould be used in speaking about numbers of individual things or people: I've fewer books than she has; There were fewer than 50 people at the meeting.

lesson ['lesn] noun 1 something which is learned or taught: The lesson which we learned from the experience was never to trust anyone. □ leçon
2 a period of teaching: during the French lesson. □ leçon
3 a part of the Bible read in church: He was asked to read the lesson on Sunday morning. □ leçon

lest [lest] conjunction in case: He was scared lest he should fail his exam. □ de peur de/que

let[1] [let] – present participle 'letting: past tense, past participle let – verb 1 to allow or permit: She refused to let her children go out in the rain; Let me see your drawing. □ laisser
2 to cause to: I will let you know how much it costs. □ faire en sorte que
3 used for giving orders or suggestions: If they will not work, let them starve; Let's (= let us) leave right away!
let alone not to mention; without taking into consideration: There's no room for all the adults, let alone the children. □ sans parler de
let (someone or something) alone/be to leave alone; not to disturb or worry: Why don't you let him be when he's not feeling well!; Do let your father alone. □ laisser tranquille
let down 1 to lower: She let down the blind. □ baisser
2 to disappoint or fail to help when necessary etc: You must give a film show at the party – you can't let the children down (noun 'let-down); She felt he had let her down by not coming to see her perform. □ décevoir (n: déception)
3 to make longer: She had to let down the child's skirt. □ (r)allonger
let fall to drop: She was so startled she let fall everything she was carrying. □ lâcher
let go (of) to stop holding (something): Will you let go of my coat!; When he was nearly at the top of the rope he suddenly let go and fell. □ lâcher
let in, out to allow to come in, go out: Let me in!; I let the dog out. □ faire entrer/sortir
let in for to involve (someone) in: I didn't know what I was letting myself in for when I agreed to do that job. □ s'engager (à/dans)
let in on to allow to share (a secret etc): We'll let her in on our plans. □ mettre au courant
let off 1 to fire (a gun) or cause (a firework etc) to explode: He let the gun off accidentally. □ faire partir, faire éclater
2 to allow to go without punishment etc: The policewoman let him off (with a warning). □ laisser partir
let up to become less strong or violent; to stop: I wish the rain would let up (noun 'let-up). □ diminuer
let well alone to allow things to remain as they are, in order not to make them worse. □ le mieux est l'ennemi du bien

let[2] [let] – present participle 'letting: past tense, past participle let – verb to give the use of (a house etc) in return for payment: She lets her house to visitors in the summer. □ louer

let to, rent (out) to mean to allow the use of (a house *etc* that one owns) to (someone) in return for payment: *to let/rent (out) one's flat to visitors.*

rent from means to give payment for one's use of (a house *etc*) to (the owner): *I rent my flat from a landlord who lives abroad.*

lethal ['liːθəl] *adjective* causing death; enough to kill: *a lethal dose of poison.* □ **mortel**

lethargy ['leθədʒi] *noun* lack of interest or energy. □ **léthargie**

le'thargic [-'θaː-] *adjective.* □ **léthargique**

letter ['letə] *noun* 1 a mark expressing a sound: *the letters of the alphabet.* □ **lettre**

2 a written message, *especially* sent by post in an envelope: *She slowly took the letter from its envelope; Did you post my letter?* □ **lettre**

'lettering *noun* 1 the way in which letters are formed: *the art of lettering.* □ **lettrage**

2 letters which have been drawn, painted *etc*: *He repainted the lettering over the shop door.* □ **lettrage**

'letterbox *noun* 1 a slit in a door (sometimes with a box behind it) through which mail from the post is put: *He put the card through the letterbox.* □ **boîte à/aux lettres**

2 a mailbox. □ **boîte à/aux lettres**

letter opener *noun* knife used for opening envelopes. □ **coupe-papier**

to the letter precisely; according to every detail: *He followed his father's instructions to the letter.* □ **à la lettre**

lettuce ['letis] *noun* a type of green plant with large leaves used as a salad. □ **laitue**

leukaemia [luːˈkiːmiə] *noun* a disease that causes white blood cells to multiply abnormally in the body. □ **leucémie**

level ['levl] *noun* 1 height, position, strength, rank *etc*: *The level of the river rose; a high level of intelligence.* □ **niveau**

2 a horizontal division or floor: *the third level of the multi-storey parking area.* □ **niveau**

3 a kind of instrument for showing whether a surface is level: *a spirit level.* □ **niveau**

4 a flat, smooth surface or piece of land: *It was difficult running uphill but he could run fast on the level.* □ **niveau**

■ *adjective* 1 flat, even, smooth or horizontal: *a level surface*; *a level spoonful* (= an amount which just fills the spoon to the top of the sides). □ **plat, ras**

2 of the same height, standard *etc*: *The top of the kitchen sink is level with the windowsill; The scores of the two teams are level.* □ **au niveau de, à égalité (avec)**

3 steady, even and not rising or falling much: *a calm, level voice.* □ **assuré**

■ *verb – past tense, past participle* 'levelled, 'leveled –

1 to make flat, smooth or horizontal: *He levelled the soil.* □ **aplanir**

2 to make equal: *Her goal levelled the scores of the two teams.* □ **égaliser**

3 (*usually with* **at**) to aim (a gun *etc*): *He levelled his pistol at the target.* □ **braquer (sur)**

4 to pull down: *The bulldozer levelled the block of flats.*

□ **raser**

'levelness *noun.* □ **nature unie**

level crossing a place where a road crosses a railway without a bridge. □ **passage à niveau**

level-'headed *adjective* calm and sensible. □ **équilibré**

do one's level best to do one's very best. □ **faire de son mieux**

level off to make or become flat, even, steady *etc*: *After rising for so long, prices have now levelled off.* □ **(se) stabiliser**

level out to make or become level: *The road levels out as it comes down to the plain.* □ **devenir plat**

on a level with level with: *His eyes were on a level with the shop counter.* □ **au niveau de, au ras de**

on the level fair; honest. □ **régulier**

lever ['liːvə] *noun* 1 a bar of wood, metal *etc* used to lift heavy weights: *A crowbar is a kind of lever; You must use a coin as a lever to get the lid of that tin off.* □ **levier, manette**

2 a bar or handle for operating a machine *etc*: *This is the lever that switches on the power.* □ **levier**

■ *verb* to move with or as if with a lever: *She levered the lid off with a coin.* □ **soulever qqch. en se servant d'un levier**

'leverage [-ridʒ] *noun* the power gained by the use of a lever. □ **force (de levier)**

levy ['levi] *verb* to raise or collect (*especially* an army or a tax): *A tax was levied on tobacco.* □ **prélever, percevoir**

■ *noun – plural* 'levies – 1 soldiers or money collected by order: *a levy on imports.* □ **levée, taxation**

2 the act of levying. □ **levée, taxation**

lexicon ['leksikən, -kon] *noun* a dictionary. □ **lexique**

liable ['laiəbl] *adjective* 1 (with **to**) tending to have, get, suffer from *etc*: *This road is liable to flooding; He is liable to pneumonia.* □ **susceptible de, sujet à**

2 possibly or probably about (to do something or to happen): *Watch the milk – it's liable to boil over.* □ **qui risque de**

,lia'bility *noun.* □ **responsabilité**

liaison [liːˈeizon] *noun* a contact or communication: *liaison between parents and teachers*; (*also adjective*) *a liason officer.* □ **liaison**

liaise [liːˈeiz] *verb* to communicate or make contact (with) *especially* as an official duty. □ **assurer la liaison avec qqn**

liar *see* lie[1].

libel ['laibəl] *noun* the legal term for something written which is harmful to a person's reputation. □ **écrit diffamatoire**

■ *verb – past tense, past participle* 'libelled, 'libeled – to damage the reputation of (someone) by libel. □ **diffamer (par écrit)**

'libellous *adjective.* □ **diffamatoire**

'libellously *adverb.* □ **calomnieusement**

liberal ['libərəl] *adjective* 1 generous: *She gave me a liberal helping of apple pie; She was very liberal with her money.* □ **généreux**

2 tolerant; not criticizing or disapproving: *The headmaster is very liberal in his attitude to young people.* □

tolérant
3 (*also noun*) (*especially with capital*) in politics, (a person belonging to a party) favouring liberty for the individual. □ **libéral**
libe'rality [-'ra-] *noun*. □ **libéralité**
'**liberally** *adverb*. □ **libéralement**
liberate ['libəreit] *verb* to set free: *The prisoners were liberated by the new government*. □ **libérer**
libe'ration *noun*. □ **libération**
'**liberator** *noun*. □ **libérateur, trice**
liberty ['libəti] *noun* 1 freedom from captivity or from slavery: *She ordered that all prisoners should be given their liberty*. □ **liberté**
2 freedom to do as one pleases: *Children have a lot more liberty now than they used to*. □ **liberté**
3 (*especially with* **take**) too great freedom of speech or action: *I think it was (taking) a liberty to ask her such a question!* □ **liberté**
'**liberties** *noun plural* privileges, rights *etc*: *civil liberties*. □ **libertés**
take the liberty of to do without permission: *I took the liberty of moving the papers from your desk – I hope you don't mind*. □ **prendre la liberté de**
library ['laibrəri] – *plural* '**libraries** – *noun* (a building or room containing) a collection of books or of gramophone records *etc*: *He works in the public library; She has a fine library of books about art*. □ **bibliothèque**
li'brarian [-'breə-] *noun* a person who is employed in a library. □ **bibliothécaire**
lice *see* **louse**.
licence, license ['laisəns] *noun* a (printed) form giving permission to do something (*eg* to drive a car, sell alcohol *etc*): *a driving licence*. □ **permis**
'**licence plate** *noun* one of the metal plates carried on the front and back of a motor vehicle showing the registration number of the vehicle. □ **plaque d'immatriculation**
'**license** *verb* to give a licence to or permit: *She is licensed to sell alcohol*. □ **autoriser**
'**licensed** *adjective* (of a shop, hotel *etc*) legally allowed to sell alcohol to customers: *a licensed grocer*. □ **qui détient une licence (de)**
licen'see *noun* a person to whom a licence (*especially* to keep a licensed hotel or public house) has been given. □ **détenteur, trice d'une licence/d'un permis**

licence is a noun: a **licence** (not **license**) to sell alcohol. **license** is a verb: **licensed** (not **licenced**) to drive a goods vehicle.

lichee *see* **lychee**.
lichen ['laikən] *noun* any of a large group of tiny plants which grow over stones, trees *etc*. □ **lichen**
lick [lik] *verb* to pass the tongue over: *The dog licked her hand*. □ **lécher**
■ *noun* 1 an act of licking: *The child gave the ice cream a lick*. □ **coup de langue**
2 a hasty application (of paint): *These doors could do with a lick of paint*. □ **petit coup**
lick into shape to put into a better or more efficient form. □ **mettre au point**

licorice *see* **liquorice**.
lid [lid] *noun* 1 a cover for a pot, box *etc*: *She lifted the lid of the box and looked inside*. □ **couvercle**
2 an eyelid: *The infection has not affected the eye itself although the lid is swollen*. □ **paupière**
lie[1] [lai] *noun* a false statement made with the intention of deceiving: *It would be a lie to say I knew, because I didn't*. □ **mensonge**
■ *verb* – *present participle* '**lying**: *past tense, past participle* **lied** – to say *etc* something which is not true, with the intention of deceiving: *There's no point in asking him – he'll just lie about it*. □ **mentir**
liar ['laiə] *noun* a person who tells lies, *especially* as a habit: *You can't trust what she says – she's such a liar*. □ **menteur, euse**

see also **lay**[1].

lie[2] [lai] – *present participle* '**lying**: *past tense* **lay** [lei]: *past participle* **lain** [lein] – *verb* 1 to be in or take a more or less flat position: *She went into the bedroom and lay on the bed; The book was lying in the hall*. □ **(s')allonger**
2 to be situated; to be in a particular place *etc*: *The farm lay three kilometres from the sea; His interest lies in farming*. □ **(se) trouver, résider**
3 to remain in a certain state: *The shop is lying empty now*. □ **rester**
4 (*with* **in**) (of feelings, impressions *etc*) to be caused by or contained in: *His charm lies in his honesty*. □ **résider (dans)**
lie back to lean back on a support: *He lay back against the pillows and went to sleep*. □ **(se) renverser (en arrière)**
lie down to take a flat or horizontal position: *The man lay down; My hair won't lie down*. □ **(s')étendre**
lie in to stay in bed late in the morning: *I like to lie in until nine on a Saturday*. □ **faire la grasse matinée**
lie in wait (for) to be waiting to catch or attack: *They lay in wait at the corner of the street and attacked him on his way home*. □ **(se) tenir à l'affût**
lie low to stay quiet or hidden: *The criminal lay low until the police stopped looking for him*. □ **rester caché**
lie with (of a choice, duty *etc*) to be the responsibility of: *The decision lies with you*. □ **incomber à**
take lying down to accept or suffer (something) without arguing, complaining or trying to avoid it. □ **accepter sans broncher**

see also **lay**[1].

lieutenant [ləf'tenənt] *noun* (*often abbreviated to* **Lt.**, **Lieut.**, *when written*) 1 in the army, the rank next below captain. □ **lieutenant**
2 in the navy, the rank next below lieutenant-commander. □ **second**
life [laif] – *plural* **lives** [laivz] – *noun* 1 the quality belonging to plants and animals which distinguishes them from rocks, minerals *etc* and things which are dead: *Doctors are fighting to save the child's life*. □ **vie**
2 the period between birth and death: *She had a long and happy life*. □ **vie**

3 liveliness: *She was full of life and energy.* □ **vie**

4 a manner of living: *She lived a life of ease and idleness.* □ **vie, existence**

5 the period during which any particular state exists: *He had many different jobs during his working life.* □ **vie**

6 living things: *It is now believed that there is no life on Mars; animal life.* □ **vie**

7 the story of a life: *She has written a life of Churchill.* □ **biographie**

8 life imprisonment: *He was given life for murder.* □ **à vie**

'lifeless *adjective* 1 dead: *a lifeless body.* □ **sans vie**

2 not lively; uninteresting: *The actress gave a lifeless performance.* □ **sans vigueur**

'lifelike *adjective* like a living person, animal *etc*: *The statue was very lifelike; a lifelike portrait.* □ **ressemblant**

life-and-'death *adjective* serious and deciding between life and death: *a life-and-death struggle.* □ **à mort**

'lifebelt *noun* a ring or belt filled with air or made of a material which floats, for keeping a person afloat. □ **bouée/gilet de sauvetage**

'lifeboat *noun* a boat for saving shipwrecked people. □ **canot de sauvetage**

'lifebuoy *noun* a buoy intended to support a person in the water till he can be rescued. □ **bouée de sauvetage**

'life cycle *noun* the various stages through which a living thing passes: *the life cycle of the snail.* □ **cycle de vie**

life expectancy the (average) length of time a person can expect to live. □ **espérance de vie**

'lifeguard *noun* a person employed to rescue and rescue swimmers at a swimming pool, beach *etc*. □ **surveillant, ante de plage**

'life jacket *noun* a sleeveless jacket filled with material that will float, for keeping a person afloat. □ **gilet de sauvetage**

'lifeline *noun* a rope for support in dangerous operations or thrown to rescue a drowning person. □ **corde d'assurance**

'lifelong *adjective* lasting the whole length of a life: *a lifelong friendship.* □ **de toujours**

'life-saving *noun* the act or skill of rescuing people from drowning: *The boy is being taught life-saving.* □ **secourisme, sauvetage**

'life-size(d) *adjective, adverb* (of a copy, drawing *etc*) as large as the original: *a life-sized statue.* □ **grandeur nature**

'lifetime *noun* the period of a person's life: *She saw many changes in her lifetime.* □ **vie**

as large as life in person; actually: *I went to the party and there was John as large as life.* □ **en personne**

bring to life to make lively or interesting: *Her lectures really brought the subject to life.* □ **rendre vivant**

come to life to become lively or interesting: *The play did not come to life until the last act.* □ **commencer à s'animer**

for life until death: *They became friends for life.* □ **pour toujours**

the life and soul of the party a person who is very active, enthusiastic, amusing *etc* at a party. □ **boute-en-train**

not for the life of me not even if it was necessary in order to save my life: *I couldn't for the life of me remember his name!* □ **absolument pas**

not on your life! certainly not!: *'Will you get married?' 'Not on your life!'* □ **jamais de la vie**

take life to kill: *It is a sin to take life.* □ **tuer**

take one's life to kill oneself. □ **se suicider**

take one's life in one's hands to take the risk of being killed. □ **risquer sa vie**

lift [lift] *verb* 1 to raise or bring to a higher position: *The box was so heavy I couldn't lift it.* □ **soulever**

2 to take and carry away: *He lifted the table through into the kitchen.* □ **porter**

3 (of mist *etc*) to disappear: *By noon, the fog was beginning to lift.* □ **se lever**

4 to rise: *The airplane lifted into the air.* □ **(s')élever**

■ *noun* 1 the act of lifting: *a lift of the eyebrows.* □ **haussement**

2 ('elevator') a small enclosed platform *etc* that moves up and down between floors carrying goods or people: *Since she was too tired to climb the stairs, she went up in the lift.* □ **ascenseur**

3 a ride in someone's car *etc*: *Can I give you a lift into town?* □ **trajet dans la voiture de qqn**

4 a raising of the spirits: *Her success in the exam gave her a great lift.* □ **stimulant**

lift off (of a rocket *etc*) to leave the ground (*noun* **'lift-off**). □ **décoller**

ligament ['ligəmənt] *noun* a piece of tough substance that joins together the bones of the body: *She pulled a ligament in her knee when she fell.* □ **ligament**

light¹ [lait] *noun* 1 the brightness given by the sun, a flame, lamps *etc* that makes things able to be seen: *It was nearly dawn and the light was getting stronger; Sunlight streamed into the room.* □ **lumière**

2 something which gives light (*eg* a lamp): *Suddenly all the lights went out.* □ **lumière**

3 something which can be used to set fire to something else; a flame: *Have you got a light* (= a match *etc*) *for my cigarette?* □ **feu**

4 a way of viewing or regarding: *He regarded her action in a favourable light.* □ **jour**

■ *adjective* 1 having light; not dark: *The studio was a large, light room.* □ **clair**

2 (of a colour) pale; closer to white than black: *light green.* □ **clair**

■ *verb* – *past tense, past participle* **lit** [lit], **'lighted** – 1 to give light to: *The room was lit only by candles.* □ **éclairer**

2 to (make something) catch fire: *He lit the gas; I think this match is damp, because it won't light.* □ **(s')allumer**

'lightness¹ *noun*. □ **clarté**

'lighten¹ *verb* to make or become brighter: *The white ceiling lightened the room; The sky was lightening.* □ **(s')éclairer**

'lighter *noun* something used for lighting (a cigarette *etc*). □ **briquet**

'lighting *noun* a means of providing light: *The lighting was so bad in the restaurant that we could hardly see.* □ **éclairage**

lighthouse *noun* a building built on rocks, coastline *etc* with a (flashing) light to guide or warn ships. □ **phare**

'light-year *noun* the distance light travels in a year (nearly 9.5 million million kilometres). □ **année-lumière**

bring to light to reveal or cause to be noticed: *The scandal was brought to light by the investigations of a journalist.* □ **mettre en lumière**

come to light to be revealed or discovered: *The manuscript came to light in a box of books at an auction.* □ **être découvert**

in the light of taking into consideration (*eg* new information): *The theory has been abandoned in the light of more recent discoveries.* □ **à la lumière de**

light up 1 to begin to give out light: *Evening came and the streetlights lit up.* □ **s'allumer**

2 to make, or become full of light: *The powerful searchlight lit up the building; She watched the house light up as everyone awoke.* □ **(s')illuminer**

3 to make someone happy: *Her face lit up when she saw him; A sudden smile lit up her face.* □ **(s')éclairer**

see the light 1 to be born, discovered, produced *etc*: *After many problems his invention finally saw the light (of day).* □ **voir le jour**

2 to be converted to someone else's point of view *etc*. □ **se convertir (à)**

set light to to cause to begin burning: *He set light to the pile of rubbish in his garden.* □ **mettre le feu à qqch.**

light² [lait] *adjective* **1** easy to lift or carry; of little weight: *I bought a light suitcase for plane journeys.* □ **léger**

2 easy to bear, suffer or do: *Next time the punishment will not be so light.* □ **léger**

3 (of food) easy to digest: *a light meal.* □ **léger**

4 of less weight than it should be: *The load of grain was several kilograms light.* □ **trop léger de**

5 of little weight: *Aluminium is a light metal.* □ **léger**

6 lively or agile: *She was very light on her feet.* □ **au pas léger**

7 cheerful; not serious: *light music.* □ **léger**

8 little in quantity; not intense, heavy, strong *etc*: *light rain.* □ **petit**

9 (of soil) containing a lot of sand. □ **meuble**

'lightly *adverb*. □ **légèrement**

'lightness² *noun*. □ **légèreté**

'lighten² *verb* to make or become less heavy: *She lightened her suitcase by taking out several pairs of shoes; The postman's bag of parcels lightened as he went from house to house.* □ **(s')alléger**

,light-'fingered *adjective* inclined to steal things. □ **chapardeur**

,light-'headed *adjective* dizzy and giddy. □ **écervelé**

,light'hearted *adjective* happy and free from anxiety; not grave or serious: *a lighthearted mood.* □ **enjoué**

'lightweight *adjective* light in weight: *a lightweight raincoat.* □ **léger**

get off lightly to escape or be allowed to go without severe punishment *etc*. □ **s'en tirer à bon compte**

make light of to treat (problems *etc*) as unimportant. □ **prendre à la légère**

travel light to travel with little luggage. □ **voyager avec peu de bagages**

lighten *see* **light¹, light².**

lighter *see* **light¹.**

lightning ['laitniŋ] *noun* a flash of electricity between clouds or from a cloud to earth during a storm, *usually* followed by thunder: *The house was struck by lightning.* □ **éclair, foudre**

---

a flash of **lightning** (not **lightening**).
lightening is the present participle of **lighten**, to make or become lighter.

---

lightning rod *noun* a metal pole, usually attached to a roof, that conducts lightning away from other structures: *Fortunately, the lightning struck the lightning rod instead of our house.* □ **paratonnerre**

like¹ [laik] *adjective* the same or similar: *They're as like as two peas.* □ **pareil à**

■ *preposition* the same as or similar to; in the same or a similar way as: *He climbs like a cat; She is like her mother.* □ **comme**

■ *noun* someone or something which is the same as or good *etc* as another: *You won't see his like/their like again.* □ **son pareil; chose pareille**

■ *conjunction* in the same or a similar way as: *No one does it like he does.* □ **comme**

'likely *adjective* **1** probable: *the likely result; It's likely that she'll succeed.* □ **probable**

2 looking *etc* as if it might be good, useful, suitable *etc*: *a likely spot for a picnic; She's the most likely person for the job.* □ **propice, convenable**

'likelihood *noun* probability. □ **probabilité**

'liken *verb* to think or speak of as being similar; to compare: *She likened the earth to an apple.* □ **comparer**

'likeness *noun* **1** (a) similarity or resemblance: *The likeness between them is amazing.* □ **ressemblance**

2 a representation of a a person *etc* in a photographic or painted portrait *etc*: *That photo of Mary is a good likeness.* □ **portrait ressemblant**

'likewise *adverb* **1** in the same or a similar manner: *He ignored her, and she ignored him likewise.* □ **pareillement**

2 also: *.Mr. Brown came, likewise Mrs. Smith.* □ **aussi**

like-'minded *adjective* having a similar opinion or purpose. □ **du même avis**

a likely story! I don't believe it! □ **en voilà une bonne!**

as likely as not probably: *As likely as not, she won't remember to come.* □ **vraisemblablement**

be like someone to be typical of someone: *It isn't like him to be late.* □ **ressembler à qqn**

feel like to be inclined, willing or anxious to (do or have something): *I don't feel like going out; I expect he feels like a cup of tea.* □ **avoir envie de**

he *etc* **is likely to** it is probable that he *etc* will: *He is likely to fail.* □ **il est probable qu'il...**

look like 1 to appear similar to: *She looks very like her mother.* □ **ressembler à**

2 to show the effects, signs or possibility of: *It looks* *like rain.* □ **avoir l'air de**

not likely! certainly not!: *'Would you put your head in a lion's mouth?' 'Me? Not likely!'* □ **jamais de la vie!**

like² [laik] *verb* **1** to be pleased with; to find pleasant or agreeable: *I like him very much; I like the way you've decorated this room.* □ **aimer**

2 to enjoy: *I like gardening.* □ **aimer**

'lik(e)able *adjective* (of a person) agreeable and attractive. □ **agréable**

'liking *noun* **1** a taste or fondness (for): *He has too great a liking for chocolate.* □ **goût (pour)**

2 satisfaction: *Is the meal to your liking?* □ **(à votre) goût**

should/would like want: *I would like to say thank you; Would you like a cup of tea?* □ **vouloir**

take a liking to to begin to like: *I've taken a liking to him.* □ **se prendre d'amitié pour qqn**

lilac ['lailək] *noun* **1** a type of small tree with bunches of white or pale purple flowers. □ **lilas**

2 (*also adjective*) (of) a pale, *usually* pinkish, purple colour: *lilac sheets.* □ **lilas**

lilt [lilt] *noun* (a tune *etc* with) a strong rhythm. □ **rythme, cadence**

lily ['lili] – *plural* **'lilies** – *noun* a type of tall plant grown from a bulb, with white or coloured flowers. □ **lys**

lily of the valley [lili ʌv ðə valiz] *noun* a fragrant plant with small white bell-shaped flowers: *The whole path up to the house smells wonderful every year when the lily of the valley blooms.* □ **muguet**

limb [lim] *noun* **1** an arm or leg. □ **membre**

2 a branch. □ **(grosse) branche**

out on a limb on one's own and in a dangerous or disadvantageous position. □ **dans une situation délicate**

limber ['limbə] : **limber up** to exercise so as to become able to move easily. □ **faire des exercices d'assouplissement**

lime¹ [laim] *noun* the white substance left after heating limestone, used in making cement. □ **chaux**

'limestone *noun* a kind of rock. □ **calcaire**

'limelight: in the limelight attracting the public's attention. □ **en vedette**

lime² [laim] *noun* **1** a type of small, very sour, yellowish-green citrus fruit related to the lemon. □ **lime**

2 (*also adjective*) (of) the colour of this fruit: *lime walls.* □ **lime**

lime³ [laim] *noun* a tree with rough bark and small heart-shaped leaves. □ **tilleul**

limelight *see* **lime¹**.

limerick ['limərik] *noun* a type of humorous poem with five lines, the third and fourth lines being shorter than the others. □ **poème humoristique**

limit ['limit] *noun* **1** the farthest point or place; the boundary: *There was no limit to her ambition.* □ **limite**

2 a restriction: *We must put a limit on our spending.* □ **restriction**

■ *verb* to set a restriction on: *We must limit the amount of time we spend on this work.* □ **limiter**

,limi'tation *noun* **1** an act of limiting. □ **limitation**

2 a lack, *eg* of a particular facility, ability *etc*: *We all have our limitations.* □ **limite**

'limited *adjective* **1** (*negative* **unlimited**) not very great, large *etc*; restricted: *My experience is rather limited.* □ **limité**

2 (*with capital, abbreviated to* **Ltd.** *when written*) a word used in the titles of certain companies: *West. and R. Chambers Ltd.* □ **ltée**

'limitless *adjective*. □ **illimité**

limousine ['liməziːn] *noun* a kind of large car *especially* one with a screen separating the front seat from the back. □ **limousine**

limp¹ [limp] *adjective* lacking stiffness or strength; drooping: *a limp lettuce; a limp excuse.* □ **mou, faible**

limp² [limp] *verb* to walk in an uneven manner (*usually* because one has hurt one's foot or leg): *He twisted his ankle and came limping home.* □ **boîter**

■ *noun* the act of limping: *He walks with a limp.* □ **claudication**

limpet ['limpit] *noun* a type of small, cone-shaped shellfish that fastens itself very firmly to rocks. □ **bernique**

limpid [limpid] *adjective* clear or transparent; able to be seen through: *Pat could see rocks at the bottom of the limpid pond.* □ **limpide**

line¹ [lain] *noun* **1** (a piece of) thread, cord, rope *etc*: *She hung the washing on the line; a fishing rod and line.* □ **corde, ligne**

2 a long, narrow mark, streak or stripe: *She drew straight lines across the page; a dotted/wavy line.* □ **ligne**

3 outline or shape *especially* relating to length or direction: *The ship had very graceful lines; A dancer uses a mirror to improve his line.* □ **ligne**

4 a groove on the skin; a wrinkle. □ **ride**

5 a row or group of objects or persons arranged side by side or one behind the other: *The children stood in a line; a line of trees.* □ **rang, rangée**

6 a short letter: *I'll drop him a line.* □ **mot**

7 a series or group of persons which come one after the other *especially* in the same family: *a line of kings.* □ **lignée**

8 a track or direction: *She pointed out the line of the new road; a new line of research.* □ **tracé, direction**

9 the railway or a single track of the railway: *Passengers must cross the line by the bridge only.* □ **voie**

10 a continuous system (*especially* of) pipes, electrical or telephone cables *etc*) connecting one place with another: *a pipeline; a line of communication; All (telephone) lines are engaged.* □ **pipeline; ligne**

11 a row of written or printed words: *The letter contained only three lines; a poem of sixteen lines.* □ **ligne**

12 a regular service of ships, aircraft *etc*: *a shipping line.* □ **ligne**

13 a group or class (of goods for sale) or a field of activity, interest *etc*: *This has been a very popular new line; Computers are not really my line.* □ **gamme de produits; domaine**

14 an arrangement of troops, *especially* when ready to fight: *fighting in the front line.* □ **ligne**

■ *verb* **1** to form lines along: *Crowds lined the pavement to see the Queen.* □ **s'aligner (le long de)**

2 to mark with lines. □ **ligner**

lineage ['liniidʒ] *noun* ancestry. □ **lignage, lignée**

linear ['liniə] *adjective* of, consisting of or like a line or lines. □ **linéaire**

lined[1] *adjective* having lines: *lined paper; a lined face.* □ **ligné; ridé**

'**liner**[1] *noun* a ship or aircraft of a regular line or company: *They all sailed to America in a large liner.* □ **paquebot**

lines *noun plural* the words an actor has to say: *He had difficulty remembering his lines.* □ **texte, rôle**

'**linesman** ['lainz-] *noun* in sport, a judge or umpire at a boundary line. □ **juge de ligne**

in line for likely to get or to be given something: *He is in line for promotion.* □ **être sur les rangs (pour)**

in, out of line with in or out of agreement with: *His views are out of line with those of his colleagues.* □ **en accord (en désaccord) avec**

line up 1 to form a line: *The children lined up ready to leave the classroom; She lined up the chairs.* □ **(s')aligner, (se) mettre en rangs**

2 to collect and arrange in readiness: *We've lined up several interesting guests to appear on the program* (*noun* '**line-up**). □ **trouver**

3 to stand one behind the other in an orderly manner: *None of us can get into the store before it opens so just stop pushing and line up.* □ **faire la queue**

read between the lines to understand something (from a piece of writing *etc*) which is not actually stated. □ **lire entre les lignes**

line[2] [lain] *verb* **1** to cover on the inside: *He lined the box with newspaper.* □ **doubler, tapisser**

2 to put a lining in: *She lined the dress with silk.* □ **doubler**

lined[2] *adjective* (*negative* **unlined**) having a lining: *a lined skirt.* □ **doublé**

'**liner**[2] *noun* something used for lining: *a dustbin liner.* □ **sac, garnissage**

'**lining** *noun* **1** (a) covering on the inside: *The basket had a padded lining.* □ **revêtement intérieur**

2 a fairly exact copy (of a piece of clothing) attached to the inside to help keep its shape *etc*: *The lining of my jacket is torn.* □ **doublure**

linen ['linin] *noun* **1** (*also adjective*) (of) cloth made of flax used to make sheets, tablecloths, tea towels *etc*: *This handkerchief is made of linen; linen sheets.* □ **(de) lin**

2 articles made of linen or, now more usually, cotton: *table linen; bed linen.* □ **linge**

liner *see* **line**[1], **line**[2].

linger ['liŋgə] *verb* **1** to remain, last or continue for a long time or after the expected time: *The smell of the bad fish lingered for days.* □ **persister**

2 to proceed slowly or delay: *We lingered in the hall, looking at the pictures.* □ **s'attarder**

lingerie ['lãʒəriː] *noun* women's underwear. □ **lingerie**

linguist ['liŋgwist] *noun* a person who studies language and/or is good at languages. □ **linguiste**

lin'guistic *adjective* of languages. □ **linguistique**

lin'guistics *noun singular* the science of languages. □ **linguistique**

lining *see* **line**[2].

link [liŋk] *noun* **1** a ring of a chain: *There was a worn link in the chain and it broke; an important link in the chain of the evidence.* □ **maillon, chaînon**

2 anything connecting two things: *His job was to act as a link between the government and the press.* □ **lien, intermédiaire**

■ *verb* to connect as by a link: *The new train service links the suburbs with the heart of the city.* □ **relier**

link up to join or be joined closely or by a link: *An electrician called to link up our house to the main electricity supply* (*noun* '**link-up**). □ **relier**

links [liŋks] *noun plural* **1** a stretch of more or less flat ground along a seashore. □ **dunes**

2 (*often with singular verb*) a golf course. □ **terrain de golf**

linoleum [li'nouliəm] *noun* (*abbreviated to* **lino** ['lainou]) a type of smooth, hard-wearing covering for floors. □ **lino(léum)**

lint [lint] *noun* **1** linen in the form of a soft fluffy material for putting over wounds. □ **ouate**

2 very small pieces of fluff from cotton *etc*. □ **peluche**

lion ['laiən] – *feminine* '**lioness** – *noun* a type of large, flesh-eating animal of the cat family, the male of which has a long, coarse mane. □ **lion, lionne**

the lion's share the largest share. □ **la part du lion**

lip [lip] *noun* **1** either of the folds of flesh which form the edge of the mouth: *She bit her lip.* □ **lèvre**

2 the edge of something: *the lip of a cup.* □ **bord**

-lipped: *a thin-lipped mouth.* □ **aux lèvres (...)**

'**lip-read** *verb* (of a deaf person) to understand what a person is saying by watching the movement of his lips. □ **lire sur les lèvres**

'**lipstick** *noun* (a stick of) colouring for the lips. □ **rouge à lèvres**

pay lip service to to show respect to, or approval of, in word only, without sincerely feeling it. □ **dire pour la forme**

liquefy *see* **liquid**.

liqueur [li'kjuə] *noun* a strong, very sweet alcoholic drink. □ **liqueur**

liquid ['likwid] *adjective* able to flow; not solid, but not a gas: *liquid nitrogen; The ice cream has become liquid.* □ **liquide**

■ *noun* a substance which flows, like water: *a clear liquid.* □ **liquide**

liquefy ['likwifai] *verb* to make or become liquid: *The butter had liquefied in the heat.* □ **(se) liquéfier**

'**liquidate** [-deit] *verb* **1** to close, and finish the affairs of (a business *etc* that has no money to continue). □ **liquider**

2 to get rid of. □ **liquider**

,**liqui'dation** *noun*. □ **liquidation**

'**liquidator** *noun*. □ **liquidateur, trice**

'**liquidize, 'liquidise** *verb* to make (food *etc*) into a liquid or semi-liquid substance by grinding it up in a liquidizer. □ **liquéfier**

liquor ['likə] *noun* strong alcoholic drink. □ **spiritueux**

liquorice ['likəris] *noun* a plant with a sweet root, and a black, sticky type of sweet made from it. □ **réglisse**

lira ['liərə] – *plural* **lire** ['liərei] – *noun* the standard unit of Italian currency. □ **lire**

lisp [lisp] *verb* to say *th* for *s* or *z* because of being unable to pronounce these sounds correctly. □ **zézayer**
■ *noun* the act or habit of lisping: *She has a lisp.* □ **zézaiement**

list[1] [list] *noun* a series *eg* of names, prices *etc* written down or said one after the other: *a shopping list; We have a long list of people who are willing to help.* □ **liste**
■ *verb* to place in a list: *He listed the things he had to do.* □ **faire la liste de**

list[2] [list] *verb* to lean over to one side: *The ship is listing.* □ **gîter**
■ *noun*: *The ship had a heavy list.* □ **gîte**

listen ['lisn] *verb* 1 (*often with* to) to give attention so as to hear (what someone is saying *etc*): *I told her three times, but she wasn't listening; Do listen to the music!* □ **écouter**
2 (*with* to) to follow the advice of: *If she'd listened to me, she wouldn't have got into trouble.* □ **écouter**
listener *noun* someone who hears or pays close attention to sounds: *Megan is a good listener and knows exactly what the teacher wants her to do.* □ **auditeur**
listen in on to listen intentionally to (a private conversation *etc*). □ **écouter qqn secrètement**

listless ['listlis] *adjective* tired and without energy or interest: *listless children.* □ **indolent**
'**listlessly** *adverb.* □ **avec indolence**
'**listlessness** *noun.* □ **indolence**

lit *see* light[1], light[3].

liter *see* litre.

literacy *see* literate.

literal ['litərəl] *adjective* 1 following the exact meaning with no exaggeration: *the literal truth.* □ **littéral, réel**
2 understanding the meaning by taking one word at a time: *a literal translation.* □ **littéral**
'**literalness** *noun.* □ **littéralité**
'**literally** *adverb: We had literally a minute to catch the train.* □ **littéralement**

literary ['litərəri] *adjective* 1 concerning literature or the writing of books: *a literary magazine.* □ **littéraire**
2 (of a person) knowledgeable about books. □ **cultivé**

literate ['litərət] *adjective* 1 able to read and write. □ **qui sait lire et écrire**
2 clever and having read a great deal. □ **cultivé**
'**literacy** *noun.* □ **aptitude à lire et à écrire**

literature ['litrətʃə] *noun* 1 poems, novels, plays *etc* in verse or prose, *especially* if of fine quality. □ **littérature**
2 written work that gives information about something: *I don't understand what the insurance agent said; is there any literature about the policy that I can read?* □ **documentation**

lithe [laið] *adjective* (used *especially* of the human body) bending easily; flexible: *as lithe as a cat.* □ **agile, souple**
'**litheness** *noun.* □ **agilité**

litigation [liti'geiʃən] *noun* a private law-suit. □ **litige**

litre ['liːtə] *noun* a measure of (*usually* liquid) capacity: *a litre of wine.* □ **litre**

litter ['litə] *noun* 1 an untidy mess of paper, rubbish *etc*: *Put your litter in that bin.* □ **ordures**
2 a heap of straw *etc* for animals to lie on *etc*. □ **litière**
3 a number of animals born to the same mother at the same time: *a litter of kittens.* □ **portée**
■ *verb* to cover (the ground *etc*) with scattered objects: *Papers littered the table.* □ **couvrir**

little ['litl] *adjective* 1 small in size: *He is only a little boy; when she was little* (= a child). □ **petit**
2 small in amount; not much: *He has little knowledge of the difficulties involved.* □ **peu (de)**
3 not important: *I did not expect her to make a fuss about such a little thing.* □ **sans importance**
■ *pronoun* (only) a small amount: *He knows little of the real world.* □ **peu de chose (sur)**
■ *adverb* 1 not much: *I go out little nowadays.* □ **peu**
2 only to a small degree: *a little-known fact.* □ **peu**
3 not at all: *He little knows how ill he is.* □ **loin de**
a little 1 a short time or distance: *Move a little to the right!* □ **un peu**
2 a small quantity of something: *She has a little money to spare; 'Is there any soup left?' 'Yes, a little.'* □ **un peu**
3 slightly: *She was a little frightened.* □ **un peu**
little by little gradually: *Little by little we began to get to know him.* □ **petit à petit**
make little of 1 to treat as unimportant *etc*: *He made little of his injuries.* □ **faire peu de cas de qqch.**
2 not to be able to understand: *I could make little of his instructions.* □ **ne pas comprendre grand chose à**

---

little means 'not much': *You have little reason to boast.*
a little means 'some', 'a small quantity': *There's a little milk left.*

---

live[1] [liv] *verb* 1 to have life; to be alive: *This poison is dangerous to everything that lives.* □ **vivre**
2 to survive: *The doctors say he is very ill, but they think he will live; It was difficult to believe that she had lived through such an experience.* □ **survivre**
3 to have one's home or dwelling (in a particular place): *She lives next to the church; They went to live in Bristol/in a huge house.* □ **vivre, habiter**
4 to pass (one's life): *He lived a life of luxury; She lives in fear of being attacked.* □ **vivre**
5 (*with* by) to make enough money *etc* to feed and house oneself: *He lives by fishing.* □ **vivre (de)**
-**lived** *adjective* having (a certain type of) life: *long-lived.* □ **à la vie (...)**
'**living** *adjective* 1 having life; being alive: *a living creature; The aim of the project was to discover if there was anything living on Mars.* □ **vivant**
2 now alive: *the greatest living artist.* □ **vivant**
■ *noun* the money *etc* needed to feed and house oneself and keep oneself alive: *He earns his living driving a taxi; She makes a good living as an author.* □ **gagner (sa vie)**
'**living room** *noun* the room of a house *etc* in which the occupants of the house usually sit during their leisure time. □ **salle de séjour, salon**
live and let live to tolerate other people's actions and expect them to tolerate one's own. □ **il faut se montrer**

tolérant

live down to live through the shame of (a foolish act *etc*) till it is forgotten. □ **faire oublier à la longue**

live in, out to have one's home at, away from, the place where one works: *All the hotel staff live in; The nurse chose to live out.* □ **être logé et nourri; ne pas être logé**

live on 1 to keep oneself alive by eating: *He lives on fish and potatoes.* □ **se nourrir de**

2 to be supported (financially) by: *He lives on $40 a week.* □ **vivre avec**

live up to to behave in a manner worthy of: *He found it difficult to live up to his reputation as a hero.* □ **vivre en accord avec**

live with to share accommodations; to reside in the same apartment or house: *Kelly lived with Sam and one other roommate in an apartment.* □ **habiter chez**

(with)in living memory within a period recent enough to be remembered by someone still alive: *It was the worst harvest in living memory.* □ **de mémoire d'homme**

live² [laiv] *adjective* **1** having life; not dead: *a live mouse.* □ **vivant**

2 (of a radio or television broadcast *etc*) heard or seen as the event takes place; not recorded: *I watched a live performance of my favourite opera on television; Was the performance live or recorded?* □ **en direct**

3 full of energy, and capable of becoming active: *a live bomb.* □ **actif, amorcé, branché**

4 burning: *a live coal.* □ **ardent**

■ *adverb* (of a radio or television broadcast *etc*) as the event takes place: *The competition will be broadcast live.* □ **en direct**

'lively *adjective* active; full of life, high spirits or movement: *She took a lively interest in us; The music is bright and lively.* □ **plein d'entrain**

'liveliness *noun.* □ **entrain**

'livestock *noun* domestic animals, *especially* horses, cattle, sheep, and pigs. □ **bétail**

live wire 1 a wire charged with electricity. □ **fil sous tension**

2 a person who is full of energy and enthusiasm: *He is very quiet, but his sister is a real live wire.* □ **personne qui pète le feu**

livelihood ['laivlihud] *noun* a means of living, *especially* of earning enough money to feed oneself *etc*. □ **gagne-pain**

liveliness, lively *see* live².

liver ['livə] *noun* **1** a large organ in the body which purifies the blood. □ **foie**

2 this organ in certain animals used as food. □ **foie**

lives *see* life.

livestock *see* live².

living *see* live¹.

lizard ['lizəd] *noun* any of several types of *usually* small, four-footed reptile. □ **lézard**

lo [lou] : **lo and behold** an expression indicating surprise *etc* at seeing or finding something. □ **et voilà que...**

load [loud] *noun* **1** something which is being carried: *The truck had to stop because its load had fallen off; She*

was carrying a load of groceries. □ **charge, chargement**

2 as much as can be carried at one time: *two truckloads of earth.* □ **chargement**

3 a large amount: *He talked a load of rubbish; We ate loads of ice cream.* □ **un (des) tas de**

4 the power carried by an electric circuit: *The wires were designed for a load of 15 amps.* □ **charge**

■ *verb* **1** to take or put on what is to be carried (*especially* if heavy): *They loaded the luggage into the car; The truck was loading when they arrived.* □ **charger**

2 to put ammunition into (a gun): *He loaded the revolver and fired.* □ **charger**

3 to put film into (a camera). □ **charger**

'loaded *adjective* **1** carrying a load: *a loaded van.* □ **chargé**

2 (of a gun) containing ammunition: *a loaded pistol.* □ **chargé**

3 (of a camera) containing film. □ **chargé**

loaf¹ [louf] – *plural* **loaves** [louvz] – *noun* a shaped mass of bread: *a sliced loaf.* □ **pain, miche (de pain)**

loaf² [louf] *verb* (*with* **about** *or* **around**) to pass time without doing anything in particular: *They were loafing about (the street).* □ **paresser**

'loafer *noun: an idle loafer.* □ **fainéant, ante**

loan [loun] *noun* **1** anything lent, *especially* money: *I shall ask the bank for a loan.* □ **prêt, emprunt**

2 the act of lending: *I gave him the loan of my bicycle.* □ **prêt**

■ *verb* to lend: *Can you loan me a pen?* □ **prêter**

loathe [louð] *verb* to hate very much. □ **détester**

'loathing *noun* great dislike and disgust. □ **dégoût**

'loathsome *adjective* horrible. □ **répugnant**

loaves *see* loaf¹.

lob [lob] *noun* a slow, high throw, hit *etc* of a ball *etc*. □ **lob**

■ *verb* – *past tense, past participle* **lobbed** – to throw or strike (a ball *etc*) so that it moves high and slowly: *She lobbed the ball over the net.* □ **faire un lob**

lobby ['lobi] – *plural* **'lobbies** – *noun* **1** a (small) entrance-hall: *a hotel lobby.* □ **hall, vestibule**

2 a group of people who try to influence the Government *etc* in a certain way or for a certain purpose. □ **groupe de pression**

■ *verb* to try to influence (the Government *etc*). □ **faire pression sur**

lobe [loub] *noun* **1** the soft lower part of the ear. □ **lobe**

2 a division of the lungs, brain *etc*. □ **lobe**

lobster ['lobstə] *noun* a type of shellfish with large claws. □ **homard**

local ['loukəl] *adjective* belonging to a certain place or district: *The local shops are very good; local problems.* □ **local, du quartier**

'locally *adverb.* □ **localement**

locality [lə'kaləti] – *plural* **lo'calities** – *noun* a district: *Public transport is a problem in this locality.* □ **localité**

locate [lə'keit] *verb* **1** to set in a particular place or position: *The kitchen is located in the basement.* □ **situer**

2 to find the place or position of: *He located the street he was looking for on the map.* □ **repérer**

lo'cation [-'keiʃən] *noun* **1** position or situation. □ **situ-**

ation, emplacement

2 the act of locating. □ **repérage**

on location (of filming) in natural surroundings outside the studio. □ **en extérieur**

lock[1] [lok] *noun* **1** a mechanism for fastening doors *etc*: *He put the key in the lock.* □ **serrure**

2 a closed part of a canal for raising or lowering boats to a higher or lower part of the canal. □ **écluse**

3 the part of a gun by which it is fired. □ **percuteur**

4 a tight hold (in wrestling *etc*). □ **clef**

■ *verb* to fasten or become fastened with a lock: *She locked the drawer; This door doesn't lock.* □ **fermer à clef**

'**locker** *noun* a small cupboard, *especially* for sports equipment. □ **casier**

'**locket** [-kit] *noun* a little ornamental case hung around the neck: *a gold locket containing a piece of his hair.* □ **médaillon**

'**locksmith** *noun* a person who makes and mends locks. □ **serrurier, ière**

lock in to prevent from getting out of a building *etc* by using a lock: *She found she was locked in, and had to climb out of the window.* □ **enfermer (à l'intérieur)**

lock out to prevent from getting into a building *etc* by using a lock: *Don't lock yourself out (of the house) by forgetting to take your key with you.* □ **enfermer dehors**

lock up 1 to confine or prevent from leaving or being taken away by using a lock: *to lock up a prisoner/one's jewellery.* □ **mettre sous clef**

2 to lock whatever should be locked: *He locked up and left the shop about 5:30 p.m.* □ **(tout) fermer (à clef)**

lock[2] [lok] *noun* **1** a piece of hair: *She cut off a lock of his hair.* □ **mèche**

2 (*in plural*) hair: *curly brown locks.* □ **cheveux**

locomotive [louka'moutiv] *noun* a railway engine. □ **locomotive**

,**loco'motion** [-'mouʃən] *noun* the process of moving from place to place. □ **locomotion**

locum ['loukəm] *noun* a person who takes the place of another (*especially* a doctor, dentist *etc*) for a time. □ **remplaçant, ante**

locust ['loukəst] *noun* a type of large insect of the grasshopper family, found in Africa and Asia, which moves in very large groups and destroys growing crops by eating them. □ **sauterelle**

lodge [lodʒ] *noun* **1** a small house, *especially* one at a gate to the grounds of a large house. □ **pavillon (de gardien)**

2 a room at a college gate *etc* for an attendant: *the porter's lodge.* □ **loge**

■ *verb* **1** to live in rooms for which one pays, in someone else's house: *He lodges with the Smiths.* □ **habiter (chez)**

2 to make or become fixed: *The bullet was lodged in his spine.* □ **(se) loger**

3 to make (an objection, an appeal *etc*) formally or officially. □ **présenter, formuler**

'**lodger** *noun* a person who lives in a room or rooms, for which he pays, in someone else's house: *She rented*

a room to a lodger. □ **pensionnaire**

'**lodging 1** (*often in plural*) a room or rooms hired in someone else's house: *She lives in lodgings.* □ **chambre meublée, logement**

2 a place to stay: *He paid the landlady for board and lodging.* □ **pension**

loft [loft] *noun* a room or space under a roof: *They kept a lot of spare furniture in the loft.* □ **grenier**

'**lofty** *adjective* **1** very high: *a lofty building.* □ **élevé**

2 haughty or proud: *a lofty attitude.* □ **hautain**

'**loftily** *adverb.* □ **avec hauteur**

'**loftiness** *noun.* □ **hauteur, noblesse**

log [log] *noun* **1** a thick piece of unshaped wood: *The trees were sawn into logs and taken to the sawmill.* □ **rondin, bûche**

2 a logbook: *The captain of the ship entered the details in the log.* □ **journal de bord**

■ *verb – past tense, past participle* **logged** – to write down or record in a logbook (*especially* the distance covered during a journey). □ **inscrire au journal de bord**

'**logbook** *noun* an official record of the journey of a ship or airplane: *All the details of the flight were entered in the logbook.* □ **livre de bord; carnet de vol**

logarithm ['logəriðəm] *noun* (*abbreviated to* **log** [log]) the number of times *eg 10* must be multiplied by itself to produce a particular number: $10 \times 10 \times 10$ or $10^3 = 1,000$, so 3 is here the logarithm of 1,000. □ **logarithme**

loggerheads ['logəhedz]: **at loggerheads** quarrelling: *They're always at loggerheads with their neighbours.* □ **à couteaux tirés (avec)**

logic ['lodʒik] *noun* (the study and art of) reasoning correctly. □ **logique**

'**logical** *adjective* (thinking or acting) according to the rules of logic: *It is logical to assume that you will get a higher salary if you are promoted; She is always logical in her thinking.* □ **logique**

'**logically** *adverb.* □ **logiquement**

loin [loin] *noun* the back of an animal when cut into pieces for food. □ **filet, longe**

'**loincloth** *noun* a piece of cloth worn around the hips, *especially* in India. □ **pagne**

loiter ['loitə] *verb* to proceed, work *etc* slowly or to stand doing nothing in particular: *They were loitering outside the ship.* □ **traîner**

loll [lol] *verb* **1** to sit or lie lazily: *to loll in a chair; You'll get nothing done if you loll about all day.* □ **se prélasser**

2 (of the tongue) to hang down or out: *The dog lay down with his tongue lolling.* □ **pendre**

lollipop ['lolipop] *noun* a large sweet on a stick for sucking. □ **suçon, sucette**

lolly ['loli] – *plural* '**lollies** – *noun* **1** a lollipop, or a similar type of sweet made of ice cream *etc*: *an ice lolly.* □ **esquimau**

2 a slang word for money. □ **fric**

lone [loun] *adjective* solitary, without companions, by itself *etc*: *a lone figure on the beach.* □ **solitaire**

'**lonely** *adjective* **1** lacking or wanting companionship: *Aren't you lonely, living by yourself?* □ **(qui se sent)**

seul
2 (of a place) far away from busy places, having few people: *a lonely island.* □ **isolé**
'**loneliness** *noun.* □ **solitude**
'**lonesome** *adjective* lonely; solitary: *She feels lonesome when her brothers are at school.* □ **solitaire**
'**lonesomeness** *noun.* □ **solitude**
long[1] [lɒŋ] *adjective* 1 measuring a great distance from one end to the other: *a long journey; a long road; long legs.* □ **long**
2 having a great period of time from the first moment to the last: *The book took a long time to read; a long conversation; a long delay.* □ **long**
3 measuring a certain amount in distance or time: *The wire is two centimetres long; The television program was just over an hour long.* □ **de long, durant**
4 away, doing or using something *etc* for a great period of time: *Will you be long?* □ **pour longtemps**
5 reaching to a great distance in space or time: *She has a long memory.* □ **bon**
■ *adverb* 1 a great period of time: *This happened long before you were born.* □ **longtemps avant**
2 for a great period of time: *Have you been waiting long?* □ **longtemps**
long-distance call *noun* a telephone call that is outside the immediate area; a call for which the telephone company sets extra charges: *The operator said it was a long-distance call and to press "1" before dialing the number; This is a long-distance call so I need some more money for the public telephone.* □ **interurbain**
,**long-drawn-'out** *adjective* taking a needlessly long time: *long-drawn-out discussions.* □ **interminable**
'**longhand** *noun* ordinary writing as opposed to shorthand. □ **écriture non abrégée**
long house in tribal societies, a long rectangular dwelling shared by several families, *especially* in south-east Asia and amongst North American Indians. □ **grande maison**
long jump a sports contest in which people jump as far as possible. □ **saut en longueur**
long-playing record (*usually* abbreviated to **LP**) a gramophone record which plays for a long time. □ **microsillon**
,**long-'range** *adjective* 1 able to reach a great distance: *long-range rockets.* □ **à longue portée**
2 taking into consideration a long period of time: *a long-range weather forecast.* □ **à long terme**
,**long-'sighted** *adjective* having difficulty in seeing close objects clearly. □ **hypermétrope; presbyte**
,**long-'sightedness** *noun.* □ **hypermétropie; presbytie**
,**long-'suffering** *adjective* patiently enduring a great deal of trouble. □ **d'une patience à toute épreuve**
,**long-'winded** *adjective* (of a speaker or his speech) tiresomely long. □ **intarissable**
as long as/so long as 1 provided only that: *As/So long as you're happy, it doesn't matter what you do.* □ **tant que**
2 while; during the time that: *As long as he's here I'll have more work to do.* □ **aussi longtemps que**
before (very) long soon: *Come in and wait – he'll be*

here before long! □ **avant longtemps**
in the long run in the end: *We thought we would save money, but in the long run our spending was about the same as usual.* □ **en fin de compte**
the long and the short of it the whole story in a few words. □ **le fin mot de l'histoire**
no longer not now as in the past: *This cinema is no longer used.* □ **(ne) plus**
so long! goodbye! □ **salut!**
long[2] [lɒŋ] *verb* (*often with* **for**) to wish very much: *He longed to go home; I am longing for a drink.* □ **avoir très envie de qqch.**
'**longing** *noun* a great desire or wish for something: *He looked at the cakes with longing.* □ **envie**
'**longingly** *adverb*: *She looked longingly at the chocolate.* □ **avec envie**
longevity [lɒnˈdʒevəti] *noun* great length of life. □ **longévité**
longitude [ˈlɒŋɡitjuːd] *noun* the distance, measured in degrees on the map, that a place is east or west of a standard north-south line, *usually* that which passes through Greenwich: *What is the latitude and longitude of that town?* □ **longitude**
,**longi'tudinal** *adjective.* □ **longitudinal**
,**longi'tudinally** *adverb.* □ **longitudinalement**
look [luk] *verb* 1 to turn the eyes in a certain direction so as to see, to find, to express *etc*: *He looked out of the window; I've looked everywhere, but I can't find him; He looked at me (angrily).* □ **regarder**
2 to seem: *It looks as if it's going to rain; She looks sad.* □ **sembler, paraître**
3 to face: *The house looks west.* □ **donner sur**
■ *noun* 1 the act of looking or seeing: *Let me have a look!* □ **coup d'œil**
2 a glance: *a look of surprise.* □ **regard**
3 appearance: *The house had a look of neglect.* □ **air**
-**looking** having a certain appearance: *good-looking; strange-looking.* □ **à l'air (...)**
looks *noun plural* (attractive) appearance: *She lost her looks as she grew older; good looks.* □ **beauté**
,**looker-'on** *noun* a person who is watching something happening; an onlooker. □ **spectateur, trice**
'**looking glass** *noun* a mirror. □ **miroir**
'**lookout** *noun* 1 a careful watch: *a sharp lookout*; (*also adjective*) *a lookout post.* □ **(de) guet**
2 a place from which such a watch can be kept. □ **poste de guet**
3 a person who has been given the job of watching: *There was a shout from the lookout.* □ **guetteur, euse**
by the look(s) of judging from the appearance of (someone or something) it seems likely or probable: *By the looks of him, he won't live much longer; It's going to rain by the look of it.* □ **à le/la voir, de toute apparence**
look after to attend to or take care of: *to look after the children.* □ **avoir soin (de)**
look ahead to consider what will happen in the future. □ **penser à l'avenir**
look down one's nose at to regard with contempt. □ **regarder de haut**
look down on to regard as inferior: *She looks down on*

her husband's relations. □ **mépriser**

look for to search for: *She lost her handbag and wasted ten minutes looking for it.* □ **chercher**

look forward to to wait with pleasure for: *I am looking forward to seeing you/to the holidays.* □ **attendre avec impatience**

look here! give your attention to this: *Look here! Isn't that what you wanted?*; *Look here, Mary, you're being unfair!* □ **écoutez! dites donc!**

look in on to visit briefly: *I decided to look in on Paul and Carol on my way home.* □ **passer voir**

look into to inspect or investigate closely: *The manager will look into your complaint.* □ **examiner**

look on 1 to watch something: *No, I don't want to play – I'd rather look on.* □ **être spectateur, trice**
2 (*with* **as**) to think of or consider: *I have lived with my aunt since I was a baby, and I look on her as my mother.* □ **considérer**

look out (*usually with* **for**) to watch: *She was looking out for him from the window.* □ **guetter**

look out! beware! take care! □ **attention!**

look over to examine: *We have been looking over the new house.* □ **visiter**

look through to look at or study briefly: *I've looked through your notes.* □ **parcourir**

look up 1 to improve: *Things have been looking up lately.* □ **s'améliorer**
2 to pay a visit to: *I looked up several old friends.* □ **aller voir**
3 to search for in a book of reference: *You should look the word up (in a dictionary).* □ **chercher**
4 to consult (a reference book): *I looked up the encyclopedia.* □ **consulter**

look up to to respect the conduct, opinions *etc* of: *He has always looked up to his father.* □ **avoir du respect pour qqn**

loom[1] [luːm] *noun* a machine in which thread is woven into a fabric. □ **métier à tisser**

loom[2] [luːm] *verb* (*often with* **up**) to appear indistinctly, often threateningly: *A huge ship loomed (up) in the fog.* □ **apparaître indistinctement**

loon [luːn] *noun* a large diving water bird with webbed feet and a distinctive call: *We heard the call of the loon on the lake in the early morning.* □ **huard**

loony [luːniː] *noun* **1** a Canadian coin equal to one dollar; a Canadian one dollar coin with a picture of a loon on it: *Robin asked Richard to change 100 pennies for a loony.* □ **un dollar canadien**
2 *see* **lunatic**.

loop [luːp] *noun* **1** a doubled-over part of a piece of rope, chain *etc*: *She made a loop in the string.* □ **boucle**
2 a U-shaped bend in a river *etc*. □ **méandre**
■ *verb* to fasten with, or form into, a loop or loops: *He looped the rope around a post.* □ **faire/passer une boucle**

loose [luːs] *adjective* **1** not tight; not firmly stretched: *a loose coat*; *This belt is loose.* □ **ample, lâche, relâché**
2 not firmly fixed: *This button is loose.* □ **décousu**
3 not tied; free: *The horses are loose in the field.* □ **lâché (en liberté)**

4 not packed; not in a packet: *loose biscuits.* □ **en vrac**

'**loosely** *adverb*. □ **de manière lâche**

'**looseness** *noun*. □ **relâchement**

'**loosen** *verb* **1** to make or become loose: *She loosened the string*; *The screw had loosened and fallen out.* □ **(se) desserrer**
2 to relax (*eg* a hold): *He loosened his grip.* □ **relâcher**

,loose-'leaf *adjective* (of a notebook *etc*) made so that pages can easily be added or removed. □ **à feuilles mobiles**

break loose to escape: *The prisoner broke loose.* □ **(s') échapper**

let loose to free from control: *The circus trainer has let the lions loose.* □ **lâcher**

a **loose** (not **lose**) screw.

loot [luːt] *noun* something which is stolen: *The thieves got away with a lot of loot.* □ **butin**
■ *verb* to rob or steal from (a place): *The soldiers looted the shops of the captured town.* □ **piller**

lop [lop] – *past tense, past participle* **lopped** – *verb* to cut off (parts) from *eg* a tree: *We lopped several branches from the tree*; *She lopped a dollar off the price.* □ **émonder; réduire**

lope [loup] *verb* to run with long steps. □ **avancer en bondissant**

lord [loːd] *noun* **1** a master; a man or animal that has power over others or over an area: *The lion is lord of the jungle.* □ **seigneur**
2 (*with capital when used in titles*) in the United Kingdom *etc* a nobleman or man of rank. □ **lord**
3 (*with capital*) in the United Kingdom, used as part of several official titles: *the Lord Mayor.* □ **Lord**

'**lordly** *adjective* grand or proud: *a lordly attitude.* □ **noble, arrogant**

'**lordliness** *noun*. □ **arrogance**

'**Lordship** *noun* (*with* **His, Your** *etc*) a word used in speaking to, or about, a man with the title 'Lord' and also certain judges who do not have this title: *Thank you, Your Lordship.* □ **Monsieur le (...); Excellence**

the Lord God; Christ. □ **le Seigneur**

lord it over to act like a lord or master towards: *Don't think you can lord it over us.* □ **traiter avec arrogance**

lore [loː] *noun* knowledge handed down on a subject: *the lore of the sea.* □ **traditions**

lose [luːz] – *past tense, past participle* **lost** [lost] – *verb* **1** to stop having; to have no longer: *She has lost interest in her work*; *I have lost my watch*; *He lost hold of the rope.* □ **perdre**
2 to have taken away from one (by death, accident *etc*): *She lost her father last year*; *The ship was lost in the storm*; *He has lost his job.* □ **perdre**
3 to put (something) where it cannot be found: *My secretary has lost your letter.* □ **perdre**
4 not to win: *I always lose at cards*; *She lost the race.* □ **perdre**
5 to waste or use more (time) than is necessary: *He lost no time in informing the police of the crime.* □ **perdre**

'**loser** *noun* a person who loses: *The losers congratulated the winners.* □ **perdant, ante**

loss [los] *noun* **1** the act or fact of losing: *suffering from loss of memory*; *the loss* (= death) *of our friend.* □ **perte**

2 something which is lost: *It was only after he was dead that we realized what a loss he was.* □ **perte**

3 the amount (*especially* of money) which is lost: *a loss of $500.* □ **perte**

lost *adjective* **1** missing; no longer to be found: *a lost ticket.* □ **perdu**

2 not won: *The game is lost.* □ **perdu**

3 wasted; not used properly: *a lost opportunity.* □ **perdu**

4 no longer knowing where one is, or in which direction to go: *I don't know whether to turn left or right – I'm lost.* □ **perdu**

at a loss not knowing what to do, say *etc*: *He was at a loss for words to express his gratitude.* □ **embarrassé**

a bad, good loser someone who behaves badly or well when he loses a game *etc.* □ **beau (mauvais) joueur**

lose oneself in to have all one's attention taken up by: *to lose oneself in a book.* □ **s'absorber dans**

lose one's memory to stop being able to remember things. □ **perdre la mémoire**

lose out to suffer loss or be at a disadvantage. □ **être perdant**

lost in having one's attention wholly taken up by: *She was lost in thought.* □ **absorbé dans**

lost on wasted, having no effect, on: *The joke was lost on him.* □ **sans effet sur**

---

to **lose** (not **loose**) the match.

---

lot [lot] *noun* **1** a person's fortune or fate: *It seemed to be her lot to be always unlucky.* □ **destinée**

2 a separate part: *She gave one lot of clothes to a rummage sale and threw another lot away.* □ **lot**

3 one article or several, sold as a single item at an auction: *Are you going to bid for lot 28?* □ **lot**

lots *noun plural* a large quantity or number: *lots of people*; *He had lots and lots of food left over from the party.* □ **beaucoup de**

a lot a large quantity or number: *What a lot of letters!* □ **beaucoup de**

draw/cast lots *see* **draw**.

lotion ['louʃən] *noun* a liquid for soothing or cleaning the skin: *hand-lotion.* □ **lotion**

lottery ['lotəri] – *plural* **'lotteries** – *noun* the sharing out of money or prizes won by chance, through drawing lots: *They held a public lottery in aid of charity.* □ **loterie**

lotus ['loutəs] *noun* a type of waterlily found in Egypt and India. □ **lotus**

loud [laud] *adjective* **1** making a great sound; not quiet: *a loud voice*; *loud music.* □ **fort**

2 showy; too bright and harsh: *loud colours*; *a loud shirt.* □ **criard, voyant**

'loudly *adverb.* □ **bruyamment, fort**

'loudness *noun.* □ **grand bruit**

,loud'hailer *noun* a simple type of loudspeaker: *The police used a loud-hailer to tell the crowd to get back.* □ **porte-voix**

,loud'speaker *noun* **1** an instrument for increasing the loudness of sounds so that they can be heard further away: *The politician addressed the crowds from his car*

through a loudspeaker. □ **haut-parleur**

2 a speaker in a radio, record player *etc.* □ **haut-parleur, enceinte acoustique**

out loud not silently; with sound or voice: *John was thinking about a joke, but didn't realize he had said it out loud until everyone laughed.* □ **à voix haute**

lounge [laundʒ] *verb* **1** to lie back in a casual manner: *lounging on a sofa.* □ **se prélasser**

2 to move about lazily; to be inactive: *I spent the day lounging about the house.* □ **flâner**

■ *noun* a sitting-room, *eg* in a hotel: *They watched television in the hotel lounge.* □ **salon**

louse [laus] – *plural* **lice** [lais] – *noun* a type of wingless, bloodsucking insect, sometimes found on the bodies of animals and people. □ **poux**

lousy ['lauzi] *adjective* **1** having lice. □ **pouilleux**

2 really terrible: *I'm a lousy cook.* □ **minable**

'lousiness *noun.* □ **état pouilleux**

lout [laut] *noun* a clumsy, ill-mannered boy or man. □ **lourdaud, aude**

'loutish *adjective.* □ **lourdaud**

love [lʌv] *noun* **1** a feeling of great fondness or enthusiasm for a person or thing: *She has a great love of music*; *her love for her children.* □ **amour**

2 strong attachment with sexual attraction: *They are in love with one another.* □ **amour**

3 a person or thing that is thought of with (great) fondness (used also as a term of affection): *Ballet is the love of her life*; *Goodbye, love!* □ **passion; chéri, ie**

4 a score of nothing in tennis: *The present score is fifteen love* (written 15–0). □ **(à) zéro**

■ *verb* **1** to be (very) fond of: *He loves his children dearly.* □ **aimer**

2 to take pleasure in: *They both love dancing.* □ **aimer**

'lovable *adjective* (*negative* **unlovable**) easy to love or like; attractive: *a lovable child.* □ **adorable, aimable**

'lovely *adjective* (*negative* **unlovely**) beautiful; attractive: *She is a lovely girl*; *She looked lovely in that dress.* □ **ravissant**

2 delightful: *Someone told me a lovely joke last night, but I can't remember it*; *a lovely meal.* □ **excellent**

'loveliness *noun.* □ **charme**

'lover *noun* **1** a person who enjoys or admires or has a special affection for something: *an art lover*; *He is a lover of sport*; *an animal lover.* □ **amateur, eure; amoureux, euse**

2 a person who is having a love affair with another. □ **amant, maîtresse**

'loving *adjective.* □ **aimant**

'lovingly *adverb.* □ **avec amour**

love affair a (temporary and often sexual) relationship between two people who are in love but not married. □ **liaison (amoureuse)**

'love-letter *noun* a letter expressing love. □ **lettre d'amour**

'lovesick *adjective* sad because of being in love: *a lovesick youth*; *love sick glances.* □ **qui se languit d'amour**

fall in love (with) to develop feelings of love and sexual attraction (for): *He fell in love with her straightaway.* □ **tomber amoureux de, s'éprendre de**

for love or money in any way at all: *We couldn't get a taxi for love or money.* □ **pour rien au monde**

make love to have sexual intercourse. □ **faire l'amour**

there's no love lost between them they dislike one another. ■ **ils ne peuvent pas se sentir**

low[1] [lou] *adjective* **1** not at or reaching up to a great distance from the ground, sea level *etc*: *low hills*; *a low ceiling*; *This chair is too low for the child.* □ **bas**

2 making little sound; not loud: *She spoke in a low voice.* □ **bas**

3 at the bottom of the range of musical sounds: *That note is too low for a female voice.* □ **bas**

4 small: *a low price.* □ **bas**

5 not strong; weak or feeble: *The fire was very low.* □ **bas**

6 near the bottom in grade, rank, class *etc*: *low temperatures*; *the lower classes.* □ **bas**

■ *adverb* in or to a low position, manner or state: *The ball flew low over the net.* □ **bas**

'lower *verb* **1** to make or become less high: *She lowered her voice.* □ **baisser**

2 to let down: *He lowered the blinds.* □ **baisser**

'lowly *adjective* of low rank; humble. □ **humble**

'lowliness *noun.* □ **humilité**

'lowdown *adjective* mean; contemptible: *a lowdown thief.* □ **méprisable**

'lowland *adjective* of or concerning lowlands: *lowland districts.* □ **plaine**

'lowlander *noun* a person who lives in the lowlands. □ **habitant, ante de la plaine**

'lowlands *noun plural* land which is low compared with other, higher land. □ **basses terres**

'low-lying *adjective* (of land) at a height not much above sea level. □ **bas**

low tide/water the time when the sea is lowest at a particular place during ebb-tide: *There is one metre of water in the harbour, even at low water.* □ **marée basse**

be low on not to have enough of: *I'll have to go to the supermarket – we're low on coffee and sugar.* □ **être à court de**

low[2] [lou] *verb* to make the noise of cattle; to moo: *The cows were lowing.* □ **meugler**

lower[1] ['lauə] *verb* (of the sky *etc*) to become dark or threatening. □ **(s') assombrir**

'lowering *adjective.* □ **menaçant**

lower[2] *see* **low**[1].

loyal ['loiəl] *adjective* faithful: *a loyal friend.* □ **loyal**

'loyally *adverb.* □ **loyalement**

'loyalty *noun.* □ **loyauté**

lozenge ['lozindʒ] *noun* **1** a small sweet for sucking: *peppermint lozenges.* □ **pastille**

2 a diamond-shaped figure. □ **losange**

lubricate ['luːbrikeit] *verb* to oil (a machine *etc*) to make it move more easily and smoothly. □ **lubrifier**

,lubri'cation *noun.* □ **lubrification**

'lubricant *noun* something (oil *etc*) which lubricates. □ **lubrifiant**

luck [lʌk] *noun* **1** the state of happening by chance: *Whether you win or not is just luck – there's no skill involved.* □ **chance, hasard**

2 something good which happens by chance: *She has all the luck!* □ **chance**

'luckless *adjective* unfortunate: *luckless children.* □ **malchanceux**

'lucky *adjective* **1** having good luck: *He was very lucky to escape alive.* □ **qui a de la chance**

2 bringing good luck: *a lucky number*; *a lucky charm.* □ **qui porte chance**

lucky charm *noun* any trinket or token believed to bring good luck: *Conrad thought his four-leaf clover was a lucky charm and he brought it to every exam.* □ **porte-bonheur**

'luckily *adverb.* □ **heureusement**

'luckiness *noun.* □ **chance**

bad luck! an expression of sympathy for someone who has failed or been unlucky. □ **pas de chance!**

good luck! an expression of encouragement made to someone who is about to take part in a competition, sit an exam *etc*: *She wished him good luck.* □ **bonne chance!**

worse luck! most unfortunately!: *He's allowing me to go, but he's coming too, worse luck!* □ **tant pis!**

lucrative ['luːkrətiv] *adjective* (of a job *etc*) bringing in a lot of money; profitable. □ **lucratif**

ludicrous ['luːdikrəs] *adjective* completely ridiculous. □ **ridicule**

'ludicrously *adverb.* □ **ridiculement**

'ludicrousness *noun.* □ **aspect ridicule**

lug [lʌg] – *past tense, past participle* **lugged** – *verb* to drag with difficulty: *She lugged the heavy trunk across the floor.* □ **traîner**

luggage ['lʌgidʒ] *noun* the suitcases, trunks *etc* of a traveller: *He carried her luggage to the train*; (*also adjective*) *a luggage compartment.* □ **(à) bagage(s)**

lukewarm ['luːkwoːm] *adjective* **1** slightly warm: *lukewarm water.* □ **tiède**

2 (of *eg* interest, support *etc*) not very enthusiastic. □ **tiède**

lull [lʌl] *verb* to make calm or quiet: *The sound of the waves lulled him to sleep.* □ **calmer, endormir**

■ *noun* a temporary period of calm. □ **accalmie**

lullaby ['lʌləbai] – *plural* **'lullabies** [-baiz] – *noun* a song sung to make children go to sleep. □ **berceuse**

lumbago [lʌm'beigou] *noun* pain in the lower part of the back. □ **lumbago**

lumber[1] ['lʌmbə] *noun* timber sawn up. □ **bois de charpente**

■ *verb* to give (someone) an unwanted responsibility: *to lumber someone with a job.* □ **mettre sur les bras**

'lumberjack [-dʒak] *noun* a person employed to cut down, saw up and move trees. □ **bûcheron, onne**

lumber jacket *noun* an informal short wool coat in a plaid pattern: *Rod wore a lumber jacket and a warm cap for the sleigh ride.* □ **blouson**

lumber[2] ['lʌmbə] *verb* to move about heavily and clumsily. □ **marcher pesamment**

luminous ['luːminəs] *adjective* giving out light; faintly shining so as to be visible in the dark: *a luminous clock-face.* □ **lumineux**

,lumi'nosity [-'no-] *noun.* □ **luminosité**

lump [lʌmp] *noun* 1 a small solid mass of no particular shape: *The custard was full of lumps and no one would eat it.* □ **grumeau**
2 a swelling: *She had a lump on her head where she had hit it.* □ **bosse**
3 a small cube-shaped mass of sugar. □ **morceau**
■ *verb* (*usually with* **together**) to treat or think of as (all) alike. □ **mettre dans le même sac**
'**lumpy** *adjective* containing lumps: *lumpy custard.* □ **grumeleux**
'**lumpiness** *noun.* □ **consistance grumeleuse**
lump sum an amount of money given all at once, not in parts over a period of time. □ **somme forfaitaire**
if you don't like it, you can lump it whether you like the situation or not, you will have to endure it. □ **si ça ne vous plaît pas, tant pis!**

lunacy ['luːnəsi] *noun* insanity; madness. □ **folie**
'**lunatic** [-tik] *adjective, noun* (*abbreviation* (*usually unkind*) **loony** ['luːni] – *plural* '**loonies**) (a person who is) insane or crazy: *Only a lunatic would do such a thing!* □ **fou**

lunar *adjective* of the moon: *a lunar eclipse.* □ **lunaire, de lune**

lunar landing [luːnər landiŋ] *noun* a putting down or coming to a stop on the surface of the moon: *The space ship made a lunar landing and the astronauts walked on the surface of the moon.* □ **alunissage**

lunatic *see* **lunacy.**

lunch [lʌntʃ], *also* **luncheon** ['lʌntʃən] *noun* the meal eaten in the middle of the day: *Doctors say lunch should be the largest meal of the day and not dinner.* □ **dîner**
■ *verb* to eat this meal: *We lunched on the train.* □ **dîner**
'**lunchtime** *noun* the time between 12:00 p.m. and 2:00 p.m., when people eat lunch. □ **heure du dîner**
out to lunch crazy, loosing touch with reality. □ **débloquer un peu**

lung [lʌŋ] *noun* one of the pair of organs of breathing, in man and other animals. □ **poumon**

lunge [lʌndʒ] *verb* to make a sudden strong or violent forward movement: *Her attacker lunged at her with a knife.* □ **faire un mouvement brusque en avant**
■ *noun* a movement of this sort: *He made a lunge at her.* □ **brusque mouvement en avant**

lurch [ləːtʃ] *verb* to move suddenly or unevenly forward; to roll to one side. □ **faire une embardée, vaciller**
■ *noun* such a movement: *The train gave a lurch and started off.* □ **embardée**
leave in the lurch to leave (a person *etc*) in a difficult situation and without help. □ **laisser dans le pétrin**

lure [luə] *noun* attraction; something very attractive or tempting: *The lure of her father's good cooking brought her back home.* □ **attrait**
■ *verb* to tempt or attract: *The bright lights of the city lured him away from home.* □ **attirer**

lurid ['luərid] *adjective* 1 (too) brightly coloured or vivid: *a lurid dress/painting/sky.* □ **criard, voyant**
2 unpleasantly shocking: *the lurid details of his accident.* □ **horrible**
'**luridly** *adverb.* □ **sinistrement**
'**luridness** *noun.* □ **aspect sinistre**

lurk [ləːk] *verb* to wait in hiding *especially* with a dishonest or criminal purpose: *She saw someone lurking in the shadows.* □ **se tapir, être tapi**

luscious ['lʌʃəs] *adjective* very sweet, juicy and delicious: *a luscious peach.* □ **succulent**
'**lusciousness** *noun.* □ **succulence**

lush [lʌʃ] *adjective* green and fertile: *lush meadows.* □ **luxuriant**

lust [lʌst] *noun* (a) very strong desire: *a lust for power.* □ **désir ardent (de)**
'**lustful** *adjective.* □ **lascif**
'**lustfully** *adverb.* □ **lascivement**
'**lusty** *adjective* 1 strong and loud: *The baby gave a lusty yell.* □ **vigoureux**
2 strong and healthy: *a lusty young man.* □ **vigoureux**
'**lustily** *adverb.* □ **vigoureusement**
'**lustiness** *noun.* □ **vigueur**

lustre ['lʌstə] *noun* shininess or brightness: *Her hair had a brilliant lustre.* □ **brillant**
'**lustrous** [-trəs] *adjective.* □ **lustré**

lusty *see* **lust.**

luxury ['lʌkʃəri]– *plural* '**luxuries** – *noun* 1 great comfort *usually* amongst expensive things: *They live in luxury*; (*also adjective*) *gold jewellery and other luxury goods.* □ **(de) luxe**
2 something pleasant but not necessary, and often rare and expensive: *We're going to give up all those luxuries and only spend money on essentials.* □ **luxe**
luxurious [lʌgˈzjuəriəs] *adjective* supplied with luxuries: *a really luxurious flat/life.* □ **luxueux**
lu'xuriously *adverb.* □ **luxueusement**
lu'xuriousness *noun.* □ **luxe**

lychee, lichee ['laitʃiː, 'liː-] *noun* (a Chinese tree bearing) a small round fruit with white juicy pulp. □ **litchi**

lying *see* **lie¹, lie².**

lyric ['lirik] *adjective* (of poetry) expressing the poet's personal feeling. □ **lyrique**
■ *noun* 1 a lyric poem. □ **poème lyrique**
2 (*in plural*) the words of a song: *The tune is good, but I don't like the lyrics.* □ **paroles**

Mm

mac [mak] short for **macintosh**.

macabre [mə'kaːbr] *adjective* weird, unearthly or horrible: *macabre horror stories.* □ **macabre**

macaroni [makə'rouni] *noun* a form of pasta, pressed out to form tubes, and dried: *The macaroni is overcooked.* □ **macaroni**

mace[1] [meis] *noun* **1** a metal or metal-headed war club, often with spikes. □ **massue**
2 an ornamental rod used as a mark of authority on ceremonial occasions. □ **masse**

mace[2] [meis] *noun* a type of spice obtained from the same fruit as nutmeg. □ **macis**

machine [mə'ʃiːn] *noun* **1** a working arrangement of wheels, levers or other parts, driven *eg* by human power, electricity *etc*, or operating electronically, producing power and/or motion for a particular purpose: *a sewing machine.* □ **machine**
2 a vehicle, *especially* a motorbike: *That's a fine machine you have!* □ **machine, appareil**
■ *verb* **1** to shape, make or finish with a power-driven tool: *The articles are machined to a smooth finish.* □ **usiner**
2 to sew with a sewing machine: *You should machine the seams.* □ **coudre à la machine**

ma'chinery *noun* **1** machines in general: *Many products are made by machinery rather than by hand.* □ **machinerie**
2 the workings or processes: *the machinery of government.* □ **rouages**

ma'chinist *noun* a person skilled in the use of machines, *eg* a sewing machine, or electrical tools: *She's a machinist in a clothes factory.* □ **opérateur, trice**

ma'chine gun *noun* an automatic gun that fires very rapidly. □ **mitrailleuse**
■ *verb: He machine-gunned a crowd of defenseless villagers.* □ **mitrailler**

machine tool a power-driven machine that shapes metal, wood, or plastics by cutting, pressing, or drilling. □ **machine-outil**

> **machinery** does not have a plural.

mackerel ['makrəl] – *plurals* '**mackerel**, '**mackerels** – *noun* **1** a type of edible sea fish, bluish green with wavy markings: *They are fishing for mackerel*; *two mackerels.* □ **maquereau**
2 its flesh as food: *fried mackerel.* □ **maquereau**

mackintosh ['makintoʃ] *noun* a waterproof overcoat, *especially* made of plastic material. □ **imperméable**

macramé [mə'kraːmi] *noun* the craft of tying thread, string *etc* in decorative knots. □ **macramé**

mad [mad] *adjective* **1** mentally disturbed or insane: *Ophelia went mad*; *You must be mad.* □ **fou**
2 (*sometimes with* **at** *or* **with**) very angry: *She was mad at me for losing my keys.* □ **furieux (contre)**
3 (*with* **about**) having a great liking or desire for: *I'm just mad about Harry.* □ **fou (de), emballé (par)**

'**madly** *adverb*. □ **follement**

'**madness** *noun*. □ **folie, insanité**

'**madden** *verb* to make mad or very angry: *The animal was maddened by the pain.* □ **rendre fou**

'**maddening** *adjective* likely to cause anger: *maddening delays.* □ **exaspérant**

'**maddeningly** *adverb*. □ **à rendre fou**

'**madman** – *plural* '**madmen**: *feminine* '**madwoman** – *plural* '**madwomen** – *noun* a person who is insane: *He drove/fought like a madman.* □ **fou, folle**

like mad wildly, desperately, very quickly *etc*: *struggling/trying/running like mad.* □ **comme un perdu**

madam ['madəm] – *plurals* **madams, mesdames** [mei'dam] – *noun* a polite form of address to a woman. □ **madame**

madden, maddening, maddeningly *see* **mad**.

made *see* **make**.

Madonna [mə'donə] *noun* (*with* **the**) the Virgin Mary, mother of Christ, *especially* as shown in works of art: *a painting of the Madonna and Child.* □ **Madone**

madrigal ['madrigəl] *noun* a type of song for several voices singing unaccompanied in harmony. □ **madrigal**

maestro ['maistrou] – *plural* '**maestros** – *noun* (a title given to) a master in one of the arts, *especially* a musical composer or conductor. □ **maestro**

magazine [magə'ziːn] *noun* **1** (*abbreviation* **mag** [mag]) a publication issued regularly containing articles, stories *etc* by various writers: *women's magazines*; (*also adjective*) *a magazine article.* □ **magazine, revue**
2 a compartment in or on a gun that holds cartridges. □ **magasin**
3 a storeroom for ammunition, explosives *etc*. □ **poudrière**

maggot ['magət] *noun* the worm-like grub or larva of a fly, *especially* a bluebottle. □ **asticot**

magic ['madʒik] *noun* **1** (the charms, spells *etc* used in) the art or practice of using supernatural forces: *The prince was turned by magic into a frog.* □ **magie**
2 the art of producing illusions by tricks: *The conjuror's magic delighted the children.* □ **magie**
3 fascination or great charm: *the magic of Sonia Delaunay's paintings.* □ **enchantement**
■ *adjective* used in or using magic: *a magic wand*; *a magic spell.* □ **magique**

'**magical** *adjective* **1** produced by, or as if by, the art of magic: *magical power.* □ **magique**
2 fascinating; charming or very beautiful: *a magical experience.* □ **enchanteur**

'**magically** *adverb*. □ **magiquement**

ma'gician [mə'dʒiʃən] *noun* a person skilled in the art of magic: *They hired a magician to entertain the children.* □ **magicien, ienne**

magistrate ['madʒistreit] *noun* a person who has power to put the laws into force and sentence those guilty of lesser crimes. □ **magistrat**

magma [magma] *noun* very hot, soft material beneath the surface of the earth: *Igneous rock and lava from a volcano are both formed from magma.* □ **magma**

magnanimous [mag'nanimərs] *adjective* noble and generous: *a magnanimous gesture.* □ **magnanime**

mag'nanimously *adverb.* □ **magnanimement**

magnanimity [magnə'nimɪti] *noun.* □ **magnanimité**

magnate ['magneit] *noun* a man of wealth or power: *He is a rich shipping magnate.* □ **magnat**

magnesium [mag'niːziəm] *noun* a silver white metallic element that burns with a bright, white light. □ **magnésium**

magnet ['magnit] *noun* a piece of iron, or of certain other materials, that attracts or repels other pieces of iron *etc*. □ **aimant**

mag'netic [-'ne-] *adjective* **1** of, or having the powers of, or operating by means of, a magnet or magnetism: *magnetic force.* □ **magnétique**

2 strongly attractive: *a magnetic personality.* □ **magnétique**

mag'netically *adverb.* □ **magnétiquement**

'magnetism *noun* **1** power of attraction: *his personal magnetism.* □ **magnétisme**

2 (the science of) magnets and their power of attraction: *the magnetism of the earth.* □ **magnétisme**

'magnetize, 'magnetise *verb* **1** to make magnetic: *You can magnetize a piece of iron.* □ **magnétiser**

2 to attract or influence strongly: *She's the kind of person who can magnetize others.* □ **magnétiser**

magnetic field the area in which the pull of a magnet, or thing acting like a magnet, is felt: *the earth's magnetic field.* □ **champ magnétique**

magnetic north the direction, either east or west of the true north, in which a magnetized needle points. □ **nord magnétique**

magnificent [məg'nifisnt] *adjective* great and splendid: *a magnificent costume; a magnificent performance.* □ **magnifique**

mag'nificently *adverb.* □ **magnifiquement**

mag'nificence *noun.* □ **magnificence**

magnify ['magnifai] *verb* to cause to appear greater: *A telescope magnifies an image; to magnify one's troubles.* □ **grossir, exagérer**

,magnifi'cation [-fi-] *noun* **1** the act of magnifying (something). □ **grossissement**

2 the power of magnifying: *the magnification of a pair of binoculars.* □ **grossissement**

3 the extent to which something (*eg* a photograph) has been magnified: *The magnification is ten times (10X).* □ **grossissement**

'magnifying glass *noun* a piece of glass with curved surfaces that makes an object looked at through it appear larger: *This print is so small that I need a magnifying glass to read it.* □ **loupe**

magnitude ['magnitjuːd] *noun* **1** importance: *a decision of great magnitude.* □ **importance**

2 size: *a star of great magnitude.* □ **magnitude**

magpie ['magpai] *noun* a black and white bird of the crow family, known for its habit of collecting shiny objects. □ **pie**

mahjong(g) [maː'dʒɒŋ] *noun* an old Chinese game played with small painted tiles. □ **ma(h)-jong**

mahogany [mə'hɒgəni] *noun* **1** the wood of a tropical American tree, much used for making furniture: *This table is made of mahogany; (also adjective) a mahogany*

table. □ **(en) acajou**

2 (*also adjective*) (of) its dark brown colour. □ **acajou**

3 (*also* **mahogany tree**) the tree. □ **acajou**

maid [meid] *noun* a female servant: *The maid answered the door.* □ **domestique**

maiden ['meidən] *noun* a (young) unmarried woman: *the village maidens.* □ **jeune fille**

maiden name a woman's surname before her marriage: *Mrs. Johnson's maiden name was Scott.* □ **nom de jeune fille**

maiden voyage a ship's first voyage. □ **premier voyage**

mail [meil] *noun* letters, parcels *etc* by post: *Her secretary opens her mail.* □ **courrier**

■ *verb* to send by post. □ **poster**

'mailbag *noun* a bag for letters *etc*: *The letters are put into mailbags and sent to London by train.* □ **sac postal**

'mailbox *noun* a box used to send or receive letters: *The postman delivered two letters today; he put them in the mailbox.* □ **boîte aux lettres**

'mailman [-man] *noun* a postman. □ **facteur, trice; postier, postière**

maim [meim] *verb* to injure badly, *especially* with permanent effects: *The hunter was maimed for life.* □ **estropié**

main [mein] *adjective* chief, principal or most important: *the main purpose; the main character in the story.* □ **principal**

■ *noun* (*also* **mains**) the chief pipe or cable in a branching system of pipes or cables: *The water's been turned off at the main(s); (also adjective) the mains electricity supply.* □ **conduite maîtresse**

'mainly *adverb* more (of) the thing mentioned than anything else; mostly or largely: *This skirt is mainly dark grey.* □ **principalement**

'mainland *noun* a large piece of land as compared with neighbouring islands: *Britain is not part of the mainland of Europe.* □ **continent**

'mainspring *noun* the chief spring, *especially* the spring that causes the wheels to move in a watch or clock. □ **ressort principal**

'mainstream *noun* the chief direction or trend of a system of theories, developments *etc*: *the mainstream of traditional art.* □ **courant dominant**

maintain [mein'tein] *verb* **1** to continue: *How long can you maintain this silence?* □ **maintenir**

2 to keep in good condition: *She maintains her car very well.* □ **entretenir**

3 to pay the expenses of: *How can you maintain three children on your small salary?* □ **subvenir aux besoins de**

4 to continue to argue or believe (that): *I maintain that the theory is true.* □ **soutenir**

'maintenance [-tənəns] *noun* **1** the process of keeping something in good condition: *car maintenance.* □ **entretien**

2 the act of maintaining (a point of view *etc*). □ **maintien**

maisonette [meizə'net] *noun* (used *especially* by estate agents *etc*) a flat or apartment on two floors or stories. □ **(appartement en) duplex**

maize [meiz] *noun* (**corn, Indian corn**) an important cereal, grown *especially* in America. □ **maïs**

majesty ['madʒəsti] – *plural* '**majesties** – *noun* 1 greatness; impressive dignity: *the majesty of God*. □ **majesté** 2 (*with capital: with* **His, Her, Your** *etc*) a title used when speaking to or of a king or queen: *Her Majesty the Queen*; *Their Majesties*; *Your Majesty*. □ **Sa/Votre Majesté**

ma'**jestic** [-'dʒes-] *adjective* having great dignity: *He looked truly majestic*. □ **majestueux**
ma'**jestically** *adverb*. □ **majestueusement**

major ['meidʒə] *adjective* great, or greater, in size, importance *etc*: *major and minor roads*; *a major discovery*. □ **majeur**
■ *noun* (*often abbreviated to* **Maj.** *when written*) the rank next below lieutenant-colonel. □ **commandant, ante**

ma'**jority** [mə'dʒo-] – *plural* ma'**jorities** – *noun* 1 the greater number: *The majority of people*. □ **majorité** 2 the difference between a greater and a smaller number: *The Democratic Party won by/with a majority of six hundred votes*. □ **majorité**
,**major** '**general** *noun* (*often abbreviated to* **Maj. Gen.** *when written*) (in the Canadian army, (a person of) the rank next below lieutenant-general. □ **général, ale de division**
the age of majority legal adulthood: *He has not yet reached the age of majority*. □ **majorité**

make [meik] – *past tense, past participle* **made** [meid] – *verb* 1 to create, form or produce: *God made the Earth*; *She makes all her own clothes*; *He made it out of paper*; *to make a muddle/mess of the job*; *to make lunch/coffee*; *We made an arrangement/agreement/deal/bargain*. □ **faire**
2 to compel, force or cause (a person or thing to do something): *They made her do it*; *He made me laugh*. □ **faire**
3 to cause to be: *I made it clear*; *You've made me very unhappy*. □ **rendre**
4 to gain or earn: *He makes $100 a week*; *to make a profit*. □ **gagner, faire**
5 (of numbers *etc*) to add up to; to amount to: *2 and 2 make(s) 4*. □ **faire**
6 to become, turn into, or be: *She'll make an excellent teacher*. □ **faire**
7 to estimate as: *I make the total 483*. □ **estimer (à)**
8 to appoint, or choose, as: *She was made manager*. □ **nommer**
9 used with many nouns to give a similar meaning to that of the verb from which the noun is formed: *He made several attempts* (= attempted several times); *They made a left turn* (= turned left); *He made* (= offered) *a suggestion/proposal/bid*; *Have you any comments to make?* □ **faire (...)**
■ *noun* a (*usually* manufacturer's) brand: *What make is your new car?* □ **marque**
'**maker** *noun* a person who makes: *a toolmaker*; *a dressmaker*. □ **fabricant, ante**
'**making** *noun* the process of producing or forming something: *glassmaking*; (*also adjective*) *the roadmaking industry*. □ **(de) fabrication**

,**make-be'lieve** *noun* the act or art of pretending and imagining: *a world of make-believe*; (*also adjective*) *a make-believe world*. □ **semblant; imaginaire**
'**makeshift** *adjective* temporary and *usually* of poor quality: *a makeshift garden shed*. □ **de fortune**
'**makeup** *noun* 1 cosmetics applied to the face *etc*: *She never wears any makeup*. □ **maquillage**
2 the set, or combination, of characteristics or ingredients that together form something, *eg* a personality; composition: *Violence is just not part of his makeup*. □ **constitution, caractère**
have the makings of to have the clear ability for becoming: *Your son has the makings of an engineer*. □ **avoir l'étoffe de**
in the making being made or formed at this very moment: *A revolution is in the making*. □ **en formation**
make a/one's bed to tidy and straighten the sheets, blankets *etc* on a bed after it has been used: *The children make their own beds every morning*. □ **faire le/son lit**
make believe to pretend (that): *The children made believe they were animals*. □ **faire semblant (de)**
make do (*with* **with**) to use something as a poor quality or temporary alternative to the real thing: *There's no meat, so we'll have to make do with potatoes*. □ **se contenter de**
make easier to enable or facilitate: *Lena's job interview was made easier by the fact that she knew several of the people interviewing her*. □ **faciliter**
make for to go towards: *We're making for home*. □ **se diriger vers**
make it to be successful: *After twenty years, we've finally made it*. □ **réussir**
make up 1 to become friends again after a quarrel: *It's time you two made up* (*with each other*). □ **se réconcilier**
2 to give compensation or make amends for something: *I'm sorry – I'll make it up to you somehow*. □ **dédommager**
make (something) of (something) to understand (something) by or from (something): *What do you make of all this?* □ **comprendre (à)**
make out 1 to see, hear or understand: *She could make out a ship in the distance*. □ **discerner**
2 to make it seem that: *He made out that he was earning a huge amount of money*. □ **prétendre**
3 to write or fill in: *The doctor made out a prescription*. □ **faire**
make up 1 to invent: *He made up the whole story*. □ **inventer**
2 to compose or be part(s) of: *The group was made up of doctors and lawyers*. □ **composer**
3 to complete: *We need one more player – will you make up the number(s)?* □ **compléter**
4 to apply cosmetics to (the face): *I don't like to see women making up* (*their faces*). □ **(se) maquiller**
5 to become friends again (after a quarrel *etc*): *They've finally made up* (*their disagreement*). □ **se réconcilier**
make up for to supply a reward, substitute *etc* for disappointment, damage, loss (of money or time) *etc*: *Next week we'll try to make up for lost time*. □ **compenser**
make up one's mind to make a decision: *He finally*

made up his mind about the job. □ **se décider**

make up to to try to gain the favour or love of by flattery *etc*: *We're always making up to the teacher by bringing her presents.* □ **courtiser qqn**

---

made of is used in speaking of the material from which an object is constructed *etc*: *This table is made of wood/plastic/ steel.*

made from is used in speaking of the raw material from which something has been produced by a process of manufacture: *Paper is made from wood/rags.*

---

malady ['malədi] – *plural* **'maladies** – *noun* an illness or disease: *He is suffering from some strange malady.* □ **maladie**

malaria [mə'leəriə] *noun* a fever caused by the bite of a certain type of mosquito. □ **malaria**

male [meil] *noun, adjective* 1 (a person, animal *etc*) of the sex having testes or an organ or organs performing a similar function; not (of) the sex which carries the young until birth *etc*: *the male of the species*; *the male rabbit.* □ **mâle**

2 (a plant) having flowers with stamens which can fertilize female flowers. □ **mâle**

malevolent [mə'levələnt] *adjective* wishing evil to others: *The wicked old man gave a malevolent smile.* □ **malveillant**

ma'levolently *adverb.* □ **avec malveillance**

ma'levolence *noun.* □ **malveillance**

malfunction [mal'fʌŋkʃən] *noun* faulty performance or a faulty process: *There's a malfunction in the main engine.* □ **mauvais fonctionnement**

malice ['malis] *noun* the wish to harm other people *etc*: *There was no malice intended in what she said.* □ **méchanceté**

mal'icious [-ʃəs] *adjective*: *She took a malicious pleasure in hurting others.* □ **méchant**

ma'liciously *adverb.* □ **avec méchanceté**

malign [mə'lain] *verb* to say unpleasant things about (someone or something), *especially* without reason: *He's always maligning his wife when she isn't there.* □ **dire du mal de**

malignant [mə'lignənt] *adjective* 1 (of people, their actions *etc*) intending, or intended, to do harm: *a malignant remark.* □ **malveillant**

2 (of a tumour, disease *etc*) likely to become worse and cause death: *She died of a malignant tumour.* □ **malin**

ma'lignantly *adverb.* □ **méchamment**

malinger [mə'liŋgə] *verb* to pretend to be unwell *eg* in order to avoid work: *He says he's ill, but I think he's just malingering.* □ **tirer au flanc**

ma'lingerer *noun.* □ **tire-au-flanc**

mallet ['malit] *noun* 1 a type of small wooden hammer: *We hammered the tent pegs into the ground with a mallet.* □ **maillet**

2 a long-handled wooden hammer for playing croquet or polo. □ **maillet**

malnutrition [malnjuːtriʃən] *noun* (a medical condition resulting from) eating too little or getting too little nourishing food: *About half of the population is suffering from malnutrition.* □ **sous-alimentation**

malt [moːlt] *noun* 1 barley or other grain soaked in water, allowed to sprout, and dried in a kiln, used in making beer, whisky *etc*. □ **malt**

2 a variety of malt whisky: *This pub sells fifteen different malts.* □ **(whisky) pur malt**

mamma, mama [mə'maː] *noun* a (name for one's) mother. □ **maman**

mammal ['maməl] *noun* any member of the class of animals (including man) in which the females feed the young with their own milk: *Monkeys are mammals.* □ **mammifère**

mam'malian [-'mei-] *adjective.* □ **mammifère**

mammary ['maməri] *adjective* of the breasts or milk glands: *the mammary glands.* □ **mammaire**

mammoth ['maməθ] *noun* a large hairy elephant of a kind no longer found living. □ **mammouth**

■ *adjective* very large (and often very difficult): *a mammoth project/task.* □ **géant**

man [man] – *plural* **men** [men] – *noun* 1 an adult male human being: *Hundreds of men, women and children*; *a four-man team.* □ **homme**

2 human beings taken as a whole; the human race: *the development of man.* □ **homme**

3 obviously masculine male person. □ **(vrai) homme**

4 a word sometimes used in speaking informally or giving commands to someone: *Get on with your work, man, and stop complaining!* □ **(mon) vieux**

5 an ordinary soldier, who is not an officer: *officers and men.* □ **soldat**

6 a piece used in playing chess or draughts: *I took three of his men in one move.* □ **pièce; pion**

■ *verb* – *past tense, past participle* **manned** – to supply with men (*especially* soldiers): *The colonel manned the guns with soldiers from our regiment.* □ **pourvoir en personnel**

-man [-mən, -man] a person (formerly *usually* used for either sex; currently, often replaced by **-person** when the person referred to can be of either sex) who performs a particular activity, as in **postman, milkman, chairman** *etc*.

'manhood *noun* 1 (of a male) the state of being adult, physically (and mentally) mature *etc*: *He died before he reached manhood.* □ **âge d'homme**

2 manly qualities: *He took her refusal to marry him as an insult to his manhood.* □ **virilité**

man'kind *noun* the human race as a whole: *He worked for the benefit of all mankind.* □ **humanité**

'manly *adjective* having the qualities thought desirable in a man, *ie* strength, determination, courage *etc*: *He is strong and manly.* □ **viril**

'manliness *noun.* □ **virilité**

manned *adjective* supplied with men: *a manned spacecraft.* □ **doté de personnel**

'man-eating *adjective* which will eat people: *a man-eating tiger.* □ **mangeur d'hommes**

'man-eater *noun.* □ **mangeur d'hommes**

man'handle *verb* 1 to move, carry *etc* by hand: *When the crane broke down, they had to manhandle the crates on to the boat.* □ **manutentionner**

2 to treat roughly: *You'll break all the china if you man-*

Mammals

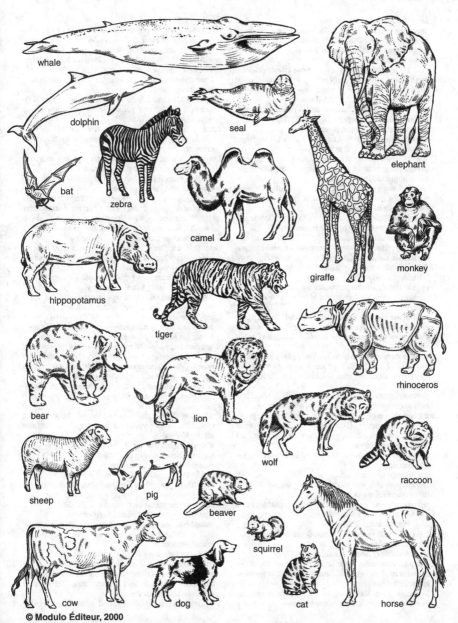

whale

dolphin

seal

elephant

bat

zebra

camel

giraffe

monkey

hippopotamus

tiger

rhinoceros

bear

lion

wolf

raccoon

sheep

pig

beaver

squirrel

cow

dog

cat

horse

handle it like that! □ **maltraiter**

'**manhole** *noun* a hole (*usually* in the middle of a road or pavement) through which someone may go to inspect sewers *etc*. □ **bouche (d'égout)**

,**man-'made** *adjective* made, happening or formed by man, not by natural means: *a man-made lake.* □ **artificiel**

'**manpower** *noun* the number of people available for employment *etc*: *There's a shortage of manpower in the building industry.* □ **main-d'œuvre**

'**manservant** – *plural* '**menservants** – *noun* a male servant (*especially* one employed as a valet): *They have only one manservant.* □ **valet de chambre**

'**mansize(d)** *adjective* of a size suitable for a man; large: *a mansized breakfast.* □ **grand**

'**manslaughter** *noun* the crime of killing someone, without intending to do so: *I was found guilty of manslaughter.* □ **homicide involontaire**

'**menfolk** *noun plural* male people, *especially* male relatives: *The women accompanied their menfolk.* □ **hommes (de la famille)**

'**menswear** ['menz-] *noun* clothing for men: *Do you sell menswear?* □ **vêtements pour hommes**

as one man simultaneously; together: *They rose as one man to applaud his speech.* □ **comme un seul homme**

the man in the street the ordinary, typical, average man: *The man in the street often has little interest in politics.* □ **l'homme de la rue**

man of letters a writer and/or scholar: *Shakespeare was perhaps Britain's greatest man of letters.* □ **homme de lettres**

man of the world a sophisticated man who is not likely to be shocked or surprised by most things: *You can speak freely – we're all men of the world.* □ **homme d'expérience**

man to man as one man to another; openly or frankly: *They talked man to man about their problems*; (*also adjective*) *a man to man discussion.* □ **d'homme à homme**

to a man every one, without exception: *They voted to a man to accept the proposal.* □ **jusqu'au dernier**

manage ['manidʒ] *verb* **1** to be in control or charge of: *My lawyer manages all my legal affairs/money.* □ **gérer**

2 to be manager of: *Kate manages the local football team.* □ **administrer**

3 to deal with, or control: *She's good at managing people.* □ **diriger**

4 to be able to do something; to succeed or cope: *Will you manage to repair your bicycle?*; *Can you manage (to eat) some more meat?* □ **réussir**

'**manageable** *adjective* (*negative* **unmanageable**) **1** that can be controlled: *The children are not very manageable.* □ **maniable**

2 that can be done: *Are you finding this work manageable?* □ **faisable**

,**managea'bility** *noun.* □ **maniabilité**

'**management** *noun* **1** the art of managing: *The management of this company is a difficult task.* □ **gestion, administration**

2 *or noun plural* the managers of a firm *etc* as a group: *The management has/have agreed to pay the workers*

more. □ **direction**

'**manager** *noun* a person who is in charge of *eg* a business, football team *etc*: *the manager of the new store.* □ **directeur, trice, gérant, ante**

mandarin ['mandərin] *noun* **1** (*also* **mandarin orange**) a type of small orange. □ **mandarine**

2 an official of high rank in the Chinese Empire. □ **mandarin**

mandolin, mandoline ['mandəlin] *noun* a musical instrument similar to a guitar: *He played a tune on the mandolin.* □ **mandoline**

mane [mein] *noun* the long hair on the back of the neck of a horse, lion *etc*: *The male of the lion has a mane.* □ **crinière**

manger ['meindʒə] *noun* a box or trough in which food for horses and cattle is placed. □ **mangeoire**

mangle ['mangl] *verb* **1** to crush to pieces: *The car was badly mangled in the accident.* □ **écraser**

2 to spoil (*eg* a piece of music) by bad mistakes *etc*: *He mangled the music by his terrible playing.* □ **massacrer**

mango ['mangou] – *plural* '**mango(e)s** – *noun* **1** the yellowish fruit of an Indian tropical tree. □ **mangue**

2 (*also* **mango tree**) the tree. □ **manguier**

mangosteen ['mangəstiːn] *noun* **1** the dark brown, orange-shaped fruit of an East Indian tree. □ **mangouste**

2 the tree. □ **mangoustan**

mangrove ['mangrouv] *noun* a tropical evergreen tree growing in or near water. □ **palétuvier**

mania ['meiniə] *noun* **1** a form of mental illness in which the sufferer is overactive, overexcited, and unreasonably happy. □ **manie**

2 an unreasonable enthusiasm for something: *He has a mania for fast cars.* □ **manie**

'**maniac** [-ak] *noun* an insane (and dangerous) person; a madman: *He drives like a maniac.* □ **maniaque**

manic ['manik] *adjective* **1** of, or suffering from, mania: *She's in a manic state.* □ **maniaque**

2 extremely energetic, active and excited: *The new manager is one of those manic people who can't rest even for a minute.* □ **excité**

manicure ['manikjuə] *verb* to care for (the hands and nails): *She manicures her nails every night.* □ **(se) faire les ongles/mains**

■ *noun* a treatment for the hands and nails: *I'm going for a manicure.* □ **soin des mains**

'**manicurist** *noun.* □ **manucure**

manifest ['manifest] *verb* to show (clearly): *She manifested her character in her behaviour.* □ **manifester**

■ *adjective* easily seen by the eye or understood by the mind; obvious: *manifest stupidity.* □ **évident**

'**manifestly** *adverb.* □ **manifestement**

,**manife'station** *noun* **1** an obvious or clear example: *This is another manifestation of their ignorance.* □ **manifestation**

2 the act of showing clearly. □ **manifestation**

manifesto [mani'festou] – *plural* ,**mani'festo(e)s** – *noun* a public *usually* written announcement of policies and intentions, *especially* by a political party: *the socialist manifesto.* □ **manifeste**

manipulate [mə'nipjuleit] *verb* **1** to handle *especially* skilfully: *I watched her manipulating the controls of the aircraft.* □ **manipuler**

2 to manage or influence cleverly (and dishonestly): *A clever lawyer can manipulate a jury.* □ **manœuvrer** ma,nipu'lation *noun.* □ **manœuvre** ma'nipulator *noun.* □ **manipulateur, trice**

manner ['manə] *noun* 1 a way in which anything is done *etc*: *She greeted me in a friendly manner.* □ **manière**

2 the way in which a person behaves, speaks *etc*: *I don't like her manner.* □ **comportement**

3 (*in plural*) (polite) behaviour, *usually* towards others: *Why don't they teach their children (good) manners?* □ **manières**

-'**mannered** having, or showing, manners of a certain kind: *a well-/bad-mannered person.* □ **élevé**

'**mannerism** *noun* an odd and obvious habit in a person's behaviour, speech *etc*: *He scratches his ear when he talks and has other mannerisms.* □ **tic, manie**

all manner of all kinds of: *He has all manner of problems.* □ **toutes sortes de**

in a manner of speaking in a certain way: *I suppose, in a manner of speaking, I am an engineer.* □ **pour ainsi dire**

manoeuvre [mə'nuːvə] *noun* 1 a planned movement (of troops, ships, aircraft, vehicles *etc*): *Can you perform all the manoeuvres required by the driving test?* □ **manœuvre**

2 a skilful or cunning plan or action: *His appointment was the result of many cunning manoeuvres.* □ **manœuvre**

■ *verb* to (cause to) perform manoeuvres: *I had difficulty manoeuvring my car into the narrow space.* □ **faire manœuvrer**

mansion ['manʃən] *noun* a large (luxurious) house: *They own a country mansion.* □ **hôtel particulier; manoir**

mantelpiece ['mantlpiːs], **mantelshelf** ['mantlʃelf], **mantel** ['mantl], *noun* the shelf above a fireplace: *She put the card on her mantelpiece.* □ **tablette de cheminée**

manual ['manjuəl] *adjective* 1 of the hand or hands: *manual skills/labour.* □ **manuel**

2 working with the hands: *a manual worker.* □ **manuel**

3 worked or operated by the hand: *a car with a manual gearbox.* □ **manuel**

■ *noun* 1 a handbook *eg* of technical information about a machine *etc*: *an instruction manual.* □ **manuel**

2 a keyboard of an organ *etc*. □ **clavier**

'**manually** *adverb* by hand: *You have to operate this sewing machine manually – it is not electric.* □ **manuellement**

manufacture [manju'faktʃə] *verb* 1 to make, *originally* by hand but now *usually* by machinery and in large quantities: *This firm manufactures cars at the rate of two hundred per day.* □ **fabriquer**

2 to invent (something false): *He manufactured an excuse for being late.* □ **fabriquer**

■ *noun* the process of manufacturing: *the manufacture of glass.* □ **fabrication**

,**manu'facturer** *noun* a person or firm that manufactures goods: *She is a carpet manufacturer.* □ **fabricant, ante**

manure [mə'njuə] *noun* a mixture containing animal dung, spread on soil to help produce better crops *etc*: *The farmer is putting manure on his fields.* □ **fumier**

■ *verb* to treat (soil or plants) with manure: *The farmer has been manuring the fields.* □ **fumer**

manuscript ['manjuskript] *noun* 1 the handwritten or typed material for a book *etc*, *usually* prepared for printing: *The publishers have lost the manuscript of my book.* □ **manuscrit**

2 a book or document written by hand: *a collection of manuscripts and printed books.* □ **manuscrit**

many ['meni] – *comparative* **more** [moː]: *superlative* **most** [moust] – *adjective* a great number of: *Many languages are spoken in Africa; There weren't very many people; You've made a great/good many mistakes.* □ **beaucoup**

■ *pronoun* a great number: *A few people survived, but many died.* □ **beaucoup**

many- having a great number of (something): *many-coloured; many-sided.* □ **à beaucoup de, multi-**

many a a great number of: *I've told him many a time to be more polite.* □ **maint**

---

many means a great number (of): *many cars; Some are full, but many are empty.*
much means a great amount (of): *much effort; It doesn't say much.*

---

map [map] *noun* 1 a drawing or plan, in outline, of (any part of) the surface of the earth, with various features shown (*usually* roads, rivers, seas, towns *etc*): *a map of the world; a road map.* □ **carte**

2 a similar type of drawing showing *eg* the surface of the moon, the position of the stars in the sky *etc*. □ **carte**

■ *verb – past tense, past participle* **mapped** – to make a map of (an area): *Africa was mapped by many different explorers.* □ **dresser la carte de**

map out to plan (a route, course of action *etc*) in detail: *to map out a route/journey.* □ **(se) tracer**

mar [maː] – *past tense, past participle* **marred** – *verb* to spoil or damage (enjoyment, beauty *etc*): *Her beauty was marred by a scar on her cheek.* □ **gâter**

marathon ['marəθən] *noun* a long-distance footrace, *usually* 42km 195m: *She came third in the marathon; (also adjective) a marathon race/discussion.* □ **marathon**

marble ['maːbl] *noun* 1 a kind of hard, *usually* highly polished stone, cold to the touch: *This table is made of marble; (also adjective) a marble statue.* □ **(de/en) marbre**

2 a small hard ball of glass used in children's games: *The little boy rolled a marble along the ground.* □ **bille**

'**marbled** *adjective* having irregular streaks of different colours, like some types of marble: *marbled stonework.* □ **marbré**

'**marbles** *noun singular* any of several games played with marbles: *The girls were playing marbles.* □ **billes**

March [maːtʃ] *noun* the third month of the year, the month following February. □ **mars**

march [maːtʃ] *verb* 1 to (cause to) walk at a constant rhythm, and often in step with others: *Soldiers were*

marching along the street. □ **(faire) marcher au pas**
2 to go on steadily: *Time marches on.* □ **s'écouler**
■ *noun* 1 (the) act of marching: *a long march; the march of time.* □ **marche**
2 a piece of music for marching to: *The band played a march.* □ **marche**

mare [meə] *noun* a female horse. □ **jument**

margarine ['maːdʒəriːn] *noun* (*abbreviation* **marge** [maːdʒ]) a butter-like substance made mainly from vegetable fats: *We use margarine instead of butter.* □ **margarine**

margin ['maːdʒin] *noun* 1 the blank edge around a page of writing or print: *Please write your comments in the margin.* □ **marge**
2 an edge or border: *the margin of the lake.* □ **bord**
3 something extra, beyond what should be needed: *Leave a wide margin for error!* □ **marge**
'**marginal** *adjective* small and almost non-existent or unimportant: *a marginal improvement.* □ **marginal**

marijuana, marihuana [mari'waːnə] *noun* a type of drug (illegal in many countries) made from the dried flowers and leaves of the hemp plant. □ **marijuana**

marine [mə'riːn] *adjective* of the sea: *marine animals; marine law.* □ **marin**
■ *noun* a soldier serving on board a ship: *I have joined the marines.* □ **fusilier marin**
mariner ['marinə] *noun* a sailor: *a master mariner.* □ **marin**

marionette [mariə'net] *noun* a type of puppet moved by strings. □ **marionnette**

marital ['maritl] *adjective* of marriage: *marital relations* (= the relationship between a married couple). □ **conjugal**

maritime ['maritaim] *adjective* 1 of the sea, shipping *etc*: *maritime law.* □ **maritime**
2 lying near the sea, and therefore having a navy, merchant shipping *etc*: *a maritime nation.* □ **maritime**

mark[1] [maːk] *noun* (*also* **Deutsche Mark, Deutschmark** ['doitʃmaːk]) the standard unit of currency in the Federal Republic of Germany. □ **mark**

mark[2] [maːk] *noun* 1 a sign or spot that can be seen, *eg* on a person's or animal's body: *My dog has a white mark on his nose.* □ **marque**
2 a point given as a reward for good work *etc*: *She got good marks in the exam.* □ **point, note**
3 a stain: *That spilt coffee has left a mark on the carpet.* □ **tache**
4 a sign used as a guide to position *etc*: *There's a mark on the map showing where the church is.* □ **signe**
5 a cross or other sign used instead of a signature: *He couldn't sign his name, so he made his mark instead.* □ **croix**
6 an indication or sign of a particular thing: *a mark of respect.* □ **marque**
■ *verb* 1 to put a mark or stain on, or to become marked or stained: *Every pupil's coat must be marked with his name; That coffee has marked the tablecloth; This white material marks easily.* □ **(se) marquer, (se) tacher**
2 to give marks to (a piece of work): *I have forty exam papers to mark tonight.* □ **corriger**

3 to show; to be a sign of: *X marks the spot where the treasure is buried.* □ **indiquer**
4 to note: *Mark it down in your notebook.* □ **noter**
5 (in football *etc*) to keep close to (an opponent) so as to prevent his getting the ball: *Your job is to mark the centre forward.* □ **marquer**
marked *adjective* obvious or easily noticeable: *There has been a marked improvement in her work.* □ **marqué**
'**markedly** [-kid-] *adverb* noticeably: *It's markedly easier to do it by this method.* □ **visiblement**
'**marker** *noun* 1 a person who marks *eg* the score at games. □ **marqueur, euse**
2 something used for marking, *eg* in scoring, showing the position of something *etc*: *The area is indicated by large green markers.* □ **marque, jalon**
3 a type of pen, *usually* with a thick point. □ **marqueur indélébile**
'**marksman** ['maːks-] – *plural* '**marksmen** – *noun* a person who shoots well: *The police marksman did not kill the criminal – he wounded him in the leg to prevent him escaping.* □ **tireur, euse d'élite**
'**marksmanship** *noun* a person's skill as a marksman. □ **adresse au tir**
leave/make one's mark to make a permanent or strong impression: *The horrors of the war have left their mark on the children.* □ **s'imposer**
mark out 1 to mark the boundary of (*eg* a football pitch) by making lines *etc*: *The pitch was marked out with white lines.* □ **délimiter**
2 to select or choose for some particular purpose *etc* in the future: *He had been marked out for an army career from early childhood.* □ **désigner**
mark time to move the feet up and down as if marching, but without going forward: *He's only marking time in this job till he gets a better one.* □ **marquer le pas**

market ['maːkit] *noun* 1 a public place where people meet to buy and sell or the public event at which this happens: *He has a clothes stall in the market.* □ **marché**
2 (a place where there is) a demand for certain things: *There is a market for cotton goods in hot countries.* □ **marché**
■ *verb* to (attempt to) sell: *I produce the goods and my sister markets them all over the world.* □ **vendre**
'**marketable** *adjective* wanted by the public and therefore able to be sold: *a marketable product.* □ **vendable**
'**marketing** *noun* (the study of) the processes by which anything may be sold: *She is in charge of marketing*; (*also adjective*) *marketing methods.* □ **marketing**
,**market-'garden** *noun* a garden where fruit and vegetables are grown for sale. □ **jardin maraîcher**
'**marketplace, ,market'square** *noun* the open space or square in a town in which a market is held. □ **(place du) marché**
market price/value the price at which a thing is being sold at a particular time: *What's the current market price of gold?* □ **prix du marché; valeur marchande**
market research investigation of the habits and preferences of the public in choosing what goods to buy: *She does market research for a cosmetics firm.* □ **étude de marché**

be on the market to be for sale: *Her house has been on the market for months.* □ **être en vente**

marmalade ['maːməleid] *noun* a type of jam made from oranges, lemons or grapefruit. □ **confiture (d'agrumes)**

maroon[1] [mə'ruːn] *noun* a dark brownish-red colour: *a deep shade of maroon*; (*also adjective*) *a large maroon car.* □ **bordeaux**

maroon[2] [mə'ruːn] *verb* 1 to put (someone) on shore on a lonely island from which he cannot escape. □ **abandonner (dans une île déserte)**

2 to leave (someone) in a helpless, lonely or uncomfortable position: *I was marooned on a lonely country road.* □ **abandonner**

marquee [maː'kiː] *noun* a very large tent used for circuses, parties *etc*: *They hired a marquee for their party.* □ **grande tente**

marriage ['maridʒ] *noun* 1 the ceremony by which a man and woman become husband and wife: *Their marriage took place last week*; (*also adjective*) *the marriage ceremony.* □ **mariage**

2 the state of being married; married life: *Their marriage lasted for thirty happy years.* □ **mariage**

3 a close joining together: *the marriage of his skill and her judgment.* □ **alliance**

'**marriageable** *adjective* suitable, or at a proper age, for marriage: *He has four marriageable sons*; *marriageable age.* □ **mariable**

marriage licence a paper giving official permission for a marriage to take place. □ **certificat de publication des bans**

marrow *noun* 1 the soft substance in the hollow parts of bones: *Beef marrow is needed for this dish.* □ **moelle**

2 (*American* **squash**) a large, green, thick-skinned vegetable, or its flesh as food. □ **courge(tte)**

marry ['mari] *verb* 1 to take (a person) as one's husband or wife: *John married my sister*; *They married in church.* □ **épouser, se marier**

2 (of a clergyman *etc*) to perform the ceremony of marriage between (two people): *The priest married them.* □ **marier**

3 to give (a son or daughter) as a husband or wife: *He married his son to a rich woman.* □ **marier**

'**married** *adjective*: *She has two married daughters.* □ **marié**

marsh [maːʃ] *noun* (an area of) soft wet land: *The heavy rainfall turned the land into a marsh.* □ **marécage, marais**

'**marshy** *adjective*. □ **marécageux**

'**marshiness** *noun*. □ **état marécageux**

marshal ['maːʃəl] *noun* 1 an official who arranges ceremonies, processions *etc*. □ **maître des cérémonies**

2 an official with certain duties in the lawcourts. □ **marshal**

3 the head of a police or fire department. □ **capitaine de gendarmerie/des pompiers**

■ *verb* – *past tense, past participle* '**marshalled**, '**marshaled** – 1 to arrange (forces, facts, arguments *etc*) in order: *Give me a minute to marshal my thoughts.* □ **rassembler**

2 to lead or show the way to: *We marshalled the whole*

group into a large room. □ **canaliser, faire entrer**

marshmallow [maːʃ'məlou] *noun* a puffy gelatine sweet made with sugar and corn starch and usually white in colour: *Most campers like to roast marshmallows on a stick held over the fire.* □ **guimauve**

marsupial [maː'sjuːpiəl] *noun, adjective* (an animal) having a pouch in which to carry its young: *The kangaroo is a marsupial.* □ **marsupial**

martial ['maːʃəl] *adjective* 1 warlike or fond of fighting: *a martial nation.* □ **guerrier**

2 belonging to or suitable for war: *martial music.* □ **martial**

martial law the ruling of a country by the army in time of war or great national emergency, when ordinary law does not apply: *The country is now under martial law.* □ **loi martiale**

Martian [maːʃən] *adjective* of the planet Mars or its presumed inhabitants: *There are 686.9 days in the Martian year.* □ **Martien**

■ *noun* a supposed inhabitant of the planet Mars: *Many people believe that Martians are little green creatures who travel in flying saucers.* □ **Martien**

martyr ['maːtə] *noun* 1 a person who suffers death or hardship for what he or she believes: *St Joan is said to have been a martyr.* □ **martyr, yre**

2 a person who continually suffers from a disease, difficulty *etc*: *She is a martyr to rheumatism.* □ **personne qui souffre beaucoup de**

■ *verb* to put (someone) to death or cause (him) to suffer greatly for his beliefs: *Saint Joan was martyred by the English.* □ **martyriser**

'**martyrdom** *noun* the suffering or death of a martyr. □ **martyre**

marvel ['maːvəl] *noun* something or someone astonishing or wonderful: *the marvels of the circus*; *He's a marvel at producing delicious meals.* □ **merveille**

■ *verb* – *past tense, past participle* '**marvelled**, '**marveled** – (*often with* **at**) to feel astonishment or wonder (at): *They marvelled at the fantastic sight.* □ **s'émerveiller (de)**

'**marvellous**, '**marvelous** *adjective* 1 wonderful: *The Alps are a marvellous sight.* □ **merveilleux**

2 very good in some way; excellent: *a marvellous idea.* □ **formidable**

'**marvellously** *adverb*. □ **merveilleusement**

marzipan ['maːzi'pan] *noun, adjective* (of) a sweet paste made of crushed almonds and sugar, used in decorating cakes, making sweets *etc*. □ **(à la) pâte d'amandes**

mascot ['maskət] *noun* a person, animal or thing supposed to bring good luck. □ **mascotte**

masculine ['maskjulin] *adjective* 1 of the male sex: *masculine qualities.* □ **masculin**

2 in certain languages, of one of *usually* two or three genders of nouns *etc*: *Is the French word for 'door' masculine or feminine?* □ **masculin**

,**mascu'linity** *noun*. □ **masculinité**

mash [maʃ] *verb* to crush into small pieces or a soft mass: *Put in some butter when you mash the potatoes.* □ **broyer**

■ *noun* mashed potato: *sausage and mash.* □ **purée de**

pommes de terre

mask [mɑːsk] *noun* something, *eg* a covering resembling a face, used for hiding or protecting the whole or part of the face: *The thief wore a black mask*; *Her face was a mask*; *under the mask of friendship.* □ **masque**
■ *verb* to hide or disguise: *He managed to mask his feelings.* □ **masquer**

mason ['meisn] *noun* (*usually* '**stonemason**) a skilled worker or builder in stone. □ **maçon, maçonne**
'**masonry** *noun* stone(work): *He was killed by falling masonry.* □ **maçonnerie**

masquerade [maskə'reid] *noun* (a) pretence or disguise: *Her show of friendship was just (a) masquerade.* □ **mascarade**
■ *verb* (*with* **as**) to pretend to be, *usually* intending to deceive: *The criminal was masquerading as a respectable businessman.* □ **se faire passer pour**

mass[1] [mas] *noun* **1** a large lump or quantity, gathered together: *a mass of concrete/ people.* □ **amas**
2 a large quantity: *I've masses of work/things to do.* □ **masse**
3 the bulk, principal part or main body: *The mass of people are in favour of peace.* □ **la plus grande partie**
4 (a) measure of the quantity of matter in an object: *The mass of the rock is 500 kilograms.* □ **masse**
■ *verb* to bring or come together in large numbers or quantities: *The troops massed for an attack.* □ **(se) masser**
■ *adjective* of large quantities or numbers: *mass murder*; *a mass meeting.* □ **(de/en) masse**
,**mass-pro'duced** *adjective* (of goods) all exactly the same and produced in great numbers or quantity: *mass-produced plastic toys.* □ **fabriqué en série**
,**mass-pro'duce** *verb.* □ **fabriquer en série**
,**mass pro'duction** *noun.* □ **fabrication en série**
the mass media those channels of communication (TV, radio, newspapers *etc*) that reach large numbers of people. □ **media**

mass[2] [mas] *noun* **1** (a) celebration, *especially* in the Roman Catholic church, of Christ's last meal (**Last Supper**) with his disciples: *What time do you go to Mass?* □ **messe**
2 a setting to music of some of the words used in this service. □ **messe**

massacre ['masəkə] *noun* **1** the killing of a large number of *usually* people, *especially* with great cruelty. □ **massacre**
2 a very bad defeat: *That last game was a complete massacre.* □ **massacre**
■ *verb* to kill (large numbers) cruelly. □ **massacrer**

massage ['masɑːʒ] *verb* to treat (a person's body or part of it) by rubbing *etc* to ease and remove pain or stiffness: *She massaged my sore back.* □ **masser**
■ *noun* (a) treatment by massaging: *Her ankle was treated by massage.* □ **massage**
masseur [ma'səː] – *feminine* **masseuse** [ma'səːz] – *noun* a person who gives massage. □ **masseur, euse**

massive ['masiv] *adjective* huge or heavy: *a massive building*; *a massive burden of taxation.* □ **massif**
'**massively** *adverb.* □ **massivement**

'**massiveness** *noun.* □ **aspect massif**

mast [mɑːst] *noun* a long upright pole *especially* for carrying the sails of a ship, an aerial, flag *etc*: *The sailor climbed the mast.* □ **mât**
-**masted** having (a certain number of) masts: *single-masted*; *four-masted.* □ **à (...) mât(s)**

master ['mɑːstə] – *feminine* **mistress** ['mistris] – *noun* **1** a person or thing that commands or controls: *I'm master in this house!* □ **maître**
2 an owner (of dog *etc*): *The dog ran to its master.* □ **maître**
3 a male teacher: *the Maths master.* □ **professeur**
4 the commander of a merchant ship: *the ship's master.* □ **capitaine**
5 a person very skilled in an art, science *etc*: *She's a real master at painting.* □ **maître**
6 (*with capital*) a polite title for a boy, in writing or in speaking: *Master John Smith.* □ **monsieur**
■ *adjective* (of a person in a job) fully qualified, skilled and experienced: *a master builder/mariner/plumber.* □ **maître**
■ *verb* **1** to overcome (an opponent, handicap *etc*): *She has mastered her fear of heights.* □ **surmonter**
2 to become skilful in: *I don't think I'll ever master arithmetic.* □ **apprendre**
'**masterful** *adjective* showing the power, authority or determination of a master: *a masterful woman.* □ **dominateur**
'**masterfully** *adverb.* □ **de manière dominatrice**
'**masterfulness** *noun.* □ **caractère dominateur**
'**masterly** *adjective* showing the skill of a master: *His handling of the situation was masterly.* □ **magistral**
'**masterliness** *noun.* □ **caractère magistral**
'**mastery** *noun* (*usually with* **over** *or* **of**) control, great skill or knowledge: *We have gained mastery over the enemy.* □ **maîtrise (de)**
master key a key which opens a number of locks. □ **passe-partout**
'**mastermind** *noun* the person planning and controlling an undertaking or scheme: *He was the mastermind behind the scheme.* □ **cerveau**
■ *verb* to plan (such a scheme): *Who masterminded the robbery?* □ **organiser**
'**masterpiece** *noun* a piece of work or art worthy (to be called the greatest achievement) of a master: *She considers this picture her masterpiece.* □ **chef-d'œuvre**
master stroke a very clever thing to do: *This sudden, unexpected attack was a master stroke.* □ **coup de maître**
master switch a switch for controlling a number of other switches: *There is a master switch that controls all the electricity.* □ **commutateur principal**
master of ceremonies (*abbreviation* **MC**) a person who announces the various stages of an entertainment, formal social gathering, series of speakers at a dinner *etc*: *The master of ceremonies introduced the speaker.* □ **maître, maîtresse des cérémonies**

mastiff ['mastif] *noun* a type of powerful dog, formerly used in hunting. □ **mastiff**

mat [mat] *noun* a flat piece of material (rushes, rubber, carpet, cork *etc*) for wiping shoes on, covering a floor, or various other purposes: *Wipe your shoes on the doormat; a table mat.* □ **(petit) tapis**

'**matted** *adjective* in a thick untidy mess: *matted hair.* □ **emmêlé**

'**matting** *noun* a material used for making mats: *coconut matting.* □ **fibres végétales**

matador ['matədɔː] *noun* the man who kills the bull in a bullfight. □ **matador**

match[1] [matʃ] *noun* a short piece of wood or other material tipped with a substance that catches fire when rubbed against a rough or specially prepared surface: *She struck a match.* □ **allumette**

'**matchbox** *noun* a box for holding matches. □ **boîte à allumettes**

match[2] [matʃ] *noun* **1** a contest or game: *a football/rugby/chess match.* □ **match**

2 a thing that is similar to or the same as another in some way(s) *eg* in colour or pattern: *These trousers are not an exact match for my jacket.* □ **chose qui va bien avec**

3 a person who is able to equal another: *She has finally met her match at arguing.* □ **égal**

4 a marriage or an act of marrying: *I hoped to arrange a match for my daughter.* □ **mariage**

■ *verb* **1** to be equal or similar to something or someone in some way *eg* in colour or pattern: *That dress matches her red hair.* □ **aller bien avec**

2 to set (two things, people *etc*) to compete: *He matched his skill against the champion's.* □ **opposer**

matched *adjective* paired or joined together, *eg* in marriage, or as contestants in a competition *etc*: *a well matched couple; The competitors were evenly matched.* □ **assorti**

'**matchless** *adjective* having no equal: *a woman of matchless beauty.* □ **sans égal**

'**matchmaker** *noun* someone who tries to arrange marriages between people. □ **marieur, euse**

mate [meit] *verb* **1** to come, or bring (animals *etc*), together for breeding: *The bears have mated and produced a cub.* □ **(s')accoupler**

2 (*chess*) to checkmate (someone). □ **mettre échec et mat**

■ *noun* **1** an animal *etc* with which another is paired for breeding: *Some birds sing in order to attract a mate.* □ **mâle/femelle**

2 a husband or wife. □ **mari/femme**

3 a companion or friend: *We've been mates for years.* □ **camarade**

4 a fellow workman or assistant: *a carpenter's mate.* □ **aide**

5 a merchant ship's officer under the master or captain: *the first mate.* □ **second, onde**

6 in chess, checkmate. □ **mat**

material [mə'tiəriəl] *noun* **1** anything out of which something is, or may be, made: *Tables are usually made from solid material such as wood.* □ **matériau**

2 cloth: *I'd like three metres of blue woollen material.* □ **tissu**

■ *adjective* **1** consisting of solid(s), liquid(s), gas(es) or any combination of these: *the material world.* □ **matériel**

2 belonging to the world; not spiritual: *He wanted material things like money, possessions and power.* □ **matériel**

3 essential or important: *evidence that is material to his defence.* □ **essentiel**

ma'terially *adverb* to a great or important extent: *Circumstances have changed materially.* □ **sensiblement**

ma'terialize, ma'terialise *verb* **1** to take solid or bodily form: *The figure materialized as we watched with astonishment.* □ **se matérialiser**

2 (of something expected or hoped for) to happen: *I don't think her plans will materialize.* □ **se réaliser**

ma,teriali'zation, ma,teriali'sation *noun.* □ **matérialisation**

maternal [mə'təːnl] *adjective* **1** of or like a mother: *maternal feelings.* □ **maternel**

2 related on the mother's side of the family: *my maternal grandfather.* □ **maternel**

ma'ternally *adverb.* □ **maternellement**

maternity [mə'təːnəti] *noun* (*usually as adjective*) the state of being or becoming a mother: *a maternity hospital; maternity clothes.* □ **(de) maternité**

mathematics [maθə'matiks] *noun singular* (*abbreviation* **maths** [maθs], **math** [maθ]) the science or branch of knowledge dealing with measurements, numbers and quantities. □ **mathématiques**

,**mathe'matical** *adjective* **1** of or done by mathematics: *mathematical tables.* □ **mathématique**

2 very exact or accurate: *mathematical precision.* □ **mathématique**

,**mathe'matically** *adverb.* □ **mathématiquement**

,**mathema'tician** [-'tiʃən] *noun* **1** a person who is good at mathematics: *For a young boy, he's quite a mathematician!* □ **mathématicien, ienne**

2 someone who works in mathematics: *She is a mathematician with a local engineering firm.* □ **mathématicien, ienne**

matinée ['matinei] *noun* a performance at a theatre, circus, cinema *etc* held in the afternoon or morning. □ **matinée**

matriarch ['meitriaːk] *noun* a woman who is head and ruler of her family or of a tribe. □ **femme chef de famille/tribu**

,**matri'archal** *adjective* of, like, ruled by *etc* a matriarch or matriarchs: *a matriarchal society* (= a society dominated by women). □ **matriarcal**

matriculate [mə'trikjuleit] *verb* to (cause to) become a member of a university *etc* by being enrolled. □ **(s')inscrire**

ma,tricu'lation *noun.* □ **inscription**

matrimony ['matriməni] *noun* the state of being married: *holy matrimony.* □ **mariage**

,**matri'monial** [-'mou-] *adjective.* □ **matrimonial**

matron ['meitrən] *noun* **1** a senior nurse in charge of a hospital. □ **infirmier en chef, infirmière en chef**

2 a dignified married woman: *Her behaviour shocked all the middle class matrons in the neighbourhood.* □ **mère de famille**

'matronly *adjective* 1 dignified and calm. □ **(très) digne**
2 rather fat: *a matronly figure.* □ **corpulent**

matter ['matə] *noun* 1 solids, liquids and/or gases in any
form, from which everything physical is made: *The
entire universe is made up of different kinds of matter.*
□ **matière**

2 a subject or topic (of discussion *etc*): *a private matter; money matters.* □ **sujet**

3 pus: *The wound was infected and full of matter.* □ **pus**

■ *verb* to be important: *That car matters a great deal to
him; It doesn't matter.* □ **avoir de l'importance**

,matter-of-'fact *adjective* keeping to the actual facts;
not fanciful, emotional or imaginative: *a matter-of-fact
account/statement/ opinion/attitude.* □ **terre-à-terre**

be the matter (*often with* with) to be the/a trouble, difficulty or thing that is wrong: *Is anything the matter?*;
What's the matter with you? □ **ce qui ne va pas**

a matter of course something that one expects to happen, be done *etc*: *You don't have to ask her – she'll do it
as a matter of course.* □ **tout naturellement**

a matter of opinion something about which different
people have different opinions or views: *Whether she's
clever or not is a matter of opinion.* □ **affaire d'opinion**

no matter it is not important: *'He's not here.' 'No matter, I'll see him later.'* □ **peu importe**

no matter who, what, where *etc* whoever, whatever,
wherever *etc*: *No matter what happens, I'll go.* □ **qui/
quoi/où que ce soit**

mattress ['matris] *noun* a thick, firm layer of padding,
covered in cloth *etc*, for lying on, *usually* as part of a
bed. □ **matelas**

mature [mə'tjuə] *adjective* 1 (having the qualities of
someone who, or something that, is) fully grown or
developed: *a very mature person.* □ **mûr**

2 (of cheese, wine *etc*) ready for eating or drinking: *a
mature cheese.* □ **fait; bon à boire**

■ *verb* 1 to make or become mature: *She matured early.*
□ **(faire) mûrir**

2 (of an insurance policy) to become due to be paid: *My
insurance policy matures when I reach sixty-five.* □
arriver à échéance

ma'turely *adverb.* □ **mûrement**

ma'turity *noun.* □ **maturité**

ma'tureness *noun.* □ **maturité**

maul [mɔːl] *verb* (*especially* of an animal) to injure (a
person or animal) *usually* badly: *He was badly mauled
by an angry lion.* □ **lacérer**

mausoleum [mɔːsə'liəm] *noun* a very fine tomb, often
with a monument: *They buried the duchess in the mausoleum.* □ **mausolée**

mauve [mouv] *noun, adjective* (of) a pale purple colour.
□ **mauve**

maxim ['maksim] *noun* a saying, general truth or rule
giving a guide to good behaviour: *'He who hesitates is
lost' is a well-known maxim.* □ **maxime**

maximum ['maksiməm] *adjective* greatest: *This requires
maximum effort/the maximum amount of effort.* □ **maximum**

■ *noun – plurals* 'maximums, 'maxima [-mə] – the
greatest number or quantity or the highest point or de-

gree: *Two hundred an hour is the maximum we can produce.* □ **maximum**

may [mei] 1 to have the permission to: *You may go home
now.* □ **pouvoir**

2 used to express a possibility in the present or future:
She may be here, I don't know. □ **se pouvoir que**

3 used to express a wish: *May you live a long and happy
life.* □ **fasse le ciel que**

may as well might as well. □ **autant dire**

may have used to express a possibility in the past: *He
may have been here, but we cannot be sure.* □ **il se peut
que**

May [mei] *noun* the fifth month of the year, the month
following April. □ **mai**

May Day the first day of May, an *especially* socialist
holiday or festival in many countries. □ **le Premier Mai**

'maypole *noun* a decorated pole for dancing around on
May Day. □ **mai**

maybe ['meibiː] *adverb* it is possible (that); perhaps:
Maybe I'll come, and maybe I won't. □ **peut-être**

mayday ['meidei] *noun* the international distress signal
sent out by ships and aircraft: *The ship sent out a mayday
(signal) before it sank.* □ **S.O.S.**

mayonnaise [meiə'neiz] *noun* a thick sauce made of egg
yolk, oil, vinegar or lemon and seasoning, and often
used on salads. □ **mayonnaise**

mayor [meə] *noun* (*especially* in England, Ireland and
the United States) the chief public official of a city, town.
□ **mairesse**

'mayoress *noun* 1 a mayor's wife: *The mayor and
mayoress attended the dinner.* □ **femme du maire**

2 a female mayor: *She has just been elected mayoress.*
□ **mairesse**

lord mayor in Britain the mayor of some capital and
other cities: *The Lord Mayor of London.* □ **lord-maire**

maze [meiz] *noun* a deliberately confusing series of paths,
often surrounded by walls or hedges, from which it's
difficult to find the way out: *I'm lost in a maze of rules
and regulations.* □ **labyrinthe**

me [miː] *pronoun* (used as the object of a verb or preposition and sometimes instead of **I**) the word used by a
speaker or writer when referring to himself: *He hit me;
Give that to me; It's me; She can go with John and me.*
□ **m', me, moi**

meadow ['medou] *noun* (*often in plural*) a field of grass,
usually on low ground: *There were cows in the meadow.*
□ **pré**

meagre ['miːgə] *adjective* poor or not enough: *meagre
strength.* □ **maigre**

'meagrely *adverb.* □ **maigrement**

'meagreness *noun.* □ **maigreur**

meal[1] [miːl] *noun* the food taken at one time: *She eats
three meals a day.* □ **repas**

meal[2] [miːl] *noun* the edible parts of grain ground to a
coarse powder: *a sack of meal; oatmeal.* □ **farine**

'mealy *adjective* like, or containing, meal. □ **farineux**

mean[1] [miːn] *adjective* 1 not generous (with money *etc*):
He's very mean (with his money/over pay). □ **avare**

2 likely or intending to cause harm or annoyance: *It is
mean to tell lies.* □ **méchant**

3 bad-tempered, vicious or cruel: *a mean mood.* □ **méchant**

4 (of a house *etc*) of poor quality; humble: *a mean dwelling.* □ **misérable**

'**meanly** *adverb*. □ **chichement**

'**meanness** *noun*. □ **avarice**

mean² [miːn] *adjective* 1 (of a statistic) having the middle position between two points, quantities *etc*: *the mean value on a graph.* □ **moyen**

2 average: *the mean annual rainfall.* □ **moyen**

■ *noun* something that is midway between two opposite ends or extremes: *Three is the mean of the series one to five.* □ **milieu**

mean³ [miːn] – *past tense, past participle* **meant** [ment] – *verb* 1 to (intend to) express, show or indicate: *'Vacation' means 'holiday'; What do you mean by (saying/doing) that?* □ **vouloir dire**

2 to intend: *I meant to go to the exhibition but forgot; For whom was that letter meant?; He means (= is determined) to be a rich man some day.* □ **avoir l'intention**

'**meaning** *noun* the sense in which a statement, action, word *etc* is (intended to be) understood: *What is the meaning of this phrase?; What is the meaning of her behaviour?* □ **sens**

■ *adjective* (of a look, glance *etc*) showing a certain feeling or giving a certain message: *The teacher gave the boy a meaning look when he arrived late.* □ **éloquent**

'**meaningful** *adjective* (often used loosely) important in some way: *a meaningful statement/relationship.* □ **significatif**

'**meaningless** *adjective* without meaning or reason; of no importance: *meaningless chatter.* □ **dénué de sens**

be meant to to be required or supposed; to have to: *The child is meant to be asleep!* □ **être censé**

mean well to have good intentions: *She meant well by what she said.* □ **avoir de bonnes intentions**

meander [mi'andə] *verb* 1 (of a river) to flow slowly along with many bends and curves: *The stream meandered through the meadows.* □ **serpenter**

2 (of people *etc*) to wander about in various directions: *His writing meanders all over the page.* □ **vagabonder**

means¹ [miːnz] *noun singular or plural* the instrument(s), method(s) *etc* by which a thing is, or may be, done or made to happen: *By what means can we find out?* □ **moyen(s)**

by all means yes, of course: *If you want to use the telephone, by all means do.* □ **certainement**

by means of using: *We escaped by means of a secret tunnel.* □ **au moyen de**

by no means 1 definitely not: *'Can I go home now?' 'By no means!'* □ **certainement pas**

2 (*also* **not by any means**) not at all: *I'm by no means certain to win.* □ **nullement**

means² [miːnz] *noun plural* money available or necessary for living *etc*: *She's a person of considerable means* (= She has plenty of money). □ **moyens, ressources**

a man of means a wealthy or rich man. □ **homme très aisé**

meantime ['miːntaim] *adverb, noun* (in the) time or period between: *I'll hear her account of the matter later*

– *meantime, I'd like to hear yours.* □ **en attendant**

meanwhile ['miːnwail] *adverb* during this time; at the same time: *The child had gone home; meanwhile, his mother was searching for him in the street.* □ **entre temps**

measles ['miːzlz] *noun singular* an infectious disease accompanied by red spots on the skin: *People usually get measles in childhood.* □ **rougeole**

measure ['meʒə] *noun* 1 an instrument for finding the size, amount *etc* of something: *a glass measure for liquids; a tape-measure.* □ **instrument de mesure**

2 a unit: *The metre is a measure of length.* □ **mesure**

3 a system of measuring: *dry/liquid/square measure.* □ **mesure**

4 a plan of action or something done: *We must take (= use, or put into action) certain measures to stop the increase in crime.* □ **mesure**

5 a certain amount: *a measure of sympathy.* □ **un(e) certain(e)**

■ *verb* 1 to find the size, amount *etc* of (something): *She measured the table.* □ **mesurer**

2 to show the size, amount *etc* of: *A thermometer measures temperature.* □ **indiquer**

3 (*with* **against, besides** *etc*) to judge in comparison with: *I measured my skill in cooking against my friend's.* □ **comparer (avec)**

4 to be a certain size: *This table measures two metres by one metre.* □ **mesurer**

'**measurement** *noun* 1 size, amount *etc* found by measuring: *What are the measurements of this room?* □ **mesure(s)**

2 the sizes of various parts of the body, *usually* the distance around the chest, waist and hips: *What are your measurements, sir?* □ **mensurations**

3 the act of measuring: *We can find the size of something by means of measurement.* □ **mesurage**

beyond measure very great: *I'm offering you riches beyond measure!* □ **sans bornes**

for good measure as something extra or above the minimum necessary: *The shopkeeper weighed out the sweets and put in a few more for good measure.* □ **pour faire bonne mesure**

full measure (no less than) the correct amount: *We must ensure that customers get full measure.* □ **bonne mesure**

made to measure (of clothing) made to fit the measurements of a particular person: *Was your jacket made to measure?; (also adjective) a made-to-measure suit.* □ **fait sur mesure**

measure out to mark (off), weigh (out) a certain distance, amount: *He measured out a kilogram of sugar.* □ **mesurer**

measure up (*often with* **to**) to reach a certain required standard: *John's performance doesn't measure up (to the others).* □ **être à la hauteur**

meat [miːt] *noun* the flesh of animals or birds used as food: *She does not eat meat; (also adjective) What did you have for the meat course?* □ **(de) viande**

'**meaty** *adjective* 1 full of (animal) meat: *a meaty soup/stew.* □ **plein de viande**

2 (tasting, smelling *etc*) like meat: *This smells meaty.* □

de viande

mechanic [mi'kanik] *noun* a skilled worker who repairs or maintains machinery. □ **mécanicien, ienne**

me'chanical *adjective* **1** having to do with machines: *mechanical engineering.* □ **mécanique**

2 worked or done by machinery: *a mechanical sweeper.* □ **mécanique**

3 done *etc* without thinking, from force of habit: *a mechanical action.* □ **machinal**

me'chanically *adverb.* □ **mécaniquement**

me'chanics *noun singular* **1** the science of the action of forces on objects: *He is studying mechanics.* □ **mécanique**

2 the art of building machines: *She applied her knowledge of mechanics to designing a new wheelchair.* □ **mécanique**

■ *noun plural* the ways in which something works or is applied: *the mechanics of the legal system.* □ **mécanisme**

'mechanism ['me-] *noun* a (*usually* small) piece of machinery: *a watch mechanism.* □ **mécanisme**

'mechanize, 'mechanise ['me-] *verb* **1** to introduce machinery into (an industry *etc*): *We've mechanized the entire process.* □ **mécaniser**

2 to supply (troops) with motor vehicles. □ **motoriser**

,mechani'zation, ,mechani'sation *noun.* □ **mécanisation**

medal ['medl] *noun* a piece of metal with a design, inscription *etc* stamped on it, given as a reward for bravery, long service, excellence *etc*, or made to celebrate a special occasion: *She won a medal in the War.* □ **médaille**

'medallist, 'medalist *noun* a person who has won a medal in a competition *etc*. □ **médaillé, ée**

meddle ['medl] *verb* to interfere: *She was always trying to meddle.* □ **s'ingérer**

'meddler *noun.* □ **personne qui se mêle de tout**

'meddlesome *adjective* fond of meddling: *a meddlesome young man.* □ **indiscret**

mediate ['miːdieit] *verb* to try to settle a dispute between people who are disagreeing: *The United States is trying to mediate (in the dispute) between these two countries.* □ **agir en médiateur, trice**

,medi'ation *noun.* □ **médiation**

'mediator *noun.* □ **médiateur, trice**

medical ['medikəl] *adjective* of healing, medicine or doctors: *medical care; medical insurance.* □ **médical**

■ *noun* a medical examination. □ **examen médical**

'medically *adverb.* □ **médicalement**

medicated ['medikeitid] *adjective* having a healing or health-giving substance mixed in: *Medicated shampoo.* □ **médicamenteux**

medicine ['medsin] *noun* **1** a substance, *especially* a liquid for swallowing, that is used to treat or keep away disease or illness: *a dose of medicine.* □ **médicament**

2 the science of curing people who are ill, or making their suffering less (*especially* by means other than surgery): *She is studying medicine.* □ **médecine**

medicinal [mə'disinl] *adjective* **1** having the power to heal and used as a medicine: *medicinal substances.* □ **médicinal**

2 of healing: *for medicinal purposes.* □ **médicinal**

me'dicinally *adverb.* □ **médicalement**

medieval, mediaeval [medi'iːvəl] *adjective* of, or belonging to, the Middle Ages: *medieval plays/music.* □ **médiéval**

mediocre [miːdi'oukə] *adjective* not very good or great; ordinary: *a mediocre performance/effort.* □ **médiocre**

,medi'ocrity [-'o-] *noun.* □ **médiocrité**

meditate ['mediteit] *verb* **1** to think deeply: *She was meditating on her troubles.* □ **réfléchir**

2 to spend short, regular periods in deep (*especially* religious) thought: *He meditates twice a day.* □ **méditer**

,medi'tation *noun.* □ **méditation**

'meditative [-tətiv] *adjective* thoughtful: *a meditative mood.* □ **méditatif**

'meditatively *adverb.* □ **d'un air méditatif**

medium ['miːdiəm] – *plurals* **media** [-diə], **mediums** – *noun* **1** something by or through which an effect is produced: *Air is the medium through which sound is carried.* □ **moyen**

2 (*especially in plural*) a means (*especially* radio, television and newspapers) by which news *etc* is made known: *the news media.* □ **média**

3 a person through whom spirits of dead people are said to speak: *I know a medium who says she can communicate with Napoleon.* □ **médium**

4 a substance in which specimens are preserved, bacteria grown *etc*. □ **milieu**

■ *adjective* middle or average in size, quality *etc*: *Would you like the small, medium or large packet?* □ **moyen**

medley ['medli] *noun* a piece of music put together from a number of other pieces: *She sang a medley of old songs.* □ **pot-pourri**

meek [miːk] *adjective* humble and not likely to complain, argue, react strongly *etc*: *a meek little man.* □ **doux**

'meekly *adverb.* □ **doucement**

'meekness *noun.* □ **douceur**

meet [miːt] – *past tense, past participle* **met** [met] – *verb* **1** to come face to face with (*eg* a person whom one knows), by chance: *She met a man on the train.* □ **(se) rencontrer**

2 (*sometimes, especially American, with* **with**) to come together with (a person *etc*), by arrangement: *The committee meets every Monday.* □ **se rejoindre, se réunir**

3 to be introduced to (someone) for the first time: *Come and meet my wife.* □ **faire la connaissance de**

4 to join: *Where do the two roads meet?* □ **se rencontrer**

5 to be equal to or satisfy (*eg* a person's needs, requirements *etc*): *Will there be sufficient stocks to meet the public demand?* □ **satisfaire à**

6 to come into the view, experience or presence of: *A terrible sight met him/his eyes when he opened the door.* □ **frapper**

7 to come to or be faced with: *He met his death in a car accident.* □ **faire face à**

8 (*with* **with**) to experience or suffer; to receive a particular response: *She met with an accident; The scheme met with their approval.* □ **avoir, recevoir**

9 to answer or oppose: *We will meet force with greater force.* □ **répondre à**

■ *noun* a gathering, *especially* of sportsmen: *The local huntsmen are holding a meet this week.* □ **réunion**

'**meeting** *noun* 1 an act of meeting: *The meeting between my mother and him was not friendly.* □ **rencontre**

2 a gathering of people for discussion or another purpose: *to attend a committee meeting.* □ **réunion**

meet (someone) halfway to respond to (someone) by making an equal effort or a compromise: *I'll invest $5,000 in this idea if you meet me halfway and do the same.* □ **faire la moitié du chemin**

mega- [megə] 1 a million, as in **megaton.** □ **méga-**

2 (*also* **megalo-** [megəlou]) large or great, as in **megalomania.** □ **mégalo-**

megalomania [megələ'meiniə] *noun* the idea, *usually* false, that one is great or powerful, combined with a passion for more greatness or power. □ **mégalomanie** ,**megalo'maniac** [-ak] *adjective, noun* (of) a person having megalomania: *That country is in the power of a dangerous megalomaniac.* □ **mégalomane**

megaphone ['megəfoun] *noun* a funnel-shaped device for speaking through, that causes sounds to be made louder and/or sent in a given direction: *She shouted instructions to the crowd through a megaphone.* □ **porte-voix**

megaton ['megətʌn] *adjective* (*usually with a number*) (of a bomb) giving an explosion as great as that of a million tons of TNT: *a five-megaton bomb.* □ **de** (...) **mégatonne**

melancholy ['melənkəli] *noun* depression or sadness: *He was overcome by a deep feeling of melancholy.* □ **mélancolie**

■ *adjective* sad; showing or causing sadness: *melancholy eyes.* □ **mélancolique**

mellow ['melou] *adjective* 1 (of character) made softer and more mature, relaxed *etc* by age and/or experience: *Her personality became more mellow as middle age approached.* □ **mûri**

2 (of sound, colour, light *etc*) soft, not strong or unpleasant: *The lamplight was soft and mellow.* □ **doux**

3 (of wine, cheese *etc*) kept until the flavour has developed fully: *a mellow burgundy.* □ **moelleux, velouté**

■ *verb* to make or become softer or more mature: *Old age has mellowed him.* □ **mûrir**

'**mellowness** *noun.* □ **douceur**

melodrama ['melədrɑːmə] *noun* 1 a (type of) play in which emotions and the goodness or wickedness of the characters are exaggerated greatly. □ **mélodrame**

2 (an example of) behaviour similar to a play of this sort: *He makes a melodrama out of everything that happens.* □ **mélo**

,**melodra'matic** [-drə'ma-] *adjective.* □ **mélodramatique**

,**melodra'matically** *adverb.* □ **d'un air/d'un ton mélodramatique**

melody ['melədi] – *plural* '**melodies** – *noun* 1 a tune: *She played Irish melodies on the harp.* □ **mélodie**

2 the principal part in a piece of harmonized music: *The sopranos sang the melody, and the other voices added the harmony.* □ **mélodie**

me'**lodic** [-'lo-] *adjective* of melody: *a melodic style.* □

me**lodique**

me'**lodious** ['lou-] *adjective* pleasing to the ear; tuneful: *melodious tunes.* □ **mélodieux**

me'**lodiously** *adverb.* □ **mélodieusement**

me'**lodiousness** *noun.* □ **caractère mélodieux**

melon ['melən] *noun* 1 a large, sweet fruit with many seeds. □ **melon**

2 its firm yellow or red flesh as food: *We started the meal with melon*; (*also adjective*) *a melon seed.* □ **(de) melon**

melt [melt] *verb* to (cause to) become soft or liquid, or to lose shape, *usually* by heating/being heated: *The ice has melted*; *My heart melted when I saw how sorry he was.* □ **(faire) fondre**

'**melting-point** *noun* the temperature at which a given solid melts: *The melting-point of ice is 0°C.* □ **point de fusion**

member ['membə] *noun* 1 a person who belongs to a group, club, society, trade union *etc*: *The association has three thousand members.* □ **membre**

2 short for **Member of Parliament.** □ **député, ée**

'**membership** *noun* 1 the state of being a member: *membership of the Communist Party.* □ **adhésion**

2 a group of members: *a society with a large membership.* □ **effectif**

3 the amount of money paid to a society *etc* in order to become a member: *The membership has increased to $5 this year.* □ **cotisation**

membrane ['membrein] *noun* a thin film or layer of tissue that covers or lines parts of the body, forms the outside of cells *etc*. □ **membrane**

memento [mə'mentou] – *plural* me'**mento(e)s** – *noun* something kept or given as a reminder or souvenir: *They gave her a small gift as a memento.* □ **souvenir**

memo ['memou] short for **memorandum.** □ **mémo**

memoirs ['memwaːz] *noun plural* a person's written account of his own life; an autobiography: *When I retire, I'm going to write my memoirs.* □ **mémoires**

memorable ['memərəbl] *adjective* worthy of being remembered: *a memorable event.* □ **mémorable**

memorandum [memə'randəm] – *plurals* ,**memo'randums,** ,**memo'randa** [-də] (*often abbreviated to* **memo** ['memou] – *plural* '**memos**) – *noun* 1 a note to help one to remember: *He wrote a memo*; (*also adjective*) *a memo pad.* □ **note**

2 a (brief) written statement about a particular matter, often passed around between colleagues: *a memorandum on Thursday's meeting.* □ **note de service**

memorial [mi'moːriəl] *noun* something (*eg* a monument) that honours or commemorates people or events of the past: *a memorial to Sir Winston Churchill*; *a war memorial.* □ **monument**

memory ['meməri] – *plural* '**memories** – *noun* 1 the power to remember things: *a good memory for details.* □ **mémoire**

2 the mind's store of remembered things: *Her memory is full of interesting stories.* □ **mémoire**

3 something remembered: *memories of her childhood.* □ **souvenir**

4 the time as far back as can be remembered: *the great-*

est fire in memory. □ **de mémoire d'homme**

'memorize, 'memorise *verb* to learn (something) so well that one can remember all of it without looking: *She memorized the directions.* □ **mémoriser**

from memory by remembering; without using a book *etc* for reference: *He said the whole poem from memory.* □ **de mémoire**

in memory of/to the memory of as a reminder or memorial of: *They built a monument in memory of their dead leader.* □ **à la mémoire de**

menace ['menəs] *noun* **1** something likely to cause injury, damage *etc: Traffic is a menace on narrow roads.* □ **menace**

2 a threat or show of hostility: *His voice was full of menace.* □ **menace**

■ *verb* to threaten: *menaced by danger.* □ **menacer**

'menacing *adjective* threatening to harm: *a menacing weapon.* □ **menaçant**

'menacingly *adverb.* □ **d'un air/ton menaçant**

menagerie [mi'nadʒəri] *noun* (a place for keeping) a collection of wild animals. □ **ménagerie**

mend [mend] *verb* **1** to put (something broken, torn *etc*) into good condition again; to repair: *Can you mend this broken chair?* □ **réparer**

2 to grow better, *especially* in health: *My broken leg is mending very well.* □ **aller mieux**

■ *noun* a repaired place: *This shirt has a mend in the sleeve.* □ **reprise**

'mending *noun* **1** the act of repairing: *the mending of the chair.* □ **réparation**

2 things needing to be mended, *especially* by sewing: *Put your torn shirt with my pile of mending!* □ **raccomodage**

meningitis [menin'dʒaitis] *noun* a serious disease in which there is inflammation of the membranes around the brain or spinal cord. □ **méningite**

menstruate ['menstrueit] *verb* to discharge blood monthly from the uterus: *Many girls begin to menstruate at the age of 12 or 13.* □ **avoir ses règles**

,menstru'ation *noun.* □ **menstruation**

mental ['mentl] *adjective* **1** of the mind: *mental illnesses/disorders.* □ **mental**

2 done or made by the mind: *mental arithmetic; a mental picture.* □ **mental**

3 for those who are ill in mind: *a mental hospital.* □ **psychiatrique**

4 suffering from an illness of the mind: *a mental patient.* □ **mental**

men'tality [-'ta-] *noun* (a level of) mental power: *low mentality.* □ **mentalité, intelligence**

'mentally *adverb* in the mind: *She's mentally incapable of understanding; He is mentally ill.* □ **mentalement**

menthol ['menθəl] *noun* a sharp-smelling substance got from peppermint oil used to help give relief from colds *etc: If you have a cold put some menthol in boiling water and breathe in the steam; Some cigarettes contain menthol.* □ **menthol**

'mentholated [-leitid] *adjective* containing menthol: *mentholated cigarettes.* □ **mentholé**

mention ['menʃən] *verb* **1** to speak of or refer to: *He*

mentioned the plan. □ **parler de**

2 to remark or say *usually* briefly or indirectly: *She mentioned (that) she might be leaving.* □ **mentionner**

■ *noun* (*often with* **of**) a (*usually* brief) remark (about): *No mention was made of this matter.* □ **mention**

not to mention used to emphasize something important or to excuse oneself for mentioning something relatively unimportant: *He is rich and clever, not to mention handsome.* □ **sans compter**

menu ['menjuː] *noun* (a card with) a list of dishes that may be ordered at a meal: *What's on the menu today?* □ **menu**

mercenary ['məːsinəri] *adjective* too strongly influenced by desire for money: *a mercenary attitude.* □ **intéressé**

■ *noun – plural* **'mercenaries** – a soldier from one country who hires his services to another country: *Mercenaries are fighting in Africa.* □ **mercenaire**

merchandise ['məːtʃəndaiz] *noun* goods to be bought and sold: *This store sells merchandise from all over the world.* □ **marchandises**

merchant ['məːtʃənt] *noun* a trader, *especially* wholesale, in goods of a particular kind: *timber/ tea/wine merchants.* □ **marchand, ande**

merchant marine, navy, service the ships of a country that are employed in trading, and their crews: *His son has joined the merchant navy.* □ **marine marchande**

merchant ship a ship involved in trade. □ **navire marchand**

mercury ['məːkjuri] *noun* an element, a poisonous, silvery, liquid metal used *especially* in thermometers *etc.* □ **mercure**

mercy ['məːsi] – *plural* **'mercies** – *noun* **1** kindness towards a person, *especially* an enemy, who is in one's power: *He showed his enemies no mercy.* □ **pitié**

2 a piece of good luck or something for which one should be grateful: *It was a mercy that it didn't rain.* □ **chance**

'merciful *adjective* willing to forgive or to punish only lightly: *a merciful judge.* □ **miséricordieux, clément**

'mercifully *adverb.* □ **miséricordieusement**

'merciless *adjective* without mercy; cruel: *merciless criticism.* □ **impitoyable**

'mercilessly *adverb.* □ **sans pitié**

at the mercy of wholly in the power of, liable to be harmed by: *A sailor is at the mercy of the sea.* □ **à la merci de**

have mercy on to give kindness to (an enemy *etc* who is in one's power): *Have mercy on me!* □ **avoir pitié de**

mere [miə] *adjective* no more than or no better than: *a mere child; the merest suggestion of criticism.* □ **simple**

'merely *adverb* simply or only: *I was merely asking a question.* □ **seulement**

merge [məːdʒ] *verb* **1** to (cause to) combine or join: *The sea and sky appear to merge at the horizon.* □ **(se) mêler**

2 (*with* **into**) to change gradually into something else: *Summer slowly merged into autumn.* □ **se fondre (dans)**

3 (*with* **into** *etc*) to disappear into (*eg* a crowd, background *etc*): *She merged into the crowd.* □ **se perdre (dans)**

'merger *noun* a joining together of business firms:

There's been a merger between two companies. □ **fusion**

meridian [mə'ridiən] *noun* an imaginary line on the earth's surface passing through the poles and any given place; any line of longitude. □ **méridien**

meringue [mə'raŋ] *noun* (a cake made from) a crisp cooked mixture of sugar and white of eggs. □ **meringue**

merit ['merit] *noun* **1** the quality of worth, excellence or praiseworthiness: *She reached her present position through merit.* □ **mérite**

2 a good point or quality: *His speech had at least the merit of being short.* □ **mérite**

■ *verb* to deserve as reward or punishment: *Your case merits careful consideration.* □ **mériter**

,meri'torious [-'tɔː-] *adjective* deserving reward or praise: *a meritorious performance.* □ **méritant, méritoire**

mermaid ['mɔːmeid] – *masculine* 'merman [-man] – *noun* an imaginary sea creature with a human body down to the waist and a fish's tail. □ **sirène**

merry ['meri] *adjective* cheerful; noisily or laughingly lively *etc*: *merry children; a merry party.* □ **joyeux**

'merrily *adverb.* □ **joyeusement**

'merriness *noun.* □ **caractère joyeux**

'merriment *noun* fun and laughter: *There was a great deal of merriment at the party.* □ **gaîté**

'merry-go-round *noun* (,carou'sel) a revolving ring of toy horses *etc* on which children ride at a fair. □ **manège**

'merrymaking *noun* cheerful celebration: *all the merrymaking at Christmas.* □ **réjouissances**

'merrymaker *noun.* □ **fêtard, arde**

mesdames *see* **madam**.

mesh [meʃ] *noun* **1** (one of) the openings between the threads of a net: *a net of (a) very fine (= small) mesh.* □ **maille**

2 (*often in plural*) a network: *A fly was struggling in the meshes of the spider's web.* □ **réseau**

■ *verb* (of teeth on *eg* gear wheels) to become engaged with each other: *The teeth on these two cogwheels mesh when they go round.* □ **s'engrener**

mesmerize, mesmerise ['mezməraiz] *verb* to hypnotize: *The child was mesmerized (= fascinated) by the television screen.* □ **hypnotiser**

'mesmerism *noun.* □ **mesmérisme**

mess [mes] *noun* a state of disorder or confusion; an untidy, dirty or unpleasant sight or muddle: *This room is in a terrible mess!; She looked a mess; The spilt food made a mess on the carpet.* □ **désordre, gâchis**

■ *verb* (*with* with) to meddle, or to have something to do with: *She's always messing with the television set.* □ **tripoter**

'messy *adjective* dirty: *a messy job.* □ **sale**

'messily *adverb.* □ **avec désordre**

'messiness *noun.* □ **désordre**

'mess-up *noun* a muddle or state of confusion: *There has been a mess-up in the timetable.* □ **gâchis**

make a mess of 1 to make dirty, untidy or confused: *The heavy rain has made a real mess of the garden.* □ **salir, gâcher**

2 to do badly: *He made a mess of his essay.* □ **gâcher**

3 to spoil or ruin (*eg* one's life): *I made a mess of my life by drinking too much.* □ **gâcher**

mess about/around 1 to behave in a foolish or annoying way: *The children were shouting and messing about.* □ **chahuter, embêter**

2 to work with no particular plan in a situation that involves mess: *I love messing about in the kitchen.* □ **bricoler**

3 (*with* with) to meddle or interfere with: *Who's been messing about with my papers?* □ **déranger**

4 to upset or put into a state of disorder or confusion: *The wind messed her hair about.* □ **chambarder**

mess up to spoil; to make a mess of: *Don't mess the room up!* □ **gâcher, mettre en désordre**

message ['mesidʒ] *noun* **1** a piece of information spoken or written, passed from one person to another: *I have a message for you from Mrs. Johnston.* □ **message**

2 the instruction or teaching of a moral story, religion, prophet *etc*: *What message is this story trying to give us?* □ **message**

'messenger [-sindʒə] *noun* a person who carries letters, information *etc* from place to place: *The king's messenger brought news of the army's defeat.* □ **messager, ère**

Messiah [mə'saiə] *noun* (*with* the) Jesus Christ. □ **Messie**

metal ['metl] *noun, adjective* **1** (of) any of a group of substances, *usually* shiny, that can conduct heat and electricity and can be hammered into shape, or drawn out in sheets, bars *etc*: *Gold, silver and iron are all metals.* □ **(de/en) métal**

2 (of) a combination of more than one of such substances: *Brass is a metal made from copper and zinc.* □ **métal**

me'tallic [-'ta-] *adjective* **1** made of metal: *a metallic element.* □ **métallique**

2 like a metal (*eg* in appearance or sound): *metallic blue; a metallic noise.* □ **métallique**

metamorphosis [metə'mɔːfəsis] – *plural* ,meta'morphoses [-siːz] – *noun* (a) marked change of form, appearance, character *etc*: *a caterpillar's metamorphosis into a butterfly.* □ **métamorphose**

metaphor ['metəfə] *noun* a form of expression (not using 'like' or 'as') in which a quality or characteristic is given to a person or thing by using a name, image, adjective *etc* normally used of something else which has similar qualities *etc*: *'He's a tiger when he's angry' is an example of (a) metaphor.* □ **métaphore**

,meta'phoric(al) [-'fo-] *adjective* of, like or using metaphors: *metaphorical language.* □ **métaphorique**

,meta'phorically *adverb.* □ **métaphoriquement**

meteor ['miːtiə] *noun* (*also* **shooting star**) a small mass or body travelling very quickly through space which appears very bright after entering the earth's atmosphere. □ **météore**

,mete'oric [-'o-] *adjective* (of success *etc*) rapid and often only lasting for a short time: *a meteoric rise to fame.* □ **fulgurant**

'meteorite [-rait] *noun* a small meteor that has fallen to earth. □ **météorite**

meteorology [miːtiə'rolədʒi] *noun* the study of weather and climate. □ **météorologie**

,meteo'rologist *noun*. □ météorologue

,meteoro'logical [-'lo-] *adjective*: *meteorological charts*. □ météorologique

meter ['miːtə] *noun* 1 an instrument for measuring, *especially* quantities of electricity, gas, water *etc*: *If you want to know how much electricity you have used you will have to look at the meter.* □ compteur
2 (*American*) see metre¹, metre².

■ *verb* to measure (*especially* electricity *etc*) by using a meter: *This instrument meters rainfall.* □ mesurer

method ['meθəd] *noun* 1 the way in which one does something: *I don't like his methods of training workers.* □ méthode
2 an orderly or fixed series of actions for doing something: *Follow the method set down in the instruction book.* □ méthode
3 good sense and a definite plan: *Her work seems to lack method.* □ méthode

me'thodical [-'θo-] *adjective* (*negative* unmethodical)
1 arranged or done in an orderly manner or according to a plan: *a methodical search.* □ méthodique
2 (in the habit of) acting in a planned, orderly way: *a methodical person/nature.* □ méthodique

me'thodically *adverb*. □ méthodiquement

meticulous [mi'tikjuləs] *adjective* very careful, almost too careful (about small details): *He paid meticulous attention to detail.* □ méticuleux

me'ticulously *adverb*. □ méticuleusement

metre¹ ['miːtə] *noun* (*often abbreviated* m *when written*) the chief unit of length in the metric system: *This table is one metre broad.* □ mètre

metric ['metrik] *adjective* of the metre or metric system: *Are these scales metric?* □ métrique

the metric system a system of weights and measures based on multiples of ten (*eg* 1 metre = 100 centimetres, 1 centimetre = 10 millimetres *etc*). □ système métrique

metre² ['miːtə] *noun* (in poetry) the regular arrangement of syllables that are stressed or unstressed, long or short: *The metre of this passage is typical of George Eliot.* □ mètre

'metrical ['me-] *adjective* of or in poetry: *The translation is not metrical – it is in prose.* □ métrique

metronome ['metrənoum] *noun* an instrument that can be set to make a ticking noise at different speeds to mark musical time. □ métronome

metropolis [mə'tropəlis] *noun* a large city, *especially* the chief city of a country: *London is England's metropolis.* □ métropole

metropolitan [metrə'politən] *adjective* of or in a capital city: *the metropolitan area/police.* □ métropolitain

mew [mjuː] *verb* to make the cry of a (young) cat: *The kittens mewed.* □ miauler

■ *noun* such a cry. □ miaulement

mezzo ['metsou], mezzo-soprano [metsousə'praːnou] – *plurals* 'mezzos, ,mezzo-so'pranos – *noun* (a person having) a singing voice between soprano and alto. □ mezzo-soprano

miaow [mi'au] *verb* to make the cry of a cat: *The cat miaowed all night.* □ miauler

■ *noun* such a cry. □ miaulement

mice *see* mouse.

micro- [maikrou] 1 very small: *micro computer*; *microprint*; *micro-organism.* □ micro-
2 one millionth part: *microvolt* (= one millionth of a volt). □ micro-

microbe ['maikroub] *noun* a very tiny living thing invisible to the naked eye, *especially* a germ causing disease. □ microbe

microcomputer [maikroukəm'pjuːtə] *noun* a very small computer containing tiny pieces of silicon *etc* ('microchips) designed to act as complex electronic circuits. □ micro-ordinateur

microfilm ['maikrəfilm] *noun* film on which documents, books *etc* are recorded very much smaller than actual size. □ microfilm

microphone ['maikrəfoun] *noun* (*abbreviation* mike [maik]) an electronic instrument for picking up sound waves to be broadcast, recorded or amplified as in radio, the telephone, a tape-recorder *etc*: *Speak into the microphone.* □ micro(phone)

microscope ['maikrəskoup] *noun* an instrument which makes very small objects able to be seen magnifying them greatly: *Germs are very small, and can only be seen with the aid of a microscope.* □ microscope

,micro'scopic [-'sko-] *adjective* seen only by the aid of a microscope: *microscopic bacteria.* □ microscopique

,micro'scopically *adverb*. □ microscopiquement

mid [mid] *adjective* at, or in, the middle of: *a midweek football match*; *in mid air*; *a mid-air collision between two aircraft.* □ mi-, au milieu de, en plein

'mid-'fielders in football *etc*, the players in the middle area of the pitch. □ demi

midday [mid'dei] *noun* the middle of the day; twelve o'clock: *We'll meet you at midday*; (*also adjective*) *a midday meal.* □ (de) midi

middle ['midl] *noun* 1 the central point or part: *the middle of a circle.* □ milieu
2 the central area of the body; the waist: *You're getting rather fat around your middle.* □ taille

■ *adjective* equally distant from both ends: *the middle seat in a row.* □ du milieu

'middling *adjective* average: *He's neither tall nor short, but of middling height.* □ moyen

middle age the years between youth and old age: *She is well into middle age.* □ âge mûr

,middle-'aged *adjective*. □ d'un certain âge

Middle Ages (*with* the) the time between the end of the Roman Empire and the Renaissance. □ moyen-âge

Middle East (*with* the) Egypt and the countries of Asia west of Pakistan. □ Moyen-Orient

'middleman [-man] *noun* a dealer who buys goods from the person who makes or grows them, and sells them to shopkeepers or to the public; a wholesaler: *You can save money by buying direct from the factory and cutting out the middleman.* □ intermédiaire

be in the middle of (doing) something to be busily occupied doing something: *Please excuse my appearance, I was in the middle of washing my hair.* □ être en train de

midget ['mɪdʒit] *noun* a person who is fully developed but has not grown to normal height. □ **nain, naine**

midnight ['mɪdnaɪt] *noun* twelve o'clock at night: *I'll go to bed at midnight*; (*also adjective*) *a midnight attack.* □ **(de) minuit**

midriff ['mɪdrɪf] *noun* the middle of the body just below the ribs. □ **diaphragme, estomac**

midst [mɪdst]: **in the midst of 1** among or in the centre of: *in the midst of a crowd of people.* □ **au milieu de**
2 at the same time as: *in the midst of all these troubles.* □ **pendant**
in our, your, their midst among, or in the same place as, us, you or them: *Large buildings keep rising in our midst.* □ **parmi**

midsummer [mid'sʌmə] *noun* the middle of summer: *It happened in midsummer*; (*also adjective*) *a midsummer day.* □ **cœur de l'été; estival**

midway [mid'wei] *adjective, adverb* in the middle of the distance or time between two points; halfway: *the midway point.* □ **à mi-chemin**

midwife ['mɪdwaɪf] – *plural* **'midwives** [-waɪvz] – *noun* a person (*usually* a trained nurse) who helps at the birth of children. □ **sage-femme**
mid'wifery [mid'wi-] *noun.* □ **obstétrique**

midwinter [mid'wintə] *noun* the middle of winter: *He arrived in midwinter*; (*also adjective*) *on a midwinter day.* □ **cœur de l'hiver; hivernal**

might¹ [mait] – *negative short form* **mightn't** ['maitnt] –
1 *past tense* of **may**: *I thought I might find you here*; *They might come if you offered them a meal.* □ **se pouvoir que**
2 used instead of 'may', *eg* to make a possibility seem less likely, or a request for permission more polite: *She might win if she tries hard*; *Might I speak to you for a few minutes, please?* □ **se pouvoir que; permettez que...**
3 used in suggesting that a person is not doing what he should: *You might help me clean the car!* □ **pouvoir au moins**
might as well used to suggest that there is no good reason for not doing something: *I might as well do it all at once.* □ **faire aussi bien de**
might have 1 used to suggest that something would have been possible if something else had been the case: *You might have caught the bus if you had run.* □ **il aurait été possible que... si**
2 used to suggest that a person has not done what he should: *You might have told me!* □ **aurais dû au moins**
3 used to show that something was a possible action *etc* but was in fact not carried out or done: *I might have gone, but I decided not to.* □ **il aurait été possible que... mais**
4 used when a person does not want to admit to having done something: *'Have you seen this man?' 'I might have.'* □ **c'est possible**
I *etc* **might have known** (often used in annoyance) I *etc* ought to have known, thought, guessed *etc* that something was or would be the case: *I might have known you would lose the key!* □ **j'aurais dû me douter**

might² [mait] *noun* power or strength: *The might of the*

opposing army was too great for us.* □ **force, puissance**

'mighty *adjective* having great power: *a mighty nation.* □ **puissant**
'mightily *adverb.* □ **puissamment**
'mightiness *noun.* □ **puissance**

migraine ['miːɡreɪn] *noun* (an attack of) a type of very severe headache, often accompanied by vomiting and difficulty in seeing: *She suffers from migraine.* □ **migraine**

migrate [mai'ɡreit] *verb* **1** (of certain birds and animals) to travel from one region to another at certain times of the year: *Many birds migrate in the early winter.* □ **émigrer**
2 (of people) to change one's home to another country or (regularly) from place to place: *The Gothic peoples who overwhelmed the Roman Empire migrated from the East.* □ **émigrer**
mi'gration *noun.* □ **migration**
'migrant ['mai-] *noun* a person, bird or animal that migrates or has migrated: *The swallow is a summer migrant to Britain*; (*also adjective*) *migrant workers.* □ **migrant, ante; migrateur**
'migratory ['maiɡrə-] *adjective.* □ **migrateur, migratoire**

mike *see* **microphone**.

mild [maild] *adjective* **1** (of a person or his personality) gentle in temper or behaviour: *such a mild man.* □ **doux**
2 (of punishment *etc*) not severe: *a mild sentence.* □ **léger**
3 (of weather *especially* if not in summer) not cold; rather warm: *a mild spring day.* □ **doux**
4 (of spices, spiced foods *etc*) not hot: *a mild curry.* □ **peu épicé**
'mildly *adverb.* □ **doucement**
'mildness *noun.* □ **douceur**

mile [mail] *noun* (*sometimes abbreviated to* **m** *when written*) a measure of length equal to 1,760 yards (1.61 km): *We walked ten miles today*; *70 miles per hour* (sometimes written **mph**); *a ten-mile hike.* □ **mille**
'milestone *noun* **1** a stone set up to show distances in miles to various places. □ **borne routière**
2 a very important event: *The discovery of penicillin was a milestone in medical history.* □ **jalon**

militant ['militənt] *adjective* wishing to take, or taking, strong or violent action: *militant workers.* □ **militant**
'militantly *adverb.* □ **avec combativité**
'militancy *noun.* □ **militantisme**

military ['militəri] *adjective* of soldiers or armed forces generally, or war: *military supplies/discipline/power.* □ **militaire**

milk [milk] *noun* a white liquid produced by female mammals as food for their young: *The commonest source of milk is the cow.* □ **lait**
■ *verb* to obtain milk from: *The farmer milks his cows each day.* □ **traire**
'milky *adjective* **1** containing milk: *milky coffee.* □ **lacté, au lait**
2 like milk in appearance: *A milky substance.* □ **laiteux**
'milkiness *noun.* □ **aspect laiteux**
'milkmaid *noun* formerly, a woman employed to milk

cows by hand. □ **trayeuse**

'**milkman** *noun* a person who delivers milk. □ **laitier**

'**milkshake** *noun* a drink made by shaking up milk and a particular flavouring: *I'd like a chocolate/strawberry milkshake.* □ **lait fouetté**

milk tooth one of the first set of a baby's teeth: *The child's milk teeth started to come out when he was six years old.* □ **dent de lait**

the Milky Way (*also* **the Galaxy**) a huge collection of stars stretching across the sky. □ **Voie lactée**

mill [mil] *noun* **1** a machine, sometimes now electrical, for grinding coffee, pepper *etc* by crushing it between rough, hard surfaces: *a coffee mill*; *a pepper mill.* □ **moulin**

2 a building where grain is ground: *The farmer took her corn to the mill.* □ **minoterie**

3 a building where certain types of things are manufactured: *A woollen mill*; *a steel mill.* □ **fabrique**

■ *verb* **1** to grind or press: *This flour was milled locally.* □ **moudre**

2 (*usually with* **about** *or* **around**) (of crowds) to move about in a disorganized way: *There's a huge crowd of people milling around outside.* □ **grouiller autour**

'**miller** *noun* a person who works a grain mill. □ **meunier, ère**

'**millstone** *noun* **1** one of the two large, heavy stones used in an old-fashioned mill for grinding grain. □ **meule**

2 (*usually with* **around one's/the neck**) something that is a heavy burden or responsibility, and prevents easy progress: *She regarded her brother as a millstone around her neck.* □ **boulet**

millennium [mi'leniəm] – *plural* **mil'lennia** [-niə] – *noun* a period of a thousand years: *Almost two millennia have passed since the birth of Christ.* □ **millénaire**

millet ['milit] *noun* a type of grain used as food: *The farmer grows millet.* □ **millet**

million ['miljən] – *plurals* '**million** (**1**, **2**), '**millions** (**2**, **3**) – noun **1** (preceded by **a**, a number, or a word signifying a quantity) the number 1 000 000: *a million*; *one million*; *five million.* □ **million**

2 the figure 1 000 000. □ **un million**

3 a million dollars: *Her fortune amounts to several million(s).* □ **million**

■ *adjective* (preceded by **a**, a number, or a word signifying a quantity) 1 000 000 in number: *six million people.* □ **million**

'**million-** having a million (of something): *a million-dollar banknote.* □ **d'un million de**

,**millio'naire** [-'neə] – *feminine* **millio'nairess** – *noun* a person having a million dollars *etc* or more. □ **millionnaire, milliardaire**

'**millionth** *noun* **1** one of a million equal parts. □ **millionième**

2 the last of a million (people, things *etc*) or (the person, thing *etc*) in an equivalent position: *the millionth* (*car*). □ **millionième**

millipede ['milipiːd] *noun* a small many-legged creature with a long round body. □ **mille-pattes**

mime [maim] *noun* **1** the art of using movement to perform the function of speech, *especially* in drama: *She is*

studying mime. □ **mime**

2 a play in which no words are spoken and the actions tell the story: *The children performed a mime.* □ **mimodrame**

3 an actor in such a play; someone who practises this art: *Marcel Marceau is a famous mime.* □ **mime**

■ *verb* to act, *eg* in such a play, using movements rather than words: *I mimed my love for you by holding my hands over your heart.* □ **mimer**

mimic ['mimik] – *past tense, past participle* '**mimicked** – *verb* to imitate (someone or something), *especially* with the intention of making him or it appear ridiculous or funny: *The comedian mimicked the Prime Minister's way of speaking.* □ **imiter**

■ *noun* a person who mimics: *Children are often good mimics.* □ **imitateur, trice**

'**mimicry** *noun.* □ **imitation**

mimosa [mi'mouzə] *noun* a plant with small flowers and fern-like leaves which close when touched (also called **sensitive plant**). □ **mimosa**

minaret [minə'ret] *noun* a tower on a mosque from which the call to prayer is sounded. □ **minaret**

mince [mins] *verb* **1** to cut into small pieces or chop finely: *Would you like me to mince the meat for you?* □ **hacher**

2 to walk with short steps, in an unpleasantly dainty or delicate way: *She minced over to him.* □ **marcher à petits pas maniérés**

■ *noun* meat (*usually* beef) chopped up into small pieces: *mince and potatoes.* □ **viande hachée**

'**mincer** *noun* a machine for mincing meat *etc*: *Could you put the meat in the mincer?* □ **hachoir**

'**mincing** *adjective* too dainty or prim: *He walked with little mincing steps.* □ **affecté**

'**mincingly** *adverb.* □ **d'une manière affectée**

'**mincemeat** *noun* a mixture of raisins, other fruits *etc*, *usually* with suet (used in baking ,**mince-'pies**). □ **hachis de fruits secs**

mind [maind] the power by which one thinks *etc*; the intelligence or understanding: *The child already has the mind of an adult.* □ **esprit, intelligence**

■ *verb* **1** to look after or supervise (*eg* a child): *mind the baby.* □ **surveiller**

2 to be upset by; to object to: *You must try not to mind when he criticizes your work.* □ **être dérangé, se refuser (à)**

3 to be careful of: *Mind* (= be careful not to trip over) *the step!* □ **prendre garde (à)**

4 to pay attention to or obey: *You should mind your parents' words/advice.* □ **prêter attention (à)**

■ *interjection* be careful!: *Mind! There's a car coming!* □ **attention**

-minded having a (certain type of) mind, as in **narrow-minded, like-minded.** □ **qui est... d'esprit**

'**mindless** *adjective* stupid and senseless: *mindless violence.* □ **stupide**

'**mindlessly** *adverb.* □ **stupidement**

'**mindlessness** *noun.* □ **stupidité**

'**mindreader** *noun* a person who claims to know other people's thoughts. □ **liseur, euse de pensées**

be out of one's mind to be mad: *He must be out of his mind!* □ **avoir perdu la raison**

do you mind! used to show annoyance, stop someone doing something *etc*: *Do you mind! That's my foot you're standing on!* □ **dis/dites donc!**

have a good mind to to feel very much inclined to (do something): *I've a good mind to tell your father what a naughty girl you are!* □ **avoir bien envie de**

have (half) a mind to to feel (slightly) inclined to (do something): *I've half a mind to take my holidays in winter this year.* □ **avoir presque envie de**

in one's mind's eye in one's imagination: *If you try hard, you can see the room in your mind's eye.* □ **en imagination**

in one's right mind sane: *No one in his right mind would behave like that.* □ **sain d'esprit**

keep one's mind on to give all one's attention to: *Keep your mind on what you're doing!* □ **se concentrer sur**

know one's own mind (*usually in negative*) to know what one really thinks, wants to do *etc*: *She doesn't know her own mind yet about abortion.* □ **savoir ce que l'on veut**

make up one's mind to decide: *They've made up their minds to stay in Africa.* □ **se décider (à)**

mind one's own business to attend to one's own affairs, not interfering in other people's: *Go away and mind your own business!* □ **s'occuper de ses affaires**

never mind don't bother; it's all right: *Never mind, I'll do it myself.* □ **ça ne fait rien**

on one's mind making one anxious, worried *etc*: *She has a lot on her mind.* □ **sur la conscience**

put (someone) in mind of to remind (someone) of: *This place puts me in mind of a book I once read.* □ **rappeler**

speak one's mind to say frankly what one means or thinks: *You must allow me to speak my mind.* □ **dire sa pensée**

take/keep one's mind off to turn one's attention from; to prevent one from thinking about: *A good holiday will take your mind off your troubles.* □ **se changer les idées**

to my mind in my opinion: *To my mind, you're better off working here than in most other places.* □ **à mon avis**

mine[1] [main] *pronoun* something which belongs to me: *Are these pencils yours or mine?*; *Sheila is a friend of mine* (= one of my friends). □ **mien, mienne, les miens, les miennes**

---

mine: *This pencil isn't yours – it's mine* (not *my one*).

---

mine[2] [main] *noun* 1 a place (*usually* underground) from which metals, coal, salt *etc* are dug: *a coalmine*; *My father worked in the mines.* □ **mine**

2 a type of bomb used underwater or placed just beneath the surface of the ground: *The ship has been blown up by a mine.* □ **mine**

■ *verb* 1 to dig (for metals *etc*) in a mine: *Coal is mined near here.* □ **extraire**

2 to place explosive mines in: *They've mined the mouth of the river.* □ **miner**

3 to blow up with mines: *His ship was mined.* □ **miner**

'**miner** *noun* a person who works in a mine, in Britain usually a coalminer. □ **mineur, euse**

'**mining** *noun*. □ **exploitation minière**

'**minefield** *noun* an area of ground or water which is full of explosive mines. □ **champ de mines**

mineral ['minərəl] *noun* a substance (metals, gems, coal, salt *etc*) found naturally in the earth and mined: *What minerals are mined in that country?*; (*also adjective*) *mineral ores.* □ **minéral**

mineral water a type of water containing small quantities of health-giving minerals. □ **eau minérale**

mingle ['miŋgl] *verb* to mix: *They mingled with the crowd.* □ **mêler**

'**mingled** *adjective*. □ **mêlé**

mini ['mini] *noun* 1 short for **miniskirt**. □ **mini**

2 (*with capital*: ®) a type of small car. □ **Mini**

■ *adjective* (*or part of a word*) small: *a mini dictionary*; *a minibus.* □ **mini-**

miniature ['minitʃə] *adjective* smaller than normal, often very small: *a miniature radio.* □ **miniature**

■ *noun* 1 a very small painting of a person. □ **miniature**

2 a copy or model of something, made on a small scale. □ **modèle réduit**

minibus ['minibʌs] *noun* a small bus, *usually* with only a dozen seats or so: *The school choir hired a minibus.* □ **minibus**

minim ['minim] *noun* a musical note roughly equal to a slow walking step in length. □ **blanche**

minimum ['miniməm] *adjective* smallest or lowest (possible, obtained, recorded *etc*): *the minimum temperature last night.* □ **minimum**

■ *noun* – *plurals* '**minimums, 'minima** [-mə] – the smallest possible number, quantity *etc* or the lowest level: *Tickets will cost a minimum of $20.* □ **minimum**

'**minimal** *adjective* very small indeed: *minimal expense.* □ **minime**

'**minimize, 'minimise** *verb* 1 to make as little as possible: *to minimize the danger.* □ **réduire au minimum**

2 to cause to seem little or unimportant: *He minimized the help he had received.* □ **minimiser**

minion ['minjən] *noun* a slave-like follower or employee. □ **larbin**

miniskirt ['miniskəːt] *noun* (*abbreviation* **mini** ['mini]) a short skirt the hem of which is well above the knees. □ **mini-jupe**

minister ['ministə] *noun* 1 a clergyman in certain branches of the Christian Church: *He is a minister in the Presbyterian church.* □ **pasteur**

2 (the title of) the head of any of the divisions or departments of a government: *the Minister for Education.* □ **ministre**

■ *verb* (*with to*) to give help (to): *She ministered to his needs.* □ **donner des soins (à)**

ministerial [mini'stiəriəl] *adjective* of or concerning ministers: *ministerial duties.* □ **ministériel, sacerdotal**

'**ministry** – *plural* '**ministries** – *noun* 1 the profession, duties or period of service of a minister of religion: *His ministry lasted for fifteen years.* □ **ministère, sacerdoce**

2 a department of government or the building where its employees work: *the Transport Ministry.* □ **ministère**

mink [miŋk] *noun* 1 a small weasel-like kind of animal. □ **vison**

2 its fur: *a hat made of mink*; (*also adjective*) *a mink coat*. □ **(de) vison**

3 a mink coat: *She wore her new mink.* □ **vison**

minor ['mainə] *adjective* less, or little, in importance, size *etc*: *Always halt when driving from a minor road on to a major road*; *She has to go into hospital for a minor operation.* □ **secondaire, mineur, petit**

■ *noun* a person who is not yet legally an adult. □ **mineur, eure**

mi'nority [mi'no-, mai'no-] *noun* a small number; less than half: *Only a minority of people live in the countryside*; *a racial/political minority.* □ **minorité**

be in the minority to be in the smaller of two groups: *Women were in the minority* (= There were more men than women) *at the meeting.* □ **être en minorité**

minstrel ['minstrəl] *noun* a musician who went about the country in medieval times, reciting or singing poems. □ **ménestrel**

mint[1] [mint] *noun* a place where money is made by the government. □ **(hôtel de la) Monnaie**

■ *verb* to manufacture (money): *When were these coins minted?* □ **frapper**

in mint condition fresh; unused; in perfect condition. □ **à l'état neuf**

mint[2] [mint] *noun* 1 a plant with strong-smelling leaves, used as a flavouring. □ **menthe**

2 (*also* 'peppermint) (a sweet with) the flavour of these leaves: *a box of mints*; (*also adjective*) *mint chocolate.* □ **bonbon à la menthe; à la menthe**

minuet [minju'et] *noun* (a piece of music to accompany) an old type of graceful dance. □ **menuet**

minus ['mainəs] *preposition* used to show subtraction: *Ten minus two equals eight* (10 − 2 = 8). □ **moins**

■ *noun* (*also* **minus sign**) a sign (−) used to show subtraction or negative quality. □ **moins**

■ *adjective* negative or less than zero: *a minus number*; *Twelve from ten equals minus two* (10 − 12 = −2). □ **négatif**

minute[1] ['minit] *noun* 1 the sixtieth part of an hour; sixty seconds: *It is twenty minutes to eight*; *The journey takes thirty minutes*; *a ten-minute delay.* □ **minute**

2 in measuring an angle, the sixtieth part of a degree; sixty seconds: *an angle of 47° 50′* (= forty-seven degrees, fifty minutes). □ **minute**

3 a very short time: *Wait a minute*; *It will be done in a minute.* □ **minute**

4 a particular point in time: *At that minute, the telephone rang.* □ **instant**

5 (*in plural*) the notes taken at a meeting recording what was said: *The chairwoman asked for this decision to be recorded in the minutes.* □ **procès-verbal, compte rendu**

minute hand the larger of the two pointers on a clock or watch, which shows the time in minutes past the hour. □ **grande aiguille**

the minute (that) as soon as: *Telephone me the minute he arrives!* □ **dès que**

to the minute (of time) exactly; precisely: *The cooking time must be correct to the minute.* □ **montre en main**

up to the minute most modern or recent: *Her clothes are always right up to the minute*; *up to the minute clothes.* □ **(du) dernier cri**

minute[2] [mai'njuːt] *adjective* 1 very small: *The diamonds in the brooch were minute.* □ **minuscule**

2 paying attention to the smallest details: *minute care.* □ **minutieux**

mi'nutely *adverb*. □ **minutieusement**

mi'nuteness *noun*. □ **minutie**

miracle ['mirəkl] *noun* 1 something which man is not normally capable of making happen and which is therefore thought to be done by a god or God: *Christ's turning of water into wine was a miracle.* □ **miracle**

2 a fortunate happening that has no obvious natural cause or explanation: *It's a miracle he wasn't killed in the plane crash.* □ **miracle**

mi'raculous [-'rakju-] *adjective*: *a miraculous recovery.* □ **miraculeux**

mi'raculously *adverb*. □ **miraculeusement**

mirage ['miraːʒ] *noun* an illusion of an area of water in the desert or on a road *etc*. □ **mirage**

mirror ['mirə] *noun* a piece of glass or metal having a surface that reflects an image: *I spend a lot of time looking in the mirror.* □ **miroir**

■ *verb* to reflect as a mirror does: *The smooth surface of the lake mirrored the surrounding mountains.* □ **refléter**

mirth [məːθ] *noun* laughter or amusement. □ **gaîté**

misadventure [misəd'ventʃə] *noun* an unlucky happening or accident. □ **mésaventure**

misapprehension [misapri'henʃən] *noun* misunderstanding. □ **malentendu**

misbehave [misbi'heiv] *verb* to behave badly: *If you misbehave, I'll send you to bed.* □ **se conduire mal**

,misbe'haviour [-'heivjə] *noun*. □ **mauvaise conduite**

miscalculate [mis'kalkjuleit] *verb* to calculate or estimate wrongly: *I miscalculated the bill.* □ **mal calculer**

mis,calcu'lation *noun*. □ **erreur de calcul**

miscarriage ['miskaridʒ] 1 in pregnancy, the loss of the baby from the womb before it is able to survive. □ **fausse couche**

2 a failure: *a miscarriage of justice* (= a wrong judgment). □ **erreur, échec**

miscellaneous [misə'leiniəs] *adjective* composed of several kinds; mixed: *a miscellaneous collection of pictures.* □ **varié, divers**

miscellany [mi'seləni] – *plural* **miscellanies** – *noun* a collection or mixture of things. □ **collection**

mischance [mis'tʃaːns] *noun* (a piece of) bad luck. □ **malchance**

mischief ['mistʃif] *noun* 1 action or behaviour (*especially* of children) that causes small troubles or annoyance to others: *That boy is always up to some mischief.* □ **sottise**

2 evil, damage or harm. □ **tort, dommage**

make mischief to cause trouble *etc*. □ **créer des ennuis**

'mischievous [-vəs] *adjective*: *a mischievous child.* □ **espiègle**

'mischievously *adverb*. □ **malicieusement**

misconception [miskən'sepʃən] *noun* a wrong idea or impression. □ **idée/opinion fausse**

misconduct [mis'kondʌkt] *noun* bad behaviour. □ **inconduite**

misdeed [mis'diːd] *noun* a bad deed. □ **méfait**

misdirect [misdi'rekt, -dai-] *verb* to direct wrongly: *She was misdirected, and ended up in the wrong street.* □ **mal renseigner**

miser ['maizə] *noun* a mean person who lives very poorly in order to store up wealth: *That old miser won't give you a cent!* □ **avare**
'**miserly** *adjective*. □ **avare**
'**miserliness** *noun*. □ **avarice**

miserable ['mizərəbl] *adjective* **1** very unhappy; *We've been miserable since my sister went away.* □ **(très) malheureux**
2 very poor in quantity or quality: *The house was in a miserable condition.* □ **misérable**
'**miserably** *adverb*. □ **misérablement**

misery ['mizəri] – *plural* '**miseries** – *noun* (something that causes) unhappiness: *the misery of the fatherless children*; *Forget your miseries and come out with me!* □ **malheureux**

misfire [mis'faiə] *verb* **1** (of a gun, bomb *etc*) to fail to explode or catch fire. □ **faire long feu**
2 (of a motor engine) to fail to ignite properly. □ **avoir des ratés**
3 (of a plan *etc*) to go wrong. □ **rater**

misfit ['misfit] *noun* a person who is not able to live or work happily with others. □ **inadapté, ée**

misfortune [mis'foːtʃən] *noun* (a piece of) bad luck: *I had the misfortune to break my leg.* □ **malchance, infortune**

misgiving [mis'givin] *noun* (*especially in plural*) (a feeling of) fear or doubt. □ **appréhension**

mishap ['mishap] *noun* an unlucky accident. □ **mésaventure**

misinform [misin'foːm] *verb* to give wrong information to. □ **mal renseigner**

misjudge [mis'dʒʌdʒ] *verb* to have an unfairly low opinion of (a person). □ **sous-estimer**

mislay [mis'lei] – *past tense, past participle* **mis'laid** – *verb* to lose: *I seem to have mislaid my wallet.* □ **égarer**

mislead [mis'liːd] – *past tense, past participle* **mis'led** [-'led] – *verb* to give a wrong idea to: *Her friendly attitude misled me into thinking I could trust her.* □ **tromper**
mis'leading *adjective*: *a misleading remark.* □ **trompeur**

misplace [mis'pleis] *verb* **1** to lose, mislay. □ **égarer**
2 to give (trust, love) to the wrong person: *Your trust in him was misplaced.* □ **mal placer**

misprint ['misprint] *noun* a mistake in printing: *This newspaper is full of misprints.* □ **coquille**

mispronounce [misprə'nauns] *verb* to pronounce (words *etc*) wrongly. □ **mal prononcer**
'**mispro,nunci'ation** [-nʌnsi-] *noun*. □ **faute de prononciation**

Miss [mis] *noun* **1** a polite title given to an unmarried female, either in writing or in speech: *Miss Wilson*; *the Misses Wilson*; *Could you ask Miss Smith to type this*

letter?; *Excuse me, miss; could you tell me how to get to Princess Road?* □ **Mademoiselle**
2 a girl or young woman: *She's a cheeky little miss!* □ **petite/jeune fille**

miss [mis] *verb* **1** to fail to hit, catch *etc*: *The arrow missed the target.* □ **manquer**
2 to fail to arrive in time for: *He missed the 8 o'clock train.* □ **rater**
3 to fail to take advantage of: *You've missed your opportunity.* □ **manquer**
4 to feel sad because of the absence of: *You'll miss your friends when you go to live abroad.* □ **regretter**
5 to notice the absence of: *I didn't miss my purse till several hours after I'd dropped it.* □ **remarquer l'absence/la disparition de**
6 to fail to hear or see: *He missed what you said because he wasn't listening.* □ **manquer**
7 to fail to go to: *I'll have to miss my lesson next week, as I'm going to the dentist.* □ **manquer**
8 to fail to meet: *We missed you in the crowd.* □ **rater**
9 to avoid: *The thief only just missed being caught by the police.* □ **échapper à**
10 (of an engine) to misfire. □ **avoir des ratés**
■ *noun* a failure to hit, catch *etc*: *two hits and two misses.* □ **coup raté/manqué**

missing *adjective* not in the usual place or not able to be found: *The child has been missing since Tuesday*; *I've found those missing papers.* □ **disparu**
go missing to be lost: *A group of climbers has gone missing in the Himalayas.* □ **se perdre**
miss out 1 to omit or fail to include: *I missed her out (of the list).* □ **oublier**
2 (*often with* **on**) to be left out of something: *George missed out (on all the fun) because of his broken leg.* □ **ne pas profiter de**
miss the boat to be left behind, miss an opportunity *etc*: *I meant to send her a birthday card but I missed the boat – her birthday was last week.* □ **manquer le coche**

misshapen [mis'ʃeipən] *adjective* badly formed: *a misshapen tree.* □ **difforme**

missile ['misail] *noun* **1** a weapon or object which is thrown or fired from a gun, bow *etc*. □ **projectile**
2 a rocket-powered weapon carrying an explosive charge: *a ground-to-air missile.* □ **missile**
guided missile a rocket-powered missile which is directed to its target by a built-in device or by radio waves *etc*. □ **missile téléguidé**

missing *see* **miss.**

mission ['miʃən] *noun* **1** a purpose for which a person or group of people is sent: *His mission was to seek help.* □ **mission**
2 the purpose for which (one feels) one was born: *She regards it as her mission to help the cause of world peace.* □ **mission**
3 a group of people sent to have political and/or business discussions: *a Chinese trade mission.* □ **mission**
4 a place where missionaries live. □ **mission**
5 a group of missionaries: *a Catholic mission.* □ **mission**
'**missionary** – *plural* '**missionaries** – *noun* a person who

is sent to teach and spread a particular religion. □ **missionnaire**

misspell [mis'spel] – *past tense, past participles* ,mis'spelt,,mis'spelled – *verb* to spell wrongly. □ **mal orthographier**

mist [mist] *noun* a cloud of moisture in the air but very close to the ground, which makes it difficult to see any distance: *The hills are covered in thick mist.* □ **brume** 'mistily *adverb*. □ **dans la brume** 'misty *adjective*. □ **brumeux** 'mistiness *noun*. □ **état brumeux** **mist over, up** to become covered (as if) with mist: *The mirror misted over*; *The windshield misted up.* □ **s'embuer**

mistake [mi'steik] – *past tense* **mi'stook** [-'stuk]: *past participle* **mi'staken** – *verb* 1 (*with* **for**) to think that (one person or thing) is another: *I mistook you for my brother in this bad light.* □ **prendre pour, confondre avec**
2 to make an error about: *They mistook the date, and arrived two days early.* □ **se tromper sur**
■ *noun* a wrong act or judgment: *a spelling mistake*; *It was a mistake to trust him*; *I took your umbrella by mistake – it looks like mine.* □ **erreur, faute**
mi'staken *adjective* wrong: *You are mistaken if you think he's clever.* □ **erroné**
mi'stakenly *adverb*. □ **par erreur**
by mistake unintentionally or accidentally: *Maheesh wanted to save his work on the computer, but by mistake he pressed the wrong key and everything was deleted.* □ **par mégarde**

Mister ['mistə] *noun* (*abbreviated to* **Mr.** *when written*) a polite title given to a male adult, either in writing or in speech: *Good morning, Mr. Smith*; *Ask Mr. Jones.* □ **Monsieur**

mistletoe ['misltou] *noun* a plant with white berries, used in Christmas decorations. □ **gui**

mistress ['mistris] *noun* 1 a woman who is the lover of a man to whom she is not married. □ **maîtresse**
2 a female teacher: *the games mistress.* □ **institutrice, professeure**
3 a woman who commands, controls or owns: *a dog and his mistress.* □ **maîtresse**
4 a female employer (of a servant): *The servant stole her mistress's jewellery.* □ **maîtresse**

mistrust [mis'trʌst] *verb* to have no confidence or trust in. □ **se méfier de**
■ *noun* lack of confidence in something. □ **méfiance** ,mis'trustful *adjective*. □ **méfiant** ,mis'trustfully *adverb*. □ **avec méfiance**

misty *see* **mist**.

misunderstand [misʌndə'stand] – *past tense, past participle* ,misunder'stood [-'stud] – *verb* to take a wrong meaning from: *She misunderstood what I said.* □ **mal comprendre**
,misunder'standing *noun* 1 (a) confusion or mistake: *a misunderstanding about the date of the meeting.* □ **erreur, méprise**
2 a slight quarrel. □ **malentendu**

misuse [mis'juːs] *noun* (a) wrong or bad use: *the misuse*

of company money; *The machine was damaged by misuse.* □ **mauvais usage**
,mis'use [-'juːz] *verb* 1 to use wrongly. □ **faire un mauvais usage de**
2 to treat badly. □ **maltraiter**

mite [mait] *noun* 1 a tiny person or child. □ **petit, ite**
2 a type of very small insect. □ **mite**

miter *see* **mitre**.

mitre ['maitə] *noun* a type of headdress worn by archbishops and bishops. □ **mitre**

mitten ['mitn] *noun* (*also* **mitt** [mit]) 1 a kind of glove with two sections, one for the thumb and the other for the fingers: *a pair of mittens.* □ **mitaine, moufle**
2 a type of glove with separate sections for each finger, reaching only to halfway down the fingers. □ **mitaine**

mix [miks] *verb* 1 to put or blend together to form one mass: *She mixed the butter and sugar together*; *He mixed the blue paint with the yellow paint to make green paint.* □ **mélanger, mêler, malaxer**
2 to prepare or make by doing this: *She mixed the cement in a bucket.* □ **préparer**
3 to go together or blend successfully to form one mass: *Oil and water don't mix.* □ **se mélanger**
4 to go together socially: *People of different races were mixing together happily.* □ **se mêler**
■ *noun* 1 the result of mixing things or people together: *London has an interesting racial mix.* □ **mélange**
2 a collection of ingredients used to make something: (a) *cake-mix.* □ **préparation**
mixed *adjective* 1 consisting of different kinds: *I have mixed feelings about leaving home*; *mixed races*; *a mixed population.* □ **mélangé, mêlé**
2 done, used *etc* by people of different sexes: *mixed tennis.* □ **mixte**
'mixer *noun* a person or thing that mixes; a thing which is used for mixing: *an electric food mixer.* □ **mélangeur**
mixture ['mikstʃə] *noun* 1 the result of mixing things or people together: *a mixture of eggs, flour and milk.* □ **mélange**
2 a number of things mixed together and used for a given purpose: *The doctor gave the baby some cough mixture.* □ **préparation**
3 the act of mixing. □ **mélange**
'mix up *noun* a confused situation *etc*: *a mix up over the concert tickets.* □ **confusion**
be mixed up (in, with) to be involved: *He was mixed up in that burglary/with some drug addicts.* □ **être mêlé (à)**
mix up 1 to blend together: *I need to mix up another tin of paint.* □ **mélanger**
2 to confuse or muddle: *I'm always mixing the twins up.* □ **confondre**
3 to confuse or upset: *You've mixed me up completely with all this information.* □ **embrouiller**

moan [moun] *verb* 1 to make a low sound of grief, pain *etc*: *The wounded soldier moaned.* □ **gémir**
2 to complain: *They're always moaning about how hard they have to work.* □ **maugréer**
■ *noun* a sound (as if) of grief, pain *etc*: *a moan of pain*; *the moan of the wind.* □ **gémissement**

moat [mout] *noun* a deep ditch, dug around a castle *etc*, usually filled with water. □ **fossés**

mob [mob] *noun* a noisy, violent or disorderly crowd of people: *He was attacked by an angry mob.* □ **cohue**

■ *verb – past tense, past participle* **mobbed** – (of a crowd) to surround and push about in a disorderly way: *The singer was mobbed by a huge crowd of his fans.* □ **assaillir**

mobile ['moubail] *adjective* 1 able to move: *The van supplying country districts with library books is called a mobile library; The old lady is no longer mobile – she has to stay in bed all day.* □ **mobile**

2 able to move or be moved quickly or easily: *Most of the furniture is very light and mobile.* □ **transportable**

3 (of someone's features or face) changing easily in expression. □ **changeant**

mo'bility [-'bi-] *noun*. □ **mobilité**

'mobilize, 'mobilise [-bi-] *verb* to make (*especially* troops, an army *etc*), or become, ready for use or action. □ **mobiliser**

,mobili'zation, ,mobili'sation [-bi-] *noun.* □ **mobilisation**

mobile home ['moubail houm] *noun* a wheeled vehicle for living, which can be pulled by a car or truck: *This summer the family will rent a mobile home and travel across the country.* □ **grande caravane**

moccasin ['mokəsin] *noun* a type of shoe, made of soft leather, traditionally worn by American Indians; an imitation of it. □ **mocassin**

mock [mok] *verb* to laugh at or cause to seem ridiculous: *They mocked my efforts at cooking.* □ **se moquer de**

■ *adjective* pretended or not real: *a mock battle; He looked at me in mock horror.* □ **simulé**

'mockery *noun* an act of making fun of something: *She could not bear the mockery of the other children.* □ **moquerie**

'mocking *adjective*: *a mocking laugh.* □ **moqueur**

'mockingly *adverb.* □ **par moquerie**

mode [moud] *noun* 1 a manner of doing something: *an unusual mode of expression.* □ **mode, manière**

2 a kind or type: *modes of transport.* □ **mode**

3 a fashion: *Large hats are the latest mode.* □ **mode**

'modish *adjective* fashionable and smart. □ **à la mode**

'modishly *adverb.* □ **à la mode**

model ['modl] *noun* 1 a copy or representation of something *usually* on a much smaller scale: *a model of the Taj Mahal*; (*also adjective*) *a model airplane.* □ **maquette, modèle (réduit)**

2 a particular type or design of something, *eg* a car, that is manufactured in large numbers: *Our Renault car is the 1983 model.* □ **modèle**

3 a person who wears clothes *etc* so that possible buyers can see them being worn: *He has a job as a male fashion model.* □ **mannequin**

4 a person who is painted, sculpted, photographed *etc* by an artist, photographer *etc*: *I work as an artist's model.* □ **modèle**

5 something that can be used to copy from. □ **modèle**

6 a person or thing which is an excellent example: *She is a model of politeness*; (*also adjective*) *model behaviour.* □ **modèle**

■ *verb – past tense, past participle* **'modelled, 'modeled** – 1 to wear (clothes *etc*) to show them to possible buyers: *They model (underwear) for a living.* □ **être mannequin**

2 to work or pose as a model for an artist, photographer *etc*: *She models at the local art school.* □ **poser**

3 to make models (of things or people): *to model (the heads of famous people) in clay.* □ **modeler**

4 to form (something) into a (particular) shape: *She modelled the clay into the shape of a penguin; She models herself on her older sister.* □ **modeler, prendre modèle sur**

'modelling, 'modeling *noun.* □ **modelage**

modem ['moudəm] *noun* a part or attachment of a computer that sends and receives messages using the telephone line; a device that enables a computer to send information to another computer: *Janice can e-mail David because her computer has a built-in-modem.* □ **modem**

moderate ['modəreit] *verb* to make or become less extreme: *He was forced to moderate his demands; Gradually the pain moderated.* □ **(se) modérer**

■ [-rət] *adjective* 1 keeping within reasonable limits; not extreme: *The prices were moderate; moderate opinions.* □ **modéré**

2 medium or average; not particularly good: *workmanship of moderate quality.* □ **moyen**

■ *noun* a person whose views are not extreme: *Politically, she's a moderate.* □ **modéré, ée**

'moderately *adverb.* □ **modérément**

'moderateness [-rət-] *noun.* □ **modération**

,mode'ration *noun* 1 the quality of being moderate: *Alcohol isn't harmful if it's taken in moderation.* □ **modération**

2 (an) act of moderating: *There has been some moderation in the force of the gale.* □ **modération**

modern ['modən] *adjective* belonging to the present or to recent times; not old or ancient: *modern furniture/clothes.* □ **moderne**

mo'dernity [-'dəː-] *noun.* □ **modernité**

'modernness *noun.* □ **modernité**

'modernize, 'modernise *verb* to bring up to date: *We should modernize the education system.* □ **moderniser**

,moderni'zation, ,moderni'sation *noun.* □ **modernisation**

modern language a language spoken nowadays (as opposed to ancient Greek, Latin *etc*). □ **langue vivante**

modest ['modist] *adjective* 1 not having, or showing, too high an opinion of one's abilities *etc*: *He's very modest about his success.* □ **modeste**

2 decent, or showing good taste; not shocking: *modest clothing.* □ **réservé, pudique**

3 not very large; moderate: *I'm a person of modest ambitions.* □ **modeste**

'modestly *adverb.* □ **modestement**

'modesty *noun.* □ **modestie, pudeur**

modicum ['modikəm] *noun* a small quantity. □ **minimum**

modify ['modifai] *verb* to change the form or quality of, *usually* slightly: *We had to modify the original design.* □ **modifier**

,modifi'cation [-fi-] *noun.* □ **modification**

modish *see* **mode**.

module ['modju:l] *noun* a self-contained unit forming *eg* part of a building, spacecraft *etc: a lunar module.* □ **module**

mohair ['mouheə] *noun* **1** the long silken hair of a type of goat. □ **mohair**

2 (*also adjective*) (of) a type of cloth or wool made from it: *a mohair jersey.* □ **(de/en) mohair**

moist [moist] *adjective* damp; slightly wet: *moist, fertile soil.* □ **moite**

'moistly *adverb.* □ **caractère moite**

'moistness *noun.* □ **moiteur**

moisten ['moisn] *verb* to wet slightly: *He moistened (= licked) his lips.* □ **humecter**

moisture ['moistʃə] *noun* (the quality of) dampness: *This soil needs moisture.* □ **humidité**

'moisturize, 'moisturise [-stʃə-] *verb* to keep the moisture in (skin): *This cream is used to moisturize the skin.* □ **hydrater**

'moisturizer, 'moisturiser *noun.* □ **produit hydratant**

molar ['moulə] *noun* a back tooth which is used for grinding food. □ **molaire**

molasses [mə'lasiz] *noun* treacle. □ **mélasse**

mold *see* **mould**.

mole[1] [moul] *noun* a small, permanent, *usually* dark, spot on the skin. □ **grain de beauté**

mole[2] [moul] *noun* a small burrowing animal with very small eyes and soft fur. □ **taupe**

'molehill *noun* a little heap of earth dug up by a mole while tunnelling. □ **taupinière**

make a mountain out of a molehill to exaggerate the importance of a problem *etc.* □ **se faire une montagne d'un rien**

molecule ['molikju:l] *noun* the group of atoms that is the smallest unit into which a substance can be divided without losing its basic nature or identity. □ **molécule**

mo'lecular [-'le-] *adjective.* □ **moléculaire**

molehill *see* **mole**[2].

molest [mə'lest] *verb* to annoy or interfere with (a person) especially sexually: *The criminal was charged with molesting a young woman.* □ **importuner**

mollify ['molifai] *verb* to calm, soothe or lessen the anger of. □ **apaiser**

,mollifi'cation [-fi-] *noun.* □ **apaisement**

molten ['moultən] *adjective* (of a solid) in a liquid state, having been melted: *molten rock.* □ **fondu, en fusion**

moment ['moumənt] *noun* **1** a very short space of time: *I'll be ready in a moment; after a few moments' silence.* □ **moment, instant**

2 a particular point in time: *At that moment, the telephone rang.* □ **moment, instant**

'momentary *adjective* lasting for only a moment: *a momentary feeling of fear.* □ **momentané**

'momentarily [moumən'te-] *adverb.* □ **momentanément**

mo'mentous [-'men-] *adjective* of great importance: *a momentous event.* □ **capital**

mo'mentously *adverb.* □ **de façon importante**

at the moment at this particular time; now: *She's rather busy at the moment.* □ **en ce moment**

the moment (that) exactly when: *I want to see him the moment he arrives.* □ **dès que**

momentum [mə'mentəm] *noun* the amount or force of motion in a moving body. □ **quantité de mouvement**

monarch ['monək] *noun* a king, queen, emperor, or empress. □ **monarque**

'monarchy – *plural* **'monarchies** – *noun* (a country *etc* that has) government by a monarch. □ **monarchie**

monastery ['monəstəri] – *plural* **'monasteries** – *noun* a house in which a community of monks lives. □ **monastère**

mo'nastic [-'na-] *adjective* of, or like, monks or monasteries: *the monastic way of life.* □ **monastique**

Monday ['mʌndi] *noun* the second day of the week, the day following Sunday. □ **lundi**

monetary ['mʌnitəri] *adjective* of, or consisting of, money: *monetary problems.* □ **monétaire**

money ['mʌni] *noun* coins or banknotes used in trading: *Have you any money in your purse?; The desire for money is a cause of much unhappiness.* □ **argent**

'moneybox *noun* a box for saving money in. □ **tirelire**

'moneylender *noun* a person who lends money and charges interest. □ **prêteur, euse sur gages**

lose, make money to make a loss or a profit: *This film is making a lot of money in America.* □ **perdre/gagner de l'argent**

mongrel ['mʌngrəl] *noun adjective* (an animal, *especially* a dog) bred from different types. □ **bâtard**

monitor ['monitə] *noun* **1** a senior pupil who helps to see that school rules are kept. □ **chef de classe**

2 any of several kinds of instrument *etc* by means of which something can be constantly checked, *especially* a small screen in a television studio showing the picture which is being transmitted at any given time. □ **moniteur**

3 a device that accepts video signals from a computer and displays information on a screen: *Sally's monitor is very large so that she can more easily see her graphic designs; The monitor is out of focus.* □ **moniteur**

■ *verb* to act as, or to use, a monitor; to keep a careful check on: *These machines/technicians monitor the results constantly.* □ **contrôler, surveiller**

monk [mʌnk] *noun* a member of a male religious group, who lives in a monastery, away from the rest of society. □ **moine**

monkey ['mʌnki] *noun* **1** an animal of the type most like man, *especially* those which are small and have long tails (*ie* not the apes). □ **singe**

2 a mischievous child: *Their son is a little monkey.* □ **polisson, onne**

■ *verb* (*especially with* **with**) to meddle or interfere: *Who's been monkeying (about) with the television set?* □ **tripoter**

monkey business michievous or illegal happenings *etc.* □ **singeries, combines**

mono ['monou] *adjective* (of records, record playing

equipment *etc*) using one channel only; not stereo. □ **monophonique**

monocle ['monəkl] *noun* a lens or eyeglass for one eye only. □ **monocle**

monogram ['monəgram] *noun* a single design made up of several letters (often a person's initials). □ **monogramme**

monologue ['monəlog] *noun* a long speech by one person *eg* in a film, play *etc*. □ **monologue**

monoplane ['monəplein] *noun* an airplane (*usually* small) with one set of wings. □ **monoplan**

monopoly [mə'nopəli] – *plural* **mo'nopolies** – *noun* the sole right of making or selling something *etc*: *This firm has a local monopoly of soap-manufacturing.* □ **monopole**

mo'nopolize, mo'nopolise *verb* **1** to have a monopoly of or over: *They've monopolized the fruit canning industry.* □ **monopoliser**

2 to take up the whole of (*eg* someone's attention): *She tries to monopolize the teacher's attention.* □ **monopoliser**

monorail ['monəreil] *noun* a system of railways with trains which run hanging from, or along the top of, one rail. □ **monorail**

monotonous [mə'notənəs] *adjective* lacking in variety; dull: *a monotonous piece of music.* □ **monotone**

mo'notonously *adverb*. □ **de façon monotone**

mo'notony *noun*. □ **monotonie**

monsoon [mon'suːn] *noun* **1** a wind that blows in Southern Asia, from the southwest in summer, from the northeast in winter. □ **mousson**

2 the rainy season caused by the southwest monsoon. □ **mousson (d'été)**

monster ['monstə] *noun* **1** (*also adjective*) (something) of unusual size, form or appearance: *a monster tomato.* □ **monstre**

2 a huge and/or horrible creature: *prehistoric monsters.* □ **monstre**

3 a very evil person: *The man must be a monster to treat his children so badly!* □ **monstre**

'monstrous *adjective* **1** huge and often unpleasant. □ **monstrueux, colossal**

2 shocking: *a monstrous lie.* □ **monstrueux**

'monstrously *adverb*. □ **monstrueusement**

month [mʌnθ] *noun* one of the twelve divisions of the year (January, February *etc*), varying in length between 28 and 31 days. □ **mois**

'monthly *adjective* happening, being published *etc* once a month: *a monthly magazine.* □ **mensuel**

■ *adverb* once a month: *The magazine is published monthly.* □ **mensuellement**

a month of Sundays an extremely long time. □ **une éternité**

monument ['monjumənt] *noun* something built in memory of a person or event, *eg* a building, tomb *etc*: *They erected a monument in her honour.* □ **monument**

,monu'mental [-'men-] *adjective* of great size or scale: *a monumental achievement.* □ **monumental**

moo [muː] – *3rd person singular present tense* **moos**: *past tense, past participle* **mooed** – *verb* to make the sound of a cow. □ **meugler**

■ *noun* such a sound. □ **meuglement**

mood [muːd] *noun* the state of a person's feelings, temper, mind *etc* at a particular time: *What kind of mood is she in?*; *I'm in a bad mood today.* □ **humeur**

'moody *adjective* often bad-tempered: *a moody child.* □ **maussade**

'moodily *adverb*. □ **d'un air maussade**

'moodiness *noun*. □ **humeur maussade**

moon [muːn] *noun* **1** the heavenly body that moves once around the earth in a month and reflects light from the sun: *The moon was shining brightly; Spacemen landed on the moon.* □ **lune**

2 any of the similar bodies moving around the other planets: *the moons of Jupiter.* □ **lune**

'moonless *adjective* (of a night) dark and having no moonlight. □ **sans lune**

'moonbeam *noun* a beam of light reflected from the moon. □ **rayon de lune**

'moonlight *noun, adjective* (made with the help of) the light reflected by the moon: *The sea looked silver in the moonlight*; *a moonlight raid.* □ **(au) clair de lune**

'moonlit *adjective* lit by the moon: *a moonlit hillside.* □ **éclairé par la lune**

moon about/around to wander around as if dazed, *eg* because one is in love. □ **flâner**

moor[1] [muə] *noun* a large stretch of open, unfarmed land with poor soil often covered with heather, coarse grass *etc*. □ **lande**

'moorland *noun* a stretch of moor. □ **lande, bruyère**

moor[2] [muə] *verb* to fasten (a ship *etc*) by a rope, cable or anchor: *We moored (the yacht) in the bay.* □ **amarrer**

'mooring *noun* the act, or a means, of fastening a ship: *The mooring broke.* □ **amarrage, amarres**

'moorings *noun plural* the place where a ship is anchored or fastened. □ **mouillage**

moose [muːs] – *plural* **moose** – *noun* a type of large deer found in North America, and also in northern Europe where it is known as the elk. □ **original**

mop [mop] *noun* **1** a pad of sponge, or a bunch of pieces of coarse string or yarn *etc*, fixed on a handle, for washing floors, dishes *etc*. □ **vadrouille**

2 a thick mass of hair: *a mop of dark hair.* □ **tignasse**

3 an act of mopping: *He gave the floor a quick mop.* □ **coup de vadrouille**

■ *verb* – *past tense, past participle* **mopped** – **1** to rub or wipe with a mop: *She mopped the kitchen floor.* □ **essuyer**

2 to wipe or clean (*eg* a face covered with sweat): *He mopped his brow.* □ **éponger**

mop up to clean away using a mop, cloth *etc*: *I mopped up the mess with my handkerchief.* □ **essuyer, éponger**

mope [moup] *verb* to be depressed and mournful. □ **broyer du noir**

moped ['mouped] *noun* a pedal cycle which has a small motor. □ **vélomoteur**

moral ['morəl] *adjective* of, or relating to, character or behaviour *especially* right behaviour: *high moral standards*; *She leads a very moral* (= good) *life.* □ **moral**

■ *noun* the lesson to be learned from something that

happens, or from a story: *The moral of this story is that crime doesn't pay.* □ **morale**

'**morally** *adverb.* □ **moralement**

mo'rality *noun.* □ **moralité**

morals *noun plural* one's principles and behaviour: *He has no morals and will do anything for money.* ⌐ **moralité, mœurs**

morale [mə'rɑːl] *noun* the level of courage and confidence in *eg* an army, team *etc*: *In spite of the defeat, morale was still high.* □ **moral**

morass [mə'ras] *noun* a bog or swamp. □ **marécage**

more [mɔː] – *comparative of* **many, much** – *adjective* **1** a greater number or quantity of: *I've more pencils than he has.* □ **plus (de)**

2 an additional number or quantity of: *We need some more milk.* □ **d'autres, encore**

■ *adverb* **1** used to form the comparative of many adjectives and adverbs, *especially* those of more than two syllables: *She can do it more easily that I can; He is much more intelligent than they are.* □ **plus**

2 to a greater degree or extent: *I'm exercising a little more now than I used to.* □ **davantage**

3 again: *We'll play it once more.* □ **encore**

■ *pronoun* **1** a greater number or quantity: *'Are there a lot of people?' 'There are far more than we expected.'* □ **plus**

2 an additional number or amount: *We've run out of paint. Will you go and get some more?* □ **encore, davantage**

more'over *adverb* also; what is more important: *I don't like the idea, and moreover, I think it's illegal.* □ **de plus, d'ailleurs**

any more any longer; nowadays: *She doesn't go any more, but she used to go twice a week.* □ **plus**

more and more increasingly: *It's becoming more and more difficult to see.* □ **de plus en plus**

more or less approximately or almost: *They've more or less finished the job; The distance is ten kilometres, more or less.* □ **plus ou moins**

the more ... the more/less: *The more I see her, the more/less I like her.* □ **plus... plus/moins**

what is/what's more moreover: *They came home after midnight, and what's more, they were drunk.* □ **qui plus est**

morgue [mɔːg] *noun* a building where people who have been found dead are laid until they are identified *etc*. □ **morgue**

morn [mɔːn] *noun* morning. □ **matin**

morning ['mɔːniŋ] *noun* the first part of the day, approximately up to noon: *this morning; tomorrow morning.* □ **matin(ée)**

in the morning the period of time in the early part of the day; the hours approximately between dawn and noon: *Cara swam in the morning then ate lunch and studied in the afternoon.* □ **avant-midi**

morning glory any of various vines with funnel-shaped purple, blue, pink or white flowers that bloom early in the day. □ **belle-de-jour**

'**morning dress** *noun* a man's morning coat and striped trousers. □ **habit**

morose [mə'rous] *adjective* angry and silent. □ **morose**

mo'rosely *adverb.* □ **d'un air morose**

mo'roseness *noun.* □ **morosité**

morphia ['mɔːfiə], **morphine** ['mɔːfiːn] *nouns* a drug used to cause sleep or deaden pain. □ **morphine**

Morse [mɔːs] *noun* a code for signalling and telegraphy in which each letter is made up of dots and dashes, or short and long sounds or flashes of light. □ **morse**

morsel ['mɔːsəl] *noun* a small piece of something, *especially* food: *a tasty morsel of fish for the cat.* □ **bouchée**

mortal ['mɔːtl] *adjective* **1** liable to die; unable to live for ever: *Man is mortal.* □ **mortel**

2 of or causing death: *a mortal illness*; *mortal enemies* (= enemies willing to fight each other till death); *mortal combat.* □ **mortel**

■ *noun* a human being: *All mortals must die sometime.* □ **mortel, elle**

mor'tality [-'ta-] *noun* **1** the state of being mortal. □ **mortalité**

2 (*also* **mortality rate**) the number of deaths in proportion to the population; the death rate: *infant mortality.* □ **(taux de) mortalité**

'**mortally** *adverb* in such a way as to cause death: *She has been mortally wounded.* □ **mortellement**

mortal sin (*especially* in Roman Catholicism) a very serious sin, as a result of which the soul is damned for ever. □ **péché mortel**

mortar[1] ['mɔːtə] *noun* a mixture of cement, sand and water, used in building *eg* to hold bricks in place. □ **mortier**

mortar[2] ['mɔːtə] *noun* a type of short gun for firing shells upwards, in close-range attacks. □ **mortier**

mortar[3] ['mɔːtə] *noun* a dish in which to grind substances, *especially* with a pestle. □ **mortier**

mortarboard ['mɔːtəbɔːd] *noun* a type of cap with a square flat top, worn on formal occasions at universities. □ **mortier**

mortgage ['mɔːgidʒ] *noun* a legal agreement by which a sum of money is lent for the purpose of buying buildings, land *etc*. □ **hypothèque**

■ *verb* to offer (buildings *etc*) as security for a loan. □ **hypothéquer**

mortician [mɔː'tiʃən] *noun* an undertaker. □ **entrepreneur, eure de pompes funèbres**

,**mortifi'cation** [-fi-] *noun.* □ **mortification**

mortuary [mɔːtʃuəri] – *plural* '**mortuaries** – *noun* a building or room *eg* in a hospital, where dead bodies are kept before burial or cremation. □ **morgue**

mosaic [mə'zeiik] *noun* (the art of making) a design formed by fitting together small pieces of coloured marble, glass *etc*. □ **mosaïque**

Moslem *see* **Muslim.**

mosque [mosk] *noun* a Muslim place of worship. □ **mosquée**

mosquito [mə'skiːtou] – *plural* **mo'squito(e)s** – *noun* any of several types of small insect, which suck blood from animals and people and in this way transmit diseases such as malaria. □ **moustique**

moss [mos] *noun* (any variety of) a type of small flowerless plant, found in damp places, forming a soft green covering on tree trunks *etc: The bank of the river was covered in moss*. □ **mousse**

'**mossy** *adjective*. □ **moussu, mousseux**

most [moust] – *superlative of* **many, much** (*often with* **the**) – *adjective* **1** (the) greatest number or quantity of: *Which of the students has read the most books?*; *Reading is what gives me most enjoyment*. □ **le plus (de)**
2 the majority or greater part of: *Most boys like playing football*; *Most modern music is difficult to understand*. □ **la plupart (de)**
■ *adverb* **1** used to form the superlative of many adjectives and adverbs, *especially* those of more than two syllables: *Of all the women I know, she's the most beautiful*; *the most delicious cake I've ever tasted*; *We see her mother or father sometimes, but we see her grandmother most frequently*. □ **le/la/les plus**
2 to the greatest degree or extent: *They like sweets and biscuits but they like ice cream most of all*. □ **le plus**
3 very or extremely: *I'm most grateful to you for everything you've done*; *a most annoying child*. □ **très**
4 almost: *Most everyone I know has read that book*. □ **presque**
■ *pronoun* **1** the greatest number or quantity: *I ate two cakes, but Mary ate more, and John ate (the) most*. □ **le plus**
2 the greatest part; the majority: *He'll be at home for most of the day*; *Most of these students speak English*; *Everyone is leaving – most have gone already*. □ **la plus grande partie (de), la majorité**
'**mostly** *adverb* to the greatest degree or extent, or for most of the time; mainly: *The air we breathe is mostly nitrogen and oxygen*; *Mostly I go to the library rather than buy books*. □ **surtout, la plupart du temps**
at (the) most taking the greatest estimate: *There were no more than fifty people in the audience at (the) most*. □ **(tout) au plus**
for the most part mostly: *For the most part, the passengers on the ship were Swedes*. □ **pour la plupart**
make the most of (something) to take advantage of (an opportunity *etc*) to the greatest possible extent: *You'll only get one chance, so you'd better make the most of it!* □ **profiter (au maximum) de**

motel [mou'tel] *noun* a hotel which caters particularly for motorists. □ **motel**

moth [moθ] – *plural* **moths** [moθs] – *noun* **1** any of a large number of insects, rather like butterflies but with wider bodies, seen mostly at night and attracted by light. □ **papillon de nuit**
2 a clothes moth: *The moths have been at my evening dress*. □ **mite**
clothes moth a type of moth whose larva feeds on cloth and makes holes. □ **mite**
'**mothball** *noun* a small ball of a chemical used to protect clothes from clothes moths. □ **boule antimite**
'**moth-eaten** *adjective* (of cloth) eaten by moths: *a moth-eaten blanket*. □ **mité**

mother ['mʌðə] *noun* **1** a female parent, *especially* human: *John's mother lives in Manchester*; *(also adjective) The mother bird feeds her young*. □ **mère**
2 (*often with capital*: *also* **Mother Superior**) the fe-

male leader of a group of nuns. □ **Mère**
■ *verb* to care for as a mother does; to protect (sometimes too much): *His wife tries to mother him*. □ **dorloter**
'**motherhood** *noun* the state of being a mother. □ **maternité**
'**motherless** *adjective* having no mother: *The children were left motherless by the accident*. □ **sans mère**
'**motherly** *adjective* like a mother; of, or suitable to, a mother: *a motherly person*; *motherly love*. □ **maternel**
'**motherliness** *noun*. □ **affection maternelle**
'**mother country**, '**motherland** [-land] *nouns* the country where one was born. □ **patrie**
'**mother-in-law** – *plural* '**mothers-in-law** – *noun* the mother of one's husband or wife. □ **belle-mère**
,**mother-of-'pearl** *noun, adjective* (of) the shining, hard, smooth substance on the inside of certain shells. □ **(de) nacre**
'**mother tongue** *noun* a person's native language: *My mother tongue is Hindi*. □ **langue maternelle**

motion ['mouʃən] *noun* **1** the act or state of moving: *the motion of the planets*; *He lost the power of motion*. □ **mouvement**
2 a single movement or gesture: *He summoned the waiter with a motion of the hand*. □ **geste**
3 a proposal put before a meeting: *She was asked to speak against the motion in the debate*. □ **motion**
■ *verb* to make a movement or sign *eg* directing a person or telling him to do something: *She motioned (to) her to come nearer*. □ **faire signe (de)**
'**motionless** *adjective* not moving: *a motionless figure*. □ **immobile**
'**motion picture** a cinema film. □ **film**
in motion moving: *Don't jump on the bus while it is in motion*. □ **en mouvement/marche**

motive ['moutiv] *noun* something that makes a person choose to act in a particular way; a reason: *What was his motive for murdering the old lady?* □ **motif**
'**motivate** [-veit] *verb* to cause to act in a particular way: *He was motivated by jealousy*. □ **pousser**
moti'vation *noun*. □ **motivation**

motor ['moutə] *noun* a machine, *usually* a gas engine or an electrical device, that gives motion or power: *a washing-machine has an electric motor*; *(also adjective) a motor boat/vehicle*. □ **(à) moteur**
'**motorist** *noun* a person who drives a car: *The motorist could not avoid hitting the dog*. □ **automobiliste**
'**motorize**, '**motorise** *verb* **1** to fit a motor to (*eg* a bicycle). □ **munir d'un moteur**
2 to supply (*eg* troops) with motor vehicles: *Many army units have been motorized*. □ **motoriser**
'**motorcade** [-keid] *noun* a procession in which everyone goes by car. □ **cortège d'automobiles**
'**motorbike**, '**motorcycle** *nouns* any of several types of *usually* heavy bicycle moved by a motor. □ **moto(cyclette)**
'**motor car** a vehicle on four wheels, moved by a motor, but not a truck or van; an automobile, car. □ **auto(mobile)**
'**motorcyclist** *noun* a person who rides a motorbike: *The motorcyclist was injured in the road accident*. □

motocycliste

mottled ['motld] *adjective* marked with spots or patches of many colours or shades: *mottled leaves*. □ **tacheté**

motto ['motou] – *plural* '**mottoes** – *noun* 1 (a short sentence or phrase which expresses) a principle of behaviour *etc*: '*Honesty is the best policy' is my motto*; *a school motto*. □ **devise**

2 a printed saying *etc*, often found inside a Christmas cracker. □ **devise de diablotin**

mould¹, mold¹ [mould] *noun* 1 (soil which is full of) rotted leaves *etc*. □ **terreau, humus**

2 a growth on stale food *etc*: *This bread is covered with mould*. □ **moisissure**

'**mouldy** *adjective* (of food *etc*) covered with mould: *mouldy cheese*; *The bread has gone mouldy*. □ **moisi**
'**mouldiness** *noun*. □ **moisi(ssure)**

mould², mold² [mould] *noun* 1 a shape into which a substance in liquid form is poured so that it may take on that shape when it cools and hardens: *a jelly mould*. □ **moule**

2 something, *especially* a food, formed in a mould. □ **gâteau**

■ *verb* 1 to form in a mould: *The metal is moulded into long bars*. □ **mouler**

2 to work into a shape: *He moulded the clay into a ball*. □ **modeler**

3 to make the shape of (something): *She moulded the figure out of/in clay*. □ **façonner, former**

moult [moult] *verb* (of birds, dogs or cats, snakes *etc*) to shed feathers, hair, a skin *etc*. □ **muer**

mound [maund] *noun* a small hill or heap of earth *etc*: *a grassy mound*; *a mound of rubbish*. □ **monticule**

mount [maunt] *verb* 1 to get or climb up (on or on to): *He mounted the platform*; *She mounted (the horse) and rode off*. □ **monter**

2 to rise in level: *Prices are mounting steeply*. ■ **monter**

3 to put (a picture *etc*) into a frame, or stick it on to card *etc*. □ **monter, coller sur carton**

4 to hang or put up on a stand, support *etc*: *He mounted the tiger's head on the wall*. □ **fixer (sur un support)**

5 to organize: *The army mounted an attack*; *to mount an exhibition*. □ **monter**

■ *noun* 1 a thing or animal that one rides, *especially* a horse. □ **monture**

2 a support or backing on which anything is placed for display: *Would this picture look better on a red mount or a black one?* □ **support**

'**mounted** *adjective* on horseback: *mounted policemen*. □ **monté**

'**Mountie** [-ti] *noun* a member of the Royal Canadian Mounted Police. □ **membre de la police montée (canadienne)**

Mount [maunt] *noun* a mountain: *Mount Everest*. □ **mont**

mountain ['mauntən] *noun* a high hill: *Mount Everest is the highest mountain in the world*; (*also adjective*) *a mountain stream*. □ **(de) montagne**

,**mountai'neer** *noun* a person who climbs mountains, *especially* with skill, or as his occupation. □ **alpiniste**

,**mountai'neering** *noun* mountain-climbing. □ **alpinisme**

'**mountainous** *adjective* full of mountains: *The country is very mountainous*. □ **montagneux**

'**mountainside** *noun* the slope of a mountain: *The avalanche swept the climbers down the mountainside*. □ **versant d'une montagne**

'**mountaintop** *noun* the summit of a mountain. □ **sommet d'une montagne**

mourn [mɔːn] *verb* to have or show great sorrow *eg* for a person who has died: *She mourned (for) her dead son*. □ **pleurer**

'**mourner** *noun*: *The mourners stood around the graveside*. □ **personne qui suit le cortège funèbre**

'**mournful** *adjective* feeling or showing sorrow: *a mournful expression*. □ **affligé, lamentable**

'**mournfully** *adverb*. □ **tristement**

'**mourning** *noun* 1 grief shown *eg* because of someone's death. □ **deuil**

2 black or dark-coloured clothes suitable for a mourner: *She was wearing mourning*. □ **vêtements de deuil**

mouse [maus] – *plural* **mice** [mais] – *noun* 1 any of several types of small furry gnawing animal with a long tail, found in houses and in fields. □ **souris**

2 a hand-held device that when activated by a button controls aactions on a computer screen: *The teacher taught the class how to use the mouse in order to move the cursor around the computer screen*; *When John clicked on OPEN with the mouse, the game started*. □ **souris**

'**mousy** *adjective* 1 (of hair) dull brown in colour. □ **châtain terne**

2 timid; uninteresting: *a mousy little woman*. □ **effacé**

'**mousehole** *noun* a hole made or used by mice. □ **trou de souris**

'**mousetrap** *noun* a mechanical trap for a mouse. □ **souricière**

mousse [muːs] *noun* a dish made from flavoured cream *etc*, whipped and eaten cold. □ **mousse**

moustache, mustache [məˈstaːʃ, ˈmʌstaʃ] *noun* the hair on the upper lip of a man: *Young Tom has grown a moustache*. □ **moustache**

mouth [mauθ] – *plural* **mouths** [mauðz] – *noun* 1 the opening in the head by which a human or animal eats and speaks or makes noises: *What has the baby got in its mouth?* □ **bouche, gueule**

2 the opening or entrance *eg* of a bottle, river *etc*: *the mouth of the harbour*. □ **goulot, embouchure**

■ [mauð] *verb* to move the lips as if forming (words), but without making any sound: *She mouthed the words to me so that no one could overhear*. □ **former des mots avec les lèvres sans émettre de son**

'**mouthful** *noun* as much as fills the mouth: *a mouthful of soup*; *I ate the cake in two mouthfuls*. □ **gorgée, bouchée**

'**mouth organ** *noun* a small musical instrument played by blowing or sucking air through its metal pipes. □ **harmonica**

'**mouthpiece** *noun* 1 the piece of a musical instrument *etc* which is held in the mouth: *the mouthpiece of a horn*. □ **bec, embouchure**

2 the part of a telephone *etc* into which one speaks. □

microphone

'**mouthwash** *noun* an antiseptic liquid used for cleaning out the mouth. □ **gargarisme, rince-bouche**

move [muːv] *verb* 1 to (cause to) change position or go from one place to another: *He moved his arm*; *Don't move!*; *Please move your car*. □ **bouger**

2 to change houses: *We're moving on Saturday*. □ **déménager**

3 to affect the feelings or emotions of: *I was deeply moved by the film*. □ **émouvoir**

■ *noun* 1 (in board games) an act of moving a piece: *You can win this game in three moves*. □ **coup**

2 an act of changing homes: *How did your move go?* □ **déménagement**

'**movable**, '**moveable** *adjective*. □ **mobile**

mover *noun* a person or company that professionally moves furniture and other goods from one location or building to another: *Use a reliable mover who can transport all your belongings without breaking anything*. □ **déménageur**

'**movement** *noun* 1 (an act of) changing position or going from one point to another: *The animal turned sideways with a swift movement*. □ **mouvement**

2 activity: *In this play there is a lot of discussion but not much movement*. □ **mouvement**

3 the art of moving gracefully or expressively: *She teaches movement and drama*. □ **expression corporelle**

4 an organization or association: *the Scout movement*. □ **mouvement**

5 the moving parts of a watch, clock *etc*. □ **mouvement**

6 a section of a large-scale piece of music: *the third movement of Beethoven's Fifth Symphony*. □ **mouvement**

7 a general tendency towards a habit, point of view *etc*: *There's a movement towards simple designs in clothing these days*. □ **mouvement**

movie [-vi] *noun* 1 a cinema film: *a horror movie*. □ **film**

2 (*in plural*: *with* **the**) the cinema and films in general: *to go to the movies*. □ **cinéma**

'**moving** *adjective* having an effect on the emotions *etc*: *a very moving speech*. □ **émouvant**

'**movingly** *adverb*. □ **d'une manière émouvante**

get a move on to hurry or move quickly: *Get a move on, or you'll be late!* □ **se remuer**

make a move 1 to move at all: *If you make a move, I'll shoot you!* □ **faire un geste**

2 (*with* **for** *or* **towards**) to move (in the direction of): *He made a move for the door*. □ **esquisser un mouvement (vers)**

move along to keep moving, not staying in one place: *The police told the crowd to move along*. □ **circuler**

move heaven and earth to do everything that one possibly can. □ **remuer ciel et terre**

move house to change one's home or place of residence: *They're moving house next week*. □ **déménager**

move in to go into and occupy a house *etc*: *We can move in on Saturday*. □ **emménager**

move off (of vehicles *etc*) to begin moving away: *The bus moved off just as I got to the bus stop*. □ **démarrer,**

s'en aller

move out to leave, cease to live in, a house *etc*: *She has to move out before the new owners arrive*. □ **déménager**

move up to move in any given direction so as to make more space: *Move up and let me sit down, please*. □ **se pousser**

on the move 1 moving from place to place: *With my kind of job, I'm always on the move*. □ **en marche**

2 advancing or making progress: *The frontiers of scientific knowledge are always on the move*. □ **en marche**

movie *see* **move**.

mow [mou] *– past tense* **mowed**: *past participles* **mowed, mown** *– verb* to cut (grass *etc*) with a scythe or mower: *He mowed the lawn*. □ **faucher; tondre**

lawn 'mower *noun* a machine for cutting grass. □ **tondeuse (à gazon)**

mow down to kill in large numbers: *Our troops were mown down by machine gun fire*. □ **faucher**

Mr. *see* **Mister**.

Mrs. ['misiz] *noun* a polite title given to a married woman, in writing or in speaking: *Please come in, Mrs. Anderson*. □ **Mme**

Ms. [miz] *noun* a polite title given, *especially* in writing, to a woman, whether married or unmarried: *Ms. Johnson*. □ **Mme**

much [mʌtʃ] *– comparative* **more** [moː]: *superlative* **most** [moust] *– adjective* a (great) amount or quantity of: *This job won't take much effort*; *I found it without much difficulty*; *How much sugar is there left?*; *There's far too much salt in my soup*; *He ate so much ice cream that he was sick*; *Take as much money as you need*; *After much discussion they decided to go*. □ **beaucoup (de)**

■ *pronoun* a large amount; a great deal: *She didn't say much about it*; *Much of this trouble could have been prevented*; *Did you eat much?*; *not much*; *too much*; *as much as I wanted*; *How much did you eat?*; *Only this/that/so much*; *How much is* (= What is the price of) *that fish?*; *Please tidy your room – it isn't much to ask*. □ **beaucoup**

■ *adverb* 1 (by) a great deal; (by) far: *She's much prettier than I am*; *He isn't much older than you*; *How much further must we walk?*; *much more easily*; *He's much the best person to ask*. □ **beaucoup (plus)**

2 to a great extent or degree: *He will be much missed*; *We don't see her much* (= often); *I thanked her very much*; *much too late*; *I've much too much to do*; *The accident was as much my fault as his*; *Much to my dismay, she began to cry*. □ **beaucoup, très**

be not much of a to be not a very good thing of a particular kind: *I'm not much of a photographer*; *That wasn't much of a lecture*. □ **ne pas être extraordinaire comme**

be too much for to overwhelm; to be too difficult *etc* for: *Is the job too much for you?* □ **dépasser**

make much of 1 to make a fuss of (a person) or about (a thing). □ **faire grand cas de**

2 to make sense of; to understand: *I couldn't make much of the film*. □ **comprendre**

much as although: *Much as I should like to come,*

I can't. □ **bien que**
much the same not very different: *The patient's condition is still much the same.* □ **presque le même**
nothing much nothing important, impressive *etc*: *'What are you doing?' 'Nothing much.'* □ **pas grand-chose**
not much nothing important, impressive *etc*: *My car isn't much to look at but it's fast.* □ **pas très**
so much for that's all that can be said about: *So much for that – let's talk about something else; He arrived half an hour late – so much for his punctuality!* □ **voilà pour, voilà ce qu'on appelle**
think too much of to have too high an opinion of: *They think too much of themselves.* □ **avoir une trop haute idée de**
without so much as without even: *She took my umbrella without so much as asking.* □ **sans même**

see also **many**.

muck [mʌk] *noun* dung, filth, rubbish *etc*: *farm yard muck.* □ **saletés**
'**mucky** *adjective*. □ **sale, boueux**
muck about/around 1 to do things without any definite plan. □ **bricoler**
2 to fool around. □ **perdre son temps**
muck out to clean (a stable). □ **nettoyer**
mucus ['mjuːkəs] *noun* the fluid from the nose. □ **mucus**
mud [mʌd] *noun* wet soft earth. □ **boue**
'**muddy** *adjective* covered with or containing mud: *muddy boots/water.* □ **boueux**
■ *verb* to make muddy: *You've muddied the floor!* □ **salir**
'**mud flat** *noun (often in plural)* an area of muddy seaside land which is covered with water at high tide. □ **banc de boue**
'**mudguard** *noun* a shield or guard over the wheel of a car, bicycle *etc* to keep mud, rainwater *etc* from splashing upwards. □ **garde-boue**
'**mud skipper** *noun* a small fish found in shallow coastal waters, able to jump about and climb low rocks to look for food. □ **gobie marcheur**
muddle ['mʌdl] *verb* to confuse or mix up: *Don't talk while I'm counting, or you'll muddle me.* □ **embrouiller**
■ *noun* a state of confusion: *These papers keep getting in a muddle.* □ **fouillis**
'**muddled** *adjective*: *muddled thinking.* □ **embrouillé**
'**muddle-headed** *adjective* incapable of clear thinking: *I was told I'm muddle-headed.* □ **brouillon**
muddle along/through to progress in spite of one's unsatisfactory methods and foolish mistakes. □ **se débrouiller tant bien que mal**
muddle up to confuse (*eg* two different things): *I'm always muddling the twins up; I've muddled up these book orders.* □ **confondre**
muffin ['mʌfin] *noun* a type of round, flat cake eaten hot with butter. □ **muffin**
muffle ['mʌfl] *verb* to deaden the sound of: *They used a gag to muffle his cries.* □ **assourdir**
'**muffler** *noun* **1** a scarf worn around the neck. □ **cache-col**

2 a silencer on a motor vehicle. □ **silencieux**
mug[1] [mʌg] *noun* a type of cup with *usually* tall, more or less vertical sides: *a mug of coffee.* □ **chope, gobelet**
'**mugful** *noun*: *two mugfuls of coffee.* □ **chope**
mug[2] [mʌg] *noun* a slang word for the face. □ **gueule**
mug[3] [mʌg] – *past tense, past participle* **mugged** – *verb* to attack and *usually* rob: *He was mugged when coming home late at night.* □ **agresser**
'**mugger** *noun* a person who attacks others in this way. □ **agresseur**
mulberry ['mʌlbəri] – *plural* '**mulberries** – *noun* **1** a type of tree on whose leaves silkworms feed. □ **mûrier**
2 its (*usually* purple) fruit. □ **mûre**
mule[1] [mjuːl] *noun* an animal whose parents are a horse and an ass, known for its habit of being stubborn. □ **mule**
'**mulish** *adjective* stubborn. □ **têtu**
mule[2] [mjuːl] *noun* a loose, backless slipper. □ **mule**
mullet ['mʌlit] *noun* an edible fish found in coastal waters. □ **mulet**
multicoloured [mʌlti'kʌləd] *adjective* having many colours: *a multicoloured shirt.* □ **multicolore**
multimillionaire [mʌltimiljə'neə] *noun* a person who has wealth valued at several million dollars *etc*. □ **multimillionnaire**
multiple ['mʌltipl] *adjective* **1** having, or affecting, many parts: *She suffered multiple injuries when she fell out of the window.* □ **multiple**
2 involving many things of the same sort: *Fifteen vehicles were involved in the multiple crash on the highway.* □ **multiple**
■ *noun* a number that contains another number an exact number of times: *65 is a multiple of 5.* □ **multiple**
multiply ['mʌltiplai] *verb* **1** to add a number to itself a given number of times and find the total: *4 + 4 + 4 or 4 multiplied by 3 or 4 × 3 = 12.* □ **multiplier**
2 to (cause to) increase in number, *especially* by breeding: *Rabbits multiply very rapidly.* □ **(se) multiplier**
,**multipli'cation** [-pli-] *noun* the act of multiplying numbers. □ **multiplication**
multiracial [mʌlti'reiʃəl] *adjective* including, for, or of, people of many races: *Britain is becoming more and more multiracial.* □ **multiracial**
multi-storey, multi-story [mʌlti'stoːri] *adjective* having many floors or storeys: *a multi-storey parking lot.* □ **à étages**
multitude ['mʌltitjuːd] *noun* a great number or crowd: *a multitude of reasons; multitudes of people.* □ **multitude**
mum, mummy[1] ['mʌm(i)] – *plural* '**mummies** – *noun* a child's name for his or her mother: *Goodbye, Mum(my)!; Where's your mum(my), Kate?* □ **maman**
mumble ['mʌmbl] *verb* to speak (words) in such a way that they are difficult to hear: *I mumbled (a few words) quietly to myself.* □ **marmotter, balbutier**
mummy[1] *see* mum.
mummy[2] ['mʌmi] – *plural* '**mummies** – *noun* a dead human body preserved *eg* by the ancient Egyptians by wrapping in bandages and treating with spice, wax *etc*. □ **momie**

mumps ['mʌmps] *noun singular* a contagious disease causing painful swelling at the sides of the neck and face. □ **oreillons**

munch [mʌntʃ] *verb* to chew (something) with the lips closed: *She was munching her breakfast.* □ **mastiquer, mâchonner**

municipal [mju'nisipəl] *adjective* of, or controlled or owned by, the government of a city or town: *the municipal buildings.* □ **municipal**

mu'**nicipally** *adverb.* □ **à l'échelon municipal**

munitions [mju'niʃənz] *noun plural* weapons and ammunition used in war. □ **munitions**

mural ['mjuərəl] *noun* a painting that is painted directly on to a wall. □ **peinture murale**

murder ['mɔːdə] *noun* **1** (an act of) killing a person on purpose and illegally: *The police are treating his death as a case of murder; an increase in the number of murders.* □ **meurtre**

2 any killing or causing of death that is considered as bad as this: *the murder of innocent people by terrorists.* □ **meurtre**

■ *verb* to kill (a person) on purpose and illegally: *He murdered two children.* □ **assassiner**

'**murderer** – *feminine* '**murderess** – *noun*: *Murderers are no longer hanged in Britain.* □ **meurtrier, ière**

'**murderous** *adjective* intending, or capable of, murder: *There was a murderous look in her eye.* □ **meurtrier**

'**murderously** *adverb.* □ **d'une façon meurtrière**

murmur ['mɔːmə] *noun* a quiet, indistinct sound, *eg* that of running water or low voices: *the murmur of the sea; There was a low murmur among the crowd.* □ **murmure**

■ *verb* to make such a sound: *The child murmured (something) in his sleep.* □ **murmurer**

'**murmuring** *adjective.* □ **murmurant**

muscle ['mʌsl] *noun* any of the bundles of fibres in the body which, by contracting or relaxing, cause movement of the body: *He has well-developed muscles in his arms.* □ **muscle**

muscular ['mʌskjulə] *adjective* **1** of, or relating to, muscle(s): *great muscular strength.* □ **musculaire**

2 having well-developed muscles; strong: *She is tall and muscular.* □ **musclé**

muscle in (*often with* **on**) to gain entry, or gain a share of something by force: *The large firms have muscled in on all the important contracts.* □ **s'immiscer**

muse [mjuːz] *verb* to think about a matter *usually* without serious concentration. □ **songer**

museum [mju'ziəm] *noun* a place where collections of things of artistic, scientific or historic interest are set out for show. □ **musée**

mush [mʌʃ] *noun* something soft and wet: *The potatoes have turned to mush after being boiled for so long.* □ **bouillie**

'**mushy** *adjective.* □ **spongieux**

mushroom ['mʌʃrum] *noun* a type of fungus, *usually* shaped like an umbrella, many varieties of which are edible. □ **champignon**

■ *verb* to grow in size very rapidly: *The town has mushroomed since all the new industry was brought in.* □ **pousser comme un champignon**

music ['mjuːzik] *noun* **1** the art of arranging and combining sounds able to be produced by the human voice or by instruments: *He prefers classical music to popular music; She is studying music; (also adjective) a music lesson.* □ **(de) musique**

2 the written form in which such tones *etc* are set down: *The pianist has forgotten to bring her music.* □ **musique**

'**musical** *adjective* **1** of or producing music: *a musical instrument.* □ **de musique**

2 like music, *especially* in being pleasant to hear: *a musical voice.* □ **musical**

3 (of a person) having a talent for music: *Their children are all musical.* □ **musical**

■ *noun* a film or play that includes a large amount of singing, dancing *etc.* □ **comédie musicale**

'**musically** *adverb.* □ **musicalement**

musician [mju'ziʃən] *noun* **1** a person who is skilled in music: *The conductor of this orchestra is a fine musician.* □ **musicien, ienne**

2 a person who plays a musical instrument: *This show has ten singers, twenty dancers and fifty musicians.* □ **musicien, ienne**

musket ['mʌskit] *noun* an old type of gun once carried by foot-soldiers. □ **mousquet**

,**muske'teer** *noun* a soldier armed with a musket. □ **mousquetaire**

Muslim ['muzlim], **Moslem** ['mozləm] *noun, adjective* (a person) of the religion known as Islam. □ **musulman, ane**

muslin ['mʌzlin] *noun, adjective* (of) a type of fine soft cotton cloth. □ **mousseline**

mussel ['mʌsl] *noun* a variety of edible shellfish with a shell in two parts. □ **moule**

must [mʌst] – *negative short form* '**mustn't** [-snt] – *verb* **1** used with another verb to express need: *We must go to the shops to get milk.* □ **devoir**

2 used, *usually* with another verb, to suggest a probability: *They must be finding it very difficult to live in such a small house.* □ **devoir**

3 used, *usually* with another verb, to express duty, an order, rule *etc*: *You must come home before midnight; All competitors must be under 15 years of age.* □ **devoir**

■ *noun* something necessary, essential, or not to be missed: *This new tent is a must for the serious camper.* □ **chose indispensable**

must have used to state a probability about something in the past: *He must have been very young when he got married.* □ **avoir dû**

mustache *see* **moustache.**

mustard ['mʌstəd] *noun* a type of seasoning with a hot taste made from the seeds of the mustard plant. □ **moutarde**

muster ['mʌstə] *verb* **1** to gather together (*especially* soldiers for duty or inspection). □ **rassembler**

2 to gather (courage, energy *etc*): *He mustered his energy for a final effort.* □ **rassembler**

mustn't *see* **must.**

musty ['mʌsti] *adjective* damp or stale in smell or taste: *musty old books.* □ **moisi**

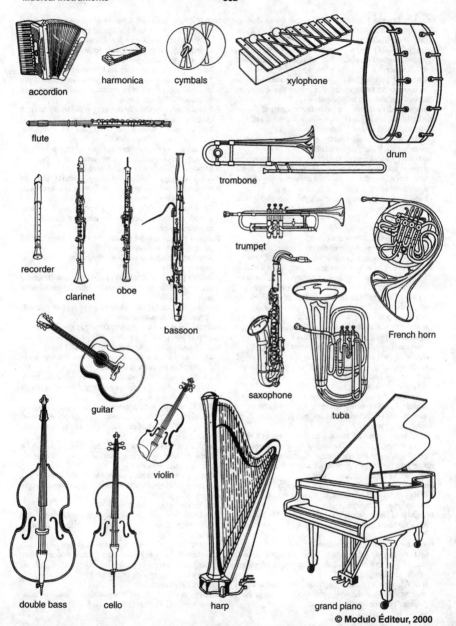

accordion

harmonica

cymbals

xylophone

drum

flute

trombone

recorder

clarinet

oboe

bassoon

trumpet

French horn

guitar

saxophone

tuba

violin

double bass

cello

harp

grand piano

mute [mjuːt] *adjective* 1 unable to speak; dumb. □ **muet**
2 silent: *She gazed at him in mute horror.* □ **muet**
3 (of a letter) not sounded in certain words: *The word 'dumb' has a mute 'b' at the end.* □ **muet**
'**mutely** *adverb.* □ **en silence**

mutiny ['mjuːtini] – *plural* '**utinies** – *noun* (a) refusal to obey one's senior officers in the navy or other armed services: *There has been a mutiny on HMS Tigress; The sailors were found guilty of mutiny.* □ **mutinerie**
■ *verb* (of sailors *etc*) to refuse to obey commands from those in authority: *The sailors mutinied because they did not have enough food.* □ **se mutiner**
muti'neer *noun* a person who mutinies. □ **mutin**
'**mutinous** *adjective*: *mutinous sailors.* □ **mutiné**

mutter ['mʌtə] *verb* to utter words in a quiet voice *especially* when grumbling *etc*. □ **marmonner**
■ *noun* such a sound: *He spoke in a mutter.* □ **marmonnement**

mutton ['mʌtn] *noun* the flesh of sheep, used as food. □ **mouton**

mutual ['mjuːtʃuəl] *adjective* 1 given *etc* by each of two or more to the other(s): *mutual help; Their dislike was mutual.* □ **mutuel**
2 common to, or shared by, two or more: *a mutual friend.* □ **mutuel**
'**mutually** *adverb.* □ **mutuellement**

muzzle ['mʌzl] *noun* 1 the jaws and nose of an animal such as a dog. □ **museau**
2 an arrangement of straps *etc* around the muzzle of an animal to prevent it from biting. □ **muselière**
3 the open end of the barrel of a gun *etc*. □ **bouche**
■ *verb* to put a muzzle on (a dog *etc*). □ **museler**

my [mai] *adjective* of or belonging to me: *That is my book; I hurt my leg; She borrowed my pen.* □ **mon/ma/mes**
■ *interjection* used to express surprise: *My, how you've grown!* □ **par exemple!**

my'self *pronoun* 1 used as the object of a verb or preposition when the speaker or writer is the object of an action he or she performs: *I cut myself while shaving; I looked at myself in the mirror.* □ **me, moi**
2 used to emphasize **I, me** or the name of the speaker or writer: *I myself can't tell you, but my friend will; I don't intend to go myself.* □ **moi-même**

see also **mine**[1].

mynah (*also* **myna**) ['mainə] *noun* a small tropical bird that can mimic human speech. □ **martin**

myopia [mai'oupiə] *noun* short-sightedness: *She suffers from myopia.* □ **myopie**
my'opic [-'o-] *adjective*: *a myopic young man; a myopic condition; She's slightly myopic.* □ **myope**

myself *see* my.

mystery ['mistəri] – *plural* '**mysteries** – *noun* 1 something that cannot be, or has not been, explained: *the mystery of how the universe was formed; the mystery of his disappearance; How she passed her exam is a mystery to me.* □ **mystère**
2 the quality of being impossible to explain, understand *etc*: *Her death was surrounded by mystery.* □ **mystère**
my'sterious [-'stiəriəs] *adjective* difficult to understand or explain, or full of mystery: *mysterious happenings; He's being very mysterious* (= refuses to explain fully) *about what his work is.* □ **mystérieux**
my'steriously *adverb.* □ **mystérieusement**

mystify ['mistifai] *verb* to be impossible (for someone) to explain or understand: *I was mystified by his behaviour.* □ **rendre perplexe**

myth [miθ] *noun* an ancient, fictional story, *especially* one dealing with gods, heroes *etc*. □ **mythe**
'**mythical** *adjective.* □ **mythique**
'**mythically** *adverb.* □ **de façon mythique**
mythology [mi'θolədʒi] *noun* (a collection of) myths. □ **mythologie**
,**mytho'logical** [-'lo-] *adjective.* □ **mythologique**

Nn

nab [nab] – *past tense, past participle* **nabbed** – *verb* to take, catch or get hold of: *The police nabbed the thief.* □ **attraper**

nag [nag] – *past tense, past participle* **nagged** – *verb* (*often with* **at**) to complain or criticize continually: *I nag (at) them to stop the noise.* □ **harceler**
'**nagging** *adjective* continuously troublesome: *a nagging worry/pain.* □ **tenace**

nail [neil] *noun* **1** a piece of horn-like substance which grows over the ends of the fingers and toes to protect them: *I've broken my nail; toe nails; Don't bite your finger nails.* □ **ongle**
2 a thin pointed piece of metal used to fasten pieces of wood *etc* together: *He hammered a nail into the wall and hung a picture on it.* □ **clou**
■ *verb* to fasten with nails: *She nailed the picture to the wall.* □ **clouer**
'**nail brush** *noun* a small brush used for cleaning one's nails. □ **brosse à ongles**
'**nail file** *noun* a small instrument with a rough surface, used for smoothing or shaping the edges of one's finger nails. □ **lime à ongles**
'**nail polish**, '**nail varnish** *nouns* a substance used to colour and/or varnish one's nails. □ **vernis à ongles**
'**nail scissors** *noun plural* scissors for trimming one's nails. □ **ciseaux à ongles**
hit the nail on the head to be absolutely accurate (in one's description of something or someone, in an estimate of something *etc*). □ **mettre le doigt dessus**

naïve, naive [nai'iːv] *adjective* **1** simple and straightforward in one's way of thinking, speaking *etc*. □ **naïf**
2 ignorantly simple. □ **ingénu**
na'ïvely *adverb*. □ **naïvement, ingénument**

naked ['neikid] *adjective* **1** without clothes: *a naked child.* □ **nu**
2 openly seen, not hidden: *the naked truth.* □ **à découvert**
3 (of a flame *etc*) uncovered or unprotected: *Naked lights are dangerous.* □ **nu**
'**nakedly** *adverb*. □ **à nu**
'**nakedness** *noun*. □ **nudité**
the naked eye the eye unaided by any artificial means such as a telescope, microscope *etc*: *Germs are too small to be seen by the naked eye.* □ **l'œil nu**

name [neim] *noun* **1** a word by which a person, place or thing is called: *My name is Rachel; She knows all the flowers by name.* □ **nom**
2 reputation; fame: *He has a name for honesty.* □ **réputation**
■ *verb* **1** to give a name to: *They named the child Thomas.* □ **nommer**
2 to speak of or list by name: *He could name all the kings of England.* □ **nommer**
'**nameless** *adjective* **1** not having a name: *a nameless fear.* □ **sans nom**
2 not spoken of by name: *The author of the book shall be nameless.* □ **anonyme**

'**namely** *adverb* that is: *Only one student passed the exam, namely Jane.* □ **à savoir**
'**nameplate** *noun* a piece of metal, plastic *etc* with a name on it: *You will know his office by the nameplate on the door.* □ **plaque**
'**namesake** *noun* a person with the same name as oneself. □ **homonyme**
call (someone) names to insult (someone) by applying rude names to him. □ **traiter de tous les noms**
in the name of by the authority of: *I arrest you in the name of the Queen.* □ **au nom de**
make a name for oneself to become famous, get a (*usually* good) reputation *etc*: *She made a name for herself as a concert pianist.* □ **se faire un nom**
name after, name for to give (a child or a thing) the name of (another person): *Peter was named after his father.* □ **donner (à qqn) le nom de**

nanny ['nani] – *plural* '**nannies** – *noun* a children's nurse. □ **nurse, nounou**
nanny-goat ['nanigout] *noun* a female goat. □ **chèvre**

nap [nap] *noun* a short sleep: *She always has a nap after lunch.* □ **(petit) somme, sieste**
catch (someone) napping to catch (someone) unprepared for a particular emergency *etc*. □ **prendre au dépourvu**

napalm ['neipaːm] *noun* petrol in a jelly-like form, used in bombs to cause fire. □ **napalm**

nape [neip] *noun* the back of the neck: *His hair curled over the nape of his neck.* □ **nuque**

napkin ['napkin] *noun* (*also* **table napkin**) a small piece of cloth or paper for protecting the clothes from drips *etc* and for wiping the lips at meals. □ **serviette (de table)**

narcotic [naːˈkotik] *noun* a type of drug that stops pain or makes one sleep, often addictive when taken in large doses. □ **narcotique**

narrate [nəˈreit] *verb* to tell (a story): *She narrated the events of the afternoon.* □ **raconter**
nar'ration *noun*. □ **narration**
narrative ['narətiv] *noun* a story: *an exciting narrative.* □ **récit**
nar'rator *noun* a person who tells a story. □ **narrateur, trice**

narrow ['narou] *adjective* **1** having or being only a small distance from side to side: *a narrow road; The bridge is too narrow for large trucks to cross.* □ **étroit**
2 only just managed: *a narrow escape.* □ **réussi de justesse**
3 (of ideas, interests or experience) not extensive enough. □ **borné**
■ *verb* to make or become narrow: *The road suddenly narrowed.* □ **(se) rétrécir**
'**narrowly** *adverb* closely; only just: *The ball narrowly missed his head.* □ **de justesse**
'**narrows** *noun plural* a narrow sea-passage; a channel or strait. □ **passage étroit**
,**narrow-'minded** *adjective* unwilling to accept ideas different from one's own. □ **à l'esprit étroit**

nasal ['neizəl] *adjective* **1** of the nose: *a nasal infection.* □ **nasal**

2 sounding through the nose: *a nasal voice*. □ **nasal**

nasty ['nɑːsti] *adjective* **1** unpleasant to the senses: *a nasty smell*. □ **désagréable**

2 unfriendly or unpleasant in manner: *They were very nasty to me*. □ **déplaisant**

3 wicked; evil: *He has a nasty temper*. □ **mauvais**

4 (of weather) very poor, cold, rainy *etc*. □ **mauvais**

5 (of a wound, cut *etc*) serious: *That dog gave her a nasty bite*. □ **vilain**

6 awkward or very difficult: *a nasty situation*. □ **pénible**

'**nastily** *adverb*. □ **désagréablement**

'**nastiness** *noun*. □ **méchanceté**

nation ['neiʃən] *noun* **1** a group of people living in a particular country, forming a single political and economic unit. □ **nation**

2 a large number of people who share the same history, ancestors, culture *etc* (whether or not they all live in the same country): *the Jewish nation*. □ **peuple**

national ['naʃənəl] *adjective* of or belonging to a particular nation: *national government*; *national pride*. □ **national**

'**nationally** *adverb*. □ **nationalement**

'**nationalism** ['na-] *noun* **1** a sense of pride in the history, culture, achievements *etc* of one's nation. □ **nationalisme**

2 the desire to bring the people of one's nation together under their own government. □ **nationalisme**

'**nationalist** ['na-] *noun*. □ **nationaliste**

,**nationa'listic** *adjective*. □ **nationaliste**

nationality [naʃə'naləti] – *plural* natio'**nalities** – *noun* (the state of belonging to) a particular nation: *'What nationality are you?' 'I'm German'*; *You can see (people of) many nationalities in London*. □ **nationalité**

'**nationalize**, '**nationalise** ['na-] *verb* to make (*especially* an industry) the property of the nation as a whole rather than the property of an individual. □ **nationaliser**

,**nationali'zation**, ,**nationali'sation** *noun*. □ **nationalisation**

national anthem a nation's official song or hymn. □ **hymne national**

national service in some countries, a period of compulsory service in the armed forces. □ **service militaire**

,**nation'wide** *adjective, adverb* (happening *etc*) throughout the whole nation: *a nationwide broadcast*; *They travelled nationwide*. □ **affectant la nation entière; à travers tout le pays**

native ['neitiv] *adjective* **1** where one was born: *my native land*. □ **natal**

2 belonging to that place: *my native language*. □ **natal**

3 belonging by race to a country: *a native Englishwoman*. □ **de souche**

4 belonging to a person naturally: *native intelligence*. □ **naturel**

■ *noun* **1** a person born in a certain place: *a native of Scotland*; *a native of London*. □ **autochtone**

2 one of the original inhabitants of a country *eg* before the arrival of explorers, immigrants *etc*: *Columbus thought the natives of America were Indians*. □ **indigène**

native speaker a person who has spoken a particular language ever since he was able to speak at all: *I am a*

native speaker of English; *a native Spanish speaker*. □ **locuteur natif**

native to (of plants and animals) belonging originally to a particular place: *These birds are native to Australia*. □ **originaire de**

the Nativity [nə'tivəti] the birth of Christ. □ **Nativité**

natter ['natə] *verb* to chatter or talk continuously, *usually* about unimportant things. □ **jacasser**

natural ['natʃərəl] *adjective* **1** of or produced by nature, not made by men: *Coal, oil etc are natural resources*; *Wild animals are happier in their natural state than in a zoo*. □ **naturel**

2 born in a person: *natural beauty*; *She had a natural ability for music*. □ **naturel, inné**

3 (of manner) simple, without pretence: *a nice, natural smile*. □ **naturel**

4 normal; as one would expect: *It's quite natural for a boy of his age to be interested in girls*. □ **naturel, normal**

5 of a musical note, not sharp or flat: *G natural is lower in pitch than G sharp*. □ **naturel**

■ *noun* **1** a person who is naturally good at something. □ **un, une (...) né, ée**

2 in music (a sign ( ) indicating) a note which is not to be played sharp or flat. □ **bécarre, note naturelle**

'**naturalist** *noun* a person who studies animal and plant life. □ **naturaliste**

'**naturally** *adverb* **1** of course; as one would expect: *Naturally I didn't want to risk missing the train*. □ **naturellement**

2 by nature; as a natural characteristic: *She is naturally kind*. □ **de nature**

3 normally; in a relaxed way: *Although he was nervous, he behaved quite naturally*. □ **avec naturel**

natural gas gas suitable for burning, found underground or under the sea. □ **gaz naturel**

natural history the study of plants and animals. □ **histoire naturelle**

natural resources sources of energy, wealth *etc* which occur naturally and are not made by man, *eg* coal, oil, forests *etc*. □ **ressources naturelles**

nature ['neitʃə] *noun* **1** the physical world, *eg* trees, plants, animals, mountains, rivers *etc*, or the power which made them: *the beauty of nature*; *the forces of nature*; *the study of nature*. □ **nature**

2 the qualities born in a person; personality: *She has a generous nature*. □ **nature**

3 quality; what something is or consists of: *What is the nature of your work?* □ **nature**

4 a kind, type *etc*: *bankers and other people of that nature*. □ **sorte, nature**

-natured having a certain type of personality: *good-natured*; *ill-natured*. □ **au naturel (...)**

in the nature of having the qualities of: *His words were in the nature of a threat*. □ **une sorte de**

naught [nɔːt] *noun* nothing. □ **rien, zéro**

naughty ['nɔːti] *adjective* (*usually* of children) badly-behaved: *a naughty boy*; *It is naughty to kick other children*. □ **vilain**

'**naughtily** *adverb*. □ **avec malice**

'**naughtiness** *noun.* □ **mauvaise conduite**

nausea ['nɔːzɪə,] *noun* a feeling of sickness. □ **nausée**

nauseate ['nɔːzɪeɪt] *verb* to make (someone) feel nausea. □ **écœurer**

nautical ['nɔːtɪkəl] *adjective* of ships or sailors: *nautical language.* □ **nautique, naval**

naval *see* **navy.**

nave [neɪv] *noun* the middle or main part of a church. □ **nef**

navel [neɪvəl] *noun* the small hollow in the front of the abdomen, just below the middle of the waist. □ **nombril**

navigate ['navɪgeɪt] *verb* **1** to direct, guide or move (a ship, aircraft *etc*) in a particular direction: *I navigated the ship through the dangerous rocks.* □ **naviguer**
2 to find or follow one's route when in a ship, aircraft, car *etc*: *If I drive will you navigate?* □ **lire la carte**
'**navigable** *adjective* (*negative* **unnavigable**) able to be travelled along: *a navigable river.* □ **navigable**
,**navi'gation** *noun* the art or skill of navigating. □ **navigation**
'**navigator** *noun* a person who navigates. □ **navigateur, trice**

navy ['neɪvɪ] – *plural* '**navies** – *noun* **1** a country's warships and the people who work in and with them: *Russia has one of the largest navies in the world; I joined the navy fifteen years ago.* □ **marine**
2 (*also adjective*) (*also* **navy blue**) (of) a dark blue colour: *a navy (blue) jersey.* □ **bleu marine**
'**naval** *adjective* of the navy: *naval uniform; a naval officer.* □ **naval**

near [nɪə] *adjective* **1** not far away in place or time: *The station is quite near; Christmas is getting near.* □ **proche**
2 not far away in relationship: *He is a near relation.* □ **proche**
■ *adverb* **1** to or at a short distance from here or the place mentioned: *He lives quite near.* □ **près**
2 (*with* **to**) close to: *Don't sit too near to the window.* □ **près de**
■ *preposition* at a very small distance from (in place, time *etc*): *She lives near the church; It was near midnight when they arrived.* □ **près de**
■ *verb* to come near (to): *The roads became busier as they neared the town; as evening was nearing.* □ **(s')approcher**
'**nearly** *adverb* not far from; almost: *nearly one o'clock; He has nearly finished.* □ **presque**
'**nearness** *noun.* □ **proximité**

nearby [nɪə'baɪ] *adverb* close to here or the place mentioned: *He lives nearby; a cottage with a stream running nearby.* □ **près**
'**nearside** *adjective* (of the side of a vehicle *etc*) furthest from the centre of the road. □ **côté droit**
,**near'sighted** *adjective* short-sighted. □ **myope**
a near miss something that is almost a hit, success *etc*. □ **quasi-collision**

neat [niːt] *adjective* **1** tidy; well-ordered, with everything in the right place: *a neat house; She is very neat and tidy.* □ **propre, bien tenu**
2 skilfully done: *She has made a neat job of the repair.* □ **très bien/bon**

3 (of drink, *especially* alcoholic) without added water: *neat whisky.* □ **sec**
'**neatness** *noun.* □ **netteté**
'**neatly** *adverb* tidily or skilfully: *Please write neatly.* □ **soigneusement**

necessary ['nesɪsərɪ] *adjective* needed; essential: *Is it necessary to sign one's name?; I shall do all that is necessary.* □ **nécessaire**
,**neces'sarily** [-'se-] *adverb.* □ **nécessairement, forcément**

necessitate [nɪ'sesɪteɪt] *verb* to make necessary: *Rebuilding the castle would necessitate spending a lot of money.* □ **rendre nécessaire, nécessiter**

necessity [nɪ'sesətɪ] – *plural* **ne'cessities** – *noun* something needed or essential: *Food is one of the necessities of life.* □ **nécessité**

neck [nek] *noun* **1** the part of the body between the head and chest: *She wore a scarf around her neck.* □ **cou**
2 the part of an article of clothing that covers that part of the body: *The neck of that shirt is dirty.* □ **col**
3 anything like a neck in shape or position: *the neck of a bottle.* □ **col, goulot**
'**necklace** [-ləs] *noun* a string of jewels, beads *etc* worn around the neck: *a diamond necklace.* □ **collier**
'**neckline** *noun* the edge of a piece of clothing at or around a person's neck: *The dress has a very low neckline.* □ **encolure**
'**necktie** *noun* a man's tie. □ **cravate**
neck and neck (in a race) exactly equal: *The horses were neck and neck as they came up to the finish.* □ **à égalité**

nectar ['nektə] *noun* **1** the sweet liquid collected by bees to make honey. □ **nectar**
2 a delicious drink. □ **nectar**

née [neɪ] *adjective* born; used to state what a woman's name was before she married: *Mrs. Jane Brown, née Black.* □ **née**

need [niːd] – *negative short form* **needn't** ['niːdnt] – *verb*
1 to require: *This page needs to be checked again; This page needs checking again; Do you need any help?* □ **avoir besoin de**
2 to be obliged: *You need to work hard if you want to succeed; They don't need to come until six o'clock; She needn't have given me such an expensive present.* □ **avoir besoin de, falloir**
■ *noun* **1** something essential, that one must have: *Food is one of our basic needs.* □ **besoin**
2 poverty or other difficulty: *Many people are in great need.* □ **besoin**
3 a reason: *There is no need for panic.* □ **besoin**
'**needless** *adjective, adverb* unnecessary: *You are doing a lot of needless work; Needless to say, he couldn't do it.* □ **inutile**
'**needlessly** *adverb.* □ **inutilement**
'**needy** *adjective* poor: *You must help needy people.* □ **nécessiteux**
a need for a lack of; a requirement for: *There is an urgent need for teachers in this city.* □ **besoin de**
in need of requiring; having a lack of: *We're in need of more money; You're badly in need of a haircut.* □

besoin de

needle ['niːdl] *noun* **1** a small, sharp piece of steel with a hole (called an eye) at one end for thread, used in sewing *etc*: *a sewing needle*. □ **aiguille**
2 any of various instruments of a long narrow pointed shape: *a knitting needle*; *a hypodermic needle*. □ **aiguille**
3 (in a compass *etc*) a moving pointer. □ **aiguille**
4 the thin, sharp-pointed leaf of a pine, fir *etc*. □ **aiguille**
'needlework *noun* work done with a needle *ie* sewing, embroidery *etc*. □ **travaux d'aiguille**

needn't *see* **need**.

negative ['negətiv] *adjective* **1** meaning or saying 'no'; denying something: *a negative answer*. □ **négatif**
2 expecting to fail: *a negative attitude*. □ **négatif**
3 less than zero: *–4 is a negative or minus number*. □ **négatif**
4 having more electrons than normal: *The battery has a negative and a positive terminal*. □ **négatif**
■ *noun* **1** a word *etc* by which something is denied: *'No' and 'never' are negatives*. □ **négation**
2 the photographic film, from which prints are made, on which light and dark are reversed: *I gave away the print, but I still have the negative*. □ **négatif**
'negatively *adverb*. □ **négativement**

neglect [ni'glekt] *verb* **1** to treat carelessly or not give enough attention to: *He neglected his work*. □ **négliger**
2 to fail (to do something): *He neglected to answer the letter*. □ **négliger**
■ *noun* lack of care and attention: *The garden is suffering from neglect*. □ **manque de soins**
neglect oneself *verb* to pay little attention to one's own care or well-being: *Doug neglected himself, not caring if his clothes were clean or his hair was washed*. □ **se négliger**

negligence ['neglidʒəns] *noun* carelessness: *The accident was caused by the driver's negligence*. □ **négligence**
'negligent *adjective*. □ **négligent**
'negligently *adverb*. □ **négligemment**

negotiate [ni'gouʃieit] *verb* **1** to bargain or discuss a subject in order to agree. □ **négocier**
2 to arrange (a treaty, payment *etc*), *usually* after a long discussion. □ **négocier**
3 to get past (an obstacle or difficulty). □ **franchir**
ne'gotiator *noun*. □ **négociateur, trice**
ne,goti'ation *noun*: *Negotiations ended without any settlement being reached*; *The dispute was settled by negotiation*. □ **négociation**

Negro ['niːgrou] – *feminine* **'Negress**: *plural* **'Negroes** – *noun* (*usually considered offensive*) a name for a person belonging to or descended from the black-skinned race from the area of Africa south of the Sahara. □ **Noir, Noire**

neigh [nei] *verb* to utter the cry of a horse: *They could hear the horses neighing*. □ **hennir**
■ *noun* such a cry: *The horse gave a neigh*. □ **hennissement**

neighbour, neighbor ['neibə] *noun* a person who lives near oneself: *my next-door neighbour*. □ **voisin, ine**
'neighbourhood *noun* **1** a district or area, *especially* in a town or city: *a poor neighbourhood*. □ **quartier**
2 a district or area surrounding a particular place: *She lives somewhere in the neighbourhood of the station*. □ **voisinage**
'neighbouring *adjective* near or next in place: *France and Belgium are neighbouring countries*. □ **voisin**
'neighbourly *adjective* (*negative* **unneighbourly**) friendly: *a very neighbourly person*. □ **amical**

neither ['naiðə, 'niːðə(r)] *adjective, pronoun* not the one nor the other (of two things or people): *Neither window faces the sea*; *Neither of them could understand Italian*. □ **ni l'un ni l'autre, aucun des deux**
neither ... nor used to introduce alternatives which are both negative: *Neither Joan nor David could come*; *He can neither read nor write*. □ **ni...ni**

As with **either ... or**, the verb usually follows the noun or pronoun that comes closest to it: *Neither Kate nor I am responsible*; *Neither she nor her children speak English*.

neon ['niːon] *noun* an element, a colourless gas used in certain forms of electric lighting, *eg* advertising signs. □ **néon**

nephew ['nefjuː] – *feminine* **niece** [niːs] – *noun* the son or daughter of a brother or sister: *My sister's two sons are my nephews, and I am their uncle*. □ **neveu, nièce**

nerve [nəːv] *noun* **1** one of the cords which carry messages between all parts of the body and the brain. □ **nerf**
2 courage: *She must have needed a lot of nerve to do that*; *He lost his nerve*. □ **courage**
3 rudeness: *What nerve!* □ **toupet**
■ *verb* to force (oneself) to have enough courage (to do something): *He nerved himself to climb the high tower*. □ **s'armer de courage**
nerves *noun plural* the condition of being too easily excited or upset: *She suffers from nerves*. □ **nervosité**
'nervous *adjective* **1** of the nerves: *the nervous system*. □ **nerveux**
2 rather afraid: *She was nervous about travelling by air*; *a nervous young man*. □ **inquiet**
'nervously *adverb*. □ **nerveusement**
'nervousness *noun*. □ **nervosité**
'nervy *adjective* excitable: *The horse is rather nervy*. □ **énervé**
'nerviness *noun*. □ **énervement**
'nerve-racking *adjective* causing great anxiety or nervousness: *a nerve-racking experience*. □ **angoissant**
nervous breakdown a period of mental illness caused by a time of great strain. □ **dépression nerveuse**
nervous system the brain, spinal cord and nerves of a person or animal. □ **système nerveux**
get on someone's nerves to irritate someone: *His behaviour really gets on my nerves*. □ **taper sur les nerfs de**

nest [nest] *noun* a structure or place in which birds (and some animals and insects) hatch or give birth to and look after their young: *The swallows are building a nest under the roof of our house*; *a wasp's nest*. □ **nid**
■ *verb* to build a nest and live in it: *A pair of robins are nesting in that bush*. □ **faire son nid, nicher**

'nestling [-liŋ] noun a young bird (still in the nest). □ oisillon

'nest-egg noun a sum of money saved up for the future. □ pécule

nestle ['nesl] verb 1 to lie close together as if in a nest: *The children nestled together for warmth.* □ se blottir 2 to settle comfortably: *She nestled into the cushions.* □ se pelotonner

nestling see nest.

net[1] [net] noun (any of various devices for catching creatures, *eg* fish, or for any of a number of other purposes, consisting of) a loose open material made of knotted string, thread, wire *etc*: *a fishing-net; a hair-net; a tennis-net; (also adjective) a net curtain.* □ (de/au) filet
■ verb – past tense, past participle 'netted – to catch in a net: *They netted several tons of fish.* □ prendre au filet

'netting noun material made in the form of a net: *wire netting.* □ tulle, treillis

'netball noun a team-game in which a ball is thrown into a net hanging high up on a pole. □ netball

'network noun 1 anything in the form of a net, *ie* with many lines crossing each other: *A network of roads covered the countryside.* □ réseau
2 a widespread organization: *a radio network.* □ réseau

net[2] [net] adjective 1 (of a profit *etc*) remaining after all expenses *etc* have been paid: *The net profit from the sale was $200.* □ net
2 (of the weight of something) not including the packaging or container: *The sugar has a net weight of 1 kilogram; The sugar weighs one kilogram net.* □ net

netball see net[1].

netting see net[1].

nettle ['netl] noun a type of plant covered with hairs that cause a painful rash if touched. □ ortie

network see net[1].

neuter ['njuːtə] adjective 1 in certain languages, of the gender which is neither masculine nor feminine: *a neuter noun.* □ neutre
2 without sex: *Worker bees are neuter, being neither male nor female.* □ neutre

neutral ['njuːtrəl] adjective 1 not taking sides in a quarrel or war: *A neutral country was asked to help settle the dispute.* □ neutre
2 (of colour) not strong or definite: *Grey is a neutral colour.* □ neutre
3 (in electricity) neither positively nor negatively charged. □ neutre
■ noun 1 (a person belonging to) a nation that takes no part in a war or quarrel. □ (habitant, ante d'un) pays neutre
2 the position of the gear of an engine in which no power passes to the wheels *etc*: *I put the car into neutral.* □ point mort

neu'trality [-'tra-] noun the state of being neutral. □ neutralité

'neutralize, 'neutralise verb to make useless or harmless *usually* by causing an opposite effect. □ neutraliser

neutron ['njuːtron] noun one of the particles which make

up the nucleus of an atom. □ neutron

never ['nevə] adverb not ever; at no time: *I shall never go there again; Never have I been so angry; his never-failing kindness.* □ jamais

,never'more adverb never again. □ jamais plus

,neverthe'less [-ðə'les] adverb in spite of that: *I am feeling ill, but I shall come with you nevertheless.* □ malgré tout

new [njuː] adjective 1 having only just happened, been built, made, bought *etc*: *She is wearing a new dress; We are building a new house.* □ neuf
2 only just discovered, experienced *etc*: *Flying in an airplane was a new experience for her.* □ nouveau
3 changed: *He is a new man.* □ nouveau
4 just arrived *etc*: *The schoolchildren teased the new boy.* □ nouveau
■ adverb freshly: *new-laid eggs.* □ frais

'newly adverb only just; recently: *She is newly married; Her hair is newly cut.* □ récemment

newborn baby *noun* an infant or very young child a few days old: *The mother wrapped a blanket around her newborn baby to take her home from the hospital.* □ nouveau-né

'newcomer noun a person who has just arrived: *He is a newcomer to this district.* □ nouveau venu, nouvelle venue

,new'fangled [-'faŋgld] adjective (of things, ideas *etc*) too new to be considered reliable: *newfangled machines.* □ trop moderne

new to having no previous experience of: *He's new to this kind of work.* □ novice (dans)

news [njuːz] noun singular a report of, or information about, recent events: *You can hear the news on the radio at 9 o'clock; Is there any news about your friend?; (also adjective) a news broadcast.* □ (de) nouvelles; (d')informations; actualités

'newsy adjective full of news: *a newsy letter.* □ plein de nouvelles

'newsagent noun (also news dealer) a person who has a shop selling newspapers (and *usually* other goods). □ marchand, ande de journaux

'newscast noun a broadcast of news in a radio or television program. □ (bulletin d')informations; actualités télévisées

'newscaster noun a person who presents a news broadcast. □ présentateur, trice

'newsletter noun a sheet containing news issued to members of a group, organization *etc*. □ bulletin

'newspaper noun a paper, printed daily or weekly, containing news *etc*: *a daily newspaper.* □ journal

news is singular: *No news is good news.*

newt [njuːt] noun a type of small animal which lives on land and in water. □ triton

next [nekst] adjective nearest in place, time *etc*: *When you have called at that house, go on to the next one; The next person to arrive late will be sent away; Who is next on the list?* □ prochain, suivant, voisin
■ adverb immediately after in place or time: *John arrived first and Jane came next.* □ ensuite

■ *pronoun* the person or thing nearest in place, time *etc*: *Finish one question before you begin to answer the next*; *One minute he was sitting beside me – the next he was lying on the ground.* □ **le suivant, la suivante**

next best, biggest, oldest *etc* the one immediately after the best, biggest, oldest *etc*: *I can't go to Paris so London is the next best place.* □ **le plus (...) après**

next door *adverb* in the next house: *I live next door (to Mrs. Smith).* □ **à côté**

next to 1 beside: *She sat next to me.* □ **auprès de, à côté de**

2 closest to: *In height, George comes next to me.* □ **juste après**

3 more or less; pretty well: *My writing is next to illegible.* □ **pratiquement**

next to last not the final one, but the one beside that; the second to the end; one before the last: *Margot is the last one in line and Peter, who is standing just in front of her, is the next to last.* □ **avant-dernier**

nib [nib] *noun* (*also* '**pen-nib**) the pointed, metal part of a fountain-pen or other pen from which the ink flows. □ **(bec de) plume**

-nibbed: *a fine-nibbed pen.* □ **à plume (...)**

nibble ['nibl] *verb* to take very small bites (of): *She was nibbling (at) a biscuit.* □ **grignoter**

■ *noun* a small bite: *Have a nibble of this cake.* □ **bouchée**

nice [nais] *adjective* 1 pleasant; agreeable: *nice weather*; *a nice person.* □ **beau, gentil**

2 used jokingly: *We're in a nice mess now.* □ **beau, joli**

3 exact; precise: *a nice sense of timing.* □ **précis**

'**nicely** *adverb.* □ **bien, gentiment**

nicety ['naisəti] – *plural* '**niceties** – *noun* a precise or delicate detail. □ **raffinement**

to a nicety exactly: *She judged the distance to a nicety.* □ **exactement**

niche [nitʃ, niːʃ] *noun* 1 a hollow in a wall for a statue, ornament *etc*. □ **niche**

2 a suitable place in life: *He found his niche in engineering.* □ **voie**

Nichrome® ['naikroum] *noun* an alloy consisting of 60% nickel, 16% chromium and 24% iron. □ **nichrome**

nick [nik] *noun* a small cut: *There was a nick in the door-post.* □ **entaille**

■ *verb* to make a small cut in something: *He nicked his chin while he was shaving.* □ **faire une entaille**

in the nick of time at the last possible moment; just in time: *She arrived in the nick of time.* □ **juste à temps**

nickel ['nikl] *noun* 1 an element, a greyish-white metal used *especially* for mixing with other metals and for plating. □ **nickel**

2 a five cent coin. □ **pièce de cinq cents**

nickname ['nikneim] *noun* an informal name given in affection, admiration, dislike *etc*: *Wellington's nickname was 'the Iron Duke'.* □ **surnom, diminutif**

■ *verb* to give a nickname to: *We nicknamed her 'Foureyes' because she wore spectacles.* □ **surnommer**

nicotine ['nikətiːn] *noun* a harmful substance contained in tobacco. □ **nicotine**

niece *see* **nephew.**

niggardly ['nigədli] *adjective* not generous; unwilling to give or spend money: *He's niggardly with his money*; *a niggardly gift.* □ **chiche**

nigh [nai] *adverb* an old word for near. □ **près (de)**

'**well-nigh** nearly; almost: *It was well-nigh midnight when she arrived.* □ **presque**

night [nait] *noun* 1 the period from sunset to sunrise: *We sleep at night*; *They talked all night (long)*; *He travelled by night and rested during the day*; *The days were warm and the nights were cool*; (*also adjective*) *She is doing night work.* □ **(de) nuit**

2 the time of darkness: *In the Arctic in winter, night lasts for twenty-four hours out of twenty-four.* □ **nuit**

'**nightly** *adjective, adverb* every night: *a nightly news program*; *He goes there nightly.* □ **(de) tous les soirs**

'**nightclub** *noun* a club open at night for drinking, dancing, entertainment *etc*. □ **boîte de nuit**

'**nightfall** *noun* the beginning of night; dusk. □ **tombée de la nuit**

'**nightgown** *noun* a garment for wearing in bed. □ **chemise de nuit**

'**nightmare** *noun* a frightening dream: *I had a nightmare about being strangled.* □ **cauchemar**

'**nightmarish** *adjective.* □ **cauchemardesque**

'**night school** *noun* (a place providing) educational classes held in the evenings for people who are at work during the day. □ **école du soir**

'**night shift** 1 (a period of) work during the night: *I'm on (the) night shift this week.* □ **poste de nuit**

2 the people who work during this period: *We met the night shift leaving the factory.* □ **équipe de nuit**

'**nighttime** *noun* the time when it is night: *Owls are usually seen at nighttime.* □ **nuit**

,**night'watchman** *noun* a person who looks after a building *etc* during the night. □ **gardien, ienne de nuit**

nightingale ['naitiŋgeil] *noun* a type of small bird with a beautiful song. □ **rossignol**

nil [nil] *noun* (in scoring) nothing; zero: *Leeds United won two-nil/by two goals to nil.* □ **rien, zéro**

nimble ['nimbl] *adjective* quick and light in movement: *a nimble jump.* □ **agile, preste**

'**nimbly** *adverb.* □ **agilement, prestement**

nine [nain] *noun* 1 the number or figure 9. □ **neuf**

2 the age of 9. □ **neuf**

■ *adjective* 1 9 in number. □ **neuf**

2 aged 9. □ **neuf**

nine- having nine (of something): *a nine-page booklet.* □ **à neuf (...)**

ninth *noun* 1 one of nine equal parts. □ **neuvième**

2 (*also adjective*) the last of nine (people, things *etc*); the next after the eighth. □ **neuvième**

'**nine-year-old** *noun* a person or animal that is nine years old. □ **(individu, etc.) âgé de neuf ans**

■ *adjective* (of a person, animal or thing) that is nine years old. □ **de neuf ans**

ninepins ['nainpinz] *noun singular* a game in which nine bottle-shaped objects are knocked over with a ball: *a game of ninepins*; *Ninepins is a very good game.* □ **(jeu de) quilles**

nineteen [nain'tiːn] *noun* 1 the number or figure 19. □

dix-neuf
2 the age of 19. □ **dix-neuf ans**
■ *adjective* 1 19 in number. □ **dix-neuf**
2 aged 19. □ **dix-neuf**
nineteen- having nineteen (of something): *a nineteen-page document.* □ **à dix-neuf (...)**
,nine'teenth *noun* 1 one of nineteen equal parts. □ **dix-neuvième**
2 (*also adjective*) the last of nineteen (people, things *etc*); the next after the eighteenth. □ **dix-neuvième**
,nine'teen-year-old *noun* a person or animal that is nineteen years old. □ **(individu, etc.) âgé de dix-neuf ans**
■ *adjective* (of a person, animal or thing) that is nineteen years old. □ **de dix-neuf ans**
talk nineteen to the dozen to talk (to one another) continually or for a long time. □ **jacasser à qui mieux mieux**
ninety ['nainti] *noun* 1 the number or figure 90. □ **quatre-vingt-dix**
2 the age of 90. □ **quatre-vingt-dix ans**
■ *adjective* 1 90 in number. □ **quatre-vingt-dix**
2 aged 90. □ **de quatre-vingt-dix ans**
'nineties *noun plural* 1 the period of time between one's ninetieth and one hundredth birthdays. □ **entre quatre-vingt-dix et cent ans**
2 the range of temperatures between ninety and one hundred degrees. □ **dans les quatre-vingt-dix degrés**
3 the period of time between the ninetieth and one hundredth years of a century. □ **les années quatre-vingt-dix**
'ninetieth *noun* 1 one of ninety equal parts. □ **quatre-vingt-dixième**
2 (*also adjective*) the last of ninety (people, things *etc*); the next after the eighty-ninth. □ **quatre-vingt-dixième**
ninety- having ninety (of something): *a ninety-dollar fine.* □ **de quatre-vingt-dix (...)**
'ninety-year-old *noun* a person or animal that is ninety years old. □ **nonagénaire**
■ *adjective* (of a person, animal or thing) that is ninety years old. □ **nonagénaire**
nip [nip] – *past tense, past participle* **nipped** – *verb* 1 to press between the thumb and a finger, or between claws or teeth, causing pain; to pinch or bite: *A crab nipped her toe; The dog nipped his ankle.* □ **pincer; donner un coup de dent**
2 to cut with such an action: *He nipped the wire with the pliers; He nipped off the heads of the flowers.* □ **sectionner**
3 to sting: *Iodine nips when it is put on a cut.* □ **piquer**
4 to move quickly; to make a quick, *usually* short, journey: *I'll just nip into this shop for cigarettes; He nipped over to Paris for the week-end.* □ **faire un saut à**
5 to stop the growth of (plants *etc*): *The frost has nipped the roses.* □ **brûler**
■ *noun* 1 the act of pinching or biting: *His dog gave her a nip on the ankle.* □ **pincement; petit coup de dent**
2 a sharp stinging quality, or coldness in the weather: *a nip in the air.* □ **froid, piquant**
3 a small drink, *especially* of spirits. □ **petit verre**
'nippy *adjective* 1 (of the weather) cold. □ **âpre**

2 quick-moving; nimble: *a nippy little car.* □ **rapide, preste**
nip (something) in the bud to stop (something) as soon as it starts: *The managers nipped the strike in the bud.* □ **étouffer dans l'œuf**
nipa ['niːpə] *noun* a tropical palm tree with large feathery leaves used for thatching, mats *etc*. □ **nipah**
nipple ['nipl] *noun* 1 the darker, pointed part of a woman's breast from which a baby sucks milk; the equivalent part of a male breast. □ **mamelon**
2 the rubber mouthpiece of a baby's feeding-bottle; a teat. □ **tétine**
nippy *see* nip.
nit [nit] *noun* the egg of a louse or other small insect (*eg* found in a person's hair). □ **lente**
nitrate *see* nitrogen.
nitrogen ['naitrədʒən] *noun* an element, a type of gas making up nearly four-fifths of the air we breathe. □ **azote**
'nitrate *noun* any of several substances containing nitrogen often used as soil fertilizers. □ **nitrate**
no [nou] *adjective* 1 not any: *We have no food; No other person could have done it.* □ **pas de, aucun**
2 not allowed: *No smoking.* □ **défense de**
3 not a: *He is no friend of mine; This will be no easy task.* □ **ne pas, aucun**
■ *adverb* not (any): *He is no better at golf than swimming; She went as far as the shop and no further.* □ **pas, non**
■ *interjection* a word used for denying, disagreeing, refusing *etc*: *'Do you like travelling?' 'No, (I don't).'; No, I don't agree; 'Will you help me?' 'No, I won't.'* □ **non**
■ *noun plural* **noes** 1 a refusal: *She answered with a definite no.* □ **non**
2 a vote against something: *The noes have won.* □ **non**
'nobody *pronoun* no person; no one: *Nobody likes him.* □ **personne**
■ *noun* a very unimportant person: *She's just a nobody.* □ **moins que rien**
'no one *pronoun* no person; nobody: *She will see no one; No one is to blame.* □ **personne**
there's no saying, knowing *etc* it is impossible to say, know *etc*: *There's no denying it; There's no knowing what she will say.* □ **impossible de...**
nobility *see* noble.
noble ['noubl] *adjective* 1 honourable; unselfish: *a noble mind; a noble deed.* □ **noble**
2 of high birth or rank: *a noble family; of noble birth.* □ **noble**
■ *noun* a person of high birth: *The nobles planned to murder the king.* □ **noble**
no'bility [-'bi-] *noun* 1 the state of being noble: *the nobility of his mind/birth.* □ **noblesse**
2 nobles *ie* dukes, earls *etc*: *The nobility supported the king during the revolution.* □ **noblesse**
'nobly *adverb*: *He worked nobly for the cause of peace.* □ **noblement**
'nobleman – *feminine* 'noblewoman – *noun* a noble: *The queen was murdered by a nobleman at her court.* □ **noble**

nobody *see* **no.**

nocturnal [nok'tə:nl] *adjective* 1 active at night: *The owl is a nocturnal bird.* □ **nocturne**
2 happening at night: *a nocturnal encounter.* □ **nocturne**

nod [nod] – *past tense, past participle* 'nodded – *verb* 1 to make a quick forward and downward movement of the head to show agreement, as a greeting *etc*: *I asked her if she agreed and she nodded (her head); He nodded to the man as he passed him in the street.* □ **faire un signe de (la) tête**
2 to let the head fall forward and downward when sleepy: *Grandmother sat nodding by the fire.* □ **somnoler**
■ *noun* a nodding movement of the head: *He answered with a nod.* □ **signe de (la) tête**
nod off to fall asleep: *He nodded off while she was speaking to him.* □ **s'assoupir**

node [noud] *noun* 1 a small swelling *eg* in an organ of the body. □ **nodule**
2 a place, often swollen, where a leaf is attached to a stem. □ **nœud**

Noel, Noël [nou'el] *noun* an old word for Christmas. □ **Noël**

noise [noiz] *noun* 1 a sound: *I heard a strange noise outside; the noise of gunfire.* □ **bruit**
2 an unpleasantly loud sound: *I hate noise.* □ **bruit**
'noiseless *adjective* without any sound: *noiseless footsteps.* □ **silencieux**
'noiselessly *adverb.* □ **silencieusement**
'noisy *adjective* making a loud noise: *noisy children; a noisy engine.* □ **bruyant**
'noisily *adverb.* □ **bruyamment**

nomad ['noumad] *noun* one of a group of people with no permanent home who travel about with their sheep, cattle *etc*: *Many of the people of central Asia are nomads.* □ **nomade**
no'madic *adjective.* □ **nomade**
no'madically *adverb.* □ **de façon nomade**

no man's land ['noumanzland] *noun* land which no one owns or controls, *especially* between opposing armies. □ **zone neutre**

nominal ['nominəl] *adjective* 1 in name only, not in reality: *He is only the nominal head of the firm.* □ **de nom, nominal**
2 very small: *She had to pay only a nominal fine.* □ **insignifiant**

nominate ['nomineit] *verb* to name (someone) for possible election to a particular job *etc*: *They nominated him as captain.* □ **nommer**
,nomi'nation *noun* 1 the act of nominating: *the nomination of a president.* □ **nomination**
2 a suggestion of a particular person for a post *etc*: *We've had four nominations for the job.* □ **proposition**
,nomi'nee *noun* a person who is nominated for a job *etc*. □ **personne nommée**

non- [non] used with many words to change their meanings to the opposite; not. □ **non-**

nonagenarian [nonədʒi'neəriən] *noun* a person who is between ninety and ninety-nine years old. □ **nonagénaire**

non-alcoholic ['nonalkə'holik] *adjective* (of a drink) not

containing any alcohol. □ **non alcoolisé**

nonchalant ['nonʃələnt] *adjective* feeling or showing no excitement, fear or other emotion. □ **nonchalant**
'nonchalantly *adverb.* □ **nonchalamment**
'nonchalance *noun.* □ **nonchalance**

non-commissioned [nonkə'miʃənd] *adjective* not holding a commission (*ie* in the army, below the rank of second lieutenant). □ **non breveté, sous-conducteur**

non-conductor [,nonkən'dʌktə] *noun* a substance *etc* that does not easily conduct heat or electricity. □ **non conducteur**

nondescript ['nondiskript] *adjective* having no noticeable, interesting or memorable characteristics: *a nondescript sort of building.* □ **quelconque**

none [nʌn] *pronoun* not one; not any: *'How many tickets have you got?' 'None'; She asked me for some food but there was none in the house; None of us have/has seen him; None of your cheek!* (= Don't be cheeky!). □ **aucun**
■ *adverb* not at all: *She is none the worse for her accident.* □ **pas plus/moins**
none but only: *None but the brave deserve our respect.* □ **seul**
,none'the'less nevertheless; in spite of this: *She had a headache, but she wanted to come with us nonetheless.* □ **néanmoins**

> **none** can be followed by a singular or plural verb: *None of the children like(s) the new teacher.*

nonetheless *see* **none.**

non-existent [nonig'zistənt] *adjective* not existing; not real: *He is afraid of some non-existent monster.* □ **inexistant**
,non-ex'istence *noun.* □ **non-existence**

non-fiction [non'fikʃən] *noun* books, magazines *etc* giving facts, information *etc, ie* not stories, novels, plays, poetry: *I read a lot of non-fiction.* □ **ouvrages généraux**

non-flammable [non'flaməbl] *adjective* non-inflammable: *Babies' clothes should be non-flammable.* □ **ininflammable**

non-inflammable [nonin'flaməbl] *adjective* not able to burn or be set alight: *non-inflammable material; Asbestos is non-inflammable.* □ **ininflammable, ignifuge**

nonplussed [non'plʌst] *adjective* completely puzzled; bewildered. □ **dérouté**

non-resident [non'rezidənt] *adjective* not living in (a school *etc*): *We have several non-resident members of staff.* □ **non résidant**

nonsense ['nons'ns, -sens] *noun* foolishness; foolish words, actions *etc*; something that is ridiculous: *He's talking nonsense; The whole book is a lot of nonsense; What nonsense!* □ **absurdité(s)**
,non'sensical [-'sen-] *adjective.* □ **absurde**

non-starter [non'sta:tə] *noun* a horse or person that, though entered for a race, does not run. □ **non-partant**

non-stick [non'stik] *adjective* (of a pan *etc*) treated, *usually* by covering with a special substance, so that food *etc* will not stick to it: *a non-stick frying-pan.* □ **qui n'attache pas**

non-stop [non'stop] *adjective* continuing without a stop:

non-stop entertainment; *Is this train non-stop?* □ **sans arrêt, direct**

non-violence [non'vaiələns] *noun* the refusal to use any violent means in order to gain political, social *etc* aims. □ **non-violence**

,**non-'violent** *adjective.* □ **non violent**

noodle ['nuːdl] *noun* a strip of paste *usually* made with water, flour and egg: *fried noodles.* □ **nouille(s)**

nook [nuk] *noun* a quiet, dark corner or place. □ **(re)coin**

every nook and cranny everywhere: *They searched in every nook and cranny.* □ **tous les coins et recoins**

noon [nuːn] *noun* twelve o'clock midday: *They arrived at noon.* □ **midi**

noose [nuːs] *noun* 1 a loop in rope, wire *etc* that becomes tighter when pulled. □ **nœud coulant**

2 such a loop in a rope used for hanging a person. □ **nœud coulant**

nor [noː] *conjunction* and not: *She did not know then what had happened, nor did she ever find out*; *I'm not going, nor is Joan.* □ **d'ailleurs, non plus**

normal ['noːməl] *adjective* usual; without any special characteristics or circumstances: *How much work do you do on a normal day?*; *normal people*; *His behaviour is not normal.* □ **normal, régulier**

nor'mality [-'ma-] *noun.* □ **normalité**

normally *adverb* 1 in a usual, ordinary way: *He was behaving quite normally yesterday.* □ **normalement**

2 usually; most often: *I normally go home at 4 o'clock.* □ **normalement**

north [noːθ] *noun* 1 the direction to the left of a person facing the rising sun, or any part of the earth lying in that direction: *She faced towards the north*; *The wind is blowing from the north*; *I used to live in the north of England.* □ **nord**

2 (*also* N) one of the four main points of the compass. □ **nord**

■ *adjective* 1 in the north: *on the north bank of the river.* □ **septentrional**

2 from the direction of the north: *a north wind.* □ **du nord**

■ *adverb* towards the north: *The stream flows north.* □ **vers le nord**

'**northerly** [-ðə-] *adjective* 1 (of a wind *etc*) coming from the north: *a northerly breeze.* □ **du nord**

2 looking, lying *etc* towards the north: *in a northerly direction.* □ **au/vers le nord**

'**northern** [-ðən] *adjective* of the north or the North. □ **du nord, septentrional**

'**northerner** [-ðə-] *noun* a person who lives, or was born, in a northern region or country. □ **habitant, ante du Nord**

'**northernmost** [-ðən-] *adjective* being furthest north: *the northernmost point of the coast.* □ **à l'extrême nord**

'**northward** *adjective* towards the north: *in a northward direction.* □ **au nord**

'**northward(s)** *adverb* towards the north: *They were travelling northwards.* □ **vers le nord**

'**northbound** *adjective* travelling northwards: *the northbound railway-line.* □ **en direction du nord**

,**north'east/,north'west** *nouns, adjective* (in or from) the direction midway between north and east or north and west, or any part of the earth lying in that direction: *the northeast counties*; *a northwest wind.* □ **(du) nord-est; (du) nord-ouest**

■ *adverb* towards the northeast or northwest: *The building faces northwest.* □ **au/vers le nord-est; au/vers le nord-ouest**

,**north'easterly/,north'westerly** *adjective* 1 (of a wind *etc*) coming from the northeast or northwest: *a north-easterly wind.* □ **du nord-est; du nord-ouest**

2 looking, lying *etc* towards the northeast or northwest: *a northwesterly direction.* □ **au/vers le nord-est; au/vers le nord-ouest**

,**north'eastern/,north'western** *adjective* of the northeast or northwest. □ **nord-est; nord-ouest**

the North Pole the northern end of the imaginary line through the earth, around which it turns. □ **pôle Nord**

nose [nouz] *noun* 1 the part of the face by which people and animals smell and *usually* breathe: *I held the flower to my nose*; *I punched the man on the nose.* □ **nez**

2 the sense of smell: *Police dogs have good noses and can follow criminals' trails.* □ **odorat**

3 the part of anything which is like a nose in shape or position: *the nose of an airplane.* □ **nez**

■ *verb* 1 to make a way by pushing carefully forward: *The ship nosed (its way) through the ice.* □ **(s')avancer avec précaution**

2 to look or search as if by smelling: *She nosed about (in) the cupboard.* □ **fureter**

-**nosed**: *a long-nosed dog.* □ **au nez (...)**

'**nos(e)y** *adjective* taking too much interest in other people and what they are doing: *Our nos(e)y neighbours are always looking in through our windows.* □ **curieux, fureteur**

'**nosily** *adverb.* □ **indiscrètement**

'**nosiness** *noun.* □ **indiscrétion**

'**nose-bag** *noun* food-bag for horses, hung over the head. □ **musette (mangeoire)**

'**nosedive** *noun* a dive or fall with the head or nose first: *The airplane did a nosedive into the sea.* □ **piqué**

■ *verb* to make such a dive: *Suddenly the plane nosedived.* □ **descendre en piqué**

follow one's nose to go straight forward. □ **continuer tout droit**

lead by the nose to make (a person) do whatever one wants. □ **mener par le bout du nez**

nose out to find (as if) by smelling: *The dog nosed out its master's glove.* □ **flairer**

pay through the nose to pay a lot, or too much. □ **payer le prix fort**

turn up one's nose at to treat with contempt: *He turned up his nose at the school dinner.* □ **faire le dégoûté devant**

under (a person's) (very) nose right in front of (a person): *The book was right under my very nose*; *He stole the money from under my very nose.* □ **(en plein) sous le nez**

nosegay ['nouzgei] *noun* a bunch of sweet-smelling flowers. □ **petit bouquet**

nostalgia [no'staldʒə] *noun* a longing for past times: *She*

felt a great nostalgia for her childhood. □ **nostalgie**
no'stalgic *adjective*. □ **nostalgique**
no'stalgically *adverb*. □ **nostalgiquement**

nostril ['nostril] *noun* one of the two openings in the
nose through which one breathes, smells *etc*. □ **narine**

not [not] *adverb* 1 (*often abbreviated to* **n't**) a word used
for denying, forbidding, refusing, or expressing the opposite of something: *I did not see her; I didn't see him;
He isn't here; Isn't she coming?; They told me not to go;
Not a single person came to the party; We're going to
London, not Paris; That's not true!* □ **ne...pas**
2 used with certain verbs such as **hope, seem, believe,
expect** and also with **be afraid**: *'Have you got much
money?' 'I'm afraid not'; 'Is she going to fail her exam?'
'I hope not'.* □ **non**
not at all it does not matter; it is not important *etc*:
'Thank you for helping me.' 'Not at all.' □ **de rien**

notable *etc see* **note.**

notation [nə'teiʃən] *noun* (the use of) a system of signs
representing numbers, musical sounds *etc*: *musical/
mathematical notation.* □ **notation**

notch [notʃ] *noun* a small V-shaped cut: *He cut a notch
in his stick.* □ **coche**
■ *verb* to make a notch in. □ **encocher**

note [nout] *noun* 1 a piece of writing to call attention to
something: *She left me a note about the meeting.* □ **note**
2 (*in plural*) ideas for a speech, details from a lecture
etc written down in short form: *The students took notes
on the professor's lecture.* □ **notes**
3 a written or mental record: *Have you kept a note of
his name?* □ **note**
4 a short explanation: *There is a note at the bottom of
the page about that difficult word.* □ **note**
5 a short letter: *She wrote a note to her friend.* □ **mot**
6 (**bill**) a piece of paper used as money; a banknote: *a
five-dollar note.* □ **billet**
7 a musical sound: *The song ended on a high note.* □
note
8 a written or printed symbol representing a musical
note. □ **note**
9 an impression or feeling: *The conference ended on a
note of hope.* □ **note**
■ *verb* 1 (*often with* **down**) to write down: *He noted
(down) her telephone number in his diary.* □ **noter**
2 to notice; to be aware of: *He noted a change in her
behaviour.* □ **remarquer**
'notable *adjective* worth taking notice of; important:
There were several notable people at the meeting. □
notable
,nota'bility *noun*. □ **notabilité**
'notably *adverb* 1 in particular: *Several people offered
to help, notably Mrs. Brown.* □ **notamment**
2 in a noticeable way: *Her behaviour was notably different from usual.* □ **notablement**
'noted *adjective* well-known: *a noted author; This town
is noted for its cathedral.* □ **célèbre**
'notebook *noun* a small book in which to write notes. □
carnet, calepin
'notepaper *noun* paper for writing letters. □ **papier à
lettres**

'noteworthy *adjective* worthy of notice; remarkable. □
remarquable
'noteworthiness *noun*. □ **importance**
take note of to notice and remember: *He took note of
the change in her appearance.* □ **prendre note de**

nothing ['nʌθiŋ] *pronoun* no thing; not anything: *There
was nothing in the cupboard; I have nothing new to
say.* □ **rien**
■ *noun* the number 0; nought: *a telephone number with
three nothings in it.* □ **zéro**
■ *adverb* not at all: *He's nothing like his father.* □ **en
rien**
'nothingness *noun* the state of being nothing or of not
existing; emptiness. □ **néant**
come to nothing to fail: *Her plans came to nothing.* □
ne pas aboutir
for nothing 1 free; without payment: *I'll do that job for
you for nothing.* □ **pour rien**
2 without result; in vain: *I've been working on this book
for six years, and all for nothing!* □ **inutilement**
have nothing to do with 1 to avoid completely: *After I
came out of prison, many of my friends would have nothing to do with me.* □ **ignorer**
2 (also **be nothing to do with**) to be something that a
person ought not to be interested in: *This letter has/is
nothing to do with you.* □ **n'avoir rien à voir avec**
make nothing of not to understand: *I can make nothing of this letter.* □ **ne rien comprendre à**
mean nothing to not to be understandable to: *These
mathematical figures mean nothing to me.* □ **ne rien
vouloir dire**
next to nothing almost nothing: *The child was wearing next to nothing.* □ **presque rien**
nothing but just; only: *The fellow's nothing but a fool!*
□ **rien que**
nothing doing! an expression used to show a strong or
emphatic refusal: *'Would you like to go to the meeting
instead of me?' 'Nothing doing!'* □ **pas question!**
there is nothing to it it is easy: *You'll soon see how to
do this job – there's nothing to it!* □ **c'est facile (comme
tout)**
think nothing of not to consider difficult, unusual *etc*:
*My father thought nothing of walking 8 kilometres to
school when he was a boy.* □ **trouver (tout) naturel de**
to say nothing of as well as; and in addition: *When
they come to stay with us, they bring all their clothes
with them, to say nothing of their three dogs.* □ **sans
parler de**

notice ['noutis] *noun* 1 a written or printed statement to
announce something publicly: *He stuck a notice on the
door, saying that he had gone home; They put a notice
in the paper announcing the birth of their daughter.* □
avis, entrefilet
2 attention: *I'll bring the problem to his notice as soon
as possible.* □ **attention**
3 warning given *especially* before leaving a job or dismissing someone: *Her employer gave her a month's
notice; The cook gave in her notice; Please give notice
of your intentions.* □ **préavis, congé**
■ *verb* to see, observe, or keep in one's mind: *I noticed*

a book on the table; *He noticed her leave the room; Did he say that? I didn't notice.* □ **(s')apercevoir, remarquer, constater**
'**noticeable** *adjective* (likely to be) easily noticed: *There's a slight stain on this dress but it's not really noticeable.* □ **visible**
'**noticeably** *adverb*: *This ball of wool is noticeably darker than these others.* □ **visiblement**
'**noticed** *adjective* (*negative* **unnoticed**). □ **remarqué**
'**notice board** ('**bulletin board**) *noun* a *usually* large board *eg* in a hall, school *etc* on which notices are put. □ **panneau d'affichage**
at short notice without much warning time for preparation *etc*: *She had to make the speech at very short notice when her boss suddenly fell ill.* □ **à la dernière minute**
take notice of to pay attention to: *I never take any notice of what my father says; Take no notice of gossip.* □ **tenir compte de**
notify ['noutifai] *verb* to inform or warn about something: *He notified the headmistress of his intentions; If there has been an accident you must notify the police.* □ **avertir**
,notifi'cation [-fi-] *noun*. □ **avis**
notion ['nouʃən] *noun* 1 understanding: *I've no notion what she's talking about.* □ **idée, notion**
2 an uncertain belief; an idea: *He has some very odd notions.* □ **idée**
3 a desire for something or to do something: *He had a sudden notion to visit his aunt.* □ **idée**
notorious [nə'to:riəs] *adjective* well-known for badness or wickedness: *a notorious murderer.* □ **notoire**
notoriety [noutə'raiəti] *noun*. □ **(triste) notoriété**
no'toriously *adverb*. □ **notoirement**
notwithstanding [notwið'standiŋ] *preposition* in spite of: *Notwithstanding the bad weather, the ship arrived on time.* □ **en dépit de**
nougat ['nʌgət, 'nu:gɑ:] *noun* a sticky kind of sweet containing nuts *etc*. □ **nougat**
nought [no:t] *noun* 1 nothing. □ **rien**
2 the figure 0: *The number contained five noughts.* □ **zéro**
noun [naun] *noun* a word used as the name of a person, animal, place, state or thing: *The words 'girl', 'James' and 'happiness' are all nouns.* □ **nom**
nourish ['nʌriʃ] *verb* to cause or help to grow, become healthy *etc*. □ **nourrir**
'**nourishing** *adjective* giving the body what is necessary for health and growth: *nourishing food.* □ **nourrissant**
'**nourishment** *noun* something that nourishes; food: *Plants draw nourishment from the earth.* □ **nourriture**
novel[1] ['novəl] *noun* a book telling a long story in prose: *the novels of Charles Dickens.* □ **roman**
'**novelist** *noun* the writer of a novel: *Virginia Woolf was a great novelist.* □ **romancier, ière**
novel[2] ['novəl] *adjective* new and strange: *a novel idea.* □ **original**
'**novelty** – *plural* '**novelties** – *noun* 1 newness and strangeness: *It took her a long time to get used to the*

novelty of her surroundings. □ **étrangeté**
2 something new and strange: *Snow is a novelty to people from hot countries.* □ **innovation**
3 a small, cheap manufactured thing sold as a toy or souvenir: *a stall selling novelties.* □ **article de fantaisie**
November [nə'vembə] *noun* the eleventh month of the year, the month following October. □ **novembre**
novice ['novis] *noun* 1 a beginner in any skill *etc*. □ **novice**
2 a monk or nun who has not yet taken all his or her vows. □ **novice**
now [nau] *adverb* 1 (at) the present period of time: *I am now living in England.* □ **à présent**
2 at once; immediately: *I can't do it now – you'll have to wait.* □ **maintenant**
3 (at) this moment: *He'll be at home now; From now on, I shall be more careful about what I say to her.* □ **maintenant; à partir de maintenant**
4 (in stories) then; at that time: *We were now very close to the city.* □ **alors**
5 because of what has happened *etc*: *I now know better than to trust her.* □ **dans ces circonstances**
6 a word in explanations, warnings, commands, or to show disbelief: *Now this is what happened; Stop that, now!; Do be careful, now.* □ **bon! allons!**
■ *conjunction* (*often with* that) because or since something has happened, is now true *etc*: *Now that you are here, I can leave; Now you have left school, you will have to find a job.* □ **maintenant que**
'**nowadays** *adverb* at the present period of time: *Food is very expensive nowadays.* □ **actuellement**
for now: *That will be enough for now – we'll continue our conversation tomorrow.* □ **pour l'instant**
just now a moment ago: *I saw him just now in the street.* □ **à l'instant**
(every) now and then/again sometimes; occasionally: *We go to the theatre (every) now and then.* □ **de temps à autre, par moment**
now, now! an expression used to warn or rebuke: *Now, now! Behave yourself!* □ **allons, allons!**
now playing being currently shown or being presented for a limited time as a movie or play: *The movie that is now playing was advertised on a poster outside the theatre* □ **à l'affiche**
now then an expression used for calming people *etc*: *'Now then,' said the policeman, 'what's going on here?'* □ **bon**
nowhere ['nouweə] *adverb* in or to no place; not anywhere: *It was nowhere to be found; 'Where have you been?' 'Nowhere in particular.'* □ **nulle part**
nowhere near not nearly: *We've nowhere near enough money to buy a car.* □ **loin de**
nozzle ['nozl] *noun* a narrow end-piece fitted to a pipe, tube *etc*: *The fireman pointed the nozzle of the hosepipe at the fire.* □ **douille, bec, gicleur**
-n't *see* not.
nucleus ['nju:kliəs] – *plural* '**nuclei** [-kliai] – *noun* 1 the central part of an atom. □ **noyau**
2 the part of a plant or animal cell that controls its development. □ **nucléus, noyau**

nuclear ['njuːkliə] *adjective* **1** using atomic energy: *a nuclear power station.* □ **nucléaire**
2 of a nucleus. □ **nucléaire**
nuclear disarmament the act of ceasing to store atomic weapons. □ **désarmement nucléaire**
nuclear energy atomic energy. □ **énergie nucléaire**
nuclear reactor an apparatus for producing nuclear energy. □ **réacteur nucléaire**

nude [njuːd] *adjective* without clothes; naked. □ **nu**
■ *noun* a photograph, picture *etc* of an unclothed human figure. □ **nu**
'**nudism** *noun* the practice of not wearing clothes *usually* because it is thought to be healthy. □ **nudisme**
'**nudist** *noun.* □ **nudiste**
'**nudity** *noun* the state of not wearing clothes. □ **nudité**
in the nude without clothes. □ **nu**

nudge [nʌdʒ] *noun* a gentle push *usually* with the elbow: *He gave her a nudge.* □ **(petit) coup de coude**
■ *verb* to hit gently, *usually* with the elbow: *She nudged him in the ribs.* □ **pousser du coude**

nudism *etc see* nude.

nugget ['nʌɡit] *noun* a lump, *especially* of gold. □ **pépite**

nuisance ['njuːsns] *noun* a person or thing that is annoying or troublesome: *That child is a terrible nuisance.* □ **plaie, fléau**

numb [nʌm] *adjective* not able to feel or move: *My arm has gone numb; She was numb with cold.* □ **engourdi**
■ *verb* to make numb: *The cold numbed his fingers.* □ **engourdir**
'**numbly** *adverb.* □ **d'une manière engourdie**
'**numbness** *noun.* □ **engourdissement**

number ['nʌmbə] *noun* **1** (*sometimes abbreviated to* **no** – *plural* **nos** – *when written in front of a figure*) a word or figure showing *eg* how many of something there are, or the position of something in a series *etc*: *Seven was often considered a magic number; Answer nos 1–10 of exercise 2.* □ **nombre; numéro**
2 a (large) quantity or group (of people or things): *She has a number of records; There were a large number of people in the room.* □ **un grand nombre de**
3 one issue of a magazine: *the autumn number.* □ **numéro**
4 a popular song or piece of music: *He sang his most popular number.* □ **numéro**
■ *verb* **1** to put a number on: *She numbered the pages in the top corner.* □ **numéroter**
2 to include: *He numbered her among his closest friends.* □ **compter**
3 to come to in total: *The group numbered ten.* □ **compter**
'**numberless** *adjective* very many. □ **innombrable**
his *etc* **days are numbered** he *etc* won't last much longer. □ **ses jours sont comptés**
without number very many: *I've told him times without number* (= very often) *not to do that.* □ **innombrable**

a number of, meaning 'several', is plural: *A number of boys are absent today.*
the number of, meaning 'the total quantity of' is singular: *The number of girls in the class is small.*

numeral ['njuːmərəl] *noun* a figure used to express a number: *1, 10, 50 are Arabic numerals; I, X, L are Roman numerals.* □ **chiffre**
nu'merical [-'me-] *adjective* of, using or consisting of numbers: *a numerical code.* □ **numérique**
nu'merically *adverb.* □ **numériquement**

numerate ['njuːmərət] *adjective* having a basic understanding of mathematics and science. □ **qui a le sens des mathématiques/sciences**
numerical *etc see* numeral.

numerous ['njuːmərəs] *adjective* very many: *His faults are too numerous to mention.* □ **nombreux**

nun [nʌn] *noun* a member of a female religious community. □ **religieuse**
'**nunnery** – *plural* '**nunneries** – *noun* a house in which a group of nuns live; a convent. □ **couvent**

nuptial ['nʌpʃəl] *adjective* of marriage. □ **nuptial**

nurse [nəːs] *noun* **1** a person who looks after sick or injured people in hospital: *She wants to be a nurse.* □ **infirmier, ière**
2 a person, *usually* a woman, who looks after small children: *The children have gone out with their nurse.* □ **nurse**
■ *verb* **1** to look after sick or injured people, *especially* in a hospital: *He was nursed back to health.* □ **soigner**
2 to give (a baby) milk from the breast. □ **allaiter**
3 to hold with care: *She was nursing a kitten.* □ **bercer (dans ses bras)**
4 to have or encourage (feelings *eg* of anger or hope) in oneself. □ **nourrir**
'**nursery** – *plural* '**nurseries** – *noun* **1** a room *etc* for young children. □ **chambre d'enfants**
2 a place where young plants are grown. □ **pépinière**
'**nursing** *noun* the profession of a nurse who cares for the sick. □ **profession d'infirmier, ière**
'**nursemaid** *noun* a nurse who looks after small children. □ **bonne d'enfants**
'**nurseryman** *noun* a person who runs, or works in, a nursery for plants. □ **pépiniériste**
nursery rhyme a short, simple poem for children. □ **comptine**
nursery school a school for very young children. □ **jardin d'enfants, école maternelle**
'**nursing home** *noun* a small private hospital. □ **clinique**

nurture ['nəːtʃə] *verb* to encourage the growth and development of (a child, plant *etc*). □ **élever**
■ *noun* care; help in growing or developing. □ **soins, nourriture**

nut [nʌt] *noun* **1** a fruit consisting of a single seed in a hard shell: *a hazel-nut; a walnut.* □ **fruit à écale**
2 a small round piece of metal with a hole through it, for screwing on the end of a bolt to hold pieces of wood, metal *etc* together: *a nut and bolt.* □ **écrou**
'**nutty** *adjective* **1** containing, or tasting of, nuts: *a nutty flavour.* □ **aux noisettes, au goût de noisette**
2 a slang word for mad: *He's quite nutty.* □ **cinglé**
'**nutcracker** *noun* (*usually in plural*) an instrument for cracking nuts open: *a pair of nutcrackers.* □ **casse-noisettes**

'**nutshell** *noun* the hard covering of a nut. □ **coquille de noix**

in a nutshell expressed, described *etc* very briefly: *I'll tell you the story in a nutshell.* □ **en un mot**

nutmeg ['nʌtmeg] *noun* a hard seed ground into a powder and used as a spice in food. □ **(noix) muscade**

nutritious [njuˈtriʃəs] *adjective* valuable as food; nourishing. □ **nutritif; nourrissant**

nutrient ['njuːtriənt] *noun* a substance which gives nourishment: *This food contains important nutrients.* □ **élément nutritif**

'**nutriment** *noun* nourishment; food. □ **nourriture**

nu'trition *noun* (the act of giving or getting) nourishment, or the scientific study of this. □ **nutrition**

nu'tritional *adjective*. □ **alimentaire**

nutshell, nutty *see* **nut**.

nuzzle ['nʌzl] *verb* to press, rub or caress with the nose: *The horse nuzzled (against) her cheek.* □ **faire des caresses à qqn**

nylon ['nailən] *noun, adjective* (of) a type of material made from chemicals and used for clothes, ropes, brushes *etc*: *a nylon shirt.* □ **(de/en) nylon**

'**nylons** *noun plural* stockings made of nylon: *three pairs of nylons.* □ **bas de nylon**

nymph [nimf] *noun* a goddess or spirit of the rivers, trees *etc*. □ **nymphe**

Oo

o [ou] *interjection* an expression used when speaking to a person, thing *etc*. □ **ô!**
See also **oh**.

oaf [ouf] *noun* a stupid or clumsy person: *That stupid oaf is always knocking things over.* □ **balourd, ourde**
'**oafish** *adjective*. □ **mufle**

oak [ouk] *noun* a type of large tree with hard wood. □ **chêne**
■ *adjective: trees in an oak wood; a room with oak panelling.* □ **chêne**

oar [oɪ] *noun* a long piece of wood with a flat end for rowing a boat. □ **aviron, rame**

oasis [ou'eisis] – *plural* o'**ases** [-siːz] – *noun* an area in a desert where water is found: *The travellers stopped at an oasis.* □ **oasis**

oath [ouθ] – *plural* **oaths** [ouθs, ouðz] – *noun* **1** a solemn promise: *He swore an oath to tell the truth.* □ **serment**
2 a word or phrase used when swearing: *curses and oaths.* □ **juron**
on/under oath having sworn an oath to tell the truth in a court of law: *The witness is on/under oath.* □ **sous serment**

oats [outs] *noun plural or singular* a type of cereal plant or its grain (seeds): *a field of oats; Horses eat oats.* □ **avoine**

obedience, obedient *see* **obey**.

obese [ə'biːs] *adjective* (of people) very fat. □ **obèse**
o'**besity** *noun: Obesity is a danger to health.* □ **obésité**

obey [ə'bei] *verb* to do what one is told to do: *I obeyed the order.* □ **obéir (à)**
obedience [ə'biːdjəns] *noun* **1** the act of obeying: *obedience to an order.* □ **obéissance**
2 willingness to obey: *They showed great obedience.* □ **soumission**
o'**bedient** *adjective: an obedient and well-behaved child.* □ **obéissant**
o'**bediently** *adverb*. □ **docilement**

obituary [ə'bitjuəri] – *plural* o'**bituaries** – *noun* a notice (*eg* in a newspaper) of a person's death, often with an account of his life and work. □ **nécrologie**

object¹ ['obdʒikt] *noun* **1** a thing that can be seen or felt: *There were various objects on the table.* □ **objet**
2 an aim or intention: *His main object in life was to become rich.* □ **but**
3 the word or words in a sentence or phrase which represent(s) the person or thing affected by the action of the verb: *He hit me; You can eat what you like.* □ **complément (d'objet)**

object² [əb'dʒekt] *verb* (*often with* **to**) to feel or express dislike or disapproval: *She wanted us to travel on foot but I objected (to that).* □ **désapprouver, s'objecter à**
objection [əb'dʒekʃən] *noun* **1** an expression of disapproval: *She raised no objection to the idea.* □ **objection**
2 a reason for disapproving: *My objection is that he is too young.* □ **objection**
ob'**jectionable** [-'dʒekʃə-] *adjective* unpleasant: *a very*

objectionable person. □ **désagréable**
ob'**jectionably** *adverb*. □ **désagréablement**

objective [əb'dʒektiv] *noun* a thing aimed at: *Our objective is freedom.* □ **objectif**
■ *adjective* not influenced by personal opinions *etc: She tried to take an objective view of the situation.* □ **objectif**
ob'**jectively** *adverb: He considered the problem objectively.* □ **objectivement**

oblige [ə'blaidʒ] *verb* **1** to force to do something: *She was obliged to go; The police obliged him to leave.* □ **obliger à**
2 to do (someone) a favour or service: *Could you oblige me by carrying this, please?* □ **rendre service (à)**
obligation [obli'geiʃən] *noun* a promise or duty: *You are under no obligation to buy this.* □ **obligation**
obligatory [ə'bligətəri] *adjective* compulsory: *Attendance at tonight's meeting is obligatory.* □ **obligatoire**
o'**bligatorily** *adverb*. □ **obligatoirement**
o'**bliging** *adjective* willing to help other people: *He'll help you – he's very obliging.* □ **obligeant, serviable**
o'**bligingly** *adverb*. □ **obligeamment**

oblique [ə'bliːk] *adjective* **1** sloping: *She drew an oblique line from one corner of the paper to the other.* □ **oblique**
2 not straight or direct: *He made an oblique reference to his work.* □ **indirect**
o'**bliquely** *adverb*. □ **obliquement**

obliterate [ə'blitəreit] *verb* **1** to cover, to prevent from being visible: *The sand-storm obliterated his footprints.* □ **effacer**
2 to destroy completely: *The town was obliterated by the bombs.* □ **rayer**

oblivious [ə'bliviəs] *adjective* unaware of or not paying attention to: *I was oblivious of what was happening; She was oblivious to our warnings.* □ **oublieux, inconscient**
o'**bliviously** *adverb*. □ **sans se rendre compte de**

oblong ['oblɒŋ] *noun* a two-dimensional, rectangular figure, but with one pair of opposite sides longer than the other pair. □ **rectangle**
■ *adjective* shaped like this: *an oblong table.* □ **rectangulaire**

obnoxious [əb'nɒkʃəs] *adjective* offensive: *an obnoxious person; The smell of that mixture is really obnoxious.* □ **odieux, nauséabond**
ob'**noxiously** *adverb*. □ **odieusement**

oboe ['oubou] *noun* a type of high-pitched woodwind musical instrument. □ **hautbois**
'**oboist** *noun*. □ **hautboïste**

obscene [əb'siːn] *adjective* disgusting, *especially* sexually: *obscene photographs.* □ **obscène**
ob'**scenely** *adverb*. □ **obscènement**
obscenity [-'se-] – *plural* ob'**scenities** – *noun* an obscene act or word(s): *He shouted obscenities at the police.* □ **obscénité**

obscure [əb'skjuə] *adjective* **1** not clear; difficult to see: *an obscure corner of the library.* □ **obscur**
2 not well-known: *an obscure author.* □ **obscur**
3 difficult to understand: *an obscure poem.* □ **obscur**
■ *verb* to make obscure: *A large tree obscured the view.*

School

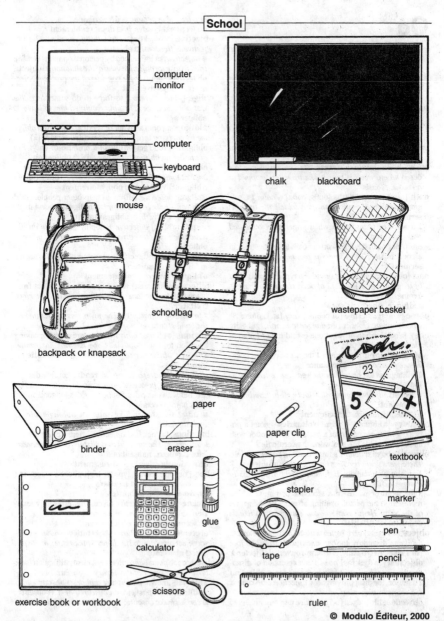

computer monitor

computer

keyboard

mouse

chalk

blackboard

backpack or knapsack

schoolbag

wastepaper basket

paper

paper clip

textbook

binder

eraser

exercise book or workbook

calculator

glue

stapler

marker

tape

pen

pencil

scissors

ruler

□ **obscurcir**
ob'scurely *adverb.* □ **obscurément**
ob'scurity *noun.* □ **obscurité**
obsequious [əb'siːkwiəs] *adjective* too humble or too ready to agree with someone: *He bowed in an obsequious manner.* □ **obséquieux**
ob'sequiously *adverb.* □ **obséquieusement**
ob'sequiousness *noun.* □ **obséquiosité**
observe [əb'zəːv] *verb* 1 to notice: *I observed her late arrival.* □ **remarquer**
2 to watch carefully: *She observed his actions with interest.* □ **observer**
3 to obey: *We must observe the rules.* □ **observer**
4 to make a remark: *'It's a lovely day', he observed.* □ **faire observer**
ob'servance *noun* 1 the act of obeying rules *etc*: *the observance of the law.* □ **observation**
2 the act of observing (a tradition *etc*): *the observance of religious holidays.* □ **observance**
ob'servant *adjective* quick to notice: *An observant girl remembered the car's registration number.* □ **observateur**
,**obser'vation** [ob-] *noun* 1 the act of noticing or watching: *She is in hospital for observation.* □ **observation, surveillance**
2 a remark. □ **observation**
ob'servatory – *plural* **ob'servatories** – *noun* a place for observing and studying the stars, weather *etc*. □ **observatoire**
ob'server *noun* a person who observes. □ **observateur, trice**
obsess [əb'ses] *verb* to occupy (someone's mind) too much: *He is obsessed by the fear of death.* □ **obséder**
ob'session [-ʃən] *noun*: *an obsession about motorbikes.* □ **obsession**
ob'sessional [-ʃə-] *adjective*: *obsessional behaviour.* □ **obsessionnel**
ob'sessive [-siv] *adjective*: *obsessive about cleanliness.* □ **obsédant**
ob'sessively *adverb.* □ **d'une manière obsédante**
ob'sessiveness *noun.* □ **caractère obsédant**
obsolescent [obsə'lesnt] *adjective* going out of use: *obsolescent slang.* □ **vieilli**
,**obso'lescence** *noun.* □ **vieillissement**
obsolete ['obsəliːt, obsə'liːt] *adjective* no longer in use: *obsolete weapons.* □ **dépassé, périmé**
obstacle ['obstəkl] *noun* something which prevents progress: *His inability to learn foreign languages was an obstacle to his career.* □ **obstacle**
obstacle race a race in which runners have to climb over, crawl through *etc* obstacles such as tires, nets *etc*. □ **course d'obstacles**
obstetrics [ob'stetriks] *noun singular* the science of helping women before, during, and after, the birth of babies. □ **obstétrique**
obstetrician [obstə'triʃən] *noun* a doctor who specializes in obstetrics. □ **obstétricien, ienne**
obstinate ['obstinət] *adjective* refusing to yield, obey *etc*: *She won't change her mind – she's very obstinate.* □ **obstiné**

'**obstinacy** [-nəsi] *noun.* □ **obstination**
'**obstinately** *adverb.* □ **obstinément**
obstruct [əb'strʌkt] *verb* 1 to block or close: *The road was obstructed by a fallen tree.* □ **obstruer**
2 to stop (something) moving past or making progress: *The crashed truck obstructed the traffic.* □ **obstruer**
ob'struction [-ʃən] *noun* something that obstructs: *an obstruction in the pipe.* □ **obstruction**
ob'structive *adjective* inclined to cause trouble and difficulties: *an obstructive personality.* □ **qui suscite des obstacles**
obtain [əb'tein] *verb* to get; to become the possessor of: *She obtained a large sum of money by buying and selling houses.* □ **obtenir**
ob'tainable *adjective* (*negative* **unobtainable**). □ **qu'on peut obtenir**
obtrusive [əb'truːsiv] *adjective* (*negative* **unobtrusive**) too noticeable: *Loud music can be very obtrusive.* □ **indiscret**
ob'trusively *adverb.* □ **indiscrètement**
ob'trusiveness *noun.* □ **indiscrétion**
obtuse [əb'tjuːs] *adjective* (of an angle) greater than a right-angle. □ **obtus**
obvious ['obviəs] *adjective* easily seen or understood; evident: *It was obvious that she was ill; an obvious improvement.* □ **évident**
'**obviously** *adverb* it is obvious (that something is the case): *Obviously, I'll need some help.* □ **évidemment**
occasion [ə'keiʒən] *noun* 1 a particular time: *I've heard you speak on several occasions.* □ **occasion**
2 a special event: *The wedding was a great occasion.* □ **événement**
oc'casional *adjective* happening, done *etc* now and then: *I take an occasional trip to New York.* □ **qui a lieu de temps en temps**
oc'casionally *adverb* now and then: *I occasionally go to the theatre.* □ **de temps en temps**
occult [ə'kʌlt]: **the occult** supernatural practices, ceremonies *etc*: *He has made a study of witches, magic and the occult.* □ **le surnaturel, les sciences occultes**
occupy ['okjupai] *verb* 1 to be in or fill (time, space *etc*): *A table occupied the centre of the room.* □ **occuper**
2 to live in: *The family occupied a small flat.* □ **occuper**
3 to capture: *The soldiers occupied the town.* □ **occuper**
'**occupant** *noun* a person who occupies (a house *etc*), not necessarily the owner of the house. □ **occupant, ante**
,**occu'pation** *noun* 1 a person's job or work. □ **métier, profession**
2 the act of occupying (a house, town *etc*). □ **occupation**
3 the period of time during which a town, house *etc* is occupied: *During the occupation, there was a shortage of food.* □ **occupation**
,**occu'pational** *adjective* of, or caused by, a person's job: *an occupational disease.* □ **qui a rapport au métier/à la profession**
'**occupier** *noun* an occupant. □ **occupant, ante**
occur [ə'kəː] – *past tense, past participle* **oc'curred** – *verb* 1 to take place: *The accident occurred yesterday*

astronaut

carpenter

chef

dentist

doctor

farmer

firefighter

hairdresser

journalist or reporter

lawyer

mail carrier

mechanic

musician

nurse

photographer

pilot

plumber

police officer

teacher

veterinarian

waitress

© Modulo Éditeur, 2000

morning. □ **se produire**

2 (*with* **to**) to come into one's mind: *An idea occurred to her*; *It occurred to me to visit my parents.* □ **venir à l'esprit (de)**

3 to be found: *Oil occurs under the sea.* □ **se trouver**

oc'currence [-'kʌ-, (*American*) -'kɔː-] *noun: a strange occurrence.* □ **événement**

> **occurrence, occurred** and **occurring** have two **r**s.

ocean ['ouʃən] *noun* **1** the salt water that covers most of the earth's surface. □ **océan**

2 one of its five main divisions: *the Atlantic Ocean.* □ **océan**

o'clock [ə'klɔk] *adverb* used, in stating the time, to refer to a particular hour: *It's five o'clock.* □ **heure(s)**
■ *adjective: the three o'clock train.* □ **heure(s)**

octagon ['oktəgən, -gon] *noun* two-dimensional figure with eight sides. □ **octogone**

octagonal [ok'tagənl] *adjective* having eight sides: *an octagonal figure.* □ **octagonal**

octave ['oktiv] *noun* in music, a series or range of eight notes. □ **octave**

octet [ok'tet] *noun* a group of eight musicians, eight lines in a poem *etc.* □ **octuor, huitain**

October [ok'toubə] *noun* the tenth month of the year, the month following September. □ **octobre**

octogenarian [oktədʒi'neəriən] *noun* a person between eighty and eighty-nine years old. □ **octogénaire**

octopus ['oktəpəs] *noun* a type of sea-creature with eight tentacles. □ **pieuvre**

oculist ['okjulist] *noun* a doctor who specializes in diseases of the eyes. □ **oculiste**

odd [od] *adjective* **1** unusual; strange: *She's wearing very odd clothes*; *a very odd young man.* □ **bizarre**

2 (of a number) that cannot be divided exactly by 2: *5 and 7 are odd* (*numbers*). □ **impair**

3 not one of a pair, set *etc*: *an odd shoe.* □ **dépareillé**

4 occasional; free: *odd moments.* □ **perdu**

'oddity – *plural* **'oddities** – *noun* a strange person or thing: *He's a bit of an oddity.* □ **excentrique; bizarrerie**

'oddly *adverb* strangely: *She is behaving very oddly.* □ **bizarrement**

'oddment *noun* a piece left over from something: *an oddment of material.* □ **fin de série, coupon**

odds *noun plural* **1** chances; probability: *The odds are that she will win.* □ **chances**

2 a difference in strength, in favour of one side: *They are fighting against heavy odds.* □ **avantage**

odd jobs (*usually* small) jobs of various kinds, often done for other people: *He's unemployed, but earns some money by doing odd jobs for old people.* □ **petits travaux, bricolage**

odd job man a person employed to do such jobs. □ **homme à tout faire**

be at odds to be quarrelling: *He has been at odds with his sister for years.* □ **être brouillé**

oddly enough it is strange or remarkable (that): *I saw John this morning. Oddly enough, I was just thinking I hadn't seen him for a long time.* □ **bizarrement**

odd man out/odd one out **1** a person or thing that is

different from others: *In this test, you have to decide which of these three objects is the odd one out.* □ **exception**

2 a person or thing that is left over when teams *etc* are made up: *When they chose the two teams, I was the odd man out.* □ **(personne, chose) en surnombre**

odds and ends small objects *etc* of different kinds: *There were various odds and ends lying about on the table.* □ **objets divers**

what's the odds? the probability in favor or against some results: *What's the odds that we'll win the bet?* □ **quelles sont les chances?**

ode [oud] *noun* a poem written to a person or thing: *'Ode to a Nightingale' was written by John Keats.* □ **ode**

odious ['oudiəs] *adjective* hateful; disgusting: *She is an odious young woman.* □ **odieux, détestable**

'odiously *adverb*. □ **odieusement**

'odiousness *noun*. □ **(caractère) odieux**

odour ['oudə] *noun* a smell (*usually* particularly good or bad): *the sweet odour of roses.* □ **odeur**

'odourless *adjective*. □ **inodore**

of [ov] *preposition* **1** belonging to: *a friend of mine.* □ **de**

2 away from (a place *etc*); after (a given time): *within five kilometres of Montreal*; *within a year of his death.* □ **de**

3 written *etc* by: *the plays of Shakespeare.* □ **de**

4 belonging to or forming a group: *He is one of my friends.* □ **de**

5 showing: *a picture of my father.* □ **de**

6 made from; consisting of: *a dress of silk*; *a collection of pictures.* □ **en, de**

7 used to show an amount, measurement of something: *a litre of gasoline*; *five bags of coal.* □ **de**

8 about: *an account of her work.* □ **de**

9 containing: *a box of chocolates.* □ **de**

10 used to show a cause: *She died of hunger.* □ **de**

11 used to show a loss or removal: *She was robbed of her jewels.* □ **de**

12 used to show the connection between an action and its object: *the smoking of a cigarette.* □ **de**

13 used to show character, qualities *etc*: *a man of courage.* □ **de**

off [of] *adverb* **1** away (from a place, time *etc*): *He walked off*; *She cut her hair off*; *The holidays are only a week off*; *She took off her coat.*

2 not working; not giving power *etc*: *The water's off*; *Switch off the light.* □ **en panne; hors circuit**

3 not at work: *He's taking tomorrow off*; *She's off today.* □ **en congé**

4 completely: *Finish off your work.* □ **complètement**

5 not as good as usual, or as it should be: *His work has gone off recently*; (*also adjective*) *an off day.* □ **médiocre**

6 (of food) rotten: *This milk has gone off – we can't drink it*; (*also adjective*) *That meat is certainly off.* □ **pourri**

7 out of a vehicle, train etc: *The bus stopped and we got off.* □ **hors de**

8 cancelled: *The marriage is off.* □ **annulé**
■ *preposition* **1** away from; down from: *It fell off the table*; *a kilometre off the coast*; *She cut about five cen-*

timetres off my hair. □ **de**

2 not wanting or allowed to have (food *etc*): *The child is off his food.* □ **sans appétit**

3 out of (a vehicle, train *etc*): *We got off the bus.* □ **hors de**

,**off'chance** *noun* a slight chance: *We waited, on the off-chance (that) he might come.* □ **au cas où**

,**off-'colour** *adjective* not very well: *She's a bit off-colour this morning.* □ **patraque**

,**offhand** *adjective* acting or speaking so casually that one is being rude: *offhand behaviour.* □ **cavalier**

■ *adverb* without thinking about something first: *I can't tell you the answer offhand.* □ **spontanément**

,**offhandedly** *adverb.* □ **cavalièrement**

,**offhandedness** *noun.* □ **désinvolture, sans-gêne**

,**offshore** *adjective* 1 in or on the sea, not far from the coast: *offshore oil wells.* □ **côtier, en mer**

2 (of winds) blowing away from the coast, out to sea. □ **de terre**

,**offside** *adverb* (in football, hockey *etc*) in a position (not allowed by the rules) between the ball and the opponents' goal: *The referee disallowed the goal because one of the players was offside.* □ **hors-jeu**

■ *adjective* (of a vehicle *etc*) on the side nearest to the centre of the road: *the front offside wheel.* □ **de gauche**

,**off-'white** *adjective* not quite white, *eg* slightly yellow *etc*: *an off-white dress.* □ **blanc cassé**

badly, well off poor, rich: *The family was quite well off.* □ **dans la gêne; aisé**

be off with you! go away! □ **allez-vous en! va-t-en!**

in the offing about to happen: *She has a new job in the offing.* □ **en vue**

off and on/on and off sometimes; occasionally: *I see him off and on at the club.* □ **de temps à autre**

the off season the period, at a hotel, holiday resort *etc*, when there are few visitors: *It's very quiet here in the off season*; *(also adjective) off-season rates.* □ **(de) morte-saison; hors-saison**

offal ['ofəl] *noun* the parts of an animal *eg* the heart, liver *etc* which are considered as food for people. □ **abats**

offend [ə'fend] *verb* 1 to make feel upset or angry: *If you don't go to her party she will be offended*; *My criticism offended her.* □ **offenser, choquer**

2 to be unpleasant or disagreeable: *Cigarette smoke offends me.* □ **choquer**

of'fence, of'fense *noun* 1 (any cause of) anger, displeasure, hurt feelings *etc*: *That rubbish dump is an offence to the eye.* □ **sujet de mécontentement/déplaisir**

2 a crime: *The police charged him with several offences.* □ **infraction**

of'fender *noun* a person who offends, *especially* against the law. □ **délinquant, ante, contrevenant, ante**

of'fensive [-siv] *adjective* 1 insulting: *offensive remarks.* □ **offensant**

2 disgusting: *an offensive smell.* □ **repoussant**

3 used to attack: *an offensive weapon.* □ **offensif**

■ *noun* an attack: *They launched an offensive against the invading army.* □ **offensive**

of'fensively *adverb.* □ **d'une manière offensante**

of'fensiveness *noun.* □ **nature offensante**

be on the offensive to be making an attack: *She always expects people to criticize her and so she is always on the offensive.* □ **être en position d'attaque**

take offence *(with* **at***)* to be offended (by something): *He took offence at what she said.* □ **s'offenser de**

offer ['ofə] – *past tense, past participle* '**offered** – *verb* 1 to put forward (a gift, suggestion *etc*) for acceptance or refusal: *She offered the man a cup of tea*; *He offered her \$20 for the picture.* □ **offrir, proposer**

2 to say that one is willing: *He offered to help.* □ **offrir (de)**

■ *noun* 1 an act of offering: *an offer of help.* □ **offre, proposition**

2 an offering of money as the price of something: *They made an offer of \$50,000 for the house.* □ **offre**

'**offering** *noun* 1 a gift: *a birthday offering.* □ **don, cadeau**

2 money given during a religious service: *a church offering.* □ **offrande**

on offer for sale, often cheaply: *That shop has chairs on offer at \$20 each.* □ **en promotion**

office ['ofis] *noun* 1 the room or building in which the business of a firm is done: *The firm's head offices are in New York*; *(also adjective) office furniture.* □ **(de) bureau**

2 the room in which a particular person works: *the bank manager's office.* □ **bureau**

3 a room or building used for a particular purpose: *Train tickets are bought at the ticket-office.* □ **bureau**

4 a position of authority, *especially* in or as a government: *Our party has not been in office for years*; *the office of mayor.* □ **charge, fonction**

'**officer** *noun* 1 a person holding a commission in the army, navy or air force: *a naval officer.* □ **officier**

2 a person who carries out a public duty: *a police-officer.* □ **fonctionnaire**

office automation *noun* the practice or technique of running an office using highly efficient devices such as computers, fax machines, photocopiers and so on: *Office automation has made the work easier, but has resulted in the firing of many staff members.* □ **bureautique**

official [ə'fiʃəl] *adjective* 1 of or concerning a position of authority: *official powers*; *official uniform.* □ **officiel**

2 done or confirmed by people in authority *etc*: *the official result of the race.* □ **officiel**

■ *noun* a person who holds a position of authority: *a government official.* □ **fonctionnaire**

officially [ə'fiʃəli] *adverb* 1 *(negative* **unofficially***)* as an official: *She attended the ceremony officially.* □ **à titre officiel**

2 formally: *The new library was officially opened yesterday.* □ **officiellement**

3 according to what is announced publicly (though not necessarily true in fact): *Officially she is on holiday – actually she is working on a new book.* □ **officiellement**

officiate [ə'fiʃieit] *verb* to do the duty or service of an office or official position: *The new clergyman officiated at the wedding.* □ **officier**

officious [ə'fiʃəs] *adjective* offering help *etc* in order to interfere: *They are so officious that I do not let them visit my house.* □ **trop empressé**

of'ficiously *adverb*. □ **avec un empressement excessif**

of'ficiousness *noun*. □ **excès d'empressement**

'office-holder *noun* a person who holds a position of authority in a society *etc*. □ **membre du bureau**

through the (kind) offices of with the help of: *I got the job through the kind offices of a friend.* □ **par l'entremise de**

often ['ofn] *adverb* many times: *I often go to the theatre*; *I should see him more often.* □ **souvent**

every so often sometimes; occasionally: *I meet her at the club every so often.* □ **de temps en temps**

ogre ['ougə] *noun* in fairy stories, a frightening, cruel giant. □ **ogre**

oh [ou] *interjection* an expression of surprise, admiration *etc*: *Oh, what a lovely present!* □ **oh!, ah!** *See also* **o**.

oil [oil] *noun* a *usually* thick liquid that will not mix with water, obtained from plants, animals and minerals: *olive oil*; *whale oil*; *vegetable oil*; *cooking oil*; *I put some oil on the hinges of the door*; *The car's engine is in need of oil.* □ **huile**

■ *verb* to put oil on or into: *The machine will work better if it's oiled.* □ **graisser**

oils *noun plural* oil paint: *She paints in oils.* □ **huile**

'oily *adjective* **1** of, like or covered with oil: *an oily liquid*; *an oily rag.* □ **huileux, gras**

2 trying to be too friendly or polite: *The waiters in that restaurant are too oily.* □ **mielleux**

'oilfield *noun* a place where mineral oil is found: *There are oilfields in the North Sea.* □ **gisement pétrolifère**

oil paint paint made with oil: *Some artists prefer to use oil paint(s).* □ **peinture à huile**

oil painting a picture painted with oil paints. □ **peinture à l'huile**

oil palm a palm tree whose fruit and seeds yield oil. □ **palmier à huile**

'oil rig *noun* a structure used to drill oil wells: *The ship sailed past an enormous oil rig.* □ **derrick**

'oil tanker *noun* a ship used for carrying oil: *An oil tanker has run aground near here.* □ **pétrolier**

'oil well *noun* a hole drilled into the earth or the sea-bed to obtain petroleum. □ **puits de pétrole**

strike oil to find oil under the ground: *After drilling for several months, they finally struck oil*; *We've struck oil* (= found what we have been looking for) *in our search for a suitable house.* □ **trouver du pétrole**

ointment ['ointmənt] *noun* any greasy substance rubbed on the skin to heal injuries *etc*. □ **onguent**

O.K., okay [ou'kei] *interjection, adjective, adverb* all right: *Will you do it? O.K., I will*; *Is my dress O.K.?*; *That's O.K. with/by me* (= I agree). □ **d'accord!; très bien**

■ *noun* approval: *He gave the plan his O.K.* □ **accord**

old [ould] *adjective* **1** advanced in age: *an old man*; *He is too old to live alone.* □ **vieux**

2 having a certain age: *He is thirty years old.* □ **âgé de**

3 having existed for a long time: *an old building*; *Those trees are very old.* □ **vieux**

4 no longer useful: *She threw away the old shoes.* □ **vieux**

5 belonging to times long ago: *old civilizations like that of Greece.* □ **ancien**

old age the later part of a person's life: *She wrote most of her poems in her old age.* □ **vieillesse**

,old-'fashioned *adjective* in a style common some time ago: *old-fashioned clothes*; *Her hairstyle is very old-fashioned.* □ **démodé**

old hand a person who is very experienced: *He's an old hand at this sort of job.* □ **vieux routier**

old maid an unmarried woman who is past the usual age of marriage. □ **vieille fille**

the old old people: *hospitals for the old.* □ **les gens âgés**

olive ['oliv] *noun* **1** a type of edible fruit which is used as a garnish *etc* and which gives oil used for cooking: *He put an olive in her cocktail*; *(also adjective) an olive tree*; *olive oil.* □ **(d')olive**

2 the tree on which it grows: *a grove of olives.* □ **olivier**

3 *(also* **olive-green***)* the brownish-green or yellowish-green colour of the fruit: *They painted the room olive*; *(also adjective) She wore an olive-green hat.* □ **(vert) olive**

4 *(also* **'olive-wood***)* the wood of the tree. □ **(bois d')olivier**

olive branch a sign of a wish for peace: *The government held out the olive branch to its opponents.* □ **rameau d'olivier**

Olympic [ə'limpik]: **the Olympic Games** *(also* **the Olympics***)* a sports competition held once every four years for amateur competitors from all parts of the world. □ **les Jeux olympiques**

ombudsman ['ombudzmən] *noun* an official appointed to look into complaints *especially* against a government. □ **médiateur, protecteur du citoyen**

omelette, omelet ['omlit] *noun* eggs beaten and fried sometimes with vegetables, meat *etc*: *a mushroom omelette.* □ **omelette**

omen ['oumən] *noun* a sign of a future event: *Long ago, storms were regarded as bad omens.* □ **augure**

ominous ['ominəs] *adjective* giving a suggestion or warning about something bad that is going to happen: *an ominous cloud*; *an ominous silence.* □ **de mauvais augure**

'ominously *adverb*. □ **sinistrement**

omit [ə'mit] – *past tense, past participle* **o'mitted** – *verb* **1** to leave out: *You can omit the last chapter of the book.* □ **omettre**

2 not to do: *I omitted to tell him about the meeting.* □ **omettre/négliger de**

o'mission [-ʃən] *noun* **1** something that has been left out: *I have made several omissions in the list of names.* □ **omission**

2 the act of omitting: *the omission of his name from the list.* □ **omission**

omitted and omitting have two ts.

omnibus ['omnibəs] *noun* **1** a large book containing a number of books, stories *etc*: *a Jane Austen omnibus*;

(*also adjective*) *an omnibus edition of Jane Austen's novels.* □ **recueil**
2 an old word for a bus. □ **omnibus**

omnipotent [om'nipətənt] *adjective* having absolute, unlimited power: *the omnipotent power of God.* □ **tout-puissant**
om'**nipotently** *adverb.* □ **de manière toute-puissante**
om'**nipotence** *noun.* □ **toute-puissance**

on [on] *preposition* 1 touching, fixed to, covering *etc* the upper or outer side of: *The book was lying on the table; He was standing on the floor; She wore a hat on her head.* □ **sur**
2 in or into (a vehicle, train *etc*): *We were sitting on the bus; I got on the wrong bus.* □ **dans**
3 at or during a certain day, time *etc*: *on Monday; On his arrival, he went straight to bed.* □ **à**
4 about: *a book on the theatre.* □ **sur, de**
5 in the state or process of: *He's on holiday.*
6 supported by: *She was standing on one leg.* □ **sur**
7 receiving, taking: *on drugs; on a diet.*
8 taking part in: *She is on the committee; Which detective is working on this case?* □ **dans; sur**
9 towards: *They marched on the town.* □ **sur**
10 near or beside: *a shop on the main road.* □ **sur, au bord de**
11 by means of: *He played a tune on the violin; I spoke to him on the telephone.* □ **à**
12 being carried by: *The thief had the stolen jewels on him.* □ **sur**
13 when (something is, or has been, done): *On investigation, there proved to be no need to panic.* □ **à**
14 followed by: *disaster on disaster.* □ **après**
■ *adverb* 1 (*especially* of something being worn) so as to be touching, fixed to, covering *etc* the upper or outer side of: *She put her hat on.* □ **mis sur**
2 used to show a continuing state *etc*, onwards: *She kept on asking questions; They moved on.* □ **sans discontinuer**
3 (*also adjective*) (of electric light, machines *etc*) working: *The television is on; Turn/Switch the light on.* □ **en marche, allumé**
4 (*also adjective*) (of films *etc*) able to be seen: *There's a good film on at the cinema this week.* □ **à l'affiche**
5 (*also adjective*) in or into a vehicle, train *etc*: *The bus stopped and we got on.* □ **à bord**
■ *adjective* 1 in progress: *The game was on.* □ **en cours**
2 not cancelled: *Is the party on tonight?* □ **toujours tenir**
'**oncoming** *adjective* approaching: *oncoming traffic.* □ **qui approche**
'**ongoing** *adjective* continuing: *an ongoing argument.* □ **en cours**
'**onward(s)** *adverb* moving forward (in place or time): *They marched on and on; on and onward(s).* □ **plus loin, désormais**
be on to (someone) to have discovered (a person's) trick, secret *etc*: *The thieves realized that the police were on to them.* □ **découvrir**
on and on used with certain verbs to emphasize the length of an activity: *She kept on and on asking questions.* □ **sans arrêt**

on time at the right time: *He got here on time.* □ **à l'heure**
on to/onto to a position on: *She lifted it onto the table.* □ **sur**

once [wʌns] *adverb* 1 a single time: *He did it once; If I could see her once again I would be happy.* □ **une fois**
2 at a time in the past: *I once wanted to be a dancer.* □ **autrefois**
■ *conjunction* when; as soon as: *Once (it had been) unlocked, the door opened easily.* □ **une fois que**
at once immediately: *Go away at once!* □ **tout de suite**
(**just**) **for once** as an exception: *Why can't you be nice to her for once?* □ **(juste) pour une fois**
once and for all once and finally: *Once and for all, I refuse!* □ **une fois pour toutes**
once in a while occasionally: *I meet him once in a while at the club.* □ **de temps à autre**

oncoming *see* **on**.

one [wʌn] *noun* 1 the number or figure 1: *One and one is two (1 + 1 = 2).* □ **un**
2 the age of 1: *Babies start to talk at one.* □ **un an**
■ *pronoun* 1 a single person or thing: *She's the one I like the best; I'll buy the red one.* □ **un, une**
2 anyone; any person: *One can see the city from here.* □ **on**
■ *adjective* 1 1 in number: *one person; He took one book.* □ **un**
2 aged 1: *The baby will be one tomorrow.* □ **qui a un an**
3 of the same opinion *etc*: *We are one in our love of freedom.* □ **unis**
one- having one (of something): *a one-legged man.* □ **d'un/à un seul**
one'self *pronoun* 1 used as the object of a verb, the subject of which is **one**: *One should wash oneself every morning.* □ **se, soi-même**
2 used in emphasis: *One always has to do these things oneself.* □ **soi(-même)**
one-'off *noun, adjective* (something) made, intended *etc* for one occasion only: *It's just a one-off arrangement.* □ **exceptionnel**
one-'sided *adjective* 1 with one person or side having a great advantage over the other: *a one-sided contest.* □ **inégal**
2 representing only one aspect of a subject: *a one-sided discussion.* □ **partial**
one-'way *adjective* 1 in which traffic can move in one direction only: *a one-way street.* □ **à sens unique**
2 valid for travel in one direction only: *a one-way ticket.* □ **simple**
one year old *noun* a person or animal that is one year old. □ **(individu, etc.) âgé d'un an**
■ *adjective* (of a person, animal or thing) that is one year old. □ **d'un an**
all one just the same: *It's all one to me what she does.* □ **tout un**
be one up on (a person) to have an advantage over (someone): *We brought out a book on this before our rivals so we're one up on them.* □ **marquer un point sur (qqn)**
not be oneself to look or feel ill, anxious *etc*: *I'd better*

go home – I'm not myself today. □ **se sentir mal fichu**
one and all all (of a group): *This was agreed by one and all.* □ **tous sans exception**
one another used as the object of a verb when an action takes place between people *etc*: *They hit one another.* □ **l'un l'autre**
one by one (of a number of people, things *etc*) one after the other: *He examined all the vases one by one.* □ **un par un**
one or two a few: *I don't want a lot of nuts – I'll just take one or two.* □ **un ou deux**

> **one of** is followed by a plural noun or pronoun, but takes a singular verb: *One of the girls works as a hairdresser; One of them is ill.*

onerous ['ounərəs] *adjective* hard to bear or do: *an onerous task.* □ **pénible**
ongoing *see* on.
onion ['ʌnjən] *noun* a type of vegetable with an eatable bulb which has a strong taste and smell: *pickled onions; Put plenty of onion in the stew.* □ **oignon**
onlooker ['onlukə] *noun* a person who watches something happening: *A crowd of onlookers had gathered around the two men who were fighting.* □ **spectateur, trice**
only ['ounli] *adjective* without any others of the same type: *She has no brothers or sisters – she's an only child; the only book of its kind.* □ **unique, seul**
■ *adverb* **1** not more than: *We have only two cups left; She lives only a kilometre away.* □ **ne...que, seulement**
2 alone: *Only you can do it.* □ **seul**
3 showing the one action done, in contrast to other possibilities: *I only scolded the child – I did not smack him.* □ **seulement**
4 not longer ago than: *I saw her only yesterday.* □ **pas plus tard que**
5 showing the one possible result of an action: *If you do that, you'll only make him angry.* □ **seulement**
■ *conjunction* except that, but: *I'd like to go, only I have to work.* □ **mais**
only too very: *I'll be only too pleased to come.* □ **que trop**
onset ['onset] *noun* a beginning: *the onset of a cold.* □ **commencement**
onslaught ['onslo:t] *noun* a fierce attack: *an onslaught on the enemy troops.* □ **assaut**
onus ['ounəs] *noun* the responsibility: *The onus is on her to prove her theory.* □ **responsabilité**
onward(s) *see* on.
onyx ['oniks] *noun* a type of precious stone with layers of different colours: *The ashtray is made of onyx; (also adjective) an onyx ashtray.* □ **(d') onyx**
ooze [uz] *verb* **1** to flow slowly: *The water oozed through the sand.* □ **suinter**
2 to have (something liquid) flowing slowly out: *His arm was oozing blood.* □ **suinter**
■ *noun* liquid, slippery mud: *The river bed was thick with ooze.* □ **vase, boue**
'oozy *adjective.* □ **vaseux; suintant**
opacity *see* opaque.

opal ['oupəl] *noun* a type of *usually* bluish-white or milky white precious stone, with slight traces or streaks of various other colours: *There are three opals in her brooch; (also adjective) an opal necklace.* □ **(d')opale**
opaque [ə'peik, ou-] *adjective* not transparent: *an opaque liquid.* □ **opaque**
o'paqueness *noun.* □ **opacité**
opacity [ə'pasəti] *noun.* □ **opacité**
open ['oupən] *adjective* **1** not shut, allowing entry or exit: *an open box; The gate is wide open.* □ **ouvert**
2 allowing the inside to be seen: *an open book.* □ **ouvert**
3 ready for business *etc*: *The shop is open on Sunday afternoons; After the fog had cleared, the airport was soon open again; The gardens are open to the public.* □ **ouvert**
4 not kept secret: *an open show of affection.* □ **manifeste**
5 frank: *He was very open with me about his work.* □ **franc**
6 still being considered *etc*: *Leave the matter open.* □ **en suspens**
7 empty, with no trees, buildings *etc*: *I like to be out in the open country; an open space.* □ **ras, vague**
■ *verb* **1** a to make or become open: *He opened the door; The door opened; The new shop opened last week.* □ **(s')ouvrir**
2 to begin: *He opened the meeting with a speech of welcome.* □ **ouvrir**
'opener *noun* something that opens (something): *a can-opener.* □ **ouvre-...**
'opening *noun* **1** a hole; a clear or open space: *an opening in the fence/forest.* □ **ouverture; brèche, clairière**
2 a beginning: *the opening of the film; (also adjective) the chairwoman's opening remarks.* □ **début; préliminaire**
3 the act of becoming or making open, the ceremony of making open: *the opening of a flower/shop/door; the opening of the new theatre.* □ **ouverture, inauguration**
4 an opportunity for work: *There are good openings in the automobile industry.* □ **débouché**
'openly *adverb* frankly: *She talked very openly about it.* □ **ouvertement**
'open air *adjective* outside: *an open air meeting.* □ **en/de plein air**
,open-'minded *adjective* willing to consider new ideas: *an open-minded approach to the problem.* □ **à l'esprit ouvert**
,open-'plan *adjective* (of a building) built with few walls inside: *an open-plan office.* □ **à aire ouverte**
be an open secret to be known to many people although supposed to be a secret: *It's an open secret that she's getting married next week.* □ **être le secret de Polichinelle**
bring (something) out into the open to make (something) public: *This affair has been kept a secret for too long – it's time it was brought out into the open.* □ **porter sur la place publique, divulguer**
in the open outside; in the open air: *It's very healthy for children to be able to play in the open.* □ **au grand air**
in the open air not in a building: *If it doesn't rain, we'll*

have the party in the open air. □ **en plein air**

keep/have an open mind to have a willingness to listen to or accept new ideas, other people's suggestions *etc* (*eg* before making a decision): *It doesn't seem to be a very good plan, but I think we should keep an open mind about it for the time being.* □ **réserver son jugement**

open on to (of a door *etc*) to open towards: *Our front door opens straight on to the street.* □ **donner sur**

the open sea any area of sea far from land: *When they reached the open sea, they were faced with large waves.* □ **la haute mer**

open to 1 likely or willing to receive: *open to charges of corruption*; *open to suggestions from any member of staff.* □ **accessible/ouvert à**

2 possible: *There are only two courses of action open to us.* □ **possible**

open up 1 to open (a shop *etc*): *I open up the shop at nine o'clock every morning.* □ **(s')ouvrir**

2 to open (a box *etc*) completely: *I opened up the parcel.* □ **ouvrir, défaire**

3 to open the (main) door of a building *etc*: '*Open up!*' *shouted the policeman.* '*We know you are in there!*' □ **ouvrir**

with open arms in a very friendly way: *They received their visitors with open arms.* □ **à/les bras ouverts**

opera ['opərə] *noun* a musical drama in which the dialogue is sung: *an opera by Verdi.* □ **opéra**

,**ope'ratic** [-'ra-] *adjective* of, or relating to, opera: *an operatic society*; *an operatic singer.* □ **d'opéra**

opera glasses binoculars for use in a theatre. □ **jumelles de théâtre**

'**opera house** *noun* a theatre in which operas are performed. □ **(théâtre de l') opéra**

operate ['opəreit] *verb* **1** to act or work: *The sewing-machine isn't operating properly.* □ **marcher, fonctionner**

2 to do or perform a surgical operation: *The surgeon operated on her for appendicitis.* □ **opérer**

,**ope'ration** *noun* **1** an action or process, *especially* when planned: *a rescue operation.* □ **opération**

2 the process of working: *Our plan is now in operation.* □ **marche, fonctionnement**

3 the act of surgically cutting a part of the body in order to cure disease: *an operation for appendicitis.* □ **opération**

4 (*often in plural*) the movement, fighting *etc* of armies: *The general was in command of operations in the north.* □ **opération**

,**ope'rational** *adjective* in good working order. □ **opérationnel, en état de marche**

'**operative** [-rətiv] *adjective* in action, having effect: *Many old laws are still operative.* □ **en vigueur**

'**operator** *noun* **1** a person who works a machine: *a lift operator.* □ **opérateur, trice**

2 a person who connects telephone calls: *Ask the operator to connect you to that number.* □ **téléphoniste**

'**operating room** *noun* the room in a hospital in which operations are performed. □ **salle d'opération**

opiate *see* **opium.**

opinion [ə'pinjən] *noun* **1** what a person thinks or believes: *My opinions about education have changed.* □ **opinion**

2 a (professional) judgment, *usually* of a doctor, lawyer *etc*: *I wanted a second opinion on my illness.* □ **avis**

3 what one thinks of the worth or value of someone or something: *I have a very high opinion of her work.* □ **opinion**

be of the opinion (that) to think: *He is of the opinion that nothing more can be done.* □ **être d'avis que**

in my, your *etc* **opinion** according to what I, you *etc* think: *In my opinion, she's right.* □ **à mon/votre, etc. avis**

a matter of opinion something about which different people (may) have different opinions: *Whether it is better to marry young or not is a matter of opinion.* □ **affaire d'opinion**

opium ['oupiəm] *noun* a drug made from the dried juice of a type of poppy. □ **opium**

opiate ['oupiət] *noun* any drug containing opium, used to make a person sleep: *The doctor gave him an opiate.* □ **opiacé**

opponent [ə'pounənt] *noun* a person who opposes: *an opponent of the government*; *She beat her opponent by four points.* □ **adversaire**

opportunity [opə'tjuːnəti] – *plural* **oppor'tunities** – *noun* a chance to do or a time for doing (something): *an opportunity to go to Rome*; *You've had several opportunities to ask him.* □ **occasion**

oppor'tune *adjective* coming at the right time: *an opportune remark.* □ **opportun**

oppor'tunely *adverb.* □ **opportunément**

oppor'tuneness *noun.* □ **opportunité**

oppor'tunist *noun* a person who takes advantage of any circumstance which will help him personally: *a political opportunist.* □ **opportuniste**

oppor'tunism *noun.* □ **opportunisme**

oppose [ə'pouz] *verb* **1** to resist or fight against (someone or something) by force or argument: *We oppose the government on this matter.* □ **s'opposer à**

2 to act or compete against: *Who is opposing him in the election?* □ **faire opposition à**

as opposed to separate or distinct from; in contrast with: *It happened in the late afternoon, as opposed to the evening.* □ **par opposition à**

opposite ['opəzit] *adjective* **1** being on the other side of: *on the opposite side of town.* □ **opposé**

2 completely different: *The two men walked off in opposite directions.* □ **opposé**

■ *preposition, adverb* on the opposite side of (something) in relation to something else: *He lives in the house opposite (mine).* □ **en face de, vis-à-vis de; (d')en face**

■ *noun* something that is completely different: *Hate is the opposite of love.* □ **contraire**

opposition [opə'ziʃən] *noun* **1** the act of resisting or fighting against by force or argument: *There is a lot of opposition to her ideas.* □ **opposition**

2 the people who are fighting or competing against: *In war and business, one should always get to know one's opposition.* □ **adversaire**

oppress [ə'pres] *verb* 1 to govern cruelly: *The king oppressed his people.* □ **opprimer**

2 to worry or depress: *The thought of leaving her oppressed me.* □ **oppresser**

op'**pression** [-ʃən] *noun*: *After five years of oppression, the peasants revolted.* □ **oppression**

op'**pressive** [-siv] *adjective* oppressing; cruel; hard to bear: *oppressive laws.* □ **tyrannique, oppressif, accablant**

op'**pressively** *adjective*. □ **d'une manière oppressive**

op'**pressiveness** *noun*. □ **caractère oppressif**

op'**pressor** *noun* a ruler who oppresses his people; a tyrant. □ **oppresseur**

opt [opt]: **opt out** (*often with of*) to choose or decide not to do something or take part in something: *You promised to help us, so you can't opt out (of it) now.* □ **choisir de ne pas participer (à)**

optician [op'tiʃən] *noun* a person who makes and sells spectacles and optical instruments: *The optician mended my spectacles.* □ **opticien, ienne**

optical ['optikəl] *adjective* of or concerning sight or what one sees: *The two objects in the picture appear to be the same size, but this is just an optical illusion* (= they are not actually the same size); *microscopes and other optical instruments.* □ **(d')optique**

optics ['optiks] *noun singular* the science of light. □ **optique**

optimism ['optimizəm] *noun* a state of mind in which one always hopes or expects that something good will happen: *Even when it was obvious to the others that he was not going to succeed he was full of optimism.* □ **optimisme**

'**optimist** *noun*. □ **optimiste**

,opti'**mistic** *adjective* always hoping or believing that something good will happen: *an optimistic person/attitude.* □ **optimiste**

opti'**mistically** *adverb*. □ **avec optimisme**

option ['opʃən] *noun* choice: *You have no option but to obey her.* □ **choix**

'**optional** *adjective* a matter of choice: *Music is optional at our school; an optional subject.* □ **facultatif**

opulent ['opjulənt] *adjective* luxurious; rich: *They lived in opulent surroundings.* □ **opulent**

'**opulently** *adverb*. □ **avec opulence**

'**opulence** *noun*. □ **opulence**

or [oz] *conjunction* 1 used to show an alternative: *Is that your book or is it mine?* □ **ou**

2 because if not: *Hurry or you'll be late.* □ **sinon**

or so about; approximately: *I bought a dozen or so (books).* □ **environ**

oracle ['orəkl] *noun* 1 a very knowledgeable person: *I don't know the answer to this problem, so I'd better go and ask the oracle.* □ **oracle**

2 in former times, a holy place where a god was believed to give answers to questions: *the oracle at Delphi.* □ **oracle**

oral ['ozrəl] *adjective* 1 spoken, not written: *an oral examination.* □ **oral**

2 of or by the mouth: *oral hygiene; an oral contraceptive.* □ **oral, buccal**

■ *noun* a spoken examination: *She passed the written exam, but failed her oral.* □ **oral**

'**orally** *adverb*: *medicine to be taken orally.* □ **oralement, par voie orale**

orange ['orindʒ] *noun* 1 a type of juicy citrus fruit with a thick reddish-yellow skin: *I'd like an orange;* (*also adjective*) *an orange tree.* □ **(d')orange**

2 the colour of this fruit. □ **orange**

■ *adjective* 1 of the colour orange: *an orange dress.* □ **orange**

2 with the taste of orange juice: *an orange drink.* □ **à l'orange, d'orange**

orangutan ['ozraŋ'uːtan] *noun* a type of large, man-like ape. □ **orang-outang**

oration [ə'reiʃən] *noun* a formal, public speech, especially in fine, beautiful language: *a funeral oration.* □ **discours solennel**

orator ['orətə] *noun* a person who makes public speeches, *especially* very eloquent ones. □ **orateur, trice**

'**oratory** ['orə-] *noun* the art of speaking well in public. □ **art oratoire**

ora'**torical** *adjective*. □ **oratoire**

orbit ['ozbit] *noun* the path in which something moves around a planet, star *etc, eg* the path of the Earth around the Sun or of a spacecraft around the Earth: *The spaceship is in orbit around the moon.* □ **orbite**

■ *verb* to go around in space: *The spacecraft orbits the Earth every 24 hours.* □ **décrire une orbite (autour de)**

orchard ['oztʃəd] *noun* a garden or other area in which fruit trees are grown: *a cherry orchard.* □ **verger**

orchestra ['ozkəstrə] *noun* a (*usually* large) group of musicians playing together, led by a conductor. □ **orchestre**

or'**chestral** [-'kes-] *adjective* for, or given by, an orchestra: *orchestral music; an orchestral concert.* □ **orchestral, symphonique**

orchid ['ozkid] *noun* a kind of plant *usually* having brightly-coloured or unusually-shaped flowers. □ **orchidée**

ordain [oz'dein] *verb* to make (someone) a priest, minister *etc, usually* by a church ceremony: *He was ordained a priest.* □ **ordonner**

ordeal [oz'dizl] *noun* a difficult, painful experience: *Being kidnapped was an ordeal for the child.* □ **(rude) épreuve**

order ['ozdə] *noun* 1 a statement (by a person in authority) of what someone must do; a command: *She gave me my orders.* □ **ordre**

2 an instruction to supply something: *orders from Germany for special gates.* □ **commande**

3 something supplied: *Your order is nearly ready.* □ **commande**

4 a tidy state: *The house is in (good) order.* □ **ordre**

5 a system or method: *I must have order in my life.* □ **ordre**

6 an arrangement (of people, things *etc*) in space, time *etc: in alphabetical order; in order of importance.* □ **ordre**

7 a peaceful condition: *law and order.* □ **ordre**

8 a written instruction to pay money: *a banker's order.* □ **mandat**

9 a group, class, rank or position: *This is a list of the various orders of plants*; *the social order.* □ **ordre**

10 a religious society, *especially* of monks: *the Benedictine order.* □ **ordre**

■ *verb* 1 to tell (someone) to do something (from a position of authority): *He ordered me to stand up.* □ **ordonner**

2 to give an instruction to supply: *I have ordered some new furniture from the shop*; *He ordered a steak.* □ **commander**

3 to put in order: *Should we order these alphabetically?* □ **organiser**

'**orderly** *adjective* well-behaved; quiet: *an orderly queue of people.* □ **discipliné**

■ *noun – plural* '**orderlies** – 1 a hospital attendant who does routine jobs. □ **aide-infirmier, ière**

2 a soldier who carries an officer's orders and messages. □ **ordonnance**

'**orderliness** *noun.* □ **(habitudes d')ordre**

'**order form** *noun* a form on which a customer's order is written. □ **bon de commande**

in order 1 correct according to what is regularly done, *especially* in meetings *etc*: *It is quite in order to end the meeting now.* □ **dans les règles**

2 in a good efficient state: *Everything is in order for the party.* □ **en ordre**

in order (that) so that: *She checked all her figures again in order that the report might be as accurate as possible.* □ **pour/afin que**

in order to for the purpose of: *I went home in order to change my clothes.* □ **pour/afin de**

made to order made when and how a customer wishes: *curtains made to order.* □ **fait sur commande**

on order having been ordered but not yet supplied: *We don't have any copies of this book at the moment, but it's on order.* □ **commandé**

order about to keep on giving orders (to someone): *I'm tired of him ordering me about all the time.* □ **commander**

out of order 1 not working (properly): *The machine is out of order.* □ **détraqué, hors d'usage**

2 not correct according to what is regularly done, *especially* in meetings *etc*: *He was out of order in saying that.* □ **contraire aux règles**

a tall order a difficult job or task: *Asking us to finish this by Friday is a bit of a tall order.* □ **beaucoup**

ordinal ['ɔːdɪnl]: **ordinal numbers** the numbers which show order in a series *ie* first, second, third *etc*. □ **(nombre) ordinal**

See also **cardinal**.

ordinary ['ɔːdənərɪ] *adjective* 1 usual; normal: *She was behaving in a perfectly ordinary manner.* □ **ordinaire, normal**

2 not unusually good *etc*: *Some people like his poetry but I think it's rather ordinary.* □ **ordinaire, moyen**

'**ordinarily** *adverb* usually. □ **ordinairement**

out of the ordinary unusual: *I don't consider her behaviour at all out of the ordinary.* □ **exceptionnel**

ordination [ɔːdɪ'neɪʃən] *noun* the act of making (a person) a priest, minister *etc*, or the ceremony at which this is done. □ **ordination**

ore [ɔː] *noun* any mineral, rock *etc* from which a metal is obtained: *iron ore.* □ **minerai**

organ[1] ['ɔːgən] *noun* 1 a part of the body or of a plant which has a special purpose: *the reproductive organs.* □ **organe**

2 a means of spreading information, *eg* a newspaper: *an organ of the Communist Party.* □ **organe**

or'ganic [-'ga-] *adjective* 1 of or concerning the organs of the body: *organic diseases.* □ **organique**

2 of, found in, or produced by, living things: *Organic compounds all contain carbon.* □ **organique**

3 (of food) grown without the use of artificial fertilizers. □ **naturel**

or'ganically *adverb.* □ **organiquement**

organ[2] ['ɔːgən] *noun* a *usually* large musical instrument similar to a piano, with or without pipes: *She plays the organ*; *an electric organ.* □ **orgue**

'**organist** *noun* a person who plays the organ: *the organist in the church.* □ **organiste**

organic *see* **organ**[1].

organism ['ɔːgənɪzəm] *noun* a *usually* small living animal or plant: *A pond is full of organisms.* □ **organisme**

organize, organise ['ɔːgənaɪz] *verb* 1 to arrange or prepare (something), *usually* requiring some time or effort: *They organized a conference.* □ **organiser**

2 to make into a society *etc*: *He organized the workers into a trade union.* □ **organiser, (se) syndiquer**

'**organizer, 'organiser** *noun.* □ **organisateur, trice**

,**organi'zation, ,organi'sation** *noun* 1 a group of people working together for a purpose: *a business organization.* □ **organisation**

2 the act of organizing: *Efficiency depends on the organization of one's work.* □ **organisation**

3 the state of being organized: *This report lacks organization.* □ **organisation**

'**organized, 'organised** *adjective* 1 efficient: *She's a very organized person.* □ **organisé**

2 well-arranged: *an organized report.* □ **méthodique**

3 having been planned: *an organized protest.* □ **organisé**

orgy ['ɔːdʒɪ] – *plural* '**orgies** – *noun* a wild party or celebration: *a drunken orgy.* □ **orgie**

Orient ['ɔːrɪənt]: **the Orient** the east (China, Japan *etc*): *the mysteries of the Orient.* □ **Orient**

,**ori'ental** [-'en-] *adjective* in or from the east: *oriental art.* □ **oriental, d'Orient**

■ *noun* a person who comes from the east. □ **Oriental, ale**

orientate ['ɔːrɪənteɪt],**orient** ['ɔːrɪənt] *verb* 1 to get (oneself) used to unfamiliar surroundings, conditions *etc*. □ **(s')orienter**

2 to find out one's position in relation to something else: *The hikers tried to orientate themselves before continuing their walk.* □ **s'orienter**

,**orien'tation** *noun.* □ **orientation**

origin ['ɔrɪdʒɪn] *noun* the place or point from which anything first comes; the cause: *the origin(s) of the English language*; *the origin of the disagreement.* □ **origine**

o'riginal [ə'ri-] *adjective* **1** existing at the beginning; first: *This part of the house is new but the rest is original.* □ **originel**

2 (able to produce ideas which are) new, fresh or not thought of before: *original ideas*; *He has a very original mind.* □ **original**

3 (of a painting *etc*) by the artist *etc*, from which copies may be made: *The original painting is in the museum, but there are hundreds of copies.* □ **original**

■ *noun* **1** the earliest version: *This is the original – all the others are copies.* □ **original**

2 a model from which a painting *etc* is made: *She is the original of the famous portrait.* □ **original**

o,rigi'nality [ərid3i'na-] *noun*: *His writing shows originality.* □ **originalité**

o'riginally *adverb*. □ **à l'origine**

originate [ə'rid3ineit] *verb* to bring or come into being: *That style of painting originated in China.* □ **donner naissance à, prendre naissance**

'origins *noun plural* a person's place of birth, family background *etc*: *He tried to hide his origins.* □ **origines**

ornament ['ɔːnəmənt] *noun* something decorative, intended to make a room *etc* more beautiful: *china ornaments.* □ **ornement**

■ [ɔːnə'ment] *verb* to decorate: *The church was richly ornamented.* □ **décorer**

,ornamen'tation *noun*. □ **décoration**

,orna'mental [-'men-] *adjective* used for ornament: *an ornamental pool in the garden.* □ **ornemental**

ornate [ɔː'neit] *adjective* with a lot of ornament: *an ornate doorway.* □ **très orné**

or'nately *adverb*. □ **avec une profusion d'ornements**

or'nateness *noun*. □ **ornementation exagérée**

ornithology [ɔːni'θolədʒi] *noun* the scientific study of birds and their behaviour: *She is interested in ornithology.* □ **ornithologie**

ornitho'logical [-'lo-] *adjective*. □ **ornithologique**

orni'thologist *noun*. □ **ornithologue**

orphan ['ɔːfən] *noun* a child who has lost both parents (rarely only one parent): *That little girl is an orphan*; *(also adjective) an orphan child.* □ **orphelin, ine**

'orphanage [-nidʒ] *noun* a home for orphans. □ **orphelinat**

orthodox ['ɔːθədoks] *adjective* **1** (of beliefs *etc*) generally accepted: *orthodox views.* □ **orthodoxe**

2 (of people) holding such beliefs: *She is very orthodox in her approach to grammar.* □ **orthodoxe**

orthop(a)edics [ɔːθə'piːdiks] *noun singular* the branch of medicine which concerns diseases and injuries of the bones: *She specialized in orthopaedics.* □ **orthopédie**

ortho'p(a)edic *adjective*. □ **orthopédique**

ostensible [o'stensəbl] *adjective* (of reasons *etc*) apparent, but not necessarily true: *Illness was the ostensible reason for his absence, but in fact he was just lazy.* □ **prétendu**

o'stensibly *adverb*. □ **en apparence**

ostentatious [osten'teiʃəs] *adjective* behaving, done *etc* in such a way as to be seen by other people and to impress them: *Their style of living is very ostentatious.* □ **ostentatoire**

,osten'tation *noun*. □ **ostentation**

,osten'tatiousness *noun*. □ **ostentation**

,osten'tatiously *adverb*. □ **avec ostentation**

ostracize, ostracise ['ostrəsaiz] *verb* to refuse to accept (someone) in society or a group: *His former friends ostracized him because of his rudeness.* □ **frapper d'ostracisme**

'ostracism *noun*. □ **ostracisme**

ostrich ['ostritʃ] *noun* a type of large bird which cannot fly. □ **autruche**

other ['ʌðə] **1** *adjective, pronoun* the second of two: *I have lost my other glove*; *I've got one of my gloves but I can't find the other* (one). □ **autre**

2 *adjective, pronoun* those people, things *etc* not mentioned, present *etc*; additional: *Some of them have arrived – where are the others?*; *The baby is here and the other children are at school.* □ **autre**

3 *adjective* (with **day, week** *etc*) recently past: *I saw him just the other day/morning.* □ **autre**

'otherwise *adverb* **1** in every other way except this: *She has a big nose but otherwise she is very good-looking.* □ **autrement**

2 doing, thinking *etc* something else: *I am otherwise engaged this evening.* □ **à autre chose**

■ *conjunction* or else; if not: *Take a taxi – otherwise you'll be late.* □ **sinon, autrement**

no/none other than the very same person as: *The man who had sent the flowers was none other than the man she had spoken to the night before.* □ **nul autre que**

other than except: *There was no one there other than an old woman.* □ **autrement que**

somehow or other in some way or by some means not known or decided: *I'll finish this job on time somehow or other.* □ **d'une manière ou d'une autre**

someone/something or other a person or thing that is not known: *Someone or other broke that window.* □ **quelqu'un/quelque chose**

somewhere or other in one place if not in another; in some place not known or decided: *She must have hidden it somewhere or other.* □ **quelque part**

otter ['otə] *noun* a type of small furry river animal that eats fish. □ **loutre**

ought [ɔːt] – *negative short form* **oughtn't** ['ɔːtnt] – *verb* (usually with **to**) **1** used to indicate duty; should: *You ought to help them*; *He oughtn't to have done that.* □ **devoir**

2 used to indicate something that one could reasonably expect; should: *He ought to have been able to do it.* □ **devoir**

ounce [auns] *noun* (*usually abbreviated to* **oz** *when written*) a unit of weight, 28.35 grams. □ **once**

our [auə] *adjective* belonging to us: *This is our house.* □ **notre**

ours [auəz] *pronoun* the one(s) belonging to us: *The house is ours.* □ **le nôtre**

our'selves *pronoun* **1** used as the object of a verb when the person speaking and other people are the object of an action *etc* they perform: *We saw ourselves in the mirror.* □ **nous**

2 used to emphasize **we, us** or the names of the speaker and other people performing an action *etc*: *We ourselves played no part in this.* □ **nous-mêmes**

3 without help *etc*: *We'll just have to finish the job ourselves.* □ **nous-mêmes, tout seuls**

oust [aust] *verb* to force out (and take the place of): *She ousted him as leader of the party.* □ **évincer**

out [aut] **1** *adverb, adjective* not in a building *etc*; from inside a building *etc*; in(to) the open air: *The children are out in the garden*; *They went out for a walk.* □ **dehors**

2 *adverb* from inside (something): *He opened the desk and took out a pencil.* □ **sortir**

3 *adverb, adjective* away from home, an office *etc*: *We had an evening out*; *The manager is out.* □ **dehors, sorti**

4 *adverb, adjective* far away: *The ship was out at sea*; *He went out to India.* □ **au large; en route vers**

5 *adverb* loudly and clearly: *He shouted out the answer.* □ **fort, tout haut**

6 *adverb* completely: *She was tired out.* □ **complètement**

7 *adverb, adjective* not correct: *My calculations seem to be out.* □ **faux**

8 *adverb, adjective* free, known, available *etc*: *She let the cat out*; *The secret is out.* □ **connu**

9 *adverb, adjective* (in games) having been defeated: *The batsman was (caught) out.* □ **éliminé**

10 *adverb, adjective* on strike: *The women walked out in protest.* □ **en grève**

11 *adverb, adjective* no longer in fashion: *Long hair is definitely out.* □ **démodé**

12 *adverb, adjective* (of the tide) with the water at or going to its lowest level: *The tide is (going) out.* □ **bas**

13 *adjective* unacceptable: *That suggestion is right out.* □ **inacceptable**

■ (*as part of a word*) **1** not inside or near, as in **outlying.** □ **ex- ... excentrique**

2 indicating outward movement, as in **outburst.** □ **ex- ... explosion**

3 indicating that the action goes further or beyond a normal action, as in **outshine.** □ **sur- ... surpasser**

'outer *adjective* outside; far from (the centre of) something: *outer space.* □ **extérieur**

'outermost *adjective* nearest the edge, outside *etc*: *the outermost ring on the target.* □ **le plus à l'extérieur**

'outing *noun* a *usually* short trip, made for pleasure: *an outing to the seaside.* □ **sortie, randonnée**

'outward *adjective* **1** on or towards the outside; able to be seen: *Judging by his outward appearance, he's not very rich*; *no outward sign of unhappiness.* □ **(vers l')extérieur**

2 (of a journey) away from: *The outward journey will be by sea, but they will return home by air.* □ **d'aller**

'outwardly *adverb* in appearance: *Outwardly he is cheerful, but he is really a very unhappy person.* □ **en apparence**

'outwards *adverb* towards the outside edge or surface: *Moving outwards from the centre of the painting, we see that the figures become smaller.* □ **vers l'extérieur**

'out-and-out *adjective* very bad: *an out-and-out liar.* □ **fieffé**

out of date *see* **date.**

,out-of-the-'way *adjective* difficult to reach or arrive at: *an out-of-the-way place.* □ **perdu**

be out for to be wanting or intending to get: *She is out for revenge.* □ **vouloir, chercher**

be out to to be determined to: *She is out to win the race.* □ **être résolu à**

out of 1 from inside: *He took it out of the bag.* □ **hors de**

2 not in: *Mr. Smith is out of the office*; *out of danger*; *out of sight.* □ **hors de**

3 from among: *Four out of five people like this song.* □ **sur**

4 having none left: *She is quite out of breath.* □ **sans**

5 because of: *She did it out of curiosity/spite.* □ **par**

6 from: *He drank the lemonade straight out of the bottle.* □ **à même qqch.**

out of doors outside: *We like to eat out of doors in summer.* □ **au grand air**

out of it 1 not part of a group, activity *etc*: *I felt a bit out of it at the party.* □ **en marge, de trop**

2 no longer involved in something: *That was a crazy scheme – I'm glad to be out of it.* □ **plus dans le coup**

out of the way 1 remote, removed from great population: *We had a pic-nic at an out of the way spot in the country.* □ **éloigné**

2 unusual: *There was nothing out of the way about what she said.* □ **insolite**

outback ['autbak] *noun* (in Australia) the country areas away from the coast and cities. □ **intérieur du pays**

outboard ['autbɔːd]: **outboard motor/engine** a motor or engine fixed on to the outside of a boat. □ **hors-bord**

outbreak ['autbreik] *noun* a sudden beginning (*usually* of something unpleasant): *the outbreak of war.* □ **déclenchement**

outburst ['autbɜːst] *noun* an explosion, *especially* of angry feelings: *a sudden outburst (of rage).* □ **explosion**

outcast ['autkaːst] *noun* a person who has been driven away from friends *etc*: *an outcast from society.* □ **paria**

outcome ['autkʌm] *noun* the result: *What was the outcome of your discussion?* □ **résultat**

outcry ['autkrai] *noun* a show of disapproval *etc*, *especially* by the general public: *There was a great outcry about the inadequate train service.* □ **tollé**

outdo [aut'duː] – *past tense* **out'did** [-'did]: *past participle* **out'done** [-'dʌn] – *verb* to do better than: *I worked very hard as I did not want to be outdone by anyone.* □ **surpasser**

outdoor ['autdɔː] *adjective* done, for use *etc* outside, not in a building: *outdoor shoes.* □ **de plein air**

out'doors *adverb* outside; not in a building *etc*: *We spend a lot of time outdoors.* □ **dehors, à l'extérieur**

outer, outermost *see* **out.**

outfit ['autfit] *noun* a set of clothes, *especially* for a particular occasion: *a wedding outfit.* □ **tenue, toilette**

outgoing [aut'gouiŋ] *adjective* **1** friendly: *a very outgoing personality.* □ **sociable**

2 going out; leaving: *the outgoing president.* □ **sortant, en partance**

outgrow [aut'grou] – *past tense* **out'grew** [-'gruː]: *past* *participle* **out'grown** – *verb* to grow too big or too old for: *My daughter has outgrown all her clothes.* □ **devenir trop grand pour**

outing *see* **out**.

outlaw ['autlɔː] *noun* a criminal, *especially* one who is punished by being refused the protection of the law. □ **hors-la-loi**

■ *verb* to make (someone) an outlaw. □ **mettre hors la loi**

outlay ['autlei] *noun* money spent: *an outlay of $500 on furniture.* □ **dépenses, mise de fonds**

outlet ['autlit] *noun* a way or passage outwards or for releasing: *That pipe is an outlet from the main tank; an outlet for her energy.* □ **déversoir; débouché**

outline ['autlain] *noun* 1 the line forming, or showing, the outer edge of something: *She drew the outline of the face first, then added the features.* □ **contour**

2 a short description of the main details of a plan *etc*: *Don't tell me the whole story, just give me an outline.* □ **plan, grandes lignes**

■ *verb* to draw or give the outline of. □ **tracer le contour de, exposer les grandes lignes de**

outlook ['autluk] *noun* 1 a view: *Their house has a wonderful outlook.* □ **vue**

2 a person's view of life *etc*: *He has a strange outlook (on life).* □ **point de vue**

3 what is likely to happen in the future: *The weather outlook is bad.* □ **perspectives**

outlying ['autlaiiŋ] *adjective* distant, far from a city *etc*: *outlying villages.* □ **écarté, isolé**

outnumber [aut'nʌmbə] *verb* to be more (in number) than: *The boys in the class outnumber the girls.* □ **être plus nombreux que**

out of date *see* **date**.

out-patient ['autpeiʃənt] *noun* a person who comes to hospital for treatment but does not stay there overnight. □ **malade en consultation externe**

■ *adjective*: *an out-patient department.*

outpost ['autpoust] *noun* a distant place: *The island was an outpost of the nation.* □ **avant-poste**

output ['autput] *noun* the quantity of goods, amount of work produced: *The output of this factory has increased by 20%; His output is poor.* □ **production, rendement**

outrage ['autreidʒ] *noun* a wicked act, *especially* of great violence: *the outrages committed by the soldiers; The decision to close the road is a public outrage.* □ **atrocité; scandale**

■ *verb* to hurt, shock or insult: *She was outraged by his behaviour.* □ **outrager**

out'rageous *adjective* noticeably terrible: *an outrageous hat; outrageous behaviour.* □ **monstrueux**

out'rageously *adverb*. □ **outrageusement**

out'rageousness *noun*. □ **caractère outrageant**

outright [aut'rait] *adverb* 1 honestly: *I told him outright what I thought.* □ **franchement**

2 immediately: *He was killed outright.* □ **sur le coup**

■ ['autrait] *adjective* without any exception or doubt: *He is the outright winner.* □ **absolu, incontesté**

outset ['autset] *noun* the beginning of something: *Our policy has to be clear from the outset.* □ **début**

outshine [aut'ʃain] – *past tense, past participle* **out'shone** [-'ʃɔn] – *verb* to be brighter than: *She outshone all the other students.* □ **éclipser**

outside ['autsaid] *noun* the outer surface: *The outside of the house was painted white.* □ **extérieur**

■ ['autsaid] *adjective* 1 of, on, or near the outer part of anything: *the outside door.* □ **extérieur**

2 not part of (a group, one's work *etc*): *We shall need outside help; She has a lot of outside interests.* □ **indépendant, de l'extérieur**

3 (of a chance *etc*) very small. □ **très faible**

■ [aut'said] *adverb* 1 out of, not in a building *etc*: *He went outside; She stayed outside.* □ **dehors**

2 on the outside: *The house looked beautiful outside.* □ **à l'extérieur**

■ [aut'said] *preposition* on the outer part or side of; not inside or within: *He stood outside the house; She did that outside working hours.* □ **hors de, en dehors de**

out'sider *noun* 1 a person who is not part of a group *etc*. □ **étranger, ère**

2 (in a race *etc*) a runner who is not expected to win: *The race was won by a complete outsider.* □ **outsider**

at the ,out'side at the most: *I shall be there for an hour at the outside.* □ **au plus**

outsize ['autsaiz] *adjective* (for people who are) bigger than usual: *outsize clothes.* □ **grande taille**

outskirts ['autskɔːts] *noun plural* the outer parts or area, *especially* of a town: *I live on the outskirts of Montreal.* □ **banlieue**

outsmart [autsmart] *verb* to outwit or to get the better of someone by being clever about something: *The magician outsmarted the audience by changing the tricks and no one could figure them out.* □ **déjouer**

outspoken [aut'spoukən] *adjective* saying exactly what one thinks: *She's a very outspoken person.* □ **qui ne mâche pas ses mots**

outstanding [aut'standiŋ] *adjective* 1 excellent; very good: *an outstanding student.* □ **exceptionnel**

2 not yet paid, done *etc*: *You must pay all outstanding bills.* □ **impayé**

out'standingly *adverb*: *outstandingly good.* □ **remarquablement**

outstrip [aut'strip] – *past tense, past participle* **out'stripped** – *verb* to go much faster than: *He outstripped the other runners.* □ **devancer**

outward(s), outwardly *see* **out**.

outweigh [aut'wei] *verb* to be greater or more than: *The advantages outweigh the disadvantages.* □ **l'emporter sur**

outwit [aut'wit] – *past tense, past participle* **out'witted** – *verb* to defeat (someone) by being cleverer than he is: *She managed to outwit the police and escape.* □ **se montrer plus malin que**

ova *see* **ovum**.

oval ['ouvəl] *adjective* shaped like an egg: *an oval table.* □ **ovale**

■ *noun* an oval shape: *He drew an oval.* □ **ovale**

ovary ['ouvəri] – *plural* **'ovaries** – *noun* the part of the female body in which eggs are formed. □ **ovaire**

ovation [ə'veiʃən, ou-] *noun* cheering or applause *etc* to express approval, welcome *etc*: *They gave the president a standing ovation* (= They stood and applauded him). □ **ovation**

oven ['ʌvn] *noun* a closed box-like space, *usually* part of a cooker, which is heated for cooking food: *She put the cake into the oven.* □ **four**

over ['ouvə] *preposition* **1** higher than; above in position, number, authority *etc*: *Hang that picture over the fireplace*; *He's over 90 years old.* □ **au-dessus de, par-dessus, plus de**

2 from one side to another, on or above the top of; on the other side of: *He jumped over the gate*; *She fell over the cat.* □ **sur, par-dessus, de l'autre côté**

3 covering: *She put her handkerchief over her face.* □ **sur**

4 across: *You find people like him all over the world.* □ **partout**

5 about: *a quarrel over money.* □ **à propos de**

6 by means of: *He spoke to her over the telephone.* □ **à**

7 during: *Over the years, she grew to hate her husband.* □ **au cours de**

8 while having *etc*: *He fell asleep over his dinner.* □ **sur**

■ *adjective* **1** higher, moving *etc* above: *The plane flew over about an hour ago.* □ **au-dessus de**

2 used to show movement, change of position: *He rolled over on his back*; *She turned over the page.* □ **de l'autre côté**

3 across: *He went over and spoke to them.* □ **là-bas**

4 downwards: *He fell over.* □ **vers le bas**

5 higher in number *etc*: *for people aged twenty and over.* □ **plus**

6 through from beginning to end, carefully: *Read it over*; *Talk it over between you.* □ **complètement, en détail**

■ *adjective* finished: *The affair is over now.* □ **fini**

■ *noun* (in cricket) a certain number of balls bowled from one end of the wicket: *She bowled thirty overs in the match.* □ **série de...**

■ (*as part of a word*) **1** too (much), as in **overdo**.

2 in a higher position, as in **overhead**.

3 covering, as in **overcoat**.

4 down from an upright position, as in **overturn**.

5 completely, as in **overcome**.

over again once more: *Play the tune over again.* □ **encore (une fois)**

over all *see* **overall** below.

over and done with finished; no longer important: *He has behaved very wickedly in the past but that's all over and done with now.* □ **fini et bien fini**

to speak **over twenty** (not **twenty over**) languages.

overall ['ouvərɔːl] *adjective* complete, including everything: *What is the overall cost of the scheme?* □ **total**

■ [ouvər'ɔːl] *adverb* (*also* **over all**) complete, including everything: *What will the scheme cost overall?* □ **au total**

'**overalls** *noun plural* a type of trousers or suit made of hard-wearing materials worn *usually* over ordinary clothes by workmen *etc* to protect them from dirt *etc*: *The painter put on his overalls before starting work*; *I'll need a clean pair of overalls tomorrow.* □ **salopette**

overarm ['ouvəraːm] *adjective, adverb* (of a throw) with the hand and arm moving around above the shoulder: *She bowled overarm*; *an overarm throw.* □ **par-dessus l'épaule**

overbalance [ouvə'baləns] *verb* to lose balance and fall: *He overbalanced on the edge of the cliff and fell into the sea below.* □ **perdre l'équilibre**

overbearing [ouvə'beəriŋ] *adjective* too sure that one is right: *I disliked her overbearing manner.* □ **arrogant**

overboard ['ouvəbɔːd] *adverb* over the side of a ship or boat into the water: *He jumped overboard.* □ **par-dessus bord**

overcast [ouvə'kaːst] *adjective* cloudy: *on a slightly overcast day.* □ **couvert**

overcharge [ouvə'tʃaːdʒ] *verb* to charge too much: *I have been overcharged for these goods.* □ **faire payer trop cher**

overcoat ['ouvəkout] *noun* a *usually* heavy coat worn over all other clothes *especially* in winter. □ **manteau**

overcome [ouvə'kʌm] *adjective* helpless; defeated by emotion *etc*: *overcome with grief; I felt quite overcome.* □ **accablé**

■ *verb* – *past tense* ,over'came [-'keim]: *past participle* ,over'come – to defeat or conquer: *She finally overcame her fear of the dark.* □ **vaincre, surmonter**

overcrowded [ouvə'kraudid] *adjective* having too many people on or in: *overcrowded buses/cities.* □ **bondé, surpeuplé**

,over'crowding *noun* the state of being overcrowded: *There is often overcrowding in cities.* □ **surpeuplement**

overdo [ouvə'duː] – *past tense* ,over'did [-'did]: *past participle* over'done [-'dʌn] – *verb* **1** to do, say (something) in an exaggerated way *etc*: *They overdid the sympathy.* □ **exagérer**

2 to cook for too long: *The meat was rather overdone.* □ **trop cuire**

overdose ['ouvədous] *noun* too great an amount (of medicine): *an overdose of sleeping-pills.* □ **surdose**

overdraft ['ouvədraːft] *noun* the amount of money by which a bank account is overdrawn: *a large overdraft.* □ **découvert**

overdrawn [ouvə'drɔːn] *adjective* having taken more money out of one's account than it had in it: *My account is overdrawn.* □ **à découvert**

overdue [ouvə'djuː] *adjective* **1** late: *The train is overdue.* □ **en retard**

2 (of bills, cheques *etc*) not yet paid, done, delivered *etc*, although the date for doing this has passed: *overdue library books.* □ **impayé, en retard**

overestimate [ouvər'estimeit] *verb* to estimate, judge *etc* (something) to be greater, larger or more important than it is: *He overestimates his own ability.* □ **surestimer**

overflow [ouvə'flou] *verb* to flow over the edge or limits (of): *The river overflowed (its banks)*; *The crowd overflowed into the next room.* □ **déborder (de)**

■ ['ouvəflou] *noun* **1** a flowing over of liquid: *I put a bucket under the pipe to catch the overflow*; (*also adjective*) *an overflow pipe.* □ **trop-plein**

2 an overflow pipe. □ **déversoir**

overgrown [ouvə'groun] *adjective* **1** full of plants that have grown too large or thick: *Our garden is overgrown with weeds.* □ **envahi (par la végétation)**

2 grown too large: *an overgrown puppy.* □ **qui a trop grandi**

overhaul [ouvə'hoːl] *verb* to examine carefully and repair: *I had my car overhauled at the garage.* □ **réviser**

■ ['ouvəhoːl] *noun: a complete overhaul.* □ **révision**

overhead [ouvə'hed] *adverb, adjective* above; over one's head: *The plane flew overhead; an overhead bridge.* □ **au-dessus (de nos têtes); aérien**

overhear [ouvə'hiə] – *past tense, past participle* ,**over'heard** [-'həːd] – *verb* to hear (what one was not intended to hear): *She overheard two people talking in the next room.* □ **entendre (par hasard)**

overjoyed [ouvə'dʒɔid] *adjective* full of joy; very glad: *She was overjoyed to hear of his safe arrival.* □ **enchanté**

overlap [ouvə'lap] – *past tense, past participle* ,**over'lapped** – *verb* to extend over and cover a part of: *The pieces of cloth overlapped (each other).* □ **(se) chevaucher**

■ ['ouvəlap] *noun: an overlap of two centimetres.* □ **chevauchement**

overload [ouvə'loud] *verb* to fill with too much of something: *The truck overturned because it had been overloaded.* □ **surcharger**

overlook [ouvə'luk] *verb* **1** to look down on: *The house overlooked the river.* □ **avoir vue sur, dominer**

2 to take no notice of: *We shall overlook your lateness this time.* □ **fermer les yeux sur**

overnight [ouvə'nait] *adjective, adverb* **1** for or during the night: *an overnight bag.* □ **d'une/de nuit; (pendant) la nuit**

2 very quick(ly): *He was an overnight success.* □ **du jour au lendemain**

overpass [ouvə'paːs] *noun* a bridge-like part of a road *etc* which passes over another road, a railway *etc*: *an overpass across the road.* □ **pont autoroutier, viaduc**

overpower [ouvə'pauə] *verb* to defeat or make helpless or captive by a greater strength: *The police overpowered the thieves.* □ **vaincre, maîtriser**

,**over'powering** *adjective* very strong: *That smell is quite overpowering.* □ **irrésistible, suffocant**

overrate [ouvə'reit] *verb* to think that something is better, stronger, more valuable *etc* than it really is: *Her beauty is overrated.* □ **surestimer**

overreact [ouvəri'akt] *verb* to react too much: *She overreacts to criticism.* □ **réagir de manière excessive**

,**overre'action** [-ʃən] *noun.* □ **réaction excessive**

overrule [ouvə'ruːl] *verb* to go against a judgment that has already been made: *The judge overruled the previous decision.* □ **casser**

overrun [ouvə'rʌn] – *present participle* ,**over'running**: *past tense* ,**over'ran** [-'ran]: *past participle* ,**over'run** – *verb* **1** to fill, occupy or take possession of: *The house was overrun with mice.* □ **envahir, occuper**

2 to continue longer than intended: *The program overran by five minutes.* □ **dépasser le temps alloué**

overseas ['ouvəsiːz] *adjective,* [ouvə'siːz] *adverb* across the sea; abroad: *He went overseas; overseas trade.* □ **d'outre-mer; outre-mer**

oversee [ouvə'siː] – *past tense* ,**over'saw** [-'sɔː]: *past participle* ,**over'seen** – *verb* to supervise: *He oversees production at the factory.* □ **surveiller**

overseer ['ouvəsiə] *noun: The overseer reported her for being late.* □ **contremaître**

overshadow [ouvə'ʃadou] *verb* to make less important *especially* by being much better than: *With her beauty and wit she quite overshadowed her sister.* □ **éclipser**

overshoot [ouvə'ʃuːt] – *past tense, past participle* ,**over'shot** [-'ʃot] – *verb* to go farther than (the point one was aiming at): *The plane overshot the runway.* □ **dépasser**

oversight ['ouvəsait] *noun* a failure to notice: *Due to an oversight, we have not paid the bill.* □ **inadvertance, oubli**

oversleep [ouvə'sliːp] – *past tense, past participle* ,**over'slept** [-'slept] – *verb* to sleep longer than one intended: *He overslept and missed the train.* □ **se réveiller (trop) tard**

overspend [ouvə'spend] – *past tense, past participle* ,**over'spent** [-t] – *verb* to spend too much money: *He overspent on his new house.* □ **trop dépenser**

overt [ou'vəːt] *adjective* not hidden or secret: *overt opposition to a plan.* □ **déclaré**

o'vertly *adverb.* □ **ouvertement**

overtake [ouvə'teik] – *past tense* ,**over'took** [-'tuk]: *past participle* ,**over'taken** – *verb* to pass (a car *etc*) while driving *etc*: *He overtook a police-car.* □ **dépasser**

overtax [ouvə'taks] *verb* to put too great a strain on: *You overtaxed your strength.* □ **abuser de**

overthrow [ouvə'θrou] – *past tense* ,**over'threw** [-'θruː]: *past participle* ,**overthrown** – *verb* to defeat and force out of power: *The government has been overthrown.* □ **renverser**

overtime ['ouvətaim] *noun* time spent in working beyond one's set number of hours *etc*: *She did five hours' overtime this week.* □ **heures supplémentaires**

overtones ['ouvətounz] *noun plural* suggestions; hints: *There were overtones of discontent in his speech.* □ **accents**

overture ['ouvətjuə] *noun* a piece of music played as an introduction to an opera *etc*. □ **ouverture**

overturn [ouvə'təːn] *verb* to turn over: *They overturned the boat; The car overturned.* □ **faire chavirer, (se) retourner**

overweight [ouvə'weit] *adjective* too heavy; too fat: *If I eat too much I soon get overweight.* □ **trop gros**

overwhelm [ouvə'welm] *verb* to defeat or overcome: *She was overwhelmed with work/grief.* □ **écraser**

,**over'whelming** *adjective* very great: *an overwhelming victory.* □ **écrasant**

overwork [ouvə'wəːk] *noun* the act of working too hard: *It's overwork that made him ill.* □ **surmenage**

,**over'worked** *adjective* made to work too hard: *His staff are overworked.* □ **surmené**

ovum ['ouvəm] – *plural* **ova** ['ouvə] – *noun* the egg from which the young of people and animals develop. □ **ovule**

owe [ou] *verb* to be in debt to: *I owe (her) $10.* □ **devoir**

'**owing** *adjective* still to be paid: *There is some money still owing (to us).* □ **dû**

owing to because of: *Owing to the rain, the football has been cancelled.* □ **en raison de**

> **owing to** is used to mean 'because of': *The shop is closed owing to* (not *due to*) *the manager's illness.*
> **due to** is used to mean 'caused by': *The accident was believed to be due to his negligence.*

owl [aul] *noun* a type of bird that flies at night and feeds on small birds and animals. □ **hibou**

own [oun] *verb* **1** to have as a possession: *I own a car.* □ **posséder**
2 to admit that something is true: *I own that I have not been working very hard.* □ **avouer**
■ *adjective, pronoun* belonging to (the person stated): *The house is my own*; *I saw it with my own eyes.* □ **propre**
'**owner** *noun* a person who owns something: *Are you the owner of that car?* □ **propriétaire**
'**ownership** *noun*. □ **(droit de) propriété**
get one's own back to revenge oneself: *He has beaten me this time, but I'll get my own back* (*on him*). □ **prendre sa revanche**
own up (*often with* **to**) to admit that one has done something: *I owned up to having broken the window.* □ **avouer**

ox [oks] – *plural* '**oxen** – *noun* **1** a castrated bull used (formerly in Britain and still in some countries) to pull carts, ploughs *etc*: *an ox-drawn cart.* □ **bœuf**
2 any bull or cow. □ **bovidé**

oxygen ['oksidʒən] *noun* an element, a gas without taste, colour or smell, forming part of the air: *She died from lack of oxygen.* □ **oxygène**
oxygen mask a mask through which a person can breathe oxygen. □ **masque à oxygène**

oyster ['oistə] *noun* a type of shellfish eaten as food, and from which pearls are formed. □ **huître**
oyster bed a place in the sea where oysters breed or are bred. □ **banc d'huîtres**

ozone ['ouzoun] *noun* a type of oxygen. □ **ozone**

Pp

pace [peis] *noun* 1 a step: *He took a pace forward.* □ **pas**
2 speed of movement: *a fast pace.* □ **allure**
■ *verb* to walk backwards and forwards (across): *She paced up and down.* □ **faire les cent pas**
'**pacemaker** *noun* 1 an electronic device to make the heart beats regular or stronger. □ **stimulateur cardiaque**
2 a person who sets the speed of a race. □ **meneur, euse de train**
keep pace with to go as fast as: *She kept pace with the car on her motorbike.* □ **aller à la même allure que**
pace out to measure by walking along, across *etc* with even steps: *She paced out the room.* □ **mesurer (une distance) au pas**
put someone *etc* **through his** *etc* **paces** to make someone *etc* show what he *etc* can do: *He put his new car through its paces.* □ **mettre qqn à l'épreuve**
set the pace to go forward at a particular speed which everyone else has to follow: *Her experiments set the pace for future research.* □ **régler l'allure**

pacify ['pasifai] *verb* to make calm or peaceful: *She tried to pacify the quarrelling children.* □ **apaiser**
pacifier *noun* a soother in the shape of a nipple used to comfort babies: *If we can't find the baby's pacifier, she'll cry all night.* □ **sucette**
,**pacifi'cation** [-fi-] *noun.* □ **pacification**
'**pacifism** *noun* the belief that all war is wrong and that one must not take part in it. □ **pacifisme**
'**pacifist** *noun* a person who believes in pacifism: *As a pacifist he refused to fight in the war.* □ **pacifiste**

pack [pak] *noun* 1 things tied up together or put in a container, *especially* to be carried on one's back: *He carried his luggage in a pack on his back.* □ **paquet, sac**
2 a set of (fifty-two) playing cards: *a pack of cards.* □ **jeu (de cartes)**
3 a number or group of certain animals: *a pack of wolves/ a wolf-pack.* □ **bande**
4 a packet: *a pack of cigarettes.* □ **paquet**
■ *verb* 1 to put (clothes *etc*) into a bag, suitcase or trunk for a journey: *I've packed all I need and I'm ready to go.* □ **mettre (dans une valise, etc.)**
2 to come together in large numbers in a small space: *They packed into the hall to hear his speech.* □ **s'entasser**
'**packing** *noun* 1 the act of putting things in bags, cases *etc: She has done her packing tonight as she is leaving in the morning.* □ **empaquetage**
2 the materials (paper, string *etc*) used to wrap things for posting *etc: He unwrapped the vase and threw away the packing.* □ **emballage**
'**packing-case** *noun* a (large) wooden box in which goods are packed and sent from place to place. □ **caisse d'emballage**
packed containing as many people as possible: *The theatre/meeting was packed.* □ **bondé**
pack off to send away, *usually* quickly and without wasting time: *They packed the children off to bed early.*

□ **expédier**
pack up to put into containers in order to take somewhere else: *She packed up the contents of her house.* □ **emballer**

package ['pakidʒ] *noun* things wrapped up and tied (for posting *etc*); a parcel: *a package of books.* □ **paquet**
■ *verb* to wrap up into a package: *He packaged (up) the clothes.* □ **empaqueter, emballer**
package holiday, package tour a holiday or tour for which one pays the organizer a fixed price which includes everything (travel, hotel, food *etc*): *It is cheaper to go on a package holiday.* □ **voyage à prix forfaitaire**

packet ['pakit] *noun* a small *often* flat, *usually* paper or cardboard container, especially one in which food is sold or in which small objects are sent through the post: *a packet of biscuits.* □ **paquet**

pact [pakt] *noun* an agreement, *especially* if formal and/ or between the representatives of nations: *They made a pact to help each other.* □ **pacte**

pad¹ [pad] *noun* 1 a soft, cushion-like object made of or filled with a soft material, used to prevent damage by knocking, rubbing *etc: He knelt on a pad to clean the floor.* □ **coussinet**
2 sheets of paper fixed together: *a writing-pad.* □ **blocnotes**
3 a platform from which rockets are sent off: *a launching-pad.* □ **rampe (de lancement)**
■ *verb* – *past tense, past participle* '**padded** – to put a pad in or on (for protection, to make big enough *etc*): *The shoes were too big so she padded them with cottonwool.* □ **rembourrer**
'**padding** *noun* material used to make a pad to protect, fill *etc: He used old blankets as padding.* □ **rembourrage**

pad² [pad] – *past tense, past participle* '**padded** – *verb* to walk softly: *The dog padded along the road.* □ **marcher à pas feutrés**

paddle¹ ['padl] *verb* to walk about in shallow water: *The children went paddling in the sea.* □ **barboter**

paddle² ['padl] *noun* a short, light oar, often with a blade at each end of the shaft, used in canoes *etc.* □ **pagaie**
■ *verb* to move with a paddle: *She paddled the canoe along the river.* □ **pagayer**
'**paddleboat** *noun* a boat driven by paddlewheels. □ **bateau à aubes**
'**paddlewheel** *noun* a large wheel fitted with flat pieces of wood, attached to the side or stern of a boat and turned to make it move through the water. □ **roue à aubes**

> to **paddle** (not **pedal**) a canoe.

paddock ['padək] *noun* a small field, containing grass and *usually* near a house or stable, in which horses *etc* are often kept. □ **enclos**

paddy field ['padifi:ld] *noun* a field, often flooded with water, in which rice is grown. □ **rizière**

padlock ['padlɔk] *noun* a (*usually* metal) movable lock with a U-shaped bar which can be passed through a ring, chain *etc* and locked: *He has put a padlock on the gate.* □ **cadenas**
■ *verb* to fasten with a padlock: *She padlocked her bike.*

□ **cadenasser**

paediatrics *see* **pediatrics.**

pagan ['peigən] *adjective* not belonging to any of the major world religions: *pagan tribes*; *pagan gods.* □ **païen**

■ *noun* a person who does not belong to any of the major world religions. □ **païen, ïenne**

'**paganism** *noun.* □ **paganisme**

page¹ [peidʒ] *noun* one side of a sheet of paper in a book, magazine *etc*: *page ninety-four*; *a three-page letter.* □ **page**

page² [peidʒ] *noun* **1** (in hotels) a boy who takes messages, carries luggage *etc*. □ **chasseur**

2 (*also* '**page boy**) a boy servant. □ **page**

■ *verb* to try to find someone in a public place by calling out his name (often through a loud-speaker system): *I could not see my friend in the hotel, so I had him paged.* □ **(faire) appeler**

pageant ['padʒənt] *noun* **1** a dramatic performance made up of different, *usually* historical scenes, often performed during a procession: *The children performed a historical pageant.* □ **spectacle historique**

2 any fine show or display: *a pageant of colour.* □ **féerie**

'**pageantry** *noun* splendid and colourful show or display: *I love the pageantry of royal processions.* □ **pompe**

pagoda [pə'goudə] *noun* a Chinese temple, built in the shape of a tall tower, each storey of which has its own narrow strip of overhanging roof. □ **pagode**

paid *see* **pay.**

pail [peil] *noun* a bucket: *Fetch a pail of water.* □ **seau**

pain [pein] *noun* hurt or suffering of the body or mind: *a pain in the chest.* □ **douleur, peine**

■ *verb* to cause suffering or upset to (someone): *It pained her to admit that she was wrong.* □ **faire souffrir, peiner**

pained *adjective* showing or expressing pain: *a pained expression.* □ **peiné**

'**painful** *adjective* causing pain: *a painful injury.* □ **douloureux**

'**painfully** *adverb.* □ **douloureusement**

'**painless** *adjective* without pain: *painless childbirth.* □ **indolore**

'**painlessly** *adverb.* □ **sans douleur**

'**painkiller** *noun* a drug *etc* which lessens or removes pain. □ **calmant**

'**painstaking** ['peinz-] *adjective* going to great trouble and taking great care: *a painstaking student.* □ **appliqué, soigneux**

a pain in the neck a person who is constantly annoying: *People who are always complaining are a pain in the neck.* □ **casse-pieds**

take pains to take great trouble and care (to do something): *She took great pains to make sure we enjoyed ourselves.* □ **se donner du mal pour**

paint [peint] *noun* a colouring substance in the form of liquid or paste: *The artist's clothes were covered in paint*; (*also adjective*) *a paint pot.* □ **(de) peinture**

■ *verb* **1** to spread paint carefully on (wood, walls *etc*): *He is painting the kitchen.* □ **peindre, peinturer**

2 to make a picture (of something or someone) using

paint: *She painted her mother and father.* □ **peindre**

'**painter** *noun* **1** a person whose job is to put paint on things, *especially* walls, doors *etc* in houses: *We employed a painter to paint the outside of the house.* □ **peintre**

2 an artist who makes pictures in paint: *Who was the painter of this portrait?* □ **(artiste) peintre**

'**painting** *noun* **1** the act or art of using paint: *Painting is very relaxing.* □ **peinture**

2 a painted picture: *There were four paintings (hanging) on the wall.* □ **peinture**

'**paintbox** *noun* a (small) box containing different paints for making pictures. □ **boîte de couleurs**

'**paintbrush** *noun* a brush used for putting on paint. □ **pinceau**

pair [peə] *noun* **1** a set of two of the same thing which are (intended to be) used *etc* together: *a pair of shoes/gloves.* □ **paire**

2 a single thing made up of two parts: *a pair of scissors*; *a pair of pants.* □ **paire**

3 two people, animals *etc*, often one of either sex, who are thought of together for some reason: *a pair of giant pandas*; *John and James are the guilty pair.* □ **couple**

■ *verb* to make into a pair: *She was paired with my brother in the tennis match.* □ **faire la paire**

---

pair is singular: *That pair of trousers needs mending*; *There is a pair of gloves on the table.*

---

pal [pal] *noun* an informal word for a friend: *My son brought a pal home for tea.* □ **copain, ine**

'**pally** *adjective* friendly: *They've become very pally.* □ **copain avec qqn**

palace ['paləs] *noun* a large and magnificent house, *especially* one lived in by a king or queen: *Buckingham Palace.* □ **palais**

palatial [pə'leiʃəl] *adjective* large and magnificent, as (in) a palace: *They lived in a palatial house*; *palatial rooms.* □ **grandiose**

palate ['palət] *noun* **1** the top of the inside of the mouth. □ **palais**

2 the ability to tell good wine, food *etc* from bad: *He has a good palate for wine.* □ **palais (fin)**

palatial *see* **palace.**

pale [peil] *adjective* **1** (of a person, his face *etc*) having less colour than normal: *a pale face*; *She went pale with fear.* □ **pâle**

2 (of a colour) closer to white than black; not dark: *pale green.* □ **pâle**

■ *verb* to become pale: *She paled at the bad news.* □ **pâlir**

'**paleness** *noun.* □ **pâleur**

palette ['palit] *noun* a small flat piece of wood *etc*, with a hole for the thumb, on which an artist mixes his colours. □ **palette**

pall¹ [poːl] *noun* the (*usually* dark-coloured) cloth which covers a coffin at a funeral: *a pall of purple-velvet*; *A pall of smoke hung over the town.* □ **drap mortuaire, voile**

pall² [poːl] *verb* to become boring or uninteresting: *Loud music soon palls.* □ **lasser**

pallid ['palid] *adjective* unpleasantly pale (*usually* suggesting ill-health): *He looked pallid and sickly.* □ **blême**
'pallor *noun* unpleasant paleness: *an unhealthy pallor.* □ **pâleur**
pally *see* pal.
palm[1] [paːm] *noun* the inner surface of the hand between the wrist and the fingers: *She held the mouse in the palm of her hand.* □ **paume**
  palm (something) off on (someone) to get rid of (an undesirable thing or person) by giving, selling *etc* to (someone else): *They palmed off their unwelcome guests on the people next door.* □ **refiler**
palm[2] [paːm] *noun* (*also* **palm tree**) a kind of tall tree, with broad, spreading leaves, which grows in hot countries: *a coconut palm.* □ **palmier, cocotier**
palpitate ['palpiteit] *verb* (of the heart) to beat rapidly. □ **palpiter**
,palpi'tations *noun plural* an attack of rapid beating of the heart. □ **palpitations**
pamper ['pampə] *verb* to treat with great kindness and give a great many special things to (a person): *The child was pampered by his parents.* □ **dorloter**
pamphlet ['pamflit] *noun* a small paper-covered book *usually* giving information, expressing an opinion on a popular subject *etc*: *a political pamphlet.* □ **opuscule, pamphlet**
pan[1] [pan] *noun* a metal pot used for cooking food: *a frying-pan; a saucepan.* □ **casserole**
'pancake *noun* a thin cake *usually* made of milk, flour and eggs and fried in a pan *etc*. □ **crêpe**
pan[2] [pan] – *past tense, past participle* **panned** – *verb* to move (a film or television camera) so as to follow a moving object or show a wide view: *The camera panned slowly across to the other side of the street.* □ **panoramiquer**
pan- [pan] all; whole: *pan-American.* □ **pan**
panama [panə'maː] *noun* (*often* **panama hat**) a hat made of straw-like material, worn in hot weather. □ **panama**
pancreas ['paŋkriəs] *noun* a part of the body which helps in the digestion of food. □ **pancréas**
panda ['pandə] *noun* (*often* **giant panda**) a large black and white bear-like animal of the raccoon family, which lives in the mountains of China. □ **panda**
pandemonium [pandi'mouniəm] *noun* a state of noise and confusion: *There was pandemonium in the classroom before the teacher arrived.* □ **vacarme**
pander ['pandə]: **pander to** to give in to (a desire, *especially* if unworthy): *Some newspapers pander to people's interest in crime and violence.* □ **encourager bassement**
pane [pein] *noun* a flat piece of glass: *a window-pane.* □ **vitre**
panel ['panl] *noun* **1** a flat, straight-sided piece of wood, fabric *etc* such as is put into a door, wall, dress *etc*: *a door-panel.* □ **pan(neau)**
  2 a group of people chosen for a particular purpose *eg* to judge a contest, take part in a quiz or other game: *I will ask some questions and the panel will try to answer them.* □ **jury, comité**
'panelled *adjective* made of or surrounded with panels

(*usually* of wood): *a panelled door; oak-panelled.* □ **lambrissé**
'panelling *noun* (wood used for) panels covering the walls of a room *etc*: *oak panelling.* □ **boiserie(s)**
pang [paŋ] *noun* a sudden sharp pain: *a pang of hunger/grief/regret.* □ **douleur**
panic ['panik] *noun* (a) sudden great fear, *especially* that spreads through a crowd *etc*: *The fire caused a panic in the city.* □ **panique**
  ■ *verb* – *past tense, past participle* **'panicked** – to make or become so frightened that one loses the power to think clearly: *He panicked at the sight of the audience.* □ **paniquer**
'panicky *adjective* inclined to panic: *She gets panicky in an exam; in a panicky mood.* □ **sujet à la panique**
pannier ['paniə] *noun* one of a pair of baskets, bags *etc* carried on either side of the back of a horse, bicycle, motorbike *etc*. □ **panier**
panorama [panə'raːmə] *noun* a wide view, of a landscape *etc*: *There is a wonderful panorama from that hill.* □ **panorama**
,pano'ramic [-'ra-] *adjective* of or like a panorama: *a panoramic view.* □ **panoramique**
pansy ['panzi] – *plural* **'pansies** – *noun* a kind of small flower. □ **pensée**
pant [pant] *verb* **1** to gasp for breath: *He was panting heavily as he ran.* □ **haleter**
  2 to say while gasping for breath: *'Wait for me!' she panted.* □ **dire en haletant**
panther ['panθə] *noun* **1** a leopard, *especially* a large one. □ **panthère**
  2 a puma. □ **couguar**
panties *noun* a short undergarment worn by women. □ **culotte, slip**
pantomime ['pantəmaim] *noun* a play performed at Christmas time, *usually* based on a popular fairy tale, with music, dancing, comedy *etc*. □ **spectacle de Noël**
pantry ['pantri] – *plural* **'pantries** – *noun* a room for storing food: *The house had a large kitchen with a pantry.* □ **garde-manger**
pants [pants] *noun plural* trousers. □ **pantalon**
papa [pə'paː] *noun* a father: *You must ask your papa; Where are you, Papa?* □ **papa**
papacy ['peipəsi] *noun* **1** the position or power of the pope: *The papacy is the central authority of the Roman Catholic church.* □ **papauté**
  2 government by popes: *the history of the papacy.* □ **papauté**
papal ['peipl] *adjective* of the pope: *papal authority.* □ **papal**
papaya [pə'paiə] *noun* a tropical tree or its fruit. □ **papaye**
paper ['peipə] *noun* **1** the material on which these words are written, made from wood, rags *etc* and used for writing, printing, wrapping parcels *etc*: *I need paper and a pen to write a letter;* (*also adjective*) *a paper bag.* □ **(en/de) papier**
  2 a single (often printed or typed) piece of this: *There were papers all over his desk.* □ **(feuille de) papier**
  3 a newspaper: *Have you read the paper?* □ **journal**
  4 a group of questions for a written examination: *The*

Latin paper was very difficult. □ **épreuve**
5 (*in plural*) documents proving one's identity, nationality *etc*: *The policeman demanded my papers.* □ **papiers (d'identité)**
'**papery** *adjective* like paper: *papery leaves.* □ **mince comme le papier**
'**paperback** *noun* a book with a paper cover. □ **livre de poche**
■ *adjective*: *paperback novels.* □ **de poche**
'**paper clip** *noun* a small, *usually* metal clip for holding papers together: *She attached her note to the papers with a paper clip.* □ **trombone**
'**paperweight** *noun* a small, heavy object which can be put on top of pieces of paper to keep them in place, also used as an ornament. □ **presse-papiers**
'**paperwork** *noun* the part of a job which consists of keeping files, writing letters *etc*: *I spend most of my time on paperwork.* □ **travail de bureau**
papier-mâché [papiei'maʃei] *noun, adjective* (of) a substance consisting of paper mixed together with some kind of glue, which can be made into models, bowls, boxes *etc*. □ **carton-pâte**
paprika ['paprikə] *noun* a type of red pepper powder used in cooking. □ **paprika**
par [paː] *noun* the normal level, standard, value *etc*. □ **au pair**
below par/not up to par not up to the usual standard: *Your work is not up to par this week.* □ **médiocre**
on a par with equal to: *As a writer she is on a par with the great novelists.* □ **au niveau de**
parable ['parəbl] *noun* a story (*especially* in the Bible) which is intended to teach a lesson: *Jesus told parables.* □ **parabole**
parachute ['parəʃuːt] *noun* an umbrella-shaped piece of light, strong cloth *etc* beneath which a person *etc* is tied with ropes so that he *etc* can come slowly down to the ground from a great height: *They made the descent from the plane by parachute*; (*also adjective*) *a parachute-jump.* □ **(en) parachute**
■ *verb* to come down to the ground using a parachute: *The troops parachuted into France.* □ **descendre en parachute**
'**parachutist** *noun* a person who uses a parachute. □ **parachutiste**
parade [pə'reid] *noun* **1** a line of people, vehicles *etc* moving forward in order often as a celebration of some event: *a circus parade.* □ **défilé**
2 an arrangement of soldiers in a particular order: *The troops are on parade.* □ **parade**
■ *verb* **1** to march in a line moving forward in order: *They paraded through the town.* □ **défiler**
2 to arrange soldiers in order: *The colonel paraded his soldiers.* □ **faire défiler**
3 to show or display in an obvious way: *She paraded her new clothes in front of her friends.* □ **exhiber**
paradise ['parədais] *noun* **1** a place or state of great happiness: *It's paradise to be by a warm fire on a cold night.* □ **paradis**
2 (*with capital*) heaven: *When we die, we go to Paradise.* □ **paradis**

paradox ['parədoks] *noun* a statement *etc* that seems to contradict itself but which is nevertheless true: *If your birthday is on February 29 you could state the paradox that you are thirteen years old although you have only had three birthdays.* □ **paradoxe**
,**para'doxical** *adjective*. □ **paradoxal**
,**para'doxically** *adverb*. □ **paradoxalement**
paraffin ['parəfin] *noun* a kind of oil which is used as a fuel: *This heater burns paraffin*; (*also adjective*) *a paraffin lamp.* □ **pétrole**
paragon ['parəgən, -gon] *noun* a perfect example of a good quality *etc*: *She is a paragon of virtue.* □ **modèle**
paragraph ['parəgraːf] *noun* a part of a piece of writing, marked by beginning the first sentence on a new line and *usually* leaving a short space at the beginning of the line: *There are a couple of paragraphs about football on page three of today's paper.* □ **paragraphe**
parallel ['parəlel] *adjective* **1** (of straight lines) going in the same direction and always staying the same distance apart: *The road is parallel to/with the river.* □ **parallèle (à)**
2 alike (in some way): *There are parallel passages in the two books.* □ **similaire**
■ *adverb* in the same direction but always about the same distance away: *We sailed parallel to the coast for several days.* □ **parallèlement à**
■ *noun* **1** a line parallel to another: *Draw a parallel to this line.* □ **parallèle**
2 a likeness or state of being alike: *Is there a parallel between the British Empire and the Roman Empire?* □ **analogie**
3 a line drawn from east to west across a map *etc* at a fixed distance from the equator: *The border between Canada and the United States follows the forty-ninth parallel.* □ **parallèle**
■ *verb* to be equal to: *His stupidity can't be paralleled.* □ **égaler qqch.**
para'llelogram [-əgram] *noun* a four-sided figure with opposite sides equal and parallel. □ **parallélogramme**
paralysis [pə'raləsis] *noun* a loss of the ability to move: *The paralysis affects his legs.* □ **paralysie**
paralyse, paralyze ['parəlaiz] *verb* to make unable to move: *paralysed with fear.* □ **paralyser**
paralytic [parə'litik] *adjective*. □ **paralytique**
paranoia [parə'noiə] *noun* a type of mental illness in which a person has fixed and unreasonable ideas that he or she is very important, or that other people are being unfair or unfriendly to him or her. □ **paranoïa**
,**para'noiac** [-'noːzik], '**paranoid** [-noid] *noun, adjective*. □ **paranoïaque**
parapet ['parəpit] *noun* a low wall along the edge of a bridge, balcony *etc*. □ **parapet**
paraphernalia [parəfə'neiliə] *noun* a (large) collection of (small) objects, often the tools *etc* for a job or hobby: *a photographer's paraphernalia.* □ **attirail**
paraphrase ['parəfreiz] *verb* to repeat, in speech or writing, in different words: *She paraphrased the poem in modern English.* □ **paraphraser**
■ *noun* something which repeats something else in different words: *She made a paraphrase of the poem.* □

paraphrase

parasite ['parəsait] *noun* an animal or plant that lives on another animal or plant without giving anything in return: *Fleas are parasites; He is a parasite on society.* □ **parasite**

,**para'sitic** *adjective*. □ **parasite (de)**

parasol ['parəsol] *noun* a light umbrella used as a protection against the sun. □ **parasol**

paratroops ['parətru:ps] *noun plural* soldiers who are trained to drop by parachute into enemy territory. □ **parachutistes**

'**paratrooper** *noun*. □ **parachutiste**

parcel ['pa:sl] *noun* thing(s) wrapped and tied, *usually* to be sent by post: *I got a parcel in the post today.* □ **colis**

parch [pa:tʃ] *verb* to make hot and very dry: *The sun parched the earth.* □ **dessécher**

parched *adjective* 1 hot and dry: *Nothing could grow in the parched land.* □ **desséché**

2 thirsty: *Can I have a cup of tea – I'm parched!* □ **qui meurt de soif**

parchment ['pa:tʃmənt] *noun* a (piece of a) material used for writing on, made from animal skin: *Medieval men often wrote on parchment.* □ **parchemin**

pardon ['pa:dn] *verb* 1 to forgive: *Pardon my asking, but can you help me?* □ **pardonner**

2 to free (from prison, punishment *etc*): *The judge pardoned the prisoners.* □ **gracier**

■ *noun* 1 forgiveness: *He prayed for pardon for his wickedness.* □ **pardon?**

2 a (document) freeing from prison or punishment: *He was granted a pardon.* □ **grâce, amnistie**

■ *interjection* used to indicate that one has not heard properly what was said: *Pardon? Could you repeat that last sentence?* □ **pardon?**

beg someone's pardon to say one is sorry (*usually* for having offended someone else *etc*): *I've come to beg (your) pardon for being so rude this morning.* □ **demander pardon à**

I beg your pardon I'm sorry: *I beg your pardon – what did you say? I wasn't listening.* □ **je vous demande pardon**

pardon me *interjection* expressing a polite apology, *especially* for not agreeing with someone: *Pardon me for interrupting you.* □ **excusez-moi**

parent ['peərənt] *noun* 1 one of the two persons *etc* (one male and one female) who are jointly the cause of one's birth. □ **père (ou) mère**

2 a person with the legal position of a mother or father *eg* by adoption. □ **père adoptif (ou) mère adoptive**

'**parentage** [-tidʒ] *noun* family or ancestry: *a woman of unknown parentage.* □ **parents**

parental [pə'rentl] *adjective: parental responsibility.* □ **des parents**

'**parenthood** *noun* the state of being a parent. □ **paternité, maternité**

parenthesis [pə'renθəsis] – *plural* **pa'rentheses** [-si:z] – *noun* 1 a word or group of words within a sentence, which gives a comment *etc* and *usually* separates from the rest of the sentence by brackets, dashes *etc*: *I asked*

Lucy (my friend Lucy Smith) to come and see me. □ **parenthèse**

2 a round bracket used to mark the seperate part of such a sentence. □ **parenthèse**

parenthetical [parən'θetikəl] *adjective*: *a parenthetical remark.* □ **entre parenthèses**

in parentheses said, written *etc* as a parenthesis. □ **entre parenthèses**

pariah [pə'raiə] *noun* a person driven out of a group or community; an outcast: *Because of his political beliefs he became a pariah in the district.* □ **paria**

parish ['pariʃ] *noun* a district or area with a particular church and priest or minister: *Our house is in the parish of St Mary('s)*; (*also adjective*) *parish affairs.* □ **paroisse; paroissial**

park [pa:k] *noun* 1 a public piece of ground with grass and trees: *The children go to the park every morning to play.* □ **parc**

2 the land surrounding a large country house: *Deer run wild in the park surrounding the mansion.* □ **parc**

■ *verb* to stop and leave (a car *etc*) for a time: *She parked in front of our house.* □ **stationner, garer**

'**parking lot** *noun* an area for parking vehicles. □ **parc de stationnement**

'**parking meter** *noun* a coin-operated meter beside which a car may be parked for the number of minutes or hours shown on the meter. □ **parcomètre**

parliament ['pa:ləmənt] *noun* the highest law-making council of a nation – in Canada, the House of Commons and the Senate, considered together: *an Act of Parliament.* □ **parlement**

,**parlia'mentary** [-'men-] *adjective*. □ **parlementaire**

parlour ['pa:lə] *noun* 1 a room in a (*usually* small) house used for sitting in and for entertaining guests. □ **(petit) salon**

2 room(s) for customers *usually* of firms providing particular services: *a beauty parlour; a funeral parlour.* □ **salon**

'**parlourmaid** *noun* a female servant who opens the door to visitors, serves tea *etc*. □ **bonne**

parody ['parədi] – *plural* '**parodies** – *noun* 1 an amusing imitation of a serious author's style of writing: *She writes parodies of John Donne's poems.* □ **parodie**

2 a very bad imitation: *a parody of the truth.* □ **parodie**

■ *verb* to make a parody of (something or someone). □ **parodier**

paroxysm ['parəksizəm] *noun* a sudden sharp attack (of pain, rage, laughter *etc*): *a paroxysm of coughing/fury.* □ **paroxysme, crise**

parquet ['pa:kei] *noun* a type of floor-covering made of pieces of wood arranged in a design: *flooring made of parquet*; (*also adjective*) *a parquet floor.* □ **parquet**

parricide ['parisaid] *noun* 1 the murder of a parent or near relative. □ **parricide**

2 a person who does such a murder. □ **parricide**

parrot ['parət] *noun* a kind of bird found in warm countries, *especially* in South America, with a hooked bill and *usually* brightly-coloured feathers, that can be taught to imitate human speech. □ **perroquet**

parsley ['pa:sli] *noun* a kind of herb used in cookery to decorate or add flavour to food. □ **persil**

parsnip ['paːsnip] *noun* 1 a plant with a yellowish-white root used as a vegetable. □ **panais**

2 the root. □ **panais**

parson ['paːsn] *noun* 1 the priest, minister *etc* of a parish, *usually* of the Church of England. □ **pasteur**

2 any priest, minister *etc*. □ **ecclésiastique**

'**parsonage** [-nidʒ] *noun* the house in which the parson of a parish lives. □ **presbytère**

part [paːt] *noun* 1 something which, together with other things, makes a whole; a piece: *We spent part of the time at home and part at the seaside.* □ **partie**

2 an equal division: *He divided the cake into three parts.* □ **part(ie)**

3 a character in a play *etc*: *She played the part of the Juliet.* □ **rôle**

4 the words, actions *etc* of a character in a play *etc*: *He learned his part quickly.* □ **rôle**

5 in music, the notes to be played or sung by a particular instrument or voice: *the violin part.* □ **partie**

6 a person's share, responsibility *etc* in doing something: *He played a great part in the government's decision.* □ **part**

■ *verb* to separate; to divide: *They parted (from each other) at the gate.* □ **(se) séparer**

'**parting** *noun* 1 the act of leaving someone, saying goodbye *etc*: *Their final parting was at the station.* □ **séparation**

2 a line dividing hair brushed in opposite directions on the head. □ **raie**

'**partly** *adverb* to a certain extent but not completely: *She was tired, partly because of the journey and partly because of the heat.* □ **en partie**

,**part-'time** *adjective, adverb* not taking one's whole time; for only a few hours or days a week: *a part-time job; She works part-time.* □ **à temps partiel**

in part partly: *He agreed that he was in part responsible for the accident.* □ **en partie**

part company 1 to go in different directions: *We parted company at the bus-stop.* □ **se quitter**

2 to leave each other or end a friendship, partnership *etc.* □ **se séparer**

part of speech one of the groups into which words are divided (*eg* noun, verb, adjective *etc*). □ **catégorie grammaticale**

part with to give away or be separated from: *He doesn't like parting with money.* □ **se défaire (de)**

take in good part to accept without being hurt or offended: *She took their jokes in good part.* □ **prendre du bon côté**

take someone's part to support someone (in an argument *etc*): *She always takes his part.* □ **prendre le parti de**

take part in to be one of a group of people doing something, to take an active share in (*eg* playing a game, performing a play, holding a discussion *etc*): *He never took part in arguments.* □ **prendre part à**

partake [paː'teik] – *past tense* **partook** [-'tuk]: *past participle* **par'taken** – *verb* to take part: *They all partook in the final decision.* □ **prendre part à**

partial ['paːʃəl] *adjective* 1 not complete; in part only: *a partial success; partial payment.* □ **partiel**

2 having a liking for (a person or thing): *She is very partial to cheese.* □ **qui a un faible pour**

,**parti'ality** [-ʃi'aləti] *noun* 1 a liking for: *He has a partiality for cheese.* □ **faible (pour, envers)**

2 the preferring of one person or side more than another: *He could not help showing his partiality for/towards his own team.* □ **partialité (pour)**

participate [paː'tisipeit] *verb* to be one of a group of people actively doing something: *Did you participate in the discussion?* □ **participer (à)**

par,tici'pation *noun*. □ **participation**

par'ticipant, par'ticipator *nouns* a person who participates (in a particular activity): *the participants in the Olympic Games.* □ **participant, ante**

particle ['paːtikl] *noun* a very small piece: *a particle of dust.* □ **particule**

particular [pə'tikjulə] *adjective* 1 of a single definite person, thing *etc* thought of separately from all others: *this particular man/problem.* □ **particulier**

2 more than ordinary: *Please take particular care of this letter.* □ **particulier**

3 difficult to please: *She is very particular about her food.* □ **exigeant**

par'ticularly *adverb* more than usually: *She was particularly pleased to see her brother.* □ **particulièrement**

par'ticulars *noun plural* facts or details: *You must give them all the particulars about the accident.* □ **détails**

in particular more than others: *I liked this book in particular.* □ **en particulier**

partisan [paːti'zan] *noun* 1 a strong and enthusiastic supporter of a person, political party, idea or philosophy *etc*: *Every movement has its partisans;* (*also adjective*) *partisan feelings.* □ **partisan, ane**

2 a member of a group organized to fight against an enemy which has occupied their country. □ **partisan**

partition [pə'tiʃən] *noun* 1 something that divides, *eg* a light, often temporary, wall between rooms: *The office was divided in two by a wooden partition.* □ **cloison**

2 the act of dividing; the state of being divided: *the partition of India.* □ **partage, partition**

■ *verb* to divide: *They partitioned the room (off) with a curtain.* □ **partager**

partner ['paːtnə] *noun* 1 a person who shares the ownership of a business *etc* with one or more others: *She was made a partner in the firm.* □ **associé, ée**

2 one of two people who dance, play in a game *etc* together: *a tennis/dancing partner.* □ **partenaire; cavalier, ière**

■ *verb* to be a partner to (someone): *He partnered his wife in the last dance.* □ **s'associer à (qqn)**

'**partnership** *noun* 1 the state of being or becoming partners: *a business partnership; She entered into partnership with her brother.* □ **association**

2 people playing together in a game: *The champions were defeated by the partnership of Jones and Smith in the men's doubles.* □ **tandem**

partridge [paːtridʒ] *noun* a game bird such as a grouse: *In the olden days, hunters went into the forest in search* *of partridge to roast for dinner.* □ **perdrix**

party ['pɑːti] – *plural* **'parties** – *noun* **1** a meeting of guests for entertainment, celebration *etc*: *a birthday party*; *She's giving/having a party tonight*; (*also adjective*) *a party dress.* □ **fête (de)**
2 a group of people with a particular purpose: *a party of tourists.* □ **groupe**
3 a group of people with the same ideas and purposes, *especially* political: *a political party.* □ **parti**

pass [pɑːs] *verb* **1** to move towards and then beyond (something, by going past, through, by, over *etc*): *I pass the shops on my way to work*; *The procession passed along the corridor.* □ **passer (devant), dépasser**
2 to move, give *etc* from one person, state *etc* to another: *They passed the photographs around*; *The tradition is passed (on/down) from father to son.* □ **transmettre**
3 to go or be beyond: *This passes my understanding.* □ **dépasser**
4 (of vehicles *etc* on a road) to overtake: *The sports car passed me at a dangerous bend in the road.* □ **dépasser**
5 to spend (time): *They passed several weeks in the country.* □ **passer**
6 (of an official group, government *etc*) to accept or approve: *The government has passed a resolution.* □ **voter**
7 to give or announce (a judgment or sentence): *The magistrate passed judgment on the prisoner.* □ **rendre**
8 to end or go away: *Her sickness soon passed.* □ **passer**
9 to (judge to) be successful in (an examination *etc*): *I passed my driving test.* □ **réussir un examen**
■ *noun* **1** a narrow path between mountains: *a mountain pass.* □ **passage**
2 a ticket or card allowing a person to do something, *eg* to travel free or to get in to a building: *You must show your pass before entering.* □ **laissez-passer**
3 a successful result in an examination, *especially* when below a distinction, honours *etc*: *There were ten passes and no fails.* □ **succès**
4 (in ball games) a throw, kick, hit *etc* of the ball from one player to another: *The centre-forward made a pass towards the goal.* □ **passe**
'passable *adjective* **1** fairly good: *a passable tennis player.* □ **passable**
2 (of a river, road *etc*) able to be passed, travelled over *etc*: *The mud has made the roads no longer passable.* □ **praticable**
'passing *adjective* **1** going past: *a passing car.* □ **qui passe**
2 lasting only a short time: *a passing interest.* □ **passager**
3 (of something said) casual and not made as part of a serious talk about the subject: *a passing reference.* □ **en passant**
,passer'by – *plural* **,passers'by** – *noun* a person who is going past a place when something happens: *He asked the passersby if they had seen the accident.* □ **passant, ante**
'password *noun* a secret word by which those who know it can recognize each other and be allowed to go past, enter *etc*: *He was not allowed into the army camp be-*

cause he did not know the password. □ **mot de passe**
in passing while doing or talking about something else; without explaining fully what one means: *He told her the story, and said in passing that he did not completely believe it.* □ **en passant**
let (something) pass to ignore something rather than take the trouble to argue: *I'll let that pass.* □ **ne pas relever**
pass as/for to be mistaken for or accepted as: *Some man-made materials could pass as silk*; *His nasty remarks pass for wit among his admirers.* □ **passer pour**
pass away to die: *Her grandmother passed away last night.* □ **mourir**
pass the buck to give the responsibility or blame for something to someone else: *He always passes the buck if he is asked to do anything.* □ **mettre sur le dos de qqn**
pass by to go past (a particular place): *I was passing by when the bride arrived at the church*; *She passed by the hospital on the way to the library.* □ **passer (à côté de)**
pass off (of sickness, an emotion *etc*) to go away: *By the evening, her sickness had passed off and she felt better.* □ **se passer**
pass (something or someone) off as to pretend that (something or someone) is (something or someone else): *He passed himself off as a journalist.* □ **(se) faire passer pour**
pass on 1 to give to someone else (*usually* something which one has been given by a third person): *I passed on his message.* □ **faire passer**
2 to die: *His mother passed on yesterday.* □ **mourir**
pass out 1 to faint: *I feel as though I'm going to pass out.* □ **perdre connaissance**
2 to give to several different people: *The teacher passed out books to her class.* □ **distribuer**
pass over to ignore or overlook: *They passed him over for promotion.* □ **passer par-dessus le dos de qqn**
pass up not to accept (a chance, opportunity *etc*): *He passed up the offer of a good job.* □ **laisser passer**

> **passed** is the past tense of **to pass**: *She passed the scene of the accident.*
> **past** means up to and beyond: *She walked past the shops.*

passage ['pasidʒ] *noun* **1** a long narrow way through, *eg* a corridor through a building: *There was a dark passage leading down to the river between tall buildings.* □ **passage**
2 a part of a piece of writing or music: *That is my favourite passage from the Bible.* □ **passage**
3 (*usually* of time) the act of passing: *the passage of time.* □ **passage**
4 a journey by boat: *He paid for his passage by working as a steward.* □ **traversée**
passenger ['pasindʒə] *noun* a person who travels in any vehicle, boat, airplane *etc* (not the driver or anyone working there): *a passenger on a train*; (*also adjective*) *a passenger train.* □ **(de) passager, ère**
passion ['paʃən] *noun* very strong feeling, *especially* of anger or love: *He argued with great passion*; *He has a*

passion for chocolate. □ **passion**

'**passionate** [-nət] *adjective* having very strong feelings; intense or emotional: *a passionate woman*; *passionate hatred.* □ **passionné**

passive ['pasiv] *adjective* **1** showing no interest, emotion *etc*, or not resisting an attack *etc*: *The villagers showed passive resistance to the enemy* (= They opposed their authority by disobedience *etc*, not by active opposition). □ **passif**

2 of the form of the verb used when the subject receives the action of the verb: *The boy was bitten by the dog.* □ **passif**

'**passively** *adverb.* □ **passivement**

'**passiveness** *noun.* □ **passivité**

pas'**sivity** *noun.* □ **passivité**

passport ['paːspoːt] *noun* a document of identification, necessary for foreign travel: *a Canadian passport.* □ **passeport**

past [paːst] *adjective* **1** just finished: *the past year.* □ **passé**

2 over, finished or ended, of an earlier time than the present: *The time for discussion is past.* □ **écoulé**

3 (of the tense of a verb) indicating action in the past: *In 'She did it', the verb is in the past tense.* □ **passé**

■ *preposition* **1** up to and beyond; by: *He ran past me.* □ **devant**

2 after: *It's past six o'clock.* □ **passé**

■ *adverb* up to and beyond (a particular place, person *etc*): *The soldiers marched past.* □ **au delà de, plus loin que**

■ *noun* **1** a person's earlier life or career, *especially* if secret or not respectable: *I never spoke about my past.* □ **passé**

2 the past tense: *a verb in the past.* □ **passé**

the past the time which was before the present: *In the past, houses were built of wood or stone.* □ **passé**

see also **passed**.

pasta ['pastə] *noun* a dough used in Italian cooking for making spaghetti, macaroni *etc*. □ **pâtes**

paste [peist] *noun* **1** a soft, damp mixture, *especially* one made up of glue and water and used for sticking pieces of paper *etc* together. □ **colle**

2 a mixture of flour, fat *etc* used for making pies, pastry *etc*. □ **pâte**

3 a mixture made from some types of food: *almond paste.* □ **pâte**

pastel ['pastəl] *adjective* (of colours) pale, containing a lot of white: *a soft pastel green.* □ **pastel**

■ *noun* **1** a kind of coloured pencil, made with chalk, which makes a pale colour. □ **pastel**

2 a picture drawn with this kind of pencil. □ **pastel**

pasteurize, pasteurise ['pastʃəraiz] *verb* to heat food, *especially* milk, for a time to kill germs in it. □ **pasteuriser**

,**pasteuri'zation,** ,**pasteuri'sation** *noun.* □ **pasteurisation**

pastille ['pastəl] *noun* a small sweet often containing medicine (*usually* for infections of the mouth or throat *etc*): *throat pastilles.* □ **pastille**

pastime ['paːstaim] *noun* an occupation which one en-

joys and takes part in in one's spare time; a hobby: *Playing chess is his favourite pastime.* □ **passe-temps**

pastor ['paːstə] *noun* a minister of religion, *especially* of the Protestant church. □ **pasteur**

'**pastoral** *adjective* **1** of country life: *a pastoral scene.* □ **pastoral**

2 of a pastor, or his work: *pastoral responsibilities.* □ **pastoral**

pastry ['peistri] – *plural* '**pastries** – *noun* **1** flour dough used in making pies, tarts *etc*. □ **pâte**

2 a pie, tart *etc* made with this: *Danish pastries.* □ **pâtisserie**

pasture ['paːstʃə] *noun* a field or area of ground covered with grass for cattle *etc* to eat: *The horses were out in the pasture.* □ **pâturage**

pat [pat] *noun* **1** a light, gentle blow or touch, *usually* with the palm of the hand and showing affection: *He gave the child a pat on the head.* □ **petite tape**

2 (of butter) a small piece; a lump. □ **noix (de beurre), motte**

■ *verb* – *past tense, past participle* '**patted** – to strike gently with the palm of the hand, *usually* as a sign of affection: *He patted the horse's neck.* □ **flatter (de la main)**

■ *adverb* (*often* **down pat**) memorized, prepared and ready to be said: *She had the answer (down) pat.* □ **par cœur, exactement**

patch [patʃ] *noun* **1** a piece of material sewn on to cover a hole: *He sewed a patch on the knee of his jeans.* □ **pièce**

2 a small piece of ground: *a vegetable patch.* □ **carré**

■ *verb* to mend (clothes *etc*) by sewing on pieces of material: *She patched the (hole in the) child's trousers.* □ **rapiécer**

'**patchy** *adjective* not all the same; varying in quality: *patchy work.* □ **inégal**

'**patchiness** *noun.* □ **manque d'unité**

'**patchwork** *noun* cloth made by sewing small pieces of material together: *a skirt made of patchwork*; (*also adjective*) *a patchwork quilt.* □ **(en) patchwork**

patch up 1 to mend, *especially* quickly and temporarily: *She patched up the roof with bits of wood.* □ **rafistoler**

2 to settle (a quarrel): *They soon patched up their disagreement.* □ **se raccommoder**

patent ['peitənt] *noun* an official licence from the government giving one person or business the right to make and sell a particular article and to prevent others from doing the same: *She took out a patent on her design*; (*also adjective*) *a patent process.* □ **brevet (d'invention); breveté**

■ *verb* to obtain a patent for; *He patented his new invention.* □ **faire breveter**

paternal [pə'təːnl] *adjective* **1** of or like a father: *paternal feelings.* □ **paternel**

2 among one's father's relatives: *Her paternal grandmother.* □ **paternel**

pa'**ternity** *noun* the fact or state of being a father. □ **paternité**

path [paːθ] – *plural* **paths** [paːðz] – *noun* **1** a way made

across the ground by the passing of people or animals: *There is a path through the fields*; *a mountain path.* □ **sentier**
2 (any place on) the line along which someone or something is moving: *He stood right in the path of the bus.* □ **chemin, trajectoire**
'**pathway** *noun* a path. □ **sentier**

pathetic [pə'θetik] *adjective* 1 causing pity: *The lost dog was a pathetic sight.* □ **pathétique**
2 weak and useless: *a pathetic attempt.* □ **pitoyable**
pa'**thetically** *adverb.* □ **pathétiquement**

pathology [pə'θɔlədʒi] *noun* the science of diseases. □ **pathologie**
pa'**thologist** *noun.* □ **pathologiste**
,patho'**logical** *adjective.* □ **pathologique**
,patho'**logically** *adverb.* □ **pathologiquement**

patient ['peiʃənt] *adjective* suffering delay, pain, irritation *etc* quietly and without complaining: *It will be your turn soon – you must just be patient!* □ **patient**
■ *noun* a person who is being treated by a doctor, dentist *etc*: *The hospital had too many patients.* □ **patient, ente**
'**patiently** *adverb.* □ **patiemment**
'**patience** *noun* the ability or willingness to be patient: *Patience is a virtue.* □ **patience**

patriarch ['peitriaːk] *noun* 1 the male head of a family or tribe. □ **patriarche**
2 *especially* in the Eastern Orthodox Church, a high-ranking bishop. □ **patriarche**
,patri'**archal** *adjective* of, like, ruled by *etc* a patriarch or patriarchs: *a patriarchal society/church.* □ **patriarcal**

patricide ['patrisaid] *noun* 1 the act of killing one's father. □ **parricide**
2 a person who does such an act. □ **parricide**

patrimony ['patriməni] *noun* property passed on to a person by his or her father or ancestors: *This farm is part of my patrimony.* □ **patrimoine**

patriot ['peitriət] *noun* a person who loves (and serves) his or her country: *Many terrorists consider themselves to be patriots fighting for freedom.* □ **patriote**
patriotic [patri'ɔtik, pei-] *adjective* (*negative* **unpatriotic**) having or showing great love for one's country: *He is so patriotic that he refuses to buy anything made abroad.* □ **patriotique**
,patri'**otically** *adverb.* □ **patriotiquement**
'**patriotism** ['pa-, 'pei-] *noun* (the showing of) great love for one's country. □ **patriotisme**

patrol [pə'troul] – *past tense, past participle* pa'**trolled** – *verb* to watch or protect (an area) by moving continually around or through it: *Soldiers patrolled the streets.* □ **patrouiller**
■ *noun* 1 a group of people *etc* who patrol an area: *They came across several army patrols in the hills.* □ **patrouille**
2 the act of watching or guarding by patrolling: *The soldiers went out on patrol*; (*also adjective*) *patrol duty.* □ (de) **patrouille**

patron ['peitrən] *noun* 1 a person who supports (often with money) an artist, musician, writer, form of art *etc*: *She's a patron of the arts.* □ **mécène**

2 a (regular) customer of a shop *etc*: *The manager said that he knew all his patrons.* □ **client, ente**
patronage ['patrənidʒ, 'pei-] *noun* the support given by a patron. □ **mécénat**
'**patronize**, '**patronise** ['pa-, 'pei-] *verb* 1 to behave towards (someone) in a way which is kind and friendly but which nevertheless shows that one thinks oneself to be more important, clever *etc* than that person: *He's a nice fellow but he does patronize his assistants.* □ **traiter avec condescendance**
2 to visit (a shop, theatre, society *etc*) regularly: *That's not a shop I patronize nowadays.* □ **fréquenter**
'**patronizing**, '**patronising** *adjective.* □ **condescendant**
'**patronizingly**, '**patronisingly** *adverb.* □ **d'un air condescendant**
patron saint a saint who protects a particular person, group of people, country *etc*: *St Andrew is the patron saint of Scotland.* □ **saint patron, sainte patronne**

patter ['patə] *verb* (of rain, footsteps *etc*) to make a quick, tapping sound: *She heard the mice pattering behind the walls.* □ **crépiter**
■ *noun* the sound made in this way: *the patter of rain on the roof.* □ **crépitement**

pattern ['patən] *noun* 1 a model or guide for making something: *a dress-pattern.* □ **patron**
2 a repeated decoration or design on material *etc*: *The dress is nice but I don't like the pattern.* □ **motif**
3 an example suitable to be copied: *the pattern of good behaviour.* □ **modèle**
'**patterned** *adjective* with a decoration or design on it; not plain: *Is her new carpet patterned?* □ **à motifs**

paunch [pɔːntʃ] *noun* a large, round stomach: *He developed quite a paunch.* □ **bedaine**
'**paunchy** *adjective* having a paunch: *He's become quite paunchy.* □ **bedonnant**

pauper ['pɔːpə] *noun* a very poor person: *Her husband died a pauper.* □ **indigent, ente**

pause [pɔːz] *noun* 1 a short stop, break or interval (while doing something): *There was a pause in the conversation.* □ **pause**
2 the act of making a musical note or rest slightly longer than normal, or a mark showing that this is to be done. □ **point d'orgue, pause**
■ *verb* to stop talking, working *etc* for a short time: *They paused for a cup of tea.* □ **faire une pause**

pave [peiv] *verb* to cover (a street, path *etc*) with (*usually* large) flat stones, concrete *etc* to make a flat surface for walking on *etc*: *She wants to pave the garden.* □ **paver**
'**pavement** *noun* (*also* '**sidewalk**) a paved surface, *especially* a paved footpath along the sides of a road for people to walk on. □ **trottoir**
'**paving stone** *noun* a large flat stone or piece of concrete used for paving. □ **pavé**

pavilion [pə'viljən] *noun* a building at exposition or trade show housing exhibits. □ **pavillon**

paw [pɔː] *noun* the foot of an animal with claws or nails: *The dog had a thorn in its paw.* □ **patte**
■ *verb* 1 (of an animal) to touch, hit *etc* (*usually* several times) with a paw or paws: *The cat was pawing (at) the*

dead mouse. □ **donner des coups de patte à**

2 (of an animal) to hit (the ground, *usually* several times) with a hoof, *usually* a front hoof: *The horse pawed (at) the ground.* □ **piaffer**

pawn [pɔːn] *verb* to give (an article of value) to a pawn-broker in exchange for money (which may be repaid at a later time to get the article back): *I had to pawn my watch to pay the bill.* □ **mettre en gage**

■ *noun* 1 in chess, one of the small pieces of lowest rank. □ **pion**

2 a person who is used by another person for his own gain, advantage *etc*: *She was a pawn in his ambitious plans.* □ **jouet**

'**pawnbroker** *noun* a person who lends money in ex-change for pawned articles. □ **prêteur, euse sur gages**

'**pawnshop** *noun* a pawnbroker's place of business. □ **maison de prêt sur gages**

in pawn having been pawned: *Her watch is in pawn.* □ **en gage**

pay [pei] – *past tense, past participle* **paid** – *verb* 1 to give (money) to (someone) in exchange for goods, serv-ices *etc*: *She paid $5 for the book.* □ **payer**

2 to return (money that is owed): *It's time you paid your debts.* □ **payer**

3 to suffer punishment (for): *You'll pay for that remark!* □ **payer**

4 to be useful or profitable (to): *Crime doesn't pay.* □ **payer**

5 to give (attention, homage, respect *etc*): *Pay atten-tion!; to pay one's respects.* □ **faire, présenter**

■ *noun* money given or received for work *etc*; wages: *How much pay do you get?* □ **salaire**

'**payable** *adjective* which may be or must be paid: *The account is payable at the end of the month.* □ **payable**

pay'ee *noun* a person to whom money is (to be) paid. □ **bénéficiaire**

'**payment** *noun* 1 money *etc* paid: *The radio can be paid for in ten weekly payments.* □ **paiement**

2 the act of paying: *She gave me a book in payment for my kindness.* □ **paiement**

'**pay packet** *noun* an envelope containing a person's wages: *The manager handed out the pay packets.* □ **enveloppe de paie**

'**payroll** *noun* 1 a list of all the workers in a factory *etc*: *We have 450 people on the payroll.* □ **liste de paye**

2 the total amount of money to be paid to all the work-ers: *The thieves stole the payroll.* □ **frais de personnel**

pay back 1 to give back (to someone something that one has borrowed): *I'll pay you back as soon as I can.* □ **rembourser**

2 to punish: *I'll pay you back for that!* □ **faire payer à**

pay off 1 to pay in full and discharge (workers) because they are no longer needed: *Hundreds of steel-workers have been paid off.* □ **licencier**

2 to have good results: *Her hard work paid off.* □ **être rentable**

pay up to give (money) to someone, *eg* in order to pay a debt: *You have three days to pay up* (= You must pay up within three days). □ **s'acquitter (de)**

put paid to to prevent a person from doing (something

he or she planned or wanted to do): *The rain put paid to our visit to the zoo.* □ **foutre en l'air les projets de qqn**

pea [piː] *noun* 1 the round seed of a kind of climbing plant, eaten as a vegetable: *We had roast beef, potatoes and peas for dinner.* □ **(petit) pois**

2 the plant which produces these seeds: *We planted peas and beans this year.* □ **pois**

peace [piːs] *noun* 1 (*sometimes with* a) (a time of) free-dom from war; (a treaty or agreement which brings about) the end or stopping of a war: *Does our country want peace or war?*; (*also adjective*) *a peace treaty.* □ **(de) paix**

2 freedom from disturbance; quietness: *I need some peace and quiet.* □ **paix**

'**peaceable** *adjective* liking peace; not fighting, quar-relling *etc*: *She's a peaceable person.* □ **pacifique**

'**peaceably** *adverb.* □ **pacifiquement**

'**peaceful** *adjective* quiet; calm; without worry or dis-turbance: *It's very peaceful in the country.* □ **paisible**

'**peacefully** *adverb.* □ **paisiblement**

'**peacefulness** *noun.* □ **paix**

'**peacemaker** *noun* a person who tries to make peace between enemies, people who are quarrelling *etc*: *When my brother and sister quarrel I act as peacemaker.* □ **pacificateur, trice**

'**peace offering** *noun* something offered or given to make peace: *She took him a drink as a peace offering.* □ **cadeau de réconciliation**

'**peacetime** *noun* a time when there is no war: *Even in peacetime, a soldier's life is hard.* □ **temps de paix**

at peace not at war; not fighting: *The two countries were at peace.* □ **en paix**

in peace 1 without disturbance: *Why can't you leave me in peace?* □ **en paix**

2 not wanting to fight: *They said they came in peace.* □ **dans des dispositions pacifiques**

make peace to agree to end a war: *The two countries finally made peace (with each other).* □ **faire la paix**

peace of mind freedom from worry *etc*. □ **tranquillité d'esprit**

peach [piːtʃ] *noun* 1 a kind of juicy, soft-skinned fruit: *She doesn't like peaches*; (*also adjective*) *a peach tree.* □ **(de) pêche**

2 (*also adjective*) (of) the orange-pink colour of the fruit: *Would you call that colour peach?*; *The walls are painted peach.* □ **(couleur) pêche**

peacock ['piːkɔk] – *feminine* '**peahen** [-hen] – *noun* a kind of large bird, the male of which is noted for its magnificent tail-feathers. □ **paon, paonne**

peak [piːk] *noun* 1 the pointed top of a mountain or hill: *snow-covered peaks.* □ **pic**

2 the highest, greatest, busiest *etc* point, time *etc*: *She was at the peak of her career.* □ **sommet**

3 the front part of a cap which shades the eyes: *The boy wore a cap with a peak.* □ **visière**

■ *verb* to reach the highest, greatest, busiest *etc* point, time *etc*: *Prices peaked in July and then began to fall.* □ **atteindre son maximum**

'**peaked** *adjective* having a peak: *a peaked cap.* □ **à visière; pointu**

'peaky *adjective* looking pale and unhealthy: *You look peaky today.* □ **pâlot**

peal [piːl] *noun* **1** the ringing of (a set of) bells. □ **carillon**
2 a set of (*usually* church) bells. □ **carillon**
3 a loud noise: *peals of laughter/thunder.* □ **coup (de tonnerre)**

■ *verb* to (cause to) ring or sound loudly: *Thunder pealed through the valley.* □ **retentir**

peanut ['piːnʌt] *noun* a type of nut that looks rather like a pea. □ **cacahuète, arachide**

pear [peə] *noun* a type of fruit of the apple family, round at the bottom and narrowing towards the stem or top: *She's very fond of pears*; (*also adjective*) *a pear tree.* □ **(de) poire**

'pear-shaped *adjective.* □ **en forme de poire**

pearl [pəːl] *noun* a valuable, hard, round object formed by oysters and several other shellfish: *The necklace consists of three strings of pearls*; (*also adjective*) *a pearl necklace.* □ **(de) perle (s)**

'pearly *adjective* like pearls: *pearly teeth.* □ **perlé**
'pearl-diver, 'pearl-fisher *nouns* a person who dives or fishes for pearls. □ **pêcheur, euse de perles**

peasant ['peznt] *noun* a person who lives and works on the land, *especially* in a poor, primitive or underdeveloped area: *Many peasants died during the drought*; (*also adjective*) *a peasant farmer.* □ **paysan, anne**

'peasantry *noun* peasants as a group; the peasants of a particular place: *What part did the peasantry play in the Russian revolution?* □ **paysannerie**

pebble ['pebl] *noun* a small, *usually* smooth stone: *small pebbles on the beach.* □ **caillou, galet**

'pebbly *adjective.* □ **caillouteux**

peck [pek] *verb* **1** (of birds) to strike or pick up with the beak, *usually* in order to eat: *The birds pecked at the corn*; *The bird pecked his hand.* □ **picorer**
2 to eat very little: *She just pecks (at) her food.* □ **chipoter**
3 to kiss quickly and briefly: *She pecked her mother on the cheek.* □ **bécoter**

■ *noun* **1** a tap or bite with the beak: *The bird gave him a painful peck on the hand.* □ **coup de bec**
2 a brief kiss: *a peck on the cheek.* □ **bécot**

'peckish *adjective* rather hungry: *I feel a bit peckish.* □ **qui a le ventre creux**

pectoral ['pektərəl] *adjective* of or on the breast or chest: *the pectoral muscles.* □ **pectoral**

peculiar [piˈkjuːljə] *adjective* **1** strange; odd: *peculiar behaviour.* □ **bizarre**
2 belonging to one person, place or thing in particular and to no other: *customs peculiar to France.* □ **propre à**
pe,culi'arity [-'a-] – *plural* **pe,culi'arities** – *noun.* □ **particularité**
pe'culiarly *adverb.* □ **bizarrement**

pedal ['pedl] *noun* a lever worked by the foot, as on a bicycle, piano, organ *etc*: *the brake pedal in a car.* □ **pédale**

■ *verb* – *past tense, past participle* **'pedalled, 'pedaled** – to move (something) by means of pedals: *She pedalled (her bicycle) down the road.* □ **pédaler**

---

to **pedal** (not **paddle**) a bicycle.

---

pedant ['pedənt] *noun* **1** a person who makes a great show of his knowledge. □ **pédant, ante**
2 a person who attaches too much importance to minor details. □ **formaliste**
pe'dantic [-'dan-] *adjective.* □ **pédant**
pe'dantically *adverb.* □ **pédantesquement**
'pedantry *noun.* □ **pédanterie**

peddle ['pedl] *verb* to go from place to place or house to house selling (small objects): *Gypsies often peddle (goods) from door to door.* □ **colporter**

'pedlar, 'peddler *noun* a person who peddles: *I bought it from a pedlar.* □ **colporteur, euse**

pedestal ['pedistl] *noun* the foot or base of a column, statue *etc*: *The statue fell off its pedestal.* □ **piédestal**

pedestrian [piˈdestriən] *noun* a person who travels on foot: *Three pedestrians were hit by the car.* □ **piéton, onne**

■ *adjective* ordinary; rather boring or unexciting: *It is a pedestrian play.* □ **prosaïque**

pediatrics [piːdiˈatriks] *noun singular* the study of the illnesses of children. □ **pédiatrie**
,pedi'atric *adjective*: *pediatric illnesses.* □ **de pédiatrie, infantile**
,pedia'trician [-ʃən] *noun* a doctor who specializes in treating and studying children's illnesses. □ **pédiatre**

pedigree ['pedigriː] *noun* **1** a list of the ancestors from whom a person or animal is descended: *a dog's pedigree.* □ **pedigree**
2 distinguished descent or ancestry: *a man of pedigree.* □ **ascendance distinguée**

■ *adjective* (of an animal) purebred; from a long line of ancestors of the same breed: *a herd of pedigree cattle.* □ **de (pure) race**

pedlar *see* **peddle.**

peek [piːk] *verb* to look, *especially* quickly and in secret: *He opened the door slightly and peeked out*; *Cover your eyes and don't peek.* □ **jeter un coup d'œil (furtif) (à)**

■ *noun* a quick look: *Take a peek through the window.* □ **coup d'œil (furtif)**

peel [piːl] *verb* **1** to take off the skin or outer covering of (a fruit or vegetable): *She peeled the potatoes.* □ **peler**
2 to take off or come off in small pieces: *The paint is beginning to peel (off).* □ **peler, (s')écailler**

■ *noun* the skin of certain fruits, *especially* oranges, lemons *etc*. □ **écorce**

'peeler *noun* a tool *etc* that peels (something): *a potato-peeler.* □ **éplucheur**

'peelings *noun plural* the strips or pieces of skin peeled off an apple, potato *etc*: *potato peelings.* □ **épluchures**

peep[1] [piːp] *verb* **1** to look through a narrow opening or from behind something: *She peeped through the window.* □ **regarder qqch. à la dérobée**
2 to look quickly and in secret: *He peeped at the answers at the back of the book.* □ **jeter un coup d'œil furtif**

■ *noun* a quick look (*usually* in secret): *She took a peep at the visitor.* □ **coup d'œil discret/furtif**

'**peephole** *noun* a hole (in a door *etc*) through which one can look. □ **trou (pour épier)**

peep[2] [piːp] *verb* to make a high pitched sound: *The car horns were peeping.* □ **crier**

■ *noun* such a sound: *the peep of a car horn.* □ **cri**

peer[1] [piə] *noun* 1 a nobleman (in Britain, one from the rank of baron upwards). □ **pair**

2 a person's equal in rank, merit or age: *The child was disliked by his peers*; (*also adjective*) *He is more advanced than the rest of his peer group.* □ **(de) pair(s)**

'**peerage** [-ridʒ] *noun* 1 a peer's title or status: *He was granted a peerage.* □ **pairie (obtention du titre de pair)**

2 (often with *plural* verb when considered as a number of separate individuals) all noblemen considered as a group: *The peerage has/have many responsibilities.* □ **noblesse**

'**peeress** *noun* 1 the wife or widow of a peer. □ **pairesse**

2 a woman who is a peer in her own right. □ **pairesse**

'**peerless** *adjective* without equal; better than all others: *Sir Galahad was a peerless knight.* □ **sans pareil**

peer[2] [piə] *verb* to look with difficulty: *She peered at the small writing.* □ **scruter**

peevish ['piːviʃ] *adjective* easily made angry; irritable; frequently complaining: *a peevish person.* □ **grincheux**

'**peevishly** *adverb.* □ **avec (mauvaise) humeur**

'**peevishness** *noun.* □ **mauvaise humeur**

peeved *adjective* angry; annoyed: *She was peeved about it.* □ **fâché**

peg [peg] *noun* 1 a *usually* short, not very thick, piece of wood, metal *etc* used to fasten or mark something: *There were four pegs stuck in the ground.* □ **piquet**

2 a hook on a wall or door for hanging clothes *etc* on: *Hang your clothes on the pegs in the cupboard.* □ **patère**

3 (*also* '**clothes-peg**) a wooden or plastic clip for holding clothes *etc* to a rope while drying. □ **pince à linge**

■ *verb – past tense, past participle* **pegged** – to fasten with a peg: *She pegged the clothes on the washing-line.* □ **accrocher**

take (someone) down a peg (or two) to make (a proud person) more humble: *We must find some way of taking him down a peg or two.* □ **remettre (qqn) à sa place**

pelican ['pelikən] *noun* a kind of large water-bird with a large beak with a pouch for carrying fish. □ **pélican**

pellet ['pelit] *noun* a little ball or similarly-shaped object: *He bought a box of lead pellets for his gun.* □ **boulette, grain**

pell-mell [pel'mel] *adverb* quickly and in disorder or great confusion: *The children rushed in pell-mell.* □ **pêle-mêle**

pelmet ['pelmit] *noun* a strip of cloth, wood *etc* hiding a curtain rail. □ **lambrequin**

pelt [pelt] *verb* 1 to throw (things) at: *The children pelted each other with snowballs.* □ **lancer**

2 to run very fast: *She pelted down the road.* □ **courir à toutes jambes**

3 (of rain; sometimes also of hailstones) to fall very heavily: *You can't leave now – it's pelting (down).* □ **pleuvoir des cordes, pleuvoir à verse**

at full pelt (running) as fast as possible: *They set off down the road at full pelt.* □ **à fond de train**

pelvis ['pelvis] *noun* the framework of bone around the body below the waist. □ **bassin**

'**pelvic** *adjective.* □ **pelvien**

pen[1] [pen] *noun* a small enclosure, *usually* for animals: *a sheep-pen.* □ **enclos**

pen[2] [pen] *noun* an instrument for writing in ink: *My pen needs a new nib.* □ **plume**

'**penknife** *noun* a pocket knife with blades which fold into the handle. □ **canif**

'**pen name** *noun* a name used by a writer instead of his own name: *Samuel Clemens used the pen name of Mark Twain.* □ **pseudonyme, nom de plume**

'**pen pal** *nouns* a *usually* young person (*usually* living abroad) with whom another (*usually* young) person regularly exchanges letters: *My daughter has pen pals in India and Spain.* □ **correspondant, ante**

penalize, penalise ['piːnəlaiz] *verb* 1 to punish (someone) for doing something wrong (*eg* breaking a rule in a game), *eg* by the loss of points *etc* or by the giving of some advantage to an opponent: *The child was penalized for his untidy handwriting.* □ **pénaliser**

2 to punish (some wrong action *etc*) in this way: *Any attempt at cheating will be heavily penalized.* □ **punir**

penalty ['penlti] – *plural* '**penalties** – *noun* 1 a punishment for doing wrong, breaking a contract *etc*: *They did wrong and they will have to pay the penalty; The death penalty has been abolished in this country.* □ **pénalité, peine**

2 in *sport etc*, a disadvantage *etc* that must be suffered for breaking the rules *etc*: *The referee awarded the team a penalty*; (*also adjective*) *a penalty kick* (= in football, a chance to kick the ball towards the goal from a spot in front of the goal without being tackled by members of the other team). □ **pénalité**

penance ['penəns] *noun* punishment that a person suffers willingly to show that he or she is sorry for something wrong he or she has done: *He did penance for his sins.* □ **pénitence**

pence *see* **penny.**

pencil ['pensl] *noun* 1 a long, thin instrument (*usually* of wood) containing a thin stick of graphite or some similar solid substance for writing or drawing: *This pencil needs sharpening/to be sharpened; She wrote in pencil*; (*also adjective*) *a pencil sharpener.* □ **crayon**

2 pencil consisting of a metal or plastic case containing a lead that is pushed forward by a screwing mechanism. □ **porte-mine**

■ *verb – past tense, past participle* '**pencilled, 'penciled** – to write or draw with a pencil: *She pencilled an outline of the house.* □ **écrire/dessiner au crayon**

pendant ['pendənt] *noun* 1 an ornament hung from a necklace: *a pendant hanging from a silver chain.* □ **pendentif**

2 the ornament and the necklace together: *She fastened a gold pendant around her neck.* □ **pendentif**

pendulum ['pendjuləm] *noun* a swinging weight, *eg* that which operates the mechanism of a clock: *The little girl watched the pendulum swing back and forwards*; (*also adjective*) *a pendulum clock.* □ **(à/de) balancier**

penetrate ['penitreit] *verb* to move, go or make a way into, past, or through (something): *The bullet penetrated* his shoulder; *Their minds could not penetrate the mystery.* □ **pénétrer**

'**penetrating** *adjective* **1** (of a voice, sound *etc*) loud and clear; easily heard: *a penetrating voice.* □ **pénétrant** **2** (of a glance, stare *etc*) hard and searching, as if trying, or able, to see into a person's mind: *a penetrating glance.* □ **pénétrant**

'**penetratingly** *adverb.* □ **avec pénétration**

,**pene'tration** *noun.* □ **pénétration**

penguin ['pengwin] *noun* a large sea-bird which is found in Antarctic regions and which cannot fly. □ **pingouin**

penicillin [peni'silin] *noun* a kind of antibiotic medicine which kills many harmful bacteria: *The doctor gave her penicillin*; (*also adjective*) *penicillin injections.* □ **(de) pénicilline**

peninsula [pə'ninsjulə] *noun* a piece of land that is almost surrounded by water: *the Malay peninsula.* □ **péninsule, presqu'île**

pe'ninsular *adjective* of or like a peninsula. □ **péninsulaire**

penis ['piːnis] *noun* the male sexual organ in humans and many animals. □ **pénis**

penitentiary [pənətən'ʃəriz] *noun* a jail or prison: *The murderer was tried for his crime and sentenced to 12 years in the penitentiary.* □ **pénitencier**

pennant ['penənt], (*also* **pennon** ['penən]) *noun* a small flag, *usually* in the shape of a long narrow triangle: *The girl had fastened a brightly-coloured pennant to the front of her bike.* □ **flamme**

penny ['peni] – *plurals* '**pennies** – *noun* **1** in Canadian currency, the hundredth part of $1: *It costs seventy-five pennies*; *Oranges, 12¢ each.* □ **penny** **2** in certain countries, a coin of low value. □ **sou, cent** **3** the value of such a coin. □ **penny, cent**

'**penniless** *adjective* very poor; with little or no money: *a penniless old man.* □ **sans le sou**

pension ['penʃən] *noun* a sum of money paid regularly to a widow, a person who has retired from work, a soldier who has been seriously injured in a war *etc*: *He lives on his pension*; *a retirement pension.* □ **pension, rente**

'**pensioner** *noun* a person who receives a pension, *especially* (**old age pensioner**) one who receives a retirement pension. □ **pensionné, ée**

pension off to allow to retire, or to dismiss, with a pension: *They pensioned him off when they found a younger man for the job.* □ **mettre à la retraite**

pensive ['pensiv] *adjective* thinking deeply (about something): *a pensive mood.* □ **pensif**

'**pensively** *adverb.* □ **pensivement**

'**pensiveness** *noun.* □ **air pensif**

pentagon ['pentəgən, -gon] *noun* a 5-sided geometrical figure. □ **pentagone**

pen'tagonal [-'ta-] *adjective.* □ **pentagonal**

pentathlon [pen'taθlən] *noun* a competition in the Olympic games *etc* which consists of contests in swimming, cross-country riding and running, fencing and pistol-shooting. □ **pentathlon**

penthouse ['penthaus] *noun* a (*usually* luxurious) flat at the top of a building: *That apartment building has a* beautiful penthouse; (*also adjective*) *a penthouse flat.* □ **appartement de terrasse**

people ['piːpl] *noun plural* **1** persons: *There were three people in the room.* □ **personne** **2** men and women in general: *People often say such things.* □ **gens** **3** (*noun singular*) a nation or race: *all the peoples of this world.* □ **peuple**

the people the ordinary people of a country as opposed to the aristocracy *etc*: *government for the people by the people.* □ **peuple**

> **people** is usually plural: *The people waiting at the airport were impatient.*
> **people** is singular, and has the plural **peoples**, when it means a nation: *a defeated people*; *the peoples of eastern Europe.*

pep [pep] *noun* an informal word for energy: *full of pep.* □ **entrain**

'**pep talk** *noun* a talk intended to arouse enthusiasm, or to make people work harder, better *etc*: *The director gave all the staff a pep talk.* □ **discours d'encouragement**

pepper ['pepə] *noun* **1** the dried, powdered berries of a certain plant, used for seasoning food: *white/black pepper*; *This soup has too much pepper in it.* □ **poivre** **2** the plant bearing these berries: *a pepper plant.* □ **poivrier** **3** any of several red, yellow, or green, hollow seed-containing fruits used as food: *red peppers stuffed with rice.* □ **piment, poivron** **4** any of the plants which bear these. □ **poivron, piment** ■ *verb* **1** to put pepper in or on (some food): *You don't have to pepper the soup.* □ **poivrer** **2** (*with* with) to throw, fire *etc* many, *usually* small, objects at (someone): *He peppered them with bullets.* □ **mitrailler**

'**peppery** *adjective* **1** (of food) containing a lot of pepper: *The soup is too peppery.* □ **poivré** **2** easily made angry: *a peppery man.* □ **colérique**

'**peppercorn** *noun* the berry of the pepper plant. □ **grain de poivre**

'**pepper mill** *noun* a small container in which peppercorns are ground into a powder. □ **moulin à poivre**

'**peppermint** *noun* **1** a flavouring taken from a type of plant and used in sweets *etc*. □ **menthe (poivrée)** **2** (*sometimes abbreviated to* **mint**) a sweet flavoured with peppermint: *The little girl had a bag of peppermints.* □ **bonbon à la menthe**

per [pər] *preposition* **1** out of: *We have less than one mistake per page.* □ **par** **2** for each: *The dinner will cost $15 per person.* □ **par** **3** in each: *six times per week.* □ **par**

per cent [pə'sent] *adverb, noun* (*often written* % *with figures*) (of numbers, amounts *etc*) stated as a fraction of one hundred: *Twenty-five per cent of one hundred and twenty is thirty*; *25% of the people did not reply to our letters.* □ **pour cent**

perceive [pə'siːv] *verb* to be or become aware of (something); to understand; to realize: *She perceived that he* was tired. □ **s'apercevoir**

percentage [pə'sentidʒ] *noun* **1** an amount, number or rate given as a fraction of one hundred: *We've expressed all these figures as percentages.* □ **pourcentage**

2 a part or proportion of something: *A large percentage of the population can't read or write.* □ **proportion**

perception [pə'sepʃən] *noun* the ability to see, understand *etc* clearly: *a woman of great perception.* □ **perspicacité**

per'ceptive [-tiv] *adjective* able to see, understand *etc* clearly: *a very perceptive man.* □ **perspicace**

per'ceptively *adverb.* □ **avec perspicacité**

per'ceptiveness *noun.* □ **perspicacité**

perch [pəːtʃ] *noun* **1** a branch *etc* on which a bird sits or stands: *The pigeon would not fly down from its perch.* □ **perchoir**

2 any high seat or position: *He looked down from his perch on the roof.* □ **perchoir**

■ *verb* **1** (of birds) to go to (a perch); to sit or stand on (a perch): *The bird flew up and perched on the highest branch of the tree.* □ **se percher**

2 to put, or be, in a high seat or position: *He perched the child on his shoulder; They perched on the fence.* □ (se) **percher**

percussion [pə'kʌʃən] *noun* **1** (in an orchestra, the group of people who play) musical instruments in which the sound is produced by striking them *eg* drums, cymbals *etc*: *He plays (the) percussion in the orchestra; (also adjective) a percussion instrument.* □ **(à/de) percussion**

2 the striking of one hard object against another: *A gun is fired by means of percussion.* □ **percussion**

per'cussionist *noun* a person who plays percussion instruments in an orchestra *etc*. □ **percussionniste**

perennial [pə'reniəl] *noun, adjective* (a plant) which lasts for more than two years: *Daffodils are perennial plants; They are perennials.* □ **vivace**

perfect ['pəːfikt] *adjective* **1** without fault or flaw; excellent: *a perfect day for a holiday; a perfect rose.* □ **parfait**

2 exact: *a perfect copy.* □ **parfait**

3 very great; complete: *a perfect stranger.* □ **tout à fait**

■ [pə'fekt] *verb* to make perfect: *She went to France to perfect her French.* □ **perfectionner**

per'fection [-ʃən] *noun* the state of being perfect: *Absolute perfection in a dictionary is rare.* □ **perfection**

per'fectionist [-ʃə-] *noun* a person who is only satisfied if what he is doing is perfect: *She's a perfectionist – her work is perfect in every detail.* □ **perfectionniste**

'perfectly *adverb* **1** without mistakes or flaws: *She performed the dance perfectly.* □ **parfaitement**

2 very; completely: *She was perfectly happy.* □ **parfaitement**

perforate ['pəːfəreit] *verb* to make a hole or holes in, *especially* a line of small holes in paper, so that it may be torn easily: *Sheets of postage stamps are perforated.* □ **perforer**

'perforated *adjective.* □ **perforé**

,perfo'ration *noun* **1** a small hole, or a number or line of small holes, made in a sheet of paper *etc*: *The pur-pose of the perforation(s) is to make the paper easier to tear.* □ **perforation**

2 the act of perforating or being perforated. □ **perforation**

perform [pə'foːm] *verb* **1** to do, *especially* with care or as a duty: *The doctor performed the operation.* □ **exécuter**

2 to act (in the theatre *etc*) or do anything musical, theatrical *etc* to entertain an audience: *The company will perform a Greek play; She performed on the violin.* □ **jouer**

per'formance *noun* **1** the doing of something: *He is very conscientious in the performance of his duties.* □ **exécution**

2 the way in which something or someone performs: *His performance in the exams was not very good.* □ **performance**

3 something done on stage *etc*: *The company gave a performance of 'Othello'; His last three performances have not been very good.* □ **représentation**

per'former *noun* a person who performs, *especially* theatrically or musically. □ **interprète**

perfume ['pəːfjuːm] *noun* **1** a sweet smell or fragrance: *the perfume of roses.* □ **parfum**

2 a liquid, cream *etc* which has a sweet smell when put on the skin, hair, clothes *etc*: *She loves French perfume(s).* □ **parfum**

■ [pə'fjuːm] *verb* **1** to put perfume on or in: *She perfumed her hair.* □ **parfumer**

2 to give a sweet smell to: *Flowers perfumed the air.* □ **embaumer**

per'fumery [-'fjuː-] – *plural* **per'fumeries** – *noun* a shop where perfume is sold or a factory where it is made. □ **parfumerie**

perhaps [pə'haps] *adverb* possibly: *Perhaps it will rain.* □ **peut-être**

peril ['peril] *noun* great danger: *You are in great peril; The explorers knew they would face many perils.* □ **péril**

'perilous *adjective* very dangerous: *a perilous journey.* □ **périlleux**

'perilousness *noun.* □ **danger**

'perilously *adverb* dangerously: *He came perilously close to death.* □ **périlleusement**

perimeter [pə'rimitə] *noun* the outside edge of any area: *the perimeter of the city; the perimeter of a circle.* □ **périmètre**

period ['piəriəd] *noun* **1** any length of time: *a period of three days; a period of waiting.* □ **période**

2 a stage in the Earth's development, an artist's development, in history *etc*: *the Pleistocene period; the modern period.* □ **ère, période**

3 the punctuation mark (.), put at the end of a sentence; a full stop. □ **point (final)**

■ *adjective* (of furniture, costumes *etc*) of or from the same or appropriate time in history; antique or very old: *period costumes; His house is full of period furniture* (= antique furniture). □ **d'époque**

,peri'odic [-'o-] *adjective* **1** happening, done *etc* occasionally: *He suffers from periodic fits of depression.* □ **périodique**

2 (*also* ,**peri'odical**) happening, done *etc* at regular intervals: *periodical reports.* □ **périodique**

,**peri'odically** *adverb*: *We see each other periodically.* □ **périodiquement**

,**peri'odical** [-'o-] *noun* a magazine which is issued regularly (every week, month *etc*). □ **périodique**

■ *adjective see* **periodic**.

periphery [pə'rifəri] *noun* (*usually in singular with* **the**) the edge (of something): *The shops are on the periphery of the housing estate.* □ **périphérie**

pe'ripheral *adjective.* □ **périphérique**

periscope ['periskoup] *noun* a tube containing mirrors, through which a person can look in order to see things which cannot be seen from the position the person is in, *especially* one used in submarines when under water to allow a person to see what is happening on the surface of the sea. □ **périscope**

perish ['periʃ] *verb* to die, *especially* in war, accident *etc*: *Many people perished in the earthquake.* □ **périr**

'**perishable** *adjective* (*especially* of food) likely to go bad quickly: *Butter is perishable.* □ **périssable**

periwinkle ['periwiŋkl] *noun* a blue-flowered trailing plant. □ **pervenche**

perk [pəːk]: **perk up** to recover one's energy or cheerfulness: *I gave her a cup of tea and she soon perked up.* □ **se ragaillardir**

perky *adjective* lively; cheerful: *You're in a perky mood.* □ **guilleret**

'**perkily** *adverb.* □ **avec entrain**

'**perkiness** *noun.* □ **entrain**

perm [pəːm] *noun* a permanent wave in a person's hair: *She's had a perm.* □ **permanente**

■ *verb* to give a permanent wave to (hair): *She's had her hair permed.* □ **faire une permanente (à)**

permanent ['pəːmənənt] *adjective* lasting; not temporary: *After many years of travelling, they made a permanent home in England.* □ **permanent**

'**permanently** *adverb.* □ **de façon permanente**

'**permanence** *noun.* □ **permanence**

permanent wave *noun* (*usually abbreviated to* **perm** [pəːm]) a wave or curl put into a person's hair by a special process and *usually* lasting for several months. □ **permanente**

permeate ['pəːmieit] *verb* (of a liquid, gas *etc*) to pass or spread into or through: *The water had permeated (through/into) the soil.* □ **s'infiltrer**

permit [pə'mit] – *past tense, past participle* **per'mitted** – *verb* **1** to agree to (another person's action); to allow or let (someone do something): *Permit me to answer your question; Smoking is not permitted.* □ **permettre**

2 to make possible: *My aunt's legacy permitted me to go to America.* □ **permettre (de)**

■ ['pəːmit] *noun* a written order allowing a person to do something: *We have a permit to export our product.* □ **permis, laissez-passer**

permission [pə'miʃən] *noun* a written, spoken *etc* agreement that someone may do something: *She gave me permission to leave.* □ **permission**

permutation [pəːmju'teiʃən] *noun* a particular order in which things are arranged: *We can write down these*

numbers in various permutations. □ **arrangement**

perpendicular [pəːpən'dikjulə] *adjective* standing, rising *etc* straight upwards; vertical: *a perpendicular cliff.* □ **perpendiculaire**

,**perpen'dicularly** *adverb.* □ **perpendiculairement**

perpetual [pə'petʃuəl] *adjective* lasting for ever or for a long time; occurring repeatedly over a long time: *He lives in perpetual fear of being discovered; perpetual noise.* □ **perpétuel**

per'petually *adverb.* □ **perpétuellement**

perplex [pə'pleks] *verb* to puzzle or confuse (someone); to make (someone) unable to understand: *He was perplexed by my questions.* □ **rendre perplexe**

per'plexed *adjective.* □ **perplexe**

per'plexedly [-'pleksid-] *adverb.* □ **avec perplexité**

per'plexity *noun*: *She stood there in perplexity.* □ **perplexité**

persecute ['pəːsikjuːt] *verb* to make (someone) suffer, *especially* because of their opinions or beliefs: *They were persecuted for their religion.* □ **persécuter**

,**perse'cution** *noun.* □ **persécution**

'**persecutor** *noun.* □ **persécuteur, trice**

persevere [pəːsi'viə] *verb* to continue to (try to) do something in spite of difficulties: *She persevered in her task.* □ **persévérer**

,**perse'verance** *noun.* □ **persévérance**

persist [pə'sist] *verb* to keep doing, thinking *etc* in spite of opposition or difficulty; to continue asking, persuading *etc*: *It will not be easy but you will succeed if you persist; He didn't want to tell her, but she persisted (in asking).* □ **persister**

per'sistent *adjective*: *She was persistent in her demands/denials; persistent questions.* □ **persistant**

per'sistently *adverb.* □ **avec persistance**

per'sistence *noun.* □ **persistance**

person ['pəːsn] – *plural* **people** ['piːpl], '**persons** – *noun*

1 a human being: *There's a person outside who wants to speak to you.* □ **personne**

2 a person's body: *He never carried money on his person* (= with him; in his pockets *etc*). □ **soi**

'**personal** *adjective* **1** one's own: *This is her personal opinion; The matter will have my personal attention.* □ **personnel**

2 private: *This is a personal matter between him and me.* □ **personnel**

3 in person: *The Prime Minister will make a personal appearance.* □ **en personne**

4 (making remarks which are) insulting, *especially* about a person's appearance *etc*: *personal remarks; Don't be personal!* □ **personnel**

,**perso'nality** – *plural* **perso'nalities** – *noun* **1** a person's characteristics (of the mind, the emotions *etc*) as a whole: *a likeable/forceful* (= strong) *personality.* □ **personnalité**

2 strong, distinctive (*usually* attractive) character: *He is not handsome but he has a lot of personality.* □ **personnalité**

3 a well-known person: *a television personality;* (*also adjective*) *a personality cult* (= very great, *usually* too great, admiration for a person, *usually* a political leader).

□ **(de la) personnalité**

'**personally** *adverb* **1** in one's own opinion: *Personally, I prefer the other.* □ **personnellement**

2 doing something oneself, not having or letting someone else do it on one's behalf: *He thanked me personally.* □ **personnellement**

personal pronoun a pronoun which refers to the first, second or third persons: *I am going; He told him; She saw you.* □ **pronom personnel**

in person personally; one's self, not represented by someone else: *The Queen was there in person; I'd like to thank him in person.* □ **en personne**

personnel [pɔːsə'nel] *noun* the people employed in a firm, factory, shop *etc*; the staff: *Our personnel are very highly trained; (also adjective) a personnel manager.* □ **(de) personnel**

perspective [pə'spektiv] *noun* **1** the way of drawing solid objects, natural scenes *etc* on a flat surface, so that they appear to have the correct shape, distance from each other *etc*: *Early medieval paintings lacked perspective.* □ **perspective**

2 a picture or view of something: *I would like a clearer perspective of the situation.* □ **perspective**

in/out of perspective 1 (of an object in a painting, photograph *etc*) having, or not having, the correct size, shape, distance *etc* in relation to the rest of the picture: *These houses don't seem to be in perspective in your drawing.* □ **en perspective; qui manque de perspective**

2 with, or without, a correct or sensible understanding of something's true importance: *Try to get these problems in(to) perspective; Keep things in perspective.* □ **en perspective**

perspire [pə'spaiə] *verb* to lose moisture through the skin when hot; to sweat: *She was perspiring in the heat.* □ **transpirer**

,**perspi'ration** [pəːspi-] *noun* the moisture lost when perspiring: *The perspiration was running down his face.* □ **transpiration**

persuade [pə'sweid] *verb* **1** to make (someone) (not) do something, by arguing with him or advising him: *We persuaded her (not) to go.* □ **persuader (de)**

2 to make (someone) certain (that something is the case); to convince: *We eventually persuaded her that we were serious.* □ **convaincre**

per'suasion [-ʒən] *noun* the act of persuading: *He gave in to our persuasion and did what we wanted him to do.* □ **persuasion**

per'suasive [-siv] *adjective* able to persuade: *He is a persuasive speaker; His arguments are persuasive.* □ **persuasif**

per'suasively *adverb.* □ **de manière persuasive**

per'suasiveness *noun.* □ **force de persuasion**

pertinent [pəːtənənt] *adjective* relevant, appropriate, having to do with the matter at hand: *The teacher asked the students to stop talking unless they had some pertinent information about the work they were doing.* □ **pertinent**

pertinently *adverb* appropriately, relating to or to do with: *The question was pertinently asked at just the right time.* □ **pertinemment**

perturb [pə'təːb] *verb* to make (someone) worried or anxious: *His threats didn't perturb her in the least.* □ **inquiéter, perturber**

perverse [pə'vəːs] *adjective* **1** continuing to do, think *etc* something which one knows, or which one has been told, is wrong or unreasonable: *a perverse child.* □ **pervers**

2 deliberately wrong; unreasonable: *perverse behaviour.* □ **obstiné (dans le mal)**

per'versely *adverb.* □ **par esprit de contradiction**

per'verseness *noun.* □ **obstination, perversité**

per'versity *noun.* □ **obstination, perversité**

pervert [pə'vəːt] *verb* **1** to change (something) from what is normal or right: *to pervert the course of justice.* □ **fausser**

2 to lead (someone) to crime or to evil or immoral (*especially* sexually immoral) acts: *The man was accused of trying to pervert children.* □ **pervertir, dépraver**

■ ['pəːvəːt] *noun* a person who does perverted (*especially* sexually immoral) acts. □ **pervers, erse**

per'version [-ʃən] *noun* **1** (the) act of perverting: *a perversion of justice.* □ **perversion**

2 a perverted act: *He is capable of any perversion.* □ **perversion**

per'verted *adjective.* □ **perverti**

peseta [pə'seitə] *noun* the standard unit of currency in Spain. □ **peseta**

peso ['peisou] – *plural* '**pesos** – *noun* the standard unit of currency in many South and Central American countries and in the Philippines. □ **peso**

pessimism ['pesimizəm] *noun* the state of mind of a person who always expects bad things to happen. □ **pessimisme**

'**pessimist** *noun* a person who thinks in this way: *She is such a pessimist that she always expects the worst.* □ **pessimiste**

,**pessi'mistic** *adjective.* □ **pessimiste**

,**pessi'mistically** *adverb.* □ **avec pessimisme**

pest [pest] *noun* **1** a creature that is harmful or destructive, *eg* a mosquito, a rat *etc*. □ **animal/insecte nuisible**

2 a troublesome person or thing: *He is always annoying me – he is an absolute pest!* □ **peste**

'**pesticide** [-tisaid] *noun* a substance that kills animal and insect pests. □ **pesticide, insecticide**

pester ['pestə] *verb* to annoy (someone) frequently or continually: *He pestered me with questions; He pestered her to help him.* □ **importuner**

pestilence ['pestiləns] *noun* any type of deadly epidemic disease, *especially* bubonic plague. □ **peste**

pestle ['pesl] *noun* a tool like a small club, used for pounding things to powder, *especially* in a mortar: *He ground the nutmeg to a powder with a mortar and pestle.* □ **pilon**

pet [pet] *noun* **1** a tame animal *etc*, *usually* kept in the home: *She keeps a rabbit as a pet; (also adjective) a pet rabbit/goldfish.* □ **animal familier**

2 (*especially* of children) a delightful or lovely person (used also as a term of affection): *Isn't that baby a pet?; Would you like some ice cream, pet?* □ **chou**

■ *adjective* favourite; greatest: *What is your pet ambition/hate?* □ **favori**

■ *verb – past tense, past participle* '**petted** – to stroke or caress (an animal) in a loving way: *The old lady sat by the fire petting her dog.* □ **caresser**

pet name a particular name used to express affection: *His pet name for her was 'Kitten'.* □ **diminutif**

pet shop a store where birds, fish, small animals and pet supplies are sold: *Andrew bought a rabbit at the same pet shop where I got my cat.* □ **animalerie**

petal ['petl] *noun* one of the *usually* brightly coloured leaf-like parts of a flower: *This rose has yellow petals edged with pink.* □ **pétale**

peter ['piːtə]: **peter out** to come gradually to an end: *As the river dried up our water-supply petered out; Their enthusiasm gradually petered out.* □ **tarir, s'épuiser**

petite [pə'tiːt] *adjective* (of women and girls) small and neat: *That girl is very petite.* □ **menue**

petition [pə'tiʃən] *noun* a formal request made to someone in authority and *usually* signed by a large number of people. □ **pétition**

■ *verb* to make such a request: *They petitioned the government for the release of the prisoners.* □ **adresser une pétition à**

pe'**titioner** *noun.* □ **pétitionnaire**

petrify ['petrifai] *verb* to make (someone) very frightened; to terrify: *The thought of having to make a speech petrified him.* □ **pétrifier**

petro- [petrou] of or related to petrol, as in **petrochemical.** □ **pétro-**

petrochemical [petrə'kemikəl] *noun* any chemical obtained from petroleum or natural gas: *the petrochemical industry.* □ **pétrochimique**

petrol ['petrəl] *noun* (**gas** *or* **gasoline**) a liquid got from petroleum, used as fuel for cars *etc*: *I'll stop at the next garage and buy more petrol;* (*also adjective*) *a petrol engine.* □ **(à) essence**

petroleum [pə'trouliəm] *noun* oil in its raw, unrefined form, which is found in natural wells below the earth's surface and from which petrol, paraffin *etc* are obtained. □ **pétrole**

petroleum jelly a soft substance got from petroleum, used *eg* in ointments. □ **vaseline**

petrol pump (gasoline pump) an apparatus at a gas station which pumps gasoline into cars *etc*, and which measures the amount of gas it pumps. □ **pompe à essence**

petrol station (gas station) a garage where gasoline is sold. □ **station-service**

petticoat ['petikout] *noun* an underskirt: *a lace-trimmed petticoat.* □ **jupon**

petty ['peti] *adjective* 1 of very little importance; trivial: *petty details.* □ **insignifiant**

2 deliberately nasty for a foolish or trivial reason: *petty behaviour.* □ **mesquin**

'**pettily** *adverb.* □ **avec mesquinerie**

'**pettiness** *noun.* □ **mesquinerie**

petty cash money used for small, everyday expenses in an office *etc*. □ **petite caisse**

pew [pjuː] *noun* a seat or bench in a church. □ **banc**

(d'église)

pewter ['pjuːtə] *noun, adjective* (of) a metal made by mixing tin and lead: *That mug is (made of) pewter; a pewter mug.* □ **(en/d') étain**

phantom ['fantəm] *noun* a ghost: *The castle is said to be haunted by a phantom.* □ **fantôme**

pharmacy ['faːməsi] – *plural* '**pharmacies** – *noun* 1 the preparation of medicines: *She is studying pharmacy.* □ **pharmacie**

2 a shop *etc* where medicines are sold or given out: *the hospital pharmacy.* □ **pharmacie**

,**pharma'ceutical** [-'sjuːtikəl] *adjective.* □ **pharmaceutique**

'**pharmacist** *noun* (**'druggist**) a person who prepares and sells medicines; a chemist. □ **pharmacien, enne**

phase [feiz] *noun* 1 a stage in the development of something: *We are entering a new phase in the war.* □ **phase**

2 one in a series of regular changes in the shape or appearance of something (*especially* the moon or a planet): *the phases of the moon.* □ **phase**

pheasant ['feznt] – *plurals* '**pheasants,** '**pheasant** – *noun* 1 a type of long-tailed bird, the male of which has brightly-coloured feathers and certain types of which are often shot for sport: *a brace of pheasant(s); two pheasants.* □ **faisan, ane**

2 (the flesh of) the bird as food: *We had roast pheasant for dinner.* □ **faisan**

phenomenon [fə'nomənən, -non] – *plural* phe'**nomena** [-nə] – *noun* a natural fact or event that is seen or happens regularly or frequently: *Magnetic attraction is an interesting phenomenon.* □ **phénomène**

phe'**nomenal** *adjective* very unusual; remarkable: *a phenomenal amount of money.* □ **phénoménal**

phe'**nomenally** *adverb.* □ **phénoménalement**

phew [fjuː] *interjection* a word or sound used to express disgust, tiredness, relief *etc*: *Phew!* □ **pouah! ouf!**

philanthropy [fi'lanθrəpi] *noun* love for mankind, *usually* as shown by money given to, or work done for, other people: *She shows her philanthropy by helping people who have been in prison.* □ **philantropie**

philanthropic [filən'θropik] *adjective* giving money or other help *etc* to others: *a philanthropic person; a philanthropic act.* □ **philantropique**

phi'**lanthropist** *noun* a philanthropic person. □ **philanthrope**

philately [fi'latəli] *noun* the study and collecting of postage-stamps. □ **philatélie**

,**phila'telic** [-'te-] *adjective.* □ **philatélique**

phi'**latelist** *noun.* □ **philatéliste**

philosophy [fi'losəfi] – *plural* phi'**losophies** – *noun* 1 the search for knowledge and truth, *especially* about the nature of man and his behaviour and beliefs: *moral philosophy.* □ **philosophie**

2 a particular system of philosophical theories: *I have a very simple philosophy* (= attitude to life) – *enjoy life!* □ **philosophie**

phi'**losopher** *noun* a person who studies philosophy, *especially* one who develops a particular set of theories: *Rousseau was a famous philosopher.* □ **philosophe**

,**philo'sophical,** ,**philo'sophic** [-'so-] *adjective* 1 of philosophy: *a philosophical discussion*; *philosophical works*. □ **philosophique**

2 (of a person) calm, not easily upset or worried: *He's had a lot of bad luck, but he's philosophical about it.* □ **philosophe**

,philo'sophically *adverb*. □ **philosophiquement**

phi'losophize, phi'losophise *verb* to think about or discuss the nature of man, the purpose of life *etc*: *He spends all his time philosophizing and never does any work.* □ **philosopher**

phlegm [flem] *noun* thick, slimy liquid brought up from the throat by coughing. □ **flegme**

phlegmatic [fleg'matik] *adjective* calm; not easily excited: *She's very phlegmatic – nothing would ever make her panic.* □ **flegmatique**

phobia ['foubiə] *noun* an intense fear or hatred of something: *She has a phobia about birds.* □ **phobie**

phoenix ['fi:niks] *noun* a mythological bird that burns itself and is born again from its own ashes. □ **phénix**

phone [foun] *noun* a telephone: *We were talking on the phone.* □ **téléphone**

■ *verb* to telephone (a person, message or place): *I'll phone you this evening.* □ **téléphoner**

phone up to (try to) speak to (someone) by means of the telephone: *I'll phone (him) up and ask about it.* □ **téléphoner**

phonetic [fə'netik] *adjective* relating to the sounds of (a) language: *She's making a phonetic study of the speech of the deaf.* □ **phonétique**

pho'netics *noun singular* the study of the sounds of language. □ **phonétique**

■ *noun singular, noun plural* (a system of) symbols used to show the pronunciation of words. □ **phonétique**

phon(e)y ['founi] *adjective* not genuine; fake; false: *a phoney French accent.* □ **faux**

■ *noun* a person who is not what he pretends to be: *He's not a real doctor – he's a phoney.* □ **charlatan**

phonics ['founiks *or* 'foniks] *noun plural* the science of sound, or of spoken sounds. □ **phonique**

photo ['foutou] – *plural* '**photos** – *noun* a photograph. □ **photo**

photocopy ['foutəkopi] – *plural* '**photocopies** – *noun* a copy of a document *etc* made by a machine which photographs it: *I'll get some photocopies made of this letter.* □ **photocopie**

■ *verb* to make a copy in this way: *Will you photocopy this letter for me?* □ **photocopier**

'**photocopier** *noun* a machine that makes photocopies. □ **photocopieur**

photograph ['foutəgra:f] *noun* (*abbreviation* **photo** ['foutou]) a picture taken by a camera, using the action of light on film or plates covered with certain chemicals: *I took a lot of photographs during my holiday.* □ **photographie**

■ *verb* to take a photograph or photographs of (a person, thing *etc*): *He spends all his time photographing old buildings.* □ **photographier**

photographer [fə'togrəfə] *noun*: *She is a professional photographer.* □ **photographe**

,photo'graphic [-'gra-] *adjective* of photographs or pho-

tography: *a photographic record of his journey.* □ **photographique**

photography [fə'togrəfi] *noun* the act of taking photographs: *She's very keen on photography.* □ **photographie**

Photostat® ['foutəstat] *noun* (a copy made by) a type of camera for producing copies of documents *etc*. □ **photocopie**

phrase [freiz] *noun* **1** a small group of words (*usually* without a finite verb) which forms part of an actual or implied sentence: *He arrived after dinner.* □ **syntagme**

2 a small group of musical notes which follow each other to make a definite individual section of a melody: *the opening phrase of the overture.* □ **phrase**

■ *verb* to express (something) in words: *I phrased my explanations in simple language.* □ **exprimer**

phraseology [freizi'olədʒi] *noun* the manner of putting words and phrases together to express oneself: *Her phraseology shows that she is a foreigner.* □ **phraséologie**

'**phrasing** *noun* **1** phraseology. □ **phraséologie**

2 the act of putting musical phrases together either in composing or playing. □ **phrasé**

'**phrase book** *noun* a book (*eg* for tourists) which contains and translates useful words and phrases in a foreign language. □ **recueil d'expressions**

phrasal verb a phrase consisting of a verb and adverb or preposition, which together function as a verb: '*Leave out', 'go without', 'go away', are phrasal verbs.* □ **verbe à postposition**

physical ['fizikəl] *adjective* **1** of the body: *Playing football is one form of physical exercise.* □ **physique**

2 of things that can be seen or felt: *the physical world.* □ **matériel**

3 of the laws of nature: *It's a physical impossibility for a man to fly like a bird.* □ **physique**

4 relating to the natural features of the surface of the Earth: *physical geography.* □ **physique**

5 relating to physics: *physical chemistry.* □ **physique**

'**physically** *adverb*. □ **physiquement**

physician [fi'ziʃən] *noun* a doctor who specializes in medical rather than surgical treatment of patients: *She completed her studies and is now a practising physician.* □ **médecin**

physics ['fiziks] *noun singular* the study of natural phenomena such as heat, light, sound, electricity, magnetism *etc* but not *usually* chemistry or biology: *Physics is his main subject at university.* □ **physique**

'**physicist** [-sist] *noun* a person who studies, or is an expert in, physics. □ **physicien, ienne**

physiotherapy [fizio'θerəpi] *noun* the treatment of injuries by physical exercise, massage *etc*, not drugs. □ **physiothérapie**

,physio'therapist *noun*. □ **physiothérapeute**

physique [fi'zi:k] *noun* the structure of a person's body: *He has a poor/powerful physique.* □ **physique**

piano [pi'anou] – *plural* **pi'anos** – *noun* a large musical instrument played by pressing keys which make hammers strike stretched wires: *She plays the piano very well*; (*also adjective*) *piano music.* □ **(de) piano**

pianist ['piənist] *noun* a person who plays the piano. □

pianiste
pi,ano-ac'cordion *noun* a type of accordion with a keyboard like that of a piano. □ **accordéon à clavier**
pianoforte [pianou'fo:ti] *noun* a piano. □ **piano**
grand piano a large piano in which the wires are stretched horizontally. □ **piano à queue**
piccolo ['pikalou] – *plural* 'piccolos – *noun* a kind of small, high-pitched flute: *She plays the piccolo.* □ **piccolo**
pick[1] [pik] *verb* **1** to choose or select: *Pick the one you like best.* □ **choisir**
2 to take (flowers from a plant, fruit from a tree *etc*), usually by hand: *The little girl sat on the grass and picked flowers.* □ **cueillir**
3 to lift (someone or something): *He picked up the child.* □ **soulever, prendre**
4 to unlock (a lock) with a tool other than a key: *When she found that she had lost her key, she picked the lock with a hair-pin.* □ **crocheter (une serrure)**
5 to select or choose at random: *Lindsay won the car when her name was picked out of a hat.* □ **piger**
■ *noun* **1** whatever or whichever a person wants or chooses: *Take your pick of these prizes.* □ **choix**
2 the best one(s) from or the best part of something: *These grapes are the pick of the bunch.* □ **le meilleur**
'pickpocket *noun* a person who steals from people's pockets: *He kept his wallet in his hand because he knew there would be pickpockets in the crowd.* □ **voleur, euse à la tire**
'pickup *noun* **1** a type of small truck or van. □ **camion-plateau**
2 the part of a record player that holds the stylus. □ **tourne-disque**
pick and choose to select or choose very carefully: *When I'm buying apples, I like to pick and choose (the ones I want).* □ **sélectionner**
pick at to eat very little of (something): *He was not very hungry, and just picked at the food on his plate.* □ **chipoter**
pick someone's brains to ask (a person) questions in order to get ideas, information *etc* from him which one can use oneself: *You might be able to help me with this problem – can I come and pick your brains for a minute!* □ **faire appel aux lumières de qqn**
pick holes in to criticize or find faults in (an argument, theory *etc*): *He sounded very convincing, but I'm sure one could pick holes in what he said.* □ **trouver à redire**
pick off to shoot (*especially* people in a group) one by one: *He picked off the enemy soldiers.* □ **abattre (successivement)**
pick on 1 to choose (someone) to do a *usually* difficult or unpleasant job: *Why do they always pick on me to do the washing-up?* □ **choisir**
2 to speak to or treat (a person) angrily or critically: *Don't pick on me – it wasn't my fault.* □ **harceler**
pick out 1 to choose or select: *She picked out one dress that she particularly liked.* □ **choisir**
2 to see or recognize (a person, thing *etc*): *She must be among those people getting off the train, but I can't pick her out.* □ **identifier**

3 to play (a piece of music), *especially* slowly and with difficulty, *especially* by ear, without music in front of one: *I don't really play the piano, but I can pick out a tune on one with one finger.* □ **retrouver (un air)**
pick someone's pocket to steal something from a person's pocket: *My wallet is gone – someone has picked my pocket!* □ **pratiquer le vol à la tire**
pick a quarrel/fight with (someone) to start a quarrel, argument or fight with (someone) on purpose: *He was angry because I beat him in the race, and he tried to pick a fight with me afterwards.* □ **chercher querelle/la bagarre**
pick up 1 to learn gradually, without formal teaching: *I never studied Italian – I just picked it up when I was in Italy.* □ **apprendre**
2 to let (someone) into a car, train *etc* in order to take him somewhere: *I picked her up at the station and drove her home.* □ **prendre**
3 to get (something) by chance: *I picked up a bargain at the shops today.* □ **dénicher**
4 to right (oneself) after a fall *etc*; to stand up: *He fell over and picked himself up again.* □ **se relever**
5 to collect (something) from somewhere: *I ordered some meat from the butcher – I'll pick it up on my way home tonight.* □ **(passer) prendre**
6 (of radio, radar *etc*) to receive signals: *We picked up a foreign broadcast last night.* □ **capter**
7 to find; to catch: *We lost his trail but picked it up again later; The police picked up the criminal.* □ **retrouver; arrêter**
pick up speed to go faster; to accelerate: *The car picked up speed as it drove down the hill.* □ **prendre de la vitesse**
pick one's way to walk carefully (around or between something one wishes to avoid touching *etc*): *She picked her way between the puddles.* □ **avancer avec précaution parmi**
pick[2] [pik] *noun* (*also* 'pickaxe – *plural* 'pickaxes) a tool with a heavy metal head pointed at one or both ends, used for breaking hard surfaces *eg* walls, roads, rocks *etc*. □ **pic**
pickaxe *see* pick[2].
picket ['pikit] *noun* **1** (any one of) a number of people employed at a factory *etc* who are on strike and who try to persuade workers not to go to work there, not to deliver goods there *etc*: *The men set up a picket to stop trucks getting into the factory; (also adjective) a picket line.* □ **piquet de grève**
2 a soldier or a small group of soldiers on special duty, usually to guard against a sudden attack by the enemy: *The commander placed pickets at various points around the camp; (also adjective) picket duty.* □ **détachement**
■ *verb* **1** to place a group of soldiers, strikers *etc* somewhere as a picket: *The strikers' leaders decided to picket the factory; The commander picketed the camp.* □ **organiser un piquet/cordon de**
2 to act as a picket (at): *In this country, strikers have the legal right to picket; The soldiers picketed the camp.* □ **faire du piquetage**
pickle ['pikl] *noun* **1** a vegetable or vegetables preserved

(see below)

in vinegar, salt water *etc*: *Do you want some pickle(s) on your salad?* □ **marinade(s)**

2 trouble; an unpleasant situation: *She got herself into a real pickle.* □ **mariner**

■ *verb* to preserve in vinegar, salt water *etc*: *I think I will pickle these cucumbers.* □ **mariner**

picnic ['piknik] *noun* a very informal meal eaten in the open air, *usually* as part of a trip, outing *etc*: *We'll go to the seaside and take a picnic*; *Let's go for a picnic!*; *(also adjective)* a picnic lunch. □ **pique-nique**

■ *verb* – *past tense, past participle* '**picnicked** – to have a picnic: *We picnicked on the beach.* □ **pique-niquer**

pictorial [pik'tɔːriəl] *adjective* **1** having many pictures: *a pictorial magazine.* □ **illustré**

2 consisting of a picture or pictures: *a pictorial map.* □ **en images**

pi'ctorially *adverb.* □ **en images**

picture ['piktʃə] *noun* **1** a painting or drawing: *This is a picture of my mother.* □ **peinture, illustration**

2 a photograph: *I took a lot of pictures when I was on holiday.* □ **photo**

3 a cinema film: *There's a good picture on at the cinema tonight.* □ **film**

4 *(with the)* a symbol or perfect example (of something): *She looked the picture of health/happiness.* □ **image**

5 *(with a)* a beautiful sight: *She looked a picture in her new dress.* □ **avoir un air ravissant**

6 a clear description: *She gave me a good picture of what was happening.* □ **description**

■ *verb* to imagine: *I can picture the scene.* □ **se représenter**

put (someone)/be in the picture to give or have all the necessary information (about something): *She put me in the picture about what had happened.* □ **mettre au courant**

the pictures the cinema: *We went to the pictures last night, but it wasn't a very good film.* □ **cinéma**

picturesque [piktʃə'resk] *adjective* (of places) pretty and interesting: *a picturesque village.* □ **pittoresque**

,**pictu'resquely** *adverb.* □ **de manière pittoresque**
,**pictu'resqueness** *noun.* □ **pittoresque**

pidgin ['pidʒən] *noun* any of a number of languages which consist of a mixture of English, French, Portuguese *etc* and some non-European *(especially* African) language: *Beach-la-mar is a pidgin spoken in parts of the southern Pacific Ocean*; *(also adjective)* pidgin English. □ **pidgin**

pie [pai] *noun* food baked in a covering of pastry: *a steak/apple pie.* □ **tarte**

pie in the sky something good promised for the future but which one is not certain or likely to get: *He says he will get a well-paid job but it's just pie in the sky.* □ **des châteaux en Espagne**

piebald ['paibɔːld] *adjective (usually* of horses) black and white in patches. □ **pie**

piece [piːs] *noun* **1** a part of anything: *a piece of cake*; *She examined it carefully piece by piece* (= each piece separately). □ **morceau**

2 a single thing or example of something: *a piece of paper*; *a piece of news.* □ **morceau; fragment**

3 a composition in music, writing (an article, short story *etc*), drama, sculpture *etc*: *She wrote a piece on social reform in the local newspaper.* □ **pièce; article**

4 a coin of a particular value: *a five cent piece.* □ **pièce**

5 in chess, draughts and other games, a small shape made of wood, metal, plastic *etc* that is moved according to the rules of the game. □ **pion**

,**piece'meal** *adverb* a little bit at a time; not as a whole: *She did the work piecemeal.* □ **par bouts**

■ *adjective* done *etc* in this way: *He has a rather piecemeal way of working.* □ **décousu, sans méthode**

go (all) to pieces (of a person) to collapse physically or nervously: *He went to pieces when his wife died.* □ **s'effondrer**

in pieces 1 with its various parts not joined together: *The bed is delivered in pieces and the customer has to put it together himself.* □ **en pièces détachées**

2 broken: *The vase was lying in pieces on the floor.* □ **en (mille) morceaux**

piece together to put (the pieces of something) together: *They tried to piece together the fragments of the broken vase.* □ **rassembler**

to pieces into separate, *usually* small pieces, or into the various parts from which (something) is made: *It was so old, it fell to pieces when I touched it.* □ **en morceaux**

pier [piə] *noun* a platform of stone, wood *etc* stretching from the shore into the sea, a lake *etc*, used as a landing-place for boats or as a place of entertainment: *The passengers stepped down on to the pier.* □ **jetée**

pierce [piəs] *verb* **1** (of pointed objects) to go into or through (something): *The arrow pierced his arm*; *A sudden light pierced the darkness.* □ **percer**

2 to make a hole in or through (something) with a pointed object: *Pierce the lid before removing it from the jar.* □ **percer**

'**piercing** *adjective* **1** loud; shrill: *a piercing scream.* □ **perçant**

2 (of cold weather, winds *etc*) sharp; intense: *a piercing wind*; *piercing cold.* □ **pénétrant**

3 looking intently or sharply as though able to see through things: *piercing eyes*; *a piercing glance.* □ **perçant**

'**piercingly** *adverb.* □ **d'une voix perçante**
'**piercingness** *noun.* □ **caractère pénétrant**

piety *see* **pious.**

pig [pig] *noun* **1** a kind of farm animal whose flesh is eaten as pork, ham and bacon: *He keeps pigs.* □ **porc**

2 an offensive word for an unpleasant, greedy or dirty person: *You pig!* □ **cochon, onne**

'**piggy** – *plural* '**piggies** – *noun* a child's word for a (little) pig. □ **cochonnet**

■ *adjective* like a pig's: *piggy eyes.* □ **de cochon, porcin**
'**piglet** [-lit] *noun* a baby pig. □ **porcelet**

'**piggyback** *adverb* (of a child) carried on the back: *He carried the boy piggyback.* □ **sur le dos**

■ *noun* a ride on someone's back: *Give me a piggyback, Daddy.* □ **un tour sur le dos de qqn**

,**pig'headed** *adjective* stubborn: *a pigheaded idiot.* □ **entêté**

,**pig'headedness** *noun.* □ **entêtement**

'pigskin *noun, adjective* (of) a kind of leather made from the skin of a pig: *Her purse was (made of) pigskin.* □ **peau de porc**

'pigsty – *plural* **'pigsties, 'pigstyes** – *noun* **1** a building in which pigs are kept. □ **porcherie**
2 a dirty, untidy place: *This room is a pigsty!* □ **soue**
pigswill *see* **swill**.

'pigtail *noun* a plait *usually* worn at the back of the head: *She wears her hair in pigtails.* □ **natte**

pigs might fly said of something very unlikely to happen: *'We might have fine weather for our holidays.' 'Yes, and pigs might fly!'* □ **quand les poules auront des dents**

pigeon ['pidʒən] *noun* any of several kinds of bird of the dove family. □ **pigeon**
'pigeonhole *noun* a small compartment for letters, papers *etc* in a desk *etc* or eg hung on the wall of an office, staffroom *etc*: *He has separate pigeonholes for bills, for receipts, for letters from friends and so on.* □ **casier**
,pigeon-'toed *adjective* (of a person or his manner of walking) with toes turned inwards: *a pigeon-toed person/walk.* □ **les pieds tournés en dedans**

piglet *see* **pig**.

pigment ['pigmənt] *noun* **1** any substance used for colouring, making paint *etc*: *People used to make paint and dyes from natural pigments.* □ **pigment**
2 a substance in plants or animals that gives colour to the skin, leaves *etc*: *Some people have darker pigment in their skin than others.* □ **pigment**
,pigmen'tation *noun* colouring (of skin *etc*): *Some illnesses cause a loss of pigmentation.* □ **pigmentation**

pigmy *see* **pygmy**.

pike [paik] – *plural* **pike** – *noun* a large fierce freshwater fish. □ **brochet**

pilaff ['pi'laf] *noun* a dish of rice, meat *etc* seasoned with spices. □ **pilaf**

pile¹ [pail] *noun* **1** a (large) number of things lying on top of each other in a tidy or untidy heap; a (large) quantity of something lying in a heap: *There was a neat pile of books in the corner of the room; There was pile of rubbish at the bottom of the garden.* □ **pile**
2 a large quantity, *especially* of money: *He must have piles of money to own a car like that.* □ **paquet**
■ *verb* to make a pile of (something); to put (something) in a pile: *She piled the boxes on the table.* □ **empiler**
'pileup *noun* an accident or crash involving *usually* several vehicles: *There has been a serious pileup on the highway, involving three cars and a truck.* □ **carambolage**
pile up to make or become a pile; to accumulate: *He piled up the earth at the end of the garden; The rubbish piled up in the kitchen.* □ **(s')entasser**

pile² [pail] *noun* a large pillar or stake driven into the ground as a foundation for a building, bridge *etc*: *The entire city of Venice is built on piles.* □ **pilot(is), pieu**
'piledriver *noun* a machine for driving piles into the ground. □ **sonnette**

pile³ [pail] *noun* the thick soft surface of carpets and some

kinds of cloth *eg* velvet: *The rug has a deep/thick pile.* □ **poil (d'un tapis), (tissus à) poil**

pilfer ['pilfə] *verb* to steal (small things): *He pilfered enough pieces of wood from the factory to make a chair.* □ **chaparder**
'pilferage *noun.* □ **chapardage**
'pilferer *noun.* □ **chapardeur, euse**

pilgrim ['pilgrim] *noun* a person who travels to a holy place: *Every year thousands of pilgrims visit Jerusalem.* □ **pèlerin, ine**
'pilgrimage [-midʒ] *noun* a journey to a holy place: *She went on a pilgrimage to Lourdes.* □ **pèlerinage**

pill [pil] *noun* a small ball or tablet of medicine, to be swallowed: *She took a pill; sleeping-pills.* □ **pilule**

pillar ['pilə] *noun* an upright post used in building as a support or decoration: *The hall was surrounded by stone pillars.* □ **pilier**

pillion ['piljən] *noun* a passenger seat on a motorcycle: *He drove the motorbike and she sat on the pillion;* (*also adjective*) *a pillion passenger/seat.* □ **siège arrière; de derrière**

pillow ['pilou] *noun* a kind of cushion for the head, *especially* on a bed. □ **oreiller**
■ *verb* to rest (one's head): *He pillowed his head on her breast.* □ **reposer**
'pillowcase *nouns* a cover for a pillow: *They bought linen sheets and pillowcases.* □ **taie d'oreiller**

pilot ['pailət] *noun* **1** a person who flies an airplane: *The pilot and crew were all killed in the air crash.* □ **pilote**
2 a person who directs a ship in and out of a harbour, river, or coastal waters. □ **pilote**
■ *adjective* experimental: *a pilot scheme* (= one done on a small scale, *eg* to solve certain problems before a larger, more expensive project is started). □ **pilote**
■ *verb* to guide as a pilot: *He piloted the ship/plane.* □ **piloter**
'pilot light *noun* a small gas light *eg* on a gas stove, which burns continuously and is used to light the main gas jets when they are turned on. □ **veilleuse**

pimple ['pimpl] *noun* a small round swelling on the skin: *I had a pimple on my nose.* □ **bouton**
'pimpled/'pimply *adjective* having pimples: *a pimpled/pimply face.* □ **boutonneux**

pin [pin] *noun* **1** a short, thin, pointed piece of metal used *eg* to hold pieces of fabric, paper *etc* together, *especially* when making clothes: *The papers are fastened together by a pin.* □ **épingle**
2 a similar but more ornamental object: *a hat-pin.* □ **épingle**
3 a bottle-shaped marker or target usually made of wood and used in a bowling game: *Gail won the game when her bowling ball hit every pin.* □ **quille**
■ *verb* – *past tense, past participle* **pinned** – **1** to fasten with a pin: *She pinned the material together.* □ **épingler**
2 to hold by pressing against something: *The fallen tree pinned him to the ground.* □ **immobiliser**
'pincushion *noun* a small cushion or similar object into which pins are pushed for keeping. □ **pelote à épingles**
'pinhole *noun* a hole made by a pin: *A pinhole camera does not need a lens.* □ **trou d'épingle**

'pinpoint verb to place or show very exactly: *She pinpointed the position on the map.* □ **mettre le doigt sur (qqch.)**

'pin-up noun **1** a picture of an attractive girl (or man), often pinned on a wall: *He has dozens of pin-ups in his room*; *(also adjective) a pin-up boy.* □ **pin up**

2 the girl (or man): *She's the favourite pin-up of the soldiers.* □ **pin up**

pin down to make (someone) give a definite answer, statement, opinion or promise: *I can't pin him down to a definite date for his arrival.* □ **obliger à**

pins and needles a tingling feeling in one's hands, arms, feet or legs: *I've got pins and needles in my arm.* □ **fourmi(llement)s**

pinafore ['pinəfɔ:] noun a kind of apron covering the clothes above and below the waist: *The children wore pinafores at nursery school.* □ **tablier (d'écolier)**

pincers ['pinsəz] noun plural **1** a tool for gripping things tightly: *She used (a pair of) pincers.* □ **tenailles**

2 the claws of lobsters, crabs *etc.* □ **pinces**

pinch [pintʃ] verb **1** to squeeze or press tightly (flesh), *especially* between the thumb and forefinger: *He pinched her arm.* □ **pincer**

2 to hurt by being too small or tight: *My new shoes are pinching (me).* □ **serrer**

3 to steal: *Who pinched my bicycle?* □ **piquer**

■ noun **1** an act of pinching; a squeeze or nip: *He gave her a pinch on the cheek.* □ **pincement**

2 a very small amount; what can be held between the thumb and forefinger: *a pinch of salt.* □ **pincée**

pinched adjective (of a person's face) looking cold, pale or thin because of cold, poverty *etc*: *Her face was pinched with cold.* □ **aux traits tirés**

feel the pinch to be in difficulty because of lack of money. □ **être serré**

pine[1] [pain] noun **1** any of several kinds of evergreen trees with cones (**'pine-cones**) and needlelike leaves (**'pine-needles**). □ **pin**

2 its wood: *The table is made of pine*; *(also adjective) a pine table.* □ **(de) pin**

pine[2] [pain] verb **1** (often with **away**) to lose strength, become weak (with pain, grief *etc*): *Since his death she has been pining (away).* □ **dépérir**

2 (usually with **for**) to want (something) very much; to long (for someone or something, or to do something): *He knew that his wife was pining for home.* □ **languir pour**

pineapple ['painapl] noun a type of large tropical fruit shaped like a large pine-cone, or the plant which produces it. □ **ananas**

ping [piŋ] noun a sharp, ringing sound such as that of a glass being lightly struck, or a stretched wire, thread *etc* being pulled and released: *His knife struck the wineglass with a loud ping.* □ **tintement**

■ verb to make such a sound: *The glass pinged.* □ **tinter**

ping-pong ['piŋpoŋ] noun **1** the game of table tennis: *Do you play ping-pong?* □ **ping-pong**

2 (®) in the United States, the equipment used in table tennis. □ **ping-pong**

pink [piŋk] noun, adjective **1** (of) (any shade of) a colour

between red and white: *a dress of pink satin.* □ **rose**

2 (of) the colour of healthy skin: *pink cheeks*; *Her cheeks are pink with health.* □ **rose**

'pinkness noun. □ **(couleur) rose**

'pinkish adjective fairly pink; close to pink: *The flowers of this plant are pinkish in colour.* □ **rosâtre**

pinnacle ['pinəkl] noun **1** a tall thin spire built on the roof of a church, castle *etc.* □ **pinacle**

2 a high pointed rock or mountain: *It was a dangerous pinnacle to climb.* □ **pic**

3 a high point of achievement, success *etc*): *She has reached the pinnacle of her career.* □ **apogée**

pint [paint] noun a unit for measuring liquids, one-eighth of a gallon (in Britain, 0.57 litre; in the United States, 0.47 litre): *a pint of milk/beer.* □ **pinte**

pioneer [paiə'niə] noun **1** a person who goes to a new, often uninhabited or uncivilized (part of a) country to live and work there: *The American pioneers*; *(also adjective) a pioneer family.* □ **pionnier, ière**

2 a person who is the first to study some new subject, or use or develop a new technique *etc*: *Lister was one of the pioneers of modern medicine.* □ **pionnier, ière, précurseur**

■ verb to be the first to do or make: *Who pioneered the use of vaccine for preventing polio?* □ **lancer, ouvrir la voie (de)**

pious ['paiəs] adjective having or showing strong religious feelings, reverence for or devotion to God *etc*: *a pious woman/attitude.* □ **pieux**

'piously adverb. □ **pieusement**

piety ['paiəti] noun. □ **piété**

pip [pip] noun a seed of a fruit: *an orange/apple pip.* □ **pépin**

pipe [paip] noun **1** a tube, *usually* made of metal, earthenware *etc*, through which water, gas *etc* can flow: *a water pipe*; *a drainpipe.* □ **tuyau**

2 a small tube with a bowl at one end, in which tobacco is smoked: *He smokes a pipe*; *(also adjective) pipe tobacco.* □ **(à) pipe**

3 a musical instrument consisting of a hollow wooden, metal *etc* tube through which the player blows or causes air to be blown in order to make a sound: *He played a tune on a bamboo pipe*; *an organ pipe.* □ **pipeau**

■ verb **1** to convey gas, water *etc* by a pipe: *Water is piped to the town from the reservoir.* □ **amener (par un tuyau)**

2 to play (music) on a pipe or pipes: *He piped a tune.* □ **jouer (sur un pipeau, une cornemuse)**

3 to speak in a high voice, make a high-pitched sound: *'Hello,' the little girl piped.* □ **dire d'une voix flûtée**

'piper noun a person who plays a pipe or pipes, *especially* the bagpipes. □ **joueur, euse de cornemuse**

pipes noun plural **1** bagpipes or some similar instrument: *He plays the pipes.* □ **cornemuse**

2 a set of musical pipes joined together to form a single instrument: *the pipes of Pan.* □ **flûte (de Pan)**

'piping noun **1** the act of playing a musical pipe or pipes. □ **action de jouer du pipeau/de la cornemuse**

2 the act or process of conveying water, gas *etc* by means of) a length of pipe or number of pipes: *lead* *piping*; *Piping the oil ashore will not be easy.* □ **canalisation**

■ *adjective* (of a sound) high-pitched: *a piping voice.* □ **flûté**

pipe dream an idea which can only be imagined, and which would be impossible to carry out: *For most people a journey around the world is only a pipe dream.* □ **château en Espagne**

'**pipeline** *noun* a long line of pipes used for conveying oil, gas, water *etc*: *an oil pipeline across the desert.* □ **oléoduc, pipeline**

piping hot very hot: *piping hot soup.* □ **brûlant**

piquant ['piːkənt] *adjective* sharp in taste; appetizing: *a piquant sauce*; *a piquant* (= exciting or interesting) *situation.* □ **piquant**

'**piquantly** *adverb.* □ **de façon piquante**

'**piquancy** *noun.* □ **goût piquant**

pique [piːk] *noun* anger caused by one's pride being hurt: *She walked out of the room in a fit of pique.* □ **dépit**

pirate ['paiərət] *noun* 1 a person who attacks and robs ships at sea: *Their ship was attacked by pirates*; (*also adjective*) *a pirate ship.* □ **pirate**

2 a person who does something without legal right, *eg* publishes someone else's work as his own or broadcasts without a licence: *a pirate radio-station.* □ **pirate**

■ *verb* to publish, broadcast *etc* without the legal right to do so: *The dictionary was pirated and sold abroad.* □ **pirater**

'**piracy** *noun* the act(s) of a pirate: *He was accused of piracy on the high seas*; *Publishing that book under his own name was piracy.* □ **piraterie**

pirouette [piru'et] *noun* a dancer's quick turning movement: *The ballerina did/danced a pirouette.* □ **pirouette**

■ *verb* to do one or a series of these movements: *She pirouetted across the stage.* □ **pirouetter**

pistachio [pi'staːʃiou] – *plural* **pis'tachios** – *noun* a greenish nut used as flavouring for food. □ **pistache**

pistol ['pistl] *noun* a small gun, held in one hand when fired: *He shot himself with a pistol.* □ **pistolet**

piston ['pistən] *noun* (in engines, pumps *etc*) a round piece *usually* of metal that fits inside a cylinder and moves up and down or backwards and forwards inside it. □ **piston**

pit[1] [pit] *noun* 1 a large hole in the ground: *The campers dug a pit for their rubbish.* □ **fosse**

2 a place from which minerals are dug, *especially* a coal-mine: *a chalk-pit*; *He works at/down the pit.* □ **puits, carrière**

3 a place beside a motor race track for repairing and refuelling racing cars: *The leading car has gone into the pit(s).* □ **stand de ravitaillement**

4 a section at the front of the theatre, usually near the stage: *Our seats were directly behind the orchestra pit.* □ **parterre**

■ *verb – past tense, past participle* '**pitted** – (*with against*) to set (a person or thing) against another in a fight, competition *etc*: *He was pitted against a much stronger man.* □ **opposer (à)**

'**pitfall** *noun* a possible danger: *She has managed to avoid most of the pitfalls of life.* □ **piège**

pit[2] [pit] *noun* the hard stone of a peach, cherry *etc*. □ **noyau**

■ *verb – past tense, past participle* '**pitted** – to remove the stone from (a peach, cherry *etc*). □ **dénoyauter**

pitch[1] [pitʃ] *verb* 1 to set up (a tent or camp): *They pitched their tent in the field.* □ **dresser**

2 to throw: *She pitched the stone into the river.* □ **lancer**

3 to (cause to) fall heavily: *He pitched forward.* □ **tomber**

4 (of a ship) to rise and fall violently: *The boat pitched up and down on the rough sea.* □ **tanguer**

5 to set (a note or tune) at a particular level: *She pitched the tune too high for my voice.* □ **donner le ton**

■ *noun* 1 the field or ground for certain games: *a cricket-pitch*; *a football pitch.* □ **terrain**

2 the degree of highness or lowness of a musical note, voice *etc*. □ **hauteur**

3 an extreme point or intensity: *His anger reached such a pitch that he hit him.* □ **degré**

4 the act of pitching or throwing or the distance something is pitched: *That was a long pitch.* □ **lancer**

5 (of a ship) the act of pitching. □ **tangage**

-**pitched** of a (certain) musical pitch: *a high-pitched/low-pitched voice.* □ **de registre (aigu, grave...)**

'**pitcher** *noun* a person who pitches *especially* (in baseball) the player who throws the ball. □ **lanceur, euse**

pitched battle a battle between armies that have been prepared and arranged for fighting beforehand: *They fought a pitched battle.* □ **bataille rangée**

'**pitchfork** *noun* a large long-handled fork for lifting and moving hay. □ **fourche**

pitch[2] [pitʃ] *noun* a thick black substance obtained from tar: *as black as pitch.* □ **bitume**

,**pitch-'black**, ,**pitch-'dark** *adjective* as black, or dark, as pitch; completely black or dark: *Outside the house it was pitch-black*; *It's a pitch-dark night.* □ **noir comme du jais**

pitcher[1] *see* **pitch**[1].

pitcher[2] ['pitʃə] *noun* a large jug: *a pitcher of water.* □ **cruche**

piteous *see* **pity**.

pith [piθ] *noun* 1 the white substance between the peel of an orange, lemon *etc* and the fruit itself. □ **peau blanche**

2 the soft substance in the centre of the stems of plants. □ **moelle**

3 the most important part of anything: *the pith of the argument.* □ **essence**

pitiable, pitiful, pitiless *see* **pity**.

pitter-patter [pitə'patə] *noun* a light, tapping sound: *the pitter-patter of rain on a window.* □ **crépitement**

■ *verb* to make such a sound. □ **crépiter**

■ *adverb* while making this sound: *The mouse ran pitter-patter across the floor.* □ **trottinement**

pity ['piti] *noun* 1 a feeling of sorrow for the troubles and sufferings of others: *She felt a great pity for him.* □ **pitié**

2 a cause of sorrow or regret: *What a pity (that) she can't come.* □ **dommage**

■ *verb* to feel pity for (someone): *She pitied him*; *She is to be pitied.* □ **avoir pitié de**

piteous ['pitiəs] *adjective* pitiful: *a piteous cry/sight.* □
pitoyable
'**piteously** *adverb*. □ **pitoyablement**
'**piteousness** *noun*. □ **état piteux**
'**pitiable** *adjective* pitiful: *He was in a pitiable condition*; *He made a pitiable attempt*. □ **pitoyable**
'**pitiably** *adverb*. □ **pitoyablement**
'**pitiful** *adjective* 1 very sad; causing pity: *a pitiful sight.*
□ **lamentable**
2 very poor, bad *etc*; causing contempt: *a pitiful attempt*;
a pitiful amount of money. □ **pitoyable**
'**pitifully** *adverb*. □ **pitoyablement**
'**pitifulness** *noun*. □ **état pitoyable**
'**pitiless** *adjective* without pity: *pitiless cruelty.* □
impitoyable
'**pitilessly** *adverb*. □ **impitoyablement**
'**pitilessness** *noun*. □ **absence de pitié**
'**pityingly** *adverb* in a way which shows that one feels
pity for someone: *She looked at him pityingly.* □ **avec
pitié**
have pity on to feel pity for (someone because of something): *Have pity on the old man.* □ **avoir pitié de**
take pity on to act kindly, or relent, towards (someone), from a feeling of pity: *She took pity on the hungry
children and gave them food.* □ **prendre pitié de**
pivot ['pivət] *noun* the pin or centre on which anything
balances and turns. □ **pivot**
■ *verb – past tense, past participle* '**pivoted** – (*with* **on**)
to turn (on): *The door pivoted on a central hinge.* □
pivoter
pixy (*plural* '**pixies**), **pixie** ['piksi] *noun* a kind of fairy. □
lutin, fée
pizza ['pi:tsə] *noun* a flat piece of dough spread with
tomato, cheese *etc* and baked. □ **pizza**
pizzicato [pitsi'ka:tou] *adjective, adverb* played by
plucking the strings of a musical instrument, not using
the bow. □ **pizzicato**
placard ['plaka:d] *noun* a notice printed on *eg* wood or
cardboard and carried, hung *etc*, in a public place: *The
protesters were carrying placards denouncing the government's policy.* □ **pancarte**
placate [plə'keit] *verb* to stop (an angry person) feeling
angry: *He placated her with an apology.* □ **apaiser**
place [pleis] *noun* 1 a particular spot or area: *a quiet place
in the country*; *I spent my holiday in various different
places.* □ **endroit**
2 an empty space: *There's a place for your books on
this shelf.* □ **place**
3 an area or building with a particular purpose: *a marketplace.* □ **place**
4 a seat (in a theatre, train, at a table *etc*): *She went to
her place and sat down.* □ **place**
5 a position in an order, series, queue *etc*: *She got the
first place in the competition*; *I lost my place in the
queue.* □ **place**
6 a person's position or level of importance in society
etc: *She has taken her place among the famous writers
of the world.* □ **place**
7 a point in the text of a book *etc*: *The wind was blowing the pages of my book and I kept losing my place.* □

page
8 duty or right: *It's not my place to tell him he's wrong.*
□ **rôle**
9 a job or position in a team, organization *etc*: *She's got
a place in the team*; *She's hoping for a place on the
staff.* □ **poste**
10 house; home: *Come over to my place.* □ **chez soi**
11 (*often abbreviated to* **Pl.** *when written*) a word used
in the names of certain roads, streets or squares. □ **place**
12 a number or one of a series of numbers following a
decimal point: *Make the answer correct to four decimal places.* □ **place décimale**
■ *verb* 1 to put: *She placed it on the table*; *He was placed
in command of the army.* □ **placer**
2 to remember who a person is: *I know I've seen her
before, but I can't quite place her.* □ **remettre**
'**place name** *noun* the name of a town, hill, valley *etc*.
□ **nom de lieu**
go places to be successful, *especially* in one's career:
That young woman is sure to go places. □ **aller loin**
in the first, second *etc* **place** expressions used to show
steps in an argument, explanation *etc*: *He decided not
to buy the house, because in the first place it was too
expensive, and in the second place it was too far from
his office.* □ **d'abord....ensuite...**
in place in the proper position; tidy: *He left everything
in place.* □ **en place, à sa place**
in place of instead of: *We advise discussion in place of
argument*; *Judy couldn't go, so I went in her place.* □
au lieu de, à (sa) place
out of place 1 not suitable (to the occasion *etc*): *His
clothes are quite out of place at a formal dinner.* □
déplacé
2 not in the proper position; untidy: *Although he had
had to run most of the way, he arrived with not a hair
out of place.* □ **déplacé**
put oneself in someone else's place to imagine what it
would be like to be someone else: *If you put yourself in
his place, you can understand why he is so careful.* □ **se
mettre à la place de**
put (someone) in his place to remind (someone), often
in a rude or angry way, of his lower social position, or
lack of importance, experience *etc*. □ **remettre (qqn) à
sa place**
take place to happen: *What took place after that?* □ **se
passer**
take the place of to be used instead of, or to be a substitute for: *I don't think television will ever take the place
of books.* □ **remplacer**
placid ['plasid] *adjective* calm and not easily disturbed
or upset: *a placid child.* □ **placide**
'**placidly** *adverb*. □ **placidement**
'**placidness** *noun*. □ **placidité**
plague [pleig] *noun* 1 *especially* formerly, an extremely
infectious and deadly disease, *especially* one carried by
fleas from rats. □ **peste**
2 a large and annoying quantity: *a plague of flies.* □
invasion
■ *verb* to annoy or pester continually or frequently: *The
child was plaguing her with questions.* □ **harceler**

plaice [pleis] – *plural* **plaice** – *noun* a type of flat fish. □ **plie**

plain [plein] *adjective* **1** simple or ordinary; without ornament or decoration: *plain living; good, plain food.* □ **simple**

2 easy to understand; clear: *Her words were quite plain.* □ **clair**

3 absolutely open or honest, with no attempt to be tactful: *I'll be quite plain with you; plain speaking.* □ **franc**

4 obvious: *It's plain (to see) you haven't been practising your music.* □ **évident, clair**

5 not pretty: *a rather plain girl.* □ **quelconque**

■ *noun* **1** a large flat level piece of land: *the plains of central Canada.* □ **plaine**

2 a kind of knitting stitch. □ **maille à l'endroit**

'plainly *adverb*. □ **simplement; clairement**

'plainness *noun*. □ **simplicité; clarté**

plain chocolate dark chocolate not containing milk. □ **chocolat à croquer**

plain clothes ordinary clothes, not a uniform: *Detectives usually wear plain clothes; (also adjective) a plain-clothes job.* □ **vêtements civils; en civil**

plain sailing progress without difficulty. □ **(chose) qui va comme sur des roulettes**

,plain-'spoken *adjective* speaking plainly, not trying to be tactful. □ **direct**

plaintiff ['pleintif] *noun* a person who starts a legal case against another. □ **plaignant, ante**

plaintive ['pleintiv] *adjective* sounding sad or sorrowful: *a plaintive cry.* □ **plaintif**

'plaintively *adverb*. □ **plaintivement**

'plaintiveness *noun*. □ **ton plaintif**

plait [plat] *noun* **1** a length of hair arranged by dividing it into sections and passing these over one another in turn: *She wore her hair in a long plait.* □ **tresse**

2 a similar arrangement of any material: *a plait of straw.* □ **tresse**

■ *verb* to arrange in this way: *She plaited three strips of leather to make a belt; She plaited her hair.* □ **tresser**

plan [plan] *noun* **1** an idea of how to do something; a method of doing something: *If everyone follows this plan, we will succeed; I have worked out a plan for making a lot of money.* □ **plan, projet**

2 an intention or arrangement: *My plan is to rob a bank and leave the country quickly; What are your plans for tomorrow?* □ **plan, projet**

3 a drawing, diagram *etc* showing a building, town *etc* as if seen from above: *These are the plans of/for our new house; a street-plan.* □ **plan**

■ *verb – past tense, past participle* **planned** – **1** (*sometimes with* **on**) to intend (to do something): *We are planning on going to Italy this year; We were planning to go last year but we hadn't enough money; They are planning a trip to Italy.* □ **projeter (de)**

2 to decide how something is to be done; to arrange (something): *We are planning a party; We'll have to plan very carefully if we are to succeed.* □ **organiser, planifier**

3 to design (a building, town *etc*): *This is the architect who planned the building.* □ **dresser les plans de**

'planner *noun* a person who plans (*especially* buildings *etc*): *a town-planner.* □ **planificateur, trice**

'planning *noun* the act of planning: *town-planning.* □ **planification**

go according to plan to happen as arranged or intended: *The journey went according to plan.* □ **se dérouler comme prévu**

plan ahead to plan something a long time before it will happen *etc*. □ **arranger d'avance**

plane[1] [plein] *noun* **1** an airplane. □ **avion**

2 a level or standard: *Man is on a higher plane (of development) than the apes.* □ **plan, niveau**

3 in geometry, a flat surface. □ **plan**

■ *verb* to move smoothly over the surface (of water *etc*). □ **planer**

plane[2] [plein] *noun* a carpenter's tool for making a level or smooth surface. □ **rabot**

■ *verb* to make (a surface) level, smooth or lower by using a plane. □ **raboter**

plane[3] [plein] *noun* a type of tree with broad leaves. □ **platane**

planet ['planit] *noun* any of the bodies (*eg* the Earth) which move around the Sun or around another star: *Mars and Jupiter are planets, but the Moon is not.* □ **planète**

'planetary *adjective*. □ **planétaire**

plank [plaŋk] *noun* a long, flat piece of wood: *The floor was made of planks.* □ **planche**

plankton ['plaŋktən] *noun* very tiny living creatures floating in seas, lakes *etc*. □ **plancton**

planner *see* **plan**.

plant [plɑːnt] *noun* **1** anything growing from the ground, having a stem, a root and leaves: *flowering/tropical plants.* □ **plante**

2 industrial machinery: *engineering plant.* □ **installation, équipement**

3 a factory. □ **usine**

■ *verb* **1** to put (something) into the ground so that it will grow: *We have planted vegetables in the garden.* □ **planter**

2 to make (a garden *etc*); to cause (a garden *etc*) to have (plants *etc*) growing in it: *The garden was planted with shrubs; We're going to plant an orchard.* □ **planter (de/en)**

3 to place heavily or firmly: *He planted himself between her and the door.* □ **(se) planter**

4 to put in someone's possession, *especially* as false evidence: *He claimed that the police had planted the weapon on his brother.* □ **cacher (pour faire incriminer)**

plan'tation [plan-] *noun* **1** a place that has been planted with trees. □ **plantation**

2 a piece of land or estate for growing certain crops, *especially* cotton, sugar, rubber, tea and tobacco: *He owned a rubber plantation in Malaysia.* □ **plantation**

'planter *noun* the owner of a plantation for growing tea, rubber *etc*: *a tea-planter.* □ **planteur, euse**

plantation, planter *see* **plant**.

plaque [plɑːk] *noun* **1** a plate of metal *etc* fixed to a wall *etc* as a memorial: *Her name was inscribed on a brass plaque.* □ **plaque**

2 a china *etc* ornament for fixing on the wall. □ **plaque**

3 a deposit of saliva and bacteria which forms on the teeth. □ **plaque**

plasma ['plazmə] *noun* the liquid part of blood and certain other fluids produced by the body. □ **plasma**

plaster ['plɑːstə] *noun* **1** (*also adjective*) (of) a substance put on walls, ceilings *etc* which dries to form a hard smooth surface: *He mixed up some plaster to repair the wall*; *a plaster ceiling*. □ **(de) plâtre**

2 (*also adjective*) (*also* **plaster of Paris**) (of) a similar quick-drying substance used for supporting broken limbs, making models *etc*: *She's got her arm in plaster*; *a plaster model*. □ **(en/de) plâtre**

3 (*also* '**sticking-plaster**) (a piece of) sticky tape (sometimes with a dressing) used to cover a wound *etc*: *You should put a plaster on that cut*. □ **pansement adhésif**

■ *verb* **1** to put plaster on: *They plastered the walls*. □ **plâtrer**

2 to spread or apply rather too thickly: *She'd look nicer if she didn't plaster so much make-up on her face*. □ **(se) mettre une épaisse couche de**

'**plasterer** *noun* a person whose job is to put plaster on walls, ceilings *etc*. □ **plâtrier, ière**

plastic ['plastik] *noun, adjective* (of) any of many chemically manufactured substances that can be moulded when still soft: *This cup is made of plastic*; *a plastic cup*. □ **plastique**

■ *adjective* easily made into different shapes. □ **plastique, malléable**

plastic surgery surgery to repair or replace damaged skin, or to improve the appearance *usually* of the face (*noun* **plastic surgeon**). □ **chirurgie esthétique; chirurgien, ienne esthétique**

Plasticine® ['plastisiːn] *noun* a coloured substance like clay used for modelling *especialy* by children. □ **pâte à modeler**

plate [pleit] *noun* **1** a shallow dish for holding food *etc*: *china plates*. □ **assiette**

2 a sheet of metal *etc*: *The ship was built of steel plates*. □ **plaque**

3 articles made of, or plated with, *usually* gold or silver: *a collection of gold plate*. □ **argenterie**

4 a flat piece of metal inscribed with *eg* a name, for fixing to a door, or with a design *etc*, for use in printing. □ **plaque**

5 an illustration in a book, *usually* on glossy paper: *The book has ten full-colour plates*. □ **planche**

6 (*also* **dental plate**) a piece of plastic that fits in the mouth with false teeth attached to it. □ **dentier**

7 a sheet of glass *etc* coated with a sensitive film, used in photography. □ **plaque**

'**plated** *adjective* covered with a thin layer of a different metal: *gold-plated dishes*. □ **plaqué**

'**plateful** *noun* the complete contents of a plate: *a plateful of potatoes*; *two platefuls of chips*. □ **assiett(é)e**

'**plating** *noun* a thin covering of metal: *silver-plating*. □ **placage**

plate glass a kind of glass made in thick sheets for windows, mirrors *etc*. □ **verre à vitre (très épais)**

plateau ['platou] – *plurals* '**plateaus**, '**plateaux** [-z] –

noun an area of high flat land; a mountain with a wide, flat top. □ **plateau**

platform ['platfɔːm] *noun* **1** a raised part of a floor *eg* in a hall, for speakers, entertainers *etc*: *The orchestra arranged themselves on the platform*. □ **estrade, tribune**

2 the raised area between or beside the lines in a railway station: *They waited on the platform for their train to arrive*; *The Montreal train will leave from platform 6*. □ **quai, plate-forme**

plating *see* plate.

platinum ['platinəm] *noun, adjective* (of) an element, a heavy, valuable grey metal, often used in making jewellery: *a platinum ring*. □ **(de) platine**

platoon [plə'tuːn] *noun* a section of a company of soldiers. □ **section**

platter ['platə] *noun* a kind of large, flat plate: *a wooden platter*. □ **plat**

plausible ['plɔːzəbl] *adjective* **1** seeming reasonable or convincing: *a plausible excuse*. □ **plausible, vraisemblable**

2 clever at talking persuasively but not to be trusted: *a plausible fellow*. □ **convaincant**

play [plei] *verb* **1** to amuse oneself: *The child is playing in the garden*; *He is playing with his toys*; *The little girl wants to play with her friends*. □ **jouer, s'amuser**

2 to take part in (games *etc*): *He plays football*; *He is playing in goal*; *Here's a pack of cards – who wants to play (with me)?*; *I'm playing golf with him this evening*. □ **jouer (à)**

3 to act in a play *etc*; to act (a character): *She's playing Lady Macbeth*; *The company is playing in Montreal this week*. □ **jouer**

4 (of a play *etc*) to be performed: *'Oklahoma' is playing at the local theatre*. □ **jouer**

5 to (be able to) perform on (a musical instrument): *She plays the piano*; *Who was playing the piano this morning?*; *He plays (the oboe) in an orchestra*. □ **jouer (de)**

6 (*usually with* **on**) to carry out or do (a trick): *She played a trick on me*. □ **jouer (un tour à)**

7 (of light) to pass with a flickering movement: *The firelight played across the ceiling*. □ **chatoyer**

8 to put down or produce (a playing card) as part of a card game: *She played the seven of hearts*. □ **jouer**

■ *noun* **1** recreation; amusement: *A person must have time for both work and play*. □ **jeu, amusement**

2 an acted story; a drama: *Shakespeare wrote many great plays*. □ **pièce (de théâtre)**

3 the playing of a game: *At the start of today's play, England was leading India by fifteen runs*. □ **match**

4 freedom of movement (*eg* in part of a machine). □ **jeu**

'**player** *noun*. □ **joueur, euse**

'**playable** *adjective* (*negative* **unplayable**) (of a ground, pitch *etc*) not good enough for a game to be played on it: *Because of the rain the referee decided the ground was not playable*. □ **en bonne condition**

'**playful** *adjective* **1** happy; full of the desire to play: *a playful kitten*. □ **enjoué**

2 joking; not serious: *a playful remark*. □ **espiègle**

'**playfully** *adverb*. □ **en badinant**

'**playfulness** *noun*. □ **badinage**

'**playboy** *noun* a rich man who spends his time and money on pleasure. □ **séducteur**

'**playground** *noun* an area in which children can play in a park, outside a school *etc*. □ **cour de récréation**

'**playing card** *noun* one of a pack of cards used in card games. □ **carte à jouer**

'**playing field** *noun* a field which is specially prepared and used for sport. □ **terrain de jeu/sport**

'**playmate** *noun* a childhood friend. □ **(petit(e)) camarade**

'**playschool** *noun* an informal nursery school. □ **garderie**

'**plaything** *noun* a toy. □ **jouet**

'**playtime** *noun* a set time for children to play (at school *etc*): *The children go outside at playtime.* □ **récréation**

'**playwright** *noun* a person who writes plays: *She is a famous playwright.* □ **dramaturge**

at play playing: *children at play.* □ **en train de jouer**

bring/come into play to (cause to) be used or exercised: *The job allowed her to bring all her talents into play.* □ **mettre/entrer en jeu**

child's play something that is very easy: *Of course you can do it – it's child's play!* □ **jeu d'enfant**

in play, out of play (of a ball) according to the rules of the game, (not) in a position where it can be hit, kicked *etc*. □ **en jeu; hors jeu**

play at 1 to pretend to be *etc*: *The children were playing at cowboys and Indians.* □ **jouer à**

2 used when asking angrily what someone is doing: *What does he think he's playing at* (= doing)? □ **jouer à**

play back to play (music, speech *etc*) on a record or tape after it has just been recorded (*noun* '**play-back**). □ **(ré)écouter; réécoute**

play down to try to make (something) appear less important: *He played down the fact that he had failed the exam.* □ **minimiser**

play fair to act honestly and fairly. □ **jouer franc jeu**

play for time to delay an action, decision *etc* in the hope that conditions will improve. □ **essayer de gagner du temps**

play havoc with to cause a lot of damage to: *The storm played havoc with the farmer's crops.* □ **ravager**

play into someone's hands to do exactly what an opponent or enemy wants one to do. □ **faire le jeu de**

play off (in games) to play a final deciding game after a draw (*noun* '**play-off**). □ **jouer la finale**

play off against to set (one person) against (another) in order to gain an advantage: *He played his father off against his mother to get more pocket money.* □ **opposer (qqn à qqn)**

play on to make use of (someone's feelings, fears *etc*): *He played on my sympathy until I lent him $10.* □ **jouer sur**

play a, no part in (not) to be one of the people who are doing (something): *He played no part in the robbery.* □ **(ne pas) prendre part à**

play safe to take no risks. □ **ne pas prendre de risques**

play the game to act fairly and honestly. □ **jouer le jeu**

play up to be troublesome or disobedient: *The children are playing up today.* □ **faire des siennes**

plea [pliː] *noun* 1 a prisoner's answer to a charge: *He made a plea of (not) guilty.* □ **défense**

2 an urgent request: *The hospital sent out a plea for blood-donors.* □ **appel urgent (à)**

plead [pliːd] – *past tense, past participles* '**pleaded** – *verb* 1 (of a prisoner) to answer a charge, saying whether one is guilty or not: *'How does the prisoner plead?' 'He pleads guilty.'* □ **plaider**

2 to present a case in court: *My lawyer will plead my case; My lawyer will plead for me.* □ **plaider**

3 (*often with* **with**) to make an urgent request: *He pleaded with me not to go; He pleaded to be allowed to go.* □ **supplier (de)**

pleasant ['pleznt] *adjective* giving pleasure; agreeable: *a pleasant day/person.* □ **agréable**

'**pleasantly** *adverb*. □ **agréablement, aimablement**

'**pleasantness** *noun*. □ **amabilité; agrément**

please [pliːz] *verb* 1 to do what is wanted by (a person); to give pleasure or satisfaction to: *You can't please everyone all the time; It pleases me to read poetry.* □ **plaire (à)**

2 to choose, want, like: *She does as she pleases.* □ **plaire**

■ *adverb* a word added to an order or request in order to be polite: *Please open the window; Close the door, please; Will you please come with me?* □ **s'il te/vous plaît**

pleased *adjective* happy; satisfied: *Aren't you pleased about moving house?; She was pleased with the dress.* □ **content**

'**pleasing** *adjective* giving pleasure; attractive: *a pleasing view.* □ **agréable**

'**pleasingly** *adverb*. □ **agréablement**

if you please please: *Come this way, if you please.* □ **s'il te/vous plaît**

please yourself do what you choose: *I don't think you should go, but please yourself.* □ **faire à sa guise**

pleasure ['pleʒə] *noun* something that gives one enjoyment; joy or delight: *the pleasures of country life; I get a lot of pleasure from listening to music.* □ **plaisir**

'**pleasurable** *adjective* giving pleasure; agreeable: *a pleasurable pastime.* □ **agréable**

'**pleasurably** *adverb*. □ **agréablement**

take pleasure in to get enjoyment from: *He takes great pleasure in annoying me.* □ **prendre plaisir à**

pleat [pliːt] *noun* a fold sewn or pressed into cloth *etc*: *a skirt with pleats.* □ **pli**

■ *verb* to make pleats in. □ **plisser**

'**pleated** *adjective*: *a pleated skirt.* □ **plissé**

plectrum ['plektrəm] *noun* a small piece of plastic *etc* for plucking the strings of a guitar. □ **plectre**

pled *see* **plead**.

pledge [pledʒ] *noun* 1 a promise: *She gave me her pledge.* □ **promesse, parole**

2 something given by a person who is borrowing money *etc* to the person he has borrowed it from, to be kept until the money *etc* is returned: *He borrowed $20 and left his watch as a pledge.* □ **gage**

3 a sign or token: *They exchanged rings as a pledge of their love.* □ **gage**

■ *verb* 1 to promise: *She pledged her support.* □

promettre
2 to give to someone when borrowing money *etc*: *to pledge one's watch*. □ **mettre en gage**

plenty ['plenti] *pronoun* 1 a sufficient amount; enough: *I don't need any more books – I've got plenty*; *We've got plenty of time to get there.* □ **(bien) assez de**

2 a large amount: *She's got plenty of money.* □ **beaucoup (de)**

■ *adjective*: *That's plenty, thank you!* □ **ça suffit**

'plenteous [-tiəs] *adjective* plentiful. □ **abondant**

'plentiful *adjective* existing in large amounts: *a plentiful supply.* □ **abondant**

pliable ['plaiəbl] *adjective* easily bent: *pliable wire.* □ **flexible**

,plia'bility *noun.* □ **flexibilité, souplesse**

pliers ['plaiəz] *noun plural* a kind of tool used for gripping, bending or cutting wire *etc*: *She used a pair of pliers to pull the nail out*; *Where are my pliers?* □ **pince(s)**

plight [plait] *noun* a (bad) situation or state: *He was in a terrible plight, as he had lost all his money.* □ **situation critique**

plod [plod] – *past tense, past participle* 'plodded – *verb* 1 to walk heavily and slowly: *The man plodded down the street.* □ **marcher lourdement/péniblement**

2 to work slowly but thoroughly: *They plodded on with the work.* □ **travailler laborieusement**

plonk [plɔŋk] *verb* to place or put noisily and rather clumsily: *He plonked his books on the table*; *She plonked herself down in front of the fire.* □ **poser bruyamment; (se) laisser tomber dans/sur**

plop [plop] *noun* the sound of a small object falling into water *etc*: *The raindrop fell into her teacup with a plop.* □ **plouf**

■ *verb* – *past tense, past participle* **plopped** – to fall with this sound: *A stone plopped into the pool.* □ **faire plouf**

plot [plot] *noun* 1 a plan, *especially* for doing something evil; a conspiracy: *a plot to assassinate the President.* □ **complot**

2 the story of a play, novel *etc*: *The play has a very complicated plot.* □ **intrigue**

3 a small piece of land *eg* for use as a gardening area or for building a house on. □ **terrain**

■ *verb* – *past tense, past participle* 'plotted – 1 to plan to bring about (something evil): *They were plotting the death of the king.* □ **comploter**

2 to make a plan, map, graph *etc* of: *The navigator plotted the course of the ship.* □ **tracer**

plough, plow [plau] *noun* a type of farm tool pulled through the top layer of the soil to turn it over. □ **charrue**

■ *verb* 1 to turn over (the earth) with such a tool: *The farmer was ploughing (in) a field.* □ **labourer**

2 to travel with difficulty, force a way *etc*: *The ship ploughed through the rough sea*; *I've all this work to plough through.* □ **avancer péniblement, peiner sur**

3 to crash: *The truck ploughed into the back of a bus.* □ **défoncer**

ploy [ploi] *noun* 1 a plan; a manoeuvre: *She uses various ploys for getting her own way.* □ **stratagème**

2 a piece of business; a little task: *The children were off on some ploy of their own.* □ **passe-temps**

pluck [plʌk] *verb* 1 to pull: *She plucked a grey hair from her head*; *He plucked at my sleeve.* □ **arracher**

2 to pull the feathers off (a chicken *etc*) before cooking it. □ **plumer**

3 to pick (flowers *etc*). □ **cueillir**

4 to pull hairs out of (eyebrows) in order to improve their shape. □ **épiler**

5 to pull and let go (the strings of a musical instrument). □ **pincer**

■ *noun* courage *She showed a lot of pluck.* □ **courage**

'plucky *adjective* courageous: *a plucky young fellow.* □ **courageux**

'pluckily *adverb.* □ **avec courage**

'pluckiness *noun.* □ **courage**

pluck up (the) **courage, energy** *etc* to gather up one's courage *etc* (to do something): *She plucked up (the) courage to ask a question.* □ **trouver le courage de**

plug [plʌg] *noun* 1 a device for putting into a mains socket in order to allow an electric current to flow through the appliance to which it is attached by cable: *She changed the plug on the electric kettle.* □ **prise (de courant)**

2 an object shaped for fitting into the hole in a bath or sink to prevent the water from running away, or a piece of material for blocking any hole. □ **bouchon**

■ *verb* – *past tense, past participle* **plugged** – to block (a hole) by putting a plug in it: *He plugged the hole in the window with a piece of newspaper.* □ **boucher**

plug in to connect up (an electrical apparatus) by inserting its plug into a socket: *Could you plug in the electric kettle?* □ **brancher**

plum [plʌm] *noun* a type of fruit, *usually* dark-red or purple, with a stone in the centre. □ **prune**

plum cake/pudding (a) cake or pudding containing raisins, currants *etc*. □ **gâteau aux raisins; plum-pudding**

plumage ['pluːmidʒ] *noun* the feathers of a bird or birds: *The peacock has (a) brilliant plumage.* □ **plumage**

plumber ['plʌmə] *noun* a person who fits and mends domestic water, gas and sewage pipes: *Send for a plumber – we have a leaking pipe.* □ **plombier, ière**

'plumbing *noun* 1 the system of pipes in a building *etc*: *We shall have to have the plumbing repaired.* □ **plomberie**

2 the fitting and repairing *etc* of pipes. □ **plomberie**

plume [pluːm] *noun* a large decorative feather: *She wore a plume in her hat.* □ **plume(t)**

plummet ['plʌmit] – *past tense, past participle* 'plummeted – *verb* (of a heavy weight) to fall or drop swiftly: *The rock plummeted to the bottom of the cliff.* □ **tomber à pic**

plump[1] ['plʌmp] *adjective* pleasantly fat and rounded; well filled out: *plump cheeks.* □ **grassouillet**

plumply *adverb.* □ **rondement**

'plumpness *noun.* □ **rondeur(s)**

plump up to shake (pillows *etc*) to restore their shape. □ **faire bouffer**

plump[2] [plʌmp]: **plump for** to choose or decide on: *She finally plumped for a house in the country.* □ **se décider**

pour

plunder ['plʌndə] *verb* to rob or steal from (a place): *The soldiers plundered and looted (the city).* □ **piller**
■ *noun* the things stolen: *They ran off with their plunder.* □ **butin**
'plunderer *noun.* □ **pillard, arde**

plunge [plʌndʒ] *verb* 1 to throw oneself down (into deep water *etc*); to dive: *She plunged into the river.* □ **plonger**
2 to push (something) violently or suddenly into: *He plunged a knife into the meat.* □ **enfoncer**
■ *noun* an act of plunging; a dive: *She took a plunge into the pool.* □ **plongeon**
'plunger *noun* an instrument for clearing blocked pipes *etc* by suction. □ **ventouse**
take the plunge to (decide to) start doing something new or difficult. □ **se jeter à l'eau**

plural ['pluərəl] *noun, adjective* (in) the form of a word which expresses more than one: *'Mice' is the plural of 'mouse'; a plural noun/verb; Is the verb in the singular or the plural?* □ **pluriel**

plus [plʌs] *preposition* used to show addition: *Two plus three equals five (2 + 3 = 5).* □ **plus**
■ *noun* (*also* **plus sign**) a sign (+) used to show addition or positive quality. □ **(signe) plus**
■ *adjective* positive or more than zero: *a plus quantity*; *The temperature was plus fifteen degrees.* □ **positif; au-dessus de zéro**

plutonium [pluː'touniəm] *noun* a radioactive element used in many nuclear processes. □ **plutonium**

ply[1] [plai] *verb* 1 an old word for to work at: *He plies his trade as weaver.* □ **exercer (un métier)**
2 to use (a tool *etc*) vigorously. □ **manier vigoureusement**
3 to keep supplying: *They plied their guests with drink.* □ **fournir sans arrêt**
ply[2] [plai] *noun* a thickness, layer or strand, as in *three-ply/two-ply wool.* □ **épaisseur, fil**
'plywood *noun, adjective* (of) a material made up of thin layers of wood glued together: *a plywood box.* □ **contre-plaqué**

pneumatic [nju'matik] *adjective* 1 filled with air: *pneumatic tires.* □ **pneumatique**
2 worked by air: *a pneumatic pump/drill.* □ **pneumatique**
pneu'matically *adverb.* □ **pneumatiquement**

pneumonia [nju'mouniə] *noun* an illness in which the lungs become inflamed. □ **pneumonie**

poach[1] [poutʃ] *verb* to cook (*eg* an egg without its shell, a fish *etc*) in boiling liquid, *especially* water or milk. □ **pocher**
poached *adjective*: *a poached egg.* □ **poché**
poach[2] [poutʃ] *verb* to hunt (game) or catch (fish) illegally on someone else's land. □ **braconner**
poacher *noun.* □ **braconnier**

pocket ['pokit] *noun* 1 a small bag sewn into or on to clothes, for carrying things in: *He stood with his hands in his pockets; a coat pocket; (also adjective) a pocket-handkerchief, a pocket knife.* □ **(de) poche**
2 a small bag attached to the corners and sides of a billiard-table *etc* to catch the balls. □ **poche**

3 a small isolated area or group: *a pocket of warm air.* □ **poche**
4 (a person's) income or amount of money available for spending: *a range of prices to suit every pocket.* □ **bourse**
■ *verb* 1 to put in a pocket: *She pocketed her wallet; She pocketed the red ball.* □ **mettre dans la/sa poche**
2 to steal: *Be careful he doesn't pocket the silver.* □ **empocher**
'pocketful *noun* the amount contained by a pocket: *a pocketful of coins.* □ **poche pleine**
'pocketbook *noun* a wallet for holding papers. □ **portefeuille**
'pocket money *noun* money for personal use, *especially* a child's regular allowance: *She gets $2 a week pocket money.* □ **argent de poche**
'pocket-size(d) *adjective* small enough to carry in one's pocket: *a pocket-size(d) dictionary.* □ **de poche**

pockmark ['pokmaːk] *noun* a scar or small dent in the skin caused by smallpox *etc*. □ **marque de petite vérole**
'pockmarked *adjective.* □ **grêlé**

pod [pod] *noun* the long seed-case of the pea, bean *etc*. □ **cosse**

podgy ['podʒi], **pudgy** ['pʌdʒi] *adjective* plump; fat. □ **rondelet**
'podginess, 'pudginess *noun.* □ **rondeur**

podium ['poudiəm] *noun* a platform on which a lecturer, musical conductor *etc* stands. □ **podium**

poem ['pouim] *noun* a piece of writing arranged in lines which *usually* have a regular rhythm and often rhyme. □ **poème**

poet ['pouit] – *feminine* **'poet, 'poetess** – *noun* a person who writes poems. □ **poète, poétesse**
poetic [pou'etik] *adjective* of, like, or suitable for, a poem: *a poetic expression.* □ **poétique**
po'etically *adverb.* □ **poétiquement**
'poetry *noun* 1 poems in general: *He writes poetry.* □ **poésie**
2 the art of composing poems: *Poetry comes naturally to some people.* □ **poésie**

point [point] *noun* 1 the sharp end of anything: *the point of a pin; a sword point; at gunpoint* (= threatened by a gun). □ **pointe**
2 a piece of land that projects into the sea *etc*: *The ship came around Lizard Point.* □ **pointe**
3 a small round dot or mark (.): *a decimal point; five point three six* (= 5.36); *In punctuation, a point is another name for a full stop.* □ **point**
4 an exact place or spot: *When we reached this point of the journey we stopped to rest.* □ **point**
5 an exact moment: *Her husband walked in at that point.* □ **moment précis**
6 a place on a scale *especially* of temperature: *the boiling-point of water.* □ **point**
7 a division on a compass *eg* north, south-west *etc*. □ **point**
8 a mark in scoring a competition, game, test *etc*: *She has won by five points to two.* □ **point**
9 a particular matter for consideration or action: *The first point we must decide is, where to meet; That's a*

good point; *You've missed the point*; *That's the whole point*; *We're wandering away from the point.* □ **point; propos**

10 (a) purpose or advantage: *There's no point (in) asking me – I don't know.* □ **sens, raison**

11 a personal characteristic or quality: *We all have our good points and our bad ones.* □ **qualités; défauts**

■ *verb* **1** to aim in a particular direction: *He pointed the gun at me.* □ **braquer (un revolver sur)**

2 to call attention to something *especially* by stretching the index finger in its direction: *She pointed (her finger) at the door*; *She pointed to a sign.* □ **montrer du doigt**

'**pointed** *adjective* having a sharp end: *a pointed nose*; *pointed shoes.* □ **pointu**

'**pointer** *noun* **1** a long stick used to indicate places on a large map *etc.* □ **baguette**

2 an indicator on a dial: *The pointer is on/at zero.* □ **aiguille**

3 a hint; a suggestion: *Give me some pointers on how to do it.* □ **conseil**

'**pointless** *adjective* having no meaning or purpose: *a pointless journey.* □ **futile, vain**

'**pointlessly** *adverb.* □ **en vain**

points *noun plural* **1** a movable section of rails which allow a train to cross over other lines or pass from one line to another: *The points had to be changed before the train could continue.* □ **aiguillage**

2 the solid tips in the toes of ballet shoes: *She can dance on her points.* □ **pointes**

be on the point of to be about to (do something): *I was on the point of going out when the telephone rang.* □ **être sur le point de**

come to the point 1 (*also* **get to the point**) to reach the most important consideration in a conversation *etc*: *He talked and talked but never came to the point.* □ **(en) venir au fait**

2 (*only with* it *as subject*) to arrive at the moment when something must be done: *He always promises to help, but when it comes to the point he's never there.* □ **quand vient le temps (de)**

make a point of to be especially careful to (do something): *I'll make a point of asking her today.* □ **se faire un devoir de**

make one's point to state one's opinion persuasively. □ **faire ressortir un argument**

point out to indicate or draw attention to: *He pointed out his house to her*; *I pointed out that we needed more money.* □ **faire remarquer**

point one's toes to stretch the foot out, shaping the toes into a point, when dancing *etc.* □ **faire des pointes**

point-blank [point'blaŋk] *adjective, adverb* **1** (in shooting) very close: *He fired at him at point-blank range.* □ **à bout portant**

2 abrupt(ly); without warning or explanation: *He asked her point-blank how old she was.* □ **de but en blanc**

poise [poiz] *verb* to balance: *He poised himself on the diving-board.* □ **(se) tenir en équilibre**

■ *noun* **1** balance and control in bodily movement: *Good poise is important for a dancer.* □ **équilibre**

2 dignity and self-confidence: *He lost his poise for a moment.* □ **assurance**

poised *adjective* **1** staying in a state of balance and stillness: *The car was poised on the edge of the cliff.* □ **en équilibre (sur)**

2 having the body in a state of tension and readiness to act: *The animal was poised ready to leap.* □ **prêt à bondir sur**

poison ['poizn] *noun* any substance which causes death or illness when taken into the body: *She killed herself by taking poison*; *(also adjective) poison gas.* □ **poison**

■ *verb* **1** to kill or harm with poison: *He poisoned his uncle.* □ **empoisonner**

2 to put poison into (food *etc*): *He poisoned his coffee.* □ **mettre du poison dans**

'**poisoner** *noun.* □ **empoisonneur, euse**

'**poisonous** *adjective* containing or using poison: *That fruit is poisonous*; *a poisonous snake.* □ **vénéneux, venimeux**

'**poisonously** *adverb.* □ **de manière venimeuse**

poison-pen letter an anonymous letter saying wicked things about a person *etc.* □ **lettre anonyme venimeuse**

poke [pouk] *verb* **1** to push something into; to prod: *He poked a stick into the hole*; *He poked her in the ribs with his elbow.* □ **enfoncer (dans)**

2 to make (a hole) by doing this: *She poked a hole in the sand with her finger.* □ **faire un trou dans**

3 to (cause to) protrude or project: *She poked her head in at the window*; *His foot was poking out of the blankets.* □ **dépasser (de)**

■ *noun* an act of poking; a prod or nudge: *She gave me a poke in the arm.* □ **coup**

'**poker** *noun* a (*usually* metal) rod for stirring up a fire. □ **tisonnier**

'**poky, pokey** *adjective* (of a room *etc*) small, with not enough space. □ **exigu**

poke about/around to look or search for something among other things. □ **fourrager (dans)**

poke fun at to laugh at unkindly: *The children often poked fun at him because of his stammer.* □ **se moquer de**

poke one's nose into to interfere with other people's business: *He is always poking his nose into my affairs.* □ **fourrer son nez dans**

poker[1] ['poukə] *noun* a kind of card game *usually* played for money. □ **poker**

poker[2]**, poky** *see* **poke.**

polar *see* **pole**[1].

pole[1] [poul] *noun* **1** the north or south end of the Earth's axis: *the North/South Pole.* □ **pôle**

2 the points in the heavens opposite the Earth's North and South Poles, around which stars seem to turn. □ **pôle**

3 either of the opposite ends of a magnet: *The opposite poles of magnets attract each other.* □ **pôle**

4 either of the opposite terminals of an electric battery: *the positive/negative pole.* □ **pôle**

'**polar** *adjective* of the earth's North or South Pole or the region around it: *the polar ice-cap*; *the polar region.* □ **polaire**

polar bear a type of bear found near the North Pole. □ **ours polaire**

be poles apart to be as different or as far apart as possible. □ **être aux antipodes (l'un de l'autre)**

pole² [poul] *noun* a long, thin, rounded piece of wood, metal *etc*: *a telegraph pole*; *a tent pole*. □ **poteau, mât**

'pole vault *noun* (in athletics *etc*) a type of jump made with the help of a pole. □ **saut à la perche**

police [pə'liːs] *noun plural* the men and women whose job is to prevent crime, keep order, see that laws are obeyed *etc*: *Call the police!*; *The police are investigating the matter*; *(also adjective)* *the police force, a police officer*. □ **(de) police**

■ *verb* to supply (a place) with police: *We cannot police the whole area*. □ **envoyer des agents**

police dog a dog trained to work with policemen (in tracking criminals, finding drugs *etc*). □ **chien policier**

po'liceman, po'licewoman *nouns* a member of the police. □ **policier, ière**

police officer *noun* someone on a police force especially trained to keep the peace: *Billy saw someone steal a car and called a police officer to stop the crime and arrest the thief*. □ **agent de police**

police station the office or headquarters of a local police force: *The lost dog was taken to the police station*. □ **poste de police**

policy¹ ['poləsi] – *plural* **'policies** – *noun* a planned or agreed course of action *usually* based on particular principles: *the government's policies on education*. □ **politique**

policy² ['poləsi] – *plural* **'policies** – *noun* a (written) agreement with an insurance company: *an insurance policy*. □ **police**

polio ['pouliou] (short for **poliomyelitis** [poulioumaiə'laitis]) *noun* a disease of the spinal cord often causing paralysis. □ **polio**

polish ['poliʃ] *verb* **1** to make smooth and shiny by rubbing: *He polished his shoes*. □ **cirer, polir**

2 (*especially* with **up**) to improve: *Polish up your English!* □ **perfectionner**

■ *noun* **1** smoothness and shininess: *There's a wonderful polish on this old wood*. □ **poli**

2 a kind of liquid, or other substance used to make something shiny: *furniture polish*; *silver polish*. □ **cire**

'polished *adjective* (*negative* **unpolished**). □ **(non) poli**

polish off to finish: *She polished off the last of the ice cream*. □ **finir**

polite [pə'lait] *adjective* having or showing good manners; courteous: *a polite child*; *a polite apology*. □ **poli**

po'litely *adverb*. □ **poliment**

po'liteness *noun*. □ **politesse**

politics ['politiks] *noun singular or plural* the science or business of, or ideas about, or affairs concerning, government. □ **politique**

po'litical *adjective* of, or concerning, politics: *for political reasons*; *political studies*. □ **politique**

po'litically *adverb*. □ **politiquement**

,poli'tician [-'tiʃən] *noun* a person whose job is politics; a member of parliament. □ **politicien, ienne**

political asylum protection given by a government to a foreigner who has left his own country for political reasons. □ **asile politique**

political prisoner a person who has been imprisoned for political reasons and not for any crime. □ **prisonnier, ière politique**

polka ['polkə] *noun* (a piece of music for) a type of quick, lively dance. □ **polka**

poll [poul] *noun* **1** an election: *They organized a poll to elect a president*. □ **élection**

2 the number of votes: *There has been a heavy poll* (= a large number of votes). □ **suffrages**

3 (*also* **opinion poll**) a test of public opinion by asking people questions. □ **sondage**

■ *verb* to receive a number of votes: *She polled fifty per cent of the votes*. □ **obtenir des votes**

'polling booth *noun* a small place or stall where one can mark one's voting paper. □ **isoloir**

'polling station *noun* a place where one goes to vote. □ **bureau de vote**

go to the polls to have an election. □ **aller aux urnes**

pollen ['polən] *noun* the powder inside a flower which fertilizes other flowers: *Bees carry pollen from flower to flower*. □ **pollen**

pollinate ['poləneit] *verb* to make (a plant) fertile by carrying pollen to it from another flower: *Insects pollinate the flowers*. □ **féconder**

,polli'nation *noun*. □ **pollinisation**

pollute [pə'luːt] *verb* to make dirty: *Chemicals are polluting the air*. □ **polluer**

pol'lution [-ʃən] *noun*. □ **pollution**

polo ['poulou] *noun* a game like hockey, played on horseback. □ **polo**

poltergeist ['poltəgaist, 'poul-] *noun* a kind of ghost that moves furniture *etc*. □ **esprit frappeur**

polygon ['poligən, -gon] *noun* a two-dimensional figure with many angles and sides. □ **polygone**

po'lygonal [-'li-] *adjective*. □ **polygonal**

polytechnic [poli'teknik] *noun* a school or college in which technical subjects, *eg* engineering and building, are taught. □ **(école) polytechnique**

polythene ['poliθiːn] *noun, adjective* (of) any of several types of plastic that can be moulded when hot: *It's made of polythene*; *a polythene bag*. □ **polyéthylène**

pomegranate ['pomigranət] *noun* a type of fruit with a thick skin and many seeds. □ **grenade**

pomelo ['poməlou] – *plural* **'pomelos** – *noun* a large tropical citrus fruit similar to a grapefruit. □ **pomelo**

pomp [pomp] *noun* solemn stateliness and magnificence, *eg* at a ceremonial occasion: *The Queen arrived with great pomp and ceremony*. □ **pompe**

'pompous *adjective* too grand in manner or speech: *The headmaster is inclined to be a bit pompous*. □ **pompeux**

'pompously *adverb*. □ **pompeusement**

'pompousness *noun*. □ **emphase**

pom'posity [-'po-] *noun*. □ **suffisance, emphase**

pomposity *see* pomp.

poncho ['pontʃou] – *plural* **'ponchos** – *noun* a garment made of, or like, a blanket, with a hole for the head. □ **poncho**

pond [pond] *noun* a small lake or pool: *the village pond*.

□ **mare, étang**

ponder ['pondə] *verb* to consider carefully: *She pondered the suggestion.* □ **réfléchir (à/sur)**

pong pong [poŋpoŋ] *noun* a tropical tree with white scented flowers and round fruits with a fibrous husk. □ **pong pong**

pontiff ['pontif] *noun* (in the Roman Catholic church) a bishop, *especially* the Pope. □ **pontife**

pontoon[1] [pon'tuːn] *noun* one of the flat-bottomed boats used to support a temporary roadway (a **pontoon bridge**) across a river *etc*. □ **ponton**

pontoon[2] [pon'tuːn] *noun* a kind of card-game. □ **vingt-et-un**

pony ['pouni] – *plural* '**ponies** – *noun* a small horse: *The child was riding a brown pony.* □ **poney**

'**ponytail** *noun* (a kind of hairstyle with the) hair tied in a bunch at the back of the head. □ **queue de cheval**

poodle ['puːdl] *noun* a breed of dog whose curly hair is often clipped in a decorative way. □ **caniche**

pool[1] [puːl] *noun* 1 a small area of still water: *The rain left pools in the road.* □ **flaque**

2 a similar area of any liquid: *a pool of blood/oil.* □ **flaque**

3 a deep part of a stream or river: *He was fishing (in) a pool near the river-bank.* □ **trou d'eau**

4 a swimming pool: *They spent the day at the pool.* □ **piscine**

pool[2] [puːl] *noun* a stock or supply: *We put our money into a general pool.* □ **cagnotte, fonds commun**

■ *verb* to put together for general use: *We pooled our money and bought a van that we could all use.* □ **mettre en commun**

(football) pools *noun plural* organized gambling on the results of football matches. □ **concours de pronostics**

poor [puə] *adjective* 1 having little money or property: *She is too poor to buy clothes for the children; the poor nations of the world.* □ **pauvre**

2 not good; of bad quality: *His work is very poor; a poor effort.* □ **médiocre**

3 deserving pity: *Poor fellow!* □ **pauvre**

'**poorness** *noun*. □ **pauvreté**

'**poorly** *adverb* not well; badly: *a poorly written essay.* □ **pauvrement**

■ *adjective* ill: *He is very poorly.* □ **malade**

pop[1] [pop] *noun* 1 a sharp, quick, explosive noise, such as that made by a cork as it comes out of a bottle: *The paper bag burst with a loud pop.* □ **pan!**

2 fizzy drink: *a bottle of pop.* □ **boisson gazeuse**

■ *verb – past tense, past participle* **popped** – 1 to (cause to) make a pop: *He popped the balloon; My balloon has popped.* □ **(faire) éclater**

2 to spring upwards or outwards: *His eyes nearly popped out of his head in amazement.* □ **sortir tout à coup, surgir**

3 to go quickly and briefly somewhere: *She popped out to buy a newspaper.* □ **sortir**

4 put quickly: *She popped the letter into her pocket.* □ **fourrer**

'**popcorn** *noun* a kind of corn that bursts open when it is heated, and is eaten either sweetened or salted. □ **maïs**

à **éclater**

'**popgun** *noun* a toy gun that fires pellets by means of compressed air. □ **pistolet à bouchon/air**

pop up to appear: *I never know where he'll pop up next.* □ **surgir**

pop[2] [pop] *adjective* (short for **popular**) 1 (of music) written, played *etc* in a modern style. □ **pop**

2 of, or related to, pop music: *a pop group; a pop singer; pop records.* □ **pop**

pope [poup] *noun* (*often with capital*) the bishop of Rome, head of the Roman Catholic church: *A new Pope has been elected.* □ **pape**

poppy ['popi] – *plural* '**poppies** – *noun* a type of plant with large, *usually* red flowers. □ **pavot**

populace ['popjuləs] *noun* the people (of a country *etc*). □ **peuple**

popular ['popjulə] *adjective* 1 liked by most people: *a popular holiday resort; a popular person; She is very popular with children.* □ **populaire**

2 believed by most people: *a popular theory.* □ **à la mode**

3 of the people in general: *popular rejoicing.* □ **populaire**

4 easily read, understood *etc* by most people: *a popular history of Canada.* □ **de vulgarisation**

'**popularly** *adverb* amongst, or by, most people: *She was popularly believed to have magical powers.* □ **communément**

'**popu'larity** [-'la-] *noun* the state of being well liked. □ **popularité**

'**popularize**, '**popularise** *verb* to make popular or widely known: *She did much to popularize women's sport.* □ **populariser**

populate ['popjuleit] *verb* (*usually in passive*) to fill with people: *That part of the world used to be populated by wandering tribes.* □ **peupler**

,**popu'lation** *noun* the people living in a particular country, area *etc*: *the population of Montreal is 2 million; a rapid increase in population.* □ **population**

'**populous** *adjective* full of people: *a populous area.* □ **populeux**

---

population is singular: *The population of the city increases in the summer.*

---

porcelain ['poːsəlin] *noun, adjective* (of) a kind of fine china: *That dish is made of porcelain; a porcelain figure.* □ **(en) porcelaine**

porch [poːtʃ] *noun* 1 a covered entrance to a building: *They waited in the porch until it stopped raining.* □ **porche**

2 a veranda. □ **véranda**

porcupine ['poːkjupain] *noun* a kind of gnawing animal covered with long prickles (called quills), and larger than a hedgehog. □ **porc-épic**

pore[1] [poː] *noun* a tiny hole, *especially* of a sweat gland in the skin. □ **pore**

'**porous** *adjective* allowing liquid to pass through: *porous clay.* □ **poreux**

pore[2] [poː]: **pore over** to study with great attention: *She pored over her books.* □ **s'absorber dans**

pork [poːk] *noun* the flesh of a pig used as food. □ **porc**

pornography [poːˈnogrəfi] *noun* literature, pictures, films *etc* that are indecent in a sexual way. □ **pornographie**

pornographic [poːnəˈgrafik] *adjective*. □ **pornographique**

porous *see* **pore**[1].

porpoise [ˈpoːpəs] *noun* a type of blunt-nosed sea animal of the dolphin family. □ **marsouin**

porridge [ˈporidʒ] *noun* a food made from oatmeal boiled in water or milk. □ **porridge, bouillie d'avoine**

port[1] [poːt] *noun* 1 (*usually without* **a** *or* **the**) a harbour: *The ship came into port.* □ **port**

2 a town with a harbour: *the port of Hull.* □ **port**

port[2] [poːt] *noun* the left side of a ship or aircraft: *The helmsman steered the ship to port;* (*also adjective*) *the port wing.* □ **(de) bâbord; (de) gauche**

port[3] [poːt] *noun* a strong, dark-red, sweet wine *originally* from Portugal. □ **porto**

portable [ˈpoːtəbl] *adjective* able to be carried, or moved easily from place to place: *a portable radio.* □ **portatif, portable**

portent [ˈpoːtent] *noun* something *usually* strange and remarkable that warns of some future happening: *strange signs and portents.* □ **présage**

porter [ˈpoːtə] *noun* 1 a person whose job is to carry luggage in a railway station *etc: The old lady could not find a porter to carry her suitcase from the train.* □ **porteur, euse**

2 a person whose job is to carry things *eg* in rough country where there is no other form of transport: *He set off into the jungle with three porters.* □ **porteur, euse**

3 a doorman or attendant in a hotel *etc: a hospital porter.* □ **portier, ière**

portfolio [poːtˈfouliou] – *plural* **port'folios** – *noun* 1 a case for carrying papers, drawings *etc.* □ **porte-documents**

2 the post or job of a government minister. □ **portefeuille**

porthole [ˈpoːthoul] *noun* a small, *usually* round, window in a ship. □ **hublot**

portico [ˈpoːtikou] – *plural* **portico(e)s** – *noun* a row of pillars supporting a roof, *usually* forming a porch to a building. □ **portique**

portion [ˈpoːʃən] *noun* 1 a part: *Read this portion of the book.* □ **partie**

2 a share: *Her portion of the money amounted to $200.* □ **part**

3 an amount of food *usually* for one person: *a portion of salad.* □ **portion**

portion out to divide into portions or shares: *The money was portioned out between the three children.* □ **répartir**

portrait [ˈpoːtrət] *noun* 1 a drawing, painting, photograph *etc* of a person: *She had her portrait painted by a famous artist.* □ **portrait**

2 a written description of a person, place *etc: a book called 'A portrait of Montreal'.* □ **portrait**

portray [poːˈtrei] *verb* 1 to make a portrait of: *In this painting, the king is portrayed sitting on his throne.* □ **faire le portrait de**

2 to act the part of: *the actor who portrays Hamlet.* □ **jouer**

portrayal [poːˈtreiəl] *noun* the act of portraying. □ **représentation, portrait**

pose[1] [pouz] *noun* 1 a position or attitude of the body: *a relaxed pose.* □ **pose**

2 a false manner or way of behaving assumed in order to impress others; a pretence: *His indignation was only a pose.* □ **affectation**

■ *verb* 1 to position oneself *eg* for a photograph to be taken: *She posed in the doorway.* □ **poser**

2 (*with* **as**) to pretend to be: *He posed as a doctor.* □ **se faire passer pour**

pose[2] [pouz] *verb* to set or offer (a question or problem) for answering or solving: *She posed a difficult question; This poses a problem.* □ **poser**

posh [poʃ] *adjective* of a superior type or class: *a posh family; posh clothes.* □ **chic**

position [əˈziʃən] *noun* 1 a way of standing, sitting *etc: She lay in an uncomfortable position.* □ **position**

2 a place or situation: *The house is in a beautiful position.* □ **emplacement**

3 a job; a post: *She has a good position with a local bank.* □ **poste**

4 a point of view: *Let me explain my position on employment.* □ **position**

■ *verb* to put or place: *She positioned the lamp in the middle of the table.* □ **placer**

be in, out of position to be (not) in the right place: *Is everything in position for the photograph?* □ **être en place; n'ôtre pas à sa place**

positive [ˈpozətiv] *adjective* 1 meaning or saying 'yes': *a positive answer; They tested the water for the bacteria and the result was positive* (= the bacteria were present). □ **positif**

2 definite; leaving no doubt: *positive proof.* □ **indéniable**

3 certain or sure: *I'm positive she's right.* □ **certain**

4 complete or absolute: *His work is a positive disgrace.* □ **vrai**

5 optimistic and prepared to make plans for the future: *Take a more positive attitude to life.* □ **positif**

6 not showing any comparison; not comparative or superlative. □ **positif**

7 (of a number *etc*) greater than zero. □ **positif**

8 having fewer electrons than normal: *In an electrical circuit, electrons flow to the positive terminal.* □ **positif**

■ *noun* 1 a photographic print, made from a negative, in which light and dark are as normal. □ **positif**

2 (an adjective or adverb of) the positive (not comparative or superlative) degree. □ **affirmatif**

'positiveness *noun*. □ **certitude**

'positively *adverb* 1 in a positive way: *He stated positively that he was innocent.* □ **formellement**

2 absolutely; completely: *He is positively the nastiest person I know.* □ **assurément**

posse [ˈposi] *noun* (*especially American*) a group or body of policemen *etc.* □ **détachement (de policiers)**

possess [pəˈzes] *verb* to own or have: *How much money does he possess?* □ **posséder**

pos'session [-ʃən] *noun* 1 something which is owned by a person, country *etc: She lost all her possessions in*

the fire. □ **possession**
2 the state of possessing. □ **possession**
pos'sessive [-siv] *adjective* 1 showing that someone or something possesses an object *etc*: *'Yours', 'mine', 'his', 'hers', 'theirs' are possessive pronouns; 'your', 'my', 'his', 'their' are possessive adjectives.* □ **possessif**
2 acting as though things and people are one's personal possessions: *a possessive mother.* □ **possessif**
pos'sessively *adverb.* □ **de manière possessive**
pos'sessiveness *noun.* □ **possessivité**
pos'sessor *noun: He is the proud possessor of a new car.* □ **propriétaire, possesseur**
possible ['posəbl] *adjective* 1 able to happen or be done: *It's possible that the train will be delayed; We'll come as soon as possible; I'll do everything possible; She did the only possible thing in the circumstances.* □ **possible**
2 satisfactory; acceptable: *I've thought of a possible solution to the problem.* □ **possible**
,possi'bility – *plural* **possi'bilities** – *noun* something that is possible; the state of being possible; (a) likelihood: *There isn't much possibility of that happening; There's a possibility of war; The plan has possibilities* (= looks as if it may be a good one). □ **possiblité**
'possibly *adverb* 1 perhaps: *'Will you have time to do it?' 'Possibly.'* □ **peut-être (bien), possiblement**
2 in a way or manner that is possible: *I'll come as fast as I possibly can; I can't possibly eat any more; Could you possibly lend me your pen?* □ **en son possible**
post¹ [poust] *noun* a long piece of wood, metal *etc*, usually fixed upright in the ground: *The notice was nailed to a post; a gate-post; the winning-post.* □ **poteau**
be first past the post to win. □ **être premier au fil d'arrivée**
keep (somebody) posted to give regular information to (a person). □ **tenir au courant**
post² [poust] *noun* (the system of collecting, transporting and delivering) letters, parcels *etc*: *I sent the book by post; Has the post arrived yet?; Is there any post for me?* □ **poste, courrier**
■ *verb* to send (a letter *etc*) by post: *She posted the parcel yesterday.* □ **poster**
'postage [-tidʒ] *noun* (the money paid for) the sending of a letter *etc* by post: *The postage was $1.20.* □ **tarif postal**
'postal *adjective* of, or concerning, the system of sending letters *etc*: *the postal service.* □ **postal**
postage stamp a small printed label fixed to a letter, parcel *etc* to show that postage has been paid. □ **timbre-poste**
postal code (*also* **postcode**) *noun* a set of letters and numbers added to the address on a letter or to make delivery easier. □ **code postal**
postbox ['pousboks] *noun* (*also* **'mailbox**) a box into which letters *etc* are put to be collected (and sent to their destination). □ **boîte aux lettres**
postcard ['pouskɑːd] *noun* a card on which a message may be sent by post, often with a picture on one side (a **picture postcard**): *She sent me a postcard of the Taj Mahal when she was in India.* □ **carte postale**
postcode ['pouskoud] *noun* a set of letters and numbers

added to the address on a letter to make delivery easier. □ **code postal**
,post-'free *adjective, adverb* without charge for sending by post: *You can send it post-free.* □ **franco**
,post-'haste *adverb* very quickly: *She travelled post-haste to Montreal.* □ **en toute hâte**
postman ['pousmən] *noun* (*also* **'mailman**) a person whose job is to (collect and) deliver letters *etc: Has the postman been this morning yet?* □ **facteur, trice**
postmark ['pousmɑːk] *noun* a mark put on a letter at a post office, showing the date and place of posting, and cancelling the postage stamp: *The postmark read 'Beirut'.* □ **cachet de la poste**
postmaster ['pousmɑːstə] – *feminine* **postmistress** ['pousmistris] – *noun* the manager of a post office. □ **receveur/euse des postes**
post office an office for receiving and dispatching letters, parcels *etc: Where is the nearest post office?* □ **bureau de poste**
post³ [poust] *noun* 1 a job: *She has a post in the government; a teaching post.* □ **poste**
2 a place of duty: *The soldier remained at his post.* □ **poste**
3 a settlement, camp *etc* especially in a distant or unpopulated area: *a trading-post.* □ **comptoir**
■ *verb* to send somewhere on duty: *He was posted abroad.* □ **poster, affecter**
post⁴ [poust] *noun:* **the first/last post** in the army, the morning/evening bugle-call. □ **première/dernière sonnerie de clairon**
postage, postal, postcard, postcode *see* **post².**
poster ['poustə] *noun* a large notice or advertisement for sticking on a wall *etc: Have you seen the posters advertising the circus?* □ **affiche**
posterior [pə'stiəriə] *adjective* coming, or situated behind. □ **postérieur**
posterity [po'sterəti] *noun* people coming after; future generations: *The treasures must be kept for posterity.* □ **postérité**
post-free *see* **post².**
post-graduate [pous'gradjuət] *adjective* (of studies *etc*) done *etc* after a (first) university degree. □ **de deuxième et troisième cycles**
■ *noun* a student doing post-graduate studies. □ **étudiant, ante de deuxième ou troisième cycle**
post-haste *see* **post².**
posthumous ['postjuməs] *adjective* 1 happening, coming *etc* to a person after his death: *the posthumous publication of his book.* □ **posthume**
2 (of a child) born after its father has died. □ **né orphelin de père**
'posthumously *adverb.* □ **après la mort (de qqn)**
postman, postmark, postmaster, postmistress *see* **post².**
post-mortem [pous'mɔːtəm] *noun* a medical examination of a dead body in order to find out the cause of death. □ **autopsie**
postnatal [pous'neitl] *adjective* concerned with, or happening, in the period after birth. □ **post-natal**
post office *see* **post².**

postpone [pəs'poun] *verb* to cancel until a future time: *The football match has been postponed (till tomorrow).* □ **ajourner**

post'ponement *noun*. □ **ajournement**

postscript ['pousskript] *noun* (*often abbreviated to* **P.S.**) a part added to a letter after the writer has signed it. □ **post-scriptum (P.-S.)**

posture ['postʃə] *noun* 1 the way in which a person places or holds his body when standing, sitting, walking *etc*: *Good posture is important for a dancer.* □ **posture**

2 a position or pose: *She knelt in an uncomfortable posture.* □ **position**

postwar [poust'woː] *adjective* of, or belonging to, the time after a war: *postwar depression.* □ **d'après-guerre**

posy ['pouzi] – *plural* **'posies** – *noun* a small bunch of flowers: *a posy of primroses.* □ **petit bouquet (de fleurs)**

pot [pot] *noun* any one of many kinds of deep container used in cooking, for holding food, liquids *etc* or for growing plants: *a cooking-pot; a plant-pot; a jam-pot; The waiter brought her a pot of tea.* □ **pot**

■ *verb* – *past tense, past participle* **'potted** – to plant in a pot. □ **mettre en pot**

'potted *adjective* 1 (of food) pressed into a pot or jar in order to preserve it: *potted meat.* □ **en pot/terrine**

2 contained in a pot: *a potted plant.* □ **en pot**

3 brief; summarized: *a potted history of North America.* □ **condensé**

'pothole *noun* 1 a hole or cave made in rock by the action of swirling water. □ **marmite de géants**

2 a hole worn in a road-surface. □ **nid-de-poule**

'potshot *noun* an easy or casual shot that doesn't need careful aim: *He took a potshot at a bird on the fence.* □ **tir à vue de nez**

pot luck a meal where each guest brings a dish. □ **à la fortune du pot**

pot-belly *noun* an extended or very large, round abdomen; a paunch caused by overeating or drinking: *Allan drank so much beer he has a pot-belly and none of his jeans fit.* □ **bedaine**

potassium [pə'tasiəm] *noun* a silvery-white element. □ **potassium**

potato [pə'teitou] – *plural* **po'tatoes** – *noun* 1 a type of plant with round underground stems (called **tubers**) which are used as a vegetable. □ **pomme de terre**

2 the tuber or tubers: *She bought 2 kilograms of potatoes.* □ **pomme de terre**

potato chip a thin, crisp, fried slice of potato: *a packet of (potato) crisps.* □ **croustilles**

potent ['poutənt] *adjective* powerful; strong: *a potent drink.* □ **puissant**

'potency *noun*. □ **puissance**

potential [pə'tenʃəl] *adjective* possible; that may develop into the thing mentioned: *That hole in the road is a potential danger.* □ **en puissance**

■ *noun* the possibility, or likelihood, of successful development (in a particular way): *The land has great farming potential; She shows potential as a teacher.* □ **potentiel**

po'tentially *adverb*. □ **en puissance**

pothole *etc see* **pot**.

potion ['pouʃən] *noun* a drink containing *eg* medicine or poison, or having a magic effect: *a love-potion.* □ **potion, philtre**

potter¹ ['potə] *noun* a person who makes plates, cups, vases *etc* out of clay and fires them in an oven (called a **kiln**). □ **potier, ière**

'pottery *noun* 1 articles made by fired clay: *He is learning how to make pottery.* □ **poterie**

2 (*plural* **'potteries**) a place where articles of fired clay are made: *He is working in the pottery.* □ **atelier de poterie**

3 the art of making such articles: *She is learning pottery.* □ **poterie**

potter² [potə] *verb* to wander about doing small jobs or doing nothing important: *I spent the afternoon pottering (about).* □ **flâner, s'amuser à des riens**

potty ['poti] *adjective* mad; crazy: *He must be potty to do that!* □ **cinglé**

pouch [pautʃ] *noun* 1 a small bag: *a tobacco-pouch.* □ **sac(oche), blague**

2 something bag-like: *This animal stores its food in two pouches under its chin.* □ **poche**

3 the pocket of skin in which the young of certain kinds of animal, *eg* the kangaroo, are reared. □ **poche**

pouffe, pouf [puːf] *noun* a large firm kind of cushion used as a seat. □ **pouf**

poulterer *see* **poultry**.

poultry ['poultri] *noun* farmyard birds, *eg* hens, ducks, geese, turkeys: *They keep poultry.* □ **volaille**

'poulterer *noun* a person who sells poultry (and game) as food: *We ordered a turkey from the poulterer.* □ **marchand, ande de volailles**

pounce [pauns] *verb* to jump suddenly, in order to seize or attack: *The cat waited beside the bird-cage, ready to pounce.* □ **bondir**

■ *noun* an act of pouncing; a sudden attack: *The cat made a pounce at the bird.* □ **bond (sur)**

pounce on to leap upon (*eg* one's prey) in order to attack or grab it: *The tiger pounced on its victim.* □ **bondir sur**

pound¹ [paund] *noun* 1 (*also* **pound sterling**: *usually abbreviated to* **#** *when written with a number*) the standard unit of British currency, 100 (new) pence. □ **livre sterling**

2 (*usually abbreviated to* **lb(s)** *when written with a number*) a measure of weight (0.454 kilograms). □ **livre**

pound² [paund] *noun* an enclosure or pen into which stray animals are put: *a dog-pound.* □ **fourrière**

pound³ [paund] *verb* 1 to hit or strike heavily; to thump: *He pounded at the door; The children were pounding on the piano.* □ **frapper fermement (sur qqch.)**

2 to walk or run heavily: *He pounded down the road.* □ **marcher/courir d'un pas lourd**

3 to break up (a substance) into powder or liquid: *She pounded the dried herbs.* □ **piler, broyer**

pour [poː] *verb* 1 to (cause to) flow in a stream: *She poured the milk into a bowl; Water poured down the wall; People were pouring out of the factory.* □ **verser, se déverser**

2 (*only with* **it** *as subject*) to rain heavily: *It was pour-*

ing this morning. □ **tomber à verse**
pout [paut] *verb* (of a sulky child *etc*) to push the lips out as a sign of displeasure. □ **faire la moue**
■ *noun* this expression of the face. □ **moue**
poverty ['povəti] *noun* the condition of being poor: *They lived in extreme poverty; the poverty of the soil.* □ **pauvreté**
powder ['paudə] *noun* 1 any substance in the form of fine particles: *soap powder; milk-powder.* □ **poudre**
2 a special kind of substance in this form, used as a cosmetic *etc*: *face-powder; talcum powder.* □ **poudre**
3 formerly, gunpowder: *powder and shot.* □ **poudre**
■ *verb* to put powder on (one's face or body): *She powdered her nose.* □ **poudrer**
'**powdered** *adjective* in the form of fine particles of dust: *powdered chocolate.* □ **en poudre**
'**powdery** *adjective* like powder: *powdery soil.* □ **poudreux**
powder puff a piece of very soft material used to apply face-powder *etc*. □ **houppe(tte)**
power ['pauə] *noun* 1 (an) ability: *A witch has magic power; A cat has the power of seeing in the dark; He no longer has the power to walk.* □ **pouvoir, faculté**
2 strength, force or energy: *muscle power; water-power; (also adjective) a power tool* (= a tool operated by electricity *etc*, not by hand). □ **puissance**
3 authority or control: *political groups fighting for power; How much power does the Queen have?; I have him in my power at last.* □ **pouvoir**
4 a right belonging to *eg* a person in authority: *The police have the power of arrest.* □ **pouvoir**
5 a person with great authority or influence: *He is quite a power in the town.* □ **personne influente**
6 a strong and influential country: *the Western powers.* □ **puissance**
7 the result obtained by multiplying a number by itself a given number of times: $2 \times 2 \times 2$ *or* 2^3 *is the third power of 2, or 2 to the power of 3.* □ **puissance**
'**powered** *adjective* supplied with mechanical power: *The machine is powered by electricity; an electrically-powered machine.* □ **actionné (mécaniquement, électriquement...)**
'**powerful** *adjective* having great strength, influence *etc*: *a powerful engine; He's powerful in local politics.* □ **puissant**
'**powerfully** *adverb*. □ **puissamment**
'**powerfulness** *noun*. □ **puissance**
'**powerless** *adjective* having no power: *The king was powerless to prevent the execution.* □ **impuissant**
'**powerlessness** *noun*. □ **impuissance**
power cut, failure a break in the electricity supply: *We had a power cut last night.* □ **panne de courant**
,**power-'driven** *adjective* worked by electricity or other mechanical means, not by hand. □ **à moteur**
power station a building where electricity is produced. □ **centrale électrique**
be in power (of a political party) to be the governing party. □ **être au pouvoir**
practicable ['praktikəbl] *adjective* able to be used or done: *a practicable plan.* □ **réalisable**

'**practicably** *adverb*. □ **de manière faisable**
'**practicableness** *noun*. □ **praticabilité**
,**practica'bility** *noun*. □ **praticabilité**
practical ['praktikəl] *adjective* 1 concerned with the doing of something: *practical difficulties; Her knowledge is practical rather than theoretical.* □ **pratique**
2 (of a thing, idea *etc*) useful; effective: *You must try to find a practical answer to the problem.* □ **pratique**
3 (*negative* **unpractical**) (of a person) able to do or deal with things well or efficiently: *She can look after herself – she's a very practical child.* □ **qui a le sens pratique**
,**practi'cality** ['ka-] *noun*. □ **sens pratique**
'**practically** *adverb* 1 almost: *The room was practically full.* □ **pratiquement**
2 in a practical way: *Practically, it's more difficult than you think.* □ **en pratique**
practical joke a *usually* irritating joke consisting of an action done to someone, rather than a story told: *He nailed my chair to the floor as a practical joke.* □ **farce**
practice ['praktis] *noun* 1 the actual doing of something, as opposed to the theory or idea: *In theory the plan should work, but in practice there are a lot of difficulties.* □ **pratique**
2 the usual way(s) of doing things: (a) habit or custom: *It was her usual practice to rise at 6:00.* □ **habitude**
3 the repeated performance or exercise of something in order to learn to do it well: *She has musical talent, but she needs a lot of practice; Have a quick practice before you start.* □ **exercice, entraînement**
4 a doctor's or lawyer's business: *She has a practice in Southampton.* □ **clientèle, cabinet**
be in/out of practice (not) having had a lot of practice recently: *I haven't played the piano for months – I'm very out of practice.* □ **être bien entraîné; être rouillé**
make a practice of to do (something) habitually: *She makes a practice of arriving late at parties.* □ **avoir l'habitude de**
put into practice to do, as opposed to planning *etc*: *He never gets the chance to put his ideas into practice.* □ **mettre en pratique**

practice is a noun: **practice** (not **practise**) makes perfect.

practise ['praktis] *verb* 1 to do exercises to improve one's performance in a particular skill *etc*: *She practises the piano every day; You must practise more if you want to enter the competition.* □ **(s')entraîner**
2 to make (something) a habit: *to practise self-control.* □ **(s')exercer (à)**
3 to do or follow (a profession, *usually* medicine or law): *She practises (law) in Montreal.* □ **exercer, pratiquer**
'**practised** *adjective* skilled through much practice: *a practised performer.* □ **expérimenté**

practise is a verb: to **practise** (not **practice**) the guitar.

practitioner *see* general practitioner.
prairie ['preəri] *noun* (*often in plural*) in North America, an area of flat, treeless, grass-covered land. □ **prairie**
praise [preiz] *verb* 1 to express admiration or approval of;

to commend: *He praised her singing.* □ **faire l'éloge de**
2 to glorify (God) by singing hymns *etc: Praise the Lord!*
□ **glorifier**
■ *noun* the expression of approval or honour: *She has received a lot of praise for her musical skill.* □ **éloge(s), louange(s)**
'**praiseworthy** *adjective* deserving praise: *a praiseworthy attempt.* □ **digne d'éloges**

pram [pram] *noun* (*also* **baby carriage**) a kind of small carriage on wheels for carrying a baby, pushed by its mother *etc.* □ **landau**

prance [praːns] *verb* (*eg* of horses) to dance or jump about. □ **caracoler**

prank [praŋk] *noun* a trick; a practical joke. □ **farce, tour**

prattle ['pratl] *verb* to talk or chatter about unimportant things or like a child. □ **babiller, jacasser**
■ *noun* childish talk; chatter. □ **babil(lage)**

prawn [proːn] *noun* a type of edible shellfish like the shrimp. □ **crevette**

pray [prei] *verb* 1 to speak reverently to God or a god in order to express thanks, make a request *etc: Let us pray*; *She prayed to God to help her.* □ **prier**
2 to hope earnestly: *Everybody is praying for rain.* □ **prier (pour)**
'**prayer** *noun* (an) act of praying: *a book of prayer*; *The child said his prayers*; *My prayers have been answered* (= I've got what I desired). □ **prière**

> **pray** is a verb: to **pray** (not **prey**) for peace.

preach [priːtʃ] *verb* 1 to give a talk (called a sermon), *usually* during a religious service, about religious or moral matters: *The vicar preached (a sermon) on/about pride.* □ **prêcher**
2 to speak to someone as though giving a sermon: *Don't preach at me!* □ **sermonner**
3 to advise: *He preaches caution.* □ **prêcher**
'**preacher** *noun.* □ **prédicateur, trice**

prearranged [priːə'reindʒd] *adjective* arranged or agreed previously: *At a prearranged signal, they all rose to their feet.* □ **fixé à l'avance**

precarious [pri'keəriəs] *adjective* insecure; risky or dangerous. □ **précaire**
pre'**cariously** *adverb.* □ **précairement**
pre'**cariousness** *noun.* □ **précarité**

precaution [pri'koːʃən] *noun* care taken to avoid accidents, disease *etc: They took every precaution to ensure that their journey would be safe and enjoyable.* □ **précaution**
pre'**cautionary** *adjective.* □ **préventif**

precede [pri'siːd] *verb* to go, happen *etc* before: *She preceded him into the room.* □ **précéder**
precedence ['presidəns] *noun* (the right of) going before in order of importance *etc: This matter is urgent and should be given precedence over others at the moment.* □ **préséance, priorité**
,**precedent** ['presidənt] *noun* a past action, *especially* a legal decision, which may act as a guide or rule in the future. □ **précédent**
pre'**ceding** *adjective: on the preceding page.* □

précédent

precinct ['priːsiŋkt] *noun* 1 (*often in plural*) the space surrounding a building *etc* (originally within walls or boundaries): *the cathedral precincts.* □ **enceinte**
2 an administrative district: *a police precinct.* □ **circonscription**
pedestrian/shopping precinct an area of shops where no cars are allowed. □ **zone piétonnière**

precious ['preʃəs] *adjective* of great value: *precious jewels.* □ **précieux**
precious metal a valuable metal such as gold, silver or platinum. □ **métal précieux**
precious stone a jewel; a gem: *diamonds, emeralds and other precious stones.* □ **pierre précieuse**
precious few/little very few/little: *I've precious little money left.* □ **bien/fort peu (de)**

precipice ['presipis] *noun* a steep cliff. □ **précipice**
precipitous [pri'sipitəs] *adjective* very steep. □ **escarpé**

precipitate [pri'sipiteit] *verb* to hasten the occurrence of an event.
■ *noun* the substance that settles at the bottom of a liquid. □ **précipité**
precipitous *see* **precipice**.

précis ['preisiz] *– plural* '**précis** [-z] *– noun* a summary of a piece of writing. □ **résumé**

precise [pri'sais] *adjective* 1 exact: *Give me her precise words*; *precise instructions*; *a precise translation.* □ **précis**
2 careful to be accurate and exact in manner, speech *etc: She is always very precise.* □ **précis**
pre'**ciseness** *noun.* □ **précision**
pre'**cisely** *adverb* 1 exactly: *at midday precisely*; *Precisely what do you mean?*; *He spoke very precisely.* □ **précisément**
2 used to express complete agreement: *'So you think we should wait until tomorrow?' 'Precisely.'* □ **précisément**
pre'**cision** [-'siʒən] *noun* exactness; accuracy: *He spoke with great precision*; *(also adjective) precision tools* (= tools used for obtaining very accurate results). □ **(de) précision**

predator ['predətə] *noun* a bird, *eg* a hawk, or animal, *eg* a lion, that attacks and kills others for food. □ **prédateur, de proie**
'**predatory** *adjective* living by attacking and feeding on others: *a predatory animal.* □ **prédateur, de proie**

predecessor ['priːdisesə] *noun* 1 someone who has had a particular job or position before: *She was my predecessor as manager.* □ **prédécesseur**
2 an ancestor: *My predecessors came from Scotland.* □ **ancêtres**

predicament [pri'dikəmənt] *noun* an unfortunate or difficult situation. □ **situation difficile**

predicate ['predikət] *noun* what is said about the subject of a sentence: *We live in Toronto*; *The president of the republic died.* □ **prédicat**

predict [pri'dikt] *verb* to say in advance; to foretell: *He predicted a change in the weather.* □ **prédire**
pre'**dictable** *adjective* (*negative* **unpredictable**) able to be foretold: *Her anger was predictable.* □ **prévisible**

pre'diction [-ʃən] *noun*: *I'm making no predictions about the result of the race.* □ **prédiction**

predominate [pri'dominei̯t] *verb* to be the stronger or greater in amount, size, number *etc*: *In this part of the country industry predominates (over agriculture).* □ **prédominer (sur)**

pre'dominant *adjective* stronger, more numerous, more noticeable *etc*: *The English language is predominant in America.* □ **prédominant**

pre'dominantly *adverb*. □ **de façon prédominante**

pre'dominance *noun*. □ **prédominance**

preen [priːn] *verb* 1 (of birds) to arrange (the feathers): *The sea-gulls were preening themselves/their feathers.* □ **lisser ses plumes**

2 used unkindly, meaning to attend to one's appearance: *The woman was preening herself in front of the mirror.* □ **se pomponner**

prefabricated [priːˈfabrikei̯tid] *adjective* (of a building *etc*) made of parts manufactured in advance and ready to be put together: *prefabricated bungalows.* □ **préfabriqué**

preface ['prefəs] *noun* an introduction to a book *etc*: *The preface explained how to use the dictionary.* □ **préface**

prefect ['priːfekt] *noun* 1 one of a number of senior pupils having special powers in a school *etc*. □ **élève (chargé de la discipline)**

2 in some countries, an administrative official. □ **préfet**

prefer [pri'fəː] – *past tense, past participle* pre'ferred – *verb* to like better: *Which do you prefer – tea or coffee?*; *I prefer reading to watching television*; *She would prefer to come with you rather than stay here.* □ **préférer**

'preferable ['pre-] *adjective* more desirable: *Is it preferable to write or make a telephone call?* □ **préférable**

'preferably *adverb*. □ **de préférence**

'preference ['pre-] *noun* (a) choice of, or (a) liking for, one thing rather than another: *He likes most music but he has a preference for classical music.* □ **préférence**

I **prefer** applies to (not **than**) oranges.
preferable, adjective, is spelt with **-r-**.
preference, noun, is spelt with **-r-**.
preferred and **preferring** are spelt with **-rr-**.

---

prefix ['priːfiks] *noun* a syllable or syllables put at the beginning of another word to change its meaning: *dislike*; *unemployed*; *remake*; *ineffective.* □ **préfixe**

pregnant ['pregnənt] *adjective* carrying unborn young in the womb. □ **enceinte**

'pregnancy (*plural* 'pregnancies) *noun*. □ **grossesse**

prehensile [pri'hensai̯l] *adjective* able to take hold of something: *Most monkeys have prehensile tails.* □ **préhensile**

prehistoric [priːiˈstorik] *adjective* of, or belonging to, the time before recorded history: *a prehistoric monster.* □ **préhistorique**

prehistory *noun* the time period before events and happenings were recorded: *Archeologists have found dinosaur bones that date back to prehistory before much was known about early man.* □ **préhistoire**

prejudge [priːˈdʒʌdʒ] *verb* to make a decision about something before hearing all the facts. □ **préjuger**

prejudice ['predʒədis] *noun* (an) opinion or feeling for or *especially* against something, formed unfairly or unreasonably *ie* without proper knowledge: *The jury must listen to his statement without prejudice*; *Is racial prejudice* (= dislike of people because of their race) *increasing in this country?* □ **préjugé**

■ *verb* 1 to cause to feel prejudice for or against something. □ **prévenir (contre)**

2 to harm or endanger (a person's position, prospects *etc*) in some way: *Your terrible handwriting will prejudice your chances of passing the exam.* □ **faire du tort à, porter préjudice à**

'prejudiced *adjective* having or showing prejudice: *a prejudiced attitude to people of other races*; *Don't be so prejudiced.* □ **qui a des préjugés (sur, contre)**

preliminary [pri'liminəri] *adjective* coming before, and preparing for, something: *The chairman made a few preliminary remarks before introducing the speaker.* □ **préliminaire**

prelude ['preljuːd] *noun* 1 an event *etc* that goes before, and acts as an introduction to, something. □ **prélude**

2 a piece of music played as an introduction to the main piece. □ **prélude**

premature [premə'tʃuə] *adjective* happening *etc* before the right or expected time: *a premature birth*; *The baby was three weeks premature.* □ **prématuré**

,prema'turely *adverb*. □ **prématurément**

premeditated [pri'medi̯tei̯tid] *adjective* thought out in advance; planned: *premeditated murder.* □ **prémédité**

premier ['premiə] *adjective* first or leading: *Italy's premier industrialist.* □ **premier**

■ *noun* a prime minister: *the French premier.* □ **premier ministre**

première ['premiə] *noun* the first performance of a play, film *etc*. □ **première**

premises ['premisiz] *noun plural* (a part of) a building and the area of ground belonging to it: *These premises are used by the local football team.* □ **lieux, locaux**

premonition [premə'niʃən] *noun* a feeling that something (*especially* something unpleasant) is going to happen. □ **pressentiment**

preoccupy [pri'okjupai̯] *verb* to engage or occupy (a person's mind *etc*) or the attention of (someone) completely: *His mind was preoccupied with plans for his holiday.* □ **préoccuper**

pre,occu'pation *noun*. □ **préoccupation**

prepaid *see* prepay.

prepare [pri'peə] *verb* to make or get ready: *Have you prepared your speech for Thursday?*; *My mother prepared a meal*; *He prepared to go out*; *Prepare yourself for a shock.* □ **(se) préparer**

preparation [prepə'rei̯ʃən] *noun* 1 the act of preparing: *You can't pass an exam without preparation.* □ **préparation**

2 something done to prepare: *She was making hasty preparations for her departure.* □ **préparatif(s)**

preparatory [-'parə-] *adjective* acting as an introduction or in order to prepare for something: *Political leaders have agreed to meet for preparatory talks about an end to the war.* □ **préparatoire**

pre'pared *adjective* (*negative* **unprepared**) made ready. □ **préparé**

preparatory school [-'parə-] a private school which educates children in preparation for a senior school (*abbreviation* **prep school** [prep-]). □ **école préparatoire (aux grandes écoles secondaires)**

be prepared (of a person) to be ready (for something, to do something *etc*): *We must be prepared for a disappointment*; *I'm not prepared* (= willing) *to lend him more money*; *The motto of the Scouts is 'Be Prepared!'.* □ **être prêt (pour, à)**

prepay [priː'pei] – *past tense, past participle* ‚**pre'paid** – *verb* to pay in advance. □ **payer (d'avance)**

‚**pre'payment** *noun.* □ **paiement anticipé**

preposition [prepə'ziʃən] *noun* a word put before a noun or pronoun to show how it is related to another word: *through the window*; *in the garden*; *written by me.* □ **préposition**

‚**prepo'sitional** *adjective.* □ **prépositionnel**

preposterous [pri'postərəs] *adjective* very foolish; ridiculous. □ **absurde, grotesque**

pre'posterously *adverb.* □ **grotesquement**

prerequisite [priə'rekwizit] *noun, adjective* (something that is) necessary for something else to be done or happen: *An interest in children is* (*a*) *prerequisite for a teacher.* □ **préalable**

prerogative [prə'rogətiv] *noun* a special right or privilege belonging to a person because of his rank, position *etc*. □ **prérogative**

prescribe [prə'skraib] *verb* to advise or order (the use of): *My doctor prescribed some pills for my cold*; *Here is a list of books prescribed by the examiners for the exam.* □ **prescrire**

pre'scription [-'skrip-] *noun* **1** a doctor's (*usually* written) instructions for the preparing and taking of a medicine: *She gave me a prescription to give to the chemist.* □ **ordonnance**

2 the act of prescribing. □ **prescription**

presence ['prezns] *noun* **1** the state, or fact, of being present: *The committee requests your presence at Thursday's meeting.* □ **présence**

2 a striking, impressive manner or appearance: *The headmistress certainly has presence.* □ **présence**

in the presence of while (someone) is present: *This document must be signed in the presence of a witness*; *Don't talk about it in my mother's presence.* □ **en présence de**

presence of mind calmness and the ability to act sensibly (in an emergency *etc*): *He showed great presence of mind in the face of danger.* □ **présence d'esprit**

present[1] ['preznt] *adjective* **1** being here, or at the place, occasion *etc* mentioned: *My father was present on that occasion*; *Who else was present at the wedding?*; *Now that the whole class is present, we can begin the lesson.* □ **présent**

2 existing now: *the present moment*; *the present prime minister.* □ **actuel**

3 (of the tense of a verb) indicating action now: *In the sentence 'She wants a chocolate', the verb is in the present tense.* □ **présent**

'**presently** *adverb* **1** soon: *She will be here presently.* □ **bientôt**

2 at the present time: *The manager is presently on holiday.* □ **en ce moment, présentement**

the present the time now: *Forget the past – think more of the present and the future!* □ **présent**

at present at the present time: *He's away from home at present.* □ **actuellement, présentement**

for the present as far as the present time is concerned: *You've done enough work for the present.* □ **pour le moment**

present[2] [pri'zent] *verb* **1** to give, *especially* formally or ceremonially: *The child presented a bunch of flowers to the Queen*; *He was presented with a gold watch when he retired.* □ **offrir (à)**

2 to introduce: *May I present my wife* (*to you*)? □ **présenter (à)**

3 to arrange the production of (a play, film *etc*): *The Elizabethan Theatre Company presents 'Hamlet', by William Shakespeare.* □ **présenter**

4 to offer (ideas *etc*) for consideration, or (a problem *etc*) for solving: *She presents* (= expresses) *her ideas very clearly*; *The situation presents a problem.* □ **présenter**

5 to bring (oneself); to appear: *He presented himself at the dinner table half an hour late.* □ **se présenter**

pre'senter *noun.* □ **présentateur, trice**

pre'sentable *adjective* suitable to be seen, introduced *etc*: *You don't look very presentable in those clothes.* □ **présentable**

‚**presen'tation** [pre-] *noun* **1** the act of presenting: *the presentation of the prizes*; *the presentation of a new play*; (*also adjective*) *a presentation ceremony*; *a presentation gold watch.* □ **(de) présentation**

2 the manner in which written work *etc* is presented or set out: *Try to improve the presentation of your work.* □ **présentation**

3 a performance, or set of repeated performances, of a play, opera *etc*: *This is the best presentation of 'Macbeth' that I've ever seen.* □ **représentation**

present arms to hold a rifle upright in front of one, as a salute. □ **présenter les armes**

present[3] ['preznt] *noun* a gift: *a wedding present*; *birthday presents.* □ **cadeau**

presently *see* present[1]. □

preserve [pri'zəːv] *verb* **1** to keep safe from harm: (*May*) *Heaven preserve us from danger!* □ **préserver/protéger (contre)**

2 to keep in existence: *They have managed to preserve many old documents.* □ **conserver**

3 to treat (food), *eg* by cooking it with sugar, so that it will not go bad: *What is the best method of preserving raspberries?* □ **conserver**

■ *noun* **1** an activity, kind of work *etc* in which only certain people are allowed to take part. □ **chasse gardée**

2 a place where game animals, birds *etc* are protected: *a game preserve.* □ **réserve**

3 jam: *blackberry jam and other preserves.* □ **confiture**

‚**preser'vation** [pre-] *noun* the action of preserving or the state or process of being preserved. □ **conservation**

pre'servative [-vətiv] *noun* something that preserves, *especially* that prevents food *etc* from going bad: *a chemical preservative.* □ **agent de conservation**

preside [pri'zaid] *verb* to be the chairman of a meeting *etc*: *The prime minister presided at/over the meeting.* □ **présider**

presidency ['prezidənsi] – *plural* **'presidencies** – *noun* **1** the rank or office of a president: *His ambition is the presidency.* □ **présidence** **2** the period of time for which somebody is president: *during the presidency of Dwight D. Eisenhower.* □ **présidence**

president ['prezidənt] *noun* **1** the leading member of a club, association *etc*: *She was elected president of the Music Society.* □ **président, ente** **2** the leader of a republic: *the President of the United States.* □ **président, ente** **presidential** [prezi'denʃəl] *adjective*: *a presidential election.* □ **présidentiel**

press [pres] *verb* **1** to use a pushing motion (against): *Press the bell twice!; The children pressed close to their mother.* □ **appuyer sur, presser** **2** to squeeze; to flatten: *The grapes are pressed to extract the juice.* □ **écraser, presser** **3** to urge or hurry: *He pressed her to enter the competition.* □ **pousser à** **4** to insist on: *The printers are pressing their claim for higher pay.* □ **presser qqn de** **5** to iron: *Your trousers need to be pressed.* □ **repasser** ■ *noun* **1** an act of pressing: *He gave her hand a press; You had better give your shirt a press.* □ **pression; repassage** **2** (*also* **'printing press**) a printing machine. □ **presse** **3** newspapers in general: *It was reported in the press*; (*also adjective*) *a press photographer.* □ **(de) presse** **4** the people who work on newspapers and magazines; journalists: *The press is/are always interested in the private lives of famous people.* □ **presse** **5** a device or machine for pressing: *a wine-press; a flower-press.* □ **pressoir** **'pressing** *adjective* urgent: *a pressing invitation.* □ **urgent, pressant** **press conference** a meeting in which information is given to journalists. □ **conférence de presse** **'press clipping** *noun* an article cut out of a newspaper or magazine. □ **coupure de presse** **be hard pressed** to be in difficulties: *He's hard pressed financially.* □ **être à la dernière extrémité** **be pressed for** to be short of: *I must hurry – I'm pressed for time.* □ **être à court de** **press for** to try to get; to keep demanding: *The miners are pressing for higher wages.* □ **réclamer avec insistance** **press forward/on** to continue (in spite of difficulties): *She pressed on with her work.* □ **persévérer dans**

pressure ['preʃə] *noun* **1** (the amount of force exerted by) the action of pressing: *to apply pressure to a cut to stop bleeding; A barometer measures atmospheric pressure.* □ **pression** **2** (a) strain or stress: *The pressures of her work are some-*

times too much for her. □ **pression** **3** strong persuasion; compulsion or force: *She agreed under pressure.* □ **(sous) pression** **'pressurize, 'pressurise** *verb* **1** to fit (an airplane *etc*) with a device that keeps air pressure normal: *The cabins have all been pressurized.* □ **pressuriser** **2** to force: *She was pressurized into giving up her job.* □ **forcer à, contraindre de** **pressure cooker** a type of saucepan in which food is cooked quickly by steam kept under great pressure. □ **autocuiseur**

prestige [pre'stiːʒ] *noun* reputation or influence due to success, rank *etc*. □ **prestige**

presume [prə'zjuːm] *verb* **1** to believe that something is true without proof; to take for granted: *When I found the room empty, I presumed that you had gone home*; *'Has she gone?' 'I presume so.'* □ **présumer, supposer** **2** to be bold enough to (act without the right, knowledge *etc* to do so): *I wouldn't presume to advise someone as clever as you.* □ **se permettre de** **pre'sumably** *adverb* I presume: *She's not in her office – presumably she went home early.* □ **vraisemblablement** **pre'sumption** [-'zʌmp-] *noun* **1** something presumed: *She married again, on the presumption that her first husband was dead.* □ **présomption** **2** unsuitable boldness, *eg* in one's behaviour towards another person. □ **impertinence** **pre'sumptuous** [-'zʌmptjuəs] *adjective* impolitely bold. □ **impertinent** **pre'sumptuousness** *noun*. □ **impertinence**

pretend [pri'tend] *verb* **1** to make believe that something is true, in play: *Let's pretend that this room is a cave!*; *Pretend to be a lion!; He wasn't really angry – he was only pretending.* □ **faire semblant (de, que)** **2** to try to make it appear (that something is true), in order to deceive: *He pretended that he had a headache; She was only pretending to be asleep; I pretended not to understand.* □ **faire semblant, prétendre** **pre'tense, pre'tence** [-s] *noun* (an) act of pretending: *Under the pretense of friendship, he persuaded her to lend him money.* □ **prétexte** **false pretenses** acts or behaviour intended to deceive: *He got the money under false pretenses.* □ **moyens frauduleux**

pretext ['priːtekst] *noun* a reason given in order to hide the real reason; an excuse. □ **prétexte**

pretty ['priti] *adjective* **1** (not *usually* of boys and men) pleasing or attractive: *a pretty girl/tune/picture/dress.* □ **joli** **2** used jokingly: *This is a pretty mess!* □ **beau, joli** ■ *adverb* rather: *That's pretty good; He's pretty old now.* □ **assez, plutôt** **'prettily** *adverb*. □ **joliment** **'prettiness** *noun*. □ **joliesse** **pretty much the same, alike** *etc* more or less the same, alike *etc*. □ **à peu près pareil** **pretty well** nearly: *I've pretty well finished.* □ **à peu près**

prevail [pri'veil] *verb* **1** (*with* **over** *or* **against**) to win or succeed: *With God's help we shall prevail over sin and wickedness*; *Truth must prevail in the end.* □ **l'emporter (de, sur)**

2 to be most usual or common: *This mistaken belief still prevails in some parts of the country.* □ **avoir cours**

pre'vailing *adjective* 1 most frequent: *The prevailing winds are from the west.* □ **dominant**

2 common or widespread at the present time: *the prevailing mood of discontent among young people.* □ **du jour**

prevalent ['prevələnt] *adjective* common; widespread: *Lung diseases used to be prevalent among miners.* □ **fréquent**

prevalence ['prevələns] *noun.* □ **prédominance**

prevail on, upon to persuade: *Can I prevail on you to stay for supper?* □ **persuader de**

prevent [pri'vent] *verb* to stop (someone doing something or something happening): *He prevented me from going.* □ **empêcher (de)**

pre'vention [-ʃən] *noun* the act of preventing: *a society for the prevention of road accidents.* □ **prévention**

pre'ventive [-tiv] *adjective* that helps to prevent illness *etc*: *preventive medicine.* □ **préventif**

preview ['pri:vju:] *noun* a viewing of a performance, exhibition *etc* before it is open to the public. □ **avant-première**

previous ['pri:viəs] *adjective* earlier in time or order: *on a previous occasion*; *the previous owner of the house.* □ **précédent**

'previously *adverb.* □ **auparavant**

previous to before: *They told their families about their engagement previous to publishing it in the newspaper.* □ **avant de**

prey [prei] – *plural* **prey** – *noun* a bird or animal, birds or animals, that is/are hunted by other birds or animals for food: *The lion tore at its prey.* □ **proie**

beast/bird of prey an animal, *eg* the lion, or a bird, *eg* the eagle, that kills and eats others. □ **prédateur/oiseau de proie**

prey on, upon to attack as prey: *Hawks prey upon smaller birds.* □ **faire sa proie de**

prey is a noun or a verb: a bird of **prey** *(not* **pray**); *to* **prey on** *(not* **pray on***) smaller creatures.*

price [prais] *noun* 1 the amount of money for which a thing is or can be bought or sold; the cost: *The price of the book was $10.* □ **prix**

2 what one must give up or suffer in order to gain something: *Loss of freedom is often the price of success.* □ **prix**

■ *verb* 1 to mark a price on: *I haven't priced these articles yet.* □ **marquer le prix de**

2 to find out the price of: *He went into the furniture shop to price the beds.* □ **s'informer du prix de**

'priceless *adjective* 1 too valuable to have a price: *priceless jewels.* □ **inestimable**

2 very funny: *a priceless story.* □ **impayable**

'pricey *adjective* expensive. □ **cher**

at a price at a high price: *We can get dinner at this hotel – at a price.* □ **en y mettant le prix**

beyond/without price very precious: *Good health is beyond price.* □ **qui n'a pas de prix**

prick [prik] *verb* to pierce slightly or stick a sharp point into: *She pricked her finger on a pin*; *He pricked a hole in the paper.* □ **piquer, percer**

■ *noun* 1 (a pain caused by) an act of pricking: *You'll just feel a slight prick in your arm.* □ **piqûre**

2 a tiny hole made by a sharp point: *a pin-prick.* □ **trou (d'épingle)**

prick (up) one's ears (of an animal) to raise the ears in excitement, attention *etc*: *The dog pricked up its ears at the sound of the doorbell.* □ **dresser l'oreille**

prickle ['prikl] *noun* 1 a sharp point growing on a plant or animal: *A hedgehog is covered with prickles.* □ **piquant**

2 a feeling of being pricked: *a prickle of fear.* □ **(sensation de) picotement**

'prickly *adjective* 1 covered with prickles: *Holly is a prickly plant.* □ **épineux, hérissé**

2 pricking; stinging: *a prickly rash.* □ **cuisant**

'prickliness *noun.* □ **hérissement**

pride [praid] *noun* 1 a feeling of pleasure and satisfaction at one's achievements, possessions, family *etc*: *She looked with pride at her beautiful daughters.* □ **fierté**

2 personal dignity: *His pride was hurt by her criticism.* □ **fierté, amour-propre**

3 a group (of lions or of peacocks): *a pride of lions.* □ **troupe**

4 a high or exaggerated opinion of one's dignity or character; an extreme regard for one's own importance or position: *Darren's stubbornness and pride stopped him from apologizing when he was wrong.* □ **orgueil**

be the pride and joy of to be the object of the pride of: *She was her parents' pride and joy.* □ **être la fierté de**

the pride of the finest thing in (a certain group *etc*): *The pride of our collection is this painting.* □ **joyau**

pride of place the most important place: *They gave pride of place at the exhibition to a Chinese vase.* □ **place d'honneur**

pride oneself on to take pride in, or feel satisfaction with (something one has done, achieved *etc*): *She prides herself on her driving skill.* □ **être fier de**

take pride in to feel pride about: *You should take more pride in* (= care more for) *your appearance.* □ **prendre soin de**

priest [pri:st] *noun* 1 (in the Christian Church, *especially* the Roman Catholic, Orthodox and Anglican churches) a clergyman. □ **prêtre**

2 (*feminine* **'priestess**) (in non-Christian religions) an official who performs sacrifices *etc* to the god(s). □ **prêtre, esse**

'priesthood *noun* 1 priests in general: *the Anglican priesthood.* □ **clergé**

2 the office or position of a priest: *He was called to the priesthood.* □ **prêtrise**

prig [prig] *noun* a person who is too satisfied with his/her own behaviour, beliefs *etc*. □ **poseur, euse**

'priggish *adjective.* □ **suffisant**

'priggishly *adverb.* □ **d'une manière suffisante**

'priggishness *noun.* □ **suffisance**

prim [prim] *adjective* (of a person, behaviour *etc*) too formal and correct: *a prim manner*; *a prim old lady*. □ **guindé**
'**primly** *adverb*. □ **d'une manière guindée**
'**primness** *noun*. □ **façons compassées**
prima ['priːmə]: **prima ballerina** the leading female dancer in a ballet company. □ **danseuse étoile**
prima donna [-'dɒnə] a leading female opera singer. □ **prima donna**
primaeval *see* primeval.
primary *see* prime[1].
primate[1] ['praimeit] *noun* an archbishop. □ **primat**
primate[2] ['praimət] *noun* a member of the highest order of mammals, *ie* man, monkeys, apes, lemurs. □ **primate**
prime[1] [praim] *adjective* **1** first or most important: *the prime minister*; *a matter of prime importance*. □ **premier**
2 best: *in prime condition*. □ **parfait**
■ *noun* the best part (of a person's *etc* life, *usually* early middle age): *She is in her prime*; *the prime of life*. □ **fleur de l'âge**
'**primary** *adjective* **1** first or most important: *his primary concern*. □ **principal**
2 of the first level or stage: *a primary school*. □ **primaire**
'**primarily** [prai'me-] *adverb* chiefly; in the first place: *I wrote the play primarily as a protest, and only secondarily as entertainment*. □ **principalement**
primary colours (of pigments, but not of light) those colours from which all others can be made, *ie* red, blue and yellow. □ **couleurs fondamentales**
prime minister the chief minister of a government. □ **premier ministre**
prime number a number that can only be divided without a remainder by itself and 1, *eg* 3, 5, 7, 31. □ **nombre premier**
prime[2] [praim] *verb* to prepare (something) by putting something into or on it: *He primed* (= put gunpowder into) *his gun*; *You must prime* (= treat with primer) *the wood before you paint it*. □ **amorcer, apprêter**
'**primer** *noun* **1** a book that gives basic information about a subject. □ **manuel d'introduction**
2 a substance put on a surface to prime it before painting. □ **apprêt**
primitive ['primətiv] *adjective* **1** belonging to the earliest times: *primitive stone tools*. □ **primitif**
2 simple or rough: *He made a primitive boat out of some pieces of wood*. □ **primitif**
primrose ['primrouz] *noun* **1** a kind of pale yellow spring flower common in woods and hedges. □ **primevère**
2 (*also adjective*) (of) its colour: *primrose walls*. □ (**jaune**) **primevère**
prince [prins] *noun* **1** a male member of a royal family, *especially* the son of a king or queen: *Prince Charles*. □ **prince**
2 the ruler of some states or countries: *Prince Rainier of Monaco*. □ **prince**
'**princely** *adjective* **1** of a prince: *princely duties*. □ **princier**
2 magnificent; splendid: *a princely gift*. □ **princier**

princess [prin'ses, 'prinsəs] *noun* **1** the wife or widow of a prince. □ **princesse**
2 a woman of the same rank as a prince in her own right: *Princess Anne*. □ **princesse**
princi'pality [-'pa-] – *plural* ,**princi'palities** – *noun* a state or country ruled by a prince. □ **principauté**
principal ['prinsəpəl] *adjective* most important: *Shipbuilding was one of Egypt's principal industries*. □ **principal**
■ *noun* **1** the head of a school, college or university. □ **directeur, trice**
2 a leading actor, singer or dancer in a theatrical production. □ **premier rôle**
3 the amount of money in a bank *etc* on which interest is paid. □ **capital**
'**principally** *adverb* mostly; chiefly: *I am principally concerned with teaching English*. □ **principalement**

the **principal** (not **principle**) dancer.
principal (not **principle**) of the college.

principality *see* prince.
principle ['prinsəpəl] *noun* **1** a general truth, rule or law: *the principle of gravity*. □ **principe**
2 the theory by which a machine *etc* works: *the principle of the jet engine*. □ **principe**
'**principles** *noun plural* one's own personal rules or standards of behaviour: *It is against my principles to borrow money*. □ **principes**
in principle in general, as opposed to in detail. □ **en principe**
on principle because of one's principles: *I never borrow money, on principle*. □ **par principe**

high moral **principles** (not **principals**).

print [print] *noun* **1** a mark made by pressure: *a footprint*; *a fingerprint*. □ **trace, empreinte**
2 printed lettering: *I can't read the print in this book*. □ **caractères**
3 a photograph made from a negative: *I entered three prints for the photographic competition*. □ **épreuve**
4 a printed reproduction of a painting or drawing. □ **gravure**
■ *verb* **1** to mark (letters *etc*) on paper (by using a printing press *etc*): *The invitations will be printed on white paper*. □ **imprimer**
2 to publish (a book, article *etc*) in printed form: *Her new novel will be printed next month*. □ **publier**
3 to produce (a photographic image) on paper: *She develops and prints her own photographs*. □ **tirer une épreuve**
4 to mark designs on (cloth *etc*): *When the cloth has been woven, it is dyed and printed*. □ **imprimer**
5 to write, using capital letters: *Please print your name and address*. □ **écrire en majuscules**
'**printer** *noun* a person who prints books, newspapers *etc*. □ **imprimeur**
'**printing** *noun* the work of a printer. □ **impression**
'**printing press** *noun* (*also* **press**) a machine for printing. □ **presse typographique**
'**printout** *noun* the printed information given by a com-

puter. □ **impression**

in/out of print (of books) available/unavailable to be bought from the publisher: *That book has been out of print for years.* □ **disponible; épuisé**

prior[1] ['praiə] *adjective* **1** already arranged for the same time: *a prior engagement.* □ **antérieur**

2 more important: *He gave up his job as he felt his health had a prior claim on his attention.* □ **prioritaire**

pri'ority [-'o-] **1** the right to be or go first: *An ambulance may have priority over other traffic.* □ **priorité**

2 (*plural* **pri'orities**) something that must be considered or done first: *Our (first) priority is to feed the hungry.* □ **priorité**

prior to before: *Prior to working in America, he had travelled in Europe.* □ **avant de**

prior[2] ['praiə] – *feminine* '**prioress** – *noun* the head of a priory. □ **prieur, eure**

'**priory** – *plural* '**priories** – *noun* a building in which a community of monks or nuns live. □ **prieuré**

prise, prize [praiz] *verb* to use force to dislodge (something) from its position: *She prised open the lid with a knife.* □ **forcer, ouvrir de force**

prism ['prizm] *noun* **1** a solid figure whose sides are parallel and whose two ends are the same in shape and size. □ **prisme**

2 a glass object of this shape, *usually* with triangular ends, which breaks up a beam of white light into the colours of the rainbow. □ **prisme**

pris'matic [-'ma-] *adjective*. □ **prismatique**

prison ['prizn] *noun* a building in which criminals are kept; a jail: *He was sent to prison*; *He is in prison.* □ **prison**

'**prisoner** *noun* anyone who has been captured and is held against his will as a criminal, in a war *etc*: *The prisoners escaped from jail.* □ **prisonnier, ière**

prisoner of war – *plural* **prisoners of war** – a member of the armed forces captured in a war. □ **prisonnier de guerre**

take, keep, hold prisoner to (capture and) confine (a person) against his will: *Many soldiers were killed and the rest taken prisoner*; *She was kept prisoner in a locked room.* □ **faire prisonnier**

private ['praivət] *adjective* **1** of, for, or belonging to, one person or group, not to the general public: *The headmaster lives in a private apartment in the school*; *in my private* (= personal) *opinion*; *This information is to be kept strictly private*; *You shouldn't listen to private conversations.* □ **privé**

2 having no public or official position or rank: *It is your duty as a private citizen to report this matter to the police.* □ **simple (citoyen, enne)**

■ *noun* in the army, an ordinary soldier, not an officer. □ **(simple) soldat**

privacy ['privəsi] *noun* the state of being away from other people's sight or interest: *in the privacy of your own home.* □ **intimité**

'**privately** *adverb*. □ **en privé**

private enterprise the management and financing of industry *etc* by individual persons or companies and not by the state. □ **entreprise privée**

private means money that does not come from one's work but from investment, inheritance *etc*. □ **fortune personnelle**

in private with no one else listening or watching; not in public: *May I speak to you in private?* □ **en privé**

privation [prai'veiʃən] *noun* poverty; hardship. □ **privation**

privilege ['privəlidʒ] *noun* (a) favour or right available, or granted, to only one person, or to a small number of people: *Senior students are usually allowed certain privileges.* □ **privilège, passe-droit**

'**privileged** *adjective*. □ **privilégié**

privy ['privi]: **privy council** a group of statesmen appointed as advisers to a king or queen. □ **conseil privé**

prize[1] [praiz] *noun* **1** a reward for good work *etc*: *She was awarded a lot of prizes at school.* □ **prix**

2 something won in a competition *etc*: *I've won first prize!*; (*also adjective*) *a prize* (= having won, or worthy of, a prize) *bull.* □ **prix; primé**

■ *verb* to value highly: *She prized my friendship above everything else.* □ **attacher beaucoup de prix à**

prize[2] *see* **prise.**

pro[1] [prou] short for **professional.**

pro[2] [prou]: **pros and cons** [prouzən'konz] the arguments for and against: *Let's hear all the pros and cons before we make a decision.* □ **le pour et le contre**Brit

pro- [prou] in favour of: **pro-American.** □ **pro-**

probable ['probəbl] *adjective* that may be expected to happen or be true; likely: *the probable result*; *Such an event is possible but not probable.* □ **probable**

'**probably** *adverb*: *I'll probably telephone you this evening.* □ **probablement**

proba'bility – *plural* **proba'bilities** – *noun* **1** the state or fact of being probable; likelihood: *There isn't much probability of that happening.* □ **probabilité**

2 an event, result *etc* that is probable: *Let's consider the probabilities.* □ **probabilité**

in all probability most probably; most likely. □ **selon toute probabilité**

probation [prə'beiʃən, prou-] *noun* **1** the system allowing people who have broken the law to go free on condition that they commit no more crimes and report regularly to a social worker. □ **(mise en) liberté surveillée**

2 (in certain jobs) a period of time during which a person is carefully watched to see that he is capable of the job. □ **stage**

pro'bationary *adjective*. □ **d'essai**

be/put on probation to (cause to) undergo a period of probation. □ **être/mettre en stage probatoire**

probe [proub] *noun* **1** a long thin instrument used by doctors to examine a wound *etc*. □ **sonde**

2 an investigation: *a police probe into illegal activities.* □ **enquête**

■ *verb* **1** to investigate: *He probed into his private life.* □ **enquêter (sur)**

2 to examine (as if) with a probe: *The doctor probed the wound*; *He probed about in the hole with a stick.* □ **sonder**

problem ['probləm] *noun* **1** a difficulty; a matter about which it is difficult to decide what to do: *Life is full of* *problems*; (*also adjective*) *a problem child.* □ **problème; difficile**

2 a question to be answered or solved: *mathematical problems.* □ **problème**

‚proble'matic(al) [-'ma-] *adjective.* □ **problématique**

proboscis [prə'bosis] *noun* a nose, or mouth-part in certain animals, insects *etc.* □ **trompe**

procedure [prə'siːdʒə] *noun* the order or method of doing something: *They followed the usual procedure(s).* □ **procédure**

pro'cedural *adjective.* □ **de procédure**

proceed [prə'siːd] *verb* **1** to go on; to continue: *They proceeded along the road*; *They proceeded with their work.* □ **avancer**

2 to follow a course of action: *I want to make a cupboard, but I don't know how to proceed.* □ **procéder**

3 to begin (to do something): *They proceeded to ask a lot of questions.* □ **commencer (à)**

4 to result: *Fear often proceeds from ignorance.* □ **provenir (de)**

5 to take legal action (against): *The police decided not to proceed against her.* □ **engager des poursuites (contre)**

pro'ceedings *noun plural* **1** the things said and done at a meeting of a society *etc.* □ **débats**

2 a legal action: *We shall start proceedings against him if the bill is not paid.* □ **poursuites**

proceeds ['prousiːdz] *noun plural* money or profit made (from a sale *etc*): *They gave the proceeds of the sale to charity.* □ **produit**

process ['prouses, 'pro-] *noun* **1** a method or way of manufacturing things: *We are using a new process to make glass.* □ **procédé**

2 a series of events that produce change or development: *The process of growing up can be difficult for a child; the digestive processes.* □ **processus**

3 a course of action undertaken: *Carrying him down the mountain was a slow process.* □ **opération**

■ *verb* to deal with (something) by the appropriate process: *Have your photographs been processed?*; *The information is being processed by computer.* □ **développer; traiter**

'processed *adjective* (of food) treated in a special way: *processed cheese/peas.* □ **préparé industriellement**

in the process of in the course of: *He is in the process of changing jobs*; *These goods were damaged in the process of manufacture.* □ **en train de, au cours de**

procession [prə'seʃən] *noun* a line of people, vehicles *etc* moving forward in order, *especially* for a ceremonial purpose: *The procession moved slowly through the streets.* □ **cortège**

proclaim [prə'kleim, prou-] *verb* to announce or state publicly: *He was proclaimed the winner.* □ **proclamer**

procla'mation [proklə-] *noun* **1** an official, *usually* ceremonial, announcement made to the public: *a royal proclamation.* □ **proclamation**

2 the act of proclaiming. □ **proclamation**

procrastinate [prə'krastineit] *verb* to delay or put off doing something: *Stop procrastinating and do it now!* □ **remettre à plus tard**

procure [prə'kjuə] *verb* to get or obtain: *She managed to procure a car.* □ **(se) procurer**

prod [prod] – *past tense, past participle* **'prodded** – *verb* **1** to push with something pointed; to poke: *He prodded her arm with his finger.* □ **pousser**

2 to urge or encourage: *He prodded her into action.* □ **pousser (qqn à faire qqch.)**

■ *noun* an act of prodding: *She gave him a prod.* □ **petit coup (de doigt, etc.)**

prodigal ['prodigəl] *adjective* spending (money *etc*) too extravagantly; wasteful. □ **prodigue**

'prodigally *adverb.* □ **avec prodigalité**

‚prodi'gality [-'ga-] *noun.* □ **prodigalité**

prodigy ['prodidʒi] – *plural* **'prodigies** – *noun* something strange and wonderful: *A very clever child is sometimes called a child prodigy; prodigies of nature.* □ **prodige**

produce [prə'djuːs] *verb* **1** to bring out: *She produced a letter from her pocket.* □ **sortir (de)**

2 to give birth to: *A cow produces one or two calves a year.* □ **donner naissance à**

3 to cause: *Her joke produced a shriek of laughter from the children.* □ **provoquer, occasionner**

4 to make or manufacture: *The factory produces furniture.* □ **produire**

5 to give or yield: *The country produces enough food for the population.* □ **produire**

6 to arrange and prepare (a theatre performance, film, television program *etc*): *The play was produced by Henry Dobson.* □ **mettre en scène; produire; réaliser**

■ ['prodjuːs] *noun* something that is produced, *especially* crops, eggs, milk *etc* from farms: *agricultural/farm produce.* □ **produits (alimentaires/agricoles)**

pro'ducer *noun* a person who produces a play, film *etc* but is *usually* not responsible for instructing the actors. □ **producteur, trice**

product ['prodʌkt] *noun* **1** a result: *The plan was the product of hours of thought.* □ **produit, résultat**

2 something manufactured: *The firm manufactures metal products.* □ **produit**

3 the result of multiplying one number by another: *The product of 9 and 2 is 18.* □ **produit**

pro'duction [-'dʌkʃən] *noun* **1** the act or process of producing something: *car-production; The production of the film cost a million dollars.* □ **production**

2 the amount produced, *especially* of manufactured goods: *The new methods increased production.* □ **production**

3 a particular performance, or set of repeated performances, of a play *etc*: *I prefer this production of 'Hamlet' to the one I saw two years ago.* □ **mise en scène**

pro'ductive [-'dʌktiv] *adjective* (*negative* **unproductive**) producing a lot; fruitful: *productive land; Our discussion was not very productive.* □ **fertile, fructueux**

productivity [prodək'tivəti] *noun* the rate or efficiency of work *especially* in industrial production. □ **productivité**

profess [prə'fes] *verb* **1** to state or declare openly. □ **professer**

2 to claim or pretend: *He professed to be an expert.* □

prétendre

pro'fession [-ʃən] *noun* 1 an occupation or job that needs special knowledge, *eg* medicine, law, teaching, engineering *etc*. □ **profession**

2 the people who have such an occupation: *the legal profession*. □ **profession**

3 an open statement or declaration. □ **déclaration**

pro'fessional [-ʃə-] *adjective* (*negative* **unprofessional**) 1 of a profession: *professional skill*. □ **professionnel**

2 of a very high standard: *a very professional performance*. □ **excellent**

3 earning money by performing, or giving instruction, in a sport or other activity that is a pastime for other people; not amateur: *a professional musician/golfer*. □ **professionnel**

■ *noun* (*abbreviation* **pro** [prou]) a person who is professional: *a golf professional/pro*. □ **professionnel, elle**

pro'fessionally *adverb*. □ **professionnellement**

professor [prə'fesə] *noun* (*often abbreviated to* **Prof.** *when written*) 1 a university teacher who is the head of a department: *He is a professor of English at Leeds*; *Professor Jones*. □ **professeur, eure titulaire**

2 a university teacher. □ **professeur, eure**

,profes'sorial [profə'sɔː-] *adjective*. □ **professoral**

pro'fessorship *noun* the post of a professor. □ **chaire**

proficient [prə'fiʃənt] *adjective* skilled; expert. □ **(très) compétent (en)**

pro'ficiently *adverb*. □ **avec ne grande compétence**

pro'ficiency *noun*. □ **grande compétence**

profile ['proufail] *noun* the view of a face, head *etc* from the side; a side view: *She has a beautiful profile*. □ **profil**

profit ['profit] *noun* 1 money which is gained in business *etc*, *eg* from selling something for more than one paid for it: *I made a profit of $8,000 on my house*; *She sold it at a huge profit*. □ **profit, bénéfice**

2 advantage; benefit: *A great deal of profit can be had from travelling abroad*. □ **profit**

■ *verb* – *past tense, past participle* **'profited** – (*with* **from** *or* **by**) to gain profit(s) from: *The business profited from its exports*; *He profited by his opponent's mistakes*. □ **tirer profit de**

'profitable *adjective* (*negative* **unprofitable**) giving profit: *The deal was quite profitable*; *a profitable experience*. □ **profitable**

'profitably *adverb*. □ **avec profit**

profound [prə'faund] *adjective* 1 deep: *profound sleep*. □ **profond**

2 showing great knowledge or understanding: *a profound remark*. □ **profond**

pro'foundly *adverb*. □ **profondément**

pro'fundity [-'fʌn-] *noun*. □ **profondeur**

profuse [prə'fjuːs] *adjective* (too) plentiful; excessive: *profuse thanks*. □ **abondant**

pro'fusely *adverb*. □ **en abondance**

pro'fusion [-ʒən] *noun* (*sometimes with* **a**) (too) great abundance: *a profusion of flowers*. □ **profusion**

program, programme ['prougram] *noun* 1 (a booklet or paper giving the details of) the planned events in an entertainment *etc*: *According to the program, the show begins at 8:00*. □ **programme**

2 a plan or scheme: *a program of reforms*. □ **programme**

3 'program a set of data, instructions *etc* put into a computer. □ **programme**

'program *verb* – *present participle* **'programming, 'programing**: *past tense, past participle* **'programmed, 'programed** – to give information, instructions *etc* to (a machine, *especially* a computer, so that it can do a particular job). □ **programmer**

'programmer *noun* a person who prepares a program for a computer. □ **programmeur, euse**

programming *noun* the plan for radio or television shows: *The programming on the CBC concentrates on shows with Canadian content*. □ **programmation**

progress ['prougres] *noun* 1 movement forward; advance: *the progress of civilization*. □ **progrès**

2 improvement: *The students are making* (*good*) *progress*. □ **progrès**

■ [prə'gres] *verb* 1 to go forward: *We had progressed only a few kilometres when the car broke down*. □ **avancer**

2 to improve: *Your French is progressing*. □ **faire des progrès**

pro'gressive [-siv] *adjective* 1 developing and advancing by stages: *a progressive illness*. □ **progressif**

2 using, or favouring, new methods: *progressive education*; *The new headmaster is very progressive*. □ **progressiste**

pro'gressively *adverb*. □ **progressivement**

pro'gressiveness *noun*. □ **progressivité**

in progress happening; taking place: *There is a meeting in progress*. □ **en cours**

prohibit [prə'hibit] *verb* to forbid: *Smoking is prohibited*. □ **interdire**

prohibition [proui'biʃən] *noun* 1 the act of prohibiting: *We demand the prohibition by the government of the sale of this drug*. □ **interdiction**

2 a rule, law *etc* forbidding something: *The headmaster issued a prohibition against bringing knives into school*. □ **interdiction**

project ['prodʒekt] *noun* 1 a plan or scheme: *a building project*. □ **projet**

2 a piece of study or research: *I am doing a project on Italian art*. □ **étude (sur)**

■ [prə'dʒekt] *verb* 1 to throw outwards, forwards or upwards: *The missile was projected into space*. □ **projeter**

2 to stick out: *A sharp rock projected from the sea*. □ **faire saillie**

3 to plan or propose. □ **projeter (de)**

pro'jectile [-tail] *noun* something that is thrown, *usually* as a weapon. □ **projectile**

pro'jection [-ʃən] *noun*. □ **projection**

pro'jector *noun* a machine for projecting films on to a screen. □ **projecteur**

prologue ['proulog] *noun* an introduction, *especially* to a play. □ **prologue**

prolong [prə'loŋ] *verb* to make longer: *Please do not prolong the discussion unnecessarily*. □ **prolonger**

prolongation [proulɔŋ'geiʃən] *noun*. □ **prolongation**

pro'longed *adjective* very long: *prolonged discussions*.

□ **prolongé**

prom [prom] *see* **promenade**.

promenade [promə'naːd] *noun* (*abbreviation* **prom** [prom]) a level road for the public to walk along, *usually* beside the sea: *They went for a walk along the promenade.* □ **promenade**

prominent ['prominənt] *adjective* 1 standing out; projecting: *prominent front teeth.* □ **proéminent**

2 easily seen: *The tower is a prominent landmark.* □ **marquant**

3 famous: *a prominent politician.* □ **important, très en vue**

'**prominently** *adverb.* □ **bien en vue**

'**prominence** *noun.* □ **importance**

promise ['promis] *verb* 1 to say, or give one's word (that one will, or will not, do something *etc*): *I promise (that) I won't be late; I promise not to be late; I won't be late, I promise (you)!* □ **promettre (de)**

2 to say or give one's assurance that one will give: *He promised me a new bike.* □ **promettre**

3 to show signs of future events or developments: *This situation promises well for the future.* □ **promettre**

■ *noun* 1 something promised: *She made a promise; I'll go with you – that's a promise!* □ **promesse**

2 a sign of future success: *She shows great promise in her work.* □ **avenir**

'**promising** *adjective* showing promise; likely to be good: *She's a promising pianist; Her work is promising.* □ **prometteur**

promontory ['proməntəri] – *plural* '**promontories** – *noun* a piece of land that projects from the coastline. □ **promontoire**

promote [prə'mout] *verb* 1 to raise (to a higher rank or position): *She was promoted to head teacher.* □ **promouvoir**

2 to encourage, organize, or help the progress of: *He worked hard to promote peace/this scheme.* □ **promouvoir**

3 to encourage the buying of; to advertise: *We are promoting a new brand of soap-powder.* □ **promouvoir**

pro'**moter** *noun.* □ **organisateur, trice**

pro'**motion** [-ʃən] *noun* 1 the raising of a person to a higher rank or position: *She has just been given (a) promotion.* □ **promotion**

2 encouragement (of a cause, charity *etc*): *the promotion of world peace.* □ **promotion**

3 the activity of advertising a product *etc*: *He is against the promotion of cigarettes.* □ **promotion**

prompt[1] [prompt] *adjective* acting, or happening, without delay or punctually: *a prompt reply; I'm surprised that she's late. She's usually so prompt.* □ **prompt, ponctuel**

'**promptly** *adverb* 1 immediately: *She promptly accepted my offer.* □ **promptement**

2 punctually: *They arrived promptly.* □ **à l'heure**

'**promptness** *noun.* □ **promptitude**

at one/two *etc* **o'clock prompt** punctually at one/two *etc* o'clock. □ **pile**

prompt[2] [prompt] *verb* 1 to persuade to do something: *What prompted you to say that?* □ **pousser à**

2 to remind (*especially* an actor) of the words that he is to say: *Several actors forgot their words and had to be prompted.* □ **souffler**

'**prompter** *noun.* □ **souffleur, euse**

prone [proun] *adjective* 1 lying flat, *especially* face downwards. □ **couché sur le ventre**

2 (*with* **to**) inclined to; likely to experience *etc*: *He is prone to illness.* □ **prédisposé à**

prong [proŋ] *noun* a spike of a fork. □ **dent**

pronged *adjective*: *a pronged instrument; a two-pronged fork.* □ **à dents**

pronoun ['prounaun] *noun* a word used instead of a noun (or a phrase containing a noun): *'He', 'it', 'who', and 'anything' are pronouns.* □ **pronom**

pronounce [prə'nauns] *verb* 1 to speak (words or sounds, *especially* in a certain way): *He pronounced my name wrongly; The 'b' in 'lamb' and the 'k' in 'knob' are not pronounced.* □ **prononcer**

2 to announce officially or formally: *He pronounced judgment on the prisoner.* □ **prononcer**

pro'**nounceable** *adjective* (*negative* **unpronounceable**) able to be pronounced. □ **prononçable**

pro'**nounced** *adjective* noticeable; definite: *He walks with a pronounced limp.* □ **prononcé**

pro'**nouncement** *noun* an announcement. □ **déclaration**

pro,nunci'**ation** [-nʌnsi-] *noun* the act, or a way, of saying a word *etc*: *He had difficulty with the pronunciation of her name.* □ **prononciation**

proof [pruːf] *noun* 1 (a piece of) evidence, information *etc* that shows definitely that something is true: *We still have no proof that he is innocent.* □ **preuve**

2 a first copy of a printed sheet, that can be corrected before the final printing: *She was correcting the proofs of her novel.* □ **épreuve**

3 in photography, the first print from a negative. □ **épreuve**

-**proof** able to withstand or avoid something: *waterproof covering.* □ **à l'épreuve de**

prop[1] [prop] *noun* a support: *The ceiling was held up with wooden props.* □ **support**

■ *verb* – *past tense, past participle* **propped** – to lean (something) against something else: *She propped her bicycle against the wall.* □ **appuyer (contre)**

prop up to support (something) in an upright position, or stop it from falling: *We had to prop up the roof; She propped herself up against the wall.* □ **appuyer**

prop[2] *see* **property**.

propaganda [propə'gandə] *noun* the activity of spreading particular ideas, opinions *etc* according to an organized plan, *eg* by a government; the ideas *etc* spread in this way: *political propaganda.* □ **propagande**

propagate ['propəgeit] *verb* 1 to spread (news *etc*). □ **(se) propager**

2 to (make plants) produce seeds. □ **(se) propager**

,propa'**gation** *noun.* □ **propagation**

propel [prə'pel] – *past tense, past participle* **pro'pelled** – *verb* – to drive forward, *especially* mechanically: *The boat is propelled by a diesel engine.* □ **propulser**

pro'**peller** *noun* a device, consisting of revolving blades, used to drive a ship or an aircraft. □ **hélice**

pro'pulsion [-'pʌlʃən] *noun* the process of propelling or being propelled: *jet-propulsion.* □ **propulsion**

proper ['propə] *adjective* **1** right, correct, or suitable: *That isn't the proper way to clean the windows; You should have done your schoolwork at the proper time – it's too late to start now.* □ **correct**
2 complete or thorough: *Have you made a proper search?* □ **convenable**
3 respectable or well-mannered: *Such behaviour isn't quite proper.* □ **comme il faut**
'**properly** *adverb* **1** correctly or rightly: *She can't pronounce my name properly.* □ **convenablement**
2 completely or thoroughly: *I didn't have time to read the book properly.* □ **complètement**
proper noun/name a noun or name which names a particular person, thing or place (beginning with a capital letter): *'Mary' and 'New York' are proper nouns.* □ **nom propre**

property ['propəti] – *plural* '**properties** – *noun* **1** something that a person owns: *These books are my property.* □ **propriété**
2 land or buildings that a person owns: *She has property in Scotland.* □ **propriété**
3 a quality (*usually* of a substance): *Hardness is a property of diamonds.* □ **propriété**
4 (*usually abbreviated to* **prop** [prop]) a small piece of furniture or an article used by an actor in a play. □ **accessoire**

prophecy ['profəsi] – *plural* '**prophecies** – *noun* **1** the power of foretelling the future. □ **prophétie**
2 something that is foretold: *He made many prophecies about the future.* □ **prophétie**
'**prophesy** [-sai] *verb* to foretell: *He prophesied (that there would be) another war.* □ **prédire**
'**prophet** [-fit] – *feminine* '**prophetess** – *noun* **1** a person who (believes that he) is able to foretell the future. □ **prophète, prophétesse**
2 a person who tells people what God wants, intends *etc*: *the prophet Isaiah.* □ **prophète, prophétesse**
pro'phetic [-'fe-] *adjective*. □ **prophétique**
pro'phetically *adverb*. □ **prophétiquement**

prophecy is a noun: Her **prophecy** (not **prophesy**) came true.
prophesy is a verb: to **prophesy** (not **prophecy**) the future.

proportion [prə'poːʃən] *noun* **1** a part (of a total amount): *Only a small proportion of the class passed the exam.* □ **proportion, pourcentage**
2 the (correct) quantity, size, number *etc* (of one thing compared with that of another): *For this dish, the butter and flour should be in the proportion of three to four (= eg 300 grams of butter with every 400 grams of flour).* □ **proportion**
pro'portional *adjective*. □ **proportionnel**
pro'portionally *adverb*. □ **proportionnellement**
pro'portionate [-nət] *adjective* being in correct proportion: *Are his wages really proportionate to the amount of work he does?* □ **proportionné (à)**
pro'portionately *adverb*. □ **proportionnellement**

be, get *etc* **in proportion (to)** to (cause to) have a correct relationship (to each other or something else): *In drawing a person, it is difficult to get all the parts of the body in proportion.* □ **être bien proportionnée; respecter les proportions**
be, get *etc* **out of (all) proportion (to)** to (cause to) have an incorrect relationship (to each other or something else): *An elephant's tail seems out of (all) proportion to the rest of its body.* □ **être disproportionné à/ avec; ne pas respecter les proportions**
in proportion to in relation to; in comparison with: *You spend far too much time on that work in proportion to its importance.* □ **en proportion de**

propose [prə'pouz] *verb* **1** to offer for consideration; to suggest: *I proposed my friend for the job; Who proposed this scheme?* □ **proposer**
2 to intend: *He proposes to build a new house.* □ **(se) proposer de**
3 to make an offer of marriage: *He proposed (to me) last night and I accepted him.* □ **demander qqn en mariage**
pro'posal *noun* **1** something proposed or suggested; a plan: *proposals for peace.* □ **proposition**
2 an offer of marriage: *She received three proposals.* □ **demande en mariage**
3 the act of proposing. □ **proposition**
proposition [propə'ziʃən] *noun* **1** a proposal or suggestion. □ **proposition**
2 a thing or situation that must be done or dealt with: *a difficult proposition.* □ **affaire**

proprietor [prə'praiətə] – *feminine* **pro'prietress** – *noun* an owner, *especially* of a shop, hotel *etc*. □ **propriétaire**
propriety [prə'praiəti] *noun* correctness of behaviour; decency; rightness. □ **bienséance**
propulsion *see* **propel**.
prose [prouz] *noun* writing that is not in verse; ordinary written or spoken language. □ **prose**
prosecute ['prosikjuːt] *verb* to bring a legal action against: *He was prosecuted for theft.* □ **poursuivre**
,**prose'cution** *noun* **1** (an) act of prosecuting or process of being prosecuted: *He faces prosecution for drunken driving; There are numerous prosecutions for this offence every year.* □ **poursuites judiciaires**
2 the person/people bringing a legal action, including the lawyer(s) representing them: *First the prosecution stated its case, then the defence.* □ **plaignant(s)**
prospect ['prospekt] *noun* **1** an outlook for the future; a view of what one may expect to happen: *She didn't like the prospect of going abroad; a job with good prospects.* □ **perspectives d'avenir**
2 a view or scene: *a fine prospect.* □ **vue, perspective**
■ [prə'spekt] *verb* to make a search (for gold *etc*): *He is prospecting for gold.* □ **prospecter**
prospector [prə'spektə] *noun* a person who prospects for gold *etc*. □ **prospecteur, trice; chercheur, euse d'or**
prospectus [prə'spektəs] *noun* a booklet giving information about a school, organization *etc*. □ **prospectus**
prosper ['prospə] *verb* to do well; to succeed: *Her business is prospering.* □ **prospérer**
pro'sperity [-'spe-] *noun* success; wealth: *We wish you*

happiness and prosperity. □ **prospérité**
'**prosperous** *adjective* successful, *especially* in business: *a prosperous businessman.* □ **prospère**
'**prosperously** *adverb.* □ **de manière prospère**
prostitute ['prostitjuːt] *noun* a person who has sexual intercourse for payment. □ **prostitué, ée**
,**prosti'tution** *noun.* □ **prostitution**
prostrate ['prostreit] *adjective* 1 lying flat, *especially* face downwards. □ **couché à plat ventre**
2 completely exhausted or overwhelmed: *prostrate with grief.* □ **accablé (de, par)**
■ [prə'streit] *verb* 1 to throw (oneself) flat on the floor, *especially* in respect or reverence: *They prostrated themselves before the emperor.* □ **se prosterner**
2 to exhaust or overwhelm: *prostrated by the long journey.* □ **accabler**
pro'stration *noun.* □ **prostration; prosternement**
protect [prə'tekt] *verb* to guard or defend from danger; to keep safe: *She protected the children from every danger; Which type of helmet protects the head best?; He wore a fur jacket to protect himself against the cold.* □ **protéger (de, contre)**
pro'tected *adjective* (of certain animals or birds) protected by law from being shot *etc.* □ **protégé**
pro'tection [-ʃən] *noun* 1 the act of protecting or state of being protected: *He ran to his mother for protection; This type of lock gives extra protection against burglary.* □ **protection**
2 something that protects: *The trees were a good protection against the wind.* □ **protection**
pro'tective [-tiv] *adjective* giving, or intended to give, protection: *protective clothing/glasses.* □ **protecteur, de protection**
pro'tector *noun.* □ **protecteur, trice**
protein ['proutiːn] *noun* any of a large number of substances present in milk, eggs, meat *etc*, which are necessary as part of the food of human beings and animals. □ **protéine**
protest [prə'test] *verb* 1 to express a strong objection: *They are protesting against the new law.* □ **protester (contre)**
2 to state or declare definitely, *especially* in denying something: *She protested that she was innocent.* □ **protester (de)**
■ ['proutest] *noun* a strong statement or demonstration of objection or disapproval: *She made no protest; (also adjective) a protest march.* □ **(de) protestation**
pro'tester *noun.* □ **protestataire**
Protestant ['protistənt] *noun, adjective* (a member of) any of the Christian churches that separated from the Roman Catholic church at or after the Reformation. □ **protestant, ante**
'**Protestantism** *noun.* □ **protestantisme**
proton ['prouton] *noun* a particle with a positive electrical charge, forming part of the nucleus of an atom. □ **proton**
protoplasm ['proutəplazəm] *noun* the half-liquid substance that is found in all living cells. □ **protoplasme**
prototype ['proutətaip] *noun* the first or original model from which others are copied. □ **prototype**

protractor [prə'traktə] *noun* an instrument for drawing and measuring angles. □ **rapporteur**
protrude [prə'truːd] *verb* to stick out; to project: *His teeth protrude.* □ **faire saillie, avancer**
proud [praud] *adjective* 1 feeling pleasure or satisfaction at one's achievements, possessions, connections *etc*: *She was proud of her new house; She was proud of her daughter's achievements; He was proud to play football for the school.* □ **fier (de)**
2 having a (too) high opinion of oneself; arrogant: *She was too proud to talk to us.* □ **orgueilleux**
3 wishing to be independent: *He was too proud to accept help.* □ **fier**
4 splendid or impressive: *The assembled fleet was a proud sight.* □ **superbe**
'**proudly** *adverb.* □ **fièrement**
do (someone) proud to be a source of pride for someone: *Our son does us proud.* □ **rendre fier de qqn**
prove [pruːv] *verb* 1 to show to be true or correct: *This fact proves his guilt; He was proved guilty; Can you prove your theory?* □ **prouver**
2 to turn out, or be found, to be: *Her suspicions proved (to be) correct; This tool proved very useful.* □ **(s')avérer**
'**proven** *adjective* (*especially* in law) proved. □ **(é)prouvé**
proverb ['provəːb] *noun* a well-known saying that gives good advice or expresses a supposed truth: *Two common proverbs are 'Many hands make light work' and 'Don't count your chickens before they're hatched!'* □ **proverbe**
pro'verbial *adjective.* □ **proverbial**
pro'verbially *adverb.* □ **proverbialement**
provide [prə'vaid] *verb* 1 to give or supply: *She provided the wine for the meal; She provided them with a bed for the night.* □ **fournir**
2 (with **for**) to have enough money to supply what is necessary: *He is unable to provide for his family.* □ **subvenir aux besoins (de)**
pro'vided, pro'viding *conjunction* if; on condition (that): *We can buy it provided/providing (that) we have enough money.* □ **pourvu que**
province ['provins] *noun* a division of a country, empire *etc*: *Britain was once a Roman province.* □ **province**
pro'vincial [-'vinʃəl] *adjective.* □ **provincial**
provision [prə'viʒən] *noun* 1 the act of providing: *The government are responsible for the provision of education for all children.* □ **fait d'assurer**
2 an agreed arrangement. □ **disposition, clause**
3 a rule or condition. □ **stipulation**
■ *verb* to supply (*especially* an army) with food. □ **ravitailler**
pro'visional *adjective* temporary; appointed, arranged *etc* only for the present time: *a provisional government.* □ **provisoire**
pro'visionally *adverb.* □ **provisoirement**
pro'visions *noun plural* (a supply of) food: *The campers got their provisions at the village shop.* □ **provisions**
make provision for to provide what is necessary for: *You should make provision for your old age.* □ **pourvoir**

aux besoins de

provoke [prə'vouk] *verb* **1** to make angry or irritated: *Are you trying to provoke me?* □ **provoquer**
2 to cause: *His words provoked laughter.* □ **provoquer**
3 to cause (a person *etc*) to react in an angry way: *He was provoked into hitting him.* □ **provoquer**

provocation [provə'keiʃən] *noun* the act of provoking or state of being provoked. □ **provocation**

pro'vocative [-'vokətiv] *adjective* likely to rouse feeling, *especially* anger or sexual interest: *provocative remarks*; *a provocative pose.* □ **provocant, provocateur**

pro'vocatively *adverb.* □ **d'une manière provocante/ provocatrice**

prow [prau] *noun* the front part of a ship; the bow. □ **proue**

prowess ['prauis] *noun* skill or ability: *athletic prowess.* □ **prouesse**

prowl [praul] *verb* to move about stealthily in order to steal, attack, catch *etc*: *Tigers were prowling in the jungle.* □ **rôder**
'prowler *noun.* □ **rôdeur, euse**
be on the prowl to be prowling: *Pickpockets are always on the prowl.* □ **rôder**

proximity [prok'siməti] *noun* nearness: *Their house is in close proximity to ours.* □ **(à) proximité (de)**

prudent ['pruːdənt] *adjective* wise and careful: *a prudent person/attitude.* □ **prudent**
'prudently *adverb.* □ **prudemment**
'prudence *noun* wisdom and caution. □ **prudence**

prune[1] [pruːn] *verb* to trim (a tree *etc*) by cutting off unnecessary twigs and branches: *He pruned the roses.* □ **émonder, tailler**

prune[2] [pruːn] *noun* a dried plum. □ **pruneau**

pry [prai] *verb* to try to find out about something that is secret, *especially* other people's affairs: *He is always prying into my business.* □ **fouiner**

psalm [saːm] *noun* a sacred song, *especially* one from the Book of Psalms in the Bible. □ **psaume**

pseudonym ['sjuːdənim] *noun* a false name used by an author: *She wrote under a pseudonym.* □ **pseudonyme**

psychiatry [sai'kaiətri] *noun* the treatment of mental illness. □ **psychiatrie**
psychiatric [saiki'atrik] *adjective.* □ **psychiatrique**
psy'chiatrist *noun* a doctor who treats mental illness. □ **psychiatre**

psychic(al) ['saikik(əl)] *adjective* concerned with the mind, *especially* with supernatural influences and forces that act on the mind and senses. □ **psychique**

psychoanalyse, psychoanalyze [saikou'anəlaiz] *verb* to treat (a person suffering from mental illness) by discussing events in his/her past life which may have caused it. □ **psychanalyser**
,psychoa'nalysis [-'naləsis] *noun.* □ **psychanalyse**
,psycho'analyst [-list] *noun* a person who gives this treatment. □ **psychanalyste**

psychology [sai'kolədʒi] *noun* the study or science of the human mind. □ **psychologie**
,psycho'logical [-'lo-] *adjective* of the mind, or of psychology. □ **psychologique**
,psycho'logically *adverb.* □ **psychologiquement**

psy'chologist *noun* a person whose work is to study the human mind. □ **psychologue**

pub [pʌb] *noun* a house or bar where alcoholic drinks are sold to the public (abbreviation of *public house*). □ **débit de boissons**

puberty ['pjuːbəti] *noun* the time when a child's body becomes sexually mature. □ **puberté**

public ['pʌblik] *adjective* of, for, or concerning, the people (of a community or nation) in general: *a public library*; *a public meeting*; *Public opinion turned against him*; *The public announcements are on the back page of the newspaper*; *This information should be made public and not kept secret any longer.* □ **public**
'publicly *adverb.* □ **publiquement**

pu'blicity [-'blisə-] *noun* **1** advertising: *There is a lot of publicity about the dangers of smoking.* □ **publicité**
2 the state of being widely known: *Film stars usually like publicity.* □ **publicité**

'publicize, 'publicise [-saiz] *verb* to make widely known; to advertise: *We are publicizing a new product.* □ **faire de la publicité pour**

public holiday a day on which all (or most) shops, offices and factories are closed for a holiday. □ **fête légale**

public relations the attitude, understanding *etc* between a firm, government *etc* and the public. □ **relations publiques**

public spirit a desire to do things for the good of the community. □ **civisme**

,public-'spirited *adjective.* □ **dévoué au bien public**

public transport the bus, tram and train services provided by a state or community for the public. □ **transports en commun**

in public in front of other people, not in private: *They are always quarrelling in public.* □ **en public**

the public people in general: *This swimming pool is open to the public every day.* □ **le public**

public opinion poll a way of finding out public opinion by questioning a certain number of people. □ **sondage d'opinion**

> **the public** is singular: *The public is entitled to know the facts.*

publication [pʌbli'keiʃən] *noun* **1** the act of publishing or announcing publicly: *the publication of a new novel*; *the publication of the facts.* □ **publication**
2 something that has been published *eg* a book or magazine: *recent publications.* □ **publication, parution**

publish ['pʌbliʃ] *verb* **1** to prepare, print and produce for sale (a book *etc*): *Her new novel is being published this month.* □ **publier**
2 to make known: *They published their engagement.* □ **rendre public, annoncer**
'publisher *noun* a person who publishes books *etc.* □ **éditeur, trice**
'publishing *noun* the business of a publisher. □ **édition**
publishing house a business that prints and sells books for the public to buy: *The author stayed with the same publishing house for every novel.* □ **imprimerie**

puck [pʌk] *noun* a hard, black, rubber disk used for passing and scoring goals in the game of hockey: *The puck* *bounced off the hockey player's stick and went into the net.* □ **rondelle**

pucker ['pʌkə] *verb* to make or become wrinkled. □ **(se) plisser**

■ *noun* a wrinkle or fold. □ **pli, ride**

pudding ['pudiŋ] *noun* any of several types of soft sweet foods made with eggs, flour, milk *etc*: *sponge pudding*; *rice pudding.* □ **pouding**

puddle ['pʌdl] *noun* a small, *usually* dirty, pool (of water): *It had been raining, and there were puddles in the road.* □ **flaque d'eau**

pudgy *see* **podgy.**

puff [pʌf] *noun* 1 a small blast of air, wind *etc*; a gust: *A puff of wind moved the branches.* □ **souffle, bouffée**
2 any of various kinds of soft, round, light or hollow objects: *a powder puff*, *(also adjective) puff sleeves.* □ **houppe(tte); manche bouffante**

■ *verb* 1 to blow in small blasts: *Stop puffing cigarette smoke into my face!*; *He puffed at his pipe.* □ **tirer/ émettre des bouffées de fumée**
2 to breathe quickly, after running *etc*: *He was puffing as he climbed the stairs.* □ **haleter**

puffed *adjective* short of breath; breathing quickly: *I'm puffed after running so fast!* □ **essoufflé**

'puffy *adjective* swollen, *especially* unhealthily: *a puffy face/ankle.* □ **bouffi, boursouflé**

puff pastry a light, flaky type of pastry. □ **pâte feuilletée**

puff out to cause to swell or expand: *The bird puffed out its feathers*; *He puffed out his cheeks.* □ **gonfler**

puff up to swell: *Her eye (was all) puffed up after the wasp stung her.* □ **enfler**

pug [pʌg] *noun* a kind of small dog with a flat nose. □ **carlin**

pull [pul] *verb* 1 to (try to) move something *especially* towards oneself *usually* by using force: *She pulled the chair towards the fire*; *She pulled at the door but couldn't open it*; *Help me to pull off my boots off*; *This railway engine can pull twelve carriages.* □ **(re)tirer (sur)**
2 *(with at or on)* in *eg* smoking, to suck at: *She pulled at her cigarette.* □ **tirer sur**
3 to row: *He pulled towards the shore.* □ **ramer**
4 (of a driver or vehicle) to steer or move in a certain direction: *The car pulled in at the garage*; *I pulled into the side of the road*; *The train pulled out of the station*; *The motorbike pulled out to overtake*; *He pulled off the road.* □ **entrer dans**

■ *noun* 1 an act of pulling: *I felt a pull at my sleeve.* □ **traction**
2 a pulling or attracting force: *magnetic pull*; *the pull (= attraction) of the sea.* □ **attraction**
3 influence: *She thinks she has some pull with the head-master.* □ **influence**

pull apart/to pieces to tear or destroy completely by pulling. □ **mettre en pièces**

pull down to destroy or demolish (buildings). □ **démolir**

pull a face/faces (at) to make strange expressions with the face *eg* to show disgust, or to amuse: *The children were pulling faces at each other*; *He pulled a face when he smelt the fish.* □ **faire des grimaces (à)**

pull a gun *etc* **on** to produce and aim a gun *etc* at (a

person). □ **braquer un revolver sur**

pull off to succeed in doing: *She's finally pulled it off!* □ **réussir (son coup)**

pull on to put on (a piece of clothing) hastily: *She pulled on a sweater.* □ **enfiler**

pull oneself together to control oneself; to regain one's self-control: *At first she was terrified, then she pulled herself together.* □ **(se) ressaisir**

pull through to (help to) survive an illness *etc*: *He is very ill, but he'll pull through*; *The expert medical treatment pulled him through.* □ **(se) tirer d'affaire**

pull up (of a driver or vehicle) to stop: *He pulled up at the traffic lights.* □ **(s')arrêter**

pull one's weight to take one's fair share of work, duty *etc*. □ **faire sa part du travail**

pull someone's leg *see* **leg.**

pulley ['puli] *noun* a wheel over which a rope *etc* can pass in order to lift heavy objects. □ **poulie**

pullover ['puləuvə] *noun* a knitted garment for the top part of the body; a sweater. □ **pullover**

pulp [pʌlp] *noun* 1 the soft, fleshy part of a fruit. □ **pulpe**
2 a soft mass of other matter, *eg* of wood *etc* from which paper is made: *wood-pulp.* □ **pulpe**

■ *verb* to make into pulp: *The fruit was pulped and bottled.* □ **réduire en pulpe**

'pulpy *adjective* of or like pulp. □ **pulpeux**

pulpit ['pulpit] *noun* a raised box or platform in a church, where the priest or minister stands, *especially* to preach the sermon. □ **chair**

pulse [pʌls] *noun* the regular beating of the heart, which can be checked by feeling the pumping action of the artery in the wrist: *The doctor felt/took her pulse.* □ **pouls**

■ *verb* to throb. □ **battre**

pulsate ['pʌlseit] *verb* to beat or throb. □ **battre**

pulsation [pʌl'seiʃən] *noun.* □ **pulsation**

pulverize, pulverise ['pʌlvəraiz] *verb* to make or crush into dust or powder. □ **pulvériser**

,pulveri'zation, ,pulveri'sation *noun.* □ **pulvérisation**

puma ['pju:mə] *noun* *(also cougar* ['ku:gə]) a type of wild animal like a large cat, found in America. □ **puma**

pumice ['pʌmis] *noun* a light kind of solidified lava. □ **ponce**

pumice stone *noun* (a piece of) this type of stone used for cleaning and smoothing the skin *etc*. □ **pierre ponce**

pummel ['pʌml] – *past tense, past participle* **'pummelled, 'pummeled** – *verb* to beat again and again with the fists. □ **rouer de coups**

pump [pʌmp] *noun* 1 a machine for making water *etc* rise from under the ground: *Every village used to have a pump from which everyone drew their water.* □ **pompe**
2 a machine or device for forcing liquid or gas into, or out of, something: *a bicycle pump* (for forcing air into the tires). □ **pompe**

■ *verb* 1 to raise or force with a pump: *Oil is being pumped out of the ground.* □ **pomper**
2 to get information from by asking questions: *He tried to pump me about the exam.* □ **tirer les vers du nez**

pump up to inflate (tires *etc*) with a pump. □ **gonfler**

pumpkin ['pʌmpkin] *noun* a kind of large, round, thick-skinned yellow fruit, eaten as food. □ **citrouille**

pun [pʌn] *noun* a type of joke in which words are used that have a similar sound, but a different meaning: *One example of a pun would be 'A pun is a punishable offence'.* □ **calembour**

■ *verb – past tense, past participle* **punned** – to make a pun. □ **faire un/des jeu(x) de mots**

punch¹ [pʌntʃ] *noun* a kind of drink made of spirits or wine, water and sugar *etc*. □ **punch**

punch² [pʌntʃ] *verb* to hit with the fist: *He punched him on the nose.* □ **donner un coup de poing à**

■ *noun* 1 a blow with the fist: *He gave him a punch.* □ **coup de poing**

2 the quality of liveliness in speech, writing *etc*. □ **vigueur**

'**punch-drunk** *adjective* (of a boxer) dizzy from being continually hit. □ **sonné**

'**punchline** the funny sentence or phrase that ends a joke: *She always laughs before she gets to the punchline.* □ **conclusion (comique)**

'**punch-up** *noun* a fight (using fists). □ **baggare**

punch³ [pʌntʃ] *noun* a tool or device for making holes in leather, paper *etc*. □ **poinçon(neuse)**

■ *verb* to make holes in with such a tool. □ **poinçonner**

Punch [pʌntʃ] *noun* the name of a comic figure in a puppet show (traditionally known as a ˌPunch and 'Judy show). □ **Polichinelle**

as pleased as Punch very pleased. □ **heureux comme un roi**

punctual ['pʌŋktʃuəl] *adjective* arriving *etc* on time; not late: *Please be punctual for your appointment; She's a very punctual person.* □ **ponctuel**

ˌpunctu'ality [-'a-] *noun*. □ **ponctualité**

'**punctually** *adverb* on time: *She arrived punctually.* □ **à l'heure**

punctuate ['pʌŋktʃueit] *verb* to divide up sentences *etc* by commas, full stops, colons *etc*. □ **ponctuer**

punctuation *noun* 1 the act of punctuating. □ **ponctuation**

2 the use of punctuation marks. □ **ponctuation**

punctuation mark any of the symbols used for punctuating, *eg* comma, full stop, question mark *etc*. □ **signe de ponctuation**

puncture ['pʌŋktʃə] *verb* to make or get a small hole in: *Some glass on the road punctured my new tire.* □ **crever**

■ *noun* a hole in a tire: *My car has had two punctures this week.* □ **crevaison**

pungent ['pʌndʒənt] *adjective* (of a taste or smell) sharp and strong. □ **piquant**

'**pungently** *adverb*. □ **de façon mordante, piquante**

punish ['pʌniʃ] *verb* 1 to cause to suffer for a crime or fault: *He was punished for stealing the money.* □ **punir**

2 to give punishment for: *The teacher punishes disobedience.* □ **punir**

'**punishable** *adjective* (of offences *etc*) able or likely to be punished by law: *Driving without a licence is a punishable offence.* □ **punissable**

'**punishment** *noun* 1 the act of punishing or process of being punished. □ **punition**

2 suffering, or a penalty, imposed for a crime, fault *etc*: *He was sent to prison for two years as (a) punishment.*

□ **punition, peine**

punitive ['pjuːnətiv] *adjective* giving punishment. □ **de punition**

punt [pʌnt] *noun* a type of flat-bottomed boat with square ends, moved by pushing against the bottom of the river *etc* with a pole. □ **bac**

■ *verb* to travel in a punt: *They punted up the river.* □ **aller en bac**

puny ['pjuːni] *adjective* small and weak: *a puny child.* □ **chétif**

'**punily** *adverb*. □ **chétivement**

'**puniness** *noun*. □ **chétivité**

pup [pʌp] *noun* 1 (*also* **puppy** ['pʌpi] – *plural* '**puppies**) a young dog: *a sheepdog pup(py).* □ **chiot**

2 the young of certain other animals: *a seal pup.* □ **jeune (animal)**

pupa ['pjuːpə] – *plural* '**pupae** [-piː] – *noun* the form that an insect takes when it is changing from a larva (*eg* a caterpillar) to its perfect form (*eg* a butterfly); a chrysalis. □ **chrysalide**

pupil¹ ['pjuːpl] *noun* a person who is being taught by a teacher or tutor: *The school has 2000 pupils.* □ **écolier, ière**

pupil² ['pjuːpl] *noun* the round opening in the middle of the eye through which the light passes. □ **pupille**

puppet ['pʌpit] *noun* a doll that can be moved *eg* by wires, or by putting the hand inside the body. □ **marionnette**

'**puppetry** *noun* the art of making puppets and producing puppet shows. □ **art des marionnettes**

'**puppet show** *noun* a play *etc* performed by puppets. □ **spectacle de marionnettes**

puppy *see* pup.

purchase ['pɔːtʃəs] *verb* to buy: *I purchased a new house.* □ **acheter**

■ *noun* 1 anything that has been bought: *She carried her purchases home in a bag.* □ **achat**

2 the act of buying: *The purchase of a car should never be a hasty matter.* □ **achat**

'**purchaser** *noun* a buyer. □ **acheteur, euse**

pure ['pjuə] *adjective* 1 not mixed with anything especially dirty or less valuable: *pure gold.* □ **pur**

2 clean, *especially* morally: *pure thoughts.* □ **pur**

3 complete; absolute: *a pure accident.* □ **pur**

4 (of sounds) clear; keeping in tune: *She sang in a high pure tone.* □ **pur**

'**purely** *adverb*. □ **purement**

'**pureness** *noun*. □ **pureté**

'**purity** *noun*. □ **pureté**

'**purify** [-fai] *verb* to make pure: *What is the best way to purify the air?* □ **purifier**

ˌpurifi'cation [-fi-] *noun*. □ **purification**

ˌpure-'blooded *adjective* of unmixed race: *a pure-blooded Englishman.* □ **pur**

ˌpure'bred *adjective* (of animals) of unmixed breed; thoroughbred: *a purebred Arabian horse.* □ **de race, pur sang**

pure and simple (*used after a noun*) nothing but: *It was an accident pure and simple.* □ **pur et simple**

purée ['pjuərei] *noun* any of several types of food made into a soft pulp: *tomato purée.* □ **purée**

purge [pɜːdʒ] *verb* 1 to make (something) clean by clearing it of everything that is bad, not wanted *etc*. □ **purger**
2 to rid (a political party *etc*) of disloyal members. □ **purger**

■ *noun* an act of purging. □ **purge**

purgative ['pɜːgətiv] *noun, adjective* (a medicine) which clears waste matter out of the body. □ **purgatif**

purification, purify *see* **pure.**

puritan ['pjuəritən] *noun* 1 a person who is strict and disapproves of many kinds of enjoyment. □ **puritain, aine**
2 formerly, in England and America, a member of a religious group wanting to make church worship *etc* simpler and plainer. □ **puritain, aine**

,puri'tanical [-'ta-] *adjective*. □ **puritain**

purity *see* **pure.**

purl [pɜːl] *noun* a kind of knitting stitch. □ **maille à l'envers**

purple ['pɜːpl] *noun, adjective* (of) a dark colour made by mixing blue and red. □ **violet**

purpose ['pɜːpəs] *noun* 1 the reason for doing something; the aim to which an action *etc* is directed: *What is the purpose of your visit?* □ **but, objet**
2 the use or function of an object: *The purpose of this lever is to stop the machine in an emergency.* □ **utilité**
3 determination: *a man of purpose.* □ **détermination**

'purposeful *adjective* having a definite purpose: *with a purposeful look on his face.* □ **déterminé**

'purposefully *adverb*. □ **délibérément**

'purposeless *adjective* having no purpose: *purposeless destruction.* □ **inutile**

'purposely *adverb* intentionally: *He did it purposely to attract my attention.* □ **exprès**

,purpose-'built *adjective* made or built for a particular need or purpose: *People who use wheelchairs sometimes live in purpose-built houses.* □ **fonctionnalisé**

on purpose intentionally: *Did you break the cup on purpose?* □ **exprès**

serve a purpose to be useful in some way. □ **servir à qqch.**

to no purpose with no useful results. □ **en pure perte**

purr [pɜː] *verb* to make the low, murmuring sound of a cat when it is pleased. □ **ronronner**

■ *noun* such a sound. □ **ronron (nement)**

purse [pɜːs] *noun* 1 a small bag for carrying money: *I looked in my purse for some change.* □ **porte-monnaie**
2 a handbag. □ **sac à main**

■ *verb* to close (the lips) tightly: *She pursed her lips in anger.* □ **(se) pincer (les lèvres)**

'purser *noun* the officer in charge of a ship's money, supplies *etc*. □ **commissaire du bord**

pursue [pə'sjuː] *verb* 1 to follow *especially* in order to catch or capture; to chase: *They pursued the thief through the town.* □ **poursuivre**
2 to occupy oneself with (studies, enquiries *etc*); to continue: *She is pursuing her studies at the University.* □ **poursuivre**

pur'suer *noun*. □ **poursuivant, ante**

pursuit [pə'sjuːt] *noun* 1 the act of pursuing: *The thief ran down the street with a policeman in (hot) pursuit.* □ **poursuite**
2 an occupation or hobby: *holiday pursuits.* □ **activité**

pus [pʌs] *noun* a thick, yellowish liquid that forms in infected wounds *etc*. □ **pus**

push [puʃ] *verb* 1 to press against something, in order to (try to) move it further away: *He pushed the door open; She pushed him away; He pushed against the door with his shoulder; The line can't move any faster, so stop pushing!; I had a good view of the race till someone pushed in front of me.* □ **pousser**
2 to try to make (someone) do something; to urge on, *especially* foolishly: *She pushed him into applying for the job.* □ **pousser (à)**
3 to sell (drugs) illegally. □ **revendre de la drogue**

■ *noun* 1 a movement of pressure against something; a thrust: *She gave him a push.* □ **poussée**
2 energy and determination: *She has enough push to do well in her job.* □ **dynamisme**

be pushed for to be short of; not to have enough of: *I'm a bit pushed for time.* □ **manquer de**

push around to treat roughly: *He pushes his younger brother around.* □ **maltraiter**

push off to go away: *I wish you'd push off!* □ **ficher le camp**

push on to go on; to continue: *Push on with your work.* □ **continuer**

push over to cause to fall; to knock down: *He pushed me over.* □ **faire tomber**

puss [pus], **pussy** ['pusi] – *plural* 'pussies – *noun* a cat. □ **minet, ette**

'pussyfoot *verb* to behave in a wary or timid way. □ **ne pas se mouiller**

put [put] – *present participle* 'putting: *past tense, past participle* put – *verb* 1 to place in a certain position or situation: *She put the plate in the cupboard; Did you put any sugar in my coffee?; He put his arm around her; I'm putting a new lock on the door; You're putting too much strain on that rope; When did the Russians first put a man into space?; You've put me in a bad temper; Can you put (= translate) this sentence into French?* □ **mettre**
2 to submit or present (a proposal, question *etc*): *I put several questions to him; She put her ideas before the committee.* □ **soumettre**
3 to express in words: *She put her refusal very politely; Children sometimes have such a funny way of putting things!* □ **exprimer**
4 to write down: *I'm trying to write a letter to her, but I don't know what to put.* □ **écrire**
5 to sail in a particular direction: *We put out to sea; The ship put into harbour for repairs.* □ **prendre le large; rentrer**

'put-on *adjective* pretended; not genuine: *a put-on foreign accent; Her accent sounded put-on.* □ **feint**

a put-up job something done to give a false appearance, in order to cheat or trick someone. □ **coup monté**

put about to spread (news *etc*). □ **faire courir**

put across to convey or communicate (ideas *etc*) to others: *She's very good at putting her ideas across.* □

communiquer

put aside 1 to abandon (work *etc*) temporarily: *She put aside her needlework.* □ **mettre de côté**

2 to save or preserve for the future: *He tries to put aside a little money each month.* □ **mettre de côté**

put away to return to its proper place, *especially* out of sight: *She put her clothes away in the drawer.* □ **ranger**

put back to return to its proper place: *Did you put my keys back?* □ **remettre en/à sa place**

put down 1 to lower: *The teacher asked the pupil to put his hand down.* □ **baisser**

2 to place on the floor or other surface, out of one's hands: *Put that knife down immediately!* □ **poser**

3 to subdue (a rebellion *etc*). □ **mater**

4 to kill (an animal) painlessly when it is old or very ill. □ **faire piquer, abattre**

put down for to write the name of (someone) on a list *etc* for a particular purpose: *You have been put down for the one hundred metres' race.* □ **inscrire**

put one's feet up to take a rest. □ **se reposer un peu**

put forth (of plants *etc*) to produce (leaves, shoots *etc*). □ **produire**

put in 1 to insert or install: *We're having a new shower put in.* □ **(faire) installer**

2 to do (a certain amount of work *etc*): *He put in an hour's training today.* □ **produire**

put off 1 to delay; to postpone: *He put off leaving/his departure till Thursday.* □ **retarder**

2 to cancel an arranged meeting *etc* with (a person): *I had to put the Browns off because I had 'flu.* □ **décommander**

3 to cause (a person) to feel disgust or dislike (for): *The cheese looked nice but the smell put me off; The conversation about illness put me off my dinner.* □ **dégoûter (de)**

put on 1 to switch on (a light *etc*): *Put the light on!* □ **allumer**

2 to dress oneself in: *Which shoes are you going to put on?* □ **mettre**

3 to add or increase: *The car put on speed; I've put on weight.* □ **prendre**

4 to present or produce (a play *etc*): *They're putting on 'Hamlet' next week.* □ **présenter**

5 to provide (*eg* transport): *They always put on extra buses between 8:00 and 9:00.* □ **mettre en service**

6 to make a false show of; to pretend: *She said she felt ill, but she was just putting it on.* □ **simuler**

7 to bet (money) on: *I've put a dollar on that horse to win.* □ **miser sur**

put out 1 to extend (a hand *etc*): *He put out his hand to steady her.* □ **tendre**

2 (of plants *etc*) to produce (shoots, leaves *etc*). □ **produire**

3 to extinguish (a fire, light *etc*): *The fire brigade soon put out the fire.* □ **éteindre**

4 to issue, give out: *They put out a distress call.* □ **lancer**

5 to cause bother or trouble to: *Don't put yourself out for my sake!* □ **se déranger**

6 to annoy: *I was put out by his decision.* □ **déranger**

The job of the fire brigade is to **put out** (not **put off**) fires.

put through 1 to arrange (a deal, agreement *etc*). □ **conclure**

2 to connect by telephone: *I'm trying to put you through (to Ottawa).* □ **mettre en communication avec**

put together to construct: *The vase broke, but I managed to put it together again.* □ **réparer, recoller**

put up 1 to raise (a hand *etc*). □ **lever**

2 to build; to erect: *They're putting up some new houses.* □ **construire**

3 to fix on a wall *etc*: *She put the poster up.* □ **accrocher (au mur)**

4 to increase (a price *etc*): *They're putting up the fees again.* □ **augmenter**

5 to offer or show (resistance *etc*): *He's putting up a brave fight.* □ **se défendre**

6 to provide (money) for a purpose: *He promised to put up the money for the scheme.* □ **fournir**

7 to provide a bed *etc* for (a person) in one's home: *Can you put us up next Thursday night?* □ **loger**

put up to to persuade (a person) to do something: *Who put you up to writing that letter?* □ **pousser à**

put up with to bear patiently: *I cannot put up with all this noise.* □ **supporter, endurer**

putrefy ['pjuːtrəfai] *verb* to make or go bad or rotten: *The meat putrefied in the heat.* □ **(se) putréfier**

putrid ['pjuːtrid] *adjective* (smelling) rotten: *putrid fish.* □ **pourri**

putt [pʌt] *verb* (in golf) to send a ball gently forward when aiming for the hole. □ **putter**

'**putter** *noun* a golf-club used for putting. □ **fer droit**

putty ['pʌti] *noun* a type of paste made from ground chalk and oil, used to fix glass in windows *etc*. □ **mastic**

puzzle ['pʌzl] *verb* **1** to perplex, baffle or bewilder: *The question puzzled them; What puzzles me is how he got here so soon.* □ **rendre perplexe**

2 to think long and carefully about a problem *etc*: *I puzzled over the sum for hours.* □ **essayer de résoudre**

■ *noun* **1** a problem that causes a lot of thought: *Her behaviour was a puzzle to him.* □ **énigme**

2 a kind of game or toy to test one's thinking, knowledge or skill: *a jig-saw puzzle; a crossword puzzle.* □ **casse-tête**

'**puzzling** *adjective* difficult to understand: *a puzzling remark.* □ **curieux**

puzzle out to solve (a problem *etc*). □ **élucider**

pygmy, pigmy ['pigmi] – *plural* '**pygmies**, '**pigmies** – *noun* a member of an African race of very small people. □ **pygmée**

pyjamas [pə'dʒɑːməz] *noun plural* a suit for sleeping, consisting of trousers and a jacket: *two pairs of pyjamas.* □ **pyjama**

pylon ['pailən] *noun* **1** a tall steel tower for supporting electric power cables. □ **pylône**

2 a guiding mark at an airfield. □ **pylône**

pyramid ['pirəmid] *noun* **1** a solid shape *usually* with a square or triangular base, and sloping triangular sides meeting in a point. □ **pyramide**

2 an ancient tomb built in this shape in Egypt. □ **pyramide**

pyre ['paiə] *noun* a pile of wood on which a dead body is ceremonially burned: *a funeral pyre.* □ **bûcher funéraire**

pyrotechnics [pairə'tekniks] *noun plural* (a display of) fireworks. □ **feux d'artifice**

python ['paiθən] *noun* a type of large non-poisonous snake that twists around its prey and crushes it. □ **python**

Qq

quack [kwak] *noun* the cry of a duck. ▫ **couin-couin**
■ *verb* to make such a sound: *The ducks quacked noisily as they swam across the pond.* ▫ **faire couin-couin**
quad *see* **quadrangle, quadruplet**.
quadrangle ['kwodraŋgl] *noun* (*abbreviation* **quad** [kwod]) a four-sided open space surrounded by buildings, *especially* in a school, college *etc*. ▫ **cour**
quadrilateral [kwodri'latərəl] *noun* a two-dimensional figure with four straight sides. ▫ **quadrilatère**
quadruped ['kwodruped] *noun* a four-footed animal: *An elephant is a quadruped.* ▫ **quadrupède**
quadruple [kwo'druːpl] *adjective* **1** four times as much or as many. ▫ **quadruple**
2 made up of four parts *etc*. ▫ **quadruple**
■ *verb* to make or become four times as great. ▫ **quadrupler**
quadruplet [kwo'druːplit] *noun* (*abbreviation* **quad** [kwod]) one of four children born at the same time to one mother. ▫ **quadruplés**
quadruplicate [kwə'druːplikət]: **in quadruplicate** in four identical copies: *Please fill out this form in quadruplicate.* ▫ **en quatre exemplaires**
quail [kweil] *verb* to draw back in fear; to shudder: *The little boy quailed at the teacher's angry voice.* ▫ **reculer (devant)**
quaint [kweint] *adjective* pleasantly odd or strange, *especially* because of being old-fashioned: *quaint customs.* ▫ **au charme vieillot**
'quaintly *adverb*. ▫ **d'une façon pittoresque**
'quaintness *noun*. ▫ **caractère vieillot**
quake [kweik] *verb* **1** (of people) to shake or tremble, *especially* with fear. ▫ **trembler**
2 (of the ground) to shake: *The ground quaked under their feet.* ▫ **trembler**
■ *noun* an earthquake. ▫ **tremblement de terre**
qualify ['kwolifai] *verb* **1** to cause to be or to become able or suitable for: *A degree in English does not qualify you to teach English; She is too young to qualify for a place in the team.* ▫ **qualifier**
2 (*with* **as**) to show that one is suitable for a profession or job *etc*, *especially* by passing a test or examination: *I hope to qualify as a doctor.* ▫ **obtenir le diplôme de**
3 (*with* **for**) to allow, or be allowed, to take part in a competition *etc*, *usually* by reaching a satisfactory standard in an earlier test or competition: *She failed to qualify for the long jump.* ▫ **se qualifier pour**
4 (of an adjective) to describe, or add to the meaning of: *In 'red books', the adjective 'red' qualifies the noun 'books'.* ▫ **qualifier**
,qualifi'cation [-fi-] *noun* **1** (the act of gaining) a skill, achievement *etc* (*eg* an examination pass) that makes (a person) able or suitable to do a job *etc*: *What qualifications do you need for this job?* ▫ **compétence(s)**
2 something that gives a person the right to do something. ▫ **diplôme**
3 a limitation to something one has said or written: *I think this is an excellent piece of work – with certain*

qualifications. ▫ **restriction**
'qualified *adjective* (*negative* **unqualified**) having the necessary qualification(s) to do (something): *a qualified engineer.* ▫ **qualifié**
'qualifying *adjective* in which players, teams *etc* attempt to qualify for a competition *etc*: *Our team was beaten in the qualifying round.* ▫ **de qualification**
quality ['kwoləti] – *plural* **'qualities** – *noun* **1** the extent to which something has features which are good or bad *etc, especially* features which are good: *We produce several different qualities of paper; In this firm, we look for quality rather than quantity; (also adjective) quality goods.* ▫ **(de) qualité**
2 some (*usually* good) feature which makes a person or thing special or noticeable: *Kindness is a human quality which everyone admires.* ▫ **qualité**
qualm [kwaːm] *noun* a feeling of uncertainty about whether one is doing right: *She had no qualms about reporting her husband's crime to the police.* ▫ **scrupule**
quandary ['kwondəri] – *plural* **'quandaries** – *noun* a state of uncertainty; a situation in which it is difficult to decide what to do. ▫ **embarras**
quantity ['kwontəti] *noun* the size, weight, number *etc* of something, *especially* a large size *etc*: *What quantity of paper do you need?; I buy these goods in quantity; a small quantity of cement; large quantities of tinned food.* ▫ **quantité**
quantity surveyor a person who is responsible for estimating the quantities of building materials needed for constructing something, and their probable cost. ▫ **métreur vérificateur**
an unknown quantity a person or thing whose characteristics, abilities *etc* cannot be predicted. ▫ **une inconnue**
quarantine ['kworəntiːn] *noun* **1** the keeping away from other people or animals of people or animals that might be carrying an infectious disease: *My dog was in quarantine for six months.* ▫ **quarantaine**
2 the period in or for which this is done: *The quarantine for a dog entering Britain from abroad is six months.* ▫ **quarantaine**
■ *verb* to put (a person or animal) in quarantine. ▫ **mettre en quarantaine**
quarrel ['kworəl] *noun* an angry disagreement or argument: *I've had a quarrel with my girlfriend.* ▫ **dispute**
■ *verb* – *past tense, past participle* **'quarrelled, 'quarreled** – to have an angry argument (with someone): *I've quarrelled with my girlfriend; My girlfriend and I have quarrelled.* ▫ **(se) disputer (avec)**
'quarrelsome *adjective* inclined to quarrel: *quarrelsome children.* ▫ **querelleur**
'quarrelsomeness *noun*. ▫ **humeur querelleuse**
quarry[1] ['kwori] – *plural* **'quarries** – *noun* a place, *usually* a very large hole in the ground, from which stone is got for building *etc*. ▫ **carrière**
■ *verb* to dig (stone) in a quarry. ▫ **extraire**
quarry[2] ['kwori] – *plural* **'quarries** – *noun* **1** a hunted animal or bird. ▫ **gibier**
2 someone or something that is hunted, chased or eagerly looked for. ▫ **proie**

quarter ['kwɔːtə] *noun* **1** one of four equal parts of something which together form the whole (amount) of the thing: *There are four of us, so we'll cut the cake into quarters; It's (a) quarter past/after four; In the first quarter of the year her firm made a profit; The shop is about a quarter of a kilometre away; an hour and a quarter; two and a quarter hours.* □ **quart**

2 in the United States and Canada, (a coin worth) twenty-five cents, the fourth part of a dollar. □ **vingt-cinq cents**

3 a district or part of a town *especially* where a particular group of people live: *He lives in the Polish quarter of the town.* □ **quartier**

4 a direction: *People were coming at me from all quarters.* □ **de toutes parts**

5 mercy shown to an enemy. □ **grâce**

6 the leg of a *usually* large animal, or a joint of meat which includes a leg: *a quarter of beef; a bull's hindquarters.* □ **quartier**

7 the shape of the moon at the end of the first and third weeks of its cycle; the first or fourth week of the cycle itself. □ **quartier**

8 one of four equal periods of play in some games. □ **quart**

9 a period of study at a college *etc usually* 10 to 12 weeks in length. □ **trimestre**

■ *verb* **1** to cut into four equal parts: *We'll quarter the cake and then we'll all have an equal share.* □ **couper en quatre**

2 to divide by four: *If we each do the work at the same time, we could quarter the time it would take to finish the job.* □ **diviser en quatre**

3 to give (*especially* a soldier) somewhere to stay: *The soldiers were quartered all over the town.* □ **cantonner**

'**quarterly** *adjective* happening, published *etc* once every three months: *a quarterly journal; quarterly payments.* □ **trimestriel**

■ *adverb* once every three months: *We pay our electricity bill quarterly.* □ **trimestriellement**

■ *plural* '**quarterlies** – *noun* a magazine *etc* which is published once every three months. □ **publication trimestrielle**

'**quarters** *noun plural* a place to stay *especially* for soldiers. □ **quartiers**

'**quarterdeck** *noun* the part of the upper deck of a ship between the stern and the mast nearest it. □ **gaillard d'arrière**

,**quarter-'final** *noun* (*often in plural*) the third-last round in a competition. □ **quart de finale**

,**quarter-'finalist** *noun.* □ **quart de finaliste**

'**quartermaster** *noun* an officer whose job is to provide soldiers with food, transport, a place to live *etc.* □ **intendant militaire**

at close quarters close to; close together: *The soldiers were fighting with the enemy at close quarters.* □ **au corps-à-corps**

quartet [kwɔː'tet] *noun* **1** a group of four singers or people playing musical instruments. □ **quatuor**

2 a piece of music written for such a group: *a Mozart quartet.* □ **quatuor**

quartz [kwɔːts] *noun, adjective* (of) a kind of hard substance found in rocks, often in the form of crystals. □ **(de, en) quartz**

quasar ['kweisɑː] *noun* a star-like object which gives out light and radio waves. □ **quasar**

quaver ['kweivə] *verb* (*especially* of a sound or a person's voice) to shake or tremble: *The old man's voice quavered.* □ **chevroter**

■ *noun* **1** a shaking or trembling: *There was a quaver in her voice.* □ **tremblement**

2 a note equal to half a crotchet in length. □ **croche**

quay [kiː] *noun* a solid, *usually* stone, landing-place, where boats are loaded and unloaded: *The boat is moored at the quay.* □ **quai**

'**quayside** *noun* the side or edge of a quay: *The boat was tied up at the quayside.* □ **à quai**

queasy ['kwiːzi] *adjective* feeling as if one is about to be sick: *The motion of the boat made her feel queasy.* □ **qui a mal au cœur**

Quebecer [kwibekə] *noun* a native of Quebec; someone who comes from Quebec: *Rhena was a Quebecer, born in Montreal.* □ **Québécois**

queen [kwiːn] *noun* **1** a woman who rules a country, who inherits her position by right of birth: *the Queen of England; Queen Elizabeth II.* □ **reine**

2 the wife of a king: *The king and his queen were both present.* □ **reine**

3 a woman who is in some way important, excellent or special: *a beauty queen; a movie queen.* □ **reine**

4 a playing card with a picture of a queen on it: *I have two aces and a queen.* □ **dame**

5 an important chess-piece: *a bishop, a king and a queen.* □ **reine**

6 the egg-laying female of certain kinds of insect (*especially* bees, ants and wasps). □ **reine**

'**queenly** *adjective* of, like or suitable for, a queen. □ **de reine**

queen mother the mother of the reigning king or queen, who was herself once a queen. □ **reine mère**

queer [kwiə] *adjective* **1** odd, strange or unusual: *queer behaviour; queer noises in the middle of the night.* □ **bizarre**

2 offensive term used to describe homosexuals. □ **tapette**

'**queerly** *adverb.* □ **bizarrement**

'**queerness** *noun.* □ **bizarrerie**

quell [kwel] *verb* **1** to put an end to (a rebellion *etc*) by force. □ **réprimer**

2 to put an end to, or take away (a person's fears *etc*). □ **calmer**

quench [kwentʃ] *verb* **1** to drink enough to take away (one's thirst): *I had a glass of lemonade to quench my thirst.* □ **étancher, désaltérer**

2 to put out (a fire): *The firemen were unable to quench the fire.* □ **éteindre**

query ['kwiəri] – *plural* '**queries** – *noun* **1** a question: *In answer to your query about hotel reservations I am sorry to tell you that we have no vacancies.* □ **question**

2 a question mark: *You have omitted the query.* □ **point d'interrogation**

■ *verb* **1** to question (a statement *etc*): *I think the waiter has added up the bill wrongly – you should query it.* □

mettre en doute

2 to ask: *'What time does the train leave?' she queried.* □ **demander**

quest [kwest] *noun* a search: *the quest for gold; the quest for truth.* □ **recherche**

question ['kwestʃən] *noun* **1** something which is said, written *etc* which asks for an answer from someone: *The question is, do we really need a computer?* □ **question**

2 a problem or matter for discussion: *There is the question of how much to pay him.* □ **question**

3 a single problem in a test or examination: *We had to answer four questions in three hours.* □ **question**

4 criticism; doubt; discussion: *He is, without question, the best man for the job.* □ **(hors de tout) doute**

5 a suggestion or possibility: *There is no question of our dismissing him.* □ **(être) question**

■ *verb* **1** to ask (a person) questions: *I'll question him about what he was doing last night.* □ **interroger, questionner**

2 to regard as doubtful: *He questioned her right to use the money.* □ **mettre en doute**

'questionable *adjective* **1** doubtful; uncertain. □ **discutable**

2 probably not true, honest, respectable: *questionable behaviour.* □ **douteux**

'questionably *adverb.* □ **de manière contestable**

'questionableness *noun.* □ **caractère douteux**

question mark a mark (?) used in writing to indicate a question. □ **point d'interrogation**

,question'naire [-'neə] *noun* a written list of questions to be answered by a large number of people to provide information for a survey or report. □ **questionnaire**

in question being talked about: *The matter in question can be left till next week.* □ **en question**

out of the question not to be thought of as possible; not to be done: *It is quite out of the question for you to go out tonight.* □ **hors de question**

queue [kju:] *noun* a line of people waiting for something or to do something: *a queue for the bus.* □ **file d'attente**

■ *verb* to stand in a queue: *We had to queue to get into the cinema; We had to queue for the cinema.* □ **faire la queue (pour)**

queue up to form, or stand in, a queue: *We queued up for tickets.* □ **faire la queue (pour)**

quick [kwik] *adjective* **1** done, said, finished *etc* in a short time: *a quick trip into town.* □ **rapide**

2 moving, or able to move, with speed: *She's a very quick walker; I made a grab at the dog, but it was too quick for me.* □ **rapide**

3 doing something, able to do something, or done, without delay; prompt; lively: *He is always quick to help; a quick answer; She's very quick at arithmetic.* □ **rapide**

■ *adverb* quickly: *Come quick – something terrible has happened!.* □ **vite**

'quickly *adverb.* □ **vite**

'quicken *verb* to make or become quicker: *He quickened his pace.* □ **accélérer**

'quickness *noun.* □ **rapidité**

'quicklime *noun* lime which has not been mixed with

water. □ **chaux vive**

'quicksand *noun* (an area of) loose, wet sand that sucks in anyone or anything that stands on it. □ **sables mouvants**

'quicksilver *noun* mercury. □ **mercure**

,quick-'tempered *adjective* easily made angry. □ **soupe au lait**

,quick-'witted *adjective* thinking very quickly: *a quick-witted policeman.* □ **à l'esprit vif**

,quick-'wittedly *adverb.* □ **avec de la vivacité d'esprit**

,quick-'wittedness *noun.* □ **vivacité d'esprit**

quiet ['kwaiət] *adjective* **1** not making very much, or any, noise; without very much, or any, noise: *Tell the children to be quiet; It's very quiet out in the country; a quiet person.* □ **tranquille, retiré**

2 free from worry, excitement *etc*: *I live a very quiet life.* □ **tranquille**

3 without much movement or activity; not busy: *We'll have a quiet afternoon watching television.* □ **tranquille**

4 (of colours) not bright. □ **discret**

■ *noun* a state, atmosphere, period of time *etc* which is quiet: *In the quiet of the night; All I want is peace and quiet.* □ **silence, calme**

■ *verb* (*often with* **down**) to quieten. □ **(se) calmer**

'quieten *verb* **1** (*often with* **down**) to make or become quiet: *I expect you to quieten down when I come into the classroom.* □ **(se) calmer**

2 to remove or lessen (a person's fears, doubts *etc*). □ **apaiser**

'quietly *adverb.* □ **silencieusement**

'quietness *noun.* □ **silence, calme**

keep quiet about to say nothing about; to keep secret: *I'd like you to keep quiet about the child's father being in prison.* □ **garder pour soi**

on the quiet secretly; without letting anyone find out: *He went out of the office to enjoy a cigarette on the quiet.* □ **en cachette**

> **quiet** is an adjective: *She has a quiet voice; Keep quiet.*
> **quite** is an adverb: *This book is quite good.*

quill [kwil] *noun* **1** a large feather, *especially* the feather of a goose, made into a pen. □ **plume (d'oie)**

2 one of the sharp spines of certain animals (*eg* the porcupine). □ **piquant**

quilt [kwilt] *noun* a bedcover filled with down, feathers *etc*. □ **édredon**

'quilted *adjective* made of two layers of material (often decoratively) stitched together with padding between them: *a quilted jacket.* □ **matelassé**

quin [kwin] *see* **quintuplet**.

quince [kwins] *noun* a fruit with a sharp taste, used in making jam *etc*. □ **coing**

quinine ['kwini:n] *noun* a bitter-tasting drug got from the bark of a type of tree, used as a medicine, *especially* for malaria. □ **quinine**

quintet [kwin'tet] *noun* **1** a group of five singers or people playing musical instruments. □ **quintette**

2 a piece of music written for such a group. □ **quintette**

quintuplet [kwin'tju:plit] *noun* (*abbreviation* **quin** [kwin]) one of five children born to one mother at the same time. □ **quintuplés**

quip [kwip] *noun* a quick, witty remark: *She is very good at making clever quips.* □ **trait d'esprit**

■ *verb – past tense, past participle* **quipped** – *verb* to make a quip or quips. □ **lancer avec esprit**

quirk [kwəːk] *noun* a strange or unusual feature of a person's behaviour *etc.* □ **excentricité**

quit [kwit] – *past tense, past participles* **'quitted, quit** – *verb* to leave, stop, or resign from *etc*: *I'm going to quit teaching*; *They have been ordered to quit the house by next week.* □ **abandonner**

be quit of to be rid of: *I am glad to be quit of that job.* □ **être débarrassé de**

quite [kwait] *adverb* **1** completely; entirely: *This is quite impossible.* □ **tout à fait**

2 fairly; rather; to a certain extent: *It's quite warm today*; *She's quite a good artist*; *I quite like the idea.* □ **assez, plutôt**

■ *interjection* exactly; indeed; I agree: *'I think he is being unfair to her.' 'Quite.'* □ **d'accord, en effet**

see also **quiet.**

quiver[1] ['kwivə] *verb* to tremble or shake: *The leaves quivered in the breeze.* □ **frémir**

■ *noun* a quivering sound, movement *etc.* □ **frémissement**

quiver[2] ['kwivə] *noun* a long, narrow case for carrying arrows in. □ **carquois**

quiz [kwiz] – *plural* **'quizzes** – *noun* a game or competition in which knowledge is tested by asking questions:

a television quiz; *a general-knowledge quiz.* □ **jeu questionnaire**

'quizmaster *noun* a question-master. □ **animateur, trice**

quoits [koits] *noun singular* a game in which rings of metal, rope *etc*, called **quoits**, are thrown on to one or more small rods or hooks. □ **jeu de palet**

quorum ['kwoːrəm] *noun* the smallest number of members necessary at a meeting before any business can be done. □ **quorum**

quota ['kwoutə] *noun* the part, share or amount allotted to each member of a group *etc.* □ **quota; quote-part**

quote [kwout] *verb* **1** to repeat the exact words of a person as they were said or written: *to quote Shakespeare/ Shakespeare's words/from Shakespeare, 'Is this a dagger which I see before me?'* □ **citer**

2 to name (a price). □ **établir (un prix)**

3 to mention or state in support of an argument: *to quote an example.* □ **citer**

quo'tation *noun* **1** a person's exact words, as repeated by someone else: *a quotation from Elizabeth Browning.* □ **citation**

2 a price mentioned (for a job *etc*). □ **devis estimatif**

3 the act of quoting. □ **citation**

quotation marks marks ('''' or '') used to show that a person's words are being repeated exactly: *He said 'I'm going out.'* □ **guillemets**

quotient [kwouʃənt] *noun* the answer to a division problem in mathematics, the number of times one number can be divided into another: *In the example: 8 divided by 2, the quotient is 4.* □ **quotient**

Rr

rabbi ['rabai] *noun* a Jewish priest or teacher of the law. □ **rabbin**

rabbit ['rabit] *noun* a type of small long-eared burrowing animal, found living wild in fields or sometimes kept as a pet. □ **lapin, ine**

rabble ['rabl] *noun* a noisy, disorderly crowd. □ **cohue**

rabies ['reibiːz] *noun* a disease that causes madness (and *usually* death) in dogs and other animals (including humans). □ **rage**

raccoon, racoon [rə'kuːn, ra-] *noun* a type of small, furry, North American animal, with a striped, bushy tail. □ **raton laveur**

race¹ [reis] *noun* a competition to find who or which is the fastest: *a horse race*. □ **course**
■ *verb* 1 to (cause to) run in a race: *I'm racing my horse on Saturday; The horse is racing against five others*. □ **(faire) courir**
2 to have a competition with (someone) to find out who is the fastest: *I'll race you to that tree*. □ **faire une course avec**
3 to go *etc* quickly: *She raced along the road on her bike*. □ **filer (à toute allure)**
'**racer** *noun* a car, bicycle *etc* built for competitive racing. □ **voiture/vélo de course**
'**race car** *noun* a car specially designed and built for racing. □ **voiture de course**
'**racecourse** *noun* (a place with) a course over which horse races are run. □ **champ de courses**
'**racehorse** *noun* a horse bred and used for racing. □ **cheval de course**
'**racetrack** *noun* (a place with) a course over which races are run by cars, dogs, athletes *etc*. □ **piste**
a race against time a desperate attempt to do something before a certain time. □ **course contre la montre**
the races a meeting for horse-racing. □ **les courses (de chevaux)**

race² [reis] *noun* 1 any one section of mankind, having a particular set of characteristics which make it different from other sections: *the Mongolian race; the white races; (also adjective) race relations*. □ **race; racial**
2 the fact of belonging to any of these various sections: *the problem of race*. □ **race(s)**
3 a group of people who share the same culture, language *etc; the Anglo-Saxon race*. □ **race**
'**racial** ['reiʃəl] *adjective* of, or having to do with, race or a particular race: *racial characteristics; racial discrimination/hatred*. □ **racial**
'**racialism** ['reiʃə-], '**racism** *noun* 1 the belief that some races are better than others. □ **racisme**
2 prejudice against someone on the grounds of his race. □ **racisme**
'**racialist** ['reiʃə-], '**racist** *noun, adjective: racist attitudes*. □ **raciste**
the human race mankind. □ **la race humaine**
of mixed race having ancestors (*especially* parents) from two or more different human races. □ **métissé**

rack¹ [rak] *noun* a frame or shelf in or on which objects

(*eg* letters, plates, luggage *etc*) are put until they are wanted or needed: *Put these tools back in the rack; Put your bag in the luggage rack*. □ **porte-outils; étagère; porte-bagages, etc.**

rack² [rak]: **rack one's brains** to think desperately hard. □ **se creuser la tête**

rack³ [rak]: **go to rack and ruin** to get into a state of neglect and decay. □ **tomber en ruine**

racket¹, racquet ['rakit] *noun* a wooden or metal frame strung with catgut or nylon, used in tennis and other games: *tennis racket; squash racket; badminton racket*. □ **raquette**

racket² ['rakit] *noun* 1 a great deal of noise: *What a racket the children are making!* □ **vacarme**
2 a dishonest way of making money: *the drug racket*. □ **combine louche**

racoon *see* **raccoon**.

racquet *see* **racket¹**.

racy ['reisi] *adjective* lively: *a racy style of writing*. □ **plein de verve**
'**racily** *adverb*. □ **avec verve**
'**raciness** *noun*. □ **verve**

radar ['reidaː] *noun* a method of showing the direction and distance of an object by means of radio waves which bounce off the object and return to their source. □ **radar**

radiant ['reidiənt] *adjective* 1 showing great joy: *a radiant smile*. □ **radieux**
2 sending out rays of heat, light *etc* or carried, sent *etc* in the form of, or by means of, rays of heat, light *etc*. □ **rayonnant**
'**radiantly** *adverb*. □ **d'un air radieux**
'**radiance** *noun: the radiance of her smile*. □ **éclat**

radiate ['reidieit] *verb* 1 to send out rays of (light, heat *etc*): *A fire radiates heat*. □ **irradier**
2 to go out or be sent out in rays, or in many directions from a central point: *Heat radiates from a fire; All the roads radiate from the centre of the town*. □ **rayonner (de)**
,**radi'ation** *noun* rays of light, heat *etc* or of any radioactive substance. □ **radiation**
'**radiator** *noun* 1 a type of apparatus for heating a room. □ **radiateur**
2 an apparatus in a car which, with a fan, cools the engine. □ **radiateur**

radical ['radikəl] *adjective* 1 relating to the basic nature of something: *radical faults in the design*. □ **fondamental**
2 thorough; complete: *radical changes*. □ **radical**
3 wanting or involving great or extreme political, social or economic changes. □ **radical**
■ *noun* a person who wants radical political changes. □ **radical, ale**
'**radically** *adverb*. □ **radicalement**

radio ['reidiou] – *plural* '**radios** – *noun* (an apparatus for) the sending and receiving of human speech, music *etc: a pocket radio; The concert is being broadcast on radio; I heard about it on the radio; (also adjective) a radio program, radio waves*. □ **(de) radio**
■ *verb* – *3rd person singular present tense* '**radios**: *past*

tense, past participle 'radioed – to send (a message) by radio: *When someone on the island is ill, we have to radio (to) the mainland for a doctor; An urgent message was radioed to us this evening.* □ **envoyer un message radio**

radioactive [reidiou'aktiv] *adjective* **1** (of some substances, *eg* uranium) giving off rays which can be dangerous, but which can also be used in *eg* medicine: *radioactive metals.* □ **radioactif**

2 containing radioactive substances: *radioactive waste/ dust.* □ **radioactif**

,radioac'tivity *noun.* □ **radioactivité**

radiograph ['reidiəgraːf] *noun* a photograph taken by means of X-rays or other rays. □ **radiographie**

,radi'ographer [-'o-] *noun* a person who makes such photographs. □ **radiologue**

radi'ography [-'o-] *noun.* □ **radiographie**

radiology [reidi'olədʒi] *noun* **1** the branch of medicine involving the use of radioactive substances and radiation in the diagnosis (and treatment) of diseases. □ **radiologie**

2 the scientific study of (the use of) radioactive substances and radiation. □ **radiologie**

,radi'ologist *noun.* □ **radiologue**

radiotherapy [reidiou'θerəpi] *noun* the treatment of disease by X-rays and other forms of radiation. □ **radiothérapie**

radish ['radiʃ] *noun* a plant with a red-skinned white root used as food. □ **radis**

radium ['reidiəm] *noun* a radioactive metallic element, used in treating certain diseases. □ **radium**

radius ['reidiəs] *noun* **1** (*plural* 'radiuses) the area within a given distance from a central point: *They searched within a radius of one kilometre from the school.* □ **rayon**

2 (*plural* 'radii [-diai]) a straight line from the centre of a circle to its circumference. □ **rayon**

raffia ['rafiə] *noun* (strips of) fibre from the leaves of a type of palm tree, used for making mats, baskets *etc.* □ **raphia**

raffle ['rafl] *noun* a way of raising money by selling numbered tickets, one or more of which win a prize: *I won this doll in a raffle; (also adjective) raffle tickets.* □ **(de)loterie**

■ *verb* to give as the prize in a raffle: *They raffled a bottle of whisky to raise money for cancer research.* □ **mettre qqch. en loterie**

raft [raːft] *noun* a number of logs, planks *etc* fastened together and used as a boat. □ **radeau**

rafter ['raːftə] *noun* a beam supporting the roof of a house. □ **chevron**

rag [rag] *noun* a piece of old, torn or worn cloth: *I'll polish my bike with this old rag.* □ **guenille, lambeau**

'ragged ['ragid] *adjective* **1** dressed in old, worn or torn clothing: *a ragged beggar.* □ **déguenillé**

2 torn: *ragged clothes.* □ **en loques**

3 rough or uneven; not straight or smooth: *a ragged edge.* □ **déchiqueté**

'raggedly *adverb.* □ **irrégulièrement, (vêtu) de guenilles**

'raggedness *noun.* □ **rugosité, délabrement**

rags *noun plural* old, worn or torn clothes: *The beggar was dressed in rags.* □ **haillons**

ragamuffin ['ragəmʌfin] *noun* a ragged, dirty person, *especially* a child. □ **va-nu-pieds**

rage [reidʒ] *noun* **1** (a fit of) violent anger: *He flew into a rage; He shouted with rage.* □ **rage**

2 violence; great force: *the rage of the sea.* □ **furie**

■ *verb* **1** to act or shout in great anger: *He raged at his dog.* □ **être furieux**

2 (of wind, storms *etc*) to be violent; to blow with great force: *The storm raged all night.* □ **faire rage**

3 (of battles, arguments *etc*) to be carried on with great violence: *The battle raged for two whole days.* □ **faire rage**

4 (of diseases *etc*) to spread quickly and affect many people: *Fever was raging through the town.* □ **faire des ravages**

'raging *adjective* violent; extreme: *raging toothache; a raging storm.* □ **violent, déchaîné**

(all) the rage very much in fashion. □ **grande vogue**

raid [reid] *noun* a sudden, short and *usually* unexpected attack: *The enemy made a raid on the docks; The police carried out a raid on the gambling den.* □ **raid**

■ *verb* **1** to make a raid on: *The police raided the gambling club.* □ **faire une descente dans**

2 to take things from: *I'm hungry – let's raid the fridge.* □ **faire une razzia**

'raider *noun*: *The raiders burned down all the houses.* □ **pillard**

rail [reil] *noun* **1** a (*usually* horizontal) bar of metal, wood *etc* used in fences *etc*, or for hanging things on: *Don't lean over the rail; a curtain-rail; a towel-rail.* □ **barre, tringle**

2 (*usually in plural*) a long bar of steel which forms the track on which trains *etc* run. □ **rail(s)**

■ *verb* (*usually with* in *or* off) to surround with a rail or rails: *We'll rail that bit of ground off to stop people walking on it.* □ **entourer d'une grille, d'une clôture**

'railing *noun* (*usually in plural*) a fence or barrier of (*usually* vertical) metal or wooden bars: *They've put railings up all around the park.* □ **grille, clôture**

'railroad *noun* a railway. □ **chemin de fer**

'railway, 'railroad *noun* **1** a track with (*usually* more than one set of) two (or sometimes three) parallel steel rails on which trains run: *They're building a new railway; (also adjective) a railway station.* □ **(de) chemin de fer**

2 (*sometimes in plural*) the whole organization which is concerned with the running of trains, the building of tracks *etc*: *He has a job on the railway; The railways are very badly run in some countries.* □ **chemin(s) de fer**

by rail by or on the railway: *goods sent by rail.* □ **par voie ferrée**

rain [rein] *noun* **1** water falling from the clouds in liquid drops: *We've had a lot of rain today; walking in the rain; We had flooding because of last week's heavy rains.* □ **pluie**

2 a great number of things falling like rain: *a rain of arrows.* □ **pluie**

■ *verb* **1** (*only with* **it** *as subject*) to cause rain to fall: *I think it will rain today.* □ **pleuvoir**

2 to (cause to) fall like rain: *Arrows rained down on the soldiers.* □ **pleuvoir**

'**rainy** *adjective* having (many) showers of rain: *a rainy day*; *the rainy season*; *rainy weather.* □ **pluvieux, des pluies**

'**raininess** *noun.* □ **pluviosité**

'**rainbow** *noun* the coloured arch sometimes seen in the sky opposite the sun when rain is falling. □ **arc-en-ciel**

'**raincoat** *noun* a waterproof coat worn to keep out the rain. □ **imperméable**

'**raindrop** *noun* a single drop of rain. □ **goutte de pluie**

'**rainfall** *noun* the amount of rain that falls in a certain place in a certain time: *We haven't had much rainfall this year*; *the annual rainfall.* □ **précipitation(s)**

'**rain gauge** *noun* an instrument for measuring rainfall. □ **pluviomètre**

'**rain-tree** *noun* a tropical tree of the mimosa family, whose pods are eaten by cattle. □ **pithécolobium**

keep, save *etc* **for a rainy day** to keep (*especially* money) until one needs it or in case one may need it. □ **garder pour les mauvais jours**

rain cats and dogs to rain very hard. □ **pleuvoir à seaux**

the rains (in tropical countries) the rainy season. □ **saison des pluies**

(as) right as rain perfectly all right; completely well. □ **en parfait état/parfaite santé**

raise [reiz] *verb* **1** to move or lift to a high(er) position: *Raise your right hand*; *Raise the flag.* □ **lever**

2 to make higher: *If you paint your flat, that will raise the value of it considerably*; *We'll raise that wall about 20 centimetres.* □ **hausser**

3 to grow (crops) or breed (animals) for food: *We don't raise pigs on this farm.* □ **élever**

4 to rear, bring up (a child): *She has raised a large family.* □ **élever**

5 to state (a question, objection *etc* which one wishes to have discussed): *Has anyone in the audience any points they would like to raise?* □ **soulever**

6 to collect; to gather: *We'll try to raise money*; *The revolutionaries managed to raise a small army.* □ **recueillir; rassembler**

7 to cause: *His remarks raised a laugh.* □ **provoquer**

8 to cause to rise or appear: *The car raised a cloud of dust.* □ **produire**

9 to build (a monument *etc*): *They've raised a statue of Robert Burns/in memory of Robert Burns.* □ **élever**

10 to give (a shout *etc*). □ **pousser**

■ *noun* an increase in wages or salary: *I'm going to ask the boss for a raise.* □ **augmentation**

raise someone's hopes to make someone more hopeful than he or she was. □ **donner de l'espoir à**

raise hell/Cain/the roof *etc* to make a great deal of noise. □ **faire un bruit de tous les diables**

raise someone's spirits to make someone less unhappy. □ **remonter le moral à qqn**

raisin ['reizən] *noun* a dried grape: *She put raisins and sultanas in the cake.* □ **raisin sec**

rajah ['raːdʒə] *noun* an Indian king or prince. □ **radjah**

rake [reik] *noun* **1** a tool which consists of a *usually* metal bar with teeth at the end of a long handle, used for smoothing earth, gathering *eg* leaves together *etc*. □ **râteau**

2 any similar tool: *a croupier's rake in a casino.* □ **râteau**

3 the act of raking: *to give the soil a rake.* □ **coup de râteau**

■ *verb* **1** to smooth or gather with a rake: *I'll rake these grass-cuttings up later.* □ **ratisser**

2 (*often with* **out**) to remove the ashes from (a fire) with a poker *etc*. □ **enlever les cendres du feu**

3 to fire guns at (a target) from one end of it to the other: *The soldiers raked the entire village with machine-gun fire.* □ **mitrailler**

rake through to make a thorough search: *I'm raking through these boxes of old clothes.* □ **fouiller dans**

rake up to find out and tell or remind people about (something, *usually* something unpleasant that would be better forgotten). □ **attiser (une ancienne querelle)**

rally ['rali] *verb* **1** to come or bring together again: *The general tried to rally his troops after the defeat*; *The troops rallied around the general.* □ **(se) rallier**

2 to come or bring together for a joint action or effort: *The supporters rallied to save the club from collapse*; *The politician asked his supporters to rally for the cause.* □ **(se) rallier**

3 to (cause to) recover health or strength: *She rallied from her illness.* □ **se remettre de**

■ *noun* – *plural* '**rallies** – **1** a *usually* large gathering of people for some purpose: *a Scouts' rally.* □ **ralliement**

2 a meeting (*usually* of cars or motorcycles) for a competition, race *etc*. □ **rallye**

3 an improvement in health after an illness. □ **retour à la santé**

4 (in tennis *etc*) a (*usually* long) series of shots before the point is won or lost. □ **échange**

rally around to come together for a joint action or effort, *especially* of support: *When John's business was in difficulty, his friends all rallied around (to help) him.* □ **se regrouper autour (de qqn)**

ram [ram] *noun* **1** a male sheep. □ **bélier**

2 something heavy, *especially* a part of a machine, used for ramming. □ **bélier**

■ *verb* – *past tense, past participle* **rammed** – **1** (of ships, cars *etc*) to run into, and cause damage to: *The destroyer rammed the submarine*; *His car rammed into/against the car in front of it.* □ **éperonner, emboutir**

2 to push down, into, on to *etc* with great force: *We rammed the fence-posts into the ground.* □ **enfoncer**

ramble ['rambl] *verb* **1** to go for a long walk or walks, *usually* in the countryside, for pleasure. □ **partir en randonnée**

2 to speak in an aimless or confused way. □ **divaguer, radoter**

■ *noun* a long walk, *usually* in the countryside, taken for pleasure. □ **randonnée**

'**rambler** *noun* **1** a climbing plant (*usually* a rose). □ **rosier grimpant**

2 a person who goes walking in the country for pleasure. □ **promeneur, euse**

'**rambling** adjective **1** aimless and confused; not keeping to the topic: *a long, rambling speech.* □ **décousu**
2 built (as if) without any plan, stretching in various directions: *a rambling old house.* □ **plein de coins et de recoins**
3 (of plants, *usually* roses) climbing. □ **grimpant**
ramble on to talk for a long time in an aimless or confused way. □ **discourir longuement et sans cohérence**
rambutan ['rambutan] *noun* a sweet, juicy red or yellow fruit with one seed and a hairy rind. □ **ramboutan**
ramp [ramp] *noun* a sloping surface between places, objects *etc* which are at different levels: *The car drove up the ramp from the quay to the ship.* □ **rampe (d'accès)**
rampage [ram'peidʒ] *verb* to rush about angrily, violently or in excitement: *The elephants rampaged through the jungle.* □ **parcourir avec rage**
be/go on the rampage ['rampeidʒ] to rush about angrily, violently or in excitement, often causing great destruction. □ **être déchaîné**
rampant ['rampənt] *adjective* very common and uncontrolled: *Vandalism is rampant in the town.* □ **qui sévit**
rampart ['rampaːt] *noun* (*often in plural*) a mound or wall for defence: *The defenders were drawn up on the ramparts.* □ **rempart**
ramshackle ['ramʃakl] *adjective* badly made; likely to fall to pieces: *a ramshackle car.* □ **délabré**
ran *see* run.
ranch [raːntʃ] *noun* a farm, *especially* one in North America for rearing cattle or horses. □ **ranch**
rancid ['ransid] *adjective* (of food, *especially* butter) tasting or smelling bad. □ **rance**
rand [rand] – *plural* **rand(s)** – *noun* the standard unit of South African currency. □ **rand**
random ['randəm] *adjective* done *etc* without any particular plan or system; irregular: *The opinion poll was based on a random sample of adults.* □ **aléatoire**
'**randomly** *adverb.* □ **au hasard**
at random without any particular plan or system: *The police were stopping cars at random and checking their brakes*; *Choose a number at random.* □ **au hasard**
rang *see* ring².
range [reindʒ] *noun* **1** a selection or variety: *a wide range of books for sale*; *She has a very wide range of interests.* □ **assortiment, variété**
2 the distance over which an object can be sent or thrown, sound can be heard *etc*: *What is the range of this missile?*; *We are within range of/beyond the range of/out of range of their guns.* □ **(à/hors de) portée (de)**
3 the amount between certain limits: *I'm hoping for a salary within the range $30,000 to $34,000*; *the range of a person's voice between his highest and lowest notes.* □ **(de l')ordre (de); étendue**
4 a row or series: *a mountain range.* □ **chaîne**
5 in the United States, land, *usually* without fences, on which cattle *etc* can graze. □ **prairie**
6 a place where a person can practise shooting *etc*; *a rifle range.* □ **champ de tir**
7 a large kitchen stove with a flat top. □ **cuisinière**
■ *verb* **1** to put in a row or rows: *The two armies were*

ranged on opposite sides of the valley. □ **(se) ranger**
2 to vary between certain limits: *Weather conditions here range between bad and dreadful/from bad to dreadful.* □ **varier (entre...et)**
3 to go, move, extend *etc*: *Her talk ranged over a number of topics.* □ **couvrir**
'**ranger** *noun* **1** a person who looks after a forest or park. □ **garde forestier**
2 a soldier who is a member of a specially trained force; a commando. □ **garde monté**
rank¹ [raŋk] *noun* **1** a line or row (*especially* of soldiers or taxis): *The officer ordered the front rank to fire.* □ **rang(ée), file**
2 (in the army, navy *etc*) a person's position of importance: *He was promoted to the rank of sergeant/colonel.* □ **rang**
3 a social class: *the lower social ranks.* □ **classe**
■ *verb* to have, or give, a place in a group, according to importance: *I would rank her among our greatest writers*; *Apes rank above dogs in intelligence.* □ **(se) classer**
the rank and file 1 ordinary people. □ **le peuple**
2 ordinary soldiers, not officers. □ **les hommes de troupe**
rank² [raŋk] *adjective* **1** complete; absolute: *rank stupidity*; *The race was won by a rank outsider.* □ **absolu**
2 unpleasantly stale and strong: *a rank smell of tobacco.* □ **rance**
'**rankness** *noun.* □ **odeur rance**
ransack ['ransak] *verb* **1** to search thoroughly in: *She ransacked the whole house for her keys.* □ **fouiller à fond**
2 loot, plunder: *The army ransacked the conquered city.* □ **piller**
ransom ['ransəm] *noun* a sum of money *etc* paid for the freeing of a prisoner: *They paid a ransom of $40,000*; (*also adjective*) *They paid $40,000 in ransom money.* □ **rançon**
■ *verb* **1** to pay money *etc* to free (someone). □ **payer la rançon de qqn**
2 to keep (a person) as a prisoner until a sum of money *etc* is paid for his or her release. □ **mettre à rançon**
hold to ransom to keep (a person) as a prisoner until a sum of money *etc* is paid for his or her release. □ **rançonner**
rant [rant] *verb* to talk angrily: *He's still ranting (and raving) about the damage to his car.* □ **fulminer**
rap [rap] *noun* a quick, brief knock or tap: *She heard a rap on the door.* □ **coup sec**
■ *verb* – *past tense, past participle* **rapped** – to hit or knock quickly and briefly: *I rapped the child's fingers with a ruler*; *She rapped on the table and called for silence.* □ **taper sur**
rap out to say quickly: *He rapped out his orders.* □ **lancer**
rapacious [rə'peiʃəs] *adjective* greedy (*especially* for money); eager to seize as much as possible. □ **rapace**
ra'paciously *adverb.* □ **avec rapacité**
ra'paciousness *noun.* □ **rapacité**
ra'pacity [-'pasə-] *noun.* □ **rapacité**
rape [reip] *noun* **1** the crime of having sexual intercourse

with a woman against her will. □ **viol**

2 the act of causing great damage, destruction *etc* to land *etc*. □ **viol**

■ *verb* 1 to force (a woman) to have sexual intercourse against her will. □ **violer**

2 to cause great damage, destruction *etc* to (countryside *etc*). □ **violer**

'**rapist** *noun* a man who rapes a woman. □ **violeur**

rapid ['rapid] *adjective* quick; fast: *She made some rapid calculations*; *She looked feverish and had a rapid pulse*. □ **rapide**

'**rapidly** *adverb*. □ **rapidement**

ra'**pidity** *noun*. □ **rapidité**

'**rapidness** *noun*. □ **rapidité**

'**rapids** *noun plural* a place in a river where the water flows quickly, often having dangerous rocks in mid-stream. □ **rapides**

rapier ['reipiə] *noun* a type of long thin sword. □ **rapière**

rapist *see* **rape**.

rapt [rapt] *adjective* fascinated (*usually* in admiration): *She listened to the speaker with rapt attention*. □ **ravi**

rapture ['raptʃə] *noun* great delight. □ **ravissement**

'**rapturous** *adjective* showing great delight: *They gave her a rapturous welcome*. □ **enthousiaste**

'**rapturously** *adverb*. □ **avec beaucoup d'enthousiasme**

in raptures greatly delighted: *She was in raptures about her beautiful new car*. □ **ravi, enchanté**

rare ['reə] *adjective* 1 not done, found, seen *etc* very often; uncommon: *a rare flower*; *a rare occurrence*. □ **rare**

2 (of meat) only slightly cooked: *I like my steak rare*. □ **saignant**

'**rareness** *noun*. □ **rareté**

'**rarely** *adverb* not often: *I rarely go to bed before midnight*. □ **rarement**

'**rarity** *noun* 1 the state of being uncommon. □ **rareté**

2 (*plural* '**rarities**) something which is uncommon: *This stamp is quite a rarity*. □ **rareté**

raring ['reəriŋ] **raring to go** very keen to begin, go *etc*. □ **trépignant d'impatience**

rascal ['raːskəl] *noun* a cheeky or naughty person, *especially* a child: *a cheeky little rascal*. □ **coquin, ine**

'**rascally** *adjective*. □ **de coquin, ine**

rash[1] [raʃ] *adjective* acting, or done, with little caution or thought: *a rash person/action/statement*; *It was rash of you to leave your present job without first finding another*. □ **imprudent**

'**rashly** *adverb*. □ **imprudemment**

'**rashness** *noun*. □ **imprudence**

rash[2] [raʃ] *noun* a large number of red spots on the skin: *That child has a rash – is it measles?* □ **éruption**

rasher ['raʃə] *noun* a thin slice (of bacon or ham). □ **tranche de lard**

raspberry ['raːzbəri] – *plural* '**raspberries** – *noun* a type of edible red berry. □ **framboise**

rasping ['raːspiŋ] *adjective* (of a sound, voice *etc*) harsh, rough and unpleasant. □ **grinçant**

rat [rat] *noun* 1 a small animal with a long tail, like a mouse but larger: *The rats have eaten holes in those bags of flour*. □ **rat**

2 an offensive word for an unpleasant and untrustworthy person. □ **salaud**

■ *verb* – *past tense, past participle* '**ratted** – 1 to break an agreement, promise *etc*. □ **manquer à**

2 to betray one's friends, colleagues *etc*: *The police know we're here. Someone must have ratted*. □ **dénoncer**

rat race the fierce, unending competition for success *etc*. □ **recherche effrénée de la réussite**

smell a rat to have a feeling that something is not as it should be; to have suspicions. □ **soupçonner qqch.**

rate [reit] *noun* 1 the number of occasions within a given period of time when something happens or is done: *a high (monthly) accident rate in a factory*. □ **taux, pourcentage**

2 the number or amount of something (in relation to something else); a ratio: *There was a failure rate of one pupil in ten in the exam*. □ **pourcentage**

3 the speed with which something happens or is done: *She works at a tremendous rate*; *the rate of increase/expansion*. □ **vitesse**

4 the level (of pay), cost *etc* (of or for something): *What is the rate of pay for this job?* □ **tarif**

5 (*usually in plural*) a tax, *especially*, in United Kingdom, paid by house-owners *etc* to help with the running of their town *etc*. □ **impôts locaux**

■ *verb* to estimate or be estimated, with regard to worth, merit, value *etc*: *I don't rate this book very highly*; *He doesn't rate very highly as a dramatist in my estimation*. □ **assigner une valeur à; être évalué**

'**rating** *noun* 1 (*usually in plural*) the position of importance, popularity *etc* (of a person, thing *etc*): *This television program has had some very bad ratings recently*. □ **cote**

2 an ordinary sailor, as opposed to an officer. □ **matelot**

at this, at that rate if this or if that is the case; if this or if that continues: *She says that she isn't sure whether we'll be allowed to finish, but at that rate we might as well not start*. □ **à ce compte-là**

rate of exchange the relative values of the currencies of two or more countries: *I want to change some dollars into francs – what is the rate of exchange?* □ **taux de change**

rather ['raːθə] *adverb* 1 to a certain extent; slightly; a little: *She's rather nice*; *That's a rather silly question/ rather a silly question*; *I've eaten rather more than I should have*. □ **plutôt, un peu**

2 more willingly; preferably: *I'd rather do it now than later*; *Can we do it now rather than tomorrow?*; *I'd rather not do it at all*; *I would/had rather you didn't do that*; *Wouldn't you rather have this one?*; *I'd resign rather than do that*. □ **plutôt (que)**

3 more exactly; more correctly: *She agreed, or rather she didn't disagree*; *One could say she was foolish rather than wicked*. □ **plutôt (que)**

ratify ['ratifai] *verb* to approve and agree to formally and officially, *especially* in writing. □ **ratifier**

,**ratifi'cation** *noun*. □ **ratification**

rating *see* **rate**.

ratio ['reiʃiou] – *plural* '**ratios** – *noun* the amount or

ration ['raʃən] *noun* a measured amount of food *etc* allowed during a particular period of time: *The soldiers were each given a ration of food for the day.* □ **ration**

■ *verb* to allow only a certain amount of (food *etc*) to a person or animal during a particular period of time: *During the oil shortage, gas was rationed.* □ **rationner**

'**rations** *noun plural* the amount of food allowed to a soldier *etc.* □ **rations**

ration out to give or allow a ration of (food *etc*), *eg* to a number of people. □ **rationner**

rational ['raʃənl] *adjective* **1** able to think, reason and judge *etc*: *Man is a rational animal.* □ **raisonnable, doué de raison**

2 sensible; reasonable; logical; not (over-) influenced by emotions *etc*: *There must be a rational explanation for those strange noises.* □ **rationnel**

'**rationally** *adverb.* □ **rationnellement**

,**ration'ality** *noun.* □ **rationalité**

rattle [ratl] *verb* **1** to (cause to) make a series of short, sharp noises by knocking together: *The cups rattled as he carried the tray in; The strong wind rattled the windows.* □ **(faire) cliqueter**

2 to move quickly: *The car was rattling along at top speed.* □ **passer à toute vitesse**

3 to upset and confuse (a person): *Don't let her rattle you – she likes annoying people.* □ **bouleverser qqn**

■ *noun* **1** a series of short, sharp noises: *the rattle of cups.* □ **bruit**

2 a child's toy, or a wooden instrument, which makes a noise of this sort: *The baby waved its rattle.* □ **crécelle**

3 the bony rings of a rattlesnake's tail. □ **sonnettes**

'**rattling** *adjective* fast; lively: *The car travelled at a rattling pace.* □ **(grande) vitesse**

'**rattlesnake** *noun* a type of poisonous American snake with bony rings in its tail which rattle. □ **serpent à sonnettes**

rattle off to say quickly and *usually* without any feeling or expression: *The boy rattled off the poem.* □ **débiter (à toute allure)**

rattle through to say or do (something) quickly: *The teacher rattled through his explanation so quickly that no one could understand him.* □ **débiter (à toute allure)**

raucous ['rɔːkəs] *adjective* hoarse or harsh (and *usually* loud); *a raucous voice.* □ **rauque**

'**raucously** *adverb.* □ **d'une voix rauque**

'**raucousness** *noun.* □ **ton rauque**

ravage ['ravidʒ] *verb* (of enemies, invaders *etc*) to cause great damage or destruction in, or to plunder (a town, country *etc*). □ **ravager**

rave [reiv] *verb* **1** to talk wildly because, or as if, one is mad. □ **délirer**

2 to talk very enthusiastically: *She's been raving about this new record she's heard.* □ **s'extasier sur**

'**raving**: **raving mad** so mad as to be raving. □ **à lier**

raven ['reivən] *noun* a large black bird of the crow family. □ **corbeau**

ravenous ['ravənəs] *adjective* very hungry. □ **vorace**

'**ravenously** *adverb.* □ **voracement**

'**ravenousness** *noun.* □ **voracité**

ravine [rə'viːn] *noun* a deep narrow valley. □ **ravin**

ravioli [ravi'ouli] *noun* small envelopes of pasta containing minced meat. □ **ravioli**

ravishing ['raviʃiŋ] *adjective* extremely delightful; very lovely: *She looks ravishing tonight.* □ **ravissant**

'**ravishingly** *adverb.* □ **de façon ravissante**

raw [rɔː] *adjective* **1** not cooked: *raw onions/meat.* □ **cru**

2 not prepared or refined; in the natural state: *raw cotton; What raw materials are used to make plastic?* □ **brut**

3 with the skin rubbed and sore: *My heel is raw because my shoe doesn't fit properly.* □ **à vif**

4 untrained; inexperienced: *raw recruits.* □ **inexpérimenté**

'**rawness** *noun.* □ **crudité**

a raw deal unfair treatment. □ **sale coup**

ray [rei] *noun* **1** a narrow beam (of light, heat *etc*): *the sun's rays; X-rays; heat-rays; a ray of light.* □ **rayon**

2 a slight amount (of hope *etc*). □ **lueur**

rayon ['reion] *noun, adjective* (of) a type of artificial silk: *a rayon scarf.* □ **rayonne**

raze, (*rare*) **rase** [reiz] *verb* to destroy completely, *especially* by fire: *to raze a city to the ground.* □ **raser**

razor ['reizə] *noun* an instrument for shaving, having a sharp cutting edge, blade (a **razor blade**), or electrically-powered revolving cutters. □ **rasoir**

,**razor-'sharp** *adjective* as sharp as a razor. □ **tranchant comme un rasoir**

reach [riːtʃ] *verb* **1** to arrive at (a place, age *etc*): *We'll never reach Montreal before dark; Money is not important when you reach my age; The noise reached our ears; Has the total reached a thousand dollars yet?; Have they reached an agreement yet?* □ **arriver/parvenir à**

2 to (be able to) touch or get hold of (something): *My keys have fallen down this hole and I can't reach them.* □ **atteindre**

3 to stretch out one's hand in order to touch or get hold of something: *He reached (across the table) for another cake; She reached out and took the book; He reached across/over and slapped him.* □ **étendre (le bras)**

4 to make contact with; to communicate with: *If anything happens you can always reach me by phone.* □ **contacter**

5 to stretch or extend: *My property reaches from here to the river.* □ **s'étendre**

■ *noun* **1** the distance that can be travelled easily: *My house is within (easy) reach (of Montreal).* □ **portée; proche de**

2 the distance one can stretch one's arm: *I keep medicines on the top shelf, out of the children's reach; My keys are down that hole, just out of reach (of my fingers); The boxer has a very long reach.* □ **portée**

3 (*usually in plural*) a straight part of a river, canal *etc*: *the lower reaches of the Thames.* □ **partie droite d'un fleuve entre deux coudes**

react [ri'akt] *verb* **1** to behave in a certain way as a result of something: *How did he react when you called him a fool?*; *He reacted angrily to the criticism*; *Hydrogen reacts with oxygen to form water.* □ **réagir**

2 (*with* **against**) to behave or act in a certain way in order to show rejection of: *Young people tend to react against their parents.* □ **réagir (contre)**

3 (*with* **to**) to be affected, *usually* badly, by (a drug *etc*): *I react very badly to penicillin.* □ **réagir (à)**

re'action [-ʃən] *noun* 1 the act of reacting: *What was his reaction to your remarks?*; *I get a bad reaction from penicillin*; *I'd like to ask you for your reactions to these suggestions.* □ **réaction**

2 a change of opinions, feelings *etc* (*usually* against someone or something): *The new government was popular at first, but then a reaction began.* □ **réaction**

3 a process of change which occurs when two or more substances are put together: (*a*) *nuclear reaction*; *a chemical reaction between iron and acid.* □ **réaction**

re'actionary [-ʃə-] *adjective*, *noun* (*plural* re'actionaries) (a person) opposed to change and progress or favouring a return to things as they were. □ **réactionnaire**

re'actor *noun* (*also* **nuclear reactor**) an apparatus in which nuclear energy is produced which can be used as a source of power, *eg* when converted into electricity. □ **réacteur (nucléaire)**

read [riːd] – *past tense, past participle* read [red] – *verb* 1 to look at and understand (printed or written words or other signs): *Have you read this letter?*; *Can your little girl read yet?*; *Can anyone here read Chinese?*; *to read music*; *I can read* (= understand without being told) *her thoughts/mind.* □ **lire**

2 to learn by reading: *I read in the paper today that the government is going to cut taxes again.* □ **lire**

3 to read aloud, *usually* to someone else: *I read my daughter a story before she goes to bed*; *I read to her before she goes to bed.* □ **faire la lecture à**

4 to pass one's time by reading books *etc* for pleasure *etc*: *I don't have much time to read these days.* □ **lire**

5 to study (a subject) at a university *etc*. □ **étudier**

6 to look at or be able to see (something) and get information from it: *I can't read the clock without my glasses*; *The nurse read the thermometer.* □ **voir; lire**

7 to be written or worded; to say: *His letter reads as follows: 'Dear Sir,...'* □ **être rédigé**

8 (of a piece of writing *etc*) to make a (good, bad *etc*) impression: *This report reads well.* □ **se lire**

9 (of dials, instruments *etc*) to show a particular figure, measurement *etc*: *The thermometer reads –5 °C.* □ **indiquer**

10 to (cause a word, phrase *etc* to) be replaced by another, *eg* in a document or manuscript: *There is one error on this page – For 'two yards', read 'two metres'*; *'Two yards long' should read 'two metres long'.* □ **au lieu de..., lire**

■ *noun* the act, or a period, of reading: *I like a good read before I go to sleep.* □ **lecture**

'readable *adjective* (*negative* **unreadable**) 1 easy or pleasant to read: *I don't usually enjoy poetry but I find these poems very readable.* □ **agréable à lire**

2 able to be read: *Your handwriting is scarcely readable.* □ **lisible**

'readableness *noun*. □ **lisibilité**

,reada'bility *noun*. □ **lisibilité**

'reader *noun* 1 a person who reads books, magazines *etc*: *She's a keen reader.* □ **lecteur, trice**

2 a person who reads a particular newspaper, magazine *etc*: *The editor asked readers to write to him with their opinions.* □ **lecteur, trice**

3 a reading book, *especially* for children or for learners of a foreign language: *a Latin reader.* □ **livre de lecture**

'readership *noun* the (number of) people who read a newspaper, magazine *etc*. □ **nombre de lecteurs**

'reading *noun* 1 the act of reading. □ **lecture**

2 the reading of something aloud, as a (public) entertainment: *a poetry reading.* □ **séance de lecture**

3 the ability to read: *The boy is good at reading.* □ **lecture**

4 the figure, measurement *etc* on a dial, instrument *etc*: *The reading on the thermometer was –5 °C.* □ **relevé**

reading- 1 for the purpose of reading: *reading-glasses*; *a reading room in a library.* □ **de lecture**

2 for learning to read: *a reading book.* □ **de lecture**

'readout – *plural* 'readouts – *noun* data produced by a computer, *eg* on magnetic or paper tape. □ **lecture**

read between the lines to look for or find information (*eg* in a letter) which is not actually stated. □ **lire entre les lignes**

read off to read from a dial, instrument *etc*: *The engineer read off the temperatures one by one.* □ **relever**

read on to continue to read; to read further: *She paused for a few moments, and then read on.* □ **continuer à lire**

read out to read aloud: *Read out the answers to the questions.* □ **lire à voix haute**

read over/through to read from beginning to end: *I'll read through your manuscript, and let you know if I find any mistakes.* □ **lire en entier**

re-address [riːə'dres] *verb* to change the address on (a letter *etc*): *This letter is for the person who used to live here – I'll re-address it and send it to her.* □ **faire suivre**

readily, readiness *see* ready.

reading *see* read.

readjust [riːə'dʒʌst] *verb* (*with* **to**) to get used again to (something one has not experienced for a time): *Some soldiers find it hard to readjust to civilian life when they leave the army.* □ **(se) réadapter (à)**

,rea'djustment *noun*. □ **réadaptation**

ready ['redi] *adjective* 1 (*negative* **unready**) prepared; able to be used *etc* immediately or when needed; able to do (something) immediately or when necessary: *I've packed our cases, so we're ready to leave*; *Is tea ready yet?*; *Your coat has been cleaned and is ready* (*to be collected*). □ **prêt (à)**

2 (*negative* **unready**) willing: *I'm always ready to help.* □ **prêt (à)**

3 quick: *You're too ready to find faults in other people*; *He always has a ready answer.* □ **prompt**

4 likely, about (to do something): *My head feels as if it's*

ready to burst. □ **prêt à, sur le point de**

'readiness *noun.* □ **promptitude**

'readily *adverb* **1** willingly: *I'd readily help you.* □ **volontiers**

2 without difficulty: *I can readily answer all your questions.* □ **facilement**

ready cash ready money. □ **argent liquide**

,ready-'made *adjective* (*especially* of clothes) made in standard sizes, and for sale to anyone who wishes to buy, rather than being made for one particular person: *a ready-made suit.* □ **tout fait**

ready money coins and banknotes: *I want to be paid in ready money, not by cheque.* □ **espèces**

,ready-to-'wear *adjective* (of clothes) ready-made. □ **prêt à porter**

in readiness ready: *I want everything in readiness for her arrival.* □ **prêt**

real [riəl] *adjective* **1** which actually exists: *There's a real monster in that cave.* □ **vrai, réel**

2 not imitation; genuine: *real leather; Is that diamond real?* □ **vrai**

3 actual: *He may own the factory, but it's his manager who is the real boss.* □ **véritable**

4 great: *a real surprise/problem.* □ **vrai**

■ *adverb* very; really: *a real nice house.* □ **très; vraiment**

'realist *noun* a person who sees, or claims to see, life as it is, without being affected by emotion *etc.* □ **réaliste**

'realism *noun.* □ **réalisme**

,rea'listic *adjective* (*negative* **unrealistic**) **1** showing things as they really are: *a realistic painting.* □ **réaliste**

2 taking a sensible, practical view of life: *I'd like to think we'd sell five of these a day, but it would be more realistic to say two.* □ **réaliste**

,rea'listically *adverb.* □ **d'une façon réaliste**

reality [ri'aləti] *noun* **1** that which is real and not imaginary: *It was a relief to get back to reality after hearing the ghost story.* □ **réalité, réel**

2 the state of being real. □ **réalité**

3 (*often in plural* – **re'alities**) a fact: *Death and sorrow are two of the grim realities of human existence.* □ **réalité**

'really *adverb* **1** in fact: *He looks a fool but he is really very clever.* □ **en réalité, réellement**

2 very: *That's a really nice hat!* □ **vraiment**

■ *interjection* an expression of surprise, protest, doubt *etc*: *'I'm going to be the next manager.' 'Oh really?'; Really! You mustn't be so rude!* □ **vraiment**

real estate (the buying and selling of) land and houses. □ **immobilier**

real estate agent a person who arranges the sale or renting of houses. □ **agent(e) immobilier(ière)**

for real genuine; true: *He says he's got a new bike, but I don't know if that's for real.* □ **pour de vrai**

in reality really; actually: *He pretends to be busy, but in reality he has very little to do.* □ **en réalité**

realism, reality *etc* see **real**.

realize, realise ['riəlaiz] *verb* **1** to know; to understand: *I realize that I can't have everything I want; I realized my mistake.* □ **comprendre**

2 to make real; to make (something) come true: *She realized her ambition to become an astronaut; My worst fears were realized.* □ **réaliser**

3 to make (money) by selling something: *He realized $60,000 on the sale of his apartment.* □ **réaliser (des profits)**

,reali'zation, ,reali'sation *noun* the act of realizing: *the realization of his mistake/hopes.* □ **prise de conscience; réalisation**

really see **real**.

realm [relm] *noun* **1** a kingdom. □ **royaume**

2 an area of activity, interest *etc*: *She's well-known in the realm of sport.* □ **domaine**

ream [ri:m] *noun* a measure for paper, equal to 480 sheets. □ **rame**

reap [ri:p] *verb* to cut and gather (corn *etc*): *The farmer is reaping the wheat.* □ **moissonner**

'reaper *noun* a person or machine that reaps. □ **moissonneur, euse**

reappear [ri:ə'piə] *verb* to appear again: *The boy disappeared behind the wall, and reappeared a few metres away.* □ **réapparaître**

,reap'pearance *noun.* □ **réapparition**

rear¹ [riə] *noun* **1** the back part of something: *There is a second bathroom at the rear of the house; The enemy attacked the army in the rear.* □ **arrière**

2 the buttocks, bottom: *The horse kicked him in his rear.* □ **derrière**

■ *adjective* positioned behind: *the rear wheels of the car.* □ **de derrière**

,rear 'admiral *noun* in the navy, (a person of) the rank above commodore. □ **contre-amiral**

'rearguard *noun singular* or *noun plural* (the group of) soldiers who protect the rear of an army (*eg* when it is retreating). □ **arrière-garde**

rear² [riə] *verb* **1** to feed and care for (a family, animals *etc* while they grow up): *She has reared six children; He rears cattle.* □ **élever**

2 (*especially* of a horse) to rise up on the hind legs: *The horse reared in fright as the car passed.* □ **(se) cabrer**

3 to raise (the head *etc*): *The snake reared its head.* □ **(se) dresser**

rear up 1 (*especially* of horses) to rear. □ **(se) cabrer**

2 of problems *etc*) to appear. □ **surgir**

rearm [ri:'ɑːm] *verb* to give or get weapons again, *especially* weapons of a new type. □ **réarmer**

re'armament [-məmənt] *noun.* □ **réarmement**

rearrange [ri:ə'reindʒ] *verb* to change the position of; to arrange differently: *We'll rearrange the chairs.* □ **réarranger**

,rear'rangement *noun.* □ **réagencement; remaniement**

reason ['ri:zn] *noun* **1** something which makes something happen, describes why it happened, should happen or is going to happen *etc*: *What is the reason for this noise?; What is your reason for going to Ottawa?; The reason (why) I am going is that I want to.* □ **raison**

2 the power of the mind to think, form opinions and judgments *etc*: *Only man has reason – animals have not.* □ **raison**

■ *verb* **1** to (be able to) think, form opinions and judgments *etc*: *Man alone has the ability to reason.* □ **raisonner**

2 to argue; to work out after some thought: *She reasoned that if he had caught the 6:30 train, he would not be home before 8:00.* □ **argumenter; raisonner**

'reasonable *adjective* **1** sensible: *a reasonable suggestion.* □ **raisonnable**

2 willing to listen to argument; acting with good sense: *You will find her very reasonable.* □ **raisonnable**

3 fair; correct; which one should or could accept: *Is $10 a reasonable price for this book?* □ **raisonnable**

4 satisfactory; as much as one might expect or want: *There was a reasonable number of people at the meeting.* □ **raisonnable**

'reasonableness *noun.* □ **caractère raisonnable**

'reasonably *adverb*: *She behaved very reasonably*; *The car is reasonably priced*; *The meeting was reasonably well attended.* □ **raisonnablement**

'reasoning *noun* the act or process of reaching a decision, conclusion *etc*: *I don't understand his reasoning at all.* □ **raisonnement**

have reason to (believe, think *etc*) to feel justified in (believing *etc*): *I have (good) reason to think that he is lying.* □ **avoir des raisons de (croire, penser, etc.)**

it stands to reason it is obvious or logical: *If you go to bed so late it stands to reason that you will be tired next morning.* □ **il va de soi que**

listen to reason to allow oneself to be persuaded to do something more sensible than what one was going to do; to pay attention to common sense. □ **entendre raison**

lose one's reason to become insane. □ **perdre la raison**

reason with to argue with (a person) in order to persuade him or her to be more sensible: *We tried to reason with the worried mother but she went out alone in the storm to look for the child.* □ **raisonner qqn**

see reason to (be persuaded to) be more sensible than one is or has been. □ **entendre raison**

within reason within the limits of good sense: *I'll do anything/go anywhere within reason.* □ **dans des limites raisonnables**

reassemble [riːəˈsembl] *verb* **1** to put (things) together after taking them apart: *The mechanic took the engine to pieces, then reassembled it.* □ **remonter**

2 to come together again: *The tourists went off sightseeing, then reassembled for their evening meal.* □ **(se) rassembler**

reassure [riəˈʃuə] *verb* to take away the doubts or fears of: *The woman was worried about the dangers of taking aspirins, but her doctor reassured her.* □ **rassurer**

,reas'surance *noun* **1** the process of reassuring or being reassured. □ **réconfort**

2 something said *etc* that makes a person feel reassured: *She wants reassurance*; *Despite her reassurances, I'm still not happy.* □ **paroles rassurantes**

,reas'suring *adjective*: *the doctor's reassuring remarks.* □ **rassurant**

,reas'suringly *adverb.* □ **d'une manière rassurante**

rebate [ˈriːbeit] *noun* a part of a payment, tax *etc* which is given back to the person paying it. □ **remise**

rebel [ˈrebl] *noun* **1** a person who opposes or fights against

people in authority, *eg* a government: *The rebels killed many soldiers*; *(also adjective) rebel troops.* □ **rebelle**

2 a person who does not accept the rules of normal behaviour *etc*: *My son is a bit of a rebel.* □ **rebelle**

■ [rəˈbel] *verb – past tense, past participle* **re'belled** – to fight (against people in authority): *The people rebelled against the dictator*; *Teenagers often rebel against their parents' way of life.* □ **se rebeller contre**

rebellion [rəˈbeljən] *noun* **1** an open or armed fight against a government *etc*. □ **rébellion**

2 a refusal to obey orders or to accept rules *etc*. □ **révolte**

rebellious [rəˈbeljəs] *adjective* rebelling or likely to rebel: *rebellious troops/children.* □ **rebelle, insoumis**

re'belliously *adverb.* □ **en rebelle**

re'belliousness *noun.* □ **esprit de rébellion**

rebound [riˈbaund] *verb* to bounce back: *The ball rebounded off the wall.* □ **rebondir**

on the rebound [ˈriːbaund] as (something) bounces back: *She caught the ball on the rebound.* □ **au rebond**

rebuff [riˈbʌf] *noun* an unkind or unfriendly refusal or rejection. □ **rebuffade**

■ *verb* to reject or refuse in an unkind of unfriendly way: *He rebuffed all the attempts of his friends to help him.* □ **repousser**

rebuke [rəˈbjuːk] *verb* to speak severely to (a person), because he or she has done wrong: *The boy was rebuked by his teacher for cheating.* □ **réprimander**

■ *noun* (stern) words spoken to a person, because he or she has done wrong. □ **réprimande**

recall [riˈkɔːl] *verb* **1** to order (a person *etc*) to return: *She had been recalled to her former post.* □ **se rappeler**

2 to remember: *I don't recall when I last saw her.* □ **se rappeler**

■ *noun* **1** an order to return: *the recall of soldiers to duty.* □ **rappel**

2 [ˈriːkɔːl] the ability to remember and repeat what one has seen, heard *etc*: *She has total recall.* □ **mémoire**

recapitulate [riːkəˈpitjuleit] *verb* (*abbreviation* **recap** [ˈriːkap] – *past tense, past participle* **'recapped**) to go over again (the chief points of a statement, argument *etc*). □ **récapituler**

'reca,pitu'lation (*abbreviation* **'recap**) *noun.* □ **récapitulation**

recapture [riˈkaptʃə] *verb* **1** to capture again: *The soldiers recaptured the city*; *The prisoners were recaptured.* □ **recapturer**

2 to convey (the feeling of something from the past): *to recapture the atmosphere of medieval London.* □ **recréer**

■ *noun* the process of recapturing or being recaptured. □ **reprise**

recede [riˈsiːd] *verb* **1** to go or move back: *When the rain stopped, the floods receded*; *His hair is receding from his forehead.* □ **reculer**

2 to become distant: *The coast receded behind us as we sailed away.* □ **s'éloigner**

receipt [rəˈsiːt] *noun* **1** the act of receiving or being received: *Please sign this form to acknowledge receipt of the money.* □ **réception**

2 a written note saying that money *etc* has been received: *I paid the bill and he gave me a receipt.* □ **reçu**

receive [rə'siːv] *verb* 1 to get or be given: *She received a letter*; *They received a good education.* □ **recevoir**
2 to have a formal meeting with: *The Pope received the Queen in the Vatican.* □ **recevoir**
3 to allow to join something: *She was received into the group.* □ **recevoir, accueillir**
4 to greet, react to, in some way: *The news was received in silence*; *The townspeople received the heroes with great cheers.* □ **recevoir, accueillir**
5 to accept (stolen goods) *especially* with the intention of reselling (them). □ **receler**
re'ceiver *noun* 1 the part of a telephone which is held to one's ear. □ **récepteur**
2 an apparatus for receiving radio or television signals. □ **récepteur**
3 a person who receives stolen goods. □ **receleur, euse**
4 a person who is appointed to take control of the business of someone who has gone bankrupt. □ **syndic**
5 a stereo amplifier with a built-in radio. □ **(poste) récepteur**

> receive is spelt with **-ei-**.

recent ['riːsnt] *adjective* happening, done *etc* not long ago: *Things have changed in recent weeks*; *recent events.* □ **récent**
'**recently** *adverb*: *She came to see me recently.* □ **récemment**
receptacle [rə'septəkl] *noun* a container of some kind: *A trash can is a receptacle for rubbish.* □ **récipient**
reception [rə'sepʃən] *noun* 1 the act of receiving or being received: *Her speech got a good reception.* □ **réception, accueil**
2 a formal party or social gathering to welcome guests: *a wedding reception.* □ **réception**
3 the quality of radio or television signals: *Radio reception is poor in this area.* □ **réception**
4 the part of a hotel, hospital *etc* where visitors enter and are attended to. □ **réception**
re'ceptionist *noun* a person who is employed (*eg* in a hotel, office *etc*) to answer the telephone, attend to guests, clients *etc*. □ **réceptionniste**
receptive [rə'septiv] *adjective* (of people, their minds *etc*) quick to understand and accept new ideas *etc*. □ **réceptif**
recess [ri'ses, 'riːses] *noun* 1 a part of a room set back from the main part; an alcove: *We can put the dining table in that recess.* □ **recoin; alcôve**
2 the time during which Parliament or the law-courts do not work: *Parliament is in recess.* □ **intersession**
3 a short period of free time between school classes. □ **récréation**
recession [rə'seʃən] *noun* a temporary fall in a country's or the world's business activities. □ **récession**
recipe ['resəpi] *noun* a set of instructions on how to prepare and cook something: *a recipe for curry*; (*also adjective*) *a recipe book.* □ **(de) recette**
recipient [rə'sipiənt] *noun* a person who receives something: *the recipient of a letter.* □ **récipiendaire; destinataire**
recite [rə'sait] *verb* to repeat aloud from memory: *to re-*

cite a poem. □ **réciter**
re'cital *noun* 1 a public performance (of music or songs) usually by one person or a small number of people: *a recital of Schubert's songs.* □ **récital**
2 the act of reciting. □ **récitation**
,**reci'tation** [resi-] *noun* 1 a poem *etc* which is recited: *a recitation from Shakespeare.* □ **récitation**
2 the act of reciting. □ **récitation**
reckless ['rekləs] *adjective* very careless; acting or done without any thought of the consequences: *a reckless driver*; *reckless driving.* □ **téméraire**
'**recklessly** *adverb*. □ **témérairement**
'**recklessness** *noun*. □ **témérité**
reckon ['rekən] *verb* 1 to consider: *She is reckoned (to be/as/as being) the best pianist in Britain.* □ **considérer**
2 to think; to have decided; to intend: *Do you reckon we'll succeed?*; *Is she reckoning on coming?* □ **penser**
'**reckoning** *noun* 1 calculation; counting: *By my reckoning, we must be about eight kilometres from the town.* □ **calcul**
2 the settling of debts *etc*. □ **règlement**
day of reckoning the time when one has to pay for, or be punished for, one's mistakes, crimes *etc*. □ **le jour du Jugement**
reckon on to depend on or expect: *I was reckoning on meeting her tonight.* □ **s'attendre à**
reckon up to count or calculate: *to reckon up the total cost.* □ **calculer**
reckon with to be prepared for; to take into consideration: *I didn't reckon with all these problems*; *He's a man to be reckoned with* (= a powerful man). □ **tenir compte**
reclaim [ri'kleim] *verb* 1 to ask for (something one owns which has been lost, stolen *etc* and found by someone else): *A wallet has been found and can be reclaimed at the manager's office.* □ **réclamer**
2 to make (wasteland) fit for use; to get back (land) from under the sea *etc* by draining *etc*. □ **rendre cultivable; assécher (du terrain)**
,**recla'mation** [reklə-] *noun*. □ **réclamation**
recline [rə'klain] *verb* to lean or lie on one's back or side: *The invalid was reclining on the sofa.* □ **être allongé**
reclining chair an armchair with a back which can be made to slope backwards. □ **fauteuil inclinable**
recluse [rə'kluːs] *noun* a person who lives alone and avoids other people. □ **reclus, use**
recognize, recognise ['rekəgnaiz] *verb* 1 to see, hear *etc* (a person, thing *etc*) and know who or what that person, thing *etc* is, because one has seen or heard him, her or it *etc* before: *I recognized her voice/handwriting*; *I recognized him by his voice.* □ **reconnaître**
2 to admit, acknowledge: *Everyone recognized her skill.* □ **reconnaître**
3 to be willing to have political relations with: *Many countries were unwilling to recognize the new republic.* □ **reconnaître**
4 to accept as valid, well-qualified *etc*: *I don't recognize the authority of this court.* □ **reconnaître**
,**recog'nizable**, ,**recog'nisable** *adjective* (*negative* **un-recognizable**). □ **reconnaissable**
,**recog'nizably**, ,**recog'nisably** *adverb*. □ **de manière**

reconnaissable

,recog'nition [-'niʃən] *noun* the act or state of recognizing or being recognized: *They gave the boy a medal in recognition of his courage; I said hello to her but she showed no recognition.* □ **(signe de) reconnaissance**

recoil [rə'koil] *verb* **1** to move back or away, *usually* quickly, in horror or fear: *He recoiled at/from the sight of the murdered child.* □ **reculer (devant)**

2 (of guns when fired) to jump back. □ **reculer**

■ ['riːkoil] *noun* the act of recoiling. □ **recul**

recollect [rekə'lekt] *verb* to remember: *I don't recollect having seen her before.* □ **se souvenir de**

,recol'lection [-ʃən] *noun* **1** the act or power of recollecting. □ **mémoire**

2 something that is remembered: *My book is called 'Recollections of Childhood'.* □ **souvenir**

recommend [rekə'mend] *verb* **1** to advise: *The doctor recommended a long holiday.* □ **recommander**

2 to suggest as being particularly good, particularly suitable *etc*: *He recommended her (to me) for the job.* □ **recommander**

,recommen'dation *noun* **1** the act of recommending: *I gave her the job on his recommendation.* □ **recommandation**

2 something recommended: *The recommendations of the committee.* □ **recommandation**

recompense ['rekəmpens] *noun* money *etc* given to someone in return for his or her trouble, inconvenience or effort. □ **récompense, dédommagement**

■ *verb* to give (someone) money *etc* in return for effort, inconvenience *etc*: *The nobleman recompensed his followers for their loyalty.* □ **récompenser**

reconcile ['rekənsail] *verb* **1** to cause (people) to become friendly again, *eg* after they have quarrelled: *Why won't you be reconciled (with him)?* □ **(se) réconcilier (avec)**

2 to bring (two or more different aims, points of view *etc*) into agreement: *The unions want high wages and the bosses want high profits – it's almost impossible to reconcile these two aims.* □ **concilier**

3 to (make someone) accept (a situation, fact *etc*) patiently: *Her mother didn't want the marriage to take place but she is reconciled to it now.* □ **se résigner à**

'recon,cili'ation [-sili-] *noun*: *There has been a reconciliation between her and her husband; an act of reconciliation.* □ **réconciliation**

recondition [riːkən'diʃən] *verb* to put in good condition again by cleaning, repairing *etc*. □ **remettre à neuf/ en état**

,recon'ditioned *adjective*: *a reconditioned television set.* □ **remis à neuf**

reconnaissance [rə'konəsəns] *noun* (the act of making) a study (of land, enemy troops *etc*) to obtain information, *eg* before a battle. □ **reconnaissance**

reconnoitre [rekə'noitə] *verb* to make a reconnaissance of (land, enemy troops *etc*). □ **reconnaître (le terrain)**

reconsider [riːkən'sidə] *verb* to think about again and possibly change one's opinion, decision *etc*: *Please reconsider your decision to leave the firm.* □ **reconsidérer**

'recon,side'ration *noun*. □ **reconsidération**

reconstitute [riː'konstitjuːt] *verb* to put or change (some-

thing) back to its original form *eg* by adding liquid: *to reconstitute dried milk.* □ **reconstituer**

re,consti'tution *noun*. □ **reconstitution**

reconstruct [riːkən'strʌkt] *verb* to create a complete description or idea, on the basis of certain known facts: *Let us try to reconstruct the crime.* □ **reconstituer**

,recon'struction [-ʃən] *noun*. □ **reconstruction**

record ['rekoːd, -kəd] *noun* **1** a written report of facts, events *etc*: *historical records; I wish to keep a record of everything that is said at this meeting.* □ **rapport écrit, procès-verbal**

2 a round flat piece of (*usually* black) plastic on which music *etc* is recorded: *a record of Beethoven's Sixth Symphony.* □ **disque**

3 (in races, games, or almost any activity) the best performance so far; something which has never yet been beaten: *He holds the record for the 1,000 metres; The record for the high jump was broken/beaten this afternoon; He claimed to have eaten fifty sausages in a minute and asked if this was a record;* (*also adjective*) *a record score.* □ **record**

4 the collected facts from the past of a person, institution *etc*: *This school has a very poor record of success in exams; He has a criminal record.* □ **dossier**

■ [rə'koːd] *verb* **1** to write a description of (an event, facts *etc*) so that they can be read in the future: *The decisions will be recorded in the minutes of the meeting.* □ **consigner**

2 to put (the sound of music, speech *etc*) on a record or tape so that it can be listened to in the future: *I've recorded the whole concert; Don't make any noise when I'm recording.* □ **enregistrer**

3 (of a dial, instrument *etc*) to show (a figure *etc*) as a reading: *The thermometer recorded 30°C yesterday.* □ **enregistrer**

4 to give or show, *especially* in writing: *to record one's vote in an election.* □ **enregistrer**

re'corder *noun* **1** a type of musical wind instrument, made of wood, plastic *etc*. □ **flûte à bec**

2 an instrument for recording on to tape. □ **magnétophone**

re'cording *noun* something recorded on tape, a record *etc*: *This is a recording of Beethoven's Fifth Symphony.* □ **enregistrement**

'record player *noun* an electrical instrument which reproduces the sounds recorded on records. □ **tourne-disque**

in record time very quickly. □ **en un temps record**

off the record (of information, statements *etc*) not intended to be repeated or made public: *The Prime Minister admitted off the record that the country was going through a serious crisis.* □ **à titre officieux**

on record recorded: *This is the coldest winter on record.* □ **attesté**

recount [ri'kaunt] *verb* to tell (a story *etc*) in detail: *She recounted her adventures.* □ **raconter**

re-count [riː'kaunt] *verb* to count again. □ **recompter**

■ ['riːkaunt] *noun* a second count: *a re-count of votes.* □ **recomptage**

recover [rə'kʌvə] *verb* **1** to become well again; to return

to good health *etc*: *She is recovering from a serious illness; The country is recovering from an economic crisis.* □ **recouvrer (la santé)**
2 to get back: *The police have recovered the stolen jewels; She will recover the cost of the repairs through the insurance.* □ **récupérer**
3 to get control of (one's actions, emotions *etc*) again: *The actor almost fell over but quickly recovered (his balance).* □ **se reprendre**
re'covery *noun* (an) act or process of recovering: *The patient made a remarkable recovery after his illness; the recovery of stolen property.* □ **recouvrement**
re-cover [riːˈkʌvə] *verb* to put a new cover on: *This chair needs to be re-covered.* □ **recouvrir**
re-create [riːkriˈeit] *verb* to describe or show realistically: *In the film, they had tried to recreate the horrors of the war.* □ **recréer**
‚re-cre'ation *noun*. □ **recréation**
recreation [rekriˈeiʃən] *noun* (a) pleasant activity which one enjoys doing in one's spare time (*eg* a sport, hobby): *I have little time for recreation; amusements and recreations.* □ **divertissement**
‚recre'ational *adjective*. □ **de récréation**
recreation ground a piece of land for playing sports, games *etc* on. □ **terrain de jeux**
recruit [rəˈkruːt] *noun* **1** a person who has (just) joined the army, air force *etc*. □ **recrue**
2 a person who has (just) joined a society, group *etc*: *Our party needs new recruits before the next election.* □ **recrue**
■ *verb* to cause to join the army, a society *etc*: *We must recruit more troops; Can't you recruit more members to the music society?* □ **recruter**
re'cruitment *noun*. □ **recrutement**
rectangle [ˈrektaŋgl] *noun* a two-dimensional, four-sided figure with opposite sides equal and all its angles right angles. □ **rectangle**
rec'tangular [-gjulə] *adjective*. □ **rectangulaire**
rectify [ˈrektifai] *verb* to put right or correct (a mistake *etc*): *We shall rectify the error as soon as possible.* □ **rectifier**
‚recti'fiable *adjective*. □ **rectifiable**
‚rectifi'cation [-fi-] *noun*. □ **rectification**
rector [ˈrektə] *noun* **1** in certain churches, a clergyman or priest in charge of a parish *etc*. □ **pasteur**
2 the head of a university, school or college. □ **directeur (d'une école secondaire), recteur (d'une université)**
rectum [ˈrektəm] *noun* the lower part of the alimentary canal, through which waste substances pass from the intestines. □ **rectum**
recumbent [rəˈkʌmbənt] *adjective* lying down. □ **couché**
recuperate [rəˈkjuːpəreit] *verb* to recover, *eg* after an illness. □ **se rétablir**
re,cupe'ration *noun*. □ **rétablissement**
recur [riˈkəː] – *past tense, past participle* **re'curred** – *verb* to happen again; to come back again: *This problem keeps recurring.* □ **se reproduire**
re'currence [-ˈkʌ-] *noun*: *He has had several recurrences of his illness.* □ **récurrence**

re'current [-ˈkʌ-] *adjective* happening often or regularly: *a recurrent nightmare.* □ **récurrent**
recycle [riːˈsaikl] *verb* to use again; to reuse or transform rather than throw away: *When Donald outgrew his clothes, he recycled everything by giving them to his younger brother to wear; The firm recycled old drink boxes, turning them into containers for plants.* □ **recycler**
recycling *noun* the technique or practice of reusing or transforming something rather than throwing it away: *Recycling makes good sense because there is a shortage of land for garbage dumps.* □ **recyclage**
red [red] *noun, adjective* **1** (of) the colour of blood: *a red car/dress/cheeks; Her eyes were red with crying.* □ **rouge**
2 (of hair or fur) (of) a colour which varies between a golden brown and a deep reddish-brown. □ **roux**
3 (a) communist: *Red China; A lot of his university friends are Reds.* □ **communiste**
'redden [red] *verb* **1** to make or become red or redder: *to redden the lips with lipstick.* □ **rougir**
2 to blush: *She reddened as she realized her mistake.* □ **rougir**
'reddish *adjective* slightly red: *reddish hair.* □ **rougeâtre**
'redness *noun*. □ **rougeur; rousseur**
'redcurrant *noun* a type of garden bush grown for its small red fruit. □ **groseille (rouge)**
'redhead *noun* a person with red hair. □ **roux, rousse; rouquin, ine**
red herring 1 something that leads people away from the main point in a discussion. □ **diversion**
2 a false clue or line of enquiry. □ **diversion**
‚red-'hot *adjective* (of metal *etc*) so hot that it is glowing red: *red-hot steel; This iron is red-hot.* □ **chauffé au rouge**
red-letter day a day which will always be remembered because of something especially good that happened on it. □ **jour mémorable**
red tape annoying and unnecessary rules and regulations. □ **paperasserie**
be in the red to be in debt. □ **être à découvert/en déficit**
catch red-handed to find (a person) in the act of doing wrong: *The police caught the thief red-handed.* □ **pris en flagrant délit**
the Red Army the army of the former USSR. □ **l'armée rouge**
see red to become angry: *When he started criticizing my work, I really saw red.* □ **voir rouge**
redeem [rəˈdiːm] *verb* **1** to buy back (something that has been pawned): *I'm going to redeem my gold watch.* □ **dégager**
2 to set (a person) free by paying a ransom; (of Jesus Christ) to free (a person) from sin. □ **racheter**
3 to compensate for or cancel out the faults of: *His willingness to work redeemed him in her eyes.* □ **racheter**
Re'deemer *noun* (*often with* **the**) Jesus Christ. □ **Rédempteur**
redemption [rəˈdempʃən] *noun*: *the redemption of man by Christ.* □ **rédemption**
past/beyond redemption too bad to be redeemed or

485

improved. □ **irrémédiable, irrécupérable**
redeeming feature a good quality that somewhat makes up for the bad qualities in a person or thing. □ **qualité qui rachète les défauts**
redirect [riːdi'rekt] *verb* to put a new address on, and post (a letter *etc*). □ **faire suivre**
redo [riː'duː] – *past tense* **redid** [riː'did]: *past participle* **redone** [riː'dʌn]* – *verb* to do again: *Your homework will have to be redone.* □ **refaire**
redouble [ri'dʌbl] *verb* to make twice as great: *She redoubled her efforts.* □ **redoubler**
redoubtable [rə'dautəbl] *adjective* (of a person) brave; bold. □ **redoutable**
redress [rə'dres] *verb* to set right or compensate for: *The company offered the woman a large sum of money to redress the harm that their product had done to her.* □ **redresser**
■ *noun* (money *etc* which is paid as) compensation for some wrong that has been done. □ **réparation**
redress the balance to make things equal again. □ **rétablir l'équilibre**
redskin *see* **red.**
reduce [rə'djuːs] *verb* **1** to make less, smaller *etc*: *The shop reduced its prices; The train reduced speed.* □ **réduire**
2 to lose weight by dieting: *I must reduce my weight to get into that dress.* □ **maigrir**
3 to drive, or put, into a particular (bad) state: *The bombs reduced the city to ruins; She was so angry, she was almost reduced to tears; During the famine, many people were reduced to eating grass and leaves.* □ **réduire (en/à)**
re'ducible *adjective*. □ **réductible**
re'duction [-'dʌk-] *noun*: *The government promised a reduction in prices later; price reductions.* □ **réduction**
redundant [rə'dʌndənt] *adjective* (of workers) no longer employed because there is no longer any job for them where they used to work: *Fifty men have just been made redundant at the local factory.* □ **licencié**
re'dundancy – *plural* **re'dundancies** – *noun*: *There have been a lot of redundancies at the local factory recently; the problem of redundancy.* □ **licenciement**
reed [riːd] *noun* **1** a kind of tall, stiff grass growing on wet or marshy ground: *reeds along a river-bank.* □ **roseau**
2 a thin piece of cane or metal in certain wind instruments (*eg* the oboe, clarinet) which vibrates and makes a sound when the instrument is played. □ **anche**
reef [riːf] *noun* a line of rocks *etc* just above or below the surface of the sea: *The ship got stuck on a reef.* □ **récif**
reek [riːk] *noun* a strong, *usually* unpleasant smell. □ **puanteur**
■ *verb* to smell strongly (of something). □ **puer**
reel [riːl] *noun* **1** a round wheel-shaped or cylindrical object of wood, metal *etc* on which thread, film, fishing-lines *etc* can be wound: *a reel of sewing-cotton; She changed the reel in the projector.* □ **bobine**
2 (the music for) a type of lively Scottish, Irish or American dance: *The fiddler played a reel; to dance*

a reel. □ **reel**
■ *verb* to stagger; to sway; to move in an unsteady way: *The drunk man reeled along the road; My brain was reeling with all the information that he gave me.* □ **tituber**
reel in to pull (*eg* a fish out of the water) by winding the line to which it is attached on to a reel. □ **ramener**
reel off to say or repeat quickly and easily, without pausing: *She reeled off the list of names.* □ **débiter**
re-elect [riːi'lekt] *verb* to elect again: *They have re-elected her to Parliament.* □ **réélire**
,re-e'lection [-ʃən] *noun*. □ **réélection**
re-enter [riː'entə] *verb* to enter again: *The spaceship will re-enter the Earth's atmosphere tomorrow.* □ **rentrer**
,re-'entry *noun*: *The spaceship's re-entry will take place tomorrow afternoon at two o'clock.* □ **rentrée**
refectory [rə'fektəri] *noun* a dining-hall for monks, students *etc*. □ **réfectoire**
refer [rə'fəː] – *past tense, past participle* **re'ferred** – *verb* (*with* **to**) **1** to talk or write (about something); to mention: *He doesn't like anyone referring to his wooden leg; I referred to your theories in my last book.* □ **faire allusion à**
2 to relate to, concern, or apply to: *My remarks refer to your last letter.* □ **renvoyer à**
3 to send or pass on to someone else for discussion, information, a decision *etc*: *The case was referred to a higher law-court; I'll refer you to the managing director.* □ **envoyer à**
4 to look for information (in something): *If I'm not sure how to spell a word, I refer to a dictionary.* □ **consulter**
referee [refə'riː] *noun* **1** a person who controls boxing, football *etc* matches, makes sure that the rules are not broken *etc*: *The referee sent two of the players off the field.* □ **arbitre**
2 a person who is willing to provide a note about one's character, ability *etc, eg* when one applies for new job. □ **répondant, ante**
■ *verb* – *past tense, past participle* **,refe'reed** – to act as a referee for a match: *I've been asked to referee (a football match) on Saturday.* □ **arbitrer**
reference ['refərəns] *noun* **1** (an) act of referring (to something); a mention (of something): *She made several references to her latest book; With reference to your request for information, I regret to inform you that I am unable to help you.* □ **référence; concernant**
2 a note about one's character, ability *etc, eg* when one applies for a new job: *Our new secretary had excellent references from her previous employers.* □ **références**
3 an indication in a book, report *etc*, showing where one got one's information or where further information can be found. □ **référence**
reference book a book which is not usually read from beginning to end but which is consulted occasionally for information, *eg* a dictionary or encyclopaedia. □ **ouvrage de référence**
reference library a library of books to be looked at for information but not borrowed. □ **bibliothèque de consultation**

> **reference**, noun, is spelt with **-r-**.
> **referred** and **referring** are spelt with **-rr-**.

referendum [refə'rendəm] – *plurals* ,refe'rendums, ,refe'renda [-də] – *noun* a general vote made by the people of a country *etc* for or against a particular government proposal *etc*. □ **référendum**

refill ['riːfil] *noun* the amount (*usually* in a container) of some material needed to fill up some object which becomes empty through use: *I must go and buy some refills for my pen*. □ **recharge**
■ [riː'fil] *verb* to fill up again: *He refilled his pipe*. □ **remplir de nouveau**

refine [rə'fain] *verb* 1 to make (a substance *eg* sugar) pure by taking out dirt, waste substances *etc*: *Oil is refined before it is used*. □ **raffiner**
2 to improve: *We have refined our techniques considerably since the work began*. □ **perfectionner**
re'fined *adjective* (*negative* **unrefined**) 1 very polite; well-mannered; elegant. □ **raffiné**
2 having been refined: *refined sugar*. □ **raffiné**
re'finement *noun* 1 good manners, good taste, polite speech *etc*. □ **raffinement**
2 (an) improvement: *to make refinements*. □ **perfectionnement**
re'finery – *plural* **re'fineries** – *noun* a place where sugar or oil *etc* is refined: *an oil refinery*. □ **raffinerie**

refit [riː'fit] – *past tense, past participle* ,re'fitted – *verb* to repair or fit new parts to (a ship): *They are refitting the liner*. □ **réparer**

reflect [rə'flekt] *verb* 1 to send back (light, heat *etc*): *The white sand reflected the sun's heat*. □ **renvoyer, refléter**
2 (of a mirror *etc*) to give an image of: *She was reflected in the mirror/water*. □ **réfléchir**
3 to think carefully: *Give her a minute to reflect (on what she should do)*. □ **réfléchir (à)**
re'flecting *adjective* able to reflect (light *etc*): *a reflecting surface*. □ **réfléchissant**
reflection, reflexion [rə'flekʃən] *noun*: *She looked at her reflection in the water*; *After reflection I felt I had made the wrong decision*; *The book is called 'Reflections of a Politician'*. □ **reflet; réflexion**
re'flective [-tiv] *adjective* 1 thoughtful: *a reflective mood*. □ **réfléchi; de réflexion**
2 reflecting: *Reflective licence plates*. □ **réfléchissant**
re'flectively *adverb*. □ **avec réflexion**
re'flector *noun* something, *especially* of glass or metal, that reflects light, heat *etc*. □ **réflecteur**

reflex ['riːfleks] *noun, adjective* (an action which is) automatic or not intended: *The doctor tapped the patient's knee in order to test his reflexes*; *a reflex action*. □ **réflexe**

reflexion *see* **reflect**.

reflexive [rə'fleksiv] *adjective* 1 (of a pronoun) showing that the object of a verb is the same person or thing as the subject: *In 'He cut himself', 'himself' is a reflexive pronoun*. □ **réfléchi**
2 (of a verb) used with a reflexive pronoun: *In 'control yourself!', 'control' is a reflexive verb*. □ **réfléchi**

reform [rə'foːm] *verb* 1 to improve or remove faults from:

The criminal's wife stated that she had made great efforts to reform her husband. □ **réformer; corriger**
2 to give up bad habits, improve one's behaviour *etc*: *He admitted that he had been a criminal, but said that he intended to reform*. □ **se corriger**
■ *noun* 1 the act of improving: *the reform of our political system*. □ **réforme**
2 an improvement: *He intends to make several reforms in the prison system*. □ **réforme**
,refor'mation [refə-] *noun*. □ **réforme**
re'formed *adjective* (*negative* **unreformed**) improved, *especially* in behaviour. □ **amendé**
re'former *noun* a person who wishes to bring about improvements: *one of the reformers of our political system*. □ **réformateur, trice**

refrain[1] [rə'frein] *noun* a line of words or music repeated regularly in a song, *especially* at the end of or after each verse; a chorus. □ **refrain**

refrain[2] [rə'frein] *verb* (with **from**) not to do; to avoid: *You are asked to refrain from smoking/from (drinking) alcohol*. □ **s'abstenir (de)**

refresh [rə'freʃ] *verb* to give new strength and energy to; to make (a person *etc*) feel less hot, tired *etc, eg* after or during a period of hard work: *This glass of cool lemonade will refresh you*. □ **revigorer; rafraîchir**
re'freshing *adjective* 1 giving new strength and energy; having a cooling and relaxing effect: *a refreshing drink of cold water*. □ **revigorant; rafraîchissant**
2 particularly pleasing because different from normal: *It is refreshing to hear a politician speak so honestly*. □ **réconfortant**
re'freshingly *adverb*. □ **d'une manière qui fait du bien**
re'freshments *noun plural* food and drink served *eg* at a meeting: *Light refreshments are available in the other room*. □ **rafraîchissements**
refresh someone's memory to remind (someone) of the facts and details of something. □ **rafraîchir la mémoire de**

refrigerator [rə'fridʒəreitə] *noun* (*also* **fridge** [fridʒ]: a machine which keeps food cold and so prevents it from going bad: *Milk should be kept in the refrigerator*. □ **réfrigérateur**
re'frigerate *verb* to keep (food) cold to prevent it from going bad: *Meat should be refrigerated*. □ **réfrigérer**
re,frige'ration *noun*. □ **réfrigération**

refuel [riː'fjuəl] – *past tense, past participle* **re'fuelled**, **re'fueled** – *verb* to supply (an airplane *etc*) with more fuel: *The plane has to be refuelled every thousand kilometres*; *The plane stopped to refuel*. □ **ravitailler (en carburant)**

refuge ['refjuːdʒ] *noun* (a place which gives) shelter or protection from danger, trouble *etc*: *The escaped prisoner sought refuge in the church*. □ **refuge**
,refu'gee *noun* a person who seeks shelter *especially* in another country, from war, disaster, or persecution: *Refugees were pouring across the frontier*; (*also adjective*) *a refugee camp*. □ **(de) réfugié, ée**

refund [ri'fʌnd] *verb* to pay back: *When the concert was cancelled, the people who had bought tickets had their money refunded*. □ **rembourser**

■ ['riːfʌnd] *noun* the paying back of money: *They demanded a refund.* □ **remboursement**

refuse[1] [rə'fjuːz] *verb* **1** not to do what one has been asked, told or is expected to do: *He refused to help me; She refused to believe what I said; When I asked him to leave, he refused.* □ **refuser de**

2 not to accept: *He refused my offer of help; They refused our invitation; She refused the money.* □ **refuser**

3 not to give (permission *etc*): *I was refused admittance to the meeting.* □ **refuser**

re'fusal *noun: I was surprised at his refusal to help me; When we sent out the wedding invitations, we had several refusals.* □ **refus**

refuse[2] ['refjuːs] *noun* rubbish; waste material from *eg* a kitchen. □ **ordures**

refuse collector, refuse collection vehicle a person who collects, a vehicle for collecting, rubbish. □ **éboueur, euse; camion à ordures**

refute [rə'fjuːt] *verb* to prove that (a person, statement *etc*) is wrong: *You can easily refute his argument.* □ **réfuter**

re'futable *adjective.* □ **réfutable**

,refu'tation [refju-] *noun.* □ **réfutation**

regain [ri'gein] *verb* **1** to get back again: *The champion was beaten in January but regained the title in March.* □ **regagner**

2 to get back to (a place): *The swimmer was swept out to sea, but managed to regain the shore.* □ **regagner**

regal ['riːɡəl] *adjective* of, like, or suitable for, a king or queen: *She has a regal appearance; regal robes.* □ **royal**

regally *adverb.* □ **royalement**

regalia [rə'geiliə] *noun singular or noun plural* **1** objects (*eg* the crown and sceptre) which are a sign of royalty, used *eg* at a coronation. □ **insignes royaux**

2 any ornaments, ceremonial clothes *etc* which are worn as a sign of a person's importance or authority. □ **insignes**

regard [rə'ɡaːd] *verb* **1** (*with* **as**) to consider to be: *I regard his conduct as totally unacceptable.* □ **considérer**

2 to think of as being very good, important *etc*; to respect: *She is very highly regarded by her friends.* □ **tenir en (...) estime**

3 to think of (with a particular emotion or feeling): *I regard him with horror; She regards the child's behaviour with amusement.* □ **considérer**

4 to look at: *She regarded me over the top of her glasses.* □ **regarder**

5 to pay attention to (advice *etc*). □ **tenir compte de**

■ *noun* **1** thought; attention: *He ran into the burning house without regard for his safety.* □ **égard**

2 sympathy; care; consideration: *He shows no regard for other people.* □ **égard(s)**

3 good opinion; respect: *I hold her in high regard.* □ **estime**

re'garding *preposition* about; concerning: *Have you any suggestions regarding this project?* □ **concernant**

re'gardless *adjective, adverb* not thinking or caring about costs, problems, dangers *etc: There may be difficulties but I shall carry on regardless (of the consequences).* □ **sans souci de; quand même**

re'gards *noun plural* greetings; good wishes: *Give my regards to your mother; He sent her his regards.* □ **amitiés**

as regards as far as (something) is concerned: *As regards the meeting tomorrow, I hope as many people will attend as possible.* □ **pour ce qui est de**

with regard to about; concerning: *I have no complaints with regard to her work.* □ **concernant**

> **with regards** is sometimes used in ending a letter.
> **with regard to** means 'about'.

regatta [rə'ɡatə] *noun* a meeting for yacht or (*usually* small) boat races. □ **régate(s)**

regent ['riːdʒent] *noun* a person who governs in place of a king or queen: *The prince was only two years old when the king died, so his uncle was appointed regent.* □ **régent, ente**

régime, regime [rei'ʒiːm] *noun* a (system of) government: *a Communist régime.* □ **régime**

regiment ['redʒimənt] *noun* a body of soldiers commanded by a colonel. □ **régiment**

■ [-ment] *verb* to organize or control (people) very strictly: *Children in schools are no longer regimented as they used to be.* □ **enrégimenter**

,regimen'tation *noun.* □ **régimentation**

,regi'mental [-'men-] *adjective* of a regiment. □ **régimentaire**

region ['riːdʒən] *noun* a part of a country, the world *etc: Do you know this region well?; in tropical regions.* □ **région**

'regional *adjective: regional variations in speech.* □ **régional**

'regionally *adverb.* □ **régionalement**

in the region of about; around; near: *The cost of the new building will be somewhere in the region of $200,000.* □ **aux alentours de**

register ['redʒistə] *noun* a written list, record *etc: a school attendance register; a register of births, marriages and deaths.* □ **registre**

■ *verb* **1** to write or cause to be written in a register: *to register the birth of a baby.* □ **enregistrer**

2 to write one's name, or have one's name written, in a register *etc: They arrived on Friday and registered at the Hilton Hotel.* □ **s'inscrire, se faire inscrire**

3 to insure (a parcel, letter *etc*) against loss in the post. □ **recommander**

4 (of an instrument, dial *etc*) to show (a figure, amount *etc*): *The thermometer registered 25°C.* □ **marquer**

'registered *adjective: a registered letter.* □ **recommandé**

,regi'strar [-'straː] *noun* **1** a person whose duty it is to keep a register (*especially* of births, marriages and deaths). □ **teneur, euse des registres (de l'état civil)**

2 in the United Kingdom *etc* one of the grades of hospital doctors. □ **interne**

'registry – *plural* **'registries** – *noun* an office or place where registers are kept. □ **bureau d'enregistrement**

register office/registry office an office where records of births, marriages *etc* are kept and where marriages may be performed. □ **bureau de l'état civil**

registration a permit issued by the government that

states who owns a particular automobile: *Ruthanne didn't have her registration or driver's licence when she was stopped by the police.* □ **immatriculation**

registration number (*also* **licence number**) the letters and numbers which a car, bus *etc* has on a plate at the front and rear. □ **numéro d'immatriculation**

regret [rə'gret] – *past tense, past participle* **re'gretted** – *verb* to be sorry about: *I regret my foolish behaviour; I regret that I missed the concert; I regret missing the concert; I regret to inform you that your application for the job was unsuccessful.* □ **regretter**

■ *noun* a feeling of sorrow, or of having done something wrong: *I have no regrets/I feel no regret about what I did; It was with deep regret that I heard the news of his death.* □ **regret**

re'gretful *adjective* feeling regret. □ **plein de regret**

re'gretfully *adverb* with regret: *Regretfully, we have had to turn down your offer.* □ **à regret**

re'grettable *adjective*: *a regrettable mistake.* □ **regrettable**

re'grettably *adverb*. □ **regrettablement**

> **regrettable** is spelt with two ts.

regular ['regjulə] *adjective* **1** usual: *Saturday is his regular day for shopping; That isn't our regular postman, is it?* □ **habituel**

2 normal: *He's too handicapped to attend a regular school.* □ **ordinaire**

3 occurring, acting *etc* with equal amounts of space, time *etc* between: *They placed guards at regular intervals around the camp; Is his pulse regular?* □ **régulier**

4 involving doing the same things at the same time each day *etc*: *a man of regular habits.* □ **régulier**

5 frequent: *She's a regular visitor; She's one of our regular customers.* □ **habituel**

6 permanent; lasting: *She's looking for a regular job.* □ **permanent**

7 (of a noun, verb *etc*) following one of the usual grammatical patterns of the language: *'Walk' is a regular verb, but 'go' is an irregular verb.* □ **régulier**

8 the same on both or all sides or parts; neat; symmetrical: *a girl with regular features; A square is a regular figure.* □ **régulier**

9 of ordinary size: *I don't want the large size of packet – just give me the regular one.* □ **ordinaire**

10 (of a soldier) employed full-time, professional; (of an army) composed of regular soldiers. □ **régulier**

■ *noun* **1** a soldier in the regular army. □ **soldat, ate de métier**

2 a regular customer (*eg* at a bar). □ **habitué, ée**

,regu'larity [-'la-] *noun*. □ **régularité**

'regularly *adverb* **1** at regular times, places *etc*: *Her heart was beating regularly.* □ **régulièrement**

2 frequently: *She comes here regularly.* □ **régulièrement**

'regulate [-leit] *verb* **1** to control: *We must regulate our spending; Traffic lights are used to regulate traffic.* □ **régler**

2 to adjust (a piece of machinery *etc*) so that it works at a certain rate *etc*: *Can you regulate this watch so that it keeps time accurately?* □ **régler**

,regu'lation *noun* **1** a rule or instruction: *There are certain regulations laid down as to how this job should be done, and these must be obeyed; (also adjective) Please use envelopes of the regulation size.* □ **règlement; réglementaire**

2 the act of regulating: *the regulation of a piece of machinery.* □ **réglage**

'regulator [-lei-] *noun* a thing that regulates (a piece of machinery *etc*). □ **régulateur**

regurgitate [ri'gə:dʒiteit] *verb* to bring back (food) into the mouth after it has been swallowed. □ **régurgiter**

re,gurgi'tation *noun*. □ **régurgitation**

rehabilitate [ri:ə'biliteit] *verb* to bring (a criminal or someone who has been ill) back to a normal life, normal standards of behaviour *etc* by treatment or training. □ **réhabiliter, rééduquer**

'reha,bili'tation *noun*. □ **réhabilitation**

rehearse [rə'hə:s] *verb* to practise (a play, piece of music *etc*) before performing it in front of an audience: *You must rehearse the scene again.* □ **répéter**

re'hearsal *noun* **1** the act of rehearsing. □ **répétition**

2 a performance done for practice: *I want the whole cast at tonight's rehearsal.* □ **répétition**

dress rehearsal a final rehearsal (of a play, opera *etc*) in which the actors or singers wear their costumes *etc*. □ **répétition générale**

rehouse [ri:'hauz] *verb* to provide with a new or different house: *After the fire, the family had to be rehoused.* □ **reloger**

reign [rein] *noun* the time during which a king or queen rules: *in the reign of Queen Victoria.* □ **règne**

■ *verb* **1** to rule, as a king or queen: *The king reigned (over his people) for forty years.* □ **régner**

2 to be present or exist: *Silence reigned at last.* □ **régner**

rein [rein] *noun* **1** (*usually in plural*) one of two straps attached to a bridle for guiding a horse. □ **rêne**

2 (*in plural*) straps fitted around a toddler so that he can be prevented from straying in the street *etc*. □ **rênes**

rein in to stop or restrain (a horse *etc*) by pulling on its reins. □ **serrer la bride à**

reincarnation [ri:inka:'nei∫ən] *noun* the rebirth of the soul in another body after death. □ **réincarnation**

reindeer ['reindiə] – *plural* **'reindeer** – *noun* a kind of large deer found in Northern Europe, Asia and America. □ **renne**

reinforce [ri:in'fɔ:s] *verb* to make stronger: *I've reinforced the elbows of this jacket with leather patches; Extra troops will be sent to reinforce the army.* □ **renforcer**

,rein'forcement *noun* **1** the act of reinforcing. □ **renforcement**

2 (*in plural*) men added to an army *etc* in order to strengthen it: *As the enemy attacks increased, the general called for reinforcements.* □ **renforts**

reject [rə'dʒekt] *verb* to refuse to accept: *She rejected his offer of help; He asked her to marry him, but she rejected him.* □ **rejeter**

■ ['ri:dʒekt] *noun* something that is rejected because it is faulty *etc*. □ **article de rebut**

re'jection [-∫ən] *noun* (an) act of rejecting. □ **rejet**

rejoice [rə'dʒois] *verb* to feel or show great happiness: *They rejoiced at the victory.* □ **se réjouir de**
re'joicing *noun* the act of feeling or showing great joy; celebrations: *There was great rejoicing at the news of the victory; The rejoicings over the birth of the baby lasted well into the night.* □ **réjouissance**

rejoinder [rə'dʒoində] *noun* an answer. □ **repartie**

rejuvenate [rə'dʒuːvəneit] *verb* to make young again. □ **rajeunir**
re,juve'nation *noun.* □ **rajeunissement**

relapse [rə'laps] *verb* to return to a former bad or undesirable state (*eg* ill health, bad habits). □ **faire une rechute**
■ *noun* a return to a former bad or undesirable state, *especially* ill health. □ **rechute**

relate [rə'leit] *verb* **1** to tell (a story *etc*): *She related all that had happened to her.* □ **raconter**
2 (*with* **to**) to be about, concerned or connected with: *Have you any information relating to the effect of penicillin on mice?* □ **se rapporter à**
3 (*with* **to**) to behave towards: *She finds it difficult to relate normally to her mother.* □ **entrer en rapport avec**
re'lated *adjective* **1** belonging to the same family (as): *I'm related to the Prime Minister; The Prime Minister and I are related.* □ **apparenté (à)**
2 connected: *other related topics.* □ **connexe**
re'lation *noun* **1** a person who belongs to the same family as oneself either by birth or because of marriage: *uncles, aunts, cousins and other relations.* □ **parent, parente**
2 a relationship (between facts, events *etc*). □ **relation**
3 (*in plural*) contact and communications between people, countries *etc*: *to establish friendly relations.* □ **relation(s)**
re'lationship *noun* **1** the friendship, contact, communications *etc* which exist between people: *She finds it very difficult to form lasting relationships.* □ **relation**
2 the fact that, or the way in which, facts, events *etc* are connected: *Is there any relationship between crime and poverty?* □ **relation**
3 the state of being related by birth or because of marriage. □ **lien de parenté**
relative ['relətiv] *noun* a member of one's family; a relation: *All her relatives attended the funeral.* □ **parent, parente**
■ *adjective* **1** compared with something else, or with each other, or with a situation in the past *etc*: *the relative speeds of a car and a train; She used to be rich but now lives in relative poverty.* □ **relatif**
2 (of a pronoun, adjective or clause) referring back to something previously mentioned: *the girl who sang the song.* □ **relatif**
relatively ['relətivli] *adverb* when compared to someone or something else: *She seems relatively happy now; This is a fairly unimportant problem, relatively speaking.* □ **relativement**

relax [rə'laks] *verb* **1** to make or become less tight or tense or less worried *etc*; to rest completely: *The doctor gave him a drug to make him relax; Relax your shoulders; He relaxed his grip for a second and the rope was*

dragged out of his hand. □ **(se) relaxer/relâcher**
2 to make or become less strict or severe: *The rules were relaxed because of the Queen's visit.* □ **relâcher**
,relax'ation [riːlaks-] *noun*: *I play golf for relaxation; Golf is one of my favourite relaxations.* □ **détente**

relay [ri'lei] – *past tense, past participle* **re'layed** – *verb* to receive and pass on (news, a message, a television program *etc*). □ **retransmettre**
■ *noun* ['riːlei] (the sending out of) a radio, television *etc* signal or program which has been received (from another place). □ **relais**
relay race a race between teams of runners, swimmers *etc*, in which the members of the team run, swim *etc* one after another, each covering one part of the total distance to be run, swum *etc*. □ **course de relais**
in relays in groups which perform some job, task *etc* one after another, one group starting when another group stops: *During the flood, firemen and policemen worked in relays to rescue people who were trapped.* □ **par relais**

release [rə'liːs] *verb* **1** to set free; to allow to leave: *He was released from prison yesterday; I am willing to release her from her promise to me.* □ **libérer**
2 to stop holding *etc*; to allow to move, fall *etc*: *He released (his hold on) the rope.* □ **lâcher**
3 to move (a catch, brake *etc*) which prevents something else from moving, operating *etc*: *She released the handbrake and drove off.* □ **desserrer**
4 to allow (news *etc*) to be made known publicly: *The list of winners has just been released.* □ **autoriser la publication de**
5 to offer (a film, record *etc*) to the general public: *Their latest record will be released next week.* □ **sortir**
■ *noun* **1** the act of releasing or being released: *After his release, the prisoner returned to his home town; the release of a new film; (also adjective) the release catch.* □ **libération; sortie; de déclenchement**
2 something that is released: *This record is their latest release; The Government issued a press release (= a statement giving information about something, sent or given to newspapers, reporters *etc*).* □ **nouveauté; communiqué**

relegate ['religeit] *verb* to put down to a lower grade, position *etc*: *The local football team has been relegated to the Second Division.* □ **reléguer**
,rele'gation *noun.* □ **relégation**

relent [rə'lent] *verb* to become less severe or unkind; to agree after refusing at first: *At first she wouldn't let them go to the cinema, but in the end she relented.* □ **se laisser fléchir**
re'lentless *adjective* without pity; not allowing anything to keep one from what one is doing or trying to do: *The police fight a relentless battle against crime.* □ **implacable**
re'lentlessly *adverb.* □ **implacablement**
re'lentlessness *noun.* □ **implacabilité**

relevant ['reləvənt] *adjective* connected with or saying something important about what is being spoken about or discussed: *I don't think his remarks are relevant (to our discussion); Any relevant information should be given to the police.* □ **pertinent (à)**

'relevance *noun*. □ **pertinence**

reliable, reliance *etc see* **rely**.

relic ['relik] *noun* 1 something left from a past time: *relics of an ancient civilization.* □ **vestige**

2 something connected with, *especially* the bones of, a dead person (*especially* a saint). □ **relique**

relief [rə'liːf] *noun* 1 a lessening or stopping of pain, worry, boredom *etc*: *When one has a headache, an aspirin brings relief; She gave a sigh of relief; It was a great relief to find nothing had been stolen.* □ **soulagement**

2 help (*eg* food) given to people in need of it: *famine relief;* (*also adjective*) *A relief fund has been set up to send supplies to the refugees.* □ **(de) secours**

3 a person who takes over some job or task from another person, *usually* after a given period of time: *The bus-driver was waiting for his relief;* (*also adjective*) *a relief driver.* □ **(de) relève**

4 the act of freeing a town *etc* from siege: *the relief of Mafeking.* □ **relève**

5 a way of carving *etc* in which the design is raised above the level of its background: *a carving in relief.* □ **relief**

re'lieve [-v] *verb* 1 to lessen or stop (pain, worry *etc*): *The doctor gave him some drugs to relieve the pain; to relieve the hardship of the refugees.* □ **soulager**

2 to take over a job or task from: *You guard the door first, and I'll relieve you in two hours.* □ **relayer**

3 to dismiss (a person) from his job or position: *He was relieved of his post/duties.* □ **relever (de)**

4 to take (something heavy, difficult *etc*) from someone: *May I relieve you of that heavy case?; The new gardener relieved the old man of the burden of cutting the grass.* □ **débarrasser de**

5 to come to the help of (a town *etc* which is under siege or attack). □ **secourir**

re'lieved *adjective* no longer anxious or worried: *I was relieved to hear you had arrived safely.* □ **soulagé**

religion [rə'lidʒən] *noun* 1 a belief in, or the worship of, a god or gods. □ **religion**

2 a particular system of belief or worship: *Christianity and Islam are two different religions.* □ **religion**

re'ligious *adjective* 1 of religion: *religious education; a religious leader/instructor.* □ **religieux**

2 following the rules, forms of worship *etc* of a religion: *a religious woman.* □ **religieux**

re'ligiously *adverb*. □ **religieusement**

re'ligiousness *noun*. □ **piété**

relinquish [rə'liŋkwiʃ] *verb* to give up: *The dictator was forced to relinquish control of the country.* □ **renoncer à**

relish ['reliʃ] *verb* to enjoy greatly: *She relishes her food; I relished the thought of telling my husband about my promotion.* □ **savourer**

■ *noun* 1 pleasure; enjoyment: *She ate the food with great relish; I have no relish for such a boring task.* □ **plaisir**

2 a strong flavour, or a sauce *etc* for adding flavour. □ **assaisonnement**

reluctant [rə'lʌktənt] *adjective* unwilling: *He was reluctant to accept the medal for his bravery.* □ **peu disposé à**

re'luctantly *adverb*. □ **à contrecœur**

re'luctance *noun*: *I don't understand her reluctance to go.* □ **répugnance**

rely [rə'lai] *verb* 1 to depend on or need: *The people on the island relied on the supplies that were brought from the mainland; I am relying on you to help me.* □ **compter sur**

2 to trust (someone) to do something; to be certain that (something will happen): *Can he rely on him to keep a secret?; She can be relied on; That is what will probably happen, but we can't rely on it.* □ **compter sur, se fier à**

re'liable [-'lai-] *adjective* (*negative* **unreliable**) able to be trusted: *Is she reliable?; Is this information reliable?* □ **fiable**

re,lia'bility *noun*. □ **sérieux**

re'liably [-'lai-] *adverb* from a reliable source; by a reliable person: *I am reliably informed that the Prime Minister is going to resign.* □ **de source sûre**

re'liance [-'lai-] *noun*: *a country's reliance on aid from other countries; a child's reliance on its mother.* □ **dépendance (de)**

re'liant *adjective*. □ **dépendant, confiant**

remain [rə'mein] *verb* 1 to be left: *Only two tins of soup remain; Very little remained of the cinema after the fire; A great many things still remain to be done.* □ **rester**

2 to stay; not to leave: *I shall remain here.* □ **rester**

3 to continue to be: *The problem remains unsolved.* □ **rester**

re'mainder [-də] *noun* the amount or number that is left when the rest has gone, been taken away *etc*: *I've corrected most of the essays – the remainder will get done tomorrow.* □ **reste**

re'mains *noun plural* 1 what is left after part has been taken away, eaten, destroyed *etc*: *the remains of a meal.* □ **restes**

2 a dead body: *to dispose of someone's remains.* □ **restes**

remand [rə'maːnd] *verb* to send (a person who has been accused of a crime) back to prison until more evidence can be collected. □ **renvoyer (un prévenu) à une autre audience**

remark [rə'maːk] *noun* a comment; something said: *The chairman made a few remarks, then introduced the speaker.* □ **remarque**

■ *verb* to say; to comment: *'She's a good-looking girl,' he remarked; She remarked that he was good-looking; He remarked on her good looks.* □ **faire remarquer, faire une/des remarque(s) sur**

re'markable *adjective* unusual; worth mentioning; extraordinary: *What a remarkable coincidence!; She really is a remarkable woman; It is quite remarkable how alike the two children are.* □ **remarquable**

re'markably *adverb*: *Their replies were remarkably similar.* □ **remarquablement**

remedy ['remədi] – *plural* '**remedies** – *noun* a cure for an illness or something bad: *I know a good remedy for toothache.* □ **remède**

■ *verb* to put right: *These mistakes can be remedied.* □

remédier à

remedial [rə'miːdiəl] *adjective* able to, or intended to, put right or to correct or cure: *She does remedial work with the less clever children; remedial exercises.* □ **réparateur, correctif**

remember [ri'membə] *verb* **1** to keep in the mind, or to bring back into the mind after forgetting for a time: *I remember you – we met three years ago; I remember watching the first men landing on the moon; Remember to telephone me tonight; I don't remember where I hid it.* □ **se rappeler**
2 to reward or make a present to: *She remembered her in her will.* □ **se souvenir de**
3 to pass (a person's) good wishes (to someone): *Remember me to your parents.* □ **rappeler au bon souvenir de**
re'membrance *noun* the act of remembering or reminding: *a statue erected in remembrance of the dead.* □ **souvenir**

remind [rə'maind] *verb* **1** to tell (someone) that there is something he or she ought to do, remember *etc*: *Remind me to post that letter; She reminded me of my promise.* □ **rappeler qqch. à qqn**
2 to make (someone) remember or think of (a person, thing *etc*): *She reminds me of her sister; This reminds me of my schooldays.* □ **rappeler**
re'minder *noun* something said, done, written, noticed *etc* that reminds one to do something: *Leave the bill on the table as a reminder that I still have to pay it.* □ **aide-mémoire**

remit [rə'mit] – *past tense, past participle* **re'mitted** – *verb* to send (money) *usually* in payment for something. □ **remettre**
re'mission [-ʃən] *noun* **1** a lessening in the severity of an illness *etc*. □ **rémission**
2 a shortening of a person's prison sentence. □ **remise de peine**
3 the act of remitting. □ **remise**
re'mittance *noun* (the sending of) money in payment for something. □ **versement**

remnant ['remnənt] *noun* a small piece or amount or a small number left over from a larger piece, amount or number: *The shop is selling remnants of cloth at half price; the remnant of the army.* □ **restant**

remorse [rə'moːs] *noun* regret about something wrong or bad which one has done. □ **remords**
re'morseful *adjective* feeling remorse. □ **plein de remords**
re'morsefully *adverb*. □ **avec remords**
re'morseless *adjective* cruel; without pity: *a remorseless tyrant.* □ **impitoyable**
re'morselessly *adverb*. □ **impitoyablement**

remote [rə'mout] *adjective* **1** far away in time or place; far from any (other) village, town *etc*: *a remote village in New South Wales; a farmhouse remote from civilization.* □ **lointain**
2 distantly related: *a remote cousin.* □ **éloigné**
3 very small or slight: *a remote chance of success; He hasn't the remotest idea what is going on.* □ **faible**
re'motely *adverb*. □ **au loin; faiblement**

re'moteness *noun*. □ **éloignement; faible degré (de)**
remote control the control of *eg* a switch or other device from a distance, by means of radio waves *etc*: *The model plane is operated by remote control.* □ **télécommande**

remove [rə'muːv] *verb* **1** to take away: *Will someone please remove all this rubbish!; He removed all the evidence of his crimes; I can't remove this stain from my shirt; He has been removed from his post as minister of education.* □ **enlever**
2 to take off (a piece of clothing): *Please remove your hat.* □ **ôter**
3 to move to a new house *etc*: *She has removed to Vancouver.* □ **déménager**
re'movable *adjective*. □ **mobile**
re'moval *noun* the act of removing or the state of being removed, *especially* the moving of furniture *etc* to a new home: *After his removal from power, the dictator was sent into exile; Our removal is to take place on Monday;* *(also adjective)* *a removal van.* □ **renvoi; (de) déménagement**
re'mover *noun* a person or thing that removes: *a stain remover; a firm of furniture removers.* □ **détachant; déménageur, euse**

remunerate [rə'mjuːnəreit] *verb* to pay (someone) for something he has done. □ **rémunérer**
re,mune'ration *noun*. □ **rémunération**
re'munerative [-rətiv] *adjective* bringing a good profit. □ **rémunérateur**

render ['rendə] *verb* **1** to cause to become: *Her remarks rendered me speechless.* □ **rendre**
2 to give or produce (a service, a bill, thanks *etc*). □ **présenter**
3 to perform (music *etc*). □ **interpréter**

rendezvous ['rondivuː] – *plural* **'rendezvous** [-vuːz] – *noun* **1** an agreement to meet someone somewhere: *They had made a rendezvous to meet at midnight.* □ **rendez-vous**
2 the place where such a meeting is to be: *The park was the lovers' usual rendezvous.* □ **rendez-vous**
3 the meeting itself: *The rendezvous took place at midnight.* □ **rendez-vous**
4 a place where a certain group of people meet or go regularly: *This pub is the rendezvous for the local artists and poets.* □ **rendez-vous**

renew [rə'njuː] *verb* **1** to begin, do, produce *etc* again: *She renewed her efforts; We must renew our attack on drug abuse.* □ **renouveler**
2 to cause (*eg* a licence) to continue for another or longer period of time: *My driver's licence has to be renewed in October.* □ **renouveler**
3 to make new or fresh or as if new again: *The panels on the doors have all been renewed.* □ **remplacer**
re'newable *adjective*. □ **renouvelable**
re'newal *noun*. □ **renouvellement**

renounce [ri'nauns] *verb* **1** to give up (a title, claim, intention *etc*) *especially* formally or publicly: *He renounced his claim to the throne.* □ **renoncer à**
2 to say *especially* formally or publicly that one will no longer have anything to do with (something): *I have*

renounced alcohol. □ **renoncer à**

renunciation [rinʌnsi'eiʃən] noun. □ **renonciation (à)**

renovate ['renəveit] verb to make as good as new again: to renovate an old building. □ **rénover**

'**renovator** noun. □ **rénovateur, trice**

,**reno'vation** noun. □ **rénovation**

renown [rə'naun] noun fame. □ **renom**

re'**nowned** adjective famous: She is renowned for her paintings; a renowned actress. □ **renommé**

rent[1] [rent] noun money paid, usually regularly, for the use of a house, shop, land etc which belongs to someone else: The rent for this flat is $50 a week. □ **loyer**

■ verb to pay or receive rent for the use of a house, shop, land etc: We rent this flat from Mr. Smith; Mr. Smith rents this flat to us. □ **louer (à)**

'**rental** noun 1 money paid as rent. □ **loyer**

2 the act of renting. □ **location**

,**rent-'free** adverb without payment of rent: He lives there rent-free. □ **sans payer de loyer**

■ adjective for which rent does not need to be paid: a rent-free flat. □ **gratuit**

rent out to allow people to use (a house etc which one owns) in exchange for money. □ **louer**

---

see also **let**.

---

rent[2] [rent] noun an old word for a tear (in clothes etc). □ **déchirure**

renunciation see **renounce**.

reorganize, reorganise [riːˈoːgənaiz] verb to organize differently; to put in a different order: We'll have to reorganize our filing system. □ **réorganiser**

re,**organi'zation, re,organi'sation** noun. □ **réorganisation**

rep see **representative**.

repaid see **repay**.

repair [ri'peə] verb 1 to mend; to make (something) that is damaged or has broken down work again; to restore to good condition: to repair a broken lock/torn jacket. □ **réparer**

2 to put right or make up for: Nothing can repair the harm done by your foolish remarks. □ **réparer**

■ noun 1 (often in plural) the act of repairing something damaged or broken down: I put my car into the garage for repairs; The bridge is under repair. □ **réparation**

2 a condition or state: The road is in bad repair; The house is in a good state of repair. □ **état**

re'**pairable** adjective (negative **unrepairable**) able to be mended. □ **réparable**

reparable ['repərəbl] adjective able to be put right. □ **réparable**

,**repa'ration** [repə-] noun 1 the act of making up for something wrong that has been done. □ **réparation**

2 money paid for this purpose. □ **réparation**

re'**pairman** [-man] noun a person who repairs televisions etc. □ **réparateur, trice**

repay [ri'pei] – past tense, past participle **repaid** [ri'peid] – verb to pay back: When are you going to repay the money you borrowed?; I must find a way of repaying her kindness/repaying her for her kindness. □ **rendre**

re'**payment** noun. □ **remboursement**

repeal [rə'piːl] verb to make (a law etc) no longer valid. □ **abroger**

■ noun the act of repealing a law etc. □ **abrogation**

repeat [rə'piːt] verb 1 to say or do again: Would you repeat those instructions, please? □ **répéter**

2 to say (something one has heard) to someone else, sometimes when one ought not to: Please do not repeat what I've just told you. □ **répéter**

3 to say (something) one has learned by heart: to repeat a poem. □ **réciter**

■ noun something which is repeated: I'm tired of seeing all these repeats on television; (also adjective) a repeat performance. □ **reprise**

re'**peated** adjective said, done etc many times: In spite of repeated warnings, he went on smoking. □ **répété**

re'**peatedly** adverb many times: I've asked her for it repeatedly. □ **à maintes reprises**

repetition [repə'tiʃən] noun (an) act of repeating. □ **répétition**

repetitive [rə'petətiv] adjective doing, saying, the same thing too often: His speeches are very repetitive; My job is a bit repetitive. □ **répétitif**

re'**petitively** adverb. □ **de façon répétitive**

re'**petitiveness** noun. □ **caractère répétitif**

repeat oneself to repeat what one has already said: Listen carefully because I don't want to have to repeat myself. □ **se répéter**

---

to **repeat** (not **repeat again**) the lessons.

---

repel [rə'pel] – past tense, past participle re'**pelled** – verb 1 to resist or fight (an enemy) successfully: to repel invaders. □ **repousser**

2 to cause a feeling of dislike or disgust: She was repelled by his dirty appearance. □ **dégoûter**

3 to force to move away: Oil repels water. □ **repousser**

repent [rə'pent] verb 1 (especially in religion) to be sorry for one's past sins. □ **se repentir**

2 (with of) to wish that one had not done, made etc: He repented of his generosity. □ **se repentir (de)**

re'**pentance** noun. □ **repentir**

re'**pentant** adjective (negative **unrepentant**): a repentant sinner. □ **repentant**

repetition, repetitive see **repeat**.

replace [rə'pleis] verb 1 to put, use etc (a person, thing etc), or to be put, used etc, in place of another: I must replace that broken lock; He replaced the cup he broke with a new one; Cars have replaced horses as the normal means of transport. □ **remplacer**

2 to put (something) back where it was: Please replace the books on the shelves. □ **replacer**

re'**placeable** adjective. □ **remplaçable**

re'**placement** noun: I must find a replacement for my secretary – she's leaving next week. □ **remplaçant, ante**

replay [riː'plei] verb to play (a football match etc) again (eg because neither team won): The match ended in a draw – it will have to be replayed. □ **rejouer**

■ ['riːplei] noun a replayed football match etc. □ **match rejoué**

replenish [rə'pleniʃ] verb to fill up again; to fill up (one's

supply of something) again: *We must replenish our stock of coal*. □ **remplir (de nouveau); se réapprovisionner**
re'**plenishment** *noun*. □ **remplissage**

replica ['replikə] *noun* an exact copy, *especially* of a work of art. □ **réplique**

reply [rə'plai] *verb* to answer: *'I don't know,' he replied*; *Should I reply to his letter?*; *She replied that she had never seen the man before*; *She replied by shrugging her shoulders*. □ **répondre**

■ *noun* – *plural* re'**plies** – 1 an answer: *'I don't know,' was his reply*; *I'll write a reply to his letter*. □ **réponse**
2 the act of answering: *What did he say in reply (to your question)?* □ **réponse**

---

to **reply to** a letter (not reply a letter).

---

report [rə'poːt] *noun* 1 a statement or description of what has been said, seen, done *etc*: *a child's school report*; *a police report on the accident*. □ **rapport**
2 rumour; general talk: *According to report, the manager is going to resign*. □ **rumeur**
3 a loud noise, *especially* of a gun being fired. □ **détonation**
4 a detailed and public account or observation of an event, occurrence or happening: *There is a report on world poverty tonight on the news*. □ **reportage**
■ *verb* 1 to give a statement or description of what has been said, seen, done *etc*: *A serious accident has just been reported*; *He reported on the results of the conference*; *Our spies report that troops are being moved to the border*; *His speech was reported in the newspaper*. □ **rendre compte de qqch.**
2 to make a complaint about; to give information about the misbehaviour *etc* of: *The boy was reported to the headmaster for being rude to a teacher*. □ **signaler**
3 to tell someone in authority about: *He reported the theft to the police*. □ **signaler**
4 to go (to a place or a person) and announce that one is there, ready for work *etc*: *The boys were ordered to report to the police station every Saturday afternoon*; *Report to me when you return*; *How many policemen reported for duty?* □ **se présenter (à)**
re'**porter** *noun* a person who writes articles and reports for a newspaper: *Reporters and photographers rushed to the scene of the fire*. □ **reporter**
re**ported speech** indirect speech. □ **discours indirect**
re**port back** to come again and report (to someone); to send a report (to someone): *He was asked to study the matter in detail and report back to the committee*. □ **présenter son rapport à**

repose [rə'pouz] *noun* rest; calm; peacefulness. □ **repos**

reprehensible [repri'hensəbl] *adjective* deserving blame: *a reprehensible act*. □ **répréhensible**
,repre'**hensibly** *adverb*. □ **de façon répréhensible**

represent [reprə'zent] *verb* 1 to speak or act on behalf of: *You have been chosen to represent our association at the conference*. □ **représenter**
2 to be a sign, symbol, picture *etc* of: *In this play, the man in black represents Death and the young girl Life*. □ **représenter**
3 to be a good example of; to show or illustrate: *What*

he said represents the feelings of many people*. □ **représenter**
,represen'**tation** *noun* 1 the act of representing or the state of being represented. □ **représentation**
2 a person or thing that represents: *These primitive statues are intended as representations of gods and goddesses*. □ **représentation**
3 (*often in plural*) a strong appeal, demand or protest. □ **représentation**
,repre'**sentative** [-tətiv] *adjective* 1 being a good example (of something); typical: *We need opinions from a representative sample of people*; *Is this poem representative of his work?* □ **représentatif**
2 carried on by elected people: *representative government*. □ **représentatif**
■ *noun* 1 (*also* **rep** [rep]) a person who represents a business; a travelling salesman: *Our representative will call on you this afternoon*. □ **représentant, ante**
2 a person who represents a person or group of people: *A Member of Parliament is the representative of the people in his constituency*. □ **représentant, ante, député, ée**

repress [rə'pres] *verb* to keep (an impulse, a desire to do something *etc*) under control: *He repressed a desire to fire the man*. □ **réprimer**
re'**pression** [-ʃən] *noun*. □ **répression**
re'**pressive** [-siv] *adjective* severe; harsh. □ **répressif**
re'**pressiveness** *noun*. □ **caractère répressif**

reprieve [rə'priːv] *verb* to pardon (a criminal) or delay his punishment: *The murderer was sentenced to death, but later reprieved*. □ **accorder un sursis ou une commutation de peine**
■ *noun* the act of pardoning a criminal or delaying his or her punishment; the order to do this. □ **grâce, sursis**

reprimand [repri'maːnd, 'reprimand] *verb* (*especially* of a person in authority) to speak or write angrily or severely to (someone) because he has done wrong; to rebuke: *The soldier was severely reprimanded for being drunk*. □ **réprimander**
■ ['reprimaːnd] *noun* angry or severe words; a rebuke: *He was given a severe reprimand*. □ **réprimande**

reprint [riː'print] *verb* to print more copies of (a book *etc*): *We are reprinting her new novel already*. □ **réimprimer**
■ ['riːprint] *noun* a copy of a book *etc* made by reprinting the original without any changes. □ **réimpression**

reprisal [rə'praizəl] *noun* something bad done to someone in return for something bad he has done to one; an act of revenge. □ **représailles**

reproach [rə'proutʃ] *verb* to rebuke or blame but *usually* with a feeling of sadness and disappointment rather than anger: *She reproached me for not telling her about my money troubles*; *There is no need to reproach yourself – you did the best you could*. □ **reprocher à**
■ *noun* (an) act of reproaching: *a look of reproach*; *She didn't deserve that reproach from you*. □ **reproche**
re'**proachful** *adjective* showing or expressing reproach: *a reproachful look*; *reproachful words*. □ **réprobateur**
re'**proachfully** *adverb*. □ **avec reproche**

reproduce [riːprə'djuːs] *verb* 1 to make or produce a

copy of; to make or produce again: *Good as the film is, it fails to reproduce the atmosphere of the book; A record player reproduces the sound which has been recorded on a record.* □ **reproduire**
2 (of humans, animals and plants) to produce (young, seeds *etc*): *How do fish reproduce?* □ **se reproduire**
,**repro'duction** [-'dʌk-] *noun* **1** the act or process of re-producing: *She is studying reproduction in rabbits.* □ **reproduction**
2 a copy (of a work of art *etc*): *These paintings are all reproductions.* □ **reproduction**
,**repro'ductive** [-'dʌktiv] *adjective* of or for reproduc-tion: *the reproductive organs of a rabbit.* □ **reproducteur**

reproof [rə'pruːf] *noun* (an) act of rebuking or reproach-ing: *a glance of stern reproof; He has received several reproofs for bad behaviour.* □ **réprimande**
reprove [rə'pruːv] *verb* to tell (a person) that he has done wrong: *The teacher reproved the girls for coming late to school.* □ **réprimander**
re'**proving** *adjective: a reproving look.* □ **réprobateur**
re'**provingly** *adverb.* □ **d'un air de reproche**

reptile ['reptail] *noun* any of the group of cold-blooded animals to which snakes, lizards, crocodiles *etc* belong. □ **reptile**
rep'**tilian** [-'ti-] *adjective.* □ **reptilien**

republic [rə'pʌblik] *noun* (a country with) a form of government in which there is no king or queen, the power of government, law-making *etc* being given to one or more elected representatives (*eg* a president, members of a parliament *etc*): *The United States is a republic – the United Kingdom is not.* □ **république**
re'**publican** *adjective* **1** of a republic: *a republican form of government.* □ **républicain**
2 (*also noun*) (a person) who supports a republican form of government: *He is not a monarchist – he is a repub-lican; my republican friends.* □ **républicain, aine**

repulse [rə'pʌls] *verb* **1** to repel (an enemy). □ **repousser**
2 to refuse to accept *eg* help from, or be friendly to. □ **repousser**
■ *noun* (an) act of repulsing. □ **refus**
repulsion [rə'pʌlʃən] *noun* disgust. □ **répulsion**
repulsive [rə'pʌlsiv] *adjective* horrible; disgusting. □ **repoussant**
re'**pulsively** *adverb.* □ **d'une façon repoussante**
re'**pulsiveness** *noun.* □ **caractère repoussant**

reputation [repju'teiʃən] *noun* the opinion which peo-ple in general have about a person *etc*, a persons's abili-ties *etc*: *That firm has a good/bad reputation; She has made a reputation for herself as an expert in comput-ers; He has the reputation of being difficult to please; The scandal damaged his reputation.* □ **réputation**
'**reputable** *adjective* respectable; well thought of: *Is that a reputable firm?* □ **honorable; de bonne réputation**
reputed [ri'pjuːtid] *adjective* generally reported and believed: *He is reputed to be very wealthy.* □ **réputé**
live up to one's reputation to behave or do as people expect one to. □ **soutenir sa réputation**

request [ri'kwest] *noun* **1** the act of asking for some-thing: *I did that at her request; After frequent requests,*

she eventually agreed to sing. □ **requête**
2 something asked for: *The next record I will play is a request.* □ **demande**
■ *verb* to ask (for) something; *People using this library are requested not to talk; Many people have requested this next song.* □ **demander (à)**
by request when or because one is asked to: *I'm sing-ing this next song by request.* □ **sur demande**
on request when requested: *Buses only stop here on request.* □ **sur demande**

requiem ['rekwiem] *noun* (a piece of music written for) a mass for the souls of the dead. □ **requiem**

require [ri'kwaiə] *verb* **1** to need: *Is there anything else you require?* □ **avoir besoin de**
2 to ask, force or order to do something: *You are re-quired by law to send your children to school; I will do everything that is required of me.* □ **exiger**
re'**quirement** *noun* something that is needed, asked for, ordered *etc*: *It is a legal requirement that all cars have brakes which work; Our firm will be able to supply all your requirements.* □ **exigence**

rescue ['reskjuː] *verb* to get or take out of a dangerous situation, captivity *etc*: *The lifeboat was sent out to res-cue the sailors from the sinking ship.* □ **secourir**
■ *noun* (an) act of rescuing or state of being rescued: *The lifeboat crew performed four rescues last week; After his rescue, the climber was taken to hospital; They came quickly to our rescue.* □ **sauvetage**
'**rescuer** *noun.* □ **sauveteur**

research [ri'səːtʃ, 'riːsəːr(r)tʃ] *noun* a close and careful study to find out (new) facts or information: *She is en-gaged in cancer research; Her researches resulted in some amazing discoveries; (also adjective) a research student.* □ **(de) recherche**
■ [ri'səːr(r)tʃ] *verb* to carry out such a study: *She's re-searching (into) Thai poetry.* □ **faire des recherches**
re'**searcher** [ri'səːtʃə, 'riːsəːrtʃər] *noun.* □ **chercheur, euse**

resemble [rə'zembl] *verb* to be like or look like: *He doesn't resemble either of his parents.* □ **ressembler à**
re'**semblance** *noun: I can see some resemblance(s) be-tween him and his father.* □ **ressemblance**

resent [ri'zent] *verb* to feel annoyed about (something) because one thinks it is unfair, insulting *etc*: *I resent his interference in my affairs.* □ **s'offenser de qqch.**
re'**sentful** *adjective* having or showing such a feeling of annoyance: *She feels resentful that her sister mar-ried before she did.* □ **froissé; plein de ressentiment**
re'**sentfully** *adverb.* □ **avec ressentiment**
re'**sentfulness** *noun.* □ **ressentiment**
re'**sentment** *noun: He has a feeling of resentment against the police after the way he was treated by them.* □ **ressentiment**

reserve [rə'zəːv] *verb* **1** to ask for or order to be kept for the use of a particular person, often oneself: *The res-taurant is busy on Saturdays, so I'll phone up today and reserve a table.* □ **réserver**
2 to keep for the use of a particular person or group of people, or for a particular use: *These seats are reserved for the committee members.* □ **réserver**

■ *noun* **1** something which is kept for later use or for use when needed: *The farmer kept a reserve of food in case he was cut off by floods.* □ **réserve**
2 a piece of land used for a special purpose *eg* for the protection of animals: *a wild-life reserve; a nature reserve.* □ **réserve**
3 the habit of not saying very much, not showing what one is feeling, thinking *etc*; shyness. □ **réserve**
4 (*often in plural*) soldiers, sailors *etc* who do not belong to the regular full-time army, navy *etc* but who are called into action when needed *eg* during a war. □ **réserviste(s)**
,**reser'vation** [rezə-] *noun* **1** the act of reserving: *the reservation of a room.* □ **réservation**
2 something (*eg* a table in a restaurant) which has been reserved: *Have you a reservation, Sir?* □ **réservation**
3 a doubt. □ **réserve**
4 a piece of land set aside for a particular purpose: *an Indian reservation in the United States.* □ **réserve**
re'served *adjective* not saying very much; not showing what one is feeling, thinking *etc*: *a reserved manner.* □ **réservé**
have, keep *etc* **in reserve** to have or keep (something) in case or until it is needed: *If you go to America please keep some money in reserve for your fare home.* □ **avoir/ garder en réserve**
reservoir ['rezəvwɑː] *noun* a place, *usually* a man-made lake, where water for drinking *etc* is stored. □ **réservoir**
resident ['rezidənt] *noun* a person who lives or has his home in a particular place: *a resident of Edinburgh.* □ **habitant, ante**
■ *adjective* **1** living or having one's home in a place: *She is now resident abroad.* □ **résident**
2 living, having to live, or requiring a person to live, in the place where he or she works: *a resident caretaker.* □ **résident, à demeure**
reside [rə'zaid] *verb* to live or have one's home in a place: *She now resides abroad.* □ **résider**
'**residence** *noun* **1** a person's home, *especially* the grand house of someone important. □ **résidence**
2 the act of living in a place, or the time of this: *during her residence in Spain.* □ **séjour**
'**residency** – *plural* '**residencies** – *noun* the home of the governor *etc* in a colony *etc*. □ **résidence officielle**
,**resi'dential** [-'denʃəl] *adjective* **1** (of an area of a town *etc*) containing houses rather than offices, shops *etc*: *This district is mainly residential; a residential neighbourhood/area.* □ **résidentiel**
2 requiring a person to live in the place where he or she works: *a residential post.* □ **qui demande résidence**
3 of, concerned with, living in a place. □ **résidentiel**
in residence (*especially* of someone important) staying in a place, sometimes to perform some official duties: *The Queen is in residence here this week.* □ **en résidence**
take up residence to go and live (in a place, building *etc*): *She has taken up residence in France.* □ **établir sa demeure**
residue ['rezidjuː] *noun* what remains or is left over. □ **résidu**

residual [rə'zidjuəl] *adjective.* □ **résiduel**
resign [rə'zain] *verb* **1** to leave a job *etc*: *If he criticizes my work again I'll resign; She resigned (from) her post.* □ **démissionner**
2 (*with* **to**) to make (oneself) accept (a situation, fact *etc*) with patience and calmness: *He has resigned himself to the possibility that he may never walk again.* □ **se résigner (à)**
resignation [rezig'neiʃən] *noun* **1** the act of resigning. □ **démission**
2 a letter *etc* stating that one is resigning: *You will receive my resignation tomorrow.* □ **démission**
3 (the state of having or showing) patient, calm acceptance (of a situation, fact *etc*): *He accepted his fate with resignation.* □ **résignation**
re'signed *adjective* (*often with* **to**) having or showing patient, calm acceptance (of a fact, situation *etc*): *She is resigned to her fate.* □ **résigné (à)**
resin ['rezin] *noun* a sticky substance produced by certain trees (*eg* firs, pines) and some other plants. □ **résine**
'**resinous** *adjective.* □ **résineux**
resist [rə'zist] *verb* **1** to fight against, *usually* successfully: *The soldiers resisted the enemy attack; He tried to resist arrest; It's hard to resist temptation.* □ **résister (à)**
2 to be able to stop oneself doing, taking *etc* (something): *I couldn't resist kicking him when he bent down; I just can't resist strawberries.* □ **résister (à)**
3 to be unaffected or undamaged by: *a metal that resists rust/acids.* □ **résister (à)**
re'sistance *noun* **1** the act of resisting: *The army offered strong resistance to the enemy;* (*also adjective*) *a resistance force.* □ **(de) résistance**
2 the ability or power to be unaffected or undamaged by something: *resistance to disease.* □ **résistance**
3 the force that one object, substance *etc* exerts against the movement of another object *etc.* □ **résistance**
re'sistant *adjective*: *This breed of cattle is resistant to disease; heat-resistant table-mats.* □ **résistant (à)**
resolution [rezə'luːʃən] *noun* **1** a firm decision (to do something): *She made a resolution to get up early.* □ **résolution**
2 an opinion or decision formally expressed by a group of people, *eg* at a public meeting: *The meeting passed a resolution in favour of allowing men to join the society.* □ **résolution**
3 resoluteness. □ **résolution**
4 the act of resolving (a problem *etc*). □ **solution**
'**resolute** [-luːt] *adjective* doing what one has decided to do, in spite of opposition, criticism *etc*: *a resolute attitude.* □ **résolu**
'**resolutely** *adverb.* □ **résolument**
'**resoluteness** *noun.* □ **résolution**
resolve [rə'zolv] *verb* **1** to make a firm decision (to do something): *I've resolved to stop smoking.* □ **prendre la résolution de**
2 to pass (a resolution): *It was resolved that women should be allowed to join the society.* □ **prendre une résolution**
3 to take away (a doubt, fear *etc*) or produce an answer

to (a problem, difficulty *etc*). □ **résoudre**
■ *noun* **1** determination to do what one has decided to do: *She showed great resolve*. □ **détermination**
2 a firm decision: *It is her resolve to become a director of this firm*. □ **résolution**
resolved [rə'zɔlvd] *adjective* determined: *I am resolved to go and nothing will stop me*. □ **résolu (à)**
resonant ['rezənənt] *adjective* (of sounds) loud; echoing; easily heard. □ **résonant**
'**resonance** *noun*. □ **résonance**
resort [rə'zɔːt] *verb* (*with* to) to begin to use, do *etc* as a way of solving a problem *etc* when other methods have failed: *He couldn't persuade people to do what he wanted, so he resorted to threats of violence*. □ **avoir recours (à)**
■ *noun* a place visited by many people (*especially* for holidays): *Brighton is a popular (holiday) resort*. □ **lieu de vacances**
as a last resort when all other methods *etc have failed*: *If we can't get the money in any other way, I suppose we could, as a last resort, sell the car*. □ **en dernier ressort, au pis-aller**
resound [rə'zaund] *verb* to sound loudly or for a long time: *The audience's cheers resounded through the hall*. □ **retentir, résonner**
re'sounding *adjective* **1** loud: *resounding cheers*. □ **retentissant**
2 very great; complete: *a resounding victory/success*. □ **retentissant**
re'soundingly *adverb*. □ **d'une manière retentissante**
resource [rə'zɔːs] *noun* **1** (*usually in plural*) something that gives help, support *etc* when needed; a supply; a means: *We have used up all our resources*; *We haven't the resources at this school for teaching handicapped children*. □ **ressource(s)**
2 (*usually in plural*) the wealth of a country, or the supply of materials *etc* which bring this wealth: *This country is rich in natural resources*. □ **ressources**
3 the ability to find ways of solving difficulties: *She is full of resource*. □ **ressources**
re'sourceful *adjective* good at finding ways of solving difficulties, problems *etc*. □ **ingénieux, débrouillard**
re'sourcefully *adverb*. □ **d'une manière ingénieuse**
re'sourcefulness *noun*. □ **ingéniosité**
respect [rə'spekt] *noun* **1** admiration; good opinion: *She is held in great respect by everyone*; *He has no respect for politicians*. □ **respect**
2 consideration; thoughtfulness; willingness to obey *etc*: *He shows no respect for his parents*. □ **respect**
3 a particular detail, feature *etc*: *These two poems are similar in some respects*. □ **égard**
■ *verb* **1** to show or feel admiration for: *I respect you for what you did*. □ **respecter**
2 to show consideration for, a willingness to obey *etc*: *One should respect other people's feelings/property*. □ **respecter**
re'spectable *adjective* **1** having a good reputation or character: *a respectable family*. □ **respectable**
2 correct; acceptable: *respectable behaviour*. □ **convenable**

3 (of clothes) good enough or suitable to wear: *You can't go out in those torn trousers – they're not respectable*. □ **convenable**
4 large, good *etc* enough; fairly large, good *etc*: *Four goals is a respectable score*. □ **respectable**
re'spectably *adverb*. □ **convenablement**
re,specta'bility *noun*. □ **respectabilité**
re'spectful *adjective* having or showing respect. □ **respectueux (envers/à l'egard de)**
re'spectfully *adverb*. □ **respectueusement**
re'spectfulness *noun*. □ **respect**
re'specting *preposition* about; concerning: *Respecting your salary, we shall come to a decision later*. □ **en ce qui concerne**
re'spective [-tiv] *adjective* belonging to *etc* each person or thing mentioned: *Peter and Jodie went to their respective homes*. □ **respectif**
re'spectively [-tiv-] *adverb* referring to each person or thing mentioned, in the order in which they are mentioned: *Jodie, James and John were first, second and third, respectively*. □ **respectivement**
re'spects *noun plural* greetings: *She sends her respects to you*. □ **respects, hommages**
pay one's respects (to someone) to visit (a person) as a sign of respect to him. □ **présenter ses respects à**
with respect to about; concerning: *With respect to your request, we regret that we are unable to assist you in this matter*. □ **concernant**
respire [rə'spaiə] *verb* to breathe. □ **respirer**
respiration [respə'reiʃən] *noun* breathing. □ **respiration**
respirator ['respə] *noun* **1** a sort of mask worn to purify the air breathed in *eg* by firemen. □ **masque à gaz**
2 a piece of apparatus used to help very ill or injured people to breathe. □ **respirateur**
respiratory ['respərətəri] *adjective* related to breathing: *respiratory diseases*. □ **respiratoire**
respite ['respait] *noun* a pause or rest. □ **répit**
resplendent [rə'splendənt] *adjective* very bright or splendid in appearance. □ **resplendissant**
re'splendently *adverb*. □ **avec splendeur**
re'splendence *noun*. □ **splendeur**
respond [rə'spond] *verb* (*with* to) **1** to answer with words, a reaction, gesture *etc*: *He didn't respond to my question; I smiled at her, but she didn't respond*. □ **répondre, réagir**
2 to show a good reaction *eg* to some course of treatment: *His illness did not respond to treatment by drugs*. □ **répondre à**
3 (of vehicles *etc*) to be guided easily by controls: *The pilot said the plane did not respond to the controls*. □ **répondre à**
re'sponse [-s] *noun* **1** a reply or reaction: *Our letters have never met with any response*; *My suggestions met with little response*. □ **réponse, réaction**
2 (*usually in plural*) in church services, a part spoken by the congregation rather than the priest. □ **répons**
re,sponsi'bility [-sə-] *plural* **-bilities** – *noun* **1** something which a person has to look after, do *etc*: *She takes her responsibilities very seriously*. □

responsabilité
2 the state of having important duties: *a position of responsibility*. □ **responsabilité**
3 the state of being responsible: *his responsibility for the accident*. □ **responsabilité**
re'sponsible [-səbl] *adjective* 1 having a duty to see that something is done *etc*: *We'll make one person responsible for buying the food for the trip*. □ **responsable**
2 (of a job *etc*) having many duties *eg* the making of important decisions: *The job of manager is a very responsible post*. □ **comportant des responsabilités**
3 (*with* for) being the cause of something: *Who is responsible for the stain on the carpet?* □ **responsable de**
4 (of a person) able to be trusted; sensible: *We need a responsible person for this job*. □ **digne de confiance**
5 (*with* for) able to control, and fully aware of (one's actions): *The lawyer said that at the time of the murder, his client was not responsible for his actions*. □ **responsable (de)**
re'sponsibly [-sə-] *adverb* in a trustworthy or serious way: *Do try to behave responsibly*. □ **avec sérieux**
re'sponsive [-siv] *adjective* (*negative* **unresponsive**): *a responsive, kindly girl*; *a responsive smile*; *The disease is responsive to treatment*. □ **qui réagit bien (à)**
re'sponsively *adverb*. □ **avec sympathie**
re'sponsiveness *noun*. □ **bonne réaction à**
rest[1] [rest] *noun* 1 a (*usually* short) period of not working *etc* after, or between periods of, effort; (a period of) freedom from worries *etc*: *Digging the garden is hard work – let's stop for a rest*; *Let's have/take a rest*; *I need a rest from all these problems – I'm going to take a week's holiday*. □ **repos**
2 sleep: *He needs a good night's rest*. □ **sommeil**
3 something which holds or supports: *a book-rest*; *a headrest on a car seat*. □ **support, appui**
4 a state of not moving: *The machine is at rest*. □ **(au) repos**
■ *verb* 1 to (allow to) stop working *etc* in order to get new strength or energy: *We've been walking for four hours – let's stop and rest*; *Stop reading for a minute and rest your eyes*; *Let's rest our legs*. □ **(se) reposer**
2 to sleep; to lie or sit quietly in order to get new strength or energy, or because one is tired: *Mother is resting at the moment*. □ **(se) reposer**
3 to (make or allow to) lean, lie, sit, remain *etc* on or against something: *Her head rested on his shoulder*; *He rested his hand on her arm*; *Her gaze rested on the jewels*. □ **(re)poser, (s')appuyer (sur)**
4 to relax, be calm *etc*: *I will never rest until I know the murderer has been caught*. □ **être calme, tranquille**
5 to (allow to) depend on: *Our hopes now rest on her, since all else has failed*. □ **reposer sur**
6 (*with* with) (of a duty *etc*) to belong to: *The choice rests with you*. □ **appartenir à**
'restful *adjective* 1 bringing rest: *a restful holiday*. □ **reposant**
2 (of colours, music *etc*) causing a person to feel calm and relaxed: *Some people find blue a restful colour*; *After a hard day's work, I like to listen to some restful music*. □ **reposant**

3 relaxed: at rest: *The patient seems more restful now*. □ **tranquille, reposé**
'restfully *adverb*. □ **paisiblement**
'restfulness *noun*. □ **tranquillité**
'restless *adjective* 1 always moving; showing signs of worry, boredom, impatience *etc*: *a restless child*; *She's been doing the same job for years now and she's beginning to get restless*. □ **agité**
2 during which a person does not sleep: *a restless night*. □ **agité**
'restlessly *adverb*. □ **nerveusement**
'restlessness *noun*. □ **nervosité**
'restroom *noun* a toilet in a theatre, factory *etc*. □ **toilettes**
at rest free from pain, worry *etc*. □ **tranquille**
come to rest to stop moving: *The ball came to rest under a tree*. □ **s'arrêter**
lay to rest to bury (someone) in a grave. □ **porter en terre**
let the matter rest to stop discussing *etc* a matter. □ **en rester là**
rest assured to be certain: *You may rest assured that we will take your views into consideration*. □ **être assuré/certain que**
set someone's mind at rest to take away a person's worries about something. □ **tranquilliser qqn**
rest[2] [rest]: **the rest** 1 what is left when part of something is taken away, finished *etc*: *the rest of the meal*. □ **reste**
2 all the other people, things *etc*: *Jack went home, but the rest of us went to the cinema*. □ **(nous/les) autres**
restaurant ['restront, -tərənt] *noun* a place where meals may be bought and eaten. □ **restaurant**
restitution [resti'tjuːʃən] *noun* the act of giving back to a person *etc* what has been taken away, or the giving of money *etc* to pay for damage, loss or injury. □ **restitution**
restive ['restiv] *adjective* beginning to show displeasure, impatience, boredom *etc eg* at delay, discipline *etc*; restless. □ **impatient, nerveux**
'restively *adverb*. □ **nerveusement**
'restiveness *noun*. □ **nervosité**
restore [rə'stoːr] *verb* 1 to repair (a building, a painting, a piece of furniture *etc*) so that it looks as it used to or ought to. □ **restaurer**
2 to bring back to a normal or healthy state: *The patient was soon restored to health*. □ **rétablir**
3 to bring or give back: *to restore law and order*; *The police restored the stolen cars to their owners*. □ **rétablir, rendre**
4 to bring or put (a person) back to a position, rank *etc* he once had: *He was asked to resign but was later restored to his former job as manager*. □ **rétablir**
,resto'ration [restə-] *noun*: *The building was closed for restoration(s)*. □ **restauration**
re'storer *noun* a person or thing that restores: *a furniture-restorer*. □ **restaurateur, trice**
restrain [rə'strein] *verb* to prevent from doing something; to control: *He was so angry he could hardly restrain himself*; *He had to be restrained from hitting the man*; *He restrained his anger with difficulty*. □ **(se) contenir/**

retenir

re'strained *adjective* controlling, or able to control, one's feelings. □ **maître de soi**

restrict [rə'strikt] *verb* 1 to keep within certain limits: *I try to restrict myself/my smoking to five cigarettes a day; Use of the parking lot is restricted to senior staff.* □ **restreindre, limiter (à)**

2 to make less than usual, desirable *etc*: *She feels this new law will restrict her freedom.* □ **limiter**

re'stricted *adjective* 1 limited; narrow, small: *a restricted space.* □ **restreint**

2 to which entry has been restricted to certain people: *The battlefield was a restricted zone.* □ **restreint**

3 in which certain restrictions (*eg* a speed limit) apply: *a restricted area.* □ **réglementé, limité**

re'striction [-ʃən] *noun* 1 a rule *etc* that limits or controls: *Even in a free democracy a person's behaviour must be subject to certain restrictions.* □ **restriction, limitation**

2 the act of restricting: *restriction of freedom.* □ **réduction**

re'strictive [-tiv] *adjective* restricting or intended to restrict. □ **restrictif**

result [rə'zʌlt] *noun* 1 anything which is due to something already done: *Her deafness is the result of a car accident; He went deaf as a result of an accident; She tried a new method, with excellent results; He tried again, but without result.* □ **résultat**

2 the answer to a sum *etc*: *Add all these figures and tell me the result.* □ **résultat**

3 the final score: *What was the result of Saturday's match?* □ **résultat**

4 (*often in plural*) the list of people who have been successful in a competition, of subjects a person has passed or failed in an examination *etc*: *She had very good exam results; The results will be published next week.* □ **résultats**

■ *verb* 1 (*often with* from) to be caused (by something): *We will pay for any damage which results (from our experiments).* □ **résulter de**

2 (*with* in) to cause or have as a result: *The match resulted in a draw.* □ **se terminer (par)**

resume [rə'zjuːm] *verb* to begin again after stopping: *After tea, the meeting resumed; We'll resume the meeting after tea.* □ **reprendre**

resumption [rə'zʌmpʃən] *noun.* □ **reprise**

resurrection [rezə'rekʃən] *noun* the process of being brought to life again after death. □ **résurrection**

resuscitate [rə'sʌsəteit] *verb* to bring (a person) back to consciousness. □ **réanimer**

re,susci'tation *noun.* □ **réanimation**

retail ['riːteil] *verb* to sell (goods) (*usually* in small quantities) to the person who is going to use them (rather than to someone who is going to sell them to someone else). □ **vendre au détail**

■ *adjective* relating to the sale of goods in this way: *a retail price.* □ **au/de détail**

'retailer *noun* a person who sells goods retail; a shopkeeper. □ **détaillant, ante**

retain [rə'tein] *verb* 1 to continue to have, use, remem-

ber *etc*; to keep in one's possession, memory *etc*: *He finds it difficult to retain information; These dishes don't retain heat very well.* □ **retenir, conserver**

2 to hold (something) back or keep (something) in its place: *This wall was built to retain the water from the river in order to prevent flooding.* □ **retenir**

retake [riː'teik] – *past tense* ,re'took [-'tuk]: *past participle* ,re'taken – *verb* 1 to capture again: *The soldiers retook the fort.* □ **reprendre**

2 to film (part of a film *etc*) again. □ **tourner à nouveau (une scène)**

■ ['riːteik] *noun* the filming of part of a film again: *the fourth retake.* □ **nouvelle prise de vues**

retaliate [rə'talieit] *verb* to do something unpleasant to a person in return for something unpleasant he has done to one: *If you insult him, he will retaliate.* □ **rendre la pareille (à qqn)**

re,tali'ation *noun.* □ **vengeance**

retard [rə'taːd] *verb* to make slower or later: *The country's economic progress was retarded by strikes; The baby's development was retarded by an accident he had shortly after birth.* □ **retarder**

,retar'dation [riːtaː-] *noun.* □ **retard**

re'tarded *adjective*: *a mentally retarded child.* □ **arriéré**

retention [rə'tenʃən] *noun* the act of retaining: *the retention of information.* □ **conservation**

re'tentive [-tiv] *adjective* able to retain: *a retentive memory.* □ **fidèle**

retina ['retinə] *noun* the part of the back of the eye that receives the image of what is seen. □ **rétine**

retinue ['retinjuː] *noun* the servants, officials *etc* who accompany a person of importance. □ **suite**

retire [rə'taiə] *verb* 1 stop working permanently, *usually* because of age: *He retired at the age of sixty-five.* □ **prendre sa retraite**

2 to leave; to withdraw: *When she doesn't want to talk to anyone, she retires to her room and locks the door; We retired to bed at midnight; The troops were forced to retire to a safer position.* □ **se retirer, partir**

re'tired *adjective* having stopped working: *My father is retired now; a retired professor.* □ **retraité**

re'tirement *noun* 1 the act of retiring from work: *It is not long till her retirement.* □ **retraite**

2 a person's life after retiring from work: *He's enjoying his retirement.* □ **retraite**

re'tiring *adjective* shy: *a very quiet, retiring person.* □ **réservé**

retook see **retake**.

retort [rə'toːt] *verb* to make a quick and clever or angry reply: *'You're too old', she said. 'You're not so young yourself', she retorted.* □ **répliquer**

■ *noun* such a reply. □ **réplique, riposte**

retrace [ri'treis] *verb* to go back along (a path *etc*) one has just come along: *She lost her keys somewhere on the way to the station, and had to retrace her steps/ journey until she found them.* □ **revenir sur ses pas, rebrousser chemin**

retract [rə'trakt] *verb* to pull, or be pulled, into the body *etc*: *A cat can retract its claws; A cat's claws can retract.* □ **rétracter**

re'traction [-ʃən] *noun*. □ **rétraction**

re'tractable *adjective* able to be pulled up or in: *An airplane has retractable wheels.* □ **escamotable**

retreat [rə'triːt] *verb* 1 to move back or away from a battle (*usually* because the enemy is winning): *After a hard struggle, they were finally forced to retreat.* □ **battre en retraite**

2 to withdraw; to take oneself away: *She retreated to the peace of her own room.* □ **se retirer (vers/dans)**

■ *noun* 1 the act of retreating (from a battle, danger *etc*): *After the retreat, the soldiers rallied once more.* □ **retraite**

2 a signal to retreat: *The bugler sounded the retreat.* □ **retraite**

3 (a place to which a person can go for) a period of rest, religious meditation *etc*: *She has gone to a retreat to pray.* □ **retraite**

retribution [retri'bjuːʃən] *noun* punishment, *especially* deserved. □ **châtiment**

retrieve [rə'triːv] *verb* 1 to get back (something which was lost *etc*): *My hat blew away, but I managed to retrieve it*; *Our team retrieved its lead in the second half.* □ **récupérer, retrouver**

2 (of *usually* trained dogs) to search for and bring back (birds or animals that have been shot by a hunter). □ **rapporter**

re'trieval *noun*. □ **récupération**

re'triever *noun* a breed of dog trained to find and bring back birds and animals that have been shot. □ **chien d'arrêt**

return [rə'tɔːn] *verb* 1 to come or go back: *She returns home tomorrow*; *He returned to London from Paris yesterday*; *The pain has returned.* □ **revenir, retourner**

2 to give, send, put *etc* (something) back where it came from: *She returned the book to its shelf*; *Don't forget to return the books you borrowed.* □ **remettre, rendre**

3 *I'll return to this topic in a minute.* □ **revenir**

4 to do (something) which has been done to oneself: *She hit him and he returned the blow*; *He said how nice it was to see her again, and she returned the compliment.* □ **rendre**

5 (of voters) to elect (someone) to Parliament. □ **élire**

6 (of a jury) to give (a verdict): *The jury returned a verdict of not guilty.* □ **rendre**

7 (in tennis *etc*) to hit (a ball) back to one's opponent: *She returned his serve.* □ **renvoyer**

■ *noun* 1 the act of returning: *On our return, we found the house had been burgled*; (*also adjective*) *a return journey.* □ **(de) retour**

2 a round trip ticket, a return ticket: *Do you want a single or a return?* □ **billet d'aller et retour**

re'turnable *adjective* that can be or that must be returned. □ **consigné**

return match a second match played between the same (teams of) players: *We played the first match on our football pitch – the return match will be on theirs.* □ **match revanche**

return ticket a round trip ticket, allowing a person to travel to a place and back again to where he started. □ **billet d'aller et retour**

by return (mail) by the very next post: *Please send me your reply by return (mail).* □ **par retour du courrier**

in return (for) as an exchange (for something): *We'll send them whisky and they'll send us vodka in return: They'll send us vodka in return for whisky.* □ **en échange (de)**

many happy returns (of the day) an expression of good wishes said to a person on his birthday: *He visited his mother on her birthday to wish her many happy returns.* □ **bon anniversaire**

---

to **return** (not **return back**) someone's book.

---

reunion [riːˈjuːnjən] *noun* 1 a meeting of people who have not met for some time: *We attended a reunion of former pupils of our school.* □ **réunion, retrouvailles**

2 the act of reuniting or state of being reunited. □ **réunion**

reunite [riːjuˈnait] *verb* to bring or come together after being separated: *The family was finally reunited after the war*; *The children were reunited with their parents.* □ **réunir**

rev [rev] – *past tense, past participle* **revved** – (*often rev up*) *verb* to increase the speed of revolution of (a car engine *etc*): *He revved the engine (up)*; *He was revving up in the yard.* □ **emballer le moteur**

revs *noun plural* revolutions (of a car engine *etc*): *thirty revs a second.* □ **tours**

reveal [rə'viːl] *verb* 1 to make known: *All their secrets have been revealed.* □ **révéler**

2 to show; to allow to be seen: *He scraped away the top layer of paint from the picture, revealing an earlier painting underneath.* □ **laisser voir**

re'vealing *adjective* allowing or causing something to be known or seen: *a revealing statement.* □ **révélateur, éloquent**

reveille [ri'vali] *noun* a bugle call at daybreak to waken soldiers. □ **réveil**

revel ['revl] – *past tense, past participle* **'revelled**, **'reveled** – *verb* (*with in*) to take great delight in something: *He revels in danger.* □ **se délecter (de)**

■ *noun* (*usually in plural*) noisy, lively enjoyment: *midnight revels.* □ **réjouissances**

'reveller *noun*. □ **bambocheur, euse**

'revelry – *plural* **'revelries** – *noun* (*often in plural*) noisy, lively enjoyment: *midnight revelries.* □ **festivités**

revelation [revə'leiʃən] *noun* 1 the act of revealing secrets, information *etc*: *the revelation of the true facts.* □ **révélation**

2 something made known: *amazing revelations.* □ **révélation**

revelry *see* revel.

revenge [rə'vendʒ] *noun* 1 harm done to another person in return for harm which he has done (to oneself or to someone else): *The man told the manager he would get/ have his revenge on the company for dismissing him*; *His revenge was to burn down the factory.* □ **vengeance**

2 the desire to do such harm: *The man said he had burned down the factory out of revenge/in revenge for being dismissed.* □ **vengeance; pour se venger de**

■ *verb* (*with* **on**) to get (one's) revenge: *He revenged himself on his enemies*; *I'll soon be revenged on you all*. □ **se venger (de)**

revenue ['revinjuː] *noun* money which comes to a person *etc* from any source or sources (*eg* property, shares), *especially* the money which comes to a government from taxes *etc*. □ **revenu**

reverberate [rivəːbvəːeit] *verb* to sound again or re-echo: *The sound of the African drums reverberated in my ears long after the concert was over*. □ **résonner**

revere [rə'viə] *verb* to feel or show great respect for: *The students revere the professor*. □ **vénérer**

reverence ['revərəns] *noun* great respect: *She was held in reverence by those who worked for her*. □ **vénération**

Reverend ['revərənd] *noun* (*usually abbreviated to* **Rev.** *when written*) a title given to a clergyman: (*the*) *Rev. John Brown*. □ **le révérend**

reverent ['revərənt] *adjective* showing great respect: *A reverent silence followed the professor's lecture*. □ **respectueux**

'reverently *adverb*. □ **respectueusement**

reverie ['revəri] *noun* **1** a state of pleasant dreamy thought: *He was lost in reverie*. □ **rêverie**

2 (*usually in plural*) a day-dream: *pleasant reveries*. □ **rêverie**

reverse [rə'vəːs] *verb* **1** to move backwards or in the opposite direction to normal: *She reversed* (*the car*) *into the garage*; *She reversed the film through the projector*. □ **faire marche arrière; inverser**

2 to put into the opposite position, state, order *etc*: *This jacket can be reversed* (= worn inside out). □ **retourner**

3 to change (a decision, policy *etc*) to the exact opposite: *The man was found guilty, but the judges in the appeal court reversed the decision*. □ **réformer, révoquer**

■ *noun* **1** (*also adjective*) (the) opposite: *'Are you hungry?' 'Quite the reverse – I've eaten far too much!'*; *I take the reverse point of view*. □ **contraire, inverse**

2 a defeat; a piece of bad luck. □ **revers**

3 (a mechanism *eg* one of the gears of a car *etc* which makes something move in) a backwards direction or a direction opposite to normal: *He put the car into reverse*; (*also adjective*) *a reverse gear*. □ **marche arrière**

4 (*also adjective*) (of) the back of a coin, medal *etc*: *the reverse* (*side*) *of a coin*. □ **revers**

re'versal *noun*: *a reversal of her previous decision*. □ **revirement (d'opinion)**

re'versed *adjective* in the opposite state, position, order *etc*: *Once she worked for me. Now our positions are reversed and I work for her*. □ **reversé, inverse**

re'versible *adjective* **1** able to be reversed. □ **réversible**

2 (of clothes) able to be worn with either side out: *Is that raincoat reversible?* □ **réversible**

reverse the charges to make a telephone call (a **reverse-charge call**) which is paid for by the person who receives it instead of by the caller. □ **appeler (appel) à frais virés**

reversion *see* **revert**.

revert [rə'vəːt] *verb* to come or go back (to a previous state, point in a discussion *etc*). □ **revenir (à)**

re'version [-ʃən] *noun*. □ **retour, réversion**

review [rə'vjuː] *noun* **1** a written report on a book, play *etc* giving the writer's opinion of it. □ **compte rendu**

2 an inspection of troops *etc*. □ **revue**

■ *verb* **1** to make or have a review of: *The book was reviewed in yesterday's paper*; *The Queen reviewed the troops*. □ **faire la critique de; passer en revue**

2 to reconsider: *We'll review the situation at the end of the month*. □ **réexaminer**

re'viewer *noun* a person who reviews books *etc*: *Who was the reviewer of the biography of Churchill?* □ **critique (littéraire)**

revise [rə'vaiz] *verb* **1** to correct faults and make improvements in (a book *etc*): *This dictionary has been completely revised*. □ **réviser, revoir**

2 to study one's previous work, notes *etc* in preparation for an examination *etc*: *You'd better start revising* (*your Latin*) *for your exam*. □ **réviser**

3 to change (one's opinion *etc*). □ **réviser**

revision [rə'viʒən] *noun*. □ **révision**

revive [rə'vaiv] *verb* **1** to come, or bring, back to consciousness, strength, health *etc*: *They attempted to revive the woman who had fainted*; *She soon revived*; *The flowers revived in water*; *to revive someone's hopes*. □ **ranimer, rétablir**

2 to come or bring back to use *etc*: *This old custom has recently* (*been*) *revived*. □ **rétablir**

re'vival *noun* **1** the act of reviving or state of being revived: *the revival of the invalid/of our hopes*. □ **retour à la vie; réveil**

2 (a time of) new or increased interest in something: *a religious revival*. □ **renouveau (religieux)**

3 (the act of producing) an old and almost forgotten play, show *etc*. □ **reprise**

revoke [rə'vouk] *verb* to change (a decision); to make (a law *etc*) no longer valid. □ **révoquer, abroger**

revocation [revə'keiʃən] *noun*. □ **abrogation**

revolt [rə'voult] *verb* **1** to rebel (against a government *etc*): *The army revolted against the dictator*. □ **se révolter/rebeller contre**

2 to disgust: *His habits revolt me*. □ **dégoûter**

■ *noun* **1** the act of rebelling: *The peasants rose in revolt*. □ **révolte**

2 a rebellion. □ **révolte**

re'volted *adjective* having a feeling of disgust: *I felt quite revolted at the sight*. □ **dégoûté**

re'volting *adjective* causing a feeling of disgust: *revolting food*. □ **répugnant**

revolution [revə'luːʃən] *noun* **1** (the act of making) a successful, violent attempt to change or remove a government *etc*: *the American Revolution*. □ **révolution**

2 a complete change in ideas, methods *etc*: *There's been a complete revolution in the way things are done in this office*. □ **révolution**

3 a complete circle or turn around a central point, axis *etc* (*eg* as made by a record turning on a record player, or the Earth moving on its axis or around the Sun. □ **tour, révolution**

,revo'lutionary *adjective* **1** involving or causing great changes in ideas, methods *etc*: *a revolutionary new proc-*

ess for making paper. □ **révolutionnaire**
2 of a revolution against a government *etc: revolutionary activities.* □ **révolutionnaire**
■ *noun – plural* **revo'lutionaries** – a person who takes part in, or is in favour of, (a) revolution. □ **révolutionnaire**
,**revo'lutionize**, ,**revo'lutionise** *verb* to cause great changes in (ideas, methods *etc*): *This new machinery will revolutionize the paper-making industry.* □ **révolutionner**

revolve [rə'volv] *verb* to move, roll or turn (in a complete circle) around a central point, axis *etc: A wheel revolves on its axle; This disc can be revolved; The Moon revolves around the Earth; The Earth revolves about the Sun and also revolves on its axis.* □ **(faire) tourner**
re'volver *noun* a type of pistol: *She shot him with a revolver.* □ **revolver**
re'volving *adjective: revolving doors.* □ **pivotant, tournant**

revue [rə'vjuː] *noun* an amusing, not very serious, theatre show. □ **revue, spectacle (de music-hall)**

reward [rə'woːd] *noun* 1 something given in return for or got from work done, good behaviour *etc: He was given a gold watch as a reward for his services to the firm; Apart from the salary, teaching children has its own particular rewards.* □ **récompense**
2 a sum of money offered for finding a criminal, lost or stolen property *etc: A reward of $100 has been offered to the person who finds the diamond brooch.* □ **récompense**
■ *verb* to give a reward to someone for something: *He was rewarded for his services; Her services were rewarded.* □ **récompenser**
re'warding *adjective* (*negative* **unrewarding**) giving pleasure, satisfaction *etc: a rewarding job.* □ **qui vaut la peine**

reword [riː'woːd] *verb* to say or write with different words: *to reword a sentence.* □ **exprimer en d'autres termes; recomposer**

rewrite [riː'rait] – *past tense* **rewrote** [ri'rout]: *past participle* **re'written** [ri'ritn] – *verb* to write again. □ **récrire**

rhapsody ['rapsədi] – *plural* **'rhapsodies** – *noun* an expression of strong feeling or excitement in *eg* music or speech. □ **rhapsodie**

rheumatism ['ruːmətizəm] *noun* a disease which causes stiffness and pain in one's joints. □ **rhumatisme**
rheu'matic [-'ma-] *adjective.* □ **rhumatisant, rhumatismal**

rhino ['rainou] – *plural* **'rhinos** – short for **rhinoceros.**

rhinoceros [rai'nosərəs] – *plurals* **rhi'noceroses, rhi'noceros** – *noun* a type of large thick-skinned animal with one or two horns on its nose. □ **rhinocéros**

rhombus ['rombəs] *noun* an equilateral parallelogram, other than a square. □ **losange**

rhododendron [roudə'dendrən] *noun* a type of flowering shrub with thick evergreen leaves and large flowers. □ **rhododendron**

rhubarb ['ruːbaːb] *noun* a large-leaved garden plant, the stalks of which can be cooked and eaten. □ **rhubarbe**

rhyme [raim] *noun* 1 a short poem: *a book of rhymes for*

children. □ **vers, poème**
2 a word which is like another in its final sound(s): '*Beef*' and '*leaf*' *are rhymes.* □ **rime**
3 verse or poetry using such words at the ends of the lines: *To amuse her colleagues she wrote her report in rhyme.* □ **en vers rimés**
■ *verb* (of words) to be rhymes: '*Beef*' *rhymes with* '*leaf*'; '*Beef*' *and* '*leaf*' *rhyme.* □ **rimer**

rhythm ['riðəm] *noun* 1 a regular, repeated pattern of sounds, stresses or beats in music, poetry *etc: Just listen to the rhythm of those drums; complicated rhythms.* □ **rythme**
2 a regular, repeated pattern of movements: *The rowers lost their rhythm.* □ **rythme**
3 an ability to sing, move *etc* with rhythm: *That girl has got rhythm.* □ **rythme**
'rhythmic, **'rhythmical** *adjective* of or with rhythm: *rhythmic movement; The dancing was very rhythmical.* □ **rythmé, rythmique**
'rhythmically *adverb.* □ **de façon rythmée**

rib [rib] *noun* 1 any one of the bones which curve around and forward from the backbone, enclosing the heart and lungs. □ **côte**
2 one of the curved pieces of wood which are joined to the keel to form the framework of a boat. □ **membrure**
3 a vertical raised strip in *eg* knitted material, or the pattern formed by a row of these. □ **côte**
4 any of a number of things similar in shape, use *etc* to a rib, *eg* one of the supports for the fabric of an airplane wing or of an umbrella. □ **nervure; baleine**
ribbed *adjective* having ribs: *a ribbed pattern.* □ **à côtes, nervures**
'ribbing *noun* a pattern or arrangement of ribs. □ **nervurage, côtes**

ribbon ['ribən] *noun* a long narrow strip of material used in decorating clothes, tying hair *etc: a blue ribbon; four metres of red ribbon.* □ **ruban**

rice [rais] *noun* a plant, grown in well-watered ground in tropical countries, whose seeds are used as food. □ **riz**

rich [ritʃ] *adjective* 1 wealthy; having a lot of money, possessions *etc: a rich man/country.* □ **riche**
2 (*with* **in**) having a lot (of something): *This part of the country is rich in coal.* □ **riche en**
3 valuable: *a rich reward; rich materials.* □ **riche, somptueux**
4 containing a lot of fat, eggs, spices *etc: a rich sauce.* □ **riche**
5 (of clothes, material *etc*) very beautiful and expensive. □ **luxueux**
'richly *adverb.* □ **richement**
'richness *noun.* □ **richesse**
'riches *noun plural* wealth. □ **richesse(s)**

rickety ['rikəti] *adjective* not well built; unsteady; likely to fall over or collapse: *a rickety table.* □ **délabré, branlant**

rickshaw ['rikʃoː] *noun* in Japan *etc*, a small two-wheeled carriage pulled by a man. □ **pousse-pousse**

ricochet ['rikəʃei] – *past tense, past participle* **'ricocheted** [-ʃeid] – *verb* to hit something and bounce away at an angle: *The bullet ricocheted off the wall.* □ **ricocher**

rid [rid] – *present participle* '**ridding**: *past tense, past participle* **rid** – *verb (with of)*; to free (someone *etc*) from: *We must try to rid the town of rats.* □ **débarrasser (de)**

be rid of, get rid of to have removed, to remove; to free oneself from: *I thought I'd never get rid of these weeds*; *I'm rid of my debts at last.* □ **se débarrasser de, être débarrassé de**

good riddance ['ridəns] I am happy to have got rid of it, him *etc*: *I've thrown out all those old books, and good riddance (to the lot of them)!* □ **bon débarras**
ridden *see* ride.

riddle[1] ['ridl] *noun* a puzzle *usually* in the form of a question, which describes an object, person *etc* in a mysterious or misleading way: *Can you guess the answer to this riddle?*; *The answer to the riddle 'What flies for ever, and never rests?' is 'The wind'.* □ **devinette**

riddle[2] ['ridl] *verb* to make (something) full of holes: *They riddled the car with bullets.* □ **cribler**

ride [raid] – *past tense* **rode** [roud]: *past participle* **ridden** ['ridn] – *verb* **1** to travel or be carried (in a car, train *etc* or on a bicycle, horse *etc*): *He rides to work every day on an old bicycle*; *The horsemen rode past.* □ **aller (à bicyclette, à cheval)**

2 to (be able to) ride on and control (a horse, bicycle *etc*): *Can you ride a bicycle?* □ **monter à**

3 to take part (in a horse-race *etc*): *He's riding in the first race.* □ **courir**

4 to go out regularly on horseback (*eg* as a hobby): *My daughter rides every Saturday morning.* □ **monter à cheval**

■ *noun* **1** a journey on horseback, on a bicycle *etc*: *She likes to go for a long ride on a Sunday afternoon.* □ **promenade à cheval, à bicyclette**

2 a *usually* short period of riding on or in something: *Can I have a ride on your bike?* □ **tour**
'**rider** *noun.* □ **cavalier, ière**

'**riding school** *noun* a place where people are taught to ride horses. □ **école d'équitation**

ridge [ridʒ] *noun* **1** a long narrow piece of ground *etc* raised above the level of the ground *etc* on either side of it. □ **crête**

2 a long narrow row of hills. □ **chaîne**

3 anything like a ridge in shape: *A ridge of high pressure is a long narrow area of high pressure as shown on a weather map.* □ **ligne**

4 the top edge of something where two sloping surfaces meet, *eg* on a roof. □ **arête, faîte**

ridiculous [rə'dikjuləs] *adjective* very silly; deserving to be laughed at: *That's a ridiculous suggestion*; *You look ridiculous in that hat!* □ **ridicule**
ri'diculously *adverb.* □ **ridiculement**
ri'diculousness *noun.* □ **ridicule**
ridicule ['ridikjuːl] *verb* to laugh at; to mock: *They ridiculed him because he was wearing one brown shoe and one black shoe.* □ **tourner en ridicule**

■ *noun* laughter at someone or something; mockery: *Despite the ridicule of his neighbours he continued to build a spaceship in his garden.* □ **raillerie**

rife [raif] *adjective (especially* of bad or dangerous things)

very widespread: *After the failure of the harvest, disease and starvation were rife.* □ **qui sévit**

rifle ['raifl] *noun* a gun with a long barrel, fired from the shoulder: *The soldiers are being taught to shoot with rifles.* □ **fusil, carabine**

■ *verb* **1** to search (through something): *The thief rifled through the drawers.* □ **dévaliser**

2 to steal: *The document had been rifled.* □ **rafler**
'**rifle range** *noun* a place for rifle practice. □ **champ/stand de tir**

rift [rift] *noun* **1** a split or crack. □ **fissure**

2 a disagreement between friends. □ **désaccord**

rig [rig] – *past tense, past participle* **rigged** – *verb* to fit (a ship) with ropes and sails. □ **gréer**

■ *noun* **1** an oil-rig. □ **derrick**

2 any special equipment, tools *etc* for some purpose. □ **équipement**

3 the arrangement of sails *etc* of a sailing-ship. □ **gréement**
'**rigging** *noun* the ropes *etc* which control a ship's masts and sails. □ **gréement**

rig up to build *usually* quickly with whatever material is available: *They rigged up a rough shelter with branches and mud.* □ **bricoler avec des moyens de fortune**

right [rait] *adjective* **1** on or related to the side of the body which in most people has the more skilful hand, or to the side of a person or thing which is toward the east when that person or thing is facing north (opposite to **left**): *When I'm writing, I hold my pen in my right hand.* □ **droit**

2 correct: *Put that book back in the right place*; *Is that the right answer to the question?* □ **bon**

3 morally correct; good: *It's not right to let thieves keep what they have stolen.* □ **bien**

4 suitable; appropriate: *He's not the right man for this job*; *When would be the right time to ask her?* □ **approprié**

■ *noun* **1** something a person is, or ought to be, allowed to have, do *etc*: *Everyone has the right to a fair trial*; *You must fight for your rights*; *You have no right to say that.* □ **droit**

2 that which is correct or good: *Who's in the right in this argument?* □ **vrai**

3 the right side, part or direction: *Turn to the right*; *Take the second road on the right.* □ **droite**

4 in politics, the people, group, party or parties holding the more traditional beliefs *etc*. □ **droite**

■ *adverb* **1** exactly: *She was standing right here.* □ **exactement**

2 immediately: *I'll go right after lunch*; *I'll come right down.* □ **tout de suite**

3 close: *She was standing right beside me.* □ **exactement**

4 completely; all the way: *The bullet went right through his arm.* □ **complètement**

5 to the right: *Turn right.* □ **à droite**

6 correctly: *Have I done that right?*; *I don't think this sum is going to turn out right.* □ **bien, juste**

■ *verb* **1** to bring back to the correct, *usually* upright, position: *The boat tipped over, but righted itself again.*

□ **(se) redresser**
2 to put an end to and make up for something wrong that has been done: *He's like a medieval knight, going about the country looking for wrongs to right.* □ **redresser**

■ *interjection* I understand; I'll do what you say *etc*: '*I want you to type some letters for me.*' '*Right, I'll do them now.*' □ **bien**

righteous ['raitʃəs] *adjective* **1** (of anger *etc*) justifiable: *righteous indignation.* □ **justifié**
2 living a good moral life: *a righteous woman.* □ **juste**
3 good; morally right: *a righteous action.* □ **vertueux**
'**righteously** *adverb.* □ **vertueusement**
'**righteousness** *noun.* □ **droiture**
'**rightful** *adjective* proper; correct; that ought to be or has a right to be something: *He is the rightful king of this country.* □ **légitime**
'**rightfully** *adverb*: *It rightfully belongs to me, although she has it at the moment.* □ **légitimement**
'**rightly** *adverb* **1** justly, justifiably; it is right, good or just that (something is the case): *He was punished for his stupidity and rightly; Rightly or wrongly she refused to speak to him.* □ **à raison, à juste titre**
2 correctly; accurately: *They rightly assumed that she would refuse to help.* □ **avec raison**
'**rightness** *noun* the state of being good or morally correct: *They believe in the rightness of their cause.* □ **justesse**
rights *noun plural* the legal right given in return for a sum of money to produce *eg* a film from a book: *She has sold the film rights of her new book to an American company.* □ **droits**
right angle an angle of ninety degrees, like any of the four angles in a square. □ **angle droit**
'**right-angled** *adjective* having a right angle: *a right-angled triangle.* □ **à angle droit**
'**right-hand** *adjective* **1** at the right; to the right of something else: *the top right-hand drawer of my desk.* □ **de droite**
2 towards the right: *a right-hand bend in the road.* □ **à/ vers la droite**
,**right-'handed** *adjective* (of people) using the right hand more easily than the left, *eg* for writing: *The majority of people are right-handed.* □ **droitier**
right wing the members of a political party who hold more traditional opinions: *She's on the right wing of the Labour Party.* □ **aile droite**
■ *adjective* (,**right-'wing**) (having opinions which are) of this sort. □ **de droite**
,**right-'winger** *noun.* □ **homme, femme de droite**
be right *verb* to be correct about something or to make a good decision: *If ou think 2 + 2 = 4, you are right.* □ **avoir raison**
by rights rightfully: *By rights, I ought to be in charge of this department.* □ **en toute justice**
get, keep on the right side of to make (someone) feel, or continue to feel, friendly or kind towards oneself: *If you want a raise, you'd better get on the right side of the boss.* □ **s'insinuer/rester dans les bonnes grâces de**
get right to understand, do, say *etc* (something) cor-

rectly: *Did I get the answer right?* □ **comprendre, dire qqch. correctement**
go right to happen as expected, wanted or intended; to be successful or without problems: *Nothing ever goes right for him.* □ **aller bien (pour)**
not in one's right mind, not (quite) right in the head (slightly) mad: *He can't be in his right mind – making incredible suggestions like that!* □ **ne pas avoir toute sa raison**
put right 1 to repair; to remove faults *etc* in (something): *There is something wrong with this kettle – can you put it right?* □ **arranger, réparer**
2 to put an end to or change (something that is wrong): *You've made a mistake in that sum – you'd better put it right.* □ **corriger**
3 to put (a watch, clock *etc*) to the correct time. □ **remettre à l'heure**
4 to correct (someone who has made a mistake): *I thought the meeting was at 2:30, but she put me right.* □ **détromper**
5 to make healthy again: *That medicine will soon put you right.* □ **rétablir**
put/set right to put back into the correct order, state *etc*: *The room was in a dreadful mess, and it took us the whole day to set it right.* □ **mettre en ordre**
right away immediately; at once. □ **tout de suite**
right-hand man a person's most trusted and useful assistant. □ **bras droit (de qqn)**
right now immediately. □ **immédiatement**
right of way 1 the right of the public to use a path that goes across private property. □ **droit de passage**
2 (,**right-of-'way** – *plural* '**rights-of-'way**) a road or path over private land, along which the public have a right to walk. □ **droit de passage**
3 the right of one car *etc* to move first *eg* when crossing an intersection, or going around a traffic circle: *It was your fault that our cars crashed – I had right of way.* □ **priorité**
serve right to be the punishment deserved by: *If you fall and hurt yourself, it'll serve you right for climbing up there when I told you not to.* □ **c'est bien fait (pour qqn)**

rigid ['ridʒid] *adjective* **1** completely stiff; not able to be bent (easily): *An iron bar is rigid.* □ **rigide**
2 very strict, and not likely to change: *rigid rules; rigid discipline; rigid views on education; a stern, rigid headmaster.* □ **inflexible, sévère**
'**rigidly** *adverb.* □ **inflexiblement**
'**rigidness, ri'gidity** *noun.* □ **rigidité**
rigour ['rigə] *noun* **1** strictness; harshness. □ **rigueur**
2 (*also* '**rigours** *noun plural*) (of weather *etc*) the state of being very bad or unpleasant, or the hardship caused by this: *the rigour(s) of life in the Arctic Circle.* □ **rigueur(s)**
'**rigorous** *adjective* **1** strict: *a rigorous training.* □ **rigoureux**
2 harsh; unpleasant: *a rigorous climate.* □ **rigoureux**
'**rigorously** *adverb.* □ **rigoureusement**
'**rigorousness** *noun.* □ **rigueur**
rim [rim] *noun* an edge or border: *the rim of a wheel; the*

504

rim of a cup. □ **jante; bord**

'**rimless** *adjective* without a rim: *rimless spectacles.* □ **sans monture**

rimmed *adjective*: *horn-rimmed spectacles*; *Her eyes were red-rimmed from crying.* □ **à monture (de/en); bordé (de)**

rind [raind] *noun* a thick, hard outer layer or covering, *especially* the outer surface of cheese or bacon, or the peel of fruit: *bacon-rind*; *lemon-rind.* □ **couenne, peau, écorce**

ring[1] [riŋ] *noun* **1** a small circle *eg* of gold or silver, sometimes having a jewel set in it, worn on the finger: *a wedding ring*; *She wears a diamond ring.* □ **anneau, bague**

2 a circle of metal, wood *etc* for any of various purposes: *a key ring*; *The trap door had a ring attached for lifting it.* □ **anneau**

3 anything which is like a circle in shape: *The children formed a ring around their teacher*; *The hot teapot left a ring on the polished table.* □ **cercle, rond**

4 an enclosed space for boxing matches, circus performances *etc*: *the circus-ring*; *The crowd cheered as the boxer entered the ring.* □ **ring**

5 a small group of people formed for business or criminal purposes: *a drugs ring.* □ **gang**

■ *verb – past tense, past participle* **ringed** *– verb* **1** to form a ring around. □ **entourer**

2 to put, draw *etc* a ring around (something): *He has ringed all your errors.* □ **entourer**

3 to put a ring on the leg of (a bird) as a means of identifying it. □ **baguer**

'**ringlet** [-lit] *noun* a long curl of hair. □ **frisette**

'**ring finger** *noun* the finger on which the wedding ring is worn (*usually* the third finger of the left hand). □ **annulaire**

'**ringleader** *noun* the leader of a group of people who are doing something wrong: *The teacher punished the ring-leader.* □ **meneur, euse**

'**ringmaster** *noun* a person who is in charge of performances in a circus ring. □ **maître de cirque**

run rings around to be very much better at doing something than; to beat easily. □ **battre à plate couture**

ring[2] [riŋ] *– past tense* **rang** [raŋ]: *past participle* **rung** [rʌŋ] *– verb* **1** to (cause to) sound: *The doorbell rang*; *She rang the doorbell*; *The telephone rang.* □ **sonner**

2 (*often with* **up**) to telephone (someone): *I'll ring you (up) tonight.* □ **donner un coup de téléphone à**

3 (*often with* **for**) to ring a bell (*eg* in a hotel) to tell someone to come, to bring something *etc*: *She rang for the maid.* □ **sonner**

4 (of certain objects) to make a high sound like a bell: *The glass rang as she hit it with a metal spoon.* □ **tinter**

5 to be filled with sound: *The hall rang with the sound of laughter.* □ **résonner, retentir**

6 (*often with* **out**) to make a loud, clear sound: *Her voice rang through the house*; *A shot rang out.* □ **retentir**

■ *noun* **1** the act or sound of ringing: *the ring of a telephone.* □ **sonnerie**

2 a telephone call: *I'll give you a ring.* □ **coup de téléphone**

3 a suggestion, impression or feeling: *Her story has a ring of truth about it.* □ **air, accent**

ring a bell to have been seen, heard *etc* before, but not remembered in detail: *Her name rings a bell, but I don't remember where I've heard it before.* □ **rappeler qqch. à qqn**

ring back to telephone (someone who has telephoned): *If she is busy at the moment, she can ring me back*; *He'll ring back tomorrow.* □ **rappeler qqn**

ring true to sound true: *His story does not ring true.* □ **sonner juste**

rink [riŋk] *noun* **1** (*usually* '**ice-rink**') (a building containing) an area of ice, for ice-skating, ice hockey *etc*. □ **patinoire**

2 (a building containing) a smooth floor for roller-skating. □ **salle de patinage à roulettes**

rinse [rins] *verb* **1** (*often with* **out**) to wash (clothes *etc*) in clean water to remove soap *etc*: *After washing the towels, rinse them (out).* □ **rincer**

2 to clean (a cup, one's mouth *etc*) by filling with clean water *etc* and then emptying the water out: *The dentist asked me to rinse my mouth out.* □ **(se) rincer**

■ *noun* **1** the act of rinsing: *Give the cup a rinse.* □ **rinçage**

2 a liquid used for changing the colour of hair: *a blue rinse.* □ **rinçage**

riot ['raiət] *noun* a noisy disturbance created by a *usually* large group of people: *The protest march developed into a riot.* □ **émeute**

■ *verb* to form or take part in a riot: *The protesters were rioting in the street.* □ **manifester avec violence**

'**rioter** *noun*. □ **manifestant, ante**

'**riotous** *adjective* **1** starting, or likely to start, a riot: *a riotous crowd.* □ **tumultueux**

2 very active, noisy and cheerful: *a riotous party.* □ **tapageur**

'**riotously** *adverb*. □ **tumultueusement**

'**riotousness** *noun*. □ **turbulence**

run riot to behave wildly; to go out of control. □ **se déchaîner**

rip [rip] *– past tense, past participle* **ripped** *– verb* **1** to make or get a hole or tear in by pulling, tearing *etc*: *He ripped his shirt on a branch*; *Her shirt ripped.* □ **(se) déchirer**

2 to pull (off, up *etc*) by breaking or tearing: *The roof of the car was ripped off in the crash*; *to rip up floorboards*; *She ripped open the envelope.* □ **arracher, déchirer**

■ *noun* a tear or hole: *a rip in my shirt.* □ **déchirure**

ripe [raip] *adjective* (*negative* **unripe**) (of fruit, grain *etc*) ready to be gathered or eaten: *ripe apples/corn.* □ **mûr**

'**ripeness** *noun*. □ **maturité**

'**ripen** *verb* to make or become ripe or riper: *The sun ripened the corn*; *The corn ripened in the sun.* □ **(faire) mûrir**

ripe (old) age a very old age: *She lived to the ripe (old) age of ninety-five.* □ **âge avancé (de)**

ripple ['ripl] *noun* a little wave or movement on the surface of water *etc*: *He threw the stone into the pond, and watched the ripples spread across the water.* □ **ondulation**

■ *verb* to (cause to) have ripples: *The grass rippled in the wind*; *The wind rippled the grass.* □ **(faire) onduler**

rise [raiz] – *past tense* **rose** [rouz]: *past participle* **risen** ['rizn'] – *verb* **1** to become greater, larger, higher *etc* to increase: *Food prices are still rising*; *His temperature rose*; *If the river rises much more, there will be a flood*; *Her voice rose to a scream*; *Bread rises when it is baked*; *His spirits rose at the good news.* □ **augmenter; monter; lever**

2 to move upwards: *Smoke was rising from the chimney*; *The birds rose into the air*; *The curtain rose to reveal an empty stage.* □ **s'élever; se lever**

3 to get up from bed: *She rises every morning at six o'clock.* □ **se lever**

4 to stand up: *The children all rose when the headmaster came in.* □ **se lever**

5 (of the sun *etc*) to appear above the horizon: *The sun rises in the east and sets in the west.* □ **se lever**

6 to slope upwards: *Hills rose in the distance*; *The ground rises at this point.* □ **s'élever, monter**

7 to rebel: *The people rose (up) in revolt against the dictator.* □ **se soulever contre**

8 to move to a higher rank, a more important position *etc*: *He rose to the rank of colonel.* □ **s'élever**

9 (of a river) to begin or appear: *The Rhône rises in the Alps.* □ **prendre sa source**

10 (of wind) to begin; to become stronger: *Don't go out in the boat – the wind has risen.* □ **se lever**

11 to be built: *Office blocks are rising all over the town.* □ **s'élever**

12 to come back to life: *Jesus has risen.* □ **ressusciter**

■ *noun* **1** (the) act of rising: *He had a rapid rise to fame*; *a rise in prices.* □ **ascension, montée**

2 a slope or hill: *The house is just beyond the next rise.* □ **côte**

3 the beginning and early development of something: *the rise of the Roman Empire.* □ **essor**

'**rising** *noun* **1** the act or rising: *the rising of the sun.* □ **lever**

2 a rebellion: *The king executed those who took part in the rising.* □ **soulèvement**

■ *adjective*: *the rising sun*; *rising prices*; *the rising generation*; *a rising young politician.* □ **levant; en hausse; montant**

early, late riser a person who gets out of bed early or late in the day. □ **lève-tôt; lève-tard**

give rise to to cause: *This plan has given rise to various problems.* □ **donner lieu/naissance à**

rise to the occasion to be able to do what is required in an emergency *etc*: *She had never had to make a speech before, but she rose to the occasion magnificently.* □ **se montrer à la hauteur (des circonstances)**

risk [risk] *noun* (a person, thing *etc* which causes or could cause) danger or possible loss or injury: *She thinks we shouldn't go ahead with the plan because of the risks involved/because of the risk of failure.* □ **risque**

■ *verb* **1** to expose to danger; to lay open to the possibility of loss: *He would risk his life for his friend*; *He risked all his money betting on that horse.* □ **risquer**

2 to take the chance of (something bad happening): *He*

was willing to risk death to save his friend; *I'd better leave early as I don't want to risk being late for the play.* □ **risquer (de)**

'**risky** *adverb* possibly causing or bringing loss, injury *etc*: *Motor-racing is a risky business.* □ **risqué**

at (a person's) own risk with the person agreeing to accept any loss, damage *etc* involved: *Cars may be parked here at their owner's risk.* □ **aux risques et périls de**

at risk in danger; likely to suffer loss, injury *etc*: *Heart disease can be avoided if people at risk take medical advice.* □ **exposé**

at the risk of with the possibility of (loss, injury, trouble *etc*): *He saved the little girl at the risk of his own life*; *At the risk of offending you, I must tell you that I disapprove of your behaviour.* □ **au risque de**

run/take the risk (of) to do something which involves a risk: *I took the risk of buying that dress for you – I hope it fits*; *He didn't want to run the risk of losing his money.* □ **courir/prendre le risque (de)**

take risks/take a risk to do something which might cause loss, injury *etc*: *One cannot be successful in business unless one is willing to take risks.* □ **prendre un/des risque(s)**

risotto [rə'zotou] – *plural* **ri'sottos** – *noun* (a dish of) rice cooked with onions, cheese *etc*. □ **risotto**

rite [rait] *noun* a solemn ceremony, *especially* a religious one: *marriage rites.* □ **rite**

ritual ['ritʃuəl] *noun* (a particular set of) traditional or fixed actions *etc* used in a religious *etc* ceremony: *Christian rituals*; *the ritual of the Roman Catholic church.* □ **rite, rituel**

■ *adjective* forming (part of) a ritual or ceremony: *a ritual dance/sacrifice.* □ **rituel**

rival ['raivəl] *noun* a person *etc* who tries to compete with another; a person who wants the same thing as someone else: *For students of English, this dictionary is without a rival*; *The two brothers are rivals for the girl next door – they both want to marry her*; (*also adjective*) *rival companies*; *rival teams.* □ **rival, ale**

■ *verb* – *past tense, past participle* '**rivalled**, '**rivaled** – to (try to) be as good as someone or something else: *He rivals his brother as a chess-player*; *Nothing rivals football for excitement and entertainment.* □ **rivaliser (avec qqn)**

'**rivalry** – *plural* '**rivalries** – *noun* the state of or an instance of being rivals: *the rivalry/rivalries between business companies.* □ **rivalité**

river ['rivə] *noun* a large stream of water flowing across country: *The Thames is a river*; *the river Thames*; *the Hudson River*; (*also adjective*) *a river animal.* □ **(de) rivière; fleuve; (adj.) fluvial**

'**riverbed** *noun* the ground over which a river runs. □ **lit de rivière/fleuve**

'**riverside** *noun* the ground along or near the side of a river: *He has a bungalow on the riverside.* □ **(au) bord de l'eau**

rivet ['rivit] *noun* a sort of metal nail; a bolt for fastening plates of metal together *eg* when building the sides of a ship. □ **rivet**

■ *verb – past tense, past participle* '**riveted** – **1** to fasten with rivets: *They riveted the sheets of metal together.* □ **riveter**
2 to fix firmly: *He stood riveted to the spot with fear*; *His eyes were riveted on the television.* □ **clouer, river (sur)**
'**riveter** *noun.* □ **riveteuse**

road [roud] *noun* **1** a strip of ground *usually* with a hard level surface for people, vehicles *etc* to travel on: *This road takes you past the school*; *(also adjective)* road safety. □ **route; (adj.) routier**
2 (*often abbreviated to* **Rd** *when written*) used in the names of roads or streets: *Her address is 24 School Road.* □ **Rte**
3 a route; the correct road(s) to follow in order to arrive somewhere: *We'd better look at the map because I'm not sure of the road.* □ **route, chemin**
4 a way that leads to something: *the road to peace*; *He's on the road to ruin.* □ **chemin (de)**
'**roadblock** *noun* a barrier put across a road (*eg* by the police) in order to stop or slow down traffic: *to set up a roadblock.* □ **barrage routier**
road map a map showing the roads of (part of) a country. □ **carte routière**
'**roadside** *noun* the ground beside a road: *flowers growing by the roadside*; *(also adjective)* a roadside café. □ **(au) bord de la route**
'**roadway** *noun* the part of a road on which cars *etc* travel: *Don't walk on the roadway.* □ **chaussée**
'**roadworks** *noun plural* the building or repairing of a road: *The traffic was held up by the roadworks.* □ **travaux d'entretien des routes**
'**roadworthy** *adjective* good enough or safe to be used on the road: *Is this car roadworthy?* □ **en état de marche**
'**roadworthiness** *noun.* □ **bon état de marche**
by road in a truck, car *etc*: *We'll send the furniture by road rather than by rail*; *We came by road.* □ **par la route**

roam [roum] *verb* to walk about without any fixed plan or purpose; to wander: *He roamed from town to town*; *She roamed (over) the hills.* □ **errer**
'**roamer** *noun.* □ **vagabond, onde**

roar [roː] *verb* **1** to give a loud deep cry; to say loudly; to shout: *The lions roared*; *The sergeant roared (out) his commands.* □ **rugir, hurler**
2 to laugh loudly: *The audience roared (with laughter) at the man's jokes.* □ **rire à gorge déployée**
3 to make a loud deep sound: *The cannons/thunder roared.* □ **gronder**
4 to make a loud deep sound while moving: *He roared past on his motorbike.* □ **gronder, vrombir**
■ *noun* **1** a loud deep cry: *a roar of pain/laughter*; *the lion's roars.* □ **rugissement; hurlement**
2 a loud, deep sound: *the roar of traffic.* □ **grondement**
do a roaring trade to have a very successful business; to sell a lot of something: *She's doing a roaring trade in/selling home-made cakes.* □ **faire des affaires d'or**

roast [roust] *verb* **1** to cook or be cooked in an oven, or over or in front of a fire *etc*: *to roast a chicken over the fire*; *The beef was roasting in the oven.* □ **(faire) rôtir/griller**
2 to heat (coffee-beans) before grinding. □ **torréfier**
■ *adjective* roasted: *roast beef/chestnuts.* □ **rôti, grillé**
■ *noun* meat that has been roasted or is for roasting: *She bought a roast*; *a delicious roast.* □ **rôti**
'**roasting** *adjective* very hot: *It's roasting outside.* □ **torride**

rob [rob] – *past tense, past participle* **robbed** – *verb* **1** to steal from (a person, place *etc*): *He robbed a bank/an old lady*; *I've been robbed!* □ **voler, dévaliser**
2 (*with of*) to take (something) away from; to deprive of: *An accident robbed him of his sight at the age of 21.* □ **priver de, ôter à**
'**robber** *noun*: *The bank robbers got away with nearly $50,000.* □ **voleur, euse**
'**robbery** – *plural* '**robberies** – *noun* the act of robbing: *Robbery is a serious crime*; *He was charged with four robberies.* □ **vol**

---

to rob a bank or a person; to **steal** a watch, pencil, money *etc*.

---

robe [roub] *noun* **1** (*often in plural*) a long, loose piece of clothing: *Many Arabs still wear robes*; *a baby's christening-robe.* □ **robe**
2 (*usually in plural*) a long, loose piece of clothing worn as a sign of a person's rank *eg* on official occasions: *a judge's robes.* □ **toge, vêtement de cérémonie**
3 a loose garment worn casually; a dressing gown: *She wore a robe over her nightdress*; *a bathrobe.* □ **peignoir**
robed *adjective* wearing robes: *judges robed in black.* □ **en robe/toge**

robin ['robin] *noun* **1** a small European bird with a red breast. □ **rouge-gorge**
2 an American thrush with an orange-red breast. □ **merle américain**

robot ['roubot] *noun* a machine which behaves, works, and often looks like a human being. □ **robot**

robust [rə'bʌst] *adjective* strong; healthy: *a robust child.* □ **robuste**
ro'bustly *adverb.* □ **vigoureusement**
ro'bustness *noun.* □ **robustesse**

rock¹ [rok] *noun* **1** (a large lump or mass of) the solid parts of the surface of the Earth: *The ship struck a rock and sank*; *the rocks on the seashore*; *He built his house on solid rock.* □ **roc(her)**
2 a large stone: *The climber was killed by a falling rock.* □ **roche**
3 a type of hard candy: *a stick of Edinburgh rock.* □ **sucre d'orge**
'**rockery** – *plural* '**rockeries** – *noun* a heap of rocks in a garden with earth between them in which small plants are grown. □ **rocaille**
'**rocky** *adjective*: *a rocky coastline.* □ **rocheux**
'**rockiness** *noun.* □ **nature rocheuse**
,**rock-'bottom** *noun, adjective* (at) the lowest level possible: *Prices have reached rock-bottom*; *rock-bottom prices.* □ **(au) niveau le plus bas**
'**rock garden** *noun* a rockery. □ **(jardin de) rocaille**
'**rock plant** *noun* any plant which grows among rocks

eg on mountains, often also grown in rockeries. □ **plante de rochers/de rocaille**

on the rocks in a state of ruin or of great financial difficulty: *Their marriage is on the rocks; The firm is on the rocks.* □ **en déconfiture**

rock² [rok] *verb* **1** to (cause to) swing gently backwards and forwards or from side to side: *The mother rocked the cradle; This cradle rocks.* □ **(se) balancer**

2 to swing (a baby) gently in one's arms to comfort it or make it sleep. □ **bercer**

3 to shake or move violently: *The earthquake rocked the building.* □ **ébranler**

'**rocker** *noun* **1** one of *usually* two curved supports on which a cradle, rocking chair *etc* rocks. □ **bascule**

2 a rocking chair. □ **berceuse**

'**rocky** *adjective* which rocks or shakes; unsteady; unsafe. □ **chancelant**

'**rockiness** *noun*. □ **caractère branlant**.

'**rocking chair** *noun* a chair which rocks backwards and forwards on rockers. □ **berceuse**

'**rocking horse** *noun* a toy horse which rocks backwards and forwards on rockers. □ **cheval à bascule**

off one's rocker mad; crazy. □ **cinglé**

rock³ [rok] *noun* (*also* **rock music**) music or songs with a strong, heavy beat and *usually* a simple melody: *She likes rock*; (*also adjective*) *a rock band.* □ **(de) rock**

,**rock'n''roll** *noun* (*also* ,**rock-and-'roll**) a simpler, earlier form of rock music. □ **rock and roll**

rocket ['rokit] *noun* **1** a tube containing materials which, when set on fire, give off a jet of gas which drives the tube forward, *usually* up into the air, used *eg* as a firework, for signalling, or for launching a spacecraft. □ **fusée, roquette**

2 a spacecraft launched in this way: *The Americans have sent a rocket to Mars.* □ **fusée**

■ *verb – past tense, past participle* '**rocketed** – to rise or increase very quickly: *Bread prices have rocketed.* □ **monter en flèche**

rocky *see* **rock¹**, **rock²**.

rod [rod] *noun* a long thin stick or piece of wood, metal *etc*: *an iron rod; a fishing-rod; a measuring-rod.* □ **tige, baguette, canne, règle**

rode *see* **ride**.

rodent ['roudənt] *noun* any of a number of types of animal with large front teeth for gnawing, *eg* squirrels, beavers, rats *etc*. □ **rongeur**

rodeo ['roudiou] – *plural* '**rodeos** – *noun especially* in the United States, a show or contest of riding, lassoing *etc*. □ **rodéo**

roe¹ [rou] *noun* the eggs of fish: *cod roe.* □ **œufs (de poissons)**

roe² [rou]: '**roe deer** – *plurals* '**roe deer**, '**roe deers** – *noun* a small deer found in Europe and Asia. □ **chevreuil**

rogue [roug] *noun* **1** a dishonest person: *I wouldn't buy a car from a rogue like him.* □ **gredin**

2 a mischievous person, *especially* a child: *She's a little rogue sometimes.* □ **polisson, onne**

role [roul] *noun* **1** a part played by an actor or actress in a play *etc*: *He is playing the rôle of King Lear.* □ **rôle**

2 the actions or functions of a person in some activity:

He played the rôle of peacemaker in the dispute. □ **rôle**

roll¹ [roul] *noun* **1** anything flat (*eg* a piece of paper, a carpet) rolled into the shape of a tube, wound around a tube *etc*: *a roll of kitchen foil; a toilet-roll.* □ **rouleau**

2 a small piece of baked bread dough, used *eg* for sandwiches: *a cheese roll.* □ **petit pain**

3 an act of rolling: *Our dog loves a roll on the grass.* □ **roulade**

4 a ship's action of rocking from side to side: *She said that the roll of the ship made her feel ill.* □ **roulis**

5 a long low sound: *the roll of thunder.* □ **roulement**

6 a thick mass of flesh: *I'd like to get rid of these rolls of fat around my waist.* □ **bourrelet**

7 a series of quick beats (on a drum). □ **roulement**

■ *verb* **1** to move by turning over like a wheel or ball: *The coin/pencil rolled under the table; He rolled the ball towards the puppy; The ball rolled away.* □ **rouler**

2 to move on wheels, rollers *etc*: *The children rolled the cart up the hill, then let it roll back down again.* □ **(faire) rouler**

3 to form (a piece of paper, a carpet) into the shape of a tube by winding: *to roll the carpet back.* □ **(en)rouler**

4 (of a person or animal in a lying position) to turn over: *The doctor rolled the patient (over) on to his side; The dog rolled on to its back.* □ **rouler**

5 to shape (clay *etc*) into a ball or cylinder by turning it about between the hands: *He rolled the clay into a ball.* □ **rouler**

6 to cover with something by rolling: *When the little girl's dress caught fire, they rolled her in a blanket.* □ **enrouler**

7 to make (something) flat or flatter by rolling something heavy over it: *to roll a lawn; to roll pastry (out).* □ **rouler; étendre (au rouleau)**

8 (of a ship) to rock from side to side while travelling forwards: *The storm made the ship roll.* □ **rouler**

9 to make a series of low sounds: *The thunder rolled; The drums rolled.* □ **gronder, rouler**

10 to move (one's eyes) around in a circle to express fear, surprise *etc*. □ **rouler**

11 to travel in a car *etc*: *We were rolling along merrily when a tire burst.* □ **rouler**

12 (of waves, rivers *etc*) to move gently and steadily: *The waves rolled in to the shore.* □ **déferler**

13 (of time) to pass: *Months rolled by.* □ **s'écouler**

'**roller** *noun* **1** any of a number of tube-shaped objects, or machines fitted with one or more such objects, for flattening, crushing, printing *etc*: *a garden roller; a roadroller.* □ **rouleau**

2 a small tube-shaped object on which hair is wound to curl it. □ **rouleau**

3 a small solid wheel or cylinder on which something can be rolled along. □ **rouleau**

4 a long large wave on the sea. □ **lame de houle**

'**rolling** *adjective* (of a landscape) having low hills and shallow valleys, without steep slopes. □ **onduleux**

'**roller skate** *noun* a skate with wheels instead of a blade: *a pair of roller skates.* □ **patin à roulettes**

■ *verb* to move on roller skates: *You shouldn't roller skate on the pavement.* □ **faire du patin à roulettes**

'**rolling pin** *noun* a *usually* wooden roller for flattening out dough. □ **rouleau (à pâtisserie)**

roll in *verb* to come in or be got in large numbers or amounts: *I'd like to own a chain store and watch the money rolling in.* □ **affluer**

roll up 1 to form into a roll: *to roll up the carpet*; *She rolled up her sleeves.* □ **rouler; retrousser**

2 to arrive: *John rolled up ten minutes late.* □ **arriver**

3 (*especially*) shouted to a crowd at a fair *etc*) to come near: *Roll up! Roll up! Come and see the bearded lady!* □ **approchez!**

roll[2] [roul] *noun* a list of names, *eg* of pupils in a school *etc*: *There are nine hundred pupils on the roll.* □ **liste**

'**roll call** *noun* an act of calling names from a list, to find out if anyone is missing *eg* in a prison or school class. □ **appel**

Roman ['roumən] *adjective* **1** connected with Rome, *especially* ancient Rome: *Roman coins.* □ **romain**

2 (*no capital*) (of printing) in ordinary upright letters like these. □ **romain**

■ *noun* a person belonging to Rome, *especially* to ancient Rome. □ **romain, aine**

Roman alphabet the alphabet in which Western European languages such as English are written. □ **alphabet romain**

Roman Catholic (*also* **Catholic**) (a member) of the Christian church which recognizes the Pope as its head. □ **catholique**

Roman Catholicism (*also* **Catholicism**) the beliefs, government *etc* of the Roman Catholic Church. □ **l'Eglise catholique (romaine)**

Roman numerals I,II,III *etc*, as opposed to the Arabic numerals 1,2,3 *etc*. □ **chiffre romain**

romance [rə'mans] *noun* **1** the relationship, actions *etc* of people who are in love: *It was a beautiful romance, but it didn't last.* □ **amour, idylle**

2 a story about such a relationship *etc, especially* one in which the people, events *etc* are more exciting *etc* than in normal life: *She writes romances.* □ **roman d'amour (à l'eau de rose)**

3 this kind of excitement: *She felt her life was lacking in romance.* □ **romanesque**

ro'mantic [-tik] *adjective* **1** (*negative* **unromantic**) (of a story) about people who are in love: *a romantic novel.* □ **romantique**

2 causing or feeling love, *especially* the beautiful love described in a romance: *Her husband is very romantic – he brings her flowers every day*; *romantic music.* □ **romantique**

3 too concerned with love and excitement: *His head is full of romantic notions.* □ **romantique**

ro'mantically *adverb.* □ **de façon romantique**

romp [romp] *verb* **1** to play in a lively way, *especially* by running about, jumping *etc*: *The children and their dog were romping about on the grass.* □ **jouer bruyamment**

2 to progress quickly and easily: *Some people find these problems difficult but he just romps through them.* □ **accomplir sans effort**

■ *noun* the act of romping: *The children had a romp in the grass.* □ **jeux bruyants**

roof [ruːf] *noun* the top covering of a building *etc*: *a flat roof*; *a tiled roof*; *the roof of a car.* □ **toit**

■ *verb* to cover with a roof: *They'll finish roofing the house next week.* □ **couvrir**

go through the roof/hit the roof to become very angry. □ **piquer une crise**

roof of the mouth the upper part of the mouth. □ **palais**

rook [ruk] *noun* **1** a kind of crow. □ **corneille**

2 (*usually* '**castle**) a chess-piece. □ **tour**

room [ruːm (*in compounds* rum, ruːm)] *noun* **1** one part of a house or building, *usually* used for a particular purpose: *This house has six rooms*; *a bedroom*; *a dining-room.* □ **pièce; chambre; salle (à manger)**

2 the space or area in which a person, thing *etc* is or could be put *etc*: *The bed takes up a lot of room*; *There's no room for you in our car*; *We'll move the bookcase to make room for the television.* □ **place**

3 a need or possibility (for something): *There is room for improvement in his work.* □ **place**

-roomed: *a four-roomed house.* □ **de (...) pièces**

'**roomful** *noun*: *She didn't feel like facing a roomful of people.* □ **pleine salle (de)**

rooms *noun plural* a set of rented rooms for living in. □ **appartement**

'**roomy** *adjective* having plenty of room: *roomy cupboards.* □ **spacieux**

'**roommate** *noun* a person who shares a room with another person *eg* in a hostel for students *etc*. □ **camarade de chambre**

roost [ruːst] *noun* a branch *etc* on which a bird rests at night. □ **perchoir**

■ *verb* (of birds) to sit or sleep on a roost. □ **se percher**

'**rooster** *noun* a farmyard cock. □ **coq**

rule the roost to be the person in a group, family *etc* whose orders, wishes *etc* are obeyed. □ **faire la loi**

root[1] [ruːt] *noun* **1** the part of a plant that grows under the ground and draws food and water from the soil: *Trees often have deep roots*; *Carrots and turnips are edible roots.* □ **racine**

2 the base of something growing in the body: *the roots of one's hair/teeth.* □ **racine**

3 cause; origin: *Love of money is the root of all evil*; *We must get at the root of the trouble.* □ **origine, racine**

4 (*in plural*) family origins: *Our roots are in Scotland.* □ **racines, origines**

■ *verb* to (make something) grow roots: *These plants aren't rooting very well*; *She rooted the plants in compost.* □ **(s')enraciner**

root beer a kind of non-alcoholic drink made from the roots of certain plants. □ **racinette**

root crop plants with roots that are grown for food: *The farm has three fields of root crops.* □ **racines alimentaires**

root out 1 to pull up or tear out by the roots: *The gardener began to root out the weeds.* □ **arracher, déraciner**

2 to get rid of completely: *We must do our best to root out poverty.* □ **extirper**

take root to grow firmly; to become established: *The plants soon took root.* □ **prendre racine**

root² [ruːt] *verb* **1** to poke about in the ground: *The pigs were rooting about for food.* □ **fouiller (avec le museau)** **2** to search by turning things over *etc*: *She rooted about in the cupboard.* □ **fouiller**

rope [roup] *noun* (a) thick cord, made by twisting together lengths of hemp, nylon *etc*: *She tied it with a (piece of) rope; a skipping rope.* □ **corde**
■ *verb* **1** to tie or fasten with a rope: *She roped the suitcase to the roof of the car.* □ **attacher avec une corde** **2** to catch with a rope; to lasso: *to rope a calf.* □ **prendre au lasso**
,**rope 'ladder** *noun* a ladder made of rope. □ **échelle de corde**
rope in to include; to persuade to join in: *We roped her in to help.* □ **enrôler qqn**
rope off to put a rope around or across (a place) in order to prevent people going in: *The end of the room was roped off for the most important guests.* □ **réserver au moyen d'une corde**

rosary ['rouzəri] – *plural* '**rosaries** – *noun* (a string of beads representing) a group of prayers, used by Roman Catholics. □ **chapelet**

rose¹ [rouz] *noun* **1** a kind of brightly-coloured, *usually* sweet-scented flower, *usually* with sharp thorns. □ **rose** **2** (*also adjective*) (of) a pink colour: *Her dress was pale rose.* □ **rose**
rosebush *noun* a thorny plant that produces fragrant flowers called roses: *Rosebushes need to be pruned after the roses die.* □ **rosier**
rosette [rə'zet] *noun* a badge or decoration in the shape of a rose, made of coloured ribbon *etc*. □ **rosette, chou**
'**rosy** *adjective* **1** rose-coloured; pink: *rosy cheeks.* □ **rose, rosé**
2 bright; hopeful: *Her future looks rosy.* □ **brillant**
'**rosily** *adverb*. □ **d'un ton rosé**
'**rosiness** *noun*. □ **roseur**
'**rosewood** *noun, adjective* (of) a dark wood used for making furniture: *a rosewood cabinet.* □ **bois de rose**
look at/see through rose-coloured spectacles/glasses to take an over-optimistic view of. □ **voir (tout/la vie) en rose**

rose² *see* **rise.**

rosette *see* **rose¹.**

rosin ['rozin] *noun* the hardened resin of some trees, used on the bows of stringed musical instruments. □ **colophane**

roster ['rostə] *noun* a list showing the work, duties *etc* that people are to do: *a duty roster.* □ **liste, tableau**

rostrum ['rostrəm] *noun* a platform on which a public speaker stands. □ **tribune**

rosy *see* **rose¹.**

rot [rot] – *past tense, past participle* '**rotted** – *verb* to make or become bad or decayed: *The fruit is rotting on the ground; Water rots wood.* □ **(faire) pourrir**
■ *noun* **1** decay: *The floorboards are affected by rot.* □ **pourriture**
2 nonsense: *Don't talk rot!* □ **bêtises**
'**rotten** *adjective* **1** (of meat, fruit *etc*) having gone bad; decayed: *rotten vegetables.* □ **pourri, gâté**
2 bad; mean: *What rotten luck!; It was a rotten thing to*

do. □ **mauvais, sale**
'**rottenness** *noun*. □ **pourriture**
'**rotter** *noun* a mean, bad person: *an absolute rotter.* □ **bon à rien**

rotary ['routəri] *adjective* turning like a wheel: *a rotary movement.* □ **rotatif**
rotate [rə'teit, 'routeit] *verb* to turn like a wheel: *She rotated the handle; The earth rotates.* □ **(faire) tourner**
ro'**tation** *noun*. □ **rotation**
rotor ['routə] *noun* the rotating part of an engine, especially the blades of a helicopter. □ **rotor**

rotten, rotter *see* **rot.**

rouble ['ruːbl] *noun* the standard unit of Russian currency. □ **rouble**

rough [rʌf] *adjective* **1** not smooth: *Her skin felt rough.* □ **rugueux, rêche**
2 uneven: *a rough path.* □ **accidenté**
3 harsh; unpleasant: *a rough voice; She's had a rough time since her husband died.* □ **brusque; rude**
4 noisy and violent: *rough behaviour.* □ **violent, brutal**
5 stormy: *The sea was rough; rough weather.* □ **houleux, mauvais**
6 not complete or exact; approximate: *a rough drawing; a rough idea/estimate.* □ **ébauché, approximatif**
■ *noun* **1** a violent bully: *a gang of roughs.* □ **voyou**
2 uneven or uncultivated ground on a golf course: *I lost my ball in the rough.* □ **rough**
'**roughly** *adverb*. □ **brutalement**
'**roughness** *noun*. □ **rudesse**
'**roughage** [-fidʒ] *noun* substances in food, *eg* bran or fibre, which help digestion. □ **aliments de lest**
'**roughen** *verb* to make or become rough: *The sea roughened as the wind rose.* □ **devenir rude/houleux**
rough diamond a person of fine character but rough manners. □ **personne aimable sous des dehors frustes**
,**rough-and-'ready** *adjective* **1** not carefully made or finished, but good enough: *a rough-and-ready meal.* □ **de fortune**
2 (of people) friendly enough but without politeness *etc*. □ **sans façon**
,**rough-and-'tumble** *noun* friendly fighting between children *etc*. □ **bagarre**
rough out to draw or explain roughly: *I roughed out a diagram; She roughed out her plan.* □ **ébaucher**

roulette [ru'let] *noun* a game of chance, played with a ball on a revolving wheel. □ **roulette**

round [raund] *adjective* **1** shaped like a circle or globe: *a round hole; a round stone; This plate isn't quite round.* □ **rond**
2 rather fat; plump: *a round face.* □ **rond**
■ *noun* **1** a complete circuit: *a round of drinks* (= one for everyone present); *a round of golf.* □ **tournée; partie**
2 a regular journey one takes to do one's work: *a postman's round.* □ **tournée**
3 a burst of cheering, shooting *etc*: *They gave her a round of applause; The soldier fired several rounds.* □ **salve**
4 a single bullet, shell *etc*: *five hundred rounds of ammunition.* □ **balle, obus**
5 a stage in a competition *etc*: *The winners of the first round will go through to the next.* □ **manche**

6 a type of song sung by several singers singing the same tune starting in succession. □ **canon**

■ *verb* to go around: *The car rounded the corner.* □ **tourner**

'**rounded** *adjective* curved; like part of the line forming a circle: *a rounded arch.* □ **arrondi**

'**roundly** *adverb* plainly; rudely: *He rebuked her roundly.* □ **rondement**

'**roundness** *noun.* □ **rondeur**

rounds *noun plural* a doctor's visits to his patients: *The doctor is (out) on his rounds.* □ **visite(s)**

'**all-round** *adjective* complete: *It was an all-round success.* □ **complet**

■ *adjective* not direct: *a roundabout route.* □ **détourné**

round figures/numbers the nearest convenient or easily remembered numbers: *Tell me the cost in round figures* (ie $20 rather than $19.87). □ **chiffre rond**

,**round-'shouldered** *adjective* with stooping shoulders. □ **voûté**

round trip 1 a journey to a place and back again (**round trip ticket** a ticket for such a journey). □ **aller et retour**

2 a trip to several places and back, taking a circular route. □ **aller et retour**

round off 1 to make something smooth *etc: He rounded off the sharp corners with a file.* □ **arrondir**

2 to complete successfully: *She rounded off her career by becoming president.* □ **achever**

round on to turn to face (a person) suddenly, *especially* angrily. □ **s'en prendre à qqn**

round up to collect together: *The farmer rounded up the sheep* (noun '**round-up**). □ **rassembler; (n.) rassemblement**

rouse [rauz] *verb* **1** to awaken: *I'll rouse you at 6 o'clock.* □ **réveiller**

2 to stir or excite: *Her interest was roused by what he said.* □ **éveiller**

'**rousing** *adjective* stirring; exciting: *a rousing speech.* □ **vibrant**

rout [raut] *verb* to defeat (an army *etc*) completely. □ **mettre en déroute**

■ *noun* a complete defeat. □ **débandade**

route [ruːt] *noun* a way of getting somewhere; a road: *Our route took us through the mountains.* □ **chemin, itinéraire**

■ *verb* to arrange a route for: *Heavy traffic was routed around the outside of the town.* □ **faire passer (par)**

route march a long march for soldiers in training. □ **marche d'entraînement**

routine [ruː'tiːn] *noun* a regular, fixed way of doing things: *one's daily routine; One needs some routine.* □ **routine**

■ *adjective* regular; ordinary: *routine work.* □ **courant, habituel**

rove [rouv] *verb* to wander; to roam: *He roved (through) the streets.* □ **vagabonder**

'**rover** *noun.* □ **vagabond, onde**

'**roving** *adjective*: *a roving band of robbers.* □ **vagabond**

row[1] [rou] *noun* a line: *two rows of houses; They were*

sitting in a row; They sat in the front row in the theatre. □ **rang(ée)**

row[2] [rou] *verb* **1** to move (a boat) through the water using oars: *He rowed (the dinghy) up the river.* □ **ramer**

2 to transport by rowing: *He rowed them across the lake.* □ **faire traverser en canot**

■ *noun* a trip in a rowing boat: *They went for a row on the river.* □ **promenade en canot**

'**rower** *noun* a person who rows; an oarsman. □ **rameur, euse**

'**rowing boat**, '**rowboat** *noun* a boat which is moved by oars. □ **canot, chaloupe**

row[3] [rau] *noun* **1** a noisy quarrel: *They had a terrible row; a family row.* □ **dispute, prise de bec**

2 a continuous loud noise: *They heard a row in the street.* □ **vacarme**

rowdy ['raudi] *adjective* noisy and rough: *rowdy children.* □ **tapageur**

'**rowdily** *adverb.* □ **de manière tapageuse**

'**rowdiness** *noun.* □ **tapage**

royal ['roiəl] *adjective* **1** of, concerning *etc* a king, queen *etc: the royal family; His Royal Highness Prince Charles.* □ **royal**

2 magnificent: *a royal feast.* □ **royal**

'**royally** *adverb.* □ **royalement**

'**royalist** *noun* a person who supports a king or queen: *The republicans fought the royalists.* □ **royaliste**

'**royalty** – *plural* '**royalties** – *noun* **1** a payment made to a writer, recording artist *etc* for every book, record *etc* sold. □ **redevance, droits d'auteur**

2 the state of being royal, or royal people in general: *The commands of royalty must be obeyed.* □ **royauté; membres de la famille royale**

royal blue (of) a bright, darkish blue: *a royal-blue dress.* □ **bleu roi**

rub [rʌb] – *past tense, past participle* **rubbed** – *verb* to move against the surface of something else, pressing at the same time: *He rubbed his eyes; The horse rubbed its head against my shoulder; The back of the shoe is rubbing against my heel.* □ **frotter**

■ *noun* an act of rubbing: *He gave the teapot a rub with a polishing cloth.* □ **coup (de torchon)**

rub down to dry (a horse) after exercise by rubbing. □ **bouchonner (un cheval)**

rub it in to keep reminding someone of something unpleasant. □ **insister (lourdement)**

rub out to remove (a mark, writing *etc*) with a rubber; to erase. □ **effacer**

rub shoulders with to meet or mix with (other people). □ **côtoyer**

rub the wrong way to annoy or irritate (someone). □ **prendre à rebrousse-poil**

rubber ['rʌbə] *noun* **1** (*also adjective*) (of) a strong elastic substance made from the juice of certain plants (*especially* the **rubber tree**), or an artificial substitute for this: *Tires are made of rubber; rubber boots.* □ **(de) caoutchouc**

2 (*also* e'**raser**) a piece of rubber used to rub out pencil *etc* marks: *a pencil, a ruler and a rubber.* □ **gomme à effacer**

'**rubbery** *adjective* like rubber. □ **caoutchouteux**

rubber band an elastic band. □ **élastique**

rubber stamp an instrument with rubber figures, letters *etc* which is used to stamp a name, date *etc* on books or papers. □ **tampon**

rubbish ['rʌbiʃ] *noun* **1** waste material; things that have been or are to be thrown away: *Our rubbish is taken away twice a week*; (*also adjective*) *a rubbish bin/bag.* □ **(à) ordures**

2 nonsense: *Don't talk rubbish!* □ **absurdités**

rubble ['rʌbl] *noun* small pieces of stone, brick *etc*. □ **gravats**

ruby ['ruːbi] – *plural* '**rubies** – *noun* **1** a kind of deep red precious stone: *a ring set with rubies*; (*also adjective*) *a ruby necklace.* □ **(de) rubis**

2 (*also adjective*) (of) its colour: *a ruby dress.* □ **rubis, vermeil**

rucksack ['rʌksak] *noun* a type of bag carried on the back by walkers, climbers *etc*. □ **sac à dos**

rudder ['rʌdə] *noun* **1** a flat piece of wood, metal *etc* fixed to the back of a boat for steering. □ **gouvernail**

2 a similar device on an aircraft. □ **gouvernail**

ruddy ['rʌdi] *adjective* **1** (of the face) rosy and showing good health: *ruddy cheeks.* □ **rouge de santé**

2 red: *The sky was filled with a ruddy glow.* □ **rougeoyant**

rude [ruːd] *adjective* **1** not polite; showing bad manners: *rude behaviour.* □ **grossier, mal élevé**

2 vulgar; indecent: *rude pictures.* □ **indécent**

'**rudely** *adverb*. □ **grossièrement**

'**rudeness** *noun*. □ **grossièreté**

'**rudiments** ['ruːdimənts] *noun plural* the first simple facts or rules of anything: *to learn the rudiments of cookery.* □ **rudiments**

rudi'mentary [-'men-] *adjective* primitive or undeveloped: *rudimentary tools.* □ **rudimentaire**

rueful ['ruːful] *adjective* regretful; sorrowful. □ **lugubre**

'**ruefully** *adverb*. □ **d'un air lugubre**

'**ruefulness** *noun*. □ **air lugubre**

ruffian ['rʌfiən] *noun* a violent, brutal person: *He was attacked by a gang of ruffians.* □ **voyou**

ruffle ['rʌfl] *verb* to make wrinkled or uneven, *especially* hair, feathers *etc*: *The wind ruffled her hair*; *The bird ruffled its feathers in anger.* □ **ébouriffer, hérisser**

rug [rʌg] *noun* a mat for the floor; a small carpet. □ **carpette**

Rugby, rugby ['rʌgbi] *noun* (*also* **Rugby/rugby football**: *abbreviation* **rugger** ['rʌgə]) a kind of football using an oval ball which can be carried. □ **rugby**

rugged ['rʌgid] *adjective* **1** rocky; uneven: *rugged mountains.* □ **déchiqueté, accidenté**

2 strong; tough: *a rugged character*; *He had rugged good looks*; *He is tall and rugged.* □ **rude**

'**ruggedly** *adverb*. □ **d'une manière rude**

'**ruggedness** *noun*. □ **rudesse**

rugger ['rʌgə] *see* **Rugby/rugby**.

ruin ['ruːin] *noun* **1** a broken, collapsed or decayed state: *the ruin of a city.* □ **ruine**

2 a cause of collapse, decay *etc*: *Drink was his ruin.* □ **perte**

3 financial disaster; complete loss of money: *The company is facing ruin.* □ **ruine**

■ *verb* **1** to cause ruin to: *The scandal ruined his career.* □ **ruiner**

2 to spoil; to treat too indulgently: *You are ruining that child!* □ **gâter**

,**rui'nation** *noun*. □ **ruine**

'**ruined** *adjective* **1** collapsed; decayed: *ruined houses.* □ **en ruine**

2 completely spoiled: *My dress is ruined!* □ **gâché**

'**ruins** *noun plural* collapsed and decayed buildings: *the ruins of the castle.* □ **ruines**

in ruins in a ruined state: *The town lay in ruins.* □ **en ruine**

rule [ruːl] *noun* **1** government: *under foreign rule.* □ **autorité**

2 a regulation or order: *school rules.* □ **règlement**

3 what usually happens or is done; a general principle: *He is an exception to the rule that fat people are usually happy.* □ **règle**

4 a general standard that guides one's actions: *I make it a rule never to be late for appointments.* □ **règle**

■ *verb* **1** to govern: *The king ruled (the people) wisely.* □ **gouverner**

2 to decide officially: *The judge ruled that the witness should be heard.* □ **décider**

3 to draw (a straight line): *She ruled a line across the page.* □ **tirer à la règle**

ruled *adjective* having straight lines drawn across: *ruled paper.* □ **ligné**

'**ruler** *noun* **1** a person who governs: *the ruler of the state.* □ **souverain, aine; chef (d'État)**

2 a long narrow piece of wood, plastic *etc* for drawing straight lines: *I can't draw straight lines without a ruler.* □ **règle**

'**ruling** *adjective* governing: *the ruling party.* □ **au pouvoir, régnant**

■ *noun* an official decision: *The judge gave his ruling.* □ **décision, jugement**

as a rule usually: *I don't go out in the evening as a rule.* □ **en règle générale**

rule off to draw a line in order to separate: *She ruled off the rest of the page.* □ **tirer une ligne (sur, sous)**

rule out to leave out; not to consider: *We mustn't rule out the possibility of bad weather.* □ **exclure**

rum [rʌm] *noun* a type of alcoholic drink, a spirit made from sugar cane: *a bottle of rum.* □ **rhum**

rumba ['rʌmbə] *noun* (a piece of music for) a South American dance. □ **rumba**

rumble ['rʌmbl] *verb* to make a low grumbling sound: *Thunder rumbled in the distance.* □ **gronder**

■ *noun* this kind of sound: *the rumble of thunder.* □ **grondement**

rummage ['rʌmidʒ] *verb* to search by turning things out or over: *She rummaged in the drawer for a clean shirt.* □ **fouiller (dans)**

■ *noun* a thorough search. □ **fouille**

rumour ['ruːmə] *noun* **1** a piece of news or a story passed from person to person, which may not be true: *I heard a rumour that you had got a new job.* □ **rumeur**

2 general talk or gossip: *Don't listen to rumour.* □ **rumeur**

rump [rʌmp] *noun* the hind part of an animal's body. □ **croupe**

rumpus ['rʌmpəs] *noun* a noisy disturbance; an uproar. □ **chahut**

run [rʌn] – *present participle* **'running** – *past tense* **ran** [ran]: *past participle* **run** – *verb* 1 (of a person or animal) to move quickly, faster than walking: *She ran down the road.* □ **courir**

2 to move smoothly: *Trains run on rails.* □ **marcher, rouler**

3 (of water *etc*) to flow: *Rivers run to the sea*; *The tap is running.* □ **couler**

4 (of a machine *etc*) to work or operate: *The engine is running*; *She ran the motor to see if it was working.* □ **marcher, fonctionner**

5 to organize or manage: *She runs the business very efficiently.* □ **diriger**

6 to race: *Is your horse running this afternoon?* □ **courir**

7 (of buses, trains *etc*) to travel regularly: *The buses run every half hour*; *The train is running late.* □ **assurer le service**

8 to last or continue; to go on: *The play ran for six weeks.* □ **tenir l'affiche**

9 to own and operate: *He runs his own business; The car is running well.* □ **exploiter, fonctionner**

10 (of colour) to spread: *When I washed my new dress the colour ran.* □ **déteindre**

11 to move (something): *She ran her fingers through his hair*; *He ran his eyes over the letter.* □ **passer**

12 (in certain phrases) to be or become: *The river ran dry*; *My blood ran cold* (= I was afraid). □ **devenir**

■ *noun* 1 the act of running: *She went for a run before breakfast.* □ **course**

2 a trip or drive: *We went for a run in the country.* □ **promenade**

3 a length of time (for which something continues): *He's had a run of bad luck.* □ **période**

4 a ladder (in a stocking *etc*): *I've got a run in my tights.* □ **échelle**

5 the free use (of a place): *He gave me the run of his house.* □ **entière disposition**

6 an enclosure or pen: *a chicken-run.* □ **poulailler**

'runner *noun* 1 a person who runs: *There are five runners in this race.* □ **coureur, euse**

2 the long narrow part on which a sled *etc* moves: *He polished the runners of the sled.* □ **patin**

3 a long stem of a plant which puts down roots. □ **stolon**

'running *adjective* 1 of or for running: *running shoes.* □ **de course**

2 continuous: *a running commentary on the football match.* □ **commentaire suivi**

■ *adverb* one after another; continuously: *We travelled for four days running.* □ **d'affilée**

'runny *adjective* liquid; watery: *Do you like your egg yolk firm or runny?*; *The baby has a runny nose.* □ **(trop) liquide**

'runaway *noun* a person, animal *etc* that runs away: *The police caught the two runaways*; (*also adjective*) *a*

runaway horse. □ **fugitif, ive**

,runner-'up *noun* a person, thing *etc* that is second in a race or competition: *My friend won the prize and I was the runner-up.* □ **second, onde**

'runway *noun* a wide path from which aircraft take off and on which they land: *The plane landed on the runway.* □ **piste (d'envol/d'atterrissage)**

in, out of the running having (no) chance of success: *She's in the running for the job of director.* □ **qui a des chances; qui n'a aucune chance (de)**

on the run escaping; running away: *He's on the run from the police.* □ **en fuite**

run across to meet: *I ran across an old friend.* □ **rencontrer qqn par hasard**

run after to chase: *The dog ran after a cat.* □ **courir après**

run aground (of a ship) to become stuck on rocks *etc*. □ **s'échouer**

run along to go away: *Run along now, children!* □ **se sauver**

run away 1 to escape: *He ran away from school.* □ **s'enfuir**

2 (*with* with) to steal: *He ran away with all her money.* □ **s'enfuir (avec)**

3 (*with* with) to go too fast *etc* to be controlled by: *The horse ran away with him.* □ **s'emballer**

run down 1 when a person's health weakens due to sickness and fatigue: *Paul has been working overtime for months and now he is run down.* □ **surmener, épuiser**

2 (of a vehicle or driver) to knock down: *I was run down by a bus.* □ **renverser**

3 to speak badly of: *He is always running me down.* □ **dénigrer**

run for to stand for election for: *He is running for president.* □ **se présenter à**

run for it to try to escape: *Quick – run for it!* □ **se sauver**

run into 1 to meet: *I ran into her in the street.* □ **tomber sur**

2 to crash into or collide with: *The car ran into a lamppost.* □ **rentrer dans**

run its course to develop or happen in the usual way: *The fever ran its course.* □ **suivre son cours**

run off 1 to print or copy: *I want 500 copies run off at once.* □ **tirer**

2 (*with* with) to steal or take away: *He ran off with my wife.* □ **partir avec**

run out 1 (of a supply) to come to an end: *The food has run out.* □ **s'épuiser**

2 (*with* of) to have no more: *We've run out of money.* □ **manquer de**

run over 1 (of a vehicle or driver) to knock down or drive over: *Don't let the dog out of the garden or he'll get run over.* □ **écraser**

2 to repeat for practice: *Let's run over the plan again.* □ **revoir**

run a temperature to have a fever. □ **avoir (de la fièvre)**

run through to look at, deal with *etc*, one after another:

She ran through their instructions. □ **parcourir**
run to to have enough money for: *We can't run to a new car this year.* □ **pouvoir se permettre (d'acheter)**
run up 1 to hoist (a flag). □ **hisser**
2 to make quickly or roughly: *I can run up a dress in a couple of hours.* □ **confectionner**
3 to collect up, accumulate (debts): *He ran up an enormous bill.* □ **laisser accumuler**
run wild to go out of control: *They let their children run wild; The garden was running wild.* □ **faire le fou; retourner à l'état sauvage**
rung[1] [rʌŋ] *noun* a step on a ladder: *a missing rung.* □ **barreau**
rung[2] *see* **ring**.
runny *see* **run**.
runway *see* **run**.
rupee [ru'piː] *noun* the standard unit of currency in India, Pakistan and Sri Lanka *etc.* □ **roupie**
rupture ['rʌptʃə] *noun* a tearing or breaking. □ **rupture; hernie**
■ *verb* to break or tear. □ **(se) rompre**
rural ['ruərəl] *adjective* of the countryside: *a rural area.* □ **rural**
ruse [ruːz] *noun* a clever trick or plan. □ **ruse**
rush[1] [rʌʃ] *verb* to (make someone or something) hurry or go quickly: *She rushed into the room; She rushed him to the doctor.* □ **se précipiter; emmener d'urgence**
■ *noun* **1** a sudden quick movement: *They made a rush for the door.* □ **ruée**
2 a hurry: *I'm in a dreadful rush.* □ **urgence**
rush hour a period when there is a lot of traffic on the roads, *usually* when people are going to or leaving work. □ **heure de pointe**
rush[2] [rʌʃ] *noun* a tall grass-like plant growing in or near water: *They hid their boat in the rushes.* □ **jonc**
Russian [rʌʃən] *adjective* of Russia or its inhabitants: *Many Russian men and women skate well; Russian circuses often have trained bears.* □ **Russe**
■ *noun* a native of Russia; the language of Russia: *The Russian was wearing heavy Cossack boots to protect*

his feet from the cold; The trade agreement was written in Russian and in English. □ **Russe**
rust [rʌst] *noun* the reddish-brown substance which forms on iron and steel, caused by air and moisture: *The car was covered with rust.* □ **rouille**
■ *verb* to (cause to) become covered with rust: *The rain has rusted the gate; There's a lot of old metal rusting in the garden.* □ **(se) rouiller**
'rustproof *adjective* that will not (allow) rust: *rustproof paint.* □ **inoxydable**
'rusty *adjective* **1** covered with rust: *a rusty old bicycle.* □ **rouillé**
2 not as good as it was because of lack of practice: *My French is rusty.* □ **rouillé**
'rustily *adverb.* □ **en grinçant**
'rustiness *noun.* □ **rouille**
rustic ['rʌstik] *adjective* **1** of the countryside: *rustic life.* □ **campagnard**
2 roughly made: *a rustic fence.* □ **rustique**
rustle ['rʌsl] *verb* **1** to (make something) make a soft, whispering sound: *The wind rustled in the trees; She rustled her papers.* □ **bruire; froisser**
2 to steal (cattle *etc*). □ **voler**
'rustler *noun* a person who steals cattle *etc.* □ **voleur de bétail**
rustle up to get or make quickly: *He rustled up a meal.* □ **préparer à la hâte**
rut [rʌt] *noun* a deep track made by a wheel *etc* in soft ground: *The road was full of ruts.* □ **ornière**
'rutted *adjective* having ruts: *a deeply-rutted path.* □ **sillonné d'ornières**
in a rut having a fixed, monotonous way of life: *I felt that I was in a rut, so I changed my job.* □ **encroûté**
ruthless ['ruːθlis] *adjective* without pity: *a ruthless attack; a ruthless tyrant.* □ **impitoyable**
'ruthlessly *adverb.* □ **impitoyablement**
'ruthlessness *noun.* □ **caractère impitoyable**
rye [rai] *noun* a kind of cereal. □ **seigle**
rye bread a kind of bread made with flour made from rye. □ **pain de seigle**

Ss

Sabbath ['sabəθ] *noun* (*usually with* **the**) a day of the week regularly set aside for religious services and rest – among the Jews, Saturday; among most Christians, Sunday. □ **sabbat; dimanche**

saber *see* **sabre.**

sable ['seibl] *noun* **1** a kind of small animal found in Arctic regions, valued for its glossy fur. □ **zibeline, martre** **2** its fur: *Artists' brushes are sometimes made of sable*; (*also adjective*) *a sable coat.* □ **(de) zibeline; en poil de martre**

sabotage ['sabətɑːʒ] *noun* the deliberate destruction in secret of machinery, bridges, equipment *etc*, by *eg* enemies in wartime, dissatisfied workers *etc*. □ **sabotage** ■ *verb* to destroy, damage or cause to fail by sabotage. □ **saboter**

,**sabo'teur** [-'təː] *noun* a person who sabotages: *The soldiers shot the three saboteurs.* □ **saboteur, euse**

sabre, saber ['seibə] *noun* a type of curved sword, used by cavalry. □ **sabre**

saccharine ['sakərin] *noun* a very sweet substance used instead of sugar. □ **saccharine** ■ *adjective* something that is excessively sweet or sentimental. □ **édulcoré**

sachet [sa'ʃei] *noun* a (small) sealed packet containing a product in liquid or powder form: *a sachet of shampoo.* □ **sachet**

sack[1] [sak] *noun* a large bag of coarse cloth, strong paper or plastic: *The potatoes were put into sacks.* □ **sac** '**sacking** *noun* a type of coarse cloth for making sacks. □ **toile à sacs** '**sackcloth** *noun* a type of coarse cloth formerly worn as a sign of mourning or of sorrow for sin. □ **sac**

sack[2] [sak] *verb* **1** to dismiss (a person) from his job: *One of the workmen was sacked for drunkenness.* □ **congédier** **2** to rob, plunder or take something violently especially after a battle victory: *The enemy soldiers went through the whole area, burning and sacking the villages along the way.* □ **saccager** **get the sack** to be sacked: *I'll get the sack if I arrive at the office late!* □ **être mis à la porte**

sacrament ['sakrəmənt] *noun* in the Christian church, a ceremony regarded as especially sacred, *eg* marriage, or baptism. □ **sacrement** ,**sacra'mental** [-'men-] *adjective.* □ **sacramentel**

sacred ['seikrid] *adjective* **1** of God or a god; (that must be respected because) connected with religion or with God or a god: *Temples, mosques, churches and synagogues are all sacred buildings.* □ **sacré** **2** (of a duty *etc*) which must be done *etc eg* because of respect for someone: *She considered it a sacred duty to fulfil her dead father's wishes.* □ **sacré** '**sacredness** *noun.* □ **caractère sacré** **nothing is sacred** to (him, them *etc*) he, they *etc* have no respect for anything. □ **rien n'est sacré pour**

sacrifice ['sakrifais] *noun* **1** the act of offering something (*eg* an animal that is specially killed) to a god: *A lamb was offered in sacrifice.* □ **sacrifice** **2** the thing that is offered in this way. □ **sacrifice** **3** something of value given away or up in order to gain something more important or to benefit another person: *Her parents made sacrifices to pay for her education.* □ **sacrifice** ■ *verb* **1** to offer as a sacrifice: *He sacrificed a sheep in the temple.* □ **sacrifier** **2** to give away *etc* for the sake of something or someone else: *He sacrificed his life trying to save the children from the burning house.* □ **sacrifier** ,**sacri'ficial** [-'fiʃəl] *adjective: sacrificial victims.* □ **sacrificiel** ,**sacri'ficially** *adverb.* □ **en guise de sacrifice**

sacrilege ['sakrəlidʒ] *noun* the act of using a holy thing or place in a wicked way: *Robbing a church is considered (a) sacrilege.* □ **sacrilège** '**sacri'legious** [-'lidʒəs] *adjective.* □ **sacrilège** ,**sacri'legiously** *adverb.* □ **d'une manière sacrilège** ,**sacri'legiousness** *noun.* □ **caractère sacrilège**

sad [sad] *adjective* unhappy or causing unhappiness: *She's sad because her son is ill; a sad face.* □ **triste** '**sadness** *noun.* □ **tristesse** '**sadden** *verb* to make or become sad: *She was saddened by her son's ingratitude.* □ **(s')attrister** '**sadly** *adverb: She stared sadly at the ruins of her house.* □ **tristement**

saddle ['sadl] *noun* a seat for a rider: *The bicycle saddle is too high.* □ **selle** ■ *noun* (*negative* **unsaddle**) to put a saddle on: *He saddled his horse and rode away.* □ **seller**

safari [sə'fɑːri] *noun* an expedition or tour, *especially* in Africa, for hunting or observing animals: *A safari was organized to the lion reserve; We often went out on safari.* □ **safari** **safari park** a large area of land reserved for wild animals, in which they can move freely and be seen by the public who *usually* drive through the park in cars. □ **réserve d'animaux sauvages**

safe[1] [seif] *adjective* **1** (*negative* **unsafe**) protected, or free (from danger *etc*): *The children are safe from danger in the garden.* □ **à l'abri (de)** **2** providing good protection: *You should keep your money in a safe place.* □ **sûr** **3** unharmed: *The missing child has been found safe and well.* □ **sauf** **4** not likely to cause harm: *These pills are not safe for children.* □ **sans danger** **5** (of a person) reliable: *a safe driver; He's a very fast driver but he's safe enough.* □ **fiable** '**safeness** *noun.* □ **sécurité** '**safely** *adverb* without harm or risk: *She got home safely.* □ **sans accident** '**safety** *noun* **1** the state of being safe: *I worry about the children's safety on these busy roads; a place of safety;* (*also adjective*) *safety goggles; safety helmet.* □ **(de) sécurité** **2** the part on the handle of a gun that keeps it from firing: *The police officer was trained to keep the safety on his gun when he was not using it.* □ **sûreté**

3 a safe place away from danger: *The girl was rescued from the overturned boat and brought to safety*. □ **sûreté**
'**safeguard** *noun* anything that gives security or protection: *a safeguard against burglary*. □ **garantie (contre)**
■ *verb* to protect: *Put a good lock on your door to safeguard your property*. □ **protéger**
'**safety belt** *noun* a fixed belt in a car or aircraft used to keep a passenger from being thrown out of the seat in an accident, crash *etc*. □ **ceinture de sécurité**
safety lamp a type of lamp used in mines that does not set fire to any inflammable gases there. □ **lampe de sûreté**
'**safety pin** *noun* a pin that has a cover over its point when it is closed. □ **épingle de sûreté**
safety valve a valve *eg* on a pressure cooker that opens if the pressure of the steam in it becomes too great. □ **soupape de sûreté**
be on the safe side to avoid risk or danger: *I'll lock the door just to be on the safe side*. □ **pour plus de sûreté**
safe and sound unharmed: *He returned safe and sound.* □ **sain et sauf**
safe² [seif] *noun* a heavy metal chest or box in which money *etc* can be locked away safely: *There is a small safe hidden behind that picture on the wall.* □ **coffrefort**
saffron ['safrən] *noun* 1 a yellow colouring and flavouring substance used in cooking: *We added some saffron to the rice.* □ **safran**
2 an orange-yellow colour. □ **jaune safran**
■ *adjective: Many Buddhist monks wear saffron robes.* □ **safran**
sag [sag] – *past tense, past participle* **sagged** – *verb* to bend, hang down, *especially* in the middle: *There were so many books on the shelf that it sagged.* □ **(s')affaisser (sous un poids)**
saga ['sɑːgə] *noun* a long, detailed story: *I expect he told you the saga of his troubles.* □ **saga**
sagacious [sə'geiʃəs] *adjective* showing intelligence, wisdom and good judgment: *The old priest was learned and sagacious.* □ **sagace, avisé**
sa'gaciously *adverb*. □ **avec sagacité**
sagacity [sə'gasəti] *noun*. □ **sagacité**
sage¹ [seidʒ] *noun* a plant whose leaves are used as flavouring in cooking. □ **sauge**
sage² [seidʒ] *noun* a wise man: *the sages of past centuries.* □ **sage**
■ *adjective* wise: *sage advice.* □ **sage**
'**sagely** *adverb*. □ **sagement**
sago ['seigou] *noun* a starchy substance obtained from inside the trunk of certain palm trees; (*also adjective*): *sago pudding*. □ **sagou**
said [sed] *verb see* **say**.
sail [seil] *noun* 1 a sheet of strong cloth spread to catch the wind, by which a ship is driven forward. □ **voile**
2 a journey in a ship: *a sail in his yacht; a week's sail to the island.* □ **voyage en bateau**
3 an arm of a windmill. □ **aile**
■ *verb* 1 (of a ship) to be moved by sails: *The yacht sailed away.* □ **aller à la voile**
2 to steer or navigate a ship or boat: *She sailed (the*

boat) to the island. □ **piloter**
3 to go in a ship or boat (with or without sails): *I've never sailed through the Mediterranean.* □ **naviguer, voguer**
4 to begin a voyage: *The ship sails today; My aunt sailed today.* □ **prendre la mer**
5 to travel on (the sea *etc*) in a ship: *He sailed the North Sea.* □ **naviguer**
6 to move steadily and easily: *Clouds sailed across the sky; She sailed through her exams; She sailed into the room.* □ **filer**
'**sailing** *noun* the activity or sport of navigating a ship or boat that has sails: *Sailing is one of his hobbies.* □ **navigation (à voile)**
'**sailboat** *noun* a boat with a mast and large canvas sheet or sail to catch the wind: *When the wind blew, the sailboat glided over the water.* □ **voilier**
sailing- having a sail or sails: *sailing-boat.* □ **à voiles**
'**sailor** *noun* a member of a ship's crew whose job is helping to sail a ship. □ **marin, matelot**
in full sail with all the sails spread: *The ship was in full sail.* □ **toutes voiles dehors**
saint [seint, (*before a name*) snt] *noun* 1 (*often abbreviated to* **St**, *especially when used in the names of places, plants etc*) a title given *especially* by the Roman Catholic and Orthodox churches to a very good or holy person after his death: *Saint Matthew; St John's Road.* □ **saint, sainte**
2 a very good, kind person: *You really are a saint to put up with her.* □ **saint, sainte**
'**saintly** *adjective: She led a saintly life; a saintly expression.* □ **(de) saint, sainte**
'**saintliness** *noun*. □ **sainteté**
sake [seik]: **for the sake of 1** in order to benefit: *He bought a house in the country for the sake of his wife's health.* □ **dans l'intérêt de qqn**
2 because of a desire for: *For the sake of peace, he said he agreed with her.* □ **pour l'amour de**
salad ['saləd] *noun* (a dish of) mixed raw vegetables. □ **salade**
fruit salad a mixture of chopped fruits *usually* eaten as a dessert. □ **salade de fruits**
salad dressing a sauce for putting on salad, *usually* consisting of oil and vinegar and sometimes spices. □ **vinaigrette**
salary ['saləri] – *plural* '**salaries** – *noun* a fixed, regular *usually* monthly payment for work: *Secretarial salaries in Toronto are quite high.* □ **salaire**
sale [seil] *noun* 1 the act of giving something to someone in exchange for money: *the sale of a house; Sales of cars have increased.* □ **vente**
2 in a shop *etc*, an offer of goods at lowered prices for a short time: *I bought my dress in a sale.* □ **solde**
3 an event at which goods are sold: *an auction sale; a book sale.* □ **vente**
'**saleroom** *noun* a room or building where public auctions are held: *Her furniture was taken to the saleroom.* □ **salle des ventes**
'**salesperson** ['seilz-] *noun* a person who sells, or shows, goods to customers in a shop *etc*. □ **vendeur, euse**

'salesmanship ['seilz-] *noun* the art of persuading people to buy things. □ **art de la vente**

for sale intended to be sold: *Have you any pictures for sale?* □ **à vendre**

salient ['seiliənt] *adjective* main; chief; most noticeable: *What were the salient points of her speech?* □ **saillant**

saliva [sə'laivə] *noun* the liquid that forms in the mouth to help digestion. □ **salive**

salivate ['saliveit] *verb* to produce saliva, *especially* in large amounts. □ **saliver**

sallow ['salou] *adjective* (of a complexion) pale or yellowish, not pink. □ **jaunâtre**

'sallowness *noun.* □ **teint jaunâtre**

sally ['sali] – *plural* **'sallies** – *noun* a sudden act of rushing out (*eg* from a fort) to make an attack. □ **sortie**

sally forth (of soldiers) to rush out to make an attack: *They sallied forth against the enemy.* □ **faire une sortie**

salmon ['samən] – *plural* **'salmon** – *noun* a type of large fish with orange-pink flesh. □ **saumon**

salon [sə'lon] *noun* a name sometimes given to a place where hairdressing *etc* is done: *a beauty salon; My hairdresser has opened a new salon.* □ **salon de coiffure**

saloon [sə'lu:n] *noun* a bar or tavern modelled after the local drinking and gambling establishments of the Old West: *The backdrop for the play was an old style Western saloon.* □ **bar, saloon**

salt [so:lt] *noun* **1** (*also* **common salt**) sodium chloride, a white substance frequently used for seasoning: *The soup needs more salt.* □ **sel**

2 any other substance formed, like common salt, from a metal and an acid. □ **sel**

3 a sailor, *especially* an experienced one: *an old salt.* □ **(vieux) loup de mer**

■ *adjective* containing, tasting of, preserved in salt: *salt water; salt pork.* □ **salé**

■ *verb* to put salt on or in: *Have you salted the potatoes?* □ **saler**

'salted *adjective* (*negative* **unsalted**) containing or preserved with salt: *salted butter; salted beef.* □ **salé**

'saltness *noun.* □ **salure, salinité**

'salty *adjective* containing or tasting of salt: *Tears are salty water.* □ **salé**

'saltiness *noun.* □ **salure, salinité**

'saltcellar *noun* a shaker or container that holds salt: *Thai dropped the saltcellar and spilled salt all over the table.* □ **salière**

bath salts a *usually* perfumed mixture of certain salts added to bath water. □ **sels de bain**

the salt of the earth a very good or worthy person: *People like her are the salt of the earth.* □ **le sel de la terre**

take (something) with a grain/pinch of salt to receive (a statement, news *etc*) with a slight feeling of disbelief: *I took his story with a pinch of salt.* □ **prendre (qqch.) avec un grain de sel**

salute [sə'lu:t] *verb* **1** (*especially* in the forces) to raise the (*usually* right) hand to the forehead to show respect: *They saluted their commanding officer.* □ **saluer**

2 to honour by firing *eg* large guns: *They saluted the Queen by firing one hundred guns.* □ **saluer**

■ *noun* an act of saluting: *The officer gave a salute; a 21-gun salute.* □ **salut, salve**

salvage ['salvidʒ] *verb* to save from loss or destruction in a fire, shipwreck *etc*: *She salvaged her books from the burning house.* □ **sauver**

■ *noun* **1** the act of salvaging. □ **sauvetage**

2 property *etc* which has been salvaged: *Was there any salvage from the wreck?* □ **objets récupérés**

salvation [sal'veiʃən] *noun* **1** in religion, the freeing of a person from sin or the saving of his or her soul. □ **salut**

2 the cause, means, or act of saving: *This delay was the salvation of the army.* □ **salut**

salve [sav] *noun* (an) ointment to heal or soothe: *lip-salve.* □ **onguent**

salver ['salvə] *noun* a small tray, often made of silver: *He received a silver salver as a retirement present.* □ **plateau (de métal, etc.)**

same [seim] *adjective* (*usually* with **the**) **1** alike; very similar: *The houses in this road are all the same; You have the same eyes as your sister (has).* □ **semblable**

2 not different: *My friend and I are the same age; She went to the same school as me.* □ **même**

3 unchanged: *My opinion is the same as it always was.* □ **même**

■ *pronoun* (*usually* with **the**) the same thing: *She sat down and we all did the same.* □ **de même**

■ *adverb* (*usually* with **the**) in the same way: *I don't feel the same about you as I did.* □ **pareillement**

all/just the same nevertheless: *I'm sure I locked the door, but, all the same, I think I'll go and check.* □ **tout de même**

at the same time 1 together. □ **en même temps**

2 nevertheless: *Mountain climbing is fun, but at the same time we must not forget the danger.* □ **néanmoins**

be all the same to to be a matter of no importance to: *I'll leave now, if it's all the same to you.* □ **être égal à**

same here I think, feel *etc* the same: *'This job bores me.' 'Same here.'* □ **pareillement**

sampan ['sampan] *noun* a small flat-bottomed Chinese boat. □ **sampan**

sample ['sa:mpl] *noun* a part taken from something to show the quality of the whole: *samples of the artist's work;* (*also adjective*) *a sample tube of ointment.* □ **échantillon**

■ *verb* to test a sample of: *She sampled my cake.* □ **tester un échantillon**

samsu ['samsu:] *noun* a Chinese alcoholic drink made from rice or millet. □ **alcool de riz ou de millet**

sanatorium [sanə'to:riəm] – *plurals* **,sana'toriums, ,sana'toria** [-riə] – *noun* **1** a hospital, *especially* for people with certain diseases of the lungs or for people who are recovering from an illness. □ **sanatorium**

2 a place in a school, college *etc* for those who are ill. □ **infirmerie**

sanctify ['saŋktifai] *verb* to make sacred, holy or free from sin. □ **sanctifier**

,sanctifi'cation [-fi-] *noun.* □ **sanctification**

sanctimonious [saŋkti'mouniəs] *adjective* trying to appear full of holiness or goodness: *a sanctimonious expression.* □ **moralisateur**

,**sancti'moniously** *adverb.* □ **d'une manière moralisatrice**

,**sancti'moniousness** *noun.* □ **fausse dévotion**

sanction ['saŋkʃən] *noun* permission or approval: *The soldier's action did not have the sanction of his commanding officer.* □ **approbation**

■ *verb* to permit or agree to: *We cannot sanction the use of force.* □ **approuver**

sanctuary ['saŋktʃuəri] – *plural* '**sanctuaries** – *noun* 1 a holy or sacred place: *the sanctuary of the god Apollo.* □ **sanctuaire**

2 a place of safety from *eg* arrest: *In earlier times a criminal could use a church as a sanctuary.* □ **refuge**

3 an area of land in which the killing of wild animals *etc* is forbidden: *a bird sanctuary.* □ **réserve**

sand [sand] *noun* 1 a large amount of tiny particles of crushed rocks, shells *etc*, found on beaches *etc*. □ **sable**

2 an area of sand, *especially* on a beach: *We lay on the sand.* □ **plage**

■ *verb* to smooth with *eg* sand-paper: *The floor should be sanded before you varnish it.* □ **sabler, poncer**

'**sandy** *adjective* 1 filled or covered with sand: *a sandy beach.* □ **sablonneux**

2 (of hair) yellowish-red in colour: *She has fair skin and sandy hair.* □ **blond roux**

sandbank ['sanbaŋk] *noun* a bank of sand formed by tides and currents. □ **banc de sable**

sandcastle ['sankaːsl] *noun* a pile of sand, sometimes made to look like a castle, built *especially* by children on beaches. □ **château de sable**

sandpaper ['sanpeipə] *noun* a type of paper with sand glued to it, used for smoothing and polishing. □ **papier de verre**

■ *verb* to make smooth with sandpaper. □ **poncer**

sandshoes ['sanʃuːz] *noun plural* soft light shoes, often with rubber soles. □ **espadrilles**

sandstone ['sanstoun] *noun* a soft type of rock made of layers of sand pressed together. □ **grès**

sandstorm ['sanstoːrm] *noun* a storm of wind, carrying with it clouds of sand: *We were caught in a sandstorm in the desert.* □ **tempête de sable**

sandal ['sandl] *noun* a type of light shoe, the sole of which is held on to the foot by straps: *a pair of sandals.* □ **sandale**

sandwich ['sanwitʃ] *noun* slices of bread *etc* with food between: *cheese sandwiches.* □ **sandwich**

■ *verb* to place or press between two objects *etc*: *His car was sandwiched between two trucks.* □ **serrer entre**

sane [sein] *adjective* 1 not mad: *in a perfectly sane state of mind.* □ **sain d'esprit**

2 sensible: *a very sane person.* □ **sensé**

'**sanely** *adverb.* □ **raisonnablement**

'**sanity** ['sa-] *noun* the state or quality of being sane: *I am concerned about her sanity.* □ **santé mentale**

sang *see* **sing**.

sanitarium [sani'teəriəm] – *plurals* ,**sani'tariums**, ,**sani'taria** – *noun* (*North American*) a sanatorium. □ **sanatorium**

sanitary ['sanitəri] *adjective* 1 of or concerning conditions or arrangements that encourage good health. □ **sanitaire**

2 free from dirt and germs: *The conditions in that camp are not sanitary.* □ **sanitaire**

,**sani'tation** *noun* the arrangements for protecting health, *especially* drainage. □ **système sanitaire; hygiène publique**

sanity *see* **sane**.

sank *see* **sink**.

sap[1] [sap] *noun* the liquid in trees, plants *etc*: *The sap flowed out when he broke the stem of the flower.* □ **sève**

sap[2] [sap] – *past tense, past participle* **sapped** – *verb* to weaken or destroy (a person's strength, confidence, courage *etc*): *The disease slowly sapped his strength.* □ **saper**

sapling ['sapliŋ] *noun* a young tree. □ **jeune arbre**

sapphire ['safaiə] *noun* a kind of dark-blue precious stone: *a gold brooch set with a sapphire;* (*also adjective*) *a sapphire ring.* □ **(de) saphir**

sarcasm ['saːkazəm] *noun* (the use of) unpleasant remarks intended to hurt a person's feelings. □ **sarcasme**

sar'castic [-'kas-] *adjective* containing, or using, sarcasm: *a sarcastic person.* □ **sarcastique**

sar'castically *adverb.* □ **sarcastiquement**

sardine [saːˈdiːn] *noun* a young pilchard, often packed in oil in small tins. □ **sardine**

sari ['saːriː] *noun* a garment worn by Hindu women, a long cloth wrapped around the waist and passed over the shoulder. □ **sari**

sarong [səˈroŋ] (in Singapore and Malaysia **sarung**) *noun* a kind of skirt worn by Malay men and women. □ **paréo**

sash[1] [saʃ] *noun* a broad band of cloth worn around the waist, or over one shoulder: *a white dress with a red sash at the waist.* □ **ceinture (d'étoffe), écharpe**

sash[2] [saʃ] *noun* a frame fitted with glass, forming part of a window: *the lower sash.* □ **châssis (d'une fenêtre à guillotine)**

sat *see* **sit**.

Satan ['seitən] *noun* the Devil; the spirit of evil. □ **Satan**

satanic [səˈtanik, (*American*) sei-] *adjective.* □ **satanique**

satchel ['satʃəl] *noun* small bag for schoolbooks *etc*. □ **sac**

satellite ['satəlait] *noun* 1 a smaller body that revolves around a planet: *The Moon is a satellite of the Earth.* □ **satellite**

2 a man-made object fired into space to travel around usually the Earth: *a weather satellite.* □ **satellite**

3 a state *etc* controlled by a more powerful neighbouring state: *Russia and her satellites.* □ **satellite**

satin ['satin] *noun* a closely woven type of silk with a shiny surface: *The baby's skin was as smooth as satin;* (*also adjective*) *a satin dress.* □ **(de) satin**

satire ['sataiə] *noun* (a piece of) writing *etc* that makes someone look foolish: *a satire on university life.* □ **satire**

sa'tirical [-'ti-] *adjective* 1 of satire: *satirical writing.* □ **satirique**

2 mocking: *in a satirical mood.* □ **satirique**

'**satirist** [-'ti-] *noun* a person who writes or performs satire(s). □ **auteur, eure satirique**

'satirize, 'satirise [-ti-] *verb* to make look foolish by using satire. □ **faire la satire de**

satisfy ['satisfai] *verb* 1 to give (a person) enough of what is wanted or needed to take away hunger, curiosity *etc*: *The apple didn't satisfy my hunger; I told her enough to satisfy her curiosity.* □ **satisfaire**

2 to please: *She is very difficult to satisfy.* □ **satisfaire**

,satis'faction [-'fakʃən] *noun* 1 the act of satisfying or state of being satisfied: *the satisfaction of desires.* □ **satisfaction**

2 pleasure or contentment: *Your success gives me great satisfaction.* □ **satisfaction**

,satis'factory [-'faktəri] *adjective* (*negative* **unsatisfactory**) giving satisfaction; good enough to satisfy: *Your work is not satisfactory; The condition of the sick woman is satisfactory.* □ **satisfaisant**

,satis'factorily [-'faktə-] *adverb.* □ **de manière satisfaisante**

'satisfied *adjective* (*sometimes with* **with**) pleased: *I'm satisfied with her progress; a satisfied customer.* □ **satisfait**

'satisfying *adjective* pleasing: *The story had a satisfying ending.* □ **satisfaisant**

saturate ['satʃəreit] *verb* 1 to make very wet: *Saturate the earth around the plants.* □ **imbiber**

2 to fill completely: *The market has been saturated with paintings like that.* □ **saturer**

satu'ration *noun.* □ **saturation**

Saturday ['satədei] *noun* the seventh day of the week, the day following Friday: *I'll see you on Saturday*; (*also adjective*) *on Saturday morning.* □ **samedi**

sauce [sɔːs] *noun* a *usually* thick liquid that is poured over other food in order to add moisture and flavour: *tomato sauce; an expert at making sauces.* □ **sauce**

'saucy *adjective* slightly rude: *a saucy remark.* □ **impertinent**

'saucily *adverb.* □ **avec impertinence**

'sauciness *noun.* □ **impertinence**

'saucepan [-pan] *noun* a deep pan *usually* with a long handle for boiling or stewing food. □ **casserole**

saucer ['sɔːsə] *noun* a small shallow dish for placing under a cup: *Could you bring me another cup and saucer?* □ **soucoupe**

saucy *see* sauce.

sauna ['sɔːnə] *noun* (a building or room equipped for) a Finnish form of steam bath: *They have a sauna in their house; They had a refreshing sauna.* □ **sauna**

saunter ['sɔːntə] *verb* (*often with* **along, off, past** *etc*) to walk or stroll about without much purpose or hurry: *I was working in the garden when she sauntered by.* □ **se balader**

■ *noun* a walk or stroll. □ **balade**

sausage ['sosidʒ] *noun* (a section of) minced meat seasoned and pushed into a tube of animal gut or a similar material: *We had sausages for breakfast; garlic sausage.* □ **saucisse**

,sausage 'roll *noun* a piece of sausage meat cooked in a roll of pastry: *They had sausage rolls at the children's party.* □ **friand**

sauté [sou'tei] *adjective* fried lightly and quickly: *sauté potatoes.* □ **sauté**

■ *verb – past tense, past participle* **'sauté(e)d** – to fry in this way. □ **(faire) sauter**

savage ['savidʒ] *adjective* 1 uncivilized: *savage tribes.* □ **primitif**

2 fierce and cruel: *The elephant can be quite savage; bitter and savage remarks.* □ **féroce**

■ *verb* to attack: *He was savaged by wild animals.* □ **attaquer férocement**

■ *noun* 1 a person in an uncivilized state: *tribes of savages.* □ **primitif**

2 a person who behaves in a cruel, uncivilized way: *I hope the police catch the savages who attacked the old lady.* □ **sauvage**

'savagely *adverb.* □ **sauvagement**

'savageness *noun.* □ **sauvagerie**

'savagery *noun.* □ **sauvagerie**

savanna(h) [sə'vanə] *noun* a grassy plain with few trees: *the savanna(h)s of Central America.* □ **savane**

save¹ [seiv] *verb* 1 to rescue or bring out of danger: *He saved his friend from drowning; The house was burnt but she saved the pictures.* □ **sauver**

2 to keep (money *etc*) for future use: *She's saving (her money) to buy a bicycle; They're saving for a house.* □ **économiser**

3 to prevent the using or wasting of (money, time, energy *etc*): *Frozen foods save a lot of trouble; I'll telephone and that will save me writing a letter.* □ **épargner**

4 in football *etc*, to prevent the opposing team from scoring a goal: *The goalkeeper saved six goals.* □ **empêcher de marquer**

5 to free from the power of sin and evil. □ **délivrer**

■ *noun* (in football *etc*) an act of preventing the opposing team from scoring a goal. □ **arrêt (du ballon)**

'saver *noun* a person or thing that saves, avoids waste *etc*: *The telephone is a great time-saver.* □ **économiseur**

'saving *noun* a way of saving money *etc* or the amount saved in this way: *It's a great saving to be able to make one's own clothes.* □ **économie**

'savings *noun plural* money saved up: *She keeps her savings in the bank.* □ **économies**

saviour, savior ['seivjə] *noun* 1 (*usually with capital*) a person or god who saves people from sin, hell *etc*. □ **Sauveur**

2 a person who rescues a person *etc* from danger *etc*: *He was the saviour of his country.* □ **sauveur**

saving grace a good quality that makes up for a fault: *His speeches are boring but they have the saving grace of being short.* □ **chose qui rachète**

savings account an account in a bank or post office on which interest is paid. □ **compte d'épargne**

savings bank a bank that receives small savings and gives interest. □ **caisse d'épargne**

save up to save: *He's been saving up for a new bike.* □ **économiser**

save² [seiv] *preposition, conjunction* except: *All save her had gone; We have no news save that the ship reached port safely.* □ **sauf (que)**

savour, savor ['seivə] *verb* to eat, drink *usually* slowly in order to appreciate taste or quality: *She savoured the delicious soup.* □ **savourer**

'**savoury** *adjective* having a *usually* salty or sharp, but not sweet, taste or smell: *a savoury omelette.* □ **salé**

■ *noun* something savoury served with *eg* alcoholic drinks. □ **amuse-gueule salé**

savour of to have a suggestion or give an impression of (*usually* something bad): *Their action savours of rebellion.* □ **sentir qqch.**

saw[1] *see* **see**.

saw[2] [sɔː] *noun* a tool for cutting, having a toothed edge: *He used a saw to cut through the branch.* □ **scie**

■ *verb* – *past tense* **sawed**: *past participles* **sawn, sawed** – to cut with a saw: *He sawed the log in two.* □ **scier**

'**sawdust** *noun* a dust of tiny fragments of wood, made by sawing. □ **sciure**

'**sawmill** *noun* a place in which wood is mechanically sawn. □ **scierie**

■ *adjective*: *a sawmill worker.* □ **de scierie**

saxophone ['saksəfoun] *noun* a type of musical instrument with a curved metal tube, played by blowing. □ **saxophone**

saxophonist [sak'sofənist] *noun*. □ **saxophoniste**

say [sei] – *3rd person singular present tense* **says** [sez]: *past tense, past participle* **said** [sed] – *verb* **1** to speak or utter: *What did you say?; She said 'Yes'.* □ **dire**

2 to tell, state or declare: *She said how she had enjoyed meeting me; She is said to be very beautiful.* □ **dire**

3 to repeat: *The child says her prayers every night.* □ **dire**

4 to guess or estimate: *I can't say when she'll return.* □ **dire**

■ *noun* the right or opportunity to state one's opinion: *I haven't had my say yet; We have no say in the decision.* □ **(avoir) droit au chapitre**

'**saying** *noun* something often said, *especially* a proverb *etc*. □ **dicton**

have (something, nothing *etc*) **to say for oneself** to be able/unable to explain one's actions *etc*: *Your work is very careless – what have you to say for yourself?* □ **avoir à dire en sa faveur**

I wouldn't say no to I would like: *I wouldn't say no to an ice cream.* □ **n'être pas de refus**

(let's) say roughly; approximately; about: *You'll arrive there in, (let's) say, three hours.* □ **disons**

say the word I'm ready to obey your wishes: *If you'd like to go with me, say the word.* □ **n'avoir qu'un mot à dire**

that is to say in other words; I mean: *She was here last Thursday, that's to say the 4th of June.* □ **c'est-à-dire**

scab [skab] *noun* **1** a crust formed over a sore or wound. □ **croûte**

2 any of several diseases of animals or plants. □ **gale**

3 a worker who refuses to join a strike. □ **briseur, euse de grève**

'**scabby** *adjective*. □ **galeux**

scabbard ['skabəd] *noun* a case in which the blade of a sword is kept. □ **gaine, fourreau**

scaffold ['skafəld] *noun* a raised platform *especially* for use formerly when putting a criminal *etc* to death. □ **échafaud**

'**scaffolding** *noun* an erection of metal poles and wooden planks used by men at work on (the outside of) a building. □ **échafaudage**

scald [skɔːld] *verb* **1** to hurt with hot liquid or steam: *She scalded her hand with boiling water.* □ **ébouillanter**

2 in cooking, to heat (*eg* milk) to just below boiling-point. □ **frémir**

■ *noun* a hurt caused by hot liquid or steam. □ **brûlure (par l'eau)**

'**scalding** *adjective* (of a liquid) hot enough to scald. □ **bouillant**

scale[1] [skeil] *noun* **1** a set of regularly spaced marks made on something (*eg* a thermometer or a ruler) for use as a measure; a system of numbers, measurement *etc*: *This thermometer has two scales marked on it, one in Fahrenheit and one in Centigrade.* □ **graduation**

2 a series or system of items of increasing or decreasing size, value *etc*: *a wage/salary scale.* □ **échelle**

3 in music, a group of notes going up or down in order: *The girl practised her scales on the piano.* □ **gamme**

4 the size of measurements on a map *etc* compared with the real size of the country *etc* shown by it: *In a map drawn to the scale 1:50 000, one centimetre represents half a kilometre.* □ **échelle**

5 the size of an activity: *These guns are being manufactured on a large scale.* □ **échelle**

scale[2] [skeil] *verb* to climb (a ladder, cliff *etc*): *The prisoner scaled the prison walls and escaped.* □ **escalader**

scale[3] [skeil] *noun* any of the small thin plates or flakes that cover the skin of fishes, reptiles *etc*: *A herring's scales are silver in colour.* □ **écaille**

'**scaly** *adjective* (of fish *etc*) covered with scales. □ **écailleux**

scales [skeilz] *noun plural* a *usually* small weighing-machine: *kitchen scales; a set of scales.* □ **balance**

scallop, also **scollop** ['skoləp] *noun* an edible shellfish that has a pair of hinged, fan-shaped shells. □ **coquille Saint-Jacques**

'**scalloped** *adjective* (of the edge of a garment *etc*) cut into curves and notches: *The collar of the blouse has a scalloped edge.* □ **festonné**

scalp [skalp] *noun* **1** the skin of the part of the head usually covered by hair: *Rub the shampoo well into your scalp.* □ **cuir chevelu**

2 the skin and hair of the top of the head: *Some North American Indians used to cut the scalps from their prisoners.* □ **scalp**

■ *verb* to cut the scalp from: *The Indians killed and scalped him.* □ **scalper**

scalpel ['skalpəl] *noun* a small knife with a thin blade, used in surgical operations. □ **scalpel**

scaly *see* **scale**[3].

scamper ['skampə] *verb* to run quickly and lightly: *The mouse scampered away when it saw me.* □ **détaler**

scan [skan] – *past tense, past participle* **scanned** – *verb*
1 to examine carefully: *She scanned the horizon for any sign of a ship.* □ **scruter**

2 to look at quickly but not in detail: *She scanned the newspaper for news of the murder.* □ **parcourir**

3 to pass radar beams *etc* over: *The area was scanned for signs of enemy aircraft.* □ **balayer**

4 to fit into a particular rhythm or metre: *The second line of that verse doesn't scan properly.* □ **(se) scander**

'**scanner** *noun* a machine *etc* that scans. □ **scanner**

scandal ['skandl] *noun* **1** something that is considered shocking or disgraceful: *The price of such food is a scandal.* □ **scandale**

2 an outburst of public indignation caused by something shocking or disgraceful: *Her love affair caused a great scandal amongst the neighbours*; *They kept the matter secret, in order to avoid a scandal.* □ **scandale**

3 gossip: *all the latest scandal.* □ **ragots**

'**scandalize, 'scandalise** *verb* to shock or horrify: *Their behaviour used to scandalize the neighbours.* □ **scandaliser**

'**scandalous** *adjective* **1** shocking or disgraceful. □ **scandaleux**

2 (of stories *etc*) containing scandal. □ **à scandale**

'**scandalously** *adverb* in a disgraceful way. □ **scandaleusement**

scant [skant] *adjective* hardly enough; not very much: *scant attention*; *scant experience.* □ **insuffisant; peu abondant**

'**scanty** *adjective* small in size; hardly enough: *scanty clothing.* □ **minuscule, insuffisant**

'**scantiness** *noun.* □ **insuffisance**

'**scantily** *adverb: scantily dressed.* □ **insuffisamment**

scapegoat ['skeipgout] *noun* a person who is blamed or punished for the mistakes of others: *The manager of the football team was made a scapegoat for the team's failure, and was forced to resign.* □ **bouc émissaire**

scar [skaː] *noun* the mark that is left by a wound or sore: *a scar on the arm where the dog bit him.* □ **cicatrice**

■ *verb – past tense, past participle* **scarred** – to mark with a scar: *He recovered from the accident but his face was badly scarred.* □ **marquer d'une cicatrice**

scarce [skeəs] *adjective* not many or enough in number: *Paintings by this artist are very scarce*; *Food is scarce because of the drought.* □ **rare**

'**scarcely** *adverb* **1** only just; not quite: *Speak louder please – I can scarcely hear you*; *scarcely enough money to live on.* □ **à peine**

2 used to suggest that something is unreasonable: *You can scarcely expect me to work when I'm ill.* □ **sûrement (pas)**

'**scarcity** *noun* (a) lack or shortage: *a scarcity of work/ jobs*; *times of scarcity.* □ **rareté**

make oneself scarce to run away or stay away, especially in order to avoid trouble: *As soon as the police arrived, he made himself scarce.* □ **s'esquiver**

scare [skeə] *verb* to startle or frighten: *You'll scare the baby if you shout*; *His warning scared him into obeying him.* □ **faire peur (à)**

■ *noun* **1** a feeling of fear or alarm: *The noise gave me a scare.* □ **peur**

2 a feeling of fear or panic among a large number of people: *a smallpox scare.* □ **panique**

scared *adjective* frightened: *I'm scared of spiders*; *a scared little girl.* □ **qui a peur (de), apeuré**

'**scarecrow** *noun* a figure set up *eg* in a field, to scare away birds and stop them from eating the seeds *etc*. □ **épouvantail**

'**scaremonger** *noun* a person who spreads alarming rumours. □ **alarmiste**

scare away/off to make go away or stay away because of fear: *The birds were scared away by the dog.* □ **faire fuir**

scarf [skaːf] – *plurals* **scarves** [skaːvz], **scarfs** – *noun* a long strip of material to wear around one's neck. □ **écharpe**

scarlet ['skaːlit] *noun, adjective* (of) a bright red colour: *scarlet poppies*; *She blushed scarlet.* □ **écarlate**

scarlet fever an infectious fever *usually* with a sore throat and red rash. □ **scarlatine**

scathing ['skeiðiŋ] *adjective* cruel, bitter, or hurtful: *scathing comments*; *He was very scathing about her book.* □ **cinglant**

'**scathingly** *adverb.* □ **d'une manière cinglante**

scatter ['skatə] *verb* **1** to (make) go or rush in different directions: *The sudden noise scattered the birds*; *The crowds scattered when the bomb exploded.* □ **(se) disperser**

2 to throw loosely in different directions: *The load from the overturned truck was scattered over the road.* □ **éparpiller**

'**scattered** *adjective* occasional; not close together: *Scattered showers are forecast for this morning*; *The few houses in the valley are very scattered.* □ **épars**

'**scattering** *noun* a small amount scattered here and there: *a scattering of sugar.* □ **petite quantité**

'**scatterbrain** *noun* a forgetful or unreliable person. □ **écervelé, ée**

'**scatterbrained** *adjective.* □ **écervelé**

scavenge ['skavindʒ] *verb* to search for useful or usable objects, food *etc* amongst rubbish *etc*. □ **fouiller les poubelles**

'**scavenger** *noun.* □ **éboueur, euse; fouilleur, euse d'ordures**

scenario [siːn] *noun* **1** an outline of a play including the story, characters, scenery and costumes: *The director explained the whole scenario of the play to the actors.* □ **scénario**

2 a sequence or possible sequence of events: *What about a scenario where I take you to dinner then you take me to lunch?* □ **scénario**

scene [siːn] *noun* **1** the place where something real or imaginary happens: *A murderer sometimes revisits the scene of his crime*; *The scene of this opera is laid/set in Switzerland.* □ **scène**

2 an incident *etc* which is seen or remembered: *She recalled scenes from her childhood.* □ **incident**

3 a show of anger: *I was very angry but I didn't want to make a scene.* □ **scène**

4 a view of a landscape *etc*: *The sheep grazing on the hillside made a peaceful scene.* □ **tableau**

5 one part or division of a play *etc*: *The hero died in the first scene of the third act of the play.* □ **scène**

6 the setting or background for a play *etc*: *Scene-changing must be done quickly.* □ **décor(s)**

7 a particular area of activity: *the academic/business scene*. □ **scène**

'**scenery** *noun* **1** the painted background for a play *etc* on a stage: *The scenery looked rather shabby*. □ **décor(s)**
2 the general appearance of a landscape *etc*: *beautiful scenery*. □ **paysage**

'**scenic** *adjective* **1** of scenery, real or theatrical: *clever scenic effects in the film*. □ **scénique**
2 having beautiful scenery: *a scenic highway*. □ **touristique**

behind the scenes out of sight of the audience or public. □ **dans les coulisses**

come on the scene to arrive: *We were enjoying ourselves till she came on the scene*. □ **faire son apparition**

> **scenery** is never used in the plural.

scent [sent] *verb* **1** to discover by the sense of smell: *The dog scented a cat*. □ **flairer**
2 to suspect: *As soon as he came into the room I scented trouble*. □ **flairer**
3 to cause to smell pleasantly: *The roses scented the air*. □ **parfumer**
■ *noun* **1** a (*usually* pleasant) smell: *This rose has a delightful scent*. □ **senteur, odeur**
2 a trail consisting of the smell which has been left and may be followed: *The dogs picked up the man's scent and then lost it again*. □ **piste**
3 a liquid with a pleasant smell; perfume. □ **parfum**

'**scented** *adjective* (*negative* **unscented**) sweet-smelling: *scented soap*. □ **parfumé**

put/throw (someone) off the scent to give (a person) wrong information so that he or she will not find the person, thing *etc* he or she is looking for: *She told the police a lie in order to throw them off the scent*. □ **dérouter**

scepter *see* **sceptre**.

sceptic *see* **skeptic**.

sceptre ['septə] *noun* the ornamental rod carried by a monarch on ceremonial occasions as a sign of power. □ **sceptre**

schedule ['skedju:l] *noun* a statement of details, *especially* of timing of activities, or of things to be done: *a work schedule for next month*. □ **plan, horaire**
■ *verb* to plan the time of (an event *etc*): *The meeting is scheduled for 9:00*. □ **inscrire à l'horaire**

scheme [ski:m] *noun* **1** a plan or arrangement; a way of doing something: *a colour scheme for the room*; *There are various schemes for improving the roads*. □ **plan**
2 a (*usually* secret) dishonest plan: *His schemes to steal the money were discovered*. □ **combine**
■ *verb* to make (*especially* dishonest) schemes: *He was punished for scheming against the President*; *They have all been scheming for my dismissal*. □ **comploter**

'**schemer** *noun: He's a dangerous schemer*. □ **intrigant, ante**

'**scheming** *adjective* having or making (*usually* secret) dishonest plans: *a scheming woman*. □ **intrigant**

schizophrenia [skitsə'fri:niə] *noun* a form of insanity in which the patient becomes severely withdrawn from reality, has delusions *etc*. □ **schizophrénie**
,**schizo'phrenic** [-'fre-] *adjective*. □ **schizophrène**

scholar ['skolə] *noun* **1** a person of great knowledge and learning: *a fine classical scholar*. □ **érudit, ite**
2 a person who has been awarded a scholarship: *As a scholar, you will not have to pay college fees*. □ **boursier, ière**

'**scholarly** *adjective* having or showing knowledge: *a scholarly person*; *a scholarly book*. □ **érudit, savant**

'**scholarliness** *noun*. □ **érudition**

'**scholarship** *noun* **1** knowledge and learning: *a woman of great scholarship*. □ **érudition**
2 money awarded to a good student to enable him or her to go on with further studies: *She was awarded a travel scholarship*. □ **bourse**

school[1] [sku:l] *noun* **1** a place for teaching *especially* children: *She goes to the school*; *He's not at university – he's still at school*; *She's still in school*. □ **école**
2 the pupils of a school: *The behaviour of this school in public is sometimes not very good*. □ **école**
3 a series of meetings or a place for instruction *etc*: *She runs a sewing school*; *a driving school*. □ **cours; école**
4 a department of a university or college dealing with a particular subject: *the School of Mathematics*. □ **institut, département**
5 a university or college. □ **faculté**
6 a group of people with the same ideas *etc*: *There are two schools of thought about the treatment of this disease*. □ **école**
■ *verb* to train through practice: *We must school ourselves to be patient*. □ **apprendre à**

'**schoolbag** *noun* a bag for carrying books *etc* to and from school: *She had a schoolbag on her back*. □ **sac d'écolier**

'**schoolboy**, '**schoolgirl** *nouns* a boy or girl who goes to school. □ **écolier, ière**

'**schoolchild** – *plural* '**schoolchildren** – *noun* a child who goes to school. □ **écolier, ière**

'**school day** *noun* a day on which children go to school: *On a school day I get up at seven o'clock*. □ **jour d'école**

'**school days** *noun plural* the time of a person's life during which he goes to school. □ **années d'école**

'**schoolmaster** – *feminine* '**schoolmistress** – *noun* a person who teaches in school. □ **maître, maîtresse d'école**

'**schoolmate** *noun* a schoolfellow, *especially* a friend. □ **camarade de classe**

'**schoolteacher** *noun* a person who teaches in a school. □ **instituteur, trice**

school[2] [sku:l] *noun* a group of certain kinds of fish, whales or other water animals swimming about: *a school of porpoises*. □ **banc; bande**

schooner ['sku:nə] *noun* a type of fast sailing-ship with two or more masts. □ **goélette**

science ['saiəns] *noun* **1** knowledge gained by observation and experiment. □ **science**
2 a branch of such knowledge *eg* biology, chemistry, physics *etc*. □ **science**
3 these sciences considered as a whole: *My daughter prefers science to languages*. □ **sciences**

,**scien'tific** [-'ti-] *adjective* **1** of science: *scientific dis-*

coveries. □ **scientifique**

2 (*negative* **unscientific**) following the rules of science: *scientific methods.* □ **scientifique**

,scien'tifically [-'ti-] *adverb.* □ **scientifiquement**

'scientist *noun* a person who studies one or more branches of science. □ **scientifique**

science fiction stories dealing with future times on Earth or in space. □ **science-fiction**

scintillating ['sintileitiŋ] *adjective* witty; very clever and amusing: *She was in a scintillating mood; scintillating wit.* □ **étincelant**

scissors ['sizəz] *noun plural* a type of cutting instrument with two blades: *a pair of scissors.* □ **ciseaux**

scoff [skof] *verb* (*sometimes with* at) to express scorn: *She scoffed at my poem.* □ **se moquer (de)**

scold [skould] *verb* to criticize or blame loudly and angrily: *She scolded the child for coming home so late.* □ **gronder**

'scolding *noun* a stern or angry rebuke: *I got a scolding for doing careless work.* □ **réprimande**

scollop *see* scallop.

scone [skon, skoun] *noun* a kind of small, flat cake made of flour and fat: *scones and jam.* □ **petit pain au lait**

scoop [sku:p] *noun* 1 any of several types of spoon-like tool, used for lifting, serving *etc*: *a grain scoop; an ice cream scoop.* □ **pelle, cuiller**

2 a piece of news *etc* that one newspaper gets and prints before the others: *The reporter was sure that he had a scoop for his paper.* □ **primeur**

■ *verb* to move with, or as if with, a scoop: *He scooped the crumbs together with his fingers.* □ **ramasser**

scoot [sku:t] *verb* (*often with* along, away, past *etc*) to move (away) fast: *He scooted down the road.* □ **filer**

'scooter *noun* 1 a type of small motor-bicycle. □ **scooter**

2 a child's two-wheeled toy vehicle propelled by the foot. □ **trottinette**

scope [skoup] *noun* 1 (*often with* for) the opportunity or chance to do, use or develop: *There's no scope for originality in this job.* □ **possibilité**

2 the area or extent of an activity *etc*: *Few things are beyond the scope of a child's imagination.* ■ **limites**

scorch [skɔ:tʃ] *verb* to burn slightly: *She scorched her dress with the iron; That material scorches easily.* □ **brûler légèrement**

■ *noun* a mark made *eg* on cloth by scorching: *scorch-marks.* □ **brûlure légère**

'scorching *adjective* very hot. □ **brûlant**

score [skɔ:] – *plurals* scores, (after a number or a word signifying a quantity) score – *noun* 1 the number of points, goals *etc* gained in a game, competition *etc*: *The soccer score is 13 to 5.* □ **score**

2 a written piece of music showing all the parts for instruments and voices: *the score of an opera.* □ **partition**

3 a set or group of twenty: *There was barely a score of people there.* □ **vingtaine**

■ *verb* 1 to gain (goals *etc*) in a game *etc*: *He scored two goals before halftime.* □ **marquer**

2 (*sometimes with* off *or* out) to remove (*eg* a name) from *eg* a list by putting a line through it: *Please could*

you score my name off (the list)?; Is that word meant to be scored out? □ **rayer**

3 to keep score: *Will you score for us, please?* □ **marquer les points**

'scorer *noun* 1 a person who scores points, goals *etc*: *Our team scored two goals – Smith and Brown were the scorers.* □ **marqueur, euse (de buts)**

2 a person who writes down the score during *eg* a cricket match. □ **marqueur, euse**

'scoreboard *noun* a *usually* large board on which the score is shown at a cricket match, a quiz-program *etc*. □ **tableau**

scores (of) very many: *She received scores of letters about her radio program.* □ **des tas de**

settle old scores to get revenge for past wrongs: *I have some old scores to settle with you.* □ **régler des vieux comptes**

scorn [skɔ:n] *noun* contempt or disgust: *He looked at my drawing with scorn.* □ **mépris**

■ *verb* to show contempt for; to despise: *They scorned my suggestion.* □ **mépriser; dédaigner**

'scornful *adjective* 1 feeling or showing scorn: *a scornful expression/remark.* □ **méprisant**

2 making scornful remarks: *He was rather scornful about your book.* □ **méprisant**

'scornfully *adverb.* ■ **avec mépris**

'scornfulness *noun.* □ **mépris, dédain**

scorpion ['skɔ:piən] *noun* an animal of the same class as spiders that has a tail with a sting. □ **scorpion**

scotch [skotʃ] *verb* to put an end to (a rumour, plan *etc*): *They scotched his attempt to become the chairman.* □ **mettre fin à**

Scotch tape® [skotʃ teip] *noun* a kind of (transparent) adhesive tape: *She mended the torn page with Scotch tape.* □ **ruban adhésif**

scot-free [skot'fri:] *escape/get off/go scot free* to be or remain unhurt or unpunished: *The car was badly damaged in the accident, but the driver escaped scot-free.* □ **indemne**

Scottish [skotiʃ] *adjective* of Scotland or its inhabitants: *Many young children from Scotland learn Scottish country dancing; Scottish children practise playing the bagpipes too.* □ **écossais**

Scot *noun* a native of Scotland: *A Scot wears a plaid skirt called a kilt.* ■ **Écossais**

scoundrel ['skaundrəl] *noun* a very wicked person: *She knew he was a scoundrel even before she married him.* □ **vaurien**

scour¹ ['skauə] *verb* to clean by hard rubbing. □ **récurer**

scour² ['skauə] *verb* to make a thorough search of: *They scoured the woods for the child.* □ **fouiller**

scourge [skə:dʒ] *noun* a cause of great suffering to many people: *Vaccination has freed us from the scourge of smallpox.* □ **fléau**

scout [skaut] *noun* 1 a person, aircraft *etc* sent out to bring in information, spy *etc*: *The scouts reported that there were Indians nearby.* □ **éclaireur, euse**

2 (*with capital*: *formerly* **Boy Scout**) a member of the Scout Movement, an organization of boys formed to develop alertness and strong character. □ **scout**

■ *verb* to act as a scout or spy: *A party was sent ahead to scout.* □ **aller en reconnaissance**

scowl [skaul] *verb* to wrinkle the brow in displeasure: *He scowled furiously (at her).* □ **froncer les sourcils**

■ *noun* angry expression on the face. □ **air menaçant**

Scrabble® ['skrabl] *noun* a kind of word-building game. □ **scrabble**

scrabble ['skrabl] *verb* (*usually with* **about** *or* **around**) to make scratching noises or movements: *He was scrabbling about looking for the money he had dropped.* □ **gratter à la recherche de**

scraggy ['skragi] *adjective* unattractively thin: *a scraggy neck.* □ **décharné**

'**scragginess** *noun.* □ **aspect décharné**

scramble ['skrambl] *verb* 1 to crawl or climb quickly, using arms and legs: *They scrambled up the slope; He scrambled over the rocks.* □ **grimper à quatre pattes**

2 to move hastily: *She scrambled to her feet.* □ **bouger précipitamment**

3 (*with* **for**) to rush, or struggle with others, to get: *The boys scrambled for the ball.* □ (**se**) **bousculer pour avoir qqch.**

4 to distort (a telephone message *etc*) so that it can only be received and understood with a special receiver. □ **brouiller**

■ *noun* (*sometimes with* **for**) an act of scrambling; a rush or struggle: *There was a scramble for the best bargains.* □ **ruée, bousculade**

'**scrambler** *noun* a device for scrambling telephone messages. □ **brouilleur**

scrambled egg(s) beaten eggs cooked with milk and butter until thick. □ **œufs brouillés**

scrap[1] [skrap] *noun* 1 a small piece or fragment: *a scrap of paper.* □ **bout**

2 (*usually in plural*) a piece of food left over after a meal: *They gave the scraps to the dog.* □ **restes**

3 waste articles that are only valuable for the material they contain: *The old car was sold as scrap;* (*also adjective*) *scrap metal.* □ **ferraille**

4 a picture *etc* for sticking into a scrapbook. □ (**dé**)**coupure**

■ *verb – past tense, past participle* **scrapped** – to discard: *They scrapped the old television set; She decided to scrap the whole plan.* □ **mettre au rebut/rancart**

'**scrappy** *adjective* made up of bits and pieces: *a scrappy meal.* □ **fait de restes**

'**scrappily** *adverb.* □ **par fragments**

'**scrappiness** *noun.* □ **caractère décousu**

'**scrapbook** *noun* a book with blank pages on which to stick pictures *etc: The actor kept a scrapbook of newspaper cuttings about his career.* □ **album (de découpures, etc.)**

scrap heap a heap of waste material, unwanted objects *etc.* □ **tas de ferraille**

scrap[2] [skrap] *noun* a fight: *He tore his jacket in a scrap with another boy.* □ **bagarre**

■ *verb – past tense, past participle* **scrapped** – to fight: *The dogs were scrapping over a bone.* □ **se bagarrer**

scrape [skreip] *verb* 1 to rub against something sharp or rough, *usually* causing damage: *He drove too close to*

the wall *and scraped his car.* □ **érafler**

2 to clean, clear or remove by rubbing with something sharp: *He scraped his boots clean; He scraped the paint off the door.* □ **racler**

3 to make a harsh noise by rubbing: *Stop scraping your feet!* □ **traîner des pieds, grincer**

4 to move along something while just touching it: *The boat scraped against the landing-stage.* □ **frôler**

5 to make by scraping: *The dog scraped a hole in the sand.* □ **faire en grattant**

■ *noun* 1 an act or sound of scraping. □ **raclement, grattement**

2 a mark or slight wound made by scraping: *a scrape on the knee.* □ **éraflure, égratignure**

3 a situation that may lead to punishment: *The child is always getting into scrapes.* □ **ennuis**

'**scraper** *noun* a tool or instrument for scraping, *especially* one for scraping paint and wallpaper off walls *etc.* □ **grattoir**

scrape the bottom of the barrel to (be obliged to) use the least useful, efficient, person or thing available: *We're short of players for the game but including John would really be scraping the bottom of the barrel.* □ **racler les fonds de tiroir**

scrape through to only just avoid failing: *She scraped through her exams.* □ **passer de justesse**

scrape together/up to manage (with difficulty) to find (enough): *I'll try to scrape a team together for tomorrow's game.* □ **réunir (à grand-peine)**

scrappy *see* scrap[1].

scratch [skratʃ] *verb* 1 to mark or hurt by drawing a sharp point across: *The cat scratched my hand; How did you scratch your leg?; I scratched myself on a rose bush.* □ **égratigner**

2 to rub to relieve itching: *You should try not to scratch insect bites.* □ (**se**) **gratter**

3 to make by scratching: *She scratched her name on the rock with a sharp stone.* □ **graver**

4 to remove by scratching: *She threatened to scratch his eyes out.* □ **arracher**

5 to withdraw from a game, race *etc: That horse has been scratched.* □ **retirer**

■ *noun* 1 a mark, injury or sound made by scratching: *covered in scratches; a scratch at the door.* □ **éraflure; grattement**

2 a slight wound: *I hurt myself, but it's only a scratch.* □ **éraflure**

3 in certain races or competitions, the starting point for people with no handicap or advantage. □ **ligne de départ**

'**scratchy** *adjective.* □ **rugueux**

'**scratchiness** *noun.* □ **rugosité**

scratch the surface to deal too slightly with a subject: *We started to discuss the matter, but only had time to scratch the surface.* □ **effleurer (un sujet)**

start from scratch to start (an activity *etc*) from nothing, from the very beginning, or without preparation: *He now has a very successful business but he started from scratch.* □ **partir de zéro**

up to scratch at or to the required or satisfactory standard: *Your work does not come up to scratch.* □

à la hauteur

scrawl [skrɔːl] *verb* to write untidily or hastily: *I scrawled a hasty note to her.* □ **griffonner**

■ *noun* untidy or bad handwriting: *I hope you can read this scrawl.* □ **gribouillage**

scrawny ['skrɔːni] *adjective* thin, bony and wrinkled: *a scrawny neck.* □ **décharné**

'scrawniness *noun.* □ **caractère décharné**

scream [skriːm] *verb* to cry or shout in a loud shrill voice because of fear or pain or with laughter; to make a shrill noise: *He was screaming in agony; 'Look out!' she screamed; We screamed with laughter.* □ **hurler**

■ *noun* 1 a loud, shrill cry or noise. □ **cri perçant**

2 a cause of laughter: *She's an absolute scream.* □ **tordant**

screech [skriːtʃ] *verb* to make a harsh, shrill cry, shout or noise: *She screeched (abuse) at him; The car screeched to a halt.* □ **pousser des cris perçants; crisser**

■ *noun* a loud, shrill cry or noise: *screeches of laughter; a screech of brakes.* □ **cri perçant; crissement**

screed [skriːd] *noun* a long report, letter *etc*: *He wrote screeds about the conference.* □ **brique**

screen [skriːn] *noun* 1 a flat, movable, often folding, covered framework for preventing a person *etc* from being seen, for decoration, or for protection from heat, cold *etc*: *Screens were put around the patient's bed; a tapestry fire-screen.* □ **paravent**

2 anything that so protects *etc* a person *etc*: *He hid behind the screen of bushes; a smokescreen.* □ **écran**

3 the surface on which films or television pictures appear: *cinema/television/radar screen.* □ **écran**

■ *verb* 1 to hide, protect or shelter: *The tall grass screened him from view.* □ **cacher; abriter**

2 to make or show a cinema film. □ **porter à l'écran; projeter**

3 to test for loyalty, reliability *etc*. □ **passer au crible**

4 to test for a disease: *Women should be regularly screened for cancer.* □ **examiner**

'screenplay *noun* the script of a film. □ **scénario**

the screen cinema or television films: *You can see him on the screen quite often; (also adjective) screen actors.* □ **(de l')écran**

screw [skruː] *noun* 1 a type of nail that is driven into something by a firm twisting action: *I need four strong screws for fixing the cupboard to the wall.* □ **vis**

2 an action of twisting a screw *etc*: *He tightened it by giving it another screw.* □ **tour de vis**

■ *verb* 1 to fix, or be fixed, with a screw or screws: *He screwed the handle to the door; The handle screws on with these screws.* □ **(se) visser**

2 to fix or remove, or be fixed or removed, with a twisting movement: *Make sure that the hook is fully screwed in; He screwed off the lid.* □ **(dé)visser**

'screwdriver *noun* a kind of tool for turning screws. □ **tournevis**

have a screw loose (of a person) to be a bit mad. □ **être un peu fêlé**

put the screws on to use force or pressure in dealing with a person: *If he won't give us the money, we'll have to put the screws on (him).* □ **forcer la main à**

screw up 1 to twist or wrinkle (the face or features): *The baby screwed up its face and began to cry.* □ **(se) crisper**

2 to crumple: *She screwed up the letter.* □ **froisser**

scribble ['skribl] *verb* 1 to write quickly or carelessly: *He scribbled a message.* □ **griffonner**

2 to make meaningless marks with a pencil *etc*: *That child has scribbled all over the wall.* □ **gribouiller**

■ *noun* 1 untidy, careless handwriting. □ **gribouillis**

2 a mark *etc* made by scribbling. □ **gribouillage**

'scribbler *noun.* □ **gribouilleur, euse**

scrimp [skrimp] *verb* **scrimp and save** to be mean or very careful with money: *She scrimps and saves for her sons' education.* □ **économe; économiser sur tout**

script [skript] *noun* the text of a play, talk *etc*: *Have the actors all got their scripts?* □ **texte**

'scriptwriter *noun* a person who writes the texts for radio or television programs. □ **scénariste**

scripture ['skriptʃə] *noun* 1 the sacred writings of a religion: *Buddhist and Hindu scriptures.* □ **écriture(s)**

2 **the Bible.** □ **Écriture sainte**

'scriptural *adjective.* □ **biblique**

scroll [skrəul] *noun* a roll of paper or parchment with writing on it. □ **rouleau**

scrounge [skraundʒ] *verb* to get by begging from someone else: *May I scrounge some coffee?* □ **taper (de)**

'scrounger *noun.* □ **tapeur, euse**

scrub [skrʌb] – *past tense, past participle* **scrubbed** – *verb* 1 to rub hard in order to clean: *She's scrubbing the floor.* □ **frotter (à la brosse)**

2 to remove by scrubbing: *She scrubbed the mess off the carpet.* □ **enlever en frottant**

3 to cancel: *We planned to go but had to scrub the idea.* □ **annuler**

■ *noun* 1 an act of scrubbing. □ **récurage**

2 an area covered with low trees and dense bushes or shrubs: *There is thick scrub that you can't walk through without getting scratched and cut by branches and thorns.* □ **broussaille**

'scrubbrush *noun* a brush with short stiff bristles for scrubbing. □ **brosse dure (à récurer)**

scruff [skrʌf]: **the scruff of the neck** the back of the neck by which an animal can be grasped or lifted: *She picked up the cat by the scruff of the neck.* □ **peau (du cou)**

scruffy ['skrʌfi] *adjective* dirty and untidy: *a scruffy person; Their house is a bit scruffy.* □ **négligé, crasseux**

scrum [skrʌm] *noun* in rugby football, a struggle for the ball by the rival forwards hunched tightly around it. □ **mêlée**

scrupulous ['skruːpjuləs] *adjective* careful in attending to detail, doing nothing wrong, dishonest *etc*: *She is scrupulous in her handling of the accounts; scrupulous attention to instructions.* □ **scrupuleux**

'scrupulously *adverb.* □ **scrupuleusement**

'scrupulousness *noun.* □ **esprit scrupuleux**

scrutiny ['skruːtəni] *noun* careful, detailed examination or inspection: *Famous people live their lives under continuous public scrutiny.* □ **examen minutieux**

'scrutinize, 'scrutinise *verb* to examine carefully: *She* *scrutinized the coin with a magnifying-glass.* □ **scruter**

scuffle ['skʌfl] *noun* a confused fight *usually* between a few people using their fists, feet *etc*: *The two men quarrelled and there was a scuffle.* □ **bagarre, mêlée**

scull [skʌl] *noun* a short, light oar. □ **aviron**

■ *verb* to move a boat with a pair of these or with an oar worked at the stern of the boat. □ **ramer**

scullery ['skʌləri] – *plural* 'sculleries – *noun* a room for rough kitchen work such as cleaning pots, pans *etc*. □ **arrière-cuisine**

sculptor ['skʌlptə] – *feminine* 'sculptress – *noun* an artist who carves or models in stone, clay, wood *etc*. □ **sculpteur, eure**

'**sculpture** [-tʃə] *noun* 1 the art of modelling or carving figures, shapes *etc*: *She went to art school to study painting and sculpture.* □ **sculpture**

2 work done by a sculptor: *These statues are all examples of ancient Greek sculpture.* □ **sculpture**

scum [skʌm] *noun* 1 dirty foam that forms on the surface of a liquid: *The pond was covered with (a) scum.* □ **écume**

2 bad, worthless people: *People of that sort are the scum of the earth.* □ **rebut, crapule**

3 despicable, bad or worthless people: *Taylor's gang beat up children, took drugs, stole from the blind and were considered the scum of the earth.* □ **crapule**

4 someone or something low class or vulgar: *The X-rated video was scum.* □ **ordure**

scurf [skəːf] *noun* dandruff: *Some shampoos help to get rid of scurf.* □ **pellicules**

'**scurfy** *adjective*. □ **pelliculeux**

scurrilous ['skʌriləs, *(American)* 'skəː-] *adjective* insulting or abusive: *a scurrilous poem.* □ **grossier**

'**scurrilously** *adverb*. □ **grossièrement**

'**scurrilousness** *noun*. □ **grossièreté**

scurry ['skʌri] *verb* (*usually with* **away, off** *etc*) to run with short, quick steps: *It began to rain and we scurried home.* □ **se précipiter**

■ *noun* an act or a noise of hurrying: *a scurry of feet.* □ **galopade**

scuttle[1] ['skʌtl] *verb* to hurry with short, quick steps. □ **courir précipitamment**

scuttle[2] ['skʌtl] *verb* (of a ship's crew) to make a hole in (the ship) in order to sink it: *The sailors scuttled the ship to prevent it falling into enemy hands.* □ **saborder**

scythe [saið] *noun* a tool with a long, curved blade for cutting tall grass *etc*. □ **faux**

■ *verb* to cut (grass *etc*) with a scythe. □ **faucher**

sea [siː] *noun* 1 (*often with* **the**) the mass of salt water covering most of the Earth's surface: *I enjoy swimming in the sea; over land and sea; The sea is very deep here; (also adjective) A whale is a type of large sea animal.* □ **mer; marin**

2 a particular area of sea: *the Baltic Sea; These fish are found in tropical seas.* □ **mer**

3 a particular state of the sea: *mountainous seas.* □ **mer**

'**seaward(s)** *adverb* towards the sea; away from the land: *The yacht left the harbour and sailed seawards.* □ **vers le large**

'**seaboard** *noun* the seacoast: *the eastern seaboard of*

the United States. □ **littoral**

sea breeze a breeze blowing from the sea towards the land. □ **brise du large**

'**seafaring** *adjective* of work or travel on ships: *a seafaring man.* □ **marin**

'**seafood** *noun* fish, *especially* shellfish. □ **fruits de mer**

■ *adjective*: *seafood restaurants.* □ **de fruits de mer**

'**seafront** *noun* a promenade or part of a town with its buildings facing the sea. □ **front de mer**

'**sea-going** *adjective* designed and equipped for travelling on the sea: *a sea-going yacht.* □ **marin**

'**seagull** *noun* a gull. □ **mouette, goéland**

'**sea landing** *noun* a setting down or stop upon water: *The airplane ran out of fuel and made an emergency sea landing.* □ **amerrissage**

sea level the level of the surface of the sea used as a base from which the height of land can be measured: *three hundred metres above sea level.* □ **niveau de la mer**

'**sea lion** *noun* a type of large seal. □ **otarie**

'**seaman** – *plural* 'seamen – *noun* a sailor, *especially* a member of a ship's crew who is not an officer. □ **marin**

'**seaport** *noun* a port on the coast. □ **port de mer**

'**seashell** *noun* the (empty) shell of a sea creature. □ **coquillage**

'**seashore** *noun* the land close to the sea. □ **rivage**

'**seasick** *adjective* ill because of the motion of a ship at sea: *Were you seasick on the voyage?* □ **qui a le mal de mer**

'**seasickness** *noun*. □ **mal de mer**

'**seaside** *noun* (*usually with* **the**) a place beside the sea: *We like to go to the seaside in the summer.* □ **bord de mer**

'**seaweed** *noun* plants growing in the sea: *The beach was covered with seaweed.* □ **algue(s)**

'**seaworthy** *adjective* (*negative* **unseaworthy**) (of a ship) suitably built and in good enough condition to sail at sea. □ **en état de naviguer**

'**seaworthiness** *noun*. □ **bon état de navigabilité**

at sea 1 on a ship and away from land: *He has been at sea for four months.* □ **en mer**

2 puzzled or bewildered: *Can I help you? You seem all at sea.* □ **perdu**

go to sea to become a sailor: *He wants to go to sea.* □ **devenir marin**

put to sea to leave the land or a port: *They planned to put to sea the next day.* □ **prendre la mer**

seal[1] [siːl] *noun* 1 a piece of wax or other material bearing a design, attached to a document to show that it is genuine and legal. □ **sceau**

2 a piece of wax *etc* used to seal a parcel *etc*. □ **cachet**

3 (something that makes) a complete closure or covering: *Paint and varnish act as protective seals for woodwork.* □ **joint hermétique**

■ *verb* 1 to mark with a seal: *The document was signed and sealed.* □ **cacheter**

2 (*negative* **unseal**) to close completely: *She licked and sealed the envelope; All the air is removed from a can of food before it is sealed.* □ **sceller**

3 to settle or decide: *This mistake sealed his fate.* □

régler

'**sealing wax** *noun* a type of wax for sealing letters *etc*. □ **cire à cacheter**

seal of approval official approval: *Doctors have now given this new drug their seal of approval.* □ **approbation**

seal off to prevent all approach to, or exit from, (an area): *The police have sealed off the area where the murdered girl was found.* □ **mettre un cordon autour de**

set one's seal to to give one's authority or agreement to: *She set her seal to the proposals for reforms.* □ **autoriser**

seal² [siːl] *noun* any of several types of sea animal, some furry, living partly on land. □ **phoque**

'**sealskin** *noun, adjective* (of) the fur of the furry type of seal: *sealskin boots; made of sealskin.* □ **(en peau) de phoque**

seam [siːm] *noun* 1 the line formed by the sewing together of two pieces of cloth *etc*. □ **couture**

2 the line where two things meet or join: *Water was coming in through the seams of the boat.* □ **joint**

3 a thin line or layer of coal *etc* in the earth: *a coal seam.* □ **veine**

■ *verb* to sew a seam in: *I've pinned the skirt together but I haven't seamed it yet.* □ **faire une couture à**

'**seamstress** ['sem-] *noun* a woman who earns her living by sewing. □ **couturière**

the seamy side (of life) the roughest, most unpleasant side or aspect of human life. □ **l'envers du décor**

seaman *see* **sea.**

seance ['seiâns] *noun* a meeting of people trying to obtain messages from the spirits of dead people: *She claims to have spoken to Napoleon at a seance.* □ **séance de spiritisme**

search [saːtʃ] *verb* 1 (*often with* **for**) to look for something by careful examination: *Have you searched through your pockets thoroughly?; I've been searching for that book for weeks.* □ **chercher**

2 (of the police *etc*) to examine, looking for *eg* stolen goods: *He was taken to the police station, searched and questioned.* □ **fouiller**

■ *noun* an act of searching: *Her search did not take long.* □ **recherche**

'**searcher** *noun*. □ **chercheur, euse**

'**searching** *adjective* trying to find out the truth by careful examination: *She gave me a searching look.* □ **scrutateur**

'**searchingly** *adverb*. □ **d'un œil scrutateur**

'**searchlight** *noun* a strong light with a beam that can be turned in any direction, used *eg* to see enemy airplanes in the sky. □ **projecteur**

search party a group of people looking for a missing person: *When the climbers failed to return, a search party was sent out.* □ **expédition de secours**

search warrant a warrant giving legal permission to the police to search a house *etc*. □ **mandat de perquisition**

in search of searching for: *We went in search of a restaurant.* □ **à la recherche de**

season ['siːzn] *noun* 1 one of the main divisions of the year according to the regular variation of the weather, length of day *etc*: *The four seasons are spring, summer, autumn and winter; The monsoon brings the rainy season.* □ **saison**

2 the usual, proper or suitable time for something: *the football season.* □ **saison**

■ *verb* 1 to add salt, pepper, mustard *etc* to: *She seasoned the meat with plenty of pepper.* □ **assaisonner**

2 to let (wood) be affected by rain, sun *etc* until it is ready for use. □ **laisser vieillir, conditionner**

'**seasonable** *adjective* (*negative* **unseasonable**) (of weather) of the kind that is to be expected for a particular time of year. □ **(hors) de saison**

'**seasonal** *adjective* done at a particular season only: *seasonal work as a waitress; seasonal sports.* □ **saisonnier**

'**seasoned** *adjective* experienced: *seasoned political campaigners.* □ **expérimenté**

'**seasoning** *noun* something used to season food: *Salt and pepper are used as seasonings.* □ **assaisonnement**

season ticket a ticket (*usually* for travel) that can be used repeatedly during a certain period: *a three-month season ticket.* □ **(carte d')abonnement**

in season (of food) available, ready for eating: *That fruit is not in season just now.* □ **de saison**

out of season not in season. □ **hors de saison**

seat [siːt] *noun* 1 something for sitting on: *Are there enough seats for everyone?* □ **siège**

2 the part of a chair *etc* on which the body sits: *This chair-seat is broken.* □ **siège**

3 (the part of a garment covering) the buttocks: *I've got a sore seat after all that horse riding; a hole in the seat of his trousers.* □ **derrière; fond**

4 a place in which a person has a right to sit: *two seats for the play; a seat in Parliament; a seat on the board of the company.* □ **place; siège**

5 a place that is the centre of some activity *etc*: *Universities are seats of learning.* □ **haut lieu**

■ *verb* 1 to cause to sit down: *I seated him in the armchair.* □ **(faire) asseoir**

2 to have seats for: *Our table seats eight.* □ **permettre tant de places assises**

-**seater** having seats for: *The bus is a thirty-seater.* □ **à (...) places**

'**seating** *noun* the supply or arrangement of seats: *She arranged the seating for the lecture.* □ **répartition des places**

seat belt in a car, airplane *etc*, a safety-belt which will hold a person in his seat in an accident *etc*. □ **ceinture de sécurité**

take a seat to sit down: *Please take a seat!* □ **s'asseoir**

secluded [si'kluːdid] *adjective* not able to be seen, talked to *etc* by other people; far away from other people *etc*: *a secluded cottage.* □ **retiré**

se'clusion [-ʒən] *noun* the state of being secluded; privacy: *She wept in the seclusion of her own room.* □ **isolement; solitude**

second¹ ['sekənd] *adjective* 1 next after, or following, the first in time, place *etc*: *February is the second month of*

the year; She finished the race in second place. □
deuxième, second
2 additional or extra: *a second house in the country.* □
deuxième
3 lesser in importance, quality *etc*: *She's a member of the school's second swimming team.* □ **deuxième**
■ *adverb* next after the first: *He came second in the race.* □ **deuxième**
■ *noun* **1** a second person, thing *etc*: *You're the second to arrive.* □ **deuxième**
2 a person who supports and helps a person who is fighting in a boxing match *etc*. □ **soigneur, euse**
■ *verb* to agree with (something said by a previous speaker), *especially* to do so formally: *He proposed the motion and I seconded it.* □ **appuyer**
'**secondary** *adjective* **1** coming after, and at a more advanced level than, primary: *secondary education.* □
secondaire
2 lesser in importance: *a matter of secondary importance.* □ **secondaire**
■ *noun – plural* '**secondaries** – a secondary school. □
(école) secondaire
'**seconder** *noun* a person who seconds. □ **personne qui appuie une motion**
'**secondly** *adverb* in the second place: *I have two reasons for not buying the house – firstly, it's too big, and secondly it's too far from town.* □ **deuxièmement**
secondary colours colours got by mixing primary colours: *Orange and purple are secondary colours.* □
couleurs complémentaires
secondary school a school where subjects are taught at a more advanced level than at primary school. □ **école secondaire**
,**second-'best** *noun, adjective* next after the best; not the best: *She wore her second-best hat; I want your best work – your second-best is not good enough.* □
deuxième
,**second-'class** *adjective* **1** of or in the class next after or below the first; not of the very best quality: *a second-class restaurant; He gained a second-class honours degree in French.* □ **de deuxième classe/catégorie**
2 (for) travelling in a part of a train *etc* that is not as comfortable or luxurious as some other part: *a second-class passenger; His ticket is second-class; (also adverb) I'll be travelling second-class.* □ **(en/de) deuxième classe**
,**second-'hand** *adjective* previously used by someone else: *second-hand clothes.* □ **d'occasion, usagé**
second lieutenant a person of the rank below lieutenant: *Second Lieutenant Jones.* □ **sous-lieutenant, ante**
,**second-'rate** *adjective* inferior: *The play was pretty second-rate.* □ **médiocre**
second sight the power of seeing into the future or into other mysteries: *They asked a woman with second sight where the dead body was.* □ **clairvoyance**
second thoughts a change of opinion, decision *etc*: *I'm having second thoughts about selling the piano.* □
changement d'avis
second hand through or from another person: *I heard the news second hand.* □ **de qqn d'autre**

come off second best to be the loser in a struggle: *That cat always comes off second best in a fight.* □ **se faire battre**
every second week, month *etc* (on or during) alternate weeks, months *etc*: *She comes in every second day.* □
tous les deux (...)
second to none better than every other of the same type: *As a portrait painter, she is second to none.* □ **qui n'a pas son pareil**
second² ['sekənd] *noun* **1** the sixtieth part of a minute: *She ran the race in three minutes and forty-two seconds.* □ **seconde**
2 a short time: *I'll be there in a second.* □ **seconde**
secret ['si:krit] *adjective* hidden from, unknown to, or not told to, other people: *a secret agreement; She kept her illness secret from everybody.* □ **secret**
■ *noun* **1** something which is, or must be kept, secret: *The date of their marriage is a secret; industrial secrets.* □ **secret**
2 a hidden explanation: *I wish I knew the secret of her success.* □ **secret**
'**secrecy** *noun* the state of being or the act of keeping secret. □ **secret**
'**secretive** [-tiv] *adjective* inclined to conceal one's activities, thoughts *etc*: *secretive behaviour.* □ **réservé**
'**secretively** *adverb*. □ **d'une façon très réservée**
'**secretiveness** *noun*. □ **réserve**
'**secretly** *adverb* in such a way that others do not know, see *etc*: *She secretly copied the numbers down in her notebook.* □ **secrètement**
secret agent a spy. □ **agent secret, agente secrète**
secret police a police force whose activities are kept secret and which is concerned mostly with political crimes. □ **police secrète**
in secret secretly: *This must all be done in secret.* □ **en/ dans le secret**
keep a secret not to tell (something secret) to anyone else: *You can't trust her to keep a secret.* □ **garder un secret**
secretary ['sekrətəri] – *plural* '**secretaries** – *noun* **1** a person employed to write letters, keep records and make business arrangements *etc* for another person: *He dictated a letter to his secretary.* □ **secrétaire**
2 a (sometimes unpaid) person who deals with the official business of an organization *etc*: *The secretary read out the minutes of the society's last meeting.* □ **secrétaire**
,**secre'tarial** [-'teə-] *adjective* of a secretary or his/her duties: *trained in secretarial work; at secretarial college.* □ **de secrétaire/secrétariat**
secrete [si'kri:t] *verb* **1** (of a gland or similar organ of the body) to separate (a fluid) from the blood, store it, and give it out: *The liver secretes bile.* □ **sécréter**
2 to hide: *He secreted the money under his mattress.* □
cacher
se'cretion [-ʃən] *noun* **1** the process of secreting a fluid. □ **sécrétion**
2 a substance produced by this process: *Saliva and urine are secretions.* □ **sécrétion**
sect [sekt] *noun* a group of people within a larger, *especially* religious, group, having views different from those

of the rest of the group. □ **secte**

sec'tarian *adjective* **1** concerned with, *especially* the narrow interests of, a sect or sects: *sectarian loyalties.* □ **sectaire**

2 caused by membership of a sect: *a sectarian murder.* □ **sectaire**

■ *noun* a member of a sect. □ **membre d'une secte**

section ['sekʃən] *noun* **1** a part or division: *She divided the orange into sections*; *There is disagreement in one section of the community*; *the accounts section of the business.* □ **section**

2 a view of the inside of anything when, or as if, it is cut right through or across: *a section of the stem of a flower.* □ **coupe**

'sectional *adjective.* □ **démontable**

sector ['sektə] *noun* a section of a circle whose sides are a part of the circumference and two straight lines drawn from the centre to the circumference. □ **secteur**

secular ['sekjulə] *adjective* not spiritual or religious: *secular art/music.* □ **profane**

secure [si'kjuə] *adjective* **1** (*often with* **against** *or* **from**) safe; free from danger, loss *etc*: *Is your house secure against burglary?*; *He went on holiday, secure in the knowledge that he had done well in the exam.* □ **sûr; assuré**

2 firm, fastened, or fixed: *Is that door secure?* □ **solide**

3 definite; not likely to be lost: *She has had a secure offer of a job*; *He has a secure job.* □ **ferme; sûr**

■ *verb* **1** (with **against** *or* **from** (something bad)) to guarantee or make safe: *Keep your jewellery in the bank to secure it against theft.* □ **protéger (de)**

2 to fasten or make firm: *He secured the boat with a rope.* □ **attacher**

se'curely *adverb.* □ **solidement; sûrement**

se'curity *noun* the state of being, or making safe, secure, free from danger *etc*: *the security of a happy home*; *This alarm system will give the factory some security*; *There has to be tight security at a prison*; (*also adjective*) *the security forces; a security guard.* □ **(de) sécurité**

security risk a person considered not safe to be given a job involving knowledge of secrets because he might give secret information to an enemy *etc*. □ **personne pas sûre**

sedan [si'dan] *noun* (*American*) a covered car for four or more people. □ **berline**

sedate[1] [si'deit] *adjective* calm, serious and dignified: *a sedate, middle-aged woman.* □ **posé**

se'dately *adverb.* □ **posément**

se'dateness *noun.* □ **manière posée**

sedate[2] [si'deit] *verb* to give a sedative: *The doctor sedated her with some pills.* □ **donner un sédatif à qqn**

sedative ['sedətiv] *noun, adjective* (a medicine, drug *etc*) having a soothing or calming effect: *This medicine will have a sedative effect.* □ **calmant**

sedentary ['sedntəri] *adjective* (of a job, way of living *etc*) requiring or involving much sitting and little exercise: *a sedentary job in a tax office.* □ **sédentaire**

sediment ['sedimənt] *noun* the material that settles at the bottom of a liquid: *Her feet sank into the sediment on the river bed.* □ **sédiment**

seduce [si'djuːs] *verb* to persuade or attract into doing, thinking *etc* (something, *especially* something foolish or wrong): *She was seduced by the attractions of the big city.* □ **séduire**

se'duction [-'dʌk-] *noun* something that tempts or attracts: *the seductions of life in the big city.* □ **séduction**

seductive [si'dʌktiv] *adjective* tempting, attractive or charming: *a seductive melody.* □ **séduisant**

sedulous ['sedjuləs] *adjective* (of a person or his or her efforts *etc*) steady, earnest and persistent: *He worked with sedulous concentration.* □ **assidu**

'sedulously *adverb.* □ **avec assiduité**

see[1] [siː] – *past tense* **saw** [soː]: *past participle* **seen** – *verb* **1** to have the power of sight: *After six years of blindness, he found he could see.* □ **voir**

2 to be aware of by means of the eye: *I can see her in the garden.* □ **voir**

3 to look at: *Did you see that play on television?* □ **regarder**

4 to have a picture in the mind: *I see many difficulties ahead.* □ **entrevoir**

5 to understand: *She didn't see the point of the joke.* □ **comprendre**

6 to investigate: *Leave this here and I'll see what I can do for you.* □ **voir**

7 to meet: *I'll see you at the usual time.* □ **voir**

8 to accompany: *I'll see you home.* □ **accompagner**

see about to attend to, or deal with: *I'll see about this tomorrow.* □ **s'occuper de**

seeing that since; considering that: *Seeing that he's ill, he's unlikely to come.* □ **étant donné que**

see off to accompany (a person starting on a journey) to the airport, railway station *etc* from which he is to leave: *He saw me off at the station.* □ **reconduire**

see out to last longer than: *These old trees will see us all out.* □ **survivre à**

see through 1 to give support to (a person, plan *etc*) until the end is reached: *I'd like to see the job through.* □ **soutenir (qqn, qqch.) jusqu'au bout**

2 not to be deceived by (a person, trick *etc*): *We soon saw through him and his little plan.* □ **pénétrer (les intentions de qqn)**

see to to attend to or deal with: *I must see to the baby.* □ **s'occuper de**

I, we *etc* **will see** I, we *etc* shall wait and consider the matter later: *'May I have a new bicycle?' 'We'll see.'* □ **on verra**

see[2] [siː] *noun* the district over which a bishop or archbishop has authority. □ **évêché; archevêché**

seed [siːd] *noun* **1** the (part of) the fruit of a tree, plant *etc* from which a new plant may be grown: *sunflower seeds; grass seed.* □ **graine, pépin, semence**

2 the beginning from which anything grows: *There was already a seed of doubt in her mind.* □ **germe**

3 (in a sporting competition *etc*) a seeded player. □ **tête de série**

■ *verb* **1** (of a plant) to produce seed: *A plant seeds after it has flowered.* □ **monter en graine**

2 in golf, tennis *etc*, to arrange (good players) in a competition so that they do not compete against each other till the later rounds. □ **classer**

'**seeded** *adjective* having been seeded: *a seeded player.* □ **classé**

'**seedling** [-liŋ] *noun* a young plant just grown from a seed: *Don't walk on the lettuce seedlings!* □ **semis, plant**

'**seedy** *adjective* 1 shabby: *a rather seedy hotel.* □ **minable**

2 ill or unhealthy: *He's feeling a bit seedy.* □ **pas dans son assiette**

'**seediness** *noun*. □ **aspect miteux**

'**seedbed** *noun* ground prepared for growing seeds. □ **semis**

go to seed 1 (of a person) to become careless about one's clothes and appearance: *Don't let yourself go to seed when you reach middle age!* □ **se négliger**

2 (of a place) to become rather shabby and uncared for: *This part of town has gone to seed recently.* □ **aller à vau-l'eau**

3 (*also* **run to seed**) (of a plant) to produce seeds after flowering. □ **monter en graine**

seek [siːk] – *past tense, past participle* **sought** [soːt] – *verb* 1 (*sometimes with* **for**) to try to find, get or achieve: *He is seeking (for) an answer; You should seek your lawyer's advice; She's seeking fame in the world of television.* □ **tâcher de; rechercher**

2 to try: *These men are seeking to destroy the government.* □ **chercher à**

sought after wanted; asked for: *This book is much sought after; a much sought-after book.* □ **très recherché**

seem [siːm] *verb* to have the appearance or give the impression of being or doing: *A thin person always seems (to be) taller than he or she really is; She seems kind; He seemed to hesitate for a minute.* □ **sembler, paraître**

'**seeming** *adjective* existing in appearance, though not usually in reality: *her seeming indifference.* □ **apparent**

'**seemingly** *adverb* apparently; according to report: *Seemingly, her mother is very ill.* □ **apparemment**

'**seemly** *adjective* (*negative* **unseemly**) (of behaviour *etc*) suitable, proper or decent: *seemly conduct.* □ **convenable**

seen *see* see[1].

seep [siːp] *verb* (of liquids) to flow slowly *eg* through a very small opening: *Blood seeped out through the bandage around his head; All his confidence seeped away.* □ **filtrer**

seer [siə] *noun* a prophet. □ **prophète, prophétesse**

seesaw ['siːsoː] *noun* a long flat piece of wood, metal *etc*, balanced on a central support so that one end of it goes up as the other goes down: *The boy fell off the seesaw in the park.* □ **bascule**

■ *verb* to move up and down like a seesaw: *The boat seesawed on the crest of the wave.* □ **(se) balancer**

seething ['siːðiŋ] *adjective* 1 (*sometimes with* **with**) very crowded: *a seething mass of people; The beach is seething with people.* □ **grouillant (de)**

2 (*usually with* **with**) very excited or agitated: *seething with excitement/anger.* □ **bouillonnant (de)**

3 very angry: *He was seething when he left the meeting.* □ **furibond**

segment ['segmənt] *noun* 1 a part or section: *He divided the orange into segments.* □ **segment**

2 a part of *eg* a circle cut off by a straight line. □ **segment**

segmented [seg'mentid] *adjective* divided into segments: *An insect has a segmented body.* □ **formé de segments**

segregate ['segrigeit] *verb* to separate from others; to keep (people, groups *etc*) apart from each other: *At the swimming pool, the sexes are segregated.* □ **séparer**

,**segre'gation** [-ʃən] *noun*. □ **ségrégation**

seismic ['saizmik] *adjective* of earthquakes: *seismic disturbances.* □ **sismique**

seis'mology [-'molədʒi] *noun* the science or study of earthquakes. □ **sismologie**

,**seismo'logical** [-'lo-] *adjective*. □ **sismologique**

seis'mologist *noun*. □ **sismologue**

seize [siːz] *verb* 1 to take or grasp suddenly, *especially* by force: *She seized the gun from him; He seized her by the arm; He seized the opportunity of leaving.* □ **saisir**

2 to take, *especially* by force or by law: *The police seized the stolen property.* □ **saisir**

---

seize is spelt with **-ei-** (not **-ie-**).

'**seizure** [-ʒə] *noun* the act of seizing: *seizure of property.* □ **saisie**

seize on to accept with enthusiasm: *I suggested a cycling holiday, and he seized on the idea.* □ **sauter sur**

seize up (of machinery *etc*) to get stuck and stop working: *The car seized up yesterday.* □ **(se) bloquer**

seldom ['seldəm] *adverb* rarely; not often: *I've seldom experienced such rudeness.* □ **rarement**

select [sə'lekt] *verb* to choose or pick from among a number: *She selected a blue dress from the wardrobe; You have been selected to represent us on the committee.* □ **sélectionner**

■ *adjective* 1 picked or chosen carefully: *A select group of friends was invited.* □ **choisi**

2 intended only for carefully chosen (*usually* rich or upper-class) people: *That school is very select.* □ **sélect**

se'lection [-ʃən] *noun* 1 the act or process of selecting or being selected: *a selection of boys for the choir;* (*also adjective*) *a selection committee.* □ **sélection; (de) choix**

2 a collection or group of things that have been selected: *a selection of verses/fruit.* □ **sélection**

se'lective [-tiv] *adjective* having the power of choice and using it, *especially* carefully: *She is very selective about clothes.* □ **sélectif**

sel'lectively *adverb*. □ **sélectivement**

se'lectiveness *noun*. □ **sélectivité**

se'lector *noun* a person who chooses, *especially* athletes, a team *etc*: *The selectors have announced the cricket team to meet Australia.* □ **sélectionneur, euse**

self [self] – *plural* **selves** [selvz] – *noun* 1 a person's own body and personality. □ **la personne**

2 one's own personal interests or advantage: *He always thinks first of self.* □ **soi-même**

'**selfish** *adjective* (*negative* **unselfish**) thinking of one's own pleasure or good and not considering other people: *a selfish person/attitude.* □ **égoïste** '**selfishly** adverb. □ **égoïstement**

'**selfishness** noun. □ **égoïsme**

'**selfless** adjective utterly unselfish: *As a soldier, he showed selfless devotion to duty.* □ **désintéressé**

'**selflessly** adverb. □ **sans penser à soi**

'**selflessness** noun. □ **désintéressement**

self- [self] **1** showing that the person or thing acting is acting upon himself, herself or itself, as in **self-respect.** □ **(respect) de soi**
2 showing that the thing is acting automatically, as in **self-closing doors.** □ **auto-... automatique**
3 by oneself, as in **self-made.** □ **auto-... autodidactique**
4 in, within *etc* oneself or itself, as in **self-centred.** □ **égo-... égocentrique**

self-addressed [selfə'drest] adjective addressed to oneself: *a stamped, self-addressed envelope.* □ **adressé à soi-même**

self-assurance [selfə'ʃuərəns] noun self-confidence. □ **assurance**

,**self-as'sured** adjective. □ **sûr de soi**

self-centred [self'sentəd] adjective interested only in one's own affairs; selfish: *She's too self-centred to take any interest in my troubles.* □ **égocentrique**

self-closing [self'klouziŋ] adjective which close automatically: *self-closing doors.* □ **à fermeture automatique**

self-coloured, self-colored [self'kʌləd] adjective of one colour all over: *a self-coloured carpet.* □ **uni**

self-confidence [self'konfidəns] noun belief or trust in one's own powers: *You need plenty of self-confidence to be a good airline pilot.* □ **confiance en soi**

,**self-'confident** adjective. □ **sûr de soi**

,**self-'confidently** adverb. □ **avec assurance**

self-conscious [self'konʃəs] adjective too easily becoming shy or embarrassed when in the presence of others: *She'll never be a good teacher – she's too self-conscious.* □ **intimidé**

'**self-'consciously** adverb. □ **avec gêne**

,**self-'consciousness** noun. □ **gêne, embarras**

self-control [selfkən'troul] noun control of oneself, one's emotions and impulses: *She behaved with admirable self-control although she was very angry.* □ **maîtrise de soi, sang-froid**

self-defence, self-defense [selfdi'fens] noun defence of one's own body, property *etc* against attack: *He killed his attacker in self-defence.* □ **légitime défense**

self-employed [selfim'ploid] adjective working for oneself and not employed by someone else: *a self-employed dressmaker.* □ **(travailleur, euse) indépendant**

self-esteem [selfi'sti:m] noun a person's respect for himself or herself: *My self-esteem suffered when I failed the exam.* □ **amour-propre**

self-evident [self'evidənt] adjective clear enough to need no proof: *It is self-evident that we need food to stay alive.* □ **qui va de soi**

self-explanatory [selfik'splanətəri] adjective needing no explanation: *I think the pictures in the instruction manual are self-explanatory.* □ **qui se passe d'explication**

self-government [self'gʌvəmənt] noun government by the people of the country without outside control. □ **autonomie**

self-important [selfim'po:tənt] adjective having too high an opinion of one's own importance: *a self-important little man.* □ **suffisant**

,**self-im'portance** noun. □ **suffisance**

self-indulgent [selfin'dʌldʒənt] adjective too ready to satisfy one's own desires: *self-indulgent habits/behaviour.* □ **qui ne se refuse rien**

,**self-in'dulgence** noun. □ **amour de son propre confort**

self-inflicted [selfin'fliktid] adjective (of wounds *etc*) done to oneself: *The doctors proved that the man's injuries were self-inflicted.* □ **volontaire**

self-interest [self'intrəst] noun consideration only for one's own aims and advantages: *He acted out of self-interest.* □ **intérêt personnel**

selfish, selfless see **self.**

self-made [self'meid] adjective owing wealth or important position to one's efforts, not to advantages given by birth, education *etc*: *a self-made man.* □ **qui a réussi par lui-même**

self-portrait [self'po:trit] noun a person's portrait or description of himself or herself: *Rembrandt painted several self-portraits; The man described is a self-portrait of the author.* □ **autoportrait**

self-possessed [selfpə'zest] adjective calm, and able to act confidently in an emergency: *a calm, self-possessed person.* □ **maître de soi**

,**self-pos'session** [-ʃən] noun. □ **sang-froid**

self-preservation ['selfprezə'veiʃən] noun the natural inclination towards the protection of oneself from harm, danger *etc*: *Self-preservation is our strongest instinct.* □ **instinct de conservation**

self-raising [self'reiziŋ] adjective (of flour) already containing an ingredient to make cakes *etc* rise. □ **à levure incorporée**

self-respect [selfri'spekt] noun respect for oneself and concern for one's reputation: *Well-known personalities should have more self-respect than to take part in television advertising.* □ **respect de soi**

,**self-re'specting** adjective. □ **qui se respecte**

self-sacrifice [self'sakrifais] noun the act of sacrificing one's own desires *etc* in order to help others: *With great self-sacrifice, she gave up the holiday to care for her sick aunt.* □ **abnégation**

self-satisfied [self'satisfaid] adjective too easily pleased with oneself and one's achievements: *'Our house is the cleanest in the row,' she said in her self-satisfied way.* □ **suffisant**

'**self-,satis'faction** [-'fakʃən] noun. □ **suffisance**

self-service [self'sə:vis] noun an arrangement by which customers themselves collect the goods that they want to buy; (*also adjective*): *a self-service restaurant.* □ **libre-service**

self-sufficient [selfsə'fiʃənt] adjective not dependent on others for help *etc*: *a self-sufficient community.* □ **autosuffisant**

,**self-suf'ficiency** noun. □ **autosuffisance**

self-willed [self'wild] adjective determined to do, or have, what one wants: *I've had enough of that self-willed* *little brat.* □ **volontaire**

sell [sel] – *past tense, past participle* **sold** [sould] – *verb*
1 to give something in exchange for money: *He sold her a car; I've got some books to sell.* □ **vendre**
2 to have for sale: *The farmer sells milk and eggs.* □ **vendre**
3 to be sold: *Her book sold well.* □ **se vendre**
4 to cause to be sold: *Packaging sells a product.* □ **faire vendre**

,**sell-out** *noun* **1** an event, *especially* a concert, for which all the tickets are sold: *Her concert was a sell-out.* □ **(concert, etc.) à guichets fermés**
2 a betrayal: *The gang realized it was a sell-out and tried to escape.* □ **trahison**

be sold on to be enthusiastic about: *I'm sold on the idea of a holiday in Canada.* □ **être emballé (par)**

be sold out 1 to be no longer available: *The second-hand records are all sold out; The concert is sold out.* □ **épuisé; à guichets fermés**
2 to have no more available to be bought: *We are sold out of children's socks.* □ **être en rupture de stock**

sell down the river to betray: *The gang was sold down the river by one of its associates.* □ **trahir**

sell off to sell quickly and cheaply: *They're selling off their old stock.* □ **liquider**

sell out 1 (*sometimes with* **of**) to sell all of something: *We sold out our entire stock.* □ **liquider**
2 to be all sold: *The second-hand records sold out within minutes of the sale starting.* □ **être épuisé**

selves *see* **self.**

semaphore ['semǝfoɹ] *noun* a system of signalling with flags held in each hand: *She signalled the message to them in semaphore.* □ **sémaphore**

semblance ['semblǝns] *noun* an appearance or likeness: *I have to coach them into some semblance of a football team by Saturday.* □ **semblant**

semi- [semi] **1** half, as in **semicircle.** □ **demi-, semi-**
2 partly, as in **semi-conscious.** □ **à demi-**

semicircle ['semisɔːkl] *noun* a half circle: *The chairs were arranged in a semicircle around the speaker.* □ **demi-cercle**

,**semi'circular** [-'sǝːkju-] *adjective.* □ **semi-circulaire**

semicolon ['semikoulǝn] *noun* the punctuation mark (;) used *especially* to separate parts of a sentence which have more independence than clauses separated by a comma: *She wondered what to do; She couldn't go back; he couldn't borrow money.* □ **point-virgule**

semi-conscious [semi'konʃǝs] *adjective* partly conscious: *She was semi-conscious when they took her to the hospital.* □ **à demi conscient**

,**semi'consciousness** *noun.* □ **demi-conscience**

semi-detached [semidi'tatʃt] *adjective* (of a house) joined to another house on one side but separate on the other: *a semi-detached bungalow.* □ **jumelé**

semi-final [semi'fainl] *noun* a match, round *etc* immediately before the final: *She reached the semifinals of the competition.* □ **demi-finale**

,**semi'finalist** *noun* a person, team *etc* competing in a semi-final. □ **demi-finaliste**

seminary ['seminǝri] – *plural* **'seminaries** – *noun* a train-

ing college for Roman Catholic priests. □ **séminaire**

semi-precious [semi'preʃǝs] *adjective* (of a stone) having some value, but not considered a gem: *garnets and other semi-precious stones.* □ **(pierre) semi-précieuse**

semitone ['semitoun] *noun* half a tone in the musical scale: *F sharp is a semitone above F natural.* □ **demi-ton**

semolina [semǝ'liːnǝ] *noun* hard particles of wheat used *eg* in milk pudding. □ **semoule**

senate ['senǝt] *noun* **1** a lawmaking body, *especially* the upper house of the parliament in some countries. □ **sénat**
2 in ancient Rome, the chief legislative and administrative body. □ **sénat**

'**senator** *noun* **1** (*sometimes abbreviated to* **Sen.** *in titles*) a member of a lawmaking senate: *Senator Smith.* □ **sénateur, trice**
2 a member of a Roman senate. □ **sénateur**

send [send] – *past tense, past participle* **sent** [sent] – *verb* **1** to cause or order to go or be taken: *The teacher sent the disobedient boy to the headmaster; She sent me this book.* □ **envoyer**
2 to move rapidly or with force: *He sent the ball right into the goal.* □ **envoyer**
3 to cause to go into a certain, *usually* bad, state: *The news sent them into a panic.* □ **précipiter**

'**sender** *noun* a person who sends *eg* a letter. □ **expéditeur, trice**

send away for to order by post: *I've sent away for some things that I saw in the catalogue.* □ **commander (par la poste)**

send for to ask to come, or order to be delivered: *Her son was sent for; I'll send for a taxi.* □ **envoyer chercher, faire venir**

send in to offer or submit, *eg* for a competition: *She sent in three drawings for the competition.* □ **soumettre**

send off to accompany (a person) to the place, or be at the place, where he will start a journey: *A great crowd gathered at the station to send the football team off* (*noun* '**send-off**). □ **venir dire au revoir (à); adieux**

send off for to send away for. □ **commander (par la poste)**

send out 1 to distribute *eg* by post: *A notice has been sent out to all employees.* □ **envoyer (par la poste)**
2 (*eg* of plants) to produce: *This plant has sent out some new shoots.* □ **produire**

send (someone) packing/send (someone) about his business to send (a person) away firmly and without politeness: *He tried to borrow money from me again, but I soon sent him packing.* □ **envoyer promener**

senile ['siːnail] *adjective* showing the feebleness or childishness of old age: *a senile old woman.* □ **sénile**

se'nility [sǝ'ni-] *noun.* □ **sénilité**

senior ['siːnjǝ] *noun, adjective* (a person who is) older in years or higher in rank or authority: *Jodie is senior to me by two years; She is two years my senior; senior army officers.* □ **aîné; supérieur**

■ *adjective* (*often abbreviated to* **Snr, Sr** *or* **Sen.** *when written*) used to indicate the father of a person who is alive and who has the same name: *John Jones Senior.* □ **père**

,**seni'ority** [-ni'o-] *noun* the state of being senior: *The* *officers sat at the table in order of seniority.* □ **ancienneté**

senior citizen a person who has passed retirement age. □ **personne âgée**

> older than but **senior to.**

sensation [sen'seiʃən] *noun* **1** the ability to feel through the sense of touch: *Cold can cause a loss of sensation in the fingers and toes.* □ **sensation**

2 a feeling: *a sensation of faintness.* □ **sensation**

3 a general feeling, or a cause, of excitement or horror: *The murder caused a sensation; His arrest was the sensation of the week.* □ **sensation**

sen'sational *adjective* **1** causing great excitement or horror: *a sensational piece of news.* □ **sensationnel**

2 very good: *The film was sensational.* □ **sensationnel**

3 intended to create feelings of excitement, horror *etc*: *That magazine is too sensational for me.* □ **à sensation**

sen'sationally *adverb.* □ **d'une manière sensationnelle**

sense [sens] *noun* **1** one of the five powers (hearing, taste, sight, smell, touch) by which a person or animal feels or notices. □ **sens**

2 a feeling: *He has an exaggerated sense of his own importance.* □ **sentiment**

3 an awareness of (something): *a well-developed musical sense; She has no sense of humour.* □ **sens**

4 good judgment: *You can rely on her – she has plenty of sense.* □ **bon sens**

5 a meaning (of a word). □ **sens**

6 something which is meaningful: *Can you make sense of her letter?* □ **signification**

■ *verb* to feel, become aware of, or realize: *She sensed that they disapproved.* □ **sentir (intuitivement)**

'senseless *adjective* **1** stunned or unconscious: *The blow knocked her senseless.* □ **sans connaissance**

2 foolish: *What a senseless thing to do!* □ **insensé**

'senselessly *adverb.* □ **insensément**

'senselessness *noun.* □ **manque de bon sens**

'senses *noun plural* (*usually with* **my, his, her** *etc*) a person's normal, sane state of mind: *She must have taken leave of her senses; When he came to his senses, he was lying in a hospital bed.* □ **raison; conscience**

sixth sense an ability to feel or realize something apparently not by means of any of the five senses: *She couldn't hear or see anyone, but a sixth sense told her that she was being followed.* □ **sixième sens**

sensibility [sensi'biləti] *noun* an awareness of, or an ability to create, art, literature *etc* showing very high standards of beauty and good taste: *a writer of great sensibility.* □ **sensibilité**

,sensi'bilities *noun plural* feelings that can be easily hurt by criticism *etc*: *Do try not to offend her sensibilities.* □ **susceptibilité**

sensible ['sensəbl] *adjective* **1** wise; having or showing good judgment: *She's a sensible, reliable person; a sensible suggestion.* □ **sensé**

2 (of clothes *etc*) practical rather than attractive or fashionable: *She wears flat, sensible shoes.* □ **pratique**

'sensibly *adverb* in a sensible way: *She sensibly brought a spare pair of shoes.* □ **raisonnablement**

sensitive ['sensitiv] *adjective* **1** (*usually with* **to**) strongly or easily affected (by something): *sensitive skin; sensitive to light.* □ **sensible (à)**

2 (*usually with* **about** *or* **to**) easily hurt or offended: *She is very sensitive to criticism.* □ **sensible (à)**

3 having or showing artistic good taste: *a sensitive writer; a sensitive performance.* □ **plein de sensibilité**

'sensitively *adverb.* □ **avec sensibilité**

'sensitiveness *noun.* □ **sensibilité**

,sensi'tivity *noun.* □ **sensibilité**

sensual ['sensjuəl] *adjective* **1** of the senses and the body rather than the mind: *sensual pleasures.* □ **sensuel**

2 having or showing a fondness for bodily pleasures: *a sensual person.* □ **sensuel**

'sensually *adverb.* □ **sensuellement**

'sensu'ality [-'a-] *noun.* □ **sensualité**

sensuous ['sensjuəs] *adjective* affecting the senses pleasantly: *Her sculptures have a sensuous quality.* □ **voluptueux**

'sensuously *adverb.* □ **voluptueusement**

sent *see* **send.**

sentence ['sentəns] *noun* **1** a number of words forming a complete statement: *'I want it', and 'Give it to me!' are sentences.* □ **phrase**

2 a punishment imposed by a lawcourt: *a sentence of three years' imprisonment; He is under sentence of death.* □ **sentence**

■ *verb* (*usually with* **to**) to condemn to a particular punishment: *He was sentenced to life imprisonment.* □ **condamner (à)**

sentiment ['sentimənt] *noun* tender feeling or emotion: *a song full of patriotic sentiment.* □ **sentiment**

,senti'mental [-'men-] *adjective* **1** (*sometimes with* **about**) having, showing or causing much tender feeling: *a sentimental person; a sentimental film about a little boy and a donkey.* □ **sentimental**

2 of the emotions or feelings: *The ring has sentimental value, as my husband gave it to me.* □ **sentimental**

,senti'mentally *adverb.* □ **sentimentalement**

,sentimen'tality [-'ta-] *noun.* □ **sentimentalité**

sentinel ['sentinl] *noun* a sentry. □ **sentinelle**

sentry ['sentri] – *plural* **'sentries** – *noun* a soldier or other person on guard to stop anyone who has no right to enter, pass *etc*: *The entrance was guarded by two sentries.* □ **sentinelle**

'sentry box *noun* a small shelter for a sentry. □ **guérite**

separate ['sepəreit] *verb* **1** (*sometimes with* **into** *or* **from**) to place, take, keep or force apart: *He separated the money into two piles; A policeman tried to separate the men who were fighting.* □ **séparer**

2 to go in different directions: *We all walked along together and separated at the intersection.* □ **se séparer**

3 (of a husband and wife) to start living apart from each other by choice. □ **se séparer**

■ [-rət] *adjective* **1** divided; not joined: *He sawed the wood into four separate pieces; The garage is separate from the house.* □ **séparé (de)**

2 different or distinct: *This happened on two separate occasions; I like to keep my job and my home life separate.* □ **distinct, séparé**

'separateness *noun.* □ fait d'être séparé

'separable *adjective* that can be separated. □ **séparable**

'separately [-rət-] *adverb* in a separate way; not together. □ **séparément**

'separates [-rəts] *noun plural* garments (*eg* jerseys, skirts, trousers, blouses, shirts) that can be worn together in varying combinations. □ **coordonnés**

,sepa'ration *noun* 1 the act of separating or the state or period of being separated: *They were together again after a separation of three years.* □ **séparation**

2 a (legal) arrangement by which a husband and wife remain married but live separately. □ **séparation**

'separatist [-rə-] *noun* a person who urges separation from an established political state, church *etc.* □ **séparatiste**

'separatism *noun.* □ **séparatisme**

separate into to divide: *The house has been separated into different flats.* □ **diviser**

---

separate is spelt with **-ar-** (not **-er-**).

---

sepia ['siːpiə] *noun, adjective* (of) a brown colour: *a sepia photograph.* □ **sépia**

September [səp'tembə] *noun* the ninth month of the year, the month following August. □ **septembre**

septic ['septik] *adjective* (of a wound *etc*) full of or caused by germs that are poisoning the blood: *a septic finger*; *septic poisoning.* □ **infecté**

septic tank a tank in which sewage is partially purified by the action of bacteria. □ **fosse septique**

septuagenarian [septʃuədʒi'neəriən] *noun* a person from seventy to seventy-nine years old. □ **septuagénaire**

sepulchre, sepulcher ['sepəlkə] *noun* a tomb. □ **sépulcre**

se'pulchral [-'pʌl-] *adjective* 1 of tombs or burials. □ **sépulcral**

2 gloomy or dismal: *a deep, sepulchral voice.* □ **sépulcral**

sequel ['siːkwəl] *noun* (*sometimes with* to) 1 a result or consequence: *an unpleasant sequel to an incident.* □ **séquelles**

2 a story that is a continuation of an earlier story: *a sequel to a story about a boy called Matthew.* □ **suite**

sequence ['siːkwəns] *noun* a series of events *etc* following one another in a particular order: *He described the sequence of events leading to his dismissal from the firm*; *a sequence of numbers*; *a dance sequence.* □ **succession**

seraph ['serəf] – *plurals* 'seraphim [-fim], 'seraphs – *noun* an angel of the highest rank. □ **séraphin**

se'raphic [-'ra-] *adjective.* □ **séraphique**

serenade [serə'neid] *noun* a piece of music played or sung in the open air at night. □ **sérénade**

■ *verb* to entertain with a serenade: *The girl stood on her balcony and was serenaded by her lover.* □ **donner une sérénade à**

serene [sə'riːn] *adjective* happy and peaceful: *a calm and serene person.* □ **serein**

se'renely *adverb.* □ **sereinement**

se'reneness *noun.* □ **sérénité**

se'renity [-'re-] *noun.* □ **sérénité**

serge [səːdʒ] *noun, adjective* (of) a type of strong, *usually* woollen, cloth: *brown serge tunics.* □ **serge**

sergeant ['saːdʒənt] *noun* (*often abbreviated to* Sgt) 1 in the Canadian army or air force, the rank above corporal: *Sergeant Brown.* □ **sergent, ente**

2 (a police officer of) the rank next above constable or patrolman. □ **sergent**

sergeant-'major *noun* (*often abbreviated to* Sgt-Maj.) in the Canadian army, the highest rank of non-commissioned officer: *Sergeant-Major Brown.* □ **sergent-major**

serial *see* series.

series ['siəriːz] – *plural* 'series – *noun* a number of *usually* similar things done, produced *etc* one after another: *a series of brilliant scientific discoveries*; *Are you watching the television series on Britain's castles?*; *a series of school textbooks.* □ **série**

'serial [-riəl] *adjective* 1 of or in a series: *serial numbers on banknotes.* □ **de/en série**

2 (of a story *etc*) published or broadcast in parts. □ **en feuilleton**

■ *noun* a serial story, play *etc.* □ **feuilleton**

'serialize, 'serialise [-riə-] *verb* to publish or broadcast as a serial. □ **publier/diffuser en feuilleton**

,seriali'zation, ,seriali'sation *noun.* □ **publication/diffusion en feuilleton**

serious ['siəriəs] *adjective* 1 grave or solemn: *a quiet, serious boy*; *You're looking very serious.* □ **sérieux**

2 (*often with* about) in earnest; sincere: *Is he serious about wanting to be a doctor?* □ **sérieux**

3 intended to make people think: *She reads very serious books.* □ **sérieux**

4 causing worry; dangerous: *a serious head injury*; *The situation is becoming serious.* □ **sérieux, grave**

'seriousness *noun.* □ **sérieux**

'seriously *adverb* in a serious way; to a serious extent: *Is he seriously thinking of being an actor?*; *She is seriously ill.* □ **sérieusement**

take (someone or something) seriously 1 to regard (a person or his statement *etc*) as in earnest: *You mustn't take his jokes/promises seriously.* □ **prendre au sérieux**

2 to regard (a matter) as a subject for concern or serious thought: *He refuses to take anything seriously.* □ **prendre au sérieux**

sermon ['səːmən] *noun* a serious talk, *especially* one given in church based on or discussing a passage in the Bible: *The text for this morning's sermon is taken from the fifth chapter of Exodus.* □ **sermon**

serpent ['səːpənt] *noun* a snake. □ **serpent**

serrated ['sereitid] *adjective* notched, as the edge of a saw is: *A breadknife is often serrated.* □ **en dents de scie**

serum ['siərəm] *noun* a watery fluid which is given as an injection to fight, or give immunity from, a disease: *Diphtheria vaccine is a serum.* □ **sérum**

servant ['səːvənt] *noun* 1 a person who is hired to work for another, *especially* in helping to run a house. □ **domestique**

2 a person employed by the government, or in the administration of a country *etc*: *a public servant*; *civil serv-*

ants. □ **employé, ée (d'un service public); fonctionnaire**

serve [sɜːv] *verb* 1 to work for a person *etc eg* as a servant: *He served his master for forty years*. □ **servir**

2 to distribute food *etc* or supply goods: *She served the soup to the guests; Which shop assistant served you (with these goods)?* □ **servir**

3 to be suitable for a purpose: *This upturned bucket will serve as a seat*. □ **servir (de)**

4 to perform duties, *eg* as a member of the armed forces: *He served (his country) as a soldier for twenty years; I served on the committee for five years*. □ **servir; être membre de**

5 to undergo (a prison sentence): *He served (a sentence of) six years for armed robbery*. □ **purger (une peine)**

6 in tennis and similar games, to start the play by throwing up the ball *etc* and hitting it: *He served the ball into the net; Is it your turn to serve?* □ **servir**

■ *noun* act of serving (a ball). □ **service**

'**server** *noun* 1 (*usually in plural*) a utensil used in serving food: *salad servers*. □ **couvert à servir**

2 a person who serves (a ball). □ **serveur, euse**

'**serving** *noun* a portion of food served: *I had two servings of pie*. □ **portion**

it serves you *etc* **right** you *etc* deserve your misfortune *etc*: *He has done no work so it will serve him right if he fails his exam*. □ **c'est bien fait pour**

serve an apprenticeship to spend a (fixed) period of time as an apprentice. □ **faire son apprentissage**

serve out to distribute to each of a number of people: *She served out the pudding*. □ **servir**

serve up to start serving (a meal). □ **servir**

service ['sɜːvis] *noun* 1 the process of serving customers in a hotel, shop *etc*: *You get very slow service in that shop; (also adjective) a service charge on a hotel bill*. □ **(de) service**

2 the act of doing something to help: *She was rewarded for her service to refugees*. □ **service**

3 the condition or work of a servant: *In the last century, many young women went into service; She had been in service as a kitchen maid; She has given faithful service to the church for many years*. □ **service**

4 a check made of all parts of *eg* a car, machine *etc* to ensure that it is in a good condition: *Bring your car in for a service*. □ **entretien**

5 a regular public supply of something *eg* transport: *a good train service into the city*. □ **service**

6 a regular meeting for worship, or a religious ceremony (in church): *He attends a church service every Sunday; the marriage service*. □ **office**

7 in tennis and similar games, the act or manner of serving the ball: *She has a strong service*. □ **service**

8 a department of work or government work: *the Civil Service*. □ **service**

9 (*often in plural*) one of the three fighting forces, the army, navy or air force. □ **branche des forces armées**

10 employment in one of these: *military service*. □ **service militaire**

■ *verb* to check (a car, machine *etc*) thoroughly to ensure that it works properly. □ **faire la révision**

'**serviceable** *adjective* (*negative* **unserviceable**) 1 useful; capable of being used: *This tractor is so old it is barely serviceable now*. □ **utilisable**

2 hard-wearing: *She walks to school every day, so she must have serviceable shoes*. □ **solide**

'**serviceman** – *feminine* '**servicewoman** – *noun* a person in one of the armed services. □ **soldat, ate**

service station a gas station with facilities for servicing cars *etc*. □ **station-service**

serviette [sɜːvi'et] *noun* a table napkin: *a paper serviette*. □ **serviette (de table)**

servile ['sɜːvail] *adjective* excessively obedient or respectful: *servile obedience/flattery*. □ **servile**

'**servilely** *adverb*. □ **servilement**

ser'vility [-'vi-] *noun*. □ **servilité**

servitude ['sɜːvitjuːd] *noun* the state of being a slave: *Their lives were spent in servitude*. □ **esclavage**

session ['seʃən] *noun* 1 a meeting, or period for meetings, of a court, council, parliament *etc*: *The judge will give his summing up at tomorrow's court session*. □ **session, séance**

2 a period of time spent on a particular activity: *a filming session*. □ **séance**

3 a university or school year or one part of this: *the summer session*. □ **année/trimestre (scolaire, universitaire)**

set [set] – *present participle* '**setting**: *past tense, past participle* **set** – *verb* 1 to put or place: *She set the tray down on the table*. □ **poser**

2 to put plates, knives, forks *etc* on (a table) for a meal: *Please would you set the table for me?* □ **mettre**

3 to settle or arrange (a date, limit, price *etc*): *It's difficult to set a price on a book when you don't know its value*. □ **fixer**

4 to give a person (a task *etc*) to do: *The witch set the prince three tasks; The teacher set a test for her pupils; She should set the others a good example*. □ **donner**

5 to cause to start doing something: *His behaviour set people talking*. □ **déclencher**

6 (of the sun *etc*) to disappear below the horizon: *It gets cooler when the sun sets*. □ **se coucher**

7 to become firm or solid: *Has the concrete set?* □ **durcir**

8 to adjust (*eg* a clock or its alarm) so that it is ready to perform its function: *She set the alarm for 7:00*. □ **régler**

9 to arrange (hair) in waves or curls. □ **faire une mise en plis**

10 to fix in the surface of something, *eg* jewels in a ring. □ **poser**

11 to put (broken bones) into the correct position for healing: *They set his broken arm*. □ **remettre en place**

■ *adjective* 1 fixed or arranged previously: *There is a set procedure for doing this*. □ **établi**

2 (*often with* **on**) ready, intending or determined (to do something): *She is set on going*. □ **résolu à**

3 deliberate: *He had the set intention of hurting him*. □ **bien déterminé**

4 stiff; fixed: *She had a set smile on her face*. □ **figé**

5 not changing or developing: *set ideas*. □ **(bien) arrêté**

6 (*with* **with**) having something set in it: *a gold ring set*

with diamonds. □ **incrusté de**

■ *noun* **1** a group of things used or belonging together: *a set of carving tools*; *a complete set of (the novels of) Jane Austen.* □ **ensemble, collection**
2 an apparatus for receiving radio or television signals: *a television/radio set.* □ **poste**
3 a group of people: *the musical set.* □ **groupe**
4 the process of setting hair: *a shampoo and set.* □ **mise en plis**
5 scenery for a play or film: *There was a very impressive set in the final act.* □ **décor**
6 a group of six or more games in tennis: *She won the first set and lost the next two.* □ **set**
'**setting** *noun* **1** a background: *This castle is the perfect setting for a murder.* □ **cadre**
2 an arrangement of jewels in *eg* a ring. □ **monture**
3 music composed for a poem *etc*: *settings of folk songs.* □ **mise en musique**
'**setback** *noun* a delay in progress. □ **contretemps**
set phrase a phrase which always occurs in one form, and which cannot be changed: *'Of no fixed abode' is a set phrase.* □ **expression toute faite**
'**setting-lotion** *noun* a lotion that is used in setting the hair. □ **fixateur (pour mise en plis)**
,**set-'to** an argument or fight. □ **prise de bec, bagarre**
'**set-up** *noun* an arrangement: *There are several families living together in that house – it's a funny set-up.* □ **arrangement**
all set (*often with* **to**) ready or prepared (to do something); just on the point of (doing something): *We were all set to leave when the phone rang.* □ **prêt (à, pour)**
set about to begin: *She set about planning her holiday; How will you set about this task?* □ **se mettre à**
set (someone) **against** (someone) to cause (a person) to dislike (another person): *She set the children against their father.* □ **monter qqn contre qqn**
set aside to keep for a special use or purpose: *She set aside some cash for use at the weekend.* □ **mettre de côté**
set back to delay the progress of: *Her illness set her back a bit at school.* □ **retarder**
set down (of a bus *etc*) to stop and let (passengers) out: *The bus set us down outside the post office.* □ **déposer**
set in to begin or become established: *Boredom soon set in among the children.* □ **survenir; s'installer**
set off 1 (*sometimes with* **on**) to start a journey: *We set off to go to the beach.* □ **se mettre en route (pour)**
2 to cause to start doing something: *She had almost stopped crying, but his harsh words set her off again.* □ **déclencher**
3 to explode or ignite: *You should let your father set off all the fireworks.* □ **faire partir (une fusée)**
set (something or someone) **on** (someone) to cause (*eg* dogs) to attack (a person): *He set his dogs on me.* □ **exciter contre**
set out 1 to start a journey: *He set out to explore the countryside.* □ **se mettre en route**
2 to intend: *I didn't set out to prove him wrong.* □ **chercher à**
set to to start to do something (vigorously): *They set to,*

and finished the work the same day. □ **(s')attaquer (à)**
set up 1 to establish: *When was the organization set up?* □ **établir**
2 to arrange or construct: *She set up the apparatus for the experiment.* □ **installer**
set up camp to erect tents *etc*: *They set up camp in a field.* □ **établir un camp**
set up house to establish one's own home: *He'll soon be earning enough to set up house on his own.* □ **s'installer (dans ses meubles)**
set up shop to start a shop. □ **ouvrir un commerce/ magasin**
set upon (*also* **set on**) to attack: *He set upon me in the dark.* □ **se jeter sur**
set(t) [set] *noun* a block of stone used in street paving. □ **pavé**
settee [se'tiː] *noun* a sofa. □ **canapé**
setter ['setə] *noun* a type of large dog. □ **setter**
settle ['setl] *verb* **1** to place in a position of rest or comfort: *I settled myself in the armchair.* □ **(s')installer**
2 to come to rest: *Dust had settled on the books.* □ **se déposer (sur)**
3 to soothe: *I gave him a pill to settle his nerves.* □ **calmer**
4 to go and live: *Many Scots settled in New Zealand.* □ **s'établir**
5 to reach a decision or agreement: *Have you settled with the builders when they are to start work?; The dispute between management and employees is still not settled.* □ **décider, régler**
6 to pay (a bill). □ **régler**
'**settlement** *noun* **1** an agreement: *The two sides have at last reached a settlement.* □ **accord**
2 a small community: *a farming settlement.* □ **colonie**
'**settler** *noun* a person who settles in a country that is being newly populated: *They were among the early settlers on the east coast of America.* □ **colon**
settle down 1 to (cause to) become quiet, calm and peaceful: *He waited for the audience to settle down before he spoke; She settled the baby down at last.* □ **(se) calmer**
2 to make oneself comfortable: *She settled (herself) down in the back of the car and went to sleep.* □ **s'installer (confortablement)**
3 to begin to concentrate on something, *eg* work: *She settled down to (do) her schoolwork.* □ **se mettre (sérieusement) à**
settle in to become used to and comfortable in new surroundings. □ **s'adapter**
settle on to agree about or decide. □ **se mettre d'accord sur**
settle up to pay (a bill): *She asked the waiter for the bill, and settled up.* □ **régler**
seven ['sevn] *noun* **1** the number or figure 7. □ **sept**
2 the age of 7. □ **sept ans**
■ *adjective* **1** 7 in number. □ **sept**
2 aged 7. □ **de sept ans**
seven- having seven (of something): *a seven-sided figure.* □ **à/de sept (...)**
'**seventh** *noun* **1** one of seven equal parts. □ **septième**

2 (*also adjective*) (the) last of seven (people, things *etc*); (the) next after the sixth. □ **septième**

'seven-year-old *noun* a person or animal that is seven years old. □ **(individu, etc.) âgé de sept ans**
■ *adjective* (of a person, animal or thing) that is seven years old. □ **de sept ans**

seventeen [sevn'tiːn] *noun* **1** the number or figure 17. □ **dix-sept**

2 the age of 17. □ **dix-sept ans**
■ *adjective* **1** 17 in number. □ **dix-sept**

2 aged 17. □ **de dix-sept ans**

seventeen- having seventeen: *a seventeen-page report*. □ **à/de dix-sept (...)**

,seven'teenth *noun* **1** one of seventeen equal parts. □ **dix-septième**

2 (*also adjective*) (the) last of seventeen (people, things *etc*); (the) next after the sixteenth. □ **dix-septième**

,seven'teen-year-old *noun* a person or animal that is seventeen years old. □ **(individu, etc.) âgé de dix-sept ans**
■ *adjective* (of a person, animal or thing) that is seventeen years old. □ **de dix-sept ans**

seventy ['sevnti] *noun* **1** the number or figure 70. □ **soixante-dix**

2 the age of 70. □ **soixante-dix ans**
■ *adjective* **1** 70 in number. □ **soixante-dix**

2 aged 70. □ **de soixante-dix ans**

seventy- having seventy: *a seventy-year lease*. □ **à/de soixante-dix (...)**

'seventies *noun plural* **1** the period of time between a person's seventieth and eightieth birthdays. □ **entre soixante-dix et soixante-dix-neuf ans**

2 the range of temperatures between seventy and eighty degrees. □ **dans les soixante-dix degrés**

3 the period of time between the seventieth and eightieth years of a century. □ **de (...) soixante-dix à (...) soixante-dix-neuf**

'seventieth *noun* **1** one of seventy equal parts. □ **soixante-dixième**

2 (*also adjective*) (the) last of seventy (people, things *etc*); (the) next after the sixty-ninth. □ **soixante-dixième**

'seventy-year-old *noun* a person or animal that is seventy years old. □ **septuagénaire**
■ *adjective* (of a person, animal or thing) that is seventy years old. □ **septuagénaire**

sever ['sevə] *verb* **1** to put an end to: *He severed relations with his family*. □ **cesser, rompre**

2 to cut or break off: *His arm was severed in the accident*. □ **couper**

'severance *noun*. □ **rupture**

several ['sevrəl] *adjective* more than one or two, but not a great many: *Several weeks passed before she got a reply to her letter*. □ **plusieurs**
■ *pronoun* some or a few: *Several of them are ill; Of the eggs, several were broken*. □ **plusieurs; quelques**

severe [sə'viə] *adjective* **1** (of something unpleasant) serious; extreme: *severe shortages of food; a severe illness; Our team suffered a severe defeat*. □ **grave**

2 strict or harsh: *a severe mother; severe criticism*. □ **sévère, strict**

3 (of style in dress *etc*) very plain: *a severe hairstyle*. □ **austère**

se'verely *adverb*. □ **sévèrement**

se'verity [-'ve-] *noun: the severity of the punishment; the severity of her dress*. □ **sévérité**

sew [sou] *– past tense* **sewed**; *past participle* **sewn** *– verb* to make, stitch or attach with thread, using a needle: *She sewed the pieces together; Have you sewn my button on yet?* □ **coudre**

'sewer *noun: She's a good sewer*. □ **couseur, euse**

'sewing *noun* **1** the activity of sewing: *I was taught sewing at school*. □ **couture**

2 work to be sewn: *She picked up a pile of sewing*. □ **couture**

'sewing machine *noun* a machine for sewing. □ **machine à coudre**

sew up to fasten completely or mend by sewing. □ **fermer par une couture**

sewn up completely settled or arranged: *The contract is all sewn up*. □ **arrangé**

to sew (not sow) a button on.

sewer[1] ['sjuə] *noun* an underground pipe or channel for carrying away water *etc* from drains. □ **égout**

'sewage [-idʒ] *noun* waste matter (carried away in sewers). □ **eau(x) d'égout**

sewer[2] *see* **sew**.

sex [seks] *noun* **1** either of the two classes (male and female) into which human beings and animals are divided according to the part they play in producing children or young: *Jeans are worn by people of both sexes; What sex is the puppy?* □ **sexe**

2 the fact of belonging to either of these two groups: *discrimination on the grounds of sex*; (*also adjective*) *sex discrimination*. □ **sexe**

'sexism *noun* discrimination or restriction because of one's sex: *It is sexism when a woman is better at the job, but a man gets the promotion*. □ **sexisme**

'sexist *adjective* showing contempt for the other sex: *a very sexist remark*. □ **sexiste**

'sexless *adjective* neither male nor female. □ **asexué**

sexual ['sekʃuəl] *adjective* concerned with the production of young or children: *the sexual organs*. □ **sexuel**

'sexuality *noun* that which has to do with sex or sexual matters: *When the girl became pregnant, her parents could no longer deny her sexuality or pretend she was still a young child*. □ **sexualité**

'sexually *adverb*. □ **sexuellement**

'sexy *adjective* having sex appeal. □ **séduisant**

sex appeal the quality of being attractive to people of the other sex: *That actress has sex appeal*. □ **charme sensuel**

sexual intercourse the sexual activity between a man and woman that is necessary for the producing of children. □ **rapports sexuels**

sexagenerian [seksədʒi'neəriən] *noun* a person from sixty to sixty-nine years old. □ **sexagénaire**

sextet [seks'tet] *noun* **1** a group of six singers or musicians. □ **sextuor**

2 a piece of music composed for such a group. □ **sextuor**

sexton ['sekstən] *noun* a person who looks after a church and often is responsible for bellringing *etc*. □ **sacristain**

shabby ['ʃabi] *adjective* **1** looking old and worn: *shabby curtains*; *shabby clothes*. □ **usé**

2 wearing old or dirty clothes: *a shabby man*; *He used to be so smart but he looks shabby now*. □ **miteux**

3 (of behaviour) unworthy or mean: *That was a shabby thing to do*. □ **mesquin**

'**shabbily** *adverb*. □ **pauvrement; mesquinement**

'**shabbiness** *noun*. □ **aspect minable; mesquinerie**

shack [ʃak] *noun* a roughly-built hut: *a wooden shack*. □ **cabane**

shackles ['ʃaklz] *noun plural* a pair of iron rings joined by a chain that are put on a prisoner's wrists, ankles *etc*, to limit movement: *His captors put shackles on him*. □ **fers**

'**shackle** *verb* to put shackles on. □ **mettre les fers à**

shade [ʃeid] *noun* **1** slight darkness caused by the blocking of some light: *I prefer to sit in the shade rather than the sun*. □ **ombre, ombrage**

2 the dark parts of a picture: *light and shade in a portrait*. □ **ombre(s)**

3 something that screens or shelters from light or heat: *a large sunshade*; *a shade for a light*. □ **pare-soleil; abat-jour, store, etc.**

4 a variety of a colour; a slight difference: *a pretty shade of green*; *shades of meaning*. □ **ton**

5 a slight amount: *The weather is a shade better today*. □ **légèrement**

■ *verb* **1** (*sometimes with* **from**) to shelter from light or heat: *She put up her hand to shade her eyes*. □ **abriter**

2 to make darker: *You should shade the foreground of that drawing*. □ **ombrer**

3 (*with* **into**) to change very gradually *eg* from one colour to another. □ **(se) fondre (en)**

'**shaded** *adjective* (of parts of a picture) made darker. □ **ombré**

shades *noun plural* (*especially American*) sunglasses. □ **lunettes de soleil**

'**shading** *noun* (in a picture *etc*) the marking that shows the darker parts. □ **ombres**

'**shady** *adjective* **1** sheltered or giving shelter from heat or light: *a shady tree*; *a shady corner of the garden*. □ **ombragé**

2 dishonest: *a shady business*. □ **louche**

'**shadiness** *noun*. □ **ombre**

put in the shade to cause to seem unimportant: *She is so beautiful that she puts her sister in the shade*. □ **éclipser qqn**

shadow ['ʃadou] *noun* **1** (a patch of) shade on the ground *etc* caused by an object blocking the light: *We are in the shadow of that building*. □ **ombre**

2 (*in plural with* **the**) darkness or partial darkness caused by lack of (direct) light: *The child was afraid that wild animals were lurking in the shadows at the corner of his bedroom*. □ **obscurité**

3 a dark patch or area: *You look tired – there are shadows under your eyes*. □ **cerne**

4 a very slight amount: *There's not a shadow of doubt that he stole the money*. □ **ombre (de)**

■ *verb* **1** to hide or darken with shadow: *A broad hat shadowed her face*. □ **ombrager qqch.**

2 to follow closely, *especially* as a detective, spy *etc*: *We shadowed him for a week*. □ **filer qqn**

'**shadowy** *adjective* **1** full of shadows: *shadowy corners*. □ **sombre**

2 dark and indistinct: *A shadowy figure went past*. □ **vague**

'**shadowiness** *noun*. □ **caractère vague**

worn to a shadow made thin and weary through *eg* hard work: *She was worn to a shadow after months of nursing her sick husband*. □ **qui n'est plus que l'ombre de soi-même**

shaft [ʃɑːft] *noun* **1** the long straight part or handle of a tool, weapon *etc*: *the shaft of a golf club*. □ **manche**

2 one of two poles on a cart *etc* to which a horse *etc* is harnessed: *The horse stood patiently between the shafts*. □ **brancard**

3 a revolving bar transmitting motion in an engine: *the driving-shaft*. □ **arbre (de transmission)**

4 a long, narrow space, made for *eg* a lift in a building: *a liftshaft*; *a mineshaft*. □ **cage (d'un ascenseur), puits**

5 a ray of light: *a shaft of sunlight*. □ **rayon**

shaggy ['ʃagi] *adjective* (covered with hair, fur *etc* that is) rough and untidy in appearance: *The dog had a shaggy coat*; *a shaggy dog*. □ **hirsute**

'**shagginess** *noun*. □ **aspect hirsute**

shake [ʃeik] – *past tense* **shook** [ʃuk]: *past participle* **shaken** – *verb* **1** to (cause to) tremble or move with jerks: *The explosion shook the building*; *We were shaking with laughter*; *Her voice shook as she told me the sad news*. □ **(faire) trembler**

2 to shock, disturb or weaken: *She was shaken by the accident*; *My confidence in him has been shaken*. □ **ébranler**

■ *noun* **1** an act of shaking: *She gave the bottle a shake*. □ **secousse**

2 drink made by shaking the ingredients together vigorously: *a chocolate milk-shake*. □ **(lait) fouetté**

'**shaking** *noun* an act of shaking or state of being shaken, shocked *etc*: *They got a shaking in the crash*. □ **secousse, ébranlement**

'**shaky** *adjective* **1** weak or trembling with age, illness *etc*: *a shaky voice*; *shaky handwriting*. □ **tremblant**

2 unsteady or likely to collapse: *a shaky chair*. □ **branlant**

3 (*sometimes with* **at**) not very good, accurate *etc*: *He's a bit shaky at arithmetic*; *My arithmetic has always been very shaky*; *I'd be grateful if you would correct my rather shaky spelling*. □ **faible**

'**shakily** *adverb*. □ **en tremblant**

'**shakiness** *noun*. □ **instabilité, tremblement**

'**shake-up** *noun* a disturbance or reorganization. □ **grand remaniement**

no great shakes not very good or important: *He has written a book, but it's no great shakes*. □ **ne pas valoir grand-chose**

shake one's fist at to hold up one's fist as though threatening to punch: *He shook his fist at me when I drove into the back of his car*. □ **menacer du poing**

shake one's head to move one's head around to left and right to mean 'No': *'Are you coming?' I asked. She shook her head.* □ **faire non de la tête**

shake off to rid oneself of: *She soon shook off the illness.* □ **venir à bout de**

shake up to disturb or rouse (people) so as to make them more energetic. □ **secouer**

shale [ʃeil] *noun* a type of rock from which oil is sometimes obtained. □ **schiste (bitumineux)**

shall [ʃəl, ʃal] – *short forms* **I'll**, **we'll**: *negative short form* **shan't** [ʃaːnt] – *verb* **1** used to form future tenses of other verbs when the subject is **I** or **we**: *We shall be leaving tomorrow; I shall have arrived by this time tomorrow.* □ **-rai, -rons**
2 used to show the speaker's intention: *I shan't be late tonight.* □ **avoir l'intention de**
3 used in questions, the answer to which requires a decision: *Shall I tell her, or shan't I?; Shall we go now?* □ **oui ou non?**
4 used as a form of command: *You shall go if I say you must.* □ **avoir l'obligation de**

shallot [ʃəlɔːt] *noun* a plant that grows a cluster of bulbs and tastes similar to an onion, often used for flavouring or as a green vegetable: *There were no onions for the salad so Daniel cut a shallot and sprinkled it on the lettuce.* □ **échalotte**

shallow [ʃalou] *adjective* **1** not deep: *shallow water; a shallow pit.* □ **peu profond**
2 not able to think seriously or feel deeply: *a rather shallow personality.* □ **superficiel**
'shallowness *noun.* □ **manque de profondeur**
'shallows *noun plural* a place where the water is shallow: *There are dangerous rocks and shallows near the island.* □ **haut-fond**

sham [ʃam] *noun* something that is pretended, not genuine: *The whole trial was a sham.* □ **imposture; imitation**
■ *adjective* pretended, artificial or false: *a sham fight; Are those diamonds real or sham?* □ **faux**
■ *verb – past tense, past participle* **shammed** – to pretend (to be in some state): *He shammed sleep/anger; He shammed dead; I think she's only shamming.* □ **faire semblant (de)**

shamble [ʃambl] *verb* to walk slowly and awkwardly, (as if) not lifting one's feet properly off the ground: *The old man shambled wearily along the street.* □ **marcher en traînant les pieds**

shambles [ʃamblz] *noun singular* a confused mess; (something in) a state of disorder: *Her room was a shambles; We're in a bit of a shambles at the moment.* □ **fouillis**

shame [ʃeim] *noun* **1** (*often with* **at**) an unpleasant feeling caused by awareness of guilt, fault, foolishness or failure: *I was full of shame at my rudeness; She felt no shame at her behaviour.* □ **honte**
2 dishonour or disgrace: *The news that he had accepted bribes brought shame on his whole family.* □ **honte**
3 (*with* **a**) a cause of disgrace or a matter for blame: *It's a shame to treat a child so cruelly.* □ **honte**
4 (*with* **a**) a pity: *What a shame that she didn't get the job!* □ **dommage**
■ *verb* **1** (*often with* **into**) to force or persuade to do something by making ashamed: *He was shamed into paying his share.* □ **obliger (qqn à) en lui faisant honte**
2 to cause to have a feeling of shame: *His cowardice shamed his parents.* □ **faire honte à**
'shameful *adjective* disgraceful: *shameful behaviour.* □ **honteux**
'shamefully *adverb.* □ **honteusement**
'shamefulness *noun.* □ **honte**
'shameless *adjective* **1** without shame; blatant: *a shameless liar; shameless deception.* □ **éhonté**
2 not modest: *a shameless woman.* □ **impudique**
'shamelessly *adverb.* □ **effrontément**
'shamelessness *noun.* □ **effronterie**
'shamefaced *adjective* showing shame or embarrassment: *He was very shamefaced about his mistake.* □ **confus**

put to shame to make feel ashamed of something or to make seem to be of poor quality by showing greater excellence: *Your beautiful drawing puts me/mine to shame.* □ **faire honte à**

to my, his *etc* **shame** it is a cause of shame to me, him *etc* that: *To my shame, my daughter always beats me at chess.* □ **à (ma, etc.) grande honte**

shampoo [ʃamˈpuː] – *plural* **shampoos** – *noun* **1** a soapy liquid or other substance for washing the hair and scalp or for cleaning carpets, upholstery *etc*: *a special shampoo for greasy hair; carpet shampoo.* □ **shampooing**
2 an act of washing *etc* with shampoo: *I had a shampoo and set at the hairdresser's.* □ **shampooing**
■ *verb – past tense, past participle* **shamˈpooed** – to wash or clean with shampoo: *She shampoos her hair every day; We shampooed the rugs yesterday.* □ **faire un shampooing à**

shandy [ʃandi] – *plural* **'shandies** – *noun* a mixture of beer and lemonade or ginger beer. □ **panaché**

shank [ʃaŋk] *noun* **1** the leg, *especially* the part between the knee and foot. □ **jambe**
2 the long straight part of *eg* a nail or screw. □ **tige**

shan't *see* **shall**.

shanty [ʃanti] – *plural* **'shanties** – *noun* a roughly-built hut or shack. □ **baraque**

shape [ʃeip] *noun* **1** the external form or outline of anything: *People are all (of) different shapes and sizes; The house is built in the shape of a letter L.* □ **forme**
2 an indistinct form: *I saw a large shape in front of me in the darkness.* □ **forme indistincte**
3 condition or state: *You're in better physical shape than I am.* □ **forme**
■ *verb* **1** to make into a certain shape, to form or model: *She shaped the dough into three separate loaves.* □ **façonner, former**
2 to influence the nature of strongly: *This event shaped her whole life.* □ **déterminer, influencer**
3 (*sometimes with* **up**) to develop: *The team is shaping (up) well.* □ **prendre une tournure**
shaped *adjective* having a certain shape: *A rugby ball is egg-shaped.* □ **en forme de**
'shapeless *adjective* lacking shape: *She wears a shape-*

less, baggy coat. □ **informe**
'**shapelessness** *noun.* □ **caractère informe**
'**shapely** *adjective* well-formed and having an attractive shape: *She has long, shapely legs.* □ **bien fait**
'**shapeliness** *noun.* □ **galbe**
in any shape (or form) at all: *I don't accept bribes in any shape or form.* □ **sous quelque forme que ce soit**
out of shape not in the proper shape: *I sat on my hat and it's rather out of shape.* □ **déformé**
take shape to develop into a definite form: *My garden is gradually taking shape.* □ **prendre forme**
share [ʃeə] *noun* **1** one of the parts of something that is divided among several people *etc*: *We all had a share of the cake; We each paid our share of the bill.* □ **part**
2 the part played by a person in something done *etc* by several people *etc*: *I had no share in the decision.* □ **part**
3 a fixed sum of money invested in a business company by a '**shareholder.** □ **action**
■ *verb* **1** (*usually with* **among, between, with**) to divide among a number of people: *We shared the money between us.* □ **partager**
2 to have, use *etc* (something that another person has or uses); to allow someone to use (something one has or owns): *The students share a sitting-room; The little boy hated sharing his toys.* □ **partager**
3 (*sometimes with* **in**) to have a share of with someone else: *He wouldn't let her share the cost of the taxi.* □ **partager**
'**shareholder** *noun* a person who owns shares in a business company. □ **actionnaire**
share and share alike with everyone having an equal share: *We divided the money between us, share and share alike.* □ **à chacun sa part**
shark [ʃɑːk] *noun* a type of large, fierce, flesh-eating fish. □ **requin**
sharp [ʃɑːp] *adjective* **1** having a thin edge that can cut or a point that can pierce: *a sharp knife.* □ **aiguisé; pointu**
2 (of pictures, outlines *etc*) clear and distinct: *the sharp outline of the mountain.* □ **net**
3 (of changes in direction) sudden and quick: *a sharp left turn.* □ **brusque**
4 (of pain *etc*) keen, acute or intense: *He gets a sharp pain after eating.* □ **violent**
5 (*often with* **with**) severe: *Don't be so sharp with the child!; She got a sharp reproach from me.* □ **sévère**
6 alert: *Dogs have sharp ears.* □ **fin**
7 shrill and sudden: *a sharp cry.* □ **perçant**
8 of a musical note, raised a semitone; too high in pitch: *F sharp; That last note was sharp.* □ **diésé; trop haut**
■ *adverb* **1** punctually: *Come at six (o'clock) sharp.* □ **pile**
2 with an abrupt change of direction: *Turn sharp left here.* □ **tout à fait**
3 at too high a pitch: *You're singing sharp.* □ **trop haut**
■ *noun* a sharp note: *sharps and flats.* □ **dièse**
2 a sign (#) to show that a note is to be raised a semitone. □ **dièse**
'**sharpen** *verb* to make or grow sharp: *He sharpened*

his pencil. □ **aiguiser**
'**sharpener** *noun* an instrument for sharpening: *a pencil-sharpener.* □ **aiguisoir**
'**sharply** *adverb* in a sharp manner: *a sharply-pointed piece of glass; The road turned sharply to the left; He rebuked her sharply.* □ **brusquement**
'**sharpness** *noun.* □ **netteté**
sharp practice dishonesty or cheating. □ **procédés malhonnêtes**
,**sharp-'witted** *adjective* intelligent and alert: *a sharp-witted boy.* □ **vif**
look sharp to be quick or to hurry: *Bring me the books and look sharp (about it)!* □ **faire vite**
shatter [ˈʃatə] *verb* **1** to break in small pieces, *usually* suddenly or forcefully: *The stone shattered the window; The window shattered.* □ **(se) fracasser**
2 to upset greatly: *She was shattered by the news of his death.* □ **anéantir**
'**shattered** *adjective.* □ **fracassé; anéanti**
shave [ʃeiv] *verb* **1** to cut away (hair) from (*usually* oneself) with a razor: *He only shaves once a week.* □ **(se) raser**
2 (*sometimes with* **off**) to scrape or cut away (the surface of wood *etc*): *The joiner shaved a thin strip off the edge of the door.* □ **raboter**
3 to touch lightly in passing: *The car shaved the wall.* □ **raser**
■ *noun* (the result of) an act of shaving. □ **rasage**
'**shaven** *adjective* shaved: *He was dark and clean-shaven.* □ **rasé**
'**shavings** *noun plural* very thin strips *especially* of wood: *The glasses were packed in wood shavings.* □ **copeaux**
shawl [ʃɔːl] *noun* a piece of fabric used as a covering for the shoulders *etc*. □ **châle**
she [ʃiː] *pronoun* (used only as the subject of a verb) **1** a female person or animal already spoken about: *When the girl saw us, she asked the time.* □ **elle**
2 any female person: *She who runs the fastest will be the winner.* □ **celle (qui)**
■ *noun* a female person or animal: *Is a cow a he or a she?* □ **femelle**
sheaf [ʃiːf] – *plural* **sheaves** [ʃiːvz] – *noun* a bundle *usually* tied or held together: *a sheaf of corn/notes.* □ **gerbe; liasse**
shear [ʃiə] – *past tense* **sheared**: *past participles* **sheared, shorn** [ʃɔːn] – *verb* **1** to clip or cut wool from (a sheep). □ **tondre**
2 (*past tense* **shorn**: *often with* **off**) to cut (hair) off: *All her curls have been shorn off.* □ **couper**
3 (*past tense* **shorn**: *especially with* **of**) to cut hair from (someone): *He has been shorn (of all his curls).* □ **couper**
4 to cut or (cause to) break: *A piece of the steel girder sheared off.* □ **(se) cisailler**
shears *noun plural* a cutting-tool with two blades, like a large pair of scissors: *a pair of shears.* □ **cisailles**
sheath [ʃiːθ] – *plural* **sheaths** [ʃiːθs, ʃiːðz] – *noun* **1** a case for a sword or blade. □ **fourreau**
2 a long close-fitting covering: *The rocket is encased in*

a metal sheath. □ **gaine**

sheathe [ʃiːð] verb to put into a sheath: He sheathed his sword. □ **rengainer**

sheaves see sheaf.

shed¹ [ʃed] noun a usually small building for working in, or for storage: a wooden shed; a garden shed. □ **remise**

shed² [ʃed] – present participle **'shedding**: past tense, past participle **shed** – verb 1 to send out (light etc): The torch shed a bright light on the path ahead. □ **projeter**
2 to cast off (clothing, skin, leaves etc): Many trees shed their leaves in autumn. □ **perdre**
3 to produce (tears, blood): I don't think many tears were shed when she left. □ **verser**

shed light on to make clearer: This letter sheds light on the reasons for her departure. □ **éclairer**

she'd see have, would.

sheen [ʃiːn] noun shine or glossiness. □ **lustre, brillant**

sheep [ʃiːp] – plural **sheep** – noun a kind of animal related to the goat, whose flesh is used as food and from whose wool clothing is made: a flock of sheep. □ **mouton**

'sheepish adjective embarrassed: a sheepish expression. □ **embarrassé**

'sheepishly adverb. □ **d'un air penaud**

'sheepdog noun a dog (of a kind often) trained to work with sheep. □ **chien de berger**

sheer¹ [ʃiə] adjective 1 absolute: Her singing was a sheer delight; It all happened by sheer chance. □ **pur**
2 very steep: a sheer drop to the sea. □ **abrupt**
3 (of cloth) very thin: sheer silk. □ **extra-fin**
■ adverb vertically: The land rises sheer out of the sea. □ **à pic**

sheer² [ʃiə]: **sheer off/away** to turn aside or swerve: The speedboat sheered off course. □ **faire une embardée**

sheet [ʃiːt] noun 1 a broad piece of cloth eg for a bed: He put clean sheets on all the beds. □ **drap**
2 a large, thin, usually flat, piece: a sheet of paper/glass. □ **feuille**

,sheet 'lightning noun the kind of lightning which appears in broad flashes. □ **éclairs diffus**

sheik(h) [ʃiːk] noun an Arab chief. □ **cheik**

'sheik(h)dom noun a state ruled by a sheik(h). □ **territoire soumis à un cheik**

shelf [ʃelf] – plural **shelves** [ʃelvz] – noun a board for laying things on: There are shelves on the kitchen walls. □ **étagère, tablette**

shelve [ʃelv] verb 1 to put aside, usually for consideration, completion etc later: The project has been shelved for the moment. □ **mettre en suspens**
2 to put up shelves in. □ **garnir d'étagères**
3 (of land) to slope gradually: The land shelves towards the sea. □ **aller en pente**

shell [ʃel] noun 1 the hard outer covering of a shellfish, egg, nut etc: an eggshell; A tortoise can pull its head and legs under its shell. □ **coquille, coquillage, carapace, écale**
2 an outer covering or framework: After the fire, all that was left was the burned-out shell of the building. □ **carcasse**

3 a metal case filled with explosives and fired from a gun etc: A shell exploded right beside him. □ **obus**
■ verb 1 to remove from its shell or pod: You have to shell peas before eating them. □ **écosser, écaler**
2 to fire explosive shells at: The army shelled the enemy mercilessly. □ **bombarder**

'shellfish – plural **'shellfish** – noun any of several kinds of sea animal covered with a shell (eg oyster, crab). □ **coquillages; crustacés; fruits de mer**

come out of one's shell to become more confident and less shy. □ **sortir de sa coquille**

shell out to pay out (money): I had to shell out twenty dollars. □ **débourser**

she'll see will.

shelter ['ʃeltə] noun 1 protection against wind, rain, enemies etc: We gave the old man shelter for the night. □ **abri**
2 a building etc designed to give such protection: a bus-shelter. □ **abri**
■ verb 1 to be in, or go into, a place of shelter: He sheltered from the storm. □ **se mettre à l'abri (de)**
2 to give protection: That line of trees shelters my garden. □ **abriter**

'sheltered adjective protected from harm and unpleasantness of all kinds: a sheltered existence. □ **protégé**

shelve, shelves see shelf.

shepherd ['ʃepəd] – feminine **'shepherdess** – noun a person who looks after sheep: The shepherd and his dog gathered in the sheep. □ **berger, ère**
■ verb (often with around, in, out etc) to guide or lead carefully: She shepherded me through a maze of corridors. □ **guider**

sheriff ['ʃerif] noun in the United States, the chief law officer of a county, concerned with maintaining peace and order. □ **shérif**

sherry ['ʃeri] noun a kind of strong wine, made in Spain and often drunk before a meal. □ **xérès**

she's see be, have.

shield [ʃiːld] noun 1 a broad piece of metal, wood etc carried as a protection against weapons. □ **bouclier**
2 something or someone that protects: A thick steel plate acted as a heat shield. □ **bouclier**
3 a trophy shaped like a shield won in a sporting competition etc: My son has won the archery shield. □ **écusson**
■ verb (often with from) 1 to protect: The goggles shielded the motorcyclist's eyes from dust. □ **protéger**
2 to prevent from being seen clearly: That group of trees shields the house from the road. □ **cacher**

shift [ʃift] verb 1 to change (the) position or direction (of): We spent the whole evening shifting furniture around; The wind shifted to the west overnight. □ **déplacer**
2 to transfer: She shifted the blame on to me. □ **rejeter**
3 to get rid of: This detergent shifts stains. □ **enlever**
■ noun 1 a change (of position etc): a shift of emphasis. □ **changement**
2 a group of people who begin work on a job when another group stop work: The night shift does the heavy work. □ **équipe**

3 the period during which such a group works: *an eight-hour shift*; (*also adjective*) *shift work.* □ **quart de travail; (travail) par équipes**

'shiftless *adjective* inefficient, lazy, or without a set purpose: *He's rather shiftless – he's had four jobs in six months.* □ **fainéant**

'shiftlessness *noun.* □ **fainéantise**

'shifty *adjective* looking cunning and dishonest: *I don't trust him – he has a very shifty look.* □ **sournois**

'shiftily *adverb.* □ **sournoisement**

'shiftiness *noun.* □ **sournoiserie**

shilling ['ʃiliŋ] *noun* **1** in Britain until 1971, a coin worth one-twentieth of £1. □ **shilling**

2 in certain East African countries, a coin worth 100 cents. □ **shilling**

shimmer ['ʃimə] *verb* to shine with a quivering or unsteady light: *The moonlight shimmered on the lake.* □ **miroiter**

shin [ʃin] *noun* the front part of the leg below the knee: *He kicked him on the shins.* □ **le devant du tibia**

■ *verb – past tense, past participle* **shinned** – (*usually with* **up**) to climb by alternate movements of both arms and both legs: *She shinned up the tree.* □ **grimper**

shine [ʃain] – *past tense, past participle* **shone** [ʃɔn] – *verb* **1** to (cause to) give out light; to direct such light towards someone or something: *The light shone from the window*; *The policeman shone his torch*; *He shone a torch on the body.* □ **briller; éclairer**

2 to be bright: *She polished the silver till it shone.* □ **briller**

3 (*past tense, past participle* **shined**) to polish: *He tries to make a living by shining shoes.* □ **polir**

4 (*often with* **at**) to be very good (at something): *She shines at games*; *You really shone in yesterday's match.* □ **briller**

■ *noun* **1** brightness; the state of being well polished: *He likes a good shine on his shoes*; *a ray of sunshine.* □ **brillant**

2 an act of polishing: *I'll just give my shoes a shine.* □ **polissage**

'shining *adjective* very bright and clear; producing or reflecting light; polished: *a shining star*; *The windows were clean and shining.* □ **brillant**

'shiny *adjective* glossy; reflecting light; polished: *a shiny cover on a book*; *a shiny nose*; *shiny shoes.* □ **brillant**

'shininess *noun.* □ **aspect brillant**

shingle ['ʃiŋgl] *noun* coarse gravel: *There's too much shingle and not enough sand on this beach.* □ **(gros) cailloux**

shingles ['ʃiŋglz] *noun singular* a kind of infectious disease causing a rash of painful blisters. □ **zona**

shiny *see* **shine.**

ship [ʃip] *noun* **1** a large boat: *The ship sank and all the passengers and crew were drowned.* □ **navire**

2 any of certain types of transport that fly: *a spaceship.* □ **vaisseau**

■ *verb – past tense, past participle* **shipped** – to send or transport by ship: *The books were shipped to Australia.* □ **expédier (par bateau/mer)**

'shipment *noun* **1** a load of goods sent by sea: *a ship-ment of wine from Portugal.* □ **cargaison**

2 the sending of goods by sea. □ **expédition (par bateau/mer)**

'shipper *noun* a person who arranges for goods to be shipped: *a firm of shippers.* □ **expéditeur, trice**

'shipping *noun* ships taken as a whole: *The harbour was full of shipping.* □ **navires**

'shipbuilder *noun* a person whose business is the construction of ships: *a firm of shipbuilders.* □ **constructeur, trice de navires**

'shipbuilding *noun.* □ **construction navale**

,ship'shape *adjective* in good order: *She left everything shipshape in her room when she left.* □ **en ordre**

'shipwreck *noun* **1** the accidental sinking or destruction of a ship: *There were many shipwrecks on the rocky coast.* □ **naufrage**

2 a wrecked ship: *an old shipwreck on the shore.* □ **épave**

■ *verb*: *We were shipwrecked off the coast of Africa.* □ **faire naufrage**

'shipyard *noun* a place where ships are built or repaired. □ **chantier naval**

ship water (of a boat) to let water in over the side: *The boat shipped water and nearly capsized.* □ **embarquer (de l'eau)**

shirk [ʃəːk] *verb* to avoid doing, accepting responsibility for *etc* (something one ought to): *She shirked telling her the bad news that night.* □ **se dérober à**

'shirker *noun.* □ **tire-au-flanc**

shirt [ʃəːt] *noun* a kind of garment worn on the upper part of the body: *a casual shirt*; *a short-sleeved shirt*; *She wore black jeans and a white shirt.* □ **chemise**

in one's shirt-sleeves without a jacket or coat: *I work better in my shirt-sleeves.* □ **en bras de chemise**

shirty ['ʃəːti] *adjective* angry; bad-tempered: *He was a bit shirty with her when she arrived late.* □ **fâché; irritable**

shit [ʃit] *noun* an impolite or offensive word for the solid waste material that is passed out of the body. □ **merde**

■ *verb – present participle* **'shitting**: *past tense, past participles* **shit, shat** – to pass waste matter from the body. □ **chier**

shiver ['ʃivə] *verb* to quiver or tremble (with cold, fear *etc*). □ **frissonner**

■ *noun* an act of shivering. □ **frisson**

'shivery *adjective* inclined to shiver: *The mention of ghosts gave her a shivery feeling.* □ **qui donne le frisson**

the shivers a feeling of horror: *The thought of working for him gives me the shivers.* □ **frisson**

shoal¹ [ʃoul] *noun* a great number of fish swimming together in one place: *The fishing boats were searching for large shoals of fish.* □ **banc (de poissons)**

shoal² [ʃoul] *noun* a shallow place in the sea *etc*; a sandbank: *The boat grounded on a shoal.* □ **haut-fond; banc de sable**

shock¹ [ʃok] *noun* **1** a severe emotional disturbance: *The news gave us all a shock.* □ **choc**

2 (*often* **electric shock**) the effect on the body of an electric current: *He got a slight shock when he touched the live wire.* □ **choc**

3 a sudden blow coming with great force: *the shock of an earthquake*. □ **secousse**

4 a medical condition caused by a severe mental or physical shock: *She was suffering from shock after the crash*. □ **choc**

■ *verb* to give a shock to; to upset or horrify: *Everyone was shocked by her death*; *The amount of violence shown on television shocks me*. □ **bouleverser; choquer**

'**shocker** *noun* a very unpleasant person or thing: *This headache is a real shocker*. □ **horreur**

'**shocking** *adjective* **1** causing horror or dismay: *shocking news*. □ **bouleversant**

2 very bad: *a shocking cold*. □ **épouvantable**

'**shockingly** *adverb* **1** very: *shockingly expensive*. □ **affreusement**

2 very badly: *It was shockingly made*. □ **très mal**

'**shock absorber** *noun* a device (in a car *etc*) for reducing the effect of bumps. □ **amortisseur (de chocs)**

shock² [ʃok] *noun* a bushy mass (of hair) on a person's head. □ **tignasse**

shod *see* **shoe**.

shoddy ['ʃodi] *adjective* **1** of poor material or quality: *shoddy furniture*. □ **de camelote**

2 mean and contemptible: *a shoddy trick*. □ **minable**

'**shoddily** *adverb*. □ **mal**

'**shoddiness** *noun*. □ **mauvaise qualité**

shoe [ʃuː] *noun* **1** an outer covering for the foot: *a new pair of shoes*. □ **chaussure, soulier**

2 (*also* '**horseshoe**) a curved piece of iron nailed to the hoof of a horse. □ **fer à cheval**

■ *verb* – *present participle* '**shoeing**: *past tense, past participles* **shod** [ʃod], **shoed** – to put a shoe or shoes on (a horse *etc*). □ **chausser; ferrer**

shod [ʃod] *adjective* with a shoe or shoes on. □ **chaussé; ferré**

'**shoelace**, '**shoestring** *noun* a kind of string or cord for fastening a shoe. □ **lacet**

'**shoemaker** *noun* a person who makes, repairs, or sells shoes. □ **cordonnier, ière**

on a shoestring with or using very little money: *He has to live on a shoestring*. □ **à peu de frais**

shone *see* **shine**.

shoo [ʃuː] *interjection* an exclamation used when chasing a person, animal *etc* away. □ **ouste**

■ *verb* to chase away: *She shooed the pigeons away*. □ **chasser**

shook *see* **shake**.

shoot [ʃuːt] – *past tense, past participle* **shot** [ʃot] – *verb* **1** (*often with* **at**) to send or fire (bullets, arrows *etc*) from a gun, bow *etc*: *The enemy were shooting at us*; *He shot an arrow through the air*. □ **tirer**

2 to hit or kill with a bullet, arrow *etc*: *He went out to shoot pigeons*; *He was sentenced to be shot at dawn*. □ **tirer; fusiller**

3 to direct swiftly and suddenly: *She shot them an angry glance*. □ **lancer**

4 to move swiftly: *She shot out of the room*; *The pain shot up his leg*; *The force of the explosion shot him across the room*. □ **(s')élancer; projeter**

5 to take (*usually* moving) photographs (for a film): *That*

film was shot in Spain; *We will start shooting next week*. □ **tourner, prendre en photo**

6 to kick or hit at a goal in order to try to score. □ **tirer**

7 to kill (game birds *etc*) for sport. □ **tirer**

■ *noun* a new growth on a plant: *The deer were eating the young shoots on the trees*. □ **pousse**

shooting *noun* **1** the firing of a gun or firearm: *The shooting took place at the corner and the wounded man staggered away*. □ **fusillade**

2 the filming of a motion picture: *The shooting was scheduled for 6:00, but the actors didn't arrive until noon*. □ **tournage**

shooting star *see* **meteor**.

shoot down to hit (a plane) with *eg* a shell and cause it to crash. □ **abattre**

shoot rapids to pass through rapids (in a canoe). □ **franchir des rapides**

shoot up to grow or increase rapidly: *Prices have shot up*. □ **monter en flèche**

shop [ʃop] *noun* **1** a place where goods are sold: *a baker's shop*. □ **magasin**

2 a workshop, or a place where any kind of industry is carried on: *a machine-shop*. □ **atelier**

■ *verb* – *past tense, past participle* **shopped** – (*often* **go shopping**) to visit shops for the purpose of buying: *We shop on Saturdays*; *She goes shopping once a week*. □ **magasiner**

'**shopper** *noun* a person who is shopping: *The street was full of shoppers*. □ **acheteur, euse**

'**shopping** *noun* **1** the activity of buying goods in shops: *Have you a lot of shopping to do?*; (*also adjective*) *a shopping list*. □ **magasinage**

2 the goods bought: *He helped her carry her shopping home*; (*also adjective*) *a shopping-basket/bag*. □ **achats; (...) à provisions**

shop assistant ('**salesclerk**, **clerk**) a person employed in a shop to serve customers. □ **vendeur, euse**

shop floor the workers in a factory or workshop, as opposed to the management. □ **les ouvriers**

'**shopkeeper** *noun* a person who runs a shop of his or her own. □ **commerçant, ante**

'**shoplifter** *noun* a person who steals goods from a shop. □ **voleur, euse à l'étalage**

'**shoplifting** *noun*. □ **vol à l'étalage**

shopping bag *noun*. □ **sac (à provisions)**

shopping centre a place, often a very large building, where there is a large number of different shops. □ **centre commercial**

shop around to compare prices, quality of goods *etc* at several shops before buying anything. □ **comparer les prix**

shore [ʃoː] *noun* land bordering on the sea or on any large area of water: *a walk along the shore*; *When the ship reached Gibraltar the passengers were allowed on shore*. □ **rivage, littoral, rive**

shorn *see* **shear**.

short [ʃoːt] *adjective* **1** not long: *You look nice with your hair short*; *Do you think my dress is too short?* □ **court**

2 not tall; smaller than usual: *a short man*. □ **petit**

3 not lasting long; brief: *a short film*; *in a very short*

time; *I've a very short memory for details.* □ **court**
4 not as much as it should be: *When I checked my*
change, I found it was 20 cents short. □ **manquant**
5 (*with* of) not having enough (money *etc*): *Most of us*
are short of money these days. □ **à court de**
6 (of pastry) made so that it is crisp and crumbles easily. □ **brisé**
■ *adverb* **1** suddenly; abruptly: *She stopped short when*
she saw me. □ **net**
2 not as far as intended: *The shot fell short.* □ **ne pas**
atteindre
'**shortness** *noun.* □ **brièveté**
'**shortage** [-tidʒ] *noun* a lack; the state of not having
enough: *a shortage of water.* □ **manque, pénurie**
'**shorten** *verb* to make or become shorter: *The dress is*
too long – we'll have to shorten it. □ **raccourcir**
'**shortening** *noun* the fat used for making pastry. □
graisse végétale
'**shortly** *adverb* soon: *She will be here shortly*; *Shortly*
after that, the police arrived. □ **bientôt**
shorts *noun plural* short trousers for men or women. □
shorts
'**shortbread** *noun* a kind of crisp, crumbling biscuit. □
sablé
,**short'change** *verb* to cheat (a buyer) by giving him
too little change. □ **tromper qqn en rendant la**
monnaie
short circuit the missing out by an electric current of a
part of an electrical circuit (*verb* ,**short-'circuit**). □
court-circuit
'**shortcoming** *noun* a fault. □ **défaut**
'**shortcut** *noun* a quicker way between two places: *I'm*
in a hurry – I'll take a shortcut across the field. □
raccourci
'**shorthand** *noun* a method of writing rapidly, using
strokes, dots *etc* to represent sounds. □ **sténographie**
,**short-'handed** *adjective* having fewer workers than are
necessary or usual. □ **à court de main-d'œuvre**
'**short list** *noun* a list of candidates selected from the
total number of applicants for a job *etc*. □ **liste des**
candidats sélectionnés
■ *verb* to put on a short-list: *We've short-listed three of*
the twenty applicants. □ **retenir la candidature**
,**short-'lived** [-'laivd] *adjective* living or lasting only for
a short time: *short-lived insects*; *short-lived enthusiasm.*
□ **éphémère**
,**short-'range** *adjective* **1** not reaching a long distance:
short-range missiles. □ **à courte portée**
2 not covering a long time: *a short-range weather fore-*
cast. □ **à court terme**
,**short-'sighted** *adjective* seeing clearly only things that
are near: *I don't recognize people at a distance because*
I'm short-sighted. □ **myope**
,**short-'sightedly** *adverb.* □ **sans prévoyance**
,**short-'sightedness** *noun.* □ **myopie; imprévoyance**
,**short-'tempered** *adjective* easily made angry: *My hus-*
band is very short-tempered in the mornings. □ **irritable**
,**short-'term** *adjective* **1** concerned only with the near
future: *short-term plans.* □ **à court terme**
2 lasting only a short time: *a short-term loan.* □ **à court**

terme
for short as an abbreviation: *His name is Victor, but we*
call him Vic for short. □ **pour abréger**
go short to cause oneself not to have enough of something: *Save this carton for tomorrow, or else we'll go*
short (*of milk*). □ **manquer (de)**
in short in a few words. □ **bref**
in short supply not available in sufficient quantity:
Fresh vegetables are in short supply. □ **en quantité**
réduite
make short work of to dispose of very quickly: *The*
children made short work of the ice cream. □ **expédier**
run short 1 (of a supply) to become insufficient: *Our*
money is running short. □ **commencer à manquer (de)**
2 (*with* of) not to have enough: *We're running short of*
money. □ **être à court de**
short and sweet: *Her reply was short and sweet: 'Get*
out!' she shouted. □ **clair et net**
short for an abbreviation of: *'Phone' is short for 'tel-*
ephone'; *What is 'Ltd.' short for?* □ **abréviation de**
short of not as far as or as much as: *Our total came to*
just short of $1,000; *We stopped five kilometres short of*
Toronto. □ **presque; juste avant**
shot¹ [ʃot] *noun* **1** a single act of shooting: *She fired one*
shot. □ **coup**
2 the sound of a gun being fired: *He heard a shot.* □
coup (de feu)
3 a throw, hit, turn *etc* in a game or competition: *It's*
your shot; *Can I have a shot?*; *She played some good*
shots in that tennis match; *Good shot!* □ **coup**
4 an attempt: *I don't know if I can do that, but I'll have*
a shot (*at it*). □ **essai**
5 something which is shot or fired, *especially* small lead
bullets used in cartridges: *lead shot.* □ **plomb(s)**
6 a photograph, *especially* a scene in a film. □ **photo;**
prise de vue
7 an injection: *The doctor gave me a shot.* □ **piqûre,**
injection
8 a marksman: *He's a good shot.* □ **bon tireur, bonne**
tireuse
'**shotgun** *noun* a type of rifle that fires shot: *a double-*
barrelled shotgun. □ **fusil de chasse**
like a shot very quickly; eagerly: *She accepted my in-*
vitation like a shot. □ **sans hésiter**
a shot in the dark a guess based on little or no information: *The detective admitted that his decision to check*
the factory had just been a shot in the dark. □ **chose**
dite/faite à tout hasard
shot² *see* shoot.
should [ʃud] – *negative short form* **shouldn't** [ʃudnt] –
verb **1** *past tense of* shall: *I thought I should never see*
you again. □ **-rais, -rait, -rions, ...**
2 used to state that something ought to happen, be done
etc: *You should hold your knife in your right hand*; *You*
shouldn't have said that. □ **devoir**
3 used to state that something is likely to happen *etc*: *If*
you leave now, you should arrive there by six o'clock. □
arriver probablement
4 used after certain expressions of sorrow, surprise
etc: *I'm surprised you should think that.* □ **ne pas**

en revenir que...

5 used after *if* to state a condition: *If anything should happen to me, I want you to remember everything I have told you today.* □ **si...**

6 (*with I or* **we**) used to state that a person wishes something was possible: *I should love to go to France (if only I had enough money).* □ **si seulement...**

7 used to refer to an event *etc* which is rather surprising: *I was just about to get on the bus when who should come along but Joan, the very person I was going to visit.* □ **et voilà que...**

shoulder ['ʃouldə] *noun* **1** the part of the body between the neck and the upper arm: *He was carrying the child on his shoulders.* □ **épaule**

2 anything that resembles a shoulder: *the shoulder of the hill.* □ **épaulement**

3 the part of a garment that covers the shoulder: *the shoulder of a coat.* □ **épaule**

4 the upper part of the foreleg of an animal. □ **épaule**

■ *verb* **1** to lift on to the shoulder: *He shouldered his pack and set off on his walk.* □ **charger sur son épaule**

2 to bear the full weight of: *He must shoulder his responsibilities.* □ **endosser**

3 to make (one's way) by pushing with the shoulder: *She shouldered her way through the crowd.* □ **se frayer un chemin à coups d'épaules**

'shoulder blade *noun* the broad flat bone of the back of the shoulder. □ **omoplate**

put one's shoulder to the wheel to begin to work very hard. □ **s'atteler à la tâche**

shoulder to shoulder close together; side by side: *We'll fight shoulder to shoulder.* □ **côte à côte**

shouldn't *see* **should**.

shout [ʃaut] *noun* **1** a loud cry or call: *She heard a shout.* □ **cri**

2 a loud burst (of laughter, cheering *etc*): *A shout went up from the crowd when he scored a goal.* □ **acclamation**

■ *verb* to say very loudly: *She shouted the message across the river; I'm not deaf – there's no need to shout; Calm down and stop shouting at each other.* □ **crier, gueuler**

shove [ʃʌv] *verb* to thrust; to push: *I shoved the papers into a drawer; I'm sorry I bumped into you – somebody shoved me; Stop shoving!; He shoved (his way) through the crowd.* □ **enfoncer, pousser**

■ *noun* a push: *He gave the table a shove.* □ **poussée**

shovel ['ʃʌvl] *noun* a tool like a spade, with a short handle, used for scooping up and moving coal, gravel *etc*. □ **pelle**

■ *verb – past tense, past participle* 'shovelled, 'shoveled – to move (as if) with a shovel, *especially* in large quantities: *She shovelled snow from the path; Don't shovel your food into your mouth!* □ **pelleter; enfourner**

'shovelful *noun* the amount that can be held, carried *etc* on a shovel: *a shovelful of coal.* □ **pelletée**

show [ʃou] *– past tense* showed: *past participles* showed, shown *– verb* **1** to allow or cause to be seen: *Show me your new dress; Please show your membership card when you come to the club; Her work is showing signs*

of improvement. □ **montrer**

2 to be able to be seen: *The tear in your dress hardly shows; a faint light showing through the curtains.* □ **se voir**

3 to offer or display, or to be offered or displayed, for the public to look at: *Which picture is showing at the cinema?; They are showing a new film; Her paintings are being shown at the art gallery.* □ **jouer; passer; exposer**

4 to point out or point to: *She showed me the road to take; Show me the man you saw yesterday.* □ **montrer**

5 (*often with* **around**) to guide or conduct: *Please show this lady to the door; They showed him around (the factory).* □ **conduire qqn**

6 to demonstrate to: *Will you show me how to do it?; She showed me a clever trick.* □ **montrer**

7 to prove: *That just shows/goes to show how stupid he is.* □ **montrer**

8 to give or offer (someone) kindness *etc*: *He showed him no mercy.* □ **montrer**

■ *noun* **1** an entertainment, public exhibition, performance *etc*: *a horse show; a flower show; the new show at the theatre; a TV show.* □ **exposition, spectacle**

2 a display or act of showing: *a show of strength.* □ **démonstration**

3 an act of pretending to be, do *etc* (something): *He made a show of working, but he wasn't really concentrating.* □ **semblant/mine (de)**

4 appearance, impression: *They just did it for show, in order to make themselves seem more important than they are.* □ **pour l'effet**

5 an effort or attempt: *She put up a good show in the chess competition.* □ **(faire) bonne figure**

'showy *adjective* giving an impression of value by a bright and striking outward appearance: *His clothes are too showy for my liking.* □ **voyant**

'showiness *noun*. □ **caractère voyant**

'show business *noun* the entertainment industry, *especially* the branch of the theatre concerned with variety shows, comedy *etc*. □ **industrie du spectacle**

'showcase *noun* a glass case for displaying objects in a museum, shop *etc*. □ **vitrine**

'showdown *noun* an open, decisive quarrel *etc* ending a period of rivalry *etc*. □ **épreuve de force**

'showground *noun* an area where displays *etc* are held. □ **champ de foire**

'show jumping *noun* a competitive sport in which horses and their riders have to jump a series of artificial fences, walls *etc*. □ **concours hippique**

'showman *noun* a person who owns or manages an entertainment, a stall at a fair *etc*. □ **forain**

'showroom *noun* a room where objects for sale *etc* are displayed for people to see: *a car showroom.* □ **salle d'exposition**

give the show away to make known a secret, trick *etc*. □ **vendre la mèche**

good show! that's good! □ **bravo!**

on show being displayed in an exhibition, showroom *etc*: *There are over five hundred paintings on show here.* □ **exposé**

show off 1 to show or display for admiration: *He showed off his new car by taking it to work.* □ **en mettre plein la vue**
2 to try to impress others with one's possessions, ability *etc*: *She is just showing off – she wants everyone to know how well she speaks French* (*noun* **'show-off** a person who does this). □ **étalage de qqch.; prétentieux, euse**
show up 1 to make obvious: *This light shows up the places where I've mended this coat.* □ **faire ressortir**
2 to reveal the faults of: *Mary was so neat that she really showed me up.* □ **faire honte à**
3 to stand out clearly: *The scratches showed up on the photograph.* □ **se voir (nettement)**
4 to appear or arrive: *I waited for her, but she never showed up.* □ **venir, arriver**
shower ['ʃauə] *noun* **1** a short fall (of rain): *I got caught in a shower on my way here.* □ **averse**
2 anything resembling such a fall of rain: *a shower of sparks*; *a shower of bullets.* □ **pluie/déluge de**
3 a bath in which water is sprayed down on the bather from above: *I'm just going to have/take a shower.* □ **douche**
4 the equipment used for such a bath: *We're having a shower fitted in the bathroom.* □ **douche**
■ *verb* **1** to pour down in large quantities (on): *They showered confetti on the bride.* □ **inonder de**
2 to bathe in a shower: *He showered and dressed.* □ **prendre une douche**
'showery *adjective* raining from time to time: *showery weather.* □ **pluvieux**
'showerproof *adjective* (of material, a coat *etc*) which will not be soaked by a light shower of rain. □ **imperméable**
shown *etc see* **show**.
shrank *see* **shrink**.
shrapnel ['ʃrapnəl] *noun* small pieces of metal from an explosive shell, bomb *etc*: *His leg was torn open by shrapnel.* □ **éclats d'obus**
shred [ʃred] *noun* a long, narrow strip (*especially* very small) torn or cut: *The lion tore his coat to shreds*; *a tiny shred of material.* □ **lambeau**
■ *verb* – *past tense, past participle* **'shredded** – to cut or tear into shreds: *to shred paper.* □ **déchiqueter**
shrew [ʃruː] *noun* a type of small mouse-like animal with a long, pointed nose. □ **musaraigne**
shrewd [ʃruːd] *adjective* showing good judgment; wise: *a shrewd man*; *a shrewd choice.* □ **astucieux**
'shrewdly *adverb*. □ **astucieusement**
'shrewdness *noun*. □ **astuce**
shriek [ʃriːk] *verb* to give out, or say with, a high scream or laugh: *She shrieked whenever she saw a spider*; *shrieking with laughter.* □ **hurler, pousser un cri**
■ *noun* such a scream or laugh: *She gave a shriek as she felt someone grab her arm*; *shrieks of laughter.* □ **cri perçant**
shrill [ʃril] *adjective* high-pitched and piercing: *the shrill cry of a child.* □ **criard**
'shrilly *adverb*. □ **d'un ton perçant/aigu**
'shrillness *noun*. □ **ton perçant/aigu**
shrimp [ʃrimp] *noun* **1** a kind of small long-tailed shell-

fish. □ **crevette**
2 an unkind word for a small person. □ **nabot, ote**
shrine [ʃrain] *noun* **1** a holy or sacred place: *Many people visited the shrine where the saint lay buried.* □ **lieu saint**
2 a *usually* highly-decorated case for holding holy objects. □ **châsse**
shrink [ʃriŋk] – *past tense* **shrank** [ʃraŋk]: *past participle* **shrunk** [ʃrʌŋk] – *verb* **1** to (cause material, clothes *etc* to) become smaller: *My jersey shrank in the wash*; *Do they shrink the material before they make it up into clothes?* □ **(faire) rétrécir**
2 to move back in fear, disgust *etc* (from): *She shrank (back) from the man.* □ **reculer devant qqch.**
3 to wish to avoid something unpleasant: *I shrank from telling her the terrible news.* □ **hésiter à faire qqch.**
'shrinkage [-kidʒ] *noun* the act of shrinking, or the amount by which something shrinks. □ **rétrécissement**
shrunken ['ʃrʌŋk(ən)] *adjective* having been made or become smaller. □ **ratatiné**
shrivel ['ʃrivl] – *past tense, past participle* **'shrivelled, 'shriveled** – *verb* to make or become dried up, wrinkled and withered: *The flowers shrivelled in the heat.* □ **(se) flétrir**
shrivel up to shrivel: *The flowers shrivelled up*; *The heat shrivelled up the flowers.* □ **(se) flétrir**
shroud [ʃraud] *noun* **1** a cloth wrapped around a dead body. □ **linceul**
2 something that covers: *a shroud of mist.* □ **voile**
■ *verb* to cover or hide: *The incident was shrouded in mystery.* □ **envelopper**
shrub [ʃrʌb] *noun* a small bush or woody plant: *He has planted bushes and shrubs in his garden.* □ **arbuste**
'shrubbery – *plural* **'shrubberies** – *noun* a part of a garden where shrubs are grown. □ **(massif d') arbustes**
shrug [ʃrʌg] – *past tense, past participle* **shrugged** – *verb* to show doubt, lack of interest *etc* by raising (the shoulders): *When I asked him if he knew what had happened, he just shrugged (his shoulders).* □ **hausser les épaules**
■ *noun* an act of shrugging: *She gave a shrug of disbelief.* □ **haussement d'épaules**
shrug off to dismiss, get rid of or treat as unimportant: *She shrugged off all criticism.* □ **ignorer**
shrunk, shrunken *see* **shrink**.
shudder ['ʃʌdə] *verb* to tremble from fear, disgust, cold *etc.* □ **frissonner**
■ *noun* an act of trembling in this way: *a shudder of horror.* □ **frisson**
shuffle ['ʃʌfl] *verb* **1** to move (one's feet) along the ground *etc* without lifting them: *Do stop shuffling (your feet)!*; *The old man shuffled along the street.* □ **traîner les pieds**
2 to mix (playing cards *etc*): *It's your turn to shuffle (the cards).* □ **mêler, battre**
■ *noun* an act of shuffling: *She gave the cards a shuffle.* □ **battage**
shun [ʃʌn] – *past tense, past participle* **shunned** – *verb* to avoid or keep away from. □ **fuir**
shut [ʃʌt] – *present participle* **'shutting**: *past tense, past*

participle **shut** – *verb* **1** to move (a door, window, lid *etc*) so that it covers or fills an opening; to move (a drawer, book *etc*) so that it is no longer open: *Shut that door, please!; Shut your eyes and don't look.* □ **fermer**
2 to become closed: *The window shut with a bang.* □ **se fermer**
3 to close and *usually* lock (a building *etc*) eg at the end of the day or when people no longer work there: *The shops all shut at half past five; There's a rumour that the factory is going to be shut.* □ **fermer**
4 to keep in or out of some place or keep away from someone by shutting something: *The dog was shut inside the house.* □ **enfermer, mettre dehors**
■ *adjective* closed. □ **fermé**
shut down (of a factory *etc*) to close or be closed, for a time or permanently: *There is a rumour going around that the factory is going to (be) shut down (noun* '**shutdown**). □ **fermer (ses portes); fermeture**
shut off 1 to stop an engine working, a liquid flowing *etc*: *I'll need to shut the gas off before I repair the fire.* □ **fermer, couper**
2 to keep away (from); to make separate (from): *He shut himself off from the rest of the world.* □ **se couper de**
shut up 1 to (cause to) stop speaking: *Tell them to shut up!; That'll shut him up!* □ **(faire) taire**
2 to close and lock: *It's time to shut up the shop.* □ **fermer**
shutter ['ʃʌtə] *noun* **1** one of *usually* two *usually* wooden covers over a window: *She closed the shutters.* □ **volet, persienne**
2 the moving cover over the lens of a camera, which opens when a photograph is taken: *When the shutter opens, light is allowed into the camera and reacts with the film.* □ **obturateur**
'**shuttered** *adjective: shuttered windows.* □ **aux volets fermés**
shuttle ['ʃʌtl] *noun* **1** in weaving, a piece of equipment for carrying the thread backwards and forwards across the other threads. □ **navette**
2 a piece of machinery for making loops in the lower thread in a sewing-machine. □ **navette**
3 an air, train or other transport service *etc* which operates constantly backwards and forwards between two places: *an airline shuttle between London and Edinburgh; space shuttle* (= a craft travelling between space stations). □ **navette**
'**shuttlecock** *noun* a rounded cork *etc*, with feathers *etc* fixed in it, used in the game of badminton. □ **volant**
shy [ʃai] – *comparative* '**shyer** *or* '**shier**: *superlative* '**shyest** *or* '**shiest** – *adjective* **1** lacking confidence in the presence of others, *especially* strangers; not wanting to attract attention: *He is too shy to go to parties.* □ **timide**
2 drawing back from (an action, person *etc*): *She is shy of strangers.* □ **mal à l'aise (avec, devant)**
3 (of a wild animal) easily frightened; timid: *Deer are very shy animals.* □ **craintif**
■ *verb* (of a horse) to jump or turn suddenly aside in fear: *The horse shied at the strangers.* □ **se cabrer (devant)**

'**shyly** *adverb.* □ **timidement**
'**shyness** *noun.* □ **timidité**
sick [sik] *adjective* **1** vomiting or inclined to vomit: *He has been sick several times today; I feel sick; She's inclined to be seasick/airsick/carsick.* □ **qui a mal au cœur**
2 ill: *He is a sick man; The doctor told me that my husband is very sick and may not live very long.* □ **malade**
3 very tired (of); wishing to have no more (of): *I'm sick of doing this; I'm sick and tired of hearing about it!* □ **qui en a assez (de)**
4 affected by strong, unhappy or unpleasant feelings: *He has been sick at heart since she left.* □ **écœuré par**
5 in bad taste: *a sick joke.* □ **macabre**
'**sicken** *verb* **1** to become sick. □ **tomber malade**
2 to disgust: *The very thought sickens me.* □ **écœurer**
'**sickening** *adjective* causing sickness, disgust or weariness; very unpleasant or annoying: *There was a sickening crunch; The weather is really sickening!* □ **écœurant**
'**sickeningly** *adverb.* □ **d'une manière écœurante**
'**sickly** *adjective* **1** tending to be often ill: *a sickly child.* □ **maladif**
2 suggesting sickness; pale; feeble: *She looks sickly.* □ **pâle**
'**sickness** *noun* the state of being sick or ill: *There seems to be a lot of sickness in the town; seasickness.* □ **maladie**
'**sick leave** *noun* time taken off from work *etc* because of sickness: *She has been on sick-leave for the last three days.* □ **congé de maladie**
make (someone) sick to make (someone) feel very annoyed, upset *etc*: *It makes me sick to see him waste money like that.* □ **rendre malade**
the sick ill people: *He visits the sick.* □ **les malades**
worried sick very worried: *I'm worried sick about it.* □ **malade d'inquiétude**

---

see also **ill**.

---

sickle ['sikl] *noun* a tool with a curved blade for cutting grain *etc*. □ **faucille**
side [said] *noun* **1** (the ground beside) an edge, border or boundary line: *She walked around the side of the field; He lives on the same side of the street as me.* □ **côté**
2 a surface of something: *A cube has six sides.* □ **côté**
3 one of the two of such surfaces which are not the top, bottom, front, or back: *There is a label on the side of the box.* □ **côté**
4 either surface of a piece of paper, cloth *etc*: *Don't waste paper – write on both sides!* □ **côté**
5 the right or left part of the body: *I've got a pain in my side.* □ **côté**
6 a part or division of a town *etc*: *She lives on the north side of the town.* □ **partie**
7 a slope (of a hill): *a mountain-side.* □ **versant**
8 a point of view; an aspect: *We must look at all sides of the problem.* □ **aspect, point de vue**
9 a party, team *etc* which is opposing another: *Whose side are you on?; Which side is winning?* □ **côté**
■ *adjective* additional, but less important: *a side issue.* □ **secondaire**

-side (the ground *etc* beside) the edge of something: *He walked along the dockside/quayside*; *a roadside café.* □ **bord (de)**

-sided having (a certain number or type of) sides: *a four-sided figure.* □ **à (...) côtés**

'sidelong *adjective, adverb* from or to the side; not directly: *a sidelong glance*; *She glanced sidelong.* □ **(en) oblique, de côté**

'sideways *adjective, adverb* to or towards one side: *He moved sideways*; *a sideways movement.* □ **de côté**

'sideburns *noun plural* the *usually* short hair grown on the side of a man's face in front of the ears. □ **favoris**

side effect an additional (often bad) effect of a drug *etc*: *These pills have unpleasant side effects.* □ **effet secondaire**

'sidelight *noun* a light fixed to the side, or at the side of the front or back, of a car, boat *etc*: *He switched his sidelights on when it began to get dark.* □ **lanterne**

'sideline *noun* 1 a business *etc* carried on outside one's regular job or activity: *She runs a mail-order business as a sideline.* □ **travail complémentaire**

2 the line marking one of the long edges of a football pitch *etc*. □ **ligne latérale**

'sidelines *noun plural* the position or point of view of a person not actually taking part in a sport, argument *etc*: *He threw in the occasional suggestion from the sidelines.* □ **de l'extérieur**

side road a small, minor road. □ **petite route**

'sidestep – *past tense, past participle* 'sidestepped – *verb* 1 to step to one side: *He sidestepped as his attacker tried to grab him.* □ **esquiver**

2 to avoid: *to sidestep a problem.* □ **éviter**

'side street *noun* a small, minor street: *The woman ran down a side street and disappeared.* □ **petite rue**

'sidetrack *verb* to turn (a person) aside from what he was about to do: *I intended to write letters this evening, but was sidetracked into going to the pictures instead.* □ **détourner l'attention de qqn**

'sidewalk *noun* a pavement or footpath. □ **trottoir**

from all sides from every direction: *People were running towards him from all sides.* □ **de tous côtés**

on all sides all around: *With enemies on all sides, we were trapped.* □ **de tous côtés**

side by side beside one another; close together: *They walked along the street side by side.* □ **côte à côte**

side with to give support to in an argument *etc*: *Don't side with her against us!* □ **prendre parti pour**

take sides to choose to support a particular opinion, group *etc* against another: *Everybody in the office took sides in the dispute.* □ **prendre parti**

sidle ['saidl] *verb* to go or move in a manner intended not to attract attention or as if one is shy or uncertain: *She sidled out of the room.* □ **se faufiler**

siege [siːdʒ] *noun* an attempt to capture a fort or town by keeping it surrounded by an armed force until it surrenders: *The town is under siege.* □ **siège**

siege is spelt with -ie- (not -ei-).

sieve [siv] *noun* a container with a bottom full of very small holes, used to separate liquids from solids or small,

fine pieces from larger ones *etc*: *He poured the soup through a sieve to remove all the lumps.* □ **tamis, crible**

■ *verb* to pass (something) through a sieve. □ **tamiser, passer au crible**

sift [sift] *verb* 1 to separate by passing through a sieve *etc*: *Sift the flour before making the cake.* □ **tamiser**

2 to examine closely: *She sifted the evidence carefully.* □ **examiner minutieusement**

sigh [sai] *verb* 1 to take a long, deep-sounding breath showing tiredness, sadness, longing *etc*: *She sighed with exasperation.* □ **soupirer**

2 to say, or express, with sighs: *'I've still got several hours' work to do,' he sighed.* □ **soupirer**

■ *noun* an act of sighing. □ **soupir**

heave a sigh to sigh: *She heaved a sigh of relief when she found her purse.* □ **pousser un soupir**

sight [sait] *noun* 1 the act or power of seeing: *The blind man had lost his sight in the war.* □ **vue**

2 the area within which things can be seen by someone: *The boat was within sight of land*; *The end of our troubles is in sight.* □ **(en) vue**

3 something worth seeing: *She took her visitors to see the sights of Ottawa.* □ **attraction touristique**

4 a view or glimpse. □ **vision, aperçu**

5 something seen that is unusual, ridiculous, shocking *etc*: *She's quite a sight in that hat.* □ **quelque chose à voir!**

6 (on a gun *etc*) an apparatus to guide the eye in taking aim: *Where is the sight on a rifle?* □ **mire**

■ *verb* 1 to get a view of; to see suddenly: *We sighted the coast as dawn broke.* □ **apercevoir**

2 to look at (something) through the sight of a gun: *She sighted her prey and pulled the trigger.* □ **viser**

'sightseeing *noun* visiting the chief buildings, places of interest *etc* of an area: *They spent a lot of their holiday sightseeing in Toronto*; (*also adjective*) *a sightseeing tour.* □ **tourisme; (adj.) touristique**

'sightseer *noun.* □ **touriste**

catch sight of to get a brief view of; to begin to see: *He caught sight of her as she came around the corner.* □ **apercevoir**

lose sight of to stop being able to see: *She lost sight of him in the crowd.* □ **perdre de vue**

sign [sain] *noun* 1 a mark used to mean something; a symbol: *+ is the sign for addition.* □ **signe**

2 a notice set up to give information (a shopkeeper's name, the direction of a town *etc*) to the public: *roadsign.* □ **panneau**

3 a movement (*eg* a nod, wave of the hand) used to mean or represent something: *He made a sign to me to keep still.* □ **signe**

4 a piece of evidence suggesting that something is present or about to come: *There were no signs of life at the house and he was afraid they were away*; *Clouds are often a sign of rain.* □ **signe**

■ *verb* 1 to write one's name (on): *Sign at the bottom, please.* □ **signer**

2 to write (one's name) on a letter, document *etc*: *She signed her name on the document.* □ **signer**

3 to make a movement of the head, hand *etc* in order to

show one's meaning: *She signed to me to say nothing.*
□ **faire signe (de)**

'**signboard** *noun* a board with a notice: *In the garden was a signboard which read 'House for Sale'.* □ **écriteau, enseigne**

'**signpost** *noun* a post with a sign on it, showing the direction and distance of places: *We saw a signpost which told us we were 80 kilometres from Montreal.* □ **poteau indicateur**

sign in/out to record one's arrival or departure by writing one's name: *He signed in at the hotel when he arrived.* □ **signer le registre**

sign up 1 to join an organization or make an agreement to do something *etc* by writing one's name. □ **s'inscrire**
2 to engage for work by making a legal contract. □ **se faire embaucher (comme, en qualité de)**

signal ['signəl] *noun* **1** a sign (*eg* a movement of the hand, a light, a sound), *especially* one arranged beforehand, giving a command, warning or other message: *She gave the signal to advance.* □ **signal**
2 a machine *etc* used for this purpose: *a railway signal.* □ **signal, feu**
3 the wave, sound received or sent out by a radio set *etc*. □ **signal**

■ *verb – past tense, past participle* '**signalled**, '**signaled**
– **1** to make signals (to): *The policewoman signalled the driver to stop.* □ **faire signe (à qqn) de**
2 to send (a message *etc*) by means of signals. □ **communiquer par signaux**

'**signalman** *noun* **1** a person who operates railway signals. □ **aiguilleur, euse**
2 a person who sends signals in general: *He is a signalman in the army.* □ **signaleur, euse**

signature ['signətʃə] *noun* **1** a signed name: *That is his signature on the cheque.* □ **signature**
2 an act of signing one's name: *Signature of this document means that you agree with us.* □ **signature**

signify ['signifai] *verb* **1** to be a sign of; to mean: *His frown signified disapproval.* □ **signifier**
2 to show; to make known by a sign, gesture *etc*: *He signified his approval with a nod.* □ **signifier, indiquer**
significance [sig'nifikəns] *noun* meaning or importance: *a matter of great significance.* □ **importance**
significant [sig'nifikənt] *adjective* having a lot of meaning or importance: *There was no significant change in the patient's condition.* □ **significatif**
significantly [sig'nifikəntli] *adverb* **1** in a significant manner: *He patted his pocket significantly.* □ **d'une manière significative**
2 to an important degree: *Sales-levels are significantly lower than last year, which is very disappointing.* □ **considérablement**

silence ['sailəns] *noun* **1** (a period of) absence of sound or of speech: *A sudden silence followed her remark.* □ **silence**
2 failure to mention, tell something *etc*: *Your silence on this subject is disturbing.* □ **silence**

■ *verb* to cause to be silent: *The arrival of the teacher silenced the class.* □ **faire taire**
■ *interjection* be silent! □ **silence!**

'**silencer** *noun* a piece of equipment fitted to a gun, or ('**muffler**) in an engine, for making noise less. □ **silencieux**
'**silent** [-t] *adjective* **1** free from noise: *The house was empty and silent.* □ **silencieux**
2 not speaking: *He was silent on that subject.* □ **silencieux**
3 not making any noise: *This lift is quite silent.* □ **silencieux**
'**silently** *adverb*. □ **silencieusement**
in silence without saying anything: *The children listened in silence to the story.* □ **en silence**

silhouette [silu'et] *noun* **1** an outline drawing of a person: *A silhouette in a silver frame hung on the wall.* □ **silhouette**
2 a dark image, *especially* a shadow, seen against the light. □ **silhouette**

silk [silk] *noun* **1** very fine, soft threads made by silkworms. □ **soie**
2 thread, cloth *etc* made from this: *The dress was made of silk*; (*also adjective*) *a silk dress.* □ **(en/de) soie**
'**silky** *adjective* soft, fine and rather shiny like silk. □ **soyeux**
'**silkiness** *noun*. □ **aspect soyeux**
'**silkworm** *noun* the caterpillar of certain moths, which makes silk. □ **ver à soie**

sill [sil] *noun* a ledge of wood, stone *etc* at the foot of an opening, such as a window or a door: *The windows of the old house were loose, and the sills were crumbling.* □ **rebord**

silly ['sili] *adjective* foolish; not sensible: *Don't be so silly!*; *silly children.* □ **bête, idiot**
'**silliness** *noun*. □ **bêtise, idiotie, niaiserie**

silt [silt] *noun* fine sand and mud left behind by flowing water. □ **vase**
silt up to (cause to) become blocked by mud *etc*: *The harbour had gradually silted up, so that large boats could no longer use it.* □ **s'envaser**

silver ['silvə] *noun* **1** an element, a precious grey metal which is used in making jewellery, ornaments *etc*: *The tray was made of solid silver.* □ **argent**
2 anything made of, or looking like, silver *especially* knives, forks, spoons *etc*: *Burglars broke into the house and stole all our silver.* □ **argenterie**

■ *adjective* **1** made of, of the colour of, or looking like, silver: *a silver brooch*; *silver stars/paint.* □ **d'argent, argenté**
2 (of a wedding anniversary, jubilee *etc*) twenty-fifth: *We celebrated our silver wedding (anniversary) last month.* □ **d'argent**
'**silvery** *adjective* like silver, *especially* in colour. □ **(gris) argenté**
silver foil/paper a common type of wrapping material, made of metal and having a silvery appearance: *Chocolate bars are sold wrapped in silver paper.* □ **papier d'argent**

similar ['similə] *adjective* (*often with* **to**) alike in many (often most) ways: *My house is similar to yours*; *Our jobs are similar.* □ **semblable**
simi'larity [-'la-] (*plural* **simi'larities**) *noun*. □ **similitude**

'**similarly** *adverb* in the same, or a similar, way. □ **de la même façon**

simile ['siməli] *noun* a form of expression using 'like' or 'as', in which one thing is compared to another which it only resembles in one or a small number of ways: *'Her hair was like silk' is a simile.* □ **comparaison**

simmer ['simə] *verb* to (cause to) cook gently at or just below boiling point: *The stew simmered on the stove*; *Simmer the ingredients in water for five minutes.* □ **(faire) mijoter**

simmer down to calm down. □ **(se) calmer**

simple ['simpl] *adjective* **1** not difficult; easy: *a simple task.* □ **simple**

2 not complicated or involved: *The matter is not as simple as you think.* □ **simple**

3 not fancy or unusual; plain: *a simple dress/design*; *She leads a very simple life.* □ **simple**

4 pure; mere: *the simple truth.* □ **pur et simple**

5 trusting and easily cheated: *She is too simple to see through his lies.* □ **naïf**

6 weak in the mind; not very intelligent: *I'm afraid he's a bit simple, but he's good with animals.* □ **niais**

'**simpleton** [-tən] *noun* a foolish person. □ **niais, niaise**

simplicity [sim'plisəti] *noun* the state of being simple: *The beauty of this idea is its simplicity*; *He answered with a child's simplicity.* □ **simplicité**

,**simpli'cation** *noun* **1** the process of making simpler. □ **simplification**

2 something made simpler; a simpler form: *The Americans have made some simplifications in English spelling.* □ **simplification**

'**simplified** *adjective* made less difficult or complicated: *simplified language/tasks.* □ **simplifié**

'**simplify** [-plifai] *verb* to make simpler: *Can you simplify your language a little?* □ **simplifier**

'**simply** *adverb* **1** only: *I do it simply for the money.* □ **simplement**

2 absolutely: *simply beautiful.* □ **tout simplement**

3 in a simple manner: *She was always very simply dressed.* □ **avec simplicité**

,**simple-'minded** *adjective* of low intelligence; stupid. □ **simplet**

,**simple-'mindedness** *noun.* □ **simplicité d'esprit**

simulate ['simjuleit] *verb* to cause (something) to appear to be real *etc*: *This machine simulates the take-off and landing of an aircraft.* □ **simuler**

'**simulated** *adjective* artificial; having the appearance of: *simulated leather*; *a simulated accident.* □ **simulé, artificiel**

,**simu'lation** *noun* **1** (an act of) simulating. □ **simulation**

2 something made to resemble something else. □ **simulation**

simultaneous [saiməl'teiniəs] *adjective* happening, or done, at exactly the same time: *He fell, and there was a simultaneous gasp from the crowd.* □ **simultané**

,**simul'taneously** *adverb.* □ **simultanément**

sin [sin] *noun* wickedness, or a wicked act, *especially* one that breaks a religious law: *It is a sin to envy the possessions of other people*; *Lying and cheating are both sins.* □ **péché, mal**

■ *verb – past tense, past participle* **sinned** – to do wrong; to commit a sin, *especially* in the religious sense: *Forgive me, Father, for I have sinned.* □ **pécher (contre)**

'**sinner** *noun.* □ **pécheur, eresse**

'**sinful** *adjective* wicked. □ **coupable; honteux**

'**sinfully** *adverb.* □ **d'une façon coupable**

'**sinfulness** *noun.* □ **caractère coupable**

since *conjunction* **1** (*often with* **ever**) from a certain time onwards: *I have been at home ever since I returned from Italy.* □ **depuis (que)**

2 at a time after: *Since he agreed to come, he has become ill.* □ **depuis que**

3 because: *Since you are going, I will go too.* □ **puisque**

■ *adverb* **1** (*usually with* **ever**) from that time onwards: *We fought and I have avoided him ever since.* □ **depuis**

2 at a later time: *We have since become friends.* □ **depuis**

■ *preposition* **1** from the time of (something in the past) until the present time: *She has been very unhappy ever since her quarrel with her boyfriend.* □ **depuis**

2 at a time between (something in the past) and the present time: *I've changed my address since last year.* □ **depuis**

3 from the time of (the invention, discovery *etc* of): *the greatest invention since the wheel.* □ **depuis**

sincere [sin'siə] *adjective* **1** true; genuine: *a sincere desire*; *sincere friends.* □ **sincère**

2 not trying to pretend or deceive: *a sincere person.* □ **sincère**

sin'cerely *adverb*: *I sincerely hope that you will succeed.* □ **sincèrement**

sin'cerity [-'se-] *noun* the state of being sincere: *The sincerity of her comments was obvious to all.* □ **sincérité**

sinful *see* **sin.**

sing [siŋ] – *past tense* **sang** [saŋ]: *past participle* **sung** [sʌŋ] – *verb* to make (musical) sounds with one's voice: *He sings very well*; *She sang a Scottish song*; *I could hear the birds singing in the trees.* □ **chanter**

'**singer** *noun* a person who sings, *eg* as a profession: *Are you a good singer?*; *She's a trained singer.* □ **chanteur, euse**

'**singing** *noun* the art or activity of making musical sounds with one's voice: *Do you do much singing nowadays?*; (*also adjective*) *a singing lesson/teacher.* □ **(de) chant**

sing out to shout or call out: *Sing out when you're ready to go.* □ **appeler (en criant)**

singe [sindʒ] – *present participle* '**singeing**: *past tense, past participle* **singed** – *verb* to (cause to) burn on the surface; to scorch: *She singed her dress by pressing it with too hot an iron.* □ **roussir**

single ['siŋgl] *adjective* **1** one only: *The spider hung on a single thread.* □ **seul, unique**

2 for one person only: *a single bed/mattress.* □ **pour une personne**

3 unmarried: *a single person.* □ **célibataire**

4 for or in one direction only: *a single ticket/journey/fare.* □ **aller simple**

■ *noun* **1** a gramophone record with only one tune or song on each side: *This group have just brought out a*

new single. □ **un quarante-cinq tours**
2 a one-way ticket. □ **aller simple**
'singleness *noun.* □ **persévérance**
'singles *noun plural* **1** (*also noun singular*) in tennis *etc*, a match or matches with only one player on each side: *The men's singles are being played this week*; (*also adjective*) *a singles match.* □ **simple**
2 (*especially American*) unmarried (*usually* young) people: *a bar for singles*; (*also adjective*) *a singles holiday/club.* □ **célibataires**
'singly *adverb* one by one; separately: *They came all together, but they left singly.* □ **séparément**
,single-'breasted *adjective* (of a coat, jacket *etc*) having only one row of buttons: *a single-breasted tweed suit.* □ **droit**
,single-'handed *adjective, adverb* working *etc* by oneself, without help: *She runs the restaurant single-handed; single-handed efforts.* □ **tout seul**
single out to choose or pick out for special treatment: *He was singled out to receive special thanks for his help.* □ **choisir**
singular ['siŋgjulə] *noun* **1** (*also adjective*) (in) the form of a word which expresses only one: *'Foot' is the singular of 'feet'; a singular noun/verb; The noun 'foot' is singular.* □ **singulier**
2 the state of being singular: *Is this noun in the singular or the plural?* □ **singulier**
sinister ['sinistə] *adjective* suggesting, or warning of, evil: *sinister happenings; Her disappearance is extremely sinister.* □ **sinistre**
sink [siŋk] – *past tense* **sank** [saŋk]: *past participle* **sunk** [sʌŋk] – *verb* **1** to (cause to) go down below the surface of water *etc*: *The torpedo sank the battleship immediately; The ship sank in deep water.* □ **couler**
2 to go down or become lower (slowly): *The sun sank slowly behind the hills; Her voice sank to a whisper.* □ **baisser**
3 to (cause to) go deeply (into something): *The ink sank into the paper; He sank his teeth into an apple.* □ **entrer (dans)**
4 (of one's spirits *etc*) to become depressed or less hopeful: *My heart sinks when I think of the difficulties ahead.* □ **se démoraliser**
5 to invest (money): *He sank all his savings in the business.* □ **engloutir**
■ *noun* a kind of basin with a drain and a water supply connected to it: *He washed the dishes in the sink.* □ **évier**
'sunken *adjective* **1** sunk under water: *a sunken ship.* □ **submergé**
2 below the level of the surrounding area: *a sunken garden.* □ **en contrebas**
be sunk to be defeated, in a hopeless position *etc*: *If he finds out that we've been disobeying him, we're sunk.* □ **être perdu**
sink in 1 to be fully understood: *The news took a long time to sink in.* □ **être compris**
2 to be absorbed: *The surface water on the paths will soon sink in.* □ **être absorbé**
sinner *see* sin.

sinus ['sainəs] *noun* (*usually in plural*) an air-filled hollow in the bones of the skull, connected with the nose: *His sinuses frequently become blocked in the winter*; (*also adjective*) *She suffers from sinus trouble.* □ **(des) sinus**
sip [sip] – *past tense, past participle* **sipped** – *verb* to drink in very small mouthfuls. □ **boire à petites gorgées**
■ *noun* a very small mouthful: *She took a sip of the medicine.* □ **petite gorgée**
siphon ['saifən] *noun* **1** a bent pipe or tube through which liquid can be drawn off from one container to another at a lower level: *She used a siphon to get some gas out of the car's tank.* □ **siphon**
2 (*also* '**soda-siphon**) a glass bottle with such a tube, used for soda water. □ **siphon (d'eau gazeuse)**
■ *verb* (with **off, into** *etc*) to draw (off) through a siphon: *They siphoned the gasoline into a can.* □ **siphonner**
sir [səː] *noun* **1** a polite form of address (spoken or written) to a man: *Excuse me, sir!; She started her letter 'Dear Sirs,...'.* □ **monsieur**
2 in the United Kingdom, the title of a knight or baronet: *Sir Francis Drake.* □ **sir**
siren ['saiərən] *noun* a kind of instrument that gives out a loud hooting noise as a (warning) signal: *a factory siren.* □ **sirène**
sirloin ['səːloin] *noun* a joint of beef cut from the upper part of the back. □ **aloyau**
sisal ['saisəl] *noun, adjective* (of) a type of fibre from a kind of Central American plant, used in making ropes *etc*. □ **sisal**
sister ['sistə] *noun* **1** the title given to a female child to describe her relationship to the other children of her parents: *She's my sister; my father's sister.* □ **sœur**
2 a female member of a religious group. □ **sœur**
3 a female fellow member of any group: *We must fight for equal opportunities, sisters!* □ **camarade**
■ *adjective* closely similar in design, function *etc*: *sister ships.* □ **similaire**
'sister-in-law – *plural* 'sisters-in-law – *noun* **1** the sister of one's husband or wife. □ **belle-sœur**
2 the wife of one's brother. □ **belle-sœur**
sit [sit] – *present participle* **sitting**: *past tense, past participle* **sat** [sat] – *verb* **1** to (cause to) rest on the buttocks; to (cause to) be seated: *She likes sitting on the floor; They sat me in the chair and started asking questions.* □ **(s')asseoir; être assis**
2 to lie or rest; to have a certain position: *The parcel is sitting on the table.* □ **être posé**
3 (with **on**) to be an official member of (a board, committee *etc*): *She sat on several committees.* □ **siéger (dans); faire partie (de)**
4 (of birds) to perch: *An owl was sitting in the tree by the window.* □ **être perché**
5 to undergo (an examination). □ **se présenter à**
6 to take up a position, or act as a model, in order to have one's picture painted or one's photograph taken: *She is sitting for a portrait/photograph.* □ **poser**
7 (of a committee, parliament *etc*) to be in session: *Parliament sits from now until Christmas.* □ **siéger**

'sitter *noun* **1** a person who poses for a portrait *etc*. □ **modèle**

2 a baby-sitter. □ **gardien, ienne**

'sitting *noun* a period of continuous action, meeting *etc*: *I read the whole book at one sitting*; *The committee were prepared for a lengthy sitting.* □ **séance**

'sit-in *noun* an occupation of a building *etc* by protesters: *The students staged a sit-in.* □ **manifestation, sit-in**

'sitting room *noun* a room used mainly for sitting in. □ **salon**

sitting target, sitting duck someone or something that is in an obvious position to be attacked: *If they're reducing staff, he's a sitting target.* □ **victime toute désignée**

sit back to rest and take no part in an activity: *He just sat back and let it all happen.* □ **rester à se croiser les bras**

sit down to (cause to) take a seat, take a sitting position: *Let's sit down over here*; *He sat the child down on the floor.* □ **(s')asseoir**

sit out 1 to remain seated during a dance: *Let's sit (this one) out.* □ **sauter une danse**

2 to remain inactive and wait until the end of: *They'll try to sit out the crisis.* □ **attendre la fin de**

sit tight to keep the same position or be unwilling to move or act: *The best thing to do is to sit tight and see if things improve.* □ **ne pas bouger**

sit up 1 to rise to a sitting position: *Can the patient sit up?* □ **s'asseoir bien droit**

2 to remain awake, not going to bed: *I sat up until 3 a.m. waiting for you!* □ **veiller**

site [sait] *noun* a place where a building, town *etc* is, was, or is to be, built: *She's got a job on a building-site*; *The site for the new factory has not been decided.* □ **chantier; emplacement**

situate [sitju:eit] *verb* to place in position; to locate: *Try to situate yourself so you can see the movie screen.* □ **situer**

situation [sitju'eiʃən] *noun* **1** circumstances; a state of affairs: *an awkward situation.* □ **situation**

2 the place where anything stands or lies: *The house has a beautiful situation beside a lake.* □ **emplacement**

3 a job: *the situations-vacant columns of the newspaper.* □ **emploi**

'situated *adjective* to be found; placed: *The new school is situated on the north side of town.* □ **situé**

six [siks] *noun* **1** the number or figure 6. □ **six**

2 the age of 6. □ **six ans**

■ *adjective* **1** 6 in number. □ **six**

2 aged 6. □ **de six ans**

six- having six (of something): *a six-cylinder engine.* □ **à/de six (...)**

sixth *noun* **1** one of six equal parts. □ **sixième**

2 (*also adjective*) (the) last of six (people, things *etc*); (the) next after the fifth. □ **sixième**

'six-year-old *noun* a person or animal that is six years old. □ **(individu, etc.) âgé de six ans**

■ *adjective* (of a person, animal or thing) that is six years old. □ **de six ans**

at sixes and sevens in confusion; completely disorganized: *On the day before the wedding, the whole house was at sixes and sevens.* □ **sens dessus dessous**

sixteen [siks'ti:n] *noun* **1** the number or figure 16. □ **seize**

2 the age of 16. □ **seize ans**

■ *adjective* **1** 16 in number. □ **seize**

2 aged 16. □ **de seize ans**

sixteen- having sixteen (of something): *a sixteen-page booklet.* □ **à/de seize (...)**

‚six'teenth *noun* **1** one of sixteen equal parts. □ **seizième**

2 (*also adjective*) (the) last of sixteen (people, things *etc*); (the) next after the fifteenth. □ **seizième**

‚six'teen-year-old *noun* a person or animal that is sixteen years old. □ **(individu, etc.) âgé de seize ans**

■ *adjective* (of a person, animal or thing) that is sixteen years old. □ **de seize ans**

sixty ['siksti] *noun* **1** the number or figure 60. □ **soixante**

2 the age of 60. □ **soixante ans**

■ *adjective* **1** 60 in number. □ **soixante**

2 aged 60. □ **de soixante ans**

'sixties *noun plural* **1** the period of time between one's sixtieth and seventieth birthdays. □ **la soixantaine**

2 the range of temperatures between sixty and seventy degrees. □ **températures entre soixante et soixante-neuf degrés**

3 the period of time between the sixtieth and seventieth years of a century. □ **les années soixante**

'sixtieth *noun* **1** one of sixty equal parts. □ **soixantième**

2 (*also adjective*) (the) last of sixty (people, things *etc*); (the) next after the fifty-ninth. □ **soixantième**

sixty- having sixty (of something): *a sixty-page supplement.* □ **à/de soixante (...)**

'sixty-year-old *noun* a person or animal that is sixty years old. □ **sexagénaire**

■ *adjective* (of a person, animal or thing) that is sixty years old. □ **sexagénaire**

size [saiz] *noun* **1** largeness: *an area the size of a football pitch*; *The size of the problem alarmed us.* □ **taille, dimension(s)**

2 one of a number of classes in which shoes, dresses *etc* are grouped according to measurements: *I take size 5 in shoes.* □ **taille, grandeur**

'sizeable *adjective* fairly large: *His income is quite sizeable, now that he has been promoted.* □ **considérable**

size up to form an opinion about a person, situation *etc*: *He sized up the situation and acted immediately.* □ **jauger**

skate¹ [skeit] *noun* **1** a boot with a steel blade fixed to it for moving on ice *etc*: *I can move very fast across the ice on skates.* □ **patin**

2 a roller skate. □ **patin à roulettes**

■ *verb* **1** to move on skates: *She skates beautifully.* □ **patiner**

2 to move over, along *etc* by skating. □ **glisser**

'skater *noun*. □ **patineur, euse**

'skating rink *noun* an area of ice set aside or designed for skating on. □ **patinoire**

skate² [skeit] – *plurals* **skate, skates** – *noun* **1** a kind of large, flat fish. □ **raie**

2 its flesh, used as food. □ **raie**

skeleton ['skelitn] *noun* **1** the bony framework of an animal or person: *The archaeologists dug up the skeleton of a dinosaur.* □ **squelette**
2 any framework or outline: *the steel skeleton of a building.* □ **charpente**
skeleton key a key which can open many different locks. □ **passe-partout**

skeptic, sceptic ['skeptik] *noun* a person who is unwilling to believe: *Most people now accept this theory, but there are a few skeptics.* □ **sceptique**
'skeptical *adjective* (*often with* **about**) unwilling to believe: *They say apples clean your teeth, but I'm skeptical about that myself.* □ **sceptique**
'skeptically *adverb.* □ **sceptiquement**
'skepticism ['-sizəm] *noun* a doubting or questioning attitude: *I regard his theories with skepticism.* □ **scepticisme**

sketch [sketʃ] *noun* **1** a rough plan, drawing or painting: *He made several sketches before starting the portrait.* □ **croquis, esquisse, schéma**
2 a short (written or spoken) account without many details: *The book began with a sketch of the author's life.* □ **résumé**
3 a short play, dramatic scene *etc*: *a comic sketch.* □ **sketch, saynète**
■ *verb* **1** to draw, describe, or plan without completing the details. □ **ébaucher, esquisser**
2 to make rough drawings, paintings *etc*: *She sketches as a hobby.* □ **faire des croquis/esquisses**
'sketchy *adjective* **1** incompletely done or carried out: *a sketchy search.* □ **sommaire**
2 slight or incomplete: *a sketchy knowledge of French.* □ **incomplet**
'sketchily *adverb.* □ **incomplètement**
'sketchiness *noun.* □ **caractère incomplet**
'sketchbook *noun* a book for drawing sketches in. □ **carnet de croquis/esquisses**

skew [skjuː] *adjective* not straight or symmetrical. □ **de travers**
■ *verb* to make or be distorted, not straight. □ **fausser; biaiser**

skewer ['skjuə] *noun* a long pin of wood or metal for keeping meat together while roasting: *Put the cubes of meat on a skewer.* □ **broche(tte)**

ski [skiː] *noun* one of a pair of long narrow strips of wood *etc* that are attached to the feet for gliding over snow, water *etc*. □ **ski**
■ *verb* – *present participle* **'skiing**; *past tense, past participle* **skied** [skiːd] – to travel on or use skis *especially* as a leisure activity: *He broke his leg when he was skiing.* □ **skier**
ski- of or for the activity of skiing: *ski-suits; ski-jump.* □ **de ski**
'skier *noun*: *The slope was crowded with skiers.* □ **skieur, euse**
'skiing *noun*: *Skiing is her favourite sport*; (*also adjective*) *a skiing holiday.* □ **(de) ski**
'ski lift *noun* any of several devices used to transport skiers to the top of the hill: *The line for the ski lift was so long it took an hour to get to the top of the hill.* □

monte-pente

skid [skid] – *past tense, past participle* **'skidded** – *verb* to slide accidentally sideways: *His back wheel skidded and he fell off his bike.* □ **déraper**
■ *noun* **1** an accidental slide sideways. □ **dérapage**
2 a wedge *etc* put under a wheel to check it on a steep place. □ **cale**

skill [skil] *noun* **1** cleverness at doing something, resulting either from practice or from natural ability: *This job requires a lot of skill.* □ **adresse, habileté**
2 a job or activity that requires training and practice; an art or craft: *the basic skills of reading and writing.* □ **technique, capacité**
'skilful *adjective* having, or showing, skill: *a skilful surgeon; It was very skilful of you to repair my bicycle.* □ **habile, adroit**
'skilfully *adverb.* □ **habilement**
'skilfulness *noun.* □ **habileté**
skilled *adjective* (*negative* **unskilled**) **1** (of a person *etc*) having skill, *especially* skill gained by training: *a skilled craftsman; She is skilled at all types of dressmaking.* □ **habile (à)**
2 (of a job *etc*) requiring skill: *a skilled trade.* □ **qualifié**

> **skilful** is spelt with **-l-** (not **-ll-**).

skim [skim] – *past tense, past participle* **skimmed** – *verb* **1** to remove (floating matter, *eg* cream) from the surface of (a liquid): *Skim the fat off the gravy.* □ **écrémer; dégraisser**
2 to move lightly and quickly over (a surface): *The skier skimmed across the snow.* □ **glisser sur qqch.**
3 to read (something) quickly, missing out parts: *She skimmed (through) the book.* □ **feuilleter**
skim milk milk from which the cream has been skimmed. □ **lait écrémé**

skimp [skimp] *verb* **1** (*with* **on**) to take, spend, use, give *etc* too little or only just enough: *She skimped on meals in order to send her daughter to college.* □ **économiser, lésiner (sur)**
2 to do (a job) imperfectly: *He's inclined to skimp his work.* □ **bâcler**
'skimpy *adjective* too small; inadequate: *a skimpy dress.* □ **trop petit**
'skimpily *adverb.* □ **chichement**
'skimpiness *noun.* □ **insuffisance**

skin [skin] *noun* **1** the natural outer covering of an animal or person: *She couldn't stand the feel of wool against her skin; A snake can shed its skin.* □ **peau, épiderme**
2 a thin outer layer, as on a fruit: *a banana-skin; onion-skins.* □ **peau, pelure**
3 a (thin) film or layer that forms on a liquid: *Boiled milk often has a skin on it.* □ **peau**
■ *verb* – *past tense, past participle* **skinned** – to remove the skin from: *He skinned and cooked the rabbit.* □ **écorcher, éplucher**
'skin-diving *noun* diving and swimming under water with simple equipment (a mask, flippers *etc*). □ **plongée sous-marine**
'skin-'tight *adjective* fitting as tightly as one's skin: *skin-tight jeans; Her new sweater is skin-tight.* □ **collant**

by the skin of one's teeth very narrowly; only just: *We escaped by the skin of our teeth.* □ **de justesse**

skinny ['skini] *adjective* very thin: *Most fat people long to be skinny.* □ **(très) maigre**

'**skinniness** *noun.* □ **maigreur**

skip [skip] – *past tense, past participle* **skipped** – *verb* 1 to go along with a hop on each foot in turn: *The little girl skipped up the path.* □ **sautiller**

2 to jump over a rope that is being turned under the feet and over the head (as a children's game). □ **sauter (à la corde)**

3 to miss out (a meal, part of a book *etc*): *I skipped lunch and went shopping instead; Skip chapter two.* □ **sauter**

■ *noun* a hop on one foot in skipping. □ **petit saut/bond**

skipper ['skipə] *noun* the captain of a ship, airplane or team. □ **capitaine**

■ *verb* to act as skipper of: *Who skippered the team?* □ **commander**

skirt [skəːt] *noun* 1 a garment, worn by women, that hangs from the waist: *Was she wearing trousers or a skirt?* □ **jupe**

2 the lower part of a dress, coat *etc*: *a dress with a flared skirt.* □ **jupe**

skittle ['skitl] *noun* a bottle-shaped, *usually* wooden object used as a target for knocking over in the game of skittles. □ **quille**

'**skittles** *noun singular* a game in which the players try to knock down a number of skittles with a ball: *a game of skittles; Do you play skittles?*; *(also adjective)* a *skittles match.* □ **(de) quilles**

skulk [skʌlk] *verb* to wait about or keep oneself hidden (often for a bad purpose): *Someone was skulking in the bushes.* □ **rôder furtivement**

skull [skʌl] *noun* the bony case that encloses the brain: *He's fractured his skull.* □ **crâne**

skunk [skʌŋk] *noun* a small North American animal which defends itself by squirting out an unpleasant-smelling liquid. □ **mouffette**

sky [skai] – *plural* **skies** *(often with* **the**) – *noun* the part of space above the earth, in which the sun, moon *etc* can be seen; the heavens: *The sky was blue and cloudless; We had grey skies and rain throughout our holiday; The skies were grey all week.* □ **ciel**

,**sky-'blue** *adjective, noun* (of) the light blue colour of cloudless sky: *She wore a sky-blue dress.* □ **bleu ciel**

'**skydiving** *noun* the sport of jumping from aircraft and waiting for some time before opening one's parachute. □ **parachutisme (en chute libre)**

'**skydiver** *noun.* □ **parachutiste (faisant de la chute libre)**

,**sky-'high** *adverb, adjective* very high: *The car was blown sky-high by the explosion; sky-high prices.* □ **très haut**

'**skylight** *noun* a window in a roof or ceiling: *The attic had only a small skylight and was very dark.* □ **lucarne**

'**skyline** *noun* the outline of buildings, hills *etc* seen against the sky: *the New York skyline; I could see something moving on the skyline.* □ **profil (de l'horizon)**

'**skyscraper** *noun* a high building of very many storeys, *especially* in the United State. □ **gratte-ciel**

the sky's the limit there is no upper limit *eg* to the amount of money that may be spent: *Choose any present you like – the sky's the limit!* □ **il n'y a pas de limites**

slab [slab] *noun* a thick slice or thick flat piece of anything: *concrete slabs; a slab of cake.* □ **bloc, pavé**

slack [slak] *adjective* 1 loose; not firmly stretched: *Leave the rope slack.* □ **lâche**

2 not firmly in position: *She tightened a few slack screws.* □ **desserré**

3 not strict; careless: *He is very slack about getting things done.* □ **négligent**

4 in industry *etc*, not busy; inactive: *Business has been rather slack lately.* □ **stagnant**

'**slacken** *verb (sometimes with* **off** *or* **up**) 1 to make or become looser: *She felt his grip on her arm slacken.* □ **(se) relâcher**

2 to make or become less busy, less active or less fast: *The doctor told him to slacken up if he wanted to avoid a heart-attack.* □ **ralentir (son rythme)**

'**slackly** *adverb.* □ **mollement**

'**slackness** *noun.* □ **manque de tension**

slacks *noun plural* trousers, *usually* loose-fitting, worn informally by men or women: *a pair of slacks.* □ **pantalon**

slain *see* **slay.**

slam [slam] – *past tense, past participle* **slammed** – *verb* 1 to shut with violence *usually* making a loud noise: *The door suddenly slammed (shut); She slammed the door in my face.* □ **claquer**

2 to strike against something violently *especially* with a loud noise: *The car slammed into the wall.* □ **se fracasser contre**

■ *noun* (the noise made by) an act of closing violently and noisily: *The door closed with a slam.* □ **claquement**

slander ['slaːndə] *noun* (the act of making) an untrue spoken, not written, statement about a person with the intention of damaging that person's reputation: *That story about her is nothing but a wicked slander!* □ **calomnie; diffamation**

■ *verb* to make such statements about (a person *etc*). □ **calomnier; diffamer**

slang [slaŋ] *noun* words and phrases (often in use for only a short time) used very informally, *eg* words used mainly by, and typical of, a particular group: *army slang; teenage slang; 'stiff' is slang for 'a corpse'.* □ **argot**

■ *verb* to speak rudely and angrily to or about (someone); to abuse: *I got furious when he started slanging my mother.* □ **traiter de tous les noms**

slant [slaːnt] *verb* to be, lie *etc* at an angle, away from a vertical or horizontal position or line; to slope: *The house is very old and all the floors and ceilings slant a little.* □ **pencher**

■ *noun* a sloping line or direction: *The roof has a steep slant.* □ **pente**

'**slanting** *adjective: She has backward-slanting writing; slanting eyes.* □ **penché; bridé**

slap [slap] *noun* a blow with the palm of the hand or anything flat: *The child got a slap from his mother for* *being rude.* □ **gifle**

■ *verb – past tense, past participle* **slapped** – to give a slap to: *He slapped my face.* □ **gifler**

,slap'dash *adjective* careless and hurried: *He does everything in such a slapdash manner.* □ **négligent**

,slap-'happy *adjective* cheerfully careless; carefree: *she cooks in a very slap-happy way.* □ **insouciant**

'slapstick *noun* a kind of humour which depends for its effect on very simple practical jokes *etc: Throwing custard pies turns a play into slapstick;* (*also adjective*) *slapstick comedy.* □ **(de) grosse farce**

slash [slaʃ] *verb* **1** to make long cuts in (cloth *etc*): *He slashed his victim's face with a razor.* □ **taillader**

2 (*with* at) to strike out violently at (something): *She slashed at the bush angrily with a stick.* □ **cingler**

3 to reduce greatly: *A notice in the shop window read 'Prices slashed!'* □ **réduire**

■ *noun* **1** a long cut or slit. □ **entaille**

2 a sweeping blow. □ **entaille**

slat [slat] *noun* a thin strip of wood, metal *etc.* □ **lame(lle)**

'slatted *adjective* having, or made with, slats: *a slatted door.* □ **à lames**

slate [sleit] *noun* **1** (a piece of) a type of easily split rock of a dull blue-grey colour, used for roofing *etc: Slates fell off the roof in the wind;* (*also adjective*) *a slate roof.* □ **(d')ardoise**

2 a small writing-board made of this, used by schoolchildren. □ **ardoise**

slaughter ['slɔːtə] *noun* **1** the killing of people or animals in large numbers, cruelly and *usually* unnecessarily: *Many people protested at the annual slaughter of seals.* □ **massacre**

2 the killing of animals for food: *Methods of slaughter must be humane.* □ **abattage**

■ *verb* **1** to kill (animals) for food: *Thousands of cattle are slaughtered here every year.* □ **abattre**

2 to kill in a cruel manner, *especially* in large numbers. □ **massacrer**

3 to criticize unmercifully or defeat very thoroughly: *Our team absolutely slaughtered the other side.* □ **écraser**

'slaughterhouse *noun* a place where animals are killed in order to be sold for food; an abattoir. □ **abattoir**

slave [sleiv] *noun* **1** a person who works for a master to whom he belongs: *In the nineteenth century many Africans were sold as slaves in the United States.* □ **esclave**

2 a person who works very hard for someone else: *He has a slave who types his letters and organizes his life for him.* □ **esclave**

■ *verb* to work very hard, often for another person: *I've been slaving away for you all day while you sit and watch television.* □ **trimer**

'slavery *noun* **1** the state of being a slave. □ **esclavage**

2 the system of ownership of slaves. □ **esclavage**

3 very hard and badly-paid work: *Her job is sheer slavery.* □ **esclavage**

slay [slei] – *past tense* **slew** [sluː]: *past participle* **slain** [slein] – *verb* to kill: *Cain slew his brother Abel.* □ **tuer**

sleazy ['sliːzi] *adjective* dirty and neglected: *This area is rather sleazy.* □ **minable**

sled [sled] *noun* a vehicle, *usually* with runners, made for sliding upon snow. □ **luge, traîneau**

■ *verb* to ride on a sledge: *The children were sledding all afternoon.* □ **faire de la luge/du traîneau**

sledgehammer ['sledʒhamə] *noun* a large heavy hammer. □ **marteau de forgeron**

sleek [sliːk] *adjective* **1** (of hair, an animal's fur *etc*) smooth, soft and glossy: *The dog has a lovely sleek coat.* □ **lisse; luisant**

2 well fed and cared for: *a sleek Siamese cat lay by the fire.* □ **au poil brillant**

'sleekly *adverb.* □ **doucereusement**

'sleekness *noun.* □ **luisant**

sleep [sliːp] – *past tense, past participle* **slept** [slept] – *verb* to rest with the eyes closed and in a state of natural unconsciousness: *Goodnight – sleep well!; I can't sleep – my mind is too active.* □ **dormir**

■ *noun* (a) rest in a state of natural unconsciousness: *It is bad for you to have too little sleep, since it makes you tired; I had only four hours' sleep last night.* □ **sommeil**

'sleeper *noun* **1** a person who sleeps: *Nothing occurred to disturb the sleepers.* □ **dormeur, euse**

2 a berth or compartment for sleeping, on a railway train: *I'd like to book a sleeper on the Vancouver train.* □ **couchette**

'sleepless *adjective* without sleep: *He spent a sleepless night worrying about the situation.* □ **sans sommeil**

'sleepy *adjective* **1** inclined to sleep; drowsy: *I feel very sleepy after that long walk.* □ **somnolent**

2 not (seeming to be) alert: *She always has a sleepy expression.* □ **endormi, somnolent**

3 (of places *etc*) very quiet; lacking entertainment and excitement: *a sleepy town.* □ **endormi, somnolent**

'sleepily *adverb.* □ **d'un air/ton endormi**

'sleepiness *noun.* □ **somnolence**

'sleeping bag *noun* a kind of large warm bag for sleeping in, used by campers *etc.* □ **sac de couchage**

'sleeping pill *nouns* a kind of pill that can be taken to make one sleep: *She tried to commit suicide by swallowing an overdose of sleeping pills.* □ **somnifère**

'sleepwalk *verb* to walk about while asleep: *She was sleepwalking again last night.* □ **faire du somnambulisme**

'sleepwalker *noun.* □ **somnambule**

put to sleep 1 to cause (a person or animal) to become unconscious by means of an anaesthetic; to anaesthetize: *The doctor will give you an injection to put you to sleep.* □ **endormir**

2 to kill (an animal) painlessly, *usually* by the injection of a drug: *As she was so old and ill my cat had to be put to sleep.* □ **(faire) piquer**

sleep like a log/top to sleep very well and soundly. □ **dormir à poings fermés**

sleep in to stay in bed long after the usual time of waking and getting up: *Niven rises early everyday for school, but on the weekend he sleeps in until noon.* □ **faire la grasse matinée**

sleep off to recover from (something) by sleeping: *She's in bed sleeping off the effects of the party.* □ **faire passer qqch. (en dormant)**

sleep on to put off making a decision about (something) overnight: *I'll sleep on it and let you know tomorrow.* □ **attendre le lendemain pour prendre une décision**

sleet [sliːt] *noun* rain mixed with snow or hail: *That isn't snow – it's just sleet.* □ **neige fondante**
■ *verb* to hail or snow, with a mixture of rain: *It seems to be sleeting outside.* □ **tomber de la neige fondante**

sleeve [sliːv] *noun* **1** the part of a garment that covers the arm: *He tore the sleeve of his jacket; a dress with long/ short sleeves.* □ **manche**
2 (*also* 'record-sleeve) a stiff envelope for a gramophone record. □ **pochette**
3 something, *eg* a tubular part in a piece of machinery, that covers as a sleeve of a garment does the arm. □ **chemise**
-sleeved having (a certain kind of) sleeve(s): *a long-sleeved dress.* □ **à manches (...)**
'**sleeveless** *adjective* without sleeves: *a sleeveless dress.* □ **sans manches**
have/keep (something) up one's sleeve to keep (a plan *etc*) secret for possible use at a later time: *I'm keeping this idea up my sleeve for the time being.* □ **garder en réserve**

sleigh [slei] *noun* a *usually* large sled pulled by a horse *etc*. □ **traîneau**

slender ['slendə] *adjective* **1** thin, slim or narrow. □ **mince, svelte**
2 slight or small: *Her chances of winning are extremely slender.* □ **mince**

slept *see* sleep.

slew¹ [sluː] *verb* to (cause to) turn or swing in a certain direction: *The car skidded and slewed across the road.* □ **déraper**

slew² *see* slay.

slice [slais] *noun* **1** a thin broad piece (of something): *How many slices of meat would you like?* □ **tranche**
2 a part or share: *Who got the largest slice of the profits?* □ **part**
■ *verb* **1** to cut into slices: *He sliced the sausage/cucumber.* □ **trancher**
2 to cut (as) with a sharp blade or knife: *The blade slipped and sliced off the tip of her forefinger.* □ **couper (net)**
3 in golf *etc*, to hit (a ball) in such a way that it curves away to the right (or in the case of a left-handed player, to the left). □ **couper**
sliced *adjective* (*negative* unsliced) cut into slices: *a sliced loaf.* □ **(coupé) en tranches/rondelles**

slick¹ [slik] *adjective* clever *especially* in a sly or dishonest way; smart: *That was a very slick move!* □ **rusé**
'**slickly** *adverb.* □ **habilement**
'**slickness** *noun.* □ **ruse**

slick² [slik] *noun* (*also* 'oil-slick) a broad band of oil floating on the surface of the sea *etc*: *An oil slick is threatening the coast.* □ **nappe de pétrole**

slide [slaid] – *past tense, past participle* **slid** [slid] – *verb*
1 to (cause to) move or pass along smoothly: *He slid the drawer open; Children must not slide in the school corridors.* □ **(faire) glisser**
2 to move quietly or secretly: *I slid hurriedly past the window; He slid the book quickly out of sight under his pillow.* □ **(se) glisser**
■ *noun* **1** an act of sliding. □ **glissade/glissement**
2 a slippery track, or apparatus with a smooth sloping surface, on which people or things can slide: *The children were taking turns on the slide in the playground.* □ **toboggan**
3 a small transparent photograph for projecting on to a screen *etc*: *The lecture was illustrated with slides.* □ **diapositive**
4 a glass plate on which objects are placed to be examined under a microscope. □ **lame porte-objet**
'**slide rule** *noun* an instrument for calculating, like a ruler in shape and having a central section that slides up and down between the outer sections. □ **règle à calcul**
'**sliding door** a type of door that slides across an opening rather than swinging on a hinge. □ **porte coulissante**

slight [slait] *adjective* **1** small; not great; not serious or severe: *a slight breeze; We have a slight problem.* □ **léger, petit**
2 (of a person) slim and delicate-looking: *It seemed too heavy a load for such a slight man.* □ **frêle**
'**slightest** *adjective* (*often in negative sentences, questions etc*) least possible; any at all: *I haven't the slightest idea where he is; The slightest difficulty seems to upset her.* □ **moindre**
'**slighting** *adjective* insulting; disrespectful: *He made rather a slighting remark about her parents.* □ **désobligeant**
'**slightingly** *adverb.* □ **d'une manière désobligeante**
'**slightly** *adverb* **1** to a small extent: *I'm still slightly worried about it.* □ **un/quelque peu**
2 slenderly: *slightly built.* □ **frêle**
in the slightest (*in negative sentences, questions etc*) at all: *You haven't upset me in the slightest; That doesn't worry me in the slightest.* □ **(pas) le moins du monde**

slim [slim] *adjective* **1** not thick or fat; thin: *She has a slim, graceful figure; Taking exercise is one way of keeping slim.* □ **svelte, mince**
2 not good; slight: *There's still a slim chance that we'll find the child alive.* □ **faible**
■ *verb* – *past tense, past participle* **slimmed** – to use means (such as eating less) in order to become slimmer: *I mustn't eat cakes – I'm trying to slim.* □ **maigrir**
slim down *verb* to lose weight: *Lawrence wanted to slim down so he exercised more and ate less.* □ **amincir**
'**slimming** *noun* the process or practice of trying to become slimmer: *Slimming should be done carefully.* □ **régime (amaigrissant)**
'**slimness** *noun.* □ **minceur**

slime [slaim] *noun* thin, slippery mud or other matter that is soft, sticky and half-liquid: *There was a layer of slime at the bottom of the pond.* □ **vase**
'**slimy** *adjective* covered with, consisting of, or like, slime: *a slimy mess on the floor.* □ **visqueux**
'**sliminess** *noun.* □ **viscosité**

sling [slin] *noun* **1** a type of bandage hanging from the neck or shoulders to support an injured arm: *He had his broken arm in a sling.* □ **écharpe**
2 a band of cloth *etc* worn over the shoulder for sup-

porting a rifle *etc* on the back. □ **bandoulière**

3 a looped arrangement of ropes, chains *etc* for supporting, hoisting, carrying and lowering heavy objects. □ **élingue, cordages**

■ *verb – past tense, past participle* **slung** [slʌŋ] – **1** to throw violently: *The boy slung a stone at the dog.* □ **jeter**

2 to support, hang or swing by means of a strap, sling *etc*: *He had a camera and binoculars slung around his neck.* □ **en bandoulière**

'slingshot ['slɪŋʃot] *noun* a small forked stick with an elastic string fixed to the two prongs for firing small stones *etc*, *usually* used by children. □ **lance-pierre(s)**

slink [slɪŋk] – *past tense, past participle* **slunk** [slʌŋk] – *verb* to move as if wanting to avoid attention: *He slunk into the kitchen and stole a cake.* □ **aller furtivement**

slip[1] [slɪp] – *past tense, past participle* **slipped** – *verb* **1** to slide accidentally and lose one's balance or footing: *I slipped and fell on the path.* □ **glisser**

2 to slide, or drop, out of the right position or out of control: *The plate slipped out of my grasp.* □ **glisser entre les doigts**

3 to drop in standard: *I'm sorry about my mistake – I must be slipping!* □ **décliner, baisser**

4 to move quietly *especially* without being noticed: *She slipped out of the room.* □ **sortir (sans être vu)**

5 to escape from: *The dog had slipped its lead and disappeared.* □ **se dégager de qqch.**

6 to put or pass (something) with a quick, light movement: *She slipped the letter back in its envelope.* □ **glisser**

■ *noun* **1** an act of slipping: *Her sprained ankle was a result of a slip on the path.* □ **faux pas**

2 a *usually* small mistake: *Everyone makes the occasional slip.* □ **gaffe**

3 a kind of undergarment worn under a dress; a petticoat. □ **combinaison, jupon**

4 (*also* **'slipway**) a sloping platform next to water used for building and launching ships. □ **cale**

'slipper *noun* a loose, soft kind of shoe for wearing indoors. □ **pantoufle**

'slippery *adjective* **1** so smooth as to cause slipping: *The path is slippery – watch out!* □ **glissant**

2 not trustworthy: *He's rather a slippery character.* □ **fuyant**

'slipperiness *noun*. □ **caractère glissant/fuyant**

'slipshod *adjective* (of work *etc*) untidy; careless: *The teacher told him his work was slipshod.* □ **négligé**

give (someone) the slip to escape from or avoid (someone) in a secretive manner: *The crooks gave the policemen the slip.* □ **fausser compagnie à**

let slip 1 to miss (an opportunity *etc*): *I let the chance slip, unfortunately.* □ **laisser passer**

2 to say (something) unintentionally: *She let slip some remark about my daughter.* □ **laisser échapper**

slip into to put on (clothes) quickly: *She slipped into her nightdress.* □ **enfiler**

slip off 1 to take (clothes) off quickly: *Slip off your shoe.* □ **ôter**

2 to move away noiselessly or hurriedly: *We'll slip off*

when no one's looking. □ **s'esquiver**

slip on to put on (clothes) quickly. □ **enfiler**

slip up to make a mistake; to fail to do something: *They certainly slipped up badly over the new appointment* (*noun* **'slip-up**). □ **gaffer; gaffe**

slip[2] [slɪp] *noun* a strip or narrow piece of paper: *She wrote down his telephone number on a slip of paper.* □ **bout**

slipper, slippery *see* **slip**[1].

slit [slɪt] – *present participle* **'slitting**: *past tense, past participle* **slit** – *verb* to make a long cut in: *She slit the envelope open with a knife.* □ **fendre, couper**

■ *noun* a long cut; a narrow opening: *a slit in the material.* □ **fente, déchirure**

slither ['slɪðə] *verb* to slide or slip while trying to walk (*eg* on mud): *The dog was slithering about on the mud.* □ **glisser**

slog [slog] – *past tense, past participle* **slogged** – *verb* **1** to hit hard (*usually* without aiming carefully): *She slogged him with her handbag.* □ **donner de grands coups à**

2 to make one's way with difficulty: *We slogged on up the hill.* □ **avancer avec effort**

3 to work very hard: *She has been slogging all week at the shop.* □ **travailler dur**

■ *noun* **1** (a period of) hard work: *months of hard slog.* □ **gros travail**

2 a hard blow: *He gave the ball a slog.* □ **grand coup**

slogan ['slougən] *noun* an easily-remembered and frequently repeated phrase which is used in advertising *etc*. □ **slogan**

slop [slop] – *past tense, past participle* **slopped** – *verb* to (cause liquid to) splash, spill, or move around violently in a container: *The water was slopping about in the bucket.* □ **renverser, déborder**

'sloppy *adjective* **1** semi-liquid; tending to slop: *sloppy food.* □ **trop liquide**

2 careless and untidy; messy: *His work is sloppy.* □ **bâclé**

3 very sentimental: *That film is rather sloppy.* □ **plein de sensiblerie**

'sloppily *adverb*. □ **sans soin**

'sloppiness *noun*. □ **sensiblerie**

slope [sloup] *noun* **1** a position or direction that is neither level nor upright; an upward or downward slant: *The floor is on a slight slope.* □ **pente**

2 a surface with one end higher than the other: *The house stands on a gentle slope.* □ **inclinaison**

■ *verb* to be in a position which is neither level nor upright: *The field slopes towards the road.* □ **pencher**

'sloping *adjective*: *a sloping roof.* □ **en pente**

slot [slot] *noun* **1** a small narrow opening, *especially* one to receive coins: *I put the correct money in the slot, but the machine didn't start.* □ **fente**

2 a (*usually* regular) position (in *eg* the schedule of television/radio programs): *The early-evening comedy slot.* □ **tranche horaire**

■ *verb* – *past tense, past participle* **'slotted** – (*with* **in** *or* **into**) to fit (something) into a small space: *She slotted the last piece of the puzzle into place; I managed to slot in my tea-break between two jobs.* □ **emboîter, insérer**

slot machine a machine, *especially* one containing cigarettes, sweets *etc* for sale, worked by putting a coin in a slot. □ **distributrice (automatique)**

slouch [slautʃ] *verb* to sit, move or walk with shoulders rounded and head hanging: *He slouched sulkily out of the room*; *She was slouching in an armchair*. □ **être affalé; traîner les pieds**

slow [slou] *adjective* 1 not fast; not moving quickly; taking a long time: *a slow train*; *The service at that restaurant is very slow*; *She was very slow to offer help*. □ **lent**

2 (of a clock *etc*) showing a time earlier than the actual time; behind in time: *My watch is five minutes slow*. □ **en retard (de)**

3 not clever; not quick at learning: *He's particularly slow at arithmetic*. □ **lent**

■ *verb* to make, or become slower: *The car slowed to take the corner*. □ **ralentir**

'**slowly** *adverb*: *He slowly opened his eyes*; *She drove home slowly*. □ **lentement**

'**slowness** *noun*. □ **lenteur**

slow motion movement which is slower than normal or actual movement *especially* as a special effect in films: *Let's watch it, in slow motion*. □ **ralenti**

slow down/up to make or become slower: *The police were warning drivers to slow down*; *The fog was slowing up the traffic*. □ **ralentir**

sludge [slʌdʒ] *noun* soft, slimy mud, grease or other matter which settles at the bottom of a liquid: *The riverbed is covered with thick sludge*. □ **boue**

slug¹ [slʌg] *noun* a kind of animal like a snail. □ **limace**

'**sluggish** *adjective* moving slowly; not active or alert: *a sluggish river*; *I always feel rather sluggish in the mornings*. □ **mou**

'**sluggishly** *adverb*. □ **mollement**

'**sluggishness** *noun*. □ **mollesse**

slug² [slʌg] *noun* a piece of metal, *especially* an irregularly shaped lump used as a bullet. □ **balle**

■ *verb – past tense, past participle* **slugged** – to strike (a person) heavily *usually* causing unconsciousness: *The man had been slugged on the back of the neck with a heavy object*. □ **assommer**

sluice [sluːs] *noun* 1 (*often* '**sluice-gate**) a sliding gate for controlling a flow of water in an artificial channel: *We shall have to open the sluice*. □ **écluse**

2 the channel or the water which flows through it. □ **canal**

slum [slʌm] *noun* a group of houses, blocks of flats, street *etc* where the conditions are dirty and overcrowded and the building(s) *usually* in a bad state: *That new block of flats is rapidly turning into a slum*; *a slum dwelling*. □ **quartier misérable**

the slums the area(s) of a town *etc* where there are slums: *As a social worker, she does a lot of work in the slums*. □ **quartier misérable**

slumber ['slʌmbə] *verb* to sleep. □ **dormir (paisiblement)**

■ *noun* sleep: *She was in a deep slumber*; *I didn't want to disturb your slumbers*. □ **sommeil (paisible)**

slump [slʌmp] *verb* 1 to fall or sink suddenly and heav-

ily: *He slumped wearily into a chair*. □ **s'effondrer**

2 (of prices, stocks, trade *etc*) to become less; to lose value suddenly: *Business has slumped*. □ **s'effondrer brutalement**

■ *noun* 1 a sudden fall in value, trade *etc*: *a slump in prices*. □ **baisse soudaine**

2 a time of very bad economic conditions, with serious unemployment *etc*; a depression: *There was a serious slump in the 1930s*. □ **crise (économique)**

slung *see* **sling**.

slunk *see* **slink**.

slush [slʌʃ] *noun* 1 melting snow: *The streets are covered with slush*. □ **neige fondante**

2 (something said or written showing) weak sentimentality: *I think most romantic novels are just slush!* □ **sensiblerie**

'**slushy** *adjective*. □ **détrempé**

'**slushiness** *noun*. □ **caractère boueux**

sly [slai] *adjective* 1 cunning or deceitful: *He sometimes behaves in rather a sly manner*. □ **sournois**

2 playfully mischievous: *She made a sly reference to my foolish mistake*. □ **malin**

'**slyly**, '**slily** *adverb*. □ **sournoisement**

'**slyness** *noun*. □ **sournoiserie**

smack¹ [smak] *verb* to strike smartly and loudly; to slap: *She smacked the child's hand/bottom*. □ **donner une tape à**

■ *noun* (the sound of) a blow of this kind; a slap: *He could hear the smack of the waves against the side of the ship*. □ **claquement**

■ *adverb* directly and with force: *He ran smack into the door*. □ **en plein (dans, sur)**

a smack on the cheek a quick, loud kiss on the cheek: *He gave her a quick smack on the cheek*. □ **gros baiser**

smack² [smak] *verb* (*with* **of**) to have a suggestion of: *The whole affair smacks of prejudice*. □ **sentir (qqch.)**

■ *noun*: *There's a smack of corruption about this affair*. □ **soupçon**

small [smoːl] *adjective* 1 little in size, degree, importance *etc*; not large or great: *She was accompanied by a small boy of about six*; *There's only a small amount of sugar left*; *She cut the meat up small for the baby*. □ **petit, infime**

2 not doing something on a large scale: *He's a small businessman*. □ **petit**

3 little; not much: *You have small reason to be satisfied with yourself*. □ **peu de**

4 (of the letters of the alphabet) not capital: *The teacher showed the children how to write a capital G and a small g*. □ **minuscule**

small ads advertisements in the personal columns of a newspaper. □ **petites annonces**

small arms weapons small and light enough to be carried by a man: *They found a hoard of rifles and other small arms belonging to the rebels*. □ **armes portatives**

small change coins of small value: *a pocketful of small change*. □ **menue monnaie**

small hours the hours immediately after midnight: *She woke up in the small hours*. □ **petit matin**

'**smallpox** *noun* a type of serious infectious disease in which there is a severe rash of large, pus-filled spots that *usually* leave scars. □ **variole**

small screen television, not the cinema: *This play is intended for the small screen.* □ **petit écran**

'small-time *adjective* (of a thief *etc*) not working on a large scale: *a small-time crook/thief.* □ **médiocre**

feel/look small to feel or look foolish or insignificant: *He criticized her in front of her colleagues and made her feel very small.* □ **se sentir (tout) honteux**

smarmy ['smɑːmi] *adjective* over-respectful and inclined to use flattery: *I can't bear his smarmy manner.* □ **obséquieux**

'smarminess *noun.* □ **obséquiosité**

smart [smɑːt] *adjective* **1** neat and well-dressed; fashionable: *You're looking very smart today; a smart suit.* □ **élégant**

2 clever and quick in thought and action: *We need a smart boy to help in the shop; I don't trust some of those smart salesmen.* □ **dégourdi**

3 brisk; sharp: *She gave him a smart slap on the cheek.* □ **vif, sec**

■ *verb* **1** (of part of the body) to be affected by a sharp stinging feeling: *The thick smoke made her eyes smart.* □ **irriter**

2 to feel annoyed, resentful *etc* after being insulted *etc*: *He is still smarting from your remarks.* □ **être piqué au vif**

■ *noun* the stinging feeling left by a blow or the resentful feeling left by an insult: *He could still feel the smart of her slap/insult.* □ **douleur cuisante**

'smarten (*often with* **up**) *verb* to make or become smarter: *He has smartened up a lot in appearance lately.* □ **devenir plus élégant**

'smartly *adverb: The soldiers stood smartly to attention; She is always smartly dressed.* □ **promptement; élégamment**

'smartness *noun.* □ **promptitude; élégance**

smash [smæʃ] *verb* **1** (*sometimes with* **up**) to (cause to) break in pieces or be ruined: *The plate dropped on the floor and smashed into little pieces; This unexpected news had smashed all his hopes; He had an accident and smashed up his car.* □ **casser, briser**

2 to strike with great force; to crash: *The car smashed into a lamppost.* □ **s'écraser contre**

■ *noun* **1** (the sound of) a breakage; a crash: *A plate fell to the ground with a smash; There has been a bad car smash.* □ **fracassement; collision**

2 a strong blow: *He gave his opponent a smash on the jaw.* □ **coup violent**

3 in tennis *etc*, a hard downward shot. □ **smash**

'smashing *adjective* marvellous; splendid: *What a smashing idea!; a smashing new bike.* □ **épatant**

smash hit a song, show *etc* that is a great success: *This play was a smash hit in New York.* □ **succès foudroyant**

smear [smiə] *verb* **1** to spread (something sticky or oily) over a surface: *The little boy smeared jam on the chair.* □ **barbouiller**

2 to make or become blurred; to smudge: *She brushed against the newly painted notice and smeared the lettering.* □ **brouiller**

3 to try to discredit (a person *etc*) by slandering him: *He has been spreading false stories in an attempt to smear us.* □ **porter atteinte à (la réputation)**

■ *noun* **1** a mark made by smearing. □ **salissure**

2 a piece of slander. □ **calomnie**

smell [smel] *noun* **1** the sense or power of being aware of things through one's nose: *My sister never had a good sense of smell.* □ **odorat**

2 the quality that is noticed by using this power: *a pleasant smell; There's a strong smell of gas.* □ **odeur**

3 an act of using this power: *Have a smell of this!* □ **reniflement**

■ *verb – past tense, past participles* **smelled, smelt** [smelt] **– 1** to notice by using one's nose: *I smell gas; I thought I smelt (something) burning.* □ **sentir**

2 to give off a smell: *The roses smelt beautiful; Her hands smelt of fish.* □ **sentir**

3 to examine by using the sense of smell: *Let me smell those flowers.* □ **sentir**

-smelling having a (particular kind of) smell: *a nasty-smelling liquid; sweet-smelling roses.* □ **d'une odeur (...)**

'smelly *adjective* having a bad smell: *smelly fish.* □ **malodorant**

'smelliness *noun.* □ **mauvaise odeur**

smell out to find (as if) by smelling: *We buried the dog's bone, but he smelled it out again.* □ **découvrir (en flairant)**

smelt¹ [smelt] *verb* to melt (ore) in order to separate metal from waste. □ **fondre**

smelt² *see* **smell.**

smile [smail] *verb* to show pleasure, amusement *etc* by turning up the corners of the mouth: *He smiled warmly at her as he shook hands; They all smiled politely at the joke; He asked her what she was smiling at.* □ **sourire**

■ *noun* an act of smiling, or the resulting facial expression: *'How do you do?' she said with a smile; the happy smiles of the children.* □ **sourire**

'smiling *adjective: a happy, smiling face.* □ **souriant**

be all smiles to be, or look, very happy: *She was all smiles when she heard the good news.* □ **être tout sourire**

smirk [smɜːk] *verb* to smile in a self-satisfied or foolish manner: *He sat there smirking after the teacher had praised him.* □ **sourire d'un air suffisant**

■ *noun* a smile of this sort. □ **sourire suffisant**

smith [smiθ] *noun* **1** a blacksmith. □ **forgeron, onne**

2 a person whose job is to work with a particular metal, or make a particular type of article: *a goldsmith; a silversmith; a gunsmith.* □ **orfèvre; armurier**

smock [smɒk] *noun* a loose, shirt-like garment. □ **blouse**

smog [smɒg] *noun* fog mixed with smoke and fumes from factories, houses, vehicles *etc*: *Some big cities have a problem with smog.* □ **smog**

smoke [smouk] *noun* **1** the cloud-like gases and particles of soot given off by something which is burning: *Smoke was coming out of the chimney; She puffed cigarette smoke into my face.* □ **fumée**

2 an act of smoking (a cigarette *etc*): *I came outside for a smoke.* □ **fait de fumer**

■ *verb* **1** to give off smoke. □ **fumer**
2 to draw in and puff out the smoke from (a cigarette *etc*): *I don't smoke, but he smokes cigars.* □ **fumer**
3 to dry, cure, preserve (ham, fish *etc*) by hanging it in smoke. □ **fumer**
smoked *adjective* treated with smoke: *smoked cheese.* □ **fumé**
'**smokeless** *adjective* **1** allowing no smoke: *Our part of the town is a smokeless zone.* □ **exempt de fumée**
2 burning without smoke: *smokeless fuel.* □ **sans fumée**
'**smoker** *noun* a person who smokes cigarettes *etc*: *When did you become a smoker?; He's a pipe-smoker.* □ **fumeur, euse**
'**smoking** *noun* the habit of smoking cigarettes *etc*: *She has given up cigarette-smoking at last; Smoking can damage your health.* □ **fait de fumer**
'**smoky** *adjective* **1** filled with, or giving out (too much) smoke: *The atmosphere in the room was thick and smoky.* □ **enfumé**
2 like smoke in appearance *etc*. □ **fumeux, enfumé**
'**smokiness** *noun*. □ **atmosphère enfumée**
smoke detector a device in a building which sounds a fire alarm when smoke passes through it. □ **détecteur de fumée**
'**smokescreen** *noun* **1** a cloud of smoke used to conceal the movements of troops *etc*. □ **écran de fumée**
2 something intended to conceal one's activities *etc*. □ **écran de fumée**
go up in smoke 1 to be completely destroyed by fire: *The whole house went up in smoke.* □ **brûler complètement**
2 to vanish very quickly leaving nothing behind: *All his plans have gone up in smoke.* □ **partir en fumée**
smolder *see* **smoulder**.
smooth [smuːð] *adjective* **1** having an even surface; not rough: *Her skin is as smooth as satin.* □ **lisse**
2 without lumps: *Mix the ingredients to a smooth paste.* □ **onctueux**
3 (of movement) without breaks, stops or jolts: *Did you have a smooth flight from New York?* □ **confortable**
4 without problems or difficulties: *a smooth journey; Her progress towards promotion was smooth and rapid.* □ **sans problèmes/histoires**
5 (too) agreeable and pleasant in manner *etc*: *I don't trust those smooth salesmen.* □ **mielleux**
■ *verb* **1** (*often with* **down, out** *etc*) to make (something) smooth or flat: *She tried to smooth the creases out.* □ **défroisser**
2 (*with* **into** *or* **over**) to rub (a liquid substance *etc*) gently over (a surface): *Smooth the moisturizing cream into/over your face and neck.* □ **faire pénétrer en massant**
'**smoothen** *verb* to make smooth. □ **aplanir**
'**smoothly** *adverb*: *The plane landed smoothly; The meeting went very smoothly.* □ **en douceur**
'**smoothness** *noun*. □ **égalité; douceur**
smother ['smʌðə] *verb* **1** to kill or die from lack of air, caused *especially* by a thick covering over the mouth and nose; to suffocate: *He smothered his victim by holding a pillow over her face.* □ **étouffer**
2 to prevent (a fire) from burning by covering it thickly:

He threw sand on the fire to smother it. □ **étouffer**
3 to cover (too) thickly; to overwhelm: *When she got home her children smothered her with kisses.* □ **couvrir de**
smoulder, smolder ['smouldə] *verb* to burn slowly or without flame: *A piece of coal had fallen out of the fire and the hearthrug was smouldering.* □ **couver**
smudge [smʌdʒ] *noun* a smear or a blurred mark: *There's a smudge of ink on your nose.* □ **tache, traînée**
■ *verb* to make or become blurred or smeared. □ **salir, maculer**
'**smudgy** *adjective*. □ **taché**
'**smudginess** *noun*. □ **flou**
smug [smʌg] *adjective* well satisfied, or too obviously pleased, with oneself: *I don't like that smug little man.* □ **suffisant**
'**smugly** *adverb*. □ **d'un air suffisant**
'**smugness** *noun*. □ **suffisance**
smuggle ['smʌgl] *verb* **1** to bring (goods) into, or send them out from, a country illegally, or without paying duty: *He was caught smuggling (several thousand cigarettes through the Customs).* □ **faire de la contrebande**
2 to send or take secretly: *I smuggled some food out of the kitchen.* □ **faire entrer/sortir clandestinement**
'**smuggler** *noun* a person who smuggles. □ **contrebandier, ière**
'**smuggling** *noun*: *the laws against smuggling; drug-smuggling.* □ **contrebande (de)**
smut [smʌt] *noun* vulgar or indecent talk *etc*: *There is too much smut on television nowadays!* □ **obscénité**
'**smutty** *adjective* (of a conversation, film *etc*) indecent; vulgar: *He could not be prevented from telling smutty stories.* □ **cochon**
'**smuttiness** *noun*. □ **obscénité**
snack [snak] *noun* a light, hasty meal: *I usually have only a snack at lunchtime*; (*also adjective*) *We had a snack lunch in the pub.* □ **casse-croûte, collation**
snag [snag] *noun* **1** a difficulty or drawback: *We did not realize at first how many snags there were in our plan.* □ **obstacle**
2 a place on a garment where a thread has been torn or pulled out of place. □ **accroc**
snail [sneil] *noun* a kind of soft-bodied small crawling animal with a coiled shell: *Snails leave a silvery trail as they move along.* □ **escargot**
at a snail's pace very slowly: *The old man walked along at a snail's pace.* □ **comme un escargot**
snake [sneik] *noun* any of a group of legless reptiles with long bodies that move along on the ground with a twisting movement, many of which have a poisonous bite: *She was bitten by a snake and nearly died.* □ **serpent**
■ *verb* to move like a snake: *He snaked his way through the narrow tunnel.* □ **serpenter**
'**snakebite** *noun* the wound resulting from the bite of a snake: *What is the best treatment for (a) snakebite?* □ **morsure de serpent**
'**snake charmer** *noun* a person who can handle snakes and make them perform rhythmical movements. □ **charmeur, euse de serpent**
snap [snap] – *past tense, past participle* **snapped** – *verb*

1 (*with* at) to make a biting movement, to try to grasp with the teeth: *The dog snapped at his ankles.* □ **essayer de mordre**

2 to break with a sudden sharp noise: *He snapped the stick in half; The handle of the cup snapped off.* □ **(se) casser net (avec un bruit sec)**

3 to (cause to) make a sudden sharp noise, in moving *etc*: *The lid snapped shut.* □ **(se) fermer d'un coup sec**

4 to speak in a sharp *especially* angry way: '*Mind your own business!*' *he snapped.* □ **dire d'un ton brusque**

5 to take a photograph of: *He snapped the children playing in the garden.* □ **prendre (en photo)**

■ *noun* 1 (the noise of) an act of snapping: *There was a loud snap as his pencil broke.* □ **bruit sec**

2 a photograph; a snapshot: *He wanted to show us his holiday snaps.* □ **photo (d'amateur)**

3 a kind of simple card game: *They were playing snap.* □ **(sorte de) jeu de bataille**

■ *adjective* done, made *etc* quickly: *a snap decision.* □ **subit**

'**snappy** *adjective* 1 irritable; inclined to snap: *He is always rather snappy on a Monday morning.* □ **hargneux**

2 quick; prompt: *You'll have to be snappy if you're catching that bus!* □ **vif**

3 smart: *He's certainly a snappy dresser.* □ **pimpant**

'**snappily** *adverb*. □ **d'un ton hargneux**

'**snappiness** *noun*. □ **hargne**

'**snapshot** *noun* a photograph taken quickly and without a lot of equipment: *That's a good snapshot of the children playing in the garden.* □ **photo (d'amateur)**

snap one's fingers to make a sharp noise by moving the thumb quickly across the top joint of the middle finger, as an informal gesture *eg* to attract someone's attention, mark the rhythm in music *etc*. □ **faire claquer ses doigts**

snap up to grab eagerly: *I saw this bargain in the shop and snapped it up straight away.* □ **sauter sur**

snare [sneə] *noun* a trap for catching an animal. □ **piège**

■ *verb* to catch with a snare: *She snared a couple of rabbits.* □ **prendre au piège**

snarl [snɑːl] *verb* (of a dog *etc*) to growl angrily, showing the teeth: *The dog snarled at the burglar.* □ **gronder (en montrant les dents)**

■ *noun* an angry sound of this kind. □ **grondement féroce**

snatch [snatʃ] *verb* 1 to (try to) seize or grab suddenly: *The monkey snatched the biscuit out of my hand.* □ **s'emparer brusquement de**

2 to take quickly, when one has time or the opportunity: *She managed to snatch an hour's sleep.* □ **saisir l'occasion**

■ *noun* 1 an attempt to seize: *The thief made a snatch at her handbag.* □ **geste vif pour saisir qqch.**

2 a short piece or extract *eg* from music, conversation *etc*: *a snatch of conversation.* □ **fragment**

sneak [sniːk] *verb* 1 to go quietly and secretly, *especially* for a dishonest purpose: *She must have sneaked into my room when no one was looking and stolen the money.* □ **se faufiler furtivement**

2 to take secretly: *He sneaked the letter out of her drawer.* □ **prendre furtivement**

■ *noun* a mean, deceitful person, *especially* a telltale. □ **rapporteur, euse**

'**sneakers** *noun plural* soft shoes with soles made of rubber, rope *etc*: *She was wearing blue jeans and sneakers.* □ **(chaussures de) tennis**

'**sneaking** *adjective* (of a feeling) slight but not easy to suppress: *She knew he was wicked but she had a sneaking admiration for his courage.* □ **inavoué**

'**sneaky** *adjective*: *It was a bit sneaky of him to tell the teacher about me.* □ **sournois**

'**sneakiness** *noun*. □ **sournoiserie**

sneer [sniə] *verb* 1 to raise the top lip at one side in a kind of smile that expresses scorn: *What are you sneering for?* □ **sourire d'un air méprisant**

2 (*with* at) to show contempt for (something) by such an expression or by scornful words *etc*: *He sneered at our attempts to improve the situation.* □ **ricaner de**

3 to say with contempt: '*You haven't a chance of getting that job,*' *he sneered.* □ **dire d'un ton de mépris**

■ *noun* a scornful expression, words *etc* that express contempt. □ **sarcasme**

sneeze [sniːz] *verb* to blow out air suddenly, violently and involuntarily through the nose: *The pepper made her sneeze.* □ **éternuer**

■ *noun* an act of sneezing. □ **éternuement**

snide [snaid] *adjective* sneering or critical in a sly, not open, manner: *He made a snide remark about her relationship with the boss.* □ **sarcastique**

sniff [snif] *verb* 1 to draw in air through the nose with a slight noise. □ **renifler**

2 to do this in an attempt to smell something: *The dog sniffed me all over; He sniffed suddenly, wondering if he could smell smoke.* □ **flairer**

■ *noun* an act of sniffing. □ **reniflement**

sniff out to discover or detect (by using the sense of smell): *The police used dogs to sniff out the explosives.* □ **trouver (en flairant)**

snigger ['snigə] *verb* to laugh quietly in an unpleasant manner *eg* at someone else's misfortune: *When he fell off his chair we all sniggered.* □ **ricaner**

■ *noun* an act of sniggering. □ **ricanement**

snip [snip] – *past tense, past participle* **snipped** – *verb* to cut sharply, *especially* with a single quick action, with scissors *etc*: *I snipped off two centimetres of thread.* □ **couper (à coups de ciseaux)**

■ *noun* 1 a cut with scissors: *With a snip of her scissors she cut a hole in the cloth.* □ **petit coup de ciseaux**

2 a small piece cut off: *The floor was covered in snips of paper.* □ **petit bout**

'**snippet** [-pit] *noun* a little piece, *especially* of information, gossip *etc*: *a snippet of news.* □ **petit bout/fragment**

snipe [snaip]: **snipe at** to shoot at (someone) from a hidden position: *The rebels were sniping at the government troops.* □ **tirer (en restant caché)**

'**sniper** *noun*: *The soldier was shot by a sniper.* □ **tireur, euse embusqué, ée**

snippet *see* snip.

snob [snob] *noun* a person who admires people of high

rank or social class, and despises those in a lower class *etc* than himself: *Being a snob, he was always trying to get to know members of the royal family.* □ **snob**
'**snobbery** *noun* behaviour, talk *etc* that is typical of a snob: *She couldn't bear her father's snobbery.* □ **snobisme**
'**snobbish** *adjective*: *She always had a snobbish desire to live in an area of expensive housing.* □ **snob**
'**snobbishly** *adverb*. □ **de manière snob**
'**snobbishness** *noun*. □ **snobisme**
snooker ['snuːkə] *noun* a kind of game played on a billiard-table with fifteen red balls and seven balls of other colours: *Do you play snooker?*; *Let's have a game of snooker*; (*also adjective*) *a snooker match.* □ **(sorte de) jeu de billard**
snoop [snuːp] *verb* (*often with* **around** *or* **into**) to make secretive investigations into things that do not concern oneself: *She's always snooping into other people's business.* □ **mettre son nez dans**
snooze [snuːz] *verb* to doze or sleep lightly: *Her grandfather was snoozing in his armchair.* □ **sommeiller**
■ *noun* a short period of light sleep. □ **petit somme**
snore [snoː] *verb* to make a noise like a snort while sleeping, when one is breathing in: *He was obviously asleep because he was snoring loudly.* □ **ronfler**
■ *noun* an act of snoring. □ **ronflement**
snorkel ['snoːkəl] *noun* a tube with the end(s) above water for allowing an underwater swimmer to breathe or a submarine to take in air. □ **tuba**
snort [snoːt] *verb* **1** (*usually of animals*) to force air noisily through the nostrils, breathing either in or out: *The horses snorted impatiently.* □ **renâcler**
2 (*of people*) to make a similar noise, showing disapproval, anger, contempt, amusement *etc*: *She snorted at the very suggestion that she was tired.* □ **grogner**
■ *noun* an act of snorting: *a snort of impatience*; *She gave a snort of laughter.* □ **grognement**
snot [snot] *noun slang* the mucus or fluid inside the nose: *Francis blew the snot from her nose into her handkerchief.* □ **mucus**
snout [snaut] *noun* the projecting mouth and nose part of certain animals, *especially* of a pig. □ **museau, groin**
snow [snou] *noun* frozen water vapour that falls to the ground in soft white flakes: *We woke up to find snow on the ground*; *We were caught in a heavy snowstorm*; *About 15 centimetres of snow had fallen overnight.* □ **neige**
■ *verb* to shower down in, or like, flakes of snow: *It's snowing heavily.* □ **neiger**
'**snowy** *adjective* **1** full of, or producing a lot of, snow: *The weather has been very snowy recently.* □ **neigeux**
2 white like snow: *the old man's snowy (white) hair.* □ **(blanc) comme neige**
'**snowball** *noun* a ball of snow pressed hard together, *especially* made by children for throwing, as a game. □ **boule de neige**
'**snow-capped** *adjective* (of mountains *etc*) having tops which are covered with snow: *snow-capped peaks.* □ **couronné de neige**
snow clearing *noun* the act or practice of plowing and

removing snow: *Snow clearing takes a lot of city money but it's worth it to keep the snow plowed off the roads.* □ **déneigement**
'**snowdrift** *noun* a bank of snow blown together by the wind: *There were deep snowdrifts at the side of the road.* □ **banc de neige**
'**snowfall** *noun* **1** a fall or shower of snow that settles on the ground: *There was a heavy snowfall last night.* □ **chute de neige**
2 the amount of snow that falls in a certain place: *The snowfall last year was much higher than average.* □ **chute de neige**
'**snowflake** *noun* one of the soft, light flakes composed of groups of crystals, in which snow falls: *A few large snowflakes began to fall from the sky.* □ **flocon de neige**
snowshoe *noun* a large racket that straps onto the boot and is used to walk through deep snow: *Grace kept sinking into the deep snow and could only walk to the cabin by snowshoe.* □ **raquette**
'**snowstorm** *noun* a heavy fall of snow *especially* accompanied by a strong wind. □ **tempête de neige**
,**snow-'white** *adjective* white like snow. □ **blanc comme neige**
snowed under overwhelmed *eg* with a great deal of work: *Last week I was absolutely snowed under with work.* □ **débordé (de)**
snub [snʌb] – *past tense, past participle* **snubbed** – *verb* to treat, or speak to, in a cold, scornful way; to insult: *He snubbed me by not replying to my question.* □ **rabrouer**
■ *noun* an act of snubbing; an insult. □ **affront**
■ *adjective* (of the nose) short and slightly turned up at the end: *a snub nose.* □ **retroussé**
snuff¹ [snʌf] *noun* powdered tobacco for sniffing up into the nose: *He took a pinch of snuff.* □ **tabac à priser**
snuff² [snʌf] *verb* to snip off the burnt part of the wick of (a candle or lamp). □ **moucher**
snuff out 1 to extinguish the flame of (a candle *etc*): *She snuffed out the candle by squeezing the wick between her thumb and forefinger.* □ **moucher**
2 to (cause to) come to a sudden end: *Opposition was quickly snuffed out.* □ **étouffer**
snuffle ['snʌfl] *verb* to make sniffing noises, or breathe noisily: *He's snuffling because he has a cold.* □ **renifler**
snug [snʌg] *adjective* **1** warm, comfortable; sheltered from the cold: *The house is small but snug.* □ **confortable**
2 (of clothes *etc*) fitting closely: *This jacket is a nice snug fit.* □ **bien ajusté**
'**snuggle** *verb* to curl one's body up *especially* closely against another person, for warmth *etc*: *She snuggled up to her mother and went to sleep.* □ **se blottir (contre)**
'**snugly** *adverb* **1** tightly and neatly: *The gun fitted snugly into my pocket.* □ **bien, à l'aise**
2 comfortably or warmly: *The girl had a scarf wrapped snugly around her neck.* □ **confortablement**
'**snugness** *noun*. □ **bien-être**
so [sou] *adverb* **1** (used in several types of sentence to express degree) to this extent, or to such an extent: *'The snake was about so long,' he said, holding his hands*

about a metre apart; *Don't get so worried!*; *She was so pleased with his progress in school that she bought him a new bicycle*; *They couldn't all get into the room, there were so many of them*; *She departed without so much as* (= without even) *a goodbye*; *You've been so* (= very) *kind to me!*; *Thank you so much!* □ **tellement**

2 (used to express manner) in this/that way: *As you hope to be treated by others, so you must treat them*; *She likes everything to be (arranged) just so* (= in one particular and precise way); *It so happens that I have to go to an important meeting tonight.* □ **ainsi**

3 (used in place of a word, phrase *etc* previously used, or something previously stated) as already indicated: *'Are you really leaving your job?' 'Yes, I've already told you/said so'*; *'Is she arriving tomorrow?' 'Yes, I hope so'*; *If you haven't read the notice, please do so now*; *'Is that so* (= true)*?' 'Yes, it's really so'*; *'Was your father angry?' 'Yes, even more so than I was expecting – in fact, so much so that he refused to speak to me all day!'* □ **cela**

4 in the same way; also: *'I hope we'll meet again.' 'So do I.'*; *She has a lot of money and so has her husband.* □ **de même**

5 (used to express agreement or confirmation) indeed: *'You said you were going shopping today.' 'So I did, but I've changed my mind.'*; *'You'll need this book tomorrow, won't you?' 'So I will.'* □ **en effet**

■ *conjunction* (and) therefore: *John had a bad cold, so I took him to the doctor*; *'So you think you'd like this job, then?' 'Yes.'*; *And so they got married and lived happily ever after.* □ **donc**

,**so-'called** *adjective* wrongly described or named in such a way: *Your so-called friends have gone without you!* □ **soi-disant**

,**so-'so** *adjective* neither very good nor very bad: *His health is so-so.* □ **comme ci, comme ça**

and so on/forth and more of the same kind of thing: *She reminded me of what I owed her and so on.* □ **et ainsi de suite**

or so *see* **or.**

so as to in order to: *He sat at the front so as to be able to hear.* □ **de façon à ce que**

so far, so good all is well up to this point: *So far, so good – we've checked the equipment, and everything's ready.* □ **jusqu'ici ça va**

so that 1 with the purpose that; in order that: *I'll wash this dress so that you can wear it.* □ **pour que**

2 with the result that: *He got up very late, so that he missed the bus and was late for work.* □ **si bien que**

so to say/speak if one may use such an expression; in a way; it could be said: *The dog is, so to speak, a member of this family.* □ **pour ainsi dire**

soak [souk] *verb* **1** to (let) stand in a liquid: *He soaked the clothes overnight in soapy water.* □ **faire tremper**

2 to make very wet: *That shower has completely soaked my clothes.* □ **tremper**

3 (*with* **in, into, through** *etc*) (of a liquid) to penetrate: *The blood from his wound has soaked right through the bandage.* □ **pénétrer**

soaked *adjective* (*often with* **through**): *She got soaked*

(*through*) *in that shower.* □ **trempé**

-soaked: *rain-soaked/blood-soaked clothing.* □ **trempé (de)**

'**soaking** *adjective* very wet: *She took off her soaking garments.* □ **trempé**

soaking wet soaking; very wet: *I've washed my hair and it's still soaking wet.* □ **trempé**

soak up to draw in or suck up; to absorb: *You'd better soak that spilt coffee up with a cloth.* □ **absorber**

soap [soup] *noun* a mixture containing oils or fats and other substances, *especially* formed into small regularly-shaped pieces and used in washing: *He found a bar of soap and began to wash his hands.* □ **savon**

■ *verb* to rub with soap: *She soaped the baby all over.* □ **savonner**

'**soapy** *adjective* **1** covered with, or full of, soap: *soapy water.* □ **savonneux**

2 like soap: *This chocolate has a soapy taste.* □ **de savon**

'**soapiness** *noun.* □ **caractère savonneux**

soap opera a radio or television serial broadcast weekly, daily *etc*, *especially* one that continues from year to year, that concerns the daily life, troubles *etc* of the characters in it. □ **feuilleton sentimental**

soar [soz] *verb* to fly high: *Seagulls soared above the cliffs*; *Prices have soared recently.* □ **monter en flèche**

sob [sob] – *past tense, past participle* **sobbed** – *verb* **1** to weep noisily: *I could hear her sobbing in her bedroom.* □ **sangloter**

2 to say, while weeping: *'I can't find my mother,' sobbed the child.* □ **sangloter**

■ *noun* the loud gasp for breath made when one is weeping *etc.* □ **sanglot**

sober ['soubə] *adjective* **1** not drunk: *He was still sober when he left.* □ **qui n'a pas bu d'alcool**

2 serious in mind: *a sober mood.* □ **posé**

3 (of colour) not bright: *She wore a sober (grey) dress.* □ **sobre**

4 moderate; not overdone or too emotional: *Her account of the accident was factual and sober.* □ **mesuré**

'**sobering** *adjective*: *a sobering experience/thought.* □ **qui dégrise**

'**soberly** *adverb.* □ **avec modération, sobrement**

'**soberness** *noun* the quality which a thing, person *etc* has when sober: *soberness of mind.* □ **sobriété**

sober up to make or become (more) sober. □ **dégriser**

so-called *see* **so.**

soccer ['sokə] *noun* football played according to certain rules. □ **football**

sociable ['souʃəbl] *adjective* (*negative* **unsociable**) fond of the company of others; friendly: *He's a cheerful, sociable man.* □ **sociable**

'**sociably** *adverb.* □ **de façon sociable**

social ['souʃəl] *adjective* **1** concerning or belonging to the way of life and welfare of people in a community: *social problems.* □ **social**

2 concerning the system by which such a community is organized: *social class.* □ **social**

3 living in communities: *Ants are social insects.* □ **social**

4 concerning the gathering together of people for the

purposes of recreation or amusement: *a social club*; *His reasons for calling were purely social.* □ **social**

'**socialism** *noun* the belief or theory that a country's wealth (its land, mines, industries, railways *etc*) should belong to the people as a whole, not to private owners. □ **socialisme**

'**socialist** *noun* a person who believes in and/or practises socialism. □ **socialiste**

■ *adjective* of or concerning socialism: *socialist policies/governments.* □ **socialiste**

'**socialize, 'socialise** *verb* to mix socially (*eg* with guests at a party *etc*). □ **voir/fréquenter des gens**

'**socially** *adverb* in a social way: *I've seen her at various conferences, but we've never met socially.* □ **en société**

social work work which deals with the care of people in a community, *especially* of the poor, under-privileged *etc* (*noun* **social worker**). □ **services sociaux**

society [sə'saiəti] – *plural* **so'cieties** – *noun* 1 mankind considered as a whole: *He was a danger to society.* □ **société**

2 a particular group or part of mankind considered as a whole: *middle-class society*; *modern western societies.* □ **société**

3 an association or club: *a model railway society.* □ **association**

4 the class of people who are wealthy, fashionable or of high rank in any area: *high society.* □ **société**

5 company or companionship: *I enjoy the society of young people.* □ **compagnie**

sock [sok] *noun* a (*usually* wool, cotton or nylon) covering for the foot and ankle, sometimes reaching to the knee, worn inside a shoe, boot *etc*: *I need a new pair of socks.* □ **chaussettes**

socket ['sokit] *noun* a specially-made or specially-shaped hole or set of holes into which something is fitted: *We'll need to have a new electric socket fitted into the wall for the television plug.* □ **douille; prise de courant**

soda ['soudə] *noun* 1 the name given to several substances formed with sodium, *especially* one (washing soda or **sodium carbonate**) in the form of crystals, used for washing, or one (baking soda or **sodium bicarbonate**) used in baking. □ **(bicarbonate de) soude**

2 soda-water: *whisky and soda.* □ **soda**

3 a drink made with flavoured soda-water and *usually* ice cream. □ **soda à la crème glacée**

'**soda water** *noun* water through which the gas carbon dioxide has been passed, making it fizzy. □ **eau gazéifiée**

sodium ['soudiəm] *noun* an element from which many substances are formed, including common salt (**sodium chloride**). □ **sodium**

sodium bicarbonate/carbonate *see* **soda.**

sofa ['soufə] *noun* a kind of long seat, stuffed and with a back and arms: *We were sitting on the sofa.* □ **sofa**

soft [soft] *adjective* 1 not hard or firm; easily changing shape when pressed: *a soft cushion.* □ **mou**

2 pleasantly smooth to the touch: *The dog has a soft, silky coat.* □ **doux, soyeux**

3 not loud: *a soft voice.* □ **doux**

4 (of colour) not bright or harsh: *a soft pink.* □ **doux**

5 not strict (enough): *You are too soft with her.* □ **indulgent**

6 (of a drink) not alcoholic: *At the party they were serving soft drinks as well as wine and spirits.* □ **non alcoolisé**

7 childishly weak, timid or silly: *Don't be so soft – the dog won't hurt you.* □ **stupide**

'**softly** *adverb.* □ **doucement**

'**softness** *noun.* □ **douceur**

soften ['sofn] *verb* to make or become soft or softer, less strong or less painful: *The thick walls softened the noise of the explosion.* □ **(s')adoucir**

,**soft-'boiled** *adjective* (of eggs) slightly boiled, so that the yolk is still soft: *She likes her eggs soft-boiled.* □ **à la coque**

,**soft-'hearted** *adjective* kind-hearted and generous: *He had been given some money by a soft-hearted aunt.* □ **au cœur tendre**

,**soft-'spoken** *adjective* having a gentle voice or manner: *He was a soft-spoken man with a shy smile.* □ **à la voix douce**

'**software** *noun* computer programs, as opposed to the machines themselves ('**hardware**). □ **logiciel**

'**softwood** *noun, adjective* (of) the wood of a conebearing tree *eg* a pine: *softwood furniture.* □ **bois tendre**

have a soft spot for to have a weakness for (someone or something) because of great affection: *He's always had a soft spot for his youngest son.* □ **avoir un faible pour qqn/qqch.**

soggy ['sogi] *adjective* very wet and soft: *In the centre of the puddle was a piece of soggy cardboard.* □ **(dé)trempé**

'**sogginess** *noun.* □ **boue, sol détrempé**

soil[1] [soil] *noun* the upper layer of the earth, in which plants grow: *to plant seeds in the soil*; *a handful of soil.* □ **sol, terre**

soil[2] [soil] *verb* to dirty or stain: *Don't soil your dress with these dusty books!* □ **salir**

solar ['soulə] *adjective* having to do with, powered by, or influenced by, the sun: *the solar year*; *a solar heating system.* □ **solaire**

,**solar-'powered** *adjective.* □ **à énergie solaire**

solar system the Sun or any star and the planets which move around it. □ **système solaire**

sold *see* **sell.**

solder ['soldər] *noun* melted metal or alloy used to join one piece of metal to another. □ **soudure**

■ *verb* to join (two or more pieces of metal) with solder: *She soldered the broken wire back on to the transistor*; *I'd like to learn how to solder.* □ **souder**

'**soldering iron** *noun* a type of tool for providing the heat needed when soldering. □ **fer à souder**

soldier ['souldʒə] *noun* a member (*usually* male) of an army, often one who is not an officer: *The boy wants to be a soldier when he grows up.* □ **soldat**

soldier on to keep going despite difficulties *etc*: *There have been several power-cuts in the office, but we are trying to soldier on (despite them).* □ **persévérer (malgré tout)**

sole[1] [soul] *noun* **1** the underside of the foot, the part on which one stands and walks. □ **plante (du pied)**

2 the flat surface of a boot or shoe that covers this part of the foot. □ **semelle**

sole[2] [soul] – *plurals* **sole, soles** – *noun* **1** a type of small, flat fish: *They were fishing for sole; three soles.* □ **sole**

2 its flesh as food: *We had sole for supper.* □ **sole**

sole[3] [soul] *adjective* **1** only; single: *my sole purpose/reason.* □ **seul, unique**

2 not shared; belonging to one person or group only: *the sole rights to a book.* □ **exclusif**

'solely *adverb* only: *She is solely responsible for the crisis.* □ **seulement**

solemn ['soləm] *adjective* **1** serious and earnest: *a solemn question; She looked very solemn as she announced the bad news.* □ **grave**

2 stately; having formal dignity: *a solemn procession.* □ **solennel**

'solemnly *adverb.* □ **solennellement**

'solemnness *noun.* □ **solennité**

solemnity [sə'lemnəti] *noun* the state of being solemn: *the solemnity of the occasion.* □ **solennité**

solicit [sə'lisit] *verb* to ask (for): *People working for charities are permitted to solicit (money from) the public.* □ **solliciter (qqch. de qqn)**

so'licitor *noun* a lawyer who prepares legal documents and briefs, gives legal advice, and (in the lower courts only) speaks on behalf of his clients. □ **avocat, are**

solid ['solid] *adjective* **1** not easily changing shape; not in the form of liquid or gas: *Water becomes solid when it freezes; solid substances.* □ **solide**

2 not hollow: *The tires of the earliest cars were solid.* □ **plein**

3 firm and strongly made (and therefore sound and reliable): *That's a solid piece of furniture; Her argument is based on good solid facts/reasoning.* □ **solide**

4 completely made of one substance: *This bracelet is made of solid gold; We dug till we reached solid rock.* □ **massif**

5 without breaks, gaps or flaws: *The policemen formed themselves into a solid line; They are solid in their determination to strike.* □ **continu; inébranlable**

6 having height, breadth and width: *A cube is a solid figure.* □ **solide**

7 consecutive; without a pause: *I've been working for six solid hours.* □ **d'affilée**

■ *adverb* without interruption; continuously: *She was working for six hours solid.* □ **d'affilée**

■ *noun* a substance that is solid: *Butter is a solid but milk is a liquid.* □ **(aliment) solide**

2 a shape that has length, breadth and height. □ **solide**

,soli'darity [-'darə-] *noun* the uniting of the interests, feelings or actions (of a group): *We must try to preserve our solidarity.* □ **solidarité**

so'lidify [-difai] *verb* to make or become solid. □ **(se) solidifier**

so,lidifi'cation [-difi-] *noun.* □ **solidification**

so'lidity *noun.* □ **solidité**

'solidness *noun.* □ **solidité**

'solidly *adverb* **1** firmly; strongly: *solidly-built houses.*

□ **solidement**

2 continuously: *I worked solidly from 8:30 a.m. till lunchtime.* □ **sans interruption**

3 unanimously: *We're solidly in agreement with your suggestions.* □ **unanimement**

solid fuel a fuel, such as coal, that is solid rather than an oil or gas. □ **combustible solide**

solitary ['solitəri] *adjective* **1** alone; without companions: *a solitary traveller.* □ **solitaire**

2 living or being alone, by habit or preference: *She was a solitary person.* □ **solitaire**

3 single: *not a solitary example.* □ **unique**

'solitude [-tjuːd] *noun* the state of being alone: *He likes solitude; He lives in solitude.* □ **solitude**

solitary confinement imprisonment in a cell by oneself: *He was sentenced to six months' solitary confinement.* □ **régime cellulaire**

solo ['soulou] – *plural* **'solos** – *noun* something (*eg* a musical piece for one voice or instrument, a dance or other entertainment) in which only one person takes part: *a cello/soprano solo.* □ **solo**

■ *adjective* in which only one takes part: *a solo flight in an airplane.* □ **en solitaire**

'soloist *noun* a person who plays, sings *etc* a solo. □ **soliste**

solstice ['solstis] *noun* the time of year when there is the greatest length of daylight (**summer solstice**) or the shortest (**winter solstice**). □ **solstice**

soluble ['soljubl] *adjective* **1** able to be dissolved or made liquid: *This dye is soluble in water.* □ **soluble**

2 (of a problem, difficulty *etc*) able to be solved. □ **(ré)soluble**

solution [sə'luːʃən] *noun* **1** an answer to a problem, difficulty or puzzle: *the solution to a crossword.* □ **solution**

2 the act of finding such an answer. □ **solution**

3 a liquid with something dissolved in it: *a solution of salt and water.* □ **solution**

solve [solv] *verb* **1** to discover the answer to (a problem *etc*): *The mathematics teacher gave the children some problems to solve.* □ **résoudre**

2 to clear up or explain (a mystery, crime *etc*): *That crime has never been solved.* □ **élucider**

solvent ['solvənt] *adjective* having enough money to be able to pay all one's debts. □ **solvable**

■ *noun* a substance, *eg* petrol, that dissolves grease *etc.* □ **solvant**

sombre, somber ['sombə] *adjective* **1** dark (and gloomy): *Black is a sombre colour.* □ **sombre**

2 grave; serious: *He was in a sombre mood.* □ **sombre**

some [sʌm] *pronoun, adjective* **1** an indefinite amount or number (of): *I can see some people walking across the field; You'll need some money if you're going shopping; Some of the ink was spilt on the desk.* □ **quelque(s); un peu**

2 (said with emphasis) a certain, or small, amount or number (of): *'Has she any experience of the work?' 'Yes, she has some.'; Some people like the idea and some don't.* □ **certain(s)**

3 (said with emphasis) at least one/a few/a bit (of): *Surely* *there are some people who agree with me?; I don't need much rest from work, but I must have some.* □ **quelques; un peu**

4 certain: *He's quite kind in some ways.* □ **certain**

■ *adjective* **1** a large, considerable or impressive (amount or number of): *I spent some time trying to convince her; I'll have some problem sorting out these papers!* □ **beaucoup de**

2 an unidentified or unnamed (thing, person *etc*): *She was hunting for some book that she's lost.* □ **quelconque**

3 (used with numbers) about; at a rough estimate: *There were some thirty people at the reception.* □ **environ**

■ *adverb* somewhat; to a certain extent: *I think we've progressed some.* □ **quelque**

'**somebody** *pronoun* someone. □ **quelqu'un**

'**someday** *adverb* (also **some day**) at an unknown time in the future: *We'll manage it someday.* □ **un jour**

'**somehow** *adverb* in some way not known for certain: *I'll get there somehow.* □ **d'une manière ou d'une autre**

'**someone** *pronoun* **1** an unknown or unnamed person: *There's someone at the door – would you answer it?; We all know someone who needs help.* □ **quelqu'un**

2 a person of importance: *He thinks he is someone.* □ **quelqu'un**

'**something** *pronoun* **1** a thing not known or not stated: *Would you like something to eat?; I've got something to tell you.* □ **quelque chose**

2 a thing of importance: *There's something in what you say.* □ **quelque chose**

'**sometime** *adverb* at an unknown time in the future or the past: *We'll go there sometime next week; They went sometime last month.* □ **dans le courant de**

'**sometimes** *adverb* occasionally: *She sometimes goes to America; He goes to America sometimes; Sometimes he seems very forgetful.* □ **parfois, quelquefois**

'**somewhat** *adverb* rather; a little: *He is somewhat sad; The news puzzled me somewhat.* □ **quelque peu**

'**somewhere** *adverb* ('**someplace**) (in or to) some place not known or not named: *They live somewhere in Montreal; I won't be at home tonight – I'm going somewhere for dinner.* □ **quelque part**

mean something to have meaning; to be significant: *Do all these figures mean something?* □ **signifier quelque chose**

or something used when the speaker is uncertain or being vague: *Her name is Mary or Margaret or something.* □ **ou quelque chose comme ça**

something like 1 about: *We have something like five hundred people working here.* □ **quelque chose comme**

2 rather like: *A zebra is something like a horse with stripes.* □ **un peu comme**

something tells me I have reason to believe; I suspect: *Something tells me she's lying.* □ **quelque chose me dit (que)**

somersault ['sʌməsɔːlt] *noun* a leap or roll in which a person turns with his feet going over his head. □ **culbute**

■ *verb* to make such a leap or roll. □ **faire la culbute**

son [sʌn] *noun* a male child (when spoken of in relation to his parents): *He is the son of the manager.* □ **fils**

'**son-in-law** – *plural* '**sons-in-law** – *noun* a daughter's husband. □ **gendre**

song [sɒŋ] *noun* **1** something (to be) sung: *He wrote this song for his wife to sing.* □ **chanson**

2 singing: *She burst into song.* □ **chanson**

3 the sound(s) made by a bird: *birdsong.* □ **chant**

'**songbird** *noun* any of the types of bird which have a pleasant song. □ **oiseau chanteur**

'**songwriter** *noun* a person who writes songs (*usually* pop songs) for a living. □ **auteur, eure (de chansons)**

sonic ['sɒnik] *adjective* of, or using, sound waves. □ **sonique**

sonic boom a sudden loud noise heard when an aircraft which is travelling faster than the speed of sound passes overhead. □ **bang supersonique**

sonnet ['sɒnit] *noun* a type of poem with fourteen lines: *Milton's/Shakespeare's sonnets.* □ **sonnet**

soon [suːn] *adverb* **1** in a short time from now or from the time mentioned: *They'll be here sooner than you think; I hope he arrives soon.* □ **tôt; bientôt**

2 early: *It's too soon to tell.* □ **tôt**

3 willingly: *I would sooner stand than sit.* □ **plutôt**

as soon as (not later than the moment) when: *You may have a biscuit as soon as we get home.* □ **dès que, aussitôt que, sitôt**

no sooner ... than when ... immediately: *No sooner had we set off than we realized we'd left the dog behind.* □ **à peine ... que**

sooner or later eventually: *She'll come home sooner or later, I suppose.* □ **tôt ou tard**

the sooner the better as quickly as possible: *'When shall I tell him?' 'The sooner the better!'* □ **le plus tôt sera le mieux**

soot [sut] *noun* the black powder left after the burning of coal *etc*. □ **suie**

'**sooty** *adjective* **1** covered with soot. □ **couvert/noir de suie**

2 of the colour of soot. □ **charbonneux**

'**sootiness** *noun*. □ **noirceur**

soothe [suːð] *verb* **1** to calm, comfort or quieten (a person, his feelings *etc*): *She was so upset that it took half an hour to soothe her.* □ **calmer**

2 to ease (pain *etc*): *The medicine soothed the child's toothache.* □ **calmer**

'**soothing** *adjective*. □ **calmant**

'**soothingly** *adverb*. □ **d'une manière calmante**

sooty *see* **soot**.

sophisticated [sə'fistikeitid] *adjective* (*negative* **unsophisticated**) **1** (of a person) having a great deal of experience and worldly wisdom, knowledge of how to dress elegantly *etc*: *a sophisticated young man; She has become very sophisticated since she went to live in Montreal.* □ **élégant, raffiné**

2 suitable for, or typical of, sophisticated people: *The joke was too sophisticated for the child to understand; sophisticated clothes/hairstyles.* □ **subtil, recherché**

3 (of machines, processes *etc*) highly-developed, elaborate and produced with a high degree of skill and knowledge: *sophisticated photographic techniques.* □ **sophistiqué**

so,phisti'cation *noun*. □ **raffinement; complexité**

soprano [sə'praːnou] – *plural* so'pranos – *noun* (a singer having) a singing voice of the highest pitch for a woman. □ **soprano**

sorcery ['soːsəri] *noun* **1** the use of power gained from evil spirits. □ **sorcellerie**

2 witchcraft or magic in general. □ **sorcellerie**

'**sorcerer** – *feminine* '**sorceress** – *noun* a person who practises sorcery. □ **sorcier, ière**

sordid ['soːdid] *adjective* **1** (of a place *etc*) dirty, mean and poor: *a very sordid neighbourhood*. □ **sordide**

2 (of a person's behaviour *etc*) showing low standards or ideals *etc*; not very pleasant or admirable: *The whole affair was rather sordid*. □ **sordide**

'**sordidly** *adverb*. □ **sordidement**

'**sordidness** *noun*. □ **caractère sordide**

sore [soː] *adjective* **1** painful: *My leg is very sore*; *I have a sore leg*. □ **douloureux**

2 suffering pain: *I am still a bit sore after my operation*. □ **endolori**

3 irritated, annoyed or offended: *She is still sore about what happened*. □ **fâché, vexé**

■ *noun* a painful, injured or diseased spot on the skin: *His hands were covered with horrible sores*. □ **plaie**

'**sorely** *adverb* badly; acutely. □ **gravement**

'**soreness** *noun*. □ **irritation**

sorrow ['sorou] *noun* (something which causes) pain of mind or grief: *He felt great sorrow when she died*. □ **chagrin**

'**sorrowful** *adjective* showing or feeling sorrow: *sorrowful people*; *a sorrowful expression*. □ **chagriné**

'**sorrowfully** *adverb*. □ **avec chagrin**

'**sorrowfulness** *noun*. □ **chagrin**

sorry ['sori] *adjective* **1** used when apologizing or expressing regret: *I'm sorry (that) I forgot to return your book*; *Did I give you a fright? I'm sorry*. □ **désolé**

2 apologetic or full of regret: *I think he's really sorry for his bad behaviour*; *I'm sure you were sorry to hear about his death*. □ **désolé**

3 unsatisfactory; poor; wretched: *a sorry state of affairs*. □ **triste**

■ *interjection* **1** used when apologizing: *Did I tread on your toe? Sorry!* □ **pardon!**

2 (used when asking a person to repeat what he has said) I beg your pardon?: *Sorry (what did you say)?* □ **pardon**

be/feel sorry for to pity: *I'm/I feel really sorry for that poor woman*. □ **avoir pitié de**

sort [soːt] *noun* a class, type or kind: *I like all sorts of books*; *She was wearing a sort of crown*. □ **sorte**

■ *verb* to separate into classes or groups, putting each item in its place: *She sorted the buttons into large ones and small ones*. □ **trier (selon)**

'**sorter** *noun* a person or machine that separates and arranges, *especially* letters, postcards *etc*. □ **trieur, trieuse**

of a sort/of sorts of a (*usually* poor) kind: *She threw together a meal of sorts but we were still hungry afterwards*. □ **quelconque**

out of sorts slightly unwell: *I felt a bit out of sorts after last night's heavy meal*. □ **pas dans son assiette**

2 not in good spirits or temper: *He's been a little out of sorts since they told him to stay at home*. □ **de mauvaise humeur**

sort of rather; in a way; to a certain extent: *She was sort of peculiar!*; *I feel sort of worried about him*. □ **plutôt**

sort out 1 to separate (one lot or type of) things from a general mixture: *I'll try to sort out some books that he might like*. □ **trier**

2 to correct, improve, solve *etc*: *You must sort out your business affairs*. □ **mettre de l'ordre (dans)**

3 to attend to, *usually* by punishing or reprimanding: *I'll soon sort you out, you evil little man!* □ **régler son compte à**

sortie ['soːti] *noun* **1** a sudden raid or attacking mission. □ **sortie**

2 a short trip or expedition. □ **sortie**

SOS [esou'es] *noun* a call for help or rescue, often in code and *usually* from a distance: *Send an SOS to the mainland to tell them that we are sinking!* □ **S.O.S**

soufflé ['suːflei, suːˈflei] *noun* a kind of frothy cooked dish, made with whisked whites of egg: *I made a cheese soufflé*. □ **soufflé**

sought *see* **seek**.

soul [soul] *noun* **1** the spirit; the non-physical part of a person, which is often thought to continue in existence after he or she dies: *People often discuss whether animals and plants have souls*. □ **âme**

2 a person: *She's a wonderful old soul*. □ **personne**

3 (of an enterprise *etc*) the organizer or leader: *She is the soul of the whole movement*. □ **âme**

4 soul music. □ **soul music**

'**soulful** *adjective* full of (*usually* sad, wistful *etc*) feeling: *a soulful expression*. □ **sentimental**

'**soulfully** *adverb*. □ **de manière sentimentale**

'**soulless** *adjective* **1** (of a person) without fine feeling or nobleness. □ **sans âme**

2 (of life, a task *etc*) dull or very unimportant. □ **terre à terre**

'**soul-destroying** *adjective* (of a task *etc*) very dull, boring, repetitive *etc*. □ **abrutissant**

soul music (*also* **soul**) a type of music, descended from American Negro gospel songs, which has great emotion. □ **musique soul**

sound[1] [saund] *adjective* **1** strong or in good condition: *The foundations of the house are not very sound*; *He's 87, but he's still sound in mind and body*. □ **solide, sain**

2 (of sleep) deep: *She's a very sound sleeper*. □ **profond (sommeil)**

3 full; thorough: *a sound basic training*. □ **solide**

4 accurate; free from mistakes: *a sound piece of work*. □ **bon, solide**

5 having or showing good judgment or good sense: *His advice is always very sound*. □ **judicieux**

'**soundly** *adverb*. □ **judicieusement**

'**soundness** *noun*. □ **solidité**

sound asleep sleeping deeply: *The baby is sound asleep*. □ **profondément endormi**

sound[2] *noun* **1** the impressions transmitted to the brain by the sense of hearing: *a barrage of sound*; (*also ad-*

jective) sound waves. □ **son; sonore**

2 something that is, or can be, heard: *The sounds were coming from the garage.* □ **bruit**

3 the impression created in the mind by a piece of news, a description *etc*: *I didn't like the sound of her hairstyle at all!* □ **allure**

■ *verb* **1** to (cause something to) make a sound: *Sound the bell!*; *The bell sounded.* □ **sonner**

2 to signal (something) by making a sound: *Sound the alarm!* □ **sonner**

3 (of something heard or read) to make a particular impression; to seem; to appear: *Your singing sounded very good*; *That sounds like a train.* □ **bien sonner à l'oreille; avoir l'air (d'être)**

4 to pronounce: *In the word 'pneumonia', the letter p is not sounded.* □ **prononcer**

5 to examine by tapping and listening carefully: *She sounded the patient's chest.* □ **ausculter**

'soundless *adjective*. □ **silencieux**

'soundlessly *adverb*. □ **sans bruit**

sound effects sounds other than dialogue or music, used in films, radio *etc*. □ **bruitage**

'soundproof *adjective* not allowing sound to pass in, out, or through: *The walls are soundproof.* □ **insonorisé**

■ *verb* to make (walls, a room *etc*) soundproof. □ **insonoriser**

'soundtrack *noun* (a recording of) the music from a film: *I've just bought the sound-track of that new film.* □ **bande sonore**

sound³ [saund] *verb* to measure the depth of (water *etc.*) □ **sonder**

'sounding *noun* **1** (a) measurement of depth of water *etc*. □ **sondage**

2 a depth measured. □ **sondage**

3 (an) act of trying to find out views *etc*. □ **sondage(s)**

sound out to try to find out someone's thoughts and plans *etc*: *Will you sound out your father on this?* □ **sonder (qqn sur qqch.)**

soup [suːp] *noun* a liquid food made from meat, vegetables *etc*: *He made some chicken soup.* □ **soupe, potage**

in the soup in serious trouble: *If she's found out about it, we're all in the soup!* □ **dans de beaux draps**

sour ['sauə] *adjective* **1** having a taste or smell similar in nature to that of lemon juice or vinegar: *Unripe apples are/taste very sour.* □ **sur, acide**

2 having a similar taste as a stage in going bad: *sour milk.* □ **aigre**

3 (of a person, his character *etc*) discontented, bad-tempered or disagreeable: *She was looking very sour this morning.* □ **revêche**

■ *verb* to make or become sour. □ **s'aigrir**

'sourly *adverb*. □ **avec aigreur**

'sourness *noun*. □ **aigreur**

source [soːs] *noun* **1** the place, person, circumstance, thing *etc* from which anything begins or comes: *They have discovered the source of the trouble.* □ **source**

2 the spring from which a river flows: *the source of the Nile.* □ **source**

south [sauθ] *noun* **1** the direction to the right of a person facing the rising sun, or any part of the earth lying in

that direction: *He stood facing towards the south*; *She lives in the south of France.* □ **sud**

2 one of the four main points of the compass. □ **sud**

■ *adjective* **1** in the south: *She works on the south coast.* □ **sud, méridional**

2 from the direction of the south: *a south wind.* □ **du sud**

■ *adverb* towards the south: *This window faces south.* □ **vers le sud**

southerly ['sʌðəli] *adjective* **1** (of a wind *etc*) coming from the south: *a southerly wind.* □ **du sud**

2 looking, lying *etc* towards the south: *in a southerly direction.* □ **du sud**

southern ['sʌðən] *adjective* of the south: *Your speech sounds southern to me*; *Australia is in the southern hemisphere.* □ **méridional; sud, austral**

southerner ['sʌðənə] *noun* a person who lives, or was born, in a southern region or country. □ **méridional, ale**

southernmost ['sʌðənmoust] *adjective* being furthest south: *the southernmost point on the mainland.* □ **le plus au sud**

'southward *adjective* towards the south: *in a southward direction.* □ **(au) sud**

'southward(s) *adverb* towards the south: *We are moving southwards.* □ **vers le sud**

'southbound *adjective* travelling southwards: *southbound traffic.* □ **vers le sud**

,south'east/,south'west *nouns* the direction midway between south and east or south and west, or any part of the earth lying in that direction. □ **sud-est; sud-ouest**

■ *adjective* **1** in the southeast or southwest: *the southeast coast.* □ **sud-est; sud-ouest**

2 from the direction of the southeast or southwest: *a southeast wind.* □ **du sud-est; du sud-ouest**

■ *adverb* towards the southeast or southwest: *The gateway faces southwest.* □ **vers le sud-est; vers le sud-ouest**

,south'easterly/,south'westerly *adjectives* **1** (of a wind *etc*) coming from the southeast or southwest: *a southeasterly wind.* □ **du sud-est; du sud-ouest**

2 looking, lying *etc* towards the southeast or southwest: *a southwesterly direction.* □ **sud-est; sud-ouest**

,south'eastern/,south'western *adjectives* of the southeast or southwest: *a southwestern dialect.* □ **du sudest; du sud-ouest**

the South Pole the southern end of the imaginary line through the earth, around which it turns. □ **Pôle Sud**

souvenir ['suːvəniə] *noun* something (bought, kept or given) which reminds one of a place, person or occasion: *a souvenir of one's holiday.* □ **souvenir**

sovereign ['sovrin] *noun* a king or queen. □ **souverain, aine**

■ *adjective* (of a country) self-governing: *a sovereign state.* □ **souverain**

soviet ['souviət] *adjective* (*often with capital*) of the USSR. □ **soviétique**

■ *noun* one of the people, *especially* one of the leaders, of the USSR. □ **Soviétique**

sow¹ [sou] – *past tense* **sowed**: *past participle* **sown,**

sowed – *verb* **1** to scatter over, or put in, the ground: *I sowed lettuce in this part of the garden.* □ **semer**
2 to plant seed over: *This field has been sown with wheat.* □ **ensemencer (en)**

to sow (not sew) seed.

sow² [sau] *noun* a female pig. □ **truie**
soya bean ['soiəbiːn], **soybean** ['soibiːn] *noun* a type of bean, processed and used as a substitute for meat *etc.* □ **soja**
soy(a) sauce a sauce made from soya beans, used in Chinese *etc* cooking. □ **sauce au soja**
space [speis] *noun* **1** a gap; an empty or uncovered place: *I couldn't find a space for my car.* □ **place**
2 room; the absence of objects; the area available for use: *Have you enough space to turn around?*; *Is there space for one more?* □ **place**
3 (*often* **outer space**) the region outside the Earth's atmosphere, in which all stars and other planets *etc* are situated: *travellers through space.* □ **espace**
■ *verb* (*also* **space out**) to set (things) apart from one another: *She spaced the rows of potatoes half a metre apart.* □ **espacer**
'spacing *noun* the amount of distance left between objects, words *etc* when they are set or laid out. □ **espacement**
spacious ['speiʃəs] *adjective* providing or having plenty of room: *Their dining-room is very spacious.* □ **spacieux**
'spaciously *adverb*. □ **amplement**
'spaciousness *noun*. □ **grandes dimensions (de)**
'space-age *adjective* extremely up-to-date and advanced: *space-age technology.* □ **de l'ère spatiale**
'spacecraft *noun* a vehicle *etc*, manned or unmanned, for travelling in space. □ **engin spatial**
'spaceship *noun* a spacecraft, *especially* a manned one. □ **vaisseau spatial**
'spacesuit *noun* a suit designed to be worn by a **'spaceman.** □ **combinaison spatiale**
spade¹ [speid] *noun* a tool with a broad blade and a handle, used for digging. □ **bêche; pelle**
spade² [speid] *noun* one of the playing cards of the suit spades. □ **pique**
spades *noun plural* (sometimes treated as *noun singular*) one of the four card suits: *the ten of spades.* □ **pique**
spaghetti [spə'geti] *noun* an Italian food consisting of long strands of pasta. □ **spaghetti**
span [span] *noun* **1** the length between the supports of a bridge or arch: *The first span of the bridge is one hundred metres long.* □ **travée, portée**
2 the full time for which anything lasts: *Seventy or eighty years is the normal span of a man's life.* □ **durée**
■ *verb* – *past tense, past participle* **spanned** – to stretch across: *A bridge spans the river.* □ **traverser**
spaniel ['spanjəl] *noun* a breed of dog with large ears which hang down. □ **épagneul**
Spanish ['spaniʃ] *adjective* of Spain or its inhabitants: *Tours through Spain usually include the chance to see a Spanish bullfight; Spanish shopkeepers close their shops every afternoon.* □ **espagnol**
■ *noun* the language of Spain: *Spanish is a Romance language, similar to French.* □ **Espagnol**
spank [spaŋk] *verb* to strike or slap with the flat of the hand, *especially* on the buttocks, *usually* as a punishment: *The child was spanked for his disobedience.* □ **donner une fessée à**
■ *noun* a slap of this kind. □ **claque sur les fesses**
spar¹ [spaː] *noun* a strong, thick pole of wood or metal, *especially* one used as a ship's mast *etc.* □ **espar**
spar² [spaː] – *past tense, past participle* **sparred** – *verb* **1** to box, *usually* for practice only. □ **s'entraîner à la boxe (avec)**
2 (*usually with* **with**) to have an argument, *usually* a friendly one. □ **escarmouche amicale**
'sparring partner *noun* **1** a person with whom a boxer practises. □ **partenaire d'entraînement**
2 a person with whom one enjoys a lively argument. □ **contradicteur amical**
spare [speə] *verb* **1** to manage without: *No one can be spared from this office.* □ **se passer de**
2 to afford or set aside for a purpose: *I can't spare the time for a holiday.* □ **réserver à**
3 to treat with mercy; to avoid injuring *etc*: *'Spare us!' they begged.* □ **épargner qqn**
4 to avoid causing grief, trouble *etc* to (a person): *Break the news gently in order to spare her as much as possible.* □ **épargner**
5 to avoid using, spending *etc*: *He spared no expense in his desire to help us.* □ **ménager**
6 to avoid troubling (a person with something); to save (a person trouble *etc*): *I answered the letter myself in order to spare you the bother.* □ **épargner (qqch. à qqn)**
■ *adjective* **1** extra; not actually being used: *We haven't a spare (bed) room for guests in our house.* □ **disponible**
2 (of time *etc*) free for leisure *etc*: *What do you do in your spare time?* □ **libre**
■ *noun* **1** a spare part (for a car *etc*): *They sell spares at that garage.* □ **pièce de rechange**
2 an extra wheel *etc*, kept for emergencies. □ **roue de secours**
'sparing *adjective* careful or economical. □ **économe**
'sparingly *adverb*. □ **frugalement**
spare part a part for a machine *etc*, used to replace an identical part if it breaks *etc.* □ **pièce de rechange**
spare rib a rib of pork with only a small amount of meat left on it. □ **côte levée**
to spare in greater supply or quantity than is needed; extra: *I'll go to an exhibition if I have time to spare*; *I have enough food to spare.* □ **de reste, de trop**
spark [spaːk] *noun* **1** a tiny red-hot piece thrown off by something burning, or when two very hard (*eg* metal) surfaces are struck together: *Sparks were being thrown into the air from the burning building.* □ **étincelle**
2 an electric current jumping across a gap: *a spark from a faulty electric socket.* □ **étincelle**
3 a trace (*eg* of life, humour): *a spark of enthusiasm.* □ **étincelle**
■ *verb* **1** to give off sparks. □ **jeter des étincelles**
2 (*often with* **off**) to start (a row, disagreement *etc*): *Their action sparked off a major row.* □ **déclencher**
sparkle ['spaːkl] *noun* **1** an effect like that made by little

sparks: *There was a sudden sparkle as her diamond ring caught the light.* □ **étincellement**

2 liveliness or brightness: *She has lots of sparkle.* □ **éclat**

■ *verb* 1 to glitter, as if throwing off tiny sparks: *The snow sparkled in the sunlight.* □ **étinceler**

2 to be lively or witty: *She really sparkled at that party.* □ **briller**

'**sparkling** *adjective* 1 (of wines) giving off bubbles of gas. □ **mousseux**

2 lively: *sparkling humour/wit.* □ **pétillant**

sparrow ['sparou] *noun* a common type of small brown bird related to the finch family. □ **moineau**

sparse [spa:s] *adjective* thinly scattered: *sparse vegetation.* □ **clairsemé**

'**sparsely** *adverb.* □ **peu abondamment**

'**sparseness** *noun.* □ **faible densité**

spasm ['spazəm] *noun* a sudden uncontrollable jerking of the muscles: *A spasm of pain twisted his face for a moment.* □ **spasme**

spastic ['spastik] *noun, adjective* (a person) suffering from brain damage that causes extreme muscle spasms and/or muscular paralysis: *Their youngest child is (a) spastic.* □ **paraplégique (spasmodique)**

spat *see* **spit**.

spatula ['spatʃulə] *noun* a kind of tool with a broad blunt blade: *Spread the icing on the cake with a spatula.* □ **spatule**

spawn [spɔːn] *noun* the eggs of fish, frogs *etc*: *In the spring, the pond is full of frog-spawn.* □ **œufs**

■ *verb* (of frogs, fish *etc*) to produce spawn. □ **frayer**

speak [spiːk] – *past tense* **spoke** [spouk]: *past participle* '**spoken** ['spoukən] – *verb* 1 to say (words) or talk: *He can't speak; She spoke a few words to us.* □ **parler**

2 (*often with* to *or* with) to talk or converse: *Can I speak to/with you for a moment?; We spoke for hours about it.* □ **parler (à, avec)**

3 to (be able to) talk in (a language): *She speaks Russian.* □ **parler**

4 to tell or make known (one's thoughts, the truth *etc*): *I always speak my mind.* □ **dire**

5 to make a speech, address an audience: *The Prime Minister spoke on unemployment.* □ **parler (de)**

'**speaker** *noun* 1 a person who is or was speaking. □ **conférencier, ière**

2 (*sometimes* ,**loud**'**speaker**) the device in a radio, record player *etc* which converts the electrical impulses into audible sounds: *Our record player needs a new speaker.* □ **haut-parleur**

'**speaking** *adjective* 1 involving speech: *a speaking part in a play.* □ **parlant**

2 used in speech: *a pleasant speaking voice.* □ **agréable à entendre**

'**spoken** *adjective* produced by speaking: *the spoken word.* □ **parole**

-**spoken** speaking in a particular way: *plain-spoken; smooth-spoken.* □ **à la parole (...)**

generally speaking in general: *Generally speaking, a good education is the key to success.* □ **en général**

speak for itself/themselves to have an obvious meaning; not to need explaining: *The facts speak for themselves.* □ **se passer de commentaires**

speak out to say boldly what one thinks: *I feel the time has come to speak out.* □ **parler franchement**

speak up to speak (more) loudly: *Speak up! We can't hear you!* □ **parler (plus) fort**

to speak of worth mentioning: *He has no talent to speak of.* □ **pour ainsi dire**

spear [spiə] *noun* a type of long-handled weapon, *usually* with an iron or steel point on the end: *He was armed with a spear and a round shield.* □ **lance**

■ *verb* to pierce or kill with a spear: *She went out in a boat and speared some fish.* □ **harponner**

'**spearhead** *noun* the leading part of an attacking force. □ **fer de lance**

■ *verb* to lead (a movement, an attack *etc*). □ **être le fer de lance de**

special ['speʃəl] *adjective* 1 out of the ordinary; unusual or exceptional: *a special occasion; a special friend.* □ **spécial, exceptionnel**

2 appointed, arranged, designed *etc* for a particular purpose: *a special messenger; a special tool for drilling holes.* □ **spécial**

■ *noun* something which is special: *There's a special* (= a special train) *due through here at 5:20.* □ **spécial**

'**specialist** *noun* a person who makes a very deep study of one branch of a subject or field: *Dr. Brown is a heart specialist.* □ **spécialiste**

'**specialty** ['speʃəlti] – *plurals* '**specialties** – *noun* 1 a special product for which one is well-known: *Brown bread is this baker's specialty.* □ **spécialité**

2 a special activity, or subject about which one has special knowledge: *Her specialty is physics.* □ **spécialité**

'**specialize**, '**specialise** *verb* (*usually with* **in**) go give one's attention (to), work (in), or study (a particular job, subject *etc*): *He specializes in fixing computers.* □ **se spécialiser, être spécialisé (dans, en)**

,**speciali'zation**, ,**speciali'sation** *noun.* □ **spécialisation**

'**specialized**, '**specialised** *adjective* (of knowledge, skills *etc*) of the accurate detailed kind obtained by specializing. □ **spécialisé**

'**specially** *adverb* 1 with one particular purpose: *I picked these flowers specially for you; a splendid cake, specially made for the occasion.* □ **spécialement**

2 particularly; exceptionally: *He's a nice child, but not specially clever.* □ **particulièrement**

species ['spiːʃiːz] – *plural* **species** – *noun* 1 a group (of animals *etc*) whose members are so similar or closely related as to be able to breed together: *There are several species of zebra.* □ **espèce**

2 a kind or sort. □ **espèce**

specify ['spesifai] *verb* 1 to name as wanted or demanded. □ **préciser**

2 to make particular or definite mention of: *She specified three types of mistake which had occurred.* □ **mentionner**

specific [spə'sifik] *adjective* 1 giving all the details clearly: *specific instructions.* □ **précis**

2 particular; exactly stated or described: *Each of the bodily organs has its own specific function.* □ **spécifique**

spe'cifically *adverb*: *I specifically told you not to do* *that*; *This dictionary is intended specifically for learners of English.* □ **expressément**

specimen ['spesimin] *noun* something used as a sample (of a group or kind of something, *especially* an object to be studied or to be put in a collection): *We looked at specimens of different types of rock under the microscope.* □ **spécimen**

speck [spek] *noun* **1** a small spot or stain: *a speck of ink.* □ **petite tache**
2 a tiny piece (*eg* of dust). □ **grain**

speckle ['spekl] *noun* a little spot on a different-coloured background: *The eggs were pale blue with dark green speckles.* □ **tacheture, moucheture**
'**speckled** *adjective* marked with speckles. □ **tacheté, moucheté**

specs [speks] short for **spectacles**. □ **lunettes**

spectacle ['spektəkl] *noun* a sight, *especially* one that is very impressive or wonderful: *The royal wedding was a great spectacle.* □ **spectacle**
spec'tacular [-'takju-] *adjective* (*negative* **unspectacular**) **1** making a great show or display: *a spectacular performance.* □ **spectaculaire**
2 impressive; dramatic: *a spectacular recovery.* □ **spectaculaire**
spec'tacularly *adverb.* □ **spectaculairement**

spectacles ['spektəklz] *noun plural* glasses which a person wears to help his eyesight: *a pair of spectacles.* □ **lunettes**

spectator ['spekteitər] *noun* a person who watches (an event): *Fifty thousand spectators came to the match.* □ **spectateur, trice**
spec'tate *verb* to be a spectator (at an event). □ **participer en simple spectateur, trice**

spectre, (*American usually*) **specter** ['spektə] *noun* a ghost. □ **spectre**

spectrum ['spektrəm] – *plurals* '**spectrums**, '**spectra** [-trə] – *noun* **1** the visible spectrum. □ **spectre**
2 the full range (of something): *The actress's voice was capable of expressing the whole spectrum of emotion.* □ **spectre**
3 the entire range of radiation of different wavelengths, part of which (the **visible spectrum**) is normally visible to the naked eye. □ **spectre**
4 a similar range of frequencies of sound (the **sound spectrum**). □ **spectre**

speculate ['spekjuleit] *verb* to make guesses: *He's only speculating – he doesn't know*; *There's no point in speculating about what's going to happen.* □ **spéculer (sur)**
,**specu'lation** *noun* **1** a guess: *Your speculations were all quite close to the truth.* □ **spéculation**
2 the act of speculating: *There was great speculation as to what was happening.* □ **conjectures**

sped *see* **speed**.

speech [spiːtʃ] *noun* **1** (the act of) saying words, or the ability to say words: *Speech is one method of communication between people.* □ **parole**
2 the words said: *His speech is full of colloquialisms.* □ **langage**
3 manner or way of speaking: *Her speech is very slow.* □ **façon de parler**

4 a formal talk given to a meeting *etc*: *parliamentary speeches.* □ **discours**
'**speechless** *adjective* unable to speak, often because of surprise, shock *etc*: *He looked at her in speechless amazement.* □ **muet**
'**speechlessly** *adverb.* □ **sans un mot**
'**speechlessness** *noun.* □ **mutisme**

speed [spiːd] *noun* **1** rate of moving: *a slow speed*; *The car was travelling at high speed.* □ **vitesse**
2 quickness of moving. □ **vitesse**
■ *verb* **1** (*past tense, past participles* **sped** [sped] '**speeded**) to (cause to) move or progress quickly; to hurry: *The car sped/speeded along the highway.* □ **aller à toute vitesse**
2 (*past tense, past participle* '**speeded**) to drive very fast in a car *etc*, faster than is allowed by law: *The policewoman said that I had been speeding.* □ **faire un excès de vitesse**
'**speeding** *noun* driving at (an illegally) high speed: *He was fined for speeding.* □ **excès de vitesse**
'**speedy** *adjective* done, carried out *etc* quickly: *a speedy answer.* □ **prompt**
'**speedily** *adverb.* □ **promptement**
'**speediness** *noun.* □ **promptitude**
speedometer [spiː'domitə] *noun* an instrument on a car *etc* showing how fast one is travelling. □ **indicateur de vitesse**
speed up – *past tense, past participle* '**speeded** – **1** to increase speed: *The car speeded up as it left the town.* □ **accélérer**
2 to quicken the rate of: *We are trying to speed up production.* □ **accélérer**

spell[1] [spel] – *past tense, past participle* **spelt** [-t], **spelled** – *verb* **1** to name or give in order the letters of (a word): *I asked him to spell his name for me.* □ **épeler**
2 (of letters) to form (a word): *C-a-t spells 'cat'.* □ **donner**
3 to (be able to) spell words correctly: *I can't spell!* □ **savoir l'orthographe**
4 to mean or amount to: *This spells disaster.* □ **signifier, mener à**
'**spelling** *noun*: *Her spelling is terrible*; (*also adjective*) *The teacher gave the children a spelling lesson/test.* □ **orthographe**

spell[2] [spel] *noun* **1** a set or words which, when spoken, is supposed to have magical power: *The witch recited a spell and turned herself into a swan.* □ **formule magique**
2 a strong influence: *He was completely under her spell.* □ **charme**

spell[3] [spel] *noun* **1** a turn (at work): *Shortly afterwards I did another spell at the machine.* □ **tour (de travail)**
2 a period of time during which something lasts: *a spell of bad health.* □ **période**
3 a short time: *We stayed in the country for a spell and then came home.* □ **certain temps**

spelt *see* **spell**[1].

spend [spend] – *past tense, past participle* **spent** [-t] – *verb* **1** to use up or pay out (money): *He spends more than he earns.* □ **dépenser**

2 to pass (time): *I spent a week in Spain this summer.* □ **passer**

spent [spent] *adjective* 1 used: *a spent match.* □ **utilisé** 2 exhausted: *By the time we had done half of the job we were all spent.* □ **épuisé**

'**spendthrift** *noun* a person who spends his money freely and carelessly. □ **dépensier, ière**

sperm [spɔːm] *plural* **sperms, sperm** – *noun* 1 the fluid in a male animal *etc* that fertilizes the female egg. □ **sperme** 2 one of the fertilizing cells in this fluid. □ **sperme**

sperm whale [spɔːm weil] *noun* a type of whale or large water mammal with a distinctive square snout: *Drew saw the spray then the flippers and large square nose and jaw of a sperm whale as it rose out of the sea.* □ **cachalot**

sphere [sfiə] *noun* a solid object with a surface on which all points are an equal distance from the centre, like *eg* most types of ball. □ **sphère**

spherical ['sferikəl] *adjective* completely round, like a ball: *It is now known that the world is not flat, but spherical; a spherical object.* □ **sphérique**

spice [spais] *noun* 1 a *usually* strong-smelling, sharp-tasting vegetable substance used to flavour food (*eg* pepper or nutmeg): *We added cinnamon and other spices.* □ **épice** 2 anything that adds liveliness or interest: *Her arrival added spice to the party.* □ **piquant**

■ *verb* to flavour with spice: *The curry had been heavily spiced.* □ **épicer**

spiced *adjective* containing spice(s): *The dish was heavily spiced.* □ **épicé**

'**spicy** *adjective* tasting or smelling of spices: *a spicy cake; He complained that the sausages were too spicy for him.* □ **épicé**

'**spiciness** *noun.* □ **goût épicé**

spider ['spaidə] *noun* a kind of small creature with eight legs and no wings, which spins a web. □ **araignée**

spike [spaik] *noun* 1 a hard, thin, pointed object (of wood, metal *etc*): *The fence had long spikes on top.* □ **pointe** 2 a pointed piece of metal attached to the sole of a shoe *etc* to prevent slipping. □ **crampon**

spiked *adjective.* □ **à pointe(s)**

'**spiky** *adjective* having spikes, or points similar to spikes: *the spiky coat of a hedgehog.* □ **garni de pointes**

'**spikiness** *noun.* □ **aspect hérissé**

spill [spil] – *past tense, past participle* **spilt** [-t], **spilled** – *verb* to (cause something to) fall or run out (*usually* accidentally): *He spilt milk on the floor; Vegetables spilled out of the burst bag.* □ **(se) renverser/répandre**

spill the beans to give away a secret: *By Monday it was evident that someone had spilled the beans to the newspapers.* □ **vendre la mèche**

spin [spin] – *present participle* '**spinning**: *past tense, past participle* **spun** [spʌn] – *verb* 1 to (cause to) go around and around rapidly: *She spun around in surprise; He spun the revolving door around and around.* □ **tournoyer; (faire) tourner** 2 to form threads from (wool, cotton *etc*) by drawing out and twisting: *The old woman was spinning (wool)*

in the corner of the room. □ **filer**

■ *noun* 1 a whirling or turning motion: *The patch of mud sent the car into a spin.* □ **tournoiement** 2 a ride, *especially* on wheels: *After lunch we went for a spin in my new car.* □ **tour**

'**spinner** *noun* a person or thing that spins. □ **fileur, euse; essoreuse**

spin out to cause to last a long or longer time: *She spun out her speech for an extra five minutes.* □ **faire durer**

spinach ['spinidʒ, -nitʃ] *noun* 1 the kind of plant whose young leaves are eaten as a vegetable: *He grows spinach in his garden.* □ **épinard** 2 the leaves as food: *We had steak and spinach for dinner.* □ **épinards**

spinal *see* spine.

spindle ['spindl] *noun* a thin pin on which something turns: *I can't turn on the radio any more, because the spindle of the control knob has broken.* □ **axe**

'**spindly** *adjective* very long and thin. □ **grêle**

spine [spain] *noun* 1 the line of linked bones running down the back of humans and many animals; the backbone: *She damaged her spine when she fell.* □ **colonne vertébrale** 2 something like a backbone in shape or function: *the spine of a book.* □ **dos** 3 a thin, stiff, pointed part growing on an animal or a plant. □ **épine**

'**spinal** *adjective* of or concerned with the backbone: *a spinal injury.* □ **vertébral**

'**spineless** *adjective* 1 of an animal, having no spine; invertebrate. □ **invertébré** 2 of a person, having a weak character; easily dominated. □ **mou**

'**spiny** *adjective* full of, or covered with, spines: *a spiny cactus.* □ **épineux**

spinal cord a cord of nerve cells running up through the backbone. □ **moelle épinière**

spinner *see* spin.

spinster ['spinstə] *noun* a woman who is not married. □ **célibataire**

spiny *see* spine.

spiral ['spaiərəl] *adjective* 1 coiled around like a spring, with each coil the same size as the one below: *a spiral staircase.* □ **en spirale** 2 winding around and around, *usually* tapering to a point: *a spiral shell.* □ **en spirale**

■ *noun* 1 an increase or decrease, or rise or fall, becoming more and more rapid (*eg* in prices). □ **spirale** 2 a spiral line or object: *A spiral of smoke rose from the chimney.* □ **spirale**

■ *verb* – *past tense, past participle* '**spiralled**, '**spiraled** – to go or move in a spiral, *especially* to increase more and more rapidly: *Prices have spiralled in the last six months.* □ **monter en flèche**

'**spirally** *adverb.* □ **en spirale**

spire ['spaiə] *noun* a tall, pointed tower, *especially* one built on the roof of a church. □ **flèche**

spirit ['spirit] *noun* 1 a principle or emotion which makes someone act: *The spirit of kindness seems to be lacking in the world nowadays.* □ **esprit**

2 a person's mind, will, personality *etc* thought of as distinct from the body, or as remaining alive *eg* as a ghost when the body dies: *Our great leader may be dead, but his spirit still lives on*; *(also adjective) the spirit world*; *Evil spirits have taken possession of him.* □ **esprit; (adj.) des esprits**

3 liveliness; courage: *She acted with spirit.* □ **courage** 'spirited *adjective* full of courage or liveliness: *a spirited attack/description.* □ **fougueux; plein de verve** 'spiritedly *adverb.* □ **avec verve**

'spirits *noun plural* 1 a person's mood: *She's in good/high/low spirits* (= He's happy/very cheerful/depressed); *This news may raise his spirits.* □ **humeur; moral** 2 strong alcoholic drink, *eg* whisky, gin, vodka *etc*. □ **spiritueux**

'spiritual [-tʃul] *adjective* of one's spirit or soul, or of one's religious beliefs. □ **spirituel** 'spiritually *adverb.* □ **spirituellement**

spirit level a tool consisting of a bar containing a glass tube of liquid, for testing whether a surface is level. □ **niveau à bulle**

spit¹ [spit] *noun* (*also* **spittle** ['spitl]) the liquid that forms in the mouth. □ **salive**
■ *verb – present participle* 'spitting: *past tense, past participle* spat [spat] – 1 to throw out (spit) from the mouth: *He spat in the gutter as an indication of contempt.* □ **cracher** 2 to send (out) with force: *The fire spat (out) sparks.* □ **cracher**

spit² [spit] *noun* a type of sharp-pointed metal bar on which meat is roasted. □ **broche**

spite [spait] *noun* ill-will or desire to hurt or offend: *She neglected to give him the message out of spite.* □ **rancune**
■ *verb* to annoy, offend or frustrate, because of spite: *He only did that to spite me!* □ **contrarier** 'spiteful *adjective*: *a spiteful remark/person*; *You're being very spiteful.* □ **rancunier** 'spitefully *adverb.* □ **par rancune** 'spitefulness *noun.* □ **rancune**

in spite of 1 taking no notice of: *She went in spite of her father's orders.* □ **malgré** 2 although something has or had happened, is or was a fact *etc*: *In spite of all the rain that had fallen, the ground was still pretty dry.* □ **malgré**

spittle *see* **spit¹.**

splash [splaʃ] *verb* 1 to make wet with drops of liquid, mud *etc*, especially suddenly and accidentally: *A passing car splashed my coat (with water).* □ **éclabousser** 2 to (cause to) fly about in drops: *Water splashed everywhere.* □ **faire des éclaboussures** 3 to fall or move with splashes: *The children were splashing in the sea.* □ **patauger** 4 to display *etc* in a place, manner *etc* that will be noticed: *Posters advertising the concert were splashed all over the wall.* □ **étaler**
■ *noun* 1 a scattering of drops of liquid or the noise made by this: *She fell in with a loud splash.* □ **éclaboussement** 2 a mark made by splashing: *There was a splash of mud

on her dress.* □ **éclaboussure** 3 a bright patch: *a splash of colour.* □ **tache**

spleen [spliːn] *noun* an organ of the body, close to the stomach, which causes changes in the blood. □ **rate**

splendid ['splendid] *adjective* 1 brilliant, magnificent, very rich and grand *etc*: *He looked splendid in his robes.* □ **splendide** 2 very good or fine: *a splendid piece of work.* □ **magnifique** 'splendidly *adverb.* □ **splendidement** 'splendour [-də] *noun.* □ **splendeur** 'splendidness *noun.* □ **splendeur**

splint [splint] *noun* a piece of wood *etc* used to keep a broken arm or leg in a fixed position while it heals. □ **attelle** 'splinter *noun* a small sharp broken piece of wood *etc*: *The rough plank gave her a splinter in her finger.* □ **écharde**
■ *verb* to split into splinters: *The door splintered under the heavy blow.* □ **se fendre en éclats**

split [split] – *present participle* 'splitting: *past tense, past participle* split – *verb* 1 to cut or (cause to) break lengthwise: *to split firewood; The skirt split all the way down the back seam.* □ **(se) fendre** 2 to divide or (cause to) disagree: *The dispute split the workers into two opposing groups.* □ **diviser**
■ *noun* a crack or break: *There was a split in one of the sides of the box.* □ **fente** ,split-'level *adjective* built, made *etc* on two levels: *a split-level dining room/cooker.* □ **à palier** **split second** a fraction of a second. □ **fraction de seconde** **splitting headache** a very bad headache: *Turn down the radio – I've a splitting headache.* □ **mal de tête atroce** **the splits** the gymnastic exercise of sitting down on the floor with one leg straight forward and the other straight back: *to do the splits.* □ **grand écart**

spoil [spoil] – *past tense, past participles* spoiled, spoilt [-t] – *verb* 1 to damage or ruin; to make bad or useless: *If you touch that drawing you'll spoil it.* □ **gâcher** 2 to give (a child *etc*) too much of what he wants and possibly make his character, behaviour *etc* worse by doing so: *They spoil that child dreadfully and she's becoming unbearable!* □ **gâter** **spoils** *noun plural* profits or rewards: *the spoils of war; the spoils of success.* □ **bénéfices, butin** **spoiled** *adjective*: *He's a very spoiled child!* □ **gâté** 'spoilsport *noun* a person who spoils, or refuses to join in, the fun of others. □ **rabat-joie**

spoke¹ [spouk] *noun* one of the ribs or bars from the centre to the rim of the wheel of a bicycle, cart *etc*. □ **rayon**

spoke², spoken *see* **speak.**

spokesman ['spouksmən] – *feminine* 'spokeswoman – *noun* a person who speaks on behalf of a group of others: *Who is the spokesman for your party?* □ **porte-parole**

sponge [spʌndʒ] *noun* 1 a type of sea animal, or its soft skeleton, which has many holes and is able to suck up and hold water. □ **éponge**

2 a piece of such a skeleton or a substitute, used for washing the body *etc*. □ **éponge**

3 a sponge pudding or cake: *We had jam sponge for dessert.* □ **gâteau de Savoie**

4 an act of wiping *etc* with a sponge: *Give the table a quick sponge over, will you?* □ **coup d'éponge**

■ *verb* **1** to wipe or clean with a sponge: *She sponged the child's face.* □ **éponger**

2 to get a living, money *etc* (from someone else): *He's been sponging off/on us for years.* □ **vivre aux crochets de**

'**sponger** *noun* a person who lives by sponging on others. □ **parasite**

'**spongy** *adjective* soft and springy or holding water like a sponge: *spongy ground.* □ **spongieux**

'**spongily** *adverb*. □ **de manière spongieuse**

'**sponginess** *noun*. □ **spongiosité**

sponge cake (a) very light cake or pudding made from flour, eggs and sugar *etc*. □ **gâteau de Savoie**

sponsor ['sponsə] *verb* **1** to take on the financial responsibility for (a person, project *etc*), often as a form of advertising or for charity: *The firm sponsors several golf tournaments.* □ **commanditer**

2 to promise (a person) that one will pay a certain sum of money to a charity *etc* if that person completes a set task (*eg* a walk, swim *etc*). □ **commanditer**

■ *noun* a person, firm *etc* that acts in this way. □ **commanditaire**

'**sponsorship** *noun* (the money given as) the act of sponsoring. □ **commandite**

spontaneous [spɒn'teiniəs] *adjective* **1** said, done *etc* of one's own free will without pressure from others: *His offer was quite spontaneous.* □ **spontané**

2 natural; not forced: *spontaneous behaviour.* □ **spontané**

spon'taneously *adverb*. □ **spontanément**

spon'taneousness *noun*. □ **spontanéité**

spontaneity [spɒntə'neiəti, spɒntə'ni:əti] *noun*. □ **spontanéité**

spoof [spu:f] *noun* a ridiculous imitation, intended to be humorous. □ **attrape**

spook [spu:k] *noun* a ghost. □ **revenant, ante**

'**spooky** *adjective* eerie and suggesting the presence of ghosts: *It's very spooky walking through the graveyard at night.* □ **qui donne la chair de poule**

'**spookiness** *noun*. □ **caractère effrayant**

spool [spu:l] *noun* **1** a type of cylindrical holder: *How can I wind this film back on to its spool?* □ **bobine**

2 the amount of thread, film *etc* held by such a holder: *She used three spools of thread in one week.* □ **bobine**

spoon [spu:n] *noun* **1** an instrument shaped like a shallow bowl with a handle for lifting food (*especially* soup or pudding) to the mouth, or for stirring tea, coffee *etc*: *a teaspoon/soup-spoon.* □ **cuiller**

2 a spoonful. □ **cuillerée**

■ *verb* to lift or scoop up with a spoon: *She spooned food into the baby's mouth.* □ **nourrir à la cuiller**

'**spoonful** *noun* the amount held by a spoon: *three spoonfuls of sugar.* □ **cuillerée**

'**spoon-feed** – *past tense, past participle* '**spoon-fed** –

verb **1** to feed with a spoon. □ **nourrir à la cuiller**

2 to teach or treat (a person) in a way that does not allow him to think or act for himself. □ **mâcher le travail à**

spore [spɔ:] *noun* a tiny seedlike cell from which ferns and other types of non-flowering plant grow. □ **spore**

sport [spɔ:t] *noun* **1** games or competitions involving physical activity: *She's very keen on sport of all kinds.* □ **sport**

2 a particular game or amusement of this kind: *Hunting, shooting and fishing are not sports I enjoy.* □ **sport**

3 a good-natured and obliging person: *He's a good sport to agree to do that for us!* □ **brave garçon/fille**

4 fun; amusement: *I only did it for sport.* □ **pour rire/le plaisir**

■ *verb* to wear, *especially* in public: *He was sporting a pink tie.* □ **exhiber**

'**sporting** *adjective* **1** of, or concerned with, sports: *the sporting world.* □ **sportif**

2 (*negative* **unsporting**) showing fairness and kindness or generosity, *especially* if unexpected: *a sporting gesture.* □ **élégant**

sports *adjective* (*also* **sport**) designed, or suitable, for sport: *a sports centre; sports equipment.* □ **de sport, sportif**

sports car a small, fast car with only two seats. □ **voiture de sport**

sports jacket a type of jacket for men, designed for casual wear. □ **veste (de) sport**

'**sportsman** ['spɔ:ts-] – *feminine* '**sportswoman** – *noun* **1** a person who takes part in sports: *He is a very keen sportsman.* □ **sportif, ive**

2 a person who shows a spirit of fairness and generosity in sport: *He's a real sportsman who doesn't seem to care if he wins or loses.* □ **beau joueur**

'**sportswear** *noun* clothing designed for playing sports in. □ **vêtements de sport**

a sporting chance a reasonably good chance. □ **assez bonne chance (de)**

spot [spɒt] *noun* **1** a small mark or stain (made by mud, paint *etc*): *She was trying to remove a spot of grease from her skirt.* □ **tache**

2 a small, round mark of a different colour from its background: *His tie was blue with white spots.* □ **pois**

3 a pimple or red mark on the skin caused by an illness *etc*: *She had measles and was covered in spots.* □ **bouton**

4 a place or small area, *especially* the exact place (where something happened *etc*): *There was a large number of detectives gathered at the spot where the body had been found.* □ **endroit**

5 a small amount: *Can I borrow a spot of sugar?* □ **un peu de**

■ *verb* – *past tense, past participle* '**spotted** – **1** to catch sight of: *She spotted him eventually at the very back of the crowd.* □ **repérer**

2 to recognize or pick out: *No one watching the play was able to spot the murderer.* □ **découvrir**

'**spotless** *adjective* very clean: *a spotless kitchen.* □ **immaculé**

'spotlessly adverb. □ **d'une propreté impeccable**
'spotlessness noun. □ **propreté impeccable**
'spotted adjective marked or covered with spots: *Her dress was spotted with grease*; *a spotted tie*. □ **taché; à pois**
'spotty adjective (of people) covered with spots: *a spotty face/young man*. □ **boutonneux**
'spottiness noun. □ **caractère tacheté/inégal**
spot check an inspection made without warning, *especially* on items chosen at random from a group: *We only found out about the flaw during a spot check on goods leaving the factory*. □ **contrôle-surprise**
'spotlight noun (a lamp for projecting) a circle of light that is thrown on to a small area. □ **projecteur**
■ verb – past tense, past participle **'spotlit, 'spotlighted** – 1 to light with a spotlight: *The stage was spotlit*. □ **éclairé par un/des projecteur(s)**
2 to show up clearly or draw attention to: *The incident spotlighted the difficulties with which we were faced*. □ **mettre en vedette**
in a spot in trouble: *His failure to return the papers on time put her in a spot*. □ **dans le pétrin**
on the spot 1 at once: *She liked it so much that she bought it on the spot*; (*also adjective*) *an on-the-spot decision*. □ **sur-le-champ; immédiat**
2 in the exact place referred to; in the place where one is needed: *It was a good thing you were on the spot when he had his heart attack*; (*also adjective*) *tour on-the-spot reporter*. □ **sur place**
3 (*especially* with **put**) in a dangerous, difficult or embarrassing position: *The interviewer's questions really put the Prime Minister on the spot*. □ **dans une situation embarrassante**
spouse [spaus] noun a husband or wife. □ **époux, ouse**
spout [spaut] verb 1 to throw out or be thrown out in a jet: *Water spouted from the hole in the tank*. □ **jaillir (de)**
2 to talk or say (something) loudly and dramatically: *He started to spout poetry, of all things!* □ **déclamer**
■ noun 1 the part of a kettle, teapot, jug, water pipe *etc* through which the liquid it contains is poured out. □ **bec**
2 a jet or strong flow (of water *etc*). □ **jet**
sprain [sprein] verb to twist (a joint, *especially* the ankle or wrist) in such a way as to tear or stretch the ligaments: *She sprained her ankle yesterday*. □ **(se) fouler, se donner une entorse**
■ noun a twisting of a joint in this way. □ **foulure, entorse**
sprang see **spring**.
sprawl [sprɔːl] verb 1 to sit, lie or fall with the arms and legs spread out widely and carelessly: *Several tired-looking people were sprawling in armchairs*. □ **s'étaler**
2 (of a town *etc*) to spread out in an untidy and irregular way. □ **s'étaler**
■ noun 1 an act of sprawling: *He was lying in a careless sprawl on the sofa*. □ **attitude affalée**
2 an untidy and irregular area (of houses *etc*): *She lost her way in the grimy sprawl of the big city*. □ **étendue tentaculaire**

'sprawling adjective: *the huge, sprawling city of Los Angeles*. □ **tentaculaire**
spray [sprei] noun 1 a fine mist of small flying drops (of water *etc*) such as that given out by a waterfall: *The perfume came out of the bottle in a fine spray*. □ **(nuage de) gouttelettes; pulvérisation**
2 a device with many small holes, or other instrument, for producing a fine mist of liquid: *She used a spray to rinse her hair*. □ **vaporisateur**
3 a liquid for spraying: *He bought a can of fly-spray*. □ **bombe (d'insecticide)**
■ verb 1 to (cause liquid to) come out in a mist or in fine jets: *The water sprayed all over everyone*. □ **arroser (de fines gouttelettes), asperger**
2 to cover with a mist or with fine jets of liquid: *He sprayed the roses to kill pests*. □ **faire des pulvérisations (sur)**
spread [spred] – past tense, past participle **spread** – verb
1 to (cause to) go (often more widely or more thinly) over a surface: *She spread honey thickly on her toast*. □ **étaler**
2 to cover (a surface with something): *She spread the bread with jam*. □ **étaler**
3 to (cause to) reach a wider area, affect a larger number of people *etc*: *The news spread through the village very quickly*. □ **se répandre**
4 to distribute over a wide area, period of time *etc*: *The exams were spread over a period of ten days*. □ **étaler sur**
5 to open out: *He spread the map on the table*. □ **étaler sur**
■ noun 1 the process of reaching a wider area, affecting more people *etc*: *the spread of information/television*; *the spread of crime among schoolchildren*. □ **diffusion, propagation**
2 something to be spread on bread *etc*: *Have some chicken spread*. □ **pâte (à tartiner)**
3 the space or time covered (by something) or the extent of spreading: *a spread of several kilometres*. □ **étendue**
spread out 1 to extend or stretch out: *The fields spread out in front of him*. □ **s'étendre (sur)**
2 to distribute over a wide area or period of time: *She spread the leaflets out on the table*. □ **étaler (sur)**
3 to scatter and go in different directions, in order to cover a wider area: *They spread out and began to search the entire area*. □ **s'éparpiller**
sprig [sprig] noun a small piece of a plant; a twig. □ **brin**
spring [spriŋ] – past tense **sprang** [spraŋ]: past participle **sprung** [sprʌŋ] – verb 1 to jump, leap or move swiftly (*usually* upwards): *She sprang into the boat*. □ **sauter, bondir**
2 to arise or result from: *Her bravery springs from her love of adventure*. □ **découler de**
3 to (cause a trap to) close violently: *The trap must have sprung when the hare stepped in it*. □ **(se) refermer brusquement**
■ noun 1 a coil of wire or other similar device which can be compressed or squeezed down but returns to its

original shape when released: *a watch-spring*; *the springs in a chair.* □ **ressort**

2 the season of the year when plants begin to grow, February or March to April or May in cooler northern regions: *Spring is my favourite season.* □ **printemps**

3 a leap or sudden movement: *The lion made a sudden spring on its prey.* □ **bond**

4 the ability to stretch and spring back again: *There's not a lot of spring in this old trampoline.* □ **élasticité**

5 a small stream flowing out from the ground. □ **source**

'**springy** *adjective* 1 able to spring back into its former shape: *The grass is very springy.* □ **élastique, souple**

2 having spring: *These floorboards are springy.* □ **flexible**

'**springiness** *noun.* □ **élasticité**

sprung [sprʌŋ] *adjective* having springs: *a sprung mattress.* □ **à ressorts**

'**springboard** *noun* 1 a springy type of diving board. □ **tremplin**

2 a board on which gymnasts jump before vaulting. □ **tremplin**

spring cleaning thorough cleaning of a house *etc* especially in spring. □ **grand nettoyage de printemps**

'**springtime** *noun* the season of spring. □ **printemps**

spring up to develop or appear suddenly: *New buildings are springing up everywhere.* □ **surgir brusquement**

sprinkle ['spriŋkl] *verb* to scatter something over something else in small drops or bits: *He sprinkled salt over his food*; *He sprinkled the roses with water.* □ **saupoudrer, asperger**

'**sprinkler** *noun* an apparatus for sprinkling *eg* water over a lawn. □ **arroseur**

'**sprinkling** *noun* a small amount or a few: *There were mostly women at the meeting but there was a sprinkling of men.* □ **quelques**

sprint [sprint] *noun* 1 a run or running race performed at high speed over a short distance: *Who won the 100 metres sprint?* □ **sprint**

2 the pace of this: *He ran up the road at a sprint.* □ **à toutes jambes**

■ *verb* to run at full speed *especially* (in) a race: *He sprinted (for) the last few hundred metres.* □ **sprinter**

'**sprinter** *noun* a person who is good at sprinting. □ **sprinteur, euse**

sprite [sprait] *noun* an elf or fairy: *a water-sprite.* □ **lutin**

sprout [spraut] *verb* 1 to (cause to) develop leaves, shoots *etc*: *The trees are sprouting new leaves.* □ **pousser**

2 (of animals, birds *etc*) to develop *eg* horns, produce *eg* feathers: *The young birds are sprouting their first feathers.* □ **pousser**

■ *noun* a new shoot or bud: *bean sprouts.* □ **pousse**

sprout up (of plants or children) to grow: *That fruit bush has sprouted up fast*; *At the age of fourteen he really began to sprout up.* □ **pousser**

spruce [spruːs] *adjective* neat and smart: *You're looking very spruce today.* □ **pimpant**

■ *noun* a short-needled evergreen often used as a Christmas tree: *Charlie strung Christmas lights around the spruce tree in the backyard.* □ **épinette**

spruce up to make oneself or somebody else smarter: *I'll go and spruce up before going out.* □ **se faire (tout) beau**

sprung *see* **spring**.

spry [sprai] *adjective* lively or active: *a spry old gentleman.* □ **vif**

'**spryly** *adverb.* □ **vivement**

'**spryness** *noun.* □ **vivacité**

spun *see* **spin**.

spur [spəː] *noun* 1 a small instrument with a sharp point or points that a rider wears on his heels and digs into the horse's sides to make it go faster. □ **éperon**

2 anything that urges a person to make greater efforts: *She was driven on by the spur of ambition.* □ **aiguillon**

on the spur of the moment suddenly; without previous planning: *We decided to go to Paris on the spur of the moment.* □ **sous l'impulsion du moment**

spur on to urge a horse to go faster, using spurs, or a person to make greater efforts: *She spurred her horse on*; *The thought of the prize spurred her on.* □ **éperonner**

spurt [spəːt] *verb* (of a liquid) to spout or gush: *Blood spurted from the wound.* □ **jaillir**

■ *noun* a sudden gush or burst: *a spurt of blood/energy.* □ **jaillissement**

put a spurt on/put on a spurt to run or go faster *eg* towards the end of a race: *She put a sudden spurt on and passed the other competitors.* □ **piquer un sprint**

spy [spai] *noun* a secret agent or person employed to gather information secretly *especially* about the military affairs of other countries: *She was arrested as a spy*; *industrial spies.* □ **espion, onne**

■ *verb* 1 to be a spy: *He had been spying for the Russians for many years.* □ **espionner**

2 to see or notice: *She spied a human figure on the mountainside.* □ **apercevoir**

'**spyhole** *noun* a peep-hole. □ **petit trou**

spy on to watch (a person *etc*) secretly: *The police had been spying on the gang for several months.* □ **épier**

squabble ['skwobl] *verb* to quarrel noisily, *usually* about something unimportant: *The children are always squabbling over the toys.* □ **se quereller (à propos de)**

■ *noun* a noisy quarrel. □ **querelle**

squad [skwod] *noun* 1 a small group of soldiers drilled or working together: *The men were divided into squads to perform different duties.* □ **escouade**

2 a group of people, *especially* a working-party: *a squad of workmen.* □ **groupe**

squadron ['skwodrən] *noun* a division of a regiment, a section of a fleet, or a group of airplanes. □ **escadron; escadrille**

squalid ['skwolid] *adjective* very dirty or filthy: *The houses are squalid and overcrowded.* □ **sordide**

'**squalor** [-lə] *noun*: *They lived in squalor.* □ **misère noire**

squall [skwoːl] *noun* a sudden violent wind, *eg* bringing rain: *The ship was struck by a squall.* □ **bourrasque**

squalor *see* **squalid**.

squander ['skwondə] *verb* to waste: *He squandered all his money on gambling.* □ **dilapider**

square [skweə] *noun* 1 a four-sided two-dimensional figure with all sides equal in length and all angles right angles. □ **carré**

2 something in the shape of this. □ **carré**

3 an open place in a town, with the buildings around it. □ **place**

4 the resulting number when a number is multiplied by itself: 3×3, or $3^2 = 9$, so 9 is the square of 3. □ **carré**

■ *adjective* **1** having the shape of a square or right angle: *I need a square piece of paper*; *He has a short, square body/a square chin.* □ **carré**

2 (of business dealings, scores in games *etc*) level, even, fairly balanced *etc*: *If I pay you an extra \$5 shall we be (all) square?*; *Their scores are (all) square (= equal).* □ **quitte, à égalité**

3 measuring a particular amount on all four sides: *This piece of wood is two metres square.* □ **carré**

4 old-fashioned: *square ideas about clothes.* □ **vieux jeu**

■ *adverb* **1** at right angles, or in a square shape: *The carpet is not cut square with the corner.* □ **à angle droit (avec)**

2 firmly and directly: *She hit him square on the point of the chin.* □ **en plein**

■ *verb* **1** to give a square shape to or make square. □ **rendre carré**

2 to settle, pay *etc* (an account, debt *etc*): *I must square my account with you.* □ **régler (ses comptes avec)**

3 to (cause to) fit or agree: *His story doesn't square with the facts.* □ **cadrer avec**

4 to multiply a number by itself: *Two squared is four.* □ **élever au carré**

squared *adjective* **1** marked or ruled with squares: *squared paper.* □ **quadrillé**

2 having been squared. □ **élevé au carré**

'**squarely** *adverb* directly and firmly: *He stood squarely in front of me*; *She looked squarely at me.* □ **carrément**

square centimetre, metre *etc* (*often abbreviated to* **cm²**, **m²** *etc when written*) an area equal to a square in which each side is one centimetre, metre *etc*: *If the door is 3 metres high and 1.5 metres wide, its area is 4.5 square metres.* □ **(centimètre, mètre, etc.) carré**

square root the number which, multiplied by itself, gives the number that is being considered: *The square root of 16 is 4* ($\sqrt{16} = 4$). □ **racine carrée**

fair and square directly: *He hit him fair and square on the nose.* □ **en plein**

go back to square one to start all over again. □ **repartir à zéro**

a square deal a fair bargain; fair treatment. □ **arrangement équitable**

squash [skwɔʃ] *verb* **1** to press, squeeze or crush: *She tried to squash too many clothes into her case*; *The tomatoes got squashed (flat) at the bottom of the shopping bag.* □ **entasser; écraser**

2 to defeat (a rebellion *etc*). □ **écraser**

■ *noun* **1** a state of being squashed or crowded: *There was a great squash in the doorway.* □ **cohue**

2 (a particular flavour of) a drink containing the juice of crushed fruit: *Have some orange squash!* □ **boisson au jus de fruit**

3 (*also* **squash rackets**) a type of game played in a walled court with rackets and a rubber ball. □ **squash**

'**squashy** *adjective* soft or easily squashed: *The rain makes the fruit very squashy.* □ **mou**

squat [skwɔt] – *past tense, past participle* '**squatted** – *verb* to sit down on the heels or in a crouching position: *The beggar squatted all day in the market place.* □ **s'accroupir**

■ *adjective* short and fat; dumpy: *a squat little man*; *an ugly, squat building.* □ **courtaud, trapu**

squawk [skwɔːk] *noun* a loud harsh cry made *eg* by an excited or angry bird: *The hen gave a squawk when she saw the fox.* □ **cri rauque**

■ *verb* to make a sound of this sort. □ **pousser un/des cri(s) rauque(s)**

squeak [skwiːk] *noun* a shrill cry or sound: *the squeaks of the mice/puppies.* □ **grincement; glapissement**

■ *verb* to make a shrill cry or sound: *The door-hinge is squeaking.* □ **grincer; glapir**

'**squeaky** *adjective* making squeaks: *squeaky shoes.* □ **grinçant**

'**squeakily** *adverb*. □ **en grinçant**

'**squeakiness** *noun*. □ **caractère grinçant**

squeal [skwiːl] *noun* a long, shrill cry: *The children welcomed her with squeals of delight.* □ **cri perçant**

■ *verb* to give a cry of this sort: *The puppy squealed with pain.* □ **pousser un/des cri(s) perçant(s)**

squeeze [skwiːz] *verb* **1** to press (something) together or from all sides tightly: *He squeezed her hand affectionately*; *She squeezed the clay into a ball.* □ **presser, serrer**

2 to force (*eg* oneself) *eg* into or through a narrow space: *The dog squeezed himself/his body into the hole*; *We were all squeezed into the back seat of the car.* □ **s'introduire**

3 to force something, *eg* liquid, out of something by pressing: *She squeezed the oranges (into a jug)*; *We might be able to squeeze some more money/information out of him.* □ **presser**

■ *noun* **1** an act of squeezing: *He gave his sister an affectionate squeeze.* □ **étreinte**

2 a condition of being squeezed: *We all got into the car, but it was a squeeze.* □ **cohue**

3 a few drops produced by squeezing. □ **quelques gouttes de**

4 a time of financial restriction: *an economic squeeze.* □ **restriction**

'**squeezer** *noun* an instrument for squeezing: *a lemon squeezer.* □ **presse-fruits**

squeeze up to move closer together: *Could you all squeeze up on the bench and make room for me?* □ **se serrer**

squelch [skweltʃ] *noun* the sucking sound made by movement in a thick, sticky substance *eg* mud. □ **bruit de succion**

■ *verb* to make squelches: *He squelched across the marsh.* □ **patauger (en faisant flic flac)**

squid [skwid] – *plurals* **squid, squids** – *noun* a type of sea creature with ten tentacles. □ **calmar**

squint [skwint] *verb* **1** to have the physical defect of having the eyes turning towards or away from each other or to cause the eyes to do this: *The child squints*; *You squint when you look down at your nose.* □ **loucher**

2 (*with* **at, up at, through** *etc*) to look with half-shut or narrowed eyes: *She squinted through the telescope.* □ **plonger son regard dans**

■ *noun* 1 a squinting position of the eyes: *an eye operation to correct her squint.* □ **strabisme**

2 a glance or look at something: *Let me have a squint at that photograph.* □ **coup d'œil**

■ *adjective, adverb* (placed *etc*) crookedly or not straight: *Your hat is squint.* □ **de travers**

squirm [skwə:m] *verb* 1 to twist the body or wriggle: *He lay squirming on the ground with pain.* □ **se tortiller**

2 to be very embarrassed or ashamed: *I squirmed when I thought of how rude I'd been.* □ **ne pas savoir où se mettre**

squirrel ['skwɔːrəl] *noun* a type of animal of the rodent family, *usually* either reddish-brown or grey, with a large bushy tail. □ **écureuil**

squirt [skwɔːt] *verb* to (make a liquid *etc*) shoot out in a narrow jet: *The elephant squirted water over itself*; *Water squirted from the hose.* □ **faire gicler**

stab [stab] – *past tense, past participle* **stabbed** – *verb* to wound or pierce with a pointed instrument or weapon: *He stabbed him (through the heart/in the chest) with a dagger.* □ **poignarder**

■ *noun* an act of stabbing or a piercing blow. □ **agression au couteau**

'**stabbing** *adjective* (of pain *etc*) very acute as though caused by a stab: *He complained of a stabbing pain just before he collapsed.* □ **lancinant**

stab (someone) in the back to act treacherously towards (someone): *She's only human.* □ **poignarder qqn dans le dos**

stable[1] ['steibl] *adjective* (*negative* **unstable**) 1 firm and steady or well-balanced: *This chair isn't very stable.* □ **stable**

2 firmly established and likely to last: *a stable government.* □ **solide, stable**

3 (of a person or his character) unlikely to become unreasonably upset or hysterical: *She's the only stable person in the whole family.* □ **équilibré**

4 (of a substance) not easily decomposed. □ **stable**

stability [stə'bi-] *noun* the quality of being stable. □ **stabilité**

'**stabilize**, '**stabilise** [-bi-] *verb* to make (more) stable: *She put a wedge of paper under the table to stabilize it.* □ **stabiliser**

,**stabili'zation**, ,**stabili'sation** *noun.* □ **stabilisation**

stable[2] ['steibl] *noun* 1 a building in which horses are kept. □ **écurie**

2 (*in plural*) a horse-keeping establishment: *He runs the riding stables.* □ **manège**

stack [stak] *noun* 1 a large, *usually* neatly shaped, pile *eg* of hay, straw, wood *etc*: *a haystack.* □ **meule**

2 a set of shelves for books *eg* in a library. □ **rayon(nage)**

■ *verb* to arrange in a large, *usually* neat, pile: *Stack the books up against the wall.* □ **empiler**

stadium ['steidiəm] – *plurals* '**stadiums**, '**stadia** [-diə] – *noun* a large sports ground or racecourse *usually* with

seats for spectators: *The athletics competitions were held in the new Olympic stadium.* □ **stade**

staff[1] [staːf] *noun* or *noun plural* a group of people employed in running a business, school *etc*: *The school has a large teaching staff*; *The staff are annoyed about the changes.* □ **personnel**

■ *verb* to supply with staff: *Most of our offices are staffed by volunteers.* □ **pourvoir en personnel**

'**staffroom** *noun* a sitting-room for the staff of *eg* a school: *A meeting will be held in the staffroom.* □ **salle des professeurs**

staff[2] [staːf], **stave** [steiv] – *plural* **staves** – *noun* a set of lines and spaces on which music is written or printed. □ **portée**

stag [stag] *noun* a male deer, *especially* a red deer. □ **cerf**

stage[1] [steidʒ] *noun* a raised platform *especially* for performing or acting on, *eg* in a theatre. □ **scène**

■ *verb* 1 to prepare and produce (a play *etc*) in a theatre *etc*: *This play was first staged in 1928.* □ **mettre en scène**

2 to organize (an event *etc*): *The protesters are planning to stage a demonstration.* □ **organiser**

'**staging** *noun* 1 wooden planks *etc* forming a platform. □ **(plate-forme d') échafaudage**

2 the way in which a play *etc* is presented on a stage: *The staging was good, but the acting poor.* □ **mise en scène**

stage direction an order to an actor playing a part to do this or that: *a stage direction to enter from the left.* □ **indication scénique**

stage fright the nervousness felt by an actor *etc* when in front of an audience, *especially* for the first time: *The young actress was suffering from stage fright and could not utter a word.* □ **trac**

'**stagehand** *noun* a workman employed to help with scenery *etc*. □ **machiniste**

stage manager a person who is in charge of scenery and equipment for plays *etc*. □ **régisseur, euse**

stage[2] [steidʒ] *noun* 1 a period or step in the development of something: *The plan is in its early stages*; *At this stage, we don't know how many survivors there are.* □ **stade**

2 part of a journey: *The first stage of our journey will be the flight to Singapore.* □ **étape**

3 a section of a bus route. □ **section**

4 a section of a rocket. □ **étage**

stagger ['stagə] *verb* 1 to sway, move or walk unsteadily: *The drunk man staggered along the road.* □ **tituber**

2 to astonish: *I was staggered to hear he had died.* □ **atterrer**

3 to arrange (people's hours of work, holidays *etc*) so that they do not begin and end at the same times. □ **échelonner**

'**staggering** *adjective* causing unsteadiness, shock or astonishment: *a staggering blow on the side of the head*; *That piece of news is staggering.* □ **renversant**

staging *see* **stage**[1].

stagnant ['stagnənt] *adjective* 1 (of water) standing still rather than flowing and therefore *usually* dirty: *a stagnant pool.* □ **stagnant**

2 dull or inactive: *Our economy is stagnant.* □ **stagnant**

stagnate ['stagneit] *verb* **1** (of water) to be or become stagnant. □ **stagner**

2 to become dull and inactive. □ **être inactif**

stag'nation *noun.* □ **stagnation**

staid [steid] *adjective* (over-)serious or old-fashioned: *A person of staid appearance/habits.* □ **posé, sérieux**

stain [stein] *verb* **1** to leave a (permanent) dirty mark or coloured patch on *eg* a fabric: *The coffee I spilt has stained my trousers.* □ **tacher**

2 to become marked in this way: *Silk stains easily.* □ **se tacher**

3 to dye or colour (*eg* wood): *The wooden chairs had been stained brown.* □ **teindre**

■ *noun* a dirty mark on a fabric *etc* that is difficult or impossible to remove: *His overall was covered with paint-stains; There is not the slightest stain upon her reputation.* □ **tache**

stainless steel (of) a metal alloy composed of steel and chromium that does not rust: *a sink made of stainless steel; stainless steel knives/cutlery.* □ **acier inoxydable**

stained glass [steind glɑːs] *noun* a window, lamp or piece of art made with pieces of coloured glass: *There were beautiful stained glass windows in the church that seemed to light up when the sun shone.* □ **vitrail**

stair [steə] *noun* (any one of) a number of steps, *usually* inside a building, going from one floor to another: *He fell down the stairs.* □ **marche**

'staircase, 'stairway *nouns* a series or flight of stairs: *A dark and narrow staircase led up to the top floor.* □ **escalier**

stake[1] [steik] *noun* a strong stick or post, *especially* a pointed one used as a support or as part of a fence. □ **pieu**

stake[2] [steik] *noun* a sum of money risked in betting: *She and her friends enjoy playing cards for high stakes.* □ **enjeu, mise**

■ *verb* to bet or risk (money or something of value): *I'm going to stake $5 on that horse.* □ **miser**

at stake 1 to be won or lost: *A great deal of money is at stake.* □ **en jeu**

2 in great danger: *The peace of the country/Our children's future is at stake.* □ **en jeu**

stalactite [stə'laktait] *noun* a spike of limestone hanging from the roof of a cave *etc* formed by the dripping of water containing lime. □ **stalactite**

stalagmite [stə'lagmait] *noun* a spike of limestone rising from the floor of a cave, formed by water dripping from the roof. □ **stalagmite**

stale [steil] *adjective* **1** (of food *etc*) not fresh and therefore dry and tasteless: *stale bread.* □ **qui n'est plus frais**

2 no longer interesting: *His ideas are stale and dull.* □ **rebattu**

3 no longer able to work *etc* well because of too much study *etc*: *If she practises the piano for more than two hours a day, she will grow stale.* □ **vidé**

stalemate ['steilmeit] *noun* **1** a position in chess in which a player cannot move without putting his king in danger. □ **pat**

2 in any contest, dispute *etc*, a position in which neither side can win: *The recent discussions ended in stalemate.* □ **impasse**

stalk[1] [stoːk] *noun* the stem of a plant or of a leaf, flower or fruit: *If the stalk is damaged, the plant may die.* □ **tige**

stalk[2] [stoːk] *verb* **1** to walk stiffly and proudly, *eg* in anger: *He stalked out of the room in disgust.* □ **marcher avec raideur**

2 to move menacingly through a place: *Disease and famine stalk (through) the country.* □ **régner (sur)**

3 in hunting, to move gradually as close as possible to game, *eg* deer, trying to remain hidden: *Have you ever stalked deer/been deer-stalking?* □ **traquer**

'stalker *noun* a person who stalks game. □ **chasseur à l'affût**

stall[1] [stoːl] *noun* **1** a compartment in a cowshed *etc*: *cattle stalls.* □ **stalle**

2 a small shop or a counter or table on which goods are displayed for sale: *She bought a newspaper at the book-stall on the station; traders' stalls.* □ **éventaire, étalage**

stall[2] [stoːl] *verb* **1** (of a car *etc* or its engine) to stop suddenly through lack of power, braking too quickly *etc*: *The car stalled when I was halfway up the hill.* □ **caler**

2 (of an aircraft) to lose speed while flying and so go out of control: *The plane stalled just after takeoff and crashed on to the runway.* □ **décrocher**

3 to cause (a car *etc*, or aircraft) to do this: *Use the brake gently or you'll stall the engine.* □ **caler**

■ *noun* a dangerous loss of flying speed in an aircraft, causing it to drop: *The plane went into a stall.* □ **décrochage**

stall[3] [stoːl] *verb* to avoid making a definite decision in order to give oneself more time. □ **temporiser**

stallion ['staljən] *noun* a fully-grown male horse. □ **étalon**

stamen ['steimən] *noun* one of the thread-like spikes in a flower that bear the pollen. □ **étamine**

stamina ['staminə] *noun* strength or power to endure fatigue *etc*: *Long-distance runners require plenty of stamina.* □ **endurance**

stammer ['stamə] *noun* the speech defect of being unable to produce easily certain sounds: *'You m-m-must m-m-meet m-m-my m-m-mother' is an example of a stammer; That child has a bad stammer.* □ **bégaiement**

■ *verb* to speak with a stammer or in a similar way because of *eg* fright, nervousness *etc*: *He stammered an apology.* □ **bégayer**

'stammerer *noun* a person who has a stammer. □ **bègue**

stamp [stamp] *verb* **1** to bring (the foot) down with force (on the ground): *He stamped his foot with rage; She stamped on the insect.* □ **taper du pied sur**

2 to print or mark on to: *I stamped the date at the top of the letter; The oranges were all stamped with the exporter's name.* □ **tamponner**

3 to stick a postage stamp on (a letter *etc*): *I've addressed the envelope but haven't stamped it.* □ **timbrer**

■ *noun* **1** an act of stamping the foot: *'Give it to me!' she shouted with a stamp of her foot.* □ **trépignement**

2 the instrument used to stamp a design *etc* on a surface: *He marked the date on the bill with a rubber date-stamp.* □ **tampon**

3 a postage stamp: *She stuck the stamps on the parcel*; *He collects foreign stamps.* □ **timbre(-poste)**

4 a design *etc* made by stamping: *All the goods bore the manufacturer's stamp.* □ **estampille**

stamp out 1 to put out or extinguish (a fire) by stamping on it: *She stamped out the remains of the fire.* □ **éteindre en piétinant**

2 to crush (a rebellion *etc*). □ **écraser**

stampede [stam'piːd] *noun* a sudden wild rush of wild animals *etc*: *a stampede of buffaloes*; *The school bell rang for lunch and there was a stampede for the door.* □ **ruée**

■ *verb* to (cause to) rush in a stampede: *The noise stampeded the elephants/made the elephants stampede.* □ **jeter la panique parmi**

stance [staːns] *noun* a person's position or manner of standing, *eg* in playing golf, cricket *etc*. □ **position**

stand [stand] – *past tense, past participle* **stood** [stud] – *verb* **1** to be in an upright position, not sitting or lying: *His leg was so painful that he could hardly stand*; *After the storm, few trees were left standing.* □ **être debout**

2 (*often with* **up**) to rise to the feet: *He pushed back his chair and stood up*; *Some people like to stand (up) when the National Anthem is played.* □ **se mettre debout**

3 to remain motionless: *The train stood for an hour outside Newcastle.* □ **rester**

4 to remain unchanged: *This law still stands.* □ **maintenir**

5 to be in or have a particular place: *There is now a factory where our house once stood.* □ **s'élever**

6 to be in a particular state, condition or situation: *As matters stand, we can do nothing to help*; *How do you stand financially?* □ **dans l'état où, dans ces conditions**

7 to accept or offer oneself for a particular position *etc*: *She is standing as Parliamentary candidate for our district.* □ **être candidat (à)**

8 to put in a particular position, *especially* upright: *He picked up the fallen chair and stood it beside the table.* □ **poser (droit/debout)**

9 to undergo or endure: *He will stand (his) trial for murder*; *I can't stand her rudeness any longer.* □ **supporter**

■ *noun* **1** a position or place in which to stand ready to fight *etc*, or an act of fighting *etc*: *The guard took up his stand at the gate*; *I shall make a stand for what I believe is right.* □ **poste**

2 an object, *especially* a piece of furniture, for holding or supporting something: *a coat-stand*; *The sculpture had been removed from its stand for cleaning.* □ **support**

3 a stall where goods are displayed for sale or advertisement. □ **étalage**

4 a large structure beside a football pitch, race course *etc* with rows of seats for spectators: *The stand was crowded.* □ **tribune**

5 a witness box in a law court. □ **barre**

'standing *adjective* permanent: *The general's standing orders must be obeyed.* □ **établi**

■ *noun* **1** time of lasting: *an agreement of long standing.* □ **durée**

2 rank or reputation: *a diplomat of high standing.* □ **importance**

'stand-by – *plural* **'stand-bys** – *noun* **1** readiness for action: *Two fire-engines went directly to the fire, and a third was on stand-by* (= ready to go if ordered). □ **d'intervention**

2 something that can be used in an emergency *etc*: *Fruit is a good stand-by when children get hungry between meals.* □ **d'appoint**

■ *adjective* (of an airline passenger or ticket) costing or paying less than the usual fare, as the passenger does not book a seat for a particular flight, but waits for the first available seat. □ **sans garantie**

■ *adverb* travelling in this way: *It costs a lot less to travel stand-by.* □ **sans garantie**

'stand-in *noun* a person who takes someone else's job *etc* for a temporary period, *especially* in making films. □ **remplaçant, ante, doublure**

'standing-room *noun* space for standing only, not sitting: *There was standing-room only on the bus.* □ **place debout**

make someone's hair stand on end to frighten someone very greatly: *The horrible scream made her hair stand on end.* □ **faire dresser les cheveux sur la tête**

stand aside to move to one side or withdraw out of someone's way: *She stood aside to let me pass.* □ **s'écarter**

stand back to move backwards or away: *A crowd gathered around the injured man, but a policeman ordered everyone to stand back.* □ **reculer**

stand by 1 to watch something happening without doing anything: *I couldn't just stand by while he was drowning.* □ **rester là (à ne rien faire)**

2 to be ready to act: *The police are standing by in case of trouble.* □ **se tenir prêt à intervenir**

3 to support; to stay loyal to: *She stood by him throughout his trial.* □ **soutenir**

stand down to withdraw *eg* from a contest. □ **se désister**

stand fast/firm to refuse to yield. □ **tenir bon/ferme**

stand for 1 to be a candidate for election to: *She stood for Parliament.* □ **être candidat, ate (à, pour)**

2 to be an abbreviation for: *HQ stands for Headquarters.* □ **vouloir dire**

3 to represent: *I like to think that our school stands for all that is best in education.* □ **représenter**

4 to tolerate: *I won't stand for this sort of behaviour.* □ **tolérer**

stand in to take another person's place, job *etc* for a time: *The leading actor was ill and another actor stood in for him.* □ **remplacer**

stand on one's own (two) feet to manage one's own affairs without help. □ **voler de ses propres ailes**

stand out 1 to be noticeable: *She stood out as one of the most intelligent girls in the school.* □ **ressortir (d'entre, parmi)**

2 to go on resisting or to refuse to yield: *The garrison stood out (against the besieging army) as long as pos-*

sible. □ **tenir bon/ferme**

stand over to supervise closely: *I have to stand over him to make him do his schoolwork.* □ **surveiller**

stand up for to support or defend: *She stood up for him when the others bullied him.* □ **prendre le parti de**

stand up to to show resistance to: *He stood up to the bigger boys who tried to bully him; These chairs have stood up to very hard use.* □ **tenir tête à**

standard ['standəd] *noun* **1** something used as a basis of measurement: *The kilogram is the international standard of weight.* □ **unité**

2 a basis for judging quality, or a level of excellence aimed at, required or achieved: *You can't judge an amateur artist's work by the same standards as you would judge that of a trained artist; high standards of behaviour; His performance did not reach the required standard.* □ **critère**

3 a flag or carved figure *etc* fixed to a pole and carried *eg* at the front of an army going into battle. □ **pavillon; étendard**

■ *adjective* (accepted as) normal or usual; *The Post Office likes the public to use a standard size of envelope.* □ **normal, standard**

'**standardize**, '**standardise** *verb* to make or keep (*eg* products) of one size, shape *etc* for the sake of convenience *etc*. □ **standardiser**

,**standardi'zation**, ,**standardi'sation** *noun*. □ **standardisation**

'**standard-bearer** *noun* a person who carries a standard or banner. □ **porte-étendard**

be up to/below standard to (fail to) achieve the required standard: *Her work is well up to standard.* □ **(n')être (pas) à la hauteur**

standard of living the level of comfort and welfare achieved in any particular society. □ **niveau de vie**

standpoint ['standpoint] *noun* a point of view: *From my standpoint, 5:00 would be a suitable time.* □ **point de vue**

standstill ['standstil]: **be at, come to, reach a standstill** to remain without moving; to stop, halt *etc*: *The traffic was at a standstill.* □ **arrêt; s'immobiliser**

stank *see* **stink**.

staple[1] ['steipl] *noun* **1** a chief product of trade or industry. □ **produit/article de base**

2 a chief or main item (of diet *etc*). □ **aliment de base**

staple[2] ['steipl] *noun* **1** a U-shaped type of nail. □ **crampon**

2 a U-shaped piece of wire that is driven through sheets of paper *etc* to fasten them together. □ **agrafe**

■ *verb* to fasten or attach (paper *etc*) with staples. □ **agrafer**

'**stapler** *noun* an instrument for stapling papers *etc*. □ **agrafeuse**

star [staː] *noun* **1** the fixed bodies in the sky, which are really distant suns: *The Sun is a star, and the Earth is one of its planets.* □ **étoile**

2 any of the bodies in the sky appearing as points of light: *The sky was full of stars.* □ **étoile**

3 an object, shape or figure with a number of pointed rays, *usually* five or six, often used as a means of marking quality *etc*: *The teacher stuck a gold star on the child's neat exercise book; a four-star hotel.* □ **étoile**

4 a leading actor or actress or other well-known performer *eg* in sport *etc*: *a film/television star; a football star;* (*also adjective*) *She has had many star roles in films.* □ **vedette**

5 an actor or singer who has achieved fame and popularity: *The star of the movie got out of a limousine wearing sun glasses and waved to thousands of adoring fans.* □ **étoile**

■ *verb* – *past tense, past participle* **starred** – **1** to play a leading role in a play, film *etc*: *She has starred in two recent films.* □ **être la vedette de**

2 (of a film *etc*) to have (a certain actor *etc*) as its leading performer: *The film starred Greta Garbo.* □ **avoir pour vedette**

'**stardom** *noun* the state of being a famous performer: *to achieve stardom.* □ **célébrité**

'**starry** *adjective* full of or shining like stars: *a starry night; starry eyes.* □ **étoilé; étincelant**

'**starfish** *noun* a type of small sea creature with five points as arms. □ **étoile de mer**

'**starfruit** *noun* a juicy, yellow, oblong, tropical fruit, which, when cut across, is star-shaped. □ **carambole**

'**starlight** *noun* the light from the stars. □ **lumière des étoiles**

'**starlit** *adjective* bright with stars: *a starlit night.* □ **étoilé**

star turn the most successful or spectacular performance or item (in a show *etc*): *The acrobats were the star turn of the evening.* □ **vedette**

see stars to see flashes of light as a result of a hard blow on the head. □ **voir trente-six chandelles**

thank one's lucky stars to be grateful for one's good luck. □ **bénir son étoile (de ce que)**

starboard ['staːbəd] *noun* the right side of a ship or aircraft, from the point of view of a person looking towards the bow or front. □ **tribord**

starch [staːtʃ] *noun* **1** a white food substance found *especially* in flour, potatoes *etc*: *Bread contains starch.* □ **fécule, amidon**

2 a powder prepared from this, used for stiffening clothes. □ **amidon**

■ *verb* to stiffen (clothes) with starch. □ **empeser**

'**starchy** *adjective* like or containing starch: *cake, biscuits and other starchy foods.* □ **féculent**

'**starchiness** *noun*. □ **raideur**

stardom *see* **star**.

stare [steə] *verb* (*often with* **at**) to look at with a fixed gaze: *They stared at her clothes in amazement; Don't stare – it's rude!* □ **regarder (fixement), dévisager**

■ *noun* a staring look: *a bold stare.* □ **regard (fixe)**

stare in the face to be easy to see or obvious: *The answer to the problem was staring me in the face.* □ **crever les yeux (à)**

starfish *see* **star**.

stark [staːk] *adjective* bare, harsh or simple in a severe way: *a stark, rocky landscape.* □ **désolé**

stark crazy/mad completely mad. □ **fou à lier**

stark naked (of a person) completely naked. □ **tout nu**

starling ['staːliŋ] *noun* a type of small bird with glossy

dark feathers. □ **étourneau**
starry *see* **star.**
start[1] [staː] *verb* **1** to leave or begin a journey: *We shall have to start at 5:30 in order to get to the boat in time.*
□ **partir**
2 to begin: *He starts working at six o'clock every morning; She started to cry; She starts her new job next week; Haven't you started (on) your meal yet?; What time does the play start?* □ **commencer (à)**
3 to (cause an engine *etc* to) begin to work: *I can't start the car; The car won't start; The clock stopped but I started it again.* □ **(faire) démarrer**
4 to cause something to begin or begin happening *etc*: *One of the students decided to start a college magazine.* □ **lancer**
■ *noun* **1** the beginning of an activity, journey, race *etc*: *I told him at the start that his idea would not succeed; The runners lined up at the start; He stayed in the lead after a good start; I shall have to make a start on that work.* □ **début; départ**
2 in a race *etc*, the advantage of beginning before or further forward than others, or the amount of time, distance *etc* gained through this: *The youngest child in the race got a start of five metres; The driver of the stolen car already had twenty minutes' start before the police began the pursuit.* □ **avance**
'starter *noun* **1** a person, horse *etc* that actually runs *etc* in a race. □ **partant, ante**
2 a person who gives the signal for the race to start. □ **starter**
3 a device in a car *etc* for starting the engine. □ **démarreur**
starting line *noun* the point or mark where a race begins: *One of the runners was disqualified for crossing the starting line before the signal to begin the race.* □ **ligne de départ**
'starting point *noun* the point from which something begins. □ **point de départ**
for a start (used in argument *etc*) in the first place, or as the first point in an argument: *You can't have a new bicycle because for a start we can't afford one.* □ **pour commencer**
get off to a good, bad start to start well or badly in a race, business *etc*. □ **bien/mal commencer**
start off 1 to begin a journey: *It's time we started off.* □ **se mettre en route**
2 to cause or allow something to begin, someone to start doing something *etc*: *The money lent to her by her father started her off as a bookseller.* □ **établir**
start out to begin a journey; to start off: *We shall have to start out at dawn.* □ **se mettre en route**
start up to (cause to) begin or begin working *etc*: *The machine suddenly started up; He has started up a new boys' club.* □ **démarrer**
to start with 1 at the beginning: *He was very nervous to start with.* □ **au début**
2 as the first point (in an argument *etc*): *There are many reasons why he shouldn't get the job. To start with, he isn't qualified.* □ **d'abord**
start[2] [staː] *verb* to jump or jerk suddenly because of

fright, surprise *etc*: *The sudden noise made me start.* □ **sursauter**
■ *noun* **1** a sudden movement of the body: *She gave a start of surprise.* □ **sursaut**
2 a shock: *What a start the news gave me!* □ **choc**
startle ['staːtl] *verb* to give a shock or surprise to: *The sound startled me.* □ **faire sursauter**
starve [staːv] *verb* **1** to (cause to) die, or suffer greatly, from hunger: *In the drought, many people and animals starved (to death); They were accused of starving their prisoners.* □ **(faire) mourir de faim; affamer**
2 to be very hungry: *Can't we have supper now? I'm starving.* □ **être affamé**
star'vation *noun* a starving state: *They died of starvation.* □ **inanition**
state[1] [steit] *noun* **1** the condition in which a thing or person is: *the bad state of the roads; The room was in an untidy state; He inquired about her state of health; What a state you're in!; He was not in a fit state to take the class.* □ **état**
2 a country considered as a political community, or, as in the United States, one division of a federation: *The Prime Minister visits the Queen once a week to discuss affairs of state; The care of the sick and elderly is considered partly the responsibility of the state; (also adjective) The railways are under state control; state-controlled/owned industries.* □ **(d')État**
3 ceremonial dignity and splendour: *The Queen, wearing her robes of state, drove in a horse-drawn coach to Westminster; (also adjective) state occasions/banquets.* □ **(d')apparat**
'stately *adjective* noble, dignified and impressive in appearance or manner: *She is tall and stately; a stately house.* □ **majestueux**
'stateliness *noun*. □ **majesté**
'statesman ['steits-] *noun* a person who plays an important part in the government of a state. □ **homme, femme d'État**
'statesmanlike ['steits-] *adjective* showing the qualities of a good statesman. □ **diplomatique**
'statesmanship ['steits-] *noun* skill in directing the affairs of a state. □ **diplomatie**
get into a state to become very upset or anxious. □ **se mettre dans tous ses états**
lie in state (of a corpse) to be laid in a place of honour for the public to see, before burial. □ **être exposé en chapelle ardente**
state[2] [steit] *verb* to say or announce clearly, carefully and definitely: *You have not yet stated your intentions.* □ **déclarer, formuler**
'statement *noun* **1** the act of stating. □ **déclaration**
2 something that is stated: *The prime minister will make a statement tomorrow on the crisis.* □ **déclaration**
3 a written statement of how much money a person has, owes *etc*: *I'll look at my bank statement to see how much money is in my account.* □ **relevé**
static ['statik] *adjective* still; not moving. □ **statique**
■ *noun* atmospheric disturbances causing poor reception of radio or television programs. □ **parasites**
static (electricity) electricity that accumulates on the

surface of objects (*eg* hair, nylon garments *etc*). □ **(électricité) statique**

station ['steiʃən] *noun* 1 a place with a ticket office, waiting rooms *etc*, where trains, buses or coaches stop to allow passengers to get on or off: *a bus station; She arrived at the station in good time for her train.* □ **gare**

2 a local headquarters or centre of work of some kind: *How many fire-engines are kept at the fire station?; a radio station; Where is the police station?; military/naval stations.* □ **poste, caserne**

3 a post or position (*eg* of a guard or other person on duty): *The watchman remained at his station all night.* □ **poste**

■ *verb* to put (a person, oneself, troops *etc* in a place or position to perform some duty): *He stationed himself at the corner of the road to keep watch; The regiment is stationed abroad.* □ **(se) poster**

'**stationary** *adjective* standing still, not moving: *a stationary vehicle.* □ **stationnaire**

station wagon *noun* a car with a large area behind the seats for luggage *etc*, and a rear door. □ **familiale**

stationer ['steiʃənə] *noun* a person who sells stationery. □ **papetier, ière**

'**stationery** *noun* paper, envelopes, pens and other articles used in writing *etc*. □ **papeterie**

statistics [stə'tistiks] *noun plural* figures giving information about something: *There were 900 deaths and 20 000 injuries on the roads last year, but the statistics for the previous year were worse.* □ **statistiques**

■ *noun singular* the study of such figures. □ **statistique**

sta'**tistical** *adjective*. □ **statistique**

sta'**tistically** *adverb*. □ **statistiquement**

statistician [stati'stiʃən] *noun* a person who is an expert in statistics. □ **statisticien, ienne**

statue ['statjuː] *noun* a sculptured figure of a person, animal *etc* in bronze, stone, wood *etc*: *A statue of Nelson stands at the top of Nelson's Column; The children stood as still as statues.* □ **statue**

stature ['statʃə] *noun* 1 height of body: *a man of gigantic stature.* □ **stature**

2 importance or reputation: *a musician of stature.* □ **envergure**

status ['steitəs, 'sta-] *noun* 1 the position of a person with regard to his legal rights *etc*: *If she marries a foreigner, will her status as a Canadian citizen be affected?* □ **état civil**

2 a person's social rank. □ **statut**

status symbol a possession that indicates one's social importance: *a car, a private swimming pool and other status symbols.* □ **signe extérieur de richesse**

statute ['statjuːt] *noun* a written law of a country. □ **loi**

staunch [stoːntʃ] *adjective* firm, trusty: *a staunch friend.* □ **loyal**

'**staunchly** *adverb*. □ **loyalement**

'**staunchness** *noun*. □ **loyauté**

stave [steiv] *noun* in music, a staff. □ **portée**

stay [stei] *verb* 1 to remain (in a place) for a time, *eg* while travelling, or as a guest *etc*: *We stayed three nights at that hotel/with a friend/in Paris; Aunt Mary is coming to stay (for a week); Would you like to stay for sup-*

per?; Stay and watch that television program. □ **rester**

2 to remain (in a particular position, place, state or condition): *The doctor told her to stay in bed; He never stays long in any job; Stay away from the office till your cold is better; Why won't these socks stay up?; Stay where you are – don't move!; In 1900, people didn't realize that cars were here to stay.* □ **rester**

■ *noun* a period of staying (in a place *etc*): *We had an overnight stay/a two days' stay in Montreal.* □ **séjour**

stay behind to remain in a place after others have left it: *They all left the office at five o'clock, but she stayed behind to finish some work.* □ **rester**

stay in to remain in one's house *etc* and not go out of doors: *I'm staying in tonight to watch television.* □ **rester chez soi**

stay out to remain out of doors and not return to one's house *etc*: *The children mustn't stay out after 20:00.* □ **rester dehors**

stay put to remain where placed: *Once a child can crawl, he won't stay put for long.* □ **rester tranquille**

stay up not to go to bed: *The children wanted to stay up and watch television.* □ **veiller**

stay with to live with or share a house with somebody: *I'll stay with my aunt this year while my parents are travelling around the world.* □ **habiter chez**

steadfast ['stedfɑːst] *adjective* firm; unchanging: *a steadfast friend.* □ **constant**

'**steadfastly** *adverb*. □ **fermement**

'**steadfastness** *noun*. □ **constance**

steady ['stedi] *adjective* 1 (*negative* **unsteady**) firmly fixed, balanced or controlled: *The table isn't steady; You need a steady hand to be a surgeon.* □ **ferme**

2 regular or even: *a steady temperature; She was walking at a steady pace.* □ **régulier**

3 unchanging or constant: *steady faith.* □ **solide**

4 (of a person) sensible and hardworking in habits *etc*: *a steady young man.* □ **travailleur**

■ *verb* to make or become steady: *He stumbled but managed to steady himself; Her heartbeat gradually steadied.* □ **(se) calmer**

'**steadily** *adverb*: *His work is improving steadily.* □ **régulièrement**

'**steadiness** *noun*. □ **régularité**

steak [steik] *noun* a slice of meat (*usually* beef) or fish (often cod) for *eg* frying or stewing: *a piece of steak; two cod steaks.* □ **bifteck; tranche, darne**

steal [stiːl] – *past tense* **stole** [stoul]: *past participle* **stolen** ['stoulən] – *verb* 1 to take (another person's property), *especially* secretly, without permission or legal right: *Thieves broke into the house and stole money and jewellery; He was expelled from the school because he had been stealing (money).* □ **voler**

2 to obtain or take (*eg* a look, a nap *etc*) quickly or secretly: *He stole a glance at her.* □ **dérober**

3 to move quietly: *She stole quietly into the room.* □ **aller furtivement**

stealth [stelθ] *noun* a secret manner of acting: *If I can't get what I want openly, I get it by stealth.* □ **(à la) dérobée**

'**stealthy** *adjective* acting, or done, with stealth: *stealthy*

footsteps. □ **furtif**
'**stealthily** *adverb*. □ **furtivement**
'**stealthiness** *noun*. □ **manière furtive**
steam [stiːm] *noun* 1 a gas or vapour that rises from hot
or boiling water or other liquid: *Steam rose from the
plate of soup/the wet earth in the hot sun; a cloud of
steam*; (*also adjective*) *A sauna is a type of steam bath.*
□ **(à/de) vapeur**
2 power or energy obtained from this: *The machinery is
driven by steam; Diesel fuel has replaced steam on the
railways*; (*also adjective*) *steam power, steam engines.*
□ **(à/de) vapeur**
■ *verb* 1 to give out steam: *A kettle was steaming on the
stove.* □ **fumer**
2 (of a ship, train *etc*) to move by means of steam: *The
ship steamed across the bay.* □ **avancer (à la vapeur)**
3 to cook by steam: *The pudding should be steamed for
four hours.* □ **cuire à la vapeur**
steam-: *steam-driven/steam-powered machinery.* □ **à
la vapeur**
'**steamer** *noun* a steamboat or steamship. □ **paquebot**
'**steamy** *adjective* of, or full of, steam: *the steamy atmosphere of the laundry.* □ **humide**
'**steaminess** *noun*. □ **vapeur**
'**steamboat**, '**steamship** *nouns* a ship driven by steam.
□ **paquebot, bateau à vapeur**
steam engine a moving engine for pulling a train, or a
fixed engine, driven by steam. □ **locomotive à vapeur**
steam roller a type of vehicle driven by steam, with
wide and heavy wheels for flattening the surface of
newly-made roads *etc*. □ **rouleau compresseur**
full steam ahead at the greatest speed possible. □ **en
avant toute**
get steamed up to get very upset or angry. □ **se mettre
dans tous ses états**
get up steam to build up energy ready for effort. □ **se
chauffer**
let off steam 1 to release steam into the air. □ **lâcher
(de) la vapeur**
2 to release or get rid of excess energy, emotion *etc*:
*The children were letting off steam by running about in
the playground.* □ **se défouler**
run out of steam to lose energy, or become exhausted.
□ **s'essoufler**
steam up to (cause to) become covered with steam:
The windows steamed up/became steamed up. □
(s')embuer
under one's own steam by one's own efforts, without
help from others: *John gave me a lift in his car, but
Mary arrived under her own steam.* □ **par ses propres
moyens**
steed [stiːd] *noun* an old word for a horse for riding. □
coursier
steel [stiːl] *noun, adjective* (of) a very hard alloy of iron
and carbon, used for making tools *etc*: *tools of the finest steel; steel knives/chisels; He had a grip of steel* (= a
very strong grip). □ **(d')acier**
■ *verb* to harden and strengthen (oneself, one's nerves
etc) in preparation for doing, or resisting, something:
He steeled himself to meet the attack/to tell his wife the

truth. □ **s'armer de courage (pour)**
'**steely** *adjective* hard, cold, strong or bright like steel.
□ **d'acier**
'**steeliness** *noun*. □ **dureté, inflexibilité**
steel wool a pad, ball *etc* of steel shavings used for scour-
ing (pans *etc*) and polishing. □ **tampon d'acier**
'**steelworks** *noun plural or noun singular* a factory
where steel is made. □ **aciérie**
steep[1] [stiːp] *adjective* 1 (of *eg* a hill, stairs *etc*) rising
with a sudden rather than a gradual slope: *The hill was
too steep for me to cycle up; a steep path; a steep climb.*
□ **escarpé**
2 (of a price asked or demand made) unreasonable or
too great: *He wants rather a steep price for his house,
doesn't he?; That's a bit steep!* □ **excessif**
'**steepness** *noun*. □ **pente (raide)**
'**steeply** *adverb* in a steep or sudden way: *The path/
prices rose steeply.* □ **en flèche**
steep[2] [stiːp] to soak thoroughly. □ **tremper (dans)**
steeple ['stiːpl] *noun* a high tower of a church *etc*, usually having a spire. □ **clocher**
'**steeplechase** *noun* a race on horseback or on foot across
open country, over hedges *etc*, or over a course on which
obstacles (*eg* fences, hedges *etc*) have been made. □
course d'obstacles
steer[1] [stiə] *noun* a young ox raised to produce beef. □
bouvillon
steer[2] [stiə] *verb* to guide or control the course of (*eg* a
ship, car *etc*): *He steered the car through the narrow
streets; I steered out of the harbour; She managed to
steer the conversation towards the subject of her birthday.* □ **diriger**
'**steering** *noun* the equipment or apparatus for steering
a ship or car *etc*: *The steering is faulty.* □ **gouvernail,
direction**
'**steering wheel** *noun* the wheel in a car for steering it,
fixed to the '**steering column**, or the wheel on a ship
that is turned to control the rudder. □ **volant**
steer clear of to avoid: *I want to steer clear of trouble
if possible.* □ **se tenir à l'écart de**
stellar ['stelə] *adjective* of stars: *stellar clusters.* □
stellaire
stem[1] [stem] *noun* 1 the part of a plant that grows upward from the root, or the part from which a leaf, flower
or fruit grows; a stalk: *Poppies have long, hairy, twisting stems.* □ **tige**
2 the narrow part of various objects, *eg* of a wine-glass
between the bowl and the base: *the stem of a wine-glass/
of a tobacco-pipe.* □ **pied**
3 the upright piece of wood or metal at the bow of a
ship: *As the ship struck the rock, she shook from stem to
stern.* □ **étrave**
■ *verb* – *past tense, past participle* **stemmed** – (*with
from*) to be caused by: *Hate sometimes stems from envy.*
□ **provenir de**
-stemmed: *a thick-stemmed plant; He smoked a short-
stemmed pipe.* □ **à tige/tuyau**
stem[2] [stem] – *past tense, past participle* **stemmed** – *verb*
to stop (a flow, *eg* of blood). □ **arrêter**
stench [stentʃ] *noun* a strong, bad smell: *the stench of*

stale tobacco smoke. □ **puanteur**

stencil ['stensl] *noun* **1** a thin piece of metal or card in which a design *etc* has been cut which can be reproduced on another surface, *eg* paper, by printing or inking over the metal *etc*. □ **pochoir**
2 a piece of waxed paper into which words have been cut by a typewriter, to be reproduced by a similar process. □ **stencil**
■ *verb – past tense, past participle* 'stencilled – to produce (a design, pattern *etc*) by using a stencil. □ **marquer au pochoir**

step [step] *noun* **1** one movement of the foot in walking, running, dancing *etc*: *He took a step forward*; *walking with hurried steps*. □ **pas**
2 the distance covered by this: *He moved a step or two nearer*; *The restaurant is only a step* (= a short distance) *away*. □ **pas**
3 the sound made by someone walking *etc*: *I heard* (foot) *steps*. □ **pas**
4 a particular movement with the feet, *eg* in dancing: *The dance has some complicated steps*. □ **pas**
5 a flat surface, or one flat surface in a series, *eg* on a stair or stepladder, on which to place the feet or foot in moving up or down: *A flight of steps led down to the cellar*; *Mind the step!*; *She was sitting on the doorstep*. □ **marche**
6 a stage in progress, development *etc*: *Mankind made a big step forward with the invention of the wheel*; *His present job is a step up from his previous one*. □ **pas**
7 an action or move (towards accomplishing an aim *etc*): *That would be a foolish/sensible step to take*; *I shall take steps to prevent this happening again*. □ **mesure**
■ *verb – past tense, past participle* **stepped** – to make a step, or to walk: *She opened the door and stepped out*; *She stepped briskly along the road*. □ **marcher**
steps *noun plural* a stepladder: *May I borrow your steps?* □ **escabeau**
'stepladder *noun* a ladder with a hinged support at the back and flat steps, not rungs. □ **escabeau**
'stepping stones *noun plural* large stones placed in a shallow stream *etc*, on which a person can step when crossing. □ **pierre de gué**
in, out of step (of two or more people walking together) with, without the same foot going forward at the same time: *to march in step*; *Keep in step!*; *She got out of step*. □ **au pas; rompre le pas**
step aside to move to one side: *He stepped aside to let me pass*. □ **s'écarter**
step by step gradually: *She improved step by step*. □ **pas à pas**
step in to intervene: *The children began to quarrel, and I thought it was time I stepped in*. □ **intervenir**
step out to walk with a long(er) and (more) energetic stride. □ **allonger le pas**
step up to increase: *The firm must step up production*. □ **intensifier**
watch one's step to be careful, *especially* over one's own behaviour. □ **prendre garde**
step [step] showing a relationship not by blood but by another marriage. □ **beau/belle; demi-**

'stepfather, 'stepmother *nouns* the husband, who is not the person's father, of a person's own mother, or the wife, who is not the person's mother, of a person's own father. □ **beau-père; belle-mère**
'stepsister, 'stepbrother *nouns* a daughter or son of a person's step-father or step-mother. □ **demi-sœur/frère**
'stepson, 'stepdaughter, 'stepchild *nouns* a son or daughter from another marriage of a person's wife or husband. □ **beau-fils; belle-fille**

steppe [step] *noun* a dry, grassy plain, as in the southeast of Europe and in Asia. □ **steppe**

stereo ['steriou] *adjective* short for **stereophonic** or **steroscopic**: *a stereo recording*. □ **stéréo**
■ *noun* **1** stereophonic equipment, *especially* a record player: *Have you got* (a) *stereo?* □ **stéréo**
2 stereophonic sound or stereoscopic vision: *recorded/ filmed in stereo*. □ **chaîne**

stereophonic [steriə'fonik] *adjective* **1** (of recorded or broadcast sound) giving the effect of coming from different directions, and *usually* requiring two loudspeakers placed apart from each other. □ **stéréophonique**
2 (of equipment, apparatus *etc*) intended for recording or playing such sound. □ **stéréophonique**

stereoscopic [steriə'skopik] *adjective* (of films, pictures *etc*) filmed, shown *etc* by an apparatus taking or showing two photographs at different angles, so that a three-dimensional image is produced. □ **stéréoscopique**

stereotype ['steəːoutaip] *noun* the standard or typical idea, usually exaggerated, of what a person is supposed to be like: *Carrying maps and several cameras, Kim was the stereotype of a tourist*. □ **stéréotype**

sterile ['sterail] *adjective* **1** (of soil, plants, humans and other animals) unable to produce crops, seeds, children or young. □ **stérile**
2 free from germs: *A surgeon's equipment must be absolutely sterile*. □ **stérile**
ste'rility [-'ri-] *noun*. □ **stérilité**
'sterilize, 'sterilise [-ri-] *verb* **1** to make (a woman *etc*) sterile. □ **stériliser**
2 to kill germs in (*eg* milk) or on (*eg* surgical instruments) by boiling. □ **stériliser**
,sterili'zation, ,sterili'sation *noun*. □ **stérilisation**

sterling ['stəːliŋ] *noun* British money, *especially* in international trading *etc*. □ **livre sterling**
■ *adjective* **1** (of silver) of a certain standard of purity. □ **fin, de bon aloi**
2 (of a person or his qualities *etc*) worthy and admirable. □ **de confiance**

stern[1] [stəːn] *adjective* harsh, severe or strict: *The teacher looked rather stern*; *stern discipline*. □ **sévère**
'sternly *adverb*. □ **sévèrement**
'sternness *noun*. □ **sévérité**

stern[2] [stəːn] *noun* the back part of a ship. □ **poupe**

stethoscope ['steθəskoup] *noun* an instrument by which a doctor can listen to the beats of the heart *etc*. □ **stéthoscope**

stevedore ['stiːvədoː] *noun* a person who loads and unloads ships; a docker. □ **débardeur, euse**

stew [stjuː] *verb* to cook (meat, fruit *etc*) by slowly boiling and simmering: *She stewed apples*; *The meat was* *stewing in the pan.* □ **mijoter**

■ *noun* (a dish of) stewed meat *etc*: *I've made some beef stew.* □ **ragoût**

steward ['stjuad] – *feminine* '**stewardess** – *noun* **1** a passenger's attendant on ship or airplane: *an air stewardess.* □ **steward, hôtesse**

2 a person who helps to arrange, and is an official at, races, entertainments *etc*. □ **organisateur, trice**

3 a person who supervises the supply of food and stores in a club, on a ship *etc*. □ **agent, ente aux vivres**

4 a person who manages an estate or farm for another person. □ **intendant, ante**

stick¹ [stik] – *past tense, past participle* **stuck** [stʌk] – *verb* **1** to push (something sharp or pointed) into or through something: *She stuck a pin through the papers to hold them together*; *Stop sticking your elbow into me!* □ **enfoncer**

2 (of something pointed) to be pushed into or through something: *Two arrows were sticking in his back.* □ **transpercer**

3 to fasten or be fastened (by glue, gum *etc*): *He licked the flap of the envelope and stuck it down*; *These labels don't stick very well*; *She stuck (the broken pieces of) the vase together again*; *His brothers used to call him Bonzo and the name has stuck.* □ **coller**

4 to (cause to) become fixed and unable to move or progress: *The car stuck in the mud*; *The cupboard door has stuck*; *I'll help you with your arithmetic if you're stuck.* □ **se coincer**

'**sticker** *noun* an adhesive label or sign bearing *eg* a design, political message *etc*, for sticking *eg* on a car's window *etc*: *The car sticker read 'Blood donors needed'.* □ **autocollant**

'**sticky** *adjective* **1** able, or likely, to stick or adhere to other surfaces: *I mended the torn book with sticky tape*; *sticky sweets.* □ **collant**

2 (of a situation or person) difficult; awkward. □ **épineux**

'**stickily** *adverb*. □ **de manière collante**

'**stickiness** *noun*. □ **caractère collant**

'**sticking-plaster** *see* **plaster**.

'**stick-in-the-mud** *noun* a person who never does anything new. □ **encroûté, ée**

come to a sticky end to have an unpleasant fate or death. □ **finir mal**

stick at to persevere with (work *etc*): *He must learn to stick at his job.* □ **s'acharner à**

stick by to support or be loyal to (a person): *Her friends stuck by her when she was in trouble.* □ **soutenir**

stick it out to endure a situation for as long as necessary. □ **tenir le coup**

stick out 1 to (cause to) project: *His front teeth stick out*; *He stuck out his tongue.* □ **(se) sortir**

2 to be noticeable: *She has red hair that sticks out in a crowd.* □ **(se) sortir**

stick one's neck out to take a risk. □ **trop s'avancer**

stick to/with not to abandon: *We've decided to stick to our previous plan*; *If you stick to me, I'll stick to you.* □ **s'en tenir à**

stick together 1 to (cause to) be fastened together: *We'll stick the pieces together*; *The rice is sticking together.*

□ **coller (ensemble)**

2 (of friends *etc*) to remain loyal to each other: *They've stuck together all these years.* □ **se serrer les coudes**

stick up for to speak in defence of (a person *etc*): *When my father is angry with me, my mother always sticks up for me.* □ **prendre le parti de**

stick² [stik] *noun* **1** a branch or twig from a tree: *They were sent to find sticks for firewood.* □ **brindille**

2 a long thin piece of wood *etc* shaped for a special purpose: *She always walks with a stick nowadays*; *a walking-stick/hockey-stick*; *a drumstick*; *candlesticks.* □ **canne; baguette, etc.**

3 a long piece: *a stick of rhubarb.* □ **tige**

get (hold of) the wrong end of the stick to misunderstand a situation, something said *etc*. □ **mal comprendre**

sticky *see* **stick¹**.

stiff [stif] *adjective* **1** rigid or firm, and not easily bent, folded *etc*: *He has walked with a stiff leg since he injured his knee*; *stiff cardboard.* □ **raide**

2 moving, or moved, with difficulty, pain *etc*: *I can't turn the key – the lock is stiff*; *I woke up with a stiff neck*; *I felt stiff the day after the climb.* □ **dur; raide**

3 (of a cooking mixture *etc*) thick, and not flowing: *a stiff dough.* □ **consistant**

4 difficult to do: *a stiff examination.* □ **difficile**

5 strong: *a stiff breeze.* □ **fort**

6 (of a person or his manner *etc*) formal and unfriendly: *I received a stiff note from the bank manager.* □ **froid**

'**stiffly** *adverb*. □ **avec raideur**

'**stiffness** *noun*. □ **raideur**

'**stiffen** *verb* to make or become stiff(er): *You can stiffen cotton with starch*; *He stiffened when he heard the unexpected sound.* □ **(se) raidir**

'**stiffening** *noun* material used to stiffen something: *The collar has some stiffening in it.* □ **empois**

bore, scare stiff to bore or frighten very much. □ **ennuyer à mourir; faire une peur bleue à**

stifle ['staifl] *verb* **1** to prevent, or be prevented, from breathing (easily) *eg* because of bad air, an obstruction over the mouth and nose *etc*; to suffocate: *She was stifled to death when smoke filled her bedroom*; *I'm stifling in this heat!* □ **étouffer**

2 to extinguish or put out (flames). □ **étouffer**

3 to suppress (a yawn, a laugh *etc*). □ **réprimer**

'**stifling** *adjective* very hot, stuffy *etc*: *stifling heat*; *It's stifling in here.* □ **étouffant, irrespirable**

stile [stail] *noun* a step, or set of steps, for climbing over a wall or fence. □ **échalier**

still¹ [stil] *adjective* **1** without movement or noise: *The city seems very still in the early morning*; *Please stand/sit/keep/hold still while I brush your hair!*; *still (= calm) water/weather.* □ **immobile, tranquille**

2 (of drinks) not fizzy: *still orange juice.* □ **non gazeux**

■ *noun* a photograph selected from a cinema film: *The magazine contained some stills from the new film.* □ **photo**

'**stillness** *noun*. □ **calme**

'**stillborn** *adjective* dead when born: *a stillborn baby.* □ **mort-né**

'**still life** *noun* the representation in a photograph or painting of one or more non-living objets: *The artist painted the still life of fruit in a bowl.* □ **nature morte**

still² [stil] *adverb* **1** up to and including the present time, or the time mentioned previously: *Are you still working for the same firm?*; *By Saturday she had still not/still hadn't replied to my letter.* □ **encore**

2 nevertheless; in spite of that: *Although the doctor told him to rest, he still went on working*; *This picture is not valuable – still, I like it.* □ **quand/tout de même**

3 even: *She seemed very ill in the afternoon and in the evening looked still worse.* □ **encore**

stilts [stilts] *noun plural* **1** a pair of poles with supports for the feet, on which a person may stand and so walk raised off the ground. □ **échasses**

2 tall poles fixed under a house *etc* to support it *eg* if it is built on a steep hillside. □ **pilotis**

stimulant ['stimjulənt] *noun* something, *eg* a medicine, drink *etc* that makes one more alert: *tea, coffee and other stimulants.* □ **stimulant**

stimulate ['stimjuleit] *verb* to rouse or make more alert, active *etc*: *After listening to the violin concerto, he felt stimulated to practise the violin again.* □ **stimuler** ,stimu'lation *noun.* □ **stimulation**
'stimulating *adjective* rousing; very interesting: *a stimulating discussion.* □ **stimulant**

stimulus ['stimjuləs] – *plural* 'stimuli [-liː] – *noun* **1** something that causes a reaction in a living thing: *Light is the stimulus that causes a flower to open.* □ **stimulus**

2 something that rouses or encourages a person *etc* to action or greater effort: *Many people think that children need the stimulus of competition to make them work better in school.* □ **stimulation**

sting [stiŋ] *noun* **1** a part of some plants, insects *etc, eg* nettles and wasps, that can prick and inject an irritating or poisonous fluid into the wound. □ **piquant, dard**

2 an act of piercing with this part: *Some spiders give a poisonous sting.* □ **piqûre**

3 the wound, swelling, or pain caused by this: *You can soothe a wasp sting by putting vinegar on it.* □ **piqûre**

■ *verb – past tense, past participle* stung [stʌŋ] – **1** to wound or hurt by means of a sting: *The child was badly stung by nettles*; *Do those insects sting?* □ **piquer**

2 (of a wound, or a part of the body) to smart or be painful: *The salt water made his eyes sting.* □ **brûler**

stingy ['stindʒi] *adjective* mean or ungenerous: *My father's very stingy with his money*; *stingy portions of food.* □ **avare; chiche**
'stingily *adverb.* □ **chichement**
'stinginess *noun.* □ **avarice**

stink [stiŋk] – *past tense* stank [staŋk]: *past participle* stunk [stʌŋk] – *verb* to have a very bad smell: *That fish stinks*; *The house stinks of cats.* □ **puer**

■ *noun* a very bad smell: *What a stink!* □ **puanteur**

stir [stəː] – *past tense, past participle* stirred – *verb* **1** to cause (a liquid *etc*) to be mixed *especially* by the constant circular movement of a spoon *etc*, in order to mix it: *He put sugar and milk into his tea and stirred it*; *She stirred the sugar into the mixture.* □ **brasser**

2 to move, either slightly or vigorously: *The breeze stirred her hair*; *He stirred in his sleep*; *Come on – stir*

yourselves! □ **remuer**

3 to arouse or touch (a person or his feelings): *He was stirred by her story.* □ **remuer**

■ *noun* a fuss or disturbance: *The news caused a stir.* □ **agitation**

'stirring *adjective* exciting: *a stirring tale.* □ **passionnant**

stir up to cause (trouble *etc*): *He was trying to stir up trouble at the factory.* □ **faire de l'agitation**

stirrups ['stɔːrəps] *noun plural* a pair of metal loops hanging on straps from a horse's saddle, to support a rider's feet. □ **étriers**

stitch [stitʃ] *noun* **1** a loop made in thread, wool *etc* by a needle in sewing or knitting: *He sewed the hem with small, neat stitches*; *Bother! I've dropped a stitch.* □ **point; maille**

2 a type of stitch forming a particular pattern in sewing, knitting *etc*: *The cloth was edged in blanket stitch*; *The jersey was knitted in stocking stitch.* □ **point; maille**

3 a sharp pain in a person's side caused by *eg* running: *I've got a stitch.* □ **point de côté**

■ *verb* to sew or put stitches into: *He stitched the two pieces together*; *I stitched the button on.* □ **coudre**

'stitching *noun* stitches: *The stitching is very untidy.* □ **couture**

in stitches laughing a lot: *Her stories kept us in stitches.* □ **(rire) à se tordre**

stitch up to close by stitching: *The doctor stitched up the wound.* □ **(re)coudre; suturer**

stock [stok] *noun* **1** (*often in plural*) a store of goods in a shop, warehouse *etc*: *Buy while stocks last!*; *The tools you require are in/out of stock* (= available/not available). □ **stock**

2 a stock of something: *We bought a large stock of food for the camping trip.* □ **provision**

3 farm animals: *She would like to purchase more* (live) *stock.* □ **bétail**

4 (*often in plural*) money lent to the government or to a business company at a fixed interest: *government stock*; *He has $20,000 in stocks and shares.* □ **titre; action**

5 liquid obtained by boiling meat, bones *etc* and used for making soup *etc*. □ **bouillon**

6 the handle of a whip, rifle *etc*. □ **manche; crosse**

■ *adjective* common; usual: *stock sizes of shoes.* □ **courant**

■ *verb* **1** to keep a supply of for sale: *Does this shop stock writing paper?* □ **avoir en stock**

2 to supply (a shop, farm *etc*) with goods, animals *etc*: *She cannot afford to stock her farm.* □ **monter**

stocks *noun plural* **1** the wooden framework upon which a ship is supported when being built, repaired *etc*. □ **cale**

2 formerly a wooden frame in which a criminal was fastened as a punishment. □ **pilori**

'stockbroker *noun* a person who buys and sells stocks and shares for others. □ **courtier en valeurs mobilières**

stock exchange a place where stocks and shares are bought and sold. □ **Bourse (des valeurs)**

stock market a stock exchange, or the dealings on that. □ **marché financier**

'**stockpile** *noun* a supply of goods or materials accumulated *eg* by a government in case of war or other emergency. □ **stock de réserve**

■ *verb* to accumulate (a supply of this sort). □ **stocker**

,**stock-'still** *adjective, adverb* motionless: *He stood absolutely stock-still.* □ **cloué sur place**

'**stock-taking** *noun* a regular check of the goods in a shop, warehouse *etc*. □ **prise d'inventaire**

stock up to accumulate a supply of (something): *The girls were stocking up on/with chocolate and lemonade for their walk.* □ **faire des provisions de**

take stock to form an opinion (about a situation *etc*): *Before you decide, give yourself time to take stock (of the situation).* □ **faire le point (de)**

stockade [sto'keid] *noun* a fence of strong posts put up around an area for defence. □ **palissade**

stockbroker *see* **stock**.

stocking ['stokiŋ] *noun* one of a pair of close-fitting coverings for the legs and feet, reaching to or above the knee: *Most women prefer tights to stockings nowadays.* □ **bas**

stockpile *see* **stock**.

stocky ['stoki] *adjective* (of a person *etc*) short, often rather stout and *usually* strong: *a stocky little boy.* □ **trapu**

'**stockily** *adverb*. □ **trapu**

'**stockiness** *noun*. □ **aspect trapu**

stodge [stodʒ] *noun* heavy, solid food. □ **aliment bourratif**

'**stodgy** *adjective* 1 (of meals *etc*) consisting of stodge: *stodgy food.* □ **lourd**

2 (of people, books *etc*) dull; not lively. □ **sans imagination**

'**stodginess** *noun*. □ **lourdeur**

stoke [stouk] *verb* to put coal or other fuel on (a fire) *eg* in the furnace of a boiler *etc*: *They stoked the furnaces.* □ **alimenter**

'**stoker** *noun*. □ **chauffeur**

stoke up to stoke: *Have they stoked up (the fires)?* □ **alimenter (une chaudière)**

stole, stolen *see* **steal**.

stolid ['stolid] *adjective* (of a person *etc*) not easily excited and rather dull. □ **flegmatique**

sto'lidity *noun*. □ **flegme**

'**stolidness** *noun*. □ **flegme**

'**stolidly** *adverb*. □ **flegmatiquement**

stomach ['stʌmək] *noun* 1 the bag-like organ in the body into which food passes when swallowed, and where most of it is digested. □ **estomac**

2 the part of the body between the chest and thighs; the belly: *a pain in the stomach.* □ **ventre**

'**stomach ache** *noun* a pain in the belly. □ **mal de ventre**

stomp [stomp] *verb* to stamp or tread heavily. □ **marcher d'un pas lourd et bruyant**

stone [stoun] *noun* 1 (*also adjective*) (of) the material of which rocks are composed: *limestone; sandstone; a stone house; stone walls; In early times, men made tools out of stone.* □ **(de) pierre**

2 a piece of this, of any shape or size: *She threw a stone*

at the dog. □ **pierre**

3 a piece of this shaped for a special purpose: *a tombstone; paving-stones; a grindstone.* □ **pierre; pavé; meule (à aiguiser)**

4 a gem or jewel: *She lost the stone out of her ring; diamonds, rubies and other stones.* □ **pierre**

5 the hard shell containing the nut or seed in some fruits *eg* peaches and cherries: *a cherry-stone.* □ **noyau, pépin**

6 a piece of hard material that forms in the kidney, bladder *etc* and causes pain. □ **calcul**

■ *verb* 1 to throw stones at, *especially* as a ritual punishment: *Saint Stephen was stoned to death.* □ **lapider**

2 to remove the stones from (fruit): *He washed and stoned the cherries.* □ **dénoyauter**

'**stony** *adjective* 1 full of, or covered with, stones: *stony soil; a stony path/beach; It's very stony around here.* □ **rocailleux**

2 (of a person's expression *etc*) like stone in coldness, hardness *etc*: *She gave me a stony stare.* □ **glacial**

'**stonily** *adverb*. □ **froidement**

'**stoniness** *noun*. □ **nature pierreuse, dureté**

,**stone-'cold**, ,**stone-'dead**, ,**stone-'deaf** *adjective* completely cold, dead, or deaf: *He's almost stone-deaf; Your soup is stone-cold.* □ **complètement froid; raide mort; sourd comme un pot**

'**stoneware** *noun, adjective* (of) a hard type of pottery made of clay containing pieces of stone: *a stoneware jug.* □ **(de) grès**

'**stonework** *noun* construction done in stone, *especially* the stone parts of a building. □ **maçonnerie**

leave no stone unturned to try every possible means: *The police left no stone unturned to (try to) find the child.* □ **remuer ciel et terre (pour)**

a stone's throw a very short distance: *They live only a stone's throw away from here.* □ **à deux pas (de)**

stood *see* **stand**.

stooge [stuːdʒ] *noun* 1 a comedian's assistant who is made the object of all his jokes. □ **faire-valoir**

2 a person who is used by another to do humble or unpleasant jobs. □ **laquais**

stool [stuːl] *noun* a seat without a back: *a piano stool; a kitchen stool.* □ **tabouret**

fall between two stools to lose both of two possibilities by hesitating between them or trying for both. □ **s'asseoir entre deux chaises**

stoop [stuːp] *verb* 1 to bend the body forward and downward: *The doorway was so low that he had to stoop (his head) to go through it; She stooped down to talk to the child.* □ **se baisser**

2 to lower one's (moral) standards by doing something: *Surely she wouldn't stoop to cheating!* □ **s'abaisser à**

■ *noun* a stooping position of the body, shoulder *etc*: *Many people develop a stoop as they grow older.* □ **dos rond**

stooped *adjective*: *stooped shoulders; He is stooped with age.* □ **voûté**

stop [stop] – *past tense, past participle* **stopped** – *verb* 1 to (make something) cease moving, or come to rest, a halt *etc*: *She stopped the car and got out; This train does not stop at Birmingham; She stopped to look at* the map; *She signalled with her hand to stop the bus.* □ **(s') arrêter**

2 to prevent from doing something: *We must stop him (from) going; I was going to say something rude but stopped myself just in time.* □ **empêcher**

3 to discontinue or cease *eg* doing something: *You just can't stop talking; The rain has stopped; It has stopped raining.* □ **s'arrêter**

4 to block or close: *He stopped his ears with his hands when I started to shout at him.* □ **(se) boucher**

5 to close (a hole, *eg* on a flute) or press down (a string on a violin *etc*) in order to play a particular note. □ **boucher; presser**

6 to stay: *Will you be stopping long at the hotel?* □ **rester**

■ *noun* **1** an act of stopping or state of being stopped: *We made only two stops on our journey; Work came to a stop for the day.* □ **arrêt; halte**

2 a place for *eg* a bus to stop: *a bus stop.* □ **arrêt**

3 in punctuation, a full stop: *Put a stop at the end of the sentence.* □ **point**

4 a device on a flute *etc* for covering the holes in order to vary the pitch, or knobs for bringing certain pipes into use on an organ. □ **clef**

5 a device, *eg* a wedge *etc*, for stopping the movement of something, or for keeping it in a fixed position: *a door-stop.* □ **taquet, butoir**

'stoppage [-pidʒ] *noun* (an) act of stopping or state or process of being stopped: *The building was at last completed after many delays and stoppages.* □ **interruption**

'stopper *noun* an object, *eg* a cork, that is put into the neck of a bottle, jar, hole *etc* to close it. □ **bouchon**

'stopping *noun* a filling in a tooth: *One of my stoppings has come out.* □ **plombage**

'stopcock *noun* a tap and valve for controlling flow of liquid through a pipe. □ **robinet d'arrêt**

'stop-gap *noun* a person or thing that fills a gap in an emergency: *He was made headmaster as a stopgap till a new man could be appointed; (also adjective) stopgap arrangements.* □ **bouche-trou; intérimaire**

'stopwatch *noun* a watch with a hand that can be stopped and started, used in timing a race *etc*. □ **chronomètre**

put a stop to to prevent from continuing: *We must put a stop to this waste.* □ **mettre un terme à**

stop at nothing to be willing to do anything, however dishonest *etc*, in order to get something: *He'll stop at nothing to get what he wants.* □ **ne reculer devant rien (pour)**

stop dead to stop completely: *I stopped dead when I saw her.* □ **s'arrêter net**

stop off to make a halt on a journey *etc*: *We stopped off at Edinburgh to see the castle.* □ **faire une (courte) halte**

stop over *verb* to make a stay of a night or more: *We're planning to stop over in Amsterdam.* □ **faire escale**

■ *noun* a short stay or break during a trip: *Joyce is flying from Montreal to Scotland with a two day stop over in England; Chuck needs to eat and use the washroom so he'll make a stop over at the next service station.* □ **escale**

storage *see* **store**.

store [stoɹ] *noun* **1** a supply of *eg* goods from which things are taken when required: *They took a store of dried and canned food on the expedition; The quartermaster is the officer in charge of stores.* □ **provisions**

2 a (large) collected amount or quantity: *She has a store of interesting facts in her head.* □ **fonds**

3 a place where a supply of goods *etc* is kept; a store-house or storeroom: *It's in the store(s).* □ **entrepôt**

4 a shop: *The post office here is also the village store; a department store.* □ **magasin**

■ *verb* **1** to put into a place for keeping: *We stored our furniture in the attic while the tenants used our house.* □ **entreposer**

2 to stock (a place *etc*) with goods *etc*: *The museum is stored with interesting exhibits.* □ **contenir**

'storage [-ridʒ] *noun* the act of storing or state of being stored: *We've put our furniture into storage at a warehouse; The meat will have to be kept in cold storage (= stored under refrigeration).* □ **entreposage**

'storehouse, 'storeroom *nouns* a place or room where goods *etc* are stored: *There is a storeroom behind the shop.* □ **entrepôt**

in store 1 kept or reserved for future use: *I keep plenty of tinned food in store for emergencies.* □ **en réserve**

2 coming in the future: *There's trouble in store for her!* □ **en réserve**

set (great) store by to value highly (*eg* a person's approval *etc*). □ **faire grand cas de**

storey (*plural* **'storeys**), **story** (*plural* **'stories**) ['stoɹri] *noun* one of the floors or levels in a building: *an apartment block of seventeen storeys.* □ **étage**

-storeyed, -storied: *A two-storied house is one with a ground floor and one floor above it.* □ **à/de (...) étages**

stork [stoɹk] *noun* a type of wading bird with long beak, neck and legs. □ **cigogne**

storm [stoɹm] *noun* **1** a violent disturbance in the air causing wind, rain, thunder *etc*: *a rainstorm; a thunderstorm; a storm at sea; The roof was damaged by the storm.* □ **orage; tempête**

2 a violent outbreak of feeling *etc*: *A storm of anger greeted his speech; a storm of applause.* □ **tempête**

■ *verb* **1** to shout very loudly and angrily: *He stormed at her.* □ **tempêter contre qqn**

2 to move or stride in an angry manner: *He stormed out of the room.* □ **aller furieusement**

3 (of soldiers *etc*) to attack with great force, and capture (a building *etc*): *They stormed the castle.* □ **prendre d'assaut**

'stormy *adjective* **1** having a lot of strong wind, heavy rain *etc*: *a stormy day; stormy weather; a stormy voyage.* □ **orageux**

2 full of anger or uncontrolled feeling: *in a stormy mood; a stormy discussion.* □ **violent, orageux**

'stormily *adverb*. □ **orageusement**

'storminess *noun*. □ **caractère orageux**

'stormbound *adjective* prevented by storms from continuing with a voyage, receiving regular supplies *etc*: *stormbound ships.* □ **bloqué par la tempête**

'stormtrooper *noun* a soldier specially trained for violent and dangerous attacks. □ **soldat des troupes**

d'assaut
a storm in a teacup a fuss made over an unimportant matter. □ **une tempête dans un verre d'eau**
take by storm to capture by means of a sudden violent attack: *The invaders took the city by storm.* □ **prendre d'assaut**

story¹ ['stoːri] – *plural* 'stories – *noun* **1** an account of an event, or series of events, real or imaginary: *the story of the disaster; the story of his life; He went to the police with his story; What sort of stories do boys aged 10 like?; adventure/murder/love stories; a storybook; She's a good storyteller.* □ **histoire**
2 (used *especially* to children) a lie: *Don't tell stories!* □ **histoire**
the story goes people say: *He has been in jail or so the story goes.* □ **à ce qu'on dit**
a tall story an obviously untrue story; a lie. □ **histoire invraisemblable**

story² see storey.

stout¹ [staut] *adjective* **1** strong or thick: *a stout stick.* □ **solide**
2 brave and resolute: *stout resistance; stout opposition.* □ **énergique**
3 fat: *He's getting stout.* □ **corpulent**
,stout-'hearted *adjective* brave. □ **intrépide**

stout² [staut] *adjective* a dark, strong type of beer. □ **stout**

stove [stouv] *noun* an apparatus using coal, gas, electricity or other fuel, used for cooking, or for heating a room: *a gas/electric (cooking) stove; Put the saucepan on the stove.* □ **cuisinière, poêle**

stow [stou] *verb* to pack neatly and *especially* out of sight: *The sailor stowed his belongings in his locker.* □ **ranger**
'stowaway *noun* a person who stows away: *They found a stowaway on the ship.* □ **passager, ère clandestin, ine**
stow away **1** to hide oneself on a ship, aircraft *etc* before its departure, in order to travel on it without paying the fare: *She stowed away on a cargo ship for New York.* □ **voyager clandestinement**
2 to put or pack in a (secret) place until required: *My jewellery is safely stowed away in the bank.* □ **ranger**

straggle ['stragl] *verb* **1** to grow or spread untidily: *His beard straggled over his chest.* □ **pousser/tomber en désordre**
2 to walk too slowly to remain with a body of *eg* marching soldiers, walkers *etc.* □ **traîner en arrière**
'straggler *noun* a person who walks too slowly during a march *etc* and gets left behind: *A car was sent to pick up the stragglers.* □ **traînard, arde**
'straggly *adjective* straggling untidily: *straggly hair.* □ **en désordre**
'straggliness *noun.* □ **caractère désordonné**

straight [streit] *adjective* **1** not bent or curved: *a straight line; straight (= not curly) hair; That line is not straight.* □ **droit; raide**
2 (of a person, his behaviour *etc*) honest, frank and direct: *Give me a straight answer!* □ **franc**
3 properly or levelly positioned: *Your tie isn't straight.* □ **droit**
4 correct and tidy: *I'll never get this house straight!;*

Now let's get the facts straight! □ **en ordre; clairement**
5 (of drinks) not mixed: *a straight gin.* □ **sans eau, sec**
6 (of a face, expression *etc*) not smiling or laughing: *You should keep a straight face while you tell a joke.* □ **impassible**
7 (of an actor) playing normal characters, or (of a play) of the ordinary type – not a musical or variety show. □ **dramatique**
■ *adverb* **1** in a straight, not curved, line; directly: *Her route went straight across the desert; He can't steer straight; Keep straight on.* □ **(tout) droit; directement**
2 immediately, without any delay: *He went straight home after the meeting.* □ **tout droit**
3 honestly or fairly: *You're not playing (= behaving) straight.* □ **franc-jeu**
■ *noun* the straight part of something, *eg* of a racecourse: *She's in the final straight.* □ **ligne droite**
'straighten *verb* to make or become straight: *He straightened his tie; The road curved and then straightened.* □ **(re)mettre d'aplomb; devenir droit**
'straightness *noun.* □ **rectitude**
straight'forward *adjective* **1** without difficulties or complications; simple: *a straightforward task.* □ **simple**
2 (of a person, his manner *etc*) frank and honest: *a nice straightforward boy.* □ **honnête**
straight'forwardly *adverb.* □ **franchement**
straight'forwardness *noun.* □ **franchise**
straight talking frank discussion. □ **franc-parler**
go straight (of a former criminal) to lead an honest life. □ **rester dans le droit chemin**
straight away immediately: *Do it straight away!* □ **tout de suite**
straighten out/up: *Their house is where the lane straightens out; He was bending over his work, but straightened up when he saw me; He straightened the room up; She's trying to straighten out the facts.* □ **devenir droit; se redresser; ranger; démêler**
a straight fight an election contest involving only two candidates. □ **duel (électoral)**
straight off straight away. □ **tout de suite**

strain¹ [strein] *verb* **1** to exert oneself or a part of the body to the greatest possible extent: *He strained his ears to hear the whisper; They strained at the door, trying to pull it open; He strained to reach the rope.* □ **tendre fortement**
2 to injure (a muscle *etc*) through too much use, exertion *etc*: *He has strained a muscle in his leg; You'll strain your eyes by reading in such a poor light.* □ **forcer**
3 to force or stretch (too far): *The constant interruptions were straining his patience.* □ **pousser à bout**
4 to put (*eg* a mixture) through a sieve *etc* in order to separate solid matter from liquid: *He strained the coffee.* □ **passer, filtrer**
■ *noun* **1** force exerted: *Can nylon ropes take more strain than the old kind of rope?* □ **traction, tension**
2 (something, *eg* too much work *etc*, that causes) a state of anxiety and fatigue: *The strain of nursing her dying husband was too much for her; to suffer from strain.* □ **tension (nerveuse)**

3 (an) injury *especially* to a muscle caused by too much exertion: *muscular strain*. □ **entorse, foulure**

4 too great a demand: *These constant delays are a strain on our patience*. □ **tension**

strained *adjective* (of a person's manner, behaviour *etc*) not natural, easy or relaxed: *a strained smile*. □ **forcé**

'**strainer** *noun* a sieve or other utensil for separating solids from liquids: *a coffee-/tea-strainer*. □ **passoire**

strain off to remove (liquid) from *eg* vegetables by using a sieve *etc*: *When the potatoes were cooked, she strained off the water*. □ **égoutter**

strain² [strein] *noun* **1** a kind or breed (of animals, plants *etc*): *a new strain of cattle*. □ **race**

2 a tendency in a person's character: *I'm sure there's a strain of madness in you*. □ **prédisposition à**

3 (*often in plural*) (the sound of) a tune: *I heard the strains of a hymn coming from the church*. □ **accords, accents**

strait [streit] *noun* **1** (*often in plural*) a narrow strip of sea between two pieces of land: *the straits of Gibraltar*; *the Bering Strait*. □ **détroit**

2 (*in plural*) difficulty; (financial) need. □ **ennuis d'argent**

'**straitjacket** *noun* a type of jacket with long sleeves tied behind to hold back the arms of *eg* a violent and insane person. □ **camisole de force**

,**strait'laced** *adjective* strict and severe in attitude and behaviour. □ **collet monté**

strand¹ [strand]: **be stranded 1** (of a ship) to go aground: *The ship was stranded on the rocks*. □ **être échoué**

2 (*also* **be left stranded**) to be left helpless without *eg* money or friends: *She was left stranded in Yugoslavia without her money or her passport*. □ **abandonner sans ressources**

strand² [strand] *noun* a thin thread, *eg* one of those twisted together to form rope, string, knitting-wool *etc*, or a long thin lock of hair: *She pushed the strands of hair back from her face*. □ **brin; mèche**

strange [streindʒ] *adjective* **1** not known, seen *etc* before; unfamiliar or foreign: *What would you do if you found a strange man in your house?*; *Whenever you're in a strange country, you should take the opportunity of learning the language*. □ **inconnu; étranger**

2 unusual, odd or queer: *She had a strange look on her face*; *a strange noise*. □ **bizarre, étrange**

'**strangely** *adverb*. □ **bizarrement, étrangement**

'**strangeness** *noun*. □ **bizarrerie**

'**stranger** *noun* **1** a person who is unknown to oneself: *I've met her once before, so she's not a complete stranger (to me)*. □ **étranger, ère**

2 a visitor: *I can't tell you where the post office is – I'm a stranger here myself*. □ **visiteur, euse**

strange to say/tell/relate surprisingly: *Strange to say, he did pass his exam after all*. □ **chose étrange**

strangely enough it is strange (that): *He lives next door, but strangely enough I rarely see him*. □ **chose étrange**

strangle ['straŋgl] *verb* to kill by gripping or squeezing the neck tightly, *eg* by tightening a cord *etc* around it: *He strangled her with a nylon stocking*; *This top button is nearly strangling me!* □ **étrangler**

,**strangu'lation** [-gju-] *noun*. □ **strangulation**

strap [strap] *noun* **1** a narrow strip of leather, cloth, or other material, *eg* with a buckle for fastening something (*eg* a suitcase, wristwatch *etc*) or by which to hold, hang or support something (*eg* a camera, rucksack *etc*): *I need a new watch-strap*; *luggage straps*. □ **courroie**

2 a short looped strip of leather *etc*, hanging from the roof of a train, by which a standing passenger can support himself. □ **poignée (de cuir)**

■ *verb – past tense, past participle* **strapped** – **1** to beat (*eg* a schoolchild) on the hand with a leather strap: *He was strapped for being rude to the teacher*. □ **administrer une correction à**

2 to fasten with a strap *etc*: *The two pieces of luggage were strapped together*; *She strapped on her new watch*. □ **attacher**

'**strapping** *adjective* large and strong: *a big strapping girl*. □ **costaud**

strap in to confine with a strap, *eg* by a safety belt in a car: *I won't start this car till you've strapped yourself in*. □ **attacher (avec une sangle/ceinture)**

strap up to fasten or bind with a strap, bandage *etc*: *His injured knee was washed and neatly strapped up*. □ **bander**

stratagem ['stratədʒəm] *noun* a trick or plan. □ **stratagème**

strategy ['stratədʒi] – *plural* '**strategies** – *noun* **1** the art of planning a campaign or large military operation: *military strategy*. □ **stratégie**

2 the art of, or a scheme for, managing an affair cleverly. □ **stratégie**

stra'tegic [-'tiː-] *adjective*. □ **stratégique**

stra'tegically *adverb*. □ **stratégiquement**

'**strategist** *noun* a person who is an expert in strategy. □ **stratège**

straw [strɔː] *noun* **1** (*also adjective*) (of) the cut stalks of corn *etc*, having many uses, *eg* as bedding for cattle *etc*, making mats and other goods *etc*: *The cows need fresh straw*; *a straw hat*. □ **(de) paille**

2 a single stalk of corn: *There's a straw in your hair*; *Their offer isn't worth a straw!* □ **paille**

3 a paper or plastic tube through which to suck a drink into the mouth: *He was sipping orange juice through a straw*. □ **paille**

the last straw an additional and intolerable circumstance in a disagreeable situation: *The hotel was expensive, the food poor, and the bad weather was the last straw*. □ **la goutte d'eau qui fait déborder le vase**

strawberry ['strɔːbəri] – *plural* '**strawberries** – *noun* a type of small juicy red fruit. □ **fraise**

stray [strei] *verb* to wander, *especially* from the right path, place *etc*: *The shepherd went to search for some sheep that had strayed*; *to stray from the point*. □ **s'écarter de**

■ *noun* a cat, dog *etc* that has strayed and has no home. □ **(animal) errant**

■ *adjective* **1** wandering or lost: *stray cats and dogs*. □ **errant**

2 occasional, or not part of a general group or tendency: *The sky was clear except for one or two stray* *clouds.* □ **isolé**

streak [striːk] *noun* **1** a long, irregular mark or stripe: *There was a streak of blood on her cheek; a streak of lightning.* □ **filet**

2 a trace of some quality in a person's character *etc: He has a streak of selfishness.* □ **tendance à**

■ *verb* **1** to mark with streaks: *Her dark hair was streaked with grey; The child's face was streaked with tears.* □ **sillonné de**

2 to move very fast: *The runner streaked around the racetrack.* □ **passer comme un éclair**

'**streaky** *adjective* marked with streaks. □ **marbré**

stream [striːm] *noun* **1** a small river or brook: *He managed to jump across the stream.* □ **ruisseau**

2 a flow of *eg* water, air *etc: A stream of water was pouring down the gutter; A stream of people was coming out of the cinema; He got into the wrong stream of traffic and uttered a stream of curses.* □ **flot**

3 the current of a river *etc: He was swimming against the stream.* □ **courant**

4 in schools, one of the classes into which children of the same age are divided according to ability. □ **classe de niveau**

■ *verb* **1** to flow: *Tears streamed down his face; Workers streamed out of the factory gates; Her hair streamed out in the wind.* □ **ruisseler; sortir à flots; flotter au vent**

2 to divide schoolchildren into classes according to ability: *Many people disapprove of streaming (children) in schools.* □ **répartir par niveau**

'**streamer** *noun* a long narrow banner, or narrow paper ribbon: *The airplane dragged a streamer that read 'Come to the Festival'; The classroom was decorated with balloons and streamers.* □ **banderole**

'**streamlined** *adjective* **1** (of a plane, car, ship *etc*) shaped so as to move faster and more efficiently: *the newest, most streamlined aircraft.* □ **aérodynamique**

2 efficient and economical: *stream lined business methods.* □ **rationalisé**

street [striːt] *noun* **1** a road with houses, shops *etc* on one or both sides, in a town or village: *the main shopping street; I met her in the street.* □ **rue**

2 (*abbreviated to* **St** *when written*) used in the names of certain roads: *Her address is 4 Shakespeare St.* □ **rue**

'**streetcar** *noun* a tramcar. □ **tramway**

street directory a booklet giving an index and plans of a city's streets. □ **répertoire/index des rues**

street lamp a public light, usually on a tall pole, that shines on the sidewalk and road: *The street lamp was broken and the whole block was in darkness.* □ **lampadaire**

be streets ahead of/better than to be much better than. □ **de loin/beaucoup**

be up someone's street to be exactly suitable for someone: *That job is just up her street.* □ **dans les cordes de**

not to be in the same street as to be completely different, *usually* worse, in quality than. □ **ne pas arriver à la cheville de**

strength, strengthen *see* **strong**.

strenuous ['strenjuəs] *adjective* energetic; requiring ef-

fort or energy: *a strenuous climb; a strenuous effort.* □ **fatigant; acharné**

'**strenuously** *adverb.* □ **vigoureusement**

stress [stres] *noun* **1** the worry experienced by a person in particular circumstances, or the state of anxiety caused by this: *the stresses of modern life; Her headaches may be caused by stress.* □ **stress**

2 force exerted by (parts of) bodies on each other: *Bridge-designers have to know about stress.* □ **tension**

3 force or emphasis placed, in speaking, on particular syllables or words: *In the word 'widow' we put stress on the first syllable.* □ **accent**

■ *verb* to emphasize (a syllable *etc*, or a fact *etc*): *Should you stress the last syllable in 'violin'?; She stressed the necessity of being punctual.* □ **accentuer**

'**stress-mark** *noun* a mark (') used to show where the stress comes in a word *etc: 'hookworm; de'signer.* □ **accent**

lay/put stress on to emphasize (a fact *etc*): *He laid stress on this point.* □ **insister sur**

stretch [stretʃ] *verb* **1** to make or become longer or wider especially by pulling or by being pulled: *She stretched the piece of elastic to its fullest extent; Her scarf was so long that it could stretch right across the room; This material stretches; The dog yawned and stretched (itself); He stretched (his arm/hand) up as far as he could, but still could not reach the shelf; Ask someone to pass you the jam instead of stretching across the table for it.* □ **(s')étirer**

2 (of land *etc*) to extend: *The plain stretched ahead of them for kilometres.* □ **s'étendre**

■ *noun* **1** an act of stretching or state of being stretched: *She got out of bed and had a good stretch.* □ **étirement**

2 a continuous extent, of *eg* a type of country, or of time: *a pretty stretch of country; a stretch of bad road; a stretch of twenty years.* □ **bout/partie; période**

'**stretcher** *noun* a light folding bed with handles for carrying the sick or wounded: *The injured man was carried to the ambulance on a stretcher.* □ **brancard, civière**

'**stretchy** *adjective* (of materials *etc*) able to stretch: *a stretchy bathing-costume.* □ **extensible**

at a stretch continuously: *I can't work for more than three hours at a stretch.* □ **d'affilée**

be at full stretch to be using all one's powers, energy *etc* to the limit in doing something. □ **donner son plein**

stretch one's legs to go for a walk for the sake of exercise: *I need to stretch my legs.* □ **se dégourdir les jambes**

stretch out in moving the body, to straighten or extend: *She stretched out a hand for the child to hold; He stretched (himself) out on the bed.* □ **(s')étendre**

strew [struː] *– past tense* **strewed;** *past participle* **strewn** *– verb* to scatter: *Rubbish was strewn about on the ground; The ground was strewn with rubbish.* □ **éparpiller**

stricken ['strikən] *adjective* deeply affected, overwhelmed or afflicted: *In his youth he was stricken with a crippling disease; grief-stricken parents; panic-stricken crowds.* □ **atteint/frappé (par)**

strict [strikt] *adjective* **1** severe, stern, and compelling obedience: *This class needs a strict teacher*; *His parents were very strict with him*; *The school rules are too strict*; *strict orders.* □ **sévère, strict**
2 exact or precise: *If the strict truth were known, I was drunk, not ill.* □ **strict**
'strictness *noun.* □ **rigueur**
'strictly *adverb.* □ **strictement**
strictly speaking if we must be completely accurate, act according to rules *etc*: *Strictly speaking, he should be punished for this.* □ **à proprement parler**
stride [straid] *past tense* **strode** [stroud]: *past participle* **stridden** ['stridn] – *verb* to walk with long steps: *He strode along the path*; *She strode off in anger.* □ **marcher à grands pas**
■ *noun* a long step: *He walked with long strides.* □ **grands pas**
make great strides to progress well: *She's making great strides in her piano-playing.* □ **faire de grands progrès**
take in one's stride to accept or cope with (a matter) successfully without worrying about it: *She takes difficulties in her stride.* □ **accepter avec équanimité**
strife [straif] *noun* conflict, fighting or quarrelling: *a country torn by strife*; *industrial strife* (= disagreement between employers and workers). □ **conflit**
strike [straik] – *past tense* **struck** [strʌk]: *past participles* **struck, stricken** ['strikən] – *verb* **1** to hit, knock or give a blow to: *He struck me in the face with his fist*; *Why did you strike him?*; *The stone struck me a blow on the side of the head*; *His head struck the table as he fell*; *The tower of the church was struck by lightning.* □ **frapper**
2 to attack: *The enemy troops struck at dawn*; *We must prevent the disease striking again.* □ **attaquer**
3 to produce (sparks or a flame) by rubbing: *She struck a match/light*; *He struck sparks from the stone with his knife.* □ **faire jaillir**
4 (of workers) to stop work as a protest, or in order to force employers to give better pay: *The men decided to strike for higher wages.* □ **faire grève**
5 to discover or find: *After months of prospecting they finally struck gold/oil*; *If we walk in this direction we may strike the right path.* □ **trouver**
6 to (make something) sound: *She struck a note on the piano/violin*; *The clock struck twelve.* □ **sonner**
7 to impress, or give a particular impression to (a person): *I was struck by the resemblance between the two men*; *How does the plan strike you?*; *It/The thought struck me that she had come to borrow money.* □ **frapper**
8 to mint or manufacture (a coin, medal *etc*). □ **frapper**
9 to go in a certain direction: *She left the path and struck (off) across the fields.* □ **prendre, aller**
10 to lower or take down (tents, flags *etc*). □ **démonter; amener**
■ *noun* **1** an act of striking: *a miners' strike.* □ **grève**
2 a discovery of oil, gold *etc*: *She made a lucky strike.* □ **découverte**
'striker *noun* **1** a worker who strikes. □ **gréviste**
2 in football, a forward player. □ **buteur**
'striking *adjective* noticeable or impressive: *She is tall*

and striking; *She wears striking clothes.* □ **frappant**
'strikingly *adverb.* □ **remarquablement**
be (out) on strike (of workers) to be striking: *The electricity workers are (out) on strike.* □ **être en grève**
call a strike (of a trade union leader *etc*) to ask workers to strike. □ **lancer un ordre de grève**
come out on strike (of workers) to strike. □ **se mettre en grève**
come, be within striking distance of to come very close to. □ **à portée de**
strike at to attempt to strike, or aim a blow at (a person *etc*): *He struck at the dog with his stick.* □ **chercher à frapper**
strike an attitude/pose to place oneself in a particular *usually* rather showy pose. □ **poser**
strike a balance to reach a satisfactory middle level of compromise between two undesirable extremes. □ **trouver le juste milieu (entre)**
strike a bargain/agreement to make a bargain; to reach an agreement. □ **conclure un marché**
strike a blow for to make an effort on behalf of (a cause *etc*). □ **rompre une lance pour**
strike down to hit or knock (a person) down: *She was struck down by a car/a terrible disease.* □ **terrasser**
strike dumb to amaze: *I was struck dumb at the news.* □ **rendre qqn muet**
strike fear/terror *etc* **into** to fill (a person) with fear *etc*: *The sound struck terror into them.* □ **terroriser**
strike home (of a blow, insult *etc*) to reach the place where it will hurt most. □ **toucher juste**
strike it rich to make a lot of money. □ **faire fortune**
strike lucky to have good luck in a particular matter. □ **jouer de chance**
strike out to erase or cross out (a word *etc*): *He read the essay and struck out a word here and there.* □ **rayer**
2 to start fighting: *He's a man who strikes out with his fists whenever he's angry.* □ **donner un coup**
strike up 1 to begin to play a tune: *The band struck up (with) 'The Red Flag'.* □ **commencer à jouer**
2 to begin (a friendship, conversation *etc*): *He struck up an acquaintance with a girl on the train.* □ **lier connaissance**
string [striŋ] *noun* **1** (a piece of) long narrow cord made of threads twisted together, or tape, for tying, fastening *etc*: *a piece of string to tie a parcel*; *a ball of string*; *a puppet's strings*; *apron-strings.* □ **ficelle**
2 a fibre *etc*, *eg* on a vegetable. □ **fil**
3 a piece of wire, gut *etc* on a musical instrument, *eg* a violin: *His A–string broke*; (*also adjective*) *She plays the viola in a string orchestra.* □ **(à) corde(s)**
4 a series or group of things threaded on a cord *etc*: *a string of beads.* □ **rang**
■ *verb* – *past tense, past participle* **strung** [strʌŋ] – **1** to put (beads *etc*) on a string *etc*: *The pearls were sent to a jeweller to be strung.* □ **enfiler**
2 to put a string or strings on (*eg* a bow or stringed instrument): *The archer strung her bow and aimed an arrow at the target.* □ **monter**
3 to remove strings from (vegetables *etc*). □ **enlever les fils de**

4 to tie and hang with string *etc*: *The farmer strung up the dead crows on the fence.* □ **suspendre**

strings *noun plural* (in an orchestra, the group of people who play) stringed instruments, *ie* violins, violas, cellos and double basses: *The conductor said the strings were too loud.* □ **cordes**

'**stringy** *adjective* (especially of meat or vegetables) having a lot of tough fibres. □ **filandreux**

'**stringiness** *noun.* □ **caractère filandreux**

string bean the long, edible green or yellow pod of certain beans. □ **haricot vert**

stringed instruments musical instruments that have strings *eg* violins, guitars *etc*. □ **instruments à cordes**

have (someone) on a string to have (a person) under one's control. □ **mener par le bout du nez**

pull strings to use one's influence or that of others to gain an advantage. □ **pistonner**

pull the strings to be the person who is really, though *usually* not apparently, controlling the actions of others. □ **tirer les ficelles**

string out to stretch into a long line: *The runners were strung out along the course.* □ **(s')échelonner**

stringent ['strindʒənt] *adjective* (of rules *etc*) very strict, or strongly enforced: *There should be much more stringent laws against the dropping of rubbish in the streets.* □ **rigoureux**

'**stringently** *adverb.* □ **rigoureusement**

'**stringency** *noun* **1** the quality of being strict. □ **rigueur**

2 scarcity of money for lending *etc*: *in times of stringency*; (*also adjective*) *The government are demanding stringency measures.* □ **(d')austérité**

stringy *see* string.

strip [strip] – *past tense, past participle* **stripped** – *verb* **1** to remove the covering from something: *She stripped the old varnish off the wall; He stripped the branch (of its bark) with his knife.* □ **décaper, enlever**

2 to undress: *She stripped the child (naked) and put him in the bath; She stripped and dived into the water; They were told to strip to the waist.* □ **(se) déshabiller**

3 to remove the contents of (a house *etc*): *The house/room was stripped bare/stripped of its furnishings; They stripped the house of all its furnishings.* □ **vider**

4 to deprive (a person) of something: *The officer was stripped of his rank for misconduct.* □ **destituer**

■ *noun* **1** a long narrow piece of (*eg* cloth, ground *etc*): *a strip of paper.* □ **bande**

2 a strip cartoon. □ **bande dessinée**

3 a footballer's shirt, shorts, socks *etc*: *The team has a red and white strip.* □ **tenue**

cartoon strip a row of drawings, *eg* in a newspaper or comic strip, telling a story. □ **bande dessinée**

'**strip lighting** *noun* lighting by long tubes rather than bulbs. □ **éclairage fluorescent**

,**strip'tease** *noun* the act of removing one's clothes one by one as a theatrical entertainment. □ **effeuillage**

■ *adjective*: *a strip-tease show.* □ **d'effeuillage**

strip off to remove clothes or a covering from a thing or person: *He stripped (his clothes) off and had a shower; The doctor stripped his bandage off.* □ **enlever**

stripe [straip] *noun* **1** a band of colour *etc*: *The wallpa-*

per was grey with broad green stripes; A zebra has black and white stripes. □ **rayure**

2 a (*usually* V-shaped) badge worn on an army uniform to show rank. □ **galon**

striped *adjective* having stripes: *a striped shirt; blue-and-white-striped curtains.* □ **rayé**

'**stripy** *adjective* covered with stripes: *A tiger has a stripy coat.* □ **rayé**

stripling ['striplin] *noun* a boy or youth not yet fully grown. □ **adolescent**

strive [straiv] – *past tense* **strove** [strouv]: *past participle* **striven** ['strivn] – *verb* to try very hard or struggle: *He always strives to please his teacher.* □ **s'efforcer de**

strode *see* stride.

stroke[1] [strouk] *noun* **1** an act of hitting, or the blow given: *He felled the tree with one stroke of the axe; the stroke of a whip.* □ **coup**

2 a sudden occurrence of something: *a stroke of lightning; an unfortunate stroke of fate; What a stroke of luck to find that money!* □ **coup**

3 the sound made by a clock striking the hour: *She arrived on the stroke of* (= punctually at) *ten.* □ **coup**

4 a movement or mark made in one direction by a pen, pencil, paintbrush *etc*: *short, even pencil strokes.* □ **coup**

5 a single pull of an oar in rowing, or a hit with the bat in playing cricket. □ **coup (d'aviron)**

6 a movement of the arms and legs in swimming, or a particular method of swimming: *She swam with slow, strong strokes; Can you do breaststroke/backstroke?* □ **brassée; nage**

7 an effort or action: *I haven't done a stroke (of work) all day.* □ **effort**

8 a sudden attack of illness which damages the brain, causing paralysis, loss of feeling in the body *etc*. □ **attaque**

at a stroke with a single effort: *We can't solve all these problems at a stroke.* □ **d'un seul coup**

stroke[2] [strouk] *verb* to rub (*eg* a furry animal) gently and repeatedly in one direction, *especially* as a sign of affection: *I stroked the cat/her hair; The dog loves being stroked.* □ **caresser**

■ *noun* an act of stroking: *She gave the dog a stroke.* □ **caresse**

stroll [stroul] *verb* to walk or wander without hurry: *He strolled along the street.* □ **se promener**

■ *noun* an act of strolling: *I went for a stroll around the town.* □ **petite promenade**

stroller ['stroulr] *noun* a small wheeled chair for a child, pushed by its mother. □ **poussette**

strong [stron] *adjective* **1** firm, sound, or powerful, and therefore not easily broken, destroyed, attacked, defeated, resisted, or affected by weariness, illness *etc*: *strong furniture; a strong castle; a strong wind; She's a strong swimmer; She has a very strong will/personality; He has never been very strong* (= healthy); *He is not strong enough to lift that heavy table.* □ **fort, puissant**

2 very noticeable; very intense: *a strong colour; a strong smell; I took a strong dislike to him.* □ **fort**

3 containing a large amount of the flavouring ingredient: *strong tea*. □ **fort**

4 (of a group, force *etc*) numbering a particular amount: *An army 20,000 strong was advancing towards the town.* □ **(fort) de**

'**strongly** *adverb*. □ **fortement**

strength [streŋθ] *noun* **1** the quality of being strong: *She got her strength back slowly after her illness; I hadn't the strength to resist him.* □ **force, puissance**

2 the number of people *etc* in a force, organization *etc*, considered as an indication of its power or effectiveness: *The force is below strength.* □ **effectif(s)**

strengthen ['streŋθən] *verb* to make or become strong or stronger: *She did exercises to strengthen her muscles; The wind strengthened.* □ **renforcer**

'**strongbox** *noun* a safe or box for valuables. □ **coffre-fort**

strong drink alcoholic liquors. □ **boisson forte**

'**stronghold** *noun* a fort, fortress or castle *etc*. □ **forteresse**

strong language swearing or abuse. □ **injure**

,**strong·'minded** *adjective* having determination. □ **résolu**

strong point a quality, skill *etc* in which a person excels: *Arithmetic isn't one of my strong points.* □ **fort**

strongroom *noun* a room specially constructed for keeping valuable articles, with thick walls and a heavy steel door *etc*. □ **chambre forte**

on the strength of relying on: *On the strength of this offer of money, we plan to start building soon.* □ **sur la foi de**

strove *see* **strive**.

struck *see* **strike**.

structure ['strʌktʃə] *noun* **1** the way in which something is arranged or organized: *A flower has quite a complicated structure; the structure of a human body.* □ **structure**

2 a building, or something that is built or constructed: *The Eiffel Tower is one of the most famous structures in the world.* □ **construction**

'**structural** *adjective* of structure: *You must get permission before making structural alterations to your house.* □ **de structure**

'**structurally** *adverb*. □ **structurellement**

struggle ['strʌgl] *verb* **1** to twist violently when trying to free oneself: *The child struggled in his arms.* □ **se débattre**

2 to make great efforts or try hard: *All his life he has been struggling with illness/against injustice.* □ **se battre (contre), lutter**

3 to move with difficulty: *He struggled out of the hole.* □ **avancer péniblement**

■ *noun* an act of struggling, or a fight: *The struggle for independence was long and hard.* □ **lutte (pour)**

struggle along to have only just enough money to live. □ **subsister tant bien que mal**

strum [strʌm] – *past tense, past participle* **strummed** – *verb* to play *especially* noisily and unskilfully on a piano or stringed instrument: *to strum a tune.* □ **taper, gratter**

strung *see* **string**.

strut [strʌt] – *past tense, past participle* '**strutted** – *verb* to walk in a stiff, proud way: *The cock strutted about the farmyard; The man was strutting along looking very pleased with himself.* □ **se pavaner**

stub [stʌb] *noun* **1** a stump or short remaining end of *eg* a cigarette, pencil *etc*: *The ashtray contained seven cigarette stubs.* □ **bout, mégot**

2 the counterfoil or retained section of a cheque *etc*. □ **talon**

■ *verb* – *past tense, past participle* **stubbed** – to hurt (*especially* a toe) by striking it against something hard: *She stubbed her toe(s) against the bedpost.* □ **se cogner (un orteil contre)**

'**stubby** *adjective* being a stub, or short and thick like a stub: *a stubby tail; stubby fingers.* □ **courtaud**

stub out to extinguish (a cigarette or cigar) by pressing it against a hard surface. □ **écraser**

stubble ['stʌbl] *noun* **1** the stubs or ends of corn left in the ground when the stalks are cut. □ **chaume**

2 short coarse hairs growing *eg* on an unshaven chin. □ **barbe de plusieurs jours**

'**stubbly** *adjective*. □ **mal rasé**

stubborn ['stʌbən] *adjective* obstinate, or unwilling to yield, obey *etc*: *He's as stubborn as a donkey.* □ **têtu**

stubby *see* **stub**.

stuck *see* **stick**¹.

stud¹ [stʌd] *noun* a collection of horses and mares kept for breeding. □ **écurie**

stud² [stʌd] *noun* **1** a knob, or nail with a large head, put into the surface of something as a protection or decoration *etc*: *metal studs on the soles of football boots; a belt decorated with studs.* □ **clou (décoratif)**

2 a type of button with two heads for fastening a collar: *a collar stud.* □ **bouton de col**

■ *verb* – *past tense, past participle* '**studded** – to cover with studs: *The sky was studded with stars.* □ **parsemer**

student ['stjuːdənt] *noun* **1** an undergraduate or graduate studying for a degree at a university *etc*: *university students; a medical student; (also adjective) She is a student nurse/teacher.* □ **(d')étudiant, ante**

2 a boy or girl at school. □ **élève**

3 a person studying a particular thing: *a student of politics.* □ **étudiant, ante**

studio ['stjuːdiou] – *plural* '**studios** – *noun* **1** the workroom of an artist or photographer. □ **studio**

2 (*often plural*) a place in which cinema films are made: *This film was made at Ramrod Studios.* □ **studio**

3 a room from which radio or television programs are broadcast: *a television studio.* □ **studio**

studious ['stjuːdiəs] *adjective* spending much time in careful studying: *a studious girl.* □ **studieux**

'**studiously** *adverb*. □ **studieusement**

'**studiousness** *noun*. □ **application**

study ['stʌdi] *verb* **1** to give time and attention to gaining knowledge of a subject: *What subject is she studying?; He is studying French; She is studying for a degree in mathematics; She's studying to be a teacher.* □ **étudier**

2 to look at or examine carefully: *He studied the railway timetable; Give yourself time to study the problem* *in detail.* □ **examiner**

■ *noun* **1** the act of devoting time and attention to gaining knowledge: *She spends all her evenings in study; She has made a study of the habits of bees.* □ **étude**

2 a musical or artistic composition: *a book of studies for the piano; The picture was entitled 'Study in Grey'.* □ **étude**

3 a room in a house *etc*, in which to study, read, write *etc*: *The headmaster wants to speak to the senior pupils in his study.* □ **bureau**

stuff¹ [stʌf] *noun* **1** material or substance: *What is that black oily stuff on the beach?; The doctor gave me some good stuff for removing warts; Show them what stuff you're made of!* (= how brave, strong *etc* you are). □ **chose; produit; étoffe**

2 (unimportant) matter, things, objects *etc*: *We'll have to get rid of all this stuff when we move house.* □ **affaires**

3 an old word for cloth. □ **étoffe**

know one's stuff to be skilful and knowledgeable in one's chosen subject. □ **s'y connaître**

that's the stuff! that's just what is wanted! □ **voilà ce qu'il faut**

stuff² [stʌf] *verb* **1** to pack or fill tightly, often hurriedly or untidily: *Her drawer was stuffed with papers; She stuffed the fridge with food; The children have been stuffing themselves with ice cream.* □ **(se) bourrer (de), s'empiffrer**

2 to fill (*eg* a turkey, chicken *etc*) with stuffing before cooking. □ **farcir**

3 to fill the skin of (a dead animal or bird) to preserve the appearance it had when alive: *They stuffed the golden eagle.* □ **empailler**

'stuffing *noun* **1** material used for stuffing *eg* toy animals: *The teddy bear had lost its stuffing.* □ **rembourrage**

2 a mixture containing *eg* breadcrumbs, spices, sausage-meat *etc*, used for stuffing chickens *etc*. □ **farce**

stuff up to block: *She stuffed the hole up with some newspaper; I've got a cold and my nose is stuffed up.* □ **boucher**

stuffy ['stʌfi] *adjective* **1** (of a room *etc*) too warm, and lacking fresh air: *Why do you sit in this stuffy room all day?* □ **mal aéré**

2 formal and dull: *Must we visit those stuffy people?* □ **collet monté**

'stuffily *adverb.* □ **de manière étouffante**

'stuffiness *noun.* □ **manque d'air**

stumble ['stʌmbl] *verb* **1** to strike the foot against something and lose one's balance, or nearly fall: *She stumbled over the edge of the carpet.* □ **trébucher**

2 to walk unsteadily: *She stumbled along the track in the dark.* □ **avancer en trébuchant**

3 to make mistakes, or hesitate in speaking, reading aloud *etc*: *He stumbles over his words when speaking in public.* □ **hésiter en parlant**

'stumbling block *noun* a difficulty that prevents progress. □ **pierre d'achoppement**

stumble across/on to find by chance: *I stumbled across this book today in a shop.* □ **tomber sur**

stump [stʌmp] *noun* **1** the part of a tree left in the ground

after the trunk has been cut down: *She sat on a (tree-) stump and ate her sandwiches.* □ **souche**

2 the part of a limb, tooth, pencil *etc* remaining after the main part has been cut out or broken off, worn away *etc*. □ **moignon; chicot; bout**

3 in cricket, one of the three upright sticks forming the wicket. □ **piquet**

■ *verb* **1** to walk with heavy, stamping steps: *She stumped angrily out of the room.* □ **aller à pas lourds**

2 to puzzle or baffle completely: *I'm stumped!* □ **estomaquer**

3 in cricket, to get (a batsman who is not in his crease) out by hitting his stumps with the ball. □ **mettre hors jeu**

'stumpy *adjective* being a stump; short and thick like a stump: *The cat had a stumpy tail.* □ **trapu**

stun [stʌn] – *past tense, past participle* **stunned** – *verb* **1** to make unconscious or knock senseless *eg* by a blow on the head: *The blow stunned him.* □ **assommer**

2 to shock or astonish: *He was stunned by the news of her death.* □ **abasourdir, ahurir**

'stunning *adjective* marvellous: *a stunning dress.* □ **sensationnel**

stung *see* **sting.**

stunk *see* **stink.**

stunt¹ [stʌnt] *verb* to prevent or check the full growth or development of: *It is thought that smoking by a pregnant mother may stunt the baby's growth.* □ **arrêter la croissance de qqn, qqch.**

'stunted *adjective* not well grown: *a stunted tree.* □ **rabougri**

stunt² [stʌnt] *noun* something (daring or spectacular) done to attract attention *etc*: *One of his stunts was to cross the Niagara Falls blindfold on a tightrope.* □ **exploit**

'stuntman [-man] *noun* a person who takes the place of an actor in film sequences involving *eg* athletic skill and danger. □ **cascadeur, euse**

stupefy ['stjuːpifai] *verb* to bewilder, confuse or amaze. □ **stupéfier, ahurir**

,stupe'faction [-'fakʃən] *noun.* □ **stupéfaction**

stupendous [stjuˈpendəs] *adjective* astonishing or tremendous. □ **fantastique**

stupid ['stjuːpid] *adjective* **1** foolish; slow at understanding: *a stupid mistake; He isn't as stupid as he looks.* □ **stupide**

2 in a bewildered or dazed state: *He was (feeling) stupid from lack of sleep.* □ **hébété**

'stupidly *adverb.* □ **stupidement**

stu'pidity *noun.* □ **stupidité**

stupor ['stjuːpə] *noun* a half-conscious, dazed or bewildered condition caused by *eg* alcohol, drugs, shock *etc*: *She was in a drunken stupor.* □ **stupeur**

sturdy ['stəːdi] *adjective* **1** strong and healthy: *He is small but sturdy.* □ **vigoureux**

2 firm and well-made: *sturdy furniture.* □ **robuste**

'sturdily *adverb.* □ **avec robustesse, vigoureusement**

'sturdiness *noun.* □ **robustesse, vigueur**

sturgeon ['stəːdʒən] – *plurals* **'sturgeon, 'sturgeons** – *noun* a type of large fish from which caviar is obtained.

□ **esturgeon**

stutter ['stʌtə] *verb* to stammer: *He stutters sometimes when he's excited*; '*I've s-s-seen a gh-gh-ghost,' he stuttered.* □ **bégayer**

■ *noun* a stammer: *He has a stutter.* □ **bégaiement**

'stutterer *noun* a person who has a stammer. □ **bègue**

sty[1] [stai] *noun* a pigsty. □ **porcherie**

sty[2], **stye** [stai] – *plurals* **sties**, **styes** – *noun* a small inflamed swelling on the eyelid. □ **orgelet**

style [stail] *noun* **1** a manner or way of doing something, *eg* writing, speaking, painting, building *etc*: *different styles of architecture*; *What kind of style are you going to have your hair cut in?*; *a new hairstyle.* □ **style**

2 a fashion in clothes *etc*: *the latest Paris styles*; *I don't like the new style of shoe.* □ **mode**

3 elegance in dress, behaviour *etc*: *She certainly has style.* □ **chic**

■ *verb* **1** to arrange (hair) in a certain way: *I'm going to have my hair cut and styled.* □ **coiffer**

2 to design in a certain style: *These chairs/clothes are styled for comfort.* □ **créer**

'stylish *adjective* elegant or fashionable: *stylish clothes/furniture.* □ **élégant; à la mode**

'stylishly *adverb*. □ **élégamment**

'stylishness *noun*. □ **élégance**

'stylist *noun* a person who arranges or designs a style *especially* in hairdressing: *a hair-stylist.* □ **coiffeur, euse**

in style in a luxurious, elegant way without worrying about the expense: *The bride arrived at the church in style, in a horse-drawn carriage.* □ **en grande pompe**

stylus ['stailəs] *noun* a gramophone needle. □ **aiguille**

Styrofoam® ['stairəfoum] *noun* plastic foam used for insulation *etc*. □ **mousse de polystyrène**

suave [swaːv] *adjective* (of a man or his manner) pleasant, elegant, polite and agreeable. □ **affable**

'suavely *adverb*. □ **avec affabilité**

'suaveness *noun*. □ **affabilité**

'suavity *noun*. □ **affabilité**

sub [sʌb] *noun* short for several words *eg* **submarine**, **subscription** *etc*: *He's the commander of a sub*; *Several people still haven't paid their subs.* □ **sous-, sub-**

subaltern [sə'bɔːltərn] *noun* an officer in the army under the rank of captain. □ **(sous-)lieutenant, ante**

subcommittee [sʌbkə'miti] *noun* a committee having powers given to it by a larger committee. □ **sous-comité**

subconscious [sʌb'konʃəs] *adjective, noun* (of) those activities of the mind of which we are not aware: *I suspect that her generosity arose from a subconscious desire for praise*; *We can't control the activities of the subconscious.* □ **subconscient**

sub'consciously *adverb*. □ **subconsciemment**

subcontinent [sʌb'kontinənt] *noun* a mass of land almost the size of a continent, forming part of a larger mass of land: *the Indian Subcontinent* (= India, Pakistan and Bangladesh). □ **sous-continent**

subcontractor [sʌb'kontraktər] *noun* a person who undertakes work for a contractor and is therefore not directly employed by the person who wants such work done: *The building contractor has employed several subcontractors to build the block of flats.* □ **sous-**

traitant, ante

subdivide [sʌbdi'vaid] *verb* to divide into smaller parts or divisions: *Each class of children is subdivided into groups according to reading ability.* □ **subdiviser**

,subdi'vision [-'viʒən] *noun*. □ **subdivision**

subdue [səb'djuː] *verb* to conquer, overcome or bring under control: *After months of fighting the rebels were subdued.* □ **soumettre**

sub'dued *adjective* quiet; not bright or lively: *subdued voices*; *She seems subdued today.* □ **atténué; sans entrain**

subject ['sʌbdʒikt] *adjective* (of countries *etc*) not independent, but dominated by another power: *subject nations.* □ **assujetti**

■ *noun* **1** a person who is under the rule of a monarch or a member of a country that has a monarchy *etc*: *We are loyal subjects of the Queen*; *He is a British subject.* □ **sujet, ette**

2 someone or something that is talked about, written about *etc*: *We discussed the price of food and similar subjects*; *What was the subject of the debate?*; *The teacher tried to think of a good subject for their essay*; *I've said all I can on that subject.* □ **sujet**

3 a branch of study or learning in school, university *etc*: *He is taking exams in seven subjects*; *Mathematics is her best subject.* □ **matière**

4 a thing, person or circumstance suitable for, or requiring, a particular kind of treatment, reaction *etc*: *I don't think her behaviour is a subject for laughter.* □ **sujet (de)**

5 in English, the word(s) representing the person or thing that *usually* does the action shown by the verb, and with which the verb agrees: *The cat sat on the mat*; *He hit her because she broke his toy*; *He was hit by the ball.* □ **sujet**

■ [səb'dʒekt] *verb* **1** to bring (a person, country *etc*) under control: *They have subjected all the neighbouring states (to their rule).* □ **assujettir**

2 to cause to suffer, or submit (to something): *He was subjected to cruel treatment*; *These tires are subjected to various tests before leaving the factory.* □ **soumettre**

subjection [səb'dʒekʃən] *noun*. □ **sujétion**

subjective [səb'dʒektiv] *adjective* (of a person's attitude *etc*) arising from, or influenced by, his or her own thoughts and feelings only; not objective or impartial: *You must try not to be too subjective if you are on a jury in a court of law.* □ **subjectif**

sub'jectively *adverb*. □ **subjectivement**

subject matter the subject discussed in an essay, book *etc*. □ **sujet**

change the subject to start talking about something different: *I mentioned the money to her, but she changed the subject.* □ **changer de sujet**

subject to 1 liable or likely to suffer from or be affected by: *He is subject to colds*; *The program is subject to alteration.* □ **sujet à**

2 depending on: *These plans will be put into practice next week, subject to your approval.* □ **sous réserve de**

sub-lieutenant [sʌbluː'tenənt] *noun* (abbreviated to **Sub-Lt.**, when written) the rank below lieutenant. □

sous-lieutenant; enseigne (de vaisseau) première classe

sublime [sə'blaim] *adjective* of overwhelming greatness, grandeur, beauty *etc*. □ **sublime**
su'blimely *adverb*. □ **sublimement**
su'blimity [-'bli-] *noun*. □ **sublimité**

submarine [sʌbmə'riːn] *noun* (*abbreviation* **sub**) a ship that can travel under the surface of the sea. □ **sous-marin**
■ *adjective* existing, or intended for use *etc*, under the surface of the sea: *submarine vegetation.* □ **sous-marin**

submerge [səb'mɜːdʒ] *verb* to cover with, or sink under, water or other liquid: *I watched the submarine submerging.* □ **submerger; plonger**
sub'merged *adjective* sunk beneath the surface: *Submerged rocks are a great danger to shipping.* □ **submergé**
sub'mergence *noun*. □ **submersion**
sub'mersion [-ʒən] *noun*. □ **submersion**

submission, submissive *see* submit.

submit [səb'mit] – *past tense, past participle* **sub'mitted** – *verb* **1** to yield to control or to a particular kind of treatment by another person *etc*: *I refuse to submit to his control; The rebels were ordered to submit.* □ **se soumettre**
2 to offer (a plan, suggestion, proposal, entry *etc*): *Competitors for the painting competition must submit their entries by Friday.* □ **soumettre**
su'bmission [-ʃən] *noun* **1** the act of submitting. □ **soumission**
2 humbleness or obedience. □ **soumission**
sub'missive [-siv] *adjective* obedient and humble. □ **soumis**
sub'missively *adverb*. □ **avec soumission**
sub'missiveness *noun*. □ **soumission**

subnormal ['sʌb'nɔːməl] *adjective* below the normal level or standard: *subnormal temperatures.* □ **au-dessous de la normale**

subordinate [sə'bɔːdinət] *adjective* lower in rank, power, importance *etc*: *A colonel is subordinate to a brigadier.* □ **subordonné (à)**
■ *noun* a person who is subordinate: *to give orders to one's subordinates.* □ **subordonné, ée**
subordinate clause a clause introduced in a sentence by a conjunction *etc*, and acting as a noun, adjective or adverb: *I don't know who she is; The book that's on the table is mine; She's crying because you were unkind.* □ **proposition subordonnée**

subscribe [səb'skraib] *verb* **1** to give money, with other people, to a charity or other cause: *He subscribes to a lot of charities; We each subscribed $1 towards the present.* □ **souscrire**
2 (*with* **to**) to promise to receive and pay for a series of issues of (a magazine *etc*): *I've been subscribing to that magazine for four years.* □ **souscrire à, s'abonner**
sub'scriber *noun* a person who subscribes to a charity or a magazine *etc*. □ **souscripteur, trice, abonné, ée**
subscription [səb'skripʃən] *noun* **1** the act of subscribing. □ **souscription**
2 a sum of money that is subscribed *eg* for receiving a magazine, for a membership of a club *etc*. □

abonnement

subsequent ['sʌbsikwənt] *adjective* following or coming after: *His misbehaviour and subsequent dismissal from the firm were reported in the newspaper.* □ **subséquent**
'subsequently *adverb* afterwards: *He escaped from prison but was subsequently recaptured.* □ **subséquemment**
subsequent to after: *The child became ill subsequent to receiving an injection against measles.* □ **à la suite de**

subside [səb'said] *verb* **1** (of land, streets, buildings *etc*) to sink lower: *When a building starts to subside, cracks usually appear in the walls.* □ **s'affaisser**
2 (of floods) to become lower and withdraw: *Gradually the water subsided.* □ **baisser**
3 (of a storm, noise or other disturbance) to become quieter: *They stayed anchored in harbour till the wind subsided.* □ **se calmer**
subsidence ['sʌbsidens, səb'saidəns] *noun* the process of subsiding: *The road has had to be closed because of subsidence.* □ **affaissement**

subsidiary [səb'sidjəri] *adjective* **1** adding to, or making a contribution towards, something larger, more important *etc*: *questions that are subsidiary to the main one.* □ **subsidiaire, accessoire**
2 (of a firm, company *etc*) controlled by another, larger firm. □ **filiale**
■ *noun* – *plural* **sub'sidiaries** – something that is subsidiary: *this firm and its subsidiaries.* □ **filiale**

subsidy ['sʌbsidi] – *plural* **'subsidies** – *noun* (a sum of) money paid by a government *etc* to an industry *etc* that needs help, or to farmers *etc* to keep the price of their products low. □ **subvention**
'subsidize, 'subsidise *verb* to give a subsidy to: *Some industries are subsidized by the government.* □ **subventionner**

subsoil ['sʌbsoil] *noun* the layer of earth beneath the surface soil. □ **sous-sol**

substance ['sʌbstəns] *noun* **1** a material: *Rubber is a tough, stretchy substance obtained from the juice of certain plants.* □ **substance**
2 as a scientific term, an element, compound or mixture. □ **substance**

substandard [sʌb'standəd] *adjective* below the (officially) approved standard: *substandard working conditions.* □ **au-dessous de la norme**

substantial [səb'stanʃəl] *adjective* **1** solid or strong: *a nice substantial table.* □ **solide**
2 large: *a substantial sum of money; That meal was quite substantial.* □ **substantiel**
subs'tantially *adverb*. □ **substantiellement**
substantiate [səb'stanʃieit] *verb* to give the facts that are able to prove or support (a claim, theory *etc*): *He cannot substantiate his claim/accusation.* □ **justifier**

substitute ['sʌbstitjuːt] *verb* to put in, or to take, the place of someone or something else: *I substituted your name for mine on the list.* □ **substituer**
■ *noun* a person or thing used or acting instead of another: *Guesswork is no substitute for investigation; She*

is not well enough to play in the tennis match, so we must find a substitute; (also adjective) I was substitute headmaster for a term. □ **suppléant, ante; succédané**

,substi'tution *noun* the act of substituting, or process of being substituted. □ **substitution**

subterranean [sʌbtə'reiniən] *adjective* lying, situated or constructed underground: *subterranean passages.* □ **souterrain**

subtitle ['sʌbtaitl] *noun* **1** a second or explanatory title to a book. □ **sous-titre**
2 on a cinema film *etc*, a translation of foreign speech appearing at the bottom of the screen: *I found it difficult to read the subtitles.* □ **sous-titre**

subtle ['sʌtl] *adjective* **1** faint or delicate in quality, and therefore difficult to describe or explain: *There is a subtle difference between 'unnecessary' and 'not necessary'; a subtle flavour.* □ **subtil**
2 clever or cunning: *He has a subtle mind.* □ **fin**
subtlety ['sʌtlti] *noun.* □ **subtilité**
'subtly *adverb.* □ **subtilement**

subtract [səb'trakt] *verb* to take one number or quantity from another: *If you subtract 5 from 8, 3 is left; In their first year at school, most children learn to add and subtract.* □ **soustraire**
sub'traction [-ʃən] *noun.* □ **soustraction**

subtropical [sʌb'tropikəl] *adjective* (belonging to those areas) close to the tropical zone: *a subtropical climate.* □ **subtropical**

suburb ['sʌbəːb] *noun* (*often in plural*) an area of houses on the outskirts of a city, town *etc*: *Edgbaston is a suburb of Birmingham; They decided to move out to the suburbs.* □ **banlieue**
su'burban *adjective* of suburbs: *suburban housing.* □ **de banlieue**
su'burbia [-biə] *noun* the suburbs. □ **la banlieue**

subvert [səb'vəːt] *verb* to overthrow or ruin completely (*eg* a person's morals, loyalty, arguments, a government). □ **corrompre; renverser**
sub'version [-ʒən] *noun.* □ **subversion**
sub'versive [-siv] *adjective* likely to destroy or overthrow (government, discipline in a school *etc*): *That boy is a subversive influence in this class.* □ **subversif**

subway ['sʌbwei] *noun* **1** an underground passage *eg* for pedestrians, under a busy road: *Cross by the subway.* □ **passage souterrain**
2 an underground railway in a city: *Go by subway.* □ **métro**

succeed [sək'siːd] *verb* **1** to manage to do what one is trying to do; to achieve one's aim or purpose: *She succeeded in persuading her to do it; She's happy to have succeeded in her chosen career; She tried three times to pass his driving test, and at last succeeded; Our new teaching methods seem to be succeeding.* □ **réussir (à)**
2 to follow next in order, and take the place of someone or something else: *He succeeded his father as manager of the firm/as king; The cold summer was succeeded by a stormy autumn; If the duke has no children, who will succeed to* (= inherit) *his property?* □ **succéder (à); hériter**
success [sək'ses] *noun* **1** (the prosperity gained by) the

achievement of an aim or purpose: *He has achieved great success as an actor/in his career.* □ **succès, réussite**
2 a person or thing that succeeds or prospers: *She's a great success as a teacher.* □ **personne qui réussit**
suc'cessful [-'ses-] *adjective* (*negative* **unsuccessful**) having success: *Were you successful in finding a new house?; The successful applicant for this job will be required to start work next month; a successful career.* □ **réussi, couronné de succès**
suc'cessfully *adverb.* □ **avec succès**
succession [sək'seʃən] *noun* **1** the right of succeeding to a throne as king, to a title *etc*: *The Princess is fifth in* (*order of*) *succession* (*to the throne*). □ **succession**
2 a number of things following after one another: *a succession of bad harvests.* □ **suite**
3 the act or process of following and taking the place of someone or something else: *her succession to the throne.* □ **succession (à)**
successive [sək'sesiv] *adjective* following one after the other: *She won three successive matches.* □ **successif**
suc'cessively [-'sesiv-] *adverb.* □ **successivement**
suc'cessor [-'se-] *noun* a person who follows, and take the place of another: *Who will be appointed as the manager's successor?* □ **successeur**
in succession one after another: *five wet days in succession.* □ **à la suite**
succulent ['sʌkjulənt] *adjective* **1** (of fruit or other food *eg* meat) juicy and delicious: *a succulent peach.* □ **succulent**
2 (of plants) having thick stems and leaves that are full of moisture. □ **gras**
■ *noun* a plant of this type: *A cactus is a type of succulent.* □ **plante grasse**
'succulence *noun.* □ **succulence**

succumb [sə'kʌm] *verb* to yield: *She succumbed to temptation and ate the chocolate.* □ **succomber (à)**

such [sʌtʃ] *adjective* **1** of the same kind as that already mentioned or being mentioned: *Animals that gnaw, such as mice, rats, rabbits and weasels are called rodents; She came from Bradford or some such place; She asked to see Mr. Johnson but was told there was no such person there; I've seen several such buildings; I've never done such a thing before; doctors, dentists and such people.* □ **tel, pareil, semblable**
2 of the great degree already mentioned or being mentioned: *If you had telephoned her, she wouldn't have got into such a state of anxiety; She never used to get such bad headaches* (*as she does now*). □ **un tel**
3 of the great degree, or the kind, to have a particular result: *He shut the window with such force that the glass broke; She's such a good teacher that the headmaster asked her not to leave; Their problems are such as to make it impossible for them to live together any more.* □ **tel**
4 used for emphasis: *This is such a shock! They have been such good friends to me!* □ **tel, si**
■ *pronoun* such a person or thing, or such persons or things: *I have only a few photographs, but can show you such as I have; This isn't a good book as such* (= as

a book) *but it has interesting pictures.* □ **le peu que; en tant que tel**

'**suchlike** *adjective, pronoun* (things) of the same kind: *I don't like books about love, romance and suchlike* (*things*). □ **de ce genre**

'**such-and-such** *adjective, pronoun* used to refer to some unnamed person or thing: *Let's suppose that you go into such-and-such a shop and ask for such-and-such.* □ **tel et tel, tel ou tel**

such as it is though it scarcely deserves the name: *You can borrow my lawn mower, such as it is.* □ **pour ce que (cela) vaut**

suck [sʌk] *verb* 1 to draw liquid *etc* into the mouth: *As soon as they are born, young animals learn to suck* (*milk from their mothers*); *She sucked up the lemonade through a straw.* □ **téter; boire**

2 to hold something between the lips or inside the mouth, as though drawing liquid from it: *I told him to take the sweet out of his mouth, but he just went on sucking; He sucked the end of his pencil.* □ **sucer**

3 to pull or draw in a particular direction with a sucking or similar action: *The vacuum cleaner sucked up all the dirt from the carpet; A plant sucks up moisture from the soil.* □ **aspirer; absorber**

■ *noun* an act of sucking: *I gave him a suck of my lollipop.* □ **suçotement**

'**sucker** *noun* 1 a person or thing that sucks: *Are these insects bloodsuckers?* □ **suceur, euse**

2 an organ on an animal, *eg* an octopus, by which it sticks to objects. □ **ventouse**

3 a curved pad or disk (of rubber *etc*) that can be pressed on to a surface and stick there. □ **ventouse**

4 a side shoot coming from the root of a plant. □ **gourmand**

suckle ['sʌkl] *verb* (of a woman or female animal) to give milk from the breasts or teats to (a baby or young). □ **allaiter**

suction ['sʌkʃən] *noun* 1 the action of sucking. □ **succion**

2 the process of creating a vacuum by reducing air pressure on the surface of a liquid so that it can be drawn up into a tube *etc*, or between two surfaces, *eg* a rubber disk and a wall, so that they stick together. □ **succion**

sudden ['sʌdn] *adjective* happening *etc* quickly and unexpectedly: *a sudden attack; Her decision to get married is rather sudden!; a sudden bend in the road.* □ **soudain**

'**suddenness** *noun*. □ **soudaineté**

'**suddenly** *adverb: She suddenly woke up; Suddenly she realized that she had a gun.* □ **soudain**

all of a sudden suddenly or unexpectedly: *All of a sudden the lights went out.* □ **tout à/d'un coup**

suds [sʌdz] *noun plural* soapsuds. □ **eau savonneuse**

sue [suː] *verb* 1 to start a law case against. □ **poursuivre en justice**

2 (*with* **for**: *especially* in law) to ask for (*eg* divorce). □ **entamer des poursuites**

suede [sweid] *noun, adjective* (of) leather from a sheep or lamb *etc* with a soft, rough surface: *suede shoes.* □ **(en/de) suède**

suet ['suːit] *noun* the hard fat from around the kidneys of an ox or sheep. □ **graisse (de rognon)**

suffer ['sʌfə] *verb* 1 to undergo, endure or bear pain, misery *etc: She suffered terrible pain from her injuries; The crash killed him instantly – he didn't suffer at all; I'll make you suffer for this insolence.* □ **souffrir**

2 to undergo or experience: *The army suffered enormous losses.* □ **subir**

3 to be neglected: *I like to see you enjoying yourself, but you mustn't let your work suffer.* □ **pâtir**

4 (*with* **from**) to have or to have often (a particular illness *etc*): *She suffers from stomach-aches.* □ **souffrir (de)**

'**suffering** *noun* (a feeling of) pain or misery: *The shortage of food caused widespread suffering; She keeps complaining about her sufferings.* □ **souffrance**

suffice [sə'fais] *verb* to be enough for a purpose or person: *Will $10 suffice* (*you*) *till Monday?* □ **suffire**

sufficient *adjective* enough: *We haven't sufficient food to feed all these people; Will $10 be sufficient for your needs?* □ **assez, suffisant**

suf'ficiency *noun.* □ **quantité suffisante**

suf'ficiently *adverb.* □ **suffisamment**

suffice it to say I need only say. □ **qu'il suffise de dire**

suffix ['sʌfiks] *noun* a small part added to the end of a word that changes the meaning: *goodness; quickly; advisable; misty; yellowish.* □ **suffixe**

suffocate ['sʌfəkeit] *verb* to kill, die, cause distress to or feel distress, through lack of air or the prevention of free breathing: *A baby may suffocate if it sleeps with a pillow; The smoke was suffocating him; May I open the window? I'm suffocating.* □ **étouffer, suffoquer**

,**suffo'cation** *noun.* □ **étouffement**

suffrage ['sʌfridʒ] *noun* 1 the right to vote. □ **droit de vote**

2 voting. □ **vote, suffrage**

,**suffra'gette** [-'dʒet] *noun* one of the women who worked and fought for women's right to vote. □ **suffragette**

sugar ['ʃugə] *noun* the sweet substance that is obtained from sugar-cane, or from the juice of certain other plants, and used in cooking and for sweetening tea, coffee *etc: Do you take sugar in your coffee?* □ **sucre**

■ *verb* to sweeten, cover or sprinkle with sugar. □ **sucrer**

'**sugary** *adjective* 1 tasting of sugar, or containing a lot of sugar: *sugary foods.* □ **sucré**

2 too sweet or sentimental: *a sugary story.* □ **à l'eau de rose**

'**sugariness** *noun.* □ **goût (trop) sucré**

'**sugar cane** *noun* a type of tall grass from whose juice sugar is obtained. □ **canne à sucre**

,**sugar-'coated** *adjective* covered with icing: *sugar-coated biscuits.* □ **enrobé de sucre**

sugar lump a small cube of sugar used for sweetening tea *etc*. □ **morceau de sucre**

sugar tongs an instrument for lifting sugar lumps: *a pair of sugar tongs.* □ **pince à sucre**

suggest [sə'dʒest, (*American also*) səg-] *verb* 1 to put (an idea *etc*) before another person *etc* for consideration; to propose: *He suggested a different plan; I suggest doing it a different way; She suggested to me one* *or two suitable people for the committee*; *I suggest that we have lunch now*. □ **suggérer**

2 to put (an idea *etc*) into a person's mind; to hint: *Are you suggesting that I'm too old for the job?*; *An explanation suddenly suggested itself to me*. □ **insinuer; venir à l'esprit**

sug'gestion [-tʃən] *noun* **1** the act of suggesting. □ **suggestion**

2 something that is suggested; a proposal or idea: *Has anyone any other suggestions to make?*; *What a clever suggestion!* □ **suggestion**

3 a slight trace or sign: *There was a suggestion of boredom in his tone*. □ **trace, soupçon**

suicide ['suːisaid] *noun* **1** the/an act of killing oneself deliberately: *She committed suicide*; *an increasing number of suicides*. □ **suicide**

2 a person who kills himself or herself deliberately. □ **suicidé, ée**

,sui'cidal *adjective* **1** inclined to suicide: *She sometimes feels suicidal*. □ **suicidaire**

2 extremely dangerous, or likely to lead to death or disaster: *He was driving at a suicidal speed*. □ **suicidaire**

,sui'cidally *adverb*. □ **d'une façon suicidaire**

suit [suːt] *noun* **1** a set of clothes *usually* all of the same cloth *etc*, made to be worn together, *eg* a jacket, trousers (and waistcoat) for a man, or a jacket and skirt or trousers for a woman. □ **costume, tailleur**

2 a piece of clothing for a particular purpose: *a bathing suit*. □ **costume**

3 a case in a law court: *He won/lost his suit*. □ **procès**

4 an old word for a formal request, *eg* a proposal of marriage to a lady. □ **demande en mariage**

5 one of the four sets of playing cards – spades, hearts, diamonds, clubs. □ **couleur**

■ *verb* **1** to satisfy the needs of, or be convenient for: *The arrangements did not suit us*; *The climate suits me very well*. □ **convenir (à)**

2 (of clothes, styles, fashions *etc*) to be right or appropriate for: *Long hair suits her*; *That dress doesn't suit her*. □ **aller bien (à)**

3 to adjust or make appropriate or suitable: *He suited his speech to his audience*. □ **adapter (à)**

'suited *adjective* (*negative* **unsuited**) fitted, or appropriate (to or for): *I don't think he's suited to/for this work*. □ **fait pour**

'suitor *noun* an old word for a man who tries to gain the love of a woman. □ **soupirant**

'suitcase *noun* a case with flat sides for clothes *etc*, used by a person when travelling: *He hastily packed his (clothes in his) suitcase*. □ **valise**

follow suit to do just as someone else has done: *He went to bed and I followed suit*. □ **faire de même**

suit down to the ground (of *eg* an arrangement, fashion *etc*) to suit (a person) completely: *The dress suits her down to the ground*. □ **aller comme un gant (à)**

suit oneself to do what one wants to do. □ **faire à son gré**

suitable ['suːtəbl] *adjective* (*negative* **unsuitable**) **1** right or appropriate for a purpose or occasion: *I haven't any suitable shoes for the wedding*; *Those shoes are not*

suitable for walking in the country; *Many people applied for the job but not one of them was suitable*. □ **convenable, approprié**

2 convenient: *We must find a suitable day for our meeting*. □ **qui convient**

,suita'bility *noun*. □ **convenance**

'suitableness *noun*. □ **convenance**

'suitably *adverb*: *You're not suitably dressed*. □ **convenablement**

suite [swiːt] *noun* a number of things forming a set: *a suite of furniture*; *He has composed a suite of music for the film*. □ **ensemble; suite**

sulfur *see* **sulphur**.

sulk [sʌlk] *verb* to show anger or resentment by being silent: *He's sulking because his mother won't let him have an ice cream*. □ **bouder**

'sulky *adjective* sulking, or tending to sulk: *in a sulky mood*; *a sulky girl*. □ **boudeur**

'sulkily *adverb*. □ **en boudant**

'sulkiness *noun*. □ **bouderie**

sullen ['sʌlən] *adjective* silent and bad-tempered: *a sullen young man*; *a sullen expression*. □ **renfrogné**

'sullenly *adverb*. □ **d'un air renfrogné**

'sullenness *noun*. □ **air renfrogné**

sulphur, sulfur ['sʌlfə] *noun* a light yellow non-metallic element found in the earth, which burns with a blue flame giving off a choking smell and is used in matches, gunpowder *etc*. □ **soufre**

'sulphate [-feit] *noun* any of several substances containing sulphur, oxygen and some other element. □ **sulfate**

sultan ['sʌltən] *noun* a ruler in certain Muslim countries. □ **sultan**

sultana[1] [-'tɑːnə] *noun* the mother, wife, sister or daughter of a sultan. □ **sultane**

sultana[2] [səl'tɑːnə] *noun* a type of small, seedless raisin. □ **raisin sec de Smyrne**

sultry ['sʌltri] *adjective* **1** (of weather) hot but cloudy, and likely to become stormy. □ **étouffant**

2 (of a person, *especially* a woman) passionate. □ **sensuel**

'sultriness *noun*. □ **chaleur étouffante**

sum [sʌm] *noun* **1** the amount or total made by two or more things or numbers added together: *The sum of 12, 24, 7 and 11 is 54*. □ **somme**

2 a quantity of money: *It will cost an enormous sum to repair the swimming pool*. □ **somme (d'argent)**

3 a problem in arithmetic: *My children are better at sums than I am*. □ **problème d'arithmétique**

sum total the complete or final total: *The sum total of the damage cannot be calculated*. □ **somme totale**

sum up – *past tense, past participle* **summed** – *verb* to give the main or important points of: *He summed up the various proposals*. □ **résumer**

summary ['sʌməri] – *plural* **'summaries** – *noun* a shortened form of a statement, story *etc* giving only the main points: *A summary of his speech was printed in the newspaper*. □ **résumé, sommaire**

'summarize, 'summarise *verb* to make a summary of: *He summarized the arguments*. □ **résumer**

summer ['sʌmə] *noun* the warmest season of the year,

May or June till August in cooler northern regions: *I went to Italy last summer*; *(also adjective) summer holidays.* □ **(d') été**

'summery *adjective* like, or appropriate for, summer: *summery weather*; *summery clothes.* □ **estival**

'summer house *noun* a small building for sitting in, in a garden. □ **tonnelle**

'summertime *noun* the season of summer. □ **été**

summit ['sʌmit] *noun* the highest point: *They reached the summit of the mountain at midday*; *At the age of thirty he was at the summit of his powers as a composer.* □ **sommet**

■ *adjective* (of a conference *etc*) at the highest level of international negotiation, at which heads of state meet for discussion. □ **au sommet**

summon ['sʌmən] *verb* to order to come or appear: *He was summoned to appear in court*; *The head teacher summoned her to his room*; *A meeting was summoned.* □ **convoquer**

sump [sʌmp] *noun* the part of a motor-engine that contains the oil. □ **réservoir**

sumptuous ['sʌmptʃuəs] *adjective* expensive and splendid: *They live in sumptuous surroundings.* □ **somptueux**

sun [sʌn] *noun* **1** the round body in the sky that gives light and heat to the earth: *The Sun is nearly 150 million kilometres away from the Earth.* □ **soleil**

2 any of the fixed stars: *Do other suns have planets revolving around them?* □ **soleil**

3 light and heat from the sun; sunshine: *We sat in the sun*; *In Britain they don't get enough sun*; *The sun has faded the curtains.* □ **soleil**

■ *verb* – *past tense, past participle* **sunned** – to expose (oneself) to the sun's rays: *He's sunning himself in the garden.* □ **(s')exposer au soleil**

'sunless *adjective* without sun, or lacking sunlight: *a sunless room.* □ **sans soleil**

'sunny *adjective* **1** filled with sunshine: *sunny weather.* □ **ensoleillé**

2 cheerful and happy: *The child has a sunny nature.* □ **heureux**

'sunniness *noun.* □ **ensoleillement; gaieté**

'sunbathe *verb* to lie or sit in the sun, *especially* wearing few clothes, in order to get a suntan. □ **prendre un bain de soleil**

'sunbeam *noun* a ray of the sun. □ **rayon de soleil**

'sunburn *noun* the brown or red colour of the skin caused by exposure to the sun's rays. □ **bronzage**

'sunburned, 'sunburnt *adjective*: *sunburnt faces.* □ **bronzé**

'sundial *noun* a device, *usually* in a garden, for telling time from the shadow of a rod or plate on its surface cast by the sun. □ **cadran solaire**

'sundown *noun* sunset. □ **coucher du soleil**

'sunflower *noun* a type of large yellow flower with petals like rays of the sun, from whose seeds we get oil. □ **tournesol**

'sunglasses *noun plural* glasses of dark-coloured glass or plastic to protect the eyes in bright sunlight. □ **lunettes de soleil**

'sunlight *noun* the light of the sun: *The cat was sitting in a patch of sunlight.* □ **lumière du soleil**

'sunlit *adjective* lighted up by the sun: *a sunlit room.* □ **ensoleillé**

'sunrise *noun* the rising of the sun in the morning, or the time of this. □ **lever du soleil**

'sunset *noun* the setting of the sun, or the time of this: *the red glow of the sunset.* □ **coucher du soleil**

'sunshade *noun* a type of umbrella for sheltering a person from the sun; a parasol. □ **ombrelle; parasol**

'sunshine *noun* **1** the light of the sun: *The children were playing in the sunshine.* □ **lumière du soleil**

2 cheerfulness or happiness. □ **rayonnement**

'sunstroke *noun* a serious illness caused by being in very hot sunshine for too long. □ **insolation**

'suntan *noun* a brown colour of the skin caused by exposure to the sun: *I'm trying to get a suntan.* □ **bronzage**

catch the sun to become sunburnt. □ **prendre un coup de soleil**

under the sun in the whole world: *I'm sure that she must have visited every country under the sun.* □ **sous le soleil**

sundae ['sʌndei] *noun* a portion of ice cream served with fruit, syrup *etc*: *a fruit sundae.* □ **coupe glacée**

Sunday ['sʌndi] *noun* the first day of the week, the day following Saturday, kept for rest and worship among Christians. □ **dimanche**

Sunday best/clothes the smart garments that a person wears for special occasions. □ **habits du dimanche**

Sunday school a school attended by children on Sundays for religious instruction. □ **école du dimanche, catéchisme**

a month of Sundays a very long time. □ **éternité**

sundial *see* **sun.**

sunflower *see* **sun.**

sung *see* **sing.**

sunglasses *see* **sun.**

sunk, sunken *see* **sink.**

sunlight ... suntan *see* **sun.**

super¹ ['suːpə] *adjective* a slang word for extremely good, nice *etc*: *a super new dress.* □ **super**

super² *see* **superintendent** *under* **superintend.**

superannuate [suːpə'ranjueit] *verb* to retire (a person) from employment because of old age, *especially* with a pension. □ **mettre (qqn) à la retraite**

'super,annu'ation *noun.* □ **retraite**

superb [su'pəːb] *adjective* magnificent or excellent: *a superb view/meal.* □ **superbe, magnifique**

su'perbly *adverb.* □ **superbement, magnifiquement**

supercilious [suːpə'siliəs] *adjective* contemptuous or disdainful: *a supercilious look.* □ **hautain, dédaigneux**

,super'ciliously *adverb.* □ **avec dédain**

,super'ciliousness *noun.* □ **hauteur**

superficial [suːpə'fiʃəl] *adjective* **1** on, or affecting, the surface only: *The wound is only superficial.* □ **superficiel**

2 not thorough: *He has only a superficial knowledge of the subject.* □ **superficiel**

'super,fici'ality [-ʃi'a-] *noun.* □ **superficialité**

,super'ficially *adverb.* □ **superficiellement**

superfluous [su'pəːfluəs] *adjective* extra; beyond what is needed or wanted. □ **superflu**

superhuman [suːpə'hjuːmən] *adjective* divine, or beyond what is human: *superhuman powers; a man of superhuman strength.* □ **surhumain**

superintend [suːpərin'tend] *verb* to supervise: *An adult should be present to superintend the children's activities.* □ **surveiller**

,**superin'tendence** *noun*: *She placed her estate under the superintendence of a manager.* □ **surveillance**

,**superin'tendent** *noun* 1 a person who superintends something, or is in charge of an institution, building *etc*: *the superintendent of a hospital.* □ **directeur, trice**

2 *(abbreviation* **super**; *often abbreviated to* **Supt** *when written)* a police officer of the rank above chief inspector. □ **directeur, trice (de police)**

superior [su'piəriə] *adjective* 1 *(often with* **to**) higher in rank, better, or greater, than: *Is a captain superior to a commander in the navy?; With his superior strength he managed to overwhelm his opponent.* □ **supérieur (à)**

2 high, or above the average, in quality: *superior workmanship.* □ **supérieur**

3 *(of a person or his attitude)* contemptuous or disdainful: *a superior smile.* □ **supérieur**

■ *noun* a person who is better than, or higher in rank than, another or others: *The servant was dismissed for being rude to his superiors.* □ **supérieur, eure**

su,peri'ority [-'o-] *noun*. □ **supériorité**

superlative [su'pɔːlətiv] *adjective* (of an adjective or adverb) of the highest degree of comparison: *'Biggest' is a superlative adjective.* □ **superlatif**

■ *noun* (an adjective or adverb of) the superlative degree: *'Best' and 'worst' are the superlatives of 'good' and 'bad'; She is the prettiest girl in the room; We'll go by different roads to see who will arrive* (*the*) *soonest/ most quickly.* □ **superlatif**

superman ['suːpəman] *noun* an imagined man of the future with amazing powers: *a race of supermen.* □ **surhomme**

supermarket ['suːpəmaːkit] *noun* a large, self-service store selling food and other goods. □ **supermarché**

supernatural [suːpə'natʃərəl] *adjective* (of *eg* matters concerning ghosts *etc*) beyond what is natural or physically possible: *supernatural happenings; a creature of supernatural strength.* □ **surnaturel**

supersonic [suːpə'sonik] *adjective* faster than the speed of sound: *These planes travel at supersonic speeds.* □ **supersonique**

superstition [suːpə'stiʃən] *noun* 1 (the state of fear and ignorance resulting from) the belief in magic, witchcraft and other things that cannot he explained by reason. □ **superstition**

2 an example of this type of belief: *There is an old superstition that those who marry in May will have bad luck.* □ **superstition**

,**super'stitious** *adjective*: *superstitious beliefs; She has always been very superstitious.* □ **superstitieux**

,**super'stitiously** *adverb*. □ **superstitieusement**

supervise ['suːpəvaiz] *verb* to direct, control or be in charge of (work, workers *etc*): *She supervises the typists.* □ **diriger, surveiller, superviser**

,**super'vision** [-'viʒən] *noun* the act or work of supervising or state of being supervised: *The firm's accounts are under the personal supervision of the manager; These children should have more supervision.* □ **supervision**

'**supervisor** *noun* a person who supervises. □ **superviseur, eure; surveillant, ante**

supper ['sʌpə] *noun* a meal taken at the end of the day: *Would you like some supper?; She has invited me to supper.* □ **souper**

'**suppertime** *noun* the time in the evening when people eat supper: *I'll be back at suppertime.* □ **l'heure du souper**

supple ['sʌpl] *adjective* (of the body *etc*) bending easily: *Take exercise if you want to keep supple; supple dancers.* □ **souple**

'**suppleness** *noun*. □ **souplesse**

supplement ['sʌpləmənt] *noun* an addition made to supply something lacking, or to correct errors *etc*: *A supplement to the dictionary is to be published next year.* □ **supplément**

■ [-ment] *verb* to make, or be, an addition to: *He does an evening job to supplement his wages.* □ **ajouter à**

,**supple'mentary** [-'men-] *adjective* added to supply what is lacking; additional. □ **supplémentaire**

suppliant ['sʌpliənt] *noun* a person begging humbly and earnestly *eg* for mercy. □ **suppliant, ante**

supplication [sʌpli'keiʃən] *noun* (an) earnest prayer or entreaty. □ **supplication**

supply [sə'plai] *verb* to give or provide: *Who is supplying the rebels with guns and ammunition?; Extra paper will be supplied by the teacher if it is needed; The town is supplied with water from a reservoir in the hills; The shop was unable to supply what she wanted.* □ **fournir, approvisionner**

■ *noun* 1 the act or process of supplying. □ **approvisionnement**

2 *(often in plural)* an amount or quantity that is supplied; a stock or store: *She left a supply of food for her children when she went away for a few days; Who will be responsible for the expedition's supplies?; Fresh supplies will be arriving soon.* □ **approvisionnement, stocks**

be in short supply (of goods *etc*) to be scarce: *Bread is in short supply.* □ **être en quantité réduite**

support [sə'poːt] *verb* 1 to bear the weight of, or hold upright, in place *etc*: *That chair won't support him/his weight; He limped home, supported by a friend on either side of him.* □ **(sup)porter, soutenir**

2 to give help, or approval to: *She has always supported our cause; His family supported him in his decision.* □ **soutenir**

3 to provide evidence for the truth of: *New discoveries have been made that support his theory; The second witness supported the statement of the first one.* □ **corroborer, confirmer**

4 to supply with the means of living: *They have four children to support.* □ **subvenir aux besoins de**

■ *noun* 1 the act of supporting or state of being supported: *That type of shoe doesn't give the foot much support; The plan was cancelled because of lack of support; Her job is the family's only means of support; I would like to say a word or two in support of his proposal.* □ **soutien, appui**

2 something that supports: *One of the supports of the bridge collapsed.* □ **support**

sup'porter *noun* a person who helps or supports (a person, cause, team *etc*): *a crowd of football supporters.* □ **partisan, ane**

sup'porting *adjective* (of an actor, role *etc*) secondary to the leading actor, role *etc*: *She has had many supporting roles; a supporting cast.* □ **secondaire, de soutien**

suppose [sə'pouz] *verb* **1** to think probable; to believe or guess: *Who do you suppose telephoned today?; 'I suppose you'll be going to the meeting?' 'Yes, I suppose so/No, I don't suppose so.'; Do you suppose she'll win?; 'Surely her statement can't be correct?' 'No, I suppose not.'* □ **supposer**

2 to accept as true for the sake of argument; to consider as a possibility: *(Let's) suppose we each had $100 to spend; Suppose the train's late – what shall we do?* □ **supposer**

3 used to make a suggestion or give an order in a polite way: *Suppose we have lunch now!; Suppose you make us a cup of tea!* □ **et si...**

sup'posing if: *Supposing she doesn't come, what shall we do?* □ **à supposer que**

be supposed to (be/do *etc***) 1** to have the reputation of (being *etc*): *He's supposed to be the best doctor in the town.* □ **passer pour**

2 to be expected or obliged to (do something *etc*): *You're supposed to make your own bed every morning.* □ **être censé**

suppress [sə'pres] *verb* **1** to defeat or put a stop to (*eg* a rebellion). □ **réprimer**

2 to keep back or stifle: *She suppressed a laugh.* □ **réprimer**

3 to prevent from being published, known *etc*: *to suppress information.* □ **interdire**

sup'pression [-ʃən] *noun*. □ **suppression, interdiction**

supreme [su'priːm] *adjective* **1** the highest, greatest, or most powerful: *the supreme ruler.* □ **suprême**

2 the greatest possible: *an act of supreme courage.* □ **suprême**

su'premely *adverb*. □ **suprêmement**

supremacy [su'preməsi] *noun* the state of being the greatest or most powerful: *How did Rome maintain her supremacy over the rest of the world for so long?* □ **suprématie**

surcharge ['səːtʃaːdʒ] *noun* an extra amount of money charged: *We paid for our holiday abroad in advance but we had to pay a surcharge because of the devaluation of the dollar.* □ **surtaxe, majoration**

sure [ʃuə] *adjective* **1** (*negative* **unsure**) having no doubt; certain: *I'm sure that I gave him the book; I'm not sure where she lives/what her address is; 'There's a bus at two o'clock.' 'Are you quite sure?'; I thought the idea was good, but now I'm not so sure; I'll help you – you can be sure of that!* □ **sûr**

2 unlikely to fail (to do or get something): *He's sure to win; You're sure of a good dinner if you stay at that hotel.* □ **sûr**

3 reliable or trustworthy: *a sure way to cure hiccups; a safe, sure method; a sure aim with a rifle.* □ **sûr**

■ *adverb* certainly; of course: *Sure I'll help you!; 'Would you like to come?' 'Sure!'* □ **bien sûr, certainement, bien entendu**

'surely *adverb* **1** used in questions, exclamations *etc* to indicate what the speaker considers probable: *Surely she's finished her work by now!; You don't believe what she said, surely?* □ **sûrement; tout de même**

2 without doubt, hesitation, mistake or failure: *Slowly but surely we're achieving our aim.* □ **sûrement**

3 (in answers) certainly; of course: *'May I come with you?' 'Surely!'* □ **bien sûr**

'sureness *noun*. □ **certitude; assurance**

,sure-'footed *adjective* not likely to slip or stumble: *Goats are sure-footed animals.* □ **au pied sûr**

as sure as used in various phrases that mean 'without fail' or 'without doubt': *As sure as fate/anything/eggs are eggs, he'll be late again.* □ **aussi sûr que**

be sure to don't fail to: *Be sure to switch off the television.* □ **ne pas manquer/oublier de**

be/feel sure of oneself to be confident. □ **être/se sentir sûr de soi**

for sure definitely or certainly: *We don't know for sure that he's dead.* □ **avec certitude**

make sure to act so that, or check that, something is certain or sure: *Arrive early at the cinema to make sure of (getting) a seat!; I think he's coming today but I'll telephone to make sure (of that/that he is).* □ **s'assurer (de)**

sure enough in fact, as was expected: *I thought she'd be angry, and sure enough she was.* □ **effectivement**

surf [səːf] *noun* the foam made as waves break on rocks or on the shore: *The children were playing in the white surf.* □ **écume**

'surfing *noun* the sport of riding on a surfboard. □ **surf**

'surfboard *noun* a board on which a bather rides towards shore on the surf. □ **planche de surf**

surface ['səːfis] *noun* **1** the outside part (of anything): *Two-thirds of the earth's surface is covered with water; This road has a very uneven surface.* □ **surface**

2 the outward appearance of, or first impression made by, a person or thing: *On the surface he seems cold and unfriendly, but he's really a kind person.* □ **apparence**

■ *verb* **1** to put a surface on (a road *etc*): *The road has been damaged by frost and will have to be surfaced again.* □ **revêtir**

2 (of a submarine, diver *etc*) to come to the surface. □ **faire surface**

surface mail mail sent by ship, train *etc* and not by airplane. □ **courrier de surface**

surge [səːdʒ] *verb* (of *eg* water or waves) to move forward with great force: *The waves surged over the rocks.* □ **déferler**

■ *noun* a surging movement, or a sudden rush: *The stone hit his head and he felt a surge of pain; a sudden surge of anger.* □ **accès**

surgeon ['sɜːdʒən] *noun* 1 a doctor who treats injuries or diseases by operations in which the body sometimes has to be cut open, *eg* to remove a diseased part. □ **chirurgien, ienne**

2 a doctor in the army or navy. □ **médecin militaire**

surgery ['sɜːdʒəri] – *plural* 'surgeries – 1 the practice or art of a surgeon: *to specialize in surgery*. □ **chirurgie**

2 a doctor's or dentist's room in which he or she examines patients. □ **cabinet (de consultation)**

surgical ['sɜːdʒikəl] *adjective* of, or by means of, surgery: *surgical instruments*; *She is in need of surgical treatment*. □ **de chirurgie, chirurgical**

'**surgically** *adverb*. □ **par la chirurgie**

surly ['sɜːli] *adjective* bad-tempered or rude. □ **bourru**

'**surliness** *noun*. □ **air bourru**

surmount [sə'maunt] *verb* to overcome or deal with (problems, obstacles *etc*) successfully: *She surmounted these obstacles without trouble*. □ **surmonter**

surname ['sɜːneim] *noun* a person's family name: *The common way of addressing people is by their surnames, preceded by Mr., Mrs., Miss, Dr. etc*; *Smith is a common British surname*. □ **nom de famille**

surpass [sə'pɑːs] *verb* to be, or do, better, or more than. □ **surpasser**

surplus ['sɜːpləs] *noun* the amount left over when what is required has been used *etc*: *Canada produces a surplus of raw materials*; *(also adjective) surplus stocks*; *The country had a trade surplus* (= exported more than it imported) *last month*. □ **(en) surplus**

surprise [sə'praiz] *noun* (the feeling caused by) something sudden or unexpected: *Her statement caused some surprise*; *Your letter was a pleasant surprise*; *There were some nasty surprises waiting for her when she returned*; *He stared at her in surprise*; *To my surprise the door was unlocked*; *(also adjective) She paid them a surprise visit*. □ **surprise**

■ *verb* 1 to cause to feel surprise: *The news surprised me*. □ **surprendre**

2 to lead, by means of surprise, into doing something: *Her sudden question surprised him into betraying himself*. □ **surprendre (au point que)**

3 to find, come upon, or attack, without warning: *They surprised the enemy from the rear*. □ **surprendre**

sur'prised *adjective* showing or feeling surprise: *her surprised face*; *I'm surprised (that) she's not here*; *You behaved badly – I'm surprised at you!*; *I wouldn't be surprised if he won*. □ **surpris**

sur'prising *adjective* likely to cause surprise: *surprising news*; *It is not surprising that he resigned*. □ **surprenant, étonnant**

sur'prisingly *adverb*: *Surprisingly, he did win*. □ **étonnamment**

take by surprise 1 to catch unawares: *The news took me by surprise*. □ **prendre par surprise**

2 to capture (a fort *etc*) by a sudden, unexpected attack. □ **prendre par un coup de main**

surrender [sə'rendə] *verb* 1 to yield: *The general refused to surrender to the enemy*; *We shall never surrender!* □ **se rendre**

2 to give up or abandon: *He surrendered his claim to the throne*; *You must surrender your old passport when applying for a new one*. □ **renoncer à; rendre**

■ *noun* (an) act of surrendering: *The garrison was forced into surrender*. □ **reddition**

surround [sə'raund] *verb* 1 to be, or come, all around: *An island is surrounded by sea*; *Enemy troops surrounded the town*; *Mystery surrounds his death*. □ **entourer**

2 to enclose: *He surrounded the castle with a high wall*. □ **entourer**

sur'rounding *adjective* lying or being all around: *the village and its surrounding scenery*. □ **environnant**

sur'roundings *noun plural* 1 the scenery *etc* that is around a place: *a pleasant hotel in delightful surroundings*. □ **environs**

2 the conditions *etc* in which a person, animal *etc* lives: *He was happy to be at home again in his usual surroundings*. □ **environnement**

survey [sə'vei] *verb* 1 to look at, or view, in a general way: *He surveyed his neat garden with satisfaction*. □ **regarder**

2 to examine carefully or in detail. □ **inspecter**

3 to measure, and estimate the position, shape *etc* of (a piece of land *etc*): *They have started to survey the piece of land that the new highway will pass through*. □ **arpenter**

4 to make a formal or official inspection of (a house *etc* that is being offered for sale). □ **inspecter**

■ ['sɜːvei] *noun* 1 a look or examination; a report: *After a brief survey of the damage he telephoned the police*; *He has written a survey of crime in big cities*. □ **examen; étude**

2 a careful measurement of land *etc*. □ **relevé**

sur'veyor *noun* a person whose job is to survey buildings or land. □ **arpenteur, euse géomètre**

survive [sə'vaiv] *verb* 1 to remain alive in spite of (a disaster *etc*): *Few birds managed to survive the bad winter*; *He didn't survive long after the accident*. □ **survivre (à)**

2 to live longer than: *He died in 1940 but his wife survived him by another twenty years*; *He is survived by his wife and two sons*. □ **survivre (à)**

sur'vival *noun* the state of surviving: *the problem of survival in sub-zero temperatures*; *(also adjective) survival equipment*. □ **(de) survie**

sur'viving *adjective* remaining alive: *She has no surviving relatives*. □ **survivant**

sur'vivor *noun* a person who survives a disaster *etc*: *There were no survivors of the air crash*. □ **survivant, ante**

suspect [sə'spekt] *verb* 1 to think (a person *etc*) guilty: *Whom do you suspect (of the crime)?*; *I suspect him of killing the girl*. □ **soupçonner (de)**

2 to distrust: *I suspected her motives/air of honesty*. □ **suspecter**

3 to think probable: *I suspect that she's trying to hide her true feelings*; *I began to suspect a plot*. □ **soupçonner**

■ ['sʌspekt] *noun* a person who is thought guilty: *There are three possible suspects in this murder case*.

□ **suspect**

■ *adjective* not trustworthy: *I think his statement is suspect.* □ **suspect**

suspicion [sə'spiʃən] *noun* **1** the process of suspecting or being suspected; the/a feeling causing a person to suspect: *They looked at each other with suspicion; I have a suspicion that she is not telling the truth.* □ **soupçon**

2 a slight quantity or trace: *There was a suspicion of triumph in her tone.* □ **soupçon**

suspicious [sə'spiʃəs] *adjective* **1** having or showing suspicion: *I'm always suspicious of men like him; a suspicious glance.* □ **méfiant, soupçonneux**

2 causing or arousing suspicion: *suspicious circumstances.* □ **suspect**

suspiciously [sə'spiʃəsli] *adverb.* □ **avec méfiance, d'une manière suspecte**

su'spiciousness *noun.* □ **caractère soupçonneux/suspect**

suspend [sə'spend] *verb* **1** to hang: *The meat was suspended from a hook.* □ **suspendre**

2 to keep from falling or sinking: *Particles of dust are suspended in the air.* □ **suspendre**

3 to stop or discontinue temporarily: *All business will be suspended until after the funeral.* □ **suspendre**

4 to prevent (a person) temporarily from continuing his or her (professional) activities or having their usual privileges: *Two footballers were suspended after yesterday's match.* □ **suspendre**

su'spenders *noun plural* braces for holding up trousers. □ **bretelles**

su'spense [-s] *noun* a state of uncertainty and anxiety: *We waited in suspense for the result of the competition.* □ **angoisse**

su'spension [-ʃən] *noun* **1** the act of suspending. □ **suspension**

2 in a motor vehicle *etc*, the system of springs *etc* supporting the frame on the axles. □ **suspension**

3 a liquid with solid particles that do not sink. □ **suspension**

suspension bridge a type of bridge that has its roadway suspended from cables supported by towers. □ **pont suspendu**

suspicion, suspicious *etc see* **suspect**.

sustain [sə'stein] *verb* **1** to bear (the weight of): *The branches could hardly sustain the weight of the fruit.* □ **supporter**

2 to give help or strength to: *The thought of seeing her again sustained him throughout his ordeal.* □ **soutenir**

swag [swag] *noun* **1** stolen goods. □ **butin**

2 in Australia, a tramp's bundle. □ **baluchon**

swagger ['swagə] *verb* to walk as though very pleased with oneself: *I saw him swaggering along the street in his new suit.* □ **se pavaner**

■ *noun* a swaggering way of walking. □ **démarche fanfaronne**

swallow¹ ['swolou] *verb* **1** to allow to pass down the throat to the stomach: *Try to swallow the pill; Her throat was so painful that she could hardly swallow.* □ **avaler**

2 to accept (*eg* a lie or insult) without question or pro-

test: *You'll never get her to swallow that story!* □ **avaler**

■ *noun* an act of swallowing. □ **avalement, déglutition**

swallow one's pride to behave humbly *eg* by making an apology. □ **ravaler son amour-propre**

swallow up to cause to disappear completely: *She was swallowed up in the crowd.* □ **engloutir**

swallow² ['swolou] *noun* a type of insect-eating bird with long wings and a divided tail. □ **hirondelle**

swam *see* **swim**.

swamp [swomp] *noun* (an area of) wet, marshy ground: *These trees grow best in swamp(s).* □ **marécage**

■ *verb* to cover or fill with water: *A great wave swamped the deck.* □ **inonder**

'swampy *adjective* (of land) covered with swamp; marshy. □ **marécageux**

'swampiness *noun.* □ **caractère marécageux**

swan [swon] *noun* a large, *usually* white, water-bird of the duck family, with a long graceful neck. □ **cygne**

swan song the last work or performance of *eg* a poet, musician *etc* before his or her death or retirement. □ **chant du cygne**

swank [swaŋk] *verb* a slang word for: to behave or talk in a conceited way. □ **se donner des airs**

■ *noun* a person who swanks. □ **poseur, euse**

'swanky *adjective.* □ **poseur**

swap *see* **swop**.

swarm [swoːm] *noun* **1** a great number (of insects or other small creatures) moving together: *a swarm of ants.* □ **essaim**

2 (*often in plural*) a great number or crowd: *swarms of people.* □ **essaim, troupe**

■ *verb* **1** (of bees) to follow a queen bee in a swarm. □ **essaimer**

2 to move in great numbers: *The children swarmed out of the school.* □ **aller en masse**

3 to be full of moving crowds: *The Tower of London was swarming with tourists.* □ **fourmiller de**

swastika ['swostikə] *noun* a cross with the ends bent at right angles, adopted as the badge of the Nazi party in Germany before the Second World War. □ **croix gammée**

swat [swot] – *past tense, past participle* **'swatted** – *verb* to crush (a fly *etc*) by slapping it with something flat: *She swatted the fly with a folded newspaper.* □ **écraser (avec une tapette)**

■ *noun* an act of swatting: *She gave the wasp a swat.* □ **coup de tapette**

swathe [sweið] *verb* to wrap or bind: *Her head was swathed in a towel.* □ **envelopper**

sway [swei] *verb* **1** to (cause to) move from side to side or up and down with a swinging or rocking action: *The branches swayed gently in the breeze.* □ **se balancer**

2 to influence the opinion *etc* of: *She's too easily swayed by her feelings.* □ **influencer**

■ *noun* **1** the motion of swaying: *the sway of the ship's deck.* □ **balancement**

2 power, rule or control: *the countries under the sway of Russia.* □ **domination**

swear [sweə] – *past tense* **swore** [swoː]: *past participle* **sworn** [swoːn] – *verb* **1** to state, declare, or promise solemnly with an oath, or very definitely and positively: *The witness must swear to tell the truth*; *She swore an oath of loyalty*; *Swear never to reveal the secret*; *I could have sworn* (= I'm sure) *she was here a minute ago.* □ **jurer**

2 to use the name of God and other sacred words, or obscene words, for emphasis or abuse; to curse: *Don't swear in front of the children!* □ **jurer**

sworn [swɔːn] *adjective* **1** (of friends, enemies *etc*) (determined, as if) having taken an oath always to remain so: *They are sworn enemies.* □ **juré**

2 (of evidence, statements *etc*) given by a person who has sworn to tell the truth: *The prisoner made a sworn statement.* □ **fait sous serment**

'**swear word** *noun* a word used in cursing: '*Damn*' *is a mild swear word.* □ **juron**

swear by 1 to appeal to (*eg* God) as a witness of one's words: *I swear by Heaven that I'm innocent.* □ **jurer par**

2 to put complete trust in (a remedy *etc*): *She swears by aspirin for all the children's illnesses.* □ **ne jurer que par**

swear in to introduce (a person) into a post or office formally, by making him swear an oath: *The new Governor is being sworn in next week.* □ **faire prêter serment à**

swear to to make a solemn statement, with an oath, in support of: *I'll swear to the truth of what she said*; *I think she was here this morning, but I wouldn't like to swear to it.* □ **attester**

sweat [swet] *noun* the moisture given out through the skin: *He was dripping with sweat after running so far in the heat.* □ **sueur**

■ *verb* **1** to give out sweat: *Vigorous exercise makes you sweat.* □ **suer**

2 to work hard: *I was sweating (away) at my work from morning till night.* □ **suer sur**

'**sweater** *noun* any kind of knitted pullover or jersey. □ **tricot, chandail**

'**sweaty** *adjective* wet or stained with, or smelling of, sweat: *sweaty clothes/bodies.* □ **moite de sueur**

'**sweatiness** *noun.* □ **moiteur (de transpiration)**

a cold sweat (coldness and dampness of the skin when a person is in) a state of shock, fear *etc*. □ **sueur froide**

sweep [swiːp] *– past tense, past participle* **swept** [swept] *– verb* **1** to clean (a room *etc*) using a brush or broom: *The room has been swept clean.* □ **balayer**

2 to move as though with a brush: *She swept the crumbs off the table with her hand*; *The wave swept him overboard*; *Don't get swept away by* (= become over-enthusiastic about) *the idea!*; *She swept aside my objections.* □ **balayer**

3 to move quickly over: *The disease/craze is sweeping the country.* □ **balayer**

4 to move swiftly or in a proud manner: *High winds sweep across the desert*; *She swept into my room without knocking on the door.* □ **balayer; aller majestueusement**

■ *noun* **1** an act of sweeping, or process of being swept, with a brush *etc*: *She gave the room a sweep.* □ **balayage**

2 a sweeping movement: *He indicated the damage with a sweep of his hand.* □ **mouvement circulaire**

3 a person who cleans chimneys. □ **ramoneur, euse**

4 a sweepstake. □ **sweepstake**

'**sweeper** *noun* a person or thing that sweeps: *a road-sweeper*; *May I borrow your carpet-sweeper?* □ **balayeur, euse; balai mécanique**

'**sweeping** *adjective* **1** that sweeps: *a sweeping gesture.* □ **large**

2 (of changes *etc*) very great: *a sweeping victory*; *sweeping reforms.* □ **radical**

at one/a sweep by one action, at one time: *He sacked half of his employees at one sweep.* □ **d'un seul coup**

sweep (someone) off his feet to affect (a person) with strong emotion or enthusiasm. □ **(s')emballer**

sweep out to sweep (a room *etc*) thoroughly; to clean by sweeping: *to sweep the classroom out.* □ **balayer**

sweep the board to be very successful; to win all the prizes. □ **remporter haut la main; faire table rase**

sweep under the carpet to avoid facing, or dealing with (an unpleasant situation *etc*) by pretending it does not exist. □ **faire l'autruche**

sweep up to gather together or remove (dirt *etc*) by sweeping: *She swept up the crumbs/mess.* □ **balayer**

sweepstake [ˈswiːpsteik] *noun* a system of gambling *eg* on a horse-race, in which the person who holds a ticket for the winning horse gets all the money staked by the other ticketholders. □ **sweepstake**

sweet [swiːt] *adjective* **1** tasting like sugar; not sour, salty or bitter: *as sweet as honey*; *Children eat too many sweet foods.* □ **sucré**

2 tasting fresh and pleasant: *young, sweet vegetables.* □ **frais**

3 (of smells) pleasant or fragrant: *the sweet smell of flowers.* □ **suave**

4 (of sounds) agreeable or delightful to hear: *the sweet song of the nightingale.* □ **mélodieux**

5 attractive or charming: *What a sweet little baby!*; *a sweet face/smile*; *You look sweet in that dress.* □ **mignon**

6 kindly and agreeable: *She's a sweet girl*; *The child has a sweet nature.* □ **gentil**

■ *noun* **1** (ˈcandy) a small piece of sweet food *eg* chocolate, toffee *etc*: *a packet of sweets*; *Have a sweet.* □ **bonbon, friandise**

2 (a dish or course of) sweet food near or at the end of a meal; (a) pudding or dessert: *The waiter served the sweet.* □ **dessert**

3 dear; darling: *Hello, my sweet!* □ **chéri, ie**

'**sweeten** *verb* to make or become sweet or sweeter: *Did you sweeten* (= put sugar in) *my tea?* □ **sucrer**

'**sweetener** *noun* something that sweetens, *eg* a substance used for sweetening food: *Saccharin is an artificial sweetener, often used instead of sugar.* □ **édulcorant**

'**sweetly** *adverb* in an attractive, charming, agreeable or kindly manner: *She sang/smiled very sweetly.* □ **gentiment, agréablement**

'**sweetness** *noun.* □ **douceur, gentillesse**

'**sweetheart** *noun* **1** a boyfriend or girlfriend. □ **amoureux, euse**

2 used as an endearment for any beloved person, *eg* a child: *Goodbye, sweetheart!* □ **chéri, ie**

sweet potato (the edible tuber of) a tropical twining plant. □ **patate douce**

sweet-'smelling *adjective: sweet-smelling flowers.* □ **odorant**

sweet-'tempered *adjective* kind and friendly. □ **aimable**

swell [swel] – *past tense* **swelled**: *past participle* **swollen** ['swoulən] – *verb* to make or become larger, greater or thicker: *The insect-bite made her finger swell; The continual rain had swollen the river; I invited her to join us on the excursion in order to swell the numbers.* □ **enfler, gonfler**

■ *noun* a rolling condition of the sea, *usually* after a storm: *The sea looked fairly calm but there was a heavy swell.* □ **houle**

■ *adjective* used as a term of approval: *a swell idea; That's swell!* □ **épatant**

'swelling *noun* 1 a swollen area, *especially* on the body as a result of injury, disease *etc: She had a swelling on her arm where the wasp had stung her.* □ **enflure, gonflement**

2 the rising of the level of water in a river or stream near the point of overflowing: *The citizens were afraid the town would flood when they saw the swelling of the river.* □ **crue**

swollen ['swoulən] *adjective* increased in size, thickness *etc*, through swelling: *a swollen river; He had a swollen ankle after falling down the stairs.* □ **enflé**

,swollen-'headed *adjective* too pleased with oneself; conceited: *He's very swollen-headed about his success.* □ **prétentieux, euse**

swell out to (cause to) bulge: *The sails swelled out in the wind.* □ **(se) gonfler**

swell up (of a part of the body) to swell: *The toothache made her face swell up.* □ **enfler**

swelter ['sweltə] *verb* (of a person *etc*) to be uncomfortably hot: *I'm sweltering in this heat!* □ **étouffer de chaleur**

swept *see* **sweep.**

swerve [swəːv] *verb* to turn away (from a line or course), *especially* quickly: *The car driver swerved to avoid the dog; She never swerved from her purpose.* □ **dévier (de)**

■ *noun* an act of swerving: *The sudden swerve rocked the passengers in their seats.* □ **écart**

swift[1] [swift] *adjective* fast or quick: *a swift horse; Our methods are swift and efficient; a swift-footed animal.* □ **rapide**

'swiftly *adverb.* □ **rapidement**

'swiftness *noun.* □ **rapidité**

swift[2] [swift] *noun* a type of bird rather like a swallow. □ **martinet**

swig [swig] – *past tense, past participle* **swigged** – *verb* to drink: *He's in the bar swigging beer.* □ **boire à grands coups**

■ *noun* a long gulp: *He took a swig from the bottle.* □ **bon coup**

swill [swil] *verb* to drink greedily: *She swilled the beer without sharing.* □ **boire d'un trait**

■ *noun (also* **'pigswill)** semi-liquid food given to pigs.

□ **pâtée**

swim [swim] – *present participle* **'swimming**: *past tense* **swam** [swam]: *past participle* **swum** [swʌm] – *verb* 1 to move through water using arms and legs or fins, tails *etc: The children aren't allowed to go sailing until they've learnt to swim; I'm going/I've been swimming; She swam into the cave; They watched the fish swimming about in the aquarium.* □ **nager**

2 to cross (a river *etc*), compete in (a race), cover (a distance *etc*) by swimming: *She swam three lengths of the swimming pool; She can't swim a stroke* (= at all). □ **nager**

3 to seem to be moving around and around, as a result of dizziness *etc: His head was swimming; Everything began to swim before his eyes.* □ **tourner**

■ *noun* an act of swimming: *We went for a swim in the lake.* □ **nage**

'swimmer *noun* a person who swims or who can swim: *He's a strong swimmer.* □ **nageur, euse**

'swimming *adjective* covered with, or floating in, a liquid: *meat swimming in/with grease.* □ **baignant, nageant (dans)**

'swimming pool *nouns* an indoor or outdoor pool for swimming in. □ **piscine**

'swimming trunks *noun plural* short pants worn by boys and men for swimming. □ **maillot de bain**

'swimsuit *nouns* a (woman's) garment worn for swimming. □ **maillot de bain**

swindle ['swindl] *verb* to cheat: *That shopkeeper has swindled me!; He swindled me out of $4.* □ **escroquer**

■ *noun* an act or example of swindling; a fraud: *an insurance swindle; Our new car's a swindle – it's falling to pieces.* □ **escroquerie**

'swindler *noun* a person who swindles. □ **escroc**

swine [swain] *noun* 1 (*plural* **swine**) an old word for a pig. □ **pourceau**

2 (*plural* **swines**) an offensive word for a person who behaves in a cruel or disgusting way towards others. □ **salaud**

swing [swiŋ] – *past tense, past participle* **swung** [swʌŋ] – *verb* 1 to (cause to) move or sway in a curve (from side to side or forwards and backwards) from a fixed point: *You swing your arms when you walk; The children were swinging on a rope hanging from a tree; The door swung open; He swung the load on to his shoulder.* □ **(se) balancer**

2 to walk with a stride: *He swung along the road.* □ **marcher d'un pas rythmé**

3 to turn suddenly: *He swung around and stared at them; He is hoping to swing the voters in his favour.* □ **(se) retourner**

■ *noun* 1 an act, period, or manner, of swinging: *He was having a swing on the rope; Most golfers would like to improve their swing.* □ **balancement**

2 a swinging movement: *the swing of the dancers' skirts.* □ **balancement**

3 a strong dancing rhythm: *The music should be played with a swing.* □ **rythme entraînant**

4 a change in public opinion *etc: a swing away from the government.* □ **revirement**

5 a seat for swinging, hung on ropes or chains from a supporting frame *etc.* □ **balançoire**
'swinging *adjective* fashionable and exciting: *the swinging city of Montreal.* □ **à la mode**
swing bridge a type of bridge that swings open to let ships pass. □ **pont tournant**
swing door a door that swings open in both directions. □ **porte battante**
be in full swing to be going ahead, or continuing, busily or vigorously: *The work was in full swing.* □ **battre son plein**
get into the swing (of things) to begin to fit into a routine *etc.* □ **se mettre au courant**
go with a swing (of an organized event *etc*) to proceed or go easily and successfully. □ **très bien marcher**
swipe [swaip] *verb* to hit hard: *She swiped the tennis ball over the net; He swiped at the wasp but didn't hit it.* □ **frapper à toute volée**
■ *noun* a hard hit: *She gave the child a swipe.* □ **taloche**
swirl [swəːl] *verb* to (cause to) move quickly, with a whirling or circling motion: *The leaves were swirled along the ground by the wind.* □ **(faire) tourbillonner**
■ *noun* a whirling or circling motion or shape: *The dancers came on stage in a swirl of colour.* □ **tourbillon**
swish [swiʃ] *verb* to (cause to) move with a hissing or rustling sound: *He swished the stick about in the air.* □ **faire siffler**
■ *noun* an act, or the sound, of swishing: *The horse cantered away with a swish of its tail.* □ **bruissement**
switch [switʃ] *noun* 1 a small lever, handle or other device *eg* for putting or turning an electric current on or off: *The switch is down when the power is on and up when it's off; He couldn't find the light-switch.* □ **interrupteur, commutateur**
2 an act of turning or changing: *After several switches of direction they found themselves on the right road.* □ **changement**
3 a thin stick. □ **baguette**
■ *verb* to change, turn: *He switched the lever to the 'off' position; Let's switch over to another program; Having considered that problem, they switched their attention to other matters.* □ **changer (de); détourner**
'switchback *noun* a railway *eg* in an amusement park, or a road that has many ups and downs (and sudden turns): *Let's go along the switchback.* □ **montagnes russes**
'switchboard *noun* a board with many switches for controlling electric currents *etc*, or for making connections by telephone, *eg* within a large office *etc.* □ **tableau de distribution; standard**
switch on/off to put or turn on/off (an electric current/ light *etc*): *He switched on the light; Switch off the electricity before going on holiday.* □ **allumer; éteindre**
swivel ['swivl] *noun* a type of joint between two parts of an object (*eg* between a chair and its base) that enables one part to turn without the other. □ **pivot**
■ *verb* – *past tense, past participle* 'swivelled – to move around (as though) on a swivel: *He swivelled his chair around to face the desk.* □ **(faire) pivoter**
swollen *see* swell.

swoon [swuːn] *verb* (an old word for) to faint. □ **s'évanouir**
■ *noun* a fainting fit. □ **évanouissement**
swoop [swuːp] *verb* to rush or fly downwards: *The owl swooped down on its prey.* □ **fondre/piquer sur**
■ *noun* an act of swooping. □ **descente en piqué**
at one fell swoop all at the same time; in a single movement or action. □ **d'un seul coup**
swop, swap [swop] – *past tense, past participle* **swopped, swapped** – *verb* to exchange one thing for another: *He swopped his ball with another boy for a pistol; They swopped books with each other.* □ **échanger**
■ *noun* an exchange: *a fair swop.* □ **échange**
sword [soːd] *noun* a weapon with a long blade that is sharp on one or both edges: *He drew his sword (from its sheath) and killed the man.* □ **épée**
'swordplay *noun* the activity of fencing. □ **escrime**
'swordsman ['soːdz-] *noun* a man who can fight or fence with a sword. □ **escrimeur, euse**
'swordtail *noun* a tropical fish of fresh water, the male having a long sword-shaped tail. □ **porte-épée**
cross swords to quarrel or disagree: *I try not to cross swords with my boss.* □ **croiser le fer avec**
swore, sworn *see* swear.
swum *see* swim.
swung *see* swing.
syllable ['siləbl] *noun* a word or part of a word *usually* containing a vowel sound: *'Cheese' has one syllable, 'but-ter' two and 'mar-ga-rine' three.* □ **syllabe**
syllabic [-'la-] *adjective.* □ **syllabique**
syllabus ['siləbəs] *noun* a program or list, *eg* of a course of lectures, or of courses of study. □ **plan de cours**
symbol ['simbəl] *noun* a thing that is regarded as representing or standing for another: *The dove is the symbol of peace.* □ **symbole**
sym'bolic [-'bo-] *adjective*: *In the Christian religion, bread and wine are symbolic of Christ's body and blood.* □ **symbolique**
sym'bolically *adverb.* □ **symboliquement**
'symbolize, 'symbolise *verb* to be a symbol of or represent by a symbol: *A ring symbolizes everlasting love.* □ **symboliser**
'symbolism *noun.* □ **symbolisme**
symmetry ['simitri] *noun* the state in which two parts, on either side of a dividing line, are equal in size, shape and position. □ **symétrie**
sym'metrical [-'me-] *adjective* having symmetry: *The two sides of a person's face are never completely symmetrical.* □ **symétrique**
sym'metrically *adverb.* □ **symétriquement**
sympathy ['simpəθi] *noun* 1 a feeling of pity or sorrow for a person in trouble: *When her husband died, she received many letters of sympathy.* □ **sympathie**
2 the state or feeling of being in agreement with, or of being able to understand, the attitude or feelings of another person: *I have no sympathy with such a stupid attitude; Are you in sympathy with the strikers?* □ **(en) sympathie**
,sympa'thetic [-'θetik] *adjective* (negative **unsympathetic**) showing or feeling sympathy: *She was very sym-*

pathetic when I failed my exam; a sympathetic smile. □
compatissant; de sympathie
sympa'thetically *adverb*. □ **sympathiquement**
'sympathize, 'sympathise *verb* to show or feel sympathy to: *I find it difficult to sympathize with him when he complains so much.* □ **sympathiser**
symphony ['simfəni] – *plural* **'symphonies** – *noun* a *usually* long piece of music for an orchestra of many different instruments, in three or four movements or parts. □ **symphonie**
sym'phonic [-'fo-] *adjective*. □ **symphonique**
symptom ['simptəm] *noun* something that a person suffers from that indicates a particular disease: *abdominal pain is a symptom of appendicitis.* □ **symptôme**
,sympto'matic [-'matik] *adjective*. □ **symptomatique**
synagogue ['sinəgog] *noun* (the building used by) a gathering of Jews meeting together for worship. □ **synagogue**
synchronize, synchronise ['siŋkrənaiz] *verb* to (cause to) happen at the same time, go at the same speed *etc*, as something else: *In the film, the movements of the actors' lips did not synchronize with the sounds of their words; to synchronize watches.* □ **(se) synchroniser**
,synchroni'zation, ,synchroni'sation *noun*. □ **synchronisation**
syncopate ['siŋkəpeit] *verb* to alter the rhythm of (music) by putting the accent on beats not usually accented. □ **syncoper**
,synco'pation *noun*. □ **syncope**
syndicate ['sindikət] *noun* **1** a council or number of persons who join together to manage a piece of business. □ **syndicat**
2 a group of newspapers under the same management. □ **syndicat de distribution**
syntax ['sintaks] *noun* (the rules for) the correct arrangement of words in a sentence. □ **syntaxe**

synthesis ['sinθəsis] – *plural* **'syntheses** [-siːz] – *noun* (something produced through) the process of combining separate parts, *eg* chemical elements or substances, into a whole: *Plastic is produced by synthesis; His recent book is a synthesis of several of his earlier ideas.* □ **synthèse**
'synthesize, 'synthesise *verb* to make (*eg* a drug) by synthesis: *Some hormones can be synthesized.* □ **synthétiser**
synthetic [sin'θetik] *noun, adjective* (a substance) produced artificially by a chemical process: *nylon and other synthetic materials/synthetics.* □ **synthétique**
syphon *see* **siphon**.
syringe [si'rindʒ] *noun* an instrument for sucking up and squirting out liquids, sometimes having a needle for giving injections. □ **seringue**
■ *verb* to clean or wash *eg* ears using a syringe. □ **laver avec une seringue**
syrup ['sərəp] *noun* **1** water or the juice of fruits boiled with sugar and made thick and sticky. □ **sirop**
2 a purified form of treacle. □ **mélasse**
'syrupy *adjective* of, or like, syrup. □ **sirupeux**
system ['sistəm] *noun* **1** an arrangement of many parts that work together: *a railway system; the solar system; the digestive system.* □ **système**
2 a person's body: *Take a walk every day – it's good for the system!* □ **organisme**
3 a way of organizing something according to certain ideas, principles *etc*: *a system of government/education.* □ **système**
4 a plan or method: *What is your system for washing the dishes?* □ **méthode**
5 the quality of being efficient and methodical: *Your work lacks system.* □ **méthode**
,syste'matic [-'matik] *adjective*. □ **systématique**
,syste'matically *adverb*. □ **systématiquement**

Tt

T [tiː]: **'T-shirt** (*also* **'tee shirt**) *noun* a light shirt of knitted cotton *etc* with short sleeves. □ **tee-shirt**

ta [taː] *interjection* (used *especially* by or to young children) thank you: *The baby says 'please' and 'ta'.* □ **merci**

tab [tab] *noun* **1** a small flat piece of some material attached to, or part of, something larger, which stands up so that it can be seen, held, pulled *etc*: *You open the packet by pulling the tab.* □ **patte, languette**

2 a strip of material attached to a piece of clothing by which it can be hung up: *Hang your jacket up by the tab.* □ **attache**

3 a piece of material with a person's name or some other mark on it, attached to a piece of clothing so that its owner can be identified. □ **étiquette, marque**

tabby ['tabi] – *plural* **'tabbies** – *noun* (*also* **'tabby cat**) a *usually* grey or brown cat with darker stripes, *especially* a female one. □ **chat tigré, chatte tigrée**

table ['teibl] *noun* **1** a piece of furniture consisting of a flat, horizontal surface on legs used *eg* to put food on at meals, or for some games: *Put all the plates on the table.* □ **table**

2 a statement of facts or figures arranged in columns *etc*: *The results of the experiments can be seen in table 5.* □ **table, tableau**

3 the people sitting at a table: *The whole table heard what she said.* □ **table, tablée**

'tablecloth *noun* a cloth for covering a table, *usually* for a meal: *an embroidered tablecloth.* □ **nappe**

table linen tablecloths, napkins *etc*: *They gave us table linen as a wedding present.* □ **linge de table**

'tablespoon *noun* **1** a large spoon, used *eg* for serving food. □ **cuiller de service**

2 a tablespoonful: *Add a tablespoon of sugar.* □ **cuillerée à soupe**

'tablespoonful *noun* the amount that will fill a tablespoon: *two tablespoonfuls of jam.* □ **cuillerée à soupe**

'tableware *noun* the dishes and cutlery used at a table for meals: *The guests will be here soon so take out the tableware and set the table.* □ **vaisselle**

table tennis a game played on a table with small bats and a light ball. □ **ping-pong**

lay/set the table to put a tablecloth, plates, knives, forks *etc* on a table for a meal: *The meal is ready – will you lay the table?* □ **mettre la table**

tablet ['tablit] *noun* **1** a pill: *Take these tablets for your headache*; *a sleeping-tablet* (= a tablet to make one sleep). □ **comprimé, pastille**

2 a flat piece or bar (of soap *etc*): *I bought a tablet of soap.* □ **tablette, pain**

3 a piece of *usually* stone with a flat surface on which words are engraved *etc*: *They put up a marble tablet in memory of her father.* □ **plaque**

taboo, tabu [təˈbuː] – *plurals* **ta'boos, ta'bus** – *noun, adjective* (something) forbidden for religious reasons or because it is against social custom: *Alcohol is (a) taboo in Muslim societies.* □ **tabou**

tack [tak] *noun* **1** a short nail with a broad flat head: *a carpet-tack.* □ **punaise**

2 in sewing, a large, temporary stitch used to hold material together while it is being sewn together properly. □ **faufil**

3 in sailing, a movement diagonally against the wind: *We sailed on an easterly tack.* □ **bord(ée)**

4 a direction or course: *After they moved, their lives took a different tack.* □ **voie, direction**

■ *verb* **1** (with **down, on** *etc*) to fasten (with tacks): *I tacked the carpet down*; *She tacked the material together.* □ **clouer, faufiler**

2 (of sailing-boats) to move diagonally (backwards and forwards) against the wind: *The boat tacked into harbour.* □ **tirer une/des bordée(s)**

tackle ['takl] *noun* **1** an act of tackling: *a rugby tackle.* □ **plaquage**

2 equipment, *especially* for fishing: *fishing tackle.* □ **matériel**

3 ropes, pulleys *etc* for lifting heavy weights: *lifting tackle.* □ **appareil de levage**

4 in sailing, the ropes, rigging *etc* of a boat. □ **gréement**

■ *verb* **1** to try to grasp or seize (someone): *The policeman tackled the thief.* □ **saisir à bras le corps**

2 to deal with or try to solve (a problem); to ask (someone) about a problem: *He tackled the problem*; *She tackled the teacher about her child's work.* □ **s'attaquer à; questionner**

3 in football, hockey *etc*, to (try to) take the ball *etc* from (a player in the other team): *He tackled his opponent.* □ **plaquer**

tact [takt] *noun* care and skill in one's behaviour to people, in order to avoid hurting or offending them: *She showed tact in dealing with difficult customers.* □ **tact**

'tactful *adjective* showing tact: *a tactful person*; *tactful behaviour.* □ **délicat**

'tactfully *adverb.* □ **avec tact**

'tactfulness *noun.* □ **tact**

tactless *adjective* without tact: *a tactless person/remark.* □ **grossier**

'tactlessly *adverb.* □ **grossièrement**

'tactlessness *noun.* □ **grossièreté**

tactics ['taktiks] *noun plural* (*sometimes in singular*) the art of arranging troops, warships *etc* during a battle, in order to win or gain an advantage over one's opponents: *They planned their tactics for the election/game/meeting.* □ **tactique**

'tactical *adjective* of or concerned with tactics or successful planning: *a tactical advantage.* □ **tactique**

'tactically *adverb.* □ **tactiquement**

tac'tician [-ˈtiʃən] *noun* a person who is good at tactics or successful planning. □ **tacticien, ienne**

tadpole ['tadpoul] *noun* a young frog or toad in its first stage of development. □ **têtard**

tag [tag] *noun* **1** a label: *a price-tag*; *a name-tag.* □ **étiquette**

2 a saying or quotation that is often repeated: *a well-known Latin tag.* □ **cliché**

3 something small that is added on or attached. □ **bout**

■ *verb* – *past tense, past participle* **tagged** – to put a tag or label on something: *All the clothes have been tagged.* □ **marquer, étiqueter**

tag along (*often with* **behind** *or* **with**) to follow or go (with someone), often when one is not wanted: *We never get away from him – everywhere we go, he insists on tagging along (with us)!* □ **suivre, traîner derrière**

tag on 1 (*usually with* **at** *or* **to**) to attach (something) to something: *These comments weren't part of his speech – he just tagged them on at the end.* □ **ajouter (après coup) (à)**

2 to follow (someone) closely: *The child always tags on to her elder sister.* □ **coller aux talons de**

tail [teil] *noun* 1 the part of an animal, bird or fish that sticks out behind the rest of its body: *The dog wagged its tail; A fish swims by moving its tail.* □ **queue**

2 anything which has a similar function or position: *the tail of an airplane/comet.* □ **queue**

■ *verb* to follow closely: *The detectives tailed the thief to the station.* □ **filer**

-tailed having a (certain size, type *etc* of) tail: *a black-tailed duck; a long-tailed dog.* □ **à (la) queue (...)**

tails *noun, adverb* (on) the side of a coin that does not have the head of the sovereign *etc* on it: *She tossed the coin and it came down tails.* □ **pile**

■ *interjection* a call showing that a person has chosen that side of the coin when tossing a coin to make a decision *etc.* □ **pile**

,tail 'end *noun* the very end or last part: *the tail end of the procession.* □ **queue**

'tail light *noun* the (*usually* red) light on the back of a car, train *etc*: *She followed the tail lights of the bus.* □ **feu arrière**

tail wind a wind coming from behind: *We sailed home with a tail wind.* □ **vent arrière**

tail off 1 to become fewer, smaller or weaker (at the end): *His interest tailed off towards the end of the film.* □ **diminuer**

2 (*also* **tail away**) (of voices *etc*) to become quieter or silent: *Her voice tailed away into silence.* □ **se taire peu à peu**

tailor ['teilə] *noun* a person who cuts and makes suits, overcoats *etc*: *He has his clothes made by a London tailor.* □ **tailleur, couturière**

■ *verb* 1 to make and fit (suits, coats *etc*): *He has his suits tailored in London.* □ **faire sur mesure**

2 to make (something) fit the circumstances; to adapt: *He tailored his way of living to his income.* □ **adapter (à)**

,tailor-'made *adjective* 1 (*especially* of women's clothes) made by a tailor to fit a person exactly. □ **fait sur mesure**

2 very well suited or adapted for some purpose: *Her new job seems tailor-made for her.* □ **fait pour**

taint [teint] *verb* 1 to spoil (something) by touching it or bringing it into contact with something bad or rotten: *The meat has been tainted.* □ **gâter, corrompre**

2 to affect (someone or something) with something evil or immoral; to corrupt: *He has been tainted by his contact with criminals.* □ **corrompre**

■ *noun* a mark or trace of something bad, rotten or evil:

the taint of decay. □ **souillure, corruption**

'tainted *adjective* spoiled or corrupted: *tainted food; The nation is tainted with evil and corruption.* □ **souillé, corrompu**

take [teik] – *past tense* **took** [tuk]: *past participle* **taken** – *verb* 1 (*often with* **down, out** *etc*) to reach out for and grasp, hold, lift, pull *etc*: *She took my hand; He took the book down from the shelf; He opened the drawer and took out a gun; I've had a tooth taken out.* □ **prendre**

2 (*often with* **away, in, off, out** *etc*) to carry, conduct or lead to another place: *I took the books (back) to the library; He's taking me with him; Take her into my office; The police took him away; I took the dog out for a walk; He took her out for dinner.* □ **apporter/emporter, amener/emmener**

3 to do or perform some action: *I think I'll take a walk; Will you take a look?; to take a bath.* □ **faire; prendre**

4 to get, receive, buy, rent *etc*: *I'm taking French lessons; I'll take three kilograms of strawberries; We took a house in Montreal.* □ **prendre**

5 (*sometimes with* **back**) to agree to have; to accept: *She took my advice; They refused to take responsibility; I won't take that (insult) from you!; I'm afraid we can't take back goods bought in a sale.* □ **accepter, prendre**

6 to need or require: *How long does it take you to go home?; It takes time to do a difficult job like this.* □ **prendre**

7 to travel by (bus *etc*): *I'm taking the next train to Toronto; I took a taxi.* □ **prendre**

8 to have enough space for: *The car takes five people.* □ **contenir**

9 to make a note, record *etc*: *She took a photograph of the castle; The nurse took the patient's temperature.* □ **prendre**

10 to remove, use, occupy *etc* with or without permission: *Someone's taken my coat; He took all my money.* □ **prendre**

11 to consider (as an example): *Take John for example.* □ **prendre**

12 to capture or win: *She took the first prize.* □ **remporter**

13 (*often with* **away, from, off**) to make less or smaller by a certain amount: *Take (away) four from ten, and that leaves six.* □ **ôter, soustraire**

14 to suppose or think (that something is the case): *Do you take me for an idiot?* □ **prendre (pour)**

15 to eat or drink: *Take these pills.* □ **prendre**

16 to conduct, lead or run; to be in charge or control of: *Will you take the class/lecture/meeting this evening?* □ **se charger de**

17 to consider or react or behave to (something) in a certain way: *She took the news calmly.* □ **prendre**

18 to feel: *He took pleasure/pride/a delight/an interest in his work.* □ **éprouver**

19 to go down or go into (a road): *Take the second road on the left.* □ **prendre**

■ *noun* 1 the amount of money taken in a shop *etc*; takings: *What was the take today?* □ **recette**

2 the filming of a single scene in a cinema film: *After five takes, the director was satisfied.* □ **prise de vue(s)**

taker *noun* a person who takes (something) *especially* one who accepts an offer or takes a bet: *I offered my friends my car, but there were no takers.* □ **preneur, euse**

takings *noun plural* the amount of money taken at a concert, in a shop *etc*: *the day's takings.* □ **recette**

'take away *noun* (*American* '**carry-out** *or* '**takeout**) **1** food prepared and bought in a restaurant but taken away and eaten somewhere else *eg* at home: *I'll go and buy a take away*; (*also adjective*) *a take away meal.* □ **(plat) (préparé) à emporter**
2 a restaurant where such food is prepared and bought. □ **restaurant qui fait des plats (préparés) à emporter**

be taken up with to be busy or occupied with: *He's very taken up with his new job.* □ **être pris (par)**

be taken with/by to find pleasing or attractive: *She was very taken with the village.* □ **être séduit/emballé par**

take after to be like (someone, *especially* a parent or relation) in appearance or character: *She takes after her father.* □ **tenir de**

take back 1 to make (someone) remember or think about (something): *Meeting my old friends took me back to my childhood.* □ **rappeler**
2 to admit that what one has said is not true: *Take back what you said about my sister!* □ **retirer**

take down to make a note or record of: *He took down her name and address.* □ **noter**

take an examination/test to have one's knowledge or ability tested formally, often in writing. □ **passer un examen**

take (someone) for to believe (mistakenly) that (someone) is (someone or something else): *I took you for your sister.* □ **prendre qqn pour**

take in 1 to include: *Literature takes in drama, poetry and the novel.* □ **comprendre**
2 to give (someone) shelter: *He had nowhere to go, so I took him in.* □ **recueillir**
3 to understand and remember: *I didn't take in what she said.* □ **saisir**
4 to make (clothes) smaller: *I lost a lot of weight, so I had to take all my clothes in.* □ **rapetisser**
5 to deceive or cheat: *He took me in with his story.* □ **avoir**

take it from me (that) you can believe me when I say (that): *Take it from me – it's true.* □ **vous pouvez me croire**

take it into one's head (to) to decide (to): *She took it into her head to go to Spain.* □ **se mettre dans la tête de**

take off 1 to remove (clothes *etc*): *He took off his coat.* □ **ôter, enlever**
2 (of an aircraft) to leave the ground: *The plane took off for Rome* (*noun* '**takeoff**). □ **décoller; décollage**
3 not to work during (a period of time): *I'm taking tomorrow morning off.* □ **prendre congé**
4 to imitate someone (often unkindly): *He used to take off his teacher to make his friends laugh* (*noun* '**take-off**). □ **imiter; imitation**

take on 1 to agree to do (work *etc*); to undertake: *She took on the job.* □ **accepter, se charger de**
2 to employ: *They are taking on five hundred more men at the factory.* □ **embaucher**
3 (*with* **at**) to challenge (someone) to a game *etc*: *I'll take you on at tennis.* □ **jouer contre**
4 to get; to assume: *Her writing took on a completely new meaning.* □ **prendre**
5 to allow (passengers) to get on or in: *The bus only stops here to take on passengers.* □ **prendre**
6 to be upset: *Don't take on so!* □ **s'en faire**

take it out on to be angry with or unpleasant to because one is angry, disappointed *etc* in oneself: *You're upset, but there's no need to take it out on me!* □ **s'en prendre à**

take over 1 to take control (of): *She has taken the business over* (*noun* '**takeover**). □ **reprendre; (n.) rachat**
2 (*often with* **from**) to do (something) after someone else stops doing it: *He retired last year, and I took over (his job) from him.* □ **prendre le relais de**

'take to 1 to find acceptable or pleasing: *I soon took to her children/idea.* □ **prendre goût à, sympathiser avec**
2 to begin to do (something) regularly: *He took to smoking a pipe.* □ **se mettre à**

take up 1 to use or occupy (space, time *etc*): *I won't take up much of your time.* □ **prendre**
2 to begin doing, playing *etc*: *She has taken up the violin/teaching.* □ **se mettre à**
3 to shorten (clothes): *My skirts were too long, so I had them taken up.* □ **raccourcir**
4 to lift or raise; to pick up: *He took up the book.* □ **élever, ramasser**

take (something) upon oneself to take responsibility for: *I took it upon myself to make sure she arrived safely.* □ **prendre sur soi de**

take (something) up with (someone) to discuss (*especially* a complaint): *Take the matter up with your MP.* □ **parler (de qqch à qqn)**

see also **bring**.

talc [talk] *noun* **1** a kind of soft mineral that feels like soap. □ **talc**
2 talcum. □ **talc**

talcum ['talkəm] *noun* (*also* **talcum powder**: *often abbreviated to* **talc**) a kind of fine, *usually* perfumed, powder made from talc, used on the body. □ **talc**

tale [teil] *noun* **1** a story: *She told me the tale of her travels.* □ **conte, récit**
2 an untrue story; a lie: *He told me he had a lot of money, but that was just a tale.* □ **histoire**

talent ['talənt] *noun* a special ability or cleverness; a skill: *a talent for drawing.* □ **talent**

'talented *adjective* (*negative* **untalented**) naturally clever or skilful; having or showing great ability: *a talented pianist.* □ **talentueux**

talisman ['ta-lis-mən] *noun* an object which is supposed to have magic powers to protect its owner; a charm: *He had a rabbit's foot which he wore around his neck as a talisman.* □ **talisman**

talk [to:k] *verb* **1** to speak; to have a conversation or discussion: *We talked about it for hours; My parrot can talk* (= imitate human speech). □ **parler**

2 to gossip: *You can't stay here – people will talk!* □ **commérer**

3 to talk about: *They spent the whole time talking philosophy.* □ **parler, discuter de**

■ *noun* **1** (*sometimes in plural*) a conversation or discussion: *We had a long talk about it; The Prime Ministers met for talks on their countries' economic problems.* □ **discussion**

2 a lecture: *The doctor gave us a talk on family health.* □ **exposé**

3 gossip: *His behaviour causes a lot of talk among the neighbours.* □ **commérages**

4 useless discussion; statements of things a person says he will do but which will never actually be done: *There's too much talk and not enough action.* □ **paroles en l'air**

talkative ['to:kətiv] *adjective* talking a lot: *a talkative person.* □ **bavard**

'**talking point** *noun* something to talk about; a subject, *especially* an interesting one: *Football is the main talking point in my family.* □ **sujet de conversation**

,**talking-'to** *noun* a talk given to someone in order to scold, criticize or blame them: *I'll give that child a good talking-to when he gets home!* □ **sermon**

talk around 1 to persuade: *I managed to talk her round.* □ **convaincre**

2 to talk about (something) for a long time without reaching the most important point: *We talked round the question for hours.* □ **tourner autour de**

talk back (*often with* to) to answer rudely: *Don't talk back to me!* □ **répondre (à)**

talk big to talk as if one is very important; to boast: *He's always talking big about his job.* □ **faire l'important**

talk down to to speak to (someone) as if he/she is much less important, clever *etc*: *Children dislike being talked down to.* □ **parler à qqn comme à un enfant**

talk (someone) into/out of (doing) to persuade (someone) (not) to do (something): *She talked me into changing my job.* □ **persuader qqn de**

talk over to discuss: *We talked over the whole idea.* □ **discuter (de)**

talk sense/nonsense to say sensible, or ridiculous, things: *Don't talk nonsense; I do wish you would talk sense.* □ **parler raison; dire des idioties**

talk shop to talk about one's work: *We agreed not to talk shop at the party.* □ **parler boutique**

talks [to:ks] *noun* negotiations or communication between groups trying to settle a dispute or trying to reach an agreement on something: *Sarah had hoped that the strike would end, but talks between the union and the company dragged on.* □ **pourparler**

tall [to:l] *adjective* **1** (of people and thin or narrow objects such as buildings or trees) higher than normal: *a tall man/tree.* □ **haut, grand**

2 (of people) having a particular height: *John is only four 1.5 metres tall.* □ **mesurer**

'**tallness** *noun.* □ **hauteur, grande taille**

a tall order something very difficult to do: *Finding somewhere for fifty children to stay tonight is rather a tall order.* □ **chose difficile**

a tall story a story which is hard to believe: *She is always telling tall stories.* □ **histoire à dormir debout**

---

tall is used *especially* of people, and of other (narrow) upright objects: *a tall girl, tree, building.*
high is used of objects that are a long way off the ground, or reach a great height: *a high shelf, diving-board, mountain, wall.*

---

tally ['tali] – *plural* '**tallies** – *noun* an account: *He kept a tally of all the work he did.* □ **compte**

■ *verb* (*often with* **with**) to agree or match: *Their stories tally; His story tallies with mine.* □ **correspondre (à)**

talon ['talən] *noun* the claw of a bird of prey. □ **serre**

'**tamarind** ['tamərind] *noun* a tropical fruit, a brown pod with a juicy, spicy pulp used in medicines, drinks *etc*. □ **tamarin**

tambourine [tambə'ri:n] *noun* a shallow, one-sided drum with tinkling metal discs in the rim, held in the hand and shaken or beaten. □ **tambour de basque**

tame [teim] *adjective* **1** (of animals) used to living with people; not wild or dangerous: *She kept a tame bear as a pet.* □ **apprivoisé**

2 dull; not exciting: *My job is very tame.* □ **insipide, monotone**

■ *verb* to make tame: *It is impossible to tame some animals.* □ **apprivoiser**

'**tamely** *adverb.* □ **docilement**

'**tameness** *noun.* □ **caractère apprivoisé; insipidité**

'**tameable** *adjective* (*negative* **untameable**) able to be tamed. □ **apprivoisable**

taming *noun* the procedure and methods used to make an animal less wild: *Although the circus employees tried, the taming of the wild lion proved too much for them.* □ **dressage**

tamper ['tampə] *verb* to interfere or meddle *usually* in such a way as to damage, break, alter *etc*: *Don't tamper with the engine.* □ **toucher à**

tampon ['tampon] *noun* a piece of cottonwool *etc* inserted in a wound *etc* to absorb blood. □ **tampon**

tan [tan] – *past tense, past participle* **tanned** – *verb* **1** to make an animal's skin into leather (by treating it with certain substances). □ **tanner**

2 to (cause a person's skin to) become brown in the sun: *She was tanned by the sun.* □ **bronzer**

■ *noun, adjective* (of) a light brown colour: *tan shoes.* □ **fauve**

■ *noun* suntan tanned skin: *He came back from holiday with a tan.* □ **bronzage**

tanned *adjective* sunburnt: *a tanned face.* □ **bronzé**

'**tanner** *noun* a person who tans leather. □ **tanneur, euse**

'**tannery** – *plural* '**tanneries** – *noun* a place where leather is tanned. □ **tannerie**

tandem ['tandəm] *noun* a long bicycle with two seats and two sets of pedals, one behind the other. □ **tandem**

■ *adverb* (*usually* of two people on a tandem) one behind the other: *They rode tandem.* □ **en tandem**

tang [taŋ] *noun* a strong or sharp taste, flavour or smell: *The air had a salty tang.* □ **saveur/senteur forte (et piquante)**

tangent ['tandʒənt] *noun* a line that touches a curve but does not cut it. □ **tangente**
go off at a tangent to go off suddenly in another direction or on a different line of thought, action *etc*: *It is difficult to have a sensible conversation with him, as he keeps going off at a tangent.* □ **prendre la tangente**

tangerine [tandʒə'ri:n] *noun* a type of small orange that has a sweet taste and is easily peeled. □ **mandarine**

tangible ['tandʒəbl] *adjective* real or definite: *tangible evidence.* □ **tangible**
'**tangibly** *adverb*. □ **tangiblement**
'**tangibility** *noun*. □ **tangibilité**

tangle ['taŋgl] *noun* an untidy, confused or knotted state: *The child's hair was in a tangle.* □ **désordre, masse enchevêtrée**
■ *verb* to make or become tangled: *Don't tangle my wool when I'm knitting.* □ **(s')emmêler, (s')embrouiller**
'**tangled** *adjective* in a tangle: *tangled hair/branches*; *Her hair is always tangled.* □ **en désordre, enchevêtré**
tangle with to become involved in a quarrel or struggle with (a person *etc*): *I tangled with her over politics.* □ **avoir une prise de bec avec**

tango ['taŋgou] – *plural* '**tangos** – *noun* (music for) a type of South American dance. □ **tango**
■ *verb* – 3rd person singular present tense '**tangos**: *past tense, past participle* '**tangoed** – to perform this dance. □ **danser le tango**

tank [taŋk] *noun* **1** a large container for liquids or gas: *a hot-water/cold-water tank.* □ **réservoir, cuve**
2 a heavy steel-covered vehicle armed with guns. □ **char d'assaut**
'**tanker** *noun* **1** a ship or large truck for carrying oil. □ **pétrolier**
2 an aircraft used to transport fuel *etc*. □ **avion-ravitailleur**

tankard ['taŋkəd] *noun* a large drinking-mug of metal, glass *etc*: *a beer tankard.* □ **chope**

tantalize, tantalise ['tantəlaiz] *verb* to tease or torment (a person *etc*) by making him want something he cannot have and by keeping it just beyond his reach: *The expensive clothes in the shop-window tantalized her.* □ **exciter la convoitise de**
'**tantalizing**, '**tantalising** *adjective*: *tantalizing smells in the kitchen.* □ **tentant**

tantamount ['tantəmaunt]: **tantamount to** having the same effect as; equivalent to: *His silence is tantamount to an admission of guilt.* □ **équivalent à**

tantrum ['tantrəm] *noun* a fit of extreme rage, with *eg* shouting and stamping: *That child is always throwing tantrums.* □ **crise de rage**

tap¹ [tap] *noun* a quick touch or light knock or blow: *I heard a tap at the door.* □ **petit coup**
■ *verb* – *past tense, past participle* **tapped** – (*often with* **at, on** *or* **with**) to give a light knock (on or with something): *She tapped at/on the window.* □ **frapper doucement**
'**tap-dancing** *noun* a type of dancing performed with special shoes that make a tapping noise. □ **claquettes**
'**tap-dancer** *noun*. □ **danseur, euse à claquettes**

tap² [tap] *noun* (*American* '**faucet**) any of several types

of device (*usually* with a handle and valve that can be shut or opened) for controlling the flow of liquid or gas from a pipe, barrel *etc*: *Turn the tap off/on!* □ **manette, robinet**
■ *verb* – *past tense, past participle* **tapped** – **1** to start using (a source, supply *etc*): *The country has many rich resources that have not been tapped.* □ **exploiter**
2 to attach a device to (someone's telephone wires) in order to be able to listen to his telephone conversations: *My phone was being tapped.* □ **mettre sur écoute**

tape [teip] *noun* **1** (a piece of) a narrow strip or band of cloth used for tying *etc*: *bundles of letters tied with tape.* □ **ruban, bande**
2 a piece of this or something similar, *eg* a string, stretched above the finishing line on a race track: *The two runners reached the tape together.* □ **fil d'arrivée**
3 a narrow strip of paper, plastic, metal *etc* used for sticking materials together, recording sounds *etc*: *adhesive tape; insulating tape; I recorded the concert on tape.* □ **ruban; bande**
4 a tape measure. □ **mètre à ruban**
■ *verb* **1** to fasten or seal with tape. □ **attacher avec un ruban**
2 to record (the sound of something) on tape: *He taped the concert.* □ **enregistrer (sur bande)**
'**tape measure**, '**measuring tape** *nouns* a length of *eg* plastic, cloth or metal tape, marked with centimetres, metres *etc* for measuring. □ **mètre à ruban**
'**tape recorder** *noun* a machine which records sounds on magnetic tape and reproduces them when required. □ **magnétophone**
'**tape-record** *verb*. □ **enregistrer au magnétophone**
'**tape recording** *noun*. □ **enregistrement magnétique**

taper ['teipə] *noun* a long, thin type of candle. □ **cierge**
■ *verb* (*sometimes with* **off**) to make or become narrower or slimmer at one end: *The leaves taper (off) to a point.* □ **(s')effiler**
'**tapered**, '**tapering** *adjective* becoming narrower or slimmer at one end: *tapering fingers.* □ **fuselé**

tapestry ['tapəstri] – *plural* '**tapestries** – *noun* (a piece of) cloth into which a picture or design has been sewn or woven, hung on a wall for decoration or used to cover *eg* the seats of chairs: *Four large tapestries hung on the walls.* □ **tapisserie**

tapioca [tapi'oukə] *noun* a type of food obtained from the underground part of the cassava plant. □ **tapioca**

tar [ta:] *noun* any of several kinds of thick, black, sticky material obtained from wood, coal *etc* and used *eg* in roadmaking. □ **goudron**
■ *verb* – *past tense, past participle* **tarred** – to cover with tar: *The road has just been tarred.* □ **goudronner**
'**tarry** *adjective* of or like tar; covered with tar. □ **goudronneux, goudronné**

tarantula [tə'ran-tʃu-lə] *noun* any of several types of large hairy spider, some poisonous. □ **tarentule**

target ['ta:git] *noun* **1** a marked board or other object aimed at in shooting practice, competitions *etc* with a rifle, bow and arrow *etc*: *His shots hit the target every time.* □ **cible**
2 any object at which shots, bombs *etc* are directed: *Their*

target was the royal palace. □ **cible**

3 a person, thing *etc* against which unfriendly comment or behaviour is directed: *the target of criticism.* □ **cible**

tariff ['tarif] *noun* 1 a list of prices or charges *eg* in a hotel: *A copy of the tariff is placed in each bedroom.* □ **tableau des prix**

2 (a list of) taxes to be paid on imported or exported goods: *the customs tariff.* □ **tarif(s) douanier(s)**

tarmac ['taːmak] *noun* the surface of a road, runway at an airport *etc: The plane was waiting on the tarmac.* □ **piste**

tarmacadam [taːmə'kadəm] *noun* a mixture of small stones and tar used for road surfaces *etc.* □ **macadam**

tarnish ['taːniʃ] *verb* to (cause a metal to) become dull and stained: *Silver tarnishes easily.* □ **(se) ternir**

■ *noun* a dull, stained appearance on a metal surface. □ **ternissure**

'**tarnished** *adjective.* □ **terni**

tarpaulin [taː'poːlin] *noun* (a sheet of) a kind of strong waterproof material: *He covered his car with a (sheet of) tarpaulin.* □ **bâche (goudronnée)**

tarragon ['tarəgən] *noun* a plant with aromatic leaves used in cooking; a herb used for sauces and meat dishes: *A pinch of tarragon adds flavour to pot roast.* □ **estragon**

tarry *see* **tar.**

tart[1] [taːt] *adjective* sharp or sour in taste: *These apples taste rather tart.* □ **sur**

'**tartly** *adverb.* □ **aigrement**

'**tartness** *noun.* □ **aigreur**

tart[2] [taːt] *noun* a pie containing *eg* fruit or jam: *an apple tart.* □ **tarte**

tartan ['taːtən] *noun* 1 (woollen or other cloth woven with) a pattern of different coloured lines and broader stripes, crossing each other at right angles, *originally* used by clans of the Scottish Highlands. □ **tartan**

2 any one pattern of this sort, *usually* associated with a particular clan *etc: the Cameron tartan.* □ **tartan**

task [taːsk] *noun* a piece of *especially* hard work; a duty that must be done: *household tasks.* □ **tâche**

task force a force selected from the armed services for a special task. □ **détachement spécial**

tassel ['tasəl] *noun* a decoration, consisting of a hanging bunch of threads tied firmly at one end and loose at the other end, put *eg* on a cushion, a hat, a shawl *etc.* □ **pompon, gland**

'**tasselled** *adjective* decorated with tassels: *a tasselled hat.* □ **orné de glands**

taste [teist] *verb* 1 to be aware of, or recognize, the flavour of something: *I can taste ginger in this cake.* □ **goûter, sentir**

2 to test or find out the flavour or quality of (food *etc*) by eating or drinking a little of it: *Please taste this and tell me if it is too sweet.* □ **goûter (à)**

3 to have a particular flavour or other quality that is noticed through the act of tasting: *This milk tastes sour; The sauce tastes of garlic.* □ **avoir un goût (de)**

4 to eat (food) *especially* with enjoyment: *I haven't tasted such a beautiful curry for ages.* □ **déguster**

5 to experience: *She tasted the delights of country life.* □ **goûter**

■ *noun* 1 one of the five senses, the sense by which we are aware of flavour: *one's sense of taste; bitter to the taste.* □ **goût**

2 the quality or flavour of anything that is known through this sense: *This wine has an unusual taste.* □ **goût**

3 an act of tasting or a small quantity of food *etc* for tasting: *Do have a taste of this cake!* □ **goûter (à)**

4 a liking or preference: *a taste for music; a queer taste in books; expensive tastes.* □ **goût**

5 the ability to judge what is suitable in behaviour, dress *etc* or what is fine and beautiful: *She shows good taste in clothes; a man of taste; That joke was in good/bad taste.* □ **goût**

'**tasteful** *adjective* showing good judgment or taste: *a tasteful flower arrangement.* □ **de bon goût**

'**tastefully** *adverb.* □ **avec goût**

'**tastefulness** *noun.* □ **(bon) goût**

'**tasteless** *adjective* 1 lacking flavour: *tasteless food.* □ **fade, insipide**

2 showing a lack of good taste or judgment: *tasteless behaviour.* □ **de mauvais goût**

'**tastelessly** *adverb.* □ **sans goût**

'**tastelessness** *noun.* □ **absence/manque de goût**

-**tasting** having a (particular kind of) taste: *a sweet-tasting liquid.* □ **au goût (...)**

'**tasty** *adjective* having a good, *especially* savoury, flavour: *tasty food.* □ **savoureux**

'**tastiness** *noun.* □ **saveur agréable**

ta-ta [ta'taː] (often used to or by young children) goodbye: *Say ta-ta to Gran.* □ **au revoir!**

tatters ['tatəz] *noun plural* torn and ragged pieces: *tatters of clothing.* □ **lambeaux**

'**tattered** *adjective* ragged or torn: *a tattered cloak/book.* □ **en loques/lambeaux**

in tatters in a torn and ragged condition: *Her clothes were in tatters.* □ **en loques/lambeaux**

tattoo [tatuː] – *3rd person singular present tense* **tat'toos**: *past tense, past participle* **tat'tooed** – *verb* to make coloured patterns or pictures on part of a person's body by pricking the skin and putting in dyes: *The design was tattooed on his arm.* □ **tatouer**

■ *noun – plural* **tat'toos** – a design tattooed on the skin: *Her arms were covered with tattoos.* □ **tatouage**

tat'tooed *adjective.* □ **tatoué**

tatty ['tati] *adjective* shabby and untidy: *tatty clothes.* □ **miteux, fatigué**

taught *see* **teach.**

taunt [toːnt] *verb* to tease, or say unpleasant things to (a person) in a cruel way: *The children at school taunted him for being dirty.* □ **accabler de sarcasmes**

■ *noun* cruel, unpleasant remarks: *He did not seem to notice their taunts.* □ **sarcasme**

'**taunting** *adjective.* □ **sarcastique**

'**tauntingly** *adverb.* □ **sarcastiquement**

taut [toːt] *adjective* pulled tight: *Keep the string taut while you tie a knot in it.* □ **(bien) tendu**

'**tauten** *verb* to make or become taut: *The ropes were tautened.* □ **(se) tendre**

tavern ['tavən] *noun* an inn or public house: *The travellers stopped at a tavern for a meal and a mug of ale.* □

auberge

tawny ['tɔːni] *adjective* (*usually* of animals' fur *etc*) yellowish-brown. □ **fauve**

tax [taks] *noun* **1** money, *eg* a percentage of a person's income or of the price of goods *etc* taken by the government to help pay for the running of the state: *income tax; a tax on tobacco.* □ **taxe, impôt**
2 a strain or burden: *The continual noise was a tax on her nerves.* □ **fardeau**
■ *verb* **1** to make (a person) pay (a) tax; to put a tax on (goods *etc*): *He is taxed on his income; Alcohol is taxed.* □ **taxer, imposer**
2 to put a strain on: *Don't tax your strength!* □ **pousser à bout**
'taxable *adjective* liable to be taxed: *taxable income/goods.* □ **imposable**
tax'ation *noun* the act or system of taxing. □ **impôts**
'taxing *adjective* mentally or physically difficult: *a taxing job.* □ **éprouvant**
,tax-'free *adjective, adverb* without payment of tax: *tax-free income.* □ **exempt d'impôts**
'taxpayer *noun* a citizen who pays taxes. □ **contribuable**
'tax (someone) with to accuse (a person) of: *I taxed her with dishonesty.* □ **taxer/accuser de**

taxi ['taksi] – *plurals* **'taxis, 'taxies** – *noun* (*also* **'taxi-cab:** (*American*) **cab**) a car, *usually* fitted with a taximeter, that can be hired with its driver, *especially* for short journeys: *I took a taxi from the hotel to the station.* □ **taxi**
■ *verb* – *3rd person singular present tense* **'taxies, 'taxis:** *present participle* **'taxiing, 'taxying:** *past tense, past participle* **'taxied** – (of an airplane) to move slowly along the ground before beginning to run forward for takeoff: *The plane taxied along the runway.* □ **rouler (doucement, sur la piste)**
'taximeter *noun* (*usually abbreviated to* **meter**) an instrument *usually* fitted to taxis to show the fare owed for the distance travelled. □ **compteur (de taxi)**
taxi rank a place where taxis stand until hired: *There is a taxi rank at the railway station.* □ **station de taxis**

taxidermy ['taksidəːmi] *noun* the art of preparing and stuffing the skins of animals *etc*. □ **taxidermie**
'taxidermist *noun*. □ **taxidermiste**

tea [tiː] *noun* **1** a type of plant grown in Asia, *especially* India, Ceylon and China, or its dried and prepared leaves: *I bought half a kilogram of tea.* □ **thé**
2 a drink made by adding boiling water to these: *Have a cup of tea!* □ **thé**
3 a cup *etc* of tea: *Two teas, please!* □ **thé**
4 a small meal in the afternoon (**afternoon tea**) or a larger one in the early evening, at which tea is often drunk: *She invited him to tea.* □ **thé, goûter**
'tea bag a small bag or sachet of thin paper containing tea, on to which boiling water is poured in a pot or cup. □ **sachet de thé**
'teacup *noun* a cup, *usually* of medium size, in which tea is served. □ **tasse à thé**
'tea party – *plural* **'tea parties** – *noun* an afternoon party at which tea is *usually* served: *She has been in-*

vited to a tea party. □ **thé**
'teapot *noun* a pot with a spout used for making and pouring tea. □ **théière**
'tearoom *noun* a restaurant where tea, coffee, cakes *etc* are served. □ **salon de thé**
'tea set, 'tea service *nouns* a set of cups, saucers and plates, sometimes with a teapot and milk-jug. □ **service à thé**
'teaspoon *noun* **1** a small spoon for use with a teacup: *I need a teaspoon to stir my tea.* □ **cuiller à thé**
2 a teaspoonful: *a teaspoon of salt.* □ **cuillerée à café**
'teaspoonful *noun* an amount that fills a teaspoon: *two teaspoonfuls of salt.* □ **cuillerée à café**
'tea time *noun* the time in the late afternoon or early evening at which people take tea: *He said he would be back at tea time.* □ **heure du thé**
'tea towel *noun* a cloth for drying dishes after they have been washed *eg* after a meal. □ **torchon (à vaisselle)**

teach [tiːtʃ] – *past tense, past participle* **taught** [tɔːt] – *verb* to give knowledge, skill or wisdom to a person; to instruct or train (a person): *She teaches English/the piano; Experience has taught him nothing.* □ **enseigner, apprendre (à)**
'teacher *noun* a person who teaches, *especially* in a school. □ **enseignant, ante; professeur, eure**
teaching *noun* **1** the work of teacher: *Teaching is a satisfying job;* (*also adjective*) *the teaching staff of a school.* □ **enseignement**
2 guidance or instruction: *She followed her mother's teaching.* □ **leçons**
3 something that is taught: *one of the teachings of Christ.* □ **enseignement**

teak [tiːk] *noun* **1** a type of tree that grows in India, Malaysia, Burma *etc*. □ **teck**
2 its very hard wood: *The table is* (*made of*) *teak;* (*also adjective*) *teak furniture.* □ **(de) teck**

team [tiːm] *noun* **1** a group of people forming a side in a game: *a football team.* □ **équipe**
2 a group of people working together: *A team of doctors.* □ **équipe**
3 two or more animals working together *eg* pulling a cart, plough *etc*: *a team of horses/oxen.* □ **attelage**
team spirit willingness of each member of a team or group to work together with loyalty and enthusiasm. □ **esprit d'équipe**
'teamwork *noun* cooperation between those who are working together on a task *etc*. □ **travail en collaboration**
team up to join with another person in order to do something together: *They teamed up with another family to rent a house for the holidays.* □ **s'associer (avec)**

tear[1] [tiə] *noun* a drop of liquid coming from the eye, as a result of emotion (*especially* sadness) or because something (*eg* smoke) has irritated it: *tears of joy/laughter/rage.* □ **larme**
'tearful *adjective* **1** inclined to cry or weep; with much crying or weeping: *The child was very tearful; a tearful farewell.* □ **pleureur, larmoyant**
2 covered with tears: *tearful faces.* □ **plein/couvert de larmes**

'**tearfully** adverb. □ **en pleurant**

'**tearfulness** noun. □ **larmoiement**

tear gas a kind of gas causing blinding tears, used against eg rioters. □ **gaz lacrymogène**

'**tear-stained** adjective marked with tears: a tear-stained face. □ **barbouillé de larmes**

in tears crying or weeping: She was in tears over the broken doll. □ **en larmes/pleurs**

tear² [teə] – past tense **tore** [tɔːn]: past participle **torn** [tɔː] – verb **1** (sometimes with **off** etc) to make a split or hole in (something), intentionally or unintentionally, with a sudden or violent pulling action, or to remove (something) from its position by such an action or movement: He tore the photograph into pieces; You've torn a hole in your jacket; I tore the picture out of a magazine. □ **déchirer, arracher**

2 to become torn: Newspapers tear easily. □ **se déchirer**

3 to rush: She tore along the road. □ **foncer**

■ noun a hole or split made by tearing: There's a tear in my dress. □ **déchirure**

be torn between (one thing and another) to have a very difficult choice to make between (two things): He was torn between obedience to his parents and loyalty to his friends. □ **être déchiré entre (...) et (...)**

tear (oneself) away to leave a place, activity etc unwillingly: I couldn't tear myself away from the television. □ **s'arracher à**

tear one's hair to be in despair with impatience and frustration: Their inefficiency makes me tear my hair. □ **s'arracher les cheveux**

tear up 1 to remove from a fixed position by violence; The wind tore up several trees. □ **arracher**

2 to tear into pieces: She tore up the letter. □ **déchirer**

tease [tiːz] verb **1** to annoy or irritate on purpose: He's teasing the cat. □ **agacer**

2 to annoy or laugh at (a person) playfully: His schoolfriends tease him about his size. □ **taquiner**

■ noun a person who enjoys teasing others: He's a tease! □ **taquin, ine**

'**teaser** noun **1** a puzzle or difficult problem: This question is rather a teaser. □ **colle**

2 a person who teases. □ **taquin, ine**

'**teasingly** adverb in a teasing manner. □ **en guise de taquinerie**

teat [tiːt] noun the part of a female animal's breast or udder through which milk passes to the young; the nipple. □ **mamelon, trayon**

technical ['teknikəl] adjective **1** having, or relating to, a particular science or skill, especially of a mechanical or industrial kind: a technical college; technical skill; technical drawing. □ **technique**

2 (having many terms) relating to a particular art or science: 'Myopia' is a technical term for 'shortsightedness'. □ **technique**

3 according to strict laws or rules: a technical defeat. □ **technique**

,**techni'cality** [-'ka-] – plural ,**techni'calities** – noun **1** a technical detail or technical term: Their instructions were full of technicalities. □ **détail technique**

2 a (trivial) detail or problem, eg caused by (too) strict obedience to laws, rules etc: I'm not going to be put off by mere technicalities. □ **détail technique, point de détail**

'**technically** adverb **1** in a technical way; She described the machine in simple terms, then more technically. □ **techniquement**

2 as far as skill and technique are concerned: The pianist gave a very good performance technically, although she seemed to lack feeling for the music. □ **sur le plan technique**

3 according to strict obedience to laws or rules: Technically, you aren't allowed to do that, but I don't suppose anyone will object. □ **en principe**

tech'nician [-'niʃən] noun a person who has been trained to do something which involves some skill, eg with a piece of machinery: One of our technicians will repair the machine. □ **technicien, ienne**

technique [tek'niːk] noun the way in which a (usually skilled) process is, or should be, carried out: They admired the pianist's faultless technique. □ **technique**

technology [tek'nolədʒi] – plural **tech'nologies** – noun (the study of) science applied to practical purposes: a college of science and technology. □ **technologie**

,**techno'logical** [-'lo-] adjective. □ **technologique**

tech'nologist noun. □ **technologue**

teddy ['tedi] – plural '**teddies** – noun (also **teddy bear**) a child's stuffed toy bear. □ **ours en peluche**

tedious ['tiːdiəs] adjective boring and continuing for a long time: a tedious speech/speaker. □ **ennuyeux**

'**tediously** adverb. □ **de façon ennuyeuse**

'**tediousness** noun. □ **ennui**

'**tedium** noun boredom; tediousness: the tedium of a long journey. □ **ennui**

teem [tiːm] verb **1** (with **with**) to be full of: The pond was teeming with fish. □ **grouiller (de)**

2 to rain heavily: The rain was teeming down. □ **pleuvoir à verse**

teens [tiːnz] noun plural **1** the years of a person's life between the ages of thirteen and nineteen: She's in her teens. □ **adolescence**

2 the numbers from thirteen to nineteen. □ **nombres entre treize et dix-neuf**

'**teenage** [-eidʒ] adjective of, or suitable for, people in their teens: teenage children/clothes/behaviour. □ **d'adolescent, ente**

'**teenager** [-eidʒə] noun a person in his or her teens. □ **adolescent, ente**

teeny ['tiːni] adjective (also **teeny-weeny** [tiːni'wiːni]) an informal or child's word for tiny: There's a teeny little insect crawling up your neck. □ **tout (petit) petit**

tee shirt see **T-shirt** under **T**.

teeth, teethe, teething see **tooth**.

teetotal [tiː'toutl] adjective never taking alcoholic drink: The whole family is teetotal. □ **abstinent**

tee'totaller, tee'totaler noun a person who is teetotal. □ **abstinent, ente**

telecast ['telikaːst] noun a television broadcast. □ **émission de télévision**

■ verb to broadcast on television. □ **diffuser**

telecommunications ['telikəmjuːni'keiʃənz] noun plu-

ral the science of sending messages, information *etc* by telephone, telegraph, radio, television *etc*. □ **télécommunications**

telegram ['teligram] *noun* a message sent by telegraph: *He received a telegram saying that his mother had died.* □ **télégramme**

telegraph ['teligraːf] *noun* **1** a system of sending messages using either wires and electricity or radio: *Send it by telegraph.* □ **télégraphe**

2 an instrument for this: *Send the message on the telegraph.* □ **télégraphe**

■ *verb* **1** to send by telegraph: *He telegraphed the time of his arrival.* □ **télégraphier**

2 to inform by telegraph: *He telegraphed us to say when he would arrive.* □ **télégraphier**

te'legrapher [-'le-], **te'legraphist** [-'le-] *nouns* a person who operates a telegraph. □ **télégraphiste**

te'legraphy [-'le-] *noun* the process, science or skill of sending messages by telegraph. □ **télégraphie**

,tele'graphic [-'gra-] *adjective*. □ **télégraphique**

telegraph pole a high, wooden pole which supports telegraph wires. □ **poteau télégraphique**

telepathy [tə'lepəθi] *noun* the communication of ideas, thoughts *etc* directly from one person's mind to another person's mind without the use of hearing, sight *etc*: *She knew just what I was thinking – it must have been telepathy.* □ **télépathie**

telepathic [teli'paθik] *adjective*. □ **télépathique**

tele'pathically *adverb*. □ **par télépathie**

te'lepathist *noun* a person who studies or practises telepathy. □ **télépathe**

telephone ['telifoun] *noun* (*often abbreviated to* **phone** [foun]) an instrument for speaking to someone from a distance, using either an electric current which passes along a wire or radio waves: *She spoke to me by telephone/on the telephone*; (*also adjective*) *a telephone number/operator*. □ **(de) téléphone**

■ (*often abbreviated to* **phone** [foun]) *verb* **1** to (try to) speak to (someone) by means of the telephone: *I'll telephone you tomorrow.* □ **téléphoner (à)**

2 to send (a message) or ask for (something) by means of the telephone: *I'll telephone for a taxi.* □ **téléphoner**

3 to reach or make contact with (another place) by means of the telephone: *Can one telephone England from Australia?* □ **téléphoner (à, en, chez)**

te'lephonist [-'le-] *noun* a person who operates a telephone switchboard in a telephone exchange. □ **téléphoniste**

telephone booth, telephone box (*also* '**call box**) a small room or compartment containing a telephone for public use. □ **cabine téléphonique**

telephone directory a book containing a list of the names, addresses and telephone numbers of all the people with telephones in a particular area: *Look them up in the telephone directory.* □ **annuaire du téléphone**

telephone exchange a central control through which telephone calls are directed. □ **central téléphonique**

telephoto [teli'foutou]: **telephoto lens** a photographic lens used for taking photographs from a long distance away. □ **téléobjectif**

teleprinter ['teliprintə] *noun* telegraph system or instrument by which messages are sent out at one place, and received and printed at another. □ **télescripteur**

telescope ['teliskoup] *noun* a kind of tube containing lenses through which distant objects appear closer: *He looked at the ship through his telescope.* □ **télescope**

■ *verb* to push or be pushed together so that one part slides inside another, like the parts of a closing telescope: *The crash telescoped the railway coaches.* □ **(se) télescoper**

,tele'scopic [-'sko-] *adjective* **1** of, like, or containing, a telescope: *a telescopic sight on a rifle.* □ **télescopique**

2 made in parts which can slide inside each other: *a telescopic radio antenna.* □ **télescopique**

television ['teliviʒən] (*often abbreviated to* **TV** [tiːˈviː]) *noun* **1** the sending of pictures from a distance, and the reproduction of them on a screen: *We saw it on television.* □ **télévision**

2 (*also* **television set**) an apparatus with a screen for receiving these pictures. □ **téléviseur**

'**televise** [-vaiz] *verb* to send a picture of by television: *The football match was televised.* □ **téléviser**

tell [tel] – *past tense, past participle* **told** [tould] – *verb* **1** to inform or give information to (a person) about (something): *He told the whole story to John*; *She told John about it.* □ **raconter**

2 to order or command; to suggest or warn: *I told her to go away.* □ **demander (de)**

3 to say or express in words: *to tell lies/the truth/a story.* □ **dire**

4 to distinguish; to see (a difference); to know or decide: *Can you tell the difference between them?*; *I can't tell one from the other*; *You can tell if the meat is cooked by/from the colour.* □ **distinguer, reconnaître, voir**

5 to give away a secret: *You mustn't tell or we'll get into trouble.* □ **parler, répéter**

6 to be effective; to be seen to give (good) results: *Good teaching will always tell.* □ **se faire sentir, se reconnaître**

'**teller** *noun* a person who tells (stories): *a story-teller.* □ **(ra)conteur, euse**

'**telling** *adjective* having a great effect: *a telling argument.* □ **efficace**

'**tellingly** *adverb*. □ **efficacement**

'**telltale** *adjective* giving information (often which a person would not wish to be known): *the telltale signs of guilt.* □ **révélateur**

I told you so I told or warned you that this would happen, had happened *etc*, and I was right: *'I told you so, but you wouldn't believe me.'* □ **je vous l'avais bien dit**

tell off to scold: *The teacher used to tell me off for not doing my homework* (*noun* ,**telling-'off** : *He gave me a good telling-off*). □ **réprimander; réprimande; engueulade**

tell on 1 to have a bad effect on: *Smoking began to tell on his health.* □ **nuire (à)**

2 to give information about (a person, *usually* if they are doing something wrong): *I'm late for work – don't tell on me!* □ **dénoncer**

tell tales to give away secret or private information

about the (*usually* wrong) actions of others: *You must never tell tales.* □ **cafarder, rapporter**

tell the time to (be able to) know what time it is by looking at a clock *etc* or by any other means: *She can tell the time from the position of the sun; Could you tell me the time, please?* □ **savoir/dire l'heure**

there's no telling it is impossible to know: *There's no telling what he'll do!* □ **impossible de dire/savoir (ce que)**

you never can tell it is possible: *It might rain – you never can tell.* □ **on ne sait jamais**

temper ['tempǝ] *noun* **1** a state of mind; a mood or humour: *He's in a bad temper.* □ **humeur**

2 a tendency to become (unpleasant when) angry: *She has a terrible temper.* □ **(mauvais) caractère**

3 a state of anger: *She's in a temper.* □ **colère**

■ *verb* **1** to bring metal to the right degree of hardness by heating and cooling: *The steel must be carefully tempered.* □ **tremper**

2 to soften or make less severe: *One must try to temper justice with mercy.* □ **tempérer (par)**

-tempered having a (certain) state of mind: *good-tempered; mean-tempered; sweet-tempered.* □ **au caractère (...)**

keep one's temper not to lose one's temper: *He was very annoyed but he kept his temper.* □ **se maîtriser**

lose one's temper to show anger: *He lost his temper and shouted at me.* □ **se mettre en colère**

temperament ['tempǝrǝmǝnt] *noun* a person's natural way of thinking, behaving *etc*: *He has a sweet/nervous temperament.* □ **tempérament**

,tempera'mental [-'men-] *adjective* emotional; excitable; showing quick changes of mood. □ **capricieux, fantasque**

,tempera'mentally [-'men-] *adverb* **1** by or according to one's temperament: *He is temperamentally unsuited to this job.* □ **par nature**

2 excitably: *She behaved very temperamentally yesterday.* □ **capricieusement**

temperate ['tempǝrǝt] *adjective* (of climate) neither too hot nor too cold. □ **tempéré**

temperature ['temprǝtʃǝ] *noun* **1** the amount or degree of cold or heat: *The food must be kept at a low temperature.* □ **température**

2 a level of body heat that is higher than normal: *She had a temperature and wasn't feeling well.* □ **température, fièvre**

take someone's temperature to measure a person's body heat, using a thermometer. □ **prendre la température de**

tempest ['tempist] *noun* a violent storm, with very strong winds: *A tempest arose and they were drowned at sea.* □ **tempête**

tempestuous [tem'pestjuǝs] *adjective* **1** (of a person, behaviour *etc*) violently emotional; passionate: *a tempestuous argument/relationship.* □ **violent, passionné**

2 very stormy; of or like a tempest: *tempestuous winds.* □ **de tempête**

tem'pestuously *adverb*. □ **de manière tempétueuse**

tem'pestuousness *noun*. □ **caractère orageux/violent**

temple[1] ['templ] *noun* a building in which people worship, *usually* as part of a non-Christian religion: *a Greek/ Hindu temple.* □ **temple**

temple[2] ['templ] *noun* either of the flat parts of the head at the side of the forehead: *The stone hit him on the temple.* □ **tempe**

tempo ['tempou] – *plurals* 'tempos, (*music*) 'tempi [-piː] – *noun* the speed at which a piece of music should be or is played. □ **tempo**

temporary ['tempǝrǝri] *adjective* lasting, acting, used *etc* for a (short) time only: *a temporary job*; *She made a temporary repair.* □ **temporaire**

'temporarily *adverb*. □ **temporairement**

'temporariness *noun*. □ **caractère temporaire**

tempt [tempt] *verb* to (try to) persuade or attract to do something; to make (someone) want to do (something): *The sunshine tempted them (to go) out.* □ **tenter**

temp'tation *noun* **1** the act of tempting: *the temptation of Christ (by the Devil).* □ **tentation**

2 something that tempts: *He was surrounded by temptations.* □ **tentation**

'tempter – *feminine* 'temptress – *noun* a person who tempts. □ **tentateur, trice**

'tempting *adjective* attractive: *That cake looks tempting.* □ **tentant**

'temptingly *adverb*. □ **d'une manière tentante**

be tempted (to do something) to think that it would be pleasant, interesting *etc* to do (something): *I'm tempted to go to the party.* □ **être tenté (de)**

ten [ten] *noun* **1** the number or figure 10. □ **dix**

2 the age of 10. □ **dix ans**

■ *adjective* **1** 10 in number. □ **dix**

2 aged 10. □ **de dix ans**

about ten approximately ten in number: *There were about ten students still in the yard.* □ **dizaine**

ten- having ten (of something): *a ten-dollar fine.* □ **à dix (...)**

tenth *noun* **1** one of ten equal parts. □ **dixième**

2 (*also adjective*) the last of ten (people, things *etc*); the next after the ninth. □ **dixième**

ten-pin bowling *noun* a game in which a ball is rolled at ten skittles in order to knock down as many as possible. □ **jeu de quilles**

'ten-year-old *noun* a person or animal that is ten years old. □ **(personne, etc.) de dix ans**

■ *adjective* (of a person, animal or thing) that is ten years old. □ **de dix ans**

tenant ['tenǝnt] *noun* a person who pays rent to another for the use of a house, building, land *etc*: *She is a tenant of the estate*; (*also adjective*) *tenant farmers.* □ **locataire**

'tenanted *adjective* (*negative* untenanted) occupied; lived in: *a tenanted house.* □ **occupé, loué; (contraire): vide**

tend[1] [tend] *verb* to take care of; to look after: *A shepherd tends his sheep.* □ **garder**

'tender *noun* **1** a person who looks after something: *a bartender.* □ **gardien, ienne**

2 a small boat which carries stores or passengers to and from a larger boat. □ **bateau ravitailleur**

tend[2] [tend] *verb* **1** to be likely (to do something); to do (something) frequently: *Plants tend to die in hot weather; He tends to get angry.* □ **avoir tendance (à)**

2 to move, lean or slope in a certain direction: *This bicycle tends to(wards) the left.* □ **pencher, tirer (vers)**

'**tendency** – *plural* '**tendencies** – *noun* likelihood; inclination: *He has a tendency to forget things.* □ **tendance**

tender[1] ['tendə] *adjective* **1** soft; not hard or tough: *The meat is tender.* □ **tendre**

2 sore; painful when touched: *His injured leg is still tender.* □ **sensible, douloureux**

3 loving; gentle: *He had a tender heart.* □ **tendre**

'**tenderness** *noun.* □ **tendresse**

'**tenderly** *adverb* in a loving and gentle manner: *He kissed her tenderly.* □ **tendrement**

,**tender-'hearted** *adjective* kind and sympathetic; easily made to feel pity. □ **sensible**

,**tender-'heartedness** *noun.* □ **sensibilité**

tender[2] *see* **tend**[1].

tendon ['tendən] *noun* a strong cord joining a muscle to a bone *etc*: *She has damaged a tendon in her leg.* □ **tendon**

tennis ['tenis] *noun* (*also* **lawn tennis**) a game for two or four players who use rackets to hit a ball to each other over a net stretched across a tennis court: *Let's play (a game of) tennis*; (*also adjective*) *a tennis match.* □ **(de) tennis**

'**tennis court** *noun* a specially-marked area on which tennis is played. □ **terrain de tennis**

'**tennis racket** *noun* a racket with which one plays tennis. □ **raquette de tennis**

tenor ['tenə] *noun* (a man with) a singing voice of the highest normal pitch for an adult male. □ **ténor**

tense[1] [tens] *noun* a form of a verb that shows the time of its action in relation to the time of speaking: *a verb in the past/future/present tense.* □ **temps**

tense[2] [tens] *adjective* **1** strained; nervous: *The crowd was tense with excitement; a tense situation.* □ **crispé, tendu**

2 tight; tightly stretched. □ **tendu**

■ *verb* to make or become tense: *He tensed his muscles.* □ **(se) tendre**

'**tensely** *adverb.* □ **d'une manière tendue**

'**tenseness** *noun.* □ **tension**

'**tension** [-ʃən] *noun* **1** the state of being stretched, or the degree to which something is stretched: *the tension of the rope.* □ **tension**

2 mental strain; anxiety: *She is suffering from nervous tension; the tensions of modern life.* □ **tension (nerveuse)**

tent [tent] *noun* a movable shelter made of canvas or other material, supported by poles or a frame and fastened to the ground with ropes and pegs: *When we go on holiday, we usually sleep in a tent.* □ **tente**

tentacle ['tentəkl] *noun* a long, thin, flexible arm-like or horn-like part of an animal, used to feel, grasp *etc*: *An octopus has eight tentacles.* □ **tentacule**

tentative ['tentətiv] *adjective* **1** not final or complete; not definite: *We have made a tentative arrangement.* □ **provisoire**

2 uncertain or hesitating: *a tentative movement.* □ **hésitant**

'**tentatively** *adverb.* □ **provisoirement**

'**tentativeness** *noun.* □ **caractère provisoire**

tenterhooks ['tentəhuks]: **be on tenterhooks** to be uncertain and anxious about what is going to happen: *He was on tenterhooks about the result of the exam.* □ **charbons ardents**

tenth *see* **ten**.

tepid ['tepid] *adjective* **1** slightly or only just warm; lukewarm: *tepid water.* □ **tiède**

2 not very enthusiastic: *a tepid welcome.* □ **tiède**

'**tepidly** *adverb.* □ **sans enthousiasme**

'**tepidness** *noun.* □ **tiédeur**

te'pidity *noun.* □ **tiédeur**

tercentenary [tɜːsen'tiːnəri] – *plural* **tercen'tenaries** – *noun* a three-hundredth anniversary: *This year marks the tercentenary of the birth of one of our greatest poets.* □ **tricentenaire**

term [tɜːm] *noun* **1** a (*usually* limited) period of time: *a term of imprisonment; a term of office.* □ **peine; mandat, période**

2 a division of a school or university year: *the autumn term.* □ **trimestre**

3 a word or expression: *Myopia is a medical term for short-sightedness.* □ **terme**

terms *noun plural* **1** the rules or conditions of an agreement or bargain: *They had a meeting to arrange terms for an agreement.* □ **conditions**

2 fixed charges (for work, service *etc*): *The firms sent us a list of their terms.* □ **conditions**

3 a relationship between people: *They are on bad/ friendly terms.* □ **termes**

■ *verb* to name or call: *That kind of painting is termed 'abstract'.* □ **appeler, nommer**

come to terms 1 to reach an agreement or understanding: *They came to terms with the enemy.* □ **arriver à un accord avec**

2 to find a way of living with or tolerating (some personal trouble or difficulty): *He managed to come to terms with his illness.* □ **faire face à, s'adapter (à)**

in terms of using as a means of expression, a means of assessing value *etc*: *She thought of everything in terms of money.* □ **en fonction de, du point de vue de**

terminate ['tɜːmineit] *verb* to bring or come to an end or limit: *She terminated the conversation.* □ **mettre fin à**

termi'nation *noun.* □ **fin**

terminal ['tɜːminəl] *noun* **1** a building containing the arrival and departure areas for passengers at an airport or one in the centre of a city or town where passengers can buy tickets for air travel *etc* and can be transported by bus *etc* to an airport: *an air terminal.* □ **aérogare**

2 a *usually* large station at either end of a railway line, or one for long-distance buses: *a bus terminal.* □ **terminus**

3 in an electric circuit, a point of connection to a battery *etc*: *the positive/negative terminal.* □ **borne**

4 a device linked to a computer by which the computer can be operated. □ **terminal**

■ *adjective* (of an illness *etc*) in the final stage before death: *This ward is for patients with terminal cancer.* □

en phase terminale
'**terminally** *adverb*. □ **tous les trimestres**

terminology [təːmi'nolədʒi] – *plural* **termi'nologies** – *noun* the special words or phrases used in a particular art, science *etc*: *legal terminology*; *Every science has its own terminology*. □ **terminologie**
,**termino'logical** *adjective*. □ **terminologique**

terminus ['təːminəs] *noun* an end, *especially* of a railway or bus route: *I get off at the bus terminus*. □ **terminus**

termite ['təːmait] *noun* a pale-coloured wood-eating kind of insect, like an ant. □ **termite**

terrace ['terəs] *noun* 1 (one of a number of) raised level banks of earth *etc*, like large steps, on the side of a hill *etc*: *Vines are grown on terraces on the hillside*. □ **terrasse**
2 a row of houses connected to each other. □ **rangée de maisons**
■ *verb* to make into a terrace or terraces: *The hillside has been terraced to make new vineyards*. □ **arranger en terrasses**

terracotta [terə'kotə] *noun*, *adjective* (of) a brownish-red mixture of clay and sand used to make vases, small statues *etc*: *This vase is (made of) terracotta; a terracotta vase*. □ **(de) terre cuite**

terrible ['terəbl] *adjective* 1 very bad: *a terrible singer*; *That music is terrible!* □ **atroce**
2 causing great pain, suffering, hardship *etc*: *War is terrible*; *It was a terrible disaster*. □ **terrible**
3 causing great fear or horror: *The noise of the guns was terrible*. □ **terrible**
'**terribly** *adverb* 1 very: *She is terribly clever*. □ **à l'extrême**
2 in a terrible way: *Does your leg hurt terribly?* □ **terriblement**

terrier ['teriə] *noun* any of several breeds of small dog: *a fox-terrier*. □ **(fox-)terrier**

terrify ['terifai] *verb* to make very frightened: *She was terrified by his appearance*. □ **terrifier**
terrific [tə'rifik] *adjective* 1 marvellous; wonderful: *a terrific party*. □ **formidable**
2 very great, powerful *etc*: *He gave the ball a terrific kick*. □ **terrible**
terrifically [tə'rifikəli] *adverb* very (much): *She enjoyed herself terrifically*. □ **terriblement**
'**terrified** *adjective*: *The terrified little boy screamed*. □ **terrifié**
'**terrifying** *adjective*. □ **terrifiant**

territory ['teritəri] – *plural* '**territories** – *noun* 1 a stretch of land; a region: *They explored the territory around the North Pole*. □ **territoire**
2 the land under the control of a ruler or state: *Canadian territory*. □ **territoire**
3 an area of interest, knowledge *etc*: *Ancient history is outside my territory*. □ **domaine**
,**terri'torial** [-'toː-] *adjective* of or belonging to (*especially* national) territory: *territorial rights/claims*. □ **territorial**
territorial waters the sea close to a country, considered to belong to it. □ **eaux territoriales**

terror ['terə] *noun* 1 very great fear: *She screamed with/in terror*; *He has a terror of spiders*. □ **terreur**
2 something which makes one very afraid: *The terrors of war*. □ **terreur**
3 a troublesome person, *especially* a child: *That child is a real terror!* □ **terreur**
'**terrorism** *noun* the actions or methods of terrorists: *international terrorism*. □ **terrorisme**
'**terrorist** *noun* a person who tries to frighten people or governments into doing what he/she wants by using or threatening violence: *The plane was hijacked by terrorists*; *(also adjective) terrorist activities*. □ **terroriste**
'**terrorize**, '**terrorise** *verb* to make very frightened by using or threatening violence: *A lion escaped from the zoo and terrorized the whole town*. □ **terroriser**
,**terrori'zation**, ,**terrori'sation** *noun*. □ **soumission par le terrorisme**
'**terror-stricken** *adjective* feeling very great fear: *The children were terror-stricken*. □ **terrorisé**

tertiary ['təːʃəri] *adjective* of or at a third level, degree, stage *etc*: *Tertiary education follows secondary education*. □ **tertiaire**

test [test] *noun* 1 a set of questions or exercises intended to find out a person's ability, knowledge *etc*; a short examination: *an arithmetic/driving test*. □ **test, examen**
2 something done to find out whether a thing is good, strong, efficient *etc*: *a blood test*. □ **test, épreuve, essai**
3 an event, situation *etc* that shows how good or bad something is: *a test of his courage*. □ **test, épreuve, essai**
4 a way to find out if something exists or is present: *a test for radioactivity*. □ **test, épreuve, essai**
5 a test match. □ **match international**
■ *verb* to carry out a test or tests on (someone or something): *The students were tested on their French*; *They tested the new aircraft*. □ **interroger; essayer**
test match in cricket, (one of) a series of matches between teams from two countries. □ **match international**
test pilot a pilot who tests new aircraft. □ **pilote d'essai**
'**test tube** *noun* a glass tube closed at one end, used in chemical tests or experiments. □ **éprouvette**

testament ['testəmənt] *noun* a written statement *especially* of what one wants to be done with one's personal property after one dies: *This is his last will and testament*. □ **testament**
Old Testament, New Testament the two main parts of the Bible. □ **Ancien Testament; Nouveau Testament**

testicle ['testikl] *noun* (*usually in plural*) one of the two glands in the male body in which sperm is produced. □ **testicule**

testify ['testifai] *verb* 1 to give evidence, *especially* in a law court: *He agreed to testify on behalf of/against the accused man*. □ **témoigner**
2 to show or give evidence of; to state that (something) is so: *I will testify to her kindness*. □ **attester**

testimony ['testiməni] – *plural* '**testimonies** – *noun* the statement(s) made by a person or people who testify in a law-court: *The jury listened to her testimony*. □ **témoignage**
testi'monial [-'mouniəl] *noun* a (written) statement say-

ing what one knows about a person's character, abilities *etc*: *When applying for a job, one usually needs a testimonial from one's last employer.* □ **recommandation**

tetanus ['tetənəs] *noun* a type of serious disease, caused by an infected wound *etc*, in which certain muscles (*especially* of the jaw) become stiff. □ **tétanos**

tether ['teðə] *noun* a rope or chain for tying an animal to a post *etc*: *He put a tether on his horse.* □ **longe**
■ *verb* to tie with a tether: *She tethered the goat to the post.* □ **attacher (à)**

text [tekst] *noun* **1** in a book, the written or printed words, as opposed to the illustrations, notes *etc*: *First the text was printed, then the drawings added.* □ **texte**
2 a passage from the Bible about which a sermon is preached: *He preached on a text from St John's gospel.* □ **texte**
'textbook *noun* a book used in teaching, giving the main facts about a subject: *a history textbook.* □ **manuel**

textile ['tekstail] *noun* a cloth or fabric made by weaving: *woollen textiles*; (*also adjective*) *the textile industry.* □ **textile**

texture ['tekstʃuə] *noun* **1** the way something feels when touched, eaten *etc*: *the texture of wood, stone, skin etc.* □ **texture**
2 the way that a piece of cloth looks or feels, caused by the way in which it is woven: *the loose texture of this material.* □ **texture**

than [ðən, ðan] *conjunction, preposition* a word used in comparisons: *It is easier than I thought*; *I sing better than he does*; *He sings better than me.* □ **que**

thank [θaŋk] *verb* to express appreciation or gratitude to (someone) for a favour, service, gift *etc*: *He thanked me for the present*; *She thanked him for inviting her.* □ **remercier**
'thankful *adjective* grateful; relieved and happy: *She was thankful that the journey was over*; *a thankful sigh.* □ **reconnaissant; de gratitude/soulagement**
'thankfully *adverb.* □ **avec reconnaissance/soulagement**
'thankfulness *noun.* □ **gratitude**
'thankless *adjective* for which no one is grateful: *Collecting taxes is a thankless task.* □ **ingrat**
'thanklessly *adverb.* □ **ingratement**
'thanklessness *noun.* □ **ingratitude**
thanks *noun plural* expression(s) of gratitude: *I really didn't expect any thanks for helping them.* □ **remerciements**
■ *interjection* thank you: *Thanks (very much) for your present*; *Thanks a lot!*; *No, thanks*; *Yes, thanks.* □ **merci**
'thanksgiving *noun* the act of giving thanks, *especially* to God, *eg* in a church service: *a service of thanksgiving.* □ **action de grâce(s)**
Thanks'giving *noun* (*also* **Thanksgiving Day**) in the United States, a special day (the fourth Thursday in November) for giving thanks to God. □ **Action de Grâces**
thanks to because of: *Thanks to the bad weather, our journey was very uncomfortable.* □ **grâce à; à cause de**
thank you I thank you: *Thank you (very much) for your*

present; *No, thank you.* □ **merci**

that [ðat] – *plural* **those** [ðouz] – *adjective* used to indicate a person, thing *etc* spoken of before, not close to the speaker, already known to the speaker and listener *etc*: *Don't take this book – take that one*; *At that time, I was living in Italy*; *When are you going to return those books?* □ **ce, cet, cette, ces (là)**
■ *pronoun* used to indicate a thing *etc*, or (*in plural* or with the verb **be**) person or people, spoken of before, not close to the speaker, already known to the speaker and listener *etc*: *What is that you've got in your hand?*; *Who is that?*; *That is the Prime Minister*; *Those present at the concert included the composer and his wife.* □ **ce, cela, ça; celui, cela, celle, ceux, celles (-là)**
■ [ðət, ðat] *relative pronoun* used to refer to a person, thing *etc* mentioned in a preceding clause in order to distinguish it from others: *Where is the parcel that arrived this morning?*; *Who is the woman (that) you were talking to?* □ **qui, que**
■ [ðət, ðat] *conjunction* **1** (often omitted) used to report what has been said *etc* or to introduce other clauses giving facts, reasons, results *etc*: *I know (that) you didn't do it*; *I was surprised (that) he had gone.* □ **que**
2 used to introduce expressions of sorrow, wishes *etc*: *That I should be accused of murder!*; *Oh, that I were with her now!* □ **dire que, si seulement**
■ [ðat] *adverb* so; to such an extent: *I didn't realize she was that ill.* □ **(aus)si**
like that in that way: *Don't hold it like that – you'll break it!* □ **comme cela/ça**
that's that an expression used to show that a decision has been made, that something has been completed, made impossible *etc*: *He has said that we can't do it, so that's that.* □ **(un point) c'est tout**

thatch [θatʃ] *noun* straw, rushes *etc* used as a roofing material for houses. □ **chaume**
■ *verb* to cover the roof of (a house) with thatch. □ **couvrir de chaume**
thatched *adjective* covered with thatch: *thatched cottages.* □ **(au toit) de chaume**

that'd ['ðatəd], **that'll** ['ðatl], **that's** ['ðats] short for **that had, that would, that will, that is.**

thaw [θɔː] *verb* **1** (of ice, snow *etc*) to melt, or make or become liquid: *The snow thawed quickly.* □ **(faire) dégeler/fondre**
2 (of frozen food *etc*) to make or become unfrozen: *Frozen food must be thawed before cooking.* □ **(faire) dé(con)geler**
■ *noun* (the time of) the melting of ice and snow at the end of winter, or the change of weather that causes this: *The thaw has come early this year.* □ **dégel**

the [ðə, ði] *adjective* (The form [ðə] is used before words beginning with a consonant *eg the house* [ðəhaus] or consonant sound *eg the union* [ðə'juːnjən]; the form [ði] is used before words beginning with a vowel *eg the apple* [ði 'apl] or vowel sound *eg the honour* [ði 'onə]) **1** used to refer to a person, thing *etc* mentioned previously, described in a following phrase, or already known: *Where is the book I put on the table?*; *Who was the man you were talking to?*; *My mug is the tall blue*

one; *Switch the light off!* □ **l', le, la, les**
2 used with a singular noun or an adjective to refer to all members of a group *etc* or to a general type of object, group of objects *etc*: *The horse is a beautiful animal*; *I spoke to her on the telephone*; *He plays the piano/violin very well*. □ **l', le, la**
3 used to refer to unique objects *etc, especially* in titles and names: *the Duke of Edinburgh*; *the Atlantic (Ocean)*. □ **l', le, la**
4 used after a preposition with words referring to a unit of quantity, time *etc*: *In this job we are paid by the hour*. □ **au, (à) l', (à) la**
5 used with superlative adjectives and adverbs to denote a person, thing *etc* which is or shows more of something than any other: *He is the kindest man I know*; *We like him (the) best of all*. □ **le, la, les**
6 (*often with* **all**) used with comparative adjectives to show that a person, thing *etc* is better, worse *etc*: *She has had a week's holiday and looks* (*all*) *the better for it*. □ **le, la, les**
the ..., the ... (*with comparative adjective or adverb*) used to show the connection or relationship between two actions, states, processes *etc*: *The harder you work, the more you earn*. □ **plus (...) plus (...)**

theatre, theater ['θiətə] *noun* **1** a place where plays, operas *etc* are publicly performed. □ **théâtre**
2 plays in general; any theatre: *Are you going to the theatre tonight?* □ **théâtre**
3 (*also* **'operating theatre**) a room in a hospital where surgical operations are performed: *Take the patient to the theatre*; (*also adjective*) *a theatre nurse*. □ **(de la) salle d'opération**
the'atrical [-'a-] *adjective* **1** of theatres or acting: *a theatrical performance/career*. □ **théâtral, dramatique**
2 (behaving) as if in a play; over-dramatic: *theatrical behaviour*. □ **théâtral**
the'atrically *adverb*. □ **théâtralement**
the,atri'cality [θiatri'ka-] *noun*. □ **théâtralité**
the'atricals [-'a-] *noun plural* dramatic performances: *She's very interested in amateur theatricals*. □ **théâtre**
the theatre 1 the profession of actors: *He's in the theatre*. □ **le théâtre**
2 drama: *His special interest is the theatre*. □ **le théâtre**

thee [ðiː] *pronoun* an old word for 'you' used only when addressing one person, *especially* God (*usually* **Thee**), as the object of a verb: *We thank Thee for Thy goodness*. □ **t', te, toi**

theft [θeft] *noun* (an act of) stealing: *He was jailed for theft*. □ **vol**

their [ðeə] *adjective* **1** belonging to them: *This is their car*; *Take a note of their names and addresses*. □ **leur(s)**
2 used instead of *his, his or her etc* where a person of unknown sex or people of both sexes are referred to: *Every one should buy their own ticket*. □ **son, sa, ses, leur(s)**
theirs [ðeəz] *pronoun* a person, thing *etc* belonging to them: *The child is theirs*; *a friend of theirs* (= one of their friends). □ **le leur, la leur, les leurs**

them [ðəm, ðem] *pronoun* (used as the object of verb or preposition) **1** people, animals, things *etc* already spo-

ken about, being pointed out *etc*: *Let's invite them to dinner*; *What will you do with them?* □ **les, eux, elles, leur**
2 used instead of *him, him or her etc* where a person of unknown sex or people of both sexes are referred to: *If anyone touches that, I'll hit them*. □ **le, la, les, leur, eux**
them'selves *pronoun* **1** used as the object of a verb or preposition when people, animals *etc* are the object of actions they perform: *They hurt themselves*; *They looked at themselves in the mirror*. □ **se, eux, elles-mêmes**
2 used to emphasize **they, them** or the names of people, animals *etc*: *They themselves did nothing wrong*. □ **eux, elles-mêmes**
3 without help *etc*: *They decided to do it themselves*. □ **tout seuls, toutes seules**

theme [θiːm] *noun* **1** the subject of a discussion, essay *etc*: *The theme for tonight's talk is education*. □ **sujet**
2 in a piece of music, the main melody, which may be repeated often. □ **thème**

then [ðen] *adverb* **1** at that time in the past or future: *I was at school then*; *If you're coming next week, I'll see you then*. □ **alors, à ce moment-là**
2 used with prepositions to mean that time in the past or future: *She should be here by then*; *I'll need you before then*; *I have been ill since then*; *Until then*; *Goodbye till then!* □ **ce moment-là**
3 after that: *I had a drink, (and) then I went home*. □ **puis, ensuite**
4 in that case: *She might not give us the money and then what would we do?* □ **alors**
5 often used *especially* at the end of sentences in which an explanation, opinion *etc* is asked for, or which show surprise *etc*: *What do you think of that, then?* □ **alors**
6 also; in addition: *I have two brothers, and then I have a cousin in America*. □ **puis**
■ *conjunction* in that case; as a result: *If you're tired, then you must rest*. □ **alors**
■ *adjective* at that time (in the past): *the then Prime Minister*. □ **d'alors**

theology [θi'olədʒi] *noun* the study of God and religious belief. □ **théologie**
,theo'logical [-'lo-] *adjective*. □ **théologique**
theo'logically [-'lo-] *adverb*. □ **théologiquement**
,theo'logian [-'loudʒiən] *noun* a person who studies, or is an expert in, theology. □ **théologien, ienne**

theorem ['θiərəm] *noun especially* in mathematics, something that has been or must be proved to be true by careful reasoning: *a geometrical theorem*. □ **théorème**

theory ['θiəri] – *plural* **'theories** – *noun* **1** an idea or explanation which has not yet been proved to be correct: *There are many theories about the origin of life*; *In theory, I agree with you, but it would not work in practice*. □ **théorie**
2 the main principles and ideas in an art, science *etc* as opposed to the practice of actually doing it: *A musician has to study both the theory and practice of music*. □ **théorie**
,theo'retical [-'reti-] *adjective*. □ **théorique**
,theo'retically [-'reti-] *adverb*. □ **théoriquement**

'theorize, 'theorise *verb* to make theories: *He did not know what had happened, so he could only theorize about it.* □ **faire des théories (sur)**
'theorist *noun*. □ **théoricien, ienne**

therapy ['θerəpi] *noun* the (methods of) treatment of disease, disorders of the body *etc*: *speech therapy; physiotherapy.* □ **traitement**
'therapist *noun*. □ **thérapeute**

therapeutic [θerə'pjuːtik] *adjective* of or concerning the healing and curing of disease: *therapeutic treatment/exercises.* □ **thérapeutique**

there [ðeə, ðə] *adverb* 1 (at, in, or to) that place: *She lives there; Don't go there.* □ **y, là**
2 used to introduce sentences in which a state, fact *etc* is being announced: *There has been an accident at the factory; There seems to be something wrong; I don't want there to be any mistakes in this.* □ **il; il y a**
3 at that time; at that point in a speech, argument *etc*: *There I cannot agree with you; Don't stop there – tell me what happened next!* □ **là**
4 (with the subject of the sentence following the verb except when it is a pronoun) used at the beginning of a sentence, *usually* with **be** or **go**, to draw attention to, or point out, someone or something: *There she goes now! There it is!* □ **voilà**
5 (*placed immediately after noun*) used for emphasis or to point out someone or something: *That book there is the one you need.* □ **-là; là**
■ *interjection* 1 used to calm or comfort: *There, now. Things aren't as bad as they seem.* □ **allons**
2 used when a person has been shown to be correct, when something bad happens, or when something has been completed: *There! I told you he would do it!; There! That's that job done; There! I said you would hurt yourself!* □ **là! voilà!**

,there'bout(s) *adverb* approximately in that place, of that number, at that time *etc*: *a hundred or thereabouts; at three o'clock or thereabouts.* □ **à peu près**

therefore ['ðeəfoː] *adverb* for that reason: *He worked hard, and therefore he was able to save money.* □ **par conséquent, donc**

there's [ðeəz] short for **there is.**

thermal ['θəːməl] *adjective* of heat: *thermal springs* (= natural springs of warm or hot water); *thermal units.* □ **thermal; thermique**

thermometer [θə'momitə] *noun* an instrument (*usually* a thin, glass tube with *eg* mercury in it) used for measuring temperature, *especially* body temperature: *The nurse took his temperature with a thermometer.* □ **thermomètre**

Thermos (flask)® ['θəːməs (flaːsk)] *noun* a type of vacuum-flask: *He had some tea in a Thermos (flask).* □ **bouteille isolante**

thermostat ['θəːməstat] *noun* an apparatus which automatically controls the temperature of a room, of water in a boiler *etc* by switching a heater or heating system on or off. □ **thermostat**
,thermo'static *adjective* using a thermostat: *thermostatic control.* □ **thermostatique**
,thermo'statically *adverb*. □ **par thermostat**

thesaurus [θi,soːrəs] *noun* a book which gives information (*eg* a dictionary or encyclopedia) *especially* one which lists words according to their meanings. □ **dictionnaire**

these *see* **this.**

thesis ['θiːsis] – *plural* 'theses [-siːz] – *noun* a long written essay, report *etc*, often done for a university degree: *a doctoral thesis; She is writing a thesis on the works of John Milton.* □ **thèse**

they [ðei] *pronoun* (used only as the subject of a verb) 1 persons, animals or things already spoken about, being pointed out *etc*: *They are in the garden.* □ **ils, elles**
2 used instead of **he, he or she** *etc* when the person's sex is unknown or when people of both sexes are being referred to: *If anyone does that, they are to be severely punished.* □ **il(s), elle(s)**

they'd *see* **have, would.**
they'll *see* **will.**
they're *see* **be.**
they've *see* **have.**

thick [θik] *adjective* 1 having a relatively large distance between opposite sides; not thin: *a thick book; thick walls; thick glass.* □ **épais**
2 having a certain distance between opposite sides: *It's two centimetres thick; a two-centimetre-thick pane of glass.* □ **épais de; de (...) d'épaisseur**
3 (of liquids, mixtures *etc*) containing solid matter; not flowing (easily) when poured: *thick soup.* □ **épais, consistant**
4 made of many single units placed very close together; dense: *a thick forest; thick hair.* □ **dense**
5 difficult to see through: *thick fog.* □ **opaque**
6 full of, covered with *etc*: *The room was thick with dust; The air was thick with smoke.* □ **plein (de), couvert (de)**
7 stupid: *Don't be so thick!* □ **bête**
■ *noun* the thickest, most crowded or active part: *in the thick of the forest; in the thick of the fight.* □ **le plus épais de; en plein cœur de**
'thickly *adverb*. □ **en une couche épaisse**
'thickness *noun*. □ **épaisseur**
'thicken *verb* to make or become thick or thicker: *We'll add some flour to thicken the soup; The fog thickened and we could no longer see the road.* □ **(s')épaissir**
,thick-'skinned *adjective* not easily hurt by criticism or insults: *You won't upset her – she's very thick-skinned.* □ **peu sensible**
thick and fast frequently and in large numbers: *The bullets/insults were flying thick and fast.* □ **dru**
through thick and thin whatever happens; in spite of all difficulties: *They were friends through thick and thin.* □ **contre vents et marées**

thicket ['θikit] *noun* a group of trees or bushes growing closely together: *He hid in a thicket.* □ **fourré**

thief [θiːf] – *plural* thieves [θiːvz] – *noun* a person who steals: *The thief got away with all my money.* □ **voleur, euse**

thieve [θiːv] *verb* to steal: *He is always thieving my pencils.* □ **voler**

thigh [θai] *noun* the part of the leg between the knee and

hip. □ **cuisse**

thimble ['θimbl] *noun* a kind of metal or plastic capital to protect the finger and push the needle when sewing. □ **dé (à coudre)**

thin [θin] *adjective* 1 having a short distance between opposite sides: *thin paper*; *The walls of these houses are too thin.* □ **mince**

2 (of people or animals) not fat: *She looks thin since her illness.* □ **mince, maigre**

3 (of liquids, mixtures *etc*) not containing any solid matter; rather lacking in taste; (tasting as if) containing a lot of water or too much water: *thin soup.* □ **clair, liquide**

4 not set closely together; not dense or crowded: *His hair is getting rather thin.* □ **clairsemé**

5 not convincing or believable: *a thin excuse.* □ **peu convaincant**

■ *verb – past tense, past participle* **thinned** – to make or become thin or thinner: *The crowd thinned after the parade was over.* □ **(s')éclaircir; (se) disperser**

'**thinly** *adverb.* □ **de façon clairsemée**

'**thinness** *noun.* □ **minceur**

thin air nowhere: *She disappeared into thin air.* □ **sans laisser de traces**

,**thin-'skinned** *adjective* sensitive; easily hurt or upset: *Be careful what you say – she's very thin-skinned.* □ **susceptible**

thin out to make or become less dense or crowded: *The trees thinned out near the river.* □ **(s')éclaircir**

thine *see* **thy.**

thing [θiŋ] *noun* 1 an object; something that is not living: *What do you use that thing for?* □ **chose**

2 a person, *especially* a person one likes: *She's a nice old thing.* □ **personne, créature**

3 any fact, quality, idea *etc* that one can think of or refer to: *Music is a wonderful thing*; *I hope I haven't done the wrong thing*; *That was a stupid thing to do.* □ **chose**

things *noun plural* things, *especially* clothes, that belong to someone: *Take all your wet things off.* □ **affaires**

first thing (in the morning *etc*) early in the morning just after getting up, starting work *etc*: *I'll do it first thing (in the morning).* □ **demain à la première heure**

last thing (at night *etc*) late at night, just before stopping work, going to bed *etc*: *She always has a cup of tea last thing at night.* □ **juste avant de se coucher**

the thing is ... the important fact or question is; the problem is: *The thing is, is he going to help us?* □ **la question est**

think [θiŋk] – *past tense, past participle* **thought** [θɔːt] – *verb* 1 (*often with* **about**) to have or form ideas in one's mind: *Can babies think?*; *I was thinking about my mother.* □ **penser (à)**

2 to have or form opinions in one's mind; to believe: *He thinks (that) the world is flat*; *What do you think of his poem?*; *What do you think about her suggestion?*; *He thought me very stupid.* □ **penser (à, de)**

3 to intend or plan (to do something), *usually* without making a final decision: *I must think what to do*; *I was thinking of/about going to Ottawa next week.* □ **penser/réfléchir (à)**

4 to imagine or expect: *I never thought to see you again*; *Little did he think that I would be there as well.* □ **penser**

■ *noun* the act of thinking: *Go and have a think about it.* □ **pensée, réflexion**

'**thinker** *noun* a person who thinks, *especially* deeply and constructively: *She's one of the world's great thinkers.* □ **penseur, euse**

-**thought-out** planned: *a well-thought-out campaign.* □ **préparé, élaboré**

think better of 1 to think again and decide not to; to reconsider: *He was going to ask for more money, but he thought better of it.* □ **se raviser**

2 to think that (someone) could not be so bad *etc*: *I thought better of you than to suppose you would do that.* □ **avoir une meilleure opinion de qqn**

think highly, well, badly *etc* **of** to have a good, or bad, opinion of: *She thought highly of him and his poetry.* □ **avoir une bonne opinion, une mauvaise opinion (de)**

think little of/not think much of to have a very low opinion of: *He didn't think much of what I had done*; *She thought little of my work.* □ **ne pas avoir une bonne opinion de**

think of 1 to remember to do (something); to keep in one's mind; to consider: *You always think of everything!*; *Have you thought of the cost involved?* □ **penser à**

2 to remember: *I couldn't think of her name when I met her at the party.* □ **se rappeler de**

3 (*with* **would, should, not, never** *etc*) to be willing to do (something): *I would never think of being rude to her*; *He couldn't think of leaving her.* □ **songer à**

think out to plan; to work out in the mind: *She thought out the whole operation.* □ **planifier**

think over to think carefully about; to consider all aspects of (an action, decision *etc*): *He thought it over, and decided not to go.* □ **bien réfléchir (à)**

think twice (*often with* **about**) to hesitate before doing (something); to decide not to do (something one was intending to do): *I would think twice about going, if I were you.* □ **y regarder à deux fois avant de**

think up to invent; to devise: *She thought up a new process.* □ **inventer**

think the world of to be very fond of: *He thinks the world of his wife.* □ **adorer**

third [θɔːd] *noun* 1 one of three equal parts. □ **tiers**

2 (*also adjective*) the last of three (people, things *etc*); the next after the second. □ **troisième**

■ *adverb* in the third position: *John came first in the race, and I came third.* □ **troisième**

'**thirdly** *adverb* in the third place: *Firstly, I haven't enough money*; *secondly, I'm too old*; *and thirdly it's raining.* □ **troisièmement**

,**third 'class** *adjective, adverb* of or in the class next after or below the second. □ **de troisième classe**

third degree a severe method of questioning people, sometimes using torture *etc*: *The police gave him the third degree.* □ **cuisiner, passer à tabac**

third party a third person who is not directly involved in an action, contract *etc*: *Was there a third party present when you and she agreed to the sale?* □ **tiers, tierce personne**

,third-'rate *adjective* of very bad quality: *a third-rate performance*. □ **de dernier ordre**

the **Third World** the developing countries, those not part of or aligned with the two main powers: *the needs of the Third World*. □ **tiers monde**

thirst [θəːst] *noun* **1** a feeling of dryness (in the mouth) caused by a lack of water or moisture: *I have a terrible thirst*. □ **soif**

2 a strong and eager desire for something: *thirst for knowledge*. □ **soif**

■ *verb* to have a great desire for: *He's thirsting for revenge*. □ **avoir soif de**

'**thirsty** *adjective* **1** suffering from thirst: *I'm so thirsty – I must have a drink*. □ **assoiffé**

2 causing a thirst: *Digging the garden is thirsty work*. □ **qui donne soif**

'**thirstily** *adverb*. □ **à longs traits**

'**thirstiness** *noun*. □ **soif**

thirteen [θəːˈtiːn] *noun* **1** the number or figure 13. □ **treize**

2 the age of 13. □ **treize ans**

■ *adjective* **1** 13 in number. □ **treize**

2 aged 13. □ **de treize ans**

thirteen- having thirteen (of something): *a thirteen-year campaign*. □ **à/de treize (...)**

,thir'teenth *noun* **1** one of thirteen equal parts. □ **treizième**

2 (*also adjective*) the last of thirteen (people, things *etc*); the next after the twelfth. □ **treizième**

,thir'teen-year-old *noun* a person or animal that is thirteen years old. □ **(individu, etc.) âgé de treize ans**

■ *adjective* (of a person, animal or thing) that is thirteen years old. □ **de treize ans**

thirty [ˈθəːti] *noun* **1** the number or figure 30. □ **trente**

2 the age of 30. □ **trente ans**

■ *adjective* **1** 30 in number. □ **trente**

2 aged 30. □ **de trente ans**

'**thirties** *noun plural* **1** the period of time between one's thirtieth and fortieth birthdays. □ **trentaine**

2 the range of temperatures between thirty and forty degrees. □ **températures entre 30 et 39 degrés**

3 the period of time between the thirtieth and fortieth years of a century. □ **années trente**

'**thirtieth** *noun* **1** one of thirty equal parts. □ **trentième**

2 (*also adjective*) the last of thirty (people, things *etc*); the next after the twenty-ninth. □ **trentième**

thirty- having thirty (of something): *a thirty-dollar fine*. □ **de trente (...)**

'**thirty-year-old** *noun* a person or animal that is thirty years old. □ **(individu, etc.) âgé de trente ans**

■ *adjective* (of a person, animal or thing) that is thirty years old. □ **de trente ans**

this [ðis] – *plural* **these** [ðiːz] – *adjective* **1** used to indicate a person, thing *etc* nearby or close in time: *This book is better than that (one)*; *I prefer these trousers*. □ **ce, cet, cette, ces**

2 used in stories to indicate a person, thing *etc* that one is describing or about to describe: *Then this man arrived*. □ **un, une; ce, cette**

■ *pronoun* used for a thing *etc* or a person nearby or

close in time: *Read this – you'll like it*; *This is my friend John Smith*. □ **ce, ceci**

■ *adverb* so; to this degree: *I didn't think it would be this easy*. □ **(aus)si**

like this in this way: *It would be quicker if you did it like this*. □ **comme ceci**

thistle [ˈθisl] *noun* a type of prickly plant with purple flowers, which grows in fields *etc*. □ **chardon**

tho' [ðou] short for **though**.

thorn [θɔːn] *noun* a hard, sharp point sticking out from the stem of certain plants: *She pricked her finger on a thorn*. □ **épine**

'**thorny** *adjective* **1** full of or covered with thorns: *a thorny branch*. □ **épineux**

2 difficult, causing trouble *etc*: *a thorny problem*. □ **épineux**

thorough [ˈθʌrou] *adjective* **1** (of a person) very careful; attending to every detail: *a thorough worker*. □ **consciencieux**

2 (of a task *etc*) done with a suitably high level of care, attention to detail *etc*: *Her work is very thorough*. □ **minutieux**

3 complete; absolute: *a thorough waste of time*. □ **complet**

'**thoroughly** *adverb* **1** with great care, attending to every detail: *She doesn't do her job very thoroughly*. □ **à fond**

2 completely: *He's thoroughly stupid/bored*. □ **complètement, tout à fait**

'**thoroughness** *noun* care; attention to detail. □ **minutie**

'**thoroughfare** [-feə] *noun* **1** a public road or street: *Don't park your car on a busy thoroughfare*. □ **voie publique**

2 (the right of) passage through: *A sign on the gate said 'No Thoroughfare'*. □ **passage interdit**

those *see* **that**.

thou [ðau] *pronoun* an old word for 'you' used only when addressing one person, *especially* God (*usually* **Thou**), as the subject of a verb: *Thou, O God ...*; *thou villain!* □ **tu, toi**

though [ðou] *conjunction* (*rare abbreviation* **tho'**) despite the fact that; although: *She went out, (even) though it was raining*. □ **bien que, quoique**

■ *adverb* however: *I wish I hadn't done it, though*. □ **cependant, pourtant**

as though as if: *You sound as though you've caught a cold*. □ **comme si**

thought [θɔːt] *verb see* **think**.

■ *noun* **1** something that one thinks; an idea: *I had a sudden thought*. □ **pensée**

2 the act of thinking; consideration: *After a great deal of thought we decided to emigrate to America*. □ **réflexion**

3 general opinion: *scientific thought*. □ **pensée**

'**thoughtful** *adjective* **1** (appearing to be) thinking deeply: *You look thoughtful*; *a thoughtful mood*. □ **pensif**

2 thinking of other people; consideration: *It was very thoughtful of you to do that*. □ **gentil, délicat**

'**thoughtfully** *adverb*. □ **pensivement; gentiment**

'**thoughtfulness** *noun*. □ **caractère réfléchi; gentillesse**

'**thoughtless** *adjective* not thinking about other people; showing no thought, care or consideration; inconsider-

ate: *thoughtless words.* □ **irréfléchi; indélicat**
'thoughtlessly *adverb.* □ **à la légère**
'thoughtlessness *noun.* □ **étourderie; indélicatesse**
thousand ['θauzənd] – *plurals* **'thousand, 'thousands** –
noun 1 the number 1000: *one thousand; two thousand;
several thousand.* □ **mille**
2 the figure 1000. □ **mille**
3 a thousand dollars: *This cost us several thousand(s).*
□ **mille**
■ *adjective* 1000 in number: *a few thousand people; I
have a couple of thousand dollars.* □ **mille**
thousand- having a thousand (of something): *a thousand kilometre journey.* □ **à/de mille (...)**
'thousandth *noun* 1 one of a thousand equal parts. □
millième
2 (*also adjective*) the last of a thousand (people, things
etc) or (the person, thing *etc*) in an equivalent position.
□ **millième**
thousands of 1 several thousand: *He's got thousands of
dollars in the bank.* □ **milliers (de)**
2 lots of: *I've read thousands of books.* □ **milliers (de)**
thrash [θraʃ] *verb* 1 to strike with blows: *The child was
soundly thrashed.* □ **battre**
2 to move about violently: *The wounded animal thrashed
about/around on the ground.* □ **se débattre**
3 to defeat easily, by a large margin: *Our team was
thrashed eighteen-nil.* □ **battre à plates coutures**
'thrashing *noun* a physical beating: *He needs a good
thrashing!* □ **correction**
thread [θred] *noun* 1 a thin strand of cotton, wool, silk
etc, especially when used for sewing: *a needle and some
thread.* □ **fil**
2 the spiral ridge around a screw: *This screw has a worn
thread.* □ **filetage**
3 the connection between the various events or details
(in a story, account *etc*): *I've lost the thread of what
she's saying.* □ **fil**
■ *verb* 1 to pass a thread through: *I cannot thread this
needle; The child was threading beads.* □ **enfiler**
2 to make (one's way) through: *She threaded her way
through the crowd.* □ **se faufiler**
'threadbare *adjective* (of material) worn thin; shabby:
a threadbare jacket. □ **élimé**
threat [θret] *noun* 1 a warning that one is going to hurt
or punish someone: *He will certainly carry out his threat
to harm you.* □ **menace**
2 a sign of something dangerous or unpleasant which
may be, or is, about to happen: *a threat of rain.* □ **menace**
3 a source of danger: *His presence is a threat to our
plan/success.* □ **menace**
'threaten *verb* to make or be a threat (to): *She threatened to kill herself; He threatened me with violence/
with a gun; A storm is threatening.* □ **menacer (de)**
three [θriː] *noun* 1 the number or figure 3. □ **trois**
2 the age of 3. □ **trois ans**
■ *adjective* 1 3 in number. □ **trois**
2 aged 3. □ **de trois ans**
three- having three (of something): *a three-page letter.*
□ **de trois (...)**

,three-di'mensional *adjective* (*abbreviation* **3–D**) having three dimensions, *ie* height, width and depth. □
tridimensionnel
three-'quarter *adjective* not quite full-length: *a three-
quarter (-length) coat.* □ **(de) trois-quarts**
'three-year-old *noun* a person or animal that is three
years old. □ **(individu, etc.) âgé de trois ans**
■ *adjective* (of a person, animal or thing) that is three
years old. □ **de trois ans**
thresh [θreʃ] *verb* to beat (the stalks of corn) in order to
extract the grain. □ **battre**
threshold ['θreʃould] *noun* 1 (a piece of wood or stone
under) a doorway forming the entrance to a house *etc*:
She paused on the threshold and then entered. □ **seuil**
2 beginning: *She is on the threshold of a brilliant career.* □ **seuil**
threw *see* **throw**.
thrift [θrift] *noun* careful spending of money, or using
of food or other resources, so that one can save or have
some left in reserve; economy: *She is noted for her thrift
but her husband is very extravagant.* □ **économie**
'thrifty *adjective* showing thrift: *a thrifty manager.* □
économe
'thriftily *adverb.* □ **avec économie**
'thriftiness *noun.* □ **économie**
thrill [θril] *verb* to (cause someone to) feel excitement:
She was thrilled at/by the invitation. □ **exciter**
■ *noun* 1 an excited feeling: *a thrill of pleasure/expec-
tation.* □ **émotion, frisson**
2 something which causes this feeling: *Meeting the
Queen was a great thrill.* □ **émotion**
'thriller *noun* an exciting novel or play, *usually* about
crime, detectives *etc*: *I always take a thriller to read on
the train.* □ **roman/pièce à suspense**
'thrilling *adjective* exciting. □ **palpitant**
thrive [θraiv] *verb* to grow strong and healthy: *Children
thrive on milk; The business is thriving.* □ **prospérer**
'thriving *adjective* successful: *a thriving industry.* □
florissant
thro' [θruz] short for **through**.
throat [θrout] *noun* 1 the back part of the mouth connecting the openings of the stomach, lungs and nose:
She has a sore throat. □ **gorge**
2 the front part of the neck: *She wore a silver brooch at
her throat.* □ **gorge**
-throated having (a certain type of) throat: *a red-
throated bird.* □ **à gorge (...)**
'throaty *adjective* (of a voice) coming from far back in
the throat; deep and hoarse. □ **de gorge**
'throatily *adverb.* □ **d'une façon gutturale**
'throatiness *noun.* □ **qualité gutturale**
throb [θrob] *noun* – *past tense, past participle* **throbbed** –
verb 1 (of the heart) to beat: *Her heart throbbed with
excitement.* □ **battre**
2 to beat regularly like the heart: *The engine was throbbing gently.* □ **vibrer, palpiter**
3 to beat regularly with pain; to be very painful: *His
head is throbbing (with pain).* □ **élancer**
■ *noun* a regular beat: *the throb of the engine/her heart/
her sore finger.* □ **vibration; battement; élancement**

throne [θroun] *noun* **1** the ceremonial chair of a king, queen *etc*, pope or bishop. □ **trône**
2 the king or queen: *He swore allegiance to the throne.* □ **trône**

throng [θroŋ] *noun* a crowd: *Throngs of people gathered to see the actress.* □ **foule**
■ *verb* to crowd or fill: *People thronged the streets to see the president.* □ **se presser (vers, dans)**

throttle ['θrotl] *noun* (in engines, the lever attached to) the valve controlling the flow of steam, gas *etc*: *The car went faster as he opened the throttle.* □ **accélérateur, arrivée de gaz**
■ *verb* to choke (someone) by gripping the throat: *This scarf is throttling me!* □ **étrangler**

through [θruː] *preposition* **1** into from one direction and out of in the other: *The water flows through a pipe.* □ **dans, à travers**
2 from side to side or end to end of: *He walked (right) through the town.* □ **d'un bout à l'autre**
3 from the beginning to the end of: *She read through the magazine.* □ **en entier**
4 because of: *He lost his job through his own stupidity.* □ **à cause de**
5 by way of: *He got the job through a friend.* □ **par l'intermédiaire de, par l'entremise de**
6 from... to (inclusive): *I go to work Monday through Friday.* □ **de (...) à (...) (inclus)**
■ *adverb* into and out of; from one side or end to the other; from beginning to end: *He went straight/right through.* □ **à travers, de part en part**
■ *adjective* **1** (of a bus or train) that goes all the way to one's destination, so that one doesn't have to change (buses or trains): *There isn't a through train – you'll have to change.* □ **direct**
2 finished: *Are you through yet?* □ **qui a fini**
through'out *preposition* **1** in all parts of: *They searched throughout the house.* □ **partout dans**
2 from start to finish of: *She complained throughout the journey.* □ **tout le long de**
■ *adverb* in every part: *The house was furnished throughout.* □ **entièrement**
all through 1 from beginning to end of: *The baby cried all through the night.* □ **du début à la fin (de)**
2 in every part of: *Road conditions are bad all through the country.* □ **dans tout, partout**
soaked, wet through very wet: *His coat was wet through.* □ **trempé**
through and through completely: *He was a gentleman through and through.* □ **complètement**
through with finished with: *Are you through with the newspaper yet?* □ **qui a terminé**

throw [θrou] – *past tense* **threw** [θruː]: *past participle* **thrown** – *verb* **1** to send through the air with force; to hurl or fling: *He threw the ball to her/threw her the ball.* □ **jeter, lancer**
2 (of a horse) to make its rider fall off: *My horse threw me.* □ **désarçonner**
3 to puzzle or confuse: *He was completely thrown by her question.* □ **désarçonner**
4 (in wrestling, judo *etc*) to wrestle (one's opponent) to

the ground. □ **envoyer au tapis**
■ *noun* an act of throwing: *That was a good throw!* □ **lancer**
throw away 1 to get rid of: *She always throws away her old clothes.* □ **jeter**
2 to lose through lack of care, concern *etc*: *Don't throw your chance of promotion away by being careless.* □ **gâcher**
throw doubt on to suggest or hint that (something) is not true: *The latest scientific discoveries throw doubt on the original theory.* □ **jeter le doute sur**
throw in to include or add as a gift or as part of a bargain: *When I bought his car he threw in the radio and a box of tools.* □ **ajouter (par-dessus le marché)**
throw light on to help to solve or give information on (a mystery, puzzle, problem *etc*): *Can anyone throw any light on the problem?* □ **éclaircir**
throw oneself into to begin (doing something) with great energy: *She threw herself into her work with enthusiasm.* □ **se lancer**
throw off 1 to get rid of: *She finally managed to throw off her cold; They were following us but we threw them off.* □ **se débarrasser de**
2 to take off very quickly: *He threw off his coat and sat down.* □ **enlever à la hâte**
throw open to open suddenly and wide: *She threw open the door and walked in.* □ **ouvrir tout grand**
throw out to get rid of by throwing or by force: *He was thrown out of the meeting; The committee threw out the proposal.* □ **jeter**
throw a party to hold, organize *etc* a party: *They threw a party for her birthday.* □ **organiser une fête**
throw up 1 a slang expression for to vomit: *She had too much to eat, and threw up on the way home.* □ **vomir**
2 to give up or abandon: *He threw up his job.* □ **lâcher**
3 to build hurriedly: *They threw up a temporary building.* □ **construire à la hâte**
throw one's voice to make one's voice appear to come from somewhere else, *eg* the mouth of a ventriloquist's dummy. □ **faire du ventriloquisme**

thru [θruː] (*American*) short for **through.**

thrust [θrʌst] – *past tense, past participle* **thrust** – *verb* to push suddenly and violently: *He thrust his spade into the ground; She thrust forward through the crowd.* □ **enfoncer**
■ *noun* **1** a sudden violent forward movement: *The army made a sudden thrust through the country.* □ **poussée**
2 a force pushing forward: *the thrust of the engines.* □ **poussée**
thrust on/upon to bring (something or someone) forcibly to someone's notice, into someone's company *etc*: *He thrust $100 on me; She is always thrusting herself on other people; Fame was thrust upon him.* □ **imposer (à)**

thud [θʌd] *noun* a dull sound like that of something heavy falling to the ground: *He dropped the book with a thud.* □ **bruit sourd**
■ *verb* – *past tense, past participle* '**thudded** – to move or fall with such a sound: *The tree thudded to the ground.* □ **faire un bruit sourd**

thug [θʌg] *noun* a violent, brutal person: *Where are the young thugs who robbed the old man?* □ **voyou**

thumb [θʌm] *noun* **1** the short thick finger of the hand, set at a different angle from the other four. □ **pouce**

2 the part of a glove covering this finger. □ **pouce**

■ *verb* (*often with* **through**) to turn over (the pages of a book) with the thumb or fingers: *She was thumbing through the dictionary.* □ **feuilleter**

'**thumbnail** *noun* the nail on the thumb. □ **ongle du pouce**

'**thumbprint** *noun* a mark made by pressing the thumb on to a surface, sometimes used as means of identification. □ **empreinte du pouce**

,**thumbs-'up** *noun* a sign expressing a wish for good luck, success *etc*: *He gave me the thumbs-up.* □ **signe de bonne chance**

'**thumbtack** (*also* '**drawing pin**) *noun* a pin with a broad, flat head used for fastening paper to a board *etc*.a pin with a broad, flat head used for fastening paper to a board *etc.*: *She hung the picture on the wall with thumbtacks.* □ **punaise**

under someone's thumb controlled or greatly influenced by someone: *They are completely under the president's thumb.* □ **mené par le bout du nez**

thump [θʌmp] *noun* (the sound of) a heavy blow or hit: *They heard a thump on the door; He gave him a thump on the head.* □ **bruit sourd et lourd**

■ *verb* to hit, move or fall with, or make, a dull, heavy noise. □ **marteler**

thunder ['θʌndə] *noun* **1** the deep rumbling sound heard in the sky after a flash of lightning: *a clap/peal of thunder; a thunderstorm.* □ **tonnerre**

2 a loud rumbling: *the thunder of horses' hooves.* □ **tonnerre**

■ *verb* **1** to sound, rumble *etc*: *It thundered all night.* □ **tonner**

2 to make a noise like thunder: *The tanks thundered over the bridge.* □ **tonner**

'**thundering** *adjective* very great: *a thundering idiot.* □ **énorme**

'**thunderous** *adjective* like thunder: *a thunderous noise.* □ **tonitruant**

'**thunderously** *adverb*. □ **comme le tonnerre**

'**thundery** *adjective* warning of, or likely to have or bring, thunder: *thundery clouds/weather.* □ **orageux, d'orage**

'**thunderbolt** *noun* **1** a flash of lightning immediately followed by thunder. □ **éclair**

2 a sudden great surprise: *Her arrival was a complete thunderbolt.* □ **coup de tonnerre**

thunderstorm *noun* a heavy downpour with rumbling of thunder often following flashes of lightning: *The heavy rain and the sound of the thunderstorm frightened the children.* □ **orage**

Thursday ['θəːzdi] *noun* the fifth day of the week, the day following Wednesday: *She came on Thursday; (also adjective) Thursday evening.* □ **(de) jeudi**

thus [ðʌs] *adverb* (referring to something mentioned immediately before or after) in this or that way or manner: *She spoke thus; Thus, she was able to finish the*

work quickly. □ **ainsi**

thwart [θwɔːt] *verb* **1** to stop or hinder (someone) from doing something: *He doesn't like to be thwarted.* □ **contrarier**

2 to prevent (something being done by someone): *All her attempts to become rich were thwarted.* □ **contrecarrer**

thy [ðai] *adjective* an old word for 'your' used only when addressing one person, *especially* God: *thy father.* □ **ton, ta, tes**

thine [ðain] *pronoun* an old word for 'yours' used only when addressing one person, *especially* God: *Thine is the glory.* □ **le tien, la tienne, les tiens, les tiennes**

■ *adjective* the form of **thy** used before a vowel or vowel sound: *Thine anger is great; thine honour.* □ **ton, ta, tes**

thy'self *pronoun* an old word for 'yourself': *Look at thyself.* □ **te, toi-même**

thyme [taim] *noun* a type of sweet-smelling herb used to season food. □ **thym**

thyself *see* thy.

tiara [ti'ɑːrə] *noun* a jewelled ornament for the head, similar to a crown. □ **diadème**

tibia ['tibiə] *noun* the larger of the two bones between the knee and ankle: *a broken tibia.* □ **tibia**

tic [tik] *noun* a nervous, involuntary movement or twitch of a muscle, *especially* of the face: *She has a nervous tic below her left eye.* □ **tic**

tick¹ [tik] *noun* **1** a regular sound, *especially* that of a watch, clock *etc*. □ **tic-tac**

2 a moment: *Wait a tick!* □ **instant**

■ *verb* to make a sound like this: *Your watch ticks very loudly!* □ **tictaquer**

tick² [tik] *noun* a mark (√) used to show that something is correct, has been noted *etc*. □ **coche**

■ *verb* (*often with* **off**) to put this mark beside an item or name on a list *etc*: *She ticked everything off on the list.* □ **cocher**

tick (someone) off, give (someone) a ticking off to scold someone: *The teacher gave me a ticking off for being late.* □ **engueuler, passer un savon à**

tick over to run quietly and smoothly at a gentle pace: *The car's engine is ticking over.* □ **tourner au ralenti**

tick³ [tik] *noun* a type of small, blood-sucking insect: *Our dog has ticks.* □ **tique**

ticket ['tikit] *noun* **1** a piece of card or paper which gives the holder a certain right, *eg* of travel, entering a theatre *etc*: *a bus-ticket; a cinema-ticket.* □ **billet**

2 a notice advising of a minor driving offence: *a parking-ticket.* □ **contravention**

3 a card or label stating the price *etc* of something. □ **étiquette**

tickle ['tikl] *verb* **1** to touch (sensitive parts of someone's skin) lightly, often making the person laugh: *He tickled me/my feet with a feather.* □ **chatouiller**

2 (of a part of the body) to feel as if it is being touched in this way: *My nose tickles.* □ **chatouiller**

3 to amuse: *The funny story tickled him.* □ **amuser**

■ *noun* **1** an act or feeling of tickling. □ **chatouillement**

2 a feeling of irritation in the throat (making one cough).

□ **chatouillement, irritation**

'**ticklish** *adjective* **1** easily made to laugh when tickled: *Are you ticklish?* □ **chatouilleux**

2 not easy to manage; difficult: *a ticklish problem/situation.* □ **délicat**

be tickled pink to be very pleased. □ **être aux anges**

tidal *see* **tide.**

tidbit *see* **titbit.**

tide [taid] *noun* the regular, twice-a-day ebbing and flowing movement of the sea: *It's high/low tide*; *The tide is coming in/going out.* □ **marée**

'**tidal** *adjective* of or affected by tides: *tidal currents*; *a tidal river.* □ **de (la) marée**

tidal wave an enormous wave in the sea, caused by an earthquake *etc.* □ **raz-de-marée**

tidings ['taidiŋz] *noun plural* news: *They brought tidings of a great victory.* □ **nouvelle(s)**

tidy ['taidi] *adjective* **1** (*negative* **untidy**) in good order; neat: *a tidy room/person*; *His hair never looks tidy.* □ **net, ordonné**

2 fairly big: *a tidy sum of money.* □ **coquet**

■ *verb* (*sometimes with* **up, away** *etc*) to put in good order; to make neat: *She tidied (away) his papers*; *She was tidying the room (up) when her mother arrived.* □ **ranger**

'**tidily** *adverb.* □ **soigneusement**

'**tidiness** *noun.* □ **ordre, propreté**

tie [tai] – *present participle* '**tying**: *past tense, past participle* **tied** – *verb* **1** (*often with* **to, on** *etc*) to fasten with a string, rope *etc*: *He tied the horse to a tree*; *The parcel was tied with string*; *I don't like this job – I hate being tied to a desk.* □ **attacher**

2 to fasten by knotting; to make a knot in: *He tied his shoelaces.* □ **nouer**

3 to be joined by a knot *etc*: *The belt of this dress ties at the front.* □ **se nouer**

4 to score the same number of points *etc* (in a game, competition *etc*): *Three people tied for first place.* □ **être à égalité**

■ *noun* **1** a strip of material worn tied around the neck under the collar of a shirt: *He wore a shirt and tie.* □ **cravate**

2 something that joins: *the ties of friendship.* □ **lien**

3 an equal score or result (in a game, competition *etc*); a draw. □ **match nul**

4 a game or match to be played. □ **match de championnat**

be tied up 1 to be busy; to be involved (with): *I can't discuss this matter just now – I'm tied up with other things.* □ **être pris/occupé**

2 (*with* **with**) to be connected with. □ **être lié à**

tie (someone) down to limit someone's freedom *etc*: *Her work tied her down.* □ **assujettir**

tie in/up to be linked or joined (logically): *This doesn't tie in (with what he said before).* □ **correspondre à**

tier [tiə] *noun* a row of seats: *They sat in the front/first tier.* □ **rangée**

tiff [tif] *noun* a slight quarrel: *She's had a tiff with her boy-friend.* □ **prise de bec**

tiger ['taigə] – *feminine* '**tigress** – *noun* a large wild animal of the cat family, with a striped coat. □ **tigre; tigresse**

tight [tait] *adjective* **1** fitting very or too closely: *I couldn't open the box because the lid was too tight*; *My trousers are too tight.* □ **serré**

2 stretched to a great extent; not loose: *He made sure that the ropes were tight.* □ **tendu**

3 (of control *etc*) strict and very careful: *She keeps (a) tight control over her emotions.* □ **strict**

4 not allowing much time: *We hope to finish this next week but the schedule's a bit tight.* □ **serré**

■ *adverb* (*also* '**tightly**) closely; with no extra room or space: *The bags were packed tight/tightly packed.* □ **bien serré**

-tight sealed so as to keep (something) in or out, as in **airtight, watertight.** □ **hermétique, étanche**

'**tighten** *verb* to make or become tight or tighter. □ **tendre**

'**tightness** *noun.* □ **étroitesse; sévérité**

tights *noun plural* a close-fitting (*usually* nylon or woollen) garment covering the feet, legs and body to the waist: *She bought three pairs of tights.* □ **collant**

,**tight-'fisted** *adjective* mean and ungenerous with money: *a tight-fisted employer.* □ **radin**

'**tightrope** *noun* a tightly-stretched rope or wire. □ **corde raide**

a tight corner/spot a difficult position or situation: *His refusal to help put her in a tight corner/spot.* □ **situation difficile**

tighten one's belt to make sacrifices and reduce one's standard of living: *If the economy gets worse, we shall just have to tighten our belts.* □ **se serrer la ceinture**

tigress *see* **tiger.**

tile [tail] *noun* **1** a piece of baked clay used in covering roofs, walls, floors *etc*: *Some of the tiles were blown off the roof during the storm.* □ **tuile; carreau**

2 a similar piece of plastic material used for covering floors *etc.* □ **carreau**

■ *verb* to cover with tiles: *We had to have the roof tiled.* □ **couvrir de tuiles, de carreaux**

tiled *adjective* covered with tiles. □ **recouvert de tuiles, de carreaux**

till¹ [til] *preposition, conjunction* to the time of or when: *I'll wait till six o'clock*; *Go on till you reach the station.* □ **jusqu'à (ce que)**

till² [til] *noun* (in a shop *etc*) a container or drawer in which money is put and registered. □ **(tiroir-)caisse**

tiller ['tilə] *noun* the handle or lever used to turn the rudder of a boat. □ **barre**

tilt [tilt] *verb* to go or put (something) into a sloping or slanting position: *He tilted his chair backwards*; *The lamp tilted and fell.* □ **pencher, incliner**

■ *noun* a slant; a slanting position: *The table is at a slight tilt.* □ **inclinaison**

(at) full tilt at full speed: *She rushed down the street at full tilt.* □ **à fond de train**

timber ['timbə] *noun* **1** wood, *especially* for building: *This house is built of timber.* □ **bois de construction**

2 trees suitable for this: *a hundred acres of good timber.* □ **arbres, bois**

3 a wooden beam used in the building of a house, ship *etc*. □ **poutre, madrier**

time [taim] *noun* 1 the hour of the day: *What time is it?*; *Can your child tell the time yet?* □ **heure**

2 the passage of days, years, events *etc*: *time and space*; *Time will tell*. □ **temps**

3 a point at which, or period during which, something happens: *at the time of his wedding*; *breakfast-time*. □ **moment, époque**

4 the quantity of minutes, hours, days *etc*, *eg* spent in, or available for, a particular activity *etc*: *This won't take much time to do*; *I enjoyed the time I spent in Paris*; *At the end of the exam, the supervisor called 'Your time is up!'* □ **temps**

5 a suitable moment or period: *Now is the time to ask him*. □ **moment**

6 one of a number occasions: *He's been to France four times*. □ **fois**

7 a period characterized by a particular quality in a person's life, experience *etc*: *He went through an unhappy time when she died*; *We had some good times together*. □ **période, temps**

8 the speed at which a piece of music should be played; tempo: *in slow time*. □ **tempo**

■ *verb* 1 to measure the time taken by (a happening, event *etc*) or by (a person, in doing something): *She timed the journey*. □ **chronométrer**

2 to choose a particular time for: *You timed your arrival beautifully!* □ **choisir le moment de**

'**timeless** *adjective* 1 not belonging to, or typical of, any particular time: *timeless works of art*. □ **intemporel**

2 never-ending: *the timeless beauty of Venice*. □ **éternel**

'**timelessly** *adverb*. □ **de façon intemporelle; éternellement**

'**timelessness** *noun*. □ **intemporalité; éternité**

'**timely** *adjective* coming at the right moment: *Your arrival was most timely*. □ **opportun**

'**timeliness** *noun*. □ **à-propos**

'**timer** *noun* 1 a person who, or a device which, measures the time taken by anything. □ **chronométreur, euse; chronomètre**

2 a clock-like device which sets something off or switches something on or off at a given time. □ **minuterie**

times *noun plural* 1 a period; an era: *We live in difficult times*. □ **période, temps (pl.)**

2 in mathematics, used to mean multiplied by: *Four times two is eight*. □ **fois**

'**timing** *noun* 1 the measuring of the amount of time taken. □ **chronométrage**

2 the regulating of speech or actions to achieve the best effect: *All comedians should have a good sense of timing*. □ **minutage**

time bomb a bomb that has been set to explode at a particular time. □ **bombe à retardement**

time-consuming *adjective* requiring or using up a lot of time: *The job was more time-consuming than Rachel thought and was not finished on time*. □ **laborieux**

time limit *noun* a fixed length of time during which something must be done and finished: *The examination has a time limit of three hours*. □ **limitation de temps**

time off a break from work or duties: *During his time off, Kevin went to a wedding in Spain*. □ **congé**

time out a short, brief break during an activity: *The coach called, "Time out!" and the game stopped for the injured player to leave the field*. □ **pause**

'**timetable** *noun* a list of the times of trains, school classes *etc*. □ **horaire**

all in good time soon enough. □ **chaque chose en son temps**

all the time continually. □ **tout le temps**

at times occasionally; sometimes. □ **parfois**

be behind time to be late. □ **être en retard**

for the time being meanwhile: *I am staying at home for the time being*. □ **pour le moment**

from time to time occasionally; sometimes: *From time to time she brings me a present*. □ **de temps en temps**

in good time early enough; before a set time (for an appointment *etc*): *We arrived in good time for the concert*. □ **à temps; en avance**

in time 1 early enough: *He arrived in time for dinner*; *Are we in time to catch the train?* □ **à temps**

2 (*with* **with**) at the same speed or rhythm: *They marched in time with the music*. □ **en mesure**

no time (at all) a very short time indeed: *The journey took no time (at all)*. □ **rien de temps**

one, two *etc* **at a time** singly, or in groups of two etc: *They came into the room three at a time*. □ **(un, deux, etc.) à la fois**

on time at the right time: *The train left on time*. □ **à l'heure**

save, waste time to avoid spending time; to spend time unnecessarily: *Take my car instead of walking, if you want to save time*; *We mustn't waste time discussing unimportant matters*. □ **gagner/perdre du temps**

take one's time to do something as slowly as one wishes. □ **prendre son temps**

time and (time) again again and again; repeatedly: *I asked her time and (time) again not to do that*. □ **maintes et maintes fois**

timid ['timid] *adjective* easily frightened; nervous; shy: *A mouse is a timid creature*. □ **timide, craintif, peureux**

'**timidly** *adverb*. □ **timidement, craintivement**

ti'**midity** *noun*. □ **timidité, caractère craintif**

'**timidness** *noun*. □ **timidité, caractère craintif**

tin [tin] *noun* 1 an element, a silvery white metal: *Is that box made of tin or steel?* □ **étain; fer-blanc**

2 (*also* **can**) a container, *usually* for food, made of '**tin plate**, thin sheets of iron covered with tin or other metal: *a tin of fruit*; *a biscuit-tin*. □ **boîte (en fer-blanc)**

■ *adjective* made of tin or tin plate: *a tin plate*. □ **de fer-blanc**

tinned *adjective* (of food) sealed in a tin for preservation *etc*: *tinned foods*. □ **en boîte/conserve**

'**tinfoil** *noun* tin or other metal in the form of very thin sheets, used for wrapping *etc*: *I'm going to bake the ham in tinfoil*. □ **papier d'aluminium**

tinge [tindʒ] *noun* a trace, or slight amount, of a colour: *Her hair had a tinge of red*. □ **teinte, nuance**

tingle ['tiŋgl] *verb* to feel a prickling sensation: *The cold* *wind made my face tingle; My fingers were tingling with cold.* □ **picoter; piquer**

■ *noun* this feeling. □ **picotement**

tinker ['tiŋkə] *noun* a person who travels around like a gypsy, mending kettles, pans *etc.* □ **rétameur, euse ambulant, ante**

■ *verb* (*often with* **about** *or* **around**) to fiddle, or work in an unskilled way, with machinery *etc: She enjoys tinkering around (with car engines).* □ **bricoler**

tinkle ['tiŋkl] *verb* to (cause to) make a sound of, or like, the ringing of small bells: *The doorbell tinkled.* □ **(faire) tinter**

■ *noun* this sound: *I heard the tinkle of breaking glass.* □ **tintement**

tinsel ['tinsəl] *noun* a sparkling, glittering substance used for decoration: *The Christmas tree was decorated with tinsel.* □ **clinquant**

'**tinselly** *adjective.* □ **clinquant**

tint [tint] *noun* a variety, or shade, of a colour. □ **nuance, teinte**

■ *verb* to colour slightly: *She had her hair tinted red.* □ **teinter (de)**

tiny ['taini] *adjective* very small: *a tiny insect.* □ **minuscule**

tip[1] [tip] *noun* the small or thin end, point or top of something: *the tips of my fingers.* □ **bout, pointe**

■ *verb – past tense, past participle* **tipped** – to put, or form, a tip on: *The spear was tipped with an iron point.* □ **garnir le bout de**

tipped *adjective* having a tip of a particular kind: *filter-tipped cigarettes; a white-tipped tail.* □ **à bout (...)**

,**tip-'top** *adjective* excellent: *The horse is in tip-top condition.* □ **excellent**

be on the tip of one's tongue to be almost, but *usually* not, spoken or said: *Her name is on the tip of my tongue* (= I can't quite remember it); *It was on the tip of my tongue to tell him* (= I almost told him). □ **être sur le bout de la langue**

tip[2] [tip] – *past tense, past participle* **tipped** – *verb* **1** to (make something) slant: *The boat tipped to one side.* □ **(faire) pencher**

2 to empty (something) from a container, or remove (something) from a surface, with this kind of motion: *He tipped the water out of the bucket.* □ **verser**

3 to dump (rubbish): *People have been tipping their rubbish in this field.* □ **déverser**

■ *noun* a place where rubbish is thrown: *a refuse/rubbish tip.* □ **dépotoir**

tip over to knock or fall over; to overturn: *He tipped the lamp over; She put the jug on the end of the table and it tipped over.* □ **(faire) basculer**

tip[3] [tip] *noun* a gift of money given to a waiter *etc*, for personal service: *I gave him a generous tip.* □ **pourboire**

■ *verb – past tense, past participle* **tipped** – to give such a gift to. □ **donner un pourboire à**

tip[4] [tip] *noun* a piece of useful information; a hint: *He gave me some good tips on/about gardening.* □ **conseil, tuyau**

tip off to give information or a hint to; to warn: *He tipped me off about her arrival* (*noun* '**tip off**). □

prévenir/avertir de; (n.) avertissement

tipsy ['tipsi] *adjective* slightly drunk. □ **éméché**

'**tipsily** *adverb.* □ **comme une personne ivre**

'**tipsiness** *noun.* □ **ivresse**

tiptoe ['tiptou] *verb* to walk on the toes, *usually* in order to be quiet: *He tiptoed past her bedroom door.* □ **marcher sur la pointe des pieds**

walk, stand *etc* **on tiptoe(s)** to walk, stand *etc* on the toes: *He stood on tiptoe(s) to reach the shelf.* □ **marcher/se mettre sur la pointe des pieds**

tire[1] ['taiə] *noun* a thick, rubber, *usually* air-filled strip around the edge of the wheel of a car, bicycle *etc: The tires of this car don't have enough air in them.* □ **pneu**

tire[2] ['taiə] *verb* to make, or become, physically or mentally in want of rest, because of lack of strength, patience, interest *etc*; to weary: *Walking tired her; He tires easily.* □ **(se) fatiguer, lasser**

tired *adjective* **1** wearied; exhausted: *She was too tired to continue; a tired child.* □ **fatigué**

2 (*with* **of**) no longer interested in; bored with: *I'm tired of (answering) stupid questions!* □ **fatigué (de)**

'**tiredness** *noun.* □ **fatigue**

'**tireless** *adjective* never becoming weary or exhausted; never resting: *a tireless worker; tireless energy/enthusiasm.* □ **infatigable**

'**tirelessly** *adverb.* □ **inlassablement**

'**tirelessness** *noun.* □ **infatigabilité**

'**tiresome** *adjective* troublesome; annoying. □ **ennuyeux**

'**tiresomely** *adverb.* □ **d'une façon ennuyeuse**

'**tiresomeness** *noun.* □ **caractère ennuyeux**

'**tiring** *adjective* causing (physical) tiredness: *I've had a tiring day; The journey was very tiring.* □ **fatigant**

tire out to tire or exhaust completely: *The hard work tired him out.* □ **épuiser**

tissue ['tiʃuː] *noun* **1** (one of the kinds of) substance of which the organs of the body are made: *nervous tissue; the tissues of the body.* □ **tissu**

2 (a piece of) thin soft paper used for wiping the nose *etc: He bought a box of tissues for his cold.* □ **papier-mouchoir**

tissue paper very thin paper, used for packing, wrapping *etc.* □ **papier de soie**

tit[1] [tit] *noun* any of several kinds of small bird: *a blue tit.* □ **mésange**

tit[2] [tit]: **tit for tat** [tat] blow for blow; repayment of injury with injury: *He tore my dress, so I spilt ink on his suit. That's tit for tat.* □ **œil pour œil, dent pour dent**

titbit ['titbit], **tidbit** ['tidbit] *noun* a tasty little piece of food: *He gave the dog a titbit.* □ **friandise**

title ['taitl] *noun* **1** the name of a book, play, painting, piece of music *etc: The title of the painting is 'A Winter Evening'.* □ **titre**

2 a word put before a person's name to show rank, honour, occupation *etc: Sir John; Lord Henry; Captain Smith; Professor Brown; Dr. (Doctor) Peter Jones.* □ **titre**

'**titled** *adjective* having a title that shows noble rank: *a titled lady.* □ **titré**

title deed a document that proves legal ownership: *I have the title deeds of the house.* □ **titre de propriété**

title page the page at the beginning of a book on which are the title, the author's name *etc*. □ **page de titre**

title rôle the rôle or part in a play of the character named in the title: *He's playing the title rôle in 'Hamlet'.* □ **rôle principal**

titter ['titə] *verb* to giggle: *He tittered nervously.* □ **rire sottement**

■ *noun* a giggle. □ **petit rire sot**

TNT [tiːzen'tiː] *noun* a type of explosive material: *The bridge was blown up with TNT.* □ **TNT**

to [tə,tu] *preposition* 1 towards; in the direction of: *I cycled to the station; The book fell to the floor; I went to the concert/lecture/play.* □ **à, vers**

2 as far as: *Her story is a lie from beginning to end.* □ **jusqu'à**

3 until: *Did you stay to the end of the concert?* □ **jusqu'à**

4 sometimes used to introduce the indirect object of a verb: *She sent it to us; You're the only person I can talk to.* □ **à**

5 used in expressing various relations: *Listen to me!; Did you reply to his letter?; Where's the key to this door?; He sang to (the accompaniment of) his guitar.* □ **à; de**

6 into a particular state or condition: *She tore the letter to pieces.* □ **en**

7 used in expressing comparison or proportion: *She's junior to me; Your skill is superior to mine; We won the match by 5 goals to 2.* □ **que; à**

8 showing the purpose or result of an action *etc*: *She came quickly to my assistance; To my horror, he took a gun out of his pocket.* □ **à**

9 [tə] used before an infinitive *eg* after various verbs and adjectives, or in other constructions: *I want to go!; She asked me to come; She worked hard to* (= in order to) *earn a lot of money; These buildings were designed to* (= so as to) *resist earthquakes; She opened her eyes to find him standing beside her; I arrived too late to see her.* □ **de; pour**

10 used instead of a complete infinitive: *He asked her to stay but she didn't want to.*

■ [tuz] *adverb* 1 into a closed or almost closed position: *She pulled/pushed the door to.* □ **de; fermer**

2 used in phrasal verbs and compounds: *He came to* (= regained consciousness); *They set to* (= They began). □ **à**

to and fro [tuːən'frou] backwards and forwards: *they ran to and fro in the street.* □ **de long en large**

toad [toud] *noun* a kind of reptile, like a large frog. □ **crapaud**

'toadstool *noun* any of several kinds of mushroom-like fungi, often poisonous. □ **champignon (vénéneux)**

toast¹ [toust] *verb* to make (bread *etc*) brown in front of direct heat: *We toasted slices of bread for tea.* □ **griller**

■ *noun* bread that has been toasted: *She always has two pieces of toast for breakfast.* □ **rôtie**

'toasted *adjective* heated by direct heat, *eg* under a grill: *toasted cheese; Do you like your bread toasted?* □ **passé sous le gril, grillé**

'toaster *noun* an electric machine for toasting bread. □ **grille-pain**

'toastrack *noun* a small stand in which slices of toast can be served: *Put the toastrack on the table.* □ **porte-toast**

toast² [toust] *verb* to drink ceremonially in honour of, or to wish success to (someone or something): *We toasted the bride and bridegroom/the new ship.* □ **porter un toast (à)**

■ *noun* 1 an act of toasting: *Let's drink a toast to our friends!* □ **toast**

2 the wish conveyed, or the person *etc* honoured, by such an act. □ **toast; personne qui est l'objet d'un toast**

tobacco [tə'bakou] – *plural* **tobaccos** – *noun* (a type of plant that has) leaves that are dried and used for smoking in pipes, cigarettes, cigars *etc*, or as snuff: *Tobacco is bad for your health.* □ **tabac**

to'bacconist [-nist] *noun* a person who sells tobacco, cigarettes *etc*. □ **marchand, ande de tabac**

toboggan [tə'bogən] *noun* a kind of light sledge. □ **luge**

■ *verb* to go on a toboggan: *We went tobogganing.* □ **faire de la luge**

today [tə'dei] *noun, adverb* 1 (on) this day: *Today is Friday; Here is today's newspaper; I'm working today.* □ **aujourd'hui**

2 (at) the present time: *Life is easier today than a hundred years ago.* □ **aujourd'hui**

toddle [todl] *verb* (*especially* of a very young child) to walk unsteadily: *The child is toddling.* □ **trottiner**

'toddler *noun* a very young child (who has just begun to be able to walk). □ **bambin, ine**

toddy ['todi] *noun* a drink made of spirits, sugar, hot water *etc*. □ **grog**

toe [tou] *noun* 1 one of the five finger-like end parts of the foot: *These tight shoes hurt my toes.* □ **orteil**

2 the front part of a shoe, sock *etc*: *There's a hole in the toe of my sock.* □ **bout**

'toenail *noun* the nail that grows on one's toes: *He was cutting his toenails.* □ **ongle d'orteil**

toe the line to act according to the rules. □ **se mettre au pas**

toffee ['tofi] *noun* (a piece of) a kind of sticky sweet made of sugar and butter: *Have a (piece of) toffee.* □ **caramel (au beurre)**

toga ['tougə] *noun* the loose outer garment worn by a citizen of ancient Rome. □ **toge**

together [tə'geðə] *adverb* 1 with someone or something else; in company: *They travelled together.* □ **ensemble**

2 at the same time: *They all arrived together.* □ **ensemble**

3 so as to be joined or united: *She nailed/fitted/stuck the pieces of wood together.* □ **ensemble**

4 by action with one or more other people: *Together we persuaded him.* □ **ensemble**

to'getherness *noun* the state of being close together: *Their evenings around the fire gave them a feeling of togetherness.* □ **union**

together with in company with; in addition to: *My knowledge, together with his money, should be very useful.* □ **ainsi que**

toil [toil] *verb* 1 to work hard and long: *She toiled all day* *in the fields.* □ **travailler dur**

2 to move with great difficulty: *He toiled along the road with all his luggage.* □ **avancer avec peine**

■ *noun* hard work: *He slept well after his hours of toil.*

□ **(dur) travail**

toilet ['toilit] *noun* (a room containing) a receptacle for the body's waste matter, *usually* with a supply of water for washing this away; a lavatory: *Do you want to go to the toilet?*; *Where is the ladies' toilet?*; (*also adjective*) *a toilet seat.* □ **toilettes; toilette**

'**toilet paper** *noun* paper for use in a toilet. □ **papier hygiénique**

'**toilet roll** *noun* a roll of toilet paper. □ **rouleau de papier hygiénique**

'**toilet water** *noun* a type of perfumed liquid for the skin. □ **eau de toilette**

token ['toukən] *noun* **1** a mark or sign: *Wear this ring, as a token of our friendship.* □ **signe, marque**

2 a card or piece of metal, plastic *etc,* for use instead of money: *The shopkeeper will exchange these tokens for goods to the value of $10.* □ **jeton; coupon, bon**

told *see* tell.

tolerate ['toləreit] *verb* to bear or endure; to put up with: *I couldn't tolerate his rudeness.* □ **tolérer**

'**tolerable** *adjective* **1** able to be borne or endured: *The heat was barely tolerable.* □ **tolérable**

2 quite good: *The food was tolerable.* □ **acceptable**

'**tolerance** *noun* **1** the ability to be fair and understanding to people whose ways, opinions *etc* are different from one's own: *We should always try to show tolerance to other people.* □ **tolérance**

2 the ability to resist the effects of *eg* a drug: *If you take a drug regularly, your body gradually acquires a tolerance of it.* □ **tolérance**

'**tolerant** *adjective* showing tolerance: *He's very tolerant towards his neighbours.* □ **tolérant**

'**tolerantly** *adverb.* □ **avec tolérance**

,**tole'ration** *noun* **1** the act of tolerating: *His toleration of her behaviour amazed me.* □ **tolérance**

2 tolerance, *especially* in religious matters: *The government passed a law of religious toleration.* □ **tolérance**

toll¹ [toul] *verb* to ring (a bell) slowly: *The church bell tolled solemnly.* □ **sonner**

toll² [toul] *noun* **1** a tax charged for crossing a bridge, driving on certain roads *etc*: *All cars pay a toll of $1*; (*also adjective*) *a toll bridge.* □ **(à) péage**

2 an amount of loss or damage suffered, *eg* as a result of disaster: *Every year there is a heavy toll of human lives on the roads.* □ **dommages, victimes**

tomato [tə'meitou] – *plural* to'**matoes** – *noun* **1** a type of fleshy, juicy fruit, *usually* red, used in salads, sauces *etc*: *We had a salad of lettuce, tomatoes and cucumbers*; (*also adjective*) *tomato sauce.* □ **(à la) tomate**

2 the plant which bears these. □ **tomate**

tomb [tuːm] *noun* a hole or vault in the ground in which a dead body is put; a grave: *She was buried in the family tomb.* □ **tombe(au)**

'**tombstone** *noun* an ornamental stone placed over a grave on which the dead person's name *etc* is engraved.

□ **pierre tombale**

tomboy ['tomboi] *noun* a girl who likes rough games and activities: *She's a real tomboy!* □ **garçon manqué**

tomcat ['tomkat] *noun* a male cat. □ **matou**

tomorrow [tə'morou] *noun, adverb* **1** (on) the day after today: *Tomorrow is Saturday*; *The news will be announced tomorrow.* □ **demain**

2 (in) the future: *tomorrow's world.* □ **demain**

tom-tom ['tomtom] *noun* a kind of drum *usually* beaten with the hands. □ **tam-tam**

ton [tʌn] *noun* **1** a unit of weight equal to 907.19 kg; a **metric ton** (*also* **tonne** [tʌn]) is 1000 kilograms: *It weighs a ton and a half; a three-ton weight.* □ **tonne**

2 a unit of space in a ship (1000 kg). □ **tonneau**

'**tonnage** [-nidʒ] *noun* the space available on a ship, measured in tons. □ **tonnage**

tons *noun plural* a lot: *I've got tons of letters to write.* □ **des tonnes de**

tonal *see* tone.

tone [toun] *noun* **1** (the quality of) a sound, *especially* a voice: *He spoke in a low/angry/gentle tone*; *She told me about it in tones of disapproval*; *That singer/violin/piano has very good tone.* □ **ton, timbre**

2 a shade of colour: *various tones of green.* □ **ton**

3 firmness of body or muscle: *Your muscles lack tone – you need exercise.* □ **tonus**

4 in music, one of the larger intervals in an octave *eg* between C and D. □ **ton**

■ *verb* to fit in well; to blend: *The brown sofa tones (in) well with the walls.* □ **s'harmoniser (avec)**

'**tonal** *adjective* of musical tones. □ **tonal**

'**toneless** *adjective* without tone; with no variation in sound *etc*: *She spoke in a toneless voice.* □ **atone**

'**tonelessly** *adverb.* □ **sans timbre**

tone down to make or become softer, less harsh *etc*: *He toned down some of his criticisms.* □ **(s')atténuer, (s')adoucir**

tongs [toŋz] *noun plural* an instrument for holding and lifting objects: *sugar-tongs*; *a pair of tongs.* □ **pince(s)**

tongue [tʌŋ] *noun* **1** the fleshy organ inside the mouth, used in tasting, swallowing, speaking *etc*: *The doctor looked at her tongue.* □ **langue**

2 the tongue of an animal used as food. □ **langue**

3 something with the same shape as a tongue: *a tongue of flame.* □ **langue**

4 a language: *English is his mother-tongue/native tongue*; *a foreign tongue.* □ **langue**

tonic ['tonik] *noun* **1** (a) medicine that gives strength or energy: *The doctor prescribed a (bottle of) tonic.* □ **tonique**

2 (*also* '**tonic water**) water containing quinine, often drunk with gin *etc*: *I'd like a gin and tonic.* □ **soda tonique**

tonight [tə'nait] *noun, adverb* (on) the night of this present day: *Here is tonight's weather forecast*; *I'm going home early tonight.* □ **ce soir**

tonnage, tonne *see* ton.

tonsil ['tonsil] *noun* either of two lumps of tissue at the back of the throat: *He had to have his tonsils (taken)* *out.* □ **amygdale**

,tonsil'litis [tonsi'laitis] *noun* painful inflammation of the tonsils: *She had/was suffering from tonsillitis.* □ **amygdalite**

too [tuː] *adverb* **1** to a greater extent, or more, than is required, desirable or suitable: *He's too fat for his clothes*; *I'm not feeling too well.* □ **trop**
2 in addition; also; as well: *My husband likes cycling, and I do, too.* □ **aussi**

took *see* **take.**

tool [tuːl] *noun* an instrument for doing work, *especially* by hand: *hammers, saws and other tools*; *the tools of his trade*; *Advertising is a powerful tool.* □ **outil, instrument**

toot [tuːt] *noun* a quick blast of a trumpet, car-horn *etc*. □ **note, coup**
■ *verb* to blow or sound a horn *etc*: *He tooted (on) the horn.* □ **donner une note, un coup de**

tooth [tuːθ] – *plural* **teeth** [tiːθ] – *noun* **1** any of the hard, bone-like objects that grow in the mouth and are used for biting and chewing: *She has had a tooth out at the dentist's.* □ **dent**
2 something that looks or acts like a tooth: *the teeth of a comb/saw.* □ **dent**

teethe [tiːð] *verb* (of a baby) to grow one's first teeth: *He cries a lot because he's teething.* □ **faire ses dents**
toothed *adjective* having teeth: *a toothed wheel.* □ **denté**
'toothless *adjective* without teeth: *a toothless old woman.* □ **édenté**
'toothy *adjective* showing a lot of teeth: *a toothy grin.* □ **découvrant largement les dents**
'toothache *noun* a pain in a tooth: *He has/is suffering from toothache.* □ **mal de dents**
'toothbrush *noun* a brush for cleaning the teeth. □ **brosse à dents**
'toothpaste *noun* a kind of paste used to clean the teeth: *a tube of toothpaste.* □ **dentifrice**
'toothpick *noun* a small piece of wood, plastic *etc* for picking out food *etc* from between the teeth. □ **cure-dents**
be, get *etc* **long in the tooth** (of a person or animal) to be, become *etc*, old: *I'm getting a bit long in the tooth to climb mountains.* □ **ne plus être (tout) jeune**
a fine-tooth comb a comb with the teeth set close together, for removing lice, dirt *etc* from hair *etc*. □ **peigne fin**
a sweet tooth a liking for sweet food: *My friend has a sweet tooth.* □ **amour des sucreries**
tooth and nail fiercely and with all one's strength: *They fought tooth and nail.* □ **de toutes ses forces**

top[1] [top] *noun* **1** the highest part of anything: *the top of the hill*; *the top of her head*; *The book is on the top shelf.* □ **haut; sommet; du haut**
2 the position of the cleverest in a class *etc*: *He's at the top of the class.* □ **en tête (de)**
3 the upper surface: *the table-top.* □ **dessus**
4 a lid: *I've lost the top to this jar*; *a bottle-top.* □ **couvercle, bouchon**
5 a (woman's) garment for the upper half of the body; a blouse, sweater *etc*: *I bought a new skirt and top.* □

haut
■ *adjective* having gained the most marks, points *etc*, *eg* in a school class: *He's top (of the class) again.* □ **en tête (de)**
■ *verb* – *past tense, past participle* **topped** – **1** to cover on the top: *She topped the cake with cream.* □ **surmonter, recouvrir**
2 to rise above; to surpass: *Our exports have topped $100,000.* □ **dépasser**
3 to remove the top of. □ **étêter**
'topless *adjective* **1** having no top. □ **sans haut**
2 very high. □ **d'une hauteur démesurée**
'topping *noun* something that forms a covering on top of something, *especially* food: *a tart with a topping of cream.* □ **garniture**
top hat (*abbreviation* **topper** ['topə]) a man's tall hat, worn as formal dress. □ **haut-de-forme**
,top-'heavy *adjective* having the upper part too heavy for the lower: *That pile of books is top-heavy – it'll fall over!* □ **trop lourd du haut**
,top 'secret *adjective* very secret. □ **ultra-secret**
at the top of one's voice very loudly: *They were shouting at the top(s) of their voices.* □ **à tue-tête**
be/feel *etc* **on top of the world** to feel very well and happy: *She's on top of the world – she's just got hired.* □ **être aux anges**
from top to bottom completely: *They've painted the house from top to bottom.* □ **de fond en comble**
the top of the ladder/tree the highest point in one's profession. □ **haut de l'échelle**
top up to fill (a cup *etc* that has been partly emptied) to the top: *Let me top up your glass/drink.* □ **remplir à nouveau**

top[2] [top] *noun* a kind of toy that spins. □ **toupie**
sleep like a top to sleep very well: *The child slept like a top after a day on the beach.* □ **dormir comme un loir**

topaz ['toupaz] *noun* a kind of precious stone, of various colours. □ **topaze**

topi, topee ['toupi] *noun* a helmet-like hat worn in hot countries as protection against the sun. □ **casque colonial**

topic ['topik] *noun* something spoken or written about; a subject: *They discussed the weather and other topics.* □ **sujet**
'topical *adjective* of interest at the present time. □ **d'actualité**
'topically *adverb*. □ **de manière actuelle**

topless *see* **top**[1].

topper short for **top hat.**

topping *see* **top**[1].

topple ['topl] *verb* to (make something) fall: *She toppled the pile of books*; *The child toppled over.* □ **renverser; basculer**

topsyturv(e)y [topsi'təːvi] *adjective, adverb* upside down; in confusion: *Everything was turned topsyturvy.* □ **sens dessus dessous**

torch [toːtʃ] *noun* **1** (*American* **'flashlight**) a small portable light worked by an electric battery: *He shone his torch into her face.* □ **lampe de poche**

2 a piece of wood *etc* set on fire and carried as a light. □ **flambeau**

tore *see* **tear**².

torment ['tɔːment] *noun* 1 (a) very great pain, suffering, worry *etc*: *He was in torment.* □ **tourment**
2 something that causes this. □ **tourment**

■ [tɔː'ment] *verb* to cause pain, suffering, worry *etc* to: *She was tormented with worry/toothache.* □ **tourmenter**
tor'mentor [-'men-] *noun* a person who torments. □ **tourmenteur, euse**

torn *see* **tear**².

tornado [tɔː'neidou] – *plural* **tor'nadoes** – *noun* a violent whirlwind that can cause great damage: *The village was destroyed by a tornado.* □ **tornade**

torpedo [tɔː'piːdou] – *plural* **tor'pedoes** – *noun* an underwater missile fired at ships: *an enemy torpedo.* □ **torpille**

■ *verb* 3rd person singular present tense **torpedoes**: *past tense, past participle* **tor'pedoed** – to attack, damage or destroy with torpedoes: *The ship was torpedoed.* □ **torpiller**

torrent ['tɔrənt] *noun* a rushing stream: *The rain fell in torrents; She attacked him with a torrent of abuse.* □ **torrent**

torrential [tə'renʃəl] *adjective* of, or like, a torrent: *torrential rain; The rain was torrential.* □ **torrentiel**

torrid ['tɔrid] *adjective* 1 very hot: *the torrid zone* (= the area of the world on either side of the equator). □ **torride**
2 passionate: *a torrid love affair.* □ **passionné**

torso ['tɔːsou] – *plural* **'torsos** – *noun* the body, excluding the head and limbs: *He had a strong torso.* □ **torse**

tortoise ['tɔːtəs] *noun* a kind of four-footed, slow-moving reptile covered with a hard shell. □ **tortue**

torture ['tɔːtʃə] *verb* to treat (someone) cruelly or painfully, as a punishment, or in order to make him/her confess something, give information *etc*: *He tortured his prisoners; She was tortured by rheumatism/jealousy.* □ **torturer**

■ *noun* 1 the act or practice of torturing: *The king would not permit torture.* □ **torture**
2 (something causing) great suffering: *the torture of waiting to be executed.* □ **torture**

toss [tɔs] *verb* 1 to throw into or through the air: *She tossed the ball up into the air.* □ **lancer**
2 (*often with* **about**) to throw oneself restlessly from side to side: *She tossed about all night, unable to sleep.* □ **se tourner et se retourner**
3 (of a ship) to be thrown about: *The boat tossed wildly in the rough sea.* □ **tanguer**
4 to throw (a coin) into the air and decide a matter according to (a correct guess about) which side falls uppermost: *They tossed a coin to decide which of them should go first.* □ **jouer à pile ou face**

■ *noun* an act of tossing. □ **lancer**

toss up to toss a coin to decide a matter: *We tossed up (to decide) whether to go to the play or the ballet.* □ **jouer à pile ou face**

win/lose the toss to guess rightly or wrongly which side of the coin will fall uppermost: *He won the toss so he started the game of cards first.* □ **gagner/perdre à pile ou face**

tot¹ [tɔt] *noun* 1 a small child: *a tiny tot.* □ **bambin**
2 a small amount of alcoholic drink: *a tot of whisky.* □ **goutte, larme**

tot² [tɔt] – *past tense, past participle* **'totted: tot up** to add up: *She totted up the figures on the bill.* □ **additionner**

total ['toutəl] *adjective* whole; complete: *What is the total cost of the holiday?; The car was a total wreck.* □ **total, complet**

■ *noun* the whole amount, *ie* of various sums added together: *The total came to/was $10.* □ **total**

■ *verb* – *past tense, past participle* **'totalled** – to add up or amount to: *The doctor's fees totalled $20.* □ **s'élever à**

'totally *adverb* completely: *I was totally unaware of his presence.* □ **totalement**

total up to add up: *He totalled up (the amount he had sold) at the end of the week.* □ **totaliser**

tote [tout] *verb* to carry: *He was toting a pile of books about with him.* □ **trimballer**

totem ['toutəm] *noun* (an image of) an animal or plant used as the badge or sign of a tribe, among North American Indians *etc*. □ **totem**

totem pole a large wooden pole on which totems are carved and painted. □ **totem**

totter ['tɔtə] *verb* to move unsteadily as if about to fall: *The building tottered and collapsed; He tottered down the road.* □ **vaciller, chanceler**

touch [tʌtʃ] *verb* 1 to be in, come into, or make, contact with something else: *Their shoulders touched; He touched the water with his foot.* □ **(se) toucher (à)**
2 to feel (lightly) with the hand: *He touched her cheek.* □ **toucher**
3 to affect the feelings of; to make (someone) feel pity, sympathy *etc*: *I was touched by her generosity.* □ **toucher**
4 to be concerned with; to have anything to do with: *I wouldn't touch a job like that.* □ **être touché, concerné (par)**

■ *noun* 1 an act or sensation of touching: *I felt a touch on my shoulder.* □ **toucher**
2 (*often with* **of**) one of the five senses, the sense by which we feel things: *the sense of touch; The stone felt cold to the touch.* □ **(le) toucher**
3 a mark or stroke *etc* to improve the appearance of something: *The painting still needs a few finishing touches.* □ **touche**
4 skill or style: *She hasn't lost her touch as a writer.* □ **touche, patte**
5 (in football) the ground outside the edges of the pitch (which are marked out with **'touchlines**): *He kicked the ball into touch.* □ **touche**

'touching *adjective* moving; causing emotion: *a touching story.* □ **touchant**

'touchingly *adverb* in a moving way, so as to cause emotion: *Her face was touchingly childlike.* □ **de manière touchante**

'touchy *adjective* easily annoyed or offended: *You're very touchy today; in rather a touchy mood.* □ **sus-**

ceptible

'**touchily** *adverb*. □ **avec humeur**

'**touchiness** *noun*. □ **susceptibilité**

in touch (with) in communication (with): *I have kept in touch with my school-friends.* □ **en contact (avec)**

lose touch (with) to stop communicating (with): *I used to see her quite often but we have lost touch.* □ **perdre le contact (avec)**

out of touch (with) 1 not in communication (with). □ **coupé (de)**

2 not sympathetic or understanding (towards): *Older people sometimes seem out of touch with the modern world.* □ **coupé (de)**

a touch a small quantity or degree: *The soup needs a touch of salt; a touch of imagination.* □ **soupçon**

touch down 1 (of aircraft) to land: *The plane should touch down at 2 o'clock.* □ **atterrir**

2 in rugby football, to put the ball on the ground behind the opposite team's goal line (*noun* '**touchdown**). □ **marquer un essai; (n.) essai**

touch off to make (something) explode: *a spark touched off the gunpowder; Her remark touched off an argument.* □ **faire exploser; déclencher**

touch up to improve *eg* paintwork, a photograph *etc* by small touches: *The photograph had been touched up.* □ **retoucher**

touch wood (*used as an interjection*) to touch something made of wood superstitiously, in order to avoid bad luck: *None of the children has ever had a serious illness, touch wood!* □ **toucher du bois**

tough [tʌf] *adjective* **1** strong; not easily broken, worn out *etc*: *Plastic is a tough material.* □ **solide**

2 (of food *etc*) difficult to chew. □ **difficile**

3 (of people) strong; able to bear hardship, illness *etc*: *She must be tough to have survived such a serious illness.* □ **robuste, tenace**

4 rough and violent: *It's a tough neighbourhood.* □ **violent**

5 difficult to deal with or overcome: *a tough problem; The competition was really tough.* □ **dur**

■ *noun* a rough, violent person; a bully. □ **dur, dure**

'**toughness** *noun*. □ **dureté, ténacité**

'**toughen** *verb* to make or become tough. □ **(se) durcir, (s')endurcir**

tough luck bad luck: *That was tough luck.* □ **pas de chance**

get tough (with someone) to deal forcefully with or refuse to yield to (a person): *When he started to argue, I got tough with him.* □ **se montrer dur avec**

toupee [tuːˈpei] *noun* a small wig. □ **postiche**

tour [tuə] *noun* **1** a journey to several places and back: *They went on a tour of Italy.* □ **voyage, visite, tournée**

2 a visit around a particular place: *She took us on a tour of the house and gardens.* □ **visite**

3 an official period of time of work *usually* abroad: *She did a tour of duty in Fiji.* □ **poste**

■ *verb* to go on a tour (around): *to tour Europe.* □ **visiter**

'**tourism** *noun* the industry dealing with tourists *ie* hotels, catering *etc*: *Tourism is an important part of our economy.* □ **tourisme**

'**tourist** *noun* a person who travels for pleasure: *Montreal is usually full of tourists; (also adjective) the tourist industry.* □ **touriste; (adj.) touristique**

tournament [ˈtuənəmənt] *noun* a competition in which many players compete in many separate games: *I'm playing in the next tennis tournament.* □ **tournoi**

tourniquet [ˈtuənikei] *noun* a bandage, or other device, tied very tightly around an injured arm or leg to prevent too much blood being lost. □ **garrot**

tousle [tozzəl] *verb* to make the hair untidy; *His brother tousled his hair, now he looks funny.* □ **ébouriffer**

tout [taut] *verb* to go about in search of buyers, jobs, support, votes *etc*: *The taxi-driver drove around touting for custom.* □ **solliciter**

tow [tou] *verb* to pull (a ship, barge, car, trailer *etc*) by a rope, chain or cable: *The tugboat towed the ship out of the harbour; The car broke down and had to be towed to the garage.* □ **remorquer**

■ *noun* (an) act of towing or process of being towed: *Give us a tow!* □ **remorquage**

'**towline/'tow rope** *nouns* a rope *etc* used in towing. □ **câble de remorquage**

towards, toward [toːrd(z)] *preposition* **1** (moving, facing *etc*) in the direction of: *He walked toward the door; She turned towards him.* □ **vers**

2 in relation to: *What are your feelings towards him?* □ **envers**

3 as a contribution or help to: *Here's $3 towards the cost of the journey.* □ **pour (contribuer à)**

4 (of time) near: *Towards night-time, the weather worsened.* □ **vers**

towel [ˈtauəl] *noun* a piece of any of several types of absorbent cloth or paper for drying oneself, dishes *etc* after washing *etc*: *After her swim she dried herself with a towel; a roll of paper kitchen towels.* □ **serviette; torchon**

■ *verb* – *past tense, past participle* '**towelled**, '**toweled** – to rub with a towel. □ **essuyer avec une serviette**

'**towelling** *noun* a kind of rough cloth from which towels *etc* are made. □ **tissu éponge**

tower [ˈtauə] *noun* a tall, narrow (part of a) building, especially (of) a castle: *the Tower of London; a church-tower.* □ **tour**

■ *verb* to rise high: *She is so small that he towers above her.* □ **dominer de toute sa hauteur**

'**towering** *adjective* **1** very high: *towering cliffs.* □ **élevé**

2 (of rage, fury *etc*) very violent or angry: *He was in a towering rage.* □ **noir**

'**tower-block** *noun* a very high block of flats, offices *etc*: *They live in a tower-block.* □ **tour**

towline *see* **tow**.

town [taun] *noun* **1** a group of houses, shops, schools *etc*, that is bigger than a village but smaller than a city: *I'm going into town to buy a dress; He's in town doing some shopping.* □ **(petite) ville**

2 the people who live in such a group of houses *etc*: *The whole town turned out to greet the heroes.* □ **ville**

3 towns in general as opposed to the countryside: *Do you live in the country or the town?* □ **ville**

town centre the main shopping and business area of a town: *You can get a bus from the town centre.* □ **centre-ville**

town hall the building in which the official business of a town is done. □ **hôtel de ville**

townhouse a single family house that is attached to a similar house on one or both sides: *Our home is in the middle of a row of townhouses.* □ **maison de ville**

'townsfolk, 'townspeople *noun plural* the people living in a town. □ **citadins, ines**

go to town to do something very thoroughly or with great enthusiasm or expense: *He really went to town on (preparing) the meal.* □ **mettre le paquet**

toxic ['toksik] *adjective* poisonous: *toxic substances.* □ **toxique**

toy [toi] *noun* an object made for a child to play with: *She got lots of toys for Christmas; a toy soldier.* □ **jouet**
■ *verb* (*with* **with**) to play with in an idle way: *He wasn't hungry and sat toying with his food.* □ **chipoter**

trace [treis] *noun* 1 a mark or sign left by something: *There were traces of egg on the plate; There's still no trace of the missing child.* □ **trace**
2 a small amount: *Traces of poison were found in the cup.* □ **trace**
■ *verb* 1 to follow or discover by means of clues, evidence *etc*: *The police have traced her to London; The source of the infection has not yet been traced.* □ **retrouver**
2 to make a copy of (a picture *etc*) by putting transparent paper over it and drawing the outline *etc*: *I traced the map.* □ **calquer, tracer**

'tracing *noun* a copy made by tracing: *I made a tracing of the diagram.* □ **calque, tracé**

trace elements elements that are needed in small quantities for the growing and developing of animal and plant life. □ **oligo-élément**

'tracing paper *noun* thin transparent paper used for tracing. □ **papier-calque**

track [trak] *noun* 1 a mark left, *especially* a footprint *etc*: *They followed the lion's tracks.* □ **trace**
2 a path or rough road: *a mountain track.* □ **piste**
3 (*also* **'racetrack**) a course on which runners, cyclists *etc* race: *a running track*; (*also adjective*) *the 100 metres sprint and other track events.* □ **piste; (d')athlétisme**
4 a railway line. □ **voie (ferrée)**
■ *verb* to follow (*eg* an animal) by the marks, footprints *etc* that it has left: *They tracked the wolf to its lair.* □ **suivre la trace (de)**

'track suit *noun* a warm suit worn by athletes *etc* when exercising, or before and after performing. □ **survêtement**

in one's tracks where one stands or is: *He stopped dead in his tracks.* □ **sur place**

keep/lose track of (not) to keep oneself informed about (the progress or whereabouts of): *I've lost track of what is happening.* □ **rester au courant de, en contact avec; ne plus être au courant de, en contact avec**

make tracks (for) to depart, or set off (towards): *We ought to be making tracks (for home).* □ **filer**

track down to pursue or search for (someone or something) until it is caught or found: *I managed to track down an old copy of the book.* □ **(finir par) trouver**

tract [trakt] *noun* 1 a piece of land. □ **étendue**
2 a system formed by connected parts of the body: *the digestive tract.* □ **système; appareil**
3 a short essay or booklet. □ **tract**

tractor ['trakta] *noun* a motor vehicle for pulling *especially* agricultural machinery: *I can drive a tractor.* □ **tracteur**

trade [treid] *noun* 1 the buying and selling of goods: *Japan does a lot of trade with Britain.* □ **commerce**
2 (a) business, occupation, or job: *She's in the jewellery trade.* □ **métier, profession**
■ *verb* 1 (*often with* **in** *or* **with**) to buy and sell: *They made a lot of money by trading; They trade in fruit and vegetables.* □ **commercer**
2 to exchange: *I traded my watch for a bicycle.* □ **échanger**

'trader *noun* a person who trades. □ **commerçant, ante**

'trademark, 'tradename *nouns* an officially registered mark or name belonging to a particular company, and not to be used by anyone else, that is put on all goods made by the company. □ **marque déposée**

'tradesman ['treidz-] *noun* 1 a shopkeeper. □ **commerçant, ante**
2 a workman in a skilled job: *I cannot mend the television-set – I'll have to send for a tradesman.* □ **spécialiste**

trade(s) union a group of workers of the same trade who join together to bargain with employers for fair wages, better working conditions *etc*. □ **syndicat**

trade(s) unionist a member of a trade(s) union (*noun* **trade(s) unionism**). □ **syndicaliste; syndicalisme**

trade wind a wind that blows towards the equator (from the north-east and south-east). □ **(vent) alizé**

trade in to give (something) as part-payment for something else: *We decided to trade in our old car and get a new one* (*noun* **'trade in**). □ **faire reprendre; (n.) reprise**

tradition [trə'diʃən] *noun* 1 (the process of passing on from generation to generation) customs, beliefs, stories *etc*: *These songs have been preserved by tradition.* □ **tradition**
2 a custom, belief, story *etc* that is passed on. □ **tradition**

tra'ditional *adjective*. □ **traditionnel**

tra'ditionally *adverb*. □ **traditionnellement**

traffic ['trafik] *noun* 1 vehicles, aircraft, ships *etc* moving about: *There's a lot of traffic on the roads/on the river.* □ **circulation, trafic**
2 trade, *especially* illegal or dishonest: *the drug traffic.* □ **trafic**
■ *verb* – *past tense, past participle* **'trafficked** – to deal or trade in, *especially* illegally or dishonestly: *They were trafficking in smuggled goods.* □ **faire le commerce/trafic de, trafiquer**

traffic circle a circular piece of ground when several roads must meet, and around which traffic must travel. □ **rond-point**

'trafficker *noun a usually* illegal or dishonest dealer: *a* *trafficker in drugs.* □ **trafiquant, ante**

traffic island a small pavement in the middle of a road, for pedestrians to stand on on their way across. □ **refuge**

traffic jam a situation in which large numbers of road vehicles are prevented from proceeding freely. □ **embouteillage**

traffic lights lights of changing colours for controlling traffic at road crossings *etc: Turn left at the traffic lights.* □ **feux (de circulation)**

traffic warden *see* **warden**.

tragedy ['tradʒədi] – *plural* '**tragedies** – *noun* 1 (a) drama about unfortunate events with a sad outcome: *'Hamlet' is one of Shakespeare's tragedies.* □ **tragédie**

2 an unfortunate or sad event: *His early death was a great tragedy for his family.* □ **tragédie**

'**tragic** *adjective* 1 sad; unfortunate: *I heard of the tragic death of her daughter.* □ **tragique**

2 of tragedy or tragedies: *a tragic hero.* □ **tragique**

trail [treil] *verb* 1 to drag, or be dragged, along loosely: *Garments were trailing from the suitcase.* □ **traîner**

2 to walk slowly and *usually* wearily: *She trailed down the road.* □ **aller en traînant les pieds**

3 to follow the track of: *The herd of reindeer was being trailed by a pack of wolves.* □ **suivre la piste (de)**

■ *noun* 1 a track (of an animal): *The trail was easy for the hunters to follow.* □ **piste**

2 a path through a forest or other wild area: *a mountain trail.* □ **sentier**

3 a line, or series of marks, left by something as it passes: *There was a trail of blood across the floor.* □ **traînée**

'**trailer** *noun* 1 a vehicle pulled behind a car: *We carry our luggage in a trailer.* □ **remorque**

2 a caravan. □ **caravane, roulotte**

3 a short film advertising a complete film. □ **bande-annonce**

train¹ [trein] *noun* 1 a railway engine with its carriages and/or trucks: *I caught the train to Toronto.* □ **train**

2 a part of a long dress or robe that trails behind the wearer: *The bride wore a dress with a train.* □ **traîne**

3 a connected series: *Then began a train of events which ended in disaster.* □ **suite**

4 a line of animals carrying people or baggage: *a mule train; a baggage train.* □ **train**

train² [trein] *verb* 1 to prepare, be prepared, or prepare oneself, through instruction, practice, exercise *etc*, for a sport, job, profession *etc: I was trained as a teacher; The race-horse was trained by my uncle.* □ **(se) former; (s')entraîner**

2 to point or aim (a gun, telescope *etc*) in a particular direction: *He trained the gun on/at the soldiers.* □ **pointer (sur)**

3 to make (a tree, plant *etc*) grow in a particular direction. □ **faire grimper**

trained *adjective* (*negative* **untrained**) having had teaching: *She's a trained nurse; a well-trained dog.* □ **qualifié, dressé**

,**trai'nee** *noun* a person who is being trained: *He's a trainee with an industrial firm; (also adjective) a trainee teacher.* □ **stagiaire, apprenti, ie**

'**trainer** *noun* 1 a person who prepares people or animals for sport, a race *etc*. □ **entraîneur, euse**

2 an aircraft used for training pilots. □ **avion-école**

'**training** *noun* 1 preparation for a sport: *She has gone into training for the race.* □ **entraînement**

2 the process of learning (the practical side of) a job: *It takes many years of training to be a doctor.* □ **formation**

trait [treit] *noun* a particular quality of a person's character: *Patience is one of his good traits.* □ **trait (de caractère)**

traitor ['treitə] *noun* a person who changes to the enemy's side or gives away information to the enemy: *He was a traitor to his country.* □ **traître, traîtresse**

tram [tram] *noun* (*also* '**tramcar**: *American* '**streetcar**) a long car running on rails and *usually* driven by electric power, for carrying passengers *especially* along the streets of a town. □ **tramway**

'**tramway** *noun* a system of tracks for trams. □ **voie de tramway**

tramp [tramp] *verb* 1 to walk with heavy footsteps: *He tramped up the stairs.* □ **marcher à pas lourds**

2 to walk *usually* for a long distance: *She loves tramping over the hills.* □ **faire de la randonnée pédestre**

■ *noun* 1 a person with no fixed home or job, who travels around on foot and *usually* lives by begging: *He gave his old coat to a tramp.* □ **vagabond, onde; clochard, arde**

2 a long walk. □ **randonnée**

3 the sound of heavy footsteps. □ **martèlement (de pas)**

4 (*also* **tramp steamer**) a small cargo-boat with no fixed route. □ **tramp**

trample ['trampl] *verb* to tread heavily (on): *The horses trampled the grass (underfoot).* □ **piétiner**

trampoline ['trampəli:n] *noun* a horizontal framework across which a piece of canvas *etc* is stretched, attached by springs, for gymnasts *etc* to jump on: *Children love jumping on trampolines.* □ **trampoline**

tramway *see* **tram**.

trance [tra:ns] *noun* a sleep-like or half-concious state: *The hypnotist put her into a trance.* □ **transe**

tranquil ['traŋkwil] *adjective* quiet; peaceful: *Life in the country is not always tranquil.* □ **tranquille**

'**tranquilly** *adverb*. □ **tranquillement**

tran'quillity *noun*. □ **tranquillité**

'**tranquillizer**, '**tranquilliser** *noun* a drug *especially* a pill to calm the nerves or cause sleep: *He took a tranquillizer.* □ **tranquillisant**

---

tranquillity is spelt with two **l**s.

---

trans- [trans, tranz] across or through. □ **trans-**

transact [tran'sakt] *verb* to do or carry out (business). □ **traiter**

tran'saction [-ʃən] *noun* 1 a particular piece of business; a business deal. □ **transaction, opération**

2 the act of transacting: *The transaction of the deal took several days.* □ **transaction**

transatlantic [tranzət'lantik] *adjective* crossing the Atlantic Ocean: *transatlantic flights/telephone calls.* □ **transatlantique**

transcontinental ['tranzkonti'nentl] *adjective* crossing a continent: *a transcontinental railway.* □ **transcontinental**

transfer [trans'fə:] – *past tense, past participle* **trans'ferred** – *verb* **1** to remove to another place: *He transferred the letter from his briefcase to his pocket.* □ **transférer**

2 to (cause to) move to another place, job, vehicle *etc*: *I'm transferring/They're transferring me to the Bangkok office.* □ **muter, transférer**

3 to give to another person, *especially* legally: *I intend to transfer the property to my son.* □ **transférer**

■ *noun* ['transfə:] **1** the act of transferring: *The manager arranged for his transfer to another football club.* □ **transfert, mutation**

2 a design, picture *etc* that can be transferred from one surface to another, *eg* from paper to material as a guide for embroidery. □ **décalcomanie**

trans'ferable *adjective* that can be transferred from one place or person to another: *This ticket is not transferable* (= may not be used except by the person to whom it is issued). □ **transférable, transmissible**

transform [trans'fo:m] *verb* to change the appearance or nature of completely: *She transformed the old kitchen into a beautiful sitting-room; His marriage has transformed him.* □ **transformer**

,transfor'mation *noun* **1** the act of transforming or process of being transformed: *the transformation of water into ice.* □ **transformation**

2 a change: *The event caused a transformation in her character.* □ **transformation**

trans'former *noun* an apparatus for changing electrical energy from one voltage to another. □ **transformateur**

transfuse [trans'fju:z] *verb* to transfer (the blood of one person) into the veins of another. □ **transfuser**

trans'fusion [-ʒən] *noun* **1** a quantity of blood transferred from one person to another: *She was given a blood transfusion.* □ **transfusion**

2 the act or process of transferring blood from one person to another. □ **transfusion**

transistor [tran'sistə] *noun* **1** a small electronic device that controls the flow of an electric current. □ **transistor**

2 (*also* **transistor radio**) a portable radio that uses these: *She took her transistor everywhere with her.* □ **transistor**

transit ['transit] *noun* the carrying or movement of goods, passengers *etc* from place to place: *The goods have been lost in transit.* □ **transit**

transition [tran'ziʃən] *noun* (a) change from one place, state, subject *etc* to another: *The transition from child to adult can be difficult.* □ **transition**

tran'sitional *adjective* of or concerning transition: *a transitional stage/period.* □ **transitoire**

transitive ['transitiv] *adjective* (of a verb) having an object: *She hit the ball; Open the door!* □ **transitif**

translate [trans'leit] *verb* to put (something said or written) into another language: *She translated the book from French into English.* □ **traduire**

trans'lation *noun* **1** the act of translating: *The transla-tion of poetry is difficult.* □ **traduction**

2 a version of a book, something said *etc*, in another language: *She gave me an Italian translation of the Bible.* □ **traduction**

trans'lator *noun* a person who translates. □ **traducteur, trice**

translucent [trans'lu:snt] *adjective* allowing light to pass through, but not transparent: *translucent silk.* □ **translucide**

trans'lucence *noun.* □ **translucidité**

trans'lucency *noun.* □ **translucidité**

transmit [tranz'mit] – *past tense, past participle* **trans'mitted** – *verb* **1** to pass on: *He transmitted the message; Insects can transmit disease.* □ **transmettre**

2 to send out (radio or television signals, programs *etc*): *The program will be transmitted at 17:00.* □ **transmettre**

trans'mission [-ʃən] *noun* **1** the act of transmitting: *the transmission of disease/radio signals.* □ **transmission**

2 a radio or television broadcast. □ **transmission**

trans'mitter *noun* an apparatus for transmitting, or a person who transmits: *a radio transmitter.* □ **transmetteur, trice**

transparent [trans'parənt, -'peə-] *adjective* able to be seen through: *The box has a transparent lid.* □ **transparent**

trans'parently *adverb.* □ **de manière transparente**

trans'parency [-'pa-] – *plural* **trans'parencies** – *noun* **1** the state of being transparent: *the transparency of the water.* □ **transparence**

2 a photograph printed on transparent material, a slide: *I took some transparencies of the cathedral.* □ **diapositive**

transplant [trans'pla:nt] *verb* **1** to remove (an organ of the body) and put it into another person or animal: *Doctors are able to transplant kidneys.* □ **transplanter, greffer**

2 to remove (skin) and put it on another part of the body. □ **transplanter, greffer**

3 to plant in another place: *We transplanted the rose-bush (into the back garden).* □ **transplanter**

■ ['transpla:nt] *noun* **1** an operation in which an organ or skin is transplanted: *She had to have a kidney trans-plant.* □ **transplantation, greffe**

2 an organ, skin, or a plant that is transplanted: *The trans-plant was rejected by the surrounding tissue.* □ **transplant, greffon**

transport [trans'po:t] *verb* to carry (goods, passengers *etc*) from one place to another: *The goods were trans-ported by air; A bus transported us from the airport to the city.* □ **transporter**

■ ['transpo:t] *noun* the process of transporting or being transported: *road transport; My husband is using my car, so I have no (means of) transport.* □ **transport**

trans'portable *adjective* able to be transported. □ **transportable**

,transpor'tation *noun* transport. □ **transport**

trans'porter *noun* someone or something that trans-ports, *especially* a heavy vehicle for carrying large goods. □ **transporteur**

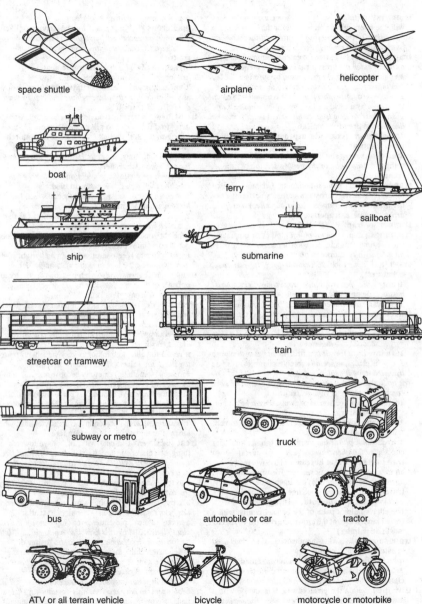

space shuttle

airplane

helicopter

boat

ferry

sailboat

ship

submarine

streetcar or tramway

train

subway or metro

truck

bus

automobile or car

tractor

ATV or all terrain vehicle

bicycle

motorcycle or motorbike

transvestite [tranzvestait] *noun* someone who dresses with the intent of being mistaken for the other sex: *No one knew Devon was a transvestite until they saw him putting on a wig and a dress.* □ **travesti**

trap [trap] *noun* 1 a device for catching animals: *She set a trap to catch the bear*; *a mousetrap.* □ **piège**
2 a plan or trick for taking a person by surprise: *She led him into a trap*; *He fell straight into the trap.* □ **piège**
■ *verb* – *past tense, past participle* **trapped** – to catch in a trap or by a trick: *He lives by trapping animals and selling their fur*; *She trapped him into admitting that he liked her.* □ **prendre au piège**
'**trapper** *noun* a person who traps animals and sells their fur. □ **trappeur, euse**
'**trap door** *noun* a small door, or opening, in a floor or ceiling: *A trap door in the ceiling led to the attic.* □ **trappe**

trapeze [trə'piːz] *noun* a horizontal bar hung on two ropes, on which gymnasts or acrobats perform: *They performed on the trapeze*; (*also adjective*) *a trapeze artist.* □ **trapèze; trapéziste**

trapper *see* **trap.**

trappings ['trapiŋz] *noun plural* clothes or ornaments suitable for a particular occasion or person: *all the trappings of royalty.* □ **ornements**

trash [traʃ] *noun* rubbish: *Throw it away! It's just trash.* □ **ordures**
'**trashy** *adjective* worthless: *trashy jewellery/novels/music.* □ **de pacotille/camelote**
'**trash can** (*American*) a dustbin. □ **poubelle**

travel ['travl] – *past tense, past participle* '**travelled**, '**traveled** – *verb* 1 to go from place to place; to journey: *I travelled to Scotland by train*; *He has to travel a long way to school.* □ **voyager**
2 to move: *Light travels in a straight line.* □ **se déplacer**
3 to visit places, *especially* foreign countries: *He has travelled a great deal.* □ **voyager**
■ *noun* the act of travelling: *Travel to and from work can be very tiring.* □ **voyage, trajet**
'**traveller** *noun* a person who travels: *a weary traveller.* □ **voyageur, euse**
'**travelogue** *noun* a film, article, talk *etc* about travels. □ **documentaire touristique**
'**travels** *noun plural* the visiting of foreign countries *etc*: *She's off on her travels again.* □ **voyage(s)**
travel agency, travel bureau a place where one can arrange journeys, book tickets *etc*: *We went to the travel agency to book our holidays.* □ **agence de voyages**
travel agent a person in charge of, or working in, a travel agency. □ **agent, ente de voyages**
traveller's palm a palm of the banana family, with a row of large leaves at the crown. □ **arbre du voyageur (sorte de palmier)**

trawl [troːl] *noun* a wide-mouthed, bag-shaped net used to catch sea fish. □ **chalut**
■ *verb* to fish with a trawl. □ **pêcher au chalut**
'**trawler** *noun* a fishing-boat used in trawling. □ **chalutier**

tray [trei] *noun* a flat piece of wood, metal *etc* with a low edge, for carrying dishes *etc*: *She brought in the*
tea on a tray; *a tea-tray.* □ **plateau**

treacherous ['tretʃərəs] *adjective* 1 betraying or likely to betray: *a treacherous person/act.* □ **traître**
2 dangerous: *The roads are treacherous in winter.* □ **traître**
'**treacherously** *adverb.* □ **traîtreusement**
'**treacherousness** *noun.* □ **traîtrise**
'**treachery** *noun* (an act of) betraying someone; disloyalty: *His treachery led to the capture and imprisonment of his friend.* □ **traîtrise**

tread [tred] – *past tense* **trod** [trod]: *past participle* **trodden** ['trodn] – *verb* 1 to place one's feet on: *He threw his cigarette on the ground and trod on it.* □ **marcher (sur)**
2 to walk on, along, over *etc*: *He trod the streets looking for a job.* □ **marcher**
3 to crush by putting one's feet on: *We watched them treading the grapes.* □ **écraser du pied**
■ *noun* 1 a way of walking or putting one's feet: *I heard his heavy tread.* □ **pas**
2 the grooved and patterned surface of a tire: *The tread has been worn away.* □ **bande de roulement**
3 the horizontal part of a step or stair on which the foot is placed. □ **marche, giron**
tread water to keep oneself afloat in an upright position by moving the legs (and arms). □ **nager debout**

treason ['triːzn] *noun* (*also* **high treason**) disloyalty to, or betrayal of, one's own country: *They were convicted of (high) treason.* □ **trahison**

treasure ['treʒə] *noun* 1 a store of money, gold, jewels *etc*: *The miser kept a secret hoard of treasure*; (*also adjective*) *a treasure chest.* □ **trésor**
2 something very valuable: *Our babysitter is a real treasure!* □ **trésor**
■ *verb* 1 to value; to think of as very valuable: *I treasure the hours I spend in the country.* □ **tenir à**
2 to keep (something) carefully because one values it: *I treasure the book you gave me.* □ **garder précieusement**
'**treasured** *adjective* regarded as precious; valued: *The photograph of her son is her most treasured possession.* □ **précieux**
'**treasurer** *noun* the person in a club, society *etc*, who looks after the money. □ **trésorier, ière**

treat [triːt] *verb* 1 to deal with, or behave towards (a thing or person), in a certain manner: *The soldiers treated me very well*; *The police are treating her death as a case of murder.* □ **traiter**
2 to try to cure (a person or disease, injury *etc*): *They treated her for a broken leg.* □ **traiter**
3 to put (something) through a process: *The woodwork has been treated with a new chemical.* □ **traiter**
4 to buy (a meal, present *etc*) for (someone): *I'll treat you to lunch*; *She treated herself to a new car.* □ **offrir**
5 to write or speak about; to discuss. □ **traiter de**
■ *noun* something that gives pleasure, *eg* an arranged outing, or some special food: *He took them to the theatre as a treat.* □ **gâterie**
'**treatment** *noun* (an) act or manner of treating: *This chair seems to have received rough treatment*; *This patient/disease requires urgent treatment.* □ **traitement**

treatise ['tri:tis] *noun* a long, detailed, formal piece of writing on some subject: *She wrote a treatise on methods of education.* □ **traité**

treaty ['tri:ti] – *plural* '**treaties** – *noun* a formal agreement between states or governments: *They signed a peace treaty.* □ **traité**

treble ['trebl] *noun, adjective* (something that is) three times as much, many *etc* as something else, or as the normal: *He earns treble what I do.* □ **triple**
■ *verb* to make, or become, three times as much: *He trebled his earnings*; *Her income has trebled.* □ **tripler**
'**trebly** *adverb*. □ **triplement**

tree [tri:] *noun* the largest kind of plant, with a thick, firm, wooden stem and branches: *We have three apple trees growing in our garden.* □ **arbre**
'**treetop** *noun* the top of a tree: *the birds in the treetops.* □ **cime (d'un arbre)**
'**tree trunk** *noun* the trunk of a tree. □ **tronc (d'arbre)**

trek [trek] – *past tense, past participle* **trekked** – *verb* to make a long, hard journey. □ **faire une (dure) randonnée**
■ *noun* a long, hard journey: *a trek through the mountains*; *a trek around the supermarket.* □ **randonnée, expédition**

tremble ['trembl] *verb* to shake *eg* with cold, fear, weakness *etc*: *She trembled with cold*; *His hands trembled as he lit a cigarette.* □ **trembler**
■ *noun* a shudder; a tremor: *a tremble of fear*; *The walls gave a sudden tremble as the truck passed by.* □ **tremblement**

tremendous [trə'mendəs] *adjective* very large; very great: *That required a tremendous effort*; *The response to our appeal was tremendous.* □ **énorme, prodigieux**
tre'mendously *adverb* very: *It's tremendously interesting*; *He's tremendously strong.* □ **énormément, prodigieusement**

tremor ['tremə] *noun* a shaking or quivering: *Earth tremors* (= slight earthquakes) *were felt in Sicily yesterday.* □ **tremblement**

trench [trentʃ] *noun* a long narrow ditch dug in the ground, *especially* as a protection for soldiers against gunfire: *The soldiers returned to the trenches.* □ **tranchée**

trend [trend] *noun* a general direction or tendency: *She follows all the latest trends in fashion*; *an upward trend in share prices.* □ **tendance**
'**trendy** *adjective* following the latest fashions: *trendy people/clothes*; *Her mother tries to be trendy.* □ **à la mode**

trespass ['trespəs] *verb* to enter illegally: *You are trespassing (on my land).* □ **s'introduire sans permission**
■ *noun* the act of trespassing. □ **entrée non autorisée**
'**trespasser** *noun* a person who trespasses. □ **intrus, use**

trestle ['tresl] *noun* a wooden support with legs: *The platform was on trestles*; *(also adjective) a trestle table.* □ **tréteau**

trial ['traiəl] *noun* 1 an act of testing or trying; a test: *Give the new car a trial*; *The disaster was a trial of her courage.* □ **essai, épreuve**
2 a legal process by which a person is judged in a court of law: *Their trial will be held next week.* □ **procès**
3 a (source of) trouble or anxiety: *My son is a great trial (to me).* □ **souci**
trial run a rehearsal, first test *etc* of anything, *eg* a play, car, piece of machinery *etc*. □ **essai**
on trial 1 the subject of a legal action in court: *She's on trial for murder.* □ **jugé**
2 undergoing tests or examination: *We've had a new television installed, but it's only on trial.* □ **à l'essai**
trial and error the trying of various methods, alternatives *etc* until the right one happens to appear or be found: *They didn't know how to put in a central-heating system, but they managed it by trial and error.* □ **tâtonnements**

triangle ['traiaŋgl] *noun* 1 a two-dimensional figure with three sides and three angles. □ **triangle**
2 a musical instrument consisting of a triangular metal bar that is struck with a small hammer. □ **triangle**
tri'angular [-gju-] *adjective* in the shape of a triangle: *a triangular road-sign*; *It is triangular in shape.* □ **triangulaire**

tribe [traib] *noun* 1 a race of people, or a family, who are all descended from the same ancestor: *the tribes of Israel.* □ **tribu**
2 a group of families, *especially* of a primitive or wandering people, ruled by a chief: *the desert tribes of Africa.* □ **tribu**
'**tribal** *adjective* of a tribe or tribes: *tribal lands/customs*; *the tribal system.* □ **tribal**
'**tribesman** ['traibz-] *noun* a man who belongs to a tribe: *an African tribesman.* □ **membre d'une (de la) tribu**

tribunal [trai'bju:nl] *noun* a group of people appointed to give judgment, *especially* on official decisions: *The case was dealt with by a tribunal.* □ **tribunal**

tributary ['tribjutəri] – *plural* '**tributaries** – *noun* a stream flowing into a river: *The River Thames has many tributaries*; *(also adjective) tributary streams.* □ **affluent; tributaire**

tribute ['tribju:t] *noun* (an) expression of praise, thanks *etc*: *This statue has been erected as a tribute to a great man*; *We must pay tribute to her great courage.* □ **tribut**
be a tribute to to be the (praiseworthy) result of: *The success of the scheme is a tribute to his hard work.* □ **témoigner de**

trick [trik] *noun* 1 something which is done, said *etc* in order to cheat or deceive someone, and sometimes to frighten them or make them appear stupid: *The message was just a trick to get her to leave the room.* □ **ruse, tour**
2 a clever or skilful action (to amuse *etc*): *The magician performed some clever tricks.* □ **tour, truc**
■ *adjective* intended to deceive or give a certain illusion: *trick photography.* □ **truqué**
'**trickery** *noun* the act of deceiving or cheating: *She could not stand his trickery.* □ **tromperie**
'**trickster** *noun* a cheat. □ **tricheur, euse**
'**tricky** *adjective* difficult: *a tricky problem/job*; *a tricky person to deal with.* □ **difficile**
'**trickily** *adverb*. □ **difficilement**
'**trickiness** *noun*. □ **difficulté**

do the trick to do or be what is necessary: *I need a piece of paper. This old envelope will do the trick!* □ **faire l'affaire**

play a trick/tricks on to do something which is amusing to oneself because it deceives or frightens (someone else), or makes them appear stupid: *He played a trick on her by jumping out from behind a wall as she passed.* □ **jouer un tour**

a trick of the trade one of the ways of being successful in a job *etc*: *Remembering the customers' names is one of the tricks of the trade.* □ **ficelle du métier**

trickle ['trikl] *verb* to flow in small amounts: *Blood was trickling down her face.* □ **dégoutter**

■ *noun* a small amount: *a trickle of water; At first there was only a trickle of people but soon a crowd arrived.* □ **un peu, un petit nombre**

tricky *see* **trick**.

tricycle ['traisikl] *noun* a kind of cycle with three wheels. □ **tricycle**

trier, tries *see* **try**.

trifle ['traifl] *noun* 1 anything of very little value: *$100 is a trifle when one is very rich.* □ **bagatelle**
2 (a dish of) a sweet pudding made of sponge-cake, fruit, cream *etc*: *I'm making a trifle for dessert.* □ **diplomate**
'**trifling** *adjective* unimportant: *a trifling amount of money.* □ **insignifiant**

trigger ['trigə] *noun* 1 a small lever on a gun, which is pulled to make the gun fire: *He aimed the rifle at her but did not pull the trigger.* □ **détente, gâchette**
2 anything which starts a series of actions or reactions. □ **déclencheur**

■ *verb* (*often with* **off**) to start (a series of events): *The attack triggered (off) a full-scale war.* □ **déclencher**

trilogy ['trilədʒi] – *plural* '**trilogies** – *noun* a group of three plays, novels *etc* by the same author which are parts of the same story or are written about the same subject. □ **trilogie**

trim [trim] – *past tense, past participle* **trimmed** – *verb* 1 to cut the edges or ends of (something) in order to make it shorter and/or neat: *He's trimming the hedge; He had his hair trimmed.* □ **tailler**
2 to decorate (a dress, hat *etc*, *usually* around the edges): *She trimmed the sleeves with lace.* □ **border (de)**
3 to arrange (the sails of a boat *etc*) suitably for the weather conditions. □ **orienter**

■ *noun* a haircut: *He went to the hairdresser's for a trim.* □ **coupe (de cheveux)**

■ *adjective* neat and tidy: *a trim appearance.* □ **net, soigné**

'**trimly** *adverb*. □ **soigneusement**
'**trimness** *noun*. □ **aspect net**
'**trimming** *noun* 1 something added as a decoration: *lace trimming.* □ **garniture**
2 (*usually in plural*) a piece cut off; an end or edge. □ **chutes**

in (good) trim in good condition: *Her figure's in good trim after all those exercises.* □ **en bon état, bonne forme**

trinket ['triŋkit] *noun* a small (*usually* cheap) ornament or piece of jewellery: *That shop sells postcards and trin-*

kets. □ **babiole**

trio ['triːou] – *plural* '**trios** – *noun* 1 a group of three (people or things). □ **trio**
2 (a piece of music for) three players: *A trio was playing in the hotel lounge; a trio by Mozart.* □ **trio**

trip [trip] – *past tense, past participle* **tripped** – *verb* 1 (*often with* **up** *or* **over**) to (cause to) catch one's foot and stumble or fall: *She tripped and fell; She tripped over the carpet.* □ **trébucher**
2 to walk with short, light steps: *She tripped happily along the road.* □ **marcher d'un pas léger**

■ *noun* a journey or tour: *She went on/took a trip to Paris.* □ **voyage**

'**tripper** *noun* a person who has made a journey for pleasure: *The resort was full of trippers.* □ **touriste**

triple ['tripl] *adjective* 1 three times (as big, much *etc* as usual): *He received triple wages for all his extra work; a triple whisky.* □ **triple**
2 made up of three (parts *etc*): *a triple agreement.* □ **triple**

■ *verb* to make or become three times as much, big *etc*; to treble: *She tripled her income; Her income tripled in ten years.* □ **tripler**

■ *noun* three times the (usual) amount: *If you work the bank holiday, you will be paid triple.* □ **triple**

'**triplet** [-lit] *noun* one of three children or animals born to the same mother at the same time: *She's just had triplets.* □ **triplés, ées**

triplicate ['triplikət]: **in triplicate** on three separate copies (of the same form *etc*): *Fill in the form in triplicate.* □ **en trois exemplaires**

tripod ['traipod] *noun* a stand with three legs, *especially* for a camera. □ **trépied**

trishaw ['traiʃɔː] *noun* a small, light vehicle with three wheels for carrying people or goods, pedalled by the operator. □ **triporteur**

trite [trait] *adjective* (of a remark, saying *etc*) already said in exactly the same way so often that it no longer has any worth, effectiveness *etc*: *His poetry is full of trite descriptions of nature.* □ **banal**
'**tritely** *adverb*. □ **banalement**
'**triteness** *noun*. □ **banalité**

triumph ['traiʌmf] *noun* 1 a great victory or success: *The battle ended in a triumph for the Romans.* □ **triomphe**
2 a state of happiness, celebration, pride *etc* after a success: *They went home in triumph.* □ **triomphe**

■ *verb* to win a victory: *The Romans triumphed (over their enemies).* □ **triompher (de)**

tri'umphal *adjective* having to do with (a) triumph: *a triumphal battle.* □ **triomphal**

tri'umphant *adjective* (glad and excited because of) having won a victory, achieved something difficult *etc*: *She gave a triumphant shout.* □ **triomphant**
tri'umphantly *adverb*. □ **triomphalement**

trivia ['trivia] *noun plural* unimportant matters or details: *I haven't time to worry about such trivia.* □ **broutilles**

'**trivial** *adjective* 1 of very little importance: *trivial details.* □ **insignifiant**

2 (*especially* of people) only interested in unimportant things; not at all serious: *He's a very trivial person.* □ **frivole**

'**trivially** *adverb.* □ **banalement**

,**trivi'ality** [-'a-] *noun* 1 the state of being trivial. □ **banalité**

2 (*plural* trivi'alities) something which is trivial: *He is always worrying about some triviality or other.* □ **banalité**

trod, trodden *see* **tread.**

troll [troul] *noun* an imaginary creature of human-like form, very ugly and evil-tempered. □ **troll**

trolley ['troli] *noun* 1 a type of small cart for carrying things *etc*: *He quickly filled the trolley with groceries.* □ **chariot**

2 (*also* '**tea trolley,** '**teacart**) a small cart, *usually* consisting of two or three trays fixed on a frame, used for serving tea, food *etc*: *They brought the tea in on a trolley.* □ **table roulante**

'**trolley bus** *noun* a bus which is driven by power from an overhead wire to which it is connected. □ **trolleybus**

trombone [trom'boun] *noun* a type of brass musical wind instrument, on which the pitch of notes is altered by sliding a tube in and out: *He plays the trombone; He played a tune on his trombone.* □ **trombone**

trom'bonist *noun* a person who plays the trombone. □ **tromboniste**

troop [truːp] *noun* 1 a group of ordinary soldiers. □ **troupe**

2 a crowd or collection (of people or animals): *A troop of visitors arrived.* □ **groupe**

■ *verb* to go in a group: *They all trooped into his office.* □ **entrer, aller en groupe**

'**trooper** *noun* an ordinary soldier. □ **soldat (de cavalerie)**

troops *noun plural* soldiers. □ **troupes**

trophy ['troufi] – *plural* '**trophies** – *noun* 1 a prize for winning in a sport *etc*: *They won a silver trophy for shooting.* □ **trophée**

2 something which is kept in memory of a victory, success *etc*. □ **trophée**

tropic ['tropik] *noun* either of two imaginary circles running around the earth at about 23 degrees north (**Tropic of Cancer**) or south (**Tropic of Capricorn**) of the equator. □ **tropique (du cancer/du capricorne)**

'**tropics** *noun plural* the hot regions between or (*loosely*) near these lines: *The ship is heading for the tropics.* □ **tropiques**

'**tropical** *adjective* 1 of the tropics: *The climate there is tropical.* □ **tropical**

2 growing *etc* in hot countries: *tropical plants.* □ **tropical**

'**tropically** *adverb.* □ **comme sous les tropiques**

trot [trot] – *past tense, past participle* '**trotted** – *verb* (of a horse) to move with fairly fast, bouncy steps, faster than a walk but slower than a canter or gallop: *The horse trotted down the road; The child trotted along beside her mother.* □ **trotter**

■ *noun* the pace at which a horse or rider *etc* moves when trotting: *They rode at a trot.* □ **trot**

'**trotter** *noun* a pig's foot. □ **pied de porc**

trouble ['trʌbl] *noun* 1 (something which causes) worry, difficulty, work, anxiety *etc*: *She never talks about her troubles; We've had a lot of trouble with our children; I had a lot of trouble finding the book you wanted.* □ **problème**

2 disturbances; rebellion, fighting *etc*: *It occurred during the time of the troubles in Cyprus.* □ **troubles**

3 illness or weakness (in a particular part of the body): *He has heart trouble.* □ **maladie**

■ *verb* 1 to cause worry, anger or sadness to: *She was troubled by the news of her sister's illness.* □ **troubler**

2 used as part of a very polite and formal request: *May I trouble you to close the window?* □ **déranger**

3 to make any effort: *He didn't even trouble to tell me what had happened.* □ **se donner la peine de**

'**troubled** *adjective* (*negative* **untroubled**) 1 worried or anxious: *He is obviously a troubled man.* □ **préoccupé**

2 disturbed and not peaceful: *troubled sleep.* □ **agité**

'**troublesome** *adjective* causing worry or difficulty: *troublesome children/tasks.* □ **pénible**

'**troublemaker** *noun* a person who continually (and *usually* deliberately) causes worry, difficulty or disturbance to other people: *Beware of her – she is a real troublemaker.* □ **fauteur, trice de troubles**

trough [trof] *noun* 1 a long, low, open container for animals' food or water: *a drinking-trough for the cattle.* □ **auge**

2 a low part between two waves (in the sea *etc*): *The boat went down into a trough.* □ **creux (d'une vague)**

3 an area of low pressure in the atmosphere, *usually* causing rain. □ **dépression**

trounce [trauns] *verb* to beat or defeat completely: *Our football team was trounced.* □ **battre à plates coutures**

troupe [truːp] *noun* a performing group (of actors, dancers *etc*): *a circus troupe.* □ **troupe**

'**trouper** *noun* 1 a member of a group of this kind. □ **membre d'une troupe**

2 a hard-working colleague. □ **bourreau de travail**

trousers ['trauzɔz] *noun plural* an outer garment for the lower part of the body, covering each leg separately: *He wore (a pair of) black trousers; She was dressed in trousers and a sweater.* □ **pantalon**

trouser- (of trousers: *a trouser button; That dog has torn my trouser leg.* □ **de pantalon**

trout [traut] – *plural* **trout** – *noun* 1 a type of freshwater fish of the salmon family: *She caught five trout.* □ **truite**

2 its flesh, used as food: *Have some more trout!* □ **truite**

trowel ['trauəl] *noun* 1 a tool like a small shovel, used in gardening: *He filled the flowerpot with earth, using a trowel.* □ **déplantoir**

2 a tool with a flat blade, for spreading mortar, plaster *etc*. □ **truelle**

truant ['truːənt] *noun* someone who stays away from school *etc* without permission: *The truants were caught and sent back to school.* □ **enfant qui fait l'école buissonnière**

'**truancy** *noun*: *Truancy is a great problem in some schools.* □ **absence non autorisée (d'un écolier)**

play truant to be a truant and stay away from school

etc: *He was always playing truant (from school)*. □ **faire l'école buissonnière**

truce [truːs] *noun* a (*usually* temporary) rest from fighting, agreed to by both sides. □ **trêve**

truck [trʌk] *noun* 1 a railway vehicle for carrying goods. □ **wagon à plateforme**

2 any of various kinds of large sturdy road vehicle used for a variety of purpose: *She drives a truck*; (*also adjective*) *a truck-driver*. □ **(de) camion**

3 a motor vehicle for carrying heavy loads: *She has a licence to drive a truck*; *a coal-truck*. □ **camion**

truck-driver *noun*. □ **camionneur, euse**

truculent ['trʌkjulənt] *adjective* (of a person) aggressive and inclined to argue. □ **agressif**

trudge [trʌdʒ] *verb* to walk with slow, tired steps: *She trudged wearily up the hill*. □ **se traîner**

■ *noun* such a walk or way of walking. □ **marche pénible**

true [truː] *adjective* 1 (*negative* **untrue**) telling of something that really happened; not invented; agreeing with fact; not wrong: *That is a true statement*; *Is it true that you did not steal the ring?* □ **vrai**

2 (*negative* **untrue**) accurate: *They don't have a true idea of its importance*. □ **exact**

3 (*negative* **untrue**) faithful; loyal: *She has been a true friend*. □ **fidèle**

4 properly so called: *A spider is not a true insect*. □ **véritable**

'**trueness** *noun*. □ **vérité**

'**truly** *adverb* 1 really: *I truly believe that this decision is the right one*. □ **vraiment**

2 in a true manner: *He loved her truly*. □ **vraiment**

trump [trʌmp] *noun* in some card games, any card of a suit which has been declared to rank higher than the other suits: *This time, hearts are trumps*; (*also adjective*) *a trump card*. □ **(d')atout**

■ *verb* to defeat (an ordinary card) by playing a card from the trump suit: *She trumped (my king) with a heart*. □ **prendre avec l'atout**

trumpet ['trʌmpit] *noun* 1 a brass musical wind instrument with a high, clear tone: *He plays the trumpet*; *He played a tune on his trumpet*. □ **trompette**

2 the cry of an elephant: *The elephant gave a loud trumpet*. □ **barrissement**

■ *verb* to make a noise like a trumpet. □ **trompeter**

'**trumpeter** *noun* a person who plays the trumpet. □ **trompettiste**

blow one's own trumpet to boast, praise oneself greatly *etc*. □ **se vanter**

truncated ['trʌŋkeitid] *adjective* shortened by cutting off a part, *especially* the end: *a truncated version of the play*. □ **tronqué**

truncheon ['trʌntʃən] *noun* a short heavy stick, carried *especially* by British policemen. □ **matraque**

trundle ['trʌndl] *verb* to (cause to) roll slowly and heavily along on wheels: *She trundled the wheelbarrow down the garden*; *The huge truck trundled along the road*. □ **(faire) rouler (bruyamment)**

trunk [trʌŋk] *noun* 1 the main stem (of a tree): *The trunk of this tree is five metres thick*. □ **tronc**

2 a large box or chest for packing or keeping clothes *etc* in: *She packed her trunk and sent it to Canada by sea*. □ **malle**

3 an elephant's long nose: *The elephant sucked up water into its trunk*. □ **trompe**

4 the body (not including the head, arms and legs) of a person (and certain animals): *He had a powerful trunk, but thin arms*. □ **tronc**

5 a storage space (of a car): *Put your baggage in the trunk*. □ **coffre**

trunks *noun plural* short trousers or pants worn by boys or men, *especially* the type used for swimming: *swimming-trunks*; *He wore only a pair of bathing-trunks*. □ **maillot de bain**

truss [trʌs] *verb* to tie or bind tightly: *She trussed the chicken and put it in the oven*; *The burglars trussed up the guards*. □ **ficeler**

trust [trʌst] *verb* 1 to have confidence or faith; to believe: *She trusted (in) them*. □ **avoir confiance (en)**

2 to give (something to someone), believing that it will be used well and responsibly: *I can't trust him with my car*; *I can't trust my car to him*. □ **confier (qqch à qqn)**

3 to hope or be confident (that): *I trust (that) you had/will have a good journey*. □ **espérer**

■ *noun* 1 belief or confidence in the power, reality, truth, goodness *etc* of a person or thing: *The firm has a great deal of trust in your ability*; *trust in God*. □ **confiance**

2 charge or care; responsibility: *The child was placed in my trust*. □ **charge**

3 a task *etc* given to a person by someone who believes that they will do it, look after it *etc* well: *She holds a position of trust in the firm*. □ **charge**

4 arrangement(s) by which something (*eg* money) is given to a person to use in a particular way, or to keep until a particular time: *The money was to be held in trust for her children*; (*also adjective*) *a trust fund*. □ **(en) fiducie**

5 a group of business firms working together: *The companies formed a trust*. □ **trust**

,**trus'tee** *noun* a person who keeps and takes care of something (*especially* money or property) for someone else. □ **fiduciaire**

'**trustworthy** *adjective* (*negative* **untrustworthy**) worthy of trust: *Is your friend trustworthy?* □ **digne de confiance**

'**trustworthiness** *noun*. □ **fidélité**

'**trusty** *adjective* able to be trusted or depended on: *a trusty sword*; *a trusty friend*. □ **fidèle**

'**trustily** *adverb*. □ **fidèlement**

'**trustiness** *noun*. □ **fidélité**

truth [truːθ] – *plural* **truths** [truːðz, truːθs] – *noun* 1 trueness; the state of being true: *I am certain of the truth of his story*; *'What is truth?' asked the philosopher*. □ **vérité**

2 the true facts: *I don't know, and that's the truth!*; *Tell the truth about it*. □ **vérité**

'**truthful** *adjective* (*negative* **untruthful**) 1 (of a person) telling the truth: *She's a truthful child*. □ **franc**

2 true: *a truthful account of what happened*. □ **véridique**

'**truthfully** *adverb*. □ **véridiquement**

'**truthfulness** *noun*. □ **véracité**

tell the truth to confess or make a true statement. □ **dire la vérité**

to tell the truth really; actually: *To tell the truth I forgot it was your birthday last week.* □ **à dire vrai**

try [trai] *verb* **1** to attempt or make an effort (to do, get *etc*): *He tried to answer the questions; Let's try and climb that tree!* □ **essayer (de)**

2 to test; to make an experiment (with) in order to find out whether something will be successful, satisfactory *etc*: *She tried washing her hair with a new shampoo; Have you tried the local beer?* □ **essayer (de)**

3 to judge (someone or their case) in a court of law: *The prisoners were tried for murder.* □ **juger**

4 to test the limits of; to strain: *You are trying my patience.* □ **mettre à l'épreuve**

■ *noun* – *plural* **tries** – **1** an attempt or effort: *Have a try (at the exam). I'm sure you will pass.* □ **tentative**

2 in rugby football, an act of putting the ball on the ground behind the opponents' goal-line: *Our team scored three tries.* □ **essai**

'**trier** *noun* a person who keeps on trying, who does not give up: *He's not very good, but he's a trier.* □ **personne persévérante**

'**trying** *adjective* **1** difficult; causing strain or anxiety: *Having to stay such a long time in hospital must be very trying.* □ **pénible**

2 (of people) stretching one's patience to the limit; annoying: *She's a very trying woman!* □ **pénible**

try on to put on (clothes *etc*) to see if they fit: *He tried on a new hat.* □ **essayer**

try out to test (something) by using it: *We are trying out new teaching methods.* □ **essayer**

tsar, czar, tzar [zaː] *noun* (the status of) any of the former emperors of Russia: *He was crowned tsar; Tsar Nicholas.* □ **tsar**

T-shirt *see* **T**.

tub [tʌb] *noun* **1** a round (*usually* wooden) container for keeping water, washing clothes *etc*: *a huge tub of water.* □ **cuve**

2 a bath: *She was sitting in the tub.* □ **baignoire**

3 a small round container for ice cream *etc*. □ **contenant**

'**tubby** *adjective* rather fat; plump: *She was rather tubby as a child but she is very slim now.* □ **grassouillet**

tuba ['tjuːbə] *noun* a large brass musical wind instrument giving a low-pitched range of notes: *He plays the tuba.* □ **tuba**

tubby *see* **tub**.

tube [tjuːb] *noun* **1** a long, low cylinder-shaped object through which liquid can pass; a pipe: *The water flowed through a rubber tube; a glass tube.* □ **tube, tuyau**

2 an organ of this kind in animals or plants. □ **tube**

3 an underground railway (*especially* in London): *I go to work on the tube/by tube; (also adjective) a tube train/station.* □ **(de) métro**

4 a container for a semi-liquid substance which is got out by squeezing: *I must buy a tube of toothpaste.* □ **tube**

'**tubing** *noun* (material for) a length or system of tubes: *two metres of tubing.* □ **tube(s), tuyau(x)**

'**tubular** [-bjulə] *adjective* **1** made of, or consisting of tubes: *tubular steel.* □ **tubulaire**

2 shaped like a tube: *The container is tubular in shape.* □ **tubulaire**

tuber ['tjuːbə] *noun* a swelling on the stem or root of a plant, in which food is stored: *Potatoes are the tubers of the potato plant.* □ **tubercule**

tuberculosis [tjubəːkju'lousis] *noun* (*often abbreviated to* **TB** [tiːˈbiː]) an infectious disease *usually* affecting the lungs: *He suffers from/has tuberculosis.* □ **tuberculose**

tubing, tubular *see* **tube**.

tuck [tʌk] *noun* **1** a fold sewn into a piece of material: *Her dress had tucks in the sleeves.* □ **rempli**

2 sweets, cakes *etc*: *Schoolboys used to spend their money on tuck; (also adjective) a tuck shop.* □ **(de) friandises**

■ *verb* to push, stuff *etc*: *He tucked his shirt into his trousers.* □ **mettre**

tuck in 1 to gather bedclothes *etc* closely around: *I said goodnight and tucked her in.* □ **border**

2 to eat greedily or with enjoyment: *They sat down to breakfast and started to tuck in straight away.* □ **manger à belles dents**

Tuesday ['tjuːzdi] *noun* the third day of the week, the day following Monday: *She came on Tuesday; (also adjective) Tuesday evening.* □ **(de) mardi**

tuft [tʌft] *noun* a small bunch or clump (of grass, hair, feathers *etc*): *She sat down on a tuft of grass.* □ **touffe**

'**tufted** *adjective* having or growing in tufts: *a tufted carpet; tufted grass.* □ **en touffe(s)**

tug [tʌg] – *past tense, past participle* **tugged** – *verb* to pull (something) sharply and strongly: *She tugged (at) the door but it wouldn't open.* □ **tirer (sur)**

■ *noun* **1** a strong, sharp pull: *He gave the rope a tug.* □ **traction**

2 a tugboat. □ **remorqueur**

'**tugboat** *noun* a small boat with a very powerful engine, for towing larger ships. □ **remorqueur**

,**tug-of-'war** *noun* a competition in which two people or teams pull at opposite ends of a rope, trying to pull their opponents over a centre line. □ **souque à la corde**

tuition [tju'iʃən] *noun* teaching, *especially* private: *He gives music tuition/tuition in music.* □ **cours particulier**

tulip ['tjuːlip] *noun* a kind of plant with brightly-coloured cup-shaped flowers, grown from a bulb. □ **tulipe**

tumble ['tʌmbl] *verb* to (cause to) fall, *especially* in a helpless or confused way: *She tumbled down the stairs; The box suddenly tumbled off the top of the wardrobe.* □ **(faire) culbuter, dégringoler, débouler**

■ *noun* a fall: *She took a tumble on the stairs.* □ **dégringolade**

'**tumbler** *noun* **1** a large drinking glass: *a tumbler of whisky.* □ **verre (droit)**

2 a tumblerful. □ **plein verre (de)**

'**tumblerful** *noun* the amount contained by a tumbler: *two tumblerfuls of water.* □ **plein verre (de)**

,**tumble'dryer** *noun* a machine for drying clothes by tumbling them around and blowing hot air into them. □ **sécheuse**

tummy ['tʌmi] – *plural* '**tummies** – *noun* a (*especially* child's) word for stomach: *She has a pain in her tummy*; (*also adjective*) *a tummy-ache*. □ **(de) ventre**

tumour, tumor ['tjuːmə] *noun* an abnormal (dangerous) mass of tissue growing on or in the body: *a brain tumour*; *The surgeon removed a tumour from her bladder*. □ **tumeur**

tumult ['tjuːmʌlt] *noun* a great noise (*usually* made by a crowd): *He could hear a great tumult in the street*. □ **tumulte**

tu'multuous [-tʃuəs] *adjective* with great noise or confusion: *The crowd gave him a tumultuous welcome*; *tumultuous applause*. □ **tumultueux**

tu'multuously *adverb*. □ **tumultueusement**

tuna (fish) ['tuːnə (fiʃ)] – *plurals* '**tuna**, '**tuna fish**, '**tunas** – *also* (**tunny (fish)** ['tʌni(fiʃ)] – *plurals* '**tunnies**, '**tunny**, '**tunny fish**) – *noun* 1 a kind of large sea-fish of the mackerel family. □ **thon**

2 its flesh, used as food. □ **thon**

tune [tjuːn] *noun* musical notes put together in a particular (melodic and pleasing) order; a melody: *He played a tune on the violin*. □ **air**

■ *verb* 1 to adjust (a musical instrument, or its strings *etc*) to the correct pitch: *The orchestra tuned their instruments*. □ **accorder**

2 to adjust a radio so that it receives a particular station: *The radio was tuned to a German station*. □ **régler (sur)**

3 to adjust (an engine *etc*) so that it runs well. □ **mettre au point**

'**tuneful** *adjective* having a good, clear, pleasant *etc* tune: *That song is very tuneful*. □ **mélodieux**

'**tunefully** *adverb*. □ **mélodieusement**

'**tunefulness** *noun*. □ **caractère mélodieux**

'**tuneless** *adjective* without a good *etc* tune; unmusical: *The child was singing in a tuneless voice*. □ **discordant**

'**tunelessly** *adverb*. □ **faux**

'**tunelessness** *noun*. □ **discordance**

'**tuner** *noun* 1 (*also* **pi'ano tuner**) a person whose profession is tuning pianos. □ **accordeur, euse**

2 the dial on a radio *etc* used to tune in to the different stations. □ **réglage de syntonisation**

3 a radio which is part of a stereo system. □ **syntonisateur**

change one's tune to change one's attitude, opinions *etc*. □ **changer de ton**

in tune 1 (of a musical instrument) having been adjusted so as to give the correct pitches: *Is the violin in tune with the piano?* □ **accordé**

2 (of a person's singing voice) at the same pitch as that of other voices or instruments: *Someone in the choir isn't (singing) in tune*. □ **juste**

out of tune not in tune. □ **faux**

tune in to tune a radio (to a particular station or program): *We usually tune (the radio) in to the news*. □ **régler (sur)**

tune up (of an orchestra *etc*) to tune its instruments. □ **accorder**

tunic ['tjuːnik] *noun* 1 a soldier's or policeman's jacket. □ **tunique**

2 a loose garment worn *especially* in ancient Greece and Rome. □ **tunique**

3 a similar type of modern garment. □ **tunique**

tunnel ['tʌnl] *noun* a (*usually* man-made) underground passage, *especially* one cut through a hill or under a river: *The road goes through a tunnel under the river*. □ **tunnel**

■ *verb* – *past tense, past participle* '**tunnelled**, '**tunneled** – to make a tunnel: *They escaped from prison by tunnelling under the walls*. □ **creuser un tunnel**

tunny (fish) *see* **tuna (fish)**.

turban ['təːbən] *noun* a long piece of cloth worn wound around the head, *especially* by men belonging to certain of the races and religions of Asia. □ **turban**

turbine ['təːbain] *noun* a type of motor, operated by the action of water, steam, gas *etc*: *a steam turbine*. □ **turbine**

turbo- [təːbou] having a turbine engine: *a turbojet (aircraft)*. □ **turbo-**

turbulent ['təːbjulənt] *adjective* violently disturbed or confused: *The seas are turbulent*; *the turbulent years of war*. □ **agité, turbulent**

'**turbulently** *adverb*. □ **tumultueusement**

'**turbulence** *noun*. □ **turbulence**

turf [təːf] – *plural* **turfs** [-fs], **turves** [-vz] – *noun* 1 rough grass and the earth it grows out of: *She walked across the springy turf*. □ **gazon**

2 (a *usually* square piece of) grass and earth: *We laid turf in our garden to make a lawn*. □ **(plaque de) gazon**

■ *verb* 1 to cover with turf(s): *We are going to turf that part of the garden*. □ **gazonner**

2 to throw: *We turfed him out of the house*. □ **jeter**

turkey ['təːki] *noun* 1 a kind of large farmyard bird. □ **dindon, dinde**

2 its flesh used as food, eaten *especially* at Christmas or (in the United States) Thanksgiving: *We had turkey for dinner*. □ **dinde**

turmoil ['təːmoil] *noun* a state of wild confused movement or disorder: *The crowd/Her mind was in (a) turmoil*. □ **émoi**

turn [təːn] *verb* 1 to (make something) move or go around; to revolve: *The wheels turned*; *She turned the handle*. □ **tourner**

2 to face or go in another direction: *He turned and walked away*; *She turned towards him*. □ **(se) tourner**

3 to change direction: *The road turned to the left*. □ **tourner**

4 to direct; to aim or point: *He turned his attention to his work*. □ **tourner (vers)**

5 to go around: *They turned the corner*. □ **tourner**

6 to (cause something to) become or change to: *You can't turn lead into gold*; *At what temperature does water turn into ice?* □ **(se) changer (en)**

7 to (cause to) change colour to: *Her hair turned white*; *The shock turned his hair white*. □ **(faire) devenir**

■ *noun* 1 an act of turning: *She gave the handle a turn*. □ **tour**

2 a winding or coil: *There are eighty turns of wire on this antenna*. □ **spire**

3 (*also* '**turning**) a point where one can change direction, *eg* where one road joins another: *Take the third*

turn(ing) on/to the left. □ **tournant**

4 one's chance or duty (to do, have *etc* something shared by several people): *It's your turn to choose a record; You'll have to wait your turn in the bathroom.* □ **tour**

5 one of a series of short circus or variety acts, or the person or persons who perform it: *The show opened with a comedy turn.* □ **numéro**

'**turning point** *noun* a place where a turn is made: *the turning point in the race; a turning point in her life.* □ **tournant, moment décisif**

'**turnover** *noun* **1** the total value of sales in a business during a certain time: *The firm had a turnover of $100,000 last year.* □ **chiffre d'affaires**

2 the rate at which money or workers pass through a business. □ **mouvement, renouvellement**

'**turnstile** *noun* a revolving gate which allows only one person to pass at a time, *usually* after payment of entrance fees *etc*: *There is a turnstile at the entrance to the football ground.* □ **tourniquet**

'**turntable** *noun* the revolving part of a record player on which the record rests while it is being played: *She put another record on the turntable so that people could dance to the music.* □ **platine (tourne-disque)**

'**turn-up** *noun* a piece of material which is folded up at the bottom of a trouser-leg: *Trousers with turn-ups are not fashionable at the moment.* □ **revers**

by turns *see* **in turn**.

do (someone) a good turn to do something helpful for someone: *She did me several good turns.* □ **rendre (un) service (à)**

in turn, by turns one after another, in regular order: *They answered the teacher's questions in turn.* □ **à tour de rôle**

out of turn out of the correct order. □ **mal à propos**

take a turn for the better, worse (of things or people) to become better or worse: *Her fortunes have taken a turn for the better; Her health has taken a turn for the worse.* □ **s'améliorer; s'aggraver**

take turns (of two or more people) to do something one after the other, not at the same time: *They took turns to look after the baby.* □ **faire (qqch.) à tour de rôle**

turn a blind eye to pretend not to see or notice (something): *Because he works so hard, his boss turns a blind eye when he comes in late.* □ **fermer les yeux (sur)**

turn against to become dissatisfied with or hostile to (people or things that one previously liked *etc*): *He turned against his friends.* □ **se retourner contre**

turn away to move or send away: *He turned away in disgust; The police turned away the crowds.* □ **(se) détourner**

turn back to (cause to) go back in the opposite direction: *He got tired and turned back; The travellers were turned back at the frontier.* □ **revenir; refouler**

turn down 1 to say 'no' to; to refuse: *He turned down her offer/request.* □ **refuser**

2 to reduce (the level of light, noise *etc*) produced by (something): *Please turn down (the volume on) the radio – it's far too loud!* □ **baisser**

turn in to hand over (a person or thing) to people in authority: *They turned the escaped prisoner in to the*

police. □ **livrer**

turn loose to set free: *She turned the horse loose in the field.* □ **libérer, lâcher**

turn off 1 to cause (water, electricity *etc*) to stop flowing: *I've turned off the water/the electricity.* □ **fermer, éteindre**

2 to turn (a tap, switch *etc*) so that something stops: *I turned off the tap.* □ **fermer, éteindre**

3 to cause (something) to stop working by switching it off: *She turned off the light/the oven.* □ **fermer, éteindre**

turn on 1 to make water, electric current *etc* flow: *She turned on the water/the gas.* □ **ouvrir, allumer**

2 to turn (a tap, switch *etc*) so that something works: *I turned on the tap.* □ **ouvrir, allumer**

3 to cause (something) to work by switching it on: *He turned on the radio.* □ **ouvrir, allumer**

4 to attack: *The dog turned on him.* □ **attaquer**

turn out 1 to send away; to make (someone) leave. □ **faire sortir**

2 to make or produce: *The factory turns out ten finished articles an hour.* □ **produire**

3 to empty or clear: *I turned out the cupboard.* □ **vider**

4 (of a crowd) to come out; to get together for a (public) meeting, celebration *etc*: *A large crowd turned out to see the procession.* □ **venir**

5 to turn off: *Turn out the light!* □ **fermer, éteindre**

6 to happen or prove to be: *She turned out to be right; It turned out that he was right.* □ **se révéler**

turn over to give (something) up (to): *She turned the money over to the police.* □ **rendre, remettre**

turn up 1 to appear or arrive: *He turned up at our house.* □ **venir, arriver**

2 to be found: *Don't worry – it'll turn up again.* □ **se retrouver**

3 to increase (the level of noise, light *etc*) produced by (something): *Turn up (the volume on) the radio.* □ **augmenter, mettre plus fort**

turnip [ˈtəːnip] *noun* **1** a type of plant with a large round root: *a field of turnips.* □ **navet**

2 the root used as food: *Would you like some turnip?* □ **navet**

turnstile, turntable *see* **turn**.

turpentine [ˈtəːpəntain] *noun* a type of oil used for thinning certain kinds of paint, cleaning paint-brushes *etc*. □ **térébenthine**

turquoise [ˈtəːkwoiz] *noun* **1** a kind of greenish-blue precious stone: *The ring was set with a turquoise.* □ **turquoise**

2 (*also adjective*) (of) its colour: *(a) pale turquoise (dress).* □ **turquoise**

turret [ˈtʌrit] *noun* **1** a small tower: *A fortress often has turrets.* □ **tourelle**

2 steel protecting gunners on a tank, plane etc. □ **tourelle**

turtle *noun* a kind of large tortoise, *especially* one living in water. □ **tortue de mer**

'**turtleneck** *noun* (a garment, *especially* a sweater, with) a high close-fitting neck: *She was wearing a turtleneck; (also adjective) a turtleneck sweater.* □ **(à) col roulé**

turtle soup soup made from the flesh of a type of turtle. □ **consommé à la tortue**

turves *see* turf.

tusk [tʌsk] *noun* one of a pair of large curved teeth which project from the mouth of certain animals *eg* the elephant, walrus, wild boar *etc*. □ **défense**

tut(-tut) (*sometimes* [tʌt('tʌt)]) *interjection* used in writing to represent the sound used to express disapproval, mild annoyance *etc*. □ **ta, ta, ta!**

tutelage ['tjuːtəlij] *noun* 1 guardianship. □ **tutelle** 2 tuition, instruction. □ **leçons, instruction**

tutor ['tjuːtə] *noun* 1 a teacher of a group of students in a college or university. □ **chargé, ée de classe**
2 a privately-employed teacher: *His parents employed a tutor to teach him Greek*. □ **précepteur, trice**
3 a book which teaches a subject, *especially* music: *I bought a violin tutor*. □ **méthode**
■ *verb* to teach: *She tutored the child in mathematics*. □ **enseigner, donner des cours particuliers à**
tu'torial [-'tɔː-] *adjective* of or concerning a tutor. □ **(de/du) chargé de classe**
■ *noun* a lesson by a tutor at a college or university: *We have lectures and tutorials in history*. □ **travaux pratiques**

tutu ['tuːtuː] *noun* a female ballet dancer's short stiff skirt. □ **tutu**

twang [twaŋ] *noun* a sound of or like a tightly-stretched string breaking or being plucked: *The string broke with a sharp twang*. □ **son de corde pincée**
■ *verb* to make a twang: *He twanged his guitar; The wire twanged*. □ **pincer (les cordes de)**

tweak [twiːk] *verb* to pull with a sudden jerk. □ **tirer, tordre**
■ *noun* a sudden sharp pull: *He gave her nose a playful tweak*. □ **torsion**

tweed [twiːd] *noun, adjective* (of) a kind of woollen cloth with a rough surface: *His suit was (made of) tweed; a tweed jacket*. □ **(de) tweed**

tweezers ['twiːzəz] *noun plural* a tool for gripping or pulling hairs, small objects *etc*: *She used a pair of tweezers to pluck her eyebrows*. □ **pinces à épiler**

twelve [twelv] *noun* 1 the number or figure 12. □ **douze** 2 the age of 12. □ **douze ans**
■ *adjective* 1 12 in number. □ **douze**
2 aged 12. □ **de douze ans**
twelve- having twelve (of something): *a twelve-week delay*. □ **de douze (...)**
'twelfth [-fθ] *noun* 1 one of twelve equal parts. □ **douzième**
2 (*also adjective*) (the) last of twelve (people, things *etc*); (the) next after the eleventh. □ **douzième**
'twelve-year-old *noun* a person or animal who is twelve years old. □ **(individu, etc.) âgé de douze ans**
■ *adjective* (of a person, animal or thing) that is twelve years old. □ **de douze ans**

twenty ['twenti] *noun* 1 the number or figure 20. □ **vingt** 2 the age of 20. □ **vingt ans**
■ *adjective* 1 20 in number. □ **vingt**
2 aged 20. □ **de vingt ans**
'twenties *noun plural* 1 the period of time between one's twentieth and thirtieth birthdays. □ **vingtaine**
2 the range of temperatures between twenty and thirty

degrees. □ **température entre vingt et vingt-neuf degrés**
3 the period of time between the twentieth and thirtieth years of a century. □ **les années vingt**
'twentieth *noun* 1 one of twenty equal parts. □ **vingtième**
2 (*also adjective*) (the) last of twenty (people, things *etc*); (the) next after the nineteenth. □ **vingtième**
twenty- having twenty (of something). □ **à/de vingt (...)**
'twenty-year-old *noun* a person who is twenty years old. □ **(individu, etc.) âgé de vingt ans**
■ *adjective* (of a person or thing) twenty years old. □ **de vingt ans**

twice [twais] *adverb* 1 two times: *I've been to London twice*. □ **deux fois**
2 two times the amount of: *She has twice his courage*. □ **deux fois plus (de)**
3 two times as good *etc* as: *He is twice the man you are*. □ **deux fois mieux**
think twice about (doing) something to be very careful about considering (doing) something: *I wouldn't think twice about sacking him*. □ **y réfléchir à deux fois**

twiddle ['twidl] *verb* to twist (something) around and around: *She twiddled the knob on the radio*. □ **tripoter**

twig [twig] *noun* a small branch of a tree: *The ground was covered with broken twigs*. □ **brindille**

twilight ['twailait] *noun* 1 (the time of) the dim light just before the sun rises or just after it sets. □ **aube naissante; crépuscule**
2 the time when the full strength or power of something is decreasing: *in the twilight of his life*. □ **crépuscule, déclin**

twin [twin] *noun* 1 one of two children or animals born of the same mother at the same time: *She gave birth to twins; (also adjective) They have twin daughters*. □ **jumeau, elle**
2 one of two similar or identical things: *Her dress is the exact twin of mine*. □ **jumeau**

twine [twain] *noun* a strong kind of string made of twisted threads: *He tied the parcel with twine*. □ **ficelle**
■ *verb* (*negative* **untwine**) to twist: *The ivy twined around the tree*. □ **s'enrouler (autour de)**

twinge [twindʒ] *noun* a sudden sharp pain: *He felt a twinge (of pain) in his neck; a twinge of regret*. □ **élancement**

twinkle ['twiŋkl] *verb* 1 to shine with a small, slightly unsteady light: *The stars twinkled in the sky*. □ **scintiller**
2 (of eyes) to shine in this way *usually* to express amusement: *Her eyes twinkled mischievously*. □ **pétiller**
■ *noun* 1 an expression of amusement (in one's eyes). □ **pétillement**
2 the act of twinkling. □ **scintillement**

twirl [twɜːl] *verb* to (cause to) turn around (and around); to spin: *She twirled her hair around her finger*. □ **(faire) tourner, (se) tortiller**
■ *noun* an act of twirling. □ **tournoiement**

twist [twist] *verb* 1 to turn around (and around): *She twisted the knob; The road twisted through the mountains*. □ **tourner, (s')enrouler, (s')entortiller**

2 to wind around or together: *He twisted the pieces of string (together) to make a rope*. □ **tresser**

3 to force out of the correct shape or position: *The heat of the fire twisted the metal*; *He twisted her arm painfully*. □ **tordre**

■ *noun* 1 the act of twisting. □ **torsion**

2 a twisted piece of something: *She added a twist of lemon to her drink*. □ **tortillon**

3 a turn, coil *etc*: *There's a twist in the rope*. □ **tortillon**

4 a change in direction (of a story *etc*): *The story had a strange twist at the end*. □ **coup de théâtre**

'**twisted** *adjective* bent out of shape: *a twisted branch*; *a twisted report*. □ **tordu; déformé**

'**twister** *noun* a dishonest or deceiving person. □ **escroc**

twit [twit] *noun* a fool or idiot: *Stupid twit!* □ **crétin, ine**

twitch [twitʃ] *verb* 1 to (cause to) move jerkily: *His hands were twitching*. □ **donner, avoir un mouvement convulsif**

2 to give a little pull or jerk to (something): *She twitched my sleeve*. □ **tirer d'un coup sec**

■ *noun* a twitching movement. □ **coup sec**

twitter ['twitə] *noun* a light, repeated chirping sound, *especially* made by (small) birds: *She could hear the twitter of sparrows*. □ **pépiement**

■ *verb* to make such a noise. □ **pépier**

two [tuː] *noun* 1 the number or figure 2. □ **deux**

2 the age of 2. □ **deux ans**

■ *adjective* 1 2 in number. □ **deux**

2 aged 2. □ **de deux ans**

two- having two (of something): *a two-door car*. □ **à/ de deux (...)**

,**two-'faced** *adjective* deceitful: *a two-faced person*. □ **hypocrite**

,**two-'handed** *adjective*, *adverb* (to be used, played *etc*) with two hands: *a two-handed stroke*. □ **à deux mains**

twosome *noun* two people; a couple: *They usually travel in a twosome*. □ **paire, couple**

,**two-'way** *adjective* able to act, operate, be used *etc* in two ways or directions: *two-way traffic*; *a two-way radio*. □ **à deux sens, bilatéral**

'**two-year-old** *noun* a person or animal that is two years old. □ **(individu, etc.) âgé de deux ans**

■ *adjective* (of a person, animal or thing) that is two years old. □ **de deux ans**

in two (broken) in two pieces: *The magazine was torn in two*. □ **en deux**

tycoon [tai'kuːn] *noun* a rich and powerful businessman: *an oil tycoon*. □ **magnat**

tying *see* **tie**.

type¹ [taip] *noun* a kind, sort; variety: *What type of house would you prefer to live in?*; *They are marketing a new type of washing powder*. □ **type, sorte, genre**

type² [taip] *noun* 1 (a particular variety of) metal blocks with letters, numbers *etc* used in printing: *Can we have the headline printed in a different type?* □ **caractère**

2 printed letters, words *etc*: *I can't read the type – it's too small*. □ **caractères**

■ *verb* to write (something) using a typewriter: *Can you type?*; *I'm typing a letter*. □ **dactylographier**

'**typing, typewriting** *noun* writing produced by a typewriter: *fifty pages of typing*. □ **dactylographie**

'**typist** *noun* a person whose job is to type: *She works as a typist*; *He is a typist in a publishing firm*. □ **dactylo**

'**typewriter** *noun* a machine with keys for printing letters on a piece of paper: *a portable/an electric typewriter*. □ **machine à écrire**

typhoid (fever) ['taifoid] *noun* a dangerous type of infectious disease, caused by germs in food or drinking water: *He died of typhoid (fever)*. □ **(fièvre) typhoïde**

typhoon [tai'fuːn] *noun* a violent sea-storm occurring in the East: *They were caught in a typhoon in the China seas*. □ **typhon**

typhus ['taifəs] *noun* a dangerous type of infectious disease, spread by lice: *She is suffering from typhus*. □ **typhus**

typical ['tipikəl] *adjective* (*negative* **untypical**) having or showing the usual characteristics (of): *He is a typical Englishman*; *They're typical civil servants*. □ **typique**

'**typically** *adverb*. □ **typiquement**

typify ['tipifai] *verb* to be a very good example of: *Vandalism at football matches typifies the modern disregard for law and order*. □ **être caractéristique de**

typing, typist *see* **type²**.

tyrant ['taiərənt] *noun* a cruel and unjust ruler: *The people suffered under foreign tyrants*. □ **tyran**

tyrannical [ti'ranikəl], **tyrannous** ['tirənəs] *adjective* of or like a tyrant: *a tyrannical ruler*; *His actions were tyrannous*. □ **tyrannique**

ty'rannically, 'tyrannously *adverb*. □ **tyranniquement**

tyrannize, tyrannise ['ti-] *verb* to rule or treat (a person or people) cruelly and unjustly: *He tyrannizes his family*. □ **tyranniser**

'**tyranny** ['ti-] *noun* an action, or the method of ruling, of a tyrant: *People will always resist tyranny*. □ **tyrannie**

tzar *see* **tsar**.

Uu

u [juː]: **'U-turn** *noun* a turn, in the shape of the letter U, made by a motorist *etc* in order to reverse his or her direction. □ **demi-tour**

udder ['ʌdə] *noun* the bag-like part of a cow, goat *etc*, with teats that supply milk for their young or for humans: *The cow has a diseased udder.* □ **pis**

ugh! [əːx(x), ʌ(x)] *interjection* expressing disgust: *Ugh! The cat has been sick!* □ **pouah!**

ugly ['ʌgli] *adjective* **1** unpleasant to look at: *It is rather an ugly house.* □ **laid**
2 unpleasant, nasty or dangerous: *ugly black clouds*; *The crowd was in an ugly mood.* □ **menaçant**
'ugliness *noun.* □ **laideur**

ulcer ['ʌlsə] *noun* a kind of sore that does not heal easily, on the skin or inside the body: *a mouth/stomach ulcer.* □ **ulcère**

ultimate ['ʌltimət] *adjective* last or final. □ **ultime**
'ultimately *adverb* in the end: *We hope ultimately to be able to buy a house of our own.* □ **ultimement**

ultimatum [ʌlti'meitəm] – *plural* ,ulti'matums – *noun* a final demand made by one person, nation *etc* to another, with a threat to stop peaceful discussion and declare war *etc* if the demand is ignored: *An ultimatum has been issued to them to withdraw their troops from our territory.* □ **ultimatum**

ultra- [ʌltrə] **1** beyond, as in **ultraviolet.** □ **ultra-... ultraviolet**
2 very or excessively: *She's ultra-cautious when she drives a car.* □ **ultra-, hyper-**

ultrasonic [ʌltrə'sonik] *adjective* (of sound waves *etc*) beyond the range of human hearing: *ultrasonic vibrations.* □ **ultrasonique**

ultraviolet [ʌltrə'vaiəlit] *adjective* (of light) consisting of rays from the invisible part of the spectrum beyond the purple, that have an effect on the skin, *eg* causing suntan. □ **ultraviolet**

umbrella [ʌm'brelə] *noun* an apparatus for protecting a person from the rain, made of a folding covered framework attached to a stick with a handle: *Take an umbrella – it's going to rain.* □ **parapluie**

umpire ['ʌmpaiə] *noun* in cricket, tennis *etc*, a person who supervises a game, makes sure that it is played according to the rules, and decides doubtful points: *Tennis players usually have to accept the umpire's decision.* □ **arbitre**
■ *verb* to act as umpire: *Have you umpired a tennis match before?* □ **arbitrer**

unable [ʌn'eibl] *adjective* without enough strength, power, skill, opportunity, information *etc* to be able (to do something): *I am unable to get out of bed*; *I shall be unable to meet you for lunch today.* □ **incapable de**

unaccountable [ʌnə'kauntəbl] *adjective* that cannot be explained: *her unaccountable absence.* □ **inexplicable**
,**unac'countably** *adverb* in a way that cannot be explained: *He was unaccountably late/ill.* □ **inexplicablement**

unadulterated [ʌnə'dʌltəreitid] *adjective* pure, or not mixed with anything else: *a feeling of unadulterated hatred.* □ **pur**

unaffected [ʌnə'fektid] *adjective* **1** of (a person, his or her feelings *etc*) not moved or affected: *The child seemed unaffected by his father's death.* □ **indifférent (à)**
2 (of an arrangement *etc*) not altered: *It has been raining heavily, but this evening's football arrangements are unaffected.* □ **inchangé**

unafraid [ʌnə'freid] *adjective* not afraid. □ **sans peur**

unanimous [ju'nanimǝs] *adjective* having, or showing, complete agreement: *The whole school was unanimous in its approval of the headmaster's plan.* □ **unanime**
u'nanimously *adverb.* □ **à l'unanimité**
una'nimity [juːnə-] *noun* complete agreement: *Unanimity among politicians is rare.* □ **unanimité**

unarmed [ʌn'aːmd] *adjective* without weapons or other means of defence: *The gangster shot an unarmed policeman*; *Judo is a type of unarmed fighting.* □ **désarmé; sans armes**

unashamedly [ʌnə'ʃeimidli] *adverb* showing no shame or embarrassment: *They were weeping unashamedly.* □ **sans honte**

unattached [ʌnə'tatʃt] *adjective* not married or engaged to be married: *Some people gives up hope of marriage if they are still unattached at the age of thirty.* □ **sans attache**

unattended [ʌnə'tendid] *adjective* not under the care or supervision of anybody: *It is dangerous to leave small children unattended in the house.* □ **sans surveillance**

unauthorized, unauthorised [ʌn'oːθəraizd] *adjective* not having the permission of the people in authority: *unauthorized use of the firm's equipment.* □ **non autorisé**

unaware [ʌnə'weə] *adjective* not aware or not knowing: *I was unaware of the man's presence.* □ **ignorant de, inconscient de**
take (someone) unawares to surprise or startle (someone): *He came into the room so quietly that he took me unawares.* □ **prendre qqn à l'improviste**

unbalanced [ʌn'balənst] *adjective* **1** without the proper amount of attention being given to everything: *If we don't hear both sides of the argument, we'll get an unbalanced view of the situation.* □ **mal équilibré**
2 disordered in the mind; not quite sane: *The murderer was completely unbalanced.* □ **déséquilibré**

unbar [ʌn'baː] – *past tense, past participle* **un'barred** – *verb* to open (a door, gate, entrance *etc*) by moving the bars that are keeping it closed: *She unlocked and unbarred the door.* □ **débarrer**

unbearable [ʌn'beərəbl] *adjective* too painful, unpleasant *etc* to bear or to tolerate: *I am suffering from unbearable toothache.* □ **insupportable, insoutenable**
un'bearably *adverb*: *unbearably painful*; *unbearably rude.* □ **insupportablement**

unbelievable [ʌnbi'liːvəbl] *adjective* too bad, good *etc* to be believed in: *unbelievable rudeness*; *Her good luck is unbelievable!* □ **incroyable**
,**unbe'lievably** *adverb.* □ **incroyablement**

unbolt [ʌn'boult] *verb* to open the bolt of (*eg* a door): *The shopkeeper unbolted the door and let the custom-*

ers enter. □ **déverrouiller**

unborn [ʌn'bɔːn] *adjective* (of a baby) still in the mother's womb: *When she was involved in a car accident the doctor was worried in case her unborn baby had been injured.* □ **à naître**

unbreakable [ʌnbreikəbl] *adjective* being unable to be smashed, splintered or divided up into smaller parts: *The child had unbreakable toys that could be dropped without being damaged.* □ **incassable**

unbuckle [ʌn'bʌkl] *verb* to undo the buckle or buckles of: *He unbuckled his belt.* □ **déboucler**

unbutton [ʌn'bʌtn] *verb* to unfasten the buttons of: *She unbuttoned her coat.* □ **déboutonner**

uncalled for [ʌn'kɔːldfɔː] *adjective* (of actions, remarks *etc*) unnecessary and *usually* rude: *Some of her comments are a bit uncalled for.* □ **déplacé**

uncanny [ʌn'kani] *adjective* strange or mysterious: *She looks so like her sister that it's quite uncanny.* □ **mystérieux**

un'cannily *adverb*. □ **mystérieusement**

unceasing [ʌn'siːsiŋ] *adjective* never stopping: *his unceasing efforts to help the sick and wounded.* □ **incessant**

un'ceasingly *adverb*. □ **sans cesse**

uncertain [ʌn'səːtn] *adjective* 1 (of a person) not sure; not definitely knowing: *I'm uncertain of my future plans*; *The government is uncertain what is the best thing to do.* □ **incertain (de)**

2 not definitely known or settled: *My plans are still uncertain*; *The uncertain weather delayed our departure.* □ **incertain**

un'certainly *adverb*. □ **d'une manière hésitante**

uncivil [ʌn'sivl] *adjective* rude: *He apologized for being uncivil to her.* □ **impoli (envers)**

un'civilly *adverb*. □ **impoliment**

uncle ['ʌŋkl] *noun* the brother of a person's father or mother, or the husband of an aunt: *He's my uncle*; *Hallo, Uncle Jim!* □ **oncle**

unclean [ʌn'kliːn] *adjective* (*eg* of food) not pure: *The Jews are not allowed to eat pork, as pigs are considered unclean.* □ **impur**

uncoil [ʌn'koil] *verb* to straighten from a coiled position: *The snake uncoiled (itself).* □ **(se) dérouler**

uncomfortable [ʌn'kʌmfətəbl] *adjective* 1 not relaxed: *He looked uncomfortable when she mentioned the subject.* □ **mal à l'aise**

2 producing a bad physical feeling: *That's a very uncomfortable chair.* □ **inconfortable**

un'comfortably *adverb*. □ **inconfortablement**

uncommon [ʌn'komən] *adjective* rare; unusual: *This type of animal is becoming very uncommon.* □ **rare**

un'commonly *adverb* very; unusually: *an uncommonly clever person.* □ **singulièrement**

uncompromising [ʌn'komprəmaiziŋ] *adjective* keeping firmly to a particular attitude, policy *etc*: *You should not adopt such an uncompromising attitude.* □ **intransigeant**

unconcern [ʌnkən'səːn] *noun* lack of interest or anxiety: *He received the news of his failure with apparent unconcern.* □ **indifférence**

,**uncon'cerned** *adjective*. □ **indifférent**

'**uncon,cernedly** [-nid-] *adverb*. □ **d'un air indifférent**

unconditional [ʌnkən'diʃənl] *adjective* complete and absolute, and not dependent on certain terms or conditions: *The victorious side demanded unconditional surrender.* □ **inconditionnel**

,**uncon'ditionally** *adverb*. □ **inconditionnellement**

unconfirmed [ʌnkən'fɔːmd] *adjective* not yet shown or proved to be true: *There are unconfirmed reports of another earthquake in China.* □ **non confirmé**

unconscious [ʌn'konʃəs] *adjective* 1 senseless or stunned, *eg* because of an accident: *She was unconscious for three days after the crash.* □ **inconscient**

2 not aware: *He was unconscious of having said anything rude.* □ **inconscient (de)**

3 unintentional: *Her prejudice is quite unconscious.* □ **inconscient**

■ *noun* the deepest level of the mind, the processes of which are revealed only through *eg* psychoanalysis: *the secrets of the unconscious.* □ **inconscient**

un'consciously *adverb* unintentionally, or without being aware: *She unconsciously addressed me by the wrong name.* □ **inconsciemment**

un'consciousness *noun*. □ **inconscience; perte de connaissance**

uncover [ʌn'kʌvə] *verb* to remove the cover from: *His criminal activities were finally uncovered.* □ **découvrir**

uncurl [ʌn'kəːl] *verb* to straighten from a curled position: *The hedgehog slowly uncurled (itself).* □ **(se) dérouler**

uncut [ʌn'kʌt] *adjective* 1 (of a book, film *etc*) not shortened. □ **sans coupures**

2 (of a diamond *etc*) not yet cut into shape for using in jewellery *etc*. □ **non taillé**

undaunted [ʌn'dɔːntid] *adjective* fearless; not discouraged: *He was undaunted by his failure.* □ **intrépide, nullement ébranlé par**

undecided [ʌndi'saidid] *adjective* 1 (of a person) unable to make a decision about something. □ **indécis**

2 (of a matter) not settled: *The date of the meeting is still undecided.* □ **en suspens**

under ['ʌndə] *preposition* 1 in or to a position lower than, or covered by: *Your pencil is under the chair*; *Strange plants grow under the sea.* □ **sous, au-dessous (de)**

2 less than, or lower in rank than: *Children under five should not cross the street alone*; *You can do the job in under an hour.* □ **(de) moins de**

3 subject to the authority of: *As a foreman, he has about fifty workers under him.* □ **sous les ordres (de)**

4 used to express various states: *The fort was under attack*; *The business improved under the new management*; *The matter is under consideration/discussion.* □ **sous, en**

■ *adverb* in or to a lower position, rank *etc*: *The swimmer surfaced and went under again*; *children aged seven and under.* □ **sous, au-dessous (de)**

under- 1 beneath, as in **underline**. □ **sous-... souligner**

2 too little, as in **underpay**. □ **sous-... sous-payer**

3 lower in rank: *the under-manager.* □ **sous-... sous-directeur**

4 less in age than: *a nursery for under-fives* (= children aged four and under). □ **de moins de**

undercarriage [ˈʌndəkaridʒ] *noun* the landing-gear of an aircraft: *The pilot had some difficulty in lowering the undercarriage.* □ **train d'atterrissage**

underclothes [ˈʌndəklouz] *noun plural* underwear: *Have you packed my underclothes?* □ **sous-vêtements**
'underclothing *noun* underclothes. □ **sous-vêtements**

undercover [ˈʌndəˈkʌvə] *adjective* working or done in secret: *She is an undercover agent for the Americans.* □ **clandestin**

undercut [ʌndəˈkʌt] – *past tense, past participle* ˌunderˈcut – *verb* to sell goods *etc* at a lower price than (a competitor): *Japanese car-exporters are able to undercut British automobile manufacturers.* □ **vendre moins cher que**

underdog [ˈʌndədog] *noun* a weak person who is dominated by someone else, or who is the loser in a struggle: *He always likes to help the underdog.* □ **perdant, ante; défavorisé, ée**

underestimate [ʌndərˈestimeit] *verb* to estimate (a person, a thing *etc*) at less than his, or her or its real amount, value, strength *etc*: *Never underestimate your opponent!* □ **sous-estimer**

underfed [ʌndəˈfed] *adjective* not given enough to eat: *That child looks underfed.* □ **sous-alimenté**

underfoot [ʌndəˈfut] *adjective* on the ground under the feet of anyone walking: *It is not actually raining just now but it is very wet underfoot.* □ **par terre**

undergarment [ˈʌndəgɑːmənt] *noun* an article of clothing worn under the outer clothes. □ **sous-vêtement**

undergo [ʌndəˈgou] – *past tense* ˌunderˈwent [-ˈwent] – *past participle* ˌunderˈgone [-ˈgon] – *verb* **1** to experience or endure: *They underwent terrible hardships.* □ **subir**
2 to go through (a process): *The car is undergoing tests/repairs*; *She has been undergoing medical treatment.* □ **subir**

undergraduate [ʌndəˈgradjuət] *noun* a student who is studying for his or her first degree. □ **étudiant, ante du premier cycle (universitaire)**

underground [ʌndəˈgraund] *adjective* below the surface of the ground: *underground railways*; *underground streams.* □ **souterrain**
■ *adverb* **1** (to a position) under the surface of the ground: *Rabbits live underground.* □ **sous (la) terre**
2 into hiding: *He will go underground if the police start looking for him.* □ **dans la clandestinité**
■ [ˈʌndəgraund] *noun* (ˈsubway) an underground railway: *She hates travelling by/on the underground.* □ **métro**

undergrowth [ˈʌndəgrouθ] *noun* low bushes or large plants growing among trees: *She tripped over in the thick undergrowth.* □ **sous-bois**

underline [ʌndəˈlain] *verb* **1** to draw a line under: *He wrote down the title of his essay and underlined it.* □ **souligner**
2 to emphasize or stress: *In her speech she underlined several points.* □ **souligner**

undermine [ʌndəˈmain] *verb* **1** to make (*eg* a building)

insecure by digging away or destroying the base or foundations: *The road was being undermined by a stream.* □ **miner**
2 to weaken (*eg* a person's health or authority): *Constant hard work had undermined her health.* □ **miner**

underneath [ʌndəˈniːθ] *preposition, adverb* at or to a lower position (than); beneath: *She was standing underneath the light*; *Have you looked underneath the bed?* □ **sous, au-dessous de**
■ *noun* the part or side beneath: *Have you ever seen the underneath of a bus?* □ **dessous**

undernourished [ʌndəˈnʌriʃt] *adjective* suffering from lack of food or nourishment. □ **sous-alimenté**

underpay *see* **underpay**.

underpants [ˈʌndəpants] *noun plural* a short undergarment worn (*usually* by men) over the buttocks: *a clean pair of underpants.* □ **caleçon**

underpay [ʌndəˈpei] – *past tense, past participle* ˌunderˈpaid – *verb* to pay (a person) too little: *They claim that they are underpaid and overworked.* □ **sous-payer**

underrate [ʌndəˈreit] *verb* to underestimate. □ **sous-estimer**

undersell [ʌndəˈsel] – *past tense, past participle* ˌunderˈsold [-ˈsould] – *verb* to sell goods at a lower price than (a competitor). □ **vendre moins cher que**

underside [ˈʌndəsaid] *noun* the lower surface; the part or side lying beneath. □ **dessous**

undersold *see* **undersell**.

understand [ʌndəˈstand] – *past tense, past participle* ˌunderˈstood [-ˈstud] – *verb* **1** to see or know the meaning of (something): *I can't understand her absence*; *Speak slowly to foreigners so that they'll understand you.* □ **comprendre**
2 to know (*eg* a person) thoroughly: *She understands children/dogs.* □ **comprendre**
3 to learn or realize (something), *eg* from information received: *At first I didn't understand how ill she was*; *I understood that you were planning to leave today.* □ **comprendre**
ˌunderˈstandable *adjective* that can be understood: *His anger is quite understandable.* □ **compréhensible**
ˌunderˈstanding *adjective* (of a person) good at knowing how other people feel; sympathetic: *an understanding person; Try to be more understanding!* □ **compréhensif**
■ *noun* **1** the power of thinking clearly: *a man of great understanding.* □ **intelligence**
2 the ability to sympathize with another person's feelings: *His kindness and understanding were a great comfort to her.* □ **compréhension**
3 a (state of) informal agreement: *The two men have come to/reached an understanding after their disagreement.* □ **entente**
make (oneself) understood to make one's meaning or intentions clear: *He tried speaking German to them, but couldn't make himself understood.* □ **se faire comprendre**

understate [ʌndəˈsteit] *verb* to state less than the truth about (something): *She has understated her difficulties.*

□ **minimiser**

,under'statement noun: It's an understatement to say he's foolish – he's quite mad. □ **affirmation en dessous de la vérité**

understood see **understand**.

understudy ['ʌndəstʌdi] verb to study (a part in a play, opera etc) so as to be able to take the place of (another actor, singer etc). □ **doubler**

■ noun – plural **'understudies** – a person who understudies: He was ill, so his understudy had to take the part. □ **doublure**

undertake [ʌndə'teik] – past tense **,under'took** [-'tuk], past participle **,under'taken** – verb 1 to accept (a duty, task, responsibility etc): She undertook the job willingly. □ **se charger de**

2 to promise (eg to do something): He has undertaken to appear at the police court tomorrow. □ **promettre**
'undertaker [-teikə] noun a person who organizes funerals. □ **entrepreneur, eure de pompes funèbres**
,under'taking noun 1 a task or piece of work: I didn't realize what a large undertaking this job would be. □ **entreprise**

2 a promise: He made an undertaking that he would pay the money back. □ **promesse**

undertook see **undertake**.

undertow [ʌndə:tou] noun a pull under the water caused by a current running swiftly in an opposite direction; the flow of water out toward the sea when a wave breaks on the beach: There is a strong undertow at the pier and several people have drowned trying to swim back to shore. □ **ressac**

underwear ['ʌndəweə] noun clothes worn under the outer clothes: She washed her skirt, blouse and underwear. □ **sous-vêtements**

underwent see **undergo**.

underworld ['ʌndəwə:ld] noun the part of the population that gets its living from crime etc: A member of the underworld told the police where the murderer was hiding. □ **pègre**

undesirable [ʌndi'zairəbl] adjective 1 not wanted: These pills can have some undesirable effects. □ **non souhaité**
2 unpleasant or objectionable: his undesirable friends; undesirable behaviour/habits. □ **indésirable**

undid see **undo**.

undivided [ʌndi'vaidid] adjective (of attention etc) not distracted; wholly concentrated: Please give the matter your undivided attention. □ **tout, entier**

undo [ʌn'du:] – past tense **un'did** [-'did]; past participle **un'done** [-'dʌn] – verb 1 to unfasten or untie: Could you undo the knot in this string? □ **défaire**
2 to reverse, or destroy, the effect of: The evil that he did can never be undone. □ **(se) défaire**
un'doing noun (the cause of) ruin or disaster: Gambling was her undoing. □ **perte**
un'done [-'dʌn] adjective (of work, a task etc) not done, or not finished: I don't like going to bed leaving jobs/work undone. □ **pas fait; inachevé**

undoubted [ʌn'dautid] adjective not doubted or denied: the undoubted excellence of the work. □ **indubitable**
un'doubtedly adverb definitely: 'Is he mistaken?' 'Undoubtedly!' □ **indubitablement**

undress [ʌn'dres] verb 1 to take the clothes off (a person): She undressed the child; Undress yourself and get into bed. □ **déshabiller**
2 to undress oneself: I undressed and went to bed. □ **se déshabiller**

undue [ʌn'dju:] adjective too great; more than is necessary: You show undue caution in distrusting him. □ **indu**
un'duly adverb: You were unduly severe with the child. □ **indûment**

unearth [ʌn'ə:θ] verb to discover (something) or remove it from a place where it is put away or hidden: During his studies, he unearthed several new facts about the history of the place. □ **déterrer, dénicher**

unearthly [ʌn'ə:θli] adjective 1 supernatural, mysterious or frightening: an unearthly sight. □ **surnaturel**
2 outrageous or unreasonable: He telephoned at the unearthly (= very early) hour of 6:30. □ **indu**

uneasy [ʌn'i:zi] adjective 1 (of a person or a situation etc) troubled, anxious or unsettled: When her son did not return, she grew uneasy. □ **inquiet**
2 nervous or shy about something: Ruth was always a bit uneasy at parties and found it hard to think of anything to say. □ **gêné**
un'ease noun uneasiness. □ **inquiétude**
un'easily adverb in an uneasy or embarrassed way: He glanced uneasily at her. □ **avec inquiétude; timidement**
un'easiness noun the state of being uneasy: I could not understand her apparent uneasiness. □ **inquiétude**

unemployed [ʌnim'ploid] adjective not having, or not able to find, work: She has been unemployed for three months. □ **au chômage**
■ noun plural people who are unemployed: The numbers of (the) unemployed are still increasing. □ **chômeurs, euses**
,unem'ployment noun 1 the state of being unemployed: If the factory is closed, many workers will face unemployment. □ **chômage**
2 the numbers of people without work: Unemployment has reached record figures this year. □ **chômage**

unending [ʌn'endiŋ] adjective never finishing: their unending struggle for survival. □ **sans fin**

unequal [ʌn'i:kwəl] adjective not equal in quantity, quality etc: They got unequal shares of/an unequal share in the money. □ **inégal**
un'equally adverb. □ **inégalement**

unerring [ʌn'ə:riŋ] adjective (always) accurate: She threw the spear with unerring aim. □ **infaillible**
un'erringly adverb. □ **infailliblement**

uneven [ʌn'i:vn] adjective 1 not even: The road surface here is very uneven. □ **inégal**
2 (of work etc) not all of the same quality: His work is very uneven. □ **inégal**
un'evenness noun. □ **inégalité**
un'evenly adverb in an uneven or unequal way: The teams are unevenly matched. □ **inégalement**

unexpected [ʌnik'spektid] adjective not expected, eg because sudden: Her promotion was quite unexpected. □ **inattendu**
unexpectedly adverb. □ **à l'improviste**

unfailing [ʌn'feiliŋ] *adjective* constant: *Her unfailing courage inspired us all.* □ **sans défaillance**
un'failingly *adverb* constantly: *She is unfailingly polite.* □ **infailliblement**
unfair [ʌn'feə] *adjective* not fair or just: *He has received unfair treatment.* □ **injuste**
un'fairly *adverb.* □ **injustement**
un'fairness *noun.* □ **injustice**
unfaithful [ʌn'feiθful] *adjective* not loyal and true. □ **infidèle**
unfamiliar [ʌnfə'miljə] *adjective* 1 not well-known: *He felt nervous about walking along unfamiliar streets.* □ **inconnu**
2 not knowing about: *I am unfamiliar with the plays of Shakespeare.* □ **qui ne connaît pas (bien)**
unfa'miliarly *adverb.* □ **d'une manière peu connue**
unfamili'arity *noun.* □ **aspect étrange**
unfasten [ʌn'faːsn] *verb* to undo (something that is fastened): *He unfastened (the buttons of) his jacket.* □ **détacher**
unfit [ʌn'fit] *adjective* 1 not good enough; not in a suitable state: *She has been ill and is quite unfit to travel.* □ **inapte (à)**
2 (of a person, dog, horse *etc*) not as strong and healthy as is possible: *You become unfit if you don't take regular exercise.* □ **pas en forme**
un'fitness *noun.* □ **mauvaise santé; inaptitude**
unflagging [ʌn'flagiŋ] *adjective* not tiring or losing vigour: *her unflagging energy.* □ **inépuisable**
unflappable [ʌn'flapəbl] *adjective* able to remain calm in a crisis. □ **imperturbable**
unflinching [ʌn'flintʃiŋ] *adjective* not yielding *etc* because of pain, danger, difficulty *etc*: *her unflinching courage/determination.* □ **résolu**
un'flinchingly *adverb.* □ **résolument**
unfold [ʌn'fould] *verb* 1 to open and spread out (a map *etc*): *He sat down and unfolded his newspaper.* □ **déplier**
2 to (cause to) be revealed or become known: *She gradually unfolded her plan to them.* □ **révéler**
unforgettable [ʌnfə'getəbl] *adjective* never able to be forgotten: *The experience was unforgettable.* □ **inoubliable**
,unfor'gettably *adverb.* □ **d'une manière inoubliable**
unfortunate [ʌn'foːtʃənət] *adjective* 1 unlucky: *She has been very unfortunate.* □ **malchanceux**
2 regrettable: *He has an unfortunate habit of giggling all the time.* □ **regrettable**
un'fortunately *adverb: I'd like to help but unfortunately I can't.* □ **malheureusement**
unfounded [ʌn'faundid] *adjective* not based on facts or reality: *The rumours are completely unfounded.* □ **sans fondement**
ungainly [ʌn'geinli] *adjective* awkward, clumsy or ungraceful: *They are rather large and ungainly.* □ **gauche**
un'gainliness *noun.* □ **gaucherie**
ungracious [ʌn'greiʃəs] *adjective* rude; impolite: *It was rather ungracious of you to refuse his invitation.* □ **impoli**
un'graciously *adverb.* □ **avec mauvaise grâce**

ungrateful [ʌn'greitful] *adjective* not showing thanks for kindness: *It will look very ungrateful if you don't write and thank him.* □ **ingrat**
unguarded [ʌn'gaːdid] *adjective* 1 without protection: *The castle gate was never left unguarded.* □ **sans surveillance**
2 careless: *an unguarded remark.* □ **imprudent**
unhappy [ʌn'hapi] *adjective* 1 sad or miserable: *He had an unhappy childhood.* □ **malheureux**
2 regrettable: *He has an unhappy knack of always saying the wrong thing.* □ **fâcheux**
un'happiness *noun.* □ **peine**
un'happily *adverb* 1 in a sad or miserable way: *He stared unhappily at her angry face.* □ **tristement**
2 unfortunately: *Unhappily, I shan't be able to see you tomorrow.* □ **malheureusement**
unharmed [ʌn'haːmd] *adverb* not injured; not damaged: *Jaleel was in a terrible accident, yet he walked away unharmed without so much as a scratch.* □ **indemne**
unhealthy [ʌn'helθi] *adjective* 1 not healthy: *He is fat and unhealthy – he doesn't take enough exercise.* □ **en mauvaise santé**
2 dangerous: *The situation was getting unhealthy.* □ **malsain; dangereux**
3 unwholesome or mentally, emotionally or psychologically sick: *The coach showed an unhealthy interest in young boys.* □ **insalubre; malsain**
un'healthily *adverb.* □ **de façon maladive, malsaine**
un'healthiness *noun.* □ **mauvaise santé; caractère malsain**
unholy [ʌn'houli] *adjective* 1 disrespectful or irreverent: *shrieks of unholy laughter.* □ **irrespectueux**
2 outrageous or unreasonable: *an unholy din.* □ **indu**
unhook [ʌn'huk] *verb* to take or release (something) from a hook: *She unhooked the picture from the wall.* □ **décrocher (de)**
unhoped for [ʌnhoupd four] *adjective* not expected; not planned for or anticipated: *Winning the lottery was an unhoped for piece of luck before our trip.* □ **inespéré**
unicorn ['juːnikoːn] *noun* in mythology, an animal like a horse, but with one straight horn on the forehead. □ **licorne**
unidentified [ʌnai'dentifaid] *adjective* not identified: *an unidentified victim.* □ **non identifié**
unidentified flying object (*often abbreviated to* **UFO** [juːef'ou, 'juːfou]) an object from outer space, *eg* a flying saucer. □ **objet volant non identifié (O.V.N.I.)**
unification *see* **unify**.
uniform ['juːnifoːm] *adjective* the same always or everywhere; not changing or varying: *The sky was a uniform grey.* □ **uniforme**
■ *noun* (a set of) clothes worn by *eg* soldiers, children at a particular school *etc*: *Full uniform must be worn; The new uniforms will arrive tomorrow.* □ **uniforme**
'uniformed *adjective* (*eg* of police) wearing a uniform, not plain clothes. □ **en uniforme**
,uni'formity *noun* the condition of being uniform: *The houses in the street had no uniformity of appearance.* □ **uniformité**
'uniformly *adverb* in a uniform way: *The essays were*

uniformly dull. □ **uniformément**

unify ['juːnifai] *verb* to combine into a single whole: *The country consisted of several small states and was unified only recently.* □ **unifier**

,unifi'cation [-fi-] *noun.* □ **unification**

uninhibited [ʌnin'hibitid] *adjective* expressing feelings *etc* freely and without embarrassment: *uninhibited people/behaviour.* □ **sans inhibitions**

unintelligible [ʌnin'teliʒəbl] *adjective* not able to be understood: *unintelligible writing/words.* □ **inintelligible**

uninterested [ʌn'intristid] *adjective* not having or showing any interest: *I told him the news but he seemed uninterested.* □ **indifférent**

uninterrupted [ʌnintə'rʌptid] *adjective* **1** continuing without pause: *four hours of uninterrupted rain.* □ **ininterrompu**

2 (of a view) not blocked by anything: *We have an uninterrupted view of the sea.* □ **ininterrompu**

uninvited [ʌnin'vaitid] *adjective* **1** without an invitation: *uninvited guests.* □ **non invité**

2 not required or encouraged: *his uninvited interference.* □ **importun**

union ['juːnjən] *noun* **1** the act of uniting or process of being united: *Union between the two countries would be impossible.* □ **union**

2 the state of being united, *eg* in marriage, friendship *etc*: *Their marriage was a perfect union.* □ **union**

3 states, countries *etc* forming a single political group: *The Union of Soviet Socialist Republics.* □ **union**

4 a club or association: *trade unions.* □ **syndicat**

Union Jack (*usually with* **the**) the national flag of the United Kingdom. □ **Union Jack**

unique [juː'niːk] *adjective* being the only one of its kind, or having no equal: *Her style is unique.* □ **unique**

unisex ['juːniseks] *adjective* (of clothes *etc*) in a style that can be worn by both men and women: *unisex clothes; a unisex hairstyle.* □ **unisexe**

unison ['juːnisn] *noun* **1** an identical musical note, or series of notes, produced by several voices singing, or instruments playing, together: *They sang in unison.* □ **unisson**

2 agreement: *They acted in unison.* □ **(à l')unisson**

unit ['juːnit] *noun* **1** a single thing, individual *etc* within a group: *The building is divided into twelve different apartments or living units.* □ **unité**

2 an amount or quantity that is used as a standard in a system of measuring or coinage: *The dollar is the standard unit of currency in America.* □ **unité**

3 the smallest whole number, 1, or any number between 1 and 9: *In the number 23, 2 is a ten, and 3 is a unit.* □ **unité**

unite [ju'nait] *verb* **1** to join together, or to make or become one: *England and Scotland were united under one parliament in 1707; He was united with his friends again.* □ **(s')unir; (s')unifier**

2 to act together: *Let us unite against the common enemy.* □ **s'unir**

u'nited *adjective* **1** joined into a political whole: *the United States of America.* □ **uni**

2 joined together by love, friendship *etc*: *They're a very united pair/family.* □ **uni**

3 made as a result of several people *etc* working together for a common purpose: *Let us make a united effort to make our business successful.* □ **conjugué**

unity ['juːnəti] *– plural* **'unities** *– noun* **1** the state of being united or in agreement: *When will men learn to live in unity with each other?* □ **unité**

2 singleness, or the state of being one complete whole: *Unity of design in his pictures is this artist's main aim.* □ **unité**

3 something arranged to form a single complete whole: *This play is not a unity, but a series of unconnected scenes.* □ **unité**

universe ['juːnivɔːs] *noun* everything – earth, planets, sun, stars *etc* – that exists anywhere: *Somewhere in the universe there must be another world like ours.* □ **univers**

,uni'versal *adjective* affecting, including *etc* the whole of the world or all or most people: *English may become a universal language that everyone can learn and use.* □ **universel**

,uni'versally *adverb.* □ **universellement**

,univer'sality [-'sa-] *noun.* □ **universalité**

university [juːni'vɔːsəti] *– plural* **uni'versities** *– noun* (the buildings or colleges of) a centre of advanced education and research, that has the power to grant degrees: *He'll have four years at university after he leaves school*; (*also adjective*) *a university student.* □ **(d')université; universitaire**

unjust [ʌn'dʒʌst] *adjective* not just; unfair: *Your suspicions are unjust.* □ **injuste**

unkind [ʌn'kaind] *adjective* cruel or harsh: *You were very unkind to her.* □ **méchant**

unknowingly [ʌn'nouiŋli] *adverb* without being aware: *She had unknowingly given the patient the wrong medicine.* □ **inconsciemment**

un'known *adjective* **1** not known: *her unknown helper.* □ **inconnu**

2 not famous; not well-known: *That actor was almost unknown before he played that part.* □ **inconnu**

unless [ən'les] *conjunction* **1** if not: *Don't come unless I telephone.* □ **à moins que**

2 except when: *The directors have a meeting every Friday, unless there is nothing to discuss.* □ **à moins que**

unlike [ʌn'laik] *adjective* **1** different (from): *I never saw twins who were so unlike (each other); Unlike poles of a magnet attract each other.* □ **différent**

2 not typical or characteristic of: *It is unlike Mary to be so silly.* □ **qui ne ressemble pas à**

unlikely [ʌn'laikli] *adjective* not likely or probable: *an unlikely explanation for his absence; She's unlikely to arrive before 19:00; It is unlikely that she will come.* □ **improbable**

unload [ʌn'loud] *verb* to remove (cargo) from (*eg* a ship, vehicle *etc*): *The men were unloading the ship.* □ **décharger**

unlock [ʌn'lok] *verb* to open (something locked): *Unlock this door, please!* □ **ouvrir, déverrouiller**

unlucky [ʌn'lʌki] *adjective* not lucky or fortunate: *I am* *unlucky – I never win at cards.* □ **malchanceux**

un'luckily *adverb* unfortunately: *Unluckily he has hurt his hand and cannot play the piano.* □ **malheureusement**

unmanned [ʌn'mand] *adjective* (of *eg* an aircraft or spacecraft) automatically controlled and therefore without a crew: *unmanned flights to Mars.* □ **inhabité**

unmistakable [ʌnmi'steikəbl] *adjective* very clear; impossible to mistake: *Her meaning was unmistakable.* □ **clair; indubitable**

unmoved [ʌn'muːvd] *adjective* not affected or moved in feelings, determination *etc*: *He was unmoved by her tears.* □ **insensible**

unnatural [ʌn'natʃərəl] *adjective* strange or queer: *an unnatural silence.* □ **anormal**

un'naturally *adverb.* □ **anormalement**

unnecessary [ʌn'nesəsəri] *adjective* **1** not necessary: *It is unnecessary to waken her yet.* □ **inutile**

2 that might have been avoided: *Your mistake caused a lot of unnecessary work in the office.* □ **inutile**

un,neces'sarily *adverb*: *He was unnecessarily rude.* □ **inutilement**

unobtrusive [ʌnəb'truːsiv] *adjective* not too obvious or noticeable: *She is quiet and unobtrusive.* □ **discret**

,unob'trusively *adverb*: *unobtrusively dressed.* □ **discrètement**

unoccupied [ʌn'okjupaid] *adjective* **1** empty or vacant: *The room/seat was unoccupied.* □ **inoccupé**

2 not busy: *I paint in my unoccupied hours/when I'm otherwise unoccupied.* □ **libre**

unpack [ʌn'pak] *verb* **1** to take out (things that are packed): *He unpacked his clothes.* □ **dépaqueter**

2 to take (clothes *etc*) out of (a case *etc*): *Have you unpacked (your case)?* □ **défaire**

unpick [ʌn'pik] *verb* to take out stitches from (something sewn or knitted): *She unpicked the seam of the dress.* □ **découdre**

unpleasant [ʌn'pleznt] *adjective* disagreeable: *an unpleasant task/smell.* □ **désagréable**

un'pleasantly *adverb.* □ **désagréablement**

unplug [ʌn'plʌg] *– past tense, past participle* un'plugged *– verb* **1** to take the plug out of. □ **déboucher**

2 to disconnect from the electricity supply: *He unplugged the television.* □ **débrancher**

unpopular [ʌn'popjulə] *adjective* generally disliked: *an unpopular person/law; He was unpopular at school.* □ **impopulaire**

un,popu'larity [-'la-] *noun.* □ **impopularité**

unpractical [ʌn'praktikəl] *adjective* (of a person) not good at practical tasks: *They're so unpractical that they can't even change an electric plug.* □ **qui n'a pas l'esprit pratique**

unprecedented [ʌn'presidəntid] *adjective* never known to have happened before: *Such an action by a prime minister is unprecedented.* □ **sans précédent, inouï**

unprofessional [ʌnprə'feʃənl] *adjective* **1** (of a person's conduct) not according to the (*usually* high) standards required in his or her profession: *The doctor was dismissed from his post for unprofessional conduct.* □ **contraire au code professionnel**

2 (of a piece of work *etc*) not done with the skill of a trained person: *This repair looks a bit unprofessional.* □ **d'amateur**

unpublished [ʌnp̩ʌbliʃd] *adjective* not in printed form such as a book or magazine for the public to buy: *Although no one had bought the manuscript, Gary's unpublished writing was just as good as his published book.* □ **inédit**

unqualified [ʌn'kwolifaid] *adjective* **1** not having the necessary qualifications (*eg* for a job): *unqualified teachers/nurses; He is unqualified for the job.* □ **non qualifié**

2 complete; without limits: *She deserves our unqualified praise.* □ **sans réserve**

unquestionable [ʌn'kwestʃənəbl] *adjective* that cannot be doubted; completely certain: *unquestionable proof.* □ **incontestablement**

un'questionably *adverb* certainly: *Unquestionably, he deserves to be punished.* □ **indiscutablement**

un'questioning *adjective* (done *etc*) without any disagreement or protest: *unquestioning obedience/belief.* □ **inconditionnel**

unravel [ʌn'ravəl] *– past tense* un'ravelled, un'raveled *– verb* **1** to take (*eg* string, thread *etc*) out of its tangled condition; to disentangle: *She could not unravel the tangled thread.* □ **démêler**

2 (*especially* of a knitted fabric) to undo or become undone: *My knitting (got) unravelled when it fell off the needles.* □ **(se) défaire**

3 to solve (a problem, mystery *etc*): *Is there no-one who can unravel this mystery?* □ **dénouer**

unreal [ʌn'riəl] *adjective* not existing in fact: *He lives in an unreal world imagined by himself.* □ **irréel**

,unre'ality [ʌnri'a-] *noun.* □ **irréalité**

unreasonable [ʌn'riːzənəbl] *adjective* **1** not guided by good sense or reason: *It is unreasonable to expect children to work so hard.* □ **déraisonnable**

2 excessive, or too great: *That butcher charges unreasonable prices.* □ **excessif**

unreserved [ʌnri'zəːvd] *adjective* **1** (of a seat *etc*) not reserved: *These seats are unreserved.* □ **non réservé**

2 complete: *The committee gave her suggestion unreserved approval.* □ **sans réserve**

3 frank: *She had a cheerful, unreserved nature.* □ **ouvert**

,unre'servedly [-vid-] *adverb* **1** completely; utterly: *We are unreservedly delighted/relieved about the result.* □ **entièrement**

2 frankly: *She spoke unreservedly.* □ **franchement**

unrest [ʌn'rest] *noun* a state of trouble or discontent, especially among a group of people: *political unrest.* □ **agitation**

unrivalled, unrivaled [ʌn'raivəld] *adjective* having no equal or rival: *She is unrivalled as a Shakespearian actress.* □ **sans rival**

unroll [ʌn'roul] *verb* to open from a rolled position: *He unrolled the mattress.* □ **(se) dérouler**

unruly [ʌn'ruːli] *adjective* uncontrollable or disorderly: *unruly teenagers/behaviour.* □ **indiscipliné**

un'ruliness *noun.* □ **indiscipline**

unsavoury [ʌn'seivəri] *adjective* very unpleasant or disgusting: *I have heard some unsavoury stories about that man.* □ **répugnant**

unscramble [ʌn'skræmbl] *verb* to decode (a message) or make clear the words of (a telephone message). □ **déchiffrer**

unscrew [ʌn'skruː] *verb* to remove or loosen (something) by taking out screws, or with a twisting or screwing action: *She unscrewed the cupboard door; Can you unscrew this lid?* □ **dévisser, desserrer**

unscrupulous [ʌn'skruːpjuləs] *adjective* having no conscience or scruples; wicked: *He is an unscrupulous rogue.* □ **sans scrupules**

unsettle [ʌn'setl] *verb* to disturb or upset: *Will a change of schools unsettle the child?* □ **perturber**

un'**settled** *adjective* 1 (of weather) changeable. □ **instable**

2 anxious or restless: *in an unsettled mood.* □ **agité**

unsightly [ʌn'saitli] *adjective* ugly: *Those new buildings are very unsightly.* □ **laid**

unspeakable [ʌn'spiːkəbl] *adjective* that cannot be expressed in words, *especially* because too bad to describe: *his unspeakable cruelty/rudeness.* □ **inexprimable**

un'**speakably** *adverb*: *The house is unspeakably filthy.* □ **d'une façon inexprimable**

unstop [ʌn'stop] – *past tense, past participle* un'**stopped** – *verb* to remove a blockage from (*eg* a drain): *The plumber has unstopped the pipe.* □ **déboucher**

unstrap [ʌn'stræp] – *past tense, past participle* un'**strapped** – *verb* to unfasten the strap of: *She unstrapped her suitcase.* □ **défaire la courroie de**

unstuck [ʌn'stʌk]: **come unstuck** 1 to stop sticking: *The label has come unstuck.* □ **(se) décoller**

2 to fail: *Our plans have come unstuck.* □ **tomber à l'eau**

unsuccessful [ʌnsəksesful] *adjective* having not achieved something; unfruitful: *Norma made one unsuccessful attempt to skate then gave up completely.* □ **infructueux**

unsuspected [ʌnsə'spektid] *adjective* not imagined or known to exist: *She had unsuspected talents.* □ **insoupçonné**

,unsu'**specting** *adjective* not aware of (coming) danger: *He stole all her money and she was completely unsuspecting.* □ **sans méfiance**

untangle [ʌn'tæŋgl] *verb* to take (*eg* string, thread *etc*) out of its tangled condition; to disentangle: *She tried to untangle her hair.* □ **démêler**

unthinkable [ʌn'θiŋkəbl] *adjective* too outrageous to be considered: *It would be unthinkable to ask her to do that.* □ **impensable**

un'**thinking** *adjective* showing lack of thought or consideration: *His unthinking words had hurt her deeply.* □ **irréfléchi**

untidy [ʌn'taidi] *adjective* disordered; in a mess: *His room is always very untidy; an untidy person.* □ **en désordre; négligé**

untie [ʌn'tai] *verb* to loosen or unfasten: *She untied the string from the parcel.* □ **détacher**

until [ən'til] *preposition, conjunction* to the time of or when: *She was here until one o'clock; I won't know until*

I get a letter from him. □ **jusqu'à (ce que)**

> **until** is spelt with one **l**.

untiring [ʌn'taiəriŋ] *adjective* (of a person or his or her efforts *etc*) never stopping or ceasing because of weariness: *her untiring efforts/energy.* □ **infatigable**

un'**tiringly** *adverb*. □ **infatigablement**

unto ['ʌntu] *preposition* an old word for 'to'. □ **à**

untrue [ʌn'truː] *adjective* not true; false: *The statement is untrue.* □ **faux**

un'truth [-θ] *noun* a lie or false statement: *His autobiography contains many untruths.* □ **fausseté**

untwist [ʌn'twist] *verb* to straighten from a twisted position: *She untwisted the wire.* □ **détordre**

unusual [ʌn'juːʒuəl] *adjective* 1 not usual; rare; uncommon: *It is unusual for him to arrive late; He has an unusual job.* □ **exceptionnel, inhabituel**

2 unprecedented; odd; not expected: *The judge made the unusual recommendation to set the prisoner free.* □ **insolite**

un'**usually** *adverb*: *She is unusually cheerful today.* □ **exceptionnellement**

unutterable [ʌn'ʌtərəbl] *adjective* 1 (of a feeling) too strong to be expressed: *To his unutterable horror, the ground began to shake.* □ **indescriptible**

2 too bad to describe: *What unutterable rudeness!* □ **indescriptible**

unveil [ʌn'veil] *verb* 1 to remove a veil (from *eg* a face): *After the marriage ceremony, the bride unveils (her face).* □ **dévoiler**

2 to uncover (a new statue *etc*) ceremonially: *The prime minister was asked to unveil the plaque on the wall of the new college.* □ **dévoiler**

unwary [ʌn'weəri] *adjective* not cautious: *If you are unwary he will cheat you.* □ **imprudent**

un'**warily** *adverb*. □ **imprudemment**

un'**wariness** *noun*. □ **imprudence**

unwelcome [ʌn'welkəm] *adjective* received unwillingly or with disappointment: *unwelcome news/guests; I felt that we were unwelcome.* □ **importun**

unwell [ʌn'wel] *adjective* not in good health: *She felt unwell this morning.* □ **souffrant**

unwieldy [ʌn'wiːldi] *adjective* large and awkward to carry or manage: *A piano is an unwieldy thing to move.* □ **encombrant**

un'**wieldiness** *noun*. □ **manque de maniabilité**

unwilling [ʌn'wiliŋ] *adjective* not willing; reluctant: *She's unwilling to accept the money.* □ **peu disposé à**

un'**willingness** *noun*. □ **refus; mauvaise grâce**

un'**willingly** *adverb*: *He did agree to go, but rather unwillingly.* □ **à contrecœur**

unwind [ʌn'waind] – *past tense, past participle* un'**wound** [-'waund] – *verb* 1 to take or come out of a coiled or wound position: *He unwound the bandage from his ankle.* □ **(se) dérouler**

2 to relax after a period of tension: *Give me a chance to unwind!* □ **se détendre**

unwise [ʌn'waiz] *adjective* not wise; foolish: *an unwise suggestion; It was rather unwise of you to agree to do that.* □ **imprudent**

un'wisely *adverb.* □ **imprudemment**

unworthy [ʌnˈwəːði] *adjective* **1** shameful or disgraceful: *That was an unworthy act/thought.* □ **indigne**

2 not deserving: *Such a remark is unworthy of notice*; *He's unworthy to have the same name as his father.* □ **indigne (de)**

3 less good than should be expected from (*eg* a person): *Such bad behaviour is unworthy of him.* □ **indigne de**

un'worthily *adverb.* □ **indignement**

un'worthiness *noun.* □ **indignité**

unwound *see* **unwind.**

unwrap [ʌnˈrap] – *past tense, past participle* **un'wrapped** – *verb* to open (something wrapped or folded): *She unwrapped the gift.* □ **ouvrir**

unzip [ʌnˈzip] – *past tense, past participle* **un'zipped** – *verb* to undo the zip of: *Will you unzip this dress please?* □ **ouvrir la fermeture à glissière (de)**

up [ʌp] *adverb, adjective* **1** to, or at, a higher or better position: *Is the elevator going up?*; *The office is up on the top floor*; *She looked up at him*; *The price of coffee is up again.* □ **en/au/vers le haut**

2 erect: *Sit/Stand up*; *He got up from his chair.* □ **droit, levé**

3 out of bed: *What time do you get up?*; *I'll be up all night finishing this work.* □ **debout, éveillé**

4 to the place or person mentioned or understood: *A taxi drove up and she got in*; *She came up (to me) and shook hands.* □ **près de, à**

5 into the presence, or consideration, of a person, group of people *etc*: *She brought up the subject during the conversation.* □ **à l'attention de**

6 to an increased degree *eg* of loudness, speed *etc*: *Please turn the radio up a little!*; *Speak up! I can't hear you*; *Hurry up!* □ **plus (haut, fort, vite, etc.)**

7 used to indicate completeness; throughly or finally: *You'll end up in hospital if you don't drive more carefully*; *She locked up the house*; *Help me wash up the dishes!*; *I've used up the whole supply of paper*; *He tore up the letter.* □ **finalement; complètement**

■ *preposition* **1** to or at a higher level on: *He climbed up the tree.* □ **en/au/vers le haut**

2 (at a place) along: *They walked up the street*; *Their house is up the road.* □ **le long de**

3 towards the source of (a river): *When do the salmon start swimming up the river?* □ **en amont**

■ *verb – past tense, past participle* **upped** – to increase (a price *etc*): *They upped the price that they wanted for their house.* □ **augmenter**

'upward *adjective* going up or directed up: *They took the upward path*; *an upward glance.* □ **montant; vers le haut**

'upward(s) *adverb* (facing) towards a higher place or level: *He was lying on the floor face upwards*; *The path led upwards.* □ **vers le haut**

,up-and-'coming *adjective* (of *eg* a person starting a career) progressing well: *an up-and-coming young doctor.* □ **plein d'avenir**

,up'hill *adverb* up a slope: *We travelled uphill for several hours.* □ **en montant**

■ *adjective* **1** sloping upwards; ascending: *an uphill road/journey.* □ **montant**

2 difficult: *This will be an uphill struggle.* □ **difficile**

,up'stairs *adverb* on or to an upper floor: *His room is upstairs*; *She went upstairs to her bedroom.* □ **à/vers l'étage supérieur, là-haut**

■ *noun – plural* **up'stairs** – the upper floor(s): *The ground floor needs painting, but the upstairs is nice*; (*also adjective*) *an upstairs sitting-room.* □ **étage; d'en haut**

up'stream *adverb* towards the upper part or source of a stream, river *etc*: *Salmon swim upstream to lay their eggs.* □ **à contre-courant**

be up and about to be out of bed: *I've been up and about for hours*; *Is she up and about again after her accident?* □ **être sur pied**

be up to 1 to be busy or occupied with (an activity *etc*): *What is he up to now?* □ **être occupé à**

2 to be capable of: *He isn't quite up to the job.* □ **à la hauteur (de)**

3 to reach the standard of: *This work isn't up to your best.* □ **être à la hauteur (de)**

4 to be the duty or privilege of: *It's up to you to decide*; *The final choice is up to him.* □ **appartenir à**

up to as far, or as much, as: *She counted up to 100*; *Up to now, the work has been easy.* □ **jusqu'à**

upbringing [ˈʌpbriŋiŋ] *noun* (an example of) the process of bringing up a child: *He had a stern upbringing.* □ **éducation**

update [ʌpˈdeit] *verb* to make (something) suitable for the present time by adapting it to recent ideas *etc*: *Dictionaries constantly need to be updated.* □ **mettre à jour**

upheaval [ʌpˈhiːvəl] *noun* a great change or disturbance: *Moving house causes a great upheaval.* □ **bouleversement**

upheld *see* **uphold.**

uphold [ʌpˈhould] – *past tense, past participle* **up'held** [-'held] – *verb* **1** to support (a person's action): *His family upholds (him in) his present action.* □ **soutenir**

2 to confirm (*eg* a claim, legal judgment *etc*): *The decision of the judge was upheld by the court.* □ **confirmer**

3 to maintain (*eg* a custom): *The old traditions are still upheld in this village.* □ **maintenir**

upholster [ʌpˈhoulstə] *verb* to fit (seats) with springs, stuffing, covers *etc*: *She upholstered the chair.* □ **rembourrer**

up'holstered *adjective*: *upholstered chairs.* □ **rembourré**

up'holsterer *noun* a person who makes, repairs or sells upholstered furniture. □ **rembourreur, euse**

up'holstery *noun* **1** the business or process of upholstering. □ **rembourrage**

2 the springs, coverings *etc* of *eg* a chair: *luxurious upholstery.* □ **rembourrage, capitonnage**

upkeep [ˈʌpkiːp] *noun* (the cost of) the process of keeping *eg* a house, car *etc* in a good condition: *They can no longer afford the upkeep of this house.* □ **entretien**

upon [əˈpon] *preposition* on: *She sat upon the floor*; *Please place it upon the table*; *Upon arrival, they went in search of a hotel.* □ **sur; à**

upon my word! an exclamation indicating surprise *etc*.

□ **ma parole!**

upper ['ʌpə] *adjective* higher in position, rank *etc*: *the upper floors of the building*; *He has a scar on his upper lip*. □ **supérieur**

■ *noun* (*usually in plural*) the part of a shoe above the sole: *There's a crack in the upper*. □ **empeigne**

'uppermost *adjective* highest: *in the uppermost room of the castle*. □ **le plus élevé**

■ *adverb* in the highest place or position: *Thoughts of him were upper-most in her mind*. □ **au premier plan de**

upper class (of) the highest rank of society; (of) the aristocracy: *The upper classes can no longer afford to have many servants*; *She speaks with an upper-class accent*. □ **aristocratie; aristocratique**

get/have the upper hand (of/over someone) to have or win an advantage over: *Our team managed to get the upper hand in the end*. □ **prendre/avoir le dessus (sur)**

uppercut ['ʌpəkʌt] *noun* in boxing *etc*, a blow aimed upwards, *eg* to the chin. □ **uppercut**

upright ['ʌprait] *adjective* **1** (*also adverb*) standing straight up; erect or vertical: *He placed the books upright in the bookcase*; *She stood upright*; *a row of upright posts*. □ **droit; vertical**

2 (of a person) just and honest: *an upright, honourable man*. □ **honnête**

■ *noun* an upright post *etc* supporting a construction: *When building the fence, place the uprights two metres apart*. □ **montant**

uprising ['ʌpraiziŋ] *noun* a rebellion or revolt: *The Hungarian uprising was quickly suppressed*. □ **soulèvement**

uproar ['ʌprɔː] *noun* (an outbreak of) noise, shouting *etc*: *The whole town was in (an) uproar after the football team's victory*. □ **tumulte**

up'roarious *adjective* very noisy, *especially* with much laughter: *The team were given an uproarious welcome*. □ **tumultueux**

up'roariously *adverb*. □ **tumultueusement**

uproot [ʌp'ruːt] *verb* to pull (a plant *etc*) out of the earth with the roots: *I uprooted the weeds and burnt them*. □ **déraciner**

upset [ʌp'set] – *past tense, past participle* **up'set** – *verb* **1** to overturn: *He upset a glass of wine over the table*. □ **renverser**

2 to disturb or put out of order: *Her illness has upset all our arrangements*. □ **bouleverser**

3 to distress: *His friend's death upset him very much*. □ **bouleverser**

■ *adjective* disturbed or distressed: *Is he very upset about failing his exam?* □ **fâché**

■ ['ʌpset] *noun* a disturbance: *He has a stomach upset*; *I couldn't bear the upset of moving house again*. □ **dérangement**

upshot ['ʌpʃot]: **the upshot** the result or end (of a matter): *What was the final upshot of that affair?* □ **résultat**

upside down [ʌpsai'daun] *adverb* **1** with the top part underneath: *The plate was lying upside down on the floor*. □ **à l'envers**

2 into confusion: *The burglars turned the house upside down*. □ **sens dessus dessous**

upstart ['ʌpstaːt] *noun* a person who has risen quickly to wealth or power but seems to lack dignity or ability: *I shall leave the firm if that little upstart becomes manager*. □ **parvenu, ue**

uptake ['ʌpteik]: **quick, slow on the uptake** quick or slow to understand: *She's inexperienced, but very quick on the uptake*. □ **avoir/n'avoir pas l'esprit vif**

uranium [ju'reiniəm] *noun* a radioactive element. □ **uranium**

urban ['əːbən] *adjective* of, consisting of, or living in, a city or town: *He dislikes urban life*; *urban traffic*. □ **urbain**

urchin ['əːtʃin] *noun* a mischievous, *usually* dirty or ragged, child, *especially* a boy: *He was chased by a crowd of urchins*. □ **gamin**

urge [əːdʒ] *verb* **1** to try to persuade or request earnestly (someone to do something): *He urged her to drive carefully*, 'Come with me,' *he urged*. □ **exhorter**

2 to try to convince a person of (*eg* the importance of, or necessity for, some action): *She urged (on them) the necessity for speed*. □ **pousser (à)**

■ *noun* a strong impulse or desire: *I felt an urge to call him*. □ **forte envie (de)**

urge on to drive or try to persuade (a person *etc*) to go on or forwards: *He urged himself on in spite of his weariness*. □ **presser**

urgent ['əːdʒənt] *adjective* needing immediate attention: *There is an urgent message for the doctor*. □ **urgent**

'urgently *adverb*. □ **d'urgence**

'urgency *noun* need for immediate action, speed *etc*: *This is a matter of great urgency*. □ **urgence**

urine ['juːrin] *noun* the waste fluid passed out of the body of animals from the bladder. □ **urine**

'urinary *adjective*: *a urinary infection*. □ **urinaire**

'urinate ['juərineit] *verb* to pass urine from the bladder. □ **uriner**

urn [əːn] *noun* **1** a tall vase or other container, *especially* for holding the ashes of a dead person: *a stone-age burial urn*. □ **urne**

2 a large metal container with a tap, in which tea or coffee is made *eg* in a canteen *etc*: *a tea-urn*. □ **fontaine (à thé)**

us [ʌs] *pronoun* (used as the object of a verb or preposition) the speaker or writer plus one or more other people: *She gave us a present*; *A plane flew over us*. □ **nous**

use[1] [juːz] *verb* **1** to employ (something) for a purpose: *What did you use to open the can?*; *Use your common sense!* □ **utiliser, employer**

2 to consume: *We're using far too much electricity*. □ **consommer**

'usable *adjective* that can be used: *Are any of these clothes usable?* □ **utilisable**

used *adjective* **1** employed or put to a purpose: *This road is not used any more*. □ **utilisé**

2 not new: *used cars*. □ **d'occasion**

'user *noun* a person who uses something: *road-users*; *electricity users*. □ **utilisateur, trice; usager, ère**

used to (something) ['juːstu] accustomed to: *She isn't used to such hard work*. □ **habitué à**

used to ['juːstu] – *negative short forms* **usedn't to,**

usen't to ['juːsntu] – (I, he *etc*) was in the habit of (doing something); (I, he *etc*) was (usually) in a particular position, state *etc*: *I used to swim every day*; *She used not to be so forgetful*; *They used to play golf, didn't they?*; *Didn't you use(d) to live near me?*; *There used to be a butcher's shop there, didn't there?* □ **avoir l'habitude de; il y avait**

use² [juːs] *noun* **1** the act of using or state of being used: *The use of force to persuade workers to join a strike cannot be justified*; *This telephone number is for use in emergencies.* □ **usage, utilisation**
2 the/a purpose for which something may be used: *This little knife has plenty of uses*; *I have no further use for these clothes.* □ **usage**
3 (often in questions or with negatives) value or advantage: *Is this coat (of) any use to you?*; *It's no use offering to help when it's too late.* □ **utilité**
4 the power of using: *She lost the use of her right arm as a result of the accident.* □ **usage**
5 permission, or the right, to use: *They let us have the use of their car while they were away.* □ **usage**
'useful *adjective* helpful or serving a purpose well: *a useful tool/dictionary*; *She made herself useful by doing the accounting for her mother.* □ **utile**
'usefulness *noun.* □ **utilité**
'usefully *adverb* in a useful way: *He spent the day usefully in repairing the car.* □ **utilement**
'useless *adjective* having no use or no effect: *Why don't you throw away those useless things?*; *We can't do it – it's useless to try.* □ **inutile**
be in use to be used: *How long has the gymnasium been in use?* □ **utilisé**
out of use obsolete or no longer used: *These textbooks have been out of use for some time.* □ **inutilisé, désuet**
come in useful to become useful: *My French came in useful on holiday.* □ **rendre service (à)**
have no use for to despise: *I have no use for such silliness/silly people.* □ **n'avoir que faire de**
it's no use it's impossible or useless: *He tried in vain to do it, then said 'It's no use.'* □ **c'est impossible; c'est inutile**
make (good) use of, put to (good) use: *He makes use of his training*; *He puts his training to good use in that job.* □ **tirer parti de, mettre à profit**
use(d)n't see use¹.

usher ['ʌʃə] – *feminine* ,ushe'rette [-'ret] – *noun* a person who shows people to their seats in a theatre *etc*. □ **placeur, euse; ouvreur, euse**
■ *verb* to lead, escort: *The waiter ushered her to a ta-*

ble. □ **conduire jusqu'à**
usual ['juːʒuəl] *adjective* done, happening *etc* most often; customary: *Are you going home by the usual route?*; *There are more people here than usual*; *Such behaviour is quite usual with children of that age*; *As usual, he was late.* □ **habituel**
'usually *adverb* on most occasions: *We are usually at home in the evenings*; *Usually we finish work at 5 o'clock.* □ **d'habitude, habituellement**
usurp [ju'zəːp] *verb* to take (another person's power, position *etc*) without the right to do so: *The king's uncle tried to usurp the throne*; *I shall not allow him to usurp my authority.* □ **usurper**
u'surper *noun.* □ **usurpateur, trice**
utensil [ju'tensl] *noun* an instrument or vessel used in everyday life: *pots and pans and other kitchen utensils.* □ **ustensile**
uterus ['juːtərəs] *noun* the womb. □ **utérus**
utility [ju'tiləti] – *plural* u'tilities – *noun* **1** usefulness: *Some kitchen gadgets have only a limited utility.* □ **utilité**
2 a useful public service, *eg* the supply of water, gas, electricity *etc*. □ **service public**
u,tili'tarian *adjective* useful rather than ornamental: *Our plates and glasses are utilitarian rather than beautiful.* □ **utilitaire**
utilize, utilise ['juːtilaiz] *verb* to find a useful purpose for (something): *The extra money is being utilized to buy books for the school library.* □ **utiliser**
,utili'zation, ,utili'sation *noun.* □ **utilisation**
utmost ['ʌtmoust] *adjective* **1** most distant: *the utmost ends of the earth.* □ **le plus éloigné**
2 greatest possible: *Take the utmost care!* □ **le plus grand (possible)**
do one's utmost to make the greatest possible effort: *She has done her utmost to help him.* □ **faire tout son possible (pour)**
Utopia [juː'toupiə] *noun* an imaginary country that has a perfect social and political system. □ **Utopie**
U'topian *adjective* (of *eg* plans for benefiting mankind) desirable, but idealistic and impossible: *Utopian schemes.* □ **utopique**
utter¹ ['ʌtə] *adjective* complete or total: *There was utter silence*; *utter darkness.* □ **complet, total**
'utterly *adverb* completely or totally: *She was utterly unaware of her danger.* □ **totalement**
utter² ['ʌtə] *verb* to produce (sounds, *eg* cries, words *etc*) with the mouth: *She uttered a sigh of relief*; *She didn't utter a single word of encouragement.* □ **pousser; prononcer**

Vv

v *see* **versus.**

V- [viː] shaped like a V: *a V-neck(ed) pull-over.* □ **en V**

vac [vak] short for **vacation**: *the summer vac.* □ **vacances**

vacant ['veikənt] *adjective* **1** empty or unoccupied: *a vacant chair; Are there any rooms vacant in this hotel?* □ **vacant, inoccupé**

2 showing no thought, intelligence or interest: *a vacant stare.* □ **vide**

'**vacancy** – *plural* '**vacancies** – *noun* **1** an unoccupied post: *We have a vacancy for a typist.* □ **poste vacant**

2 the condition of being vacant; emptiness: *The vacancy of his expression made me doubt if he was listening.* □ **vide**

'**vacantly** *adverb* absent-mindedly; without concentration: *He stared vacantly out of the window.* □ **distraitement**

vacation [vei-'keiʃən] *noun* a holiday: *a summer vacation.* □ **vacances**

■ *verb* (*American*) to take a holiday: *She vacationed in Paris last year.* □ **passer des vacances**

on vacation not working; having a holiday: *She has gone to Italy on vacation.* □ **en vacances**

vacationer *noun* someone who is on holiday; a person who is on a trip: *Many vacationers have their trips spoiled by losing their luggage.* □ **vacancier**

vaccine ['vaksiːn] *noun* a substance made from the germs that cause a particular disease, *especially* smallpox, and given to a person or animal to prevent him or her from catching that disease. □ **vaccin**

'**vaccinate** [-ksi-] *verb* to protect (a person *etc*) against a disease by putting vaccine into his or her blood: *Has your child been vaccinated against smallpox?* □ **vacciner (contre)**

,**vacci'nation** [-ksi-] *noun* (an) act of vaccinating or process of being vaccinated: *I'm to have a vaccination tomorrow; Vaccination was introduced in the eighteenth century.* □ **vaccination**

vacuum ['vakjum] *noun* **1** a space from which (almost) all air or other gas has been removed. □ **vide**

2 short for **vacuum cleaner.** □ **aspirateur**

■ *verb* to clean (something) using a vacuum cleaner: *They vacuumed the carpet.* □ **passer l'aspirateur**

vacuum cleaner a machine that cleans carpets *etc* by sucking dust *etc* into itself. □ **aspirateur**

('**vacuum)flask** *noun* a container with double walls that have a vacuum between them to keep the contents from losing or gaining heat: *a (vacuum-)flask of hot coffee.* □ **bouteille isolante**

vagabond ['vagəbond] *noun* an old word for a person having no settled home, or roving from place to place, *especially* in an idle or disreputable manner: *rogues and vagabonds.* □ **vagabond, onde**

vagrant ['veigrənt] *noun* a person who has no fixed home; a tramp. □ **itinérant, ante; vagabond, onde**

'**vagrancy** *noun* the state of being a vagrant: *Vagrancy is a crime in some countries.* □ **vagabondage**

vague [veig] *adjective* **1** not clear, distinct or definite:

Through the fog we saw the vague outline of a ship; He has only a vague idea of how this machine works. □ **vague**

2 (of people) imprecise, or impractical and forgetful: *He is always very vague when making arrangements.* □ **vague**

'**vagueness** *noun.* □ **vague, imprécision**

'**vaguely** *adverb* **1** in a vague manner: *I remember her very vaguely.* □ **vaguement**

2 slightly: *She felt vaguely irritated; I feel vaguely uneasy.* □ **vaguement**

vain [vein] *adjective* **1** having too much pride in one's appearance, achievements *etc*; conceited: *They're very vain about their good looks.* □ **vaniteux**

2 unsuccessful: *He made a vain attempt to reach the drowning woman.* □ **vain**

3 empty; meaningless: *vain threats; vain promises.* □ **vide**

'**vainly** *adverb* unsuccessfully: *She searched vainly for the treasure.* □ **vainement**

vanity ['vanəti] *noun* **1** excessive admiration of oneself; conceit: *Vanity is their chief fault.* □ **vanité**

2 worthlessness or pointlessness: *the vanity of human ambition.* □ **vanité**

in vain with no success: *He tried in vain to open the locked door.* □ **en vain**

vale [veil] *noun* a valley. □ **vallée**

valentine ['valəntain] *noun* a sweetheart chosen, or a card, love letter *etc* sent, on St. Valentine's Day, February 14: *Will you be my valentine?; He sent her a valentine; (also adjective) a valentine card.* □ **personne aimée; de la Saint-Valentin**

valet ['valit, 'valei] *noun* a manservant who looks after his master's clothes *etc*: *His valet laid out his evening suit.* □ **valet de chambre**

valiant ['valiənt] *adjective* (of a person, his or her actions *etc*) brave, courageous or heroic: *valiant deeds; He was valiant in battle.* □ **brave**

'**valiantly** *adverb.* □ **bravement**

valid ['valid] *adjective* **1** (of reasons, arguments *etc*) true; reasonable or acceptable: *That is not a valid excuse.* □ **valable**

2 legally effective; having legal force: *She has a valid passport.* □ **valide**

'**validly** *adverb.* □ **valablement**

valise [və'liːs] *noun* a type of soft bag in which clothes and personal items are carried when travelling. □ **sac de voyage**

valley ['vali] *noun* a stretch of flat, low land between hills or mountains, *usually* drained by a river and its tributaries: *a beautiful green valley between the mountains.* □ **vallée**

valour ['valə] *noun* courage or bravery, *especially* in battle: *He displayed his valour on the battlefield.* □ **bravoure**

value ['valjuː] *noun* **1** worth, importance or usefulness: *Her special knowledge was of great value during the war; She sets little value on wealth.* □ **valeur; utilité**

2 price: *What is the value of that stamp?* □ **valeur**

3 purchasing power: *Are those coins of any value?* □

valeur
4 fairness of exchange (for one's money *etc*): *You get good value for money at this supermarket!* □ **achat avantageux**
5 the length of a musical note. □ **valeur**
■ *verb* 1 to suggest a suitable price for: *This painting has been valued at $50,000.* □ **évaluer (à)**
2 to regard as good or important: *He values your advice very highly.* □ **valoriser**
'**valuable** *adjective* having high value: *a valuable painting.* □ **de valeur**
'**valuables** *noun plural* things of special value: *She keeps her jewellery and other valuables in a locked drawer.* □ **objets de valeur**
'**valued** *adjective* regarded as valuable or precious: *What is your most valued possession?* □ **précieux**
'**valueless** *adjective* having no value; worthless: *The necklace is completely valueless.* □ **sans valeur**
'**values** *noun plural* standards or principles: *People have very different moral values.* □ **valeurs**
valve [valv] *noun* 1 a device for allowing a liquid or gas to pass through an opening in one direction only. □ **valve, soupape**
2 a structure with the same effect in an animal body: *Valves in the heart control the flow of blood in the human body.* □ **valvule**
3 a type of electronic component found in many, *especially* older, types of television, radio *etc*. □ **lampe**
vampire ['vampaiə] *noun* a dead person who is imagined to rise from the grave at night and suck the blood of sleeping people. □ **vampire**
van [van] *noun* a vehicle for carrying goods on roads or railways: *She drives a van*; (*also adjective*) *a van-driver*; *a vanload of waste paper.* □ **(de) camion(nette)**
vandal ['vandəl] *noun* a person who purposely and pointlessly damages or destroys public buildings or other property: *Vandals have damaged this telephone kiosk.* □ **vandale**
'**vandalism** *noun* the behaviour of a vandal: *All the telephones are out of order owing to vandalism.* □ **vandalisme**
'**vandalize, 'vandalise** *verb*: *The lift in our block of flats has been vandalized.* □ **saccager**
vanguard ['vanga:d] *noun* 1 the part of an army going in front of the main body. □ **avant-garde**
2 the leaders in any movement: *We're in the vanguard of the movement for reform!* □ **avant-garde**
vanilla [və'nilə] *noun* a flavouring obtained from a tropical orchid, and used in ice-cream and other foods: *vanilla ice-cream.* □ **(à la) vanille**
vanish ['vaniʃ] *verb* to become no longer visible, *especially* suddenly: *The ship vanished over the horizon*; *Our hopes suddenly vanished.* □ **disparaître**
vanity *see* **vain**.
vanquish ['vaŋkwiʃ] *verb* to defeat or conquer: *You must vanquish your fears.* □ **vaincre**
vapour, vapor ['veipə] *noun* 1 the gas-like form into which a substance can be changed by heating: *water vapour.* □ **vapeur**
2 mist, fumes or smoke in the air: *Near the marshes the*

air was filled with a strange-smelling vapour. □ **vapeur**
'**vaporize, 'vaporise** *verb* to (cause to) change into a gas-like state. □ **(se) vaporiser**
variable, variation *see* **vary**.
variegated ['veərigeitid] *adjective* (of leaves *etc*) varied in colour. □ **multicolore**
variety [və'raiəti] – *plural* **va'rieties** – *noun* 1 the quality of being of many different kinds or of being varied: *There's a great deal of variety in this job.* □ **variété**
2 a mixed collection or range: *The children got a variety of toys on their birthdays.* □ **grand choix (de)**
3 a sort or kind: *They grow fourteen different varieties of rose.* □ **variété**
4 a type of mixed theatrical entertainment including dances, songs, short sketches *etc*: *I much prefer operas to variety*; (*also adjective*) *a variety show.* □ **(de) variétés**
various ['veəriəs] *adjective* 1 different; varied: *His reasons for leaving were many and various.* □ **varié**
2 several: *Various people have told me about you.* □ **différent**
'**variously** *adverb*. □ **diversement**
varnish ['va:niʃ] *noun* 1 a *usually* clear sticky liquid which gives protection and a glossy surface to wood, paint *etc*. □ **vernis**
2 the glossy surface given by this liquid: *Be careful or you'll take the varnish off the table!* □ **vernis**
■ *verb* to cover with varnish: *Don't sit on that chair – I've just varnished it.* □ **vernir**
vary ['veəri] *verb* to make, be or become different: *These apples vary in size from small to medium.* □ **varier**
'**variable** *adjective* 1 that may be varied: *The machine works at a variable speed.* □ **variable**
2 (of *eg* winds, weather *etc*) liable or likely to change: *British weather is very variable.* □ **changeant**
■ *noun* something that varies, *eg* in quantity, value, effect *etc*: *Have you taken all the variables into account in your calculations?* □ **variable**
'**variably** *adverb*. □ **variablement**
,**varia'bility** – *plural* **varia'bilities** – *noun*. □ **variabilité**
,**vari'ation** *noun* 1 the extent to which a thing changes: *In the desert there are great variations in temperature.* □ **variation**
2 one of a series of musical elaborations made on a basic theme or melody: *Brahms' variations on Haydn's 'St Anthony's Chorale'.* □ **variation**
'**varied** *adjective*: *She has had a very varied career.* □ **varié**
variety store [vəraiəti: stour] *noun* a small grocery store that sells convenience or everyday items such as bread and milk: *Grace stopped at the variety store on the corner to buy a pair of pantyhose.* □ **dépanneur**
vase [veis] *noun* a type of jar or jug used mainly as an ornament or for holding cut flowers: *a vase of flowers.* □ **vase**
vast [va:st] *adjective* of very great size or amount: *He inherited a vast fortune.* □ **immense**
'**vastness** *noun*. □ **immensité**
vat [vat] *noun* a large vessel or tank, *especially* one for holding fermenting spirits. □ **cuve**

vaudeville ['vɔːdəvil] *noun* the type of theatre show in which there is a variety of short acts; music-hall: *There are very few theatres now where vaudeville is performed.* □ **(spectacle de) variétés**

vault[1] [vɔːlt] *noun* **1** (a room, *especially* a cellar, with) an arched roof or ceiling: *the castle vaults.* □ **cave voûtée** **2** an underground room, *especially* for storing valuables: *The thieves broke into the bank vaults.* □ **chambre forte** **3** a burial chamber, often for all the members of a family: *She was buried in the family vault.* □ **caveau** '**vaulted** *adjective* **1** (of a roof or ceiling) arched. □ **voûté, en voûte** **2** (of a building *etc*) having an arched roof or ceiling. □ **voûté, en voûte**

vault[2] [vɔːlt] *noun* a leap aided by the hands or by a pole: *With a vault he was over the fence and away.* □ **saut** ■ *verb* to leap (over): *She vaulted (over) the fence.* □ **sauter**

VCR (Video Cassette Recorder) device connected to a television for recording programs or for viewing recorded movies or programs: *Put the movie in the VCR so that we can watch it.* □ **magnétoscope**

veal [viːl] *noun* the flesh of a calf, used as food: *We had veal for dinner.* □ **veau**

veer [viə] *verb* to change direction suddenly: *The car veered across the road to avoid hitting a small boy.* □ **virer**

vegetable ['vedʒtəbl] *noun* **1** a plant or part of a plant, other than a fruit, used as food: *We grow potatoes, beans and other vegetables*; *(also adjective) vegetable oils.* □ **(à, de, aux) légume(s)** **2** a plant: *Grass is a vegetable, gold is a mineral and a human being is an animal.* □ **végétal** ,**vege'tarian** [vedʒi-] *noun* a person who does not eat meat of any kind: *Has he always been a vegetarian?*; *(also adjective) This is a vegetarian dish.* □ **végétarien, ienne** ,**vege'tarianism** *noun.* □ **végétarisme** **vegetate** ['vedʒiteit] *verb* to live an idle, boring and pointless life: *I would like to get a job – I don't want to vegetate.* □ **végéter** ,**vege'tation** [vedʒi-] *noun* plants in general; plants of a particular region or type: *tropical vegetation.* □ **végétation**

vehicle ['viəkl] *noun* any means of transport on land, *especially* on wheels, *eg* a car, bus, bicycle *etc*. □ **véhicule**

veil [veil] *noun* a piece of thin cloth worn over the face or head to hide, cover, or protect it: *Some women wear veils for religious reasons, to prevent strangers from seeing their faces*; *a veil of mist over the mountains*; *a veil of secrecy.* □ **voile** ■ *verb* to cover with a veil. □ **voiler** **veiled** *adjective* **1** wearing, or covered by, a veil: *a veiled lady*; *The bride was veiled.* □ **voilé** **2** (only slightly) disguised: *a veiled threat.* □ **voilé**

vein [vein] *noun* **1** any of the tubes that carry the blood back to the heart. □ **veine** **2** a similar-looking line on a leaf. □ **nervure**

velocity [və'lɒsəti] *noun* speed, *especially* in a given direction. □ **vélocité**

velvet ['velvit] *noun, adjective* (of) a type of cloth made from silk *etc* with a soft, thick surface: *Her dress was made of velvet; a velvet jacket.* □ **(de) velours** '**velvety** *adjective.* □ **velouté**

vendetta [ven'detə] *noun* a fierce, often violent, long-lasting dispute: *There has been a bitter vendetta between the two families for many years.* □ **vendetta**

venerate ['venəreit] *verb* to respect; to honour greatly: *In some countries, old people are venerated more than in others.* □ **vénérer** '**venerable** *adjective* worthy of great respect because of age or for special goodness: *a venerable old man.* □ **vénérable** ,**vene'ration** *noun: His pupils regarded him with veneration.* □ **vénération**

Venetian [və'niːʃən]: **Venetian blind** a window blind made of thin, movable, horizontal strips of wood, metal or plastic: *We have put up Venetian blinds to stop our neighbours looking in our front windows.* □ **store vénitien**

vengeance ['vendʒəns] *noun* harm done in return for injury received; revenge. □ **vengeance**

venison ['venisn] *noun* the flesh of deer, used as food: *We had roast venison for dinner*; *(also adjective) venison stew.* □ **(de) gibier; venaison**

venom ['venəm] *noun* **1** the poison produced by some snakes, scorpions *etc*, transmitted by biting or stinging: *the venom of a cobra.* □ **venin** **2** great ill-feeling, anger *etc*: *He spoke with venom.* □ **venin** '**venomous** *adjective* **1** (of snakes *etc*) poisonous: *venomous reptiles.* □ **venimeux** **2** (of people, their words etc) full of ill-feeling: *a venomous speech.* □ **venimeux** '**venomously** *adverb.* □ **avec venin**

vent [vent] *noun* a hole to allow air, smoke *etc* to pass out or in: *an air-vent.* □ **évent** ■ *verb* to give expression or an outlet to (an emotion *etc*): *He was angry with himself and vented his rage on his son by beating him violently.* □ **décharger (sur)** **give vent to** to express (an emotion *etc*) freely: *He gave vent to his anger in a furious letter to the newspaper.* □ **donner libre cours à**

ventilate ['ventileit] *verb* to allow fresh air to enter (*eg* a room). □ **ventiler** ,**venti'lation** *noun* the act or means of ventilating or the state of being ventilated: *There was no window in the room, and no other (means of) ventilation.* □ **ventilation** '**ventilator** *noun* a device for ventilating a room *etc*. □ **ventilateur**

ventriloquist [ven'trilɑkwist] *noun* a professional entertainer who can speak so that his or her voice seems to come from some other person or place, *especially* from a dummy which he or she controls. □ **ventriloque** **ven'triloquism** *noun.* □ **ventriloquie**

venture ['ventʃə] *noun* an undertaking or scheme that involves some risk: *her latest business venture.* □ **entreprise (risquée)**

cabbage

corn

leek

beans

radish

carrot

cauliflower

broccoli

eggplant

pepper

artichoke

onion

garlic

lettuce

mushroom

tomato

sweet potato

potato

beet

cucumber

celery

asparagus

peas

© Modulo Éditeur, 2000

■ *verb* **1** to dare to go: *Every day the child ventured further into the forest.* □ **s'aventurer**

2 to dare (to do (something), especially to say (something)): *He ventured to kiss her hand; I ventured (to remark) that her skirt was too short.* □ **se risquer à**

3 to risk: *He decided to venture all his money on the scheme.* □ **risquer**

veranda(h) [vəˈrandə] *noun* (*also* **porch**) a kind of covered balcony, with a roof extending beyond the main building supported by light pillars. □ **véranda**

verb [vəːb] *noun* the word or phrase that gives the action, or asserts something, in a sentence, clause *etc*: *I saw her; She ran away from me; I have a feeling; What is this?* □ **verbe**

'**verbal** *adjective* **1** of, or concerning, verbs: *verbal endings such as '-fy', '-ize'.* □ **verbal**

2 consisting of, or concerning, spoken words: *a verbal warning/agreement.* □ **verbal**

'**verbally** *adverb* in or by speech, not writing: *I replied to the invitation verbally.* □ **verbalement**

verdict ['vəːdikt] *noun* **1** the decision of a jury at the end of a trial: *The jury brought in a verdict of guilty.* □ **verdict**

2 an opinion or decision reached after consideration: *The competitors are still waiting for the verdict of the judges.* □ **verdict**

verge [vəːdʒ] *noun* the (grass) edging of a garden bed, a road *etc*: *It's illegal to drive on the grass verge.* □ **bord**

■ *verb* to be on the border (of): *She is verging on insanity.* □ **frôler**

verify ['verifai] *verb* to confirm the truth or correctness of (something): *Can you verify her statement?* □ **vérifier**

'**verifiable** *adjective.* □ **vérifiable**

,**verifi'cation** [-fi-] *noun.* □ **vérification**

vermilion [vəˈmiljən] *noun, adjective* (of) a bright red colour. □ **vermillon**

vermin ['vəːmin] *noun* undesirable or troublesome pests such as fleas, rats, or mice: *Farmers are always having trouble with various types of vermin; It is vermin such as these men that are trying to destroy society.* □ **vermine**

vernacular [vəˈnakjulə] *adjective* colloquial or informally conversational: *vernacular speech/language.* □ **vernaculaire**

■ *noun* the common informal language of a country *etc* as opposed to its formal or literary language: *They spoke to each other in the vernacular of the region.* □ **langue vernaculaire**

versatile ['vəːsətail] *adjective* **1** (of people *etc*) able to turn easily and successfully from one task, activity or occupation to another: *a versatile entertainer; He will easily get another job – he is so versatile.* □ **aux talents variés**

2 (of a material *etc*) capable of being used for many purposes: *a versatile tool.* □ **polyvalent**

,**versa'tility** [-ti-] *noun.* □ **souplesse**

verse [vəːs] *noun* **1** a number of lines of poetry, grouped together and forming a separate unit within the poem, song, hymn *etc*: *This song has three verses.* □ **strophe**

2 a short section in a chapter of the Bible. □ **verset**

3 poetry, as opposed to prose: *She expressed her ideas in verse.* □ **vers**

version ['vəːʒən] *noun* an account from one point of view: *The boy gave his version of what had occurred.* □ **version**

versus ['vəːsəs] *preposition* (*often abbreviated to* **v** *or* **vs** *when written*) against: *the England v Wales rugby match.* □ **contre**

vertebra ['vəːtibrə] – *plural* **vertebrae** [-briː] – *noun* any of the bones of the spine: *She has a broken vertebra.* □ **vertèbre**

'**vertebrate** [-brət] *noun, adjective* (an animal) having a backbone: *Insects are not vertebrates.* □ **vertébré**

vertical ['vəːtikəl] *adjective* standing straight up at right angles to the earth's surface, or to a horizontal plane or line; upright: *The hillside looked almost vertical.* □ **vertical**

'**vertically** *adverb.* □ **verticalement**

vertigo ['vəːtigou] *noun* dizziness, *especially* as brought on by fear of heights: *Keep them back from the edge of the cliff – they suffer from vertigo.* □ **vertige**

very ['veri] *adverb* **1** to a great degree: *She's very clever; You came very quickly; I'm not feeling very well.* □ **très**

2 absolutely; in the highest degree: *The very first thing you must do is ring the police; She has a car of her very own.* □ **tout; de loin**

■ *adjective* **1** exactly or precisely the thing, person *etc* mentioned: *You're the very person I want to see; At that very minute the door opened.* □ **même**

2 extreme: *at the very end of the day; at the very top of the tree.* □ **tout (à)**

3 used for emphasis in other ways: *The very suggestion of a sea voyage makes them feel seasick.* □ **seul**

very well used to express (reluctant) agreement to a request *etc*: *'Please be home before midnight.' 'Very well.'* □ **très bien**

vessel ['vesl] *noun* **1** a container, *usually* for liquid: *a plastic vessel containing acid.* □ **récipient**

2 a ship: *a 10 000-ton grain-carrying vessel.* □ **vaisseau**

vest [vest] *noun* **1** a kind of sleeveless shirt worn under a shirt, blouse *etc*: *He was dressed only in (a) vest and underpants.* □ **camisole**

2 a waistcoat: *jacket, vest and trousers*; (*also adjective*) *a vest pocket.* □ **(de) gilet**

vet[1] *see* **veterinary**.

vet[2] [vet] – *past tense, past participle* '**vetted** – *verb* to investigate carefully (and pass as satisfactory): *Every member of staff has been vetted by our security department before he starts work here.* □ **examiner de près**

veteran ['vetərən] *noun, adjective* **1** a person who is (old and) experienced as a soldier *etc* or in some other occupation: *a veteran footballer/entertainer.* □ **vétéran**

2 a person who has been in the army *etc*: *war veterans.* □ **ancien combattant**

veterinary [vetəˈrinəri] *adjective* of, or concerning, the treatment of diseases in animals: *veterinary medicine; veterinary care.* □ **vétérinaire**

veterinarian, veterinary surgeon [vetəriˈneəriən] *noun* (*both often abbreviated to* **vet** [vet]) a doctor for animals. □ **vétérinaire**

veto ['viːtou] – *3rd person singular present tense* **'vetoes**: *past tense, past participle* **'vetoed** – *verb* to forbid, or refuse to consent to: *They vetoed your suggestion.* □ **mettre son veto à**
■ *noun* – *plural* **'vetoes** – (*also* **power of veto**) the power or right to refuse or forbid: *the chairman's (power of) veto.* □ **(droit de) veto**

vex [veks] *verb* to annoy or distress (a person): *There were no other problems to vex us.* □ **vexer**
vex'ation *noun* **1** the state of being vexed. □ **vexation**
2 a cause of annoyance or trouble: *minor worries and vexations.* □ **vexation**

via ['vaiə] *preposition* by way of: *We went to America via Japan; The news reached me via my aunt.* □ **par, via**

viaduct ['vaiədʌkt] *noun* a *usually* long bridge carrying a road or railway over a valley *etc.* □ **viaduc**

vibrate [vai'breit, 'vaibreit] *verb* to (cause to) shake, tremble, or move rapidly back and forth: *Every sound that we hear is making part of our ear vibrate; The engine has stopped vibrating.* □ **(faire) vibrer**
vi'bration [-'brei-] *noun* (an) act of vibrating: *This building is badly affected by the vibration of all the heavy traffic that passes.* □ **vibration**

vicar ['vikə] *noun* a clergyman of the Church of England. □ **pasteur (anglican)**
'vicarage [-ridʒ] *noun* the house of a vicar. □ **presbytère**

vice¹, vise [vais] *noun* a kind of strong tool for holding an object firmly, *usually* between two metal jaws: *The carpenter held the piece of wood in a vice; He has a grip like a vice.* □ **étau**

vice² [vais] *noun* **1** a serious moral fault: *Continual lying is a vice.* □ **vice**
2 a bad habit: *Smoking is not one of my vices.* □ **défaut**

vice- [vais] second in rank and acting as deputy for: *the Vice-President; the vice-chairman.* □ **vice-**

vice versa [vaisi'vəːsə] *adverb* (of two things or people) the other way around: *Dogs often chase cats but not usually vice versa.* □ **vice versa**

vicinity [vi'sinəti] *noun* a neighbourhood or local area: *Are there any cinemas in the/this vicinity?* □ **voisinage**

vicious ['viʃəs] *adjective* evil; cruel; likely to attack or cause harm: *Keep back from that dog – it's vicious.* □ **méchant**
'viciously *adverb.* □ **méchamment**
'viciousness *noun.* □ **méchanceté**

victim ['viktim] *noun* a person who receives ill-treatment, injury *etc.*: *a murder victim; Food is being sent to the victims of the disaster.* □ **victime**

victor ['viktə] *noun* the person who wins a battle or other contest. □ **vainqueur**
vic'torious [-'toː-] *adjective* successful or winning: *the victorious army; Which team was victorious?* □ **victorieux**
vic'toriously *adverb.* □ **victorieusement**
'victory – *plural* **'victories** – *noun* (a) defeat of an enemy or rival: *Our team has had two defeats and eight victories; At last they experienced the joy of victory.* □ **victoire**

Victorian [vik'toːriən] *adjective* **1** of the reign of Queen Victoria (1837–1901): *Victorian writers; Victorian households/furniture.* □ **victorien**
2 (of an attitude towards morals *etc*) strict and conservative: *a Victorian attitude to life.* □ **victorien**
■ *noun* a person living in Queen Victoria's reign: *The Victorians were great engineers and industrialists.* □ **victorien, ienne**

video ['vidiou] – *plural* **'videos** – *noun* **1** the recording or broadcasting (by means of a **video recorder**) of television pictures and sound. □ **vidéophonie**
2 a videotape. □ **bande magnétoscopique**
3 a video recorder. □ **magnétoscope**
■ *verb* to record on a video recorder or videotape: *She videoed the television programme on volcanoes.* □ **enregistrer au magnétoscope**
'videotape ['vidiouteip] *noun* recording tape carrying pictures and sound. □ **vidéocassette**

vie [vai] – *present participle* **'vying** ['vaiiŋ]: *past tense, past participle* **vied** – *verb* to compete with: *The two parents vied with each other in their attempts to gain the children's love.* □ **rivaliser**

view [vjuː] *noun* **1** (an outlook on to, or picture of) a scene: *Your house has a fine view of the hills; She painted a view of the harbour.* □ **vue**
2 an opinion: *Tell me your view/views on the subject.* □ **opinion**
3 an act of seeing or inspecting: *We were given a private view of the exhibition before it was opened to the public.* □ **visite**
■ *verb* to look at, or regard (something): *She viewed the scene with astonishment.* □ **regarder**
'viewer *noun* **1** a person who watches television: *This programme has five million viewers.* □ **téléspectateur, trice**
2 a device with a magnifying lens, and often with a light, used in viewing transparencies. □ **visionneuse**
'viewpoint *noun* a point of view: *I am looking at the matter from a different viewpoint.* □ **point de vue**
in view of taking into consideration; because of: *In view of the committee's criticisms of him, he felt he had to resign.* □ **vu, étant donné**
on view being shown or exhibited: *There's a marvellous collection of prints on view at the gallery.* □ **exposé**
point of view a way or manner of looking at a subject, matter *etc*: *You must consider everyone's point of view before deciding.* □ **point de vue**

vigilance ['vidʒiləns] *noun* watchfulness or readiness for danger: *He watched her with the vigilance of a hawk.* □ **vigilance**
'vigilant *adjective.* □ **vigilant**

vigour, vigor ['vigə] *noun* strength and energy: *He began his new job with enthusiasm and vigour.* □ **vigueur**
'vigorous *adjective*: *a vigorous dance.* □ **vigoureux**
'vigorously *adverb.* □ **vigoureusement**

> The adjective is always spelt **vigorous**.

vile [vail] *adjective* horrible; wicked; disgusting: *That was a vile thing to say!; The food tasted vile.* □ **abominable**
'vilely *adverb.* □ **bassement**

'**vileness** *noun.* □ **bassesse**

villa ['vilə] *noun* a type of detached or semi-detached (*usually* luxury) house, in the country or suburbs, or used for holidays at the seaside: *They have a villa at the seaside.* □ **villa**

village ['vilidʒ] *noun* **1** a group of houses *etc* which is smaller than a town: *They live in a little village; (also adjective) a village school.* □ **(du) village**

2 the people who live in such a group of houses: *The whole village turned out to see the celebrations.* □ **village**

'**villager** *noun* a person who lives in a village. □ **villageois, oise**

villain ['vilən] *noun* a person who is wicked or of very bad character: *the villain of the play/story.* □ **méchant, ante**

'**villainous** *adjective.* □ **infâme**

'**villainy** – *plural* '**villainies** – *noun* (an instance of) wickedness: *His villainy was well known.* □ **infamie**

vine [vain] *noun* **1** a type of climbing plant which bears grapes. □ **vigne**

2 any climbing or trailing plant. □ **plante grimpante**

'**vineyard** ['vin-] *noun* an area which is planted with grape vines: *We spent the summer touring the French vineyards.* □ **vignoble**

vinegar ['vinigə] *noun* a sour liquid made from wine, beer *etc*, used in seasoning or preparing food: *Mix some oil and vinegar as a dressing for the salad.* □ **vinaigre**

vintage ['vintidʒ] *noun* (a wine from) the grape-harvest of a certain (particularly good) year: *What vintage is this wine?; a vintage year* (= a year in which good wine was produced); *vintage port* (= port from a vintage year). □ **(bonne) année**

viola [vi'oulə] *noun* a type of musical instrument very similar to, but slightly larger than, the violin: *She plays the viola in the school orchestra.* □ **alto**

violent ['vaiələnt] *adjective* **1** having, using, or showing, great force: *There was a violent storm at sea; a violent earthquake; He has a violent temper.* □ **violent**

2 caused by force: *a violent death.* □ **violent**

'**violently** *adverb.* □ **violemment**

'**violence** *noun* great roughness and force, often causing severe physical injury or damage: *I was amazed at the violence of his temper; They were terrified by the violence of the storm.* □ **violence**

violet ['vaiəlit] *noun* **1** a kind of small bluish-purple flower. □ **violette**

2 (*also adjective*) (of) a bluish-purple colour. □ **violet**

violin [vaiə'lin] *noun* a type of musical instrument with four strings, played with a bow: *She played the violin in the school orchestra; Can you play that on the violin?* □ **violon**

,**vio'linist** *noun* a violin player: *She is a leading violinist.* □ **violoniste**

violoncello [vaiələn'tʃelou] *noun* full form of **cello**. □ **violoncelle**

,**violon'cellist** *noun* full form of **cellist**. □ **violoncelliste**

viper ['vaipə] *noun* an adder. □ **vipère**

virgin ['vəːdʒin] *noun* a person, *especially* a woman, who has had no sexual intercourse: *She was still a virgin when she married.* □ **vierge**

'**virginal** *adjective* of a virgin: *Their face had a virginal look.* □ **virginal**

vir'ginity *noun* the state of being a virgin. □ **virginité**

virile [virail] *adjective* **1** manly; refering to masculine strength or energy: *In Greek legends, Hercules is a virile hero with extreme physical power.* □ **viril**

2 having sexual ability to father many children: *Claude is a virile man who has already had nine children.* □ **viril**

virility [vərilətiː] *noun* **1** the state of being virile; the state of having extreme vigor or strength: *Weight lifting will increase your strength and virility.* □ **virilité**

2 the state of being sexually and physically able to have many children: *Paul thought of himself as a virile man and proved his virility by fathering ten children.* □ **virilité**

virtual [virtʃuəl] *adjective* in effect, as good as although not actually so; of images generated by computer: *Sarah was reduced to virtual poverty after losing her job; With the special glasses, we experienced virtual reality and felt as though we were actually walking on the surface of the moon.* □ **virtuel**

'**virtually** ['vəːtʃuəli] *adverb* **1** certainly or effectively: *The band at the dance was virtually unknown.* □ **virtuellement**

2 more or less, though not strictly speaking; in effect: *He was virtually penniless.* □ **pratiquement**

virtue ['vəːtʃuː] *noun* **1** a good moral quality: *Honesty is a virtue.* □ **vertu**

2 a good quality: *The house is small, but it has the virtue of being easy to clean.* □ **avantage**

3 goodness of character *etc*: *She is a person of great virtue.* □ **vertu, mérite**

'**virtuous** *adjective* morally good: *She is a virtuous young woman.* □ **vertueux**

'**virtuously** *adverb.* □ **vertueusement**

'**virtuousness** *noun.* □ **vertu**

virtuoso [vəːtʃu'ousou] – *plurals* ,**virtu'osos**, **virtu'osi** – *noun* a person who knows a great deal about *eg* music, painting, *especially* a skilled performer: *He's a virtuoso on the violin; (also adjective) a virtuoso pianist/performance.* □ **(de) virtuose**

,**virtu'osity** [-'o-] *noun* great skill in one of the fine arts: *I am impressed by the virtuosity of that musician.* □ **virtuosité**

virus ['vaiərəs] *noun* any of various types of germs that are a cause of disease. □ **virus**

■ *adjective: He is suffering from a virus infection.* □ **viral**

visa ['viːzə] *noun* a mark or stamp put on a passport by the authorities of a country to show that the bearer may travel to, or in, that country: *I have applied for a visa for the United States.* □ **visa**

viscount ['vaikaunt] *noun* a nobleman next in rank below an earl. □ **vicomte**

'**viscountess** *noun* **1** the wife or widow of a viscount. □ **vicomtesse**

2 a woman of the same rank as a viscount. □ **vicomtesse**

vise see **vice¹**.

visible ['vizǝbl] *adjective* able to be seen: *The house is visible through the trees; The scar on her face is scarcely visible now.* □ **visible**

'**visibly** *adverb.* □ **visiblement**

,**visi'bility** *noun* the range of distance over which things may be (clearly) seen: *Visibility is poor today; Visibility in the fog was down to ten metres in places.* □ **visibilité**

vision ['viʒǝn] *noun* 1 something seen in the imagination or in a dream: *God appeared to him in a vision.* □ **vision**

2 the ability to see or plan into the future: *Politicians should be people of vision.* □ **clairvoyance**

3 the ability to see or the sense of sight: *He is slowly losing his vision.* □ **vue**

visit ['vizit] *verb* 1 to go to see (a person or place): *We visited my parents at the weekend; They visited the ruins at Pompei while they were on holiday.* □ **visiter**

2 to stay in (a place) or with (a person) for a time: *Many birds visit (Canada) only during the summer months.* □ **séjourner (à/chez)**

■ *noun* an act of going to see someone or something for pleasure, socially, professionally *etc*, or going to stay for a time: *We went on a visit to my aunt's; the children's visit to the museum.* □ **visite**

'**visitor** *noun* a person who visits, socially or professionally: *I'm expecting visitors from America; We're having visitors next week.* □ **visiteur, euse**

visual ['viʒuǝl] *adjective* of sight or the process of seeing: *strange visual effects.* □ **visuel**

'**visually** *adverb.* □ **visuellement**

vital ['vaitl] *adjective* 1 essential; of the greatest importance: *Speed is vital to the success of our plan; It is vital that we arrive at the hospital soon.* □ **vital**

2 lively and energetic: *a vital person/personality.* □ **vif**

,**vi'tality** [-'ta-] *noun* liveliness and energy: *a girl of tremendous vitality.* □ **vitalité**

vitamin ['vaitǝmin] *noun* any of a group of substances necessary for healthy life, different ones occurring in different natural things such as raw fruit, dairy products, fish, meat *etc*: *A healthy diet is full of vitamins; Vitamin C is found in fruit and vegetables;* (*also adjective*) *vitamin pills.* □ **(de) vitamine**

vivacious [vi'veiʃǝs] *adjective* lively and bright: *She is vivacious and attractive.* □ **vif**

vi'vaciously *adverb.* □ **avec vivacité**
vi'vaciousness *noun.* □ **vivacité**

vivid ['vivid] *adjective* 1 (of colours *etc*) brilliant; very bright: *The door was painted a vivid yellow; The trees were vivid in their autumn colours.* □ **vif**

2 clear; striking: *I have many vivid memories of that holiday; a vivid image/description.* □ **clair; frappant**

3 (of the imagination) active; lively: *She has a vivid imagination.* □ **vif**

'**vividly** *adverb.* □ **vivement**

'**vividness** *noun.* □ **vivacité**

vixen ['viksn] *noun* a female fox: *The vixen was followed by her cubs.* □ **renarde**

vocabulary [vǝ'kabjulǝri] – *plural* **vo'cabularies** – *noun*

1 words in general: *This book contains some difficult vocabulary.* □ **vocabulaire**

2 (the stock of) words known and used *eg* by one person, or within a particular trade or profession: *He has a vocabulary of about 20 000 words; the specialized vocabulary of nuclear physics.* □ **vocabulaire**

3 a list of words in alphabetical order with meanings *eg* added as a supplement to a book dealing with a particular subject: *This edition of Shakespeare's plays has a good vocabulary at the back.* □ **lexique**

vocal ['voukǝl] *adjective* 1 of, or concerning, the voice: *vocal music.* □ **vocal**

2 (of a person) talkative; keen to make one's opinions heard by other people: *She's always very vocal at meetings.* □ **qui se fait entendre**

vo'cally *adverb.* □ **à haute voix; oralement**

'**vocalist** *noun* a singer: *a female vocalist.* □ **chanteur, euse**

vocal cords folds of membrane in the larynx that produce the sounds used in speech, singing *etc* when vibrated. □ **cordes vocales**

vocation [vou'keiʃǝn] *noun* 1 a feeling of having been called (by God), or born *etc*, to do a particular type of work: *He had a sense of vocation about his work as a doctor.* □ **vocation**

2 the work done, profession entered *etc* (as a result of such a feeling): *Law is her vocation; Many people regard teaching as a vocation.* □ **vocation**

vodka ['vodkǝ] *noun* an alcoholic spirit made from rye or sometimes from potatoes, originating in Russia. □ **vodka**

vogue [voug] *noun* a fashion: *Short hair is the vogue.* □ **mode**

in vogue fashionable: *The French style of dress is in vogue just now.* □ **à la mode**

voice [vois] *noun* 1 the sounds from the mouth made in speaking or singing: *He has a very deep voice; She spoke in a quiet/loud/angry/kind voice.* □ **voix**

2 the voice regarded as the means of expressing opinion: *The voice of the people should not be ignored; the voice of reason/conscience.* □ **voix**

■ *verb* 1 to express (feelings *etc*): *He voiced the discontent of the whole group.* □ **exprimer**

2 to produce the sound of (*especially* a consonant) with a vibration of the vocal cords as well as with the breath: *'Th' should be voiced in 'this' but not in 'think'.* □ **sonoriser**

voiced *adjective* (*negative* **unvoiced**). □ **sonore**
'**voiceless** *adjective.* □ **sans voix**

be in good voice to have one's voice in good condition for singing or speaking: *The choir was in good voice tonight.* □ **être en voix**

lose one's voice to be unable to speak *eg* because of having a cold, sore throat *etc*: *When I had 'flu I lost my voice for three days.* □ **perdre la voix**

raise one's voice to speak more loudly than normal *especially* in anger: *I don't want to have to raise my voice to you again.* □ **élever la voix**

void [void] *adjective* 1 not valid or binding: *The treaty has been declared void.* □ **nul**

2 (*with* **of**) lacking entirely: *a statement void of mean-*

ing. □ **vide de**

■ *noun* a huge empty space, *especially* (*with* **the**) outer space: *The rocket shot up into the void*; *Her death left a void in her husband's life.* □ **vide**

volcano [vol'keinou] – *plural* **vol'canoes** – *noun* a hill or mountain with an opening through which molten rock, ashes *etc* periodically erupt, or have erupted in the past, from inside the earth: *The village was destroyed when the volcano erupted.* □ **volcan**

vol'canic [-'ka-] *adjective* of, like, or produced by, a volcano: *volcanic rock.* □ **volcanique**

volley ['voli] *noun* 1 in tennis, the hitting of a ball before it bounces. □ **volée**

2 a burst of firing *etc*: *a volley of shots*; *a volley of questions/curses.* □ **volée**

■ *verb* 1 to hit (a ball *etc*) before it bounces: *He volleyed the ball back to his opponent.* □ **attraper à la volée**

2 to fire a rapid burst of (bullets, questions *etc*). □ **tirer une volée, lâcher un torrent de**

'volleyball *noun* a game in which a ball is volleyed over a high net, using the hands. □ **volley-ball**

volt [voult] *noun* (*often abbreviated to* **V**) the unit used in measuring the force driving electricity through a circuit, or the strength of an electric current. □ **volt**

'voltage [-tidʒ] *noun* (a) force measured in volts: *Low voltage reduces the current, making the lights burn dimly.* □ **voltage**

volume ['voljum] *noun* 1 a book: *This library contains over a million volumes.* □ **volume**

2 one of a series of connected books: *Where is volume fifteen of the encyclopedia?* □ **volume**

3 the amount of space occupied by something, expressed in cubic measurement: *What is the volume of the gas tank?* □ **volume**

4 amount: *A large volume of work remains to be done.* □ **quantité**

5 level of sound *eg* on a radio, television *etc*: *Turn up the volume on the radio.* □ **volume**

voluntary ['volǝntǝri] *adjective* 1 done, given *etc* by choice, not by accident or because of being forced: *Their action was completely voluntary – nobody asked them to do that.* □ **volontaire**

2 run, financed *etc* by such actions, contributions *etc*: *He does a lot of work for a voluntary organization.* □ **bénévole**

voluntarily ['volǝntǝrǝli, volǝn'terǝli] *adverb*. □ **volontairement**

volunteer [volǝn'tiǝ] *verb* 1 to offer oneself for a particular task, of one's own free will: *He volunteered to act as messenger*; *She volunteered for the dangerous job.* □ **se porter volontaire**

2 to offer (*eg* an opinion, information *etc*): *Two or three people volunteered suggestions.* □ **offrir**

■ *noun* a person who offers to do, or does, something (*especially* who joins the army) of his or her own free will: *If we can get enough volunteers we shall not force people to join the Army.* □ **volontaire**

vomit ['vomit] *verb* to throw out (the contents of the stomach or other matter) through the mouth; to be sick:

Whenever the ship started to move they felt like vomiting. □ **vomir**

■ *noun* food *etc* ejected from the stomach. □ **vomi(ssure)**

voodoo ['vuːduː] *noun* a type of witchcraft originally practised by certain Negro races in the West Indies. □ **vaudou**

vote [vout] *noun* (the right to show) one's wish or opinion, *eg* in a ballot or by raising a hand *etc*, *especially* at an election or in a debate: *In Britain, the vote was given to women over twenty-one in 1928*; *Nowadays everyone over eighteen has a vote*; *A vote was taken to decide the matter.* □ **vote; droit de vote**

■ *verb* 1 to cast or record one's vote: *She voted for the Conservative candidate*; *I always vote Labour*; *I shall vote against the restoration of capital punishment.* □ **voter**

2 to allow, by a vote, the provision of (something) *eg* to someone, for a purpose *etc*: *They were voted $5,000 to help them in their research.* □ **voter**

'voter *noun* a person who votes or has the right to vote. □ **électeur, trice**

vote of confidence a vote taken to establish whether the government or other authority still has the majority's support for its policies. □ **vote de confiance**

vote of thanks an invitation, *usually* in the form of a short speech, to an audience *etc* to show gratitude to a speaker *etc* by applauding *etc*: *Mrs. Smith proposed a vote of thanks to the organizers of the concert.* □ **motion de remerciements**

vouch [vautʃ] *verb* 1 to say that one is sure that something is fact or truth: *Will you vouch for the truth of the statement?* □ **garantir**

2 to guarantee the honesty *etc* of (a person): *My friends will vouch for me.* □ **répondre de**

'voucher *noun* a piece of paper which confirms that a sum of money has been, or will be, paid: *a sales voucher.* □ **reçu, bon de caisse**

vow [vau] *noun* a solemn promise, *especially* one made to God: *The monks have made/taken a vow of silence*; *marriage vows.* □ **vœu**

■ *verb* 1 to make a solemn promise (that): *He vowed that he would die rather than surrender.* □ **jurer (de/que)**

2 to threaten: *She vowed revenge on all her enemies.* □ **jurer (de/que)**

vowel ['vauǝl] *noun* 1 in English and many other languages, the letters *a, e, i, o, u.* □ **voyelle**

2 (*also* **vowel sound**) any of the sounds represented by these five letters or by *y*, or by combination of these with each other and/or *w*. □ **voyelle**

voyage ['voiidʒ] *noun* a *usually* long journey, *especially* by sea: *The voyage to America used to take many weeks.* □ **traversée**

■ *verb* to make such a journey: *They voyaged for many months.* □ **voyager (par mer)**

'voyager *noun* an old word for a person making a voyage, or who has made several voyages. □ **voyageur, euse**

vs *see* **versus**.

vulgar ['vʌlgǝ] *adjective* 1 not generally socially accept-

able, decent or polite; ill-mannered: *Such behaviour is regarded as vulgar.* □ **vulgaire**
2 of the common or ordinary people: *the vulgar tongue/ language.* □ **vulgaire**
'vulgarly *adverb.* □ **vulgairement**
vul'garity [-'ga-] – *plural* **vul'garities** – *noun* (an example of) bad manners, bad taste *etc*, in *eg* speech, behaviour *etc*: *the vulgarity of his language.* □ **vulgarité**

vulnerable ['vʌlnərəbl] *adjective* unprotected against attack; liable to be hurt or damaged: *Small animals are often vulnerable to attack.* □ **vulnérable**
,vulnera'bility *noun.* □ **vulnérabilité**
vulture ['vʌltʃə] *noun* a type of large bird of prey feeding chiefly on dead bodies. □ **vautour**
vying *see* **vie**.

Ww

waddle ['wodl] *verb* to take short steps and move from side to side in walking (as a duck does): *The ducks waddled across the road; The young child waddled down the street.* □ **(se) dandiner**
■ *noun* a clumsy, rocking way of walking. □ **dandinement**

wade [weid] *verb* 1 to go or walk (through water, mud *etc*) with some difficulty: *She waded across the river towards me; I've finally managed to wade through that boring book I had to read.* □ **patauger (dans)**
2 to cross (a river *etc*) by wading: *We'll wade the stream at its shallowest point.* □ **passer à gué**
'**wader** *noun* any of several types of bird that wade in search of food. □ **échassier**

wafer ['weifə] *noun* a type of very thin biscuit, often eaten with ice-cream. □ **gaufrette**
,**wafer-'thin** *adjective* extremely thin. □ **mince comme une pelure d'oignon**

waffle ['wofl] *verb* to talk on and on foolishly, pretending that one knows something which one does not: *This lecturer will waffle on for hours.* □ **parler pour ne rien dire**
■ *noun* talk of this kind: *His speech was pure waffle; He has no idea what he's talking about.* □ **verbiage**

wag [wag] – *past tense, past participle* **wagged** – *verb* (especially of a dog's tail) to (cause to) move to and fro, *especially* from side to side: *The dog wagged its tail with pleasure.* □ **remuer**
■ *noun* a single wagging movement: *The dog's tail gave a feeble wag.* □ **frétillement**

wage[1] [weidʒ] *verb* to carry on or engage in (*especially* a war): *The North waged war on/against the South.* □ **faire (la guerre)**

wage[2] [weidʒ] *noun* (*also* '**wages** *noun plural*) a regular, *usually* weekly rather than monthly, payment for the work that one does: *He spends all his wages on books; What is her weekly wage?* □ **salaire, paye**
'**wage packet** *noun* 1 the packet in which wages are paid: *The cashier puts the workmen's money in wage packets.* □ **enveloppe de paye**
2 wages: *Because of heavier taxation, my wage packet has been getting smaller.* □ **paye**

wager ['weidʒə] *noun* a bet: *We made a wager that he would win.* □ **pari**
■ *verb* to bet (something) on the chance of something happening: *I'll wager (ten dollars) that I can jump further than you.* □ **parier, gager**

waggle ['wagl] *verb* to (cause to) move from side to side: *His beard waggled as he ate.* □ **remuer**
■ *noun* such a movement. □ **remuement**

wagon, waggon ['wagən] *noun* 1 a type of four-wheeled vehicle for carrying heavy loads: *a hay wagon.* □ **chariot, charrette**
2 an open railway carriage for goods: *a goods wagon.* □ **wagon (de marchandises)**

waif [weif] *noun* a stray, uncared-for child: *a poor little waif.* □ **enfant abandonné**

wail [weil] *verb* to utter sorrowful or complaining cries: *The child is wailing over its broken toy.* □ **se lamenter**
■ *noun* a long cry: *wails of grief; I heard the wail of a police siren.* □ **hurlement**

waist [weist] *noun* 1 (the measurement around) the narrow part of the human body between the ribs and hips: *She has a very small waist.* □ **(tour de) taille**
2 the narrow middle part of something similar, *eg* a violin, guitar *etc*. □ **échancrure**
3 the part of an article of clothing which goes around one's waist: *Can you take in the waist of these trousers?* □ **ceinture**
'**waisted** *adjective* shaped to fit around the waist: *a waisted jacket.* □ **cintré**
waistband ['weisband] *noun* the part of a pair of trousers, skirt *etc* which goes around the waist: *The waistband of this skirt is too tight.* □ **ceinture**
waistcoat ['weiskout] *noun* (*American* **vest**) a short, *usually* sleeveless jacket worn immediately under the outer jacket: *a three-piece suit consists of trousers, jacket and waistcoat.* □ **gilet**

wait [weit] *verb* 1 (*with* **for**) to remain or stay (in the same place or without doing anything): *Wait (for) two minutes (here) while I go inside; I'm waiting for John (to arrive).* □ **attendre**
2 (*with* **for**) to expect: *I was just waiting for that pile of dishes to fall!* □ **(s')attendre (à)**
3 (*with* **on**) to serve dishes, drinks *etc* (at table): *This servant will wait on your guests; He waits at table.* □ **servir**
■ *noun* an act of waiting; a delay: *There was a long wait before they could get on the train.* □ **attente**
'**waiter** – *feminine* '**waitress** – *noun* a person who serves people with food *etc* at table: *She is a waitress in a café; Which waiter served you in the restaurant?* □ **serveur, euse**
'**waiting list** *noun* a list of the names of people who are waiting for something: *She is on the waiting list for medical treatment.* □ **liste d'attente**
'**waiting room** *noun* a room in which people may wait (*eg* at a station, doctor's office *etc*). □ **salle d'attente**

waive [weiv] 1 to give up or not insist upon (*eg* a claim or right): *He waived his claim to all the land north of the river.* □ **renoncer (à)**
2 not to demand or enforce (a fine, penalty *etc*): *The judge waived the sentence and let him go free.* □ **abandonner**

wake[1] [weik] – *past tense* **woke** [wouk], (*rare*) **waked**: *past participle* **woken** ['woukən], (*rare*) **waked** – *verb* to bring or come back to consciousness after being asleep: *She woke to find that it was raining; Go and wake the others, will you?* □ **(se) réveiller**
'**wakeful** *adjective* 1 not asleep; not able to sleep: *a wakeful child.* □ **(bien) éveillé**
2 (of a night) in which one gets little sleep: *We spent a wakeful night worrying about her.* □ **(nuit) blanche**
'**wakefully** *adverb*. □ **sans dormir**
'**wakefulness** *noun*. □ **insomnie; vigilance**
'**waken** *verb* to wake: *What time are you going to waken him?; I wakened early.* □ **(se) réveiller**

wake up 1 to wake: *Wake up! You're late*; *The baby woke up in the middle of the night.* □ **(se) réveiller**

2 to become aware of: *It is time you woke up to the fact that you are not working hard enough.* □ **prendre conscience de**

wake² [weik] *noun* a strip of smooth-looking or foamy water left behind a ship. □ **sillage**

in the wake of immediately behind or after: *Our tiny boat was caught in the wake of the huge ship.* □ **dans le sillage de**

walk [wo:k] *verb* **1** (of people or animals) to (cause to) move on foot at a pace slower than running, never having both or all the feet off the ground at once: *He walked across the room and sat down*; *How long will it take to walk to the station?*; *She walks her dog in the park every morning.* □ **marcher; promener**

2 to travel on foot for pleasure: *We're going walking in the hills for our holidays.* □ **se promener (à pied)**

3 to move on foot along: *It's dangerous to walk the streets of New York alone after dark.* □ **marcher (dans)**

■ *noun* **1** (the distance covered during) an outing or journey on foot: *She wants to go for/to take a walk*; *It's a long walk to the station.* □ **promenade; marche**

2 a way or manner of walking: *I recognised her walk.* □ **démarche**

3 a route for walking: *There are many pleasant walks in this area.* □ **itinéraire**

'walker *noun* a person who goes walking for pleasure: *We met a party of walkers as we were going home.* □ **promeneur, euse**

,walkie-'talkie *noun* a portable two-way radio: *The soldiers spoke to each other on the walkie-talkie.* □ **émetteur-récepteur portatif**

'walking stick *noun* a stick used (*especially* as an aid to balance) when walking: *The old lady has been using a walking stick since she hurt her leg.* □ **canne**

Walkman® *noun* a small portable radio that plays tapes and is equipped with earphones: *Bud listens to his Walkman when he jogs so his music will not disturb anyone else.* □ **baladeur**

'walkover *noun* an easy victory: *It was a walkover! We won 8–nil.* □ **victoire facile**

'walkway *noun* a path *etc* for pedestrians only. □ **passage pour piétons**

walk all over (someone) to pay no respect to (a person's) rights, feelings *etc*: *He'll walk all over you if you let him.* □ **marcher sur les pieds de**

walk off with 1 to win easily: *He walked off with all the prizes at the school sports.* □ **gagner haut la main**

2 to steal: *The thieves have walked off with my best silver and china.* □ **voler, piquer**

walk of life a way of earning one's living; an occupation or profession: *People from all walks of life went to the minister's funeral.* □ **profession, métier**

walk on air to feel extremely happy *etc*: *She's walking on air since he asked her to marry him.* □ **être aux anges**

walkout *noun* a strike; a protest by workers resulting in the disruption of work: *Although the strike vote hasn't been called yet, everyone anticipates a walkout by noon today.* □ **débrayage**

wall [wo:l] *noun* **1** something built of stone, brick, plaster, wood *etc* and used to separate off or enclose something: *There's a wall at the bottom of the garden*: *The Great Wall of China*; *a garden wall.* □ **mur(aille)**

2 any of the sides of a building or room: *One wall of the room is yellow – the rest are white.* □ **mur**

■ *verb* (*often with* **in**) to enclose (something) with a wall: *We've walled in the playground to prevent the children getting out.* □ **entourer d'un mur**

walled *adjective*: *a walled city.* □ **fortifié, entouré d'un mur**

-walled having (a certain type or number of) wall(s): *a high-walled garden.* □ **à (...) mur(s)**

'wallpaper *noun* paper used to decorate interior walls of houses *etc*: *My wife wants to put wallpaper on the walls but I would rather paint them.* □ **papier peint**

■ *verb* to put such paper on: *I have wallpapered the front room.* □ **tapisser**

,wall-to-'wall *adjective* (of a carpet *etc*) covering the entire floor of a room *etc*. □ **moquette**

have one's back to the wall to be in a desperate situation: *The army in the south have their backs to the wall, and are fighting a losing battle.* □ **avoir le dos au mur**

up the wall crazy: *This business is sending/driving me up the wall!* □ **fou**

wallet ['wolit] *noun* **1** a small (*usually* folding) case made of soft leather, plastic *etc*, carried in the pocket and used for holding (*especially* paper) money, personal papers *etc*: *He has lost all his money – his wallet has been stolen.* □ **portefeuille**

2 a similar case containing other things: *a plastic wallet containing a set of small tools.* □ **trousse**

wallop ['woləp] *verb* to strike (something or someone) hard: *He walloped the desk with his fist*; *I'll wallop you if you do that again!* □ **cogner, taper (sur)**

■ *noun* a heavy or powerful blow: *He gave John a wallop right on the chin.* □ **gros coup**

wallow ['wolou] *verb* to roll about with enjoyment: *This, hippopotamus wallowed in the mud.* □ **se vautrer (dans)**

■ *noun* an act of wallowing. □ **fait de se vautrer**

walnut ['wo:lnʌt] *noun* **1** a type of tree whose wood is used for making furniture *etc*. □ **noyer**

2 the nut produced by this tree. □ **noix**

3 (*also adjective*) (of) the wood of the tree: *a walnut table.* □ **en/de noyer**

walrus ['wo:lrəs] – *plurals* **'walruses, 'walrus** – *noun* a type of large sea animal with huge tusks, related to the seal. □ **morse**

waltz [wo:lts] *noun* (a piece of music for) a type of slow ballroom dance performed by couples: *The band is playing a waltz*; (*also adjective*) *waltz music.* □ **(de) valse**

■ *verb* **1** to dance a waltz (with): *Can you waltz?*; *She waltzed her partner around the room.* □ **valser (avec)**

2 to move cheerfully or with confidence: *He waltzed into the room and told us that he was getting married the next day.* □ **(entrer) d'un pas joyeux**

wan [won] *adjective* pale and sickly-looking: *She still looks wan after her illness.* □ **pâle**

'wanly *adverb*. □ **faiblement**

'wanness *noun*. □ **pâleur**

wand [wond] *noun* a long slender rod *eg* used as the symbol of magic power by conjurors, fairies *etc*: *In the story, the fairy waved her magic wand and the frog became a prince.* □ **baguette (magique)**

wander ['wondə] *verb* **1** to go, move, walk *etc* (about, in or on) from place to place with no definite destination in mind: *I'd like to spend a holiday wandering through France*; *The mother wandered the streets looking for her child.* □ **errer (dans), (se) promener**

2 to go astray or move away from the proper place or home: *His mind wanders*; *My attention was wandering.* □ **(s')égarer**

■ *noun* an act of wandering: *He's gone for a wander around the shops.* □ **tour**

'**wanderer** *noun.* □ **vagabond, onde**

'**wanderlust** *noun* the wish to travel: *She's always travelling – her wanderlust will never be satisfied.* □ **passion du voyage**

wane [wein] *verb* (of the moon) to appear to become smaller as less of it is visible. □ **décroître**

on the wane becoming less: *His power is on the wane.* □ **en déclin**

wangle ['waŋgl] *verb* to obtain or achieve (something) by trickery: *He got us seats for the concert – I don't know how he wangled it.* □ **(se) débrouiller (pour avoir)**

want [wont] *verb* **1** to be interested in having or doing, or to wish to have or do (something); to desire: *Do you want a cigarette?*; *She wants to know where he is*; *He wants to go home.* □ **vouloir**

2 to need: *This wall wants a coat of paint.* □ **avoir besoin de**

3 to lack: *This house wants none of the usual modern features but I do not like it*; *The people will want (= be poor) no longer.* □ **manquer (de)**

■ *noun* **1** something desired: *The child has a long list of wants.* □ **demande**

2 poverty: *They have lived in want for many years.* □ **pauvreté**

3 a lack: *There's no want of opportunities these days.* □ **manque (de)**

'**wanted** *adjective* **1** being searched for by the police because of having committed a criminal act: *She is a wanted woman*; *He is wanted for murder.* □ **recherché**

2 (*negative* **unwanted**) (of people) needed; cared for: *Old people must be made to feel wanted.* □ **utile; dont on a besoin**

want for to lack: *She wants for nothing.* □ **manquer de**

wanton ['wontən] *adjective* **1** without reason; motiveless: *wanton cruelty*; *the wanton destruction of property.* □ **gratuit**

2 (of a person) immoral: *wanton young women.* □ **dévergondé**

'**wantonly** *adverb.* □ **gratuitement**

'**wantonness** *noun.* □ **gratuité**

war [woː] *noun* (an) armed struggle, *especially* between nations: *Their leader has declared war on Britain*; *The larger army will win the war*; *the horrors of war*; (*also adjective*) *He is guilty of war crimes.* □ **(de) guerre**

■ *verb – past tense, past participle* **warred** – to fight: *The two countries have been warring constantly for generations.* □ **(se) faire la guerre**

'**warlike** *adjective* (*negative* **unwarlike**) fond of, or likely to begin, war: *a warlike nation.* □ **belliqueux**

'**warrior** ['wo-] *noun* a soldier or skilled fighting man, *especially* in primitive societies: *The chief of the tribe called his warriors together*; (*also adjective*) *a warrior prince.* □ **guerrier, ière**

war correspondent a newspaper reporter who writes articles on a war *especially* from the scene of fighting. □ **correspondant, ante de guerre**

'**war cry** – *plural* '**war cries** – *noun* a shout used in battle as an encouragement to the soldiers: *'For king and country' was the war cry of the troops as they faced the enemy.* □ **cri de guerre**

'**war dance** *noun* a dance performed by the people of some primitive societies before going to war. □ **danse guerrière**

'**warfare** *noun* fighting, as in a war: *He refused to fight, because he has religious objections to warfare.* □ **guerre**

'**warhead** *noun* the explosive section of a missile, torpedo *etc*: *nuclear warheads.* □ **ogive**

'**warhorse** *noun* a horse used in battle. □ **cheval de bataille**

'**warlord** *noun* a very powerful military leader. □ **seigneur de la guerre**

'**warmonger** *noun* a person who encourages war(s), often for personal reasons. □ **belliciste**

'**warpaint** *noun* paint applied to the face *etc* by the people of some primitive societies before going into battle. □ **peinture de guerre**

'**warship** *noun* a ship used in war or defence. □ **navire de guerre**

'**wartime** *noun* the time during which a country, a people *etc* is at war: *There is a great deal of hardship and misery in wartime*; (*also adjective*) *a wartime economy.* □ **(temps) de guerre**

war of nerves a war, contest *etc* in which each side tries to win by making the other nervous, *eg* by bluff, rather than by actually fighting: *That game of chess was a war of nerves.* □ **guerre des nerfs**

warble ['woːbl] *verb* to sing in a trembling voice, as some birds do: *The bird was warbling (his song) on a high branch.* □ **gazouiller**

■ *noun* an act, or the sound, of warbling: *the warble of a bird in summer.* □ **gazouillement**

'**warbler** *noun* any of several kinds of small singing bird. □ **fauvette**

ward [woːd] *noun* **1** a room with a bed or beds for patients in a hospital *etc*: *He is in a surgical ward of the local hospital.* □ **salle**

2 a person who is under the legal control and care of someone who is not his or her parent or (a **ward of court**) of a court: *She was made a ward of court so that she could not marry until she was eighteen.* □ **pupille (sous tutelle judiciaire)**

'**warder** *noun* a person who guards prisoners in a jail: *He shot a warder and escaped from jail.* □ **gardien, ienne de prison**

warden ['woːdn] *noun* **1** the person in charge of an old people's home, a student residence *etc*: *The warden has* *reported that two students are missing from the hostel.* □ **directeur, trice**

2 (*also* **traffic warden**) a person who controls parking and the flow of traffic in an area: *If the (traffic) warden finds your car parked there you will be fined.* □ **patrouilleur, euse**

3 a person who has been appointed to look after the civil population in case of *eg* air raids (an **air raid warden**). □ **préposé, ée à la défense passive**

4 (*also* **game warden**) a person who guards a game reserve. □ **gardien, ienne**

wardrobe ['wɔːdroub] *noun* **1** a cupboard in which clothes may be hung: *Hang your suit in the wardrobe.* □ **garde-robe**

2 a stock of clothing: *She bought a complete new wardrobe in Paris.* □ **garde-robe, armoire**

-ward(s) [wəd(z)] in a (certain) direction, as in **backward(s), homeward(s).** □ **vers**

-ware [weə] manufactured articles (made of a particular material): *silverware/glassware.* □ **articles de/en**

wares *noun plural* articles for sale: *a tradesman selling his wares.* □ **marchandises**

warehouse *noun* a building in which goods are stored: *a furniture warehouse.* □ **entrepôt**

warm [wɔːm] *adjective* **1** moderately, or comfortably, hot: *Are you warm enough, or shall I close the window?*; *a warm summer's day.* □ **(assez) chaud**

2 (of clothes) protecting the wearer from the cold: *a warm jumper.* □ **chaud**

3 welcoming, friendly, enthusiastic *etc*: *a warm welcome*; *a warm smile.* □ **chaleureux**

4 tending to make one hot: *This is warm work!* □ **qui donne chaud**

5 (of colours, *especially* the pale ones) enriched by a certain quantity of red or pink, or (of red *etc*) rich and bright: *a warm red*; *I don't want white walls – I want something warmer.* □ **chaud**

■ *verb* **1** to make moderately hot: *He warmed his hands in front of the fire.* □ **(se) (ré)chauffer**

2 to become friendly or enthusiastic (about): *She warmed to his charm.* □ **se sentir attiré (par)**

■ *noun* an act of warming: *Give your hands a warm in front of the fire.* □ **(se) réchauffer**

'warmly *adverb.* □ **chaudement**

warmness *noun.* □ **chaleur**

'warmth [-θ] *noun* the state of being warm: *the warmth of the fire*; *The actor was delighted by the warmth of the applause*; *The warmth of her smile made me feel welcome.* □ **chaleur**

,warm-'blooded *adjective* **1** having a blood temperature greater than that of the surrounding atmosphere: *warm-blooded animals such as man.* □ **à sang chaud**

2 enthusiastic; passionate: *When I was young and warm-blooded, I was passionate about many things that don't interest me now.* □ **enthousiaste**

,warm'hearted *adjective* kind and affectionate: *a warmhearted old lady*; *a warmhearted action.* □ **chaleureux**

,warm'heartedness *noun.* □ **chaleur**

warm up to make or become warm: *The room will soon*

warm up; *Have a cup of coffee to warm you up.* □ **(se) réchauffer**

warn [wɔːn] *verb* **1** to tell (a person) in advance (about a danger *etc*): *Black clouds warned us of the approaching storm*; *They warned her that she would be ill if she didn't rest.* □ **prévenir (de)**

2 to advise (someone against doing something): *I was warned about/against speeding by the policeman*; *They warned him not to be late.* □ **avertir (de)**

'warning *noun* **1** an event, or something said or done, that warns: *He gave her a warning against driving too fast*; *His heart attack will be a warning to him not to work so hard.* □ **avertissement**

2 advance notice or advance signs: *The earthquake came without warning.* □ **avertissement**

■ *adjective* giving a warning: *She received a warning message.* □ **d'avertissement**

'warningly *adverb: She looked warningly at the naughty boy.* □ **en signe d'avertissement**

warp[1] [wɔːp] *verb* **1** to make or become twisted out of shape: *The door has been warped by all the rain we've had lately.* □ **gauchir**

2 to cause to think or act in an abnormal way: *His experiences had warped his judgment/mind.* □ **fausser**

■ *noun* the shape into which something is twisted by warping: *The rain has given this wood a permanent warp.* □ **gauchissement**

warped *adjective.* □ **tordu, faussé**

warp[2] [wɔːp] *noun* (*usually with* **the**) the set of threads lying lengthwise in a loom during weaving (the other being the **weft** [weft]). □ **chaîne**

warrant ['worənt] *verb* **1** to justify: *A slight cold does not warrant your staying off work.* □ **justifier**

2 an old word to state confidently or (be willing to) bet that: *I'll warrant he's gone riding instead of doing his work.* □ **assurer (que)**

■ *noun* something that gives authority, *especially* a legal document giving the police the authority for searching someone's house, arresting someone *etc*: *The police have a warrant for his arrest.* □ **mandat**

warren ['worən] *noun* a place where many rabbits have their burrows. □ **terrier**

warrior *see* **war.**

wart [wɔːt] *noun* a small hard growth on the skin: *He has warts on his fingers.* □ **verrue**

wary ['weəri] *adjective* cautious or on one's guard (about or concerning): *a wary animal*; *Be wary of lending money to her.* □ **prudent; méfiant**

'warily *adverb.* □ **avec prudence**

'wariness *noun.* □ **prudence**

was *see* **be.**

wash [woʃ] *verb* **1** to clean (a thing or person, *especially* oneself) with (soap and) water or other liquid: *How often do you wash your hair?*; *You wash (the dishes) and I'll dry*; *We can wash in the stream.* □ **(se) laver**

2 to be able to be washed without being damaged: *This fabric doesn't wash very well.* □ **supporter le lavage**

3 to flow (against, over *etc*): *The waves washed (against) the ship.* □ **clapoter (contre)**

4 to sweep (away *etc*) by means of water: *The floods*

have washed away hundreds of houses. □ **emporter**

■ *noun* **1** an act of washing: *He's just gone to have a wash.* □ **(faire sa) toilette**

2 things to be washed or being washed: *Your sweater is in the wash.* □ **lavage**

3 the flowing or lapping (of waves *etc*): *the wash of waves against the rocks.* □ **clapotis**

4 a liquid with which something is washed: *a mouthwash.* □ **liquide (de nettoyage)**

5 a thin coat (of water-colour paint *etc*), *especially* in a painting: *The background of the picture was a pale blue wash.* □ **lavis**

6 the waves caused by a moving boat *etc*: *The rowing-boat was tossing about in the wash from the ship's propellers.* □ **remous, sillage**

'washable *adjective* able to be washed without being damaged: *Is this dress washable?* □ **lavable**

'washer *noun* **1** a person or thing (*eg* a machine) that washes: *They've just bought an automatic dish-washer.* □ **laveur, euse; lave-vaisselle**

2 a flat ring of rubber, metal *etc* to keep nuts or joints tight: *Our tap needs a new washer.* □ **rondelle**

'washing *noun* **1** (an) act of cleaning by water: *I don't mind washing, but I hate ironing.* □ **lessive**

2 clothes washed or to be washed: *I'll hang the washing out to dry.* □ **linge**

,washed 'out *adjective* **1** completely lacking in energy *etc*: *I feel quite washed out today.* □ **épuisé**

2 (of garments *etc*) pale, having lost colour as a result of washing: *She wore a pair of old, washed out jeans.* □ **délavé**

'washerwoman, washerman *nouns* a person who is paid to wash clothes. □ **blanchisseur, euse**

'wash (hand) basin a basin in which to wash one's face and hands: *We are having a new washhand basin installed in the bathroom.* □ **(cuvette de) lavabo**

'washing machine *noun* an electric machine for washing clothes: *She has an automatic washing machine.* □ **machine à laver**

'washing powder *noun* a powdered detergent used when washing clothes. □ **détergent**

,washing-'up *noun* dishes *etc* cleaned or to be cleaned after a meal *etc*: *I'll help you with the washing-up.* □ **vaisselle**

'washout *noun* (an idea, project, person *etc* which is) a complete failure: *He was a complete washout as a secretary.* □ **fiasco, nullité**

'washroom *noun* a lavatory. □ **toilettes**

wash up 1 to wash dishes *etc* after a meal: *I'll help you wash up; We've washed the plates up.* □ **laver (la vaisselle)**

2 to wash one's hands and face. □ **(se) débarbouiller**

3 to bring up on to the shore: *The ship was washed up on the rocks; A lot of rubbish has been washed up on the beach.* □ **rejeter (sur le rivage)**

wasn't *see* be.

wasp [wosp] *noun* a type of winged insect having a sting and a slender waist. □ **guêpe**

'waspish *adjective* (of a person) unpleasant in manner, temper *etc*: *a nasty, waspish young woman.* □ **grincheux**

'waspishly *adverb*. □ **d'un ton aigre**

'waspishness *noun*. □ **aigreur**

waste [weist] *verb* to fail to use (something) fully or in the correct or most useful way: *You're wasting my time with all these stupid questions.* □ **gaspiller**

■ *noun* **1** material which is or has been made useless: *industrial waste from the factories*; (*also adjective*) *waste material.* □ **déchets, rebut**

2 (the) act of wasting: *That was a waste of an opportunity.* □ **gaspillage**

3 a huge stretch of unused or infertile land, or of water, desert, ice *etc*: *the Arctic wastes.* □ **terres désolées**

'wastage [-tidʒ] *noun* loss by wasting; the amount wasted: *Of the total amount, roughly 20% was wastage.* □ **perte**

'wasteful *adjective* involving or causing waste: *Throwing away that bread is wasteful.* □ **gaspilleur**

'wastefully *adverb*. □ **en gaspillant**

'wastefulness *noun*. □ **manque d'économie**

waste paper paper which is thrown away as not being useful: *Offices usually have a great deal of waste paper.* □ **papier (à jeter)**

wastepaper basket ['weispeipə] a basket or other (small) container for waste paper: *Put those old letters in the wastepaper basket.* □ **corbeille à papier**

waste pipe ['weispaip] a pipe to carry off waste material, or water from a sink *etc*: *The kitchen waste pipe is blocked.* □ **(tuyau de) vidange**

waste away to decay; to lose weight, strength and health *etc*: *She is wasting away because she has a terrible disease.* □ **dépérir**

watch [wotʃ] *noun* **1** a small instrument for telling the time by, worn on the wrist or carried in the pocket of a waistcoat *etc*: *He wears a gold watch; a wrist-watch.* □ **montre**

2 a period of standing guard during the night: *I'll take the watch from two o'clock till six.* □ **garde**

3 in the navy *etc*, a group of officers and men who are on duty at a given time: *The night watch come(s) on duty soon.* □ **quart**

■ *verb* **1** to look at (someone or something): *He was watching her carefully ; She is watching television.* □ **regarder**

2 to keep a lookout (for): *They've gone to watch for the ship coming in; Could you watch for the postman?* □ **guetter**

3 to be careful of (someone or something): *Watch (that) you don't fall off!; Watch him! He's dangerous.* □ **faire attention (de/à)**

4 to guard or take care of: *Watch the prisoner and make sure she doesn't escape; Please watch the baby while I go shopping.* □ **surveiller**

5 to wait for (a chance, opportunity *etc*): *Watch your chance, and then run.* □ **attendre**

'watcher *noun*. □ **observateur, trice**

'watchful *adjective* alert and cautious: *watchful eyes; If you are watchful you will not be robbed.* □ **vigilant**

'watchfully *adverb*. □ **avec vigilance**

'watchfulness *noun*. □ **vigilance**

'watchdog *noun* a dog which guards someone's property *etc*: *We leave a watchdog in our office at night to scare away thieves.* □ **chien de garde**

'watchmaker *noun* a person who makes and repairs watches, clocks *etc*. □ **horloger, ère**

'watchman *noun* (*often* ,night 'watchman) a man employed to guard a building *etc* against thieves, *especially* at night: *The bank-robbers shot the (night) watchman.* □ **gardien, ienne (de nuit)**

'watchtower *noun* an old word for a tower on which a lookout is posted. □ **tour de guet**

'watchword *noun* a motto or slogan used by members of a group of people who think (or act) alike: *Let freedom be our watchword!* □ **mot d'ordre**

keep watch to be on guard: *He kept watch while the other soldiers slept.* □ **monter la garde**

watch one's step to be careful what one does or says: *He's in a bad mood, so watch your step and don't say anything wrong!* □ **faire attention**

watch out (*with* **for**) to be careful (of): *Watch out for the cars!*; *Watch out! The police are coming!* □ **faire attention (à)**

watch over to guard or take care of: *The mother bird is watching over her young.* □ **veiller (sur)**

water ['wɔːtə] *noun* a colourless, transparent liquid compound of hydrogen and oxygen, having no taste or smell, which turns to steam when boiled and to ice when frozen: *She drank two glasses of water*; *'Are you going swimming in the sea?' 'No, the water's too cold'*; *Each bedroom in the hotel is supplied with hot and cold running water*; (*also adjective*) *The plumber had to turn off the water supply in order to repair the pipe*; *transport by land and water.* □ **eau**

■ *verb* **1** to supply with water: *He watered the plants.* □ **arroser**

2 (of the mouth) to produce saliva: *Her mouth watered at the sight of all the food.* □ **saliver**

3 (of the eyes) to fill with tears: *The dense smoke made his eyes water.* □ **pleurer**

'waters *noun plural* a body of water such as the sea, a river *etc*: *the stormy waters of the bay.* □ **eaux**

'watery *adjective* **1** like water; diluted: *a watery fluid.* □ **aqueux; liquide**

2 (of eyes) full of fluid *eg* because of illness, cold winds *etc*. □ **larmoyant**

3 (of a colour) pale: *eyes of a watery blue.* □ **délavé**

'wateriness *noun*. □ **caractère aqueux**

water boatman a water insect with oarlike back legs that propel it through the water. □ **notonecte**

'waterborne *adjective* carried or transmitted by water: *Typhoid is a waterborne disease.* □ **d'origine hydrique**

'water closet *noun* (*abbreviation* **WC**) a lavatory. □ **toilettes**

'watercolour *noun* a type of paint which is thinned with water instead of oil. □ **aquarelle**

'watercress *noun* a herb which grows in water and is often used in salads. □ **cresson (de fontaine)**

'waterfall *noun* a natural fall of water from a height such as a rock or a cliff. □ **chute**

'waterfowl *noun* or *noun plural* a bird or birds which live on or beside water. □ **oiseau(x) aquatique(s)**

'waterfront *noun* that part of a town *etc* which faces the sea or a lake: *She lives on the waterfront.* □ **front de mer**

'waterhole *noun* a spring or other place where water can be found in a desert or other dry country: *The elephant drank from the waterhole.* □ **mare**

water hyacinth a floating water plant with violet or blue flowers. □ **lis d'eau**

'watering can *noun* a container used when watering plants. □ **arrosoir**

water level the level of the surface of a mass of water: *The water level in the reservoir is sinking/rising.* □ **niveau d'eau**

'waterlily – *plural* **'waterlilies** – *noun* a water plant with broad flat floating leaves. □ **nénuphar**

'waterlogged *adjective* (of ground) soaked in water. □ **détrempé**

water main a large underground pipe carrying a public water supply. □ **conduite principale**

'watermelon a type of melon with green skin and red flesh. □ **melon d'eau**

'waterproof *adjective* not allowing water to soak through: *waterproof material.* □ **imperméable**

■ *noun* a coat made of waterproof material: *She was wearing a waterproof.* □ **imperméable**

■ *verb* to make (material) waterproof. □ **imperméabiliser**

'watershed *noun* an area of high land from which rivers flow in different directions into different basins. □ **ligne de partage des eaux**

'water-skiing *noun* the sport of skiing on water, towed by a motor-boat. □ **ski nautique**

'water-ski *verb*. □ **faire du ski nautique**

'watertight *adjective* made in such a way that water cannot pass through. □ **étanche**

water vapour water in the form of a gas, produced by evaporation. □ **vapeur d'eau**

'waterway *noun* a channel, *eg* a canal or river, along which ships can sail. □ **voie navigable**

'waterwheel *noun* a wheel moved by water to work machinery *etc*. □ **roue hydraulique**

'waterworks *noun plural* or *noun singular* a place in which water is purified and stored before distribution to an area. □ **ouvrages de purification de l'eau**

hold water to be convincing: *His explanation won't hold water.* □ **tenir debout**

in(to) deep water in(to) trouble or danger: *I got into deep water during that argument.* □ **en mauvaise posture**

water down to dilute: *This milk has been watered down.* □ **diluer**

watt [wɔt] *noun* (*abbreviated to* **W** when written) a unit of power, *especially* of heat or light. □ **watt**

wave [weiv] *noun* **1** a moving ridge, larger than a ripple, moving on the surface of water: *rolling waves*; *a boat tossing on the waves.* □ **vague**

2 a vibration travelling *eg* through the air: *radio waves*; *sound waves*; *light waves.* □ **onde**

3 a curve or curves in the hair: *Are those waves natural?* □ **ondulation**

4 a (*usually* temporary) rise or increase: *the recent crime wave*; *a wave of violence*; *The pain came in waves.* □ **vague**

5 an act of waving: *She recognized me, and gave me a wave.* □ **signe de la main**

■ *verb* **1** to move backwards and forwards or flutter: *The flags waved gently in the breeze.* □ **flotter (au vent)**

2 to (cause hair to) curve first one way then the other: *He's had his hair waved*; *Her hair waves naturally.* □ **onduler**

3 to make a gesture (of greeting *etc*) with (*eg* the hand): *She waved to me across the street*; *Everyone was waving handkerchiefs in farewell*; *They waved goodbye.* □ **saluer d'un signe de la main, faire signe à**

'**wavy** *adjective* (of hair) full of waves: *His hair is wavy but his sister's hair is straight.* □ **ondulé**

'**waviness** *noun.* □ **ondulation(s)**

'**wave(band)** *noun* a range of wavelengths on which *eg* radio signals are broadcast. □ **bande de fréquences**

'**wavelength** *noun* the distance from any given point on one (radio *etc*) wave to the corresponding point on the next. □ **longueur d'ondes**

wave aside to dismiss (a suggestion *etc*) without paying much attention to it. □ **écarter d'un geste**

waver ['weivə] *verb* to be unsteady or uncertain: *He wavered between accepting and refusing.* □ **hésiter**

wax[1] [waks] *noun* **1** the sticky, fatty substance of which bees make their cells; beeswax. □ **cire**

2 the sticky, yellowish substance formed in the ears. □ **cire**

3 a manufactured, fatty substance used in polishing, to give a good shine: *furniture wax.* □ **cire**

4 (*also adjective*) (*also* '**candle wax**) (of) a substance made from paraffin, used in making candles, models *etc*, that melts when heated: *a wax model.* □ **(en/de) cire**

5 sealing wax. □ **cire à cacheter**

■ *verb* to smear, polish or rub with wax. □ **cirer**

waxed *adjective* having a coating of wax: *waxed paper.* □ **ciré**

'**waxen**, '**waxy** *adjective.* □ **cireux**

'**waxwork** *noun* a wax model (*usually* of a well-known person). □ **statue en cire**

'**waxworks** *noun plural* an exhibition of such models. □ **musée de cire**

wax[2] [waks] *verb* **1** (of the moon) to appear to grow in size as more of it becomes visible. □ **croître**

2 an old word for to grow or increase. □ **croître**

way [wei] *noun* **1** an opening or passageway: *This is the way in/out*; *There's no way through.* □ **entrée; sortie; issue**

2 a route, direction *etc*: *Which way shall we go?*; *Which is the way to Princes Street?*; *His house is on the way from here to the school*; *Will you be able to find your/ the way to my house?*; *Your house is on my way home*; *The errand took me out of my way*; *a highway*; *a railway.* □ **direction; chemin**

3 used in the names of roads: *His address is 21 Melville Way.* □ **chemin**

4 a distance: *It's a long way to the school*; *The nearest*

shops are only a short way away. □ **loin; près**

5 a method or manner: *What is the easiest way to write a book?*; *I know a good way of doing it*; *He's got a funny way of talking*; *This is the quickest way to chop onions.* □ **manière, moyen**

6 an aspect or side of something: *In some ways this job is quite difficult*; *In a way I feel sorry for him.* □ **façon**

7 a characteristic of behaviour; a habit: *He has some rather unpleasant ways.* □ **manière**

8 used with many verbs to give the idea of progressing or moving: *He pushed his way through the crowd*; *They soon ate their way through the food.* □ **(se) frayer un chemin; venir à bout (de)**

■ *adverb* by a long distance or time; far: *The winner finished the race way ahead of the other competitors*; *It's way past your bedtime.* □ **(de) loin**

'**wayfarer** *noun* a traveller, *especially* on foot. □ **voyageur, euse**

'**wayside** *noun* the side of a road, path *etc*: *We can stop by the wayside and have a picnic*; (*also adjective*) *a wayside inn.* □ **bord de la route**

be/get on one's way to start or continue a walk, journey *etc*: *Well, thanks for the cup of tea, but I must be on my way now.* □ **se mettre en route**

by the way incidentally, in passing, while I remember *etc*: *By the way, did you know he was getting married?* □ **en passant**

fall by the wayside (of projects, ideas *etc*) to be abandoned; to fail. □ **rester en plan**

get/have one's own way to do, get *etc* what one wants: *You can't always have your own way.* □ **obtenir ce que l'on désire**

get into/out of the way of (doing) something to become accustomed to (not) doing; to get into/out of the habit of doing: *They got into the way of waking up late when they were on holiday.* □ **prendre/perdre l'habitude de**

go out of one's way to do more than is really necessary: *He went out of his way to help us.* □ **se donner du mal pour**

have a way with to be good at dealing with or managing: *She has a way with children.* □ **savoir s'y prendre avec**

have it one's own way to get one's own way: *Oh, have it your own way – I'm tired of arguing.* □ **faire à (sa) tête**

in a bad way unwell; in poor condition: *The patient is in a bad way.* □ **(aller) mal**

in, out of the/someone's way (not) blocking someone's progress, or occupying space that is needed by someone: *Don't leave your bicycle where it will get in the way of pedestrians*; *Will I be in the/your way if I work at this table?*; *'Get out of my way!' he said rudely.* □ **(ne pas/être) dans les jambes de qqn**

lose one's way to stop knowing where one is, or in which direction one ought to be going: *I lost my way through the city.* □ **se perdre**

make one's way 1 to go: *They made their way towards the centre of the town.* □ **se diriger (vers)**

2 to get on in the world. □ **faire son chemin**

make way (for) to stand aside and leave room (for): *The crowd parted to make way for the ambulance.* □ **laisser passer**

under way moving, in progress *etc*: *Her plans are under way.* □ **en cours**

way of life a manner of spending one's life: *I enjoy farming – it's a pleasant way of life.* □ **mode de vie**

ways and means methods, *especially* of providing money. □ **ressources**

waylay [wei'lei] – *past tense, past participle* **way'laid** – *verb* to ambush: *He was waylaid by a crowd of angry demonstrators.* □ **attaquer**

wayward ['weiwəd] *adjective* (of a child *etc*) self-willed and rebellious. □ **rebelle**

WC *see* **water closet** *under* **water**.

we [wiː] *pronoun* (used only as the subject of a verb) the word used by a speaker or writer in mentioning himself or herself together with other people: *We are going home tomorrow.* □ **nous**

weak [wiːk] *adjective* **1** lacking in physical strength: *Her illness has made her very weak.* □ **faible**

2 not strong in character: *I'm very weak when it comes to giving up cigarettes.* □ **sans volonté**

3 (of a liquid) diluted; not strong: *weak tea.* □ **faible**

4 (of an explanation *etc*) not convincing. □ **peu convaincant**

5 (of a joke) not particularly funny. □ **plat**

'weakly *adverb*. □ **faiblement**

'weaken *verb* to (cause to) become weak, *especially* in physical strength or character: *The patient has weakened*; *The strain of the last few days has weakened him.* □ **(s')affaiblir**

'weakling [-liŋ] *noun* a weak person, animal, or plant: *She married a weakling.* □ **être faible**

'weakness *noun* **1** the state of being weak. □ **faiblesse**

2 something weak or faulty; a defect: *weaknesses of character*; *Smoking is one of my weaknesses.* □ **faiblesse**

have a weakness for to have a liking for: *She has a weakness for chocolate biscuits.* □ **avoir un faible pour**

wealth [welθ] *noun* **1** riches: *He is a man of great wealth.* □ **fortune**

2 a great quantity (of): *a wealth of information.* □ **abondance**

'wealthy *adjective* having much money and/or many possessions; rich: *She is a wealthy young widow.* □ **riche**

wean [wiːn] *verb* to cause (a child or young animal) to become used to food other than the mother's milk: *The baby has been weaned (on to solid foods).* □ **sevrer**

weapon ['wepən] *noun* any instrument or means which is used for one's own defence or for attacking others: *Rifles, arrows, atom bombs and tanks are all weapons*; *The police are looking for the murder weapon*; *Surprise is our best weapon.* □ **arme**

wear [weə] – *past tense* **wore** [woː]: *past participle* **worn** [woːn] – *verb* **1** to be dressed in or carry on (a part of) the body: *She wore a white dress*; *Does he usually wear spectacles?* □ **porter**

2 to arrange (one's hair) in a particular way: *She wears her hair in a pony-tail.* □ **porter**

3 to have or show (a particular expression): *He wore an*

angry expression. □ **avoir**

4 to (cause to) become thinner *etc* because of use, rubbing *etc*: *This carpet has worn in several places*; *This sweater is wearing thin at the elbows.* □ **(s')user**

5 to make (a bare patch, a hole *etc*) by rubbing, use *etc*: *I've worn a hole in the elbow of my jacket.* □ **faire**

6 to stand up to use: *This material doesn't wear very well.* □ **résister (à l'usure)**

■ *noun* **1** use as clothes *etc*: *I use this suit for everyday wear*; *Those shoes won't stand much wear.* □ **vêtement**

2 articles for use as clothes: *casual wear*; *sportswear*; *leisure wear.* □ **vêtements (de)**

3 (*sometimes* **wear and tear**) damage due to use: *The hall carpet is showing signs of wear.* □ **usure**

4 ability to withstand use: *There's plenty of wear left in it yet.* □ **usage**

'wearable *adjective* (*negative* **unwearable**) fit to be worn: *My only wearable coat is at the cleaners.* □ **mettable**

'wearer *noun*: *a dress that makes the wearer feel elegant.* □ **personne qui porte (...)**

'wearing *adjective* exhausting: *I've had rather a wearing day.* □ **épuisant**

worn [woːn] *adjective* damaged as a result of use: *a badly-worn carpet.* □ **usé**

wear away to make or become damaged, thinner, smoother *etc* through use, rubbing *etc*: *The steps have (been) worn away in places.* □ **(s')user**

wear off to become less: *The pain is wearing off.* □ **disparaître**

wear out to (cause to) become unfit for further use: *My socks have worn out*; *I've worn out my socks.* □ **(s')user**

worn out **1** so damaged by use as to be unfit for further use: *These shoes are worn out*; *a worn-out sweater.* □ **usé jusqu'à la corde**

2 very tired: *His wife is worn out after looking after the children.* □ **épuisé**

weary ['wiəri] *adjective* tired; with strength or patience exhausted: *a weary sigh*; *He looks weary*; *I am weary of his jokes.* □ **fatigué**

■ *verb* to (cause to) become tired: *The patient wearies easily*; *Don't weary the patient.* □ **(se) fatiguer**

'wearily *adverb*. □ **avec lassitude**

'weariness *noun*. □ **fatigue**

'wearisome *adjective* causing weariness: *a wearisome journey.* □ **fatigant**

'wearisomely *adverb*. □ **péniblement**

weasel ['wiːzl] *noun* a type of small flesh-eating animal with a long slender body. □ **belette**

weather ['weðə] *noun* conditions in the atmosphere, *especially* as regards heat or cold, wind, rain, snow *etc*: *The weather is too hot for me*; *stormy weather*; (*also adjective*) *a weather chart/report, the weather forecast.* □ **temps; météo**

■ *verb* **1** to affect or be affected by exposure to the air, resulting in drying, change of colour, shape *etc*: *The wind and sea have weathered the rocks quite smooth.* □ **éroder**

2 to survive safely: *The ship weathered the storm although she was badly damaged.* □ **réchapper (à)**

'weatherbeaten *adjective* showing effects of exposure to the weather: *a weatherbeaten face*. □ **hâlé, usé**

'weathercock, 'weathervane *nouns* a piece of metal (often in the form of a farmyard cock), placed on top of a building, which turns to show the direction of the wind. □ **girouette**

make heavy weather of to find it very (often unnecessarily) difficult to do (something): *She's making heavy weather of typing that letter.* □ **se compliquer la vie pour**

under the weather in poor health: *I'm feeling under the weather this week.* □ **ne pas se sentir en forme**

---

weather refers to climate: *fine weather.*
whether is a conjunction: *Do you know whether he is coming?*

---

weave [wiːv] – *past tense* **wove** [wouv]: *past participle* **woven** ['wouvən] – *verb* **1** to make by crossing strands in a pattern: *to weave cloth.* □ **tisser**

2 to tell (an interesting story). □ **inventer**

3 (*past tense, past participle* **weaved**) to move backwards and forwards or from side to side: *The cyclist weaved in and out of the traffic.* □ **(se) faufiler**

'weaver *noun.* □ **tisserand, ande**

web [web] *noun* **1** a type of trap for flies *etc* made of fine silk threads, spun by a spider *etc*: *a spider's web.* □ **toile**

2 the skin between the toes of a waterfowl. □ **palmure**

webbed *adjective* (of ducks' *etc* feet) joined between the toes by a web. □ **palmé**

'webbing *noun* a tough woven fabric used in making belts, straps, upholstery *etc*. □ **toile forte en bande**

'web-'footed, ,web-'toed *adjective* having webbed feet. □ **palmipède**

wed [wed] – *past tense, past participles* **'wedded, wed** – *verb* to marry. □ **(se) marier (avec)**

'wedding *noun* a marriage ceremony: *The wedding will take place on Saturday*; (*also adjective*) *a wedding-cake*; *her wedding-day*; *a wedding-ring.* □ **mariage, noces**

we'd *see* **have, would.**

wedge [wedʒ] *noun* **1** a piece of wood or metal, thick at one end and sloping to a thin edge at the other, used in splitting wood *etc* or in fixing something tightly in place: *She used a wedge under the door to prevent it swinging shut.* □ **coin; cale**

2 something similar in shape: *a wedge of cheese.* □ **morceau**

■ *verb* to fix or become fixed by, or as if by, a wedge or wedges: *He is so fat that he got wedged in the doorway.* □ **(se) coincer**

wedlock ['wedlok] *noun* the state of being married. □ **mariage**

Wednesday ['wenzdi] *noun* the fourth day of the week, the day following Tuesday. □ **mercredi**

weed [wiːd] *noun* any wild plant, *especially* when growing among cultivated plants or where it is not wanted: *The garden is full of weeds.* □ **mauvaise herbe**

■ *verb* to remove weeds (from): *to weed the garden.* □ **désherber**

'weedkiller *noun* a chemical *etc* used to kill weeds. □ **herbicide**

weed out to remove (things which are unwanted) from a group or collection. □ **trier et jeter**

week [wiːk] *noun* **1** any sequence of seven days, *especially* from Sunday to Saturday: *It's three weeks since I saw her.* □ **semaine**

2 the five days from Monday to Friday inclusive: *He can't go during the week, but he'll go on Saturday or Sunday.* □ **semaine**

3 the amount of time spent working during a period of seven days: *He works a forty-eight-hour week.* □ **semaine (de)**

'weekly *adjective* happening, published *etc* once a week: *a weekly magazine.* □ **hebdomadaire**

■ *adverb* once a week: *The newspaper is published weekly.* □ **hebdomadairement**

■ *noun* – *plural* **'weeklies** – a publication coming out once a week: *Is this newspaper a weekly or a daily?* □ **hebdomadaire**

'weekday *noun* any day except a Saturday or Sunday: *Our office is open only on weekdays*; (*also adjective*) *weekday flights.* □ **jour ouvrable**

,week'end *noun* the period from the end of one working week until the beginning of the next (*ie* Saturday and Sunday, or Friday evening to Sunday evening): *We spent a weekend in Paris*; (*also adjective*) *a weekend trip.* □ **(de) fin de semaine**

a week last Friday *etc* the Friday *etc* before last: *She died a week last Tuesday.* □ **il y a une semaine**

a week today, tomorrow, (on/next) Friday *etc* a week from today, tomorrow, Friday *etc*: *I'm going away a week tomorrow*; *Could we meet a week (on/next) Monday?* □ **dans une semaine**

weep [wiːp] – *past tense, past participle* **wept** [wept] – *verb* to shed tears: *She wept when she heard the terrible news*; *They wept tears of happiness.* □ **pleurer**

weft *see* **warp**[2].

weigh [wei] *verb* **1** to find the heaviness of (something) by placing it on a scale: *He weighed himself on the bathroom scales*; *You must have your luggage weighed at the airport.* □ **(se) peser**

2 to be equal to in heaviness: *This parcel weighs one kilogram*; *How much/What does this box weigh?* □ **peser**

3 to be a heavy burden to: *She was weighed down with two large suitcases.* □ **peser sur**

weight [weit] *noun* **1** the amount which a person or thing weighs: *He's put on a lot of weight* (= got much fatter) *over the years.* □ **poids**

2 a piece of metal *etc* of a standard weight: *two kilograms weight.* □ **poids**

3 burden; load: *You have taken a weight off my mind.* □ **poids**

4 importance: *Her opinion carries a lot of weight.* □ **poids**

■ *verb* **1** to attach, or add, a weight or weights to: *The plane is weighted at the nose so that it balances correctly in flight.* □ **lester**

2 to hold down by attaching weights: *They weighted the balloon to prevent it from flying away.* □ **retenir/ maintenir avec un poids**

'weightless *adjective* not affected by the earth's gravity

pull: *The astronauts became weightless on going into orbit around the earth.* □ **en état d'apesanteur**
'**weightlessness** *noun.* □ **apesanteur**
'**weighty** *adjective* 1 important: *a weighty reason.* □ **de poids**
2 heavy. □ **pesant**
'**weightily** *adverb.* □ **pesamment**
'**weightiness** *noun.* □ **importance, lourdeur**
'**weighing machine** *noun* a (public) machine for weighing people, loads *etc*: *I weighed myself on the weighing-machine at the railway station.* □ **balance**
weigh anchor to lift a ship's anchor in preparation for sailing. □ **lever l'ancre**
weigh in to find one's weight before a fight, after a horse-race *etc* (*noun* '**weigh-in**). □ **peser; se faire peser**
weigh out to measure out by weighing: *He weighed out six kilograms of sand.* □ **peser**
weigh up to calculate, estimate; to consider: *He weighed up his chances of success.* □ **calculer**
weir [wiə] *noun* a dam across a river, with a drop on one side. □ **barrage**
weird [wiəd] *adjective* odd or very strange: *a weird story*; *She wears weird clothes.* □ **bizarre, étrange**
'**weirdly** *adverb.* □ **bizarrement**
'**weirdness** *noun.* □ **étrangeté**
welcome ['welkəm] *adjective* received with gladness and happiness: *She will make you welcome*; *He is a welcome visitor at our house*; *The extra money was very welcome*; *The holiday made a welcome change.* □ **bienvenu**
■ *noun* reception; hospitality: *We were given a warm welcome.* □ **accueil**
■ *verb* to receive or greet with pleasure and gladness: *We were welcomed by our hosts*; *She will welcome the chance to see you again.* □ **accueillir; (se) réjouir (de)**
■ *interjection* used to express gladness at someone's arrival: *Welcome to Britain!* □ **bienvenue**
'**welcoming** *adjective*: *a welcoming smile.* □ **accueillant**
be welcome to to be gladly given permission to (have, do or accept something): *You're welcome to stay as long as you wish.* □ **être invité de bon cœur (à)**
you're welcome! that's quite all right, no thanks are necessary: *'Thanks !' 'You're welcome!'* □ **(il n'y a) pas de quoi**
weld [weld] *verb* to join (pieces of metal) by pressure, often using heat, electricity *etc*. □ **souder**
■ *noun* a joint made by welding. □ **soudure**
'**welder** *noun.* □ **soudeur, euse**
welfare ['welfeə] *noun* mental and physical health; living conditions: *Who is looking after the child's welfare?* □ **bien-être**
welfare state a country which runs insurance schemes for its inhabitants, supplying them with free medical care, pensions *etc*. □ **Etat-providence**
well[1] [wel] *noun* 1 a lined shaft made in the earth from which to obtain water, oil, natural gas *etc*. □ **puits**
2 the space around which a staircase winds: *He fell down the stair-well.* □ **cage (d'escalier)**
■ *verb* (of water from the earth or of tears) to flow freely: *Tears welled up in her eyes.* □ **monter (à)**

well[2] [wel] – *comparative* **better** ['betə]: *superlative* **best** [best] – *adjective* 1 healthy: *I don't feel very/at all well*; *He doesn't look very well*; *She's been ill but she's quite well now.* □ **bien**
2 in a satisfactory state or condition: *All is well now.* □ **bien**
■ *adverb* 1 in a good, correct, successful, suitable *etc* way: *He's done well to become a millionaire at thirty*; *She plays the piano well*; *Mother and baby are both doing well*; *How well did he do in the exam?* □ **bien; bien (réussir)**
2 with good reason; with justice: *You may well look ashamed – that was a cruel thing to do*; *You can't very well refuse to go.* □ **bien**
3 with approval or praise: *She speaks well of you.* □ **en bien**
4 used (*with eg* **damn, jolly** *etc*) for emphasis: *You can jolly well do it yourself!* □ **bien**
5 thoroughly: *Examine the car well before you buy it.* □ **attentivement**
6 to a great or considerable extent: *He is well over fifty.* □ **largement**
■ *interjection* 1 used to express surprise *etc*: *Well ! I'd never have believed it!* □ **eh bien**
2 used when re-starting a conversation, starting an explanation *etc*: *Do you remember John Watson? Well, he's become a teacher.* □ **eh bien**
well- 1 in a good, satisfactory *etc* way *etc*, as in **well-behaved.** □ **bien**
2 very much, as in **well-known.** □ **bien**
,**well-be'haved** *adjective* behaving correctly: *well-behaved children.* □ **sage**
,**well-'being** *noun* welfare: *She is always very concerned about her mother's well-being.* □ **bien-être**
,**well-'bred** *adjective* (of a person) having good manners. □ **bien élevé**
,**well-'built** *adjective* muscular; having a strong, handsome figure. □ **bien bâti**
,**well-'earned** *adjective* thoroughly deserved: *a well-earned rest.* □ **bien mérité**
,**well-'educated** *adjective* educated to a good standard. □ **instruit**
,**well-'fed** *adjective* correctly and sufficiently fed. □ **bien nourri**
,**well-'groomed** *adjective* of smart, tidy appearance. □ **soigné**
,**well-in'formed** *adjective* having or showing a thorough knowledge: *a well-informed person/essay.* □ **bien informé**
,**well-'known** *adjective* familiar or famous: *a well-known TV personality.* □ **célèbre**
,**well-'made** *adjective*: *a well-made table.* □ **bien fait**
,**well-'mannered** *adjective* polite. □ **bien élevé**
,**well 'off** *adjective* 1 rich: *He is very well off*; *a well off young lady.* □ **aisé**
2 fortunate: *You do not know when you are well off.* □ **aisé, bien nanti**
,**well-'read** [-'red] *adjective* having read many books *etc*; intelligent. □ **cultivé**
,**well-'spoken** *adjective* (of a person) speaking with a

pleasing voice, in a grammatically correct way *etc*. □ **qui parle bien**

,**well-to-'do** *adjective* having enough money to live comfortably. □ **aisé**

,**well-wisher** *noun* a person who wishes one success *etc*. □ **personne qui veut du bien (à); admirateur, trice**

as well in addition; too: *If you will go, I'll go as well*. □ **aussi**

as well as in addition to: *She works in a restaurant in the evenings as well as doing a full-time job during the day*. □ **en plus de**

be just as well to be fortunate; to be no cause for regret: *It's just as well (that) you didn't go – the meeting was cancelled*. □ **aussi bien que**

be as well to to be advisable or sensible: *It would be as well to go by train – the roads are flooded*. □ **valoir mieux**

very well fine, okay: *Have you finished? Very well, you may go now*. □ **très bien**

well done! used in congratulating a person: *I hear you won the competition. Well done!* □ **bravo!**

well enough fairly, but not particularly, well. □ **pas trop mal**

well up in knowing a great deal about: *He's very well up in financial matters*. □ **bien renseigné**

we'll *see* **will, shall.**

wellingtons ['weliŋtənz] *noun plural* rubber boots loosely covering the calves of the legs. □ **bottes de caoutchouc**

welt [welt] *noun* a band or strip fastened to an edge of an article of clothing for strength or for ornament. □ **bordure**

went *see* **go.**

wept *see* **weep.**

were, we're, weren't *see* **be.**

werewolf [weəwulf] *noun* (*also* **werwolf**) an imaginary animal believed to have once been human but is now wolf or able to take the form of a wolf: *In the legend, a young man turned into a vicious werewolf whenever the moon was full*. □ **loup-garou**

west [west] *noun* 1 the direction in which the sun sets or any part of the earth lying in that direction: *They travelled towards the west*; *The wind is blowing from the west*; *in the west of Britain*. □ **ouest**

2 (*often with capital: also* **W**) one of the four main points of the compass. □ **ouest**

■ *adjective* 1 in the west: *She's in the west wing of the hospital*. □ **ouest**

2 from the direction of the west: *a west wind*. □ **(d')ouest**

■ *adverb* towards the west: *The cliffs face west*. □ **à l'ouest**

'**westerly** *adjective* 1 (of a wind, breeze *etc*) coming from the west: *a westerly wind*. □ **d'ouest**

2 looking, lying *etc* towards the west: *moving in a westerly direction*. □ **vers l'ouest**

'**western** *adjective* of the west or the West: *Western customs/clothes*. □ **(de l')ouest, occidental**

■ *noun* a film or novel about the Wild West: *Most westerns are about cowboys and Red Indians*. □ **western**

'**westernmost** *adjective* furthest west: *the westernmost*

point. □ **le plus à l'ouest**

'**westward** *adjective* towards the west: *in a westward direction*. □ **vers l'ouest**

'**westward(s)** *adverb* towards the west: *We journeyed westwards for two weeks*. □ **en direction de l'ouest**

go west to become useless; to be destroyed: *I'm afraid this jacket has finally gone west*; *That's all hopes of winning gone west*. □ **être foutu**

the West Europe and North and South America. □ **l'Ouest, Occident**

the Wild West the western United States, before the establishment of law and order. □ **le Far West**

wet [wet] *adjective* 1 containing, soaked in, or covered with, water or another liquid: *We got soaking wet when it began to rain*; *His shirt was wet through with sweat*; *wet hair*; *The car skidded on the wet road*. □ **mouillé**

2 rainy: *a wet day*; *wet weather*; *It was wet yesterday*. □ **pluvieux**

■ *verb* – *present tense* '**wetting**: *past tense, past participles* **wet, 'wetted** – to make wet: *She wet her hair and put shampoo on it*; *The baby has wet himself/his nappy/the bed*. □ **mouiller**

■ *noun* 1 moisture: *a patch of wet*. □ **humidité**

2 rain: *Don't go out in the wet*. □ **pluie**

'**wetness** *noun*. □ **humidité**

wet blanket a depressing companion. □ **rabat-joie**

'**wet nurse** *noun* a woman employed to breast-feed someone else's baby. □ **nourrice**

'**wetsuit** *noun* a rubber suit for wearing in cold conditions when diving *etc*. □ **combinaison de plongée**

wet snow *noun* a snowfall that is partially melted and damp: *The hills were covered with slush and our skis stuck in the heavy wet snow*. □ **neige fondante**

wet through soaked to the skin. □ **trempé jusqu'aux os**

we've *see* **have.**

whack [wak] *verb* to strike smartly, making a loud sound: *His father whacked him for misbehaving*. □ **donner un grand coup (à)**

■ *noun* a blow: *His father gave him a whack across the ear*. □ **claque**

whale [weil] *noun* a type of very large mammal that lives in the sea. □ **baleine**

'**whalebone** *noun, adjective* (of) a light bendable substance got from the upper jaw of certain whales. □ **fanon de baleine**

whale oil oil obtained from the fatty parts of a whale. □ **huile de baleine**

have a whale of a time to enjoy oneself very much. □ **s'amuser énormément**

wharf [wo:f] – *plurals* **wharfs, wharves** [wo:vz] – *noun* a platform alongside which ships are moored for loading and unloading. □ **quai**

what [wot] *pronoun, adjective* 1 used in questions *etc* when asking someone to point out, state *etc* one or more persons, things *etc*: *What street is this?*; *What's your name/address/telephone number?*; *What time is it?*; *What (kind of) bird is that?*; *What is she reading?*; *What did you say?*; *What is this cake made of?*; '*What do you want to be when you grow up?*' '*A doctor*.'; *Tell me what* *you mean*; *I asked him what clothes I should wear.* □ **quel; qu'est-ce que; ce que**

2 (*also adverb*) used in exclamations of surprise, anger *etc*: *What clothes she wears!*; *What a fool he is!*; *What naughty children they are!*; *What a silly book this is!*; *What* (*on earth/in the world/ever*) *is happening?* □ **quel; qu'est-ce que; quoi**

■ *relative pronoun* **1** the thing(s) that: *Did you find what you wanted?*; *These tools are just what I need for this job*; *What that child needs is a good spanking!* □ **ce que**

2 (*also relative adjective*) any (things or amount) that; whatever: *I'll lend you what clothes you need*; *Please lend me what you can.* □ **le, la, les; ce que**

what'ever *relative adjective, relative pronoun* any (thing(s) or amount) that: *I'll lend you whatever* (*books*) *you need.* □ **tout (...) que**

■ *adjective, pronoun* no matter what: *You have to go on, whatever* (*trouble*) *you meet*; *Whatever* (*else*) *you do, don't say that!* □ **quoi que**

■ *adjective* whatsoever; at all: *I had nothing whatever to do with that.* □ **absolument**

■ *pronoun* (*also* **what ever**) used in questions or exclamations to express surprise *etc*: *Whatever will he say when he hears this?* □ **qu'est-ce que (...) bien**

'whatnot *noun* such things: *She told me all about publishing and whatnot.* □ **truc**

'what's his/her/its *etc* **name** *noun* used in referring vaguely to a person or thing: *Where does what's his name live?* □ **chose**

,whatso'ever [-sou-] *adjective* at all: *That's nothing whatsoever to do with me.* □ **du tout**

know what's what to be able to tell what is important. □ **connaître son affaire**

what about? **1** used in asking whether the listener would like (to do) something: *What about a glass of milk?*; *What about going to the cinema?* □ **et si...?**

2 used in asking for news or advice: *What about your new book?*; *What about the other problem?* □ **qu'en est-il de...?**

what ... for 1 why(?): *What did he do that for?* □ **pourquoi**

2 for what purpose(?): *What is this switch for?* □ **à quoi sert**

what have you and similar things; and so on: *clothes, books and what have you.* □ **et que sais-je encore**

what if? what will or would happen if...?: *What if he comes back?* □ **et si...?**

what...like? used when asking for information about someone or something: *'What does it look like?' 'It's small and square.'*; *'What's her mother like?' 'Oh, she's quite nice.'*; *We may go — it depends* (*on*) *what the weather's like.* □ **à quoi ressemble...**

what of it? used in replying, to suggest that what has been done, said *etc* is not important: *'You've offended her.' 'What of it?'* □ **et après?**

what with because of: *What with taking no exercise and being too fat, he had a heart attack.* □ **étant donné**

what'll ['wotl], **what's** [wots] short for **what shall/what will, what is/what has.**

wheat [wiːt] *noun* a type of grain from which flour, much

used in making bread, cakes *etc*, is obtained. □ **blé**

'wheaten *adjective* made of wheat: *a wheaten loaf.* □ **de blé**

wheel [wiːl] *noun* **1** a circular frame or disc turning on a rod or axle, on which vehicles *etc* move along the ground: *A bicycle has two wheels, a tricycle three, and most cars four*; *a cartwheel.* □ **roue**

2 any of several things similar in shape and action: *a potter's wheel*; *He was found drunk at the wheel* (= steering-wheel) *of his car.* □ **tour, volant**

■ *verb* **1** to cause to move on wheels: *She wheeled her bicycle along the path.* □ **(faire) rouler, pousser**

2 to (cause to) turn quickly: *He wheeled around and slapped me.* □ **(se) retourner (brusquement)**

3 (of birds) to fly in circles. □ **tournoyer**

wheeled *adjective*: *a wheeled vehicle.* □ **à roues**

-wheeled *adjective*: *a four-wheeled vehicle.* □ **à (...) roues**

'wheelbarrow *noun* a small carrier with one wheel at the front, and two legs and two handles at the back: *She used a wheelbarrow to move the manure to the back garden.* □ **brouette**

'wheelchair *noun* a chair with wheels, used for moving from place to place by invalids or those who cannot walk. □ **fauteuil roulant**

'wheelhouse *noun* the shelter in which a ship's steering wheel is placed. □ **timonerie**

'wheelwright *noun* a craftsman who makes wheels. □ **charron**

wheeze [wiːz] *verb* to breathe with a hissing sound and with difficulty. □ **respirer bruyamment**

■ *noun* such a sound. □ **respiration bruyante**

'wheezy *adjective.* □ **asthmatique**

'wheezily *adverb.* □ **comme un asthmatique**

'wheeziness *noun.* □ **caractère asthmatique**

when [wen] *adverb* at what time(?): *When did you arrive?*; *When will you see her again?*; *I asked him when the incident had occurred*; *Tell me when to jump.* □ **quand**

■ [wɔn, wen] *conjunction* **1** (at or during) the time at which: *It happened when I was abroad*; *When you see her, give her this message*; *When I've finished, I'll telephone you.* □ **quand, lorsque**

2 in spite of the fact that; considering that: *Why do you walk when you have a car?* □ **alors que**

whence [wens] *adverb* from what place or circumstance (?); from where (?). □ **d'où**

when'ever *conjunction* **1** at any time that: *Come and see me whenever you want to.* □ **toutes les fois que, n'importe quand**

2 at every time that: *I go to the theatre whenever I get the chance.* □ **chaque fois que**

where [weə] *adverb* (to or in) which place (?): *Where are you going* (*to*)*?*; *Do you know where we are?*; *Where does he get his ideas from?*; *We asked where to find a good restaurant.* □ **où**

■ *relative pronoun* ((to or in) the place) to or in which: *It's nice going on holiday to a place where you've been before*; *This is the town where I was born*; *It's still where it was*; *I can't see her from where I am.* □ **où**

,wherea'bouts *adverb* near or in what place(?): *Wherea-*

bouts is it?; *I don't know whereabouts it is.* □ **où (donc)**
'whereabouts *noun singular or noun plural* the place where a person or thing is: *I don't know his whereabouts.* □ **lieu où se trouve (qqn/qqch)**
where'as *conjunction* when in fact; but on the other hand: *He thought I was lying, whereas I was telling the truth.* □ **tandis que**
where'by *relative pronoun* by which. □ **par quoi; par quel moyen...**
,whereu'pon *conjunction* at or after which time, event *etc*: *He insulted her, whereupon she slapped him.* □ **après quoi; et sur ce**
wher'ever *relative pronoun* 1 no matter where: *I'll follow you wherever you may go*; *Wherever he is he will be thinking of you.* □ **n'importe/partout où**
2 (to or in) any place that: *Go wherever she tells you to go.* □ **(là) où**
■ *adverb* (*also* **where ever**) used in questions or exclamations to express surprise *etc*: *Wherever did she get that hat?* □ **mais où donc**
where's short for **where is, where has.**

whet [wet] – *past tense, past participle* **'whetted** – *verb*
1 to sharpen (a tool) by rubbing it on a grindstone or whetstone. □ **aiguiser**
2 to make (one's appetite) keen. □ **aiguiser**
'whetstone *noun* a stone for sharpening the blades of knives *etc*. □ **pierre à aiguiser**
whether ['weðə] *conjunction* if: *I don't know whether it's possible.* □ **si**
whether ... or introducing alternatives: *He can't decide whether to go or not/whether or not to go*; *Whether you like the idea or not, I'm going ahead with it*; *Decide whether you're going or staying.* □ **si (...) ou non; que (...) ou (non)**

see also **weather.**

whey [wei] *noun* the watery part of milk separated from the curd (the thick part), *especially* in making cheese. □ **petit-lait**
which [witʃ] *adjective, pronoun* used in questions *etc* when asking someone to point out, state *etc* one or more persons, things *etc* from a particular known group: *Which (colour) do you like best?*; *Which route will you travel by?*; *At which station should I change trains?*; *Which of the two girls do you like better?*; *Tell me which books you would like*; *Let me know which train you'll be arriving on*; *I can't decide which to choose.* □ **quel; lequel, laquelle**
■ *relative pronoun* (used to refer to a thing or things mentioned previously to distinguish it or them from others: able to be replaced by **that** except after a preposition: able to be omitted except after a preposition or when the subject of a clause) (the) one(s) that: *This is the book which/that was on the table*; *This is the book (which/that) you wanted*; *A scalpel is a type of knife which/that is used by surgeons*; *The chair (which/that) you are sitting on is broken*; *The documents for which they were searching have been recovered.* □ **qui; que; lequel**
■ *relative adjective, relative pronoun* used, after a

comma, to introduce a further comment on something: *My new car, which I paid several thousand dollars for, is not running well*; *He said he could speak Russian, which was untrue*; *My father may have to go into hospital, in which case he won't be going on holiday.* □ **(ce) que/qui; auquel (cas)**
which'ever *relative adjective, relative pronoun* 1 any (one(s)) that: *I'll take whichever (books) you don't want*; *The prize will go to whichever of them writes the best essay.* □ **celui, celle (qui/que)**
2 no matter which (one(s)): *Whichever way I turned, I couldn't escape.* □ **quel que soit**
which is which(?) which is one and which is the other (?): *Mary and Susan are twins and I can't tell which is which.* □ **lequel est lequel**

whiff [wif] *noun* a sudden puff (of air, smoke, smell *etc*): *a whiff of gasoline*; *a whiff of cigar smoke.* □ **odeur, bouffée**
while [wail] *conjunction* (*also* **whilst** [wailst]) 1 during the time that: *I saw him while I was out walking.* □ **pendant que**
2 although: *While I sympathize, I can't really do very much to help.* □ **bien que**
■ *noun* a space of time: *It took me quite a while*; *It's a long while since we saw her.* □ **(assez) longtemps; quelque temps**
while away to pass (time) without boredom: *He whiled away the time by reading.* □ **(faire) passer**
worth one's while worth one's time and trouble: *It's not worth your while reading this book, because it isn't accurate.* □ **qui vaut la peine (de)**
whim [wim] *noun* 1 a sudden desire or change of mind: *I am tired of that child's whims.* □ **caprice**
2 a sudden fancy or spur-of-the-moment desire: *On a sudden whim, Francine dyed her hair blue.* □ **lubie**
whimper ['wimpə] *verb* to cry with a low, shaky or whining voice: *I heard a puppy/a child whimpering.* □ **gémir, pleurnicher**
■ *noun* a cry of this kind: *The dog gave a little whimper.* □ **gémissement**
whine [wain] *verb* 1 to utter a complaining cry or a cry of suffering: *The dog whines when it's left alone in the house.* □ **gémir**
2 to make a similar noise: *I could hear the engine whine.* □ **gémir**
3 to complain unnecessarily: *Stop whining about how difficult this job is!* □ **se lamenter (sur/à propos de)**
■ *noun* such a noise: *the whine of an engine.* □ **plainte stridente**
'whiningly *adverb*. □ **d'un ton geignard**
whinny ['wini] *verb* to make the cry of a horse: *The horse whinnied when it saw its master.* □ **hennir**
■ *noun* – *plural* **'whinnies** – such a cry. □ **hennissement**
whip [wip] *noun* 1 a long cord or strip of leather attached to a handle, used for punishing people, driving horses *etc*: *She carries a whip but she would never use it on the horse.* □ **fouet**
2 in parliament, a member chosen by his party to make sure that no one fails to vote on important questions. □ **whip**

■ *verb – past tense, past participle* **whipped** – **1** to strike with a whip: *He whipped the horse to make it go faster; The criminals were whipped.* □ **fouetter**

2 to beat (eggs *etc*). □ **fouetter**

3 to move fast *especially* with a twisting motion like a whip: *Suddenly he whipped around and saw me; He whipped out a revolver and shot her.* □ **(se) retourner brusquement; sortir vivement**

'**whiplash** *noun* (the action of) the lash or cord of a whip. □ **coup de fouet**

whip up 1 to whip: *I'm whipping up eggs for the dessert.* □ **battre au fouet**

2 to produce or prepare quickly: *I'll whip up a meal in no time.* □ **préparer en vitesse**

whippet ['wipit] *noun* a type of racing dog. □ **whippet**

whir(r) [wəɪ] – *past tense, past participle* **whirred** – *verb* to make, or move with, a buzzing sound, *especially* as of something turning through the air: *The propellers whirred and we took off.* □ **vrombir**

■ *noun* such a sound. □ **vrombissement**

whirl [wəɪl] *verb* to move rapidly (around, away *etc*): *She whirled around when I called her name; The wind whirled my hat away before I could grab it.* □ **se retourner brusquement; tourbillonner**

■ *noun* **1** an excited confusion: *a whirl of activity; My head's in a whirl – I can't believe it's all happening!* □ **tourbillon**

2 a rapid turn. □ **tourbillon; tournoiement**

'**whirlpool** *noun* a circular current in a river or sea, caused by opposing tides, winds or currents. □ **tourbillon**

'**whirlwind** *noun* a violent circular current of wind with a whirling motion. □ **tornade**

whirr *see* **whir(r)**.

whisk [wisk] *verb* **1** to sweep, or cause to move, rapidly: *He whisked the dirty dishes off the table; He whisked her off to the doctor.* □ **faire disparaître à toute allure; emmener immédiatement**

2 to beat (eggs *etc*) with a fork or whisk. □ **battre**

■ *noun* **1** a rapid, sweeping motion. □ **coup (de)**

2 a kitchen tool made of wire *etc*, for beating eggs, cream *etc*. □ **fouet**

whisker ['wiskə] *noun* **1** *in plural* a man's moustache, beard and/or sideburns. □ **barbe, moustaches, favoris**

2 (*usually in plural*) one of the long hairs between the nose and the mouth of a cat *etc*. □ **moustaches**

'**whiskered**, '**whiskery** *adjective*. □ **à barbe/moustache/favoris**

miss *etc* **by a whisker** to manage only barely to miss *etc*. □ **manquer d'un poil**

whisky, whiskey ['wiski] *noun* a type of alcoholic drink made from grain. □ **whisky**

whisper ['wispə] *verb* **1** to speak or say very softly: *You'll have to whisper or she'll hear you; 'Don't tell him,' she whispered.* □ **chuchoter**

2 (of trees *etc*) to make a soft sound in the wind: *The leaves whispered in the breeze.* □ **murmurer**

■ *noun* a very quiet sound, *especially* something said: *They spoke in whispers.* □ **murmure**

'**whisperer** *noun*. □ **chuchoteur, euse**

whist [wist] *noun* a type of card game. □ **whist**

whistle ['wisl] *verb* **1** to make a shrill, often musical, sound by forcing one's breath between the lips or teeth: *Can you whistle?; He whistled to attract my attention; She whistled a happy tune.* □ **siffler**

2 to make such a sound with a device designed for this: *The electric kettle's whistling; The referee whistled for half-time.* □ **siffler**

3 to make a shrill sound in passing through the air: *The bullet whistled past his head.* □ **passer en sifflant**

4 (of the wind) to blow with a shrill sound. □ **siffler**

■ *noun* **1** the sound made by whistling: *She gave a loud whistle to her friend across the road.* □ **(coup de) sifflet**

2 a musical pipe designed to make a whistling noise. □ **pipeau**

3 an instrument used by policemen, referees *etc* to make a whistling noise: *The referee blew her whistle at the end of the game.* □ **sifflet**

white [wait] *adjective* **1** of the colour of the paper on which these words are printed: *The bride wore a white dress.* □ **blanc**

2 having light-coloured skin, through being of European *etc* descent: *the first white man to explore Africa.* □ **blanc**

3 abnormally pale, because of fear, illness *etc*: *He went white with shock.* □ **blême**

4 with milk in it: *A white coffee, please.* □ **(au) lait**

■ *noun* **1** the colour of the paper on which these words are printed: *White and black are opposites.* □ **blanc**

2 a white-skinned person: *racial trouble between blacks and whites.* □ **blanc, blanche**

3 (*also* '**egg white**) the clear fluid in an egg, surrounding the yolk: *This recipe tells you to separate the yolks from the whites.* □ **blanc (d'œuf)**

4 (of an eye) the white part surrounding the pupil and iris: *The whites of her eyes are bloodshot.* □ **blanc**

'**whiten** *verb* to make or become white or whiter: *He used a little bleach to whiten the sheets.* □ **blanchir**

'**whiteness** *noun*. □ **blancheur**

'**whitening** *noun* a substance used to make certain things (*eg* tennis shoes) white again. □ **blanc**

'**whitish** *adjective* fairly white; close to white. □ **blanchâtre**

,**white-'collar** *adjective* (of workers, jobs *etc*) not manual; (working) in an office *etc*. □ **de bureau**

white elephant a useless, unwanted possession. □ **objet superflu**

white horse *noun* (*usually in plural*) a wave that has a crest of white foam. □ **mouton(s)**

,**white-'hot** *adjective* (of metals) so hot that they have turned white: *a white-hot poker.* □ **chauffé à blanc**

white lie an not very serious lie: *I'd rather tell my mother a white lie than tell her the truth and upset her.* □ **pieux mensonge**

'**whitewash** *noun* a mixture of *usually* lime and water, used for whitening walls. □ **lait/blanc de chaux**

■ *verb* to cover with whitewash. □ **blanchir à la chaux**

'**whitewashed** *adjective*. □ **blanchi à la chaux**

white wine *see* **wine**.

whither ['wiðə] *relative pronoun, adverb* to which

place(?). □ **où**

whiting ['waitiŋ] – *plurals* '**whiting, whitings** – *noun* a type of small fish related to the cod. □ **merlan**

whittle ['witl] *verb* to cut or shape (*eg* a stick) with a knife. □ **tailler au couteau**

whizz [wiz] *verb* to fly through the air with a hissing sound: *The arrow whizzed past his shoulder*. □ **passer en sifflant**

who [hu:] *pronoun* (used as the subject of a verb) what person(s)(?): *Who is that woman in the green hat?*; *Who did that?*; *Who won?*; *Do you know who all these people are?* □ **(qui est-ce) qui**

■ *relative pronoun* 1 (used to refer to a person or people mentioned previously to distinguish him or them from others: used as the subject of a verb: (*usually* replaceable by **that**) (the) one(s) that: *The man who/that telephoned was a friend of yours*; *A doctor is a person who looks after people's health*. □ **qui**

2 used, after a comma, to introduce a further comment on a person or pronoun: *His mother, who by that time was tired out, gave him a smack*. □ **qui**

who'ever *relative pronoun* any person or people that: *Whoever gets the job will have a lot of work to do*. □ **quiconque**

■ *pronoun* 1 no matter who: *Whoever rings, tell him/them I'm out*. □ **qui que ce soit**

2 (also **who ever**) used in questions to express surprise *etc*: *Whoever said that?* □ **qui donc**

whom [hu:m] *pronoun* (used as the object of a verb or preposition, but in everyday speech sometimes replaced by **who**) what person(s)(?): *Whom/who do you want to see?*; *Whom/who did you give it to?*; *To whom shall I speak?* □ **que, qui**

■ *relative pronoun* (used as the object of a verb or preposition but in everyday speech sometimes replaced by **who**) 1 (used to refer to a person or people mentioned previously, to distinguish him or them from others: able to be omitted or replaced by **that** except when following a preposition) (the) one(s) that: *The man* (*whom/that*) *you mentioned is here*; *Today I met some friends* (*whom/that*) *I hadn't seen for ages*; *This is the woman to whom I gave it*; *This is the man* (*whom/who/that*) *I gave it to*. □ **que, (à) qui**

2 used, after a comma, to introduce a further comment on a person or people: *My father, whom I'd like you to meet one day, is interested in your work*. □ **qui, que know who's who** to know which people are important. □ **connaître les personnes influentes**

who'd short for **who would, who should, who had**.

whole [houl] *adjective* 1 including everything and/or everyone; complete: *The whole staff collected the money for your present*; *a whole pineapple*. □ **(tout) entier**

2 not broken; in one piece: *She swallowed the biscuit whole*. □ **(en) entier**

■ *noun* 1 a single unit: *The different parts were joined to form a whole*. □ **tout**

2 the entire thing: *We spent the whole of one week sunbathing on the beach*. □ **totalité; tout**

'**wholeness** *noun*. □ **intégralité**

'**wholly** *adverb* completely or altogether: *I am not wholly*

certain yet. □ **complètement, tout à fait**

,**whole'hearted** *adjective* sincere and enthusiastic: *wholehearted support*. □ **sans réserve(s)**

'**wholemeal** *noun* flour made from the entire wheat grain or seed: *wholemeal flour/bread*. □ **complet**

on the whole taking everything into consideration: *Our trip was successful on the whole*. □ **dans l'ensemble**

whole note ['houl nout] *noun* in music, a note equal in length to two half notes. □ **ronde**

wholesale ['houlseil] *adjective* 1 (*also adverb*) buying and selling goods on a large scale, *usually* from a manufacturer and to a retailer: *a wholesale business*; *He buys the materials wholesale*. □ **en/de gros**

2 on a large scale: *the wholesale slaughter of innocent people*. □ **systématique**

'**wholesaler** *noun* a person who buys and sells goods wholesale. □ **grossiste**

wholesome ['houlsəm] *adjective* healthy; causing good health: *wholesome food*; *wholesome exercise*. □ **sain; salutaire**

'**wholesomely** *adverb*. □ **sainement**

'**wholesomeness** *noun*. □ **nature saine**

who'll short for **who shall, who will**.

whom *see* **who**.

whoop [wu:p, hu:p] *noun* 1 a loud cry of delight, triumph *etc*: *a whoop of joy*. □ **cri**

2 the noisy sound made when breathing in after prolonged coughing. □ **sifflement**

■ *verb* to give a loud cry of delight, triumph *etc*. □ **pousser des cris**

'**whooping cough,** '**hooping cough** ['hu:-] *noun* an infectious disease with violent bouts of coughing followed by a whoop. □ **coqueluche**

who's short for **who is, who has**.

whose [hu:z] *adjective, pronoun* belonging to which person(?): *Whose is this jacket?*; *Whose* (*jacket*) *is this?*; *Whose car did you come back in?*; *In whose house did this incident happen?*; *Tell me whose* (*pens*) *these are*. □ **à qui; de qui**

■ *relative adjective, relative pronoun* of whom or which (the): *Show me the boy whose father is a policeman*; *What is the name of the woman whose book this is?* □ **dont; à qui**

why [wai] *adverb* for which reason (?): '*Why did you hit the child?*'; '*He hit the child.*' '*Why?*'; '*Why haven't you finished?*'; '*I haven't finished.*' '*Why not?*'; '*Let's go to the cinema.*' '*Why not?*' (= Let's!); *Tell me why you came here*. □ **pourquoi**

■ *relative pronoun* for which: *Give me one good reason why I should help you!* □ **pour lequel, pour laquelle**

wick [wik] *noun* the twisted threads of cotton *etc* in a candle, lamp *etc*, which draw up the oil or wax into the flame. □ **mèche**

wicked ['wikid] *adjective* evil; sinful: *He is a wicked man*; *That was a wicked thing to do*. □ **méchant, mauvais**

'**wickedly** *adverb*. □ **méchamment**

'**wickedness** *noun*. □ **méchanceté**

wicker ['wikə] *adjective* (of *eg* a chair or basket) made of twigs, rushes *etc* woven together. □ **en/d'osier**

'**wickerwork** *noun* articles made in this way. □ **vannerie**

wide [waid] *adjective* **1** great in extent, *especially* from side to side: *wide streets*; *Her eyes were wide with surprise.* □ **large**

2 being a certain distance from one side to the other: *This material is three metres wide; How wide is it?* □ (de) **large**

3 great or large: *She won by a wide margin.* □ **grand**

4 covering a large and varied range of subjects *etc*: *a wide experience of teaching.* □ **grand**

■ *adverb* with a great distance from top to bottom or side to side: *He opened his eyes wide.* □ **tout grand**

'**widely** *adverb*. □ **largement**

'**widen** *verb* to make, or become, wide or wider: *They have widened the road; The lane widens here.* □ **(s')élargir**

'**wideness** *noun*. □ **largeur**

width [widθ] *noun* **1** size from side to side: *What is the width of this material?; This fabric comes in three different widths.* □ **largeur**

2 the state of being wide. □ **largeur**

,**wide-'ranging** *adjective* (of interests *etc*) covering a large number of subjects *etc*. □ **varié**

'**widespread** *adjective* spread over a large area or among many people: *widespread hunger and disease.* □ **très répandu**

give a wide berth (to) to keep well away from: *I give people with colds a wide berth/give a wide berth to people with colds.* □ **se tenir à bonne distance (de)**

wide apart a great (or greater than average) distance away from one another: *He held his hands wide apart.* □ **très écarté**

wide awake fully awake. □ **bien (r)éveillé**

wide open fully open: *The door was wide open; Her eyes are wide open but she seems to be asleep.* □ **grand ouvert**

widow ['widou] *noun* a woman whose husband is dead: *My brother's widow has married again.* □ **veuve**

■ *verb* to cause to become a widow or widower: *She/ He was widowed in 1943.* □ **devenir veuf, veuve**

'**widower** *noun* a man whose wife is dead. □ **veuf**

width *see* **wide.**

wield [wiːld] *verb* **1** to use: *He can certainly wield an axe.* □ **manier**

2 to have and use: *to wield authority.* □ **exercer**

wife [waif] – *plural* **wives** [waivz] – *noun* the woman to whom one is married: *Come and meet my wife; He is looking for a wife.* □ **femme**

old wives' tale a superstitious and misleading story. □ **conte de bonne femme**

wig [wig] *noun* an artificial covering of hair for the head: *Does she wear a wig?* □ **perruque, postiche**

wiggle ['wigl] *verb* to waggle or wriggle: *He wiggled his hips.* □ **tortiller (de)**

'**wiggly** *adjective* not straight; going up and down, from side to side *etc*: *a wiggly line.* □ **ondulé**

wigwam ['wigwaːm] *noun* a North American Indian tent made of skins *etc*. □ **wigwam**

wild [waild] *adjective* **1** (of animals) not tamed: *wolves and other wild animals.* □ **sauvage**

2 (of land) not cultivated. □ **sauvage**

3 uncivilized or lawless; savage: *wild tribes.* □ **sauvage**

4 very stormy; violent: *a wild night at sea; a wild rage.* □ **déchaîné; fou**

5 mad, crazy, insane *etc*: *wild with hunger; wild with anxiety.* □ **délirant (de); fou (de)**

6 rash: *a wild hope.* □ **fou, extravagant**

7 not accurate or reliable: *a wild guess.* □ **en l'air, au hasard**

8 very angry. □ **(fou) furieux**

'**wildly** *adverb*. □ **furieusement**

'**wildness** *noun*. □ **aspect sauvage**

'**wildfire: spread like wildfire** (of *eg* news) to spread extremely fast. □ **se répandre comme une traînée de poudre**

'**wildfowl** *noun plural* wild birds, *especially* water birds such as ducks, geese *etc*. □ **oiseau(x) sauvage(s)**

,**wild 'goose chase** an attempt to catch or find something one cannot possibly obtain. □ **quête impossible**

'**wildlife** *noun* wild animals, birds, insects *etc* collectively: *to protect wildlife.* □ **faune**

in the wild (of an animal) in its natural surroundings: *Young animals have to learn to look after themselves in the wild.* □ **à l'état sauvage**

the wilds the uncultivated areas (of a country *etc*): *They're living out in the wilds of Australia somewhere.* □ **régions sauvages**

the Wild West *see* **west.**

wilderness ['wildənəs] *noun* (a) desert or wild area of a country *etc*. □ **lieux sauvages**

wilful *see* **will.**

will [wil] *noun* **1** the mental power by which one controls one's thought, actions and decisions: *Do you believe in freedom of the will?* □ **volonté**

2 (control over) one's desire(s) or wish(es); determination: *It was done against her will; He has no will of his own – he always does what the others want; Children often have strong wills; He has lost the will to live.* □ **volonté, désir**

3 (a legal paper having written on it) a formal statement about what is to be done with one's belongings, body *etc* after one's death: *Have you made a will yet?* □ **testament**

■ *verb* – *short forms* **I'll** [ail], **you'll** [juːl], **he'll** [hiːl], **she'll** [ʃiːl], **it'll** ['itl], **we'll** [wiːl], **they'll** [ðeil]: *negative short form* **won't** [wount] – **1** used to form future tenses of other verbs: *We'll go at six o'clock tonight; Will you be here again next week?; Things will never be the same again; I will have finished the work by tomorrow evening.* □ **-rai, -ras, -ra, ...**

2 used in requests or commands: *Will you come into my office for a moment, please?; Will you please stop talking!* □ **vouloir**

3 used to show willingness: *I'll do that for you if you like; I won't do it!* □ **vouloir (bien)**

4 used to state that something happens regularly, is quite normal *etc*: *Accidents will happen.* □ **il arrive que**

'**wilful** *adjective* **1** obstinate. □ **entêté**

2 intentional: *wilful damage to property.* □ **volontaire**

'**wilfully** *adverb*. □ **avec entêtement**

'**wilfulness** *noun.* □ **entêtement**

-**willed**: *weak-willed/strong-willed people.* □ **de forte volonté/sans volonté**

'**willing** *adjective* ready to agree (to do something): *a willing helper; She's willing to help in any way she can.* □ **disposé/prêt (à)**

'**willingly** *adverb.* □ **de bon cœur**

'**willingness** *noun.* □ **bonne volonté**

'**willpower** *noun* the determination to do something: *I don't have the willpower to stop smoking.* □ **volonté**

at will as, or when, one chooses. □ **à volonté**

with a will eagerly and energetically: *They set about (doing) their tasks with a will.* □ **avec détermination**

willow ['wilou] *noun* a type of tree with long, slender branches. □ **saule**

wilt [wilt] *verb* (of flowers) to droop: *The plants are wilting because they haven't been watered.* □ **(se) faner**

'**wily** ['waili] *adjective* crafty, cunning, sly *etc*: *a wily old fox; He is too wily for the police to catch him.* □ **rusé**

'**wiliness** *noun.* □ **ruse**

wimp [wimp] *noun* someone who is not at all brave; a person unable to stand up for their opinions, a coward: *The principal is such a wimp that he is afraid to discipline students who cheat.* □ **poule mouillée**

win [win] – *present participle* '**winning**: *past tense, past participle* **won** [wʌn] – *verb* **1** to obtain (a victory) in a contest; to succeed in coming first in (a contest), *usually* by one's own efforts: *She won a fine victory in the election; Who won the war/match?; He won the bet; She won (the race) in a fast time/by a clear five metres.* □ **gagner**

2 to obtain (a prize) in a competition *etc, usually* by luck: *to win first prize; I won $5 in the crossword competition.* □ **gagner**

3 to obtain by one's own efforts: *He won her respect over a number of years.* □ **gagner**

■ *noun* a victory or success: *She's had two wins in four races.* □ **victoire**

'**winner** *noun.* □ **gagnant, ante**

'**winning** *adjective* **1** victorious or successful: *the winning candidate.* □ **gagnant**

2 attractive or charming: *a winning smile.* □ **irrésistible**

'**winning post** *noun* in horse-racing, a post marking the place where a race finishes. □ **poteau d'arrivée**

win over to succeed in gaining the support and sympathy of: *At first he refused to help us but we finally won him over.* □ **convaincre**

win the day to gain a victory; to be successful. □ **l'emporter**

win through to succeed in getting (to a place, the next stage *etc*): *It will be a struggle, but we'll win through in the end.* □ **y arriver**

wince [wins] *verb* to start or jump with pain: *She winced as the dentist touched her broken tooth.* □ **(se) crisper**

winch [wintʃ] *noun* a type of powerful machine for hoisting or hauling heavy loads. □ **treuil**

■ *verb* to hoist (up) or haul (in) using a winch. □ **soulever/déplacer avec un treuil**

wind[1] [wind] *noun* **1** (an) outdoor current of air: *The wind is strong today; There wasn't much wind yesterday; Cold*

winds blow across the desert. □ **vent**

2 breath: *Climbing these stairs takes all the wind out of me.* □ **souffle**

3 air or gas in the stomach or intestines: *His stomach pains were due to wind.* □ **gaz**

■ *verb* to cause to be out of breath: *The heavy blow winded him.* □ **couper le souffle (à)**

■ *adjective* (of a musical instrument) operated or played using air pressure, *especially* a person's breath. □ **à vent**

'**windy** *adjective*: *a windy hill-top; a windy day; It's windy today.* □ **venteux, exposé aux vents**

'**windiness** *noun.* □ **caractère venteux**

'**windfall** *noun* **1** an apple *etc* blown from a tree. □ **fruit(s) abattu(s) par le vent**

2 any unexpected gain or success. □ **aubaine**

'**windmill** *noun* a machine with sails that work by wind power, for grinding corn or pumping water. □ **moulin à vent**

'**windpipe** *noun* the passage for air between mouth and lungs. □ **trachée**

'**windshield** *noun* a transparent (*usually* glass) screen above the dashboard of a car. □ **pare-brise**

'**windsock** *noun* a device for indicating the direction and speed of wind on an airfield. □ **manche à air**

'**windswept** *adjective* exposed to the wind and showing the effects of it: *windswept hair; a windswept landscape.* □ **ébouriffé; exposé aux vents**

get the wind up to become nervous or anxious: *She got the wind up when she realized how close we were to the edge.* □ **avoir la frousse**

get wind of to get a hint of or hear indirectly about. □ **avoir vent de**

get one's second wind to recover one's natural breathing after breathlessness. □ **retrouver son souffle**

in the wind about to happen: *A change of policy is in the wind.* □ **dans l'air**

like the wind very quickly: *The horse galloped away like the wind.* □ **comme le vent**

wind[2] [waind] – *past tense, past participle* **wound** [waund] – *verb* **1** to wrap around in coils: *He wound the rope around his waist and began to climb.* □ **enrouler**

2 to make into a ball or coil: *to wind wool.* □ **enrouler**

3 (of a road *etc*) to twist and turn: *The road winds up the mountain.* □ **serpenter**

4 to tighten the spring of (a clock, watch *etc*) by turning a knob, handle *etc*: *I forgot to wind my watch.* □ **remonter**

'**winder** *noun* a lever or instrument for winding, on a clock or other mechanism. □ **remontoir**

'**winding** *adjective* full of bends *etc*: *a winding road.* □ **sinueux**

wind up **1** to turn, twist or coil; to make into a ball or coil: *My ball of wool has unravelled – could you wind it up again?* □ **enrouler; bobiner**

2 to wind a clock, watch *etc*: *She wound up the clock.* □ **remonter**

3 to end: *I think it's time to wind the meeting up.* □ **clore**

be/get wound up to be, or get, in a very excited or anxious state. □ **être énervé**

window ['windou] *noun* an opening in the wall of a building *etc* which is fitted with a frame of wood, metal *etc* containing glass or similar material, that can be seen through and *usually* opened: *I saw her through the window*; *Open/Close the window*; *goods displayed in a shop-window*. □ **fenêtre; vitrine**

'**window box** *noun* a box on a window-ledge, in which plants may be grown. □ **jardinière**

'**window dressing** *noun* the arranging of goods in a shop window. □ **composition d'étalage**

'**window dresser** *noun*. □ **étalagiste**

'**window frame** *noun* the wooden or metal frame of a window. □ **châssis (de fenêtre)**

'**window ledge** *noun* a ledge at the bottom of a window (*usually* on the outside). □ **rebord de fenêtre**

'**windowpane** *noun* one of the sheets of glass in a window. □ **vitre**

'**window shopping** *noun* looking at things in shop windows, but not actually buying anything. □ **lèche-vitrine**

'**windowsill** *noun* a ledge at the bottom of a window (inside or outside). □ **appui/rebord de fenêtre**

windpipe *etc see* **wind**¹.

wine [wain] *noun* a type of alcoholic drink made from the fermented juice of grapes or other fruit: *two bottles of wine; a wide range of inexpensive wines*. □ **vin**

wing [wiŋ] *noun* 1 one of the arm-like limbs of a bird or bat, which it *usually* uses in flying, or one of the similar limbs of an insect: *The eagle spread his wings and flew away; The bird cannot fly as it has an injured wing; These butterflies have red and brown wings*. □ **aile**

2 a similar structure jutting out from the side of an airplane: *the wings of a jet*. □ **aile**

3 a section built out to the side of a (*usually* large) house: *the west wing of the hospital*. □ **aile**

4 any of the corner sections of a motor vehicle: *The rear left wing of the car was damaged in the accident*. □ **aile**

5 a section of a political party or of politics in general: *the Left/Right wing*. □ **aile**

6 one side of a football *etc* field: *He made a great run down the left wing*. □ **aile**

7 in rugby and hockey, a player who plays mainly down one side of the field. □ **ailier**

8 in the air force, a group of three squadrons of aircraft. □ **escadre/brigade aérienne**

winged *adjective* having wings: *a winged creature*. □ **ailé**

-**winged**: *a four-winged insect*. □ **à (...) ailes**

'**winger** *noun* in football *etc*, a player who plays mainly down one side of the field. □ **ailier**

'**wingless** *adjective*. □ **sans ailes**

wings *noun plural* the sides of a theatre stage: *She waited in the wings*. □ **coulisses**

wing commander in the air force, the rank above squadron leader. □ **lieutenant-colonel**

'**wingspan** *noun* the distance from the tip of one wing to the tip of the other when outstretched (of birds, airplanes *etc*). □ **envergure**

on the wing flying, *especially* away: *The wild geese are on the wing*. □ **en vol**

take under one's wing to take (someone) under one's

protection. □ **prendre sous son aile**

wink [wiŋk] *verb* 1 to shut and open an eye quickly in friendly greeting, or to show that something is a secret *etc*: *He winks at all the girls who pass; Her father winked at her and said 'Don't tell your mother about her present.'* □ **faire un clin d'œil (à)**

2 (of *eg* lights) to flicker and twinkle. □ **clignoter**

■ *noun* an act of winking: *'Don't tell anyone I'm here', he said with a wink*. □ **clin d'œil**

forty winks a short sleep: *Father often has forty winks in his armchair after lunch*. □ **petit somme**

winkle¹ ['wiŋkl] *verb* to force (something out of something) gradually and with difficulty: *She winkled the shell out from the rock ; He tried to winkle some information out of her*. □ **extraire**

winkle² ['wiŋkl] *noun* (*also* '**periwinkle** ['peri-]) a type of small shellfish, shaped like a small snail, eaten as food. □ **bigorneau**

winning *etc see* **win**.

winnow ['winou] *verb* to separate the chaff from (the grain) by wind. □ **vanner**

winter ['wintə] *noun* the coldest season of the year, November or December till January or February in cooler northern regions: *We often have snow in winter*; (*also adjective*) *winter evenings*. □ **(d')hiver**

'**wintry** *adjective* like winter in being very cold: *a wintry day; wintry weather*. □ **hivernal**

'**wintriness** *noun*. □ **caractère hivernal**

winter sports sports played in the open air on snow and ice, *eg* skiing, tobogganing *etc*. □ **sports d'hiver**

'**wintertime** *noun* the season of winter. □ **hiver**

wipe [waip] *verb* 1 to clean or dry by rubbing with a cloth, paper *etc*: *Would you wipe the table for me?* □ **essuyer**

2 to remove by rubbing with a cloth, paper *etc*: *The child wiped her tears away with her handkerchief; Wipe that writing off (the blackboard); Please wipe up that spilt milk*. □ **essuyer, effacer**

■ *noun* an act of cleaning by rubbing: *Give the table a wipe*. □ **coup de torchon**

'**wiper** *noun* (*also* **windscreen wiper**) a moving arm for clearing rain *etc* from a vehicle's windscreen. □ **essuie-glace**

wipe out 1 to clean the inside of (a bowl *etc*) with a cloth *etc*. □ **bien essuyer**

2 to remove; to get rid of: *You must try to wipe out the memory of these terrible events*. □ **effacer**

3 to destroy completely: *They wiped out the whole regiment in one battle*. □ **anéantir**

wire ['waiə] *noun* 1 (*also adjective*) (of) metal drawn out into a long strand, as thick as string or as thin as thread: *We need some wire to connect the battery to the rest of the circuit; a wire fence*. □ **fil (métallique/électrique); grillage**

2 a single strand of this: *There must be a loose wire in my radio somewhere*. □ **fil**

3 the metal cable used in telegraphy: *The message came over the wire this morning*. □ **télégraphe**

4 a telegram: *Send me a wire if I'm needed urgently*. □ **télégramme**

■ *verb* **1** to fasten, connect *etc* with wire: *The house has been wired (up), but the electricity hasn't been connected yet.* □ **pourvoir d'une installation électrique**

2 to send a telegram to: *Wire me if anything important happens.* □ **télégraphier (à)**

3 to send (a message) by telegram: *You can wire the details to my brother in New York.* □ **télégraphier**

'**wireless** *noun* an older word for (a) radio. □ **radio**

'**wiring** *noun* the (system of) wires used in connecting up a circuit *etc*. □ **installation électrique**

high wire a high tightrope: *acrobats on the high wire.* □ **corde raide**

,**wire 'netting** *noun* a material with wide mesh woven of wire, used in fencing *etc*. □ **grillage**

wiry ['waiəri] *adjective* (of a person, his body *etc*) slim but strong. □ **sec et nerveux**

wise [waiz] *adjective* **1** having gained a great deal of knowledge from books or experience or both and able to use it well. □ **sage**

2 sensible: *You would be wise to do as she suggests*; *a wise decision.* □ **sage, (bien) avisé**

'**wisely** *adverb*. □ **sagement**

wisdom ['wizdəm] *noun*: *Wisdom comes with experience.* □ **sagesse**

wisdom tooth ['wizdəm-] any one of the four back teeth cut after childhood, *usually* about the age of twenty. □ **dent de sagesse**

'**wisecrack** *noun* a joke. □ **pointe**

wise guy a person who (shows that he) thinks that he is smart, knows everything *etc*. □ **malin**

be wise to to be fully aware of: *He thinks I'm going to give him some money, but I'm wise to his plan.* □ **se rendre compte de**

none the wiser not knowing any more than before: *She tried to explain the rules to me, but I'm none the wiser.* □ **pas plus avancé**

put (someone) wise to tell, inform (someone) of the real facts. □ **mettre au courant**

-wise [waiz] **1** in respect of or as regards: *This new idea may prove to be difficult costwise.* □ **en ce qui concerne**

2 in a (particular) way: *The stripes run crosswise.* □ **à la manière de**

wish [wiʃ] *verb* **1** to have and/or express a desire: *There's no point in wishing for a miracle*; *Touch the magic stone and wish*; *He wished that she would go away*; *I wish that I had never met him.* □ **souhaiter (que)**

2 to require (to do or have something): *Do you wish to sit down, sir?*; *We wish to book some seats for the theatre*; *I'll cancel the arrangement if you wish.* □ **vouloir**

3 to say that one hopes for (something for someone): *I wish you the very best of luck.* □ **souhaiter (qqch à qqn)**

■ *noun* **1** a desire or longing, or the thing desired: *It's always been my wish to go to South America some day.* □ **souhait**

2 an expression of desire: *The fairy granted her three wishes*; *Did you make a wish?* □ **vœu**

3 (*usually in plural*) an expression of hope for success *etc* for someone: *He sends you his best wishes.* □ **vœux**

'**wishing well** *noun* a well which is supposed to have the power of granting any wish made when one is beside it. □ **fontaine magique**

wisp [wisp] *noun* thin strand: *a wisp of hair*; *a wisp of smoke.* □ **brin, fil**

'**wispy** *adjective*: wispy hair. □ **fin**

wistful ['wistful] *adjective* thoughtful and rather sad, (as if) longing for something with little hope: *The dog looked into the butcher's window with a wistful expression on his face.* □ **mélancolique**

'**wistfully** *adverb*. □ **avec mélancolie**

'**wistfulness** *noun*. □ **air mélancolique**

wit [wit] *noun* **1** humour; the ability to express oneself in an amusing way: *His plays are full of wit*; *I admire her wit.* □ **esprit**

2 a person who expresses himself in a humorous way, tells jokes *etc*: *He's a great wit.* □ **homme, femme d'esprit**

3 common sense, inventiveness *etc*: *He did not have the wit to defend himself.* □ **bon sens**

'**witless** *adjective* crazy, stupid *etc*. □ **stupide**

-witted having understanding or intelligence of a certain kind: *quick-/sharp-witted.* □ **à l'esprit (...)**

'**witticism** [-sizəm] *noun* a witty remark *etc*. □ **mot d'esprit**

'**witty** *adjective* clever and amusing: *a witty person*; *witty remarks.* □ **spirituel**

'**wittily** *adverb*. □ **avec beaucoup d'esprit**

'**wittiness** *noun*. □ **humour**

at one's wits' end utterly confused and desperate. □ **à bout de ressources**

keep one's wits about one to be cautious, alert and watchful. □ **rester attentif**

live by one's wits to live by cunning rather than by hard work. □ **vivre d'expédients**

(frighten/scare) out of one's wits (to frighten) (almost) to the point of madness: *The sight of the gun in her hand scared me out of my wits.* □ **faire une peur bleue (à)**

witch [witʃ] *noun* a woman who is supposed to have powers of magic, *usually* through working with the devil. □ **sorcière**

'**witchcraft** *noun* magic practised by a witch *etc*. □ **sorcellerie**

'**witch doctor** *noun* in some African tribes, a person whose profession is to cure illness and keep away evil magical influences. □ **sorcier**

with [wið] *preposition* **1** in the company of; beside; among; including: *I was walking with my mother*; *Do they enjoy playing with each other?*; *He used to play football with the Arsenal team*; *Put this book with the others.* □ **avec**

2 by means of; using: *Mend it with this glue*; *Cut it with a knife.* □ **avec**

3 used in expressing the idea of filling, covering *etc*: *Fill this jug with milk*; *She was covered with mud.* □ **de**

4 used in describing conflict: *They quarrelled with each other*; *She fought with my brother.* □ **avec**

5 used in descriptions of things: *a man with a limp*; *a girl with long hair*; *a stick with a handle*; *Treat this book with care.* □ **avec**

6 as the result of: *He is shaking with fear.* □ **de**

7 in the care of: *Leave your case with the porter.* □ **à**

8 in relation to; in the case of; concerning: *Be careful with that!*; *What's wrong with you?*; *What shall I do with these books?* □ **avec**

9 used in expressing a wish: *Down with fascism!*; *Up with Manchester United!* □ **à/au...**

withdraw [wið'drɔː] – *past tense* **with'drew** [-'druː]: *past participle* **with'drawn** – *verb* **1** to (cause to) move back or away: *The army withdrew from its position*; *He withdrew his troops*; *They withdrew from the competition.* □ **(se) retirer**

2 to take back (something one has said): *She withdrew her remarks, and apologized*; *He later withdrew the charges he'd made against her.* □ **retirer**

3 to remove (money from a bank account *etc*): *I withdrew all my savings and went abroad.* □ **retirer**

with'drawal *noun.* □ **retrait**

with'drawn *adjective* (of a person) not responsive or friendly. □ **renfermé**

wither ['wiðə] *verb* (of plants *etc*) to (cause to) fade, dry up, or decay: *The plants withered because they had no water*; *The sun has withered my plants.* □ **(se) faner**

withhold [wið'hould] – *past tense, past participle* **with'held** [-'held] – *verb* to refuse to give: *to withhold permission.* □ **refuser**

within [wi'ðin] *preposition* inside (the limits of): *She'll be here within an hour*; *I could hear sounds from within the building*; *His actions were within the law* (= not illegal). □ **à l'intérieur de**

■ *adverb* inside: *Car for sale. Apply within.* □ **à l'intérieur**

without [wi'ðaut] *preposition* **1** in the absence of; not having: *They went without you*; *I could not live without her*; *We cannot survive without water.* □ **sans**

2 not: *He drove away without saying goodbye*; *You can't walk along this street without meeting someone you know.* □ **sans**

without the knowledge of unknown to; ignorant of or unaware of: *Anil wanted to become a dancer and he did it without the knowledge of his dad.* □ **à l'insu de; sans savoir**

withstand [wið'stand] – *past tense, past participle* **with'stood** [-'stud] – *verb* to oppose or resist (successfully): *They withstood the siege for eight months.* □ **résister (à); soutenir**

witness ['witnəs] *noun* **1** a person who has seen or was present at an event *etc* and so has direct knowledge of it: *Someone must have seen the accident but the police can find no witnesses.* □ **témoin**

2 a person who gives evidence, *especially* in a law court. □ **témoin**

3 a person who adds his signature to a document to show that he considers another signature on the document to be genuine: *You cannot sign your will without witnesses.* □ **témoin**

■ *verb* **1** to see and be present at: *This lady witnessed an accident at three o'clock this afternoon.* □ **être témoin de**

2 to sign one's name to show that one knows that (some-

thing) is genuine: *He witnessed my signature on the new agreement.* □ **attester l'authenticité de**

'witness box/'witness stand *noun* the stand from which a witness gives evidence in a court of law. □ **barre des témoins**

bear witness to give evidence: *She will bear witness to his honesty.* □ **témoigner (de)**

witty *etc see* **wit**.

wives *see* **wife**.

wizard ['wizəd] *noun* a man who is said to have magic powers: *a fairy-story about a wizard.* □ **magicien**

wobble ['wobl] *verb* to rock unsteadily from side to side: *The bicycle wobbled and the child fell off.* □ **ballotter**

■ *noun* a slight rocking, unsteady movement: *This wheel has a bit of a wobble.* □ **tremblement**

'wobbly *adjective.* □ **branlant**

'wobbliness *noun.* □ **caractère branlant**

woe [wou] *noun* (a cause of) grief or misery: *He has many woes*; *She told a tale of woe.* □ **malheur**

'woeful *adjective* miserable; unhappy: *a woeful expression.* □ **air affligé**

'woefully *adverb.* □ **d'un air affligé**

'woefulness *noun.* □ **affliction**

'woebegone [-bigon] *adjective* sad-looking: *a woebegone face.* □ **désolé**

woke, woken *see* **wake**[1].

wolf [wulf] – *plural* **wolves** [wulvz] – *noun* a type of wild animal of the dog family, *usually* found hunting in packs. □ **loup, louve**

■ *verb* to eat greedily: *He wolfed (down) his breakfast and hurried out.* □ **engloutir**

'wolf cub *noun* **1** a young wolf. □ **louveteau**

2 an old name for a Cub Scout. □ **louveteau**

'wolf whistle *noun* a whistle impolitely made by a man to express his admiration of a woman's appearance. □ **sifflement admiratif**

keep the wolf from the door to keep away hunger or want. □ **mettre à l'abri du besoin**

woman ['wumən] – *plural* **women** ['wimin] – *noun* **1** an adult human female: *His sisters are both grown women now*; *(also adjective) a woman doctor*; *women doctors.* □ **femme(-)**

2 a female domestic daily helper: *We have a woman who comes in to do the cleaning.* □ **femme de ménage**

-woman sometimes used instead of **-man** when the person performing an activity is a woman, as in **chairwoman.** □ **femme**

'womanhood *noun* the state of being a woman: *She will reach womanhood in a few years' time.* □ **féminité**

'womankind, womenkind ['wimin-] *nouns* women generally. □ **les femmes**

'womanly *adjective* (showing qualities) natural or suitable to a woman: *a womanly figure*; *womanly charm.* □ **féminin**

'womanliness *noun.* □ **féminité**

'womenfolk ['wimin-] *noun plural* female people, *especially* female relatives. □ **les femmes**

womb [wuːm] *noun* the part of the body of a female mammal in which the young are developed and kept until birth. □ **utérus**

won *see* **win**.

wonder ['wʌndə] *noun* **1** the state of mind produced by something unexpected or extraordinary: *He was full of wonder at the amazing sight.* □ **émerveillement**
2 something strange, unexpected or extraordinary: *the Seven Wonders of the World*; *You work late so often that it's a wonder you don't take a bed to the office!* □ **merveille**
3 the quality of being strange or unexpected: *The wonder of the discovery is that it was only made ten years ago.* □ **merveille**
■ *verb* **1** to be surprised: *Caroline is very fond of John – I shouldn't wonder if she married him.* □ **(s')étonner**
2 to feel curiosity or doubt: *Have you ever wondered about his reasons for wanting this money?* □ **se poser des questions (sur)**
3 to feel a desire to know: *I wonder what the news is.* □ **(se) demander**
'wonderful *adjective* arousing wonder; extraordinary, especially in excellence: *a wonderful opportunity*; *a wonderful present*; *She's a wonderful person.* □ **merveilleux**
'wonderfully *adverb.* □ **merveilleusement**
'wonderingly *adverb* with great curiosity and amazement: *The children gazed wonderingly at the puppets.* □ **avec étonnement**
'wonderland [-land] *noun* a land or place full of wonderful things. □ **pays merveilleux**
'wondrous ['wʌndrəs] *adjective* wonderful. □ **merveilleux**
no wonder it isn't surprising: *No wonder you couldn't open the door – it was locked!* □ **rien d'étonnant à ce que**

won't *see* **will**.

woo [wuː] – *3rd person singular present tense* **woos**: *past tense, past participle* **wooed** – *verb* (of a man) to seek as a wife: *He wooed the daughter of the king.* □ **faire la cour (à)**
'wooer *noun.* □ **prétendant**

wood [wud] *noun* **1** (*also adjective*) (of) the material of which the trunk and branches of trees are composed: *My desk is (made of) wood*; *She gathered some wood for the fire*; *I like the smell of a wood fire.* □ **(de) bois**
2 (*often in plural*) a group of growing trees: *They went for a walk in the woods.* □ **bois**
3 a golf-club whose head is made of wood. □ **bois**
'wooded *adjective* (of land) covered with trees: *a wooded hillside.* □ **boisé**
'wooden *adjective* made of wood: *three wooden chairs.* □ **en/de bois**
'woody *adjective* **1** covered with trees: *woody countryside.* □ **boisé**
2 (of a smell *etc*) of or like wood. □ **de/du bois**
'woodcutter *noun* a person whose job is felling trees. □ **bûcheron, onne**
'woodland *noun* land covered with woods: *a stretch of woodland.* □ **région boisée**
'woodlouse – *plural* **'woodlice** – *noun* a tiny creature with a jointed shell, found under stones *etc*. □ **cloporte**
'woodpecker *noun* a type of bird which pecks holes in

the bark of trees, searching for insects. □ **pic**
'woodwind [-wind] *noun* (in an orchestra, the group of people who play) wind instruments made of wood. □ **bois**
'woodwork *noun* **1** the art of making things from wood; carpentry: *She did woodwork at school.* □ **ébénisterie, menuiserie**
2 the wooden part of any structure: *The woodwork in the house is rotting.* □ **boiserie, charpente**
'woodworm – *plurals* **'woodworm, woodworms** – *noun* the larva of a certain type of beetle, which bores into wood and destroys it. □ **ver du bois**
out of the wood(s) out of danger. □ **tiré d'embarras**

wool [wul] *noun, adjective* (of) the soft hair of sheep and some other animals, often made into yarn *etc* for knitting or into fabric for making clothes *etc*: *I wear wool in winter*; *knitting-wool*; *a wool blanket.* □ **(de/en) laine**
'woollen *adjective* made of wool: *a woollen hat.* □ **de/en laine**
'woollens *noun plural* clothes (*especially* jumpers *etc*) made of wool: *Woollens should be washed by hand.* □ **lainages**
'woolly *adjective* made of, or like, wool: *a woolly jumper/rug.* □ **de/en laine; laineux**
■ *noun – plural* **'woollies** – a knitted garment. □ **lainages**
'woolliness *noun.* □ **caractère confus**
pull the wool over someone's eyes to deceive someone. □ **en faire accroire (à)**

word [wəːd] *noun* **1** the smallest unit of language (whether written, spoken or read). □ **mot**
2 a (brief) conversation: *I'd like a (quick) word with you in my office.* □ **mot**
3 news: *When you get there, send word that you've arrived safely.* □ **nouvelles**
4 a solemn promise: *He gave her his word that it would never happen again.* □ **parole**
■ *verb* to express in written or spoken language: *How are you going to word the letter so that it doesn't seem rude?* □ **formuler**
'wording *noun* the manner of expressing something, the choice of words *etc*. □ **formulation**
,word-'perfect *adjective* repeated, or able to repeat something, precisely in the original words: *a word-perfect performance*; *He wants to be word-perfect by next week's rehearsal.* □ **sur le bout des doigts**
by word of mouth by one person telling another in speech, not in writing: *She got the information by word of mouth.* □ **verbalement**
get a word in edgeways to break into a conversation *etc* and say something. □ **placer un mot**
in a word to sum up briefly: *In a word, I don't like him.* □ **en un mot**
keep, break one's word to keep or fail to keep one's promise. □ **tenir/manquer (à sa) parole**
take (someone) at his word to believe (someone) without question and act according to his words. □ **prendre (qqn) au mot**
take someone's word for it to assume that what someone says is correct (without checking). □ **croire (qqn) sur parole**

word for word in the exact, original words: *That's precisely what he told me, word for word.* □ **mot pour mot**
wore *see* wear.
work [wəːk] *noun* **1** effort made in order to achieve or make something: *She has done a lot of work on this project.* □ **travail**
2 employment: *I cannot find work in this town.* □ **travail**
3 a task or tasks; the thing that one is working on: *Please clear your work off the table.* □ **travail**
4 a painting, book, piece of music *etc*: *the works of Van Gogh/Shakespeare/Mozart; This work was composed in 1816.* □ **œuvre**
5 the product or result of a person's labours: *Her work has shown a great improvement lately.* □ **travail**
6 one's place of employment: *He left (his) work at 5:30 p.m.; I don't think I'll go to work tomorrow.* □ **travail**
■ *verb* **1** to (cause to) make efforts in order to achieve or make something: *She works at the factory three days a week; He works his employees very hard; I've been working on/at a new project.* □ **(faire) travailler (sur/à)**
2 to be employed: *Are you working just now?* □ **travailler**
3 to (cause to) operate (in the correct way): *He has no idea how that machine works/how to work that machine; That machine doesn't/won't work, but this one's working.* □ **(faire) fonctionner**
4 to be practicable and/or successful: *If my scheme works, we'll be rich!* □ **marcher**
5 to make (one's way) slowly and carefully with effort or difficulty: *She worked her way up the rock face.* □ **progresser (lentement)**
6 to get into, or put into, a stated condition or position, slowly and gradually: *The wheel worked loose.* □ **devenir peu à peu**
7 to make by craftsmanship: *The ornaments had been worked in gold.* □ **façonner**
-work 1 (the art of making) goods of a particular material: *He learns woodwork at school; This shop sells basketwork.* □ **travail de**
2 parts of something, *eg* a building, made of a particular material: *The stonework/woodwork/paintwork needs to be renewed.* □ **ouvrage de...**
'workable *adjective* (of a plan) able to be carried out. □ **réalisable**
'worker *noun* **1** a person who works or who is employed in an office, a factory *etc*: *office workers; car workers.* □ **employé, ée; travailleur, euse**
2 a manual worker rather than an office worker *etc*. □ **ouvrier, ière**
3 a person who works (hard *etc*): *She's a slow/hard worker.* □ **travailleur, euse**
co-worker *noun* one of the people who work in the same place of employment as oneself: *His co-workers teased him about being the boss's favourite.* □ **camarade de travail**
works *noun singular or noun plural* a factory *etc*: *The steelworks is/are closed for the holidays.* □ **usine**
■ *noun plural* **1** the mechanism (of a watch, clock *etc*):

The works are all rusted. □ **mécanisme**
2 deeds, actions *etc*: *She's devoted her life to good works.* □ **œuvres**
'work basket, 'workbox *etc nouns* a basket, box *etc* for holding thread, needlework *etc*. □ **corbeille à ouvrage**
'workbook *noun* a book of exercises *usually* with spaces for answers. □ **cahier d'exercices**
'workforce *noun* the number of workers (available for work) in a particular industry, factory *etc*. □ **main-d'œuvre**
working class the section of society who work with their hands, doing manual labour. □ **classe ouvrière**
working day, 'workday *nouns* **1** a day on which one goes to work, and is not on holiday. □ **jour ouvrable**
2 the period of actual labour in a normal day at work: *My working day is eight hours long.* □ **journée de travail**
working hours the times of day between which one is at work: *Normal working hours are nine-to-five.* □ **heures de travail**
'working party, 'work party *nouns* a group of people gathered together (*usually* voluntarily) to perform a particular physical task: *They organized a work-party to clear the canal of weeds.* □ **équipe; groupe de travail**
working week the five days from Monday to Friday inclusive when people go to work. □ **semaine de travail**
'workman, 'workwoman *noun* a person who does manual work: *the workmen on a building site.* □ **ouvrier, ière**
'workmanlike *adjective* **1** suitable to a good workman: *a workmanlike attitude.* □ **professionnel**
2 well performed: *a workmanlike job.* □ **bien fait**
'workmanship *noun* the skill of a qualified workman; skill in making things. □ **métier; maîtrise professionnelle**
'workout *noun* a period of hard physical exercise for the purpose of keeping fit *etc*. □ **séance d'entraînement**
'workshop *noun* **1** a room or building, *especially* in a factory *etc* where construction and repairs are carried out. □ **atelier**
2 a course of experimental work for a group of people on a particular project. □ **atelier**
at work working: *She's writing a novel and she likes to be at work (on it) by eight o'clock every morning.* □ **au travail**
get/set to work to start work: *Could you get to work painting that ceiling?; I'll have to set to work on this mending this evening.* □ **se mettre au travail**
go to work on to begin work on: *We're thinking of going to work on an extension to the house.* □ **entreprendre**
have one's work cut out to be faced with a difficult task: *You'll have your work cut out to beat the champion.* □ **avoir du pain sur la planche**
in working order (of a machine *etc*) operating correctly. □ **en état de marche**
out of work having no employment: *He's been out of work for months.* □ **au chômage**

work of art a painting, sculpture *etc*. □ **œuvre d'art**

work off to get rid of (something unwanted or unpleasant) by taking physical exercise *etc*: *He worked off his anger by running around the garden six times.* □ **se débarrasser de**

work out 1 to solve or calculate correctly: *I can't work out how many should be left.* □ **résoudre**

2 to come to a satisfactory end: *Don't worry – it will all work out (in the end).* □ **(s')arranger**

3 to perform physical exercises. □ **(s')entraîner**

work up 1 to excite or rouse gradually: *She worked herself up into a fury (adjective ,*worked '*up: Don't get so worked up!).* □ **s'échauffer; dans tous ses états**

2 to raise or create: *I just can't work up any energy/ appetite/enthusiasm today.* □ **arriver à avoir**

work up to to progress towards and prepare for: *Work up to the difficult exercises gradually.* □ **progresser graduellement**

work wonders to produce marvellous results: *These pills have worked wonders on my rheumatism.* □ **faire des miracles**

world [wɜːld] *noun* 1 the planet Earth: *every country of the world.* □ **monde**

2 the people who live on the planet Earth: *The whole world is waiting for a cure for cancer.* □ **monde**

3 any planet *etc*: *people from other worlds.* □ **monde**

4 a state of existence: *Many people believe that after death the soul enters the next world; Do concentrate! You seem to be living in another world.* □ **monde**

5 an area of life or activity: *the insect world; the world of the international businessman.* □ **monde**

6 a great deal: *The holiday did her a/the world of good.* □ **le plus grand bien**

7 the lives and ways of ordinary people: *He's been a monk for so long that he knows nothing of the (outside) world.* □ **monde**

'worldly *adjective* of or belonging to this world; not spiritual: *worldly pleasures.* □ **de ce monde, terrestre**

'worldliness *noun*. □ **attachement aux biens de ce monde**

,world'wide *adjective, adverb* (extending over or found) everywhere in the world: *a worldwide sales network; Their products are sold worldwide.* □ **mondial; dans le monde entier**

the best of both worlds the advantages of both the alternatives in a situation *etc* in which one can normally only expect to have one: *A woman has the best of both worlds when she has a good job and a happy family life.* □ **gagner sur les deux tableaux**

for all the world exactly, quite *etc*: *What a mess you're in! You look for all the world as if you'd had an argument with an express train.* □ **exactement**

out of this world unbelievably marvellous: *The concert was out of this world.* □ **sensationnel**

what in the world(?) used for emphasis when asking a question: *What in the world have you done to your hair?* □ **que diable**

worm [wɜːm] *noun* a kind of small creeping animal with a ringed body and no backbone; an earth-worm. □ **ver (de terre)**

■ *verb* 1 to make (one's way) slowly or secretly: *She wormed her way to the front of the crowd.* □ **(se) faufiler**

2 to get (information *etc*) with difficulty (out of someone): *It took me hours to worm the true story out of him.* □ **soutirer (qqch. à qqn)**

worn *see* wear.

worry ['wʌri] *verb* 1 to (cause to) feel anxious: *His dangerous driving worries me; His mother is worried about his education; There's no need to worry just because he's late.* □ **(s')inquiéter**

2 to annoy; to distract: *Don't worry me just now – I'm busy!* □ **harceler, embêter**

3 to shake or tear with the teeth *etc* as a dog does its prey *etc*. □ **jouer (avec)**

■ *noun* (a cause of) anxiety: *That boy is a constant (source of) worry to his mother!; Try to forget your worries.* □ **souci, inquiétude, tracas**

'worried *adjective* (*negative* **unworried**): *a worried look.* □ **inquiet**

worse [wɜːs] *adjective* 1 bad to a greater extent: *My exam results were bad but his were much worse (than mine).* □ **pire (que)**

2 not so well: *I feel worse today than I did last week.* □ **moins bien (que)**

3 more unpleasant: *Waiting for exam results is worse than sitting the exams.* □ **pire (que)**

■ *adverb* not so well: *He behaves worse now than he did as a child.* □ **moins bien (que)**

■ *pronoun* someone or something which is bad to a greater extent than the other (of two people, things *etc*): *the worse of the two alternatives.* □ **le, la pire (de)**

'worsen *verb* to (cause to) grow worse: *The situation has worsened.* □ **empirer**

none the worse for not in any way harmed by: *The child was lost in the supermarket but fortunately was none the worse for his experience.* □ **pas plus mal**

the worse for wear becoming worn out: *These chairs are the worse for wear.* □ **usé à la corde**

worship ['wɜːʃip] – *past tense, past participle* 'worshipped, 'worshiped – *verb* 1 to pay great honour to: *to worship God.* □ **adorer**

2 to love or admire very greatly: *She worships her older brother.* □ **adorer**

■ *noun* the act of worshipping: *A church is a place of worship; the worship of God/of money.* □ **culte**

'worshipper *noun*. □ **fidèle**

worst [wɜːst] *adjective* bad to the greatest extent: *That is the worst book I have ever read.* □ **pire**

■ *adverb* in the worst way or manner: *This group performed worst (of all) in the test.* □ **le plus mal**

■ *pronoun* the thing, person *etc* which is bad to the greatest extent: *the worst of the three; His behaviour is at its worst when he's with strangers; At the worst they can only fine you.* □ **le, la pire (de); au pire**

do one's worst to do the most evil *etc* thing that one can. □ **faire de son pire**

get the worst of to be defeated in (a fight *etc*). □ **avoir le dessous**

if the worst comes to the worst if the worst possible thing happens: *If the worst comes to the worst you can*

sell your house. □ **en mettant les choses au pire**
the worst of it is (that) the most unfortunate *etc* aspect
of the situation is (that). □ **le pire est que**
worth [wɔːθ] *noun* value: *These books are of little or no*
worth; She sold fifty dollars' worth of tickets. □ **valeur**
■ *adjective* 1 equal in value to: *Each of these stamps is*
worth a cent. □ **valoir**
2 good enough for: *His suggestion is worth consider-*
ing: The exhibition is well worth a visit. □ **qui vaut**
'worthless *adjective* of no value: *worthless old coins.* □
sans valeur
'worthlessly *adverb.* □ **d'une manière qui ne vaut rien**
'worthlessness *noun.* □ **absence (totale) de valeur**
'worthy [-ði] *adjective* 1 good and deserving: *I will-*
ingly give money to a worthy cause. □ **valable, noble**
2 (*with* of) deserving: *She was not worthy of the honour*
given to her. □ **digne de**
3 (*with* of) typical of, suited to, or in keeping with: *a*
performance worthy of a champion. □ **digne (de)**
4 of great enough importance *etc*: *He was not thought*
worthy to be presented to the king. □ **digne (de)**
■ *noun* – *plural* **'worthies** – a highly respected person.
□ **notable**
'worthily *adverb.* □ **dignement**
'worthiness *noun.* □ **caractère digne**
-worthy 1 deserving; fit for: *a blameworthy act.* □ **digne**
de
2 fit for its appropriate use: *a seaworthy ship.* □ **en état**
de...
worth'while *adjective* deserving attention, time and
effort *etc*: *a worthwhile cause*; *It isn't worthwhile to*
ask him – he'll only refuse. □ **qui vaut la peine (de)**
for all one is worth using all one's efforts, strength *etc*:
She swam for all she was worth towards the shore. □ **de**
toutes ses forces
would [wud] – *short forms* **I'd** [aid], **you'd** [juːd], **he'd**
[hiːd], **she'd** [ʃiːd], **it'd** ['itəd], **we'd** [wiːd], **they'd**
[ðeid]: *negative short form* **wouldn't** ['wudnt] – *verb* 1
past tense of **will**: *He said he would be leaving at nine*
o'clock the next morning; *I asked if she'd come and*
mend my television set; *I asked him to do it, but he*
wouldn't; I thought you would have finished by now. □
-rais, -rais, -rait, ...
2 used in speaking of something that will, may or might
happen (*eg* if a certain condition is met): *If I asked her*
to the party, would she come?; *I would have come to*
the party if you'd asked me; I'd be happy to help you. □
-rais, -rais, -rait...
3 used to express a preference, opinion *etc* politely: *I*
would do it this way; *It'd be a shame to lose the oppor-*
tunity; I'd prefer to go tomorrow rather than today. □
-rais, -rais, -rait ...
4 used, said with emphasis, to express annoyance: *I've*
lost my car-keys – that would happen! □ **ça devait**
arriver
'would-be *adjective* trying, hoping, or merely pretending, to be: *a would-be poet.* □ **qui se veut, soi-disant**
would you used to introduce a polite request to someone to do something: (*Please*) *would you close the door?*
□ **voudriez-vous**

wouldn't *see* would.
wound[1] *see* wind[2].
wound[2] [wuːnd] *noun* a physical hurt or injury: *The*
wound that he had received in the war still gave him
pain occasionally; She died from a bullet-wound. □
blessure
■ *verb* 1 to hurt or injure physically: *He didn't kill the*
animal – he just wounded it; She was wounded in the
battle. □ **blesser**
2 to hurt (someone's feelings): *to wound someone's*
pride. □ **blesser**
'wounded *adjective* having been injured, *especially* in
war *etc*: *the wounded man.* □ **blessé**
■ *noun plural* wounded people, *especially* soldiers: *How*
many wounded are there? □ **blessés**
wove, woven *see* weave.
wrangle ['raŋgl] *verb* to quarrel or argue angrily. □ **(se)**
disputer
■ *noun* an angry argument. □ **dispute**
wrap [rap] – *past tense, past participle* **wrapped** – *verb*
1 to roll or fold (around something or someone): *He*
wrapped his handkerchief around his bleeding finger.
□ **enrouler (autour de)**
2 to cover by folding or winding something around: *He*
wrapped the book (up) in brown paper; She wrapped
the baby up in a warm shawl. □ **envelopper**
■ *noun* a warm covering to put over one's shoulders. □
châle
'wrapper *noun* a paper cover for a sweet, packet of cigarettes *etc*: *a sweet-wrapper.* □ **papier (d'emballage)**
'wrapping *noun* something used to wrap or pack something in: *Christmas wrappings.* □ **papier d'emballage**
wrapped up in giving all one's attention to: *She's very*
wrapped up in her work these days. □ **absorbé (par)**
wrap up to dress warmly: *You have to wrap up well if*
you visit England in winter; Wrap the child up well. □
(s')emmitoufler
wrath [raθ] *noun* violent anger. □ **colère**
'wrathful *adjective.* □ **courroucé**
wreath [riːθ] – *plural* **wreaths** [riːθs, riːðz] – *noun* 1 a
circular garland of flowers or leaves, placed at a grave,
or put on someone's shoulders or head after his/her victory *etc*: *We put a wreath of flowers on her mother's*
grave. □ **couronne**
2 a drift or curl of smoke, mist *etc*: *wreaths of smoke.* □
spirale, filet
wreathe [riːð] *verb* to cover: *faces wreathed in smiles.*
□ **rayonnant**
wreck [rek] *noun* 1 a very badly damaged ship: *The divers*
found a wreck on the sea-bed. □ **épave**
2 something in a very bad condition: *an old wreck of a*
car, I feel a wreck after cleaning the house. □ **ruine**
3 the destruction of a ship at sea: *The wreck of the Royal*
George. □ **naufrage**
■ *verb* to destroy or damage very badly: *The ship was*
wrecked on rocks in a storm; My son has wrecked my
car; You have wrecked my plans. □ **détruire, démolir**
'wreckage [-kidʒ] *noun* the remains of something
wrecked: *After the accident, the wreckage (of the cars)*
was removed from the highway. □ **débris**

wren [ren] *noun* a type of very small bird. □ **roitelet**
wrench [rentʃ] *verb* 1 to pull with a violent movement:
She wrenched the gun out of my hand. □ **arracher**
2 to sprain: *to wrench one's shoulder.* □ **(se) fouler**
■ *noun* 1 a violent pull or twist. □ **violent mouvement
de torsion**
2 a type of strong tool for turning nuts, bolts *etc.* □ **clef
(à molette)**
throw a wrench in the works to frustrate or ruin (a
plan, system *etc*). □ **mettre des bâtons dans les roues
(de)**
wrestle ['resl] *verb* 1 to struggle physically (with someone), *especially* as a sport. □ **lutter**
2 to struggle (with a problem *etc*): *I've been wrestling
with the office accounts.* □ **se (dé)battre (avec)**
'**wrestler** *noun* a person who takes part in the sport of
wrestling. □ **lutteur, euse**
wrestling *noun* a sport where two opponents struggle
with their hands and attempt to bring the other's shoulder to the ground: *Harold won the wrestling by pressing Duncan's shoulder to the mat.* □ **lutte**
wretch [retʃ] *noun* 1 a miserable, unhappy creature: *The
poor wretch!* □ **malheureux, euse**
2 a name used in annoyance or anger: *You wretch!* □
scélérat, ate
wretched ['retʃid] *adjective* 1 very poor or miserable:
They live in a wretched little house. □ **misérable**
2 used in annoyance: *This wretched machine won't work!*
□ **maudit**
'**wretchedly** *adverb.* □ **misérablement**
'**wretchedness** *noun.* □ **misère**
wriggle ['rigl] *verb* to twist to and fro: *The child kept
wriggling in his seat; How are you going to wriggle out
of this awkward situation?* □ **(se) tortiller, frétiller; (se)
sortir/dépêtrer de**
■ *noun* a wriggling movement. □ **tortillement,
frétillement**
'**wriggler** *noun.* □ **enfant qui remue sans cesse**
wring [riŋ] – *past tense, past participle* **wrung** [rʌŋ] –
verb 1 to force (water) from (material) by twisting or
by pressure: *He wrung the water from his soaking-wet
shirt.* □ **essorer**
2 to clasp and unclasp (one's hands) in desperation, fear
etc. □ **(se) tordre les mains (de désespoir)**
'**wringer** *noun* a machine for forcing water from wet
clothes. □ **essoreuse**
wringing wet soaked through: *The clothes are wringing wet; wringing-wet clothes.* □ **trempé**
wrinkle ['riŋkl] *noun* a small crease on the skin (*usually*
on one's face): *Her face is full of wrinkles.* □ **ride**
■ *verb* to (cause to) become full of wrinkles or creases:
The damp had wrinkled the pages. □ **rider; plisser**
'**wrinkled** *adjective* full of wrinkles: *a wrinkled face.* □
ridé
wrist [rist] *noun* the (part of the arm at the) joint between hand and forearm: *I can't play tennis – I've hurt
my wrist.* □ **poignet**
'**wristwatch, 'wristletwatch** [-lit-] *nouns* a watch worn
on the wrist. □ **montre-bracelet**
write [rait] – *past tense* **wrote** [rout]: *past participle*

written ['ritn] – *verb* 1 to draw (letters or other forms
of script) on a surface, *especially* with a pen or pencil
on paper: *They wrote their names on a sheet of paper;
The child has learned to read and write; Please write
in ink.* □ **écrire**
2 to compose the text of (a book, poem *etc*): *She wrote
a book on prehistoric monsters.* □ **écrire**
3 to compose a letter (and send it): *He has written a
letter to me about this matter; I'll write you a long letter about my holiday; I wrote to you last week.* □ **écrire**
'**writer** *noun* a person who writes, *especially* for a living: *Dickens was a famous English writer; the writer of
this letter.* □ **écrivain, aine**
'**writing** *noun* letters or other forms of script giving the
written form of (a) language: *the Chinese form of writing; I can't read your writing.* □ **écriture**
'**writings** *noun plural* the collected books, poems, correspondence *etc* of a particular (*usually* famous) person: *the writings of Plato.* □ **écrits**
written ['ritn] *adjective* in writing: *a written message.*
□ **écrit**
'**writing paper** *noun* paper for writing letters *etc* on:
writing paper and envelopes. □ **papier à lettres**
write down to record in writing: *She wrote down every
word he said.* □ **mettre par écrit**
write out to copy or record in writing: *Write this exercise out in your neatest handwriting.* □ **transcrire**
writhe [raið] *verb* to twist violently to and fro, *especially* in pain or discomfort: *to writhe in agony; She
writhed about when I tickled her.* □ **(se) tordre**
wrong [roŋ] *adjective* 1 having an error or mistake(s);
incorrect: *The child gave the wrong answer; We went in
the wrong direction.* □ **mauvais**
2 incorrect in one's answer(s), opinion(s) *etc*; mistaken:
*I thought Singapore was south of the Equator, but I was
quite wrong.* □ **dans l'erreur**
3 not good, not morally correct *etc*: *It is wrong to steal.*
□ **mal**
4 not suitable: *He's the wrong man for the job.* □ **mauvais**
5 not right; not normal: *There's something wrong with
this engine; What's wrong with that child – why is she
crying?* □ **qui ne va pas**
■ *adverb* incorrectly: *I think I may have spelt her name
wrong.* □ **mal**
■ *noun* that which is not morally correct: *He does not
know right from wrong.* □ **mal**
■ *verb* to insult or hurt unjustly: *You wrong me by suggesting that I'm lying.* □ **faire du tort à**
'**wrongful** *adjective* not lawful or fair: *wrongful dismissal from a job.* □ **injuste**
'**wrongfully** *adverb.* □ **injustement**
'**wrongfulness** *noun.* □ **injustice**
'**wrongly** *adverb* 1 incorrectly: *The letter was wrongly
addressed.* □ **mal**
2 unjustly: *I have been wrongly treated.* □ **injustement**
'**wrongdoer** *noun* a person who does wrong or illegal
things: *The wrongdoers must be punished.* □ **malfaiteur,
trice**
'**wrongdoing** *noun.* □ **méfaits**
be wrong *verb* to be mistaken about something; to have

an opinion that is not correct: *Nancy thought the book would have a happy ending, but she was wrong.* □ **avoir tort**

do (someone) wrong to insult (someone), treat (someone) unfairly *etc.* □ **mal agir (envers)**

do wrong to act incorrectly or unjustly: *You did wrong to punish him.* □ **mal agir (en)**

go wrong 1 to go astray, badly, away from the intended plan *etc*: *Everything has gone wrong for her in the past few years.* □ **mal tourner**

2 to stop functioning properly: *The machine has gone wrong – I can't get it to stop!* □ **se détraquer**

3 to make a mistake: *Where did I go wrong in that sum?* □ **se tromper**

in the wrong guilty of an error or injustice: *She is completely blameless. You're the one who's in the wrong!* □ **dans son tort**

wrote *see* **write.**

wrung *see* **wring.**

wry [rai] *adjective* slightly mocking: *a wry smile.* □ **ironique**

'**wryly** *adverb.* □ **avec une ironie désabusée**

Xx

X-rays [eks'reiz] *noun plural* rays which can pass through many substances impossible for light to pass through, and which produce a picture of the object through which they have passed. □ **rayon(s) X**

,**X-'ray** *noun* (the process of taking) a photograph using X-rays: *I'm going to hospital for an X-ray*; *We'll take an X-ray of your chest*; *(also adjective) an X-ray photograph.* □ **radiographie**

■ *verb* to take a photograph of using X-rays: *They X-rayed my arm to see if it was broken.* □ **radiographier**

Xerox® ['ziərɒks] *noun* **1** a type of photographic process used for copying documents. □ **photocopie**
2 a copying-machine using this process. □ **photocopieuse**
3 a photocopy (of something) made by such a process. □ **photocopie**

■ *verb* to photocopy (something) using this process. □ **photocopier**

Xmas ['krisməs] short for **Christmas**.

xylophone ['zailəfoun] *noun* a musical instrument consisting of wooden or metal slats of various lengths, which produce different notes when struck by wooden hammers. □ **xylophone**

Yy

yacht [jɔt] *noun* a boat or small ship, usually with sails, often with an engine, built and used for racing or cruising: *We spent our holidays on a friend's yacht*; (*also adjective*) *a yacht race.* □ **(de) yacht**
'**yachting** *noun* the pastime of sailing in a yacht. □ **navigation de plaisance**
'**yachtsman** ['jɔts-] *noun* a person who sails a yacht: *a keen yachtsman.* □ **plaisancier, ière**
yacht club a club for yacht-owners. □ **club nautique**

yak [jak] – *plurals* **yaks, yak** – *noun* a type of long-haired ox, found in Tibet. □ **ya(c)k**

yam [jam] *noun* any of several kinds of potato-like tropical plants used as food. □ **igname**

yank [jaŋk] *noun* a sudden sharp pull; a jerk: *She gave the rope a yank.* □ **secousse**
■ *verb* to pull suddenly and sharply: *She yanked the child out of the mud.* □ **tirer (d'un coup sec)**

Yank [jaŋk] *noun* an impolite word for a person from the United States of America. □ **Ricain(e)**
Yankee ['jaŋki] *noun, adjective* a more affectionate word for (an) American. □ **Yankee; yankee**

yap [jap] – *past tense, past participle* **yapped** – *verb* (of a puppy or small dog) to give a high-pitched bark. □ **japper**
■ *noun* a short, high-pitched bark: *The puppy gave a yap.* □ **jappement**

yard¹ [jɑːd] *noun* (*often abbreviated to* **yd**) an old unit of length equal to 0.9144 metres. □ **verge**

yard² [jɑːd] *noun* **1** an area of (enclosed) ground beside a building: *Leave your bicycle in the yard*; *a school-yard*; *a courtyard.* □ **cour**
2 an area of enclosed ground used for a special purpose: *a shipyard*; *a dockyard.* □ **chantier**

yarn¹ [jɑːn] *noun* wool, cotton *etc* spun into thread: *knitting-yarn*; *a length of yarn.* □ **fil**

yarn² [jɑːn] *noun* an old word for a story or tale: *She told us interesting yarns about her travels.* □ **longue histoire**

yashmak ['jaʃmak] *noun* a veil worn by Moslem women, covering the face below the eyes. □ **litham**

yawn [jɔːn] *verb* to stretch the mouth wide and take a deep breath when tired or bored: *She yawned and fell asleep.* □ **bâiller**
■ *noun* an act of yawning: *a yawn of boredom.* □ **bâillonnement**
'**yawning** *adjective* wide open: *a yawning gap.* □ **béant**

ye [jiː] *pronoun* an old word for **you**, occurring as the subject of a sentence. □ **vous**

year [jiə] *noun* **1** the period of time the earth takes to go once around the sun, about 365 days: *We lived here for five years, from November 1968 to November 1973*; *a two-year delay.* □ **an**
2 the period from January 1 to December 31, being 365 days, except in a leap year, when it is 366 days: *in the year 1945.* □ **année**
'**yearly** *adjective* happening *etc* every year: *We pay a yearly visit to my aunt.* □ **annuel**
■ *adverb* every year: *The festival is held yearly.* □ **annuellement**
'**yearbook** *noun* a book of information which is updated and published every year: *a students' year-book.* □ **annuaire**
all (the) year round, long *etc* throughout the whole year: *The weather is so good here that we can swim all (the) year round.* □ **toute l'année**

yearn [jəːn] *verb* to feel a great desire; to long: *to yearn for an end to the war.* □ **aspirer à**
'**yearning** *noun* (a) strong desire. □ **aspiration**

yeast [jiːst] *noun* a substance which causes fermentation, used in making beer, bread *etc*. □ **levure**

yell [jel] *noun* a loud, shrill cry; a scream: *a yell of pain.* □ **hurlement**
■ *verb* to make such a noise: *She yelled at him to be careful.* □ **hurler**

yellow ['jelou] *adjective, noun* (of) the colour of gold, the yolk of an egg *etc*: *a yellow dress*; *yellow sands*; *Yellow is my favourite colour.* □ **jaune**
■ *verb* to make or become yellow: *It was autumn and the leaves were beginning to yellow.* □ **jaunir**
'**yellowness** *noun*. □ **ton jaune**

yelp [jelp] *verb* (of a dog *etc*) to give a sharp, sudden cry: *The dog yelped with pain.* □ **japper**
■ *noun* a sharp, sudden cry: *The dog gave a yelp of pain.* □ **jappement**

yen [jen] – *plural* **yen** – *noun* the standard unit of Japanese currency. □ **yen**

yes [jes] *interjection* used to express agreement or consent: *Yes, that is true*; *Yes, you may go.* □ **oui**

yesterday ['jestədi] *noun, adverb* (on) the day before today: *Yesterday was a tiring day*; *She went home yesterday.* □ **hier**

yet [jet] *adverb* **1** up till now: *She hasn't telephoned yet*; *Have you finished yet?*; *We're not yet ready.* □ **jusqu'à présent**
2 used for emphasis: *He's made yet another mistake/yet more mistakes.* □ **encore**
3 (*with a comparative adjective*) even: *a yet more terrible experience.* □ **encore**
■ *conjunction* but; however: *He's pleasant enough, yet I don't like him.* □ **pourtant**
as yet up to the time referred to, *usually* the present: *I haven't had a book published as yet.* □ **encore, jusqu'ici**

yew [juː] *noun* a type of evergreen tree with dark leaves and red berries. □ **if**

yield [jiːld] *verb* **1** to give up; to surrender: *He yielded to the other man's arguments*; *She yielded all her possessions to the state.* □ **céder**
2 to give way to force or pressure: *At last the door yielded.* □ **céder**
3 to produce naturally, grow *etc*: *How much milk does that herd of cattle yield?* □ **produire**
■ *noun* the amount produced by natural means: *the annual yield of wheat.* □ **rendement**

yodel ['joudl] – *past tense, past participle* '**yodelled**, '**yodeled** – *verb* to sing (a melody *etc*), changing frequently from a normal to a very high-pitched voice and back again. □ **yodler**
'**yodeller** *noun*. □ **yodleur, euse**

yoga ['yougə] *noun* 1 any of several systems of physical exercises based on a Hindu system of philosophy and meditation. □ **yoga**

2 the philosophy (*usually* including the meditation and exercises). □ **yoga**

'**yogi** [-gi] *noun* a person who practises and/or teaches the yoga philosophy. □ **yogi**

yogourt, yog(h)urt ['jou-gət] *noun* a type of semi-liquid food made from fermented milk. □ **yogourt**

yoke [jouk] *noun* 1 a wooden frame placed over the necks of oxen to hold them together when they are pulling a cart *etc.* □ **joug**

2 a frame placed across a person's shoulders, for carrying buckets *etc.* □ **palanche**

3 something that weighs people down, or prevents them being free: *the yoke of slavery.* □ **joug**

4 the part of a garment that fits over the shoulders and around the neck: *a black dress with a white yoke.* □ **empiècement**

■ *verb* to join with a yoke: *He yoked the oxen to the plough.* □ **mettre au joug**

yolk [jouk] *noun* (*also* '**egg yolk**) the yellow part of an egg: *The child will only eat the yolk of an egg – she won't eat the white.* □ **jaune (d'œuf)**

you [juː] *pronoun* 1 (used as the subject or object of a verb, or as the object of a preposition) the person(s) *etc* spoken or written to: *You look well!*; *I asked you a question*; *Do you all understand?*; *Who came with you?* □ **vous; tu/toi/te**

2 used with a noun when calling someone something, *especially* something unpleasant: *You idiot!*; *You fools!* □ **espèce de**

you'd *see* have, would.

you'll *see* will.

young [jʌŋ] *adjective* in the first part of life, growth, development *etc*; not old: *a young person*; *Young babies sleep a great deal*; *A young cow is called a calf.* □ **jeune**

■ *noun plural* the group of animals or birds produced by parents: *Most animals defend their young.* □ **petits**

'**youngster** *noun* a young person: *A group of youngsters were playing football.* □ **jeune**

the young young people in general. □ **les jeunes**

your [jɔː] *adjective* belonging to you: *your house/car.* □ **votre/vos; ton/ta/tes**

yours [juərz] *pronoun* something belonging to you: *This book is yours*; *Yours is on that shelf.* □ **le/la/les vôtre(s); le tien, la tienne, les tiens, les tiennes**

your'self – *plural* **your'selves** [-'selvz] – *pronoun* 1 used as the object of a verb or preposition when the person(s) spoken or written to is/are the object(s) of an action he, she or they perform(s): *Why are you looking at yourselves in the mirror?*; *You can dry yourself with this towel.* □ **vous(-même(s)); toi(-même); te**

2 used to emphasize you: *You yourself can't do it, but you could ask someone else to do it.* □ **même**

3 without help *etc*: *You can jolly well do it yourself!* □ **tout seul**

yours (**faithfully, sincerely, truly**) expressions written before one's signature at the end of a letter. □ **vôtre, à vous**

you're *see* be.

youth [juːθ] – *plural* **youths** [juːðz] – *noun* 1 (the state of being in) the early part of life: *Enjoy your youth!*; *She spent her youth in America.* □ **jeunesse**

2 a boy of fifteen to twenty years old approximately: *He and two other youths were kicking a football about.* □ **jeune homme**

3 young people in general: *Some people say that today's youth has/have no sense of responsibility.* □ **jeunesse**

'**youthful** *adjective* 1 young: *The girl looked very youthful.* □ **jeune**

2 energetic, active, young-looking *etc*: *Exercise will keep you youthful.* □ **jeune**

3 of youth: *youthful pleasures.* □ **juvénile**

'**youthfully** *adverb.* □ **en jeune homme/fille**

'**youthfulness** *noun.* □ **jeunesse**

youth hostel a place for young people, *especially* hikers, on holiday, where cheap and simple accommodation is provided (*noun* **youth hosteller**). □ **auberge de jeunesse**

you've *see* have.

yo-yo, Yo-yo® ['joujou] *noun* a type of toy, consisting of a pair of discs made of wood, metal *etc* with a groove between them around which a piece of string is tied, the toy being made to run up and down the string: *going up and down like a yo-yo.* □ **yo-yo**

yuan [ju'an] – *plural* **yu'an** – *noun* the standard unit of currency in the People's Republic of China. □ **yuan**

Zz

zeal [ziːl] *noun* enthusiasm or keenness. □ **zèle**
zealous ['zeləs] *adjective* enthusiastic; keen: *He is a zealous supporter of our cause.* □ **zélé**
'**zealously** *adverb.* □ **avec zèle**

zebra ['ziːbrə, 'zeb-] – *plural* '**zebras**, '**zebra** – *noun* a kind of striped animal of the horse family, found wild in Africa: *two zebras; a herd of zebra.* □ **zèbre**
zebra crossing a place, marked in black and white stripes, where traffic stops for pedestrians to cross a street. □ **passage pour piétons**

zenith ['zeniθ] *noun* the highest point: *The sun reaches its zenith at midday.* □ **zénith**

zero ['ziərou] – *plural* '**zeros** – *noun* **1** the number or figure 0: *Three plus zero equals three; The figure 100 has two zeros in it.* □ **zéro**
2 the point on a scale (*eg* on a thermometer) which is taken as the standard on which measurements may be based: *The temperature was 5 degrees above/below zero.* □ **zéro**
3 the exact time fixed for something to happen, *eg* an explosion, the launching of a spacecraft *etc*: *It is now 3 minutes to zero.* □ **l'heure H**

zest [zest] *noun* keen enjoyment: *She joined in the games with zest.* □ **entrain, enthousiasme**

zigzag ['zigzag] *adjective* (of a line, road *etc*) having sharp bends or angles from side to side: *a zigzag path through the woods.* □ **zigzag**
■ *verb – past tense, past participle* '**zigzagged** – to move in a zigzag manner: *The road zigzagged through the mountains.* □ **zigzaguer**

zinc [ziŋk] *noun* a bluish-white metallic element. □ **zinc**

zip¹ [zip] *noun* **1** (*also* '**zipper**) a zip fastener. □ **fermeture à glissière**
2 a whizzing sound: *They heard the zip of a flying bullet.* □ **sifflement**
■ *verb – past tense, past participle* **zipped** – **1** to fasten with a zip fastener: *She zipped up her trousers; This dress zips at the back.* □ **fermer une fermeture à glissière**
2 to move with a whizzing sound: *A bullet zipped past his head.* □ **siffler**
zip fastener (*usually* **zip** *or* '**zipper**) a device for fastening clothes *etc*, in which two rows of metal or nylon teeth are made to fit each other when a sliding tab is pulled along them. □ **fermeture à glissière**

zip² [zip]: **zip code** in the United States, a postal code, having the form of a five-figure number, placed at the end of an address. □ **code postal**

zombie ['zombi] *noun* a slow-moving person of very little intelligence. □ **imbécile**

zone [zoun] *noun* **1** an area or region, *usually* of a country, town *etc, especially* one marked off for a special purpose: *a no-parking zone; a traffic-free zone.* □ **zone**
2 any of the five bands into which the earth's surface is divided according to temperature: *The tropical zone is the area between the Tropic of Capricorn and the Tropic of Cancer.* □ **zone**

zoo [zuː] *noun* (*short for* **zoological garden**) a place where wild animals are kept for the public to see, and for study, breeding *etc*. □ **zoo**

zoology [zu'olədʒi] *noun* the scientific study of animals. □ **zoologie**
,**zoo'logical** [zuə'lo-] *adjective.* □ **zoologique**
,**zoo'logically** [-'lo-] *adverb.* □ **zoologiquement**
zo'ologist *noun.* □ **zoologiste**

zoom [zuːm] *noun* a loud, low-pitched buzzing noise: *the zoom of (an) aircraft.* □ **vrombissement**
■ *verb* to move very quickly with this kind of noise: *The motorbike zoomed past us.* □ **passer en trombe**
zoom lens a type of camera lens which can make a distant object appear gradually closer without moving the camera. □ **focale variable**
zoom in to direct a camera (on to an object *etc*) and use a zoom lens to make it appear to come closer: *Film the whole building first, then zoom in on the door.* □ **faire un zoom (sur)**

INDEX
FRANÇAIS / ANGLAIS

Aa

à at, on, to, unto
à aire ouverte open-plan
à autre chose otherwise
à bas down with
à bon marché cheaply, inexpensively
à bord on
à bord (de) aboard
à bout portant point-blank
à bras ouverts with open arms
à bras-le-corps bodily
à califourchon astride
à cause de on account of, because of, through
à ce compte-là at that rate, at this rate
à ce jour to date
à cet égard on that score
à charge dependent
à cheval on horseback
à cœur ouvert heart-to-heart
à condition que on condition that
à contre-courant upstream
à contrecœur unwillingly, grudgingly, reluctantly
à côté next door
à côté de beside, next to
à court de short
à court terme short-term
à découvert naked, overdrawn
à défaut de failing
à demi half
à demi conscient semi-conscious
à destination de destined
à deux doigts de within an inch of
à deux sens two-way
à dire vrai to tell the truth
à domicile at home
à double tranchant cut both ways
à droite right
à égalité even, neck and neck
à feuilles mobiles loose-leaf
à feuilles persistantes evergreen
à flot afloat
à fond in depth, to the full, inside out, thoroughly
à fond de train at full pelt, (at) full tilt
à force de by dint of
à/de gauche left-hand
à gauche left
à guichets fermés booked up, sell-out
à haute voix aloud, vocally
à jour up to date
à l'abri (de) safe (from)
à l'affiche on

à l'agonie at death's door
à l'aise comfortable, at ease
à l'amiable amicably
à l'antenne on the air
à l'avenir in future
à l'écart (de) aloof
à l'encontre de counter
à l'envers inside out, upside down
à l'esprit étroit narrow-minded
à l'esprit ouvert open-minded
à l'esprit vif quick-witted
à l'essai on trial
à l'est eastward
à l'état neuf in mint condition
à l'étranger abroad
à l'exception de except for
à l'excès to a fault
à l'exclusion de excluding
à l'extérieur outside
à l'extrême in the extreme, terribly
à l'extrême nord northernmost
à l'heure on time, promptly, on time
à l'heure juste on the hour
à l'instant just now
à l'intérieur in, indoors
à l'intérieur (de) inside of
à l'intérieur (des terres) inland
à l'inverse conversely
à l'orange orange
à l'origine originally
à l'unanimité unanimously
à la dérive adrift
à la dernière minute at the eleventh hour, at short notice
à la disposition de at one's disposal
à la file in single file
à la hâte hastily, hurriedly, in a hurry, in haste
à la hauteur up to scratch
à la légère heedlessly, thoughtlessly
à la lettre to the letter
à la longue in due course
à la lumière de in the light of
à la main by hand
à la mémoire de in memory of, to the memory of
à la merci de at the mercy of
à la mode fashionable, in, in fashion
à la place (de) instead, instead of
à la portée de la main on hand
à la santé de here's to
à la suite de following, subsequent to
à l'improviste unexpectedly
à long terme long-range
à longue portée long-range
à main levée freehand, a show of hands

à maintes reprises repeatedly
à même qqch. out of
à merveille famously
à mi-chemin half-way, midway
à moins que unless
à moitié half
à mon avis to my mind
à moteur power-driven
à mourir to death
à nu bareback, nakedly
à part except for
à part entière fully-fledged
à pas de géant by leaps and bounds
à peine hardly, scarcely
à peu près pretty well, thereabout(s)
à pic sheer
à pied on foot
à plat flat
à plein temps full-time
à plein volume at full blast
à portée (de la main) at one's elbow, handy
à portée de voix hearing
à première vue on the face of it
à présent now
à propos by the way, incidentally
à propos de concerning, over
à proprement parler strictly speaking
à proximité close at hand
à quatre foursome
à quatre pattes on all fours
à rebours backwards
à reculons backwards
à regret regretfully
à ressorts sprung
à sang froid cold-blooded
à savoir namely
à sens unique one-way
à temps in good time, in time
à temps partiel part-time
à tête chercheuse homing
à titre officiel officially
à titre officieux off the record
à tour de rôle in turn, by turns
à tout jamais evermore
à tout prendre all in all
à tout prix at all costs
à toute allure flat out, headlong, hotfoot
à toute épreuve foolproof
à tue-tête at the top of one's voice
à voix basse under one's breath
à/de gauche left-hand
à/les bras ouverts with open arms
à/vers l'est east
à-coup jolt
à-propos aptness, timeliness
abaisser à, s' stoop

abandon abandonment, disuse
abandonné abandoned, derelict, deserted, disused
abandonner abandon, desert, ditch, forsake, quit, waive
abasourdir dum(b)found, stun
abat-jour lampshade
abats giblets, offal
abattage slaughter
abattement dejection
abattoir abattoir, slaughter-house
abattre bring down, butcher, chop, cut down, fell, hew
abattre shoot down, slaughter
abattu dejected, downcast, down-in-the-mouth
abbaye abbey
abbé abbot
abbesse abbess
abcès abscess, gumboil
abdication abdication
abdiquer abdicate
abdomen abdomen
abdominal abdominal
abeille bee, honeybee
abhorrer abhor
abîme abyss, chasm
abîmer damage
abnégation self-sacrifice
aboiement bark
abolir abolish
abolition abolition
abominable abominable, infamous
abominablement abominably, abysmally, fiendishly
abomination abomination
abominer abominate
abondamment abundantly
abondance abundance, copiousness
abondant plenteous, plentiful, profuse, abundant
abonder en abound (in, with)
abonnement subscription
abonner, s' subscribe
aborigène aborigine
aboyer bark, bay
abrasif abrasive
abrégé abridged
abréger abbreviate, abridge
abréviation abbreviation
abri bunker, cover, shelter
abri anti nucléaire bunker
abricot apricot
abriter shade, shelter
abrogation repeal, revocation
abroger repeal
abrupt sheer, abrupt
abruti dopey, soul-destroying
absence absence
absent absent, faraway

absentéisme absenteeism
absentéiste absentee
absenter, s' absent
absolu absolute, direct, outright, rank
absolument absolutely, just
absolument pas not for the life of me
absolution absolution
absorbant absorbent
absorbé deep, engrossed
absorbé (par) intent (on), wrapped up (in)
absorber absorb, soak up
absorber dans, s' lose oneself in, pore (over)
absorption absorption
absoudre absolve
abstenir (de), s' abstain, refrain (from)
abstention abstention
abstinence abstinence
abstinent teetotal
abstrait abstract
abstrus abstruse
absurde absurd, cockeyed, nonsensical, preposterous
absurdement absurdly
absurdité absurdity, absurdness, nonsense
absurdités nonsense, rubbish
abuser de abuse, overtax
abuser de la bonté de impose (on)
académie academy
académiquement academically
acajou mahogany
accablant damning
accablé overcome, prostrate
accabler (de) assail, bear down on, prostrate
accalmie lull
accaparer hog
accéder (à) accede (to)
accélérateur accelerator, throttle
accélération acceleration
accélérer accelerate, expedite, quicken, speed up
accent (tonique) accent
accent accent, emphasis, stress, stress-mark
accents overtones
accentuer accent, stress
acceptable acceptable, admissible, tolerable
acceptation acceptance
accepter accept, fall in with, take, take on
accepter sans broncher take lying down
accepter un pari take a bet

accès access, fit, surge
accessibilité accessibility
accessible accessible, approachable, open to
accessoire accessory, attachment, frill, property
accident accident, crash
accident mortel fatality
accidenté broken, bumpy, rough
accidentel accidental
acclamation acclaim, acclamation, cheer
acclamer acclaim
acclimatation acclimatization
acclimater (à), (s') acclimatize
accolade(s) bracket
accommodant accommodating, compliant
accommoder de, s' make the best of it
accompagnateur, trice accompanist, courier
accompagnement accompaniment
accompagner accompany, come along
accompli accomplished, consummate
accomplir accomplish, fulfil
accomplir sans effort romp
accomplissement accomplishment, fulfilment
accord accord, agreement, chord, settlement
accordé in tune
accordéon accordion
accordéon à clavier piano-accordion
accorder accord, award, grant, hang together, tune, tune up
accorder (avec), s' correspond (to)
accorder, (s') hang together
accordeur, euse tuner
accords strain
accoster accost
accouchement childbirth, confinement, delivery
accoucher deliver, give birth
accoudoir arm
accoupler, (s') mate
accoutrement get-up
accoutumance (à) familiarization
accrédité accredited
accroc snag
accroché hooked (on)
accrocher hang, hook
accrocher (à), s' cling (to)
accrocher à, s' hang on
accrocher (au mur) put up
accroissement increase
accroître, (s') increase, build up

accroupir, s' crouch, squat
accueil reception, welcome
accueillant welcoming
accueillir greet, receive, welcome
acculé cornered
acculer corner
accumulateur accumulator
accumulation accumulation
accumuler amass, accumulate
accusation accusation, charge, incrimination
accusé, ée the accused, defendant
accuser charge
accuser (de) accuse (of)
accuser réception de acknowledge
acharné furious, hellbent on
acharner à, s' stick at
acharner inutilement, s' flog a dead horse
achat purchase
achat avantageux value
acheter buy, purchase
acheteur, euse purchaser, shopper
achevé complete
achèvement completion
achever finish off, round off
acide acid
acidité acidity
acier steel
aciérie steelworks
acné acne
acolyte cohort, henchman
acompte deposit, down payment
acoustique acoustic, acoustics
acquérir acquire, develop
acquiescer acquiesce
acquisition accession, acquisition
acquittement acquittal
acquitter acquit, pay up
acquitter de, s' discharge
âcre acrid
acrobate acrobat
acrobatie(s) acrobatics, aerobatics
acrobatique acrobatic
acte act
acteur actor
actif active, assets, energetic, live
action action, deed, share
actionnaire shareholder
actionner drive
activement actively, busily, hotly
activité activeness, activity
actrice actress
actualités news
actuel present, currently
actuellement nowadays, at present
acuité acuteness
acupuncture acupuncture
adaptabilité adaptability
adaptable adaptable

adaptateur adaptor
adaptation adaptation
adapter arrange, tailor
adapter (à), (s') adapt
adapter, s' find one's feet, settle in
addition addition, check
additionner add, tot
adhérence adhesion
adhérer à adhere (to)
adhésif adhesive
adhésion adherence, membership
adieu farewell
adjacent adjacent
adjectif adjective
adjectival adjectival
adjoint, ointe deputy, assistant
admettre admit
administrateur, trice administrator, executive, governor
administratif administrative
administration administration, government
administrer administer, administrate, manage
admirable admirable
admirablement admirably
admirateur admiring, admirer
admiration admiration
admirativement admiringly
admirateur, trice admirer, fan
admirer admire
admissibilité eligibility
admissible eligible
admission entrance, intake
adolescence adolescence, teens
adolescent stripling
adolescent, ente adolescent, teenager
adonné (à) addicted (to)
adopter adopt
adoptif adoptive
adoption adoption
adorable adorable, darling, dear, lovable
adorablement adorably
adoration adoration
adorer adore, idolize, think the world of, worship
adoucir, (s') soften, tone down
adoucissant balmy
adoucissement balminess
adresse address, adroitness, deftness, skill
adresser à address, apply (for)
adroit adroit, deft
adroitement adroitly, deftly
adulation adulation
adulte adult, grown
adultère adultery
adverbe adverb

adverbial adverbial
adverbialement adverbially
adversaire adversary, opponent, opposition
adversité adversity
aérer air
aérien aerial
aérodrome aerodrome
aérodynamique streamlined
aérogare terminal
aérogramme air letter
aéroglisseur hovercraft
aéronautique aeronautics, aeronautical, aviation
aéroport airport
aérosol aerosol
affabilité affability, suaveness, suavity
affable affable, bland, suave
affaiblir, s' fade (away)
affaire business, case, proposition, stuff, things
affaire(s) affair, business
affaissement subsidence
affaisser, (s') fall away
affaler, (s') flop
affamé famished, hungry
affectation pose
affecter affect, allocate
affecter (à) assign
affection affection, fondness
affectueusement affectionately, fondly
affectueux affectionate
affiche bill, poster
affiliation affiliation
affilié affiliated, associate
affirmatif affirmative, positive
affirmation affirmation, claim
affirmer affirm, assert
affirmer, s' assert oneself
affliction affliction, distress
affligé cursed with, grief-stricken, mournful
affligeant distressing
affliger afflict, distress, grieve
affluent tributary
affluer flock, roll in
afflux influx
affolé distracted
affranchir frank
affréter charter
affreux atrocious, ghastly, horrible, horrid
affront affront, snub
affrontement clash, encounter
affronter breast, clash, confront, face
afin de in order to
agaçant annoying, irritating

agacé annoyed
agacer irritate, tease
âge age
âge mûr middle age
agence de voyages travel agency, travel bureau
agenouiller, (s') kneel (down)
agent, ente agent
agent, ente de bord flight attendant
agent de décomposition decomposer
agent, ente de police police officer
agent, ente de voyages travel agent
agent, ente double double agent
agent, ente immobilier, ière real estate agent
agent secret secret agent
agente électorale canvasser
aggraver aggravate
agile agile, lithe, nimble
agilement nimbly
agilité agility, litheness
agir act, act on
agir réciproquement interact
agitateur, trice agitator
agitation agitation, choppiness, stir, unrest
agité agitated, choppy, restless, troubled, turbulent, unsettled
agiter agitate
agneau lamb
agonie agony
agrafe staple
agrafeuse stapler
agrandir enlarge, extend
agrandissement enlargement
agréable agreeable, enjoyable, lik(e)able, pleasant, pleasing, pleasurable
agréablement agreeably, pleasantly, pleasingly, pleasurably
agresser assault, mug
agresseur, euse aggressor, assailant, mugger
agressif aggressive, belligerent, truculent
agression aggression
agressivement aggressively
agressivité aggressiveness
agricole agricultural
agriculture agriculture
agrumes citrus fruit
ahurir stun, stupefy
aide aid, assistance, help, mate
aide-infirmier, ière orderly
aide-mémoire reminder
aider aid, assist, help
aigle eagle
aigre sour
aigreur sourness, tartness, waspishness

aigrir embitter, sour
aigu acute, high, high-pitched
aiguille hand, needle, pointer, stylus
aiguille à tricoter knitting needle
aiguilleur, euse signalman
aiguillon goad, spur
aiguisé sharp
aiguiser sharpen, whet
aiguisoir sharpener
ail garlic
aile fender, wing
ailleurs elsewhere
ailleurs, d' moreover
aimable amiable, genial, lovable, sweet-tempered
aimablement affably, amiably, genially, kindly, pleasantly
aimant loving, magnet
aimer enjoy, like, love
aine groin
aîné senior, elder, eldest
ainsi thus
ainsi que together with
air comprimé compressed air
air(s) air, look, tune
aire area, apron
aisance facility, fluency
aisé comfortable, effortless, well-off
aisselle armpit
ajournement adjournment, postponement
ajourner adjourn, postpone
ajourner à adjourn
ajout addition
ajouter (à) add (to), supplement
ajusté close
ajuster (à) adjust (to)
alarmant alarming
alarmer alarm
alarmiste scaremonger
album album, scrapbook
alcalin alkaline
alcool alcohol
alcoolique alcoholic, drunkard
alcoolisé alcoholic
alcoolisme alcoholism
alcôve alcove
aléatoire random
alentour around
alerte alarm, alert
alerter alert
alezan chestnut
algèbre algebra
algébrique algebraic
algue(s) algae, seaweed
alias alias
alibi alibi
aliénation alienation, derangement
aliéné deranged

aliéner, s' alienate
aligner align, draw up, line up
aligner (le long de), s' line
aligner (sur), s' align
aligner, (s') line up
aliment(s) foodstuff
alimentaire nutritional
aliments de lest roughage
alinéa indentation
alité laid up
alizé trade wind
allaiter breastfeed, nurse, suckle
allant bounce, go
allée aisle, drive, alley
allégation allegation
alléger, (s') lighten
allègre blithe, blithely
allégresse elation, exhilaration
alléguer allege
aller go
aller à la dérive drift
aller à toute allure hurtle
aller à vau-l'eau go to seed
aller aux urnes go to the polls
aller avec go with
aller bien (à) suit
aller bien avec match
aller chercher fetch, get
aller comme un gant suit (someone) down to the ground, fit like a glove
aller et retour round trip
aller furieusement storm
aller jusqu'au bout go the whole hog, go through with
aller jusqu'au fond de get to the bottom of
aller (à bicyclette) ride
aller loin go far, go places
aller trop loin go too far
aller voir call on
allergie allergy
allergique allergic
alliage alloy
alliance alliance
allié allied
alliée ally
allier (à) ally
allier avec, s' gang up with
alligator alligator
allocation allocation, allowance
allongé elongated
allongement elongation
allonger (de l'argent) fork out
allonger le pas step out
allonger, (s') lie
allouer (à) allocate
allumage ignition
allumer kindle, light, put on, switch on/off

allumer, s' light up
allumette match
allure pace
allusion allusion, hint
almanach almanac
alors then
alouette lark
aloyau sirloin
alphabet ABC, alphabet
alphabétique alphabetical
alphabétiquement alphabetically
alpin alpine
alpinisme mountaineering
alpiniste mountaineer
altéré corrupt
alternance alternation
alternative alternative
alterné alternate
alterner alternate
altitude altitude, elevation
alto alto, viola
aluminium aluminum
alvéolé cellular
amabilité geniality, pleasantness
amaigri emaciated
amaigrissement emaciation
amalgame cement
amande almond, kernel
amandier almond (tree)
amant lover
amarrage mooring
amarrer berth, moor
amas mass
amasser gather
amateur lover, fan
amateur, trice amateur
ambassade embassy
ambigu ambiguous
ambiguïté ambiguity
ambitieusement ambitiously
ambitieux ambitious
ambition aim, ambition, ambitiousness
ambre amber
ambulance ambulance
âme soul
amélioration improvement
améliorer improve on, take a turn for the better
améliorer, (s') better, improve, look up
amende fine
amener bring
amer bitter
amèrement bitterly
amertume bitterness
ameublement furnishings
ami, ie friend
amiante asbestos
amical amicable, friendly,

neighbourly
amie girlfriend
amiral, ale admiral
amitié friendship
ammoniac/ammoniaque ammonia
amnésie amnesia
amnistie amnesty
amoncellement drift
amortir break, cushion, deaden
amortisseur (de chocs) shock-absorber
amour darling, dear, love
amoureux, euse lover, sweetheart
ampère ampere
amphibie amphibian, amphibious
amphithéâtre amphitheatre
ample full, loose
amplement amply, spaciously
ampleur extent
amplificateur amplifier, booster
amplification amplification
amplifier amplify
ampoule blister, bulb
amputation amputation
amputer amputate
amusant amusing, funny
amuse-gueule appetizer
amusement amusement, gaiety
amuser amuse, entertain, tickle
amuser, (s') amuse, enjoy oneself, play
amygdale tonsil
amygdalite tonsillitis
an year
analphabétisme illiteracy
analyse analysis
analyser analyse
analyste analyst
analytique analytical
ananas pineapple
anarchie anarchy
anarchisme anarchism
anarchiste anarchist
anatomie anatomy
anatomique anatomical
anatomiquement anatomically
anatomiste anatomist
ancestral ancestral
ancêtre(s) ancestor, forebears, forefathers, predecessor
anche reed
ancien ancient, antique, early, former, late, old
ancien combattant veteran
ancienneté seniority
ancre anchor
âne ass, donkey, jackass
anéantir annihilate, dash, shatter, wipe out
anéantissement annihilation

anecdote anecdote
anémie anemia
anémié bloodless
anémique anemic
anesthésie anaesthesia
anesthésier anaesthetic
anesthésique anaesthetic
anesthésiste anaesthetist
ange angel
angélique angelic, cherubic
Anglais English
angle angle
angliciser anglicize
angoissant anxious, nerve-racking
angoisse anguish, distraught, suspense
anguille eel
angularité angularity
anguleux angular
anicroche hitch
animal animal, beast
animal nuisible pest
animateur, trice animator, disc jockey, television show host, quizmaster/mistress
animation animation
animé animated, busy
animer animate, enliven
animosité animosity
annales annals
anneau ring
année year
année-lumière light year
annexe annex
annexion annexation
anniversaire anniversary, birthday
annonce ad, advert, announcement, intimation
annoncer advertise, announce, call, herald, intimate
annonceur, euse advertiser
annuaire directory
annuel annual, yearly
annuellement annually, yearly
annulaire ring finger
annulation annulment, cancellation
annulé off
annuler annul, call off, cancel, cancel out, invalidate, scrub
anomalie handicap
anonymat anonymity
anonyme anonymous, nameless
anonymement anonymously
anormal abnormal, unnatural
anormalement abnormally, unnaturally
anse cove, creek, handle, inlet
antagonisme antagonism
antagoniste antagonist, antagonistic
antarctique Antarctic

antenne antenna, feeler
antérieur prior
anthologie anthology
anthracite anthracite
anthropologie anthropology
anthropologique anthropological
anthropologue anthropologist
anti- anti-
antiaérien anti-aircraft
antibiotique antibiotic
anticipé advance
antidater backdate
antidote antidote
antigel antifreeze
antilope antelope
antique antique
antiquité antiquity, antique
antiseptique antiseptic
antisocial antisocial
antonyme antonym
anxiété anxiety
anxieux anxious
août August
apaisement appeasement,
  mollification
apaiser appease, mollify, pacify,
  placate, quieten
aparté aside
apathie apathy
apathique apathetic, inert
apercevoir catch sight of, sight,
  notice, spy
apercevoir, s' perceive
apéritif appetizer
apeuré scared
aplanir flatten, level, smoothen
aplatir, s' grovel
apogée pinnacle
apostolique apostolic
apostrophe apostrophe
apothéose grand finale
apôtre apostle
apparaître appear, emerge
apparaître indistinctement loom
appareil aircraft, apparatus,
  appliance, device, machine
appareil acoustique hearing aid
appareil de levage tackle
appareil-photo camera
apparemment apparently,
  seemingly
apparence appearance, guise,
  surface
apparent apparent, seeming
apparenté (à) akin, related
apparition appearance, emergence
appartement apartment, flat
appartenir à belong
appât bait
appauvrir impoverish

appauvrissement impoverishment
appel appeal, call, roll call
appeler call
appendice appendix
appendicite appendicitis
appétissant appetizing
appétit appetite
applaudir applaud, clap
applaudissement applause
applicabilité applicability
applicable (à) applicable
application application, diligence,
  studiousness
appliqué diligent, painstaking
appliquer administer, apply,
  enforce
apporter bring, take (away, in, off,
  out)
apposer affix
appréciable appreciable
appréciateur appreciative
apprécier appreciate
appréhender apprehend
appréhensif apprehensive
appréhension apprehension,
  apprehensiveness, misgiving
apprendre learn, instruct
apprenti, ie apprentice
apprentissage apprenticeship
apprêt dressing, primer
apprêter dress
apprivoisable tameable
apprivoisé tame
apprivoiser tame
approbation approbation, approval,
  endorsement, favour, sanction
approche approach, come, draw up
approcher, (s') near
approfondi intimate
approfondir, s' deepen
approprié fitting, right
approprié (à) appropriate
approuver approve, countenance,
  endorse, hold with, sanction
approvisionnement catering,
  supply
approvisionner supply
approximatif approximate, rough
approximation approximation
approximativement approximately
appui support, rest
appui de fenêtre windowsill
appui-tête headrest
appuyer favour, prop up, second,
  rest
appuyer (à/contre/sur), (s') lean
  (against/on), press
âpre nippy
après after
après-midi afternoon

après (d') according to
aptitude bent
aptitude (à) aptitude
aquarium aquarium
aquatique aquatic
arabe Arabic
arable arable
arachide peanut
araignée spider
arbalète crossbow
arbitrage arbitration
arbitraire arbitrary, arbitrarily
arbitre arbitrator, referee, umpire
arbitrer arbitrate, referee, umpire
arbre tree, evergreen
arbre de Noël Christmas tree
arbre (de transmission) shaft
arbre généalogique family tree
arbuste shrub
arc arc, arch, bow
arc-en-ciel rainbow
archange archangel
archéologie archaeology
archéologique archaeological
archéologue archaeologist
archer, ère archer
archet bow
archevêque archbishop
archipel archipelago
architecte architect
architectural architectural
architecture architecture
archives archives
archiviste archivist
arctique Arctic
ardemment ardently, eagerly,
  keenly
ardent ardent, blazing, live
ardeur ardour, fire
ardoise slate
ardu arduous
arène arena, bullring
argent funds, money, silver
argent liquide cash, ready cash
argenté silvery
argenterie silver
argile clay
argot slang
argument argument, reason
aride arid, dry
aridité aridity, aridness
aristocrate aristocrat
aristocratie aristocracy
aristocratique aristocratic
aristocratiquement aristocratically
arithmétique arithmetic,
  arithmetical
arme weapon
armé armed
arme à feu firearm, gun

armée army
armement armament
armer arm
armer de courage, s' nerve, steel
armer, (s') arm
armes arms
armistice armistice
armoire cabinet, closet, cupboard, wardrobe
armoiries arms, coat of arms, crest
armure armour
aromatique aromatic
arôme aroma
arpenter survey
arqué bandy
arquer arch
arracher dig up, extract, gouge, pluck, rip, tear (off)
arracher les cheveux, s' tear one's hair
arrangement arrangement, permutation, set-up
arranger arrange, put right
arranger d'avance plan ahead
arrestation arrest
arrêt arrest, catch, decree, halt, stop
arrêt du cœur heart failure
arrêter arrest, break off, cast off, stem
arrêter net, s' stop dead
arrêter, (s') draw up, halt, pull up, stop
arriération backwardness
arriéré arrears, backward, retarded
arrière back, rear
arrière-cour backyard
arrière-cuisine scullery
arrière-garde rearguard
arrière-pays hinterland
arrière-plan background
arrière-train hindquarters
arrivant, ante arrival, comer
arrivée arrival, finish
arriver appear, arrive, come about, get, happen, reach, show up
arriver à get, figure out
arriver à échéance mature
arriver à un accord avec come to terms
arrogance arrogance, lordliness
arrogant arrogant, overbearing
arrondi rounded
arrondir round off
arroser hose, spray, water
arroseur sprinkler
arsenal armoury, arsenal
arsenic arsenic
art art, artistry
art de la vente salesmanship
art dramatique drama

art oratoire oratory
artère artery
artériel arterial
arthrite arthritis
arthritique arthritic
article article, item
article défini definite article
articles goods
articulation articulation, enunciation, joint
articulé jointed
articuler articulate, enunciate
artificiel artificial, man-made
artificiellement artficially
artillerie artillery
artisan, ane artisan, craftsman/woman
artiste artist, artiste, artistic, entertainer
artistique artistic
artistiquement artistically
as ace
ascendant ascendancy/ascendency
ascenseur elevator, lift
ascension ascent, rise
ascète ascetic
ascétique ascetic
ascétiquement ascetically
ascétisme asceticism
asexué sexless
asile asylum
aspect aspect, side
asperger spray
asphalte asphalt
asphyxier gas
aspirateur vacuum, vacuum cleaner
aspiration aspiration, yearning
aspirer à aspire to, yearn
aspirine aspirin
assaillir beset, besiege, mob
assaisonnement seasoning
assaisonner season
assassin assassin, cutthroat
assassinat assassination
assassiner assassinate, murder
assault assault, onslaught
assemblée assembly, council
assembler, (s') assemble, gather
assentiment assent
asseoir seat, sit
asseoir, (s') sit, sit down, take a seat
assertion assertion, contention
assez enough, fairly, pretty, quite
assidu sedulous
assiduité attendance
assiégé beleaguered
assiéger besiege
assiette plate, plateful
assiettée plateful

assignation à résidence house arrest
assigner (à) assign
assimilation assimilation
assimiler assimilate, identify
assistant, ante assistant, helper
assister à attend
association fellowship, partnership
associé associate, partner
associer associate, connect
associer à (qqn), s' partner
associer (avec), s' team up
assoiffé thirsty
assombrir, (s') cloud, darken, lower
assombrissement gloominess
assommant deadly
assommer knock, knock out, lay out, slug, stun
assorti assorted, matched
assortiment assortment, range
assoupir, s' doze off, nod off
assourdir deafen, muffle
assourdissant deafening
assujetti subject
assujettir tie (someone) down
assumer assume
assurance poise, self-assurance
assurance(s) assurance, insurance
assuré assertive, confident, level
assurément positively
assurer assure, insure, warrant
assurer (de), s' make sure
assurer (que), (s') ensure, make certain
astérisque asterisk
asthmatique asthmatic
asthme asthma
astreignant exacting
astrologie astrology
astrologique astrological
astrologue astrologer
astronaute astronaut
astronome astronomer
astronomie astronomy
astronomique astronomic(al)
astuce artfulness, astuteness, gimmick, shrewdness
astucieusement artfully, cunningly, shrewdly
astucieux cunning, shrewd
atelier shop, workshop
athée atheist, atheistic
athéisme atheism
athlète athlete
athlétique athletic
athlétisme athletics
atlas atlas
atmosphère atmosphere, flavour
atmosphérique atmospheric
atome atom

atomique atomic
atone toneless
atours array, finery
atout asset, trump
atroce agonizing, atrocious, excruciating, terrible
atrocement agonizingly
atrocité atrociousness, atrocity, outrage
attachant appealing, endearing
attache anchor, clamp, clip, fatener, tab
attaché fast
attaché (à) attached (to), devoted (to)
attachement attachment, dedication
attacher attach, clip, fasten, hitch, lash, strap, strap in, tether, tie
attaque attack, dose, fit, stroke
attaquer attack, eat into, strike
attaquer (à main armée) hold up
attaquer à s' attack, come to grips with, go at, grapple, set with
attarder, s' linger
atteindre attain, get at, hit, reach
atteindre en moyenne average
atteindre le sommet de breast
atteindre sa majorité (come of) age
atteint/frappé (par) stricken
attelage coupling, team
atteler à la tâche, s' put one's shoulder to the wheel
attendre anticipate, await, expect, hang on, wait, want
attendre à, s' bargain for, reckon on, wait (for)
attendre avec impatience look forward to
attentat attempt
attentat à l'ordre public breach of the peace
attente expectancy, expectation, wait
attentif (à) attentive
attention attention, beware, carefulness, look out, notice
attentivement attentively, intently
atténuer, (s') tone down
atterré aghast
atterrer stagger
atterrir land, touch down
atterrissage landing
attesté on record
attester swear to, testify
attifer get up
attirail paraphernalia
attirer attract, draw, entice, lure
attirer l'attention de catch someone's eye

attirer, (s') incur
attiser fan
attitude attitude
attraction attraction, draw
attrait appeal, attractiveness, desirability, enticement, lure
attrape catch, spoof
attrape-nigaud con
attraper catch, get, nab
attraper son coup de mort catch one's death (of cold)
attrayant attractive, enticing
attribuer allot, ascribe
attribuer (à) attribute, credit (with)
attribut attribute
attrister, (s') sadden
attrouper, s' crowd
au bord de on
au bout du rouleau on one's last legs
au cas où in case, in the event of
au centuple hundredfold
au coin du feu fireside
au corps-à-corps at close quarters
au courant in the know
au cours de in the course of
au début at first, initially
au dépourvu off guard
au fond at heart
au grand air in the open, out of doors
au hasard at random, haphazardly, randomly
au lieu de in place of, instead of
au loin away
au milieu de in the midst of
au moyen de by means of
au niveau de on a par with
au nom de in the name of
au pair par
au paroxysme at fever pitch
au pas de course at the double
au petit bonheur haphazard
au pied de la lettre at face value
au pis-aller as a last resort
au plus at the outside
au pouvoir ruling
au rabais cut-price
au ras de on a level with
au rebond on the rebound
au regard perçant hawk-eyed
au repos idle
au revoir goodbye
au risque de at the risk of
au (strict) minimum to the bone
au total overall
au-delà de beyond
au-dessous de below, under, underneath
au-dessus de above, over

au-dessus de ses moyens beyond one's means
au-dessus de tout soupcon in the clear
aubaine bonus, boon, windfall
aube cock crow, dawn, twilight
aubépine hawthorn
auberge inn, tavern
auberge de jeunesse youth hostel
aubergine eggplant
aubergiste innkeeper
aucun any, no, none
audace audacity, boldness, daring
audacieux audacious, daring
audibilité audibility
audible audible
audience audience
audio(-) audio-, audiovisual
audiotypiste audiotypist
auditif aural
audition audition, hearing
auditoire audience
auge trough
augmentation appreciation, augmentation, increment, raise, raise
augmenter augment, deepen, put up, rise, turn up, up
augure omen
aujourd'hui today
aumône alms
aumônier chaplain
auparavant previously
auprès de beside
aura aura
auréole halo
aurore dawn
ausculter sound
aussi also, as, likewise, too
aussi loin que as far as
aussi longtemps que as long as, so long as
aussitôt que immediatly, as soon as
austère austere, severe
austérité austerity, stringency
autel altar
auteur, eure author
authenticité authenticity
authentique authentic, genuine
auto(-) auto-
auto car, motor car
auto-stoppeur, euse hitch hiker
autobiographie autobiography
autobiographique autobiographic(al)
autobus bus
autocar coach
autochtone aboriginal, native
autocollant sticker
autocrate autocrat

autocratie autocracy
autocratique autocratic
autocuiseur pressure cooker
autographe autograph
automate automaton
automatique automatic
automatiquement automatically
automatisation automation
automatisé automated
automne autumn, fall
automobile automobile
automobiliste motorist
autonome autonomous
autonomie autonomy, home rule
autoportrait self-portrait
autopsie autopsy, post mortem, postmortem
autorisation authorization, clearance
autorisé authoritative
autoriser authorize, entitle, license, set one's seal to
autoritaire authoritarian, bossy, dogmatic
autoritarisme bossiness
autorité authority, rule
autoroute freeway, highway
autosuffisance self-sufficiency
autosuffisant self-sufficient
autour about, around
autre another, other
autrefois formerly, once
autrement otherwise
autruche ostrich
aux dépens de at the expense of
aux extrêmes to extremes
aux frais de at the expense of
aux risques et périls de at (a person's) own risk
aux soins de care of
aux talents variés versatile
aux trousses (de) in hot pursuit
aux yeux de in the eyes of
auxiliaire auxiliary
avalanche avalanche
avaler drink in, swallow
avance advance, lead, start
avancé advanced
avance lead, start
avancer advance, bring forward, go along, proceed, progress
avancer en bondissant lope
avancer petit à petit edge, inch
avant before, forward, front
avant de previous to, prior to
avant longtemps before (very) long
avant-bras forearm
avant-garde advance, vanguard
avant-goût foretaste

avant-poste outpost
avant-première preview
avant-propos foreword
avant-scène apron
avant-toit eaves
avantage advantage, good, virtue
avantageusement advantageously
avantageux advantageous
avare avaricious, grasping, mean, miser, miserly, stingy
avarice avarice, meanness, miserliness, stinginess
avarier, s' go off
avec with
avec amour lovingly
avec colère irascibly
avec effusion effusively
avec envie longingly
avec extase ecstatically
avec les hommages de with compliments
avec naturel naturally
avec robustesse sturdily
avec soin diligently
avènement accession, advent
avenir future, promise
aventure adventure, venture
aventureusement adventurously
aventureux adventurous
aventurier, ière adventurer
avenue avenue
avérer, (s') prove
averse downpour, shower
aversion aversion, dislike
avertir caution, notify, warn
avertissement caution, warning
avertisseur d'incendie fire alarm
aveu admission, confession
aveuglant blinding, dazzling, glaring
aveugle blind, implicit
aveuglément blindly, implicitly
aveugler dazzle, glare
aviateur militaire airman
aviateur, trice flyer, flier
aviation aviation
avide acquisitive, avid, covetous, greedy
avidement avidly, covetously, greedily
avidité avidity, greed, greediness
avion airplane, plane, jet
avion de ligne airliner
avion-école trainer
avion-ravitailleur tanker
aviron oar, scull
avis estimation, notice, notification, opinion
avisé acute, astute, cautious

aviser acquaint
avocat avocado
avocat, ate barrister, counsel, lawyer, solicitor
avoine oats
avoir have
avoir à l'œil keep an eye on
avoir affaire à to do with
avoir besoin de need, require, want
avoir bien envie de have a good mind to
avoir bon espoir hope for the best
avoir confiance (en) trust
avoir cours prevail
avoir de l'importance matter
avoir de la fièvre run a temperature
avoir des haut-le-cœur gag
avoir du chagrin grieve
avoir du respect pour qqn look up to
avoir envie (de) fancy, feel like, take one's fancy
avoir envie de have a hankering for, feel like
avoir faim de hunger
avoir grand besoin (de qqch.) hard up
avoir l'air de look like
avoir l'avantage (sur) have an/the advantage (over)
avoir l'étoffe de have the makings of
avoir l'habitude de make a practice of, used to
avoir l'impression de feel as if/as though
avoir l'impressiom (que) feel
avoir l'impression que be under the impression (that), feel
avoir l'intention (de) mean, intend
avoir la vie dure diehard
avoir le dessus get the best of
avoir le hoquet hiccup, hiccough
avoir les compétences pour have what it takes
avoir les moyens (de) afford
avoir lieu hold
avoir perdu la raison be out of one's mind
avoir peur (de) fear
avoir pitié de be/feel sorry for, have mercy on, have pity on, pity
avoir (qqch.) à cœur have at heart
avoir (qqch.) à voir (avec) have to do with
avoir recours (à) resort (to)
avoir soin (de) look after
avoir tendance (à) be inclined to, tend
avoir un compte à régler avec qqn have a bone to pick with (someone)

avoir un faible pour qqn/qqch
have a soft spot for
avoir un goût (de) taste (of)
avoir un rapport avec have to do
with (a person or thing)
avoir une bonne opinion think
highly, well

avoir une envie folle de die
avoir une prise de bec avec tangle
with
avoir une trop haute idée de think
too much of
avoir vue sur overlook
avortement abortion

avorter abort
avoué, ée attorney
avouer confess, own, own up (to)
avril April
axe axis, spindle
axiome axiom
azote nitrogen

Bb

babil prattle
babillage babble, prattle
babiller prattle
babiole trinket
babouin baboon
bac ferry
bâcle bar
bâclé sloppy
bâcler skimp
bacon bacon
bactérie(s) bacteria
bactériologie bacteriology
bactériologique bacteriological
bactériologiste bacteriologist
badinage playfulness
badminton badminton
bafouiller babble
bagage(s) baggage, luggage
bagarre brawl, dust-up, rough-and-tumble, scrap, scuffle
bagarrer, se scrap
bagatelle trifle
bague ring
baguer ring
baguette baton, chopstick, pointer, wand
baie bay, berry
baignade bathing, dip
baigner bathe
baigneur, euse bather
baignoire bath, bathtub, tub
bail lease
bâillement yawn
bâiller yawn
bâillon gag
bain bath, bathe
baïonnette bayonet
baiser kiss
baisse decline, drop
baisser come down, decline, fall, incline, let down, lower, put down, sink
baisser, se stoop
bal ball, dance
balade jaunt, saunter
balader, se saunter
balafre gash
balai broom
balance balance, scales, weighing-machine
balancement sway, swing
balancer, (se) rock, seesaw, sway, swing
balancier pendulum
balancoire swing
balayer brush, sweep
balayeur, euse sweeper

balbutier mumble
balcon balcony
baldaquin canopy
baleine whale
balise beacon
balle bale, ball, bullet, slug
ballerine ballerina
ballet ballet
ballon balloon
ballot bundle
balourd oaf
balsa balsa
baluchon swag
bambin tot, toddler
bambocheur, euse reveller
bambou bamboo
banal commonplace, corny, trite
banalement tritely, trivially
banalité triteness, triviality
banane banana
banc bank, bench, pew
banc d'huîtres oyster bed
banc de boue mudflat
banc de neige snowdrift
banc de poissons shoal
banc de sable sandbank, shoal
banc des accusés dock
bande band, gang, strip
bande dessinée comic strip, strip cartoon
bande magnétoscopique video
bande sonore soundtrack
bandeau blindfold, headband
bander strap up
banderole banner, streamer
bandit bandit, gunman
bandit de grand chemin highwayman
bandoulière sling
banjo banjo
banlieue outskirts, suburb
banlieusard, arde commuter
bannière banner
bannir banish
bannissement banishment
banque bank
banquet banquet, dinner
banquier, ière banker
baptême baptism
baptiser baptize, christen
baptismal baptismal
bar bar, saloon, pub
baraque booth, shanty
baratte churn
barbare barbarous, barbarian
barbarie barbarousness
barbe beard, whisker
barbe à papa cotton candy
barbecue barbecue
barbelé barbed wire

barbillon barb
barboter dabble, paddle
barbouiller smear
barbu bearded
baril barrel
barmaid barmaid, barman
baromètre barometer, glass
barométrique barometric
baron, onne baron
barrage barrage, dam, weir
barrage routier roadblock
barre bar, helm, rail, stand, tiller
barreau banister, rung
barrer cross
barreur, euse coxswain
barricade barricade
barrière barrier
barrissement trumpet
bas base, hose, low, stocking
bas les pattes! hands off!
bas de nylon nylons
bas prix cheapness
basalte basalt
bascule rocker, seesaw
basculer tip over
base base, basis, footing
baser found
baser (sur/à) base (on)
basket(-ball) basketball
basse bass, farmyard
bassement basely, despicably, vilely
basses terres lowlands
bassesse baseness, vileness
basset allemand dachshund
bassin basin, dock, pelvis
basson bassoon
bastion bastion
bataille battle, fight
bataille rangée pitched battle
bataillon battalion
bâtard bastard, mongrel
bateau boat
bateau à aubes paddleboat
bateau de plaisance launch
bateau-maison houseboat
batik batik
bâtiment building
bâtir build
bâtisse building
bâton bat, baton
bâton d'encens joss stick
bâton de golf golf club
battage shuffle
battement flap
batterie battery
batteur beater, drummer
battre beat, break, cream, defeat, pulsate, pulse, struggle, thrash, thresh, throb, whisk

battre à plate couture beat hollow, run rings round, trounce
battre (des ailes) flap
battre des ailes flutter
battre du tambour drum
battre en duel, se duel
battre en retraite beat a (hasty) retreat, retreat
battre le fer pendant qu'il est chaud strike while the iron is hot
battre, (se) battle, fight
battre son plein be in full swing
battu beaten, defeated
baume balm, balsam
bavard chatty, garrulous, talkative
bavarder gossip
baver dribble
bavette bib
bazar bazaar
béant gaping, yawning
beau beautiful, fair, fine, good-looking, handsome, nice, pretty
beau-fils stepson
beau-frère brother-in-law
beau-père father-in-law, stepfather
beaucoup far, many
beaucoup (de) a good deal/a great deal of, a lot, lots, much, plenty of
beauté beauty, handsomeness
beaux atours glad rags
beaux jours heyday
beaux-arts art, fine art
bébé baby
bec beak, bill, mouthpiece, spout
bec Bunsen bunsen
bec de gaz burner
bécarre natural
bêche spade
bêcher dig
bécot peck
bécoter peck
bedaine paunch
bedonnant paunchy
bégaiement stammer, stutter
bégayer gibber, stammer, stutter
bégonia begonia
bègue stammerer, stutterer
beige beige
beigne donut, doughnut
bêler bleat
bélier ram
belle-fille daughter-in-law, stepdaughter
belle-mère mother-in-law, stepmother
belle-sœur sister-in-law
belligérance belligerence
belligérant belligerent
belliqueux bellicose
bémol flat

bénédicité grace
bénédiction benediction, blessing, godsend
bénéfices spoils
bénéficiaire beneficiary, payee
bénévole voluntary
bénin benign
bénir bless
béquille crutch
ber cradle
bercer cradle, rock
bercer (dans ses bras) nurse
berceuse lullaby, rocker, rocking chair
berger shepherd
bergère shepherdess
berline sedan
bernacle barnacle
bernard-l'ermite hermit crab
berner fool
bernique limpet
besoin need
besoin de a need for, in need of
best-seller bestseller
bestial beastly
bestialité beastliness
bétail livestock
bête beast, brute, dense, dumb, silly, thick
bêtise rot, silliness
béton concrete
beurre butter
beurré buttery
beurrer butter
beuverie carousal
bibliographie bibliography
bibliothécaire librarian
bibliothèque bookcase, library
biblique biblical, scriptural
bicarbonate de soude soda
bicentenaire bicentenary
biceps biceps
biche doe, hind
bicyclette bicycle
bidon churn
bien well
bien en main in hand
bien en vue prominently
bien entendu sure
bien mérité hard-earned
bien que although, if, though
bien s'entendre agree
bien sûr of course
bien-être ease, snugness
bienfait shapely
bienfaiteur, trice benefactor
bienfaits benefit
biens effects, estate
bienséance propriety
bientôt presently, shortly, soon

bienveillance benevolence, goodwill, good will, graciousness, kindliness
bienveillant benevolent, kindly
bienvenu acceptable, welcome
bière beer
biffer cross out
bifteck steak
bifurquer branch, fork
bigame bigamist, bigamous
bigamie bigamy
bigot bigot, bigoted
bigoterie bigotry
bihebdomadaire bi-weekly
bijoutier, ière jeweller
bijoux jewellery
bikini bikini
bilan balance sheet
bilan de santé checkup
bilatéral bilateral
bile bile, gall
bilieux bilious
bilingue bilingual
billard billiards
bille marble
billet bill, ticket
billet de banque banknote
billot block
bimensuel bi-monthly, bi-weekly, fortnightly
bimestriel bi-monthly
binaire binary
binette hoe
bingo bingo
biochimie biochemistry
biochimique biochemical
biochimiste biochemist
biodégradable biodegradable
biographe biographer
biographie biography, life
biographique biographic(al)
biologie biology
biologique biological
biologiste biologist
bionique bionic
bip beep, beeper
bipède biped
biper beep, beeper
bis encore
bisannuel biennial
biscuit biscuit, cookie
biseau bevel
biseauté bevelled
bison bison, buffalo
bitume bitumen, pitch
bitumineux bituminous
bizarre bizarre, odd, peculiar, queer, strange, weird
bizarrement funnily, oddly, peculiarly, strangely, weirdly

bizarrerie queerness, strangeness
black-out blackout
blague joke, lark
blagueur, euse joker
blaireau badger
blâme censure
blâmer blame, censure
blanc blank, white
blanc comme neige snow-white
blanche minim
blanchir launder, whiten
blanchisserie laundry
blanchisseur, euse laundress
blasphématoire blasphemous
blazer blazer
blé grain, wheat
blé d'Inde corn
blême pallid, white
blessant cutting, hurtful
blessé hurt, injured, wounded
blesser hurt, injure, wound
blessure wound
bleu blue, blueness, blueprint,
  bruise
bleuâtre bluish
blindage armour
blindé armoured
blizzard blizzard
bloc bloc, block
bloc-notes pad
blocus bloc
blond blond, fair
blond roux sandy
blonde blonde
blondeur fairness
bloquer block, bloc
bloquer, (se) jam, seize up
blottir (contre), se snuggle
blottir, se huddle, nestle
blouse smock
bluff bluff
boa boa
bobine bobbin, coil, reel, spool
bobsleigh bobsleigh
bocal jar
bœuf beef, bullock, ox
boghei buggy
bohémien, ienne gypsy, gipsy
boire drink
boire à (la santé de) drink to, drink
  (to) the health of
boire à petites gorgées sip
boire (comme un trou) booze
boire d'un trait swill
bois antler, wood, woodwind
bois de charpente lumber
bois de chauffage firewood
bois de construction timber
bois de rose rosewood

bois flotté driftwood
boiserie(s) panelling, woodwork
boisson beverage, drink
boisson gazeuse soft-drink
boîte box, case
boîte à surprise jack-in-the-box
boîte à thé caddy
boîte à/aux lettres letterbox,
  mailbox
boîte de conserve can
boîte de couleurs paintbox
boîte de nuit nightclub
boîte de vitesses gearbox
boîte noire black box
boîte postale box number
boiter limp
boiterie lameness
boiteux lame
boîtier housing
bol basin, bowl
boléro bolero
bombardement bombardment
bombarder blitz, bomb, bombard,
  shell
bombardier bomber
bombe bomb, bombshell
bombé domed
bombe à hydrogène hydrogen
  bomb
bombe à retardement time bomb
bombe atomique A-bomb, atom(ic)
  bomb
bombe (d'insecticide) spray
bombe H H-bomb
bon good, right, sound
bon, bonne à rien good-for-
  nothing, no good
bon de commande order form
bon débarras good riddance
bon état de marche roadworthiness
bon marché cheap, inexpensive
bon pour good for
bon sens sense, wit, common sense
bon teint fast
bonbon candy, sweet
bonbon à la menthe peppermint
bond bounce, jump, limp, spring
bond (sur) pounce
bondé crowded, overcrowded,
  packed (out)
bondir bound, pounce
bonheur happiness
bonne parlourmaid
bonne chance good luck
bonne d'enfants nursemaid
bonne forme in (good) trim
bonne humeur good humour
bonnes œuvres good works
bonnet bonnet, cap
bonneterie hosiery

bonsaï bonsai
bonté goodness
bookmaker bookmaker
boomerang boomerang
bord border, brim, edge, lip,
  margin, verge
bord de la route roadside
bord de mer seaside
border edge, fringe, tuck in
bordure border, edging, fringe
bordure de trottoir curb, sidewalk
borne terminal
borné dim, narrow
borne routière milestone
bosse bump, dent, dint, hump,
  lump, dent
bossu, ue humpback, hunchback
botanique botany, botanic(al)
botaniste botanist
botte boot
bouc billy-goat
bouc émissaire scapegoat
boucanier buccaneer
bouché blocked
bouche mouth
bouche d'égout manhole
bouche d'incendie hydrant
bouche-à-bouche kiss of life
bouche-pores filler
bouche-trou stopgap
bouchée gulp, morsel, mouthful,
  nibble
boucher bung, choke, clog, cork,
  plug, stop up, stuff up
boucher, ère butcher
bouchon bottleneck, cork, plug,
  stopper
bouchon d'air airlock
bouchonner (un cheval) rub down
boucle buckle, curl, loop
bouclé curly
bouclier shield
bouddhisme Buddhism
bouddhiste Buddhist
bouder sulk
bouderie sulkiness
boudeur sulky
boue mud, sludge, sogginess
bouée de sauvetage buoy, lifebuoy
boueux muddy
bouffant baggy
bouffe grub
bouffée drag
bouffi puffy
bouffon clownish, jester
bouffonneries antics
bougainvillée bougainvillaea
bougeotte the fidgets
bouger budge, move
bouger (sans cesse) fidget

bougie candle
bougon grumpy
bougonner (contre) grumble
bouillant scalding
bouillie mush
bouillir boil
bouilloire kettle
bouillon broth
bouillonnant (de) seething (with)
boulanger, ère baker
boulangerie baker, bakery
boule ball, bowl
boule antimites mothball
boule de gomme gum
boule de neige snowball
bouleau birch
boulet millstone
boulette dumpling, pellet
bouleversant shocking
bouleversement upheaval
bouleverser confuse, shock, upset
boulon bolt
bouquet bouquet
bourde howler
bourdon bumblebee
bourdonnement buzz, drone, hum
bourdonner buzz, drone, hum
bourgeon bud
bourrasque squall
bourreau executioner, hangman
bourreau de travail glutton, trouper
bourrelet roll
bourrer (de), (se) stuff
bourru crusty, gruff, surly
bourse exchange, pocket, scholarship
boursier, ière scholar
bousculé hurried
bousculer hustle, jostle
boussole compass
bout end, hunk, scrap, stub, tip
boute-en-train the life and soul of the party
bouteille bottle, cylinder
bouteille consignée empty
bouteille isolante Thermos (flask)
bouteur bulldozer
boutique (de luxe) boutique
bouton button, pimple, spot
bouton de manchettes cufflinks
boutonner button
boutonneux pimpled, pimply, spotty
boutonnière buttonhole
bouture cutting
bouvillon bullock, steer
bovidé ox
boxe boxing
boxeur boxer

boyau d'arrosage hose
boycottage boycott
boycotter boycott
bracelet bangle, bracelet
braconner poach
braconnier poacher
braguette fly
braiement bray
braille braille
brailler bawl
braire bray
braise embers
brancard shaft
branche bough, branch, limb
brancher plug in
brandir brandish, flourish
branlant shaky
braquer (un revolver sur) point (a gun) at
bras arm
bras dessus, bras dessous arm-in-arm
bras droit (de qqn) right-hand man
brasier blaze
brassard armband
brasse breaststroke, fathom
brassée armful
brasser brew, stir
brasserie brewery
brasseur, euse brewer
bravade bravado
brave brave, gallant, valiant
bravement bravely, gallantly, valiantly
braver brave
bravo bravo, good for you
bravoure bravery, gallantry, valour
brebis ewe
brebis galeuse black sheep
brèche breach, hole
bredouillement gabble
bredouiller gabble, jabber
bref brief, in short
bretelles braces, suspenders
brevet commission, patent
bric-à-brac jumble, junk
bricolage do-it-yourself
bricoler tinker
bride bridle
bridge bridge
brièvement briefly
brièveté shortness
brigade brigade
brillamment brilliantly
brillant bright, brilliant, shining, shiny
brillant brilliance, gloss, lustre, shine
briller shine, sparkle
brin sprig, strand, wisp

brin de causette gossip
brindille stick, twig
brioche bun
brique screed
briquet lighter
brisant breaker
brise breeze
brise-lames breakwater
briser break, fracture
briser la glace break the ice
briser le cœur de break someone's heart
briseur, euse de grève scab
brocart brocade
broche brooch, skewer, spit
brochet pike
brochette kebab
brochure brochure
brocoli broccoli
broder embroider
broderie embroidery
bronchite bronchitis
bronchitique bronchitic
bronzage sunburn, suntan, tan
bronze bronze
bronzé bronzed, brown, sunburned, sunburnt, tanned
bronzer tan
brossage brush
brosse brush
brosse à cheveux hairbrush, brush
brosse à dents toothbrush
brosse à ongles nail brush
brosser brush
brouette barrow
brouhaha hubbub
brouillard fog
brouille disagreement
brouiller blur, jam, scramble, smear
brouilleur scrambler
brouillon draft, muddle-headed
brousse bush
brouter browse, crop, graze
broyer mash
broyeur, euse grinder
bruine drizzle
bruissement swish
bruit cheep, noise, rattle, sound
bruit éclatant blare
bruit sourd thud
bruitage sound effects
brûlant piping hot, scorching
brûler burn
brûler légèrement scorch
brûlure burn, scald
brûlure légère scorch
brûlures d'estomac heartburn
brume mist, haze
brumeux foggy, hazy, misty
brun brown

brunir brown
brusque abrupt, brusque, curt, gruff, rough, sharp
brusquement abruptly, brusquely, sharply
brusquerie abruptness, bluntness, brusqueness, curtness
brut blunt, crude, gross, raw
brutalement roughly
brutaliser bully, kick about/around
brute beast, brute
brute (tyrannique) bully
bruyamment loudly, noisily
bruyant noisy

bruyère heather
bûche log
bûcher funéraire pyre
bûcheron, onne lumberjack, woodcutter
budget budget
buffet buffet
buffle buffalo
buisson bush
bulbe bulb
bulbeux bulbous
bulle bubble
bulletin bulletin, newsletter, newscast
bungalow bungalow

bureau agency, bureau, den, desk, office, study
bureau de location rental-office
bureau de poste post office
bureau de vote polling station
bureaucratie bureaucracy
bureaucratique bureaucratic
buste bust
but end, goal, object, purpose
butin booty, haul, loot, plunder, swag
butor boor
butte hillock
buvard blotter, blotting paper

Cc

c'est facile (comme tout) there is nothing to it
c'est vite dit! easier said than done
c'est-à-dire that is to say
cà et là here and there, hither and thither
cabane cabin, shack
cabine booth, cabin, cubicle
cabine de pilotage flight deck
cabine téléphonique telephone booth, telephone box
cabinet (ministériel) cabinet
câble cable
câble de remorquage towline, towrope
câble de remorque hawser
câbler cable
câblogramme cable
caboteur coaster
cabrer, (se) rear up
cacahuète peanut
cacao cocoa
cacatoès cockatoo
caché hidden
cache-cache hide-and-seek
cache-col muffler
cachemire cashmere
cacher hold back, interrupt, keep back, screen, secrete, shield
cacher, (se) hide
cachet seal
cacheter seal
cachette hiding, hiding place
cachot (souterrain) dungeon
cachottier cagey
cactus cactus
cadavre body, corpse
caddie caddie, caddy
cadeau gift, present
cadenas padlock
cadet, ette cadet, junior
cadran dial
cadre frame, square
cafard the blues
café coffee, coffee shop
café-restaurant cafe
caféine caffeine
cafétéria cafeteria
cafetière coffee pot
caftan caftan, kaftan
cage cage, coop
cage (d'un ascenseur) shaft
cagneux knock-kneed
cagnotte kitty
cahier book
cahier d'exercices workbook
cailler curdle

caillot clot
caillou pebble
caisse case, crate
caisse d'épargne savings bank
caisse (de sortie) checkout
caisse (enregistreuse) cash register
caissier, ière cashier
cajoler cajole, coax
cajou cashew
calamité calamity
calamiteux calamitous
calcaire limestone
calcium calcium
calcul calculation, computation, reckoning
calculable calculable
calculatrice calculator
calculer calculate, compute, reckon up
cale hold, skid, slip
caleçon underpants
calembour pun
calendrier calendar
caler stall
calibre bore, calibre, gauge
calice chalice
câlin cuddle
calleux horny
calligraphie calligraphy
calmant painkiller, sedative, soothing
calmar squid
calme calm, calmness, composed, composure, cool, cool-headed, stillness
calmement calmly, coolly
calmer calm, edge, lull, quell, settle, soothe
calmer, (se) calm down, compose, cool down, ease, quiet, quieten, settle down, simmer down
calomnie slander, smear
calomnier slander
calomnieusement libellously
calorie calorie
calorifique calorific
calque tracing
calquer trace
calvitie baldness
calypso calypso
camarade comrade, fellow, mate
camarade de chambre roommate
camarade de classe classmate, schoolmate
camarade de travail co-worker
camaraderie comradeship, fellowship
cambriolage burglary, housebreaking
cambrioler burgle

cambrioleur, euse burglar, housebreaker
cambrure arch
caméléon chameleon
camélia camellia
caméra cine-camera, camera
camion truck
camion-plateau pick-up
camionnette van
camionneur, euse truck driver
camisole vest
camisole de force straitjacket
camouflage camouflage
camoufler camouflage
camp camp
campagnard rustic
campagne campaign, country, countryside
campement camp, encampment
camper camp
campeur, euse camper
camphre camphor
camping camping
campus campus
canal canal, channel, sluice
canal d'écoulement drain
canalisation piping
canaliser channel, marshal
canapé couch, settee
canard duck
canari canary
cancan cancan
cancer cancer
cancéreux cancerous
cancre dunce
candidat, ate applicant, candidate, entrant, entry
candidature application, candidacy
cane duck
caneton duckling
caniche poodle
canif penknife
canin canine
cannabis cannabis
canne cane, stick, walking stick
canne à pêche fishing rod
canne à sucre sugar cane
cannelé grooved
cannelle cinnamon
cannibale cannibal, cannibalistic
cannibalisme cannibalism
canoë canoe
canoéiste canoeist
canon barrel, cannon, canon, round
canonique canonical
canonisation canonization
canoniser canonize
canonnière gunboat
canot dinghy, rowing boat, rowboat
canot de sauvetage lifeboat

cantine canteen
cantique hymn
cantonner billet, quarter
canyon canyon
caoutchouc india-rubber, rubber
caoutchouc mousse foam rubber
caoutchouteux rubbery
cap cape, head
capable able, capable
capable de equal to, good for
capacité ability, capability, capacity
cape cape, cloak
capillaire capillary
capitaine captain, master, skipper
capitaine de port harbour-master
capital capital, momentous,
  principal
capitale capital
capitalisme capitalism
capitaliste capitalist
capitulation caitulation
capituler capitulate
caporal, ale corporal
capot hood
caprice caprice, whim
capricieusement capriciously,
  temperamentally
capricieux capricious,
  temperamental
capsule cap, capsule
capter pick up
captif, ive captive
captiver captivate, enthral
captivité captivity
capture capture
capuchon cowl, hood
caquet cackle
car for
carabine à air comprimé air gun
caracoler prance
caractère character, disposition,
  type
caractères print
caractérisation characterization
caractériser characterize
caractéristique characteristic,
  feature
carafe carafe
carambolage pileup
carambole starfruit
caramel caramel, toffee
caramel écossais butterscotch
carat carat
caravane camper, caravan, trailer
carbone carbon, carbon copy
carboniser char
carburant fuel
carburateur carburetor
carcasse carcass, hulk, shell
cardiaque cardiac

cardinal cardinal
caresse caress, stroke
caresser caress, fondle, pet, stroke
cargaison cargo, shipment
cargo freighter
caricature caricature
caricaturiste caricaturist, cartoonist
carie caries, decay
carillon chime, peal
carillonner chime
carnage carnage
carnassier carnivore
carnaval carnival
carnet notebook
carnivore animal eater, carnivorous
carotte carrot
carpe carp
carquois quiver
carré square
carré au chocolat brownie
carreau diamond
carrefour crossroads, intersection
carrément squarely
carrière career, quarry
carrosse coach
carrosserie bodywork
carroussel carousel
carte card, chart, map
carte à jouer playing card
carte bancaire bank card
carte blanche a free hand
carte d'identité identity card
carte postale postcard
carte routière road map
cartel combine
cartilage cartilage, gristle
cartographe cartographer
cartographie cartography
cartographique cartographic
carton card, cardboard, carton
carton-pâte papier-mache
cartouche cartridge
cas case
cas limite borderline
cas urgent/imprévu emergency
cascade cascade
cascadeur stuntman
caserne barracks
caserne de pompier fire station
casier locker, pigeonhole
casino casino
casque crash-helmet, helmet
casquette cap
cassant brittle
cassé broken
casse cassia
casse-cou dare-devil
casse-croûte snack
casse-noisettes nutcracker
casse-pieds a pain in the neck

casse-tête jigsaw (puzzle), puzzle
casser crack, overrule, smash
casserole pan, saucepan
cassette cassette
cassure breakage
castagnettes castanets
caste caste
castor beaver
castration castration
castrer castrate
cataclysme cataclysm
cataclysmique catalysmic
catalogue catalogue
catalyseur catalyst
catalytique catalytic
catamaran catamaran
catapulter catapult
cataracte cataract
catastrophe catastrophe
catastrophique catastrophic
catéchisme catechism
catégorie category
catégorique emphatic
catégoriquement emphatically,
  flatly
cathédrale cathedral
catholicisme Catholicism
catholique Catholic, Roman
  Catholic
cauchemar nightmare
cauchemardesque nightmarish
cause cause
causer cause
caustique caustic
cautériser cauterize
caution bail
cavalerie cavalry
cavalier cavalier, escort, horseman,
  knight
cavalier, ière rider
cavalièrement offhandedly
cave cellar
caveau vault
caverne cavern
caverneux cavernous, hollow
caviar caviar(e)
cavité cavity
cécité blindness
céder yield
cèdre cedar
ceinture belt, girdle, waist
ceinturé belted
ceinture (d'étoffe) sash
ceinture de sécurité safety belt,
  seat belt
ceinturer belt
célèbre celebrated, famous, noted
célébrer commemorate
célébrité celebrity, stardom
céleri celery

céleste celestial, heavenly
célibat celibacy
célibataire bachelor, celibate, single, spinster
cellulaire cellular
cellule cell
cellulose cellulose
cendre ash, cinder
cendres ashes
cendrier ashtray
censeur, eure censor
censure censorship
censurer censor
cent cent, hundred
centenaire centenary, centenarian
centième hundredth
centigrade centigrade
centimètre centimetre
central central, telephone exchange
centrale électrique power station
centralement centrally
centralisation centralization
centraliser centralize
centre centre
centre commercial emporium, shopping centre
centre d'activité hub
centre-ville downtown, town centre
centrifuge centrifugal
cependant however, though
céramique ceramic
cerceau hoop
cercle circle, club, ring
cercueil casket, coffin
céréale cereal
cérébral cerebral
cérémonial ceremonial
cérémonie ceremony
cérémonieusement formally
cérémonieux ceremonious
cerf kite, stag
cerf-volant kite
cerise cherry
cerne shadow
certain certain, positive, some
certainement by all means, certainly, sure
certificat certificate
certification certification
certifier certify
certitude certainty, cinch, positiveness, sureness
cerveau brain
cervidé deer
cessation cessation
cesser cease, give up, sever, go off
c'est-à-dire that is to say
chacal jackal
chacun apiece, each
chacun de every

chagrin grief, heartache, heartbreak, sorrow, sorrowfulness
chagriné aggrieved, sorrowful
chahut bedlam, rumpus
chahuter mess about/around
chaîne chain, channel, ridge
chaînes bond, fetter
chair flesh
chair de poule goosebumps
chaire chair, professorship, pulpit
chaise chair
chaise électrique electric chair
chaise haute high chair
chaise-longue deck chair
chaland barge
châle shawl
chalet chalet, cottage
chaleur heat, heatedness, warmness
chaleureux hearty, warm
chaloupe rowboat
chalumeau blowtorch
chalut trawl
chalutier trawler
chamailler, se hassle
chambarder mess about/around
chambre chamber
chambre à coucher bedroom
chambre à gaz gas chamber
chambre d'enfants nursery
chambre forte strongroom, vault
chambre meublée lodging
chameau camel
chamois huff, chamois
champ field
champ de bataille battlefield
champ de courses racecourse
champ de mines minefield
champ de tir rifle range
champ magnétique magnetic field
champagne champagne
champignon fungus, mushroom, toadstool
champion, onne champion
championnat championship
chance break, chance, luck, luckiness, mercy
chancelant groggy, rocky
chancelier, ière chancellor
chances odds
chanceux lucky
chandail sweater
chandelier candlestick
chandelle candle
change exchange
changeant changeable, mobile, variable
changement break, change, shift, switch
changement d'avis a change of heart

changement de vitesse gear
changer exchange, switch
changer d'avis change one's mind
changer de conduite turn over a new leaf
changer de main change hands
changer de ton change one's tune
changer (en), (se) change/turn into
changer les idées, se take/keep one's mind off
chanoine canon
chanson song
chansonnette ditty
chant song
chantage blackmail
chanter harmonize, sing
chanteur, euse singer, vocalist
chanteur, euse de charme crooner
chantier construction site, yard
chantier naval dockyard, shipyard
chanvre hemp
chaos chaos
chaotique chaotic
chaotiquement chaotically
chapardage pilferage
chaparder pilfer
chapardeur, euse pilferer
chapeau hat
chapeau melon bowler
chapelet rosary
chapelier, ière hatter
chapelle chapel
chapelure breadcrumbs
chaperon chaperone
chapiteau capital
chapitre chapter
chaque each, either
chaque chose en son temps all in good time
chaque fois (que) every time, whenever
char chariot, tank
charabia gibberish
charade charades
charbon coal
charbon de bois charcoal
charbons ardents tenterhooks
charcuterie delicatessen
chardon thistle
charge charge, laden, load, office, trust
chargé loaded
chargé, ée de classe tutor
charger charge, load
charger de, se take, take charge, take on, undertake
charger qqn de burden
chargeur cartridge
chariot carriage, cart, trolley, wagon

chariot élévateur fork-lift truck
charitable charitable
charitablement charitably
charité charity
charlatan phon(e)y
charmant charming, delightful
charme charm, comeliness, enthralment, glamour, loveliness, spell
charmer charm, enchant
charnu fleshy
charpente framework, skeleton
charpenterie carpentry
charpentier, ière carpenter
charrette cart, wagon
charrier cart
charrue plough
charte charter
chasse chase, flush, hunt, hunting
chasse gardée preserve
chasser chase, exclude, hunt, shoo
chasseur fighter, huntsman, page
chasseur, euse/chasseresse hunter
châssis chassis, sash, window-frame
chaste chaste
chasteté chasteness, chastity
chasuble jumper
chat cat
châtaigne chestnut
châtain chestnut
château castle
château de sable sandcastle
château en Espagne pipe dream
châtier chasten, chastise
châtiment chastisement, retribution
chaton kitten
chatouillement tickle
chatouiller tickle
chatouilleux ticklish
chatoyer play
chaud hot, warm
chaudement warmly
chaudière boiler, furnace
chaudron cauldron
chauffage heating
chauffage central central heating
chauffé heated
chauffé à blanc white hot
chauffe-eau heater
chauffe-plat hot-plate
chauffer get up steam, hot up
chauffeur, euse chauffeur
chaume stubble, thatch
chaussé shod
chaussée causeway, roadway
chausser shoe
chaussettes sock
chaussure footwear, shoe

chaussure de gymnastique gym shoe
chauve bald
chauve-souris bat
chauvin chauvinistic, chauvinist
chauvinisme chauvinism
chaux lime
chaux vive quicklime
chavirer capsize
chef chef, chief, chieftain, commander, head, leader
chef d'orchestre conductor
chef de file exponent
chef de train conductor, guard
chef-d'œuvre masterpiece
cheik sheik(h)
chemin lane, path, road, route, way
chemin de fer railroad, railway
cheminée chimney, funnel
chemise folder, shirt, sleeve
chemise de nuit nightgown
chemisier blouse
chenal channel
chêne oak
chenil kennel
chenille caterpillar
chèque check, cheque
chèque en blanc blank cheque
chéquier cheque book
cher dear, expensive, pricey
chercher ask for, fish for, hunt for, look for, search, seek
chercher dans tous les coins hunt high and low
chercher querelle/la bagarre pick a quarrel/fight with (someone)
chercheur, euse researcher, searcher
chéri darling
chéri, ie darling, honey, sweet, sweetheart
chérir cherish
cherté costliness
chérubin cherub
chétif puny
chétivement punily
chétodon angelfish
cheval horse
cheval de bataille charger
cheval de course racehorse
cheval de selle hack
cheval-vapeur horsepower
chevaleresque chivalrous
chevalet bridge, easel
chevalier knight
chevauchement overlap
chevaucher, (se) overlap
chevet bedside
cheveux hair, lock
cheville ankle

chèvre goat, nanny-goat
chevreau kid
chevreuil roe, roe deer
chevroter quaver
chez (soi) home
chic chic, posh, style
chiche niggardly
chichement meanly, skimpily, stingily
chicorée chicory
chien dog
chien courant foxhound
chien de berger sheepdog
chien de garde watchdog
chien de traîneau husky
chien-chaud hot dog
chienne bitch
chier shit
chiffon duster
chiffre digit, figure, numeral
chiffre d'affaires turnover
chiffre romain Roman numerals
chiffre rond round figures/numbers
chimie chemistry
chimique chemical
chimiste chemist
chimpanzé chimpanzee
chiot pup
chipoter peck, pick at
chiquenaude flip
chirurgical surgical
chirurgie surgery
chirurgie esthétique plastic surgery
chirurgien, ienne surgeon
chlore chlorine
chloroforme chloroform
chlorophylle chlorophyll
choc jolt, shock, start
chocolat chocolate
chœur choir, chorus
choisir choose, pick, single out
choisir de faire qqch. elect
choisir de ne pas participer (à) opt out (of)
choisir le moment de time
choix choice, option, pick
choléra cholera
chômage unemployment
chômeurs, euses the unemployed
chope mug, mugful, tankard
choquer offend
choral choral
choriste chorister
chose affair, thing
chou cabbage
chou-fleur cauliflower
choucas jackdaw
chrétien Christian
christianisme Christianity

chromatique chromatic
chrome chrome, chromium
chronique chronic, chronicle, column
chroniquement chronically
chroniqueur, euse chronicler, columnist
chronologie chronology
chronologique chronological
chronologiquement chronologically
chronométrage timing
chronomètre stopwatch
chronométrer clock, time
chronométreur, euse timer
chrysalide chrysalis, pupa
chrysanthème chrysanthemum
chuchoter whisper
chut! hush
chute downfall, fall, flop, waterfall
chute de neige snowfall
chutney chutney
ci-après hereafter
ci-inclus herein
ci-joint herewith
cible butt, target
cicatrice scar
cidre cider
ciel heaven, sky
cierge taper
cigale cicada
cigare cigar
cigarette cigarette, fag
cigogne stork
cil eyelash, lash
cime d'un arbre treetop
ciment cement
cimetière cemetery, churchyard, graveyard
cimier crest
cinéma cinema, movie theatre, the movies, the pictures
cinétique kinetic
cinglant biting, scathing
cinglé batty, cracked, nutty, off one's rocker, potty
cingler slash
cinq five
cinquantaine fifties
cinquante fifty
cinquantième fiftieth
cinquième fifth
cintré arched, waisted
cintre hanger
circoncire circumcise
circoncision circumcision
circonférence circumference, girth
circonscription constituency, precinct
circonspection caginess

circonstance circumstance
circuit circuit
circulaire circular
circularité circularity
circulation circulation, flow, traffic
circulatoire circulatory
circuler circulate, get around, move along
circumnavigation circumnavigation
cire polish, wax
ciré waxed
cire à cacheter sealing wax
cire d'abeille beeswax
cirer polish, wax
cireux waxen, waxy
cirque circus
cisailler, (se) shear
cisailles shears
ciseau(x) chisel, scissors
ciseaux à ongles nail scissors
ciseler chisel
citadelle citadel
citadins, ines townsfolk, townspeople
citation quotation
cité city
citer quote
citerne cistern
citoyen, enne citizen
citoyenneté citizenship
citrique citric
citron lemon
citronnade lemonade
citronnelle lemon grass
citrouille pumpkin
civière stretcher
civil civil
civilisation civilization
civiliser civilize
civique civic, civil
civisme public spirit
clair clear, distinct, explicit, light, plain, unmistakable, vivid
clair de lune moonlight
clair et net short and sweet
clairement clearly
clairière clearing
clairon bugle
clairsemé sparse, thin
clairvoyance second sight, vision
clameur clamour
clan clan
clandestin clandestine, undercover
clapier hutch
clapoter (contre) lap
claque box, buffet
claque sur les fesses spank
claquement bang, clap, crack, slam, smack

claquemurer coop up
claquer bang, slam
claquettes tap dancing
clarification clarification
clarifier clarify
clarinette clarinet
clarinettiste clarinettist
clarté clarity, distinctness, explicitness, lightness
classe class, classroom, grade, rank
classé seeded
classer class, classify, file, grade
classer par catégories categorize
classer, (se) rank
classeur filing cabinet
classification classification, gradation
classique classical, classic, formal
claudication limp
clause clause
claustrophobe claustrophobic
claustrophobie claustrophobia
clavecin harpsichord
clavicule collar bone
clavier keyboard, manual
clef clef, key, lock
clef à écrous clef, key, lock, spanner
clef à molette wrench
clémence clemency, forgiveness
clément clement
clergé clergy, priesthood
clérical clerical
cliché cliche, tag
client, ente client, customer, fare, patron
clientèle clientele, custom, goodwill, good will, practice
cligner des yeux blink
clignotant flashing
clignotement (des yeux) blink
clignoter flicker, wink
climat climate
climatique climatic
climatisation air conditioning
climatisé air-conditioned
climatiseur air conditioner
clin d'œil wink
clinique clinic, clinical, nursing home
clinquant tinsel, tinselly
clipper clipper
clique clique
cliqueter clank, click, rattle
cliquetis clank, jingle
clivage cleavage
clochard, arde down-and-out, tramp
cloche bell
clocher belfry, steeple

cloison bulkhead, partition
cloître cloister
cloque blister
clôture enclosure, fence
clôturer fence
clou highlight, nail
clou de girofle clove
cloué au lit bedridden
clouer nail, rivet, tack
clown clown
club club
club nautique yacht club
coaguler clot
coalition coalition
coassement croak
coasser croak
cobalt cobalt
cobaye guinea pig
cobra cobra
cocaïne cocaine
cocarde cockade
coccinelle ladybug
coche notch, tick
cocher coachman, tick (off)
cochon smutty
cochon, onne pig
cochonnet piggy
cockpit cockpit
cocon cocoon
cocotte casserole
code cipher, code
code de la route Highway Code
code postal postal code, zip code
coder code
coercition coercion
cœur core, heart
cœur gros a heavy heart
coexistence coexistence
coexister coexist
coffre chest, trunk
coffre-fort safe, strongbox
coffret casket
cognac cognac
cogner (contre/dans), (se) bump
cogner dans, (se) blunder
cohérence coherence, consistency
cohérent coherent, consistent
cohorte cohort
cohue crush, mob, rabble, squash
coiffer style
coiffeur barber
coiffeur, euse hairdresser, stylist
coiffeuse dressing table
coiffure coiffure, hairdo, hairdressing, hairstyle, headdress
coin angle, corner, wedge
coincer jam, stick, wedge
coïncidence coincidence
coïncider (avec) coincide (with)
coing quince

coke coke
col collar, neck
col bleu bluecollar
col de pasteur dog collar
col roulé turtleneck
coléoptère beetle
colère anger, temper, wrath
colérique peppery
coleus coleus
colique colic
colis parcel
collaborateur, trice collaborator
collaboration collaboration
collaborer collaborate
collage collage
collant jammy, skin tight, sticky, tights
collation snack
colle glue, gum, paste
collectif collective
collection array, collection, miscellany
collectionneur, euse collector
collectivement collectively
collège academy
collègue colleague
coller adhere, glue, gum, stick
coller à cleave to
coller aux talons de tag on
collet monté straitlaced
collier collar, necklace
colline hill
collision collision
colombe dove
côlon colon
colon colonist, settler
colonel, elle colonel
colonial colonial
colonialisme colonialism
colonialiste colonialist
colonie colony, settlement
colonisation colonization
coloniser colonize
colonnade colonnade
colonne column
colonne vertébrale backbone, spine
coloquinte bittergourd
colorant colouring
coloré coloured, colourful
colorier colour in
colossal colossal
colporter hawk, peddle
colporteur, euse hawker, pedlar
coma coma
combat action, bout, combat, conflict, fight
combattant, ante combatant, fighter
combattre combat, fight
combinaison combination, slip

combinaison de plongée wetsuit
combinaison spatiale spacesuit
combine fiddle, scheme
combiner combine
comble acme, heaped, height
comblé fulfilled
combustible combustible, fuel
combustion combustion
combustion interne internal combustion
comédie comedy
comestibilité edibility
comestible edible
comète comet
comique comedy, comedian, comic, comical, laughable
comité committee
commandant, ante commandant, major
commandant en chef commander in chief
commande commission, control, order
commandé on order
commandement commandment
commandement d'une équipe captaincy
commander command, order, order about, send away for
commander (par la poste) send off for
commanditer sponsor
commanditaire backer, sponsor
commandite sponsor
commando commando
comme as, as if/as though, like, like that
comme ci, comme ça so-so
comme de l'eau hand over fist
comme des pains chauds like hot cakes
comme il faut proper
comme larrons en foire like a house on fire
comme sur des roulettes like clockwork
comme un perdu like mad
comme un seul homme as one man
commémoratif commemorative
commémoration commemoration
commémorer commemorate
commencement beginning, commencement, onset
commencer commence, enter on/upon
commencer (à) begin, proceed, start
commencer à s'animer come to life
comment how, comment

commentaire commentary
commentateur, trice commentator
commenter comment, commentate
commérages gossip, talk
commerçant, ante shopkeeper, trader, tradesman
commerce business, commerce, trade
commerce des tissus drapery
commercer deal, trade
commercial commercial
commercialiser commercialize
commère gossip
commérer gossip, talk
commettre commit
commisération commiseration
commissaire commissioner
commissaire-priseur, euse auctioneer
commission commission, errand
commode bureau, convenient
commodément conveniently
commodité convenience
commodités amenity
commodore commodore
commotion (cérébrale) concussion
commotionné concussed
commuer commute
commun common, joint
communautaire communal
communauté community
commune commune
communicatif communicative, forthcoming
communication communication
communion communion
communiqué bulletin, communiqué
communiquer communicate, impart, put across/over
communisme communism
communiste communist, red
commutateur switch
compact compact
compagnie companionship, company, society
compagnie aérienne airline
compagnon brother, companion
comparable comparable
comparaison comparison, simile
comparaître appear
comparatif comparative
comparer liken, measure
comparer, (se) compare
compartiment compartment
comparution appearance
compas compass, dividers
compassé formal
compassion compassion
compatibilité compatibility
compatible consistent, compatible

compatissant compassionate, sympathetic
compatriote compatriot, countryman
compensateur compensatory
compenser compensate, make good, make up for
compétence competence, qualification
compétence (en) expertness
compétent able, competent, good
compétition contest
compilateur, trice compiler
compilation compilation
complément complement
complémentaire complementary
complet all-round, complete, exhaustive, thorough, utter
complètement completely, dead, full, off, over, properly, thoroughly, through and through, wholly
compléter complement, finish off, make up
complexe complex
complexité abstruseness, complexity, intricacy
complication complication
complice accessory, accomplice, confederate
compliment compliment
compliqué complicated, elaborate, intricate, involved
compliquer complicate
complot plot, scheme
comportement behaviour, demeanour, manner
comporter carry, act
comporter, se behave
composé compound
composer compose, dial
compositeur, trice composer
composition composition
compost compost
compréhensible comprehensible, understandable
compréhensif understanding
compréhension apprehension, comprehension, grasp, understanding
comprendre apprehend, catch, comprehend, comprise, conceive, fathom, get, realize, take in, understand
compresseur air pump
compressible compressible
compression compression
comprimé tablet
comprimer compress
compromettant incriminating
compromettre jeopardize

compromis compromise
comptabilité accountancy
comptable accountant
comptant cash
compte account, count
compte d'épargne savings account
compte rendu account, review
compter carry weight, count, number
compter sur bank on, count on, rely
compteur clock, meter
compteur à gaz gas meter
compteur de taxi taximeter
comptine nursery rhyme
comptoir counter, godown, post
comte count, earl
comté county
comtesse countess
concave concave
concavité concavity
concentration concentration
concentré concentrated, evaporated
concentrer condense, focus
concentrer, (se) concentrate
concentrer (sur), se centre, keep one's mind on
concentrique concentric
concept concept
conception conception, design
concernant regarding, with regard to
concerner concern, to do with
concert chorus, concert
concerté concerted
concerto concerto
concession concession
concevable conceivable
concevoir conceive, design
concierge caretaker, janitor, janitress
conciliant conciliatory
conciliation conciliation
concilier conciliate, reconcile
concilier, se conciliate
concis concise
concision brevity, conciseness
conclave conclave
concluant conclusive
conclure clinch, close, conclude, gather
conclure un marché strike a bargain/agreement
conclusion conclusion
concombre cucumber
concorder (avec) accord
concours competition
concret concrete
concurrence competition
concurrent, ente competitor, contestant

concurrentiel competitive
condamnation condemnation, conviction
condamner condemn, damn, doom, sentence
condensation condensation
condensé potted
condenser condense
condescendance condescension
condescendant condescending, patronizing
condescendre (à) condescend (to)
condiment condiment
condition condition
conditionnel conditional
conditionnellement conditionally
conditionner condition, season
condoléances condolence
conducteur conductor
conducteur, trice driver
conducteur, trice de char charioteer
conduction conduction
conductrice conductress
conduire conduct, lead
conduire à lead up to
conduire bien, se behave
conduire (en voiture) drive
conduire jusqu'à usher
conduire mal, se misbehave
conduire qqn show
conduit(e) duct
conduite behaviour, conduct
cône cone
confédération confederacy, confederation
conférence lecture
conférencier, ière lecturer, speaker
conférer bestow
confesseur confessor
confession confession
confessionnal confessional
confettis confetti
confiance confidence, faith, hopefulness, trust
confiance en soi self-confidence
confiant confiding
confidentiel confidential, confidentially
confidentiellement confidentially, in confidence
confier consign, trust
confier (à) confide
confier à qqn entrust
confiné confined
confirmation confirmation, corroboration
confirmer bear out, confirm, corroborate, uphold
confiscation confiscation

confiseries confectionery
confisqué forfeit
confisquer confiscate
confit candied
confiture jam, preserve
confiture d'agrumes marmalade
conflit clash, strife
conflit (d'opinions) conflict
confluence confluence
confondre confound, confuse, mix up, muddle up
conformément (à) (in) accordance (with)
conformer, se conform
conformer (à), se abide by
conformité compliance, conformity
confort comfort, cosiness
confortable comfortable, smooth, snug
confortablement comfortably, snugly
confrérie brotherhood, fraternity
confrontation confrontation
confronter (avec) confront (with)
confus abashed, confused, shamefaced
confusément confusedly
confusion bewilderment, confusion, distraction, mix up
congé holiday, notice
congédier dismiss, get the boot, sack
congélateur deep freeze, freezer
congeler deep freeze, freeze
congénital congenital
congénitalement congenitally
congrès conference, congress, convention
congruent congruent
congruité congruity
conifère conifer
conique conical
conjectural conjectural
conjecture conjecture, guesswork
conjecturer conjecture
conjectures speculation
conjonction conjunction
conjugaison conjugation
conjugal conjugal, marital
conjugué united
conjuguer conjugate
connaissance acquaintance, consciousness, grip, knowledge
connaissances techniques know-how
connaisseur, euse connoisseur, judge
connaître be acquainted with, know
connaître son affaire know what's what
connexe related

connexion connection
connivence connivance
conquérant, ante conqueror
conquérir conquer
conquête conquest
consacrer consecrate, devote, give up, go in for
consacrer, (se) dedicate
consciemment consciously
conscience conscience, conscientiousness
conscience (de qqch.) awareness
consciencieusement conscientiously
consciencieux conscientious, thorough
conscient conscious
conscient (de) alive to, aware
conscription conscription, draft
conscrit, ite conscript
consécration consecration
consécutif consecutive
consécutivement consecutively
conseil advice, council, counsel, hint, pointer, tip
conseillé advisable
conseiller de advise, counsel
conseiller, ère adviser, advisor, councillor, counsellor
consensus consensus
consentant acquiescent
consentement acquiescence, consent
consentir (à) agree, consent
conséquence consequence
conservateur conservative
conservateur, trice curator, custodian, diehard
conservation preservation, retention
conservatisme conservatism
conservatoire conservatory
conserve conserve
conserver keep, preserve, store up
conserverie cannery
considérable considerable, sizeable
considérablement considerably, significantly
considération consideration
considérer consider, look on, reckon, regard
considérer comme admis take for granted
considérer comme normal take for granted
consigné returnable
consigner record
consistance consistency
consistant thick
consister consist

consolation consolation
consoler console
consolidation consolidation
consolider consolidate
consommateur, trice consumer
consommation consumption, consummation
consommer consume, consummate, use
consonne consonant
consortium consortium
conspirateur, trice conspirator
conspiration conspiracy
conspirer conspire
constamment always
constance constancy, steadfastness
constant constant, steadfast
constater notice
constellation constellation, galaxy
consternation consternation, dismay
consterner dismay
constipation constipation
constipé constipated
constituer constitute
constitutif constituent
constitution constitution, establishment, make-up
constitutionnel constitutional
constitutionnellement constitutionally
constructeur, trice builder, constructor
constructeur, trice de navires shipbuilder
constructif constructive
construction building, construction, erection, structure
construction navale shipbuilding
construire build, construct, put up
construire à la hâte throw up
construire, se go up
consul, ule consul
consulaire consular
consulat consulate
consultatif advisory
consultation consultation
consulter consult, look up, refer
consumer consume
contact contact
contacter contact, reach
contagieux catching, contagious, infectious
contagion contagion
contamination contamination
contaminer contaminate
conte tale
contemplatif contemplative
contemplation contemplation
contemplativement

contemplatively
contempler contemplate
contemporain, aine contemporary
contenance front
contenant tub
conteneur container
contenir confine, contain, hold, store
contenir/retenir, (se) restrain
content gratified, pleased
contentement de soi complacence
contenter, se make do
contenter (de), se content
contenu content
contestation contention
contester dispute
conteur, euse teller
contexte context
continence continence
continent continent, mainland
continental continental
contingent contingent
continu continuous, solid
continuel ceaseless, continual, eternal, everlasting
continuellement continuously, for ever, forever
continuer carry on, continue, get on, go on, keep going, keep on, push on
continuer (à/de) keep, keep going
continuer sa route drive on
continuité continuity
contorsion contortion
contorsionniste contortionist
contour contour, outline
contourner bypass
contraceptif contraceptive
contraception contraception
contracter contract, incur
contraction contraction
contradiction contradiction
contradictoire contradictory
contraindre coerce, compel, force
contrainte compulsion
contraire contrary, converse, opposite, reverse
contraire aux règles out of order
contrairement (à) contrary (to)
contrariant contrary
contrarier antagonize, spite, thwart
contrariété chagrin
contraste contrast
contrat contract
contravention ticket
contre against, versus
contre vents et marées through thick and thin
contre-amiral rear admiral
contre-attaque counterattack

contre-interrogatoire cross examination
contre-torpilleur destroyer
contrebalancer counteract
contrebande contraband, smuggling
contrebandier, ière smuggler
contrebasse double bass
contrecarrer thwart
contredire contradict
contrefaire counterfeit, fake, forge
contrefort buttress, foothill
contremaître foreman, overseer
contremaîtresse forewoman
contreplaqué plywood
contrer counter
contretemps setback
contrevenir (à) contravene
contribuable taxpayer
contribuer contribute
contribution contribution
contrit contrite
contrition contriteness, contrition
contrôle checkpoint, control, spot check
contrôler control, monitor
contrôleur, euse controller
controverse controversy
convaincant convincing, plausible
convaincre convince, persuade, talk round, win over
convalescence convalescence
convalescent, ente convalescent
convection convection
convenable decent, fit, proper, respectable, seemly, suitable
convenablement appropriately, decently, decorously, properly, respectably, suitably
convenance etiquette, expediency, suitability, suitableness
convenances form
convenir (à) fit, suit
convention compact, convention
conventionnel conventional
convenu appointed
convergence convergence
convergent convergent
converger converge
conversation conversation
converser converse
conversion conversion
converti, ie convert
convertibilité convertibility
convertir, (se) convert
convexe convex
conviction conviction
convoi convoy
convoiter covet
convoitise covetousness

convoquer call, convene, have up, summon
convoyeur conveyor belt
convulser, (se) convulse
convulsif convulsive
convulsion convulsion
convulsivement convulsively
coopératif co-operative
coopération co-operation
coopérer co-operate
coordination coordination
coordonner coordinate
copain buddy, chum, pal
copeaux shavings
copie copy, duplicate
copier copy, crib
copieusement copiously
copieux copious, hearty, lavish
copra copra
coq cock, rooster
coq nain bantam
coque hull
coquet tidy
coquetel cocktail
coquetier egg cup
coquillage seashell, shellfish
coquille misprint, shell
coquille d'œuf eggshell
coquille de (noix) nutshell
coquille Saint-Jacques scallop
coquin, ine rascal
cor corn, horn
cor d'harmonie horn
corail coral
corbeau raven
corbillard hearse
corde cord, line, rope
corde de tente guy
corde raide tightrope
cordes strings
cordial cordial, hearty
cordialement cordially
cordialité cordiality, heartiness
cordon cordon, drawstring
cordonnier, ière cobbler, shoemaker
corne horn
corné horny
corne de brume fog horn
cornée cornea
corneille crow, rook
cornemuse bagpipes, pipes
corner corner
cornet cone
cornu horned
coronaire coronary
coroner coroner
corporel corporal
corps body, corps
corps célestes heavenly bodies

corps et âme heart and soul
corps législatif legislature
corps à corps hand to hand
corpulence corpulence
corpulent corpulent, matronly, stout
correct proper, correctly
correctement correctly
correctif corrective
correction correction, correctness, emendation
correspondance correspondence
correspondant corresponding
correspondant, ante correspondent, penfriend, pen pal
correspondre correspond, tally
correspondre à answer, tie in/up
corrida bullfight
corridor corridor, hall
corriger amend, correct, emend, mark, put right, reform
corroborer support
corroder corrode
corrompre corrupt, subvert
corrompu corrupt
corrosif corrosive
corrosion corrosion
corruptibilité corruptibility
corruptible corruptible
corruption bribery, corruption, graft
corsage bodice
corset corset
cortège cavalcade, cortege, procession
corvée bee, chore, drag, drudgery, grind
corvette duffel coat, duffle coat
cosmique cosmic
cosmonaute cosmonaut
cosmopolite cosmopolitan
cosmos cosmos
cosse pod
costaud beefy, hefty, strapping
costume costume, suit
côte coast, rib, rise
cote rating
côté side
côte à côte abreast, shoulder to shoulder, side by side
côte levée spare rib
côtelette chop, cutlet
côtier coastal, inshore, offshore
cotisation membership
coton cotton
côtoyer rub shoulders with
cottage cottage
cotte de mailles chain mail
cou neck
cou-de-pied instep

couche coat, covering, diaper, layer, napkin
couché à plat ventre prostrate
couché sur le ventre prone
coucher lay, go to bed
coucher, se go down
couchette berth, bunk, cot, sleeper
coucou cuckoo
coude elbow
coudre sew, stitch, stitch up
couenne rind
couette duvet
couguar panther
couin-couin quack
couler cast, flow, sink
couleur colour
couleurs fondamentales primary colours
coulisses wings
coup bash, blast, blow, coup, hit, jab, knock, poke, shot, stroke
coup d'État coup, coup d'état
coup d'envoi kick off
coup d'œil glance, glimpse, look, squint
coup d'œil furtif peek, peep
coup de bec peck
coup de chance fluke
coup de coude nudge
coup de feu gunshot, shot
coup de fil call
coup de fouet lash
coup de klaxon hoot
coup de langue lick
coup de main hand
coup de maître master stroke
coup de pied kick
coup de poing punch
coup de téléphone ring
coup de tête header
coup de théâtre twist
coup de tonnerre peal, thunderbolt
coup droit forehand
coup interdit foul
coup léger dab
coup violent bang
coupable culpable, culprit, guilty, sinful
coupé coupe
coupe cup, section
coupe (de cheveux) haircut, trim
coupe-papier letter opener
couper clip, cut, cut off, dock, sever, shear, slice, shut off
couper en cubes dice
couper en dégradé layer
couper en deux bisect, halve
couper en quatre quarter
couper en tranches/rondelles slice
couper la parole à cut short

couper les cheveux en quatre split hairs
couperet cleaver
couple couple, pair
coupon coupon
coups de feu gunfire
coupure cut, cutting, scrap
coupure (de presse) clipping, press clipping
cour court, courtship, courtyard, quadrangle, yard
cour de justice law court
cour de récréation playground
courage cheer, courage, fortitude, heart, nerve, pluck, pluckiness, spirit
courageusement courageously, gamely
courageux courageous, plucky
couramment fluently
courant common, current, routine, stream
courant dominant mainstream
courbe bend, curve, curvy
courbé crooked, curved
courber crook
courbure curvature
coureur, euse runner
courge(tte) marrow
courir pelt, ride, run
courir après go after
courir deux lièvres à la fois have several/too many irons in the fire
courir le risque (de) run/take the risk (of)
couronne coronet, crown, wreath
couronnement coronation
couronner crown
courrier correspondence, mail
courroie belt, strap
cours class, course, school
cours par correspondance correspondence course
course race, run
course contre la montre a race against time
course de haies obstacle race, steeplechase
coursier steed
court short
court-circuit short circuit
courtaud squat, stubby
courtepointe counterpane
courtier broker
courtisan courtier
courtiser court, make up to
courtois gracious, civilly
courtoisement civilly
courtoisie chivalry, civility, courtliness, courtesy

couseur, euse sewer
cousin, ine cousin
coussin cushion, pad
coûte que coûte by hook or by crook
couteau knife
coutelas cutlass
coûter cost
coûteux costly
couture seam, sewing, stitching
couturier, ière dressmaker
couturière seamstress
couvent convent, convent school, nunnery
couver brood, incubate
couvercle lid, top
couvert overcast
couverture blanket, cover, coverage
couveuse incubator
couvre-chef headgear
couvre-feu curfew
couvre-lit bedcover, bedspread, coverlet
couvrir coat, cover, litter, roof
cover-girl cover girl
crabe crab
cracher belch, spit out
craie chalk
craindre (que) fear
crainte fear
crainte révérentielle awe
craintif fearful, shy
cramoisi crimson
crampe cramp
crampon spike, staple
cramponner clamp
cran grit, guts
crâne skull
crapaud toad
crapule scum
craquelin cracker
craquer crack
crasse grime
crasseux filthy, grubby
cratère crater
cravache crop
cravate necktie, tie
crayeux chalky
crayon pencil
crayon de couleur crayon
créancier, ière creditor
créateur creative, creator
créateur, trice designer
création creation
créativité creativity
créature being, creature
crécelle rattle
crèche crib
crédibilité credibility, credit

crédit credit
credo creed
crédule credulous, gullible
crédulité credulousness, gullibility
créer create
crème cream
crème glacée ice, ice cream
crémerie dairy
crémeux creamy
créosote creosote
crêpe crepe, pancake
crépitement crackle, pitter-patter
crépiter crackle, pitter-patter
crépu crinkly, frizzy
crépuscule dusk, twilight
crescendo crescendo
cresson cress, watercress
crête comb, crest, ridge
crétin, ine blockhead, cretin
creuser burrow, dig, excavate, hollow out
creuser la tête, se rack one's brain
creuser un tunnel tunnel
creuset crucible
creux crook, depression, dip, hollow, hollowness
crevaison puncture
crevasse crevasse
crevé dog-tired, fagged out
crever puncture, stare in the face
crevette prawn, shrimp
cri call, cry, peep, shout
cri de l'oie honk
cri perçant scream, screech, shriek
criard garish, gaudy, loud, lurid, shrill
cribler riddle
cric jack
crier cry, holler, peep, shout
crime crime, enormity, felony, foul play, enormity
criminel criminal, felon
criminellement criminally
crinière mane
crise attack, crisis, depression
crise de cœur heart attack
crise de nerfs hysterics
crise de rage tantrum
crise économique slump
crispé tense
crisper contort, screw up
crissement crunch
cristal crystal
cristallin crystalline, lens
cristallisation crystallization
cristalliser, (se) crystallize
critère criterion, standard
critique acute, appreciation, critic, critical, criticism, reviewer
critiquer criticize

croc fang
croche quaver
crochet fang, hook
crochet (faire au) crochet
crochu hooked
crocodile crocodile
croire believe, credit, expect, fancy, hold
croisade crusade
croiser le fer avec cross swords
croiser, (se) cross
croiseur cruiser
croisière cruise
croissance growth
croissant crescent, croissant
croître grow
croix cross, mark
croix gammée swastika
croquant crisp, crunchy, gristly
croque-mitaine bogeyman
croquer crunch
croquet croquet
croquis sketch
crosse butt
crottes droppings
croupe rump
croupier, ière croupier
croustillant crisp
croustille chip, crisp, potato chip
croûte crust, scab
croûton crouton
croyable believable, credible
croyance(s) belief
croyant, ante believer
cru raw
cruauté cruelty
cruche crock, jug, pitcher
crucial crucial
crucifier crucify
crucifix crucifix

crucifixion crucifixion
crudité crudity, rawness
cruel cruel, heartless, inhumane
cruellement cruelly
crustacé crustacean
crypte crypt
cube cube
cubique cubic
cueillir pick, pluck
cuiller spoon
cuiller de service tablespoon
cuillerée spoon, spoonful
cuillerée à soupe tablespoon, tablespoonful
cuir leather, scalp
cuir chevelu scalp
cuirassé battleship
cuire cook, fire
cuire à la vapeur steam
cuire au four bake
cuisine cookery, cuisine, galley, kitchen
cuisiner grill
cuisinier, ière cook
cuisinière cooker, range, stove
cuisse thigh
cuisson baking
cuissot haunch
cuit baked, done
cuivré brassy
cuivre copper
cuivres brass
cul bum
cul par-dessus tête head over heels
cul-de-sac cul-de-sac, dead end
culasse breech
culbute somersault, tumble
culminer culminate
culot brass neck, cheek
culotte breeches, knickers, panties,

pants
culotte de cheval jodhpurs
culpabilité culpability, guilt, guiltiness
culte cult, worship
culte des héros hero-worship
cultivé cultivated, cultured, literary, literate, well-read
cultiver cultivate, farm
culture cultivation, culture
culture générale general knowledge
culturel cultural
cumulatif cumulative
curatif curative
cure-dents toothpick
curieusement curiously
curieux curious, nos(e)y, puzzling
curiosité curio, curiosity
curry curry, curry powder
cursif cursive
cuticules cuticle
cuve tub, vat
cuvette basin, bulb
cyanure cyanide
cycle cycle
cycle de vie life cycle
cyclique cyclic
cycliste cyclist
cyclone cyclone
cygne swan
cylindre cylinder
cylindrique cylindrical
cymbale cymbal
cynique cynical, cynic
cyniquement cynically
cynisme cynicism
cyprès cypress

Dd

d'abord first, to begin with, to start with
d'accord all right, O.K., okay, quite
d'affilée at a stretch, on end, running, solid
d'ailleurs more'over
d'après according to
d'avance in advance, beforehand
d'est east, easterly
d'habitude usually
d'homme à homme man to man
d'occasion second-hand, used
d'or golden
d'un bout à l'autre all over, through
d'un certain âge middle-aged
d'un commun accord with one accord
d'un coup d'œil at a glance
d'un seul coup all at once, at a stroke
dactylo typist
dactylographie typing, typewriting
dactylographier type
daltonien colour blind
dame dame, lady, queen
dames checquers
damné damned, bloody
damner damn
dandiner (se) waddle
danger danger, hazard, jeopardy, perilousness
dangereux dangerous
dans amid, amidst, in, inside, into, on, through
dans ce cas in that case, in that event
dans de beaux draps in deep water, in the soup
dans l'attente expectantly
dans l'ensemble altogether
dans l'intérêt de in the interest(s) of
dans la crainte de in fear of
dans la gêne badly off
dans la même galère in the same boat
dans la mesure où insofar as, in so far as
dans la poche in the bag
dans le feu (de l'action) in the heat of (the moment)
dans le mille spot on
dans le pétrin in a spot
dans les coulisses behind the scenes
dans les parages around
dans les règles in order

dans son élément in one's element
dans son (propre) intérêt in one's (own) interest
dans tout all through
dans une large mesure largely
danse dance
danse folklorique country dance
danser dance
danseur, euse dancer
danseur, euse à claquettes tap dancer
danseur, euse de ballet ballet dancer
danseuse étoile prima
dard dart
date date
dater date
datte date
dauphin dolphin
davantage further, more
dé dice
de from, of, to
dé à coudre thimble
de bon augure auspicious
de bon cœur willingly
de bon goût tasteful
de bonne heure early
de bonne humeur good-humoured
de bonne/mauvaise grâce with (a) good/bad grace
de but en blanc point-blank
de cérémonie/soirée formal
de concert avec in association with, in concert
de côté aside, sideways
de dernier ordre third-rate
de derrière hind
de direction executive
de façon tatillonne fussily
de fond en comble from top to bottom
de fortune makeshift, rough-and-ready
de garde on call, on duty
de grande classe high-class
de haut niveau high-level
de haute puissance high-powered
de justesse narrowly, by the skin of one's teeth
de l'autre côté (de) across
de l'autre côté de beyond
de l'aveu général admittedly
de loin easily, by far
de long en large backwards and forwards, to and fro
de luxe de luxe
de mauvais augure ominous
de mauvais goût tasteless
de mauvaise foi insincere
de mauvaise grâce grudgingly

de mauvaise humeur out of sorts
de mauvaise qualité cheap
de mémoire d'homme (with)in living memory
de nature naturally
de notoriété publique common knowledge
de part en part through
de peur de for fear of
de plein air open air
de plein gré of one's own accord
de plus besides, furthermore
de plus en plus increasingly, more and more
de préférence preferably
de première main at first hand
de près closely
de quelque manière que however
de race bred, purebred
de reste over, (and) to spare
de retour back
de saison seasonable, in season
de sang-froid in cold blood
de son propre chef off one's own bat
de souche native
de source sûre (straight) from the horse's mouth
de temps à autre every now and then, every now and again, (every) now and then/again, off and on/on and off, once in a while
de temps en temps every so often, from time to time, occasionally
de toujours lifelong
de tout cœur heartily, with all one's heart
de tout repos gilt-edged
de toute évidence evidently
de toute facon anyhow, anyway, either way
de toutes ses forces like grim death, tooth and nail
de travers amiss, crooked, skew, squint
de très loin far and away
de va-et-vient back and forth
de/du retour homeward
débandade rout
débarcadère landing, landing stage
débardeur, euse docker, stevedore
débarquement disembarkation, landing
débarquer disembark, drop, land
débarrassé de free
débarrasser clear, clear out
débarrasser (de) rid of
débarrasser de, se be rid off, dispose of, get rid of, throw off
débarrer unbar

débat debate, disputation, opening, outset, start
débats proceedings
débattre debate, hit out
débattre, se struggle, thrash
débauché debauched, dissolute
débauche debauchery, dissoluteness
débiliter debilitate
débit debit
débiter debit, reel off
débiteur, trice debtor
débloquer un peu out to lunch
débordé (de) snowed under
déborder de bubble over
débouché opening
déboucher unplug, unstop
déboucler unbuckle
débouler tumble down
débourser shell out
debout on end, up
déboutonner unbutton
débraillé dishevelled, disheveled
débrancher disconnect, unplug
débrayer come out
débris wreckage
débrouillard resourceful
débrouiller, se fend, get by
débrouiller tant bien que mal, se muddle along/through
débusquer flush
début(s) debut
débutant, ante beginner, learner
décadence decadence
décadent decadent
décalage lag
décalcomanie transfer
décamper clear off
décaper strip
décapitation decapitation
décapiter decapitate
décapotable convertible
décédé deceased
décembre December
décence decency
décennie decade
décent decent
déception anticlimax, disappointment
décerner award, honour
décès death
décevant disappointing
décevoir disappoint, let down
déchaîné out of control
déchaîner, se run riot
décharger unload, vent
décharné bony, scraggy, scrawny
déchets waste
déchiffrer decipher, unscramble
déchiqueté jagged, ragged, rugged

déchiqueter shred
déchirant harrowing
déchirer tear up, rip
déchirer, se tear
déchirure rip, tear
décibel decibel
décidé decisive, determined
décidé (à) intent on
décider fix on, rule, settle
décider (de) choose, decide
décider pour, se plump
décider, se make up one's mind
décilitre decilitre
décimal decimal
décimalisation decimalization
décimaliser decimalize
décimation decimation
décimer decimate
décisif decisive
décision adjudication, decision, ruling
déclamer declaim, downgrade, spout
déclaration declaration, profession, pronouncement, statement
déclaré overt
déclarer declare, state
déclarer coupable convict
déclasser downgrade
déclenchement outbreak
déclencher activate, spark, touch off, trigger
déclencheur trigger
déclin decline, twilight
décliner decline, ebb
décocher let fly
décoder decipher, decode
décoller blast off, lift off, take off, unstuck
décoloration discolouration
décolorer, (se) bleach, discolour
décombres debris
décommander put off
décomposer, se decompose
décomposition decomposition
déconcerté taken aback
déconcerter baffle, bewilder, discomfit, disconcert
déconfit crestfallen
décongeler defrost, thaw
déconseillé (de) inadvisable
déconsidérer discredit
décor set
décor(s) scene, scenery
décorateur, trice decorator
décoratif decorative
décoration decoration, ornamentation
décoration (intérieure) interior decoration

décorer decorate, ornament
décortiquer husk
décorum decorum
découdre unpick
découler de spring from
découper carve, cut
découragé cheesed off, despondent, dispirited, downhearted
découragement despondency, discouragement
décourager deter, discourage, dishearten
décousu loose, piecemeal, rambling
découvert overdraft
découverte discovery, strike
découvrir discover, find, find out, be on to (someone), spot, uncover
décret decree, edict
décréter decree
décrire characterize, depict, describe
décrocher (de) unhook
décroître diminish, fall off, wane
déçu disappointed
dédaigner despise, disdain
dédaigneusement disdainfully, fastidiously
dédaigneux contemptuous, disdainful
dédain disdain
dedans inside
dédicace dedication, autograph
dédicacer autograph
dédier dedicate
dédommager compensate, make it up
déduction deduction, inference
déduire deduce, deduct, infer
défaire open up, undo
défaire, se come apart
défaite defeat
défaitisme defeatism
défaitiste defeatist
défaut blemish, defect, failing, fault, flaw, impediment, shortcoming, vice
défaveur disfavour
défavorable adverse
défavorablement adversely
défavorisé deprived
défection defection
défectueux defective, deficient, faulty, flawed
défectuosité flaw
défendable arguable
défendre defend, forbid, hold
défendre, se put up
défense championship, defence, plea, tusk
défenseur advocate, defender

défensif defensive
déférence deference
déferler roll, surge
défi challenge, dare, defiance
défiance distrustfulness
déficit deficit
défier challenge, dare, defy
défiguration disfigurement
défigurer deface, disfigure
défilé parade
défiler parade
définir define
définissable definable
définitif final
définition definition
déflation deflation
défoncer bash, plough
défoncer, se freak out
déformation distortion
déformé deformed, out of shape
déformer deform, distort
déformer, se buckle
défouler, se let off steam
défroisser smooth down/out
défunt deceased
dégagement clearance, extrication
dégager give out, disengage
dégager, se clear
dégât damage
dégel thaw
dégeler thaw
dégénéré degenerate
dégénérer degenerate
dégingandé gangling
dégivrer defrost
déglutition swallow
dégonfler deflate
dégonfler, se chicken out, funk, get cold feet
dégourdi smart
dégourdir les jambes, se stretch one's legs
dégoût disgust, distaste, loathing
dégoûtant beastly, disgusting, foul
dégoûté revolted
dégoûter disgust, repel, revolt
dégoûter (de) put off
dégoutter drip, trickle
dégradant degrading
dégrader degrade
dégrader, se go down
degré degree
dégringolade tumble
dégriser sober up
déguenillé ragged
déguisement disguise, fancy dress
déguiser, (se) disguise
déguster taste
dehors out, outdoors, outside
déjà already

déjections cast
déjeuner breakfast
délabré ramshackle, rickety
délabrement disrepair
délaissé desolate, friendless
délavé washed-out
délecter (de), se revel
délégation delegation, deputation
délégué, ée delegate
déléguer delegate, depute
délibérément purposefully
délicat delicate, fine, tactful, ticklish
délicatement delicately, gingerly
délicatesse daintiness, delicacy
délice delight
délicieusement deliciously, delightfully
délicieux delicious
délimiter mark out
délinquant, ante offender
délirant delirious
délirer rave
délit de fuite hit and run
délivrer save
déloyal disloyal, faithless
déloyalement disloyally
déloyauté disloyalty, faithlessness
delta delta
déluge deluge, flood
demain tomorrow
demande call, demand, proposal, request, want
demander ask, ask for, enquire, inquire, query
demander (à) request
demander (de) tell (to)
demander des nouvelles de ask after, inquire (after)
demander, se debate
démangeaison itch, itchiness
démanger itch
démaquillant cleanser
démarche gait, walk
démarche(s) approach
démarrer start, start up
démarreur starter
démasquer find out
démêlage disentanglement
démêler unravel, untangle
démêler, (se) disentangle
déménagement move
déménager move, move out
démener, se bustle
dément insane
démentir belie
démesurément exorbitantly
demi-cercle semicircle
demi-conscience semi-consciousness

demi-finale semifinal
demi-finaliste semi-finalist
demi-frère half-brother, stepbrother
demi-jour gloom
demi-sœur half-sister, stepsister
demi-ton semitone
demi-tour around, u turn
demie half
démis out of joint, resignation
démissionner resign
démocrate democrat, democratic
démocratie democracy
démocratique democratic
démocratiquement democratically
démodé dated, dowdy, old-fashioned, out of date, out of fashion
demoiselle damsel
demoiselle d'honneur bridesmaid
démolir demolish, pull down
démolition demolition
démon demon, devil, fiend
démonstration demonstration, display, exhibition, show
démontable sectional
démonter deflate, dismantle, take apart
démontrer demonstrate
démoraliser demoralize
dénégation denial
dénicher dig out, hunt out, pickup, run to earth
dénigrement denigration
dénigrer denigrate, run down
dénoncer denounce, inform against/on, rat, tell on
dénonciation denunciation
dénoter denote
dénouer unravel
dénoyauter pit, stone
dense dense, thick
densité density
dent cog, prong, tooth
dent de lait milk tooth
dentaire dental
denté toothed
dentelé indented
dentelle lace
dentelure indentation
dentier dental plate, dentures
dentifrice toothpaste
dentiste dentist
dentisterie dentistry
dénudé bare
dépanner help out
dépaqueter unpack
dépareillé odd
départ departure, going
département department
dépassé obsolete

dépasser exceed, overshoot, top
dépecé jointed
dépecer joint
dépêche dispatch
dépêcher, se hurry, hurry up
dépendance addiction
dépendant reliant
dépendant (de) dependent
dépendre de depend, hinge on
dépense excessive extravagance
dépenser expend, lay out, spend
dépenser/donner sans compter lavish
dépenses expenditure, outlay
dépensier extravagant, spendthrift
dépérir pine
dépit pique
déplacé improper, out of place, uncalled for
déplacement displacement
déplacer displace, shift
déplacer, se travel
déplaire displease
déplaisant nasty
déplaisir displeasure
déplantoir trowel
dépliant leaflet
déplier unfold
déplorable deplorable
déplorer deplore
déposer deposit, lay down
déposer à la banque bank
déposséder dispossess
dépôt deposit
dépotoir dump, tip
dépouiller de, se cast
dépourvu (de) devoid (of)
dépraver pervert
déprécier belittle
dépression depression, trough
dépression atmosphérique depression
dépression nerveuse nervous breakdown
déprimant depressing
déprimé blue, depressed
déprimer depress, get down
de proie predator
depuis since, all along
depuis le tout début from the word go
député, ée congressman, congresswoman, Member of Parliament, representative
déraciner root out, uproot
déraisonnable unreasonable
dérangement disturbance, inconvenience, upset
déranger disturb, intrude, put out, trouble

dérapage skid
déraper skid, slew
déridage facelift
dérision derision
dérisoire derisive, derisory
dérivation bypass, derivation
dérivé derivative
dérive fin, leeway
dériver drift
dériveur dinghy
dernier final, last
dernier cri up to the minute
dérobée stealth
dérober back out, steal
dérober, se back out, fence
dérouler comme prévu, se go according to plan
dérouler, (se) uncoil, uncurl, unroll, unwind
déroutant baffling
dérouté nonplussed
dérouter put/throw (someone) off the scent
derrick rig
derrière after, backside, behind, bottom, rear, seat
derrière le dos (de qqn) behind someone's back
dès que as soon as, immediately, the minute (that), the moment (that)
des tas de hundreds of, scores (of)
désabusement disillusionment
désabuser disillusion
désaccord difference, disagreement, discrepancy, division, friction
désagréable disagreeable, distasteful, ill-tempered/ill-natured, nasty, objectionable, unpleasant
désagréablement disagreeably, nastily, objectionably, unpleasantly
désagrément annoyance
désaltérer quench
désamorcer defuse
désapprobateur disapproving
désapprobation disapproval
désapprouver disapprove, frown on/upon, object
désarçonner throw
désarmant disarming
désarmé unarmed
désarmement disarmament
désarmer disarm
désarroi disarray
désastre disaster
désastreux disastrous
désavantage disadvantage, handicap
désavantageux disadvantageous

désavouer disown
descendant downward, descendant
descendre descend, dismount, ebb
descendre (de) alight, be descended from
descendre en piqué nosedive
descente chute, descent, drop, swoop
description description, picture
déséquilibré unbalanced
désert deserted, desert
déserter defect, desert
déserteur deserter
désertion desertion
désespéré desperate, hopeless
désespérément desperately
désespérer (de), (se) despair
désespoir despair, desperation, hopelessness
déshabiller undress, strip
déshonneur disgrace, dishonour
déshonorant discreditable, dishonourable
déshonorer dishonour
déshydratation dehydration
déshydrater dehydrate
désignation designation
désigné designate
désigner designate, mark out
désincarné disembodied
désinfectant disinfectant
désinfecter disinfect
désintégration disintegration
désintégrer, (se) disintegrate
désintéressé disinterested, selfless
désintéressement selflessness
désintéresser de, se lose interest
désinvolte airy, flippant, glib, jaunty
désinvolture airiness, casualness, flippancy, jauntiness, offhandedness
désir desire
désirable desirable
désirer desire, hanker
désireux de eager
désister, se stand down
désobéir disobey
désobéissance disobedience
désobéissant disobedient
désobligeant slighting
désodorisant deodorant
désolation desolation
désolé afraid, desolate, sorry, stark
désordonné disorderly
désordre clutter, disarrangement, disorder, mess, messiness, tangle
désorganisation disorganization
désorganisé disorganized
désormais henceforth

désosser bone, fillet
despote despot
despotique despotic
despotiquement despotically
despotisme despotism
desséché desiccated, parched
dessécher bake, parch
dessécher, se dry up
dessein design
desserré slack
desserrer, (se) loosen
dessert dessert, sweet
dessin design, drawing
dessin animé cartoon
dessinateur draftsman
dessinatrice draftswoman
dessiner draw, landscape
dessous underneath, underside
dessus top
destin destiny, fate
destinataire addressee
destination destination
destiné (à) destined, fated
destinée lot
destituer depose
destructeur, trice destructive
destructif destructive
destruction destruction
désuni broken
détachable detachable
détachant remover
détaché detached
détachement detachment, draft
détachement spécial task force
détacher detach, unfasten, untie
détail detail, technicality
détaillant, ante retailer
détaillé detailed
détails particulars
détaler scamper
détecter detect
détendre, se unwind
détenir detain, hold
détente relaxation, trigger
détention custody, detention
détenu, ue convict, detainee, inmate
détergent detergent
détérioration deterioration, impairment
détériorer deteriorate, impair
détermination determination, purpose, resolve
déterminé definite, determined, purposeful
déterminer determine
déterrer dig out, unearth
détestable detestable
détester detest, dislike, hate, loathe
détonateur detonator, fuse

détonation detonation, report
détoner detonate
détordre untwist
détour detour
détourné circuitous, devious, indirect, roundabout
détournement hijack, embezzlement
détourner avert, divert, embezzle, head off, hijack, turn away
détours deviousness
détracteur, trice critic
détraqué haywire, out of order
détrempe distemper
détrempe slushy, waterlogged
détresse distress
détriment detriment
détroit channel, strait
détromper put right
détruire destroy, wreck
dette debt, indebtedness
deuil bereavement, mourning
deux two
deuxième latter, second, second-best
deuxièmement secondly
deux-points colon
dévaliser rifle, rob
dévaluation devaluation
dévaluer devalue
devancer outstrip
devant at the front of, front, in front (of)
dévastateur devastating
dévaster devastate, lay waste
développement development
développer amplify, develop, enlarge on, process
devenir become, get, go, grow, grow up, turn
devenir ami, ie avec make friends (with)
devenir fou furieux (run) amok
devenir membre de join
dévergondé abandoned, wanton
déverrouiller unbolt, unlock
déverser tip
déversoir outlet, overflow
déviation deflection, diversion
dévidoir hose reel
dévier deflect, swerve
devin diviner
deviner guess
devinette riddle
devis estimatif quotation
devise motto
dévisser unscrew
dévoiler expose, unveil
devoir duty, must, ought, owe
devoirs (à la maison) homework

dévorer devour
dévot devout
dévoué dedicated, devoted
dévouement devotion
dextérité dexterity
diabète diabetes
diabétique diabetic
diable devil
diablotin imp
diabolique fiendish
diaboliquement fiendishly
diadème tiara
diagnostic diagnosis
diagnostiquer diagnose
diagonale diagonal
diagramme diagram
dialecte dialect
dialogue dialogue
diamant diamond
diamètre diameter
diaphragme midriff
diapositive slide, transparency
diarrhée diarrhoea
dictateur, trice dictator
dictature dictatorship
dictée dictation
dicter dictate
diction diction
dictionnaire dictionary, thesaurus
dicton saying
dièse sharp
dieu deity, god
diffamatoire libellous
diffamer (par écrit) libel
différence difference
différenciation differentiation
différent unlike, various
différent (de) different
différer defer, differ
différer d'opinion (avec) dissent
difficile difficult, fastidious, hard, heavy, tough, tricky
difficilement ill, trickily
difficulté arduousness, difficulty, trickiness
difforme misshapen
difformité crookedness, deformity
diffuser beam, broadcast, diffuse, telecast
diffusion spread
digérer digest, keep down
digestible digestible
digestif digestive
digestion digestion
digne decorous, dignified, worthy
digne d'éloges praiseworthy
digne de deserving, dependable
digne de confiance responsible, trustworthy
dignitaire dignitary

dignité dignity
digression digression
digue dyke, dike, embankment
dilapider squander
dilatation enlargement, expansion
dilaté distended
dilater, (se) dilate, expand
dilemme dilemma
dilué dilute
diluer dilute, water down
dilution dilution
dimanche Sunday
dimension dimension, size
diminué diminished
diminuer abate, decrease, diminish, dwindle, fall away, lessen, let up, tail off
diminuer de moitié halve
diminutif pet name, nickname
diminution abatement, decrease, diminution
dindon turkey
dîner dine, dinner, lunch
dîner en ville/dehors dine on, dine out
dîneur, euse diner
dingo dingo
dinosaure dinosaur
diocèse diocese
diphtérie diphtheria
diphtongue diphthong
diplomate diplomat, trifle
diplomatie diplomacy, statesmanship
diplomatique diplomatic, statesmanlike
diplomatiquement diplomatically
diplôme degree, diploma, qualification
dire say, speak, tell
dire ce qu'on a sur le cœur get something off one's chest
dire d'un ton brusque snap
dire du mal de malign
dire la bonne aventure tell (someone's) fortune
dire la vérité tell the truth
dire sa pensée speak one's mind
direct direct, forthright
directement directly, straight
directeur, trice director, head, headmaster, manager, principal superintendent, warden
direction direction, leadership, management, way
directionnel directional
directive directive, guideline
dirigeable airship
diriger carry on, conduct, direct, manage, run, steer, supervise

diriger droit sur, se make a beeline for
diriger (automatiquement) sur/ vers, (se) home in on
diriger vers, se make for
discernement judiciousness
discerner discern, make out
disciple disciple, follower
disciplinaire disciplinary
discipline discipline
discipliné orderly
discipliner, (se) discipline
discordance tunelessness
discordant discordant, jarring, tuneless
discorde discord
discothèque discotheque
discours address, speech
discours solennel oration
discrédit discredit, disrepute
discréditer discredit
discret quiet, unobtrusive
discrètement unobtrusively
discrétion discreetness, discretion
discrimination discrimination
discussion discussion, talk
discutable debatable, disputable
discuter discuss, talk over
discuter de talk about
diseur, euse de bonne aventure fortune teller
disgrâce disgrace
disgracier disgrace
dislocation dislocation
disloquer dislocate
disparaître die, die out, disappear, vanish
disparition disappearance, extinction
disparu extinct, missing
dispenser dispense, excuse
disperser, (se) disband, disperse, scatter, thin
dispersion dispersal
disponibilité availability
disponible available, at hand, in hand, spare
disposer array, dispose
dispositif contrivance
disposition frame of mind, provision
disproportionné (à/avec) disproportionate
dispute dispute, quarrel, row
disputer, se dispute
disputer, (se) fight
disputer (sur), se argue
disqualification disqualification
disqualifier disqualify
disque album, disc, disk, discus, record

disquette floppy disk
dissection dissection
dissemblable dissimilar
dissemblance dissimilari
dissension dissension
dissentiment dissent
disséquer dissect
dissidence dissidence
dissident, ente dissident
dissimulation concealment, cover-up
dissimuler conceal, disguise, gloss over
dissiper dispel
dissocier dissociate
dissolution dissolution
dissonance discord
dissoudre, (se) dissolve
dissuader dissuade
dissuasion dissuasion
distance distance
distant aloof, distant
distillateur distiller
distillation distillation
distiller distil
distillerie distillery
distinct distinct, separate
distinctement distinctly
distinctif distinctive
distinction distinction, eminence, honour
distinctivement distinctively
distinguable distinguishable
distingué cultivated, distinguished, gentlemanly
distinguer differentiate, tell apart
distinguer (entre) discriminate
distinguer, se distinguish
distraction absent-mindedness, amusement, distraction, diversion, entertainment
distraire distract
distrait absent-minded, distracted
distraitement absentmindedly, vacantly
distrayant entertaining
distribuer dish out, give out, hand out, issue, pass out
distributif countable
distribution cast, distribution
distributrice (automatique) slot machine
divaguer ramble
divan divan
divergence divergence
divergent divergent
diverger diverge
divers diverse, diversely
diversement variously
diversifier, (se) diversify

diversion diversion, red herring
diversité diverseness, diversity
divertir divert
divertissant entertaining
divertissement act, entertainment, recreation
dividende dividend
divin divine, heavenly
divination divination
divinité divinity
diviser separate up, split
diviser en quatre quarter
diviser, (se) divide
diviseur factor
divisible divisible
division division, league
divisionnaire divisional
divorce divorce
divulguer leak
dix ten
dix-huit eighteen
dix-neuf nineteen
dix-sept seventeen
dixième tenth
docile docile
docilement docilely, obediently, tamely
docilité docility
docteur, eure doctor
doctorat doctorate
doctrine doctrine
document document
documentaire documentary
documentaire touristique travelogue
dogmatiquement dogmatically
dogme dogma
doigt digit, finger
dollar dollar
domaine domain, field, realm, territory
dôme dome
domestication domestication
domestique domestic, help, maid, servant
domestiqué domesticated
dominance dominance
dominant commanding, dominant, prevailing
dominateur domineering, masterful
domination domination, dominion, sway
dominer dominate, tower
dominion dominion
domino domino
dommage damage, pity
dommage (que) too bad
dommages et intérêts damage
don bounty, contribution, donation, gift, offering

donateur, trice contributor, donor
donc hence, therefore
donnant donnant give and take
donne deal
donné given
données data, input
donner allow, give, lend
donner asile (à) harbour
donner de l'espoir à raise someone's hopes
donner des airs, se put on airs/give oneself airs, swank
donner des détails sur elaborate
donner des instructions à brief, instruct
donner des soins (à) minister
donner du mal pour, se take pains
donner l'exemple set (someone) an example
donner l'heure exacte keep time
donner la chair de poule make someone's flesh creep
donner la peine (de), se bother
donner le rôle de cast
donner libre cours à indulge, give vent to
donner lieu (à) give rise to
donner naissance à bear, originate, produce
donner naissance (à) give birth (to)
donner son accord (à) assent (to)
donner son plein be at full stretch
donner sur face, open onto
donner un bain à bath
donner un coup de couteau knife
donner un coup de main give/lend a helping hand
donner un coup de pied (à) kick
donner un coup de poing à punch
donner un cours/une leçon lecture
donner un pourboire à tip
donner une entorse, se sprain
donner une fessée à spank
donner une râclée belt
donneur, euse dealer
donneur, euse de sang blood donor
doper dope
dorer bask, gild
dorloter coddle, cosset, mother, pamper
dormeur, euse sleeper
dormir sleep, sleep like a log/top
dormir comme un loir sleep like a top
dormir (paisiblement) slumber
dorsal dorsal
dortoir dormitory
dorure gilt
dos back, spine
dos d'âne humpback

dose dose
dossier brief, dossier, file, record
dot dowry, endowment
doter (de) endow
douane customs
doublage dubbing
double double, dual, duplicate
doublé lined
double jeu double-dealing
doubler double, dub, line
doublure lining, understudy
doucement easy, gently, meekly, mildly, softly
doucereusement sleekly
douceur blandness, gentleness, meekness, mellowness, mildness, softness, sweetness
douche shower
douche (froide) damper
doué apt, brainy, gifted, great
douille nozzle, socket
douillet cozy
douillettement cozily
douleur ache, pain, pang
douloureusement distressingly, painfully
douloureux painful, sore
doute doubt, dubiety, question
douter (que/de) doubt
douteux doubtful, dubious, questionable
doux cuddly, fresh, gentle, meek, mellow, mild, soft
douzaine dozen
douze twelve
douzième twelfth
doyen dean
drachme drachma
dragon dragon
draguer drag, dredge
dragueur dredger
drainage drainage
drainer drain
dramatique dramatic, straight
dramatisation dramatization
dramatiser dramatize
dramaturge dramatist, playwright
drame drama
drap sheet, pall
drapeau colours, flag
draper drape
dressé trained
dresser erect
dresser à la propreté housetrain
dresser la carte de chart, map
dresser, (se) rear
dresseur, euse (de chiens) handler
dribbler dribble
drogue dope, drug
drogué, ée junkie

droguer drug
droit erect, right, straight, up, upright
droit de passage right of way
droit de veto veto
droit de vote franchise, suffrage
droit(s) copyright, due, entitlement, rights
droite right
droitier right-handed
droiture righteousness
drôle comic, funny
dru thick and fast
dû due, owing
du début à la fin (de) all through
du fond du cœur from the bottom of one's heart
du jour au lendemain overnight
du même avis like-minded
du milieu environmental

du moins at least
du tout at all
du/au monde on earth
duc duke
ducal ducal
duché dukedom
duchesse duchess
ductile ductile
duel duel
dune dune
duo duet
dupe dupe
duplicateur duplicator, stiff, tough
dur callous, hard
dur (au toucher) harsh
dur d'oreille hard of hearing
durabilité durability
durable durable, lasting
durant during
durcir harden, set

durcir, (se) toughen
dure besogne graft
durée duration, span, standing
durement callously, harshly
durer last
dureté callousness, hardness, harshness, steeliness, stoniness, toughness
durione durian
duvet down, fuzz
duveteux downy, fluffy
dynamique dynamic, dynamics
dynamiquement dynamically
dynamisme drive, push
dynamite dynamite
dynamo dynamo
dynastie dynasty
dynastique dynastic
dysenterie dysentery

Ee

eau water
eau de Cologne eau de cologne
eau de javel bleach
eau de toilette toilet water
eau de vaisselle dishwater
eau douce fresh water
eau gazéifiée soda water
eau minérale mineral water
eaux territoriales territorial waters
ébaucher rough out, sketch
ébène ebony
éberlué flabbergasted
éblouir dazzle
éblouissant dazzling
éboueur, euse refuse collector,
  scavenger
ébouillanter scald
ébouriffer ruffle
ébranler jar, shake
ébrécher chip
ébréchure chip
écaille scale
écailler, (s') flake, peel
écailleux scaly
écale shell
écarlate scarlet
écart deviation, swerve
écarté outlying
écartement gauge
écarter d'un geste wave aside
écarter de, s' stray
écarter, s' deviate, stand aside, step
  aside
ecchymose bruise
ecclésiastique clergyman,
  ecclesiastic(al), parson
ecchymose bruise
écervelé flighty, light-headed,
  scatterbrained, scatterbrain
échafaud scaffold
échafaudage scaffolding
échancrure(s) indentation
échange exchange, interchange,
  swap, swop
échangeable (contre) exchangeable
échanger change, exchange, swap,
  swop, trade
échangeur interchange
échantillon cross-section, sample
échappement exhaust
échapper (à) break away, elude,
  escape
échapper, (s') break loose, escape,
  get away
écharde splinter
écharpe scarf, sling
échasses stilts

échassier wader
échec check, failure
échec et mat checkmate
échecs chess
échelle ladder, scale
échelle de corde rope ladder
échelonner stagger, string out
écheveau hank
écho(s) echo, gossip column
échoué aground, high and dry
échouer break down, draw a blank,
  fall through, ground
échouer (à) fail
échouer, s' run aground
éclaboussement splash
éclabousser splash
éclaboussure splash
éclair bolt, eclair, flash, lightning,
  thunderbolt
éclairage lighting
éclairant illuminating
éclaircir throw light on, thin
éclaircir, (s') clear up, thin out
éclaircissement(s) enlightenment
éclairé enlightened
éclairer light, shed light on
éclairer (aux projecteurs)
  floodlight
éclairer (qqn sur qqch.) enlighten
éclairer, (s') brighten, lighten, light
  up
éclaireur, euse scout
éclat brightness, brilliance, glint,
  sparkle
éclat de rire guffaw
éclatant brilliant
éclatement blowout, burst
éclater bang, burst, explode, pop
éclats d'obus shrapnel
éclipse eclipse, outshine
éclipser overshadow, put in the
  shade
éclore hatch
écluse lock, sluice
écœurant disgusting, sickening
écœuré par sick
écœurement disgust
écœurer disgust, nauseate, sicken
école school
école d'équitation riding school
école du soir night school
école maternelle kindergarten
école primaire primary school,
  elementary school
école secondaire high school
écolier, ière pupil, schoolchild
écologie ecology
écologique ecological
écologiquement ecologically
écologiste ecologist

économe economical, sparing,
  thrifty
économie economy, saving, thrift,
  thriftiness
économies savings
économie politique economics
économique economic
économiquement economically
économiser economize, save, save
  up, skimp on
économiseur saver
économiste economist
écoper bale
écorce bark, crust, peel
écorcher bark, graze, jar, skin
écorchure abrasion, graze
écorné dog-eared
écosser shell
écouler elapse
écouler, s' drain, elapse, intervene
écourter curtail
écouter hear, listen
écouter (indiscrètement)
  eavesdrop
écouteurs headphones
écoutille hatchway
écran screen
écrasant crushing, grinding,
  overwhelming
écraser crush, dwarf, grind down,
  mangle, overwhelm, press, run
  over, smash, stamp out, stub out
écraser du pied tread
écraser, s' crash
écrémer cream, skim
écrevisse crayfish
écrier, s' exclaim
écrire write
écrire en vitesse dash off
écrire/dessiner au crayon pencil
écrit diffamatoire libel
écriteau signboard
écrits writings
écriture entry, hand, handwriting,
  scripture, writing
écrivain, aine writer
écrou nut
écrouler, s' collapse
écume lather, scum, surf, froth
écureuil squirrel
écurie stable, stud
écusson shield
eczéma eczema
édenté toothless
édifice edifice
éditeur, trice publisher
édition edition, publishing
édition spéciale extra
éditorial editorial, leader
édredon eiderdown, quilt

éducatif educational
éducation breeding, upbringing
édulcorant sweetener
effacé mousy
effacer efface, erase, obliterate, rub out, wipe, wipe out
effectif membership
effectivement sure enough
effectuer effect
efféminé effeminate
effervescence effervescence, ferment
effervescent effervescent
effet effect, effects
efficace effective, effectual, efficacious, efficient, telling
efficacement effectively, efficiently, tellingly
efficacité efficacy, efficiency
effigie effigy
effiler, (s') taper
effilocher, (s') fray
efflanqué lanky
effleurer (un sujet) scratch the surface
effluent effluent
effondrer, s' cave in, collapse, give way, go (all) to pieces, slump
efforcer (de), s' endeavour
efforcer de, s' strive
efforcer, (s') exert
effort effort, exertion, haul, stroke
effrayant fearful, frightening
effrayé afraid, frightened
effrayer frighten
effronté brash, brazen, cheeky, impudent
effrontément impudently, shamelessly
effronterie cheekiness, effrontery, gall, impudence, shamelessness
effroyable frightful
effusion de sang bloodshed
égal even, fifty-fifty
égal, ale equal
également equally, evenly
égaler equal
égaliser equalise, equalize, even, even out, even up, level
égalité equality, evenness, smoothness
égard regard, respect
égaré astray
égarer mislay, misplace, wander
égayer, s' cheer up
églefin haddock
église church
égo ego
égocentrique egocentric, self-centred

égoïsme egoism, selfishness
égoïste egoist, egoistic, egoistical, selfish
égoïstement selfishly
égout sewer, drain
égoutter strain off
égouttoir draining board
égratigner scratch
éhonté shameless
éjecter, (s') eject
élaboration elaboration
élaborer hammer out
élan dart, elk
élancement twinge
élancer shoot, throb
élargir, s' broaden
élasticité elasticity, give, spring, springiness
élastique elastic, elastic band, rubber band, springy
électeur, trice constituent, elector, voter
élection(s) election
élection poll
élections election
électoral electoral
électorat electorate
électricien, ienne electrician
électricité electricity
électrification electrification
électrifié electrified
électrifier electrify
électrique electric, electrical
électriquement electrically
électrisant electric, electrifying
électriser electrify
électrocuter electrocute
électrode electrode
électroménager appliance
électron electron
électronique electronic, electronics
élégamment fashionably, stylishly
élégance elegance, stylishness
élégant elegant, smart, sophisticated, sporting, stylish
élégie elegy
élément element
élément nutritif nutrient
élémentaire basic, elementa
éléphant elephant
élevage culture
élévation elevation
élevé lofty, towering
élève student
élève officier cadet
élever breed, bring up, foster, nurture, raise, rear, take up
élever à, s' total
élever au carré square
élever la voix raise one's voice

élever, (s') lift
élever, s' ascend, lift, rise
élimé threadbare
élimination elimination
éliminer eliminate, knock out
élingue sling
élire elect
élite elite
élixir elixir
elle she, it, her
elles they, them
ellipse ellipse
elliptique elliptical
élocution elocution
éloge(s) praise
éloigné distant, out of the way, remote
éloignement remoteness
éloigner (de), s' get off
éloquemment eloquently
éloquence eloquence
éloquent eloquent, meaning
élucider puzzle out, solve
émaciation gauntness
émacié gaunt
émail enamel
émanation emanation
émancipation emancipation
émanciper emancipate
emballage packing
emballer pack up, sweep (someone) off his feet
emballer, s' bolt
embarcadère jetty
embarcation craft
embardée lurch
embargo embargo
embarquement embarkation
embarquer, (s') embark
embarras difficulty, discomfiture, embarrassment, fix, quandary
embarrassant, ante embarrassing
embarrassé at a loss, sheepish
embarrasser embarrass
embaucher engage, hire, take on
embaumer embalm, perfume
embellir beautify
embêter hassle, worry
emblématique emblematic
emblème emblem
embobiner get round
emboîter slot
embonpoint fatness
embouteillage jam, traffic jam
emboutir ram
embranchement fork
embrasé alight
embrasser, (s') kiss
embrayage, (pédale d') clutch
embrouillé garbled, muddled

embrouiller confuse, mix up, muddle, tangle
embryologie embryology
embryologique embryological
embryologiste embryologist
embryon embryo
embryonnaire embryonic
embuer fog, cloud
embuer, (s') steam up, mist over/up
embuscade ambush
éméché tipsy
émeraude emerald
émerger emerge
émeri emery
émerveillement wonder
émerveiller (de), s' marvel (at)
émetteur-récepteur portatif walkie-talkie
émettre emit
émeute riot
émietter, (s') crumble
émigrant, ante emigrant
émigration emigration
émigrer emigrate, migrate
éminent eminent
émission broadcast, telecast
emmagasiner stock up
emmêlé matted
emmêler entangle, tangle
emménager move in
emmener take (away, out)
emmener d'urgence rush
emmitoufler, s' wrap up
émoi flurry, fluster, flutter, turmoil
émonder lop, prune
émotif emotional
émotion emotion, feeling, thrill
émoussé blunt
émousser blunt
émouvant moving
émouvoir move
empailler stuff
empaler (sur) impale
empaquetage packing
empaqueter bundle, package
emparer brusquement de, s' snatch
emparer de, s' hijack
empêcher inhibit, interfere with, prevent, stop
empêcher qqn d'entrer keep out
empêcher qqn de sortir keep in
empereur emperor
empeser starch
emphase pompousness
empiètement (sur) encroachment
empiéter sur encroach
empiffrer (s') stuff
empiler pile, stack
empiler (de) heap

empire empire
empirer empire, go from bad to worse, worsen
emplacement position, site, situation
emploi employment, situation
employé employed, employee
employé, ée (de bureau) clerk
employé, ée de maison domestic help
employer employ, use
employeur, euse employer
emplumé feathered
emplumer feather
empocher pocket
empoigner grasp
empois stiffening
empoisonner poison
empoisonneur, euse poisoner
emporter carry off, take away, take out
empourprer, s' flame
empreinte impression, imprint
empreinte de pied footmark, footprint
empreinte digitale fingerprint
empreinte du pouce thumbprint
empressement alacrity
empresser (de), s' hasten
emprise hold
emprisonnement confinement, imprisonment
emprisonner gaol, imprison, jail
emprunt borrowing, loan
emprunter borrow
emprunteur, euse borrower
émulation emulation
émulsion emulsion
en abondance profusely
en accord (en désaccord) avec in (out of) line with
en activité active
en amont up
en apparence ostensibly, outwardly
en appeler à appeal
en arrière backward
en attendant meantime
en aucun cas on no account
en aval downstream
en avance fast
en avant forth, forward
en avant (de) ahead
en avoir assez fed up
en bas downstairs
en berne at half mast
en bonne santé healthy
en bonnes mains in good hands
en bouton in bud
en cachette on the quiet
en cas de in case of

en ce moment at the moment
en ce qui concerne respecting
en chair et en os in the flesh
en chaleur in/on heat
en colère angry
en congé off
en connaissance de cause with one's eyes open
en conséquence accordingly
en contact (avec) in touch (with)
en contrebas sunken
en cours in progress, on, ongoing, under way
en déclin on the ebb
en dents de scie serrated
en dépit de in the face of, notwithstanding
en dernier last
en désaccord avec out of line with
en déséquilibre off balance
en désordre helter-skelter, straggly, tangled
en détail in detail
en deuil bereaved
en direct live
en disgrâce in the doghouse
en douceur smoothly
en échange (de) in return (for)
en éclaireur in advance
en effet indeed
en émoi agog
en entier in full
en état d'arrestation under arrest
en état de marche in action, functional, roadworthy
en face de facing, opposite
en faillite bankrupt
en fait actually, as a matter of fact, in fact, in point of fact
en faveur de in favour of
en feu/flammes on fire
en fin de compte after all, in the end, in the event, in the long run
en finir avec have done with, hear/see the last of
en flammes ablaze
en flèche steeply
en fleur in flower
en fonction de in terms of
en formation in the making
en forme fit
en friche fallow
en fuite on the run
en gage in pawn
en général at large, generally speaking, in general
en gros in bulk, wholesale
en haut above
en herbe budding
en imagination in one's mind's eye

en jeu at stake, in play
en l'air aloft
en larmes/pleurs in tears
en liberté at large
en lieu sûr out of harm's way
en long et en large at length
en loques/lambeaux tattered, in tatters
en marche on the move, on
en marge out of it
en mauvaise santé unhealthy
en même temps at the same time
en (mille) morceaux in pieces
en moins de inside
en mouvement/marche in motion
en ordre in order, shipshape
en paix at peace, in peace
en panne dead, off
en particulier in particular
en partie partly, in part
en passant by the way, in passing
en personne as large as life, in person
en phase terminale terminal
en pièces détachées in pieces
en pied full-length
en plan high and dry
en plein fair and square, full, square
en plein air in the open air
en pleurant tearfully
en plomb leaden
en plus de as well as
en poudre powdered
en premier lieu firstly
en prendre à, s' get at, go on at, round on
en préparation afoot
en principe in principle, technically
en privé privately, in private
en profondeur in-depth
en promotion on offer
en proportion de in proportion to
en public in public
en puissance potential, potentially
en pure perte to no purpose
en question in question
en raison de owing to
en réalité in effect, in reality, really
en règle générale as a general rule, as a rule
en réserve in store
en résidence in residence
en résumé in brief
en retard belated, in arrears, late, overdue
en route (pour) en route
en sang bloody
en silence dumbly, in silence, mutely
en son for intérieur inwardly

en suspens (in) abeyance, open, undecided
en tant que as
en temps voulu duly
en tenir à, s' stick to/with
en tête (de) at the top
en tirer à bon compte, s' get off lightly
en tout in all
en tout premier lieu first and foremost
en toute bonne foi in (all) good faith
en toute justice by right(s)
en un mot in a nutshell
en un temps record in record time
en uniforme uniformed
en vacances on holiday, on vacation
en vain in vain
en vedette in the limelight
en venir au fait come to the point, get down to brass tacks
en vigueur active, effective, in effect, in, into force, operative
en voie de développement emergent
en vol airborne, in flight
en vrac loose
en vrille beady
en vue in the offing, with an eye to something
en-tête heading
en/au/vers le haut up
en/hors de service in/out of commission
encadrer frame
encaisser cash
encan auction
encapuchonné hooded
enceinte compound, expectant, precinct, pregnant
encens incense
encercler circle, encircle, hem in
enchaîner chain
enchanté enchanted, overjoyed
enchanté de enamoured
enchantement magic
enchanter delight, enrapture
enchanteur bewitching, enchanter, magical
enchère bidding
enchevêtrement entanglement
enclencher, (s') interlock
enclin à given (to)
enclos enclosure, paddock, pen
enclume anvil
encocher notch
encolure neckline
encombrant cumbersome, unwieldy

encombré cluttered, congested
encombrement congestion
encore again, even, over again, still, yet
encorner gore
encourageant encouraging, hopeful
encouragement encouragement, incentive
encourager cheer, encourage, hearten
encourager (à) encourage
encrassé grimy
encre ink
encrier inkpot, inkwell
encyclopédie encyclop(a)edia
encyclopédique encyclop(a)edic
endémique endemic
endetté in debt
endiguer dam
endimancher, s' dress up
endoctrinement indoctrination
endoctriner indoctrinate
endolori sore
endommagé damaged
endommager damage
endormi asleep, sleepy
endormir put to sleep, fall asleep
endormir, s' drop off
endosser endorse, shoulder
endroit place, spot
endurance endurance, stamina
endurer put up with
endurcir, (s') toughen
énergie energy
énergie nucléaire atomic energy, atomic power, nuclear energy
énergique drastic, energetic, stout
énergiquement energetically
énervé edgy, fidget, nervy, on edge
énervement edginess, nerviness
enfance childhood, boyhood
enfant child, kid
enfant abandonnée, ée waif
enfant adoptif, ive foster-child
enfantillage childishness
enfantin babyish, childish
enfer hell
enfermé closeted
enfermer confine, shut
enfermer (à l'intérieur) lock in
enfermer dans encase
enfiler draw on, pull on, slip into, slip on, string, thread
enfin at (long) last, at length, finally, lastly
enflammé inflamed
enflammer fire, inflame
enflammer, (s') catch fire, flare up, ignite
enflé swollen

enfler puff up, swell
enflure swelling
enfoncer break down, dig, embed, fix, jab, plunge, ram, shove, stick, thrust
enfoncer (dans) poke
enfouir bury
enfreindre infringe
enfuir, s' run away
enfuir (de), s' fly
enfuir (ensemble), s' elope
enfumé smoky
engagé (à) committed
engageant engaging
engagement involvement
engager engage, commit
engager, (s') contract, enlist, join up
engager (à/dans), s' let in for
engager des poursuites (contre) proceed
engendrer father
engin spatial spacecraft
engloutir engulf, gobble, gulp, swallow up
engouement craze
engourdi asleep, numb
engourdir numb
engourdissement numbness
engrais fertilizer
engraisser fatten
engrenage gear
engrenner, s' engage
engueulade telling-off
engueuler tick (someone) off, give (someone) a ticking off
énigmatique cryptic, enigmatic
énigme enigma, puzzle
enivrant intoxicating
enivrer, (s') intoxicate
enjeu stake
enjoindre (de) bid
enjôleur beguiling
enjoliver embellish
enjoliveur hubcap
enjoué kittenish, lighthearted
enlèvement abduction, clearance, disposal
enlever abduct, clear out, get off, remove, strip, throw off
enluminé illuminated
enluminure illumination
ennemi hostile
ennemi, ie enemy, foe
ennuager, s' cloud
ennui boredom, bother, tediousness, tedium
ennuyer bore, bother
ennuyeux boring, dreary, dull, flat, tedious, tiresome

énorme enormous, huge, thundering, tremendous
énormément no end (of), hugely, tremendously
énormité enormity, exorbitance, flagrancy, hugeness
enquête inquest, inquiry, investigation, probe
enquête sur le terrain fieldwork
enquêter (sur) enquire, inquire, investigate, probe
enquêteur, euse investigator
enraciner, (s') root
enrégimenter regiment
enregistrement recording, tape-recording
enregistrer record, register, tape, tape-record
enregistrer au magnétoscope video
enrichir enrich
enrôler conscript, rope in, enroll
enroué hoarse, husky
enrouement hoarseness, huskiness
enrouler coil, roll, wind wind up
enrouler, s' curl
ensanglanté bloody
enseignant, ante teacher
enseigne signboard
enseignement instruction, teaching
enseignement supérieur higher education
enseigner teach, tutor
ensemble complex, ensemble, jointly, set, suite, together
ensemencer (en) sow
ensoleillé sunny, sunlit
ensoleillement sunniness
ensorceler bewitch, enchant
ensorcellement enchantment
ensuite next, then
entaille hack, nick, slash
entasser cramp, crush, heap, squash
entasser, (s') bunch, pack, pile up
entasser (dans), s' crowd
entendre hear, get along
entendre à rire take a joke
entendre avec, s' fit in
entendre bien (avec), s' get on (with), hit it off
entendre par hasard overhear
entendre raison listen to reason, see reason
entendu knowing
entente concord, understanding
enterrement burial, interment
enterrer bury, inter
enterrer la hache de guerre bury the hatchet
en-tête heading

entêté pigheaded, wilful
entêtement pigheadedness, wilfulness
enthousiasme enthusiasm, enthuse, zest
enthousiaste enthusiast, rapturous, warm-blooded
entier entire, full, whole
entièrement altogether, entirely, throughout, unreservedly
entonnoir filler, funnel
entorse strain
entortillement kink
entourage entourage
entourer enclose, ring, surround
entracte intermission, interval
entrailles bowel, entrails, guts
entrain dash, gusto, liveliness, pep, perkiness, zest
entraînement training
entraîner bring about, lead
entraîner, s' practise, train, work out
entraîneur, euse coach, instructor, trainer
entrave drag, fetter
entraver hamper, impede
entre among, amongst, between
entre les mains de at the hands of, in the hands of
entre nous between you and me
entre-temps meanwhile
entrebâillement crack
entrechoquer, s' clash
entrecroisé criss-cross
entrée admission, admittance, entrance, entree, entry, hall, way
entrée non autorisée trespass
entrelacer, (s') entwine
entremets dessert
entreposage storage
entreposer store
entrepôt store, storehouse, storeroom, warehouse
entrepreneur, eure contractor, entrepreneur
entrepreneur, eure de pompes funèbres undertaker
entreprise concern, enterprise, undertaking
enterprise privée private enterprise
enterprise risquée gamble, venture
entrer (dans) enter, enter into
entrer dans l'histoire go down, make history
entrer dans les détails de elaborate
entrer en collision collide
entrer en rapport avec relate (to)
entrer en scène come on
entrer en service enter

entrer en vigueur come into effect
entrer par effraction (dans) break in (to)
entrer par une oreille et sortir par l'autre go in one ear and out the other
entretenir confer, keep, keep up, maintain
entretien keep, maintenance, service, upkeep
entrevoir see
entrevue interview
entrouvert ajar
énumération enumeration
énumérer enumerate
envahir invade, overrun
envahisseur, euse invader
enveloppe envelope, husk
enveloppe de paie pay packet, wage packet
envelopper envelop, wrap
envenimer, (s') fester
envergure stature, winspan
envers toward, towards
enviable enviable
envie envy, fancy, longing
envier begrudge, envy
environ about, or so, round about
environnant surrounding
environnement environment, surroundings
environs surroundings
envisager envisage
envoi consignment
envoyé, ée envoy
envoyer send, refer
envoyer chercher send for
envoyer (par la poste) send out
envoyer promener send (someone) packing
épagneul spaniel
épais crass, thick
épaisseur ply, thickness
épaissir, (s') thicken
épanouir, s' blossom
épanouissement blossoming
épargne savings
épargner save, spare
éparpiller scatter, strew
éparpiller, s' spread out
épars scattered
épatant smashing, swell
épaule shoulder
épave shipwreck, wreck
épée sword
épeler spell
éperdument head over heels
éperon spur
éphémère short-lived
épi ear

épicé hot, spiced, spicy
épice spice
épicer spice
épicerie groceries
épicier, ière grocer
épidémie epidemic
épiderme skin
épier spy on
épilepsie epilepsy
épileptique epileptic
épiler pluck
épinard spinach
épine spine, thorn
épineux knotty, prickly, spiny, sticky, thorny
épingle pin
épingle de sûreté safety pin
épisode episode, instalment
éplucheur peeler
épluchures peelings
éponge sponge
épopée epic
époque age, epoch, era
épouser marry
épousseter dust, dust down
épouvantable appalling, awful, dreadful, fearful, frightful, shocking
épouvantablement appallingly
épouvantail fright, scarecrow
épouvanter appal
époux, ouse consort, spouse
éprendre de (s') fall in love with
épreuve event, experience, paper, print, proof, test
épreuve de force showdown
épreuve(s) hardship
éprouvant taxing
éprouver encounter, experience
éprouvette test-tube
épuisant gruelling
épuisé exhausted, fatigued, jaded, rundown, spent, washed-out, worn out
épuisement exhaustion
épuiser drain, exhaust, tire out, run out
équateur equator
équation equation
équatorial equatorial
équerre (à dessin) set-square
équestre equestrian
équilatéral equilateral
équilibre balance, equilibrium, footing, poise
équilibré level-headed
équilibrer, (s') balance
équinoxe equinox
équipage crew
équipe crew, gang, shift, team

équipe de nuit night shift
équipement equipment, gear, kit, rig
équiper fit, fit out
équiper (de) equip
équitable equitable
équitablement equitably
équitation horse-riding
équité equity
équivalent equivalent, tantamount
équivaloir amount to
érafler scrape
éraflure scrape, scratch
ère era, period
éreintant backbreaking
ermitage hermitage
ermite hermit
érosion erosion
érotique erotic
errant stray
erratum erratum
errer roam, wander
erreur error, miscarriage, mistake, misunderstanding
erreur de calcul miscalculation
erroné mistaken
érudit scholarly, scholar
érudition scholarliness, scholarship
éruption blowout, eruption, rash
escabeau steps, stepladder
escadron squadron
escalade escalation
escalader climb, scale
escale (faire) stop over
escalier staircase, stairway
escalier de secours fire escape
escalier roulant escalator
escamotable retractable
escargot snail
escarpé craggy, precipitous, steep
esclavage bondage, servitude, slavery
esclave slave
escorter escort
escouade squad
escrime fencing, sword-play
escroc con man, swindler, twister
escroquer con, swindle
escroquerie con, swindle
espace gap, space
espace (à remplir) blank
espacement spacing
espacer space
espadrille(s) sandshoes
espèce(s) species
espérance de vie life expectancy
espérance(s) expectation, hope
espérer hope, trust
espérer en dépit de tout hope against hope

espiègle impish, mischievous, playful
espion, onne spy
espionnage espionage
espionner spy
esplanade esplanade
espoir hope
esprit head, mind, spirit
esprit d'équipe team spirit
esprit d'imitation imitativeness
esprit d'initiative enterprise
esprit d'invention inventiveness
esprit de contradiction contrariness
esquisser draft
esquiver dodge, duck, sidestep
esquiver, s' make oneself scarce, slip off
essai effort, shot, touch down, trial, try
essaim hive, swarm
essayage fitting
essayer try on, try out
essayer (de) try
essayer d'égaler emulate
essayer de gagner du temps play for time
essayer de résoudre puzzle
essence essence, gasoline
essentiel essential, gist
essentiellement essentially
essieu axle
essor rise
essorer wring
essoreuse dryer, wringer
essoufflé breathless, puffed, out of breath
essoufflement breathlessness
essouffler, s' run out of steam
essui-glace wiper
essuyer brush away, dry, mop, towel, wipe
est east
estafette dispatch rider
estampille stamp
esthétique cosmetic
estimation estimate
estime esteem, regard
estimer count, esteem, estimate
estival summery
estomac stomach
estomaquer stump
estrade platform
estropié maim
estropier cripple, disable, lame
estuaire estuary
esturgeon sturgeon
et and, and so on/forth
et caetera etcetera
établi bench, established

établir ascertain, determine, establish, lay down, start off, quote, settle
établir, s' establish, settle
établissement establishment, institution
étage floor, stage, storey
étagère shelf
étain pewter, tin
étalage stand
étalagiste window dresser
étaler lay out, splash, spread, spread out
étaler, s' sprawl
étalon stallion
étamine stamen
étanche watertight
étancher quench
étang pond
étant donné given, seeing that
étape leg, stage
état state, status
étau vice
été summer, summertime
éteindre extinguish, put off, put out, quench
éteindre, s' die away, go out
éteint extinct
étendard standard
étendre, (s') extend, lie down, stretch, stretch out
étendue expanse, extent, spread, tract
éternel eternal, timeless
éternellement eternally, everlastingly
éternité age, a month of Sundays, eternity
éternuement sneeze
éternuer sneeze
éther ether
ethnique ethnic
ethnologie ethnology
ethnologique ethnological
ethnologue ethnologist
étincelant scintillating
étinceler sparkle
étincelle spark, sparkle
étiqueter brand, label
étiquette label, tab, tag, ticket
étirement stretch
étirer, (s') stretch
étoile star
étoilé starlit, starry
étoile de cinéma filmstar
étoile de mer starfish
étonnamment amazingly, surprisingly
étonnant astonishing, surprising
étonnement astonishment

étonner astonish, surprise, wonder
étouffant stifling
étouffement suffocation
étouffer hush up, smother, snuff out, stifle, suffocate
étouffer de chaleur swelter
étourderie thoughtlessness
étourdi dizzy, foolish, forgetful
étourdir daze
étourneau starling
étrange strange, weird
étrangement eerily, strangely
étranger (à) foreign
étranger, ère alien, foreigner, outsider, stranger
étrangeté eeriness, novelty, weirdness
étrangler strangle, throttle
étrangleur choke
étrave stem
être be
être à court de be low on, run short
être à égalité tie
être à l'origine de be at the bottom of
être à la hauteur be up to, make the grade, measure up
être à la tête (de) head
être absorbé sink in
être au pied du mur have one's back to the wall
être aux anges be tickled pink, be/feel at top of the world, walk on air
être aux prises engage
être brouillé be at odds
être capable de have it in oneself
être d'accord avec agree, go along with
être d'avis que be of the opinion (that)
être dans... jusqu'au cou be up to the eyes in
être de mèche avec be hand in glove (with someone)
être débarrassé de be quit of, be rid of
être découvert come to light
être dépourvu de be lacking
être destiné à intend (for)
être disposé à be inclined to
être dur avec be hard on
être emballé (par) be sold on, enthuse
être en désaccord (avec) disagree (with)
être en face de face
être en forme be in good form
être en minorité be in the minority
être en place be in position
être en position d'attaque be on the offensive

être en retard be behind time, fall behind
être en rupture de stock be sold out
être en voix be in good voice
être énervé be/get wound up
être fier de pride oneself on
être florissant flourish
être hors de propos be beside the point
être hors de soi fume
être humain human being
être injuste envers be hard on, do (someone) an injustice
être l'artisan de engineer
être le secret de Polichinelle be an open secret
être ligué avec qqn be in league with
être mêlé (à) be mixed up with
être mêlé à to do with
être obligé (de) have to
être occupé à be up to
être originaire de hail from
être plus nombreux que outnumber
être pour qqch. dans have a hand in (something)
être résolu à be out to
être serré feel the pinch
être sur le point de be about to, be on the point of
être sur les rangs (pour) in line for
être tout oreilles be all ears
être/se mettre dans le pétrin be in/get into hot water
étreindre embrace, hug
étreinte embrace, hug, squeeze
étriers stirrups
étriller curry
étroit narrow
étroitesse tightness
étude study
étude (sur) project
études education
étudiant, ante student
étudier explore, study
étudier en détail go into
étui de revolver holster
eucalyptus eucalyptus
euphémique euphemistic
euphémisme euphemism
euthanasie euthanasia
eux them
évacuation evacuation
évacuer evacuate, expel
évader, s' break out
évader (de), s' escape
évaluation assessment, evaluation
évaluer assess, estimate, evaluate,

gauge
évaluer (à) value at
évangélique evangelical
évangéliste evangelist
évangile gospel
évanouir, s' faint, swoon
évanouissement faint, swoon
évaporation evaporation
évaporer, (s') evaporate
évaser, (s') flare
évasif evasive
évasion escape
évasivement evasively
évêché see
éveillé awake, wakeful
éveiller arouse, rouse
événement event, happening, occasion, occurrence
évent blowhole, vent
éventail fan
éventaire stall
éventé flat
éventer, (s') fan
éventualité contingency, eventuality
évêque bishop
évidemment evidently, obviously
évident apparent, evident, manifest, obvious
évier sink
évincer oust
éviter avoid, evade, fight shy of, sidestep
évocateur evocative
évocation evocation
évoluer evolve
évolution evolution
évolutionniste evolutionary
évoquer evoke
exact accurate, correct, exact, true
exactement accurately, exactly, just, to a nicety
exactitude accuracy, exactness
exagération exaggeration
exagérer exaggerate, overdo
exalté, ée hothead
exalter elevate, extol, glorify
examen examination, survey
examen minutieux scrutiny
examen(s) (de fin d'études) finals
examinateur, trice examiner
examiner examine, go into, go over, look into, screen, study
examiner (de près) inspect, vet
exaspérant infuriating, maddening
exaspération aggravation, exasperation
exaspérer aggravate, exasperate, gall
excavatrice digger, excavator

excédent (de) excess
excellence excellence
excellent capital, excellent, lovely, professional, tip-top
exceller (en) excel
excentricité crankiness, eccentricity, quirk
excentrique crank, cranky, eccentric, oddity
exception exception, odd man out/odd one out
exceptionnel bumper, exceptional, out of the ordinary, outstanding, special, unusual
exceptionnellement exceptionally, unusually
excès excess
excessif excessive, extravagant, steep, unreasonable
excessivement excessively
excitabilité excitability
excitant exciting
excitation excitement
excité excited, manic
exciter excite, thrill
exciter la convoitise de tantalize
exclamation ejaculation, exclamation, interjection
exclamer, s' ejaculate, exclaim
exclure rule out
exclure (de) bar, except, exclude
exclusif cliqu(e)y, cliquish, exclusive, sole
exclusion exclusion
exclusivement exclusively
excrément excrement
excréter excrete
excrétion excretion
excroissance growth
excursion excursion, hike
excursionniste hiker
excusable excusable
excuse(s) apology, excuse
excuser apologize, excuse
exécrable accursed
exécuter execute, perform, put to death
exécuteur, trice testamentaire executor
exécutif executive
exécution execution, performance
exemplaire copy, exemplary
exemple example, illustration, instance
exempté (de) exempt
exempter (de) exempt
exemption exemption
exercer exercise, exert, wield
exercer (à), s' practise
exercer (un métier) ply

exercice drill, exercise, exertion, practice
exhalation exhalation
exhiber parade, sport
exhiber rapidement flash
exhortation exhortation
exhorter exhort, urge
exhumation exhumation
exhumer exhume
exigeant demanding, particular
exigence demand, requirement
exiger call for, demand, expect, require
exigu poky, pokey
exil exile
existence being, existence
exister exist
exode exodus
exorbitant exorbitant, extortionate
exorciser exorcize, exorcise
exorcisme exorcism
exorciste exorcist
exotique exotic
expansif effusive
expatrié, ée expatriate
expédier dispatch, pack off
expédier par exprès express
expéditeur, trice sender, shipper
expéditif expeditious
expédition dispatch, expedition
expédition de secours search party
expéditionnaire expeditionary
expéditivement expeditiously
expérience experience, experiment
expérimental experimental
expérimentalement experimentally
expérimentation experimentation
expérimenté experienced, practised, seasoned
expérimenter experiment
expert adept, assessor, consultant, expert
expert (à/en) adept

expiration expiration
expirer exhale, expire, lapse
explicable explicable
explicatif explanatory, illustrative
explication elucidation, explanation
explicite express
explicitement explicitly
expliquer elucidate, explain, expound, have it out
exploit exploit, stunt
exploitation exploitation
exploitation (agricole) farming
exploiter exploit, harness, tap
explorateur, trice explorer
exploration exploration
exploratoire exploratory
explorer explore
exploser blow up, explode, go off
explosif explosive
explosion blast, blaze, explosion, outburst
exportateur, trice exporter
exportation export
exporter export
exposant index, exhibitor
exposé dissertation, exposition, on show, on view, talk
exposer display, exhibit, expose
exposition aspect, display, exhibition, exposure, show
exprès deliberately, on purpose, purposely
express express, expressly
expressément specifically
expressif expressive
expression expression
expression fractionnaire improper fraction
expression toute faite set phrase
expressivité expressiveness
exprimer air, embody, express, phrase, voice
exprimer, (s') express

expulser deport, eject, expel
expulser (de) evict, expel
expulsion deportation, ejection, eviction, expulsion
exquis exquisite
extase ecstasy
extasié ecstatic
extasier sur, s' rave
extensible stretchy
extension extension
extérieur exterior, outer, outside
extérieurement externally
extermination extermination
exterminer exterminate, kill off
externat day school
externe external
extincteur extinguisher, fire-extinguisher
extinction extinction
extirper fish out, root out
extorquer extort
extorsion extortion
extraction extraction
extrader extradite
extradition extradition
extraire extract, quarry, winkle
extrait excerpt, extract
extraordinaire extraordinary, fantastic
extraordinairement extraordinarily, fantastically
extraterrestre extraterrestrial
extravagant fanciful
extrême extreme
extrêmement exceedingly, extremely, highly
extrémisme extremism
extrémiste extreme, extremist
extrémité(s) extremity
extroverti, ie extrovert
exubérance exuberance
exubérant exuberant, gushing
exultation exultation

Ff

fable fable

fabricant, ante maker, manufacturer

fabrication fabrication, making, manufacture

fabrication en série mass production

fabrique mill, manufacture

fabriquer en série mass-produce

fabuleusement fabulously

fabuleux fabulous

fac-similé facsimile

façade facade, frontage

face face, heads

face à face face to face

facétieusement facetiously

facétieux facetious

facette facet

fâché angry, displeased, peeved, shirty, sore, upset

fâcher (avec), se fall out (with)

facial facial

facile easy, fluent

facile à retenir catchy

facile à vivre good-natured

facilement easily, readily

facilité ease, easiness, facility

façon fashion

façon de gift of the gab

façon de parler figure of speech

façonner mould, shape

facteur factor, mailman, postman

factice dummy

faction faction

facture bill, invoice

facturer (à) bill

facultatif optional

faculté faculty, school

fade tasteless

faible dim, faint, feeble, helpless, slim, weak

faible lueur glimmer

faiblement dimly, faintly, feebly, wanly, weakly

faiblesse debility, dimness, faintness, helplessness, weakness

faiblir flag

faïence earthenware

faille fault

failli, ie bankrupt

faillible fallible

faillir fail

faillite bankruptcy, crash

faim hunger, hungriness

fainéant bone idle, idle, shiftless

fainéant, ante drone, layabout, lazy-bones, loafer

fainéantise shiftlessness

faire do, make

faire (tout) beau, se spruce up

faire à son gré suit oneself

faire allusion (à) allude (to), refer (to)

faire appel appeal, draw on

faire attention pay heed to, take care, take heed of, watch one's step

faire bien comprendre (qqch. à qqn) impress (on, upon)

faire campagne pour canvass (for)

faire chanter blackmail

faire chavirer overturn

faire claquer ses doigts snap one's fingers

faire comprendre, (se) get across, get over, get through, make (oneself) understood

faire concurrence aux voisins keep up with the Joneses

faire contre mauvaise fortune bon cœur grin and bear it, make the best of a bad job, put a good face on it

faire couin-couin quack

faire de grands progrès make great strides

faire de l'escrime fence

faire de l'exercice exercise

faire de la contrebande smuggle

faire de la course de haies hurdle

faire de la prestidigitation conjure

faire de son mieux do one's best, do one's level best

faire démarrer (qqch.) get (something) off the ground

faire des affaires d'or do a roaring trade

faire des caresses à qqn nuzzle

faire des fouilles (dans) excavate

faire des grimaces make/pull a face, pull a face/faces (at)

faire des histoires fuss

faire des progrès get ahead, progress

faire des recherches research

faire don de donate

faire du bien à benefit

faire du bon travail cover ground

faire du mal (à) harm, hurt

faire du piquetage picket

faire du somnanbulisme sleepwalk

faire du stop hitch hike

faire du tort à prejudice

faire durer eke

faire écho à echo

faire échouer foil, frustrate

faire enrager enrage

faire entrer qqch. dans la tête de qqn hammer

faire entrer/sortir let in/out

faire éruption erupt

faire escale stop over

faire étalage de flaunt

faire face (à) come to terms, cope, face the music, face up to

faire faillite crash

faire faire ses études à educate

faire fête à fawn

faire feu fire

faire fonction de act as

faire fortune strike it rich

faire gicler squirt

faire grand cas de make much of, set (great) store by

faire honte à disgrace, shame, put to shame

faire irruption burst

faire l'affaire fill the bill, do the trick

faire l'amour make love

faire l'autruche bury one's head in the sand

faire l'école buissonnière play truant

faire l'éloge de praise

faire l'honneur de honour

faire l'imbécile fool (about/around)

faire l'important talk big

faire l'interprète interpret

faire la connaissance de meet, make someone's acquaintance

faire la critique de review

faire la différence (entre) differentiate (between)

faire la grasse matinée lie in

faire la grève perlée go slow

faire la liste de list

faire la loi dictate, lay down the law, rule the roost

faire la moue pout

faire la paix make peace

faire la quête pass/send round the hat

faire la queue (pour) queue, queue up

faire la sourde oreille à turn a deaf ear to

faire le commerce de deal

faire le dégoûté devant turn up one's nose at

faire le jeu de play into someone's hands

faire le pitre play the fool

faire le plein fill up

faire le portrait de portray

faire le(s) fou(s) lark about/around

faire le/son lit make a/one's bed

faire les choses à moitié do things by halves

faire long feu misfire
faire mal ache
faire marcher qqn have on, lead on, pull someone's leg
faire match nul draw
faire naufrage shipwreck
faire opposition à oppose
faire partie (de) belong, crew (for), form
faire partir (une fusée) set off
faire passer pour, (se) masquerade, pass (something or someone) off as, pose
faire payer charge
faire peu de cas de qqch. make little of
faire peur (à) scare
faire plaisir, se indulge
faire pression sur lobby
faire rage rage
faire remarquer point out
faire sa part do one's bit, keep one's end up
faire saillie project, protrude
faire sauter blast
faire semblant (de) feign, make believe, pretend, sham
faire sensation make a hit with
faire signe à beckon, flag down, gesture, wave
faire son chemin make one's way
faire son effet take effect
faire son nid nest
faire souffrir hurt, pain
faire suivre forward, re-address
faire surface surface
faire table rase de make a clean sweep
faire taire silence
faire tinter clink, tinkle
faire tomber pushover
faire (tout) beau, se spruce up
faire tout son possible (pour) do one's utmost (to)
faire un brin de toilette freshen (up)
faire un devoir de, se make a point of
faire un double de duplicate
faire un exemple de make an example of
faire un flop flop
faire un lob lob
faire un nom, se make a name for oneself
faire un peu de (en amateur) dabble
faire un saut à nip
faire un signe de (la) tête nod
faire un trou dans poke

faire un/des jeu(x) de mots pun
faire une descente dans raid
faire une digression digress
faire une embardée lurch, sheer
faire une gaffe blunder, drop a brick/drop a clanger
faire une injection inject
faire une razzia raid
faire une rechute relapse
faire vieux, se get on
faire vite make haste
faire-valoir stooge
faire/passer une boucle loop
faisabilité feasibility
faisable feasible, manageable
faisan, ane pheasant
fait fact
fait à la hâte hasty
fait à la main handmade
fait à la maison homemade
fait pour suited
fait sur commande made to order
fait sur mesure made to measure, tailor-made
faîte crown, ridge
faits et gestes doings
falaise cliff
fallacieux fallacious
falsification falsification
falsifier falsify
familial domestic
familiale station wagon
familiariser (avec) familiarize (with)
familiarité familiarity
familier chatty, colloquial, familiar, informal
familièrement colloquially, familiarly
famille family, folks, kin
famine famine
fanatique fanatic, fanatical
fanatiquement fanatically
fanatisme fanaticism
faner, (se) wilt, wither
fanfare brass band, fanfare
fantaisie fancy, fantasy
fantasque fanciful
fantastique fantastic, stupendous
fantomatique ghostly
fantôme ghost, phantom
faon fawn
farce farce, practical joke, prank, stuffing
farceur, euse joker
farcir stuff
fard blush
fard à paupières eyeshadow
fardeau burden, tax
farine flour, meal

farine de maïs cornflour, cornstarch
farineux mealy
fascinant fascinating
fascination fascination
fasciner fascinate
fasciste fascist
fatal fatal
fatalement fatally
fatalisme fatalism
fataliste fatalist, fatalistic
fatidique fateful
fatigant strenuous, tiring
fatigue fatigue, tiredness, weariness
fatigué tired, weary
fatiguer, (se) tire, weary
fauché broke
faucher mow, mow down, scythe
faucille sickle
faucon falcon, hawk
faufil tack
faufiler, se thread, weave, worm
faune faun, fauna, wildlife
faussé warped
fausse alerte false alarm
fausse couche miscarriage
faussement deceitfully, erroneously
fausser pervert, skew
fausser compagnie à give (someone) the slip
fausset falsetto
fausseté deceitfulness, erroneousness, falsity, untruth
faute fault, lapse, mistake
faute de prononciation mispronunciation
fauteuil armchair, easy chair
fauteuil roulant bathchair, wheeelchair
fauteur, trice de troubles troublemaker
fautif at fault
fauve fawn, tan, tawny
faux bogus, counterfeit, erroneous, fake, false, forgery, out of tune, phon(e)y, scythe, sham, untrue
faux col head
faux départ false start
faux nom alias
faux-bourdon drone
faveur favour
favorable favourably
favorablement favourably
favori favourite, sideburns
favoriser foster, further
favoritisme favouritism
faïence earthenware
fébrile feverish
fèces feces
fécond fertile

féconder pollinate
fécule starch
féculent starchy
fédéral federal
fédération federation
fédéré federated
fée fairy
feindre counterfeit
feint assumed, put-on
feinte blind
fêlé cracked
fêler, (se) crack
félicitations congratulation, felicitations
félicité blessedness, felicity
féliciter congratulate
félin cat, feline
fêlure crack
femelle female
féminin feminine
féminisme feminism
féministe feminist
féminité femininity, womanliness
femme wife, woman
femme de chambre chambermaid
fémur femur
fendre cleave, slit
fendre, (se) split
fenêtre window
fente chink, slit, slot, split
féodal feudal, feudalism
fer iron
fer à cheval horseshoe
fer à repasser iron
fer à souder soldering iron
fer droit putter
ferler (une voile) furl
fermé exclusive, shut
ferme farm, secure, steady
ferme (avec dépendances) homestead
ferme laitière dairy farm
fermement firmly, steadfastly
fermentation fermentation
fermenter ferment
fermer close, close down, close up, shut, shut off, shut up, turn off, turn out
fermer à clef lock
fermer d'un coup sec, (se) snap
fermer les yeux sur close one's eyes to, overlook, turn a blind eye
fermer (ses portes) shut down
fermeté decisiveness
fermeture closure
fermeture éclair zip, zip fastener, zipper
fermier, ière farmer
fermoir clasp
féroce ferocious, fierce, savage

férocement ferociously, fiercely
férocité ferocity
ferraille scrap
fers irons, shackles
fertile fertile, productive
fertilisation fertilization
fertiliser fertilize
fertilité fertility
fervent devout, fervent, keen
ferveur fervour
fesse buttock
fessée hiding
festin feast
festival festival
festivité festivity, revelry
festonné scalloped
festoyer feast
fête celebration, feast, festival, party
fête légale public holiday
fêter celebrate
fétiche charm, fetish
fétide fetid
feu fire, light
feu arrière tail light
feu avant headlight
feu d'artifice firework
feu de camp campfire
feu (de joie) bonfire
feu vert the green light
feuillage foliage
feuille leaf, sheet
feuille d'or gold leaf
feuille/papier d'aluminium foil
feuilleter browse, dip into, flip, thumb
feuilleton serial, soap opera
feuillu leafy
feutre felt
feux d'artifice pyrotechnics
feux de circulation traffic lights
fève bean
février February
fiable reliable, safe
fiançailles betrothal, engagement
fiancé betrothed, engaged
fiancé, ée fiancé
fiancer (à) betroth (to)
fiasco fiasco
fibre fibre
fibre de verre fibreglass
fibres végétales matting
fibreux fibrous
ficeler truss
ficelle string, twine
ficher de, se not care a hoot/two hoots
ficher le camp push off
fichier file
fichu down the drain

fictif fictitious
fidèle accurate, constant, faithful, retentive, true, trusty, worshipper
fidèlement faithfully, trustily
fidélité allegiance, faithfulness, fidelity, trustworthiness, trustiness
fiduciaire trustee
fiducie trust
fier proud
fier (se) to rely on
fièrement proudly
fierté pride
fiesta fiesta
fièvre fever, temperature
fiévreusement feverishly
fiévreux feverish
fifre fife
figer, (se) congeal
figer sur place freeze
figue fig
figurant, ante extra
figuré figurative
figure figure
figure de proue figurehead
figurer figure
figurine figurine
fil cord, flex, grain, string, thread, wire, yarn
filament filament
filandreux stringy
file file, queue
filer fly, make tracks (for), scoot, spin, tail
filer (à toute allure) race
filer qqn shadow
filet fillet, loin, net, streak, wreath
filetage thread
filial filial
filiale subsidiary
filière channel
fille daughter, girl
filleul godchild, goddaughter
film film, motion picture, movie, picture
filmer film
fils son
fils de la vierge gossamer
filtre filter
filtrer seep, strain
fin acute, close, delicate, end, ending, fine, subtle, termination, wispy
fin d'alerte all-clear
finale final, finale
finalement eventually, finally
finaliser finalize
finaliste finalist
finalité finality
finance finance
financier financial, financier

financièrement financially
fin de semaine weekend
finesse finesse, keenness
fini done, finish, finished, finite, over
finir close, end, finish, finish up
finir mal come to a sticky end
finir par end up, grow on
fiole flask
fioriture flourish
firmament firmament
firme firm
fission fission
fissure cleft, rift
fixation fixation
fixe fixed, immovable
fixé à l'avance prearranged
fixement fixedly
fixer appoint, crystallize, fix, gaze, set
fixer une limite, (se) draw the line
flacon flask
flagellation flogging
flagrant blatant, flagrant, glaring
flair flair
flairer nose out, scent, sniff
flamant flamingo
flambeau torch
flamber flame
flamboiement blaze
flamboyant flamboyant, flaming
flamboyer flare
flamme flame, pennant
flanc flank
flanelle flannel
flâner dawdle, lounge, potter
flânerie dawdling
flâneur, euse dawdler
flanquer flank, catch
flaque pool, puddle
flash flashlight
flasque flabby, floppy
flatter butter up, flatter, pat
flatterie flattery
flatteur complimentary, flatterer
fléau evil, scourge
flèche arrow, jib, spire
fléchir flex
flegmatique phlegmatic, stolid
flegmatiquement stolidly
flegme phlegm, stolidity, stolidness
flétrir, (se) shrivel, shrivel up
fleur bloom, blossom, flower
fleur de l'âge prime
fleuret foil
fleuri flowered, flowery
fleurir bloom, blossom, flower
fleuriste florist
fleuve river
flexibilité pliability

flexible flexible, pliable, springy
flic cop, copper
flirt flirtation, flirt
flirteur flirt, flirtatious
flocon flake, snowflake
floconneux flaky, fuzzy
flop flop
floraison bloom
floral floral
flore flora
florin guilder
florissant flourishing, thriving
flot stream
flottabilité buoyancy
flotte fleet, float
flotter float, flop
flotter (au vent) wave
flotteur float
flottille flotilla
flou cloudy, fuzzy, fuzziness, smudginess
fluide fluid
fluidité fluidity
fluor fluoride, fluorine
fluorescence fluorescence
fluorescent fluorescent
flûte flute
flûte à bec recorder
flûtiste flautist
flux flux
foc jib
focale variable zoom lens
fœtal foetal
fœtus foetus
foi belief, faith
foie liver
foin hay
foire fair, bomb
fois time
folâtrement friskily
folâtrer frisk, frolic
folie craziness, folly, insanity, lunacy, madness
folio folio
folklore folklore
follement crazily, madly
fomenter ferment
foncé dark
foncer dart, tear
fonceur, euse go-getter
foncièrement fundamentally
fonction function
fonctionnaire civil servant, officer, official
fonctionnalisé purpose-built
fonctionnel functional
fonctionner function, work
fond background, bottom
fond (du problème) kernel
fondamental fundamental, radical

fondant fudge
fondateur, trice founder
fondation founding, foundation, institution
fondement(s) fundamental
fonder establish, found, ground, institute
fonder sur, (se) go by
fonderie foundry
fondre melt, smelt
fondre (dans), se merge (into)
fondre sur bear down on
fonds fund
fondu molten
fongicide fungicide
fontaine fountain
fonte cast iron
football football, soccer
forain, aine showman
forcé bound to forced, strained
force emphasis, force, might, strength
force de persuasion persuasiveness
forcément necessarily
forceps forceps
forcer prise, strain
forcer (à) force, pressurize
forcer la main (à) force someone's hand, put the screws on
forces (armées) forces
forer bore
forestier forestry
forêt forest
forge forge
forger forge
forgeron, onne blacksmith
formalité formality
format format, formation
formation formation, training
forme form, shape
formellement positively
former form, mould, shape, train
formidable fabulous, grand, marvellous, terrific
formidablement formidably
formulaire form
formulation wording
formule formula, spell
formuler draw up, state
fort fort, hard, high, loud, strong
fortement firmly, strongly
forteresse fortress, stronghold
fortification(s) fortification
fortifié walled
fortifier fortify
fortuit casual, incidental
fortune fortune, wealth
fortune personnelle private means
forum forum
fossé ditch

fosse pit
fosse septique septic tank
fossés moat
fossette dimple
fossile fossil
fossiliser fossilize
fossoyeur, euse gravedigger
fou bishop, crazy, fool, lunatic, mad, wild
fou à lier stark crazy/mad
fou d'inquiétude frantic
fou de joie delirious
foudre lightning
foudroyer du regard glare
fouet whip, whisk
fouetter flog, lash, whip
fougère fern
fougueux high-spirited, spirited
fouille(s) excavation
fouiller fish, go through, grub, root, scour, search
fouiller à fond ransack
fouiller (dans) rummage
fouiller les poubelles scavenge
fouiller (pour trouver) forage
fouillis jumble, muddle, shambles
fouiner pry
foulard cravat, headscarf, headsquare
foule army, crowd, host, throng
foulure sprain
four kiln, oven
fourche pitchfork
fourchette fork
fourchu forked
fourgon float
fourmi ant
fourmilière anthill
fourmiller de swarm
fournir furnish, provide, put up, supply
fourrage feed, fodder, forage
fourreau scabbard, sheath
fourrer son nez dans poke one's nose into
fourreur, euse furrier
fourrière pound
fourrure(s) fur
foutaise hogwash
foyer fireplace, focus, hearth, home, hostel
fracas clatter, crash
fracassé shattered
fracassement smash
fracasser, (se) crash, shatter
fraction fraction
fraction de seconde split second
fraction décimale decimal fraction
fracture fracture
fragile breakable, flimsy, fragile

fragilité brittleness, fragility, frailty
fragment snatch
fragmenter, (se) fragment
fraîcheur cool, coolness
fraîchir freshen
frais cool, expense, expenses, fresh, new, sweet
frais de transport haulage
fraise strawberry
framboise raspberry
franc above-board, direct, franc, frank, open, plain, straight, truthful
franc jeu fair play, straight
franc-parler straight talking
franchement downright, honestly, outright, straightforwardly, unreservedly
franchir negotiate
franchise candour, directness, straightforwardness
franco post-free
Franco- Franco-
frange bangs
frappant bold, striking
frapper clip, hit, knock, strike
frapper à toute volée swipe
frapper au-dessous de la ceinture hit below the belt
frapper avec un bâton bat
frapper d'ostracisme ostracize
frapper doucement tap
frapper fermement (sur qqch.) pound
frapper violemment bang
fraternel fraternal
fraternellement fraternally
fraternité brotherhood
fraude fraud
fraudeur, euse embezzler
frauduleux fraudulent
frayer spawn
frayer un passage, (se) fight one's way
fredaine escapade
fredonner croon, hum
frein brake
freiner brake
frêle frail, slight
frelon hornet
frémir quiver, scald
frénésie frenzy
frénétique frenzied
frénétiquement deliriously, frantically, frenziedly
fréquemment frequently
fréquence frequency
fréquent frequent, prevalent
fréquentation company
fréquenter associate (with), frequent, go around with, haunt

fréquenter, (se) go steady
frère brother
frère adoptif foster-brother
fresque fresco
fret freight, fry
frétillement wriggles
frétiller wriggle
friable crumbly
friand de fond of
friandise candy, sweet, titbit, tuck
fric lolly
frictionner chafe
fringant dashing, frisky
friper, se crumple
frire fry
frise frieze, curl
friser frizz
frisette ringlet
frisson shiver, shudder
frissonner shiver, shudder
frite French fries
frivole frivolous, trivial
frivolement frivolously
frivolité frivolousness, frivolity
froid chill, chilly, chilliness, cold, cool, frigid, nip
froidement coldly
froideur coldness
froissé huff, huffy
froisser screw up, crease
froisser, se crinkle, crush
frôler brush, graze, scrape, verge
fromage cheese
fronce gather
froncer gather, frown
froncer les sourcils knit one's brows, scowl
fronde slingshot
front brow, face, forehead, front
front de mer seafront
frontal frontal
frontière border, boundary, frontier
frontispice frontispiece
frottement friction
frotter rub, scrub
froussard jittery
fructueux fruitful
frugalement sparingly
fruit fruit
fruité fruity
fruits de mer seafood
frustration frustration
frustré frustrated
frustrer frustrate
fugitif, ive fugitive, runaway
fugue (amoureuse) elopement
fuir flee, leak, shun
fuite evasion, flight, leak, leakage
fulgurant meteoric
fulminer rant, fume

fumée fume, smoke
fumer smoke
fumeur, euse smoker
fumeux smoky
fumier dung, manure
funèbre funereal
funérailles funeral
funiculaire funicular
furet ferret
fureter ferret (about), nose

fureur fury
furibond seething
furie rage, like fury
furieux blazing, furious, irate, mad, wild
furoncle boil
furtif furtive, stealthy
furtivement stealthily
fusée rocket
fuselage fuselage

fuselé tapered, tapering
fusible fuse
fusil rifle
fusion fusion, merger
fusionner fuse
futile futile, pointless
futilité futility
futur future
fuyant slippery

Gg

gâcher make a mess of, mess up, spoil, throw away
gâchette trigger
gâchis mess-up
gadget gadget
gaffe blunder, boob, gaffe, slip
gaffer blunder, slip up
gage forfeit, pledge
gageure bet
gager wager, bet
gagnant, ante winner
gagne-pain bread and butter, livelihood
gagner gain, gain ground, win
gagner le gros lot hit the jackpot
gagner (sa vie) earn
gagner/perdre du temps save/waste time
gai gay
gaiement cheerily, gaily
gaieté gaiety
gaillard d'arrière quarterdeck
gain gain
gaieté cheerfulness, cheeriness, jolliness, merriment, mirth
gala gala
galaxie galaxy
galbe shapeliness
gale scab
galère galley
galerie (marchande) gallery, arcade
galeux scabby
galion galleon
gallon gallon
galon stripe
galop gallop
galopade scurry
galopant galloping
galoper gallop
galvaniser galvanize
gambade caper
gambader gambol
gambit gambit
gamin urchin
gamme scale
gamme de produits line
gang ring
gangrène gangrene
gangreneux gangrenous
gangster gangster, hoodlum
gant glove
gant de boxe boxing glove
garage garage
garantie guarantee
garantie (contre) safeguard
garantir guarantee, vouch

garce bitch
garçon boy, lad
garçon d'écurie groom
garçon d'honneur best man
garçon manqué tomboy
garde custody, guard, keeping, watch
garde d'enfants babysitter
garde d'honneur guard of honour
garde du corps bodyguard
garde forestier forester, ranger
garde monté ranger
garde-à-vous attention
garde-boue mudguard
garde-chasse gamekeeper, game warden
garde-côte coastguard
garde-feu fender
garde-manger larder, pantry
garde-robe wardrobe
gardenparty garden party
garder babysit, guard, hold, hold down, keep, tend
garder la main keep one's hand in
garder la tête froide keep one's head
garder pour soi keep quiet about, keep (something) to oneself, keep (something) under one's hat
garder précieusement treasure
garder, se keep
garder secret keep it dark
garder son sang-froid keep one's cool
garder un secret keep a secret
garderie creche, playschool
gardien de but goalkeeper
gardien, ienne de nuit night watchman
gardien, ienne attendant, babysitter, guardian, keeper, sitter, tender
gardien, ienne de prison gaoler, jailer, jailor, warden
gare station
garer park
gargariser, se gargle
gargarisme mouthwash
garnir garnish
garnison garrison
garniture garnish, topping, trimming
garrot tourniquet
gars guy
gas-oil diesel fuel/oil
gaspillage waste
gaspiller fritter, waste
gaspilleur wasteful
gastrique gastric
gastronomique gastronomic

gâté spoilt
gâteau cake, mould
gâteau au fromage cheesecake
gâteau de Savoie sponge cake
gâter blemish, indulge, mar, ruin, spoil, taint
gâterie goody, treat
gauche gauche, gawky, left, ungainly
gaucher left-handed
gaucherie ungainliness
gauchir warp
gauchissement warp
gaufrette wafer
gaz gas, wind
gaz carbonique carbon dioxide
gaz de combat tear gas
gaz lacrymogène tear gas
gaz naturel natural gas
gaze gauze
gazelle gazelle
gazeux gaseous, gassy
gazon grass, turf
gazouiller babble, chirp, warble
gazouillis chirp
géant giant, mammoth
géant, ante giant
geisha geisha
gel freeze, frost
gélatine gelatine
gelé frostbitten, frozen
gelée jelly
geler freeze, freeze up, ice over/up
gelure frostbite
gémir groan, moan, whimper, whine
gémissement groan, moan, whimper
gênant awkward, bothersome
gencive(s) gum
gendre son-in-law
gêné embarrassed
gène gene
gêne self-consciousness
généalogie genealogy
généalogique genealogical
généalogiste genealogist
gêner embarrass
général all-round, blanket, broad, general
général, ale general
généralement generally
généralisation generalization
généraliser generalize
génération generation
génératrice generator
généreusement generously, handsomely
généreux free, generous, liberal
générique credits, generic

générosité bounty, generosity
genêt broom
génétique genetic, genetics
genévrier juniper
génie genius
génisse heifer
génitif genitive
génocide genocide
genou knee, lap
genre form, gender, kind, type
gens folk, people
gentil kind, nice, sweet, thoughtful
gentillesse amiability, kindness
gentiment kindly, sweetly
gentleman gentleman
géographe geographer
géographie geography
géographique geographic(al)
géographiquement geographically
géologie geology
géologique geological
géologiquement geologically
géologue geologist
géométrie geometry
géométrique geometric(al)
gérant(e) manager
gerbe sheaf
gercé chapped
gérer administer, manage
gériatrie geriatrics
gériatrique geriatric
germe germ, seed
germer germinate
germination germination
geste gesture, motion
gesticuler gesticulate
gestion management
geyser geyser
ghetto ghetto
gibbon gibbon
gibet gallows, gibbet
gibier game, quarry, venison
gicleur jet, nozzle
gifle cuff, slap
gifler cuff, slap
gigantesque gigantic
gigue jig
gilet vest, waistcoat
gilet (de laine) cardigan
gilet de sauvetage life jacket
gin gin
girafe giraffe
gisement deposit, field
gisement pétrolifère oilfield
gîter heel, list
givre frost
glaçage glaze, icing
glacé glacé, icy
glace glass, ice
glacer ice

glacial Arctic, freezing, frigid, frosty, icy
glacialement frigidly, frostily
glacier glacier
glaçon ice cube, icicle
gladiateur gladiator
glande gland
glandulaire glandular
glaner glean
glas knell
glissade slide
glissant greasy, slippery
glissement glide, landslide
glisser glide, skate, slide, slip
glisser (sans bruit), (se) creep
glisser sur qqch. skim
glisser un mot en faveur de put in a good word for
glissoire chute
globalement globally
globe globe
globe oculaire eyeball
globe-trotter globetrotter
globulaire globular
gloire glory, honour, illustriousness
glorieusement gloriously
glorieux glorious
glorification glorification
glorifier glorify, praise
glossaire glossary
glouglouter gobble
gloussement cackle, cluck
glousser cackle, chuckle, cluck
glouton, onne glutton
gloutonnerie gluttony
gluant glutinous
glucose glucose
glycérine glycerin(e)
gnou gnu
gobelet beaker, mug
gobie goby
goéland seagull
goélette schooner
goinfrer, se hog
golf golf
golfe gulf
golfeur, euse golfer
gomme gum
gomme à effacer eraser, rubber
gomme à mâcher chewing gum, gum
gommeux gummy
gond hinge
gondole gondola
gondolier, ière gondolier
gonflable inflatable
gonflement inflation, swelling
gonfler blow up, bulge, inflate, puff out, pump up, swell out
gong gong

gorge gorge, throat
gorgée draft, mouthful
gorger de, se gorge
gorille gorilla
goudron tar
gouge gouge
goulot mouth
gourde gourd
gourdin club
gourmand greedy
gourmandise gluttony
gourmet gourmet
gousse clove
goût taste, tastefulness
goût (pour) liking (for)
goûter tea, taste
goutte dribble, drip, drop, tot
gouttelette droplet
gouttière drainpipe, gutter
gouvernail rudder, steering
gouvernante housekeeper
gouvernement administration, government
gouvernemental governmental
gouverner govern, rule
gouverneur, eure governor
grâce grace, gracefulness, pardon, quarter, reprieve
grâce à thanks to
gracier pardon
gracieusement gracefully
gracieux comely, graceful
gradation gradation
graduation graduation, scale
graduel gradual
graduellement gradually
graduer calibrate, graduate
graffiti graffiti
grain bean, grain, speck
grain de beauté beauty spot, mole
grain de poivre peppercorn
graine seed
graisse fattiness, grease
graisse (de rôti) dripping
graisse végétale shortening
graisser grease, oil
graisseux greasy
graminée grass
grammaire grammar
grammatical grammatical
grammaticalement grammatically
gramme gram(me)
grand good, grand, great, grown-up, high, large, mansize(d), tall, wide
grand écart the splits
grand film feature
grand livre ledger
grand magasin department store, emporium, general store

grand vent gale
grand-maman granny
grand-mère grandmother
grand-papa grandad
grand-père grandfather
grand-route highway
grande activité hustle
grande aiguille minute hand
grande maison long house
grande tente marquee
grandement greatly
grandeur greatness, grandeur, largeness, size
grandeur nature full-scale, life-size(d)
grandiose grandiose, palatial
grandir grow, increase
grands-parents grandparent
grange barn
granit granite
granulé granulated
granule granule
granuleux granular
graphique chart, graph, graphic
graphiquement graphically
graphite graphite
grappe bunch
gras bold, fat, fatty, succulent
grassouillet plump, tubby
gratitude gratitude, thankfulness
gratte-ciel skyscraper
gratter, (se) scratch
grattoir scraper
gratuit free, gratuitous, wanton
gratuité gratuitousness, wantoness
gratuitement gratuitously, wantonly
gravats rubble
grave bad, deep, grave, grievous, serious, severe, solemn
graveleux gritty
gravement gravely, sorely
graver brand, engrave, scratch
graver (dans) impress
graveur, euse engraver
gravier gravel
gravité gravity
gravure print
gredin rogue
gréement rig, rigging, tackle
gréer rig
greffe graft
grégaire gregarious
grêle hail, spindly
grêler hail
grêlon hailstone
grenade grenade, pomegranate
grenier attic, garret, loft
grenier à blé granary
grenouille frog

grès sandstone, stoneware
grésillant crackly
grève strike
grève de la faim hunger strike
gréviste striker
gribouillage scrawl, scribble
gribouiller scribble
gribouilleur, euse scribbler
gribouillis scribble
grief grievance, grouse
griffe claw
griffonnage (distrait) doodle
griffonner scrawl, scribble
griffonner (distraitement) doodle
grignoter nibble
gril grill
grillage grating
grille grid, railing
grille (de foyer) grate
grille-pain toaster
griller broil, grill, toast
grillon cricket
grimacer make/pull a face, pull faces (at)
grimpant rambling
grimper clamber, climb, creep, escalate, shin
grimper en flèche boom
grimpeur, euse climber
grinçant creaky, grating, grinding, rasping, squeaky
grincement creak, squeak
grincer creak, grind, squeak
grincheux crotchety, peevish
grippe influenza
gris grey
gris argenté silvery
grisâtre greyish
grisonnant grey
grisonner grey
grog toddy
grognement growl, grunt, snort
grogner growl, grunt, snort
grognon fretful, grouchy
grommeler grunt
grondement boom, grumble, roar, rumble
grondement féroce snarl
gronder chide, grumble, roar, rumble, scold
gros big, fat, heavy
gros gibier big game
gros lot jackpot
gros plan close-up
gros rire belly laugh
gros titre headline
groseille redcurrant, gooseberry
grossesse pregnancy
grossier boorish, coarse, crass, gross, rude, scurrilous, tactless

grossièrement coarsely, grossly, rudely, scurrilously, tactlessly
grossièreté bad language, coarseness, crudeness, rudeness, scurrilousness, tactlessness
grossièreté verbale abusiveness
grossir magnify
grossissement magnification
grossiste wholesaler
grotesque farcical, grotesque
grotesquement grotesquely, preposterously
grotte cave
grouillant (de) alive (with), seething (with)
grouiller, se jump to it
groupe group, party, squad, troop
groupe de pression lobby
groupe sanguin blood group/type
groupement conglomeration
grouper, (se) group
grouper (autour de), se cluster (round)
grue crane
grumeau lump
grumeleux lumpy
grutier, ière crane driver
gué ford
guenille rag
guépard cheetah
guêpe wasp
guérillero guer(r)illa
guérir cure, heal
guérissable curable
guérisseur, euse healer
guérite sentry box
guerre war, warfare
guerre bactériologique biological warfare
guerre civile civil war
guerre des nerfs war of nerves
guerre froide cold war
guerrier martial
guerrier, ière warrior
guetter look out (for), watch
guetteur, euse lookout
gueule mouth, mug
gueule de bois hangover
gueuler shout
gui mistletoe
guichet (de location) box office
guide Girl Guide, guide
guider guide, shepherd
guidon handlebars
guillemets quotation marks
guilleret perky
guillotine guillotine
guimbarde crock
guindé prim
guirlande garland

guitare guitar
guitariste guitarist
guppy guppy
gymkhana gymkhana

gymnase gym, gymnasium
gymnaste gymnast
gymnastique gymnastic,
gymnastics

gynécologie gynecology
gynécologue gynecologist

Hh

habile clever, dext(e)rous, skilful, skilled

habilement ably, skilfully, slickly

habileté ability, handiness, skilfulness

habillé dressed

habillement attire

habiller, (s') clothe, dress

habit habitable, morning dress

habit(s) habit

habitable habitable, inhabitable

habitant, ante citizen, inhabitant, resident

habitant, ante de la plaine lowlander

habitant, ante du Nord northerner

habitat habitat

habitation dwelling, habitation

habiter dwell, inhabit

habiter (chez) lodge (with)

habitude custom, habit, practice

habitué à accustomed to, used to (something)

habituel accustomed, customary, habitual, regular, usual

habituellement customarily, habitually, usually

habituer à get (someone) into the habit of

habituer (à), (s') accustom

hache axe

hacher chop, hack, mince

hachette hatchet

hachoir chopper, mincer

hagard drawn, haggard

haie hedge, hedgerow, hurdle

haillons rags

haine breath, hatred

haïr hate

hâlé weatherbeaten

haleine breath

haleter gasp, pant, puff

hall foyer, hall, lobby

hallucination delusion, hallucination

halo halo

halte halt

hamac hammock

hambourgeois hamburger

hameçon hook

hamster hamster

hanche haunch, hip

handicap handicap

handicapé handicapped, disabled

handicaper handicap

hangar hangar

hanté haunted

hanter haunt

harangue harangue

harcèlement harassment

harceler badger, goad, harass, harry, nag, pick on, worry

hardi bold

hardiment boldly

harem harem

hareng herring

hargne snappiness

hargneux snappy

haricot bean

haricot(s) vert(s) French beans, string bean

harmonica harmonica, mouth organ

harmonie harmony, harmoniousness

harmonieusement harmoniously

harmonieux harmonious

harmonique harmonic

harmonisation harmonization

harmoniser, (s') harmonize, tone

harnacher harness

harnais harness

harpe harp

harpiste harpist

harpon harpoon, spear

hasard chance, fortune

haschisch hashish

hâte haste, hurry

hâter (se) accelerate, hasten, hurry

hâtif cursory

hâtivement cursorily

haussement lift

haussement d'épaules shrug

hausser raise

hausser les sourcils raise one's eyebrows

haut head, high, tall, top

haut de l'échelle the top of the ladder/tree

haut fourneau blast furnace

haut la main with flying colours, hands down

haut les mains! hands up!

haut placé exalted

haut-de-forme top hat

haut-parleur loudspeaker, speaker

hautain haughty, lofty, supercilious

hautbois oboe

hautboïste oboist

haute mer the high seas

haute-fidélité hi-fi, high fidelity

hauteur height, highness, loftiness, pitch, tallness

haut-parleur loud speaker

havre haven

havresac Knapsack

hebdomadaire weekly

hebdomadairement weekly

hébété dazed, stupid

hectare hectare

hélas! alas!

héler hail

hélice propeller

hélicoptère chopper, helicopter

hélium helium

hello hello

hémisphère hemisphere

hémisphérique hemispherical

hémoglobine haemoglobin

hémorragie haemorrhage

hennir neigh, whinny

hennissement neigh, whinnies

héraldique heraldic

héraut herald

herbe grass, herb

herbeux grassy

herboriste herbalist

héréditaire hereditary

hérédité heredity

hérésie heresy

hérétique heretic, heretical

hérissé bristly

hérissement prickliness

hérisser fluff

hérisson hedgehog

héritage heirloom, inheritance, legacy

hériter (de) inherit

héritier, ière heir, heiress

hermétique airtight

hermine ermine

héroïne heroin, heroine

héroïque heroic

héroïquement heroically

héroïsme heroism

héron heron

héros hero

hertz hertz

hésitant dubious, faltering, hesitant, tentative

hésitation hesitancy

hésiter falter, hang back, hover (between)

hésiter (à) hesitate

hêtre beech

heure hour, time

heure de pointe rush hour

heure du coucher bedtime

heure du dîner lunchtime

heures supplémentaires overtime

heureusement fortunately, luckily

heureux fortunate, happy

heureux comme un roi as pleased as Punch

heurter go against, hit, knock (against, on)

heurtoir knocker

hexagone hexagon
hibernation hibernation
hiberner hibernate
hibiscus hibiscus
hibou owl
hideur hideousness
hideusement hideously
hideux hideous
hier yesterday
hiérarchie hierarchy
hiérarchique hierarchical
hiéroglyphe(s) hieroglyphics
hilare hilarious
hilarité hilarity
hindou Hindu
hippie hippie, hippy
hippopotame hippopotamus
hirondelle swallow
hirsute shaggy
hisser hoist, run up
histoire history, story, tale
histoire à dormir debout cock-and-bull story, a tall story
histoire naturelle natural history
histoires fuss
historien, ienne historian
historique historic, historical
historiquement historically
hiver winter, wintertime
hivernal wintery
hockey hockey
holocauste holocaust
homard lobster
homicide homicide, homicidal
homicide involontaire manslaughter
hommage homage
homme fellow, man
homme à tout faire handyman, odd job man
homme de barre helmsman
homme de lettres man of letters
homme des cavernes caveman
homme dominateur he-man
homme-grenouille frogman
homme/femme d'affaires businessman, businesswoman
homologue counterpart
homonyme homonym, namesake
homosexualité homosexuality
homosexuel, elle homosexual
honnête honest, straightforward, upright
honnêtement honestly
honnêteté honesty
honneur glory, honour
honneurs honours
honorable creditable, honourable, reputable
honorablement creditably

honoraire honorary
honoraires fee
honorer honour
honoris causa honorary
honte disgrace, shame, shamefulness
honteusement disgracefully, shamefully
honteux ashamed, disgraceful, shameful
hôpital hospital, infirmary
hoquet gasp, hiccup
horaire hourly, timetable
horde horde
horizon horizon
horizontal horizontal
horizontalement horizontally
horloge clock
horloge de parquet grandfather clock
horloge/montre à affichage numérique digital clock/watch
horloger, ère watchmaker
hormone hormone
horoscope horoscope
horreur abhorrence, eyesore, ghastliness, horror
horrible ghastly, gruesome, horrible, horrid, lurid
horriblement horribly
horrifiant horrifying
horrifier horrify
hors d'usage out of action, out of order
hors de off, out of, outside
hors de propos irrelevantly
hors de question out of the question
hors de saison out of season
hors des sentiers battus off the beaten track
hors faculté extramural
hors-bord outboard
hors-d'œuvre hors d'oeuvre
hors-jeu offside
hors-la-loi outlaw
hors-saison the off season
hors taxe duty-free
horticole horticultural
horticulture horticulture
hospitalier hospitable
hospitalisation hospitalization
hospitaliser hospitalize
hospitalité hospitableness, hospitality
hostile hostile
hostilité enmity, hostility
hostilités hostilities
hôte host
hôtel hotel

hôtel de ville hall, town hall
hôtelier, ière hotelier
hôtesse de l'air air hostess
houblon hop
houle swell
houlette crook
houleux billowy
houppe(tte) powder puff, puff
hourra hurrah, hurray, hoorah, hooray
houx holly
hublot porthole
huée hoot, jeer
huer boo, hoot, jeer
huile oil, oils
huile capillaire hair oil
huile de foie de morue cod-liver oil
huile de ricin castor oil
huileux oily
huilier cruet
huit eight
huitième eighth
huître oyster
hululement hoot
hululer hoot
humain human, humane
humainement humanly
humanité humaneness, humanity, mankind
humble humble, lowly
humblement humbly
humecter dampen, moisten
humeur mood, spirits, temper
humide damp, humid, steamy
humidité damp, dampness, humidity, moisture, wet, wetness
humiliant humiliating
humiliation humiliation
humilier humble, humiliate
humilité humbleness, humility, lowliness
humoriste humorist
humoristique humorous
humour humour, humorousness, wittiness
humus humus
huppé crested
hurluberlu eccentric
hurlement bellow, howl, wail, yell
hurler bellow, blast, howl, scream, shriek, yell
hutte hut
hybride cross, cross-, crossbreed
hydrate de carbone carbohydrate
hydrater moisturize
hydraulique hydraulic, hydraulics
hydrauliquement hydraulically
hydro-électricité hydroelectricity
hydro-électrique hydroelectric
hydrogène hydrogen

hyène hyena, hyaena
hygiène hygiene
hygiénique hygienic
hygiéniquement hygienically
hymne anthem, national anthem
hypermétrope longsighted,
  farsighted
hypermétropie longsightedness,
  farsighted

hypnose hypnosis
hypnotique hypnotic
hypnotiser hypnotize, mesmerize
hypnotiseur hypnotist
hypnotisme hypnotism
hypocrisie hypocrisy
hypocrite double-dealing,
  hypocrite, hypocritical, two-faced
hypocritiquement hypocritically

hypodermique hypodermic
hypothèque mortgage
hypothéquer mortgage
hypothèse assumption, hypothesis
hypothétique hypothetical
hypothétiquement hypothetically
hystérie hysteria
hystérique hysterical
hystériquement hysterically

Ii

iceberg iceberg
ici here, hither
ici et là about, around
icône icon, ikon
idéal ideal
idéalement ideally
idéalisation idealization
idéaliser idealize
idéalisme idealism
idéaliste idealist, idealistic
idée idea, inkling, notion
idée dominante keynote
idée géniale brainwave
idée/opinion fausse misconception
identification identification
identifier identify, pick out
identifier à, (s') identify oneself with
identifier avec, (s') identify with
identique identical
identiquement identically
identité identity
idiomatique idiomatic
idiome idiom
idiot idiotic
idiot, ote ass, cretin, half-wit, idiot, jackass
idiotement idiotically
idolâtre idolatrous
idolâtrer hero-worship
idolâtrie idolatry
idole idol
if yew
igloo igloo
igname yam
ignare clueless, ignorant
ignifuge non-inflammable
ignoble ignoble
ignoblement ignobly
ignorance ignorance
ignorant illiterate, unaware
ignorant (de) ignorant (of)
ignorer have nothing to do with, ignore
iguane iguana
île island, isle
illégal illegal
illégalement illegally
illégalité illegality, lawlessness
illégitime illegitimate
illégitimement illegitimately
illégitimité illegitimacy
illettré illiterate
illicite illicit
illicitement illicitly
illimité boundless, limitless
illisibilité illegibility

illisible illegible
illisiblement illegibly
illogique illogical
illogiquement illogically
illogisme illogicality
illumination(s) illumination
illuminer illuminate, light up
illusion illusion
illusionniste illusionist
illustrateur, trice illustrator
illustration illustration, picture
illustré illustrated, pictorial
illustre illustrious
illustrer exemplify, illustrate
ils, elles they
image image, picture
image floue blur
imaginaire fictional, fictitious, imaginary
imaginatif imaginative
imagination fancy, imagination
imaginer dream up, imagine
imbécile clot, fat-head, imbecile, zombie
imbécillité idiocy, imbecility
imbiber saturate
imitateur, trice imitator, mimic
imitatif imitative
imitation imitation, mimicry
imiter copy, imitate, mimic, take off
immaculé immaculate, spotless
immangeable inedible
immaturité immaturity
immédiat immediate, instant
immédiatement directly, immediately, instantly, right now, this instant
immense immense, vast
immensément immensely
immensité immensity, vastness
immerger immerse
immersion immersion
immeuble block, building
immigrant, ante immigrant
immigration immigration
imminence imminence
imminent imminent
immobile immobile, motionless, still
immobilier real estate
immobiliser immobilize, pin
immobiliser, s' standstill
immobilité immobility
immoral immoral
immoralement immorally
immoralité immorality
immortaliser immortalize
immortalité immortality
immortel immortal

immunisation immunization
immunisé (contre) immune (to, from)
immuniser (contre) immunize (to, from)
immunité immunity
impact impact
impair odd
imparfait imperfect
imparfaitement imperfectly
impartial impartial
impartialement fairly, impartially
impartialité impartiality
impasse blind alley, deadlock, stalemate
impassible impassive, straight
impassiblement impassively
impatiemment impatiently
impatience impatience
impatient impatient, restive
impatient (de) in a hurry (to)
impatienter, s' chafe
impayable priceless
impayé outstanding, overdue
impeccable flawless, immaculate
impénétrable impenetrable
impensable unthinkable
impératif imperative
impératrice empress
imperceptibilité inaudibility
imperfection imperfection
impérial imperial
impérialisme imperialism
impérialiste imperialist
impérieux imperious
imperméable raincoat, showerproof, waterproof
impersonnalité impersonality
impersonnel impersonal
impersonnellement impersonally
impertinence impertinence, presumption, presumptuousness, sauciness
impertinent presumptuous, saucy
impertinent (envers) impertinent (to)
imperturbable unflappable
impétueusement impetuously
impétueux hotheaded, impetuous
impétuosité impetuosity
impitoyable hard-hearted, pitiless, remorseless, ruthless
impitoyablement pitilessly, remorselessly, ruthlessly
implacabilité relentlessness
implacable fierce, implacable, relentless
implacablement implacably, relentlessly
implantation implantation

implanter implant
impliquer imply
implorer crave, implore
impoli discourteous, impolite, ungracious
impoli (envers) uncivil (to)
impoliment impolitely, uncivilly
impolitesse discourtesy, impoliteness, incivility
impopulaire unpopular
impopularité unpopularity
importance greatness, importance, magnitude, noteworthiness, prominence, significance, standing, weightiness
important important, prominent
importateur, trice importer
importation(s) import, importation
importer import
importun uninvited, unwelcome
importuner annoy, bother, molest, pester
imposable taxable
imposant commanding, imposing
imposer command, exact, impose, thrust on/upon
imposer, s' gain ground, assert oneself
imposition imposition
impossibilité impossibility
impossible impossible
imposteur fake, fraud, impostor
imposture sham
impôt sur le revenu income tax
impôts taxation
impraticabilité impracticability
impraticable impassable, impracticable
imprécis imprecise
imprécision imprecision
impression fancy, feeling, impression, printing, printout
impressionnant impressive
impressionner impress
imprimer impress, imprint, print
imprimeur printer
improbable improbable, unlikely
impromptu impromptu
improvisation improvisation
improviser improvise
improviste (à l') unexpectedly
imprudemment imprudently, rashly, unwarily, unwisely
imprudence imprudence, incautiousness, rashness, unwariness
imprudent imprudent, incautious, indiscreet, rash, unguarded, unwary, unwise
impudent barefaced

impudeur immodesty
impudique immodest, shameless
impudiquement immodestly
impuissance powerlessness
impuissant powerless
impulsif impulsive
impulsion impulse
impulsivement impulsively
impulsivité impulsiveness
impur impure, unclean
impureté impurity
in vogue, modish, modishly, popular
inaccessibilité inaccessibility
inaccessible inaccessible
inachevé undone
inactif inactive
inaction inaction
inactivité inactivity, inertness
inadapté, ée misfit
inadmissibilité inadmissibility
inadmissible inadmissible
inadvertance oversight
inanimé inanimate
inanition starvation
inapparent inconspicuous
inapte (à) unfit (to)
inattendu chance, unexpected
inattentif inattentive
inattention inattention, inattentiveness
inaudible inaudible
inaugural inaugural
inauguration inauguration
inaugurer inaugurate
incalculable incalculable
incandescent incandescent
incantation incantation
incapable (de) incapable (of)
incapable de unable
incapacité failure, inability
incapacité (de) incapability (of)
incarnation incarnation
incarné incarnate
incendiaire incendiary
incendie conflagration, fire
incendie criminel arson
incertain doubtful, uncertain
incertitude doubtfulness, dubiousness, indecision
incessant constant, incessant, unceasing
inchangé unaffected
incident incident, scene
incinérateur incinerator
incinération cremation, incineration
incinérer cremate, incinerate
incision incision
incisive incisor

incitation (à) incitement (to)
inciter (à) abet (to), incite (to)
inclinaison gradient, slope, tilt
inclination inclination
incliner cock, tilt
inclure include
inclus inclusive
inclusion inclusion
incohérence incoherence
incohérent incoherent
incolore colourless
incomber à fall to, lie with
incombustible incombustible
incommensurable immeasurable
incommodité discomfort
incomparable incomparable
incomparablement incomparably
incompatibilité incompatibility
incompatible incompatible
incompétence incompetence
incompétent incompetent, ineffectual
incomplet incomplete, sketchy
incompréhensible incomprehensible
inconcevable inconceivable
inconditionnel unconditional, unquestioning
inconditionnellement unconditionally
inconduite misconduct
inconfort discomfort
inconfortable uncomfortable
inconfortablement uncomfortably
incongru incongruous
incongruité incongruity, incongruousness
inconnu strange, unfamiliar, unknown
inconsciemment unconsciously, unknowingly
inconscience unconsciousness
inconscient insensible, unconscious
inconsistance inconsistency
inconsolable inconsolable
inconstance fickleness
inconstant fickle, inconstant
incontestable indisputable, unquestionable
incontrôlable out of hand
inconvenance impropriety
inconvénient drawback, inconvenient
incorporer incorporate
incorrect incorrect
incorrection incorrectness
incorrigible incorrigible
incorruptibilité incorruptibility
incorruptible incorruptible
incrédibilité incredibility

incrédule incredulous
incrédulité disbelief, incredulity
incriminer incriminate
incroyable incredible, unbelievable
incroyablement incredibly, unbelievably
incrustation inlay
incrusté inlaid, set (with)
incubation incubation
incuber incubate
inculquer implant (into), instil (into)
incurable incurable
indécence indecency
indécent indecent, rude
indéchiffrable indecipherable
indécis in doubt, fluid, indecisive, undecided
indécision indecision
indéfini indefinite
indélébile indelible
indemne scot-free
indemnité compensation
indéniable positive
indépendamment (de) independently (of)
indépendance independence
indépendant (de) independent (de)
indescriptible unutterable
indésirable undesirable
indestructible indestructible
indéterminé indefinite
index forefinger, index, index finger
indicateur de vitesse speedometer
indicateur, trice informer
indicatif indicative
indication indication
indice clue
indiciblement inexpressibly
indifféremment indifferently
indifférence disregard, indifference, unconcern
indifférenciable (de) indistinguishable (from)
indifférent indifferent, unconcerned, uninterested
indifférent (à) indifferent (to), unaffected (by)
indigène native
indigent, ente pauper, poor
indigeste indigestible
indigestion indigestion
indignation indignation
indigné indignant
indigne unworthy
indignement unworthily
indignité unworthiness
indiquer indicate, mark
indiquer le chemin de direct

indirect indirect, oblique
indiscipline indiscipline, unruliness
indiscipliné insubordinate, unruly
indiscret indiscreet, meddlesome, obtrusive
indiscrètement nosily, obtrusively
indiscrétion indiscretion, nosiness, obtrusiveness
indiscutablement unquestionably
indispensable indispensable
indistinct indistinct
indistinctement indistinctly
individu individual
individuel individual
indivisibilité indivisibility
indivisible indivisible
indolence listlessness
indolent listless
indolore painless
indu undue, unearthly, unholy
indubitable undoubted
indubitablement beyond doubt, undoubtedly
indulgence indulgence, lenience,
indulgent forgiving, indulgent, lenient, soft
indûment unduly
industrialisé industrialised, industrialized
industrie industry
industrie lourde heavy industry
industriel industrial, industrialist
inébranlable immovable, solid
inefficace ineffective, ineffectual, inefficient
inefficacement inefficiently
inefficacité ineffectiveness, ineffectualness, inefficiency
inégal inconsistent, one-sided, patchy, unequal, uneven
inégalement unequally, unevenly
inégalité inequality, unevenness
inéligibilité ineligibility
inépuisable inexhaustible, unflagging
inerte inert
inertie inertia
inestimable invaluable, priceless
inévitabilité inevitability
inévitable inescapable, inevitable
inévitablement inevitably
inexact inaccurate, inexact
inexactitude inaccuracy, inexactness
inexcusable inexcusable
inexcusablement inexcusably
inexistant non-existent
inexpérience inexperience
inexpérimenté green, inexperienced, raw

inexplicable inexplicable, unaccountable
inexplicablement inexplicably, unaccountably
inexpressif blank
inexprimable inexpressible, unspeakable
infaillibilité infallibility
infaillible infallible, unerring
infailliblement infallibly, unerringly, unfailingly
infâme infamous, villainous
infamie infamy, villainy
infanterie infantry
infarctus (du myocarde) coronary, coronary thrombosis
infatigabilité tirelessness
infatigable tireless, untiring
infatigablement untiringly
infécond barren
infect foul
infecter infect
infection infection
inférieur à inferior to
infériorité inferiority
infertile infertile
infertilité infertility
infestation infestation
infester (de) infest (with)
infidèle unfaithful
infidélité infidelity
infiltrer (dans), (s') infiltrate (into)
infiltrer, (s') filter
infiltrer, s' permeate
infime fractional, small
infini immeasurable, infinite
infiniment dearly, immeasurably, infinitely
infinité infinity
infinitif infinitive
infinitude infiniteness
infirme infirm
infirmerie infirmary, sanatorium
infirmier, ière nurse
infirmier en chef head nurse
infirmité disability, infirmity
inflammabilité inflammability
inflammable flammable, inflammable
inflammation inflammation
inflation inflation
inflationnaire inflationary
inflexibilité inflexibility
inflexible adamant, grim, inflexible, rigid
inflexiblement inflexibly, rigidly
infliction infliction
infliger (à) inflict (on)
influence influence, pull
influencer bias, sway

influent influential
influer sur influence, affect
informateur, trice informant
information information, news
informatique data-processing
informatiser computerize
informe shapeless, informal
informer (de) advise (of), inform (of)
informer (de, sur), s' enquire (about)
infortune misfortune
infraction contravention, offence
infrarouge infrared
ingénierie engineering
ingénieur civil engineer
ingénieur, eure engineer
ingénieusement cleverly, ingeniously
ingénieux clever, ingenious, resourceful
ingéniosité cleverness, ingeniousness, ingenuity, resourcefulness
ingénu naive
ingérence interference
ingrat thankless, ungrateful
ingratement thanklessly
ingratitude ingratitude, thanklessness
ingrédient ingredient
inhabité unmanned
inhabituel unusual
inhalateur inhaler
inhalation inhalation
inhibé inhibited
inhibition inhibition
inhospitalier inhospitable
inhumain inhuman
inhumainement inhumanely
inhumanité inhumanity
ininflammable non-flammable
inintelligible unintelligible
ininterrompu uninterrupted
iniquité iniquity
initial initial
initiation initiation
initiative initiative
initié, ée initiate
initier initiate, introduce to
injecté de sang bloodshot
injection injection, shot
injure abuse, insult, strong language
injurier abuse, insult
injurieusement abusively
injurieux abusive, insulting
injuste unfair, unjust, wrongful
injustement unfairly, wrongfully, wrongly

injustice injustice, unfairness, wrongfulness
inlassablement tirelessly
inné inborn, natural
innocemment harmlessly, innocently
innocence innocence
innocent innocent
innocuité harmlessness
innombrable countless, innumerable, numberless, without number
innovateur, trice innovator
innovation innovation, novelty
innover break new ground
inoccupé unoccupied, vacant
inodore odourless
inoffensif harmless, innocuous, inoffensive
inondation flood, inundation
inonder deluge, flood, inundate, swamp
inonder de shower
inopérable inoperable
inopportunité inadvisability
inorganique inorganic
inoubliable unforgettable
inouï unprecedented, incredible
inoxydable rustproof
inquiet insecure, nervous, uneasy
inquiétant eerie
inquiéter disquiet, perturb
inquiéter, (s') worry
inquiétude concern, disquiet, unease, uneasiness, worry
inquiétude(s) alarm
insaisissable elusive
insalubre insanitary
insalubrité insanitariness
insanité insanity, madness
insatiabilité insatiableness
insatiable insatiable
insatiablement insatiably
insatisfait frustrated
inscription enrolment, inscription, matriculation
inscrire enter, inscribe
inscrire (à) put down for
inscrire (à), (s') check in, enter (for)
inscrire au journal de bord log
inscrire, (s') enrol, matriculate
inscrire, s' register, sign up
insecte bug, insect
insecticide insecticide
insectivore insectivorous
insécurité insecurity
insensé insane, senseless
insensibilité heartlessness, insensitivity

insensible insensitive, unmoved
insensible à insensitive to
inséparable inseparable
insérer insert
insertion insertion
insigne badge, insignia
insignes regalia
insignifiance insignificance
insignifiant insignificant, nominal, petty, trifling, trivial
insinuation implication
insinuer suggest
insipide bland, tame
insistance emphasis
insister (lourdement) rub it in
insister sur lay/put stress on
insolation sunstroke
insolemment insolently
insolence insolence
insolent insolent
insolite out of the way
insolubilité insolubility
insoluble insoluble
insomniaque insomniac
insomnie insomnia, wakefulness
insondable abysmal, bottomless, impenetrable
insonorisé soundproof
insonoriser soundproof
insouciant carefree, happy-go-lucky
insouciant (de) heedless (of)
insoumis rebellious
insoupçonné unsuspected
insoutenable unbearable
inspecter inspect, survey
inspecteur, trice inspector
inspection inspection
inspiration inspiration
inspirer inspire
instabilité instability, shakiness
instable unsettled
installation installation, plant
installation à demeure fixture
installation électrique wiring
installations facility, fitting
installer fit, install, set up
installer, (s') settle
installer (confortablement), s' settle down
instant instant, minute
instantané instant, instantaneous
instantanément instantaneously
instaurer initiate
instigation instigation
instinct instinct
instinct de possession acquisitiveness
instinct grégaire herd instinct
instinctif instinctive

instinctivement instinctively
institut institute, school
instituteur, trice schoolteacher
institutionnel institutional
institutrice mistress
instructif informative, instructive
instruction(s) instruction
instructions briefing, direction
instruire educate
instruit well-educated
instrument instrument
instrument de musique instrument
instrumental instrumental
instrumentiste instrumentalist
instrument(s) à cordes stringed
  instruments
insubordination insubordination
insuffisamment insufficiently,
  scantily
insuffisance inadequacy,
  insufficiency, scantiness,
  skimpiness
insuffisant inadequate, insufficient,
  scant
insulaire insular, islander
insuline insulin
insultant insulting
insulter insult
insulte(s) brickbat, insult
insupportable dreadful, impossible,
  unbearable
insupportablement unbearably
insurgé, ée insurgent
insurger (contre), s' take up arms
  (against)
insurmontable insuperable
intact intact
intarissable inexhaustible, long-
  winded
intégration integration
intégrer, (s') integrate
intégrité integrity
intellectuel intellectual
intelligemment intelligently
intelligence brain, intellect,
  intelligence, understanding
intelligent bright, clever, intelligent
intelligibilité intelligibility
intelligible intelligible
intelligiblement intelligibly
intemporalité timelessness
intemporel timeless
intendant, ante steward
intendant militaire quartermaster
intense deep, intense
intensément intensely
intensif crash, intensive
intensifier heighten, step up
intensité depth, intenseness,
  intensity, intensiveness

intensivement intensively
intenter (une action) file
intention intent, intention
intentionnel intentional
intentionnellement intentionally
interaction interaction
intercéder intercede
intercepter collar, intercept
interception interception
intercession intercession
interchangeable interchangeable
interdiction ban, prohibition
interdire ban, prohibit, suppress
interdit forbidden, no-go
interdit (à) out of bounds (for)
intéressant interesting
intéressé interested
intéressé par interested in
intéresser (à) interest (in), take an
  interest (in)
intérêt personnel self-interest
intérêt(s) interest
intérieur domestic, indoor, inland,
  inner, inside, interior, internal
intérieurement internally
interjection interjection
intermède interlude
intermédiaire intermediary,
  intermediate, middleman
interminable endless, long-drawn-
  out
intermittent intermittent
international international
internationalement internationally
interne intern, internal
internement committal, internment
interner intern
interphone intercom
interprétation interpretation
interprète exponent, interpreter,
  performer
interpréter interpret, render
interrogateur, trice interrogator
interrogatif interrogative
interrogation interrogation
interrogatoire examination
interroger examine, interrogate,
  question, test
interrompu brooken
interrompre abort, break, break
  in(to), butt in, cut short,
  discontinue, interrupt
interrupteur switch
interruption discontinuation,
  interruption, stoppage
intersecter, (s') intersect
intersection crossing, intersection
intervalle interval, lapse
intervenir chip in, cut in, step in,
  intervene

intervenir (auprès de) intercede
  (with)
intervention intervention
interviewer interview
intervieweur, euse interviewer
intestin gut, intestine
intestinal intestinal
intestins bowel
intime bosom, close, intimate,
  inward
intimement intimately
intimidation intimidation
intimidé self-conscious
intimider cow, intimidate
intimité intimacy, privacy
intituler entitle, head
intolérable intolerable
intolérablement intolerably
intolérance intolerance
intolérant (de) intolerant (of)
intonation intonation
intoxiqué, ée addict
intransigeant uncompromising
intransitif intransitive
intransitivement intransitively
intrépide fearless, intrepid, stout-
  hearted, undaunted
intrépidement fearlessly, intrepidly
intrépidité intrepidity
intrigant intriguing, scheming
intrigant, ante schemer
intrigue action, intrigue, plot
introduction introduction
introduire introduce
intronisation enthronement
introniser enthrone
introverti, ie introvert
intrus, use gate crasher, intruder,
  trespasser
intrusion intrusion
intuition hunch, intuition
inutile needless, purposeless,
  unnecessary, useless
inutilement needlessly, for nothing,
  unnecessarily
invalide cripple, disabled
invalidité disablement, invalidity
invariable invariable
invariablement invariably
invasion invasion, plague
inventaire inventory
inventer concoct, cook up, devise,
  fabricate, invent, make up, think
  up, weave
inventeur, trice inventor
inventif inventive
invention contrivance, fabrication,
  figment, invention
inverse anti-, invert, counter-
inversion inversion

invertébré invertebrate, spineless
investir invest
investissement investment
investisseur, euse investor
investiture investiture
invétéré confirmed
invincibilité invincibility
invincible invincible
invinciblement invincibly
invisibilité invisibility
invisible invisible
invisiblement invisibly
invitant inviting
invitation invitation
invité, ée guest
inviter ask, invite
invocation invocation
involontaire involuntary
involontairement involuntarily
invoquer invoke
invraisemblable improbable
invraisemblablement improbably
invraisemblance improbability
invulnérable invulnerable
iode iodine
irascibilité irascibility
irascible irascible
iris iris, iridescence
irisé iridescent
ironie irony

ironique ironic(al)
ironiquement ironically
irradier radiate
irréalisable impracticable
irréalité unreality
irréconciliable incompatible
irréel unreal
irréfléchi hasty, thoughtless, unthinking
irrégularité irregularity
irrégulier erratic, irregular
irrégulièrement erratically, irregularly
irrémédiablement irreparably
irremplaçable irreplaceable
irréparable irreparable, irretrievable
irréparablement irretrievably
irréprochable blameless, faultless
irréprochablement faultlessly
irrésistible irrepressible, irresistible, overpowering, winning
irrésistiblement irresistibly
irrésolu indecisive, hesitant
irrespect disrespect
irrespecteusement disrespectfully
irrespectueux disrespectful, unholy
irrespirable stiffling
irresponsabilité irresponsibility
irresponsable irresponsible

irresponsablement irresponsibly
irrévérence irreverence
irrévérencieusement irreverently
irrévérencieux irreverent
irréversible irreversible
irrigation irrigation
irriguer irrigate
irritabilité irritableness
irritable irritable, short-tempered
irritation irritation, soreness
irrité angry
irriter chafe, irritate, put someone's back up, smart
islamique Islamic
isolation insulation
isolé isolated, lonely
isolement isolation, seclusion
isoler insulate, isolate
isoloir polling booth
issue exit, way
isthme isthmus
italique italic, italics
itinéraire itinerary
itinérant itinerant, vagrant
ivoire ivory
ivre drunk
ivresse drunkenness, intoxication, tipsiness
ivrogne drunk

Jj

jabot crop
jacassement chatter
jacasser chatter, natter
jacasser à qui mieux mieux talk nineteen to the dozen
jacinthe hyacinth
jade jade
jaguar jaguar
jaillir gush, spout, spurt
jaillissement gush, spurt
jais jet
jalon milestone
jalousement jealously
jalousie envy, jealousy
jaloux (de) envious, jealous (of)
jamais ever, never
jamais de la vie not on your life!, not likely!
jamais plus nevermore
jambe leg, shank
jambon ham
jamboree jamboree
jante rim
janvier January
jappement yap, yelp
japper yap, yelp
jaquette jacket
jardin garden(s)
jardinage gardening
jardin botanique botanic(al) garden(s)
jardin d'enfants nursery school
jardin maraîcher market garden
jardiner garden
jardinier, ière gardener, landscape gardener
jargon cant, jargon
jarret hock
jars gander
jauge gauge
jauger size up
jaunâtre sallow
jaune yellow
jaune d'oeuf yolk
jaunir yellow
jaunisse jaundice
javelot javelin
jazz jazz, jazzy
jean denim, jeans
jeannette brownie
jeep jeep
jersey jersey
jet jet, spout
jetable disposable
jetée pier

jeter cast, cast aside, chuck, discard, dump, sling, throw, throw away, throw out, turf
jeter de la poudre aux yeux de qqn throw dust in someone's eyes
jeter des flammes flame
jeter le doute sur throw doubt on
jeter sur, se fall on/upon, go at, go for
jeter un coup d'œil glimpse, glance
jeter un coup d'œil furtif peek, peep
jeton chip, counter, token
jeu action, gambling, game, pack, play
jeu brutal horseplay
jeu d'enfant child's play, cinch
jeu (de cartes) deck, pack (of cards)
jeu de dames chequers
jeu de fléchettes darts
jeu de quilles ninepins, ten-pin bowling
jeu questionnaire quiz
jeudi Thursday
jeûne fast, fasting
jeune juvenile, young, youngster, youthful
jeune fille girl, lass, maiden
jeune homme lad, youth
jeune marié, ée bridegroom, bride
jeune/futur marié groom
jeûner fast
jeunesse youth, youthfulness
jockey jockey
joie gladness, glee, joy
joindre fold, join
joindre (à) enclose
joindre les deux bouts make (both) ends meet
joindre, se join (up)
joint join, seam
joint à allied (with)
joint hermétique seal
jointure knuckle
joker joker
joli handsome, nice, pretty
joliesse prettiness
joliment prettily
jonc bulrush, rush
jonction junction
jongler juggle
jongleur, euse juggler
jonque junk
jonquille daffodil
joue cheek
jouer act, enact, gamble, perform, play, play at
jouer à pile ou face toss, toss up
jouer au golf golf

jouer aux dés dice
jouer avec le feu play with fire
jouer contre take on
jouer d'oreille play by ear
jouer des coudes elbow
jouer du violon fiddle
jouer franc jeu play fair
jouer la comédie put on an act
jouer le jeu play the game
jouer sur un pipeau pipe
jouer un tour play a hoax on, play a trick/tricks on
jouet plaything, toy
joueur, euse gambler, player
joueur, euse de cornemuse piper
joug yoke
jouir (de) enjoy
jour day, daylight, light
jour après jour day by day, day in day out
jour d'école school day
journal diary, journal, newspaper, paper
journal de bord log
journal officiel gazette
journalisme journalism
journaliste journalist
journalistique journalistic
journée day
jovial breezy, convivial, jolly, jovial
jovialement convivially, jovially
jovialité conviviality, joviality
joyau gem
joyeusement cheerfully, gleefully, happily, joyfully, joyously, merrily
joyeux cheerful, cheery, glad, gleeful, joyful, joyous, merry
jubilant jubilant
jubilé jubilee
judiciaire judicial
judicieusement judiciously, soundly
judicieux judicious, sound
judo judo
juge adjudicator, judge, justice, on trial
jugé on trial
juge de ligne linesman
jugement judg(e)ment
juger adjudicate, deem, judge, try
juillet July
juin June
juke-box jukebox
jumeau, elle twin
jumelé semi-detached
jumelles binoculars, field-glasses
jumelles de théâtre opera glasses
jument mare
jungle jungle
junte junta

jupe skirt
jupe-culotte culotte
jupon petticoat, slip
juré sworn, juror
jurer swear, vow
jurer par swear by
juridiction jurisdiction
juridique legal
juridiquement judicially
jurisprudence jurisprudence
juron oath, swear-word
jury jury, panel
jury d'accusation grand jury

jus juice
jusqu'à as far as to, up to
jusqu'à (ce que) till, until
jusqu'à présent yet
jusqu'à un certain point to some
  degree, to a certain extent/to some
  extent
jusqu'au bout to the last
jusqu'aux os to the bone
jusqu'ici so far, hither to
juste correct, fair, in tune, just,
  righteous
juste à temps in the nick of time

juste après next to
juste ciel! goodness gracious,
  goodness me, gracious
juste pour une fois just for once
justesse adequacy, rightness
justice justness, justice
justifiable justifiable
justification justification
justifié righteous
justifier explain away, justify,
  substantiate, warrant
juteux juicy
juvénile youthful

Kk

kaki khaki
kaléidoscope kaleidoscope
kaléidoscopique kaleidoscopic
kangourou kangaroo
kapok kapok
karaté karate

kayak kayak
kermesse fête
kérosène kerosene
ketchup ketchup
kidnapper kidnap
kilo(gramme) kilogram(me)
kilomètre kilometre
kilowatt kilowatt
kilt kilt

kimono kimono
kiosque kiosk
kit kit
kiwi kiwi
klaxon horn, honk
klaxonner honk, hoot
koala koala (bear)
kyste cyst

Ll

l'emporter sur get the better of, outweigh
l'un l'autre each other, one another
l'un(e) ou l'autre either
là here
là-haut upstairs
la dernière chose que... the last thing
la goutte qui fait déborder le vase the last straw
la main dans la main hand in hand
la plupart (de) most, the best part of
la tête la première headfirst
laboratoire laboratory
laborieusement arduously, laboriously
laborieux laborious, difficult
labourer plough
labyrinthe labyrinth, maze
lac lake
lacer lace
lacérer maul
lacet lace, shoelace
lâche cowardly, loose, slack
lâcher blurt, let fall, let go (of), let loose, release, throw up
lâcheté cowardice, cowardliness
lacté milky
lady lady
lagune lagoon
laïc layman
laid homely, ugly, unsightly
laideur ugliness
laine wool
laine d'agneau lambswool
laineux fleecy, wooly
laïque lay
laisse lead, leash
laisser leave, let
laisser aller, se let one's hair down
laisser aller à, se indulge in
laisser dans le pétrin leave in the lurch
laisser distancer, (se) drop back
laisser entrer admit
laisser le bénéfice du doute (à qqn) give (someone) the benefit of the doubt
laisser partir let off
laisser passer pass up, let slip, make way (for)
laisser tomber drop, jilt
laisser tranquille leave alone, let (someone or something) alone/be
laissez-passer pass
lait milk

lait fouetté milkshake
laiterie dairy
laiteux milky
laitier milkman
laiton brass
laitue lettuce
lambeau rag, shred, tatters
lambiner dally
lambrequin pelmet
lambrissé panelled
lame billow, blade, slat
lamelle gill, slat
lamentable mournful, pitiful
lamentation lament, lamentation
lamenter sur, (se) lament, wail
lampe lamp, valve
lampe de poche flashlight, torch
lampe de sûreté safety lamp
lance lance, spear
lance-pierre slingshot
lancement launch
lancer cast, fling, heave, launch, pitch, put out, shoot, toss
lancer avec esprit quip
lancer, se throw oneself into
lancer dans, se embark on, launch into, launch out
lancer un défi à fly in the face of
lancer (violemment) hurl
lanceur, euse pitcher
lancinant stabbing
landau baby carriage, pram
lande moor, moorland
langage language, speech
langue language, tongue
langue maternelle mother tongue
langue morte dead language
langue vernaculaire vernacular
langue vivante modern language
languir pour pine (for)
languir, (se) languish
languissamment languidly
languissant depressed, languid
lanière lash
lanterne lantern, sidelight
laper lap, lap up
lapider stone
lapin, ine rabbit
laquais stooge
laque lacquer
larbin minion
larder (de) lard
large broad, wide
largement widely
largeur breadth, width
larguer jettison, cast off
larme tear
larmoiement tearfulness
larmoyant watery
larvaire larval

larve grub, larva
lascif lustful
lascivement lustfully
laser laser
lasser pall, tire
lasso lasso
latent latent
latéral lateral, sideline
latéralement laterally
latex latex
latin Latin
latino-américain Latin American
latitude latitude
latrines latrine
latte batten, floorboard
laurier bay, laurel
lavable washable
lavabo basin
lavage wash
lavande lavender
lave lava
lavement enema
lave-vaisselle washer
laver (la vaisselle) wash up
laver, (se) wash
laverie automatique laund(e)rette
laveur, euse washer
lavis wash
laxatif laxative
le comble the end
le dernier cri the last word
le dernier mot the last word
le fin mot de l'histoire the long and the short of it
le lendemain de Noël Boxing day
le long de along, alongside
le moins (de/que) least
le plus most, uppermost
le plus (de) most
le pour et le contre pros and cons
le sort en est jeté the die is cast
lèche-vitrine window shopping
lécher lick
lécher les bottes de qqn fawn (upon)
leçon lesson, teaching
lecteur, trice reader
lecture reading
légal forensic, legal
légalement lawfully, legally
légaliser legalize
légalité legality
légation legation
légendaire legendary
légende caption, fable, key, legend
léger flimsy, fluffy, light, lightweight, mild, slight
légèrement faintly, lightly
légèreté lightness
légiférer legislate

légion legion
législateur, trice legislator
législatif legislative
légitime lawful, legitimate, rightful
légitime défense self-defence
légitimement legitimately, rightfully
légitimité legitimacy
legs bequest
léguer bequeath, leave
légumes verts greens
lent slow
lente nit
lentement slowly
lenteur slowness
lentille lens, lentil
léopard leopard
lèpre leprosy
lépreux, euse leper
lésion injury
lessive washing, laundry
léthargie lethargy
léthargique lethargic
lettrage lettering
lettre letter
lettre d'amour love letter
lettres arts
leucémie leukaemia
lève-tôt early riser
lever raise
lever du jour daybreak, daylight
lever l'ancre weigh anchor
lever, (se) arise, get up, lift, rise
levier crowbar, lever
levier de vitesse gear lever/change/stick
lèvre lip
lévrier greyhound
levure baking powder, yeast
lexique lexicon, vocabulary
lézard lizard
liaison affair, communications, liaison, love affair
libellule damselfly, dragonfly
libéral liberal
libéralement liberally
libéralité liberality
libérateur, trice liberator
libération discharge, liberation, release
libérer discharge, free, liberate, release, turn loose
liberté freedom, liberty
liberté d'expression free speech
liberté surveillée probation
libertés civiques civil liberties/rights
libraire bookseller
librairie bookshop, bookstore
libre free, spare, unoccupied

libre arbitre free will
libre-échange free trade
libre-service cash and carry, self-service
librement freely
licenciement redundancy
licencier lay off, dismiss
lichen lichen
licorne unicorn
licou halter
lie dregs
liège cork
lien bond, contact, link, tie
lier bind
lierre ivy
lieu de naissance birthplace
lieue league
lieutenant lieutenant
lieux premises
lièvre hare
ligament ligament
lignage lineage
ligne fishing line, line
ligné lined, ruled
ligne de conduite course
ligne de départ scratch
ligne droite straight
lignée line
ligner line
ligue league
liguer, se band, gang up on
lilas lilac
limace slug
lime file, lime
lime à ongles emery board, nail file
limer, (se) file
limitation limitation
limitation/contrôle des naissances birth control, family planning
limite borderline, bound, limit, limitation
limité limited
limiter keep down, limit
limites scope
limonade lemonade
limousine limousine
limpide crystal clear
limpidité clarity
lin linen, shroud
linéaire linear
linge linen
lingerie lingerie
lingot ingot
linguiste linguist
linguistique linguistic, linguistics
lino(léum) linoleum
lion lion
liquéfier liquidize, liquefy
liqueur liqueur
liquidateur, trice liquidator

liquidation liquidation
liquide fluid, liquid, watery
liquider liquidate, sell off, sell out
lire à voix haute readout
lire entre les lignes read between the lines
lire la carte navigate
lire, (se) read
lire sur les lèvres lip-read
lisibilité legibility, readableness, readability
lisible legible, readable
lisiblement legibly
lisse sleek, smooth
lisser ses plumes preen
liste list, roll, roster
liste d'attente waiting list
liste de paye payroll
liste noire blacklist
lit bed
lit de camp camp bed, cot
lit de mort deathbed
lit de rivière/fleuve riverbed
litchi lychee, lichee
literie bedding
litière litter
litige litigation
litre litre
littéraire literary
littéral literal
littéralement literally
littéralité literalness
littérature literature
littoral coast, coastal, seaboard, shore
livraison delivery
livre book, pound
livre de cuisine cookbook
livre de lecture reader
livre de poche paperback
livre relié hardback
livre sterling pound, sterling
livrer deliver, turn in
livret de banque bank book
lobe lob, lobe
local local
localement locally
localité locality
locataire tenant
location hire, rental
locomotion locomotion
locomotive engine, locomotive
locomotive à vapeur steam engine
locution idiomatique idiom
logarithme logarithm
loge box, dressing room, lodge
logement accommodation, housing, lodging
loger accommodate, house, lodge, put up

logiciel software
logique logical
logiquement logically
loi act, law, legislation
loi martiale martial law
loin afar, far
loin de far from, nowhere near
lointain far, faraway, remote
loisir leisure
long long
longe tether
longévité longevity
longitude longitude
longitudinal longitudinal
longitudinalement longitudinally
longtemps long
longueur length
longueur d'ondes wavelength
loquacité garrulity, garrulousness
loquet latch, catch
lord lord
lorgner leer
losange diamond, lozenge, rhombus
lot lot
loterie lottery, raffle
lotion lotion
lotion capillaire conditioner
lotissement estate
lotus lotus
louable commendable, laudable

louablement laudably
louange commendation, praise
louangeur adulatory
louche doubtful, fishy, ladle, shady
loucher squint
louer lease, let, rent, rent out
loup wolf
loupe magnifying glass
lourd heavy, stodgy
lourdaud loutish, lout
lourdement heavily
lourdeur heaviness, stodginess, weightiness
loutre otter
louve wolf
louveteau cub
loyal loyal, staunch
loyalement loyally, staunchly
loyauté loyalty, staunchness
loyer rent, rental
lubrifiant lubricant
lubrification lubrication
lubrifier lubricate
lucarne skylight
lucratif lucrative
lueur gleam, ray
luge sledge, toboggan
lugubre dismal, rueful
lugubrement dismally
luire gleam, glint

luire faiblement glimmer
luisant sleekness
lumbago lumbago
lumière light
lumineux luminous
luminosité luminosity
lunaire lunar
lundi Monday
lune moon
lune de miel honeymoon
lunettes glasses, specs, spectacles
lunettes de protection goggles
lunettes de soleil shades, sunglasses
lustre chandelier, glossiness, lustrous, sheen
lustré glossy
lutin elf, goblin, pixy, sprite
lutrin lectern
lutte fight, struggle
lutter (contre) contend (with) fight, struggle
luxe luxury, luxuriousness
luxe inouï the lap of luxury
luxueusement luxuriously
luxueux luxurious, rich
luxuriant lush
lyrique lyric
lys lily

Mm

macabre grisly, macabre, sick
macadam tarmacadam
macaroni macaroni
mâcher chew
machin contraption
machinal automatic, mechanical
machine machine
machine à coudre sewing machine
machine à écrire typewriter
machine à laver washing machine
machine-outil machine tool
machinerie machinery
machiniste stagehand
mâchoire chop, jaw
mâchonner champ, munch
macis mace
maçon bricklayer, mason
maçonnerie masonry, stonework
macramé macrame
madame madam
mademoiselle miss
madrigal madrigal
maestro maestro
magasin magazine, shop, store
magasinage shopping
magasiner shop
magazine magazine
magicien, ienne magician, wizzard
magie magic
magie noire black art/magic
magique magic
magiquement magically
magistral masterly
magistrat magistrate
magma jumble
magnanime magnanimous
magnanimement magnanimously
magnanimité magnanimity
magnat baron, magnate, tycoon
magnésium magnesium
magnétique magnetic
magnétiquement magnetically
magnétiser magnetize
magnétisme magnetism
magnétophone recorder, tape
  recorder
magnétoscope video recorder,
  VCR
magnificence magnificence
magnifique grand, magnificent,
  splendid
magnifiquement finely,
  magnificently
magnitude magnitude
mai May
maigre lean, meagre, skinny, thin
maigrement meagerly

maigreur leanness, meagreness,
  skinniness
maigrir reduce, slim
maille mesh
maillet mallet
maillon link
maillot leotard
maillot de bain swimming trunks,
  swimsuit, trunks
main hand
main d'applaudissement vote of
  thanks
main-d'œuvre labour, manpower,
  workforce
maintenant now
maintenir maintain, uphold
maintenir en équilibre balance
maintainir, (se) hold off
maintes et maintes fois time and
  (time) again
maintien carriage, maintenance
maire mayor, mayoress
mais but, only
maïs corn
maïs à éclater popcorn
maison home, house, household
maisonnée household
maître master, schoolmaster
maître de soi restrained, self-
  possessed
maître-chanteur blackmailer
maîtresse mistress
maîtrise (de) mastery
maîtrise de soi self-control
maîtriser contain, control
majesté majesty, stateliness
majestueusement majestically
majestueux august, majestic,
  stately
majeur major
majorité majority
majuscule capital
mal badly, evil, harm, ill, wrong
mal à l'aise ill at ease,
  uncomfortable
mal à propos out of turn
mal calculer miscalculate
mal d'oreille(s) earache
mal de dents toothache
mal de mer seasickness
mal de tête headache
mal de ventre stomach ache
mal du pays homesickness
mal élevé ill-bred, ill-mannered
malade bad, ill, invalid, poorly, sick
maladie complaint, disease, illness,
  malady, sickness, trouble
maladif sickly
maladresse awkwardness,
  clumsiness

maladroit awkward, clumsy,
  inexpert
maladroitement awkwardly,
  clumsily, inexpertly, lamely
malaise indisposition
malaria malaria
malaxer mix
malchance mischance, misfortune
malchanceux down on one's luck,
  luckless, unfortunate, unlucky
mâle male
malédiction curse
malentendu misapprehension,
  misunderstanding
malfaiteur, trice wrongdoer, crook
malgré despite, in spite of
malgré tout even so, nevertheless
malhabile awkward
malheur curse, woe
malheureusement unfortunately,
  unhappily, unluckily
malheureux ill-fated, unhappy,
  wretch
malhonnête crooked, dishonest, on
  the fiddle
malhonnêtement dishonestly
malhonnêteté dishonesty
malicieusement mischievously
malin foxy, malignant, sly, wise
  guy, clever
malle trunk
malodorant smelly
malpropre dirty, grubby
malsain unhealthy
malt malt
maltraiter ill-treat, ill-use, knock
  about/around, manhandle, misuse,
  push around
malveillance ill will, malevolence
malveillant malevolent, malignant
maman mamma, mama, mum,
  mummy
mamelon nipple, teat
mammaire mammary
mammifère mammal, mammalian
mammouth mammoth
manche shaft, sleeve
manchette cuff, feature, headline
mandarin mandarin
mandarine tangerine
mandat draft, order, term, warrant
mandat de perquisition search
  warrant
mandat-poste postal order
mandataire attorney
mandoline mandolin, mandoline
manège carousel, merry-go-round,
  stable
manette tap, lever
mangeable eatable

mangeoire manger
manger eat
manger à la fortune du pot take pot luck
mangeur d'hommes man-eater, man-eating
mangouste mangosteen
mangue mango
manguier mango
maniabilité manageability
maniable manageable
maniaque maniac, manic
manie mania
manier handle
manière manner, way
manifestant, ante demonstrator, rioter
manifestation demonstration, display, manifestation, sit-in
manifeste manifesto, open
manifestement evidently, manifestly
manifester demonstrate, manifest
manigances goings-on
manioc cassava
manipulateur, trice manipulator
manipuler handle, manipulate
mannequin dummy, model
manœuvre exercise, gambit, manipulation, mœuvre
manœuvrer manipulate
manque deficiency, irrelevance, lack, shortage, want
manque d'à-propos irrelevancy
manque d'air stuffiness
manque de mesure excessiveness
manque de naturel artificiality
manque de soins neglect
manquer miss, go short
manquer (à) fail
manquer (de) fall short, lack, run out, want, want for
manteau coat, overcoat
manucure manicurist
manuel handbook, manual, textbook
manuel d'introduction primer
manuellement manually
manufacture factory
manuscrit copy, handwritten, manuscript
manutentionner manhandle
maquereau mackerel
maquette model
maquillage makeup
maquiller, (se) makeup
marais marsh
marante arrowhead
marathon marathon
marbre marble

marbré marbled, streaky
marc (de café) grounds
marchand, ande dealer, merchant
marchand, ande de journaux newsagent
marchand, ande de légumes greengrocer
marchand, ande de nouveautés draper
marchand, ande de tabac tobacconist
marchand, ande de volailles poulterer
marchander bargain, haggle
marchandise commodity, goods, merchandise, wares
marché bargain, deal, market
marche march, stair, step, walk
marche arrière reverse
marché commun the Common Market
marché financier stock market
marché noir black market
marcher go, operate, run, step, walk
marcher à grands pas stride
marcher à pas lourds clump, tramp
marcher au pas march
marcher d'un pas léger trip
marcher en file indienne file
marcher pesamment lumber
marcher rondement hum
marcher (sur) tread
marcher sur la pointe des pieds tiptoe, walk on tiptoe(s)
marcher sur les pieds de walk all over (someone)
marcher sur les traces de follow in someone's footsteps
marcher tranquillement amble
mardi Tuesday
mare pond, waterhole
marécage bog, fen, marsh, morass, swamp
marécageux boggy, marshy, swampy
marée tide
marée descendante ebb tide
marée haute high tide, high water
marée montante flood tide
marelle hopscotch
margarine margarine
marge allowance, margin
marge (de sécurité) leeway
marginal marginal, dropout
marguerite daisy
mari husband, mate
mariable marriageable
mariage marriage, match,

matrimony, wedding, wedlock
marié married
marier marry
marier (avec), (se) wed, marry
marieur, euse matchmaker
marijuana marijuana, marihuana
marin marine, mariner, sailor, seafaring, sea-going, seaman
marinade(s) pickle
marine fleet, navy
marine marchande merchant marine
mariner pickle
marionnette marionette, puppet
maritime maritime
mark mark
marketing marketing
marmonnement mutter
marmonner mutter
marmotter mumble
marotte a bee in one's bonnet
marquant prominent
marque make, mark, marker
marqué marked
marque de fabrique brand
marque déposée trademark
marquer mark, score, tag
marquer au fer rouge brand
marquer le pas mark time
marquer un point sur (qqn) be one up on (a person)
marqueur, euse marker, scorer
marqueur indélébile marker
marraine godmother
marron brown, chestnut
mars March
marsouin porpoise
marsupial marsupial
marteau hammer
marteler hammer, thump
martial martial
martin-pêcheur kingfisher
martyr martyr, martyrdom
martyriser martyr
mascarade masquerade
mascotte mascot
masculin masculine
masque mask
masque à gaz gas mask, respirator
masque à oxygène oxygen mask
masquer blot out, cloak, mask
massacre massacre, slaughter
massacrer butcher, mangle, slaughter
massage massage
masse bulk, mace, mass
masser, (se) massage, mass
massette cattail
masseur, euse masseur
massicot guillotine

massif massive, solid
massivement massively
massue mace
mastic putty
mastiff mastiff
mastiquer munch
mastodonte hulk
mât flagpole, flagstaff, mast
mat mate
mât de charge derrick
matador matador
match match, play
match de boxe boxing match
match international test, test match
match nul draw, tie
matelas mattress
matelassé quilted
matelot rating, sailor
mater put down
matérialisation materialization
matérialiser, se materialize
matériau material
matériel material, physical, tackle
maternel maternal, motherly
maternellement maternally
maternité motherhood
mathématicien, ienne mathematician
mathématique mathematical, mathematics
mathématiquement mathematically
matière matter, subject
matière grasse fat
matin morn, morning
matinée matinée
matou tomcat
matraque truncheon
matraquer club
matriarcal matriarchal
matrice die
matrimonial matrimonial
maturité maturity, matureness, ripeness
maudire curse
maudit accursed, damned
maugréer moan
mausolée mausoleum
maussade dull, glum, moody
mauvais bad, dirty, evil, ill, nasty, rotten, wrong
mauvais caractère irritability
mauvais service disservice
mauvais traitement ill-treatment
mauvais usage misuse
mauvaise conduite misbehaviour, naughtiness
mauvaise herbe weed
mauvaise humeur bile,

grumpiness, huffiness, peevishness
mauvaise santé unfitness
mauve mauve
maxime maxim
maximum all-out, maximum
mayonnaise mayonnaise
méandre loop
mécanicien, ienne engine driver, mechanic
mécanicien, ienne (de la marine) engineer
mécanique mechanical, mechanics
mécaniquement mechanically
mécanisation mechanization
mécaniser mechanize
mécanisme clockwork, gear, mechanics, mechanism, works
mécénat patronage
mécène patron
méchamment malignantly, viciously, wickedly
méchanceté badness, evilness, nastiness, viciousness, wickedness
méchant bad, catty, malicious, mean, unkind, vicious, wicked
méchant, ante evil doer, villain
mèche lock
mécontent discontented, disgruntled
mécontentement annoyance, discontent, discontentment, dissatisfaction
mécontenter dissatisfy
médaille medal
médaillé, ée medallist
médaillon inset, locket
médecin doctor, physician
médecine medicine
média mass media, medium
médiateur ombudsman
médiateur, trice mediator
médiation mediation
médical medical
médicalement medically, medicinally
médicament drug, medicine
médicamenteux medicated
médicinal medicinal
médiéval medieval, mediaeval
médiocre below par/not up to par, indifferent, mediocre, poor, second-rate
médiocrité mediocrity
médire backbite
médisance backbiting
méditatif meditative
méditation meditation
méditer meditate
médium medium
méduse jellyfish

méfait misdeed, wrongdoing
méfiance distrust, mistrust
méfiant distrustful, mistrustful, suspicious
méfier, se distrust
méfier de, se mistrust
mégalomane megalomaniac
mégalomanie megalomania
mégatonne megaton
mégot butt, fag-end
meilleur better
mélancolie melancholy
mélancolique melancholy, wistful
mélange blend, mix, mixture
mélangé mixed
mélange blend, mix
mélanger mix, blend, jumble
mélanger, se mix
mélangeur blender, mixer
mélasse molasses, syrup
mêlé mingled, mixed
mêlée scrum, scuffle
mêler mingle, mix
mêler (à) embroil, involve
mêler, se merge, mix
mélèze larch
mélo melodrama
mélodie melody
mélodieusement melodiously, tunefully
mélodieux melodious, sweet, tuneful
mélodique melodic
mélodramatique melodramatic
mélodrame melodrama
melon melon
membrane membrane
membre limb, member
membrure rib
même even, same
même si even if
mémo memo
mémoire memoirs, memory, recall, recollection
mémorable memorable
mémoriser memorize
menaçant grim, lowering, menacing, ugly
menace menace, threat
menacer menace, threaten
menacer du poing shake one's fist at
ménage establishment, housework
ménager husband, spare
ménagère housewife
ménagerie menagerie
mendiant, ante beggar
mendier beg
mené par le bout du nez henpecked

mener go, lead
mener à bien carry out
mener campagne agitate
mener en bateau lead up the garden path
mener par le bout du nez have (someone) on a string, lead by the nose
mener une campagne électorale electioneer
ménestrel minstrel
meneur, euse leader, ringleader
méningite meningitis
menottes handcuffs
mensonge fairy story, falsehood, fib, lie
menstruation menstruation
mensuel monthly
mensurations measurement
mental mental
mentalement mentally
mentalité mentality
menteur, euse liar
menthe mint
menthe poivrée peppermint
menthol menthol
mentholé mentholated
mention distinction, mention
mentionner mention, specify
mentir lie
menton chin
menu menu
menu fretin small fry
menuet minuet
menuiserie wooodwork
menuisier, ière carpenter
mépris contempt, scorn, scornfulness
méprisable contemptible, despicable, lowdown
méprisant scornful
mépriser despise, look down on, scorn
mer sea
mercantilisme commercialism
mercenaire mercenary
merci thanks, thank you
mercredi Wednesday
mercure mercury, quicksilver
merde shit
mère mother, matron
méridien meridian
méridional South, southern
méridional, ale southerner
meringue meringue
méritant meritorious
mérite merit
mériter deserve, earn, merit
méritoire deserving
merlan whitling
merle blackbird

merle américain robin
merveille dream, marvel, wonder
merveilleusement marvellously, wonderfully
merveilleux great, marvellous, wonderful, wondrous
mésange tit
mésaventure misadventure, mishap
mesmérisme mesmerism
mesquin petty, shabby
mesquinerie pettiness
message communication, message
messager, ère courier, messenger
messe mass
mesurage measurement
mesure bar, measure, measurement, step
mesuré deliberate, sober
mesurer gauge, measure, measure out, meter, tall
métal metal
métal précieux precious metal
métallique metallic
métamorphose metamorphosis
métaphore metaphor
métaphorique metaphoric(al)
métaphoriquement figuratively, metaphorically
météo weather
météore meteor
météorite meteorite
météorologie meteorology
météorologique meteorological
météorologue meteorologist
méthode method, system, tutor
méthodique methodical, organized
méthodiquement methodically
méticuleusement meticulously
méticuleux meticulous
métier business, craft, occupation, trade, walk of life, workmanship
métier à tisser loom
métissé of mixed race, crossbred
mètre metre, tape
mètre à ruban measuring tape, tape, tape measure
métrique metric, metrical
métro subway, tube, underground
métronome metronome
métropole metropolis
métropolitain metropolitan
mets dish
mets délicat delicacy
mettable wearable
mettre change, get into, get on, lay, put, put on
mettre à jour update
mettre à l'abri, se shelter
mettre à l'aise, se make oneself at home

mettre à l'épreuve try
mettre à la retraite pension off
mettre à la terre earth
mettre à nu lay bare
mettre à pied axe
mettre à, se get down to, go about, get about, take to, take up
mettre au courant fill in, let in on, put (someone)/be in the picture
mettre au courant, se acquaint, get into the swing (of things)
mettre au pas, se toe the line
mettre au point focus, lick into shape, tune
mettre au rebut/rancart scrap
mettre au travail, se get/set to work
mettre bas foal
mettre d'accord sur, se settle on
mettre d'aplomb straighten
mettre dans la tête de, se take it into one's head (to)
mettre dans le même sac lump together
mettre dans tous ses états, se get into a state, get steamed up
mettre dans une valise pack
mettre de côté lay aside, lay by, put aside, set aside
mettre de l'ordre (dans) sort out
mettre debout, se stand
mettre des bâtons dans les roues throw a spanner in the works
mettre échec et mat mate
mettre en application put into effect
mettre en apprentissage (chez) apprentice
mettre en boîte box
mettre en cage cage
mettre en code, (se) dip
mettre en colère, se lose one's temper
mettre en commun pool
mettre en conserve can
mettre en danger endanger
mettre en déroute rout
mettre en désordre disarrange
mettre en doute challenge, query, question
mettre en frais pour, se do (someone) proud
mettre en fuite put to flight
mettre en gage pawn, pledge
mettre en grève, se come out on strike
mettre en italique italicize
mettre en lumière bring to light
mettre en ordre put/set right
mettre en pièces pull apart/to pieces

mettre en pot pot
mettre en pratique put into practice
mettre en quarantaine quarantine
mettre en quatre (pour), se bend/fall over backwards
mettre en rade lay up
mettre en rangs, (se) line up
mettre en route, se set off, set out, start off, start out
mettre en scène produce, stage
mettre en valeur enhance
mettre en vedette feature, highlight, spotlight
mettre entre parenthèses bracket
mettre fin à put an end to, terminate
mettre hors la loi outlaw
mettre l'adresse sur address
mettre la main sur get one's hands on, lay (one's) hands on
mettre la table lay/set the table
mettre le doigt dessus hit the nail on the head
mettre le doigt sur put one's finger on, pinpoint
mettre le feu à qqch. set fire to (something), set light to, set
mettre le paquet go to town
mettre les pieds dans les plats, (se) put one's foot in it
mettre par écrit write down
mettre son nez dans snoop
mettre son veto à veto
mettre sous clef lock up
mettre sur écoute tap
mettre sur le compte de qqn charge
mettre sur le dos de qqn pass the buck
mettre sur le même pied equate
mettre tous ses œufs dans le même panier put all one's eggs in one basket
mettre un terme à call a halt (to), put a stop to
mettre/entrer en jeu bring/come into play
meublé furnished
meuble de rangement cabinet
meubler furnish
meuglement moo
meugler low, moo
meule millstone, stack
meule de foin hayrick
meule à aiguiser grindstone
meunier, ère miller
meurtre murder
meurtrier murderous, murderer
mezzo-soprano mezzo

mi-temps halftime
miaulement mew, miaow
miauler mew, miaow
micro- micro-
micro(phone) microphone
micro-ordinateur microcomputer
microbe bug, germ, microbe
microfilm microfilm
microphone microphone, mouthpiece
microscope microscope
microscopique microscopic
microsillon long-playing record
midi midday, noon
miel honey
mielleux oily, smooth
miette crumb
miettes de pain breadcrumbs
mieux better
mignon cute, dainty, sweet
migraine migraine
migrant, ante migrant
migrateur migratory
migration migration
mijoter simmer, stew
mijoter un mauvais coup be up to no good
milieu element, environment, mean, medium, middle
militaire military
militant camaigner, militant
militantisme militancy
mille mile, thousand
mille-pattes centipede, millipede
millénaire millennium
millet millet
milliard billion
millième thousandth
milliers (de) thousands of
million million
millionième millionth
millionnaire millionaire
mime mime
mimodrame mime
mimosa mimosa
minable bum, dingy, lousy, seedy, shoddy, sleazy
minaret minaret
mince slender, slim, thin
mince comme une pelure d'oignon wafer-thin
minceur slimness, thinness
mine aspect, countenance, lead, mine
mine d'or bonanza, gold mine
mine de charbon coalmine, colliery
mine terrestre land mine
miner mine, undermine
minerai ore

minéral mineral
minet, ette puss
mineur (de charbon) collier
mineur, eure minor, miner
mini mini
mini-jupe miniskirt
miniature miniature
minibus minibus
minime minimal
minimiser minimize, play down, understate
minimum minimum
ministère ministry
ministériel ministerial
ministre minister
minorité minority
minoterie mill
minuit midnight
minuscule diminutive, minute, scanty, small, tiny
minutage timing
minute minute
minuterie timer
minutie minuteness, thoroughness
minutieusement elaborately, minutely
minutieux elaborate, minute, thorough
miracle miracle
miraculeusement miraculously
miraculeux miraculous
mirage mirage
mire sight
miroir looking glass, mirror
miroiter shimmer
mise stake
mise à mort kill
mise en application enforcement
mise en scène production, staging
miser stake
miser sur back, put on
misérable abject, mean, miserable, wretched
misérablement abjectly, miserably, wretchedly
misère misery, squalor, wretchedness
miséricordieusement mercifully
miséricordieux gracious, merciful
missile missile
missile téléguidé guided missile
mission mission
missionnaire missionary
mitaine mitten
mite mite, moth
mité moth-eaten
miteux disreputable, down-at-heel, shabby, tatty
mitrailler machine gun, pepper, rake

mitrailleuse machine gun
mitre mitre
mixte mixed
mobile mobile, movable, moveable, removable
mobilier furniture
mobilisation mobilization
mobiliser mobilize
mobilité mobility
mocassin moccasin
mode fashion, mode, style, vogue
mode de vie way of life
modelage modelling
modèle model, pattern, sitter
modèle réduit miniature
modeler model, mould
modération moderateness, moderation
modéré easy, moderate
modérer allay, damp down, curb, moderate
modérer, se moderate
moderne modern, up to date
modernisation modernization
moderniser modernize
modernité modernity, modernness
modeste humble, modest
modestement modestly
modestie demureness, modesty
modification alteration, modification
modifier alter, modify
module module
moelle marrow, pith
moelle épinière spinal cord
moelleux mellow
moi-même myself
moignon stump
moindre, le/la lesser
moine monk
moins less, lesser, minus
mois month
moisi mould, mouldy, musty
moisissure mouldiness
moissonner reap
moissonneur, euse harvester, reaper
moissonneuse-batteuse combine harvester
moite clammy, moist
moite de sueur sweaty
moiteur moistness
moitié half
moitié-moitié fifty-fifty, half-and-half
molaire molar
moléculaire molecular
molécule molecule
mollement slackly, sluggishly
mollesse sluggishness
mollet calf

moment moment, time
moment précis point
momentané momentary
momentanément momentarily
momie mummy
mon Dieu! goodness, heavens
monarchie monarchy
monarque monarch
monastère monastery
monastique monastic
monde world
mondial worldwide
monétaire monetary
moniteur monitor, counsellor
monnaie change, currency
monnaie décimale decimal currency
monocle monocle
monogramme monogram
monologue monologue
monoplan monoplane
monopole monopoly
monopoliser monopolize
monorail monorail
monotone humdrum, monotonous
monotonie monotony
monsieur gentleman, sir
monstre fiend, horror, monster
monstrueusement monstrously
monstrueux monstrous, outrageous
mont Mount, mountain
montagne mountain
montagneux hilly, mountainous
montant rising, upright
montant de porte gate post
monté mounted
montée ascent, climb
monter assemble, climb, flow, go up, mount
monter à la tête go to someone's head
monter à, se amount
monter en flèche rocket, shoot up, soar, spiral
monter en graine go to seed
monter la garde stand guard, keep watch
monter les mailles cast on
monter qqn contre qqn set (someone) against (someone)
monter un bateau hoax
monter un coup (contre) frame
monteur, euse fitter
monticule mound
montre watch
montre en main to the minute
montre-bracelet wristwatch
montrer display, exhibit, point, show
monture mount, setting

monument memorial, monument
monumental monumental
moquer (de), (se) flout, gibe, jeer, jibe, joke, laugh at, make fun of, mock, poke fun at, scoff
moquerie jibe, gibe, mockery
moqueur derisive, mocking
moral ethical, moral, morale
morale ethics, moral
moralisateur sanctimonious
moralité morality, morals
morceau cut, fragment, lump, piece
mordant acid, biting, caustic
mordre bite
mordre la poussière bite the dust
mordu fiend, freak
morgue morgue, mortuary
morose morose
morosité moroseness
morphine morphia
mors bit
morse Morse, walrus
morsure bite
mort dead, death
mort-né stillborn
mortalité mortality
mortel deadly, lethal, mortal
mortellement deadly, mortally
mortier mortar, mortarboard
mortification mortification
morue cod
mosaïque mosaic
mosquée mosque
mot note, word
mot d'ordre watchword
mot de passe password
mot pour mot word for word
motel motel
motet anthem
moteur engine, motor
moteur diesel diesel engine
motif design, grounds, motive, pattern
motion motion
motion de remerciements vote of thanks
motivation motivation
moto(cyclette) motorbike, motorcycle
motoculteur cultivator
motocycliste motorcyclist
motoriser mechanize, motorize
mots croisés crossword (puzzle)
motte clod
mou limp, sluggish, soft, spineless, squashy
mouche fly
mouche bleue bluebottle
mouche commune housefly
moucher snuff, snuff out

moucheron gnat
moucheté flecked
mouchoir handkerchief
moudre grind, mill
moue pout
mouette gull, seagull
mouffette skunk
mouillage anchorage, moorings
mouillé wet
mouiller wet
moule cast, mould, mussel
mouler mould
moulin mill
moulin à poivre pepper mill
moulin à vent windmill
mourir die, pass away, pass on
mourir d'envie de be gasping for, itch
mourir de faim starve
mousquet musket
mousquetaire musketeer
mousse foam, froth, lather, moss, mousse
mousseline chiffon, muslin
mousser foam
mousseux frothy, sparkling, mossy
mousson monsoon
moussu mossy
moustache moustache, whiskers
moustique mosquito
moutarde mustard
mouton mutton, sheep
mouvement motion, movement, turnover
mouvementé eventful

moyen average, mean, medium, middling, moderate, ordinary, way
Moyen Âge Middle Ages
moyenne average
moyens means
moyeu hub
mucus mucus
muer break, moult
muet dumb, mute, speechless
muffin muffin
mufle oafish
mugir hoot, howl
mule mule, mullet
multicolore multicoloured, variegated
multimillionnaire multimillionaire
multiple multiple
multiplication multiplication
multiplier multiply
multiracial multiracial
multitude multitude
municipal municipal
munitions ammunition, munitions
mûr mature, ripe
mur wall
muraille wall
mûre mulberry
mûrement maturely
mûri mellow
mûrier mulberry
mûrir mature, mellow, ripen
murmurant murmuring
murmure murmur, whisper
murmurer whisper
musaraigne shrew

muscle brawn, muscle
musclé brawny, muscular
musculaire muscular
museau muzzle, snout
musée museum
museler muzzle
muselière muzzle
musette (mangeoire) nose bag
musical musical
musicalement musically
musicien, cienne musical, musician
musique music
musique de chambre chamber music
musulman, ane Muslim
muter transfer
mutin mutineer
mutiné mutinous
mutiner, se mutiny
mutinerie mutiny
mutisme dumbness, speechlessness
mutuel mutual
mutuellement mutually
myope myopic, nearsighted, short-sighted
myopie myopia, shortsightedness
mystère mystery
mystérieusement enigmatically, mysteriously, uncannily
mystérieux mysterious, uncanny
mystifier bamboozle, fox
mythe myth
mythique mythical
mythologie mythology
mythologique mythological

Nn

n'arriver à rien get nowhere

n'avoir qu'une parole be as good as one's word

n'avoir rien à voir have nothing to do with

n'importe comment anyhow, hit-or-miss

n'importe lequel des deux either

n'importe où wherever

n'importe quand whenever

n'importe quel any

n'importe qui anybody, anyone

n'importe quoi anything

nabot, ote shrimp

nacelle gondola

nacre mother-of-pearl

nage swim

nage sur le dos backstroke

nageoire fin, flipper

nager swim

nageur, euse swimmer

naïf naïve, naive, simple

nain dwarf, midget

naissance birth

naître be born

naïvement naïvely

napalm napalm

nappe tablecloth

narcotique narcotic

narine nostril

narrateur, trice narrator

narration narration

nasal nasal

natal native

nation nation

national national

nationalement nationally

nationalisation nationalization

nationaliser nationalize

nationalisme nationalism

nationaliste nationalist, nationalistic

nationalité nationality

natte pigtail

naturaliste naturalist

nature fibre, nature

nature saine wholesomeness

naturel ease, easy, native, natural, organic

naturellement naturally

naufrage shipwreck, wreck

naufragé, ée castaway

nausée nausea

nautique nautical

naval naval

navet turnip

navette shuttle

navigable navigable

navigateur, trice navigator

navigation navigation, sailing

navigation de plaisance shuttle, yachting

naviguer navigate, sail

navire boat, ship

navire de guerre warship

navire marchand merchant ship

ne pas avoir le cœur de not have the heart to

ne pas convenir (à) (de) disagree (with)

ne pas démordre (de) stick to one's guns

ne pas être à la hauteur fall down

ne pas laisser chômer keep someone hopping

ne pas pouvoir se sentir there's no love lost between them

ne pas se fatiguer take it easy

ne pas se mouiller pussyfoot

ne pas tenir compte de discount

ne pas trop en mettre go easy on

ne tenir aucun compte de disregard

néanmoins nonetheless, none the less

néant nothingness

nécessaire necessary

nécessairement necessarily

nécessité necessity

nécessiter involve, necessitate

nécessiteux needy

nécrologie obituary

nectar nectar

nef nave

négatif minus, negative

négation negative

négativement negatively

négligé careless, scruffy, slipshod

négligemment carelessly, negligently

négligence carelessness, negligence

négligent negligent, slack

négliger neglect, omit

négliger, se go to seed

négociateur, trice negotiator

négociation negotiation

négocier negotiate

neige snow

neige fondante slush, wet snow

neiger snow

neigeux snowy

nénuphar waterlily

néon neon

nerf nerve

nerveusement nervously, restlessly, restively

nerveux excitable, highly-strung, jumpy, nervous

nervosité nerves, nervousness, restlessness, restiveness

nervure vein

net clean, clear-cut, flat, net, sharp, tidy, trim

nettement cleanly, definitely

netteté neatness

nettoyer clean, clean up, cleanse, muck out

nettoyer (à fond) do out

nettoyer à sec dry clean

nettoyeur, euse cleaner

neuf new, nine

neutraliser neutralize

neutralité neutrality

neutre neuter, neutral

neutron neutron

neuvième ninth

neveu nephew

nez nose

ni l'un ni l'autre neither

ni... ni neither ... nor

niais simple, simpleton

niaiserie silliness

niche kennel, niche

nichée brood

nickel nickel

nicotine nicotine

nid nest

nièce niece

nier deny

nigaud, aude booby

nitrate nitrate

niveau level, plane

niveau à bulle spirit level

niveau d'eau water level

niveau de la mer sea level

niveler even

noble high, lordly, noble, nobleman, noblewoman

noblement nobly

noblesse kingliness, nobility, peerage

noce(s) wedding

nocivité hurtfulness

nocturne nocturnal

nodule node

Noël Noel, Christmas

nœud bow, hitch, knot, node

nœud coulant noose

noir black, dark, glowering

noir d'ébène ebony

noir d'encre inky

noir de jais jet black

noir sur blanc in black and white

noirceur blackness, sootiness

noircir black, blacken

noisetier hazel

noisette hazel, hazelnut

noix walnut

noix de cajou cashew
noix de coco coconut
nom name, noun
nom de baptême christian name
nom de famille surname
nom de jeune fille maiden name
nom de lieu place name
nom de plume pen name
nom propre proper noun/name
nomade nomad, nomadic
nombre number
nombre à deux chiffres double figures
nombre ordinal ordinal number
nombre premier prime number
nombreux numerous
nombril navel
nominal nominal
nomination appointment, nomination
nommer appoint, name, nominate
non no, not
non alcoolisé non-alcoholic
non compris exclusive of, not included
non plus either
non résidant non-resident
non valable invalid
non violent non-violent
non conducteur non-conductor
non-existence non-existence
non-violence non-violence
nonagénaire ninety-year-old, nonagenarian
nonchalamment nonchalantly
nonchalance nonchalance
nonchalant nonchalant
nord north
nord magnétique magnetic north
normal natural, normal, standard

normalement normally
normalité normality
nostalgie nostalgia
nostalgique nostalgic
nostalgiquement nostalgically
notabilité notability
notable notable
notablement notably
notamment notably
notation notation
note chit, grade, memorandum, note, toot, mark
note de service memorandum
note en bas de page footnote
noter jot, mark, note, take down
notion notion
notoire notorious
notoirement notoriously
notonecte water boatman
nouer knot, tie
noueux gnarled, knobbly, knotty
nougat nougat
nouille noodle
nourri au sein breastfed
nourrice wet nurse
nourrir entertain, feed, nourish, nurse
nourrir (de), se feed (on)
nourrir de, se live on
nourrissant nourishing
nourrisson infant
nourriture food, nourishment, nutriment
nouveau fresh, new
nouveau départ a clean slate
nouveau venu newcomer
nouveauté release
nouvelle(s) tidings
nouvellement freshly
nouvelles news, word

novembre November
novice novice
novice (dans) new to
noyau nucleus, pit, stone
noyer walnut
noyer, (se) drown
nu bare, in the nude, naked, nude
nu-pieds barefoot(ed)
nu-tête bareheaded
nuage cloud
nuageux cloudy
nuance tint
nucléaire nuclear
nucléus nucleus
nudisme nudism
nudiste nudist
nudité bareness, nakedness, nudity
nuée cloud
nuire (à) tell on
nuisible detrimental, harmful
nuisible (à) injurious (to)
nuit night, nighttime
nul drawn, void
nul autre que no/none other than
nulle part nowhere
nullité washout
numérique digital, numerical
numériquement numerically
numéro issue, number
numéro d'immatriculation registration number
numéroter number
nuptial nuptial
nuque nape
nurse nanny, nurse
nutritif nutritious
nutrition nutrition
nylon nylon
nymphe nymph

Oo

oasis oasis
obéir (à) obey
obéissance obedience
obéissant biddable, obedient
obèse gross, obese
obésité obesity
objecter à, s' take exception to/at, object to
objectif objective
objection objection
objectivement objectively
objet object
objets de valeur valuables
obligation commitment, duty, obligation
obligatoire compulsory, obligatory
obligatoirement compulsorily, obligatorily
obligeamment obligingly
obligeant obliging
obliger accommodate, oblige
oblique oblique, sidelong
obliquement obliquely
oblitérer cancel
obscène bawdy, filthy, obscene
obscènement obscenely
obscénité obscenity, smut, smuttiness
obscur obscure
obscurément obscurely
obscurité darkness, duskiness, obscurity, shadow
obsédant obsessive
obséder obsess
obséquieusement obsequiously
obséquieux obsequious, smarmy
obséquiosité obsequiousness, smarminess
observance observance
observateur observant, observer, watcher
observation observance, observation
observatoire observatory
observer eye, observe
obsession obsession
obsessionnel obsessional
obstacle bar, barrier, hindrance, hurdle, impediment, obstacle, snag
obstétricien, ienne obstetrician
obstétrique midwifery, obstetrics
obstination obstinacy, perversity, perverness
obstiné obstinate
obstinément obstinately
obstruction obstruction
obstruer obstruct

obtenir get, obtain
obtenir ce que l'on désire get/have one's own way
obtenir son diplôme graduate
obturateur shutter
obturer fill
obtus obtuse
obus shell
occasion chance, occasion, opportunity
occasion unique golden opportunity
occasionner entail, cause, produce
Occident the West
occupant, ante occupant, occupier
occupation occupation
occupé busy, engaged, tenanted
occuper employ, occupy
occuper (à), s' busy (with)
occuper de, s' attend, care for, deal with, see about, see to
occuper de ses affaires, s' mind one's own business
océan ocean
octave octave
octobre October
octogénaire eighty-year-old, octogenarian
octogonal octagonal
octogone octagon
octroi bestowal
octuor octet
oculaire eyepiece
oculiste oculist
ode ode
odeur odour, scent, smell, whiff
odieusement hatefully, obnoxiously, odiously
odieux hateful, obnoxious, odious
odieux (à) abhorrent (to)
odorant fragrant, sweet-smelling
odorat nose, smell
œcuménique ecumenical
œil eye
œil au beurre noir black eye
œillet eyelet
œsophage gullet
œuf egg
œuf de Pâques easter egg
œufs spawn
œufs brouillés scrambled egg(s)
œufs (de poissons) roe
œuvre handywork, work
œuvre d'art work of art
offensant offensive
offensé injured
offenser affront, offend
offenser de, s' resent, take offence of
offensif offensive
offensive offensive

office service
officiel formal, official
officiellement officially
officier officer, officiate
offrande offering
offre bid, offer
offrir gift, offer, treat, volunteer
offrir à extend
offrir (à) present
ogive warhead
ogre ogre
oie goose
oignon onion
oindre anoint
oiseau bird
oiseau de basse-cour fowl
oiseau de volière cagebird
oiseau(x) aquatique(s) waterfowl
oiseau(x) sauvage(s) wildfowl
oiseau-mouche hummingbird
oisillon chick, fledg(e)ling, nestling
oison gosling
oléoduc pipeline
oligo élément trace elements
olive olive
olivier olive
olympiques (jeux) Olympics
ombragé shady
ombrage shade
ombrager shadow
ombre shade, shadiness, shadow, sunshade
ombrer shade
ombres shading
omelette omelette, omelet
omettre omit
omission omission
omnibus omnibus
omoplate shoulder blade
once ounce
oncle uncle
onctueux smooth
onde wave
onde électromagnétique electromagnetic waves
ondulation(s) curl, curliness, ripple, wave, waviness
ondulé corrugated, wavy, wiggly
onduler ripple, wave
onduleux rolling
ongle fingernail, nail
ongle d'orteil toenail
ongle du pouce thumbnail
onguent ointment, salve
onyx onyx
onze eleven
onzième eleventh
opacité opaqueness, opacity
opale opal
opaque opaque, thick

opéra opera, opera house
opérateur, trice machinist, operator
opération operation, process
opérationnel operational
opercule gill cover
opérer operate
opiacé opiate
opinion opinion, view
opium opium
opportun expedient, opportune, timely
opportunément opportunely
opportunisme opportunism
opportuniste opportunist
opportunité advisability, appropriateness, expedience, opportuneness
opposé opposite
opposé à averse to
opposer match, oppose
opposition opposition
oppresser oppress
oppresseur oppressor
oppression oppression
opprimé downtrodden
opprimer oppress
opticien, ienne optician
optimisme optimism
optimiste optimist, optimistic
optique optics
opulence opulence
opulent opulent
opuscule pamphlet
or gold
oracle oracle
orage storm
orageusement stormily
orageux stormy, thundery
oral oral
oralement orally
orang-outang orangutan
orange orange
orateur, trice orator
oratoire oratorical
orbite orbit
orchestral orchestral
orchestre band, orchestra
orchidée orchid
ordinaire ordinary
ordinairement ordinarily
ordinateur computer
ordination ordination
ordonnance orderly, prescription
ordonner command, direct, ordain, order
ordre command, order, orderliness, tidiness
ordre du jour agenda
ordures garbage, litter, refuse, rubbish, trash

oreille ear
oreille indiscrète eavesdropper
oreiller pillow
oreillons mumps
orfèvre goldsmith, smith
organe organ
organique organic
organiquement organically
organisateur, trice organizer, promoter, steward, stewardess
organisation organization
organisé organized
organiser get up, mastermind, order, organize, plan
organiser une fête throw a party
organiser, (s') form
organisme organism, system
organiste organist
orge barley
orgelet sty
orgie orgy
orgue organ
orgueilleux proud, conceited
Orient the East
oriental eastern, oriental
orientation direction, orientation
orienter, (s') orientate
originaire de native to
original novel, original
originalité originality
origine extraction, origin, root
originel original
origines origins
orignal moose
orme elm
ornement adornment, embellishment, ornament
ornemental ornamental
ornementation exagérée ornateness
orner adorn, embellish
ornière rut
ornithologie ornithology
ornithologique ornithological
ornithologue ornithologist
orphelin, ine orphan
orphelinat orphanage
orteil toe
orthodoxe orthodox
orthographe spelling
orthopédie orthop(a)edics
orthopédique orthop(a)edic
ortie nettle
os bone
osé off colour
oser dare
ossature frame
osseux angular, bony
ostentation ostentation, ostentatiousness

ostentatoire ostentatious
ostracisme ostracism
otage hostage
otarie sea lion
ôter remove, slip off, take, take off
ou or, either...or
où where, wherever
où, d' whence
où (donc) whereabouts
ouate cottonwool, lint
oublier forget, leave out, miss out
oublier, (s') forget
oublieux oblivious
ouest west
ouest, à l' west
ouest, d' westerly
ouest, de l' western
oui yes
ouï-dire hearsay
ouïe hearing
ouïes gill
ouragan hurricane
ourlet hem
ours bear
ours en peluche teddy (bear)
ours gris (d'Amérique) grizzly
ours polaire polar bear
ouste shoo
outil implement, tool
outrage contempt, outrage
outrageusement outrageously
outre-mer overseas
outrecuidant cocksure
ouvert free, open
ouvert à tous free-for-all
ouvertement openly, overtly
ouverture aperture, opening, overture
ouvrage de -work
ouvre-boîte(s) can opener
ouvrier labourer
ouvrir answer, open, turn on
ouvrir (en un tournemain) flick
ouvrir la marche lead on
ouvrir le feu (sur) open fire (on)
ouvrir, (s') open, open up
ouvrir tout grand throw open
ouvrir un commerce/magasin set up shop
ouvrir une brèche dans breach
ouvrir violemment, (s') burst open
ovaire ovary
ovale oval
ovation ovation
ovule egg, ovum
oxyde de carbone carbon monoxide
oxygène oxygen
ozone ozone

Pp

pacificateur, trice peacemaker
pacification pacification
pacifique peaceable
pacifiquement peaceably
pacifisme pacifism
pacifiste pacifist
pacte pact
pagaie paddle
paganisme paganism
pagayer paddle
page leaf, page
page de garde flyleaf
page de titre title page
pagne loincloth
pagode pagoda
paiement payment
païen, ïenne heathen, pagan
paillasson doormat
paille straw
pain bread, cake, loaf
pain d'épice gingerbread
pain de seigle rye bread
pair even, peer
paire brace, pair, twosome
paisible peaceful
paisiblement peacefully, restfully
paix peace, peacefulness
palais palace, palate, roof of the mouth
palais de justice courthouse
pale blade
pâle chalky, pale, sickly, wan
palette palette
palétuvier mangrove
pâleur paleness, pallor, wanness
palier landing
pâlir pale
palissade hoarding, stockade
palme attap, atap, flipper
palmé webbed
palmier palm, plam tree
palmipède web-footed
palmure web
pâlot peaky
palourde clam
palper feel
palpitant thrilling, exciting
palpitation flutter, palpitations
palpiter palpitate
pamplemousse grapefruit
pan flap
panaché shandy
panais parsnip
panama panama
pancarte placard
pancréas pancreas
panda panda

panégyrique eulogy
panier basket, hamper, pannier
panique flap, panic, scare
paniquer flap, panic
panne breakdown, failure
panne de courant blackout, power cut
panneau board, panel, sign
panneau d'affichage billboard, notice board
panorama panorama
panoramique panoramic
pansement bandage, dressing
pansement adhésif plaster
panser dress, groom
pantalon pants, slacks, trousers
panthère panther
pantoufle slipper
panure breadcrumbs
paon peacock
papa dad, daddy, papa
papal papal
papauté papacy
papaye papaya
pape pope
papeterie stationery
papetier, ière stationer
papier paper
papier à lettres notepaper, writing paper
papier carbone carbon paper
papier d'aluminium tinfoil
papier de soie tissue paper
papier de verre sandpaper
papier hygiénique toilet paper
papier quadrillé graph paper
papier-calque tracing paper
papier-mouchoir tissue
papier peint wallpaper
papiers (d'identité) papers
papillon butterfly
papillon de nuit moth
paprika paprika
paquebot liner, steamer
Pâques Easter
paquet bunch, pack, package, packet, pile
par by, per, via
par à-coups by fits and starts
par cœur by heart
par conséquent consequently, therefore
par égard pour in deference to
par erreur mistakenly
par exemple for example, for instance
par habitude from force of habit
par hasard accidentally, by any chance, casually
par ici hereabout(s)

par ignorance ignorantly
par inadvertance inadvertently
par intervalles intermittently, at intervals
par l'entremise de through, by/ through the agency of, through the (kind) offices of
par l'intermédiaire de through
par la présente hereby
par la suite afterwards
par mégarde inadvertently
par moment at times, every now and then/again
par nature temperamentally
par opposition à as opposed to
par pitié for goodness' sake
par porteur by hand
par principe on principle
par ses propres moyens under one's own steam
par terre underfoot
par un heureux hasard by chance
par-ci par-là here and there
par-dessus bord overboard
par-dessus la tête up to one's ears (in)
par-dessus tout above all
parabole parable
parachute chute, parachute
parachutisme skydiving
parachutiste parachutist, paratrooper, skydiver
parade parade
paradis heaven, paradise
paradoxal paradoxical
paradoxalement paradoxically
paradoxe paradox
paragraphe paragraph
paraître appear, come out
parallèle parallel
parallélogramme parallelogram
paralyser cripple, paralyse
paralysie paralysis
paralytique paralytic
paranoïa paranoia
paranoïaque paranoiac
parapet parapet
parapher initial
paraphrase paraphrase
parapluie umbrella
parasite parasite, sponger
parasites interference, static
parasol parasol
paravent screen
parc grounds, park
parc à gibier game reserve
parc de stationnement car park, parking lot
parce que because
parcelle allotment, atom

parchemin parchment
parcomètre parking meter
parcourir cover, look through, run through
pardon forgiveness, pardon
pardonner condone, forgive, pardon
pare-brise windshield
pare-chocs bumper
pare-étincelles fire-guard
pareil à like
pareillement alike, likewise
parent kin, relation, relative
parent adoptif foster-parent
parent, ente kinsman, kinswoman
parenthèse parenthesis
parents kinsfolk, kindred, parentage
parer, se array
paresse idleness, laziness
paresser idle, loaf
paresseusement idly, lazily
paresseux idler, lazy
parfait perfect
parfaitement eminently, excellently, ideally, perfectly
parfois at times, sometimes
parfum flavouring, fragrance, perfume, scent
parfumé scented
parfumer flavour, perfume, scent
parfumerie perfumery
pari bet, outcast, wager
paria pariah
parier (sur) bet, wager
parlement parliament
parlementaire parliamentary
parler speak, talk
parler à tort et à travers talk through one's hat
parler boutique talk shop
parler franchement speak out
parler (plus) fort speak up
parmi amidst, among, amongst
parodie charade, parody
parodier parody
paroisse parish
parole faith, speech, word
parole d'honneur word of honour
paroles lyric, talk
paroxysme paroxysm
parquet parquet
parrain godfather
parricide parricide, patricide
part(ie) part
part part, portion, share, slice
partage partition
partager distribute, double up, partition, share
partager également go halves with

partant, ante starter
partenaire partner
parterre bed, flower bed
parti party
parti pris bias
partial bias(s)ed, one-sided
partialité partiality
participant, ante participant, participator
participation interest, participation
participer (à) enter into, participate
particularité peculiarity
particule fleck, particle
particulier individual, particular
particulièrement especially, particularly
partie game, portion, side
partiel partial
partir come out, depart, go, go off, start
partir de zéro start from scratch
partir en coup de vent dash off
partir (en voiture) drive off
partisan(s) following
partisan, ane adherent, devotee, partisan, supporter
partition score, partition
partout all over, everywhere, high and low, throughout
parution publication
parvenir à arrive at
parvenu, ue upstart
pas pace, step, tread
pas à pas step by step
pas de chance hard luck, tough luck
pas de porte doorstep
pas en forme unfit
pas la moindre chance not a dog's chance
pas le moins du monde not in the least
pas question! nothing doing!
passable fair, passable
passage pass, passage
passage à niveau level crossing
passage étroit narrows
passage pour piétons zebra crossing
passager passing
passant, ante passerby
passe pass
passé past
passe-droit privilege
passe-partout master key, skeleton key
passe-plat hatch
passe-temps hobby, pastime
passeport passport
passer fill in, go, pass, spend

passer (à côté de) pass by
passer à gué ford
passer au crible screen
passer au jet hose down
passer au peigne fin comb
passer comme un éclair flash (by)
passer de commentaires, se speak for itself/themselves
passer de justesse scrape through
passer de, se dispense with, do without, go without, spare
passer des vacances vacation
passer devant lead the way
passer en revue inspect
passer en trombe zoom
passer graduellement à grade
passer l'aspirateur vacuum
passer les menottes à handcuff
passer par-dessus le dos de qqn pass over
passer pour pass as/for
passer prendre call for
passer, se happen
passer un examen take an examination/test
passer un savon à haul (someone) over the coals
passer voir drop by, drop in, look in on
passerelle bridge, gangplank
passif passive
passion love, passion
passionnant enthralling, gripping, stirring
passionné heated, hot-blooded, passionate, torrid
passionné de keen on
passivement passively
passivité passiveness, passivity
passoire colander, strainer
pastel pastel
pasteur minister, parson, pastor, rector
pasteurisation pasteurization
pasteuriser pasteurize
pastille lozenge, pastille
pastoral pastoral
patauger flounder, splash, wade
patchwork patchwork
pâté blot
pâte dough, pastry
pâte à modeler plasticine
pâte à tarte crust
pâte d'amandes marzipan
pâte feuilletée puff pastry
patère peg
paternel fatherly, paternal
paternité fatherhood, parenthood, paternity
pâtes pasta

pathétique pathetic
pathétiquement pathetically
pathologie pathology
pathologique pathological
pathologiquement pathologically
pathologiste pathologist
patiemment patiently
patience forbearance, patience
patient forbearing, patient
patienter hold on
patin runner, skate
patin à roulettes roller skate
patiner skate
patineur, euse skater
patinoire ice rink, rink, skatingrink
pâtir suffer
pâtisserie pastry
pâtissier, ière confectioner
pâtre herdsman
patriarche patriarch
patrie home, homeland, mother
    country, motherland
patrimoine heritage, patrimony
patriote patriot
patriotique patriotic
patriotiquement patriotically
patriotisme patriotism
patron pattern
patron, onne boss, landlord
patrouille patrol
patrouiller patrol
patrouilleur, euse warden
patte leg, paw, tab
patte de devant foreleg
pâturage pasture
paume hand, palm
paupière eyelid, lid
pause break, intermission, pause
pauvre poor
pauvrement poorly, shabbily
pauvreté poorness, poverty, want
pavaner, se strut, swagger
pavé paving stone, set(t)
paver pave
pavillon hall
pavillon (de gardien) lodge
pavot poppy
payable payable
paye wage packet, wages
payer pay
payer la note foot the bill
payer le prix fort pay through the
    nose
payer pour answer for
pays country, land
paysage landscape, scenery
paysagisme landscape gardening
paysan, anne peasant
paysannerie peasantry
péage toll

peau hide, skin
peau de daim buckskin
peau de porc pigskin
pêche peach
péché sin
pêche à la ligne angling
pêcher angle, fish
pêcher au chalut trawl
pécher (contre) sin
pêcheur fisherman
pécheur, eresse sinner
pêcheur, euse (à la ligne) angler
pêcheur, euse de perles pearl diver,
    pearl fisher
pectoral pectoral
pécule nest egg
pédagogique educational
pédagogue education(al)ist
pédale pedal
pédaler pedal
pédant pedantic, pedant
pédanterie pedantry
pédiatre paediatrician
pédiatrie paediatrics
pédicure chiropodist
pedigree pedigree
pègre underworld
peigne comb
peigner comb
peignoir robe
peindre colour, paint
peine pain, penalty, punishment,
    unhappiness
peiné pained
peintre painter
peinture colour, paint, painting,
    picture
peinture à l'eau emulsion paint
peinture à l'huile oil painting, oil
    paint
peinture laquée enamel
peinture murale mural
peinturer paint
pelage coat
pêle-mêle pell-mell
peler peel
pèlerin, ine pilgrim
pèlerinage pilgrimage
pélican pelican
pelle scoop, shovel
pelle à poussière dustpan
pelletée shovelful
pelleter shovel
pellicule film
pellicules dandruff, scurf
pelliculeux scurfy
pelote à épingles pincushion
peloton d'exécution firing squad
pelotonner, se nestle
pelouse green, lawn

peluche fluff, lint
pelure skin
pelvien pelvic
pénaliser penalize
pénalité penalty
penchant inclination, leaning
pencher lean, slant, slope, tilt, tip
pencher, (se) droop
pendaison hanging
pendaison de crémaillère
    housewarming
pendant during, for, in the midst of
pendant que while
pendentif pendant
pendre dangle, hang, loll
pénétrant penetrating, piercing
pénétrer penetrate, soak
pénible nasty, onerous,
    troublesome, trying, difficult
péniche barge
pénicilline penicillin
péninsulaire peninsular
péninsule peninsula
pénis penis
pénitence penance
penny penny
pensée pansy, think, thought
penser figure, reckon, think
penser à consider, look ahead, think
    of
penseur, euse thinker
pensif pensive, thoughtful
pension board, boarding house,
    lodging, pension
pension de famille guesthouse
pensionnaire boarder, lodger
pensionnat boarding school
pensionné, ée pensioner
pensivement pensively,
    thoughtfully
pentagonal pentagonal
pentagone pentagon
pentathlon pentathlon
pente descent, grade, gradient, hill,
    incline, slant, slope, steepness
pénurie shortage
pépiement twitter
pépier twitter
pépin pip, seed, stone
pépinière nursery
pépiniériste nurseryman
pépite nugget
perçant keen, piercing, sharp
percé leaky
perce-oreille earwig
percée breakthrough
percer drill, lance, pierce
perceuse drill
perche bass, perch
percher, se perch, roost

perchoir perch, roost
percussion percussion
percuter crash
percuteur lock
perdant, ante loser, underdog
perdre forfeit, lose
perdre connaissance pass out
perdre courage lose heart
perdre (dans), se merge (into)
perdre de vue lose sight of
perdre du terrain lose ground
perdre l'équilibre overbalance
perdre la face lose face
perdre la maîtrise de lose one's grip
perdre la mémoire lose one's memory
perdre la raison lose one's reason
perdre la tête lose one's head
perdre la voix lose one's voice
perdre le contact (avec) lose touch (with)
perdre le goût de go off
perdre, se go missing
perdre son sang-froid lose one's cool
perdre son temps idle away, muck about/around
perdu lost, odd
père father, senior
perfection perfection, refinement
perfectionner perfect, polish, refine
perfectionniste perfectionist
perforation perforation
perforé perforated
perforer perforate
performance performance
péricliter go to the dogs
péril hazardousness, peril
périlleusement perilously
périlleux hazardous, perilous
périmé out of date
périmètre perimeter
période period, run, spell, time
période glaciaire ice age
périodique periodic, periodical
péripétie épisode
périphérie periphery
périphérique peripheral
périr perish
périscope periscope
périssable perishable
perle bead
perlé pearly
perles pearl
permanence permanence
permanent permanent
permanente perm, permanent wave
permettre allow, permit
permettre de, se presume

permis licence, permit
permission leave, permission
pérorer hold forth
perpendiculaire perpendicular
perpendiculairement perpendicularly
perpétuel perpetual
perpétuellement perpetually
perplexe perplexed
perplexité perplexity
perroquet parrot
perruche budgerigar
perruque wig
persécuter persecute
persécuteur, trice persecutor
persécution persecution
persévérance perseverance
persévérer persevere, press forward/on
persienne shutter
persil parsley
persistance persistence
persistant persistent
persister linger, persist
personnage character
personnalité personality
personne individual, nobody, no one, people, person, thing
personne à charge charge, dependant
personne âgée senior citizen
personne de couleur coloured person
personne déplacée displaced person
personnel individual, personal, personnel, staff
personnellement personally
personnification embodiment, impersonation
personnifier impersonate
perspective outlook, perspective
perspectives d'avenir prospect
perspicace perceptive
perspicacité insight, perception, perceptiveness
persuader get, persuade
persuader (de) argue
persuader de prevail on/upon
persuader qqn de talk (someone) into/out of (doing)
persuasif persuasive
persuasion persuasion
perte loss, undoing, wastage
pertinemment aptly
pertinence relevance
pertinent apt, relevant
perturbateur disruptive
perturbation disruption
perturber disrupt, perturb, unsettle

pervenche periwinkle
pervers perverse, pervert
perversion perversion
perversité perversity, perverseness
perverti perverted
pervertir pervert
pesamment weightily
pesant heavy, weighty
pesanteur gravity
peser weigh, weigh in, weigh out
peseta peseta
peso peso
pessimisme pessimism
pessimiste pessimist, pessimistic
peste pest, pestilence, plague
pesticide pesticide
pétale petal
pétard banger, cracker, firecracker
pétillant bubbly, fizzy, sparkling
pétillement fizz, twinkle
pétiller bubble, effervesce, fizz, twinkle
petit little, short, small
petit à petit by degrees, little by little
petit bouquet (de fleurs) posy
petit chausson bootee
petit coup (de doigt) prod
petit(e) camarade playmate
petit somme doze
petit-enfant grandchild
petit-fils grandson
pétite aiguille hour hand
petite caisse petty cash
petite enfance infancy
petite-fille granddaughter
pétition petition
pétitionnaire petitioner
pétrifier petrify
pétrin jam, pickle
pétrir knead
pétrochimique petrochemical
pétrole petroleum
pétrolier oil tanker, tanker
peu few, little
peu à peu bit by bit
peu approprié inappropriate
peu concluant inconclusive
peu disposé à unwilling
peu importe no matter
peu profond shallow
peuple nation, people, populace
peupler populate
peur fear, fright, scare
peureux chicken-hearted, timid, coward
peut-être maybe, perhaps
peut-être (bien) possibly
phallocrate male chauvinist
phare headlamp, lighthouse

pharmaceutique pharmaceutical
pharmacie dispensary, drugstore, pharmacy
pharmacien, ienne pharmacist
phase phase
phénix phoenix
phénoménal phenomenal
phénomène phenomenon, freak
philanthrope philanthropist
philanthropie philanthropy
philanthropique philanthropic
philatélie philately
philatélique philatelic
philatéliste philatelist
philosophe philosopher
philosopher philosophize
philosophie philosophy
philosophique philosophical, philosophic
philosophiquement philosophically
phobie phobia
phonétique phonetic, phonetics
phonique phonics
phonographe gramophone
phoque seal
photo photo, picture, shot, snap
photo d'amateur snapshot
photocopie photocopy, Photostat
photocopier photocopy
photocopieur copier, photocopier
photographe photographer
photographie photograph, photography
photographier photograph
photographique photographic
phrase phrase, sentence
phrasé phrasing
phraséologie phraseology, phrasing
physicien, ienne physicist
physiothérapeute physiotherapist
physiothérapie physiotherapy
physique bodily, physical, physics, physique
physiquement physically
piaffer paw
pianiste pianist
piano piano, pianoforte
piano à queue grand piano
piaulement cheep
piauler cheep
pic pinnacle
piccolo piccolo
picorer peck
picotement tingle
picoter tingle
pidgin pidgin
pie magpie, piebald
pièce apartment, chamber, component, patch, piece, play, room

pièce à conviction exhibit
pièce de monnaie coin
pièce de rechange spare, spare part
pièce de théâtre drama, play
pied foot, leg, stem
piédestal pedestal
piège decoy, pitfall, snare, trap
pierre flint, stone
pierre d'achoppement stumbling block
pierre gemme gemstone
pierre ponce pumice stone
pierre précieuse gem, jewel, precious stone
pierre tombale gravestone, headstone, tombstone
piété godliness, piety, religiousness
piétiner trample
piéton, onne pedestrian
piètre lame
pieu stake
pieusement piously
pieuvre octopus
pieux godly, pious
pigeon pigeon
piger catch on
pigiste freelance
pigment pigment
pignon gable
pilaf pilaff
pilaf de poisson kedgeree
pile pile
pile ou face heads or tails
pile(s) battery
piler pound
pilier pillar
pillard raider, plunderer
piller loot, plunder, ransack
pilon drumstick, pestle
pilori stocks
pilot(is) pile
pilote pilot
pilote d'essai test pilot
piloter pilot, sail
pilotis pile, stilts
pilule pill
piment pepper
piment fort chilli, chili
pimpant snappy, spruce
pin pine
pinacle pinnacle
pince claw, pliers
pince à épiler tweezers
pince(s) tongs
pince-sans-rire dry
pinceau paintbrush
pincée pinch
pincement nip, pinch
pincer nip, pinch
pincer (les lèvres), (se) purse

pinces pincers
ping-pong ping-pong, table tennis
pingouin penguin
pinson finch
pinte pint
piolet ice axe
pion man, pawn, piece
pionnier, ière pioneer
pipe pipe
pipeau pipe, whistle
pipeline line, pipeline
piquant keen, piquant, prickle, pungent, quill, spice, sting
piqué nosedive
pique spade
pique-nique picnic
pique-niquer picnic
piquer nip, pinch, prick, sting
piquer une crise go through the roof/hit the roof
piquet peg, picket
piqûre injection, prick, shot, sting
pirate hijacker, pirate
pirater pirate
piraterie piracy
pire worse, worst
pirouette pirouette
pis udder
pisciculteur, trice fish farmer
piscine pool, swimming pool
pissenlit dandelion
pistache pistachio
piste lead, racetrack, scent, tarmac, track, trail
piste (d'envol/d'atterrissage) runway
pistolet pistol
pistolet à air popgun
piston piston
pistonner pull strings
pitié mercy, pity
pitoyable pathetic, piteous, pitiable, pitiful
pitoyablement piteously, pitiably, pitifully
pittoresque graphic, picturesque, picturesqueness
pivot pivot, swivel
pivotant revolving
pivoter pivot, swivel
pizza pizza
pizzicato pizzicato
placage plating
placard closet, cupboard
place place, room, seat, space, square
placement investment
placeur, euse usher
placide placid
placidement placidly

placidité placidness
plafond ceiling
plage beach
plaider argue, plead
plaie nuisance, sore
plaignant, ante plaintiff
plaignant(s) prosecution
plaindre, se complain
plaine lowland, plain
plainte complaint
plaintif plaintive
plaintivement plaintively
plaire please
plaire à appeal
plaisancier yachtsman
plaisanter jest, joke, kid
plaisanterie crack, jest
plaisir enjoyment, fun, kick, pleasure, relish
plaisir anticipé anticipation
plan layout, outline, plan, schedule, scheme
plan de cours syllabus
planche board, plank
planche à repasser ironing board
planche de surf surfboard
plancher floor
plancton plankton
planer plane
planétaire planetary
planète planet
planeur glider
planificateur, trice planner
planification planning
planifier plan, think out
plant seedling
plantation plantation
plante plant
plante annuelle annual
plante du pied sole
planter plant
planteur, euse planter
plantureux, euse buxom
plaquage tackle
plaque nameplate, plaque, plate, tablet
plaqué plated
plaque d'immatriculation licence plate
plaquer tackle
plasma plasma
plastic gelignite
plastique plastic
plat dish, even, flat, lank, platter
platane plane
plate-bande border, flower bed
plate-forme platform
plateau plateau, tray
plateau (de métal) salver
platine platinum

plâtre plaster, cast
plâtrer plaster
plâtrier, ière plasterer
plausible plausible
plectre plectrum
plein full, solid
plein air open air
plein d'astuces gimmicky
plein d'avenir up-and-coming
plein d'entrain lively
plein d'espoir hopeful
plein d'initiative enterprising
plein de full of
plein/couvert de larmes tearful
pleine longueur full-length
pleine louche (de) ladleful
pleine lune full moon
pleinement fully
plénitude completeness
pleurer cry, mourn, water, weep
pleureur tearful
pleurs cry
pleuvoir rain
pleuvoir à seaux pelt (down), rain cats and dogs
pleuvoir à verse teem
pli crease, fold, pleat, pucker
pliant collapsible, folding
plié folded
plie plaice
plier bend, fold
plier, se collapse, double up
plissé pleated
plisser pleat, pucker
plomb lead
plombage filling, stopping
plomberie plumbing
plombier, ière plumber
plonge dishwashing
plongée sous-marine skin diving
plongeoir diving board
plongeon dive, header, plunge
plonger dive, plunge
plonger dans l'eau duck
plongeur, euse diver
pluie hail, rain, wet
plumage plumage
plume feather, pen, plume
plume (d'oie) quill
plumer pluck
plumet plume
plumeux feathery
pluriel plural
plus more, plus
plus bas below
plus dans le coup out of it
plus loin further, onward(s)
plus ou moins give or take, more or less
plus petit que less

plus tard later on
plusieurs several
plutonium plutonium
plutôt rather
pluvieux rainy, showery, wet
pluviomètre rain gauge
pluviosité raininess
pneu tire
pneumatique pneumatic
pneumonie pneumonia
poché poached
poche pocket, pouch
pocher poach
pochette sleeve
pochoir stencil
podium podium
podologie chiropody
poêle à frire frying pan
poème poem, lyric
poésie poetry
poète poet
poétique poetic
poétiquement poetically
poids weight
poids lourd heavyweight
poignard dagger
poignarder qqn dans le dos stab (someone) in the back
poignée handful, knob
poignée (d'épée) hilt
poignée de main handshake
poignée de porte doorknob
poignet wrist
poil bristle, fur, hair
poilu hairy
poinçon(neuse) punch
poinçonner punch
poindre dawn
poing fist
point dot, full stop, mark, period, point, stitch, stop
point culminant climax, culmination
point d'ébullition boiling point
point d'exclamation exclamation mark
point d'interrogation query, question mark
point d'orgue pause
point de congélation freezing point
point de fusion melting point
point de mire focus
point de repère landmark
point de vue angle, outlook, point of view, standpoint, viewpoint
point mort neutral
point noir blackhead
point-virgule semicolon
pointe point, spike
pointe de flèche arrowhead

pointer clock in, out/on, off
pointes points
pointillé dotted
pointu peaked, pointed
poire pear
poireau leek
poireauter kick one's heels
pois pea, spot
poison poison
poisson fish
poisson rouge goldfish
poisson-chat catfish
poissonnerie fishmarket
poissonnier, ière fish merchant, fishmonger
poitrine bosom, breast, bust, chest
poivre pepper
poivré peppery
poivrer pepper
poivrier pepper
poivron pepper
poker poker
polaire polar
pôle pole
poli civil, courteous, polish, polite
police police, policy
police d'assurance insurance policy
police secrète secret police
policier, ière detective, policeman, policewoman
poliment courteously, politely
polio polio
polir burnish, polish, shine
polissage shine
polisson, onne rogue
politesse courteousness, grace, politeness
politicien, enne politician
politique policy, politics, political
politiquement politically
polka polka
pollen pollen
pollinisation pollination
polluer pollute
pollution pollution
polo polo
poltron coward, cowardly
polyéthylène polythene
polygonal polygonal
polygone polygon
polypore bracket fungus
polytechnique polytechnic
polyvalent versatile
pomme apple
pomme de discorde a bone of contention
pomme de terre potato
pompe pageantry, pomp, pump
pompe à incendie fire engine

pomper pump
pompette slightly drunk
pompeusement pompously
pompeux pompous
pompier, ière firefighter
pompiers (sapeurs-) fire brigade
pompon tassel
pomponner, se preen
poncer sand
poncho poncho
ponctualité punctuality
ponctuation punctuation
ponctuel punctual
ponctuer punctuate
pondeuse layer
pondre lay
poney pony
pont bridge, deck
pont aérien airlift
pont autoroutier overpass
pont d'envol flight deck
pont-levis drawbridge
pontife pontiff
ponton pontoon
populaire folk, popular
populariser popularize
popularité popularity
population population
populeux populous
porc hog, pig, pork
porc-épic porcupine
porcelaine bone china, china, porcelain
porcelet piglet
porche archway, porch
porcherie pigsty, sty
porcin piggy
pore pore
poreux porous
pornographie pornography
pornographique dirty, pornographic
porridge porridge
port harbour, port
port de mer seaport
port franc entrepot
portable portable
portatif portable
porte door, gate, gateway
porte-avions aircraft carrier
porte-documents briefcase, portfolio
porte-étendard standard-bearer
porte-monnaie purse
porte-parole spokesman
porte-voix loudhailer, megaphone
portée litter, reach, staff, stave
portée de voix earshot
portefeuille billfold, pocketbook, portfolio, wallet

porter bear, carry, have on, lift
porter à l'écran screen
porter des fruits bear fruit
porter en terre lay to rest
porter un jugement (sur) pass judgment (on)
porter un toast (à) toast
porter volontaire, se volunteer
porteur, euse bearer, porter
portier doorman, porter
portion helping, portion, serving
portique gantry, portico
porto port
portrait image, portrait, portrayal
pose exposure, pose
posé sedate, sober
posément deliberately, sedately
poser lay, pose, put down, set, sit, stand
poser son regard sur lay/set eyes on
poser sur, se alight (on)
poseur swanky
poseur, euse de bombes bomber
positif positive
position bearings, position, posture, stance
posologie dosage
posséder hold, own, possess
possesseur possessor
possessif possessive
possession possession
possibilité possibility
possible open to, possible
possiblement possibly
postnatal postnatal
post-scriptum postscript
postal postal
poste place, position, post, stand, station, tour
poste aérienne airmail
poste d'essence gas station
poste de guet lookout
poste de nuit night shift
poste de police police station
poste vacant vacancy
poster, (se) post, station
postérieur posterior
postérité posterity
posthume posthumous
postiche toupee, wig
postier mailman
postsynchroniser dub
postsynchronisation dubbing
postuler apply for
posture posture
pot jar, pot
pot (à fleurs) flowerpot
pot-de-vin bribe
pot-pourri medley

potage soup
potassium potassium
poteau pole, post
poteau (de but) goalpost
potelé chubby
potentiel potential
poterie pottery
potier, ière potter
potion potion
pou head louse
poubelle garbage can, trash can
pouce inch, thumb
pouding pudding
poudre powder
poudre (à canon) gunpowder
poudre de riz face powder
poudrer powder
poudrerie blizzard
poudreux powdery
poudrier compact
poudrière magazine
pouf pouffe, pouf
pouilleux lousy
poulain colt, foal
poule hen
poulet(te) chicken
pouliche filly
poulie pulley
pouls pulse
poumon lung
poupe stern
poupée doll, dolly
pour in one's favour, for
pour ainsi dire in a manner of
  speaking
pour de bon for good, for keeps
pour deux personnes double
pour impressionner for effect
pour l'amour du ciel/de Dieu! for
  heaven's sake
pour l'instant for now
pour le mieux for the best
pour le moment for the present, for
  the time being
pour le plaisir for the hell of it
pour rien for nothing, for love or
  money
pour rire in fun
pour s'amuser for fun
pour toujours for ever/forever, for
  life
pour/afin de in order to
pour/afin que in order (that)
pourboire gratuity, tip
pourceau swine
pourcent percent
pourcentage percentage, rate
pourchasser hound, hunt
pourquoi why
pourri bad, putrid, rotten

pourrir rot
pourrissement decay
pourriture rot, rottenness
poursuite chase, pursuit
poursuites proceedings,
  prosecution
poursuivant, ante pursuer
poursuivre chase, give chase,
  follow up, prosecute, pursue, sue
pourtant yet
pourvoir à cater
pourvoir aux besoins de make
  provision for
pourvoir (de) furnish
pourvu que provided, providing
pousse growth, sprout
pousse-mine pencil
pousse-pousse rickshaw
poussée heave, hoist, push, shove,
  thrust
pousser grow, impel, prod, push,
  sprout, sprout up, urge, utter
pousser à egg, press, prod, prompt,
  put up to
pousser à bout strain, tax
pousser du coude nudge
pousser, se move up
pousser un soupir heave a sigh
poussette stroller
poussière dust, grit
poussiéreux dusty
poussin chick
poutre beam, girder, timber
pouvoir can, control, may, power
pouvoir que, se might
pouvoir s'attendre à in for
pouvoir se permettre (de) afford
poux louse
prairie grassland, prairie, range
praticabilité practicableness,
  practicability
praticable passable
pratique convenient, handy, hard-
  headed, practical, practice, sensible
pratiquement as good as, next to,
  practically, virtually
pratiquer practise
pré meadow
préalable prerequisite
préavis notice
précaire precarious
précairement precariously
précarité precariousness
précaution precaution
précédemment previously
précédent precedent, preceding,
  previous
précéder precede
précepteur, trice tutor
précieux precious, treasured,

valued
précipice precipice
précipitation hastiness, rainfall
précipité precipitate
précipiter, se dash, fling, rush,
  scurry
précis nice, precise, specific
précisément precisely
préciser specify
précision preciseness, precision
précocité earliness
précurseur forerunner
prédateur predator, predatory
prédécesseur predecessor
prédicat predicate
prédicateur, trice preacher
prédiction prediction
prédire foretell, predict, prophesy
prédisposé à prone (to)
prédisposition à strain
prédominance predominance,
  prevalence
prédominant predominant
prédominer (sur) predominate
préfabriqué prefabricated
préface preface
préférable better, preferable
préféré, ée favourite
préférence favour, preference
préférer (à) prefer
préfet prefect
préfixe prefix
préhensile prehensile
préhistorique prehistoric
préjugé prejudice
préjuger prejudge
prélasser, se loll, lounge
prélever levy
préliminaire preliminary
prélude prelude
prématuré early, premature
prématurément prematurely
prémédité premeditated
premier premier, prime
premier, ière first
premier ministre premier, prime
  minister
premier plan foreground
premier-né first-born
première premiere
premiers soins first aid
prendre assume, catch on, gain, get
  up, take, take on, take up
prendre à la légère make light of
prendre à rebrousse-poil rub the
  wrong way
prendre au dépourvu catch out,
  catch (someone) napping, catch
  (someone) on the hop
prendre au filet net

prendre au lasso lasso, rope
prendre au piège snare, trap
prendre au sérieux/à cœur take to heart
prendre congé take off, take one's leave (of)
prendre conscience de wake up
prendre d'amitié pour qqn, se take a liking to
prendre d'assaut storm, take by storm
prendre de la valeur appreciate
prendre de la vitesse get up, pick up speed
prendre du bon côté take in good part
prendre du retard fall behind
prendre en bonne part take (something) in good part
prendre en considération take into consideration
prendre en grippe take a dislike to
prendre en main take in hand
prendre en photo shoot a picture of
prendre feu go up in smoke/flames
prendre forme form, take shape
prendre garde beware, watch one's step
prendre garde (à) mind
prendre goût à take a fancy to, take to
prendre l'avantage/le dessus (sur) have/get/gain the upper hand
prendre la direction take charge
prendre la fuite make a break for it
prendre la liberté de take the liberty of
prendre la mer sail, put to sea
prendre la tangente go off at a tangent
prendre la température de take someone's temperature
prendre le parti de stand up for, stick up for, take someone's part
prendre le relais de take over
prendre les devants jump the gun
prendre note de take note of
prendre par surprise take by surprise
prendre part à go in for, join in, take part in, partake
prendre parti take sides, side with
prendre peur take fright
prendre plaisir à delight, take pleasure in
prendre pour mistake (for)
prendre qqn à l'improviste take (someone) unawares
prendre (qqn) au mot take (someone) at his/her word

prendre qqn pour take (someone) for
prendre racine take root
prendre sa retraite retire
prendre sa source rise
prendre, (se) catch
prendre ses aises take one's ease
prendre ses jambes à son cou take to one's heels
prendre soin de take care of
prendre son temps take one's time
prendre sur soi de take (something) upon oneself
prendre (trop) à cœur take to heart
prendre un bain de soleil sunbathe
prendre un coup de soleil catch the sun
prendre un risque take a gamble
prendre un/des risque(s) take risks/take a risk
prendre une douche shower
prendre/garder en otage take/hold (someone) hostage
preneur, euse taker
prénom first name
préoccupation consideration, preoccupation
préoccupé troubled
préoccuper preoccupy
préparatif(s) preparation, arrangements
préparation concoction, preparation
préparatoire preparatory
préparé prepared
préparer dispense, edit, fix, mix
préparer à la hâte rustle up
préparer, (se) prepare
préparer (mentalement) pour, se brace (for)
préposé, ée attendant
préposition preposition
prépositionnel prepositional
prépuce foreskin
prérogative prerogative
près near, nearby, nigh
près (de) close, close to, near, up to
présage portent
présager bode
presbyte far-sighted
presbytère parsonage, vicarage
prescrire prescribe
préséance precedence
présence presence
présence d'esprit presence of mind
présent in attendance, present
présentable presentable
présentateur, trice announcer, newscaster

présentation introduction, presentation
présentement at present, presently
présenter lodge, present, introduce
présenter, se present
présenter à, se run for
présenter les armes present arms
préserver conserve
présidence chair, chairmanship, presidency
président chairman, president
présidente chairwoman, president
présidentiel presidential
présider chair, preside
présomption presumption
presque almost, hardly, nearly
presque rien next to nothing
presqu'île peninsula
pressant insistent, pressing
pressé in a hurry
presse press
presse typographique printing press, press
presse-fruits squeezer
presse-papiers paperweight
pressentiment foreboding, premonition
presser hustle, press, squeeze, throng, urge on
pression press, pressure
pressoir press
pressuriser pressurize
preste nimble
prestement alertly, nimbly
prestidigitateur, trice conjuror
prestige prestige
présumer presume
prêt all set, in readiness, loan, ready
prêt à game, ready (to)
prêt-à-porter ready-to-wear
prêt-à-manger fast food(s)
prête-nom figurehead
prétendant, ante claimant, contender, wooer
prétendre claim, make out, profess, pretend, allege
prétendu ostensible
prétentieux, euse show off, swollen-headed
prêter lend, loan
prêter à, (se) lend itself to
prêter attention à attend (to)
prêter attention (à) mind
prêteur, euse sur gages moneylender, pawnbroker
prétexte pretence, pretext
prêtre, esse priest
prêtrise priesthood
preuve evidence, proof
prévenance(s) attentiveness

prévenant considerate
prévenir avert, prejudice
prévenir (de) warn
prévenir/avertir de tip off
préventif precautionary, preventive
prévention prevention
prévisible foreseeable, predictable
prévision forecast
prévoir anticipate, arrange, forecast, foresee
prévoyance foresight, forethought
prévu d'avance foregone
prier pray
prière prayer
prieur, eure prior
prieuré priory
prima donna prima donna
primaire primary
primate primate
prime bonus
primeur scoop
primevère primrose
primitif primitive, savage
prince prince
princesse princess
princier princely
principal chief, main, primary, principal
principalement mainly, primarily, principally
principauté principality
principe principle, principles
printemps spring, springtime
prioritaire prior
priorité priority, right of way
pris de vertige dizzy
pris en flagrant délit catch red-handed
prise catch, grip, hold, intake, plug, set-to
prise de bec row, tiff
prise de conscience realization
prise de courant plug, power point
prise de vue(s) take
prise électrique socket
prismatique prismatic
prisme prism
prison gaol, jail, prison
prisonnier, ière captive, prisoner
prisonnier, ière de guerre prisoner of war
prisonnier, ière politique political prisoner
privation deprivation, privation
privé private
privé de bereft (of)
priver (de) deprive (of)
privilège privilege
privilégié privileged
prix charge, cost, price, prize

prix de consolation booby prize
prix du marché market price/value
prix/taux fixe flat rate
probabilité likelihood, probability
probable likely, probable
probablement probably
problématique problematic(al)
problème problem, trouble
procédé process
procéder proceed
procédure procedure
procès lawsuit, suit, trial
procès-verbal minutes, record
processus process
prochain forthcoming, next
proche near
proclamation proclamation
proclamer proclaim
procurer fix (someone) up with (something), get, procure
procurer, (se) procure
prodigalité lavishness, prodigality
prodige prodigy
prodigieux fantastic, tremendous
prodigieusement tremendously
prodigue lavish, prodigal
producteur, trice grower, producer
production output, production
productivité productivity
produire generate, produce, put forth, turn out, yield
produire, se occur
produit product, stuff
produit chimique chemical
produits (alimentaires/agricoles) produce
proéminent prominent
profane lay, secular
professer profess
professeur, eure master, professor, teacher
profession profession
professionnel, le professional
professionnellement professionally
professoral professorial
profil profile
profit gain, profit
profitable profitable
profiter (au maximum) de make the most of (something)
profiter de take advantage of
profond deep, inner, profound
profondément deeply, profoundly
profondeur deepness, depth, profundity
profondeurs depths
profusion profusion
programme program
programmer program
programmeur, euse programmer

progrès advance, development, progress
progresser get on, make headway
progressif progressive
progressiste progressive
progressivement progressively
proie prey, quarry
projecteur floodlight, projector, searchlight, spotlight
projectile missile, projectile
projection projection
projet project, plan
projeter project, shed
projeter (un rayon de lumière) flash
prologue prologue
prolongation prolongation
prolongé prolonged
prolonger prolong
promenade promenade, run, walk
promenade à cheval ride
promenade au grand air airing
promenade en canot row
promenade en voiture drive
promener, (se) stroll, wander
promeneur, euse rambler, walker
promesse pledge, promise, undertaking
prometteur hopeful, promising
promettre pledge, promise, undertake
promontoire headland, promontory
promotion promotion
promouvoir elevate, promote
prompt early, prompt, ready, speedy
promptement promptly, smartly, speedily
promptitude alertness, promptness, readiness, smartness, speediness
promulgation enactment
pronom pronoun
prononçable pronounceable
prononcé pronounced
prononcer deliver, pronounce, sound
prononciation pronunciation
propagande propaganda
propagation propagation
propager, (se) propagate
prophète prophet, seer
prophétie prophecy
prophétique prophetic
prophétiquement prophetically
propice favourable, likely
proportion percentage, proportion, ratio
proportionné (à) proportionate
proportionnel proportional

proportionnellement proportionally, proportionately
propos point
proposer offer, propose
proposition clause, nomination, proposal
propre clean, neat, own
propreté cleanliness
propriétaire householder, landlord, owner, possessor, proprietor
propriétaire terrien landowner
propriété estate, property
propulser propel
propulsion propulsion
propulsion par réaction jet propulsion
prosaïque pedestrian
prose prose
prospecter prospect
prospecteur, trice prospector
prospectus handbill, handout, leaflet, prospectus
prospère flourishing, prosperous
prospérer flourish, make good, prosper, thrive
prospérité prosperity
prosterner, se prostrate
prostitué, ée prostitute
prostitution prostitution
prostration prostration
protecteur protective, protector
protection protection
protégé protected, sheltered
protéger protect, safeguard, secure, shield
protéger (de) keep off
protéine protein
protestant, ante Protestant
protestantisme Protestantism
protestataire protester
protestation protest, hullabaloo
protester protest
proton proton
protoplasme protoplasm
prototype prototype
proue bow, prow
prouesse prowess
prouver prove
provenir (de) emanate, proceed (from), stem from

proverbe proverb
proverbial proverbial
proverbialement proverbially
providentiel heaven-sent
province province
provincial provincial
provision stock, groceries
provisions provisions
provisoire provisional, tentative
provisoirement provisionally, tentatively
provocant provocative
provocateur, trice challenger
provocation provocation
provoquer incite, produce, provoke
proximité closeness, nearness
prudemment cautiously, guardedly, prudently
prudence caution, prudence, wariness
prudent careful, cautious, chary, guarded, prudent, wary
prune plum, prune
psalmodie chant
psaume psalm
pseudonyme pen name, pseudonym
psychanalyse analysis, psychoanalysis
psychanalyser psychoanalyse
psychanalyste analyst, psychoanalyst
psychiatre analyst, psychiatrist
psychiatrie psychiatry
psychiatrique mental, psychiatric
psychique psychic(al)
psychologie psychology
psychologique psychological
psychologiquement psychologically
psychologue psychologist
puanteur reek, stench, stink
puberté puberty
public common, extramural, public
publication publication
publicité commercial, publicity
publier print, publish
publiquement publicly
puce flea
puceron aphid, greenfly
pudeur modesty

pudique modest
puer reek, stink
puéril juvenile
puérilement childishly
puis then
puisque since
puissamment mightily, powerfully
puissance input, mightiness, potency, power, powerfulness, strength
puissant mighty, potent, powerful, strong
puits pit, well
puits de pétrole oil well
pull-over pullover
pulpe flesh, pulp
pulpeux pulpy
pulsation pulsation
pulvérisation pulverization, spray
pulvériser grind up, pulverize
puma cougar, puma
punaise bedbug, bug, drawing pin, tack, thumbtack
punch punch
punir discipline, penalize, punish
punissable punishable
punition punishment
pupille eyeball, pupil
pupitre desk
pur clean, pure, pure-blooded, unadulterated
pur et simple pure and simple
purée puree, mash
purement purely
pureté pureness
purgatif purgative
purge purge
purger (une peine) serve
purification purification
purifier purify
puritain puritanical, puritan
pus matter, pus
putréfier, (se) putrefy
putter putt
pygmée pygmy, pigmy
pyjama pyjamas
pylône pylon
pyramide pyramid
python python

Qq

qu'est-ce que what
quadragénaire forty-year-old
quadrilatère quadrilateral
quadrillé squared
quadrupède quadruped
quadruple quadruple
quai platform, quay, wharf
quais dock
qualifié eligible, good, qualified, skilled, trained
qualifier qualify
qualité grade, quality
quand when
quand bien même even though
quand les poules auront des dents pigs might fly
quant à as for, as to
quantité quantity, volume
quarantaine quarantine
quarante forty
quarantième fortieth
quart quarter
quart de finale quarter-final
quart de finaliste quarter-finalist
quart de travail shift
quartier neighbourhood, quarter
quartier général headquarters

quartiers quarters
quartz quartz
quasar quasar
quasi-collision near miss
quasiment almost
quatorze fourteen
quatorzième fourteenth
quatre four
quatre-vingt-dix ninety
quatre-vingt-dixième ninetieth
quatre-vingtième eightieth
quatre-vingts eighty
quatrième fourth
quatuor quartet
que than, to, what, which
Québécois, oise Quebecer
quel what
quel que soit whichever
quelconque nondescript, of a sort/ of sorts
quelqu'un anybody, anyone, somebody, someone, someone or other
quelque chose anything, something
quelquefois sometimes, at times
quelque part anywhere, somewhere, somewhere or other
quelque peu somewhat
quelque(s) some
quelques(-uns) a few

querelle argument, feud, squabble
quereller (se) fight
querelleur contentious, quarrelsome
question issue, query, question
questionnaire questionnaire
questionner question
queue tail, tail end
queue-de-cheval ponytail
qui who
quiconque whoever
qui plus est what is/what's more
quille keel, skittle
quincaillerie hardware
quinine quinine
quintette quintet
quintuplés quintuplet
quinzaine fortnight
quinze fifteen
quinzième fifteenth
quitter square, leave
quitter la maison leave home
quitter, (se) part company (with)
quoi what
quoique although, though
quoi qu'il arrive come what may
quorum quorum
quota quota
quotidien daily, everyday
quotidiennement daily

Rr

rabais discount
rabat-joie spoilsport, wet blanket
rabattre sur, se fall back on
rabbin rabbi
rabot plane
raboter shave
raboteux bumpy
rabougri stunted
rabrouer snub
raccommodage mending
raccommoder, se patch up
raccord joint
raccourci shortcut
raccourcir shorten, take up
raccourcissement curtailment
raccrocher hang up
raccrocher à, se clutch
raccrocher à n'importe quoi, se clutch at straws
raccrocher (au nez de) hang up
race breed, race, strain
racheter redeem
racial racial
racine root
racine carrée square root
racine cubique cube root
racines alimentaires root crop
racinette root beer
racisme racialism, racism
raciste racialist
raclée beating
raclement scrape
racler scrape
racler les fonds de tiroir scrape the bottom of the barrel
raconter narrate, recount, relate, tell
raconter des blagues fib
radar radar
radeau raft
radiateur fire, radiator
radiation radiation
radical radical
radicalement drastically, radically
radiesthésie divining
radieux bright, radiant
radin tight-fisted
radio radio, wireless
radioactif radioactive
radioactivité radioactivity
radiodiffusion broadcasting
radiographie radiograph, X-ray
radiographier X-ray
radiologie radiology
radiologue radiographer
radiothérapie radiotherapy
radis radish

radium radium
radjah rajah
radoter ramble
rafale flurry, gust
raffiné courtly, refined
raffinement nicety, refinement, sophistication
raffiner refine
raffinerie refinery
raffoler de dote
rafistoler cobble, patch up
rafler rifle
rafraîchir la mémoire de refresh someone's memory
rafraîchissements refreshments
ragaillardir, (se) exhilarate, perk
rage rabies, rage
ragots scandal
ragoût stew
raid raid
raid aérien air raid
raide mort stone-dead
raideur formality, starchiness, stiffness
raidir, (se) stiffen
raie parting, skate
rail rail
raillerie ridicule
railleur jeering
rainure groove
raisin grape
raisin sec currant, raisin
raison case, cause, reason, senses
raison valable justification
raisonnable rational, reasonable
raisonnablement reasonably, sanely, sensibly
raisonnement reasoning
raisonner reason
raisonner qqn reason with
raisonneur argumentative
rajeunir rejuvenate
rajeunissement rejuvenation
ralenti slow motion
ralentir decelerate, slow, slow down/up
ralentir (son rythme) slacken
ralentissement deceleration
ralliement rally
rallier, se rally
rallonge leaf
rallonger lengthen, let down
rallye rally
ramassage collection
ramassis huddle
rame oar
rameau d'olivier olive branch
ramener bring back
ramer pull, row, scull
rameur, euse rower

ramoneur, euse sweep
rampe banister, footlight
rampe (d'accès) ramp
rampe de lancement launching pad, pad
ramper crawl, creep
rance rancid, rank
ranch ranch
rançon ransom
rançonner hold to ransom
rancune grudge, ill feeling, spite, spitefulness
rancunier spiteful
randonnée hike, ramble, tramp, trek, outing
rang line, rank, row, string
ranger clear up, put away, stow, tidy, arrange
ranger, (se) bring round, revive
ranimer bring round, revive
rapace rapacious
rapacité rapaciousness, rapacity
râpe grater
râper grate
raphia raffia
rapide casual, fast, nippy, quick, rapid, swift
rapidement fast, in a hurry, rapidly, swiftly
rapides rapids
rapidité dispatch, fastness, quickness, rapidity, rapidness, swiftness
rapiécer patch
rappel curtain call, recall
rappeler recall, remind, take back
rappeler, se remember
rappeler de, se think of
rappeler qqch. à qqn ring a bell
rappeler qqn ring back
rapport report, record
rapporter bring back, fetch, tell tales
rapporter à, se relate to
rapporteur sneak
rapports sexuels intercourse, sexual intercourse
rapproché close-set
rapprocher close up
raquette racket
rare few and far between, infrequent, rare, scarce, uncommon
rarement rarely, seldom
rareté infrequence, rareness, rarity, scarcity
ras open
rasé shaven
raser level, raze, shave
raser, (se) shave
raseur, euse bore

rasoir razor
rassemblement assembly
rassembler assemble, muster, piece together, round up
rassembler, (se) collect, congregate, gather together, reassemble
rassembler autour (de), se gather round
rassembler (en troupeau), (se) herd
rassurant reassuring
rassurer reassure
rat rat
rat de bibliothèque bookworm
ratatiné shrunken
raté abortive, failure
rate spleen
râteau rake
rater fluff, flunk, misfire, miss
ratification ratification
ratifier ratify
ration ration
rationalisé streamlined
rationalité rationality
rationnel rational
rationnellement rationally
rationner ration, ration out
ratisser rake
raton laveur raccoon, racoon
rattraper catch up, gain on
rauque raucous
ravage havoc, play havoc with
ravager ravage
ravaler son amour-propre swallow one's pride
ravi rapt, in raptures
ravin ravine, gully
ravioli ravioli
raviser, se think better of
ravissant lovely, ravishing
ravissement enchantment, rapture
ravisseur, euse captor, kidnapper
ravitailler provision, refuel
ravitailler en combustible, (se) fuel
rayé striped, stripy
rayer delete, obliterate, score, strike out
rayon beam, bookshelf, radius, ray, shaft, spoke, stack
rayon de lune moonbeam
rayon de miel comb, honeycomb
rayon de soleil sunbeam
rayon(s) X X-ray(s)
rayonnage stack
rayonnant radiant
rayonne rayon
rayonner beam, glow, radiate
rayons gamma gamma

rayure bar, stripe
raz-de-marée tidal wave
réacteur reactor
réacteur nucléaire nuclear reactor
réaction reaction
réaction excessive overreaction
réactionnaire reactionary
réadaptation readjustment
réadapter (à), (se) readjust
réagencement rearrangement
réagir react
réagir à react to
réagir (contre) react against
réalisable feasible, practicable
réalisation fruition
réaliser achieve, realize
réaliser, se come into one's own, materialize
réalisme realism
réaliste realist, realistic
réalité actuality, reality
réanimation resuscitation
réanimer resuscitate
réapparaître reappear
réapparition reappearance
réarmement rearmament
réarmer rearm
réarranger rearrange
rébarbatif forbidding
rebattu stale
rebelle rebel, rebellious, wayward
rebeller contre, se rebel (against)
rébellion rebellion
rebondir bounce, rebound
rebord flange, ledge, sill
rebord de fenêtre window ledge, windowsill
rebuffade rebuff
rebut dregs, dud, waste
recaler fail
récapitulation recapitulation
récapituler go over, recapitulate
recapturer recapture
receler receive
receleur, euse receiver
récemment lately, latterly, newly, recently
recensement census
récent recent
récepteur receiver
réceptif receptive
réception do, receipt, reception
réceptionniste receptionist
récession recession
recette recipe, take, takings
recevoir entertain, get, receive
recharge refill
réchauffer (se) warmup
recherche hunt, quest, research, search

recherché wanted
rechercher seek
rechigner à grudge
rechute relapse
récidiviste gaolbird, jailbird
récif reef
récipiendaire recipient
récipient container, receptacle, vessel
récit narrative, recital
récital recital
récitation recital
réciter recite, repeat
réclamation claim, reclamation
réclame advertisement
réclamer claim, demand, reclaim
réclamer avec insistance press for
reclus, use recluse
recoin nook, recess
récolte harvest
récolter harvest
recommandation recommendation, testimonial
recommandé registered
recommander commend, recommend
recommander (de) advocate
récompense award, recompense, reward
récompenser recompense, reward
recomposer reword
recompter recount
réconciliation reconciliation
réconcilier, se make it up
réconcilier (avec), (se) reconcile
reconduire see off
réconfort comfort, reassurance
réconfortant comforting, heartwarming, refreshing
reconnaissable recognizable
reconnaissance acknowledg(e)ment, appreciation, recognition, reconnaissance
reconnaissant grateful, thankful
reconnaître acknowledge, concede, grant, know, recognize
reconnu accepted
reconsidération reconsideration
reconsidérer reconsider
reconstituer reconstitute, reconstruct
reconstitution reconstitution
reconstruction reconstruction
record record
recouvrement recovery
recouvrement de sol flooring
recouvrer (la santé) recover
recouvrir blanket, floor, re-cover
recouvrir d'un tapis carpet
récréation playtime, recess, re-creation

recréer recapture, re-create
récrire rewrite
recrue recruit
recrutement engagement, recruitment
recruter enlist, recruit
rectangle oblong, rectangle
rectangulaire oblong, rectangular
recteur, trice chancellor
rectifiable rectifiable
rectification rectification
rectifier calibrate, rectify
rectitude straightness
rectum rectum
reçu receipt, voucher
recueil omnibus
recueil d'expressions phrase book
recueillir raise, take in, collect
recul kick, recoil
reculer fall back, get back, kick, quail, recede, recoil, stand back
reculer (devant) cringe
récupération retrieval
récupérer get back, recover, retrieve
récurage scrub
récurer scour
récurrence recurrence
récurrent recurrent
recycler recycle
rédacteur, trice editor
rédaction composition, essay
reddition surrender
rédemption redemption
redevable (à qqn de qqch.) indebted
redevance royalty
redoubler redouble
redoutable formidable, redoubtable
redouter dread
redresser, se redress, draw up, right, straighten out/up
réductible reducible
réduction depletion, reduction, restriction
réduire cut, cut back, cut down, damp down, deplete, dim, reduce
réduire au minimum minimize
réduire en pulpe pulp
réel actual, fact, real
réélection re-election
réélire re-elect
réellement actually, really
réexaminer review
refaire redo
réfectoire refectory
référence reference
référendum referendum
refermer brusquement, (se) spring
refiler (qqch. à qqn) fob off with

réfléchi reflective, reflexive
réfléchir cogitate, meditate, reflect, think
réfléchir à consider
réfléchir (à/sur) ponder (on)
réfléchissant reflecting, reflective
réflecteur reflector
reflet reflection, reflexion
refléter mirror, reflect
réflexe reflex
réflexion cogitation, reflection, thought
réformateur, trice reformer
réforme reform, reformation
réformer reform, reverse
refouler bottle up
refrain chorus, jingle, refrain
réfrigérateur refrigerator
réfrigération refrigeration
réfrigérer refrigerate
refroidir cool down
refroidir, (se) cool, dampen
refroidissement chill
refuge island, refuge, sanctuary, traffic island
réfugié, ée refugee
refus denial, refusal, unwillingness
refuser decline, deny, refuse, turn down, withhold
refuser de refuse
réfutable refutable
réfutation refutation
réfuter disprove, refute
regagner regain
regard look
regard fixe gaze, stare
regard furieux glare
regard mauvais leer
regarder look, regard, see, view, watch
regarder de haut look down one's nose at
regarder (fixement) stare
regarder qqch. à la dérobée peep
régate(s) regatta
régent, ente regent
régime diet, regime
régime cellulaire solitary confinement
régiment regiment
régimentaire regimental
régimentation regimentation
région country, district, region
régional regional
régionalement regionally
régir govern
régisseur, euse stage manager
registre damper, register
réglable adjustable
réglage adjustment, regulation

règle rule, ruler
règle à calcul slide rule
règlement reckoning, regulation, rule
réglementé restricted
régler adjust, regulate, set, settle up
régler des vieux comptes settle old scores
régler la note check out
régler (sur) tune, tune in
réglisse liquorice
règne kingdom, reign
régner reign
regorger (de) abound (in, with)
regret regret
regrettable regrettable, unfortunate
regrettablement regrettably
regretter miss, regret
régularité regularity, steadiness
régulateur regulator
régulier even, normal, regular, steady
régulièrement consistently, regularly, steadily
régurgitation regurgitation
régurgiter regurgitate
réhabilitation rehabilitation
réhabiliter rehabilitate
réimpression reprint
réimprimer reprint
rein kidney
réincarnation reincarnation
reine queen
reine de beauté beauty queen
reine mère queen mother
reine-claude greengage
rejet rejection
rejeter cast off, disallow, reject
rejoindre, (se) join
rejouer replay
réjouir gladden, make someone's day
réjouir de, se exult, rejoice
réjouissance rejoicing
réjouissances jamboree, jubilation, merry making, revel
relâché lax, loose
relâchement laxity, laxness, looseness
relâcher loosen, relax, set free, slacken
relâcher, se slacken
relais relay
relatif comparative, relative
relation connection, contact, relation, relationship
relations dealing, intercourse
relations industrielles industrial relations
relations publiques public relations

relativement comparatively, relatively
relaxer, (se) relax
relayer relieve
relégation relegation
reléguer relegate
relevé reading, statement, survey
relève relief
relever, se pick up, read off
relief relief
relier bind, connect, join, link up
relieur, euse bookbinder
religieuse nun
religieusement religiously
religieux religious
religion religion
relique relic
reliure binding, bookbinding
reloger rehouse
reluire glisten
remarquable noteworthy, remarkable
remarquablement conspicuously, outstandingly, remarkably, strikingly
remarqué noticed
remarque remark
remarquer note, notice, observe
remblayer bank
rembourrage padding, stuffing, upholstery
rembourré upholstered
rembourrer pad, upholster
rembourreur, euse upholsterer
remboursement refund, repayment
rembourser pay back, refund
remède cure, remedy
remédier à remedy
remerciements thanks
remercier thank
remettre give in, hand in, remit return
remettre à neuf/en recondition
remettre à plus tard procrastinate
remettre en place set
remettre en/à sa place put back
remettre (qqn) à sa place take (someone) down a peg (or two), put (someone) in his or her place
remettre, (se) get over
remis à neuf reconditioned
remise rebate, remission, shed
remise de diplômes graduation
rémission remission
remontant booster
remonter reassemble, wind
remonter le moral de qqn raise someone's spirits
remontoir winder
remords remorse

remorquage tow
remorque trailer
remorquer tow
remorqueur tug, tugboat
remous backwash
rempart bulwark, rampart
remplaçable replaceable
remplaçant, ante locum, replacement, stand in
remplacer displace, fill in, replace, stand in, take the place of
rempli filled
remplir fill, fill in, refill
remplissage replenishment
remporter sweep the board, take
remue-ménage bustle
remuer stir, wag, waggle
remuer ciel et terre (pour) leave no stone unturned, move heaven and earth
rémunérateur remunerative
rémunération emolument, remuneration
rémunérer remunerate
renâcler snort
renard fox
renarde vixen
rencontre encounter, meeting
rencontrer encounter, fall in with
rencontrer par hasard chance on/ upon
rencontrer qqn par hasard run across
rencontrer, (se) meet
rendement yield, output
rendez-vous appointment, date, rendezvous
rendre give back, render, repay, turn over
rendre aveugle blind
rendre (bien) compte de, se appreciate
rendre cher (à) endear
rendre compte de account for, report
rendre fier de qqn do someone proud
rendre fou madden
rendre furieux infuriate
rendre justice à qqn give (someone) his or her due
rendre l'âme give up the ghost
rendre la pareille (à qqn) retaliate
rendre nécessaire necessitate
rendre perplexe puzzle
rendre public publish
rendre qqn capable de enable
rendre, se give in, give up, surrender
rendre ridicule, se make a fool of oneself

rendre service (à) come in useful, do (someone) a good turn, oblige
rêne rein
renfermé airless, close, withdrawn
renflement bulge
renfoncement indent, indentation
renfoncer indent
renforcement reinforcement
renforcer reinforce, strengthen
renforts reinforcement
renfrogné sullen
rengaine catchphrase
renier disown
reniflement smell, sniff
renifler sniff, snuffle
renne reindeer
renom fame, renown
renommé renowned
renommée fame
renoncer forswear, give up as a bad job
renoncer à give up, relinquish, renounce, surrender, waive
renonciation (à) renunciation
renouveau (religieux) revival
renouvelable renewable
renouveler renew
renouvellement renewal
rénovateur, trice renovator
rénovation facelift, renovation
rénover renovate
renseignement information, intelligence
renseigner, se make inquiries
renseigner sur, se check up (on)
rentable economic
rente pension
rentrée comeback, re-entry
rentrer re-enter
renversant staggering, amazing
renverser knock, knock over, overthrow, topple, upset
renverser, se spill
renverser (en arrière), se lie back
renvoi cross-reference, dismissal, expulsion
renvoyer dismiss, echo, fire, reflect, return, send down
renvoyer à cross-refer, refer
renvoyer (de) expel
réorganisation reorganization
réorganiser reorganise, reorganize
repaire hideout, den
répandre distribute, spill
répandre, se disperse, spread
réparable repairable, reparable
réparateur remedial
réparation mending, redress, repair, reparation

réparer make amends, cobble, fix, mend, repair
répartie rejoinder
répartir distribute, portion out
repartir à zéro go back to square one
repas meal
repassage ironing
repasser iron, press
repentant repentant
repentir repentance
repentir, se repent
repentir de, se repent (of)
repérage location
repérer locate, spot
repérer, se find/get one's bearings
répertoire A-Z/A to Z, catalogue, fund
répertoire géographique gazetteer
répéter go over, rehearse, repeat
répétitif repetitive
répétition rehearsal, repetition
répétition générale dress rehearsal
répit grace, respite
replier fold
réplique cue, replica, retort
répliquer retort
répondre answer, reply, respond
répondre à answer, fill, respond, talk back
répondre de answer for, vouch
réponse answer, response
reportage article
reporter reporter
repos repose, rest
reposant restful
reposer pillow, rest
reposer, se rest
reposer sur ses lauriers, se rest on one's laurels
repoussant offensive, repulsive
repousser beat off, fight off, rebuff, repel, repulse
repoussoir foil
répréhensible reprehensible
reprendre retake, take over
reprendre connaissance come round, come to
reprendre courage take heart
reprendre, se recover
représailles reprisal
représentant, ante agent, representative
représentatif representative
représentation performance, representation
représenter act on behalf of/act for, depict, represent
répressif repressive
répression repression

réprimande admonition, lecture, rebuke, reprimand, reproof, scolding
réprimander admonish, rebuke, reprimand, reprove, tell off
réprimer quell, repress, suppress
reprise recapture, repeat, resumption, revival, trade in
réprobateur reproachful, reproving
reproche reproach
reprocher fault, find fault with
reprocher à blame, reproach
reproducteur reproductive
reproduction duplication, reproduction
reproduire reproduce
reproduire, se breed, recur
reptile reptile
reptilien reptilian
républicain, aine republican
république republic
répugnance disinclination, reluctance
répugnant loathsome, revolting, unsavoury
répulsion repulsion
réputation character, name, reputation
réputé reputed
requête request
requiem requiem
requin shark
réquisitionner commandeer
réseau mesh, network
réservation booking, reservation
réserve aloofness, forest, hoard, preserve, reserve, reservation, reserved, sanctuary, secretiveness
réservé demure, modest, reserved, retiring, secretive
réserve d'animaux sauvages safari park
réserver book, reserve
réserver à spare
réserver (pour) earmark
réserver son jugement keep/have an open mind
réservoir dam, reservoir, sump, tank
résidence residence
résident resident
résidentiel residential
résider reside
résider (dans) lie (in)
résidu residue
résignation resignation
résigné (à) resigned (to)
résigner à, se reconcile, resign
résine resin
résineux resinous

résistance element, fight, resistance
résistant durable, resistant
résister hold, resist
résolu determined, firm, resolute, set, strong-minded, unflinching
résolument resolutely, unflinchingly
résolution resolution, resoluteness, resolve
résonance resonance
résonant resonant
résonner resound, ring
résoudre resolve, solve
resquiller jump the line
respect respect, respectfulness
respect de soi self-respect
respectabilité respectability
respectable respectable
respecter respect
respectif respective
respectivement respectively
respectueusement respectfully, reverently
respectueux dutiful, respectful, reverent
respectueux des lois law-abiding
respectueux envers/à l'égard de respectful
respirateur respirator
respiration breath, respiration
respiration artificielle artificial respiration
respiratoire respiratory
respirer breathe, inhale, respire
resplendir blaze
resplendissant ablaze, resplendent
responsabilité blame, concern, liability, onus, responsibility
responsable responsible, in charge of
responsable (de) answerable (to, from)
ressac backwash
ressaisir, (se) pull oneself together
ressemblance likeness, resemblance
ressemblant lifelike, like
ressembler à look like, resemble
ressembler à qqn be like someone
ressentiment resentfulness, resentment
ressentir feel
ressort spring
ressortir (d'entre) stick out, stand out
ressource resource, means
ressources naturelles natural resources
ressusciter rise
restant remnant

restaurant restaurant
restaurateur, trice restorer
restauration restoration
restaurer restore
restauvolant drive-in
reste remainder, rest
rester lie, remain, stand, stay
rester à l'écart de keep out of
rester au courant de keep track of
rester bouche bée gape
rester caché lie low
rester dans le droit chemin go straight
rester dehors stay out
rester tranquille stay put
rester valable hold good
restes remains, scrap
restitution restitution
restreindre curb, restrict
restreint confined, restricted
restrictif restrictive
restriction limit, qualification, restriction
résultat outcome, result, upshot
résulter (de) ensue, result
résumé abridg(e)ment, abstract, precis, sketch, summary
résumer sum up, summarize
résurrection resurrection
rétablir restore, put right
rétablir, se recover, recuperate
rétablissement recuperation
rétameur, euse ambulant, ante tinker
retard lateness, retardation
retardement delay
retarder delay, hold back, put off, retard, set back
retenir book, carry forward, hold, hold back, keep, keep back, retain
retenir son souffle hold one's breath
retentir blare, jangle, peal, resound, ring
retentissant resounding
rétine retina
retiré quiet, secluded
retirer draw, draw out, retire, take back, withdraw
retirer (vers/dans), se retreat
retombées radioactives fallout
retoucher touch up
retour homecoming, return, reversion
retourner return, reverse
retourner, (se) swing
retourner contre, se turn against
rétracter, (se) retract, eat one's words
rétractation retraction

retrait withdrawl
retraité retired
retraite retirement, retreat, superannuation
retrancher excise
retransmettre relay
rétrécir narrow, shrink
rétrécissement shrinkage
rétrogradation demotion
rétrograder demote
retroussé snub
retrouvailles reunion
retrouver trace
retrouver, se end up, land, turn up
réunion gathering, get together, meet, meeting, reunion
réunir, (se) get together, meet, reunite
réussi successful
réussi de justesse narrow
réussir bring off, come off, get there, make it, manage, succeed
réussir (son coup) pull off
réussite achievement, success
rêvasser daydream
rêve dream
revêche cantankerous, sour
réveiller awake, rouse
réveiller, (se) awake, wake up
réveiller trop tard, se oversleep
révélateur revealing, telltale
révélation disclosure, eye-opener, revelation
révéler disclose, reveal, unfold
revenant, ante spook
revendication claim, demand
revendiquer assert, claim
revendre de la drogue push
revenir return, revert, turn back, amount
revenir à amount, go back
revenir sur go back on, harp on (about)
revenir sur ses pas double back
revenu income, revenue
rêver (de/que) dream (of)
réverbère lamppost
révérence curtsey, curtsy
révérend Reverend
rêverie daydream, dream, reverie
revers backhand, cuff, lapel, reverse, turn-up
reversé reversed
réversible reversible
revêtir surface
revêtu clad
rêveur dreamer, dreamy
rêveusement dreamily
revigorant refreshing
revigorer refresh

revirement reversal, swing
réviser brush up, overhaul, revise
révision overhaul, revision
revoir revise, run over
révoltant appalling
révolte rebellion, revolt
révolter contre, se revolt (against)
révolution revolution
révolutionnaire revolutionary
révolutionner revolutionize
révoquer revoke
revue inspection, journal, magazine, review
rez-de-chaussée ground floor
rhapsodie rhapsody
rhinocéros rhinoceros
rhododendron rhododendron
rhubarbe rhubarb
rhum rum
rhumatisant rheumatic
rhumatismal rheumatic
rhumatisme rheumatism
rhume cold
rhume des foins hay fever
ricanement snigger
ricaner snigger, sneer
riche affluent, rich, wealthy
richement richly
richesse affluence, richness
richesse(s) riches
ricocher glance off, ricochet
ride furrow, line, wrinkle
ridé wrinkled
rideau curtain, drapes
rider furrow, wrinkle
ridicule foolish, ludicrous, ridiculous, ridiculousness
ridiculement laughably, ludicrously, ridiculously
ridiculiser make a fool of, ridicule
rien naught, nil, nothing, nought
rien que nothing but
rigide inflexible, rigid
rigidité rigidness, rigidity
rigoureusement rigorously, stringently
rigoureux close, exact, hard, rigorous, stringent
rigueur rigour, rigorousness, strictness, stringency
rime rhyme
rimer rhyme
rinçage rinse
rincer (se) rinse
rince-bouche mouthwash
ring ring
riposter, se défendre fight back
rire laugh, laughter
rire à gorge déployée roar
rire bruyamment guffaw

rire de deride
rire nerveusement giggle
rire nerveux giggle
rire sottement titter
risée laughing stock
risible laughable
risotto risotto
risque chance, risk
risqué chancy, dicey, risky
risquer hazard, risk, venture
risquer sa vie dice with death, take one's life in one's hands
rite ritual
rivage seashore, shore
rival, ale rival
rivaliser vie
rivaliser (avec) compete, rival
rivalité competition, rivalry
rive bank, shore
rivet rivet
riveter rivet
riveteuse riveter
rivière river
riz rice
rizière paddy field
robe dress, frock, robe
robe de chambre dressing gown
robe du soir evening dress
robe (de soirée) gown
robinet tap
robot robot
robuste burly, hardy, healthy, robust, sturdy, tough
robustesse hardiness, robustness, sturdiness
rocaille rockery, rock garden
rocailleux stony
roche rock
rocher boulder, rock
rocheux rocky
rock and roll rock'n roll
rodéo rodeo
rôder prowl
rôder autour de hover
rôdeur, euse prowler
roi king
rôle part, place, role
rôle principal lead, title role
roman fiction, novel
roman d'amour (à l'eau de rose) romance
romance ballad
romancier, ière novelist
romanesque romance
romantique romantic
rompre break, rupture
ronchonnement grumble
rond round
rond-point traffic circle

ronde beat, semibreve
rondelet podgy
rondement plumply, roundly
rondeur plumpness, podginess, pudginess, roundness
rondin log
ronflement snore
ronfler snore
rongé par les soucis careworn
ronger erode, gnaw
ronger son frein champ at the bit
rongeur rodent
ronron(nement) purr
ronronner purr
rosâtre pinkish
rose pink, rose
rosé rosy
rose des vents compass rose
roseau reed
rosée dew
rosette rosette
roseur rosiness
rosser give (someone) a hammering
rossignol nightingale
rot belch, burp
rotatif rotary
roter belch, burp
rôti roast
rôtie toast
rôtir roast
rotor rotor
rotule kneecap
roturier, ière commoner
rouble rouble
roue à aubes paddlewheel
roue de charrette cartwheel
roue de secours spare
rouer de coups beat up, pummel
rouge flushed, red
rouge à lèvres lipstick
rouge-gorge robin
rougeâtre reddish
rougeoiement glow
rougeole measles
rougeoyant fiery, ruddy
rougeoyer glow
rougeur blush, flush, redness
rougir blush, flush, redden
rouille blight, rust, rustiness
rouillé rusty
rouiller rust
roulade roll
rouleau coil, roll, roller, scroll
rouleau (à pâtisserie) rolling pin
rouleau compresseur steam roller
rouleau de papier hygiénique toilet roll
roulement roll
roulement à billes ball bearings

rouler roll
roulette castor, caster, roulette
roulis roll
roulotte trailer
roupie rupee
roupillon forty winks
rouspétance grouch
rouspéter grouch, grouse
rouspéteur, euse grouch
rouquin, ine redhead
roussir singe
route lane, road
routine routine
roux foxy, ginger, red, redhead
royal kingly, regal, royal
royalement regally, royally
royaliste royalist
royaume kingdom, realm
royauté royalty
ruban ribbon, tape
ruban adhésif Scotch tape
rubis ruby
ruche beehive, hive
rucher apiary
rude rough, rugged, crude
rudesse roughness, ruggedness
rudimentaire crude, rudimentary
rudiments ABC, elements, essential, rudiments
rue lane, street
ruée rush, scramble, stampede
ruée vers l'or gold rush
ruelle alley
rugby rugby
rugir roar
rugissement roar
rugosité raggedness, scratchiness
rugueux rough, scratchy
ruine doom, ruin, ruination
ruiner bankrupt, beggar, ruin
ruisseau brook, creek, stream
ruisseler stream
rumba rumba
rumeur report, rumour
rumeur publique grapevine
ruminer cud
ruminer (sur) brood
rupture rupture, severance
rural rural
rusé artful, crafty, slick, wily
ruse craft, craftiness, cunning, guile, ruse, slickness, trick, wiliness
rustique rustic
rustre bumpkin
rutilant glowing
rythme beat, lilt, rhythm
rythmique rhythmic, rhythmical

Ss

s'il vous plaît please
sabbat Sabbath
sable sand
sablé shortbread
sabler sand
sables mouvants quicksands
sablier hourglass
sablonneux sandy
saborder scuttle
sabot clog, hoof
sabotage sabotage
saboter sabotage
saboteur, euse saboteur
sabre sabre, axe
sabrer (dans) axe
sac bag, kitbag, pouch, sack, sackcloth, satchel
sac à dos haversack, knapsack, rucksack
sac à main handbag, purse
sac (à provisions) shopping bag
sac d'écolier schoolbag
sac de couchage sleeping bag
sac de marin duffel bag
sac de voyage valise
sac postal mailbag
saccadé jerky
saccager vandalize
saccharine saccharin(e)
sachet sachet
sacramentel sacramental
sacré sacred
sacrement sacrament
sacrifice sacrifice
sacrificiel sacrificial
sacrifier sacrifice
sacrilège sacrilege, sacrilegious
sacristain sexton
safari safari
safran saffron
saga saga
sagace sagacious
sagacité sagacity
sage discreet, good, sage, well-behaved, wise
sage-femme midwife
sagement sagely, wisely
sagesse discretion, hindsight, wisdom
sagou sago
saignant bleeding, rare
saignée drain
saigner bleed
saillant salient
sain sound
sain d'esprit in one's right mind, sane

sain et sauf safe and sound
saindoux lard
sainement wholesomely
saint blessed, hallowed, holy, saint
sainteté holiness, saintliness
saisie seizure
saisir grab, seize, take in, tackle
saisir de, se grab
saisir l'allusion take a/the hint
saisir le truc (pour faire qqch.) get the hang of
saison season
saisonnier seasonal
salade salad
salade de chou coleslaw
salade de fruits fruit salad
salaire earnings, pay, salary, wage, wages
salaud rat, swine
salé briny, salted, salty, savoury
sale dirty, messy, mucky
saler salt
saleté dirt, dirtiness, filth, grubbiness
saletés muck
salir make a mess of, muddy, smudge, soil
salir, (se) dirty
salissure smear
salive saliva, spit
saliver salivate
salle auditorium, hall, house, room, ward
salle à manger dining room
salle d'attente waiting room
salle d'exposition showroom
salle d'opération operating room
salle de bains bathroom
salle de bal ballroom
salle de quilles bowling alley
salle de séjour living room
salle des accidentés casualty department
salon drawing room, living room, lounge, parlour, salon, sitting room
salon de thé tearoom
saloon saloon
salopette dungarees, overalls
salubre healthy
salubrité healthiness
saluer acknowledge, greet, hail, salute
salure saltness
salut bow, hail, salute, salvation
salut! hi, so long!
salutation greeting
salve burst, round
samedi Saturday
sampan sampan
sanatorium sanatorium, sanitarium
sanctification sanctification

sanctifier sanctify
sanctuaire sanctuary
sandale sandal
sandwich sandwich
sang blood
sang (coagulé) gore
sang-froid self-control, self-possession, coolness
sanglant bloody, gory
sangle girth
sanglier boar
sanglot sob
sangloter sob
sangsue leech
sanguinaire bloodthirsty
sanitaire sanitary
sans without
sans-abri homeless
sans arrêt ceaselessly, non-stop, on and on
sans aucun doute doubtless
sans avenir dead end
sans bornes beyond measure
sans cérémonie informally
sans cervelle empty-headed
sans cesse constantly, continually, incessantly, unceasingly
sans compter lavishly
sans connaissance senseless
sans conviction half-heartedly
sans défense defenceless
sans dormir wakefully
sans doute no doubt
sans effet lost on, of no avail, to no avail
sans effort effortlessly
sans égal matchless
sans égards inconsiderate
sans enthousiasme half-hearted, tepidly
sans espoir hopeless, hopelessly
sans façon rough and ready
sans faute without fail
sans fin unending
sans fond bottomless
sans fondement baseless, idle, unfounded
sans gêne inconsiderate
sans goût tastelessly
sans importance little, neither here nor there
sans le sou penniless
sans loi lawless
sans nom nameless
sans ornements bald
sans pareil beyond compare, peerless
sans parler de to say nothing of
sans pitié cold-blooded, heartlessly, mercilessly

sans précédent unprecedented
sans préparation extempore
sans prétentions/façons homely
sans rapport avec la question irrelevant
sans ressources helplessly
sans rire in earnest
sans scrupules unscrupulous
sans tenir compte de irrespective of
sans timbre tonelessly
sans valeur valueless
sans vie lifeless
sans vigueur lifeless
sans volonté weak
santé health, sanity
saper sap
saphir sapphire
sapin fir
sarbacane blowpipe
sarcasme sarcasm, sneer, taunt
sarcastique sarcastic, snide, taunting
sarcastiquement sarcastically, tauntingly
sarcler hoe
sardine sardine
sari sari
satanique satanic
satellite satellite
satin satin
satire satire
satirique satirical
satisfaction satisfaction
satisfaire answer, satisfy
satisfaire à fulfil, meet
satisfaisant satisfactory, satisfying
satisfait content, contented, satisfied
saturation saturation
saturer saturate
sauce dressing, sauce
sauce au jus gravy
saucière (gravy) boat
saucisse frankfurter, sausage
sauf apart from, but, excepted, excepting, safe, save
sauf (que) except
sauge sage
saule willow
saumâtre brackish
saumon salmon
saumure brine
sauna sauna
saupoudrer dredge, sprinkle
saut jump, vault
saut (à cloche-pied) hop
saut à la perche pole vault
saut en hauteur high jump
saut en longueur long jump

sauté sauté
saute-mouton leapfrog
sauter fuse, hop, jump, saute, skip, spring, vault
sauter de joie jump for joy
sauter en parachute bale out
sauter (par-dessus) leap
sauter sur seize on, snap up
sauterelle grasshopper, locust
sautillement hop
sautiller hop, jig, jiggle, skip
sauvage antisocial, savage, wild
sauvagement savagely
sauvagerie savageness, savagery
sauver salvage, save
sauver la face save one's face
sauver, se escape, run along, run for it
sauvetage rescue, salvage
sauveteur rescuer
sauveur saviour
savane savanna(h)
savant learned
saveur flavour, tastiness
savoir can, know, know how to, knowledge, learning
savoir sur le bout des doigts know backwards
savoir know-how
savon soap
savonner soap
savonneux soapy
savourer glory, relish, savour
savoureux tasty
saxophone saxophone
saxophoniste saxophonist
scalp scalp
scalpel scalpel
scalper scalp
scandale scandal
scandaleusement scandalously
scandaleux scandalous
scandaliser scandalize
scander chant, scan
scanner scanner
scaphandre autonome aqualung
scarabée beetle
scarlatine scarlet fever
sceau seal
sceller seal
scénario screenplay
scénariste scriptwriter
scène scene, stage
scénique scenic
scepticisme scepticism
sceptique sceptic, sceptical
sceptiquement sceptically
sceptre sceptre
schéma sketch
schiste (bitumineux) shale

schizophrène schizophrenic
schizophrénie schizophrenia
scie saw
scie à métaux hacksaw
sciemment knowingly
science science
scientifique scientific, scientist
scientifiquement scientifically
scier saw
scierie sawmill
scintillant glittering
scintillement glitter, twinkle
scintiller glitter, twinkle
sciure filings, sawdust
scooter scooter
score score
scorpion scorpion
scout scout
scrabble Scrabble
scrupule qualm
scrupuleusement scrupulously
scrupuleux scrupulous
scrutateur searching
scruter peer, scan, scrutinize
sculpter carve
sculpteur, eure sculptor
sculpture carving, sculpture
séance session, sitting
séance d'entraînement workout
seau bucket, pail
sec dry
séché dried
sèche-cheveux hair-dryer
sécher blot, dry off
sécheresse drought, dryness
sécheuse tumbledryer
séchoir dryer
second lieutenant, mate, second
secondaire minor, secondary, side
seconde second
secouer agitate, jog, joggle, jolt, shake up
secourir relieve, rescue
secourisme life-saving
secours help
secousse hitch, jerk, shake, shock, yank
secret secret, secrecy
secrétaire secretary
secrètement secretly
sécréter secrete
sécrétion secretion
sectaire sectarian
secte denomination, sect
secteur area, sector
section section
sectionner nip
séculaire age-old
sécurité safeness, security
sédentaire sedentary

sédiment sediment
séducteur playboy
séduction glamour, seduction
séduire ensnare, seduce
séduisant alluring, attractive, glamorous, seductive, sexy
segment segment
ségrégation segregation
seiche cuttlefish
seigle rye
seigneur lord
sein breast
séisme earthquake
seize sixteen
seizième sixteenth
séjour residence, stay
séjourner (à/chez) visit
sel salt
sélect exclusive, select
sélectif selective
sélection selection
sélectionner pick and choose, select
sélectionneur, euse selector
sélectivement selectively
sélectivité selectiveness
selle saddle
selon according to
selon toute probabilité in all probability
sels de bain bath salts
semaine week
sémaphore semaphore
semblable alike, same, similar
semblant make-believe, semblance
sembler appear, look, seem
semelle sole
semence seed
semer sow
semestriel biannual, half-yearl
semestriellement biannually
semi-circulaire semicircular
séminaire seminary
semis seedbed, seedling
semoule semolina
sénat senate
sénateur, trice senator
sénile senile
sénilité senility
sens meaning, point, sense
sens commun common sense
sens dessus dessous at sixes and sevens, topsyturv(e)y, upside down
sens (général) drift
sens pratique practicality
sensation feeling, sensation
sensationnel gorgeous, out of this world, sensational, stunning
sensé sane, sensible
sensibilité sensibility, sensitiveness, sensitivity, tender-heartedness

sensibilité (à) appreciation
sensible sensitive, tender, tender-hearted
sensible à sensitive
sensiblement appreciably, materially
sensiblerie sloppiness, slush
sensualité sensuality
sensuel sensual
sensuellement sensually
sentence sentence
senteur scent
sentier path, pathway, trail
sentier pédestre footpath
sentiment feeling, sense, sentiment
sentimental sentimental, soulful
sentimentalement sentimentally
sentimentalité sentimentality
sentinelle sentinel, sentry
sentir feel, smell
sentir à l'aise, se be/feel at home
sentir attiré (par/vers), se fancy
sentir honteux, se feel/look small
sentir (intuitivement) sense
sentir mal fichu, se not be oneself
sentir qqch. savour of
sentir, se feel
sentir, (se) feel like
séparable separable
séparation detachment, division, parting, separation
séparatisme separatism
séparatiste separatist
séparément individually, separately, singly
séparer cut off, divorce, segregate, separate, separate out
séparer, se part, part company
sépia sepia
sept seven
septembre September
septentrional north
septième seventh
septuagénaire septuagenarian, seventy-year-old
sépulcral sepulchral
sépulcre sepulchre
séquelles sequel
séraphin seraph
séraphique seraphic
serein serene
sereinement serenely
sérénade serenade
sérénité sereneness
serge serge
sergent, ente sergeant
sergent-major sergeant-major
série chain, series
sérieusement badly, earnestly, in earnest, seriously

sérieux businesslike, earnest, earnestness, grave, serious, seriousness
seringue syringe
serment oath
sermon sermon, talking-to
sermonner preach
serpent serpent, snake
serpent à sonnettes rattlesnake
serpenter meander, snake, wind
serre conservatory, greenhouse, talon
serré talon
serre (chaude) hothouse
serrement de gorge gulp
serrer clasp, clench, constrict, pinch, squeeze
serrer entre sandwich
serrer la ceinture, se tighten one's belt
serrer la main, (se) shake hands with (someone)
serrer la vis (à) clampdown
serrer les coudes, se stick together
serrer les dents grit
serrer (les uns contre les autres), se huddle
serrer, se squeeze up
serrure lock
serrurier, ière locksmith
sérum serum
serveur, euse server, waiter, waitress
serviable obliging
service department, favour, serve, service
service de santé health service
service de renseignements intelligence
service militaire national service, service
service public utility
services sociaux social work
serviette towel
serviette (de table) napkin, serviette
servile servile
servilement servilely
servilité servility
servir serve, serve a purpose, wait (on)
servir de, se apply
ses quatre vérités (à qqn) home truth
session, séance session
set set
setter setter
seuil threshold
seul alone, lonely, only, single, sole
seulement merely, only, solely

sève sap
sévère harsh, severe, sharp, stern, strict
sévèrement severely, sternly
sévérité severity, sternness
sevrer wean
sexagénaire sexagenerian, sixty-year-old
sexe sex
sexiste sexist
sextuor sextet
sexuel sexual
sexuellement sexually
seyant becoming
shampooing shampoo
shérif sheriff
si if
si seulement if only
siècle century
siège seat, siege
siéger sit
sieste nap
sifflement hiss
siffler hiss, whistle
sifflet catcall, hiss, whistle
signal signal
signal d'alarme alarm
signaler report
signature signature
signe evidence, mark, sign, token
signe de la main wave
signe de (la) tête nod
signe de ponctuation punctuation mark
signer sign
signet bookmark
significatif meaningful, significant
signification sense
signifier signify, spell
silence hush, quiet, quietness, silence
silencieusement noiselessly, quietly, silently
silencieux hushed, muffler, noiseless, silencer, silent, soundless
silex flint
silhouette figure, silhouette
sillage wake, wash
sillon furrow, streak
sillonner de streak
silo elevator
similaire sister
similitude similarity
simple mere, one-way, plain, simple, straightforward
simple d'esprit half-witted
simplement plainly, simply
simplet simple-minded
simplicité homeliness, informality, plainness, simplicity

simplification simplification
simplifié simplified
simplifier simplify
simulation simulation
simulé feigned, mock, simulated
simuler put on, simulate
simultané concurrent, simultaneous
simultanéité concurrence
simultanément concurrently, simultaneously
sincère candid, genuine, guileless, heartfelt, sincere
sincèrement candidly, frankly, genuinely, guilelessly, sincerely
sincérité candidness, guilelessness, sincerity
singe ape, monkey
singeries monkey business
singulier singular
singulièrement uncommonly
sinistre baleful, grim, sinister
sinistrement balefully, grimly, luridly, ominously
sinon or, or else, otherwise
sinueux winding
sinus sinus
siphon siphon
sirène hooter, mermaid, siren
sirop syrup
sirop pour la toux cough-syrup
sirupeux syrupy
sisal sisal
sismique seismic
sismologie seismology
sismologique seismological
sismologue seismologist
sitôt as soon as
situation location, situation
situation critique plight
situation difficile predicament, a tight corner/spot
situé situated
situer locate
six six
sixième sixth
sixième sens sixth sense
sketch sketch
ski ski
skier ski
skieur, euse skier
slip briefs
slogan chant, slogan
smash smash
smog smog
smoking dinnerjacket
snob snob, snobbish
snobisme snobbery, snobbishness
sobre abstemious, sober
sobrement abstemiously, soberly
sobriété abstemiousness, soberness

sociable companionable, gregarious, outgoing, sociable
social social
socialisme socialism
socialiste socialist
société association, brotherhood company, society
socque clog
soda soda
soda au gingembre ginger ale, ginger beer
soda tonique tonic
sodium sodium
sœur sister
sœur adoptive foster sister
sofa sofa
soi-disant so-called
soie silk
soigneux painstaking
soif thirst, thirstiness
soigné formal, well-groomed
soigner attend, doctor, nurse, take care of
soigneur, euse second
soigneusement carefully, neatly, tidily, trimly
soigneux painstaking
soin care
soins attention, nurture
soir eve, evening
soirée evening
soixante sixty
soixantième sixtieth
soja soya bean
sol ground, soil
solaire solar
soldat man, private, serviceman, soldier, trooper
solde balance, sale
solderie cash and carry
sole sole
soleil sun, sunshine
solennel solemn
solennellement ceremoniously, solemnly
solennité solemnness, solemnity
solidarité solidarity
solide firm, hard-wearing, hearty, hefty, secure, solid, stable, steady, stout, substantial, tough
solidement securely, solidly
solidification solidification
solidifier, (se) solidify
solidité solidity, solidness, soundness
solitaire lone, lonesome, solitary
solitude loneliness, lonesomeness, solitude
solliciter court, invite, solicit, tout
solo solo, soloist

solstice solstice
soluble soluble
solution answer, resolution, solution
solvabilité credit
solvable solvent
solvant solvent
sombre dusky, gloomy, shadowy, sombre
sombrer go down
sommaire brief, sketchy, summary
somme amount, nap, snooze, sum
somme forfaitaire lump sum
sommeil rest, sleep
sommeil (paisible) slumber
sommeiller doze, snooze
sommet apex, brow, height, peak, summit
somnambule sleepwalker
somnifère sleeping pill, sleeping-tablet
somnolence drowsiness, sleepiness
somnolent drowsy
somnoler nod
somptueux sumptuous
son sound
son métallique clang
sondage poll, sounding
sondage d'opinion public opinion poll
sonde probe, sound
songe dream
songer daydream, muse, think of
sonique sonic
sonner chime, ring, sound, toll
sonnerie ring
sonnet sonnet
sonnette bell, piledriver, rattle
sonore voiced
sonoriser voice
sophisme fallacy
sophistiqué sophisticated
soprano soprano
sorcellerie sorcery, witchcraft
sorcier, ière sorcerer
sorcière hag, witch
sordide sordid, squalid
sordidement sordidly
sort fate, outgoing
sorte kind, nature, sort
sorti out
sortie exit, outing, sortie
sortilège charm
sortir come up with, exit, get out, go out
sortir (de chez soi) leave home
sortir de sa coquille come out of one's shell
sortir de ses gonds fly off the handle

sortir (sans être vu) slip
sortir, (se) stick out
sosie double
sottise mischief
sou penny
souche stump
souci care, trial
soucier (de), se care
soucoupe saucer
soucoupe volante flying saucer
soudain abrupt, sudden, suddenly
soudaineté suddenness
souder knit, solder, weld
soudeur, euse welder
soudoyer bribe
soudure solder, weld
soue pigsty
souffle puff
soufflé soufflé
souffler blow, breathe, prompt
soufflet bellows
souffleur, euse prompter
souffrance suffering
souffrant indisposed, unwell
souffrir ail, suffer
soufre sulphur
souhait wish
souhaiter qqch à qqn wish
souhaiter (que) wish
souillé tainted
souiller foul
souillure taint
soûl drunk
soulagé relieved
soulagement alleviation, relief
soulager alleviate, ease, help, relieve
soulèvement rising, uprising
soulever bring up, lift, pick, raise
soulever contre, se rise against
soulever, (se) heave
soulever/remuer à la fourche fork
soulier shoe
souligner emphasize, underline
soumettre bring forward, put, subdue, subject, submit
soumettre (à), se comply
soumettre, se submit
soumis submissive, obedience
soumission obedience, submission, submissiveness
soumissionner bid
soupape de sûreté safety valve
soupçon dash, hint, smack, suspicion
soupçonner de suspect
soupçonner qqch. smell a rat
soupe soup
soupe au lait quick-tempered
souper supper

soupir sigh
soupirant suitor
soupirer sigh
souple flexible, supple
souplesse flexibility, suppleness, versatility
souque à la corde tug-of-war
source fountain, head, source, spring
sourcil brow, eyebrow
sourd deaf
sourd comme un pot stone-deaf
sourd-muet deaf-mute
souriant smiling
souricière mousetrap
sourire smile
sourire épanoui grin
souris mouse
sournois sly, sneaky
sournoisement shiftily, slily, slyly
sournoiserie shiftiness, slyness, sneakiness
sous beneath, under, underneath
sous condition on approval
sous forme de in the form of
sous la garde de in (someone's) care
sous la main on hand
sous le feu de under fire
sous le nez under (a person's) (very) nose
sous les ordres (de) under
sous les yeux (de) before/under one's very eyes
sous réserve de subject to
sous serment on/under oath
sous-alimentation malnutrition
sous-alimenté underfed, undernourished
sous-bois undergrowth
sous-comité subcommittee
sous-continent subcontinent
sous-entendre get at
sous-estimer misjudge, underestimate, underrate
sous-lieutenant sub-lieutenant, second lieutenant
sous-marin deep sea, submarine
sous-payer underpay
sous-produit by-product
sous-sol basement, subsoil
sous-titre subtitle
sous-traitant, ante subcontractor
sous-vêtement underclothes, undergarment, underwear
souscripteur, trice subscriber
souscription subscription
souscrire à, s'abonner subscribe to
soustraction subtraction
soustraire subtract

soutane cassock
soutenir argue, back, bolster, contend, maintain, stand by, stick by, sustain, uphold, withstand
soutenir (que) insist
souterrain subterranean, underground
soutien support
soutien (de famille) breadwinner
soutien-gorge brassiere
souvenir keepsake, memento, memory, recollection, remembrance, souvenir
souvenir de, se recollect, remember
souvenir que, se keep in mind
souvent often
souverain, aine ruler, sovereign
soviétique soviet
soyeux silky, soft
spacieux commodious, roomy, spacious
spaghetti spaghetti
spasme spasm
spatule spatula
spécial especial, special
spécialement specially, especially
spécialisation specialization
spécialisé specialized
spécialiser, se specialize
spécialiste consultant, specialist, tradesman
spécialité specialty
spécifique specific
spécimen example, specimen
spectacle entertainment, spectacle
spectacle de cabaret cabaret
spectacle de marionnettes puppet show
spectaculaire dramatic, spectacular
spectaculairement spectacularly
spectateur, trice bystander, looker-on, onlooker, spectator
spectre spectre, spectrum
spéculation speculation
spéculer (sur) speculate
sperme sperm
sphère globe, sphere
sphérique spherical
spirale spiral
spire turn
spirituel spiritual, witty
spirituellement spiritually
spiritueux liquor, spirits
splendeur glory, grandeur, resplendence, splendour, splendidness
splendide gorgeous, splendid
splendidement splendidly
spongieux mushy, spongy
spongiosité sponginess

spontané spontaneous, spontaneousness
spontanéité spontaneousness, spontaneity
spontanément offhand, spontaneously
spore spore
sport casual, sport
sportif sporting, sportsman
sportive sportswoman
sprint sprint
sprinteur, euse sprinter
squash squash
squelette skeleton
stabilisation stabilization
stabiliser level off, stabilize
stabilité stability
stable stable
stade stadium, stage
stage probation
stagiaire trainee
stagnant stagnant
stagnation stagnation
stagner stagnate
stalactite stalactite
stalagmite stalagmite
stalle stall
stand de ravitaillement pit
stand de tir rifle range
standard switchboard, standard
standardisation standardization
standardiser standardize
station de taxis taxi rank
stationnement (parc de) parking lot
stationner park
station-service gas station, service station
statique static
statisticien, ienne statistician
statistique statistics, statistical
statistiquement statistically
statistiques statistics
statue image, statue
stature stature
statut status
stellaire stellar
stencil stencil
sténographie shorthand
steppe steppe
stéréo stereo
stéréophonique stereophonic
stéréoscopique stereoscopic
stérile barren, infertile, sterile
stérilisation sterilization
stériliser sterilize
stérilité barrenness, sterility
stéthoscope stethoscope
steward steward
stigmatiser brand

stimulant lift, stimulant, stimulating
stimulateur cardiaque pacemaker
stimulation stimulation, stimulus
stimuler inspire, stimulate
stimulus stimulus
stipulation provision
stock stock
stocker hoard, stockpile
stolon runner
store blind
store vénitien Venetian blind
stout stout
strabisme squint
strangulation strangulation
stratagème ploy, stratagem
stratège strategist
stratégie strategy
stratégique strategic
stratégiquement strategically
stress stress
strict hard and fast, severe, strict, tight
strictement strictly
strophe verse
structure frame, structure
structurellement structurally
studieusement studiously
studieux studious
studio studio
stupéfaction amazement, daze, stupefaction
stupéfait bemused
stupéfiant amazing, astounding
stupéfier amaze, astound, bowl over, stupefy
stupeur stupor
stupide brainless, mindless, soft, stupid, witless
stupidement foolishly, mindlessly, stupidly
stupidité foolishness, mindlessness, stupidity
style style
stylisme designing
stylo fountain pen
stylo-bille ballpoint
suave sweet
subalterne inferior
subconsciemment subconsciously
subconscient subconscious
subdiviser subdivide
subdivision subdivision
subir go through, suffer, undergo
subit snap
subjectif subjective
subjectivement subjectively
sublime sublime
sublimement sublimely
submergé sunken

submerger submerge
submersion submergence, submersion
subordonné, ée subordinate
subséquemment subsequently
subséquent subsequent
subsister exist, eke
substance substance
substantiel substantial
substantiellement substantially
substituer substitute
substitution substitution
subtil fine, sophisticated, subtle
subtilement subtly
subtilité subtlety
subtropical subtropical
subvenir aux besoins (de) maintain, support, provide (for
subvention grant, subsidy
subventionner subsidize
subversif subversive
subversion subversion
suc juice
succéder (à) succeed
succès hit, success
successeur successor
successif successive
succession sequence, succession
successivement successively
succion suction
succomber (à) succumb (to)
succulence lusciousness
succulent luscious, succulent
succursale branch
sucer suck
sucette lollipop
suceur, euse sucker
suçon lollipop
sucre sugar
sucré sugary, sweet
sucre d'orge barley sugar, rock
sucre en poudre caster
sucrer sugar, sweeten
sud south
suède suede
suer sweat
sueur sweat
suffire hold out, suffice
suffire pour tout le monde go round
suffisamment adequately, sufficiently
suffisance pomposity, priggishness, self-importance, self-satisfaction, smugness
suffisant adequate, bumptious, cocky, priggish, self-important, self-satisfied, smug, sufficient
suffixe suffix
suffoquer choke, suffocate

suffrages poll
suffragette suffragette
suggérer suggest
suggestion suggestion
suicidaire suicidal
suicide suicide
suicider (se) to take one's life
suie soot
suinter exude, ooze
suite continuation, follow-up, succession, train
suites aftermath
suivant following
suivre act on, follow, trail
suivre (de près) follow up
suivre la trace (de) track
suivre son cours run its course
suivre un régime diet
sujet matter, subject matter, theme, topic
sujet à subject to
sujet de conversation talking point
sujet de mécontentement/déplaisir offence
sujet, ette subject
sujétion subjection
sulfate sulphate
sultan sultan, sultana
superbe gallant, glorious, proud, superb
superbement superbly
superficialité superficiality
superficiel shallow, superficial
superficiellement superficially
superflu inessential, superfluous
supérieur superior, upper
supériorité superiority
superlatif superlative
supermarché supermarket
supersonique supersonic
superstitieusement superstitiously
superstitieux superstitious
superstition superstition
superviser supervise
superviseur, eure supervisor
supervision supervision
suppléant acting, substitute
supplément extra, supplement
supplémentaire additional, extra, supplementary
suppliant appealing, suppliant
supplication entreaty, supplication
supplier beseech, entreat
supplier (de) beg, plead (with)
support bracket, mount, prop, rest, stand, support
supportable bearable, endurable
supporter abide, bear, endure, put up with, stand, support, sustain
supporter patiemment bear with

supposer assume, expect, guess, imagine, suppose
supposition guess
suppression deletion, eradication, excision, suppression
supprimer cut, do away with, eradicate
suppuration discharge
suprématie supremacy
suprême supreme
sur about, on, on to/onto, over, sour, tart, upon
sûr safe, secure, sure
sûr de soi self-assured, self-confident
sur demande by request, on demand, on request
sur l'honneur on one's honour
sur-le-champ on the spot
sur le coup outright
sur le déclin downhill
sur le fait in the act (of)
sur le qui-vive on the alert
sur le tard latterly
sur place on the spot, in one's tracks
sur ses gardes on guard
surabondance glut
surcharger overload
surdité deafness
surdose overdose
sureau elder
sûrement surely
surestimer overestimate, overrate
surf surfing
surface surface
surgir pop up, rear up
surgir brusquement spring up
surhomme superman
surhumain superhuman
surmenage overwork
surmené overworked, rundown
surmonter master, surmount, top
surnaturel supernatural, unearthly
surnom nickname
surnommer dub, nickname
surpasser excel, outdo, surpass
surpeuplement overcrowding
surplus surplus
surprenant surprising
surprendre catch, creep up on, surprise
surpris surprised
surprise surprise
sursaut jump, start
sursauter jump, start
surtaxe surcharge
surtout mostly
surveillance guard, invigilation, superintendence

surveillant, ante invigilator, lifeguard, supervisor
surveiller guard, keep an eye on, keep guard (on), invigilate, mind, oversee, superintend, supervise, watch
survenir arise, crop up
survêtement track suit
survie survival
survivant, ante survivor
survivre live, survive
survivre à see out
susceptibilité sensibilities, touchiness
susceptible huffy, thin-skinned, touchy
susceptible de apt, liable
susciter evoke, excite
susciter l'espoir chez raise someone's hopes
susdit aforesaid
suspect suspect, suspicious
suspecter suspect
suspendre hang, hang up, string, suspend

suspension suspension
svelte slender, slim
sweepstake sweep, sweepstake
syllabe syllable
syllabique syllabic
sylviculture forestry
symbole symbol
symbolique symbolic
symboliquement symbolically
symboliser symbolize
symbolisme symbolism
symétrie symmetry
symétrique symmetrical
symétriquement symmetrically
sympathie fellow feeling, sympathy
sympathique congenial
sympathiquement sympathetically
sympathiser sympathize
symphonie symphony
symphonique symphonic
symptomatique symptomatic
symptôme symptom
synagogue synagogue
synchronisation synchronization
synchroniser, (se) synchronize

syncope blackout, syncopation
syncoper syncopate
syndic receiver
syndicalisme trade(s) unionism
syndicaliste trade(s) unionist
syndicat syndicate, trade(s) union, union
syndiquer, (se) organize
syntagme phrase
syntaxe syntax
synthèse synthesis
synthétique synthetic
synthétiser synthesize
syntonisateur tuner
systématique systematic
systématiquement systematically
système system, tract
système métrique metric system
système monétaire coinage
système nerveux nervous system
système sanguin bloodstream
système sanitaire sanitation
système solaire solar system

Tt

tabac tobacco
tabac à priser snuff
table table
table de salle à manger dining table
table des matières contents
tableau (noir) blackboard
tableau chalkboard, scene, scoreboard
tableau de bord dashboard
tableau des prix tariff
tableau noir blackboard
tablée table
tablette shelf
tablier apron
tablier (d'écolier) pinafore
tabou taboo, tabu
tabouret stool
tâche assignment, job, task
tache blotch, mark, smudge, splash, spot, stain
taché smudgy, spotted
taché d'encre inky
tache de rousseur freckle
taché de rousseur freckled, freckly
taché de sang bloodstained
tache de vin birthmark
tacher blot, stain
tâcher de seek
tacher, (se) mark
tacheté mottled, speckled
tacheture speckle
tact tact, tactfulness
tacticien, ienne tactician
tactique tactics, tactical
tactiquement tactically
taie d'oreiller pillowcase/pillowslip
taillader slash
taille clip, middle, size, trim, waist
tailler, se carve out
tailler au couteau whittle
tailleur cutter, tailor
taire shut up, tail off
talc talc, talcum
talent accomplishment, faculty, talent
talentueux talented
talisman talisman
taloche clip, swipe
talon heel
talonner dog
talus bank
tam-tam tom-tom
tamarin tamarind
tambour drum
tambour de basque tambourine
tambouriner drum

tamia chipmunk
tamis sieve
tamiser sift
tampon buffer, rubber stamp, stamp, tampon
tampon d'acier steel wool
tamponner dab, stamp
tandem partnership, tandem
tandis que as
tangage pitch
tangente tangent
tangibilité tangibility
tangible tangible
tangiblement tangibly
tango tango
tanguer pitch, toss
tanière den, earth, lair
tanné leathery
tanner tan
tannerie tannery
tanneur, euse tanner
tant bien que mal after a fashion
tant que as long as, so long as
tante aunt
taon horsefly
tapage disturbance, rowdiness
tapageur flashy, riotous, rowdy
tape-à-l'œil eye-catching
taper sur rap
taper sur les nerfs de get on someone's nerves, grate
tapette queer
tapioca tapioca
tapir, se lurk
tapis carpet, mat
tapisser wallpaper
tapisserie tapestry
taquet stop
taquin, ine tease, teaser
taquiner tease
taquinerie banter
tarabiscoté fussy
tard late
tarentule tarantula
tarif rate, tariff
tarif postal postage
tarir peter (out)
tartan tartan
tarte pie, tart
tas batch, heap, pile
tas de ferraille scrap heap
tasse cup
tâter feel
tâter le terrain see how the land lies
tatillon finicky, fussy
tâtonnements trial and error
tâtonner fumble, grope
tatouage tattoo
tatoué tattooed

tatouer tattoo
taudis hovel
taupe mole
taupinière molehill
taux rate
taux de change rate of exchange
taux de natalité birthrate
taxable dutiable
taxation levy
taxe duty, excise, tax
taxer impose, tax, tax (someone) with
taxi cab, taxi
taxidermie taxidermy
taxidermiste taxidermist
technicien, ienne technician
technique skill, technical, technique
techniquement technically
technologie technology
technologique technological
technologue technologist
teck teak
tee-shirt T-shirt
teindre dye, stain
teint colouring
teinte hue, tinge, tint
teinture dye
teinture d'iode iodine
télécommande remote control
télécommunications telecommunications
télégramme telegram, wire
télégraphe telegraph, wire
télégraphie telegraphy
télégraphier telegraph, wire
télégraphique telegraphic
télégraphiste telegrapher
téléobjectif telephoto
télépathe telepathist
télépathie telepathy
télépathique telepathic
téléphone phone, telephone
téléphoner phone, phone up, telephone
téléphoner à call, call up, give (someone) a call
téléphoniste operator, telephonist
télescope telescope
télescopique telescopic
téléscripteur teleprinter
télésiège chairlift
téléspectateur, trice viewer
téléviser televise
téléviseur television
télévision television
tellement so
téméraire daredevil, foolhardy, reckless
témérairement recklessly

témérité foolhardiness, recklessness
témoignage testimony
témoigner hear witness, testify
témoigner de be a tribute to
témoin witness
témoin oculaire eyewitness
tempe temple
tempérament temperament
température heat, temperature
tempéré temperate
tempérer temper
tempête tempest
tempête dans un verre d'eau a storm in a teacup
tempête de neige snowstorm
tempête de sable sandstorm
temple temple
tempo tempo, time
temporaire casual, temporary
temporairement temporarily
temporiser stall
temps tense, time, weather
tenace dogged, nagging, tough
ténacité doggedness, toughness
tenailles pincers
tendance tendency, trend
tendon tendon
tendre extend, fond, tender, tighten
tendre, (se) tauten, tense
tendre une embuscade à ambush
tendrement tenderly
tendresse tenderness
tendu keyed up, taut, tight
ténèbres darkness
teneur content
tenir endure, keep, last out
tenir à treasure
tenir à distance, (se) keep at arm's length, keep one's distance
tenir à l'affût, (se) lie in wait (for)
tenir à l'écart de, se steer clear of
tenir à l'écart, se keep oneself to oneself
tenir au courant keep (somebody) posted
tenir au courant de, se keep abreast of
tenir au repos, se stand at ease
tenir bon hold one's ground, hold one's own
tenir bon/ferme stand fast/firm, stand out
tenir compagnie à qqn keep (someone) company
tenir compte reckon with, take account of something
tenir compte de allow, consider, make allowance for, regard, take notice of

tenir de take after
tenir en équilibre, (se) poise
tenir l'affiche run
tenir la maison (de) keep house (for)
tenir le coup bear up, stick it out
tenir par la main, se hold hands (with someone)
tenir parole deliver the goods, keep one's word
tenir pour acquis take for granted
tenir (qqch. de qqn) inherit
tenir sa langue hold one's tongue
tenir, (se) hold
tenir tête à stand up to
tenir, (se) hold
tennis tennis
ténor tenor
tension stress, tenseness, tension
tension artérielle blood pressure
tension nerveuse tension
tentaculaire sprawling
tentacule tentacle
tentant tantalizing, tempting
tentateur, trice tempter
tentation temptation
tentative attempt, endeavour, try
tente tent
tenter attempt, have a crack, tempt
tenter de attempt, have a crack (at)
tenture(s) drapery, hangings
tenu par l'honneur à (in) honour bound
tenue outfit
tenue de soirée evening dress
térébenthine turpentine
terme term, terms
terminal terminal
terminer complete, finish off, get through
terminer, (se) break up
terminologie terminology
terminologique terminological
terminus terminal, terminus
termite termite
terne colourless, drab
terni tarnished
ternir, (se) tarnish
terrain course, field, ground, land, pitch
terrain d'aviation airfield
terrain de camping campsite
terrain de golf golf course, links
terrain de jeux playing field, recreation ground
terrain de tennis tennis court
terrasse terrace
terrasser devastate, floor, strike down
terre earth, land, soil, ground

terre cuite terracotta
terre ferme dry land
terre-à-terre down to earth, matter of fact, soulless
terreau mould
terrestre earthly
terreur dread, terror
terreux ashen
terrible awful, dire, formidable, terrible, terrific
terriblement awfully, dreadfully, fearfully, frightfully, terribly, terrifically
terrier burrow, terrier, warren
terrifiant horrific, terrifying
terrifié terrified
terrifier terrify
territoire territory
territorial territorial
terrorisé terror-stricken
terroriser strike fear/terror, terrorize
terrorisme terrorism
terroriste terrorist
tertiaire tertiary
test test
testament testament, will
testicule testicle
tétanos tetanus
têtard tadpole
tête head, lead
tête de série seed
téter suck
tétine dummy, nipple
têtu mulish, stubborn
texte lines, script, text
textile textile
texture texture
thé tea
théâtral dramatic, theatrical
théâtralement theatrically
théâtralité theatricality
théâtre drama, theatre, theatricals
théière teapot
thème theme
théologie divinity, theology
théologien, ienne theologian
théologique theological
théologiquement theologically
théorème theorem
théoricien, ienne theorist
théorie theory
théorique theoretical
théoriquement theoretically
thérapeute therapist
thérapeutique therapeutic
thermal thermal
thermomètre thermometer
thermomètre centigrade centigrade thermometer

thermostat thermostat
thermostatique thermostatic
thèse thesis
thon tuna (fish)
thym thyme
tibia tibia
tic mannerism, tic
tiède lukewarm, tepid
tiédeur half-heartedness, tepidness, tepidity
tiers third, third party
tiers-monde Third World
tige rod, shank, stalk, stem, stick
tignasse mop, shock
tigre tiger
tigresse tigress
tilleul lime
timbale kettledrum
timbre buzzer, stamp, tone
timbre-poste postage stamp
timbrer stamp
timide bashful, shy, timid
timidement bashfully, coyly, diffidently, shyly, timidly
timidité bashfulness, coyness, shyness, timidity, timidness
timonerie wheelhouse
tintement clink, ping, tinkle
tinter clink, ring
tique tick
tir à l'arc archery
tir de mines blasting
tirage draught, draw, impression
tirant d'eau draught
tiré d'affaire off the hook
tiré d'embarras out of the wood
tiré par les cheveux far-fetched
tire-au-flanc shirker
tire-bouchon corkscrew
tirelire moneybox
tirer derive, discharge, drag, draw, extricate, fire, haul, pull, shoot, tug, tweak
tirer au sort draw/cast lots
tirer d'affaire, (se) pull through
tirer de elicit (from)
tirer des bouffées de fumée puff
tirer la chasse (d'eau) flush
tirer les ficelles pull the strings
tirer les vers du nez pump
tirer parti de make (good) use of, put to (good)
tirer profit de benefit, cash in on, profit (by, from)
tirer son chapeau à take one's hat off to
tirer sur fire (at, on), pull (at, on)
tirer une conclusion de draw a conclusion from
tirer une ligne (sur) rule off

tiret dash
tireur, euse d'élite marksman
tireur, euse embusqué, ée sniper
tiroir drawer
tisonnier poker
tisser weaver
tisserand, ande weaver
tissu cloth, fabric, material, tissue
tissu éponge towelling
titre stock, title
titré titled
titre de propriété title deed
titubation grogginess
tituber reel, stagger
toast toast
toboggan slide
toge gown, toga
tohu-bohu hubbub
toile canvas, web
toile d'araignée cobweb
toilette toilet, wash
toilettes bathroom, cloakroom, convenience, lavatory, restroom, water closet
toilettes pour hommes gents
toison fleece
toit roof
tolérable tolerable
tolérance tolerance, toleration
tolérant liberal, tolerant
tolérer stand for, tolerate
tollé outcry
tomate tomato
tombe grave, tomb
tombée de la nuit nightfall
tomber fall
tomber à l'eau go by the board, unstuck
tomber à pic plummet
tomber à plat fall flat
tomber à verse lash, pour
tomber amoureux de fall for, fall in love (with)
tomber dans lapse
tomber dans l'oreille d'un sourd fall on deaf ears
tomber dans le panneau fall for
tomber dans les pommes keel over
tomber en panne break down, fail
tomber en ruine go to rack and ruins
tomber entre les mains de fall into the hands (of someone)
tomber goutte à goutte dribble
tomber malade be taken ill, sicken
tomber malade de be/go down with
tomber sans connaissance black out

tomber sur chance on/upon, come upon, happen (up) on, stumble across/on
ton shade, tone
tonal tonal
tondeuse clipper
tondeuse à gazon lawn mower
tondre cut, fleece, mow, shear
tonique keynote, tonic
tonitruant thunderous
tonnage tonnage
tonne ton
tonneau barrel, cask, drum, ton
tonner boom, thunder
tonnerre thunder
tonus tone
topaze topaz
tordant scream
tordre twist, writhe
tordu twisted, warped
torero bullfighter
tornade tornado, whirlwind
torpille torpedo
torréfier roast
torrent flot, torrent
torrentiel torrential
torride roasting, torrid
torse torso
torsion tweak, twist
tort harm, mischief
tortillement wriggle
tortiller, se squirm, wiggle, wriggle
tortillon twist
tortue tortoise, turtle
tortueusement crookedly
torture torture
torturer torture
tôt early
tôt ou tard sooner or later
total aggregate, gross, overall, total
totalement totally, utterly
totaliser total up
totalité entirety, whole
totem totem, totem pole
touchant touching
touche key, touch
toucher finger, touch
toucher (à) adjoin, tamper
toucher du bois touch wood
toucher juste strike home
touffe tuft
touffu bushy
toujours always, ever
toupet nerve
toupie top
tour castle, circuit, hoax, joke, lathe, ride, spin, tower, turn, wheel
tour à tour alternately
tour d'habitation high-rise
tour de contrôle control tower

tour de passe-passe hocus-pocus
tour de piste lap
tour de taille waist
tour de vis screw
tour du chapeau hat trick
tourbillon eddy, swirl, whirl, whirlpool
tourbillonner eddy, swirl, whirl
tourelle turret
tourisme sight-seeing, tourism
touriste sight-seer, tourist, tripper
touristique scenic
tourment torment
tourmenteur, euse tormentor
tournant curve, turn, turning point
tourne-disque pickup, record player
tournée circuit, round, tour
tourner curve, rotate, round, spin, turn, twirl, twist
tourner au ralenti idle, tick over
tourner autour (de) circle, hang about/around
tourner autour de talk around
tourner autour du pot beat about the bush
tourner en ridicule ridicule
tourner les talons turn on one's heel
tourner mal come to grief
tournesol sunflower
tournevis screwdriver
tourniquet turnstile
tournoi tournament
tournoiement spin, twirl, whirl
tournoyer spin
tous les coins et recoins every nook and cranny
tous les deux alternate
tous les soirs nightly
tous sans exception one and all
tousser cough
tout all, every, everything, whole
tout à/d'un coup all at once, all of a sudden
tout à fait quite, wholly
tout à l'heure just now
tout aussi every bit as
tout compris all in
tout d'abord first of all
tout de même all/just the same, honestly
tout de suite at once, right away, straight away, straight off
toutefois although
tout haut out
tout le long de throughout
tout le monde everybody, everyone
tout le temps all the time
tout près at hand

tout seul by oneself, itself
tout son soûl to one's heart's content
tout-puissant almighty, omnipotent
toutefois although
toutes les fois que whenever
toute-puissance omnipotence
toutes sortes de all manner of
toutes voiles dehors in full sail
toux cough
toxicomane drug addict
toxique toxic
trac stage fright
tracas worry
tracassé harassed
tracasser ail, bug
tracasser (pour), (se) fret
tracé line, tracing
trace print, suggestion, trace, track
tracer plot, trace
trachée windpipe
tract tract
tracteur tractor
traction strain, tug
tradition tradition
traditionnel traditional
traditionnellement traditionally
traditions lore
traducteur, trice translator
traduction translation
traduire translate
traduire en justice bring to justice
trafic traffic
traficoter fiddle
trafiquant, ante trafficker
trafiquant du marché noir black marketeer
trafiquer doctor, traffic
tragédie tragedy
tragique tragic
trahir betray, double-cross, sell down the river
trahison betrayal, sellout, treason
train train
train d'atterrissage landing gear, undercarriage
traînard, arde straggler
traîne train, sleigh
traîneau sledge, sleigh
traînée trail
traîner drag, loiter, lug, trail
traîner derrière lag
traîner des pieds scrape
traîner en arrière straggle
traîner en longueur drag
traîner la jambe hobble
traîner les pieds shuffle
traîner, se crawl, trudge
traire milk
trait characteristic, feature, quip

trait d'union hyphen
trait de caractère trait
traité treatise, treaty
traitement therapy, treatment
traiter handle, transact, treat
traiter de deal with
traiter de tous les noms call (someone) names
traiter en ami(e) befriend
traiteur, euse caterer
traître betrayer, traitor, treacherous
traîtreusement treacherously
trajectoire path
tramer, (se) hatch
trampoline trampoline
tramway streetcar, tram
tranchant edge
tranche slice, trench
trancher slice
tranquille cushy, easy, quiet, restful, tranquil
tranquillement tranquilly
tranquillisant tranquillizer
tranquilliser qqn set someone's mind at rest
tranquillité restfulness, tranquillity
tranquillité d'esprit peace of mind
transaction transaction
transatlantique transatlantic
transcontinental transcontinental
transcrire write out
transe trance
transférable transferable
transférer convey, transfer
transfert transfer
transformable convertible
transformateur transformer
transformation transformation
transformer convert, transform
transfuser transfuse
transfusion transfusion
transgresser infringe
transgression infringement
transistor transistor
transit transit
transitif transitive
transition transition
transitoire transitional
translucide translucent
translucidité translucence
transmetteur, trice transmitter
transmettre hand down, pass, transmit
transmission transmission
transparence clearness, transparency
transparent clear, transparent
transpercer stick
transpiration perspiration
transpirer perspire

transplant transplant
transport carriage, conveyance, freight, transport, transportation
transportable mobile, transportable
transporté de joie elated
transporter carry, convey, entrance, haul, transport
transporter d'urgence hurry
transporteur transporter
transporteur, euse conveyor, haulier
transports en commun public transport
trapèze trapeze
trappe trap door
trapu chunky, stocky, stumpy
traquer hunt down, stalk
travail handiwork, industry, job, labour, work
travail de bureau paperwork
travail manuel handicraft
travail préparatoire groundwork
travaillé en relief embossed
travailler labour, work
travailler à la pige freelance
travailler dur toil
travailleur industrious, steady
travailleur, euse worker
travailleur, euse indépendant, ante self-employed
travailliste labour
travaux d'aiguille needlework
travaux pratiques tutorial
travée bay, span
traversée crossing, passage, voyage
traverser cross, ferry, span
traversier ferry
traversin bolster
trayeuse milkmaid
trébucher stumble, trip (up, over)
treize thirteen
treizième thirteenth
trèfle clover
tremblant shaky
tremblement quaver, tremble, tremor, wobble
tremblement de terre earthquake, quake
trembler quake, shake, tremble
trempé soaked, wringing wet
trempé jusqu'aux os wet through
tremper dip, drench, soak, steep, temper
trempette dip
tremplin springboard
trentaine thirties
trente thirty
trentième thirtieth
trépidant frantic, hectic
trépied tripod

trépignement stamp
très most, very
très bien all right, very well
très bon marché dirt cheap
très mal shockingly
trésor treasure
trésorier, ière treasurer
tressaillir flinch
tresse braid, plait
tresser braid, plait, twist
tréteau trestle
treuil hoist, winch
trêve truce
triangle triangle
tribal tribal
tribord starboard
tribu tribe
tribunal court, tribunal
tribune gallery, grandstand, rostrum, stand
tribut tribute
tricentenaire tercentenary
tricher cheat
tricheur, euse cheat, trickster
tricot knitting, sweater
tricoter knit
tricoteur, euse knitter
tricycle tricycle
tridimensionnel three-dimensional
trié sur le volet hand-picked
trier sort
trieur sorter
trilogie trilogy
trimballer cart, tote
trimer drudge, slave
trimestre quarter, term
trimestriel quarterly
trio trio
triomphal triumphal
triomphalement triumphantly
triomphant exultant, triumphant
triomphe triumph
triompher (de) triumph
triple treble, triple
triplement trebly
tripler treble, triple
triplés, ées triplet
triporteur trishaw
tripoter fiddle, mess, monkey (with), twiddle
triste cheerless, doleful, dreary, forlorn, gloomy, sad, sorry
tristement dolefully, drearily, forlornly, mournfully, sadly
tristesse dolefulness, dreariness, gloom, sadness
triton newt
troc barter
trois three
trois-quarts three-quarter

troisième third
troisièmement thirdly
trolleybus trolley bus
trombone paper clip, trombone
tromboniste trombonist
trompe proboscis, trunk
tromper beguile, deceive, hoodwink, mislead
tromper, (se) delude, err, go wrong
tromper sur, se mistake
tromperie deceit, deception, trickery
trompeter trumpet
trompette trumpet
trompettiste trumpeter
trompeur deceitful, deceptive, misleading
trompeusement deceptively
tronc trunk
tronc d'arbre tree trunk
trône throne
tronqué truncated
trop (de) excess (of)
trop empressé officious
trop-plein overflow
trophée trophy
tropical tropical
tropique tropic
troquer (contre) barter
trot trot, toddle
trotter trot
trottinette scooter
trottoir pavement, sidewalk
trou eye, hole
trou d'eau pool
trou d'épingle pinhole, prick
trou de serrure keyhole
trou de souris mousehole
trou pour épier peephole
troublé confused
trouble disorder, disturbance, trouble
troubler disturb, fluster, trouble
trouer hole
trouille funk
troupe chorus, pride, troop, troupe
troupeau flock, herd
troupes troops
trousse wallet
trouvaille find
trouver find, line up, strike
trouver à redire pick holes in
trouver du pétrole strike oil
trouver le courage de pluck up (the) courage, energy
trouver le juste milieu strike a balance
trouver moyen de (faire) contrive
trouver, se occur
truc device, dodge, knack, trick

truelle trowel
truie sow
truite trout
truqué fixed
trust trust
tsar czar, tsar, tzar
tuba snorkel, tuba
tube tube, tubing
tubercule tuber
tuberculose tuberculosis
tubulaire tubular
tuer destroy, kill, slay, take life
tuer le temps kill time
tueur, euse killer
tuile tile
tulipe tulip
tulle netting

tumeur tumour
tumulte commotion, tumult, uproar
tumultueusement riotously,
　　tumultuously, turbulently,
　　uproariously
tumultueux disorderly, riotous,
　　tumultuous, uproarious
tunique tunic
tunnel tunnel
turban turban
turbine turbine
turbulence riotousness, turbulence
turbulent boisterous
turquoise turquoise
tutelle guardianship, tutelage
tuteur, trice guardian
tutu tutu

tuyau pipe
tuyau d'arrosage hose
tweed tweed
tympan drum, eardrum
type chap, guy, type
typhon typhoon
typhus typhus
typique characteristic, typical
typiquement characteristically,
　　typically
tyran tyrant
tyrannie high-handedness, tyranny
tyrannique high-handed,
　　oppressive, tyrannical
tyranniquement high-handedly
　　tyrannically, tyrannously
tyranniser tyrannize

Uu

ulcère ulcer
ultimatum ultimatum
ultime ultimate
ultimement ultimately
ultra-secret top secret
ultrasonique ultrasonic
ultraviolet ultraviolet
un jour one day, some day
un ou deux one or two
un par un one by one
un petit peu (de) dab (of)
un peu bit, a little
un peu partout here, there and
  everywhere
un peu tard belatedly
un/quelque peu slightly
unanime unanimous
unanimité unanimity
une chance sur deux an even
  chance
une fois once
une fois pour toute once and for all
une fois que once

uni self-coloured, united
unification unification
unifié corporate
unifier unify, unite
uniforme uniform
uniformément uniformly
uniformité uniformity
union togetherness, union
unique solitary, unique, only
uniquement exclusively
unir, (s') join forces, unite
unisexe unisex
unisson unison
unité credit, unit
univers universe
universalité universality
universel global, universal
universellement universally
universitaire academic
université university
uppercut uppercut
uranium uranium
urbain urban
urgence rush, urgency
urgent pressing, urgent
urinaire urinary

urine urine
uriner urinate
urne urn
usage convention, use
usagé second hand
usé bare, shabby
usine factory, plant
usine à gaz gasworks
usiner machine
ustensile utensil
usure fatigue
usurpateur, trice usurper
usurper usurp
utérus uterus
utile helpful, useful
utilement helpfully, usefully
utilisable serviceable, usable
utilisateur, trice user
utilisation utilization
utilisé spent, used
utiliser use, utilize
utilitaire utilitarian
utilité helpfulness, purpose, use,
  usefulness, utility
utopique Utopian

Vv

va-nu-pieds ragamuffin
vacances holiday, vacation
vacancier, ière holydaymaker
vacant vacant
vacarme din, hullaballoo, pandemonium, racket, row
vaccin vaccine
vaccination inoculation, vaccination
vacciner (contre) inoculate, vaccinate
vache bitchy, cow
vache laitière dairy cow
vacher, ère cowherd
vaciller flicker, totter
vadrouille mop
vadrouiller gad
vagabond, onde hobo, roamer, rover, roving, tramp, vagabond, wanderer
vagabondage vagrancy
vagabonder knock about/around, meander, rove
vague hazy, shadowy, vague, vagueness, wave
vague de chaleur heat wave
vaguement vaguely
vain empty, fruitless, idle, vain
vaincre overcome, overpower, vanquish
vainement fruitlessly, vainly
vainqueur conqueror, victor, winner
vaisseau ship, vessel
vaisseau sanguin blood vessel
vaisseau spatial spaceship
vaisselier dresser
vaisselle tableware, dishes
valable valid, worthy
valablement validly
valet jack, knave
valet de chambre manservant, valet
valet de pied footman
valeur denomination, value, worth
valeur nominale face value
valeurs values
valide valid
valise grip, suitcase
vallée vale, valley
valoir worth
valoir, mieux be as well to
valoir, se nothing/not much to choose between
valoriser value
valse waltz
valser waltz
valve valve

valvule valve
vampire vampire
vandale vandal
vandalisme vandalism
vanille vanilla
vanité conceit, vanity
vaniteux conceited, vain
vanner winnow
vannerie basketry, wickerwork
vantard boastful
vantardise boasting, boastfulness
vanter (de), se boast, brag
vanter, se boast, brag, blow one's own trumpet
vapeur steam, steaminess, vapour
vaporeux filmy, frothy
vaporisateur spray
vaporiser, (se) vaporize
variabilité variability
variable variable
variablement variably
variation variation
varicelle chicken pox
varié miscellaneous, various, varied
varier vary
variété variety
variole smallpox
vase ooze, silt, slime, vase
vase à bec beaker
vaseline petroleum jelly
vaseux oozy
vasque bath
vaste capacious, comprehensive, extensive
vaudou voodoo
vaurien bum, scoundrel
vautour vulture
veau calf, veal
vedette star, star turn
végétal vegetable
végétarien, ienne vegetarian
végétarisme vegetarianism
végétation vegetation
végéter vegetate
véhicule vehicle
veille eve
veiller sit up, stay up, watch over
veilleuse pilot light
veine seam, vein
vêler calve
vélo cycle
vélocité velocity
vélomoteur moped
velours velvet
velours côtelé cord
velouté creamy, creaminess, velvety
velu hairy
venaison venison
vendable marketable
vendetta vendetta

vendeur, euse assistant, clerk, salesman, saleswoman, shop assistant
vendre cash in, market, sell, sell up
vendre au détail retail
vendre la mèche let the cat out of the bag, give the show away, spill the beans
vendredi Friday
vénéneux poisonous
vénérable venerable
vénération reverence, veneration
vénérer revere, venerate
vengeance retaliation, revenge, vengeance
venger avenge
venger de, (se) be/get even with, revenge (on)
vengeur avenger
venimeux venomous
venin venom
venir come, turn out, turn up
venir à bout de shake off
venir à l'esprit (de) occur (to)
venir subitement à l'esprit dawn on
vent wind
vent arrière tail wind
vent contraire headwind
vente sale
venteux breezy, gusty, windy
ventilateur fan, ventilator
ventilation ventilation
ventiler ventilate
ventouse plunger, sucker
ventre belly, stomach, tummy
ventriloque ventriloquist
ventriloquie ventriloquism
venue arrival, coming
ver worm
ver à soie silkworm
ver de terre earthworm
ver luisant glowworm
véracité truthfulness
véranda porch, veranda(h)
verbal verbal
verbalement by word of mouth, verbally
verbe verb
verbillage waffle
verdâtre greenish
verdict verdict
verge yard
verger orchard
verglacé icy
verglas ice storm
véridique truthful
véridiquement truthfully
vérifiable ascertainable, verifiable
vérificateur, trice auditor

vérification check, verification
vérification des comptes audit
vérifier check, check out, verify
vérifier des comptes audit
véritable real, true
vérité trueness, truth
vermeil ruby
vermillon vermilion
vermine vermin
vernaculaire vernacular
vernir varnish
vernis glaze, varnish
vernis à ongles nail polish, nail varnish
vernisser glaze
verre drink, glass
verre à pied goblet
verre de contact contact lens
verre (droit) tumbler
verrou bolt
verrue wart
vers around, rhyme, toward, towards, verse
vers l'est easterly, eastward(s)
vers l'intérieur inward, inwards
vers le bas down, downward(s)
vers le haut upward(s)
vers le large seaward(s)
versant side
versement instalment, remittance
versement d'un acompte deposit
verser empty, pour, tip
verset verse
version version
vert green, immature
vertébral spinal
vertèbre vertebra
vertébré vertebrate
vertical vertical
verticalement vertically
vertige(s) dizziness, giddiness, vertigo
vertigineusement dizzily, giddily
vertigineux dizzy
vertu virtue, virtuousness
vertueusement righteously, virtuously
vertueux righteous, virtuous
verve raciness
vésicule biliaire gall bladder
vessie bladder
veste coat, sports jacket
vestiaire cloakroom, dressing room
vestibule hallway, lobby
vestige relic
veston coat, jacket
vêtement garment
vêtements clothes, clothing, dress
vêtements de sport sportswear
vêtements de travesti drag

vêtements pour hommes menswear
vétéran veteran
vétérinaire veterinary, veterinary surgeon, vet
vêtir attire, dress
vêtu clad
veuf widower
veuve widow
vexation vexation
vexer vex
viaduc overpass, viaduct
viande meat
viande hachée mince
vibration throb, vibration
vibrer throb, vibrate
vicaire curate
vice vice
vice versa vice versa
vicomte viscount
vicomtesse viscountess
victime casualty, victim
victoire victory
victorien Victorian
victorieusement victoriously
victorieux victorious
victuailles eatable
vide bare, blank, emptiness, vacancy, vacant, vacuum, vain, void
vide (de) empty
vide de void of
vidéocassette videotape
vidéophonie video
vider drain, gut, turn out
vider, (se) empty
vider son verre drink up
vie life, lifetime
vie de chien a dog's life
vie de famille domesticity
vieille fille old maid
vieillesse old age
vieilli obsolescent, out of date
vieillir age
vieillissement obsolescence
vieillot antiquated
vierge virgin
vieux aged, ancient, has-been, old
vieux jeu square
vieux routier old hand
vif bright, brisk, sharp-witted, smart, snappy, spry, vital, vivacious
vigilance vigilance, watchfulness
vigilant alert, heedful, vigilant, watchful
vigne grapevine, vine
vignoble vineyard
vigoureusement forcefully, robustly, strenuously, vigorously
vigoureux forceful, lusty, sturdy,

vigorous
vigueur lustiness, punch, vigour
vilain nasty, naughty
villa villa
village village
villageois, oise villager
ville city, town
vin wine
vinaigre vinegar
vinaigrette salad dressing
vingt twenty
vingt-et-un pontoon
vingtaine score, twenties
vingtième twentieth
viol rape
violemment violently
violence violence
violent fiery, high, raging, rough, sharp, stormy, tempestuous, tough, violent
violenter assault
violer rape
violet purple, violet
violette violet
violeur rapist
violon fiddle, violin
violoncelle cello, violoncello
violoncelliste cellist, violoncellist
violoneux, euse fiddler
violoniste violinist
vipère viper
virage bend
viral virus
virer veer
virer de bord go about
virginal virginal
virginité virginity
virgule comma
viril manly
virilité manhood, manliness
virtuosité virtuosity
virus virus
vis screw
vis-à-vis de opposite
visa visa
visage face
viscosité gumminess, sliminess
viser aim, take aim, sight
viser à aim to/at
visibilité visibility
visible noticeable, visible
visiblement markedly, noticeably, visibly
visière peak
vision sight, vision
visionneuse viewer
visite call, rounds, view, visit
visiter look over, tour, visit
visiteur, euse caller, stranger, visitor

vison mink
visqueux slimy
visser, (se) screw
visuel visual
visuellement visually
vital vital
vitalité vitality
vitamine vitamin
vite fast, quickly
vitesse rate, speed
vitre glaze, pane, windowpane
vitreux glassy
vitrier, ière glazier
vitrine showcase
vivace perennial
vivacité high spirits, spryness, vivaciousness, vividness
vivacité d'esprit quick-wittedness
vivant alive, animate, live, living
vivement acutely, briskly, hotly, spryly, vividly
vivifiant bracing, exhilarating, invigorating
vivifier invigorate
vivre live
vivre en accord avec live up to
vivre en marge de la société drop out
vocabulaire vocabulary
vocal vocal
vocation vocation
vociférant clamorous
vodka vodka
vœu vow, wish
vœux greetings
voguer sail
voie lane, line, track
voie aérienne airway
voie de tramway tramway
voie express expressway
voie publique thoroughfare
voie navigable waterway
voilà there
voile sail, sailing, shroud, veil
voilé veiled
voiler veil
voir see
voir double see double
voir le jour see the light

voir les choses du même œil see eye to eye
voir rouge see red
voir (tout/la vie) en rose look at/ see through rose-coloured glasses
voisin neighbour, neighbouring
voisinage neighbourhood, vicinity
voiture car, carriage
voiture de course race car
voiture de louage hackney
voiture de sport sports car
voix voice
voix traînante drawl
vol flight, robbery
vol à l'étalage shoplifting
vol à main armée holdup
vol à voile gliding
vol nolisé charter
volaille poultry
volant flounce, frill, shuttlecock, steering wheel
volcan volcano
volcanique volcanic
volée flight, volley
voler fly, rob, steal, thieve, walk of with
voler de ses propres ailes stand on one's own (two) feet
volet shutter
voleur, euse robber, thief
voleur, euse à l'étalage shoplifter
volière aviary
volley-ball volleyball
volontaire headstrong, self-inflicted, self-willed, voluntary, volunteer, willful
volontairement voluntarily
volonté will, willpower
volontiers freely, readily
volt volt
voltage voltage
voltigement flitting
voltiger flit, flutter, hover
volume volume
volumineux bulky
voluptueusement sensuously
voluptueux sensuous
vomi sick, vomit
vomir disgorge, throw up, vomit

vomissure sick
vorace ravenous
voracement hungrily, ravenously
voracité ravenousness
vote ballot, suffrage, vote
vote de confiance vote of confidence
voter pass, vote
vouloir want
vouloir à tout prix set one's heart on
vouloir dire intend, mean
vouloir en venir (à) be driving at
voulu deliberate
voûte arch, hunched up
voûté hunched up, round-shouldered, stooped, vaulted
voyage journey, tour, travel, trip
voyager journey, travel
voyager clandestinement stow away
voyager (par mer) voyage
voyageur, euse traveller, voyager, wayfarer
voyageur, euse de commerce commercial traveller
voyance clairvoyance
voyant jazzy, showy
voyant, ante clairvoyant
voyelle vowel
voyou hoodlum, hooligan, rough, ruffian, thug
vrai positive, real, right, true
vraiment indeed, really, truly
vraisemblable plausible
vraisemblablement as likely as not, presumably
vrombissement zoom
vu in view of, inasmuch as, in as much as
vue eyesight, outlook, prospect, sight, view, vision
vue d'ensemble bird's-eye view
vue en élévation elevation
vulgaire common, vulgar
vulgairement vulgarly
vulgarité vulgarity
vulnérabilité vulnerability
vulnérable vulnerable

Ww

wagon carriage, coach
wagon-restaurant diner, dining car
watt watt
western western
whisky whiskey
whist whist
wigwam wigwam

Xx

xérès sherry
xylophone xylophone

Yy

yacht yacht
yack yak
Yankee Yankee
yen yen
yo-yo yo-yo
yodler yodel
yodleur, euse yodeller
yoga yoga
yogi yogi
yogourt yogurt

Zz

zèbre zebra
zèle zeal
zélé officious, zealous
zénith zenith
zéro nothing, nought, zero
zézaiement lisp
zézayer lisp
zibeline sable
zigzag zigzag
zigzaguer zigzag
zinc zinc
zona shingles
zone area, belt, zone
zone industrielle industrial estate
zone neutre no man's land
zoo zoo
zoologie zoology
zoologique zoological
zoologiquement zoologically
zoologiste zoologist

GRAMMATICAL
NOTES

Nouns

Singular and Plural

Nouns Always in the Singular and Used with a Singular Verb

advice	equipment	machinery	stationery
baggage	furniture	mud	traffic
clothing	knowledge	music	
dirt	lightning	rust	
dust	luggage	scenery	

Nouns Always in the Plural and Used with a Plural Verb

clothes	pincers	scissors	tights
congratulations	pliers	shorts	trousers
hackles	pyjamas	spectacles	tweezers
pants	riches	thanks	

Nouns with the Same Form in Singular and Plural

cod	salmon	trout	hovercraft
deer	sheep	aircraft	spacecraft

Nouns with a Plural Form but Used with a Singular Verb

billiards	checkers	mumps
bowls	measles	news

Gender

Masculine and Feminine Genders

The **masculine gender** denotes the class of persons and animals that are **male**.
The **feminine gender** denotes the class of persons and animals that are **female**.

Nouns with a Completely Different Masculine and Feminine Form

Masculine	Feminine	Masculine	Feminine
bachelor	spinster	landlord	landlady
boy	girl	man	woman
bridegroom	bride	nephew	niece
brother	sister	sir	madam
comedian	comedienne	son	daughter
father	mother	uncle	aunt
fiancé	fiancée	widower	widow
gentleman	lady	bull	cow
hero	heroine	cock	hen
husband	wife	dog	bitch
king	queen	drake	duck

Nouns with the Feminine Form Ending in -ess

Masculine	Feminine	Masculine	Feminine
emperor	empress	lion	lioness
god	goddess	master	mistress
heir	heiress	prince	princess
host	hostess	tiger	tigress

Names for Jobs

Masculine	Feminine	Masculine	Feminine
actor	actress	schoolmaster	schoolmistress
conductor	conductress (on a bus *etc*)	salesman	saleswoman
manager	manageress	steward	stewardess
policeman	policewoman	waiter	waitress

Common Gender

1. The **common gender** denotes the class of persons that can be male or female.

adult	cousin	parent	pupil
athlete	friend	passenger	tourist
baby	guest	person	worker
child	motorist	principal	

2. Most words for jobs are of common gender.

-er/-or	-ist	-ant/ent	-ician	-person
builder	artist	accountant	dietician	chairperson
conductor	chemist	civil servant	musician	salesperson
(of an orchestra)	dentist	president	physician	
director	journalist	shop assistant	technician	
doctor	scientist	student		
driver		travel agent		
editor				
teacher				
writer				

Neuter Gender

The **neuter gender** denotes the class of things without sex that can be referred to as 'it', *eg* chair, table, book, plant etc; but a baby or animal can also be referred to as 'it'.

Adjectives

Comparison of Adjectives

Adjectives have three degrees of comparison.

1. The positive degree
The positive degree is the simple form of the adjective and is used to describe a noun.

- John is **tall**.
- This table is **high**.
- This house is **expensive**.

2. The comparative degree
The comparative degree is used to compare two persons or things.

- Mr White is **fatter** than Mr Brown.
- The red car is **better** than the blue one.
- The ring is **more expensive** than the watch.

3. The superlative degree
The superlative degree is used to compare three or more persons or things.

- Michael is the **most hardworking** pupil in this class.
- That dictionary is the **thickest** book on the shelf.
- Among the pupils, Gwen has the **most** money in the bank.

How to Form the Comparative and Superlative Degrees of Adjectives

One-Syllable Adjectives

Positive	Comparative = Adjective + **-er**	Superlative = Adjective + **-est**
bright	brighter	brightest
dear	dearer	dearest
warm	warmer	warmest

Adjectives Ending in **-e**

Positive	Comparative = Adjective + **-r**	Superlative = Adjective + **-st**
ripe	riper	ripest
pale	paler	palest
true	truer	truest

Adjectives with a Single Vowel and Ending with a Single Consonant

Positive	Comparative = last consonant doubles + **-er**	Superlative = last consonant doubles + **-est**
red	redder	reddest
big	bigger	biggest
fat	fatter	fattest

Adjectives with Two or More Syllables

Positive	Comparative = more + adjective	Superlative = most + adjective
attractive	more attractive	most attractive
beautiful	more beautiful	most beautiful
careful	more careful	most careful

Two-Syllable Adjectives (and Some One-Syllable Adjectives) Ending in -y

Positive	Comparative = Adjective changes y to i + -er	Superlative = Adjective changes y to i + -est
angry	angrier	angriest
busy	busier	busiest
dirty	dirtier	dirtiest
dry	drier	driest

Exceptions

Positive	Comparative = Adjective + -er or -r	Superlative = Adjective + -est or -st
clever	cleverer	cleverest
common	commoner	commonest
handsome	handsomer	handsomest
narrow	narrower	narrowest
pleasant	pleasanter	pleasantest
polite	politer	politest
quiet	quieter	quietest
shallow	shallower	shallowest
simple	simpler	simplest
stupid	stupider	stupidest
wicked	wickeder	wickedest

Adjectives with Irregular Comparative and Superlative Forms

Positive	Comparative	Superlative
far	farther/further	farthest/furthest
bad	worse	worst
good	better	best
little	less	least
many	more	most
much	more	most
some	more	most

Adverbs

Comparison of Adverbs

Adverbs have three degrees of comparison.

1. The positive degree
The positive degree is the simple form of the adverb.

> - The monkeys chattered **noisily**.
> - The baby slept **soundly**.
>
> - The jewels sparkled **brilliantly**.

2. The comparative degree
The comparative degree is used to compare two actions.

> - I walk **faster** than you.
> - Mr Black does his work **more carefully** than Mr Green does.
> - Marty dances **more gracefully** than Anne.

3. The superlative degree
The superlative degree is used to compare three or more actions.

> - Linda can run **fastest** among the girls.
> - She spoke **most politely** to me.
>
> - He came **earliest** of all.

How to Form the Comparative and Superlative Degrees of Adverbs

Positive	Comparative = More + Adverb	Superlative = Most + Adverb
angrily	more angrily	most angrily
sweetly	more sweetly	most sweetly
warmly	more warmly	most warmly

One-Syllable Adverbs

Positive	Comparative = Adverb + **-er**	Superlative = Adverb + **-est**
fast	faster	fastest
near	nearer	nearest
soon	sooner	soonest

Adverbs with Irregular Comparative and Superlative Forms

Positive	Comparative	Superlative
badly	worse	worst
far	farther/further	farthest/furthest
little	less	least
much	more	most
well	better	best

Punctuation

(.) A period is used at the end of a statement and often after a command.

• This is a good essay.	• Show it to the headmaster tomorrow.

(?) A question mark comes after a question.

• Would you make a copy for me?	• Don't you want to come with me?

(!) An exclamation mark comes after an exclamation or interjection, and sometimes after a command.

• Hello!	• Dont't forget what I said!

Capital Letters

Use a **capital letter** at the beginning of a sentence, for names, for the word 'I' and for the months of the year and the days of the week:

> Tell Amy that I can meet her in London at the British Museum on Saturday 20th April.

(,) A comma shows a slight break in a sentence. It is used, for instance:

a) between two clauses joined by *but* or *or* if the second one has a subject:
   I'll come and see you tonight, but I don't want to be out too late.

b) after a subordinate clause:
   When he returned, I made a cup of tea.

c) around the kind of relative clause that gives additional information (but not around the kind that just identifies a person or thing):
   His brother, who was getting angry, gave him a slap. (But no commas in *Those people who would like tickets should write to the secretary.*)

d) around a descriptive or explanatory phrase referring to a person or thing:
   Mr Jones, the headmaster of our school, told me to write to you.

e) after introductory words, or around words that form a comment:
   However, I wasn't late after all.
   I must leave now, unfortunately.
   Philip, I'm sorry to say, has been neglecting his homework.

f) before *please*, after *yes* and *no*, and before or after the name of the person who is being spoken to:
   Can you lend me a pencil, please?
   Yes, I can.
   Don't cry, Mary.

g) in a list of more than two things and often between adjectives before a noun, where there are two or more:
   a pen, a pencil and an eraser
   a hot, dusty day (but no commas in a *pretty little girl*, because *little girl* is regarded as a single unit)

(:) A **colon** is used to introduce the answer that the first part of the sentence expects:

- There's one thing I'd really like: a new bicycle.
- You'll need the following: cardboard, glue and scissors.

(;) A **semicolon** separates parts of a sentence that are equally important and are not linked by *and*, *but*, *or*, etc. Sometimes a semicolon is used to separate items in a list:

- One bag of chips is enough; to eat two would be greedy.
- I have three ambitions: to visit India and see the Taj Mahal; to fly a plane; to write a book.

(' ') **Quotation marks** are used before and after direct speech; a **comma** is usually put before or after the direct speech:

- Mary said, 'You're late.'
- 'You're late,' said Mary.

(') An **apostrophe** is used:

---
a) to form possessive nouns; it is placed before the *s* with singular nouns and with plural nouns not ending in -*s*, and after the *s* with plural nouns ending in -*s*:
  - Anne's book; the children's toys; the twins' bedroom.

b) in short forms, showing where part of a word has been left out:
  - I've only two dollars left.
  - Aren't you going too?

(-) A **hyphen** is used:

---
a) in compound adjectives placed before the noun:
  - a six-page essay; a five-year-old child; a well-deserved reward.

b) sometimes with a prefix:
  - The votes must be re-counted. She is my co-worker.

Question tags

Question tags are placed at the end of statements to turn them into questions.

Negative tags are placed after positive statements and **positive tags** after negative statements.

Some people incorrectly use the single tag 'isn't it' after all statements. Thus we get sentences like:

He has gone home, isn't it?   She is pretty, isn't it?   You are Mrs Grey, isn't it?

Correct Question Tags

Positive statement	Negative tag	Negative statement	Positive tag
This bag is yours,	**isn't** it?	This bag isn't yours,	**is** it?
Those books are new,	**aren't** they?	Those books aren't new,	**are** they?
Mary was absent,	**wasn't** she?	Mary wasn't absent,	**was** she?
The boys were late,	**weren't** they?	The boys weren't late,	**were** they?
John has done it,	**hasn't** he?	John hasn't done it,	**has** he?
They have seen it,	**haven't** they?	They haven't seen it,	**have** they?
She will help us,	**won't** she?	She won't help us,	**will** she?
There will be a show,	**won't** there?	There won't be a show,	**will** there?
You can carry it,	**can't** you?	You can't carry it,	**can** you?
They could do it,	**couldn't** they?	They couldn't do it,	**could** they?
She must be here,	**musn't** she?	She musn't be there,	**must** she?
Children like sweets,	**don't** they?	They don't like sweets,	**do** they?
Jane works hard,	**doesn't** she?	Tom doesn't work hard,	**does** he?
David lost the game,	**didn't** he?	He didn't lose the game,	**did** he?

Verbs

Common Irregular Verbs

Infinitive	Past tense	Past participle	Infinitive	Past tense	Past participle
arise	arose	arisen	bless	blessed	blessed
awake	awoke	awoken	blow	blew	blown
be	was, were	been	break	broke	broken
bear	bore	borne	breed	bred	bred
beat	beat	beaten	bring	brought	brought
become	became	become	build	built	built
begin	began	begun	burn	burnt or	burnt or
bend	bent	bent		burned	burned
beseech	besought or	besought or	burst	burst	burst
	beseeched	beseeched	buy	bought	bought
bet	bet or betted	bet or betted	catch	caught	caught
bid	bade or bid	bade or bid	choose	chose	chosen
		or bidden	come	came	come
bite	bit	bitten	cost	cost	cost
bleed	bled	bled	creep	crept	crept